Anthology of American Literature

Ninth Edition

Volume II

George McMichael *California State University, Hayward*
James S. Leonard *The Citadel*
Shelley Fisher Fishkin *Stanford University*
David Bradley *University of Oregon*
Dana D. Nelson *Vanderbilt University*
Joseph Csicsila *Eastern Michigan University*

PEARSON
Prentice Hall

Upper Saddle River, New Jersey 07458

Library of Congress Cataloging-in-Publication Data

Anthology of American literature/George McMichael . . . [et al.].—9th ed.
p. cm.
Includes bibliographical references and index.
ISBN 0-13-221647-7 (v. 2)
1. American literature. 2. United States—Literary collections. I. McMichael, George L.
PS507.A68 2007
810.8—dc22

2006017742

Editorial Director: Leah Jewell
Acquisitions Editor: Vivian Garcia
Editorial Assistant: Christina Volpe
Director of Marketing: Brandy Dawson
Marketing Assistant: Christina Volpe
Production Liaison: Barbara Reilly
Prepress and Manufacturing Buyer: Christina Amato
Cover Art Director: Jayne Conte
Cover Design: Bruce Kenselaar
Cover Image: Ward Schumaker/Theispot.com
Composition/Full-Service Project Management: Kari Callaghan Mazzola and John P. Mazzola
Printer/Binder: Courier Companies, Inc.
Cover Printer: Phoenix Color Corp.

This book was set in 10/11 New Baskerville.

Grateful acknowledgment is made to the copyright holders on pages 2399–2408, which are hereby a continuation of this copyright page.

Pearson Education LTD.
Pearson Education Singapore, Pte. Ltd
Pearson Education, Canada, Ltd
Pearson Education—Japan
Pearson Education Australia PTY, Limited
Pearson Education North Asia Ltd
Pearson Educación de Mexico, S.A. de C.V.
Pearson Education Malaysia, Pte. Ltd
Pearson Education, Upper Saddle River, NJ

PEARSON
Prentice
Hall

10 9 8 7 6 5 4 3 2 1
ISBN 13: 978-0-13-221647-0
ISBN 10: 0-13-221647-7

Contents

Preface

For three decades, students and instructors have relied on the McMichael *Anthology of American Literature* as a reliable source of literary texts, annotations, and contextual information. The McMichael anthology has secured its reputation with a solid core of writers and works, and has enhanced that reputation with quality ancillaries, including the Pick-a-Penguin Program, the American Literature Database, a text-specific Companion Website™, and Research Navigator™. Because it allows such flexibility in meeting individual course needs, *Anthology of American Literature* is truly a complete American Literature resource.

In revising Volume II of this ninth edition, we have continued to follow the principles of selection that have made the previous editions so successful:

- We have selected works primarily for their literary significance.
- We have represented authors by offering extensive samplings of their works.
- We have included, where possible, long works in their entirety.
- We have provided clear, concise, and informative introductions and headnotes that are appropriate for student readers.
- We have explained unfamiliar terms and allusions through in-text references and footnotes.
- We have presented author bibliographies that are selective and current.

Authors and works in the anthology follow a generally chronological order. In deciding on a standard text from among the various editions available for selections, we have chosen, whenever possible, the edition most respected by modern scholars. The text reprinted is identified at the end of the headnote for each author. Spelling and punctuation are, in some instances, regularized and modernized to correct obvious errors and to suit the reader's convenience. An editorial excision of less than one paragraph is indicated by an ellipsis (. . .); excisions of a paragraph or more are indicated by a centered ellipsis:

. . .

The date on the left immediately following each literary selection indicates the date of composition when known; dates on the right indicate the date or dates of publication.

New to the Ninth Edition

Building on the anthology's solid foundation, we were able to make numerous enhancements to the content:

- We have updated and revised period introductions and headnotes.
- We have created new sections on "Reading the Historical Context" and "Reading the Critical Context" to collect pertinent works in those categories by authors (such as Mark Twain, Henry James, and T. S. Eliot) represented by more copious selections elsewhere in the anthology and by newly represented authors (such as Albion Tourgée, Martin Luther King, and Tim O'Brien) whose writings provide valuable context for the anthology's literary selections.
- We have included new headnotes and selections for Albion Tourgée, Anna Julia Cooper, Abraham Cahan, Paul Laurence Dunbar, O. Henry (William Sydney Porter), Owen Wister, James Weldon Johnson, Gertrude Simmons Bonnin (Zitkala Sa), Carl Sandburg, Sinclair Lewis, Edgar Lee Masters, Anzia Yazierska, Edna St. Vincent Millay, Martin Luther King, Tim O'Brien, Ann Petry, Shirley Jackson, Joseph Heller, William Styron, N. Scott Momaday, James Welch, James Alan McPherson, David Bradley, Gloria Anzaldúa, August Wilson, Frederick Busch, Simon Ortiz, and Sherman Alexie.
- We have added new works or expanded existing ones by Mark Twain, Walt Whitman, Mary E. Wilkins Freeman, Sarah Orne Jewett, Charles Waddell Chesnutt, Ambrose Bierce, Charlotte Perkins Gilman, Kate Chopin, Stephen Crane, Jack London, Theodore Dreiser, W. E. B. Du Bois, Willa Cather, Sherwood Anderson, Wallace Stevens, Jean Toomer, Zora Neale Hurston, F. Scott Fitzgerald, William Faulkner, John Steinbeck, Eudora Welty, Richard Wright, John Updike, Alice Walker, and Toni Morrison.
- In two instances we have departed from the standard anthology format of grouping works by individual authors in order to present unified samplings of edited collections that were pivotal in helping to define important literary movements. These are *The New Negro* (1925), edited by Alain Locke, which was an important cornerstone of the Harlem Renaissance, and *Black Fire: An Anthology of Afro-American Writing* (1968), edited by Amiri Baraka (LeRoi Jones) and Larry Neal, which was an important defining element of the Black Arts Movement.
- We have revamped the treatment of Native American authors, moving away from the "myths and legends" motif that predominated in previous editions and toward an emphasis on specifically identifiable speakers and authors firmly anchored in the historical context. Only one "myths and legends" entry is retained: *Diné bahane': The Navajo Creation Story,* which has been moved from the beginning of Volume I to the last section of Volume II in recognition of its continuing vital role as an oral tradition in the daily life of a culture that has no written language. In keeping with this, a late twentieth-century translation of the selection is used.

Anthology of American Literature also offers design features that make it more accessible to students. The typeface for the headnotes and the literary selections is easy to read. Updated chronological charts offer students at-a-glance information about authors' lives and works, as well as key historical, political, technological, and cultural contexts.

A Complete American Literature Resource

How does the McMichael *Anthology of American Literature* offer more of what students and instructors want for their American Literature courses?

Pick a Penguin Program

Prentice Hall is proud to announce an agreement with Penguin Putnam that allows us to package—at substantial discounts—the most popular American Literature trade paperbacks with the McMichael *Anthology of American Literature.* Ask your Prentice Hall sales representative for details and for a listing of available American Literature titles.

American Literature Database

Now instructors can customize course material with the Pearson Custom Library of American Literature. A database featuring more than 1,700 literary works, the Pearson Custom Library of American Literature gives instructors the flexibility to choose other selections that they might want to use along with the McMichael anthology. For details, visit <http://www.pearsoncustom.com/database/americanlit>, or contact your Prentice Hall sales representative.

American Literature Online

The expanded Companion Website™ at <www.prenhall.com/mcmichael> offers an interactive experience for students and instructors. Weblinks, interactive timelines, author profiles, essay questions, and general resources all make the McMichael Companion Website™ an excellent resource for in-class discussions and out-of-class research.

Instructor's Manual

This instructor supplement provides background information on every writer in the anthology and offers discussion topics and analytical questions to help promote class discussion. The Instructor's Manual also provides alternate tables of contents organized by literary types and genres as well as literary themes and topics to offer professors additional options for grouping the selections. To order this supplement, contact your local Prentice Hall sales representative. (ISBN 978-0-13-224280-6)

Teacher's Edition

This casebound version of the text is offered as a courtesy to adopters. It is identical to the student version in terms of content, but offers a hard cover to help prevent wear and tear on the text. To order this special Teacher's Edition, contact your local Prentice Hall sales representative. (ISBN 978-0-13-221648-7)

Research Navigator™

Research Navigator™ is an ideal tool for instructors and students who need more resources for research. Available for qualified adopters, Research Navigator™ offers coverage of the research-writing process with three databases of source material, including EBSCO's *ContentSelect™*, *The New York Times* Search-by-Subject Archive, and a Literature Link Library. Take a tour on the Web at <http://www.researchnavigator.com>.

Acknowledgments

We would like to thank the countless instructors, students, and editorial and production teams who have contributed their time and ideas to *Anthology of American Literature.* For the ninth edition, thanks is particularly extended to Libby Walker, Christine Wharton, Philip Leon, James Hutchisson, Licia Calloway, David Allen, and Sean Heuston of The Citadel; Larry Carlson and Scott Peeples of the College of Charleston; and James Wharton Leonard of Duke University. We also wish to thank the reviewers who provided us with valuable feedback: Ann Baker of North Carolina State University, David Stout of Luzerne County Community College, David Thibodaux of University of Louisiana–Lafayette, Katherine Grimes of Ferrum College, and Phillip Sterling of Ferris State University.

We would also like to express our gratitude to the Prentice Hall publishing team: Vivian Garcia, Leah Jewell, Ann Marie McCarthy, Barbara Reilly, and Christina Volpe. Additionally, we would like to thank our production editor, Kari Callaghan Mazzola of Big Sky Composition, and our permissions specialist, Michael Farmer.

THE EDITORS

About the Editors

JAMES S. LEONARD is Professor and Chair of the Department of English at The Citadel. He is the editor of *Making Mark Twain Work in the Classroom* (1999), coeditor of *Author-ity and Textuality: Current Views of Collaborative Writing* (1994) and *Satire or Evasion? Black Perspectives on Huckleberry Finn* (1992), coauthor of *The Fluent Mundo: Wallace Stevens and the Structure of Reality* (1988), editor of the *Mark Twain Circular* (since 1987), managing editor of *The Mark Twain Annual* (since 2004), and a major contributor to *The Greenwood Encyclopedia of Poets and Poetry* (2006) and *American History Through Literature* (2005). He is also the author of essays on other American literary figures such as Ralph Waldo Emerson, Herman Melville, Walt Whitman, Emily Dickinson, Henry James, and Eudora Welty. He received his Ph.D. from Brown University in 1983.

SHELLEY FISHER FISHKIN is Professor of English and Director of American Studies at Stanford University. She is the author, editor, or co-editor of forty books, including the award-winning *Was Huck Black? Mark Twain and African American Voices* (1993) and *From Fact to Fiction: Journalism and Imaginative Writing in America* (1988), as well as *Lighting Out for the Territory* (1997), *The Oxford Mark Twain* (1996), *The Historical Guide to Mark Twain* (2002), *Is He Dead? A Comedy in Three Acts by Mark Twain* (2004), *People of the Book: Thirty Scholars Reflect on Their Jewish Identity* (with Jeffrey Rubin-Dorsky) (1996), *Listening to Silences: New Essays in Feminist Criticism* (with Elaine Hedges) (1994), and *Sport of the Gods and Other Essential Writings by Paul Laurence Dunbar* (with David Bradley) (2005). She has also published more than eighty articles, essays, or reviews in publications including *American Quarterly, American Literature, Journal of American History, American Literary History,* and the *New York Times Book Review,* and has lectured on American literature in Belgium, Canada, Chile, China, France, Ireland, Israel, Italy, Japan, Korea, Mexico, the Netherlands, Portugal, Russia, Taiwan, Turkey, the United Kingdom, and throughout the United States.

A member of the first class of women to graduate from Yale College, she stayed on at Yale to earn her M.A. in English and her Ph.D. in American

Studies. Before her arrival at Stanford, she directed the Poynter Fellowship in Journalism at Yale and taught American Studies and English at the University of Texas at Austin, where she chaired the American Studies Department. She co-founded the Charlotte Perkins Gilman Society and is a past president of the Mark Twain Circle of America and the American Studies Association.

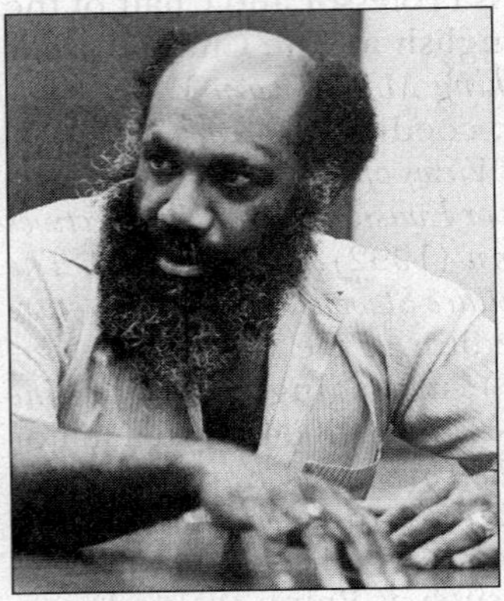

DAVID BRADLEY earned a B.A. in Creative Writing at the University of Pennsylvania in 1972 and an M.A. in United States Studies at the University of London in 1974. A Professor of English at Temple University from 1976 to 1997, Bradley has been a visiting professor at the San Diego State University, the University of California–San Diego, the Massachusetts Institute of Technology, Colgate University, the College of William & Mary, the City College of the City University of New York, and the Michener Center for Writers at the University of Texas, Austin. He is currently an Associate Professor of Fiction in the Creative Writing Program at the University of Oregon.

Bradley has read and lectured extensively in the United States and also in Japan, Korea, Pakistan, the United Kingdom, South Africa, and Australia. He is the author of two novels, *South Street* (1975) and *The Chaneysville Incident* (1981), which was awarded the 1982 PEN/Faulkner Award and an Academy Award from the American Academy and Institute of Arts and Letters. His nonfiction has appeared in *Esquire, Redbook, The New York Times, The Los Angeles Times,* and *The New Yorker.* In addition, he is a recipient of fellowships from the John Simon Guggenheim Foundation and the National Endowment for the Arts. His most recent publication is semi-scholarly: *Sport of the Gods and Other Essential Writings by Paul Laurence Dunbar,* which he co-edited with Shelley Fisher Fishkin. His current works-in-progress include a creative nonfiction book, *The Bondage Hypothesis: Meditations on Race, History, and America,* a novel-in-stories, *Raystown,* and an essay collection, *Lunch Bucket Pieces: New and Selected Creative Nonfiction.*

DANA D. NELSON received her Ph.D. from Michigan State, and she is the Gertrude Conaway Vanderbilt Professor of English and American Studies at Vanderbilt University. She is the author of *The Word in Black and White: Reading "Race" in American Literature, 1638–1867* (1992) and *National Manhood: Capitalist Citizenship and the Imagined Fraternity of White Men* (1998), as well as editor of several reprint editions of nineteenth-century American female writers (including Rebecca Rush, Lydia Maria Child, Fanny Kemble, and Frances Butler Leigh). Her teaching interests include comparative

American colonial literatures, developing democracy in the eighteenth and nineteenth centuries, ethnic and minority literatures, women's literature, and frontier representations in literature.

She has served or is serving on numerous editorial boards, including *American Literature, Early American Literature, American Literary History, Arizona Quarterly,* and *American Quarterly.* She is an active member of the Modern Language Association and the American Studies Association. She is currently working on two books: The first argues that presidentialism is bad for U.S. democracy, and the second studies developing practices and representations of democracy in the late British colonies and the early United States.

JOSEPH CSICSILA is Associate Professor of English Language and Literature at Eastern Michigan University. He is the author of *Canons by Consensus: Critical Trends and American Literature Anthologies* (2004), the first systematic study of American literature textbooks used by college instructors in the past century. Csicsila is a specialist in nineteenth- and early twentieth-century American literature and culture, and his essays on Mark Twain, Mary Wilkins Freeman, William Faulkner, and other American literary figures have appeared in numerous journals. Currently he serves as Executive Coordinator of the Mark Twain Circle of America.

The Literature of the Late Nineteenth Century

By the end of the Civil War (1861–1865), powerful forces had emerged that would dominate life in twentieth-century America. The Emancipation Proclamation and the Thirteenth Amendment to the U.S. Constitution had legally freed African Americans from nearly four centuries of bondage in America. The industrial North had triumphed over the agrarian South. From that victory came a society based on mass labor and mass consumption. Steam power began to replace water power, and machines driven by steam engines supplanted traditional hand labor in factories and on farms. In the 1770s, Thomas Jefferson had voiced the hope that the majority of Americans would never be "occupied at a work bench, for those who labor in the earth are the chosen people of God." But after 1865, the United States ceased to be the white agrarian democracy that Jefferson had cherished. It became instead the most heavily industrialized nation in the world, and its people in ever-greater numbers ceased to "labor in the earth" and moved to towns and cities to labor on the machines of new industries.

The Effects of Industrialization

As industrialism spread, the nature of labor changed. Machines displaced most of the hand labor previously required in manufacturing. Independent, skilled handcraftsmen became obsolete, unable to compete with machines operated by semiskilled laborers twenty-four hours a day, seven days a week. And the machines, with their great cost and high efficiency, came to be seen by mill owners and factory managers as far more valuable and useful than the workers who ran them. As a result, traditional relationships between employers and craftsmen weakened and grew more impersonal. In giant corporations that employed hundreds, even thousands, the workers no longer knew their customers, no longer even saw their employers. Nonetheless, great numbers of men, women, and children—native-born and foreign-born—flocked to American cities, drawn by hopes for steady factory work and high factory pay.

Power Surges

In the cities—swollen with growing numbers of the poor and unskilled—great political change was taking place. As more people of the urban underclasses sought, and found, power at the polls, the centers of political power shifted. Traditional political alliances weakened and new political groups emerged, taking their power from, and proclaiming their devotion to, the laboring classes.

Amid the upheavals of the time, the art of political patronage and graft rose to new heights in the United States, causing the first grand age of American civic corruption. Confused voters, new to the ballot box, elected big-city bosses and their henchmen who flourished on kickbacks and fraud, boldly collected their boodle, and scoffed at the law. In six years, during the 1860s and 1870s, New York's "Boss" William Tweed and his "Tweed Ring" of municipal crooks cost the city of New York an estimated two hundred million dollars, equal to more than two billion dollars in the 1990s. And during the presidency of Ulysses S. Grant (1869–1877) the crimes of high federal officials were exposed in scandals then unequaled in the history of the United States. The actions of Grant in protecting his political cronies and ignoring their blatant misdeeds led many Americans to conclude that the president of the United States was himself a common thief. American government, at all levels, seemed overrun with rascals.

During the Civil War the power of the national government dramatically expanded. For the first time, federal authority intruded directly into the lives of the majority of the people. The war brought the first national conscription laws and marked the first time that federal income taxes were levied. It also brought about the issuance of the first national currency—paper money backed by the federal government rather than by individual states and local banks. Rapid growth of federal power brought benefits and troubles. In 1865, the first official step toward nationwide racial equality was made when the Thirteenth Amendment to the Constitution was adopted, abolishing slavery within the United States, except as punishment for a crime. And the federal government used its powers to encourage business growth and the exploitation of natural resources, creating vast new wealth.

But great riches and economic power were, as always, concentrated in the hands of the few: bankers and industrialists who touted the glories of "business and bustle," business luminaries who revered the virtues of self-help. The laudatory term "Captain of Industry" was coined in the 1880s as business and financial tycoons came for the first time to be celebrated as national heroes, as models for young men who hoped to rise in the world through luck and pluck. It was the beginning of what Mark Twain called "The Gilded Age," an age of extremes—of decline and progress, of poverty and wealth, of gloom and hope.

Mass Communication and Migration

In the last half of the nineteenth century, Americans ceased to be isolated from the world and from each other. Coast-to-coast overland mail service began in 1858—a letter could be sent from St. Louis to San Francisco in as little as four weeks. In 1860, the Pony Express cut that time to ten and a half days. And within a year a message could be sent from New York to San Francisco in seconds, on the new telegraph line that spanned the nation in 1861. A transatlantic telegraph cable joined America and Europe in 1866. Ten years later, Alexander Graham Bell patented his invention of the telephone. By 1900 the United States had 1,356,000 telephones—twice as many as all of Europe.

If the telegraph and the telephone helped to bring Americans closer together, the railroads finally "united" the United States. The first railroad, the Baltimore and Ohio, began operation in 1830 with 13 miles of track. In 1869, the first transcontinental railroad was completed, linking the Atlantic and the Pacific. Five years later railroad mileage exceeded 74,000 miles, and the United States had the most extensive railroad system in the world. By 1889, the trip across the continent that had taken as much as five months by wagon during the Gold Rush of 1849 could now be made in trains (with Pullman sleepers and dining cars) in 108 hours—little more than four days.

With the building of the railroads came rapid commercial development. Vast new lands reached by rail lines were put under the plow, bringing enormous increases in farm products. The production of livestock and wheat doubled, tripled, and even quadrupled. New Yorkers could now eat beef shipped in newly invented refrigerator cars all the way from the slaughterhouses of Chicago; Floridians could buy inexpensive flour from mills in Minneapolis. Enterprising merchants like Richard Sears and Montgomery Ward created nationwide retail organizations that could undersell local shopkeepers. The clothing, household goods, and farm equipment once made locally by costly handwork were replaced by inexpensive, mass-produced goods made from standardized patterns in centralized factories. The nation was becoming a single giant marketplace, and retail stores that sold ready-made clothes and prepackaged foods began to resemble the stores of modern America, where the same goods, displayed in the same ways, are sold from one end of the land to the other. Indisputably, the coming of the railroads changed how Americans worked, where they lived, how they ate, how they dressed. In 1883, the railroads even changed the way Americans kept time when the more than fifty-six time zones in the United States were reduced to four to promote greater efficiency in scheduling railroad traffic.

As transportation became more convenient, better, and cheaper, the nation's people became increasingly mobile. In the last surge of westward expansion, mass numbers of Americans and immigrant Europeans, lured by the promise of free land, migrated to the Great Plains and the mountain states—extending the United States from the Atlantic to the Pacific. Vast areas were no longer unknown and unexplored; by 1890, "the frontier"—the westward-moving line of settlement begun three hundred years before on the Atlantic Coast—ceased to exist, although its influence would remain, shaping the life of the nation and inspiring legends, novels, and western movies by which the world would come to know America.

Westward expansion brought more land for white settlers and a broader material base for national power, but at great costs for some. The fabled "closing of the American frontier" brought the subjugation of Native American tribes and an institutionalized attack on their cultures, culminating projects that had begun in the seventeenth century among the colonizing powers. Following the U.S. Civil War, the cultures of America's plains Indians were especially vibrant, in part because they made productive use of horses, guns, tools, and other goods they had purchased in trade with Europeans since early contact. But the combined onslaught of a concerted U.S. war against them in the 1870s and 1880s, the ongoing ravages of smallpox, white hunters' mercenary destruction of the buffalo, and growing incursions fueled by white settlers' land hunger, gold fever and Indian-hating attitudes, succeeded in bringing once-proud and powerful Indian tribes into formal "submission" and onto reservations—often at a distance from their traditional lands—designated for them by the U.S. government.

The age that saw the final subjugation of the Indians and the ending of the frontier was also an age of steel and steam, electricity and oil. From the Civil War to World War I, steel production in the United States increased more than six hundred times, and steelmaking became the nation's dominant industry. Alternating electrical current was introduced in 1886. Incandescent lamps illuminated the cities with electricity provided by giant, steam-driven dynamos. The tallow candles and whale-oil lamps of rural America were replaced by lanterns filled with inexpensive kerosene made from crude oil. The American petroleum industry began, and with it came the age of the automobile.

From 1870 to 1890, the total population of the United States doubled. Villages became towns, towns became cities, and cities grew to a size and with a speed that would have astonished the Founding Fathers. From 1860 to 1910, Philadelphia's population tripled, New York City's quadrupled, and Chicago's increased twenty times to 2 million, making it the nation's second-largest city.

As the population doubled, the national income quadrupled, and by the mid-1890s the United States could boast four thousand millionaires. The rich prospered mightily, and prodigious fortunes were piled up by industrial and banking magnates such as John D. Rockefeller, Andrew Carnegie, and J. Pierpont Morgan. The growth of big business and big industry also widened further the gulf between the rich and the poor, giving rise to reform movements and labor unions that voiced the grievances of debt-ridden farmers and immigrant workers who lived in city slums and labored in giant, impersonal factories.

Broadening Civil Rights

Following the Civil War, the Congress of the United States passed a stringent series of Reconstruction Acts to force its will upon the South and to protect black freedmen. Voting rights were established for black men, along with the right to testify in courts, to serve on juries, to own property, and to hold public office. But by 1877, with the end of Reconstruction and the withdrawal from the South of the last federal occupying troops, most of the newly won rights for blacks began to erode. Well before the end of the century, poll taxes and literacy tests were legalized and used to disqualify black voters. Separate and unequal schools and public facilities were created; legal rights were denied in both the North and the South. Thousands of black Americans were lynched in the last decades of the nineteenth century. White supremacy was firmly re-established, and blacks were segregated to lives of poverty and indignity.

With the success of the abolitionist movement, white women continued to press for full political enfranchisement. Women entered the workforce in growing numbers, although many would only be able to find work performing menial tasks. When the doors of higher education finally opened to upper-class white women, many intended to improve their circumstances by attending the new all-female colleges, including Vassar, Wellesley, and Smith. Even with these improvements, however, women would not gain the right to vote from the federal government until 1922.

Immigration dropped sharply during the Civil War, but after the 1880s a rising tide of foreigners, beckoned by the American promise of jobs and political freedom, came to the New World at such a rate that by 1910 more than a third of the population of America's largest cities was foreign-born. Large-scale immigration and technical advancements in industry and agriculture increased the need for literacy, creating a demand for widespread public education. In the fifty years following the Civil War, the number of high schools in the United

States increased thirty-five times. Higher education ceased to be a privilege limited to children of the well-to-do. Under the Morrill Act of 1862, millions of acres of federal land were given to the states for the establishment of public "land-grant" universities for "the liberal and practical education of the industrial classes."

Developing Cultural Ideals

Increased wealth, and the desire for its conspicuous display, gave rise to a gingerbread era of American design whose prime function was to attract attention. American millionaires built Gothic and Romanesque mansions and decorated them with towers, domes, columns, stained-glass windows, and ornamental gimcracks of wood and iron. Looking across the Atlantic for cultural guidance, they filled their rooms with imported European art, adopted European dress styles and manners, sent their sons to Europe for an education, eagerly married off their daughters to European noblemen (many of them impoverished, some of them bogus), attended theatrical productions in which British actors performed, and listened to music written by European composers.

After 1865, a strong national tradition in painting began to develop, apparent in the work of such artists as Thomas Eakins, who realistically portrayed the America he saw around him and who urged his students "to remain in America, to peer deeper into the heart of American life." But numerous artists saw opportunity elsewhere and preferred to lead expatriate lives in Europe. Among them were the most renowned American painters of the period: James McNeill Whistler and John Singer Sargent. In a land of triumphant materialism, high culture had little impact on the mass of the people, who sought and found their entertainment in circuses, in vaudeville shows, in the new professional sports, and, after the 1890s, in motion-picture theaters named "nickelodeons" after their five-cent admission fee.

Literary Pursuits: Romanticism, Realism, and Naturalism

In the latter half of the nineteenth century, technical improvements in printing, lower costs for paper, and the rise of national corporations that could pour money into newspaper and magazine advertisements caused the growth of a great variety of low-cost, general-interest publications. From 1865 to 1905, the total number of periodicals published in the United States increased from about 700 to more than 6,000, all trying to satisfy the appetites of a vast new reading audience that was hungry for news articles, essays, fiction, and poems.

At this time, women became the nation's dominant cultural force and ladies' journalism began to flourish. In 1891, the *Ladies Home Journal* (founded in 1883) became the first American magazine with a circulation exceeding half a million; by 1905, its circulation had reached a full million. A new generation of women authors appeared whose poetry and fiction was published in popular ten-cent monthly and weekly magazines. Harriet Beecher Stowe, the author of *Uncle Tom's Cabin* (1852), had become an American institution and the most famous literary woman in the world. Other writers, including Sarah Orne Jewett, Kate Chopin, Mary Wilkins Freeman, and Louisa May Alcott published widely and achieved significant readerships as well.

Americans continued to read the works of Irving, Cooper, Hawthorne, and Poe, but by the 1870s, Hawthorne and Thoreau had died; Emerson, Lowell, Longfellow, Holmes, and Whittier had passed their literary zeniths. Melville, living in obscurity, had ceased to publish his fiction. Only Whitman continued to offer a new literary vision to the world, issuing a fifth edition of *Leaves of Grass* in 1870 and publishing *Democratic Vistas* in 1871. As New England's cultural dominance waned, New York replaced Boston as the nation's literary center, drawing writers from New England, the South, and the West to the publishing houses and periodicals of the nation's largest city.

New writers appeared, among them Bret Harte, William Dean Howells, and Mark Twain, whose background and training, unlike those of the older generation they displaced, were middle-class and journalistic rather than genteel or academic. Influenced by such Europeans as Zola, Flaubert, Balzac, Dostoyevsky, and Tolstoy, America's new and noteworthy authors sought to portray American life as they saw it, insisting that the ordinary and the local were just as suitable for artistic portrayal as the magnificent and the remote.

As in most literary rebellions, the new literature rose out of the authors' desire to renovate the literary theories of a previous age. The realists had what Henry James called "a powerful impulse to mirror the unmitigated realities of life." Earlier in the nineteenth century, James Fenimore Cooper had insisted on the author's right to avoid representations of "squalid misery" and to present instead an idealized and "poetic" portrait of life. But by the end of the nineteenth century the realists, and the literary naturalists who followed them, had turned away from the portrayal of idealized characters and events. Instead, they sought to describe the wide range of American experience and to present the subtleties of human personality, to portray characters who were neither all good nor all bad.

Realism had originated in France as *réalisme*, a literary doctrine that called for "reality and truth" in the depiction of ordinary life. Realism first appeared in the United States in the literature of local color, an amalgam of romantic plots and realistic descriptions of things immediately observable: the dialects, customs, sights, and sounds of regional America. Bret Harte in the 1860s was the first American writer of local color to achieve wide popularity. He presented stories about western mining towns populated by colorful gamblers, outlaws, and scandalous women. Thereafter editors—ever sensitive to public taste—demanded regional stories and tales of the life of America's Westerners, Southerners, and Easterners; writers such as Bret Harte, Harriet Beecher Stowe, Kate Chopin, Joel Chandler Harris, and Mark Twain provided them. Local-color fiction reached its peak of popularity in the 1880s.

The arbiter of nineteenth-century literary realism in America was William Dean Howells. He defined realism as "nothing more and nothing less than the truthful treatment of material," and he best exemplified his theories in such novels as *A Modern Instance* (1882), *The Rise of Silas Lapham* (1885), and *A Hazard of New Fortunes* (1890). Howells spoke for a generation of writers who found their subject matter in the experiences of the American middle class, describing their home lives, jobs, social customs, successes, and failures. The bulk of America's literary realism was limited to optimistic treatment of the surface of life. Yet the greatest of America's realists, Henry James and Mark Twain, moved well beyond a surface portrayal of nineteenth-century America. James probed deeply into the individual psychology of his characters, writing in a rich and intricate style that supported his intense scrutiny of complex human experience. Twain, breaking out of the limits of local-color fiction, wrote *Huckleberry Finn* (1884). The book was highly praised, and although Twain engaged issues of race, slavery, and unexamined white privilege, he, like most white writers of this time, wrote from the ideological perspective of his own culture—a society where people of color rarely appeared and were always subordinate. The suffering and oppression of Native Americans, African Americans, Chinese immigrants, and others were invisible in most white literary production. Readers had to look to the works of writers like Zitkala-Sa (Lakota Sioux), Sui Sin Far, Ida B. Wells-Barnet, Charles Chesnutt, and Frances E. W. Harper for reflections of the lives of Americans of color.

In the 1880s, Howells spoke out against the writing of a bleak fiction of failure and despair. He called for the treatment of the "smiling aspects of life" as being the more "American," insisting that America was truly a land of hope and of possibility that should be reflected in its literature. But at the end of the century came a generation of writers whose ideas of the workings of the universe and whose perception of society's disorders led them to naturalism, a new and harsher realism. America's literary naturalists scorned the idea that literature should present comforting moral truths. Instead, naturalist writers attempted to achieve extreme objectivity and frankness, presenting characters of low social and economic classes who were dominated by their environment and heredity. Naturalists emphasized that the world was amoral, that men and women had no free will, that their lives were controlled by heredity and the environment, that religious "truths" were illusory, that the destiny of humanity was misery in life and oblivion in death.

Naturalism, like realism, had come from Europe. In America it had been shaped by the Civil War, and by the teachings of Charles Darwin. Darwinism suggested that people are dominated by the irresistible forces of evolution. The pessimism and deterministic ideas of naturalism pervaded the works of such writers as Stephen Crane, Frank Norris, Jack London, Henry Adams, Charlotte Perkins Gilman, and Theodore Dreiser. They wrote detailed descriptions of the lives of the downtrodden; they offered frank treatment of human passion and sexuality; they portrayed men and women overwhelmed by the blind forces of nature—all of which had a powerful influence on modern writers.

Realism and naturalism remained popular with writers at the turn of the century. Writers of the early 1900s, including Edwin Arlington Robinson, Willa Cather, Robert Frost, and William Faulkner, achieved great success by depicting a "real" America and celebrating what they perceived to be commonplace truths of a new land and a new people. As the twentieth century progressed, these voices would be heard among others, including those of American blacks and other marginalized peoples, in mainstream America.

You can find more general resources about this period on our Companion Website™ at <www.prenhall.com/mcmichael>.

International Affairs, Exploration, Settlement, and Science

1867 Typewriter invented
1867 U.S. buys Alaska from Russia for $7.2 million
1867 British establish The Dominion of Canada. Alfred Nobel patents dynamite
1868 First commercial typewriter patented

1869 Vacuum cleaner invented
1869 Transcontinental railroad completed

1870 National census: population 39,818,494

1871 Charles Darwin publishes *The Descent of Man*

1876 General Custer and 265 men killed at Little Bighorn, Montana
1876 Alexander Graham Bell patents the telephone

Politics and Government

1861–1865 American Civil War
1862 First Federal income tax
1862 Lincoln issues Emancipation Proclamation
1863 Lincoln delivers Gettysburg Address
1864 Lincoln reelected
1865 Lee surrenders at Appomatox
1865 Lincoln assassinated. Andrew Johnson becomes president
1865 13th Amendment abolishes slavery

1867 U.S. buys Alaska for $7.2 million
1867 Reconstruction begins in American South

1868 Congress approves 8-hour day for federal employees
1868 14th Amendment grants black Americans citizenship
1868 U.S. Grant elected president. Reelected 1872
1869 Wyoming passes first U.S. woman-suffrage law

1870 Virginia, Mississippi, Texas, and Georgia readmitted to the Union

Society and Culture

1862 Julia Ward Howe publishes "The Battle Hymn of the Republic"

1863 Lincoln's "Gettysburg Address"

1865 Mark Twain publishes "The Celebrated Jumping Frog of Calaveras County"

1866 Whittier publishes *Snow-Bound*

1868 Louisa May Alcott publishes *Little Women*

1869 Mark Twain publishes *Innocents Abroad*
1869 First professional baseball team, Cincinnati Red Stockings, established
1869 First intercollegiate football game. Rutgers defeats Princeton

1872 Mark Twain publishes *Roughing It*
1876 National Baseball League founded
1876 Mark Twain publishes *Tom Sawyer*

International Affairs, Exploration, Settlement, and Science

1878 Bicycles first manufactured in U.S.
1878 Edison patents phonograph
1879 Edison invents workable incandescent lightbulb
1880 First important gold strike in Alaska
1881 First electric light power plant built, in New York
1882 Indian chief Geronimo captured; Plains Indian warfare ends
1883 Brooklyn Bridge completed
1884 Hiram Maxim invents machine gun
1884 Steam turbine invented
1885 Automobile invented
1887 First true golf course built
1888 First successful electric trolley line opened. First Kodak hand camera developed
1890 As settlement expands, American frontier disappears. National census: 62,947,714

Politics and Government

1877 Reconstruction ends. All federal troops withdrawn from the South
1877 Chief Joseph leads Nez Percé Indians in battles with U.S. Army
1880 Chinese Treaty (limiting immigration) signed
1881 President Garfield assassinated. Chester Arthur becomes president
1883 Standard time zones established in U.S.
1884–1888 Woman Suffragettes form Equal Rights party, nominate woman candidate for president
1888 Department of Labor established
1889 Indian Territory (Oklahoma) opened to white settlement
1890 Sherman Anti-Trust Act passed

Society and Culture

1877 American Museum of Natural History opens in New York City
1877 Philadelphia Conservatory of Music founded
1878 Henry James publishes *Daisy Miller*
1879 Henry George publishes *Progress and Poverty*
1880 Salvation Army established in U.S.
1880 Metropolitan Museum of New York City opens
1880 Joel Chandler Harris publishes *Uncle Remus*
1881 American Red Cross formed
1881 Boston Symphony founded
1883 New York Metropolitan Opera House opens
1884 Mark Twain publishes *Huckleberry Finn*
1885 First "skyscraper" built in Chicago
1886 Statue of Liberty dedicated
1886 American Federation of Labor formed
1889 First All-American football team selected

International Affairs, Exploration, Settlement, and Science

1891 Edison patents motion-picture camera
1891 First zipper patented

1893 Cherokee Strip in Oklahoma opened for settlement

1895 King Gillette invents safety razor

1896 First public exhibition of motion pictures
1897 First American subway opens, in Boston
1897–1898 Gold Rush to the Canadian Klondike
1898 Spain cedes Guam, Puerto Rico, and the Philippines to the U.S. for $20 million

Politics and Government

1892 Grover Cleveland elected president

1894 Coxey's Army of protesters marches on Washington, D.C.
1894 U.S. recognizes Republic of Hawaii

1896 Rural free delivery of U.S. mail begins

1898 U.S. Battleship *Maine* blows up in Havana, Cuba harbor
1898–1899 Spanish-American War

Society and Culture

1891 James Naismith invents basketball
1891 International Copyright Law established

1893 Chicago World's Columbian Exposition

1894 Labor Day declared legal holiday

1895 Stephen Crane publishes *The Red Badge of Courage*

1897 Library of Congress completed

1898 First show of American Impressionist painters

1899 Scott Joplin introduces ragtime to white Americans
1899 Coca-Cola first bottled
1899 Sigmund Freud publishes *The Interpretation of Dreams*

*William Cullen Bryant	1794–1878
*Ralph Waldo Emerson	1803–1882
*Nathaniel Hawthorne	1804–1864
*James Russell Lowell	1819–1891
*Herman Melville	1819–1891
*Walt Whitman	1819–1892
*Emily Dickinson	1830–1886
Mark Twain	1835–1910
Bret Harte	1836–1902
William Dean Howells	1837–1920
Henry Adams	1838–1918
Ambrose Bierce	1842–1914
Henry James	1843–1916
George Washington Cable	1844–1925
Joel Chandler Harris	1848–1908
Sarah Orne Jewett	1849–1909
Kate Chopin	1851–1904
Mary E. Wilkins Freeman	1852–1930
Charles Waddell Chesnutt	1858–1932
Charlotte Perkins Gilman	1860–1935
Edith Wharton	1862–1937
Frank Norris	1870–1902
Stephen Crane	1871–1900
Theodore Dreiser	1871–1945
Jack London	1876–1916

*Indicates authors who are covered in *Anthology of American Literature, Volume I.*

Reading the Historical Context

The Civil War of 1861–1865 was a national trauma of huge proportions. In its aftermath Mark Twain and Albion Tourgée, among many others, attempted to bring to light its causes, its far-reaching effects, and the problems involved in "reconstructing" not only the ravaged South but the war-torn American psyche. In the following two excerpts, Twain concentrates on what he saw as the frame of mind that led the South into its disastrous stand in defense of its slaveholding tradition, while Tourgée concentrates on the scandalous violence perpetrated after the war by groups such as the Ku Klux Klan in an attempt to block the Reconstruction plans of the Republican Party and return the South, insofar as possible, to its antebellum condition.

Mark Twain (Samuel L. Clemens)
1835–1910

Samuel Langhorne Clemens, better known by his pen-name Mark Twain, was born in Missouri, a slaveholding state, and grew up there. As a young man he became a riverboat pilot on the Mississippi and continued in that occupation until a blockade of the river during the Civil War made it impossible for him to continue. Many years later, in the 1880s, Twain, by then a famous writer of novels and travel books, returned to the Mississippi, traveled along its length, and wrote a new travel book called Life on the Mississippi, *which was published in 1883. It was something of a hodgepodge, as his travel books tended to be, of descriptions of scenery and culture, reminiscences of the past, amusing anecdotes, and essays on various subjects. In the following excerpt from* Life on the Mississippi, *Twain focuses on the Southern fascination with the novels of Sir Walter Scott and finds in that a suggestive correlation with what he sees as a fatal flaw in the traditional Southern culture.*

TEXT: *Life on the Mississippi*, 1883.

from *LIFE ON THE MISSISSIPPI*

[SIR WALTER SCOTT AND THE SOUTHERN CHARACTER][1]

The largest annual event in New Orleans is a something which we arrived too late to sample—the Mardi-Gras festivities. I saw the procession of the Mystic Crew of Comus there, twenty-four years ago—with knights and nobles and so on, clothed in silken and golden Paris-made gorgeousnesses, planned and bought for that single night's use; and in their train all manner of giants, dwarfs, monstrosities, and other diverting grotesquerie—a startling and wonderful sort

[1]This excerpt is taken from Chapter 46 (Enchantments and Enchanters) of *Life on the Mississippi*.

of show, as it filed solemnly and silently down the street in the light of its smoking and flickering torches; but it is said that in these latter days the spectacle is mightily augmented, as to cost, splendor, and variety. There is a chief personage—"Rex"; and if I remember rightly, neither this king nor any of his great following of subordinates is known to any outsider. All these people are gentlemen of position and consequence; and it is a proud thing to belong to the organization; so the mystery in which they hide their personality is merely for romance's sake, and not on account of the police.

Mardi-Gras is of course a relic of the French and Spanish occupation; but I judge that the religious feature has been pretty well knocked out of it now. Sir Walter[2] has got the advantage of the gentlemen of the cowl and rosary, and he will stay. His medieval business, supplemented by the monsters and the oddities, and the pleasant creatures from fairy-land, is finer to look at than the poor fantastic inventions and performances of the reveling rabble of the priest's day, and serves quite as well, perhaps, to emphasize the day and admonish men that the grace-line between the worldly season and the holy one is reached.

This Mardi-Gras pageant was the exclusive possession of New Orleans until recently. But now it has spread to Memphis and St. Louis and Baltimore. It has probably reached its limit. It is a thing which could hardly exist in the practical North; would certainly last but a very brief time; as brief a time as it would last in London. For the soul of it is the romantic, not the funny and the grotesque. Take away the romantic mysteries, the kings and knights and big-sounding titles, and Mardi-Gras would die, down there in the South. The very feature that keeps it alive in the South—girly-girly romance—would kill it in the North or in London. Puck and Punch, and the press universal, would fall upon it and make merciless fun of it, and its first exhibition would be also its last.

Against the crimes of the French Revolution and of Bonaparte may be set two compensating benefactions: the Revolution broke the chains of the *ancien régime* and of the Church, and made of a nation of abject slaves a nation of freemen; and Bonaparte instituted the setting of merit above birth, and also so completely stripped the divinity from royalty, that whereas crowned heads in Europe were gods before, they are only men, since, and can never be gods again, but only figureheads, and answerable for their acts like common clay. Such benefactions as these compensate the temporary harm which Bonaparte and the Revolution did, and leave the world in debt to them for these great and permanent services to liberty, humanity, and progress.

Then comes Sir Walter Scott with his enchantments, and by his single might checks this wave of progress, and even turns it back; sets the world in love with dreams and phantoms; with decayed and swinish forms of religion; with decayed and degraded systems of government; with the sillinesses and emptinesses, sham grandeurs, sham gauds, and sham chivalries of a brainless and worthless long-vanished society. He did measureless harm; more real and lasting harm, perhaps, than any other individual that ever wrote. Most of the world has now outlived good part of these harms, though by no means all of them; but in our South they flourish pretty forcefully still. Not so forcefully as half a generation ago, perhaps, but still forcefully. There, the genuine and wholesome civilization of the nineteenth century is curiously confused and commingled

[2]British novelist Sir Walter Scott (1771–1832).

with the Walter Scott Middle-Age sham civilization; and so you have practical, common-sense, progressive ideas, and progressive works; mixed up with the duel, the inflated speech, and the jejune[3] romanticism of an absurd past that is dead, and out of charity ought to be buried. But for the Sir Walter disease, the character of the Southerner—or Southron, according to Sir Walter's starchier way of phrasing it—would be wholly modern, in place of modern and medieval mixed, and the South would be fully a generation further advanced than it is. It was Sir Walter that made every gentleman in the South a Major or a Colonel, or a General or a Judge, before the war; and it was he, also, that made these gentlemen value these bogus decorations. For it was he that created rank and caste down there, and also reverence for rank and caste, and pride and pleasure in them. Enough is laid on slavery, without fathering upon it these creations and contributions of Sir Walter.

Sir Walter had so large a hand in making Southern character, as it existed before the war, that he is in great measure responsible for the war. It seems a little harsh toward a dead man to say that we never should have had any war but for Sir Walter; and yet something of a plausible argument might, perhaps, be made in support of that wild proposition. The Southerner of the American Revolution owned slaves; so did the Southerner of the Civil War: but the former resembles the latter as an Englishman resembles a Frenchman. The change of character can be traced rather more easily to Sir Walter's influence than to that of any other thing or person.

One may observe, by one or two signs, how deeply that influence penetrated, and how strongly it holds. If one take up a Northern or Southern literary periodical of forty or fifty years ago, he will find it filled with wordy, windy, flowery "eloquence," romanticism, sentimentality—all imitated from Sir Walter, and sufficiently badly done, too—innocent travesties of his style and methods, in fact. This sort of literature being the fashion in both sections of the country, there was opportunity for the fairest competition; and as a consequence, the South was able to show as many well-known literary names, proportioned to population, as the North could.

But a change has come, and there is no opportunity now for a fair competition between North and South. For the North has thrown out that old inflated style, whereas the Southern writer still clings to it—clings to it and has a restricted market for his wares, as a consequence. There is as much literary talent in the South, now, as ever there was, of course; but its work can gain but slight currency under present conditions; the authors write for the past, not the present; they use obsolete forms, and a dead language. But when a Southerner of genius writes modern English, his book goes upon crutches no longer, but upon wings; and they carry it swiftly all about America and England, and through the great English reprint publishing houses of Germany—as witness the experience of Mr. Cable and Uncle Remus, two of the very few Southern authors who do not write in the Southern style. Instead of three or four widely-known literary names, the South ought to have a dozen or two—and will have them when Sir Walter's time is out.

A curious exemplification of the power of a single book for good or harm is shown in the effects wrought by "Don Quixote" and those wrought by "Ivanhoe."

[3]Childish.

The first swept the world's admiration for the medieval chivalry-silliness out of existence; and the other restored it. As far as our South is concerned, the good work done by Cervantes is pretty nearly a dead letter, so effectually has Scott's pernicious work undermined it.

1883

Albion Tourgée 1838–1905

Albion Tourgée was born in Ohio and lived in the Northern states before the Civil War. During the war he served as a soldier for the North, suffering both serious injuries and capture by the South. When the war ended he moved to North Carolina, where he became a judge and a political activist who supported Reconstruction policies but also tried to gain economic concessions to help the Southern states recover. In 1879 he published the book on which his literary reputation principally rests, A Fool's Errand, by One of the Fools, *which features descriptions of post-Civil War racial violence in the South by such groups as the Ku Klux Klan. In the following year he brought out a second edition of* A Fool's Errand, *with a second part, titled* The Invisible Empire, *attached.* The Invisible Empire, *a nonfiction work, offered statistical and documentary support for his contention that the fictional events portrayed in* A Fool's Errand *were based on the fact of racial violence that he had been exposed to during his time in North Carolina. The following selection (Chapters 2 and 3) from* The Invisible Empire *offers an explanation of the nature and background of the Ku Klux Klan and other related groups blamed for racial violence in the post-war South.*

TEXT: *A Fool's Errand. By One of the Fools. A Novel. Together with Part II, The Invisible Empire, An Historical Review of the Epoch on Which This Tale Is Based,* 1880.

from *THE INVISIBLE EMPIRE*

CHAPTER II

THE METHOD OF INQUIRY

In considering the actual condition of the South, it should be remembered that with the Southern people political prejudice is the strongest possible passion which can be aroused, and that such prejudice has very naturally been at fever-heat since the close of the war.

It should also be remembered that the orators and writers of the South have, with rare exceptions, been all upon one side of the political controversies of the day. Four-fifths of the whites of the South—in many sections nine-tenths, and not unfrequently a greater proportion of them—have been solidly arrayed against the remainder of their own race and the colored people. The white Republicans of the South must be rated below the average of their fellow-citizens in respect to wealth and intelligence, and especially in the matter of property. It is not probable that at any time more than one-fifth of the education and wealth of the South was held by Republicans. The press was almost entirely in the hands of the Democrats because a Republican press had small means of existence. To the class that tried to accept the new order of things, therefore, the power of utterance, the capacity for that continuous reiteration of facts which finally dins them into the public ear and fastens them upon the public conscience, was almost entirely denied. The press of the South is not representative of them, their thoughts, experiences, and desires, and indeed has never claimed to be. From the first it has declared itself to be the champion and representative of the "white people of the South," meaning that portion of the white race which did not coöperate politically with the blacks. It is consequently of little use to turn to their columns for testimony upon this subject, though we may notice some unconscious revelations which are startling in their character.

The great reservoir of undigested facts pertinent to this matter is the Report of the Joint Congressional Committee on the Ku-Klux Conspiracy, embracing thirteen closely printed octavo volumes, containing more than six thousand large pages, or the equivalent of *twenty-five thousand of the pages of this book.*

This exhaustless store of evidence is the result of an inquiry which was concluded in 1872, and was chiefly concerned with the events of the previous four years.

Just here it may be well to state a fact which has generally escaped the memory of Northern men who have not been especially concerned in political life, viz.: that the first State governments which went into operation under the Reconstruction Acts of Congress were organized about the first of July, 1868. Before that time the Johnsonian Provisional Governments were in operation, while the commanders of the various Military Districts had supervisory and discretionary power to modify or set aside their acts when deemed by them unjust and oppressive.[1] During this time there was, in effect, but one party at the South. The colored men had not then been admitted to the right of suffrage, and the old property qualifications in several of the States still applied to the white voters. The power of these Provisional Governments was solely in the hands of the majority of white voters, while the representation in the legislatures was based on population; the Union element of those States thus being in a minority so hopeless as to render it powerless for good or evil. Whatever struggle there was at the ballot-box was entirely local in its character, and almost always between individuals of varying shades of the same political faith. The administration of government and the enforcement of law during this time was lodged in the magistracy and officers appointed by these Provisional Governments, except in the few instances where they were superseded by appointees of the military commanders of the respective districts.

The Republican party was first organized in the South in the spring and summer of 1867 (just two years after the close of the war), and colored men first voted under the Reconstruction Acts at the elections held for delegates to Constitutional Conventions in the several States in the fall of that year.

Thus, it will be seen that the negro did not become a potential factor in Southern politics until the fall of 1867, and that no governments were organized through his influence or under Republican auspices until the midsummer of

[1]The Johnsonian Provisional Governments were state governments directly mandated by the Federal government, under President Andrew Johnson, for temporary governance immediately after the Civil War.

1868. These facts will be found to be of prime importance in considering the matters which will be laid before the reader, since they give a key, otherwise difficult to obtain, to the motive and spirit of the actors in the scenes of violence which marked these years and in various forms have continued until the present. Every reader should therefore fix in his mind at the outset these three points:

1. From the Surrender, in April, 1865, until July, 1868, the Provisional or Johnsonian State Governments existed at the South, with supervisory power in the commander of the Military District after the spring of 1867.
2. The Republican party was organized at the South in the spring of 1867, and colored men first voted in the fall of that year.
3. The first Reconstructionary Governments were organized, and the States readmitted under them, in July, 1868.

With these preliminary facts well in mind, we will go forward upon our path of inquiry. And if it seems to be a limited one, confined to the disclosure of a single line of development—the history, in fact, of the Ku-Klux organization—the reader will remember that this immense and efficient enginery, which in a few months overspread a territory larger than modern Europe, powerful enough to cope with a nation of conquerors, and exact enough to catch and grind to powder the most insignificant individual obnoxious to its hate, was the organic representative of the ideas, the sentiments, the intentions, and the determination of "the South." It is to be studied as an authenticated type, a recognized exponent.

The vast volume of the testimony taken by the Congressional Committee referred to, as well as the fact that their report proper presented no adequate summary or analysis of its character (as indeed it would be nearly impossible to do within the compass of such a report), has prevented the facts appearing therein from becoming generally known. Besides that, the nation had supped full of horrors in the decade of civil strife which it had just passed through, and the public mind was anxious to escape the consideration of such apparently remediless evils. It is none of our present purpose to attempt to summarize the entire contents of those volumes, but only to present extracts from the testimony which may serve to further illustrate and substantiate the narrative presented in the first part of this volume,[2] and to give some reasonable analysis of the underlying spirit, motive, and—so to speak—principle, that moved half a million men to these deeds of savagery. These instances, the striking similarity of many of which to the incidents already narrated will be noted at once, are taken chiefly from those volumes of the Report which embrace the inquiry relating to the States of Georgia and Alabama. They are but samples even of those, culled almost at random from pages overloaded with like testimony. They are but isolated cries which come up from a few individuals out of the thousands who lay stricken on the field where the hostile "civilizations" met in silent and unnoted but yet woeful conflict. These States are selected because they have usually been accounted as among the more peaceful. They have witnessed no wholesale slaughters like those of New Orleans and Memphis, of Hamburg and Ellenton. But the motive power is everywhere the same, and the few citations

[2]That is, Tourgée's novel *A Fool's Errand, by One of the Fools.*

here made will suffice to show the spirit, causes, and consequences of these acts, and direct the mind of every honest-minded citizen to the consideration of the remedy already suggested, as the true and only cure for the ills delineated.

In every instance the name of the witness and the volume and page on which his testimony may be found will be given, and in most cases also a brief statement of his standing and antecedents. The purpose is to invite scrutiny and awaken thought, and not to present argument or engage in controversy. The past is dead. Its acts are buried. The late Reverdy Johnson, when appearing as counsel for certain of the perpetrators, horrified by the testimony adduced in the course of the trial, threw up his hands and exclaimed: "It is simple savagery, for which there can be no excuse or palliation." We may echo this candid cry; and yet it would be an act of ghoulish horror to drag these things again to the light of day, were it not that the spirit which prompted, permitted, and excused such acts is but a part of that development which is termed "Southern civilization," and the effects of which are everywhere to be seen. As such, it constitutes a part of the present, and typifies a spirit which may at any moment burst forth afresh in the future.

The opinion has been ventured in "A Fool's Errand" that only GENERAL EDUCATION—*universal enlightenment of whites and blacks alike*—can be relied upon to change the spirit which moved these horrors, and that it is the first great duty of the Nation to provide for such enlightenment. How this may be done is a question for further consideration; but that it must be done, the history of freedom and Christian civilization as contrasted with this record leaves little in doubt. We ask any reader to consider the pages which follow and then deny that doctrine if he can—if he dare!

CHAPTER III

Rise, Scope, and Purpose of the Ku-Klux Klan

Referring to "A Fool's Errand," from page 170 onwards, and especially pages 244 to 252, for a general description of the rise of organized terrorism in the South, let us examine it more specifically. "The Ku-Klux," as a generic term, embraced the various orders of "The Constitutional Union Guards," "The White Brotherhood," "The Society of the Pale Faces," "The Knights of the White Camelia," "The Invisible Empire," and an order the name of which was represented in their printed documents only by stars, which Gen. N. B. Forrest[3] and other members declared had no name. Whether these various orders were different degrees of one organization, or were merely different names for the same thing in different localities, it is impossible to say. It would seem, from all that has become known, that the "Invisible Empire" was a higher grade, a more important and thoroughly guarded degree than the others—a ruling, controlling, and select circle, within and above the more numerous and popular grades of the order. It is a somewhat peculiar fact that though the signs, passwords, and

[3]Nathan Bedford Forrest (1821–1877) was a Confederate general renowned for brilliance as a cavalry officer. Although not the originator of the Ku Klux Klan, he lent it respectability by accepting appointment as its Grand Wizard. Under pressure from President Ulysses S. Grant, he later repudiated Klan violence and ordered its leaders to cease their operations.

general methods of procedure of the other branches of the Ku-Klux organizations were obtained from many sources, the information in regard to this was very scanty and unsatisfactory. A few admitted themselves to be members of it, but little if anything has ever been learned in regard to its organization and plan of operations. It was known to be an existent fact all over the South, and was generally believed by the members of the other kindred orders to be the directing and controlling central circle of them all.

This view is greatly strengthened by the fact that they all seem to have had a common origin, and all who speak with regard to the report in reference to its source accord the credit of its institution and supreme headship to Gen. N. B. Forrest, the noted Confederate cavalry general and the ill-famed hero of the massacre of Fort Pillow.[4]

From his own testimony, it appears that the order was first instituted in Tennessee during the year 1866, though it does not seem to have extended much beyond that State or to have attracted general public attention until about the first of 1868.[5] In January, 1868, so far as appears, the name *Ku-Klux Klan* first became a part of our printed vocabulary. In February of that year, the newspapers of the North began to herald its doings through the country as a huge joke which certain pretended ghostly night-riders were playing upon the ignorant freedmen of the South, making them believe that they were the spirits of slain Confederates hailing from hell and slain in some great battle, which was almost always Shiloh, a fact which in itself marks the South-Western origin of the invention. At this time the illustrated newspapers began to teem with caricatures of the disguised horsemen and frightened darkies; and the peculiar *clucks* which were used by them as a signal, and from which the organization has taken its best-known name, became familiar about this time to the street Arabs of the Northern cities. The country regarded it as a broad farce, not by any means accepting the old apothegm that "one might as well be killed as scared to death." It was thought to be a very pleasant and innocent amusement for the chivalry of the South to play upon the superstitious fears of the recently emancipated colored people. The nation held its sides with laughter, and the Ku-Klux took heart from these cheerful echoes and extended their borders without delay. It must be stated here, however, in palliation of this conduct of the North, that the previous murders and outrages by organized bands in Tennessee, reported by that wisest and noblest of our soldiers, Gen. Geo. H. Thomas, were not then known to have been committed by these men, and were not connected in the minds of the laughers with the grotesque uniforms of the Klan.

Between January and May of 1868, General Forrest seems to have visited nearly all of the Southern States, and immediately after his visit in each State there was a sudden and widespread reign of Ku-Klux horrors. He was in Georgia in February, and in North Carolina in March, 1868; both of which periods are fixed by the testimony as the dates on which the Ku-Klux was first heard of in those regions.

[4]Fort Pillow was a fort in western Tennessee, on the Mississippi River, which Forrest captured in April 1864. Union soldiers reported—apparently accurately, though it was denied by the Confederate forces—that many Union soldiers, especially black soldiers fighting for the North, were murdered by the Confederate soldiers after they had surrendered.

[5]The Ku Klux Klan was founded, as Tourgée correctly suggests, in 1866 in Pulaski, Tennessee by six young Confederate sympathizers.

WALTER BROCK, a lawyer and farmer of Haralson County, Ga., native of Arkansas and forty-three years old, giving a conversation with one Daniel Dodson, a confessed Ku-Klux, says:

"He told me that Wm. Pond commanded the den, but they had recently turned him out and put in another: he did not know who he was. He said they had each to pay his dollar, initiation-fee or something of that sort, and they paid it, and Billy failed to account for it to General Forrest, and they turned him out. . . . He told me that Gen. Forrest was the chief of the order." (*Reports,* Vol. 7: pp. 1012–1017.)

The first operation on the part of the Ku-Klux in Georgia was the killing of Senator Ashburn at Columbus, on the 31st of March, 1868. Rev. J. H. Caldwell, native of South Carolina, and Judge of the District Court for the 37th senatorial district of Georgia, testifies:

"Q.—Did you see any prominent person here from a neighboring State, about that time, who had been publicly rumored to be a prominent officer of the order?

"A.—Yes, sir; several—one in particular. . . . General Forrest. . . . I saw him and was introduced to him about the close of the convention, which adjourned on the 11th of March." (Vol. 6: pp. 432–433.)

Many other witnesses testify to the same general report. Gen. Forrest, in his own testimony, is careful not to deny such report, but tries to leave the inference that what he knew of the order was merely incidental. He says, however:

"I was getting at that time from one hundred to one hundred and fifty letters a day, and had a private secretary writing all the time. I was receiving letters from all over the Southern States, men complaining, whose friends had been killed or families insulted and they were writing to me to know what they ought to do." (Vol. 13: p. 9.)

This would be a very natural thing, if he were the "Grand Wizard of the Empire" (mentioned in the very interesting "Prescript" or constitution of the order, annexed to his testimony and beginning on page 35 of Vol. 13), whose duties are described in Art. IV as follows:

"DUTIES OF OFFICERS. *Grand Wizard.* Art. IV., Sec. 1. It shall be the duty of the Grand Wizard, who is the supreme officer of the empire, to communicate with and receive reports from the Grand Dragons of Realms as to the condition, strength, efficiency, and progress of the *s within their respective realms; and he shall communicate from time to time to all subordinate *s through the Grand Dragons the condition, strength, efficiency and progress of the *s throughout his vast empire, and such other information as he may deem expedient to impart. And it shall further be his duty to keep by his G. Scribe a list of the names (without any caption or explanation whatever) of the Grand Dragons of the different realms of his empire, and shall number such realms with the Arabic numerals, 1, 2, 3, &c., *ad finem.* And he shall instruct his Grand Exchequer as to the appropriation and disbursement which he shall make of the revenue of the *s that comes to his hands. He shall have the sole power to issue copies of this Prescript, through his subalterns and deputies, for the organization and establishment of subordinate *s. And he shall have the further power to appoint his Genii, also a Grand Scribe and a Grand Exchequer for his department, and to appoint and ordain Special Deputy Grand Wizards to assist him in the more rapid and effectual dissemination and establishment of *s throughout his Empire. He is further empowered to appoint and instruct deputies to organize and control realms, dominions, provinces, and dens, until the same shall elect a Grand Dragon, a Grand Titan, a Grand Giant, and a Grand Cyclops, in the manner hereinafter provided."

It is strongly in confirmation of Forrest's connection with the order, that that officer upon cross-examination was quite *unable to remember the name of his secretary,* did not know where he then was, and had not heard of him in eighteen months. However, with the amount of correspondence Gen. Forrest had on hand we may very well rely upon his statement in a letter under date of September 3d, 1868, as to the extent of the order.

Said he, "It was reported, and I believed the report, that there are *forty thousand* Ku-Klux in Tennessee; and I believe the organization stronger in other States." (Vol. 13: p. 35.)

Many witnesses testify to the numbers in the different States as reported by members of the band, all agreeing in the main with the above estimate. When the bill for amnesty to all who had been guilty of Ku-Klux outrages was before the Legislature of North Carolina in 1873, it was openly admitted and urged as an argument in favor of the passage of the bill that there were "from thirty to forty thousand members of the Klan" in that State. The general belief was that there were not less than *five hundred thousand* in the entire South. This belief is fully sustained by Gen. Forrest's estimate, which there is no doubt he stood in a position to make very accurate.

With the foregoing ideas as to the origin of this formidable "Empire," the vast area of territory it controlled and the magnificent army that served its behests, we naturally ask what was the impelling cause of this effort, and what the practical end to be gained by it.

There are several modes of getting a clear idea as to the aims of the organization. It is evident that no one motive was at the bottom of it, except the very broad and general one of an organized hostility to the elevation of the colored race, and, by consequence, to any and all things that might contribute to that—the Reconstruction Acts, negro suffrage, colored schools, Northern immigration with its revolutionary and "radical" ideas, and so on.

One of the plainest and most probable accounts of how and why the spread of this organization was welcomed by Southern men, of the better as well as of the lower grades, may be found in the testimony given before the committee by the Rev. A. S. LAKIN, who was in 1867 appointed by Archbishop Clark to go on traveling commission as Presiding Elder of the M. E. Church, in Montgomery District of Alabama, taking the names of Presiding Elders and preachers, with the amounts of money due to each, as their reports had been obstructed, drafts abstracted, and preachers were suffering. He traveled 650 miles throughout Northern Alabama in the saddle.

"In my travels," he says, "I put up with some of the leading men of the State, and learned from them this fact: that they never would submit; that they never would yield; they had lost their property, their reputation; and, last and worst of all, their slaves were made their equals, or were likely to be, and perhaps their superiors, to rule over them. In extended conversations with them I inquired how we would help ourselves. They said there was an organization, already very extensive and that would spread over the Southern States, that would rid them of this terrible calamity. I stated that we would be arrested and punished; that the government would visit upon us probably heavier punishments than any we had experienced. They said they could rule that and control it. I asked how, and they replied, 'Why, suppose a man drops out here'—meaning that they would kill him; 'while that is being investigated, another will drop out here, and there, and yonder, until the cases are so frequent and numerous that we will overwhelm the courts, and nothing can withstand the omnipotence of popular sentiment and public opinion.' I gathered these facts from various sources; they seemed to be patent. On my arrival at Huntsville, after this long and tedious tour, I learned of the organization of the Ku-Klux Klan. It answered precisely the description and seemed to answer precisely the design expressed by these leading men." (Vol. 8: pp. 111–112.)

1880

Reading the Critical Context

The period from the end of the Civil War until about 1900 is often termed the "Age of Realism" because the fiction of the period was dominated by a reaction against the idealizing tendencies of the romantic literature of the previous literary period, and by a turn toward fiction that would accurately portray the lives, actions, and speech of real human beings in such situations as they could reasonably be expected to encounter. Among the leading practitioners and theorists of this turn toward "realism" in fiction were William Dean Howells, Henry James, and Mark Twain. The essays that follow give concise representations of their ideas about the value of fiction and the standards to which they believed it should be held.

William Dean Howells 1837–1920

William Dean Howells was perhaps the most influential American literary figure of the late nineteenth century. A prolific novelist, he was also associate editor and then editor of the Atlantic Monthly *and later a columnist for* Harper's Magazine. *Both his own practice as a novelist and his essays articulating his literary principles, which became the mainstream principles of American literary realism, strongly impacted the writing of American fiction of his time and generated vigorous opposition from fiction writers and critics who regarded his realistic credo as a formula for soulless fiction. The following excerpts from his book of essays titled* Criticism and Fiction *set forth his objections to romanticism and his conception of what an "American realism" should be like.*

TEXT: *Criticism and Fiction*, 1891.

from *CRITICISM AND FICTION*[1]

II

[THE IDEAL GRASSHOPPER]

"As for those called critics," the author [Edmund Burke] says, "they have generally sought the rule of the arts in the wrong place; they have sought among poems, pictures, engravings, statues, and buildings; but art can never give the rules that make an art. This is, I believe, the reason why artists in general, and poets principally, have been confined in so narrow a circle; they have been rather imitators of one another than of nature. Critics follow them, and therefore can do little as guides. I can judge but poorly of anything while I measure it by no other standard than itself. The true standard of the arts is in every man's power; and an easy observation of the most common, sometimes of the meanest things, in nature will give the truest lights, where the greatest sagacity and industry that slights such observation must leave us in the dark, or, what is worse, amuse and mislead us by false lights."[2]

If this should happen to be true—and it certainly commends itself to acceptance—it might portend an immediate danger to the vested interests of criticism, only that it was written a hundred years ago; and we shall probably have the "sagacity and industry that slights the observation" of nature long enough yet to allow most critics the time to learn some more useful trade than criticism as they pursue it. Nevertheless, I am in hopes that the communistic era in taste foreshadowed by Burke is approaching, and that it will occur within the lives of men now overawed by the foolish old superstition that literature and art are anything but the expression of life, and are to be judged by any other test than that of their fidelity to it. The time is coming, I hope, when each new author, each new artist, will be considered, not in his proportion to any other author or artist, but in his relation to the human nature, known to us all, which it is his privilege, his high duty, to interpret. "The true standard of the artist is in every man's power" already, as Burke says; Michelangelo's[3] "light of the piazza," the glance of the common eye, is and always was the best light on a statue; Goethe's[4] "boys and blackbirds" have in all ages been the real connoisseurs of berries; but hitherto the mass of common men have been afraid to apply their own simplicity, naturalness, and honesty to the appreciation of the beautiful. They have always cast about for the instruction of some one who professed to know better, and who browbeat wholesome common-sense into the self-distrust that ends in sophistication. They have fallen generally to the worst of this bad species, and have been "amused[5] and misled" (how pretty that quaint old use of amuse is!) "by the false lights" of critical vanity and self-righteousness.

[1]A collection of essays selected from those published (1886 to 1891) in Howells's column, "The Editor's Study," in *Harper's Magazine*.

[2]From *Philosophical Inquiry into the Origins of Our Ideas on the Sublime and Beautiful* (1756) by Edmund Burke (1729–1797), British statesman and orator.

[3]Italian painter and sculptor (1475–1564).

[4]Johann Wolfgang von Goethe (1749–1832), German author.

[5]In the earlier meaning of "deceived."

They have been taught to compare what they see and what they read, not with the things that they have observed and known, but with the things that some other artist or writer has done. Especially if they have themselves the artistic impulse in any direction they are taught to form themselves, not upon life, but upon the masters who became masters only by forming themselves upon life. The seeds of death are planted in them, and they can produce only the still-born, the academic. They are not told to take their work into the public square and see if it seems true to the chance passer, but to test it by the work of the very men who refused and decried any other test of their own work. The young writer who attempts to report the phrase and carriage of every-day life, who tries to tell just how he has heard men talk and seen them look, is made to feel guilty of something low and unworthy by the stupid people who would like to have him show how Shakespeare's men talked and looked, or Scott's, or Thackeray's, or Balzac's, or Hawthorne's, or Dickens's;[6] he is instructed to idealize his personages, that is, to take the life-likeness out of them, and put the book-likeness into them. He is approached in the spirit of the wretched pedantry into which learning, much or little, always decays when it withdraws itself and stands apart from experience in an attitude of imagined superiority, and which would say with the same confidence to the scientist: "I see that you are looking at a grasshopper there which you have found in the grass, and I suppose you intend to describe it. Now don't waste your time and sin against culture in that way. I've got a grasshopper here, which has been evolved at considerable pains and expense out of the grasshopper in general; in fact, it's a type. It's made up of wire and cardboard, very prettily painted in a conventional tint, and it's perfectly indestructible. It isn't very much like a real grasshopper, but it's a great deal nicer, and it's served to represent the notion of a grasshopper ever since man emerged from barbarism. You may say that it's artificial. Well, it is artificial; but then it's ideal too; and what you want to do is to cultivate the ideal. You'll find the books full of my kind of grasshopper, and scarcely a trace of yours in any of them. The thing that you are proposing to do is commonplace; but if you say that it isn't commonplace, for the very reason that it hasn't been done before, you'll have to admit that its photographic."

As I said, I hope the time is coming when not only the artist, but the common, average man, who always "has the standard of the arts in his power," will have also the courage to apply it, and will reject the ideal grasshopper wherever he finds it, in science, in literature, in art, because it is not "simple, natural, and honest," because it is not like a real grasshopper. But I will own that I think the time is yet far off, and that the people who have been brought up on the ideal grasshopper, the heroic grasshopper, the impassioned grasshopper, the self-devoted, adventureful, good old romantic cardboard grasshopper, must die out before the simple, honest, and natural grasshopper can have a fair field. I am in no haste to compass the end of these good people, whom I find in the mean time very amusing. It is delightful to meet one of them, either in print or out of it—some sweet elderly lady or excellent gentleman whose youth was pastured on the literature of thirty or forty years ago—and to witness the confidence with which they preach their favorite authors as all the law and the

[6]Sir Walter Scott (1771–1832), Scottish novelist; William Makepeace Thackeray (1811–1863), English novelist; Honore de Balzac (1799–1850), French novelist; Charles Dickens (1812–1870), English novelist.

prophets. They have commonly read little or nothing since, or, if they have, they have judged it by a standard taken from these authors, and never dreamed of judging it by nature; they are destitute of the documents in the case of the later writers; they suppose that Balzac was the beginning of realism, and that Zola[7] is its wicked end; they are quite ignorant, but they are ready to talk you down, if you differ from them, with an assumption of knowledge sufficient for any occasion. The horror, the resentment, with which they receive any question of their literary saints is genuine; you descend at once very far in the moral and social scale, and anything short of offensive personality is too good for you; it is expressed to you that you are one to be avoided, and put down even a little lower than you have naturally fallen.

These worthy persons are not to blame; it is part of their intellectual mission to represent the petrifaction of taste, and to preserve an image of a smaller and cruder and emptier world than we now live in, a world which was feeling its way towards the simple, the natural, the honest, but was a good deal "amused and misled" by lights now no longer mistakable for heavenly luminaries. They belong to a time, just passing away, when certain authors were considered authorities in certain kinds, when they must be accepted entire and not questioned in any particular. Now we are beginning to see and to say that no author is an authority except in those moments when he held his ear close to Nature's lips and caught her very accent. These moments are not continuous with any authors in the past, and they are rare with all. Therefore I am not afraid to say now that the greatest classics are sometimes not at all great, and that we can profit by them only when we hold them, like our meanest contemporaries, to a strict accounting, and verify their work by the standard of the arts which we all have in our power, the simple, the natural, and the honest.

Those good people, those curious and interesting if somewhat musty backnumbers, must always have a hero, an idol of some sort, and it is droll to find Balzac, who suffered from their sort such bitter scorn and hate for his realism while he was alive, now become a fetich in his turn, to be shaken in the faces of those who will not blindly worship him. But it is no new thing in the history of literature: whatever is established is sacred with those who do not think. At the beginning of the century, when romance was making the same fight against effete classicism which realism is making to-day against effete romanticism, the Italian poet Monti[8] declared that "the romantic was the cold grave of the Beautiful," just as the realistic is now supposed to be. The romantic of that day and the real of this are in certain degree the same. Romanticism then sought, as realism seeks now, to widen the bounds of sympathy, to level every barrier against aesthetic freedom, to escape from the paralysis of tradition. It exhausted itself in this impulse; and it remained for realism to assert that fidelity to experience and probability of motive are essential conditions of a great imaginative literature. It is not a new theory, but it has never been universally characterized literary endeavor. When realism becomes false to itself, when it heaps up facts merely, and maps life instead of picturing it, realism will perish too. Every true realist instinctively knows this, and it is perhaps the reason why he is careful of every fact, and feels himself bound to express or to indicate its meaning at the

[7]Emile Zola (1840–1902), French naturalistic writer.
[8]Vincenzo Monti (1754–1828), Italian poet.

risk of overmoralizing. In life he finds nothing insignificant; all tells for destiny and character; nothing that God has made is contemptible. He cannot look upon human life and declare this thing or that thing unworthy of notice, any more than the scientist can declare a fact of the material world beneath the dignity of his inquiry. He feels in every nerve the equality of things and the unity of men; his soul is exalted, not by vain shows and shadows and ideals, but by realities, in which alone the truth lives. In criticism it is his business to break the images of false gods and misshapen heroes, to take away the poor silly toys that many grown people would still like to play with. He cannot keep terms with Jack the Giant-killer or Puss in Boots, under any name or in any place, even when they appear as the convict Vautrec, or the Marquis de Montrivaut, or the Sworn Thirteen Noblemen.[9] He must say to himself that Balzac, when he imagined these monsters, was not Balzac, he was Dumas;[10] he was not realistic, he was romantic.

XXI

[AMERICAN FICTION]

It is no doubt such work as Mr. James's that an English essayist (Mr. E. Hughes[11]) has chiefly in mind, in a study of the differences of the English and American novel. He defines the English novel as working from within outwardly, and the American novel as working from without inwardly. The definition is very surprisingly accurate; and the critic's discovery of this fundamental difference is carried into particulars with a distinctness which is as unfailing as the courtesy he has in recognizing the present superiority of American work. He seems to think, however, that the English principle is the better, though why he should think so he does not make so clear. It appears a belated and rather voluntary effect of patriotism, disappointing in a philosopher of his degree; but it does not keep him from very explicit justice to the best characteristics of our fiction. "The American novelist is distinguished for the intellectual grip which he has of his characters. . . . He penetrates below the crust, and he recognizes no necessity of the crust to anticipate what is beneath. . . . He utterly discards heroics; he often even discards anything like a plot. . . . His story proper is often no more than a natural predicament. . . . It is no stage view we have of his characters, but one behind the scenes. . . . We are brought into contact with no strained virtues, illumined by strained light upon strained heights of situation. . . . Whenever he appeals to the emotions it would seem to be with an appeal to the intellect too. . . . because he weaves his story of the finer, less self-evident though common threads of human nature, seldom calling into play the grosser and more powerful strain. . . . Everywhere in his pages we come across acquaintances undisguised. . . . The characters in an American novel are never unapproachable to the reader. . . . The naturalness, with the every-day atmosphere which surrounds it, is one great charm of the American

[9]Characters in a series of novels, known as La Comedie humaine, by Balzac.
[10]Alexandre Dumas père (1803–1870), French romantic novelist, author of *The Count of Monte Cristo* and *The Three Musketeers*.
[11]Eilian Hughes, English literary critic, author of *Some Aspects of Humanity* (1889).

novel. . . . It is throughout examinative, discursory, even more—quizzical. Its characters are undergoing, at the hands of the author, calm, interested observation. . . . He is never caught identifying himself with them; he must preserve impartiality at all costs . . . but . . . the touch of nature is always felt, the feeling of kinship always follows. . . . The strength of the American novel is its optimistic faith. . . . If out of this persistent hopefulness it can evolve for men a new order of trustfulness, a tenet that between man and man there should be less suspicion, more confidence, since human nature sanctions it, its mission will have been more than an aesthetic, it will have been a moral one."

Not all of this will be found true of Mr. James, but all that relates to artistic methods and characteristics will, and the rest is true of American novels generally. For the most part in their range and tendency they are admirable. I will not say they are all good, or that any of them is wholly good; but I find in nearly every one of them a disposition to regard our life without the literary glasses so long thought desirable, and to see character, not as it is in other fiction, but as it abounds outside of all fiction. This disposition sometimes goes with poor enough performance, but in some of our novels it goes with performance that is excellent; and at any rate it is for the present more valuable than evenness of performance. It is what relates American fiction to the only living movement in imaginative literature, and distinguishes by a superior freshness and authenticity any group of American novels from a similarly accidental group of English novels, giving them the same good right to be as the like number of recent Russian novels, French novels, Spanish novels, Italian novels, Norwegian novels. It is the difference of the American novelist's ideals from those of the English novelist that gives him his advantage, and seems to promise him the future. The love of the passionate and the heroic, as the Englishman has it, is such a crude and unwholesome thing, so deaf and blind to all the most delicate and important facts of art and life, so insensible to the subtle values in either that its presence or absence makes the whole difference, and enables one who is not obsessed by it to thank Heaven that he is not as that other man is.

There can be little question that many refinements of thought and spirit which every American is sensible of in the fiction of this continent, are necessarily lost upon our good kin beyond seas, whose thumb-fingered apprehension requires something gross and palpable for its assurance of reality. This is not their fault, and I am not sure that it is wholly their misfortune: they are made so as not to miss what they do not find, and they are simply content without those subtleties of life and character which it gives us so keen a pleasure to have noted in literature. If they perceive them at all it is as something vague and diaphanous, something that filmily wavers before their sense and teases them, much as the beings of an invisible world might mock one of our material frame by intimations of their presence. It is with reason, therefore, on the part of an Englishman, that Mr. Henley[12] complains of our fiction as a shadow-land, though we find more and more in it the faithful report of our life, its motives and emotions, and all the comparatively etherealized passions and ideals that influence it.

In fact, the American who chooses to enjoy his birthright to the full, lives in a world wholly different from the Englishman's, and speaks (too often through

[12]William Ernest Henley (1849–1903), English poet and critic.

his nose) another language: he breathes a rarefied and nimble air full of shining possibilities and radiant promises which the fog-and-soot-clogged lungs of those less-favored islanders struggle in vain to fill themselves with. But he ought to be modest in his advantage, and patient with the coughing and sputtering of his cousin who complains of finding himself in an exhausted receiver[13] on plunging into one of our novels. To be quite just to the poor fellow, I have had some such experience as that myself in the atmosphere of some of our more attenuated romances.

Yet every now and then I read a book with perfect comfort and much exhilaration, whose scenes the average Englishman would gasp in. Nothing happens; that is, nobody murders or debauches anybody else; there is no arson or pillage of any sort; there is not a ghost, or a ravening beast, or a hair-breadth escape, or a shipwreck, or a monster of self-sacrifice, or a lady five thousand years old in the whole course of the story; "no promenade, no band of music, nossing!" as Mr. Du Maurier's Frenchman said of the meet for a fox-hunt.[14] Yet it is all alive with the keenest interest for those who enjoy the study of individual traits and general conditions as they make themselves known to American experience.

These conditions have been so favorable hitherto (though they are becoming always less so) that they easily account for the optimistic faith of our novel which Mr. Hughes notices. It used to be one of the disadvantages of the practice of romance in America, which Hawthorne more or less whimsically lamented, that there were so few shadows and inequalities in our broad level of prosperity; and it is one of the reflections suggested by Dostoïevsky's[15] novel, The Crime and the Punishment, that whoever struck a note so profoundly tragic in American fiction would do a false and mistaken thing—as false and as mistaken in its way as dealing in American fiction with certain nudities which the Latin peoples seem to find edifying. Whatever their deserts, very few American novelists have been led out to be shot, or finally exiled to the rigors of a winter at Duluth; and in a land where journeymen carpenters and plumbers strike for four dollars a day the sum of hunger and cold is comparatively small, and the wrong from class to class has been almost inappreciable, though all this is changing for the worse. Our novelists, therefore, concern themselves with the more smiling aspects of life, which are the more American, and seek the universal in the individual rather than the social interests. It is worth while, even at the risk of being called commonplace, to be true to our well-to-do actualities; the very passions themselves seem to be softened and modified by conditions which formerly at least could not be said to wrong any one, to cramp endeavor, or to cross lawful desire. Sin and suffering and shame there must always be in the world, I suppose, but I believe that in this new world of ours it is still mainly from one to another one, and oftener still from one to one's self. We have death too in America, and a great deal of disagreeable and painful disease, which the multiplicity of our patent medicines does not seem to cure; but this is tragedy that comes in the very nature of things, and is not peculiarly American, as the large, cheerful average of health and success and happy life is. It will not do to boast, but it is well to be true to the facts, and to see that, apart from these purely mortal troubles, the race

[13]I.e., in a vacuum, an empty jar.

[14]In *Pictures of English Society* (1884) by George du Maurier (1834–1896), English illustrator and novelist.

[15]Fyodor Dostoyevsky (1821–1881), Russian novelist.

here has enjoyed conditions in which most of the ills that have darkened its annals might be averted by honest work and unselfish behavior.

Fine artists we have among us, and right-minded as far as they go; and we must not forget this at evil moments when it seems as if all the women had taken to writing hysterical improprieties, and some of the men were trying to be at least as hysterical in despair of being as improper. If we kept to the complexion of a certain school—which sadly needs a school-master—we might very well be despondent; but, after all, that school is not representative of our conditions or our intentions. Other traits are much more characteristic of our life and our fiction. In most American novels, vivid and graphic as the best of them are, the people are segregated if not sequestered, and the scene is sparsely populated. The effect may be in instinctive response to the vacancy of our social life, and I shall not make haste to blame it. There are few places, few occasions among us, in which a novelist can get a large number of polite people together, or at least keep them together. Unless he carries a snap-camera his picture of them has no probability; they affect one like the figures perfunctorily associated in such deadly old engravings as that of "Washington Irving and his Friends." Perhaps it is for this reason that we excel in small pieces with three or four figures, or in studies of rustic communities, where there is propinquity if not society. Our grasp of more urbane life is feeble; most attempts to assemble it in our pictures are failures, possibly because it is too transitory, too intangible in its nature with us, to be truthfully represented as really existent.

I am not sure that the Americans have not brought the short story nearer perfection in the all-round sense than almost any other people, and for reasons very simple and near at hand. It might be argued from the national hurry and impatience that it was a literary form peculiarly adapted to the American temperament, but I suspect that its extraordinary development among us is owing much more to more tangible facts. The success of American magazines, which is nothing less than prodigious, is only commensurate with their excellence. Their sort of success is not only from the courage to decide what ought to please, but from the knowledge of what does please; and it is probable that, aside from the pictures, it is the short stories which please the readers of our best magazines. The serial novels they must have, of course; but rather more of course they must have short stories, and by operation of the law of supply and demand, the short stories, abundant in quantity and excellent in quality, are forthcoming because they are wanted. By another operation of the same law, which political economists have more recently taken account of, the demand follows the supply, and short stories are sought for because there is a proven ability to furnish them, and people read them willingly because they are usually very good. The art of writing them is now so disciplined and diffused with us that there is no lack either for the magazines or for the newspaper "syndicates" which deal in them almost to the exclusion of the serials. In other countries the feuilleton[16] of the journals is a novel continued from day to day, but with us the papers, whether daily or weekly, now more rarely print novels, whether they get them at first hand from the writers, as a great many do, or through the syndicates, which purvey a vast variety of literary wares, chiefly for the Sunday editions of the city journals. In the country papers the short story takes place of the chapters of a serial which used to be given.

1891

[16]A literary composition, often a story or chapter of a novel, published in a newspaper.

Henry James 1843–1916

Henry James, besides being one of the most respected American writers of novels and short stories, was a major theoretician in the art of fictional narrative. "The Art of Fiction," the essay presented here, is his most famous work in that arena, but in addition he produced prefaces to his novels and other essays on the subject of fiction-writing that not only helped to define realism but also established some of the fundamental tenets that later flowered in the works and theoretical documents of the early twentieth century—what has come to be known as the Modernist Era of American literature. "The Art of Fiction" is important for its description of the artistic process, its claim for literary fiction as a legitimate art form, and its analysis of what makes art in general, and literary fiction in particular, worthwhile.

TEXT: *Partial Portraits,* 1888.

THE ART OF FICTION

I should not have affixed so comprehensive a title to these few remarks, necessarily wanting in any completeness upon a subject the full consideration of which would carry us far, did I not seem to discover a pretext for my temerity in the interesting pamphlet lately published under this name by Mr. Walter Besant.[1] Mr. Besant's lecture at the Royal Institution[2]—the original form of his pamphlet—appears to indicate that many persons are interested in the art of fiction, and are not indifferent to such remarks, as those who practise it may attempt to make about it. I am therefore anxious not to lose the benefit of this favourable association, and to edge in a few words under cover of the attention which Mr. Besant is sure to have excited. There is something very encouraging in his having put into form certain of his ideas on the mystery of story-telling.

It is a proof of life and curiosity—curiosity on the part of the brotherhood of novelists as well as on the part of their readers. Only a short time ago it might have been supposed that the English novel was not what the French call *discutable.*[3] It had no air of having a theory, a conviction, a consciousness of itself behind it—of being the expression of an artistic faith, the result of choice and comparison. I do not say it was necessarily the worse for that: it would take much more courage than I possess to intimate that the form of the novel as Dickens and Thackeray (for instance) saw it had any taint of incompleteness. It was, however, *naif*[4] (if I may help myself out with another French word); and evidently if it be destined to suffer in any way for having lost its *naïveté* it has now an idea of making sure of the corresponding advantages. During the period I have alluded to there was a comfortable, good-humoured feeling abroad that a novel is a novel, as a pudding is a pudding, and that our only business with it could be to swallow it. But within a year or two, for some reason or other, there have been signs of returning animation—the era of discussion would appear to

[1]Sir Walter Besant (1836–1901), English novelist, historian, and literary critic.
[2]In London. [3]French: debatable, discussable. [4]French: naive.

have been to a certain extent opened. Art lives upon discussion, upon experiment, upon curiosity, upon variety of attempt, upon the exchange of views and the comparison of standpoint; and there is a presumption that those times when no one has anything particular to say about it, and has no reason to give for practice or preference, though they may be times of honour, are not times of development—are times, possibly even, a little of dulness. The successful application of any art is a delightful spectacle, but the theory too is interesting; and though there is a great deal of the latter without the former I suspect there has never been a genuine success that has not had a latent core of conviction. Discussion, suggestion, formulation, these things are fertilising when they are frank and sincere. Mr. Besant has set an excellent example in saying what he thinks, for his part, about the way in which fiction should be written, as well as about the way in which it should be published; for his view of the "art," carried on into an appendix, covers that too. Other labourers in the same field will doubtless take up the argument, they will give it the light of their experience, and the effect will surely be to make our interest in the novel a little more what it had for some time threatened to fail to be—a serious, active, inquiring interest, under protection of which this delightful study may, in moments of confidence, venture to say a little more what it thinks of itself.

It must take itself seriously for the public to take it so. The old superstition about fiction being "wicked" has doubtless died out in England; but the spirit of it lingers in a certain oblique regard directed toward any story which does not more or less admit that it is only a joke. Even the most jocular novel feels in some degree the weight of the proscription that was formerly directed against literary levity: the jocularity does not always succeed in passing for orthodoxy. It is still expected, though perhaps people are ashamed to say it, that a production which is after all only a "make-believe" (for what else is a "story"?) shall be in some degree apologetic—shall renounce the pretension of attempting really to represent life. This, of course, any sensible, wide-awake story declines to do, for it quickly perceives that the tolerance granted to it on such a condition is only an attempt to stifle it disguised in the form of generosity. The old evangelical hostility to the novel, which was as explicit as it was narrow, and which regarded it as little less favourable to our immortal part than a stage-play, was in reality far less insulting. The only reason for the existence of a novel is that it does attempt to represent life. When it relinquishes this attempt, the same attempt that we see on the canvas of the painter, it will have arrived at a very strange pass. It is not expected of the picture that it will make itself humble in order to be forgiven; and the analogy between the art of the painter and the art of the novelist is, so far as I am able to see, complete. Their inspiration is the same, their process (allowing for the different quality of the vehicle), is the same, their success is the same. They may learn from each other, they may explain and sustain each other. Their cause is the same, and the honour of one is the honour of another. The Mahometans think a picture an unholy thing, but it is a long time since any Christian did,[5] and it is therefore the more odd that in the Christian mind the traces (dissimulated though they may be) of a suspicion of the sister art should linger to this day. The only effectual way to lay it

[5]Figural representation was forbidden in early Islam, a tradition that continues in many Islamic countries. Similarly, the early Christian church opposed the creation and worship of religious portraits (icons) as a form of idolatry.

to rest is to emphasise the analogy to which I just alluded—to insist on the fact that as the picture is reality, so the novel is history. That is the only general description (which does it justice) that we may give of the novel. But history also is allowed to represent life; it is not, any more than painting, expected to apologise. The subject-matter of fiction is stored up likewise in documents and records, and if it will not give itself away, as they say in California, it must speak with assurance, with the tone of the historian. Certain accomplished novelists have a habit of giving themselves away which must often bring tears to the eyes of people who take their fiction seriously. I was lately struck, in reading over many pages of Anthony Trollope,[6] with his want of discretion in this particular. In a digression, a parenthesis or an aside, he concedes to the reader that he and this trusting friend are only "making believe." He admits that the events he narrates have not really happened, and that he can give his narrative any turn the reader may like best. Such a betrayal of a sacred office seems to me, I confess, a terrible crime; it is what I mean by the attitude of apology, and it shocks me every whit as much in Trollope as it would have shocked me in Gibbon or Macaulay.[7] It implies that the novelist is less occupied in looking for the truth (the truth, of course I mean, that he assumes, the premises that we must grant him, whatever they may be), than the historian, and in doing so it deprives him at a stroke of all his standing-room. To represent and illustrate the past, the actions of men, is the task of either writer, and the only difference that I can see is, in proportion as he succeeds, to the honour of the novelist, consisting as it does in his having more difficulty in collecting his evidence, which is so far from being purely literary. It seems to me to give him a great character, the fact that he has at once so much in common with the philosopher and the painter; this double analogy is a magnificent heritage.

It is of all this evidently that Mr. Besant is full when he insists upon the fact that fiction is one of the *fine* arts, deserving in its turn of all the honours and emoluments that have hitherto been reserved for the successful profession of music, poetry, painting, architecture. It is impossible to insist too much on so important a truth, and the place that Mr. Besant demands for the work of the novelist may be represented, a trifle less abstractly, by saying that he demands not only that it shall be reputed artistic, but that it shall be reputed very artistic indeed. It is excellent that he should have struck this note, for his doing so indicates that there was need of it, that his proposition may be to many people a novelty. One rubs one's eyes at the thought; but the rest of Mr. Besant's essay confirms the relation. I suspect in truth that it would be possible to confirm it still further, and that one would not be far wrong in saying that in addition to the people to whom it has never occured that a novel ought to be artistic, there are a great many others who, if this principle were urged upon them, would be filled with an indefinable mistrust. They would find it difficult to explain their repugnance, but it would operate strongly to put them on their guard. "Art," in our Protestant communities, where so many things have got so strangely twisted about, is supposed in certain circles to have some vaguely injurious effect upon those who make it an important consideration, who let it weigh in the balance. It is assumed to be opposed in some mysterious manner to morality, to amusement, to instruction. When it is embodied in the work of the painter

[6]Anthony Trollope (1815–1882), English novelist.
[7]Edward Gibbon (1737–1794) and Thomas Babington Macaulay (1800–1859), English historians.

(the sculptor is another affair!) you know what it is: it stands there before you, in the honesty of pink and green and a gilt frame; you can see the worst of it at a glance, and you can be on your guard. But when it is introduced into literature it becomes more insidious—there is danger of its hurting you before you know it. Literature should be either instructive or amusing, and there is in many minds an impression that these artistic preoccupations, the search for form, contribute to neither end, interfere indeed with both. They are too frivolous to be edifying, and too serious to be diverting; and they are moreover priggish and paradoxical and superfluous. That, I think, represents the manner in which the latent thought of many people who read novels as an exercise in skipping would explain itself if it were to become articulate. They would argue, of course, that a novel ought to be "good," but they would interpret this term in a fashion of their own, which indeed would vary considerably from one critic to another. One would say that being good means representing virtuous and aspiring characters, placed in prominent positions; another would say that it depends on a "happy ending," on a distribution at the last of prizes, pensions, husbands, wives, babies, millions, appended paragraphs, and cheerful remarks. Another still would say that it means being full of incident and movement, so that we shall wish to jump ahead, to see who was the mysterious stranger, and if the stolen will was ever found, and shall not be distracted from this pleasure by any tiresome analysis or "description." But they would all agree that the "artistic" idea would spoil some of their fun. One would hold it accountable for all the description, another would see it revealed in the absence of sympathy. Its hostility to a happy ending would be evident, and it might even in some cases render any ending at all impossible. The "ending" of a novel is, for many persons, like that of a good dinner, a course of dessert and ices, and the artist in fiction is regarded as a sort of meddlesome doctor who forbids agreeable aftertastes. It is therefore true that this conception of Mr. Besant's of the novel as a superior form encounters not only a negative but a positive indifference. It matters little that as a work of art it should really be as little or as much of its essence to supply happy endings, sympathetic characters, and an objective tone, as if it were a work of mechanics: the association of ideas, however incongruous, might easily be too much for it if an eloquent voice were not sometimes raised to call attention to the fact that it is at once as free and as serious a branch of literature as any other.

Certainly this might sometimes be doubted in presence of the enormous number of works of fiction that appeal to the credulity of our generation, for it might easily seem that there could be no great character in a commodity so quickly and easily produced. It must be admitted that good novels are much compromised by bad ones, and that the field at large suffers discredit from overcrowding. I think, however, that this injury is only superficial, and that the superabundance of written fiction proves nothing against the principle itself. It has been vulgarised, like all other kinds of literature, like everything else today, and it has proved more than some kinds accessible to vulgarisation. But there is as much difference as there ever was between a good novel and a bad one: the bad is swept with all the daubed canvases and spoiled marble into some unvisited limbo, or infinite rubbish-yard beneath the back-windows of the world, and the good subsists and emits its light and stimulates our desire for perfection. As I shall take the liberty of making but a single criticism of Mr. Besant, whose tone is so full of the love of his art, I may as well have done with it at once. He seems to me to mistake in attempting to say so definitely beforehand what sort of an affair the good novel will be. To indicate the danger of such an error as that has been the purpose of these few pages; to suggest that certain traditions on the subject, applied *priori,* have already had much to answer for, and that the good health of an art which undertakes so immediately to reproduce life must demand that it be perfectly free. It lives upon exercise, and the very meaning of exercise is freedom. The only obligation to which in advance we may hold a novel, without incurring the accusation of being arbitrary, is that it be interesting. That general responsibility rests upon it, but it is the only one I can think of. The ways in which it is at liberty to accomplish this result (of interesting us) strike me as innumerable, and such as can only suffer from being marked out or fenced in by prescription. They are as various as the temperament of man, and they are successful in proportion as they reveal a particular mind, different from others. A novel is in its broadest definition a personal, a direct impression of life; that, to begin with, constitutes its value, which is greater or less according to the intensity of the impression. But there will be no intensity at all, and therefore no value, unless there is freedom to feel and say. The tracing of a line to be followed, of a tone to be taken, of a form to be filled out, is a limitation of that freedom and a suppression of the very thing that we are most curious about. The form, it seems to me, is to be appreciated after the fact; then the author's choice has been made, his standard has been indicated; then we can follow lines and directions and compare tones and resemblances. Then in a word we can enjoy one of the most charming of pleasures, we can estimate quality, we can apply the test of execution. The execution belongs to the author alone; it is what is most personal to him, and we measure him by that. The advantage, the luxury, as well as the torment and responsibility of the novelist, is that there is no limit to what he may attempt as an executant—no limit to his possible experiments, efforts, discoveries, successes. Here it is especially that he works, step by step, like his brother of the brush, of whom we may always say that he has painted his picture in a manner best known to himself. His manner is his secret, not necessarily a jealous one. He cannot disclose it as a general thing if he would; he would be at a loss to teach it to others. I say this with a due recollection of having insisted on the community of method of the artist who paints a picture and the artist who writes a novel. The painter *is* able to teach the rudiments of his practice, and it is possible, from the study of good work (granted the aptitude), both to learn how to paint and to learn how to write. Yet it remains true, without injury to the *rapprochement,*[8] that the literary artist would be obliged to say to his pupil much more than the other, "Ah, well, you must do it as you can!" It is a question of degree, a matter of delicacy. If there are exact sciences, there are also exact arts, and the grammar of painting is so much more definite that it makes the difference.

I ought to add, however, that if Mr. Besant says at the beginning of his essay that the "laws of fiction may be laid down and taught with as much precision and exactness as the laws of harmony, perspective, and proportion," he mitigates what might appear to be extravagance by applying his remark to "general" laws, and by expressing most of these rules in a manner with which it would certainly be unaccommodating to disagree. That the novelist must write from his experience, that his "characters must be real and such as might be met

[8]French: comparison.

with in actual life;" that "a young lady brought up in a quiet country village should avoid descriptions of garrison life," and "a writer whose friends and personal experiences belong to the lower middle-class should carefully avoid introducing his characters into society;" that one should enter one's notes in a common-place book; that one's figures should be clear in outline; that making them clear by some trick of speech or of carriage is a bad method, and "describing them at length" is a worse one; that English Fiction should have a "conscious moral purpose;" that "it is almost impossible to estimate too highly the value of careful workmanship—that, is, of style;" that "the most important point of all is the story," that "the story is everything": these are principles with most of which it is surely impossible not to sympathise. That remark about the lower middle-class writer and his knowing his place is perhaps rather chilling; but for the rest I should find it difficult to dissent from any one of these recommendations. At the same time, I should find it difficult positively to assent to them, with the exception, perhaps, of the injunction as to entering one's notes in a common-place book. They scarcely seem to me to have the quality that Mr. Besant attributes to the rules of the novelist—the "precision and exactness" of "the laws of harmony, perspective, and proportion." They are suggestive, they are even inspiring, but they are not exact, though they are doubtless as much so as the case admits of: which is proof of that liberty of interpretation for which I just contended. For the value of these different injunctions—so beautiful and so vague—is wholly in the meaning one attaches to them. The characters, the situation, which strike one as real will be those that touch and interest one most, but the measure of reality is very difficult to fix. The reality of Don Quixote or of Mr. Micawber[9] is a very delicate shade; it is a reality so coloured by the author's vision that, vivid as it may be, one would hesitate to propose it as a model: one would expose one's self to some very embarrassing questions on the part of a pupil. It goes without saying that you will not write a good novel unless you possess the sense of reality; but it will be difficult to give you a recipe for calling that sense into being. Humanity is immense, and reality has a myriad forms; the most one can affirm is that some of the flowers of fiction have the odour of it, and others have not; as for telling you in advance how your nosegay should be composed, that is another affair. It is equally excellent and inconclusive to say that one must write from experience; to our supposititious aspirant such a declaration might savour of mockery. What kind of experience is intended, and where does it begin and end? Experience is never limited, and it is never complete; it is an immense sensibility, a kind of huge spiderweb of the finest silken threads suspended in the chamber of consciousness, and catching every airborne particle in its tissue. It is the very atmosphere of the mind; and when the mind is imaginative—much more when it happens to be that of a man of genius—it takes to itself the faintest hints of life, it converts the very pulses of the air into revelations. The young lady living in a village has only to be a damsel upon whom nothing is lost to make it quite unfair (as it seems to me) to declare to her that she shall have nothing to say about the military. Greater miracles have been seen than that, imagination assisting, she should speak the truth about some of these gentlemen. I remember an English novelist, a woman of genius, telling

[9]The hero of Cervantes's *Don Quixote* (written 1605–1615) and a character in Dickens's *David Copperfield* (written 1849–1850), respectively.

me that she was much commended for the impression she had managed to give in one of her tales of the nature and way of life of the French Protestant youth. She had been asked where she learned so much about this recondite being, she had been congratulated on her peculiar opportunities. These opportunities consisted in her having once, in Paris, as she ascended a staircase, passed an open door where, in the household of a *pasteur*,[10] some of the young Protestants were seated at table round a finished meal. The glimpse made a picture; it lasted only a moment, but that moment was experience. She had got her direct personal impression, and she turned out her type. She knew what youth was, and what Protestantism; she also had the advantage of having seen what it was to be French, so that she converted these ideas into a concrete image and produced a reality. Above all, however, she was blessed with the faculty which when you give it an inch takes an ell, and which for the artist is a much greater source of strength than any accident of residence or of place in the social scale. The power to guess the unseen from the seen, to trace the implication of things, to judge the whole piece by the pattern, the condition of feeling life in general so completely that you are well on your way to knowing any particular corner of it—this cluster of gifts may almost be said to constitute experience, and they occur in country and in town, and in the most differing stages of education. If experience consists of impressions, it may be said that impressions *are* experience, just as (have we not seen it?) they are the very air we breathe. Therefore, if I should certainly say to a novice, "Write from experience and experience only," I should feel that this was rather a tantalising monition if I were not careful immediately to add, "Try to be one of the people on whom nothing is lost!"

I am far from intending by this to minimise the importance of exactness—of truth of detail. One can speak best from one's own taste, and I may therefore venture to say that the air of reality (solidity of specification) seems to me to be the supreme virtue of a novel—the merit on which all its other merits (including that conscious moral purpose of which Mr. Besant speaks) helplessly and submissively depend. If it be not there they are all as nothing, and if these be there, they owe their effect to the success with which the author has produced the illusion of life. The cultivation of this success, the study of this exquisite process, form, to my taste, the beginning and the end of the art of the novelist. They are his inspiration, his despair, his reward, his torment, his delight. It is here in very truth that he competes with life; it is here that he competes with his brother the painter in *his* attempt to render the look of things, the look that conveys their meaning, to catch the colour, the relief, the expression, the surface, the substance of the human spectacle. It is in regard to this that Mr. Besant is well inspired when he bids him take notes. He cannot possibly take too many. He cannot possibly take enough. All life solicits him, and to "render" the simplest surface, to produce the most momentary illusion, is a very complicated business. His case would be easier, and the rule would be more exact, if Mr. Besant had been able to tell him what notes to take. But this, I fear, he can never learn in any manual; it is the business of his life. He has to take a great many in order to select a few, he has to work them up as he can, and even the guides and philosophers who might have most to say to him must leave him

[10]French: pastor.

alone when it comes to the application of precepts, as we leave the painter in communion with his palette. That his characters "must be clear in outline," as Mr. Besant says—he feels that down to his boots; but how he shall make them so is a secret between his good angel and himself. It would be absurdly simple if he could be taught that a great deal of "description" would make them so, or that on the contrary the absence of description and the cultivation of dialogue, or the absence of dialogue and the multiplication of "incident," would rescue him from his difficulties. Nothing, for instance, is more possible than that he be of a turn of mind for which this odd, literal opposition of description and dialogue, incident and description, has little meaning and light. People often talk of these things as if they had a kind of internecine distinctness, instead of melting into each other at every breath, and being intimately associated parts of one general effort of expression. I cannot imagine composition existing in a series of blocks, nor conceive, in any novel worth discussing at all, of a passage of description that is not in its intention narrative, a passage of dialogue that is not in its intention descriptive, a touch of truth of any sort that does not partake of the nature of the incident, or an incident that derives its interest from any other source than the general and only source of the success of a work of art—that of being illustrative. A novel is a living thing, all one and continuous, like any other organism, and in proportion as it lives will it be found, I think, that in each of the parts there is something of each of the other parts. The critic who over the close texture of a finished work shall pretend to trace a geography of items will mark some frontiers as artificial, I fear, as any that have been known to history. There is an old-fashioned distinction between the novel of character and the novel of incident which must have cost many a smile to the intending fabulist who was keen about his work. It appears to me as little to the point as the equally celebrated distinction between the novel and the romance—to answer as little to any reality. There are bad novels and good novels, as there are bad pictures and good pictures; but that is the only distinction in which I see any meaning, and I can as little imagine speaking of a novel of character as I can imagine speaking of a picture of character. When one says picture one says of character, when one says novel one says of incident, and the terms may be transposed at will. What is character but the determination of incident? What is incident but the illustration of character? What is either a picture or a novel that is *not* of character? What else do we seek in it and find in it? It is an incident for a woman to stand up with her hand resting on a table and look out at you in a certain way; or if it be not an incident I think it will be hard to say what it is. At the same time it is an expression of character. If you say you don't see it (character in *that—allons donc!*),[11] this is exactly what the artist who has reasons of his own for thinking he *does* see it undertakes to show you. When a young man makes up his mind that he has not faith enough after all to enter the church as he intended, that is an incident, though you may not hurry to the end of the chapter to see whether perhaps he doesn't change once more. I do not say that these are extraordinary or startling incidents. I do not pretend to estimate the degree of interest proceeding from them, for this will depend upon the skill of the painter. It sounds almost puerile to say that some incidents are intrinsically much more important than others, and I need not

[11]French: nonsense!

take this precaution after having professed my sympathy for the major ones in remarking that the only classification of the novel that I can understand is into that which has life and that which has it not.

The novel and the romance, the novel of incident and that of character—these clumsy separations appear to me to have been made by critics and readers for their own convenience, and to help them out of some of their occasional queer predicaments, but to have little reality or interest for the producer, from whose point of view it is of course that we are attempting to consider the art of fiction. The case is the same with another shadowy category which Mr. Besant apparently is disposed to set up—that of the "modern English novel"; unless indeed it be that in this matter he has fallen into an accidental confusion of standpoints. It is not quite clear whether he intends the remarks in which he alludes to it to be didactic or historical. It is as difficult to suppose a person intending to write a modern English as to suppose him writing an ancient English novel: that is a label which begs the question. One writes the novel, one paints the picture, of one's language and of one's time, and calling it modern English will not, alas! make the difficult task any easier. No more, unfortunately, will calling this or that work of one's fellow-artist a romance—unless it be, of course, simply for the pleasantness of the thing, as for instance when Hawthorne gave this heading to his story of *Blithedale*.[12] The French, who have brought the theory of fiction to remarkable completeness, have but one name for the novel, and have not attempted smaller things in it, that I can see, for that. I can think of no obligation to which the "romancer" would not be held equally with the novelist; the standard of execution is equally high for each. Of course it is of execution that we are talking—that being the only point of a novel that is open to contention. This is perhaps too often lost sight of, only to produce interminable confusions and cross-purposes. We must grant the artist his subject, his idea, his *donnée*:[13] our criticism is applied only to what he makes of it. Naturally I do not mean that we are bound to like it or find it interesting: in case we do not our course is perfectly simple—to let it alone. We may believe that of a certain idea even the most sincere novelist can make nothing at all, and the event may perfectly justify our belief; but the failure will have been a failure to execute, and it is in the execution that the fatal weakness is recorded. If we pretend to respect the artist at all, we must allow him his freedom of choice, in the face, in particular cases, of innumerable presumptions that the choice will not fructify. Art derives a considerable part of its beneficial exercise from flying in the face of presumptions, and some of the most interesting experiments of which it is capable are hidden in the bosom of common things. Gustave Flaubert has written a story about the devotion of a servant-girl to a parrot,[14] and the production, highly finished as it is, cannot on the whole be called a success. We are perfectly free to find it flat, but I think it might have been interesting; and I, for my part, am extremely glad he should have written it; it is a contribution to our knowledge of what can be done—or what cannot. Ivan Turgénieff has written a tale about a deaf and dumb serf and a lap-dog[15] and the thing is touching, loving, a little masterpiece. He struck the note of life where Gustave Flaubert missed it—he flew in the face of a presumption and achieved a victory.

[12] *The Blithedale Romance* (1852). [13] French: fundamental idea, theme.
[14] "Un Coeur simple" (1877), by the French novelist Gustave Flaubert (1821–1880).
[15] "Mumu" (1856), by the Russian novelist Ivan Turgenev (1818–1883).

Nothing, of course, will ever take the place of the good old fashion of "liking" a work of art or not liking it: the most improved criticism will not abolish that primitive, that ultimate test. I mention this to guard myself from the accusation of intimating that the idea, the subject, of a novel or a picture, does not matter. It matters, to my sense, in the highest degree, and if I might put up a prayer it would be that artists should select none but the richest. Some, as I have already hastened to admit, are much more remunerative than others, and it would be a world happily arranged in which persons intending to treat them should be exempt from confusions and mistakes. This fortunate condition will arrive only, I fear, on the same day that critics become purged from error. Meanwhile, I repeat, we do not judge the artist with fairness unless we say to him, "Oh, I grant you your starting-point, because if I did not I should seem to prescribe to you, and heaven forbid I should take that responsibility. If I pretend to tell you what you must not take, you will call upon me to tell you then what you must take; in which case I shall be prettily caught. Moreover, it isn't till I have accepted your data that I can begin to measure you. I have the standard, the pitch; I have no right to tamper with your flute and then criticise your music. Of course I may not care for your idea at all; I may think it silly, or stale, or unclean; in which case I wash my hands of you altogether. I may content myself with believing that you will not have succeeded in being interesting, but I shall, of course, not attempt to demonstrate it, and you will be as indifferent to me as I am to you. I needn't remind you that there are all sorts of tastes: who can know it better? Some people, for excellent reasons, don't like to read about carpenters; others, for reasons even better, don't like to read about courtesans. Many object to Americans. Others (I believe they are mainly editors and publishers) won't look at Italians. Some readers don't like quiet subjects; others don't like bustling ones. Some enjoy a complete illusion, others the consciousness of large concessions. They choose their novels accordingly, and if they don't care about your idea they won't, *a fortiori,*[16] care about your treatment."

So that it comes back very quickly, as I have said, to the liking: in spite of M. Zola,[17] who reasons less powerfully than he represents,[18] and who will not reconcile himself to this absoluteness of taste, thinking that there are certain things that people ought to like, and that they can be made to like. I am quite at a loss to imagine anything (at any rate in this matter of fiction) that people *ought* to like or dislike. Selection will be sure to take care of itself, for it has a constant motive behind it. That motive is simply experience. As people feel life, so they will feel the art that is most closely related to it. This closeness of relation is what we should never forget in talking of the effort of the novel. Many people speak of it as a factitious, artificial form, a product of ingenuity, the business of which is to alter and arrange the things that surround us, to translate them into conventional, traditional moulds. This, however, is a view of the matter which carries us but a very short way, condemns the art to an eternal repetition of a few familiar *clichés*, cuts short its development, and leads us straight up to a dead wall. Catching the very note and trick, the strange irregular rhythm of life, that is the attempt whose strenuous force keeps Fiction upon her feet. In proportion as in what she offers us we see life

[16]Latin: with greater reason. [17]Émile Zola (1840–1902), French novelist and critic.
[18]I.e., his critical arguments are less powerful than his fiction.

without rearrangement do we feel that we are touching the truth; in proportion as we see it *with* rearrangement do we feel that we are being put off with a substitute, a compromise and convention. It is not uncommon to hear an extraordinary assurance of remark in regard to this matter of rearranging, which is often spoken of as if it were the last word of art. Mr. Besant seems to me in danger of falling into the great error with his rather unguarded talk about "selection." Art is essentially selection, but it is a selection whose main care is to be typical, to be inclusive. For many people art means rose-coloured window-panes, and selection means picking a bouquet for Mrs. Grundy.[19] They will tell you glibly that artistic considerations have nothing to do with the disagreeable, with the ugly; they will rattle off shallow commonplaces about the province of art and the limits of art till you are moved to some wonder in return as to the province and the limits of ignorance. It appears to me that no one can ever have made a seriously artistic attempt without becoming conscious of an immense increase—a kind of revelation—of freedom. One perceives in that case—by the light of a heavenly ray—that the province of art is all life, all feeling, all observation, all vision. As Mr. Besant so justly intimates, it is all experience. That is a sufficient answer to those who maintain that it must not touch the sad things of life, who stick into its divine unconscious bosom little prohibitory inscriptions on the end of sticks, such as we see in public gardens—"It is forbidden to walk on the grass; it is forbidden to touch the flowers; it is not allowed to introduce dogs or to remain after dark; it is requested to keep to the right." The young aspirant in the line of fiction whom we continue to imagine will do nothing without taste, for in that case his freedom would be of little use to him; but the first advantage of his taste will be to reveal to him the absurdity of the little sticks and tickets. If he have taste, I must add, of course he will have ingenuity, and my disrespectful reference to that quality just now was not meant to imply that it is useless in fiction. But it is only a secondary aid; the first is a capacity for receiving straight impressions.

Mr. Besant has some remarks on the question of "the story" which I shall not attempt to criticise, though they seem to me to contain a singular ambiguity, because I do not think I understand them. I cannot see what is meant by talking as if there were a part of a novel which is the story and part of it which for mystical reasons is not—unless indeed the distinction be made in a sense in which it is difficult to suppose that any one should attempt to convey anything. "The story," if it represents anything, represents the subject; the idea, the *donnée* of the novel; and there is surely no "school"—Mr. Besant speaks of a school—which urges that a novel should be all treatment and no subject. There must assuredly be something to treat; every school is intimately conscious of that. This sense of the story being the idea, the starting-point, of the novel, is the only one that I see in which it can be spoken of as something different from its organic whole; and since in proportion as the work is successful the idea permeates and penetrates it, informs and animates it, so that every word and every punctuation-point contribute directly to the expression, in that proportion do we lose our sense of the story being a blade which may be drawn

[19]I.e., submitting to convention and prudish taste. Mrs. Grundy, a character in *Speed the Plow* (1798), a play by Thomas Morton (1764–1838), has come to stand as a symbol of those interested only in the "safe" aspects of life and art.

more or less out of its sheath. The story and the novel, the idea and the form, are the needle and thread, and I never heard of a guild of tailors who recommend the use of the thread without the needle, or the needle without the thread. Mr. Besant is not the only critic who may be observed to have spoken as if there were certain things in life which constitute stories, and certain others which do not. I find the same odd implication in an entertaining article in the *Pall Mall Gazette,* devoted, as it happens, to Mr. Besant's lecture. "The story is the thing!" says this graceful writer, as if with a tone of opposition to some other idea. I should think it was, as every painter who, as the time for "sending in"[20] his picture looms in the distance, finds himself still in quest of a subject—as every belated artist not fixed about his theme will heartily agree. There are some subjects which speak to us and others which do not, but he would be a clever man who should undertake to give a rule—an index expurgatorius[21]—by which the story and the no-story should be known apart. It is impossible (to me at least) to imagine any such rule which shall not be altogether arbitrary. The writer in the *Pall Mall* opposes the delightful (as I suppose) novel of *Margot la Balafrée*[22] to certain tales in which "Bostonian nymphs" appear to have "rejected English dukes for psychological reasons." I am not acquainted with the romance just designated, and can scarcely forgive the *Pall Mall* critic for not mentioning the name of the author, but the title appears to refer to a lady who may have received a scar in some heroic adventure. I am inconsolable at not being acquainted with this episode, but am utterly at a loss to see why it is a story when the rejection (or acceptance) of a duke is not, and why a reason, psychological or other, is not a subject when a cicatrix[23] is. They are all particles of the multitudinous life with which the novel deals, and surely no dogma which pretends to make it lawful to touch the one and unlawful to touch the other will stand for a moment on its feet. It is the special picture that must stand or fall, according as it seem to possess truth or to lack it. Mr. Besant does not, to my sense, light up the subject by intimating that a story must, under penalty of not being a story, consist of "adventures." Why of adventures more than of green spectacles? He mentions a category of impossible things, and among them he places "fiction without adventure." Why without adventure, more than without matrimony, or celibacy, or parturition,[24] or cholera, or hydropathy,[25] or Jansenism?[26] This seems to me to bring the novel back to the hapless little *rôle* of being an artificial, ingenious thing—bring it down from its large, free character of an immense and exquisite correspondence with life. And what *is* adventure, when it comes to that, and by what sign is the listening pupil to recognise it? It is an adventure—an immense one—for me to write this little article; and for a Bostonian nymph to reject an English duke is an adventure only less stirring, I should say, than for an English duke to be rejected by a Bostonian nymph. I see dramas within dramas in that, and innumerable points of view. A psychological reason is, to my imagination, an object adorably

[20]Submitting for exhibition.

[21]Latin: expurgatory index; here used to mean a standard by which to judge.

[22]A novel (1884) by Fortuné du Boisgobey (1821–1891), French romantic novelist. "Balafrée" means "the scar-faced woman."

[23]Scar. [24]Childbirth. [25]The use of water to treat disease.

[26]Doctrines of Bishop Cornelis Jansen (1585–1638), Dutch theologian who taught an extreme form of predestination and emphasized the saving power of divine grace.

pictorial; to catch the tint of its complexion—I feel as if that idea might inspire one to Titianesque[27] efforts. There are few things more exciting to me, in short, than a psychological reason, and yet, I protest, the novel seems to me the most magnificent form of art. I have just been reading, at the same time, the delightful story of *Treasure Island*, by Mr. Robert Louis Stevenson[28] and, in a manner less consecutive, the last tale from M. Edmond de Goncourt, which is entitled *Chérie*.[29] One of these works treats of murders, mysteries, islands of dreadful renown, hairbreadth escapes, miraculous coincidences and buried doubloons. The other treats of a little French girl who lived in a fine house in Paris, and died of wounded sensibility because no one would marry her. I call *Treasure Island* delightful, because it appears to me to have succeeded wonderfully in what it attempts; and I venture to bestow no epithet upon *Chérie*, which strikes me as having failed deplorably in what it attempts—that is in tracing the development of the moral consciousness of a child. But one of these productions strikes me as exactly as much of a novel as the other, and as having a "story" quite as much. The moral consciousness of a child is as much a part of life as the islands of the Spanish Main, and the one sort of geography seems to me to have those "surprises" of which Mr. Besant speaks quite as much as the other. For myself (since it comes back in the last resort, as I say, to the preference of the individual), the picture of the child's experience has the advantage that I can at successive steps (an immense luxury, near to the "sensual pleasure" of which Mr. Besant's critic in the *Pall Mall* speaks) say Yes or No, as it may be, to what the artist puts before me. I have been a child in fact, but I have been on a quest for a buried treasure only in supposition, and it is a simple accident that with M. de Goncourt I should have for the most part to say No. With George Eliot,[30] when she painted that country with a far other intelligence, I always said Yes.

The most interesting part of Mr. Besant's lecture is unfortunately the briefest passage—his very cursory allusion to the "conscious moral purpose" of the novel. Here again it is not very clear whether he be recording a fact or laying down a principle; it is a great pity that in the latter case he should not have developed his idea. This branch of the subject is of immense importance, and Mr. Besant's few words point to considerations of the widest reach, not to be lightly disposed of. He will have treated the art of fiction but superficially who is not prepared to go every inch of the way that these considerations will carry him. It is for this reason that at the beginning of these remarks I was careful to notify the reader that my reflections on so large a theme have no pretension to be exhaustive. Like Mr. Besant, I have left the question of the morality of the novel till the last, and at the last I find I have used up my space. It is a question surrounded with difficulties, as witness the very first that meets us, in the form of a definite question, on the threshold. Vagueness, in such a discussion, is fatal, and what is the meaning of your morality and your conscious moral purpose? Will you not define your terms and explain how (a novel being a picture) a picture can be either moral or immoral?

[27]In the manner of the Venetian painter Titian (1477?–1576), who was renowned for his realism and rich coloring.

[28]English writer (1850–1894), author of *Treasure Island* (1883).

[29]Novel (1884) by Edmond Huot de Goncourt (1822–1896).

[30]George Eliot (Mary Ann Evans), English novelist (1819–1880). James refers to her novel *Silas Marner* (1861).

You wish to paint a moral picture or carve a moral statue: will you not tell us how you would set about it? We are discussing the Art of Fiction; questions of art are questions (in the widest sense) of execution; questions of morality are quite another affair, and will you not let us see how it is that you find it so easy to mix them up? These things are so clear to Mr. Besant that he has deduced from them a law which he sees embodied in English Fiction, and which is "a truly admirable thing and a great cause for congratulation." It is a great cause for congratulation indeed when such thorny problems become as smooth as silk. I may add that in so far as Mr. Besant perceives that in point of fact English Fiction has addressed itself preponderantly to these delicate questions he will appear to many people to have made a vain discovery. They will have been positively struck, on the contrary, with the moral timidity of the usual English novelist; with his (or with her) aversion to face the difficulties with which on every side the treatment of reality bristles. He is apt to be extremely shy (whereas the picture that Mr. Besant draws is a picture of boldness), and the sign of his work, for the most part, is a cautious silence on certain subjects. In the English novel (by which of course I mean the American as well), more than in any other, there is a traditional difference between that which people know and that which they agree to admit that they know, that which they see and that which they speak of, that which they feel to be a part of life and that which they allow to enter into literature. There is the great difference, in short, between what they talk of in conversation and what they talk of in print. The essence of moral energy is to survey the whole field, and I should directly reverse Mr. Besant's remark and say not that the English novel has a purpose, but that it has a diffidence. To what degree a purpose in a work of art is a source of corruption I shall not attempt to inquire; the one that seems to me least dangerous is the purpose of making a perfect work. As for our novel, I may say lastly on this score that as we find it in England to-day it strikes me as addressed in a large degree to "young people," and that this in itself constitutes a presumption that it will be rather shy. There are certain things which it is generally agreed not to discuss, not even to mention, before young people. That is very well, but the absence of discussion is not a symptom of the moral passion. The purpose of the English novel—"a truly admirable thing, and a great cause for congratulation"—strikes me therefore as rather negative.

There is one point at which the moral sense and the artistic sense lie very near together; that is in the light of the very obvious truth that the deepest quality of a work of art will always be the quality of the mind of the producer. In proportion as that intelligence is fine will the novel, the picture, the statue partake of the substance of beauty and truth. To be constituted of such elements is, to my vision, to have purpose enough. No good novel will ever proceed from a superficial mind; that seems to me an axiom which, for the artist in fiction, will cover all needful moral ground: if the youthful aspirant take it to heart it will illuminate for him many of the mysteries of "purpose." There are many other useful things that might be said to him, but I have come to the end of my article, and can only touch them as I pass. The critic in the *Pall Mall Gazette*, whom I have already quoted, draws attention to the danger, in speaking of the art of fiction, of generalising. The danger that he has in mind is rather, I imagine, that of particularising, for there are some comprehensive remarks which, in addition to those embodied in Mr. Besant's suggestive lecture, might without fear of misleading him be addressed to the ingenuous student. I should remind him first of the magnificence of the form that is open to him, which offers to sight so few restrictions and such innumerable opportunities. The other arts, in comparison, appear confined and hampered; the various conditions under which they are exercised are so rigid and definite. But the only condition that I can think of attaching to the composition of the novel is, as I have already said, that it be sincere. This freedom is a splendid privilege, and the first lesson of the young novelist is to learn to be worthy of it. "Enjoy it as it deserves," I should say to him; "take possession of it, explore it to its utmost extent, publish it, rejoice in it. All life belongs to you, and do not listen either to those who would shut you up into corners of it and tell you that it is only here and there that art inhabits, or to those who would persuade you that this heavenly messenger wings her way outside of life altogether, breathing a superfine air, and turning away her head from the truth of things. There is no impression of life, no manner of seeing it and feeling it, to which the plan of the novelist may not offer a place; you have only to remember that talents so dissimilar as those of Alexandre Dumas and Jane Austen, Charles Dickens and Gustave Flaubert have worked in this field with equal glory. Do not think too much about optimism and pessimism; try and catch the colour of life itself. In France to-day we see a prodigious effort (that of Émile Zola, to whose solid and serious work no explorer of the capacity of the novel can allude without respect) we see an extraordinary effort vitiated by a spirit of pessimism on a narrow basis. M. Zola is magnificent, but he strikes an English reader as ignorant; he has an air of working in the dark; if he had as much light as energy, his results would be of the highest value. As for the aberrations of a shallow optimism, the ground (of English fiction especially) is strewn with their brittle particles as with broken glass. If you must indulge in conclusions, let them have the taste of a wide knowledge. Remember that your first duty is to be as complete as possible—to make as perfect a work. Be generous and delicate and pursue the prize."

1884 1888

Mark Twain (Samuel L. Clemens)
1835–1910

Mark Twain, never a man to avoid head-on confrontations, made his most notable contribution to literary theory by taking on one of the most honored figures of American romanticism: James Fenimore Cooper. While Twain's intention in "Fenimore Cooper's Literary Offences" is partly comic, it also offers some entirely serious principles about the qualities that good fiction should exhibit—qualities such as realistic dialogue and characterization, believable events, economy of style, and avoidance of inconsistencies. It might fairly be said that in reporting Cooper's defects, Twain at times employs gross exaggeration, but whether Cooper is guilty as charged or not, Twain's analysis of his shortcomings employs well-articulated principles that effectively represent the literary realist's approach to fiction-writing.

TEXT: "Fenimore Cooper's Literary Offences," *North American Review,* July 1895.

FENIMORE COOPER'S LITERARY OFFENCES[1]

The Pathfinder and *The Deerslayer* stand at the head of Cooper's novels as artistic creations. There are others of his works which contain parts as perfect as are to be found in these, and scenes even more thrilling. Not one can be compared with either of them as a finished whole.

The defects in both of these tales are comparatively slight. They were pure works of art.—*Prof. Lounsbury*[2]

The five tales reveal an extraordinary fulness of invention.

. . . One of the very greatest characters in fiction, "Natty Bumppo." . . .

The craft of the woodsman, the tricks of the trapper, all the delicate art of the forest, were familiar to Cooper from his youth up.—*Prof. Brander Matthews.*[3]

Cooper is the greatest artist in the domain of romantic fiction yet produced by America.—*Wilkie Collins*[4]

It seems that it was far from right for the Professor of English Literature in Yale, the Professor of English Literature in Columbia, and Wilkie Collins, to deliver opinions on Cooper's literature without having read some of it. It would have been much more decorous to keep silent and let persons talk who have read Cooper.

Cooper's art has some defects. In one place in *Deerslayer,* and in the restricted space of two-thirds of a page, Cooper has scored 114 offences against literary art out of a possible 115. It breaks the record.

There are nineteen rules governing literary art in the domain of romantic fiction—some say twenty-two. In *Deerslayer* Cooper violated eighteen of them. These eighteen require:

1. That a tale shall accomplish something and arrive somewhere. But the *Deerslayer* tale accomplishes nothing and arrives in the air.
2. They require that the episodes of a tale shall be necessary parts of the tale, and shall help to develop it. But as the *Deerslayer* tale is not a tale, and accomplishes nothing and arrives nowhere, the episodes have no rightful place in the work, since there was nothing for them to develop.
3. They require that the personages in a tale shall be alive, except in the case of corpses, and that always the reader shall be able to tell the corpses from the others. But this detail has often been overlooked in the *Deerslayer* tale.
4. They require that the personages in a tale, both dead and alive, shall exhibit a sufficient excuse for being there. But this detail also has been overlooked in the *Deerslayer* tale.

[1]James Fenimore Cooper (1789–1851), American novelist, author of the Leatherstocking Tales: *The Deerslayer* (1841), *The Last of the Mohicans* (1826), *The Pathfinder* (1840), *The Pioneers* (1823), and *The Prairie* (1827).

[2]Thomas R. Lounsbury (1838–1915), author of *James Fenimore Cooper* (1882).

[3]Brander Matthews (1852–1929), who had recently written a laudatory essay on the occasion of the centennial of Cooper's birth.

[4]English novelist (1824–1889).

5. They require that when the personages of a tale deal in conversation, the talk shall sound like human talk, and be talk such as human beings would be likely to talk in the given circumstances, and have a discoverable meaning, also a discoverable purpose, and a show of relevancy, and remain in the neighborhood of the subject in hand, and be interesting to the reader, and help out the tale, and stop when the people cannot think of anything more to say. But this requirement has been ignored from the beginning of the *Deerslayer*, tale to the end of it.
6. They require that when the author describes the character of a personage in his tale, the conduct and conversation of that personage shall justify said description. But this law gets little or no attention in the *Deerslayer* tale, as "Natty Bumppo's[5] case will amply prove.
7. They require that when a personage talks like an illustrated, gilt-edged, tree-calf,[6] hand-tooled, seven-dollar Friendship's Offering[7] in the beginning of a paragraph, he shall not talk like a negro minstrel in the end of it. But this rule is flung down and danced upon in the *Deerslayer* tale.
8. They require that crass stupidities shall not be played upon the reader as "the craft of the woodsman, the delicate art of the forest," by either the author or the people in the tale. But this rule is persistently violated in the *Deerslayer* tale.
9. They require that the personages of a tale shall confine themselves to possibilities and let miracles alone; or, if they venture a miracle, the author must so plausibly set it forth as to make it look possible and reasonable. But these rules are not respected in the *Deerslayer* tale.
10. They require that the author shall make the reader feel a deep interest in the personages of his tale and in their fate; and that he shall make the reader love the good people in the tale and hate the bad ones. But the reader of the *Deerslayer* tale dislikes the good people in it, is indifferent to the others, and wishes they would all get drowned together.
11. They require that the characters in a tale shall be so clearly defined that the reader can tell beforehand what each will do in a given emergency. But in the *Deerslayer* tale this rule is vacated.

In addition to these large rules there are some little ones. These require that the author shall

12. *Say* what he is proposing to say, not merely come near it.
13. Use the right word, not its second cousin.
14. Eschew surplusage.
15. Not omit necessary details.
16. Avoid slovenliness of form.
17. Use good grammar.
18. Employ a simple and straightforward style.

Even these seven are coldly and persistently violated in the *Deerslayer* tale.

[5]The hero of the Leatherstocking Tales.
[6]Calfskin chemically treated to produce a treelike design and used for elegant bookbinding.
[7]Gift books, typically filled with lofty, sentimental literature and high-toned language.

Cooper's gift in the way of invention was not a rich endowment: but such as it was he liked to work it, he was pleased with the effects, and indeed he did some quite sweet things with it. In his little box of stage properties he kept six or eight cunning devices, tricks, artifices for his savages and woodsmen to deceive and circumvent each other with, and he was never so happy as when he was working these innocent things and seeing them go. A favorite one was to make a moccasined person tread in the tracks of the moccasined enemy, and thus hide his own trail. Cooper wore out barrels and barrels of moccasins in working that trick. Another stage-property that he pulled out of his box pretty frequently was his broken twig. He prized his broken twig above all the rest of his effects, and worked it the hardest. It is a restful chapter in any book of his when somebody doesn't step on a dry twig and alarm all the reds and whites for two hundred yards around. Every time a Cooper person is in peril, and absolute silence is worth four dollars a minute, he is sure to step on a dry twig. There may be a hundred handier things to step on, but that wouldn't satisfy Cooper. Cooper requires him to turn out and find a dry twig; and if he can't do it, go and borrow one. In fact the Leather Stocking Series ought to have been called the Broken Twig Series.

I am sorry there is not room to put in a few dozen instances of the delicate art of the forest, as practiced by Natty Bumppo and some of the other Cooperian experts. Perhaps we may venture two or three samples. Cooper was a sailor—a naval officer; yet he gravely tells us how a vessel, driving toward a lee[8] shore in a gale, is steered for a particular spot by her skipper because he knows of an *undertow* there which will hold her back against the gale and save her. For just pure woodcraft, or sailorcraft, or whatever it is, isn't that neat? For several years Cooper was daily in the society of artillery, and he ought to have noticed that when a cannon ball strikes the ground it either buries itself or skips a hundred feet or so; skips again a hundred feet or so—and so on, till it finally gets tired and rolls. Now in one place he loses some "females"—as he always calls women—in the edge of a wood near a plain at night in a fog, on purpose to give Bumppo a chance to show off the delicate art of the forest before the reader. These mislaid people are hunting for a fort. They hear a cannon-blast, and a cannon-ball presently comes rolling into the wood and stops at their feet. To the females this suggests nothing. The case is very different with the admirable Bumppo. I wish I may never know peace again if he doesn't strike out promptly and *follow the track* of that cannon-ball across the plain through the dense fog and find the fort. Isn't it a daisy? If Cooper had any real knowledge of Nature's ways of doing things, he had a most delicate art in concealing the fact. For instances: one of his acute Indian experts, Chingachgool[9] (pronounced Chicago, I think), has lost the trail of a person he is tracking through the forest. Apparently that trail is hopelessly lost. Neither you nor I could ever have guessed out the way to find it. It was very different with Chicago. Chicago was not stumped for long. He turned a running stream out of its course, and there, in the slush in its old bed, were that person's moccasin-tracks. The current did not wash them away, as it would have done in all other like cases—no, even the eternal

[8]Protected from the wind.
[9]Natty Bumppo's Indian companion in the Leatherstocking Tales.

laws of Nature have to vacate when Cooper wants to put up a delicate job of woodcraft on the reader.

We must be a little wary when Brander Matthews tells us that Cooper's books "reveal an extraordinary fulness of invention." As a rule, I am quite willing to accept Brander Matthew's literary judgments and applaud his lucid and graceful phrasing of them; but that particular statement needs to be taken with a few tons of salt. Bless your heart, Cooper hadn't any more invention than a horse; and I don't mean a high class horse, either; I mean a clothes horse. It would be very difficult to find a really clever "situation" in Cooper's books; and still more difficult to find one of any kind which he has failed to render absurd by his handling of it. Look at the episodes of "the caves"; and at the celebrated scuffle between Maqua[10] and those others on the table-land a few days later; and at Hurry Harry's[11] queer water-transit from the castle to the ark; and at Deerslayer's half hour with his first corpse; and at the quarrel between Hurry Harry and Deerslayer later; and at—but choose for yourself; you can't go amiss.

If Cooper had been an observer, his inventive faculty would have worked better, not more interestingly, but more rationally, more plausibly. Cooper's proudest creations in the way of "situations" suffer noticeably from the absence of the observer's protecting gift. Cooper's eye was splendidly inaccurate. Cooper seldom saw anything correctly. He saw nearly all things as through a glass eye, darkly. Of course a man who cannot see the commonest little everyday matters accurately is working at a disadvantage when he is constructing a "situation." In the *Deerslayer* tale Cooper has a stream which is fifty feet wide, where it flows out of a lake; it presently narrows to twenty as it meanders along for no given reason, and yet, when a stream acts like that it ought to be required to explain itself. Fourteen pages later the width of the brook's outlet from the lake has suddenly shrunk thirty feet and become the "narrowest part of the stream." This shrinkage is not accounted for. The stream has bends in it, a sure indication that it has alluvial banks, and cuts them; yet these bends are only thirty and fifty feet long. If Cooper had been a nice and punctilious observer he would have noticed that the bends were oftener nine hundred feet long than short of it.

Cooper made the exit of that stream fifty feet wide in the first place, for no particular reason; in the second place, he narrowed it to less than twenty to accommodate some Indians. He bends a "sapling" to the form of an arch over this narrow passage, and conceals six Indians in its foliage. They are "laying" for a settler's scow or ark which is coming up the stream on its way to the lake; it is being hauled against the stiff current by a rope whose stationary end is anchored in the lake; its rate of progress cannot be more than a mile an hour. Cooper describes the ark, but pretty obscurely. In the matter of dimensions "it was little more than a modern canal boat." Let us guess, then, that it was about 140 feet long. It was of "greater breadth than common." Let us guess, then, that it was about sixteen feet wide. This leviathan had been prowling down bends which were but a third as long as itself, and scraping between banks where it had only two feet of space to spare on each side. We cannot too much

[10]Magua, a Huron chief in *The Last of the Mohicans.*
[11]Henry March, a white hunter in *The Deerslayer.*

admire this miracle. A low-roofed log dwelling occupies "two-thirds of the ark's length"—a dwelling ninety feet long and sixteen feet wide, let us say—a kind of vestibule train. The dwelling has two rooms—each forty-five feet long and sixteen feet wide, let us guess. One of them is the bed-room of the Hutter girls, Judith and Hetty; the other is the parlor, in the day time, at night it is papa's bed chamber. The ark is arriving at the stream's exit, now, whose width has been reduced to less than twenty feet to accommodate the Indians—say to eighteen. There is a foot to spare on each side of the boat. Did the Indians notice that there was going to be a tight squeeze there? Did they notice that they could make money by climbing down out of that arched sapling and just stepping aboard when the ark scraped by? No; other Indians would have noticed these things, but Cooper's Indians never notice anything. Cooper thinks they are marvellous creatures for noticing, but he was almost always in error about his Indians. There was seldom a sane one among them.

The ark is 140 feet long; the dwelling is 90 feet long. The idea of the Indians is to drop softly and secretly from the arched sapling to the dwelling as the ark creeps along under it at the rate of a mile an hour, and butcher the family. It will take the ark a minute and half to pass under. It will take the 90-foot dwelling a minute to pass under. Now, then, what did the six Indians do? It would take you thirty years to guess, and even then you would have to give it up, I believe. Therefore, I will tell you what the Indians did. Their chief, a person of quite extraordinary intellect for a Cooper Indian, warily watched the canal boat as it squeezed along under him, and when he had got his calculations fined down to exactly the right shade, as he judged, he let go and dropped, and *missed the house!* That is actually what he did. He missed the house, and landed in the stern of the scow. It was not much of a fall, yet it knocked him silly. He lay there unconscious. If the house had been 97 feet long, he would have made the trip. The fault was Cooper's, not his. The error lay in the construction of the house. Cooper was no architect.

There still remained in the roost five Indians. The boat has passed under and is now out of their reach. Let me explain what the five did—you would not be able to reason it out for yourself. No. 1 jumped for the boat, but fell in the water astern of it. Then No. 2 jumped for the boat, but fell in the water still further astern of it. Then No. 3 jumped for the boat, and fell a good way astern of it. Then No. 4 jumped for the boat, and fell in the water *away* astern. Then even No. 5 made a jump for the boat—for he was a Cooper Indian. In the matter of intellect, the difference between a Cooper Indian and the Indian that stands in front of the cigar shop is not spacious. The scow episode is really a sublime burst of invention; but it does not thrill, because the inaccuracy of the details throws a sort of air of fictitiousness and general improbability over it. This comes of Cooper's inadequacy as an observer.

The reader will find some examples of Cooper's high talent for inaccurate observation in the account of the shooting match in *The Pathfinder.* "A common wrought nail was driven lightly into the target, its head having been first touched with paint." The color of the paint is not stated—an important omission, but Cooper deals freely in important omissions. No, after all, it was not an important omission; for this nail head is *a hundred yards* from the marksman and could not be seen by them at that distance no matter what its color might be. How far can the best eyes see a common house fly? A hundred yards? It is quite impossible. Very well, eyes that cannot see a house fly that is a hundred yards away cannot see an ordinary nail head at that distance, for the size of the two objects is the same. It takes a keen eye to see a fly or a nail head at fifty yards—one hundred and fifty feet. Can the reader do it?

The nail was lightly driven, its head painted, and game called. Then the Cooper miracles began. The bullet of the first marksman chipped an edge of the nail head; the next man's bullet drove the nail a little way into the target—and removed all the paint. Haven't the miracles gone far enough now? Not to suit Cooper; for the purpose of this whole scheme is to show off his prodigy, Deerslayer-Hawkeye-Long-Rifle-Leather-Stocking-Pathfinder-Bumppo[12] before the ladies.

> "Be all ready to clench it, boys!" cried out Pathfinder, stepping into his friend's tracks the instant they were vacant. "Never mind a new nail; I can see that, though the paint is gone, and what I can see, I can hit at a hundred yards, though it were only a mosquito's eye. Be ready to clench!"
>
> The rifle cracked, the bullet sped its way and the head of the nail was buried in the wood, covered by the piece of flattened lead.

There, you see, is a man who could hunt flies with a rifle, and command a ducal salary in a Wild West show to-day, if we had him back with us.

The recorded feat is certainly surprising, just as it stands; but it is not surprising enough for Cooper. Cooper adds a touch. He had made Pathfinder do this miracle with another man's rifle, and not only that, but Pathfinder did not have even the advantage of loading it himself. He had everything against him, and yet he made that impossible shot, and not only made it, but did it with absolute confidence, saying, "Be ready to clench." Now a person like that would have undertaken that same feat with a brickbat, and with Cooper to help he would have achieved it, too.

Pathfinder showed off handsomely that day before the ladies. His very first feat was a thing which no Wild West show can touch. He was standing with the group of marksmen, observing—a hundred yards from the target, mind: one Jasper raised his rifle and drove the centre of the bull's-eye. Then the quartermaster fired. The target exhibited no result this time. There was a laugh. "It's a dead miss," said Major Lundie. Pathfinder waited an impressive moment or two, then said in that calm, indifferent, know-it-all way of his, "No, Major—he has covered Jasper's bullet, as will be seen if any one will take the trouble to examine the target."

Wasn't it remarkable! How *could* he see that little pellet fly through the air and enter that distant bullet-hole? Yet that is what he did; for nothing is impossible to a Cooper person. Did any of those people have any deep-seated doubts about this thing? No; for that would imply sanity, and these were all Cooper people.

> The respect for Pathfinder's skill and for his *quickness and accuracy of sight* (the italics are mine) was so profound and general, that the instant he made this declaration the spectators began to distrust their own opinions, and a dozen rushed

[12]Names given Nathaniel Bumppo in the various Leatherstocking Tales

> to the target in order to ascertain the fact. There, sure enough, it was found that the quartermaster's bullet had gone through the hole made by Jasper's, and that, too, so accurately as to require a minute examination to be certain of the circumstance, which, however, was soon clearly established by discovering one bullet over the other in the stump against which the target was placed.

They made a "minute" examination; but never mind; how could they know that there were two bullets in that hole without digging the latest one out? for neither probe nor eyesight could prove the presence of any more than one bullet. Did they dig? No; as we shall see. It is the Pathfinder's turn now; he steps out before the ladies, takes aim, and fires.

But alas! here is a disappointment; an incredible, an unimaginable disappointment—for the target's aspect is unchanged; there is nothing there but that same old bullet hole!

> "If one dared to hint at such a thing," cried major Duncan, "I should say that the Pathfinder has also missed the target."

As nobody had missed it yet, the "also" was not necessary; but never mind about that, for the Pathfinder is going to speak.

> "No; no, Major," said he, confidently, "that *would* be a risky declaration. I didn't load the piece, and can't say what was in it, but if it was lead, you will find the bullet driving down those of the Quartermaster and Jasper, else is not my name Pathfinder."

Is the miracle sufficient as it stands? Not for Cooper. The Pathfinder speaks again, as he "now slowly advances towards the stage occupied by the females:"

> "That's not all, boys, that's not all; if you find the target touched at all, I'll own to a miss. The Quartermaster cut the wood, but you'll find no wood cut by that last messenger."

The miracle is at last complete. He knew—doubtless *saw*—at the distance of a hundred yards—that his bullet had passed into the hole *without fraying the edges.* There were now three bullets in that one hole—three bullets imbedded processionally in the body of the stump back of the target. Everybody knew this—somehow or other—and yet nobody had dug any of them out to make sure. Cooper is not a close observer, but he is interesting. He is certainly always that, no matter what happens. And he is more interesting when he is not noticing what he is about than when he is. This is a considerable merit.

The conversations in the Cooper books have a curious sound in our modern ears. To believe that such talk really ever came out of people's mouths would be to believe that there was a time when time was of no value to a person who thought he had something to say; when it was the custom to spread a two-minute remark out to ten; when a man's mouth was a rolling-mill[13] and busied itself all day long in turning four-foot pigs of thought into thirty-foot

[13]A mill where "pigs" (ingots of metal) are shaped into railroad rails.

bars of conversational railroad iron by attenuation; when subjects were seldom faithfully stuck to, but the talk wandered all around and arrived nowhere; when conversations consisted mainly of irrelevancies, with here and there a relevancy, a relevancy with an embarrassed look, as not being able to explain how it got there.

Cooper was certainly not a master in the construction of dialogue. Inaccurate observation defeated him here as it defeated him in so many other enterprises of his. He even failed to notice that the man who talks corrupt English six days in the week must and will talk it on the seventh, and can't help himself. In the *Deerslayer* story he lets Deerslayer talk the showiest kind of book talk sometimes, and at other times the basest of base dialects. For instance, when some one asks him if he has a sweetheart, and if so, where she abides, this is the majestic answer:

> "She's in the forest—hanging from the boughs of the trees, in a soft rain—in the dew on the open grass—the clouds that float about in the blue heavens—the birds that sing in the woods—the sweet springs where I slake my thirst—and in all the other glorious gifts that come from God's Providence!"

And he preceded that, a little before, with this:

> "It consarns me as all things that touches a fri'nd consarns a fri'nd."

And this is another of his remarks:

> "If I was Injin born, now, I might tell of this, or carry in the scalp and boast of the expl'ite afore the whole tribe; or if my inimy had only been a bear"—and so on.

We cannot imagine such a thing as a veteran Scotch Commander-in-Chief comporting himself in the field like a windy melodramatic actor, but Cooper could. On one occasion Alice and Cora were being chased by the French through a fog in the neighborhood of their father's fort.[14]

> *"Point de quartier aux coquins!"*[15] cried an eager pursuer, who seemed to direct the operations of the enemy.
>
> "Stand firm and be ready, my gallant 6oths!" suddenly exclaimed a voice above them; "wait to see the enemy; fire low, and sweep the glacis."[16]
>
> "Father! father!" exclaimed a piercing cry out the mist; "it is I! Alice! thy own Elsie! spare, O! save your daughters!"
>
> "Hold!" shouted the former speaker, in the awful tones of parental agony, the sound reaching even to the woods, and rolling back in solemn echo. "'Tis she! God has restored me my children! Throw open the sallyport,[17] to the field, 6oths, to the field; pull not a trigger, lest ye kill my lambs! Drive off these dogs of France with your steel."

[14]In *The Last of the Mohicans.* [15]French: "Show the rascals no mercy!"
[16]Cleared field that slopes away from a fortress wall.
[17]Small door in a fortress wall, from which troops "sally forth" to battle.

Cooper's word-sense was singularly dull. When a person has a poor ear for music he will flat and sharp right along without knowing it. He keeps near the tune, but it is *not* the tune. When a person has a poor ear for words, the result is a literary flatting and sharping; you perceive what he is intending to say, but you also perceive that he doesn't *say* it. This is Cooper. He was not a word-musician. His ear was satisfied with the *approximate* word. I will furnish some circumstantial evidence in support of this charge. My instances are gathered from half a dozen pages of the tale called *Deerslayer.* He uses "verbal," for "oral"; "precision," for "facility"; "phenomena," for "marvels"; "necessary," for "predetermined"; "unsophisticated," for "primitive"; "preparation," for "expectancy"; "rebuked," for "subdued"; "dependent on," for "resulting from"; "fact," for "condition"; "fact," for "conjecture"; "precaution," for "caution"; "explain," for "determine"; "mortified," for "disappointed"; "meretricious," for "factitious"; "materially," for "considerably"; "decreasing," for "deepening"; "increasing," for "disappearing"; "embedded," for "enclosed"; "treacherous," for "hostile"; "stood," for "stooped"; "softened," for "replaced"; "rejoined," for "remarked"; situation," for "condition"; "different," for "differing"; "insensible," for "unsentient"; "brevity," for "celerity"; "distrusted," for "suspicious"; "mental imbecility," for "imbecility"; "eyes," for "sight"; "counteracting," for "opposing"; "funeral obsequies," for "obsequies."

There have been daring people in the world who claimed that Cooper could write English, but they are all dead now—all dead but Lounsbury. I don't remember that Lounsbury makes the claim in so many words, still he makes it, for he says that *Deerslayer* is a "pure work of art." Pure, in that connection, means faultless—faultless in all details—and language is a detail. If Mr. Lounsbury had only compared Cooper's English with the English which he writes himself—but it is plain that he didn't; and so it is likely that he imagines until this day that Cooper's is as clean and compact as his own. Now I feel sure, deep down in my heart, that Cooper wrote about the poorest English that exists in our language, and that the English of *Deerslayer* is the very worst that even Cooper ever wrote.

I may be mistaken, but it does seem to me that *Deerslayer* is not a work of art in any sense; it does seem to me that it is destitute of every detail that goes to the making of a work of art; in truth, it seems to me that *Deerslayer* is just simply a literary *delirium tremens.*[18]

A work of art? It has no invention; it has no order, system, sequence or result; it has no lifelikeness, no thrill, no stir, no seeming of reality; its characters are confusedly drawn, and by their acts and words they prove that they are not the sort of people the author claims that they are; its humor is pathetic; it pathos is funny; its conversations are—oh! indescribable; its love-scenes odious; its English a crime against the language.

Counting these out, what is left is Art. I think we must all admit that.

1895

[18]A violent delirium caused by excessive alcohol consumption.

Literature of the Late Nineteenth Century

Walt Whitman 1819–1892

In 1855, after first reading Leaves of Grass, *Ralph Waldo Emerson wrote to Walt Whitman, "I am not blind to the worth of the wonderful gift of* Leaves of Grass. *I find it the most extraordinary piece of wit and wisdom that America has yet contributed. . . . I greet you at the beginning of a great career, which yet must have had a long foreground somewhere, for such a start."*

Whitman was thirty-six years old then, and nothing in his "long foreground" suggested that he would write an important book of American poetry. He had been born in 1819 in a rural village on Long Island, New York. His parents were semiliterate and could give him little more than a basic understanding of political liberalism and a deistic faith shaped by the teachings of Quakerism. He had only five or six years of formal schooling, but he was a voracious reader of nineteenth-century novels, English romantic poetry, the "classics" of European literature, and the New Testament. His teachers characterized him as a "dreamy and impractical youth," and he drifted through a series of jobs as an office boy, a printer, and a country schoolteacher. He had a natural talent for journalism. For a short time, he edited a Long Island weekly newspaper, and when he was twenty-two and attracted to the bohemian life of Manhattan, he went to New York City.

In the city, Whitman worked as a printer, as an editor, and as a freelance journalist contributing essays, short stories, and poems to the popular newspapers and magazines of the 1840s. When he was twenty-seven, he became editor of the Brooklyn Daily Eagle, *but after only two years he was dismissed because of his radically liberal political views. Next, he made a brief visit to New Orleans, but he soon returned to New York City, where he opened a printing office and stationery store and began to write poetry. In 1855 he published the first edition of* Leaves of Grass. *It contained twelve poems that reportedly Whitman himself had set in type and printed at his own expense. Few copies of his slim book of poetry were sold, yet those who read it were rarely indifferent. His apparently formless free-verse departures from poetic convention, his incantations and boasts, his homoerotic sexuality,and his exotic and vulgar language caused critics steeped in the gentilities of the nineteenth century to label his work a "poetry of barbarism" and warn that it was "not to be read aloud to a mixed audience." At best, the reviewers judged the poems "gross yet elevated," "superficial yet profound," a "mixture of Yankee transcendentalism and New York rowdyism." At worst, Whitman's "leaves" were called "noxious weeds," "spasmodic idiocy," "a mass of stupid filth." Ralph Waldo Emerson found the poetry "extraordinary"; John Greenleaf Whittier judged it "loose, lurid, and impious" and threw his gift-copy into the fireplace; and Fanny Fern gave it public approval. From 1857 to 1859, Whitman edited the Brooklyn* Times, *and, undaunted by the critical response to the first edition, he reworked* Leaves of Grass, *publishing expanded second and third editions in 1856 and 1860. When the Civil War began, he traveled south to Washington, D.C., where he obtained an appointment as a government clerk and worked as a volunteer nurse, a "wound-dresser," in nearby military hospitals. While living in Washington, he published* Drum-Taps *(1865), Civil War poems that he gathered into the fourth edition of* Leaves of Grass *(1867). By the time Whitman had published the fifth edition (1871), his poetry had begun to receive increasing critical recognition in England as well as in America. He had come to see his work as a single "poem" to be revised and improved over a lifetime, but in 1873, when he was fifty-four, he suffered a paralytic stroke. Living at his brother's home in Camden, New Jersey, and cared for by a small group of devoted friends, Whitman spent most of the remaining nineteen years of his life revising successive editions of* Leaves of Grass *until the final version was published shortly before his death in 1892.*

The more than 400 poems that had appeared in the nine editions of Leaves of Grass *printed in Whitman's lifetime were unprecedented in American literature. They were a compound of commonplaces, of disorganized and raw experience, of sentimentalism, and of true poetic inspiration. They had ecstatic perceptions of humans and nature, united and divine. Whitman had an expansive vision, an urgent desire to incorporate the entire American experience into his life and into poetry. He aspired to be a cosmic consciousness, to experience and glorify all humanity and all human qualities, including "sex, womanhood, maternity, lusty animations, organs, acts."*

Walt Whitman had yearned to be the "bard of democracy," a public poet celebrated by democratic men and women "en-masse," but while he lived, the bulk of his poetry was read only by literary enthusiasts and intellectuals. In his final years, Whitman's devoted followers solemnized him as "The Good Gray Poet." He became a national figure, America's whiskery sage, but the wide popularity he had yearned to have nonetheless escaped him. He was defeated in his greatest literary ambitions, yet his poems came to exert tremendous influence on modern American poetry, including the history of the gay male literary tradition. Whitman had been a radically new poet, had made his own rhythms, created his own mythic world, and in writing his sprawling epic of American democracy he helped make possible the free-verse unorthodoxies and the private literary intensities of a modern world that would one day come to honor him as one of its great poets.

FURTHER READING: *The Complete Writings of Walt Whitman,* ed. R. Bucke, T. Harned, and H. Traubel, 10 vols., 1902; *The Collected Writings of Walt Whitman,* 22 vols., ed. G. Allen et al., 1961–1984; *Complete Poetry and Selected Prose,* 1995; *Selected Letters of Walt Whitman,* ed. E. Miller, 1995; G. Allen, *The Solitary Singer: A Critical Biography of Walt Whitman,* 1955, 1967; R. Asselineau, *The Evolution of Walt Whitman,* 2 vols., 1960, 1962; J. Kaplan, *Walt Whitman: A Life,* 1980; D. Reynolds, *Walt Whitman's America: A Cultural Biography,* 1995; R. Chase, *Walt Whitman Reconsidered,* 1955; J. Miller, *A Critical Guide to "Leaves of Grass,"* 1957; *The Americanness of Walt Whitman,* ed. L. Marx, 1960; H. Waskow, *Whitman: Explorations in Form,* 1966; E. Miller, *Walt Whitman's Poetry,* 1968, 1969; *A Century of Whitman Criticism,* ed. E. Miller, 1969; G. Allen, *A Reader's Guide to Walt Whitman,* 1970; J. Rubin, *The Historic Whitman,* 1973; F. Stovall, *The Foreground of Leaves of Grass,* 1974; S. Black, *Whitman's Journey into Chaos,* 1975; G. Allen, *The New Walt Whitman Handbook,* 1975; S. Giantvalley, *Walt Whitman, 1838–1839: A Reference Guide,* 1981; P. Zweig, *Walt Whitman: The Making of the Poet,* 1984; T. Wynn, *The Lunar Light of Whitman's Poetry,* 1987; G. Hutchinson, *The Ecstatic Whitman,* 1986; K. Larson, *Whitman's Drama of Consensus,* 1988; B. Erkkila, *Whitman the Political Poet,* 1989; K. Price, *Whitman and Tradition,* 1990; E. Greenspan, *Walt Whitman and the American Reader,* 1990; M. Moon, *Disseminating Whitman,* 1991; M. Bauerlein, *Whitman and the American Idiom,* 1991; B. Fone, *Masculine Landscapes: Walt Whitman and the Homoerotic Text,* 1992; T. Nathanson, *Whitman's Presence: Body, Voice, and Writing in* Leaves of Grass, 1992; *The Continuing Presence of Walt Whitman,* ed. R. Martin, 1992; E. Greenspan, *Cambridge Companion to Walt Whitman,* 1995; *Walt Whitman and the World,* eds. E. Folsom and G. Allen, 1995; E. Ingvar, *Whitman Between Impressionism and Expressionism,* 1995; *Walt Whitman: The Contemporary Reviews,* ed K. Price, 1996; B. Erkkila and J. Grossman, *Breaking Ground,* 1996; G. Allen and E. Folsom, *Walt Whitman and the World,* 1995; J. Krieg, *A Whitman Chronology,* 1998; J. Perlman, E. Folsom, and D. Campion, *Walt Whitman: The Measure of His Song,* 1998; *Walt Whitman: An Encyclopedia,* ed. J.

LeMaster and D. Kummings, 1998; J. Loving, *Walt Whitman: Song of Himself,* 1999; V. Pollak, *The Erotic Whitman,* 2000; S. Mack, *The Pragmatic Whitman,* 2002.

TEXTS: *Leaves of Grass,* 1891; *The Collected Writings of Walt Whitman: The Early Poems and the Fiction,* Vol. II, ed. F. Stovall, 1964; *Leaves of Grass: Comprehensive Reader's Edition,* ed. H. Blodgett and S. Bradley, 1965.

PREFACE TO THE 1855 EDITION OF *LEAVES OF GRASS*[1]

America does not repel the past or what it has produced under its forms or amid other politics or the idea of castes or the old religions. . . . accepts the lesson with calmness . . . is not so impatient as has been supposed that the slough[2] still sticks to opinions and manners and literature while the life which served its requirements has passed into the new life of the new forms . . . perceives that the corpse is slowly borne from the eating and sleeping rooms of the house . . . perceives that it waits a little while in the door . . . that it was fittest for its days . . . that its action has descended to the stalwart and wellshaped heir who approaches . . . and that he shall be fittest for his days.

The Americans of all nations at any time upon the earth have probably the fullest poetical nature. The United States themselves are essentially the greatest poem. In the history of the earth hitherto the largest and most stirring appear tame and orderly to their ampler largeness and stir. Here at last is something in the doings of man that corresponds with the broadcast doings of the day and night. Here is not merely a nation but a teeming nation of nations. Here is action untied from strings necessarily blind to particulars and details magnificently moving in vast masses. Here is the hospitality which forever indicates heroes. . . . Here are the roughs and beards and space and ruggedness and nonchalance that the soul loves. Here the performance disdaining the trivial unapproached in the tremendous audacity of its crowds and groupings and the push of its perspective spreads with crampless and flowing breath and showers its prolific and splendid extravagance. One sees it must indeed own the riches of the summer and winter, and need never be bankrupt while corn grows from the ground or the orchards drop apples or the bays contain fish or men beget children upon women.

Other states indicate themselves in their deputies. . . . but the genius of the United States is not best or most in its executives or legislatures, nor in its ambassadors or authors or colleges or churches or parlors, nor even in its newspapers or inventors . . . but always most in the common people. Their manners speech dress friendships—the freshness and candor of their physiognomy—the picturesque looseness of their carriage . . . their deathless attachment to freedom—their aversion to anything indecorous or soft or mean—the practical acknowledgment of the citizens of one state by the citizens of all other states—the fierceness of their roused resentment—their curiosity and welcome of novelty—

[1]The first (1855) edition of *Leaves of Grass* contained a dozen poems and a preface in which Whitman declared his literary philosophy. Later editions omitted the 1855 Preface, but portions were incorporated in poems subsequently added to the text. The marks of ellipsis (. . .) are Whitman's, as are the eccentric spellings.

[2]Dead tissue, such as the cast-off skin of a snake.

their self-esteem and wonderful sympathy—their susceptibility to a slight—the air they have of persons who never knew how it felt to stand in the presence of superiors—the fluency of their speech—their delight in music, the sure symptom of manly tenderness and native elegance of soul . . . their good temper and openhandedness—the terrible significance of their elections—the President's taking off his hat to them not they to him—these too are unrhymed poetry. It awaits the gigantic and generous treatment worthy of it.

The largeness of nature or the nation were monstrous without a corresponding largeness and generosity of the spirit of the citizen. Not nature nor swarming states nor streets and steamships nor prosperous business nor farms nor capital nor learning may suffice for the ideal of man . . . nor suffice the poet. No reminiscences may suffice either. A live nation can always cut a deep mark and can have the best authority the cheapest . . . namely from its own soul. This is the sum of the profitable uses of individuals or states and of present action and grandeur and of the subjects of poets.—As if it were necessary to trot back generation after generation to the eastern records! As if the beauty and sacredness of the demonstrable must fall behind that of the mythical! As if men do not make their mark out of any times! As if the opening of the western continent by discovery and what has transpired since in North and South America were less than the small theatre of the antique or the aimless sleepwalking of the middle ages! The pride of the United States leaves the wealth and finesse of the cities and all returns of commerce and agriculture and all the magnitude of geography or shows of exterior victory to enjoy the breed of fullsized men or one fullsized man unconquerable and simple.

The American poets are to enclose old and new for America is the race of races. Of them a bard[3] is to be commensurate with a people. To him the other continents arrive as contributions . . . he gives them reception for their sake and his own sake. His spirit responds to his country's spirit. . . . he incarnates its geography and natural life and rivers and lakes. Mississippi with annual freshets and changing chutes, Missouri and Columbia and Ohio and Saint Lawrence with the falls and beautiful masculine Hudson, do not embouchure[4] where they spend themselves more than they embouchure into him. The blue breadth over the inland sea of Virginia and Maryland and the sea off Massachusetts and Maine and over Manhattan bay and over Champlain and Erie and over Ontario and Huron and Michigan and Superior, and over the Texan and Mexican and Floridian and Cuban seas and over the seas off California and Oregon, is not tallied by the blue breadth of the waters below more than the breadth of above and below is tallied by him. When the long Atlantic coast stretches longer and the Pacific coast stretches longer he easily stretches with them north or south. He spans between them also from east to west and reflects what is between them. On him rise solid growths that offset the growths of pine and cedar and hemlock and liveoak and locust and chestnut and hickory and limetree and cottonwood and tuliptree and cactus and wildvine and tamarind and persimmon. . . . and tangles as tangled as any canebrake or swamp. . . . and forests coated with transparent ice and icicles hanging from the boughs and crackling in the wind. . . . and sides and peaks of mountains. . . . and pasturage sweet and free as savannah or upland or prairie. . . . with flights and songs and screams

[3]The poet-singer of a tribe or nation. [4]Pour out, as from a river mouth.

that answer those of the wildpigeon and highhold[5] and orchard oriole and coot and surf-duck and redshouldered-hawk and fish-hawk and white-ibis and indian-hen and cat-owl and water-pheasant and qua-bird and pied-sheldrake and blackbird and mockingbird and buzzard and condor and night-heron and eagle. To him the hereditary countenance descends both mother's and father's. To him enter the essences of the real things and past and present events—of the enormous diversity of temperature and agriculture and mines—the tribes of red aborigines—the weatherbeaten vessels entering new ports or making landings on rocky coasts—the first settlements north or south—the rapid stature and muscle—the haughty defiance of '76,[6] and the war and peace and formation of the constitution. . . . the union always surrounded by blatherers and always calm and impregnable—the perpetual coming of immigrants—the wharf hem'd cities and superior marine—the unsurveyed interior—the loghouses and clearings and wild animals and hunters and trappers. . . . the free commerce—the fisheries and whaling and golddigging—the endless gestation of new states—the convening of Congress every December,[7] the members duly coming up from all climates and the uttermost parts. . . . the noble character of the young mechanics[8] and of all free American workmen and workwomen. . . . the general ardor and friendliness and enterprise—the perfect equality of the female with the male. . . . the large amativeness[9]—the fluid movement of the population—the factories and mercantile life and laborsaving machinery—the Yankee swap[10]—the New-York firemen and the target excursion[11]—the southern plantation life—the character of the northeast and of the northwest and southwest—slavery and the tremulous spreading of hands to protect it, and the stern opposition to it which shall never cease till it ceases or the speaking of tongues and the moving of lips cease. For such the expression of the American poet is to be transcendent and new. It is to be indirect and not direct or descriptive or epic. Its quality goes through these to much more. Let the age and wars of other nations be chanted and their eras and characters be illustrated and that finish the verse. Not so the great psalm of the republic. Here the theme is creative and has vista. Here comes one among the wellbeloved stonecutters and plans with decision and science and sees the solid and beautiful forms of the future where there are now no solid forms.

Of all nations the United States with veins full of poetical stuff most need poets and will doubtless have the greatest and use them the greatest. Their Presidents shall not be their common referee so much as their poets shall. Of all mankind the great poet is the equable man. Not in him but off from him things are grotesque or eccentric or fail of their sanity. Nothing out of its place is good and nothing in its place is bad. He bestows on every object or quality its fit proportions neither more nor less. He is the arbiter of the diverse and he is the key. He is the equalizer of his age and land. . . . he supplies what wants supplying and checks what wants checking. If peace is the routine out of him speaks the spirit of peace, large, rich, thrifty, building vast and populous cities, encouraging agriculture and the arts and commerce—lighting the study of man, the soul, immortality—federal, state or municipal government, marriage,

[5]Woodpecker. [6]The Declaration of Independence.
[7]In the nineteenth century the Congress of the United States convened in December.
[8]Manual workers, artisans. [9]Phrenological term signifying a capacity for loving others.
[10]Bargain. [11]Trip to a shooting meet.

health, freetrade, intertravel by land and sea. . . . nothing too close, nothing too far off . . . the stars not too far off. In war he is the most deadly force of the war. Who recruits him recruits horse and foot[12] . . . he fetches parks[13] of artillery the best that engineer ever knew. If the time becomes slothful and heavy he knows how to arouse it . . . he can make every word he speaks draw blood. Whatever stagnates in the flat[14] of custom or obedience or legislation he never stagnates. Obedience does not master him, he masters it. High up out of reach he stands turning a concentrated light . . . he turns the pivot with his finger . . . he baffles the swiftest runners as he stands and easily overtakes and envelopes them. The time straying toward infidelity and confections and persiflage he withholds by his steady faith . . . he spreads out his dishes . . . he offers the sweet firm-fibred meat that grows men and women. His brain is the ultimate brain. He is no arguer . . . he is judgment. He judges not as the judge judges but as the sun falling around a helpless thing. As he sees the farthest he has the most faith. His thoughts are the hymns of the praise of things. In the talk on the soul and eternity and God off of his equal plane he is silent. He sees eternity less like a play with a prologue and denouement. . . . he sees eternity in men and women . . . he does not see men and women as dreams or dots. Faith is the antiseptic of the soul . . . it pervades the common people and preserves them . . . they never give up believing and expecting and trusting. There is that indescribable freshness and unconsciousness about an illiterate person that humbles and mocks the power of the noblest expressive genius. The poet sees for a certainty how one not a great artist may be just as sacred and perfect as the greatest artist. . . . . . The power to destroy or remould is freely used by him but never the power of attack. What is past is past. If he does not expose superior models and prove himself by every step he takes he is not what is wanted. The presence of the greatest poet conquers . . . not parleying or struggling or any prepared attempts. Now he has passed that way see after him! there is not left any vestige of despair or misanthropy or cunning or exclusiveness or the ignominy of a nativity or color or delusion of hell or the necessity of hell. . . . . and no man thenceforward shall be degraded for ignorance or weakness or sin.

The greatest poet hardly knows pettiness or triviality. If he breathes into any thing that was before thought small it dilates with the grandeur and life of the universe. He is a seer. . . . he is individual . . . he is complete in himself. . . . the others are as good as he, only he sees it and they do not. He is not one of the chorus. . . . he does not stop for any regulation . . . he is the president of regulation. What the eyesight does to the rest he does to the rest. Who knows the curious mystery of the eyesight? The other senses corroborate themselves, but this is removed from any proof but its own and foreruns the identities of the spiritual world. A single glance of it mocks all the investigations of man and all the instruments and books of the earth and all reasoning. What is marvellous? what is unlikely? what is impossible or baseless or vague? after you have once just opened the space of a peachpit and given audience to far and near to the sunset and had all things enter with electric swiftness softly and duly without confusion or jostling or jam.

The land and sea, the animals fishes and birds, the sky of heaven and the orbs, the forests mountains and rivers, are not small themes . . . but folks expect

[12]Horse soldiers (cavalry) and foot soldiers (infantry). [13]Depots, assembly areas.
[14]Shoal, marsh.

of the poet to indicate more than the beauty and dignity which always attach to dumb real objects . . . . they expect him to indicate the path between reality and their souls. Men and women perceive the beauty well enough . . probably as well as he. The passionate tenacity of hunters, wood men, early risers, cultivators of gardens and orchards and fields, the love of healthy women for the manly form, seafaring persons, drivers of horses, the passion for light and the open air, all is an old varied sign of the unfailing perception of beauty and of a residence of the poetic in outdoor people. They can never be assisted by poets to perceive . . . some may but they never can. The poetic quality is not marshalled in rhyme or uniformity or abstract addresses to things nor in melancholy complaints or good precepts, but is the life of these and much else and is in the soul. The profit of rhyme is that it drops seeds of a sweeter and more luxuriant rhyme, and of uniformity that it conveys itself into its own roots in the ground out of sight. The rhyme and uniformity of perfect poems show the free growth of metrical laws and bud from them as unerringly and loosely as lilacs or roses on a bush, and take shapes as compact as the shapes of chestnuts and oranges and melons and pears, and shed the perfume impalpable to form. The fluency and ornaments of the finest poems or music or orations or recitations are not independent but dependent. All beauty comes from beautiful blood and a beautiful brain. If the greatnesses are in conjunction in a man or woman it is enough. . . . the fact will prevail through the universe. . . . but the gaggery[15] and gilt of a million years will not prevail. Who troubles himself about his ornaments or fluency is lost. This is what you shall do: Love the earth and sun and the animals, despise riches, give alms to every one that asks, stand up for the stupid and crazy, devote your income and labor to others, hate tyrants, argue not concerning God, have patience and indulgence toward the people, take off your hat to nothing known or unknown or to any man or number of men, go freely with powerful uneducated persons and with the young and with the mothers of families, read these leaves in the open air every season of every year of your life, re-examine all you have been told at school or church or in any book, dismiss whatever insults your own soul, and your very flesh shall be a great poem and have the richest fluency not only in its words but in the silent lines of its lips and face and between the lashes of your eyes and in every motion and joint of your body. . . . . . . The poet shall not spend his time in unneeded work. He shall know that the ground is always ready ploughed and manured. . . . others may not know it but he shall. He shall go directly to the creation. His trust shall master the trust of everything he touches. . . . and shall master all attachment.

The known universe has one complete lover and that is the greatest poet. He consumes an eternal passion and is indifferent which chance happens and which possible contingency of fortune or misfortune and persuades daily and hourly his delicious pay. What balks or breaks others is fuel for his burning progress to contact and amorous joy. Other proportions of the reception of pleasure dwindle to nothing to his proportions. All expected from heaven or from the highest he is rapport with in the sight of the daybreak or a scene of the winter woods or the presence of children playing or with his arm round the neck of a man or woman. His love above all love has leisure

[15]Sham.

and expanse. . . . he leaves room ahead of himself. He is no irresolute or suspicious lover . . . he is sure . . . he scorns intervals. His experience and the showers and thrills are not for nothing. Nothing can jar him. . . . suffering and darkness cannot—death and fear cannot. To him complaint and jealousy and envy are corpses buried and rotten in the earth. . . . he saw them buried. The sea is not surer of the shore or the shore of the sea than he is of the fruition of his love and of all perfection and beauty.

The fruition of beauty is no chance of hit or miss . . . it is inevitable as life. . . . it is exact and plumb as gravitation. From the eyesight proceeds another eyesight and from the hearing proceeds another hearing and from the voice proceeds another voice eternally curious of the harmony of things with man. To these respond perfections not only in the committees that were supposed to stand for the rest but in the rest themselves just the same. These understand the law of perfection in masses and floods . . . that its finish is to each for itself and onward from itself . . . that it is profuse and impartial . . . that there is not a minute of the light or dark nor an acre of the earth or sea without it—nor any direction of the sky nor any trade or employment nor any turn of events. This is the reason that about the proper expression of beauty there is precision and balance . . . one part does not need to be thrust above another. The best singer is not the one who has the most lithe and powerful organ . . . the pleasure of poems is not in them that take the handsomest measure and similes and sound.

Without effort and without exposing in the least how it is done the greatest poet brings the spirit of any or all events and passions and scenes and persons some more and some less to bear on your individual character as you hear or read. To do this well is to compete with the laws that pursue and follow time. What is the purpose must surely be there and the clue of it must be there. . . . and the faintest indication is the indication of the best and then becomes the clearest indication. Past and present and future are not disjoined but joined. The greatest poet forms the consistence of what is to be from what has been and is. He drags the dead out of their coffins and stands them again on their feet. . . . he says to the past, Rise and walk before me that I may realize you. He learns the lesson. . . . he places himself where the future becomes present. The greatest poet does not only dazzle his rays over character and scenes and passions . . . he finally ascends and finishes all . . . he exhibits the pinnacles that no man can tell what they are for or what is beyond. . . . he glows a moment on the extremest verge. He is most wonderful in his last half-hidden smile or frown . . . by that flash of the moment of parting the one that sees it shall be encouraged or terrified afterward for many years. The greatest poet does not moralize or make applications of morals . . . he knows the soul. The soul has that measureless pride which consists in never acknowledging any lessons but its own. But it has sympathy as measureless as its pride and the one balances the other and neither can stretch too far while it stretches in company with the other. The inmost secrets of art sleep with the twain. The greatest poet has lain close betwixt both and they are vital in his style and thoughts.

The art of art, the glory of expression and the sunshine of the light of letters is simplicity. Nothing is better than simplicity . . . nothing can make up for excess or for the lack of definiteness. To carry on the heave of impulse and pierce intellectual depths and give all subjects their articulations are powers neither common nor very uncommon. But to speak in literature with the perfect rectitude and insousiance[16] of the movements of animals and the unimpeachableness of the sentiment of trees in the woods and grass by the roadside is the flawless triumph of art. If you have looked on him who has achieved it you have looked on one of the masters of the artists of all nations and times. You shall not contemplate the flight of the graygull over the bay or the mettlesome action of the blood horse or the tall leaning of sunflowers on their stalk or the appearance of the sun journeying through heaven or the appearance of the moon afterward with any more satisfaction than you shall contemplate him. The greatest poet has less a marked style and is more the channel of thoughts and things without increase or diminution, and is the free channel of himself. He swears to his art, I will not be meddlesome, I will not have in my writing any elegance or effort or originality to hang in the way between me and the rest like curtains. I will have nothing hang in the way, not the richest curtains. What I tell I tell for precisely what it is. Let who may exalt or startle or fascinate or sooth[17] I will have purposes as health or heat or snow has and be as regardless of observation. What I experience or portray shall go from my composition without a shred of my composition. You shall stand by my side and look in the mirror with me.

The old red blood and stainless gentility of great poets will be proved by their unconstraint. A heroic person walks at his ease through and out of that custom or precedent or authority that suits him not. Of the traits of the brotherhood of writers savans[18] musicians inventors and artists nothing is finer than silent defiance advancing from new free forms. In the need of poems philosophy politics mechanism science behaviour, the craft of art, an appropriate native grand-opera, shipcraft, or any craft, he is greatest forever and forever who contributes the greatest original practical example. The cleanest expression is that which finds no sphere worthy of itself and makes one.

The messages of great poets to each man and woman are, Come to us on equal terms, Only then can you understand us, We are no better than you, What we enclose you enclose, What we enjoy you may enjoy. Did you suppose there could be only one Supreme? We affirm there can be unnumbered Supremes, and that one does not countervail another any more than one eyesight countervails another . . . and that men can be good or grand only of the consciousness of their supremacy within them. What do you think is the grandeur of storms and dismemberments and the deadliest battles and wrecks and the wildest fury of the elements and the power of the sea and the motion of nature and of the throes of human desires and dignity and hate and love? It is that something in the soul which says, Rage on, Whirl on, I tread master here and everywhere, Master of the spasms of the sky and of the shatter of the sea, Master of nature and passion and death, And of all terror and all pain.

The American bards shall be marked for generosity and affection and for encouraging competitors . . They shall be kosmos[19] . . without monopoly or secresy[20] . . glad to pass any thing to any one . . hungry for equals night and day. They shall not be careful of riches and privilege. . . . they shall be riches and privilege. . . . they shall perceive who the most affluent man is. The most affluent man is he that confronts all the shows he sees by equivalents out of the

[16]Insouciance, lack of concern.
[17]Changed to "soothe" in later texts.
[18]Savants, sages.
[19]Cosmos.
[20]Changed to "secrecy" in later texts.

stronger wealth of himself. The American bard shall delineate no class of persons nor one or two out of the strata of interests nor love most nor truth most nor the soul most nor the body most. . . . and not be for the eastern states more than the western or the northern states more than the southern.

Exact science and its practical movements are no checks on the greatest poet but always his encouragement and support. The outset and remembrance are there . . . there the arms that lifted him first and brace[21] him best. . . . there he returns after all his goings and comings. The sailor and traveler . . the anatomist, chemist, astronomer, geologist, phrenologist, spiritualist, mathematician, historian and lexicographer are not poets, but they are the lawgivers of poets and their construction underlies the structure of every perfect poem. No matter what rises or is uttered they sent the seed of the conception of it . . . of them and by them stand the visible proofs of souls . . . . . always of their fatherstuff[22] must be begotten the sinewy races of bards. If there shall be love and content between the father and the son and if the greatness of the son is the exuding of the greatness of the father there shall be love between the poet and the man of demonstrable science. In the beauty of poems are the tuft and final applause of science.

Great is the faith of the flush of knowledge and of the investigation of the depths of qualities and things. Cleaving and circling here swells the soul of the poet yet it[23] president of itself always. The depths are fathomless and therefore calm. The innocence and nakedness are resumed . . . they are neither modest nor immodest. The whole theory of the special and supernatural and all that was twined with it or educed[24] out of it departs as a dream. What has ever happened . . . . what happens and whatever may or shall happen, the vital laws enclose all . . . . they are sufficent[25] for any case and for all cases . . . none to be hurried or retarded . . . . any miracle of affairs or persons inadmissible in the vast clear scheme where every motion and every spear of grass and the frames and spirits of men and women and all that concerns them are unspeakably perfect miracles all referring to all and each distinct and in its place. It is also not consistent with the reality of the soul to admit that there is anything in the known universe more divine than men and women.

Men and women and the earth and all upon it are simply to be taken as they are, and the investigation of their past and present and future shall be unintermitted and shall be done with perfect candor. Upon this basis philosophy speculates ever looking toward the poet, ever regarding the eternal tendencies of all toward happiness never inconsistent with what is clear to the senses and to the soul. For the eternal tendencies of all toward happiness make the only point of sane philosophy. Whatever comprehends less than that . . . whatever is less than the laws of light and of astronomical motion . . . or less than the laws that follow the thief the liar the glutton and the drunkard through this life and doubtless afterward. . . . . . or less than vast stretches of time or the slow formation of density or the patient upheaving of strata—is of no account. Whatever would put God in a poem or system of philosophy as contending against some being or influence is also of no account. Sanity and ensemble characterise the great master . . . spoilt in one principle all is spoilt. The great master has nothing to do with miracles. He sees health for himself in being one of the

[21]Changed to "braced" in later texts. [22]Seminal fluid. [23]Corrected to "is" in later texts.
[24]Brought. [25]Changed to "sufficient" in later texts.

mass. . . . he sees the hiatus in singular eminence. To the perfect shape comes common ground. To be under the general law is great for that is to correspond with it. The master knows that he is unspeakably great and that all are unspeakably great. . . . that nothing for instance is greater than to conceive children and bring them up well . . . that to be is just as great as to perceive or tell.

In the make of the great masters the idea of political liberty is indispensible. Liberty takes the adherence of heroes wherever men and women exist. . . . but never takes any adherence or welcome from the rest more than from poets. They are the voice and exposition of liberty. They out of ages are worthy the grand idea. . . . to them it is confided and they must sustain it. Nothing has precedence of it and nothing can warp or degrade it. The attitude of great poets is to cheer up slaves and horrify despots. The turn of their necks, the sound of their feet, the motions of their wrists, are full of hazard to the one and hope to the other. Come nigh them awhile and though they neither speak or advise you shall learn the faithful American lesson. Liberty is poorly served by men whose good intent is quelled from one failure or two failures or any number of failures, or from the casual indifference or ingratitude of the people, or from the sharp show of the tushes[26] of power, or the bringing to bear soldiers and cannon or any penal statutes. Liberty relies upon itself, invites no one, promises nothing, sits in calmness and light, is positive and composed, and knows no discouragement. The battle rages with many a loud alarm and frequent advance and retreat. . . . the enemy triumphs. . . . the prison, the handcuffs, the iron necklace and anklet, the scaffold, garrote and leadballs do their work. . . . the cause is asleep. . . . the strong throats are choked with their own blood. . . . the young men drop their eyelashes toward the ground when they pass each other. . . . and is liberty gone out of that place? No never. When liberty goes it is not the first to go nor the second or third to go . . it waits for all the rest to go . . it is the last . . . When the memories of the old martyrs are faded utterly away. . . . when the large names of patriots are laughed at in the public halls from the lips of the orators. . . . when the boys are no more christened after the same but christened after tyrants and traitors instead. . . . when the laws of the free are grudgingly permitted and laws for informers and bloodmoney are sweet to the taste of the people. . . . when I and you walk abroad upon the earth stung with compassion at the sight of numberless brothers answering our equal friendship and calling no man master—and when we are elated with noble joy at the sight of slaves. . . . when the soul retires in the cool communion of the night and surveys its experience and has much extasy over the word and deed that put back a helpless innocent person into the gripe of the gripers or into any cruel inferiority . . . when those in all parts of these states who could easier realize the true American character but do not yet—when the swarms of cringers, suckers,[27] doughfaces,[28] lice of politics, planners of sly involutions for their own preferment to city offices or state legislatures or the judiciary or congress or the presidency, obtain a response of love and natural deference from the people whether they get the offices or no. . . . when it is better to be a bound booby[29] and rogue in office at a high salary than the poorest free mechanic or farmer with his hat unmoved from his head and firm eyes and a candid and generous heart. . . . and when servility by town or state or the federal government

[26]Tusks, teeth. [27]Blackmailing politicians.
[28]Pliable, unprincipled men. [29]A political hack controlled by special interests.

or any oppression on a large scale or small scale can be tried on without its own punishment following duly after in exact proportion against the smallest chance of escape. . . . or rather when all life and all the souls of men and women are discharged from any part of the earth—then only shall the instinct of liberty be discharged from that part of the earth.

As the attributes of the poets of the kosmos concentre in the real body and soul and in the pleasure of things they possess the superiority of genuineness over all fiction and romance. As they emit themselves facts are showered over with light. . . . the daylight is lit with more volatile light. . . . also the deep between the setting and rising sun goes deeper many fold. Each precise object or condition or combination or process exhibits a beauty. . . . the multiplication table its—old age its—the carpenter's trade its—the grand-opera its. . . . the hugehulled cleanshaped New-York clipper at sea under steam or full sail gleams with unmatched beauty. . . . the American circles and large harmonies of government gleam with theirs. . . . and the commonest definite intentions and actions with theirs. The poets of the kosmos advance through all interpositions and coverings and turmoils and strategems to first principles. They are of use. . . . they dissolve poverty from its need and riches from its conceit. You large proprietor they say shall not realize or perceive more than any one else. The owner of the library is not he who holds a legal title to it having bought and paid for it. Any one and every one is owner of the library who can read the same through all the varieties of tongues and subjects and styles, and in whom they enter with ease and take residence and force toward paternity and maternity, and make supple and powerful and rich and large. . . . . These American states strong and healthy and accomplished shall receive no pleasure from violations of natural models and must not permit them. In paintings or mouldings or carvings in mineral or wood, or in the illustrations of books or newspapers, or in any comic or tragic prints, or in the patterns of woven stuffs or any thing to beautify rooms or furniture or costumes, or to put upon cornices or monuments or on the prows or sterns of ships, or to put anywhere before the human eye indoors or out, that which distorts honest shapes or which creates unearthly beings or places or contingencies is a nuisance and revolt. Of the human form especially it is so great it must never be made ridiculous. Of ornaments to a work nothing outre[30] can be allowed . . but those ornaments can be allowed that conform to the perfect facts of the open air and that flow out of the nature of the work and come irrepressibly from it and are necessary to the completion of the work. Most works are most beautiful without ornament . . . Exaggerations will be revenged in human physiology. Clean and vigorous children are jetted[31] and conceived only in those communities where the models of natural forms are public every day. . . . . Great genius and the people of these states must never be demeaned to romances. As soon as histories are properly told there is no more need of romances.

The great poets are also to be known by the absence in them of tricks and by the justification of perfect personal candor. Then folks echo a new cheap joy and a divine voice leaping from their brains: How beautiful is candor! All faults may be forgiven of him who has perfect candor. Henceforth let no man of us lie, for we have seen that openness wins the inner and outer world and that there is no single exception, and that never since our earth gathered itself in a mass have

[30]Extravagant. [31]I.e., produced by a jet of seminal fluid.

deceit or subterfuge or prevarication attracted its smallest particle or the faintest tinge of a shade—and that through the enveloping wealth and rank of a state or the whole republic of states a sneak or sly person shall be discovered and despised. . . . and that the soul has never been once fooled and never can be fooled. . . . and thrift without the loving nod of the soul is only a fœtid puff. . . . and there never grew up in any of the continents of the globe nor upon any planet or satellite or star, nor upon the asteroids, under the fluid wet of the sea, nor in that condition which precedes nor in any part of the ethereal space, nor in the midst of density, nor the birth of babes, nor at any time during the changes of life, nor in that condition that follows what we term death, nor in any stretch of abeyance or action afterward of vitality, nor in any process of formation or reformation anywhere, a being whose instinct hated the truth.

Extreme caution or prudence, the soundest organic health, large hope and comparison and fondness for women and children, large alimentiveness and destructiveness and causality,[32] with a perfect sense of the oneness of nature and the propriety of the same spirit applied to human affairs . . these are called up of the float[33] of the brain of the world to be parts of the greatest poet from his birth out of his mother's womb and from her birth out of her mother's. Caution seldom goes far enough. It has been thought that the prudent citizen was the citizen who applied himself to solid gains and did well for himself and his family and completed a lawful life without debt or crime. The greatest poet sees and admits these economies as he sees the economies of food and sleep, but has higher notions of prudence than to think he gives much when he gives a few slight attentions at the latch of the gate. The premises of the prudence of life are not the hospitality of it or the ripeness and harvest of it. Beyond the independence of a little sum laid aside for burial-money, and of a few clapboards around the shingles overhead on a lot[34] of American soil owned, and the easy dollars that supply the year's plain clothing and meals, the melancholy prudence of the abandonment of such a great being as a man is to the toss and pallor of years of moneymaking with all their scorching days and icy nights and all their stifling deceits and underhanded dodgings, or infinitessimals of parlors, or shameless stuffing while others starve . . and all the loss of the bloom and odor of the earth and of the flowers and atmosphere and of the sea and of the true taste of the women and men you pass or have to do with in youth or middle age, and the issuing sickness and desperate revolt at the close of a life without elevation or naivete, and the ghastly chatter of a death without serenity or majesty, is the great fraud upon modern civilization and forethought, blotching the surface and system which civilization undeniably drafts, and moistening with tears the immense features it spreads and spreads with such velocity before the reached kisses of the soul . . . Still the right explanation remains to be made about prudence. The prudence of the mere wealth and respectability of the most esteemed life appears too faint for the eye to observe at all when little and large alike drop quietly aside at the thought of the prudence suitable for immortality. What is wisdom that fills the thinness of a year or seventy or eighty years to wisdom spaced out by ages and coming back at a certain time with strong reinforcements and rich presents and

[32]Phrenological terms meaning an appetite for food, an interest in destruction, and a tendency to trace effects to their causes.

[33]Flow or fluid. [34]Small plot of land.

the clear faces of wedding-guests as far as you can look in every direction running gaily toward you? Only the soul is of itself. . . . all else has reference to what ensues. All that a person does or thinks is of consequence. Not a move can a man or woman make that affects him or her in a day or a month or any part of the direct lifetime or the hour of death but the same affects him or her onward afterward through the indirect lifetime. The indirect is always as great and real as the direct. The spirit receives from the body just as much as it gives to the body. Not one name of word or deed . . not of venereal sores or discolorations . . not the privacy of the onanist[35] . . not of the putrid veins of gluttons or rumdrinkers . . . not peculation[36] or cunning or betrayal or murder . . no serpentine poison of those that seduce women . . not the foolish yielding of women . . not prostitution . . not of any depravity of young men . . not of the attainment of gain by discreditable means . . not any nastiness of appetite . . not any harshness of officers to men or judges to prisoners or fathers to sons or sons to fathers or of husbands to wives or bosses to their boys . . not of greedy looks or malignant wishes . . . nor any of the wiles practised by people upon themselves . . . ever is or ever can be stamped on the programme but it is duly realized and returned, and that returned in further performances . . . and they returned again. Nor can the push of charity or personal force ever be any thing else than the profoundest reason, whether it bring arguments to hand or no. No specification is necessary . . to add or subtract or divide is in vain. Little or big, learned or unlearned, white or black, legal or illegal, sick or well, from the first inspiration down the windpipe to the last expiration out of it, all that a male or female does that is vigorous and benevolent and clean is so much sure profit to him or her in the unshakable order of the universe and through the whole scope of it forever. If the savage or felon is wise it is well. . . . if the greatest poet or savan is wise it is simply the same . . . if the President or chief justice is wise it is the same . . . if the young mechanic or farmer is wise it is no more or less . . if the prostitute is wise it is no more nor less. The interest will come round . . all will come round. All the best actions of war and peace . . . all help given to relatives and strangers and the poor and old and sorrowful and young children and widows and the sick, and to all shunned persons . . all furtherance of fugitives and of the escape of slaves . . all the self-denial that stood steady and aloof on wrecks and saw others take the seats of the boats . . . all offering of substance or life for the good old cause, or for a friend's sake or opinion's sake . . . all pains of enthusiasts scoffed at by their neighbors . . all the vast sweet love and precious suffering of mothers . . all honest men baffled in strifes recorded or unrecorded . . . . all the grandeur and good of the few ancient nations whose fragments of annals we inherit . . and all the good of the hundreds of far mightier and more ancient nations unknown to us by name or date or location . . . . all that was ever manfully begun, whether it succeeded or no . . . . all that has at any time been well suggested out of the divine heart of man or by the divinity of his mouth or by the shaping of his great hands . . and all that is well thought or done this day on any part of the surface of the globe . . or on any of the wandering stars or fixed stars by those there as we are here . . or that is henceforth to be well thought or done

[35]In the nineteenth century, the sin for which the Lord slew Onan (Genesis 38:9) was thought to have been masturbation.

[36]Embezzlement.

by you whoever you are, or by any one—these singly and wholly inured at their time and inure now and will inure always to the identities from which they sprung or shall spring . . . Did you guess any of them lived only its moment? The world does not so exist . . no parts palpable or impalpable so exist . . . no result exists now without being from its long antecedent result, and that from its antecedent, and so backward without the farthest mention-able spot coming a bit nearer the beginning than any other spot. . . . Whatever satisfies the soul is truth. The prudence of the greatest poet answers at last the craving and glut of the soul, is not contemptuous of less ways of prudence if they conform to its ways, puts off nothing, permits no let-up for its own case or any case, has no particular sabbath or judgment-day, divides not the living from the dead or the righteous from the unrighteous, is satisfied with the present, matches every thought or act by its correlative, knows no possible forgiveness or deputed atonement . . knows that the young man who composedly periled his life and lost it has done exceeding well for himself, while the man who has not periled his life and retains it to old age in riches and ease has perhaps achieved nothing for himself worth mentioning . . and that only that person has no great prudence to learn who has learnt to prefer real longlived things, and favors body and soul the same, and perceives the indirect assuredly following the direct, and what evil or good he does leaping onward and waiting to meet him again—and who in his spirit in any emergency whatever neither hurries or avoids death.

The direct trial of him who would be the greatest poet is today. If he does not flood himself with the immediate age as with vast oceanic tides . . . . . and if he does not attract his own land body and soul to himself and hang on its neck with incomparable love and plunge his semitic[37] muscle into its merits and demerits . . . and if he be not himself the age transfigured . . . . and if to him is not opened the eternity which gives similitude to all periods and locations and processes and animate and inanimate forms, and which is the bond of time, and rises up from its inconceivable vagueness and infiniteness in the swimming shape of today, and is held by the ductile anchors of life, and makes the present spot the passage from what was to what shall be, and commits itself to the representation of this wave of an hour and this one of the sixty beautiful children of the wave—let him merge in the general run and wait his development. . . . . Still the final test of poems or any character or work remains. The prescient poet projects himself centuries ahead and judges performer or performance after the changes of time. Does it live through them? Does it still hold on untired? Will the same style and the direction of genius to similar points be satisfactory now? Has no new discovery in science or arrival at superior planes of thought and judgment and behavior fixed him or his so that either can be looked down upon? Have the marches of tens and hundreds and thousands of years made willing detours to the right hand and the left hand for his sake? Is he beloved long and long after he is buried? Does the young man think often of him? and the young woman think often of him? and do the middleaged and the old think of him?

A great poem is for ages and ages in common and for all degrees and complexions and all departments and sects and for a woman as much as a man and a man as much as a woman. A great poem is no finish to a man or woman but

[37]Seminal.

rather a beginning. Has any one fancied he could sit at last under some due authority and rest satisfied with explanations and realize and be content and full? To no such terminus does the greatest poet bring . . . he brings neither cessation or sheltered fatness and ease. The touch of him tells in action. Whom he takes he takes with firm sure grasp into live regions previously unattained . . . . thenceforward is no rest . . . . they see the space and ineffable sheen that turn the old spots and lights into dead vacuums. The companion of him beholds the birth and progress of stars and learns one of the meanings. Now there shall be a man cohered out of a tumult and chaos . . . . the elder encourages the younger and shows him how . . . they two shall launch off fearlessly together till the new world fits an orbit for itself and looks unabashed on the lesser orbits of the stars and sweeps through the ceaseless rings and shall never be quiet again.

There will soon be no more priests. Their work is done. They may wait awhile . . perhaps a generation or two . . dropping off by degrees. A superior breed shall take their place . . . . the gangs of kosmos and prophets en masse shall take their place. A new order shall arise and they shall be the priests of man, and every man shall be his own priest. The churches built under their umbrage[38] shall be the churches of men and women. Through the divinity of themselves shall the kosmos and the new breed of poets be interpreters of men and women and of all events and things. They shall find their inspiration in real objects today, symptoms of the past and future. . . . They shall not deign to defend immortality or God or the perfection of things or liberty or the exquisite beauty and reality of the soul. They shall arise in America and be responded to from the remainder of the earth.

The English language befriends the grand American expression. . . . it is brawny enough and limber and full enough. On the tough stock of a race who through all change of circumstance was never without the idea of political liberty, which is the animus of all liberty, it has attracted the terms of daintier and gayer and subtler and more elegant tongues. It is the powerful language of resistance . . . it is the dialect of common sense. It is the speech of the proud and melancholy races and of all who aspire. It is the chosen tongue to express growth faith self-esteem freedom justice equality friendliness amplitude prudence decision and courage. It is the medium that shall well nigh express the inexpressible.

No great literature nor any like style of behaviour or oratory or social intercourse or household arrangements or public institutions or the treatment by bosses of employed people, nor executive detail or detail of the army or navy, nor spirit of legislation or courts or police or tuition or architecture or songs or amusements or the costumes of young men, can long elude the jealous and passionate instinct of American standards. Whether or no the sign appears from the mouths of the people, it throbs a live interrogation in every freeman's and freewoman's heart after that which passes by, or this built to remain. Is it uniform with my country? Are its disposals without ignominious distinctions? Is it for the evergrowing communes of brothers and lovers, large, well-united, proud beyond the old models, generous beyond all models? Is it something grown fresh out of the fields or drawn from the sea for use to me today here? I know that what answers for me an American must answer for any individual or nation that serves for a part of my materials. Does this answer?

[38]Shadow.

or is it without reference to universal needs? or sprung of the needs of the less developed society of special ranks? or old needs of pleasure overlaid by modern science and forms? Does this acknowledge liberty with audible and absolute acknowledgment, and set slavery at nought for life and death? Will it help breed one goodshaped and wellhung man, and a woman to be his perfect and independent mate? Does it improve manners? Is it for the nursing of the young of the republic? Does it solve[39] readily with the sweet milk of the nipples of the breasts of the mother of many children? Has it too the old ever-fresh forbearance and impartiality? Does it look with the same love on the last born and on those hardening toward stature, and on the errant, and on those who disdain all strength of assault outside of their own?

The poems distilled from other poems will probably pass away. The coward will surely pass away. The expectation of the vital and great can only be satisfied by the demeanor of the vital and great. The swarms of the polished deprecating and reflectors and the polite float off and leave no remembrance. America prepares with composure and goodwill for the visitors that have sent word. It is not intellect that is to be their warrant and welcome. The talented, the artist, the ingenious, the editor, the statesman, the erudite . . they are not unappreciated . . they fall in their place and do their work. The soul of the nation also does its work. No disguse can pass on it . . no disguse can conceal from it. It rejects none, it permits all. Only toward as good as itself and toward the like of itself will it advance half-way. An individual is as superb as a nation when he has the qualities which make a superb nation. The soul of the largest and wealthiest and proudest nation may well go half-way to meet that of its poets. The signs are effectual. There is no fear of mistake. If the one is true the other is true. The proof of a poet is that his country absorbs him as affectionately as he has absorbed it.

1855

SONG OF MYSELF

1

I CELEBRATE myself, and sing myself,
And what I assume you shall assume,
For every atom belonging to me as good belongs to you.

I loaf and invite my soul,
I lean and loaf at my ease observing a spear of summer grass.

My tongue, every atom of my blood, formed from this soil, this air,
Born here of parents born here from parents the same, and their parents the same,
I, now thirty-seven years old in perfect health begin,
Hoping to cease not till death.

[39]Dissolve.

Creeds and schools in abeyance,
Retiring back a while sufficed at what they are, but never forgotten,
I harbor for good or bad, I permit to speak at every hazard,
Nature without check with original energy.

2

Houses and rooms are full of perfumes, the shelves are crowded with perfumes,
I breathe the fragrance myself and know it and like it,
The distillation would intoxicate me also, but I shall not let it.

The atmosphere is not a perfume, it has no taste of the distillation, it is odorless,
It is for my mouth forever, I am in love with it,
I will go to the bank by the wood and become undisguised and naked,
I am mad for it to be in contact with me.

The smoke of my own breath,
Echoes, ripples, buzzed whispers, love-root, silk-thread, crotch and vine,
My respiration and inspiration, the beating of my heart, the passing of blood and air through my lungs,
The sniff of green leaves and dry leaves, and of the shore and dark-colored sea-rocks, and of hay in the barn,

The sound of the belched words of my voice loosed to the eddies of the wind,
A few light kisses, a few embraces, a reaching around of arms,
The play of shine and shade on the trees as the supple boughs wag,
The delight alone or in the rush of the streets, or along the fields and hill-sides,
The feeling of health, the full-noon trill, the song of me rising from bed and meeting the sun.

Have you reckoned a thousand acres much? have you reckoned the earth much?
Have you practiced so long to learn to read?
Have you felt so proud to get at the meaning of poems?

Stop this day and night with me and you shall possess the origin of all poems,
You shall possess the good of the earth and sun, (there are millions of suns left,)
You shall no longer take things at second or third hand, nor look through the eyes of the dead, nor feed on the spectres in books,
You shall not look through my eyes either, nor take things from me,
You shall listen to all sides and filter them from your self.

3

I have heard what the talkers were talking, the talk of the beginning and the end,
But I do not talk of the beginning or the end.

There was never any more inception than there is now,
Nor any more youth or age than there is now,
And will never be any more perfection than there is now,
Nor any more heaven or hell than there is now.

Urge and urge and urge,
Always the procreant urge of the world.

Out of the dimness opposite equals advance, always substance and increase, always sex,
Always a knit of identity, always distinction, always a breed of life.
To elaborate is no avail, learned and unlearned feel that it is so.

Sure as the most certain sure, plumb in the uprights, well entretied,[1] braced in the beams,
Stout as a horse, affectionate, haughty, electrical,
I and this mystery here we stand.

Clear and sweet is my soul, and clear and sweet is all that is not my soul.

Lack one lacks both, and the unseen is proved by the seen,
Till that becomes unseen and receives proof in its turn.

Showing the best and dividing it from the worst age vexes age,
Knowing the perfect fitness and equanimity of things, while they discuss I am silent, and go bathe and admire myself.

Welcome is every organ and attribute of me, and of any man hearty and clean,
Not an inch nor a particle of an inch is vile, and none shall be less familiar than the rest.

I am satisfied—I see, dance, laugh, sing;
As the hugging and loving bed-fellow[2] sleeps at my side through the night, and withdraws at the peep of the day with stealthy tread,
Leaving me baskets covered with white towels swelling the house with their plenty,
Shall I postpone my acceptation and realization and scream at my eyes,
That they turn from gazing after and down the road,
And forthwith cipher[3] and show me to a cent,
Exactly the value of one and exactly the value of two, and which is ahead?

[1]A carpenter's term meaning supported, braced.
[2]In the 1855 edition the "bed-fellow" is identified as God. [3]Calculate.

4

Trippers and askers[4] surround me,
People I meet, the effect upon me of my early life or the ward and city I live in, or the nation,
The latest dates, discoveries, inventions, societies, authors old and new,
My dinner, dress, associates, looks, compliments, dues,
The real or fancied indifference of some man or woman I love,
The sickness of one of my folks or of myself, or ill-doing or loss or lack of money, or depressions or exaltations,
Battles, the horrors of fratricidal[5] war, the fever of doubtful news, the fitful events;
These come to me days and nights and go from me again,
But they are not the Me myself.

Apart from the pulling and hauling stands what I am,
Stands amused, complacent, compassionating, idle, unitary,
Looks down, is erect, or bends an arm on an impalpable certain rest,
Looking with side-curved head curious what will come next,
Both in and out of the game and watching and wondering at it.

Backward I see in my own days where I sweated through fog with linguists and contenders,
I have no mockings or arguments, I witness and wait.

5

I believe in you my soul, the other I am must not abase itself to you,
And you must not be abased to the other.

Loaf with me on the grass, loose the stop from your throat,
Not words, not music or rhyme I want, not custom or lecture, not even the best,
Only the lull I like, the hum of your valved voice.

I mind how once we lay such a transparent summer morning,
How you settled your head athwart my hips and gently turned over upon me,
And parted the shirt from my bosom-bone, and plunged your tongue to my bare-stript heart,
And reached till you felt my beard, and reached till you held my feet.

Swiftly arose and spread around me the peace and knowledge that pass all the argument of the earth,
And I know that the hand of God is the promise of my own,
And I know that the spirit of God is the brother of my own,
And that all the men ever born are also my brothers, and the women my sisters and lovers,

[4]I.e., travelers and beggars. [5]Brother killing brother.

And that a kelson[6] of the creation is love,
And limitless are leaves stiff or drooping in the fields,
And brown ants in the little wells beneath them,
And mossy scabs of the worm fence,[7] heaped stones, elder, mullein and poke-weed.

6

A child said What is the grass? fetching it to me with full hands;
How could I answer the child? I do not know what it is any more than he.

I guess it must be the flag of my disposition, out of hopeful green stuff woven.

Or I guess it is the handkerchief of the Lord,
A scented gift and remembrancer designedly dropt,
Bearing the owner's name someway in the corners, that we may see and remark, and say Whose?

Or I guess the grass is itself a child, the produced babe of the vegetation.

Or I guess it is a uniform hieroglyphic,
And it means, Sprouting alike in broad zones and narrow zones,
Growing among black folks as among white,
Kanuck, Tuckahoe, Congressman, Cuff,[8] I give them the same, I receive them the same.

And now it seems to me the beautiful uncut hair of graves.

Tenderly will I use you curling grass,
It may be you transpire from the breasts of young men,
It may be if I had known them I would have loved them,
It may be you are from old people, or from offspring taken soon out of their mothers' laps,
And here you are the mothers' laps.

This grass is very dark to be from the white heads of old mothers,
Darker than the colorless beards of old men,
Dark to come from under the faint red roofs of mouths.

O I perceive after all so many uttering tongues,
And I perceive they do not come from the roofs of mouths for nothing.

I wish I could translate the hints about the dead young men and women,
And the hints about old men and mothers, and the offspring taken soon out of their laps.

[6] Keelson, ship timbers that brace the keel. [7] A zigzag rail fence.
[8] Kanuck: a French Canadian; Tuckahoe: a Virginian of the coastal lowlands; Cuff: an African American.

What do you think has become of the young and old men?
And what do you think has become of the women and children?

They are alive and well somewhere,
The smallest sprout shows there is really no death,
And if ever there was it led forward life, and does not wait at the end to arrest it,
And ceased the moment life appeared.

All goes onward and outward, nothing collapses,
And to die is different from what any one supposed, and luckier.

7

Has any one supposed it lucky to be born?
I hasten to inform him or her it is just as lucky to die, and I know it.

I pass death with the dying and birth with the new-washed babe, and am not contained between my hat and boots,
And peruse manifold objects, no two alike and every one good,
The earth good and the stars good, and their adjuncts all good.

I am not an earth nor an adjunct of an earth,
I am the mate and companion of people, all just as immortal and fathomless as myself,
(They do not know how immortal, but I know.)

Every kind for itself and its own, for me mine male and female,
For me those that have been boys and that love women,
For me the man that is proud and feels how it stings to be slighted,
For me the sweet-heart and the old maid, for me mothers and the mothers of mothers,
For me lips that have smiled, eyes that have shed tears,
For me children and the begetters of children.

Undrape! you are not guilty to me, nor stale nor discarded,
I see through the broadcloth and gingham whether or no,
And am around, tenacious, acquisitive, tireless, and cannot be shaken away.

8

The little one sleeps in its cradle,
I lift the gauze and look a long time, and silently brush away flies with my hand.

The youngster and the red-faced girl turn aside up the bushy hill,
I peeringly view them from the top.

The suicide sprawls on the bloody floor of the bedroom,
I witness the corpse with its dabbled hair, I note where the pistol has fallen.

The blab of the pave,[9] tires of carts, sluff[10] of boot-soles, talk of the promenaders,
The heavy omnibus,[11] the driver with his interrogating thumb, the clank of the shod horses on the granite floor,
The snow-sleighs, clinking, shouted jokes, pelts of snow-balls,
The hurrahs for popular favorites, the fury of roused mobs,
The flap of the curtained litter,[12] a sick man inside borne to the hospital,
The meeting of enemies, the sudden oath, the blows and fall,
The excited crowd, the policeman with his star quickly working his passage to the centre of the crowd,
The impassive stones that receive and return so many echoes,
What groans of over-fed or half-starved who fall sunstruck or in fits,
What exclamations of women taken suddenly who hurry home and give birth to babes,
What living and buried speech is always vibrating here, what howls restrained by decorum,
Arrests of criminals, slights, adulterous offers made, acceptances, rejections with convex lips,
I mind them or the show or resonance of them—I come and I depart.

9

The big doors of the country barn stand open and ready,
The dried grass of the harvest-time loads the slow-drawn wagon,
The clear light plays on the brown gray and green intertinged,
The armfuls are packed to the sagging mow.

I am there, I help, I came stretched atop of the load,
I felt its soft jolts, one leg reclined on the other,
I jump from the cross-beams and seize the clover and timothy,[13]
And roll head over heels and tangle my hair full of wisps.

10

Alone far in the wilds and mountains I hunt,
Wandering amazed at my own lightness and glee,
In the late afternoon choosing a safe spot to pass the night,
Kindling a fire and broiling the fresh-killed game,
Falling asleep on the gathered leaves with my dog and gun by my side.

[9]The talk of the streets. [10]Shuffling sound.
[11]A large, passenger-carrying vehicle, a bus; horse-drawn in Whitman's day.
[12]A curtained vehicle, equipped with a litter (stretcher), for transporting the sick or wounded.
[13]A coarse grass, used for fodder.

The Yankee clipper[14] is under her sky-sails,[15] she cuts the sparkle and scud,[16]
My eyes settle the land, I bend at her prow or shout joyously from the deck.

The boatmen and clam-diggers arose early and stopped for me,
I tucked my trouser-ends in my boots and went and had a good time;
You should have been with us that day round the chowder-kettle.

I saw the marriage of the trapper in the open air in the far west, the bride was a red girl,
Her father and his friends sat near cross-legged and dumbly smoking, they had moccasins to their feet and large thick blankets hanging from their shoulders,
On a bank lounged the trapper, he was dressed mostly in skins, his luxuriant beard and curls protected his neck, he held his bride by the hand,
She had long eyelashes, her head was bare, her coarse straight locks descended upon her voluptuous limbs and reached to her feet.

The runaway slave came to my house and stopped outside,
I heard his motions crackling the twigs of the woodpile,
Through the swung half-door of the kitchen I saw him limpsy[17] and weak,
And went where he sat on a log and led him in and assured him,
And brought water and filled a tub for his sweated body and bruised feet,
And gave him a room that entered from my own, and gave him some coarse clean clothes,
And remember perfectly well his revolving eyes and his awkwardness,
And remember putting plasters on the galls of his neck and ankles;
He staid with me a week before he was recuperated and passed north,
I had him sit next me at table, my fire-lock[18] leaned in the corner.

11

Twenty-eight young men bathe by the shore,
Twenty-eight young men and all so friendly;
Twenty-eight years of womanly life and all so lonesome.

She owns the fine house by the rise of the bank,
She hides handsome and richly drest aft the blinds of the window.

Which of the young men does she like the best?
Ah the homeliest of them is beautiful to her.

Where are you off to, lady? for I see you,
You splash in the water there, yet stay stock still in your room.

Dancing and laughing along the beach came the twenty-ninth bather,
The rest did not see her, but she saw them and loved them.

[14]Swift sailing vessel. [15]Upper sails. [16]Sea foam. [17]Limp. [18]Gun.

The beards of the young men glistened with wet, it ran from their long hair,
Little streams passed all over their bodies.

An unseen hand also passed over their bodies,
It descended tremblingly from their temples and ribs.

The young men float on their backs, their white bellies bulge to the sun, they do not ask who seizes fast to them,
They do not know who puffs and declines with pendant and bending arch,
They do not think whom they souse with spray.

12

The butcher-boy puts off his killing-clothes, or sharpens his knife at the stall in the market,
I loiter enjoying his repartee and his shuffle and break-down.[19]

Blacksmiths with grimed and hairy chests environ the anvil,
Each has his main-sledge, they are all out, there is a great heat in the fire.

From the cinder-strewed threshold I follow their movements,
The lithe sheer[20] of their waists plays even with their massive arms,
Overhand the hammers swing, overhand so slow, overhand so sure,
They do not hasten, each man hits in his place.

13

The negro holds firmly the reins of his four horses, the block swags[21] underneath on its tied-over chain,
The negro that drives the long dray[22] of the stone-yard, steady and tall he stands poised on one leg on the string-piece,[23]
His blue shirt exposes his ample neck and breast and loosens over his hip-band,
His glance is calm and commanding, he tosses the slouch of his hat away from his forehead,
The sun falls on his crispy hair and mustache, falls on the black of his polished and perfect limbs.
I behold the picturesque giant and love him, and I do not stop there,
I go with the team also.

[19]Popular dance steps. [20]Curve.
[21]Sways, sags heavily. [22]A sledge or wagon used for hauling heavy loads.
[23]A long support timber.

In me the caresser of life wherever moving, backward as well as forward
sluing,[24]
To niches aside and junior[25] bending, not a person or object missing,
Absorbing all to myself and for this song.

Oxen that rattle the yoke and chain or halt in the leafy shade, what is that
you express in your eyes?
It seems to me more than all the print I have read in my life.

My tread scares the wood-drake and wood-duck on my distant and day-long
ramble,
They rise together, they slowly circle around.

I believe in those winged purposes,
And acknowledge red, yellow, white, playing within me,
And consider green and violet and the tufted crown[26] intentional,
And do not call the tortoise unworthy because she is not something else,
And the jay in the woods never studied the gamut,[27] yet trills pretty well
to me,
And the look of the bay mare shames silliness out of me.

14

The wild gander leads his flock through the cool night,
Ya-honk he says, and sounds it down to me like an invitation,
The pert[28] may suppose it meaningless, but I listening close,
Find its purpose and place up there toward the wintry sky.

The sharp-hoofed moose of the north, the cat on the house-sill, the
chickadee, the prairie-dog,
The litter of the grunting sow as they tug at her teats,
The brood of the turkey-hen and she with her half-spread wings,
I see in them and myself the same old law.

The press of my foot to the earth springs a hundred affections,
They scorn the best I can do to relate them.

I am enamored of growing out-doors,
Of men that live among cattle or taste of the ocean or woods,
Of the builders and steerers of ships and the wielders of axes and mauls,
and the drivers of horses,
I can eat and sleep with them week in and week out.

[24]Turning, twisting. [25]Smaller. [26]Of the drake.
[27]Musical scale. [28]Self-assured, cocky.

What is commonest, cheapest, nearest, easiest, is Me,
Me going in for my chances, spending for vast returns,
Adorning myself to bestow myself on the first that will take me,
Not asking the sky to come down to my good will,
Scattering it freely forever.

15

The pure contralto sings in the organ loft,
The carpenter dresses his plank, the tongue of his foreplane whistles its wild ascending lisp,
The married and unmarried children ride home to their Thanksgiving dinner,
The pilot seizes the king-pin,[29] he heaves down with a strong arm,
The mate stands braced in the whale-boat, lance and harpoon are ready,
The duck-shooter walks by silent and cautious stretches,
The deacons are ordained with crossed hands at the altar,
The spinning-girl retreats and advances to the hum of the big wheel,
The farmer stops by the bars[30] as he walks on a First-day loafe[31] and looks at the oats and rye,
The lunatic is carried at last to the asylum a confirmed case,
(He will never sleep any more as he did in the cot in his mother's bed-room;)
The jour[32] printer with gray head and gaunt jaws works at his case,[33]
He turns his quid of tobacco while his eyes blur with the manuscript;
The malformed limbs are tied to the surgeon's table,
What is removed drops horribly in a pail;
The quadroon[34] girl is sold at the auction-stand, the drunkard nods by the bar-room stove,
The machinist rolls up his sleeves, the policeman travels his beat, the gate-keeper marks who pass,
The young fellow drives the express-wagon, (I love him, though I do not know him;)
The half-breed straps on his light boots to compete in the race,
The western turkey-shooting draws old and young, some lean on their rifles, some sit on logs,
Out from the crowd steps the marksman, takes his position, levels his piece;
The groups of newly-come immigrants cover the wharf or levee,
As the woolly-pates[35] hoe in the sugar-field, the overseer views them from his saddle,
The bugle calls in the ball-room, the gentlemen run for their partners, the dancers bow to each other,

[29]An extended spoke on a ship's pilot wheel. [30]Fence rails.
[31]A Sunday (from Quaker terminology) time of ease. [32]Journeyman, trained.
[33]Type case. [34]Of one-quarter black ancestry. [35]African Americans.

The youth lies awake in the cedar-roofed garret and harks to the musical rain,
The Wolverine[36] sets traps on the creek that helps fill the Huron,[37]
The squaw wrapped in her yellow-hemmed cloth is offering moccasins and bead-bags for sale,
The connoisseur peers along the exhibition-gallery with half-shut eyes bent sideways,
As the deck-hands make fast the steamboat the plank is thrown for the shore-going passengers,
The young sister holds out the skein while the elder sister winds it off in a ball, and stops now and then for the knots,
The one-year wife is recovering and happy having a week ago borne her first child,
The clean-haired Yankee girl works with her sewing-machine or in the factory or mill,
The paving-man[38] leans on his two-handed rammer, the reporter's lead flies swiftly over the note-book, the sign-painter is lettering with blue and gold,
The canal boy trots on the tow-path,[39] the book-keeper counts at his desk, the shoemaker waxes his thread,
The conductor beats time for the band and all the performers follow him,
The child is baptized, the convert is making his first professions,
The regatta is spread on the bay, the race is begun, (how the white sails sparkle!)
The drover[40] watching his drove sings out to them that would stray,
The pedler sweats with his pack on his back, (the purchaser higgling[41] about the odd cent;)
The bride unrumples her white dress, the minute-hand of the clock moves slowly,
The opium-eater reclines with rigid head and just-opened lips,
The prostitute draggles her shawl, her bonnet bobs on her tipsy and pimpled neck,
The crowd laugh at her blackguard[42] oaths, the men jeer and wink to each other,
(Miserable! I do not laugh at your oaths nor jeer you;)
The President holding a cabinet council is surrounded by the great Secretaries,
On the piazza walk three matrons stately and friendly with twined arms,
The crew of the fish-smack pack repeated layers of halibut in the hold,
The Missourian crosses the plains toting his wares and his cattle,
As the fare-collector goes through the train he gives notice by the jingling of loose change,
The floor-men are laying the floor, the tinners are tinning[43] the roof, the masons are calling for mortar,
In single file each shouldering his hod pass onward the laborers;

[36]Inhabitant of Michigan. [37]Lake Huron. [38]Street-repair man.
[39]Canal-side path for the draft animals that tow canal barges.
[40]One who drives herds of animals. [41]Bargaining.
[42]Rude, abusive. [43]I.e., tinsmiths are sealing the sheet-metal roof.

Seasons pursuing each other the indescribable crowd is gathered, it is the fourth of Seventh-month,[44] (what salutes of cannon and small arms!)
Seasons pursuing each other the plougher ploughs, the mower mows, and the winter-grain falls in the ground;
Off on the lakes the pike-fisher watches and waits by the hole in the frozen surface,
The stumps stand thick round the clearing, the squatter strikes deep with his axe,
Flatboatmen make fast towards dusk near the cotton-wood or pecan-trees,
Coon-seekers[45] go through the regions of the Red river[46] or through those drained by the Tennessee, or through those of the Arkansas,
Torches shine in the dark that hangs on the Chattahooche or Altamahaw,[47]
Patriarchs sit at supper with sons and grandsons and great-grandsons around them,
In walls of adobie, in canvas tents, rest hunters and trappers after their day's sport,
The city sleeps and the country sleeps,
The living sleep for their time, the dead sleep for their time,
The old husband sleeps by his wife and the young husband sleeps by his wife;
And these tend inward to me, and I tend outward to them,
And such as it is to be of these more or less I am,
And of these one and all I weave the song of myself.

16

I am of old and young, of the foolish as much as the wise,
Regardless of others, ever regardful of others,
Maternal as well as paternal, a child as well as a man,
Stuffed with the stuff that is coarse and stuffed with the stuff that is fine,
One of the Nation of many nations, the smallest the same and the largest the same,
A Southerner soon as a Northerner, a planter nonchalant and hospitable down by the Oconee[48] I live,
A Yankee bound my own way ready for trade, my joints the limberest joints on earth and the sternest joints on earth,
A Kentuckian walking the vale of the Elkhorn[49] in my deer-skin leggings, a Louisianian or Georgian,
A boatman over lakes or bays or along coasts, a Hoosier, Badger, Buckeye;[50]
At home on Kanadian[51] snow-shoes or up in the bush, or with fishermen off Newfoundland,
At home in the fleet of ice-boats, sailing with the rest and tacking,
At home on the hills of Vermont or in the woods of Maine, or the Texan ranch,

[44]Quaker term for July. [45]Raccoon hunters. [46]Along the Oklahoma–Texas border.
[47]Rivers in Georgia. [48]River in Georgia. [49]River in Nebraska.
[50]An inhabitant of Indiana, of Wisconsin, of Ohio, respectively.
[51]Whitman's spelling of "Canadian."

Comrade of Californians, comrade of free North-Westerners, (loving their big proportions,)
Comrade of raftsmen and coalmen, comrade of all who shake hands and welcome to drink and meat,
A learner with the simplest, a teacher of the thoughtfullest,
A novice beginning yet experient of[52] myriads of seasons,
Of every hue and caste am I, of every rank and religion,
A farmer, mechanic, artist, gentleman, sailor, quaker,
Prisoner, fancy-man,[53] rowdy, lawyer, physician, priest.

I resist any thing better than my own diversity,
Breathe the air but leave plenty after me,
And am not stuck up, and am in my place.

(The moth and the fish-eggs are in their place,
The bright suns I see and the dark suns I cannot see are in their place,
The palpable is in its place and the impalpable is in its place.)

17

These are really the thoughts of all men in all ages and lands, they are not original with me,
If they are not yours as much as mine they are nothing, or next to nothing,
If they are not the riddle and the untying of the riddle they are nothing,
If they are not just as close as they are distant they are nothing.

This is the grass that grows wherever the land is and the water is,
This the common air that bathes the globe.

18

With music strong I come, with my cornets and my drums,
I play not marches for accepted victors only, I play marches for conquered and slain persons.

Have you heard that it was good to gain the day?
I also say it is good to fall, battles are lost in the same spirit in which they are won.

I beat and pound for the dead,
I blow through my embouchures[54] my loudest and gayest for them.
Vivas[55] to those who have failed!
And to those whose war-vessels sank in the sea!
And to those themselves who sank in the sea!

[52]I.e., one who has experienced. [53]A whore's pimp.
[54]Mouthpieces of musical instruments. [55]Salutes.

And to all generals that lost engagements, and all overcome heroes!
And the numberless unknown heroes equal to the greatest heroes known!

19

This is the meal equally set, this the meat for natural hunger,
It is for the wicked just same as the righteous, I make appointments with all,
I will not have a single person slighted or left away,
The kept-woman, sponger, thief, are hereby invited,
The heavy-lipped slave is invited, the venerealee[56] is invited;
There shall be no difference between them and the rest.

This is the press of a bashful hand, this the float and odor of hair,
This the touch of my lips to yours, this the murmur of yearning,
This the far-off depth and height reflecting my own face,
This the thoughtful merge[57] of myself, and the outlet again.

Do you guess I have some intricate purpose?
Well I have, for the Fourth-month[58] showers have, and the mica on the side
 of a rock has.

Do you take it I would astonish?
Does the daylight astonish? does the early redstart twittering through the
 woods?
Do I astonish more than they?

This hour I tell things in confidence,
I might not tell everybody, but I will tell you.

20

Who goes there? hankering, gross, mystical, nude;
How is it I extract strength from the beef I eat?

What is a man anyhow? what am I? what are you?

All I mark as my own you shall offset it with your own,
Else it were time lost listening to me.

I do not snivel that snivel the world over,
That months are vacuums and the ground but wallow and filth.

Whimpering and truckling fold with powders for invalids,[59] conformity goes
 to the fourth-removed,[60]
I wear my hat as I please indoors or out.

[56]One crazed by sexual desire or disease. [57]Union, convergence. [58]April.
[59]I.e., whimpering and knuckling under are suited to combine with medicines for invalids.
[60]Those distantly separated, far removed from others.

Why should I pray? why should I venerate and be ceremonious?

Having pried through the strata, analyzed to a hair, counseled with doctors
and calculated close,
I find no sweeter fat than sticks to my own bones.

In all people I see myself, none more and not one a barley-corn less,
And the good or bad I say of myself I say of them.

I know I am solid and sound,
To me the converging objects of the universe perpetually flow,
All are written to me, and I must get what the writing means.

I know I am deathless,
I know this orbit of mine cannot be swept by a carpenter's compass,
I know I shall not pass like a child's carlacue cut with a burnt stick at night.[61]

I know I am august,
I do not trouble my spirit to vindicate itself or be understood,
I see that the elementary laws never apologize,
(I reckon I behave no prouder than the level[62] I plant my house by, after all.)

I exist as I am, that is enough,
If no other in the world be aware I sit content,
And if each and all be aware I sit content.

One world is aware and by far the largest to me, and that is myself,
And whether I come to my own to-day or in ten thousand or ten million
years,
I can cheerfully take it now, or with equal cheerfulness I can wait.

My foothold is tenoned and mortised[63] in granite,
I laugh at what you call dissolution,
And I know the amplitude of time.

21

I am the poet of the Body and I am the poet of the Soul,
The pleasures of heaven are with me and the pains of hell are with me,
The first I graft and increase upon myself, the latter I translate into new
tongue.

I am the poet of the woman the same as the man,
And I say it is as great to be a woman as to be a man,
And I say there is nothing greater than the mother of men.

[61]A momentary pattern (a curlicue) made in the dark by waving a glowing stick or ember.
[62]Carpenter's level.
[63]Carpenter's term meaning fastened together by a strong, interlocked joint.

I chant the chant of dilation or pride,
We have had ducking and deprecating about enough,
I show that size is only development.

Have you outstripped the rest? are you the President?
It is a trifle, they will more than arrive there every one, and still pass on.

I am he that walks with the tender and growing night,
I call to the earth and sea half-held by the night.

Press close bare-bosomed night—press close magnetic nourishing night!
Night of south winds—night of the large few stars!
Still nodding night—mad naked summer night.

Smile O voluptuous cool-breathed earth!
Earth of the slumbering and liquid trees!
Earth of departed sunset—earth of the mountains misty-topped!
Earth of the vitreous[64] pour of the full moon just tinged with blue!
Earth of shine and dark mottling the tide of the river!
Earth of the limpid gray of clouds brighter and clearer for my sake!

Far-swooping elbowed earth—rich apple-blossomed earth!
Smile, for your lover comes.

Prodigal, you have given me love—therefore I to you give love!
O unspeakable passionate love.

22

You sea! I resign myself to you also—I guess what you mean,
I behold from the beach your crooked fingers,
I believe you refuse to go back without feeling of me,
We must have a turn together, I undress, hurry me out of sight of the land,
Cushion me soft, rock me in billowy drowse,
Dash me with amorous wet, I can repay you.

Sea of stretched ground-swells,
Sea breathing broad and convulsive breaths,
Sea of the brine of life and of unshovelled yet always-ready graves,
Howler and scooper of storms, capricious and dainty sea,
I am integral with you, I too am of one phase and of all phases.

Partaker of influx and efflux I, extoller of hate and conciliation,
Extoller of amies[65] and those that sleep in each others' arms.

I am he attesting sympathy,
(Shall I make my list of things in the house and skip the house that supports them?)

[64]Glassy. [65]French: friends, lovers.

I am not the poet of goodness only, I do not decline to be the poet of wickedness also.

What blurt is this about virtue and about vice?
Evil propels me and reform of evil propels me, I stand indifferent,
My gait is no fault-finder's or rejecter's gait,
I moisten the roots of all that has grown.

Did you fear some scrofula[66] out of the unflagging pregnancy?
Did you guess the celestial laws are yet to be worked over and rectified?

I find one side a balance and the antipedal side a balance,
Soft doctrine as steady help as stable doctrine,
Thoughts and deeds of the present our rouse and early start.

This minute that comes to me over the past decillions,[67]
There is no better than it and now.

What behaved well in the past or behaves well today is not such wonder,
The wonder is always and always how there can be a mean man or an infidel.

23

Endless unfolding of words of ages!
And mine a word of the modern, the word En-Masse.[68]

A word of the faith that never balks,
Here or henceforward it is all the same to me, I accept Time absolutely.

It alone is without flaw, it alone rounds and completes all,
That mystic baffling wonder alone completes all.

I accept Reality and dare not question it,
Materialism first and last imbuing.

Hurrah for positive science! long live exact demonstration!
Fetch stonecrop[69] mixed with cedar and branches of lilac,
This is the lexicographer, this the chemist, this made a grammar[70] of the old cartouches,[71]
These mariners put the ship through dangerous unknown seas.
This is the geologist, this works with the scalper, and this is a mathematician.

Gentlemen, to you the first honors always!
Your facts are useful, and yet they are not my dwelling,
I but enter by them to an area of my dwelling.

[66]A disease of the lungs and lymph glands. [67]The number 1 followed by thirty-two zeros.
[68]French: All together, in a mass. [69]An herb used in folk medicine.
[70]I.e., deciphered. [71]Oval borders within which Egyptian hieroglyphs were inscribed.

Less the reminders of properties told my words,
And more the reminders they of life untold, and of freedom and extrication,
And make short account of neuters and geldings, and favor men and women fully equipped,
And beat the gong of revolt, and stop with fugitives and them that plot and conspire.

24

Walt Whitman, a kosmos,[72] of Manhattan the son,
Turbulent, fleshy, sensual, eating, drinking and breeding,
No sentimentalist, no stander above men and women or apart from them,
No more modest than immodest.

Unscrew the locks from the doors!
Unscrew the doors themselves from their jambs!

Whoever degrades another degrades me,
And whatever is done or said returns at last to me.

Through me the afflatus[73] surging and surging, through me the current and index.

I speak the password primeval, I give the sign of democracy,
By God! I will accept nothing which all cannot have their counterpart of on the same terms.

Through me many long dumb voices,
Voices of the interminable generations of prisoners and slaves,
Voices of the diseased and despairing and of thieves and dwarfs,
Voices of cycles of preparation and accretion,
And of the threads that connect the stars, and of wombs and of the father-stuff,[74]
And of the rights of them the others are down upon,
Of the deformed, trivial, flat, foolish, despised,
Fog in the air, beetles rolling balls of dung.

Through me forbidden voices,
Voices of sexes and lusts, voices veiled and I remove the veil,
Voices indecent by me clarified and transfigured.

I do not press my fingers across my mouth,
I keep as delicate around the bowels as around the head and heart,
Copulation is no more rank to me than death is.

I believe in the flesh and the appetites,
Seeing, hearing, feeling, are miracles, and each part and tag of me is a miracle.

[72]Cosmos, universe. [73]Divine spirit, poetic inspiration. [74]Semen.

Divine am I inside and out, and I make holy whatever I touch or am touched from,
The scent of these arm-pits aroma finer than prayer,
This head more than churches, bibles, and all the creeds.

If I worship one thing more than another it shall be the spread of my own body, or any part of it,
Translucent mould of me it shall be you!
Shaded ledges and rests it shall be you!
Firm masculine colter[75] it shall be you!
Whatever goes to the tilth[76] of me it shall be you!
You my rich blood! your milky stream pale strippings of my life!
Breast that presses against other breasts it shall be you!
My brain it shall be your occult convolutions!
Root of washed sweet-flag![77] timorous pond-snipe! nest of guarded duplicate eggs! it shall be you!
Mixed tussled hay of head, beard, brawn, it shall be you!
Trickling sap of maple, fiber of manly wheat, it shall be you!
Sun so generous it shall be you!
Vapors lighting and shading my face it shall be you!
You sweaty brooks and dews it shall be you!
Winds whose soft-tickling genitals rub against me it shall be you!
Broad muscular fields, branches of live oak, loving lounger in my winding paths, it shall be you!
Hands I have taken, face I have kissed, mortal I have ever touched, it shall be you.

I dote on myself, there is that lot of me and all so luscious,
Each moment and whatever happens thrills me with joy,
I cannot tell how my ankles bend, nor whence the cause of my faintest wish,
Nor the cause of the friendship I emit, nor the cause of the friendship I take again.

That I walk up my stoop, I pause to consider if it really be,
A morning-glory at my window satisfies me more than the metaphysics of books.

To behold the daybreak!
The little light fades the immense and diaphanous shadows,
The air tastes good to my palate.

Hefts[78] of the moving world at innocent gambols silently rising freshly exuding,
Scooting obliquely high and low.

Something I cannot see puts upward libidinous prongs,
Seas of bright juice suffuse heaven.

[75]Iron blade at the front of a plow. [76]Cultivation.
[77]The calamus, a plant with green flowers and aromatic roots. [78]Mass, main parts.

The earth by the sky staid with, the daily close of their junction,
The heaved challenge from the east that moment over my head,
The mocking taunt, See then whether you shall be master!

25

Dazzling and tremendous how quick the sun-rise would kill me,
If I could not now and always send sun-rise out of me.

We also ascend dazzling and tremendous as the sun,
We found our own O my soul in the calm and cool of the daybreak.

My voice goes after what my eyes cannot reach,
With the twirl of my tongue I encompass worlds and volumes of worlds.

Speech is the twin of my vision, it is unequal to measure itself,
It provokes me forever, it says sarcastically,
Walt you contain enough, why don't you let it out then?

Come now I will not be tantalized, you conceive too much of articulation,
Do you not know O speech how the buds beneath you are folded?
Waiting in gloom, protected by frost,
The dirt receding before my prophetical screams,
I underlying causes to balance them at last,
My knowledge my live parts, it keeping tally with the meaning of all things,
Happiness, (which whoever hears me let him or her set out in search of this
    day.)

My final merit I refuse you, I refuse putting from me what I really am,
Encompass worlds, but never try to encompass me,
I crowd your sleekest and best by simply looking toward you.

Writing and talk do not prove me,
I carry the plenum[79] of proof and every thing else in my face,
With the hush of my lips I wholly confound the skeptic.

26

Now I will do nothing but listen,
To accrue what I hear into this song, to let sounds contribute toward it.

I hear bravuras of birds, bustle of growing wheat, gossip of flames, clack of
    sticks cooking my meals,
I hear the sound I love, the sound of the human voice,
I hear all sounds running together, combined, fused or following,
Sounds of the city and sounds out of the city, sounds of the day and night,

[79]Fullness.

Talkative young ones to those that like them, the loud laugh of work-people at their meals,
The angry base[80] of disjointed friendship, the faint tones of the sick,
The judge with hands tight to the desk, his pallid lips pronouncing a death-sentence,
The heave'e'yo of stevedores unlading ships by the wharves, the refrain of the anchor-lifters,
The ring of alarm-bells, the cry of fire, the whirr of swift-streaking engines and hose-carts with premonitory tinkles and colored lights,
The steam-whistle, the solid roll of the train of approaching cars,
The slow march played at the head of the association marching two and two,
(They go to guard some corpse, the flag-tops are draped with black muslin.)

I hear the violoncello, ('tis the young man's heart's complaint)
I hear the keyed cornet, it glides quickly in through my ears,
It shakes mad-sweet pangs through my belly and breast.

I hear the chorus, it is a grand opera,
Ah this indeed is music—this suits me.

A tenor large and fresh as the creation fills me,
The orbic flex of his mouth is pouring and filling me full.

I hear the trained soprano (what work with hers is this?)
The orchestra whirls me wider than Uranus[81] flies,
It wrenches such ardors from me I did not know I possessed them,
It sails me, I dab with bare feet, they are licked by the indolent waves,
I am cut by bitter and angry hail, I lose my breath,
Steeped amid honeyed morphine, my windpipe throttled in fakes[82] of death,
At length let up again to feel the puzzle of puzzles,
And that we call Being.

27

To be in any form, what is that?
(Round and round we go, all of us, and ever come back thither,)
If nothing lay more developed the quahaug[83] in its callous shell were enough.

Mine is no callous shell,
I have instant conductors all over me whether I pass or stop,
They seize every object and lead it harmlessly through me.

I merely stir, press, feel with my fingers, and am happy,
To touch my person to some one else's is about as much as I can stand.

[80]Bass. [81]Planet with a large orbit.
[82]Rope coils. [83]An Atlantic clam.

28

Is this then a touch? quivering me to a new identity,
Flames and ether making a rush for my veins,
Treacherous tip of me reaching and crowding to help them,
My flesh and blood playing out lightning to strike what is hardly different
 from myself,
On all sides prurient provokers stiffening my limbs,
Straining the udder of my heart for its withheld drip,
Behaving licentious toward me, taking no denial,
Depriving me of my best as for a purpose,
Unbuttoning my clothes, holding me by the bare waist,
Deluding my confusion with the calm of the sunlight and pasture-fields,
Immodestly sliding the fellow-senses away,
They bribed to swap off with touch and go and graze at the edges of me,
No consideration, no regard for my draining strength or my anger,
Fetching the rest of the herd around to enjoy them a while,
Then all uniting to stand on a headland and worry me.

The sentries desert every other part of me,
They have left me helpless to a red marauder,
They all come to the headland to witness and assist against me.

I am given up by traitors,
I talk wildly, I have lost my wits, I and nobody else am the greatest traitor,
I went myself first to the headland, my own hands carried me there.

You villain touch! what are you doing? my breath is tight in its throat,
Unclench your floodgates, you are too much for me.

29

Blind loving wrestling touch, sheathed hooded sharp-toothed touch!
Did it make you ache so, leaving me?

Parting tracked by arriving, perpetual payment of perpetual loan,
Rich showering rain, and recompense richer afterward.

Sprouts take and accumulate, stand by the curb prolific and vital,
Landscapes projected masculine, full-sized and golden.

30

All truths wait in all things,
They neither hasten their own delivery nor resist it,
They do not need the obstetric forceps of the surgeon,
The insignificant is as big to me as any,
(What is less or more than a touch?)

Logic and sermons never convince,
The damp of the night drives deeper into my soul.

(Only what proves itself to every man and woman is so,
Only what nobody denies is so.)

A minute and a drop of me settle my brain,
I believe the soggy clods shall become lovers and lamps,
And a compend[84] of compends is the meat of a man or woman,
And a summit and flower there is the feeling they have for each other,
And they are to branch boundlessly out of that lesson until it becomes omnific,[85]
And until one and all shall delight us, and we them.

31

I believe a leaf of grass is no less than the journey work of the stars,
And the pismire[86] is equally perfect, and a grain of sand, and the egg of the wren,
And the tree-toad is a chef-d'oeuvre[87] for the highest,
And the running blackberry would adorn the parlors of heaven,
And the narrowest hinge in my hand puts to scorn all machinery,
And the cow crunching with depressed head surpasses any statue,
And a mouse is miracle enough to stagger sextillions[88] of infidels.

I find I incorporate gneiss,[89] coal, long-threaded moss, fruits, grains, esculent roots,
And am stuccoed with quadrupeds and birds all over,
And have distanced what is behind me for good reasons,
But call any thing back again when I desire it.

In vain the speeding or shyness,
In vain the plutonic rocks[90] send their old heat against my approach,
In vain the mastodon retreats beneath its own powdered bones,
In vain objects stand leagues off and assume manifold shapes,
In vain the ocean settling in hollows and the great monsters lying low,
In vain the buzzard houses herself with the sky,
In vain the snake slides through the creepers and logs,
In vain the elk takes to the inner passes of the woods,
In vain the razor-billed auk sails far north to Labrador,
I follow quickly, I ascend to the nest in the fissure of the cliff.

[84]Compendium, epitome. [85]All-creating, all-inclusive. [86]Ant.
[87]French: masterpiece. [88]The number 1 followed by twenty-one zeros.
[89]Coarse-grained rock with light and dark mineral layers, found in the United States from New England to the Rocky Mountains.
[90]Once-molten rock formed deep within the earth.

32

I think I could turn and live with animals, they are so placid and self-contained,
I stand and look at them long and long.

They do not sweat and whine about their condition,
They do not lie awake in the dark and weep for their sins,
They do not make me sick discussing their duty to God,
Not one is dissatisfied, not one is demented with the mania of owning things,
Not one kneels to another, nor to his kind that lived thousands of years ago,
Not one is respectable or unhappy over the whole earth.

So they show their relations to me and I accept them,
They bring me tokens of myself, they evince them plainly in their possession.

I wonder where they get those tokens,
Did I pass that way huge times ago and negligently drop them?

Myself moving forward then and now and forever,
Gathering and showing more always and with velocity,
Infinite and omnigenous,[91] and the like of these among them,
Not too exclusive toward the reachers of my remembrancers,
Picking out here one that I love, and now go with him on brotherly terms.

A gigantic beauty of a stallion, fresh and responsive to my caresses,
Head high in the forehead, wide between the ears,
Limbs glossy and supple, tail dusting the ground,
Eyes full of sparkling wickedness, ears finely cut, flexibly moving.

His nostrils dilate as my heels embrace him,
His well-built limbs tremble with pleasure as we race around and return.

I but use you a minute, then I resign you, stallion,
Why do I need your paces when I myself out-gallop them?
Even as I stand or sit passing faster than you.

33

Space and Time! now I see it is true, what I guessed at,
What I guessed when I loafed on the grass,
What I guessed while I lay alone in my bed,
And again as I walked the beach under the paling stars of the morning.

[91]Of all kinds.

My ties and ballasts[92] leave me, my elbows rest in sea-gaps,[93]
I skirt sierras, my palms cover continents,
I am afoot with my vision.

By the city's quadrangular houses—in log huts, camping with lumber-men,
Along the ruts of the turnpike, along the dry gulch and rivulet bed,
Weeding my onion-patch or hosing rows of carrots and parsnips, crossing savannas,[94] trailing in forests,
Prospecting, gold-digging, girdling[95] the trees of a new purchase,
Scorched ankle-deep by the hot sand, hauling my boat down the shallow river,
Where the panther walks to and fro on a limb overhead, where the buck turns furiously at the hunter,
Where the rattlesnake suns his flabby length on a rock, where the otter is feeding on fish,
Where the alligator in his tough pimples sleeps by the bayou,
Where the black bear is searching for roots or honey, where the beaver pats the mud with his paddle-shaped tail;
Over the growing sugar, over the yellow-flowered cotton plant, over the rice in its low moist field,
Over the sharp-peaked farm house, with its scalloped scum and slender shoots from the gutters,[96]
Over the western persimmon, over the long-leaved corn, over the delicate blue-flower flax,
Over the white and brown buckwheat, a hummer and buzzer[97] there with the rest,
Over the dusky green of the rye as it ripples and shades in the breeze;
Scaling mountains, pulling myself cautiously up, holding on by low scragged[98] limbs,
Walking the path worn in the grass and beat through the leaves of the brush,
Where the quail is whistling betwixt the woods and the wheat-lot,
Where the bat flies in the Seventh-month eve, where the great goldbug[99] drops through the dark,
Where the brook puts out of the roots of the old tree and flows to the meadow,
Where cattle stand and shake away flies with the tremulous shuddering of their hides,
Where the cheese-cloth hangs in the kitchen, where andirons straddle the hearth-slab, where cobwebs fall in festoons from the rafters;
Where trip-hammers crash, where the press is whirling its cylinders,
Wherever the human heart beats with terrible throes under its ribs,
Where the pear-shaped balloon is floating aloft, (floating in it myself and looking composedly down,)

[92]The ropes and heavy weights that limit the ascent of a passenger balloon.
[93]Inlets, bays. [94]Flat, tropical grasslands.
[95]Killing a tree by cutting a deep ring around the trunk.
[96]Pointed roof with sediment washed into patterns by the rain and with grass sprouting from soil deposited in the roof gutters.
[97]Hummingbird and bee. [98]Stunted. [99]A beetle.

Where the life-car[100] is drawn on the slip-noose, where the heat hatches
pale-green eggs in the dented sand,
Where the she-whale swims with her calf and never forsakes it,
Where the steam-ship trails hind-ways its long pennant of smoke,
Where the fin of the shark cuts like a black chip out of the water,
Where the half-burned brig[101] is riding on unknown currents,
Where shells grow to her slimy deck, where the dead are corrupting below;
Where the dense-starred flag is borne at the head of the regiments,
Approaching Manhattan up by the long-stretching island,
Under Niagara, the cataract falling like a veil over my countenance,
Upon a door-step, upon the horse-block[102] of hard wood outside,
Upon the race-course, or enjoying picnics or jigs or a good game of
base-ball,
At he-festivals, with blackguard gibes, ironical license, bull-dances,[103]
drinking, laughter,
At the cider-mill tasting the sweets of the brown mash, sucking the juice
through a straw,
At apple-peelings wanting kisses for all the red fruit I find,
At musters,[104] beach-parties, friendly bees,[105] huskings, house-raisings;
Where the mocking-bird sounds his delicious gurgles, cackles, screams,
weeps,
Where the hay-rick stands in the barn-yard, where the dry-stalks are scattered,
where the brood-cow waits in the hovel,
Where the bull advances to do his masculine work, where the stud to the
mare, where the cock is treading the hen,
Where the heifers browse, where geese nip their food with short jerks,
Where sun-down shadows lengthen over the limitless and lonesome
prairie,
Where herds of buffalo make a crawling spread of the square miles far and
near,
Where the humming-bird shimmers, where the neck of the long-lived swan is
curving and winding,
Where the laughing-gull scoots by the shore, where she laughs her
near-human laugh,
Where bee-hives range on a gray bench in the garden half hid by the high
weeds,
Where band-necked partridges roost in a ring on the ground with their
heads out,
Where burial coaches enter the arched gates of a cemetery,
Where winter wolves bark amid wastes of snow and icicled trees,
Where the yellow-crowned heron comes to the edge of the marsh at night
and feeds upon small crabs,
Where the splash of swimmers and divers cools the warm noon,

[100]Watertight rescue vessel pulled by rope from ship to shore.
[101]Sailing ship. [102]Mounting step.
[103]Dances where men, lacking female partners, dance with each other.
[104]Gatherings. [105]Parties where friends gather to work, like bees.

Where the katydid works her chromatic reed[106] on the walnut-tree over the well,
Through patches of citrons[107] and cucumbers with silver-wired leaves,
Through the salt-lick or orange glade, or under conical firs,
Through the gymnasium, through the curtained saloon, through the office or public hall;
Pleased with the native and pleased with the foreign, pleased with the new and old,
Pleased with the homely woman as well as the handsome,
Pleased with the quakeress as she puts off her bonnet and talks melodiously,
Pleased with the tune of the choir of the whitewashed church,
Pleased with the earnest words of the sweating Methodist preacher, impressed seriously at the camp-meeting;
Looking in at the shop-windows of Broadway the whole forenoon, flatting the flesh of my nose on the thick plate glass,
Wandering the same afternoon with my face turned up to the clouds, or down a lane or along the beach,
My right and left arms round the sides of two friends, and I in the middle;
Coming home with the silent and dark-cheeked bush-boy,[108] (behind me he rides at the drape[109] of the day,)
Far from the settlements studying the print of animals' feet, or the moccasin print,
By the cot in the hospital reaching lemonade to a feverish patient,
Nigh the coffined corpse when all is still, examining with a candle;
Voyaging to every port to dicker and adventure,
Hurrying with the modern crowd as eager and fickle as any,
Hot toward one I hate, ready in my madness to knife him,
Solitary at midnight in my back yard, my thoughts gone from me a long while,
Walking the old hills of Judaea with the beautiful gentle God by my side,
Speeding through space, speeding through heaven and the stars,
Speeding amid the seven satellites and the broad ring,[110] and the diameter of eighty thousand miles,
Speeding with tailed meteors, throwing fire-balls like the rest,
Carrying the crescent child[111] that carries its own full mother in its belly,
Storming, enjoying, planning, loving, cautioning,
Backing and filling, appearing and disappearing,
I tread day and night such roads.

I visit the orchards of spheres and look at the product,
And look at quintillions[112] ripened and look at quintillions green.

[106]I.e., sounds colorful harmonies in her throat. [107]A variety of watermelon.
[108]Wilderness boy. [109]Close.
[110]The eight major planets, including Saturn with its minute surrounding particles that appear as a broad ring.
[111]The bright, crescent portion of a new moon partially lighted by the setting sun.
[112]The number 1 followed by eighteen zeros.

I fly those flights of a fluid and swallowing soul,
My course runs below the soundings of plummets.

I help myself to material and immaterial,
No guard can shut me off, no law prevent me.

I anchor my ship for a little while only,
My messengers continually cruise away or bring their returns to me.

I go hunting polar furs and the seal, leaping chasms with a pike-pointed staff,
 clinging to topples[113] of brittle and blue.

I ascend to the foretruck,[114]
I take my place late at night in the crow's-nest,
We sail the arctic sea, it is plenty light enough,
Through the clear atmosphere I stretch around on the wonderful beauty,
The enormous masses of ice pass me and I pass them, the scenery is plain in
 all directions,
The white-topped mountains show in the distance, I fling out my fancies
 toward them,
We are approaching some great battle-field in which we are soon to be
 engaged,
We pass the colossal outposts of the encampment, we pass with still feet and
 caution,
Or we are entering by the suburbs some vast and ruined city,
The blocks and fallen architecture more than all the living cities of the
 globe.

I am a free companion, I bivouac by invading watchfires,
I turn the bridegroom out of bed and stay with the bride myself,
I tighten her all night to my thighs and lips.

My voice is the wife's voice, the screech by the rail of the stairs,
They fetch my man's body up dripping and drowned.

I understand the large hearts of heroes,
The courage of present times and all times,
How the skipper saw the crowded and rudderless wreck of the steamship,
 and Death chasing it up and down the storm,
How he knuckled tight and gave not back an inch, and was faithful of days
 and faithful of nights,
And chalked in large letters on a board, Be of good cheer, we will not desert
 you;
How he followed with them and tacked with them three days and would not
 give it up,
How he saved the drifting company at last,
How the lank loose-gowned women looked when boated from the side of
 their prepared graves,

[113]Fallen ice. [114]Platform near the top of a foremast.

How the silent old-faced infants and the lifted sick, and the sharp-lipped unshaved men;
All this I swallow, it tastes good, I like it well, it becomes mine,
I am the man, I suffered, I was there.[115]

The disdain and calmness of martyrs,
The mother of old, condemned for a witch, burnt with dry wood, her children gazing on,
The hounded slave that flags in the race, leans by the fence, blowing, covered with sweat,
The twinges that sting like needles his legs and neck, the murderous buckshot and the bullets,
All these I feel or am.

I am the hounded slave, I wince at the bite of the dogs,
Hell and despair are upon me, crack and again crack the marksmen,
I clutch the rails of the fence, my gore dribs, thinned with the ooze of my skin,[116]
I fall on the weeds and stones,
The riders spur their unwilling horses, haul close,
Taunt my dizzy ears and beat me violently over the head with whip-stocks.

Agonies are one of my changes of garments,
I do not ask the wounded person how he feels, I myself become the wounded person,
My hurts turn livid upon me as I lean on a cane and observe.

I am the mashed fireman with breast-bone broken,
Tumbling walls buried me in their debris,
Heat and smoke I inspired,[117] I heard the yelling shouts of my comrades,
I heard the distant click of their picks and shovels,
They have cleared the beams away, they tenderly lift me forth.

I lie in the night air in my red shirt, the pervading hush is for my sake,
Painless after all I lie exhausted but not so unhappy,
White and beautiful are the faces around me, the heads are bared of their fire-caps,
The kneeling crowd fades with the light of the torches.

Distant and dead resuscitate,
They show as the dial or move as the hands of me, I am the clock myself.

I am an old artillerist, I tell of my fort's bombardment,
I am there again.

Again the long roll of the drummers,
Again the attacking cannon, mortars,
Again to my listening ears the cannon responsive.

[115]The shipwreck episode is based on an actual sea disaster reported in newspapers in January 1854.
[116]I.e., my blood drips, thinned with sweat. [117]Inhaled.

I take part, I see and hear the whole,
The cries, curses, roar, the plaudits for well-aimed shots,
The ambulanza[118] slowly passing trailing its red drip,
Workmen searching after damages, making indispensable repairs,
The fall of grenades through the rent roof, the fan-shaped explosion,
The whiz of limbs, heads, stone, wood, iron, high in the air.

Again gurgles the mouth of my dying general, he furiously waves with his hand,
He gasps through the clot Mind not me—mind—the entrenchments.

34

Now I tell what I knew in Texas in my early youth,[119]
(I tell not the fall of Alamo,
Not one escaped to tell the fall of Alamo,
The hundred and fifty are dumb yet at Alamo,)
'Tis the tale of the murder in cold blood of four hundred and twelve young men.

Retreating they had formed in a hollow square with their baggage for breastworks,
Nine hundred lives out of the surrounding enemies, nine times their number, was the price they took in advance,
Their colonel was wounded and their ammunition gone,
They treated[120] for an honorable capitulation, received writing and seal, gave up their arms and marched back prisoners of war.

They were the glory of the race of rangers,
Matchless with horse, rifle, song, supper, courtship,
Large, turbulent, generous, handsome, proud, and affectionate,
Bearded, sunburnt, dressed in the free costume of hunters,
Not a single one over thirty years of age.

The second First-day morning they were brought out in squads and massacred, it was beautiful early summer,
The work commenced about five o'clock and was over by eight.

None obeyed the command to kneel,
Some made a mad and helpless rush, some stood stark and straight,
A few fell at once, shot in the temple or heart, the living and dead lay together,
The maimed and mangled dug in the dirt, the new-comers saw them there,
Some half-killed attempted to crawl away,

[118]Military ambulance.
[119]Whitman was never in Texas. The episode described below was drawn from reports of a massacre of Texans by Mexicans in the Revolution of 1836, shortly after the fall of the Alamo.
[120]Negotiated.

These were dispatched with bayonets or battered with the blunts of muskets,
A youth not seventeen years old seized his assassin till two more came to release him,
The three were all torn and covered with the boy's blood.

At eleven o'clock began the burning of the bodies;
That is the tale of the murder of the four hundred and twelve young men.

35

Would you hear of an old-time sea-fight?
Would you learn who won by the light of the moon and stars?
List to the yarn,[121] as my grandmother's father the sailor told it to me.

Our foe was no sulk in his ship I tell you, (said he,)
His was the surly English pluck, and there is no tougher or truer, and never was, and never will be;
Along the lowered eve he came horribly raking[122] us.

We closed with him, the yards entangled, the cannon touched,
My captain lashed fast[123] with his own hands.

We had received some eighteen pound shots under the water,
On our lower-gun-deck two large pieces had burst at the first fire, killing all around and blowing up overhead.

Fighting at sun-down, fighting at dark,
Ten o'clock at night, the full moon well up, our leaks on the gain, and five feet of water reported,[124]
The master-at-arms loosing the prisoners confined in the after-hold to give them a chance for themselves.

The transit to and from the magazine[125] is now stopt by the sentinels,
They see so many strange faces they do not know whom to trust.

Our frigate takes fire,
The other asks if we demand quarter?[126]
If our colors are struck[127] and the fighting done?

[121]Whitman's account is based on a letter from John Paul Jones to Benjamin Franklin (September 1779) telling of the sea battle (1779) between the British ship *Serapis* and the American ship *Bonhomme Richard* commanded by John Paul Jones.

[122]Sweeping the length of the ship with gunfire.

[123]Jones reported that he "made both ships fast" when they came together.

[124]Jones reported that during the battle, the destructive fire from the British *Serapis* caused the *Bonhomme Richard* to take "five feet of water in the hold."

[125]Gunpowder storage room. [126]Ask for clemency.

[127]During the battle, the flag of the *Bonhomme Richard* was shot away, causing the British to think the flag had been lowered as a sign of surrender.

Now I laugh content, for I hear the voice of my little captain,
We have not struck, he composedly cries, we have just begun our part of the fighting.[128]

Only three guns are in use,
One is directed by the captain himself against the enemy's main-mast,
Two well served with grape and canister[129] silence his musketry and clear his decks.

The tops[130] alone second the fire of this little battery, especially the main-top,
They hold out bravely during the whole of the action.

Not a moment's cease,
The leaks gain fast on the pumps, the fire eats toward the powder-magazine.

One of the pumps has been shot away, it is generally thought we are sinking.

Serene stands the little captain,
He is not hurried, his voice is neither high nor low,
His eyes give more light to us than our battle-lanterns.

Toward twelve there in the beams of the moon they surrender to us.

36

Stretched and still lies the midnight,
Two great hulls motionless on the breast of the darkness,
Our vessel riddled and slowly sinking, preparations to pass to the one we have conquered,
The captain on the quarter-deck coldly giving his orders through a countenance white as a sheet,
Near by the corpse of the child that served in the cabin,
The dead face of an old salt with long white hair and carefully curled whiskers,
The flames spite of all that can be done flickering aloft and below,
The husky voices of the two or three officers yet fit for duty,
Formless stacks of bodies and bodies by themselves, dabs of flesh upon the masts and spars,
Cut of cordage, dangle of rigging, slight shock of the soothe of waves,
Black and impassive guns, litter of powder-parcels, strong scent,
A few large stars overhead, silent and mournful shining,

[128]A paraphrase of Jones's words "I have not yet begun to fight."
[129]Charges of large (grape) or small (canister) iron balls.
[130]The platforms on the mastheads from which sharpshooters fired onto the enemy's deck below.

Delicate sniffs of sea-breeze, smells of sedgy grass and fields by the shore,
  death-messages given in charge to survivors,
The hiss of the surgeon's knife, the gnawing teeth of his saw,
Wheeze, cluck, swash of falling blood, short wild scream, and long, dull,
  tapering groan,
These so, these irretrievable.

37

You laggards there on guard! look to your arms!
In at the conquered doors they crowd! I am possessed!
Embody all presences outlawed or suffering,
See myself in prison shaped like another man,
And feel the dull unintermitted pain.

For me the keepers of convicts shoulder their carbines and keep watch,
It is I let out in the morning and barred at night.

Not a mutineer walks handcuffed to jail but I am handcuffed to him and
  walk by his side,
(I am less the jolly one there, and more the silent one with sweat on my
  twitching lips.)

Not a youngster is taken for larceny but I go up too, and am tried and
  sentenced.

Not a cholera patient lies at the last gasp but I also lie at the last gasp,
My face is ash-colored, my sinews gnarl, away from me people retreat.

Askers embody themselves in me and I am embodied in them,
I project[131] my hat, sit shame-faced, and beg.

38

Enough! enough! enough!
Somehow I have been stunned. Stand back!
Give me a little time beyond[132] my cuffed[133] head, slumbers, dreams, gaping,
I discover myself on the verge of a usual mistake.

That I could forget the mockers and insults!
That I could forget the trickling tears and the blows of the bludgeons and
  hammers!
That I could look with a separate look on my own crucifixion and bloody
  crowning.

[131]Hold forth. [132]I.e., time to get over, recover from. [133]Befuddled.

I remember now,
I resume the overstaid fraction,[134]
The grave of rock multiplies what has been confided to it, or to any graves,
Corpses rise, gashes heal, fastenings roll from me.

I troop forth replenished with supreme power, one of an average unending procession,
Inland and sea-coast we go, and pass all boundary lines,
Our swift ordinances on their way over the whole earth,
The blossoms we wear in our hats the growth of thousands of years.

Eleves,[135] I salute you! come forward!
Continue your annotations, continue your questionings.

39

The friendly and flowing savage, who is he?
Is he waiting for civilization, or past it and mastering it?
Is he some Southwesterner raised out-doors? is he Kanadian?
Is he from the Mississippi country? Iowa, Oregon, California?
The mountains? prairie-life, bush-life? or sailor from the sea?

Wherever he goes men and women accept and desire him,
They desire he should like them, touch them, speak to them, stay with them.

Behavior lawless as snow-flakes, words simple as grass, uncombed head, laughter, and naivete,
Slow-stepping feet, common features, common modes and emanations,
They descend in new forms from the tips of his fingers,
They are waited with the odor of his body or breath, they fly out of the glance of his eyes.

40

Flaunt of the sunshine I need not your bask—lie over!
You light surfaces only, I force surfaces and depths also.

Earth! you seem to look for something at my hands,
Say, old top-knot,[136] what do you want?

Man or woman, I might tell how I like you, but cannot,
And might tell what it is in me and what it is in you, but cannot,
And might tell that pining I have, that pulse of my nights and days.

Behold, I do not give lectures or a little charity,
When I give I give myself.

[134]Recalculate. [135]French: students.
[136]Indian, from the tuft of hair used to ornament the head.

You there, impotent, loose in the knees,
Open your scarfed chops[137] till I blow grit[138] within you,
Spread your palms and lift the flaps of your pockets,
I am not to be denied, I compel, I have stores plenty and to spare,
And any thing I have I bestow.

I do not ask who you are, that is not important to me,
You can do nothing and be nothing but what I will enfold you.

To cotton-field drudge or cleaner of privies I lean,
On his right cheek I put the family kiss,
And in my soul I swear I never will deny him.

On women fit for conception I start bigger and nimbler babes.
(This day I am jetting the stuff of far more arrogant republics.)

To any one dying, thither I speed and twist the knob of the door.
Turn the bedclothes toward the foot of the bed,
Let the physician and the priest go home.

I seize the descending man and raise him with resistless will,
O despairer, here is my neck,
By God, you shall not go down! hang your whole weight upon me.

I dilate[139] you with tremendous breath, I buoy you up,
Every room of the house do I fill with an armed force,
Lovers of me, bafflers of graves.

Sleep—I and they keep guard all night,
Not doubt, not decease shall dare to lay finger upon you,
I have embraced you, and henceforth possess you to myself,
And when you rise in the morning you will find what I tell you is so.

41

I am he bringing help for the sick as they pant on their backs,
And for strong upright men I bring yet more needed help.

I heard what was said of the universe,
Heard it and heard it of several thousand years;
It is middling well as far as it goes—but is that all?

Magnifying and applying come I,
Outbidding at the start the old cautious hucksters,[140]
Taking myself the exact dimensions of Jehovah,

[137]Lined and wrinkled cheeks, jaws. [138]Strength of spirit, courage.
[139]Inflate, expand. [140]Peddlers.

Lithographing Kronos, Zeus his son, and Hercules his grandson,
Buying drafts of Osiris, Isis, Belus, Brahma, Buddha,
In my portfolio placing Manito loose, Allah on a leaf, the crucifix engraved,
With Odin and the hideous-faced Mexitli[141] and every idol and image,
Taking them all for what they are worth and not a cent more,
Admitting they were alive and did the work of their days,
(They bore mites as for unfledged birds who have now to rise and fly and sing for themselves,)
Accepting the rough deific[142] sketches to fill out better in myself, bestowing them freely on each man and woman I see,
Discovering as much or more in a framer framing a house,
Putting higher claims for him there with his rolled-up sleeves driving the mallet and chisel,
Not objecting to special revelations, considering a curl of smoke or a hair on the back of my hand just as curious as any revelation,
Lads ahold of fire-engines and hook-and-ladder ropes no less to me than the gods of the antique wars,
Minding their voices peal through the crash of destruction,
Their brawny limbs passing safe over charred laths, their white foreheads whole and unhurt out of the flames;
By the mechanic's wife with her babe at her nipple interceding for every person born,
Three scythes at harvest whizzing in a row from three lusty angels with shirts bagged out at their waists,
The snag-toothed hostler[143] with red hair redeeming sins past and to come,
Selling all he possesses, traveling on foot to fee lawyers for his brother and sit by him while he is tried for forgery;
What was strewn in the amplest strewing the square rod about me, and not filling the square rod then,
The bull and the bug never worshipped half enough,
Dung and dirt more admirable than was dreamed,
The supernatural of no account, myself waiting my time to be one of the supremes,
The day getting ready for me when I shall do as much good as the best, and be as prodigious;
By my life-lumps![144] becoming already a creator,
Putting myself here and now to the ambushed womb of the shadows.

42

A call in the midst of the crowd,
My own voice, orotund sweeping and final.

Come my children,
Come my boys and girls, my women, household and intimates,

[141]Whitman's list of gods includes those from Greek, Egyptian, Babylonian, and Norse mythology and from Judaism, Christianity, Hinduism, Buddhism, and Islam. Manito was a nature god of the Algonquian Indians; Mexitli, an Aztec god of war.

[142]Divine. [143]Stablemen. [144]Testicles.

Now the performer launches his nerve, he has passed his prelude on the reeds within.

Easily written loose-fingered chords—I feel the thrum of your climax and close.
My head slues round on my neck,
Music rolls, but not from the organ,
Folks are around me, but they are no household of mine.

Ever the hard unsunk ground,
Ever the eaters and drinkers, ever the upward and downward sun, ever the air and the ceaseless tides,
Ever myself and my neighbors, refreshing, wicked, real,
Ever the old inexplicable query, ever that thorned thumb, that breath of itches and thirsts,
Ever the vexer's hoot! hoot! till we find where the sly one hides and bring him forth,
Ever love, ever the sobbing liquid of life,
Ever the bandage under the chin, ever the trestles[145] of death.

Here and there with dimes on the eyes[146] walking,
To feed the greed of the belly the brains liberally spooning,
Tickets buying, taking, selling, but in to the feast never once going,
Many sweating, ploughing, thrashing, and then the chaff for payment receiving,
A few idly owning, and they the wheat continually claiming.

This is the city and I am one of the citizens,
Whatever interests the rest interests me, politics, wars, markets, newspapers, schools,
The mayor and councils, banks, tariffs, steamships, factories, stocks, stores, real estate and personal estate.

The little plentiful manikins skipping around in collars and tailed coats
I am aware who they are, (they are positively not worms or fleas,)
I acknowledge the duplicates of myself, the weakest and shallowest is deathless with me,
What I do and say the same waits for them,
Every thought that flounders in me the same flounders in them.

I know perfectly well my own egotism,
Know my omnivorous lines and must not write any less,
And would fetch you whoever you are flush with myself.

Not words of routine this song of mine,
But abruptly to question, to leap beyond yet nearer bring;
This printed and bound book—but the printer and the printing-office boy?

[145]Trestles: supports for coffins.
[146]Whitman refers here both to the dead (whose eyelids are held shut by coins) and to the greedy.

The well-taken photographs—but your wife or friend close and solid in your arms?
The black ship mailed with iron, her mighty guns in her turrets—but the pluck of the captain and engineers?
In the houses the dishes and fare and furniture—but the host and hostess, and the look out of their eyes?
The sky up there—yet here or next door, or across the way?
The saints and sages in history—but you yourself?
Sermons, creeds, theology—but the fathomless human brain,
And what is reason? and what is love? and what is life?

43

I do not despise you priests, all time, the world over,
My faith is the greatest of faiths and the least of faiths,
Enclosing worship ancient and modern and all between ancient and modern,
Believing I shall come again upon the earth after five thousand years,
Waiting responses from oracles, honoring the gods, saluting the sun,
Making a fetish[147] of the first rock or stump, powowing with sticks in the circle of obis,[148]
Helping the llama or brahmin[149] as he trims the lamps of the idols,
Dancing yet through the streets in a phallic procession, rapt and austere in the woods a gymnosophist,[150]
Drinking mead from the skull-cap, to Shastas and Vedas[151] admirant,[152] minding the Koran,
Walking the teokallis,[153] spotted with gore from the stone and knife, beating the serpent-skin drum,
Accepting the Gospels, accepting him that was crucified, knowing assuredly that he is divine,
To the mass kneeling or the puritan's prayer rising, or sitting patiently in a pew,
Ranting and frothing in my insane crisis, or waiting dead-like till my spirit arouses me,
Looking forth on pavement and land, or outside of pavement and land,
Belonging to the winders of the circuit of circuits.

One of that centripetal and centrifugal gang I turn and talk like man leaving charges before a journey.

Down-hearted doubters dull and excluded,
Frivolous, sullen, moping, angry, affected, disheartened, atheistical,
I know every one of you, I know the sea of torment, doubt, despair and unbelief.

[147]An object of worship. [148]Magic charms.
[149]Lama, a Tibetan high priest; Brahmin, a Hindu high priest.
[150]A Hindu ascetic [151]Hindu religious teachings.
[152]French: admiring. [153]Aztec temple with sacrificial altar.

How the flukes[154] splash!
How they contort rapid as lightning, with spasms and spouts of blood!

Be at peace bloody flukes of doubters and sullen mopers,
I take my place among you as much as among any,
The past is the push of you, me, all, precisely the same,
And what is yet untried and afterward is for you, me, all, precisely the same.

I do not know what is untried and afterward,
But I know it will in its turn prove sufficient, and cannot fail.

Each who passes is considered, each who stops is considered, not single one can it fall.

It cannot fall the young man who died and was buried,
Nor the young woman who died and was put by his side,
Nor the little child that peeped in at the door, and then drew back and was never seen again,
Nor the old man who has lived without purpose, and feels it with bitterness worse than gall,
Nor him in the poor house tubercled by rum and the bad disorder,[155]
Nor the numberless slaughtered and wrecked, nor the brutish koboo[156] called the ordure[157] of humanity,
Nor the sacs[158] merely floating with open mouths for food to slip in,
Nor any thing in the earth, or down in the oldest graves of the earth,
Nor any thing in the myriads of spheres, nor the myriads of myriads that inhabit them,
Nor the present, nor the least wisp that is known.

44

It is time to explain myself—let us stand up.

What is known I strip away,
I launch all men and women forward with me into the Unknown.

The clock indicates the moment—but what does eternity indicate?

We have thus far exhausted trillions of winters and summers,
There are trillions ahead, and trillions ahead of them.

Births have brought us richness and variety,
And other births will bring us richness and variety.

[154]The tail of a whale.
[155]I.e., marked by tubercles (lesions and swellings) caused by rum and syphilis.
[156]Primitive native of Sumatra. [157]Filth, excrement.
[158]Primitive aquatic animals.

I do not call one greater and one smaller,
That which fills its period and place is equal to any.

Were mankind murderous or jealous upon you, my brother, my sister?
I am sorry for you, they are not murderous or jealous upon me,
All has been gentle with me, I keep no account with lamentation,
(What have I to do with lamentation?)

I am an acme of things accomplished, and I an encloser of things to be.

My feet strike an apex of the apices[159] of the stairs,
On every step bunches of ages, and larger bunches between the steps,
All below duly traveled, and still I mount and mount.

Rise after rise bow the phantoms behind me,
Afar down I see the huge first Nothing, I know I was even there,
I waited unseen and always, and slept through the lethargic mist,
And took my time, and took no hurt from the fetid carbon.

Long I was hugged close—long and long.

Immense have been the preparations for me,
Faithful and friendly the arms that have helped me.

Cycles ferried my cradle, rowing and rowing like cheerful boatmen,
For room to me stars kept aside in their own rings,
They sent influences to look after what was to hold me.

Before I was born out of my mother generations guided me,
My embryo has never been torpid, nothing could overlay[160] it.

For it the nebula cohered to an orb,
The long slow strata piled to rest it on,
Vast vegetables gave it sustenance,
Monstrous sauroids[161] transported it in their mouths and deposited it with
care.

All forces have been steadily employed to complete and delight me,
Now on this spot I stand with my robust soul.

45

O span of youth! ever-pushed elasticity!
O manhood, balanced, florid and full.

My lovers suffocate me,
Crowding my lips, thick in the pores of my skin,
Jostling me through streets and public halls, coming naked to me at night,

[159]Plural of "apex," the highest point. [160]Oppress, smother. [161]Prehistoric reptiles.

Crying by day, Ahoy! from the rocks of the river, swinging and chirping over my head,
Calling my name from flower-beds, vines, tangled underbrush,
Lighting on every moment of my life,
Bussing[162] my body with soft balsamic[163] busses,
Noiselessly passing handfuls out of their hearts and giving them to be mine.

Old age superbly rising! O welcome, ineffable grace of dying days!
Every condition promulges[164] not only itself, it promulges what grows after and out of itself,
And the dark hush promulges as much as any.

I open my scuttle[165] at night and see the far-sprinkled systems,
And all I see multiplied as high as I can cipher edge but the rim of the farther systems.

Wider and wider they spread, expanding, always expanding,
Outward and outward and forever outward.

My sun has his sun and round him obediently wheels,
He joins with his partners a group of superior circuit,
And greater sets follow, making specks of the greatest inside them.

There is no stoppage and never can be stoppage,
If I, you, and the worlds, and all beneath or upon their surfaces, were this moment reduced back to a pallid float,[166] it would not avail the long run,
We should surely bring up again where we now stand,
And surely go as much farther, and then farther and farther.

A few quadrillions of eras, a few octillions[167] of cubic leagues, do not hazard the span or make it impatient,
They are but parts, any thing is but a part.

See ever so far, there is limitless space outside of that,
Count ever so much, there is limitless time around that.

My rendezvous is appointed, it is certain,
The Lord will be there and wait till I come on perfect terms,
The great Camerado,[168] the lover true for whom I pine will be there.

46

I know I have the best of time and space, and was never measured and never will be measured.

[162]Kissing. [163]Fragrant with the aroma of balsam.
[164]Generates. [165]An opening in a house or roof.
[166]I.e., returned to a primordial state where all life is suspended as particles in water.
[167]The number 1 followed by twenty-seven zeros. [168]Comrade.

I tramp a perpetual journey, (come listen all!)
My signs are a rain-proof coat, good shoes, and a staff cut from the woods,
No friend of mine takes his ease in my chair,
I have no chair, no church, no philosophy,
I lead no man to a dinner-table, library, exchange,[169]
But each man and each woman of you I lead upon a knoll,
My left hand hooking you round the waist,
My right hand pointing to landscapes of continents and the public road.

Not I, not any one else can travel that road for you,
You must travel it for yourself.

It is not far, it is within reach,
Perhaps you have been on it since you were born and did not know,
Perhaps it is everywhere on water and on land.

Shoulder your duds dear son, and I will mine, and let us hasten forth,
Wonderful cities and free nations we shall fetch[170] as we go.

If you tire, give me both burdens, and rest the chuff[171] of your hand on my hip,
And in due time you shall repay the same service to me,
For after we start we never lie by again.

This day before dawn I ascended a hill and looked at the crowded heaven,
And I said to my spirit *When we become the enfolders of those orbs, and the pleasure and knowledge of every thing in them, shall we be filled and satisfied then?*
And my spirit said *No, we but level that lift[172] to pass and continue beyond.*

You are also asking me questions and I hear you,
I answer that I cannot answer, you must find out for yourself.

Sit a while dear son,
Here are biscuits to eat and here is milk to drink,
But as soon as you sleep and renew yourself in sweet clothes, I kiss you with a good-by kiss and open the gate for your egress[173] hence.

Long enough have you dreamed contemptible dreams,
Now I wash the gum from your eyes,
You must habit yourself to the dazzle of the light and of every moment of your life.

Long have you timidly waded holding a plank by the shore,
Now I will you to be a bold swimmer,
To jump off in the midst of the sea, rise again, nod to me, shout, and laughingly dash with your hair.

[169]Stock exchange. [170]Reach. [171]Heel.
[172]Rising ground. [173]Exit.

47

I am the teacher of athletes,
He that by me spreads a wider breast than my own proves the width of my own,
He most honors my style who learns under it to destroy the teacher.

The boy I love, the same becomes a man not through derived power, but in his own right,
Wicked rather than virtuous out of conformity or fear,
Fond of his sweetheart, relishing well his steak,
Unrequited love or a slight cutting him worse than sharp steel cuts,
First-rate to ride, to fight, to hit the bull's eye, to sail a skiff, to sing a song or play on the banjo,
Preferring scars and the beard and faces pitted with small-pox over all latherers,[174]
And those well-tanned to those that keep out of the sun.

I teach straying from me, yet who can stray from me?
I follow you whoever you are from the present hour,
My words itch at your ears till you understand them.

I do not say these things for a dollar or to fill up the time while I wait for a boat,
(It is you talking just as much as myself, I act as the tongue of you,
Tied in your mouth, in mine it begins to be loosened.)

I swear I will never again mention love or death inside a house,
And I swear I will never translate myself at all, only to him or her who privately stays with me in the open air.

If you would understand me go to the heights or water-shore,
The nearest gnat is an explanation, and a drop or motion of waves key,
The maul, the oar, the hand-saw, second my words.
No shuttered room or school can commune with me,
But roughs and little children better than they.

The young mechanic is closest to me, he knows me well,
The woodman that takes his axe and jug with him shall take me with him all day,
The farm-boy ploughing in the field feels good at the sound of my voice,
In vessels that sail my words sail, I go with fishermen and seamen and love them.

The soldier camped or upon the march is mine,
On the night ere the pending battle many seek me, and I do not fail them,
On that solemn night (it may be their last) those that know me seek me.
My face rubs to the hunter's face when he lies down alone in his blanket,

[174]Those who are clean-shaven.

The driver thinking of me does not mind the jolt of his wagon,
The young mother and old mother comprehend me,
The girl and the wife rest the needle a moment and forget where they are,
They and all would resume what I have told them.

48

I have said that the soul is not more than the body,
And I have said that the body is not more than the soul,
And nothing, not God, is greater to one than one's self is,
And whoever walks a furlong without sympathy walks to his own funeral
dressed in his shroud,
And I or you pocketless of a dime may purchase the pick of the earth,
And to glance with an eye or show a bean in its pod confounds the learning
of all times,
And there is no trade or employment but the young man following it may
become a hero,
And there is no object so soft but it makes a hub for the wheeled universe,
And I say to any man or woman, Let your soul stand cool and composed
before a million universes.

And I say to mankind, Be not curious about God,
For I who am curious about each am not curious about God,
(No array of terms can say how much I am at peace about God and about
death.)

I hear and behold God in every object, yet understand God not in the least,
Nor do I understand who there can be more wonderful than myself.

Why should I wish to see God better than this day?
I see something of God each hour of the twenty-four, and each moment
then,
In the faces of men and women I see God, and in my own face in the glass,
I find letters from God dropt in the street, and every one is signed by God's
name,
And I leave them where they are, for I know that wheresoe'er I go,
Others will punctually come for ever and ever.

49

And as to you Death, and you bitter hug of mortality, it is idle to try to alarm
me.

To his work without flinching the accoucheur[175] comes,
I see the elder-hand[176] pressing receiving supporting,
I recline by the sills of the exquisite flexible doors,
And mark the outlet, and mark the relief and escape.

[175]Midwife, obstetrician. [176]Left hand.

And as to you Corpse I think you are good manure, but that does not offend me,
I smell the white roses sweet-scented and growing,
I reach to the leafy lips, I reach to the polished breasts of melons.
And as to you Life I reckon you are the leavings of many deaths,
(No doubt I have died myself ten thousand times before.)

I hear you whispering there O stars of heaven,
O suns—O grass of graves—O perpetual transfers and promotions,
If you do not say any thing how can I say any thing?

Of the turbid pool that lies in the autumn forest,
Of the moon that descends the steeps of the soughing[177] twilight,
Toss, sparkles of day and dusk—toss on the black stems that decay in the muck,
Toss to the moaning gibberish of the dry limbs.

I ascend from the moon, I ascend from the night,
I perceive that the ghastly glimmer is noonday sunbeams reflected,
And debouch[178] to the steady and central from the offspring great or small.

50

There is that in me—I do not know what it is—but I know it is in me.

Wrenched and sweaty—calm and cool then my body becomes,
I sleep—I sleep long.

I do not know it—it is without name—it is a word unsaid,
It is not in any dictionary, utterance, symbol.

Something it swings on more than the earth I swing on,
To it the creation is the friend whose embracing awakes me.

Perhaps I might tell more. Outlines! I plead for my brothers and sisters.

Do you see O my brothers and sisters?
It is not chaos or death—it is form, union, plan—it is eternal life—it is Happiness.

51

The past and present wilt—I have filled them, emptied them.
And proceed to fill my next fold of the future.

[177]Sighing, moaning. [178]Emerge.

Listener up there! what have you to confide to me?
Look in my face while I snuff[179] the sidle[180] of evening,
(Talk honestly, no one else hears you, and I stay only a minute longer.)

Do I contradict myself?
Very well then I contradict myself,
(I am large, I contain multitudes.)

I concentrate toward them that are nigh, I wait on the door-slab.

Who has done his day's work? who will soonest be through with his supper?
Who wishes to walk with me?

Will you speak before I am gone? will you prove already too late?

52

The spotted hawk swoops by and accuses me, he complains of my gab and my loitering.

I too am not a bit tamed, I too am untranslatable,
I sound my barbaric yawp[181] over the roofs of the world.

The last scud[182] of day holds back for me,
It flings my likeness after the rest and true as any on the shadowed wilds,
It coaxes me to the vapor and the dusk.

I depart as air, I shake my white locks at the runaway sun,
I effuse[183] my flesh in eddies, and drift it in lacy jags.

I bequeath myself to the dirt to grow from the grass I love,
If you want me again look for me under your boot-soles.

You will hardly know who I am or what I mean,
But I shall be good health to you nevertheless,
And filter and fiber your blood.

Failing to fetch me at first keep encouraged,
Missing me one place search another,
I stop somewhere waiting for you.

1855, 1881

[179]Extinguish. [180]Fading light. [181]Loud cry, yell.
[182]Wind-driven clouds or mist. [183]Pour out.

from *INSCRIPTIONS*

TO YOU

Stranger! if you, passing, meet me, and desire to speak to me, why should you not speak to me?
And why should I not speak to you?

1860, 1860[1]

ONE'S-SELF I SING

One's-Self I sing, a simple separate person,
Yet utter the word Democratic, the word En-Masse.

Of physiology from top to toe I sing,
Not physiognomy[1] alone nor brain alone is worthy for the Muse,
I say the Form complete is worthier far,
The Female equally with the Male I sing.

Of Life immense in passion, pulse, and power,
Cheerful, for freest action form'd under the laws divine,
The Modern Man I sing.

1867, 1871

WHEN I READ THE BOOK

When I read the book, the biography famous,
And is this then (said I) what the author calls a man's life?
And so will some one when I am dead and gone write my life?
(As if any man really knew aught of my life,
Why even I myself I often think know little or nothing of my real life,
Only a few hints, a few diffused faint clews and indirections
I seek for my own use to trace out here.)

1867, 1871

I HEAR AMERICA SINGING

I hear America singing, the varied carols I hear;
Those of mechanics—each one singing his, as it should be, blithe and strong;
The carpenter singing his, as he measures his plank or beam,
The mason singing his, as he makes ready for work, or leaves off work;

[1]The first date following each of Whitman's poems indicates its first appearance in print. The second, publication in its final form.
[1]Facial features, as indications of character.

The boatman singing what belongs to him in his boat—the deckhand
singing on the steamboat deck;
The shoemaker singing as he sits on his bench—the hatter singing as he
stands;
The wood-cutter's song—the ploughboy's, on his way in the morning, or at
the noon intermission, or at sundown;
The delicious singing of the mother—or of the young wife at work—or of the
girl sewing or washing—
Each singing what belongs to her, and to none else;
The day what belongs to the day—at night, the party of young fellows,
robust, friendly,
Singing, with open mouths, their strong melodious songs.

1860, 1867

POETS TO COME

Poets to come! orators, singers, musicians to come!
Not today is to justify me, and answer what I am for;
But you, a new brood, native, athletic, continental, greater than before
known,
Arouse! Arouse—for you must justify me—you must answer.

I myself but write one or two indicative words for the future,
I but advance a moment, only to wheel and hurry back in the darkness.

I am a man who, sauntering along, without fully stopping, turns a casual look
upon you, and then averts his face,
Leaving it to you to prove and define it,
Expecting the main things from you.

1860, 1867

from *CHILDREN OF ADAM*

FROM PENT-UP ACHING RIVERS

From pent-up aching rivers,
From that of myself without which I were nothing,
From what I am determin'd to make illustrious, even if I stand sole among
men,
From my own voice resonant, singing the phallus,
Singing the song of procreation,
Singing the need of superb children and therein superb grown people,
Singing the muscular urge and the blending,
Singing the bedfellow's song, (O resistless yearning!
O for any and each the body correlative attracting!
O for you whoever you are your correlative body! O it, more than all else,
you delighting!)

From the hungry gnaw that eats me night and day,
From native moments, from bashful pains, singing them,
Seeking something yet unfound though I have diligently sought it many a long year,
Singing the true song of the soul fitful at random,
Renascent with grossest Nature or among animals,
Of that, of them and what goes with them my poems informing,
Of the smell of apples and lemons, of the pairing of birds,
Of the wet of woods, of the lapping of waves,
Of the mad pushes of waves upon the land, I them chanting,
The overture lightly sounding, the strain anticipating,
The welcome nearness, the sight of the perfect body,
The swimmer swimming naked in the bath, or motionless on his back lying and floating,
The female form approaching, I pensive, love-flesh tremulous aching,
The divine lust for myself or you or for any one making,
The face, the limbs, the index from head to foot, and what it arouses,
The mystic deliria,[1] the madness amorous, the utter abandonment,
(Hark close and still what I now whisper to you,
I love you, O you entirely possess me,
O that you and I escape from the rest and go utterly off, free and lawless,
Two hawks in the air, two fishes swimming in the sea not more lawless than we;)
The furious storm through me careering, I passionately trembling,
The oath of the inseparableness of two together, of the woman that loves me and whom I love more than my life, that oath swearing,
(O I willingly stake all for you,
O let me be lost if it must be so!
O you and I! what is it to us what the rest do or think?
What is all else to us? only that we enjoy each other and exhaust each other if it must be so;)
From the master, the pilot I yield the vessel to,
The general commanding me, commanding all, from him permission taking,
From time the programme hastening, (I have loiter'd too long as it is,)
From sex, from the warp and from the woof,[2]
From privacy, from frequent repinings alone,
From plenty of persons near and yet the right person not near,
From the soft sliding of hands over me and thrusting of fingers through my hair and beard,
From the long sustain'd kiss upon the mouth or bosom,
From the close pressure that makes me or any man drunk, fainting with excess,
From what the divine husband knows, from the work of fatherhood,
From exultation, victory and relief, from the bedfellow's embrace in the night,
From the act-poems of eyes, hands, hips and bosoms,

[1]Delusions, hallucinations.
[2]Interwoven vertical and horizontal threads of a fabric.

From the cling of the trembling arm,
From the bending curve and the clinch,
From side by side the pliant coverlet off-throwing,
From the one so unwilling to have me leave, and me just as unwilling to leave,
(Yet a moment O tender waiter, and I return,)
From the hour of shining stars and dropping dews,
From the night a moment I emerging flitting out,
Celebrate you act divine and you children prepared for,
And you stalwart loins.

1860, 1881

OUT OF THE ROLLING OCEAN THE CROWD

Out of the rolling ocean the crowd came a drop gently to me,
Whispering *I love you, before long I die,*
I have travel'd a long way merely to look on you to touch you,
For I could not die till I once look'd on you,
For I fear'd I might afterward lose you.

Now we have met, we have look'd, we are safe,
Return in peace to the ocean my love,
I too am part of the ocean my love, we are not so much separated,
Behold the great rondure,[1] the cohesion of all, how perfect!
But as for me, for you, the irresistible sea is to separate us,
As for an hour carrying us diverse, yet cannot carry us diverse forever;
Be not impatient—a little space—know you I salute the air, the ocean and the land,
Every day at sundown for your dear sake my love.

1865, 1881

AS ADAM EARLY IN THE MORNING

As Adam, early in the morning,
Walking forth from the bower, refreshed with sleep;
Behold me where I pass—hear my voice—approach,
Touch me—touch the palm of your hand to my Body as I pass;
Be not afraid of my Body.

1861, 1867

ONCE I PASS'D THROUGH A POPULOUS CITY

Once I pass'd through a populous city imprinting my brain for future use with its shows, architecture, customs, traditions,

[1]Gracefully rounded curve.

Yet now of all that city I remember only a woman I casually met there who detain'd me for love of me,
Day by day and night by night we were together—all else has long been forgotten by me,
I remember I say only that woman who passionately clung to me,
Again we wander, we love, we separate again,
Again she holds me by the hand, I must not go,
I see her close beside me with silent lips sad and tremulous.

1860, 1867

FACING WEST FROM CALIFORNIA'S SHORES

Facing west from California's shores,
Inquiring, tireless, seeking what is yet unfound,
I, a child, very old, over waves, towards the house of maternity,[1] the land of migrations, look afar,
Look off the shores of my Western sea, the circle almost circled;
For starting westward from Hindustan,[2] from the Vales of Kashmere,[3]
From Asia, from the north, from the God, the sage, and the hero,
From the south, from the flowery peninsulas and the spice islands,[4]
Long having wander'd since, round the earth having wander'd,
Now I face home again, very pleas'd and joyous,
(But where is what I started for so long ago?
And why is it yet unfound?)

1860, 1867

from *CALAMUS*[1]

IN PATHS UNTRODDEN

In paths untrodden,
In the growth of margins of pond-waters,
Escaped from the life that exhibits itself,
From all the standards hitherto publish'd, from the pleasures, profits, conformities,
Which too long I was offering to feed my soul,
Clear to me now standards not yet publish'd, clear to me that my soul,
That the soul of the man I speak for rejoices in comrades,
Here by myself away from the clank of the world,
Tallying and talk'd to here by tongues aromatic,
No longer abash'd, (for in this secluded spot I can respond as I would not dare elsewhere,)

[1]I.e., Asia, then thought to be the place of man's origin. [2]India.
[3]Mountain region of northern India. [4]The islands of Indonesia.
[1]Whitman wrote that Calamus "is the very large and aromatic grass, or rush, growing about water-ponds . . . spears about three feet high."

Strong upon me the life that does not exhibit itself, yet contains all the rest,
Resolv'd to sing no songs to-day but those of manly attachment,
Projecting them along that substantial life,
Bequeathing hence types of athletic love,
Afternoon this delicious Ninth-month[2] in my forty-first year,
I proceed for all who are or have been young men,
To tell the secret of my nights and days,
To celebrate the need of comrades.

1860, 1867

SCENTED HERBAGE OF MY BREAST

Scented herbage of my breast,
Leaves from you I glean, I write, to be persued best afterwards,
Tomb-leaves,[1] body-leaves growing up above me above death,
Perennial roots, tall leaves, O the winter shall not freeze you delicate leaves,
Every year shall you bloom again, out from where you retired you shall emerge again;
Or I do not know whether many passing by will discover you or inhale your faint odor, but I believe a few will;
O slender leaves! O blossoms of my blood! I permit you to tell in your own way of the heart that is under you,
O I do not know what you mean there underneath yourselves, you are not happiness,
You are often more bitter than I can bear, you burn and sting me,
Yet you are beautiful to me you faint tinged roots, you make me think of death,
Death is beautiful from you, (what indeed is finally beautiful except death and love?)
O I think it is not for life I am chanting here my chant of lovers, I think it must be for death,
For how calm, how solemn it grows to ascend to the atmosphere of lovers,
Death or life I am then indifferent, my soul declines to prefer,
(I am not sure but the high soul of lovers welcomes death most,)
Indeed O death, I think now these leaves mean precisely the same as you mean,
Grow up taller sweet leaves that I may see! grow up out of my breast!
Spring away from the conceal'd heart there!
Do not fold yourself so in your pink-tinged roots timid leaves!
Do not remain down there so ashamed, herbage of my breast!
Come I am determin'd to unbare this broad breast of mine, I have long enough stifled and choked;
Emblematic and capricious blades I leave you, now you serve me not;
I will say what I have to say by itself,

[2]September.
[1]Probably an allusion derived from a contemporary illustration of an Egyptian mummy from which were sprouting leaves of grain.

I will sound myself and comrades only, I will never again utter a call only
their call,
I will raise with it immortal reverberations through the States,
I will give an example to lovers to take permanent shape and will through the
States,
Through me shall the words be said to make death exhilarating,
Give me your tone therefore O death, that I may accord with it,
Give me yourself, for I see that you belong to me now above all, and are
folded inseparably together, you love and death are,
Nor will I allow you to balk me any more with what I was calling life,
For now it is convey'd to me that you are the purports essential,
That you hide in these shifting forms of life, for reasons, and that they are
mainly for you,
That you beyond them come forth to remain, the real reality,
That behind the mask of materials you patiently wait, no matter how long,
That you will one day perhaps take control of all,
That you will perhaps dissipate this entire show of appearance,
That may-be you are what it is all for, but it does not last so very long,
But you will last very long.

1860, 1881

WHAT THINK YOU I TAKE MY PEN IN HAND?

What think you I take my pen in hand to record?
The battle-ship, perfect-modeled, majestic, that I saw pass the offing today
under full sail?
The splendors of the past day? Or the splendor of the night that envelops
me?
Or the vaunted glory and growth of the great city spread around me?—No;
But I record of two simple men I saw today, on the pier, in the midst of the
crowd, parting the parting of dear friends;
The one to remain hung on the other's neck, and passionately kissed him,
While the one to depart, tightly pressed the one to remain in his arms.

1860, 1881

I SAW IN LOUISIANA A LIVE-OAK GROWING

I saw in Louisiana a live-oak growing,
All alone stood it and the moss hung down from the branches,
Without any companion it grew there uttering joyous leaves of dark green,
And its look, rude, unbending, lusty, made me think of myself,
But I wonder'd how it could utter joyous leaves standing alone there without
its friend near, for I knew I could not,
And I broke off a twig with a certain number of leaves upon it, and twined
around it a little moss,
And brought it away, and I have placed it in sight in my room,

It is not needed to remind me as of my own dear friends,
(For I believe lately I think of little else than of them,)
Yet it remains to me a curious token, it makes me think of manly love;
For all that, and though the live-oak glistens there in Louisiana solitary in a wide flat space,
Uttering joyous leaves all its life without a friend a lover near,
I know very well I could not.

1860, 1867

I HEAR IT WAS CHARGED AGAINST ME

I hear it was charged against me that I sought to destroy institutions,
But really I am neither for nor against institutions,
(What indeed have I in common with them? or what with the destruction of them?)
Only I will establish in the Mannahatta[1] and in every city of these States inland and seaboard,
And in the fields and woods, and above every keel little or large that dents the water,
Without edifices or rules or trustees or any argument,
The institution of the dear love of comrades.

1860, 1867

CROSSING BROOKLYN FERRY[1]

1

Flood-tide below me! I see you face to face!
Clouds of the west—sun there half an hour high—I see you also face to face.

Crowds of men and women attired in the usual costumes, how curious you are to me!
On the ferry-boats the hundreds and hundreds that cross, returning home, are more curious to me than you suppose,
And you that shall cross from shore to shore years hence are more to me, and more in my meditations, than you might suppose.

2

The impalpable sustenance of me from all things at all hours of the day,
The simple, compact, well-join'd scheme, myself disintegrated, every one disintegrated yet part of the scheme,

[1]Indian word from which "Manhattan" was derived.
[1]Originally titled "Sun-Down Poem."

The similitudes[2] of the past and those of the future,
The glories strung like beads on my smallest sighs and hearings, on the walk in the street and the passage over the river,
The current rushing so swiftly and swimming with me far away,
The others that are to follow me, the ties between me and them,
The certainty of others, the life, love, sight, hearing of others.

Others will enter the gates of the ferry and cross from shore to shore,
Others will watch the run of the flood-tide,
Others will see the shipping of Manhattan north and west, and the heights of Brooklyn to the south and east,
Others will see the islands large and small;
Fifty years hence, others will see them as they cross, the sun half an hour high,
A hundred years hence, or ever so many hundred years hence, others will see them,
Will enjoy the sunset, the pouring-in of the flood-tide, the falling-back to the sea of the ebb-tide.

3

It avails not, time nor place—distance avails not,
I am with you, you men and women of a generation, or ever so many generations hence,
Just as you feel when you look on the river and sky, so I felt,
Just as any of you is one of a living crowd, I was one of a crowd,
Just as you are refresh'd by the gladness of the river and the bright flow, I was refresh'd,
Just as you stand and lean on the rail, yet hurry with the swift current, I stood yet was hurried,
Just as you look on the numberless masts of ships and the thick-stemm'd pipes of steamboats, I look'd.

I too many and many a time cross'd the river of old,
Watched the Twelfth-month[3] sea-gulls, saw them high in the air floating with motionless wings, oscillating their bodies,
Saw how the glistening yellow lit up parts of their bodies and left the rest in strong shadow,
Saw the slow-wheeling circles and the gradual edging toward the south,
Saw the reflection of the summer sky in the water,
Had my eyes dazzled by the shimmering track of beams,
Look'd at the fine centrifugal spokes of light round the shape of my head in the sunlit water,
Look'd on the haze on the hills southward and south-westward,
Look'd on the vapor as it flew in fleeces tinged with violet,
Look'd toward the lower bay to notice the vessels arriving,

[2]Similarities. [3]December.

Saw their approach, saw aboard those that were near me,
Saw the white sails of schooners and sloops, saw the ships at anchor,
The sailors at work in the rigging or out astride the spars,
The round masts, the swinging motion of the hulls, the slender serpentine pennants,
The large and small steamers in motion, the pilots in their pilot-houses,
The white wake left by the passage, the quick tremulous whirl of the wheels,
The flags of all nations, the falling of them at sunset,
The scallop-edged waves in the twilight, the ladled cups, the frolicsome crests and glistening,
The stretch afar flowing dimmer and dimmer, the gray walls of the granite storehouses by the docks,
On the river the shadowy group, the big steam-tug closely flank'd on each side by the barges, the hay-boat, the belated lighter,[4]
On the neighboring shore the fires from the foundry chimneys burning high and glaringly into the night,
Casting their flicker of black contrasted with wild red and yellow light over the tops of houses, and down into the clefts of streets.

4

These and all else were to me the same as they are to you,
I loved well those cities, loved well the stately and rapid river,
The men and women I saw were all near to me,
Others the same—others who look back on me because I look'd forward to them,
(The time will come, though I stop here to-day and to-night.)

5

What is it then between us?
What is the count of the scores or hundreds of years between us?

Whatever it is, it avails not—distance avails not, and place avails not,
I too lived, Brooklyn of ample hills was mine,
I too walk'd the streets of Manhattan island, and bathed in the waters around it,
I too felt the curious abrupt questionings stir within me,
In the day among crowds of people sometimes they came upon me,
In my walks home late at night or as I lay in my bed they came upon me,
I too had been struck from the float forever held in solution,
I too had receiv'd identity by my body,
That I was I knew was of my body, and what I should be I knew I should be of my body.

[4]Barge used in loading and unloading cargo ships.

6

It is not upon you alone the dark patches fall,
The dark threw its patches down upon me also,
The best I had done seem'd to me blank and suspicious,
My great thoughts as I supposed them, were they not in reality meagre?
Nor is it you alone who know what it is to be evil,
I am he who knew what it was to be evil,
I too knitted the old knot of contrarity,
Blabb'd, blush'd, resented, lied, stole, grudg'd,
Had guile, anger, lust, hot wishes I dared not speak,
Was wayward, vain, greedy, shallow, sly, cowardly, malignant,
The wolf, the snake, the hog, not wanting[5] in me,
The cheating look, the frivolous word, the adulterous wish, not wanting,
Refusals, hates, postponements, meanness, laziness, none of these wanting,
Was one with the rest, the days and haps[6] of the rest,
Was call'd by my nighest[7] name by clear loud voices of young men as they saw
me approaching or passing,
Felt their arms on my neck as I stood, or the negligent leaning of their flesh
against me as I sat,
Saw many I loved in the street or ferry-boat or public assembly, yet never told
them a word,
Lived the same life with the rest, the same old laughing, gnawing, sleeping,
Play'd the part that still looks back on the actor or actress,
The same old role, the role that is what we make it, as great as we like,
Or as small as we like, or both great and small.

7

Closer yet I approach you,
What thought you have of me now, I had as much of you—I laid in my stores
in advance,
I consider'd long and seriously of you before you were born.

Who was to know what should come home to me?
Who knows but I am enjoying this?
Who knows, for all the distance, but I am as good as looking at you now, for
all you cannot see me?

8

Ah, what can ever be more stately and admirable to me than mast-hemm'd
Manhattan?
River and sunset and scallop-edg'd waves of flood-tide?
The sea-gulls oscillating their bodies, the hay-boat in the twilight, and the
belated lighter?

[5]Lacking. [6]Chance events. [7]Shortest or most familiar.

What gods can exceed these that clasp me by the hand, and with voices I love call me promptly and loudly by my nighest name as I approach?
What is more subtle than this which ties me to the woman or man that looks in my face?
Which fuses me into you now, and pours my meaning into you?
We understand then do we not?
What I promis'd without mentioning it, have you not accepted?
What the study could not teach—what the preaching could not accomplish is accomplish'd, is it not?

9

Flow on, river! flow with the flood-tide, and ebb with the ebb-tide!
Frolic on, crested and scallop-edg'd waves!
Gorgeous clouds of the sunset! drench with your splendor me, or the men and women generations after me!
Cross from shore to shore, countless crowds of passengers!
Stand up, tall masts of Mannahatta! stand up, beautiful hills of Brooklyn!
Throb, baffled and curious brain! throw our questions and answers!
Suspend here and everywhere, eternal float of solution!
Gaze, loving and thirsting eyes, in the house or street or public assembly!
Sound out, voices of young men! loudly and musically call me by my nighest name!
Live, old life! play the part that looks back on the actor or actress!
Play the old role, the role that is great or small according as one makes it!
Consider, you who peruse me, whether I may not in unknown ways be looking upon you;
Be firm, rail over the river, to support those who lean idly, yet haste with the hasting current;
Fly on, sea-birds! fly sideways, or wheel in large circles high in the air;
Receive the summer sky, you water, and faithfully hold it till all downcast eyes have time to take it from you!
Diverge, fine spokes of light, from the shape of my head, or any one's head, in the sunlit water!
Come on, ships from the lower bay! pass up or down, white-sail'd schooners, sloops, lighters!
Flaunt away, flags of all nations! be duly lower'd at sunset!
Burn high your fires, foundry chimneys! cast black shadows at nightfall! cast red and yellow light over the tops of the houses!
Appearances, now or henceforth, indicate what you are,
You necessary film, continue to envelop the soul,
About my body for me, and your body for you, be hung our divinest aromas,
Thrive, cities—bring your freight, bring your shows, ample and sufficient rivers,
Expand, being than which none else is perhaps more spiritual,
Keep your places, objects than which none else is more lasting.

You have waited, you always wait, you dumb, beautiful ministers,
We receive you with free sense at last, and are insatiate henceforward,

Not you any more shall be able to foil us, or withhold yourselves from us,
We use you, and do not cast you aside—we plant you permanently within us,
We fathom you not—we love you—there is perfection in you also,
You furnish your parts toward eternity,
Great or small, you furnish your parts toward the soul.

1856, 1881

from *SEA-DRIFT*

OUT OF THE CRADLE ENDLESSLY ROCKING

Out of the cradle endlessly rocking,
Out of the mocking-bird's throat, the musical shuttle,
Out of the Ninth-month[1] midnight,
Over the sterile sands and the fields beyond, where the child leaving his bed
    wander'd alone, bareheaded, barefoot,
Down from the shower'd halo,
Up from the mystic play of shadows twining and twisting as if they were alive,
Out from the patches of briers and blackberries,
From the memories of the bird that chanted to me,
From your memories sad brother, from the fitful risings and fallings I heard,
From under that yellow half-moon late-risen and swollen as if with tears,
From those beginning notes of yearning and love there in the mist,
From the thousand responses of my heart never to cease,
From the myriad thence-arous'd words,
From the word stronger and more delicious than any,
From such as now they start the scene revisiting,
As a flock, twittering, rising, or overhead passing,
Borne hither, ere all eludes me, hurriedly,
A man, yet by these tears a little boy again,
Throwing myself on the sand, confronting the waves,
I, chanter of pains and joys, uniter of here and hereafter,
Taking all hints to use them, but swiftly leaping beyond them,
A reminiscence sing.

Once Paumanok,[2]
When the lilac-scent was in the air and Fifth-month[3] grass was growing,
Up this seashore in some briers,
Two feather'd guests from Alabama, two together,
And their nest, and four light-green eggs spotted with brown,
And every day the he-bird to and fro near at hand,
And every day the she-bird crouch'd on her nest, silent, with bright eyes,
And every day I, a curious boy, never too close, never disturbing them,
Cautiously peering, absorbing, translating.

[1]September. [2]Indian name for Long Island, New York. [3]May.

Shine! shine! shine!
Pour down your warmth, great sun!
While we bask, we two together.

Two together!
Winds blow south, or winds blow north,
Day come white, or night come black,
Home, or rivers and mountains from home,
Singing all time, minding no time,
While we two keep together.

Till of a sudden,
May-be kill'd, unknown to her mate,
One forenoon the she-bird crouch'd not on the nest,
Nor return'd that afternoon, nor the next,
Nor ever appear'd again.

And thenceforward all summer in the sound of the sea,
And at night under the full of the moon in calmer weather,
Over the hoarse surging of the sea,
Or flitting from brier to brier by day,
I saw, I heard at intervals the remaining one, the he-bird,
The solitary guest from Alabama.

Blow! blow! blow!
Blow up sea-winds along Paumanok's shore;
I wait and I wait till you blow my mate to me.

Yes, when the stars glisten'd,
All night long on the prong of a moss-scallop'd stake,
Down almost amid the slapping waves,
Sat the lone singer wonderful causing tears.

He call'd on his mate,
He pour'd forth the meanings which I of all men know.

Yes my brother I know,
The rest might not, but I have treasur'd every note,
For more than once dimly down to the beach gliding,
Silent, avoiding the moonbeams, blending myself with the shadows,
Recalling now the obscure shapes, the echoes, the sounds and sights after
  their sorts,
The white arms out in the breakers tirelessly tossing,
I, with bare feet, a child, the wind wafting my hair,
Listen'd long and long.

Listen'd to keep, to sing, now translating the notes,
Following you my brother.

Soothe! soothe! soothe!
Close on its wave soothes the wave behind,

And again another behind embracing and lapping, every one close,
But my love soothes not me, not me.

Low hangs the moon, it rose late,
It is lagging—O I think it is heavy with love, with love.

O madly the sea pushes upon the land,
With love, with love.

O night! do I not see my love fluttering out among the breakers?
What is that little black thing I see there in the white?

Loud! loud! loud!
Loud I call to you, my love!
High and clear I shoot my voice over the waves,
Surely you must know who is here, is here,
You must know who I am, my love.

Low-hanging moon!
What is that dusky spot in your brown yellow?
O it is the shape, the shape of my mate!
O moon do not keep her from me any longer.

Land! land! O land!
Whichever way I turn, O I think you could give me my mate back again if you only would,
For I am almost sure I see her dimly whichever way I look.

O rising stars!
Perhaps the one I want so much will rise, will rise with some of you.

O throat! O trembling throat!
Sound clearer through the atmosphere!
Pierce the woods, the earth,
Somewhere listening to catch you must be the one I want.

Shake out carols!
Solitary here, the night's carols!
Carols of lonesome love! death's carols!
Carols under that lagging, yellow, waning moon!
O under that moon where she droops almost down into the sea!
O reckless despairing carols.

But soft! sink low!
Soft! let me just murmur,
And do you wait a moment you husky-nois'd sea,
For somewhere I believe I heard my mate responding to me,
So faint, I must be still, be still to listen,
But not altogether still, for then she might not come immediately to me.

Hither my love!
Here I am! here!

With this just-sustain'd note I announce myself to you,
This gentle call is for you my love, for you.

Do not be decoy'd elsewhere,
That is the whistle of the wind, it is not my voice,
That is the fluttering, the fluttering of the spray,
Those are the shadows of leaves.

O darkness! O in vain!
O I am very sick and sorrowful.

O brown halo in the sky near the moon, drooping upon the sea!
O troubled reflection in the sea!
O throat! O throbbing heart!
And I singing uselessly, uselessly all the night.

O past! O happy life! O songs of joy!
In the air, in the woods, over fields,
Loved! loved! loved! loved! loved!
But my mate no more, no more with me!
We two together no more.

The aria sinking,
All else continuing, the stars shining,
The winds blowing, the notes of the bird continuous echoing,
With angry moans the fierce old mother incessantly moaning,
On the sands of Paumanok's shore gray and rustling,
The yellow half-moon enlarged, sagging down, drooping, the face of the sea almost touching,
The boy ecstatic, with his bare feet the waves, with his hair the atmosphere dallying,
The love in the heart long pent, now loose, now at last tumultuously bursting,
The aria's meaning, the ears, the soul, swiftly depositing,
The strange tears down the cheeks coursing,
The colloquy there, the trio, each uttering,
The undertone, the savage old mother incessantly crying.
To the boy's soul's questions sullenly timing, some drown'd secret hissing.
To the outsetting bard.

Demon or bird! (said the boy's soul,)
Is it indeed toward your mate you sing? or is it really to me?
For I, that was a child, my tongue's use sleeping, now I have heard you,
Now in a moment I know what I am for, I awake,
And already a thousand singers, a thousand songs, clearer, louder and more sorrowful than yours,
A thousand warbling echoes have started to life within me, never to die.

O you singer solitary, singing by yourself, projecting me,
O solitary me listening, never more shall I cease perpetuating you,

Never more shall I escape, never more the reverberations,
Never more the cries of unsatisfied love be absent from me,
Never again leave me to be the peaceful child I was before what there in the night,
By the sea under the yellow and sagging moon,
The messenger there arous'd, the fire, the sweet hell within,
The unknown want, the destiny of me.

O give me the clew![4] (it lurks in the night here somewhere,)
O if I am to have so much, let me have more!
A word then, (for I will conquer it,)
The word final, superior to all,
Subtle, sent up—what is it?—I listen:
Are you whispering it, and have been all the time, you sea-waves?
Is that it from your liquid rims and wet sands?

Whereto answering, the sea,
Delaying not, hurrying not,
Whisper'd me through the night, and very plainly before daybreak,
Lisp'd to me the low and delicious word death,
And again, death, death, death, death,
Hissing melodious, neither like the bird nor like my arous'd child's heart,
But edging near as privately for me rustling at my feet,
Creeping thence steadily up to my ears and laving me softly all over,
Death, death, death, death, death.

Which I do not forget,
But fuse the song of my dusky demon and brother,
That he sang to me in the moonlight on Paumanok's gray beach,
With the thousand responsive songs at random,
My own songs awaked from that hour,
And with them the key, the word up from the waves,
The word of the sweetest song and all songs,
That strong and delicious word which, creeping to my feet,
(Or like some old crone rocking the cradle, swathed in sweet garments, bending aside,)
The sea whisper'd me.

1859, 1881

AS I EBB'D WITH THE OCEAN OF LIFE

1

As I ebb'd with the ocean of life,
As I wended the shores I know,
As I walk'd where the ripples continually wash you Paumanok,

[4]Clue.

Where they rustle up hoarse and sibilant,
Where the fierce old mother endlessly cries for her castaways,
I musing late in the autumn day, gazing off southward,
Held by this electric self out of the pride of which I utter poems,
Was seiz'd by the spirit that trails in the lines underfoot,
The rim, the sediment that stands for all the water and all the land of the globe.

Fascinated, my eyes reverting from the south, dropt, to follow those slender windrows,[1]
Chaff, straw, splinters of wood, weeds and the sea-gluten,[2]
Scum, scales from shining rocks, leaves of salt-lettuce, left by the tide,
Miles walking, the sound of breaking waves the other side of me,
Paumanok there and then as I thought the old thought of likenesses,
These you presented to me you fish-shaped island,
As I wended the shores I know,
As I walk'd with that electric self seeking types.[3]

2

As I wend to the shores I know not,
As I list to the dirge, the voices of men and women wreck'd,
As I inhale the impalpable breezes that set in upon me,
As the ocean so mysterious rolls toward me closer and closer,
I too but signify at the utmost a little wash'd-up drift,
A few sands and dead leaves to gather,
Gather, and merge myself as part of the sands and drift.

O baffled, balk'd, bent to the very earth,
Oppress'd with myself that I have dared to open my mouth,
Aware now that amid all that blab whose echoes recoil upon me I have not once had the least idea who or what I am,
But that before all my arrogant poems the real Me stands yet untouch'd, untold, altogether unreach'd,
Withdrawn far, mocking me with mock-congratulatory signs and bows,
With peals of distant ironical laughter at every word I have written,
Pointing in silence to these songs, and then to the sand beneath.
I perceive I have not really understood any thing, not a single object, and that no man ever can,
Nature here in sight of the sea taking advantage of me to dart upon me and sting me,
Because I have dared to open my mouth to sing at all.

[1]Rows heaped up by the wind or waves. [2]Thick, sticky plant substance.
[3]I.e., seeking "likenesses" of himself.

3

You oceans both, I close with you,
We murmur alike reproachfully rolling sands and drift, knowing not why,
These little shreds indeed standing for you and me and all.

You friable[4] shore with trails of debris,
You fish-shaped island, I take what is underfoot,
What is yours is mine my father.

I too Paumanok,
I too have bubbled up, floated the measureless float, and been wash'd on your shores,
I too am but a trail of drift and debris,
I too leave little wrecks upon you, you fish-shaped island.

I throw myself upon your breast my father,
I cling to you so that you cannot unloose me,
I hold you so firm till you answer me something.

Kiss me my father,
Touch me with your lips as I touch those I love,
Breathe to me while I hold you close the secret of the murmuring I envy.

4

Ebb, ocean of life, (the flow will return,)
Cease not your moaning you fierce old mother,
Endlessly cry for your castaways, but fear not, deny not me,
Rustle not up so hoarse and angry against my feet as I touch you or gather from you.

I mean tenderly by you and all,
I gather for myself and for this phantom looking down where we lead, and following me and mine.

Me and mine, loose windrows, little corpses,
Froth, snowy white, and bubbles,
(See, from my dead lips the ooze exuding at last,
See, the prismatic colors glistening and rolling,)
Tufts or straw, sands, fragments,
Buoy'd hither from many moods, one contradicting another,
From the storm, the long calm, the darkness, the swell,
Musing, pondering, a breath, a briny tear, a dab of liquid or soil,
Up just as much out of fathomless workings fermented and thrown,
A limp blossom or two, torn, just as much over waves floating, drifted at random,

[4]Crumbling.

Just as much for us that sobbing dirge of Nature,
Just as much whence we come that blare of the cloud-trumpets,
We, capricious, brought hither we know not whence, spread out before you,
You up there walking or sitting,
Whoever you are, we too lie in drifts at your feet.

1860, 1881

from *BY THE ROADSIDE*

WHEN I HEARD THE LEARN'D ASTRONOMER

When I heard the learn'd astronomer,
When the proofs, the figures, were ranged in columns before me,
When I was shown the charts and diagrams, to add, divide, and measure
them,
When I sitting heard the astronomer where he lectured with much applause
in the lecture-room,
How soon unaccountable I became tired and sick,
Till rising and gliding out I wander'd off by myself,
In the mystical moist night-air, and from time to time,
Look'd up in perfect silence at the stars.

1865, 1865

THE DALLIANCE[1] OF THE EAGLES

Skirting the river road, (my forenoon walk, my rest,)
Skyward in air a sudden muffled sound, the dalliance of the eagles,
The rushing amorous contact high in space together,
The clinching interlocking claws, a living, fierce, gyrating wheel,
Four beating wings, two beaks, a swirling mass tight grappling,
In tumbling turning clustering loops, straight downward falling,
Till o'er the river pois'd, the twain yet one, a moment's lull,
A motionless still balance in the air, then parting, talons loosing,
Upward again on slow-firm pinions, slanting, their separate diverse flight,
She hers, he his, pursuing.

1880, 1881

from *DRUM-TAPS*

BEAT! BEAT! DRUMS!

Beat! beat! drums!—blow! bugles! blow!
Through the windows—through doors—burst like a ruthless force,
Into the solemn church, and scatter the congregation,
Into the school where the scholar is studying;

[1]In the sense of amorous play and mating.

Leave not the bridegroom quiet—no happiness must he have now with his bride,
Nor the peaceful farmer any peace, ploughing his field or gathering his grain,
So fierce you whirr and pound you drums—so shrill you bugles blow.

Beat! beat! drums!—blow! bugles! blow!
Over the traffic of cities—over the rumble of wheels in the streets;
Are beds prepared for sleepers at night in the houses? no sleepers must sleep in those beds,
No bargainers' bargains by day—no brokers or speculators—would they continue?
Would the talkers be talking? would the singer attempt to sing?
Would the lawyer rise in the court to state his case before the judge?
Then rattle quicker, heavier drums—you bugles wilder blow.

Beat! beat! drums!—blow! bugles! blow!
Make no parley—stop for no expostulation,
Mind not the timid—mind not the weeper or prayer,
Mind not the old man beseeching the young man,
Let not the child's voice be heard, nor the mother's entreaties,
Make even the trestles to shake the dead where they lie awaiting the hearses,
So strong you thump O terrible drums—so loud you bugles blow.

1861, 1867

CAVALRY CROSSING A FORD

A line in long array where they wind betwixt green islands,
They take a serpentine course, their arms flash in the sun—hark to the musical clank,
Behold the silvery river, in it the splashing horses loitering stop to drink,
Behold the brown-faced men, each group, each person a picture, the negligent rest on the saddles,
Some emerge on the opposite bank, others are just entering the ford—while,
Scarlet and blue and snowy white,
The guidon flags[1] flutter gayly in the wind.

1865, 1871

BIVOUAC ON A MOUNTAIN SIDE

I see before me now a traveling army halting,
Below a fertile valley spread, with barns and the orchards of summer,
Behind, the terraced sides of a mountain, abrupt, in places rising high,
Broken, with rocks, with clinging cedars, with tall shapes dingily seen,

[1]Military flags or pennants.

The numerous camp-fires scatter'd near and far, some away up on the mountain,
The shadowy forms of men and horses, looming, large-sized, flickering,
And over all the sky—the sky! far, far out of reach, studded, breaking out, the eternal stars.

1865, 1871

VIGIL STRANGE I KEPT ON THE FIELD ONE NIGHT

Vigil strange I kept on the field one night;
When you my son and my comrade dropt at my side that day,
One look I but gave which your dear eyes return'd with a look I shall never forget,
One touch of your hand to mine O boy, reach'd up as you lay on the ground,
Then onward I sped in the battle, the even-contested battle,
Till late in the night reliev'd to the place at last again I made my way,
Found you in death so cold dear comrade, found your body son of responding kisses, (never again on earth responding,)
Bared your face in the starlight, curious the scene, cool blew the moderate night-wind,
Long there and then in vigil I stood, dimly around me the battle field spreading,
Vigil wondrous and vigil sweet there in the fragrant silent night,
But not a tear fell, not even a long-drawn sigh, long long I gazed,
Then on the earth partially reclining sat by your side leaning my chin in my hands,
Passing sweet hours, immortal and mystic hours with you dearest comrade—not a tear, not a word,
Vigil of silence, love and death, vigil for you my son and my soldier,
As onward silently stars aloft, eastward new ones upward stole,
Vigil final for you brave boy, (I could not save you, swift was your death,
I faithfully loved you and cared for you living, I think we shall surely meet again,)
Till at latest lingering of the night, indeed just as the dawn appear'd,
My comrade I wrapt in his blanket, envelop'd well his form,
Folded the blanket well, tucking it carefully over head and carefully under feet,
And there and then and bathed by the rising sun, my son in his grave, in his rude-dug grave I deposited,
Ending my vigil strange with that, vigil of night and battle-field dim,
Vigil for boy of responding kisses, (never again on earth responding,)
Vigil for comrade swiftly slain, vigil I never forget, how as day brighten'd,
I rose from the chill ground and folded my soldier well in his blanket,
And buried him where he fell.

1865, 1867

A MARCH IN THE RANKS HARD-PREST, AND THE ROAD UNKNOWN

A march in the ranks hard-prest, and the road unknown,
A route through a heavy wood with muffled steps in the darkness,
Our army foil'd with loss severe, and the sullen remnant retreating,
Till after midnight glimmer upon us the lights of a dim-lighted building,
We come to an open space in the woods, and halt by the dim-lighted building,
'Tis a large old church at the crossing roads, now an impromptu hospital,
Entering but for a minute I see a sight beyond all the pictures and poems ever made,
Shadows of deepest, deepest black, just lit by moving candles and lamps,
And by one great pitchy torch stationary with wild red flame and clouds of smoke,
By these, crowds, groups of forms vaguely I see on the floor, some in the pews laid down,
At my feet more distinctly a soldier, a mere lad, in danger of bleeding to death, (he is shot in the abdomen,)
I stanch the blood temporarily, (the youngster's face is white as a lily,)
Then before I depart I sweep my eyes o'er the scene fain[1] to absorb it all,
Faces, varieties, postures beyond description, most in obscurity, some of them dead,
Surgeons operating, attendants holding lights, the smell of ether, the odor of blood,
The crowd, O the crowd of the bloody forms, the yard outside also fill'd,
Some on the bare ground, some on planks or stretchers, some in the death-spasm sweating,
An occasional scream or cry, the doctor's shouted orders or calls,
The glisten of the little steel instruments catching the glint of the torches,
These I resume as I chant, I see again the forms, I smell the odor,
Then hear outside the orders given, *Fall in, my men, fall in;*
But first I bend to the dying lad, his eyes open, a half-smile gives he me,
Then the eyes close, calmly close, and I speed forth to the darkness,
Resuming, marching, ever in darkness marching, on in the ranks,
The unknown road still marching.

1865, 1867

A SIGHT IN CAMP IN THE DAYBREAK GRAY AND DIM

A sight in camp in the daybreak gray and dim,
As from my tent I emerge so early sleepless,
As slow I walk in the cool fresh air the path near by the hospital tent,

[1]Eager, desirous.

Three forms I see on stretchers lying, brought out there untended lying,
Over each the blanket spread, ample brownish woolen blanket,
Gray and heavy blanket, folding, covering all.

Curious I halt and silent stand,
Then with light fingers I from the face of the nearest the first just lift the blanket;
Who are you elderly man so gaunt and grim, with well-gray'd hair, and flesh all sunken about the eyes?
Who are you my dear comrade?

Then to the second I step—and who are you my child and darling?
Who are you sweet boy with cheeks yet blooming?

Then to the third—a face nor child nor old, very calm, as of beautiful yellow-white ivory;
Young man I think I know you—I think this face is the face of the Christ himself,
Dead and divine and brother of all, and here again he lies.

1865, 1867

THE WOUND-DRESSER

1

An old man bending I come among new faces,
Years looking backward resuming in answer to children,
Come tell us old man, as from young men and maidens that love me,
(Arous'd and angry, I'd thought to beat the alarum, and urge relentless war,
But soon my fingers fail'd me, my face droop'd and I resign'd myself,
To sit by the wounded and soothe them, or silently watch the dead;)
Years hence of these scenes, of these furious passions, these chances,
Of unsurpass'd heroes, (was one side so brave? the other was equally brave;)
Now be witness again, paint the mightiest armies of earth,
Of those armies so rapid so wondrous what saw you to tell us?
What stays with you latest and deepest? of curious panics,
Of hard-fought engagements or sieges tremendous what deepest remains?

2

O maidens and young men I love and that love me,
What you ask of my days those the strangest and sudden your talking recalls,
Soldier alert I arrive after a long march cover'd with sweat and dust,
In the nick of time I come, plunge in the fight, loudly shout in the rush of successful charge,
Enter the captur'd works[1]—yet lo, like a swift-running river they fade,

[1]Fortifications.

Pass and are gone they fade—I dwell not on soldiers' perils or soldiers' joys,
(Both I remember well—many the hardships, few the joys, yet I was content.)

But in silence, in dreams' projections,
While the world of gain and appearance and mirth goes on,
So soon what is over forgotten, and waves wash the imprints off the sand,
With hinged knees returning I enter the doors, (while for you up there,
Whoever you are, follow without noise and be of strong heart.)

Bearing the bandages, water and sponge,
Straight and swift to my wounded I go,
Where they lie on the ground after the battle brought in,
Where their priceless blood reddens the grass the ground,
Or to the rows of the hospital tent, or under the roof'd hospital,
To the long rows of cots up and down each side I return,
To each and all one after another I draw near, not one do I miss,
An attendant follows holding a tray, he carries a refuse pail,
Soon to be fill'd with clotted rags and blood, emptied, and fill'd again.

I onward go, I stop,
With hinged knees and steady hand to dress wounds,
I am firm with each, the pangs are sharp yet unavoidable,
One turns to me his appealing eyes—poor boy! I never knew you,
Yet I think I could not refuse this moment to die for you, if that would save
you.

3

On, on I go, (open doors of time! open hospital doors!)
The crush'd head I dress, (poor crazed hand tear not the bandage away,)
The neck of the calvalry-man with the bullet through and through I
examine,
Hard the breathing rattles, quite glazed already the eye, yet life struggles
hard,
(Come sweet death! be persuaded O beautiful death! In mercy come quickly.)

From the stump of the arm, the amputated hand,
I undo the clotted lint, remove the slough, wash off the matter and blood,
Back on his pillow the soldier bends with curv'd neck and side-falling head,
His eyes are closed, his face is pale, he dares not look on the bloody stump,
And has not yet look'd on it.

I dress a wound in the side, deep, deep,
But a day or two more, for see the frame all wasted and sinking,
And the yellow-blue countenance see.

I dress the perforated shoulder, the foot with the bullet-wound,
Cleanse the one with a gnawing and putrid gangrene, so sickening, so
offensive,
While the attendant stands behind aside me holding the tray and pail.

I am faithful, I do not give out,
The fractur'd thigh, the knee, the wound in the abdomen,
These and more I dress with impassive hand, (yet deep in my breast a fire, a burning flame.)

4

Thus in silence in dreams' projections,
Returning, resuming, I thread my way through the hospitals,
The hurt and wounded I pacify with soothing hand,
I sit by the restless all the dark night, some are so young,
Some suffer so much, I recall the experience sweet and sad,
(Many a soldier's loving arms about this neck have cross'd and rested,
Many a soldier's kiss dwells on these bearded lips.)

1865, 1881

from *MEMORIES OF PRESIDENT LINCOLN*

WHEN LILACS LAST IN THE DOORYARD BLOOM'D

1

When lilacs last in the dooryard bloom'd,
And the great star[1] early droop'd in the western sky in the night,
I mourn'd, and yet shall mourn with ever-returning spring.

Ever-returning spring, trinity sure to me you bring,
Lilac blooming perennial and drooping star in the west,
And thought of him I love.

2

O powerful western fallen star!
O shades of night—O moody, tearful night!
O great star disappear'd—O the black murk that hides the star!
O cruel hands that hold me powerless—O helpless soul of me!
O harsh surrounding cloud that will not free my soul.

3

In the dooryard fronting an old farm-house near the white-wash'd palings,
Stands the lilac-bush tall-growing with heart-shaped leaves of rich green,

[1]Venus.

With many a pointed blossom rising delicate, with the perfume strong I love,
With every leaf a miracle—and from this bush in the dooryard,
With delicate-color'd blossoms and heart-shaped leaves of rich green,
A sprig with its flower I break.

4

In the swamp in secluded recesses,
A shy and hidden bird is warbling a song.

Solitary the thrush,
The hermit withdrawn to himself, avoiding the settlements,
Sings by himself a song.

Song of the bleeding throat,
Death's outlet song of life, (for well dear brother I know,
If thou wast not granted to sing thou would'st surely die.)

5

Over the breast of the spring, the land, amid cities,
Amid lanes and through old woods, where lately the violets peep'd from the ground, spotting the gray debris,
Amid the grass in the fields each side of the lanes, passing the endless grass,
Passing the yellow-spear'd wheat, every grain from its shroud in the dark-brown fields uprisen,
Passing the apple-tree blows[2] of white and pink in the orchards,
Carrying a corpse to where it shall rest in the grave,
Night and day journeys a coffin.[3]

6

Coffin that passes through lanes and streets,
Through day and night with the great cloud darkening the land,
With the pomp of the inloop'd flags with the cities draped in black,
With the show of the States themselves as of crape-veil'd women standing,
With processions long and winding and the flambeaus[4] of the night,
With the countless torches lit, with the silent sea of faces and the unbared heads,
With the waiting depot, the arriving coffin, and the sombre faces,
With dirges through the night, with the thousand voices rising strong and solemn,
With all the mournful voices of the dirges pour'd around the coffin,

[2]Blossoms.
[3]Following Lincoln's assassination in April 1865, his body was carried on a funeral train from Washington, D.C., to Springfield, Illinois, for burial.
[4]Burning torches.

The dim-lit churches and the shuddering organs—where amid these you journey,
With the tolling tolling bells' perpetual clang,
Here, coffin that slowly passes,
I give you my sprig of lilac.

7

(Not for you, for one alone,
Blossoms and branches green to coffins all I bring,
For fresh as the morning, thus would I chant a song for you O sane and sacred death.

All over bouquets of roses,
O death, I cover you over with roses and early lilies,
But mostly and now the lilac that blooms the first,
Copious I break, I break the sprigs from the bushes,
With loaded arms I come, pouring for you,
For you and the coffins all of you O death.)

8

O western orb sailing the heaven,
Now I know what you must have meant as a month since I walk'd,
As I walk'd in silence the transparent shadowy night,
As I saw you had something to tell as you bent to me night after night,
As you droop'd from the sky low down as if to my side, (while the other stars all look'd on,)
As we wander'd together the solemn night, (for something I know not what kept me from sleep,)
As the night advanced, and I saw on the rim of the west how full you were of woe,
As I stood on the rising ground in the breeze in the cool transparent night,
As I watch'd where you pass'd and was lost in the netherward black of the night,
As my soul in its trouble dissatisfied sank, as where you sad orb,
Concluded, dropt in the night, and was gone.

9

Sing on there in the swamp,
O singer bashful and tender, I hear your notes, I hear your call,
I hear, I come presently, I understand you,
But a moment I linger, for the lustrous star has detain'd me,
The star my departing comrade holds and detains me.

10

O how shall I warble myself for the dead one there I love?
And how shall I deck my song for the large sweet soul that has gone?
And what shall my perfume be for the grave of him I love?

Sea-winds blown from east and west,
Blown from the Eastern sea and blown from the Western sea, till there on the prairies meeting,
These and with these and the breath of my chant,
I'll perfume the grave of him I love.

11

O what shall I hang on the chamber walls?
And what shall the pictures be that I hang on the walls,
To adorn the burial-house of him I love?

Pictures of growing spring and farms and homes,
With the Fourth-month[5] eve at sundown, and the gray smoke lucid and bright,
With floods of the yellow gold of the gorgeous, indolent, sinking sun, burning, expanding the air,
With the fresh sweet herbage under foot, and the pale green leaves of the trees prolific,
In the distance the flowing glaze, the breast of the river, with a wind-dapple here and there,
With ranging hills on the banks, with many a line against the sky, and shadows,
And the city at hand with dwellings so dense, and stacks of chimneys,
And all the scenes of life and the workshops, and the workmen homeward returning.

12

Lo, body and soul—this land,
My own Manhattan with spires, and the sparkling and hurrying tides, and ships,
The varied and ample land, the South and the North in the light, Ohio's shores and flashing Missouri,
And ever the far-spreading prairies cover'd with grass and corn.

Lo, the most excellent sun so calm and haughty,
The violet and purple morn with just-felt breezes,
The gentle soft-born measureless light,

[5]April.

The miracle spreading bathing all, the fulfill'd noon,
The coming eve delicious, the welcome night and the stars,
Over my cities shining all, enveloping man and land.

13

Sing on, sing on you gray-brown bird,
Sing from the swamps, the recesses, pour your chant from the bushes,
Limitless out of the dusk, out of the cedars and pines.

Sing on dearest brother, warble your reedy song,
Loud human song, with voice of uttermost woe.
O liquid and free and tender!
O wild and loose to my soul—O wondrous singer!
You only I hear—yet the star holds me, (but will soon depart,)
Yet the lilac with mastering odor holds me.

14

Now while I sat in the day and look'd forth,
In the close of the day with its light and the fields of spring, and the farmers preparing their crops,
In the large unconscious scenery of my land with its lakes and forests,
In the heavenly aerial beauty, (after the perturb'd winds and the storms,)
Under the arching heavens of the afternoon swift passing, and the voices of children and women,
The many-moving sea-tides, and I saw the ships how they sail'd,
And the summer approaching with richness, and the fields all busy with labor,
And the infinite separate houses, how they all went on, each with its meals and minutia of daily usages,
And the streets how their throbbings throbb'd, and the cities pent—lo, then and there,
Falling upon them all and among them all, enveloping me with the rest,
Appear'd the cloud, appear'd the long black trail,
And I knew death, its thought, and the sacred knowledge of death.

Then with the knowledge of death as walking one side of me,
And the thought of death close-walking the other side of me,
And I in the middle as with companions, and as holding the hands of companions,
I fled forth to the hiding receiving night that talks not,
Down to the shores of the water, the path by the swamp in the dimness,
To the solemn shadowy cedars and ghostly pines so still.

And the singer so shy to the rest receiv'd me,
The gray-brown bird I know receiv'd us comrades three,
And he sang the carol of death, and a verse for him I love.

From deep secluded recesses,
From the fragrant cedars and the ghostly pines so still,
Came the carol of the bird.

And the charm of the carol rapt me,
As I held as if by their hands my comrades in the night,
And the voice of my spirit tallied the song of the bird.

Come lovely and soothing death,
Undulate round the world, serenely arriving, arriving,
In the day, in the night, to all, to each,
Sooner or later delicate death.

Prais'd be the fathomless universe,
For life and joy, and for objects and knowledge curious,
And for love, sweet love—but praise! praise! praise!
For the sure-enwinding arms of cool-enfolding death.

Dark mother always gliding near with soft feet,
Have none chanted for thee a chant of fullest welcome?
Then I chant it for thee, I glorify thee above all,
I bring thee a song that when thou must indeed come, come unfalteringly.

Approach strong deliveress,
When it is so, when thou hast taken them I joyously sing the dead,
Lost in the loving floating ocean of thee,
Laved in the flood of thy bliss O death.

From me to thee glad serenades,
Dances for thee I propose saluting thee, adornments and feastings for thee,
And the sights of the open landscape and the high-spread sky are fitting,
And life and the fields, and the huge and thoughtful night.

The night in silence under many a star,
The ocean shore and the husky whispering wave whose voice I know,
And the soul turning to thee O vast and well-veil'd death,
And the body gratefully nestling close to thee.

Over the tree-tops I float thee a song,
Over the rising and sinking waves, over the myriad fields and the prairies wide,
Over the dense-pack'd cities all and the teeming wharves and ways,
I float this carol with joy, with joy to thee O death.

15

To the tally of my soul,
Loud and strong kept up the gray-brown bird,
With pure deliberate notes spreading filling the night.

Loud in the pines and cedars dim,
Clear in the freshness moist and the swamp-perfume,
And I with my comrades there in the night.

While my sight that was bound in my eyes unclosed,
As to long panoramas of visions.

And I saw askant[6] the armies,
I saw as in noiseless dreams hundreds of battle-flags,
Borne through the smoke of the battles and pierc'd with missiles I saw them,
And carried hither and yon through the smoke, and torn and bloody,
And at last but a few shreds left on the staffs, (and all in silence,)
And the staffs all splinter'd and broken.
I saw battle-corpses, myriads of them,
And the white skeletons of young men, I saw them,

I saw the debris and debris of all the slain soldiers of the war,
But I saw they were not as was thought,
They themselves were fully at rest, they suffer'd not,
The living remain'd and suffer'd, the mother suffer'd,
And the wife and the child and the musing comrade suffer'd,
And the armies that remain'd suffer'd.

16

Passing the visions, passing the night,
Passing, unloosing the hold of my comrades' hands,
Passing the song of the hermit bird and the tallying song of my soul,
Victorious song, death's outlet song, yet varying ever-altering song,
As low and wailing, yet clear the notes, rising and falling, flooding the night,
Sadly sinking and fainting, as warning and warning, and yet again bursting with joy,
Covering the earth and filling the spread of the heaven,
As that powerful psalm in the night I heard from recesses,
Passing, I leave thee lilac with heart-shaped leaves,
I leave thee there in the dooryard, blooming, returning with spring.

I cease from my song for thee,
From my gaze on thee in the west, fronting the west, communing with thee,
O comrade lustrous with silver face in the night.

Yet each to keep and all, retrievements out of the night,
The song, the wondrous chant of the gray-brown bird,
And the tallying chant, the echo arous'd in my soul,
With the lustrous and drooping star with the countenance full of woe,
With the holders holding my hand nearing the call of the bird,

[6]Sideways, out of the corner of the eye, with mistrust.

Comrades mine and I in the midst, and their memory ever to keep, for the dead I loved so well,
For the sweetest, wisest soul of all my days and lands—and this for his dear sake,
Lilac and star and bird twined with the chant of my soul,
There in the fragrant pines and the cedars dusk and dim.

1865–1866, 1881

from *AUTUMN RIVULETS*

THERE WAS A CHILD WENT FORTH

There was a child went forth every day,
And the first object he look'd upon, that object he became,
And that object became part of him for the day or a certain part of the day,
Or for many years or stretching cycles of years.

The early lilacs became part of this child,
And grass and white and red morning-glories, and white and red clover, and the song of the phœbe-bird,
And the Third-month lambs and the sow's pink-faint litter, and the mare's foal and the cow's calf,
And the noisy brood of the barnyard or by the mire of the pond-side,
And the fish suspending themselves so curiously below there, and the beautiful curious liquid,
And the water-plants with their graceful flat heads, all became part of him.

The field-sprouts of Fourth-month and Fifth-month became part of him,
Winter-grain sprouts and those of the light-yellow corn, and the esculent roots of the garden,
And the apple-trees cover'd with blossoms and the fruit afterward, and wood-berries, and the commonest weeds by the road,
And the old drunkard staggering home from the outhouse of the tavern whence he had lately risen,
And the schoolmistress that pass'd on her way to the school,
And the friendly boys that pass'd, and the quarrelsome boys,
And the tidy and fresh-cheek'd girls, and the barefoot negro boy and girl,
And all the changes of city and country wherever he went.

His own parents, he that had father'd him and she that had conceiv'd him in her womb and birth'd him,
They gave this child more of themselves than that,
They gave him afterward every day, they became part of him.

The mother at home quietly placing the dishes on the supper-table,
The mother with mild words, clean her cap and gown, a wholesome odor falling off her person and clothes as she walks by,

The father, strong, self-sufficient, manly, mean, anger'd, unjust,
The blow, the quick loud word, the tight bargain, the crafty lure,
The family usages, the language, the company, the furniture, the yearning and swelling heart,
Affection that will not be gainsay'd, the sense of what is real, the thought if after all it should prove unreal,
The doubts of day-time and the doubts of night-time, the curious whether and how,
Whether that which appears so is so, or is it all flashes and specks?
Men and women crowding fast in the streets, if they are not flashes and specks what are they?
The streets themselves and the façades of houses, and goods in the windows,
Vehicles, teams, the heavy-plank'd wharves, the huge crossing at the ferries,
The village on the highland seen from afar at sunset, the river between,
Shadows, aureola and mist, the light falling on roofs and gables of white or brown two miles off,
The schooner near by sleepily drooping down the tide, the little boat slack-tow'd astern,
The hurrying tumbling waves, quick-broken crests, slapping,
The strata of color'd clouds, the long bar of maroon-tint away solitary by itself, the spread of purity it lies motionless in,
The horizon's edge, the flying sea-crow, the fragrance of salt marsh and shore mud,
These became part of that child who went forth every day, and who now goes, and will always go forth every day.

1855, 1871

SPARKLES FROM THE WHEEL

1

Where the city's ceaseless crowd moves on, the live-long day,
Withdrawn, I join a group of children watching—I pause aside with them.

By the curb, toward the edge of the flagging,
A knife-grinder works at his wheel, sharpening a great knife;
Bending over, he carefully holds it to the stone—by foot and knee,
With measured tread, he turns rapidly—As he presses with light but firm hand,
Forth issue, then, in copious golden jets,
Sparkles from the wheel.

2

The scene, and all its belongings—how they seize and affect me!
The sad, sharp-chinned old man, with worn clothes, and broad shoulder-band of leather;

Myself, effusing and fluid—a phantom curiously floating—now here
absorbed and arrested;

The group, (an unminded point, set in a vast surrounding;)
The attentive, quiet children—the loud, proud, restive base of the streets;
The low, hoarse purr of the whirling stone—the light-press'd blade,
Diffusing, dropping, sideways-darting, in tiny showers of gold,
Sparkles from the wheel.

1871, 1871

WHO LEARNS MY LESSON COMPLETE?

Who learns my lesson complete?
Boss, journeyman, apprentice—churchman and atheist,
The stupid and the wise thinker—parents and offspring—merchant, clerk,
porter and customer,
Editor, author, artist, and schoolboy—draw nigh and commence;
It is no lesson—it lets down the bars to a good lesson,
And that to another, and every one to another still.

The great laws take and effuse without argument;
I am of the same style, for I am their friend,
I love them quits and quits—I do not halt, and make salaams.[1]

I lie abstracted, and hear beautiful tales of things, and the reasons
of things;
They are so beautiful, I nudge myself to listen.

I cannot say to any person what I hear—I cannot say it to myself—it is very
wonderful.

It is no small matter, this round and delicious globe, moving so exactly in its
orbit forever and ever, without one jolt, or the untruth of a single second;
I do not think it was made in six days, nor in ten thousand years, nor ten
billions of years,
Nor planned and built one thing after another, as an architect plans and
builds a house.

I do not think seventy years is the time of a man or woman,
Nor that seventy millions of years is the time of a man or woman,
Nor that years will ever stop the existence of me, or anyone else.

Is it wonderful that I should be immortal? as every one is immortal;
I know it is wonderful, but my eyesight is equally wonderful, and how I was
conceived in my mother's womb is equally wonderful;
And pass'd from a babe, in the creeping trance of a couple of summers and
winters, to articulate and walk—all this is equally wonderful.

[1]Bows.

And that my Soul embraces you this hour, and we affect each other without
ever seeing each other, and never perhaps to see each other, is every bit as
wonderful.

And that I can think such thoughts as these, is just as wonderful;
And that I can remind you, and you think them, and know them to be true,
is just as wonderful.

And that the moon spins round the earth, and on with the earth, is equally
wonderful,
And that they balance themselves with the sun and stars, is equally
wonderful.

1855, 1867

PASSAGE TO INDIA

1

Singing my days,
Singing the great achievements of the present,
Singing the strong light works of engineers,
Our modern wonders, (the antique ponderous Seven[1] outvied),
In the Old World the east the Suez canal[2]
The New by its mighty railroad spann'd,[3]
The seas inlaid with eloquent gentle wires,[4]
Yet first to sound, and ever sound, the cry with thee O soul,
The Past! the Past! the Past!

The Past—the dark unfathom'd retrospect!
The teeming gulf—the sleepers and the shadows!
The past—the infinite greatness of the past!
For what is the present after all but a growth out of the past?
(As a projectile form'd, impell'd, passing a certain line, still keeps on,
So the present, utterly form'd, impell'd by the past.)

2

Passage O soul to India!
Eclaircise[5] the myths Asiatic, the primitive fables.

Not you alone proud truths of the world,
Not you alone ye facts of modern science,
But myths and fables of eld,[6] Asia's, Africa's fables,

[1]The Seven Wonders of the Ancient World.
[2]Completed in 1867, formally opened in 1869.
[3]The transcontinental railroad was completed at Promontory, Utah, in 1869.
[4]A transatlantic cable was laid in 1866. [5]Clarify, explain. [6]Antiquity.

The far-darting beams of the spirit, the unloos'd dreams,
The deep diving bibles and legends,
The daring plots of the poets, the elder religions;
O you temples fairer than lilies pour'd over by the rising sun!
O you fables spurning the known, eluding the hold of the known, mounting
  to heaven!
You lofty and dazzling towers, pinnacled, red as roses, burnish'd with gold!
Towers of fables immortal fashion'd from mortal dreams!
You too I welcome and fully the same as the rest!
You too with joy I sing.

Passage to India!
Lo, soul, seest thou not God's purpose from the first?
The earth to be spann'd, connected by network,
The races, neighbors, to marry and be given in marriage,
The oceans to be cross'd, the distant brought near,
The lands to be welded together.
A worship new I sing,
You captain, voyagers, explorers, yours,
You engineers, you architects, machinists, yours,
You, not for trade or transportation only,
But in God's name, and for thy sake O soul.

3

Passage to India!
Lo soul for thee of tableaus twain,
I see in one the Suez canal initiated, open'd,
I see the procession of steamships, the Empress Eugenie's[7] leading the van,
I mark from on deck the strange landscape, the pure sky, the level sand in
  the distance,
I pass swiftly the picturesque groups, the workmen gather'd,
The gigantic dredging machines.

In one again, different, (yet thine, all thine, O soul, the same,)
I see over my own continent the Pacific railroad[8] surmounting every barrier,
I see continual trains of cars winding along the Platte carrying freight and
  passengers,
I hear the locomotives rushing and roaring, and the shrill steamwhistle,
I hear the echoes reverberate through the grandest scenery in the world,
I cross the Laramie plains, I note the rocks in grotesque shapes, the buttes,
I see the plentiful larkspur and wild onions, the barren, colorless,
  sage-deserts,
I see in glimpses afar or towering immediately above me the great
  mountains, I see the Wind river and the Wahsatch mountains,

[7]Empress of France, wife of Napoleon III. She was aboard the ship leading the procession at the formal opening of the Suez Canal.

[8]The transcontinental railroad linked the Atlantic and the Pacific oceans in 1869. In the remainder of the stanza, Whitman lists sites, from Nebraska to California, along the route of the railroad.

I see the Monument mountain the Eagle's Nest, I pass the Promontory, I ascend the Nevadas,
I scan the noble Elk mountain and wind around its base,
I see the Humboldt range, I thread the valley and cross the river,
I see the clear waters of Lake Tahoe, I see forests of majestic pines,
Or crossing the great desert, the alkaline plains, I behold enchanting mirages of waters and meadows,
Marking through these and after all, in duplicate slender lines,
Bridging the three or four thousand miles of land travel,
Tying the Eastern to the Western sea,
The road between Europe and Asia.

(Ah Genoese[9] thy dream! thy dream!
Centuries after thou art laid in thy grave,
The shore thou foundest verifies thy dream.)

4

Passage to India!
Struggles of many a captain, tales of many a sailor dead,
Over my mood stealing and spreading they come,
Like clouds and cloudlets in the unreach'd sky.

Along all history, down the slopes,
As a rivulet running, sinking now, and now again to the surface rising,
A ceaseless thought, a varied train—lo, soul, to thee, thy sight, they rise,
The plans, the voyages again, the expeditions;
Again Vasco de Gama[10] sails forth,
Again the knowledge gain'd, the mariner's compass,
Lands found and nations born, thou born America,
For purpose vast, man's long probation fill'd,
Thou rondure[11] of the world at last accomplish'd,

5

O vast Rondure, swimming in space,
Cover'd all over with visible power and beauty,
Alternate light and day and the teeming spiritual darkness,
Unspeakable high processions of sun and moon and countless stars above,
Below the manifold grass and waters, animals, mountains, trees,
With inscrutable purpose, some hidden prophetic intention,
Now first it seems my thought begins to span thee.

[9]Christopher Columbus, born in Genoa, Italy.
[10]Vasco da Gama. Portuguese navigator, the first European to sail from Europe, around Africa's Cape of Good Hope, to India (1497–1498).
[11]Encirclement, circumnavigation.

Down from the gardens of Asia descending radiating,
Adam and Eve appear, then their myriad progeny after them,
Wandering, yearning, curious, with restless explorations,
With questionings, baffled, formless, feverish, with never-happy hearts,
With that sad incessant refrain, *Wherefore unsatisfied soul?* and *Whither O mocking life?*

Ah who shall soothe these feverish children?
Who justify these restless explorations?
Who speak the secret of impassive earth?
Who bind it to us? what is this separate Nature so unnatural?
What is this earth to our affections? (unloving earth, without a throb to answer ours,
Cold earth, the place of graves.)

Yet soul be sure the first intent remains, and shall be carried out,
Perhaps even now the time has arrived.
After the seas are all cross'd, (as they seem already cross'd,)
After the great captains and engineers have accomplish'd their work,
After the noble inventors, after the scientists, the chemist, the geologist, ethnologist,
Finally shall come the poet worthy that name,
The true son of God shall come singing his songs.

Then not your deeds only O voyagers, O scientists and inventors, shall be justified,
All these hearts as of fretted children shall be sooth'd,
All affection shall be fully responded to, the secret shall be told,
All these separations and gaps shall be taken up and hook'd and link'd together,
The whole earth, this cold, impassive, voiceless earth, shall be completely justified,
Trinitas[12] divine shall be gloriously accomplish'd and compacted by the true son of God, the poet,
(He shall indeed pass the straits and conquer the mountains,
He shall double the cape of Good Hope to some purpose,)
Nature and Man shall be disjoin'd and diffused no more,
The true son of God shall absolutely fuse them.

6

Year at whose wide-flung door I sing!
Year of the purpose accomplish'd!
Year of the marriage of continents, climates and oceans!
(No mere doge of Venice now wedding the Adriatic,)[13]

[12]Whitman's approximate Spanish for "the Holy Trinity."

[13]The Doge (chief magistrate of the city-state of Venice, 697–1797) symbolized the union of Venice and the sea by annually casting a gold ring into the Adriatic.

I see O year in you the vast terraqueous globe given and giving all,
Europe to Asia, Africa join'd, and they to the New World,
The lands, geographies, dancing before you, holding a festival garland,
As brides and bridegrooms hand in hand.

Passage to India!
Cooling airs from Caucasus[14] far, soothing cradle of man,
The river Euphrates[15] flowing, the past lit up again.

Lo soul, the retrospect brought forward,
The old, most populous, wealthiest of earth's lands,
The streams of the Indus and the Ganges[16] and their many affluents,
(I my shores of America walking to-day behold, resuming all,)
The tale of Alexander[17] on his warlike marches suddenly dying,
On one side China and on the other side Persia and Arabia,
To the south the great seas and the bay of Bengal,
The flowing literatures, tremendous epics, religions, castes,
Old occult Brahma interminably far back, the tender and junior Buddha,
Central and southern empires and all their belongings, possessors,
The wars of Tamerlane,[18] the reign of Aurungzebe,[19]
The traders, rulers, explorers, Moslems, Venetians, Byzantium, the Arabs,
 Portuguese,

The first travelers famous yet, Marco Polo,[20] Batouta the Moor,[21]
Doubts to be solv'd, the map incognita,[22] blanks to be fill'd,
The foot of man unstay'd, the hands never at rest,
Thyself O soul that will not brook a challenge.

The mediæval navigators rise before me,
The world of 1492, with its awaken'd enterprise,
Something swelling in humanity now like the sap of the earth in spring,
The sunset splendor of chivalry declining.

And who art thou sad shade?
Gigantic, visionary, thyself a visionary,
With majestic limbs and pious beaming eyes,
Spreading around with every look of thine a golden world,
Enhuing it with gorgeous hues.

As the chief histrion,[23]
Down to the footlights walks in some great scena,[24]

[14]Mountainous area in Russia between the Black and Caspian seas.
[15]River flowing from Turkey to the Persian Gulf. [16]Rivers in India.
[17]Alexander the Great (356–323 B.C.). [18]Mongol conqueror (1336?–1405).
[19]Emperor of Hindustan (1618–1707). [20]Venetian (1254–1324), early traveler to China.
[21]Explorer of Africa and Asia (1303–1377). [22]Unknown.
[23]Actor. [24]Scene.

Dominating the rest I see the Admiral[25] himself,
(History's type[26] of courage, action, faith,)
Behold him sail from Palos[27] leading his little fleet,
His voyage behold, his return, his great fame,
His misfortunes, calumniators, behold him a prisoner, chain'd,
Behold his dejection, poverty, death.

(Curious in time I stand, noting the efforts of heroes,
Is the deferment long? bitter the slander, poverty, death?
Lies the seed unreck'd[28] for centuries in the ground? lo, to God's due occasion,
Uprising in the night, it sprouts, blooms,
And fills the earth with use and beauty.)

7

Passage indeed O soul to primal thought,
Not lands and seas alone, thy own clear freshness,
The young maturity of brood and bloom,
To realms of budding bibles.

O soul, repressless, I with thee and thou with me,
Thy circumnavigation of the world begin,
Of man, the voyage of his mind's return,
To reason's early paradise,
Back, back to wisdom's birth, to innocent intuitions,
Again with fair creation.

8

O we can wait no longer,
We too take ship O soul,
Joyous we too launch out on trackless seas,
Fearless for unknown shores on waves of ecstasy to sail,
Amid the wafting winds, (thou pressing me to thee, I thee to me, O soul,)
Caroling free, singing our song of God,
Chanting our chant of pleasant exploration.

With laugh and many a kiss,
(Let others deprecate, let others weep for sin, remorse, humiliation,)
O soul thou pleasest me, I thee.

Ah more than any priest O soul we too believe in God,
But with the mystery of God we dare not dally.

[25]Columbus. [26]Symbol, model.
[27]Spanish seaport from which Columbus sailed, August 1492. [28]Unnoticed.

O soul thou pleasest me, I thee,
Sailing these seas or on the hills, or waking in the night,
Thoughts, silent thoughts, of Time and Space and Death, like waters flowing,
Bear me indeed as through the regions infinite,
Whose air I breathe, whose ripples hear, lave me all over,
Bathe me O God in thee, mounting to thee,
I and my soul to range of thee.

O Thou transcendent,
Nameless, the fibre and the breath,
Light of the light, shedding forth universes, thou centre of them,
Thou mightier centre of the true, the good, the loving,
Thou moral, spiritual fountain—affection's source—thou reservoir,
(O pensive soul of me—O thirst unsatisfied—waitest not there?
Waitest not haply for us somewhere there the Comrade perfect?)
Thou pulse—thou motive of the stars, suns, systems,
That, circling, move in order, safe, harmonious,
Athwart the shapeless vastnesses of space,
How should I think, how breathe a single breath, how speak, if, out of myself,
I could not launch, to those, superior universes?

Swiftly I shrivel at the thought of God,
At Nature and its wonders, Time and Space and Death,
But that, I, turning, call to thee O soul, thou actual Me,
And lo, thou gently masterest the orbs,
Thou matest Time, smilest content at Death,
And fillest, swellest full the vastnesses of Space.

Greater than stars or suns,
Bounding O soul thou journeyest forth;
What love than thine and ours could wider amplify?
What aspirations, wishes, outvie thine and ours O soul?
What dreams of the ideal? what plans of purity, perfection, strength?
What cheerful willingness for others' sake to give up all?
For others' sake to suffer all?

Reckoning ahead O soul, when thou, the time achiev'd,
The seas all cross'd, weather'd the capes, the voyage done,
Surrounded, copest, frontest God, yieldest, the aim attain'd,
As fill'd with friendship, love complete, the Elder Brother found,
The Younger melts in fondness in his arms.

9

Passage to more than India!
Are thy wings plumed indeed for such far flights?
O soul, voyagest thou indeed on voyages like those?

Disportest thou on waters such as those?
Soundest below the Sanscrit and the Vedas?[29]
Then have thy bent[30] unleash'd.

Passage to you, your shores, ye aged fierce enigmas!
Passage to you, to mastership of you, ye strangling problems!
You, strew'd with the wrecks of skeletons, that, living, never reach'd you.

Passage to more than India!
O secret of the earth and sky!
Of you O waters of the sea! O winding creeks and rivers!
Of you O woods and fields! of you strong mountains of my land!
Of you O prairies! of you gray rocks!
O morning red! O clouds! O rain and snows!
O day and night, passage to you!

O sun and moon and all you stars! Sirius and Jupiter![31]
Passage to you!

Passage, immediate passage! the blood burns in my veins!
Away O soul! hoist instantly the anchor!
Cut the hawser—haul out—shake out every sail!
Have we not stood here like trees in the ground long enough?
Have we not grovel'd here long enough, eating and drinking like mere brutes?
Have we not darken'd and dazed ourselves with books long enough?

Sail forth—steer for the deep waters only,
Reckless O soul, exploring, I with thee, and thou with me,
For we are bound where mariner has not yet dared to go,
And we will risk the ship, ourselves and all.

O my brave soul!
O farther farther sail!
O daring joy, but safe! are they not all the seas of God?
O farther, farther, farther sail!

1871, 1881

THE SLEEPERS

1

I wander all night in my vision,
Stepping with light feet, swiftly and noiselessly stepping and stopping,
Bending with open eyes over the shut eyes of sleepers,

[29]Hindu scriptures, written in Sanskrit. [30]Force, energy.
[31]Sirius: the brightest star in the sky. Jupiter: the largest planet.

Wandering and confused, lost to myself, ill-assorted, contradictory,
Pausing, gazing, bending, and stopping,

How solemn they look there, stretch'd and still,
How quiet they breathe, the little children in their cradles.

The wretched features of ennuyés,[1] the white features of corpses, the livid faces of drunkards, the sick-gray faces of onanists,
The gash'd bodies on battle-fields, the insane in their strong-door'd rooms, the sacred idiots, the new-born emerging from gates, and the dying emerging from gates,
The night pervades them and infolds them.

The married couple sleep calmly in their bed, he with his palm on the hip of the wife, and she with her palm on the hip of the husband,
The sisters sleep lovingly side by side in their bed,
The men sleep lovingly side by side in theirs,
And the mother sleeps with her little child carefully wrapt.

The blind sleep, and the deaf and dumb sleep,
The prisoner sleeps well in the prison, the runaway son sleeps,
The murderer that is to be hung next day, how does he sleep?
And the murder'd person, how does he sleep?

The female that loves unrequited sleeps,
And the male that loves unrequited sleeps,
The head of the money-maker that plotted all day sleeps,
And the enraged and treacherous dispositions, all, all sleep.

I stand in the dark with drooping eyes by the worst-suffering and the most restless,
I pass my hands soothingly to and fro a few inches from them,
The restless sink in their beds, they fitfully sleep.

Now I pierce the darkness, new beings appear,
The earth recedes from me into the night,
I saw that it was beautiful, and I see that what is not the earth is beautiful.

I go from bedside to bedside, I sleep close with the other sleepers each in turn,
I dream in my dream all the dreams of the other dreamers,
And I become the other dreamers.

I am a dance—play up there! the fit is whirling me fast!

I am the ever-laughing—it is new moon and twilight,
I see the hiding of douceurs,[2] I see nimble ghosts whichever way I look,
Cache[3] and cache again deep in the ground and sea, and where it is neither ground nor sea.

[1]French: bored, vexed people. [2]Delights, pleasures. [3]Hide.

Well do they do their jobs those journeymen divine,
Only from me can they hide nothing, and would not if they could,
I reckon I am their boss and they make me a pet besides,
And surround me and lead me and run ahead when I walk,
To lift their cunning covers to signify[4] me with stretch'd arms, and resume the way;
Onward we move, a gay gang of blackguards! with mirth-shouting music and wild-flapping pennants of joy!

I am the actor, the actress, the voter, the politician,
The emigrant and the exile, the criminal that stood in the box,[5]
He who has been famous and he who shall be famous after to-day,
The stammerer, the well-form'd person, the waster or feeble person.

I am she who adorn'd herself and folded her hair expectantly,
My truant lover has come, and it is dark.

Double yourself and receive me darkness,
Receive me and my lover too, he will not let me go without him.

I roll myself upon you as upon a bed, I resign myself to the dusk.

He whom I call answers me and takes the place of my lover,
He rises with me silently from the bed.
Darkness, you are gentler than my lover, his flesh was sweaty and panting,
I feel the hot moisture yet that he left me.

My hands are spread forth, I pass them in all directions,
I would sound up the shadowy shore to which you are journeying.

Be careful darkness! already what was it touch'd me?
I thought my lover had gone, else darkness and he are one,
I hear the heart-beat, I follow, I fade away.

2

I descend my western course,[6] my sinews are flaccid,
Perfume and youth course through me and I am their wake.

It is my face yellow and wrinkled instead of the old woman's,
I sit low in a straw-bottom chair and carefully darn my grandson's stockings.

It is I too, the sleepless widow looking out on the winter midnight,
I see the sparkles of starshine on the icy and pallid earth.

A shroud I see and I am the shroud, I wrap a body and lie in the coffin,
It is dark here under ground, it is not evil or pain here, it is blank here, for reasons.

[4]Signal. [5]Courtroom dock, where the accused stands during a criminal trial.
[6]I.e., grow old.

(It seems to me that every thing in the light and air ought to be happy,
Whoever is not in his coffin and the dark grave let him know he has enough.)

3

I see a beautiful gigantic swimmer swimming naked through the eddies of the sea,
His brown hair lies close and even to his head, he strikes out with courageous arms, he urges himself with his legs,
I see his white body, I see his undaunted eyes,
I hate the swift-running eddies that would dash him head-foremost on the rocks.

What are you doing you ruffianly red-trickled waves?
Will you kill the courageous giant? will you kill him in the prime of his middle age?

Steady and long he struggles,
He is baffled, bang'd, bruis'd, he holds out while his strength holds out,
The slapping eddies are spotted with his blood, they bear him away, they roll him, swing him, turn him,
His beautiful body is borne in the circling eddies, it is continually bruis'd on rocks,
Swiftly and out of sight is borne the brave corpse.

4

I turn but do not extricate myself,
Confused, a past-reading, another, but with darkness yet.

The beach is cut by the razory ice-wind, the wreck-guns[7] sound,
The tempest lulls, the moon comes floundering through the drifts.

I look where the ship helplessly heads end on, I hear the burst as she strikes,
I hear the howls of dismay, they grow fainter and fainter.

I cannot aid with my wringing fingers,
I can but rush to the surf and let it drench me and freeze upon me.

I search with the crowd, not one of the company is wash'd to us alive,
In the morning I help pick up the dead and lay them in rows in a barn.

5

Now of the older war-days, the defeat at Brooklyn,[8]
Washington stands inside the lines, he stands on the intrench'd hills amid a crowd of officers,

[7]Guns that fire a lifeline to wrecked ships.
[8]British victory over American forces at the Battle of Brooklyn Heights, August 1776.

His face is cold and damp, he cannot repress the weeping drops,
He lifts the glass perpetually to his eyes, the color is blanch'd from his cheeks,
He sees the slaughter of the southern braves[9] confided to him by their parents.

The same at last and at last when peace is declared,
He stands in the room of the old tavern,[10] the well-belov'd soldiers all pass through,
The officers speechless and slow draw near in their turns,
The chief encircles their necks with his arm and kisses them on the cheek,
He kisses lightly the wet cheeks one after another, he shakes hands and bids good-by to the army.

6

Now what my mother told me one day as we sat at dinner together,
Of when she was a nearly grown girl living home with her parents on the old homestead.

A red squaw came one breakfast-time to the old homestead,
On her back she carried a bundle of rushes for rush-bottoming chairs,
Her hair, straight, shiny, coarse, black, profuse, half-envelop'd her face,
Her step was free and elastic, and her voice sounded exquisitely as she spoke.

My mother look'd in delight and amazement at the stranger,
She look'd at the freshness of her tall-borne face and full and pliant limbs,
The more she look'd upon her she loved her,
Never before had she seen such wonderful beauty and purity,
She made her sit on a bench by the jamb of the fireplace, she cook'd food for her,
She had no work to give her, but she gave her remembrance and fondness.

The red squaw staid all the forenoon, and toward the middle of the afternoon she went away,
O my mother was loth[11] to have her go away,
All the week she thought of her, she watch'd for her many a month,
She remember'd her many a winter and many a summer,
But the red squaw never came nor was heard of there again.

7

A show of the summer softness—a contact of something unseen—an amour of the light and air,
I am jealous and overwhelm'd with friendliness,
And will go gallivant with the light and air myself.

[9]Revolutionary soldiers from the southern colonies.
[10]Fraunces Tavern, New York City, where Washington bid farewell to his troops, in 1783.
[11]Reluctant.

O love and summer, you are in the dreams and in me,
Autumn and winter are in the dreams, the farmer goes with his thrift,
The droves[12] and crops increase, the barns are well-fill'd.

Elements merge in the night, ships make tacks in the dreams,
The sailor sails, the exile returns home,
The fugitive returns unharm'd, the immigrant is back beyond months and years,
The poor Irishman lives in the simple house of his childhood with the well-known neighbors and faces,
They warmly welcome him, he is barefoot again, he forgets he is well off,
The Dutchman voyages home, and the Scotchman and Welshman voyage home, and the native of the Mediterranean voyages home,
To every port of England, France, Spain, enter well-fill'd ships,
The Swiss foots it towards his hills, the Prussian goes his way, the Hungarian his way, and the Pole his way,
The Swede returns, and the Dane and Norwegian return.

The homeward bound and the outward bound,
The beautiful lost swimmer, the ennuyé, the onanist, the female that loves unrequited, the money-maker,
The actor and actress, those through with their parts and those waiting to commence,
The affectionate boy, the husband and wife, the voter, the nominee that is chosen and the nominee that has fail'd,
The great already known and the great any time after to-day,
The stammerer, the sick, the perfect-form'd, the homely,
The criminal that stood in the box, the judge that sat and sentenced him, the fluent lawyers, the jury, the audience,
The laugher and weeper, the dancer, the midnight widow, the red squaw,
The consumptive, the erysipalite,[13] the idiot, he that is wrong'd,
The antipodes,[14] and every one between this and them in the dark,
I swear they are averaged now—one is no better than the other,
The night and sleep have liken'd them and restored them.

I swear they are all beautiful,
Every one that sleeps is beautiful, every thing in the dim light is beautiful,
The wildest and bloodiest is over, and all is peace.

Peace is always beautiful,
The myth of heaven indicates peace and night.

The myth of heaven indicates the soul,
The soul is always beautiful, it appears more or it appears less, it comes or it lags behind,
It comes from its embower'd garden and looks pleasantly on itself and encloses the world,

[12]Herds of animals. [13]One suffering from erysipelas, infected and inflamed skin.
[14]Those living on the opposite side of the earth.

Perfect and clean the genitals previously jetting, and perfect and clean the womb cohering,
The head well-grown proportion'd and plumb, and the bowels and joints proportion'd and plumb.

The soul is always beautiful,
The universe is duly in order, every thing is in its place,
What has arrived is in its place and what waits shall be in its place,
The twisted skull waits, the watery or rotten blood waits,
The child of the glutton or venerealee waits long, and the child of the drunkard waits long, and the drunkard himself waits long,
The sleepers that lived and died wait, the far advanced are to go on in their turns, and the far behind are to come on in their turns,
The diverse shall be no less diverse, but they shall flow and unite—they unite now.

8

The sleepers are very beautiful as they lie unclothed,
They flow hand in hand over the whole earth from east to west as they lie unclothed,
The Asiatic and African are hand in hand, the European and American are hand in hand,
Learn'd and unlearn'd are hand in hand, and male and female are hand in hand,
The bare arm of the girl crosses the bare breast of her lover, they press close without lust, his lips press her neck,
The father holds his grown or ungrown son in his arms with measureless love, and the son holds the father in his arms with measureless love,
The white hair of the mother shines on the white wrist of the daughter,
The breath of the boy goes with the breath of the man, friend is inarm'd by friend,
The scholar kisses the teacher and the teacher kisses the scholar, the wrong'd is made right,
The call of the slave is one with the master's call, and the master salutes the slave,
The felon steps forth from the prison, the insane become sane, the suffering of sick persons is reliev'd,
The sweatings and fevers stop, the throat that was unsound is sound, the lungs of the consumptive are resumed, the poor distress'd head is free,
The joints of the rheumatic move as smoothly as ever, and smoother than ever,
Stiflings and passages open, the paralyzed become supple,
The swell'd and convuls'd and congested awake to themselves in condition,
They pass the invigoration of the night and the chemistry of the night, and awake.

I too pass from the night,
I stay a while away O night, but I return to you again and love you.

Why should I be afraid to trust myself to you?
I am not afraid, I have been well brought forward by you,
I love the rich running day, but I do not desert her in whom I lay so long,
I know not how I came of you and I know not where I go with you, but I know I came well and shall go well.

I will stop only a time with the night, and rise betimes,
I will duly pass the day O my mother, and duly return to you.

1855, 1881

from *WHISPERS OF HEAVENLY DEATH*

A NOISELESS PATIENT SPIDER

A noiseless patient spider,
I mark'd where on a little promontory it stood isolated,
Mark'd how to explore the vacant vast surrounding,
It launch'd forth filament, filament, filament, out of itself,
Ever unreeling them, ever tirelessly speeding them.

And you O my soul where you stand,
Surrounded, detached, in measureless oceans of space,
Ceaselessly musing, venturing, throwing, seeking the spheres to connect them,
Till the bridge you will need be form'd, till the ductile anchor hold,
Till the gossamer thread you fling catch somewhere, O my soul.

1868, 1881

from *FROM NOON TO STARRY NIGHT*

TO A LOCOMOTIVE IN WINTER

Thee for my recitative,[1]
Thee in the driving storm even as now, the snow, the winter-day declining,
Thee in thy panoply,[2] thy measur'd dual throbbing and thy beat convulsive,
Thy black cylindric body, golden brass and silvery steel,
Thy ponderous side-bars, parallel and connecting rods, gyrating, shuttling at thy sides,
Thy metrical, now swelling pant and roar, now tapering in the distance,
Thy great protruding head-light fix'd in front,
Thy long, pale, floating vapor-pennants, tinged with delicate purple,
Thy dense and murky clouds out-belching from thy smoke-stack,
Thy knitted frame, thy springs and valves, the tremulous twinkle of thy wheels,
Thy train of cars behind, obedient, merrily following,
Through gale or calm, now swift, now slack, yet steadily careering;[3]

[1]A rhythmically free, vocal narration, a recitation. [2]Suit of armor. [3]Speeding.

Type of the modern—emblem of motion and power—pulse of the continent,
For once come serve the Muse and merge in verse, even as here I see thee,
With storm and buffeting gusts of winds and falling snow,
By day the warning ringing bell to sound its notes,
By night thy silent signal lamps to swing.

Fierce-throated beauty!
Roll through my chant with all thy lawless music, thy swinging lamps at night,
Thy madly-whistled laughter, echoing, rumbling like an earthquake, rousing all,
Law of thyself complete, thine own track firmly holding,
(No sweetness debonair of tearful harp or glib piano thine,)
Thy trills of shrieks by rocks and hills return'd,
Launch'd o'er the prairies wide, across the lakes,
To the free skies unpent and glad and strong.

1876, 1881

from *DEMOCRATIC VISTAS*

America, filling the present with greatest deeds and problems, cheerfully accepting the past, including feudalism, (as, indeed, the present is but the legitimate birth of the past, including feudalism,) counts, as I reckon, for her justification and success, (for who, as yet, dare claim success?) almost entirely on the future. Nor is that hope unwarranted. To-day, ahead, though dimly yet, we see, in vistas, a copious, sane, gigantic offspring. For our New World I consider far less important for what it has done, or what it is, than for results to come. Sole among nationalities, these States have assumed the task to put in forms of lasting power and practicality, on areas of amplitude rivaling the operations of the physical kosmos, the moral political speculations of ages, long, long deferr'd, the democratic republican principle, and the theory of development and perfection by voluntary standards, and self-reliance. Who else, indeed, except the United States, in history, so far, have accepted in unwitting faith, and, as we now see, stand, act upon, and go security for, these things?

But preluding no longer, let me strike the key-note of the following strain. First premising that, though the passages of it have been written at widely different times, (it is, in fact, a collection of memoranda, perhaps for future designers, comprehenders,) and though it may be open to the charge of one part contradicting another—for there are opposite sides to the great question of democracy, as to every great question—I feel the parts harmoniously blended in my own realization and convictions, and present them to be read only in such oneness, each page and each claim and assertion modified and temper'd by the others. Bear in mind, too, that they are not the result of studying up in political economy, but of the ordinary sense, observing, wandering among men, these States, these stirring years of war and peace. I will not gloss over the appalling dangers of universal suffrage in the United States. In fact, it is to admit and face these dangers I am writing. To him or her within whose thought rages the battle, advancing, retreating, between democracy's convictions, aspirations, and the people's crudeness, vice, caprices, I mainly write this essay. I shall use the words America and democracy as convertible[1] terms. Not an ordinary one is the issue. The United States are destined either to surmount the gorgeous history of feudalism, or else prove the most tremendous failure of time. Not the least doubtful am I on any prospects of their material success. The triumphant future of their business, geographic and productive departments, on larger scales and in more varieties than ever, is certain. In those respects the republic must soon (if she does not already) outstrip all examples hitherto afforded, and dominate the world.

Admitting all this, with the priceless value of our political institutions, general suffrage, (and fully acknowledging the latest, widest opening of the doors,) I say that, far deeper than these, what finally and only is to make of our western world a nationality superior to any hitherto known, and outtopping the past, must be vigorous, yet unsuspected Literatures, perfect personalities and sociologies, original, transcendental, and expressing (what, in highest sense, are not yet express'd at all,) democracy and the modern. With these, and out of these, I promulge new races of Teachers, and of perfect Women, indispensable to endow the birth-stock of a New World. For feudalism, caste, the ecclesiastic traditions, though palpably retreating from political institutions, still hold essentially, by their spirit, even in this country, entire possession of the more important fields, indeed the very subsoil, of education, and of social standards and literature.

I say that democracy can never prove itself beyond cavil,[2] until it founds and luxuriantly grows its own forms of art, poems, schools, theology, displacing all that exists, or that has been produced anywhere in the past, under opposite influences. It is curious to me that while so many voices, pens, minds, in the press, lecture-rooms, in our Congress, &c., are discussing intellectual topics, pecuniary dangers, legislative problems, the suffrage, tariff and labor questions, and the various business and benevolent needs of America, with propositions, remedies, often worth deep attention, there is one need, a hiatus the profoundest, that no eye seems to perceive, no voice to state. Our fundamental want to-day in the United States, with closest, amplest reference to present conditions, and to the future, is of a class, and the clear idea of a class, of native authors, literatuses, far different, far higher in grade than any yet known, sacerdotal,[3] modern, fit to cope with our occasions, lands, permeating, the whole mass of American mentality, taste, belief, breathing into it a new breath of life, giving it decision, affecting politics far more than the popular superficial suffrage, with results inside and underneath the elections of Presidents or Congresses—radiating, begetting appropriate teachers, schools, manners, and, as its grandest result, accomplishing (what neither the schools nor the churches and their clergy have hitherto accomplish'd, and without which this nation will no more stand, permanently, soundly, than a house will stand without a substratum,) a religious and moral character beneath the political and productive and intellectual bases of the States. For know you not, dear, earnest reader, that the people of our land may all read and write, and may all possess the right to vote—and yet the main things may be entirely lacking?—(and this to suggest them.)

View'd, to-day, from a point of view sufficiently over-arching, the problem of humanity all over the civilized world is social and religious, and is to be finally

[1]Equivalent. [2]Argument, question. [3]Priestly.

met and treated by literature. The priest departs, the divine literatus comes. Never was anything more wanted than, to-day, and here in the States, the poet of the modern is wanted, or the great literatus of the modern. At all times, perhaps, the central point in any nation, and that whence it is itself really sway'd the most, and whence it sways others, is its national literature, especially its archetypal[4] poems. Above all previous lands, a great original literature is surely to become the justification and reliance, (in some respects the sole reliance,) of American democracy.

Few are aware how the great literature penetrates all, gives hue to all, shapes aggregates and individuals, and, after subtle ways, with irresistible power, constructs, sustains, demolishes at will. Why tower, in reminiscence, above all the nations of the earth, two special lands, petty in themselves, yet inexpressibly gigantic, beautiful, columnar? Immoral Judah[5] lives, and Greece immortal lives, in a couple of poems.

Nearer than this. It is not generally realized, but it is true, as the genius of Greece, and all the sociology, personality, politics and religion of those wonderful states, resided in their literature or esthetics, that what was afterwards the main support of European chivalry, the feudal, ecclesiastical, dynastic world over there—forming its osseous[6] structure, holding it together for hundreds, thousands of years, preserving its flesh and bloom, giving it form, decision, rounding it out, and so saturating it in the conscious and unconscious blood, breed, belief, and intuitions of men, that it still prevails powerful to this day, in defiance of the mighty changes of time—was its literature, permeating to the very marrow, especially that major part, its enchanting songs, ballads, and poems.

To the ostent[7] of the senses and eyes, I know, the influences which stamp the world's history are wars, uprisings or downfalls of dynasties, changeful movements of trade, important inventions, navigation, military or civil governments, advent of powerful personalities, conquerors, &c. These of course play their part; yet, it may be, a single new thought, imagination, abstract principle, even literary style, fit for the time, put in shape by some great literatus, and projected among mankind, may duly cause changes, growths, removals, greater than the longest and bloodiest war, or the most stupendous merely political, dynastic, or commercial overturn.

In short, as, though it may not be realized, it is strictly true, that a few first-class poets, philosophs, and authors, have substantially settled and given status to the entire religion, education, law, sociology, &c., of the hitherto civilized world, by tinging and often creating the atmospheres out of which they have arisen, such also must stamp, and more than ever stamp, the interior and real democratic construction of this American continent, to-day, and days to come. Remember also this fact of difference, that, while through the antique and through the medivæal ages, highest thoughts and ideas realized themselves, and their expression made its way by other arts, as much as, or even more than by, technical literature, (not open to the mass of persons, or even to the majority of eminent persons,) such literature in our day and for current purposes, is not only more eligible than all the other arts put together, but has become the only general means of morally influencing the world. Painting, sculpture,

[4]Original, upon which others are based. [5]Ancient kingdom in Palestine.
[6]Bony, skeletal. [7]Appearance.

and the dramatic theatre, it would seem, no longer play an indispensable or even important part in the workings and mediumship of intellect, utility, or even high esthetics. Architecture remains, doubtless with capacities, and a real future. Then music, the combiner, nothing more spiritual, nothing more sensuous, a god, yet completely human, advances, prevails, holds highest place; supplying in certain wants and quarters what nothing else could supply. Yet in the civilization of to-day it is undeniable that, over all the arts, literature dominates, serves beyond all—shapes the character of church and school—or, at any rate, is capable of doing so. Including the literature of science, its scope is indeed unparallel'd.

Before proceeding further, it were perhaps well to discriminate on certain points. Literature tills its crops in many fields, and some may flourish, while others lag. What I say in these Vistas has its main bearing on imaginative literature, especially poetry, the stock of all. In the department of science, and the specialty of journalism, there appear, in these States, promises, perhaps fulfillments, of highest earnestness, reality, and life. These, of course, are modern. But in the region of imaginative, spinal and essential attributes, something equivalent to creation is, for our age and lands, imperatively demanded. For not only is it not enough that the new blood, new frame of democracy shall be vivified[8] and held together merely by political means, superficial suffrage, legislation, &c., but it is clear to me that, unless it goes deeper, gets at least as firm and as warm a hold in men's hearts, emotions and belief, as, in their days, feudalism or ecclesiasticism, and inaugurates its own perennial sources, welling from the centre forever, its strength will be defective, its growth doubtful, and its main charm wanting. I suggest, therefore, the possibility should some two or three really original American poets, (perhaps artists or lecturers,) arise, mounting the horizon like planets, stars of the first magnitude, that, from their eminence, fusing contributions, races, far localities, &c., together they would give more compaction and more moral identity, (the quality to-day most needed,) to these States, than all its Constitutions, legislative and judicial ties, and all its hitherto political, warlike, or materialistic experiences. As, for instance, there could hardly happen anything that would more serve the States, with all their variety of origins, their diverse climes, cities, standards, &c., than possessing an aggregate of heroes, characters, exploits, sufferings, prosperity or misfortune, glory or disgrace, common to all, typical of all—no less, but even greater would it be to possess the aggregation of a cluster of mighty poets, artists, teachers, fit for us, national expressers, comprehending and effusing for the men and women of the States, what is universal, native, common to all, inland and seaboard, northern and southern. The historians say of ancient Greece, with her ever-jealous autonomies, cities, and states, that the only positive unity she ever own'd or receiv'd, was the sad unity of a common subjection, at the last, to foreign conquerors. Subjection, aggregation of that sort, is impossible to America; but the fear of conflicting and irreconcilable interiors, and the lack of a common skeleton, knitting all close, continually haunts me. Or, if it does not, nothing is plainer than the need, a long period to come, of a fusion of the States into the only reliable identity, the moral and artistic one. For, I say, the true nationality of the States, the genuine union, when we come to a mortal crisis, is, and is to be, after all, neither the written law, nor,

[8]Given life.

(as is generally supposed,) either self-interest, or common pecuniary or material objects—but the fervid and tremendous IDEA, melting everything else with resistless heat, and solving all lesser and definite distinctions in vast, indefinite, spiritual, emotional power.

It may be claim'd, (and I admit the weight of the claim,) that common and general worldly prosperity, and a populace well-to-do, and with all life's material comforts, is the main thing, and is enough. It may be argued that our republic is, in performance, really enacting to-day the grandest arts, poems, &c., by beating up the wilderness into fertile farms, and in her railroads, ships, machinery, &c. And it may be ask'd, Are these not better, indeed, for America, than any utterances even of greatest rhapsode,[9] artist, or literatus?

I too hail those achievements with pride and joy: then answer that the soul of man will not with such only—nay, not with such at all—be finally satisfied; but needs what, (standing on these and on all things, as the feet stand on the ground,) is address'd to the loftiest, to itself alone.

Out of such considerations, such truths, arises for treatment in these Vistas the important question of character, of an American stock-personality, with literatures and arts for outlets and return-expressions, and, of course, to correspond, within outlines common to all. To these, the main affair, the thinkers of the United States, in general so acute, have either given feeblest attention, or have remain'd, and remain, in a state of somnolence.

For my part, I would alarm and caution even the political and business reader, and to the utmost extent, against the prevailing delusion that the establishment of free political institutions, and plentiful intellectual smartness, with general good order, physical plenty, industry, &c., (desirable and precious advantages as they all are,) do, of themselves, determine and yield to our experiment of democracy the fruitage of success. With such advantage as present fully, or almost fully, possess'd—the Union just issued, victorious, from the struggle[10] with the only foes it need ever fear, (namely, those within itself, the interior ones,) and with unprecedented materialistic advancement—society, in these States, is canker'd, crude, superstitious, and rotten. Political, or law-made society is, and private, or voluntary society, is also. In any vigor, the element of the moral conscience, the most important, the verteber[11] to State or man, seems to me either entirely lacking, or seriously enfeebled or ungrown.

I say we had best look our times and lands searchingly in the face, like a physician diagnosing some deep disease. Never was there, perhaps, more hollowness at heart than at present, and here in the United States. Genuine belief seems to have left us. The underlying principles of the States are not honestly believ'd in, (for all this hectic glow, and these melodramatic screamings,) nor is humanity itself believ'd in. What penetrating eye does not everywhere see through the mask? The spectacle is appaling. We live in an atmosphere of hypocrisy throughout. The men believe not in the women, nor the women in the men. A scornful superciliousness rules in literature. The aim of all the *littérateurs*[12] is to find something to make fun of. A lot of churches, sects, &c., the most dismal phantasms I know, usurp the name of religion. Conversation is a mass of badinage. From deceit in the spirit, the mother of all false deeds, the offspring is already incalculable. An acute and candid person, in the revenue

[9]A singer of poems. [10]The American Civil War (1861–1865).
[11]Vertebrae. [12]I.e., literary dilettantes, superficial critics.

department in Washington, who is led by the course of his employment to regularly visit the cities, north, south and west, to investigate frauds, has talk'd much with me about his discoveries. The depravity of the business classes of our country is not less than has been supposed, but infinitely greater. The official services of America, national, state, and municipal, in all their branches and departments, except the judiciary, are saturated in corruption, bribery, falsehood, mal-administration; and the judiciary is tainted. The great cities reek with respectable as much as non-respectable robbery and scoundrelism. In fashionable life, flippancy, tepid amours, weak infidelism, small aims, or no aims at all, only to kill time. In business, (this all-devouring modern word, business,) the one sole object is, by any means, pecuniary gain. The magician's serpent in the fable ate up all the other serpents; and money-making is our magician's serpent, remaining to-day sole master of the field. The best class we show, is but a mob of fashionably dress'd speculators and vulgarians. True, indeed, behind this fantastic farce, enacted on the visible stage of society, solid things and stupendous labors are to be discover'd, existing crudely and going on in the background, to advance and tell themselves in time. Yet the truths are none the less terrible. I say that our New World democracy, however great a success in uplifting the masses out of their sloughs, in materialistic development, products, and in a certain highly-deceptive superficial popular intellectuality, is, so far, an almost complete failure in its social aspects, and in really grand religious, moral, literary, and esthetic results. In vain do we march with unprecedented strides to empire so colossal, outvying the antique, beyond Alexander's, beyond the proudest sway of Rome. In vain have we annex'd Texas, California, Alaska, and reach north for Canada and south for Cuba. It is as if we were somehow being endow'd with a vast and more and more thoroughly-appointed body, and then left with little or no soul.

Let me illustrate further, as I write, with current observations, localities, &c. The subject is important, and will bear repetition. After an absence, I am now again (September, 1870) in New York city and Brooklyn, on a few weeks' vacation. The splendor, picturesqueness, and oceanic amplitude and rush of these great cities, the unsurpass'd situation, rivers and bay, sparkling sea-tides, costly and lofty new buildings, façades of marble and iron, of original grandeur and elegance of design, with the masses of gay color, the preponderance of white and blue, the flags flying, the endless ships, the tumultuous streets, Broadway, the heavy, low, musical roar, hardly ever intermitted, even at night; the jobbers' houses, the rich shops, the wharves, the great Central park, and the Brooklyn Park of hills, (as I wander among them this beautiful fall weather, musing, watching, absorbing)—the assemblages of the citizens in their groups, conversations, trades, evening amusements, or along the by-quarters—these, I say, and the like of these, completely satisfy my senses of power, fulness, motion, &c., and give me, through such senses and appetites, and through my esthetic conscience, a continued exaltation and absolute fulfilment. Always and more and more, as I cross the East and North rivers, the ferries, or with the pilots in their pilot-houses, or pass an hour in Wall street, or the gold exchange, I realize, (if we must admit such partialisms,) that not Nature alone is great in her fields of freedom and the open air, in her storms, the shows of night and day, the mountains, forests, seas—but in the artificial, the work of man too is equally great—in this profusion of teeming humanity—in these ingenuities, streets, goods, houses, ships—these hurrying, feverish, electric crowds of men, their complicated business genius, (not least among the geniuses,) and all this mighty, many-threaded wealth and industry concentrated here.

But sternly discarding, shutting our eyes to the glow and grandeur of the general superficial effect, coming down to what is of the only real importance, Personalities, and examining minutely, we question, we ask, Are there, indeed, *men* here worthy the name? Are there athletes? Are there perfect women, to match the generous material luxuriance? Is there a pervading atmosphere of beautiful manners? Are there crops of fine youths, and majestic old persons? Are there arts worthy freedom and a rich people? Is there a great moral and religious civilization—the only justification of a great material one? Confess that to severe eyes, using the moral microscope upon humanity, a sort of dry and flat Sahara appears, these cities, crowded with petty grotesques, malformations, phantoms, playing meaningless antics. Confess that everywhere, in shop, street, church, theatre, barroom, official chair, are pervading flippancy and vulgarity, low cunning, infidelity—everywhere the youth puny, impudent, foppish, prematurely ripe—everywhere an abnormal libidinousness,[13] unhealthy forms, male, female, painted, padded, dyed, chignon'd,[14] muddy complexions, bad blood, the capacity for good motherhood deceasing or deceas'd, shallow notions of beauty, with a range of manners, or rather lack of manners, (considering the advantages enjoy'd,) probably the meanest to be seen in the world.

Of all this, and these lamentable conditions, to breathe into them the breath recuperative of sane and heroic life, I say a new founded literature, not merely to copy and reflect existing surfaces, or pander to what is called taste—not only to amuse, pass away time, celebrate the beautiful, the refined, the past, or exhibit technical, rhythmic, or grammatical dexterity—but a literature underlying life, religious, consistent with science, handling the elements and forces with competent power, teaching and training men—and, as perhaps the most precious of its results, achieving the entire redemption of woman out of these incredible holds and webs of silliness, millinery, and every kind of dyspeptic depletion—and thus insuring to the States a strong and sweet Female Race, a race of perfect Mothers—is what is needed.

And now, in the full conception of these facts and points, and all that they infer, pro and con—with yet unshaken faith in the elements of the American masses, the composites, of both sexes, and even consider'd as individuals—and ever recognizing in them the broadest bases of the best literary esthetic appreciation—I proceed with my speculations, Vistas.

First, let us see what we can make out of a brief, general, sentimental consideration of political democracy, and whence it has arisen, with regard to some of its current features, as an aggregate, and as the basic structure of our future literature and authorship. We shall, it is true, quickly and continually find the origin-idea of the singleness of man, individualism, asserting itself, and cropping forth, even from the opposite ideas. But the mass, or lump character, for imperative reasons, is to be ever carefully weigh'd, borne in mind, and provided for. Only from it, and from its proper regulation and potency, comes the other, comes the chance of individualism. The two are contradictory, but our task is to reconcile them.

. . .

[13]Lustfulness. [14]I.e., with elaborately dressed hair.

We do not, (at any rate I do not,) put it either on the ground that the People, the masses, even the best of them, are, in their latent or exhibited qualities, essentially sensible and good—nor on the ground of their rights; but that good or bad, rights or no rights, the democratic formula is the only safe and preservative one for coming times. We endow the masses with the suffrage for their own sake, no doubt; then, perhaps still more, from another point of view, for community's sake. Leaving the rest to the sentimentalists, we present freedom as sufficient in its scientific aspect, cold as ice, reasoning, deductive, clear and passionless as crystal.

Democracy too is law, and of the strictest, amplest kind. Many suppose, (and often in its own ranks the error,) that it means a throwing aside of law, and running riot. But, briefly, it is the superior law, not alone that of physical force, the body, which, adding to, it supersedes with that of the spirit. Law is the unshakable order of the universe forever; and the law over all, and law of laws, is the law of successions; that of the superior law, in time, gradually supplanting and overwhelming the inferior one. (While, for myself, I would cheerfully agree—first covenanting that the formative tendencies shall be administer'd in favor, or at least not against it, and that this reservation be closely construed—that until the individual or community show due signs, or be so minor and fractional as not to endanger the State, the condition of authoritative tutelage may continue, and self-government must abide its time.) Nor is the esthetic point, always an important one, without fascination for highest aiming souls. The common ambition strains for elevations, to become some privileged exclusive. The master sees greatness and health in being part of the mass; nothing will do as well as common ground. Would you have in yourself the divine, vast, general law? Then merge yourself in it.

And, topping democracy, this most alluring record, that it alone can bind, and ever seeks to bind, all nations, all men, of however various and distant lands, into a brotherhood, a family. It is the old, yet ever-modern dream of earth, out of her eldest and her youngest, her fond philosophers and poets. Not that half only, individualism, which isolates. There is another half, which is adhesiveness or love, that fuses, ties and aggregates, making the races comrades, and fraternizing all. Both are to be vitalized by religion, (sole worthiest elevator of man or State,) breathing into the proud, material tissues, the breath of life. For I say at the core of democracy, finally, is the religious element. All the religions, old and new, are there. Nor may the scheme step forth, clothed in resplendent beauty and command, till these, bearing the best, the latest fruit, the spiritual, shall fully appear.

. . .

The true gravitation-hold of liberalism in the United States will be a more universal ownership of property, general homesteads, general comfort—a vast, intertwining reticulation of wealth. As the human frame, or, indeed, any object in this manifold universe, is best kept together by the simple miracle of its own cohesion, and the necessity, exercise and profit thereof, so a great and varied nationality, occupying millions of square miles, were firmest held and knit by the principle of the safety and endurance of the aggregate of its middling property owners. So that, from another point of view, ungracious as it may sound, and a paradox after what we have been saying, democracy looks with the suspicious, ill-satisfied eye upon the very poor, the ignorant, and on those out of business. She asks for men and women with occupations, well-off, owners of houses and acres, and with cash in the bank—and with some cravings for literature, too; and must have them, and hastens to make them. Luckily, the seed is already well-sown, and has taken ineradicable root.

. . .

Then still the thought returns, (like the thread-passage in overtures,)[15] giving the key and echo to these pages. When I pass to and fro, different latitudes, different seasons, beholding the crowds of the great cities, New York, Boston, Philadelphia, Cincinnati, Chicago, St. Louis, San Francisco, New Orleans, Baltimore—when I mix with these interminable swarms of alert, turbulent, good-natured, independent citizens, mechanics, clerks, young persons—at the idea of this mass of men, so fresh and free, so loving and so proud, a singular awe falls upon me. I feel, with dejection and amazement, that among our geniuses and talented writers or speakers, few or none have yet really spoken to this people, created a single image-making work for them, or absorb'd the central spirit and the idiosyncrasies which are theirs—and which, thus, in highest ranges, so far remain entirely uncelebrated, unexpress'd.

Dominion strong is the body's; dominion stronger is the mind's. What has fill'd, and fills to-day our intellect, our fancy, furnishing the standards therein, is yet foreign. The great poems, Shakspere included, are poisonous to the idea of the pride and dignity of the common people, the life-blood of democracy. The models of our literature, as we get it from other lands, ultramarine,[16] have had their birth in courts, and bask'd and grown in castle sunshine; all smells of princes' favors. Of workers of a certain sort, we have, indeed, plenty, contributing after their kind; many elegant, many learn'd, all complacent. But touch'd by the national test, or tried by the standards of democratic personality, they wither to ashes. I say I have not seen a single writer, artist, lecturer, or what not, that has confronted the voiceless but ever erect and active, pervading, underlying will and typic[17] aspiration of the land, in a spirit kindred to itself. Do you call those genteel little creatures American poets? Do you term that perpetual, pistareen,[18] paste-pot work, American art, American drama, taste, verse? I think I hear, echoed as from some mountain-top afar in the west, the scornful laugh of the Genius of these States.

Democracy, in silence, biding its time, ponders its own ideals, not of literature and art only—not of men only, but of women. The idea of the women of America, (extricated from this daze, this fossil and unhealthy air which hangs about the word *lady,*) develop'd, raised to become the robust equals, workers, and, it may be, even practical and political deciders with the men—greater than man, we may admit, through their divine maternity, always their towering, emblematical attribute—but great, at any rate, as man, in all departments; or, rather, capable of being so, soon as they realize it, and can bring themselves to give up toys and fictions, and launch forth, as men do, amid real, independent, stormy life.

Then, as towards our thought's finale, (and, in that, overarching the true scholar's lesson,) we have to say there can be no complete or epical presentation of democracy in the aggregate, or anything like it, at this day, because its

[15] A recurring melodic phrase or theme, a musical leitmotif. [16] Beyond the sea.
[17] Typical. [18] Of little value.

doctrines will only be effectually incarnated in any one branch, when, in all, their spirit is at the root and centre. Far, far, indeed, stretch, in distance, our Vistas! How much is still to be disentangled, freed! How long it takes to make this American world see that it is, in itself, the final authority and reliance!

Did you, too, O friend, suppose democracy was only for elections, for politics, and for a party name? I say democracy is only of use there that it may pass on and come to its flower and fruits in manners, in the highest forms of interaction between men, and their beliefs—in religion, literature, colleges, and schools—democracy in all public and private life, and in the army and navy. I have intimated that, as a paramount scheme, it has yet few or no full realizers and believers. I do not see, either, that it owes any serious thanks to noted propagandists or champions, or has been essentially help'd, though often harm'd, by them. It has been and is carried on by all the moral forces, and by trade, finance, machinery, intercommunications, and, in fact, by all the developments of history, and can no more be stopp'd than the tides, or the earth in its orbit. Doubtless, also, it resides, crude and latent, well down in the hearts of the fair average of the American-born people, mainly in the agricultural regions. But it is not yet, there or anywhere, the fully-receiv'd, the fervid, the absolute faith.

I submit, therefore, that the fruition of democracy, on aught like a grand scale, resides altogether in the future. As, under any profound and comprehensive view of the gorgeous-composite feudal world, we see in it, through the long ages and cycles of ages, the results of a deep, integral, human and divine principle, or fountain, from which issued laws, ecclesia,[19] manners, institutes, costumes, personalities, poems, (hitherto unequall'd,) faithfully partaking of their source, and indeed only arising either to betoken it, or to furnish parts of that varied-flowing display, whose centre was one and absolute—so, long ages hence, shall the due historian or critic make at least an equal retrospect, an equal history for the democratic principle. It too must be adorn'd, credited, with its results—then, when it, with imperial power, through amplest time, has dominated mankind—has been the source and test of all the moral, esthetic, social, political, and religious expressions and institutes of the civilized world—has begotten them in spirit and in form, and has carried them to its own unprecedented heights—has had, (it is possible,) monastics and ascetics, more numerous, more devout than the monks and priests of all previous creeds—has sway'd the ages with a breadth and rectitude tallying Nature's own—has fashion'd, systematized, and triumphantly finish'd and carried out, in its own interest, and with unparallel'd success, a new earth and a new man.

Thus we presume to write, as it were, upon things that exist not, and travel by maps yet unmade, and a blank. But the throes of birth are upon us; and we have something of this advantage in seasons of strong formations, doubts, suspense—for then the afflatus of such themes haply may fall upon us, more or less; and then, hot from surrounding war and revolution, our speech, though without polish'd coherence, and a failure by the standard called criticism, comes forth, real at least as the lightnings.

And may-be we, these days, have, too, our own reward—(for there are yet some, in all lands, worthy to be so encouraged.) Though not for us the joy of entering at the last the conquer'd city—not ours the chance ever to see with

[19]Church rules, religious doctrines.

our own eyes the peerless power and splendid *eclat* of the democratic principle, arriv'd at meridian, filling the world with effulgence and majesty far beyond those of past history's kings, or all dynastic sway—there is yet, to whoever is eligible among us, the prophetic vision, the joy of being toss'd in the brave turmoil of these times—the promulgation and the path, obedient, lowly reverent to the voice, the gesture of the god, or holy ghost, which others see not, hear not—with the proud consciousness that amid whatever clouds, seductions, or heart-wearying postponements, we have never deserted, never despair'd, never abandon'd the faith.

So much contributed, to be conn'd well, to help prepare and brace our edifice, our plann'd Idea—we still proceed to give it in another of its aspects—perhaps the main, the high façade of all. For to democracy, the leveler, the unyielding principle of the average, is surely join'd another principle, equally unyielding, closely tracking the first, indispensable to it, opposite, (as the sexes are opposite,) and whose existence, confronting and ever modifying the other, often clashing, paradoxical, yet neither of highest avail without the other, plainly supplies to these grand cosmic politics of ours, and to the launch'd forth mortal dangers of republicanism, to-day or any day, the counterpart and offset whereby Nature restrains the deadly original relentlessness of all her first-class laws. This second principle is individuality, the pride and centripetal isolation of a human being in himself—identity—personalism. Whatever the name, its acceptance and thorough infusion through the organization of political commonalty now shooting Aurora-like about the world, are of utmost importance, as the principle itself is needed for very life's sake. It forms, in a sort, or is to form, the compensating balance-wheel of the successful working machinery of aggregate America.

And, if we think of it, what does civilization itself rest upon—and what object has it, with its religions, arts, schools, &c., but rich, luxuriant, varied personalism? To that, all bends; and it is because toward such result democracy alone, on anything like Nature's scale, breaks up the limitless fallows of humankind, and plants the seed, and gives fair play, that its claims now precede the rest. The literature, songs, esthetics, &c., of a country are of importance principally because they furnish the materials and suggestions of personality for the women and men of that country, and enforce them in a thousand effective ways. As the top-most claim of a strong consolidating of the nationality of these States, is, that only by such powerful compaction can the separate States secure that full and free swing within their spheres, which is becoming to them, each after its kind, so will individuality, with unimpeded branchings, flourish best under imperial republican forms.

. . .

To practically enter into politics is an important part of American personalism. To every young man, north and south, earnestly studying these things, I should here, as an offset to what I have said in former pages, now also say, that may-be to views of very largest scope, after all, perhaps the political, (perhaps the literary and sociological,) America goes best about its development its own way—sometimes, to temporary sight, appaling enough. It is the fashion among dillettantes and fops (perhaps I myself am not guiltless,) to decry the whole formulation of the active politics of America, as beyond redemption, and to be carefully kept away from. See you that you do not fall into this error. America, it may be, is doing very well upon the whole, notwithstanding these antics of the parties and their leaders, these half-brain'd nominees, the many ignorant ballots, and many elected failures and blatherers. It is the dillettantes, and all who shirk their duty, who are not doing well. As for you, I advise you to enter more strongly yet into politics. I advise every young man to do so. Always inform yourself from parties. They have been useful, and to some extent remain so; but the floating, uncommitted electors, farmers, clerks, mechanics, the masters of parties—watching aloof, inclining victory this side or that side—such are the ones most needed, present and future. For America, if eligible at all to downfall and ruin, is eligible within herself, not without; for I see clearly that the combined foreign world could not beat her down. But these savage, wolfish parties alarm me. Owning no law but their own will, more and more combative, less and less tolerant of the idea of ensemble and of equal brotherhood, the perfect equality of the States, the ever-over-arching American ideas, it behooves you to convey yourself implicitly to no party, nor submit blindly to their dictators, but steadily hold yourself judge and master over all of them.

. . .

It must still be reiterated, as, for the purpose of these memoranda, the deep lesson of history and time, that all else in the contributions of a nation or age, through its politics, materials, heroic personalities, military *eclat,* &c., remains crude, and defers, in any close and thorough-going estimate, until vitalized by national, original archetypes in literature. They only put the nation in form, finally tell anything—prove, complete anything—perpetuate anything. Without doubt, some of the richest and most powerful and populous communities of the antique world, and some of the grandest personalities and events, have, to after and present times, left themselves entirely unbequeath'd. Doubtless, greater than any that have come down to us, were among those lands, heroisms, persons, that have not come down to us at all, even by name, date, or location. Others have arrived safely, as from voyages over wide, century-stretching seas. The little ships, the miracles that have buoy'd them, and by incredible chances safely convey'd them, (or the best of them, their meaning and essence,) over long wastes, darkness, lethargy, ignorance, &c., have been a few inscriptions—a few immortal compositions, small in size, yet compassing what measureless values of reminiscence, contemporary portraitures, manners, idioms, and beliefs, with deepest inference, hint and thought, to tie and touch forever the old, new body, and the old, new soul! These! and still these! bearing the freight so dear—dearer than pride—dearer than love. All the best experience of humanity, folded, saved, freighted to us here. Some of these tiny ships we call Old and New Testament, Homer, Eschylus, Plato, Juvenal, &c., Precious minims![20] I think, if we were forced to choose, rather than have you, and the likes of you, and what belongs to, and has grown of you blotted out and gone, we could better afford, appaling as that would be, to lose all actual ships, this day fasten'd by wharf, or floating on wave, and see them, with all their cargoes, scuttled and sent to the bottom.

Gather'd by geniuses of city, race or age, and put by them in highest of art's forms, namely, the literary form, the peculiar combinations and the outshows of that city, age, or race, its particular modes of the universal attributes and

[20]Small things.

passions, its faiths, heroes, lovers and gods, wars, traditions, struggles, crimes, emotions, joys, (or the subtle spirit of these,) having been pass'd on to us to illumine our own selfhood, and its experiences—what they supply, indispensable and highest, if taken away, nothing else in all the world's boundless storehouses could make up to us, or ever again return.

For us, along the great highways of time, those monuments stand—those forms of majesty and beauty. For us those beacons burn through all the nights. Unknown Egyptians, graving hieroglyphs; Hindus, with hymn and apothegm[21] and endless epic; Hebrew prophet, with spirituality, as in flashes of lightning, conscience like red-hot iron, plaintive songs and screams of vengeance for tyrannies and enslavement; Christ, with bent head, brooding love and peace, like a dove; Greek, creating eternal shapes of physical and esthetic proportion; Roman, lord of satire, the sword, and the codex;[22]—of the figures, some far off and veil'd, others near and visible; Dante, stalking with lean form, nothing but fibre, not a grain of superfluous flesh; Angelo,[23] and the great painters, architects, musicians; rich Shakspere, luxuriant as the sun, artist and singer of feudalism in its sunset, with all the gorgeous colors, owner thereof, and using them at will; and so to such as German Kant and Hegel,[24] where they, though near us, leaping over the ages, sit again, impassive, imperturbable, like the Egyptian gods. Of these, and the like of these, is it too much, indeed, to return to our favorite figure, and view them as orbs and systems of orbs, moving in free paths in the spaces of that other heaven, the kosmic intellect, the soul?

Ye powerful and resplendent ones! ye were, in your atmospheres, grown not for America, but rather for her foes, the feudal and the old—while our genius is democratic and modern. Yet could ye, indeed, but breathe your breath of life into our New World's nostrils—not to enslave us, as now, but, for our needs, to breed a spirit like your own—perhaps, (dare we to say it?) to dominate, even destroy, what you yourselves have left! On your plane, and no less, but even higher and wider, must we mete and measure for to-day and here. I demand races of orbic bards, with unconditional uncompromising sway. Come forth, sweet democratic despots of the west!

By points like these we, in reflection, token what we mean by any land's or people's genuine literature. And thus compared and tested, judging amid the influence of loftiest products only, what do our current copious fields of print, covering in manifold forms, the United States, better, for an analogy, present, than, as in certain regions of the sea, those spreading, undulating masses of squid, through which the whale swimming, with head half out, feeds?

Not but that doubtless our current so-called literature, (like an endless supply of small coin,) performs a certain service, and may-be, too, the service needed for the time, (the preparation-service, as children learn to spell.) Everybody reads, and truly nearly everybody writes, either books, or for the magazines or journals. The matter has magnitude, too, after a sort. But is it really advancing? or, has it advanced for a long while? There is something impressive about the huge editions of the dailies and weeklies, the mountain-stacks of white paper piled in the press-vaults, and the proud, crashing, tencylinder presses, which I can stand and watch any time by the half hour. Then, (though the States in the field of imagination present not a single first-class work, not a single great literatus,)

[21]Maxim. [22]Law. [23]Michelangelo.
[24]Immanuel Kant (1724–1804) and Friedrich Hegel (1770–1831), German philosophers.

the main objects, to amuse, to titilate, to pass away time, to circulate the news, and rumors of news, to rhyme and read rhyme, are yet attain'd, and on a scale of infinity. To-day, in books, in the rivalry of writers, especially novelists, success, (so-call'd,) is for him or her who strikes the mean flat average, the sensational appetite for stimulus, incident, persiflage,[25] &c., and depicts, to the common calibre, sensual, exterior life. To such, or the luckiest of them, as we see, the audiences are limitless and profitable; but they cease presently. While this day, or any day, to workmen portraying interior or spiritual life, the audiences were limited, and often laggard—but they last forever.

Compared with the past, our modern science soars, and our journals serve—but ideal and even ordinary romantic literature, does not, I think, substantially advance. Behold the prolific brood of the contemporary novel, magazine-tale, theatre-play, &c. The same endless thread of tangled and superlative love-story, inherited, apparently from the Amadises and Palmerins[26] of the 13th, 14th, and 15th centuries over there in Europe. The costumes and associations brought down to date, the seasoning hotter and more varied, the dragons and ogres left out—but the *thing*, I should say, has not advanced—is just as sensational, just as strain'd—remains about the same, nor more, nor less.

What is the reason our time, our lands, that we see no fresh local courage, sanity, of our own—the Mississippi, stalwart Western men, real mental and physical facts, Southerners, &c., in the body of our literature? especially the poetic part of it. But always, instead a parcel of dandies and ennuyees, dapper little gentlemen from abroad, who flood us with their thin sentiment of parlors, parasols, piano-songs, tinkling rhymes, the five-hundredth importation—or whimpering and crying about something, chasing one aborted conceit after another, and forever occupied in dyspeptic amours with dyspeptic women. While, current and novel, the grandest events and revolutions, and stormiest passions of history, are crossing to-day with unparallel'd rapidity and magnificence over the stages of our own and all the continents, offering new materials, opening new vistas, with largest needs, inviting the daring launching forth of conceptions in literature, inspired by them, soaring in highest regions, serving art in its highest, (which is only the other name for serving God, and serving humanity,) where is the man of letters, where is the book, with any nobler aim than to follow in the old track, repeat what has been said before—and, as its utmost triumph, sell well, and be erudite or elegant?

Mark the roads, the processes, through which these States have arrived, standing easy, henceforth ever-equal, ever-compact, in their range to-day. European adventures? the most antique? Asiatic or African? old history—miracles—romances? Rather, our own unquestion'd facts. They hasten, incredible, blazing bright as fire. From the deeds and days of Columbus down to the present, and including the present—and especially the late Secession war[27]—when I con[28] them, I feel, every leaf, like stopping to see if I have not made a mistake, and fall'n on the splendid figments of some dream. But it is no dream. We stand, live, move, in the huge flow of our age's materialism—in its spirituality. We have had founded for us the most positive of lands. The founders have pass'd to other spheres—but what are these terrible duties they have left us?

. . .

[25]Frivolous talk. [26]European chivalric romances.
[27]The American Civil War (1861–1865). [28]Examine, study.

The old men, I remember as a boy, were always talking of American independence. What is independence? Freedom from all laws or bonds except those of one's own being, control'd by the universal ones. To lands, to man, to woman, what is there at last to each, but the inherent soul, nativity, idiocrasy, free, highest-poised, soaring its own flight, following out itself?

At present, these States, in their theology and social standards, (of greater importance than their political institutions,) are entirely held possession of by foreign lands. We see the sons and daughters of the New World, ignorant of its genius, not yet inaugurating the native, the universal, and the near, still importing the distant, the partial, and the dead. We see London, Paris, Italy—not original, superb, as where they belong—but second-hand here, where they do not belong. We see the shreds of Hebrews, Romans, Greeks; but where, on her own soil, do we see, in any faithful, highest, proud expression, America herself? I sometimes question whether she has a corner in her own house.

Not but that in one sense, and a very grand one, good theology, good art, or good literature, has certain features shared in common. The combination fraternizes, ties the races—is, in many particulars, under laws applicable indifferently to all, irrespective of climate or date, and, from whatever source, appeals to emotions, pride, love, spirituality, common to humankind. Nevertheless, they touch a man closest, (perhaps only actually touch him,) even in these, in their expression, through autochthonic[29] lights and shades, flavors, fondnesses, aversions, specific incidents, illustrations, out of his own nationality, geography, surroundings, antecedents, &c. The spirit and the form are one, and depend far more on association, identity and place, than is supposed. Subtly interwoven with the materiality and personality of a land, a race—Teuton, Turk, Californian, or what not—there is always something—I can hardly tell what it is—history but describes the results of it—it is the same as the untellable look of some human faces. Nature, too, in her stolid forms, is full of it—but to most it is there a secret. This something is rooted in the invisible roots, the profoundest meanings of that place, race, or nationality; and to absorb and again effuse it, uttering words and products as from its midst, and carrying it into highest regions, is the work, or a main part of the work, of any country's true author, poet, historian, lecturer, and perhaps even priest and philosoph. Here, and here only, are the foundations for our really valuable and permanent verse, drama, &c.

But at present, (judged by any higher scale than that which finds the chief ends of existence to be to feverishly make money during one-half of it, and by some "amusement," or perhaps foreign travel, flippantly kill time, the other half,) and consider'd with reference to purposes of patriotism, health, a noble personality, religion, and the democratic adjustments, all these swarms of poems, literary magazines, dramatic plays, resultant so far from American intellect, and the formation of our best ideas, are useless and a mockery. They strengthen and nourish no one, express nothing characteristic, give decision and purpose to no one, and suffice only the lowest level of vacant minds.

Of what is called the drama, or dramatic presentation in the United States, as now put forth at the theatres, I should say it deserves to be treated with the same gravity, and on a par with the questions of ornamental confectionery at public dinners, or the arrangement of curtains and hangings in a ball-room—

[29]Indigenous, native.

nor more, nor less. Of the other, I will not insult the reader's intelligence, (once really entering into the atmosphere of these Vistas,) by supposing it necessary to show, in detail, why the copious dribble, either of our little or well-known rhymesters, does not fulfil, in any respect, the needs and august occasions of this land. America demands a poetry that is bold, modern, and all-surrounding and kosmical, as she is herself. It must in no respect ignore science or the modern, but inspire itself with science and the modern. It must bend its vision toward the future, more than the past. Like America, it must extricate itself from even the greatest models of the past, and, while courteous to them, must have entire faith in itself, and the products of its own democratic spirit only. Like her, it must place in the van, and hold up at all hazards, the banner of the divine pride of man in himself, (the radical foundation of the new religion.) Long enough have the People been listening to poems in which common humanity, deferential, bends low, humiliated, acknowledging superiors. But America listens to no such poems. Erect, inflated, and fully self-esteeming be the chant; and then America will listen with pleased ears.

Nor may the genuine gold, the gems, when brought to light at last, be probably usher'd forth from any of the quarters currently counted on. To-day, doubtless, the infant genius of American poetic expression, (eluding those highly-refined imported and gilt-edged themes, and sentimental and butterfly flights, pleasant to orthodox publishers—causing tender spasms in the coteries, and warranted not to chafe the sensitive cuticle of the most exquisitely artificial gossamer delicacy,) lies sleeping far away, happily unrecognized and uninjur'd by the coteries, the art-writers, the talkers and critics of the saloons, or the lecturers in the colleges—lies sleeping, aside, unrecking[30] itself, in some western idiom, or native Michigan or Tennessee repartee, or stump-speech—or in Kentucky or Georgia, or the Carolinas—or in some slang or local song or allusion of the Manhattan, Boston, Philadelphia or Baltimore mechanic—or up in the Maine woods—or off in the hut of the California miner, or crossing the Rocky mountains, or along the Pacific railroad or on the breasts of the young farmers of the northwest, or Canada, or boatmen of the lakes. Rude and coarse nursing-beds, these; but only from such beginnings and stocks, indigenous here, may haply arrive, be grafted, and sprout, in time, flowers of genuine American aroma, and fruits truly and fully our own.

I say it were a standing disgrace to these States—I say it were a disgrace to any nation, distinguish'd above others by the variety and vastness of its territories, its materials, its inventive activity, and the splendid practicality of its people, not to rise and soar above others also in its original styles in literature and art, and its own supply of intellectual and esthetic masterpieces, archetypal, and consistent with itself. I know not a land except ours that has not, to some extent, however small, made its title clear. The Scotch have their born ballads, subtly expressing their past and present, and expressing character. The Irish have theirs. England, Italy, France, Spain, theirs. What has America? With exhaustless mines of the richest ore of epic, lyric, tale, tune, picture, &c., in the Four Years' War;[31] with, indeed, I sometimes think, the richest masses of material ever afforded a nation, more variegated, and on a larger scale—the first sign of proportionate, native, imaginative Soul, and first-class works to match, is, (I cannot too often repeat,) so far wanting.

[30]Disregarding. [31]The American Civil War (1861–1865).

Long ere the second centennial arrives, there will be some forty to fifty great States, among them Canada and Cuba. When the present century closes, our population will be sixty or seventy millions. The Pacific will be ours, and the Atlantic mainly ours. There will be daily electric communication with every part of the globe. What an age! What a land! Where, elsewhere, one so great? The individuality of one nation must, then, as always, lead the world. Can there be any doubt who the leader ought to be? Bear in mind, though, that nothing less than the mightiest original non-subordinated SOUL has ever really, gloriously led, or ever can lead. (This Soul—its other name, in these Vistas is LITERATURE.)

. . .

Present literature, while magnificently fulfilling certain popular demands, with plenteous knowledge and verbal smartness, is profoundly sophisticated, insane, and its very joy is morbid. It needs tally and express Nature, and the spirit of Nature, and to know and obey the standards. I say the question of Nature, largely consider'd, involves the question of the esthetic, the emotional, and the religious—and involves happiness. A fitly born and bred race, growing up in right conditions of out-door as much as in-door harmony, activity and development, would probably, from and in those conditions, find it enough merely *to live*—and would, in their relations to the sky, air, water, trees, &c., and to the countless common shows, and in the fact of life itself, discover and achieve happiness—with Being suffused night and day by wholesome extasy, surpassing all the pleasures that wealth, amusement, and even gratified intellect, erudition, or the sense of art, can give.

In the prophetic literature of these States (the reader of my speculations will miss their principal stress unless he allows well for the point that a new Literature, perhaps a new Metaphysics, certainly a new Poetry, are to be, in my opinion, the only sure and worthy supports and expressions of the American Democracy,) Nature, true Nature, and the true idea of Nature, long absent, must, above all, become fully restored, enlarged, and must furnish the pervading atmosphere to poems, and the test of all high literary and esthetic compositions. I do not mean the smooth walks, trimm'd hedges, poseys and nightingales of the English poets, but the whole orb, with its geologic history, the kosmos, carrying fire and snow, that rolls through the illimitable areas, light as a feather, though weighing billions of tons. Furthermore, as by what we now partially call Nature is intended, at most, only what is entertainable by the physical conscience, the sense of matter, and of good animal health—on these it must be distinctly accumulated, incorporated, that man, comprehending these, has in towering superaddition, the moral and spiritual consciences, indicating his destination beyond the ostensible, the mortal.

To the heights of such estimate of Nature indeed ascending, we proceed to make observations for our Vistas, breathing rarest air. What is I believe called Idealism seems to me to suggest, (guarding against extravagance, and ever modified even by its opposite,) the course of inquiry and desert of favor for our New World metaphysics, their foundation of and in literature, giving hue to all.

The elevating and etherealizing ideas of the unknown and of unreality must be brought forward with authority, as they are the legitimate heirs of the known, and of reality, and at least as great as their parents. Fearless of scoffing, and of the ostent, let us take our stand, our ground, and never desert it, to confront the growing excess and arrogance of realism. To the cry, now victorious—the cry of sense, science, flesh, incomes, farms, merchandise, logic, intellect, demonstrations, solid perpetuities, buildings of brick and iron, or even the facts of the shows of trees, earth, rocks, &c., fear not, my brethren, my sisters, to sound out with equally determin'd voice, that conviction brooding within the recesses of every envision'd soul—illusions! apparitions! figments all! True, we must not condemn the show, neither absolutely deny it, for the indispensability of its meanings; but how clearly we see that, migrate in soul to what we can already conceive of superior and spiritual points of view, and, palpable as it seems under present relations, it all and several might, nay certainly would, fall apart and vanish.

I hail with joy the oceanic, variegated, intense practical energy, the demand for facts, even the business materialism of the current age, our States. But woe to the age or land in which these things, movements, stopping at themselves, do not tend to ideas. As fuel to flame, and flame to the heavens, so must wealth, science, materialism—even this democracy of which we make so much—unerringly feed the highest mind, the soul. Infinitude the flight: fathomless the mystery. Man, so diminutive, dilates beyond the sensible universe, competes with, outcopes space and time, meditating even one great idea. Thus, and thus only, does a human being, his spirit, ascend above, and justify, objective Nature, which, probably nothing in itself, is incredibly and divinely serviceable, indispensable, real, here. And as the purport of objective Nature is doubtless folded, hidden, somewhere here—as somewhere here is what this globe and its manifold forms, and the light of day, and night's darkness, and life itself, with all its experiences, are for—it is here the great literature, especially verse, must get its inspiration and throbbing blood. Then may we attain to a poetry worthy the immortal soul of man, and which, while absorbing materials, and, in their own sense, the shows of Nature, will, above all, have, both directly and indirectly, a freeing, fluidizing, expanding, religious character, exulting with science, fructifying the moral elements, and stimulating aspirations, and meditations on the unknown.

The process, so far, is indirect, and peculiar, and though it may be suggested, cannot be defined. Observing, rapport, and with intuition, the shows and forms presented by Nature, the sensuous luxuriance, the beautiful in living men and women, the actual play of passions, in history and life—and, above all, from those developments either in Nature or human personality in which power, (dearest of all to the sense of the artist,) transacts itself—out of these, and seizing what is in them, the poet, the esthetic worker in any field, by the divine magic of his genius, projects them, their analogies, by curious removes, indirections, in literature and art. (No useless attempt to repeat the material creation, by daguerreotyping the exact likeness by mortal mental means.) This is the image-making faculty, coping with material creation, and rivaling, almost triumphing over it. This alone, when all the other parts of a specimen of literature or art are ready and waiting, can breathe into it the breath of life, and endow it with identity.

"The true question to ask," says the librarian of Congress in a paper read before the Social Science Convention at New York, October, 1869, "The true question to ask respecting a book, is, *has it help'd any human soul?*" This is the hint, statement, not only of the great literatus, his book, but of every great artist. It may be that all works of art are to be first tried by their art qualities, their image-forming talent, and their dramatic, pictorial, plot-constructing, euphonious and other talents. Then, whenever claiming to be first-class works, they are to be strictly and sternly tried by their foundation in, and radiation, in the highest sense, and always indirectly, of the ethic principles, and eligibility to free, arouse, dilate.

As, within the purposes of the Kosmos, and vivifying all meterology, and all the congeries[32] of the mineral, vegetable and animal worlds—all the physical growth and development of man, and all the history of the race in politics, religions, wars, &c., there is a moral purpose, a visible or invisible intention, certainly underlying all—its results and proof needing to be patiently waited for—needing intuition, faith, idiosyncrasy, to its realization, which many, and especially the intellectual, do not have—so in the product, or congeries of the product, of the greatest literatus. This is the last, profoundest measure and test of a first-class literary, or esthetic achievement, and when understood and put in force must fain, I say, lead to works, books, nobler than any hitherto known. Lo! Nature, (the only complete, actual poem,) existing calmly in the divine scheme, containing all, content, careless of the criticisms of a day, or these endless and wordy chatterers. And lo! to the consciousness of the soul, the permanent identity, the thought, the something, before which the magnitude even of democracy, art, literature, &c., dwindles, becomes partial, measurable—something that fully satisfies, (which those do not.) That something is the All, and the idea of All, with the accompanying idea of eternity, and of itself, the soul, buoyant, indestructible, sailing space forever, visiting every region, as a ship the sea. And again lo! the pulsations in all matter, all spirit, throbbing forever—the eternal beats, eternal systole and diastole[33] of life in things—wherefrom I feel and know that death is not the ending, as was thought, but rather the real beginning—and that nothing ever is or can be lost, nor ever die, nor soul, nor matter.

In the future of these States must arise poets immenser far, and make great poems of death. The poems of life are great, but there must be the poems of the purports of life, not only in itself, but beyond itself. I have eulogized Homer, the sacred bards of Jewry, Eschylus, Juvenal, Shakspere, &c., and acknowledged their inestimable value. But, (with perhaps the exception, in some, not all respects, of the second-mention'd,) I say there must, for future and democratic purposes, appear poets, (dare I to say so?) of higher class even than any of those—poets not only possess'd of the religious fire and abandon of Isaiah,[34] luxuriant in the epic talent of Homer, or for proud characters as in Shakspere, but consistent with the Hegelian formulas[35] and consistent with modern science. America needs, and the world needs, a class of bards who will, now and ever, so link and tally the rational physical being of man, with the ensembles of time and space, and with this vast and multiform show, Nature, surrounding him, ever tantalizing him, equally a part, and yet not a part of him, as to essentially harmonize, satisfy, and put at rest. Faith, very old, now scared away by science, must be restored, brought back by the same power that caused her departure—restored with new sway, deeper, wider, higher than ever. Surely, this

[32]Aggregation, collection.
[33]Contraction and expansion, as with the beating of the heart. [34]Hebrew prophet.
[35]The German philosopher Hegel's dialectical system of thesis, antithesis, and synthesis by which opposites are unified and something new emerges.

universal ennui, this coward fear, this shuddering at death, these low, degrading views, are not always to rule the spirit pervading future society, as it has the past, and does the present. What the Roman Lucretius[36] sought most nobly, yet all too blindly, negatively to do for his age and its successors, must be done positively by some great coming literatus, especially poet, who, while remaining fully poet, will absorb whatever science indicates, with spiritualism, and out of them, and out of his own genius, will compose the great poem of death. Then will man indeed confront Nature, and confront time and space, both with science, and *con amore,*[37] and take his right place, prepared for life, master of fortune and misfortune. And then that which was long wanted will be supplied, and the ship that had it not before in all her voyages, will have an anchor.

. . .

Arrived now, definitely, at an apex for these Vistas, I confess that the promulgation and belief in such a class or institution—a new and greater literatus order—its possibility, (nay certainty,) underlies these entire speculations—and that the rest, the other parts, as superstructures, are all founded upon it. It really seems to me the condition, not only of our future national and democratic development, but of our perpetuation. In the highly artificial and materialistic bases of modern civilization, with the corresponding arrangements and methods of living, the force-infusion of intellect alone, the depraving influences of riches just as much as poverty, the absence of all high ideals in character—with the long series of tendencies, shapings, which few are strong enough to resist, and which now seem, with steam-engine speed, to be everywhere turning out the generations of humanity like uniform iron castings—all of which, as compared with the feudal ages, we can yet do nothing better than accept, make the best of, and even welcome, upon the whole, for their oceanic practical grandeur, and their restless wholesale kneading of the masses—I say of all this tremendous and dominant play of solely materialistic bearings upon current life in the United States, with the results as already seen, accumulating, and reaching far into the future, that they must either be confronted and met by at least an equally subtle and tremendous force-infusion for purposes of spiritualization, for the pure conscience, for genuine esthetics, and for absolute and primal manliness and womanliness—or else our modern civilization, with all its improvements, is in vain, and we are on the road to a destiny, a status, equivalent, in its real world, to that of the fabled damned.

Prospecting thus the coming unsped days, and that new order in them—marking the endless train of exercise, development, unwind, in nation as in man, which life is for—we see, fore-indicated, amid these prospects and hopes, new law-forces of spoken and written language—not merely the pedagogue-forms, correct, regular, familiar with precedents, made for matters of outside propriety, fine words, thoughts definitely told out—but a language fann'd by the breath of Nature, which leaps overhead, cares mostly for impetus and effects, and for what it plants and invigorates to grow—tallies life and character, and seldomer tells a thing than suggests or necessitates it. In fact, a new theory of

[36]Roman poet (first century B.C.). His masterwork, *De Rerum Natura,* was written to counteract the despair and artificiality of his age.

[37]Italian: with love.

literary composition for imaginative works of the very first class, and especially for highest poems, is the sole course open to these States. Books are to be call'd for, and supplied, on the assumption that the process of reading is not a half-sleep, but, in highest sense, an exercise, a gymnast's struggle; that the reader is to do something for himself, must be on the alert, must himself or herself construct indeed the poem, argument, history, metaphysical essay—the text furnishing the hints, the clue, the start or frame-work. Not the book needs so much to be the complete thing, but the reader of the book does. That were to make a nation of supple and athletic minds, well-train'd, intuitive, used to depend on themselves, and not on a few coteries of writers.

Investigating here, we see, not that it is a little thing we have, in having the bequeath'd libraries, countless shelves of volumes, records, &c.; yet how serious the danger, depending entirely on them, of the bloodless vein, the nerveless arm, the false application, at second or third hand. We see that the real interest of this people of ours in the theology, history, poetry, politics, and personal models of the past, (the British islands, for instance, and indeed all the past,) is not necessarily to mould ourselves or our literature upon them, but to attain fuller, more definite comparisons, warnings, and the insight to ourselves, our own present, and our own far grander, different, future history, religion, social customs, &c. We see that almost everything that has been written, sung, or stated, of old, with reference to humanity under the feudal and oriental institutes, religions, and for other lands, needs to be re-written, re-sung, re-stated, in terms consistent with the institutions of these States, and to come in range and obedient uniformity with them.

We see, as in the universes of the material kosmos, after meteorological, vegetable, and animal cycles, man at last arises, born through them, to prove them, concentrate them, to turn upon them with wonder and love—to command them, adorn them, and carry them upward into superior realms—so, out of the series of the preceding social and political universes, now arises these States. We see that while many were supposing things established and completed, really the grandest things always remain; and discover that the work of the New World is not ended, but only fairly begun.

We see our land, America, her literature, esthetics, &c., as, substantially, the getting in form, or effusement and statement, of deepest basic elements and loftiest final meanings, of history and man—and the portrayal, (under the eternal laws and conditions of beauty,) of our own physiognomy, the subjective tie and expression of the objective, as from our own combination, continuation, and points of view—and the deposit and record of the national mentality, character, appeals, heroism, wars, and even liberties—where these, and all, culminate in native literary and artistic formulation, to be perpetuated; and not having which native, first-class formulation, she will flounder about, and her other, however imposing, eminent greatness, prove merely a passing gleam; but truly having which, she will understand herself, live nobly, nobly contribute, emanate, and, swinging, poised safely on herself, illumin'd and illuming, become a full-form'd world, and divine Mother not only of material but spiritual worlds, in ceaseless succession through time—the main thing being the average, the bodily, the concrete, the democratic, the popular, on which all the superstructures of the future are to permanently rest.

1867–1870

1871

Emily Dickinson 1830–1886

One day in April 1862, Thomas Wentworth Higginson, a poetry critic for the Atlantic Monthly, *received a letter from Emily Dickinson of Amherst, Massachusetts, asking, "Are you too deeply occupied to say if my verse is alive?" The four poems she enclosed provoked an immediate response and began a correspondence that lasted twenty-two years. Although Emily Dickinson thanked her "preceptor" Higginson for the "surgery" he performed on her poetry, she wanted his encouragement more than his advice, and she politely ignored his suggestions for regularizing her rough rhythms and imperfect rhymes and for correcting her spelling and grammar. Recognizing Emily Dickinson's poetic genius, despite her violations of poetic convention, Higginson remained her friend and adviser throughout her life, and after her death he assisted in gathering her poems for publication.*

Only eight of Emily Dickinson's poems were published while she lived, and it was not until the appearance of Poems by Emily Dickinson *(1890), four years after her death, that her work became available to the general reading public for the first time. The early critical estimates were mixed. Some reviewers found the poetry to be "balderdash" suffering from lack of rhyme, faulty grammar, and incomprehensible metaphors, a "farrago of illiterate and uneducated sentiment." But other readers found them remarkably pointed and evocative. As the years passed and as more poems were published, critical estimates grew more favorable until, with the publication of all her known poetry in* The Poems of Emily Dickinson *(1955), she had come to be regarded as one of America's most gifted poets.*

Emily Dickinson's entire life, except for brief visits to nearby Boston and to Washington, D.C., was spent in and around her birthplace, Amherst. The Dickinsons of Amherst were prominent. Her grandfather was a founder of Amherst College; for seventy years her father and then her brother, both lawyers, served as College Treasurer and Trustee. Her mother was often an invalid and required Dickinson and her sister Lavinia to run the large household.

As Emily Dickinson grew older, she increasingly withdrew from society, seldom leaving her garden and her large family house. There she wrote poems and letters to her friends and watched the life of the town from her upstairs bedroom window. Her friends, she said, were her "estate," and among them were the Reverend Charles Wadsworth and Dickinson's sister-in-law, Susan. Both of these cherished companions profoundly affected her creative and emotional life; however, many contemporary critics now accept the loving relationship between Susan and Emily as the more affecting one. Dickinson's love poems to her sister-in-law particularly reflect the passion she felt for her.

Emily Dickinson lived a more intense and passionate life than was thought by neighbors and acquaintances who saw her only as an eccentric, unmarried woman. Not even those closest to her knew fully the depth and extent of her emotions or that the nearly 1,800 poems, tied neatly in packets found after her death, would reveal an immensely complex and passionate sensibility. Dickinson's painstaking composing, revising, copying, and sewing of her poems into handmade fascicles suggest private publication and a rejection of the literary marketplace in favor of her own artistic vision. Poe strategized concerning the literary marketplace, Hawthorne unsuccessfully tried to conquer it, Stowe and Fanny Fern took it by storm, and Melville ultimately scorned it, but Dickinson chose a literary production separate from publication.

Dickinson's subjects were love, death, nature, immortality, and beauty. Written largely in meters common to Protestant hymn books, her poems employed irregular rhythms, off- or slant-rhymes, paradox, and a careful balancing of abstract Latinate and concrete Anglo-Saxon words. Many of her lyrics concentrated on the theme of death, which she typically personified as a monarch, a lord, or a kindly but irresistible lover, yet her moods varied widely, from melancholy to exuberance, grief to joy, and despair to spiritual intoxication.

Emily Dickinson's favorite authors included Shakespeare, Keats, the Brownings, Ruskin, and Sir Thomas Browne, whose uneasy balance of faith and skepticism she shared. Early in life she rebelled against the Calvinism of the Amherst Congregational Church, yet she retained the Calvinist tendency to look inwardly, and she had a Calvinist sense of both the inherent beauty and the frightening coldness of the world. Well over a century after Dickinson's death, the majority of critics read her poetry through broader lenses, uncovering new interpretations of poems under-read by contemporaries in the conventional patriarchal world of nineteenth-century New England.

FURTHER READING: *The Complete Poems of Emily Dickinson,* ed. T. Johnson, 1960, 1976; *The Manuscript Books of Emily Dickinson,* ed. R. Franklin, 1981; *New Poems of Emily Dickinson,* ed. W. Shurr, 1993; *The Letters of Emily Dickinson,* 3 vols., ed. T. Johnson, 1958; J. Leyda, *The Years and Hours of Emily Dickinson,* 2 vols., 1960; *Critical Essays on Emily Dickinson,* ed. P. Ferlazzo, 1984; V. Pollak, *Emily Dickinson: The Anxiety of Gender,* 1984; C. Wolff, *Emily Dickinson,* 1986; J. Loving, *Emily Dickinson: The Poet of the Second Story,* 1987; C. Miller, *Emily Dickinson: A Poet's Grammar,* 1987; E. Phillips, *Emily Dickinson: Personae and Performance,* 1988; G. Stonum, *The Dickinson Sublime,* 1990; J. Small, *Positive as Sound: Emily Dickinson's Rhyme,* 1990; M. Loeffelholz, *Dickinson and the Boundaries of Feminist Theory,* 1991; J. Kirby, *Emily Dickinson,* 1991; J. Farr, *The Passion of Emily Dickinson,* 1992; D. Oberhaus, *Emily Dickinson's Fascicles,* 1995; M. Werner, *Emily Dickinson's Open Folios,* 1995; *Dickinson and Audience,* ed. M. Orzeck and R. Weisbuch, 1996; D. Wardrop, *Emily Dickinson's Gothic,* 1996; R. Smith, *The Seductions of Emily Dickinson,* 1996; B. Doriani, *Emily Dickinson: Daughter of Prophecy,* 1996; E. Phillips, *Emily Dickinson: Personae and Performance,* 1997; E. Petrino, *Emily Dickinson and Her Contemporaries,* 1998; R. Lundin, *Emily Dickinson and the Art of Belief,* 1998; *An Emily Dickinson Encyclopedia,* ed. J. Donahue, 1998; J. Guthrie, *Emily Dikinson's Vision,* 1998; *The Emily Dickinson Handbook,* ed. G. Grabber, 1998; *Emily Dickinson,* ed. H. Bloom, 1999; *Emily Dickinson,* ed. Graham Clarke, 2000; A. Habeggar, *My Life Is Laid Away in Books,* 2001; D. Mitchell, *Emily Dickinson: Monarch of Perception,* 2001; *The Cambridge Companion to Emily Dickinson,* ed. W. Martin, 2002; R. Brantley, *Experience and Faith: The Late-Romantic Imagination of Emily Dickinson,* 2004; *The Emily Dickinson Handbook,* ed. G. Grabber, C. Miller, and R. Hagenbuchle, 2005; A. Borus, *A Student's Guide to Emily Dickinson,* 2005.

TEXTS: *The Poems of Emily Dickinson,* 3 vols., ed. T. Johnson, 1955; *The Letters of Emily Dickinson,* ed. T. Johnson, 1958. Some spelling has been normalized.

49[1]

I never lost as much but twice,
And that was in the sod.
Twice have I stood a beggar
Before the door of God!

[1]Few of Emily Dickinson's poems were given titles. The numbers used here are from *The Poems of Emily Dickinson,* 3 vols.; ed. T. Johnson, 1955.

Angels—twice descending
Reimbursed my store—
Burglar! Banker—Father!
I am poor once more!
1858? 1890

67

Success is counted sweetest
By those who ne'er succeed.
To comprehend a nectar
Requires sorest need.

Not one of all the purple Host
Who took the Flag today
Can tell the definition
So clear of Victory
As he defeated—dying—
On whose forbidden ear
The distant strains of triumph
Burst agonized and clear!
1859 1878

125

For each ecstatic instant
We must an anguish pay
In keen and quivering ratio
To the ecstacy.
For each beloved hour
Sharp pittances of years—
Bitter contested farthings[1]—
And Coffers heaped with Tears!
1859? 1891

130

These are the days when Birds come back—
A very few—a Bird or two—
To take a backward look.

These are the days when skies resume
The old—old sophistries[1] of June—
A blue and gold mistake.

[1]Coins of little value.
[1]Subtle, deceptive reasoning.

Oh fraud that cannot cheat the Bee—
Almost the plausibility
Induces my belief.

Till ranks of seeds their witness bear—
And softly thro' the altered air
Hurries a timid leaf.

Oh Sacrament of summer days,
Oh Last Communion[2] in the Haze—
Permit a child to join.

Thy sacred emblems to partake—
Thy consecrated bread to take
And thine immortal wine!
1859? 1890

165

A *Wounded* Deer—leaps highest—
I've heard the Hunter tell—
'Tis but the Ecstasy of *death*—
And then the Brake is still!

The *Smitten* Rock that gushes!
The *trampled* Steel that springs!
A Cheek is always redder
Just where the Hectic stings!
Mirth is the Mail of Anguish—
In which it Cautious Arm,
Lest anybody spy the blood
And "you're hurt" exclaim!
1860? 1890

185

"Faith" is a fine invention
When Gentlemen can *see*—
But Microscopes are prudent
In an Emergency.
1860? 1891

[2]In the Christian sacrament of Communion, believers are united with Christ through partaking of consecrated bread and wine.

210

The thought beneath so slight a film—
Is more distinctly seen—
As laces just reveal the surge—
Or Mists—the Appenine—
1860? 1891

214

I taste a liquor never brewed—
From Tankards scooped in Pearl—
Not all the Frankfort Berries[1]
Yield such an Alcohol!

Inebriate of Air—am I—
And Debauchee of Dew—
Reeling—thro endless summer days—
From inns of Molten Blue—

When "Landlords" turn the drunken Bee
Out of the Foxglove's door—
When Butterflies—renounce their "drams"—
I shall but drink the more!
Till Seraphs[2] swing their snowy Hats—
And Saints—to windows run—
To see the little Tippler
From Manzanilla[3] come![4]
1860? 1861, 1890

216

Safe in their Alabaster Chambers—
Untouched by Morning—
And untouched by Noon—
Lie the meek members of the Resurrection—
Rafter of Satin—and Roof of Stone!

Grand go the Years—in the Crescent—above them—
Worlds scoop their Arcs—
And Firmaments—row—

[1]Grapes grown in the region of Frankfurt am Main, Germany, and used in making a fine Rhine wine. Another version of this line reads, "Not all the Vats upon the Rhine."
[2]The highest ranking of the nine orders of angels.
[3]A sherry wine exported from Manzanilla, Spain.
[4]Two other versions of the final line exist:
"Come staggering toward the Sun."
"Leaning against the—Sun—"

Diadems—drop—and Doges[1]—surrender—
Soundless as dots—on a Disc of Snow—
1861 1890

241

I like a look of Agony,
Because I know it's true—
Men do not sham Convulsion,
Nor simulate, a Throe[1]—

The Eyes glaze once—and that is Death—
Impossible to feign
The Beads upon the Forehead
By homely Anguish strung.
1861? 1890

249

Wild Nights—Wild Nights!
Were I with thee
Wild Nights should be
Our luxury!

Futile—the Winds—
To a Heart in port—
Done with the Compass—
Done with the Chart!
Rowing in Eden—
Ah, the Sea!
Might I but moor—Tonight—
In Thee!
1861? 1891

258

There's a certain Slant of light,
Winter Afternoons—
That oppresses, like the Heft[1]
Of Cathedral Tunes—

Heavenly Hurt, it gives us—
We can find no scar,
But internal difference,
Where the Meanings, are—

[1]The chief magistrates of Venice (697–1797).
[1]A spasm.
[1]Weight.

None may teach it—Any—
'Tis the Seal Despair—
An imperial affliction
Sent us of the Air—

When it comes, the Landscape listens—
Shadows—hold their breath—
When it goes, 'tis like the Distance
On the look of Death—
1861? 1890

280

I felt a Funeral, in my Brain,
And Mourners to and fro
Kept treading—treading—till it seemed
That Sense was breaking through—

And when they all were seated,
A Service, like a Drum—
Kept beating—beating—till I thought
My Mind was going numb—

And then I heard them lift a Box
And creak across my Soul
With those same Boots of Lead, again,
Then Space—began to toll,

As all the Heavens were a Bell,
And Being, but an Ear,
And I, and Silence, some strange Race
Wrecked, solitary, here—
And then a Plank in Reason, broke,
And I dropped down, and down—
And hit a World, at every plunge,
And Finished knowing—then—
1861? 1896

287

A Clock stopped—
Not the Mantel's—
Geneva's[1] farthest skill
Can't put the puppet bowing—
That just now dangled still—

[1]Geneva, Switzerland—renowned for its clockmakers.

An awe came on the Trinket!
The Figures hunched, with pain—
Then quivered out of Decimals—
Into Degreeless Noon—

It will not stir for Doctors—
This Pendulum of snow—
This Shopman importunes it—
While cool—concernless No—

Nods from the Gilded pointers—
Nods from the Seconds slim—
Decades of Arrogance between
The Dial life—
And Him—
1861? 1896

303

The Soul selects her own Society—
Then—shuts the Door—
To her divine Majority—
Present no more—

Unmoved—she notes the Chariots—pausing—
At her low Gate—
Unmoved—an Emperor be kneeling
Upon her Mat—

I've known her—from an ample nation—
Choose One—
Then—close the Valves of her attention—
Like Stone—
1862? 1890

324

Some keep the Sabbath going to Church—
I keep it, staying at Home—
With a Bobolink for a Chorister—
And an Orchard, for a Dome—

Some keep the Sabbath in Surplice[1]—
I just wear my Wings—

[1]A loose, white robe worn by priests and others who help conduct church services.

And instead of tolling the Bell, for Church,
Our little Sexton[2]—sings.

God preaches, a noted Clergyman—
And the sermon is never long
So instead of getting to Heaven, at last—
I'm going, all along.
1860? 1864

328

A Bird came down the Walk—
He did not know I saw—
He bit an Angleworm in halves
And ate the fellow, raw,

And then he drank a Dew
From a convenient Grass—
And then hopped sidewise to the Wall
To let a Beetle pass—

He glanced with rapid eyes
That hurried all around—
They looked like frightened Beads, I thought—
He stirred his Velvet Head

Like one in danger, Cautious,
I offered him a Crumb
And he unrolled his feathers
And rowed him softer home—

Than Oars divide the Ocean,
Too silver for a seam—
Or Butterflies, off Banks of Noon
Leap, plashless[1] as they swim.
1862 1891

338

I know that He exists.
Somewhere—in Silence—
He has hid his rare life
From our gross eyes.

[2]A church employee who takes care of church property, rings the church bells, and in some parishes digs graves. Here equated with the bobolink.
[1]Splashless.

'Tis an instant's play.
'Tis a fond Ambush—
Just to make Bliss
Earn her own surprise!

But—should the play
Prove piercing earnest—
Should the glee—glaze—
In Death's—stiff—stare—

Would not the fun
Look too expensive!
Would not the jest—
Have crawled too far!
1862 1891

341

After great pain, a formal feeling comes—
The Nerves sit ceremonious, like Tombs—
The stiff Heart questions was it He, that bore,
And Yesterday, or Centuries before?

The Feet, mechanical, go round—
Of Ground, or Air, or Ought—
A Wooden way
Regardless grown,
A Quartz contentment, like a stone—

This is the Hour of Lead—
Remembered, if outlived,
As Freezing persons, recollect the Snow—
First—Chill—then Stupor—then the letting go—
1862 1929

401

What Soft—Cherubic Creatures—
These Gentlewomen are—
One would as soon assault a Plush[1]—
Or violate a Star—

Such Dimity[2] Convictions—
A Horror so refined

[1]Cloth with a long, soft pile. [2]Cotton fabric, delicate and sheer.

Of freckled Human Nature—
Of Deity—ashamed[3]—

It's such a common—Glory—
A Fisherman's—Degree—
Redemption—Brittle Lady—
Be so—ashamed of Thee—
1862? 1896

414

'Twas like a Maelstrom,[1] with a notch,
That nearer, every Day,
Kept narrowing its boiling Wheel
Until the Agony

Toyed coolly with the final inch
Of your delirious Hem—
And you dropt, lost,
When something broke—
And let you from a Dream—

As if a Goblin with a Gauge—
Kept measuring the Hours—
Until you felt your Second
Weigh, helpless, in his Paws—

And not a Sinew—stirred—could help,
And sense was setting numb—
When God—remembered—and the Fiend
Let go, then, Overcome—

As if your Sentence stood—pronounced—
And you were frozen led
From Dungeon's luxury of Doubt
To Gibbets,[2] and the Dead—

And when the Film had stitched your eyes
A Creature gasped "Reprieve"!
Which Anguish was the utterest—then—
To perish, or to live?
1862? 1945

[3]"For whosoever shall be ashamed of me and of my words, of him shall the Son of man be ashamed, when he shall come in his own glory . . ." Luke 9:26.

[1]A violent whirlpool.

[2]Wooden frameworks on which criminals are hanged and left on display as a warning.

435

Much Madness is divinest Sense—
To a discerning Eye—
Much Sense—the starkest Madness—
'Tis the Majority
In this, as All, prevail—
Assent—and you are sane—
Demur—you're straightway dangerous—
And handled with a Chain—
1862? 1890

441

This is my letter to the World
That never wrote to Me—
The simple News that Nature told—
With tender Majesty
Her Message is committed
To Hands I cannot see—
For love of Her—Sweet—countrymen—
Judge tenderly—of Me
1862 1890

448

This was a Poet—It is That
Distills amazing sense
From ordinary Meanings—
And Attar[1] so immense

From the familiar species
That perished by the Door—
We wonder it was not Ourselves
Arrested it—before—

Of Pictures, the Discloser—
The Poet—it is He—
Entitles Us—by Contrast—
To ceaseless Poverty—

Of Portion—so unconscious—
The Robbing—could not harm—
Himself—to Him—a Fortune—
Exterior—to Time—
1862? 1929

[1]Fragrant oils extracted from flowers.

449

I died for Beauty—but was scarce
Adjusted in the Tomb
When One who died for Truth, was lain
In an adjoining Room—

He questioned softly "Why I failed"?
"For Beauty," I replied—
"And I—for Truth—Themself are One—
We Bretheren, are," He said—

And so, as Kinsmen, met a Night—
We talked between the Rooms—
Until the Moss had reached our lips—
And covered up—our names—
1862? 1890

465

I heard a Fly buzz—when I died—
The Stillness in the Room
Was like the Stillness in the Air—
Between the Heaves of Storm—

The Eyes around—had wrung them dry—
And Breaths were gathering firm
For that last Onset—when the King
Be witnessed—in the Room—

I willed my Keepsakes—Signed away
What portion of me be
Assignable—and then it was
There interposed a Fly—

With Blue—uncertain stumbling Buzz—
Between the light—and me—
And then the Windows failed—and then
I could not see to see—
1862? 1896

510

It was not Death, for I stood up,
And all the Dead, lie down—
It was not Night, for all the Bells
Put out their Tongues, for Noon.

It was not Frost, for on my Flesh
I felt Siroccos[1]—crawl—
Nor Fire—for just my Marble feet
Could keep a Chancel,[2] cool—

And yet, it tasted, like them all,
The Figures I have seen
Set orderly, for Burial,
Reminded me, of mine—

As if my life were shaven,
And fitted to a frame,
And could not breathe without a key,
and 'twas like Midnight, some—

When everything that ticked—has stopped—
And Space stares all around—
Or Grisly frosts—first Autumn morns,
Repeal the Beating Ground—

But, most, like Chaos—Stopless—cool—
Without a Chance, or Spar—
Or even a Report of Land—
To justify—Despair.
1862 1891

520

I started Early—Took my Dog—
And visited the Sea—
The Mermaids in the Basement
Came out to look at me—

And Frigates[1]—in the Upper Floor
Extended Hempen Hands—
Presuming Me to be a Mouse—
Aground—upon the Sands—

But no Man moved Me—till the Tide
Went past my simple Shoe—
And past my Apron—and my Belt
And past my Bodice—too—

And made as He would eat me up—
As wholly as a Dew

[1]Hot, Mediterranean winds that originate in the Libyan deserts.
[2]Area of a church where the altar is placed.
[1]Swift-sailing ships.

Upon a Dandelion's Sleeve—
And then—I started—too—

And He—He followed—close behind—
I felt His Silver Heel
Upon my Ankle—Then my Shoes
Would overflow with Pearl—

Until We met the Solid Town—
No One He seemed to know—
And bowing—with a Mighty look—
At me—The Sea withdrew—
1862? 1891

585

I like to see it lap the Miles—
And lick the Valleys up—
And stop to feed itself at Tanks
And then—prodigious step

Around a Pile of Mountains—
And supercilious peer
In Shanties—by the sides of Roads—
And then a Quarry pare

To fit its sides
And crawl between
Complaining all the while
In horrid—hooting stanza—
Then chase itself down Hill—

And neigh like Boanerges[1]—
Then—prompter than a Star
Stop—docile and omnipotent
At its own stable door—
1862? 1891

613

They shut me up in Prose—
As when a little Girl
They put me in the Closet—
Because they liked me "still"—

[1]Hebrew: Sons of Thunder, a term used to describe loud-voiced preachers and orators.

Still! Could themself have peeped—
And seen my Brain—go round—
They might as wise have lodged a Bird
For Treason—in the Pound—

Himself has but to will
And easy as a Star
Look down upon Captivity—
And laugh—No more have I—
1862? 1935

632

The Brain—is wider than the sky—
For—put them side by side—
The one the other will contain
With ease—and You—beside—

The Brain is deeper than the sea—
For—hold them—Blue to Blue—
The one the other will absorb—
As Sponges—Buckets—do—

The Brain is just the weight of God—
For—Heft them—Pound for Pound—
And they will differ—if they do—
As Syllable from Sound—
1862? 1896

640

I cannot live with You—
It would be Life—
And Life is over there—
Behind the Shelf—
The Sexton[1] keeps the Key to—
Putting up
Our Life—His Porcelain—
Like a Cup—

Discarded of the Housewife—
Quaint—or Broke—
A newer Sevres[2] pleases—
Old Ones crack—

[1]Church official in charge of a church building and its grounds.
[2]Fine porcelain made in Sèvres, France.

I could not die—with You—
For One must wait
To shut the Other's Gaze down—
You—could not—

And I—Could I stand by
And see You—freeze—
Without my Right of Frost—
Death's privilege?

Nor could I rise—with you—
Because Your Face
Would put out Jesus'—
That new Grace

Glow plain—and foreign
On my homesick Eye—
Except that You than He
Shone closer by—

They'd judge Us—How—
For You—served Heaven—You know,
Or sought to—
I could not—

Because You saturated Sight—
And I had no more Eyes
For sordid excellence
As Paradise.

And were You lost, I would be—
Though My Name
Rang loudest
On the Heavenly fame—

And were You—saved—
And I—condemned to be
Where You were not—
That self—were Hell to Me—

So We must meet apart—
You there—I—here—
With just the Door ajar
That Oceans are—and Prayer—
And that White Sustenance—
Despair—
1862? 1890

650

Pain—has an Element of Blank—
It cannot recollect
When it begun—or if there were
A time when it was not—

It has no Future—but itself—
Its Infinite contain
Its Past—enlightened to perceive
New Periods—of Pain.
1862? 1890

657

I dwell in Possibility—
A fairer House than Prose—
More numerous of Windows—
Superior—for Doors—

Of Chambers as the Cedars—
Impregnable of Eye—
And for an Everlasting Roof
The Gambrels[1] of the Sky—

Of Visiters—the fairest—
For Occupation—This—
The spreading wide my narrow Hands
To gather Paradise—
1862? 1929

670

One need not be a Chamber—to be Haunted—
One need not be a House—
The Brain has Corridors—surpassing
Material Place—

Far safer, of a Midnight Meeting
External Ghost
Than its interior Confronting—
That Cooler Host.

[1]Angled roofs.

Far safer, through an Abbey gallop,
The Stones a'chase[1]—
Than Unarmed, one's a'self[2] encounter—
In lonesome Place—

Ourself behind ourself, concealed—
Should startle most—
Assassin hid in our Apartment
Be Horror's least.

The Body—borrows a Revolver—
He bolts the Door—
O'erlooking a superior spectre—
Or More—
1863? 1891

709

Publication—is the Auction
Of the Mind of Man—
Poverty—be justifying
For so foul a thing

Possibly—but We—would rather
From Our Garret go
White—Unto the White Creator—
Than invest—Our Snow—

Thought belong to Him who gave it—
Then—to Him Who bear
It's Corporeal illustration—Sell
The Royal Air—

In the Parcel—Be the Merchant
Of the Heavenly Grace—
But reduce no Human Spirit
To Disgrace of Price—
1863? 1929

712

Because I could not stop for Death—
He kindly stopped for me—
The Carriage held but just Ourselves—
And Immortality.

[1]I.e., in pursuit. [2]I.e., own self.

We slowly drove—He knew no haste
And I had put away
My labor and my leisure too,
For His Civility—

We passed the School, where Children strove
At Recess—in the Ring—
We passed the Fields of Gazing Grain—
We passed the Setting Sun—

Or rather—He passed Us—
The Dews drew quivering and chill—
For only Gossamer, my Gown—
My Tippet[1]—only Tulle[2]

We paused before a House that seemed
A Swelling of the Ground—
The Roof was scarcely visible—
The Cornice—in the Ground—

Since then—'tis Centuries—and yet
Feels shorter than the Day
I first surmised the Horses' Heads
Were toward Eternity—
1863? 1890

732

She rose to His Requirement—dropt
The Playthings of Her Life
To take the honorable Work
Of Woman, and of Wife—

If ought She missed in Her new Day,
Of Amplitude, or Awe—
Or first Prospective—Or the Gold
In using, wear away,

It lay unmentioned—as the Sea
Develope Pearl, and Weed,
But only to Himself—be known
The Fathoms they abide—
1863? 1890

[1]A cape or scarf. [2]Thin, net fabric.

745

Renunciation—is a piercing Virtue—
The letting go
A Presence—for an Expectation—
Not now—
The putting out of Eyes—
Just Sunrise—
Lest Day—
Day's Great Progenitor—
Outvie
Renunciation—is the Choosing
Against itself—
Itself to justify
Unto itself—
When larger function—
Make that appear—
Smaller—that Covered Vision—Here—
1863? 1929

754

My life had stood—a Loaded Gun—
In Corners—till a Day
The Owner passed—identified—
And carried Me away—

And now We roam in Sovereign Woods—
And now We hunt the Doe—
And every time I speak for Him—
The Mountains straight reply—

And do I smile, such cordial light
Upon the Valley glow—
It is as a Vesuvian[1] face
Had let its pleasure through—

And when at Night—Our good Day done—
I guard My Master's Head—
'Tis better than the Eider-Duck's[2]
Deep Pillow—to have shared—

[1]I.e., resembling Mount Vesuvius, a volcano near Naples, Italy.
[2]North American waterfowl highly prized for its soft down.

To foe of His—I'm deadly foe—
None stir the second time—
On whom I lay a Yellow Eye—
Or an emphatic Thumb—

Though I than He—may longer live
He longer must—than I—
For I have but the power to kill,
Without—the power to die—
1863? 1929

764

Presentiment—is that long Shadow—on the Lawn—
Indicative that Suns go down—

The Notice to the startled Grass
That Darkness—is about to pass—
1862? 1890

976

Death is a Dialogue between
The Spirit and the Dust.
"Dissolve" says Death—The Spirit "Sir
I have another Trust"—

Death doubts it—Argues from the Ground—
The Spirit turns away
Just laying off for evidence
An Overcoat of Clay.
1864? 1890

986

A narrow Fellow in the Grass
Occasionally rides—
You may have met Him—did you not
His notice sudden is—

The Grass divides as with a Comb—
A spotted shaft is seen—
And then it closes at your feet
And opens further on—

He likes a Boggy Acre
A Floor too cool for corn—
Yet when a Boy, and Barefoot—
I more than once at Noon
Have passed, I thought, a Whip lash
Unbraiding in the Sun
When stooping to secure it
It wrinkled, and was gone—

Several of Nature's People
I know, and they know me—
I feel for them a transport
Of cordiality—

But never met this Fellow
Attended, or alone
Without a tighter breathing
And Zero at the Bone—
1865, 1866 1891

1052

I never saw a Moor—
I never saw the Sea—
Yet know I how the Heather looks
And what a Billow be.

I never spoke with God
Nor visited in Heaven—
Yet certain am I of the spot
As if the Checks[1] were given—
1865? 1890

[1]Tokens of verification, tickets.

1078

The Bustle in a House
The Morning after Death
Is solemnest of industries
Enacted upon Earth—

The Sweeping up the Heart
And putting Love away
We shall not want to use again
Until Eternity.
1866? 1890

1129

Tell all the truth but tell it slant—
Success in Circuit lies
Too bright for our infirm Delight
The Truth's superb surprise
As Lightning to the Children eased
With explanation kind
The Truth must dazzle gradually
Or every man be blind—
1868? 1945

1207

He preached upon "Breadth" till it argued him narrow—
The Broad are too broad to define
And of "Truth" until it proclaimed him a Liar—
The Truth never flaunted a Sign—

Simplicity fled from his counterfeit presence
As Gold the Pyrites[1] would shun—
What confusion would cover the innocent Jesus
To meet so enabled a Man!
1872? 1891

[1]Iron or copper pyrites, called "fool's gold" because they resemble gold.

1463

A Route of Evanescence
With a revolving Wheel—
A Resonance of Emerald—
A Rush of Cochineal[1]—
And every Blossom on the Bush
Adjusts its tumbled Head—
The mail from Tunis,[2] probably,
An easy Morning's Ride—
1879? 1891

1545

The Bible is an antique Volume—
Written by faded Men
At the suggestion of Holy Spectres—
Subjects—Bethlehem—
Eden—the ancient Homestead—
Satan—the Brigadier—
Judas—the Great Defaulter—
David—the Troubadour—
Sin—a distinguished Precipice
Others must resist—
Boys that "believe" are very lonesome—
Other Boys are "lost"—
Had but the Tale a warbling Teller—
All the Boys would come—
Orpheus'[1] Sermon captivated—
It did not condemn—
1879–1882? 1924

1624

Apparently with no surprise
To any happy Flower
The Frost beheads it at its play—
In accidental power—

[1]A red dye. [2]City in North Africa.
[1]Legendary Greek poet and musician whose music charmed wild beasts, trees, and even rivers.

The blonde Assassin passes on—
That Sun proceeds unmoved
To measure off another Day
For an Approving God.
1884? 1890

1670

In Winter in my Room
I came upon a Worm
Pink lank and warm
But as he was a worm
And worms presume
Not quite with him at home
Secured him by a string
To something neighboring
And went along.

A Trifle afterward
A thing occurred
I'd not believe it if I heard
But state with creeping blood
A snake with mottles rare
Surveyed my chamber floor
In feature as the worm before
But ringed with power
The very string with which
I tied him—too
When he was mean and new
That string was there—

I shrank—"How fair you are!"
Propitiation's claw—
"Afraid he hissed
Of me?"
"No cordiality"—
He fathomed me—
Then to a Rhythm *Slim*
Secreted in his Form
As Patterns swim
Projected him.

That time I flew
Both eyes his way
Lest he pursue
Nor ever ceased to run

Till in a distant Town
Towns on from mine
I set me down
This was a dream—
1914

1732

My life closed twice before its close;
It yet remains to see
If immortality unveil
A third event to me,

So huge, so hopeless to conceive
As these that twice befell.
Parting is all we know of heaven,
And all we need of hell.
1896

1755

To make a prairie it takes a clover and one bee,
One clover, and a bee,
And revery.
The revery alone will do,
If bees are few.
1896

1760

Elysium is as far as to
The very nearest Room
If in that Room a Friend await
Felicity or Doom—

What fortitude the Soul contains,
That it can so endure
The accent of a coming Foot—
The opening of a Door—
1882? 1890

LETTERS TO T. W. HIGGINSON

15 April 1862

Mr Higginson,[1]

Are you too deeply occupied to say if my Verse is alive?

The Mind is so near itself—it cannot see, distinctly—and I have none to ask—

Should you think it breathed—and had you the leisure to tell me, I should feel quick gratitude—

If I make the mistake—that you dared to tell me—would give me sincerer honor—toward you—

I enclose my name—asking you, if you please—Sir—to tell me what is true?

That you will not betray me—it is needless to ask—since Honor is its own pawn—

1862 1891

25 April 1862

Mr Higginson,[1]

Your kindness claimed earlier gratitude—but I was ill—and write today, from my pillow.

Thank you for the surgery—it was not so painful as I supposed. I bring you others—as you ask—though they might not differ—

While my thought is undressed—I can make the distinction, but when I put them in the Gown—they look alike, and numb.

You asked how old I was? I made no verse—but one or two—until this winter—Sir—

[1]In place of a signature, Emily Dickinson enclosed a card (in its own envelope) on which she wrote her name. The first letter to Higginson, which begins a correspondence that lasted until the month of her death, she wrote because she had just read his "Letter to a Young Contributor," the lead article in the *Atlantic Monthly* for April, offering practical advice to beginning writers. She also enclosed four poems: "Safe in their Alabaster Chambers," "The nearest Dream recedes unrealized," "We play at Paste," and "I'll tell you how the sun rose." When Higginson first published the letter, he introduced it by saying: "On April 16, 1862, I took from the post office in Worcester, Mass., where I was then living, the following letter."

[1]Higginson says in his *Atlantic Monthly* article introducing the letter that the enclosed poems were two: "Your riches taught me poverty," and "A bird came down the walk." But the evidence after study of the folds in the letters and poems suggest that he was in error. The enclosures seem to have been: "There came a Day at Summer's full," "Of all the Sounds despatched abroad," and "South Winds jostle them." Harriet Prescott Spofford's "Circumstance" was published in the *Atlantic Monthly* for May 1860. Higginson's "Letter to a Young Contributor" quotes Ruskin and cites Sir Thomas Browne for vigor of style. The article's comment on "what a delicious prolonged perplexity it is to cut and contrive a decent *clothing of words* . . ." may explain Dickinson's phrase "While my thought is undressed." The friend who taught her "Immortality" has generally been thought to be Benjamin Franklin Newton. The two editors who recently had asked her for her mind may have been Bowles and Holland. Though Emily Dickinson frequently refers to the Brownings, she never again mentions Ruskin, and mentions Keats but twice.

I had a terror—since September—I could tell to none—and so I sing, as the Boy does by the Burying Ground—because I am afraid—You inquire my Books—For Poets—I have Keats—and Mr and Mrs Browning. For Prose—Mr Ruskin—Sir Thomas Browne—and the Revelations. I went to school—but in your manner of the phrase—had no education. When a little Girl, I had a friend, who taught me Immortality—but venturing too near, himself—he never returned—Soon after, my Tutor, died—and for several years, my Lexicon—was my only companion—Then I found one more—but he was not contented I be his scholar—so he left the Land.

You ask of my Companions Hills—Sir—and the sundown—and a Dog—large as myself, that my Father bought me—They are better than Beings—because they know—but do not tell—and the noise in the Pool, at Noon—excels my Piano. I have a Brother and Sister—My Mother does not care for thought—and Father, too busy with his Briefs—to notice what we do—He buys me many Books—but begs me not to read them—because he fears they joggle the Mind. They are religious—except me—and address an Eclipse, every morning—whom they call their "Father." But I fear my story fatigues you—I would like to learn—Could you tell me how to grow—or is it unconveyed—like Melody—or Witchcraft?

You speak of Mr Whitman—I never read his Book—but was told that he was disgraceful—

I read Miss Prescott's "Circumstance," but it followed me, in the Dark—so I avoided her—

Two Editors of Journals came to my Father's House, this winter—and asked me for my Mind—and when I asked them "Why," they said I was penurious—and they, would use it for the World—

I could not weight myself—Myself—

My size felt small—to me—I read your chapters in the Atlantic—and experienced honor for you—I was sure you would not reject a confiding question—

Is this—Sir—what you asked me to tell you?

Your friend, E—Dickinson.

1862 1891

7 June 1862

Dear friend.[1]

Your letter gave no Drunkenness, because I tasted Rum before—Domingo comes but once—yet I have had few pleasures so deep as your opinion, and if I tried to thank you, my tears would block my tongue—

My dying Tutor told me that he would like to live till I had been a poet, but Death was much of Mob as I could master—then—And when far afterward—a sudden light on Orchards, or a new fashion in the wind troubled my attention—I felt a palsy, here—the Verses just relieve—

[1]The phrase "I have no Saxon" (used near the end of this letter) means "Language fails me." She enclosed no poems in this letter.

Your second letter surprised me, and for a moment, swung—I had not supposed it. Your first—gave no dishonor, because the True—are not ashamed—I thanked you for your justice—but could not drop the Bells whose jingling cooled my Tramp—Perhaps the Balm, seemed better, because you bled me, first.

I smile when you suggest that I delay "to publish"—that being foreign to my thought, as Firmament to Fin—

If fame belonged to me, I could not escape her—if she did not, the longest day would pass me on the chase—and the approbation of my Dog, would forsake me—then—My Barefoot-Rank is better—

You think my gait "spasmodic"—I am in danger—Sir—

You think me "uncontrolled"—I have no Tribunal.

Would you have time to be the "friend" you should think I need? I have a little shape—it would not crowd your Desk—nor make much Racket as the Mouse, that dents your Galleries—

If I might bring you what I do—not so frequent to trouble you—and ask you if I told it clear—'twould be control, to me—

The Sailor cannot see the North—but knows the Needle can—

The "hand you stretch me in the Dark," I put mine in, and turn away—I have no Saxon, now—

As if I asked a common Alms,
And in my wondering hand
A Stranger pressed a Kingdom,
And I, bewildered, stand—
As if I asked the Orient
Had it for me a Morn—
And it should lift its purple Dikes,
And shatter me with Dawn!

But, will you be my Preceptor, Mr Higginson?

Your friend E Dickinson—

1862 1891

July 1862[1]

Could you believe me—without? I had no portrait, now, but am small, like the Wren, and my Hair is bold, like the Chestnut Bur—and my eyes, like the Sherry in the Glass, that the Guest leaves—Would this do just as well?

It often alarms Father—He says Death might occur, and he has Molds of all the rest—but has no Mold of me, but I noticed the Quick wore off those things, in a few days, and forestall the dishonor—You will think no caprice of me—

[1]"Pippa Passes," the first of the series in Browning's "Bells and Pomegranates," had been published in 1841. The letter enclosed four poems: "Of Tribulation these are they," "Your Riches taught me poverty," "Some keep the Sabbath going to Church," and "Success is counted sweetest."

You said "Dark." I know the Butterfly—and the Lizard—and the Orchis—

Are not those *your* Countrymen?

I am happy to be your scholar, and will deserve the kindness, I cannot repay.

If you truly consent, I recite, now—

Will you tell me my fault, frankly as to yourself, for I had rather wince, than die. Men do not call the surgeon, to commend—the Bone, but to set it, Sir, and fracture within, is more critical. And for this, Preceptor, I shall bring you—Obedience—the Blossom from my Garden, and every gratitude I know. Perhaps you smile at me. I could not stop for that—My Business is Circumference—An ignorance, not of Customs, but if caught with the Dawn—or the Sunset see me—Myself the only Kangaroo among the Beauty, Sir, if you please, it afflicts me, and I thought that instruction would take it away.

Because you have much business, beside the growth of me—you will appoint, yourself, how often I shall come—without your inconvenience. And if at any time—you regret you received me, or I prove a different fabric to that you supposed—you must banish me—

When I state myself, as the Representative of the Verse—it does not mean—me—but a supposed person. You are true, about the "perfection."

Today, makes Yesterday mean.

You spoke of Pippa Passes—I never heard anybody speak of Pippa Passes—before.

You see my posture is benighted.

To thank you, baffles me. Are you perfectly powerful? Had I a pleasure you had not, I could delight to bring it.

Your Scholar

1862 1891

August 1862

Dear friend—[1]

Are these more orderly? I thank you for the Truth—

I had no Monarch in my life, and cannot rule myself, and when I try to organize—my little Force explodes—and leaves me bare and charred—

I think you called me "Wayward." Will you help me improve?

I supposed the pride that stops the Breath, in the Core of Woods, is not of Ourself—

You say I confess the little mistake, and omit the large—Because I can see Orthography—but the Ignorance out of sight—is my Preceptor's charge—

Of "shunning Men and Women"—they talk of Hallowed things, aloud—and embarrass my Dog—He and I dont object to them, if they'll exist their side. I

[1]With this letter Dickinson enclosed two poems: "Before I got my Eye put out," and "I cannot dance upon my Toes."

think Carl[o] would please you—He is dumb, and brave—I think you would like the Chestnut Tree, I met in my walk. It hit my notice suddenly—and I thought the Skies were in Blossom—

Then there's a noiseless noise in the Orchard—that I let persons hear—You told me in one letter, you could not come to see me, "now," and I made no answer, not because I had none, but did not think myself the price that you should come so far—

I do not ask so large a pleasure, lest you might deny me—

You say "Beyond your knowledge." You would not jest with me, because I believe you—but Preceptor—you cannot mean it? All men say "What" to me, but I thought it a fashion—

When much in the Woods as a little Girl, I was told that the Snake would bite me, that I might pick a poisonous flower, or Goblins kidnap me, but I went along and met no one but Angels, who were far shyer of me, than I could be of them, so I hav'nt that confidence in fraud which many exercise.

I shall observe your precept—though I dont understand it, always.

I marked a line in One Verse—because I met it after I made it—and never consciously touch a paint, mixed by another person—

I do not let go it, because it is mine.

Have you the portrait of Mrs Browning? Persons sent me three—If you had none, will you have mine?

Your Scholar—

1862 1891

June 1869

Dear friend[1]

A Letter always feels to me like immortality because it is the mind alone without corporeal friend. Indebted in our talk to attitude and accent, there seems a spectral power in thought that walks alone—I would like to thank you for your great kindness but never try to lift the words which I cannot hold.

Should you come to Amherst, I might then succeed, though Gratitude is the timid wealth of those who have nothing. I am sure that you speak the truth, because the noble do, but your letters always surprise me. My life has been too simple and stern to embarrass any.

"Seen of Angels" scarcely my responsibility

It is difficult not to be fictitious in so fair a place, but test's severe repairs are permitted all.

[1]Dickinson echoes her opening sentence in a letter to James Clark that she wrote in 1882. This is her third refusal to go to Boston, and her second invitation to Higginson to come to Amherst, and it answers a letter written by Higginson, dated May 11, 1869. Dickinson's conviction that Higginson was the friend who saved her life must have been very deep, for she uses the same phrase in a letter written to him ten years later.

When a little Girl I remember hearing that remarkable passage and preferring the "Power," not knowing at the time that "Kingdom" and "Glory" were included.

You noticed my dwelling alone—To an Emigrant, Country is idle except it be his own. You speak kindly of seeing me. Could it please your convenience to come so far as Amherst I should be very glad, but I do not cross my Father's ground to any House or town.

Of our greatest acts we are ignorant—

You were not aware that you saved my Life. To thank you in person has been since then one of my few requests. The child that asks my flower "Will you," he says—"Will you"—and so to ask for what I want I know no other way.

You will excuse each that I say, because no other taught me?

Dickinson

1869 1891

late May 1874

I thought that being a Poem one's self precluded the writing Poems, but perceive the Mistake. It seemed like going Home, to see your beautiful thought once more, now so long forbade it—Is it Intellect that the Patriot means when he speaks of his "Native Land"? I should have feared to "quote" to you what you "most valued."

You have experienced sanctity.
It is to me untried.

Of Life to own—
From Life to draw—
But never touch the Reservoir—

You kindly ask for my Blossoms and Books—I have read but a little recently—Existence has overpowered Books. Today, I slew a Mushroom—

I felt as if the Grass was pleased
To have it intermit.
This Surreptitious Scion
Of Summer's circumspect.

The broadest words are so narrow we can easily cross them—but there is water deeper than those which has no Bridge. My Brother and Sisters would love to see you. Twice, you have gone—Master—

Would you but once come—

1874 1931

Mark Twain (Samuel L. Clemens)
1835–1910

One of America's most celebrated authors, Mark Twain launched his literary career with the publication in 1865 of "Jim Smiley and His Jumping Frog," a comic western tale that he heard in a mining camp not far from his cabin on Jackass Hill in the California gold country. Later titled "The Notorious Jumping Frog of Calaveras County," it was one of the many tall tales Twain heard in the mining camps where he had gone in 1861 when he was twenty-five. And while these tales were the fodder for his earliest work, they would prove to be only samplings of the dozens of yarns the gifted storyteller had in store for American readers.

Mark Twain's boyhood was spent in Hannibal, Missouri, a hamlet nestled on the banks of the Mississippi River, which served as the setting for many of his most famous tales. After his father's death in 1847, he left school at the age of eleven to be apprenticed to a printer. Here he developed a taste for writing and at the age of sixteen he had his first piece published in a Boston magazine. After four years as a journeyman printer, Twain set out to become a Mississippi riverboat pilot, but his career ended when the river was blockaded at the beginning of the Civil War. After a short term of soldiering as a Confederate volunteer, Twain went to Nevada, hoping to strike it rich in the silver fields. When his mining schemes failed, he joined the staff of the Virginia City Territorial Enterprise, *exchanged his real name, Samuel L. Clemens, for a pseudonym, "Mark Twain" (taken from the river leadsman's cry, meaning "two fathoms of water"), and began his career as a frontier humorist. In 1866, after six years as a miner, newspaper reporter, and lecturer in California, Nevada, and Hawaii, Twain went east, responding, he said, to "a 'call' to literature, of a low order—i.e., humorous." He took with him a reputation as "the wild humorist of the Pacific Slope" and a lively imagination that had led him to turn many of his newspaper "reports" into burlesques and comic sketches.*

While in New York, Twain was commissioned by a San Francisco paper to sail on a five-month voyage with a group of American tourists and to report their confrontations with the cultural and religious shrines of Europe and the Holy Land. On returning to America, Twain gathered his irreverent newspaper articles, revised them, and published them as Innocents Abroad *(1869). In this book Twain spares neither Europe nor America in his skewering of convention. Next came* Roughing It *(1872), a narrative of his original journey west. Both* Innocents Abroad *and* Roughing It *sold extremely well, establishing Twain as a very popular American author. His first attempt at novel writing was* The Gilded Age *(1873), on which he collaborated with the journalist and essayist Charles Dudley Warner (1829–1900). The novel gave its name to the boom times, the post-Civil War age of unbridled individualism and speculation, which it satirized. The satire was somewhat ironic, given that Twain had been living a decidedly "Gilded Age" lifestyle since his marriage to Olivia Landon (daughter of a wealthy coal merchant) in 1870.*

Twain's recollections of his early boyhood in Hannibal stirred him to write Tom Sawyer *(1876) and its sequel,* Huckleberry Finn *(1884). His memories of his three years as a "cub" and master pilot on the Mississippi inspired* Life on the Mississippi *(1883). By the time he wrote* A Connecticut Yankee in King Arthur's Court *(1889), with its angry satire on royalty, religion, and the chivalric ideals of Arthurian England, his work had become more serious and critical. By the 1890s, the amused tolerance that had once typified his writing had been displaced by increasingly bitter attacks on the injustices of society and the folly of humankind. In* Pudd'nhead Wilson *(1894) the humor was slight and the attacks on bigotry furious. By the turn of the century, with the publication of "The Man That Corrupted Hadleyburg" (1900), "To the Person Sitting in Darkness" (1901), and "The Mysterious Stranger" (1916), Twain's vision of humans as greedy, oafish, hypocritical, cruel, and predatory, was wholly apparent.*

Although traces of Twain's later pessimism are evident in his earliest works, his change from jovial humorist to despairing determinist has been explained as the result of a series of personal catastrophes. The deaths of his wife and two daughters left him embittered and lonely. The failure of his publishing firm and a series of bad financial investments brought him humiliation and bankruptcy, leading him to travel throughout the world on a lecture series to pay off his debts, a long and exhausting experience he recorded with barely disguised weariness in Following the Equator *(1897). In 1906, he began to record the details of much of the best and the worst of his life, portions of which appeared as his* Autobiography *(1924), published posthumously, as was the collection entitled* Letters from the Earth *(1962), which contained the most despairing of his pronouncements and his last raging volleys at the "damned human race."*

As a satirist, Twain employed his common, lowly characters as vernacular spokespeople to deflate the values of the official culture of his day and what he saw as the folly of American politics and imperialism. Though much of his work is weakened by the sound of his fury and his irrational quirks, other pieces, particularly his masterwork Huckleberry Finn, *clearly demonstrate the dual nature of Twain's earlier work. The novel displays the major achievements of Twain's art: the carefully controlled point of view with its implicit ironies expressed through the voice of a semiliterate boy, the masterful use of dialects, the balancing of romanticism and realism, humor and pathos, innocence and evil, all united for a journey down the river that serves as the mythic center of the novel. Originally judged to be simply another "boys' book" like* Tom Sawyer, *the story of Huck and Jim and the great river has proven to be an important literary contribution to U.S. discourse about race and slavery. Samuel Clemens's idyllic childhood on the Mississippi was set against the backdrop of slavery, and* Huckleberry Finn *reflects some of the contradictions between Mark Twain's nostalgia for his antebellum boyhood and his understanding of some of the aspects of the oppression of African Americans. Huck's famous voice is based, at least in part, on an African American boy named "Sociable Jimmy." The book is one of the first by a white American writer to depict a black character as fully human (for which Ralph Ellison praised Twain), but it also takes an ambiguous stance toward African Americans generally. What many critics see as the moral grandeur of Huck's decision to "go to hell" and help Jim escape has often seemed fatuous to many black readers. Since it was first published,* Huckleberry Finn *has been repeatedly banned in one area or another on the basis of its perceived stance on race—in some cases too progressive, in others too racist. In spite of and because of the controversy it stirs,* Huckleberry Finn *continues to be one of the most widely read novels in America.*

Through such works as Huckleberry Finn *and* Life on the Mississippi, *Twain shaped the world's view of America and had a profound impact on the development of American writing. His presentation of American material, his use of the vernacular idiom, his departures from the traditions of nineteenth-century gentility, and his sense of alienation influenced numerous American writers of the twentieth century, among them Ernest Hemingway, who voiced his opinion by writing, "All modern American literature comes from one book by Mark Twain called* Huckleberry Finn *. . . it's the best book we've had. . . . There was nothing before. There has been nothing so good since."*

FURTHER READING: W. Blair, *Mark Twain and Huck Finn,* 1960; J. Cox, *M. Twain: The Fate of Humor,* 1966; J. Kaplan, *Mr. Clemens and Mark Twain,* 1966; *The Mark Twain Papers,* ed.

R. Hirst, 1969–; *The Works of Mark Twain,* ed. J. Gerber, 1972–; L. Budd, *Our Mark Twain,* 1983; E. Emerson, *The Authentic Mark Twain,* 1984; J. Wilson, *A Reader's Guide to the Short Stories of Mark Twain,* 1987; *On Mark Twain,* ed. L. Budd and E. Cady, 1987; D. Sewall, *Mark Twain's Languages,* 1987; *Mark Twain's Own Autobiography,* ed. M. Kiskis, 1990; V. Doyno, *Writing Huck Finn,* 1991; J. Steinbrink, *Getting to Be Mark Twain,* 1991; *The Critical Response to Mark Twain's "Huckleberry Finn,"* ed. L. Champion, 1991; C. Dolmetsch, *Our Famous Guest: Mark Twain in Vienna,* 1992; *Mark Twain: Collected Tales, Sketches, Speeches, and Essays,* ed. L. Budd, 1992; H. Wonham, *Mark Twain and the Art of the Tall Tale,* 1992; *Satire or Evasion? Black Perspectives on Huckleberry Finn,* ed. J. Leonard, T. Tenney, and T. Davis, 1992; *The Mark Twain Encyclopedia,* ed. J. LeMaster and J. Wilson, 1993; J. Stahl, *Mark Twain: Culture and Gender,* 1994; G. Camfield, *Sentimental Twain,* 1994; S. Fishkin, *Was Huck Black? Mark Twain and African American Voices,* 1994; *The Adventures of Huckleberry Finn: Critical Controversies,* ed. G. Graff and J. Phelan, 1995; R. Knoper, *Acting Naturally: Mark Twain in the Culture of Performance,* 1995; *The Cambridge Companion to Mark Twain,* ed. F. Robinson, 1995; D. Florence, *Persona and Humor in Mark Twain's Early Writing,* 1995; B. Michelson, *Mark Twain on the Loose,* 1995; R. Rasmussen, *Mark Twain A to Z,* 1995; *Mark Twain's Humor,* ed. D. Sloane, 1995; R. Lowry, *"Littery Man": Mark Twain and Modern Authorship,* 1996; *The Oxford Mark Twain,* 29 vols., ed. S. Fishkin, 1996; P. Messent, *Mark Twain,* 1997; L. Skandera-Trombley, *Mark Twain in the Company of Women,* 1997; T. Quirk, *Mark Twain: A Study of the Short Fiction,* 1997; J. Chadwick-Joshua, *The Jim Dilemma: Reading Race in Huckleberry Finn,* 1998; *A Historical Guide to Mark Twain,* ed. S. Fishkin, 2002; *Constructing Mark Twain,* ed. L. Skandera-Trombley and M. Kiskis, 2002; G. Camfield, *The Oxford Reader's Companion to Mark Twain,* 2003; F. Kaplan, *The Singular Mark Twain,* 2003; L. Ziff, *Mark Twain,* 2004; R. Powers, *Mark Twain: A Life,* 2005; *A Companion to Mark Twain,* P. Messent and L. Budd, 2006.

TEXTS: "The Notorious Jumping Frog of Calaveras County," "Story of the Bad Little Boy," "Disgraceful Persecution of a Boy," and "A True Story" from *Mark Twain's Sketches: New and Old,* 1875; "Goldsmith's Friend Abroad Again" from *Galaxy,* 1870; "Sociable Jimmy" from *New York Times,* 1874; "Old Times on the Mississippi" from *Atlantic Monthly,* 1875; *Adventures of Huckleberry Finn,* 1885; "Fenimore Cooper's Literary Offences" from *How to Tell a Story and Other Essays,* 1897; "My First Lie, and How I Got Out of It" from *The Man That Corrupted Hadleyburg and Other Essays and Stories,* 1900; "To the Person Sitting in Darkness" from *North American Review,* 1901; "The War Prayer" from *Europe and Elsewhere,* 1923.

THE NOTORIOUS JUMPING FROG OF CALAVERAS[1] COUNTY

In compliance with the request of a friend of mine, who wrote me from the East, I called on good-natured, garrulous old Simon Wheeler, and inquired after my friend's friend, Leonidas W. Smiley, as requested to do, and I hereunto append the result. I have a lurking suspicion that *Leonidas W.* Smiley is a myth; that my friend never knew such a personage; and that he only conjectured that if I asked old Wheeler about him, it would remind him of his infamous *Jim* Smiley, and he would go to work and bore me to death with some exasperating reminiscence of him as long and as tedious as it should be useless to me. If that was the design, it succeeded.

[1]"Pronounced Cal-e-*va*-ras."—Twain's note. First published as "Jim Smiley and His Jumping Frog," in 1865. Later versions were titled "The Celebrated . . ." or, as here, "The Notorious Jumping Frog of Calaveras County."

I found Simon Wheeler dozing comfortably by the bar-room stove of the dilapidated tavern in the decayed mining camp of Angel's,[2] and I noticed that he was fat and bald-headed, and had an expression of winning gentleness and simplicity upon his tranquil countenance. He roused up, and gave me good day. I told him that a friend of mine had commissioned me to make some inquiries about a cherished companion of his boyhood named *Leonidas W.* Smiley—*Rev. Leonidas W.* Smiley, a young minister of the Gospel, who he had heard was at one time a resident of Angel's Camp. I added that if Mr. Wheeler could tell me anything about this Rev. Leonidas W. Smiley, I would feel under many obligations to him.

Simon Wheeler backed me into a corner and blockaded me there with his chair, and then sat down and reeled off the monotonous narrative which follows this paragraph. He never smiled, he never frowned, he never changed his voice from the gentle-flowing key to which he tuned his initial sentence, he never betrayed the slightest suspicion of enthusiasm; but all through the interminable narrative there ran a vein of impressive earnestness and sincerity, which showed me plainly that, so far from his imagining that there was anything ridiculous or funny about his story, he regarded it as a really important matter, and admired its two heroes as men of transcendent genius in *finesse.* I let him go on in his own way, and never interrupted him once.

"Rev. Leonidas W. H'm, Reverend Le—well, there was a feller here once by the name of *Jim* Smiley, in the winter of '49—or maybe it was the spring of '50—I don't recollect exactly, somehow, though what makes me think it was one or the other is because I remember the big flume[3] warn't finished when he first come to the camp; but anyway, he was the curiousest man about always betting on anything that turned up you ever see, if he could get anybody to bet on the other side; and if he couldn't he'd change sides. Any way that suited the other man would suit *him*—any way just so's he got a bet, *he* was satisfied. But still he was lucky, uncommon lucky; he most always come out winner. He was always ready and laying for a chance; there couldn't be no solit'ry thing mentioned but that feller'd offer to bet on it, and take ary side you please, as I was just telling you. If there was a horse-race, you'd find him flush or you'd find him busted at the end of it; if there was a dog-fight, he'd bet on it; if there was a cat-fight, he'd bet on it; if there was a chickenfight, he'd bet on it; why, if there was two birds setting on a fence, he would bet you which one would fly first; or if there was a camp-meeting, he would be there reg'lar to bet on Parson Walker, which he judged to be the best exhorter about here, and so he was too, and a good man. If he even see a straddle-bug[4] start to go anywheres, he would bet you how long it would take him to get to—to wherever he was going to, and if you took him up, he would foller that straddle-bug to Mexico but what he would find out where he was bound for and how long he was on the road. Lots of the boys here has seen that Smiley, and can tell you about him. Why, it never made no difference to *him*—he'd bet on *any* thing—the dangdest feller. Parson Walker's wife laid very sick once for a good while, and it seemed as if they warn't going to save her; but one morning he come in, and Smiley up and asked him

[2]Angel's Camp, a mining settlement in Calaveras County, California.

[3]An inclined waterway, usually made of wood, through which water is carried for use in hydraulic mining.

[4]A beetle with long legs, a tumble-bug.

how she was, and he said she was considerable better—thank the Lord for his inf'nite mercy—and coming on so smart that with the blessing of Prov'dence she'd get well yet; and Smiley, before he thought, says, 'Well, I'll resk two-and-a-half she don't anyway.'

"Thish-yer Smiley had a mare—the boys called her the fifteen-minute nag, but that was only in fun, you know, because of course she was faster than that—and he used to win money on that horse, for all she was so slow and always had the asthma, or the distemper, or the consumption, or something of that kind. They used to give her two or three hundred yards' start, and then pass her under way; but always at the fag end of the race she'd get excited and desperate like, and come cavorting and straddling up, and scattering her legs around limber, sometimes in the air, and sometimes out to one side among the fences, and kicking up m-o-r-e dust and raising m-o-r-e racket with her coughing and sneezing and blowing her nose—and *always* fetch up at the stand just about a neck ahead, as near as you could cipher it down.

"And he had a little small bull-pup, that to look at him you'd think he warn't worth a cent but to set around and look ornery and lay for a chance to steal something. But as soon as money was up on him he was a different dog; his under-jaw'd begin to stick out like the fo'castle of a steamboat, and his teeth would uncover and shine like the furnaces. And a dog might tackle him and bully-rag him, and bite him, and throw him over his shoulder two or three times, and Andrew Jackson—which was the name of the pup—Andrew Jackson would never let on but what *he* was satisfied, and hadn't expected nothing else—and the bets being doubled and doubled on the other side all the time, till the money was all up; and then all of a sudden he would grab that other dog jest by the j'int of his hind leg and freeze to it—not chaw, you understand, but only just grip and hang on till they throwed up the sponge, if it was a year. Smiley always come out winner on that pup, till he harnessed a dog once that didn't have no hind legs, because they'd been sawed off in a circular saw, and when the thing had gone along far enough, and the money was all up, and he come to make a snatch for his pet holt, he see in a minute how he'd been imposed on, and how the other dog had him in the door, so to speak, and he 'peared surprised, and then he looked sorter discouraged-like, and didn't try no more to win the fight, and so he got shucked out bad. He give Smiley a look, as much as to say his heart was broke, and it was *his* fault, for putting up a dog that hadn't no hind legs for him to take holt of, which was his main dependence in a fight, and then he limped off a piece and laid down and died. It was a good pup, was that Andrew Jackson, and would have made a name for hisself if he'd lived, for the stuff was in him and he had genius—I know it, because he hadn't no opportunities to speak of, and it don't stand to reason that a dog could make such a fight as he could under them circumstances if he hadn't no talent. It always makes me feel sorry when I think of that last fight of his'n, and the way it turned out.

"Well, thish-yer Smiley had rat-tarriers, and chicken cocks, and tomcats and all them kind of things, till you couldn't rest, and you couldn't fetch nothing for him to bet on but he'd match you. He ketched a frog one day, and took him home, and said he cal'lated to educate him; and so he never done nothing for three months but set in his back yard and learn that frog to jump. And you bet you he *did* learn him, too. He'd give him a little punch behind, and the next minute you'd see that frog whirling in the air like a doughnut—see him turn one summerset,[5] or maybe a couple, if he got a good start, and come down flat-footed and all right, like a cat. He got him up so in the matter of ketching flies, and kep' him in practice so constant, that he'd nail a fly every time as fur as he could see him. Smiley said all a frog wanted was education, and he could do 'most anything—and I believe him. Why, I've seen him set Dan'l Webster down here on this floor—Dan'l Webster was the name of the frog—and sing out, "Flies, Dan'l, flies!" and quicker'n you could wink he'd spring straight up and snake a fly off'n the counter there, and flop down on the floor ag'in as solid as a gob of mud, and fall to scratching the side of his head with his hind foot as indifferent as if he hadn't no idea he'd been doin' any more'n any frog might do. You never see a frog so modest and straight-for'ard as he was, for all he was so gifted. And when it come to fair and square jumping on a dead level, he could get over more ground at one straddle than any animal of his breed you ever see. Jumping on a dead level was his strong suit, you understand; and when it come to that, Smiley would ante up money on him as long as he had a red.[6] Smiley was monstrous proud of his frog, and well he might be, for fellers that had traveled and been everywheres all said he laid over any frog that ever *they* see.

"Well, Smiley kep' the beast in a little lattice box, and he used to fetch him down-town sometimes and lay for a bet. One day a feller—a stranger in the camp, he was—come acrost him with his box, and says:

"'What might it be that you've got in the box?'

"And Smiley says, sorter indifferent-like, 'It might be a parrot, or it might be a canary, maybe, but it ain't—it's only just a frog.'

"And the feller took it, and looked at it careful, and turned it round this way and that, and says, 'H'm—so 'tis. Well, what's *he* good for?'

"'Well,' Smiley says, easy and careless, 'he's good enough for *one* thing, I should judge—he can outjump any frog in Calaveras County.'

"The feller took the box again, and took another long, particular look, and give it back to Smiley, and says, very deliberate, 'Well,' he says, 'I don't see no p'ints about that frog that's any better'n any other frog.'

"'Maybe you don't,' Smiley says. 'Maybe you understand frogs and maybe you don't understand 'em; maybe you've had experience, and maybe you ain't only a amature, as it were. Anyways, I've got *my* opinion, and I'll resk forty dollars that he can outjump any frog in Calaveras County.'

"And the feller studied a minute, and then says, kinder sad-like, 'Well, I'm only a stranger here, and I ain't got no frog; but if I had a frog, I'd bet you.'

"And then Smiley says, 'That's all right—that's all right—if you'll hold my box a minute, I'll go and get you a frog.' And so the feller took the box, and put up his forty dollars along with Smiley's, and set down to wait.

"So he set there a good while thinking and thinking to himself, and then he got the frog out and prized his mouth open and took a teaspoon and filled him full of quail-shot—filled him pretty near up to his chin—and set him on the floor. Smiley he went to the swamp and slopped around in the mud for a long time, and finally he ketched a frog, and fetched him in, and give him to this feller, and says:

"Now, if you're ready, set him alongside of Dan'l, with his fore paws just even with Dan'l's, and I'll give the word.' Then he says, 'One—two—three *git!*' and

[5]Somersault. [6]A "red cent," a copper penny.

him and the feller touched up the frogs from behind, and the new frog hopped off lively, but Dan'l give a heave, and hysted up his shoulders—so—like a Frenchman, but it warn't no use—he couldn't budge; he was planted as solid as a church, and he couldn't no more stir than if he was anchored out. Smiley was a good deal surprised, and he was disgusted too, but he didn't have no idea what the matter was, of course.

"The feller took the money and started away; and when he was going out at the door, he sorter jerked his thumb over his shoulder—so—at Dan'l, and says again, very deliberate, 'Well,' he says, '*I* don't see no p'ints about that frog that's any better'n any other frog.'

"Smiley he stood scratching his head and looking down at Dan'l a long time, and at last he says, 'I do wonder what in the nation[7] that frog throw'd off for—I wonder if there ain't something the matter with him—he 'pears to look mighty baggy, somehow.' And he ketched Dan'l by the nap of the neck, and hefted him, and says, "Why blame my cats if he don't weigh five pound!" and turned him upside down and he belched out a double handful of shot. And then he see how it was, and he was the maddest man—he set the frog down and took out after that feller, but he never ketched him. And—"

[Here Simon Wheeler heard his name called from the front yard, and got up to see what was wanted.] And turning to me as he moved away, he said: "Just set where you are, stranger, and rest easy—I ain't going to be gone a second."

But, by your leave, I did not think that a continuation of the history of the enterprising vagabond *Jim* Smiley would be likely to afford me much information concerning the Rev. *Leonidas W.* Smiley, and so I started away.

At the door I met the sociable Wheeler returning, and he button-holed me and recommenced:

"Well, thish-yer Smiley had a yaller one-eyed cow that didn't have no tail, only just a short stump like a bannanner, and—"

However, lacking both time and inclination, I did not wait to hear about the afflicted cow, but took my leave.

1865 1875

STORY OF THE BAD LITTLE BOY

Once there was a bad little boy whose name was Jim—though, if you will notice, you will find that bad little boys are nearly always called James in your Sunday-school books. It was strange, but still it was true that this one was called Jim.

He didn't have any sick mother either—a sick mother who was pious and had the consumption,[1] and would be glad to lie down in the grave and be at rest but for the strong love she bore her boy, and the anxiety she felt that the world might be harsh and cold towards him when she was gone. Most bad boys in the Sunday-books are named James, and have sick mothers, who teach them to say, "Now, I lay me down," etc., and sing them to sleep with sweet, plaintive voices, and then kiss them good-night, and kneel down by the bedside and weep. But

[7]Euphemism for "damnation."
[1]Tuberculosis.

it was different with this fellow. He was named Jim, and there wasn't anything the matter with his mother—no consumption, nor anything of that kind. She was rather stout than otherwise, and she was not pious; moreover, she was not anxious on Jim's account. She said if he were to break his neck it wouldn't be much loss. She always spanked Jim to sleep, and she never kissed him good-night; on the contrary, she boxed his ears when she was ready to leave him.

Once this little bad boy stole the key of the pantry, and slipped in there and helped himself to some jam, and filled up the vessel with tar, so that his mother would never know the difference; but all at once a terrible feeling didn't come over him, and something didn't seem to whisper to him, "Is it right to disobey my mother? Isn't it sinful to do this? Where do bad little boys go who gobble up their good kind mother's jam?" and then he didn't kneel down all alone and promise never to be wicked any more, and rise up with a light, happy heart, and go and tell his mother all about it, and beg her forgiveness, and be blessed by her with tears of pride and thankfulness in her eyes. No; that is the way with all other bad boys in the books; but it happened otherwise with this Jim, strangely enough. He ate that jam, and said it was bully, in his sinful, vulgar way; and he put in the tar, and said that was bully also, and laughed, and observed "that the old woman would get up and snort" when she found it out; and when she did find it out, he denied knowing anything about it, and she whipped him severely, and he did the crying himself. Everything about this boy was curious—everything turned out differently with him from the way it does to the bad Jameses in the books.

Once he climbed up in Farmer Acorn's apple-tree to steal apples, and the limb didn't break, and he didn't fall and break his arm, and get torn by the farmer's great dog, and then languish on a sick bed for weeks, and repent and become good. Oh! no; he stole as many apples as he wanted and came down all right; and he was all ready for the dog too, and knocked him endways with a brick when he came to tear him. It was very strange—nothing like it ever happened in those mild little books with marbled backs,[2] and with pictures in them of men with swallow-tailed coats and bell-crowned hats, and pantaloons that are short in the legs, and women with the waists of their dresses under their arms, and no hoops on.[3] Nothing like it in any of the Sunday-school books.

Once he stole the teacher's pen-knife, and, when he was afraid it would be found out and he would get whipped, he slipped it into George Wilson's cap—poor Widow Wilson's son, the moral boy, the good little boy of the village, who always obeyed his mother, and never told an untruth, and was fond of his lessons, and infatuated with Sunday-school. And when the knife dropped from the cap, and poor George hung his head and blushed, as if in conscious guilt, and the grieved teacher charged the theft upon him, and was just in the very act of bringing the switch down upon his trembling shoulders, a white-haired, improbable justice of the peace did not suddenly appear in their midst, and strike an attitude and say, "Spare this noble boy—there stands the cowering culprit! I was passing the school-door at recess, and unseen myself, I saw the theft committed!" And then Jim didn't get whaled, and the venerable justice didn't read the tearful school a homily, and take George by the hand and say such a boy deserved to be exalted, and then tell him to come and make his home with

[2]Pretentious books with bindings colored to resemble marble.
[3]Twain describes the "proper" dress of genteel Americans in the mid-nineteenth century.

him, and sweep out the office, and make fires, and run errands, and chop wood, and study law, and help his wife do household labors, and have all the balance of the time to play, and get forty cents a month, and be happy. No; it would have happened that way in the books, but it didn't happen that way to Jim. No meddling old clam of a justice dropped in to make trouble, and so the model boy George got thrashed, and Jim was glad of it because, you know, Jim hated moral boys. Jim said he was "down on them milksops." Such was the coarse language of this bad, neglected boy.

But the strangest thing that ever happened to Jim was the time he went boating on Sunday, and didn't get drowned, and that other time that he got caught out in the storm when he was fishing on Sunday, and didn't get struck by lightning. Why, you might look, and look, all through the Sunday-school books from now till next Christmas, and you would never come across anything like this. Oh no; you would find that all the bad boys who go boating on Sunday invariably get drowned; and all the bad boys who get caught out in storms when they are fishing on Sunday infallibly get struck by lightning. Boats with bad boys in them always upset on Sunday, and it always storms when bad boys go fishing on the Sabbath. How this Jim ever escaped is a mystery to me.

This Jim bore a charmed life—that must have been the way of it. Nothing could hurt him. He even gave the elephant in the menagerie a plug of tobacco, and the elephant didn't knock the top of his head off with his trunk. He browsed around the cupboard after essence of peppermint, and didn't make a mistake and drink *aqua fortis.*[4] He stole his father's gun and went hunting on the Sabbath, and didn't shoot three or four of his fingers off. He struck his little sister on the temple with his fist when he was angry, and she didn't linger in pain through long summer days, and die with sweet words of forgiveness upon her lips that redoubled the anguish of his breaking heart. No; she got over it. He ran off and went to sea at last, and didn't come back and find himself sad and alone in the world, his loved ones sleeping in the quiet churchyard, and the vine-embowered home of his boyhood tumbled down and gone to decay. Ah! no; he came home as drunk as a piper, and got into the station-house[5] the first thing.

And he grew up and married, and raised a large family, and brained them all with an axe one night, and got wealthy by all manner of cheating and rascality; and now he is the infernalest wickedest scoundrel in his native village, and is universally respected, and belongs to the Legislature.

So you see there never was a bad James in the Sunday-school books that had such a streak of luck as this sinful Jim with the charmed life.

1865 1875

DISGRACEFUL PERSECUTION OF A BOY

In San Francisco, the other day, "A well-dressed boy, on his way to Sunday-school, was arrested and thrown into the city prison for stoning Chinamen."

What a commentary is this upon human justice! What sad prominence it gives to our human disposition to tyrannize over the weak! San Francisco has

[4]Nitric acid. [5]Jail.

little right to take credit to herself for her treatment of this poor boy. What had the child's education been? How should he suppose it was wrong to stone a Chinamen? Before we side against him, along with outraged San Francisco, let us give him a chance—let us hear the testimony for the defence.

He was a "well-dressed" boy, and a Sunday-school scholar, and therefore, the chances are that his parents were intelligent, well-to-do people, with just enough natural villainy in their composition to make them yearn after the daily papers, and enjoy them; and so this boy had opportunities to learn all through the week how to do right, as well as on Sunday.

It was in this way that he found out that the great commonwealth of California imposes an unlawful mining-tax upon John the foreigner, and allows Patrick the foreigner to dig gold for nothing—probably because the degraded Mongol is at no expense for whisky, and the refined Celt cannot exist without it.

It was in this way that he found out that a respectable number of the tax-gatherers—it would be unkind to say all of them—collect the tax twice, instead of once; and that, inasmuch as they do it solely to discourage Chinese immigration into the mines, it is a thing that is much applauded, and likewise regarded as being singularly facetious.

It was in this way that he found out that when a white man robs a sluice-box (by the term white man is meant Spaniards, Mexicans, Portuguese, Irish, Hondurans, Peruvians, Chileans, &c., &c.), they make him leave the camp; and when a Chinaman does that thing, they hang him.

It was in this way that he found out that in many districts of the vast Pacific coast, so strong is the wild, free love of justice in the hearts of the people, that whenever any secret and mysterious crime is committed, they say, "Let justice be done, though the heavens fall," and go straightway and swing a Chinaman.

It was in this way that he found out that by studying one half of each day's "local items," it would appear that the police of San Francisco were either asleep or dead, and by studying the other half it would seem that the reporters were gone mad with admiration of the energy, the virtue, the high effectiveness, and the dare-devil intrepidity of that very police—making exultant mention of how "the Argus-eyed officer So-and-so," captured a wretched knave of a Chinaman who was stealing chickens, and brought him gloriously to the city prison; and how "the gallant officer Such-and-such-a-one," quietly kept an eye on the movements of an "unsuspecting, almond-eyed son of Confucius" (your reporter is nothing if not facetious), following him around with that far-off look of vacancy and unconsciousness always so finely affected by that inscrutible being, the forty-dollar policeman, during a waking interval, and captured him at last in the very act of placing his hands in a suspicious manner upon a paper of tacks, left by the owner in an exposed situation; and how one officer performed this prodigious thing, and another officer that, and another the other—and pretty much every one of these performances having for a dazzling central incident a Chinaman guilty of a shilling's worth of crime, an unfortunate, whose misdemeanor must be hurraed into something enormous in order to keep the public from noticing how many really important rascals went uncaptured in the meantime, and how overrated those glorified policemen actually are.

It was in this way that the boy found out that the Legislature, being aware that the Constitution has made America an asylum for the poor and the oppressed of all nations, and that, therefore, the poor and oppressed who fly to our shelter must not be charged a disabling admission fee, made a law that every Chinaman, upon landing, must be *vaccinated* upon the wharf, and pay to the State's appointed officer *ten dollars* for the service, when there are plenty of doctors in San Francisco who would be glad enough to do it for him for fifty cents.

It was in this way that the boy found out that a Chinaman had no rights that any man was bound to respect; that he had no sorrows that any man was bound to pity; that neither his life nor his liberty was worth the purchase of a penny when a white man needed a scapegoat; that nobody loved Chinamen, nobody befriended them, nobody spared them suffering when it was convenient to inflict it; everybody, individuals, communities, the majesty of the State itself, joined in hating, abusing, and persecuting these humble strangers.

And, therefore, what *could* have been more natural than for this sunny-hearted boy, tripping along to Sunday-school, with his mind teeming with freshly-learned incentives to high and virtuous action, to say to himself—

"Ah, there goes a Chinaman! God will not love me if I do not stone him."

And for this he was arrested and put in the city jail.

Everything conspired to teach him that it was a high and holy thing to stone a Chinaman, and yet he no sooner attempts to do his duty that he is punished for it—he, poor chap, who has been aware all his life that one of the principal recreations of the police, out toward the Gold Refinery, is to look on with tranquil enjoyment while the butchers of Brannan Street set their dogs on unoffending Chinamen, and make them flee for their lives.[1]

Keeping in mind the tuition in the humanities which the entire "Pacific coast" gives its youth, there is a very sublimity of incongruity in the virtuous flourish with which the good city fathers of San Francisco proclaim (as they have lately done) that "The police are positively ordered to arrest all boys, of every description and wherever found, who engage in assaulting Chinamen."

Still, let us be truly glad they have made the order, notwithstanding its inconsistency; and let us rest perfectly confident the police are glad, too. Because there is no personal peril in arresting boys, provided they be of the small kind, and the reporters will have to laud their performances just as loyally as ever, or go without items.

The new form for local items in San Francisco will now be:—"The ever vigilant and efficient officer So-and-so succeeded, yesterday afternoon, in arresting Master Tommy Jones, after a determined resistance," etc., etc., followed by the customary statistics and final hurrah, with its unconscious sarcasm: "We are happy in being able to state that this is the forty-seventh boy arrested by this gallant officer since the new ordinance went into effect. The most extraordinary activity prevails in the police department. Nothing like it has been seen since we can remember."

1870 1875

[1]I have many such memories in my mind, but am thinking just at present of one particular one, where the Brannan Street butchers set their dogs on a Chinaman who was quietly passing with a basket of clothes on his head; and while the dogs mutilated his flesh, a butcher increased the hilarity of the occasion by knocking some of the Chinaman's teeth down his throat with half a brick. This incident sticks in my memory with a more malevolent tenacity, perhaps, on account of the fact that I was in the employ of a San Francisco journal at the time, and was not allowed to publish it because it might offend some of the peculiar element that subscribed for the paper. [Mark Twain's note]

from GOLDSMITH'S FRIEND ABROAD AGAIN[1]

Note.—No experience is set down in the following letters which had to be invented. Fancy is not needed to give variety to the history of a Chinaman's sojourn in America. Plain fact is amply sufficient.

LETTER I

Shanghai, 18—

DEAR CHING-FOO: It is all settled, and I am to leave my oppressed and overburdened native land and cross the sea to that noble realm where all are free and all equal, and none reviled or abused—America! America, whose precious privilege it is to call herself the Land of the Free and the Home of the Brave. We and all that are about us here look over the waves longingly, contrasting the privations of this our birthplace with the opulent comfort of that happy refuge. We know how America has welcomed the Germans and the Frenchmen and the stricken and sorrowing Irish, and we know how she has given them bread and work and liberty, and how grateful they are. And we know that America stands ready to welcome all other oppressed peoples and offer her abundance to all that come, without asking what their nationality is, or their creed or color. And, without being told it, we know that the foreign sufferers she has rescued from oppression and starvation are the most eager of her children to welcome us, because, having suffered themselves, they know what suffering is, and having been generously succored, they long to be generous to other unfortunates and thus show that magnanimity is not wasted upon them.

AH SONG HI

. . .

LETTER III

San Francisco, 18—

DEAR CHING-FOO: I stepped ashore jubilant! I wanted to dance, shout, sing, worship the generous Land of the Free and Home of the Brave. But as I walked from the gang-plank a man in a gray uniform[2] kicked me violently behind and told me to look out—so my employer translated it. As I turned, another officer of the same kind struck me with a short club and also instructed me to look out. I was about to take hold of my end of the pole which had mine and Hong-Wo's basket and things suspended from it, when a third officer hit me with his club to signify that I was to drop it, and then kicked me to signify that he was satisfied with my promptness. Another person came now, and searched all through

[1]Twain's title refers to *The Citizen of the World* (1762), by Oliver Goldsmith (1730–1774).
[2]A policeman.

our basket and bundles, emptying everything out on the dirty wharf. Then this person and another searched us all over. They found a little package of opium sewed into the artificial part of Hong-Wo's queue, and they took that, and also they made him prisoner and handed him over to an officer, who marched him away. They took his luggage, too, because of his crime, and as our luggage was so mixed together that they could not tell mine from his, they took it all. When I offered to help divide it, they kicked me and desired me to look out.

Having now no baggage and no companion, I told my employer that if he was willing, I would walk about a little and see the city and the people until he needed me. I did not like to seem disappointed with my reception in the good land of refuge for the oppressed, and so I looked and spoke as cheerily as I could. But he said, wait a minute—I must be vaccinated to prevent my taking the small-pox. I smiled and said I had already had the small-pox, as he could see by the marks, and so I need not wait to be "vaccinated," as he called it. But he said it was the law, and I must be vaccinated anyhow. The doctor would never let me pass, for the law obliged him to vaccinate all Chinamen and charge them *ten dollars apiece* for it, and I might be sure that no doctor who would be the servant of that law would let a fee slip through his fingers to accommodate any absurd fool who had seen fit to have the disease in some other country. And presently the doctor came and did his work and took my last penny—my ten dollars which were the hard savings of nearly a year and a half of labor and privation. Ah, if the law-makers had only known there were plenty of doctors in the city glad of a chance to vaccinate people for a dollar or two, they would never have put the price up so high against a poor friendless Irish, or Italian, or Chinese pauper fleeing to the good land to escape hunger and hard times.

AH SONG HI

LETTER IV

San Francisco, 18—

DEAR CHING FOO: I have been here about a month now, and am learning a little of the language every day. My employer was disappointed in the matter of hiring us out to service on the plantations in the far eastern portion of this continent. His enterprise was a failure, and so he set us all free, merely taking measures to secure to himself the repayment of the passage money which he paid for us. We are to make this good to him out of the first moneys we earn here. He says it is sixty dollars apiece.

We were thus set free about two weeks after we reached here. We had been massed together in some small houses up to that time, waiting. I walked forth to seek my fortune. I was to begin life a stranger in a strange land, without a friend, or a penny, or any clothes but those I had on my back. I had not any advantage on my side in the world—not one, except good health and the lack of any necessity to waste any time or anxiety on the watching of my baggage. No, I forget. I reflected that I had one prodigious advantage over paupers in other lands—I was in America! I was in the heaven-provided refuge of the oppressed and the forsaken!

Just as that comforting thought passed through my mind, some young men set a fierce dog on me. I tried to defend myself, but could do nothing. I retreated to the recess of a closed doorway, and there the dog had me at his mercy, flying at my throat and face or any part of my body that presented itself. I shrieked for help, but the young men only jeered and laughed. Two men in gray uniforms (policemen is their official title) looked on for a minute and then walked leisurely away. But a man stopped them and brought them back and told them it was a shame to leave me in such distress. Then the two policemen beat off the dog with small clubs, and a comfort it was to be rid of him, though I was just rags and blood from head to foot. The man who brought the policemen asked the young men why they abused me in that way, and they said they didn't want any of his meddling. And they said to him:

"This Ching divil comes till Ameriky to take the bread out o' dacent intilligent white men's mouths, and whin they try to defind their rights there's a dale o' fuss made about it."

They began to threaten my benefactor, and as he saw no friendliness in the faces that had gathered meanwhile, he went on his way. He got many a curse when he was gone. The policemen now told me I was under arrest and must go with them. I asked one of them what wrong I had done to anyone that I should be arrested, and he only struck me with his club and ordered me to "hold my yop." With a jeering crowd of street boys and loafers at my heels, I was taken up an alley and into a stone-paved dungeon which had large cells all down one side of it, with iron gates to them. I stood up by a desk while a man behind it wrote down certain things about me on a slate. One of my captors said:

"Enter a charge against this Chinaman of being disorderly and disturbing the peace."

I attempted to say a word, but he said:

"Silence! Now ye had better go slow, my good fellow. This is two or three times you've tried to get off some of your d_____d insolence. Lip won't do here. You've got to simmer down, and if you don't take to it paceable we'll see if we can't make you. Fat's your name?"

"Ah Song Hi."

"Alias what?"

I said I did not understand, and he said what he wanted was my *true* name, for he guessed I picked up this one since I stole my last chickens. They all laughed loudly at that.

Then they searched me. They found nothing, of course. They seemed very angry and asked who I supposed would "go my bail or pay my fine." When they explained these things to me, I said I had done nobody any harm, and why should I need to have bail or pay a fine? Both of them kicked me and warned me that I would find it to my advantage to try and be as civil as convenient. I protested that I had not meant anything disrespectful. Then one of them took me to one side and said:

"Now look here, Johnny, it's no use you playing softy wid us. We mane business, ye know; and the sooner ye put us on the scent of a V the asier ye'll save yerself from a dale of trouble. Ye can't get out o' this for anny less. Who's your frinds?"

I told him I had not a single friend in all the land of America, and that I was far from home and help, and very poor. And I begged him to let me go.

He gathered the slack of my blouse collar in his grip and jerked and shoved and hauled at me across the dungeon, and then unlocking an iron cell-gate thrust me in with a kick and said:

"Rot there, ye furrin spawn, till ye lairn that there's no room in America for the likes of ye or your nation."

AH SONG HI

. . .

LETTER VII

San Francisco, 18—

DEAR CHING FOO: I was glad enough when my case came up. An hour's experience had made me as tired of the police court as of the dungeon. I was not uneasy about the result of the trial, but on the contrary felt that as soon as the large auditory of Americans present should hear how that the rowdies had set the dogs on me when I was going peacefully along the street, and how, when I was all torn and bleeding, the officers arrested *me* and put me in jail and let the rowdies go free, the gallant hatred of oppression which is part of the very flesh and blood of every American would be stirred to its utmost, and I should be instantly set at liberty. In truth I began to fear for the other side. There in full view stood the ruffians who had misused me, and I began to fear that in the first burst of generous anger occasioned by the revealment of what they had done, they might be harshly handled, and possibly even banished from the country as having dishonored her and being no longer worthy to remain upon her sacred soil.

The official interpreter of the court asked my name, and then spoke it aloud so that all could hear. Supposing that all was now ready, I cleared my throat and began—in Chinese, because of my imperfect English:

"Hear, O high and mighty mandarin, and believe! As I went about my peaceful business in the street, behold certain men set a dog on me, and—"

"Silence!"

It was the judge that spoke. The interpreter whispered to me that I must keep perfectly still. He said that no statement would be received from me—I must only talk through my lawyer.

I had no lawyer. In the early morning a police court lawyer (termed, in the higher circles of society, a "shyster") had come into our den in the prison and offered his services to me, but I had been obliged to go without them because I could not pay in advance or give security. I told the interpreter how the matter stood. He said I must take my chances on the witnesses then. I glanced around, and my failing confidence revived.

"Call those four Chinamen yonder," I said. "They saw it all. I remember their faces perfectly. They will prove that the white men set the dog on me when I was not harming them."

"That won't work," said he. "In this country white men can testify against Chinamen all they want to, but *Chinamen ain't allowed to testify against white men!*"

What a chill went through me! And then I felt the indignant blood rise to my cheek at this libel upon the Home of the Oppressed, where all men are free and equal—perfectly equal—perfectly free and perfectly equal. I despised this Chinese-speaking Spaniard for his mean slander of the land that was sheltering and feeding him. I sorely wanted to sear his eyes with that sentence from the great and good American Declaration of Independence which we have copied in letters of gold in China and keep hung up over our family altars and in our temples—I mean the one about all men being created free and equal.

But woe is me, Ching Foo, the man was right. He was right, after all. There were my witnesses, but I could not use them. But now came a new hope. I saw my white friend come in, and I felt that he had come there purposely to help me. I may almost say I knew it. So I grew easier. He passed near enough to me to say under his breath, "Don't be afraid," and then I had no more fear. But presently the rowdies recognized him and began to scowl at him in no friendly way, and to make threatening signs at him. The two officers that arrested me fixed their eyes steadily on his; he bore it well, but gave in presently, and dropped his eyes. They still gazed at his eyebrows, and every time he raised his eyes he encountered their winkless stare—until after a minute or two he ceased to lift his head at all. The judge had been giving some instructions privately to someone for a little while, but now he was ready to resume business. Then the trial so unspeakably important to me, and freighted with such prodigious consequence to my wife and children, began, progressed, ended, was recorded in the books, noted down by the newspaper reporters, and *forgotten* by everybody but me—all in the little space of two minutes!

"Ah Song Hi, Chinaman. Officers O'Flannigan and O'Flaherty, witnesses. Come forward, Officer O'Flannigan."

OFFICER—"He was making a disturbance in Kearny street."

JUDGE—"Any witnesses on the other side?"

No response. The white friend raised his eyes—encountered Officer O'Flaherty's—blushed a little—got up and left the court-room, avoiding all glances and not taking his own from the floor.

JUDGE—"Give him five dollars or ten days."

In my desolation there was a glad surprise in the words; but it passed away when I found that he only meant that I was to be fined five dollars or imprisoned ten days longer in default of it.

There were twelve or fifteen Chinamen in our crowd of prisoners, charged with all manner of little thefts and misdemeanors, and their cases were quickly disposed of, as a general thing. When the charge came from a policeman or other white man, he made his statement and that was the end of it, unless the Chinaman's lawyer could find some white person to testify in his client's behalf; for, neither the accused Chinaman nor his countrymen being allowed to say anything, the statement of the officers or other white person was amply sufficient to convict. So, as I said, the Chinamen's cases were quickly disposed of, and fines and imprisonment promptly distributed among them. In one or two of the cases the charges against Chinamen were brought by Chinamen themselves, and in those cases Chinamen testified against Chinamen, through the interpreter; but the fixed rule of the court being that the preponderance of testimony in such cases should determine the prisoner's guilt or innocence, and there being nothing very binding about an oath administered to the lower orders of our people without the ancient solemnity of cutting off a chicken's head and burning some yellow paper at the same time, the interested parties naturally drum up a cloud of witnesses who are cheerfully willing to give evidence without ever knowing anything about the matter in hand. The judge has a custom of rattling through with as much of this testimony as his patience will stand, and then shutting off the rest and striking an average.

By noon all the business of the court was finished, and then several of us who had not fared well were remanded to prison; the judge went home; the lawyers, and officers, and spectators departed their several ways, and left the uncomely court-room to silence, solitude, and Stiggers, the newspaper reporter, which latter would now write up his items (said an ancient Chinaman to me), in the which he would praise all the policemen indiscriminately and abuse the Chinamen and dead people.

AH SONG HI
1870–1871

SOCIABLE JIMMY

[I sent the following home in a private letter, some time ago, from a certain little village. It was in the days when I was a public lecturer. I did it because I wished to preserve the memory of the most artless, sociable, and exhaustless talker I ever came across. He did not tell me a single remarkable thing, or one that was worth remembering; and yet he was himself so interested in his small marvels, and they flowed so naturally and comfortably from his lips that his talk got the upper hand of my interest, too, and I listened as one who receives a revelation. I took down what he had to say, just as he said it—without altering a word or adding one.]

I had my supper in my room this evening, (as usual,) and they sent up a bright, simple, guileless little darkey boy to wait on me—ten years old—a wide-eyed, observant little chap. I said:

"What is your name, my boy?"

"Dey calls me Jimmy, Sah, but my right name's James, Sah."

I said, "Sit down there, Jimmy—I'll not want you just yet."

He sat down in a big arm-chair, hung both his legs over one of the arms, and looked comfortable and conversational. I said:

"Did you have a pleasant Christmas, Jimmy?"

"No, sah—not zackly. I was kind o' sick den. But de res' o' de people *dey* had a good time—mos' all uv 'em had a good time. Dey all got drunk. Dey all gits drunk heah, every Christmas, and carries on and has awful good times."

"So you were sick, and lost it all. But unless you were *very* sick I should think that if you had asked the doctor he might have let you get—get—a *little* drunk—and—"

"Oh, no, Sah—I don' never git drunk—it's de *white* folks—dem's de ones I means. Pa used to git drunk, but dat was befo' I was big—but he's done quit. He don' git drunk no mo' now. Jis' takes one nip in de mawnin', now, cuz his stomach riles up, he sleeps so soun'. Jis' one nip—over to de s'loon—every mawnin'. He's powerful sickly—powerful—sometimes he can't hardly git aroun', he can't. He goes to de doctor every week—over to Ragtown. An' one time he tuck some stuff, you know, an' it mighty near *fetched* him. Ain't it dish-yer blue vittles dat's pison?—ain't dat it?—truck what you pisons cats wid?"

"Yes blue vittles [vitriol] is a very convincing article with a cat."

"Well, den, dat was it. De ole man, he tuck de bottle and shuck it, and shuck it—he seed it was blue, and he didn't know but it was blue mass, which he tuck mos' always—blue mass pills—but den he 'spected maybe dish-yer truck might be some other kin' o' blue stuff, and so he sot de bottle down, and drat if it wa'n't blue vittles, sho' nuff, when de doctor come. An' de doctor he say if he'd a tuck dat blue vittles it would a highsted him, *sho*'. People can't be too particlar 'bout sich things. Yes, in*deedy!*

"We ain't got no cats heah, 'bout dis hotel. Bill he don't like 'em. He can't stan' a cat no way. Ef he was to ketch one he'd slam it outen de winder in a minute. Yes he would. Bill's down on cats. So is de gals—waiter gals. When dey ketches a cat bummin' aroun' heah, dey jis' *scoops* him—'deed dey do. Dey snake him into de cistern—dey's been cats drownded in dat water dat's in yo' pitcher. I seed a cat in dare yistiddy—all swelled up like a pudd'n. I bet you dem gals done dat. Ma says if dey was to drownd a cat for *her,* de fust one of 'em she ketched she'd jam her into de cistern 'long wid de cat. Ma wouldn't *do* dat, I don't reckon, but 'deed an' double, she *said* she would. I can't kill a chicken—well, I kin wring its neck off, cuz dat don't make 'em no sufferin scacely; but I can't take and chop dey heads off, like some people kin. It makes me feel so—so—well, I kin see dat chicken nights so's I can't sleep. Mr. Dunlap, he's de richest man in dis town. Some people says dey's fo' thousan' people in dis town—dis city. But Bill he says dey aint but 'bout thirty-three hund'd. And Bill he knows, cuz he's lived heah all his life, do' dey *do* say he won't never set de river on fire. I don't know how dey fin' out—*I* wouldn't like to count all dem people. Some folks says dis town would be considerable bigger if it wa'n't on accounts of so much lan' all roun' it dat ain't got no houses on it." [This in perfect seriousness—dense simplicity—no idea of a joke.] "I reckon you seed dat church as you come along up street. Dat's an awful big church—awful high steeple. An' it's all solid stone, excep' jes' de top part—de steeple, I means—dat's wood. It falls off when de win' blows pooty hard, an' one time it stuck in a cow's back and busted de cow all to de mischief. It's gwine to kill some body yit, dat steeple is. A man—big man, he was—bigger'n what Bill is—he tuck it up dare and fixed it again—an' he didn't look no bigger'n a boy, he was so high up. Dat steeple's awful high. If you look out de winder you kin see it." [I looked out, and was speechless with awe and admiration—which gratified Jimmy beyond expression. The wonderful steeple was some sixty or seventy feet high, and had a clock-face on it.] "You see dat arrer on top o' dat steeple? Well, Sah, dat arrer is pooty nigh as big as dis do' [door.] I seed it when dey pulled it outen de cow. It mus' be awful to stan' in dat steeple when de clock is strikin'—dey say it is. Booms and jars so's you think the world's a comin' to an end. *I* wouldn't like to be up dare when de clock's a strikin'. Dat clock ain't jest a *striker,* like dese common clocks. It's a *bell*—jist a reglar *bell*—and it's a buster. You kin hear dat bell all over dis city. You ought to hear it boom, boom, boom, when dey's a fire. My sakes! Dey ain't got no bell like dat in Ragtown.

I ben to Ragtown, an' I ben mos' halfway to Dockery [thirty miles.] De bell in Ragtown's got so ole now she don't make no soun', scasely."

[Enter the landlord—a kindly man, verging toward fifty. My small friend, without changing position, says:]

"Bill, didn't you say dat dey was only thirty-three hund'd people in dis city?"

"Yes, about thirty-three hundred is the population now."

"Well, some folks says dey's fo' thousan'."

"Yes, I know they do; but it isn't correct."

"Bill, I don't think dis gen'lman kin eat a whole prairie-chicken, but dey *tole* me to fetch it all up."

"Yes, that's all right—he ordered it."

[Exit "Bill," leaving me comfortable; for I had been perishing to know who "Bill" was.]

"Bill he's de oldest. An' he's de bes', too. Dey's fo'teen in dis fam'ly—all boys an' gals. Bill he suppo'ts 'em all—an' he don' never complain—he's *real* good, Bill is. All dem brothers an' sisters o' his'n ain't no count—all ceptin' dat little teeny one dat fetched in dat milk. Dat's Kit, Sah. She ain't only nine year ole. But she's de mos' lady-like one in de whole bilin'. You don't never see Kit a-rairin' an' a-chargin' aroun' an' kickin' up her heels like de res' o' de gals in dis fam'ly does gen'ally. Dat was Nan dat you hearn a-cuttin' dem shines on de pi-anah while ago. An' sometimes ef she don't rastle dat pi-anah when she gits started! *Tab* can't hole a candle to *her,* but Tab kin *sing* like de very nation. She's de only one in dis family dat kin sing. You don't never hear a yelp outen Nan. Nan can't sing for shucks. I'd jes' lieves hear a tom-cat dat's got scalded. Dey's fo'-teen in dis fam'ly 'sides de ole man an' de ole 'ooman—all brothers an' sisters. But some of 'em don't live heah—do' Bill he suppo'ts 'em—lends 'em money, an' pays dey debts an' he'ps 'em along. I tell you Bill he's *real* good. Dey all gits drunk—all 'cep Bill. De ole man he gits drunk, too, same as de res' uv 'em. Bob, he don't git drunk much—jes' sloshes roun' de s'loons some, an' takes a dram sometimes. Bob he's next to Bill—'bout forty year old. Dey's all married—all de fam'ly's married—cep some of de gals. Dare's fo'teen. It's de biggest family in dese parts, dey say. Dare's Bill—Bill Nubbles—Nubbles is de name; Bill an' Griz, an' Duke, an' Bob, an' Nan, an' Tab, an' Kit, an' Sol, an' Si, an' Phil, an' Puss, an' Jake, an' Sal—Sal she's married an' got chil'en as big as I is—an' Hoss Nubbles, he's de las'. Hoss is what dey mos' always calls him, but he's got another name dat I somehow dis remember, it's so kind o' hard to git de hang of it." [Then observing that I had been taking down this extraordinary list of nicknames for adults, he said:] "But in de mawnin' I can ask Bill what's Hoss's other name, an' den I'll come up an' tell you when I fetches yo' breakfast. An' may be I done got some o' dem names mixed up, but Bill, he kin tell me. Dey's fo'teen."

By this time he was starting off with the waiter, (and a pecuniary consideration for his sociability,) and, as he went out, he paused a moment and said:

"Dad-fetch it, somehow dat other name don't come. But, anyways, you jes' read dem names over an' see if dey's fo'teen." [I read the list from the fly-leaf of Longfellow's *New-England Tragedies.*] "Dat's right, Sah. Dey's all down, I'll fetch up Hoss's other name in de mawnin', Sah. Don't you be oneasy."

[Exit, whistling "Listen to the Mockingbird."]

1874

A TRUE STORY, REPEATED WORD FOR WORD AS I HEARD IT

It was summer time, and twilight. We were sitting on the porch of the farm-house, on the summit of the hill, and "Aunt Rachel" was sitting respectfully below our level, on the steps,—for she was our servant, and colored. She was of mighty frame and stature; she was sixty years old, but her eye was undimmed and her strength unabated. She was a cheerful, hearty soul, and it was no more trouble for her to laugh than it is for a bird to sing. She was under fire, now, as usual when the day was done. That is to say, she was being chaffed without mercy, and was enjoying it. She would let off peal after peal of laughter, and then sit with her face in her hands and shake with throes of enjoyment which she could no longer get breath enough to express. At such a moment as this a thought occurred to me, and I said:

"Aunt Rachel, how is it that you've lived sixty years and never had any trouble?"

She stopped quaking. She paused, and there was a moment of silence. She turned her face over her shoulder toward me, and said, without even a smile in her voice:—

"Misto C———,[1] is you in 'arnest?"

It surprised me a good deal; and it sobered my manner and my speech, too. I said:—

"Why, I thought—that is, I meant—why, you *can't* have had any trouble. I've never heard you sigh, and never seen your eye when there wasn't a laugh in it."

She faced fairly around, now, and was full of earnestness.

"Has I had any trouble? Misto C———, I's gwyne to tell you, den I leave it to you. I was bawn down 'mongst de slaves; I knows all 'bout slavery, 'case I ben one of 'em my own se'f. Well, sah, my ole man—dat's my husban'—he was lovin' an' kind to me, jist as kind as you is to yo' own wife. An' we had chil'en—seven chil'en—an' we loved dem chil'en jist de same as you loves yo' chil'en. Dey was black, but de Lord can't make no chil'en so black but what dey mother loves 'em an' wouldn't give 'em up, no, not for anything dat's in dis whole world.

"Well sah, I was raised in ole Fo'ginny, but my mother she was raised in Mary-land; an' my *souls!* she was turrible when she'd git started! My *lan'!* but she'd make de fur fly! When she'd git into dem tantrums, she always had one word dat she said. She'd straighten herse'f up an' put her fists in her hips an' say, 'I want you to understan' dat I wa'nt bawn in the mash to be fool' by trash! I's one o' de ole Blue Hen's Chickens,[2] *I* is!' 'Ca'se, you see, dat's what folks dat's bawn in Maryland calls deyselves, an' dey's proud of it. Well, dat was her word. I don't ever forgit it, beca'se she said it so much, an' beca'se she said it one day when my little Henry tore his wris' awful, and most busted his head, right up at de top of his forehead, an' de niggers didn't fly aroun' fas' enough to 'tend to him. An' when dey talk' back at her, she up an' she says, 'Look-a-heah!' she says, 'I want you niggers to understan' dat I wa'nt bawn in de mash to be fool' by trash! I's one o' de ole Blue Hen's Chickens, *I* is!' an' den she clar' dat kitchen an' ban-dage' up de chile herse'f. So I says dat word, too, when I's riled.

"Well, bymeby my ole mistis say she's broke, an' she' got to sell all the nig-gers on de place. An' when I heah dat dey gwyne to sell us all off at oction in Richmon', oh de good gracious! I know what dat mean!"

[1]Mr. Clemens (Mark Twain's real name).

[2]A designation derived from the nickname of a famous regiment in the American Revolution.

Aunt Rachel had gradually risen, while she warmed to her subject, and now she towered above us, black against the stars.

"Dey put chains on us an' put us on a stan' as high as dis po'ch,—twenty foot high,—an' all de people stood aroun', crowds an' crowds. An' dey'd come up dah an' look at us all roun', an' squeeze our arm, an' make us git up an' walk, an' den say, 'Dis one too ole,' or 'Dis one lame,' or 'Dis one don't' mount to much.' An' dey sole my ole man, an' took him away, an' dey begin to sell my chil'en an' take *dem* away, an' I begin to cry; an' de man say, 'Shet up yo' dam blubberin',' an' hit me on de mouf wid his han'. An' when de las' one was gone but my little Henry, I grab' *him* clost up to my breas' so, an' I ris up an' says, 'You shan't take him away,' I says; 'I'll kill de man dat tetches him!' I says. But my little Henry whisper an' say, 'I gwyne to run away, an' den I work an' buy yo' freedom.' Oh, bless de chile, he always so good! But dey got him—dey got him, de men did; but I took and tear de clo'es mos' off of 'em an' beat 'em over de head wid my chain; an' *dey* give it to *me,* too, but I didn't mine dat.

"Well, dah was my ole man gone, an' all my chil'en, all my seven chil'en—an' six of 'em I hain't set eyes on ag'in to dis day, an' dat's twenty-two year ago las' Easter. De man dat bought me b'long' in Newbern, an' he took me dah. Well, bymeby de years roll on an' de waw come. My marster he was a Confedrit colonel, an' I was his family's cook. So when de Unions took dat town, dey all run away an' lef' me all by myse'f wid de other niggers in dat mons'us big house. So de big Union' officers move in dah, an' dey ask me would I cook for *dem.* 'Lord bless you,' says I, 'dat's what I's *for.*'

"Dey wa'nt no small-fry officers, mine you, dey was de biggest dey *is;* an' de way dey made dem sojers mosey roun'! De Gen'l he tole me to boss dat kitchen; an' he say, 'If anybody come meddlin' wid you, you jist make 'em walk chalk; don't you be afeared,' he say; 'you's 'mong frens, now.'

"Well, I thinks to myse'f, if my little Henry ever got a chance to run away, he'd make to de Norf, o' course. So one day I comes in dah whar de big officers was, in de parlor, an' I drops a kurtchy, so, an' I up an' tole 'em 'bout my Henry, dey a-listenin' to my troubles jist de same as if I was white folks; an' I says, 'What I come for is beca'se if he got away and got up Norf whar you gemmen comes from, you might 'a' seen him, maybe, an' could tell me so as I could fine him ag'in; he was very little, an' he had a sk-yar on his lef' wris', an' at de top of his forehead.' Den dey look mournful, an' de Gen'l say, 'How long sence you los' him?' an' I say, 'Thirteen year.' Den de Gen'l say, 'He wouldn't be little no mo', now—he's a man!'

"I never thought o' dat befo'! He was only dat little feller to *me,* yit. I never thought 'bout him growin' up an' bein' big. But I see it den. None o' de gemmen had run acrost him, so dey couldn't do nothin' for me. But all dat time, do' *I* didn't know it, my Henry *was* run off to de Norf, years an' years, an, he was a barber, too, an' worked for hisse'f. An' bymeby, when de waw come' he ups an' he says: 'I's done barberin',' he says, 'I's gwyne to fine my ole mammy, less'n she's dead.' So he sole out an' went to whar dey was recruitin', an' hired hisse'f out to de colonel for his servant; an' den he went all froo de battles everywhah, huntin' for his ole mammy; yes indeedy, he'd hire to fust one officer an' den another, tell he'd ransacked de whole Souf; but you see *I* didn't know nuffin 'bout *dis.* How was *I* gwyne to know it?

"Well, one night we had a big sojer ball; de sojers dah at Newbern[3] was always havin' balls an' carryin' on. Dey had 'em in my kitchen, heaps o' times, 'ca'se it was so big. Mine you, I was *down* on sich doin's; beca'se my place was wid de officers, an' it rasp me to have dem common sojers cavortin' roun' my kitchen like dat. But I alway' stood aroun' an' kep' things straight, I did; an' sometimes dey'd git my dander up, an' den I'd make 'em clar dat kitchen, mine I *tell* you!

"Well, one night—it was a Friday night—dey comes a whole plattoon f'm a *nigger* ridgment dat was on guard at de house,—de house was head-quarters, you know,—an' den I was jist a-*bilin'!* Mad? I was jist a-*boomin'!* I swelled aroun', an' swelled aroun'; I jist was a-itchin' for 'em to do somefin for to start me. *An'* dey was a-waltzin' an' a-dancin'! *my!* but dey was havin' a time! an' I jist a-swellin' an' a-swellin' up! Pooty soon, 'long comes *sich* a spruce young nigger a-sailin' down de room wid a yaller wench roun' de wais'; an' roun' an' roun' an' roun' dey went, enough to make a body drunk to look at 'em; an' when dey got abreas' o' me, dey went to kin' o' balancin' aroun' fust on one leg an' den on t'other, an' smilin' at my big red turban, an' makin' fun, an' I ups an' says '*Git* along wid you!—rubbage!' De young man's face kin' o' changed, all of a sudden, for 'bout a second, but den he went to smilin' ag'in, same as he was befo'. Well, 'bout dis time, in comes some niggers dat played music and b'long to de ban', an' dey *never* could git along widout puttin' on airs. An' de very fust air dey put on dat night, I lit into 'em! Dey laughed, an' dat made me wuss. De res' o' de niggers got to laughin', an' den my soul *alive* but I was hot! My eye was jist a-blazin'! I jist straightened myself up, so,—jist as I is now, plum to de ceilin', mos',—an' I digs my fists into my hips, an' I says, 'Look-a-heah!' I says, 'I want you niggers to understan' dat I wa'nt bawn in de mash to be fool' by trash! I's one o' de ole Blue Hen's Chickens, *I* is!' an' den I see dat young man stan' a-starin' an' stiff, lookin' kin' o' up at de ceilin' like he fo'got somefin, an' couldn't 'member it no mo'. Well, I jist march' on dem niggers,—so, lookin' like a gen'l,—an' dey jist cave' away befo' me an' out at de do'. An' as dis young man was a-goin' out, I heah him say to another nigger, 'Jim,' he says, 'you go 'long an' tell de cap'n I be on han' 'bout eight o'clock in de mawnin'; dey's somefin on my mine,' he says; 'I don't sleep no mo' dis night. You go 'long, he says, 'an' leave me by my own se'f.'

"Dis was 'bout one o'clock in de mawnin'. Well, 'bout seven, I was up an' on han', gittin' de officers' breakfast. I was a-stoopin' down by de stove,—jist so, same as if yo' foot was de stove,—an' I'd opened de stove do' wid my right han',—so, pushin' it back, jist as I pushes yo' foot,—an' I'd jist got de pan o' hot biscuits in my han' an' was 'bout to raise up, when I see a black face come aroun' under mine, an' de eyes a-lookin' up into mine, jist as I's a-lookin' up clost under yo' face now; an' I jist stopped *right dah,* an' never budged! jist gazed, an' gazed, so; an' de pan begin to tremble, an' all of a sudden I *knowed!* De pan drop' on de flo' an' I grab his lef' han' an' shove back his sleeve,—jist so, as I's doin' to you,—an' den I goes for his forehead an' push de hair back, so, an' 'Boy!' I says, 'if you an't my Henry, what is you doin' wid dis welt on yo' wris' an' dat sk-yar on yo' forehead? De Lord God ob heaven be praise', I got my own ag'in!'

"Oh, no, Misto C———, *I* hain't had no trouble. An' no *joy!*"

1874 1875

[3]New Bern, North Carolina.

from *OLD TIMES ON THE MISSISSIPPI*

I
[A BOY WANTS TO BE A PILOT]

When I was a boy, there was but one permanent ambition among my comrades in our village[1] on the west bank of the Mississippi River. That was, to be a steamboatman. We had transient ambitions of other sorts, but they were only transient. When a circus came and went, it left us all burning to become clowns; the first negro minstrel show that came to our section left us all suffering to try that kind of life; now and then we had a hope that if we lived and were good, God would permit us to be pirates. These ambitions faded out, each in its turn; but the ambition to be a steamboatman always remained.

Once a day a cheap, gaudy packet arrived upward from St. Louis, and another downward from Keokuk.[2] Before these events had transpired, the day was glorious with expectancy; after they had transpired, the day was a dead and empty thing. Not only the boys, but the whole village, felt this. After all these years I can picture that old time to myself now, just as it was then: the white town drowsing in the sunshine of a summer's morning; the streets empty, or pretty nearly so; one or two clerks sitting in front of the Water Street stores, with their splint-bottomed chairs tilted back against the wall, chins on breasts, hats slouched over their faces, asleep—with shingle-shavings enough around to show what broke them down; a sow and a litter of pigs loafing along the sidewalk, doing a good business in water-melon rinds and seeds; two or three lonely little freight piles scattered about the "levee;" a pile of "skids" on the slope of the stone-paved wharf, and the fragrant town drunkard asleep in the shadow of them; two or three wood flats at the head of the wharf, but nobody to listen to the peaceful lapping of the wavelets against them; the great Mississippi, the majestic, the magnificent Mississippi, rolling its mile-wide tide along, shining in the sun; the dense forest away on the other side; the "point" above the town, and the "point" below, bounding the river-glimpse and turning it into a sort of sea, and withal a very still and brilliant and lonely one. Presently a film of dark smoke appears above one of those remote "points;" instantly a negro drayman,[3] famous for his quick eye and prodigious voice, lifts up the cry, "S-t-e-a-m-boat a-comin'!" and the scene changes! The town drunkard stirs, the clerks wake up, a furious clatter of drays follows, every house and store pours out a human contribution, and all in a twinkling the dead town is alive and moving. Drays, carts, men, boys, all go hurrying from many quarters to a common centre, the wharf. Assembled there, the people fasten their eyes upon the coming boat as upon a wonder they are seeing for the first time. And the boat *is* rather a handsome sight, too. She is long and sharp and trim and pretty; she has two tall, fancy-topped chimneys, with a gilded device of some kind swung between them; a fanciful pilot-house, all glass and "gingerbread," perched on top of the "texas" deck[4] behind them; the paddle-boxes are gorgeous with a picture or with gilded rays above the boat's name; the boiler deck,

[1]Hannibal, Missouri. [2]Keokuk, Iowa, on the Mississippi River.
[3]Wagon driver. [4]Upper deck structure with the largest (hence "Texas") cabins.

the hurricane deck,[5] and the texas deck are fenced and ornamented with clean white railings; there is a flag gallantly flying from the jack-staff;[6] the furnace doors are open and the fires glaring bravely; the upper decks are black with passengers; the captain stands by the big bell, calm, imposing, the envy of all; great volumes of the blackest smoke are rolling and tumbling out of the chimneys—a husbanded grandeur created with a bit of pitch pine just before arriving at a town; the crew are grouped on the forecastle; the broad stage is run far out over the port bow, and an envied deck-hand stands picturesquely on the end of it with a coil of rope in his hand; the pent[7] steam is screaming through the gauge-cocks; the captain lifts his hand, a bell rings, the wheels stop; then they turn back, churning the water to foam, and the steamer is at rest. Then such a scramble as there is to get aboard, and to get ashore, and to take in freight and to discharge freight, all at one and the same time; and such a yelling and cursing as the mates facilitate it all with! Ten minutes later the steamer is under way again, with no flag on the jack-staff and no black smoke issuing from the chimneys. After ten more minutes the town is dead again, and the town drunkard asleep by the skids once more.

My father was a justice of the peace, and I supposed he possessed the power of life and death over all men and could hang anybody that offended him. This was distinction enough for me as a general thing; but the desire to be a steamboatman kept intruding, nevertheless. I first wanted to be a cabin-boy, so that I could come out with a white apron on and shake a table-cloth over the side, where all my old comrades could see me; later I thought I would rather be the deck-hand who stood on the end of the stage-plank with the coil of rope in his hand, because he was particularly conspicuous. But these were only day-dreams—they were too heavenly to be contemplated as real possibilities. By and by one of our boys went away. He was not heard of for a long time. At last he turned up as apprentice engineer or "striker" on a steamboat. This thing shook the bottom out of all my Sunday-school teachings. That boy had been notoriously worldly, and I just the reverse; yet he was exalted to this eminence, and I left in obscurity and misery. There was nothing generous about this fellow in his greatness. He would always manage to have a rusty bolt to scrub while his boat tarried at our town, and he would sit on the inside guard and scrub it, where we could all see him and envy him and loathe him. And whenever his boat was laid up he would come home and swell around the town in his blackest and greasiest clothes, so that nobody could help remembering that he was a steamboatman; and he used all sorts of steamboat technicalities in his talk, as if he were so used to them that he forgot common people could not understand them. He would speak of the "lab-board" side of a horse in an easy, natural way that would make one wish he was dead. And he was always talking about "St. Looy" like an old citizen; he would refer casually to occasions when he "was coming down Fourth Street," or when he was "passing by the Planter's House,"[8] or when there was a fire and he took a turn on the brakes of "the old Big Missouri;" and then he would go on and lie about how many towns the size of ours were burned down there that day. Two or three of the boys had long been persons of consideration among us because they had been to St. Louis once and

[5]Upper, promenade deck, open to the weather. [6]Short staff from which a ship's flag is flown.
[7]Confined, under high pressure. [8]Elegant St. Louis hotel.

had a vague general knowledge of its wonders, but the day of their glory was over now. They lapsed into a humble silence, and learned to disappear when the ruthless "cub"-engineer approached. This fellow had money, too, and hair oil. Also an ignorant silver watch and a showy brass watch chain. He wore a leather belt and used no suspenders. If ever a youth was cordially admired and hated by his comrades, this one was. No girl could withstand his charms. He "cut out" every boy in the village. When his boat blew up at last, it diffused a tranquil contentment among us such as we had not known for months. But when he came home the next week, alive, renowned, and appeared in church all battered up and bandaged, a shining hero, stared at and wondered over by everybody, it seemed to us that the partiality of Providence for an undeserving reptile had reached a point where it was open to criticism.

This creature's career could produce but one result, and it speedily followed. Boy after boy managed to get on the river. The minister's son became an engineer. The doctor's and the postmaster's sons became "mud clerks;" the wholesale liquor dealer's son became a bar-keeper on a boat; four sons of the chief merchant, and two sons of the county judge, became pilots. Pilot was the grandest position of all. The pilot, even in those days of trivial wages, had a princely salary—from a hundred and fifty to two hundred and fifty dollars a month, and no board to pay. Two months of his wages would pay a preacher's salary for a year. Now some of us were left disconsolate. We could not get on the river—at least our parents would not let us.

So by and by I ran away. I said I never would come home again till I was a pilot and could come in glory. But somehow I could not manage it. I went meekly aboard a few of the boats that lay packed together like sardines at the long St. Louis wharf, and very humbly inquired for the pilots, but got only a cold shoulder and short words from mates and clerks. I had to make the best of this sort of treatment for the time being, but I had comforting day-dreams of a future when I should be a great and honored pilot, with plenty of money, and could kill some of these mates and clerks and pay for them.

Months afterward the hope within me struggled to a reluctant death, and I found myself without an ambition. But I was ashamed to go home. I was in Cincinnati, and I set to work to map out a new career. I had been reading about the recent exploration of the river Amazon by an expedition sent out by our government. It was said that the expedition, owing to difficulties, had not thoroughly explored a part of the country lying about the head-waters, some four thousand miles from the mouth of the river. It was only about fifteen hundred miles from Cincinnati to New Orleans, where I could doubtless get a ship. I had thirty dollars left; I would go and complete the exploration of the Amazon. This was all the thought I gave to the subject. I never was great in matters of detail. I packed my valise, and took passage on an ancient tub called the Paul Jones, for New Orleans. For the sum of sixteen dollars I had the scarred and tarnished splendors of "her" main saloon principally to myself, for she was not a creature to attract the eye of wiser travelers.

When we presently got under way and went poking down the broad Ohio, I became a new being, and the subject of my own admiration. I was a traveler! A word never had tasted so good in my mouth before. I had an exultant sense of being bound for mysterious lands and distant climes which I never have felt in so uplifting a degree since. I was in such a glorified condition that all ignoble feelings departed out of me, and I was able to look down and pity the untraveled with a compassion that had hardly a trace of contempt in it. Still, when we stopped at villages and wood-yards, I could not help lolling carelessly upon the railings of the boiler deck to enjoy the envy of the country boys on the bank. If they did not seem to discover me, I presently sneezed to attract their attention, or moved to a position where they could not help seeing me. And as soon as I knew they saw me I gaped and stretched, and gave other signs of being mightily bored with traveling.

I kept my hat off all the time, and stayed where the wind and the sun could strike me, because I wanted to get the bronzed and weather-beaten look of an old traveler. Before the second day was half gone, I experienced a joy which filled me with the purest gratitude; for I saw that the skin had begun to blister and peel off my face and neck. I wished that the boys and girls at home could see me now.

We reached Louisville in time—at least the neighborhood of it. We stuck hard and fast on the rocks in the middle of the river and lay there four days. I was now beginning to feel a strong sense of being a part of the boat's family, a sort of infant son to the captain and younger brother to the officers. There is no estimating the pride I took in this grandeur, or the affection that began to swell and grow in me for those people. I could not know how the lordly steamboatman scorns that sort of presumption in a mere landsman. I particularly longed to acquire the least trifle of notice from the big stormy mate, and I was on the alert for an opportunity to do him a service to that end. It came at last. The riotous powwow of setting a spar was going on down on the forecastle, and I went down there and stood around in the way—or mostly skipping out of it—till the mate suddenly roared a general order for somebody to bring him a capstan bar. I sprang to his side and said: "Tell me where it is—I'll fetch it!"

If a rag-picker had offered to do a diplomatic service for the Emperor of Russia, the monarch could not have been more astounded than the mate was. He even stopped swearing. He stood and stared down at me. It took him ten seconds to scrape his disjointed remains together again. Then he said impressively: "Well, if this don't beat hell!" and turned to his work with the air of a man who had been confronted with a problem too abstruse for solution.

I crept away, and courted solitude for the rest of the day. I did not go to dinner;[9] I stayed away from supper until everybody else had finished. I did not feel so much like a member of the boat's family now as before. However, my spirits returned, in installments, as we pursued our way down the river. I was sorry I hated the mate so, because it was not in (young) human nature not to admire him. He was huge and muscular, his face was bearded and whiskered all over; he had a red woman and a blue woman tattooed on his right arm,—one on each side of a blue anchor with a red rope to it; and in the matter of profanity he was perfect. When he was getting out cargo at a landing, I was always where I could see and hear. He felt all the sublimity of his great position, and made the world feel it, too. When he gave even the simplest order, he discharged it like a blast of lightning, and sent a long, reverberating peal of profanity thundering after it. I could not help contrasting the way in which the average landsman would give an order, with the mate's way of doing it. If the landsman should wish the gang-plank moved a foot farther forward, he would probably say:

[9]The noon meal.

"James, or William, one of you push that plank forward, please;" but put the mate in his place, and he would roar out: "Here, now, start that gang-plank for'ard! Lively, now! *What*'re you about! Snatch it! *snatch* it! There! there! Aft again! aft again! Don't you hear me? Dash it to dash! are you going to *sleep* over it! '*Vast*[10] heaving. 'Vast heaving, I tell you! Going to heave it clear astern? WHERE're you going with that barrel! *for'ard* with it 'fore I make you swallow it, you dash-dash-dash-*dashed* split between a tired mud-turtle and a crippled hearse-horse!"

I wished I could talk like that.

When the soreness of my adventure with the mate had somewhat worn off, I began timidly to make up to the humblest official connected with the boat—the night watchman. He snubbed my advances at first, but I presently ventured to offer him a new chalk pipe, and that softened him. So he allowed me to sit with him by the big bell on the hurricane deck, and in time he melted into conversation. He could not well have helped it, I hung with such homage on his words and so plainly showed that I felt honored by his notice. He told me the names of dim capes and shadowy islands as we glided by them in the solemnity of the night, under the winking stars, and by and by got to talking about himself. He seemed over-sentimental for a man whose salary was six dollars a week—or rather he might have seemed so to an older person than I. But I drank in his words hungrily, and with a faith that might have moved mountains if it had been applied judiciously. What was it to me that he was soiled and seedy and fragrant with gin? What was it to me that his grammar was bad, his construction worse, and his profanity so void of art that it was an element of weakness rather than strength in his conversation? He was a wronged man, a man who had seen trouble, and that was enough for me. As he mellowed into his plaintive history his tears dripped upon the lantern in his lap, and I cried, too, from sympathy. He said he was the son of an English nobleman—either an earl or an alderman, he could not remember which, but believed he was both; his father, the nobleman, loved him, but his mother hated him from the cradle; and so while he was still a little boy he was sent to "one of them old, ancient colleges"—he couldn't remember which; and by and by his father died and his mother seized the property and "shook" him, as he phrased it. After his mother shook him, members of the nobility with whom he was acquainted used their influence to get him the position of "loblolly-boy[11] in a ship;" and from that point my watchman threw off all trammels of date and locality and branched out into a narrative that bristled all along with incredible adventures; a narrative that was so reeking with bloodshed and so crammed with hair-breadth escapes and the most engaging and unconscious personal villainies, that I sat speechless, enjoying, shuddering, wondering, worshiping.

It was a sore blight to find out afterwards that he was a low, vulgar, ignorant, sentimental, half-witted humbug, an untraveled native of the wilds of Illinois, who had absorbed wildcat literature and appropriated its marvels, until in time he had woven odds and ends of the mess into this yarn, and then gone on telling it to fledglings like me, until he had come to believe it himself.

1875

[10]"Avast": stop, halt.

[11]Boy who assists a ship's surgeon and prepares ointments and medicine (loblolly)

ADVENTURES OF HUCKLEBERRY FINN[1]

(TOM SAWYER'S COMRADE)

Scene: The Mississippi

Time: Forty to Fifty Years Ago[2]

NOTICE

Persons attempting to find a motive in this narrative will be prosecuted; persons attempting to find a moral in it will be banished; persons attempting to find a plot in it will be shot.

BY ORDER OF THE AUTHOR
PER G.G.,[3] CHIEF OF ORDNANCE.

EXPLANATORY

In this book a number of dialects are used, to wit: the Missouri negro dialect; the extremest form of the backwoods South-Western dialect; the ordinary "Pike-County"[4] dialect; and four modified varieties of this last. The shadings have not been done in a haphazard fashion, or by guess-work; but painstakingly, and with the trustworthy guidance and support of personal familiarity with these several forms of speech.

I make this explanation for the reason that without it many readers would suppose that all these characters were trying to talk alike and not succeeding.

THE AUTHOR

CHAPTER I

You don't know about me, without you have read a book by the name of "The Adventures of Tom Sawyer,"[5] but that ain't no matter. That book was made by Mr. Mark Twain, and he told the truth, mainly. There was things which he stretched, but mainly he told the truth. That is nothing. I never seen anybody but lied, one time or another, without it was Aunt Polly, or the widow, or maybe Mary.[6] Aunt Polly—Tom's Aunt Polly, she is—and Mary, and the Widow Douglas, is all told about in that book—which is mostly a true book; with some stretchers, as I said before.

Now the way that the book winds up, is this: Tom and me found the money that the robbers hid in the cave, and it made us rich. We got six thousand dollars apiece—all gold. It was an awful sight of money when it was piled up. Well,

[1]The text is taken from the first American edition (1885). A small number of typographical errors have been silently corrected.

[2]1845–1835.

[3]Twain probably refers to General (and former President) Ulysses S. Grant (1822–1885).

[4]In Missouri. [5]Published in 1876. [6]Tom Sawyer's cousin.

Judge Thatcher, he took it and put it out at interest, and it fetched u a day apiece, all the year round—more than a body could tell what to The Widow Douglas, she took me for her son, and allowed she woul ize me; but it was rough living in the house all the time, considering how dismal regular and decent the widow was in all her ways; and so when I couldn't stand it no longer, I lit out. I got into my old rags, and my sugar-hogshead[7] again, and was free and satisfied. But Tom Sawyer, he hunted me up and said he was going to start a band of robbers, and I might join if I would go back to the widow and be respectable. So I went back.

The widow she cried over me, and called me a poor lost lamb, and she called me a lot of other names, too, but she never meant no harm by it. She put me in them new clothes again, and I couldn't do nothing but sweat and sweat, and feel all cramped up. Well, then, the old thing commenced again. The widow rung a bell for supper, and you had to come to time. When you got to the table you couldn't go right to eating, but you had to wait for the widow to tuck down her head and grumble a little over the victuals, though there warn't really anything the matter with them. That is, nothing only everything was cooked by itself. In a barrel of odds and ends it is different; things get mixed up, and the juice kind of swaps around, and the things go better.

After supper she got out her book and learned me about Moses and the Bulrushers;[8] and I was in a sweat to find out all about him; but by-and-by she let it out that Moses had been dead a considerable long time; so then I didn't care no more about him; because I don't take no stock in dead people.

Pretty soon I wanted to smoke, and asked the widow to let me. But she wouldn't. She said it was a mean practice and wasn't clean, and I must try to not do it any more. That is just the way with some people. They get down on a thing when they don't know nothing about it. Here she was a bothering about Moses, which was no kin to her, and no use to anybody, being gone, you see, yet finding a power of fault with me for doing a thing that had some good in it. And she took snuff too; of course that was all right, because she done it herself.

Her sister, Miss Watson, a tolerable slim old maid, with goggles on, had just come to live with her, and took a set at me now, with a spelling-book. She worked me middling hard for about an hour, and then the widow made her ease up. I couldn't stood it much longer. Then for an hour it was deadly dull, and I was fidgety. Miss Watson would say, "Don't put your feet up there, Huckleberry;" and "don't scrunch up like that, Huckleberry—set up straight;" and pretty soon she would say, "Don't gap[9] and stretch like that, Huckleberry—why don't you try to behave?" Then she told me all about the bad place, and I said I wished I was there. She got mad, then, but I didn't mean no harm. All I wanted was to go somewheres; all I wanted was a change, I warn't particular. She said it was wicked to say what I said; said she wouldn't say it for the whole world; *she* was going to live so as to go to the good place. Well, I couldn't see no advantage in going where she was going, so I made up my mind I wouldn't try for it. But I never said so, because it would only make trouble, and wouldn't do no good.

Now she had got a start, and she went on and told me all about the good place. She said all a body would have to do there was to go around all day long

[7] A large barrel.
[8] The daughter of Pharaoh found the infant Moses in a basket of bulrushes (Exodus 2:1–10).
[9] Yawn.

with a harp and sing, forever and ever. So I didn't think much of it. But I never said so. I asked her if she reckoned Tom Sawyer would go there, and, she said, not by a considerable sight. I was glad about that, because I wanted him and me to be together.

Miss Watson she kept pecking at me, and it got tiresome and lonesome. By-and-by they fetched the niggers[10] in and had prayers, and then everybody was off to bed. I went up to my room with a piece of candle and put it on the table. Then I set down in a chair by the window and tried to think of something cheerful, but it warn't no use. I felt so lonesome I most wished I was dead. The stars was shining, and the leaves rustled in the woods ever so mournful; and I heard an owl, away off, who-whooing about somebody that was dead, and a whippowill and a dog crying about somebody that was going to die; and the wind was trying to whisper something to me and I couldn't make out what it was, and so it made the cold shivers run over me. Then away out in the woods I heard that kind of a sound that a ghost makes when it wants to tell about something that's on its mind and can't make itself understood, and so can't rest easy in its grave and has to go about that way every night grieving. I got so down-hearted and scared, I did wish I had some company. Pretty soon a spider went crawling up my shoulder, and I flipped it off and it lit in the candle; and before I could budge it was all shriveled up. I didn't need anybody to tell me that that was an awful bad sign and would fetch me some bad luck, so I was scared and most shook the clothes off of me. I got up and turned around in my tracks three times and crossed my breast every time; and then I tied up a little lock of my hair with a thread to keep witches away. But I hadn't no confidence. You do that when you've lost a horseshoe that you've found, instead of nailing it up over the door, but I hadn't ever heard anybody say it was any way to keep off bad luck when you'd killed a spider.

I set down again, a shaking all over, and got out my pipe for a smoke; for the house was all as still as death, now, and so the widow wouldn't know. Well, after a long time I heard the clock away off in the town go boom—boom—boom—twelve licks—and all still again—stiller than ever. Pretty soon I heard a twig snap, down in the dark amongst the trees—something was a stirring. I set still and listened. Directly I could just barely hear a "*me-yow me-yow!*" down there. That was good Says I, "*me-yow me-yow*" as soft as I could, and then I put out the light and scrambled out of the window onto the shed. Then I slipped down to the ground and crawled in amongst the trees, and sure enough there was Tom Sawyer waiting for me.

CHAPTER II

We went tip-toeing along a path amongst the trees back towards the end of the widow's garden, stooping down so as the branches wouldn't scrape our heads. When we was passing by the kitchen I fell over a root and made a noise. We

[10]I.e., slaves. "Nigger" (a corruption of "Negro") is considered abusive today. In pre–Civil War America it was widely used merely as a synonym for "slave." The presence of the term throughout the novel reflects Twain's effort to reproduce accurately the common speech of mid-nineteenth-century Americans, both black and white, and in its racist aspect the term provides a profoundly ironic backdrop for the novel's anti-racist revelations.

scrouched down and laid still. Miss Watson's big nigger, named Jim, was setting in the kitchen door; we could see him pretty clear, because there was a light behind him. He got up and stretched his neck out about a minute, listening. Then he says,

"Who dah?"

He listened some more; then he come tip-toeing down and stood right between us; we could a touched him, nearly. Well, likely it was minutes and minutes that there warn't a sound, and we all there so close together. There was a place on my ankle that got to itching; but I dasn't scratch it; and then my ear begun to itch; and next my back, right between my shoulders. Seemed like I'd die if I couldn't scratch. Well, I've noticed that thing plenty of times since. If you are with the quality,[11] or at a funeral, or trying to go to sleep when you ain't sleepy—if you are anywheres where it won't do for you to scratch, why you will itch all over in upwards of a thousand places. Pretty soon Jim says:

"Say—who is you? Whar is you? Dog my cats ef I didn't hear sumf'n. Well, I knows what I's gwyne to do. I's gwyne to set down here and listen tell I hears it agin."

So he set down on the ground betwixt me and Tom. He leaned his back up against a tree, and stretched his legs out till one of them most touched one of mine. My nose begun to itch. It itched till the tears come into my eyes. But I dasn't scratch. Then it begun to itch on the inside. Next I got to itching underneath. I didn't know how I was going to set still. This miserableness went on as much as six or seven minutes; but it seemed a sight longer than that. I was itching in eleven different places now. I reckoned I couldn't stand it more'n a minute longer, but I set my teeth hard and got ready to try. Just then Jim begun to breathe heavy; next he begun to snore—and then I was pretty soon comfortable agin.

Tom he made a sign to me—kind of a little noise with his mouth—and we went creeping away on our hands and knees. When we was ten foot off, Tom whispered to me and wanted to tie Jim to the tree for fun; but I said no; he might wake and make a disturbance, and then they'd find out I warn't in. Then Tom said he hadn't got candles enough, and he would slip in the kitchen and get some more. I didn't want him to try. I said Jim might wake up and come. But Tom wanted to resk it; so we slid in there and got three candles, and Tom laid five cents on the table for pay. Then we got out, and I was in a sweat to get away; but nothing would do Tom but he must crawl to where Jim was, on his hands and knees, and play something on him. I waited, and it seemed a good while, everything was so still and lonesome.

As soon as Tom was back, we cut along the path, around the garden fence, and by-and-by fetched up on the steep top of the hill the other side of the house. Tom said he slipped Jim's hat off of his head and hung it on a limb right over him, and Jim stirred a little, but he didn't wake. Afterwards Jim said the witches bewitched him and put him in a trance, and rode him all over the State, and then set him under the trees again and hung his hat on a limb to show who done it. And next time Jim told it he said they rode him down to New Orleans: and after that, every time he told it he spread it more and more, till by-and-by he said they rode him all over the world, and tired him most to death,

[11] I.e., quality people, the upper classes.

and his back was all over saddle-boils. Jim was monstrous proud about it, and he got so he wouldn't hardly notice the other niggers. Niggers would come miles to hear Jim tell about it, and he was more looked up to than any nigger in that country. Strange niggers would stand with their mouths open and look him all over, same as if he was a wonder. Niggers is always talking about witches in the dark by the kitchen fire; but whenever one was talking and letting on to know all about such things, Jim would happen in and say, "H'm! You know 'bout witches?" and that nigger was corked up and had to take a back seat. Jim always kept that five-center piece around his neck with a string and said it was a charm the devil give to him with his own hands and told him he could cure anybody with it and fetch witches whenever he wanted to, just by saying something to it; but he never told what it was he said to it. Niggers would come from all around there and give Jim anything they had, just for a sight of that five-center piece; but they wouldn't touch it, because the devil had had his hands on it. Jim was most ruined, for a servant, because he got so stuck up on account of having seen the devil and been rode by witches.

Well, when Tom and me got to the edge of the hill-top, we looked away down into the village and could see three or four lights twinkling, where there was sick folks, may be; and the stars over us was sparkling ever so fine; and down by the village was the river, a whole mile broad, and awful still and grand. We went down the hill and found Jo Harper, and Ben Rogers, and two or three more of the boys, hid in the old tanyard. So we unhitched a skiff[12] and pulled down the river two mile and a half, to the big scar on the hillside, and went ashore.

We went to a clump of bushes, and Tom made everybody swear to keep the secret, and then showed them a hole in the hill, right in the thickest part of the bushes. Then we lit the candles and crawled in on our hands and knees. We went about two hundred yards, and then the cave opened up. Tom poked about amongst the passages and pretty soon ducked under a wall where you wouldn't a noticed that there was a hole. We went along a narrow place and got into a kind of room, all damp and sweaty and cold, and there we stopped. Tom says:

"Now we'll start this band of robbers and call it Tom Sawyer's Gang. Everybody that wants to join has got to take an oath, and write his name in blood."

Everybody was willing. So Tom got out a sheet of paper that he had wrote the oath on, and read it. It swore every boy to stick to the band, and never tell any of the secrets; and if anybody done anything to any boy in the band, whichever boy was ordered to kill that person and his family must do it, and he mustn't eat and he mustn't sleep till he had killed them and hacked a cross in their breasts, which was the sign of the band. And nobody that didn't belong to the band could use that mark, and if he did he must be sued; and if he done it again he must be killed. And if anybody that belonged to the band told the secrets, he must have his throat cut, and then have his carcass burnt up and the ashes scattered all around, and his name blotted off the list with blood and never mentioned again by the gang, but have a curse put on it and be forgot, forever.

Everybody said it was a real beautiful oath, and asked Tom if he got it out of his own head. He said, some of it, but the rest was out of pirate books, and robber books, and every gang that was hightoned had it.

[12]A flat-bottomed rowboat.

Some thought it would be good to kill the *families* of boys that told the secrets. Tom said it was a good idea, so he took a pencil and wrote it in. Then Ben Rogers says:

"Here's Huck Finn, he hain't got no family—what you going to do 'bout him?"

"Well, hain't he got a father?" says Tom Sawyer.

"Yes, he's got a father, but you can't never find him, these days. He used to lay drunk with the hogs in the tanyard, but he hain't been seen in these parts for a year or more."

They talked it over, and they was going to rule me out, because they said every boy must have a family or somebody to kill, or else it wouldn't be fair and square for the others. Well, nobody could think of anything to do—everybody was stumped, and set still. I was most ready to cry; but all at once I thought of a way, and so I offered them Miss Watson—they could kill her. Everybody said:

"Oh, she'll do, she'll do. That's all right. Huck can come in."

Then they all stuck a pin in their fingers to get blood to sign with, and I made my mark on the paper.

"Now," says Ben Rogers, "what's the line of business of this Gang?"

"Nothing only robbery and murder," Tom said.

"But who are we going to rob? houses—or cattle—or——"

"Stuff! stealing cattle and such things ain't robbery, it's burglary," says Tom Sawyer. "We ain't burglars. That ain't no sort of style. We are highwaymen. We stop stages and carriages on the road, with masks on, and kill the people and take their watches and money."

"Must we always kill the people?"

"Oh, certainly. It's best. Some authorities think different, but mostly it's considered best to kill them. Except some that you bring to the cave here and keep them till they're ransomed."

"Ransomed? What's that?"

"I don't know. But that's what they do. I've seen it in books; and so of course that's what we've got to do."

"But how can we do it if we don't know what it is?"

"Why blame[13] it all, we've *got* to do it. Don't I tell you it's in the books? Do you want to go to doing different from what's in the books, and get things all muddled up?"

"Oh, that's all very fine to *say,* Tom Sawyer, but how in the nation[14] are these fellows going to be ransomed if we don't know how to do it to them? that's the thing *I* want to get at. Now what do you *reckon* it is?"

"Well, I don't know. But per'aps if we keep them till they're ransomed, it means that we keep them till they're dead."

"Now, that's something *like.* That'll answer. Why couldn't you said that before? We'll keep them till they ransomed to death—and a bothersome lot they'll be, too, eating up everything and always trying to get loose."

"How you talk, Ben Rogers. How can they get loose when there's a guard over them, ready to shoot them down if they move a peg?"

"A guard. Well that *is* good. So somebody's got to set up all night and never get any sleep, just so as to watch them. I think that's foolishness. Why can't a body take a club and ransom them as soon as they get here?"

[13]Euphemism for "damn." [14]Euphemism for "damnation."

"Because it ain't in the books so—that's why. Now Ben Rogers, do you want to do things regular, or don't you?—that's the idea. Don't you reckon that the people that made the books knows what's the correct thing to do? Do you reckon *you* can learn 'em anything? Not by a good deal. No, sir, we'll just go on and ransom them in the regular way."

"All right. I don't mind; but I say it's a fool way, anyhow. Say—do we kill the women, too?"

"Well, Ben Rogers, if I was as ignorant as you I wouldn't let on. Kill the women? No—nobody ever saw anything in the books like that. You fetch them to the cave, and you're always as polite as pie to them; and by-and-by they fall in love with you and never want to go home any more."

"Well, if that's the way, I'm agreed, but I don't take no stock in it. Mighty soon we'll have the cave so cluttered up with women, and fellows waiting to be ransomed, that there won't be no place for the robbers. But go ahead, I ain't got nothing to say."

Little Tommy Barnes was asleep, now, and when they waked him up he was scared, and cried, and said he wanted to go home to his ma, and didn't want to be a robber any more.

So they all made fun of him, and called him cry-baby, and that made him mad, and he said he would go straight and tell all the secrets. But Tom give him five cents to keep quiet, and said we would all go home and meet next week and rob somebody and kill some people.

Ben Rogers said he couldn't get out much, only Sundays, and so he wanted to begin next Sunday; but all the boys said it would be wicked to do it on Sunday, and that settled the thing. They agreed to get together and fix a day as soon as they could, and then we elected Tom Sawyer first captain and Jo Harper second captain of the Gang, and so started home.

I clumb up the shed and crept into my window just before day was breaking. My new clothes was all greased up and clayey, and I was dog-tired.

CHAPTER III

Well, I got a good going-over in the morning, from old Miss Watson, on account of my clothes; but the widow she didn't scold, but only cleaned off the grease and clay and looked so sorry that I thought I would behave a while if I could. Then Miss Watson she took me in the closet[15] and prayed, but nothing come of it. She told me to pray every day, and whatever I asked for I would get it. But it warn't so. I tried it. Once I got a fish-line, but no hooks. It warn't any good to me without hooks. I tried for the hooks three or four times, but somehow I couldn't make it work. By-and-by, one day, I asked Miss Watson to try for me, but she said I was a fool. She never told me why, and I couldn't make it out no way.

I set down, one time, back in the woods, and had a long think about it. I says to myself, if a body can get anything they pray for, why don't Deacon Winn get back the money he lost on pork? Why can't the widow get back her silver snuff-box that was stole? Why can't Miss Watson fat up? No, says I to myself,

[15]"When thou prayest, enter into thy closet. . . ." (Matthew 6:6).

there ain't nothing in it. I went and told the widow about it, and she said the thing a body could get by praying for it was "spiritual gifts." This was too many for me, but she told me what she meant—I must help other people, and do everything I could for other people, and look out for them all the time, and never think about myself. This was including Miss Watson, as I took it. I went out in the woods and turned it over in my mind a long time, but I couldn't see no advantage about it—except for the other people—so at last I reckoned I wouldn't worry about it any more, but just let it go. Sometimes the widow would take me one side and talk about Providence in a way to make a body's mouth water; but maybe next day Miss Watson would take hold and knock it all down again. I judged I could see that there was two Providences, and a poor chap would stand considerable show with the widow's Providence, but if Miss Watson's got him there warn't no help for him any more. I thought it all out, and reckoned I would belong to the widow's, if he wanted me, though I couldn't make out how he was agoing to be any better off then than what he was before, seeing I was so ignorant and so kind of low-down and ornery.

Pap he hadn't been seen for more than a year, and that was comfortable for me; I didn't want to see him no more. He used to always whale me when he was sober and could get his hands on me; though I used to take to the woods most of the time when he was around. Well, about this time he was found in the river drowned, about twelve mile above town, so people said. They judged it was him, anyway; said this drowned man was just his size, and was ragged, and had uncommon long hair—which was all like pap—but they couldn't make nothing out of the face, because it had been in the water so long it warn't much like a face at all. They said he was floating on his back in the water. They took him and buried him on the bank. But I warn't comfortable long, because I happened to think of something. I knowed mighty well that a drownded man don't float on his back, but on his face. So I knowed then, that this warn't pap, but a woman dressed up in a man's clothes. So I was uncomfortable again. I judged the old man would turn up again by-and-by, though I wished he wouldn't.

We played robber now and then about a month, and then I resigned. All the boys did. We hadn't robbed nobody, we hadn't killed any people, but only just pretended. We used to hop out of the woods and go charging down on hogdrovers and women in carts taking garden stuff to market, but we never hived[16] any of them. Tom Sawyer called the hogs "ingots," and he called the turnips and stuff "julery" and we would go to the cave and pow-wow[17] over what we had done and how many people we had killed and marked. But I couldn't see no profit in it. One time Tom sent a boy to run about town with a blazing stick, which he called a slogan (which was the sign for the Gang to get together), and then he said he had got secret news by his spies that next day a whole parcel of Spanish merchants and rich A-rabs was going to camp in Cave Hollow with two hundred elephants, and six hundred camels, and over a thousand "sumter" mules,[18] all loaded down with di'monds, and they didn't have only a guard of four hundred soldiers, and so we would lay in ambuscade, as he called it, and kill the lot and scoop the things. He said we must slick up our swords and guns, and get ready. He never could go after even a turnip-cart but he must have the swords and guns all scoured up for it; though they was only lath and broom-sticks, and you might scour at them till you rotted and then they warn't

[16]Got, captured. [17]Talk. [18]Pack mules.

worth a mouthful of ashes more than what they was before. I didn't believe we could lick such a crowd of Spaniards and A-rabs, but I wanted to see the camels and elephants, so I was on hand next day, Saturday, in the ambuscade; and when we got the word, we rushed out of the woods and down the hill. But there warn't no Spaniards and A-rabs, and there warn't no camels nor no elephants. It warn't anything but a Sunday-school picnic, and only a primer-class[19] at that. We busted it up, and chased the children up the hollow; but we never got anything but some doughnuts and jam, though Ben Rogers got a rag doll, and Jo Harper got a hymn-book and a tract; and then the teacher charged in and made us drop everything and cut. I didn't see no di'monds, and I told Tom Sawyer so. He said there was loads of them there, anyway; and he said there was A-rabs there, too, and elephants and things. I said, why couldn't we see them, then? He said if I warn't so ignorant, but had read a book called "Don Quixote,"[20] I would know without asking. He said it was all done by enchantment. He said there was hundreds of soldiers there, and elephants and treasure, and so on, but we had enemies which he called magicians, and they had turned the whole thing into an infant Sunday School, just out of spite. I said, all right, then the thing for us to do was to go for the magicians. Tom Sawyer said I was a numskull.

"Why," says he, "a magician could call up a lot of genies, and they would hash you up like nothing before you could say Jack Robinson. They are as tall as a tree and as big around as a church."

"Well," I says, "s'pose we got some genies to help *us*—can't we lick the other crowd then?"

"How you going to get them?"

"I don't know. How do *they* get them?"

"Why they rub an old tin lamp or an iron ring, and then the genies come tearing in, with the thunder and lightning a-ripping around and the smoke a-rolling, and everything they're told to do they up and do it. They don't think nothing of pulling a shot tower[21] up by the roots, and belting a Sunday-school superintendent over the head with it—or any other man."

"Who makes them tear around so?"

"Why, whoever rubs the lamp or the ring. They belong to whoever rubs the lamp or the ring, and they've got to do whatever he says. If he tells them to build a palace forty miles long, out of di'monds, and fill it full of chewing gum, or whatever you want, and fetch an emperor's daughter from China for you to marry, they've got to do it—and they've got to do it before sun-up next morning, too. And more—they've got to waltz that palace around over the country wherever you want it, you understand."

"Well," says I, "I think they are a pack of flatheads for not keeping the palace themselves 'stead of fooling them away like that. And what's more—if I was one of them I would see a man in Jericho before I would drop my business and come to him for the rubbing of an old tin lamp."

"How you talk, Huck Finn. Why, you'd *have* to come when he rubbed it, whether you wanted to or not."

[19]First grade.

[20]Cervantes' novel, published in 1605. In the novel, Don Quixote attacks a flock of sheep, later explaining that the sheep were actually an army of knights who had been transformed by a magician.

[21]A tower in which pellets are made by pouring molten lead from the top of the tower, through a sieve, into a tank of water.

"What, and I as high as a tree and as big as a church? Al
would come; but I lay I'd make that man climb the highest tr
the country."

"Shucks, it ain't no use to talk to you, Huck Finn. You don't seem to kno anything, somehow—perfect sap-head."

I thought all this over for two or three days, and then I reckoned I would see if there was anything in it. I got an old tin lamp and an iron ring and went out in the woods and rubbed and rubbed till I sweat like an Injun, calculating to build a palace and sell it; but it warn't no use, none of the genies come. So then I judged that all that stuff was only just one of Tom Sawyer's lies. I reckoned he believed in the A-rabs and the elephants, but as for me I think different. It had all the marks of a Sunday school.

CHAPTER IV

Well, three or four months run along, and it was well into the winter, now. I had been to school most all the time, and could spell, and read, and write just a little, and could say the multiplication table up to six times seven is thirty-five, and I don't reckon I could ever get any further than that if I was to live forever. I don't take no stock in mathematics, anyway.

At first I hated the school, but by-and-by I got so I could stand it. Whenever I got uncommon tired I played hookey, and the hiding I got next day done me good and cheered me up. So the longer I went to school the easier it got to be. I was getting sort of used to the widow's ways, too, and they warn't so raspy on me. Living in a house, and sleeping in a bed, pulled on me pretty tight, mostly, but before the cold weather I used to slide out and sleep in the woods, sometimes, and so that was a rest to me. I liked the old ways best, but I was getting so I liked the new ones, too, a little bit. The widow said I was coming along slow but sure, and doing very satisfactory. She said she warn't ashamed of me.

One morning I happened to turn over the salt-cellar at breakfast. I reached for some of it as quick as I could, to throw over my left shoulder and keep off the bad luck, but Miss Watson was in ahead of me, and crossed me off. She says, "Take your hands away, Huckleberry—what a mess you are always making." The widow put in a good word for me, but that warn't going to keep off the bad luck, I knowed that well enough. I started out, after breakfast, feeling worried and shaky, and wondering where it was going to fall on me, and what it was going to be. There is ways to keep off some kinds of bad luck, but this wasn't one of them kind; so I never tried to do anything, but just poked along low-spirited and on the watchout.

I went down the front garden and clumb over the stile,[22] where you go through the high board fence. There was an inch of new snow on the ground, and I seen somebody's tracks. They had come up from the quarry and stood around the stile a while, and then went on around the garden fence. It was funny they hadn't come in, after standing around so. I couldn't make it out. It was very curious, somehow. I was going to follow around, but I stooped down to look at the tracks first. I didn't notice anything at first, but next I did. There was a cross in the left boot-heel made with big nails, to keep off the devil.

[22]A set of steps up and over a fence.

I was up in a second and shinning down the hill. I looked over my shoulder every now and then, but I didn't see nobody. I was at Judge Thatcher's as quick as I could get there. He said:

"Why, my boy, you are all out of breath. Did you come for your interest?"

"No sir," I says; "is there some for me?"

"Oh, yes, a half-yearly is in, last night. Over a hundred and fifty dollars. Quite a fortune for you. You better let me invest it along with your six thousand, because if you take it you'll spend it."

"No, sir," I says, "I don't want to spend it. I don't want it at all—nor the six thousand, nuther. I want you to take it; I want to give it to you—the six thousand and all."

He looked surprised. He couldn't seem to make it out. He says:

"Why, what can you mean, my boy?"

I says, "Don't you ask me no questions about it, please. You'll take it—won't you?"

He says:

"Well I'm puzzled. Is something the matter?"

"Please take it," says I, "and don't ask me nothing—then I won't have to tell no lies."

He studied a while, and then he says:

"Oho-o. I think I see. You want to *sell* all your property to me—not give it. That's the correct idea."

Then he wrote something on a paper and read it over and says:

"There—you see it says 'for a consideration.' That means I have bought it of you and paid you for it. Here's a dollar for you. Now, you sign it."

So I signed it, and left.

Miss Watson's nigger, Jim, had a hair-ball as big as your fist, which had been took out of the fourth stomach of an ox, and he used to do magic with it. He said there was a spirit inside of it, and it knowed everything. So I went to him that night and told him pap was here again, for I found his tracks in the snow. What I wanted to know, was, what he was going to do, and was he going to stay? Jim got out his hair-ball, and said something over it, and then he held it up and dropped it on the floor. It fell pretty solid, and only rolled about an inch. Jim tried it again, and then another time, and it acted just the same. Jim got down on his knees and put his ear against it and listened. But it warn't no use; he said it wouldn't talk. He said sometimes it wouldn't talk without money. I told him I had an old slick counterfeit quarter that warn't no good because the brass showed through the silver a little, and it wouldn't pass nohow, even if the brass didn't show, because it was so slick it felt greasy, and so that would tell on it every time. (I reckoned I wouldn't say nothing about the dollar I got from the judge.) I said it was pretty bad money, but maybe the hair-ball would take it, because maybe it wouldn't know the difference. Jim smelt it, and bit it, and rubbed it, and said he would manage so the hair-ball would think it was good. He said he would split open a raw Irish potato and stick the quarter in between and keep it there all night, and next morning you couldn't see no brass, and it wouldn't feel greasy no more, and so anybody in town would take it in a minute, let alone a hair-ball. Well, I knowed a potato would do that, before, but I had forgot it.

Jim put the quarter under the hair-ball and got down and listened again. This time he said the hair-ball was all right. He said it would tell my whole fortune if I wanted it to. I says, go on. So the hair-ball talked to Jim, and Jim told it to me. He says:

"Yo' ole father doan' know, yit, what he's a-gwyne to do. Sometimes he spec he'll go 'way, en den agin he spec he'll stay. De bes' way is to res' easy en let de ole man take his own way. Dey's two angels hoverin' roun' 'bout him. One uv 'em is white en shiny, en t'other one is black. De white one gits him to go right, a little while, den de black one sail in en bust it all up. A body can't tell, yit, which one gwyne to fetch him at de las'. But you is all right. You gwyne to have considable trouble in yo' life, en considable joy. Sometimes you gwyne to git hurt, en sometimes you gwyne to git sick; but every time you's gwyne to git well agin. Dey's two gals flying' 'bout you in yo' life. One uv 'em's light en t'other one is dark. One is rich en t'other is po'. You's gwyne to marry de po' one fust en de rich one by-en-by. You wants to keep 'way fum de water as much as you kin, en don't run no resk, 'kase it's down in de bills[23] dat you's gwyne to git hung."

When I lit my candle and went up to my room that night, there set pap, his own self!

CHAPTER V

I had shut the door to. Then I turned around, and there he was. I used to be scared of him all the time, he tanned me so much. I reckoned I was scared now, too; but in a minute I see I was mistaken. That is, after the first jolt, as you may say, when my breath sort of hitched—he being so unexpected; but right away after, I see I warn't scared of him worth bothering about.

He was most fifty, and he looked it. His hair was long and tangled and greasy, and hung down, and you could see his eyes shining through like he was behind vines. It was all black, no gray; so was his long, mixed-up whiskers. There warn't no color in his face, where his face showed; it was white; not like another man's white, but a white to make a body sick, a white to make a body's flesh crawl—a tree-toad white, a fish-belly white. As for his clothes—just rags, that was all. He had one ankle resting on t'other knee; the boot on that foot was busted, and two of his toes stuck through, and he worked them now and then. His hat was laying on the floor; an old black slouch[24] with the top caved in, like a lid.

I stood a-looking at him; he set there a-looking at me, with his chair tilted back a little. I set the candle down. I noticed the window was up; so he had clumb in by the shed. He kept a-looking me all over. By-and-by he says:

"Starchy clothes—very. You think you're a good deal of a big-bug, *don't* you?"

"Maybe I am, maybe I ain't," I says.

"Don't you give me none o' your lip," says he. "You've put on considerable many frills since I been away. I'll take you down a peg before I get done with you. You're educated, too, they say; can read and write. You think you're better'n your father, now, don't you, because he can't? *I'll* take it out of you. Who

[23]I.e., decreed, predestined. [24]A felt hat with a wide brim.

told you you might meddle with such hifalut'n foolishness, hey?—who told you you could?"

"The widow. She told me."

"The widow, hey?—and who told the widow she could put in her shovel about a thing that ain't none of her business?"

"Nobody never told her."

"Well, I'll learn her how to meddle. An looky here—you drop that school, you hear? I'll learn people to bring up a boy to put on airs over his own father and let on to be better'n what *he* is. You lemme catch you fooling around that school again, you hear? Your mother couldn't read, and she couldn't write, nuther, before she died. None of the family couldn't, before *they* died. *I* can't; and here you're a-swelling yourself up like this. I ain't the man to stand it—you hear? Say—lemme hear you read."

I took up a book and begun something about General Washington and the wars. When I'd read about a half a minute, he fetched the book a whack with his hand and knocked it across the house. He says:

"It's so. You can do it. I had my doubts when you told me. Now looky here; you stop that putting on frills. I won't have it. I'll lay[25] for you, my smarty; and if I catch you about that school I'll tan you good. First you know you'll get religion, too. I never see such a son."

He took up a little blue and yaller picture of some cows and a boy, and says: "What's this?"

"It's something they give me for learning my lessons good."

He tore it up, and says—

"I'll give you something better—I'll give you a cowhide."[26]

He set there a-mumbling and a-growling a minute, and then he says—

"*Ain't* you a sweet-scented dandy, though? A bed; and bedclothes; and a look'n glass; and a piece of carpet on the floor—and your own father got to sleep with the hogs in the tanyard. I never see such a son. I bet I'll take some o'these frills out o' you before I'm done with you. Why there ain't no end to your airs—they say you're rich. Hey?—how's that?"

"I hain't got no money."

"It's a lie. Judge Thatcher's got it. You git it. I want it."

"They lie—that's how."

"Looky here—mind how you talk to me; I'm a-standing about all I can stand, now—so don't gimme no sass. I've been in town two days, and I hain't heard nothing but about you bein' rich. I heard about it away down the river, too. That's why I come. You git me that money to-morrow—I want it."

"I hain't got no money, I tell you. You ask Judge Thatcher; he'll tell you the same."

"All right. I'll ask him; and I'll make him pungle,[27] too, or I'll know the reason why. Say—how much you got in your pocket? I want it."

"I hain't got only a dollar, and I want that to—"

"It don't make no difference what you want it for—you just shell it out."

He took it and bit it to see if it was good, and then he said he was going down town to get some whiskey; said he hadn't had a drink all day. When he had got out on the shed, he put his head in again, and cussed me for putting on frills and trying to be better than him; and when I reckoned he was gone,

[25]Lie in wait. [26]A whipping with a cowhide strap. [27]Pay.

he come back and put his head in again, and told me to mind about that school, because he was going to lay for me and lick me if I didn't drop that.

Next day he was drunk, and he went to Judge Thatcher's and bullyragged[28] him and tried to make him give up the money, but he couldn't, and then he swore he'd make the law force him.

The judge and the widow went to law to get the court to take me away from him and let one of them be my guardian; but it was a new judge that had just come, and he didn't know the old man; so he said courts mustn't interfere and separate families if they could help it; said he'd druther not take a child away from its father. So Judge Thatcher and the widow had to quit on the business.

That pleased the old man till he couldn't rest. He said he'd cowhide me till I was black and blue if I didn't raise some money for him. I borrowed three dollars from Judge Thatcher, and pap took it and got drunk and went a-blowing around and cussing and whooping and carrying on; and he kept it up all over town, with a tin pan, till most midnight; then they jailed him, and next day they had him before court, and jailed him again for a week. But he said *he* was satisfied; said he was boss of his son, and he'd make it warm for *him*.

When he got out the new judge said he was agoing to make a man of him. So he took him to his own house, and dressed him up clean and nice, and had him to breakfast and dinner and supper with the family, and was just old pie to him, so to speak. And after supper he talked to him about temperance and such things till the old man cried, and said he'd been a fool, and fooled away his life; but now he was agoing to turn over a new leaf and be a man nobody wouldn't be ashamed of, and he hoped the judge would help him and not look down on him. The judge said he could hug him for them words; so *he* cried, and his wife she cried again; pap said he'd been a man that had always been misunderstood before, and the judge said he believed it. The old man said that what a man wanted that was down, was sympathy; and the judge said it was so; so they cried again. And when it was bedtime, the old man rose up and held out his hand, and says:

"Look at it gentlemen, and ladies all; take ahold of it; shake it. There's a hand that was the hand of a hog; but it ain't so no more; it's the hand of a man that's started in on a new life, and 'll die before he'll go back. You mark them words—don't forget I said them. It's a clean hand now; shake it—don't be afeard."

So they shook it, one after the other, all around, and cried. The judge's wife she kissed it. Then the old man he signed a pledge—made his mark.[29] The judge said it was the holiest time on record, or something like that. Then they tucked the old man into a beautiful room, which was the spare room, and in the night sometime he got powerful thirsty and clumb out onto the porch-roof and slid down a stanchion and traded his new coat for a jug of forty-rod,[30] and clumb back again and hada good old time; and towards daylight he crawled out again, drunk as a fiddler, and rolled off the porch and broke his left arm in two places and was most froze to death when somebody found him after sun-up. And when they come to look at that spare room, they had to take soundings[31] before they could navigate it.

[28]Scolded.
[29]I.e., signed, by making his mark, a written pledge to abstain from alcohol.
[30]Rotgut whiskey judged powerful enough to knock a man 40 rods, or 660 feet.
[31]Measure depths, go carefully.

The judge he felt kind of sore. He said he reckoned a body could reform the ole man with a shot-gun, maybe, but he didn't know no other way.

CHAPTER VI

Well, pretty soon the old man was up and around again, and then he went for Judge Thatcher in the courts to make him give up that money, and he went for me, too, for not stopping school. He catched me a couple of times and thrashed me, but I went to school just the same, and dodged him or out-run him most of the time. I didn't want to go to school much, before, but I reckoned I'd go now to spite pap. That law trial was a slow business; appeared like they warn't ever going to get started on it; so every now and then I'd borrow two or three dollars off of the judge for him, to keep from getting a cowhiding. Every time he got money he was drunk; and every time he got drunk he raised Cain around town; and every time he raised Cain he got jailed. He was just suited—this kind of thing was right in his line.

He got to hanging around the widow's too much, and so she told him at last, that if he didn't quit using[32] around there she would make trouble for him. Well, *wasn't* he mad? He said he would show who was Huck Finn's boss. So he watched out for me one day in the spring, and catched me, and took me up the river about three mile, in a skiff, and crossed over to the Illinois shore where it was woody and there warn't no houses but an old log hut in a place where the timber was so thick you couldn't find it if you didn't know where it was.

He kept me with him all the time, and I never got a chance to run off. We lived in that old cabin, and he always locked the door and put the key under his head, nights. He had a gun which he had stole, I reckon, and we fished and hunted, and that was what we lived on. Every little while he locked me in and went down to the store, three miles to the ferry, and traded fish and game for whisky and fetched it home and got drunk and had a good time, and licked me. The widow she found out where I was, by-and-by, and she sent a man over to try to get hold of me, but pap drove him off with the gun, and it warn't long after that till I was used to being where I was, and liked it, all but the cowhide part.

It was kind of lazy and jolly, laying off comfortable all day, smoking and fishing, and no books nor study. Two months or more ran along, and my clothes got to be all rags and dirt, and I didn't see how I'd ever got to like it so well at the widow's, where you had to wash, and eat on a plate, and comb up, and go to bed and get up regular, and be forever bothering over a book and have old Miss Watson pecking at you all the time. I didn't want to go back no more. I had stopped cussing, because the widow didn't like it; but now I took to it again because pap hadn't no objections. It was pretty good times up in the woods there, take it all around.

But by-and-by pap got too handy with his hick'ry, and I couldn't stand it. I was all over welts. He got to going away so much, too, and locking me in. Once he locked me in and was gone three days. It was dreadful lonesome. I judged he had got drowned and I wasn't ever going to get out any more. I was scared. I made up my mind I would fix up some way to leave there. I had tried to get

[32]Loitering.

out of that cabin many a time, but I couldn't find no way. Th
dow to it big enough for a dog to get through. I couldn't get u
was too narrow. The door was thick solid oak slabs. Pap was p
to leave a knife or anything in the cabin when he was away; I reckon I ha
ed the place over as much as a hundred times; well, I was 'most all the time at it, because it was about the only way to put in the time. But this time I found something at last; I found an old rusty wood-saw without any handle; it was laid in between a rafter and the clapboards of the roof. I greased it up and went to work. There was an old horse-blanket nailed against the logs at the far end of the cabin behind the table, to keep the wind from blowing through the chinks and putting the candle out. I got under the table and raised the blanket and went to work to saw a section of the big bottom log out, big enough to let me through. Well, it was a good long job, but I was getting towards the end of it when I heard pap's gun in the woods. I got rid of the signs of my work, and dropped the blanket and hid my saw, and pretty soon pap come in.

Pap warn't in a good humor—so he was his natural self. He said he was down to town, and everything was going wrong. His lawyer said he reckoned he would win his lawsuit and get the money, if they ever got started on the trial; but then there was ways to put it off a long time, and Judge Thatcher knowed how to do it. And he said people allowed there'd be another trial to get me away from him and give me to the widow for my guardian, and they guessed it would win, this time. This shook me up considerable, because I didn't want to go back to the widow's any more and be so cramped up and sivilized, as they called it. Then the old man got to cussing, and cussed everything and everybody he could think of, and then cussed them all over again to make sure he hadn't skipped any, and after that he polished off with a kind of a general cuss all around, including a considerable parcel of people which he didn't know the names of, and so called them what's-his-name, when he got to them, and went right along with his cussing.

He said he would like to see the widow get me. He said he would watch out, and if they tried to come any such game on him he knowed of a place six or seven mile off, to stow me in, where they might hunt till they dropped and they couldn't find me. That made me pretty uneasy again, but only for a minute; I reckoned I wouldn't stay on hand till he got that chance.

The old man made me go to the skiff and fetch the things he had got. There was a fifty-pound sack of corn meal, and a side of bacon, ammunition, and a four-gallon jug of whisky, and an old book and two newspapers for wadding,[33] besides some tow.[34] I toted up a load, and went back and set down on the bow of the skiff to rest. I thought it all over, and I reckoned I would walk off with the gun and some lines, and take to the woods when I run away. I guessed I wouldn't stay in one place, but just tramp right across the country, mostly night times, and hunt and fish to keep alive, and so get so far away that the old man nor the widow couldn't ever find me any more. I judged I would saw out and leave that night if pap got drunk enough, and I reckoned he would. I got so full of it I didn't notice how long I was staying, till the old man hollered and asked me whether I was asleep or drownded.

[33]The material used to make the plugs inserted to retain the powder charge in a muzzle-loading gun.

[34]Short fibers of flax or hemp.

I got the things all up to the cabin, and then it was about dark. When I was cooking supper the old man took a swig or two and got sort of warmed up, and went to ripping again. He had been drunk over in town, and laid in the gutter all night, and he was a sight to look at. A body would a thought he was Adam, he was just all mud.[35] Whenever his liquor begun to work, he most always went for the govment. This time he says:

"Call this a govment! why, just look at it and see what it's like. Here's the law a-standing ready to take a man's son away from him—a man's own son, which he has had all the trouble and all the anxiety and all the expense of raising. Yes, just as that man has got that son raised at last, and ready to go to work and begin to do suthin' for *him* and give him a rest, the law up and goes for him. And they call *that* govment! That ain't all, nuther. The law backs that old Judge Thatcher up and helps him to keep me out o' my property. Here's what the law does. The law takes a man worth six thousand dollars and upards, and jams him into an old trap of a cabin like this, and lets him go round in clothes that ain't fitten for a hog. They calls that govment! A man can't get his rights in a govment like this. Sometimes I've a mighty notion to just leave the country for good and all. Yes, and I *told* 'em so; I told old Thatcher so to his face. Lots of 'em heard me, and can tell what I said. Says I, for two cents I'd leave the blamed country and never come anear it agin. Them's the very words. I says, look at my hat—if you call it a hat—but the lid raises up and the rest of it goes down till it's below my chin, and then it ain't rightly a hat at all, but more like my head was shoved up through a jint o' stove-pipe. Look at it, says I—such a hat for me to wear—one of the wealthiest men in this town, if I could git my rights.

"Oh, yes, this is a wonderful govment, wonderful. Why, looky here. There was a free nigger there, from Ohio;[36] a mulatter,[37] most as white as a white man. He had the whitest shirt on you ever see, too, and the shiniest hat; and there ain't a man in that town that's got as fine clothes as what he had; and he had a gold watch and chain, and a silver-headed cane—the awfulest old gray-headed nabob[38] in the State. And what do you think? they said he was a p'fessor in a college, and could talk all kinds of languages, and knowed everything. And that ain't the wust. They said he could *vote,* when he was at home. Well, that let me out. Thinks I, what is the country a-coming to? It was 'lection day, and I was just about to go and vote, myself, if I warn't too drunk to get there; but when they told me there was a State in this country where they'd let a nigger vote, I drawed out. I says I'll never vote again. Them's the very words I said; they all heard me; and the country may rot for all me—I'll never vote agin as long as I live. And to see the cool way of that nigger—why, he wouldn't a give me the road if I hadn't shoved him out o' the way. I says to the people, why ain't this nigger put up at auction and sold?—that's what I want to know. And what do you reckon they said? Why, they said he couldn't be sold till he's been in the State six months,[39] and he hadn't been there that long yet.

[35]"And the Lord God formed man of the dust of the ground" (Genesis 2:7).
[36]Ohio had no slavery. [37]Mulatto, of mixed black and white ancestry.
[38]Man of prominence, a "swell."
[39]A reference to the fact that in some circumstances a free Negro could be legally re-enslaved.

There, now—that's a specimen. They call that a govment that can't sell a free nigger till he's been in the State six months. Here's a govment that calls itself a govment, and lets on to be a govment, and thinks it is a govment, and yet's got to set stock-still for six whole months before it can take ahold of a prowling, thieving, infernal, white-shirted free nigger, and—"

Pap was agoing on so, he never noticed where his old limber legs was taking him to, so he went head over heels over the tub of salt pork, and barked both shins, and the rest of his speech was all the hottest kind of language—mostly hove at the nigger and the govment, though he give the tub some, too, all along, here and there. He hopped around the cabin considerable, first on one leg and then on the other, holding first one shin and then the other one, and at last he let out with his left foot all of a sudden and fetched the tub a rattling kick. But it warn't good judgment, because that was the boot that had a couple of his toes leaking out of the front end of it; so now he raised a howl that fairly made a body's hair raise, and down he went in the dirt, and rolled there, and held his toes; and the cussing he done then laid over anything he had ever done previous. He said so his own self, afterwards. He had heard old Sowberry Hagan in his best days, and he said it laid over him, too; but I reckon that was sort of piling it on, maybe.

After supper pap took the jug, and said he had enough whisky there for two drunks and one delirium tremens. That was always his word. I judged he would be blind drunk in about an hour, and then I would steal the key, or saw myself out, one or t'other. He drank, and drank, and tumbled down on his blankets, by-and-by; but luck didn't run my way. He didn't go sound asleep, but was uneasy. He groaned, and moaned, and thrashed around this way and that, for a long time. At last I got so sleepy I couldn't keep my eyes open, all I could do, and so before I knowed what I was about I was sound asleep, and the candle burning.

I don't know how long I was asleep, but all of a sudden there was an awful scream and I was up. There was pap, looking wild and skipping around every which way and yelling about snakes. He said they was crawling up his leg; and then he would give a jump and scream, and say one had bit him on the cheek—but I couldn't see no snakes. He started and run round and round the cabin, hollering "take him off! take him off! he's biting me on the neck!" I never see a man look so wild in the eyes. Pretty soon he was all fagged out, and fell down panting; then he rolled over and over, wonderful fast, kicking things every which way, and striking and grabbing at the air with his hands, and screaming, and saying there was devils ahold of him. He wore out, by-and-by, and laid still a while, moaning. Then he laid stiller, and didn't make a sound. I could hear the owls and the wolves, away off in the woods, and it seemed terrible still. He was laying over by the corner. By-and-by he raised up, part way, and listened, with his head to one side. He says very low:

"Tramp—tramp—tramp; that's the dead; tramp—tramp—tramp; they're coming after me; but I won't go—Oh, they're here! don't touch me—don't! hands off!—they're cold; let go—Oh, let a poor devil alone!"

Then he went down on all fours and crawled off begging them to let him alone, and he rolled himself up in his blanket and wallowed in under the old pine table, still a-begging; and then he went to crying. I could hear him through the blanket.

By-and-by he rolled out and jumped up on his feet looking wild, and he see me and went for me. He chased me round and round the place, with a clasp-knife,[40] calling me the Angel of Death[41] and saying he would kill me and then I couldn't come for him no more. I begged, and told him I was only Huck, but he laughed *such* a screechy laugh, and roared and cussed, and kept on chasing me up. Once when I turned short and dodged under his arm he made a grab and got me by the jacket between my shoulders, and I thought I was gone; but I slid out of the jacket quick as lightning, and saved myself. Pretty soon he was all tired out, and dropped down with his back against the door, and said he would rest a minute and then kill me. He put his knife under him, and said he would sleep and get strong, and then he would see who was who.

So he dozed off, pretty soon. By-and-by I got the old split-bottom[42] chair and clumb up, as easy as I could, not to make any noise, and got down the gun. I slipped the ramrod down it to make sure it was loaded, and then I laid it across the turnip barrel, pointing towards pap, and set down behind it to wait for him to stir. And how slow and still the time did drag along.

CHAPTER VII

"Git up! what you 'bout!"

I opened my eyes and looked around, trying to make out where I was. It was after sun-up, and I had been sound asleep. Pap was standing over me, looking sour—and sick, too. He says—

"What you doin' with this gun?"

I judged he didn't know nothing about what he had been doing, so I says:

"Somebody tried to get in, so I was laying for him."

"Why didn't you roust me out?"

"Well, I tried to, but I couldn't; I couldn't budge you."

"Well, all right. Don't stand there palavering[43] all day, but out with you and see if there's a fish on the lines for breakfast. I'll be along in a minute."

He unlocked the door and I cleared out, up the river bank. I noticed some pieces of limbs and such things floating down, and a sprinkling of bark; so I know the river had begun to rise. I reckoned I would have great times, now, if I was over at the town. The June rise used to be always luck for me; because as soon as that rise begins, here comes cord-wood[44] floating down, and pieces of log rafts—sometimes a dozen logs together; so all you have to do is to catch them and sell them to the wood yards and the sawmill.

I went along up the bank with one eye out for pap and t'other one out for what the rise might fetch along. Well, all at once, here comes a canoe; just a beauty, too, about thirteen or fourteen foot long, riding high like a duck. I shot head first off of the bank, like a frog, clothes and all on, and struck out for the canoe. I just expected there'd be somebody laying down in it, because people often done that to fool folks, and when a chap had pulled a skiff out most to it

[40]A knife with a blade that folds into the clasp (handle).
[41]In folklore, the Angel of Death confronts those who are to die.
[42]I.e., with a seat of interwoven wood strips. [43]Talking idly, jabbering.
[44]Wood cut in four-foot lengths.

they'd raise up and laugh at him. But it warn't so this time. It was a dr sure enough, and I clumb in and paddled her ashore. Thinks I the old be glad when he sees this—she's worth ten dollars. But when I got to shore pap wasn't in sight yet, and as I was running her into a little creek like a gully, all hung over with vines and willows, I struck another idea; I judged I'd hide her good, and then, stead of taking to the woods when I run off, I'd go down the river about fifty mile and camp in one place for good, and not have such a rough time tramping on foot.

It was pretty close to the shanty, and I thought I heard the old man coming, all the time; but I got her hid; and then I out and looked around a bunch of willows, and there was the old man down the path a piece just drawing a bead on a bird with his gun. So he hadn't seen anything.

When he got along, I was hard at it taking up a "trot" line.[45] He abused me a little for being so slow, but I told him I fell in the river and that was what made me so long. I knowed he would see I was wet, and then he would be asking questions. We got five catfish off the lines and went home.

While we laid off, after breakfast, to sleep up, both of us being about wore out, I got to thinking that if I could fix up some way to keep pap and the widow from trying to follow me, it would be a certainer thing than trusting to luck to get far enough off before they missed me; you see, all kinds of things might happen. Well, I didn't see no way for a while, but by-and-by pap raised up a minute, to drink another barrel of water, and he says:

"Another time a man comes a-prowling round here, you roust me out, you hear? That man warn't here for no good. I'd a shot him. Next time, you roust me out, you hear?"

Then he dropped down and went to sleep again—but what he had been saying give me the very idea I wanted. I says to myself, I can fix it now so nobody won't think of following me.

About twelve o'clock we turned out and went along up the bank. The river was coming up pretty fast, and lots of drift-wood going by on the rise. By-and-by, along comes part of a log raft—nine logs fast together. We went out with the skiff and towed it ashore. Then we had dinner. Anybody but pap would a waited and see the day through, so as to catch more stuff; but that warn't pap's style. Nine logs was enough for one time; he must shove right over to town and sell. So he locked me in and took the skiff and started off towing the raft about half-past three. I judged he wouldn't come back that night. I waited till I reckoned he had got a good start, then I out with my saw and went to work on that log again. Before he was t'other side of the river I was out of the hole; him and his raft was just a speck on the water away off yonder.

I took the sack of corn meal and took it to where the canoe was hid, and shoved the vines and branches apart and put it in; then I done the same with the side of bacon; then the whisky jug; I took all the coffee and sugar there was, and all the ammunition; I took the wadding; I took the bucket and gourd, I took a dipper and a tin cup, and my old saw and two blankets, and the skillet and the coffee-pot. I took fish-lines and matches and other things—everything that was worth a cent. I cleaned out the place. I wanted an ax, but there wasn't any, only the one out at the wood pile, and I knowed why I was going to leave that. I fetched out the gun, and now I was done.

[45] A long fishing line (usually set in a stream or river) from which hooks are suspended at intervals.

I had wore the ground a good deal, crawling out of the hole and dragging out so many things. So I fixed that as good as I could from the outside by scattering dust on the place, which covered up the smoothness and the sawdust. Then I fixed the piece of log back into its place, and put two rocks under it and one against it to hold it there,—for it was bent up at that place, and didn't quite touch ground. If you stood four or five foot away and didn't know it was sawed, you wouldn't even notice it; and besides, this was the back of the cabin and it warn't likely anybody would go fooling around there.

It was all grass clear to the canoe; so I hadn't left a track. I followed around to see. I stood on the bank and looked out over the river. All safe. So I took the gun and went up a piece into the woods and was hunting around for some birds, when I see a wild pig; hogs soon went wild in them bottoms after they had got away from the prairie farms. I shot this fellow and took him into camp.

I took the ax and smashed in the door—I beat it and hacked it considerable, a-doing it. I fetched the pig in and took him back nearly to the table and hacked into his throat with the ax, and laid him down on the ground to bleed—I say ground, because it *was* ground—hard packed, and no boards. Well, next I took an old sack and put a lot of big rocks in it,—all I could drag—and I started it from the pig and dragged it to the door and through the woods down to the river and dumped it in, and down it sunk, out of sight. You could easy see that something had been dragged over the ground. I did wish Tom Sawyer was there, I know he would take an interest in this kind of business, and throw in the fancy touches. Nobody could spread himself like Tom Sawyer in such a thing as that.

Well, last I pulled out some of my hair, and bloodied the ax good, and stuck it on the back side, and slung the ax in the corner. Then I took up the pig and held him to my breast with my jacket (so he couldn't drip) till I got a good piece below the house and then dumped him into the river. Now I thought of something else. So I went and got the bag of meal and my old saw out of the canoe and fetched them to the house. I took the bag to where it used to stand, and ripped a hole in the bottom of it with the saw, for there warn't no knives and forks on the place—pap done everything with his clasp-knife, about the cooking. Then I carried the sack about a hundred yards across the grass and through the willows east of the house, to a shallow lake that was five mile wide and full of rushes—and ducks too, you might say, in the season. There was a slough or a creek leading out of it on the other side, that went miles away, I don't know where, but it didn't go to the river. The meal sifted out and made a little track all the way to the lake. I dropped pap's whetstone there too, so as to look like it had been done by accident. Then I tied up the rip in the meal sack with a string, so it wouldn't leak no more, and took it and my saw to the canoe again.

It was about dark, now; so I dropped the canoe down the river under some willows that hung over the bank, and waited for the moon to rise. I made fast to a willow; then I took a bite to eat, and by-and-by laid down in the canoe to smoke a pipe and lay out a plan. I says to myself, they'll follow the track of that sackful of rocks to the shore and then drag the river for me. And they'll follow that meal track to the lake and go browsing down the creek that leads out of it to find the robbers that killed me and took the things. They won't ever hunt the river for anything but my dead carcass. They'll soon get tired of that, and won't bother no more about me. All right; I can stop anywhere I want to. Jackson's Island is good enough for me; I know that island pretty well, and nobody ever comes there. And then I can paddle over to town, nights, and slink around and pick up things I want. Jackson's Island's the place.

I was pretty tired, and the first thing I knowed, I was asleep. When I woke up I didn't know where I was, for a minute. I set up and looked around, a little scared. Then I remembered. The river looked miles and miles across. The moon was so bright I could a counted the drift logs that went a slipping along, black and still, hundreds of yards out from shore. Everything was dead quiet, and it looked late, and *smelt* late. You know what I mean—I don't know the words to put it in.

I took a good gap and a stretch, and was just going to unhitch and start, when I heard a sound away over the water. I listened. Pretty soon I made it out. It was that dull kind of a regular sound that comes from oars working in rowlocks when it's a still night. I peeped out through the willow branches, and there it was—a skiff, away across the water. I couldn't tell how many was in it. It kept a-coming, and when it was abreast of me I see there warn't but one man in it. Thinks I, maybe it's pap, though I warn't expecting him. He dropped below me, with the current, and by-and-by he come a-swinging up shore in the easy water,[46] and he went by so close I could a reached out the gun and touched him. Well it *was* pap, sure enough—and sober, too, by the way he laid to his oars.

I didn't lose no time. The next minute I was a-spinning down stream soft but quick in the shade of the bank. I made two mile and a half, and then struck out a quarter of a mile or more towards the middle of the river, because pretty soon I would be passing the ferry landing and people might see me and hail me. I got out amongst the drift-wood and then laid down in the bottom of the canoe and let her float. I laid there and had a good rest and a smoke out of my pipe, looking away into the sky, not a cloud in it. The sky looks ever so deep when you lay down on your back in the moonshine; I never knowed it before. And how far a body can hear on the water such nights! I heard people talking at the ferry landing. I heard what they said, too, every word of it. One man said it was getting towards the long days and the short nights, now. T'other one said *this* warn't one of the short ones, he reckoned—and then they laughed, and he said it over again and they laughed again; then they waked up another fellow and told him, and laughed, but he didn't laugh; he ripped out something brisk and said let him alone. The first fellow said he 'lowed to tell it to his old woman—she would think it was pretty good; but he said that warn't nothing to some things he had said in his time. I heard one man say it was nearly three o'-clock, and he hoped daylight wouldn't wait more than about a week longer. After that, the talk got further and further away, and I couldn't make out the words any more, but I could hear the mumble; and now and then a laugh, too, but it seemed a long ways off.

I was away below the ferry now. I rise up and there was Jackson's Island, about two mile and a half down stream, heavy-timbered and standing up out of the middle of the river, big and dark and solid, like a steamboat without any lights. There warn't any signs of the bar at the head—it was all under water, now.

It didn't take me long to get there. I shot past the head at a ripping rate, the current was so swift, and then I got into the dead water[47] and landed on the side towards the Illinois shore. I run the canoe into a deep dent in the bank that I

[46]Where the current is slight. [47]I.e., without current.

out; I had to part the willow branches to get in; and when I made fast
ld a seen the canoe from the outside.

p and set down on a log at the head of the island and looked out on the big river and the black driftwood, and away over to the town, three mile away, where there was three or four lights twinkling. A monstrous big lumber raft was about a mile up stream, coming along down, with a lantern in the middle of it. I watched it come creeping down, and when it was most abreast of where I stood I heard a man say, "Stern oars, there! heave her head to stabboard!"[48] I heard that just as plain as if the man was by my side.

There was a little gray in the sky, now; so I stepped into the woods and laid down for a nap before breakfast.

CHAPTER VIII

The sun was up so high when I waked, that I judged it was after eight o'clock. I laid there in the grass and the cool shade, thinking about things and feeling rested and ruther comfortable and satisfied. I could see the sun out at one or two holes, but mostly it was big trees all about, and gloomy in there amongst them. There was freckled places on the ground where the light sifted down through the leaves, and the freckled places swapped about a little, showing there was a little breeze up there. A couple of squirrels set on a limb and jabbered at me very friendly.

I was powerful lazy and comfortable—didn't want to get up and cook breakfast. Well, I was dozing off again, when I thinks I hears a deep sound of "boom!" away up the river. I rouses up and rests on my elbow and listens; pretty soon I hears it again. I hopped up and went and looked out at a hole in the leaves, and I see a bunch of smoke laying on the water a long ways up—about abreast the ferry. And there was the ferry-boat full of people, floating along down. I knowed what was the matter, now. "Boom!" I see the white smoke squirt out of the ferry-boat's side. You see, they was firing cannon over the water, trying to make my carcass come to the top.

I was pretty hungry, but it warn't going to do for me to start a fire, because they might see the smoke. So I set there and watched the cannon-smoke and listened to the boom. The river was a mile wide, there, and it always looks pretty on a summer morning—so I was having a good enough time seeing them hunt for my remainders, if I only had a bite to eat. Well, then I happened to think how they always put quicksilver in loaves of bread and float them off because they always go right to the drownded carcass and stop there. So says I, I'll keep a lookout, and if any of them's floating around after me, I'll give them a show. I changed to the Illinois edge of the island to see what luck I could have, and I warn't disappointed. A big double loaf come along, and I most got it, with a long stick, but my foot slipped and she floated out further. Of course I was where the current set in the closest to the shore—I knowed enough for that. But by-and-by along comes another one, and this time I won. I took out the plug and shook out the little dab of quicksilver, and set my

[48]Starboard, the right-hand side of a ship viewed by an observer looking forward. Larboard, "labboard," the left-hand side.

teeth in. It was "baker's bread"[49]—what the quality eat—none of yo
down corn-pone.[50]

I got a good place amongst the leaves, and set there on a log, munching the bread and watching the ferry-boat, and very well satisfied. And then something struck me. I says, now I reckon the widow or the parson or somebody prayed that this bread would find me, and here it has gone and done it. So there ain't no doubt but there is something in that thing. That is, there's something in it when a body like the widow or the parson prays, but it don't work for me, and I reckon it don't work for only just the right kind.

I lit a pipe and had a good long smoke and went on watching. The ferry-boat was floating with the current, and I allowed I'd have a chance to see who was aboard when she come along, because she would come in close, where the bread did. When she'd got pretty well along down towards me, I put out my pipe and went to where I fished out the bread, and laid down behind a log on the bank in a little open place. Where the log forked I could peep through.

By-and-by she come along, and she drifted in so close that they could a run out a plank and walked ashore. Most everybody was on the boat. Pap, and Judge Thatcher, and Becky Thatcher, and Jo Harper, and Tom Sawyer, and his old Aunt Polly, and Sid and Mary, and plenty more. Everybody was talking about the murder, but the captain broke in and says:

"Look sharp, now; the current sets in the closest here, and maybe he's washed ashore and got tangled amongst the brush at the water's edge. I hope so, anyway."

I didn't hope so. They all crowded up and leaned over the rails, nearly in my face, and kept still, watching with all their might. I could see them first-rate, but they couldn't see me. Then the captain sung out:

"Stand away!" and the cannon let off such a blast right before me that it made me deef with the noise and pretty near blind with the smoke, and I judged I was gone. If they'd a had some bullets in, I reckon they'd a got the corpse they was after. Well, I see I warn't hurt, thanks to goodness. The boat floated on and went out of sight around the shoulder of the island. I could hear the booming, now and then, further and further off, and by-and-by after an hour, I didn't hear it no more. The island was three mile long. I judged they had got to the foot, and was giving it up. But they didn't yet a while. They turned around the foot of the island and started up the channel on the Missouri side, under steam, and booming once in a while as they went. I crossed over to that side and watched them. When they got abreast the head of the island they quit shooting and dropped over to the Missouri shore and went home to the town.

I knowed I was all right now. Nobody else would come a-hunting after me. I got my traps[51] out of the canoe and made me a nice camp in the thick woods. I made a kind of a tent out of my blankets to put my things under so the rain wouldn't get at them. I catched a cat-fish and haggled him open with my saw, and towards sundown I started my camp fire and had supper. Then I set out a line to catch some fish for breakfast.

When it was dark I set by my camp fire smoking, and feeling pretty satisfied; but by-and-by it got sort of lonesome, and so I went and set on the bank and listened to the currents washing along, and counted the stars and drift-logs and

[49]White bread, made from wheat flour, a luxury. [50]Corn bread. [51]Gear, belongings.

rafts that come down, and then went to bed; there ain't no better way to put in time when you are lonesome; you can't stay so, you soon get over it.

And so for three days and nights. No difference—just the same thing. But the next day I went exploring around down through the island. I was boss of it; it all belonged to me, so to say, and I wanted to know all about it; but mainly I wanted to put in the time. I found plenty strawberries, ripe and prime; and green summer-grapes, and green razberries; and the green blackberries was just beginning to show. They would all come handy by-and-by, I judged.

Well, I went fooling along in the deep woods till I judged I warn't far from the foot of the island. I had my gun along, but I hadn't shot nothing; it was for protection; thought I would kill some game nigh home. About this time I mighty near stepped on a good sized snake, and it went sliding off through the grass and flowers, and I after it, trying to get a shot at it. I clipped along, and all of a sudden I bounded right on to the ashes of a camp fire that was still smoking.

My heart jumped up amongst my lungs. I never waited for to look further, but uncocked my gun and went sneaking back on my tiptoes as fast as ever I could. Every now and then I stopped a second, amongst the thick leaves, and listened; but my breath come so hard I couldn't hear nothing else. I slunk along another piece further, then listened again; and so on, and so on; if I see a stump, I took it for a man; if I trod on a stick and broke it, it made me feel like a person had cut one of my breaths in two and I only got half, and the short half, too.

When I got to camp I warn't feeling very brash, there warn't much sand in my craw;[52] but I says, this ain't no time to be fooling around. So I got all my traps into my canoe again so as to have them out of sight, and I put out the fire and scattered the ashes around to look like an old last year's camp, and then clumb a tree.

I reckon I was up in the tree two hours; but I didn't see nothing, I didn't hear nothing—I only *thought* I heard and seen as much as a thousand things. Well, I couldn't stay up there forever; so at last I got down, but I kept in the thick woods and on the lookout all the time. All I could get to eat was berries and what was left over from breakfast.

By the time it was night I was pretty hungry. So when it was good and dark, I slid out from shore before moonrise and paddled over to the Illinois bank—about a quarter of a mile. I went out in the woods and cooked a supper, and I had about made up my mind I would stay there all night, when I hear a *plunkety-plunk, plunkety-plunk,* and says to myself, horses coming; and next I heard people's voices. I got everything into the canoe as quick as I could, and then went creeping through the woods to see what I could find out. I hadn't got far when I hear a man say:

"We better camp here, if we can find a good place; the horses is about beat out. Let's look around."

I didn't wait, but shoved out and paddled away easy. I tied up in the old place, and reckoned I would sleep in the canoe.

I didn't sleep much. I couldn't, somehow, for thinking. And every time I waked up I thought somebody had me by the neck. So the sleep didn't do me no good. By-and-by I says to myself, I can't live this way; I'm agoing to find out who it is that's here on the island with me; I'll find it out or bust. Well, I felt better, right off.

[52] I.e., courage in my heart.

So I took my paddle and slid out from shore just a step or two, ar the canoe drop along down amongst the shadows. The moon was sh outside of the shadows it made it most as light as day. I poked along well onto an hour, everything still as rocks and sound asleep. Well by this time I was most down to the foot of the island. A little ripply, cool breeze begun to blow, and that was as good as saying the night was about done. I give her a turn with the paddle and brung her nose to shore; then I got my gun and slipped out and into the edge of the woods. I set down there on a log and looked out through the leaves. I see the moon go off watch and the darkness begin to blanket the river. But in a little while I see a pale streak over the tree-tops, and knowed the day was coming. So I took my gun and slipped off towards where I had run across that camp fire, stopping every minute or two to listen. But I hadn't no luck, somehow! I couldn't seem to find the place. But by-and-by, sure enough, I catched a glimpse of fire, away through the trees. I went for it, cautious and slow. By-and-by I was close enough to have a look, and there laid a man on the ground. It most give me the fan-tods.[53] He had a blanket around his head, and his head was nearly in the fire. I set there behind a clump of bushes, in about six foot of him, and kept my eyes on him steady. It was getting gray daylight, now. Pretty soon he gapped, and stretched himself, and hove off the blanket, and it was Miss Watson's Jim! I bet I was glad to see him. I says:

"Hello, Jim!" and skipped out.

He bounced up and stared at me wild. Then he drops down on his knees, and puts his hands together and says:

"Doan' hurt me—don't! I hain't ever done no harm to a ghos'. I awluz liked dead people, en done all I could for 'em. You go en git in de river agin, whah you b'longs, en doan' do nuffin to Ole Jim, 'at 'uz awluz yo' fren'."

Well, I warn't long making him understand I warn't dead. I was ever so glad to see Jim. I warn't lonesome now. I told him I warn't afraid of *him* telling the people where I was. I talked along, but he only set there and looked at me; never said nothing. Then I says:

"It's good daylight. Le's get breakfast. Make up your camp fire good."

"What's de use er makin' up de camp fire to cook strawbries en sich truck?[54] But you got a gun, hain't you? Den we kin git sumfn better den strawbries."

"Strawberries and such truck," I says. "Is that what you live on?"

"I couldn' git nuffn else," he says.

"Why, how long you been on the island, Jim?"

"I come heah de night arter you's killed."

"What, all that time?"

"Yes-indeedy."

"And ain't you had nothing but that kind of rubbage to eat?"

"No, sah—nuffn else."

"Well, you must be most starved, ain't you?"

"I reck'n I could eat a hoss. I think I could. How long you ben on de islan'?"

"Since the night I got killed."

"No! W'y, what has you lived on? But you got a gun. Oh, yes, you got a gun. Dat's good. Now you kill sumfn en I'll make up de fire."

So we went over to where the canoe was, and while he built a fire in a grassy open place amongst the trees, I fetched meal and bacon and coffee,

[53] Fidgets. [54] Things, produce.

and coffee-pot and frying-pan, and sugar and tin cups, and the nigger was set back considerable, because he reckoned it was all done with witchcraft. I catched a good big cat-fish, too, and Jim cleaned him with his knife, and fried him.

When breakfast was ready, we lolled on the grass and eat it smoking hot. Jim laid it in with all his might, for he was most about starved. Then when we had got pretty well stuffed, we laid off and lazied.

By-and-by Jim says:

"But looky here, Huck, who wuz it dat 'uz killed in dat shanty, ef it warn't you?"

Then I told him the whole thing, and he said it was smart. He said Tom Sawyer couldn't get up no better plan than what I had. Then I says:

"How do you come to be here, Jim, and how'd you get here?"

He looked pretty uneasy, and didn't say nothing for a minute. Then he says:

"Maybe I better not tell."

"Why, Jim?"

"Well, dey's reasons. But you wouldn't tell on me ef I 'uz to tell you, would you, Huck?"

"Blamed if I would, Jim."

"Well, I b'lieve you, Huck. I—I *run off.*"

"Jim!"

"But mind, you said you wouldn't tell—you know you said you wouldn't tell, Huck."

"Well, I did. I said I wouldn't, and I'll stick to it. Honest *injun* I will. People would call me a low down Ab'litionist[55] and despise me for keeping mum—but don't make no difference. I ain't agoing to tell, and I ain't agoing back there anyways. So now, le's know all about it."

"Well, you see, it 'uz dis way. Ole Missus—dat's Miss Watson—she pecks on me all de time, en treats me pooty rough, but she awluz said she wouldn't sell me down to Orleans. But I noticed dey wuz a nigger trader roun' de place considable, lately, en I begin to git oneasy. Well, one night I creeps to de do', pooty late, en de do' warn't quite shet, en I hear ole missus tell de widder she gwyne to sell me down to Orleans[56] but she didn't want to, but she could git eight hund'd dollars for me, en it 'uz sich a big stack o'money she couldn' resis'. De widder she try to git her to say she wouldn' do it, but I never waited to hear de res'. I lit out mighty quick, I tell you.

"I tuck out en shin down de hill en 'spec to steal a skift 'long de sho' som'ers 'bove de town, but dey wuz people a-stirring' yit, so I hid in de ole tumble-down cooper shop[57] on de bank to wait for everybody to go 'way. Well, I wuz dah all night. Dey wuz somebody roun' all de time. 'Long 'bout six in de mawnin', skifts begin to go by, en 'bout eight er nine every skift dat went 'long wuz talkin' 'bout how yo' pap come over to de town en say you's killed. Dese las' skifts wuz full o' ladies en genlmen agoin' over for to see de place. Sometimes dey'd pull up at de sho' en take a res' b'fo' dey started acrost, so by de talk I got to know all 'bout de killin'. I 'uz powerful sorry you's killed, Huck, but I ain't no mo', now.

[55]One devoted to the abolition of slavery.
[56]I.e., be "sold down the river" to work as a field hand on a large plantation.
[57]A barrel-maker's shop.

"I laid dah under de shavins all day. I 'uz hungry, but I warn't afeared; bekase I knowed ole missus en de widder wuz goin' to start to de campmeetn'[58] right arter breakfas' en be gone all day, en dey knows I goes off wid de cattle 'bout daylight, so dey wouldn't 'spec to see me roun' de place, en so dey wouldn' miss me tell arter dark in de evenin'. De yuther servants wouldn' miss me, kase dey'd shin out en take holiday, soon as de ole folks 'uz out'n de way.

"Well, when it come dark I tuck out up de river road, en went 'bout two mile er more to whah dey warn't no houses. I'd made up my mine 'bout what I's agwyne to do. You see ef I kep' on tryin' to git away afoot, de dogs 'ud track me; ef I stole a skift to cross over, dey'd miss dat skift, you see, en dey'd know 'bout whah I'd lan' on de yuther side en whah to pick up my track. So I says, a raff is what I's arter; it doan' *make* no track.

"I see a light a-comin' roun' de p'int, bymeby, so I wade' in en shove' a log ahead o' me, en swum more'n half-way acrost de river, en got in 'mongst de driftwood, en kep' my head down low, en kinder swum agin de current tell de raff come along. Den I swum to de stern uv it, en tuck aholt. It clouded up en 'uz pooty dark for a little while. So I clumb up en laid down on de planks. De men 'uz all 'way yonder in de middle, whah de lantern wuz. De river wuz arisin' en dey wuz a good current; so I reck'n'd 'at by fo' in de mawnin' I'd be twenty-five mile down de river, en den I'd slip in, jis' b'fo' daylight, en swim asho' en take to de woods on de Illinois side.[59]

"But I didn't have no luck. When we 'uz mos' down to de head er de islan', a man begin to come aft wid de lantern. I see it warn't no use fer to wait, so I slid overboad, en struck out fer de islan'. Well, I had a notion I could lan' mos' anywhers, but I couldn't—bank too bluff. I 'uz mos' to de foot er de islan' b'fo' I foun' a good place. I went into de woods en jedged I wouldn' fool wid raffs no mo', long as dey move de lantern roun' so. I had my pipe en a plug er dogleg,[60] en some matches in my cap, en dey warn't wet, so I 'uz all right."

"And so you ain't had no meat nor bread to eat all this time? Why didn't you get mud-turkles?"

"How you gwyne to git'm? You can't slip up on um en grab um; en how's a body gwyne to hit um wid a rock? How could a body do it in de night? en I warn't gwyne to show myself on de bank in de daytime."

"Well, that's so. You've had to keep in the woods all the time, of course. Did you hear 'em shooting the cannon?"

"Oh, yes. I knowed dey was arter you. I see um go by heah; watched um thoo de bushes."

Some young birds come along, flying a yard or two at a time and lighting. Jim said it was a sign it was going to rain. He said it was a sign when young chickens flew that way, and so he reckoned it was the same way when young birds done it. I was going to catch some of them, but Jim wouldn't let me. He said it was death. He said his father laid mighty sick once, and some of them catched a bird, and his old granny said his father would die, and he did.

[58]Evangelistic religious meetings held in rural areas and attended by enthusiasts who camp nearby.

[59]In Illinois, although it was a free state, runaway slaves lacking free papers were subject to arrest and a term of indentured labor. Jim's best chance for escape was to continue down river to the confluence of the Mississippi and Ohio rivers and thence up the Ohio to a northern state. There proslavery forces were less numerous than in southern Illinois, and Jim could hope to escape to Canada through the Underground Railway.

[60]A plug of cheap leaf tobacco, twisted and bent into the shape of a dog's hind leg.

And Jim said you mustn't count the things you are going to cook for dinner, because that would bring bad luck. The same if you shook the tablecloth after sundown. And he said if a man owned a bee-hive, and that man died, the bees must be told about it before sun-up next morning, or else the bees would all weaken down and quit work and die. Jim said bees wouldn't sting idiots; but I didn't believe that, because I had tried them lots of times myself, and they wouldn't sting me.

I had heard about some of these things before, but not all of them. Jim knowed all kinds of signs. He said he knowed most everything. I said it looked to me like all the signs was about bad luck, and so I asked him if there warn't any good-luck signs. He says:

"Mighty few—an' *dey* ain' no use to a body. What you want to know when good luck's a-comin' for? want to keep it off?" And he said: "Ef you's got hairy arms en a hairy breas', it's a sign dat you's agwyne to be rich. Well, dey's some use in a sign like dat, 'kase it's so fur ahead. You see, maybe you's got to be po' a long time fust, en so you might git discourage' en kill yo'self 'f you didn' know by de sign dat you gwyne to be rich bymeby."

"Have you got hairy arms and hairy breast, Jim?"

"What's de use to ax dat question? don' you see I has?"

"Well, are you rich?"

"No, but I ben rich wunst, and gwyne to be rich agin. Wunst I had foteen dollars, but I tuck to specalat'n', en got busted out."

"What did you speculate in, Jim?"

"Well, fust I tackled stock."

"What kind of stock?"

"Why, live stock. Cattle, you know. I put ten dollars in a cow. But I ain't gwyne to resk no mo' money in stock. De cow up 'n' died on my han's."

"So you lost the ten dollars."

"No, I didn't lose it all. I on'y los' 'bout nine of it. I sole de hide en taller[61] for a dollar en ten cents."

"You had five dollars and ten cents left. Did you speculate any more?"

"Yes. You know dat one-laigged nigger dat b'longs to ole Misto Bradish? well, he sot up a bank, en say anybody dat put in a dollar git fo' dollars mo' at de en' er de year. Well, all de niggers went in, but dey didn' have much. I wuz de on'y one dat had much. So I stuck out for mo' dan fo' dollars, en I said 'f I didn' git it I'd start a bank mysef. Well o' course dat nigger want' to keep me out er de business, bekase he say dey warn't business 'nough for two banks, so he say I could put in my five dollars en he pay me thirty-five at de en' er de year.

"So I done it. Den I reck'n'd I'd inves' de thirty-five dollars right off en keep things a-movin'. Dey wuz a nigger name' Bob, dat had ketched a wood-flat,[62] en his marster didn' know it;[63] en I bought it off'n him en told him to take de thirty-five dollars when de en' er de year come; but somebody stole de wood-flat dat night, en nex' day de one-laigged nigger say de bank's busted. So dey didn' none uv us git no money."

"What did you do with the ten cents, Jim?"

[61]Tallow. [62]Flat-bottomed boat for carrying wood.
[63]Possessions of a slave were, by law, the property of the slave's owner.

"Well, I 'uz gwyne to spen' it, but I had a dream, en de dream tole me to give it to a nigger name' Balum—Balum's Ass[64] dey call him for short, he's one er dem chuckle-heads, you know. But he's lucky, dey say, en I see I warn't lucky. De dream say let Balum inves' de ten cents en he'd make a raise for me. Well, Balum he tuck de money, en when he wuz in church he hear de preacher say dat whoever give to de po' len' to de Lord, en boun' to git his money back a hund'd times. So Balum he tuck en give de ten cents to de po', en laid low to see what wuz gwyne to come of it."

"Well, what did come of it, Jim?"

"Nuffn' never come of it. I couldn' manage to k'leck dat money no way; en Balum he couldn'. I ain' gwyne to len' no mo' money 'dout I see de security. Boun' to git yo' money back a hund'd times, de preacher say! Ef I could git de ten *cents* back, I'd call it squah, en be glad er de chanst."

"Well, it's all right, anyway, Jim, long as you're going to be rich again some time or other."

"Yes—en I's rich now, come to look at it. I owns mysef, en I's wuth eight hund'd dollars. I wisht I had de money, I wouldn' want no mo'."

CHAPTER IX

I wanted to go and look at a place right about the middle of the island, that I'd found when I was exploring; so we started, and soon got to it, because the island was only three miles long and a quarter of a mile wide.

This place was a tolerable long steep hill or ridge, about forty foot high. We had a rough time getting to the top, the sides were so steep and the bushes so thick. We tramped and clumb around all over it, and by-and-by found a good big cavern in the rock, most up to the top of the side toward Illinois. The cavern was as big as two or three rooms bunched together, and Jim could stand up straight in it. It was cool in there. Jim was for putting our traps in there, right away, but I said we didn't want to be climbing up and down there all the time.

Jim said if we had the canoe hid in a good place, and had all the traps in the cavern, we could rush there if anybody was to come to the island, and they would never find us without dogs. And besides, he said them little birds had said it was going to rain, and did I want the things to get wet?

So we went back and got the canoe and paddled up abreast the cavern, and lugged all the traps up there. Then we hunted up a place close by to hide the canoe in, amongst the thick willows. We took some fish off of the lines and set them again, and begun to get ready for dinner.

The door of the cavern was big enough to roll a hogshead in, and on one side of the door the floor stuck out a little bit and was flat and a good place to build a fire on. So we built it there and cooked dinner.

We spread the blankets inside for a carpet, and eat our dinner in there. We put all the other things handy at the back of the cavern. Pretty soon it darkened up and begun to thunder and lighten; so the birds was right about it. Directly

[64]A pun on the Biblical story of Balaam who, blind to the truth, was saved from death by the ass upon which he rode (Numbers 22:21–34).

to rain, and it rained like all fury, too, and I never see the wind blow one of these regular summer storms. It would get so dark that it looked all blue-black outside, and lovely; and the rain would thrash along by so thick that the trees off a little ways looked dim and spider-webby; and here would come a blast of wind that would bend the trees down and turn up the pale underside of the leaves; and then a perfect ripper of a gust would follow along and set the branches to tossing their arms as if they were just wild; and next, when it was just about the bluest and blackest—*fst!* it was as bright as glory and you'd have a little glimpse of tree-tops a-plunging about, away off yonder in the storm, hundreds of yards further than you could see before; dark as sin again in a second, and now you'd hear the thunder let go with an awful crash and then go rumbling, grumbling, tumbling down the sky towards the under side of the world, like rolling empty barrels down stairs, where it's long stairs and they bounce a good deal, you know.

"Jim, this is nice," I says. "I wouldn't want to be nowhere else but here. Pass me along another hunk of fish and some hot corn-bread."

"Well, you wouldn't a ben here, 'f it hadn't a ben for Jim. You'd a ben down dah in de woods widout any dinner, en gittn' mos' drownded, too, dat you would, honey. Chickens knows when it's gwyne to rain, en so do de birds, chile."

The river went on raising and raising for ten or twelve days, till at last it was over the banks. The water was three or four foot deep on the island in the low places and on the Illinois bottom. On that side it was a good many miles wide; but on the Missouri side it was the same old distance across—a half a mile—because the Missouri shore was just a wall of high bluffs.

Daytimes we paddled all over the island in the canoe. It was mighty cool and shady in the deep woods even if the sun was blazing outside. We went winding in and out amongst the trees; and sometimes the vines hung so thick we had to back away and go some other way. Well, on every old broken-down tree, you could see rabbits, and snakes, and such things; and when the island had been overflowed a day or two, they got so tame, on account of being hungry, that you could paddle right up and put your hand on them if you wanted to; but not the snakes and turtles—they would slide off in the water. The ridge our cavern was in, was full of them. We could a had pets enough if we'd wanted them.

One night we catched a little section of a lumber raft—nice pine planks. It was twelve foot wide and about fifteen or sixteen foot long, and the top stood above water six or seven inches, a solid level floor. We could see saw-logs[65] go by in the daylight, sometimes, but we let them go; we didn't show ourselves in daylight.

Another night, when we was up at the head of the island, just before daylight, here comes a frame house down, on the west side. She was a two-story, and tilted over, considerable. We paddled out and got aboard—clumb in at an upstairs window. But it was too dark to see yet, so we made the canoe fast and set in her to wait for daylight.

The light begun to come before we got to the foot of the island. Then we looked in at the window. We could make out a bed, and a table, and two old

[65]Split, in preparation for sawing.

chairs, and lots of things around about on the floor; and there was clothes hanging against the wall. There was something laying on the floor in the far corner that looked like a man. So Jim says:

"Hello, you!"

But it didn't budge. So I hollered again, and then Jim says:

"De man ain't asleep—he's dead. You hold still—I go en see."

He went and bent down and looked, and says:

"It's a dead man. Yes, indeedy; naked, too. He's ben shot in de back. I reck'n he's ben dead two er three days. Come in, Huck, but doan' look at his face—it's too gashly."

I didn't look at him at all. Jim throwed some old rags over him, but he needn't done it; I didn't want to see him. There was heaps of old greasy cards scattered around over the floor, and old whisky bottles, and a couple of masks made out of black cloth; and all over the walls was the ignorantest kind of words and pictures, made with charcoal. There was two old dirty calico[66] dresses, and a sun-bonnet, and some women's under-clothes, hanging against the wall, and some men's clothing, too. We put the lot into the canoe; it might come good. There was a boy's old speckled straw hat on the floor; I took that too. And there was a bottle that had had milk in it; and it had a rag stopper for a baby to suck. We would a took the bottle, but it was broke. There was a seedy old chest, and an old hair trunk[67] with the hinges broke. They stood open, but there warn't nothing left in them that was any account. The way things was scattered about, we reckoned the people left in a hurry and warn't fixed so as to carry off most of their stuff.

We got an old tin lantern, and a butcher knife without any handle, and a bran-new Barlow knife[68] worth two bits in any store, and a lot of tallow candles, and a tin candlestick, and a gourd, and a tin cup, and a ratty old bed-quilt off the bed, and reticule[69] with needles and pins and beeswax and buttons and thread and all such truck in it, and a hatchet and some nails, and a fish-line as thick as my little finger, with some monstrous hooks on it, and a roll of buckskin, and a leather dog-collar, and a horse-shoe, and some vials of medicine that didn't have no label on them; and just as we was leaving I found a tolerable good curry-comb,[70] and Jim he found a ratty old fiddle-bow, and a wooden leg. The straps was broke off of it, but barring that, it was a good enough leg, though it was too long for me and not long enough for Jim, and we couldn't find the other one, though we hunted all around.

And so, take it all around, we made a good haul. When we was ready to shove off, we was a quarter of a mile below the island, and it was pretty broad day; so I made Jim lay down in the canoe and cover up with the quilt, because if he set up, people could tell he was a nigger a good ways off. I paddled over to the Illinois shore, and drifted most a half a mile doing it. I crept up the dead water under the bank, and hadn't no accidents and didn't see nobody. We got home all safe.

[66]Colorful, printed cotton cloth.
[67]A trunk covered with cowhide from which the hair has not been removed.
[68]A pocketknife. [69]Small bag, a purse.
[70]Metal comb used for grooming (currying) horses.

CHAPTER X

After breakfast I wanted to talk about the dead man and guess out how he come to be killed, but Jim didn't want to. He said it would fetch bad luck; and besides, he said, he might come and ha'nt us; he said a man that warn't buried was more likely to go a-ha'nting around than one that was planted and comfortable. That sounded pretty reasonable, so I didn't say no more; but I couldn't keep from studying over it and wishing I knowed who shot the man, and what they done it for.

We rummaged the clothes we'd got, and found eight dollars in silver sewed up in the lining of an old blanket overcoat. Jim said he reckoned the people in that house stole the coat, because if they'd a knowed the money was there they wouldn't a left it. I said I reckoned they killed him, too; but Jim didn't want to talk about that. I says:

"Now you think it's bad luck; but what did you say when I fetched in the snake-skin that I found on the top of the ridge day before yesterday? You said it was the worst bad luck in the world to touch a snake-skin with my hands. Well, here's your bad luck! We've raked in all this truck and eight dollars besides. I wish we could have some bad luck like this every day, Jim."

"Never you mind, honey, never you mind. Don't you git too peart.[71] It's a-comin'. Mind I tell you, it's a-comin'."

It did come, too. It was a Tuesday that we had that talk. Well, after dinner Friday, we was laying around in the grass at the upper end of the ridge, and got out of tobacco. I went to the cavern to get some, and found a rattlesnake in there. I killed him, and curled him up on the foot of Jim's blanket, ever so natural, thinking there'd be some fun when Jim found him there. Well, by night I forgot all about the snake, and when Jim flung himself down on the blanket while I struck a light, the snake's mate was there, and bit him.

He jumped up yelling, and the first thing the light showed was the varmint curled up and ready for another spring. I laid him out in a second with a stick, and Jim grabbed pap's whisky jug and begun to pour it down.

He was barefooted, and the snake bit him right on the heel. That all comes of being such a fool as to not remember that wherever you leave a dead snake its mate always comes there and curls around it. Jim told me to chop off the snake's head and throw it away, and then skin the body and roast a piece of it. I done it, and he eat it and said it would help cure him. He made me take off the rattles and tie them around his wrist, too. He said that that would help. Then I slid out quiet and throwed the snakes clear away amongst the bushes; for I warn't going to let Jim find out it was all my fault, not if I could help it.

Jim sucked and sucked at the jug, and now and then he got out of his head and pitched around and yelled; but every time he come to himself he went to sucking at the jug again. His foot swelled up pretty big, and so did his leg; but by-an-by the drunk begun to come, and so I judge he was all right; but I'd druther been bit with a snake than pap's whisky.

Jim was laid up for four days and nights. Then the swelling was all gone and he was around again. I made up my mind I wouldn't ever take aholt of a snake-skin again with my hands, now that I see what had come of it. Jim said he reckoned I would believe him next time. And he said that handling a snake-skin was

[71] Smart.

such awful bad luck that maybe we hadn't got to the end of it yet. He said he druther see the new moon over his left shoulder as much as a thousand times than take up a snake-skin in his hand. Well, I was getting to feel that way myself, though I've always reckoned that looking at the new moon over your left shoulder is one of the carelessest and foolishest things a body can do. Old Hank Bunker done it once, and bragged about it; and in less than two years he got drunk and fell off of the shot tower and spread himself out so that he was just a kind of a layer, as you may say; and they slid him edgeways between two barn doors for a coffin, and buried him so, so they say, but I didn't see it. Pap told me. But anyway, it all come of looking at the moon that way, like a fool.

Well, the days went along, and the river went down between its banks again; and about the first thing we done was to bait one of the big hooks with a skinned rabbit and set it and catch a cat-fish that was as big as a man, being six foot two inches long, and weighed over two hundred pounds. We couldn't handle him, of course; he would a flung us into Illinois. We just set there and watched him rip and tear around till he drownded. We found a brass button in his stomach, and a round ball, and lots of rubbage. We split the ball open with the hatchet, and there was a spool in it. Jim said he'd had it there a long time, to coat it over so and make a ball of it. It was as big a fish as was ever catched in the Mississippi, I reckon. Jim said he hadn't ever seen a bigger one. He would a been worth a good deal over at the village. They peddle out such a fish as that by the pound in the market house there; everybody buys some of him; his meat's as white as snow and makes a good fry.

Next morning I said it was getting slow and dull and I wanted to get a stirring up, some way. I said I reckoned I would slip over the river and find out what was going on. Jim liked that notion; but he said I must go in the dark and look sharp. Then he studied it over and said, couldn't I put on some of them old things and dress up like a girl? That was a good notion, too. So we shortened up one of the calico gowns and I turned up my trowser-legs to my knees and got into it. Jim hitched it behind with the hooks, and it was a fair fit. I put on the sun-bonnet and tied it under my chin, and then for a body to look in and see my face was like looking down a joint of stove-pipe. Jim said nobody would know me, even in the daytime hardly. I practiced around all day to get the hang of the things, and by-and-by I could do pretty well in them, only Jim said I didn't walk like a girl; and he said I must quit pulling up my gown to get at my britches pocket. I took notice, and done better.

I started up the Illinois shore in the canoe just after dark.

I started across to the town from a little below the ferry landing, and the drift of the current fetched me in at the bottom of the town. I tied up and started along the bank. There was a light burning in a light shanty that hadn't been lived in for a long time, and I wondered who had took up quarters there. I slipped up and peeped in at the window. There was a woman about forty year old in there, knitting by a candle that was on a pine table. I didn't know her face; she was a stranger, for you couldn't start[72] a face in that town that I didn't know. Now this was lucky, because I was weakening; I was getting afraid I had come; people might know my voice and find me out. But if this woman had been in such a little town two days she could tell me all I wanted to know; so I knocked at the door, and made up my mind I wouldn't forget I was a girl.

[72]Find, discover.

CHAPTER XI

"Come in," says the woman, and I did. She says:

"Take a cheer."

I done it. She looked me all over with her little shiny eyes, and says: "What might your name be?"

"Sarah Williams."

"Where 'bouts do you live? In this neighborhood?"

"No'm. In Hookerville, seven mile below. I've walked all the way and I'm all tired out."

"Hungry, too, I reckon. I'll find you something."

"No'm, I ain't hungry. I was so hungry I had to stop two miles below here at a farm; so I ain't hungry no more. It's what makes me so late. My mother's down sick, and out of money and everything, and I come to tell my uncle Abner Moore. He lives at the upper end of the town, she says, I hain't ever been here before. Do you know him?"

"No; but I don't know everybody yet. I haven't lived here quite two weeks. It's a considerable ways to the upper end of the town. You better stay here all night. Take off your bonnet."

"No," I says, "I'll rest a while, I reckon, and go on. I ain't afeard of the dark."

She said she wouldn't let me go by myself, but her husband would be in by-and-by, maybe in a hour and a half, and she'd send him along with me. Then she got to talking about her husband, and about her relations up the river, and her relations down the river, and about how much better off they used to was, and how they didn't know but they'd made a mistake coming to our town, instead of letting well alone—and so on and so on, till I was afeard *I* had made a mistake coming to her to find out what was going on in the town; but by-and-by she dropped onto pap and the murder, and then I was pretty willing to let her clatter right along. She told about me and Tom Sawyer finding the six thousand dollars[73] (only she got it ten) and all about pap and what a hard lot he was, and what a hard lot I was, and at last she got down to where I was murdered. I says:

"Who done it? We've heard considerable about these goings on, down in Hookerville, but we don't know who 'twas that killed Huck Finn."

"Well, I reckon there's a right smart chance[74] of people *here* that'd like to know who killed him. Some thinks old Finn done it himself."

"No—is that so?"

"Most everybody thought it at first. He'll never know how nigh he come to getting lynched. But before night they changed around and judged it was done by a runaway nigger named Jim."

"Why *he*——"

I stopped. I reckoned I better keep still. She run on, and never noticed I had put in at all.

"The nigger run off the very night Huck Finn was killed. So there's a reward out for him—three hundred dollars. And there's a reward out for old Finn too—two hundred dollars. You see, he come to town the morning after the

[73]The sum found by Huck and Tom, as described in *Tom Sawyer,* actually totaled $12,000.

[74]Southern dialect: a large number.

murder, and told about it, and was out with 'em on the ferry-boat hunt, and right away after he up and left. Before night they wanted to lynch him, but he was gone, you see. Well, next day they found out the nigger was gone; they found out he hadn't ben seen sence ten o'clock the night the murder was done. So then they put it on him, you see, and while they was full of it, next day back comes old Finn and went boo-hooing to Judge Thatcher to get money to hunt for the nigger all over Illinois with. The judge give him some, and that evening he got drunk and was around till after midnight with a couple of mighty hard looking strangers, and then went off with them. Well, he hain't come back sence, and they ain't looking for him back till this thing blows over a little, for people thinks now that he killed his boy and fixed things so folks would think robbers done it, and then he'd get Huck's money without having to bother a long time with a lawsuit. People do say he warn't any too good to do it. Oh, he's sly, I reckon. If he don't come back for a year, he'll be all right. You can't prove anything on him, you know; everything will be quieted down then, and he'll walk into Huck's money as easy as nothing."

"Yes, I reckon so, 'm. I don't see nothing in the way of it. Has everybody quit thinking the nigger done it?"

"Oh, no, not everybody. A good many thinks he done it. But they'll get the nigger pretty soon, now, and maybe they can scare it out of him."

"Why, are they after him yet?"

"Well, you're innocent, ain't you! Does three hundred dollars lay round every day for people to pick up? Some folks thinks the nigger ain't far from here. I'm one of them—but I hain't talked it around. A few days ago I was talking with an old couple that lives next door in the log shanty, and they happened to say hardly anybody ever goes to that island over yonder that they call Jackson's Island. Don't anybody live there? says I. No, nobody, says they. I didn't say any more, but I done some thinking. I was pretty near certain I'd seen smoke over there, about the head of the island, a day or two before that, so I says to myself, like as not that nigger's hiding over there; anyway, says I, it's worth the trouble to give the place a hunt. I hain't seen any smoke sence, so I reckon maybe he's gone, if it was him; but husband's going over to see—him and another man. He was gone up the river; but he got back to-day and I told him as soon as he got here two hours ago."

I had got so uneasy I couldn't set still. I had to do something with my hands; so I took up a needle off of the table and went to threading it. My hands shook, and I was making a bad job of it. When the woman stopped talking, I looked up, and she was looking at me pretty curious, and smiling a little. I put down the needle and thread and let on to be interested—and I was, too—and says:

"Three hundred dollars is a power of money. I wish my mother could get it. Is your husband going over there to-night?"

"Oh, yes. He went up town with the man I was telling you of, to get a boat and see if they could borrow another gun. They'll go over after midnight."

"Couldn't they see better if they was to wait till daytime?"

"Yes. And couldn't the nigger see better, too? After midnight he'll likely be asleep, and they can slip around through the woods and hunt up his camp fire all the better for the dark, if he's got one."

"I didn't think of that."

The woman kept looking at me pretty curious, and I didn't feel a bit comfortable. Pretty soon she says:

"What did you say your name was, honey?"

"M—Mary Williams."

Somehow it didn't seem to me that I said it was Mary before, so I didn't look up; seemed to me I said it was Sarah; so I felt sort of cornered, and was afeared maybe I was looking it, too. I wished the woman would say something more; the longer she set still, the uneasier I was. But now she says:

"Honey, I thought you said it was Sarah when you first come in?"

"Oh, yes'm, I did. Sarah Mary Williams. Sarah's my first name. Some calls me Sarah, some calls me Mary."

"Oh, that's the way of it?"

"Yes'm."

I was feeling better, then, but I wished I was out of there, anyway. I couldn't look up yet.

Well, the woman fell to talking about how hard times was, and how poor they had to live, and how the rats was as free as if they owned the place, and so forth, and so on, and then I got easy again. She was right about the rats. You'd see one stick his nose out of a hole in the corner every little while. She said she had to have things handy to throw at them when she was alone, or they wouldn't give her no peace. She showed me a bar of lead, twisted up into a knot, and said she was a good shot with it generly, but she'd wrenched her arm a day or two ago, and didn't know whether she could throw true, now. But she watched for a chance, and directly she banged away at a rat, but she missed him wide, and said "Ouch!" it hurt her arm so. Then she told me to try for the next one. I wanted to be getting away before the old man got back, but of course I didn't let on. I got the thing, and the first rat that showed his nose I let drive, and if he'd a stayed where he was he'd a been a tolerable sick rat. She said that that was first-rate, and she reckoned I would hive the next one. She went and got the lump of lead and fetched it back and brought along a hank of yarn, which she wanted me to help her with. I held up my two hands and she put the hank over them and went on talking about her and her husband's matters. But she broke off to say:

"Keep your eye on the rats. You better have the lead in your lap, handy."

So she dropped the lump into my lap, just at that moment, and I clapped my legs together on it and she went on talking. But only about a minute. Then she took off the hank and looked me straight in the face, but very pleasant, and says:

"Come, now—what's your real name?"

"Wh-what, mum?"

"What's your real name? Is it Bill, or Tom, or Bob?—or what is it?"

I reckon I shook like a leaf, and I didn't know hardly what to do. But I says:

"Please to don't poke fun at a poor girl like me, mum. If I'm in the way, here, I'll——"

"No, you won't. Set down and stay where you are. I ain't going to hurt you, and I ain't going to tell on you, nuther. You just tell me your secret, and trust me. I'll keep it; and what's more, I'll help you. So'll my old man, if you want him to. You see, you're a runaway 'prentice—that's all. It ain't anything. There ain't any harm in it. You've been treated bad, and you made up your mind to cut. Bless you, child, I wouldn't tell on you. Tell me all about it, now—that's a good boy."

So I said it wouldn't be no use to try to play it any longer, and I would just make a clean breast and tell her everything, but she mustn't go back on her promise. Then I told her my father and mother was dead, and the law had bound me[75] out to a mean old farmer in the country thirty mile back from the river, and he treated me so bad I couldn't stand it no longer; he went away to be gone a couple of days, and so I took my chance and stole some of his daughter's old clothes, and cleared out, and I had been three nights coming the thirty miles; I traveled nights, and hid day-times and slept, and the bag of bread and meat I carried from home lasted me all the way and I had a plenty. I said I believed my uncle Abner Moore would take care of me, and so that was why I struck out for this town of Goshen.

"Goshen, child? This ain't Goshen. This is St. Petersburg.[76] Goshen's ten mile further up the river. Who told you this was Goshen?"

"Why, a man I met at day-break this morning, just as I was going to turn into the woods for my regular sleep. He told me when the roads forked I must take the right hand, and five mile would fetch me to Goshen."

"He was drunk I reckon. He told you just exactly wrong."

"Well, he did act like he was drunk, but it ain't no matter now. I got to be moving along. I'll fetch Goshen before day-light."

"Hold on a minute. I'll put you up a snack to eat. You might want it."

So she put me up a snack, and says:

"Say—when a cow's laying down, which end of her gets up first? Answer up prompt, now—don't stop to study over it. Which end gets up first?"

"The hind end, mum."

"Well, then, a horse?"

"The for'rard end, mum."

"Which side of a tree does the most moss grow on?"

"North side."

"If fifteen cows is browsing on a hillside, how many of them eats with their heads pointed the same direction?"

"The whole fifteen, mum."

"Well, I reckon you *have* lived in the country. I thought maybe you was trying to hocus[77] me again. What's your real name, now?"

"George Peters, mum."

"Well, try to remember it, George. Don't forget and tell me it's Elexander before you go, and then get out by saying it's George-Elexander when I catch you. And don't go about women in that old calico. You do a girl tolerable poor, but you might fool men, maybe. Bless you, child, when you set out to thread a needle, don't hold the thread still and fetch the needle up to it; hold the needle still and poke the thread at it—that's the way a woman most always does; but a man always does t'other way. And when you throw at a rat or anything, hitch yourself up a tip-toe, and fetch your hand up over your head as awkward as you can, and miss your rat about six or seven foot. Throw stiff-armed from the shoulder, like there was a pivot there for it to turn on—like a girl; not from the wrist and elbow, with your arm out to one side, like a boy. And mind you, when a girl tries to catch anything in her lap, she throws her knees apart; she don't clap them together, the way you did when you catched the lump of lead. Why, I spotted you for a boy when you was threading the needle; and I contrived the other things just to make certain. Now trot along to your uncle, Sarah Mary Williams

[75]Assigned, as a ward of the court.
[76]Twain's fictional name for Hannibal, Missouri, his boyhood home. [77]Trick.

George Elexander Peters, and if you get into trouble you send word to Mrs. Judith Loftus, which is me, and I'll do what I can to get you out of it. Keep the river road, all the way, and next time you tramp, take shoes and socks with you. The river road's a rocky one, and your feet'll be in a condition when you get to Goshen, I reckon."

I went up the bank about fifty yards, and then I doubled on my tracks and slipped back to where my canoe was, a good piece below the house. I jumped in and was off in a hurry. I went up stream far enough to make the head of the island, and then started across. I took off the sun-bonnet, for I didn't want no blinders[78] on, then. When I was about the middle, I hear the clock begin to strike; so I stops and listens; the sound come faint over the water, but clear—eleven. When I struck the head of the island I never waited to blow, though I was most winded, but I shoved right into the timber where my old camp used to be, and started a good fire there on a high-and-dry spot.

Then I jumped in the canoe and dug out for our place a mile and a half below, as hard as I could go. I landed, and slopped through the timber and up the ridge and into the cavern. There Jim laid, sound asleep on the ground. I roused him out and says:

"Git up and hump yourself, Jim! There ain't a minute to lose. They're after us!"

Jim never asked no questions, he never said a word; but the way he worked for the next half an hour showed about how he was scared. By that time everything we had in the world was on our raft and she was ready to be shoved out from the willow cove where she was hid. We put out the camp fire at the cavern the first thing, and didn't show a candle outside after that.

I took the canoe out from shore a little piece and took a look, but if there was a boat around I couldn't see it, for stars and shadows ain't good to see by. Then we got out the raft and slipped along down in the shade, past the foot of the island dead still, never saying a word.

CHAPTER XII

It must a been close onto one o'clock when we got below the island at last, and the raft did seem to go mighty slow. If a boat was to come along, we was going to take to the canoe and break for the Illinois shore; and it was well a boat didn't come, for we hadn't ever thought to put the gun into the canoe, or a fishing-line or anything to eat. We was in ruther too much of a sweat to think of so many things. It warn't good judgment to put *everything* on the raft.

If the men went to the island, I just expect they found the camp fire I built, and watched it all night for Jim to come. Anyways, they stayed away from us, and if my building the fire never fooled them it warn't no fault of mine. I played it as low-down on them as I could.

When the first streak of day begun to show, we tied up to a tow-head in a big bend on the Illinois side, and hacked off cotton-wood branches with the hatchet and covered up the raft with them so she looked like there had been a cave-in in the bank there. A tow-head is a sand-bar that has cotton-woods on it as thick as harrow-teeth.[79]

[78]Attachments on a horse's bridle, to restrict vision

[79]As numerous as teeth on a harrow, a rake.

We had mountains on the Missouri shore and heavy timber on the Illinois side, and the channel was down the Missouri shore at that place, so we warn't afraid of anybody running across us. We laid there all day and watched the rafts and steamboats spin down the Missouri shore, and up-bound steamboats[80] fight the big river in the middle. I told Jim all about the time I had jabbering with that woman; and Jim said she was a smart one, and if she was to start after us herself *she* wouldn't set down and watch a camp fire—no, sir, she'd fetch a dog. Well, then, I said, why couldn't she tell her husband to fetch a dog? Jim said he bet she did think of it by the time the men was ready to start, and he believed they must a gone up town to get a dog and so they lost all that time, or else we wouldn't be here on a tow-head sixteen or seventeen mile below the village—no, indeedy, we would be in that same old town again. So I said I didn't care what was the reason they didn't get us, as long as they didn't.

When it was beginning to come on dark, we poked our heads out of the cottonwood thicket and looked up, and down, and across; nothing in sight; so Jim took up some of the top planks of the raft and built a snug wigwam to get under in blazing weather and rainy, and to keep the things dry. Jim made a floor for the wigwam, and raised it a foot or more above the level of the raft, so now the blankets and all the traps was out of the reach of steamboat waves. Right in the middle of the wigwam we made a layer of dirt about five or six inches deep with a frame around it for to hold it to its place; this was to build a fire on in sloppy weather or chilly; the wigwam would keep it from being seen. We made an extra steering oar, too, because one of the others might get broke, on a snag or something. We fixed up a short forked stick to hang the old lantern on; because we must always light the lantern whenever we see a steamboat coming down stream, to keep from getting run over; but we wouldn't have to light it for upstream boats unless we see we was in what they call a "crossing"; for the river was pretty high yet, very low banks being still a little under water; so up-bound boats didn't always run the channel, but hunted easy water.

This second night we run between seven and eight hours, with a current that was making over four miles an hour. We catched fish, and talked, and we took a swim now and then to keep off sleepiness. It was kind of solemn, drifting down the big still river, laying on our backs looking up at the stars, and we didn't ever feel like talking loud, and it warn't often that we laughed, only a little kind of a low chuckle. We had mighty good weather, as a general thing, and nothing ever happened to us at all, that night, nor the next, nor the next.

Every night we passed towns, some of them away up on black hillsides, nothing but just a shiny bed of lights, not a house could you see. The fifth night we passed St. Louis, and it was like the whole world lit up. In St. Petersburg they used to say there was twenty or thirty thousand people in St. Louis, but I never believed it till I see that wonderful spread of lights at two o'clock that still night. There warn't a sound there; everybody was asleep.

Every night, now, I used to slip ashore, towards ten o'clock, at some little village, and buy ten or fifteen cents' worth of meal or bacon or other stuff to eat; and sometimes I lifted a chicken that warn't roosting comfortable, and took him along. Pap always said, take a chicken when you get a chance, because if you don't want him yourself you can easy find somebody that does, and a

[80] Steamboats going upriver, against the current.

good deed ain't ever forgot. I never see pap when he didn't want the chicken himself, but that is what he used to say, anyway.

Mornings, before daylight, I slipped into corn fields and borrowed a watermelon, or a mushmelon, or a punkin, or some new corn, or things of that kind. Pap always said it warn't no harm to borrow things, if you was meaning to pay them back, sometime; but the widow said it warn't anything but a soft name for stealing, and no decent body would do it. Jim said he reckoned the widow was partly right and pap was partly right; so the best way would be for us to pick out two or three things from the list and say we wouldn't borrow them any more—then he reckoned it wouldn't be no harm to borrow the others. So we talked it over all one night, drifting along down the river, trying to make up our minds whether to drop the watermelons, or the cantelopes, or the mushmelons, or what. But towards daylight we got it all settled satisfactory, and concluded to drop crabapples and p'simmons. We warn't feeling just right, before that, but it was all comfortable now. I was glad the way it come out, too, because crabapples ain't ever good, and the p'simmons wouldn't be ripe for two or three months yet.

We shot a water-fowl, now and then, that got up too early in the morning or didn't go to bed early enough in the evening. Take it all around, we lived pretty high.

The fifth night below St. Louis we had a big storm after midnight, with a power of thunder and lightning, and the rain poured down in a solid sheet. We stayed in the wigwam and let the raft take care of itself. When the lightning glared out we could see a big straight river ahead, and high rocky bluffs on both sides. By-and-by says I, "Hel-*lo,* Jim, looky younder!" It was a steamboat that had killed herself on a rock. We was drifting straight down for her. The lightning showed her very distinct. She was leaning over, with part of her upper deck above water, and you could see every little chimblyguy[81] clean and clear, and a chair by the big bell, with an old slouch hat hanging on the back of it when the flashes come.

Well, it being away in the night, and stormy, and all so mysterious-like, I felt just the way any other boy would a felt when I see that wreck laying there so mournful and lonesome in the middle of the river. I wanted to get aboard of her and slink around a little, and see what there was there. So I says:

"Le's land on her, Jim."

But Jim was dead against it, at first. He says:

"I doan' want to go fool'n 'long er no wrack. We's doin' blame' well, en we better let blame' well alone, as de good book says. Like as not dey's a watchman on dat wrack."

"Watchman your grandmother," I says; "there ain't nothing to watch but the texas[82] and the pilot-house; and do you reckon anybody's going to resk his life for a texas and a pilot-house such a night as this, when it's likely to break up and wash off down the river any minute?" Jim couldn't say nothing to that, so he didn't try. "And besides," I says, "we might borrow something worth having, out of the captain's stateroom.[83] Seegars, *I* bet you—and cost five cents apiece, solid cash. Steamboat captains is always rich, and get sixty dollars

[81]Wires that brace (guy) the smoke stacks.
[82]Structure on the upper deck of a steamboat, with the biggest (hence "texas") cabins.
[83]Sleeping quarters.

a month, and *they* don't care a cent what a thing costs, you know, long as they want it. Stick a candle in your pocket; I can't rest, Jim, till we give her a rummaging. Do you reckon Tom Sawyer would ever go by this thing? Not for pie, he wouldn't. He'd call it an adventure—that's what he'd call it; and he'd land on that wreck if it was his last act. And wouldn't he throw style into it?—wouldn't he spread himself, nor nothing? Why, you'd think it was Christopher C'lumbus discovering Kingdom-Come. I wish Tom Sawyer *was* here."

Jim he grumbled a little, but give in. He said we mustn't talk any more than we could help, and then talk mighty low. The lightning showed us the wreck again, just in time, and we fetched the starboard derrick,[84] and made fast there.

The deck was high out, here. We went sneaking down the slope of it to labboard,[85] in the dark, towards the texas, feeling our way slow with our feet, and spreading our hands out to fend off the guys, for it was so dark we couldn't see no sign of them. Pretty soon we struck the forward end of the skylight, and clumb onto it; and the next step fetched us in front of the captain's door, which was open, and by Jimminy, away down through the texas-hall we see a light! and all in the same second we seem to hear low voices in yonder!

Jim whispered and said he was feeling powerful sick, and told me to come along. I says, all right; and was going to start for the raft; but just then I heard a voice wail out and say:

"Oh, please don't, boys; I swear I won't ever tell!"

Another voice said, pretty loud:

"It's a lie, Jim Turner. You've acted this way before. You always want more'n your share of the truck, and you've always got it, too, because you've swore 't if you didn't you'd tell. But this time you've said it jest one time too many. You're the meanest, treacherousest hound in this country."

By this time Jim was gone for the raft. I was just a-biling with curiosity; and I says to myself, Tom Sawyer wouldn't back out now, and so I won't either; I'm agoing to see what's going on here. So I dropped on my hands and knees, in the little passage, and crept aft in the dark, till there warn't but about one stateroom betwixt me and the cross-hall of the texas. Then, in there I see a man stretched on the floor and tied hand and foot, and two men standing over him, and one of them had a dim lantern in his hand, and the other one had a pistol. This one kept pointing the pistol at the man's head on the floor and saying—

"I'd *like* to! And I orter, too, a mean skunk!"

The man on the floor would shrivel up, and say: "Oh, please don't, Bill—I hain't ever goin' to tell."

And every time he said that, the man with the lantern would laugh, and say:

" 'Deed you *aint!* You never said no truer thing 'n that, you bet you." And once he said: "Hear him beg! and yit if we hadn't got the best of him and tied him, he'd a killed us both. And what *for?* Jist for noth'n. Jist because we stood on our *rights*—that's what for. But I lay you ain't agoin' to threaten nobody any more, Jim Turner. Put *up* that pistol, Bill."

Bill says:

"I don't want to, Jake Packard. I'm for killin' him—and didn't he kill old Hatfield jist the same way—and don't he deserve it?"

"But I don't *want* him killed, and I've got my reasons for it."

[84] Cargo boom for loading and unloading the ship.
[85] Left (port) side of a ship, looking forward.

"Bless yo' heart for them words, Jake Packard! I'll never forgit you, long's I live!" says the man on the floor, sort of blubbering.

Packard didn't take no notice of that, but hung up his lantern on a nail, and started towards where I was, there in the dark, and motioned Bill to come. I crawfished[86] as fast as I could, about two yards, but the boat slanted so that I couldn't make very good time; so to keep from getting run over and catched I crawled into a stateroom on the upper side. The man come a-pawing along in the dark, and when Packard got to my stateroom, he says:

"Here—come in here."

And in he come, and Bill after him. But before they got in, I was up in the upper berth, cornered, and sorry I come. Then they stood there, with their hands on the ledge of the berth, and talked. I couldn't see them, but I could tell where they was, by the whisky they'd been having. I was glad I didn't drink whisky; but it wouldn't made much difference, anyway, because most of the time they couldn't a treed me because I didn't breathe. I was too scared. And besides, a body *couldn't* breathe, and hear such talk. They talked low and earnest. Bill wanted to kill Turner. He says:

"He's said he'll tell, and he will. If we was to give both our shares to him *now,* it wouldn't make no difference after the row, and the way we've served him. Shore's you're born, he'll turn State's evidence, now you hear *me.* I'm for putting him out of his troubles."

"So'm I," says Packard, very quiet.

"Blame it, I'd sorter begun to think you wasn't. Well, then, that's all right. Les' go and do it."

"Hold on a minute; I hain't had my say yit. You listen to me. Shooting's good, but there's quieter ways if the thing's *got* to be done. But what *I* say, is this; it ain't good sense to go court'n around after a halter,[87] if you git at what you're up to in some way that's jist as good and at the same time don't bring you into no resks. Ain't that so?"

"You bet it is. But how you goin' to manage it this time?"

"Well, my idea is this: we'll rustle around and gether up whatever pickins we've overlooked in the staterooms, and shove for shore and hide the truck. Then we'll wait. Now I say it ain't agoin' to be more 'n two hours befo' this wrack breaks up and washes off down the river. See? He'll be drownded, and won't have nobody to blame for it but his own self. I reckon that's a considerable sight better'n killin' of him. I'm unfavorable to killin' a man as long as you can git around it; it ain't good sense, it ain't good morals. Ain't I right?"

"Yes—I reck'n you are. But s'pose she *don't* break up and wash off?"

"Well, we can wait the two hours, anyway, and see, can't we?"

"All right, then; come along."

So they started, and I lit out, all in a cold sweat, and scrambled forward. It was dark as pitch there; but I said in a kind of a coarse whisper, "Jim!" and he answered up, right at my elbow, with a sort of a moan, and I says:

"Quick, Jim, it ain't no time for fooling around and moaning; there's a gang of murderers in yonder, and if we don't hunt up their boat and set her drifting down the river so these fellows can't get away from the wreck, there's one of 'em going to be in a bad fix. But if we find their boat we can put *all* of 'em in a bad

[86]Crawled backward. [87]Hangman's noose.

fix—for the Sheriff 'll get 'em. Quick—hurry! I'll hunt the labboard side, you hunt the stabboard. You start at the raft, and—"

"Oh, my lordy, lordy! *Raf'?* Dey ain' no raf' no mo', she done broke loose en gone!—'en here we is!"

CHAPTER XIII

Well, I catched my breath and most fainted. Shut up on a wreck with such a gang as that! But it warn't no time to be sentimentering. We'd *got* to find that boat, now—had to have it for ourselves. So we went a-quaking and shaking down the stabboard side, and slow work it was, too—seemed a week before we got to the stern. No sign of a boat. Jim said he didn't believe he could go any further—so scared he hadn't hardly any strength left, he said. But I said come on, if we get left on this wreck, we are in a fix, sure. So on we prowled, again. We struck for the stern of the texas, and found it, and then scrabbled along forwards on the skylight, hanging on from shutter to shutter, for the edge of the skylight was in the water. When we got pretty close to the cross-hall door, there was the skiff, sure enough! I could just barely see her. I felt ever so thankful. In another second I would a been aboard of her; but just then the door opened. One of the men stuck his head out, only about a couple of foot from me, and I thought I was gone; but he jerked it in again, and says,

"Heave that blame lantern out o' sight, Bill!"

He flung a bag of something into the boat, and then got in himself, and set down. It was Packard. Then Bill *he* come out and got in. Packard says, in a low voice:

"All ready—shove off!"

I couldn't hardly hang onto the shutters, I was so weak. But Bill says:

"Hold on—'d you go through him?"

"No. Didn't you?"

"No. So he's got his share o' the cash, yet."

"Well, then, come along—no use to take truck and leave money."

"Say—won't he suspicion what we're up to?"

"Maybe he won't. But we got to have it anyway. Come along."

So they got out and went in.

The door slammed to, because it was on the careened side; and in a half second I was in the boat, and Jim come a tumbling after me. I out with my knife and cut the rope, and away we went!

We didn't touch an oar, and we didn't speak nor whisper, nor hardly even breathe. We went gliding swift along, dead silent, past the tip of the paddle-box, and past the stern; then in a second or two more we was a hundred yards below the wreck, and the darkness soaked her up, every last sign of her, and we was safe, and knowed it.

When we was three or four hundred yards down stream, we see the lantern show like a little spark at the texas door, for a second, and we knowed by that that the rascals had missed their boat, and was beginning to understand that they was in just as much trouble, now, as Jim Turner was.

own justice

Then Jim manned the oars, and we took out after our raft. Now was the first time that I begun to worry about the men—I reckon I hadn't had time to before. I begun to think how dreadful it was, even for murderers, to be in such a fix. I says to myself, there ain't no telling but I might come to be a murderer myself, yet, and then how would *I* like it? So says I to Jim:

"The first light we see, we'll land a hundred yards below it or above it, in a place where it's a good hiding-place for you and the skiff, and then I'll go and fix up some kind of a yarn, and get somebody to go for that gang and get them out of their scrape, so they can be hung when their time comes."

But that idea was a failure; for pretty soon it begun to storm again, and this time worse than ever. The rain poured down, and never a light showed; everybody in bed, I reckon. We boomed along down the river, watching for lights and watching for our raft. After a long time the rain let up, but the clouds staid, and the lightning kept whimpering, and by-and-by a flash showed us a black thing ahead, floating, and we made for it.

It was the raft, and mighty glad was we to get aboard of it again. We seen a light, now, away down to the right, on shore. So I said I would go for it. The skiff was half full of plunder which that gang had stole, there on the wreck. We hustled it onto the raft in a pile, and I told Jim to float along down, and show a light when he judged he had gone about two mile, and keep it burning till I come; then I manned my oars and shoved for the light. As I got down towards it, three or four more showed—up on a hillside. It was a village. I closed in above the shore-light, and laid on my oars and floated. As I went by, I see it was a lantern hanging on the jackstaff[88] of a double-hull ferry-boat. I skimmed around for the watchman, a-wondering whereabouts he slept; and by-and-by I found him roosting on the bitts,[89] forward, with his head down between his knees. I give his shoulder two or three little shoves, and begun to cry.

He stirred up, in a kind of a startlish way; but when he see it was only me, he took a good gap and stretch, and then he says:

"Hello, what's up? Don't cry, bub. What's the trouble?"

I says:

"Pap, and mam, and sis, and—"

Then I broke down. He says:

"Oh, dang it, now, *don't* take on so, we all has to have our troubles and this'n 'll come out all right. What's the matter with 'em?

"They're—they're—are you the watchman of the boat?"

"Yes," he says, kind of pretty-well-satisfied like. "I'm the captain and the owner, and the mate, and the pilot, and watchman, and head deck-hand; and sometimes I'm the freight and passengers. I ain't as rich as old Jim Hornback, and I can't be so blame' generous and good to Tom, Dick and Harry as what he is, and slam around money the way he does; but I've told him a many a time 't I wouldn't trade places with him; for, says I, a sailor's life's the life for me, and I'm derned if *I'd* live two mile out o' town, where there ain't nothing ever goin' on, not for all his spondulicks[90] and as much more on top of it. Says I——"

I broke in and says:

"They're in an awful peck of trouble, and——"

"*Who* is?"

"Why, pap, and mam, and sis, and Miss Hooker; and if you'd take your ferry-boat and go up there——"

[88]Short pole from which a flag or light can be hung.

[89]Posts fixed on the deck, to which lines can be fastened.

[90]Riches.

"Up where? Where are they?"

"On the wreck."

"What wreck?"

"Why, there ain't but one."

"What, you don't mean the *Walter Scott?*"

"Yes."

"Good land! what are they doin' *there,* for gracious sakes?"

"Well, they didn't go there a-purpose."

"I bet they didn't! Why, great goodness, there ain't no chance for 'em if they don't git off mighty quick! Why, how in the nation did they ever git into such a scrape?"

"Easy enough. Miss Hooker was a-visiting, up there to the town——"

"Yes, Booth's Landing—go on."

"She was a-visiting, there at Booth's Landing, and just in the edge of the evening she started over with her nigger woman in the horseferry,[91] to stay all night at her friend's house, Miss What-you-may-call-her, I disremember her name, and they lost their steering-oar, and swung around and went a-floating down, stern-first, about two mile, and saddle-baggsed on[92] the wreck, and the ferry man and the nigger woman and the horses was all lost, but Miss Hooker she made a grab and got aboard the wreck. Well, about an hour after dark, we come along down in our trading-scow,[93] and it was so dark we didn't notice the wreck till we was right on it; and so *we* saddlebaggsed; but all of us was saved but Bill Whipple—and oh, he *was* the best cretur!—I most wish't it had been me, I do."

"My George! It's the beatenest thing I ever struck. And *then* what did you all do?"

"Well, we hollered and took on, but it's so wide there, we couldn't make nobody hear. So pap said somebody got to get ashore and get help somehow. I was the only one that could swim, so I made a dash for it, and Miss Hooker she said if I didn't strike help sooner, come here and hunt up her uncle, and he'd fix the thing. I made the land about a mile below, and been fooling along ever since, trying to get people to do something, but they said, 'What, in such a night and such a current? there ain't no sense in it; go for the steam-ferry.' Now if you'll go, and——"

"By Jackson, I'd *like* to, and blame it I don't know but I will; but who in the dingnation's agoin' to *pay* for it? Do you reckon your pap——"

"Why *that's* all right. Miss Hooker she told me, *particular,* that her uncle Hornback——"

"Great guns! is *he* her uncle? Looky here, you break for that light over yonder-way, and turn out west when you git there, and about a quarter of a mile out you'll come to the tavern; tell 'em to dart you out to Jim Hornback's and he'll foot the bill. And don't you fool around any, because he'll want to know the news. Tell him I'll have his niece all safe before he can get to town. Hump yourself, now; I'm agoing up around the corner here, to roust out my engineer."

I struck for the light, but as soon as he turned the corner I went back and got into my skiff and bailed her out and then pulled up shore in the easy water about six hundred yards, and tucked myself in among some woodboats; for I couldn't rest easy till I could see the ferry-boat start. But take it all around, I was

[91]Ferry large enough to carry horses. [92]Wrapped around. [93]Flat-bottomed cargo boat.

feeling ruther comfortable on accounts of taking all this trouble for that gang, for not many would a done it. I wished the widow knowed about it. I judged she would be proud of me for helping these rapscallions, because rapscallions and dead beats is the kind the widow and good people takes the most interest in.

Well, before long, here comes the wreck, dim and dusky, sliding along down! A kind of cold shiver went through me, and then I struck out for her. She was very deep, and I see in a minute there warn't much chance for anybody being alive in her. I pulled all around her and hollered a little, but there wasn't any answer; all dead still. I felt a little bit heavy-hearted about the gang, but not much, for I reckoned if they could stand it, I could.

Then here comes the ferry-boat; so I shoved for the middle of the river on a long down-stream slant; and when I judged I was out of eye-reach, I laid on my oars, and looked back and see her go and smell around the wreck for Miss Hooker's remainders, because the captain would know her uncle Hornback would want them; and then pretty soon the ferry-boat give it up and went for shore, and I laid into my work and went a-booming down the river.

It did seem a powerful long time before Jim's light showed up; and when it did show, it looked like it was a thousand mile off. By the time I got there the sky was beginning to get a little gray in the east; so we struck for an island, and hid the raft, and sunk the skiff, and turned in and slept like dead people.

CHAPTER XIV

By-and-by, when we got up, we turned over the truck the gang had stole off of the wreck, and found boots, and blankets, and clothes, and all sorts of other things, and a lot of books, and a spy-glass, and three boxes of seegars. We hadn't ever been this rich before, in neither of our lives. The seegars was prime. We laid off all the afternoon in the woods talking, and me reading the books, and having a general good time. I told Jim all about what happened inside the wreck, and at the ferry-boat; and I said these kinds of things was adventures; but he said he didn't want no more adventures. He said that when I went in the texas and he crawled back to get on the raft and found her gone, he nearly died; because he judged it was all up with *him*, anyway it could be fixed; for if he didn't get saved he would get drownded; and if he did get saved, whoever saved him would send him back home so as to get the reward, and then Miss Watson would see him South, sure. Well, he was right; he was most always right; he had an uncommon level head, for a nigger.

I read considerable to Jim about kings, and dukes, and earls, and such, and how gaudy they dressed, and how much style they put on, and called each other your majesty, and your grace, and your lordship, and so on, 'stead of mister; and Jim's eyes bugged out, and he was interested. He says:

"I didn' know dey was so many un um. I hain't heard 'bout none un um, skasely, but ole King Sollermun, onless you counts dem kings dat's in a pack er k'yards. How much do a king git?"

"Get?" I says; "why, they get a thousand dollars a month if they want it; they can have just as much as they want; everything belongs to them."

"*Ain'* dat gay? En what dey got to do, Huck?"

"*They* don't do nothing! Why how you talk. They just set around."

"No—is dat so?"

"Of course it is. They just set around. Except maybe when there's a war; then they go to the war. But other times they just lazy around; or go hawking—just hawking and sp—Sh!—d' you hear a noise?"

We skipped out and looked; but it warn't nothing but the flutter of a steamboat's wheel, away down coming around the point; so we come back.

"Yes," says I, "and other times, when things is dull, they fuss with the parlyment; and if everybody don't go just so he whacks their heads off. But mostly they hang around the harem."

"Round' de which?"

"Harem."

"What's de harem?"

"The place where he keep his wives. Don't you know about the harem? Solomon had one; he had about a million wives."

"Why, yes, dat's so; I—I'd done forgot it. A harem's a bo'd'n-house, I reck'n. Mos' likely dey has rackety times in de nussery. En I reck'n de wives quarrels considable; en dat 'crease de racket. Yit dey say Sollermun de wises' man dat ever live'. I doan' take no stock in dat. Bekase why: would a wise man want to live in de mids' er sich a blimblammin' all de time? No—'deed he wouldn't. A wise man 'ud take en buil' a biler-factry; en den he could shet *down* de biler-factry when he want to res'."

"Well, but he *was* the wisest man, anyway; because the widow she told me so, her own self."

"I doan k'yer what de widder say, he *warn't* no wise man, nuther. He had some er de dad-fetchedes' ways I ever see. Does you know 'bout dat chile dat he 'uz gwyne to chop in two?"[94]

"Yes, the widow told me all about it."

"*Well,* den! Warn' dat de beatenes' notion in de worl'? You jes' take en look at it a minute. Dah's de stump, dah—dat's one er de women; heah's you—dat's de yuther one; I's Sollermun; en dish-yer dollar bill's de chile. Bofe un you claims it. What does I do? Does I shin aroun' mongs' de neighbors en fine out which un you de bill *do* b'long to, en han' it over to de right one, all safe en soun', de way dat anybody dat had any gumption would? No—I take en whack de bill in *two,* en give half un it to you, en de yuther half to de yuther woman. Dat's de way Sollermun was gwyne to do wid de chile. Now I want to ast you: what's de use er dat half a bill?—can't buy noth'n wid it. En what use is a half a chile? I would'n give a dern for a million un um."

"But hang it, Jim, you've clean missed the point—blame it, you've missed it a thousand mile."

"Who? Me? Go 'long. Doan' talk to *me* 'bout yo' pints. I reck'n I knows sense when I sees it; en dey ain' no sense in sich doin's as dat. De 'spute warn't 'bout a half a chile, de 'spute was 'bout a whole chile; en de man dat think he kin settle a 'spute 'bout a whole chile wid a half a chile, doan' know enough to come in out'n de rain. Doan' talk to me 'bout Sollermun, Huck, I knows him by de back."

"But I tell you you don't get the point."

"Blame de pint! I reck'n I knows what I knows. En mine you, de *real* pint is down furder—it's down deeper. It lays in de way Sollermun was raised. You take

[94]To halt a dispute about the parentage of a child, Solomon threatened to divide it in two, expecting the real parent to make strenuous objections (I Kings 3:16–28).

a man dat's got on'y one er two chillen; is dat man gwyne to be waseful o' chillen? No, he ain't; he can't 'ford it. *He* know how to value 'em. But you take a man dat's got 'bout five million chillen runnin' roun' de house, en it's diffunt. *He* as soon chop a chile in two as a cat. Dey's plenty mo'. A chile er two, mo'er less, warn't no consekens to Sollermun, dad fetch him!"

I never see such a nigger. If he got a notion in his head once, there warn't no getting it out again. He was the most down on Solomon of any nigger I ever see. So I went to talking about other kings, and let Solomon slide. I told about Louis Sixteenth that got his head cut off in France long time ago; and about his little boy the dolphin,[95] that would a been a king, but they took and shut him up in jail, and some say he died there.

"Po' little chap."

"But some says he got out and got away, and come to America."

"Dat's good! But he'll be pooty lonesome—dey ain' no kings here, is dey, Huck?"

"No."

"Den, he cain't git no situation. What he gwyne to do?"

"Well, I don't know. Some of them gets on the police, and some of them learns people how to talk French."

"Why, Huck, doan' de French people talk de same way we does?"

"*No*, Jim; you couldn't understand a word they said—not a single word."

"Well, now, I be ding-busted! How do dat come?"

"*I* don't know; but it's so. I got some of their jabber out of a book. Spose a man was to come to you and say *Polly-voo-franzy*[96]—what would you think?"

"I wouldn' think nuff'n; I'd take en bust him over de head. Dat is, if he warn't white. I wouldn't 'low no nigger to call me dat."

"Shucks, it ain't calling you anything. It's only saying do you know how to talk French."

"Well, den, why couldn't he *say* it?"

"Why, he *is* a-saying it. That's a Frenchman's *way* of saying it."

"Well, it's a blame' ridicklous way, en I doan' want to hear no mo' 'bout it. Dey ain' no sense in it."

"Looky here, Jim; does a cat talk like we do?"

"No, a cat don't."

"Well, does a cow?"

"No, a cow don't, nuther."

"Does a cat talk like a cow, or a cow talk like a cat?"

"No, dey don't."

"It's natural and right for 'em to talk different from each other, ain't it?"

"'Course."

"And ain't it natural and right for a cat and a cow to talk different from *us*?"

"Why, mos' sholy it is."

"Well, then, why ain't it natural and right for a *Frenchman* to talk different from us? You answer me that."

[95]The dauphin, then eldest living son of the king of France. Louis Charles (1785–1795?), son of Louis XVI, survived his father's execution during the French Revolution but died in prison. According to legend, he escaped, and numerous imposters thereafter claimed to be the dauphin and thus Louis XVII.

[96]Huck's version of French: Parlez-vous français? (Do you speak French?)

"Is a cat a man, Huck?"

"No."

"Well, den, dey ain't no sense in a cat talkin' like a man. Is a cow a man?—er is a cow a cat?"

"No, she ain't either of them."

"Well, den, she ain't got no business to talk like either one er the yuther of 'em. Is a Frenchman a man?"

"Yes."

"*Well,* den! Dad blame it, why doan' he *talk* like a man? You answer me *dat!*"

I see it warn't no use wasting words—you can't learn a nigger to argue. So I quit.

CHAPTER XV

We judged that three nights more would fetch us to Cairo,[97] at the bottom of Illinois, where the Ohio River comes in, and that was what we was after. We would sell the raft and get on a steamboat and go way up the Ohio amongst the free States, and then be out of trouble.

Well, the second night a fog begun to come on, and we made for a tow-head to tie to, for it wouldn't do to try to run in fog; but when I paddled ahead in the canoe, with the line, to make fast, there warn't anything but little saplings to tie to. I passed the line around one of them right on the edge of the cut bank,[98] but there was a stiff current, and the raft come booming down so lively she tore it out by the roots and away she went. I see the fog closing down, and it made me so sick and scared I couldn't budge for most a half a minute it seemed to me—and then there warn't no raft in sight; you couldn't see twenty yards. I jumped into the canoe and run back to the stern and grabbed the paddle and set her back a stroke. But she didn't come. I was in such a hurry I hadn't untied her. I got up and tried to untie her, but I was so excited my hands shook so I couldn't hardly do anything with them.

As soon as I got started I took out after the raft, hot and heavy, right down the tow-head. That was all right as far as it went, but the tow-head warn't sixty yards long, and the minute I flew by the foot of it I shoot out into the solid white fog, and hadn't no more idea which way I was going than a dead man.

Thinks I, it won't do to paddle; first I know I'll run into the bank or a tow-head or something; I got to set still and float, and yet it's mighty fidgety business to have to hold your hands still at such a time. I whooped and listened. Away down there, somewhere, I hears a small whoop, and up comes my spirits. I went tearing after it, listening sharp to hear it again. The next time it come. I see I warn't heading for it but heading away to the right of it. And the next time, I was heading away to the left of it—and not gaining on it much, either, for I was flying around, this way and that and t'other, but it was going straight ahead all the time.

I did wish the fool would think to beat a tin pan, and beat it all the time, but he never did, and it was the still places between the whoops that was making the trouble for me. Well, I fought along, and directly I hears the whoop *behind* me. I was tangled good, now. That was somebody else's whoop, or else I was turned around.

[97]Pronounced KAY-roh. [98]Steep bank formed by the cutting force of the river's current.

I throwed the paddle down. I heard the whoop again; it was behind me yet, but in a different place; it kept coming, and kept changing its place, and I kept answering, till by-and-by it was in front of me again and I knowed the current had swung the canoe's head down stream and I was all right, if that was Jim and not some other raftsman hollering. I couldn't tell nothing about voices in a fog, for nothing don't look natural nor sound natural in a fog.

The whooping went on, and in about a minute I come a booming down on a cut bank with smoky ghosts of big trees on it, and the current throwed me off to the left and shot by, amongst a lot of snags that fairly roared, the current was tearing by them so swift.

In another second or two it was solid white and still again. I set perfectly still, then, listening to my heart thump, and I reckon I didn't draw a breath while it thumped a hundred.

I just give up, then. I knowed what the matter was. That cut bank was an island, and Jim had gone down t'other side of it. It warn't no tow-head, that you could float by in ten minutes. It had the big timber of a regular island; it might be five or six mile long and more than a half a mile wide.

I kept quiet, with my ears cocked, about fifteen minutes, I reckon. I was floating along, of course, four or five mile an hour; yet you don't ever think of that. No, you *feel* like you are laying dead still on the water; and if a little glimpse of snag slips by, you don't think to yourself how fast *you're* going, but you catch your breath and think, my! how that snag's tearing along. If you think it ain't dismal and lonesome out in a fog that way, by yourself, in the night, you try it once—you'll see.

Next, for about a half an hour, I whoops now and then; at last I hears the answer a long ways off, and tries to follow it, but I couldn't do it, and directly I judged I'd got into a nest of tow-heads, for I had little dim glimpses of them on both sides of me, sometimes just a narrow channel between; and some that I couldn't see, I knowed was there, because I'd hear the wash of the current against the old dead brush and trash that hung over the banks. Well, I warn't long losing the whoops, down amongst the tow-heads; and I only tried to chase them a little while, anyway, because it was worse than chasing a Jack-o-lantern.[99] You never knowed a sound dodge around so, and swap places so quick and so much.

I had to claw away from the bank pretty lively, four or five times, to keep from knocking the islands out of the river; and so I judged the raft must be butting into the bank every now and then, or else it would get further ahead and clear out of hearing—it was floating a little faster than what I was.

Well, I seemed to be in the open river again, by-and-by, but I couldn't hear no sign of a whoop nowheres. I reckoned Jim had fetched up on a snag, maybe, and it was all up with him. I was good and tired, so I laid down in the canoe and said I wouldn't bother no more. I didn't want to go to sleep, of course; but I was so sleepy I couldn't help it; so I thought I would take just one little cat-nap.

But I reckon it was more than a cat-nap, for when I waked up the stars was shining bright, the fog was all gone, and I was spinning down a big bend stern first. First I didn't know where I was; I thought I was dreaming; and when things begun to come back to me, they seemed to come up dim out of last week.

[99]A will-o'-the-wisp, an elusive light.

It was a monstrous big river here, with the tallest and the thickest kind of timber on both banks; just a solid wall, as well as I could see, by the stars. I looked away down stream, and seen a black speck on the water. I took out after it, but when I got to it it warn't nothing but a couple of saw-logs made fast together. Then I see another speck, and chased that; then, another, and this time I was right. It was the raft.

When I got to it Jim was setting there with his head down between his knees, asleep, with his right arm hanging over the steering oar. The other oar was smashed off, and the raft was littered up with leaves and branches and dirt. So she'd had a rough time.

I made fast and laid down under Jim's nose on the raft, and begun to gap, and stretch my fists out against Jim, and says:

"Hello, Jim, have I been asleep? Why didn't you stir me up?"

"Goodness gracious, is dat you, Huck? En you ain' dead—you ain' drownded—you's back agin? It's too good for true, honey, it's too good for true. Lemme look at you, chile, lemme feel o' you. No, you ain' dead! you's back agin, 'live en soun', jis de same ole Huck—de same ole Huck, thanks to goodness!"

"What's the matter with you, Jim? You been a drinking?"

"Drinkin'? Has I ben a drinkin'? Has I had a chance to be a drinkin'?"

"Well, then, what makes you talk so wild?"

"How does I talk wild?"

"*How?* why, hain't you been talking about my coming back, and all that stuff, as if I'd been gone away?"

"Huck—Huck Finn, you look me in de eye; look me in de eye. *Hain't* you been gone away?"

"Gone away? Why, what in the nation do you mean? *I* hain't been gone anywheres. Where would I go to?"

"Well, looky here, boss, dey's sumf'n wrong, dey is. Is I *me,* or who *is* I? Is I heah, or whah *is* I? Now dat's what I wants to know."

"Well, I think you're here, plain enough, but I think you're a tangle-headed old fool, Jim."

"I is, is I? Well you answer me dis. Didn't you tote out de line in de canoe, fer to make fas' to de tow-head?"

"No, I didn't. What tow-head? I hain't seen no tow-head."

"You hain't seen no tow-head? Looky here—didn't de line pull loose en de raf' go a hummin' down de river, en leave you en de canoe behine in de fog?"

"What fog?"

"Why *de* fog. De fog dat's ben aroun' all night. En didn't you whoop, en didn't I whoop, tell we got mix' up in de islands en one un us got los' en t'other one was jis' as good as los', 'kase he didn't know whah he wuz? En didn't I bust up agin a lot er dem islands en have a turrible time en mos' git drowned? Now ain' dat so, boss—ain't it so? You answer me dat."

"Well, this is too many for me, Jim. I hain't seen no fog, nor no islands, nor no troubles, nor nothing. I been setting here talking with you all night till you went to sleep about ten minutes ago, and I reckon I done the same. You couldn't a got drunk in that time, so of course you've been dreaming."

"Dad fetch it, how is I gwyne to dream all dat in ten minutes?"

"Well, hang it all, you did dream it, because there didn't any of it happen."

"But Huck, it's all jis' as plain to me as——"

"It don't make no difference how plain it is, there ain't nothing in it. I know, because I've been here all the time."

Jim didn't say nothing for about five minutes, but set there studying over it. Then he says:

"Well, den, I reck'n I did dream it, Huck; but dog my cats ef it ain't de powerfullest dream I ever see. En I hain't ever had no dream b'fo' dat's tired me like dis one."

"Oh, well, that's all right, because a dream does tire a body like everything, sometimes. But this one was a staving[100] dream—tell me all about it, Jim."

So Jim went to work and told me the whole thing right through, just as it happened, only he painted it up considerable. Then he said he must start in and " 'terpret" it, because it was sent for a warning. He said the first tow-head stood for a man that would try to do us some good, but the current was another man that would get us away from him. The whoops was warnings that would come to us every now and then, and if we didn't try hard to make out to understand them they'd just take us into bad luck, 'stead of keeping us out of it. The lot of tow-heads was troubles we was going to get into with quarrelsome people and all kinds of mean folks, but if we minded our business and didn't talk back and aggravate them, we would pull through and get out of the fog and into the big clear river,[101] which was the free States, and wouldn't have no more trouble.

It had clouded up pretty dark just after I got onto the raft, but it was clearing up again, now.

"Oh, well, that's all interpreted well enough, as far as it goes, Jim," I says; "but what does *these* things stand for?"

It was the leaves and rubbish on the raft, and the smashed oar. You could see them first rate, now.

Jim looked at the trash, and then looked at me, and back at the trash again. He had got the dream fixed so strong in his head that he couldn't seem to shake it loose and get the facts back into its place again, right away. But when he did get the thing straightened around, he looked at me steady, without ever smiling, and says:

"What do dey stan' for? I's gwyne to tell you. When I got all wore out wid work, en wid de callin' for you, en went to sleep, my heart wuz mos' broke bekase you wuz los', en I didn' k'yer no mo' what become er me en de raf'. En when I wake up en fine you back agin', all safe en soun', de tears come en I could a got down on my knees en kiss' yo' foot I's so thankful. En all you wuz thinkin 'bout wuz how you could make a fool uv ole Jim wid a lie. Dat truck dah is *trash;* en trash is what people is dat puts dirt on de head[102] er dey fren's en makes 'em ashamed."

Then he got up slow, and walked to the wigwam, and went in there, without saying anything but that. But that was enough. It made me feel so mean I could almost kissed *his* foot to get him to take it back.

It was fifteen minutes before I could work myself up to go and humble myself to a nigger—but I done it, and I warn't ever sorry for it afterwards, neither. I didn't do him no more mean tricks, and I wouldn't done that one if I'd a knowed it would make him feel that way.

[100]Smashing. [101]The Ohio River.

[102]A reference to various Old Testament figures who "cast up dust upon their heads" in a gesture of submission and humiliation, as in Ezekiel 27:30.

CHAPTER XVI

We slept most all day, and started out at night, a little ways behind a monstrous long raft that was as long going by as a procession. She had four long sweeps[103] at each end, so we judged she carried as many as thirty men, likely. She had five big wigwams aboard, wide apart, and an open camp fire in the middle, and a tall flag-pole at each end. There was a power of style about her. It *amounted* to something being a raftsman on such a craft as that.

We went drifting down into a big bend, and the night clouded up and got hot. The river was very wide, and was walled with solid timber on both sides; you couldn't see a break in it hardly ever, or a light. We talked about Cairo, and wondered whether we would know it when we got to it. I said likely we wouldn't, because I had heard say there warn't but about a dozen houses there, and if they didn't happen to have them lit up, how was we going to know we was passing a town? Jim said if the two big rivers joined together there, that would show. But I said maybe we might think we was passing the foot of an island and coming into the same old river again. That disturbed Jim—and me too. So the question was, what to do? I said, paddle ashore the first time a light showed, and tell them pap was behind, coming along with a trading-scow, and was a green hand at the business, and wanted to know how far it was to Cairo. Jim thought it was a good idea, so we took a smoke on it and waited.

There warn't nothing to do, now, but to look out sharp for the town, and not pass it without seeing it. He said he'd be mighty sure to see it, because he'd be a free man the minute he seen it, but if he missed it he'd be in the slave country again and no more show[104] for freedom. Every little while he jumps up and says:

"Dah she is!"

But it warn't. It was Jack-o-lanterns, or lightning-bugs; so he set down again, and went to watching, same as before. Jim said it made him all over trembly and feverish to be so close to freedom. Well, I can tell you it made me all over trembly and feverish, too, to hear him, because I begun to get it through my head that he *was* most free—and who was to blame for it? Why, *me.* I couldn't get that out of my conscience, no how nor no way. It got to troubling me so I couldn't rest; I couldn't stay still in one place. It hadn't ever come to me before, what this thing was that I was doing. But now it did; and it staid with me, and scorched me more and more. I tried to make out to myself that *I* warn't to blame, because *I* didn't run Jim off from his rightful owner; but it warn't no use, conscience up and says, every time, "But you knowed he was running for his freedom, and you could a paddled ashore and told somebody." That was so—I couldn't get around that, noway. That was where it pinched. Conscience says to me, "What had poor Miss Watson done to you, that you could see her nigger go off right under your eyes and never say one single word? What did that poor old woman do to you, that you could treat her so mean? Why, she tried to learn you your book, she tried to learn you your manners, she tried to be good to you every way she knowed how. *That's* what she done."

I got to feeling so mean and so miserable I most wished I was dead. I fidgeted up and down the raft, abusing myself to myself, and Jim was fidgeted up and

[103]Long oars used for steering. [104]Chance.

down past me. We neither of us could keep still. Every time he danced around and says, "Dah's Cairo!" it went through me like a shot, and I thought if it *was* Cairo I reckoned I would die of miserableness.

Jim talked out loud all the time while I was talking to myself. He was saying how the first thing he would do when he got to a free State he would go to saving up money and never spend a single cent, and when he got enough he would buy his wife, which was owned on a farm close to where Miss Watson lived; and then they would both work to buy the two children, and if their master wouldn't sell them, they'd get an Ab'litionist to go and steal them.

It most froze me to hear such talk. He wouldn't ever dared to talk such talk in his life before. Just see what a difference it made in him the minute he judged he was about free. It was according to the old saying, "give a nigger an inch and he'll take an ell." Thinks I, this is what comes of my not thinking. Here was this nigger which I had as good as helped to run away, coming right out flat-footed and saying he would steal his children—children that belonged to a man I didn't even know; a man that hadn't ever done me no harm.

I was sorry to hear Jim say that, it was such a lowering of him. My conscience got to stirring me up hotter than ever, until at last I says to it, "Let up on me—it ain't too late, yet—I'll paddle ashore at the first light, and tell." I felt easy, and happy, and light as a feather, right off. All my troubles was gone. I went to looking out sharp for a light, and sort of singing to myself. By-and-by one showed. Jim sings out:

"We's safe. Huck, we's safe! Jump up and crack yo' heels, dat's de good ole Cairo at las', I jis knows it!"

I says:

"I'll take the canoe and go see, Jim. It mightn't be, you know."

He jumped and got the canoe ready, and put his old coat in the bottom for me to set on, and give me the paddle; and as I shoved off, he says:

"Pooty soon I'll be a-shout'n for joy, en I'll say, it's all on accounts o'Huck; I's a free man, en I couldn't ever ben free ef it hadn' ben for Huck; Huck done it. Jim won't ever forgit you, Huck; you's de bes' fren' Jim's ever had; en you's de *only* fren' ole Jim's got now."

I was paddling off, all in a sweat to tell on him; but when he says this, it seemed to kind of take the tuck all out of me. I went along slow then, and I warn't right down certain whether I was glad I started or whether I warn't. When I was fifty yards off, Jim says:

"Dah you goes, de ole true Huck; de on'y white genlman dat ever kep' his promise to ole Jim."

Well, I just felt sick. But I says, I *got* to do it—I can't get *out* of it. Right then, along comes a skiff with two men in it, with guns, and they stopped and I stopped. One of they says:

"What's that, yonder?"

"A piece of a raft," I says.

"Do you belong on it?"

"Yes, sir."

"Any men on it?"

"Only one, sir."

"Well, there's five niggers run off to-night, up yonder above the head of the bend. Is your man white or black?"

I didn't answer up prompt. I tried to, but the words wouldn't come. I tried, for a second or two, to brace up and out with it, but I warn't man enough—hadn't the spunk of a rabbit. I see I was weakening; so I just give up trying, and up and says—

"He's white."

"I reckon we'll go and see for ourselves."

"I wish you would," says I, "because it's pap that's there, and maybe you'd help me tow the raft ashore where the light is. He's sick—and so is mam and Mary Ann."

"Oh, the devil! we're in a hurry, boy. But I s'pose we've got to. Come—buckle to your paddle, and let's get along."

I buckled to my paddle and they laid to their oars. When we had made a stroke or two, I says:

"Pap'll be mighty much obleeged to you, I can tell you. Everybody goes away when I want them to help me tow the raft ashore, and I can't do it by myself."

"Well, that's infernal mean. Odd, too. Say, boy, what's the matter with your father?"

"It's the—a—the—well, it ain't anything, much."

They stopped pulling. It warn't but a mighty little ways to the raft, now. One says:

"Boy, that's a lie. What *is* the matter with your pap? Answer up square, now, and it'll be the better for you."

"I will, sir, I will, honest—but don't leave us, please. It's the—the—gentlemen, if you'll only pull ahead, and let me heave you the head-line,[105] you won't have to come a-near the raft—please do."

"Set her back, John, set her back!" says one. They backed water. "Keep away, boy—keep to looard.[106] Confound it, I just expect the wind has blowed it to us. Your pap's got the small-pox, and you know it precious well. Why didn't you come out and say so? Do you want to spread it all over?"

"Well," says I, a-blubbering, "I've told everybody before, and then they just went away and left us."

"Poor devil, there's something in that. We are right down sorry for you, but we—well, hang it, we don't want the small-pox, you see. Look here, I'll tell you what to do. Don't you try to land by yourself, or you'll smash everything to pieces. You float along down about twenty miles and you'll come to a town on the left-hand side of the river. It will be long after sun-up, then, and when you ask for help, you tell them your folks are all down with chills and fever. Don't be a fool again, and let people guess what is the matter. Now we're trying to do you a kindness; so you just put twenty miles between us, that's a good boy. It wouldn't do any good to land yonder where the light is—it's only a wood-yard.[107] Say—I reckon your father's poor, and I'm bound to say he's in pretty hard luck. Here—I'll put a twenty dollar gold piece on this board, and you get it when it floats by. I feel mighty mean to leave you, but my kingdom! it won't do to fool with small-pox, don't you see?"

"Hold on, Parker," says the other man, "here's a twenty to put on the board for me. Good-bye, boy, you do as Mr. Parker told you, and you'll be all right."

[105]Line attached to the prow of a boat. [106]Leeward, downwind.
[107]Refueling station for wood-burning steamboats.

"That's so, my boy—good-bye, good-bye. If you see any runaway niggers, you get help and nab them, and you can make some money by it."

"Good-bye, sir," says I, "I won't let no runaway niggers get by me if I can help it."

They went off, and I got aboard the raft, feeling bad and low, because I knowed very well I had done wrong, and I see it warn't no use for me to try to learn to do right; a body that don't get *started* right when he's little, ain't got no show—when the pinch comes there ain't nothing to back him up and keep him to his work, and so he gets beat. Then I thought a minute, and says to myself, hold on,—spose you'd a done right and give Jim up; would you felt better than what you do now? No, says I, I'd feel bad—I'd feel just the same way I do now. Well, then, says I, what's the use you learning to do right, when it's troublesome to do right and ain't no trouble to do wrong, and the wages is just the same? I was stuck. I couldn't answer that. So I reckoned I wouldn't bother no more about it, but after this always do whichever come handiest at the time.

I went into the wigwam; Jim warn't there. I looked all around; he warn't anywhere. I says:

"Jim!"

"Here I is, Huck, Is dey out o' sight yit? Don't talk loud."

He was in the river, under the stern oar, with just his nose out. I told him they was out of sight, so he come aboard. He says:

"I was a-listenin' to all de talk, en I slips into de river en was gwyne to shove for sho' if dey come aboard. Den I was gwyne to swim to de raf' agin when dey was gone. But lawsy, how you did fool 'em, Huck! Dat *wuz* de smartes' dodge! I tell you, chile, I 'speck it save' ole Jim—old Jim ain't gwyne to forgit you for dat, honey."

Then we talked about the money. It was a pretty good raise, twenty dollars apiece. Jim said we could take deck passage[108] on a steamboat now, and the money would last us as far as we wanted to go in the free States. He said twenty mile more warn't far for the raft to go, but he wished we was already there.

Towards daybreak we tied up, and Jim was mighty particular about hiding the raft good. Then he worked all day fixing things in bundles, and getting all ready to quit rafting.

That night about ten we hove in sight of the lights of a town away down in a left-hand bend.

I went off in the canoe, to ask about it. Pretty soon I found a man out in the river with a skiff, setting a trot-line. I ranged up and says:

"Mister, is that town Cairo?"

"Cairo? no. You must be a blame' fool."

"What town is it, mister?"

"If you want to know, go and find out. If you stay here botherin' around me for about a half a minute longer, you'll get something you won't want."

I paddled to the raft. Jim was awful disappointed, but I said never mind, Cairo would be the next place, I reckoned.

We passed another town before daylight, and I was going out again; but it was high ground, so I didn't go. No high ground about Cairo, Jim said. I had forgot it. We laid up for the day, on a tow-head tolerable close to the left-bank. I begun to suspicion something. So did Jim. I says:

[108]Without a private cabin, the cheapest passage.

"Maybe we went by Cairo in the fog that night."

He says:

"Doan' less talk about it, Huck. Po' niggers can't have no luck. I awluz 'spected dat rattle-snake skin warn't done wid its work."

"I wish I'd never seen that snake-skin, Jim—I do wish I'd never laid eyes on it."

"It ain't yo' fault, Huck; you didn' know. Don't you blame yo'self 'bout it."

When it was daylight, here was the clear Ohio water in shore, sure enough, and outside was the old regular Muddy! So it was all up with Cairo.[109]

We talked it all over. It wouldn't do to take to the shore; we couldn't take the raft up the stream, of course. There warn't no way but to wait for dark, and start back in the canoe and take the chances. So we slept all day amongst the cotton-wood thicket, so as to be fresh for the work, and when we went back to the raft about dark the canoe was gone!

We didn't say a word for a good while. There warn't anything to say. We both knowed well enough it was some more work of the rattle-snake skin; so what was the use to talk about it? It would only look like we was finding fault, and that would be bound to fetch more bad luck—and keep on fetching it, too, till we knowed enough to keep still.

By-and-by we talked about what we better do, and found there warn't no way but just to go along down with the raft till we got a chance to buy a canoe to go back in. We warn't going to borrow it when there warn't anybody around, the way pap would do, for that might set people after us.

So we shoved out, after dark, on the raft.

Anybody that don't believe yet, that it's foolishness to handle a snake-skin, after all that that snake-skin done for us, will believe it now, if they read on and see what more it done for us.

The place to buy canoes is off of rafts laying up at shore. But we didn't see no rafts laying up; so we went along during three hours and more. Well, the night got gray, and ruther thick, which is the next meanest thing to fog. You can't tell the shape of the river, and you can't see no distance. It got to be very late and still, and then along comes a steamboat up the river. We lit the lantern, and judged she would see it. Up-stream boats didn't generly come close to us; they go out and follow the bars and hunt for easy water under the reefs; but nights like this they bull right up the channel against the whole river.

We could hear her pounding along, but we didn't see her good till she was close. She aimed right for us. Often they do that and try to see how close they can come without touching; sometimes the wheel bites off a sweep, and then the pilot sticks his head out and laughs, and thinks he's mighty smart. Well, here she comes, and we said she was going to try to shave us; but she didn't seem to be sheering off a bit. She was a big one, and she was coming in a hurry, too, looking like a black cloud with rows of glowworms around it; but all of a sudden she bulged out, big and scary, with a long row of wide-open furnace doors shining like red-hot teeth, and her monstrous bows and guards hanging right over us. There was a yell at us, and a jingling of bells to stop the engines, a pow-wow of cussing, and whistling of steam—and as Jim went overboard on one side and I on the other, she come smashing straight through the raft.

[109]When Huck sees the clearer waters of the Ohio flowing in the Mississippi, he knows he and Jim have passed beyond the confluence of the two rivers at Cairo, where they had hoped to go up the Ohio River.

I dived—and I aimed to find the bottom, too, for a thirty-foot wheel had got to go over me, and I wanted it to have plenty of room. I could always stay under water a minute; this time I reckon I staid under water a minute and a half. Then I bounced for the top in a hurry, for I was nearly busting. I popped out to my arm-pits and blowed the water out of my nose, and puffed a bit. Of course there was a booming current; and of course that boat started her engines again ten seconds after she stopped them, for they never cared much for raftsmen; so now she was churning along up the river, out of sight in the thick weather, though I could hear her.

I sung out for Jim, about a dozen times, but I didn't get any answer; so I grabbed a plank that touched me while I was "treading water," and struck out for shore, shoving it ahead of me. But I made out to see that the drift of the current was towards the left-hand shore,[110] which meant that I was in a crossing; so I changed off and went that way.

It was one of these long, slanting, two-mile crossings; so I was a good long time in getting over. I made a safe landing, and clum up the bank. I couldn't see but a little ways, but I went poking along over rough ground for a quarter of a mile or more, and then I run across a big old-fashioned double log house[111] before I noticed it. I was going to rush by and get away, but a lot of dogs jumped out and went to howling and barking at me, and I knowed better than to move another peg.

CHAPTER XVII

In about half a minute somebody spoke out a window, without putting his head out, and says:

"Be done, boys! Who's there?"

I says:

"It's me."

"Who's me?"

"George Jackson, sir."

"What do you want?"

"I don't want nothing, sir. I only want to go along by, but the dogs won't let me."

"What are you prowling around here this time of night, for—hey?"

"I warn't prowling around, sir; I fell overboard off of the steamboat."

"Oh, you did, did you? Strike a light there, somebody. What did you say your name was?"

"George Jackson, sir. I'm only a boy."

"Look here; if you're telling the truth, you needn't be afraid—nobody 'll hurt you. But don't try to budge; stand right where you are. Rouse out Bob and Tom, some of you, and fetch the guns. George Jackson, is there anybody with you?"

"No, sir, nobody."

I heard the people stirring around in the house, now, and see a light. The man sung out:

[110]Kentucky, where the next episode takes place.

[111]A two-room log house, under a single roof and with an open passageway separating the two rooms.

"Snatch that light away, Betsy, you old fool—ain't you got any sense? Put it on the floor behind the front door. Bob, if you and Tom are ready, take your places."

"All ready."

"Now, George Jackson, do you know the Shepherdsons?"

"No, sir—I never heard of them."

"Well, that may be so, and it mayn't. Now, all ready, Step forward, George Jackson. And mind, don't you hurry—come mighty slow. If there's anybody with you, let him keep back—if he shows himself he'll be shot. Come along, now. Come slow; push the door open, yourself—just enough to squeeze in, d' you hear?"

I didn't hurry, I couldn't if I'd a wanted to. I took one slow step at a time, and there warn't a sound, only I thought I could hear my heart. The dogs were as still as the humans, but they followed a little behind me. When I got to the three log door-steps, I heard them unlocking and unbarring and unbolting. I put my hand on the door and pushed it a little and a little more, till somebody said, "There, that's enough—put your head in." I done it, but I judged they would take it off.

The candle was on the floor, and there they all was, looking at me, and me at them, for about a quarter of a minute. Three big men with guns pointed at me, which made me wince, I tell you; the oldest, gray and about sixty, the other two thirty or more—all of them fine and handsome—and the sweetest old gray-headed lady, and back of her two young women which I couldn't see right well. The old gentleman says:

"There—I reckon it's all right. Come in."

As soon as I was in, the old gentleman he locked the door and barred it and bolted it, and told the young men to come in with their guns, and they all went in a big parlor that had a new rag carpet on the floor, and got together in a corner that was out of range of the front windows—there warn't none on the side. They held the candle, and took a good look at me, and all said, "Why *he* ain't a Shepherdson—no, there ain't any Shepherdson about him." Then the old man said he hoped I wouldn't mind being searched for arms, because he didn't mean no harm by it—it was only to make sure. So he didn't pry into my pockets, but only felt outside with his hands, and said it was all right. He told me to make myself easy and at home, and tell all about myself; but the old lady says:

"Why bless you, Saul, the poor thing's as wet as he can be; and don't you reckon it may be he's hungry?"

"True for you, Rachel—I forgot."

So the old lady says:

"Betsy" (this was a nigger woman), "you fly around and get him something to eat, as quick as you can, poor thing; and one of you girls go and wake up Buck and tell him—Oh, here he is himself. Buck, take this little stranger and get the wet clothes off from him and dress him up in some of yours that's dry."

Buck looked about as old as me—thirteen or fourteen[112] or along there, though he was a little bigger than me. He hadn't on anything but a shirt, and he was very frowsy-headed. He come in gaping and digging one fist into his eyes, and he was dragging a gun along with the other one. He says:

[112]Elsewhere Twain wrote that Huck was fourteen.

"Ain't they no Shepherdsons around?"

They said, no, 'twas a false alarm.

"Well," he says, "if they'd a ben some, I reckon I'd a got one."

They all laughed, and Bob says:

"Why, Buck, they might have scalped us all, you've been so slow in coming."

"Well, nobody come after me, and it ain't right. I'm always kep' down; I don't get no show."

"Never mind, Buck, my boy," says the old man, "you'll have show enough, all in good time, don't you fret about that. Go 'long with you now, and do as your mother told you."

When we got up stairs to his room, he got me a coarse shirt and a roundabout[113] and pants of his, and I put them on. While I was at it he asked me what my name was, but before I could tell him, he started to telling me about a blue jay and a young rabbit he had catched in the woods day before yesterday, and he asked me where Moses was when the candle went out. I said I didn't know; I hadn't heard about it before, no way.

"Well, guess," he says.

"How'm I going to guess," says I, "when I never heard tell about it before?"

"But you can guess, can't you? It's just as easy."

"*Which* candle?" I says.

"Why, any candle," he says.

"I don't know where he was," says I; "where was he?"

"Why he was in the *dark!* That's where he was!"

"Well, if you knowed where he was, what did you ask me for?"

"Why, blame it, it's a riddle, don't you see? Say, how long are you going to stay here? You got to stay always. We can just have booming times—they don't have no school now. Do you own a dog? I've got a dog—and he'll go in the river and bring out chips that you throw in. Do you like to comb up, Sundays, and all that kind of foolishness? You bet I don't, but ma she makes me. Confound these ole britches, I reckon I'd better put 'em on, but I'd ruther not, it's so warm. Are you all ready? All right—come along, old hoss."

Cold corn-pone, cold corn-beef, butter and butter-milk—that is what they had for me down there, and there ain't nothing better that ever I've come across yet. Buck and his ma and all of them smoked cob pipes, except the nigger woman, which was gone, and the two young women. They all smoked and talked, and I eat and talked. The young women had quilts around them, and their hair down their backs. They all asked me questions, and I told them how pap and me and all the family was living on a little farm down at the bottom of Arkansaw, and my sister Mary Ann run off and got married and never was heard of no more, and Bill went to hunt them and he warn't heard of no more, and Tom and Mort died, and then there warn't nobody but just me and pap left, and he was just trimmed down to nothing, on account of his troubles; so when he died I took what was left, because the farm didn't belong to us, and started up the river, deck passage, and fell overboard; and that was how I come to be here. So they said I could have a home there as long as I wanted it. Then it was most daylight, and everybody went to bed, and I went to bed with Buck, and when I waked up in the morning, drat it all, I had forgot what my name was. So I laid there about an hour trying to think, and when Buck waked up, I says:

[113]A jacket.

"Can you spell, Buck?"

"Yes," he says.

"I bet you can't spell my name," says I.

"I bet you what you dare I can," says he.

"All right," says I, "go ahead."

"G-o-r-g-e J-a-x-o-n—there now," he says.

"Well," says I, "you done it, but I didn't think you could. It ain't no slouch of a name to spell—right off without studying."

I set it down, private, because somebody might want *me* to spell it, next, and so I wanted to be handy with it and rattle it off like I was used to it.

It was a mighty nice family, and a mighty nice house, too. I hadn't seen no house out in the country before that was so nice and had so much style. It didn't have an iron latch on the front door, nor a wooden one with a buckskin string, but a brass knob to turn, the same as houses in a town. There warn't no bed in the parlor, not a sign of a bed; but heaps of parlors in towns has beds in them. There was a big fireplace that was bricked on the bottom, and the bricks was kept clean and red by pouring water on them and scrubbing them with another brick; sometimes they washed them over with red water-paint that they call Spanish-brown, same as they do in town. They had big brass dog-irons[114] that could hold up a saw-log.[115] There was a clock on the middle of the mantelpiece, with a picture of a town painted on the bottom half of the glass front, and a round place in the middle of it for the sun, and you could see the pendulum swing behind it. It was beautiful to hear that clock tick; and sometimes when one of these peddlers had been along and scoured her up and got her in good shape, she would start in and strike a hundred and fifty before she got tuckered out. They wouldn't took any money for her.

Well, there was a big outlandish parrot on each side of the clock, made out of something like chalk, and painted up gaudy. By one of the parrots was a cat made of crockery, and a crockery dog by the other; and when you pressed down on them they squeaked, but didn't open their mouths nor look different nor interested. They squeaked through underneath. There was a couple of big wild-turkey-wing fans spread out behind those things. On a table in the middle of the room was a kind of a lovely crockery basket that had apples and oranges and peaches and grapes piled up in it which was much redder and yellower and prettier than real ones is, but they warn't real because you could see where pieces had got chipped off and showed the white chalk or whatever it was, underneath.

This table had a cover made out of beautiful oil-cloth, with a red and blue spread-eagle painted on it, and a painted border all around. It come all the way from Philadelphia, they said. There was some books too, piled up perfectly exact, on each corner of the table. One was a big family Bible, full of pictures. One was "Pilgrim's Progress,"[116] about a man that left his family, it didn't say why. I read considerable in it now and then. The statements was interesting, but tough. Another was "Friendship's Offering,"[117] full of beautiful stuff and poetry; but I didn't read the poetry. Another was Henry Clay's[118] Speeches, and

[114]Andirons. [115]A log long and large enough to saw into timbers and beams.
[116]A Christian allegory by the English Puritan John Bunyan (1628–1688).
[117]A gift-book collection of sentimental prose and poetry.
[118]Political leader and orator from Kentucky (1777–1852).

another was Dr. Gunn's Family Medicine,[119] which told you all about what to do if a body was sick or dead. There was a Hymn Book, and a lot of other books. And there was nice split-bottom chairs, and perfectly sound, too—not bagged down in the middle and busted, like an old basket.

They had pictures hung on the walls—mainly Washingtons and Lafayettes, and battles, and Highland Marys,[120] and one called "Signing the Declaration." There was some that they called crayons, which one of the daughters which was dead made her own self when she was only fifteen years old. They was different from any pictures I ever see before; blacker, mostly, than is common. One was a woman in a slim black dress, belted small under the arm-pits, with bulges like a cabbage in the middle of the sleeves, and a large black scoop-shovel bonnet with a black veil, and white slim ankles crossed about with black tape, and very wee black slippers, like a chisel, and she was leaning pensive on a tombstone on her right elbow, under a weeping willow, and her other hand hanging down her side holding a white handkerchief and a reticule, and underneath the picture it said "Shall I Never See Thee More Alas." Another one was a young lady with her hair all combed up straight to the top of her head, and knotted there in front of a comb like a chair-back, and she was crying into a handkerchief and had a dead bird laying on its back in her other hand with its heels up, and underneath the picture it said "I Shall Never Hear Thy Sweet Chirrup More Alas." There was one where a young lady was at a window looking up at the moon, and tears running down her cheeks; and she had an open letter in one hand with black sealing-wax showing on one edge of it, and she was mashing a locket with a chain to it against her mouth, and underneath the picture it said "And Art Thou Gone Yes Thou Art Gone Alas." These was all nice pictures, I reckon, but I didn't somehow seem to take to them, because if ever I was down a little, they always give me the fan-tods. Everybody was sorry she died, because she had laid out a lot more of these pictures to do, and a body could see by what she had done what they had lost. But I reckoned, that with her disposition, she was having a better time in the graveyard. She was at work on what they said was her greatest picture when she took sick, and every day and every night it was her prayer to be allowed to live till she got it done, but she never got the chance. It was a picture of a young woman in a long white gown, standing on the rail of a bridge all ready to jump off, with her hair all down her back, and looking up to the moon, with the tears running down her face, and she had two arms folded across her breast, and two arms stretched out in front, and two more reaching up towards the moon—and the idea was, to see which pair would look best and then scratch out all the other arms; but, as I was saying, she died before she got her mind made up, and now they kept this picture over the head of the bed in her room, and every time her birthday come they hung flowers on it. Other times it was hid with a little curtain. The young woman in the picture had a kind of a nice sweet face, but there was so many arms it made her look too spidery, seemed to me.

This young girl kept a scrap-book when she was alive, and used to paste obituaries and accidents and cases of patient suffering in it out of the *Presbyterian*

[119]A medical guide first published in 1830 and still used in 1855.

[120]Mary Campbell, the subject of several elegies by the Scottish poet Robert Burns (1759–1796). She was portrayed in numerous sentimental illustrations.

Observer, and write poetry after them out of her own head. It was very good poetry. This is what she wrote about a boy by the name of Stephen Dowling Bots that fell down a well and was drownded:

ODE TO STEPHEN DOWLING BOTS, DEC'D.[121]

And did young Stephen sicken,
And did young Stephen die?
And did the sad hearts thicken,
And did the mourners cry?

No; such was not the fate of
Young Stephen Dowling Bots;
Though sad hearts round him thickened,
'Twas not from sickness' shots.

No whooping-cough did rack his frame,
Nor measles drear, with spots;
Not these impaired the sacred name
Of Stephen Dowling Bots.

Despised love struck not with woe
That head of curly knots,
Nor stomach troubles laid him low,
Young Stephen Dowling Bots.

O no. Then list with tearful eye,
Whilst I his fate do tell.
His soul did from this cold world fly,
By falling down a well.

They got him out and emptied him;
Alas it was too late;
His spirit was gone for to sport aloft
In the realm of the good and great.

If Emmeline Grangerford could make poetry like that before she was fourteen, there ain't no telling what she could a done by-and-by. Buck said she could rattle off poetry like nothing. She didn't ever have to stop to think. He said she would slap down a line, and if she couldn't find anything to rhyme with it she would just scratch it out and slap down another one, and go ahead. She warn't particular, she could write about anything you choose to give her to write about, just so it was sadful. Every time a man died, or a woman died, or a child died, she would be on hand with her "tribute" before he was cold. She called them tributes. The neighbors said it was the doctor first, then Emmeline, then the undertaker—the undertaker never got in ahead of Emmeline but once, and then she hung fire on a rhyme for the dead person's name, which was Whistler. She warn't ever the same, after that; she never complained, but she kind of pined

[121]Deceased.

away and did not live long. Poor thing, many's the time I made myself go up to the little room that used to be hers and get out her poor old scrap-book and read in it when her pictures had been aggravating me and I had soured on her a little. I liked all that family, dead ones and all, and warn't going to let anything come between us. Poor Emmeline made poetry about all the dead people when she was alive, and it didn't seem right that there warn't nobody to make some about her, now she was gone; so I tried to sweat out a verse or two myself, but I couldn't seem to make it go, somehow. They kept Emmeline's room trim and nice and all the things fixed in it just the way she liked to have them when she was alive, and nobody ever slept there. The old lady took care of the room herself, though there was plenty of niggers, and she sewed there a good deal and read her Bible there, mostly.

Well, as I was saying about the parlor, there was beautiful curtains on the windows; white, with pictures painted on them, of castles with vines all down the walls, and cattle coming down to drink. There was a little old piano, too, that had tin pans[122] in it, I reckon, and nothing was ever so lovely as to hear the young ladies sing, "The Last Link is Broken"[123] and play "The Battle of Prague"[124] on it. The walls of all the rooms was plastered, and most had carpets on the floors, and the whole house was whitewashed on the outside.

It was a double house, and the big open place betwixt them was roofed and floored, and sometimes the table was there in the middle of the day, and it was a cool, comfortable place. Nothing couldn't be better. And warn't the cooking good, and just bushels of it too!

CHAPTER XVIII

Col. Grangerford was a gentleman, you see. He was a gentleman all over; and so was his family. He was well born, as the saying is, and that's worth as much in a man as it is in a horse, so the Widow Douglas said, and nobody ever denied that she was of the first aristocracy in our town; and pap he always said it, too, though he warn't no more quality than a mud-cat,[125] himself. Col. Grangerford was very tall and very slim, and had a darkish-paly complexion, not a sign of red in it anywheres; he was clean-shaved every morning, all over his thin face, and he had the thinnest kind of lips, and the thinnest kind of nostrils, and a high nose, and heavy eyebrows, and the blackest kind of eyes, sunk so deep back that they seemed like they was looking out of caverns at you, as you may say. His forehead was high, and his hair was black and straight, and hung to his shoulders. His hands was long and thin, and every day of his life he put on a clean shirt and a full suit from head to foot made out of linen so white it hurt your eyes to look at it; and on Sundays he wore a blue tail-coat with brass buttons on it. He carried a mahogany cane with a silver head to it. There warn't no frivolishness about him, not a bit, and he warn't ever loud. He was as kind as he

[122]Pianos in the nineteenth century were sometimes built with cymbals and bells that could be sounded by striking keys and foot pedals.

[123]A popular, sentimental song published in 1840.

[124]A piece of ranting, bombastic program music (1788) that attempted to recreate the sounds of the battle of Prague (1756), between the armies of Prussia and Austria.

[125]Catfish.

could be—you could feel that, you know, and so you had confidence. Sometimes he smiled, and it was good to see; but when he straightened himself up like a liberty-pole,[126] and the lightning began to flicker out from under his eyebrows you wanted to climb a tree first, and find out what the matter was afterwards. He didn't ever have to tell anybody to mind their manners—everybody was always good mannered where he was. Everybody loved to have him around, too; he was sunshine most always—I mean he made it seem like good weather. When he turned into a cloud-bank it was awful dark for a half minute and that was enough; there wouldn't nothing go wrong again for a week.

When him and the old lady come down in the morning, all the family got up out of their chairs and give them good-day, and didn't set down again till they had set down. Then Tom and Bob went to the sideboard where the decanters was, and mixed a glass of bitters and handed it to him, and he held it in his hand and waited till Tom's and Bob's was mixed, and then they bowed and said "Our duty to you, sir, madam;" and *they* bowed the least bit in the world and said thank you, and so they drank, all three, and Bob and Tom poured a spoonful of water on the sugar and the mite of whisky or apple brandy in the bottom of their tumblers, and give it to me and Buck, and we drank to the old people too.

Bob was the oldest, and Tom next. Tall, beautiful men with very broad shoulders and brown faces, and long black hair and black eyes. They dressed in white linen from head to foot, like the old gentleman, and wore broad Panama hats.

Then there was Miss Charlotte, she was twenty-five, and tall and proud and grand, but as good as she could be, when she warn't stirred up; but when she was, she had a look that would make you wilt in your tracks, like her father. She was beautiful.

So was her sister, Miss Sophia, but it was a different kind. She was gentle and sweet, like a dove, and she was only twenty.

Each person had their own nigger to wait on them—Buck, too. My nigger had a monstrous easy time, because I warn't used to having anybody do anything for me, but Buck's was on the jump most of the time.

This was all there was of the family, now; but there used to be more—three sons; they got killed; and Emmeline that died.

The old gentleman owned a lot of farms, and over a hundred niggers. Sometimes a stack of people would come there, horseback, from ten to fifteen mile around, and stay five or six days, and have such junketings round about and on the river, and dances and picnics in the woods, day-times, and balls at the house, nights. These people was mostly kin-folks of the family. The men brought their guns with them. It was a handsome lot of quality, I tell you.

There was another clan of aristocracy around there—five or six families—mostly of the name of Shepherdson. They was as high-toned, and well born, and rich and grand, as the tribe of Grangerfords. The Shepherdsons and the Grangerfords used the same steamboat landing, which was about two mile above our house; so sometimes when I went up there with a lot of our folks I used to see a lot of Shepherdsons there, on their fine horses.

One day Buck and me was away out in the woods, hunting, and heard a horse coming. We was crossing the road. Buck says:

"Quick! Jump for the woods!"

[126] A tall pole, often topped with a flag, used as a symbol of liberty.

We done it, and then peeped down the woods through the leaves. Pretty soon a splendid young man come galloping down the road, setting his horse easy and looking like a soldier. He had his gun across his pommel. I had seen him before. It was young Harney Shepherdson. I heard Buck's gun go off at my ear, and Harney's hat tumbled off from his head. He grabbed his gun and rode straight to the place where we was hid. But we didn't wait. We started through the woods on a run. The woods warn't thick, so I looked over my shoulder, to dodge the bullet, and twice I seen Harney cover Buck with his gun; and then he rode away the way he come—to get his hat, I reckon, but I couldn't see. We never stopped running till we got home. The old gentleman's eyes blazed a minute—'twas pleasure, mainly, I judged—then his face sort of smoothed down, and he says, kind of gentle:

"I don't like that shooting from behind a bush. Why didn't you step into the road, my boy?"

"The Shepherdsons don't, father. They always take advantage."

Miss Charlotte she held her head up like a queen while Buck was telling his tale, and her nostrils spread and her eyes snapped. The two young men looked dark, but never said nothing. Miss Sophia she turned pale, but the color came back when she found the man warn't hurt.

Soon as I could get Buck down by the corn-cribs[127] under the trees by ourselves, I says:

"Did you want to kill him, Buck?"

"Well, I bet I did."

"What did he do to you?"

"Him? He never done nothing to me."

"Well, then, what did you want to kill him for?"

"Why nothing—only it's on account of the feud."

"What's a feud?"

"Why, where was you raised? Don't you know what a feud is?"

"Never heard of it before—tell me about it."

"Well," says Buck, "a feud is this way. A man has a quarrel with another man, and kills him; then that other man's brother kills *him;* then the other brothers on both sides, goes for one another; then the *cousins* chip in—and by-and-by everybody's killed off, and there ain't no more feud. But it's kind of slow, and takes a long time."

"Has this one been going on long, Buck?"

"Well I should *reckon!* it started thirty year ago, or som'ers along there. There was trouble 'bout something and then a lawsuit to settle it; and the suit went agin one of the men, and so he up and shot the man that won the suit—which he would naturally do, of course. Anybody would."

"What was the trouble about, Buck?—land?"

"I reckon maybe—I don't know."

"Well, who done the shooting?—was it a Grangerford or a Shepherdson?"

"Laws, how do *I* know? It was so long ago."

"Don't anybody know?"

"Oh, yes, pa knows, I reckon, and some of the other old folks; but they don't know, now, what the row was about in the first place."

"Has there been many killed, Buck?"

[127]Wooden-frame structures used for drying corn.

"Yes—right smart chance of funerals. But they don't always kill. Pa's got a few buck-shot in him; but he don't mind it 'cuz he don't weigh much any- way. Bob's been carved up some with a bowie, and Tom's been hurt once or twice."

"Has anybody been killed this year, Buck?"

"Yes, we got one and they got one. 'Bout three months ago, my cousin Bud, fourteen year old, was riding through the woods, on t'other side of the river, and didn't have no weapon with him, which was blame' foolishness, and in a lonesome place he hears a horse a-coming behind him, and see old Baldy Shepherdson a-linkin' after him with his gun in his hand and his white hair a-flying in the wind; and 'stead of jumping off and taking to the brush, Bud 'lowed he could outrun him; so they had it, nip and tuck, for five mile or more, the old man a-gaining all the time; so at last Bud seen it warn't any use, so he stopped and faced around so as to have the bullet holes in front, you know, and the old man he rode up and shot him down. But he didn't git much chance to enjoy his luck, for inside of a week, our folks laid *him* out."

"I reckon that old man was a coward, Buck."

"I reckon he *warn't* a coward. Not by a blame' sight. There ain't a coward amongst them Shepherdsons—not a one. And there ain't no cowards amongst the Grangerfords, either. Why, that old man kep' up his end in a fight one day, for a half an hour, against three Grangerfords, and come out winner. They was all a-horseback; he lit off of his horse and got behind a little wood-pile, and kep' his horse before him to stop the bullets; but the Grangerfords staid on their horses and capered around the old man, and peppered away at him, and he peppered away at them. Him and his horse both went home pretty leady and crippled, but the Grangerfords had to be *fetched* home—and one of 'em was dead, and another died the next day. No, sir, if a body's out hunting for cowards, he don't want to fool away any time amongst them Shepherdsons, becuz they don't breed any of that *kind*."

Next Sunday we all went to church, about three mile, everybody a-horseback. The men took their guns along, so did Buck, and kept them between their knees or stood them handy against the wall. The Shepherdsons done the same. It was pretty ornery preaching—all about brotherly love, and such-like tiresomeness; but everybody said it was a good sermon, and they all talked it over going home, and had such a powerful lot to say about faith, and good works, and free grace,[128] and preforeordestination,[129] and I don't know what all, that it did seem to me to be one of the roughest Sundays I had run across yet.

About an hour after dinner everybody was dozing around, some in their chairs and some in their rooms, and it got to be pretty dull. Buck and a dog was stretched out on the grass in the sun, sound sleep. I went up to our room, and judged I would take a nap myself. I found that sweet Miss Sophia standing in her door, which was next to ours, and she took me in her room and shut the door very soft, and asked me if I liked her, and I said I did; and she asked me if I would do something for her and not tell anybody, and I said I would. Then she said she'd forgot her Testament, and left it in the seat at church, between two other books and would I slip out quiet and go there and fetch it to her, and not say nothing to nobody. I said I would. So I slid out and slipped off up the road, and there warn't anybody at the church, except maybe a hog or two,

[128]God's grace—election for heaven, given free, without regard for human efforts.
[129]Huck combines the religious doctrines of predestination and foreordination.

for there warn't any lock on the door, and hogs like a puncheon floor[130] in summertime because it's cool. If you notice, most folks don't go to church only when they've got to; but a hog is different.

Says I to myself something's up—it ain't natural for a girl to be in such a sweat about a Testament; so I give it a shake, and out drops a little piece of paper with "*Half-past two*" wrote on it with a pencil. I ransacked it, but couldn't find anything else. I couldn't make anything out of that, so I put the paper in the book again, and when I got home and up stairs, there was Miss Sophia in her door waiting for me. She pulled me in and shut the door; then she looked in the Testament till she found the paper, and as soon as she read it she looked glad; and before a body could think, she grabbed me and give me a squeeze, and said I was the best boy in the world, and not to tell anybody. She was mighty red in the face, for a minute, and her eyes lighted up and it made her powerful pretty. I was a good deal astonished, but when I got my breath I asked her what the paper was about, and she asked me if I had read it, and I said no, and she asked me if I could read writing, and I told her "no, only coarse-hand,"[131] and then she said the paper warn't anything but a book-mark to keep her place, and I might go and play now.

I went off down to the river, studying over this thing, and pretty soon I noticed that my nigger was following along behind. When we was out of sight of the house, he looked back and around a second, and then comes a-running, and says:

"Mars Jawge, if you'll come down into de swamp, I'll show you a whole stack o' water-moccasins."[132]

Thinks I, that's mighty curious; he said that yesterday. He oughter know a body don't love water-moccasins enough to go around hunting for them. What is he up to anyway? So I says—

"All right, trot ahead."

I followed a half a mile, then he struck out over the swamp and waded ankle deep as much as another half mile. We come to a little flat piece of land which was dry and very thick with trees and bushes and vines, and he says—

"You shove right in dah, jist a few steps, Mars Jawge, dah's whah dey is. I's seed 'm befo', I don't k'yer to see 'em no mo'."

Then he slopped right along and went away, and pretty soon the trees hid him. I poked into the place a-ways, and come to a little open patch as big as a bedroom, all hung around with vines, and found a man laying there asleep—and by jings it was my old Jim!

I waked him up, and I reckoned it was going to be a grand surprise to him to see me again, but it warn't. He nearly cried, he was so glad, but he warn't surprised. Said he swum along behind me, that night, and heard me yell every time, but dasn't answer, because he didn't want nobody to pick *him* up, and take him into slavery again. Says he—

"I got hurt a little, en couldn't swim fas', so I wuz a considable ways behine you, towards de las'; when you landed I reck'ned I could ketch up wid you on de lan' 'dout havin' to shout at you, but when I see dat house I begin to go slow. I 'uz off too far to hear what they dey say to you—I wuz 'fraid o' de dogs—

[130]A floor of rough, wooden slabs.
[131]Large, rough printing by hand.
[132]A species of poisonous snakes.

but when it 'uz all quiet agin, I knowed you's in de house, so I struck out fer de woods to wait for day. Early in de mawnin' some er de niggers come along, gwyne to de fields, en dey tuck me en showed me dis place, whah de dogs can't track me on accounts o' de water, en dey brings me truck to eat every night, en tells me how you's a gitt'n along."

"Why didn't you tell my Jack to fetch me here sooner, Jim?"

"Well, 'twarn't no use to 'sturb you, Huck, tell we could do sumfin—but we's all right, now. I ben a-buyin' pots en pans en vittles, as I got a chanst, en a patchin' up de raf', nights when——"

"*What* raft, Jim?"

"Our ole raf'."

"You mean to say our old raft warn't smashed all to flinders?"

"No, she warn't. She was tore up a good deal—one en' of her was—but dey warn't no great harm done, on'y our traps was mos' all los'. Ef we hadn' dive' so deep en swum so fur under water, en de night hadn' ben so dark, en we warn't so sk'yerd, en ben sich punkin-heads, as de sayin' is, we'd a seed de raf'. But it's jis' as well as we didn't, 'kase now she's all fixed up agin mos' as good as new, en we's got a new lot o' stuff, too, in de place o' what 'uz los'."

"Why, how did you get hold of the raft again, Jim—did you catch her?"

"How I gwyne to ketch her, en I out in de woods? No, some er de niggers foun' her ketched on a snag, along heah in de ben', en dey hid her in a crick, 'mongst de willows, en dey wuz so much jawin' 'bout which un 'um she b'long to de mos', dat I come to heah 'bout it pooty soon, so I ups en settles de trouble by tellin' 'um she don't b'long to none uv um, but to you en me; en I ast 'm if dey gwyne to grab a young white genlman's propaty, en git a hid'n for it? Den I gin 'm ten cents apiece, en dey 'uz mighty well satisfied, en wisht some mo' raf's 'ud come along en make 'm rich agin. Dey's mighty good to me, dese niggers is, en whatever I wants 'm to do fur me, I don't have to ast 'm twice, honey. Dat Jack's a good nigger, en pooty smart."

"Yes, he is. He ain't ever told me you was here; told me to come, and he'd show me a lot of water-moccasins. If anything happens, *he* ain't mixed up in it. He can say he never seen us together, and it'll be the truth."

I don't want to talk much about the next day. I reckon I'll cut it pretty short. I waked up about dawn, and was agoing to turn over and go to sleep again, when I noticed how still it was—didn't seem to be anybody stirring. That warn't usual. Next I noticed that Buck was up and gone. Well, I gets up, a-wondering, and goes down stairs—nobody around; everything as still as a mouse. Just the same outside; thinks I, what does it mean? Down by the wood-pile I comes across my Jack, and says:

"What's it all about?"

Says he:

"Don't you know, Mars Jawge?"

"No," says I, "I don't."

"Well, den, Miss Sophia's run off! 'deed she has. She run off in de night, sometime—nobody don't know jis' when—run off to git married to dat young Harney Shepherdson, you know—leastways, so dey 'spec. De fambly foun' it out, 'bout half an hour ago—maybe a little mo'—en I *tell* you dey warn't no time los. Sich another hurryin' up guns en hosses *you* never see! De women folks has gone for to stir up de relations, en ole Mars Saul en de boys tuck dey guns en rode up de river road for to try to ketch dat young man en kill him 'fo' he kin git acrost de river wid Miss Sophia. I reck'n dey's gwyne to be mighty rough times."

"Buck went off 'thout waking me up."

"Well I reck'n he *did!* Dey warn't gwyne to mix you up in it. Mars Buck he loaded up his gun en 'lowed he's gwyne to fetch home a Shepherdson or bust. Well, dey'll be plenty un 'm dah, I reck'n, en you bet you he'll fetch one ef he gits a chanst."

I took up the river road as hard as I could put. By-and-by I begin to hear guns a good ways off. When I come in sight of the log store and the woodpile where the steamboat lands, I worked along under the trees and brush till I got to a good place, and then I clumb up into the forks of a cotton-wood that was out of reach, and watched. There was a wood-rank[133] four foot high, a little ways in front of the tree, and first I was going to hide behind that; but maybe it was luckier I didn't.

There was four or five men cavorting around on their horses in the open place before the log store, cussing and yelling, and trying to get at a couple of young chaps that was behind the wood-rank alongside of the steamboat landing—but they couldn't come it. Every time one of them showed himself on the river side of the wood-pile he got shot at. The two boys was squatting back to back behind the pile, so they could watch both ways.

By-and-by the men stopped cavorting around and yelling. They started riding towards the store; then up gets one of the boys, draws a steady bead over the wood-rank, and drops one of them out of his saddle. All the men jumped off of their horses and grabbed the hurt one and started to carry him to the store; and that minute the two boys started on the run. They got half-way to the tree I was in before the men noticed. Then the men see them, and jumped on their horses and took out after them. They gained on the boys, but it didn't do no good, the boys had too good a start; they got to the wood-pile that was in front of my tree, and slipped in behind it, and so they had the bulge[134] on the men again. One of the boys was Buck, and the other was a slim young chap about nineteen years old.

The men ripped around awhile, and then rode away. As soon as they was out of sight, I sung out to Buck and told him. He didn't know what to make of my voice coming out of the tree, at first. He was awful surprised. He told me to watch out sharp and let him know when the men come in sight again; said they was up to some devilment or other—wouldn't be gone long. I wished I was out of that tree, but I dasn't come down. Buck begun to cry and rip, and 'lowed that him and his cousin Joe (that was the other young chap) would make up for this day, yet. He said his father and his two brothers was killed, and two or three of the enemy. Said the Shepherdsons laid for them, in ambush. Buck said his father and brothers ought to waited for their relations—the Shepherdsons was too strong for them. I asked him what was become of young Harney and Miss Sophia. He said they'd got across the river and was safe. I was glad of that; but the way Buck did take on because he didn't manage to kill Harney that day he shot at him—I hain't ever heard anything like it.

All of a sudden, bang! bang! bang! goes three or four guns—the men had slipped around through the woods and come in from behind without their

[133]Stack. [134]Advantage.

horses! The boys jumped for the river—both of them hurt—and a
down the current the men run along the bank shooting at them
out, "Kill them, kill them!" It made me so sick I most fell out of the tree. I ain't agoing to tell *all* that happened—it would make me sick again if I was to do that. I wished I hadn't ever come ashore that night, to see such things. I ain't ever going to get shut of them—lots of times I dream about them.

I staid in the tree till it begun to get dark, afraid to come down. Sometimes I heard guns away off in the woods; and twice I seen little gangs of men gallop past the log store with guns; so I reckoned the trouble was still agoing on. I was mighty down-hearted; so I made up my mind I wouldn't ever go anear that house again, because I reckoned I was to blame, somehow. I judged that that piece of paper meant that Miss Sophia was to meet Harney somewheres at half-past two and run off; and I judged I ought to told her father about that paper and the curious way she acted, and then maybe he would a locked her up and this awful mess wouldn't ever happened.

When I got down out of the tree, I crept along down the river bank a piece, and found the two bodies laying in the edge of the water, and tugged at them till I got them ashore; then I covered up their faces, and got away as quick as I could. I cried a little when I was covering up Buck's face, for he was mighty good to me.

It was just dark, now. I never went near the house, but struck through the woods and made for the swamp. Jim warn't on his island, so I tramped off in a hurry for the crick, and crowded through the willows, red-hot to jump aboard and get out of that awful country—the raft was gone! My souls, but I was scared! I couldn't get my breath for most a minute. Then I raised a yell. A voice not twenty-five foot from me, says—

"Good lan'! is dat you, honey? Doan' make no noise."

It was Jim's voice—nothing ever sounded so good before. I run along the bank a piece and got aboard, and Jim he grabbed me and hugged me, he was so glad to see me. He says—

"Laws bless you, chile, I 'uz right down sho' you'd dead agin. Jack's been heah, he say he reck'n you's ben shot, kase you didn' come home no mo'; so I's jes' dis minute a startin' de raf' down towards de mouf er de crick, so's to be all ready for to shove out en leave soon as Jack comes agin en tells me for certain you *is* dead. Lawsy, I's mighty glad to get you back agin, honey."

I says—

"All right—that's mighty good; they won't find me, and they'll think I've been killed, and floated down the river—there's something up there that'll help them to think so—so don't you lose no time, Jim, but just shove off for the big water[135] as fast as ever you can."

I never felt easy till the raft was two mile below there and out in the middle of the Mississippi. Then we hung up our signal lantern, and judged that we was free and safe once more. I hadn't had a bite to eat since yesterday; so Jim he got out some corn-dodgers[136] and buttermilk, and pork and cabbage, and greens—there ain't nothing in the world so good, when it's cooked right—and whilst I eat my supper we talked, and had a good time. I was powerful glad to get away from the feuds, and so was Jim to get away from the swamp. We said

[135] The main channel of the Mississippi River. [136] Hard-baked cornmeal cakes.

there warn't no home like a raft, after all. Other places do seem so cramped up and smothery, but a raft don't. You feel mighty free and easy and comfortable on a raft.

CHAPTER XIX

Two or three days and nights went by; I reckon I might say they swum by, they slid along so quiet and smooth and lovely. Here is the way we put in the time. It was a monstrous big river down there—sometimes a mile and a half wide; we run nights, and laid up and hid day-times; soon as night was most gone, we stopped navigating and tied up—nearly always in the dead water under a tow-head; and then cut young cotton-woods and willows and hid the raft with them. Then we set out the lines. Next we slid into the river and had a swim, so as to freshen up and cool off; then we set down on the sandy bottom where the water was about knee deep, and watched the daylight come. Not a sound, anywheres—perfectly still—just like the whole world was asleep, only sometimes the bull-frogs a-cluttering, maybe. The first thing to see, looking away over the water, was a kind of dull line—that was the woods on t'other side—you couldn't make nothing else out; then a pale place in the sky; then more paleness, spreading around; then the river softened up away off, and warn't black any more, but gray; you could see little dark spots drifting along, ever so far away—trading scows, and such things; and long black streaks—rafts; sometimes you could hear a sweep screaking; or jumbled up voices, it was so still, and sound come so far; and by-and-by you could see a streak on the water which you know by the look of the streak that there's a snag there in a swift current which breaks on it and makes that streak look that way; and you see the mist curl up off of the water, and the east reddens up, and the river, and you make out a log cabin in the edge of the woods, away on the bank on t'other side of the river, being a wood-yard, likely, and piled by them cheats so you can throw a dog through it anywheres;[137] then the nice breeze springs up, and comes fanning you from over there, so cool and fresh, and sweet to smell, on account of the woods and the flowers; but sometimes not that way, because they've left dead fish laying around, gars,[138] and such, and they do get pretty rank; and next you've got the full day, and everything smiling in the sun, and the song-birds just going it!

A little smoke couldn't be noticed, now, so we would take some fish off of the lines, and cook up a hot breakfast. And afterwards we would watch the lonesomeness of the river, and kind of lazy along, and by-and-by lazy off to sleep. Wake up, by-and-by, and look to see what done it, and maybe see a steamboat, coughing along up stream, so far off towards the other side you couldn't tell nothing about her only whether she was stern-wheel or side-wheel; then for about an hour there wouldn't be nothing to hear nor nothing to see—just solid lonesomeness. Next you'd see a raft sliding by, away off

[137]Woodcutters sold wood by volume to passing steamboats. By stacking their wood loosely, with large gaps, the unscrupulous tried to sell less wood for more money.

[138]A tough, inedible fish, a variety of pike.

yonder, and maybe a galoot[139] on it chopping, because they're m[illegible] doing it on a raft; you'd see the ax flash, and come down—you don't [illegible] nothing; you see that ax go up again, and by the time it's above the man's head, then you hear the *k'chunk!*—it had took all that time to come over the water. So we would put in the day, lazying around, listening to the stillness. Once there was a thick fog, and the rafts and things that went by was beating tin pans so the steamboats wouldn't run over them. A scow or a raft went by so close we could hear them talking and cussing and laughing—heard them plain; but we couldn't see no sign of them; it made you feel crawly, it was like spirits carrying on that way in the air. Jim said he believed it was spirits; but I says:

"No, spirits wouldn't say, 'dern the dern fog.'"

Soon as it was night, out we shoved; when we got her out to about the middle, we let her alone, and let her float wherever the current wanted her to; then we lit the pipes, and dangled our legs in the water and talked about all kinds of things—we was always naked, day and night, whenever the mosquitoes would let us—the new clothes Buck's folks made for me was too good to be comfortable, and besides I didn't go much on clothes, nohow.

Sometimes we'd have that whole river all to ourselves for the longest time. Yonder was the banks and the islands, across the water; and maybe a spark—which was a candle in a cabin window—and sometimes on the water you could see a spark or two—on a raft or a scow, you know; and maybe you could hear a fiddle or a song coming over from one of them crafts. It's lovely to live on a raft. We had the sky, up there, all speckled with stars, and we used to lay on our backs and look up at them, and discuss about whether they was made, or only just happened—Jim he allowed they was made, but I allowed they happened; I judged it would have took too long to *make* so many. Jim said the moon could a *laid* them; well, that looked kind of reasonable, so I didn't say nothing against it, because I've seen a frog lay most as many, so of course it could be done. We used to watch the stars that fell, too, and see them streak down. Jim allowed they'd got spoiled and was hove out of the nest.

Once or twice of a night we would see a steamboat slipping along in the dark, and now and then she would belch a whole world of sparks up out of her chimbleys, and they would rain down in the river and look awful pretty; then she would turn a corner and her lights would wink out and her pow-wow[140] shut off and leave the river still again; and by-and-by her waves would get to us, a long time after she was gone, and joggle the raft a bit, and after that you wouldn't hear nothing for you couldn't tell how long, except maybe frogs or something.

After midnight the people on shore went to bed, and then for two or three hours the shores was black—no more sparks in the cabin windows. These sparks was our clock—the first one that showed again meant morning was coming, so we hunted a place to hide and tie up, right away.

One morning about day-break, I found a canoe and crossed over a chute[141] to the main shore—it was only two hundred yards—and paddled about a mile up a crick amongst the cypress woods, to see if I couldn't get some berries. Just as I was passing a place where a kind of a cow-path crossed the crick, here comes a couple of men tearing up the path as tight as they could foot it. I thought I

[139]Fellow. [140]Engine noise. [141]A narrow channel with a swift current.

was a goner, for whenever anybody was after anybody I judged it was *me*—or maybe Jim. I was about to dig out from there in a hurry, but they was pretty close to me then, and sung out and begged me to save their lives—said they hadn't been doing nothing, and was being chased for it—said there was men and dogs a-coming. They wanted to jump right in, but I says—

"Don't you do it. I don't hear the dogs and horses yet; you've got time to crowd through the brush and get up the crick a little ways; then you take to the water and wade down to me and get in—that'll throw the dogs off the scent."

They done it, and soon as they was aboard I lit out for our towhead and in about five or ten minutes we heard the dogs and the men away off, shouting. We heard them come along towards the crick, but couldn't see them; they seemed to stop and fool around a while; then as we got further and further away all the time, we couldn't hardly hear them at all; by the time we had left a mile of woods behind us and struck the river, everything was quiet, and we paddled over to the tow-head and hid in the cotton-woods and was safe.

One of these fellows was about seventy, or upwards, and had a bald head and very gray whiskers. He had an old battered-up slouch hat on, and a greasy blue woolen shirt, and ragged old blue jeans britches stuffed into his boot tops, and home-knit galluses[142]—no, he only had one. He had an old long-tailed blue jeans coat with slick brass buttons, flung over his arm, and both of them had big fat ratty-looking carpet-bags.[143]

The other fellow was about thirty and dressed about as ornery. After breakfast we all laid off and talked, and the first thing that come out was that these chaps didn't know one another.

"What got you into trouble?" says the baldhead to t'other chap.

"Well, I'd been selling an article to take the tartar off the teeth—and it does take it off, too, and generly the enamel along with it—but I staid about one night longer than I ought to, and was just in the act of sliding out when I ran across you on the trail this side of town, and you told me they were coming, and begged me to help you to get off. So I told you I was expecting trouble myself and would scatter out *with* you. That's the whole yarn—what's yourn?"

"Well, I'd ben a-runnin' a little temperance revival thar, 'bout a week, and was the pet of the women-folks, big and little, for I was makin' it mighty warm for the rummies, I *tell* you, and takin' as much as five or six dollars a night—ten cents a head, children and niggers free—and business a growin' all the time; when somehow or another a little report got around, last night, that I had a way of puttin' in my time with a private jug, on the sly. A nigger rousted me out this mornin', and told me the people was getherin' on the quiet, with their dogs and horses, and they'd be along pretty soon and give me 'bout half an hour's start, and then run me down, if they could; and if they got me they'd tar and feather me and ride me on a rail, sure. I didn't wait for no breakfast—I warn't hungry."

"Old man," says the young one, "I reckon we might double-team[144] it together; what do you think?"

"I ain't undisposed. What's your line—mainly?"

[142]Suspenders. [143]Cheap suitcases made out of carpet remnants.
[144]Work together, like a team of horses.

"Jour[145] printer, by trade; do a little in patent medicines; theatre-actor—tragedy, you know; take a turn at mesmerism[146] and phrenology[147] when there's a chance; teach singing-geography school for a change; sling a lecture, sometimes—oh, I do lots of things—most anything that comes handy, so it ain't work. What's your lay?"[148]

"I've done considerble in the doctoring way in my time. Layin' on o' hands[149] is my best holt—for cancer, and paralysis, and sich things; and I k'n tell a fortune pretty good, when I've got somebody along to find out the facts for me. Preachin's my line, too; and workin' camp-meetin's; and missionaryin' around."

Nobody never said anything for a while; then the young man hove a sigh and says—

"Alas!"

"What're you alassin' about?" says the baldhead.

"To think I should have lived to be leading such a life, and be degraded down into such company." And he begun to wipe the corner of his eye with a rag.

"Dern your skin, ain't the company good enough for you?" says the baldhead, pretty pert and uppish.

"Yes, it *is* good enough for me; it's as good as I deserve; for who fetched me so low, when I was so high? *I* did myself. I don't blame *you,* gentlemen—far from it; I don't blame anybody. I deserve it all. Let the cold world do its worst; one thing I know—there's a grave somewhere for me. The world may go on just as it's always done, and take everything from me—loved ones, property, everything—but it can't take that. Some day I'll lie down in it and forget it all, and my poor broken heart will be at rest." He went on a-wiping.

"Drot your pore broken heart," says the baldhead; "what are you heaving your pore broken heart at *us* f'r? *We* hain't done nothing."

"No, I know you haven't. I ain't blaming you, gentlemen. I brought myself down—yes, I did it myself. It's right I should suffer—perfectly right—I don't make any moan."

"Brought you down from whar? Whar was you brought down from?"

"Ah, you would not believe me; the world never believes—let it pass—'tis no matter. The secret of my birth——"

"The secret of your birth? Do you mean to say——"

"Gentlemen," says the young man, very solemn, "I will reveal it to you, for I feel I may have confidence in you. By rights I am a duke!"

Jim's eyes bugged out when he heard that; and I reckon mine did, too. Then the baldhead says: "No! you can't mean it?"

"Yes. My great-grandfather, eldest son of the Duke of Bridgewater, fled to this country about the end of the last century, to breathe the pure air of freedom; married here, and died, leaving a son, his own father dying about the same time. The second son of the late duke seized the title and estates—the infant real duke was ignored. I am the lineal descendant of that infant—I am the rightful Duke of Bridgewater; and here am I, forlorn, torn from my high estate, hunted of men, despised by the cold world, ragged, worn, heart-broken, and degraded to the companionship of felons on a raft!"

[145]Journeyman, i.e., trained. [146]Hypnotism.
[147]Presuming to read human character from the shape of the head.
[148]Trade, profession. [149]Faith healing.

Jim pitied him ever so much and so did I. We tried to comfort him, but he said it warn't much use, he couldn't be much comforted; said if we was a mind to acknowledge him, that would do him more good than most anything else; so we said we would, if he would tell us how. He said we ought to bow, when we spoke to him, and say "Your Grace," or "My Lord," or "Your Lordship"—and he wouldn't mind it if we called him plain "Bridgewater," which he said was a title, anyway, and not a name; and one of us ought to wait on him at dinner, and do any little thing for him he wanted done.

Well, that was all easy, so we done it. All through dinner Jim stood around and waited on him, and says, "Will yo' Grace have some o' dis, or some o' dat?" and so on, and a body could see it was mighty pleasing to him.

But the old man got pretty silent, by-and-by—didn't have much to say, and didn't look pretty comfortable over all that petting that was going on around that duke. He seemed to have something on his mind. So, along in the afternoon, he says:

"Looky here, Bilgewater," he says, "I'm nation sorry for you, but you ain't the only person that's had troubles like that."

"No?"

"No, you ain't. You ain't the only person that's ben snaked[150] down wrongfully out'n a high place."

"Alas!"

"No, you ain't the only person that's had a secret of his birth." And by jings, *he* begins to cry.

"Hold! What do you mean?"

"Bilgewater, kin I trust you?" says the old man, still sort of sobbing.

"To the bitter death!" He took the old man by the hand and squeezed it, and says, "The secret of your being: speak!"

"Bilgewater, I am the late Dauphin!"

You bet you Jim and me started, this time. Then the duke says:

"You are what?"

"Yes, my friend, it is too true—your eyes is lookin' at this very moment on the pore disappeared Dauphin, Looy the Seventeen, son of Looy the Sixteen and Marry Antonette."

"You! At your age![151] No! You mean you're the late Charlemagne;[152] you must be six or seven hundred years old, at the very least."

"Trouble has done it, Bilgewater, trouble has done it; trouble has brung these gray hairs and this premature balditude. Yes, gentlemen, you see before you, in blue jeans and misery, the wanderin', exiled, trampled-on and sufferin' rightful King of France."

Well, he cried and took on so, that me and Jim didn't know hardly what to do, we was so sorry—and so glad and proud we'd got him with us, too. So we set in, like we done before with the duke, and tried to comfort *him.* But he said it warn't no use, nothing but to be dead and done with it all could do him any good; though he said it often made him feel easier and better for a while if people treated him according to his rights, and got down on one knee to speak to him, and always called him "Your Majesty," and waited on him first at meals, and didn't set down in his presence till he asked them. So Jim and me set to majestying him, and doing

[150]Brought, pulled. [151]Had he lived, the lost dauphin would have been in his fifties.
[152]The Holy Roman Emperor Charles the Great (742–814).

this and that and t'other for him, and standing up till he told us we might set down. This done him heaps of good, and so he got cheerful and comfortable. But the duke kind of soured on him, and didn't look a bit satisfied with the way things was going; still, the king acted real friendly towards him, and said the duke's great-grandfather and all the other Dukes of Bilgewater was a good deal thought of by *his* father and was allowed to come to the palace considerable; but the duke staid huffy a good while, till by-and-by the king says:

"Like as not we got to be together a blamed long time, on this h-yer raft, Bilgewater, and so what's the use o' your bein' sour? It'll only make things oncomfortable. It ain't my fault I warn't born a duke, it ain't your fault you warn't born a king—so what's the use to worry? Make the best o' things the way you find 'em, says I—that's my motto. This ain't no bad thing that we've struck here—plenty grub and an easy life—come, give us your hand, Duke, and less all be friends."

The duke done it, and Jim and me was pretty glad to see it. It took away all the uncomfortableness, and we felt mighty good over it, because it would a been a miserable business to have any unfriendliness on the raft; for what you want, above all things, on a raft, is for everybody to be satisfied, and feel right and kind towards the others.

It didn't take me long to make up my mind that these liars warn't no kings nor dukes, at all, but just low-down humbugs and frauds. But I never said nothing, never let on; kept it to myself; it's the best way; then you don't have no quarrels, and don't get into no trouble. If they wanted us to call them kings and dukes, I hadn't no objections, 'long as it would keep peace in the family; and it warn't no use to tell Jim, so I didn't tell him. If I never learnt nothing else out of pap, I learnt that the best way to get along with his kind of people is to let them have their own way.

CHAPTER XX

They asked us considerable many questions; wanted to know what we covered up the raft that way for, and laid by in the daytime instead of running—was Jim a runaway nigger? Says I—

"Goodness sakes, would a runaway nigger run *south?*"

No, they allowed he wouldn't. I had to account for things some way, so I says:

"My folks was living in Pike County, in Missouri, where I was born, and they all died off but me and pa and my brother Ike. Pa, he 'lowed he'd break up and go down and live with Uncle Ben, who's got a little one-horse place on the river, forty-four mile below Orleans. Pa was pretty poor, and had some debts; so when he'd squared up there warn't nothing left but sixteen dollars and our nigger, Jim. That warn't enough to take us fourteen hundred mile, deck passage nor no other way. Well, when the river rose, pa had a streak of luck one day; he ketched this piece of a raft; so we reckoned we'd go down to Orleans on it. Pa's luck didn't hold out; a steamboat run over the forrard corner of the raft, one night, and we all went overboard and dove under the wheel; Jim and me come up, all right, but pa was drunk, and Ike was only four years old, so they never come up no more. Well, for the next day or two we had considerable trouble, because people was always coming out in skiffs and trying to take Jim away from me, saying they believed he was a runaway nigger. We don't run day-times no more, now; nights they don't bother us."

The duke says—

"Leave me alone to cipher out a way so we can run in the daytime if we want to. I'll think the thing over—I'll invent a plan that'll fix it. We'll let it alone for to-day, because of course we don't want to go by that town yonder in daylight—it mightn't be healthy."

Towards night it begun to darken up and look like rain; the heat lightning was squirting around, low down in the sky, and the leaves was beginning to shiver—it was going to be pretty ugly, it was easy to see that. So the duke and the king went to overhauling our wigwam, to see what the beds was like. My bed was a straw tick[153]—better than Jim's, which was a corn-shuck tick; there's always cobs around about in a shuck tick, and they poke into you and hurt; and when you roll over, the dry shucks sound like you was rolling over in a pile of dead leaves; it makes such a rustling that you wake up. Well, the duke allowed he would take my bed; but the king allowed he wouldn't. He says—

"I should a reckoned the difference in rank would a sejested to you that a corn-shuck bed warn't just fitten for me to sleep on. Your Grace'll take the shuck bed yourself."

Jim and me was in a sweat again, for a minute, being afraid there was going to be some more trouble amongst them; so we was pretty glad when the duke says—

"'Tis my fate to be always ground into the mire under the iron heel of oppression. Misfortune has broken my once haughty spirit; I yield, I submit; 'tis my fate. I am alone in the world—let me suffer; I can bear it."

We got away as soon as it was good and dark. The king told us to stand well out towards the middle of the river, and not show a light till we got a long ways below the town. We come in sight of the little bunch of lights by-and-by—that was the town, you know—and slid by, about a half a mile out, all right. When we was three-quarters of a mile below, we hoisted up our signal lantern; and about ten o'clock it come on to rain and blow and thunder and lighten like everything; so the king told us to both stay on watch till the weather got better; then him and the duke crawled into the wigwam and turned in for the night. It was my watch below, till twelve,[154] but I wouldn't a turned in, anyway, if I'd had a bed; because a body don't see such a storm as that every day in the week, not by a long sight. My souls, how the wind did scream along! And every second or two there'd come a glare that lit up the white-caps for a half a mile around, and you'd see the islands looking dusty through the rain, and the trees thrashing around in the wind; then comes a *h-wack!*—bum! bum! bumble-umble-um-bum-bum-bum-bum—and the thunder would go rumbling and grumbling away, and quit—and then *rip* comes another flash and another sockdolager.[155] The waves most washed me off the raft, sometimes, but I hadn't any clothes on, and didn't mind. We didn't have no trouble about snags; the lightning was glaring and flittering around so constant that we could see them plenty soon enough to throw her head this way or that and miss them.

I had the middle watch, you know, but I was pretty sleepy by that time, so Jim he said he would stand the first half of it for me; he was always mighty good, that way, Jim was. I crawled into the wigwam, but the king and the duke had their legs sprawled around so there warn't no show for me; so I laid outside—I didn't mind the rain, because it was warm, and the waves warn't running so high, now. About

[153]Mattress. [154]I.e., Huck is off duty ("below") until the middle watch, midnight to 4 A.M.
[155]Tremendous crash, from "doxology," a hymn in praise of God and traditionally the loudest part of a church service.

two they come up again, though, and Jim was going to call me, but he changed his mind because he reckoned they warn't high enough yet to do any harm; but he was mistaken about that, for pretty soon all of a sudden along comes a regular ripper, and washed me overboard. It most killed Jim a-laughing. He was the easiest nigger to laugh that ever was, anyway.

I took the watch, and Jim he laid down and snored away; and by-and-by the storm let up for good and all; and the first cabin-light that showed, I rousted him out and we slid the raft into hiding-quarters for the day.

The king got out an old ratty deck of cards, after breakfast, and him and the duke played seven-up[156] a while, five cents a game. Then they got tired of it, and allowed they would "lay out a campaign," as they called it. The duke went down into his carpet-bag and fetched up a lot of little printed bills, and read them out loud. One bill said, "The celebrated Dr. Armand de Mantalban of Paris," would "lecture on the Science of Phrenology" at such and such a place, on the blank day of blank, at ten cents admission, and "furnish charts of character at twenty-five cents apiece." The duke said that was *him.* In another bill he was the "world renowned Shakesperean tragedian, Garrick the Younger,[157] of Drury Lane, London." In other bills he had a lot of other names and done other wonderful things, like finding water and gold with a "divining rod,"[158] "dissipating witchspells," and so on. By-and-by he says—

"But the histrionic muse is the darling. Have you ever trod the boards,[159] Royalty?"

"No," says the king.

"You shall then, before you're three days older, Fallen Grandeur," says the duke. "The first good town we come to, we'll hire a hall and do the sword-fight in Richard III, and the balcony scene in Romeo and Juliet. How does that strike you?"

"I'm in, up to the hub, for anything that will pay, Bilgewater, but you see I don't know nothing about play-actin', and hain't ever seen much of it. I was too small when pap used to have 'em at the palace. Do you reckon you can learn me?"

"Easy!"

"All right. I'm jist a-freezn' for something fresh, anyway. Less commence, right away."

So the duke he told him all about who Romeo was, and who Juliet was, and said he was used to being Romeo, so the king could be Juliet.

"But if Juliet's such a young gal, Duke, my peeled head and my white whiskers is goin' to look oncommon odd on her, maybe."

"No, don't you worry—these country jakes won't ever think of that. Besides, you know, you'll be in costume, and that makes all the difference in the world; Juliet's in a balcony, enjoying the moonlight before she goes to bed, and she's got on her night-gown and her ruffled night-cap. Here are the costumes for the parts."

He got out two or three curtain-calico suits, which he said was meedyevil armor for Richard III. and t'other chap,[160] and a long white cotton night-shirt and a ruffled night-cap to match. The king was satisfied; so the duke got out his book

[156]A card game in which the winner must score seven points.

[157]David Garrick (1717–1779), British actor, had died the previous century. There was no Garrick the Younger.

[158]A forked rod or stick believed to point magically toward water or buried treasure.

[159]Acted on the stage. [160]The Earl of Richmond.

and read the parts over in the most splendid spread-eagle[161] way, prancing around and acting at the same time, to show how it had got to be done; then he give the book to the king and told him to get his part by heart.

There was a little one-horse town about three mile down the bend, and after dinner the duke said he had ciphered out his idea about how to run in daylight without it being dangersome for Jim; so he allowed he would go down to the town and fix that thing. The king allowed he would go too, and see if he couldn't strike something. We was out of coffee, so Jim said I better go along with them in the canoe and get some.

When we got there, there warn't nobody stirring; streets empty, and perfectly dead and still, like Sunday. We found a sick nigger sunning himself in a back yard, and he said everybody that warn't too young or too sick or too old, was gone to camp-meeting, about two mile back in the woods. The king got the directions, and allowed he'd go and work that camp-meeting for all it was worth, and I might go, too.

The duke said what he was after was a printing office. We found it; a little bit of a concern, up over a carpenter shop—carpenters and printers all gone to the meeting, and no doors locked. It was a dirty, littered-up place, and had ink marks, and handbills with pictures of horses and runaway niggers on them, all over the walls. The duke shed his coat and said he was all right, now. So me and the king lit out for the camp-meeting.

We got there in about a half an hour, fairly dripping, for it was a most awful hot day. There was as much as a thousand people there, from twenty mile around. The woods was full of teams and wagons, hitched everywheres, feeding out of the wagon troughs and stomping to keep off the flies. There was sheds made out of poles and roofed over with branches, where they had lemonade and gingerbread to sell, and piles of watermelons and green corn and such-like truck.

The preaching was going on under the same kinds of sheds, only they was bigger and held crowds of people. The benches was made out of outside slabs of logs, with holes bored in the round side to drive sticks into for legs. They didn't have no backs. The preachers had high platforms to stand on, at one end of the sheds. The women had on sun-bonnets; and some had linsey-woolsey[162] frocks, some gingham ones, and a few of the young ones had on calico. Some of the young men was barefooted, and some of the children didn't have on any clothes but just a tow-linen[163] shirt. Some of the old women was knitting, and some of the young folks was courting on the sly.

The first shed we come to, the preacher was lining out a hymn.[164] He lined out two lines, everybody sung it, and it was kind of grand to hear it, there was so many of them and they done it in such a rousing way; then he lined out two more for them to sing—and so on. The people woke up more and more, and sung louder and louder; and towards the end, some begun to groan, and some begun to shout. Then the preacher begun to preach; and begun in earnest, too; and went weaving first to one side of the platform and then the other, and then a leaning down over the front of it, with his arms and his body going all the time, and shouting his words out with all his might; and every now and then he would hold up his Bible and spread it open, and kind of pass it around this way and that, shouting, "It's the brazen serpent in the wilderness! Look upon it and

[161]Ornate, exaggerated. [162]Coarse cloth of linen or cotton and wool. [163]Rough linen.
[164]Speaking out the words so the congregation, lacking hymnbooks, could follow in song.

live!" And people would shout out, "Glory!—A-a-*men!*" And so he went on, and the people groaning and crying and saying amen:

"Oh, come to the mourners' bench![165] come, black with sin! (*amen!*) come, sick and sore! (*amen!*) come, lame and halt, and blind! (*amen!*) come, pore and needy, sunk in shame! (*a-a-amen!*) come all that's worn, and soiled, and suffering!—come with a broken spirit! come with a contrite heart! come in your rags and sin and dirt! the waters that cleanse is free, the door of heaven stands open—oh, enter in and be at rest! (*a-a-men! glory, glory hallelujah!*)"

And so on. You couldn't make out what the preacher said, any more, on account of the shouting and crying. Folks got up, everywheres in the crowd, and worked their way, just by main strength, to the mourners' bench, with the tears running down their faces; and when all the mourners had got up there to the front benches in a crowd, they sung and shouted, and flung themselves down on the straw, just crazy and wild.

Well, the first I knowed, the king got agoing; and you could hear him over everybody; and next he went a-charging up on the platform and the preacher he begged him to speak to the people, and he done it. He told them he was a pirate—been a pirate for thirty years, out in the Indian Ocean, and his crew was thinned out considerable, last spring, in a fight, and he was home now, to take out some fresh men, and thanks to goodness he'd been robbed last night, and put ashore off a steamboat without a cent, and he was glad of it, it was the blessedest thing that ever happened to him, because he was a changed man now, and happy for the first time in his life; and poor as he was, he was going to start right off and work his way back to the Indian Ocean and put in the rest of his life trying to turn the pirates into the true path; for he could do it better than anybody else, being acquainted with all the pirate crews in that ocean; and though it would take him a long time to get there, without money, he would get there anyway, and every time he convinced a pirate he would say to him, "Don't you thank me, don't you give me no credit, it all belongs to them dear people in Pokeville camp-meeting, natural brothers and benefactors of the race—and that dear preacher there, the truest friend a pirate ever had!"

And then he busted into tears, and so did everybody. Then somebody sings out, "Take up a collection for him, take up a collection!" Well, a half a dozen made a jump to do it, but somebody sings out, "Let *him* pass the hat around!" Then everybody said it, the preacher too.

So the king went all through the crowd with his hat, swabbing his eyes, and blessing the people and praising them and thanking them for being so good to the poor pirates away off there; and every little while the prettiest kind of girls, with the tears running down their cheeks, would up and ask him would he let them kiss him, for to remember him by; and he always done it; and some of them he hugged and kissed as many as five or six times—and he was invited to stay a week; and everybody wanted him to live in their houses, and said they'd think it was an honor; but he said as this was the last day of the camp-meeting he couldn't do no good, and besides he was in a sweat to get to the Indian Ocean right off and go to work on the pirates.

When we got back to the raft and he come to count up, he found he had collected eighty-seven dollars and seventy-five cents. And then he had fetched away a three-gallon jug of whisky, too, that he found under a wagon when we was starting

[165]Front seats, near the pulpit, for those who mourn their sins and want to repent.

home through the woods. The king said, take it all around, it laid over any day he'd ever put in the missionarying line. He said it warn't no use talking, heathens don't amount to shucks, alongside of pirates, to work a camp-meeting with.

The duke was thinking *he'd* been doing pretty well, till the king come to show up, but after that he didn't think so so much. He had set up and printed off two little jobs for farmers, in that printing office—horse bills—and took the money, four dollars. And he had got in ten dollars' worth of advertisements for the paper, which he said he would put in for four dollars if they would pay in advance—so they done it. The price of the paper was two dollars a year, but he took in three subscriptions for half a dollar apiece on condition of them paying him in advance; they were going to pay in cord-wood and onions, as usual, but he said he had just bought the concern and knocked down the price as low as he could afford it, and was going to run it for cash. He set up a little piece of poetry, which he made, himself, out of his own head—three verses—kind of sweet and saddish—the name of it was, "Yes, crush, cold world, this breaking heart"—and he left that all set up and ready to print in the paper and didn't charge nothing for it. Well, he took in nine dollars and a half, and said he'd done a pretty square day's work for it.

Then he showed us another little job he'd printed and hadn't charged for, because it was for us. It had a picture of a runaway nigger, with a bundle on a stick, over his shoulder, and "$200 reward" under it. The reading was all about Jim, and just described him to a dot. It said he run away from St. Jacques' plantation, forty mile below New Orleans, last winter, and likely went north, and whoever would catch him and send him back, he could have the reward and expenses.

"Now," says duke, "after to-night we can run in the day-time if we want to. Whenever we see anybody coming, we can tie Jim hand and foot with a rope, and lay him in the wigwam and show this handbill and say we captured him up the river, and were too poor to travel on a steamboat, so we got this little raft on credit from our friends and are going down to get the reward. Handcuffs and chains would look better on Jim, but it wouldn't go well with the story of us being so poor. Too much like jewelry. Ropes are the correct thing—we must preserve the unities,[166] as we say on the boards."

We all said the duke was pretty smart, and there couldn't be no trouble about running day-times. We judged we could make miles enough that night to get out of the reach of the pow-wow we reckoned the duke's work in the printing office was going to make in that little town—then we could boom right along, if we wanted to.

We laid low and kept still, and never shoved out till nearly ten o'clock; then we slid by, pretty wide away from the town, and didn't hoist our lantern till we was clear out of sight of it.

When Jim called me to take the watch at four in the morning, he says—

"Huck, does you reck'n we gwyne to run acrost any mo' kings on dis trip?"

"No," I says, "I reckon not."

"Well," says he, "dat's all right, den. I doan' mine one er two kings, but dat's enough. Dis one's powerful drunk, en de duke ain' much better."

I found Jim had been trying to get him to talk French, so he could hear what it was like; but he said he had been in this country so long, and had so much trouble, he'd forgot it.

[166]The dramatic unities of time, place, and action of the neoclassic French theater.

CHAPTER XXI

It was after sun-up, now, but we went right on, and didn't tie up. The king and the duke turned out, by-and-by, looking pretty rusty; but after they'd jumped overboard and took a swim, it chippered them up a good deal. After breakfast the king he took a seat on a corner of the raft, and pulled off his boots and rolled up his britches, and let his legs dangle in the water, so as to be comfortable, and lit his pipe, and went to getting his Romeo and Juliet by heart. When he had got it pretty good, him and the duke begun to practice it together. The duke had to learn him over and over again, how to say every speech; and he made him sigh, and put his hand on his heart, and after while he said he done it pretty well; "only," he says, "you mustn't bellow out *Romeo!* that way, like a bull—you must say it soft, and sick, and languishy, so—R-o-o-meo! that is the idea; for Juliet's a dear sweet mere child of a girl, you know, and she don't bray like a jackass."

Well, next they got out a couple of long swords that the duke made out of oak laths, and begun to practice the sword-fight—the duke called himself Richard III.; and the way they laid on, and pranced around the raft was grand to see. But by-and-by the king tripped and fell overboard, and after that they took a rest, and had a talk about all kinds of adventures they'd had in other times along the river.

After dinner, the duke says:

"Well, Capet,[167] we'll want to make this a first-class show, you know, so I guess we'll add a little more to it. We want a little something to answer encores with, anyway."

"What's onkores, Bilgewater?"

The duke told him, and then says:

"I'll answer by doing the Highland fling or the sailor's hornpipe;[168] and you—well, let me see—oh, I've got it—you can do Hamlet's soliloquy."

"Hamlet's which?"

"Hamlet's soliloquy, you know; the most celebrated thing in Shakespeare. Ah, it's sublime, sublime! Always fetches the house. I haven't got it in the book—I've only got one volume—but I reckon I can piece it out from memory. I'll just walk up and down a minute, and see if I can call it back from recollection's vaults."

So he went to marching up and down, thinking, and frowning horrible every now and then; then he would hoist up his eyebrows; next he would squeeze his hand on his forehead and stagger back and kind of moan; next he would sigh, and next he'd let on to drop a tear. It was beautiful to see him. By-and-by he got it. He told us to give attention. Then he strikes a most noble attitude, with one leg shoved forwards, and his arms stretched away up, and his head tilted back, looking up at the sky; and then he begins to rip and rave and grit his teeth; and after that, all through his speech he howled, and spread around, and swelled up his chest, and just knocked the spots out of any acting ever *I* see before. This is the speech—I learned it, easy enough, while he was learning it to the king:

[167]Family name of Louis XVI.

[168]Highland fling: a lively Scottish dance. Sailor's hornpipe: a dance in which the performer, accompanied by a hornpipe, acts out the tasks of a sailor.

To be, or not to be; that is the bare bodkin
That makes calamity of so long life;
For who would fardels bear, till Birnam Wood do come to Dunsinane,
But that the fear of something after death
Murders the innocent sleep,
Great nature's second course,
And makes us rather sling the arrows of outrageous fortune
Than fly to others that we know not of.
There's the respect must give us pause:
Wake Duncan with thy knocking! I would thou couldst;
For who would bear the whips and scorns of time,
The oppressor's wrong, the proud man's contumely,
The law's delay, and the quietus which his pangs might take,
In the dead waste and middle of the night, when church-yards yawn
In customary suits of solemn black,
But that the undiscovered country from whose bourne no traveler
 returns,
Breathes forth contagion on the world,
And thus the native hue of resolution, like the poor cat i' the adage,
I sicklied o'er with care.
And all the clouds that lowered o'er our housetops,
With this regard their currents turn awry,
And lose the name of action.
'Tis a consummation devoutly to be wished. But soft you, the fair
 Ophelia:
Ope not thy ponderous and marble jaws,
But get thee to a nunnery—go![169]

Well, the old man he liked that speech, and he mighty soon got it so he could do it first rate. It seemed like he was just born for it; and when he had his hand in and was excited, it was perfectly lovely the way he would rip and tear and rair up behind when he was getting it off.

The first chance we got, the duke he had some show bills printed; and after that, for two or three days as we floated along, the raft was a most uncommon lively place, for there warn't nothing but sword-fighting and rehearsing—as the duke called it—going on all the time. One morning, when we was pretty well down the State of Arkansaw, we come in sight of a little one-horse town in a big bend; so we tied up about three-quarters of a mile above it, in the mouth of a crick which was shut in like a tunnel by the cypress trees, and all of us but Jim took the canoe and went down there to see if there was any chance in that place for our show.

We struck it mighty lucky; there was going to be a circus there that afternoon, and the country people was already beginning to come in, in all kinds of old shackly wagons, and on horses. The circus would leave before night, so our show would have a pretty good chance. The duke he hired the court house, and we went around and stuck up our bills. They read like this:

[169]The Duke's soliloquy is a hodgepodge of Shakespeare quotations from *Hamlet, Macbeth,* and *Richard III.*

Shaksperean Revival!!!
Wonderful Attraction!
For One Night Only!
The world renowned tragedians,
David Garrick, the younger, of Drury Lane Theatre, London,
and
Edmund Kean the elder,[170] of the Royal Haymarket Theatre, White-chapel, Pudding Lane, Piccadilly, London, and the
Royal Continental Theatres, in their sublime
Shaksperean Spectacle entitled
The Balcony Scene
in
Romeo and Juliet!!!
Romeo......................................Mr. Garrick.
Juliet.......................................Mr. Kean.
Assisted by the whole strength of the company
New costumes, new scenery, new appointments!
Also:
The thrilling, masterly, and blood-curdling
Broad-sword conflict
In Richard III!!!
Richard III.................................Mr. Garrick.
Richmond.............................Mr. Kean.
also:
(by special request,)
Hamlet's Immortal Soliloquy!
By the Illustrious Kean!
Done by him 300 consecutive nights in Paris!
For One Night Only,
On account of imperative European engagements!
Admission 25 cents; children and servants, 10 cents.

Then we went loafing around the town. The stores and houses was most all old shackly dried-up frame concerns that hadn't even been painted; they was set up three or four foot above ground on stilts, so as to be out of reach of the water when the river was overflowed. The houses had little gardens around them, but they didn't seem to raise hardly anything in them but jimpson weeds, and sunflowers, and ash-piles, and old curled-up boots and shoes, and pieces of bottles, and rags, and played-out tin-ware. The fences was made of different kinds of boards, nailed on at different times; and they leaned every which-way, and had gates that didn't generly have but one hinge—a leather one. Some of the fences had been whitewashed, some time or another, but the duke said it was in Clumbus's time, like enough. There was generly hogs in the garden, and people driving them out.

[170]British actor (1787?–1833).

All the stores was along one street. They had white-domestic[171] awnings in front, and the country people hitched their horses to the awning-posts. There was empty dry-goods boxes under the awnings, and loafers roosting on them all day long, whittling them with their Barlow knives; and chawing tobacco, and gaping and yawning and stretching—a mighty ornery lot. They generly had on yellow straw hats most as wide as an umbrella, but didn't wear no coats nor waistcoats; they called one another Bill, and Buck, and Hank, and Joe, and Andy, and talked lazy and drawly, and used considerable many cusswords. There was as many as one loafer leaning up against every awning-post, and he most always had his hands in his britches pockets, except when he fetches them out to lend a chaw of tobacco or scratch. What a body was hearing amongst them, all the time was—

"Gimme a chaw'v tobacker, Hank."

"Cain't—I hain't got but one chaw left. Ask Bill."

Maybe Bill he gives him a chaw; maybe he lies and says he ain't got none. Some of them kinds of loafers never has a cent in the world, nor a chaw of tobacco of their own. They get all their chawing by borrowing—they say to a fellow, "I wisht you'd len' me a chaw, Jack, I jist this minute give Ben Thompson the last chaw I had"—which is a lie, pretty much every time; it don't fool nobody but a stranger; but Jack ain't no stranger, so he says—

"*You* give him a chaw, did you? so did your sister's cat's grandmother. You pay me back the chaws you've awready borry'd off'n me, Lafe Buckner, then I'll loan you one or two ton of it, and won't charge you no back intrust, nuther."

"Well, I *did* pay you back some of it wunst."

"Yes, you did—'bout six chaws. You borry'd store tobacker and paid back nigger-head."[172]

Store tobacco is flat black plug, but these fellow mostly chaws the natural leaf twisted. When they borrow a chaw, they don't generly cut it off with a knife, but they set the plug in between their teeth, and gnaw with their teeth and tug at the plug with their hands till they get it in two—then sometimes the one that owns the tobacco looks mournful at it when it's handed back, and says, sarcastic—

"Here, gimme the *chaw,* and you take the *plug.*"

All the streets and lanes was just mud, they warn't nothing else *but* mud—mud as black as tar, and nigh about a foot deep in some places; and two or three inches deep in *all* the places. The hogs loafed and grunted around, everywheres. You'd see a muddy sow and a litter of pigs come lazying along the street and whollop herself right down in the way, where folks had to walk around her, and she'd stretch out, and shut her eyes, and wave her ears, whilst the pigs was milking her, and look as happy as if she was on salary. And pretty soon you'd hear a loafer sing out, "Hi! *so* boy! sick him, Tige!" and away the sow would go, squealing most horrible, with a dog or two swinging to each ear, and three or four dozen more a-coming; and then you would see all the loafers get up and watch the thing out of sight, and laugh at the fun and look grateful for the noise. Then they'd settle back again till there was a dog-fight. There couldn't anything wake them up all over, and make them happy all over, like a dog-fight—unless it might be putting turpentine on a stray dog and setting fire to him, or tying a tin pan to his tail and see him run himself to death.

[171]Crude canvas. [172]Cheap, leaf tobacco.

On the river front some of the houses was sticking out over the bank, and they was bowed and bent, and about ready to tumble in. The people had moved out of them. The bank was caved away under one corner of some others, and that corner was hanging over. People lived in them yet, but it was dangersome, because sometimes a strip of land as wide as a house caves in at a time. Sometimes a belt of land a quarter of a mile deep will start in and cave along and cave along till it all caves into the river in one summer. Such a town as that has to be always moving back, and back, and back, because the river's always gnawing at it.

The nearer it got to the noon that day, the thicker and thicker was the wagons and horses in the streets, and more coming all the time. Families fetched their dinners with them, from the country, and eat them in the wagons. There was considerable whisky drinking going on, and I seen three fights. By-and-by somebody sings out—

"Here comes old Boggs!—in from the country for his little old monthly drunk—here he comes, boys!"

All the loafers looked glad—I reckoned they was used to having fun out of Boggs. One of them says—

"Wonder who he's a gwyne to chaw up this time. If he'd a chawed up all the men he's ben a gwyne to chaw up in the last twenty year, he'd have considerable ruputation, now."

Another one says, "I wisht old Boggs'd threaten me, 'cuz then I'd know I warn't gwyne to die for a thousan' year."

Boggs comes a-tearing along on his horse, whooping and yelling like an Injun, and singing out—

"Cler the track, thar. I'm on the waw-path, and the price uv coffins is a gwyne to raise."

He was drunk, and weaving about in his saddle; he was over fifty year old, and had a very red face. Everybody yelled at him, and laughed at him, and sassed him, and he sassed back, and said he'd attend to them and lay them out in their regular turns, but he couldn't wait now, because he'd come to town to kill old Colonel Sherburn, and his motto was, "meat first, and spoon vittles to top off on."

He see me, and rode up and says—

"Whar'd you come f'm, boy? You prepared to die?"

Then he rode on. I was scared; but a man says—

"He don't mean nothing; he's always a carryin' on like that, when he's drunk. He's the best-naturednest old fool in Arkansaw—never hurt nobody, drunk nor sober."

Boggs rode up before the biggest store in town and bent his head down so he could see under the curtain of the awning, and yells—

"Come out here, Sherburn! Come out and meet the man you've swindled. You're the houn' I'm after, and I'm a gwyne to have you, too!"

And so he went on, calling Sherburn everything he could lay his tongue to, and the whole street packed with people listening and laughing and going on. By-and-by a proud-looking man about fifty-five—and he was a heap the best dressed man in that town, too—steps out of the store, and the crowd drops back on each side to let him come. He says to Boggs, mighty ca'm and slow—he says:

"I'm tired of this; but I'll endure it till one o'clock. Till one o'clock, mind—no longer. If you open your mouth against me once, after that time, you can't travel so far but I will find you."

Then he turns and goes in. The crowd looked mighty sober; nobody stirred, and there warn't no more laughing. Boggs rode off blackguarding Sherburn as loud as he could yell, all down the street; and pretty soon back he comes and stops before the store, still keeping it up. Some men crowded around him and tried to get him to shut up, but he wouldn't; they told him it would be one o'-clock in about fifteen minutes, and so he *must* go home—he must go right away. But it didn't do no good. He cussed away, with all his might, and throwed his hat down in the mud and rode over it, and pretty soon away he went a-raging down the street again, with his gray hair a-flying. Everybody that could get a chance at him tried their best to coax him off of his horse so they could lock him up and get him sober; but it warn't no use—up the street he would tear again, and give Sherburn another cussing. By-and-by somebody says—

"Go for his daughter!—quick, go for his daughter; sometimes he'll listen to her. If anybody can persuade him, she can."

So somebody started on a run. I walked down street a ways, and stopped. In about five or ten minutes, here comes Boggs again—but not on his horse. He was a-reeling across the street towards me, bareheaded, with a friend on both sides of him aloft of this arms and hurrying him along. He was quiet, and looked uneasy; and he warn't hanging back any, but was doing some of the hurrying himself. Somebody sings out—

"Boggs!"

I looked over there to see who said it, and it was that Colonel Sherburn. He was standing perfectly still, in the street, and had a pistol raised in his right hand—not aiming it, but holding it out with the barrel tilted up towards the sky. The same second I see a young girl coming on the run, and two men with her. Boggs and the men turned round, to see who called him, and when they see the pistol the men jumped to one side, and the pistol barrel come down slow and steady to a level—both barrels cocked. Boggs throws up both of his hands, and says, "O Lord, don't shoot!" Bang! goes the first shot, and he staggers back clawing at the air—bang! goes the second one, and he tumbles backwards onto the ground, heavy and solid, with his arms spread out. The young girl screamed out, and comes rushing, and down she throws herself on her father, crying, and saying. "Oh, he's killed him, he's killed him!" The crowd closed up around them, and shouldered and jammed one another, with their necks stretched, trying to see, and people on the inside trying to shove them back, and shouting, "Back, back! give him air, give him air!"

Colonel Sherburn he tossed his pistol onto the ground, and turned around on his heels and walked off.

They took Boggs to a little drug store, the crowd pressing around, just the same, and the whole town following, and I rushed and got a good place at the window, where I was close to him and could see in. They laid him on the floor, and put one large Bible under his head, and opened another one and spread it on his breast—but they tore open his shirt first, and I seen where one of the bullets went in. He made about a dozen long gasps, his breast lifting the Bible up when he drawed in his breath, and letting it down again when he breathed it out—and after that he laid still; he was dead.[173] Then they pulled his daughter away

[173]Twain's description of the death of Boggs closely follows the details of a murder that occurred in Hannibal in 1845. Twain's father served as judge at the subsequent trial. The defendant was acquitted.

from him, screaming and crying, and took her off. She was about sixteen, and very sweet and gentle-looking, but awful pale and scared.

Well, pretty soon the whole town was there, squirming and scrouging and pushing and shoving to get at the window and have a look, but people that had the places wouldn't give them up, and folks behind them was saying all the time, "Say, now, you've looked enough, you fellows; 'taint right and 'taint fair, for you to stay thar all the time, and never give nobody a chance; other folks has their rights as well as you."

There was considerable jawing back, so I slid out, thinking maybe there was going to be trouble. The streets was full, and everybody was excited. Everybody that seen the shooting was telling how it happened, and there was a big crowd packed around each one of these fellows, stretching their necks and listening. One long lanky man, with long hair and a big white fur stove-pipe hat on the back of his head, and a crooked-handled cane, marked out the places on the ground where Boggs stood, and where Sherburn stood, and the people following him around from one place to t'other and watching everything he done, and bobbing their heads to show they understood, and stooping a little and resting their hands on their thighs to watch him mark the places on the ground with his cane; and then he stood up straight and stiff where Sherburn had stood, frowning and having his hat-brim down over his eyes, and sung out, "Boggs!" and then fetched his cane down slow to a level, and says "Bang!" staggered backwards, says "Bang!" again, and fell down flat on his back. The people that had seen the thing said he done it perfect; said it was just exactly the way it all happened. Then as much as a dozen people got out their bottles and treated him.

Well, by-and-by somebody said Sherburn ought to be lynched. In about a minute everybody was saying it; so away they went, mad and yelling, and snatching down every clothes-line they come to, to do the hanging with.

CHAPTER XXII

They swarmed up the street towards Sherburn's house, a-whooping and yelling and raging like Injuns, and everything had to clear the way or get run over and tromped to mush, and it was awful to see. Children was heeling it ahead of the mob, screaming and trying to get out of the way; and every window along the road was full of women's heads, and there was nigger boys in every tree, and bucks and wenches[174] looking over every fence; and as soon as the mob would get nearly to them they would break and skaddle back out of reach. Lots of the women and girls was crying and taking on, scared most to death.

They swarmed up in front of Sherburn's palings as thick as they could jam together, and you couldn't hear yourself think for the noise. It was a little twenty-foot yard. Some sung out "Tear down the fence! tear down the fence!" Then there was a racket of ripping and tearing and smashing, and down she goes, and the front wall of the crowd begins to roll in like a wave.

Just then Sherburn steps out on the roof of his little front porch, with a double-barrel gun in his hand, and takes his stand, perfectly ca'm and deliberate, not saying a word. The racket stopped, and the wave sucked back.

[174]Young male and female slaves.

Sherburn never said a word—just stood there, looking down. The stillness was awful creepy and uncomfortable. Sherburn run his eye slow along the crowd; and wherever it struck, the people tried a little to outgaze him, but they couldn't; they dropped their eyes and looked sneaky. Then pretty soon Sherburn sort of laughed; not the pleasant kind, but the kind that makes you feel like when you are eating bread that's got sand in it.

Then he says, slow and scornful:

"The idea of *you* lynching anybody! It's amusing. The idea of you thinking you had pluck enough to lynch a *man!* Because you're brave enough to tar and feather poor friendless cast-out women that come along here, did that make you think you had grit enough to lay your hands on a *man?* Why a *man's* safe in the hands of ten thousand of your kind—as long as it's day-time and you're not behind him.

"Do I know you? I know you clear through. I was born and raised in the South, and I've lived in the North; so I know the average all around. The average man's a coward. In the North he lets anybody walk over him that wants to, and goes home and prays for a humble spirit to bear it. In the South one man, all by himself, has stopped a stage full of men, in the day-time, and robbed the lot. Your newspapers call you a brave people so much that you think you *are* braver than any other people—whereas you're just *as* brave, and no braver. Why don't your juries hang murderers? Because they're afraid the man's friends will shoot them in the back, in the dark—and it's just what they *would* do.

"So they always acquit; and then a *man* goes in the night, with a hundred masked cowards at his back, and lynches the rascal. Your mistake is, that you didn't bring a man with you; that's one mistake, and the other is that you didn't come in the dark, and fetch your masks. You brought *part* of a man—Buck Harkness, there—and if you hadn't had him to start you, you'd a taken it out in blowing.

"You didn't want to come. The average man don't like trouble and danger. *You* don't like trouble and danger. But if only *half* a man—like Buck Harkness, there—shouts 'Lynch him, lynch him!' you're afraid to back down—afraid you'll be found out to be what you are—*cowards*—and so you raise a yell, and hang yourselves onto that half-a-man's coat tail, and come raging up here, swearing what big things you're going to do. The pitifulest thing out is a mob; that's what an army is—a mob; they don't fight with courage that's born in them, but with courage that's borrowed from their mass, and from their officers. But a mob without any *man* at the head of it, is *beneath* pitifulness. Now the thing for *you* to do, is to droop your tails and go home and crawl in a hole. If any real lynching's going to be done, it will be done in the dark, Southern fashion; and when they come they'll bring their masks, and fetch a *man* along. Now *leave*—and take your half-a-man with you"—tossing his gun up across his left arm and cocking it, when he says this.

The crowd washed back sudden, and then broke all apart and went tearing off every which way, and Buck Harkness he heeled it after them, looking tolerable cheap. I could a staid, if I'd a wanted to, but I didn't want to.

I went to the circus, and loafed around the back side till the watchman went by, and then dived in under the tent. I had my twenty-dollar gold piece and some other money, but I reckoned I better save it, because there ain't no telling how soon you are going to need it, away from home and amongst strangers, that way. You can't be too careful. I ain't opposed to spending money on circuses, when there ain't no other way, but there ain't no use in *wasting* it on them.

It was a real bully circus. It was the splendidest sight that ever was, when they all come riding in, two and two, a gentleman and lady, side by side, the men just in their drawers and under-shirts, and no shoes nor stirrups, and resting their hands on their thighs, easy and comfortable—there must a been twenty of them—and every lady with a lovely complexion, and perfectly beautiful, and looking just like a gang of real sure-enough queens, and dressed in clothes that cost millions of dollars, and just littered with diamonds. It was a powerful fine sight; I never see anything so lovely. And then one by one they got up and stood, and went a-weaving around the ring so gentle and wavy and graceful, the men looking ever so tall and airy and straight, with their heads bobbing and skimming along, away up there under the tent-roof, and every lady's rose-leafy dress flapping soft and silky around her hips, and she looking like the most loveliest parasol.

And then faster and faster they went, all of them dancing, first one foot stuck out in the air and then the other, the horses leaning more and more, and the ring-master going round and round the centre-pole, cracking his whip and shouting "hi!—hi!" and the clown cracking jokes behind him; and by-and-by all hands dropped the reins, and every lady put her knuckles on her hips and every gentleman folded his arms, and then how the horses did lean over and hump themselves! And so, one after the other they all skipped off into the ring, and made the sweetest bow I ever see, and then scampered out, and everybody clapped their hands and went just about wild.

Well, all through the circus they done the most astonishing things; and all the time that clown carried on so it most killed the people. The ring-master couldn't ever say a word to him but he was back at him quick as a wink with the funniest things a body ever said; and how he ever *could* think of so many of them, and so sudden and so pat, was what I couldn't noway understand. Why, I couldn't a thought of them in a year. And by-and-by a drunk man tried to get into the ring—said he wanted to ride; said he could ride as well as anybody that ever was. They argued and tried to keep him out, but he wouldn't listen, and the whole show come to a standstill. Then the people begun to holler at him and make fun of him, and that made him mad, and he begun to rip and tear; so that stirred up the people, and a lot of men begun to pile down off of the benches and swarm towards the ring, saying, "Knock him down! throw him out!" and one or two women begun to scream. So, then, the ringmaster he made a little speech, and said he hoped there wouldn't be no disturbance, and if the man would promise he wouldn't make no more trouble, he would let him ride, if he thought he could stay on the horse. So everybody laughed and said all right, and the man got on. The minute he was on, the horse begun to rip and tear and jump and cavort around, with two circus men hanging onto his bridle trying to hold him, and the drunk man hanging onto his neck, and his heels flying in the air every jump, and the whole crowd of people standing up and shouting and laughing till the tears rolled down. And at last, sure enough, all the circus men could do, the horse broke loose, and away he went like the very nation, round and round the ring, with that sot laying down on him and hanging to his neck, with first one leg hanging most to the ground on one side, and then t'other one on t'other side, and the people just crazy. It warn't funny to me, though; I was all of a tremble to see his danger. But pretty soon he struggled up astraddle and grabbed the bridle, a-reeling this way and that; and the next minute he sprung up and dropped the bridle and stood! and the horse agoing like a house afire too. He just stood up there, a-sailing around as easy and comfortable as if he warn't ever drunk in his life—and then he begun to pull off his clothes and sling them. He shed them so thick they kind of clogged up the air, and altogether he shed seventeen suits. And then, there he was, slim and handsome, and dressed the gaudiest and prettiest you ever saw, and he lit into that horse with his whip and made him fairly hum—and finally skipped off to the dressing-room, and everybody just a-howling with pleasure and astonishment.

Then the ring-master he see how he had been fooled, and he *was* the sickest ring-master you ever see, I reckon. Why, it was one of his own men! He had got up that joke all out of his own head, and never let on to nobody. Well, I felt sheepish enough, to be took in so, but I wouldn't a been in that ring-master's place, not for a thousand dollars. I don't know; there may be bullier circuses than what that one was, but I never struck them yet. Anyways it was plenty good enough for *me;* and wherever I run across it, it can have all of *my* custom, every time.

Well, that night we had *our* show; but there warn't only about twelve people there, just enough to pay expenses. And they laughed all the time, and that made the duke mad; and everybody left, anyway, before the show was over, but one boy which was asleep. So the duke said these Arkansaw lunkheads couldn't come up to Shakspeare; what they wanted was low comedy—and may be something ruther worse than low comedy, he reckoned. He said he could size their style. So next morning he got some big sheets of wrapping-paper and some black paint, and drawed off some handbills and stuck them up all over the village. The bills said:

AT THE COURT HOUSE!
FOR 3 NIGHTS ONLY!
The World-Renowned Tragedians
DAVID GARRICK THE YOUNGER!
AND
EDMUND KEAN THE ELDER!
Of the London and Continental Theatres,
In their Thrilling Tragedy of
THE KING'S CAMELOPARD[175]
OR
THE ROYAL NONESUCH!!!
Admission 50 cents.

Then at the bottom was the biggest line of all—which said:

LADIES AND CHILDREN NOT ADMITTED.

"There," says he, "if that line don't fetch them, I don't know Arkansaw!"

[175]A giraffe.

CHAPTER XXIII

Well, all day him and the king was hard at it, rigging up a stage, and a curtain, and a row of candles for footlights; and that night the house was jam full of men in no time. When the place couldn't hold no more, the duke he quit tending door and went around the back way and come onto the stage and stood up before the curtain, and made a little speech, and praised up this tragedy, and said it was the most thrillingest one that ever was; and so he went on a-bragging about the tragedy and about Edmund Kean the Elder, which was to play the main principal part in it; and at last when he'd got everybody's expectations up high enough, he rolled up the curtain, and the next minute the king come a-prancing out on all fours, naked; and he was painted all over, ring-streaked-and-striped, all sorts of colors, as splendid as a rainbow. And—but never mind the rest of his outfit, it was just wild, but it was awful funny. The people most killed themselves laughing; and when the king got done capering, and capered off behind the scenes, they roared and clapped and stormed and haw-hawed till he come back and done it over again; and after that, they made him do it another time. Well, it would a made a cow laugh to see the shines that old idiot cut.

Then the duke he lets the curtain down, and bows to the people and says the great tragedy will be performed only two nights more, on accounts of pressing London engagements, where the seats is all sold already for it in Drury Lane; and then he makes them another bow, and says if he has succeeded in pleasing them and instructing them, he will be deeply obleeged if they will mention it to their friends and get them to come and see it.

Twenty people sings out:

"What, is it over? Is that *all?*"

The duke says yes. Then there was a fine time. Everybody sings out "sold,"[176] and rose up mad, and was agoing for that stage and them tragedians. But a big fine-looking man jumps up on a bench, and shouts:

"Hold on! Just a word, gentlemen." They stopped to listen. "We are sold—mighty badly sold. But we don't want to be the laughing-stock of this whole town, I reckon, and never hear the last of this thing as long as we live. *No.* What we want, is to go out of here quiet, and talk this show up, and sell the *rest* of the town! Then we'll all be in the same boat. Ain't that sensible?" ("You bet it is!—the jedge is right!" everybody sings out.) "All right, then—not a word about any sell. Go along home, and advise everybody to come and see the tragedy."

Next day you couldn't hear nothing around that town but how splendid that show was. House was jammed again, that night, and we sold this crowd the same way. When me and the king and the duke got home to the raft, we all had a supper; and by-and-by, about midnight, they made Jim and me back her out and float her down the middle of the river and fetch her in and hide her about two mile below town.

The third night the house was crammed again—and they warn't new-comers, this time, but people that was at the show the other two nights. I stood by the duke at the door, and I see that every man that went in had his pockets bulging, or something muffled up under his coat—and I see it warn't no perfumery neither, not by a long sight. I smelt sickly eggs by the barrel, and rotten

[176]"Cheated."

cabbages, and such things; and if I know the signs of a dead cat being around, and I bet I do, there was sixty-four of them went in. I shoved in there for a minute, but it was too various[177] for me, I couldn't stand it. Well, when the place couldn't hold no more people, the duke he give a fellow a quarter and told him to tend door for him a minute, and then he started around for the stage door, I after him; but the minute we turned the corner and was in the dark, he says:

"Walk fast, now, till you get away from the houses, and then shin for the raft like the dickens was after you!"

I done it, and he done the same. We struck the raft at the same time, and in less than two seconds we was gliding down stream, all dark and still, and edging towards the middle of the river, nobody saying a word. I reckoned the poor king was in for a gaudy time of it with the audience; but nothing of the sort; pretty soon he crawls out from under the wigwam, and says:

"Well, how'd the old thing pan out this time, Duke?"

He hadn't been up town at all.

We never showed a light till we was about ten mile below that village. Then we lit up and had a supper, and the king and the duke fairly laughed their bones loose over the way they'd served them people. The duke says:

"Greenhorns, flatheads! *I* knew the first house would keep mum and let the rest of the town get roped in; and I knew they'd lay for us the third night, and consider it was *their* turn now. Well, it *is* their turn, and I'd give something to know how much they'd take for it. I *would* just like to know how they're putting in their opportunity. They can turn it into a picnic, if they want to—they brought plenty provisions."

Them rapscallions took in four hundred and sixty-five dollars in that three nights. I never see money hauled in by the wagon-load like that, before.

By-and-by, when they was asleep and snoring, Jim says:

"Don't it 'spise you, de way dem kings carries on, Huck?"

"No," I says, "it don't."

"Why don't it, Huck?"

"Well, it don't, because it's in the breed. I reckon they're all alike."

"But, Huck, dese kings o' ourn is regular rapscallions; dat's jist what dey is; dey's regular rapscallions."

"Well, that's what I'm a-saying; all kings is mostly rapscallions, as fur as I can make out."

"Is dat so?"

"You read about them once—you'll see. Look at Henry the Eight; this'n's a Sunday-School Superintendent to *him*. And look at Charles Second, and Louis Fourteen, and Louis Fifteen, and James Second, and Edward Second, and Richard Third, and forty more; beside all them Saxon heptarchies[178] that used to rip around so in old times and raise Cain. My, you ought to seen old Henry the Eight when he was in bloom. He *was* a blossom. He used to marry a new wife every day, and chop off her head next morning. And he would do it just as indifferent as if he was ordering up eggs. 'Fetch up Nell Gwynn,' he says. They fetch her up. Next morning, 'Chop off her head!' And they chop it off. 'Fetch

[177] I.e., it was too much.

[178] The seven Anglo-Saxon kingdoms of England (Northumbria, Mercia, East Anglia, Essex, Kent, Sussex, and Wessex), and their period of dominance, from the sixth to the ninth century.

up Jane Shore,' he says; and up she comes. Next morning, 'Chop off her head'—'Ring up Fair Rosamun.'[179] Fair Rosamun answers the bell. Next morning, 'Chop off her head.' And he made every one of them tell him a tale every night; and he kept that up till he had hogged a thousand and one tales that way, and then he put them all in a book, and called it Domesday Book—which was a good name and stated the case.[180] You don't know kings, Jim, but I know them; and this old rip of ourn is one of the cleanest I've struck in history. Well, Henry he takes a notion he wants to get up some trouble with this country. How does he got at it—give notice?—give the country a show? No. All of a sudden he heaves all the tea in Boston Harbor overboard, and whacks out a declaration of independence, and dares them to come on. That was *his* style—he never give anybody a chance. He had suspicions of his father, the Duke of Wellington. Well, what did he do?—ask him to show up? No—drownded him in a butt of mamsey, like a cat. Spose people left money laying around where he was—what did he do? He collared it. Spose he contracted to do a thing; and you paid him, and didn't set down there and see he done it—what did he do? He always done the other thing. Spose he opened his mouth—what then? If he didn't shut it up powerful quick, he'd lose a lie, every time. That's the kind of a bug Henry was; and if we'd a had him along 'stead of our kings, he'd a fooled that town a heap worse than ourn done. I don't say that ourn is lambs, because they ain't, when you come right down to the cold facts; but they ain't nothing to *that* old ram, anyway. All I say is, kings is kings, and you got to make allowances. Take them all around, they're a mighty ornery lot. It's the way they're raised."

"But dis one do *smell* so like de nation, Huck."

"Well, they all do, Jim. *We* can't help the way a king smells; history don't tell no way."

"Now de duke, he's a tolerble likely man, in some ways."

"Yes, a duke's different. But not very different. This one's a middling hard lot, for a duke. When he's drunk, there ain't no nearsighted man could tell him from a king."

"Well, anyways, I doan' hanker for no mo' un um, Huck. Dese is all I kin stan'."

"It's the way I feel, too, Jim. But we've got them on our hands, and we got to remember what they are, and make allowances. Sometimes I wish we could hear of a country that's out of kings."

What was the use to tell Jim these warn't real kings and dukes? It wouldn't a done no good; and besides, it was just as I said; you couldn't tell them from the real kind.

I went to sleep, and Jim didn't call me when it was my turn. He often done that. When I waked up, just at day-break, he was setting there with his head down betwixt his knees, moaning and mourning to himself. I didn't take notice, nor let on. I knowed what it was about. He was thinking about his wife and his children, away up yonder, and he was low and homesick; because he hadn't ever been away from home before in his life; and I do believe he cared just as much for his people as white folks does for theirn. It don't seem natural, but I

[179]Women who were mistresses of English kings of the twelfth, fifteenth, and seventeenth centuries. None was married to King Henry VIII.

[180]Here as elsewhere, Huck mixes the events and characters of history and fiction.

reckon it's so. He was often moaning and mourning that way, nights, when he judged I was asleep, and saying, "Po' little 'Lizabeth! po' little Johnny! it's mighty hard; I spec' I ain't ever gwyne to see you no mo', no mo'!" He was a mighty good nigger, Jim was.

But this time I somehow got to talking to him about his wife and young ones; and by-and-by he says:

"What makes me feel so bad dis time, uz bekase I hear sumpn over yonder on de bank like a whack, er a slam, while ago, en it mine me er de time I treat my little 'Lizabeth so ornery. She warn't on'y 'bout fo' year ole, en she tuck de sk'yarlet-fever, an had a powful rough spell; but she got well, en one day she was a-stannin' aroun', en I says to her, I says:

"Shet de do'."

"She never done it; jis' stood dah, kiner smilin' up at me. It make me mad; en I says agin, mighty loud, I says:

" 'Doan' you hear me?—shet de do'!'

"She jis' stood de same way, kiner smilin' up. I was a-bilin'! I says: 'I lay I *make* you mine!'

"En wid dat I fetch' her a slap side de head dat sont her a-sprawlin'. Den I went into de yuther room, en 'uz gone 'bout ten minutes; en when I come back, dah was dat do' a-stannin' open *yit,* en dat chile stannin' mos' right in it, a-lookin' down and mournin', en de tears runnin' down. My, but I *wuz* mad, I was agwyne for de chile, but jis' den—it was a do' dat open innerds—jis' den, 'long come de wind en slam it to, behind de chile, ker-*blam!*—en my lan', de chile never move'! My breff mos' hop outer me; en I feel so—so—I doan' know *how* I feel, I crope out, all a-tremblin', en crope aroun' en open de do' easy en slow, en poke my head in behine de chile, sof' en still, en all uv a sudden, I says *pow!* jis' as loud as I could yell. *She never budge!* Oh, Huck, I bust out a-cryin' en grab her up in my arms, en say, 'Oh, de po' little thing! de Lord God Amighty fogive po' ole Jim, kaze he never gwyne to fogive hisself as long's he live!' Oh, she was plumb deef en dumb, Huck, plumb deef en dumb—en I'd ben a-treat'n her so!"

CHAPTER XXIV

Next day, towards night, we laid up under a little willow towhead out in the middle; where there was a village on each side of the river, and the duke and the king begun to lay out a plan for working them towns. Jim he spoke to the duke, and said he hoped it wouldn't take but a few hours, because it got mighty heavy and tiresome to him when he had to lay all day in the wigwam tied with the rope. You see, when we left him all alone we had to tie him, because if anybody happened on him all by himself and not tied, it wouldn't look much like he was a runaway nigger, you know. So the duke said it *was* kind of hard to have to lay roped all day, and he'd cipher out some way to get around it.

He was uncommon bright, the duke was, and he soon struck it. He dressed Jim up in King Lear's outfit—it was a long curtain-calico gown, and a white horse-hair wig and whiskers; and then he took his theatre-paint and painted Jim's face and hands and ears and neck all over a dead dull solid blue, like a man that's been drownded nine days. Blamed if he warn't the horriblest looking outrage I ever see. Then the duke took and wrote out a sign on a shingle so—

Sick Arab—but harmless when not out of his head.

And he nailed that shingle to a lath, and stood the lath up four or five foot in front of the wigwam. Jim was satisfied. He said it was a sight better than laying tied a couple of years every day and trembling all over every time there was a sound. The duke told him to make himself free and easy, and if anybody ever come meddling around, he must hop out of the wigwam, and carry on a little, and fetch a howl or two like a wild beast, and he reckoned they would light out and leave him alone. Which was sound enough judgment; but you take the average man, and he wouldn't wait for him to howl. Why, he didn't only look like he was dead, he looked considerable more than that.

These rapscallions wanted to try the Nonesuch again, because there was so much money in it, but they judged it wouldn't be safe, because maybe the news might a worked along down by this time. They couldn't hit no project that suited, exactly; so at last the duke said he reckoned he'd lay off and work his brains an hour or two and see if he couldn't put up something on the Arkansaw village; and the king he allowed he would drop over to t'other village, without any plan, but just trust in Providence to lead him the profitable way—meaning the devil, I reckon. We had all bought store clothes where we stopped last; and now the king put his'n on, and he told me to put mine on. I done it, of course. The king's duds was all black, and he did look real swell and starchy. I never knowed how clothes could change a body before. Why, before, he looked like the orneriest old rip that ever was; but now, when he'd take off his new white beaver[181] and make a bow and do a smile, he looked that grand and good and pious that you'd say he had walked right out of the ark, and maybe was old Leviticus[182] himself. Jim cleaned up the canoe, and I got my paddle ready. There was a big steamboat laying at the shore away up under the point, about three mile above town—been there a couple of hours, taking on freight. Says the king:

"Seein' how I'm dressed, I reckon maybe I better arrive down from St. Louis or Cincinnati, or some other big place. Go for the steamboat, Huckleberry; we'll come down to the village on her."

I didn't have to be ordered twice, to go and take a steamboat ride. I fetched the store a half a mile above the village, and then went scooting along the bluff bank in the easy water. Pretty soon we come to a nice innocent-looking young country jake setting on a log swabbing the sweat off of his face, for it was powerful warm weather; and he had a couple of big carpet-bags by him.

"Run her nose in shore," says the king. I done it. "Wher' you bound for, young man?"

"For the steamboat; going to Orleans."

"Git aboard," says the king. "Hold on a minute, my servant'll he'p you with them bags. Jump out and he'p the gentleman Adolphus"—meaning me, I see.

[181]Hat.

[182]Huck confuses Leviticus, a book of the Old Testament, with Noah, who built the ark and survived the flood.

I done so, and then we all three started on again. The young chap was mighty thankful; said it was tough work toting his baggage in such weather. He asked the king where he was going, and the king told him he'd come down the river and landed at the other village this morning, and now he was going up a few miles to see an old friend on a farm up there. The young fellow says:

"When I first see you, I says to myself, 'It's Mr. Wilks, sure, and he come mighty near getting here in time.' But then I says again, 'No, I reckon it ain't him, or else he wouldn't be paddling up the river.' You *ain't* him, are you?"

"No, my name's Blodgett—Elexander Blodgett—*Reverend* Elexander Blodgett, I spose I must say, as I'm one o' the Lord's poor servants. But still I'm jist as able to be sorry for Mr. Wilks for not arriving in time, all the same, if he's missed anything by it—which I hope he hasn't."

"Well, he don't miss any property by it, because he'll get that all right; but he's missed seeing his brother Peter die—which he mayn't mind, nobody can tell as to that—but his brother would a give anything in this world to see *him* before he died; never talked about nothing else all these three weeks; hadn't seen him since they was boys together—and hadn't ever seen his brother William at all—that's the deef and dumb one—William ain't more than thirty or thirty-five. Peter and George was the only ones that come out here; George was the married brother; him and his wife both died last year. Harvey and William's the only ones that's left now; and, as I was saying, they haven't got here in time."

"Did anybody send 'em word?"

"Oh, yes; a month or two ago, when Peter was first took; because Peter said then that he sorter felt like he warn't going to get well this time. You see, he was pretty old, and George's g'yirls was too young to be much company for him, except Mary Jane the redheaded one; and so he was kinder lonesome after George and his wife died, and didn't seem to care much to live. He most desperately wanted to see Harvey—and William too, for that matter—because he was one of them kind that can't bear to make a will. He left a letter behind for Harvey, and said he'd told in it where his money was hid, and how he wanted the rest of the property divided up so George's g'yirls would be all right—for George didn't leave nothing. And that letter was all they could get him to put a pen to."

"Why do you reckon Harvey don't come? Wher' does he live?"

"Oh, he lives in England—Sheffield—preaches there—hasn't ever been in this country. He hasn't had any too much time—and besides he mightn't a got the letter at all, you know."

"Too bad, too bad he couldn't a lived to see his brothers, poor soul. You going to Orleans, you say?"

"Yes, but that ain't only a part of it. I'm going in a ship, next Wednesday, for Ryo Janeero,[183] where my uncle lives."

"It's a pretty long journey. But it'll be lovely; I wisht I was agoing. Is Mary Jane the oldest? How old is the others?"

"Mary Jane's nineteen, Susan's fifteen, and Joann's about fourteen—that's the one that gives herself to good works and has a hare-lip."

"Poor things! to be left alone in the cold world so."

"Well, they could be worse off. Old Peter had friends, and they ain't going to let them come to no harm. There's Hobson, the Babtis' preacher; and Deacon

[183]Rio de Janeiro, Brazil.

Lot Hovey, and Ben Rucker, and Abner Shackleford, and Levi Bell, the lawyer; and Dr. Robinson, and their wives, and the widow Bartley, and—well, there's a lot of them; but these are the ones that Peter was thickest with, and used to write about sometimes, when he wrote home; so Harvey 'll know where to look for friends when he gets here."

Well, the old man he went on asking questions till he just fairly emptied that young fellow. Blamed if he didn't inquire about everybody and everything in that blessed town, and all about all the Wilkses; and about Peter's business—which was a tanner; and about George's—which was a carpenter; and about Harvey's—which was a dissentering minister;[184] and so on, and so on. Then he says:

"What did you want to walk all the way up to the steamboat for?"

"Because she's a big Orleans boat, and I was afeared she mightn't stop there. When they're deep they won't stop for a hail. A Cincinnati boat will, but this is a St. Louis one."

"Was Peter Wilks well off?"

"Oh, yes, pretty well off. He had houses and land, and it's reckoned he left three or four thousand in cash hid up som'ers."

"When did you say he died?"

"I didn't say, but it was last night."

"Funeral to-morrow, likely?"

"Yes, 'bout the middle of the day."

"Well, it's all terrible sad; but we've all got to go, one time or another. So what we want to do is to be prepared; then we're all right."

"Yes, sir, it's the best way. Ma used to always say that."

When we struck the boat, she was about done loading, and pretty soon she got off. The king never said nothing about going aboard so I lost my ride, after all. When the boat was gone, the king made me paddle up another mile to a lonesome place, and then he got ashore, and says:

"Now, hustle back, right off, and fetch the duke up here, and the new carpetbags. And if he's gone over to t'other side, go over there and git him. And tell him to git himself up regardless. Shove along, now."

I see what *he* was up to; but I never said nothing, of course. When I got back with the duke, we hid the canoe and then they set down on a log, and the king told him everything, just like the young fellow had said it—every last word of it. And all the time he was a doing it, he tried to talk like an Englishman; and he done it pretty well too, for a slouch. I can't imitate him, and so I ain't agoing to try to; but he really done it pretty good. Then he says:

"How are you on the deef and dumb, Bilgewater?"

The duke said, leave him alone for that; said he had played a deef and dumb person on the histrionic boards. So then they waited for a steamboat.

About the middle of the afternoon a couple of little boats come along, but they didn't come from high enough up the river; but a last there was a big one, and they hailed her. She sent out her yawl, and we went aboard, and she was from Cincinnati; and when they found we only wanted to go four or five mile, they was booming mad, and give us a cussing, and said they wouldn't land us. But the king was ca'm. He says:

[184]Dissenting minister, one who rejects the traditional doctrines of an established church, a nonconformist.

"If gentlemen kin afford to pay a dollar a mile apiece, to be took on and put off in a yawl, a steamboat kin afford to carry 'em, can't it?"

So they softened down and said it was all right; and when we got to the village, they yawled us ashore. About two dozen men flocked down, when they see the yawl a coming; and when the king says—

"Kin any of you gentlemen tell me wher' Mr. Peter Wilks lives?" they give a glance at one another, and nodded their heads, as much as to say, "What d' I tell you?" Then one of them says, kind of soft and gentle:

"I'm sorry, sir, but the best we can do is tell you where he *did* live yesterday evening."

Sudden as winking, the ornery old cretur went all to smash, and fell up against the man, and put his chin on his shoulder, and cried down his back, and says:

"Alas, alas, our poor brother—gone, and we never got to see him; oh, it's too, *too* hard!"

Then he turns around, blubbering, and makes a lot of idiotic signs to the duke on his hands, and blamed if *he* didn't drop a carpet-bag and bust out a-crying. If they warn't the beatenest lot, them two frauds, that ever I struck.

Well, the men gethered around, and sympathized with them, and said all sorts of kind things to them, and carried their carpet-bags up the hill for them, and let them lean on them and cry, and told the king all about his brother's last moments, and the king he told it all over again on his hands to the duke, and both of them took on about that dead tanner like they'd lost the twelve disciples. Well, if ever I struck anything like it, I'm a nigger. It was enough to make a body ashamed of the human race.

CHAPTER XXV

The news was all over town in two minutes, and you could see the people tearing down on the run, from every which way, some of them putting on their coats as they come. Pretty soon we was in the middle of a crowd, and the noise of the tramping was like a soldier-march. The windows and dooryards was full; and every minute somebody would say, over a fence:

"Is it *them?*"

And somebody trotting along with the gang would answer back and say,

"You bet it is."

When we got to the house, the street in front of it was packed, and the three girls was standing in the door. Mary Jane *was* red-headed, but that don't make no difference, she was most awful beautiful, and her face and her eyes was all lit up like glory, she was so glad her uncles was come. The king he spread his arms, and Mary Jane she jumped for them, and the hare-lip jumped for the duke, and there they *had* it! Everybody most, leastways women, cried for joy to see them meet at last and have such good times.

Then the king he hunched the duke, private—I see him do it—and then he looked around and see the coffin, over in the corner on two chairs; so then, him and the duke, with a hand across each other's shoulder, and t'other hand to their eyes, walked slow and solemn over there, everybody dropping back to give them room, and all the talk and noise stopping, people saying "Sh!" and all the men taking their hats off and drooping their heads, so you could a heard a pin fall. And when they got there, they bent over and looked in the coffin, and took one sight, and then they bust out a crying so you could a heard them to Orleans, most; and then they put their arms around each other's necks, and hung their chins over each other's shoulders; and then for three minutes, or maybe four, I never see two men leak the way they done. And mind you, everybody was doing the same; and the place was that damp I never see anything like it. Then one of them got on one side of the coffin, and t'other on t'other side, and they kneeled down and rested their foreheads on the coffin, and let on to pray all to theirselves. Well, when it come to that, it worked the crowd like you never see anything like it, and so everybody broke down and went to sobbing right out loud—the poor girls, too; and every woman, nearly, went up to the girls, without saying a word, and kissed them, solemn, on the forehead, and then put their hand on their head, and looked up towards the sky, with the tears running down, and then busted out and went off sobbing and swabbing, and give the next woman a show. I never see anything so disgusting.

Well, by-and-by the king he gets up and comes forward a little, and works himself up and slobbers out a speech, all full of tears and flapdoodle about its being a sore trial for him and his poor brother to lose the diseased and to miss seeing the diseased alive, after the long journey of four thousand mile, but it's a trial that's sweetened and sanctified to us by this dear sympathy and these holy tears, and so he thanks them out of his heart and out of his brother's heart, because out of their mouths they can't, words being too weak and cold, and all that kind of rot and slush, till it was just sickening; and then he blubbers out a pious goody-goody Amen, and turns himself loose and goes to crying fit to bust.

And the minute the words was out of his mouth somebody over in the crowd struck up the doxolojer,[185] and everybody joined in with all their might, and it just warmed you up and made you feel as good as church letting out. Music *is* a good thing; and after all that soul-butter and hogwash, I never see it freshen up things so, and sound so honest and bully.

Then the king begins to work his jaws again, and says how him and his nieces would be glad if a few of the main principal friends of the family would take supper here with them this evening, and help set up with the ashes of the diseased; and says if his poor brother laying yonder could speak, he knows who he would name, for they was names that was very dear to him, and mentioned often in his letters; and so he will name the same, to-wit, as follows, vizz:—Rev. Mr. Hobson, and Deacon Lot Hovey, and Mr. Ben Rucker, and Abner Shackleford, and Levi Bell, and Dr. Robinson, and their wives, and the widow Bartley.

Rev. Hobson and Dr. Robinson was down to the end of the town, a-hunting together; that is, I mean the doctor was shipping a sick man to t'other world, and the preacher was pinting him right. Lawyer Bell was away up to Louisville on some business. But the rest was on hand, and so they all come and shook hands with the king and thanked him and talked to him; and then they shook hands with the duke, and didn't say nothing but just kept a-smiling and bobbing their heads like a passel of sapheads whilst he made all sorts of signs with his hands and said "Goo-goo—goo-goo-goo," all the time, like a baby that can't talk.

So the king he blatted along, and managed to inquire about pretty much everybody and dog in town, by his name, and mentioned all sorts of little things

[185]Doxology, a hymn in praise of God.

that happened one time or another in the town, or to George's family, or to Peter; and he always let on that Peter wrote him the things, but that was a lie, he got every blessed one of them out of that young flathead that we canoed up to the steamboat.

Then Mary Jane she fetched the letter her uncle left behind, and the king he read it out loud and cried over it. It give the dwelling-house and three thousand dollars, gold, to the girls; and it give the tanyard (which was doing a good business), along with some other houses and land (worth about seven thousand), and three thousand dollars in gold to Harvey and William, and told where the six thousand cash was hid, down cellar. So these two frauds said they'd go and fetch it up, and have everything square and above-board; and told me to come with a candle. We shut the cellar door behind us, and when they found the bag they spilt it out on the floor, and it was a lovely sight, all of them yaller-boys.[186] My, the way the king's eyes did shine! He slaps the duke on the shoulder, and says:

"Oh, *this* ain't bully, nor noth'n! Oh, no, I reckon not! Why, Biljy, it beats the Nonesuch, *don't* it!"

The duke allowed it did. They pawed the yaller-boys, and sifted them through their fingers and let them jingle down on the floor; and the king says:

"It ain't no use talkin'; bein' brothers to a rich dead man, and representatives of furrin heirs that's got left, is the line for you and me, Bilge. Thish-yer comes of trust'n to Providence. It's the best way, in the long run. I've tried 'em all, and ther' ain't no better way."

Most everybody would a been satisfied with the pile, and took it on trust; but no, they must count it. So they counts it, and it comes out four hundred and fifteen dollars short. Says the King:

"Dern him, I wonder what he done with that four hundred and fifteen dollars?"

They worried over that a while, and ransacked all around for it. Then the duke says:

"Well, he was a pretty sick man, and likely he made a mistake—I reckon that's the way of it. The best way's to let it go, and keep still about it. We can spare it."

"Oh, shucks, yes, we can *spare* it. I don't k'yer noth'n 'bout that—it's the *count* I'm thinkin' about. We want to be awful square and open and aboveboard, here, you know. We want to lug this h-yer money up stairs and count it before everybody—then ther' ain't noth'n suspicious. But when the dead man says ther's six thous'n dollars, you know, we don't want to—"

"Hold on," says the duke. "Less make up the deffsit"—and he begun to haul out yaller-boys out of his pocket.

"It's a most amaz'n' good idea, duke—you *have* got a rattlin' clever head on you," says the king. "Blest if the old Nonesuch ain't a heppin' us out agin"—and *he* begun to haul out yaller-jackets and stack them up.

It most busted them, but they made up the six thousand clean and clear.

"Say," says the duke, "I got another idea. Le's go up stairs and count this money, and then take and *give it to the girls*."

"Good land, duke, lemme hug you! It's the most dazzling idea 'at ever a man struck. You have cert'nly got the most astonishin' head I ever see. Oh, this is the

[186]Gold coins.

boss dodge,[187] ther' ain't no mistake 'bout it. Let 'em fetch along their suspicions now, if they want to—this'll lay 'em out."

When we got up stairs, everybody gethered around the table, and the king he counted it and stacked it up, three hundred dollars in a pile—twenty elegant little piles. Everybody looked hungry at it, and licked their chops. Then they raked it into the bag again, and I see the king begin to swell himself up for another speech. He says:

"Friends all, my poor brother that lays yonder, has done generous by them that's left behind in the vale of sorrers. He has done generous by these-yer poor little lambs that he loved and sheltered, and that's left fatherless and motherless. Yes, and we that knowed him, knows that he would a done *more* generous by 'em if he hadn't ben afeard o' woundin' his dear William and me. Now, *wouldn't* he? Ther' ain't no question 'bout it, in *my* mind. Well, then—what kind o' brothers would it be, that 'd stand in his way at sech a time? And what kind o' uncles would it be that'd rob—yes, *rob*—sech poor sweet lambs as these 'at he loved so, at sech a time? If I know William—and I *think* I do—he—well, I'll jest ask him." He turns around and begins to make a lot of signs to the duke with his hands; and the duke he looks at him stupid and leather-headed a while, then all of a sudden he seems to catch his meaning, and jumps for the king, goo-gooing with all his might for joy, and hugs him about fifteen times before he lets up. Then the king says, "I knowed it; I reckon *that*'ll convince anybody the way *he* feels about it. Here, Mary Jane, Susan, Joanner, take the money—take it *all*. It's the gift of him that lays yonder, cold but joyful."

Mary Jane she went for him, Susan and the hare-lip went for the duke, and then such another hugging and kissing I never see yet. And everybody crowded up with the tears in their eyes, and most shook the hands off of them frauds, saying all the time:

"You *dear* good souls!—how *lovely!*—how *could* you!"

Well, then, pretty soon all hands got to talking about the diseased again, and how good he was, and what a loss he was, and all that; and before long a big iron-jawed man worked himself in there from outside, and stood a listening and looking, and not saying anything; and nobody saying anything to him either, because the king was talking and they was all busy listening. The king was saying—in the middle of something he's started in on—

"—they bein' partickler friends o' the diseased. That's why they're invited here this evenin'; but to-morrow we want *all* to come—everybody; for he respected everybody, he liked everybody, and so it's fitten that his funeral orgies sh'd be public."

And so he went a-mooning on and on, liking to hear himself talk, and every little while he fetched in his funeral orgies again, till the duke he couldn't stand it no more; so he writes on a little scrap of paper, "*obsequies,* you old fool," and folds it up and goes to goo-gooing and reaching it over people's heads to him. The king he reads it, and puts it in his pocket, and says:

"Poor William, afflicted as he is, his *heart's* aluz right. Asks me to invite everybody to come to the funeral—wants me to make 'em all welcome. But he needn't a worried—it was jest what I was at."

[187]Best scam.

Then he weaves along again, perfectly ca'm, and goes to dropping in his funeral orgies again every now and then, just like he done before. And when he done it the third time, he says:

"I say orgies, not because it's the common term, because it ain't—obsequies bein' the common term—but because orgies is the right term. Obsequies ain't used in England no more, now—it's gone out. We say orgies now, in England. Orgies is better, because it means the thing you're after, more exact. It's a word that's made up out'n the Greek *orgo,* outside, open, abroad; and the Hebrew *jeesum,* to plant, cover up; hence in*ter.* So, you see, funeral orgies is an open er public funeral."

He was the *worst* I ever struck. Well, the iron-jawed man he laughed right in his face. Everybody was shocked. Everybody says, "Why *doctor!*" and Abner Shackleford says:

"Why, Robinson, hain't you heard the news? This is Harvey Wilks."

The king he smiled eager, and shoved out his flapper, and says:

"*Is* it my poor brother's dear good friend and physician? I——"

"Keep your hands off of me!" says the doctor. "*You* talk like an Englishman—*don't* you? It's the worst imitation I ever heard. *You* Peter Wilks's brother. You're a fraud, that's what you are!"

Well, how they all took on! They crowded around the doctor, and tried to quiet him down, and tried to explain to him, and tell him how Harvey'd showed in forty ways that he *was* Harvey, and knowed everybody by name, and the names of the very dogs, and begged and *begged* him not to hurt Harvey's feelings and the poor girls' feelings, and all that; but it warn't no use, he stormed right along, and said any man that pretended to be an Englishman and couldn't imitate the lingo no better than what he did, was a fraud and a liar. The poor girls was hanging to the king and crying; and all of a sudden the doctor ups and turns on *them.* He says:

"I was your father's friend, and I'm your friend; and I warn you *as* a friend, and an honest one, that wants to protect you and keep you out of harm and trouble, to turn your backs on that scoundrel, and have nothing to do with him, the ignorant tramp, with his idiotic Greek and Hebrew as he calls it. He is the thinnest kind of an imposter—has come here with a lot of empty names and facts which he has picked up somewheres, and you take them for *proofs,* and are helped to fool yourselves by these foolish friends here, who ought to know better. Mary Jane Wilks, you know me for your friend, and for your unselfish friend, too. Now listen to me; turn this pitiful rascal out—I *beg* you to do it. Will you?"

Mary Jane straightened herself up, and my, but she was handsome! she says:

"*Here* is my answer." She hove up the bag of money and put it in the king's hands, and says, "Take this six thousand dollars, and invest it for me and my sisters any way you want to, and don't give us no receipt for it."

Then she put her arm around the king on one side, and Susan and the harelip done the same on the other. Everybody clapped their hands and stomped on the floor like a perfect storm, whilst the king held up his head and smiled proud. The doctor says:

"All right, I wash *my* hands of the matter. But I warn you all that a time's coming when you're going to feel sick whenever you think of this day"—and away he went.

"All right, doctor," says the king, kinder mocking him, "we'll try and get 'em to send for you"—which made them all laugh, and they said it was a prime good hit.

CHAPTER XXVI

Well when they was all gone, the king asks Mary Jane how they was off for spare rooms, and she said she had one spare room, which would do for Uncle William, and she'd give her own room to Uncle Harvey, which was a little bigger, and she would turn into the room with her sisters and sleep on a cot; and up garret was a little cubby, with a pallet in it. The king said the cubby would do for his valley—meaning me.

So Mary Jane took us up, and she showed them their rooms, which was plain but nice. She said she'd have her frocks and a lot of other traps took out of her room if they was in Uncle Harvey's way, but he said they warn't. The frocks was hung along the wall, and before them was a curtain made out of calico that hung down to the floor. There was an old hair trunk in one corner, and a guitar box in another, and all sorts of little knick-knacks and jim-cracks around, like girls brisken up a room with. The king said it was all the more homely and more pleasanter for these fixings, and so don't disturb them. The duke's room was pretty small, but plenty good enough, and so was my cubby.

That night they had a big supper, and all them men and women was there, and I stood behind the king and the duke's chairs and waited on them, and the niggers waited on the rest. Mary Jane she set at the head of the table with Susan along side of her, and said how bad the biscuits was, and how mean the preserves was, and how ornery and tough the fried chicken was—and all that kind of rot, the way women always do to force out compliments; and the people all knowed everything was tip-top, and said so—said "How *do* you get biscuits to brown so nice?" and "Where, for the land's sake *did* you get these amaz'n pickles?" and all that kind of humbug talky-talk, just the way people always does at a supper, you know.

And when it was all done, me and the hare-lip had supper in the kitchen off of the leavings, whilst the others was helping the niggers clean up the things. The hare-lip she got to pumping me about England, and blest if I didn't think the ice was getting mighty thin, sometimes. She says:

"Did you ever see the king?"

"Who? William Fourth?[188] Well, I bet I have—he goes to our church." I knowed he was dead years ago, but I never let on. So when I says he goes to our church, she says:

"What—regular?"

"Yes—regular. His pew's right over opposite ourn—on t'other side the pulpit."

"I thought he lived in London?"

"Well, he does. Where *would* he live?"

"But I thought *you* lived in Sheffield?"[189]

I see I was up a stump. I had to let on to get choked with a chicken bone, so as to get time to think how to get down again. Then I says:

[188]King of England, 1830–1837. [189]English city north of London.

"I mean he goes to our church regular when he's in Sheffield. That's only in the summer-time, when he comes there to take the sea baths."

"Why, how you talk—Sheffield ain't on the sea."

"Well, who said it was?"

"Why, you did."

"I *didn't* nuther."

"You did!"

"I didn't."

"You did."

"I never said nothing of the kind."

"Well, what *did* you say, then?"

"Said he come to take the sea *baths*—that's what I said."

"Well, then! how's he going to take the sea baths if it ain't on the sea?"

"Looky here," I says; "did you ever see any Congress water?"[190]

"Yes."

"Well, did you have to go to Congress to get it?"

"Why, no."

"Well, neither does William Fourth have to go to the sea to get a sea bath."

"How does he get it, then?"

"Gets it the way people down here gets Congress-water—in barrels. There in the palace at Sheffield they've got furnaces, and he wants his water hot. They can't bile that amount of water away off there at the sea. They haven't got no conveniences for it."

"Oh, I see, now. You might a said that in the first place and saved time."

When she said that, I see I was out of the woods again, and so I was comfortable and glad. Next she says:

"Do you go to church, too?"

"Yes—regular."

"Where do you set?"

"Why, in our pew."

"*Whose* pew?"

"Why, *ourn*—your Uncle Harvey's."

"His'n? What does *he* want with a pew?"

"Wants it to set in. What did you *reckon* he wanted with it?"

"Why, I thought he'd be in the pulpit."

Rot him, I forgot he was a preacher. I see I was up a stump again, so I played another chicken bone and got another think. Then I says:

"Blame it, do you suppose there ain't but one preacher to a church?"

"Why, what do they want with more?"

"What!—to preach before a king? I never see such a girl as you. They don't have no less than seventeen."

"Seventeen! My land! Why, I wouldn't set out such a string as that, not if I *never* got to glory. It must take 'em a week."

"Shucks, they don't *all* of 'em preach the same day—only *one* of 'em."

"Well, then, what does the rest of 'em do?"

"Oh, nothing much. Loll around, pass the plate—and one thing or another. But mainly they don't do nothing."

"Well, then, what are they *for?*"

[190]Mineral water from the Congress Spring, Saratoga, New York.

"Why, they're for *style.* Don't you know nothing?"

"Well, I don't *want* to know no such foolishness as that. How is servants treated in England? Do they treat 'em better 'n we treat our niggers?"

"*No!* A servant ain't nobody there. They treat them worse than dogs."

"Don't they give 'em holidays, the way we do, Christmas and New Year's week, and Fourth of July?"

"Oh, just listen! A body could tell *you* hain't ever been to England, by that. Why, Hare-l—why, Joanna, they never see a holiday from year's end to year's end; never go to the circus, nor theatre, nor nigger shows,[191] nor nowheres."

"Nor church?"

"Nor church."

"But *you* always went to church."

Well, I was gone up again. I forgot I was the old man's servant. But next minute I whirled in on a kind of an explanation how a valley was different from a common servant, and *had* to go to church whether he wanted to or not, and set with the family, on account of it's being the law. But I didn't do it pretty good, and when I got done I see she warn't satisfied. She says:

"Honest injun, now, hain't you been telling me a lot of lies?"

"Honest injun," says I.

"None of it at all?"

"None of it at all. Not a lie in it," says I.

"Lay your hand on this book and say it."

I see it warn't nothing but a dictionary, so I laid my hand on it and said it. So then she looked a little better satisfied, and says:

"Well, then, I'll believe some of it; but I hope to gracious if I'll believe the rest."

"What is it you won't believe, Joe?" says Mary Jane, stepping in with Susan behind her. "It ain't right nor kind for you to talk so to him, and him a stranger and so far from his people. How would you like to be treated so?"

"That's always your way, Maim—always sailing in to help somebody before they're hurt. I hain't done nothing to him. He's told some stretchers, I reckon; and I said I wouldn't swallow it all; and that's every bit and grain I *did* say. I reckon he can stand a little thing like that, can't he?"

"I don't care whether 'twas little or whether 'twas big, he's here in our house and a stranger, and it wasn't good of you to say it. If you was in his place, it would make you feel ashamed; and so you oughtn't to say a thing to another person that will make *them* feel ashamed."

"Why, Maim, he said——"

"It don't make no difference what he *said*—that ain't the thing. The thing is for you to treat him *kind,* and not be saying things to make him remember he ain't in his own country and amongst his own folks."

I says to myself, *this* is a girl that I'm letting that old reptile rob her of her money!

Then Susan *she* waltzed in; and if you'll believe me, she did give Hare-lip hark from the tomb![192]

[191]Minstrel shows.

[192]A scolding—derived from "Hark! from the tombs a doleful sound . . .," a line from the hymn "A Funeral Thought," by Isaac Watts (1674–1748), English hymnist.

Says I to myself, And this is *another* one that I'm letting him rob her of her money!

Then Mary Jane she took another inning, and went in sweet and lovely again—which was her way—but when she got done there warn't hardly anything left o' poor Hare-lip. So she hollered.

"All right, then," says the other girls, "you just ask his pardon."

She done it, too. And she done it beautiful. She done it so beautiful it was good to hear; and I wished I could tell her a thousand lies, so she could do it again.

I says to myself, this is *another* one that I'm letting him rob her of her money. And when she got through, they all jest laid theirselves out to make me feel at home and know I was amongst friends. I felt so ornery and low down and mean, that I says to myself, My mind's made up; I'll hive[193] that money for them or bust.

So then I lit out—for bed, I said, meaning some time or another. When I got by myself, I went to thinking the thing over. I says to myself, shall I go to that doctor, private, and blow on these frauds? No—that won't do. He might tell who told him; then the king and the duke would make it warm for me. Shall I go, private, and tell Mary Jane? No—I dasn't do it. Her face would give them a hint, sure; they've got the money, and they'd slide right out and get away with it. If she was to fetch in help, I'd get mixed up in the business, before it was done with, I judge. No, there ain't no good way but one. I got to steal that money, somehow; and I got to steal it some way that they won't suspicion that I done it. They've got a good thing, here; and they ain't agoing to leave till they've played this family and this town for all they're worth, so I'll find a chance time enough. I'll steal it, and hide it; and by-and-by, when I'm away down the river, I'll write a letter and tell Mary Jane where it's hid. But I better hive it to-night, if I can, because the doctor maybe hasn't let up as much as he lets on he has; he might scare them out of here, yet.

So, thinks I, I'll go and search them rooms. Up stairs the hall was dark, but I found the duke's room, and started to paw around it with my hands; but I recollected it wouldn't be much like the king to let anybody else take care of that money but his own self; so then I went to his room and begun to paw around there. But I see I couldn't do nothing without a candle, and I dasn't light one, of course. So I judged I'd got to do the other thing—lay for them, and eavesdrop. About that time, I hears their footsteps coming, and was going to skip under the bed; I reached for it, but it wasn't where I thought it would be; but I touched the curtain that hid Mary Jane's frocks, so I jumped in behind that and snuggled in amongst the gowns, and stood there perfectly still.

They come in and shut the door; and the first thing the duke done was to get down and look under the bed. Then I was glad I hadn't found the bed when I wanted it. And yet, you know, it's kind of natural to hide under the bed when you are up to anything private. They sets down, then, and the king says:

"Well, what is it? and cut it middlin' short, because it's better for us to be down there a whoopin'-up the mournin' than up here givin' 'em a chance to talk us over."

"Well, this is it, Capet. I ain't easy; I ain't comfortable. That doctor lays on my mind. I wanted to know your plans. I've got a notion, and I think it's a sound one."

[193]Secure.

"What is it, duke?"

"That we better glide out of this, before three in the morning, and clip it down the river with what we've got. Specially, seeing we got it so easy—*given* back to us, flung at our heads, as you may say, when of course we allowed to have to steal it back. I'm for knocking off and lighting out."

That made me feel pretty bad. About an hour or two ago, it would a been a little different, but now it made me feel bad and disappointed. The king rips out and says:

"What! And not sell out the rest o' the property? March off like a passel o' fools and leave eight or nine thous'n' dollars' worth o' property layin' around jest sufferin' to be scooped in?—and all good salable stuff, too."

The duke he grumbled; said the bag of gold was enough, and he didn't want to go no deeper—didn't want to rob a lot of orphans of *everything* they had.

"Why, how you talk!" says the king. "We shan't rob 'em of nothing at all but jest this money. The people that *buys* the property is the suff'rers; because as soon's it's found out 'at we didn't own it—which won't be long after we've slid—the sale won't be valid, and it'll all go back to the estate. These-yer orphans 'll git their house back agin, and that's enough for *them;* they're young and spry, and k'n easy earn a livin'. *They* ain't agoing to suffer. Why, jest think—there's thous'n's and thous'n's that ain't nigh so well off. Bless you, *they* ain't got noth'n to complain of."

Well, the king he talked him blind; so at last he give in, and said all right, but said he believed it was blame foolishness to stay, and that doctor hanging over them. But the king says:

"Cuss the doctor! What do we k'yer for *him?* Hain't we got all the fools in town on our side? and ain't that a big enough majority in any town?"

So they got ready to go down stairs again. The duke says:

"I don't think we put that money in a good place."

That cheered me up. I'd begun to think I warn't going to get a hint of no kind to help me. The king says:

"Why?"

"Because Mary Jane'll be in mourning from this out; and first you know the nigger that does up the rooms will get an order to box these duds up and put 'em away; and do you reckon a nigger can run across money and not borrow some of it?"

"Your head's level, agin, duke," says the king; and he come a fumbling under the curtain two or three foot from where I was. I stuck tight to the wall, and kept mighty still, though quivery; and I wondered what them fellows would say to me if they catched me; and I tried to think what I'd better do if they did catch me. But the king he got the bag before I could think more than about a half a thought, and he never suspicioned I was around. They took and shoved the bag through a rip in the straw tick that was under the feather bed, and crammed it in a foot or two amongst the straw and said it was all right, now, because a nigger only make up the feather bed, and don't turn over the straw tick only about twice a year, and so it warn't in no danger of getting stole, now.

But I knowed better. I had it out of there before they was half-way down stairs. I groped along up to my cubby, and hid it there till I could get a chance to do better. I judged I better hide it outside of the house somewheres, because if they missed it they would give the house a good ransacking. I knowed that very well. Then I turned in, with my clothes all on; but I couldn't a gone to sleep, if

I wanted to, I was in such a sweat to get through with the business. By-and-by I heard the king and the duke come up; so I rolled off of my pallet and laid with my chin at the top of my ladder and waited to see if anything was going to happen. But nothing did.

So I held on till all the late sounds had quit and the early ones hadn't begun, yet; and then I slipped down the ladder.

CHAPTER XXVII

I crept to their doors and listened; they was snoring, so I tip-toed along, and got down stairs all right. There warn't a sound anywheres. I peeped through a crack of the dining-room door, and see the men that was watching the corpse all sound asleep on their chairs. The door was open into the parlor, where the corpse was laying, and there was a candle in both rooms. I passed along, and the parlor door was open; but I see there warn't nobody in there but the remainders of Peter; so I shoved on by; but the front door was locked, and the key wasn't there. Just then I heard somebody coming down the stairs, back behind me. I run in the parlor, and took a swift look around, and the only place I see to hide the bag was in the coffin. The lid was shoved along about a foot, showing the dead man's face down in there, with a wet cloth over it, and his shroud on. I tucked the moneybag in under the lid, just down beyond where his hands was crossed, which made me creep, they was so cold, and then I run back across the room and in behind the door.

The person coming was Mary Jane. She went to the coffin, very soft, and kneeled down and looked in; then she put up her handkerchief and I see she begun to cry, though I couldn't hear her, and her back was to me. I slid out, and as I passed the dining-room I thought I'd make sure them watchers hadn't seen me; so I looked through the crack and everything was all right. They hadn't stirred.

I slipped up to bed, feeling ruther blue, on accounts of the thing playing out that way after I had took so much trouble and run so much resk about it. Says I, if it could stay where it is, all right; because when we get down the river a hundred mile or two, I could write back to Mary Jane, and she could dig him up again and get it; but that ain't the thing that's going to happen; the thing that's going to happen is, the money'll be found when they come to screw on the lid. Then the king 'll get it again, and it 'll be a long day before he gives anybody another chance to smouch[194] it from him. Of course I *wanted* to slide down and get it out of there, but I dasn't try it. Every minute it was getting earlier, now, and pretty soon some of them watchers would begin to stir, and I might get catched—catched with six thousand dollars in my hands that nobody hadn't hired me to take care of. I don't wish to be mixed up in no such business as that, I says to myself.

When I got down stairs in the morning, the parlor was shut up, and the watchers was gone. There warn't nobody around but the family and the widow Bartley and our tribe. I watched their faces to see if anything had been happening, but I couldn't tell.

[194]Steal.

Towards the middle of the day the undertaker come, with his man, and they set the coffin in the middle of the room on a couple of chairs, and then set all our chairs in rows, and borrowed more from the neighbors till the hall and the parlor and the dining-room was full. I see the coffin lid was the way it was before, but I dasn't go to look in under it, with folks around.

Then the people begun to flock in, and the beats[195] and the girls took seats in the front row at the head of the coffin, and for half an hour the people filed around slow, in single rank, and looked down at the dead man's face a minute, and some dropped in a tear, and it was all very still and solemn, only the girls and the beats holding handkerchiefs to their eyes and keeping their heads bent, and sobbing a little. There warn't no other sound but the scraping of the feet on the floor, and blowing noses—because people always blows them more at a funeral than they do at other places except church.

When the place was packed full, the undertaker he slid around in his black gloves with his softy soothering ways, putting on the last touches, and getting people and things all shipshape and comfortable, and making no more sound than a cat. He never spoke; he moved people around, he squeezed in late ones, he opened up passage-ways, and done it all with nods, and signs with his hands. Then he took his place over against the wall. He was the softest, glidingest, stealthiest man I ever see; and there warn' no more smile to him than there is to a ham.

They had borrowed a melodeum[196]—a sick one; and when everything was ready, a young woman set down and worked it, and it was pretty skreeky and colicky, and everybody joined in and sung, and Peter was the only one that had a good thing, according to my notion. Then the Reverend Hobson opened up, slow and solemn, and begun to talk; and straight off the most outrageous row busted out in the cellar a body ever heard; it was only one dog, but he made a most powerful racket, and he kept it up, right along; the parson he had to stand there, over the coffin, and wait—you couldn't hear yourself think. It was right down awkward, and nobody didn't seem to know what to do. But pretty soon they see that long-legged undertaker make a sign to the preacher as much to say, "Don't you worry—just depend on me." Then he stooped down and begun to glide along the wall, just his shoulders showing over the people's heads. So he glided along, and the pow-wow and racket getting more and more outrageous all the time; and at last, when he had gone around two sides of the room, he disappears down cellar. Then, in about two seconds we heard a whack, and the dog he finished up with a most amazing howl or two, and then everything was dead still, and the parson begun his solemn talk where he left off. In a minute or two here comes this undertaker's back and shoulders gliding along the wall again, and so he glided, and glided, around three sides of the room, and then rose up, and shaded his mouth with his hands, and stretched his neck out towards the preacher over the people's heads, and says, in a kind of a coarse whisper, *"He had a rat!"* Then he drooped down and glided along the wall again to his place. You could see it was a great satisfaction to the people, because naturally they wanted to know. A little thing like that don't cost nothing, and it's just the little things that makes a man to be looked up to and liked. There warn't no more popular man in town than what that undertaker was.

[195]Deadbeats, i.e., the Duke and the Dauphin. [196]A small, reed organ.

Well, the funeral sermon was very good, but pison long and tiresome; and then the king he shoved in and got off some of his usual rubbage, and at last the job was through, and the undertaker begun to sneak up on the coffin with his screw-driver. I was in a sweat then, and watched him pretty keen. But he never meddled at all; just slid the lid along, as soft as mush, and screwed it down tight and fast. So there I was! I didn't know whether the money was in there, or not. So, says I, spose somebody has hogged that bag on the sly?—now how do *I* know whether to write to Mary Jane or not? 'Spose she dug him up and didn't find nothing—what would she think of me? Blame it, I says, I might get hunted up and jailed; I'd better lay low and keep dark, and not write at all; the thing's awful mixed, now; trying to better it, I've worsened it a hundred times, and I wish to goodness I'd just let it alone, dad fetch the whole business!

They buried him, and we come back home, and I went to watching faces again—I couldn't help it, and I couldn't rest easy. But nothing come of it; the faces didn't tell me nothing.

The king he visited around, in the evening, and sweetened everybody up, and made himself ever so friendly; and he give out the idea that his congregation over in England would be in a sweat about him, so he must hurry and settle up the estate right away, and leave for home. He was very sorry he was so pushed, and so was everybody; they wished he could stay longer, but they said they could see it couldn't be done. And he said of course him and William would take the girls home with him; and that pleased everybody too, because then the girls would be well fixed, and amongst their own relations; and it pleased the girls, too—tickled them so they clean forgot they ever had a trouble in the world; and told him to sell out as quick as he wanted to, they would be ready. Them poor things was that glad and happy it made my heart ache to see them getting fooled and lied to so, but I didn't see no safe way for me to chip in and change the general tune.

Well, blamed if the king didn't bill[197] the house and the niggers and all the property for auction straight off—sale two days after the funeral; but anybody could buy private beforehand if they wanted to.

So the next day after the funeral, along about noontime, the girl's joy got the first jolt; a couple of nigger traders come along, and the king sold them the niggers reasonable, for three-day drafts[198] as they called it, and away they went, the two sons up the river to Memphis, and their mother down the river to Orleans. I thought them poor girls and them niggers would break their hearts for grief; they cried around each other, and took on so it most made me down sick to see it. The girls said they hadn't ever dreamed of seeing the family separated or sold away from the town. I can't ever get it out of my memory, the sight of them poor miserable girls and niggers hanging around each other's necks and crying; and I reckon I couldn't a stood it all but would a had to bust out and tell on our gang if I hadn't knowed the sale warn't no account and the niggers would be back home in a week or two.

The thing made a big stir in the town, too, and a good many come out flat-footed and said it was scandalous to separate the mother and the children that way. It injured the frauds some; but the old fool he bulled right along, spite of all the duke could say or do, and I tell you the duke was powerful uneasy.

[197]Advertise. [198]Bank drafts (checks) that can be cashed after three days.

Next day was auction day. About broad-day in the morning, the king and the duke come up in the garret and woke me up, and I see by their look that there was trouble. The king says:

"Was you in my room night before last?"

"No, your majesty"—which was the way I always called him when nobody but our gang warn't around.

"Was you in there yisterday er last night?"

"No, your majesty."

"Honor bright, now—no lies."

"Honor bright, your majesty, I'm telling you the truth. I hain't been near your room since Miss Mary Jane took you and the duke and showed it to you."

The duke says:

"Have you seen anybody else go in there?"

"No, your grace, not as I remember, I believe."

"Stop and think."

I studied a while, and see my chance, then I says:

"Well, I see the niggers go in there several times."

Both of them give a little jump; and looked like they hadn't ever expected it, and then like they *had*. Then the duke says:

"What, *all* of them?"

"No—leastways not all at once. That is, I don't think I ever see them all come *out* at once but just one time."

"Hello—when was that?"

"It was the day we had the funeral. In the morning. It warn't early, because I overslept. I was just starting down the ladder, and I see them."

"Well, go on, *go* on—what did they do? How'd they act?"

"They didn't do nothing. And they didn't act anyway, much, as fur as I see. They tip-toed away; so I seen, easy enough, that they'd shoved in there to do up your majesty's room, or something, sposing you was up; and found you *warn't* up, and so they was hoping to slide out of the way of trouble without waking you up, if they hadn't already waked you up."

"Great guns, *this* is a go!" says the king; and both of them looked pretty sick, and tolerable silly. They stood there a thinking and scratching their heads, a minute, and then the duke he burst into a kind of a little raspy chuckle, and says:

"It does beat all, how neat the niggers played their hand. They let on to be *sorry* they was going out of this region! and I believed they *was* sorry. And so did you, and so did everybody. Don't ever tell *me* any more that a nigger ain't got any histrionic talent. Why, the way they played that thing, it would fool *anybody*. In my opinion, there's a fortune in 'em. If I had capital and a theatre, I wouldn't want a better lay out than that—and here we've gone and sold 'em for a song. Yes, and ain't privileged to sing the song, yet. Say, where *is* that song?—that draft."

"In the bank for to be collected. Where *would* it be?"

"Well, *that's* all right then, thank goodness."

Says I, kind of timid-like:

"Is something gone wrong?"

The king whirls on me and rips out:

"None o' your business! You keep your head shet, and mind y'r own affairs—if you got any. Long as you're in this town, don't you forgit *that*, you hear?" Then he says to the duke, "We got to jest swaller it, and say noth'n: mum's the word for *us*."

As they was starting down the ladder, the duke he chuckles again, and says:
"Quick sales *and* small profits! It's a good business—yes."

The king snarls around on him and says,

"I was trying to do for the best, in sellin' 'm out so quick. If the profits has turned out to be none, lackin' considable, an none to carry, is it my fault any more'n it's yourn?"

"Well, *they'd* be in this house yet, and we *wouldn't* if I could a got my advice listened to."

The king sassed back, as much as was safe for him, and then swapped around and lit into *me* again. He give me down the banks[199] for not coming and *telling* him I see the niggers come out of his room acting that way—said any fool would a *knowed* something was up. And then waltzed in and cussed *himself* a while; and said it all come of him not laying late and taking his natural rest that morning, and he'd be blamed if he'd ever do it again. So they went off a jawing; and I felt dreadful glad I'd worked it all off onto the niggers and yet hadn't done the niggers no harm by it.

CHAPTER XXVIII

By-and-by it was getting-up time; so I come down the ladder and started for down stairs, but as I come to the girls' room, the door was open, and I see Mary Jane setting by her old hair trunk, which was open and she'd been packing things in it—getting ready to go to England. But she had stopped now, with a folded gown in her lap, and had her face in her hands, crying. I felt awful bad to see it; of course anybody would. I went in there, and says:

"Miss Mary Jane, you can't abear to see people in trouble, and *I* can't—most always. Tell me about it."

So she done it. And it was the niggers—I just expected it. She said the beautiful trip to England was most about spoiled for her; and she didn't know *how* she was ever going to be happy there, knowing the mother and the children warn't ever going to see each other no more—and then busted out bitterer than ever, and flung up her hands, and says:

"Oh, dear, dear, to think they ain't *ever* going to see each other any more!"

"But they *will*—and inside of two weeks—and I *know* it!" says I.

Laws, it was out before I could think!—and before I could budge, she throws her arms arond my neck, and told me to say it *again,* say it *again,* say it *again!*

I see I had spoke too sudden, and said too much, and was in a close place. I asked her to let me think a minute; and she set there, very impatient and excited, and handsome, but looking kind of happy and eased-up, like a person that's had a tooth pulled out. So I went to studying it out. I says to myself, I reckon a body that ups and tells the truth when he is in a tight place, is taking considerable many resks, though I ain't had no experience, and can't say for certain; but it looks so to me, anyway; and yet here's a case where I'm blest if it don't look to me like the truth is better, and actuly *safer,* than a lie. I must lay it by in my mind, and think it over some time or other, it's so kind of strange and unregular. I never see nothing like it. Well, I says to myself at last, I'm agoing

[199]A tongue-lashing.

to chance it; I'll up and tell the truth this time, though it does seem most like setting down on a kag of powder and touching it off just to see where you'll go to. Then I says:

"Miss Mary Jane, is there any place out of town a little ways, where you could go and stay three or four days?"

"Yes—Mr. Lothrop's. Why?"

"Never mind why, yet. If I'll tell you how I know the niggers will see each other again—inside of two weeks—here in this house—and *prove* how I know it—will you go to Mr. Lothrop's and stay four days?"

"Four days!" she says; "I'll stay a year!"

"All right," I says, "I don't want nothing more out of *you* than just your word—I druther have it than another man's kiss-the-Bible."[200] She smiled, and reddened up very sweet, and I says, "If you don't mind it, I'll shut the door—and bolt it."

Then I come back and set down again, and says:

"Don't you holler. Just set still, and take it like a man. I got to tell the truth, and you want to brace up, Miss Mary, because it's a bad kind, and going to be hard to take, but there ain't no help for it. These uncles of yourn ain't no uncles at all—they're a couple of frauds—regular dead beats. There, now we're over the worst of it—you can stand the rest middling easy."

It jolted her up like everything, of course; but I was over the shoal water[201] now, so I went right along, her eyes a blazing higher and higher all the time, and told her every blame thing, from where we first struck that young fool going up to the steamboat, clear through to where she flung herself onto the king's breast at the front door and he kissed her sixteen or seventeen times—and then up she jumps, with her face afire like sunset, and says:

"The brute! Come—don't waste a minute—not a *second*—we'll have them tarred and feathered, and flung in the river!"

Says I:

"Cert'nly. But do you mean, *before* you go to Mr. Lothrop's, or——"

"Oh," she says, "what am I *thinking* about!" she says, and set right down again. "Don't mind what I said—please don't—you *won't* now, *will* you?" Laying her silky hand on mine in that kind of a way that I said I would die first. "I never thought, I was so stirred up," she says; "now go on, and I won't do so any more. You tell me what to do, and whatever you say, I'll do it."

"Well," I says, "it's a rough gang, them two frauds, and I'm fixed so I got to travel with them a while longer, whether I want to or not—I druther not tell you why—and if you was to blow on them this town would get me out of their claws, and *I*'d be all right, but there'd be another person that you don't know about who'd be in big trouble. Well, we got to save *him*, hain't we? Of course. Well, then, we won't blow on them."

Saying them words put a good idea in my head. I see how maybe I could get me and Jim rid of the frauds; get them jailed here, and then leave. But I didn't want to run the raft in day-time, without anybody aboard to answer questions but me; so I didn't want the plan to begin working till pretty late to-night. I says:

"Miss Mary Jane, I'll tell you what we'll do—and you won't have to stay at Mr. Lothrop's so long, nuther. How fur is it?"

[200]Oath sworn on the Bible. [201]Past the most dangerous water, "over the worst of it."

"A little short of four miles—right out in the country, back here."

"Well, that'll answer. Now you go along out there, and lay low till nine or half-past, to-night, and then get them to fetch you home again—tell them you've thought of something. If you get here before eleven, put a candle in this window, and if I don't turn up, wait *till* eleven, and *then* if I don't turn up it means I'm gone, and out of the way, and safe. Then you come out and spread the news around, and get these beats jailed."

"Good," she says, "I'll do it."

"And if it just happens so that I don't get away, but get took up along with them, you must up and say I told you the whole thing beforehand, and you must stand by me all you can."

"Stand by you, indeed I will. They sha'n't touch a hair of your head!" she says, and I see her nostrils spread and her eyes snap when she said it, too.

"If I get away, I sha'n't be here," I says, "to prove these rapscallions ain't your uncles, and I couldn't do it if I *was* here. I could swear they was beats and bummers, that's all; though that's worth something. Well, there's others can do that better than what I can—and they're people that ain't going to be doubted as quick as I'd be. I'll tell you how to find them. Gimme a pencil and a piece of paper. There—*'Royal Nonesuch, Bricksville.'* Put it away, and don't lose it. When the court wants to find out something about these two, let them send up to Bricksville and say they've got the men that played the Royal Nonesuch, and ask for some witnesses—why, you'll have that entire town down here before you can hardly wink, Miss Mary. And they'll come a-biling, too."

I judged we had got everything fixed about right, now. So I says:

"Just let the auction go right along, and don't worry. Nobody don't have to pay for the things, and they ain't going out of this till they get that money—and the way we've fixed it the sale ain't going to count, and they ain't going to *get* no money. It's just like the way it was with the niggers—it warn't no sale, and the niggers will be back before long. Why, they can't collect the money for the *niggers,* yet—they're in the worst kind of a fix, Miss Mary."

"Well," she says. "I'll run down to breakfast now, and then I'll start straight for Mr. Lothrop's."

"'Deed, *that* ain't the ticket, Miss Mary Jane." I says, "by no manner of means; go *before* breakfast."

"Why?"

"What did you reckon I wanted you to go at all for, Miss Mary?"

"Well, I never thought—and come to think, I don't know. What was it?"

"Why, it's because you ain't one of these leather-face people. I don't want no better book than what your face is. A body can set down and read it off like coarse print. Do you reckon you can go and face your uncles, when they come to kiss you good-morning, and never—"

"There, there, don't! Yes, I'll go before breakfast—I'll be glad to. And leave my sisters with them?"

"Yes—never mind about them. They've got to stand it yet a while. They might suspicion something if all of you was to go. I don't want you to see them, nor your sisters, nor nobody in this town—if a neighbor was to ask how is your uncles this morning, your face would tell something. No, you go right along, Miss Mary Jane, and I'll fix it with all of them. I'll tell Miss Susan to give your love to your uncles and say you've went away for a few hours for to get a little rest and change, or to see a friend, and you'll be back to-night or early in the morning."

"Gone to see a friend is all right, but I won't have my love given to them."

"Well, then, it sha'n't be." It was well enough to tell *her* so—no harm in it. It was only a little thing to do, and no trouble; and it's the little things that smooths people's roads and most, down here below; it would make Mary Jane comfortable, and it wouldn't cost nothing. Then I says: "There's one more thing—that bag of money."

"Well, they've got that; and it makes me feel pretty silly to think *how* they got it."

"No, you're out, there. They hain't got it."

"Why, who's got it?"

"I wish I knowed, but I don't. I *had* it, because I stole it from them: and I stole it to give to you; and I know where I hid it, but I'm afraid it ain't there no more. I'm awful sorry, Miss Mary Jane, I'm just as sorry as I can be; but I done the best I could; I did, honest. I come nigh getting caught, and I had to shove it into the first place I come to, and run—and it warn't a good place."

"Oh, stop blaming yourself—it's too bad to do it, and I won't allow it—you couldn't help it; it wasn't your fault. Where did you hide it?"

I didn't want to set her to thinking about her troubles again; I couldn't seem to get my mouth to tell her what would make her see that corpse layin' in the coffin with that bag of money on his stomach. So for a minute I didn't say nothing—then I says:

"I'd druther not *tell* you where I put it, Miss Mary Jane, if you don't mind letting me off; but I'll write it for you on a piece of paper, and you can read it along the road to Mr. Lothrop's, if you want to. Do you reckon that'll do?"

"Oh, yes."

So I wrote: "I put it in the coffin. It was in there when you was crying there, away in the night. I was behind the door, and I was mighty sorry for you, Miss Mary Jane."

It made my eyes water a little, to remember her crying there all by herself in the night, and them devils laying there right under her own roof, shaming her and robbing her; and when I folded it up and give it to her, I see the water come into her eyes, too; and she shook me by the hand, hard, and says:

"*Good*-bye—I'm going to do everything just as you've told me; and if I don't ever see you again, I sha'n't ever forget you, and I'll think of you a many and a many a time, and I'll *pray* for you, too!"—and she was gone.

Pray for me! I reckoned if she knowed me she'd take a job that was more nearer her size. But I bet she done it, just the same—she was just that kind. She had the grit to pray for Judus if she took the notion—there warn't no backdown to her, I judge. You may say what you want to, but in my opinion she had more sand[202] in her than any girl I ever see; in my opinion she was just full of sand. It sounds like flattery, but it ain't no flattery. And when it comes to beauty—and goodness too—she lays over them all. I hain't ever seen her since that time that I see her go out of that door; no, I hain't ever seen her since, but I reckon I've thought of her a many and a many a million times, and of her saying she would pray for me; and if ever I'd a thought it would do any good for me to pray for *her*, blamed if I wouldn't a done it or bust.

Well, Mary Jane she lit out the back way, I reckon; because nobody see her go. When I struck Susan and the hare-lip, I says:

[202] Grit, courage.

"What's the name of them people over on t'other side of the river that you all goes to see sometimes?"

They says:

"There's several; but it's the Proctors, mainly."

"That's the name," I says; "I most forgot it. Well, Miss Mary Jane she told me to tell you she's gone over there in a dreadful hurry—one of them's sick."

"Which one?"

"I don't know; leastways I kinder forget; but I think it's——"

"Sakes alive, I hope it ain't *Hanner?*"

"I'm sorry to say it," I says, "but Hanner's the very one."

"My goodness—and she so well only last week! Is she took bad?"

"It ain't no name for it. They set up with her all night, Miss Mary Jane said, and they don't think she'll last many hours."

"Only think of that, now! What's the matter with her!"

I couldn't think of anything reasonable, right off that way, so I says:

"Mumps."

"Mumps your granny! They don't set up with people that's got the mumps."

"They don't, don't they? You better bet they do with *these* mumps. These mumps is different. It's a new kind, Miss Mary Jane said."

"How's it a new kind?"

"Because it's mixed up with other things."

"What other things?"

"Well, measles, and whooping-cough, and erysiplas,[203] and consumption,[204] and yaller jaunders,[205] and brain fever, and I don't know what all."

"My land! And they call it the *mumps?*"

"That's what Miss Mary Jane said."

"Well, what in the nation do they call it the *mumps* for?"

"Why, because it *is* the mumps. That's what it starts with."

"Well, ther' ain't no sense in it. A body might stump his toe, and take pison, and fall down the well, and break his neck, and bust his brains out, and somebody come along and ask what killed him, and some numskull up and say, 'Why, he stumped his *toe.*' Would ther' be any sense in that? No. And ther' ain't no sense in *this,* nuther. Is it ketching?"

"Is it *ketching?* Why, how you talk. Is a *harrow* catching?—in the dark? If you don't hitch onto one tooth, you're bound to on another, ain't you? And you can't get away with that tooth without fetching the whole harrow along, can you? Well, these kind of mumps is a kind of a harrow, as you may say—and it ain't no slouch of a harrow, nuther, you come to get it hitched on good."

"Well, it's awful, I think," says the hare-lip. "I'll go to Uncle Harvey and——"

"Oh, yes," I says, "I *would.* Of *course* I would. I wouldn't lose no time."

"Well, why wouldn't you?"

"Just look at it a minute, and maybe you can see. Hain't your uncles obleeged to get along home to England as fast as they can? And do you reckon they'd be mean enough to go off and leave you to go all that journey by yourselves? *You* know they'll wait for you. So fur, so good. Your uncle Harvey's a preacher, ain't he? Very well, then; is a *preacher* going to deceive a steamboat clerk? is he going to deceive a *ship clerk?*—so as to get them to let Miss Mary Jane go aboard? Now *you* know he ain't. What *will* he do, then? Why, he'll say,

[203]A skin disease. [204]Tuberculosis. [205]Yellow jaundice.

'It's a great pity, but my church matters has got to get along the best way they can; for my niece has been exposed to the dreadful pluribus-unum[206] mumps, and so it's my bounden duty to set down here and wait the three months it takes to show on her if she's got it.' But never mind, if you think it's best to tell your uncle Harvey——"

"Shucks, and stay fooling around here when we could all be having good times in England whilst we was waiting to find out whether Mary Jane's got it or not? Why, you talk like a muggins."[207]

"Well, anyway, maybe you better tell some of the neighbors."

"Listen at that, now. You do beat all, for natural stupidness. Can't you *see* that *they'd* go and tell? Ther' ain't no way but just to not tell anybody at *all*."

"Well, maybe you're right—yes, I judge you *are* right."

"But I reckon we ought to tell Uncle Harvey she's gone out a while, anyway, so he won't be uneasy about her."

"Yes, Miss Mary Jane she wanted you to do that. She says, 'Tell them to give Uncle Harvey and William my love and a kiss, and say I've run over the river to see Mr.—Mr.—what *is* the name of that rich family your uncle Peter used to think so much of?—I mean the one that——"

"Why, you must mean the Apthorps, ain't it?"

"Of course; bother them kind of names, a body can't ever seem to remember them, half the time, somehow. Yes, she said, say she has run over for to ask the Apthorps to be sure and come to the auction and buy this house, because she allowed her uncle Peter would rather they had it than anybody else; and she's going to stick to them till they say they'll come, and then, if she ain't too tired, she's coming home; and if she is, she'll be home in the morning anyway. She said, don't say nothing about the Proctors, but only about the Apthorps—which'll be perfectly true, because she *is* going there to speak about their buying the house; I know it, because she told me so, herself."

"All right," she said, and cleared out to lay for her uncles, and give them the love and the kisses, and tell them the message.

Everything was all right now. The girls wouldn't say nothing because they wanted to go to England; and the king and the duke would ruther Mary Jane was off working for the auction than around in reach of Doctor Robinson. I felt very good; I judged I had done it pretty neat—I reckoned Tom Sawyer couldn't a done it no neater himself. Of course he would a throwed more style into it, but I can't do that very handy, not being brung up to it.

Well, they held the auction in the public square, along towards the end of the afternoon, and it strung along, and strung along, and the old man he was on hand and looking his level piousest, up there longside of the auctioneer, and chipping in a little Scripture, now and then, or a little goody-goody saying, of some kind, and the duke he was around goo-gooing for sympathy all he knowed how, and just spreading himself generly.

But by-and-by the thing dragged through, and everything was sold. Everything but a little old trifling lot in the graveyard. So they'd got to work *that* off—I never see such a girafft as the king was for wanting to swallow *everything*. Well, whilst they was at it, a steamboat landed, and in about two minutes up

[206]High-sounding Latin, taken from the United States motto that is stamped on coins: "E Pluribus Unum," One Out of Many.

[207]Fool.

comes a crowd a whooping and yelling and laughing and carrying on, and singing out:

"*Here's* your opposition line! here's your two sets o' heirs to old Peter Wilks—and you pays your money and you takes your choice!"

CHAPTER XXIX

They was fetching a very nice looking old gentleman along, and a nice looking younger one, with his right arm in a sling. And my souls, how the people yelled, and laughed, and kept it up. But I didn't see no joke about it, and I judged it would strain the duke and the king some to see any. I reckoned they'd turn pale. But no, nary a pale did *they* turn. The duke he never let on he suspicioned what was up, but just went a goo-gooing around, happy and satisfied, like a jug that's googling out buttermilk; and as for the king, he just gazed and gazed down sorrowful on them new-comers like it give him the stomach-ache in his very heart to think there could be such frauds and rascals in the world. Oh, he done it admirable. Lots of the principal people gethered around the king, to let him see they was on his side. That old gentleman that had just come looked all puzzled to death. Pretty soon he began to speak, and I see, straight off, he pronounced *like* an Englishman, not the king's way, though the king's *was* pretty good, for an imitation. I can't give the old gent's words, nor I can't imitate him; but he turned around to the crowd, and says, about like this:

"This is a surprise to me which I wasn't looking for; and I'll acknowledge, candid and frank, I ain't very well fixed to meet it and answer it; for my brother and me has had misfortunes, he's broke his arm, and our baggage got put off at a town above here, last night in the night by a mistake. I am Peter Wilks's brother Harvey, and this is his brother William, which can't hear nor speak—and can't even make signs to amount to much, now 't he's only got one hand to work them with. We are who we say we are; and in a day or two, when I get the baggage, I can prove it. But, up till then, I won't say nothing more, but go to the hotel and wait."

So him and the new dummy[208] started off; and the king he laughs, and blethers out:

"Broke his arm—*very* likely *ain't* it?—and very convenient, too, for a fraud that's got to make signs, and hain't learnt how. Lost their baggage! That's *mighty* good!—and mighty ingenious—under the *circumstances!*"

So he laughed again; and so did everybody else, except three or four, or maybe half a dozen. One of these was that doctor; another one was a sharp looking gentleman, with a carpet-bag of the old-fashioned kind made out of carpet-stuff, that had just come off the steamboat and was talking to him in a low voice, and glancing towards the king now and then and nodding their heads—it was Levi Bell, the lawyer that was gone up to Louisville; and another one was a big rough husky that come along and listened to all the old gentleman said, and was listening to the king now. And when the king got done, this husky up and says:

"Say, looky here; if you are Harvey Wilks, when'd you come to this town?"

"The day before the funeral, friend," says the king.

[208]Deaf mute.

"But what time o' day?"

"In the evenin'—'bout an hour er two before sundown."

"*How'd* you come?"

"I come down on the *Susan Powell,* from Cincinnati."

"Well, then, how'd you come to be up the Pint in the *mornin'*—in a canoe?"

"I warn't up at the Pint in the mornin'."

"It's a lie."

Several of them jumped for him and begged him not to talk that way to an old man and preacher.

"Preacher be hanged, he's a fraud and a liar. He was up at the Pint that mornin'. I live up there, don't I? Well, I was up there, and he was up there. I *see* him there. He come in a canoe, along with Tim Collins and a boy."

The doctor he up and says:

"Would you know the boy again if you was to see him, Hines?"

"I reckon I would, but I don't know. Why, yonder he is, now. I know him perfectly easy."

It was me he pointed at. The doctor says:

"Neighbors, I don't know whether the new couple is frauds or not; but if *these* two ain't frauds, I am an idiot, that's all. I think it's our duty to see that they don't get away from here till we've looked into this thing. Come along, Hines; come along, the rest of you. We'll take these fellows to the tavern and affront them with t'other couple, and I reckon we'll find out *something* before we get through."

It was nuts for the crowd, though maybe not for the king's friends; so we all started. It was about sundown. The doctor he led me along by the hand, and was plenty kind enough, but he never let *go* my hand.

We all got in a big room in the hotel, and lit up some candles, and fetched in the new couple. First, the doctor says:

"I don't wish to be too hard on these two men, but *I* think they're frauds, and they may have complices that we don't know nothing about. If they have, won't the complices get away with that bag of gold Peter Wilks left? It ain't unlikely. If these men ain't frauds, they won't object to sending for that money and letting us keep it till they prove they're all right—ain't that so?"

Everybody agreed to that. So I judged they had our gang in a pretty tight place, right at the outstart. But the king he only looked sorrowful, and says:

"Gentlemen, I wish the money was there, for I ain't got no disposition to throw anything in the way of a fair, open, out-and-out investigation o' this misable business; but alas, the money ain't there; you k'n send and see, if you want to."

"Where is it, then?"

"Well, when my niece give it to me to keep for her, I took and hid it inside o' the straw tick o' my bed, not wishin' to bank it for the few days we'd be here, and considerin' the bed a safe place, we not bein' used to niggers, and suppos'n' 'em honest, like servants in England. The niggers stole it the very next mornin' after I had went down stairs; and when I sold 'em, I hadn't missed the money yit, so they got clean away with it. My servant here k'n tell you 'bout it, gentlemen."

The doctor and several said "Shucks!" and I see nobody didn't altogether believe him. One man asked me if I see the niggers steal it. I said no, but I see them sneaking out of the room and hustling away, and I never thought nothing, only

I reckoned they was afraid they had waked up my master and was trying to get away before he made trouble with them. That was all they asked me. Then the doctor whirls on me and says:

"Are *you* English too?"

I says yes; and him and some others laughed, and said, "Stuff!"

Well, then they sailed in on the general investigation, and there we had it, up and down, hour in, hour out, and nobody never said a word about supper, nor ever seemed to think about it—and so they kept it up, and kept it up; and it *was* the worst mixed-up thing you ever see. They made the king tell his yarn, and they made the old gentleman tell his'n; and anybody but a lot of prejudiced chuckleheads would a *seen* that the old gentleman was spinning truth and t'other one lies. And by-and-by they had me up to tell what I knowed. The king he give me a left-handed look out of the corner of his eye, and so I knowed enough to talk on the right side. I begun to tell about Sheffield, and how we lived there, and all about the English Wilkses, and so on; but I didn't get pretty fur till the doctor begun to laugh; and Levi Bell, the lawyer, says:

"Set down, my boy, I wouldn't strain myself, if I was you. I reckon you ain't used to lying, it don't seem to come handy; what you want is practice. You do it pretty awkward."

I didn't care nothing for the compliment, but I was glad to be let off, anyway.

The doctor he started to say something, and turns and says:

"If you'd been in town at first, Levi Bell——"

The king broke in and reached out his hand, and says:

"Why, is this my poor dead brother's old friend that he's wrote so often about?"

The lawyer and him shook hands, and the lawyer smiled and looked pleased, and they talked right along a while, and then got to one side and talked low; and at last the lawyer speaks up and says:

"That'll fix it. I'll take the order and send it, along with your brother's, and then they'll know it's all right."

So they got some paper and a pen, and the king he set down and twisted his head to one side, and chawed his tongue, and scrawled off something; and then they give the pen to the duke—and then for the first time, the duke looked sick. But he took the pen and wrote. So then the lawyer turns to the new old gentleman and says:

"You and your brother please write a line or two and sign your names."

The old gentleman wrote, but nobody couldn't read it. The lawyer looked powerful astonished, and says:

"Well, it beats *me*"—and snaked a lot of old letters out of his pocket, and examined them, and then examined the old man's writing, and then *them* again; and then says: "These old letters is from Harvey Wilks; and here's *these* two's handwritings, and anybody can see *they* didn't write them" (the king and the duke looked sold and foolish, I tell you, to see how the lawyer had took them in), "and here's *this* old gentleman's handwriting, and anybody can tell, easy enough, *he* didn't write them—fact is, the scratches he makes ain't properly *writing,* at all. Now here's some letters from——"

The new old gentleman says:

"If you please, let me explain. Nobody can read my hand but my brother there—so he copies for me. It's *his* hand you've got there, not mine."

"*Well!*" says the lawyer, "this *is* a state of things. I've got some of William's letters too; so if you'll get him to write a line or so we can com—"

"He *can't* write with his left hand," says the old gentleman. "If he could use his right hand, you would see that he wrote his own letters and mine too. Look at both, please—they're by the same hand."

The lawyer done it, and says:

"I believe it's so—and if it ain't so, there's a heap stronger resemblance than I'd noticed before, anyway. Well, well, well! I thought we was right on the track of a solution, but it's gone to grass, partly. But anyway, *one* thing is proved—*these* two ain't either of 'em Wilkses"—and he wagged his head towards the king and the duke.

Well, what do you think?—that muleheaded old fool wouldn't give in *then!* Indeed he wouldn't. Said it warn't no fair test. Said his brother William was the cussedest joker in the world, and hadn't *tried* to write—*he* see William was going to play one of his jokes the minute he put the pen to paper. And so he warmed up and went warbling and warbling right along, till he was actuly beginning to believe what he was saying, *himself*—but pretty soon the new old gentleman broke in, and says:

"I've thought of something. Is there anybody here that helped to lay out my br—helped to lay out the late Peter Wilks for burying?"

"Yes," says somebody, "me and Ab Turner done it. We're both here."

Then the old man turns towards the king, and says:

"Peraps this gentleman can tell me what was tatooed on his breast?"

Blamed if the king didn't have to brace up mighty quick, or he'd a squshed down like a bluff bank that the river has cut under, it took him so sudden—and mind you, it was a thing that was calculated to make most *anybody* sqush to get fetched such a solid one as that without any notice—because how was *he* going to know what was tatooed on the man? He whitened a little; he couldn't help it; and it was mighty still in there, and everybody bending a little forwards and gazing at him. Says I to myself, *Now* he'll throw up the sponge—there ain't no more use. Well, did he? A body can't hardly believe it, but he didn't. I reckon he thought he'd keep the thing up till he tired them people out, so they'd thin out, and him and the duke could break loose and get away. Anyway, he set there, and pretty soon he begun to smile, and says:

"Mf! It's a *very* tough question, *ain't* it! *Yes,* sir, I k'n tell you what's tatooed on his breast. It's jest a small, thin, blue arrow—that's what it is; and if you don't look clost, you can't see it. *Now* what do you say—hey?"

Well, *I* never see anything like that old blister for clean out-and-out cheek.

The new old gentleman turns brisk towards Ab Turner and his pard, and his eye lights up like he judged he'd got the king *this* time, and says:

"There—you've heard what he said! Was there any such mark on Peter Wilks's breast?"

Both of them spoke up and says:

"We didn't see no such mark."

"Good!" says the old gentleman. "Now, what you *did* see on his breast was a small dim P, and a B (which is an initial he dropped when he was young), and a W, with dashes between them, so: P—B—W"—and he marked them that way on a piece of paper. "Come—ain't that what you saw?"

Both of them spoke up again, and says:

"No, we *didn't.* We never seen any marks at all."

Well, everybody *was* in a state of mind, now; and they sings out:

"The whole *bilin'* of 'm's frauds! Le's duck 'em! le's drown 'em! le's ride 'em on a rail!" and everybody was whooping at once, and there was a rattling pow-wow. But the lawyer he jumps on the table and yells, and says:

"Gentlemen—gentle*men!* Hear me just a word—just a *single* word—if you PLEASE! There's one way yet—let's go and dig up the corpse and look."

That took them.

"Hooray!" they all shouted, and was starting right off; but the lawyer and the doctor sung out:

"Hold on, hold on! Collar all these four men and the boy, and fetch *them* along, too!"

"We'll do it!" they all shouted; "and if we don't find them marks we'll lynch the whole gang!"

I *was* scared, now, I tell you. But there warn't no getting away, you know. They gripped us all, and marched us right along, straight for the graveyard, which was a mile and a half down the river, and the whole town at our heels, for we made noise enough, and it was only nine in the evening.

As we went by our house I wished I hadn't sent Mary Jane out of town; because now if I could tip her the wink, she'd light out and save me, and blow on our dead-beats.

Well, we swarmed along down the river road, just carrying on like wild-cats; and to make it more scary, the sky was darking up, and the lightning beginning to wink and flitter, and the wind to shiver amongst the leaves. This was the most awful trouble and most dangersome I ever was in; and I was kinder stunned; everything was going so different from what I had allowed for; stead of being fixed so I could take my own time, if I wanted to, and see all the fun, and have Mary Jane at my back to save me and set me free when the close-fit come, here was nothing in the world betwixt me and sudden death but just them tatoo-marks. If they didn't find them—

I couldn't bear to think about it; and yet, somehow, I couldn't think about nothing else. It got darker and darker, and it was a beautiful time to give the crowd the slip; but that big husky had me by the wrist—Hines—and a body might as well try to give Goliar[209] the slip. He dragged me right along, he was so excited; and I had to run to keep up.

When they got there they swarmed into the graveyard and washed over it like an overflow. And when they got to the grave, they found they had about a hundred times as many shovels as they wanted, but nobody hadn't thought to fetch a lantern. But they sailed into digging, anyway, by the flicker of the lightning, and sent a man to the nearest house a half a mile off, to borrow one.

So they dug and dug, like everything; and it got awful dark, and the rain started, and the wind swished and swushed along, and the lightning come brisker and brisker, and the thunder boomed; but them people never took no notice of it, they was so full of this business; and one minute you could see everything and every face in that big crowd, and the shovelfuls of dirt sailing up out of the grave, and the next second the dark wiped it all out, and you couldn't see nothing at all.

At last they got out the coffin, and begun to unscrew the lid, and then such another crowding, and shouldering, and shoving as there was, to scrouge in

[209]Goliath.

and get a sight, you never see; and in the dark, that way, it was awful. Hines he hurt my wrist dreadful, pulling and tugging so, and I reckon he clean forgot I was in the world, he was so excited and panting.

All of a sudden the lightning let go a perfect sluice of white glare, and somebody sings out:

"By the living jingo, here's the bag of gold on his breast!"

Hines let out a whoop, like everybody else, and dropped my wrist and give a big surge to burst his way in and get a look, and the way I lit out and shinned for the road in the dark, there ain't nobody can tell.

I had the road all to myself, and I fairly flew—leastways I had it all to myself except the solid dark, and the now-and-then glares, and the buzzing of the rain, and the thrashing of the wind, and the splitting of the thunder; and sure as you are born I did clip it along!

When I struck the town, I see there warn't nobody out in the storm, so I never hunted for no back streets, but humped it straight through the main one; and when I begun to get towards our house I aimed my eye and set it. No light there; the house all dark—which made me feel sorry and disappointed, I didn't know why. But at last, just as I was sailing by, *flash* comes the light in Mary Jane's window! and my heart swelled up sudden, like to burst; and the same second the house and all was behind me in the dark, and wasn't ever going to be before me no more in this world. She *was* the best girl I ever see, and had the most sand.

The minute I was far enough above the town to see I could make the tow-head, I begun to look sharp for a boat to borrow; and the first time the lightning showed me one that wasn't chained, I snatched it and shoved. It was a canoe, and warn't fastened with nothing but a rope. The tow-head was a rattling big distance off, away out there in the middle of the river, but I didn't lose no time; and when I struck the raft at last, I was so fagged I would a just laid down to blow and gasp if I could afforded it. But I didn't. As I sprung aboard I sung out:

"Out with you, Jim, and set her loose! Glory be to goodness, we're shut of them!"

Jim lit out, and was a coming for me with both arms spread, he was so full of joy; but when I glimpsed him in the lightning, my heart shot up in my mouth, and I went overboard backwards; for I forgot he was old King Lear and a drownded A-rab all in one, and it most scared the livers and lights[210] out of me. But Jim fished me out, and was going to hug me and bless me, and so on, he was so glad I was back and we was shut of the king and the duke, but I says:

"Not now—have it for breakfast,[211] have it for breakfast! Cut loose and let her slide!"

So, in two seconds, away we went, a sliding down the river, and it *did* seem so good to be free again and all by ourselves on the big river and nobody to bother us. I had to skip around a bit, and jump up and crack my heels a few times, I couldn't help it; but about the third crack, I noticed a sound that I knowed mighty well—and held my breath and listened and waited—and sure enough, when the next flash busted out over the water, here they come!—and just a laying to their oars and making their skiff hum! It was the king and the duke. So I wilted right down onto the planks, then, and give up; and it was all I could do to keep from crying.

[210]I.e., "livers and lungs," hence "guts." [211]Save it for later.

CHAPTER XXX

When they got aboard, the king went for me, and shook me by the collar, and says:

"Tryin' to give us the slip, was ye, you pup! Tired of our company—hey?"

I says:

"No, your majesty, we warn't—*please* don't, your majesty!"

"Quick, then, and tell us what *was* your idea, or I'll shake the insides out o' you!"

"Honest, I'll tell you everything, just as it happened, your majesty. The man that had aholt of me was very good to me, and kept saying he had a boy about as big as me that died last year, and he was sorry to see a boy in such a dangerous fix; and when they was all took by surprise by finding the gold, and made a rush for the coffin, he lets go of me and whispers, 'Heel it, now, or they'll hang ye, sure!' and I lit out. It didn't seem no good for *me* to stay—*I* couldn't do nothing, and I didn't want to be hung if I could get away. So I never stopped running till I found the canoe; and when I got here I told Jim to hurry, or they'd catch me and hang me yet, and said I was afeard you and the duke wasn't alive, now, and I was awful sorry, and so was Jim, and was awful glad when we see you coming, you may ask Jim if I didn't."

Jim said it was so; and the king told him to shut up, and said, "Oh, yes, it's *mighty* likely!" and shook me up again, and said he reckoned he'd drownd me. But the duke says:

"Leggo the boy, you old idiot! Would *you* a done any different? Did you inquire around for *him,* when you got loose? *I* don't remember it."

So the king let go of me, and begun to cuss that town and everybody in it. But the duke says:

"You better a blame sight give *yourself* a good cussing, for you're the one that's entitled to it most. You hain't done a thing, from the start, that had any sense in it, except coming out so cool and cheeky with that imaginary blue-arrow mark. That *was* bright—it was right down bully; and it was the thing that saved us. For if it hadn't been for that, they'd a jailed us till them Englishmen's baggage come—and then—the penitentiary, you bet! But that trick took 'em to the graveyard, and the gold done us a still bigger kindness; for if the excited fools hadn't let go all holts and made that rush to get a look, we'd a slept in our cravats[212] to-night—cravats warranted to *wear,* too—longer than *we'd* need 'em."

They was still a minute—thinking—then the king says, kind of absentminded like:

"Mf! And we reckoned the *niggers* stole it!"

That made me squirm!

"Yes," says the duke, kinder slow, and deliberate, and sarcastic, "*We* did."

After about a half a minute, the king drawls out:

"Leastways—*I* did."

The duke says, the same way:

"On the contrary—*I* did."

The king kind of ruffles up, and says:

"Looky here, Bilgewater, what'r you referrin' to?"

[212] I.e., hangman's nooses.

The duke says, pretty brisk:

"When it comes to that, maybe you'll let me ask, what was *you* referring to?"

"Shucks!" says the king, very sarcastic; "but *I* don't know—maybe you was asleep, and didn't know what you was about."

The duke bristles right up, now, and says:

"Oh, let *up* on this cussed nonsense—do you take me for a blame' fool? Don't you reckon *I* know who hid that money in that coffin?"

"*Yes,* sir! I know you *do* know—because you done it yourself!"

"It's a lie!"—and the duke went for him. The king sings out:

"Take y'r hands off!—leggo my throat!—I take it all back!"

The duke says:

"Well, you just own up, first, that you *did* hide that money there, intending to give me the slip one of these days, and come back and dig it up, and have it all to yourself."

"Wait jest a minute, duke—answer me this one question, honest and fair; if you didn't put the money there, say it, and I'll b'lieve you, and take back everything I said."

"You old scoundrel, I didn't, and you know I didn't. There, now!"

"Well, then, I b'lieve you. But answer me only jest this one more—now *don't* git mad; didn't you have it in your *mind* to hook the money and hide it?"

The duke never said nothing for a little bit; then he says:

"Well—I don't care if I *did,* I didn't *do* it, anyway. But you not only had it in mind to do it, but you *done* it."

"I wisht I may never die if I done it, duke, and that's honest. I won't say I warn't *goin'* to do it, because I *was;* but you—I mean somebody—got in ahead o' me."

"It's a lie! You done it, and you got to *say* you done it, or——"

The king begun to gurgle, and then he gasps out:

"'Nough!—*I own up!*"

I was very glad to hear him say that, it made me feel much more easier than what I was feeling before. So the duke took his hands off, and says:

"If you ever deny it again, I'll drown you. It's *well* for you to set there and blubber like a baby—it's fitten for you, after the way you've acted. I never see such an old ostrich for wanting to gobble everything—and I a trusting you all the time, like you was my own father. You ought to been ashamed of yourself to stand by and hear it saddled onto a lot of poor niggers and you never say a word for 'em. It makes me feel ridiculous to think I was soft enough to *believe* that rubbage. Cuss you, I can see, now, why you was so anxious to make up the deffersit—you wanted to get what money I'd got out of the Nonesuch and one thing or another, and scoop it *all!*"

The king says, timid, and still a snuffling:

"Why, duke, it was you that said make up the deffersit, it warn't me."

"Dry up! I don't want to hear no more *out* of you!" says the duke. "And *now* you see what you *got* by it. They've got all their own money back, and all of *ourn* but a shekel[213] or two, *besides.* G'long to bed—and don't you deffersit *me* no more deffersits, long 's *you* live!"

[213]An ancient coin of the Near East; here the term is used to mean any coin that does not have high monetary value.

So the king sneaked into the wigwam, and took to his bottle for comfort; and before long the duke tackled *his* bottle; and so in about a half an hour they was as thick as thieves again, and the tighter they got, the lovinger they got; and went off a snoring in each other's arms. They both got powerful mellow, but I noticed the king didn't get mellow enough to forget to remember to not deny about hiding the money-bag again. That made me feel easy and satisfied. Of course when they got to snoring, we had a long gabble, and I told Jim everything.

CHAPTER XXXI

We dasn't stop again at any town, for days and days; kept right along down the river. We was down south in the warm weather, now, and a mighty long ways from home. We begun to come to trees with Spanish moss on them, hanging down from the limbs like long gray beards. It was the first I ever see it growing, and it made the woods look solemn and dismal. So now the frauds reckoned they was out of danger, and they begun to work the villages again.

First they done a lecture on temperance; but they didn't make enough for them both to get drunk on. Then in another village they started a dancing school; but they didn't know no more how to dance than a kangaroo does; so the first prance they made, the general public jumped in and pranced them out of town. Another time they tried a go at yellocution; but they didn't yellocute long till the audience got up and give them a solid good cussing and made them skip out. They tackled missionarying, and mesmerizering, and doctoring, and telling fortunes, and a little of everything; but they couldn't seem to have no luck. So at last they got just about dead broke, and laid around the raft, as she floated along, thinking, and thinking, and never saying nothing, by the half a day at a time, and dreadful blue and desperate.

And at last they took a change, and begun to lay their heads together in the wigwam and talk low and confidential two or three hours at a time. Jim and me got uneasy. We didn't like the look of it. We judged they was studying up some kind of worse deviltry than ever. We turned it over and over, and at last we made up our minds they was going to break into somebody's house or store, or was going into the counterfeit-money business, or something. So then we was pretty scared, and made up an agreement that we wouldn't have nothing in the world to do with such actions, and if we ever got the least show we would give them the cold shake, and clear out and leave them behind. Well, early one morning we hid the raft in a good safe place about two mile below a little bit of a shabby village, named Pikesville, and the king he went ashore, and told us all to stay hid whilst he went up to town and smelt around to see if anybody had got any wind of the Royal Nonesuch there yet. ("House to rob, you *mean,*" says I to myself; "and when you get through robbing it you'll come back here and wonder what's become of me and Jim and the raft—and you'll have to take it out in wondering.") And he said if he warn't back by mid-day, the duke and me would know it was all right, and we was to come along.

So we staid where we was. The duke he fretted and sweated around, and was in a mighty sour way. He scolded us for everything, and we couldn't seem to do nothing right; he found fault with every little thing. Something was a-brewing, sure. I was good and glad when midday come and no king; we could have a change, anyway—and maybe a chance for *the* change, on top of it. So me and the duke went up to the village, and hunted around there for the king, and by-and-by we found him in the back room of a little low doggery,[214] very tight, and a lot of loafers bullyragging him for sport, and he a cussing and threatening with all his might, and so tight he couldn't walk, and couldn't do nothing to them. The duke he begun to abuse him for an old fool, and the king begun to sass back; and the minute they was fairly at it, I lit out, and shook the reefs out of[215] my hind legs, and spun down the river road like a deer—for I see our chance; and I made up my mind that it would be a long day before they ever see me and Jim again. I got down there all out of breath but loaded up with joy, and sung out—

"Set her loose, Jim, we're all right now!"

But there warn't no answer, and nobody come out of the wigwam. Jim was gone! I set up a shout—and then another—and then another one; and run this way and that in the woods, whooping and screeching; but it warn't no use—old Jim was gone. Then I set down and cried; I couldn't help it. But I couldn't set still long. Pretty soon I went out on the road, trying to think what I better do, and I run across a boy walking, and asked him if he'd seen a strange nigger, dressed so and so, and he says:

"Yes."

"Whereabouts?" says I.

"Down to Silas Phelps's place, two mile below here. He's a runaway nigger, and they've got him. Was you looking for him?"

"You bet I ain't! I run across him in the woods about an hour or two ago, and he said if I hollered he'd cut my livers out—and told me to lay down and stay where I was; and I done it. Been there ever since; afeard to come out."

"Well," he says, "you needn't be afeard no more, becuz they've got him. He run off f'm down South, som'ers."

"It's a good job they got him."

"Well, I *reckon!* There's two hundred dollars reward on him. It's like picking up money out'n the road."

"Yes, it is—and *I* could a had it if I'd been big enough; I see him *first.* Who nailed him?"

"It was an old fellow—a stranger—and he sold out his chance in him for forty dollars, becuz he's got to go up the river and can't wait. Think o' that, now! You bet *I'd* wait, if it was seven year."

"That's me, every time," says I. "But maybe his chance ain't worth no more than that, if he'll sell it so cheap. Maybe there's something ain't straight about it."

"But it *is,* though—straight as a string. I see the handbill myself. It tells all about him, to a dot—paints him like a picture, and tells the plantation he's frum, below Newr *leans.* No-sirree-*bob,* they ain't no trouble 'bout *that* speculation, you bet you. Say, gimme a chaw tobacker, won't ye?"

I didn't have none, so he left. I went to the raft, and set down in the wigwam to think. But I couldn't come to nothing. I thought till I wore my head sore, but I couldn't see no way out of the trouble. After all this long journey, and after all we'd done for them scoundrels, here was it all come to nothing, everything

[214]Saloon. [215]Stretched out.

all busted up and ruined, because they could have the heart to serve Jim such a trick as that, and make him a slave again all his life, and amongst strangers, too, for forty dirty dollars.

Once I said to myself it would be a thousand times better for Jim to be a slave at home where his family was, as long as he'd *got* to be a slave, and so I'd better write a letter to Tom Sawyer and tell him to tell Miss Watson where he was. But I soon give up that notion, for two things: she'd be mad and disgusted at his rascality and ungratefulness for leaving her, and so she'd sell him straight down the river again; and if she didn't everybody naturally despises an ungrateful nigger, and they'd make Jim feel it all the time, and so he'd feel ornery and disgraced. And then think of *me!* It would get all around, that Huck Finn helped a nigger to get his freedom; and if I was to ever see anybody from that town again, I'd be ready to get down and lick his boots for shame. That's just the way: a person does a low-down thing, and then he don't want to take no consequences of it. Thinks as long as he can hide it, it ain't no disgrace. That was my fix exactly. The more I studied about this, the more my conscience went to grinding me, and the more wicked and low-down and ornery I got to feeling. And at last, when it hit me all of a sudden that here was the plain hand of Providence slapping me in the face and letting me know my wickedness was being watched all the time from up there in heaven, whilst I was stealing a poor old woman's nigger that hadn't ever done me no harm, and now was showing me there's One that's always on the lookout, and ain't agoing to allow no such miserable doings to go only just so fur and no further, I most dropped in my tracks I was so scared. Well, I tried the best I could to kinder soften it up somehow for myself, by saying I was brung up wicked, and so I warn't so much to blame; but something inside of me kept saying, "There was the Sunday school, you could a gone to it; and if you'd a done it they'd a learnt you, there, that people that acts as I'd been acting about that nigger goes to everlasting fire."

It made me shiver. And I about made up my mind to pray; and see if I couldn't try to quit being the kind of a boy I was, and be better. So I kneeled down. But the words wouldn't come. Why wouldn't they? It warn't no use to try and hide it from Him. Nor from *me,* neither. I knowed very well why they wouldn't come. It was because my heart warn't right; it was because I warn't square; it was because I was playing double. I was letting *on* to give up sin, but away inside of me I was holding to the biggest one of all. I was trying to make my mouth *say* I would do the right thing and the clean thing, and go and write to that nigger's owner and tell where he was; but deep down in me I knowed it was a lie—and He knowed it. You can't pray a lie—I found that out.

So I was full of trouble, full as I could be; and didn't know what to do. At last I had an idea; and I says, I'll go and write the letter—and *then* see if I can pray. Why, it was astonishing, the way I felt as light as a feather, right straight off, and my troubles all gone. So I got a piece of paper and a pencil, all glad and excited, and set down and wrote:

> Miss Watson your runaway nigger Jim is down here two mile below Pikesville and Mr. Phelps has got him and he will give him up for the reward if you send.
>
> HUCK FINN.

I felt good and all washed clean of sin for the first time I had ever felt so in my life, and I knowed I could pray now. But I didn't do it straight off, but laid

the paper down and set there thinking—thinking how good it was
pened so, and how near I come to being lost and going to hell. An
thinking. And got to thinking over our trip down the river; and I see Jim
me, all the time, in the day, and in the night-time, sometimes moonlight, sometimes storms, and we a floating along, talking, and singing, and laughing. But somehow I couldn't seem to strike no places to harden me against him, but only the other kind. I'd see him standing my watch on top of his'n, stead of calling me, so I could go on sleeping; and see him how glad he was when I come back out of the fog; and when I come to him again in the swamp, up there where the feud was; and such-like times; and would always call me honey, and pet me, and do everything he could think of for me, and how good he always was; and at last I struck the time I saved him by telling the men we had smallpox aboard, and he was so grateful, and said I was the best friend ole Jim ever had in the world, and the *only* one he's got now; and then I happened to look around, and see that paper.

It was a close place. I took it up, and held it in my hand. I was a trembling, because I'd got to decide, forever, betwixt two things, and I knowed it. I studied a minute, sort of holding my breath, and then says to myself:

"All right, then, I'll *go* to hell"—and tore it up.

It was awful thoughts, and awful words, but they was said. And I let them stay said; and never thought no more about reforming. I shoved the whole thing out of my head; and said I would take up wickedness again, which was in my line, being brung up to it, and the other warn't. And for a starter, I would go to work and steal Jim out of slavery again; and if I could think up anything worse, I would do that, too; because as long as I was in, and in for good, I might as well go the whole hog.

Then I set to thinking over how to get at it, and turned over considerable many things in my mind; and at last fixed up a plan that suited me. So then I took the bearings of a woody island that was down the river a piece, and as soon as it was fairly dark I crept out with my raft and went for it, and hid it there, and then turned in. I slept the night through, and got up before it was light, and had my breakfast, and put on my store clothes, and tied up some others and one thing or another in a bundle, and took the canoe and cleared for shore. I landed below where I judged was Phelps's place, and hid my bundle in the woods, and then filled up the canoe with water, and loaded rocks into her and sunk her where I could find her again when I wanted her, about a quarter of a mile below a little steam sawmill that was on the bank.

Then I struck up the road, and when I passed the mill I see a sign on it, "Phelps's Sawmill," and when I come to the farm-houses, two or three hundred yards further along, I kept my eyes peeled, but didn't see nobody around, though it was good daylight, now. But I didn't mind, because I didn't want to see nobody just yet—I only wanted to get the lay of the land. According to my plan, I was going to turn up there from the village, not from below. So I just took a look, and shoved along, straight for town. Well, the very first man I see, when I got there, was the duke. He was sticking up a bill for the Royal Nonesuch—three-night performance—like that other time. *They* had the cheek, them frauds! I was right on him, before I could shirk. He looked astonished, and says:

"Hel-*lo!* Where'd *you* come from?" Then he says, kind of glad and eager, "Where's the raft?—got her in a good place?"

I says:

"Why, that's just what I was agoing to ask your grace."

Then he didn't look so joyful—and says:

"What was your idea for asking *me?*" he says.

"Well," I says, "when I see the king in that doggery yesterday, I says to myself, we can't get him home for hours, till he's soberer; so I went a loafing around town to put in the time, and wait. A man up and offered me ten cents to help him pull a skiff over the river and back to fetch a sheep, and so I went along; but when we was dragging him to the boat, and the man left me aholt of the rope and went behind him to shove him along, he was too strong for me, and jerked loose and run, and we after him. We didn't have no dog, and so we had to chase him all over the country till we tired him out. We never got him till dark, then we fetched him over, and I started down for the raft. When I got there and see it was gone, I says to myself, 'they've got into trouble and had to leave; and they've took my nigger, which is the only nigger I've got in the world, and now I'm in a strange country, and ain't got no property no more, nor nothing, and no way to make my living;' so I set down and cried. I slept in the woods all night. But what *did* become of the raft then?—and Jim, poor Jim!"

"Blamed if *I* know—that is, what's become of the raft. That old fool had made a trade and got forty dollars, and when we found him in the doggery the loafers had matched half dollars with him and got every cent but what he'd spent for whisky; and when I got him home late last night and found the raft gone, we said, 'That little rascal has stole our raft and shook us, and run off down the river.'"

"I wouldn't shake my *nigger,* would I?—the only nigger I had in the world, and the only property."

"We never thought of that. Fact is, I reckon we'd come to consider him *our* nigger; yes, we did consider him so—goodness knows we had trouble enough for him. So when we see the raft was gone, and we flat broke, there warn't anything for it but to try the Royal Nonesuch another shake. And I've pegged along ever since, dry as a powder-horn. Where's that ten cents? Give it here."

I had considerable money, so I give him ten cents, but begged him to spend it for something to eat, and give me some, because it was all the money I had, and I hadn't had nothing to eat since yesterday. He never said nothing. The next minute he whirls on me and says:

"Do you reckon that nigger would blow on us? We'd skin him if he done that!"

"How can he blow? Hain't he run off?"

"No! That old fool sold him, and never divided with me, and the money's gone."

"*Sold* him?" I says, and begun to cry; "why, he was *my* nigger, and that was my money. Where is he?—I want my nigger."

"Well, you can't *get* your nigger, that's all—so dry up your blubbering. Looky here—do you think *you'd* venture to blow on us? Blamed if I think I'd trust you. Why, if you *was* to blow on us——"

He stopped, but I never see the duke look so ugly out of his eyes before. I went on a-whimpering, and says:

"I don't want to blow on nobody; and I ain't got no time to blow, nohow. I got to turn out and find my nigger."

He looked kinder bothered, and stood there with his bills fluttering on his arm, thinking, and wrinkling up his forehead. At last he says:

"I'll tell you something. We got to be here three days. If you'll promise you won't blow, and won't let the nigger blow, I'll tell you where to find him."

So I promised, and he says:

"A farmer by the name of Silas Ph——" and then he stopped. You see he started to tell me the truth; but when he stopped, that way, and begun to study and think again, I reckoned he was changing his mind. And so he was. He wouldn't trust me; he wanted to make sure of having me out of the way the whole three days. So pretty soon he says: "The man that bought him is named Abram Foster—Abram G. Foster—and he lives forty mile back here in the country, on the road to Lafayette."

"All right," I says, "I can walk it in three days. And I'll start this very afternoon."

"No you won't, you'll start *now;* and don't you lose any time about it, neither, nor do any gabbling by the way. Just keep a tight tongue in your head and move right along, and then you won't get into trouble with *us,* d'ye hear?"

That was the order I wanted, and that was the one I played for. I wanted to be left free to work my plans.

"So clear out," he says; "and you can tell Mr. Foster whatever you want to. Maybe you can get him to believe that Jim *is* your nigger—some idiots don't require documents—leastways I've heard there's such down South here. And when you tell him the handbill and the reward's bogus, maybe he'll believe you when you explain to him what the idea was for getting 'em out. Go 'long, now, and tell him anything you want to; but mind you don't work your jaw any *between* here and there."

So I left, and struck for the back country. I didn't look around, but I kinder felt like he was watching me. But I knowed I could tire him out at that. I went straight out in the country as much as a mile, before I stopped; then I doubled back through the woods towards Phelps's. I reckoned I better start in on my plan straight off, without fooling around, because I wanted to stop Jim's mouth till these fellows could get away. I didn't want no trouble with their kind. I'd seen all I wanted to of them, and wanted to get entirely shut of them.

CHAPTER XXXII

When I got there it was still and Sunday-like, and hot and sunshiny—the hands was gone to the fields; and there was them kind of faint dronings of bugs and flies in the air that makes it seem so lonesome and like everybody's dead and gone; and if a breeze fans along and quivers the leaves, it makes you feel mournful, because you feel like it's spirits whispering—spirits that's been dead ever so many years—and you always think they're talking about *you.* As a general thing it makes a body wish *he* was dead, too, and done with it all.

Phelps's was one of these little one-horse cotton plantations; and they all look alike. A rail fence round a two-acre yard; a stile, made out of logs sawed off and up-ended, in steps, like barrels of a different length, to climb over the fence with, and for the women to stand on when they are going to jump onto a horse; some sickly grass-patches in the big yard, but mostly it was bare and smooth, like an old hat with the nap rubbed off; big double log house for the white folks—hewed logs, with the chinks stopped up with mud or mortar, and these mud-stripes been whitewashed some time or another; round-log kitchen, with a big broad, open but roofed passage joining it to the house; log smoke-house back of the kitchen; three little log nigger-cabins in a row t'other side the smoke-house; one little hut all by itself away down against the back fence, and some out-buildings down a piece the other side; ash-hopper,[216] and big kettle to bile soap in, by the little hut; bench by the kitchen door, with bucket of water and a gourd; hound asleep there, in the sun; more hounds asleep, round about; about three shade-trees away off in a corner; some currant bushes and gooseberry bushes in one place by the fence; outside of the fence a garden and a water-melon patch; then the cotton fields begins; and after the fields, the woods.

I went around and clumb over the back stile by the ash-hopper, and started for the kitchen. When I got a little ways, I heard the dim hum of a spinning-wheel wailing along up and sinking along down again; and then I knowed for certain I wished I was dead—for that *is* the lonesomest sound in the whole world.

I went right along, not fixing up any particular plan, but just trusting to Providence to put the right words in my mouth when the time come; for I'd noticed that Providence always did put the right words in my mouth, if I left it alone.

When I got half-way, first one hound and then another got up and went for me, and of course I stopped and faced them, and kept still. And such another pow-wow as they made! In a quarter of a minute I was a kind of a hub of a wheel, as you may say—spokes made out of dogs—circle of fifteen of them packed together around me, with their necks and noses stretched up towards me, a barking and howling; and more a coming; you see them sailing over fences and around corners from everywheres.

A nigger woman come tearing out of the kitchen with a rolling-pin in her hand, singing out, "Begone! *you* Tige! you Spot! begon sah!" and she fetched first one and then another of them a clip and sent him howling, and then the rest followed; and the next second, half of them come back, wagging their tails around me and making friends with me. There ain't no harm in a hound, nohow.

And behind the woman comes a little nigger girl and two little nigger boys, without anything on but tow-linen shirts, and they hung onto their mother's gown, and peeped out from behind her at me, bashful, the way they always do. And here comes the white woman running from the house, about forty-five or fifty year old, bareheaded, and her spinning-stick in her hand; and behind her comes her little white children, acting the same way the little niggers was doing. She was smiling all over so she could hardly stand—and says:

"It's *you,* at last!—*ain't* it?"

I out with a "Yes'm," before I thought.

She grabbed me and hugged me tight; and then gripped me by both hands and shook and shook; and the tears come in her eyes, and run down over; and she couldn't seem to hug and shake enough, and kept saying, "You don't look as much like your mother as I reckoned you would, but law sakes, I don't care

[216]A bin for the fireplace ashes from which lye was extracted for use in making soap.

for that, I'm *so* glad to see you! Dear, dear, it does seem like I could eat you up! Children, it's your cousin Tom!—tell him howdy."

But they ducked their heads, and put their fingers in their mouths, and hid behind her. So she run on:

"Lize, hurry up and get him a hot breakfast, right away—or did you get your breakfast on the boat?"

I said I had got it on the boat. So then she started for the house, leading me by the hand, and the children tagging after. When we got there, she set me down in a split-bottomed chair, and set herself down on a little low stool in front of me, holding both of my hands, and says:

"Now I can have a *good* look at you; and laws-a-me, I've been hungry for it a many and a many a time, all these long years, and it's come at last! We been expecting you a couple of days and more. What's kep' you?—boat get aground?"

"Yes'm—she——"

"Don't say yes'm—say Aunt Sally. Where'd she get aground?"

I didn't rightly know what to say, because I didn't know whether the boat would be coming up the river or down. But I go a good deal on instinct; and my instinct said she would be coming up—from down towards Orleans. That didn't help me much, though; for I didn't know the names of bars down that way. I see I'd got to invent a bar, or forget the name of the one we got aground on—or—Now I struck an idea, and fetched it out:

"It warn't the grounding—that didn't keep us back but a little. We blowed out a cylinder-head."

"Good gracious! anybody hurt?"

"No'm. Killed a nigger."

"Well, it's lucky; because sometimes people do get hurt. Two years ago last Christmas, your uncle Silas was coming up from Newrleans on the old *Lally Rook,*[217] and she blowed out a cylinder-head and crippled a man. And I think he died afterwards. He was a Babtist. Your uncle Silas knowed a family in Baton Rouge that knowed his people very well. Yes, I remember, now he *did* die. Mortification[218] set in, and they had to amputate him. But it didn't save him. Yes, it was mortification—that was it. He turned blue all over, and died in the hope of a glorious resurrection. They say he was a sight to look at. Your uncle's been up to the town every day to fetch you. And he's gone again, not more'n an hour ago; he'll be back any minute, now. You must a met him on the road, didn't you?—oldish man, with a——"

"No, I didn't see nobody, Aunt Sally. The boat landed just at daylight, and I left my baggage on the wharf-boat[219] and went looking around the town and out a piece in the country, to put in the time and not get here too soon; and so I come down the back way."

"Who'd you give the baggage to?"

"Nobody."

"Why, child, it'll be stole!"

"Not where *I* hid it I reckon it won't," I says.

"How'd you get your breakfast so early on the boat?"

It was kinder thin ice, but I says:

[217]Named for the beautiful princess in *Lalla Rookh* (1817), a series of Oriental tales by the English poet Thomas Moore (1779–1852).

[218]Gangrene. [219]A floating dock or landing platform.

"The captain see me standing around, and told me I better have something to eat before I went ashore; so he took me in the texas to the officers' lunch,[220] and give me all I wanted."

I was getting so uneasy I couldn't listen good. I had my mind on the children all the time; I wanted to get them out to one side, and pump them a little, and find out who I was. But I couldn't get no show, Mrs. Phelps kept it up and run on so. Pretty soon she made the cold chills streak all down my back, because she says:

"But here we're a running on this way, and you hain't told me a word about Sis, nor any of them. Now I'll rest my works a little, and you start up yourn; just tell me *everything*—tell me all about 'm all—every one of 'm; and how they are, and what they're doing, and what they told you to tell me; and every last thing you can think of."

Well, I see I was up a stump—and up it good. Providence had stood by me this fur, all right, but I was hard and tight aground, now. I see it warn't a bit of use to try to go ahead—I'd *got* to throw up my hand. So I says to myself, here's another place where I got to resk the truth. I opened my mouth to begin; but she grabbed me and hustled me in behind the bed, and says:

"Here he comes! stick your head down lower—there, that'll do; you can't be seen, now. Don't you let on you're here. I'll play a joke on him. Children, don't you say a word."

I see I was in a fix, now. But it warn't no use to worry; there warn't nothing to do but just hold still, and try and be ready to stand from under when the lightning struck.

I had just one little glimpse of the old gentleman when he come in, then the bed hid him. Mrs. Phelps she jumps for him and says:

"Has he come?"

"No," says her husband.

"Good-*ness* gracious!" she says, "what in the world *can* have become of him?"

"I can't imagine," says the old gentleman; "and I must say, it makes me dreadful uneasy."

"Uneasy!" she says, "I'm ready to go distracted! He *must* a come; and you've missed him along the road. I *know* it's so—something *tells* me so."

"Why Sally, I *couldn't* miss him along the road—*you* know that."

"But oh, dear, dear, what *will* Sis say! He must a come! You must a missed him. He——"

"Oh, don't distress me any more'n I'm already distressed. I don't know what in the world to make of it. I'm at my wit's end, and I don't mind acknowledging 't I'm right down scared. But there's no hope that he's come; for he *couldn't* come and me miss him. Sally, it's terrible—just terrible—something's happened to the boat, sure!"

"Why, Silas! Look yonder!—up the road!—ain't that somebody coming?"

He sprung to the window at the head of the bed, and that give Mrs. Phelps the chance she wanted. She stooped down quick, at the foot of the bed, and give me a pull, and out I come; and when he turned back from the window, there she stood, a-beaming and a-smiling like a house afire, and I standing pretty meek and sweaty alongside. The old gentleman stared, and says:

"Why, who's that?"

[220]Mess, eating room.

"Who do you reckon 't is?"

"I hain't no idea. Who *is* it?"

"It's *Tom Sawyer!*"

By jings, I most slumped through the floor. But there warn't no time to swap knives;[221] the old man grabbed me by the hand and shook, and kept on shaking; and all the time, how the woman did dance around and laugh and cry; and then how they both did fire off questions about Sid, Mary, and the rest of the tribe.

But if they was joyful, it warn't nothing to what I was; for it was like being born again, I was so glad to find out who I was. Well, they froze to me for two hours; and at last when my chin was so tired it couldn't hardly go, any more, I had told them more about my family—I mean the Sawyer family—than ever happened to any six Sawyer families. And I explained all about how we blowed out a cylinder-head at the mouth of White River and it took us three days to fix it. Which was all right, and worked first rate; because *they* didn't know but what it would take three days to fix it. If I'd a called it a bolt-head it would a done just as well.

Now I was feeling pretty comfortable all down one side, and pretty uncomfortable all up the other. Being Tom Sawyer was easy and comfortable; and it stayed easy and comfortable till by-and-by I hear a steamboat coughing along down the river—then I says to myself, spose Tom Sawyer come down on that boat?—and spose he steps in here, any minute, and sings out my name before I can throw him a wink to keep quiet? Well, I couldn't *have* it that way—it wouldn't do at all. I must go up the road and waylay him. So I told the folks I reckoned I would go up to the town and fetch down my baggage. The old gentleman was for going along with me, but I said no, I could drive the horse myself, and I druther he wouldn't take no trouble about me.

CHAPTER XXXIII

So I started for town, in the wagon, and when I was half-way I see a wagon coming, and sure enough it was Tom Sawyer, and I stopped and waited till he come along. I says "Hold on!" and it stopped alongside, and his mouth opened up like a trunk, and staid so; and he swallowed two or three times like a person that's got a dry throat, and then says:

"I hain't ever done you no harm. You know that. So then, what you want to come back and ha'nt *me* for?"

I says:

"I hain't come back—I hain't *gone.*"

When he heard my voice, it righted him up some, but he warn't quite satisfied yet. He says:

"Don't you play nothing on me, because I wouldn't on you. Honest injun, now, you ain't a ghost?"

"Honest injun, I ain't," I says.

"Well—I—I—well, that ought to settle it, of course; but I can't somehow seem to understand it, no way. Looky here, warn't you ever murdered at *all?*"

[221] I.e., to change plans.

"No. I warn't ever murdered at all—I played it on them. You come in here and feel of me if you don't believe me."

So he done it; and it satisfied him; and he was that glad to see me again, he didn't know what to do. And he wanted to know all about it right off; because it was a grand adventure, and mysterious, and so it hit him where he lived. But I said, leave it alone till by-and-by; and told his driver to wait, and we drove off a little piece, and I told him the kind of a fix I was in, and what did he reckon we better do? He said, let him alone a minute, and don't disturb him. So he thought and thought, and pretty soon he says:

"It's all right, I've got it. Take my trunk in your wagon, and let on it's your'n; and you turn back and fool along slow, so as to get to the house about the time you ought to; and I'll go towards town a piece, and take a fresh start, and get there a quarter or a half an hour after you; and you needn't let on to know me, at first."

I says:

"All right; but wait a minute. There's one more thing—a thing that *nobody* don't know but me. And that is, there's a nigger here that I'm a trying to steal out of slavery—and his name is *Jim*—old Miss Watson's Jim."

He says:

"What! Why Jim is——"

He stopped and went to studying. I says:

"*I* know what you'll say. You'll say it's dirty low-down business; but what if it is?—*I*'m low down; and I'm agoing to steal him, and I want you to keep mum and not let on. Will you?"

His eye lit up, and he says:

"I'll *help* you steal him!"

Well, I let go all holts then, like I was shot. It was the most astonishing speech I ever heard—and I'm bound to say Tom Sawyer fell, considerable, in my estimation. Only I couldn't believe it. Tom Sawyer a *nigger stealer!*

"Oh, shucks," I says, "you're joking."

"I ain't joking, either."

"Well, then," I says, "joking or no joking, if you hear anything said about a runaway nigger, don't forget to remember that *you* don't know nothing about him, and *I* don't know nothing about him."

Then we took the trunk and put it in my wagon, and he drove off his way, and I drove mine. But of course I forgot all about driving slow, on accounts of being glad and full of thinking; so I got home a heap too quick for that length of a trip. The old gentleman was at the door, and he says:

"Why, this is wonderful. Who ever would a thought it was in that mare to do it. I wish we'd a timed her. And she hain't sweated a hair—not a hair. It's wonderful. Why, I wouldn't take a hundred dollars for that horse now; I wouldn't, honest; and yet I'd a sold her for fifteen before, and thought 'twas all she was worth."

That's all he said. He was the innocentest, best old soul I ever see. But it warn't surprising; because he warn't only just a farmer, he was a preacher, too, and had a little one-horse log church down back of the plantation, which he built it himself at his own expense, for a church and school-house, and never charged nothing for his preaching, and it was worth it, too. There was plenty other farmer-preachers like that, and done the same way, down South.

In about half an hour Tom's wagon drove up to the front stile, and Aunt Sally she see it through the window because it was only about fifty yards, and says:

"Why, there's somebody come! I wonder who 'tis? Why, I do believe it's a stranger. Jimmy" (that's one of the children), "run and tell Lize to put on another plate for dinner."

Everybody made a rush for the front door, because, of course, a stranger don't come *every* year, and so he lays over the yaller fever, for interest, when he does come. Tom was over the stile and starting for the house; the wagon was spinning up the road for the village, and we was all bunched in the front door. Tom had his store clothes on, and an audience—and that was always nuts for Tom Sawyer. In them circumstances it warn't no trouble to him to throw in an amount of style that was suitable. He warn't a boy to meeky[222] along up that yard like a sheep; no, he come ca'm and important, like the ram. When he got afront of us, he lifts his hat ever so gracious and dainty, like it was the lid of a box that had butterflies asleep in it and he didn't want to disturb them, and says:

"Mr. Archibald Nichols, I presume?"

"No, my boy," says the old gentleman, "I'm sorry to say't your driver has deceived you; Nichols's place is down a matter of three mile more. Come in, come in."

Tom he took a look back over his shoulder, and says, "Too late—he's out of sight."

"Yes, he's gone, my son, and you must come in and eat your dinner with us; and then we'll hitch up and take you down to Nichols's."

"Oh, I *can't* make you so much trouble; I couldn't think of it. I'll walk—I don't mind the distance."

"But we won't *let* you walk—it wouldn't be Southern hospitality to do it. Come right in."

"Oh, *do*," says Aunt Sally; "it ain't a bit of trouble to us, not a bit in the world. You *must* stay. It's a long, dusty three mile, and we *can't* let you walk. And besides, I've already told 'em to put on another plate, when I see you coming; so you mustn't disappoint us. Come right in, and make yourself at home."

So Tom he thanked them very hearty and handsome, and let himself be persuaded, and come in; and when he was in, he said he was a stranger from Hicksville, Ohio, and his name was William Thompson—and he made another bow.

Well, he run on, and on, and on, making up stuff about Hicksville and everybody in it he could invent, and I getting a little nervous, and wondering how this was going to help me out of my scrape: and at last, still talking along, he reached over and kissed Aunt Sally right on the mouth, and then settled back again in his chair, comfortable, and was going on talking; but she jumped up and wiped it off with the back of her hand, and says:

"You owdacious puppy!"

He looked kind of hurt, and says:

"I'm surprised at you, m'am."

"You're s'rp—Why, what do you reckin *I* am? I've a good notion to take and—say, what do you mean by kissing me?"

He looked kind of humble, and says:

"I didn't mean nothing, m'am. I didn't mean no harm. I—I—thought you'd like it."

"Why, you born fool!" She took up the spinning-stick, and it looked like it was all she could do to keep from giving him a crack with it. "What made you think I'd like it?"

[222]Come meekly.

"Well, I don't know. Only, they—they—told me you would."

"*They* told you I would. Whoever told you's *another* lunatic. I never heard the beat of it. Who's *they?*"

"Why—everybody. They all said so, m'am."

It was all she could do to hold in; and her eyes snapped, and her fingers worked like she wanted to scratch him; and she says:

"Who's 'everybody?' Out with their names—or ther'll be an idiot short."

He got up and looked distressed, and fumbled his hat, and says:

"I'm sorry, and I warn't expecting it. They told me to. They all told me to. They all said kiss her; and said she'll like it. They all said it—every one of them. But I'm sorry, m'am, and I won't do it no more—I won't, honest."

"You won't, won't you? Well, I sh'd *reckon* you won't!"

"No'm, I'm honest about it; I won't ever do it again. Till you ask me."

"Till I *ask* you! Well, I never see the beat of it in my born days! I lay you'll be the Methusalem-numskull[223] of creation before ever *I* ask you—or the likes of you."

"Well," he says "it does surprise me so. I can't make it out, somehow. They said you would, and I thought you would. But—" He stopped and looked around slow, like he wished he could run across a friendly eye, somewhere's; and fetched up on the old gentleman's, and says, "Didn't *you* think she'd like me to kiss her, sir?"

"Why, no, I—I—well, no, I b'lieve I didn't."

Then he looks on around, the same way, to me—and says:

"Tom, didn't *you* think Aunt Sally 'd open out her arms and say, 'Sid Sawyer——' "

"My land!" she says, breaking in and jumping for him, "you impudent young rascal, to fool a body so—" and was going to hug him, but he fended her off, and says:

"No, not till you've asked me, first."

So she didn't lose no time, but asked him; and hugged him and kissed him, over and over again, and then turned him over to the old man, and he took what was left. And after they got a little quiet again, she says:

"Why, dear me, I never see such a surprise. We warn't looking for *you*, at all, but only Tom. Sis never wrote to me about anybody coming but him."

"It's because it warn't *intended* for any of us to come but Tom," he says; "but I begged and begged, and at the last minute she let me come, too; so coming down the river, me and Tom thought it would be a first-rate surprise for him to come here to the house first, and for me to by-and-by tag along and drop in and let on to be a stranger. But it was a mistake, Aunt Sally. This ain't no healthy place for a stranger to come."

"No—not impudent whelps, Sid. You ought to had your jaws boxed; I hain't been so put out since I don't know when. But I don't care, I don't mind the terms—I'd be willing to stand a thousand such jokes to have you here. Well, to think of that performance! I don't deny it, I was most putrified[224] with astonishment when you give me that smack."

[223] I.e., a numbskull as old as Methuselah, the Biblical patriarch said to have lived 969 years (Genesis 5:27).

[224] Petrified, turned to stone.

We had dinner out in that broad open passage betwixt the house and the kitchen; and there was things enough on that table for seven families—and all hot, too; none of your flabby tough meat that's laid in a cupboard in a damp cellar all night and tastes like a hunk of old cold cannibal in the morning. Uncle Silas he asked a pretty long blessing over it, but it was worth it; and it didn't cool it a bit, neither, the way I've seen them kind of interruptions do, lots of times.

There was a considerable good deal of talk, all the afternoon, and me and Tom was on the lookout all the time, but it warn't no use, they didn't happen to say nothing about any runaway nigger, and we was afraid to try to work up to it. But at supper, at night, one of the little boys says:

"Pa, mayn't Tom and Sid and me go to the show?"

"No," says the old man, "I reckon there ain't going to be any; and you couldn't go if there was; because the runaway nigger told Burton and me all about that scandalous show, and Burton said he would tell the people; so I reckon they've drove the owdacious loafers out of town before this time."

So there it was!—but *I* couldn't help it. Tom and me was to sleep in the same room and bed; so, being tired, we bid good-night and went up to bed, right after supper, and clumb out of the window and down the lightning-rod, and shoved for the town; for I didn't believe anybody was going to give the king and the duke a hint, and so, if I didn't hurry up and give them one they'd get into trouble sure.

On the road Tom he told me all about how it was reckoned I was murdered, and how pap disappeared, pretty soon, and didn't come back no more, and what a stir there was when Jim run away; and I told Tom all about our Royal Nonesuch rapscallions, and as much of the raft-voyage as I had time to; and as we struck into the town and up through the middle of it—it was as much as half-after eight, then—here comes a raging rush of people, with torches, and an awful whooping and yelling, and banging tin pans and blowing horns; and we jumped to one side to let them go by; and as they went by, I see they had the king and the duke astraddle of a rail—that is, I knowed it *was* the king and the duke, though they was all over tar and feathers, and didn't look like nothing in the world that was human—just looked like a couple of monstrous big soldier-plumes.[225] Well, it made me sick to see it; and I was sorry for them poor pitiful rascals, it seemed like I couldn't ever feel any hardness against them any more in the world. It was a dreadful thing to see. Human beings *can* be awful cruel to one another.

We see we was too late—couldn't do no good. We asked some straggler about it, and they said everybody went to the show looking very innocent; and laid low and kept dark till the poor old king was in the middle of his cavortings on the stage; then somebody give a signal, and the house rose up and went for them.

So we poked along back home, and I warn't feeling so brash as I was before, but kind of ornery, and humble, and to blame, somehow—though *I* hadn't done nothing. But that's always the way; it don't make no difference whether you do right or wrong, a person's conscience ain't got no sense, and just goes for him *anyway.* If I had a yaller dog that didn't know no more than a person's conscience does, I would pison him. It takes up more room than all the rest of a person's insides, and yet ain't no good, nohow. Tom Sawyer he says the same.

[225]The decorative feathered crests on military headgear.

CHAPTER XXXIV

We stopped talking, and got to thinking. By-and-by Tom says:

"Looky here, Huck, what fools we are, to not think of it before! I bet I know where Jim is."

"No! Where?"

"In that hut down by the ash-hopper. Why, looky here. When we was at dinner, didn't you see a nigger man go in there with some vittles?"

"Yes."

"What did you think the vittles was for?"

"For a dog."

"So'd I. Well, it wasn't for a dog."

"Why?"

"Because part of it was watermelon."

"So it was—I noticed it. Well, it does beat all, that I never thought about a dog not eating watermelon. It shows how a body can see and don't see at the same time."

"Well, the nigger unlocked the padlock when he went in, and he locked it again when he come out. He fetched uncle a key, about the time we got up from table—same key, I bet. Watermelon shows man, lock shows prisoner; and it ain't likely there's two prisoners on such a little plantation, and where the people's all so kind and good. Jim's the prisoner. All right—I'm glad we found it out detective fashion; I wouldn't give shucks for any other way. Now you work your mind and study out a plan to steal Jim, and I will study out one, too; and we'll take the one we like the best."

What a head for just a boy to have! If I had Tom Sawyer's head, I wouldn't trade it off to be a duke, nor mate of a steamboat, nor clown in a circus, nor nothing I can think of. I went to thinking out a plan, but only just to be doing something; I knowed very well where the right plan was going to come from. Pretty soon, Tom says:

"Ready?"

"Yes," I says.

"All right—bring it out."

"My plan is this," I says. "We can easy find out if it's Jim in there. Then get up my canoe to-morrow night, and fetch my raft over from the island. Then the first dark night that comes, steal the key out of the old man's britches, after he goes to bed, and shove off down the river on the raft, with Jim, hiding day-times and running nights, the way me and Jim used to do before. Wouldn't that plan work?"

"*Work?* Why cert'nly, it would work, like rats a fighting. But it's too blame' simple; there ain't nothing *to* it. What's the good of a plan that ain't no more trouble than that? It's as mild as goosemilk. Why, Huck, it wouldn't make no more talk than breaking into a soap factory."

I never said nothing, because I warn't expecting nothing different; but I knowed mighty well that whenever he got *his* plan ready it wouldn't have none of them objections to it.

And it didn't. He told me what it was, and I see in a minute it was worth fifteen of mine, for style, and would make Jim just as free a man as mine would, and maybe get us all killed besides. So I was satisfied, and said we would waltz in on it. I needn't tell what it was, here, because I knowed it wouldn't stay the way it was. I knowed he would be changing it around, every which way, as we went along, and heaving in new bullinesses wherever he got a chance. And that is what he done.

Well, one thing was dead sure; and that was, that Tom Sawyer was in earnest and was actuly going to help steal that nigger out of slavery. That was the thing that was too many for me. Here was a boy that was respectable, and well brung up; and had a character to lose; and folks at home that had characters; and he was bright and not leather-headed; and knowing and not ignorant; and not mean but kind; and yet here he was, without any more pride, or rightness or feeling, than to stoop to this business, and make himself a shame and his family a shame, before everybody. I *couldn't* understand it no way at all. It was outrageous, and I knowed I ought to just up and tell him so; and so be his true friend, and let him quit the thing right where he was, and save himself. And I *did* start to tell him; but he shut me up, and says:

"Don't you reckon I know what I'm about? Don't I generly know what I'm about?"

"Yes."

"Didn't I *say* I was going to help steal the nigger?"

"Yes."

"*Well* then."

That's all he said, and that's all I said. It warn't no use to say any more; because when he said he'd do a thing, he always done it. But *I* couldn't make out how he was willing to go into this thing; so I just let it go, and never bothered no more about it. If he was bound to have it so, *I* couldn't help it.

When we got home, the house was all dark and still; so we went on down to the hut by the ash-hopper, for to examine it. We went through the yard, so as to see what the hounds would do. They knowed us, and didn't make no more noise than country dogs is always doing when anything comes by in the night. When we got to the cabin, we took a look at the front and the two sides; and on the side I warn't acquainted with—which was the north side—we found a square window-hole, up tolerable high, with just one stout board nailed across it. I says:

"Here's the ticket. This hole's big enough for Jim to get through, if we wrench off the board."

Tom says:

"It's as simple as tit-tat-toe, three-in-a-row, and as easy as playing hooky. I should *hope* we can find a way that's a little more complicated than *that,* Huck Finn."

"Well, then," I says, "how'll it do to saw him out, the way I done before I was murdered, that time?"

"That's more *like,*" he says. "It's real mysterious, and troublesome, and good," he says; "but I bet we can find a way that's twice as long. There ain't no hurry; le's keep on looking around."

Betwixt the hut and the fence, on the back side, was a lean-to, that joined the hut at the eaves, and was made out of plank. It was as long as the hut, but narrow—only about six foot wide. The door to it was at the south end, and was padlocked. Tom he went to the soap kettle, and searched around and fetched back the iron thing they lift the lid with; so he took it and prized out one of the staples. The chain fell down, and we opened the door and went in, and shut it, and struck a match, and see the shed was only built against the cabin and hadn't no connection with it; and there warn't no floor to the shed, nor nothing in it but some old rusty played-out hoes, and spades, and picks, and a crippled plow. The match went out, and so did we, and shoved in the staple again, and the door was locked as good as ever. Tom was joyful. He says:

"Now we're all right. We'll *dig* him out. It'll take about a week!"

Then we started for the house, and I went in the back door—you only have to pull a buckskin latch-string, they don't fasten the doors—but that warn't romantical enough for Tom Sawyer: no way would do him but he must climb up the lightning-rod. But after he got up half-way about three times, and missed fire and fell every time, and the last time most busted his brains out, he thought he'd got to give it up; but after he was rested, he allowed he would give her one more turn for luck, and this time he made the trip.

In the morning we was up at break of day, and down to the nigger cabins to pet the dogs and make friends with the nigger that fed Jim—if it *was* Jim that was being fed. The niggers was just getting through breakfast and starting for the fields; and Jim's nigger was piling up a tin pan with bread and meat and things; and whilst the others was leaving, the key come from the house.

This nigger had a good-natured, chuckle-headed face, and his wool was all tied up in little bunches with thread. That was to keep witches off. He said the witches was pestering him awful, these nights, and making him see all kinds of strange things, and hear all kinds of strange words and noises, and he didn't believe he was ever witched so long, before, in his life. He got so worked up, and got to running on so about his troubles, he forgot all about what he'd been agoing to do. So Tom says:

"What's the vittles for? Going to feed the dogs?"

The nigger kind of smiled around graduly over his face, like when you heave a brickbat[226] in a mud puddle, and he says:

"Yes, Mars Sid, *a* dog. Cur'us dog, too. Does you want to go en look at 'im?"

"Yes."

I hunched Tom, and whispers:

"You going, right here in the day-break? *That* warn't the plan."

"No, it warn't—but it's the plan *now.*"

So, drat him, we went along, but I didn't like it much. When we got in, we couldn't hardly see anything, it was so dark; but Jim was there, sure enough, and could see us; and he sings out:

"Why, *Huck!* En good *lan'!* ain' dat Misto Tom?"

I just knowed how it would be; I just expected it. *I* didn't know nothing to do; and if I had, I couldn't a done it; because that nigger busted in and says:

"Why, de gracious sakes! do he know you genlmen?"

We could see pretty well, now. Tom he looked at the nigger, steady and kind of wondering, and says:

"Does *who* know us?"

"Why, dish-yer runaway nigger."

"I don't reckon he does; but what put that into your head?"

"What *put* it dar? Didn' he jis' dis minute sing out like he knowed you?"

Tom says, in a puzzle-up kind of way:

"Well, that's mighty curious. *Who* sung out? *When* did he sing out? *What* did he sing out?" And turns to me, perfectly ca'm, and says, "Did *you* hear anybody sing out?"

[226]A piece of brick.

Of course there warn't nothing to be said but the one thing; so I says:

"No; *I* ain't heard nobody say nothing."

Then he turns to Jim, and looks him over like he never see him before; and says:

"Did you sing out?"

"No, sah," says Jim; "*I* hain't said nothing, sah."

"Not a word?"

"No, sah, I hain't said a word."

"Did you ever see us before?"

"No, sah; not as *I* knows on."

So Tom turns to the nigger, which was looking wild and distressed, and says, kind of severe:

"What do you reckon's the matter with you, anyway? What made you think somebody sung out?"

"Oh, it's de dad-blame' witches, sah, en I wisht I was dead, I do. Dey's awluz at it, sah, en dey do mos' kill me, dey sk'yers me so. Please to don't tell nobody 'bout it sah, er ole Mars Silas he'll scole me; 'kase he say dey *ain't* no witches. I jis' wish to goodness he was heah now—*den* what would he say! I jis' bet he couldn't fine no way to git aroun' it *dis* time. But it's awluz jis' so; people dat's *sot,* stays sot; dey won't look into nothn' en fine it out f'r deyselves, en when *you* fine it out en tell um 'bout it, dey doan' b'lieve you."

Tom give him a dime, and said we wouldn't tell nobody; and told him to buy some more thread to tie up his wool with; and then looks at Jim, and says:

"I wonder if Uncle Silas is going to hang this nigger. If I was to catch a nigger that was ungrateful enough to run away, *I* wouldn't give him up, I'd hang him:" And whilst the nigger stepped to the door to look at the dime and bite it to see if it was good, he whispers to Jim, and says:

"Don't ever let on to know us. And if you hear any digging going on nights, it's us: we're going to set you free."

Jim only had time to grab us by the hand and squeeze it, then the nigger come back, and we said we'd come again some time if the nigger wanted us to; and he said he would, more particular if it was dark, because the witches went for him mostly in the dark, and it was good to have folks around then.

CHAPTER XXXV

It would be most an hour yet till breakfast, so we left, and struck down into the wood; because Tom said we got to have *some* light to see how to dig by, and a lantern makes too much, and might get us into trouble; what we must have was a lot of them rotten chunks that's called fox-fire[227] and just makes a soft kind of a glow when you lay them in a dark place. We fetched an armful and hid it in the weeds, and set down to rest, and Tom says, kind of dissatisfied:

"Blame it, this whole thing is just as easy and awkard as it can be. And so it makes it so rotten difficult to get up a difficult plan. There ain't no watchman to be drugged—now there *ought* to be a watchman. There ain't even a dog to give a sleeping-mixture to. And there's Jim chained by one leg, with a ten-foot

[227]Luminous glow of fungi on rotting wood.

chain, to the leg of his bed: why, all you got to do is to lift up the bedstead and slip off the chain. And Uncle Silas he trusts everybody; sends the key to the punkin-headed nigger, and don't send nobody to watch the nigger. Jim could a got out of that window hole before this, only there wouldn't be no use trying to travel with a ten-foot chain on his leg. Why, drat it, Huck, it's the stupidest arrangement I ever see. You got to invent *all* the difficulties. Well, we can't help it, we got to do the best we can with the materials we've got. Anyhow, there's one thing—there's more honor in getting him out through a lot of difficulties and dangers, where there warn't one of them furnished to you by the people who it was their duty to furnish them, and you had to contrive them all out of your own head. Now look at just that one thing of the lantern. When you come down to the cold facts, we simply got to *let on* that a lantern's resky. Why, we could work with a torchlight procession if we wanted to, I believe. Now, whilst I think of it, we got to hunt up something to make a saw out of, the first chance we get."

"What do we want of a saw?"

"What do we *want* of it? Hain't we got to saw the leg of Jim's bed off, so as to get the chain loose?"

"Why, you just said a body cold lift up the bedstead and slip the chain off."

"Well, if that ain't just like you, Huck Finn. You *can* get up the infant-schooliest[228] ways of going at a thing. Why, hain't you ever read any books at all?—Baron Trenck, nor Casanova, nor Benvenuto Chelleeny, nor Henri IV.,[229] nor none of them heroes? Whoever heard of getting a prisoner loose in such an old-maidy way as that? No; the way all the best authorities does, is to saw the bed-leg in two, and leave it just so, and swallow the sawdust, so it can't be found, and put some dirt and grease around the sawed place so the very keenest seneskal[230] can't see no sign of it's being sawed, and thinks the bed-leg is perfectly sound. Then, the night you're ready, fetch the leg a kick, down she goes; slip off your chain, and there you are. Nothing to do but hitch your rope-ladder to the battlements, shin down it, break your leg in the moat—because a rope-ladder is nineteen foot too short, you know—and there's your horses and your trusty vassles, and they scoop you up and fling you across a saddle and away you go, to your native Langudoc, or Navarre,[231] or wherever it is. It's gaudy, Huck. I wish there was a moat to this cabin. If we get time, the night of the escape, we'll dig one."

I says:

"What do we want of a moat, when we're going to snake him out from under the cabin?"

But he never heard me. He had forgot me and everything else. He had his chin in his hand, thinking. Pretty soon, he sighs, and shakes his head; then sighs again, and says:

"No, it wouldn't do—there ain't necessity enough for it."

"For what?" I says.

"Why, to saw Jim's leg off," he says.

[228]"Nursery-schooliest."

[229]Baron Friedrich von Trenck (1726–1794), Giovanni Giacomo Casanova (1725–1798), Benvenuto Cellini (1500–1571), Henry IV, King of France (1589–1610). All were adventurers who attempted daring escapes.

[230]Seneschal, an official in a medieval household, a steward.

[231]Languedoc, a medieval province of southern France. Navarre, an ancient kingdom in the Pyrenees between France and Spain.

"Good land!" I says, "why, there ain't *no* necessity for it. And what would you want to saw his leg off for, anyway?"

"Well, some of the best authorities has done it. They couldn't get the chain off, so they just cut their hand off, and shoved. And a leg would be better still. But we got to let that go. There ain't necessity enough in this case; and besides, Jim's a nigger and wouldn't understand the reasons for it, and how it's the custom in Europe; so we'll let it go. But there's one thing—he can have a rope-ladder; we can tear up our sheets and make him a rope-ladder easy enough. And we can send it to him in a pie; it's mostly done that way. And I've et worse pies."

"Why, Tom Sawyer, how you talk," I says; "Jim ain't got no use for a rope-ladder."

"He *has* got use for it. How *you* talk, you better say; you don't know nothing about it. He's *got* to have a rope-ladder; they all do."

"What in the nation can he *do* with it?"

"*Do* with it? He can hide it in his bed, can't he? That's what they all do; and *he's* got to, too. Huck, you don't ever seem to want to do anything that's regular; you want to be starting something fresh all the time. Spose he *don't* do nothing with it? ain't it there in his bed, for a clew, after he's gone? and don't you reckon they'll want clews? Of course they will. And you wouldn't leave them any? That would be a *pretty* howdy-do, *wouldn't* it! I never heard of such a thing."

"Well," I says, "if it's in the regulations, and he's got to have it, all right, let him have it; because I don't wish to go back on no regulations; but there's one thing, Tom Sawyer—if we go to tearing up our sheets to make Jim a rope-ladder, we're going to get into trouble with Aunt Sally, just as sure as you're born. Now, the way I look at it, a hickry-bark ladder don't cost nothing, and don't waste nothing, and is just as good to load up a pie with, and hide in a straw tick, as any rag ladder you can start; and as for Jim, he ain't had no experience, and so *he* don't care what kind of a——"

"Oh, shucks, Huck Finn, if I was as ignorant as you, I'd keep still—that's what *I'd* do. Who ever heard of a state prisoner escaping by a hickry-bark ladder? Why, it's perfectly ridiculous."

"Well, all right, Tom, fix it your own way; but if you'll take my advice, you'll let me borrow a sheet off of the clothes-line."

He said that would do. And that give him another idea, and he says:

"Borrow a shirt, too."

"What do we want of a shirt, Tom?"

"Want it for Jim to keep a journal on."

"Journal your granny—*Jim* can't write."

"Spose he *can't* write—he can make marks on the shirt, can't he, if we make him a pen out of an old pewter spoon or a piece of an old iron barrel-hoop?"

"Why, Tom, we can pull a feather out of a goose and make him a better one; and quicker, too."

"*Prisoners* don't have geese running around the donjon-keep to pull pens out of, you muggins. They *always* make their pens out of the hardest, toughest, troublesome piece of old brass candlestick or something like that they can get their hands on; and it takes them weeks and weeks, and months and months to file it out, too, because they've got to do it by rubbing it on the wall. *They* wouldn't use a goose-quill if they had it. It ain't regular."

"Well, then, what'll we make him the ink out of?"

"Many makes it out of iron-rust and tears; but that's the common sort and women; the best authorities uses their own blood. Jim can do that; and when he wants to send any little common ordinary mysterious message to let the world know where he's captivated, he can write it on the bottom of a tin plate with a fork and throw it out of the window. The Iron Mask[232] always done that, and it's a blame' good way, too."

"Jim ain't got no tin plates. They feed him in a pan."

"That ain't anything; we can get him some."

"Can't nobody *read* his plates."

"That ain't got nothing to *do* with it, Huck Finn. All *he's* got to do is write on the plate and throw it out. You don't *have* to be able to read it. Why, half the time you can't read anything a prisoner writes on a tin plate, or anywhere else."

"Well, then what's the sense in wasting the plates?"

"Why, blame it all, it ain't the *prisoner's* plates."

"But it's *somebody's* plates, ain't it?"

"Well, spos'n it is? What does the *prisoner* care whose——"

He broke off there, because we heard the breakfast-horn blowing. So we cleared out for the house.

Along during the morning I borrowed a sheet and a white shirt off of the clothes-line; and I found an old sack and put them in it, and we went down and got the fox-fire, and put that in too. I called it borrowing, because that was what pap always called it; but Tom said it warn't borrowing, it was stealing. He said we was representing prisoners; and prisoners don't care how they get a thing so they get it, and nobody don't blame them for it, either. It ain't no crime in a prisoner to steal the thing he needs to get away with, Tom said; it's his right; and so, as long as we was representing a prisoner, we had a perfect right to steal anything on this place we had the least use for, to get ourselves out of prison with. He said if we warn't prisoners it would be a very different thing, and nobody but a mean ornery person would steal when he warn't a prisoner. So we allowed we would steal everything there was that come handy. And yet he made a mighty fuss, one day, after that, when I stole a watermelon out of the nigger patch[233] and eat it; and he made me go and give the niggers a dime, without telling them what it was for. Tom said that what he meant was, we could steal anything we *needed*. Well, I says, I needed the watermelon. But he said I didn't need it to get out of prison with, there's where the difference was. He said if I'd a wanted it to hide a knife in, and smuggle it to Jim to kill the seneskal with, it would a been all right. So I let it go at that, though I couldn't see no advantage in my representing a prisoner, if I got to set down and chaw over a lot of gold-leaf[234] distinctions like that, every time I see a chance to hog a watermelon.

Well, as I was saying, we waited that morning till everybody was settled down to business, and nobody in sight around the yard; then Tom he carried the sack into the lean-to whilst I stood off a piece to keep watch. By-and-by he come out, and we went and set down on the wood-pile, to talk. He says:

"Everything's all right, now, except tools; and that's easy fixed."

"Tools?" I says.

"Yes."

"Tools for what?"

[232]The legendary masked prisoner in the Bastille who was a character in the romantic novel *Le Vicomte de Bragelonne* (1848–1850) by Alexandre Dumas (1802–1870). Portions of the novel were translated into English in the 1850s.

[233]Slaves' garden. [234]Thin, superficial.

"Why, to dig with. We ain't agoing to *gnaw* him out, are we?"

"Ain't them old crippled picks and things in there good enough to dig a nigger out with?" I says.

He turns on me looking pitying enough to make a body cry, and says:

"Huck Finn, did you *ever* hear of a prisoner having picks and shovels, and all the modern conveniences in his wardrobe to dig himself out with? Now I want to ask you—if you got any reasonableness in you at all—what kind of a show would *that* give him to be a hero? Why, they might as well lend him the key, and done with it. Picks and shovels—why they wouldn't furnish 'em to a king."

"Well, then," I says, "if we don't want the picks and shovels, what do we want?"

"A couple of case-knives."[235]

"To dig the foundations out from under that cabin with?"

"Yes."

"Confound it, it's foolish, Tom."

"It didn't make no difference how foolish it is, it's the *right* way—and it's the regular way. And there ain't no *other* way, that ever *I* heard of, and I've read all the books that gives any information about these things. They always dig out with a case-knife—and not through dirt, mind you; generly it's through solid rock. And it takes them weeks and weeks and weeks, and for ever and ever. Why, look at one of them prisoners in the bottom dungeon of the Castle Deef,[236] in the harbor of Marseilles, that dug himself out that way; how long was *he* at it, you reckon?"

"I don't know."

"Well, guess."

"I don't know. A month and a half?"

"*Thirty-seven year*—and he come out in China. *That's* the kind. I wish the bottom of *this* fortress was solid rock."

"*Jim* don't know nobody in China."

"What's *that* got to do with it? Neither did that other fellow. But you're always a-wandering off on a side issue. Why can't you stick to the main point?"

"All right—*I* don't care where he comes out, so he *comes* out; and Jim don't, either, I reckon. But there's one thing, anyway—Jim's too old to be dug out with a case-knife. He won't last."

"Yes he will *last,* too. You don't reckon it's going to take thirty-seven years to dig out through a *dirt* foundation, do you?"

"How long will it take, Tom?"

"Well, we can't resk being as long as we ought to, because it mayn't take very long for Uncle Silas to hear from down there by New Orleans. He'll hear Jim ain't from there. Then his next move will be to advertise Jim, or something like that. So we can't resk being as long digging him out as we ought to. By rights I reckon we ought to be a couple of years; but we can't. Things being so uncertain, what I recommend is this: that we really dig right in, as quick as we can; and after that, we can *let on,* to ourselves, that we was at it thirty-seven years. Then we can snatch him out and rush him away the first time there's an alarm. Yes, I reckon that'll be the best way."

"Now, there's *sense* in that," I says. "Letting on don't cost nothing; letting on ain't no trouble; and if it's any object, I don't mind letting on we was at it a

[235]Kitchen knives, kept in a case.

[236]The Chateau d'If, a prison in *The Count of Monte Cristo* (1845) by Alexandre Dumas.

hundred and fifty year. It wouldn't strain me none, after I got my hand in. So I'll mosey along now, and smouch[237] a couple of case-knives."

"Smouch three," he says; "we want one to make a saw out of."

"Tom, if it ain't unregular and irreligious to sejest it," I says, "there's an old rusty saw-blade around yonder sticking under the weatherboarding behind the smoke-house."

He looked kind of weary and discouraged-like, and says:

"It ain't no use to try to learn you nothing, Huck. Run along and smouch the knives—three of them." So I done it.

CHAPTER XXXVI

As soon as we reckoned everybody was asleep, that night, we went down the lightning-rod, and shut ourselves up in the lean-to, and got out our pile of fox-fire, and went to work. We cleared everything out of the way, about four or five foot along the middle of the bottom log. Tom said he was right behind Jim's bed now, and we'd dig in under it, and when we got through there couldn't nobody in the cabin ever know there was any hole there, because Jim's counter-pin[238] hung down most to the ground, and you'd have to raise it up and look under to see the hole. So we dug and dug, with the case-knives, till most midnight; and then we was dog-tired, and our hands was blistered, and yet you couldn't see we'd done anything, hardly. At last I says:

"This ain't no thirty-seven year job, this is a thirty-eight year job, Tom Sawyer."

He never said nothing. But he sighed, and pretty soon he stopped digging, and then for a good little while I knowed he was thinking. Then he says:

"It ain't no use, Huck, it ain't agoing to work. If we was prisoners it would, because then we'd have as many years as we wanted, and no hurry; and we wouldn't get but a few minutes to dig, every day, while they was changing watches, and so our hands wouldn't get blistered, and we could keep it up right along, year in and year out, and do it right; and the way it ought to be done. But *we* can't fool along, we got to rush; we ain't got no time to spare. If we was to put in another night this way, we'd have to knock off for a week to let our hands get well—couldn't touch a case-knife with them sooner."

"Well, then, what we going to do, Tom?"

"I'll tell you. It ain't right, and it ain't moral, and I wouldn't like it to get out—but there ain't only just the one way; we got to dig him out with the picks, and *let on* it's case-knives."

"Now you're talking!" I says; "your head gets leveler and leveler all the time, Tom Sawyer," I says. "Picks is the thing, moral or no moral; and as for me, I don't care shucks for the morality of it, nohow. When I start in to steal a nigger, or a watermelon, or a Sunday-school book, I ain't no ways particular how it's done so it's done. What I want is my nigger; or what I want is my watermelon; or what I want is my Sunday-school book; and if a pick's the handiest thing, that's the thing I'm agoing to dig that nigger or that watermelon or that Sunday-school book out with; and I don't give a dead rat what the authorities thinks about it nuther."

[237]Steal. [238]Counterpane, bedspread.

"Well," he says, "there's excuse for picks and letting-on in a case like this; if it warn't so, I wouldn't approve of it, nor I wouldn't stand by and see the rules broke—because right is right, and wrong is wrong, and a body ain't got no business doing wrong when he ain't ignorant and knows better. It might answer for *you* to dig Jim out with a pick, *without* any letting-on, because you don't know no better; but it wouldn't for me, because I do know better. Gimme a case-knife."

He had his own by him, but I handed him mine. He flung it down, and says: "Gimme a *case-knife*."

I didn't know just what to do—but then I thought. I scratched around amongst the old tools, and got a pick-ax and give it to him, and he took it and went to work, and never said a word.

He was always just that particular. Full of principle.

So then I got a shovel, and then we picked and shoveled, turn about, and made the fur fly. We stuck to it about a half an hour, which was as long as we could stand up; but we had a good deal of a hole to show for it. When I got up stairs, I looked out at the window and see Tom doing his level best with the lightning-rod, but he couldn't come it, his hands was so sore. At last he says:

"It ain't no use, it can't be done. What you reckon I better do? Can't you think up no way?"

"Yes," I says, "but I reckon it ain't regular. Come up the stairs, and let on it's a lightning-rod."

So he done it.

Next day Tom stole a pewter spoon and a brass candlestick in the house, for to make some pens for Jim out of, and six tallow candles; and I hung around the nigger cabins, and laid for a chance, and stole three tin plates. Tom said it wasn't enough; but I said nobody wouldn't ever see the plates that Jim throwed out, because they'd fall in the dog-fennel and jimpson weeds under the window-hole—then we could tote them back and he could use them over again. So Tom was satisfied. Then he says:

"Now, the thing to study out is, how to get the things to Jim."

"Take them in through the hole," I says, "when we get it done."

He only just looked scornful, and said something about nobody ever heard of such an idiotic idea, and then he went to studying. By-and-by he said he had ciphered out two or three ways, but there warn't no need to decide on any of them yet. Said we'd got to post Jim first.

That night we went down the lightning-rod a little after ten, and took one of the candles along, and listened under the window-hole, and heard Jim snoring; so we pitched it in, and it didn't wake him. Then we whirled in with the pick and shovel, and in about two hours and a half the job was done. We crept in under Jim's bed and into the cabin, and pawed around and found the candle and lit it, and stood over Jim a while, and found him looking hearty and healthy, and then we woke him up gentle and gradual. He was so glad to see us he most cried; and called us honey, and all the pet names he could think of; and was for having us hunt up a cold chisel to cut the chain off of his leg with, right away, and clearing out without losing any time. But Tom he showed him how unregular it would be, and set down and told him all about our plans, and how we could alter them in a minute any time there was an alarm; and not to be the least afraid, because we would see he got away, *sure.* So Jim he said it was all right, and we set there and talked over old times a while, and then Tom asked a lot of questions, and when Jim told him Uncle Silas come in every day or two to pray with him, and Aunt Sally come in to see if he was comfortable and had plenty to eat, and both of them was kind as they could be, Tom says:

"*Now* I know how to fix it. We'll send you some things by them."

I said, "Don't do nothing of the kind; it's one of the most jackass ideas I ever struck;" but he never paid no attention to me; went right on. It was his way when he'd got his plans set.

So he told Jim how we'd have to smuggle in the rope-ladder pie, and other large things, by Nat, the nigger that fed him, and he must be on the lookout, and not be surprised, and not let Nat see him open them; and we would put small things in uncle's coat pockets and he must steal them out; and we would tie things to aunt's apron strings or put them in her apron pocket, if we got a chance; and told him what they would be and what they was for. And told him how to keep a journal on the shirt with his blood, and all that. He told him everything. Jim he couldn't see no sense in the most of it, but he allowed we was white folks and knowed better than him; so he was satisfied, and said he would do it all just as Tom said.

Jim had plenty corn-cob pipes and tobacco; so we had a right down good sociable time; then we crawled out through the hole, and so home to bed, with hands that looked like they'd been chawed. Tom was in high spirits. He said it was the best fun he ever had in his life, and the most intellectural; and said if he could see his way to it we would keep it up all the rest of our lives and leave Jim to our children to get out; for he believed Jim would come to like it better and better the more he got used to it. He said that in that way it could be strung out to as much as eighty year, and would be the best time on record. And he said it would make us all celebrated that had a hand in it.

In the morning we went out to the wood-pile and chopped up the brass candlestick into handy sizes, and Tom put them and the pewter spoon in his pocket. Then we went to the nigger cabins, and while I got Nat's notice off, Tom shoved a piece of candlestick into the middle of a corn-pone that was in Jim's pan, and we went along with Nat to see how it would work, and it just worked noble; when Jim bit into it it most mashed all his teeth out; and there warn't ever anything could a worked better. Tom said so himself. Jim he never let on but what it was only just a piece of rock or something like that that's always getting into bread, you know; but after that he never bit into nothing but what he jabbed his fork into it three or four places, first.

And whilst we was a standing there in the dimmish light, here comes a couple of the hounds bulging in, from under Jim's bed; and they kept on piling in till there was eleven of them, and there warn't hardly room in there to get your breath. By jings, we forgot to fasten that lean-to door. The nigger Nat he only just hollered "witches!" once, and keeled over onto the floor amongst the dogs, and begun to groan like he was dying. Tom jerked the door open and flung out a slab of Jim's meat, and the dogs went for it, and in two seconds he was out himself and back again and shut the door, and I knowed he'd fixed the other door too. Then he went to work on the nigger, coaxing him and petting him, and asking him it he'd been imagining he saw something again. He raised up, and blinked his eyes around, and says:

"Mars Sid, you'll say I's a fool, but if I didn't b'lieve I see most a million dogs, er devils, er some'n, I wisht I may die right heah in dese tracks. I did, mos' sholy. Mars Sid, I *felt* um—I *felt* um, sah; dey was all over me. Dad fetch it, I jis' wisht I could get my han's on one er dem witches jis' wunst—on'y jis' wunst—it's all I'd ast. But mos'ly I wisht dey'd leme 'lone, I does."

Tom says:

"Well, I tell you what *I* think. What makes them come here just at this runaway nigger's breakfast-time? It's because they're hungry; that's the reason. You make them a witch pie; that's the thing for *you* to do."

"But my lan', Mars Sid, how's *I* gwyne to make 'm a witch pie? I doan' know how to make it. I hain't ever hearn er sich a thing b'fo'."

"Well, then, I'll have to make it myself."

"Will you do it, honey?—will you? I'll wusshup de groun' und' yo' foot, I will!"

"All right, I'll do it, seeing it's you, and you've been good to us and showed us the runaway nigger. But you got to be mighty careful. When we come around, you turn your back; and then whatever we've put in the pan, don't you let on you see it at all. And don't you look, when Jim unloads the pan—something might happen, I don't know what. And above all, don't you *handle* the witch-things."

"*Hannel* 'm Mars Sid? What *is* you talkin' 'bout? I wouldn't lay de weight er my fingers on um, not f'r ten hund'd thous'n' billion dollars, I wouldn't."

CHAPTER XXXVII

That was all fixed. So then we went away and went to the rubbage-pile in the back yard where they keep the old boots, and rags, and pieces of bottles, and wore-out tin things, and all such truck, and scratched around and found an old tin washpan and stopped up the holes as well as we could, to bake the pie in, and took it down cellar and stole it full of flour, and started for breakfast and found a couple of shingle-nails that Tom said would be handy for a prisoner to scrabble his name and sorrows on the dungeon walls with, and dropped one of them in Aunt Sally's apron pocket which was hanging on a chair, and t'other we stuck in the band of Uncle Silas's hat, which was on the bureau, because we heard the children say their pa and ma was going to the runaway nigger's house this morning, and then went to breakfast, and Tom dropped the pewter spoon in Uncle Silas's coat pocket, and Aunt Sally wasn't come yet, so we had to wait a little while.

And when she come she was hot, and red, and cross, and couldn't hardly wait for the blessing; and then she went to sluicing out coffee with one hand and cracking the handiest child's head with her thimble with the other, and says:

"I've hunted high, and I've hunted low, and it does beat all, what *has* become of your other shirt."

My heart fell down amongst my lungs and livers and things, and a hard piece of corn-crust started down my throat after it and got met on the road with a cough and was shot across the table and took one of the children in the eye and curled him up like a fishing-worm, and let a cry out of him the size of a war-whoop, and Tom he turned kinder blue around the gills, and it all amounted to a considerable state of things for about a quarter of a minute or as much as that, and I would a sold out for half price if there was a bidder. But after that we was all right again—it was the sudden surprise of it that knocked us so kind of cold. Uncle Silas he says:

"It's most uncommon curious, I can't understand it. I know perfectly well I took it *off,* because——"

"Because you hain't got but one *on.* Just *listen* at the man! *I* know you took it off, and know it by a better way than your wool gethering memory, too, because it was on the clo'es-line yesterday—I see it there myself. But it's gone—that's the long and the short of it, and you'll just have to change to a red flann'l one till I can get time to make a new one. And it'll be the third I've made in two years; it just keep a body on the jump to keep you in shirts; and whatever you do manage to *do* with 'm all, is more'n *I* can make out. A body'd think you *would* learn to take some sort of care of 'em, at your time of life."

"I know it, Sally, and I do try all I can. But it oughtn't to be altogether my fault, because you know I don't see them nor have nothing to do with them except when they're on me; and I don't believe I've ever lost one of them *off* of me."

"Well, it ain't *your* fault if you haven't, Silas—you'd a done it if you could, I reckon. And the shirt ain't all that's gone, nuther. Ther's a spoon gone; and *that* ain't all. There was ten, and now ther's only nine. The calf got the shirt I reckon, but the calf never took the spoon, *that's* certain."

"Why, what else is gone, Sally?"

"Ther's six *candles* gone—that's what. The rats could a got the candles, and I reckon they did; I wonder they don't walk off with the whole place, the way you're always going to stop their holes and don't do it; and if they warn't fools they'd sleep in your hair, Silas—*you'd* never find it out; but you can't lay the *spoon* on the rats, and that I *know.*"

"Well, Sally, I'm in fault, and I acknowledge it; I've been remiss; but I won't let to-morrow go by without stopping up them holes."

"Oh, I wouldn't hurry, next year'll do. Matilda Angelina Araminta *Phelps!*"

Whack comes the thimble, and the child snatches her claws out of the sugar-bowl without fooling around any. Just then, the nigger woman steps onto the passage, and says:

"Missus, dey's a sheet gone."

"A *sheet* gone! Well, for the land's sake!"

"I'll stop up them holes *to-day,*" says Uncle Silas, looking sorrowful.

"Oh, *do* shet up!—spose the rats took the *sheet? Where's* it gone, Lize?"

"Clah to goodness I hain't no notion, Miss Sally. She wuz on de clo's-line yistiddy, but she doen gone; she ain' dah no mo', now."

"I reckon the world *is* coming to an end. I *never* see the beat of it, in all my born days. A shirt, and a sheet, and a spoon, and six can——"

"Missus," comes a young yaller wench, "dey's a brass cannelstick miss'n."

"Cler out from here, you hussy, er I'll take a skillet to ye!"

Well, she was just a biling. I begun to lay for a chance; I reckoned I would sneak out and go for the woods till the weather moderated. She kept a raging right along, running her insurrection all by herself, and everybody else mighty meek and quiet; and at last Uncle Silas, looking kind of foolish, fishes up that spoon out of his pocket. She stopped, with her mouth open and her hands up; and as for me, I wished I was in Jeruslem or somewheres. But not long; because she says:

"It's *just* as I expected. So you had it in your pocket all the time; and like as not you've got the other things there, too. How'd it get there?"

"I reely don't know, Sally," he says, kind of apologizing, "or you know I would tell. I was a-studying over my text in Acts Seventeen,[239] before breakfast, and I reckon it put it in there not noticing, meaning to put my Testament in, and it must be so, because my Testament ain't in, but I'll go and see, and if the Testament is where I had it, I'll know I didn't put it in, and that will show that I laid the Testament down and took up the spoon, and——"

"Oh, for the land's sake! Give a body a rest! Go 'long now, the hole kit and biling of ye; and don't come nigh me again till I've got back my peace of mind."

I'd a heard her, if she'd a said it to herself, let alone speaking it out; and I'd a got up and obeyed her, if I'd a been dead. As we was passing through the setting-room, the old man he took up his hat, and the shingle-nail fell out on the floor, and he just merely picked it up and laid it on the mantel-shelf, and never said nothing, and went out. Tom see him do it, and remembered about the spoon, and says:

"Well, it ain't no use to send things by *him* no more, he ain't reliable." Then he says: "But he done us a good turn with the spoon, anyway, without knowing it, and so we'll go and do him one without *him* knowing it—stop up his rat-holes."

There was a noble good lot of them, down cellar, and it took us a whole hour, but we done the job tight and good, and ship-shape. Then we heard steps on the stairs, and blowed out our light, and hid; and here comes the old man, with a candle in one hand and a bundle of stuff in t'other, looking as absent-minded as year before last. He went a mooning around, first to one rat-hole and then another, till he'd been to them all. Then he stood about five minutes, picking tallow-drip off of his candle and thinking. Then he turns off slow and dreamy towards the stairs, saying:

"Well, for the life of me I can't remember when I done it. I could show her now that I warn't to blame on account of the rats. But never mind—let it go. I reckon it wouldn't do no good."

And so he went on a mumbling up stairs, and then we left. He was a mighty nice old man. And always is.

Tom was a good deal bothered about what to do for a spoon, but he said we'd got to have it; so he took a think. When he had ciphered it out, he told me how we was to do; then we went and waited around the spoon-basket till we see Aunt Sally coming, and then Tom went to counting the spoons and laying them out to one side, and I slid one of them up my sleeve, and Tom says:

"Why, Aunt Sally, there ain't but nine spoons, *yet*."

She says:

"Go 'long to your play, and don't bother me. I know better, I counted 'm myself."

"Well, I've counted them twice, Aunty, and *I* can't make but nine."

She looked out of all patience, but of course she come to count—anybody would.

"I declare to gracious ther' *ain't* but nine!" she says. "Why, what in the world—plague *take* the things, I'll count 'm again."

So I slipped back the one I had, and when she got done counting, she says:

[239]Acts 17, in the New Testament, which describes the experiences of the biblical Silas.

"Hang the troublesome rubbage, ther's *ten,* now!" and she looked huffy and bothered both. But Tom says:

"Why, Aunty, *I* don't think there's ten."

"You numskull, didn't you see me *count* im?"

"I know, but——"

"Well, I'll count 'm *again.*"

So I smouched one, and they come out nine same as the other time. Well, she *was* in a tearing way—just a trembling all over, she was so mad. But she counted and counted, till she got that addled she'd start to count-in the *basket* for a spoon, sometimes; and so, three times they come out right, and three times they come out wrong. Then she grabbed up the basket and slammed it across the house and knocked the cat galley-west;[240] and she said cle'r out and let her have some peace, and if we come bothering around her again betwixt that and dinner, she'd skin us. So we had the odd spoon; and dropped it in her apron pocket whilst she was a giving us our sailing-orders, and Jim got it all right, along with her shingle-nail, before noon. We was very well satisfied with this business, and Tom allowed it was worth twice the trouble it took, because he said *now* she couldn't even count them spoons twice alike again to save her life; and wouldn't believe she'd counted them right, if she *did;* and said that after she'd about counted her head off, for the next three days, he judged she'd give it up and offer to kill anybody that wanted her to ever count them any more.

So we put the sheet back on the line, that night, and stole one out of her closet; and kept on putting it back and stealing it again, for a couple of days, till she didn't know how many sheets she had, any more, and said she didn't *care,* and warn't agoing to bullyrag[241] the rest of her soul out about it, and wouldn't count them again not to save her life, she druther die first.

So we was all right now, as to the shirt and the sheet and the spoon and the candles, by the help of the calf and the rats and the mixed-up counting; and as to the candlestick, it warn't no consequence, it would blow over by-and-by.

But that pie was a job; we had no end of trouble with that pie. We fixed it up away down in the woods, and cooked it there; and we got it done at last, and very satisfactory, too; but not all in one day; and we had to use up three washpans full of flour, before we got through, and we got burnt pretty much all over, in places, and eyes put out with the smoke; because, you see, we didn't want nothing but a crust, and we couldn't prop it up right, and she would always cave in. But of course we thought of the right way at last; which was to cook the ladder, too, in the pie. So then we laid in with Jim, the second night, and tore up the sheet all in little strings, and twisted them together, and long before daylight we had a lovely rope, that you could a hung a person with. We let on it took nine months to make it.

And in the forenoon we took it down to the woods, but it wouldn't go in the pie. Being made of a whole sheet, that way, there was rope enough for forty pies, if we'd a wanted them, and plenty left over for soup, or sausage, or anything you choose. We could a had a whole dinner.

But we didn't need it. All we needed was just enough for the pie, and so we throwed the rest away. We didn't cook none of the pies in the washpan, afraid

[240]For a loop. [241]Mistreat, punish.

the solder would melt; but Uncle Silas he had a noble brass warmingpan[242] which he thought considerable of, because it belonged to one of his ancesters with a long wooden handle that come over from England with William the Conqueror in the *Mayflower*[243] or one of them early ships and was hid away up garret with a lot of other old pots and things that was valuable, not on account of being any account because they warn't, but on account of them being relicts, you know, and we snaked her out, private, and took her down there, but she failed on the first pies, because we didn't know how, but she come up smiling on the last one. We took and lined her with dough, and set her in the coals, and loaded her up with rag-rope, and put on a dough roof, and shut down the lid, and put hot embers on top, and stood off five foot, with the long handle, cool and comfortable, and in fifteen minutes she turned out a pie that was a satisfaction to look at. But the person that et it would want to fetch a couple of kags of toothpicks along, for if that rope-ladder wouldn't cramp him down to business, I don't know nothing what I'm talking about, and lay him in enough stomach-ache to last him till next time, too.

Nat didn't look, when we put the witch-pie in Jim's pan; and we put the three tin plates in the bottom of the pan under the vittles; and so Jim got everything all right, and as soon as he was by himself he busted into the pie and hid the rope-ladder inside of his straw-tick, and scratched some marks on a tin plate and throwed it out of the window-hole.

CHAPTER XXXVIII

Making them pens was a distressid-tough job, and so was the saw; and Jim allowed the inscription was going to be the toughest of all. That's the one which the prisoner has to scrabble on the wall. But we had to have it; Tom said we'd *got* to; there warn't no case of a state prisoner not scrabbling his inscription to leave behind, and his coat of arms.

"Look at Lady Jane Grey," he says; "look at Gilford Dudley; look at old Northumberland![244] Why, Huck, spose it *is* considerble trouble?—what you going to do?—how you going to get around it? Jim's *got* to do his inscription and coat of arms. They all do."

Jim says:

"Why, Mars Tom, I hain't got no coat o' arms; I hain't got nuffn but dishyer ole shirt, en you knows I got to keep de journal on dat."

"Oh, you don't understand, Jim; a coat of arms is very different."

"Well," I says, "Jim's right, anyway, when he says he hain't got no coat of arms, because he hain't."

"I reckon *I* knowed that," Tom says, "but you bet he'll have one before he goes out of this—because he's going out *right,* and there ain't going to be no flaws in his record."

[242]Long-handled pan, filled with hot coals and used to warm a bed.

[243]William the Conquerer lived 1027–1087. The *Mayflower* carried the Pilgrims to America in 1620.

[244]In 1553, the Duke of Northumberland attempted to make his daughter-in-law, Lady Jane Grey, Queen of England. Subsequently, Northumberland, Lady Jane Grey, and Guilford Dudley, her husband, were first imprisoned and then executed.

So whilst me and Jim filed away at the pens on a brickbat apiece, Jim a making his'n out of the brass and I making mine out of the spoon, Tom set to work to think out the coat of arms. By-and-by he said he'd struck so many good ones he didn't hardly know which to take, but there was one which he reckoned he'd decide on. He says:

"On the scutcheon[245] we'll have a bend *or* in the dexter base, a saltire *murrey* in the fess, with a dog, couchant, for common charge, and under his foot a chain embattled, for slavery, with a chevron *vert* in a chief engrailed, and three invected lines on a field *azure,* with the nombril points rampant on a dancette indented; crest, a runaway nigger, *sable,* with his bundle over his shoulder on a bar sinister: and a couple of gules for supporters, which is you and me; motto, *Maggiore fretta, minore atto.* Got it out of a book—means, the more haste, the less speed."[246]

"Geewhillikins," I says, "but what does the rest of it mean?"

"We ain't got no time to bother over that," he says, "we got to dig in like all git-out."

"Well, anyway," I says, "what's *some* of it? What's a fess?"

"A fess—a fess is—*you* don't need to know what a fess is. I'll show him how to make it when he gets to it."

"Shucks, Tom," I says, "I think you might tell a person. What's a bar sinister?"

"Oh, *I* don't know. But he's got to have it. All the nobility does."

That was just his way. If it didn't suit him to explain a thing to you, he wouldn't do it. You might pump at him a week, it wouldn't make no difference.

He'd got all that coat of arms business fixed, so now he started in to finish up the rest of that part of work, which was to plan out a mournful inscription—said Jim got to have one, like they all done. He made up a lot, and wrote them out on a paper, and read them off, so:

1. *Here a captive heart busted.*
2. *Here a poor prisoner, forsook by the world and friends, fretted out his sorrowful life.*
3. *Here a lonely heart broke, and a worn spirit went to its rest, after thirty-seven years of solitary captivity.*
4. *Here, homeless and friendless, after thirty-seven years of bitter captivity, perished a noble stranger, natural son of Louis XIV.*

Tom's voice trembled, whilst he was reading them, and he most broke down. When he got done, he couldn't no way make up his mind which one for Jim to scrabble onto the wall, they was all so good; but at last he allowed he would let him scrabble them all on. Jim said it would take him a year to scrabble such a lot of truck onto the logs with a nail, and he didn't know how to make letters, besides; but Tom said he would block them out for him, and then he wouldn't have nothing to do but just follow the lines. Then pretty soon he says:

"Come to think, the logs ain't agoing to do; they don't have log walls in a dungeon: we got to dig the inscriptions into a rock. We'll fetch a rock."

[245]An armorial shield. The jumble of technical heraldic terms that follows describes a coat-of-arms made up of a shield decorated with a slanted band of speckled gold, vertical bands of red, a purple cross in the center, a lying dog at the bottom, and a green chevron at the top, all surmounted by the figure of a runaway slave.

[246]Actually, "The more fretting, the less action."

Jim said the rock was worse than the logs; he said it would take him such a pison long time to dig them into a rock, he wouldn't ever get out. But Tom said he would let me help him do it. Then he took a look to see how me and Jim was getting along with the pens. It was most pesky tedious hard work and slow, and didn't give my hands no show to get well of the sores, and we didn't seem to make no headway, hardly. So Tom says:

"I know how to fix it. We got to have a rock for the coat of arms and mournful inscriptions, and we can kill two birds with that same rock. There's a gaudy big grindstone down at the mill, and we'll smouch it, and carve the things on it, and file out the pens and the saw on it, too."

It warn't no slouch of an idea; and it warn't no slouch of a grindstone nuther; but we allowed we'd tackle it. It warn't quite midnight, yet, so we cleared out for the mill, leaving Jim at work. We smouched the grindstone, and set out to roll her home, but it was a most nation tough job. Sometimes, do what we could, we couldn't keep her from falling over, and she come mighty near mashing us, every time. Tom said she was going to get one of us, sure, before we got through. We got her half way; and then we was plumb played out, and most drownded with sweat. We see it warn't no use, we got to go and fetch Jim, so he raised up his bed and slid the chain off the bed-leg, and wrapt it round and round his neck, and we crawled out through our hole and down there, and Jim and me laid into that grindstone and walked her along like nothing; and Tom superintended. He could out-superintend any boy I ever see. He knowed how to do everything.

Our hole was pretty big, but it warn't big enough to get the grindstone through; but Jim he took the pick and soon made it big enough. Then Tom marked out them things on it with the nail, and set Jim to work on them, with the nail for a chisel and an iron bolt from the rubbage in the lean-to for a hammer, and told him to work till the rest of his candle quit on him, and then he could go to bed, and hide the grindstone under his straw tick and sleep on it. Then we helped him fix his chain back on the bed-leg, and was ready for bed ourselves. But Tom thought of something, and says:

"You got any spiders in here, Jim?"

"No, sah, thanks to goodness I hain't, Mars Tom."

"All right, we'll get you some."

"But bless you, honey, I doan' *want* none. I's afeard un um. I jis' 's soon have rattlesnakes aroun'."

Tom thought a minute or two, and says:

"It's a good idea. And I reckon it's been done. It *must* a been done; it stands to reason. Yes, it's a prime good idea. Where could you keep it?"

"Keep what, Mars Tom?"

"Why, a rattlesnake."

"De goodness gracious alive, Mars Tom! Why, if dey was a rattlesnake to come in heah, I'd take en bust right out thoo dat log wall, I would, wid my head."

"Why, Jim, you wouldn't be afraid of it, after a little. You could tame it."

"*Tame* it!"

"Yes—easy enough. Every animal is grateful for kindness and petting, and they wouldn't *think* of hurting a person that pets them. Any book will tell you that. You try—that's all I ask; just try for two or three days. Why, you can get him so, in a little while, that he'll love you; and sleep with you; and won't stay away from you a minute; and will let you wrap him round your neck and put his head in your mouth."

"*Please,* Mars Tom—doan' talk so! I can't *stan'* it. He'd *let* me shove his head in my mouf—fer a favor, hain't it? I lay he'd wait a pow'ful long time 'fo' I *ast* him. En mo' en dat, I doan' *want* him to sleep wid me."

"Jim, don't act so foolish. A prisoner's *got* to have some kind of a dumb pet, and if a rattlesnake hain't ever been tried, why, there's more glory to be gained in your being the first to ever try it than any other way you could ever think of to save your life."

"Why, Mars Tom, I doan' *want* no sich glory. Snake take 'n bite Jim's chin off, den *whah* is de glory? No, sah, I doan' want no sich doin's."

"Blame it, can't you *try?* I only want you to try—you needn't keep it up if it don't work."

"But de trouble all *done,* ef de snake bit me while's I's a tryin' him. Mars Tom, I's willin' to tackle mos' anything 'at ain't onreasonable, but ef you en Huck fetches a rattlesnake in heah for me to tame, I's gwyne to *leave,* dat's *shore.*"

"Well, then, let it go, let it go, if you're so bullheaded about it. We can get you some garter-snakes and you can tie some buttons on their tails, and let on they're rattlesnakes, and I reckon that'll have to do."

"I k'n stan' *dem,* Mars Tom, but blame' 'f I couldn't get along widout um, I tell you dat. I never knowed b'fo', 't was so much bother and trouble to be a prisoner."

"Well, it *always* is, when it's done right. You got any rats around here?"

"No, sah, I hain't seed none."

"Well, we'll get you some rats."

"Well, Mars Tom, I doan' *want* no rats. Dey's de dad-blamedest creturs to 'sturb a body, en rustle roun' over 'im, en bite his feet, when he's trying' to sleep, I ever see. No, sah, gimme g'yarter-snakes, 'f I's got to have 'm, but doan' gimme no rats. I ain' got no use f'r um, skasely."

"But Jim, you *got* to have 'em—they all do. So don't make no more fuss about it. Prisoners ain't ever without rats. There ain't no instance of it. And they train them, and pet them, and learn them tricks, and they get to be as sociable as flies. But you got to play music to them. You got anything to play music on?"

"I ain't got nuffn but a coase comb en a piece o' paper, en a juice-harp; but I reck'n dey wouldn' take no stock in a juice-harp."

"Yes they would. *They* don't care what kind of music 'tis. A jews-harp's plenty good enough for a rat. All animals likes music—in a prison they dote on it. Specially, painful music; and you can't get no other kind out of a jews-harp. It always interests them; they come out to see what's the matter with you. Yes, you're all right; you're fixed very well. You want to set on your bed, nights, before you go to sleep, and early in the mornings, and play your jews-harp; play The Last Link Is Broken—that's the thing that'll scoop a rat, quicker'n anything else: and when you've played about two minutes, you'll see all the rats, and the snakes, and spiders, and things begin to feel worried about you, and come. And they'll just fairly swarm over you, and have a noble good time."

"Yes, *dey* will, I reck'n, Mars Tom, but what kine er time is *Jim* havin'? Blest if I kin see de pint. But I'll do it ef I got to. I reck'n I better keep de animals satisfied, en not have no trouble in de house."

Tom waited to think over, and see if there wasn't nothing else; and pretty soon he says:

"Oh—there's one thing I forgot. Could you raise a flower here, do you reckon?"

"I doan' know but maybe I could, Mars Tom; but it's tolable dark in heah, en I ain' got no use f'r no flower, no how, en she'd be a pow'ful sight o' trouble."

"Well, you try it, anyway. Some other prisoners has done it."

"One er dem big cat-tail-lookin' mullen-stalks would grow in heah, Mars Tom, I reck'n, but she wouldn' be wuth half de trouble she'd coss."

"Don't you believe it. We'll fetch you a little one, and you plant it in the corner, over there, and raise it. And don't call it mullen, call it Pitchiola[247]—that's its right name, when it's in a prison. And you want to water it with your tears."

"Why, I got plenty spring water, Mars Tom."

"You don't *want* spring water; you want to water it with your tears. It's the way they always do."

"Why, Mars Tom, I lay I kin raise one er dem mullen-stalks twyste wid spring water whiles another man's a *start'n* one wid tears."

"That ain't the idea. You *got* to do it with tears."

"She'll die on my han's, Mars Tom, she sholy will; kase I doan' skasely ever cry."

So Tom was stumped. But he studied it over, and then said Jim would have to worry along the best he could with an onion. He promised he would go to the nigger cabins and drop one, private, in Jim's coffee-pot, in the morning. Jim said he would "jis' 's soon have tobacker in his coffee"; and found so much fault with it, and with the work and bother of raising the mullen, and jews-harping the rats, and petting and flattering up the snakes and spiders and things, on top of all the other work he had to do on pens, and inscriptions, and journals, and things, which made it more trouble and worry and responsibility to be a prisoner than anything he ever undertook, that Tom most lost all patience with him; and said he was just loadened down with more gaudier chances than a prisoner ever had in the world to make a name for himself, and yet he didn't know enough to appreciate them, and they was just about wasted on him. So Jim he was sorry, and said he wouldn't behave so no more, and then me and Tom shoved for bed.

CHAPTER XXXIX

In the morning we went up to the village and bought a wire rat trap and fetched it down, and unstopped the best rat hole, and in about an hour we had fifteen of the bulliest kind of ones; and then we took it and put it in a safe place under Aunt Sally's bed. But while we was gone for spiders, little Thomas Franklin Benjamin Jefferson Elexander Phelps found it there, and opened the door of it to see if the rats would come out, and they did; and Aunt Sally she come in, and when we got back she was a standing on top of the bed raising Cain, and the rats was doing what they could to keep off the dull times for her. So she took and dusted us both with the hickry, and we was as much as two hours catching another fifteen or sixteen, drat that meddlesome cub, and they warn't the likeliest, nuther, because the first haul was the pick of the flock. I never see a likelier lot of rats than what that first haul was.

[247]In the romantic novel *Picciola* (1836) by Joseph Boniface (1798–1865), a prisoner is kept alive by a plant growing in his cell.

We got a splendid stock of sorted spiders, and bugs, and frogs, and caterpillars, and one thing or another; and we like-to got a hornet's nest, but we didn't. The family was at home. We didn't give it right up, but staid with them as long as we could; because we allowed we'd tire them out or they'd got to tire us out, and they done it. Then we got allycumpain[248] and rubbed on the places, and was pretty near all right again, but couldn't set down convenient. And so we went for the snakes, and grabbed a couple of dozen garters and house-snakes, and put them in a bag, and put it in our room, and by that time it was supper time, and a rattling good honest day's work; and hungry?—oh, no, I reckon not! And there warn't a blessed snake up there, when we went back—we didn't half tie the sack, and they worked out, somehow, and left. But it didn't matter much, because they was still on the premises somewhere. So we judged we could get some of them again. No, there warn't no real scarcity of snakes about the house for a considerable spell. You'd see them dripping from the rafters and places, every now and then; and they generly landed in your plate, or down the back of your neck, and most of the time where you didn't want them. Well, they was handsome, and striped, and there warn't no harm in a million of them; but that never made no difference to Aunt Sally, she despised snakes, be the breed what they might, and she couldn't stand them no way you could fix it; and every time one of them flopped down on her, it didn't make no difference what she was doing, she would just lay that work down and light out. I never see such a woman. And you could hear her whoop to Jericho. You couldn't get her to take aholt of one of them with the tongs. And if she turned over and found one in bed, she would scramble out and lift a howl that you would think the house was afire. She disturbed the old man so, that he said he could most wish there hadn't ever been no snakes created. Why, after every last snake had been gone clear out of the house for as much as a week, Aunt Sally warn't over it yet; she warn't near over it; when she was setting thinking about something, you could touch her on the back of her neck with a feather and she would jump right out of her stockings. It was very curious. But Tom said all women was just so. He said they was made that way; for some reason or other.

We got a licking every time one of our snakes come in her way; and she allowed these lickings warn't nothing to what she would do if we ever loaded up the place again with them. I didn't mind the lickings, because they didn't amount to nothing; but I minded the trouble we had, to lay in another lot. But we got them laid in, and all the other things; and you never see a cabin as blithesome as Jim's was when they'd all swarm out for music and go for him. Jim didn't like the spiders, and the spiders didn't like Jim; and so they'd lay for him and make it mighty warm for him. And he said that between the rats, and the snakes, and the grindstone, there warn't no room in bed for him skasely; and when there was, a body couldn't sleep, it was so lively, and it was always lively, he said, because *they* never all slept at one time, but took turn about, so when the snakes was asleep the rats was on deck, and when the rats turned in the snakes come on watch, so he always had one gang under him, in his way, and t'other gang having a circus over him, and if he got up to hunt a new place, the spiders would take a chance at him as he crossed over. He said if he ever got out, this time, he wouldn't ever be a prisoner again, not for a salary.

[248]Elecampane, a medicinal herb.

Well, by the end of three weeks, everything was in pretty good shape. The shirt was sent in early, in a pie, and every time a rat bit Jim he would get up and write a little in his journal whilst the ink was fresh; the pens was made, the inscriptions and so on was all carved on the grindstone; the bed-leg was sawed in two, and we had et up the sawdust, and it give us a most amazing stomach-ache. We reckoned we was all going to die, but didn't. It was the most undigestible sawdust I ever see; and Tom said the same. But as I was saying, we'd got all the work done, now, at last; and we was all pretty much fagged out, too, but mainly Jim. The old man had wrote a couple of times to the plantation below Orleans to come and get their runaway nigger, but hadn't got no answer, because there warn't no such plantation; so he allowed he would advertise Jim in the St. Louis and New Orleans papers; and when he mentioned the St. Louis ones, it give me the cold shivers, and I see we hadn't no time to lose. So Tom said, now for the nonnamous letters.

"What's them?" I says.

"Warnings to the people that something is up. Sometimes it's done one way, sometimes another. But there's always somebody spying around, that gives notice to the governor of the castle. When Louis XVI was going to light out of the Tooleries, a servant girl done it.[249] It's a very good way, and so is the nonnamous letters. We'll use them both. And it's usual for the prisoner's mother to change clothes with him, and she stays in, and he slides out in her clothes. We'll do that too."

"But looky here, Tom, what do we want to *warn* anybody for, that something's up? Let them find it out for themselves—it's their lookout."

"Yes, I know; but you can't depend on them. It's the way they've acted from the very start—left us to do *everything*. They're so confiding and mullet-headed[250] they don't take notice of nothing at all. So if we don't *give* them notice, there won't be nobody nor nothing to interfere with us, and so after all our hard work and trouble this escape 'll go off perfectly flat: won't amount to nothing—won't be nothing *to* it."

"Well, as for me, Tom, that's the way I'd like."

"Shucks," he says, and looked disgusted. So I says:

"But I ain't going to make no complaint. Anyway that suits you suits me. What you going to do about the servant-girl?"

"You'll be her. You slide in, in the middle of the night, and hook that yaller girl's frock."

"Why, Tom, that'll make trouble next morning; because of course she prob'bly hain't got any but that one."

"I know; but you don't want it but fifteen minutes, to carry the nonnamous letter and shove it under the front door."

"All right, then, I'll do it; but I could carry it just as handly in my own togs."

"You wouldn't look like a servant-girl *then,* would you?"

"No, but there won't be nobody to see what I look like, *anyway.*"

"That ain't got nothing to do with it. The thing for us to do, is just to do our *duty,* and not worry about whether anybody *sees* us do it or not. Hain't you got no principle at all?"

[249]The Tuileries, royal residence in Paris, France (1564–1871). Following the French Revolution, King Louis XVI's plans to escape his imprisonment were said to have been revealed to the authorities by a chambermaid.

[250]Stupid.

"All right, I ain't saying nothing; I'm the servant-girl. Who's Jim's mother?"

"I'm his mother. I'll hook a gown from Aunt Sally."

"Well, then, you'll have to stay in the cabin when me and Jim leaves."

"Not much. I'll stuff Jim's clothes full of straw and lay it on his bed to represent his mother in disguise, and Jim 'll take the nigger woman's gown[251] off of me and wear it, and we'll all evade together. When a prisoner of style escapes, it's called an evasion. It's always called so when a king escapes, f'rinstance. And the same with a king's son; it don't make no difference whether he's a natural one or an unnatural one."

So Tom he wrote the nonnamous letter, and I smouched the yaller wench's frock, that night, and put it on, and shoved it under the front door, the way Tom told me to. It said:

> *Beware. Trouble is brewing. Keep a sharp lookout.*
>
> UNKNOWN FRIEND.

Next night we stuck a picture which Tom drawed in blood, of a skull and crossbones, on the front door; and next night another one of a coffin, on the back door. I never see a family in such a sweat. They couldn't been worse scared if the place had a been full of ghosts laying for them behind everything and under the beds and shivering through the air. If a door banged, Aunt Sally she jumped, and said "ouch!" if anything fell, she jumped and said "ouch!" if you happened to touch her, when she warn't noticing, she done the same; she couldn't face noway and be satisfied, because she allowed there was something behind her every time—so she was always a whirling around, sudden, and saying "ouch," and before she'd get two-thirds around, she'd whirl back again, and say it again; and she was afraid to go to bed, but she dasn't set up. So the thing was working very well, Tom said; he said he never see a thing work more satisfactory. He said it showed it was done right.

So he said, now for the grand bulge! So the very next morning at the streak of dawn we got another letter ready, and was wondering what we better do with it, because we heard them say at supper they was going to have a nigger on watch at both doors all night. Tom he went down the lightning-rod to spy around; and the nigger at the back door was asleep, and he stuck it in the back of his neck and come back. This letter said:

> *Don't betray me, I wish to be your friend. There is a desprate gang of cutthroats from over in the Ingean Territory[252] going to steal your runaway nigger to-night, and they have been trying to scare you so as you will stay in the house and not bother them. I am one of the gang, but have got religgion and wish to quit it and lead a honest life again, and will betray the helish design. They will sneak down from northards, along the fence, at midnight exact, with a false key, and go in the nigger's cabin to get him. I am to be off a piece and blow a tin horn if I see any danger; but stead of that, I will* BA *like a sheep soon as they get in and not blow at all; then whilst they are getting his chains loose, you slip there and lock them in, and can kill them at your leasure. Don't do anything but just the way I am telling you, if you do they will suspicion something and raise whoopjamboreehoo. I do not wish any reward but to know I have done the right thing.*
>
> UNKNOWN FRIEND.

[251]Some of Twain's editors have considered this an error in consistency and have corrected the text to read "Aunt Sally's gown."

[252]From 1834 to 1890, present-day Oklahoma was designated Indian Territory. During those years it was frequently used by outlaws as a refuge from state and federal authorities.

CHAPTER XL

We was feeling pretty good, after breakfast, and took my canoe and went over the river a fishing, with a lunch, and had a good time, and took a look at the raft and found her all right, and got home late to supper, and found them in such a sweat and worry they didn't know which end they was standing on, and made us go right off to bed the minute we was done supper, and wouldn't tell us what the trouble was, and never let on a word about the new letter, but didn't need to, because we knowed as much about it as anybody did, and as soon as we was half up stairs and her back was turned, we slid for the cellar cubboard and loaded up a good lunch and took it up to our room and went to bed, and got up about half-past eleven, and Tom put on Aunt Sally's dress that he stole and was going to start with the lunch, but says:

"Where's the butter?"

"I laid out a hunk of it," I says, "on a piece of a corn-pone."

"Well, you *left* it laid out, then—it ain't here."

"We can get along without it," I says.

"We can get along *with* it, too," he says; "just you slide down cellar and fetch it. And then mosey right down the lightning-rod and come along. I'll go and stuff the straw into Jim's clothes to represent his mother in disguise, and be ready to *ba* like a sheep and shove soon as you get there."

So out he went, and down cellar went I. The hunk of butter, big as a person's fist, was where I had left it, so I took up the slab of corn-pone with it on, and blowed out my light, and started up stairs, very stealthy, and got up to the main floor all right, but here comes Aunt Sally with a candle, and I clapped the truck in my hat, and clapped my hat on my head, and the next second she see me; and she says:

"You been down cellar?"

"Yes'm."

"What you been doing down there?"

"Noth'n."

"Noth'n!"

"No'm."

"Well, then, what possessed you to go down there, this time of night?"

"I don't know'm."

"You don't *know?* Don't answer me that way, Tom, I want to know what you been *doing* down there?"

"I hain't been doing a single thing, Aunt Sally, I hope to gracious if I have."

I reckoned she'd let me go, now, and as a generl thing she would; but I spose there was so many strange things going on she was just in a sweat about every little thing that warn't yard-stick straight; so she says, very decided:

"You just march into that setting-room and stay there till I come. You been up to something you no business to, and I lay I'll find out what it is before *I'm* done with you."

So she went away as I opened the door and walked into the setting-room. My, but there was a crowd there! Fifteen farmers, and every one of them had a gun. I was most powerful sick, and slunk to a chair and set down. They was setting around, some of them talking a little, in a low voice, and all of them fidgety and uneasy, but trying to look like they warn't; but I knowed they was, because they was always taking off their hats, and putting them on, and scratching their heads, and changing their seats, and fumbling with their buttons. I warn't easy myself, but I didn't take my hat off, all the same.

I did wish Aunt Sally would come, and get done with me, and lick me, if she wanted to, and let me get away and tell Tom how we'd overdone this thing, and what a thundering hornet's nest we'd got ourselves into, so we could stop fooling around, straight-off, and clear out with Jim before these rips got out of patience and come for us.

At last she come, and begun to ask me questions, but I *couldn't* answer them straight, I didn't know which end of me was up; because these men was in such a fidget now, that some was wanting to start right *now* and lay for them desperadoes, and saying it warn't but a few minutes to midnight; and others was trying to get them to hold on and wait for the sheep-signal; and here was aunty pegging away at the questions, and me a shaking all over and ready to sink down in my tracks I was that scared; and the place getting hotter and hotter, and the butter beginning to melt and run down my neck and behind my ears; and pretty soon, when one of them says, "*I'm* for going and getting in the cabin *first,* and right *now,* and catching them when they come," I most dropped; and a streak of butter come a trickling down my forehead, and Aunt Sally she see it, and turns white as a sheet, and says:

"For the land's sake what *is* the matter with the child!—he's got the brain fever as shore as you're born, and they're oozing out!"

And everybody runs to see, and she snatches off my hat, and out comes the bread, and what was left of the butter, and she grabbed me, and hugged me, and says:

"Oh, what a turn you did give me! and how glad and grateful I am it ain't no worse; for luck's against us, and it never rains but it pours, and when I see that truck I thought we'd lost you, for I knowed by the color and all, it was just like your brains would be if—Dear, dear, whyd'nt you *tell* me that was what you'd been down there for, *I* wouldn't a cared. Now cler out to bed, and don't lemme see no more of you till morning!"

I was up stairs in a second, and down the lightning-rod in another one, and shinning through the dark for the lean-to. I couldn't hardly get my words out, I was so anxious; but I told Tom as quick as I could, we must jump for it, now, and not a minute to lose—the house full of men, yonder, with guns!

His eyes just blazed; and he says:

"No!—is that so? *Ain't* it bully! Why, Huck, if it was to do over again, I bet I could fetch two hundred! If we could put it off till——"

"Hurry! *hurry!*" I says, "Where's Jim?"

"Right at your elbow; if you reach out your arm you can touch him. He's dressed, and everything's ready. Now we'll slide out and give the sheep-signal."

But then we heard the tramp of men coming to the door, and heard them begin to fumble with the padlock; and heard a man say:

"I *told* you we'd be too soon; they haven't come—the door is locked. Here, I'll lock some of you in the cabin and you lay for 'em in the dark and kill 'em when they come; and the rest scatter around a piece, and listen if you can hear 'em coming."

So in they come, but couldn't see us in the dark, and most trod on us whilst we was hustling to get under the bed. But we got under all right, and out through the hole, swift but soft—Jim first, me next, and Tom last, which was according to Tom's orders. Now we was in the lean-to, and heard trampings close by outside. So we crept to the door, and Tom stopped us there and put his eye to the crack, but couldn't make out nothing, it was so dark; and whispered and said he would listen for the steps to get further, and when he nudged us Jim must glide out first, and him last. So he set his ear to the crack and listened, and listened, and listened, and the steps a scraping around, out there, all the time; and at last he nudged us, and we slid out, and stooped down, not breathing, and not making the least noise, and slipped stealthy towards the fence, in Injun file,[253] and got to it, all right, and me and Jim over it; but Tom's britches catched fast on a splinter on the top rail, and then he hear the steps coming, so he had to pull loose, which snapped the splinter and made a noise; and as he dropped in our tracks and started, somebody sings out:

"Who's that? Answer, or I'll shoot!"

But we didn't answer; we just unfurled our heels and shoved. Then there was a rush, and a *bang, bang, bang!* and the bullets fairly whizzed around us! We heard them sing out:

"Here they are! They've broke for the river! after 'em boys! And turn loose the dogs!"

So here they come, full tilt. We could hear them, because they wore boots, and yelled, but we didn't wear no boots, and didn't yell. We was in the path to the mill; and when they got pretty close onto us, we dodged in the bush and let them go by, and then dropped in behind them. They'd had all the dogs shut up, so they wouldn't scare off the robbers; but by this time somebody had let them loose, and here they come, making pow-wow enough for a million; but they was our dogs; so we stopped in our tracks till they catch up; and when they see it warn't nobody but us, and no excitement to offer them, they only just said howdy, and tore right ahead towards the shouting and clattering; and then we up stream again and whizzed along after them till we was nearly to the mill, and then struck up through the bush to where my canoe was tied, and hopped in and pulled for dear life towards the middle of the river, but didn't make no more noise than we was obleeged to. Then we struck out, easy and comfortable, for the island where my raft was; and we could hear them yelling and barking at each other all up and down the bank, till we was so far away the sounds got dim and died out. And when we stepped onto the raft, I says:

"*Now,* old Jim, you're a free man *again,* and I bet you won't ever be a slave nomore."

"En a mighty good job it wuz, too. Huck. It 'uz planned beautiful, en it 'uz *done* beautiful; en dey ain't *nobody* kin git up a plan dat's mo' mixed-up en splendid den what dat one wuz."

We was all as glad as we could be, but Tom was the gladdest of all, because he had a bullet in the calf of his leg.

When me and Jim heard that, we didn't feel so brash as what we did before. It was hurting him considerable, and bleeding; so we laid him in the wigwam and tore up one of the duke's shirts for to bandage him, but he says:

"Gimme the rags, I can do it myself. Don't stop, now; don't fool around here, and the evasion booming along so handsome; man the sweeps, and set her loose! Boys, we done it elegant—'deed we did. I wish *we'd* a had the handling of Louis XVI., there wouldn't a been no "Son of Saint Louis, ascend to

[253]Single file.

heaven!"[254] wrote down in *his* biography: no, sir, we'd a whooped him over the *border*—that's what we'd a done with *him*—and done it just as slick as nothing at all, too. Man the sweeps—man the sweeps!"

But me and Jim was consulting—and thinking. And after we'd thought a minute, I says:

"Say it, Jim."

So he says:

"Well, den, dis is de way it look to me, Huck. Ef it wuz *him* dat 'uz bein' sot free, en one er de boys wuz to git shot, would he say, 'Go on en save me, nemmine 'bout a doctor f'r to save dis one? Is dat like Mars Tom Sawyer? Would he say dat? You *bet* he wouldn't! *Well,* den, is *Jim* gwyne to say it? No, sah—I doan' budge a step out'n dis place, 'dout a *doctor;* not if it's forty year!"

I knowed he was white inside, and I reckoned he'd say what he did say—so it was all right, now, and I told Tom I was agoing for a doctor. He raised considerble row about it, but me and Jim stuck to it and wouldn't budge; so he was for crawling out and setting the raft loose himself; but we wouldn't let him. Then he give us a piece of his mind—but it didn't do no good.

So when he see me getting the canoe ready, he says:

"Well, then, if you're bound to go, I'll tell you the way to do, when you get to the village. Shut the door, and blindfold the doctor tight and fast, and make him swear to be silent as the grave, and put a purse full of gold in his hand, and then take and lead him all around the back alleys and everywheres, in the dark, and then fetch him here in the canoe, in a roundabout way amongst the islands, and search him and take his chalk away from him, and don't give it back to him till you get him back to the village, or else he will chalk this raft so he can find it again. It's the way they all do."

So I said I would, and left, and Jim was to hide in the woods when he see the doctor coming, till he was gone again.

CHAPTER XLI

The doctor was an old man; a very nice, kind-looking old man, when I got him up. I told him me and my brother was over on Spanish Island hunting, yesterday afternoon, and camped on a piece of a raft we found, and about midnight he must a kicked his gun in his dreams, for it went off and shot him in the leg, and we wanted him to go over there and fix it and not say nothing about it, nor let anybody know, because we wanted to come home this evening, and surprise the folks.

"Who is your folks?" he says.

"The Phelpses, down yonder."

"Oh," he says. And after a minute, he says: "How'd you say he got shot?"

"He had a dream," I says, "and it shot him."

"Singular dream," he says.

So he lit up his lantern, and got his saddle-bags, and we started. But when he see the canoe, he didn't like the look of her—said she was big enough for one, but didn't look pretty safe for two. I says:

[254]A quotation from *The French Revolution* (1837) by Scottish historian Thomas Carlyle (1795–1881).

"Oh, you needn't be afeard, sir, she carried the three of us, easy enough."

"What three?"

"Why, me and Sid, and—and—and *the guns;* that's what I mean."

"Oh," he says.

But he put his foot on the gunnel, and rocked her; and shook his head, and said he reckoned he'd look around for a bigger one. But they was all locked and chained; so he took my canoe, and said for me to wait till he come back, or I could hunt around further, or maybe I better go down home and get them ready for the surprise, if I wanted to. But I said I didn't; so I told him just how to find the raft, and then he started.

I struck an idea, pretty soon. I says to myself, spos'n he can't fix that leg just in three shakes of a sheep's tail, as the saying is? spos'n it takes him three or four days? What are we going to do?—lay around there till he lets the cat out of the bag? No, sir, I know what *I'll* do. I'll wait, and when he comes back, if he says he's got to go any more, I'll get down there, too, if I swim; and we'll take and tie him, and keep him, and shove out down the river; and when Tom's done with him, we'll give him what it's worth, or all we got, and then let him get ashore.

So then I crept into a lumber pile to get some sleep; and next time I waked up the sun was away up over my head! I shot out and went for the doctor's house, but they told me he'd gone away in the night, some time or other, and warn't back yet. Well, thinks I, that looks powerful bad for Tom, and I'll dig out for the island, right off. So away I shoved, and turned the corner, and nearly rammed my head into Uncle Silas's stomach! He says:

"Why, *Tom!* Where you been all this time, you rascal?"

"I hain't been nowheres," I says, "only just hunting for the runaway nigger—me and Sid."

"Why, where ever did you go?" he says. "Your aunt's been mighty un-easy."

"She needn't," I says, "because we was all right. We followed the men and the dogs, but they out-run us, and we lost them; but we thought we heard them on the water, so we got a canoe and took out after them, and crossed over but couldn't find nothing of them; so we cruised along upshore till we got kind of tired and beat out; and tied up the canoe and went to sleep, and never waked up till about an hour ago, then we paddled over here to hear the news, and Sid's at the post-office to see what he can hear, and I'm branching out to get something to eat for us, and then we're going home."

So then we went to the post-office to get "Sid"; but just as I suspicioned, he warn't there; so the old man he got a letter out of the office, and we waited a while longer but Sid didn't come; so the old man said come along, let Sid foot it home, or canoe-it, when he got done fooling around—but we would ride. I couldn't get him to let me stay and wait for Sid; and he said there warn't no use in it, and I must come along, and let Aunt Sally see we was all right.

When we got home, Aunt Sally was that glad to see me she laughed and cried both, and hugged me, and give me one of them lickings of hern that don't amount to shucks, and said she serve Sid the same when he come.

And the place was plumb full of farmers and farmers' wives, to dinner; and such another clack a body never heard. Old Mrs. Hotchkiss was the worst; her tongue was agoing all the time. She says:

"Well, Sister Phelps, I've ransacked that-air cabin over an' I b'lieve the nigger was crazy. I says so to Sister Damrell—didn't I, Sister Damrell?—s'I, he's crazy, s'I—them's the very words I said. You all hearn me: he's crazy, s'I; everything shows it, s'I. Look at that-air grindstone, s'I; want to tell *me*'t any cretur 'ts in his right mind's agoin' to scrabble all them crazy things onto a grindstone, s'I? Here sich 'n' sich a person busted his heart; 'n' here so 'n' so pegged along for thirty-seven year, 'n' all that—natcherl son o' Louis somebody, 'n' sich ever-last'n rubbage. He's plumb crazy, s'I; it's what I says in the fust place, it's what I says in the middle, 'n' it's what I says last 'n' all the time—the nigger's crazy—crazy's Nebokoodneezer,[255] s'I."

"An' look at that air-ladder made out'n rags, Sister Hotchkiss," says old Mrs. Damrell, "what in the name o' goodness *could* he ever want of——"

"The very words I was a-sayin' no longer ago th'n this minute to Sister Utterback, 'n' she'll tell you so herself. Sh-she, look at that-air rag ladder, sh-she; 'n' s'I, yes, *look* at it, s'I—what *could* he a wanted of it, s'I. Sh-she, Sister Hotchkiss, sh-she——"

"But how in the nation'd they ever *git* that grindstone *in* there, *anyway?* 'n' who dug that-air *hole?* 'n' who——"

"My very *words,* Brer Penrod! I was a-sayin'—pass that-air sasser o' m'lasses, won't ye?—I was a-sayin' to Sister Dunlap, jist this minute, how *did* they git that grindstone in there, s'I. Without *help,* mind you—'thout *help! Thar's* wher' tis. Don't tell *me,* s'I; there *wuz* help, s'I; 'n' ther' wuz a *plenty* help, too, s'I; ther's ben a *dozen* a-helpin' that nigger, 'n' I lay I'd skin every last nigger on this place, but *I'd* find out who done it, s'I; 'n' moreover, s'I——"

"A *dozen* says you!—*forty* couldn't a done everything that's been done. Look at them case-knife saws and things, how tedious they've been made; look at that bed-leg sawed off with 'm, a week's work for six men; look at that nigger made out'n straw on the bed; and look at——"

"You may *well* say it, Brer Hightower! It's jist as I was a-sayin' to Brer Phelps, his own self. S'e, what do *you* think of it, Sister Hotchkiss, s'e? think o' what, Brer Phelps, s'I? think o' that bed-leg sawed off that a way, s'e? *think* of it, s'I? I lay it never sawed *itself* off, s'I—somebody *sawed* it, s'I; that's my opinion, take it or leave it, it mayn't be no 'count, s'I, but sich as 'tis, it's my opinion, s'I, 'n' if anybody k'n start a better one, s'I, let him *do* it, s'I, that's all. I says to Sister Dunlap, s'I——"

"Why, dog my cats, they must a ben a house-ful o'niggers in there every night for four weeks, to a done all that work, Sister Phelps. Look at that shirt—every last inch of it kivered over with secret African writ'n done with blood! Must a ben a raft uv'm at it right along, all the time, almost. Why, I'd give two dollars to have it read to me; 'n' as for the niggers that wrote it, I 'low I'd take 'n' lash 'm t'll——"

"People to *help* him, Brother Marples! Well, I reckon you'd *think* so, if you'd a been in this house for a while back. Why, they've stole everything they could lay their hands on—and we a watching, all the time, mind you. They stole that shirt right off o' the line! and as for that sheet they made the rag ladder out of ther' ain't no telling how many times they *didn't* steal that; and flour, and candles, and candlesticks, and spoons, and the old warming-pan, and most a thousand things that I disremember, now, and my new calico dress; and me, and Silas, and my Sid and Tom on the constant watch day *and* night, as I was'a telling you, and not a one of us could catch hide nor hair, nor sight nor sound of

[255]Nebuchadnezzar, King of Babylon, was deprived of his reason for failure to honor the Lord (Daniel 4:29–37).

them; and here at the last minute, lo and behold you, they slides right in under our noses, and fools us, and not only fools *us* but the Injun Territory robbers too, and actuly gets *away* with that nigger, safe and sound, and that with sixteen men and twenty-two dogs right on their very heels at that very time! I tell you, it just bangs anything I ever *heard* of. Why, *sperits* couldn't a done better, and been no smarter. And I reckon they must a *been* sperits—because, *you* know our dogs, and ther' ain't no better; well, them dogs never even got on the *track* of'm, once! You explain *that* to me, if you can!—*any* of you!"

"Well, it does beat——"

"Laws alive, I never——"

"So help me, I wouldn't a be——"

"*House* thieves as well as——"

"Goodnessgracioussakes, I'd a ben afeard to *live* in sich a——"

"'Fraid to *live!*—why, I was that scared I dasn't hardly go to bed, or get up, or lay down, or *set* down, Sister Ridgeway. Why, they'd steal the very—why, goodness sakes, you can guess what kind of a fluster *I* was in by the time midnight come, last night. I hope to gracious if I warn't afraid they'd steal some o'the family! I was just to that pass, I didn't have no reasoning faculties no more. It looks foolish enough, *now,* in the day-time; but I says to myself, there's my two poor boys asleep, 'way up stairs in that lonesome room, and I declare to goodness I was that uneasy 't I crep' up there and locked 'em in! I *did.* And anybody would. Because, you know, when you get scared, that way, and it keeps running on, and getting worse and worse, all the time, and your wits gets to addling, and you get to doing all sorts o' wild things, and by-and-by you think to yourself, spos'n *I* was a boy, and was away up there, and the door ain't locked, and you—" She stopped, looking kind of wondering, and then she turned her head around slow, and when her eye lit on me—I got up and took a walk.

Says I to myself, I can explain better how we come to not be in that room this morning, if I go out to one side and study over it a little. So I done it. But I dasn't go fur, or she'd a sent for me. And when it was late in the day, the people all went, and then I come in and told her the noise and shooting waked up me and "Sid," and the door was locked, and we wanted to see the fun, so we went down the lightning-rod, and both of us got hurt a little, and we didn't never want to try *that* no more. And then I went on and told her all what I told Uncle Silas before; and then she said she'd forgive us, and maybe it was all right enough anyway, and about what a body might expect of boys, for all boys was a pretty harum-scarum lot, as fur as she could see; and so, as long as no harm hadn't come of it, she judged she better put in her time being grateful we was alive and well and she had us still, stead of fretting over what was past and done. So then she kissed me, and patted me on the head, and dropped into a kind of a brown study; and pretty soon jumps up, and says:

"Why, lawsamercy, it's most night, and Sid not come yet! What *has* become of that boy?"

I see my chance; so I skips and says:

"I'll run right up to town and get him," I says.

"No you won't," she says. "You'll stay right wher' you are; *one's* enough to be lost at a time. If he ain't here to supper, your uncle'll go."

Well, he warn't there to supper; so right after supper uncle went.

He come back about ten, a little bit uneasy; hadn't run across Tom's track. Aunt Sally was a good *deal* uneasy; but Uncle Silas he said there warn't no occasion to be—boys will be boys, he said, and you'll see this one turn up in the morning, all sound and right. So she had to be satisfied. But she said she'd set up for him a while, anyway, and keep a light burning, so he could see it.

And then when I went up to bed she come up with me and fetched her candle, and tucked me in, and mothered me so good I felt mean, and like I couldn't look her in the face; and she sat down on the bed and talked with me a long time, and said what a splendid boy Sid was, and didn't seem to want to ever stop talking about him; and kept asking me every now and then, if I reckoned he could a got lost, or hurt, or maybe drownded, and might be laying at this minute, somewheres, suffering or dead, and she not by him to help him, and so the tears would drip down, silent, and I would tell her that Sid was all right, and would be home in the morning, sure; and she would squeeze my hand, or maybe kiss me, and tell me to say it again, and keep on saying it, because it done her good, and she was in so much trouble. And when she was going away, she looked down in my eyes, so steady and gentle, and says:

"The door ain't going to be locked, Tom; and there's the window and the rod; but you'll be good, *won't* you? And you won't go? For *my* sake."

Laws knows I *wanted* to go, bad enough, to see about Tom, and was all intending to go; but after that, I wouldn't a went, not for kingdoms.

But she was on my mind, and Tom was on my mind; so I slept very restless. And twice I went down the rod, away in the night, and slipped around front, and see her setting there by her candle in the window with her eyes towards the road and the tears in them; and I wished I could do something for her, but I couldn't, only to swear that I wouldn't never do nothing to grieve her any more. And the third time, I waked up at dawn, and slid down, and she was there yet, and her candle was most out, and her old gray head was resting on her hand, and she was asleep.

CHAPTER XLII

The old man was up town again, before breakfast, but couldn't get no track of Tom; and both of them set at the table, thinking, and not saying nothing, and looking mournful, and their coffee getting cold, and not eating anything. And by-and-by the old man says:

"Did I give you the letter?"

"What letter?"

"The one I got yesterday out of the post-office."

"No, you didn't give me no letter."

"Well, I must a forgot it."

So he rummaged his pockets, and then went off somewheres where he had laid it down, and fetched it, and give it to her. She says:

"Why, it's from St. Petersburg—it's from Sis."

I allowed another walk would do me good; but I couldn't stir. But before she could break it open, she dropped and run—for she see something. And so did I. It was Tom Sawyer on a mattress; and that old doctor; and Jim, in *her* calico dress, with his hands tied behind him; and a lot of people. I hid the letter behind the first thing that come handy, and rushed. She flung herself at Tom, crying, and says:

"Oh, he's dead, he's dead, I know he's dead!"

And Tom he turned his head a little, and muttered something or other, which showed he warn't in his right mind; then she flung up her hands, and says:

"He's alive, thank God! And that's enough!" she snatched a kiss of him, and flew for the house to get the bed ready, and scattering orders right and left at the niggers and everybody else, as fast as her tongue could go, every jump of the way.

I followed the men to see what they was going to do with Jim; and the old doctor and Uncle Silas followed after Tom into the house. The men was very huffy, and some of them wanted to hang Jim, for an example to all the other niggers around there, so they wouldn't be trying to run away, like Jim done, and making such a raft of trouble, and keeping a whole family scared most to death for days and nights. But the others said, don't do it, it wouldn't answer at all, he ain't our nigger, and his owner would turn up and make us pay for him, sure. So that cooled them down a little, because the people that's always the most anxious for to hang a nigger that hain't done just right, is always the very ones that ain't the most anxious to pay for him when they've got their satisfaction out of him.

They cussed Jim considerable, though, and give him a cuff or two, side the head, once in a while, but Jim never said nothing, and he never let on to know me, and they took him to the same cabin, and put his own clothes on him, and chained him again, and not to no bed-leg, this time, but to a big staple drove into the bottom log, and chained his hands, too, and both legs, and said he warn't to have nothing but bread and water to eat, after this, till his owner come or he was sold at auction, because he didn't come in a certain length of time, and filled up our hole, and said a couple of farmers with guns must stand watch around about the cabin every night, and bull-dog tied to the door in the daytime; and about this time they was through with the job and was tapering off with a kind of generl good-bye cussing, and then the old doctor comes and takes a look, and says:

"Don't be no rougher on him than you're obleeged to, because he ain't a bad nigger. When I got to where I found the boy, I see I couldn't cut the bullet out without some help, and he warn't in no condition for me to leave, to go and get help; and he got a little worse and a little worse, and after a long time he went out of his head, and wouldn't let me come anigh him, any more, and said if I chalked his raft he'd kill me, and no end of wild foolishness like that, and I see I couldn't do anything at all with him; so I says, I got to have *help,* somehow; and the minute I says it, out crawls this nigger from somewheres, and says he'll help, and he done it, too, and done it very well. Of course I judged he must be a runaway nigger, and there I *was!* and there I had to stick, right straight along all the rest of the days, and all night. It was a fix, I tell you! I had a couple of patients with the chills, and of course I'd of liked to run up to town and see them, but I dasn't because the nigger might get away, and then I'd be to blame; and yet never a skiff come close enough for me to hail. So there I had to stick, plumb till daylight this morning' and I never see a nigger that was a better nuss or faithfuller, and yet he was resking his freedom to do it, and was all tired out, too, and I see plain enough he'd been worked main hard, lately, I liked the nigger for that; I tell you, gentlemen, a nigger like that is worth a thousand dollars—and kind treatment, too. I had everything I needed, and the boy was doing as well there as he would a done at home—better, maybe, because it was so quiet;

but there I *was,* with both of 'm on my hands; and there I had to stick, till about dawn this morning; then some men in a skiff come by, and as good luck would have it, the nigger was setting by the pallet with his head propped on his knees, sound asleep; so I motioned them in, quiet, and they slipped up on him and grabbed him and tied him before he knowed what he was about, and we never had no trouble. And the boy being in a kind of a flightly sleep, too, we muffled the oars and hitched the raft on, and towed her over very nice and quiet, and the nigger never made the least row nor said a word, from the start. He ain't no bad nigger, gentlemen; that's what I think about him."

Somebody says:

"Well, it sounds very good, doctor, I'm obleeged to say."

Then the others softened up a little, too, and I was mightly thankful to that old doctor for doing Jim that good turn; and I was glad it was according to my judgment of him, too; because I thought he had a good heart in him and was a good man, the first time I see him. Then they all agreed that Jim had acted very well, and was deserving to have some notice took of it, and reward. So every one of them promised, right out and hearty, that they wouldn't cuss him no more.

Then they come out and locked him up. I hoped they was going to say he could have one or two of the chains took off, because they was rotten heavy, or could have meat and greens with his bread and water, but they didn't think of it, and I reckoned it warn't best for me to mix in, but I judged I'd get the doctor's yarn to Aunt Sally, somehow or other, as soon as I'd got through the breakers that was laying just ahead of me. Explanations, I mean, of how I forgot to mention about Sid being shot, when I was telling how him and me put in that drafted night paddling around hunting the runaway nigger.

But I had plenty time. Aunt Sally she stuck to the sick-room all day and all night; and every time I see Uncle Silas mooning around, I dodged him.

Next morning I heard Tom was a good deal better, and they said Aunt Sally was gone to get a nap. So I slips to the sick-room, and if I found him awake I reckoned we could put up a yarn for the family that would wash. But he was sleeping, and sleeping very peaceful, too; and pale, not fire-faced the way he was when he come. So I set down and laid for him to wake. In about a half an hour, Aunt Sally comes gliding in, and there I was, up a stump again! She motioned me to be still, and set down by me, and begun to whisper, and said we could all be joyful now, because all the symptoms was first rate, and he'd been sleeping like that for ever so long, and looking better and peacefuller all the time, and ten to one he'd wake up in his right mind.

So we set there watching, and by-and-by he stirs a bit, and opens his eyes very natural, and takes a look, and says:

"Hello, why I'm at *home!* How's that? Where's the raft?"

"It's all right," I says.

"And *Jim?*"

"The same," I says, but couldn't say it pretty brash. But he never noticed, but says:

"Good! Splendid! *Now* we're all right and safe! Did you tell Aunty?"

I was going to say yes; but she chipped in and says:

"About what, Sid?"

"Why, about the way the whole thing was done."

"What whole thing?"

"Why, *the* whole thing. There ain't but one; how we set the runaway nigger free—me and Tom."

"Good land! Set the run—What *is* the child talking about! Dear, dear out of his head again!"

"*No,* I ain't out of my HEAD; I know all what I'm talking about. We *did* set him free—me and Tom. We laid out to do it, and we *done* it. And we done it elegant, too." He'd got a start, and she never checked him up, just set and stared and stared, and let him clip along, and I see it warn't no use for *me* to put it. "Why, Aunty, it cost us a power of work—weeks of it—hours and hours, every night, whilst you was all asleep. And we had to steal candles, and the sheet, and the shirt, and your dress, and spoons, and tin plates, and case-knives, and the warming-pan, and the grind-stone, and flour, and just no end of things, and you can't think what work it was to make the saws and pens, and inscriptions, and one thing or another, and you can't think *half* the fun it was. And we had to make up the pictures of coffins and things, and nonnamous letters from the robbers, and get up and down the lightning-rod, and dig the hole into the cabin, and make the rope-ladder and send it in cooked up in a pie, and send in spoons and things to work with, in your apron pocket"—

"Mercy sakes!"

——"and load up the cabin with rats and snakes and so on, for company for Jim; and then you kept Tom here so long with the butter in his hat that you come near spilling the whole business, because the men come before we was out of the cabin, and we had to rush, and they heard us and let drive at us, and I got my share, and we dodged out of the path and let them go by, and when the dogs come they warn't interested in us, but went for the most noise, and we got our canoe, and made for the raft, and was all safe, and Jim was a free man, and we done it all by ourselves, and *wasn't* it bully, Aunty!"

"Well, I never heard the likes of it in all my born days! So it was *you,* you little rapscallions, that's been making all this trouble, and turned everybody's wits clean inside out and scared us all most to death. I've as good a notion as ever I had in my life, to take it out o' you this very minute. To think, here I've been, night after night, a—*you* just get well once, you young scamp, and I lay I'll tan the Old Harry[256] out o' both o' ye!"

But Tom, he *was* so proud and joyful, he just *couldn't* hold in, and his tongue just *went* it—she a-chipping in, and spitting fire all along, and both of them going it at once, like a cat-convention; and she says:

"*Well,* you get all the enjoyment you can out of it *now,* for mind I tell you if I catch you meddling with him again——"

"Meddling with *who?*" Tom says, dropping his smile and looking surprised.

"With *who?*" Why, the runaway nigger, of course. Who'd you reckon?"

Tom looks at me very grave, and says:

"Tom, didn't you just tell me he was all right? Hasn't he got away?"

"*Him?*" says Aunt Sally; "the runaway nigger? 'Deed he hasn't. They've got him back, safe and sound, and he's in that cabin again, on bread and water, and loaded down with chains, till he's claimed or sold!"

Tom rose square up in bed, with his eye hot, and his nostrils opening and shutting like gills, and sings out to me:

[256]The Devil.

"They hain't no *right* to shut him up! *Shove!*—and don't you lose a minute. Turn him loose! he ain't no slave; he's as free as any cretur that walks this earth!"

"What *does* this child mean?"

"I mean every word I *say,* Aunt Sally, and if somebody don't go, *I*'ll go. I've knowed him all his life, and so has Tom, there. Old Miss Watson died two months ago, and she was ashamed she ever was going to sell him down the river, and *said* so; and she set him free in her will."

"Then what on earth did *you* want to set him free for, seeing he was already free?"

"Well, that *is* a question, I must say; and *just* like women! Why, I wanted the *adventure* of it; and I'd a waded neck-deep in blood to—goodness alive, AUNT POLLY!"

If she warn't standing right there, just inside the door, looking as sweet and contented as an angel half-full of pie, I wish I may never!

Aunt Sally jumped for her, and most hugged the head off of her, and cried over her, and I found a good enough place for me under the bed, for it was getting pretty sultry, for *us,* seemed to me. And I peeped out, and in a little while Tom's Aunt Polly shook herself loose and stood there looking across at Tom over her spectacles—kind of grinding him into the earth, you know. And then she says:

"Yes, you *better* turn y'r head away—I would if I was you, Tom."

"Oh, deary me!" says Aunt Sally; "*is* he changed so? Why, that ain't *Tom,* it's Sid; Tom's—Tom's—why, where is Tom? He was here a minute ago."

"You mean where's Huck *Finn*—that's what you mean! I reckon I hain't raised such a scamp as my Tom all these years, not to know him when I *see* him. That *would* be a pretty howdy-do. Come out from under that bed, Huck Finn."

So I don it. But not feeling brash.

Aunt Sally she was one of the mixed-upset looking persons I ever see; except one, and that was Uncle Silas, when he come in, and they told it all to him. It kind of made him drunk, as you may say, and he didn't know nothing at all the rest of the day, and preached a prayer-meeting sermon that night that give him a rattling ruputation, because the oldest man in the world couldn't a understood it. So Tom's Aunt Polly, she told all about who I was, and what; and I had to up and tell how I was in such a tight place that when Mrs. Phelps took me for Tom Sawyer—she chipped in and says, "Oh, go on and call me Aunt Sally, I'm used to it, now, and 'tain't no need to change"——that when Aunt Sally took me for Tom Sawyer, I had to stand it—there warn't no other way, and I knowed he wouldn't mind, because it would be nuts for him, being a mystery, and he'd make an adventure out of it and be perfectly satisfied. And so it turned out, and he let on to be Sid, and made things as soft as he could for me.

And his Aunt Polly she said Tom was right about old Miss Watson setting Jim free in her will; and so, sure enough, Tom Sawyer had gone and took all that trouble and bother to set a free nigger free! and I couldn't ever understand, before, until that minute and that talk, how he *could* help a body set a nigger free, with his bringing-up.

Well, Aunt Polly she said that when Aunt Sally wrote to her that Tom and *Sid* had come, all right and safe, she says to herself:

"Look at that, now! I might have expected it, letting him go off that way without anybody to watch him. So now I got to go and trapse all the way down the river, eleven hundred mile, and find out what the creetur's up to, *this* time; as long as I couldn't seem to get any answer out of you about it."

"Why, I never heard nothing from you," says Aunt Sally.

"Well, I wonder! Why, I wrote to you twice, to ask you what you could mean by Sid being here."

"Well, I never got 'em, Sis."

Aunt Polly, she turns around slow and severe, and says:

"You, Tom!"

"Well—*what?*" he says, kind of pettish.

"Don't you what *me,* you impudent thing—hand out them letters."

"What letters?"

"*Them* letters. I be bound, if I have to take aholt of you I'll——"

"They're in the trunk. There, now. And they're just the same as they was when I got them out of the office. I hain't looked into them, I hain't touched them. But I knowed they'd make trouble, and I thought if you warn't in no hurry, I'd——"

"Well, you *do* need skinning, there ain't no mistake about it. And I wrote another one to tell you I was coming; and I spose he——"

"No, it come yesterday; I hain't read it yet, but *it's* all right, I've got that one."

I wanted to offer to bet two dollars she hadn't, but I reckoned maybe it was just as safe to not to. So, I never said nothing.

CHAPTER THE LAST

The first time I catched Tom, private, I asked him what was his idea, time of the evasion?—what it was he'd planned to do if the evasion worked all right and he managed to set a nigger free that was already free before? And he said, what he had planned in his head, from the start, if we got Jim out all safe, was for us to run him down the river, on the raft, and have adventures plumb to the mouth of the river, and then tell him about his being free, and take him back up home on a steamboat, in style, and pay him for his lost time, and write word ahead and get out all the niggers around, and have them waltz him into town with a torchlight procession and a brass band, and then he would be a hero, and so would we. But I reckoned it was about as well the way it was.

We had Jim out of the chains in no time, and when Aunt Polly and Uncle Silas and Aunt Sally found out how good he helped the doctor nurse Tom, they made a heap of fuss over him, and fixed him up prime, and give him all he wanted to eat, and a good time, and nothing to do. And we had him up to the sick-room; and had a high talk; and Tom give Jim forty dollars for being prisoner for us so patient, and doing it up so good, and Jim was pleased most to death, and busted out, and says:

"*Dah,* now, Huck, what I tell you?—what I tell you up dah on Jackson islan'? I *tole* you I got a hairy breas', en what's de sign un it; en I *tole* you I ben rich wunst, en gwineter to be rich *agin;* en it's come true; en heah she *is! Dah,* now! doan' talk to *me*—signs is *signs,* mine I tell you; en I knowed jis' 's well 'at I 'uz gwineter be rich agin as I's a stannin' heah dis minute!"

And then Tom he talked along, and talked along, and says le's all three slide out of here, one of these nights, and get an outfit, and go for howling adventures amongst the Injuns, over in the Terrority, for a couple of weeks or two; and I says, all right, that suits me, but I ain't got no money for to buy the outfit, and

I reckon I couldn't get none from home, because it's likely pap's been back before now, and got it all away from Judge Thatcher and drunk it up.

"No he hain't," Tom says; "it's all there, yet—six thousand dollars and more; and your pap hain't ever been back since. Hadn't when I come away, anyhow."

Jim says, kind of solemn:

"He ain't a comin' back no mo', Huck."

I says:

"Why, Jim?"

"Nemmine why, Huck—but he ain't comin' back no mo'."

But I kept at him; so at last he says:

"Doan' you 'member de house dat was float'n down de river, en dey wuz a man in dah, kivered up, en I went in en unkivered him and didn't let you come in? Well, den, you k'n git yo' money when you wants it; kase dat wuz him."

Tom's most well, now, and got his bullet around his neck on a watch-guard for a watch, and is always seeing what time it is, and so there ain't nothing more to write about, and I am rotten glad of it, because if I'd a knowed what a trouble it was to make a book I wouldn't a tackled it and ain't agoing to no more. But I reckon I got to light out for the Territory ahead of the rest, because Aunt Sally she's going to adopt me and sivilize me and I can't stand it. I been there before.

THE END. YOURS TRULY, HUCK FINN.

1876–1883 1884, 1885

MY FIRST LIE, AND HOW I GOT OUT OF IT

As I understand it, what you desire is information about "my first lie, and how I got out of it." I was born in 1835; I am well along, and my memory is not as good as it was. If you had asked about my first truth it would have been easier for me and kinder of you, for I remember that fairly well; I remember it as if it were last week. The family think it was week before, but that is flattery and probably has a selfish project back of it. When a person has become seasoned by experience and has reached the age of sixty-four, which is the age of discretion, he likes a family compliment as well as ever, but he does not lose his head over it as in the old innocent days.

I do not remember my first lie, it is too far back; but I remember my second one very well. I was nine days old at the time, and had noticed that if a pin was sticking in me and I advertised it in the usual fashion, I was lovingly petted and coddled and pitied in a most agreeable way and got a ration between meals besides.

It was human nature to want to get these riches, and I fell. I lied about the pin—advertising one when there wasn't any. You would have done it; George Washington did it, anybody would have done it. During the first half of my life I never knew a child that was able to rise above that temptation and keep from telling that lie. Up to 1867 all the civilized children that were ever born into the world were liars—including George. Then the safety-pin came in and blocked the game. But is that reform worth anything? No; for it is reform by force and has no virtue in it; it merely stops that form of lying, it doesn't impair the disposition to lie, by a shade. It is the cradle application of conversion by fire and sword, or of the temperance principle through prohibition.

To return to that early lie. They found no pin and they realized that another liar had been added to the world's supply. For by grace of a rare inspiration a quite commonplace but seldom noticed fact was borne in upon their understandings—that almost all lies are acts, and speech has no part in them. Then, if they examined a little further they recognized that all people are liars from the cradle onward, without exception, and that they begin to lie as soon as they wake in the morning, and keep it up without rest or refreshment until they go to sleep at night. If they arrived at that truth it probably grieved them—did, if they had been heedlessly and ignorantly educated by their books and teachers; for why should a person grieve over a thing which by the eternal law of his make he cannot help? He didn't invent the law; it is merely his business to obey it and keep still; join the universal conspiracy and keep so still that he shall deceive his fellow-conspirators into imagining that he doesn't know that the law exists. It is what we all do—we that know. I am speaking of the lie of silent assertion; we can tell it without saying a word, and we all do it—we that know. In the magnitude of its territorial spread it is one of the most majestic lies that the civilizations make it their sacred and anxious care to guard and watch and propagate.

For instance. It would not be possible for a humane and intelligent person to invent a rational excuse for slavery; yet you will remember that in the early days of the emancipation agitation in the North the agitators got but small help or countenance from any one. Argue and plead and pray as they might, they could not break the universal stillness that reigned, from pulpit and press all the way down to the bottom of society—the clammy stillness created and maintained by the lie of silent assertion—the silent assertion that there wasn't anything going on in which humane and intelligent people were interested.

From the beginning of the Dreyfus case to the end of it all France, except a couple of dozen moral paladins, lay under the smother of the silent-assertion lie that no wrong was being done to a persecuted and unoffending man. The like smother was over England lately, a good half of the population silently letting on that they were not aware that Mr. Chamberlain was trying to manufacture a war in South Africa and was willing to pay fancy prices for the materials.

Now there we have instances of three prominent ostensible civilizations working the silent-assertion lie. Could one find other instances in the three countries? I think so. Not so very many, perhaps, but say a billion—just so as to keep within bounds. Are those countries working that kind of lie, day in and day out, in thousands and thousands of varieties, without ever resting? Yes, we know that to be true. The universal conspiracy of the silent-assertion lie is hard at work always and everywhere, and always in the interest of a stupidity or a sham, never in the interest of a thing fine or respectable. Is it the most timid and shabby of all lies? It seems to have the look of it. For ages and ages it has mutely labored in the interest of despotisms and aristocracies and chattel slaveries, and military slaveries, and religious slaveries, and has kept them alive; keeps them alive yet, here and there and yonder, all about the globe; and will go on keeping them alive until the silent-assertion lie retires from business—the silent assertion that nothing is going on which fair and intelligent men are aware of and are engaged by their duty to try to stop.

What I am arriving at is this: When whole races and peoples conspire to propagate gigantic mute lies in the interest of tyrannies and shams, why should we care anything about the trifling lies told by individuals? Why should we try to make it appear that abstention from lying is a virtue? Why should we want to beguile ourselves in that way? Why should we without shame help the nation lie, and then be ashamed to do a little lying on our own account? Why shouldn't we be honest and honorable, and lie every time we get a chance? That is to say, why shouldn't we be consistent, and either lie all the time or not at all? Why should we help the nation lie the whole day long and then object to telling one little individual private lie in our own interest to go to bed on? Just for the refreshment of it, I mean, and to take the rancid taste out of our mouth.

Here in England they have the oddest ways. They won't tell a spoken lie—nothing can persuade them. Except in a large moral interest, like politics or religion, I mean. To tell a spoken lie to get even the poorest little personal advantage out of it is a thing which is impossible to them. They make me ashamed of myself sometimes, they are so bigoted. They will not even tell a lie for the fun of it; they will not tell it when it hasn't even a suggestion of damage or advantage in it for any one. This has a restraining influence upon me in spite of reason, and I am always getting out of practice.

Of course, they tell all sorts of little unspoken lies, just like anybody; but they don't notice it until their attention is called to it. They have got me so that sometimes I never tell a verbal lie now except in a modified form; and even in the modified form they don't approve of it. Still, that is as far as I can go in the interest of the growing friendly relations between the two countries; I must keep some of my self-respect—and my health. I can live on a pretty low diet, but I can't get along on no sustenance at all.

Of course, there are times when these people have to come out with a spoken lie, for that is a thing which happens to everybody once in a while, and would happen to the angels if they came down here much. Particularly to the angels, in fact, for the lies I speak of are self-sacrificing ones told for a generous object, not a mean one; but even when these people tell a lie of that sort it seems to scare them and unsettle their minds. It is a wonderful thing to see, and shows that they are all insane. In fact, it is a country which is full of the most interesting superstitions.

I have an English friend of twenty-five years' standing, and yesterday when we were coming down-town on top of the 'bus I happened to tell him a lie—a modified one, of course; a half-breed, a mulatto; I can't seem to tell any other kind now, the market is so flat. I was explaining to him how I got out of an embarrassment in Austria last year. I do not know what might have become of me if I hadn't happened to remember to tell the police that I belonged to the same family as the Prince of Wales. That made everything pleasant and they let me go; and apologized, too, and were ever so kind and obliging and polite, and couldn't do too much for me, and explained how the mistake came to be made, and promised to hang the officer that did it, and hoped I would let bygones be bygones and not say anything about it; and I said they could depend on me. My friend said, austerely:

"You call it a modified lie? Where is the modification?"

I explained that it lay in the form of my statement to the police.

"I didn't say I belonged to the royal family; I only said I belonged to the same family as the Prince—meaning the human family, of course; and if those people had had any penetration they would have known it. I can't go around furnishing brains to the police; it is not to be expected."

"How did you feel after that performance?"

"Well, of course I was distressed to find that the police had misunderstood me, but as long as I had not told any lie I knew there was no occasion to sit up nights and worry about it."

My friend struggled with the case several minutes, turning it over and examining it in his mind, then he said that so far as he could see the modification was itself a lie, it being a misleading reservation of an explanatory fact, and so I had told two lies instead of only one.

"I wouldn't have done it," said he; "I have never told a lie, and I should be very sorry to do such a thing."

Just then he lifted his hat and smiled a basketful of surprised and delighted smiles down at a gentleman who was passing in a hansom.

"Who was that, G——?"

"I don't know."

"Then why did you do that?"

"Because I saw he thought he knew me and was expecting it of me. If I hadn't done it he would have been hurt. I didn't want to embarrass him before the whole street."

"Well, your heart was right, G——, and your act was right. What you did was kindly and courteous and beautiful; I would have done it myself; but it was a lie."

"A lie? I didn't say a word. How do you make it out?"

"I know you didn't speak, still you said to him very plainly and enthusiastically in dumb show, 'Hello! you in town? Awful glad to see you, old fellow; when did you get back?' Concealed in your actions was what you have called 'a misleading reservation of an explanatory fact'—the fact that you had never seen him before. You expressed joy in encountering him—a lie; and you made that reservation—another lie. It was my pair over again. But don't be troubled—we all do it."

Two hours later, at dinner, when quite other matters were being discussed, he told how he happened along once just in the nick of time to do a great service for a family who were old friends of his. The head of it had suddenly died in circumstances and surroundings of a ruinously disgraceful character. If known the facts would break the hearts of the innocent family and put upon them a load of unendurable shame. There was no help but in a giant lie, and he girded up his loins and told it.

"The family never found out, G——?"

"Never. In all these years they have never suspected. They were proud of him and always had reason to be; they are proud of him yet, and to them his memory is sacred and stainless and beautiful."

"They had a narrow escape, G——."

"Indeed they had."

"For the very next man that came along might have been one of these heartless and shameless truth-mongers. You have told the truth a million times in your life, G——, but that one golden lie atones for it all. Persevere."

Some may think me not strict enough in my morals, but that position is hardly tenable. There are many kinds of lying which I do not approve. I do not like an injurious lie, except when it injures somebody else; and I do not like the lie of bravado, nor the lie of virtuous ecstasy; the latter was affected by Bryant, the former by Carlyle.

Mr. Bryant said, "Truth crushed to earth will rise again." I have taken medals at thirteen world's fairs, and may claim to be not without capacity, but I never told as big a one as that Mr. Bryant was playing to the gallery; we all do it. Carlyle said, in substance, this—I do not remember the exact words: "This gospel is eternal—that a lie shall not live." I have a reverent affection for Carlyle's books, and have read his *Revolution* eight times; and so I prefer to think he was not entirely at himself when he told that one. To me it is plain that he said it in a moment of excitement, when chasing Americans out of his back-yard with brickbats. They used to go there and worship. At bottom he was probably fond of them, but he was always able to conceal it. He kept bricks for them, but he was not a good shot, and it is matter of history that when he fired they dodged, and carried off the brick; for as a nation we like relics, and so long as we get them we do not much care what the reliquary thinks about it. I am quite sure that when he told that large one about a lie not being able to live he had just missed an American and was overexcited. He told it above thirty years ago, but it is alive yet; alive, and very healthy and hearty, and likely to outlive any fact in history. Carlyle was truthful when calm, but give him Americans enough and bricks enough and he could have taken medals himself.

As regards that time that George Washington told the truth, a word must be said, of course. It is the principal jewel in the crown of America, and it is but natural that we should work it for all it is worth, as Milton says in his "Lay of the Last Minstrel." It was a timely and judicious truth, and I should have told it myself in the circumstances. But I should have stopped there. It was a stately truth, a lofty truth—a Tower; and I think it was a mistake to go on and distract attention from its sublimity by building another Tower alongside of it fourteen times as high. I refer to his remark that he "could not lie." I should have fed that to the marines; or left it to Carlyle; it is just in his style. It would have taken a medal at any European fair, and would have got an Honorable Mention even at Chicago if it had been saved up. But let it pass; the Father of his Country was excited. I have been in those circumstances, and I recollect.

With the truth he told I have no objection to offer, as already indicated. I think it was not premeditated, but an inspiration. With his fine military mind, he had probably arranged to let his brother Edward in for the cherry-tree results, but by an inspiraton he saw his opportunity in time and took advantage of it. By telling the truth he could astonish his father; his father would tell the neighbors; the neighbors would spread it; it would travel to all firesides; in the end it would make him President, and not only that, but First President. He was a far-seeing boy and would be likely to think of these things. Therefore, to my mind, he stands justified for what he did. But not for the other Tower; it was a mistake. Still, I don't know about that; upon reflection I think perhaps it wasn't. For indeed it is that Tower that makes the other one live. If he hadn't said "I cannot tell a lie" there would have been no convulsion. That was the earthquake that rocked the planet. That is the kind of statement that lives forever, and a fact barnacled to it has a good chance to share its immortality.

To sum up, on the whole I am satisfied with things the way they are. There is a prejudice against the spoken lie, but none against any other, and by examination and mathematical computation I find that the proportion of the spoken lie to the other varieties is as 1 to 22,894. Therefore the spoken lie is of no consequence, and it is not worth while to go around fussing about it and trying to make believe that it is an important matter. The silent colossal National

Lie that is the support and confederate of all the tyrannies and shams and inequalities and unfairnesses that afflict the peoples—that is the one to throw bricks and sermons at. But let us be judicious and let somebody else begin.

And then—But I have wandered from my text. How did I get out of my second lie? I think I got out with honor, but I cannot be sure, for it was a long time ago and some of the details have faded out of my memory. I recollect that I was reversed and stretched across some one's knee, and that something happened, but I cannot now remember what it was. I think there was music; but it is all dim now and blurred by the lapse of time, and this may be only a senile fancy.

1900

TO THE PERSON SITTING IN DARKNESS

"Christmas will dawn in the United States over a people full of hope and aspiration and good cheer. Such a condition means contentment and happiness. The carping grumbler who may here and there go forth will find few to listen to him. The majority will wonder what is the matter with him and pass on."—*New York Tribune,* on Christmas Eve.

From *The Sun,* of New York:

"The purpose of this article is not to describe the terrible offences against humanity committed in the name of Politics in some of the most notorious East Side districts. *They could not be described, even verbally.* But it is the intention to let the great mass of more or less careless citizens of this beautiful metropolis of the New World get some conception of the havoc and ruin wrought to man, woman and child in the most densely populated and least known section of the city. Name, date and place can be supplied to those of little faith—or to any man who feels himself aggrieved. It is a plain statement of record and observation, written without license and without garnish.

"Imagine, if you can, a section of the city territory completely dominated by one man, without whose permission neither legitimate nor illegitimate business can be conducted; *where illegitimate business is encouraged and legitimate business discouraged;* where the respectable residents have to fasten their doors and windows summer nights and sit in their rooms with asphyxiating air and 100-degree temperature, rather than try to catch the faint whiff of breeze in their natural breathing places, the stoops of their homes; *where naked women dance by night in the streets, and unsexed men prowl like vultures through the darkness on business'* not only permitted but encouraged by the police; *where the education of infants begins with the knowledge of prostitution* and the training of little girls is training in the arts of Phryne; where *American* girls brought up with the refinements of *American* homes are imported from small towns up-State, Massachusetts, Connecticut and New Jersey, and kept as virtually prisoners as if they were locked up behind jail bars until they have lost all semblance of womanhood; *where small boys are taught to solicit for the women of disorderly houses;* where there is an organized society of young men *whose sole business in life is to corrupt young girls and turn them over to bawdy houses;* where men walking with their wives along the street are openly insulted; *where children that have adult diseases are the chief patrons of the hospitals and dispensaries;* where it is the rule, rather than the exception, that *murder, rape, robbery and theft go unpunished*—in short where the Premium of the most awful forms of Vice is the Profit of the politicians."

The following news from China appeared in *The Sun,* of New York, on Christmas Eve. The italics are mine:

"The Rev. Mr. Ament, of the American Board of Foreign Missions, has returned from a trip which he made for the purpose of collecting indemnities for damages done by Boxers. *Everywhere he went he compelled the Chinese to pay.* He says that all his native Christians are now provided for. He had 700 of them under his charge, and 300 were killed. He has *collected* 300 *taels for each* of these murders, and has *compelled full payment for all the property belonging to Christians* that was destroyed. He also assessed *fines* amounting to THIRTEEN TIMES the amount of the indemnity. *This money will be used for the propagation of the Gospel.*

"Mr. Ament declares that the compensation he has collected is *moderate,* when compared with the amount secured by the Catholics, who demand, in addition to money, *head for head.* They collect 500 taels for each murder of a Catholic. In the Wenchiu country, 680 Catholics were killed, and for this the European Catholics here demand 750,000 strings of cash and 680 *heads.*

"In the course of a conversation, Mr. Ament referred to the attitude of the missionaries toward the Chinese. He said:

" 'I deny emphatically that the missionaries are *vindictive,* that they *generally* looted, or that they have done anything *since* the siege that *the circumstances did not demand.* I criticise the Americans. *The soft hand of the Americans is not as good as the mailed fist of the Germans.* If you deal with the Chinese with a soft hand they will take advantage of it.'

"The statement that the French Government will return the loot taken by the French soldiers, is the source of the greatest amusement here. The French soldiers were more systematic looters than the Germans, and it is a fact that to-day *Catholic Christians,* carrying French flags and armed with modern guns, *are looting villages* in the Province of Chili."

By happy luck, we get all these glad tidings on Christmas Eve—just in time to enable us to celebrate the day with proper gaiety and enthusiasm. Our spirits soar, and we find we can even make jokes: Taels I win, Heads you lose.

Our Reverend Ament is the right man in the right place. What we want of our missionaries out there is, not that they shall merely represent in their acts and persons the grace and gentleness and charity and loving kindness of our religion, but that they shall also represent the American spirit. The oldest Americans are the Pawnees. Macallum's History says:

"When a white Boxer kills a Pawnee and destroys his property, the other Pawnees do not trouble to seek *him* out, they kill any white person that comes along; also, they make some white village pay deceased's heirs the full cash value of deceased, together with full cash value of the property destroyed; they also make the village pay, in addition, *thirteen times* the value of that property into a fund for the dissemination of the Pawnee religion, which they regard as the best of all religions for the softening and humanizing of the heart of man. It is their idea that it is only fair and right that the innocent should be made to suffer for the guilty, and that it is better that ninety and nine innocent should suffer than that one guilty person should escape."

Our Reverend Ament is justifiably jealous of those enterprising Catholics, who not only get big money for each lost convert, but get "head for head" besides. But he should soothe himself with the reflection that the entirety of their exactions are for their own pockets, whereas he, less selfishly, devotes only 300 taels per head to that service, and gives the whole vast thirteen repetitions of the property-indemnity to the service of propagating the Gospel. His magnanimity has won him the approval of his nation, and will get him a monument. Let him be content with these rewards. We all hold him dear for manfully defending his fellow missionaries from exaggerated charges which were beginning to distress us, but which his testimony has so considerably modified that we can now contemplate them without noticeable pain. For now we know that, even before the siege, the missionaries were not "generally" out looting, and that, "since the siege," they have acted quite handsomely, except when "circumstances" crowded them. I am arranging for the monument. Subscriptions for it can be sent to the American Board; designs for it can be sent to me. Designs must allegorically set forth the Thirteen Reduplications of the Indemnity, and the Object for which they were exacted; as Ornaments, the designs must exhibit 680 Heads, so disposed as to give a pleasing and pretty effect; for the Catholics have done nicely, and are entitled to notice in the monument. Mottoes may be suggested, if any shall be discovered that will satisfactorily cover the ground.

Mr. Ament's financial feat of squeezing a thirteen-fold indemnity out of the pauper peasants to square other people's offenses, thus condemning them and their women and innocent little children to inevitable starvation and lingering death, in order that the blood-money so acquired might be *"used for the propagation of the Gospel,"* does not flutter my serenity; although the act and the words, taken together, concrete a blasphemy so hideous and so colossal that, without doubt, its mate is not findable in the history of this or of any other age. Yet, if a layman had done that thing and justified it with those words, I should have shuddered, I know. Or, if I had done the thing and said the words myself—however, the thought is unthinkable, irreverent as some imperfectly informed people think me. Sometimes an ordained minister sets out to be blasphemous. When this happens, the layman is out of the running; he stands no chance.

We have Mr. Ament's impassioned assurance that the missionaries are not "vindictive." Let us hope and pray that they will never become so, but will remain in the almost morbidly fair and just and gentle temper which is affording so much satisfaction to their brother and champion to-day.

The following is from the *New York Tribune* of Christmas Eve. It comes from that journal's Tokio correspondent. It has a strange and impudent sound, but the Japanese are but partially civilized as yet. When they become wholly civilized they will not talk so:

> "The missionary question, of course, occupies a foremost place in the discussion. It is now felt as essential that the Western Powers take cognizance of the sentiment here, that religious invasions of Oriental countries by powerful Western organizations are tantamount to filibustering expeditions, and should not only be discountenanced, but that stern measures should be adopted for their suppression. The feeling here is that the missionary organizations constitute a constant menace to peaceful international relations."

Shall we? That is, shall we go on conferring our Civilization upon the peoples that sit in darkness, or shall we give those poor things a rest? Shall we bang right ahead in our old-time, loud, pious way, and commit the new century to the game; or shall we sober up and sit down and think it over first? Would it not be prudent to get our Civilization-tools together, and see how much stock is left on hand in the way of Glass Beads and Theology, and Maxim Guns and Hymn Books, and Trade-Gin and Torches of Progress and Enlightenment (patent adjustable ones, good to fire villages with, upon occasion), and balance the books, and arrive at the profit and loss, so that we may intelligently decide whether to continue the business or sell out the property and start a new Civilization Scheme on the proceeds?

Extending the Blessings of Civilization to our Brother who Sits in Darkness has been a good trade and has paid well, on the whole; and there is money in it yet, if carefully worked—but not enough, in my judgment, to make any considerable risk advisable. The People that Sit in Darkness are getting to be too scarce—too scarce and too shy. And such darkness as is now left is really of but an indifferent quality, and not dark enough for the game. The most of those People that Sit in Darkness have been furnished with more light than was good for them or profitable for us. We have been injudicious.

The Blessings-of-Civilization Trust, wisely and cautiously administered, is a Daisy. There is more money in it, more territory, more sovereignty, and other kinds of emolument, than there is in any other game that is played. But Christendom has been playing it badly of late years, and must certainly suffer by it, in my opinion. She has been so eager to get every stake that appeared on the green cloth, that the People who Sit in Darkness have noticed it—they have noticed it, and have begun to show alarm. They have become suspicious of the Blessings of Civilization. More—they have begun to examine them. This is not well. The Blessings of Civilization are all right, and a good commercial property; there could not be a better, in a dim light. In the right kind of a light, and at a proper distance, with the goods a little out of focus, they furnish this desirable exhibit to the Gentlemen who Sit in Darkness:

Love,	Law and Order,
Justice,	Liberty,
Gentleness,	Equality,
Christianity,	Honorable Dealing,
Protection to the Weak,	Mercy,
Temperance,	Education,—and so on.

There. Is it good? Sir, it is pie. It will bring into camp any idiot that sits in darkness anywhere. But not if we adulterate it. It is proper to be emphatic upon that point. This brand is strictly for Export—apparently. *Apparently.* Privately and confidentially, it is nothing of the kind. Privately and confidentially, it is merely an outside cover, gay and pretty and attractive, displaying the special patterns of our Civilization which we reserve for Home Consumption, while *inside* the bale is the Actual Thing that the Customer Sitting in Darkness buys with his blood and tears and land and liberty. That Actual Thing is, indeed, Civilization, but it is only for Export. Is there a difference between the two brands? In some of the details, yes.

We all know that the Business is being ruined. The reason is not far to seek. It is because our Mr. McKinley, and Mr. Chamberlain, and the Kaiser, and the

Czar and the French have been exporting the Actual Thing *with the outside cover left off.* This is bad for the Game. It shows that these new players of it are not sufficiently acquainted with it.

It is a distress to look on and note the mismoves, they are so strange and so awkward. Mr. Chamberlain manufactures a war out of materials so inadequate and so fanciful that they make the boxes grieve and the gallery laugh, and he tries hard to persuade himself that it isn't purely a private raid for cash, but has a sort of dim, vague respectability about it somewhere, if he could only find the spot; and that, by and by, he can scour the flag clean again after he has finished dragging it through the mud, and make it shine and flash in the vault of heaven once more as it had shone and flashed there a thousand years in the world's respect until he laid his unfaithful hand upon it. It is bad play—bad. For it exposes the Actual Thing to Them that Sit in Darkness, and they say: "What! Christian against Christian? And only for money? Is *this* a case of magnanimity, forbearance, love, gentleness, mercy, protection of the weak—this strange and over-showy onslaught of an elephant upon a nest of field-mice, on the pretext that the mice had squeaked an insolence at him—conduct which 'no self-respecting government could allow to pass unavenged?' as Mr. Chamberlain said. Was that a good pretext in a small case, when it had not been a good pretext in a large one?—for only recently Russia had affronted the elephant three times and survived alive and unsmitten. Is this Civilization and Progress? Is it something better than we already possess? These harryings and burnings and desert-makings in the Transvaal—is this an improvement on our darkness? Is it, perhaps, possible that there are two kinds of Civilization—one for home consumption and one for the heathen market?"

Then They that Sit in Darkness are troubled, and shake their heads; and they read this extract from a letter of a British private, recounting his exploits in one of Methuen's victories, some days before the affair of Magersfontein, and they are troubled again:

> "We tore up the hill and into the intrenchments, and the Boers saw we had them; so they dropped their guns and went down on their knees and put up their hands clasped, and begged for mercy. And we gave it them—*with the long spoon.*"

The long spoon is the bayonet. See *Lloyd's Weekly,* London, of those days. The same number—and the same column—contained some quite unconscious satire in the form of shocked and bitter upbraidings of the Boers for their brutalities and inhumanities!

Next, to our heavy damage, the Kaiser went to playing the game without first mastering it. He lost a couple of missionaries in a riot in Shantung, and in his account he made an overcharge for them. China had to pay a hundred thousand dollars apiece for them, in money; twelve miles of territory, containing several millions of inhabitants and worth twenty million dollars; and to build a monument, and also a Christian church; whereas the people of China could have been depended upon to remember the missionaries without the help of these expensive memorials. This was all bad play. Bad, because it would not, and could not, and will not now or ever, deceive the Person Sitting in Darkness. He knows that it was an overcharge. He knows that a missionary is like any other man: he is worth merely what you can supply his place for, and no more. He is useful, but so is a doctor, so is a sheriff, so is an editor; but a just Emperor does not charge war-prices for such. A diligent, intelligent, but obscure missionary, and a diligent, intelligent country editor are worth much, and we know it; but they are not worth the earth. We esteem such an editor, and we are sorry to see him go; but, when he goes, we should consider twelve miles of territory, and a church, and a fortune, over-compensation for his loss. I mean, if he was a Chinese editor, and we had to settle for him. It is no proper figure for an editor or a missionary; one can get shop-worn kings for less. It was bad play on the Kaiser's part. It got this property, true; but it *produced the Chinese revolt,* the indignant uprising of China's traduced patriots, the Boxers. The results have been expensive to Germany, and to the other Disseminators of Progress and the Blessings of Civilization.

The Kaiser's claim was paid, yet it was bad play, for it could not fail to have an evil effect upon Persons Sitting in Darkness in China. They would muse upon the event, and be likely to say: "Civilization is gracious and beautiful, for such is its reputation; but can we afford it? There are rich Chinamen, perhaps they could afford it; but this tax is not laid upon them, it is laid upon the peasants of Shantung; it is they that must pay this mighty sum, and their wages are but four cents a day. Is this a better civilization than ours, and holier and higher and nobler? Is not this rapacity? Is not this extortion? Would Germany charge America two hundred thousand dollars for two missionaries, and shake the mailed fist in her face, and send warships, and send soldiers, and say: "Seize twelve miles of territory, worth twenty millions of dollars, as additional pay for the missionaries; and make those peasants build a monument to the missionaries, and a costly Christian church to remember them by?' And later would Germany say to her soldiers: 'March through America and slay, *giving no quarter;* make the German face there, as has been our Hunface here, a terror for a thousand years; march through the Great Republic and slay, slay, slay, carving a road for our offended religion through its heart and bowels?' Would Germany do like this to America, to England, to France, to Russia? Or only to China the helpless—imitating the elephant's assault upon the field-mice? Had we better invest in this Civilization—this Civilization which called Napoleon a buccaneer for carrying off Venice's bronze horses, but which steals our ancient astronomical instruments from our walls, and goes looting like common bandits—that is, all the alien soldiers except America's; and (Americans again excepted) storms frightened villages and cables the result to glad journals at home every day: 'Chinese losses, 450 killed; ours, *one officer and two men wounded.* Shall proceed against neighboring village to-morrow, where a *massacre* is reported.' Can we afford Civilization?"

And, next, Russia must go and play the game injudiciously. She affronts England once or twice—with the Person Sitting in Darkness observing and noting; by moral assistance of France and Germany, she robs Japan of her hard-earned spoil, all swimming in Chinese blood—Port Arthur—with the Person again observing and noting; then she seizes Manchuria, raids its villages, and chokes its great river with the swollen corpses of countless massacred peasants—that astonished Person still observing and noting. And perhaps he is saying to himself: "It is yet *another* Civilized Power, with its banner of the Prince of Peace in one hand and its loot-basket and its butcher-knife in the other. Is there no salvation for us but to adopt Civilization and lift ourselves down to its level?"

And by and by comes America, and our Master of the Game plays it badly—plays it as Mr. Chamberlain was playing it in South Africa. It was a mistake to do that; also, it was one which was quite unlooked for in a Master who was playing it so well in Cuba. In Cuba, he was playing the usual and regular *American* game, and it was winning, for there is no way to beat it. The Master, contemplating Cuba, said: "Here is an oppressed and friendless little nation which is willing to fight to be free; we go partners, and put up the strength of seventy million sympathizers and the resources of the United States: play!" Nothing but Europe combined could call that hand: and Europe cannot combine on anything. There, in Cuba, he was following our great traditions in a way which made us very proud of him, and proud of the deep dissatisfaction which his play was provoking in Continental Europe. Moved by a high inspiration, he threw out those stirring words which proclaimed that forcible annexation would be "criminal aggression;" and in that utterance fired another "shot heard round the world." The memory of that fine saying will be outlived by the remembrance of no act of his but one—that he forgot it within the twelvemonth, and its honorable gospel along with it.

For, presently, came the Philippine temptation. It was strong; it was too strong, and he made that bad mistake: he played the European game, the Chamberlain game. It was a pity; it was a great pity, that error; that one grievous error, that irrevocable error. For it was the very place and time to play the American game again. And at no cost. Rich winnings to be gathered in, too; rich and permanent; indestructible; a fortune transmissible forever to the children of the flag. Not land, not money, not dominion—no, something worth many times more than that dross: our share, the spectacle of a nation of long harassed and persecuted slaves set free through our influence; our posterity's share, the golden memory of that fair deed. The game was in our hands. If it had been played according to the American rules, Dewey would have sailed away from Manila as soon as he had destroyed the Spanish fleet—after putting up a sign on shore guaranteeing foreign property and life against damage by the Filipinos, and warning the Powers that interference with the emancipated patriots would be regarded as an act unfriendly to the United States. The Powers cannot combine, in even a bad cause, and the sign would not have been molested.

Dewey could have gone about his affairs elsewhere, and left the competent Filipino army to starve out the little Spanish garrison and send it home, and the Filipino citizens to set up the form of government they might prefer, and deal with the friars and their doubtful acquisitions according to Filipino ideas of fairness and justice—ideas which have since been tested and found to be of as high an order as any that prevail in Europe or America.

But we played the Chamberlain game, and lost the chance to add another Cuba and another honorable deed to our good record.

The more we examine the mistake, the more clearly we perceive that it is going to be bad for the Business. The Person Sitting in Darkness is almost sure to say: "There is something curious about this—curious and unaccountable. There must be two Americas: one that sets the captive free, and one that takes a once-captive's new freedom away from him, and picks a quarrel with him with nothing to found it on; then kills him to get his land."

The truth is, the Person Sitting in Darkness *is* saying things like that; and for the sake of the Business we must persuade him to look at the Philippine matter in another and healthier way. We must arrange his opinions for him. I believe it can be done; for Mr. Chamberlain has arranged England's opinion of the South African matter, and done it most cleverly and successfully. He presented the facts—some of the facts—and showed those confiding people what the facts meant. He did it statistically, which is a good way. He used the formula: "Twice 2 are 14, and 2 from 9 leaves 35." Figures are effective; figures will convince the elect.

Now, my plan is a still bolder one than Mr. Chamberlain's, though apparently a copy of it. Let us be franker than Mr. Chamberlain; let us audaciously present the whole of the facts, shirking none, then explain them according to Mr. Chamberlain's formula. This daring truthfulness will astonish and dazzle the Person Sitting in Darkness, and he will take the Explanation down before his mental vision has had time to get back into focus. Let us say to him:

"Our case is simple. On the 1st of May, Dewey destroyed the Spanish fleet. This left the Archipelago in the hands of its proper and rightful owners, the Filipino nation. Their army numbered 30,000 men, and they were competent to whip out or starve out the little Spanish garrison; then the people could set up a government of their own devising. Our traditions required that Dewey should now set up his warning sign, and go away. But the Master of the Game happened to think of another plan—the European plan. He acted upon it. This was, to send out an army—ostensibly to help the native patriots put the finishing touch upon their long and plucky struggle for independence, but really to take their land away from them and keep it. That is, in the interest of Progress and Civilization. The plan developed, stage by stage, and quite satisfactorily. We entered into a military alliance with the trusting Filipinos, and they hemmed in Manila on the land side, and by their valuable help the place, with its garrison of 8,000 or 10,000 Spaniards, was captured—a thing which we could not have accomplished unaided at that time. We got their help by—by ingenuity. We knew they were fighting for their independence, and that they had been at it for two years. We knew they supposed that we also were fighting in their worthy cause—just as we had helped the Cubans fight for Cuban independence—and we allowed them to go on thinking so. *Until Manila was ours and we could get along without them.* Then we showed our hand. Of course, they were surprised—that was natural; surprised and disappointed; disappointed and grieved. To them it looked un-American; uncharacteristic; foreign to our established traditions. And this was natural, too; for we were only playing the American Game in public—in private it was the European. It was neatly done, very neatly, and it bewildered them. They could not understand it; for we had been so friendly—so affectionate, even—with those simple-minded patriots. We, our own selves, had brought back out of exile their leader, their hero, their hope, their Washington—Aguinaldo; brought him in a warship, in high honor, under the sacred shelter and hospitality of the flag; brought him back and restored him to his people, and got their moving and eloquent gratitude for it. Yes, we had been so friendly to them, and had heartened them up in so many ways! We had lent them guns and ammunition; advised with them; exchanged pleasant courtesies with them; placed our sick and wounded in their kindly care; entrusted our Spanish prisoners to their humane and honest hands; fought shoulder to shoulder with them against 'the common enemy' (our own phrase); praised their courage, praised their gallantry, praised their mercifulness, praised their fine and honorable conduct; borrowed their trenches, borrowed strong positions which they had previously captured from the Spaniard; petted them, lied to them—officially proclaiming that our land and naval forces came to give them their freedom and displace the bad Spanish Government—fooled them, used them until we needed them no longer; then derided the sucked orange and threw it away. We kept the positions which we had beguiled them of; by and by, we moved a force forward and overlapped patriot ground—a clever thought, for we needed trouble, and this would produce it. A Filipino soldier, crossing the ground, where no one had a right to forbid him, was shot by our sentry. The badgered patriots resented this with arms, without waiting to know whether Aguinaldo, who was absent, would approve or not. Aguinaldo did not approve; but that availed nothing. What we wanted, in the interest of Progress and Civilization, was the Archipelago, unencumbered by patriots struggling for independence; and War was what we needed. We clinched our opportunity. It is Mr. Chamberlain's case over again—at least in its motive and intention; and we played the game as adroitly as he played it himself."

At this point in our frank statement of fact to the Person Sitting in Darkness, we should throw in a little trade-taffy about the Blessings of Civilization—for a change, and for the refreshment of his spirit—then go on with our tale:

"We and the patriots having captured Manila, Spain's ownership of the Archipelago and her sovereignty over it were at an end—obliterated—annihilated—not a rag or shred of either remaining behind. It was then that we conceived the divinely humorous idea of *buying* both of these spectres from Spain! [It is quite safe to confess this to the Person Sitting in Darkness, since neither he nor any other sane person will believe it.] In buying those ghosts for twenty millions, we also contracted to take care of the friars and their accumulations. I think we also agreed to propagate leprosy and smallpox, but as to this there is doubt. But it is not important; persons afflicted with the friars do not mind other diseases.

"With our Treaty ratified, Manila subdued, and our Ghosts secured, we had no further use for Aguinaldo and the owners of the Archipelago. We forced a war, and we have been hunting America's guest and ally through the woods and swamps ever since."

At this point in the tale, it will be well to boast a little of our war-work and our heroisms in the field, so as to make our performance look as fine as England's in South Africa; but I believe it will not be best to emphasize this too much. We must be cautious. Of course, we must read the war-telegrams to the Person, in order to keep up our frankness; but we can throw an air of humorousness over them, and that will modify their grim eloquence a little, and their rather indiscreet exhibitions of gory exultation. Before reading to him the following display heads of the dispatches of November 18, 1900, it will be well to practice on them in private first, so as to get the right tang of lightness and gaiety into them:

"ADMINISTRATION WEARY OF PROTRACTED HOSTILITIES!"
"REAL WAR AHEAD FOR FILIPINO REBELS!"*
"WILL SHOW NO MERCY!"
"KITCHENER'S PLAN ADOPTED!"

*"Rebels!" Mumble that funny word—don't let the Person catch it distinctly.

Kitchener knows how to handle disagreeable people who are fighting for their homes and their liberties, and we must let on that we are merely imitating Kitchener, and have no national interest in the matter, further than to get ourselves admired by the Great Family of Nations, in which august company our Master of the Game has bought a place for us in the back row.

Of course, we must not venture to ignore our General MacArthur's reports—oh, why do they keep on printing those embarrassing things?—we must drop them trippingly from the tongue and take the chances:

"During the last ten months our losses have been 268 killed and 750 wounded; Filipino loss, *three thousand two hundred and twenty-seven killed,* and 694 wounded."

We must stand ready to grab the Person Sitting in Darkness, for he will swoon away at this confession, saying: "Good God, those 'niggers' spare their wounded, and the Americans massacre theirs!"

We must bring him to, and coax him and coddle him, and assure him that the ways of Providence are best, and that it would not become us to find fault with them; and then, to show him that we are only imitators, not originators, we must read the following passage from the letter of an American soldier-lad in the Philippines to his mother, published in *Public Opinion,* of Decorah, Iowa, describing the finish of a victorious battle:

"WE NEVER LEFT ONE ALIVE. IF ONE WAS WOUNDED, WE WOULD RUN OUR BAYONETS THROUGH HIM."

Having now laid all the historical facts before the Person Sitting in Darkness, we should bring him to again, and explain them to him. We should say to him:

"They look doubtful, but in reality they are not. There have been lies; yes, but they were told in a good cause. We have been treacherous; but that was only in order that real good might come out of apparent evil. True, we have crushed a deceived and confiding people; we have turned against the weak and the friendless who trusted us; we have stamped out a just and intelligent and well-ordered republic; we have stabbed an ally in the back and slapped the face of a guest; we have bought a Shadow from an enemy that hadn't it to sell; we have robbed a trusting friend of his land and his liberty; we have invited our clean young men to shoulder a discredited musket and do bandit's work under a flag which bandits have been accustomed to fear, not to follow; we have debauched America's honor and blackened her face before the world; but each detail was for the best. We know this. The Head of every State and Sovereignty in Christendom and ninety per cent. of every legislative body in Christendom, including our Congress and our fifty State Legislatures, are members not only of the church, but also of the Blessings-of-Civilization Trust. This world-girdling accumulation of trained morals, high principles, and justice, cannot do an unright thing, an unfair thing, an ungenerous thing, an unclean thing. It knows what it is about. Give yourself no uneasiness; it is all right."

Now then, that will convince the Person. You will see. It will restore the Business. Also, it will elect the Master of the Game to the vacant place in the Trinity of our national gods; and there on their high thrones the Three will sit, age after age, in the people's sight, each bearing the Emblem of his service: Washington, the Sword of the Liberator; Lincoln, the Slave's Broken Chains; the Master, the Chains Repaired.

It will give the Business a splendid new start. You will see.

Everything is prosperous, now; everything is just as we should wish it. We have got the Archipelago, and we shall never give it up. Also, we have every reason to hope that we shall have an opportunity before very long to slip out of our Congressional contract with Cuba and give her something better in the place of it. It is a rich country, and many of us are already beginning to see that the contract was a sentimental mistake. But now—right now—is the best time to do some profitable rehabilitating work—work that will set us up and make us comfortable, and discourage gossip. We cannot conceal from ourselves that, privately, we are a little troubled about our uniform. It is one of our prides; it is acquainted with honor; it is familiar with great deeds and noble; we love it, we revere it; and so this errand it is on makes us uneasy. And our flag—another pride of ours, our chiefest! We have worshipped it so; and when we have seen it in far lands—glimpsing it unexpectedly in that strange sky, waving its welcome and benediction to us—we have caught our breath, and uncovered our heads, and couldn't speak, for a moment, for the thought of what it was to us and the great ideals it stood for. Indeed, we *must* do something about these things; we must not have the flag out there, and the uniform. They are not needed there; we can manage in some other way. England manages, as regards the uniform, and so can we. We have to send soldiers—we can't get out of that—but we can disguise them. It is the way England does in South Africa. Even Mr. Chamberlain himself takes pride in England's honorable uniform, and makes the army down there wear an ugly and odious and appropriate disguise, of yellow stuff such as quarantine flags are made of, and which are hoisted to warn the healthy away from unclean disease and repulsive death. This cloth is called khaki. We could adopt it. It is light, comfortable, grotesque, and deceives the enemy, for he cannot conceive of a soldier being concealed in it.

And as for a flag for the Philippine Province, it is easily managed. We can have a special one—our States do it: we can have just our usual flag, with the white stripes painted black and the stars replaced by the skull and cross-bones.

And we do not need that Civil Commission out there. Having no powers, it has to invent them, and that kind of work cannot be effectively done by just anybody; an expert is required. Mr. Croker can be spared. We do not want the United States represented there, but only the Game.

By help of these suggested amendments, Progress and Civilization in that country can have a boom, and it will take in the Persons who are Sitting in Darkness, and we can resume Business at the old stand.

1901

THE WAR-PRAYER[1]

It was a time of great and exalting excitement. The country was up in arms, the war was on, in every breast burned the holy fire of patriotism; the drums were beating, the bands playing, the toy pistols popping, the bunched firecrackers hissing and spluttering; on every hand and far down the receding and

[1]Dictated by Twain in 1904 or 1905 and first published in 1923.

fading spread of roofs and balconies a fluttering wilderness of flags flashed in the sun; daily the young volunteers marched down the wide avenue gay and fine in their new uniforms, the proud fathers and mothers and sisters and sweethearts cheering them with voices choked with happy emotion as they swung by; nightly the packed mass-meetings listened, panting, to patriot oratory which stirred the deepest deeps of their hearts, and which they interrupted at briefest intervals with cyclones of applause, the tears running down their cheeks the while; in the churches the pastors preached devotion to flag and country, and invoked the God of Battles, beseeching His aid in our good cause in outpouring of fervid eloquence which moved every listener. It was indeed a glad and gracious time, and the half dozen rash spirits that ventured to disapprove of the war and cast a doubt upon its righteousness straightway got such a stern and angry warning that for their personal safety's sake they quickly shrank out of sight and offended no more in that way.

Sunday morning came—next day the battalions would leave for the front; the church was filled; the volunteers were there, their young faces alight with martial dreams—visions of the stern advance, the gathering momentum, the rushing charge, the flashing sabers, the flight of the foe, the tumult, the enveloping smoke, the fierce pursuit, the surrender!—then home from the war, bronzed heroes, welcomed, adored, submerged in golden seas of glory! With the volunteers sat their dear ones, proud, happy, and envied by the neighbors and friends who had no sons and brothers to send forth to the field of honor, there to win for the flag or, failing, die the noblest of noble deaths. The service proceeded; a war-chapter from the Old Testament was read; the first prayer was said; it was followed by an organ-burst that shook the building, and with one impulse the house rose, with glowing eyes and beating hearts, and poured out that tremendous invocation

> "God the all-terrible! Thou who ordainest!
> Thunder thy clarion and lightning thy sword!"

Then came the "long" prayer. None could remember the like of it for passionate pleading and moving and beautiful language. The burden of its supplication was that an ever-merciful and benignant Father of us all would watch over our noble young soldiers, and aid, comfort, and encourage them in their patriotic work; bless them, shield them in the day of battle and the hour of peril, bear them in His mighty hand, make them strong and confident, invincible in the bloody onset, help them to crush the foe, grant to them and to their flag and country imperishable honor and glory—

An aged stranger entered and moved with slow and noiseless step up the main aisle, his eyes fixed upon the minister, his long body clothed in a robe that reached to his feet, his head bare, his white hair descending in a frothy cataract to his shoulders, his seamy face unnaturally pale, pale even to ghastliness. With all eyes following him and wondering, he made his silent way; without pausing, he ascended to the preacher's side and stood there, waiting. With shut lids the preacher, unconscious of his presence, continued his moving prayer, and at last finished it with the words, uttered in fervent appeal, "Bless our arms, grant us the victory, O Lord our God, Father and Protector of our land and flag!"

The stranger touched his arm, motioned him to step aside—which the startled minister did—and took his place. During some moments he surveyed the spellbound audience with solemn eyes, in which burned an uncanny light; then in a deep voice he said—

"I come from the Throne—bearing a message from Almighty God!" The words smote the house with a shock; if the stranger perceived it he gave it no attention. "He has heard the prayer of His servant your shepherd, and will grant it if such shall be your desire after I, His messenger, shall have explained to you its import—that is to say, its full import. For it is like unto many of the prayers of men, in that it asks for more than he who utters it is aware of—except he pause and think.

"God's servant and yours has prayed his prayer. Has he paused, and taken thought? Is it one prayer? No, it is two—one uttered, the other not. Both have reached the ear of Him who heareth all supplications, the spoken and the unspoken. Ponder this—keep it in mind: if you would beseech a blessing upon yourself, beware! lest without intent you invoke a curse upon a neighbor at the same time. If you pray for the blessing of rain upon your crop which needs it, by that act you are possibly praying for a curse upon some neighbor's crop which may not need rain and can be injured by it.

"You have heard your servant's prayer—the uttered part of it. I am commissioned of God to put into words the other part of it—that part which the pastor—and also you in your hearts—fervently prayed silently. And ignorantly and unthinkingly? God grant that it was so! You heard these words: 'Grant us the victory, O Lord our God!' That is sufficient. The *whole* of the uttered prayer is compacted into those pregnant words. Elaborations were not necessary. When you have prayed for victory you have prayed for many unmentioned results which follow victory—*must* follow it, cannot help but follow it. Upon the listening spirit of God the Father fell also the unspoken part of the prayer. He commandeth me to put it into words. Listen!

"O Lord, our Father, our young patriots, idols of our hearts, go forth to battle—be Thou near them! With them—in spirit—we also go forth from the sweet peace of our beloved firesides to smite the foe. O Lord, our God, help us to tear their soldiers to bloody shreds with our shells; help us to cover their smiling fields with the pale forms of their patriot dead; help us to drown the thunder of the guns with the shrieks of their wounded, writhing in pain; help us to lay waste their humble homes with a hurricane of fire; help us to wring the hearts of their unoffending widows with unavailing grief; help us to turn them out roofless with little children to wander unfriended the wastes of their desolated land in rags and hunger and thirst, sport of the sun-flames of summer and the icy winds of winter, broken in spirit, worn with travail, imploring Thee for the refuge of the grave and denied it—for our sakes who adore Thee, Lord, blast their hopes, blight their lives, protract their bitter pilgrimage, make heavy their steps, water their way with their tears, stain the white snow with the blood of their wounded feet! We ask it, in the spirit of love, of Him Who is the Source of Love, and Who is the ever-faithful refuge and friend of all that are sore beset and seek His aid with humble and contrite hearts. Amen."

[*After a pause.*] "Ye have prayed it; if ye still desire it, speak!—The messenger of the Most High waits."

It was believed, afterwards, that the man was a lunatic, because there was no sense in what he said.

1904–1905 1923

Mary E. Wilkins Freeman
1852–1930

In the years following the Civil War, decaying villages and abandoned farms marked the landscape of rural New England. Cheap land in the West and the lure of jobs in growing industrial centers to the south drew off the stronger, younger, and more adventurous. Those who remained behind often lacked the opportunity or the will to leave. A substantial portion were unmarried women. They were so numerous that the strong-willed New England spinster, the stern old maid, became a public institution, the object of poems, jokes, songs, and newspaper cartoons. It was just such women, waiting tidily in fading New England villages, who became the subjects of Mary Wilkins Freeman's best stories.

Until her marriage in middle age to Dr. Charles Freeman of Metuchen, New Jersey, Mary Eleanor Wilkins lived in Randolph, Massachusetts, and in Brattleboro, Vermont, small towns in decline, with empty stores along the main street and silent mills along the river. She was in frail health as a girl, and in her solitude she turned naturally to reading. As a teenager she wrote and published a number of poems for children, but she decided to make writing her career when she was in her early twenties and needed a vocation to help support her family. Her love of books was equaled by a curiosity about the towns of Vermont and Massachusetts. She studied their histories, their distinctive buildings, and the dialect and character of their people.

In 1881, she received ten dollars for a poem published in a children's magazine. Her first book was a collection of children's verse, Decorative Plaques *(1883). Her first success in writing fiction for adults came in 1882 with "A Shadow Story," which won a prize of fifty dollars from a Boston weekly. Two years later, when* Harper's Bazaar *accepted "Two Old Lovers" for publication, her career was launched, and her stories were soon in demand by editors of major magazines. She drew the admiration of such literary notables as James Russell Lowell and Henry James. Her stories were republished in England, and from France came requests for permission to translate her stories into French. In all she published thirty-nine volumes. Her best were* A Humble Romance and Other Stories *(1887), and* A New England Nun and Other Stories *(1891), tales of stolid village and farm people in remote New England.*

Mary Wilkins Freeman aimed "to preserve in literature" the "old and probably disappearing ways of New England character." Her stories mix elements of romance, realism, and naturalism. She wrote of strong-minded people whose individualism earns the wrath of friends and village neighbors. She depicted the pinched and stagnating lives of hesitant lovers whose endlessly prolonged courtships are destined never to conclude in marriage. Her work is frequently compared to that of Sarah Orne Jewett. Both described the lives of the men and women of small-town New England. Both have been identified with the local color tradition in American literature—writers whose stories and sketches emphasize the character types, customs, settings, and speech of regions that in nineteenth-century America still preserved their distinct identity.

Yet Mary Freeman's writing was less concerned with locale, more concerned with character. And her writing had a sharp, ironic edge to it that Sarah Orne Jewett seldom attempted. Freeman's stories are written with greater detachment, less sympathetic musing at the dilemmas of her characters. Her view could be sharp, critical, unsparing. Lacking the lenient tenderness that Sarah Orne Jewett exhibited for the people she described, Mary Wilkins Freeman could achieve a realism that to modern eyes more clearly portrays the strength and follies of the people she lived among, a realism that justifiably brought her recognition as "the most truthful recorder in fiction of New England life."

FURTHER READING: *The Best Stories of Mary Wilkins Freeman,* ed. H. Lanier, 1927; *Selected Stories of Mary E. Wilkins Freeman,* ed. M. Pryse, 1983; *The Uncollected Stories of Mary Wilkins Freeman,* ed. M. Reichardt, 1992; *The Infant Sphinx: Collected Letters of Mary E. Wilkins Freeman,* ed. B. Kendrick, 1985; E. Foster, *Mary E. Wilkins Freeman,* 1956; L. Glasser, *In a Closet Hidden: The Life of Mary E. Wilkins Freeman,* 1996; A. Hamblen, *The New England Art of Mary E. Wilkins Freeman,* 1966; P. Westbrook, *Mary Wilkins Freeman,* 1967, 1988; *Critical Essays on Mary Wilkins Freeman,* ed. S. Marchalonis, 1991; M. Reichardt, *A Web of Relationship: Women in the Short Fiction of Mary Wilkins Freeman,* 1992; M. Reichardt, *Mary Wilkins Freeman,* 1998.

TEXTS: "A Mistaken Charity" from *A Humble Romance and Other Stories,* 1887; "A New England Nun" from *A New England Nun and Other Stories,* 1891.

A NEW ENGLAND NUN

It was late in the afternoon, and the light was waning. There was a difference in the look of the tree shadows out in the yard. Somewhere in the distance cows were lowing and a little bell was tinkling; now and then a farm-wagon tilted by, and the dust flew; some blue-shirted laborers with shovels over their shoulders plodded past; little swarms of flies were dancing up and down before the people's faces in the soft air. There seemed to be a gentle stir arising over everything for the mere sake of subsidence—a very premonition of rest and hush and night.

This soft diurnal[1] commotion was over Louisa Ellis also. She had been peacefully sewing at her sitting-room window all the afternoon. Now she quilted her needle carefully into her work, which she folded precisely, and laid in a basket with her thimble and thread and scissors. Louisa Ellis could not remember that ever in her life she had mislaid one of these little feminine appurtenances, which had become, from long use and constant association, a very part of her personality.

Louisa tied a green apron round her waist, and got out a flat straw hat with a green ribbon. Then she went into the garden with a little blue crockery bowl, to pick some currants for her tea. After the currants were picked she sat on the back door-step and stemmed them, collecting the stems carefully in her apron, and afterwards throwing them into the hen-coop. She looked sharply at the grass beside the step to see if any had fallen there.

Louisa was slow and still in her movements; it took her a long time to prepare her tea; but when ready it was set forth, with as much grace as if she had been a veritable[2] guest to her own self. The little square table stood exactly in the centre of the kitchen, and was covered with a starched linen cloth whose border pattern of flowers glistened. Louisa had a damask[3] napkin on her tea-tray, where were arranged a cut-glass tumbler full of teaspoons, a silver cream-pitcher, a china sugar-bowl, and one pink china cup and saucer. Louisa used china every day—something which none of her neighbors did. They whispered about it among themselves. Their daily tables were laid with common crockery, their sets of best china stayed in the parlor closet, and Louisa Ellis was no richer nor better bred than they. Still she would use the china. She had for her supper a glass dish full of sugared currants, a plate of little cakes, and one of light

[1]Taking place during the day. [2]True. [3]Elegant, richly patterned linen.

white biscuits. Also a leaf or two of lettuce, which she cut up daintily. Louisa was very fond of lettuce, which she raised to perfection in her little garden. She ate quite heartily, though in a delicate, pecking way; it seemed almost surprising that any considerable bulk of the food should vanish.

After tea she filled a plate with nicely baked thin corncakes, and carried them out into the back-yard.

"Cæsar!" she called. "Cæsar! Cæsar!"

There was a little rush, and the clank of a chain, and a large yellow-and-white dog appeared at the door of his tiny hut, which was half hidden among the tall grasses and flowers. Louisa patted him and gave him the corn-cakes. Then she returned to the house and washed the tea-things, polishing the china carefully. The twilight had deepened; the chorus of the frogs floated in at the open window wonderfully loud and shrill, and once in a while a long sharp drone from a tree-toad pierced it. Louisa took off her green gingham apron, disclosing a shorter one of pink and white print. She lighted her lamp, and sat down again with her sewing.

In about half an hour Joe Dagget came. She heard his heavy step on the walk, and rose and took off her pink-and-white apron. Under that was still another—white linen with a little cambric edging on the bottom; that was Louisa's company apron. She never wore it without her calico sewing apron over it unless she had a guest. She had barely folded the pink and white one with methodical haste and laid it in a table-drawer when the door opened and Joe Dagget entered.

He seemed to fill up the whole room. A little yellow canary that had been asleep in his green cage at the south window woke up and fluttered wildly, beating his little yellow wings against the wires. He always did so when Joe Dagget came into the room.

"Good-evening," said Louisa. She extended her hand with a kind of solemn cordiality.

"Good-evening, Louisa," returned the man, in a loud voice.

She placed a chair for him, and they sat facing each other, with the table between them. He sat bolt-upright, toeing out his heavy feet squarely, glancing with a good-humored uneasiness around the room. She sat gently erect, folding her slender hands in her white-linen lap.

"Been a pleasant day," remarked Dagget.

"Real pleasant," Louisa assented, softly. "Have you been haying?" she asked, after a little while.

"Yes, I've been haying all day, down in the ten-acre lot. Pretty hot work."

"It must be."

"Yes, it's pretty hot work in the sun."

"Is your mother well to-day?"

"Yes, mother's pretty well."

"I suppose Lily Dyer's with her now?"

Dagget colored. "Yes, she's with her," he answered, slowly.

He was not very young, but there was a boyish look about his large face. Louisa was not quite as old as he, her face was fairer and smoother, but she gave people the impression of being older.

"I suppose she's a good deal of help to your mother," she said, further.

"I guess she is; I don't know how mother'd get along without her," said Dagget, with a sort of embarrassed warmth.

"She looks like a real capable girl. She's pretty-looking too," remarked Louisa.

"Yes, she is pretty fair looking."

Presently Dagget began fingering the books on the table. There was a square red autograph album, and a Young Lady's Gift-Book[4] which had belonged to Louisa's mother. He took them up one after the other and opened them; then laid them down again, the album on the Gift-Book.

Louisa kept eying them with mild uneasiness. Finally she rose and changed the position of the books, putting the album underneath. That was the way they had been arranged in the first place.

Dagget gave an awkward little laugh. "Now what difference did it make which book was on top?" said he.

Louisa looked at him with a deprecating smile. "I always keep them that way," murmured she.

"You do beat everything," said Dagget, trying to laugh again. His large face was flushed.

He remained about an hour longer, then rose to take leave. Going out, he stumbled over a rug, and trying to recover himself, hit Louisa's work-basket on the table, and knocked it on the floor.

He looked at Louisa, then at the rolling spools; he ducked himself awkwardly toward them, but she stopped him. "Never mind," said she; "I'll pick them up after you're gone."

She spoke with a mild stiffness. Either she was a little disturbed, or his nervousness affected her, and made her seem constrained in her effort to reassure him.

When Joe Dagget was outside he drew in the sweet evening air with a sigh, and felt much as an innocent and perfectly well-intentioned bear might after his exit from a china shop.

Louisa, on her part, felt much as the kind-hearted, long-suffering owner of the china shop might have done after the exit of the bear.

She tied on the pink, then the green apron, picked up all the scattered treasures and replaced them in her work-basket, and straightened the rug. Then she set the lamp on the floor, and began sharply examining the carpet. She even rubbed her fingers over it, and looked at them.

"He's tracked in a good deal of dust," she murmured. "I thought he must have."

Louisa got a dust-pan and brush, and swept Joe Dagget's track carefully.

If he could have known it, it would have increased his perplexity and uneasiness, although it would not have disturbed his loyalty in the least. He came twice a week to see Louisa Ellis, and every time, sitting there in her delicately sweet room, he felt as if surrounded by a hedge of lace. He was afraid to stir lest he should put a clumsy foot or hand through the fairy web, and he had always the consciousness that Louisa was watching fearfully lest he should.

Still the lace and Louisa commanded perforce his perfect respect and patience and loyalty. They were to be married in a month, after a singular courtship which had lasted for a matter of fifteen years. For fourteen out of the fifteen years the two had not once seen each other, and they had seldom

[4] An expensive, decorative book. Widely popular in the nineteenth century, gift-books were collections of poems, essays, and fiction of elevated sentiment. They were often set out, like modern coffee-table books, as evidence of the refined gentility of the household.

exchanged letters. Joe had been all those years in Australia, where he had gone to make his fortune, and where he had stayed until he made it. He would have stayed fifty years if it had taken so long, and come home feeble and tottering, or never come home at all, to marry Louisa.

But the fortune had been made in the fourteen years, and he had come home now to marry the woman who had been patiently and unquestioningly waiting for him all that time.

Shortly after they were engaged he had announced to Louisa his determination to strike out into new fields, and secure a competency before they should be married. She had listened and assented with the sweet serenity which never failed her, not even when her lover set forth on that long and uncertain journey. Joe, buoyed up as he was by his sturdy determination, broke down a little at the last, but Louisa kissed him with a mild blush, and said good-by.

"It won't be for long," poor Joe had said, huskily; but it was for fourteen years.

In that length of time much had happened. Louisa's mother and brother had died, and she was all alone in the world. But greatest happening of all—a subtle happening which both were too simple to understand—Louisa's feet had turned into a path, smooth maybe under a calm, serene sky, but so straight and unswerving that it could only meet a check at her grave, and so narrow that there was no room for any one at her side.

Louisa's first emotion when Joe Dagget came home (he had not apprised her of his coming) was consternation, although she would not admit it to herself, and he never dreamed of it. Fifteen years ago she had been in love with him—at least she considered herself to be. Just at that time, gently acquiescing with and falling into the natural drift of girlhood, she had seen marriage ahead as a reasonable feature and a probable desirability of life. She had listened with calm docility to her mother's views upon the subject. Her mother was remarkable for her cool sense and sweet, even temperament. She talked wisely to her daughter when Joe Dagget presented himself, and Louisa accepted him with no hesitation. He was the first lover she had ever had.

She had been faithful to him all these years. She had never dreamed of the possibility of marrying any one else. Her life, especially for the last seven years, had been full of a pleasant peace, she had never felt discontented nor impatient over her lover's absence; still she had always looked forward to his return and their marriage as the inevitable conclusion of things. However, she had fallen into a way of placing it so far in the future that it was almost equal to placing it over the boundaries of another life.

When Joe came she had been expecting him, and expecting to be married for fourteen years, but she was much surprised and taken aback as if she had never thought of it.

Joe's consternation came later. He eyed Louisa with an instant confirmation of his old admiration. She had changed but little. She still kept her pretty manner and soft grace, and was, he considered, every whit as attractive as ever. As for himself, his stent[5] was done; he had turned his face away from fortune-seeking, and the old winds of romance whistled as loud and sweet as ever through his ears. All the song which he had been wont to hear in them was Louisa; he had for a long time a loyal belief that he heard it still, but finally it seemed to

[5]Stint: task, time of service.

him that although the winds sang always that one song, it had another name. But for Louisa the wind had never more than murmured; now it had gone down, and everything was still. She listened for a little while with half-wistful attention; then she turned quietly away and went to work on her wedding clothes.

Joe had made some extensive and quite magnificent alterations in his house. It was the old homestead; the newly-married couple would live there, for Joe could not desert his mother, who refused to leave her old home. So Louisa must leave hers. Every morning, rising and going about among her neat maidenly possessions, she felt as one looking her last upon the faces of dear friends. It was true that in a measure she could take them with her, but, robbed of their old environments, they would appear in such new guises that they would almost cease to be themselves. Then there were some peculiar features of her happy solitary life which she would probably be obliged to relinquish altogether. Sterner tasks than these graceful but half-needless ones would probably devolve upon her. There would be a large house to care for; there would be company to entertain; there would be Joe's rigorous and feeble old mother to wait upon; and it would be contrary to all thrifty village traditions for her to keep more than one servant. Louisa had a little still, and she used to occupy herself pleasantly in summer weather with distilling the sweet and aromatic essences from roses and peppermint and spearmint. By-and-by her still must be laid away. Her store of essences was already considerable, and there would be no time for her to distil for the mere pleasure of it. Then Joe's mother would think it foolishness; she had already hinted her opinion in the matter. Louisa dearly loved to sew a linen seam, not always for use, but for the simple, mild pleasure which she took in it. She would have been loath to confess how more than once she had ripped a seam for the mere delight of sewing it together again. Sitting at her window during long sweet afternoons, drawing her needle gently through the dainty fabric, she was peace itself. But there was a small chance of such foolish comfort in the future. Joe's mother, domineering, shrewd old matron that she was even in her old age, and very likely even Joe himself, with his honest masculine rudeness, would laugh and frown down all these pretty but senseless old maiden ways.

Louisa had almost the enthusiasm of an artist over the mere order and cleanliness of her solitary home. She had throbs of genuine triumph at the sight of the window-panes which she had polished until they shone like jewels. She gloated gently over her orderly bureau-drawers, with their exquisitely folded contents redolent with lavender and sweet clover and very purity. Could she be sure of the endurance of even this? She had visions, so startling that she half repudiated them as indelicate, of coarse masculine belongings strewn about in endless litter; of dust and disorder arising necessarily from a coarse masculine presence in the midst of all this delicate harmony.

Among her forebodings of disturbance, not the least was with regard to Cæsar. Cæsar was a veritable hermit of a dog. For the greater part of his life he had dwelt in his secluded hut, shut out from the society of his kind and all innocent canine joys. Never had Cæsar since his early youth watched at a woodchuck's hole; never had he known the delights of a stray bone at a neighbor's kitchen door. And it was all on account of a sin committed when hardly out of his puppyhood. No one knew the possible depth of remorse of which this mild-visaged, altogether innocent-looking old dog might be capable; but whether or not he had encountered remorse, he had encountered a full measure of righteous retribution. Old Cæsar seldom lifted up his voice in a growl or a bark; he was fat and sleepy; there were yellow rings which looked like spectacles around his dim old eyes; but there was a neighbor who bore on his hand the imprint of several of Cæsar's sharp white youthful teeth, and for that he had lived at the end of a chain, all alone in a little hut, for fourteen years. The neighbor, who was choleric and smarting with the pain of his wound, had demanded either Cæsar's death or complete ostracism. So Louisa's brother, to whom the dog had belonged, had built him his little kennel and tied him up. It was now fourteen years since, in a flood of youthful spirits, he had inflicted that memorable bite, and with the exception of short excursions, always at the end of the chain, under the strict guardianship of his master or Louisa, the old dog had remained a close prisoner. It is doubtful if, with his limited ambition, he took much pride in the fact, but it is certain that he was possessed of considerable cheap fame. He was regarded by all the children in the village and by many adults as a very monster of ferocity. St. George's dragon[6] could hardly have surpassed in evil repute Louisa Ellis's old yellow dog. Mothers charged their children with solemn emphasis not to go too near to him, and the children listened and believed greedily, with a fascinated appetite for terror, and ran by Louisa's house stealthily, with many sidelong and backward glances at the terrible dog. If perchance he sounded a hoarse bark, there was a panic. Wayfarers chancing into Louisa's yard eyed him with respect, and inquired if the chain were stout. Cæsar at large might have seemed a very ordinary dog, and excited no comment whatever; chained, his reputation overshadowed him, so that he lost his own proper outlines and looked darkly vague and enormous. Joe Dagget, however, with his good-humored sense and shrewdness, saw him as he was. He strode valiantly up to him and patted him on the head, in spite of Louisa's soft clamor of warning, and even attempted to set him loose. Louisa grew so alarmed that he desisted, but kept announcing his opinion in the matter quite forcibly at intervals. "There ain't a better-natured dog in town," he would say, "and it's downright cruel to keep him tied up there. Some day I'm going to take him out."

Louisa had very little hope that he would not, one of these days, when their interests and possessions should be more completely fused in one. She pictured to herself Cæsar on the rampage through the quiet and unguarded village. She saw innocent children bleeding in his path. She was herself very fond of the old dog, because he had belonged to her dead brother and he was always very gentle with her; still she had great faith in his ferocity. She always warned people not to go too near him. She fed him on ascetic fare of cornmush and cakes, and never fired his dangerous temper with heating and sanguinary diet of flesh and bones. Louisa looked at the old dog munching his simple fare, and thought of her approaching marriage and trembled. Still no anticipation of disorder and confusion in lieu of sweet peace and harmony, no forebodings of Cæsar on the rampage, no wild fluttering of her little yellow canary, were sufficient to turn her a hair's-breadth. Joe Dagget had been fond of her and working for her all these years. It was not for her, whatever came to pass, to prove untrue and break his heart. She put the exquisite little stitches into her wedding-garments, and the time went on until it was only a week before her wedding-day. It was a Tuesday evening, and the wedding was to be a week from Wednesday.

[6]According to medieval legend, the Christian hero Saint George slew a ferocious dragon, thus freeing an innocent maiden (the dragon's hostage) and ridding the land of terror.

There was a full moon that night. About nine o'clock Louisa strolled down the road a little way. There were harvest-fields on either hand, bordered by low stone walls. Luxuriant clumps of bushes grew beside the wall, and trees—wild cherry and old apple-trees—at intervals. Presently Louisa sat down on the wall and looked about her with mildly sorrowful reflectiveness. Tall shrubs of blueberry and meadow-sweet, all woven together and tangled with blackberry vines and horsebriers, shut her in on either side. She had a little clear space between them. Opposite her, on the other side of the road, was a spreading tree; the moon shone between its boughs, and the leaves twinkled like silver. The road was bespread with a beautiful shifting dapple of silver and shadow; the air was full of a mysterious sweetness. "I wonder if it's wild grapes?" murmured Louisa. She sat there some time. She was just thinking of rising, when she heard footsteps and low voices, and remained quiet. It was a lonely place, and she felt a little timid. She thought she would keep still in the shadow and let the persons, whoever they might be, pass her.

But just before they reached her the voices ceased, and the footsteps. She understood that their owners had also found seats upon the stone wall. She was wondering if she could not steal away unobserved, when the voice broke the stillness. It was Joe Dagget's. She sat still and listened.

The voice was announced by a loud sigh, which was familiar as itself. "Well," said Dagget, "you've made up your mind, then, I suppose?"

"Yes," returned another voice; "I'm going day after to-morrow."

"That's Lily Dyer," thought Louisa to herself. The voice embodied itself in her mind. She saw a girl tall and full-figured, with a firm, fair face, looking fairer and firmer in the moonlight, her strong yellow hair braided in a close knot. A girl full of a calm rustic strength and bloom, with a masterful way which might have beseemed a princess. Lily Dyer was a favorite with the village folk; she had just the qualities to arouse the admiration. She was good and handsome and smart. Louisa had often heard her praises sounded.

"Well," said Joe Dagget, "I ain't got a word to say."

"I don't know what you could say," returned Lily Dyer.

"Not a word to say," repeated Joe, drawing out the words heavily. Then there was a silence. "I ain't sorry," he began at last, "that that happened yesterday—that we kind of let on how we felt to each other. I guess it's just as well we knew. Of course I can't do anything any different. I'm going right on an' get married next week. I ain't going back on a woman that's waited for me fourteen years, an' break her heart."

"If you should jilt her to-morrow, I wouldn't have you," spoke up the girl, with sudden vehemence.

"Well, I ain't going to give you the chance," said he; "but I don't believe you would, either."

"You'd see I wouldn't. Honor's honor, an' right's right. An' I'd never think anything of any man that went against 'em for me or any other girl; you'd find that out, Joe Dagget."

"Well, you'll find out fast enough that I ain't going against 'em for you or any other girl," returned he. Their voices sounded almost as if they were angry with each other. Louisa was listening eagerly.

"I'm sorry you feel as if you must go away," said Joe, "but I don't know but it's best."

"Of course it's best. I hope you and I have got common-sense."

"Well, I suppose you're right." Suddenly Joe's voice got an undertone of tenderness. "Say, Lily," said he, "I'll get along well enough myself, but I can't bear to think—You don't suppose you're going to fret much over it?"

"I guess you'll find out I sha'n't fret much over a married man."

"Well, I hope you won't—I hope you won't, Lily. God knows I do. And—I hope—one of these days—you'll—come across somebody else—"

"I don't see any reason why I shouldn't." Suddenly her tone changed. She spoke in a sweet, clear voice, so loud that she could have been heard across the street. "No, Joe Dagget," said she, "I'll never marry any other man as long as I live. I've got good sense, an' I ain't going to break my heart nor make a fool of myself; but I'm never going to be married, you can be sure of that. I ain't that sort of a girl to feel this way twice."

Louisa heard an exclamation and a soft commotion behind the bushes; then Lily spoke again—the voice sounded as if she had risen. "This must be put a stop to," said she. "We've stayed here long enough. I'm going home."

Louisa sat there in a daze, listening to their retreating steps. After a while she got up and slunk softly home herself. The next day she did her housework methodically; that was as much a matter of course as breathing; but she did not sew on her wedding-clothes. She sat at her window and meditated. In the evening Joe came. Louisa Ellis had never known that she had any diplomacy in her, but when she came to look for it that night she found it, although meek of its kind, among her little feminine weapons. Even now she could hardly believe that she had heard aright, and that she would not do Joe a terrible injury should she break her troth-plight.[7] She wanted to sound him without betraying too soon her own inclinations in the matter. She did it successfully, and they finally came to an understanding; but it was a difficult thing, for he was as afraid of betraying himself as she.

She never mentioned Lily Dyer. She simply said that while she had no cause of complaint against him, she had lived so long in one way that she shrank from making a change.

"Well, I never shrank, Louisa," said Dagget. "I'm going to be honest enough to say that I think maybe it's better this way; but if you'd wanted to keep on, I'd have stuck to you till my dying day. I hope you know that."

"Yes, I do," said she.

That night she and Joe parted more tenderly than they had done for a long time. Standing in the door, holding each other's hands, a last great wave of regretful memory swept over them.

"Well, this ain't the way we've thought it was all going to end, is it, Louisa?" said Joe.

She shook her head. There was a little quiver on her placid face.

"You let me know if there's ever anything I can do for you," said he. "I ain't ever going to forget you, Louisa." Then he kissed her, and went down the path.

Louisa, all alone by herself that night, wept a little, she hardly knew why; but the next morning, on waking, she felt like a queen who, after fearing lest her domain be wrested away from her, sees it firmly insured in her possession.

Now the tall weeds and grasses might cluster around Cæsar's little hermit hut, the snow might fall on its roof year in and year out, but he never would go on a rampage through the unguarded village. Now the little canary might

[7]Pledge to marry.

turn itself into a peaceful yellow ball night after night, and have no need to wake and flutter with wild terror against its bars. Louisa could sew linen seams, and distil roses, and dust and polish and fold away in lavender, as long as she listed. That afternoon she sat with her needle-work at the window, and felt fairly steeped in peace. Lily Dyer, tall and erect and blooming, went past; but she felt no qualm. If Louisa Ellis had sold her birthright she did not know it, the taste of the pottage[8] was so delicious, and had been her sole satisfaction for so long. Serenity and placid narrowness had become to her as the birthright itself. She gazed ahead through a long reach of future days strung together like pearls in a rosary, every one like the others, and all smooth and flawless and innocent, and her heart went up in thankfulness. Outside was the fervid summer afternoon; the air was filled with the sounds of the busy harvest of men and birds and bees; there were halloos, metallic clatterings, sweet calls, and long hummings. Louisa sat, prayerfully numbering her days, like an uncloistered nun.

1891

A MISTAKEN CHARITY

There were in a green field a little, low, weather-stained cottage, with a foot-path leading to it from the highway several rods distant, and two old women—one with a tin pan and old knife searching for dandelion greens among the short young grass, and the other sitting on the door-step watching her, or, rather, having the appearance of watching her.

"Air there enough for a mess, Harriét?" asked the old woman on the door-step. She accented oddly the last syllable of the Harriet, and there was a curious quality in her feeble, cracked old voice. Besides the question denoted by the arrangement of her words and the rising inflection, there was another, broader and subtler, the very essence of all questioning, in the tone of her voice itself; the cracked, quavering notes that she used reached out of themselves, and asked, and groped like fingers in the dark. One would have known by the voice that the old woman was blind.

The old woman on her knees in the grass searching for dandelions did not reply; she evidently had not heard the question. So the old woman on the door-step, after waiting a few minutes with her head turned expectantly, asked again, varying her question slightly, and speaking louder:

"Air there enough for a mess, do ye s'pose, Harriét?"

The old woman in the grass heard this time. She rose slowly and laboriously; the effort of straightening out the rheumatic old muscles was evidently a painful one; then she eyed the greens heaped up in the tin pan, and pressed them down with her hand.

"Wa'al, I don't know, Charlotte," she replied, hoarsely. "There's plenty on 'em here, but I 'ain't got near enough for a mess; they do bile down so when you get 'em in the pot; an' it's all I can do to bend my j'ints enough to dig 'em."

[8]A thick soup, cooked in a pot. The reference is to the biblical Esau, who foolishly sold his birthright (inheritance) for a meal of bread and pottage (Genesis 25:29–34).

"I'd give consider'ble to help ye, Harriét," said the old woman on the door-step.

But the other did not hear her; she was down on her knees in the grass again, anxiously spying out the dandelions.

So the old woman on the door-step crossed her little shrivelled hands over her calico knees, and sat quite still, with the soft spring wind blowing over her.

The old wooden door-step was sunk low down among the grasses, and the whole house to which it belonged had an air of settling down and mouldering into the grass as into its own grave.

When Harriet Shattuck grew deaf and rheumatic, and had to give up her work as tailoress, and Charlotte Shattuck lost her eyesight, and was unable to do any more sewing for her livelihood, it was a small and trifling charity for the rich man who held a mortgage on the little house in which they had been born and lived all their lives to give them the use of it, rent and interest free. He might as well have taken credit to himself for not charging a squirrel for his tenement in some old decaying tree in his woods.

So ancient was the little habitation, so wavering and mouldering, the hands that had fashioned it had lain still so long in their graves, that it almost seemed to have fallen below its distinctive rank as a house. Rain and snow had filtered through its roof, mosses had grown over it, worms had eaten it, and birds built their nests under its eaves; nature had almost completely overrun and obliterated the work of man, and taken her own to herself again, till the house seemed as much a natural ruin as an old tree-stump.

The Shattucks had always been poor people and common people; no especial grace and refinement or fine ambition had ever characterized any of them; they had always been poor and coarse and common. The father and his father before him had simply lived in the poor little house, grubbed for their living, and then unquestioningly died. The mother had been of no rarer stamp, and the two daughters were cast in the same mould.

After their parents' death Harriet and Charlotte had lived along in the old place from youth to old age, with the one hope of ability to keep a roof over their heads, covering on their backs, and victuals in their mouths—an all-sufficient one with them.

Neither of them had ever had a lover; they had always seemed to repel rather than attract the opposite sex. It was not merely because they were poor, ordinary, and homely; there were plenty of men in the place who would have matched them well in that respect; the fault lay deeper—in their characters. Harriet, even in her girlhood, had a blunt, defiant manner that almost amounted to surliness, and was well calculated to alarm timid adorers, and Charlotte had always had the reputation of not being any too strong in her mind.

Harriet had gone about from house to house doing tailor-work after the primitive country fashion, and Charlotte had done plain sewing and mending for the neighbors. They had been, in the main, except when pressed by some temporary anxiety about their work or the payment thereof, happy and contented, with that negative kind of happiness and contentment which comes not from gratified ambition, but a lack of ambition itself. All that they cared for they had had in tolerable abundance, for Harriet at least had been swift and capable about her work. The patched, mossy old roof had been kept over their heads, the coarse, hearty food that they loved had been set on their table, and their cheap clothes had been warm and strong.

After Charlotte's eyes failed her, and Harriet had the rheumatic fever, and the little hoard of earnings went to the doctors, times were harder with them, though still it could not be said that they actually suffered.

When they could not pay the interest on the mortgage they were allowed to keep the place interest free; there was as much fitness in a mortgage on the little house, anyway, as there would have been on a rotten old apple-tree; and the people about, who were mostly farmers, and good friendly folk, helped them out with their living. One would donate a barrel of apples from his abundant harvest to the two poor old women, one a barrel of potatoes, another a load of wood for the winter fuel, and many a farmer's wife had bustled up the narrow foot-path with a pound of butter, or a dozen fresh eggs, or a nice bit of pork. Besides all this, there was a tiny garden patch behind the house, with a straggling row of currant bushes in it, and one of gooseberries, where Harriet contrived every year to raise a few pumpkins, which were the pride of her life. On the right of the garden were two old apple-trees, a Baldwin and a Porter, both yet in a tolerably good fruit-bearing state.[1]

The delight which the two poor old souls took in their own pumpkins, their apples and currants, was indescribable. It was not merely that they contributed largely towards their living; they were their own, their private share of the great wealth of nature, the little taste set apart for them alone out of her bounty, and worth more to them on that account, though they were not conscious of it, than all the richer fruits which they received from their neighbors' gardens.

This morning the two apple-trees were brave with flowers, the currant bushes looked alive, and the pumpkin seeds were in the ground. Harriet cast complacent glances in their direction from time to time, as she painfully dug her dandelion greens. She was a short, stoutly built old woman, with a large face coarsely wrinkled, with a suspicion of a stubble of beard on the square chin.

When her tin pan was filled to her satisfaction with the sprawling, spidery greens, and she was hobbling stiffly towards her sister on the door-step, she saw another woman standing before her with a basket in her hand.

"Good-morning, Harriet," she said, in a loud, strident voice, as she drew near. "I've been frying some doughnuts, and I brought you over some warm."

"I've been tellin' her it was real good in her," piped Charlotte from the door-step, with an anxious turn of her sightless face towards the sound of her sister's footstep.

Harriet said nothing but a hoarse "Good-mornin', Mis' Simonds." Then she took the basket in her hand, lifted the towel off the top, selected a doughnut, and deliberately tasted it.

"Tough," said she. "I s'posed so. If there is anything I 'spise on this airth it's a tough doughnut."

"Oh, Harriét!" said Charlotte, with a frightened look.

"They air tough," said Harriet, with hoarse defiance, "and if there is anything I 'spise on this airth it's a tough doughnut."

The woman whose benevolence and cookery were being thus ungratefully received only laughed. She was quite fleshy, and had a round, rosy, determined face.

"Well, Harriet," said she, "I am sorry they are tough, but perhaps you had better take them out on a plate, and give me my basket. You may be able to eat two or three of them if they are tough."

[1]Baldwin and Porter are varieties of apples.

"They air tough—turrible tough," said Harriet, stubbornly; but she took the basket into the house and emptied it of its contents nevertheless.

"I suppose your roof leaked as bad as ever in that heavy rain day before yesterday?" said the visitor to Harriet, with an inquiring squint towards the mossy shingles, as she was about to leave with her empty basket.

"It was turrible," replied Harriet, with crusty acquiescence—"turrible. We had to set pails an' pans everywheres, an' move the bed out."

"Mr. Upton ought to fix it."

"There ain't any fix to it; the old ruff ain't fit to nail new shingles on to; the hammerin' would bring the whole thing down on our heads," said Harriet, grimly.

"Well, I don't know as it can be fixed, it's so old. I suppose the wind comes in bad around the windows and doors too?"

"It's like livin' with a piece of paper, or mebbe a sieve, 'twixt you an' the wind an' the rain," quoth Harriet, with a jerk of her head.

"You ought to have a more comfortable home in your old age," said the visitor, thoughtfully.

"Oh, it's well enough," cried Harriet, in quick alarm, and with a complete change of tone; the woman's remark had brought an old dread over her. "The old house 'll last as long as Charlotte an' me do. The rain ain't so bad, nuther is the wind; there's room enough for us in the dry places, an' out of the way of the doors an' windows. It's enough sight better than goin' on the town." Her square, defiant old face actually looked pale as she uttered the last words and stared apprehensively at the woman.

"Oh, I did not think of your doing that," she said, hastily and kindly. "We all know how you feel about that, Harriet, and not one of us neighbors will see you and Charlotte go to the poorhouse while we've got a crust of bread to share with you."

Harriet's face brightened. "Thank ye, Mis' Simonds," she said, with reluctant courtesy. "I'm much obleeged to you an' the neighbors. I think mebbe we'll be able to eat some of them doughnuts if they air tough," she added, mollifyingly, as her caller turned down the foot-path.

"My, Harriét," said Charlotte, lifting up a weakly, wondering, peaked old face, "what did you tell her them doughnuts was tough fur?"

"Charlotte, do you want everybody to look down on us, an' think we ain't no account at all, just like any beggars, 'cause they bring us in vittles?" said Harriet, with a grim glance at her sister's meek, unconscious face.

"No, Harriét," she whispered.

"Do you want *to go to the poor-house?*"

"No, Harriét." The poor little old woman on the door-step fairly cowered before her aggressive old sister.

"Then don't hender me agin when I tell folks their doughnuts is tough an' their pertaters is poor. If I don't kinder keep up an' show some sperrit, I sha'n't think nothing of myself, an' other folks won't nuther, and fust thing we know they'll kerry us to the poorhouse. You'd 'a been there before now if it hadn't been for me, Charlotte."

Charlotte looked meekly convinced, and her sister sat down on a chair in the doorway to scrape her dandelions.

"Did you git a good mess, Harriét?" asked Charlotte, in a humble tone.

"Toler'ble."

"They'll be proper relishin' with that piece of pork Mis' Mann brought in yesterday. O Lord, Harriét, it's a chink!"

Harriet sniffed.

Her sister caught with her sensitive ear the little contemptuous sound. "I guess," she said, querulously, and with more pertinacity than she had shown in the matter of the doughnuts, "that if you was in the dark, as I am, Harriét, you wouldn't make fun an' turn up your nose at chinks. If you had seen the light streamin' in all of a sudden through some little hole that you hadn't known of before when you set down on the door-step this mornin', and the wind with the smell of the apple blows in it came in your face, an' when Mis' Simonds brought them hot doughnuts, an' when I thought of the pork an' greens jest now—O Lord, how it did shine in! An' it does now. If you was me, Harriét, you would know there was chinks."

Tears began starting from the sightless eyes, and streaming pitifully down the pale old cheeks.

Harriet looked at her sister, and her grim face softened.

"Why, Charlotte, hev it that thar *is* chinks if you want to. Who cares?"

"Thar *is* chinks, Harriét."

"Wa'al, thar *is* chinks, then. If I don't hurry, I sha'n't get these greens in in time for dinner."

When the two old women sat down complacently to their meal of pork and dandelion greens in their little kitchen they did not dream how destiny slowly and surely was introducing some new colors into their web of life, even when it was almost completed, and that this was one of the last meals they would eat in their old home for many a day. In about a week from that day they were established in the "Old Ladies' Home" in a neighboring city. It came about in this wise: Mrs. Simonds, the woman who had brought the gift of hot doughnuts, was a smart, energetic person, bent on doing good, and she did a great deal. To be sure, she always did it in her own way. If she chose to give hot doughnuts, she gave hot doughnuts; it made not the slightest difference to her if the recipients of her charity would infinitely have preferred ginger cookies. Still, a great many would like hot doughnuts, and she did unquestionably a great deal of good.

She had a worthy coadjutor in the person of a rich and childless elderly widow in the place. They had fairly entered into a partnership in good works, with about an equal capital on both sides, the widow furnishing the money, and Mrs. Simonds, who had much the better head of the two, furnishing the active schemes of benevolence.

The afternoon after the doughnut episode she had gone to the widow with a new project, and the result was that entrance fees had been paid, and old Harriet and Charlotte made sure of a comfortable home for the rest of their lives.The widow was hand in glove with officers of missionary boards and trustees of charitable institutions. There had been an unusual mortality among the inmates of the "Home" this spring, there were several vacancies, and the matter of the admission of Harriet and Charlotte was very quickly and easily arranged. But the matter which would have seemed the least difficult—inducing the two old women to accept the bounty which Providence, the widow, and Mrs. Simonds were ready to bestow on them—proved the most so. The struggle to persuade them to abandon their tottering old home for a better was a terrible one. The widow had pleaded with mild surprise, and Mrs. Simonds with benevolent determination; the counsel and reverend eloquence of the minister had been called in; and when they yielded at last it was with a sad grace for the recipients of a worthy charity.

It had been hard to convince them that the "Home" was not an almshouse under another name, and their yielding at length to anything short of actual force was only due probably to the plea, which was advanced most eloquently to Harriet, that Charlotte would be so much more comfortable.

The morning they came away, Charlotte cried pitifully, and trembled all over her little shrivelled body. Harriet did not cry. But when her sister had passed out the low, sagging door she turned the key in the lock, then took it out and thrust it slyly into her pocket, shaking her head to herself with an air of fierce determination.

Mrs. Simonds's husband, who was to take them to the depot, said to himself, with disloyal defiance of his wife's active charity, that it was a shame, as he helped the two distressed old souls into his light wagon, and put the poor little box, with their homely clothes in it, in behind.

Mrs. Simonds, the widow, the minister, and the gentleman from the "Home" who was to take charge of them, were all at the depot, their faces beaming with the delight of successful benevolence. But the two poor old women looked like two forlorn prisoners in their midst. It was an impressive illustration of the truth of the saying "that it is more blessed to give than to receive."

Well, Harriet and Charlotte Shattuck went to the "Old Ladies' Home" with reluctance and distress. They stayed two months, and then—they ran away.

The "Home" was comfortable, and in some respects even luxurious; but nothing suited those two unhappy, unreasonable old women.

The fare was of a finer, more delicately served variety than they had been accustomed to; those finely flavored nourishing soups for which the "Home" took great credit to itself failed to please palates used to common, coarser food.

"O Lord, Harriét, when I set down to the table here there ain't no chinks," Charlotte used to say. "If we could hev some cabbage, or some pork an' greens, how the light would stream in!"

Then they had to be more particular about their dress. They had always been tidy enough, but now it had to be something more; the widow, in the kindness of her heart, had made it possible, and the good folks in charge of the "Home," in the kindness of their hearts, tried to carry out the widow's designs.

But nothing could transform these two unpolished old women into two nice old ladies. They did not take kindly to white lace caps and delicate neckerchiefs. They liked their new black cashmere dresses well enough, but they felt as if they broke a commandment when they put them on every afternoon. They had always worn calico with long aprons at home, and they wanted to now; and they wanted to twist up their scanty gray locks into little knots at the back of their heads, and go without caps, just as they always had done.

Charlotte in a dainty white cap was pitiful, but Harriet was both pitiful and comical. They were totally at variance with their surroundings, and they felt it keenly, as people of their stamp always do. No amount of kindness and attention—and they had enough of both—sufficed to reconcile them to their new abode. Charlotte pleaded continually with her sister to go back to their old home.

"O Lord, Harriét, she would exclaim (by the way, Charlotte's "O Lord," which, as she used it, was innocent enough, had been heard with much disfavor in the "Home," and she, not knowing at all why, had been remonstrated with concerning it), "let us go home. I can't stay here no ways in this world. I don't like their vittles, an' I don't like to wear a cap; I want to go home and do different. The currants will be ripe, Harriét. O Lord, thar was almost a chink, thinking about 'em. I want some of 'em; an' the Porter apples will be gittin' ripe, an' we could have some apple-pie. This here ain't good; I want merlasses fur sweeting. Can't we get back no ways, Harriét? It ain't far, an' we could walk, an' they don't lock us in, nor nothin'. I don't want to die here; it ain't so straight up to heaven from here. O Lord, I've felt as if I was slantendicular from heaven ever since I've been here, an' it's been so awful dark. I ain't had any chinks. I want to go home, Harriét."

"We'll go to-morrow mornin'," said Harriet, finally; "we'll pack up our things an' go; we'll put on our old dresses, an' we'll do up the new ones in bundles, an' we'll jest shy out the back way to-morrow mornin'; an' we'll go. I kin find the way, an' I reckon we kin git thar, if it is fourteen mile. Mebbe somebody will give us a lift."

And they went. With a grim humor Harriet hung the new white lace caps with which she and Charlotte had been so pestered, one on each post at the head of the bedstead, so they would meet the eyes of the first person who opened the door. Then they took their bundles, stole slyly out, and were soon on the high-road, hobbling along, holding each other's hands, as jubilant as two children, and chuckling to themselves over their escape, and the probable astonishment there would be in the "Home" over it.

"O Lord, Harriét, what do you s'pose they will say to them caps?" cried Charlotte, with a gleeful cackle.

"I guess they'll see as folks ain't goin' to be made to wear caps agin their will in a free kentry," returned Harriet, with an echoing cackle, as they sped feebly and bravely along.

The "Home" stood on the very outskirts of the city, luckily for them. They would have found it a difficult undertaking to traverse the crowded streets. As it was, a short walk brought them into the free country road—free comparatively, for even here at ten o'clock in the morning there was considerable travelling to and from the city on business or pleasure.

People whom they met on the road did not stare at them as curiously as might have been expected. Harriet held her bristling chin high in the air, and hobbled along with an appearance of being well aware of what she was about, that led folks to doubt their own first opinion that there was something unusual about the two old women.

Still their evident feebleness now and then occasioned from one and another more particular scrutiny. When they had been on the road a half-hour or so, a man in a covered wagon drove up behind them. After he had passed them, he poked his head around the front of the vehicle and looked back. Finally he stopped, and waited for them to come up to him.

"Like a ride, ma'am?" said he, looking at once bewildered and compassionate.

"Thankee," said Harriet, "we'd be much obleeged."

After the man had lifted the old women into the wagon, and established them on the back seat, he turned around, as he drove slowly along, and gazed at them curiously.

"Seems to me you look pretty feeble to be walking far," said he. "Where were you going?"

Harriet told him with an air of defiance.

"Why," he exclaimed, "it is fourteen miles out. You could never walk it in the world. Well, I am going within three miles of there, and I can go on a little farther as well as not. But I don't see—Have you been in the city?"

"I have been visitin' my married darter in the city," said Harriet, calmly.

Charlotte started, and swallowed convulsively.

Harriet had never told a deliberate falsehood before in her life, but this seemed to her one of the tremendous exigencies of life which justify a lie. She felt desperate. If she could not contrive to deceive him in some way, the man might turn directly around and carry Charlotte and her back to the "Home" and the white caps.

"I should not have thought your daughter would have let you start for such a walk as that," said the man. "Is this lady your sister? She is blind, isn't she? She does not look fit to walk a mile."

"Yes, she's my sister," replied Harriet, stubbornly: "an' she's blind; an' my darter didn't want us to walk. She felt reel bad about it. But she couldn't help it. She's poor, and her husband's dead, an' she's got four leetle children."

Harriet recounted the hardships of her imaginary daughter with a glibness that was astonishing. Charlotte swallowed again.

"Well," said the man, "I am glad I overtook you, for I don't think you would ever have reached home alive."

About six miles from the city an open buggy passed them swiftly. In it were seated the matron and one of the gentlemen in charge of the "Home." They never thought of looking into the covered wagon—and indeed one can travel in one of those vehicles, so popular in some parts of New England, with as much privacy as he could in his tomb. The two in the buggy were seriously alarmed, and anxious for the safety of the old women, who were chuckling maliciously in the wagon they soon left far behind. Harriet had watched them breathlessly until they disappeared on a curve of the road; then she whispered to Charlotte.

A little after noon the two old women crept slowly up the foot-path across the field to their old home.

"The clover is up to our knees," said Harriet; "an' the sorrel and the white-weed; an' there's lots of yaller butterflies."

"O Lord, Harriét, thar's a chink, an' I do believe I saw one of them yaller butterflies go past it," cried Charlotte, trembling all over, and nodding her gray head violently.

Harriet stood on the old sunken door-step and fitted the key, which she drew triumphantly from her pocket, in the lock, while Charlotte stood waiting and shaking behind her.

Then they went in. Everything was there just as they had left it. Charlotte sank down on a chair and began to cry. Harriet hurried across to the window that looked out on the garden.

"The currants air ripe," said she; "*an*' them pumpkins hev run all over everything."

"O Lord, Harriét," sobbed Charlotte, "thar is so many chinks that they air all runnin' together!"

1887

Sarah Orne Jewett 1849–1909

Sarah Orne Jewett learned to observe New Englanders as she accompanied her father, a physician, on his daily rounds, visiting patients on farms and in villages near South Berwick, Maine. She was a sickly child, and her formal schooling was irregular. She compensated by reading widely in her father's substantial library: poets; French, Russian, and English novelists; and American writers such as Emerson and Lowell. But later in life she recalled, "The best of my education was received in my father's buggy and the places to which it carried me."

In 1863, after reading a book of regional tales of New England by Harriet Beecher Stowe, Sarah Orne Jewett resolved that she too would become a writer and record permanently and truly the life and the people of Maine that she knew so well. She set out to gather local legends and folk tales. She studied the manners and customs, the peculiarities of speech, and the family histories of farmers and villagers on the mainland and fishermen on the coastal isles. At fourteen she began writing tales and sketches, using pen names such as Alice Eliot or Sarah Sweet because, as she later explained, she wanted no one to know of her literary ambitions.

When she was eighteen, her first story was published, "Jenny Garrow's Lovers," an amateurish tale filled with melodrama and literary stereotypes. But two years later, in 1869, her writing had so improved that one of her stories was accepted by the illustrious Atlantic Monthly, America's most respected journal. Over the years her work continued to appear in the nation's most prestigious magazines, including the Atlantic Monthly, Scribner's, and Harper's. In 1877, she collected a series of her tales and sketches and published them under the title Deephaven. It was the first of more than twenty volumes—short stories, novels, children's books, poems—that she wrote in a career that extended into the twentieth century.

Although Sarah Orne Jewett traveled widely outside Maine, her best stories and sketches took place in her native state and portrayed the lives of the men and, more often, the women who lived in the villages and on farms of New England following the American Civil War. She rejected the disruptions and grasping values that she saw in nineteenth-century urban life, reaffirming the sturdy goodness of country ways and country people. In such fiction as "A White Heron," her most highly praised short story, she exhibits fundamental themes to which she frequently returned: the virtues of village life and unblemished nature, the tenacious resistance to change exhibited by people living in a rural backwater, and the discord brought by strangers and strange ideas.

Sarah Jewett's stories portray suffering and defeat, yet they celebrate open-hearted innocence, sympathy, kindness, understanding, and sensitivity—the values of the passing age she yearned to honor and labored to record. She was not a literary naturalist, writing of helpless people doomed by fate and harsh environment; still, she emphasized the impact of the natural world upon their lives. The sea, the rocky soil, the fields and forests of Maine, the idyllic summers and the long winters—all shape, for good or ill, the people she describes, binding them to lives they enjoy and endure.

Critics have objected that her stories stress character and scene at the expense of plot and action, that in her fiction she exhibits an extravagant compassion for her characters that frequently borders on sentimentalism. Her writing was purposely muted and pacific, and her range was narrow—Henry James called her work a "beautiful quantum of achievement." Yet the writing in her most notable single volume, The Country of the Pointed Firs (1896), has brought her praise as the creator of the "best regional fiction to have come out of nineteenth-century America." And her ability to portray the *commonplace lives of the men and women she knew—their manners, their beliefs, their New England speech—continues to attract praise and enthusiastic readers more than half a century after her death, long after the world that she described has ceased to be.*

FURTHER READING: *Deephaven and Other Stories,* ed. R. Cary, 1966; *The Uncollected Short Stories of Sarah Orne Jewett,* ed. R. Cary, 1971; *Sarah Orne Jewett: Novels and Stories,* ed. M. Bell, 1994; *Letters of Sarah Orne Jewett,* ed. A. Fields, 1911; *Sarah Orne Jewett Letters,* ed. R. Cary, 1956, 1967; F. Matthiessen, *Sarah Orne Jewett,* 1929, 1965; J. Frost, *Sarah Orne Jewett,* 1960; R. Cary, *Sarah Orne Jewett,* 1962; M. Thorp, *Sarah Orne Jewett,* 1966; *Appreciation of Sarah Orne Jewett, 29 Interpretive Essays,* ed. E. Cary, 1973; J. Donovan, *Sarah Orne Jewett,* 1980; G. Nagel, *Critical Essays on Sarah Orne Jewett,* 1984; L. Renza, *"A White Heron" and the Question of Minor Literature,* 1984; S. Sherman, *Sarah Orne Jewett: An American Persephone,* 1989; M. Mobley, *Folk Roots and Mythic Wings in Sarah Orne Jewett and Toni Morrison,* 1991; E. Silverthorne, *Sarah Orne Jewett: A Writer's Life,* 1993; P. Blanchard, *Sarah Orne Jewett: Her World and Her Work,* 1994.

TEXTS: *A White Heron and Other Stories,* 1886; *Atlantic Monthly,* July 1890.

A WHITE HERON

1. The woods were already filled with shadows one June evening, just before eight o'clock, though a bright sunset still glimmered faintly among the trunks of the trees. A little girl was driving home her cow, a plodding, dilatory, provoking creature in her behavior, but a valued companion for all that. They were going away from the western light, and striking deep into the dark woods, but their feet were familiar with the path, and it was no matter whether their eyes could see it or not.

There was hardly a night the summer through when the old cow could be found waiting at the pasture bars; on the contrary, it was her greatest pleasure to hide herself away among the high huckleberry bushes, and though she wore a loud bell she had made the discovery that if one stood perfectly still it would not ring. So Sylvia had to hunt for her until she found her, and call Co'! Co'! with never an answering Moo, until her childish patience was quite spent. If the creature had not given good milk and plenty of it, the case would have seemed very different to her owners. Besides, Sylvia had all the time there was, and very little use to make of it. Sometimes in pleasant weather it was a consolation to look upon the cow's pranks as an intelligent attempt to play hide and seek, and as the child had no playmates she lent herself to this amusement with a good deal of zest. Though this chase had been so long that the wary animal herself had given an unusual signal of her whereabouts, Sylvia had only laughed when she came upon Mistress Moolly at the swamp-side, and urged her affectionately homeward with a twig of birch leaves. The old cow was not inclined to wander farther, she even turned in the right direction for once as they left the pasture, and stepped along the road at a good pace. She was quite ready to be milked now, and seldom stopped to browse. Sylvia wondered what her grandmother would say because they were so late. It was a great while since she had left home at half past five o'clock, but everybody knew the difficulty of making this errand a short one. Mrs. Tilley had chased the hornéd torment too many summer evenings herself to blame any one else for lingering, and was only thankful as she waited that she had Sylvia, nowadays, to give such valuable assistance. The good woman suspected that Sylvia loitered occasionally on her own account; there never was such a child for straying about out-of-doors since the world was made! Everybody said that it was a good change for a little maid who had tried to grow for eight years in a crowded manufacturing town, but, as for Sylvia herself, it seemed as if she never had been alive at all before she came to live at the farm. She thought often with wistful compassion of a wretched dry geranium that belonged to a town neighbor.

"'Afraid of folks,'" old Mrs. Tilley said to herself, with a smile, after she had made the unlikely choice of Sylvia from her daughter's houseful of children, and was returning to the farm. "'Afraid of folks,' they said! I guess she won't be troubled no great with 'em up to the old place!" When they reached the door of the lonely house and stopped to unlock it, and the cat came to purr loudly, and rub against them, a deserted pussy, indeed, but fat with young robins. Sylvia whispered that this was a beautiful place to live in, and she never should wish to go home.

The companions followed the shady woodroad, the cow taking slow steps, and the child very fast ones. The cow stopped long at the brook to drink, as if the pasture were not half a swamp, and Sylvia stood still and waited, letting her bare feet cool themselves in the shoal water, while the great twilight moths struck softly against her. She waded on through the brook as the cow moved away, and listened to the thrushes with a heart that beat fast with pleasure. There was a stirring in the great boughs overhead. They were full of little birds and beasts that seemed to be wide-awake, and going about their world, or else saying goodnight to each other in sleepy twitters. Sylvia herself felt sleepy as she walked along. However, it was not much farther to the house, and the air was soft and sweet. She was not often in the woods so late as this, and it made her feel as if she were a part of the gray shadows and the moving leaves. She was just thinking how long it seemed since she first came to the farm a year ago, and wondering if everything went on in the noisy town just the same as when she was there; the thought of the great red-faced boy who used to chase and frighten her made her hurry along the path to escape from the shadow of the trees.

Suddenly this little woods-girl is horror-stricken to hear a clear whistle not very far away. Not a bird's whistle, which would have a sort of friendliness, but a boy's whistle, determined, and somewhat aggressive. Sylvia left the cow to whatever sad fate might await her, and stepped discreetly aside into the bushes, but she was just too late. The enemy had discovered her, and called out in a very cheerful and persuasive tone, "Halloa, little girl, how far is it to the road?" and trembling Sylvia answered almost inaudibly, "A good ways."

She did not dare to look boldly at the tall young man, who carried a gun over his shoulder, but she came out of her bush and again followed the cow, while he walked alongside.

"I have been hunting for some birds," the stranger said kindly, "and I have lost my way, and need a friend very much. Don't be afraid," he added gallantly. "Speak up and tell me what your name is, and whether you think I can spend the night at your house, and go out gunning early in the morning."

Sylvia was more alarmed than before. Would not her grandmother consider her much to blame? But who could have foreseen such an accident as this? It did not appear to be her fault, and she hung her head as if the stem of it were broken, but managed to answer "Sylvy," with much effort when her companion again asked her name.

Mrs. Tilley was standing in the doorway when the trio came into view. The cow gave a loud moo by way of explanation.

"Yes, you'd better speak up for yourself, you old trial! Where'd she tuck herself away this time, Sylvy?" Sylvia kept an awed silence; she knew by instinct that her grandmother did not comprehend the gravity of the situation. She must be mistaking the stranger for one of the farmer-lads of the region.

The young man stood his gun beside the door, and dropped a heavy gamebag beside it; then he bade Mrs. Tilley good-evening, and repeated his wayfarer's story, and asked if he could have a night's lodging.

"Put me anywhere you like," he said. "I must be off early in the morning, before day; but I am very hungry, indeed. You can give me some milk at any rate, that's plain."

"Dear sakes, yes," responded the hostess, whose long slumbering hospitality seemed to be easily awakened. "You might fare better if you went out on the main road a mile or so, but you're welcome to what we've got. I'll milk right off, and you make yourself at home. You can sleep on husks or feathers," she proffered graciously. "I raised them all myself. There's good pasturing for geese just below here towards the ma'sh. Now step round and set a plate for the gentleman, Sylvy!" And Sylvia promptly stepped. She was glad to have something to do, and she was hungry herself.

It was a surprise to find so clean and comfortable a little dwelling in this New England wilderness. The young man had known the horrors of its most primitive housekeeping, and the dreary squalor of that level of society which does not rebel at the companionship of hens. This was the best thrift of an old-fashioned farmstead, though on such a small scale that it seemed like a hermitage. He listened eagerly to the old woman's quaint talk, he watched Sylvia's pale face and shining gray eyes with ever growing enthusiasm, and insisted that this was the best supper he had eaten for a month; then, afterward, the new-made friends sat down in the doorway together while the moon came up.

Soon it would be berry-time, and Sylvia was a great help at picking. The cow was a good milker, though a plaguy thing to keep track of, the hostess gossiped frankly, adding presently that she had buried four children, so that Sylvia's mother, and a son (who might be dead) in California were all the children she had left. "Dan, my boy, was a great hand to go gunning," she explained sadly. "I never wanted for pa'tridges or gray squer'ls while he was to home. He's been a great wand'rer, I expect, and he's no hand to write letters. There, I don't blame him, I'd ha' seen the world myself if it had been so I could."

"Sylvia takes after him," the grandmother continued affectionately, after a minute's pause. "There ain't a foot o' ground she don't know her way over, and the wild creatur's counts her one o' themselves. Squer'ls she'll tame to come an' feed right out o' her hands, and all sorts o' birds. Last winter she got the jaybirds to bangeing[1] here, and I believe she'd a' scanted[2] herself of her own meals to have plenty to throw out amongst 'em, if I hadn't kep' watch. Anything but crows, I tell her, I'm willin' to help support,—though Dan he went an' tamed one o' them that did seem to have reason same as folks. It was round here

[1]Gathering. [2]Deprived.

a good spell after he went away. Dan an' his father they didn't hitch,—but he never held up his head ag'in after Dan had dared him an' gone off."

The guest did not notice this hint of family sorrows in his eager interest in something else.

"So Sylvy knows all about birds, does she?" he exclaimed, as he looked round at the little girl who sat, very demure but increasingly sleepy, in the moonlight. "I am making a collection of birds myself. I have been at it ever since I was a boy." (Mrs. Tilley smiled.) "There are two or three very rare ones I have been hunting for these five years. I mean to get them on my own ground if they can be found."

"Do you cage 'em up?" asked Mrs. Tilley doubtfully, in response to this enthusiastic announcement.

"Oh no, they're stuffed and preserved, dozens and dozens of them," said the ornithologist, "and I have shot or snared every one myself. I caught a glimpse of a white heron three miles from here on Saturday, and I have followed it in this direction. They have never been found in this district at all. The little white heron, it is," and he turned again to look at Sylvia with the hope of discovering that the rare bird was one of her acquaintances.

But Sylvia was watching a hop-toad in the narrow foot-path.

"You would know the heron if you saw it," the stranger continued eagerly. "A queer tall white bird with soft feathers and long thin legs. And it would have a nest perhaps in the top of a high tree, made of sticks, something like a hawk's nest."

Sylvia's heart gave a wild beat; she knew that strange white bird, and had once stolen softly near where it stood in some bright green swamp grass, away over at the other side of the woods. There was an open place where the sunshine always seemed strangely yellow and hot, where tall, nodding rushes grew, and her grandmother had warned her that she might sink in the soft black mud underneath and never be heard of more. Not far beyond were the salt marshes and beyond those was the sea, the sea which Sylvia wondered and dreamed about, but never had looked upon, though its great voice could often be heard above the noise of the woods on stormy nights.

"I can't think of anything I should like so much as to find that heron's nest," the handsome stranger was saying. "I would give ten dollars to anybody who could show it to me," he added desperately, "and I mean to spend my whole vacation hunting for it if need be. Perhaps it was only migrating, or had been chased out of its own region by some bird of prey."

Mrs. Tilley gave amazed attention to all this, but Sylvia still watched the toad, not divining, as she might have done at some calmer time, that the creature wished to get to its hole under the doorstep, and was much hindered by the unusual spectators at that hour of the evening. No amount of thought, that night, could decide how many wished-for treasures the ten dollars, so lightly spoken of, would buy.

The next day the young sportsman hovered about the woods, and Sylvia kept him company, having lost her first fear of the friendly lad, who proved to be most kind and sympathetic. He told her many things about the birds and what they knew and where they lived and what they did with themselves. And he gave her a jack-knife, which she thought as great a treasure as if she were a desert-islander. All day long he did not once make her troubled or afraid except when he brought down some unsuspecting singing creature from its bough. Sylvia would have liked him vastly better without his gun; she could not understand why he killed the very birds he seemed to like so much. But as the day waned, Sylvia still watched the young man with loving admiration. She had never seen anybody so charming and delightful; the woman's heart, asleep in the child, was vaguely thrilled by a dream of love. Some premonition of that great power stirred and swayed these young foresters who traversed the solemn woodlands with soft-footed silent care. They stopped to listen to a bird's song; they pressed forward again eagerly, parting the branches,—speaking to each other rarely and in whispers; the young man going first and Sylvia following, fascinated, a few steps behind, with her gray eyes dark with excitement.

She grieved because the longed-for white heron was elusive, but she did not lead the guest, she only followed, and there was no such thing as speaking first. The sound of her own unquestioned voice would have terrified her,—it was hard enough to answer yes or no when there was need of that. At last evening began to fall, and they drove the cow home together, and Sylvia smiled with pleasure when they came to the place where she heard the whistle and was afraid only the night before.

2. Half a mile from home, at the farther edge of the woods, where the land was highest, a great pine-tree stood, the last of its generation. Whether it was left for a boundary mark, or for what reason, no one could say; the woodchoppers who had felled its mates were dead and gone long ago, and a whole forest of sturdy trees, pines and oaks and maples, had grown again. But the stately head of this old pine towered above them all and made a landmark for sea and shore miles and miles away. Sylvia knew it well. She had always believed that whoever climbed to the top of it could see the ocean; and the little girl had often laid her hand on the great rough trunk and looked up wistfully at those dark boughs that the wind always stirred, no matter how hot and still the air might be below. Now she thought of the tree with a new excitement, for why, if one climbed it at break of day, could not one see all the world, and easily discover whence the white heron flew, and mark the place, and find the hidden nest?

What a spirit of adventure, what wild ambition! What fancied triumph and delight and glory for the later morning when she could make known the secret! It was almost too real and too great for the childish heart to bear.

All night the door of the little house stood open, and the whippoorwills came and sang upon the very step. The young sportsman and his old hostess were sound asleep, but Sylvia's great design kept her broad awake and watching. She forgot to think of sleep. The short summer night seemed as long as the winter darkness, and at last when the whippoorwills ceased, and she was afraid the morning would after all come too soon, she stole out of the house and followed the pasture path through the woods, hastening toward the open ground beyond, listening with a sense of comfort and companionship to the drowsy twitter of a half-awakened bird, whose perch she had jarred in passing. Alas, if the great wave of human interest which flooded for the first time this dull little life should sweep away the satisfactions of an existence heart to heart with nature and the dumb life of the forest!

There was the huge tree asleep yet in the paling moonlight, and small and hopeful Sylvia began with utmost bravery to mount to the top of it, with tingling, eager blood coursing the channels of her whole frame, with her bare feet and fingers, that pinched and held like bird's claws to the monstrous ladder reaching up, up, almost to the sky itself. First she must mount the white oak tree that grew alongside, where she was almost lost among the dark branches and the green leaves heavy and wet with dew; a bird fluttered off its nest, and a red squirrel ran to and fro and scolded pettishly at the harmless housebreaker. Sylvia felt her way easily. She had often climbed there, and knew that higher still one of the oak's upper branches chafed against the pine trunk, just where its lower boughs were set close together. There, when she made the dangerous pass from one tree to the other, the great enterprise would really begin.

She crept out along the swaying oak limb at last, and took the daring step across into the old pine-tree. The way was harder than she thought; she must reach far and hold fast, the sharp dry twigs caught and held her and scratched her like angry talons, the pitch made her thin little fingers clumsy and stiff as she went round and round the tree's great stem, higher and higher upward. The sparrows and robins in the woods below were beginning to wake and twitter to the dawn, yet it seemed much lighter there aloft in the pine-tree, and the child knew that she must hurry if her project were to be of any use.

The tree seemed to lengthen itself out as she went up, and to reach farther and farther upward. It was like a great main-mast to the voyaging earth; it must truly have been amazed that morning through all its ponderous frame as it felt this determined spark of human spirit creeping and climbing from higher branch to branch. Who knows how steadily the least twigs held themselves to advantage this light, weak creature on her way! The old pine must have loved his new dependent. More than all the hawks, and bats, and moths, and even the sweet-voiced thrushes, was the brave, beating heart of the solitary gray-eyed child. And the tree stood still and held away the winds that June morning while the dawn grew bright in the east.

Sylvia's face was like a pale star, if one had seen it from the ground, when the last thorny bough was past, and she stood trembling and tired but wholly triumphant, high in the tree-top. Yes, there was the sea with the dawning sun making a golden dazzle over it, and toward that glorious east flew two hawks with slow-moving pinions. How low they looked in the air from that height when before one had only seen them far up, and dark against the blue sky. Their gray feathers were as soft as moths; they seemed only a little way from the tree, and Sylvia felt as if she too could go flying away among the clouds. Westward, the woodlands and farms reached miles and miles into the distance; here and there were church steeples, and white villages; truly it was a vast and awesome world.

The birds sang louder and louder. At last the sun came up bewilderingly bright. Sylvia could see the white sails of ships out at sea, and the clouds that were purple and rose-colored and yellow at first began to fade away. Where was the white heron's nest in the sea of green branches, and was this wonderful sight and pageant of the world the only reward for having climbed to such a giddy height? Now look down again, Sylvia, where the green marsh is set among the shining birches and dark hemlocks; there where you saw the white heron once you will see him again; look, look! a white spot of him like a single floating feather comes up from the dead hemlock and grows larger, and rises, and comes close at last, and goes by the landmark pine with steady sweep of wing and outstretched slender neck and crested head. And wait! wait! do not move a foot or a finger, little girl, do not send an arrow of light and consciousness from your two eager eyes, for the heron has perched on a pine bough not far beyond yours, and cries back to his mate on the nest, and plumes his feathers for the new day!

The child gives a long sigh a minute later when a company of shouting catbirds comes also to the tree, and vexed by their fluttering and lawlessness the solemn heron goes away. She knows his secret now, the wild, light, slender bird that floats and wavers, and goes back like an arrow presently to his home in the green world beneath. Then Sylvia, well satisfied, makes her perilous way down again, not daring to look far below the branch she stands on, ready to cry sometimes because her fingers ache and her lamed feet slip. Wondering over and over again what the stranger would say to her, and what he would think when she told him how to find his way straight to the heron's nest.

"Sylvy, Sylvy!" called the busy old grandmother again and again, but nobody answered, and the small husk bed was empty, and Sylvia had disappeared.

The guest waked from a dream, and remembering his day's pleasure hurried to dress himself that it might sooner begin. He was sure from the way the shy little girl looked once or twice yesterday that she had at least seen the white heron, and now she must really be persuaded to tell. Here she comes now, paler than ever, and her worn old frock is torn and tattered, and smeared with pine pitch. The grandmother and the sportsman stand in the door together and question her, and the splendid moment has come to speak of the dead hemlock-tree by the green marsh.

But Sylvia does not speak after all, though the old grandmother fretfully rebukes her, and the young man's kind appealing eyes are looking straight in her own. He can make them rich with money; he has promised it, and they are poor now. He is so well worth making happy, and he waits to hear the story she can tell.

No, she must keep silence! What is it that suddenly forbids her and makes her dumb? Has she been nine years growing, and now, when the great world for the first time puts out a hand to her, must she thrust it aside for a bird's sake? The murmur of the pine's green branches is in her ears, she remembers how the white heron came flying through the golden air and how they watched the sea and the morning together, and Sylvia cannot speak, she cannot tell the heron's secret and give its life away.

Dear loyalty, that suffered a sharp pang as the guest went away disappointed later in the day, that could have served and followed him and loved him as a dog loves! Many a night Sylvia heard the echo of his whistle haunting the pasture path as she came home with the loitering cow. She forgot even her sorrow at the sharp report of his gun and the piteous sight of thrushes and sparrows dropping silent to the ground, their songs hushed and their pretty feathers stained and wet with blood. Were the birds better friends than their hunter might have been,—who can tell? Whatever treasures were lost to her, woodlands and summer-time, remember! Bring your gifts and graces and tell your secrets to this lonely country child!

1886

THE TOWN POOR

Mrs. William Trimble and Miss Rebecca Wright were driving along Hampden east road, one afternoon in early spring. Their progress was slow. Mrs. Trimble's sorrel horse[1] was old and stiff, and the wheels were clogged by clay mud. The frost was not yet out of the ground, although the snow was nearly gone, except in a few places on the north side of the woods, or where it had drifted all winter against a length of fence.

"There must be a good deal o' snow to the nor'ard of us yet," said weatherwise Mrs. Trimble. "I feel it in the air; 't is more than the ground-damp. We ain't goin' to have real nice weather till the up-country snow 's all gone."

"I heard say yesterday that there was good sleddin' yet, all up through Parsley," responded Miss Wright. "I should n't like to live up in them northern places. My cousin Ellen's husband was a Parsley man, an' he was obliged, as you may have heard, to go up north to his father's second wife's funeral: got back day before yesterday. 'T was about twenty-one miles, an' they started on wheels; but when they'd gone nine or ten miles, they found't was no sort o' use, an' left their wagon an' took a sleigh. The man that owned it charged 'em four an' six, too. I should n't have thought he would; they told him they was goin' to a funeral; an' they had their own buffaloes an' everything."

"Well, I expect it's a good deal harder scratchin, up that way; they have to git money where they can; the farms is very poor as you go north," suggested Mrs. Trimble kindly. "'T ain't none too rich a country where we be, but I've always been grateful I wa'n't born up to Parsley."

The old horse plodded along, and the sun, coming out from the heavy spring clouds, sent a sudden shine of light along the muddy road. Sister Wright drew her large veil forward over the high rim of her bonnet. She was not used to driving, or to being much in the open air; but Mrs. Trimble was an active business woman, and looked after her own affairs herself, in all weathers. The late Mr. Trimble had left her a good farm, but not much ready money, and it was often said that she was better off in the end than if he had lived. She regretted his loss deeply, however; it was impossible for her to speak of him, even with intimate friends, without emotion, and nobody had ever hinted that this emotion was insincere. She was most warmhearted and generous, and in her limited way played the part of Lady Bountiful[2] in the town of Hampden.

"Why, there's where the Bray girls lives, ain't it?" she exclaimed, as, beyond a thicket of witch-hazel and scruboak, they came in sight of a weatherbeaten, solitary farmhouse. The barn was too far away for thrift or comfort, and they could see long lines of light through the shrunken boards as they came nearer. The fields looked both stony and sodden. Somehow, even Parsley itself could be hardly more forlorn.

"Yes 'm," said Miss Wright, "that's where they live now, poor things. I know the place, though I ain't been up here for years. You don't suppose, Mis' Trimble—I ain't seen the girls out to meetin' all winter. I've re'lly been covetin"'—

[1]A light-brown or orange-brown horse.

[2]Lady Bountiful is a character noted for her charitable good works in the play *Beaux Stratagem,* by British playwright George Farquhar (1678–1707).

"Why, yes, Rebecca, of course we could stop," answered Mrs. Trimble heartily. "The exercises was over earlier'n I expected, an you're goin' to remain over night long o' me, you know. There won't be no tea till we git there, so we can't be late. I'm in the habit o' sendin' a basket to the Bray girls when any o' our folks is comin' this way, but I ain't been to see 'em since they moved up here. Why, it must be a good deal over a year ago. I know 't was in the late winter they had to make the move. "I' was cruel hard, I must say, an' if I had n't been down with my pleurisy[3] fever, I'd have stirred round an' done somethin' about it. There was a good deal o'sickness at the time, an'—well, 't was kind o' rushed through, breakin' of 'em up, an' lots o' folks blamed the selec'*men;* but when 't was done, 't was done, an' nobody took holt to undo it. Ann an' Mandy looked same's ever when they come to meetin', 'long in the summer,—kind o' wishful, perhaps. They've always sent me word they was gittin' on pretty comfortable."

"That would be their way," said Rebecca Wright. "They never was any hand to complain, though Mandy's less cheerful than Ann. If Mandy'd been spared such poor eyesight, an' Ann had n't got her lame wrist that wa'n't set right, they'd kep' off the town fast enough. They both shed tears when they talked to me about havin' to break up, when I went to see 'em before I went over to brother Asa's. You see we was brought up neighbors an' went to school together, the Brays an' me. 'T was a special Providence brought us home this road, I've been so covetin' a chance to git to see 'em. My lameness hampers me."

"I'm glad we come this way, myself," said Mrs. Trimble.

"I'd like to see just how they fare," Miss Rebecca Wright continued. "They give their consent to goin' on the town because they knew they'd got to be dependent, an' so they felt't would come easier for all than for a few to help 'em. They acted real dignified an' rightminded, contrary to what most do in such cases, but they was dreadful anxious to see who would bid 'em off, town-meeting day; they did so hope 't would be somebody right in the village. I just sat down an' cried good when I found Abel Janes's folks had got hold of 'em. They always had the name of bein' slack an' poor-spirited, an' they did it just for what they got out o' the town. The selectmen[4] this last year ain't what we have had. I hope they've been considerate about the Bray girls."

"I should have be'n more considerate about fetchin' of you up," apologized Mrs. Trimble. "I 've got my horse, an' you 're lame-footed; 't is too far for you to come. But time does slip away with busy folks, an' I forgit a good deal I ought to remember."

"There's nobody more considerate than you be," protested Miss Rebecca Wright.

Mrs. Trimble made no answer, but took out her whip and gently touched the sorrel horse, who walked considerably faster, but did not think it worth while to trot. It was a long, roundabout way to the house, farther down the road and up a lane.

"I never had any opinion of the Bray girls' father, leavin' 'em as he did," said Mrs. Trimble.

"He was much praised in his time, though there was always some said his early life had n't been up to the mark," explained her companion. "He was a great favorite of our then preacher, the Reverend Daniel Longbrother. They did a good deal for the parish, but they did it their own way. Deacon Bray was one

[3]An inflammation of the lining surrounding the lungs. [4]Members of the town council.

that did his part in the repairs without urging. You know 't was in his time the first repairs was made, when they got out the old soundin'-board an' them handsome square pews. It cost an awful sight o' money, too. They had n't done payin' up that debt when they set to to alter it again an' git the walls frescoed. My grandmother was one that always spoke her mind right out, an' she was dreadful opposed to breakin' up the square pews where she'd always set. They was countin' up what 't would cost in parish meetin', an' she riz right up an' said 't would n't cost nothin' to let 'em stay, an' there wa'n't a house carpenter left in the parish that could do such nice work, an' time would come when the great-grandchildren would give their eye-teeth to have the old meetin'-house look just as it did then. But haul the inside to pieces they would and did."

"There come to be a real fight over it, did n't there?" agreed Mrs. Trimble soothingly. "Well, 't wa'n't good taste. I remember the old house well. I come here as a child to visit a cousin o' mother's, an' Mr. Trimble's folks was neighbors, an' we was drawed to each other then, young 's we was. Mr. Trimble spoke of it many 's the time,—the first time he ever see me, in a leghorn hat[5] with a feather; 't was one that mother had, an' pressed over."

"When I think of them old sermons that used to be preached in that old meetin'-house of all, I'm glad it's altered over, so's not to remind folks," said Miss Rebecca Wright, after a suitable pause. "Them old brimstone discourses, you know, Mis'Trimble. Preachers is far more reasonable, nowadays. Why, I set an' thought, last Sabbath, as I listened, that if old Mr. Longbrother an' Deacon Bray could hear the difference they'd crack the ground over 'em like pole beans, an' come right up 'longside their headstones."

Mrs. Trimble laughed heartily, and shook the reins three or four times by way of emphasis. "There 's no gitting round you," she said, much pleased. "I should think Deacon Bray would want to rise, any way, if 't was so he could, an' knew how his poor girls was farin'. A man ought to provide for his folks he's got to leave behind him, specially if they're women. To be sure, they had their little home; but we've seen how, with all their industrious ways, they had n't means to keep it. I s'pose he thought he'd got time enough to lay by, when he give so generous in collections; but he did n't lay by, an' there they be. He might have took lessons from the squirrels; even them little wild creatur's makes them their winter boards, an' men-folks ought to know enough if squirrels does. 'Be just before you are generous:' that's what was always set for the B's in the copy-books, when I was to school, and it often runs through my mind."

"'As for man, his days are as grass,'—that was for A; the two go well together," added Miss Rebecca Wright soberly. "My good gracious, ain't this a starved-lookin' place? It makes me ache to think them nice Bray girls has to brook it here."

The sorrel horse, though somewhat puzzled by an unexpected deviation from his homeward way, willingly came to a stand by the gnawed corner of the dooryard fence, which evidently served as hitching-place. Two or three ragged old hens were picking about the yard, and at last a face appeared at the kitchen window, tied up in a handkerchief, as if it were a case of toothache. By the time our friends reached the side door next this window, Mrs. Janes came disconsolately to open it for them, shutting it again as soon as possible, though the air felt more chilly inside the house.

[5]A kind of straw hat.

"Take seats," said Mrs. Janes briefly. "You'll have to see me just as I be. I have been suffering these four days with the ague, and everything to do. Mr. Janes is to court, on the jury. 'T was inconvenient to spare him. I should be pleased to have you lay off your things."

Comfortable Mrs. Trimble looked about the cheerless kitchen, and could not think of anything to say; so she smiled blandly and shook her head in answer to the invitation. "We'll just set a few minutes with you, to pass the time o'day, an' then we must go in an' have a word with the Miss Brays, bein' old acquaintance. It ain't been so we could git to call on 'em before. I don't know's you're acquainted with Miss R'becca Wright. She's been out of town a good deal."

"I heared she was stopping over to Plainfields with her brother's folks," replied Mrs. Janes, rocking herself with irregular motion, as she sat close to the stove. "Got back some time in the fall. I believe?"

"Yes'm," said Miss Rebecca, with an undue sense of guilt and conviction. "We've been to the installation over to the East Parish, an' thought we'd stop in; we took this road home to see if 't was any better. How is the Miss Brays gittin' on?"

"They're well's common," answered Mrs. Janes grudgingly. "I was put out with Mr. Janes for fetchin' of 'em here, with all I 've got to do, an' I own I was kind o' surly to 'em 'long to the first of it. He gits the money from the town, an' it helps him out; but he bid 'em off for five dollars a month, an' we can't do much for 'em at no such price as that. I went an' dealt with the selec'men, an' made 'em promise to find their firewood an' some other things extra. They was glad to git rid o' the matter the fourth time I went, an' would ha' promised 'most anything. But Mr. Janes don't keep me half the time in oven-wood, he's off so much; an' we was cramped o' room, any way. I have to store things up garrit a good deal, an' that keeps me trampin' right through their room. I do the best for 'em I can, Mis' Trimble, but 't ain't so easy for me as 't is for you, with all your means to do with."

The poor woman looked pinched and miserable herself, though it was evident that she had no gift at house or home keeping. Mrs. Trimble's heart was wrung with pain, as she thought of the unwelcome inmates of such a place; but she held her peace bravely, while Miss Rebecca again gave some brief information in regard to the installation.

"You go right up them back stairs," the hostess directed at last. "I'm glad some o' you church folks has seen fit to come an' visit 'em. There ain't been nobody here this long spell, an' they've aged a sight since they come. They always send down a taste out of your baskets, Mis' Trimble, an' I relish it. I tell you. I'll shut the door after you, if you don't object. I feel every draught o' cold air."

"I've always heard she was a great hand to make a poor mouth. Wa'n't she from somewheres up Parsley way?" whispered Miss Rebecca, as they stumbled in the half-light.

"Poor meechin' body, wherever she come from," replied Mrs. Trimble, as she knocked at the door.

There was silence for a moment after this unusual sound; then one of the Bray sisters opened the door. The eager guests stared into a small, low room, brown with age, and gray, too, as if former dust and cobwebs could not be made wholly to disappear. The two elderly women who stood there looked like captives. Their withered faces wore a look of apprehension, and the room itself was more bare and plain than was fitting to their evident refinement of character and self-respect. There was an uncovered small table in the middle of the floor, with some crackers on a plate; and, for some reason or other, this added a great deal to the general desolation.

But Miss Ann Bray, the elder sister, who carried her right arm in a sling, with piteously drooping fingers, gazed at the visitors with radiant joy. She had not seen them arrive. The one window gave only the view at the back of the house, across the fields, and their coming was indeed a surprise. The next minute she was laughing and crying together. "Oh, sister!" she said, "if here ain't our dear Mis' Trimble!—an' my heart o' goodness, 't is 'Becca Wright, too! What dear good creatur's you be! I've felt all day as if somethin' good was goin' to happen, an' was just sayin' to myself 't was most sundown now, but I wouldn't let on to Mandany I'd give up hope quite yet. You see, the scissors stuck in the flour this very mornin', an' it's always a reliable sign. There, I've got to kiss ye both again!"

"I don't know where we can all set," lamented sister Mandana. "There ain't but the one chair an' the bed; t'other chair's too rickety; an' we 've been promised another these ten days; but first they've forgot it, an' next Mis' Janes can't spare it,—one excuse an' another. I'm goin' to git a stump o' wood an' nail a board on to it, when I can git outdoor again," said Mandana, in a plaintive voice. "There, I ain't goin' to complain o' nothin', now you've come," she added; and the guests sat down, Mrs. Trimble, as was proper, in the one chair.

"We've sat on the bed many's the time with you, 'Becca, an' talked over our girl nonsense, ain't we? You know where 't was,—in the little back bedroom we had when we was girls, an' used to peek out at our beaux through the strings o' mornin'-glories," laughed Ann Bray delightedly, her thin face shining more and more with joy. "I brought some o' them mornin'-glory seeds along when we come away, we'd raised 'em so many years; an' we got 'em started all right, but the hens found 'em out. I declare I chased them poor hens, foolish as 't was; but the mornin'-glories I'd counted on a sight to remind me o' home. You see, our debts was so large, after my long sickness an' all, that we did n't feel 't was right to keep back anything we could help from the auction."

It was impossible for any one to speak for a moment or two; the sisters felt their own uprooted condition afresh, and their guests for the first time really comprehended the piteous contrast between that neat little village house, which now seemed a palace of comfort, and this cold, unpainted upper room in the remote Janes farmhouse. It was an unwelcome thought to Mrs. Trimble that the well-to-do town of Hampden could provide no better for its poor than this, and her round face flushed with resentment and the shame of personal responsibility. "The girls shall be well settled in the village before another winter, if I pay their board myself," she made an inward resolution, and took another almost tearful look at the broken stove, the miserable bed, and the sisters' one hair-covered trunk, on which Mandana was sitting. But the poor place was filled with a golden spirit of hospitality.

Rebecca was again discoursing eloquently of the installation; it was so much easier to speak of general subjects, and the sisters had evidently been longing to hear some news. Since the late summer they had not been to church, and presently Mrs. Trimble asked the reason.

"Now, don't you go to pouring out our woes, Mandy!" begged little old Ann, looking shy and almost girlish, and as if she insisted upon playing that life was still all before them and all pleasure. "Don't you go to spoilin' their visit with our complaints! They know well's we do that changes must come, an' we'd been so wonted to our home things that this come hard at first; but then they felt for us. I know just as well's can be. 'Twill soon be summer again, an' 't is real pleasant right out in the fields here, when there ain't too hot a spell. I've got to know a sight o' new singin' birds since we come."

"Give me the folks I've always known," sighed the younger sister, who looked older than Miss Ann, and less even-tempered. "You may have your birds, if you want 'em. I do re'lly long to go to meetin' an' see folks go by up the aisle. Now, I will speak of it, Ann, whatever you say. We need, each of us, a pair o' good stout shoes an' rubbers,[6]—ours are all wore out; an' we've asked an' asked, an' they never think to bring 'em, an'"—

Poor old Mandana, on the trunk, covered her face with her arms and sobbed aloud. The elder sister stood over her, and patted her on the thin shoulder like a child, and tried to comfort her. It crossed Mrs. Trimble's mind that it was not the first time one had wept and the other had comforted. The sad scene must have been repeated many times in that long, drear winter. She would see them forever after in her mind as fixed as a picture, and her own tears fell fast.

"You did n't see Mis' Janes's cunning little boy, the next one to the baby, did you?" asked Ann Bray, turning round quickly at last, and going cheerfully on with the conversation. "Now, hush, Mandy, dear; they'll think you're childish! He's a dear, friendly little creatur'; an' likes to stay with us a good deal, though we feel's if 't was too cold for him, now we are waitin' to get us more wood."

"When I think of the acres o' woodland in this town!" groaned Rebecca Wright. "I believe I'm goin' to preach next Sunday, 'stead o' the minister, an' I'll make the sparks fly. I've always heard the saying, 'What's everybody's business is nobody's business,' an' I've come to believe it."

"Now, don't you, 'Becca. You've happened on a kind of a poor time with us, but we've got more belongings than you see here, an' a good large cluset, where we can store those things there ain't room to have about. You an' Miss Trimble have happened on a kind of poor day, you know. Soon's I git me some stout shoes an' rubbers, as Mandy says, I can fetch home plenty o' little dry boughs o' pine; you remember I was always a great hand to roam in the woods? If we could only have a front room, so 't we could look out on the road an' see the passin', an' was shod for meetin', I don't know's we should complain. Now we're just goin' to give you what we 've got, an' make out with a good welcome. We make more tea 'n we want in the mornin', an' then let the fire go down, since 't has been so mild. We've got a *good* cluset" (disappearing as she spoke), "an' I know this to be good tea, 'cause it's some o' yourn, Mis' Trimble. An' here are our sprigged chiny cups that R'becca knows by sight, if Mis' Trimble don't. We kep' out four of 'em, an' put the even half dozen with the rest of the auction stuff. I've often wondered who 'd got 'em, but I never asked, for fear 't would be somebody that would distress us. They was mother's, you know."

The four cups were poured, and the little table pushed to the bed, where Rebecca Wright still sat, and Mandana, wiping her eyes, came and joined her. Mrs. Trimble sat in her chair at the end, and Ann trotted about the room in pleased content for a while, and in and out of the closet, as if she still had much to do; then she came and stood opposite Mrs. Trimble. She was very short and small, and there was no painful sense of her being obliged to stand. The four cups

[6]Rubber coverings to keep the shoes dry.

were not quite full of cold tea, but there was a clean old tablecloth folded double, and a plate with three pairs of crackers neatly piled, and a small—it must be owned, a very small—piece of hard white cheese. Then, for a treat, in a glass dish, there was a little preserved peach, the last—Miss Rebecca knew it instinctively—of the household stores brought from their old home. It was very sugary, this bit of peach; and as she helped her guests and sister Mandy, Miss Ann Bray said, half unconsciously, as she often had said with less reason in the old days, "Our preserves ain't so good as usual this year; this is beginning to candy." Both the guests protested, while Rebecca added that the taste of it carried her back, and made her feel young again. The Brays had always managed to keep one or two peach-trees alive in their corner of a garden. "I've been keeping this preserve for a treat," said her friend. "I'm glad to have you eat some, 'Becca. Last summer I often wished you was home an' could come an' see us, 'stead o' being away off to Plainfields."

The crackers did not taste too dry. Miss Ann took the last of the peach on her own cracker; there could not have been quite a small spoonful, after the others were helped, but she asked them first if they would not have some more. Then there was a silence, and in the silence a wave of tender feeling rose high in the hearts of the four elderly women. At this moment the setting sun flooded the poor plain room with light; the unpainted wood was all of a golden-brown, and Ann Bray, with her gray hair and aged face, stood at the head of the table in a kind of aureole. Mrs. Trimble's face was all a-quiver as she looked at her; she thought of the text about two or three being gathered together, and was half afraid.

"I believe we ought to 've asked Mis' Janes if she would n't come up," said Ann. "She's real good feelin', but she's had it very hard, an' gits discouraged. I can't find that she's ever had anything real pleasant to look back to, as we have. There, next time we'll make a good heartenin' time for her too."

The sorrel horse had taken a long nap by the gnawed fence-rail, and the cool air after sundown made him impatient to be gone. The two friends jolted homeward in the gathering darkness, through the stiffening mud, and neither Mrs. Trimble nor Rebecca Wright said a word until they were out of sight as well as out of sound of the Janes house. Time must elapse before they could reach a more familiar part of the road and resume conversation on its natural level.

"I consider myself to blame," insisted Mrs. Trimble at last. "I have n't no words of accusation for nobody else, an' I ain't one to take comfort in calling names to the board o' selec'*men*. I make no reproaches, an' I take it all on my own shoulders; but I'm goin' to stir about me, I tell you! I shall begin early tomorrow. They're goin' back to their own house,—it's been standin' empty all winter,—an' the town's goin' to give 'em the rent an' what firewood they need; it won't come to more than the board's payin' out now. An' you an' me 'll take this same horse an' wagon, an' ride an' go afoot by turns, an' git means enough together to buy back their furniture an' whatever was sold at that plaguy auction; an' then we'll put it all back, an' tell 'em they 've got to move to a new place, an' just carry 'em right back again where they come from. An' don't you never tell, R'becca, but here I be a widow woman, layin' up what I make from my farm for nobody knows who, an' I'm goin' to do for them Bray girls all I'm a mind to. I should be sca't to wake up in heaven, an' hear anybody there ask how the Bray girls was. Don't talk to me about the town o' Hampden, an' don't ever let me hear the name o' town poor! I'm ashamed to go home an' see what's set out for supper. I wish I'd brought 'em right along."

"I was goin' to ask if we could n't git the new doctor to go up an' do somethin' for poor Ann's arm," said Miss Rebecca. "They say he's very smart. If she could get so 's to braid straw or hook rugs again, she 'd soon be earnin' a little somethin'. An' may be he could do somethin' for Mandy's eyes. They did use to live so neat an' ladylike. Somehow I could n't speak to tell 'em there that 't was I bought them six best cups an' saucers, time of the auction; they went very low, as everythin' else did, an' I thought I could save it some other way. They shall have 'em back an' welcome. You're real wholehearted, Mis' Trimble. I expect Ann'll be sayin' that her father's child'n wa'n't goin' to be left desolate, an' that all the bread he cast on the waters 's comin' back through you."

"I don't care what she says, dear creatur'!" exclaimed Mrs. Trimble. "I'm full o' regrets I took time for that installation, an' set there seepin' in a lot o' talk this whole day long, except for its kind of bringin' us to the Bray girls. I wish to my heart 't was to-morrow mornin' a'ready, an' I a-startin' for the selec'*men*."

1890

Bret Harte 1836–1902

Like many other Americans who wrote about the West, Bret Harte was originally an Easterner. Born in Albany, New York, he did not go west until 1854, following his father's death and his mother's remarriage. His reports of his early life were filled with fantasy and romance. He claimed early genius, to have been reading Shakespeare at the age of six. It is certain that he taught school for a time. He may also have prospected for gold for a short period, and there is evidence that he spent a "brief, delightful hour" in 1857 riding shotgun on a stagecoach for Wells Fargo Express. The job was as dangerous as legend and the movies have represented it: Harte's predecessor as guard was wounded by bandits; his successor was shot and killed.

Harte next became a professional writer, first for a newspaper in northern California. After he imprudently denounced a mob's massacre of sixty Indians, mostly women and children, his life was threatened, and he fled to San Francisco. There, in 1868, he became the first editor of The Overland Monthly, *a magazine that was to be influential and prosperous until he left it. He had published poems and stories prior to his employment on* The Overland Monthly, *but it was while he was its editor that he wrote the works that made him famous: "The Luck of Roaring Camp" appeared in the second issue, soon followed by "The Outcasts of Poker Flat" and his most famous poem, "Plain Language from Truthful James," usually known as "The Heathen Chinee."*

The enormous success of Harte's fiction brought him wide acclaim: Charles Dickens (Harte's favorite author) praised his writing and urged Harte to come to London to work for him; publishers from the East flooded Harte with offers. His career was at its peak: He was a famous writer and editor, he had been appointed Secretary of the U.S. Mint in San Francisco and Professor of Literature at the University of California.

In 1871, Harte accepted an unprecedented contract of ten thousand dollars from The Atlantic Monthly *for twelve "poems and sketches," and he left California for Boston, now so famous that an English newspaper issued daily accounts of his journey from coast to coast. Although he was to live nearly thirty years more, the remainder of his life was a disappointment and anticlimax. After California, his writing became self-imitative and repetitious, as he himself admitted late in his life: "I grind out the old tunes on the old organ, and gather up the coppers." Without the immediate inspiration of the West to bring energy to his stories, his sentimentality became more obvious. In his later writings, a dominant theme—moral redemption through sacrifice—was tiresomely repeated. His contract was not renewed by* The Atlantic Monthly, *and, unable to make a living from his writing, he went on a series of lecture tours, served in the U.S. diplomatic corps in Germany and Scotland, and spent the last years of his life in England. His last letters are full of his worries over money, self-pitying complaints about his health, and a grieving awareness of a wasted talent.*

In fact, Harte's talent was always minor. Even the best of his stories are overly sentimental; the characters seem deadly similar from tale to poem. Cynical gamblers, gruff but ever-loyal partners, and whores "with hearts of gold" recur again and again. Nevertheless, Harte did vividly characterize a vital period in American history—the final settlement of the West. He was the first widely acclaimed, and one of the best, local color writers who emphasized American regionalism and paved the way for the coming of literary realism. Harte's writing was noteworthy, in an age of genteel evasions, for its frequent portrayal of crucial areas of human experience—sex, love, and death—directly and openly. But perhaps above all, Harte's works and his great, though short-lived, success stand as a notable expression of the world's long-lasting fascination with life on the American frontier.

FURTHER READING: *The Works of Bret Harte,* 18 vols., 1899, 1981; *Bret Harte: Representative Selections,* ed., J. Harrison, 1941; H. Boynton, *Bret Harte,* 1903, 1973; T. Pemberton, *The Life of Bret Harte,* 1903; G. Stewart, *Bret Harte: Argonaut and Exile,* 1931; R. O'Connor, *Bret Harte,* 1966; M. Duckett, *Mark Twain and Bret Harte,* 1964; P. Morrow, *Bret Harte: Literary Critic,* 1979; L. Barnett, *Bret Harte: A Reference Guide,* 1980; G. Scharnhorst, *Bret Harte,* 1992; A. Nissen, *Bret Harte: Prince and Pauper,* 2000.

TEXT: *The Writings of Bret Harte,* 20 vols. 1896–1914.

TENNESSEE'S PARTNER

I do not think that we ever knew his real name. Our ignorance of it certainly never gave us any social inconvenience, for at Sandy Bar in 1854 most men were christened anew. Sometimes these appellatives were derived from some distinctiveness of dress, as in the case of "Dungaree Jack"; or from some peculiarity of habit, as shown in "Saleratus Bill," so called from an undue proportion of that chemical[1] in his daily bread; or from some unlucky slip, as exhibited in "The Iron Pirate," a mild, inoffensive man, who earned that baleful title by his unfortunate mispronunciation of the term "iron pyrites." Perhaps this may have been the beginning of a rude heraldry; but I am constrained to think that it was because a man's real name in that day rested solely upon his own unsupported statement. "Call yourself, Clifford, do you?" said Boston, addressing a timid new-comer with infinite scorn; "hell is full of such Cliffords!" He then introduced the unfortunate man, whose name happened to be really Clifford, as

[1]Saleratus, baking soda.

"Jay-bird Charley,"—an unhallowed inspiration of the moment, that clung to him ever after.

But to return to Tennessee's Partner, whom we never knew by any other than this relative title; that he had ever existed as a separate and distinct individuality we only learned later. It seems that in 1853 he left Poker Flat to go to San Francisco, ostensibly to procure a wife. He never got any farther than Stockton. At that place he was attracted by a young person who waited upon the table at the hotel where he took his meals. One morning he said something to her which caused her to smile not unkindly, to somewhat coquettishly break a plate of toast over his upturned, serious simple face, and to retreat to the kitchen. He followed her, and emerged a few moments later, covered with more toast and victory. That day a week they were married by a Justice of the Peace, and returned to Poker Flat. I am aware that something more might be made of this episode, but I prefer to tell it as it was current at Sandy Bar,—in the gulches and barrooms,—where all sentiment was modified by a strong sense of humor.

Of their married felicity but little is known, perhaps for the reason that Tennessee, then living with his partner, one day took occasion to say something to the bride on his own account, at which, it is said, she smiled not unkindly and chastely retreated,—this time as far as Marysville, where Tennessee followed her, and where they went to housekeeping without the aid of a Justice of the Peace. Tennessee's Partner took the loss of his wife simply and seriously, as was his fashion. But to everybody's surprise, when Tennessee one day returned from Marysville, without his partner's wife,—she having smiled and retreated with somebody else,—Tennessee's Partner was the first man to shake his hand and greet him with affection. The boys who had gathered in the cañon to see the shooting were naturally indignant. Their indignation might have found vent in sarcasm but for a certain look in Tennessee's Partner's eye that indicated a lack of humorous appreciation. In fact he was a grave man, with a steady application to practical detail which was unpleasant in a difficulty.

Meanwhile a popular feeling against Tennessee had grown up on the Bar. He was known to be a gambler; he was suspected to be a thief. In these suspicions Tennessee's Partner was equally compromised; his continued intimacy with Tennessee after the affair above quoted could only be accounted for on the hypothesis of a copartnership of crime. At last Tennessee's guilt became flagrant. One day he overtook a stranger on his way to Red Dog. The stranger afterward related that Tennessee beguiled the time with interesting anecdote and reminiscence, but illogically concluded the interview in the following words: "And now, young man, I'll trouble you for your knife, your pistols, and your money. You see your weppings might get you into trouble at Red Dog, and your money's a temptation to the evilly disposed. I think you said your address was San Francisco. I shall endeavor to call." It may be stated here that Tennessee had a fine flow of humor, which no business preoccupation could wholly subdue.

This exploit was his last. Red Dog and Sandy Bar made common cause against the highwayman. Tennessee was hunted in very much the same fashion as his prototype, the grizzly. As the toils[2] closed around him, he made a desperate dash through the Bar, emptying his revolver at the crowd before the Arcade Saloon, and so on up Grizzly Cañon; but at its farther extremity he was stopped by a small man on a gray horse. The men looked at each other a

[2]Snares, traps.

moment in silence. Both were fearless, both self-possessed and independent; and both types of a civilization that in the seventeenth century would have been called heroic, but, in the nineteenth, simply "reckless." "What have you got there?—I call," said Tennessee, quietly. "Two bowers[3] and an ace," said the stranger, as quietly, showing two revolvers and a bowie-knife. "That takes me," returned Tennessee; and with this gamblers' epigram, he threw away his useless pistol, and rode back with his captor.

It was a warm night. The cool breeze which usually sprang up with the going down of the sun behind the *chaparral*-crested mountain was that evening withheld from Sandy Bar. The little cañon was stifling with heated resinous odors, and the decaying drift-wood on the Bar sent forth faint, sickening exhalations. The feverishness of day, and its fierce passions, still filled the camp. Lights moved restlessly along the bank of the river, striking no answering reflection from its tawny current. Against the blackness of the pines the windows of the old loft above the express-office stood out staringly bright; and through their curtainless panes the loungers below could see the forms of those who were even then deciding the fate of Tennessee. And above all this, etched on the dark firmament, rose the Sierra, remote and passionless, crowned with the remoter passionless stars.

The trial of Tennessee was conducted as fairly as was consistent with a judge and jury who felt themselves to some extent obliged to justify, in their verdict, the previous irregularities of arrest and indictment. The law of Sandy Bar was implacable, but not vengeful. The excitement and personal feeling of the chase were over; with Tennessee safe in their hands they were ready to listen patiently to any defence, which they were already satisfied was insufficient. There being no doubt in their own minds, they were willing to give the prisoner the benefit of any that might exist. Secure in the hypothesis that he ought to be hanged, on general principles, they indulged him with more latitude or defence than his reckless hardihood seemed to ask. The Judge appeared to be more anxious than the prisoner, who, otherwise, unconcerned, evidently took a grim pleasure in the responsibility he had created. "I don't take any hand in this yer game," had been his invariable, but good-humored reply to all questions. The Judge—who was also his captor—for a moment vaguely regretted that he had not shot him "on sight," that morning, but presently dismissed this human weakness as unworthy of the judicial mind. Nevertheless, when there was a tap at the door, and it was said that Tennessee's Partner was there on behalf of the prisoner, he was admitted at once without question. Perhaps the younger member of the jury, to whom the proceedings were becoming irksomely thoughtful, hailed him as a relief.

For he was not, certainly, an imposing figure. Short and stout, with a square face, sunburned into a preternatural redness, clad in a loose duck "jumper," and trousers streaked and splashed with red soil, his aspect under any circumstances would have been quaint, and was now even ridiculous. As he stooped to deposit at his feet a heavy carpet-bag he was carrying, it became obvious, from partially developed legends and inscriptions, that the material with which his trousers had been patched had been originally intended for a less ambitious covering. Yet he advanced with great gravity, and after having shaken the hand of

[3]High cards.

each person in the room with labored cordiality, he wiped his serious, perplexed face on a red bandanna handkerchief, a shade lighter than his complexion, laid his powerful hand upon the table to steady himself, and thus addressed the Judge:—

"I was passin' by," he began, by way of apology, "and I thought I'd just step in and see how things was gittin' on with Tennessee thar,—my pardner. It's a hot night. I disremember any sich weather before on the Bar."

He paused a moment, but nobody volunteering any other meteorological recollection, he again had recourse to his pocket-handkerchief, and for some moments mopped his face diligently.

"Have you anything to say in behalf of the prisoner?" said the Judge, finally.

"Thet's it," said Tennessee's Partner, in a tone of relief. "I come yar as Tennessee's pardner,—knowing him nigh on four year, off and on, wet and dry, in luck and out o' luck. His ways ain't allers my ways, but thar ain't any p'ints in that young man, thar ain't any liveliness as he's been up to, as I don't know. And you sez to me, sez you,—confidential-like, and between man and man,—sez you, 'Do you know anything in his behalf?' and I sez to you, sez I,—confidential-like, as between man and man,—'What should a man know of his pardner?'"

"Is this all you have to say?" asked the Judge, impatiently, feeling, perhaps, that a dangerous sympathy of humor was beginning to humanize the Court.

"Thet's so," continued Tennessee's Partner. "It ain't for me to say anything agin' him. And now, what's the case? Here's Tennessee wants money, wants it bad, and does n't like to ask it of his old pardner. Well, what does Tennessee do? He lays for a stranger, and he fetches that stranger. And you lays for *him,* and you fetches *him;* and the honors is easy.[4] And I put it to you, bein' a far-minded man, and to you, gentlemen, all, as far-minded men, ef this is n't so."

"Prisoner," said the Judge, interrupting, "have you any questions to ask this man?"

"No! no!" continued Tennessee's Partner, hastily. "I play this yer hand alone. To come down to the bed-rock, it's just this: Tennessee, thar, has played it pretty rough and expensive-like on a stranger, and on this yer camp. And now, what's the fair thing? Some would say more; some would say less. Here's seventeen hundred dollars in coarse gold and a watch,—it's about all my pile,—and call it square!" And before a hand could be raised to prevent him, he had emptied the contents of the carpet-bag upon the table.

For a moment his life was in jeopardy. One or two men sprang to their feet, several hands groped for hidden weapons, and a suggestion to "throw him from the window" was only overridden by a gesture from the Judge. Tennessee laughed. And apparently oblivious of the excitement, Tennessee's Partner improved the opportunity to mop his face again with his handkerchief.

When order was restored, and the man was made to understand, by the use of forcible figures and rhetoric, that Tennessee's offence could not be condoned by money, his face took a more serious and sanguinary hue, and those who were nearest to him noticed that his rough hand trembled slightly on the table. He hesitated a moment as he slowly returned the gold to the carpet-bag, as if he had not yet entirely caught the elevated sense of justice which swayed the tribunal, and was perplexed with the belief that he had not offered enough. Then he turned to the Judge, and saying, "This yer is a lone hand, played alone,

[4]I.e., honor cards are equally divided; thus, everything is equal.

and without my pardner," he bowed to the jury and was about to withdraw, when the Judge called him back. "If you have anything to say to Tennessee, you had better say it now." For the first time that evening the eyes of the prisoner and his stranger advocate met. Tennessee smiled, showed his white teeth, and, saying, "Euchred,[5] old man!" held out his hand. Tennessee's Partner took it in his own, and saying, "I just dropped in as I was passin' to see how things was gettin' on," let the hand passively fall, and adding that "it was a warm night," again mopped his face with his handkerchief, and without another word withdrew.

The two men never again met each other alive. For the unparalleled insult of a bribe offered to Judge Lynch—who, whether bigoted, weak, or narrow, was at least incorruptible—firmly fixed in the mind of that mythical personage any wavering determination of Tennessee's fate; and at the break of day he was marched, closely guarded, to meet it at the top of Marley's Hill.

How he met it, how cool he was, how he refused to say anything, how perfect were the arrangements of the committee, were all duly reported, with the addition of a warning moral and example to all future evil-doers, in the Red Dog Clarion, by its editor, who was present, and to whose vigorous English I cheerfully refer the reader. But the beauty of that midsummer morning, the blessed amity of earth and air and sky, the awakened life of the free woods and hills, the joyous renewal and promise of Nature, and above all, the infinite Serenity that thrilled through each, was not reported, as not being a part of the social lesson. And yet, when the weak and foolish deed was done, and a life, with its possibilities and responsibilities, had passed out of the misshapen thing that dangled between earth and sky, the birds sang, the flowers bloomed, the sun shone, as cheerily as before; and possibly the Red Dog Clarion was right.

Tennessee's Partner was not in the group that surrounded the ominous tree. But as they turned to disperse attention was drawn to the singular appearance of a motionless donkey-cart halted at the side of the road. As they approached, they at once recognized the venerable "Jenny" and the two-wheeled cart as the property of Tennessee's Partner,—used by him in carrying dirt from his claim; and a few paces distant the owner of the equipage himself, sitting under a buckeye-tree, wiping the perspiration from his glowing face. In answer to an inquiry, he said he had come for the body of the "diseased," "if it was all the same to the committee." He did n't wish to "hurry anything"; he could "wait." He was not working that day; and when the gentlemen were done with the "diseased," he would take him. "Ef thar is any present," he added, in his simple, serious way, "as would care to jine in the fun'l, they kin come." Perhaps it was from a sense of humor, which I have already intimated was a feature of Sandy Bar,—perhaps it was from something even better than that; but two thirds of the loungers accepted the invitation at once.

It was noon when the body of Tennessee was delivered into the hands of his partner. As the cart drew up to the fatal tree, we noticed that it contained a rough, oblong box,—apparently made from a section of sluicing,[6]—and half filled with bark and the tassels of pine. The cart was further decorated with slips of willow, and made fragrant with buckeye-blossoms. When the body was deposited in the box, Tennessee's Partner drew over it a piece of tarred canvas, and gravely mounting the narrow seat in front, with his feet upon the shafts,

[5]From the card game euchre, the loser of which is "euchred."
[6]Long boards used in building water channels.

urged the little donkey forward. The equipage moved slowly on, at that decorous pace which was habitual with "Jenny" even under less solemn circumstances. The men—half curiously, half jestingly, but all good-humoredly—strolled along beside the cart; some in advance, some a little in the rear of the homely catafalque.[7] But, whether from the narrowing of the road or some present sense of decorum, as the cart passed on, the company fell to the rear in couples, keeping step, and otherwise assuming the external show of a formal procession. Jack Folinsbee, who had at the outset played a funeral march in dumb show[8] upon an imaginary trombone, desisted, from a lack of sympathy and appreciation,—not having, perhaps, your true humorist's capacity to be content with the enjoyment of his own fun.

The way led through Grizzly Cañon,—by this time clothed in funeral drapery and shadows. The redwoods, burying their moccasined feet in the red soil, stood in Indian-file along the track, trailing an uncouth benediction from their bending boughs upon the passing bier. A hare, surprised into helpless inactivity, sat upright and pulsating in the ferns by the roadside, as the *cortège* went by. Squirrels hastened to gain a secure outlook from higher boughs; and the blue-jays, spreading their wings, fluttered before them like outriders, until the outskirts of Sandy Bar were reached, and the solitary cabin of Tennessee's Partner.

Viewed under more favorable circumstances, it would not have been a cheerful place. The unpicturesque site, the rude and unlovely outlines, the unsavory details, which distinguish the nestbuilding of the California miner, were all here, with the dreariness of decay superadded. A few paces from the cabin there was a rough enclosure, which, in the brief days of Tennessee's Partner's matrimonial felicity, had been used as a garden, but was now overgrown with fern. As we approached it we were surprised to find that what we had taken for a recent attempt at cultivation was the broken soil about an open grave.

The cart was halted before the enclosure; and rejecting the offers of assistance with the same air of simple self-reliance he had displayed throughout, Tennessee's Partner lifted the rough coffin on his back, and deposited it, unaided, within the shallow grave. He then nailed down the board which served as a lid; and mounting the little mound of earth beside it, took off his hat, and slowly mopped his face with his handkerchief. This the crowd felt was a preliminary to speech; and they disposed themselves variously on stumps and boulders, and sat expectant.

"When a man," began Tennessee's Partner, slowly, "has been running free all day, what's the natural thing for him to do? Why, to come home. And if he ain't in a condition to go home, what can his best friend do? Why, bring him home! And here's Tennessee has been running free, and we brings him home from his wandering." He paused, and picked up a fragment of quartz, rubbed it thoughtfully on his sleeve, and went on: "It ain't the first time that I've packed him on my back, as you see'd me now. It ain't the first time that I brought him to this yer cabin when he could n't help himself; it ain't the first time that I and 'Jinny' have waited for him on yon hill, and picked him up and so fetched him home, when he could n't speak, and did n't know me. And now that it's the last time, why—" he paused, and rubbed the quartz gently on his sleeve—"you see it's sort of rough on his pardner. And now, gentlemen," he added, abruptly, picking up his long-handled shovel, "the fun'l's over; and my thanks, and Tennessee's thanks, to you for your trouble."

[7]Ornamental framework that carries a coffin. [8]Silently.

Resisting any proffers of assistance, he began to fill in the grave, turning his back upon the crowd, that after a few moments' hesitation gradually withdrew. As they crossed the little ridge that hid Sandy Bar from view, some, looking back, thought they could see Tennessee's Partner, his work done, sitting upon the grave, his shovel between his knees, and his face buried in his red bandanna handkerchief. But it was argued by others that you couldn't tell his face from his handkerchief at that distance; and this point remained undecided.

In the reaction that followed the feverish excitement of that day, Tennessee's Partner was not forgotten. A secret investigation had cleared him of any complicity in Tennessee's guilt, and left only a suspicion of his general sanity. Sandy Bar made a point of calling on him, and proffering various uncouth, but well-meant kindnesses. But from that day his rude health and great strength seemed visibly to decline; and when the rainy season fairly set in, and the tiny grass-blades were beginning to peep from the rocky mound above Tennessee's grave, he took to his bed.

One night, when the pines beside the cabin were swaying in the storm, and trailing their slender fingers over the roof, and the roar and rush of the swollen river were heard below, Tennessee's Partner lifted his head from the pillow, saying, "It is time to go for Tennessee; I must put 'Jinny' in the cart"; and would have risen from his bed but for the restraint. Struggling, he still pursued his singular fancy: "There, now, steady, 'Jinny,'—steady, old girl. How dark it is! Look out for the ruts,—and look out for him, too, old gal. Sometimes, you know, when he's blind drunk, he drops down right in the trail. Keep on straight up to the pine on the top of the hill. Thar—I told you so!—thar he is,—coming this way, too,—all by himself, sober, and his face a-shining. Tennessee! Pardner!"

And so they met.

1869

George Washington Cable

1844–1925

In 1875, the editor of Harper's Magazine *rejected a short story submitted by George Washington Cable. Stories for* Harper's, *the editor explained, should be "of a pleasant character," preferably "love tales," whereas Cable had shown "disagreeable aspects of human nature" that left "an unpleasant impression on the mind of the reader." It was not the first time, nor would it be the last, that Cable's writing roused genteel readers to complain of his improprieties. Yet Cable himself had standards of personal behavior so austere, so lofty, that his friend Mark Twain was moved to observe that "when it comes down to moral honesty, limpid innocence, and utterly blameless piety, the Apostles were mere policemen [compared] to Cable." Raised in a strict, religious family, Cable was devoted to daily prayer and Bible reading. Throughout his life he never smoked or drank, he refused to work or travel on Sunday, and not until he was middle-aged did he permit himself to see a play. Yet he often wrote of violence and death, of racial intermarriage, and of problems of human weakness and desire that to his own age were beyond the bounds of literary decency.*

Cable wrote of a world he knew, of Louisiana and New Orleans, where he was born and raised. His formal education was brief. In 1859, his father died, and fourteen-year-old George quit school and went to work to support his family. He worked as an office boy and then clerked in a store, all the while struggling to educate himself by studying Latin and reading history and literature. During the Civil War he enlisted in the Confederate cavalry and was twice wounded. After the war, Cable worked as a surveyor and then as a bookkeeper for a cotton merchant in New Orleans. Fascinated by New Orleans and its people, Cable began to study the early history of the city and listen to stories of its blacks and its Creoles (descendants of early Spanish and French settlers). Cable was quick to notice the possibility of using Louisiana as a source for fiction, for he was aware of a growing public interest in local color stories that displayed the speech, manners, and character types found in the different regions of the United States.

In 1873, Scribner's Monthly *published "Sieur George," the first of many short tales in which Cable described New Orleans, its ancient streets, its decaying buildings, and its colorful inhabitants. In 1879 Cable published* Old Creole Days, *a collection of his best stories, including "Sieur George," "Posson Jone," and "Belles Demoiselles Plantation." In 1880 his first and most noteworthy novel appeared,* The Grandissimes, *a story of American "intruders" into the European life of New Orleans early in the 1800s. Having achieved literary success, Cable was at last able to leave business and devote himself fully to writing. Two novels,* Madame Delphine *and* Dr. Sevier, *were published in 1881 and 1884. And he began the lectures and platform readings of his own works that brought him wide recognition throughout the United States.*

At the peak of his fame, Cable turned increasingly from fiction to pamphleteering. He attacked political corruption in the South and spoke out for civil reform and rights for blacks. Cable's stories had sometimes stirred resentment among Louisiana's proud Creoles, who were embarrassed by his stories and felt he had held them up to national ridicule. Now the Creoles were joined by others who were indignant at Cable's political attacks and at his vigorous efforts in behalf of racial justice. Cable was charged with stirring social unrest. He was called a turncoat, an "unnatural Southern growth, a bastard sprout" who took advantage of his friends and neighbors for the sake of northern readers and northern dollars. In 1884, faced with growing public hostility and social ostracism, Cable moved his family from New Orleans, eventually settling in Northampton, Massachusetts, where he was to live the rest of his life. He continued his social criticism with The Silent South *(1885), a strong indictment of the treatment given freed slaves. And he wrote* John March, Southerner *(1894), a novel set in the South during the reconstruction years immediately following the Civil War. But Cable could never equal the achievement of his early short stories and novels. His move north had separated him from the people and the scenes he knew best, and his growing willingness to adapt his work to the delicate tastes of magazine and book editors drained his writing of its former power.*

Much of Cable's work now seems melodramatic and burdened with moral teaching. Modern readers often find his dialect transcriptions to be tedious and over-detailed, his plots to be unrealistic and contrived. At its best his fiction was a blend of romance and realism. He depicted the sounds, sights, and characters of an exotic region of America. He was interested in the strange, the colorful, even the grotesque. But unlike many regional writers of his time, Cable described a world of moral complexity devoid of happy endings and certain triumphs. He was the first southern writer to deal seriously with miscegenation, the racial mixing of blacks and whites, in America. He wrote of the rise and decline of social classes and of the burdens that the past imposes on the present—vital themes that reappear in the work of such modern southern writers as Eudora Welty, Flannery O'Connor, Thomas Wolfe, and William Faulkner. Cable was a reformer, a social critic, and a historian. He sacrificed much for the cause of justice and equality in America. But his greatest achievement was his vivid depiction of his native region and its people, especially the Louisiana Creoles who once hated Cable for his descriptions of their life but who now are largely remembered as part of a bygone age that lives only in the stories and tales he wrote.

FURTHER READING: *The Negro Question: A Selection of Writings on Civil Rights in the South by George W. Cable,* ed. A. Turner, 1958; *Creoles and Cajuns: Stories of Old Louisiana,* ed. A. Turner, 1959; L. Biklé, *George W. Cable: His Life and Letters,* 1928; K. Ekström, *George W. Cable: A Study of His Early Life and Work,* 1950; A. Turner, *George W. Cable: A Biography,* 1956; P. Butcher, *George W. Cable: The Northampton Years,* 1959; A. Turner, *Mark Twain and George W. Cable,* 1960; P. Butcher, *George W. Cable,* 1962; L. Rubin, *George W. Cable,* 1969; *Critical Essays on George W. Cable,* ed. A. Turner, 1980; A. Petry, *A Genius in His Way,* 1987; G. Jones, *Strange Talk: The Politics of Dialect Literature in Gilded Age America,* 1999.

TEXT: *Old Creole Days,* 1879.

BELLES DEMOISELLES PLANTATION

The original grantee was Count———, assume the name to be De Charleu; the old Creoles[1] never forgive a public mention. He was the French king's commissary. One day, called to France to explain the lucky accident of the commissariat having burned down with his account-books inside, he left his wife, a Choctaw[2] Comptesse, behind.

Arrived at court, his excuses were accepted, and that tract granted him where afterwards stood Belles Demoiselles[3] Plantation. A man cannot remember every thing! In a fit of forgetfulness he married a French gentlewoman, rich and beautiful, and "brought her out."[4] However, "All's well that ends well;" a famine had been in the colony, and the Choctaw Comptesse had starved, leaving nought but a half-caste orphan family lurking on the edge of the settlement, bearing our French gentlewoman's own new name, and being mentioned in Monsieur's will.

And the new Comptesse—she tarried but a twelve month, left Monsieur a lovely son, and departed, led out of this vain world by the swamp-fever.

From this son sprang the proud Creole family of De Charleu. It rose straight up, up, up, generation after generation, tall, branchless, slender, palm-like; and finally, in the time of which I am to tell, flowered with all the rare beauty of a century-plant, in Artemise, Innocente, Felicité, the twins Maria and Martha, Leontine and little Septima; the seven beautiful daughters for whom their home had been fitly named Belles Demoiselles.

The Count's grant had once been a long Pointe,[5] round which the Mississippi used to whirl, and seethe, and foam, that it was horrid to behold. Big whirlpools would open and wheel about in the savage eddies under the low bank, and

[1]Descendants of early Spanish and French settlers.
[2]An Indian tribe living northeast of New Orleans. [3]French: Beautiful Maidens.
[4]I.e., brought her to America. [5]A pointed or arrow-shaped plot of land.

close up again, and others open, and spin, and disappear. Great circles of muddy surface would boil up from hundreds of feet below, and gloss over, and seem to float away,—sink, come back again under water, and with only a soft hiss surge up again, and again drift off, and vanish. Every few minutes the loamy bank would tip down a great load of earth upon its besieger, and fall back a foot,—sometimes a yard,—and the writhing river would press after, until at last the Pointe was quite swallowed up, and the great river glided by in a majestic curve, and asked no more; the bank stood fast, the "caving" became a forgotten misfortune, and the diminished grant was a long, sweeping, willowy bend, rustling with miles of sugar-cane.

Coming up the Mississippi in the sailing craft of those early days, about the time one first could descry the white spires of the old St. Louis Cathedral,[6] you would be pretty sure to spy, just over to your right under the levee,[7] Belles Demoiselles Mansion, with its broad veranda and red painted cypress roof, peering over the embankment, like a bird in the nest, half hid by the avenue of willows which one of the departed De Charleus,—he that married a Marot,—had planted on the levee's crown.

The house stood unusually near the river, facing eastward, and standing four-square, with an immense veranda about its sides, and a flight of steps in front spreading broadly downward, as we open arms to a child. From the veranda nine miles of river were seen; and in their compass, near at hand, the shady garden full of rare and beautiful flowers; farther away broad fields of cane and rice, and the distant quarters of the slaves, and on the horizon everywhere a dark belt of cypress forest.

The master was old Colonel De Charleu,—Jean Albert Henri Joseph De Charleu-Marot, and "Colonel" by the grace of the first American governor.[8] Monsieur,—he would not speak to any one who called him "Colonel,"—was a hoary-headed patriarch. His step was firm, his form erect, his intellect strong and clear, his countenance classic, serene, dignified, commanding, his manners courtly, his voice musical,—fascinating. He had had his vices,—all his life; but had borne them, as his race do, with a serenity of conscience and a cleanness of mouth that left no outward blemish on the surface of the gentleman. He had gambled in Royal Street,[9] drank hard in Orleans Street,[10] run his adversary through in the duelling-ground at Slaughter-house Point,[11] and danced and quarrelled at the St. Philippe-street-theatre quadroon balls.[12] Even now, with all his courtesy and bounty, and a hospitality which seemed to be entertaining angels, he was bitter-proud and penurious, and deep down in his hard-finished heart loved nothing but himself, his name, and his motherless children. But these!—their ravishing beauty was all but excuse enough for the unbounded idolatry of their father. Against these seven goddesses he never rebelled. Had they even required him to defraud old De Carlos—

I can hardly say.

[6]Church (1794) in the center of New Orleans.

[7]Embankment for protection against river floods.

[8]William Claiborne, appointed in March 1806 to administer the new Territory after the United States had acquired it through the Louisiana Purchase.

[9]A street of New Orleans gambling houses. [10]A street at the center of old New Orleans.

[11]A traditional duelling site, now preserved in a New Orleans city park.

[12]Elegant balls given for young women of one-quarter black ancestry.

Old De Carlos was his extremely distant relative on the Choctaw side. With this single exception, the narrow thread-like line of descent from the Indian wife, diminished to a mere strand by injudicious alliances, and deaths in the gutters of old New Orleans, was extinct. The name, by Spanish contact, had become De Carlos; but this one surviving bearer of it was known to all, and known only, as Injin Charlie.

One thing I never knew a Creole to do. He will not utterly go back on the ties of blood, no matter what sort of knots those ties may be. For one reason, he is never ashamed of his or his father's sins; and for another,—he will tell you—he is "all heart!"

So the different heirs of the De Charleu estate had always strictly regarded the rights and interests of the De Carloses, especially their ownership of a block of dilapidated buildings in a part of the city, which had once been very poor property, but was beginning to be valuable. This block had much more than maintained the last De Carlos through a long and lazy lifetime, and, as his household consisted only of himself, and an aged and crippled negress, the inference was irresistible that he "had money." Old Charlie, though by *alias* an "Injin," was plainly a dark white man, about as old as Colonel De Charleu, sunk in the bliss of deep ignorance, shrewd, deaf, and, by repute at least, unmerciful.

The Colonel and he always conversed in English. This rare accomplishment, which the former had learned from his Scotch wife,—the latter from up-river traders,—they found an admirable medium of communication, answering, better than French could, a similar purpose to that of the stick which we fasten to the bit of one horse and breast-gear of another, whereby each keeps his distance. Once in a while, too, by way of jest, English found its way among the ladies of Belles Demoiselles, always signifying that their sire was about to have business with old Charlie.

Now a long-standing wish to buy out Charlie troubled the Colonel. He had no desire to oust him unfairly; he was proud of being always fair; yet he did long to engross the whole estate under one title. Out of his luxurious idleness he had conceived this desire, and thought little of so slight an obstacle as being already somewhat in debt to old Charlie for money borrowed, and for which Belles Demoiselles was, of course, good, ten times over. Lots, buildings, rents, all, might as well be his, he thought, to give, keep, or destroy. "Had he but the old man's heritage. Ah! he might bring that into existence which his *belles demoiselles* had been begging for, 'since many years;' a home,—and such a home,— in the gay city. Here he should tear down this row of cottages, and make his garden wall; there that long rope-walk[13] should give place to vine-covered arbors; the bakery yonder should make way for a costly conservatory; that wine warehouse should come down, and the mansion go up. It should be the finest in the State. Men should never pass it, but they should say—'the palace of the De Charleus; a family of grand descent, a people of elegance and bounty, a line as old as France, a fine old man, and seven daughters as beautiful as happy; whoever dare attempt to marry there must leave his own name behind him!'

"The house should be of stones fitly set, brought down in ships from the land of 'les Yankees,' and it should have an airy belvedere,[14] with a gilded image

[13]A long room or covered walkway where fibers are twisted into lengths of rope.
[14]A gallery built on top of a house.

tip-toeing and shining on its peak, and from it you should see, far across the gleaming folds of the river, the red roof of Belles Demoiselles, the country-seat. At the big stone gate there should be a porter's lodge, and it should be a privilege even to see the ground."

Truly they were a family fine enough, and fancy-free enough to have fine wishes, yet happy enough where they were, to have had no wish but to live there always.

To those, who, by whatever fortune, wandered into the garden of Belles Demoiselles some summer afternoon as the sky was reddening towards evening, it was lovely to see the family gathered out upon the tiled pavement at the foot of the broad front steps, gayly chatting and jesting, with that ripple of laughter that comes so pleasingly from a bevy of girls. The father would be found seated in their midst, the centre of attention and compliment, witness, arbiter, umpire, critic, by his beautiful children's unanimous appointment, but the single vassal, too, of seven absolute sovereigns.

Now they would draw their chairs near together in eager discussion of some new steps in the dance, or the adjustment of some rich adornment. Now they would start about him with excited comments to see the eldest fix a bunch of violets in his button-hole. Now the twins would move down a walk after some unusual flower, and be greeted on their return with the high-pitched notes of delighted feminine surprise.

As evening came on they would draw more quietly about their paternal centre. Often their chairs were forsaken, and they grouped themselves on the lower steps, one above another, and surrendered themselves to the tender influences of the approaching night. At such an hour the passer on the river, already attracted by the dark figures of the broad-roofed mansion, and its woody garden standing against the glowing sunset, would hear the voices of the hidden group rise from the spot in the soft harmonies of an evening song; swelling clearer and clearer as the thrill of music warmed them into feeling, and presently joined by the deeper tones of the father's voice; then, as the daylight passed quite away, all would be still, and he would know that the beautiful home had gathered its nestlings under its wings.

And yet, for mere vagary, it pleased them not to be pleased.

"Arti!" called one sister to another in the broad hall, one morning,—mock amazement in her distended eyes,—"something is goin' to took place!"

"Comm-e-n-t?"[15]—long-drawn perplexity.

"Papa is goin' to town!"

The news passed up stairs.

"Inno!"—one to another meeting in a doorway,—"something is goin' to took place!"

"Qu'est-ce-que c'est!"[16]—vain attempt at gruffness.

"Papa is goin' to town!"

The unusual tidings were true. It was afternoon of the same day that the Colonel tossed his horse' bridle to his groom, and stepped up to old Charlie, who was sitting on his bench under a China-tree, his head, as was his fashion, bound in a Madras handkerchief. The "old man" was plainly under the effect of spirits, and smiled a deferential salutation without trusting himself to his feet.

[15]French: "What?" [16]French: "What is it?"

"Eh, well Charlie!"—the colonel raised his voice to suit his kinsman's deafness,—"how is those times with my friend Charlie?"

"Eh?" said Charlie, distractedly.

"Is that goin' well with my friend Charlie?"

"In de house,—call her,"—making a pretence of rising.

"*Non, non!* I don't want,"—the speaker paused to breathe—"ow is collection?"

"Oh!" said Charlie, "every day he make me more poorer!"

"What do you hask for it?" asked the planter indifferently, designating the house by a wave of his whip.

"Ask for w'at?" said Injin Charlie.

"De *house!* What you ask for it?"

"I don't believe," said Charlie.

"What you would *take* for it!" cried the planter.

"Wait for w'at?"

"What you would *take* for the whole block?"

"I don't want to sell him!"

"I'll give you *ten thousand dollah* for it."

"Ten t'ousand dollah for dis house? Oh, no, dat is no price. He is blame good old house,—dat old house." (Old Charlie and the Colonel never swore in presence of each other.) "Forty years dat old house didn't had to be paint! I easy can get fifty t'ousand dollar for dat old house."

"Fifty thousand picayunes;[17] yes," said the Colonel.

"She's a good house. Can make plenty money," pursued the deaf man.

"That's what make you so rich, eh, Charlie?"

"*Non,* I don't make nothing. Too blame clever, me, dat's de troub'. She's a good house,—make money fast like a steamboat,—make a barrel full in a week! Me, I lose money all de days. Too blame clever."

"Charlie!"

"Eh?"

"Tell me what you'll take."

"Make? I don't make *nothing.* Too blame clever."

"What will you *take?*"

"Oh! I got enough already,—half drunk now."

"What will you take for the 'ouse?"

"You want to buy her?"

"I don't know,"—(shrug),—"may*be,*—if you sell it cheap."

"She's a bully old house."

There was a long silence. By and by old Charlie commenced—

"Old Injin Charlie is a low-down dog."

"C'est vrai, oui!"[18] retorted the Colonel in an undertone.

"He's got Injin blood in him."

The Colonel nodded assent.

"But he's got some blame good blood, too, ain't it?"

The Colonel nodded impatiently.

"*Bien!*[19] Old Charlie's Injin blood says, 'sell de house, Charlie, you blame old fool!' *Mais,*[20] old Charlie's good blood says, 'Charlie! if you sell dat old house,

[17]A Spanish coin worth 6 American cents. [18]French: "That's true, yes!"
[19]French: "Right." [20]French: "But."

Charlie, you low-down old dog, Charlie, what de Compte De Charleu make for you grace-gran'-muzzer, de dev' can eat you, Charlie, I don't care.'"

"But you'll sell it anyhow, won't you, old man?"

"No!" And the *no* rumbled off in muttered oaths like thunder out on the Gulf. The incensed old Colonel wheeled and started off.

"Curl!" (Colonel) said Charlie, standing up unsteadily.

The planter turned with an inquiring frown.

"I'll trade with you!" said Charlie.

The Colonel was tempted. "'Ow'l you trade?" he asked.

"My house for yours!"

The old Colonel turned pale with anger. He walked very quickly back, and came close up to his kinsman.

"Charlie!" he said.

"Injin Charlie,"—with a tipsy nod.

But by this time self-control was returning. "Sell Belles Demoiselles to you?" he said in a high key, and then laughed "Ho, ho, ho!" and rode away.

A cloud, but not a dark one, overshadowed the spirits of Belles Demoiselles' plantation. The old master, whose beaming presence had always made him a shining Saturn, spinning and sparkling within the bright circle of his daughters, fell into musing fits, started out of frowning reveries, walked often by himself, and heard business from his overseer fretfully.

No wonder. The daughters knew his closeness in trade, and attributed to it his failure to negotiate for the Old Charlie buildings,—so to call them. They began to depreciate Belles Demoiselles. If a north wind blew, it was too cold to ride. If a shower had fallen, it was too muddy to drive. In the morning the garden was wet. In the evening the grasshopper was a burden. *Ennui*[21] was turned into capital; every headache was interpreted a premonition of ague; and when the native exuberance of a flock of ladies without a want or a care burst out in laughter in the father's face, they spread their French eyes, rolled up their little hands, and with rigid wrists and mock vehemence vowed and vowed again that they only laughed at their misery, and should pine to death unless they could move to the sweet city. "Oh! the theatre! Oh! Orleans Street! Oh! the masquerade! the Place d'Armes![22] the ball!" and they would call upon Heaven with French irreverence, and fall into each other's arms, and whirl down the hall singing a waltz, end with a grand collision and fall, and, their eyes streaming merriment, lay the blame on the slippery floor, that would some day be the death of the whole seven.

Three times more the fond father, thus goaded, managed, by accident,—business accident,—to see old Charlie and increase his offer; but in vain. He finally went to him formally.

"Eh?" said the deaf and distant relative. "For what you want him, eh? Why you don't stay where you halways be 'appy? Dis is a blame old rat-hole,—good for old Injin Charlie,—da's all. Why you don't stay where you be halways 'appy? Why you don't buy somewheres else?"

[21]Boredom.

[22]Present-day Jackson Square. A military parade ground during French control of the city, it is now a park.

"That's none of your business," snapped the planter. Truth was, his reasons were unsatisfactory even to himself.

A sullen silence followed. Then Charlie spoke:

"Well, now, look here; I sell you old Charlie's house."

"*Bien!*[23] and the whole block," said the Colonel.

"Hold on," said Charlie. "I sell you de 'ouse and de block. Den I go and git drunk, and go to sleep; de dev' comes along and says, 'Charlie! old Charlie, you blame low-down old dog, wake up! What you doin' here? Where's de 'ouse what Monsieur le Compte give your grace-gran-muzzer? Don't you see dat fine gentyman, De Charleu, done gone and tore him down and make him over new, you blame old fool, Charlie, you low-down old Injin dog!'"

"I'll give you forty thousand dollars," said the Colonel.

"For de 'ouse?"

"For all."

The deaf man shook his head.

"Forty-five!" said the Colonel.

"What a lie? For what you tell me 'What a lie?' I don't tell you no lie."

"*Non, non!* I give you *forty-five!*" shouted the Colonel.

Charlie shook his head again.

"Fifty!"

He shook it again.

The figures rose and rose to—

"Seventy-five!"

The answer was an invitation to go away and let the owner alone, as he was, in certain specified respects, the vilest of living creatures, and no company for a fine gentyman.

The "fine gentyman" longed to blaspheme,—but before old Charlie!—in the name of pride, how could he? He mounted and started away.

"Tell you what I'll make wid you," said Charlie.

The other, guessing aright, turned back without dismounting, smiling.

"How much Belles Demoiselles hoes me now?" asked the deaf one.

"One hundred and eighty thousand dollars," said the Colonel, firmly.

"Yass," said Charlie. "I don't want Belles Demoiselles."

The old Colonel's quiet laugh intimated it made no difference either way.

"But me," continued Charlie, "me,—I'm got le Compte De Charleu's blood in me, any'ow,—a litt' bit, any'ow, ain't it?"

The Colonel nodded that it was.

"*Bien!* If I go out of dis place and don't go to Belles Demoiselles, de peoples will say,—dey will say, 'Old Charlie he been all doze time tell a blame *lie!* He ain't no kin to his old grace-gran-muzzer, not a blame bit! He don't got nary drop of De Charleu blood to save his blame low-down old Injin soul!' No, sare! What I want wid money, den? No, sare! My place for yours!"

He turned to go into the house, just too soon to see the Colonel make an ugly whisk at him with his riding-whip. Then the Colonel, too, moved off.

Two or three times over, as he ambled homeward, laughter broke through his annoyance, as he recalled old Charlie's family pride and the presumption of his offer. Yet each time he could but think better of—not the offer to swap,

[23]French: "Good!"

but the preposterous ancestral loyalty. It was so much better than he could have expected from his "low-down" relative, and not unlike his own whim withal—the proposition which went with it was forgiven.

This last defeat bore so harshly on the master of Belles Demoiselles, that the daughters, reading chagrin in his face, began to repent. They loved their father as daughters can, and when they saw their pretended dejection harassing him seriously they restrained their complaints, displayed more than ordinary tenderness, and heroically and ostentatiously concluded there was no place like Belles Demoiselles. But the new mood touched him more than the old, and only refined his discontent. Here was a man, rich without the care of riches, free from any real trouble, happiness as native to his house as perfume to his garden, deliberately, as it were with premeditated malice, taking joy by the shoulder and bidding her be gone to town, whither he might easily have followed, only that the very same ancestral nonsense that kept Injin Charlie from selling the old place for twice its value prevented him from choosing any other spot for a city home.

But by and by the charm of nature and the merry hearts around him prevailed; the fit of exalted sulks passed off, and after a while the year flared up at Christmas, flickered, and went out.

New Year came and passed, the beautiful garden of Belles Demoiselles put on its spring attire; the seven fair sisters moved from rose to rose; the cloud of discontent had warmed into visible vapor in the rich sunlight of family affection, and on the common memory the only scar of last year's wound was old Charlie's sheer impertinence in crossing the caprice of the De Charleus. The cup of gladness seemed to fill with the filling of the river.

How high that river was! Its tremendous current rolled and tumbled and spun along, hustling the long funeral flotillas of drift,—and how near shore it came! Men were out day and night watching the levee. On windy nights even the old Colonel took part, and grew light-hearted with occupation and excitement, as every minute the river threw a white arm over the levee's top, as though it would vault over. But all held fast, and, as the summer drifted in, the water sunk down into its banks and looked quite incapable of harm.

On a summer afternoon of uncommon mildness, old Colonel Jean Albert Henri Joseph De Charleu-Marot, being in a mood for revery, slipped the custody of his feminine rulers and sought the crown of the levee, where it was his wont to promenade. Presently he sat upon a stone bench,—a favorite seat. Before him lay his broad-spread fields; near by, his lordly mansion; and being still,—perhaps by female contact,—somewhat sentimental, he fell to musing on his past. It was hardly worthy to be proud of. All its morning was reddened with mad frolic, and far toward the meridian it was marred with elegant rioting. Pride had kept him well-nigh useless, and despised the honors won by valor; gaming had dimmed prosperity; death had taken his heavenly wife; voluptuous ease had mortgaged his lands; and yet his house still stood, his sweet-smelling fields were still fruitful, his name was fame enough; and yonder and yonder, among the trees and flowers like angels walking in Eden, were the seven goddesses of his only worship.

Just then a slight sound behind him brought him to this feet. He cast his eyes anxiously to the outer edge of the little strip of bank between the levee's base and the river. There was nothing visible. He paused, with his ear toward the water, his face full of frightened expectation. Ha! There came a single plashing sound, like some great beast slipping into the river, and little waves in a wide semi-circle came out from under the bank and spread over the water!

"My God!"

He plunged down the levee and bounded through the low weeds to the edge of the bank. It was sheer, and the water about four feet below. He did not stand quite on the edge, but fell upon his knees a couple of yards away, wringing his hands, moaning and weeping, and staring through his watery eyes at a fine, long crevice just discernible under the matted grass, and curving outward on either hand toward the river.

"My God!" he sobbed aloud; "my God!" and even while he called, his God answered: the tough Bermuda grass stretched and snapped, the crevice slowly became a gape, and softly, gradually, with no sound but the closing of the water at last, a ton or more of earth settled into the boiling eddy and disappeared.

At the same instant a pulse of the breeze brought from the garden behind, the joyous, thoughtless laughter of the fair mistresses of Belles Demoiselles.

The old Colonel sprang up and clambered over the levee. Then forcing himself to a more composed movement, he hastened into the house and ordered his horse.

"Tell my children to make merry while I am gone," he left word. "I shall be back to-night," and the horse's hoofs clattered down a by-road leading to the city.

"Charlie," said the planter, riding up to a window, from which the old man's nightcap was thrust out, "what you say, Charlie,—my house for yours, eh, Charlie—what you say?"

"Ello!" said Charlie, "from where you come from dis time of to-night?"

"I come from the Exchange[24] in St. Louis Street." (A small fraction of the truth.)

"What you want?" said matter-of-fact Charlie.

"I come to trade."

The low-down relative drew the worsted[25] off his ears. "Oh yass," he said with an uncertain air.

"Well, old man Charlie, what you say: my house for yours,—like you said, eh, Charlie?"

"I dunno," said Charlie; "it's nearly mine now. Why you don't stay dare youse'f?"

"Because I don't want!" said the Colonel savagely. "Is dat reason enough for you? You better take me in de notion,[26] old man, I tell you,—yes!"

Charlie never winced; but how his answer delighted the Colonel! Quoth Charlie:

"I don't care—I take him!—*mais,* possession give right off."

"Not the whole plantation, Charlie; only"—

"I don't care," said Charlie; "we easy can fix dat. *Mais,* what for you don't want to keep him? I don't want him. You better keep him."

"Don't you try to make no fool of me, old man," cried the planter.

"Oh, no!" said the other. "Oh, no! but you make a fool of yourself, ain't it?"

The dumbfounded Colonel stared; Charlie went on:

[24]A saloon. [25]Wool nightcap. [26]I.e., "while I'm inclined to trade."

"Yass! Belles Demoiselles is more wort' dan tree block like dis one. I pass by dare since two weeks. Oh, pritty Belles Demoiselles! De cane was wave in de wind, de garden smell like a bouquet, de white-cap was jump up and down on de river; seven *belles demoiselles* was ridin' on horses. 'Pritty, pritty, pritty!' says old Charlie. Ah! *Monsieur le père,* 'ow 'appy, 'appy, 'appy!"

"Yass!" he continued—the Colonel still staring—"le Compte De Charleu have two familie. One was low-down Choctaw, one was high up *noblesse.* He gave the low-down Choctaw dis old rat-hole; he give Belles Demoiselles to your granfozzer; and now you don't be *satisfait.* What I'll do wid Belles Demoiselles? She'll break me in two years, yass. And what you'll do wid old Charlie's house, eh? You'll tear her down and make you'se'f a blame old fool. I rather wouldn't trade!"

The planter caught a big breathful of anger, but Charlie went straight on:

"I rather wouldn't, *mais* I will do it for you;—just the same, like Monsieur le Compte would say, 'Charlie, you old fool, I want to shange houses wid you."'

So long as the Colonel suspected irony he was angry, but as Charlie seemed, after all, to be certainly in earnest, he began to feel conscience-stricken. He was by no means a tender man, but his lately-discovered misfortune had unhinged him, and this strange, undeserved, disinterested family fealty on the part of Charlie touched his heart. And should he still try to lead him into the pitfall he had dug? He hesitated;—no, he would show him the place by broad daylight, and if he chose to overlook the "caving bank," it would be his own fault;—a trade's a trade.

"Come," said the planter, "come at my house to-night; to-morrow we look at the place before breakfast, and finish the trade."

"For what?" said Charlie.

"Oh, because I got to come in town in the morning."

"I don't want," said Charlie. "How I'm goin' to come dere?"

"I git you a horse at the liberty stable."

"Well—anyhow—I don't care—I'll go." And they went.

When they had ridden a long time, and were on the road darkened by hedges of Cherokee rose, the Colonel called behind him to the "low-down" scion:

"Keep the road, old man."

"Eh?"

"Keep the road."

"Oh, yes; all right; I keep my word; we don't goin' to play no tricks, eh?"

But the Colonel seemed not to hear. His ungenerous design was beginning to be hateful to him. Not only old Charlie's unprovoked goodness was prevailing; the eulogy on Belles Demoiselles had stirred the depths of an intense love for his beautiful home. True, if he held to it, the caving of the bank, at its present fearful speed, would let the house into the river within three months; but were it not better to lose it so, than sell his birthright? Again,—coming back to the first thought,—to betray his own blood! It was only Injin Charlie; but had not the De Charleu blood just spoken out in him? Unconsciously he groaned.

After a time they struck a path approaching the plantation in the rear, and a little after, passing from behind a clump of live-oaks, they came in sight of the villa. It looked so like a gem, shining through its dark grove, so like a great glow-worm in the dense foliage, so significant of luxury and gayety, that the poor master, from an overflowing heart, groaned again.

"What?" asked Charlie.

The Colonel only drew his rein, and, dismounting mechanically, contemplated the sight before him. The high, arched doors and windows were thrown wide to the summer air, from every opening the bright light of numerous candelabra darted out upon the sparkling foliage of magnolia and bay, and here and there in the spacious verandas a colored lantern swayed in the gentle breeze. A sound of revel fell on the ear, the music of harps; and across one window, brighter than the rest, flitted, once or twice, the shadows of dancers. But oh! the shadows flitting across the heart of the fair mansion's master!

"Old Charlie," said he, gazing fondly at his house, "You and me is both old, eh?"

"Yaas," said the stolid Charlie.

"And we has both been bad enough in our time, eh, Charlie?"

Charlie, surprised at the tender tone, repeated "Yaas."

"And you and me is mighty close?"

"Blame close, yaas."

"But you never know me to cheat, old man!"

"No,"—impassively.

"And do you think I would cheat you now?"

"I dunno," said Charlie. "I don't believe."

"Well, old man, old man,"—his voice began to quiver,—"I sha'nt cheat you now. My God!—old man, I tell you—you better not make the trade!"

"Because for what?" asked Charlie in plain anger; but both looked quickly toward the house! The Colonel tossed his hands wildly in the air, rushed forward a step or two, and giving one fearful scream of agony and fright, fell forward on his face in the path. Old Charlie stood transfixed with horror. Belles Demoiselles, the realm of maiden beauty, the home of merriment, the house of dancing, all in the tremor and glow of pleasure, suddenly sank, with one short, wild wail of terror—sunk, sunk, down, down, down, into the merciless, unfathomable flood of the Mississippi.

Twelve long months were midnight to the mind of the childless father; when they were only half gone, he took his bed; and every day, and every night, old Charlie, the "low-down," the "fool," watched him tenderly, tended him lovingly, for the sake of his name, his misfortunes, and his broken heart. No woman's step crossed the floor of the sick-chamber, whose western dormer-windows overpeered the dingy architecture of old Charlie's block; Charlie and a skilled physician, the one all interest, the other all gentleness, hope, and patience—these only entered by the door; but by the window came in a sweet-scented evergreen vine, transplanted from the caving bank of Belles Demoiselles. It caught the rays of sunset in its flowery net and let them softly in upon the sick man's bed; gathered the glancing beams of the moon at midnight, and often wakened the sleeper to look, with his mindless eyes, upon their pretty silvery fragments strewn upon the floor.

By and by there seemed—there was—a twinkling dawn of returning reason. Slowly, peacefully, with an increase unseen from day to day, the light of reason came into the eyes, and speech became coherent; but withal there came a failing of the wrecked body, and the doctor said that monsieur was both better and worse.

One evening, as Charlie sat by the vine-clad window with his fireless pipe in his hand, the old Colonel's eyes fell full upon his own, and rested there.

"Charl—," he said with an effort, and his delighted nurse hastened to the bedside and bowed his best ear. There was an unsuccessful effort or two, and then he whispered, smiling with sweet sadness,—

"We didn't trade."

The truth, in this case, was a secondary matter to Charlie; the main point was to give a pleasing answer. So he nodded his head decidedly, as who should say—"Oh yes, we did, it was a bonafide swap!" but when he saw the smile vanish, he tried the other expedient and shook his head with still more vigor, to signify that they had not so much as approached a bargain; and the smile returned.

Charlie wanted to see the vine recognized. He stepped backward to the window with a broad smile, shook the foliage, nodded and looked smart.

"I know," said the Colonel, with beaming eyes,—"many weeks."

The next day—

"Charl—"

The best ear went down.

"Send for a priest."

The priest came, and was alone with him a whole afternoon. When he left, the patient was very haggard and exhausted, but smiled and would not suffer the crucifix to be removed from his breast.

One more morning came. Just before dawn Charlie, lying on a pallet in the room, thought he was called, and came to the bedside.

"Old man," whispered the failing invalid, "is it caving yet?"

Charlie nodded.

"It won't pay you out."

"Oh, dat makes not'ing," said Charlie. Two big tears rolled down his brown face. "Dat makes not'in."

The Colonel whispered once more:

"*Mes belles demoiselles!* in paradise;—in the garden—I shall be with them at sunrise;" and so it was.

1874, 1879

Charles Waddell Chesnutt

1858–1932

Charles Waddell Chesnutt, a black man, was born free in Ohio shortly before the Civil War. He spent much of his early life in North Carolina, first as a teacher, then as a principal of a segregated high school. But Chesnutt disliked the South; he missed "civilization and companionship," and so he moved to New York in 1883. There he worked as a stenographic reporter and as an accountant, and he began to write poetry and short fiction.

In 1885 and 1886, several of his stories and poems were published in popular magazines, but he seldom received more than five or ten dollars for each. To support his family, he studied law, and he returned to Ohio, where he was admitted to the bar in 1887, scoring the highest mark of all those who took the bar examination. Black lawyers seldom prospered in nineteenth-century America, and Chesnutt was forced to make a living as a legal stenographer. But he continued writing, and recognition came swiftly when the most prestigious magazine in America, The Atlantic Monthly, *published his story "The Goophered Grapevine" in August 1887.*

Many of Chesnutt's stories were folktales in the manner of Joel Chandler Harris, and some were without apparent racial concerns or implications. Other stories dealt with racial matters in ways generally acceptable to the prejudices of the white reading public of his time. Chesnutt's recurring subjects were "passing" (blacks passing themselves off as whites—usually with disastrous results), humorous intraracial conflicts between mulattoes and full-blooded blacks, and examples of the instinctively wise (but properly subservient) black man fooling the whites. But the stories are often highly ironic, and racial issues were presented in ways that were subtle, forceful, and well ahead of their time.

By 1900, the year of the publication of his first novel, The House Behind the Cedars, *Chesnutt's racial attitudes had become increasingly militant. He condemned and satirized the South and showed that his black heroine's attempt to pass as white was clearly misguided and so led to tragedy. Chesnutt's major criticism was reserved for his novel's protagonist, who did succeed in passing and who thereafter denied his black heritage. In subsequent novels,* The Marrow of Tradition *(1901) and* The Colonel's Dream *(1905), Chesnutt's racial statements became increasingly blunt and candid. His subjects were race riots, racial injustice, and bigotry; he relied less on veiled irony and more on direct statement, and the tone of his novels became more pessimistic. Even William Dean Howells, Chesnutt's patron, criticized the bitterness of* The Marrow of Tradition, *and others said the novel was an attempt to "humiliate the whites."*

Chesnutt had great hopes for the improvement of race relations in the United States, and his novels were conscious attempts to bring such improvement about. Perhaps disillusioned by the failure of his work to lead to any marked change in the relations between blacks and whites, Chesnutt gave up writing after 1905 and retreated to the consolations of family, travel, and work. By today's standards his attitudes seem passive and dated. But his subtlety, irony, and militancy are often unperceived and undervalued, and he remains an important and pivotal figure in the development of black literature in twentieth-century America.

FURTHER READING: *The Collected Stories of Charles W. Chesnutt,* ed. W. Andrews, 1991; *The Journals of Charles W. Chesnutt,* ed. R. Brodhead, 1993; *To Be an Author: Letters of Charles Waddell Chesnutt,* eds. J. McElrath and R. Leitz, 1997; H. Chesnutt, *Charles Waddell Chesnutt: Pioneer of the Color Line,* 1952; J. Heermance, *Charles W. Chesnutt,* 1974; *The Short Fiction of Charles W. Chesnutt,* ed. S. Lyons, 1974; F. Keller, *An American Crusade: The Life of Charles Waddell Chesnutt,* 1978; S. Lyons, *Charles W. Chesnutt,* 1980; W. Andrews, *The Literary Career of Charles W. Chesnutt,* 1980; S. Render, *Charles W. Chesnutt,* 1980; H. Wonham, *Charles Waddell Chesnutt,* 1998; *Critical Essays on Charles Chesnutt,* ed. J. McElrath, 1999; D. McWilliams, *Charles W. Chesnutt and the Fictions of Race,* 2002; M. Wilson, *Whiteness in the Novels of Charles W. Chesnutt,* 2004.

TEXTS: "The Goophered Grapevine" from *The Conjure Woman,* 1899; "The Wife of His Youth" from *The Wife of His Youth and Other Stories of the Color Line,* 1899; "A Metropolitan Experience" from *The Short Fiction of Charles W. Chesnutt,* ed. S. Render, 1974.

THE GOOPHERED GRAPEVINE

Some years ago my wife was in poor health, and our family doctor, in whose skill and honesty I had implicit confidence, advised a change of climate. I shared, from an unprofessional standpoint, his opinion that the raw winds, the chill rains, and the violent changes of temperature that characterized the winters in the region of the Great Lakes tended to aggravate my wife's difficulty, and would undoubtedly shorten her life if she remained exposed to them. The doctor's advice was that we seek, not a temporary place of sojourn, but a permanent residence, in a warmer and more equable climate. I was engaged at the time in grape-culture in northern Ohio, and, as I liked the business and had given it much study, I decided to look for some other locality suitable for carrying it on. I thought of sunny France, of sleepy Spain, of Southern California, but there were objections to them all. It occurred to me that I might find what I wanted in some one of our own Southern States. It was a sufficient time after the war for conditions in the South to have become somewhat settled; and I was enough of a pioneer to start a new industry, if I could not find a place where grape-culture had been tried. I wrote to a cousin who had gone into the turpentine business in central North Carolina. He assured me, in response to my inquiries, that no better place could be found in the South than the State and neighborhood where he lived; the climate was perfect for health, and, in conjunction with the soil, ideal for grape-culture; labor was cheap, and land could be bought for a mere song. He gave us a cordial invitation to come and visit him while we looked into the matter. We accepted the invitation, and after several days of leisurely travel, the last hundred miles of which were up a river on a sidewheel steamer, we reached our destination, a quaint old town, which I shall call Patesville, because, for one reason, that is not its name. There was a red brick market-house in the public square, with a tall tower, which held a four-faced clock that struck the hours, and from which there pealed out a curfew at nine o'clock. There were two or three hotels, a court-house, a jail, stores, offices, and all the appurtenances of a county seat and a commercial emporium; for while Patesville numbered only four or five thousand inhabitants, of all shades of complexion, it was one of the principal towns in North Carolina, and had a considerable trade in cotton and naval stores.[1] This business activity was not immediately apparent to my unaccustomed eyes. Indeed, when I first saw the town, there brooded over it a calm that seemed almost sabbatic in its restfulness, though I learned later on that underneath its somnolent exterior the deeper currents of life—love and hatred, joy and despair, ambition and avarice, faith and friendship—flowed not less steadily than in livelier latitudes.

We found the weather delightful at that season, the end of summer, and were hospitably entertained. Our host was a man of means and evidently regarded our visit as a pleasure, and we were therefore correspondingly at our ease, and in a position to act with the coolness of judgment desirable in making so radical a change in our lives. My cousin placed a horse and buggy at our disposal, and himself acted as our guide until I became somewhat familiar with the country.

I found that grape-culture, while it had never been carried on to any great extent, was not entirely unknown in the neighborhood. Several planters thereabouts had attempted it on a commercial scale, in former years, with greater or less success; but like most Southern industries, it had felt the blight of war and had fallen into desuetude.

I went several times to look at a place that I thought might suit me. It was a plantation of considerable extent, that had formerly belonged to a wealthy man

[1]Pitch, turpentine, rosin, and other supplies used in maintaining wooden sailing vessels.

by the name of McAdoo. The estate had been for years involved in litigation between disputing heirs, during which period shiftless cultivation had well-nigh exhausted the soil. There had been a vineyard of some extent on the place, but it had not been attended to since the war, and had lapsed into utter neglect. The vines—here partly supported by decayed and broken-down trellises, there twining themselves among the branches of the slender saplings which had sprung up among them—grew in wild and unpruned luxuriance, and the few scattered grapes they bore were the undisputed prey of the first comer. The site was admirably adapted to grape-raising; the soil, with a little attention, could not have been better; and with the native grape, the luscious scuppernong,[2] as my main reliance in the beginning, I felt sure that I could introduce and cultivate successfully a number of other varieties.

One day I went over with my wife to show her the place. We drove out of the town over a long wooden bridge that spanned a spreading mill-pond, passed the long whitewashed fence surrounding the county fair-ground, and struck into a road so sandy that the horse's feet sank to the fetlocks. Our route lay partly up hill and partly down, for we were in the sand-hill country; we drove past cultivated farms, and then by abandoned fields grown up in scrub-oak and short-leaved pine, and once or twice through the solemn aisles of the virgin forest, where the tall pines, well-nigh meeting over the narrow road, shut out the sun, and wrapped us in cloistral solitude. Once, at a crossroads, I was in doubt as to the turn to take, and we sat there waiting ten minutes—we had already caught some of the native infection of restfulness—for some human being to come along, who could direct us on our way. At length a little negro girl appeared, walking straight as an arrow, with a piggin[3] full of water on her head. After a little patient investigation, necessary to overcome the child's shyness, we learned what we wished to know, and at the end of about five miles from the town reached our destination.

We drove between a pair of decayed gateposts—the gate itself had long since disappeared—and up a straight sandy lane, between two lines of rotting rail fence, partly concealed by jimson-weeds and briers, to the open space where a dwelling-house had once stood, evidently a spacious mansion, if we might judge from the ruined chimneys that were still standing, and the brick pillars on which the sills rested. The house itself, we had been informed, had fallen a victim to the fortunes of war.

We alighted from the buggy, walked about the yard for a while, and then wandered off into the adjoining vineyard. Upon Annie's complaining of weariness I led the way back to the yard, where a pine log, lying under a spreading elm, afforded a shady though somewhat hard seat. One end of the log was already occupied by a venerable-looking colored man. He held on his knees a hat full of grapes, over which he was smacking his lips with great gusto, and a pile of grapeskins near him indicated that the performance was no new thing. We approached him at an angle from the rear, and were close to him before he perceived us. He respectfully rose as we drew near, and was moving away, when I begged him to keep his seat.

"Don't let us disturb you," I said. "There is plenty of room for us all."

He resumed his seat with somewhat of embarrassment. While he had been standing, I had observed that he was a tall man, and, though slightly bowed by

[2]A muscadine grape. [3]Wooden pail.

the weight of years, apparently quite vigorous. He was not entirely black, and this fact, together with the quality of his hair, which was about six inches long and very bushy, except on the top of his head, where he was quite bald, suggested a slight strain of other than negro blood. There was a shrewdness in his eyes, too, which was not altogether African, and which, as we afterwards learned from experience, was indicative of a corresponding shrewdness in his character. He went on eating the grapes, but did not seem to enjoy himself quite so well as he had apparently done before he became aware of our presence.

"Do you live around here?" I asked, anxious to put him at his ease.

"Yas, sah. I lives des ober yander, behine de nex' san'-hill, on de Lumberton plank-road."

"Do you know anything about the time when this vineyard was cultivated?"

"Lawd bless you, suh, I knows all about it. Dey ain' na'er a man in dis settlement w'at won' tel you ole Julius McAdoo 'uz bawn en raise' on dis yer same plantation. Is you de Norv'n gemman w'at's gwine ter buy de ole vimya'd?"

"I am looking at it," I replied; "but I don't know that I shall care to buy unless I can be reasonably sure of making something out of it."

"Well, suh, you is a stranger ter me, en I is a stranger ter you, en we is bofe strangers ter one anudder, but 'f I 'uz in yo' place, I wouldn' buy dis vimya'd."

"Why not?" I asked.

"Well, I dunno whe'r you b'lieves in conj'in 'er not,—some er de w'ite folks don't, er says dey don't,—but de truf er de matter is dat dis yer old vimya'd is goophered."

"Is what?" I asked, not grasping the meaning of this unfamiliar word.

"Is goophered,—conju'd, bewitch'."

He imparted this information with such solemn earnestness, and with such an air of confidential mystery, that I felt somewhat interested, while Annie was evidently much impressed, and drew closer to me.

"How do you know it is bewitched?" I asked.

"I would n' spec' fer you ter b'lieve me 'less you know all 'bout de fac's. But ef you en young miss dere doan' min' lis'nin' ter a ole nigger run on a minute er two w'ile you ere restin', I kin 'splain to you how it all happen'."

We assured him that we would be glad to hear how it all happened, and he began to tell us. At first the current of his memory—or imagination—seemed somewhat sluggish; but as his embarrassment wore off, his language flowed more freely, and the story acquired perspective and coherence. As he became more and more absorbed in the narrative, his eyes assumed a dreamy expression, and he seemed to lose sight of his auditors, and to be living over again in monologue his life on the old plantation.

"Ole Mars Dugal' McAdoo," he began, "bought dis place long many years befo' de wah, en I 'member well w'en he sot out all dis yer part er de plantation in scuppernon's. De vimes growed monst'us fas', en Mars Dugal' made a thousan' gallon er scuppernon' wine eve'y year.

"Now, ef dey's an'thing a nigger lub, nex' ter 'possum, en chick'n, en watermillyums, it's scuppernon's. Dey ain' nuffin dat kin stan' up side'n de scuppernon' fer sweetness; sugar ain't a suckumstance ter scuppernon'. W'en de season is nigh 'bout ober, en de grapes begin ter swivel up des a little wid de wrinkles er ole age,—w'en de skin git sof' en brown,—den de scuppernon' make you smack yo' lip en roll yo' eye en wush fer mo'; so I reckon it ain' very stonishin' dat niggers lub scuppernon'.

"Dey wuz a sight er niggers in de naberhood er de vimya'd. Dere wuz ole Mars Henry Brayboy's niggers, en ole Mars Jeems McLean's niggers, en Mars Dugal's own niggers; den dey wuz a settlement er free niggers en po' buckrahs[4] down by de Wim'l'ton Road, en Mars Dugal' had de only vimya'd in de naberhood. I reckon it ain' so much so nowadays, but befo' de wah, in slab'ry times, a nigger did n' mine goin' fi' er ten mile in a night, w'en dey wuz sump'n good ter eat at de yuther een'.

"So atter a w'ile Mars Dugal' begin ter miss his scuppernon's. Co'se he 'cuse' de niggers er it, but dey all 'nied it ter de las'. Mars Dugal's sot spring guns[5] en steel traps, en he en de oberseah sot up nights once't er twice't, tel one night Mars Dugal'—he 'uz a monst'us keerless man—got his leg shot full er cowpeas.[6] But somehow er nudder dey couldn' nebber ketch none er de niggers. I dunner how it happen, but it happen des like I tell you, en de grapes kep' on a-goin' des de same.

"But bimbey ole Mars Dugal' fix' up a plan ter stop it. Dey wuz a conjuh 'oman livin' down 'mongs' de free niggers on de Wim'l'ton Road, en all de darkies fum Rockfish ter Beaver Crick wuz feared er her. She could wuk de mos' powerfulles' kin' er goopher,—could make people hab fits, er rheumatiz, er make 'em des dwinel away en die; en dey say she went out ridin' de niggers at night, fer she wuz a witch 'sides bein' a conjah 'oman. Mars Dugal' hearn 'bout Aun' Peggy's doins, en begun ter 'flect whe'r er no he could n' git her ter he'p him keep de niggers off'n de grapevimes. One day in spring er de year, ole miss pack' up a basket er chick'n en poun'-cake, en a bottle er scuppernon' wine, en Mars Dugal' tuk it in his buggy en driv ober ter Aun' Peggy's cabin. He tuk de basket in, en had a long talk wid Aun' Peggy.

"De nex' day Aun' Peggy come up ter de vimya'd. De niggers seed her slippin' roun', en dey soon foun' out what she 'uz doin' dere. Mars Dugal' had hi'ed her ter goopher de grapevimes. She sa'ntered 'roun' 'mongs' de vimes, en tuk a leaf fum dis one, en a grape-hull fum dat one, en a grape-seed fum anudder one; en den a little twig fum here, en a little pinch er dirt fum dere, en put it all in a big black bottle, wid a snake's toof en a speckle' hen's gall en some ha'rs fum a black cat's tail, en den fill' de bottle wid scuppernon' wine. W'en she got de goopher all ready en fix', she tuk 'n went out in de woods en buried it under de root uv a red oak tree, en den come back en tole one er de niggers she done goopher de grapevimes, en a'er a nigger w'at eat dem grapes 'ud be sho ter die inside'n twel' mont's.

"Atter dat de niggers let de scuppernon's 'lone, en Mars Dugal' did n' hab no 'casion ter fine no mo' fault; en de season wuz mos' gone, w'en a strange gemman stop at de plantation one night ter see Mars Dugal' on some business; en his coachman, seein' de scuppernon's growin' so nice en sweet, slip 'roun' behine de smoke-house, en et all de scuppernon's he could hole. Nobody did n' notice it at de time, but dat night, on de way home, de gemman's hoss runned away en kill' de coachman. W'en we hearn de noos, Aun' Lucy, de cook, she up'n say she seed de strange nigger eat'n er de scuppernon's behine de smokehouse; en den we knowed de goopher had b'en er wukkin'. Den one er de nigger chilluns runned away fum de quarters one day, en got in de scuppernon's, en died de nex' week. W'ite folks say he die' er de fevuh, but de niggers knowed

[4]Whites. [5]Guns set to fire when a trespasser trips a wire attached to the trigger.
[6]Dried peas used in place of lead buckshot in a shotgun load.

it wuz de goopher. So you k'n be sho de darkies did n' hab much ter do wid dem scuppernon' vimes.

"W'en de scuppernon' season 'uz ober fer dat year, Mars Dugal' foun' he had made fifteen hund'ed gallon er wine; en one er de niggers hearn him laffin' wid de oberseah fit ter kill, en sayin' dem fifteen hund'ed gallon er wine wuz monst'us good intrus' on de ten dollars he laid out on de vimya'd. So I 'low ez he paid Aun' Peggy ten dollars fer to goopher de grapevimes.

"De goopher did n' wuk no mo tel de nex' summer, w'en 'long to'ds de middle er de season one er de fiel' han's died; en ez dat lef' Mars Dugal' sho't er han's, he went off ter town fer ter buy anudder. He fotch de noo nigger home wid 'im. He wuz er ole nigger, er de color er a gingy-cake, en ball ez a hoss-apple on de top er his head. He wuz a peart ole nigger, do', en could do a big day's wuk.

"Now it happen dat one er de niggers on de nex' plantation, one er ole Mars Henry Brayboy's niggers, had runned away de day befo', en tuk ter de swamp, en ole Mars Dugal' en some er de yuther nabor w'ite folks had gone out wid dere guns en dere dogs fer ter he'p 'em hunt fer de nigger; en de han's on our own plantation wuz all so flusterated dat we fuhgot ter tell de noo han' 'bout de goopher on de scuppernon' vimes. Co'se he smell de grapes en see de vimes, an atter dahk de fus' thing he done wuz ter slip off ter de grapevimes 'dout sayin' nuffin ter nobody. Nex' mawnin' he tole some er de niggers 'bout de fine bait er scuppernon' he et de night befo'.

"W'en dey tole 'im 'bout de goopher on de grapevimes, he 'uz dat tarrified dat he turn pale, en look des like he gwine ter die right in his tracks. De oberseah come up en axed w'at 'uz de matter; en w'en dey tole 'im Henry be'n eatin' er de scuppernon's, en got de goopher on 'im, he gin Henry a big drink er w'iskey, en 'low dat de nex' rainy day he take 'im ober ter Aun't Peggy's, en see ef she would n' take de goopher off'n him, seein' ez he did n' know nuffin erbout it tell he done et de grapes.

"Sho nuff, it rain de nex' day, en de oberseah went over ter Aun' Peggy's wid Henry. En Aun' Peggy say dat bein' ez Henry did n' know 'bout de goopher, en et de grapes in ign'ance er de conseq'ences, she reckon she mought be able fer ter take de goopher off'n him. So she fotch out her bottle wid some conjuh medicine in it, en po'd some out in a go'd fer Henry ter drink. He manage ter git it down; he say it tas'e like whiskey wid sump'n bitter in it. She 'lowed dat 'ud keep de goopher off'n him tel de spring; but w'en de sap begin ter rise in de grapevimes he ha' ter come en see her ag'in, en she tell him w'at e's ter do.

"Nex' spring, w'en de sap commence' ter rise in de scuppernon' vime, Henry tuk a ham one night. What'd de git de ham? *I* doan know; dey wa'n't no hams on de plantation 'cep'n w'at 'uz in de smoke-house, but *I* never see Henry 'bout de smoke-house. But ez I wuz a-sayin', he tuk de ham ober ter Aun' Peggy's; en Aun' Peggy tole 'im dat w'en Mars Dugal' begin ter prune de grapevimes, he mus' go en take 'n scrape off de sap whar it ooze out'n de cut een's er de vimes, en 'n'into his ball head wid it; en ef he do dat once't a year de goopher would n' wuk agin 'im long ez he done it. En bein' ez he fotch her de ham, she fix' it so he kin eat all de scuppernon' he want.

"So Henry 'n'into his head wid de sap out'n de big grapevime des ha'f way 'twix' de quarters en de big house, en de goopher nebber wuk again him dat summer. But de beatenes' thing you eber see happen ter Henry. Up ter dat time he wuz ez ball ez a sweeten' 'tater, but des ez soon ez de young leaves begun ter come out on de grapevimes, de ha'r begun ter grow out on Henry's head, en by de middle er de summer he had de bigges' head er ha'r on de plantation. Befo' dat, Henry had tol'able good ha'r roun' de aidges, but soon ez de young grapes begun ter come, Henry's ha'r begun to quirl all up in little balls, des like dis yer reg'lar grapy ha'r, en by de time de grapes got ripe his head look des like a bunch er grapes. Combin' it did n' do no good; he wuk at it ha'f de night wid er Jim Crow,[7] en think he git it straighten' out, but in de mawnin' de grapes 'ud be dere des de same. So he gin it up, en tried ter keep de grapes down by havin' his ha'r cut sho't.

"But dat wa'n't de quares' thing 'bout de goopher. When Henry come ter de plantation, he wuz gittin' a little ole an stiff in de j'ints. But dat summer he got des ez spry en libely ez any young nigger on de plantation; fac', he got so biggity dat Mars Jackson, de oberseah, ha' ter th'eaten ter whip 'im, ef he did n' stop cuttin' up his didos en behave hisse'f. But de mos' cur'ouses' thing happen' in de fall, when de sap begin ter go down in de grapevimes. Fus', when de grapes 'uz gethered, de knots begun ter straighten out'n Henry's ha'r; en we'en de leaves begin ter fall, Henry's ha'r 'mence' ter drap out; en when de vimes 'uz bar', Henry's head wuz baller 'n it wuz in de spring, en he begin ter git ole en stiff in de j'ints ag'in, en paid no mo' 'tention ter de gals dyoin' er de whole winter. En nex' spring, w'en he rub de sap on ag'in, he got young ag'in, en so soopl en libely dat none er de young niggers on de plantation could n' jump, ner dance, ner hoe ez much cotton ez Henry. But in de fall er de year his grapes 'mence' ter straighten out, en his j'ints ter git stiff, en his ha'r drap off, en de rheumatiz begin ter wrastle wid 'im.

"Now, ef you'd 'a' knowed ole Mars Dugal' McAdoo, you'd 'a' knowed dat it ha' ter be a mighty rainy day when he could n' fine sump'n fer his niggers ter do, en it ha' ter be a mighty little hole he could n' crawl thoo, en ha' ter be a monst'us cloudy night when a dollar git by him in de dahkness; en w'en he see how Henry git young in de spring en ole in defall, he 'lowed ter hisse'f ez how he could make mo' money out'n Henry dan by wukkin' him in de cotton-fiel'. 'Long de nex' spring, atter de sap 'mence' ter rise, en Henry 'n'int 'is hed en sta'ted fer ter git young en soopl, Mars Dugal' up 'n tuk Henry ter town, en sole 'im fer fifteen hunder' dollars. Co'se de man w'at bought Henry did n' know nuffin 'bout de goopher, en Mars Dugal' did n' see no 'casion fer ter till 'im. Long to'ds de fall, w'en de sap went down, Henry begin ter git ole ag'in same ez yuzhal, en his noo marster begin ter git skeered les'n he gwine ter lose his fifteen-hunder'-dollar nigger. He sent fer a mighty fine doctor, but de med'cine did n' 'pear ter do no good; de goopher had a good holt. Henry tole de doctor 'bout de goopher, but de doctor des laff at 'im.

"One day in de winter Mars Dugal' went ter town, en wuz santerin' 'long de Main Street, when who should he meet but Henry's noo marster. Dey said 'Hoody,' en Mars Dugal' ax 'im ter hab a seegyar; en atter dey run on awhile 'bout de craps en de weather, Mars Dugal' ax 'im, sorter keerless, like ez ef he des thought of it,—

"'How you like de nigger I sole you las' spring?'

"Henry's marster shuck his head en knock de ashes off'n his seegyar.

[7]"A small card, resembling a currycomb in construction, and used by negroes in the rural districts instead of a comb."—Chesnutt's note. Card: a tool with wire teeth, used for carding (combing) fibers.

"'Spec' I made a bad bahgin when I bought dat nigger. Henry done good wuk all de summer, but sence de fall set in he 'pears ter be sorter pinin' away. Dey ain' nuffin pertickler de matter wid 'im—leastways de doctor say so—'cep'n a tech er de rheumatiz; but his ha'r is all fell out, en ef he don't pick up his strenk mighty soon, I spec' I'm gwine ter lose 'im.'

"Dey smoked on awhile, en bimeby ole mars say, "Well, a bahgin's a bahgin, but you en me is good fren's, en I doan wan' ter see you lose all de money you paid fer dat nigger; en ef w'at you say is so, en I ain't 'sputin' it, he ain't wuf much now. I 'spec's you wukked him too ha'd dis summer, er e'se de swamps down here don't agree wid de san'-hill nigger. So you des lemme know, en ef he gits any wusser I'll be willin' ter gib yer five hund'ed dollars fer 'im, en take my chances on his livin'."

"Sho 'nuff, when Henry begun ter draw up wid de rheumatiz en it look like he gwine ter die fer sho, his noo marster sen' fer Mars Dugal', en Mars Dugal' gin him what he promus, en brung Henry home ag'in. He tuk good keer uv 'im dyoin' er de winter,—give 'im w'iskey ter rub his rheumatiz, en terbacker ter smoke, en all he want ter eat,—caze a nigger w'at he could make a thousan' dollars a year off'n did n' grow on eve'y huckleberry bush.

"Nex' spring, w'en de sap ris en Henry's ha'r commence' ter sprout, Mars Dugal' sole 'im ag'in, down in Robeson County dis time; en he kep' dat sellin' business up fer five year er mo'. Henry nebber say nuffin 'bout de goopher ter his noo marsters, 'caze he know he gwine ter be tuk good keer uv de nex' winter, w'en Mars Dugal' buy him back. En Mars Dugal' made 'nuff money off'n Henry ter buy anudder plantation ober on Beaver Crick.

"But 'long 'bout de een' er dat five year dey come a stranger ter stop at de plantation. De fus' day he 'uz dere he went out wid Mars Dugal' en spent all de mawnin' lookin' ober de vimya'd, en atter dinner dey spent all de evenin' playin' kya'ds. De niggers soon 'skiver' dat he wuz a Yankee, en dat he come down ter Norf C'lina fer ter l'arn de w'ite folks how to raise grapes en make wine. He promus Mars Dugal' he c'd make de grapevimes b'ar twice't ez many grapes, en dat de noo winepress he wuz a-sellin' would make mo' d'n twice't ez many gallons er wine. En ole Mars Dugal' des drunk it all in, des 'peared ter be bewitch' wid dat Yankee. W'en de darkies see dat Yankee runnin' 'roun' de vimy'd en diggin' under de grapevimes, dey shuk dere heads, en 'lowed dat dey feared Mars Dugal' losin' his min'. Mars Dugal' had all de dirt dug away fum under de roots er all de scuppernon' vimes, an' let 'em stan' dat away fer a week er mo'. Den dat Yankee made de niggers fix up a mixtry er lime en ashes en manyo,[8] en po' it 'roun' de roots er de grapevimes. Den he 'vise Mars Dugal' fer ter trim de vimes close't, en Mars Dugal' tuck 'n done eve'ything de Yankee tole him ter do. Dyoin' all er dis time, mind yer, dis yer Yankee wuz libbin' off'n de fat er de lan', at de big house, en playin' kya'ds wid Mars Dugal' eve'y night; en dey say Mars Dugal' los' mo'n a thousan' dollars dyoin's er de week dat Yankee wuz a-ruinin' de grapevimes.

"W'en de sap ris nex' spring, ole Henry 'n'inted his head ez yuzhal, en his ha'r 'mence' ter grow des de same ez it done eve'y year. De scuppernon' vimes growed monst'us fas', en de leaves wuz greener en thicker dan dey eber be'n dyoin' my rememb'ance; en Henry's ha'r growed out thicker dan eber, en he 'peared ter git younger 'n younger, en soopler 'n soopler; en seein' ez he wuz

[8]"Manure."

sh'ot er han's dat spring, havin' tuk in consid'able noo groun', Mars Dugal' cluded he would n' sell Henry 'tel he git de crap in en de cotton chop'. So he kep' Henry on de plantation.

"But long 'bout time fer de grapes ter come on de scuppernon' vimes, dey 'peared ter come a change ober 'em; de leaves withered en swivel' up, en de young grapes turn' yaller, en bimeby eve'ybody on de plantation could see dat de whole vimya'd wuz dyin'. Mars Dugal' tuk 'n water de vimes en done all he could, but 't wa'n' no use: dat Yankee had done bus' de watermillyum. One time de vimes picked up a bit, en Mars Dugal' 'lowed dey wuz gwine ter come out ag'in; but dat Yankee done dug too close under de roots, en prune de branches too close ter de vime, en all dat lime en ashes done burn' de life out'n de vimes, en dey des kep' a-with'in' en a-swivelin'.

"All dis time de goopher wuz a-wukken'. When de vimes sta'ted ter wither, Henry 'mence' ter complain er his rheumatiz; en when de leaves begin ter dry up, his ha'r 'mence' ter drap out. When de vimes fresh' up a bit, Henry 'd git peart ag'in, en when de vimes wither' ag'in, Henry 'd git ole ag'in, en des kep' gittin' mo' en mo' fitten fer nuffin; he des pined away, en pined away, en fine'-ly tuk ter his cabin; en when de big vime whar he got de sap ter 'n'int his head withered en turned yaller en died, Henry died too,—des went out sorter like a cannel. Dey did n't 'pear ter be nuffin de matter wid 'im, 'cep'n' de rheumatiz, but his strenk des dwinnel' away 'tel he did n' hab ernuff lef' ter draw his bref. De goopher had got de under holt, en th'owed Henry dat time fer good en all.

"Mars Dugal' tuk on might'ly 'bout losin' his vimes en his nigger in de same year; en he swo' dat ef he could git holt er dat Yankee he'd wear 'im ter a frazzle, en den chaw up de frazzle; en he'd done it, too, for Mars Dugal' 'uz a monst'us brash man w'en he once git started. He sot de vimya'd out ober ag'in, but it wuz th'ee er fo' year befo' de vimes got ter b'arin' any scuppernon's.

"W'en de wah broke out, Maars Dugal' raise' a comp'ny, en went off ter fight de Yankees. He say he wuz mighty glad dat wah come, en he des want ter kill a Yankee fer eve'y dollar he los' 'long er dat grape-raisin' Yankee. En I 'spec' he would 'a' done it, too, ef de Yankees had n' s'picioned sump'n, en killed him fus'. Atter de s'render ole miss move' ter town, de niggers all scattered 'way fum de plantation, en de vimya'd ain' be'n cultervated sence."

"Is that story true?" asked Annie doubtfully, but seriously, as the old man concluded his narrative.

"It's des ez true ez I'm a-settin' here, miss. Dey's a easy way ter prove it: I kin lead de way right ter Henry's grave ober yander in de plantation buryin'-groun'. En I tell yer w'at, marster, I would n' 'vise you to buy dis yer ole vimya'd, 'caze de goopher's on it yit, en dey ain' no tellin' w'en it's gwine ter crap out."

"But I thought you said all the ole vines died."

Dey did 'pear ter die, but a few un 'em come out ag'in, en is mixed in 'mongs' de yuthers. I ain' skeered ter eat de grapes, 'caze I knows de old vimes fum de noo ones; but wid strangers dey ain' no tellin' w'at mought happen. I would n' 'vise yer ter buy dis vimya'd."

I bought the vineyard, nevertheless, and it has been for a long time in a thriving condition, and is often referred to by the local press as a striking illustration of the opportunities open to Northern capital in the development of Southern industries. The luscious scuppernong holds first rank among our grapes, though we cultivate a great many other varieties, and our income from cked and shipped to the Northern markets is quite considerable. I nave not noticed any developments of the goopher in the vineyard, although I have a mild suspicion that our colored assistants do not suffer from want of grapes during the season.

I found, when I bought the vineyard, that Uncle Julius had occupied a cabin on the place for many years, and derived a respectable revenue from the product of the neglected grapevines. This, doubtless, accounted for his advice to me not to buy the vineyard, though whether it inspired the goopher story I am unable to state. I believe, however, that the wages I paid him for his services as coachman, for I gave him employment in that capacity, were more than an equivalent for anything he lost by the sale of the vineyard.

1887

THE WIFE OF HIS YOUTH

I

Mr. Ryder was going to give a ball. There were several reasons why this was an opportune time for such an event.

Mr. Ryder might aptly be called the dean of the Blue Veins. The original Blue Veins were a little society of colored persons organized in a certain Northern city shortly after the war. Its purpose was to establish and maintain correct social standards among a people whose social condition presented almost unlimited room for improvement. By accident, combined perhaps with some natural affinity, the society consisted of individuals who were, generally speaking, more white than black. Some envious outsider made the suggestion that no one was eligible for membership who was not white enough to show blue veins. The suggestion was readily adopted by those who were not of the favored few, and since that time the society, though possessing a longer and more pretentious name, had been known far and wide as the "Blue Vein Society," and its members as the "Blue Veins."

The Blue Veins did not allow that any such requirement existed for admission to their circle, but, on the contrary, declared that character and culture were the only things considered; and that if most of their members were light-colored, it was because such persons, as a rule, had had better opportunities to qualify themselves for membership. Opinions differed, too, as to the usefulness of the society. There were those who had been known to assail it violently as a glaring example of the very prejudice from which the colored race had suffered most; and later, when such critics had succeeded in getting on the inside, they had been heard to maintain with zeal and earnestness that the society was a lifeboat, an anchor, a bulwark and a shield,—a pillar of cloud by day and of fire by night, to guide their people through the social wilderness. Another alleged prerequisite for Blue Vein membership was that of free birth; and while there was really no such requirement, it is doubtless true that very few of the members would have been unable to meet it if there had been. If there were one or two of the older members who had come up from the South and from slavery, their history presented enough romantic circumstances to rob their servile origin of its grosser aspects.

While there were no such tests of eligibility, it is true that the Blue Veins had their notions on these subjects, and that not all of them were equally liberal in regard to the things they collectively disclaimed. Mr. Ryder was one of the most conservative. Though he had not been among the founders of the society, but had come in some years later, his genius for social leadership was such that he had speedily become its recognized adviser and head, the custodian of its standards, and the preserver of its traditions. He shaped its social policy, was active in providing for its entertainment, and when the interest fell off, as it sometimes did, he fanned the embers until they burst again into a cheerful flame.

There were still other reasons for his popularity. While he was not as white as some of the Blue Veins, his appearance was such as to confer distinction upon them. His features were of a refined type, his hair was almost straight; he was always neatly dressed; his manners were irreproachable, and his morals above suspicion. He had come to Groveland a young man, and obtaining employment in the office of a railroad company as messenger had in time worked himself up to the position of stationery clerk, having charge of the distribution of the office supplies for the whole company. Although the lack of early training had hindered the orderly development of a naturally fine mind, it had not prevented him from doing a great deal of reading or from forming decidedly literary tastes. Poetry was his passion. He could repeat whole pages of the great English poets; and if his pronunciation was sometimes faulty, his eye, his voice, his gestures, would respond to the changing sentiment with a precision that revealed a poetic soul and disarmed criticism. He was economical, and had saved money; he owned and occupied a very comfortable house on a respectable street. His residence was handsomely furnished, containing among other things a good library, especially rich in poetry, a piano, and some choice engravings. He generally shared his house with some young couple, who looked after his wants and were company for him; for Mr. Ryder was a single man. In the early days of his connection with the Blue Veins he had been regarded as quite a catch, and young ladies and their mothers had manœuvred with much ingenuity to capture him. Not, however, until Mrs. Molly Dixon visited Groveland had any woman ever made him wish to change his condition to that of a married man.

Mrs. Dixon had come to Groveland from Washington in the spring, and before the summer was over she had won Mr. Ryder's heart. She possessed many attractive qualities. She was much younger than he; in fact, he was old enough to have been her father, though no one knew exactly how old he was. She was whiter than he, and better educated. She had moved in the best colored society of the country, at Washington, and had taught in the schools of that city. Such a superior person had been eagerly welcomed to the Blue Vein Society, and had taken a leading part in its activities. Mr. Ryder had at first been attracted by her charms of person, for she was very good looking and not over twenty-five; then by her refined manners and the vivacity of her wit. Her husband had been a government clerk, and at his death had left a considerable life insurance. She was visiting friends in Groveland, and, finding the town and the people to her liking, had prolonged her stay indefinitely. She had not seemed displeased at Mr. Ryder's attentions, but on the contrary had given him every proper encouragement; indeed, a younger and less cautious man would long since have spoken. But he had made up his mind, and had only to determine the time when he would ask her to be his wife. He decided to give a ball in her honor, and at some time during the evening of the ball to offer her his heart and hand. He had no special fears about the outcome, but, with a little touch of romance, he wanted the surroundings to be in harmony with his own feelings when he should have received the answer he expected.

Mr. Ryder resolved that this ball should mark an epoch in the social history of Groveland. He knew, of course,—no one could know better,—the entertainments that had taken place in past years, and what must be done to surpass them. His ball must be worthy of the lady in whose honor it was to be given, and must, by the quality of its guests, set an example for the future. He had observed of late a growing liberality, almost a laxity, in social matters, even among members of his own set, and had several times been forced to meet in a social way persons whose complexions and callings in life were hardly up to the standard which he considered proper for the society to maintain. He had a theory of his own.

"I have no race prejudice," he would say, "but we people of mixed blood are ground between the upper and the nether millstone. Our fate lies between absorption by the white race and extinction in the black. The one doesn't want us yet, but may take us in time. The other would welcome us, but it would be for us a backward step. 'With malice towards none, with charity for all,'[1] we must do the best we can for ourselves and those who are to follow us. Self-preservation is the first law of nature."

His ball would serve by its exclusiveness to counteract leveling tendencies, and his marriage with Mrs. Dixon would help to further the upward process of absorption he had been wishing and waiting for.

II

The ball was to take place on Friday night. The house had been put in order, the carpets covered with canvas, the halls and stairs decorated with palms and potted plants; and in the afternoon Mr. Ryder sat on his front porch, which the shade of a vine running up over a wire netting made a cool and pleasant lounging place. He expected to respond to the toast "The Ladies" at the supper, and from a volume of Tennyson[2]—his favorite poet—was fortifying himself with apt quotations. The volume was open at "A Dream of Fair Women." His eyes fell on these lines, and he read them aloud to judge better of their effect:—

"At length I saw a lady within call,
Stiller than chisell'd marble, standing there;
A daughter of the gods, divinely tall,
And most divinely fair."

He marked the verse, and turning the page read the stanza beginning,—

"O sweet pale Margaret,
O rare pale Margaret."[3]

[1] A passage from Abraham Lincoln's second inaugural address, delivered in March 1865, as the Civil War was ending, expressing his desire to put the divisions of the past behind and effectively reunite the nation.

[2] English poet Alfred, Lord Tennyson (1809–1892). [3] From Tennyson's poem "Margaret."

He weighed the passage a moment, and decided that it would not do. Mrs. Dixon was the palest lady he expected at the ball, and she was of a rather ruddy complexion, and of lively disposition and buxom build. So he ran over the leaves until his eye rested on the description of Queen Guinevere:—

"She seem'd a part of joyous Spring:
A gown of grass-green silk she wore,
Buckled with golden clasps before;
A light-green tuft of plumes she bore
Closed in a golden ring.

"She look'd so lovely, as she sway'd
The rein with dainty finger-tips,
A man had given all other bliss,
And all his worldly worth for this,
To waste his whole heart in one kiss
Upon her perfect lips."[4]

As Mr. Ryder murmured these words audibly, with an appreciative thrill, he heard the latch of his gate click, and a light footfall sounding on the steps. He turned his head, and saw a woman standing before his door.

She was a little woman, not five feet tall, and proportioned to her height. Although she stood erect, and looked around her with very bright and restless eyes, she seemed quite old; for her face was crossed and recrossed with a hundred wrinkles, and around the edges of her bonnet could be seen protruding here and there a tuft of short gray wool. She wore a blue calico gown of ancient cut, a little red shawl fastened around her shoulders with an old-fashioned brass brooch, and a large bonnet profusely ornamented with faded red and yellow artificial flowers. And she was very black,—so black that her toothless gums, revealed when she opened her mouth to speak, were not red, but blue. She looked like a bit of the old plantation life, summoned up from the past by the wave of a magician's wand, as the poet's fancy had called into being the gracious shapes of which Mr. Ryder had just been reading.

He rose from his chair and came over to where she stood.

"Good-afternoon, madam," he said.

"Good-evenin', suh," she answered, ducking suddenly with a quaint curtsy. Her voice was shrill and piping, but softened somewhat by age. "Is dis yere whar Mistuh Ryduh lib, suh?" she asked, looking around her doubtfully, and glancing into the open windows, through which some of the preparations for the evening were visible.

"Yes," he replied, with an air of kindly patronage, unconsciously flattered by her manner, "I am Mr. Ryder. Did you want to see me?"

"Yas, suh, ef I ain't 'sturbin' of you too much."

"Not at all. Have a seat over here behind the vine, where it is cool. What can I do for you?"

"'Scuse me, suh," she continued, when she had sat down on the edge of a chair, "'scuse me, suh, I's lookin' for my husban'. I heerd you wuz a big man an' had libbed heah a long time, an' I 'lowed you would n't min' ef I'd come

[4]From Tennyson's poem "Sir Launcelot and Queen Guinevere."

roun' an' ax you ef you'd ever heerd of a merlatter man by de name er Sam Taylor 'quirin' roun' in de chu'ches ermongs' de people fer his wife 'Liza Jane?"

Mr. Ryder seemed to think for a moment.

"There used to be many such cases right after the war," he said, "but it has been so long that I have forgotten them. There are very few now. But tell me your story, and it may refresh my memory."

She sat back farther in her chair so as to be more comfortable, and folded her withered hands in her lap.

"My name's 'Liza," she began, "'Liza Jane. W'en I wuz young I us'ter b'long ter Marse Bob Smif, down in ole Missoura. I wuz bawn down dere. W'en I wuz a gal I wuz married ter a man named Jim. But Jim died, an' after dat I married a merlatter man named Sam Taylor. Sam wuz free-bawn, but his mammy and daddy died, an' de w'ite folks 'prenticed him ter my marster fer ter work fer 'im 'tel he wuz growed up. Sam worked in de fiel', an' I wuz de cook. One day Ma'y Ann, ole miss's maid, came rushin' out ter de kitchen, an' says she, ''Liza Jane, ole marse gwine sell yo' Sam down de ribber.'

"'Go way f'm yere,' says I; 'my husban' 's free!'

"'Don' make no diff'ence. I heerd ole marse tell ole miss he wuz gwine take yo' Sam 'way wid 'im ter-morrow, fer he needed money, an' he knowed whar he could git a t'ousan' dollars fer Sam an' no questions axed.'

"W'en Sam come home f'm de fiel' dat night, I tole him 'bout ole marse gwine steal 'im, an' Sam run erway. His time wuz mos' up, an' he swo' dat w'en he wuz twenty-one he would come back an' he'p me run erway, er else save up de money ter buy my freedom. An' I know he 'd 'a' done it, fer he thought a heap er me, Sam did. But w'en he come back he did n' fin' me, fer I wuz n' dere. Ole marse had heerd dat I warned Sam, so he had me whip' an' sol' down de ribber.

"Den de wah broke out, an' w'en it wuz ober de cullud folks wuz scattered. I went back ter de ole home; but Sam wuz n' dere, an' I could n' l'arn nuffin' 'bout 'im. But I knowed he 'd be'n dere to look fer me an' had n' foun' me, an' had gone erway ter hunt fer me.

"I's be'n lookin' fer 'im eber sence," she added simply, as though twenty-five years were but a couple of weeks, "an' I knows he 's be'n lookin' fer me. Fer he sot a heap er sto' by me, Sam did, an' I know he 's be'n huntin' fer me all dese years,—'less'n he 's be'n sick er sump'n, so he could n' work, er out'n his head, so he could n' 'member his promise. I went back down de ribber, fer I 'lowed he 'd gone down dere lookin' fer me. I's be'n ter Noo Orleens, an' Atlanty, an' Charleston, an' Richmon'; an' w'en I'd be'n all ober de Souf I come ter de Norf. Fer I knows I'll fin' 'im some er dese days," she added softly, "er he'll fin' me, an' den we'll bofe be as happy in freedom as we wuz in de ole days befo' de wah." A smile stole over her withered countenance as she paused a moment, and her bright eyes softened into a far away look.

This was the substance of the old woman's story. She had wandered a little here and there. Mr. Ryder was looking at her curiously when she finished.

"How have you lived all these years?" he asked.

"Cookin', suh. I's a good cook. Does you know anybody w'at needs a good cook, suh? I's stoppin' wid a cullud fam'ly roun' de corner yonder 'tel I kin git a place."

"Do you really expect to find your husband? He may be dead long ago."

She shook her head emphatically. "Oh no, he ain' dead. De signs an' de tokens tells me. I dremp three nights runnin' on'y dis las' week dat I foun' him."

"He may have married another woman. Your slave marriage would not have prevented him, for you never lived with him after the war, and without that your marriage does n't count."

"Would n' make no diff'ence wid Sam. He would n' marry no yuther 'ooman 'tel he foun' out 'bout me. I knows it," she added. "Sump'n's be'n tellin' me all dese years dat I's gwine fin' Sam 'fo' I dies."

"Perhaps he's outgrown you, and climbed up in the world where he would n't care to have you find him."

"No, indeed, suh," she replied, "Sam ain' dat kin' er man. He wuz good ter me, Sam wuz, but he wuz n' much good ter nobody e'se, fer he wuz one er de triflin'es' han's on de plantation. I 'spec's ter haf ter suppo't 'im w'en I fin' 'im, fer he nebber would work 'less'n he had ter. But den he wuz free, an' he did n' git no pay fer his work, an' I don' blame 'im much. Mebbe he's done better sence he run erway, but I ain' 'spectin' much."

"You may have passed him on the street a hundred times during the twenty-five years, and not have known him; time works great changes."

She smiled incredulously. "I'd know 'im 'mongs' a hund'ed men. Fer dey wuz n' no yuther merlatter man like my man Sam, an' I could n' be mistook. I's toted his picture roun' wid me twenty-five years."

"May I see it?" asked Mr. Ryder. "It might help me to remember whether I have seen the original."

As she drew a small parcel from her bosom he saw that it was fastened to a string that went around her neck. Removing several wrappers, she brought to light an old-fashioned daguerreotype in a black case. He looked long and intently at the portrait. It was faded with time, but the features were still distinct, and it was easy to see what manner of man it had represented.

He closed the case, and with a slow movement handed it back to her.

"I don't know of any man in town who goes by that name," he said, "nor have I heard of any one making such inquiries. But if you will leave me your address, I will give the matter some attention, and if I find out anything I will let you know."

She gave him the number of a house in the neighborhood, and went away, after thanking him warmly.

He wrote the address on the fly-leaf of the volume of Tennyson, and, when she had gone, rose to his feet and stood looking after her curiously. As she walked down the street with mincing step, he saw several persons whom she passed turn and look back at her with a smile of kindly amusement. When she had turned the corner, he went upstairs to his bedroom, and stood for a long time before the mirror of his dressing-case, gazing thoughtfully at the reflection of his own face.

III

At eight o'clock the ballroom was a blaze of light and the guests had begun to assemble; for there was a literary programme and some routine business of the society to be gone through with before the dancing. A black servant in evening dress waited at the door and directed the guests to the dressing-rooms.

The occasion was long memorable among the colored people of the city; not alone for the dress and display, but for the high average of intelligence and culture that distinguished the gathering as a whole. There were a number of school-teachers, several young doctors, three or four lawyers, some professional singers, an editor, a lieutenant in the United States army spending his furlough in the city, and others in various polite callings; these were colored, though most of them would not have attracted even a casual glance because of any marked difference from white people. Most of the ladies were in evening costume, and dress coats and dancing pumps were the rule among the men. A band of string music, stationed in an alcove behind a row of palms, played popular airs while the guests were gathering.

The dancing began at half past nine. At eleven o'clock supper was served. Mr. Ryder had left the ballroom some little time before the intermission, but reappeared at the suppertable. The spread was worthy of the occasion, and the guests did full justice to it. When the coffee had been served, the toastmaster, Mr. Solomon Sadler, rapped for order. He made a brief introductory speech, complimenting host and guests, and then presented in their order the toasts of the evening. They were responded to with a very fair display of after-dinner wit.

"The last toast," said the toast-master, when he reached the end of the list, "is one which must appeal to us all. There is no one of us of the sterner sex who is not at some time dependent upon woman,—in infancy for protection, in manhood for companionship, in old age for care and comforting. Our good host has been trying to live alone, but the fair faces I see around me to-night prove that he too is largely dependent upon the gentler sex for most that makes life worth living,—the society and love of friends,—and rumor is at fault if he does not soon yield entire subjection to one of them. Mr. Ryder will now respond to the toast,—The Ladies."

There was a pensive look in Mr. Ryder's eyes as he took the floor and adjusted his eyeglasses. He began by speaking of woman as the gift of Heaven to man, and after some general observations on the relations of the sexes he said: "But perhaps the quality which most distinguishes woman is her fidelity and devotion to those she loves. History is full of examples, but has recorded none more striking than one which only to-day came under my notice."

He then related, simply but effectively, the story told by his visitor of the afternoon. He gave it in the same soft dialect, which came readily to his lips, while the company listened attentively and sympathetically. For the story had awakened a responsive thrill in many hearts. There were some present who had seen, and others who had heard their fathers and grandfathers tell, the wrongs and sufferings of this past generation, and all of them still felt, in their darker moments, the shadow hanging over them. Mr. Ryder went on:—

"Such devotion and confidence are rare even among women. There are many who would have searched a year, some who would have waited five years, a few who might have hoped ten years; but for twenty-five years this woman has retained her affection for and her faith in a man she has not seen or heard of in all that time.

"She came to me to-day in the hope that I might be able to help her find this long-lost husband. And when she was gone I gave my fancy rein, and imagined a case I will put to you.

"Suppose that this husband, soon after his escape, had learned that his wife had been sold away, and that such inquiries as he could make brought no information of her where abouts. Suppose that he was young, and she much older than he; that he was light, and she was black; that their marriage was a slave marriage, and legally binding only if they chose to make it so after the war. Suppose, too, that he made his way to the North, as some of us have done, and there, where he had larger opportunities, had improved them, and had in the course of all these years grown to be as different from the ignorant boy who ran away from fear of slavery as the day is from the night. Suppose, even, that he had qualified himself, by industry, by thrift, and by study, to win the friendship and be considered worthy the society of such people as these I see around me to-night, gracing my board and filling my heart with gladness; for I am old enough to remember the day when such a gathering would not have been possible in this land. Suppose, too, that, as the years went by, this man's memory of the past grew more and more indistinct, until at last it was rarely, except in his dreams, that any image of this bygone period rose before his mind. And then suppose that accident should bring to his knowledge the fact that the wife of his youth, the wife he had left behind him,—not one who had walked by his side and kept pace with him in his upward struggle, but one upon whom advancing years and a laborious life had set their mark,—was alive and seeking him, but that he was absolutely safe from recognition or discovery, unless he chose to reveal himself. My friends, what would the man do? I will presume that he was one who loved honor, and tried to deal justly with all men. I will even carry the case further, and suppose that perhaps he had set his heart upon another, whom he had hoped to call his own. What would he do, or rather what ought he to do, in such a crisis of a lifetime?

"It seemed to me that he might hesitate, and I imagined that I was an old friend, a near friend, and that he had come to me for advice; and I argued the case with him. I tried to discuss it impartially. After we had looked upon the matter from every point of view, I said to him, in words that we all know:—

'This above all: to thine own self be true,
And it must follow, as the night the day,
Thou canst not then be false to any man.'[5]

Then, finally, I put the question to him, 'Shall you acknowledge her?'

"And now, ladies and gentlemen, friends and companions, I ask you, what should he have done?"

There was something in Mr. Ryder's voice that stirred the hearts of those who sat around him. It suggested more than mere sympathy with an imaginary situation; it seemed rather in the nature of a personal appeal. It was observed, too, that his look rested more especially upon Mrs. Dixon, with a mingled expression of renunciation and inquiry.

She had listened, with parted lips and streaming eyes. She was the first to speak:

"He should have acknowledged her."

"Yes," they all echoed, "he should have acknowledged her."

[5]A piece of fatherly advice from the character Polonius to his son Laertes in *Hamlet* (Act I, scene iii, lines 78–80), by the great English dramatist William Shakespeare (1564–1616).

"My friends and companions," responded Mr. Ryder, "I thank you, one and all. It is the answer I expected, for I knew your hearts."

He turned and walked toward the closed door of an adjoining room, while every eye followed him in wondering curiosity. He came back in a moment, leading by the hand his visitor of the afternoon, who stood startled and trembling at the sudden plunge into this scene of brilliant gayety. She was neatly dressed in gray, and wore the white cap of an elderly woman.

"Ladies and gentlemen," he said, "this is the woman, and I am the man, whose story I have told you. Permit me to introduce to you the wife of my youth."

1899

A METROPOLITAN EXPERIENCE

I had come to New York to seek my fortune. The path over which I was to pursue the fickle goddess was but vaguely defined, at least in regard to details. But I knew what I wanted to do, and that was to practice my profession.

I had just finished a three years' course in a New Jersey medical college, during which time I had spent the greater part of my modest patrimony, which had consisted of three thousand dollars realized from an insurance on my father's life. My father had been a physician of fine skill, high ideals, and small practice, a not uncommon combination. I had no mother or sisters to keep me at home; our town was abundantly supplied with physicians; and, as I did not care to wait half a lifetime for a practice which would have barely supported me during the remaining half, I had determined to seek my fortune elsewhere.

On leaving a small town, it was natural that I should come to a large one. I knew that the greatest success, other things being equal, was only possible where the largest opportunities existed; and if I did not succeed in a large city, I could not reproach myself with the lack of opportunity. Hence I came to New York.

I secured board at a second-rate boarding house in the neighborhood of Washington Square. It was part of my plan of operations to study the city a while before hanging out my shingle.

With this object in view I spent a good deal of time on the streets and in public parks; and on pleasant evenings I frequently sat for an hour or two in Washington Square.[1] Seated there, on one of the public benches, often in close proximity to some bottle-nosed and ill-odored tramp, I would study the strange jumble of types in the stream of humanity that rolled through the park, which is more of a thoroughfare than a pleasure-ground.

Most of those who passed belonged to the shabbier classes of the metropolis; you could see there every variety of New Yorker, from the above-mentioned tramp to the shabby genteel clerk; only the wealthy and prosperous-looking were seldom met with.

One evening as I sat in my accustomed seat, absorbed for the moment in a calculation as to how long the human stomach could endure the food at Mrs. Van Hashelar's boarding house, I was dimly conscious of a female figure passing by. I looked up, but the lady had gone too far for me to see her face. What

[1]A section of New York City now more commonly called Greenwich Village.

I did see was a slender figure, set off by a blue silk dress of a stylish cut, and though walking somewhat briskly, borne along with a graceful motion quite different from the usual wobble of a woman in a hurry; a charming back, above which rose a well-turned neck, surmounted by a head of hair of the color poets are popularly supposed to rave about, a ruddy gold, on top of which in turn reposed a most bewitching bonnet. This somewhat elaborate description but faintly pictures the impression she made upon me at the time.

I felt a sudden desire to see the lady's face; I was sure it would be beautiful and I have always been a great admirer of beautiful women, or rather of the beautiful in women—the distinction is obvious. I rose from my seat, and started down another path, running in the same general direction as she was going, intending to execute a sort of flank movement and meet her face to face on the other side of the park, where the two paths converged after a long curve. Just as I approached the point where the paths came together the lady slipped and fell, uttering a little scream. I rushed forward and assisted her to rise.

"Are you badly hurt?" I inquired in a sympathetic voice.

"Oh, no," she replied, thanking me, "it is nothing at all." But as she started off she came near falling a second time. I caught her and placed her arm in mine.

"Shall I call a carriage?" I asked.

"Oh, no," she said, "it is hardly worthwhile. I live only a short distance, and—if you will—"

"Certainly," I said, not waiting for her to finish the sentence, "I shall be very glad to assist you."

A few minutes' walk, and one or two turns brought us to a brick house of conventional style, and I helped her up the high stoop and rang the doorbell. As she did not release my arm when the door was opened, I could do nothing less than help her into the house. I deposited my fair burden on a cushioned armchair in the parlor, and, hat in hand, was beginning an elaborate parting bow, when she exclaimed:

"Oh, do sit down and rest a moment. How tired you must be carrying poor me such a distance."

I sat down. I may say here that she was quite as pretty as I had imagined her to be.

"I suppose we ought to be introduced," she said. "I am Miss Preston."

"And I am Dr. Scott, at your service," I replied. Our conversation had not advanced beyond this preliminary stage when the doorbell rang, and the servant girl entered a moment later with a telegraph message. Excusing herself, Miss Preston hurriedly tore open the envelope and glanced at the message. Her face took on a look of concern, and she said to the servant:

"Katy, is papa at home?"

"No, ma'am, he went to Boston this afternoon."

"Then telephone Uncle George's house and see if he is at home," and when the girl had gone out she continued, turning to me: "It's all about my Cousin Harry. He is at Yale,[2] and I am afraid is just a little wild. He tells me that through an unfortunate mistake he has got into a scrape, without any fault of his own, and that if I don't send him a telegraph money order for fifty dollars by nine o'clock, he is likely to be disgraced, and perhaps expelled from college."

[2]Yale University, in New Haven, Connecticut.

I murmured my sympathy. The girl returned and announced that Uncle George had gone to Philadelphia, and would not be back until the next night. At this intelligence the expression of concern in Miss Preston's face deepened into dismay.

"Papa away—Uncle George out of town—and only twenty-five dollars in the house," she exclaimed. "Oh, what shall—"

I interrupted her: "If I can venture to offer you my assistance I shall be glad to lend you the money."

"Oh, no," she said, "I couldn't think of accepting a loan from a stranger—or, such a recent acquaintance," she corrected herself, blushing.

I assured her with some eloquence of speech that in a crisis like this the ordinary conventionalities of polite society should yield to the exigency of the moment; and in the end I persuaded her to accept a loan of twenty-five dollars.

"Papa will send a check when he returns tomorrow," she said, "or I will send the money by Katy, if you will leave me your card."

I felt for my card-case, but I had left it at home. I said it didn't matter; I often walked down that way, and would stop in in a day or two, and see if she had recovered from her injury.

"Very well," she replied with a fine blush and an entrancing smile, "I shall expect you."

I went home with my head in a whirl. What a divine creature! What beauty! What grace! What refinement of sentiment! And to think that I had been able to serve this beautiful creature and to place her under an obligation to me, and that I was expected to call again. I felt much like a knight-errant[3] of the olden time when he had rescued some captive princess, and had been rewarded for his valor with permission to wear her colors. My ecstatic condition was the more excusable by reason of the fact that I had no lady acquaintances in New York—barring Mrs. Van Hashelar—and had been for three years immersed in the dry details of my medical studies, and entirely without ladies' society.

I concluded that two days would be a reasonable time to elapse before I called to see Miss Preston. I spent the next two days in dreamland. If I sought my accustomed seat in Washington Square it was only to compare the women who passed with Miss Preston. It was very annoying to have to think of such an adorable creature in such a formal way. "Dear Miss Preston" would have looked very well on an envelope, or even as a spoken address; but to think of her as "Miss Preston" was maddening. I tried to supply the hiatus, and ran over all the pretty names I could think of without being able to decide upon any one which expressed all I thought her name ought to suggest. I suppose If I had known her name was Sarah, or Jane, or even Sarah Jane, I would have thought it very nice, but I gave up in despair the attempt to name such loveliness. To find relief from my restlessness I went up to the Astor Library[4] and tried to read a bulky treatise on macrobiosis,[5] which was my favorite study; but somehow the subject was less interesting than usual, and I finally found temporary distraction from my thoughts in Ouida's latest novel.

[3]Literally, a "wandering" knight. In medieval romances knights-errant were knights who traveled about the countryside looking for adventure, and for princesses or other noble damsels to rescue.

[4]A library in New York City founded by John Jacob Astor (1763–1848). It was a forerunner of the New York Public Library.

[5]Apparently a reference to macrobiotics, a dietary concept that especially emphasizes the health benefits of vegetables and whole grains.

The two days finally ran out, and with winged feet I sought the home of my fair acquaintance. I was at first a little doubtful about the place, as on my former visit my absorption in the young lady had been such that I had failed to notice either street or number. However, by following the same course as before, I soon found the house and rang the doorbell. A servant girl admitted me, and asking my name, ushered me into the parlor. I had been seated but a moment when a somewhat elderly woman of angular build and severe countenance entered the room. In answer to her inquiring look I said that I had called to ask how Miss Preston was.

"Miss Preston? Why, there's no Miss Preston here," she said.

I looked around the room. It was surely the same room in which I had seen her last. There was the same ugly steel engraving of Abraham Lincoln signing the Emancipation Proclamation; the same chromo of Charles Sumner[6] between the front windows, the piano occupied the same corner, and on it stood the same open sheet of music, the latest popular catch, "When the Chickens Come to Roost," or some similar title.

"But, madam," I said, "is not this the residence of Mr. Preston?"

"No, indeed," she replied, "this is Mrs. Ledbetter's boarding house."

"This is surely where I saw Miss Preston. But perhaps I am mistaken in the house, though it seems hardly possible."

"There are no Prestons in the block," she said, positively. Then a thought seemed to strike her. "Perhaps you mean Miss Weston; she and her father went away yesterday."

"Was she a blond, with dark blue eyes and very fine teeth, and did she wear a blue silk dress?" I inquired.

"Her exact description, only those fine teeth were false. They left yesterday, without paying their board bill. Twenty-six dollars, young man, is a large sum for a poor widow to be swindled out of."

I began to have an idea. "Do you know where they lived?" I asked.

"They said they were going to Boston, where they were expecting remittances, and all that. But it's my belief that they live wherever they can get board. That sort of people don't have any homes."

My idea had by this time developed into a theory. I remembered the stories I had read of the female sharpers of New York. I had been swindled. The sprained ankle was only a trap, into which I had fallen, like any common greenhorn. I made my theory known to Mrs. Ledbetter, and her opinion readily coincided with mine, which was further strengthened by several circumstances which she related. My theory became a conviction. I had been taken in, and I had myself to thank for it.

"Well, young man," said Mrs. Ledbetter, "you have my sympathy, but I don't see that that helps either of us. Where are you boarding?"

Having found out that I did not wish to change my boarding house, Mrs. Ledbetter at length permitted me to wish her good afternoon.

I was cruelly undeceived. My faith in humanity had received a shock from which I feared, in my youthful pessimism, that it would never recover. Henceforth woman lost her charm for me, and in every fair face I saw a possible Miss

[6]Charles Sumner (1811–1874) was a U.S. senator from Massachusetts. He was a very vocal opponent of slavery and a leader of the Radical Republicans. He served as a principal architect of the post–Civil War reconstruction program.

Preston. I steeled my heart against feminine attractions; I even changed my boarding house because I discovered in myself signs of weakening toward a pretty shorthand writer who came to board at Mrs. Van Hashelar's. My mind was made up; I would live and die a bachelor.

However, this sternness wore off, or, at least became softened with time, which takes the edge off the sharpest pain. I resumed my walks and character studies; but as my experience of Washington Square had been so painful I got into the habit of going up to Central Park[7] to pursue my observations. One afternoon I sat on an iron bench just at the intersection of a carriage drive and a footway reading a copy of the *Herald*,[8] which contained a graphic account of a great ball on Fifth Avenue the night before. I was wondering how long it would be before I could gain admittance to that enchanted sphere—I confess that I am given to day-dreams—when a carriage drew near, and an exclamation in a feminine voice caused me to look up. A hansom cab had stopped a few yards away, in which sat an elderly gentleman and a very good-looking young lady.

"Yes, papa," said the lady, "it is surely he; I cannot be mistaken." When she spoke I recognized Miss Preston. In the light of those eyes and the charm of that voice I forgot that I had been swindled, and blushed to the roots of my hair—I am not sure that my hair did not blush, but as it is naturally red I cannot be certain. I lifted my hat and advanced to the carriage, as her attitude showed that she expected me to do.

"Papa," she said, turning to the portly, well-dressed gentleman who sat beside her, "this is Dr. Scott, who so kindly helped me to rescue Harry from that very disagreeable predicament the other day; my papa, Mr. Preston. We have been looking for you ever since, and I have been, oh, so mortified that I could not learn your address. We got the directory and looked up all the Dr. Scotts, but could not find you. How could you be so cruel as to leave us under such a burden of obligation for so long?"

As I was trying to collect my thoughts, and to tell the truth without referring to my manifestly absurd suspicions, the portly and respectable father invited me to enter the carriage. I complied, and as we drove through the shaded drives on the beautiful metropolitan pleasure-ground, I explained that I had been unable to find the house.

"A very natural mistake," observed Mr. Preston, oracularly, "for one who is not familiar with great cities. To find a needle in a hay-mow is an easy task compared with searching for a person in New York without an address"—in which opinion I agreed with him; indeed, he could not at that moment have expressed an opinion in which I would not have concurred.

But why prolong the story? I accompanied them home; I got my money, though that was a small matter. My first visit was but one of many, and I now have an office in the basement of my father-in-law's residence. Mr. Preston is an alderman, and is interested in city contracts. He is already rich, and when his term of office expires we expect to move up on Fifth Avenue. As my wife is her father's only child, and will undoubtedly inherit his wealth, I am not obliged to enter the feverish race for money. I am at present engaged in the preparation of a work on macrobiosis which I expect will make me famous. There is but one drawback to our wedded happiness—Mr. Preston is a widower and I have no mother-in-law.

1887, 1974

[7]A large public park in New York City.
[8]A popular New York newspaper published from 1835 to 1924.

Joel Chandler Harris 1848–1908

In his Autobiography, *Mark Twain recalled that among the happiest moments of his youth were those at his uncle's farm when he listened raptly while Uncle Dan (later the model for Jim in* Huckleberry Finn*) told the "immortal tales . . . Uncle Remus Harris was to gather into his books and charm the world with." The stories of Br'er Fox and Br'er Rabbit had their origins in the folk myths of Europe and Africa, but Harris made them memorable by presenting their humorous and sometimes bitter wisdom through the character and dialect of an old, uneducated former slave, Uncle Remus.*

Written at a time when writers and readers alike were fascinated by local-color stories, Harris's tales had much the same appeal as Twain's frontier yarns, Bret Harte's tales of the Sierra miners, and Kate Chopin's portrayals of the Louisiana Creoles. And Harris's tales were object lessons not only for those who, like Br'er Rabbit, paid for their heedlessness and pride, but also for all the down-trodden who used their wits to survive and to laugh at their oppressors. Like other regionalist stories, they captured the flavor of a way of life at a single point in time, but like the best of local-color fiction, they had a peculiarly human appeal that kept them alive long after the historical and regional peculiarities they described had disappeared.

Harris took most of his stories from blacks he had known while working as a youth on a Georgia plantation. Later he became a journalist in Macon, New Orleans, and Savannah before serving twenty-four years on the staff of the Atlanta Constitution, *where he published many of the humorous stories of plantation blacks that made him famous.*

His first volume of collected tales, Uncle Remus, His Songs and Sayings, *appeared in 1880. Numerous other collections followed during the next thirty years, among them* Nights with Uncle Remus *(1883) and* Free Joe and Other Georgian Sketches *(1887), which included "Free Joe and the Rest of the World," the tragic tale of a slave who, granted his freedom, could find no place for himself in the slave-holding South before the Civil War.*

FURTHER READING: *The Complete Tales of Uncle Remus,* ed. R. Chase, 1955; R. Wiggins, *The Life of Joel Chandler Harris,* 1918; J. Harris, *The Life and Letters of Joel Chandler Harris,* 1918; A. Harlow, *Joel Chandler Harris,* 1941; S. Brooks, *Joel Chandler Harris, Folklorist,* 1950; P. Cousins, *Joel Chandler Harris: A Biography,* 1968; R. Bickley, *Joel Chandler Harris,* 1978, 1987; F. Baer, *Sources and Analogues of the Uncle Remus Tales,* 1980; *Critical Essays on Joel Chandler Harris,* ed. R. Bickley, 1981.

TEXTS: "How Mr. Rabbit Was Too Sharp for Mr. Fox," *Uncle Remus: His Songs and Sayings,* 1880; "Free Joe and the Rest of the World," *Free Joe and Other Georgian Sketches,* 1887.

HOW MR. RABBIT WAS TOO SHARP FOR MR. FOX

"Uncle Remus," said the little boy one evening, when he had found the old man with little or nothing to do, "did the Fox kill and eat the Rabbit when he caught him with the Tar-Baby?"

"Law, honey, ain't I tell you 'bout dat?" replied the old darkey, chuckling slyly. "I 'clar[1] ter gracious I ought er tole you dat, but old man Nod[2] wuz ridin'

[1]"Declare." [2]I.e., sleepiness.

on my eyeleds twel[3] a leetle mo'n[4] I'd a dis'member'd my own name, en den on to dat here come yo' mammy hollerin' atter you.

"W'at I tell you w'en I fus' begin? I tole you Brer Rabbit wuz a monstus soon[5] creetur; leas'ways dat's w'at I laid out fer ter tell you. Well, den, honey, don't you go en make no udder calkalashuns, kaze in dem days Brer Rabbit en his fambly wuz at de head er de gang w'en enny racket wuz on han', en dar dey stayed. 'Fo'[6] you begins fer ter wipe yo' eyes 'bout Brer Rabbit, you wait en see whar'bouts Brer Rabbit gwine ter fetch up at. But dat's needer yer ner dar.[7]

"W'en Brer Fox fin' Brer Rabbit mixt up wid de Tar-Baby, he feel mighty good, en he roll on de groun' en laugh. Bimeby he up'n say, sezee:

"'Well, I speck I got you dis time, Brer Rabbit', sezee; 'maybe I ain't, but I speck I is. You bin runnin' roun' here sassin' atter me a mighty long time, but I speck you done come ter de een' er de row. You bin cuttin' up yo' capers en bouncin' 'roun' in dis neighborhood ontwel[8] you come ter b'lieve yo'se'f de boss er de whole gang. En den you er allers somers[9] whar you got no bizness,' sez Brer Fox, sezee. 'Who ax you fer ter come en strike up a 'quaintance wid dish yer Tar-Baby? En who stuck you up dar whar you iz? Nobody in de roun' worl'. You des tuck en jam yo'se'f on dat Tar-Baby widout waitin' fer enny invite,' sez Brer Fox, sezee, 'en dar you is, en dar you'll stay twel I fixes up a bresh-pile and fiers her up, kaze I'm gwine ter bobbycue you dis day, sho,' sez Brer Fox, sezee.

"Den Brer Rabbit talk mighty 'umble.

"'I don't keer w'at you do wid me, Brer Fox,' sezee, 'so you don't fling me in dat brier-patch. Roas' me, Brer Fox,' sezee, 'but don't fling me in dat brier-patch,' sezee.

"'Hit's so much trouble fer ter kindle a fier,' sez Brer Fox, sezee, 'dat I speck I'll hatter hang you,' sezee.

"'Hang me des ez high as you please, Brer Fox,' sez Brer Rabbit, sezee, 'but do fer de Lord's sake don't fling me in dat brier-patch,' sezee.

"'I ain't got no string,' sez Brer Fox, sezee, 'en now I speck I'll hatter drown you,' sezee.

"'Drown me des ez deep ez you please, Brer Fox,' sez Brer Rabbit, sezee, 'but don't fling me in dat brier-patch,' sezee.

"'Dey ain't no water nigh,'[10] sez Brer Fox, sezee, 'en now I speck I'll hatter skin you,' sezee.

"'Skin me, Brer Fox,' sez Brer Rabbit, sezee, 'snatch out my eyeballs, t'ar out my years[11] by de roots, en cut off my legs,' sezee, 'but do please, Brer Fox, don't fling me in dat brier-patch,' sezee.

"Co'se[12] Brer Fox wanter hurt Brer Rabbit bad ez he kin, so he cotch 'im by de behime legs en slung 'im right in de middle er de brier-patch. Dar wuz a considerabul flutter whar Brer Rabbit struck de bushes, en Brer Fox sorter hang 'roun' fer ter see w'at wuz gwine ter happen. Bimeby he heard somebody call 'im, en way up de hill he see Brer Rabbit settin' cross-legged on a chinkapin[13] log koamin' de pitch out'n his ha'r wid a chip. Den Brer Fox know dat he bin swop off[14] mighty bad. Brer Rabbit wuz bleedzd[15] fer ter fling back some er his sass, en he holler out:

[3]"Till." [4]"More and." [5]Quick. [6]"Before." [7]"Neither here nor there."
[8]"Until." [9]"Always somewheres." [10]"Near." [11]"Ears."
[12]"Of course." [13]Chestnut. [14]Tricked. [15]Obliged.

"'Bred en bawn in a brier-patch, Brer Fox—bred en bawn in a brier-patch!' en wid dat he skip out des ez lively ez a cricket in de embers."

1880

FREE JOE AND THE REST OF THE WORLD

The name of Free Joe strikes humorously upon the ear of memory. It is impossible to say why, for he was the humblest, the simplest, and the most serious of all God's living creatures, sadly lacking in all those elements that suggest the humorous. It is certain, moreover, that in 1850 the sober-minded citizens of the little Georgian village of Hillsborough were not inclined to take a humorous view of Free Joe, and neither his name nor his presence provoked a smile. He was a black atom, drifting hither and thither without an owner, blown about by all the winds of circumstance, and given over to shiftlessness.

The problems of one generation are the paradoxes of a succeeding one, particularly if war, or some such incident, intervenes to clarify the atmosphere and strengthen the understanding. Thus, in 1850, Free Joe represented not only a problem of large concern, but, in the watchful eyes of Hillsborough, he was the embodiment of that vague and mysterious danger that seemed to be forever lurking on the outskirts of slavery, ready to sound a shrill and ghostly signal in the impenetrable swamps, and steal forth under the midnight stars to murder, rapine, and pillage—a danger always threatening, and yet never assuming shape; intangible, and yet real; impossible, and yet not improbable. Across the serene and smiling front of safety, the pale outlines of the awful shadow of insurrection sometimes fell. With this invisible panorama as a background, it was natural that the figure of Free Joe, simple and humble as it was, should assume undue proportions. Go where he would, do what he might, he could not escape the finger of observation and the kindling eye of suspicion. His lightest words were noted, his slightest actions marked.

Under all the circumstances it was natural that his peculiar condition should reflect itself in his habits and manners. The slaves laughed loudly day by day, but Free Joe rarely laughed. The slaves sang at their work and danced at their frolics, but no one ever heard Free Joe sing or saw him dance. There was something painfully plaintive and appealing in his attitude, something touching in his anxiety to please. He was of the friendliest nature, and seemed to be delighted when he could amuse the little children who had made a playground of the public square. At times he would please them by making his little dog Dan perform all sorts of curious tricks, or he would tell them quaint stories of the beasts of the field and birds of the air; and frequently he was coaxed into relating the story of his own freedom. That story was brief, but tragical.

In the year of our Lord 1840, when a negro speculator of a sportive turn of mind reached the little village of Hillsborough on his way to the Mississippi region, with a caravan of likely negroes of both sexes, he found much to interest him. In that day and at that time there were a number of young men in the village who had not bound themselves over to repentance for the various misdeeds of the flesh. To these young men the negro speculator (Major Frampton was his name) proceeded to address himself. He was a Virginian, he declared; and, to prove the statement, he referred all the festively inclined young men of

Hillsborough to a barrel of peach-brandy in one of his covered wagons. In the minds of these young men there was less doubt in regard to the age and quality of the brandy than there was in regard to the negro trader's birthplace. Major Frampton might or might not have been born in the Old Dominion—that was a matter of consideration and inquiry—but there could be no question as to the mellow pungency of the peach-brandy.

In his own estimation, Major Frampton was one of the most accomplished of men. He had summered at the Virginia Springs; he had been to Philadelphia, to Washington, to Richmond, to Lynchburg, and to Charleston, and had accumulated a great deal of experience which he found useful. Hillsborough was hid in the woods of Middle Georgia, and its general aspect of innocence impressed him. He looked on the young men who had shown their readiness to test his peach-brandy as overgrown country boys who needed to be introduced to some of the arts and sciences he had at his command. Thereupon the major pitched his tents, figuratively speaking, and became, for the time being, a part and parcel of the innocence that characterized Hillsborough. A wiser man would doubtless have made the same mistake.

The little village possessed advantages that seemed to be providentially arranged to fit the various enterprises that Major Frampton had in view. There was the auction block in front of the stuccoed court-house, if he desired to dispose of a few of his negroes; there was a quarter-track, laid out to his hand and in excellent order, if he chose to enjoy the pleasures of horse-racing; there were secluded pine thickets within easy reach, if he desired to indulge in the exciting pastime of cock-fighting; and various lonely and unoccupied rooms in the second story of the tavern, if he cared to challenge the chances of dice or cards.

Major Frampton tried them all with varying luck, until he began his famous game of poker with Judge Alfred Wellington, a stately gentleman with a flowing white beard and mild blue eyes that gave him the appearance of a benevolent patriarch. The history of the game in which Major Frampton and Judge Alfred Wellington took part is something more than a tradition in Hillsborough, for there are still living three or four men who sat around the table and watched its progress. It is said that at various stages of the game Major Frampton would destroy the cards with which they were playing, and send for a new pack, but the result was always the same. The mild blue eyes of Judge Wellington, with few exceptions, continued to overlook "hands" that were invincible—a habit they had acquired during a long and arduous course of training from Saratoga to New Orleans. Major Frampton lost his money, his horses, his wagons, and all his negroes but one, his body-servant. When his misfortune had reached this limit, the major adjourned the game. The sun was shining brightly, and all nature was cheerful. It is said that the major also seemed to be cheerful. However this may be, he visited the courthouse, and executed the papers that gave his body-servant his freedom. This being done, Major Frampton sauntered into a convenient pine thicket, and blew out his brains.

The negro thus freed came to be known as Free Joe. Compelled, under the law, to choose a guardian, he chose Judge Wellington, chiefly because his wife Lucinda was among the negroes won from Major Frampton. For several years Free Joe had what may be called a jovial time. His wife Lucinda was well provided for, and he found it a comparatively easy matter to provide for himself; so that, taking all the circumstances into consideration, it is not matter for astonishment that he became somewhat shiftless.

When Judge Wellington died, Free Joe's troubles began. The judge's negroes, including Lucinda, went to his half-brother, a man named Calderwood, who was a hard master and a rough customer generally—a man of many eccentricities of mind and character. His neighbors had a habit of alluding to him as "Old Spite"; and the name seemed to fit him so completely that he was known far and near as "Spite" Calderwood. He probably enjoyed the distinction the name gave him, at any rate he never resented it, and it was not often that he missed an opportunity to show that he deserved it. Calderwood's place was two or three miles from the village of Hillsborough, and Free Joe visited his wife twice a week, Wednesday and Saturday nights.

One Sunday he was sitting in front of Lucinda's cabin, when Calderwood happened to pass that way.

"Howdy, marster," said Free Joe, taking off his hat.

"Who are you?" exclaimed Calderwood abruptly, halting and staring at the negro.

"I'm name' Joe, marster. I'm Lucindy's ole man."

"Who do you belong to?"

"Marse John Evans is my gyardeen, marster."

"Big name—gyardeen. Show your pass."

Free Joe produced that document, and Calderwood read it aloud slowly, as if he found it difficult to get at the meaning:

"To whom it my concern: This is to certify that the boy Joe Frampton has my permission to visit his wife Lucinda."

This was dated at Hillsborough, and signed *"John W. Evans."*

Calderwood read it twice, and then looked at Free Joe, elevating his eyebrows, and showing his discolored teeth.

"Some mighty big words in that there. Evans owns this place, I reckon. When's he comin' down to take hold?"

Free Joe fumbled with his hat. He was badly frightened.

"Lucindy say she speck you wouldn't min' my comin', long ez I behave, marster."

Calderwood tore the pass in pieces and flung it away.

"Don't want no free niggers 'round here," he explained. "There's the big road. It'll carry you to town. Don't let me catch you here no more. Now, mind what I tell you."

Free Joe presented a shabby spectacle as he moved off with his little dog Dan slinking at his heels. It should be said in behalf of Dan, however, that his bristles were up, and that he looked back and growled. It may be that the dog had the advantage of insignificance, but it is difficult to conceive how a dog bold enough to raise his bristles under Calderwood's very eyes could be as insignificant as Free Joe. But both the negro and his little dog seemed to give a new and more dismal aspect to forlornness as they turned into the road and went toward Hillsborough.

After this incident Free Joe appeared to have clearer ideas concerning his peculiar condition. He realized the fact that though he was free he was more helpless than any slave. Having no owner, every man was his master. He knew that he was the object of suspicion, and therefore all his slender resources (ah! how pitifully slender they were!) were devoted to winning, not kindness and appreciation, but toleration; all his efforts were in the direction of mitigating the circumstances that tended to make his condition so much worse than that of the negroes around him—negroes who had friends because they had masters.

So far as his own race was concerned, Free Joe was an exile. If the slaves secretly envied him his freedom (which is to be doubted, considering his miserable condition), they openly despised him, and lost no opportunity to treat him with contumely. Perhaps this was in some measure the result of the attitude which Free Joe chose to maintain toward them. No doubt his instinct taught him that to hold himself aloof from the slaves would be to invite from the whites the toleration which he coveted, and without which even his miserable condition would be rendered more miserable still.

His greatest trouble was the fact that he was not allowed to visit his wife; but he soon found a way out of his difficulty. After he had been ordered away from the Calderwood place, he was in the habit of wandering as far in that direction as prudence would permit. Near the Calderwood place, but not on Calderwood's land, lived an old man named Micajah Staley and his sister Becky Staley. These people were old and very poor. Old Micajah had a palsied arm and hand; but, in spite of this, he managed to earn a precarious living with his turning-lathe.

When he was a slave Free Joe would have scorned these representatives of class known as poor white trash, but now he found them sympathetic and helpful in various ways. From the back door of their cabin he could hear the Calderwood negroes singing at night, and he sometimes fancied he could distinguish Lucinda's shrill treble rising above the other voices. A large poplar grew in the woods some distance from the Staley cabin, and at the foot of this tree Free Joe would sit for hours with his face turned toward Calderwood's. His little dog Dan would curl up in the leaves near by, and the two seemed to be as comfortable as possible.

One Saturday afternoon Free Joe, sitting at the foot of his friendly poplar, fell asleep. How long he slept, he could not tell; but when he awoke little Dan was licking his face, the moon was shining brightly, and Lucinda his wife stood before him laughing. The dog, seeing that Free Joe was asleep, had grown somewhat impatient, and he concluded to make an excursion to the Calderwood place on his own account. Lucinda was inclined to give the incident a twist in the direction of superstition.

"I' uz settn' down front er de fireplace," she said, "cookin' me some meat, w'en all of a sudden I year sumpin at de do'—scratch, scratch. I tuck'n tu'n de meat over, en make out I ain't year it. Bimeby it come dar 'gin—scratch, scratch. I up en open de do', I did, en, bless de Lord! dar wuz little Dan, en it look like ter me dat his ribs done grow terge'er. I gin 'im some bread, en den w'en he start out, I tuck'n foller 'im, kaze, I say ter myse'f, may be my nigger man mought be some'rs 'roun'. Dat ar little dog got sense, mon."

Free Joe laughed and dropped his hand lightly on Dan's head. For a long time after that he had no difficulty in seeing his wife. He had only to sit by the poplar tree until little Dan could run and fetch her. But after a while the other negroes discovered that Lucinda was meeting Free Joe in the woods, and information of the fact soon reached Calderwood's ears. Calderwood was what is called a man of action. He said nothing; but one day he put Lucinda in his buggy, and carried her to Macon, six miles away. He carried her to Macon, and came back without her; and nobody in or around Hillsborough, or in that section, ever saw her again.

For many a night after that Free Joe sat in the woods and waited. Little Dan would run merrily off and be gone a long time, but he always came back without Lucinda. This happened over and over again. The "willis-whistlers"[1] would call and call, like fantom huntsmen wandering on a far-off shore; the screech-owl would shake and shiver in the depths of the woods: the nighthawks, sweeping by on noiseless wings, would snap their beaks as though they enjoyed the huge joke of which Free Joe and little Dan were the victims; and the whip-poor-wills would cry to each other through the gloom. Each night seemed to be lonelier than the preceding, but Free Joe's patience was proof against loneliness. There came a time, however, when little Dan refused to go after Lucinda. When Free Joe motioned him in the direction of the Calderwood place, he would simply move about uneasily and whine; then he would curl up in the leaves and make himself comfortable.

One night, instead of going to the poplar tree to wait for Lucinda, Free Joe went to the Staley cabin, and, in order to make his welcome good, as he expressed it, he carried with him an armful of fat-pine splinters. Miss Becky Staley had a great reputation in those parts as a fortune-teller, and the schoolgirls, as well as older people, often tested her powers in this direction, some in jest and some in earnest. Free Joe placed his humble offering of lightwood in the chimney corner, and then seated himself on the steps, dropping his hat on the ground outside.

"Miss Becky," he said presently, "whar in de name er gracious you reckon Lucindy is?"

"Well, the Lord he'p the nigger!" exclaimed Miss Becky, in a tone that seemed to reproduce, by some curious agreement of sight with sound, her general aspect of peakedness. "Well, the Lord he'p the nigger! hain't you been a-seein' her all this blessed time? She's over at old Spite Calderwood's, if she's anywheres, I reckon."

"No'm, dat I ain't, Miss Becky. I ain't seen Lucindy in now gwine on mighty nigh a mont'."

"Well, it hain't a-gwine to hurt you," said Miss Becky, somewhat sharply. "In my day an' time it wuz allers took to be a bad sign when niggers got to honeyin' 'roun' an' gwine on."

"Yessum," said Free Joe, cheerfully assenting to the proposition—"yessum, dat's so, but me an' my ole 'oman, we 'uz raise terge'er, en dey ain't bin many days w'en we 'uz 'way fum one 'n'er like we is now."

"Maybe she's up an' took up wi' some un else," said Micajah Staley from the corner. "You know what the sayin' is: 'New master, new nigger.'"

"Dat's so, dat's de sayin', but tain't wid my ole 'oman like 'tis wid yuther niggers. Me en her wuz des natally raise up terge'er. Dey's lots likelier niggers dan w'at I is," said Free Joe, viewing his shabbiness with a critical eye, "but I knows Lucindy mos' good ez I does little Dan dar—dat I does."

There was no reply to this, and Free Joe continued:

"Miss Becky, I wish you please, ma'am, take en run yo' kyards en see sump'n n'er 'bout Lucindy; kaze ef she sick, I'm gwine dar. Dey ken take en take me up en gimme a stroppin', but I'm gwine dar."

Miss Becky got her cards, but first she picked up a cup, in the bottom of which were some coffee-grounds. These she whirled slowly round and round,

[1]Willets, large shore birds.

ending finally by turning the cup upside down on the hearth and allowing it to remain in that position.

"I'll turn the cup first," said Miss Becky, "and then I'll run the cards and see what they say."

As she shuffled the cards the fire on the hearth burned low, and in its fitful light the gray-haired, thin-featured woman seemed to deserve the weird reputation which rumor and gossip had given her. She shuffled the cards for some moments, gazing intently in the dying fire; then, throwing a piece of pine on the coals, she made three divisions of the pack, disposing them about in her lap. Then she took the first pile, ran the cards slowly through her fingers, and studied them carefully. To the first she added the second pile. The study of these was evidently not satisfactory. She said nothing, but frowned heavily; and the frown deepened as she added the rest of the cards until the entire fifty-two had passed in review before her. Though she frowned, she seemed to be deeply interested. Without changing the relative position of the cards, she ran them all over again. Then she threw a larger piece of pine on the fire, shuffled the cards afresh, divided them into three piles, and subjected them to the same careful and critical examination.

"I can't tell the day when I've seed the cards run this a-way," she said after a while. "What is an' wha ain't, I'll never tell you; but I know what the cards sez."

"W'at does dey say, Miss Becky?" the negro inquired, in a tone the solemnity of which was heightened by its eagerness.

"They er runnin' quare. These here that I'm a-lookin' at," said Miss Becky, "they stan' for the past. Them there, they er the present; and the t'others, they er the future. Here's a bundle"—tapping the ace of clubs with her thumb—"and here's a journey as plain as the nose on a man's face. Here's Lucinda—"

"Whar she, Miss Becky?"

"Here she is—the queen of spades."

Free Joe grinned. The idea seemed to please him immensely.

"Well, well, well!" he exclaimed. "Ef dat don't beat my time! De queen er spades! W'en Lucindy year dat hit'll tickle 'er, sho'!"

Miss Becky continued to run the cards back and forth through her fingers.

"Here's a bundle an' a journey, and here's Lucinda. An' here's ole Spite Calderwood."

She held the cards toward the negro and touched the king of clubs.

"De Lord he'p my soul!" exclaimed Free Joe with a chuckle. "De faver's dar.[2] Yesser, dat's him! W'at de matter 'long wid all un um, Miss Becky?"

The old woman added the second pile of cards to the first, and then the third, still running them through her fingers slowly and critically. By this time the piece of pine in the fireplace had wrapped itself in a mantle of flame, illuminating the cabin and throwing into strange relief the figure of Miss Becky as she sat studying the cards. She frowned ominously at the cards and mumbled a few words to herself. Then she dropped her hands in her lap and gazed once more into the fire. Her shadow danced and capered on the wall and floor behind her, as if, looking over her shoulder into the future, it could behold a rare spectacle. After a while she picked up the cup that had been turned on the hearth. The coffee-grounds, shaken around, presented what seemed to be a most intricate map.

[2] I.e., "the resemblance [favor] is there."

"Here's the journey," said Miss Becky, presently; "here's the big road, here's rivers to cross, here's the bundle to tote." She paused and sighed. "They hain't no names writ here, an' what it all means I'll never tell you. Cajy, I wish you'd be so good as to han' me my pipe."

"I hain't no hand wi' the kyards," said Cajy, as he handed the pipe, "but I reckin I can patch out your misinformation, Becky, bekaze the other day, whiles I was a-finishin' up Mizzers Perdue's rollin'-pin, I hearn a rattlin' in the road. I looked out, an' Spite Calderwood was a-driven' by in his buggy, an' thar sot Lucinda by him. It'd in-about drapt out er my min'."

Free Joe sat on the door-sill and fumbled at his hat, flinging it from one hand to the other.

"You ain't see em gwine back, is you, Mars Cajy?" he asked after a while.

"Ef they went back by this road," said Mr. Staley, with the air of one who is accustomed to weigh well his words, "it must 'a' bin enduring' of the time whiles I was asleep, bekaze I hain't bin no furder from my shop than to yon bed."

"Well, sir!" exclaimed Free Joe in an awed tone, which Mr. Staley seemed to regard as a tribute to his extraordinary powers of statement.

"Ef it's my beliefs you want," continued the old man, "I'll pitch 'em at you fair and free. My beliefs is that Spite Calderwood is gone an' took Lucindy outen the county. Bless your heart and soul! when Spite Calderwood meets the Old Boy[3] in the road they'll be a turrible scuffle. You mark what I tell you."

Free Joe, still fumbling with his hat, rose and leaned against the door-facing. He seemed to be embarrassed. Presently he said:

"I speck I better be gittin' 'long. Nex' time I see Lucindy, I'm gwine tell 'er w'at Miss Becky say 'bout de queen er spades—dat I is. Ef dat don't tickle 'er, dey ain't no nigger 'oman never bin tickle'."

He paused a moment, as though waiting for some remark or comment, some confirmation of misfortune, or, at the very least, some endorsement of his suggestion that Lucinda would be greatly pleased to know that she had figured as the queen of spades; but neither Miss Becky nor her brother said anything.

"One minnit ridin' in the buggy 'longside er Mars Spite, en de nex' high-falutin' 'roun' playin' de queen er spades. Mon, deze yer nigger gals gittin' up in de pictur's; dey sholy is."

With a brief "Good night, Miss Becky, Mars Cajy," Free Joe went out into the darkness, followed by little Dan. He made his way to the poplar, where Lucinda had been in the habit of meeting him, and sat down. He sat there a long time; he sat there until little Dan, growing restless, trotted off in the direction of the Calderwood place. Dozing against the poplar, in the gray dawn of the morning, Free Joe heard Spite Calderwood's fox-hounds in full cry a mile away.

"Shoo!" he exclaimed, scratching his head, and laughing to himself, "dem ar dogs is des a-warming' dat old fox up."

But it was Dan the hounds were after, and the little dog came back no more. Free Joe waited and waited, until he grew tired of waiting. He went back the next night and waited, and for many nights thereafter. His waiting was in vain, and yet he never regarded it as in vain. Careless and shabby as he was, Free Joe was thoughtful enough to have his theory. He was convinced that little Dan had

[3]Satan.

found Lucinda, and that some night when the moon was shining brightly through the trees, the dog would rouse him from his dreams as he sat sleeping at the foot of the poplar tree, and he would open his eyes and behold Lucinda standing over him, laughing merrily as of old; and then he thought what fun they would have about the queen of spades.

How many nights Free Joe waited at the foot of the poplar tree for Lucinda and little Dan no one can ever know. He kept no account of them, and they were not recorded by Micajah Staley nor by Miss Becky. The season ran into summer and then into fall. One night he went to the Staley cabin, cut the two old people an armful of wood, and seated himself on the doorsteps, where he rested. He was always thankful—and proud, as it seemed—when Miss Becky gave him a cup of coffee, which she was sometimes thoughtful enough to do. He was especially thankful on this particular night.

"You er still layin' off for to strike up wi' Lucindy out thar in the woods, I reckon," said Micajah Staley, smiling grimly. The situation was not without its humorous aspects.

"Oh, dey er comin', Mars Cajy, dey er comin', sho," Free Joe replied. "I boun' you dey'll come; en w'en dey does come, I'll des take en fetch um yer, whar you kin see um wid you own eyes, you en Miss Becky."

"No," said Mr. Staley, with a quick and emphatic gesture of disapproval. "Don't! don't fetch 'em anywheres. Stay right wi' 'em as long as may be."

Free Joe chuckled, and slipped away into the night, while the two old people sat gazing in the fire. Finally Micajah spoke.

"Look at that nigger; look at 'im. He's pine-blank as happy now as a killdee[4] by a mill-race. You can't faze 'em. I'd in-about give up my t'other hand ef I could stan' flat-tooted, an' grin at trouble like that there nigger."

"Niggers is niggers," said Miss Becky, smiling grimly, "an' you can't rub it out; yit I lay, I've seed a heap of white people lots meaner'n Free Joe. He grins—an' that's nigger—but I've ketched his under jaw a-tremblin' when Lucindy's name uz brung up. An' I tell you," she went on, bridling up a little, and speaking with almost fierce emphasis, "the Old Boy's done sharpened his claws for Spite Calderwood. You'll see it."

"Me, Rebecca?" said Mr. Staley, hugging his palsied arm; "me? I hope not."

"Well, you'll know it then," said Miss Becky, laughing heartily at her brother's look of alarm.

The next morning Micajah Staley had occasion to go into the woods after a piece of timber. He saw Free Joe sitting at the foot of the poplar, and the sight vexed him somewhat.

"Git up from there," he cried, "an' go an' arn your livin'. A mighty purty pass it's come to, when great big buck niggers can lie a-snorin' in the woods all day, when t'other folks is got to be up an' a-gwine.[5] Git up from there!"

Receiving no response, Mr. Staley went to Free Joe, and shook him by the shoulder; but the negro made no response. He was dead. His hat was off, his head was bent, and a smile was on his face. It was as if he had bowed and smiled when death stood before him, humble to the last. His clothes were ragged; his hands were rough and callous; his shoes were literally tied together with strings;

[4]A shore bird named after its shrill, two-syllable cry. It feeds at mud flats and shore lines, such as those along a mill-race—the canal that brings water to a mill wheel.

[5]"Going."

he was shabby in the extreme. A passer-by, glancing at him, could have no idea that such a humble creature had been summoned as a witness before the Lord God of Hosts.

1887

William Dean Howells 1837–1920

As a novelist, critic, and magazine editor, Howells was the leading spokesman of literary realism in nineteenth-century America. In an age of genteel authors, he was one of a new breed, like Twain and Hamlin Garland, raised in humble surroundings in America's midlands. Born in Ohio, the son of a printer, Howells was considered a small-town prodigy. By the age of seven he was setting type in his father's print shop, and though he had little formal education he remained throughout his life an omnivorous reader who could enjoy everything but historical novels, romantic fiction, and detective stories.

At twenty-one he became city editor of the Ohio State Journal *in Columbus. In 1860, he wrote a campaign biography of Lincoln, and after Lincoln was elected President, Howells was rewarded with appointment as American Consul in Venice, Italy. His life in Italy and his reading of Italian literature sharpened his taste for realistic writing and gave him the subject matter for a series of essays on Italian poets, four novels about Americans in Italy, and three travel books, including* Venetian Life *(1866), a collection of sketches that was reissued more than twenty times and was his most profitable book.*

With the end of the Civil War, Howells returned to America and moved to Boston, where he was appointed assistant editor and later editor-in-chief of the nation's most eminent journal, The Atlantic Monthly. *He came to know the literary "gods and half gods and quarter gods of New England," among them Lowell, who was amazed that such a book of "airy elegance" as* Venetian Life *could have been written by a man from "the rough-and-ready West."*

Howells' ten years as editor refined his critical sense, while his experiences as an outlander observing the domestic manners of the American middle class gave him the themes and events of his fiction of urban society. In 1872, he published his first novel, Their Wedding Journey, *and in 1881, having written more than a dozen books, six of them novels, Howells left the* Atlantic *and eventually settled in New York where he continued his prolific writing. He wrote over a hundred books—novels, collections of short stories, essays, autobiographies, and verse. His finest novel,* The Rise of Silas Lapham, *was published in 1885. His literary doctrines were partially "summed up" in* Criticism and Fiction *(1891), a selection of essays he had written for his column, "The Editor's Study," which appeared in* Harper's *from 1886 to 1892.*

Howells portrayed the American scene in mansions, summer resorts, railroad cars, and offices. He attempted to make his characters not heroic but "real," with all their virtues and all their "vacancy and tiresomeness." Much of his realism was external, characters and events viewed from without. His works rarely achieved, or sought to achieve, what modern critics think of as psychological depth. He dealt with proprieties. The evils of his characters were slight, their passions restrained, their triumphs few. He avoided the excitements and catastrophes of romanticism just as he avoided sex and sensuality and what he considered to be the sordid excesses of naturalism.

More than any other writer or critic, Howells brought the Age of Realism to America. His reviews and his personal attention had encouraged the development of Mark Twain, Stephen Crane, Hamlin Garland, and Frank Norris, and he helped introduce to America such famous writers as Ibsen, Dostoyevsky, and Tolstoy. Howells was called the literary symbol of his age; he received honorary degrees from Yale, Columbia, Princeton, and Oxford. Newspaper and magazine writers exalted him, among them Theodore Dreiser, who reported on Howells' climb up "Fame's Ladder." But by the early years of the century his "smiling" realism had been displaced by the naturalism and harsher realisms of the twentieth century; his vogue had passed, and he wrote to Henry James, "I am comparatively a dead cult with my statues cut down and the grass growing over me in the pale moonlight."

FURTHER READING: *The Writings of William Dean Howells,* 6 vols., 1900, now superseded by a new edition in progress: *A Selected Edition of W. D. Howells,* 41 vols. projected, ed. E. Cady, 1968–. *The Complete Plays of W. D. Howells,* ed. W. Meserve, 1960; M. Howells, *Life in Letters of William Dean Howells,* 2 vols., 1928, 1968; *A Realist in the American Theatre: Selected Drama Criticism of William Dean Howells,* ed. B. Murphy, 1992; J. Woodress, *Howells and Italy,* 1952; E. Carter, *Howells and the Age of Realism,* 1954; E. Cady, *The Road to Realism,* 1956, 1986; E. Cady, *The Realist at War,* 1958, 1986; V. Brooks, *Howells: His Life and World,* 1959; G. Bennett, *William Dean Howells,* 1968; E. Wagenknecht, *William Dean Howells: The Friendly Eye,* 1969; K. Lynn, *William Dean Howells, An American Life,* 1971; G. Bennett, *The Realism of William Dean Howells,* 1973; W. Alexander, *William Dean Howells: The Realist as Humanist,* 1981; K. Eble, *William Dean Howells,* 1982; E. Prioleau, *The Circle of Eros: Sexuality in the Work of William Dean Howells,* 1983; J. Crowley, *The Black Heart's Truth: The Early Career of William Dean Howells,* 1985; E. Nettels, *Language, Race, and Social Class in Howells' America,* 1988; J. Crowley, *The Mask of Fiction: Essays on W. D. Howells,* 1989; R. Olsen, *Dancing in Chains: The Youth of William Dean Howells,* 1991; J. Crowley, *The Dean of American Letters,* 1999; P. Abeln, *William Dean Howells and the Ends of Realism,* 2005; S. Goodwin and C. Dawson, *William Dean Howells: A Writer's Life,* 2005.

TEXT: *Between the Dark and the Daylight,* 1907.

EDITHA

The air was thick with the war feeling,[1] like the electricity of a storm which has not yet burst. Editha sat looking out into the hot spring afternoon, with her lips parted, and panting with the intensity of the question whether she could let him go. She had decided that she could not let him stay, when she saw him at the end of the still leafless avenue, making slowly up towards the house, with his head down and his figure relaxed. She ran impatiently out on the veranda, to the edge of the steps, and imperatively demanded greater haste of him with her will before she called aloud to him: "George!"

He had quickened his pace in mystical response to her mystical urgence, before he could have heard her; now he looked up and answered, "Well?"

"Oh, how united we are!" she exulted, and then she swooped down the steps to him. "What is it?" she cried.

"It's war," he said, and he pulled her up to him and kissed her.

[1]I.e., the emotions roused by the coming of the Spanish-American War (1898).

She kissed him back intensely, but irrelevantly, as to their passion, and uttered from deep in her throat, "How glorious!"

"It's war," he repeated, without consenting to her sense of it; and she did not know just what to think at first. She never knew what to think of him; that made his mystery, his charm. All through their courtship, which was contemporaneous with the growth of the war feeling, she had been puzzled by his want of seriousness about it. He seemed to despise it even more than he abhorred it. She could have understood his abhorring any sort of bloodshed; that would have been a survival of his old life when he thought he would be a minister, and before he changed and took up the law. But making light of a cause so high and noble seemed to show a want of earnestness at the core of his being. Not but that she felt herself able to cope with a congenital defect of that sort, and make his love for her save him from himself. Now perhaps the miracle was already wrought in him. In the presence of the tremendous fact that he announced, all triviality seemed to have gone out of him; she began to feel that. He sank down on the top step, and wiped his forehead with his handkerchief, while she poured out upon him her question of the origin and authenticity of his news.

All the while, in her duplex emotioning, she was aware that now at the very beginning she must put a guard upon herself against urging him, by any word or act, to take the part that her whole soul willed him to take, for the completion of her ideal of him. He was very nearly perfect as he was, and he must be allowed to perfect himself. But he was peculiar, and he might very well be reasoned out of his peculiarity. Before her reasoning went her emotioning: her nature pulling upon his nature, her womanhood upon his manhood, without her knowing the means she was using to the end she was willing. She had always supposed that the man who won her would have done something to win her; she did not know what, but something. George Gearson had simply asked her for her love, on the way home from a concert, and she gave her love to him, without, as it were, thinking. But now, it flashed upon her, if he could do something worthy to *have* won her—be a hero, *her* hero—it would be even better than if he had done it before asking her; it would be grander. Besides, she had believed in the war from the beginning.

"But don't you see, dearest," she said, "that it wouldn't have come to this if it hadn't been in the order of Providence? And I call any war glorious that is for the liberation of people who have been struggling for years against the cruelest oppression. Don't you think so, too?"

"I suppose so," he returned languidly. "But war! Is it glorious to break the peace of the world?"

"That ignoble peace! It was no peace at all, with that crime and shame at our very gates." She was conscious of parroting the current phrases of the newspapers, but it was no time to pick and choose her words. She must sacrifice anything to the high ideal she had for him, and after a good deal of rapid argument she ended with the climax: "But now it doesn't matter about the how or why. Since the war has come, all that is gone. There are no two sides any more. There is nothing now but our country."

He sat with his eyes closed and his head leant back against the veranda, and he remarked, with a vague smile, as if musing aloud, "Our country—right or wrong."[2]

[2]A phrase coined in 1816 by the American naval hero Stephen Decatur (1779–1820).

"Yes, right or wrong!" she returned, fervidly. "I'll go and get you some lemonade." She rose rustling, and whisked away; when she came back with two tall glasses of clouded liquid on a tray, and the ice clucking in them, he still sat as she had left him, and she said, as if there had been no interruption: "But there is no question of wrong in this case. I call it a sacred war. A war for liberty and humanity, if ever there was one. And I know you will see it just as I do, yet."

He took half the lemonade at a gulp, and he answered as he set the glass down: "I know you always have the highest ideal. When I differ from you I ought to doubt myself."

A generous sob rose in Editha's throat for the humility of a man, so very nearly perfect, who was willing to put himself below her.

Besides, she felt, more subliminally, that he was never so near slipping through her fingers as when he took that meek way.

"You shall not say that! Only, for once I happen to be right." She seized his hand in her two hands, and poured her soul from her eyes into his. "Don't you think so?" she entreated him.

He released his hand and drank the rest of his lemonade, and she added, "Have mine too," but he shook his head in answering, "I've no business to think so, unless I act so, too."

Her heart stopped a beat before it pulsed on with leaps that she felt in her neck. She had noticed that strange thing in men: they seemed to feel bound to do what they believed, and not think a thing was finished when they said it, as girls did. She knew what was in his mind, but she pretended not, as she said, "Oh, I am not sure," and then faltered.

He went on as if to himself, without apparently heeding her: "There's only one way of proving one's faith in a thing like this."

She could not say that she understood, but she did understand.

He went on again. "If I believed—if I felt as you do about this war—Do you wish me to feel as you do?"

Now she was really not sure; so she said: "George, I don't know what you mean."

He seemed to muse away from her as before. "There is a sort of fascination in it. I suppose that at the bottom of his heart every man would like at times to have his courage tested, to see how he would act."

"How can you talk in that ghastly way?"

"It *is* rather morbid. Still, that's what it comes to, unless you're swept away by ambition or driven by conviction. I haven't the conviction or the ambition, and the other thing is what it comes to with me. I ought to have been a preacher, after all; then I couldn't have asked it of myself, as I must, now I'm a lawyer. And you believe it's a holy war, Editha?" he suddenly addressed her. "Oh, I know you do! But you wish me to believe so, too?"

She hardly knew whether he was mocking or not, in the ironical way he always had with her plainer mind. But the only thing was to be outspoken with him.

"George, I wish you to believe whatever you think is true, at any and every cost. If I've tried to talk you into anything, I take it all back."

"Oh, I know that, Editha. I know how sincere you are, and how—I wish I had your undoubting spirit! I'll think it over; I'd like to believe as you do. But I don't, now; I don't, indeed. It isn't this war alone; though this seems peculiarly wanton and needless; but it's every war—so stupid; it makes me sick. Why shouldn't this thing have been settled reasonably?"

"Because," she said, very throatily again, "God meant it to be war."

"You think it was God? Yes, I suppose that is what people will say."

"Do you suppose it would have been war if God hadn't meant it?"

"I don't know. Sometimes it seems as if God had put this world into men's keeping to work it as they pleased."

"Now, George, that is blasphemy."

"Well, I won't blaspheme. I'll try to believe in your pocket Providence," he said, and then he rose to go.

"Why don't you stay to dinner?" Dinner at Balcom's Works was at one o'clock.

"I'll come back to supper, if you'll let me. Perhaps I shall bring you a convert."

"Well, you may come back, on that condition."

"All right. If I don't come, you'll understand."

He went away without kissing her, and she felt it a suspension of their engagement. It all interested her intensely; she was undergoing a tremendous experience, and she was being equal to it. While she stood looking after him, her mother came out through one of the long windows onto the veranda, with a catlike softness and vagueness.

"Why didn't he stay to dinner?"

"Because—because—war has been declared," Editha pronounced, without turning.

Her mother said, "Oh, my!" and then said nothing more until she had sat down in one of the large Shaker chairs[3] and rocked herself for some time. Then she closed whatever tacit passage of thought there had been in her mind with the spoken words: "Well, I hope *he* won't go."

"And *I* hope he *will,*" the girl said, and confronted her mother with a stormy exaltation that would have frightened any creature less unimpressionable than a cat.

Her mother rocked herself again for an interval of cogitation. What she arrived at in speech was: "Well, I guess you've done a wicked thing, Editha Balcom."

The girl said, as she passed indoors through the same window her mother had come out by: "I haven't done anything—yet."

In her room, she put together all her letters and gifts from Gearson, down to the withered petals of the first flower he had offered, with that timidity of his veiled in that irony of his. In the heart of the packet she enshrined her engagement ring which she had restored to the pretty box he had brought it to her in. Then she sat down, if not calmly yet strongly, and wrote:

"GEORGE:—I understood when you left me. But I think we had better emphasize your meaning that if we cannot be one in everything we had better be one in nothing. So I am sending these things for your keeping till you have made up your mind.

"I shall always love you, and therefore I shall never marry any one else. But the man I marry must love his country first of all, and be able to say to me,

> 'I could not love thee, dear, so much,
> Loved I not honor more.'[4]

[3]Furniture manufactured at Shaker religious communes and characterized by elegant simplicity.
[4]From "To Lucasta, Going to the Wars," by the English poet Richard Lovelace (1618–1658).

"There is no honor above America with me. In this great hour there is no other honor.

"Your heart will make my words clear to you. I had never expected to say so much, but it has come upon me that I must say the utmost. EDITHA."

She thought she had worded her letter well, worded it in a way that could not be bettered; all had been implied and nothing expressed.

She had it ready to send with the packet she had tied with red, white, and blue ribbon, when it occurred to her that she was not just to him, that she was not giving him a fair chance. He had said he would go and think it over, and she was not waiting. She was pushing, threatening, compelling. That was not a woman's part. She must leave him free, free, free. She could not accept for her country or herself a forced sacrifice.

In writing her letter she had satisfied the impulse from which it sprang; she could well afford to wait till he had thought it over. She put the packet and the letter by, and rested serene in the consciousness of having done what was laid upon her by her love itself to do, and yet used patience, mercy, justice.

She had her reward. Gearson did not come to tea, but she had given him till morning, when, late at night there came up from the village the sound of a fife and drum, with a tumult of voices, in shouting, singing, and laughing. The noise drew nearer and nearer; it reached the street end of the avenue; there it silenced itself, and one voice, the voice she knew best, rose over the silence. It fell; the air was filled with cheers; the fife and drum struck up, with the shouting, singing, and laughing again, but now retreating; and a single figure came hurrying up the avenue.

She ran down to meet her lover and clung to him. He was very gay, and he put his arm round her with a boisterous laugh. "Well, you must call me Captain now; or Cap, if you prefer; that's what the boys call me. Yes, we've had a meeting at the town-hall, and everybody has volunteered; and they selected me for captain, and I'm going to the war, the big war, the glorious war, the holy war ordained by the pocket Providence that blesses butchery. Come along; let's tell the whole family about it. Call them from their downy beds, father, mother, Aunt Hitty, and all the folks!"

But when they mounted the veranda steps he did not wait for a larger audience; he poured the story out upon Editha alone.

"There was a lot of speaking, and then some of the fools set up a shout for me. It was all going one way, and I thought it would be a good joke to sprinkle a little cold water on them. But you can't do that with a crowd that adores you. The first thing I knew I was sprinkling hell-fire on them. 'Cry havoc, and let slip the dogs of war.'[5] That was the style. Now that it had come to the fight, there were no two parties; there was one country, and the thing was to fight to a finish as quick as possible. I suggested volunteering then and there, and I wrote my name first of all on the roster. Then they elected me—that's all. I wish I had some ice-water."

She left him walking up and down the veranda, while she ran for the ice-pitcher and a goblet, and when she came back he was still walking up and down, shouting the story he had told her to her father and mother, who had come out more sketchily dressed than they commonly were by day. He drank goblet after

[5]From Shakespeare's *Julius Caesar,* Act III, Scene i, line 273.

goblet of the ice-water without noticing who was giving it, and kept on talking, and laughing through his talk wildly. "It's astonishing," he said, "how well the worse reason looks when you try to make it appear the better. Why, I believe I was the first convert to the war in that crowd to-night! I never thought I should like to kill a man; but now I shouldn't care; and the smokeless powder lets you see the man drop that you kill. It's all for the country! What a thing it is to have a country that *can't* be wrong, but if it is, is right, anyway!"

Editha had a great, vital thought, an inspiration. She set down the ice-pitcher on the veranda floor, and ran up-stairs and got the letter she had written him. When at last he noisily bade her father and mother, "Well, good-night. I forgot I woke you up; I sha'n't want any sleep myself," she followed him down the avenue to the gate. There, after the whirling words that seemed to fly away from her thoughts and refuse to serve them, she made a last effort to solemnize the moment that seemed so crazy, and pressed the letter she had written upon him.

"What's this?" he said. "Want me to mail it?"

"No, no. It's for you. I wrote it after you went this morning. Keep it—keep it—and read it sometime—" She thought, and then her inspiration came: "Read it if ever you doubt what you've done, or fear that I regret your having done it. Read it after you've started."

They strained each other in embraces that seemed as ineffective as their words, and he kissed her face with quick, hot breaths that were so unlike him, that made her feel as if she had lost her old lover and found a stranger in his place. The stranger said: "What a gorgeous flower you are, with your red hair, and your blue eyes that look black now, and your face with the color painted out by the white moonshine! Let me hold you under the chin, to see whether I love blood, you tiger-lily!" Then he laughed Gearson's laugh, and released her, scared and giddy. Within her wilfulness she had been frightened by a sense of subtler force in him, and mystically mastered as she had never been before.

She ran all the way back to the house, and mounted the steps panting. Her mother and father were talking of the great affair. Her mother said: "Wa'n't Mr. Gearson in rather of an excited state of mind? Didn't you think he acted curious?"

"Well, not for a man who'd just been elected captain and had set 'em up for the whole of Company A," her father chuckled back.

"What in the world do you mean, Mr. Balcom? Oh! There's Editha!" She offered to follow the girl indoors.

"Don't come, mother!" Editha called, vanishing.

Mrs. Balcom remained to reproach her husband. "I don't see much of anything to laugh at."

"Well, it's catching. Caught it from Gearson. I guess it won't be much of a war, and I guess Gearson don't think so, either. The other fellows will back down as soon as they see we mean it. I wouldn't lose any sleep over it. I'm going back to bed, myself."

Gearson came again next afternoon, looking pale and rather sick, but quite himself, even to his languid irony. "I guess I'd better tell you, Editha, that I consecrated myself to your god of battles last night by pouring too many libations to him down my own throat. But I'm all right now. One has to carry off the excitement, somehow."

"Promise me," she commanded, "that you'll never touch it again!"

"What! Not let the cannikin clink? Not let the soldier drink?[6] Well, I promise."

"You don't belong to yourself now; you don't even belong to *me*. You belong to your country, and you have a sacred charge to keep yourself strong and well for your country's sake. I have been thinking, thinking all night and all day long."

"You look as if you had been crying a little, too," he said, with his queer smile.

"That's all past. I've been thinking, and worshipping *you*. Don't you suppose I know all that you've been through, to come to this? I've followed you every step from your old theories and opinions."

"Well, you've had a long row to hoe."

"And I know you've done this from the highest motives—"

"Oh, there won't be much pettifogging[7] to do till this cruel war is—"

"And you haven't simply done it for my sake. I couldn't respect you if you had."

"Well, then we'll say I haven't. A man that hasn't got his own respect intact wants the respect of all the other people he can corner. But we won't go into that. I'm in for the thing now, and we've got to face our future. My idea is that this isn't going to be a very protracted struggle; we shall just scare the enemy to death before it comes to a fight at all. But we must provide for contingencies, Editha. If anything happens to me—"

"Oh, George!" She clung to him, sobbing.

"I don't want you to feel foolishly bound to my memory. I should hate that, wherever I happened to be."

"I am yours, for time and eternity—time and eternity." She liked the words; they satisfied her famine for phrases.

"Well, say eternity; that's all right; but time's another thing; and I'm talking about time. But there is something! My mother! If anything happens—"

She winced, and he laughed. "You're not the bold soldier-girl of yesterday!"

Then he sobered. "If anything happens, I want you to help my mother out. She won't like my doing this thing. She brought me up to think war a fool thing as well as a bad thing. My father was in the Civil War; all through it; lost his arm in it." She thrilled with the sense of the arm round her; what if that should be lost? He laughed as if divining her: "Oh, it doesn't run in the family, as far as I know!" Then he added, gravely: "He came home with misgivings about war, and they grew on him. I guess he and mother agreed between them that I was to be brought up in his final mind about it; but that was before my time. I only knew him from my mother's report of him and his opinions; I don't know whether they were hers first; but they were hers last. This will be a blow to her. I shall have to write and tell her—"

He stopped, and she asked: "Would you like me to write, too, George?"

"I don't believe that would do. No, I'll do the writing. She'll understand a little if I say that I thought the way to minimize it was to make war on the largest possible scale at once—that I felt I must have been helping on the war somehow if I hadn't helped keep it from coming, and I knew I hadn't; when it came, I had no right to stay out of it."

Whether his sophistries satisfied him or not, they satisfied her. She clung to his breast, and whispered, with closed eyes and quivering lips: "Yes, yes, yes!"

[6]Adapted from Shakespeare's *Othello,* Act II, Scene iii, lines 71–75.

[7]Quibbling, bickering.

"But if anything should happen, you might go to her and see what you could do for her. You know? It's rather far off; she can't leave her chair—"

"Oh, I'll go, if it's the ends of the earth! But nothing will happen! Nothing *can!* I—"

She felt herself lifted with his rising, and Gearson was saying, with his arm still round her, to her father: "Well, we're off at once, Mr. Balcom. We're to be formally accepted at the capital, and then bunched up with the rest somehow, and sent into camp somewhere, and got to the front as soon as possible. We all want to be in the van,[8] of course; we're the first company to report to the Governor. I came to tell Editha, but I hadn't got round to it."

She saw him again for a moment at the capital, in the station, just before the train started southward with his regiment. He looked well, in his uniform, and very soldierly, but somehow girlish, too, with his clean-shaven face and slim figure. The manly eyes and the strong voice satisfied her, and his preoccupation with some unexpected details of duty flattered her. Other girls were weeping and bemoaning themselves, but she felt a sort of noble distinction in the abstraction, the almost unconsciousness, with which they parted. Only at the last moment he said: "Don't forget my mother. It mayn't be such a walk-over as I supposed," and he laughed at the notion.

He waved his hand to her as the train moved off—she knew it among a score of hands that were waved to other girls from the platform of the car, for it held a letter which she knew was hers. Then he went inside the car to read it, doubtless, and she did not see him again. But she felt safe for him through the strength of what she called her love. What she called her God, always speaking the name in a deep voice and with the implication of a mutual understanding, would watch over him and keep him and bring him back to her. If with an empty sleeve, then he should have three arms instead of two, for both of hers should be his for life. She did not see, though, why she should always be thinking of the arm his father had lost.

There were not many letters from him, but they were such as she could have wished, and she put her whole strength into making hers such as she imagined he could have wished, glorifying and supporting him. She wrote to his mother glorifying him as their hero, but the brief answer she got was merely to the effect that Mrs. Gearson was not well enough to write herself, and thanking her for her letter by the hand of some one who called herself "Yrs truly, Mrs. W. J. Andrews."

Editha determined not to be hurt, but to write again quite as if the answer had been all she expected. Before it seemed as if she could have written, there came news of the first skirmish, and in the list of the killed, which was telegraphed as a trifling loss on our side, was Gearson's name. There was a frantic time of trying to make out that it might be, must be, some other Gearson; but the name and the company and the regiment and the State were too definitely given.

Then there was a lapse into depths out of which it seemed as if she never could rise again; then a lift into clouds far above all grief, black clouds, that blotted out the sun, but where she soared with him, with George—George! She had the fever that she expected of herself, but she did not die in it; she was not

[8]Vanguard, forefront.

even delirious, and it did not last long. When she was well enough to leave her bed, her one thought was of George's mother, of his strangely worded wish that she should go to her and see what she could do for her. In the exaltation of the duty laid upon her—it buoyed her up instead of burdening her—she rapidly recovered.

Her father went with her on the long railroad journey from northern New York to western Iowa; he had business out at Davenport, and he said he could just as well go then as any other time; and he went with her to the little country town where George's mother lived in a little house on the edge of the illimitable cornfields, under trees pushed to a top of the rolling prairie. George's father had settled there after the Civil War, as so many other old soldiers had done; but they were Eastern people, and Editha fancied touches of the East in the June rose overhanging the front door, and the garden with early summer flowers stretching from the gate of the paling fence.

It was very low inside the house, and so dim, with the closed blinds, that they could scarcely see one another: Editha tall and black in her crapes which filled the air with smell of their dyes; her father standing decorously apart with his hat on his forearm, as at funerals; a woman rested in a deep armchair, and the woman who had let the strangers in stood behind the chair.

The seated woman turned her head round and up, and asked the woman behind her chair: "*Who* did you say?"

Editha, if she had done what she expected of herself, would have gone down on her knees at the feet of the seated figure and said, "I am George's Editha," for answer.

But instead of her own voice she heard that other woman's voice saying: "Well, I don't know as I *did* get the name just right. I guess I'll have to make a little more light in here," and she went and pushed two of the shutters ajar.

Then Editha's father said, in his public will-now-address-a-few-remarks tone: "My name is Balcom, ma'am—Junius H. Balcom, of Balcom's Works. New York: my daughter—"

"Oh!" the seated woman broke in, with a powerful voice, the voice that always surprised Editha from Gearson's slender frame. "Let me see you. Stand round where the light can strike your face," and Editha dumbly obeyed. "So, you're Editha Balcom," she sighed.

"Yes," Editha said, more like a culprit than a comforter.

"What did you come for?" Mrs. Gearson asked.

Editha's face quivered and her knees shook. "I came—because—because George—" She could go no further.

"Yes," the mother said, "he told me he had asked you to come if he got killed. You didn't expect that, I suppose, when you sent him."

"I would rather have died myself than done it!" Editha said, with more truth in her deep voice than she ordinarily found in it. "I tried to leave him free—"

"Yes, that letter of yours, that came back with his other things, left him free."

Editha saw now where George's irony came from.

"It was not to be read before—unless—until—I told him so," she faltered.

"Of course, he wouldn't read a letter of yours, under the circumstances, till he thought you wanted him to. Been sick?" the woman abruptly demanded.

"Very sick," Editha said, with self-pity.

"Daughter's life," her father interposed, "was almost despaired of, at one time."

Mrs. Gearson gave him no heed. "I suppose you would have been glad to die, such a brave person as you! I don't believe *he* was glad to die. He was always a timid boy, that way; he was afraid of a good many things; but if he was afraid he did what he made up his mind to. I suppose he made up his mind to go, but I knew what it cost him by what it cost me when I heard of it. I had been through *one* war before. When you sent him you didn't expect he would get killed."

The voice seemed to compassionate Editha, and it was time. "No," she huskily murmured.

"No, girls don't; women don't when they give their men up to their country. They think they'll come marching back, somehow, just as gay as they went, or if it's an empty sleeve, or even an empty pantaloon, it's all the more glory, and they're so much the prouder of them, poor things!"

The tears began to run down Editha's face; she had not wept till then; but it was now such a relief to be understood that the tears came.

"No, you didn't expect him to get killed," Mrs. Gearson repeated, in a voice which was startlingly like George's again. "You just expected him to kill some one else, some of those foreigners, that weren't there because they had any say about it, but because they had to be there, poor wretches—conscripts, or whatever they call 'em. You thought it would be all right for my George, *your* George, to kill the sons of those miserable mothers and the husbands of those girls that you would never see the faces of." The woman lifted her powerful voice in a psalmlike note. "I thank my God he didn't live to do it! I thank my God they killed him first, and that he ain't livin' with their blood on his hands!" She dropped her eyes, which she had raised with her voice, and glared at Editha. "What you got that black on for?" She lifted herself by her powerful arms so high that her helpless body seemed to hang limp its full length. "Take it off, take it off, before I tear it from your back!"

The lady who was passing the summer near Balcom's Works was sketching Editha's beauty, which lent itself wonderfully to the effects of a colorist. It had come to that confidence which is rather apt to grow between artist and sitter, and Editha had told her everything.

"To think of your having such a tragedy in your life!" the lady said. She added: "I suppose there are people who feel that way about war. But when you consider the good this war has done—how much it has done for the country! I can't understand such people, for my part. And when you had come all the way out there to console her—got up out of a sick-bed! Well!"

"I think," Editha said, magnanimously, "she wasn't quite in her right mind; and so did papa."

"Yes," the lady said, looking at Editha's lips in nature and then at her lips in art, and giving an empirical touch to them in the picture. "But how dreadful of her! How perfectly—excuse me—how *vulgar!*"

A light broke upon Editha in the darkness which she felt she had been without a gleam of brightness for weeks and months. The mystery that had bewildered her was solved by the word; and from that moment she rose from grovelling in shame and self-pity, and began to live again in the ideal.

1905

Henry James 1843–1916

Like one of his own characters, Henry James was an artist reconnoitering society, a "passionate pilgrim" in search of experience. His intense perceptions of life undoubtedly owed much to his unusual upbringing. James's wealthy father provided his children with tutors and took them back and forth across the Atlantic to give them a European education and expose them to international society. As a youth, James lived in New York, Geneva, London, Paris, and Newport, Rhode Island, where he and his brother William, who later became a distinguished philosopher and psychologist, studied art and enjoyed the society of their American cousins and the children of their wealthy neighbors.

In 1862, James entered Harvard Law School but soon withdrew and embarked on a literary career. He published his first short story in 1864 at the age of twenty-one. In the next decade, spent alternately in America and Europe, he came under the influence of Flaubert, Turgenev, and Balzac.

In 1871, the Atlantic *serialized James's first novel,* Watch and Ward, *with which he hoped, but failed, to achieve fame. Years later, looking back and finding such early works "hideous," James preferred to declare that his first real novel was* Roderick Hudson *(1875). In 1876, when he was thirty-three, James settled permanently in England and, except for one long visit to the United States, remained in Europe for the rest of his life. The next decade saw the appearance of novels that brought him popular success:* The American *(1877), with its "international" theme of the traditionless American confronting the complexity of European life;* Daisy Miller *(1878), which one American critic described as "an outrage to American girlhood" but which brought James his first international fame; and* The Portrait of a Lady *(1881), the finest example of James's early work.*

The most ambitious novels of James's second period, The Bostonians *(1886),* The Princess Casamassima *(1886), and* The Tragic Muse *(1890), were failures with the public, as were his attempts, in the 1890s, to write for the stage. But James continued to write short stories and novels, and while he never recovered his early popularity, his last novels,* The Wings of the Dove *(1902),* The Ambassadors *(1903), and* The Golden Bowl *(1904), exemplify the mature and formidable style of a third literary period, which critics have come to praise as "The Major Phase."*

In 1915, James, the American expatriate, became a British subject, largely to show his support for the British cause in the First World War. His gesture was his last noteworthy symbolic achievement, for seven months later (February 1916) he died. At the time of his death, James's audience was small. Few of his works remained in print. His writing was no longer in vogue, especially in his native land where he was criticized as anti-American for portraying his fellow Americans as crass and shallow.

Readers in both England and America objected to the narrow emotional and social range of characters drawn from "the hothouse life of the leisured classes." And James was criticized, even parodied, for the obscure and costive style of his final period—a style capable of expressing great subtleties, but based on the assumption that the reader was as well-educated, as heedful of implications, and as unhurried as the author himself. James's mannered works were dismissed as "cathedrals of frosted glass," and at the end of his life James himself was forced to acknowledge that his writing had become "insurmountably unsaleable."

But unlike his contemporary Howells, James was to have his greatest influence not on his own age but on the age that followed. And since the 1930s and 1940s, his influence on writers and readers of modern fiction has grown to be immense. His twenty-two novels and over a hundred short stories, and his critical commentaries, are seen as major contributions to the art of fiction itself, helping to free the novel from its alliances with journalism and romantic storytelling. And he has come to be called the "first of the modern psychological novelists" because his novels and stories of men and women confronting complex society are chronicles of the psychological perceptions that James himself defined as the highest form of experience.

FURTHER READING: *The Complete Tales of Henry James,* 12 vols., ed. L. Edel, 1962–1965; *The Tales of Henry James,* 3 vols., ed. M. Aziz, 1973—; *The Complete Plays of Henry James,* ed. L. Edel, 1949, 1990; *The Complete Notebooks of Henry James,* ed. L. Edel and L. Powers, 1987; *The Letters of Henry James,* 4 vols., ed. L. Edel, 1975–1984; F. Mattheissen, *Henry James: The Major Phase,* 1944; F. Dupee, *Henry James,* 1951, 1956, 1965; L. Edel, *Henry James,* 5 vols., 1953–1972, 2 vols., 1977, 1 vol., 1985; S. Novick, *Henry James: The Young Master,* 1996; F. Crews, *The Tragedy of Manners: Moral Drama in the Later Novels of Henry James,* 1957; O. Cargill, *Novels of Henry James,* 1961; C. Anderson, *Person, Place, and Thing in Henry James's Novels,* 1977; S. Kappeler, *Writing and Reading in Henry James,* 1980; D. Fogel, *Henry James and the Structure of the Romantic Imagination,* 1981; R. Norrman, *The Insecure World of Henry James's Fiction,* 1982; E. Wagenknecht, *The Novels of Henry James,* 1983; A. Margolis, *Henry James and the Problem of Audience,* 1985; *Critical Essays on Henry James: The Early Novels,* ed. J. Gargano, 1987; *Critical Essays on Henry James: The Late Novels,* ed. J. Gargano, 1987; D. Smit, *The Language of a Master,* 1988; S. Mizruchi, *The Power of Historical Knowledge,* 1988; R. Gale, *A Henry James Encyclopedia,* 1989; S. Cameron, *Thinking in Henry James,* 1989; R. Hocks, *Henry James,* 1990; M. Bell, *Meaning in Henry James,* 1990; P. Horne, *Henry James and Revision,* 1991; A Tinter, *The Cosmopolitan World of Henry James,* 1991; *Henry James: A Reference Guide,* 1975–1987, ed. J. Funston, 1991; J. Woolf, *Henry James: The Major Novels,* 1991; R. Posnock, *The Trial of Curiosity: Henry James, William James, and the Challenge of Modernity,* 1991; I. Bell, *Henry James and the Past,* 1991; F. Kaplan, *Henry James: The Imagination of Genius,* 1992; *A Companion to Henry James Studies,* ed. D. Fogel, 1993; R. Jolly, *Henry James: History, Narrative, Fiction,* 1993. S. Teahan, *The Rhetorical Logic of Henry James,* 1995; *Henry James: The Contemporary Reviews,* ed. K. Hayes, 1996; S. Blair, *Henry James and the Writing of Race and Nation,* 1996; L. Gordon, *A Private Life of Henry James,* 1999; J. Tambling, *Henry James,* 2000; R. Pippin, *Henry James and Modern Moral Life,* 2001; T. Hadley, *Henry James and the Imagination of Pleasure,* 2002; E. Harden, *A Henry James Chronology,* 2005.

TEXTS: *Daisy Miller, Cornhill Magazine,* June–July, 1878; "The Real Thing," and "The Beast in the Jungle," *The Novels and Tales of Henry James,* New York Edition, 26 vols., 1907–1917.

DAISY MILLER: A STUDY[1]

PART I

At the little town of Vevey, in Switzerland, there is a particularly comfortable hotel. There are, indeed, many hotels; for the entertainment of tourists is the business of the place, which, as many travellers will remember, is seated upon the edge of a remarkably blue lake[2]—a lake that it behoves every tourist to visit. The shore of the lake presents an unbroken array of establishments of this

[1]First published in *Cornhill Magazine,* June–July 1878 (the text presented here) and later revised by James in 1909 for inclusion in *The Novels and Tales of Henry James,* New York Edition, 26 vols., 1907–1909, 1917.

[2]Lake Geneva.

order, of every category, from the "grand hotel" of the newest fashion, with a chalk-white front, a hundred balconies, and a dozen flags flying from its roof, to the little Swiss *pension*[3] of an elder day, with its name inscribed in German-looking lettering upon a pink or yellow wall, and an awkward summerhouse in the angle of the garden. One of the hotels of Vevey, however, is famous, even classical, being distinguished from many of its upstart neighbours by an air both of luxury and of maturity. In this region, in the month of June, American travellers are extremely numerous; it may be said, indeed, that Vevey assumes at this period some of the characteristics of an American watering-place. There are sights and sounds which evoke a vision, an echo, of Newport and Saratoga.[4] There is a flitting hither and thither of "stylish" young girls, a rustling of muslin flounces, a rattle of dance-music in the morning hours, a sound of high-pitched voices at all times. You receive an impression of these things at the excellent inn of the "Trois Couronnes,"[5] and are transported in fancy to the Ocean House or to Congress Hall.[6] But at the "Trois Couronnes," it must be added, there are other features that are much at variance with these suggestions: neat German waiters, who look like secretaries of legation; Russian princesses sitting in the garden; little Polish boys walking about, held by the hand, with their governors; a view of the sunny crest of the Dent du Midi[7] and the picturesque towers of the Castle of Chillon.[8]

I hardly know whether it was the analogies or the differences that were uppermost in the mind of a young American, who, two or three years ago, sat in the garden of the "Trois Couronnes," looking about him, rather idly, at some of the graceful objects I have mentioned. It was a beautiful summer morning, and in whatever fashion the young American looked at things, they must have seemed to him charming. He had come from Geneva the day before, by the little steamer, to see his aunt, who was staying at the hotel—Geneva having been for a long time his place of residence. But his aunt had a headache—his aunt had almost always a headache—and now she was shut up in her room, smelling camphor, so that he was at liberty to wander about. He was some seven-and-twenty years of age; when his friends spoke of him, they usually said that he was at Geneva, "studying." When his enemies spoke of him they said—but, after all, he had no enemies; he was an extremely amiable fellow, and universally liked. What I should say is, simply, that when certain persons spoke of him they affirmed the reason of his spending so much time at Geneva was that he was extremely devoted to a lady who lived there—a foreign lady—a person older than himself. Very few Americans—indeed I think none—had ever seen this lady, about whom there were some singular stories. But Winterbourne had an old attachment for the little metropolis of Calvinism;[9] he had been put to school there as a boy, and he had afterwards gone to college there—circumstances which had led to his forming a great many youthful friendships. Many of these he had kept, and they were a source of great satisfaction to him.

[3]A residential hotel.
[4]Newport, Rhode Island, and Saratoga Springs, New York, fashionable nineteenth-century American summer resorts.
[5]French: "Three Crowns." [6]Resort hotels at Newport and Saratoga.
[7]Mountain peak in the Swiss Alps, south of Vevey.
[8]Thirteenth-century castle on Lake Geneva, the setting for Byron's poem "The Prisoner of Chillon" (1816).
[9]The Protestant reformer John Calvin (1509–1564) lived in Geneva (1541–1564).

After knocking at his aunt's door and learning that she was indisposed, he had taken a walk about the town, and then he had come in to his breakfast. He had now finished his breakfast; but he was drinking a small cup of coffee, which had been served to him on a little table in the garden by one of the waiters who looked like an *attaché*.[10] At last he finished his coffee and lit a cigarette. Presently a small boy came walking along the path—an urchin of nine or ten. The child, who was diminutive for his years, had an aged expression of countenance, a pale complexion, and sharp little features. He was dressed in knickerbockers, with red stockings, which displayed his poor little spindleshanks;[11] he also wore a brilliant red cravat. He carried in his hand a long alpenstock,[12] the sharp point of which he thrust into everything that he approached—the flower-beds, the garden-benches, the trains of the ladies' dresses. In front of Winterbourne he paused, looking at him with a pair of bright, penetrating little eyes.

"Will you give me a lump of sugar?" he asked, in a sharp, hard little voice—a voice immature, and yet, somehow, not young.

Winterbourne glanced at the small table near him, on which his coffee-service rested, and saw that several morsels of sugar remained. "Yes, you may take one," he answered; "but I don't think sugar is good for little boys."

The little boy stepped forward and carefully selected three of the coveted fragments, two of which he buried in the pocket of his knickerbockers, depositing the other as promptly in another place. He poked his alpenstock, lance-fashion, into Winterbourne's bench, and tried to crack the lump of sugar with his teeth.

"Oh, blazes; it's har-r-d!" he exclaimed, pronouncing the adjective in a peculiar manner.

Winterbourne had immediately perceived that he might have the honour of claiming him as a fellow-countryman. "Take care you don't hurt your teeth," he said, paternally.

"I haven't got any teeth to hurt. They have all come out. I have only got seven teeth. My mother counted them last night, and one came out right afterwards. She said she'd slap me if any more came out. I can't help it. It's this old Europe. It's the climate that makes them come out. In America they didn't come out. It's these hotels."

Winterbourne was much amused. "If you eat three lumps of sugar, your mother will certainly slap you," he said.

"She's got to give me some candy, then," rejoined his young interlocutor. "I can't get any candy here—any American candy. American candy's the best candy."

"And are American little boys the best little boys?" asked Winterbourne.

"I don't know. I'm an American boy," said the child.

"I see you are one of the best!" laughed Winterbourne.

"Are you an American man?" pursued this vivacious infant. And then, on Winterbourne's affirmative reply—"American men are the best," he declared.

His companion thanked him for the compliment; and the child, who had now got astride of his alpenstock, stood looking about him, while he attacked a second lump of sugar. Winterbourne wondered if he himself had been like this in his infancy, for he had been brought to Europe at about this age.

[10]A minor diplomat, one who is "attached" to an embassy. [11]Legs.
[12]A long staff with a metal point, used in mountain climbing.

"Here comes my sister!" cried the child, in a moment. "She's an American girl."

Winterbourne looked along the path and saw a beautiful young lady advancing. "American girls are the best girls," he said, cheerfully, to his young companion.

"My sister ain't the best!" the child declared. "She's always blowing[13] at me."

"I imagine that is your fault, not hers," said Winterbourne. The young lady meanwhile had drawn near. She was dressed in white muslin, with a hundred frills and flounces, and knots of pale-coloured ribbon. She was bare-headed; but she balanced in her hand a large parasol, with a deep border of embroidery; and she was strikingly, admirably pretty. "How pretty they are!" thought Winterbourne, straightening himself in his seat, as if he were prepared to rise.

The young lady paused in front of his bench, near the parapet of the garden, which overlooked the lake. The little boy had now converted his alpenstock into a vaulting-pole, by the aid of which he was springing about in the gravel, and kicking it up not a little.

"Randolph," said the young lady, "what *are* you doing?"

"I'm going up the Alps," replied Randolph. "This is the way!" And he gave another little jump, scattering the pebbles about Winterbourne's ears.

"That's the way they come down," said Winterbourne.

"He's an American man!" cried Randolph, in his little hard voice.

The young lady gave no heed to this announcement, but looked straight at her brother. "Well, I guess you had better be quiet," she simply observed.

It seemed to Winterbourne that he had been in a manner presented. He got up and stepped slowly towards the young girl, throwing away his cigarette. "This little boy and I have made acquaintance," he said, with great civility. In Geneva, as he had been perfectly aware, a young man was not at liberty to speak to a young unmarried lady except under certain rarely-occurring conditions; but here at Vevey, what conditions could be better than these?—a pretty American girl coming and standing in front of you in a garden. This pretty American girl, however, on hearing Winterbourne's observation, simply glanced at him; she then turned her head and looked over the parapet, at the lake and the opposite mountains. He wondered whether he had gone too far; but he decided that he must advance farther, rather than retreat. While he was thinking of something else to say, the young lady turned to the little boy again.

"I should like to know where you got that pole," she said.

"I bought it!" responded Randolph.

"You don't mean to say you're going to take it to Italy."

"Yes, I am going to take it to Italy!" the child declared.

The young girl glanced over the front of her dress, and smoothed out a knot or two of ribbon. Then she rested her eyes upon the prospect again. "Well, I guess you had better leave it somewhere," she said, after a moment.

"Are you going to Italy?" Winterbourne inquired, in a tone of great respect.

The young lady glanced at him again. "Yes, sir," she replied. And she said nothing more.

"Are you—a—going over the Simplon?"[14] Winterbourne pursued, a little embarrassed.

[13]Fussing, nagging. [14]Mountain pass between Switzerland and Italy.

"I don't know," she said. "I suppose it's some mountain. Randolph, what mountain are we going over?"

"Going where?" the child demanded.

"To Italy," Winterbourne explained.

"I don't know," said Randolph. "I don't want to go to Italy. I want to go to America."

"Oh, Italy is a beautiful place!" rejoined the young man.

"Can you get candy there?" Randolph loudly inquired.

"I hope not," said his sister. "I guess you have had enough candy, and mother thinks so too."

"I haven't had any for ever so long—for a hundred weeks!" cried the boy, still jumping about.

The young lady inspected her flounces and smoothed her ribbons again; and Winterbourne presently risked an observation upon the beauty of the view. He was ceasing to be embarrassed, for he had begun to perceive that she was not in the least embarrassed herself. There had not been the slightest alteration in her charming complexion; she was evidently neither offended nor fluttered. If she looked another way when he spoke to her, and seemed not particularly to hear him, this was simply her habit, her manner. Yet, as he talked a little more, and pointed out some of the objects of interest in the view, with which she appeared quite unacquainted, she gradually gave him more of the benefit of her glance; and then he saw that this glance was perfectly direct and unshrinking. It was not, however, what would have been called an immodest glance, for the young girl's eyes were singularly honest and fresh. They were wonderfully pretty eyes; and, indeed, Winterbourne had not seen for a long time anything prettier than his fair countrywoman's various features—her complexion, her nose, her ears, her teeth. He had a great relish for feminine beauty; he was addicted to observing and analysing it; and as regards this young lady's face he made several observations. It was not at all insipid, but it was not exactly expressive; and though it was eminently delicate Winterbourne mentally accused it—very forgivingly—of a want of finish. He thought it very possible that Master Randolph's sister was a coquette;[15] he was sure she had a spirit of her own; but in her bright, sweet, superficial little visage there was no mockery, no irony. Before long it became obvious that she was much disposed towards conversation. She told him that they were going to Rome for the winter—she and her mother and Randolph. She asked him if he was a "real American;" she shouldn't have taken him for one; he seemed more like a German—this was said after a little hesitation, especially when he spoke. Winterbourne, laughing, answered that he had met Germans who spoke like Americans; but that he had not, so far as he remembered, met an American who spoke like a German. Then he asked her if she should not be more comfortable in sitting upon the bench which he had just quitted. She answered that she liked standing up and walking about; but she presently sat down. She told him she was from New York State—"if you know where that is." Winterbourne learned more about her by catching hold of her small, slippery brother and making him stand a few minutes by his side.

"Tell me your name, my boy," he said.

[15]A flirtatious tease.

"Randolph C. Miller," said the boy, sharply. "And I'll tell you her name;" and he levelled his alpenstock at his sister.

"You had better wait till you are asked!" said this young lady, calmly.

"I should like very much to know your name," said Winterbourne.

"Her name is Daisy Miller!" cried the child. "But that isn't her real name; that isn't her name on her cards."

"It's a pity you haven't got one of my cards!" said Miss Miller.

"Her real name is Annie P. Miller," the boy went on.

"Ask him *his* name," said his sister, indicating Winterbourne.

But on this point Randolph seemed perfectly indifferent; he continued to supply information with regard to his own family. "My father's name is Ezra B. Miller," he announced. "My father ain't in Europe; my father's in a better place than Europe."

Winterbourne imagined for a moment that this was the manner in which the child had been taught to intimate that Mr. Miller had been removed to the sphere of celestial rewards. But Randolph immediately added, "My father's in Schenectady. He's got a big business. My father's rich, you bet."

"Well!" ejaculated Miss Miller, lowering her parasol and looking at the embroidered border. Winterbourne presently released the child, who departed, dragging his alpenstock along the path. "He doesn't like Europe," said the young girl. "He wants to go back."

"To Schenectady, you mean?"

"Yes; he wants to go right home. He hasn't got any boys here. There is one boy here, but he always goes round with a teacher; they won't let him play."

"And your brother hasn't any teacher?" Winterbourne inquired.

"Mother thought of getting him one, to travel round with us. There was a lady told her of a very good teacher; an American lady—perhaps you know her—Mrs. Sanders. I think she came from Boston. She told her of this teacher, and we thought of getting him to travel round with us. But Randolph said he didn't want a teacher travelling round with us. He said he wouldn't have lessons when he was in the cars.[16] And we *are* in the cars about half the time. There was an English lady we met in the cars—I think her name was Miss Featherstone; perhaps you know her. She wanted to know why I didn't give Randolph lessons—give him "instruction," she called it. I guess he could give me more instruction than I could give him. He's very smart."

"Yes," said Winterbourne; "he seems very smart."

"Mother's going to get a teacher for him as soon as we get to Italy. Can you get good teachers in Italy?"

"Very good, I should think," said Winterbourne.

"Or else she's going to find some school. He ought to learn some more. He's only nine. He's going to college." And in this way Miss Miller continued to converse upon the affairs of her family, and upon other topics. She sat there with her extremely pretty hands, ornamented with very brilliant rings, folded in her lap, and with her pretty eyes now resting upon those of Winterbourne, now wandering over the garden, the people who passed by, and the beautiful view. She talked to Winterbourne as if she had known him a long time. He found it very pleasant. It was many years since he had heard a young girl talk so much. It might have been said of this unknown young lady, who had come and sat

[16]Railroad cars.

down beside him upon a bench, that she chattered. She was very quiet; she sat in a charming tranquil attitude, but her lips and her eyes were constantly moving. She had a soft, slender, agreeable voice, and her tone was decidedly sociable. She gave Winterbourne a history of her movements and intentions, and those of her mother and brother, in Europe, and enumerated, in particular, the various hotels at which they had stopped. "That English lady, in the cars," she said—"Miss Featherstone—asked me if we didn't all live in hotels in America. I told her I had never been in so many hotels in my life as since I came to Europe. I have never seen so many—it's nothing but hotels." But Miss Miller did not make this remark with a querulous accent; she appeared to be in the best humour with everything. She declared that the hotels were very good, when once you got used to their ways, and that Europe was perfectly sweet. She was not disappointed—not a bit. Perhaps it was because she had heard so much about it before. She had ever so many intimate friends that had been there ever so many times. And then she had had ever so many dresses and things from Paris. Whenever she put on a Paris dress she felt as if she were in Europe.

"It was a kind of a wishing-cap," said Winterbourne.

"Yes," said Miss Miller, without examining this analogy; "it always made me wish I was here. But I needn't have done that for dresses. I am sure they send all the pretty ones to America; you see the most frightful things here. The only thing I don't like," she proceeded, "is the society. There isn't any society; or, if there is, I don't know where it keeps itself. Do you? I suppose there is some society somewhere, but I haven't seen anything of it. I'm very fond of society, and I have always had a great deal of it. I don't mean only in Schenectady, but in New York. I used to go to New York every winter. In New York I had lots of society. Last winter I had seventeen dinners given me; and three of them were by gentlemen," added Daisy Miller. "I have more friends in New York than in Schenectady—more gentleman friends; and more young lady friends too," she resumed in a moment. She paused again for an instant; she was looking at Winterbourne with all her prettiness in her lively eyes and in her light, slightly monotonous smile. "I have always had," she said, "a great deal of gentlemen's society."

Poor Winterbourne was amused, perplexed, and decidedly charmed. He had never yet heard a young girl express herself in just this fashion; never, at least, save in cases where to say such things seemed a kind of demonstrative evidence of a certain laxity of deportment. And yet was he to accuse Miss Daisy Miller of actual or potential *inconduite,*[17] as they said at Geneva? He felt that he had lived at Geneva so long that he had lost a good deal; he had become dishabituated to the American tone. Never, indeed, since he had grown old enough to appreciate things, had he encountered a young American girl of so pronounced a type as this. Certainly she was very charming, but how deucedly sociable! Was she simply a pretty girl from New York State—were they all like that, the pretty girls who had a good deal of gentlemen's society? Or was she also a designing, an audacious, an unscrupulous young person? Winterbourne had lost his instinct in this matter, and his reason could not help him. Miss Daisy Miller looked extremely innocent. Some people had told him that, after all, American girls were exceedingly innocent; and others had told him that, after all, they were not. He was inclined to think Miss Daisy Miller was a

[17]French: misconduct.

flirt—a pretty American flirt. He had never, as yet, had any relations with young ladies of this category. He had known, here in Europe, two or three women—persons older than Miss Daisy Miller, and provided, for respectability's sake, with husbands—who were great coquettes—dangerous, terrible women, with whom one's relations were liable to take a serious turn. But this young girl was not a coquette in that sense; she was very unsophisticated; she was only a pretty American flirt. Winterbourne was almost grateful for having found the formula that applied to Miss Daisy Miller. He leaned back in his seat; he remarked to himself that she had the most charming nose he had ever seen; he wondered what were the regular conditions and limitations of one's intercourse with a pretty American flirt. It presently became apparent that he was on the way to learn.

"Have you been to that old castle?" asked the young girl, pointing with her parasol to the far-gleaming walls of the Château de Chillon.

"Yes, formerly, more than once," said Winterbourne. "You too, I suppose, have seen it?"

"No; we haven't been there. I want to go there dreadfully. Of course I mean to go there. I wouldn't go away from here without having seen that old castle."

"It's a very pretty excursion," said Winterbourne, "and very easy to make. You can drive, you know, or you can go by the little steamer."

"You can go in the cars," said Miss Miller.

"Yes; you can go in the cars," Winterbourne assented.

"Our courier[18] says they take you right up to the castle," the young girl continued. "We were going last week; but my mother gave out. She suffers dreadfully from dyspepsia. She said she couldn't go. Randolph wouldn't go either; he says he doesn't think much of old castles. But I guess we'll go this week, if we can get Randolph."

"Your brother is not interested in ancient monuments?" Winterbourne inquired, smiling.

"He says he don't care much about old castles. He's only nine. He wants to stay at the hotel. Mother's afraid to leave him alone, and the courier won't stay with him; so we haven't been to many places. But it will be too bad if we don't go up there." And Miss Miller pointed again at the Château de Chillon.

"I should think it might be arranged," said Winterbourne. "Couldn't you get some one to stay—for the afternoon—with Randolph?"

Miss Miller looked at him a moment; and then, very placidly—"I wish *you* would stay with him!" she said.

Winterbourne hesitated a moment. "I should much rather go to Chillon with you."

"With me?" asked the young girl, with the same placidity.

She didn't rise, blushing, as a young girl at Geneva would have done; and yet Winterbourne, conscious that he had been very bold, thought it possible she was offended. "With your mother," he answered very respectfully.

But it seemed that both his audacity and his respect were lost upon Miss Daisy Miller. "I guess my mother won't go after all," she said. "She don't like to ride round in the afternoon. But did you really mean what you said just now; that you would like to go up there?"

"Most earnestly," Winterbourne declared.

[18]A servant who accompanies travelers.

"Then we may arrange it. If mother will stay with Randolph, I guess Eugenio will."

"Eugenio?" the young man inquired.

"Eugenio's our courier. He doesn't like to stay with Randolph; he's the most fastidious man I ever saw. But he's a splendid courier. I guess he'll stay at home with Randolph if mother does, and then we can go to the castle."

Winterbourne reflected for an instant as lucidly as possible—"we" could only mean Miss Daisy Miller and himself. This programme seemed almost too agreeable for credence; he felt as if he ought to kiss the young lady's hand. Possibly he would have done so—and quite spoiled the project; but at this moment another person—presumably Eugenio—appeared. A tall, handsome man, with superb whiskers, wearing a velvet morning-coat and a brilliant watch-chain, approached Miss Miller, looking sharply at her companion. "Oh, Eugenio!" said Miss Miller, with the friendliest accent.

Eugenio had looked at Winterbourne from head to foot; he now bowed gravely to the young lady. "I have the honour to inform mademoiselle that luncheon is upon the table."

Miss Miller slowly rose. "See here, Eugenio," she said. "I'm going to that old castle, any way."

"To the Château de Chillon, mademoiselle?" the courier inquired. "Mademoiselle has made arrangements?" he added, in a tone which struck Winterbourne as very impertinent.

Eugenio's tone apparently threw, even to Miss Miller's own apprehension, a slightly ironical light upon the young girl's situation. She turned to Winterbourne, blushing a little—a very little. "You won't back out?" she said.

"I shall not be happy till we go!" he protested.

"And you are staying in this hotel?" she went on. "And you are really an American?"

The courier stood looking at Winterbourne, offensively. The young man, at least, thought his manner of looking an offence to Miss Miller; it conveyed an imputation that she "picked up" acquaintances. "I shall have the honour of presenting to you a person who will tell you all about me," he said smiling, and referring to his aunt.

"Oh, well, we'll go some day," said Miss Miller. And she gave him a smile and turned away. She put up her parasol and walked back to the inn beside Eugenio. Winterbourne stood looking after her; and as she moved away, drawing her muslin furbelows over the gravel, said to himself that she had the *tourmure*[19] of a princess.

He had, however, engaged to do more than proved feasible, in promising to present his aunt, Mrs. Costello, to Miss Daisy Miller. As soon as the former lady had got better of her headache he waited upon her in her apartment; and, after the proper inquiries in regard to her health, he asked her if she had observed, in the hotel, an American family—a mamma, a daughter, and a little boy.

"And a courier?" said Mrs. Costello. "Oh, yes I have observed them. Seen them—heard them—and kept out of their way." Mrs. Costello was a widow with a fortune; a person of much distinction, who frequently intimated that, if she were not so dreadfully liable to sick-headaches, she would probably have left a deeper impress upon her time. She had a long pale face, a high nose, and a

[19]French: appearance.

great deal of very striking white hair, which she wore in large puffs and *rouleaux*[20] over the top of her head. She had two sons married in New York, and another who was now in Europe. This young man was amusing himself at Hombourg,[21] and, though he was on his travels, was rarely perceived to visit any particular city at the moment selected by his mother for her own appearance there. Her nephew, who had come up to Vevey expressly to see her, was therefore more attentive than those who, as she said, were nearer to her. He had imbibed at Geneva the idea that one must always be attentive to one's aunt. Mrs. Costello had not seen him for many years, and she was greatly pleased with him, manifesting her approbation by initiating him into many of the secrets of that social sway which, as she gave him to understand, she exerted in the American capital.[22] She admitted that she was very exclusive; but, if he were acquainted with New York, he would see that one had to be. And her picture of the minutely hierarchical constitution of the society of that city, which she presented to him in many different lights, was, to Winterbourne's imagination, almost oppressively striking.

He immediately perceived, from her tone, that Miss Daisy Miller's place in the social scale was low. "I am afraid you don't approve of them," he said.

"They are very common," Mrs. Costello declared. "They are the sort of Americans that one does one's duty by not—not accepting."

"Ah, you don't accept them?" said the young man.

"I can't, my dear Frederick. I would if I could, but I can't."

"The young girl is very pretty," said Winterbourne, in a moment.

"Of course she's pretty. But she is very common."

"I see what you mean of course," said Winterbourne, after another pause.

"She has that charming look that they all have," his aunt resumed. "I can't think where they pick it up; and she dressed in perfection—no, you don't know how well she dresses. I can't think where they get their taste."

"But, my dear aunt, she is not, after all, a Comanche savage."

"She is a young lady," said Mrs. Costello, "who has an intimacy with her mamma's courier."

"An intimacy with the courier?" the young man demanded.

"Oh, the mother is just as bad! They treat the courier like a familiar friend—like a gentleman. I shouldn't wonder if he dines with them. Very likely they have never seen a man with such good manners, such fine clothes, so like a gentleman. He probably corresponds to the young lady's idea of a Count. He sits with them in the garden, in the evening. I think he smokes."

Winterbourne listened with interest to these disclosures; they helped him to make up his mind about Miss Daisy. Evidently she was rather wild. "Well," he said, "I am not a courier, and yet she was very charming to me."

"You had better have said at first," said Mrs. Costello with dignity, "that you had made her acquaintance."

"We simply met in the garden and we talked a bit."

"*Tout bonnement!*[23] And pray what did you say?"

"I said I should take the liberty of introducing her to my admirable aunt."

"I am much obliged to you."

"It was to guarantee my respectability," said Winterbourne.

[20]French: rolls, coils. [21]A German health resort.
[22]America's social capital, New York City. [23]French: "Is that so!"

"And pray who is to guarantee hers?"

"Ah, you are cruel!" said the young man. "She's a very nice young girl."

"You don't say that as if you believed it," Mrs. Costello observed.

"She is completely uncultivated," Winterbourne went on. "But she is wonderfully pretty, and, in short, she is very nice. To prove that I believe it, I am going to take her to the Château de Chillon."

"You two are going off there together? I should say it proved just the contrary. How long had you known her, may I ask, when this interesting project was formed? You haven't been twenty-four hours in the house."

"I had known her half an hour!" said Winterbourne, smiling.

"Dear me!" cried Mrs. Costello. "What a dreadful girl!"

Her nephew was silent for some moments. "You really think, then," he began, earnestly, and with a desire for trustworthy information—"you really think that——" But he paused again.

"Think what, sir?" said his aunt.

"That she is the sort of young lady who expects a man—sooner or later—to carry her off?"

"I haven't the least idea what such young ladies expect a man to do. But I really think that you had better not meddle with little American girls that are uncultivated, as you call them. You have lived too long out of the country. You will be sure to make some great mistake. You are too innocent."

"My dear aunt, I am not so innocent," said Winterbourne, smiling and curling his moustache.

"You are too guilty, then!"

Winterbourne continued to curl his moustache, meditatively. "You won't let the poor girl know you then?" he asked at last.

"Is it literally true that she is going to the Château de Chillon with you?"

"I think that she fully intends it."

"Then, my dear Frederick," said Mrs. Costello, "I must decline the honour of her acquaintance. I am an old woman, but I am not too old—thank Heaven—to be shocked!"

"But don't they all do these things—the young girls in America?" Winterbourne inquired.

Mrs. Costello stared a moment. "I should like to see my granddaughters do them!" she declared, grimly.

This seemed to throw some light upon the matter, for Winterbourne remembered to have heard that his pretty cousins in New York were "tremendous flirts." If, therefore, Miss Daisy Miller exceeded the liberal margin allowed to these young ladies, it was probable that anything might be expected of her. Winterbourne was impatient to see her again, and he was vexed with himself that, by instinct, he should not appreciate her justly.

Though he was impatient to see her, he hardly knew what he should say to her about his aunt's refusal to become acquainted with her; but he discovered, promptly enough, that with Miss Daisy Miller there was no great need of walking on tiptoe. He found her that evening in the garden, wandering about in the warm starlight, like an indolent sylph, and swinging to and fro the largest fan he had ever beheld. It was ten o'clock. He had dined with his aunt, had been sitting with her since dinner, and had just taken leave of her till the morrow. Miss Daisy Miller seemed very glad to see him; she declared it was the longest evening she had ever passed.

"Have you been all alone?" he asked.

"I have been walking round with mother. But mother gets tired walking round," she answered.

"Has she gone to bed?"

"No; she doesn't like to go to bed," said the young girl. "She doesn't sleep—not three hours. She says she doesn't know how she lives. She's dreadfully nervous. I guess she sleeps more than she thinks. She's gone somewhere after Randolph; she wants to try to get him to go to bed. He doesn't like to go to bed."

"Let us hope she will persuade him," observed Winterbourne.

"She will talk to him all she can; but he doesn't like her to talk to him," said Miss Daisy, opening her fan. "She's going to try to get Eugenio to talk to him. But he isn't afraid of Eugenio. Eugenio's a splendid courier, but he can't make much impression on Randolph! I don't believe he'll go to bed before eleven." It appears that Randolph's vigil was in fact triumphantly prolonged, for Winterbourne strolled about with the young girl for some time without meeting her mother. "I have been looking round for that lady you want to introduce me to," his companion resumed. "She's your aunt." Then, on Winterbourne's admitting the fact, and expressing some curiosity as to how she learned it, she said she heard all about Mrs. Costello from the chambermaid. She was very quiet and very *comme il faut;*[24] she wore white puffs; she spoke to no one, and she never dined at the *table d'hôte.*[25] Every two days she had a headache. "I think that's a lovely description, headache and all!" said Miss Daisy, chattering along in her thin, gay voice. "I want to know her ever so much. I know just what *your* aunt would be; I know I should like her. She would be very exclusive. I like a lady to be exclusive; I'm dying to be exclusive myself. Well, we *are* exclusive, mother and I. We don't speak to every one—or they don't speak to us. I suppose it's about the same thing. Any way, I shall be ever so glad to know your aunt."

Winterbourne was embarrassed. "She would be most happy," he said; "but I am afraid those headaches will interfere."

The young girl looked at him through the dusk. "But I suppose she doesn't have a headache every day," she said, sympathetically.

Winterbourne was silent a moment. "She tells me she does," he answered at last—not knowing what to say.

Miss Daisy Miller stopped and stood looking at him. Her prettiness was still visible in the darkness; she was opening and closing her enormous fan. "She doesn't want to know me!" she said, suddenly. "Why don't you say so? You needn't be afraid. I'm not afraid!" And she gave a little laugh.

Winterbourne fancied there was a tremor in her voice; he was touched, shocked, mortified by it. "My dear young lady," he protested, "she knows no one. It's her wretched health."

The young girl walked on a few steps, laughing still. "You needn't be afraid," she repeated. "Why should she want to know me?" Then she paused again; she was close to the parapet of the garden, and in front of her was the starlit lake. There was a vague sheen upon its surface, and in the distance were dimly-seen mountain forms. Daisy Miller looked out upon the mysterious prospect, and then she gave another little laugh. "Gracious! she *is* exclusive!" she said. Winterbourne wondered whether she was seriously wounded, and for a moment almost wished that her sense of injury might be such as to make it becoming in

[24]French: proper. [25]French: ordinary public dining table.

him to attempt to reassure and comfort her. He had a pleasant sense that she would be very approachable for consolatory purposes. He felt then, for the instant, quite ready to sacrifice his aunt, conversationally; to admit that she was a proud, rude woman, and to declare that they needn't mind her. But before he had time to commit himself to this perilous mixture of gallantry and impiety, the young lady, resuming her walk, gave an exclamation in quite another tone. "Well; here's mother! I guess she hasn't got Randolph to go to bed." The figure of a lady appeared, at a distance, very indistinct in the darkness, and advancing with a slow and wavering movement. Suddenly it seemed to pause.

"Are you sure it is your mother? Can you distinguish her in this thick dusk?" Winterbourne asked.

"Well!" cried Miss Daisy Miller, with a laugh, "I guess I know my own mother. And when she has got on my shawl, too! She is always wearing my things."

The lady in question, ceasing to advance, hovered vaguely about the spot at which she had checked her steps.

"I am afraid your mother doesn't see you," said Winterbourne. "Or perhaps," he added—thinking, with Miss Miller, the joke permissible—"perhaps she feels guilty about your shawl."

"Oh, it's a fearful old thing!" the young girl replied, serenely. "I told her she could wear it. She won't come here, because she sees you."

"Ah, then!" said Winterbourne, "I had better leave you."

"Oh, no; come on!" urged Miss Daisy Miller.

"I'm afraid your mother doesn't approve of my walking with you."

Miss Miller gave him a serious glance. "It isn't for me; it's for you—that is, it's for *her*. Well; I don't know who it's for! But mother doesn't like any of my gentlemen friends. She's right down timid. She always makes a fuss if I introduce a gentleman. But I *do* introduce them—almost always. If I didn't introduce my gentlemen friends to mother," the young girl added, in her little soft, flat monotone, "I shouldn't think I was natural."

"To introduce me," said Winterbourne, "you must know my name." And he proceeded to pronounce it.

"Oh, dear; I can't say all that!" said his companion, with a laugh. But by this time they had come up to Mrs. Miller, who, as they drew near, walked to the parapet of the garden and leaned upon it, looking intently at the lake, and turning her back on them. "Mother!" said the young girl, in a tone of decision. Upon this the elder lady turned round. "Mr. Winterbourne," said Miss Daisy Miller, introducing the young man very frankly and prettily. "Common" she was, as Mrs. Costello had pronounced her; yet it was a wonder to Winterbourne that, with her commonness, she had a singularly delicate grace.

Her mother was a small, spare, light person, with a wandering eye, a very exiguous nose, and a large forehead, decorated with a certain amount of thin, much-frizzled hair. Like her daughter, Mrs. Miller was dressed with extreme elegance; she had enormous diamonds in her ears. So far as Winterbourne could observe, she gave him no greeting—she certainly was not looking at him. Daisy was near her, pulling her shawl straight. "What are you doing, poking round here?" this young lady inquired; but by no means with that harshness of accent which her choice of words may imply.

"I don't know," said her mother, turning towards the lake again.

"I shouldn't think you'd want that shawl!" Daisy exclaimed.

"Well—I do!" her mother answered, with a little laugh.

"Did you get Randolph to go to bed?" asked the young girl.

"No; I couldn't induce him," said Mrs. Miller, very gently. "He wants to talk to the waiter. He likes to talk to that waiter."

"I was telling Mr. Winterbourne," the young girl went on; and to the young man's ear her tone might have indicated that she had been uttering his name all her life.

"Oh, yes!" said Winterbourne; "I have the pleasure of knowing your son."

Randolph's mamma was silent; she turned her attention to the lake. But at last she spoke. "Well, I don't see how he lives!"

"Anyhow, it isn't so bad as it was at Dover," said Daisy Miller.

"And what occurred at Dover?" Winterbourne asked.

"He wouldn't go to bed at all. I guess he sat up all night—in the public parlour. He wasn't in bed at twelve o'clock: I know that."

"It was half-past twelve," declared Mrs. Miller, with mild emphasis.

"Does he sleep much during the day?" Winterbourne demanded.

"I guess he doesn't sleep much," Daisy rejoined.

"I wish he would!" said her mother. "It seems as if he couldn't."

"I think he's real tiresome," Daisy pursued.

Then, for some moments, there was silence. "Well Daisy Miller," said the elder lady, presently, "I shouldn't think you'd want to talk against your own brother!"

"Well, he *is* tiresome, mother," said Daisy, quite without the asperity of a retort.

"He's only nine," urged Mrs. Miller.

"Well, he wouldn't go to that castle," said the young girl. "I'm going there with Mr. Winterbourne."

To this announcement, very placidly made, Daisy's mamma offered no response. Winterbourne took for granted that she deeply disapproved of the projected excursion; but he said to himself that she was a simple, easily-managed person, and that a few deferential protestations would take the edge from her displeasure. "Yes," he began; "Your daughter has kindly allowed me the honour of being her guide."

Mrs. Miller's wandering eyes attached themselves, with a sort of appealing air, to Daisy, who, however, strolled a few steps farther, gently humming to herself. "I presume you will go in the cars," said her mother.

"Yes; or in the boat," said Winterbourne.

"Well, of course, I don't know," Mrs. Miller rejoined. "I have never been to that castle."

"It is a pity you shouldn't go," said Winterbourne, beginning to feel reassured as to her opposition. And yet he was quite prepared to find that, as a matter of course, she meant to accompany her daughter.

"We've been thinking ever so much about going," she pursued; "but it seems as if we couldn't. Of course Daisy—she wants to go round. But there's a lady here—I don't know her name—she says she shouldn't think we'd want to go to see castles *here;* she should think we'd want to wait till we got to Italy. It seems as if there would be so many there," continued Mrs. Miller, with an air of increasing confidence. "Of course, we only want to see the principal ones. We visited several in England," she presently added.

"Ah, yes! in England there are beautiful castles," said Winterbourne. "But Chillon, here, is very well worth seeing."

"Well, if Daisy feels up to it——," said Mrs. Miller, in a tone impregnated with a sense of the magnitude of the enterprise. "It seems as if there was nothing she wouldn't undertake."

"Oh, I think she'll enjoy it!" Winterbourne declared. And he desired more and more to make it a certainty that he was to have the privilege of a *tête-à-tête*[26] with the young lady, who was still strolling along in front of them, softly vocalising. "You are not disposed, madam," he inquired, "to undertake it yourself?"

Daisy's mother looked at him, an instant, askance, and then walked forward in silence. Then—"I guess she had better go alone," she said, simply.

Winterbourne observed to himself that this was a very different type of maternity from that of the vigilant matrons who massed themselves in the forefront of social intercourse in the dark old city at the other end of the lake. But his meditations were interrupted by hearing his name very distinctly pronounced by Mrs. Miller's unprotected daughter.

"Mr. Winterbourne!" murmured Daisy.

"Mademoiselle!" said the young man.

"Don't you want to take me out in a boat?"

"At present?" he asked.

"Of course!" said Daisy.

"Well, Annie Miller!" exclaimed her mother.

"I beg you, madam, to let her go," said Winterbourne, ardently; for he had never yet enjoyed the sensation of guiding through the summer starlight a skiff freighted with a fresh and beautiful young girl.

"I shouldn't think she'd want to," said her mother. "I should think she'd rather go indoors."

"I'm sure Mr. Winterbourne wants to take me," Daisy declared. "He's so awfully devoted!"

"I will row you over to Chillon, in the starlight."

"I don't believe it!" said Daisy.

"Well!" ejaculated the elder lady again.

"You haven't spoken to me for half an hour," her daughter went on.

"I have been having some very pleasant conversation with your mother," said Winterbourne.

"Well; I want you to take me out in a boat!" Daisy repeated. They had all stopped, and she had turned round and was looking at Winterbourne. Her face wore a charming smile, her pretty eyes were gleaming, she was swinging her great fan about. No; it's impossible to be prettier than that, thought Winterbourne.

"There are half a dozen boats moored at that landing-place," he said, pointing to certain steps which descended from the garden to the lake. "If you will do me the honour to accept my arm, we will go and select one of them."

Daisy stood there smiling; she threw back her head and gave a little, light laugh. "I like a gentleman to be formal!" she declared.

"I assure you it's a formal offer."

"I was bound I would make you say something," Daisy went on.

"You see it's not very difficult," said Winterbourne. "But I am afraid you are chaffing me."

"I think not, sir," remarked Mrs. Miller, very gently.

[26]French: private talk.

"Do, then, let me give you a row," he said to the young girl.

"It's quite lovely, the way you say that!" cried Daisy.

"It will be still more lovely to do it."

"Yes, it would be lovely!" said Daisy. But she made no movement to accompany him; she only stood there laughing.

"I should think you had better find out what time it is," interposed her mother.

"It is eleven o'clock, madam," said a voice, with a foreign accent, out of the neighbouring darkness; and Winterbourne, turning, perceived the florid personage who was in attendance upon the two ladies. He had apparently just approached.

"Oh, Eugenio," said Daisy, "I am going out in a boat!"

Eugenio bowed. "At eleven o'clock, mademoiselle?"

"I am going with Mr. Winterbourne. This very minute."

"Do tell her she can't," said Mrs. Miller to the courier.

"I think you had better not go out in a boat, mademoiselle," Eugenio declared.

Winterbourne wished to Heaven this pretty girl were not so familiar with her courier; but he said nothing.

"I suppose you don't think it's proper!" Daisy exclaimed. "Eugenio doesn't think anything's proper."

"I am at your service," said Winterbourne.

"Does mademoiselle propose to go alone?" asked Eugenio of Mrs. Miller.

"Oh, no; with this gentleman!" answered Daisy's mamma.

The courier looked for a moment at Winterbourne—the latter thought he was smiling—and then, solemnly, with a bow, "As mademoiselle pleases!" he said.

"Oh, I hoped you would make a fuss!" said Daisy. "I don't care to go now."

"I myself shall make a fuss if you don't go," said Winterbourne.

"That's all I want—a little fuss!" And the young girl began to laugh again.

"Mr. Randolph has gone to bed!" the courier announced, frigidly.

"Oh, Daisy; now we can go!" said Mrs. Miller.

Daisy turned away from Winterbourne, looking at him, smiling, and fanning herself. "Good-night," she said; "I hope you are disappointed, or disgusted, or something!"

He looked at her, taking the hand she offered him. "I am puzzled," he answered.

"Well; I hope it won't keep you awake!" she said, very smartly; and, under the escort of the privileged Eugenio, the two ladies passed towards the house.

Winterbourne stood looking after them; he was indeed puzzled. He lingered beside the lake for a quarter of an hour; turning over the mystery of the young girl's sudden familiarities and caprices. But the only very definite conclusion he came to was that he should enjoy deucedly "going off" with her somewhere.

Two days afterwards he went off with her to the Castle of Chillon. He waited for her in the large hall of the hotel, where the couriers, the servants, the foreign tourists were lounging about and staring. It was not the place he should have chosen, but she had appointed it. She came tripping downstairs, buttoning her long gloves, squeezing her folded parasol against her pretty figure, dressed in the perfection of a soberly elegant travelling-costume. Winterbourne was a man of imagination and, as our ancestors used to say, sensibility;[27] as he looked at her dress and, on the great staircase, her little rapid, confiding step,

[27]I.e., sensitivity.

he felt as if there were something romantic going forward. He could have believed he was going to elope with her. He passed out with her among all the idle people that were assembled there; they were all looking at her very hard; she had begun to chatter as soon as she joined him. Winterbourne's preference had been that they should be conveyed to Chillon in a carriage; but she expressed a lively wish to go in the little steamer; she declared that she had a passion for steamboats. There was always such a lovely breeze upon the water, and you saw such lots of people. The sail was not long, but Winterbourne's companion found time to say a great many things. To the young man himself their little excursion was so much of an escapade—an adventure—that, even allowing for her habitual sense of freedom, he had some expectation of seeing her regard it in the same way. But it must be confessed that, in this particular, he was disappointed. Daisy Miller was extremely animated, she was in charming spirits; but she was apparently not at all excited; she was not fluttered; she avoided neither his eyes nor those of any one else; she blushed neither when she looked at him nor when she felt that people were looking at her. People continued to look at her a great deal, and Winterbourne took much satisfaction in his pretty companion's distinguished air. He had been a little afraid that she would talk loud, laugh overmuch, and even, perhaps, desire to move about the boat a good deal. But he quite forgot his fears; he sat smiling, with his eyes upon her face, while, without moving from her place, she delivered herself of a great number of original reflections. It was the most charming garrulity he had ever heard. He had assented to the idea that she was "common;" but was she so, after all, or was he simply getting used to her commonness? Her conversation was chiefly of what metaphysicians term the objective cast; but every now and then it took a subjective turn.

"What on *earth* are you so grave about?" she suddenly demanded, fixing her agreeable eyes upon Winterbourne's.

"Am I grave?" he asked. "I had an idea I was grinning from ear to ear."

"You look as if you were taking me to a funeral. If that's a grin, your ears are very near together."

"Should you like me to dance a hornpipe on the deck?"

"Pray do, and I'll carry round your hat. It will pay the expenses of our journey."

"I never was better pleased in my life," murmured Winterbourne.

She looked at him a moment, and then burst into a little laugh. "I like to make you say those things! You're a queer mixture!"

In the castle, after they had landed, the subjective element decidedly prevailed. Daisy tripped about the vaulted chambers, rustled her skirts in the corkscrew staircases, flirted back with a pretty little cry and a shudder from the edge of the *oubliettes,*[28] and turned a singularly well-shaped ear to everything that Winterbourne told her about the place. But he saw that she cared very little for feudal antiquities, and that the dusky traditions of Chillon made but a slight impression upon her. They had the good fortune to have been able to walk about without other companionship than that of the custodian; and Winterbourne arranged with this functionary that they should not be hurried—that they should linger and pause wherever they chose. The custodian interpreted the bargain generously—Winterbourne, on his side, had been generous—and

[28]French: oblivions, a term for prison cells sunk below floor level and with openings only at the top.

ended by leaving them quite to themselves. Miss Miller's observations were not remarkable for logical consistency; for anything she wanted to say she was sure to find a pretext. She found a great many pretexts in the rugged embrasures of Chillon for asking Winterbourne sudden questions about himself—his family, his previous history, his tastes, his habits, his intentions—and for supplying information upon corresponding points in her own personality. Of her own tastes, habits, and intentions Miss Miller was prepared to give the most definite, and indeed the most favourable, account.

"Well; I hope you know enough!" she said to her companion, after he had told her the history of the unhappy Bonivard.[29] "I never saw a man that knew so much!" The history of Bonivard had evidently, as they say, gone into one ear and out of the other. But Daisy went on to say that she wished Winterbourne would travel with them and "go round" with them; they might know something, in that case. "Don't you want to come and teach Randolph?" she asked. Winterbourne said that nothing could possibly please him so much; but that he had unfortunately other occupations. "Other occupations? I don't believe it!" said Miss Daisy. "What do you mean? You are not in business." The young man admitted that he was not in business; but he had engagements which, even within a day or two, would force him to go back to Geneva. "Oh, bother!" she said: "I don't believe it!" and she began to talk about something else. But a few moments later, when he was pointing out to her the pretty design of an antique fireplace, she broke out irrelevantly, "You don't mean to say you are going back to Geneva?"

"It is a melancholy fact that I shall have to return to Geneva tomorrow."

"Well, Mr. Winterbourne," said Daisy; "I think you're horrid!"

"Oh, don't say such dreadful things!" said Winterbourne—"just at the last!"

"The last!" cried the young girl; "I call it the first. I have half a mind to leave you here and go straight back to the hotel alone." And for the next ten minutes she did nothing but call him horrid. Poor Winterbourne was fairly bewildered; no young lady had as yet done him the honour to be so agitated by the announcement of his movements. His companion, after this, ceased to pay any attention to the curiosities of Chillon or the beauties of the lake; she opened fire upon the mysterious charmer in Geneva whom she appeared to have instantly taken it for granted that he was hurrying back to see. How did Miss Daisy Miller know that there was a charmer in Geneva? Winterbourne, who denied the existence of such a person, was quite unable to discover; and he was divided between amazement at the rapidity of her induction and amusement at the frankness of her *persiflage*.[30] She seemed to him, in all this, an extraordinary mixture of innocence and crudity. "Does she never allow you more than three days at a time?" asked Daisy, ironically. "Doesn't she give you a vacation in summer? There's no one so hard worked but they can get leave to go off somewhere at this season. I suppose, if you stay another day, she'll come after you in the boat. Do wait over till Friday, and I will go down to the landing to see her arrive!" Winterbourne began to think he had been wrong to feel disappointed in the temper in which the young lady had embarked. If he had missed the personal accent, the personal accent was now making its appearance. It sounded very distinctly,

[29]François de Bonnivard (1496?–1570), Swiss patriot jailed in the Castle of Chillon (1530–1536) and the hero of Byron's *The Prisoner of Chillon*, 1816.

[30]Banter.

at last, in her telling him she would stop "teasing" him if he would promise her solemnly to come down to Rome in the winter.

"That's not a difficult promise to make," said Winterbourne. "My aunt has taken an apartment in Rome for the winter, and has already asked me to come and see her."

"I don't want you to come for your aunt," said Daisy; "I want you to come for me." And this was the only allusion that the young man was ever to hear her make to his invidious kinswoman. He declared that, at any rate, he would certainly come. After this Daisy stopped teasing. Winterbourne took a carriage, and they drove back to Vevey in the dusk; the young girl was very quiet.

In the evening Winterbourne mentioned to Mrs. Costello that he had spent the afternoon at Chillon, with Miss Daisy Miller.

"The Americans—of the courier?" asked this lady.

"Ah, happily," said Winterbourne, "the courier stayed at home."

"She went with you all alone?"

"All alone."

Mrs. Costello sniffed a little at her smelling-bottle. "And that," she exclaimed, "is the young person whom you wanted me to know!"

PART II

Winterbourne, who had returned to Geneva the day after his excursion to Chillon, went to Rome towards the end of January. His aunt had been established there for several weeks, and he had received a couple of letters from her. "Those people you were so devoted to last summer at Vevey have turned up here, courier and all," she wrote. "They seem to have made several acquaintances, but the courier continues to be the most *intime.*[31] The young lady, however, is also very intimate with some third-rate Italians, with whom she rackets about in a way that makes much talk. Bring me that pretty novel of Cherbuliez's—'Paule Méré'[32]—and don't come later than the 23rd."

In the natural course of events, Winterbourne, on arriving in Rome, would presently have ascertained Mrs. Miller's address at the American banker's, and have gone to pay his compliments to Miss Daisy. "After what happened at Vevey I think I may certainly call upon them," he said to Mrs. Costello.

"If, after what happens—at Vevey and everywhere—you desire to keep up the acquaintance, you are very welcome. Of course a man may know every one. Men are welcome to the privilege!"

"Pray what is it that happens—here, for instance?" Winterbourne demanded.

"The girl goes about alone with her foreigners. As to what happens further, you must apply elsewhere for information. She has picked up half-a-dozen of the regular Roman fortune-hunters, and she takes them about to people's houses. When she comes to a party she brings with her a gentleman with a good deal of manner and a wonderful moustache."

"And where is the mother?"

"I haven't the least idea. They are very dreadful people."

[31]French: "intimate."

[32]Charles Victor Cherbuliez (1829–1899). French novelist, author of *Paule Méré* (1868).

Winterbourne meditated a moment. “They are very ignorant—very innocent only. Depend upon it they are not bad.”

“They are hopelessly vulgar,” said Mrs. Costello. “Whether or no being hopelessly vulgar is being ‘bad’ is a question for the metaphysicians. They are bad enough to dislike, at any rate; and for this short life that is quite enough.”

The news that Daisy Miller was surrounded by half-a-dozen wonderful moustaches checked Winterbourne’s impulse to go straightway to see her. He had perhaps not definitely flattered himself that he had made an ineffaceable impression upon her heart, but he was annoyed at hearing of a state of affairs so little in harmony with an image that had lately flitted in and out of his own meditations; the image of a very pretty girl looking out of an old Roman window and asking herself urgently when Mr. Winterbourne would arrive. If, however, he determined to wait a little before reminding Miss Miller of his claims to her considerations, he went very soon to call upon two or three other friends. One of these friends was an American lady who had spent several winters at Geneva, where she had placed her children at school. She was a very accomplished woman, and she lived in the Via Gregoriana.[33] Winterbourne found her in a little crimson drawing-room, on a third floor; the room was filled with southern sunshine. He had not been there ten minutes when the servant came in, announcing “Madame Mila!” This announcement was presently followed by the entrance of little Randolph Miller, who stopped in the middle of the room and stood staring at Winterbourne. An instant later his pretty sister crossed the threshold; and then, after a considerable interval, Mrs. Miller slowly advanced.

“I know you!” said Randolph.

“I’m sure you know a great many things,” exclaimed Winterbourne, taking him by the hand. “How is your education coming on?”

Daisy was exchanging greetings very prettily with her hostess; but when she heard Winterbourne’s voice she quickly turned her head. “Well, I declare!” she said.

“I told you I should come, you know,” Winterbourne rejoined, smiling.

“Well—I didn’t believe it,” said Miss Daisy.

“I am much obliged to you,” laughed the young man.

“You might have come to see me!” said Daisy.

“I arrived only yesterday.”

“I don’t believe that!” the young girl declared.

Winterbourne turned with a protesting smile to her mother; but this lady evaded his glance, and, seating herself, fixed her eyes upon her son. “We’ve got a bigger place than this,” said Randolph. “It’s all gold on the walls.”

Mrs. Miller turned uneasily in her chair. “I told you if I were to bring you, you would say something!” she murmured.

“I told *you!*” Randolph exclaimed. “I tell *you,* sir!” he added jocosely, giving Winterbourne a thump on the knee. “It *is* bigger, too!”

Daisy had entered upon a lively conversation with her hostess; Winterbourne judged it becoming to address a few words to her mother. “I hope you have been well since we parted at Vevey,” he said.

Mrs. Miller now certainly looked at him—at his chin. “Not very well, sir,” she answered.

[33]Fashionable street in Rome.

"She's got the dyspepsia," said Randolph. "I've got it too. Father's got it. I've got it most!"

This announcement, instead of embarrassing Mrs. Miller, seemed to relieve her. "I suffer from the liver," she said. "I think it's this climate; it's less bracing than Schenectady, especially in the winter season. I don't know whether you know we reside at Schenectady. I was saying to Daisy that I certainly hadn't found anyone like Dr. Davis, and I didn't believe I should. Oh, at Schenectady, he stands first; they think everything of him. He has so much to do, and yet there was nothing he wouldn't do for me. He said he never saw anything like my dyspepsia, but he was bound to cure it. I'm sure there was nothing he wouldn't try. He was just going to try something new when we came off. Mr. Miller wanted Daisy to see Europe for herself. But I wrote to Mr. Miller that it seems as if I couldn't get on without Dr. Davis. At Schenectady he stands at the very top; and there's a great deal of sickness there, too. It affects my sleep."

Winterbourne had a good deal of pathological gossip with Dr. Davis's patient, during which Daisy chattered unremittingly to her own companion. The young man asked Mrs. Miller how she was pleased with Rome. "Well, I must say I am disappointed," she answered. "We had heard so much about it; I suppose we had heard too much. But we couldn't help that. We had been led to expect something different."

"Ah, wait a little, and you will become very fond of it," said Winterbourne.

"I hate it worse and worse every day!" cried Randolph.

"You are like the infant Hannibal,"[34] said Winterbourne.

"No, I ain't!" Randolph declared, at a venture.

"You are not much like an infant," said his mother. "But we have seen places," she resumed, "that I should put a long way before Rome." And in reply to Winterbourne's interrogation, "There's Zurich," she concluded; "I think Zurich is lovely; and we hadn't heard half so much about it."

"The best place we've seen is the City of Richmond!" said Randolph.

"He means the ship," his mother explained. "We crossed in that ship. Randolph had a good time on the City of Richmond."

"It's the best place I've seen," the child repeated. "Only it was turned the wrong way."

"Well, we've got to turn the right way some time," said Mrs. Miller, with a little laugh. Winterbourne expressed the hope that her daughter at least found some gratification in Rome, and she declared that Daisy was quite carried away. "It's on account of the society—the society's splendid. She goes round everywhere; she has made a great number of acquaintances. Of course she goes round more than I do. I must say they have been very sociable; they have taken her right in. And then she knows a great many gentlemen. Oh, she thinks there's nothing like Rome. Of course, it's a great deal pleasanter for a young lady if she knows plenty of gentlemen."

By this time Daisy had turned her attention again to Winterbourne. "I've been telling Mrs. Walker how mean you were!" the young girl announced.

"And what is the evidence you have offered?" asked Winterbourne, rather annoyed at Miss Miller's want of appreciation of the zeal of an admirer who on his way down to Rome had stopped neither at Bologna nor at Florence, simply because of a certain sentimental impatience. He remembered that a

[34]Carthaginian general (247–183? B.C.) who as a youth swore eternal hatred of Rome.

cynical compatriot had once told him that American women—the pretty ones, and this gave a largeness to the axiom—were at once the most exacting in the world and the least endowed with a sense of indebtedness.

"Why, you were awfully mean at Vevey," said Daisy. "You wouldn't do anything. You wouldn't stay there when I asked you."

"My dearest young lady," cried Winterbourne, with eloquence, "have I come all the way to Rome to encounter your reproaches?"

"Just hear him say that!" said Daisy to her hostess, giving a twist to a bow on this lady's dress. "Did you ever hear anything so quaint?"

"So quaint, my dear?" murmured Mrs. Walker, in the tone of a partisan of Winterbourne.

"Well, I don't know," said Daisy, fingering Mrs. Walker's ribbons. "Mrs. Walker, I want to tell you something."

"Motherr," interposed Randolph, with his rough ends to his words, "I tell you you've got to go. Eugenio 'll raise something!"

"I'm not afraid of Eugenio," said Daisy, with a toss of her head. "Look here, Mrs. Walker," she went on, "you know I'm coming to your party."

"I am delighted to hear it."

"I've got a lovely dress."

"I am very sure of that."

"But I want to ask a favour—permission to bring a friend."

"I shall be happy to see any of your friends," said Mrs. Walker, turning with a smile to Mrs. Miller.

"Oh, they are not my friends," answered Daisy's mamma, smiling shyly, in her own fashion. "I never spoke to them!"

"It's an intimate friend of mine—Mr. Giovanelli," said Daisy, without a tremor in her clear little voice or a shadow on her brilliant little face.

Mrs. Walker was silent a moment, she gave a rapid glance at Winterbourne. "I shall be glad to see Mr. Giovanelli," she then said.

"He's an Italian," Daisy pursued, with the prettiest serenity. "He's a great friend of mine—he's the handsomest man in the world—except Mr. Winterbourne! He knows plenty of Italians, but he wants to know some Americans. He thinks ever so much of Americans. He's tremendously clever. He's perfectly lovely!"

It was settled that this brilliant personage should be brought to Mrs. Walker's party, and then Mrs. Miller prepared to take her leave. "I guess we'll go back to the hotel," she said.

"You may go back to the hotel, mother, but I'm going to take a walk," said Daisy.

"She's going to walk with Mr. Giovanelli," Randolph proclaimed.

"I am going to the Pincio,"[35] said Daisy, smiling.

"Alone, my dear—at this hour?" Mrs. Walker asked. The afternoon was drawing to a close—it was the hour for the throng of carriages and contemplative pedestrians. "I don't think it's safe, my dear," said Mrs. Walker.

"Neither do I," subjoined Mrs. Miller. "You'll get the fever as sure as you live. Remember what Dr. Davis told you!"

"Give her some medicine before she goes," said Randolph.

[35]One of the hills of Rome, with a panoramic view of the city.

The company had risen to its feet; Daisy, still showing her pretty teeth, bent over and kissed her hostess. "Mrs. Walker, you are too perfect," she said. "I'm not going alone; I am going to meet a friend."

"Your friend won't keep you from getting the fever," Mrs. Miller observed.

"Is it Mr. Giovanelli?" asked the hostess.

Winterbourne was watching the young girl; at this question his attention quickened. She stood there smiling and smoothing her bonnet ribbons; she glanced at Winterbourne. Then, while she glanced and smiled, she answered without a shade of hesitation, "Mr. Giovanelli—the beautiful Giovanelli."

"My dear young friend," said Mrs. Walker, taking her hand, pleadingly, "don't walk off to the Pincio at this hour to meet a beautiful Italian."

"Well, he speaks English," said Mrs. Miller.

"Gracious me!" Daisy exclaimed, "I don't want to do anything improper. There's an easy way to settle it." She continued to glance at Winterbourne. "The Pincio is only a hundred yards distant, and if Mr. Winterbourne were as polite as he pretends he would offer to walk with me!"

Winterbourne's politeness hastened to affirm itself, and the young girl gave him gracious leave to accompany her. They passed downstairs before her mother, and at the door Winterbourne perceived Mrs. Miller's carriage drawn up, with the ornamental courier whose acquaintance he had made at Vevey seated within. "Good-by, Eugenio!" cried Daisy, "I'm going to take a walk." The distance from the Via Gregoriana to the beautiful garden at the other end of the Pincian Hill is, in fact, rapidly traversed. As the day was splendid, however, and the concourse of vehicles, walkers, and loungers numerous, the young Americans found this progress much delayed. This fact was highly agreeable to Winterbourne, in spite of his consciousness of his singular situation. The slow-moving, idly-gazing Roman crowd bestowed much attention upon the extremely pretty young foreign lady who was passing through it upon his arm; and he wondered what on earth had been in Daisy's mind when she proposed to expose herself, unattended, to its appreciation. His own mission, to her sense, apparently, was to consign her to the hands of Mr. Giovanelli; but Winterbourne, at once annoyed and gratified, resolved that he would do no such thing.

"Why haven't you been to see me?" asked Daisy. "You can't get out of that."

"I have had the honour of telling you that I have only just stepped out of the train."

"You must have stayed in the train a good while after it stopped!" cried the young girl, with her little laugh. "I suppose you were asleep. You have had time to go to see Mrs. Walker."

"I knew Mrs. Walker—" Winterbourne began to explain.

"I knew where you knew her. You knew her at Geneva. She told me so. Well, you knew me at Vevey. That's just as good. So you ought to have come." She asked him no other question than this; she began to prattle about her own affairs. "We've got splendid rooms at the hotel; Eugenio says they're the best rooms in Rome. We are going to stay all winter—if we don't die of the fever; and I guess we'll stay then. It's a great deal nicer than I thought; I thought it would be fearfully quiet; I was sure it would be awfully poky. I was sure we should be going round all the time with one of those dreadful old men that explain about the pictures and things. But we only had about a week of that, and now I'm enjoying myself. I know ever so many people, and they are all so charming. The society's extremely select. There are all kinds—English, and Germans, and Italians. I think I like the English best. I like their style of conversation. But there are some lovely Americans. I never saw anything so hospitable. There's something or other every day. There's not much dancing; but I must say I never thought dancing was everything. I was always fond of conversation. I guess I shall have plenty at Mrs. Walker's—her rooms are so small." When they had passed the gate of the Pincian Gardens, Miss Miller began to wonder where Mr. Giovanelli might be. "We had better go straight to that place in front," she said, "where you look at the view."

"I certainly shall not help you to find him," Winterbourne declared.

"Then I shall find him without you," said Miss Daisy.

"You certainly won't leave me!" cried Winterbourne.

She burst into her little laugh. "Are you afraid you'll get lost—or run over? But there's Giovanelli, leaning against that tree. He's staring at the woman in the carriages: did you ever see anything so cool?"

Winterbourne perceived at some distance a little man standing with folded arms, nursing his cane. He had a handsome face, an artfully poised hat, a glass in one eye and a nosegay in his buttonhole. Winterbourne looked at him a moment and then said, "Do you mean to speak to that man?"

"Do I mean to speak to him? Why, you don't suppose I mean to communicate by signs?"

"Pray understand, then," said Winterbourne, "that I intend to remain with you."

Daisy stopped and looked at him, without a sign of troubled consciousness in her face; with nothing but the presence of her charming eyes and her happy dimples. "Well, she's a cool one!" thought the young man.

"I don't like the way you say that," said Daisy. "It's too imperious."

"I beg your pardon if I say it wrong. The main point is to give you an idea of my meaning."

The young girl looked at him more gravely, but with eyes that were prettier than ever. "I have never allowed a gentleman to dictate to me, or to interfere with anything I do."

"I think you have made a mistake," said Winterbourne. "You should sometimes listen to a gentleman—the right one."

Daisy began to laugh again. "I do nothing but listen to gentlemen!" she exclaimed. "Tell me if Mr. Giovanelli is the right one?"

The gentleman with the nosegay in his bosom had now perceived our two friends, and was approaching the young girl with obsequious rapidity. He bowed to Winterbourne as well as to the latter's companion; he had a brilliant smile, an intelligent eye; Winterbourne thought him not a bad-looking fellow. But he nevertheless said to Daisy—"No, he's not the right one."

Daisy evidently had a natural talent for performing introductions; she mentioned the name of each of her companions to the other. She strolled along with one of them on each side of her; Mr. Giovanelli, who spoke English very cleverly—Winterbourne afterwards learned that he had practised the idiom upon a great many American heiresses—addressed her a great deal of very polite nonsense; he was extremely urbane, and the young American, who said nothing, reflected upon that profundity of Italian cleverness which enables people to appear more gracious in proportion as they are more acutely disappointed. Giovanelli, of course, had counted upon something more intimate; he had not bargained for a party of three. But he kept his temper in a manner which suggested far-stretching intentions. Winterbourne flattered himself that he had taken his measure. "He is not a gentleman," said the young American; "He is only a clever imitation of one. He is a music-master, or a penny-a-liner,[36] or a third-rate artist. Damm his good looks!" Mr. Giovanelli had certainly a very pretty face; but Winterbourne felt a superior indignation at his own lovely fellow-countrywoman's not knowing the difference between a spurious gentleman and a real one. Giovanelli chattered and jested and made himself wonderfully agreeable. It was true that if he was an imitation the imitation was brilliant. "Nevertheless," Winterbourne said to himself, "a nice girl ought to know!" And then he came back to the question whether this was in fact a nice girl. Would a nice girl—even allowing for her being a little American flirt—make a rendezvous with a presumably low-lived foreigner? The rendezvous in this case, indeed, had been in broad daylight, and in the most crowded corner of Rome; but was it not impossible to regard the choice of these circumstances as a proof of extreme cynicism? Singular though it may seem, Winterbourne was vexed that the young girl, in joining her *amoroso*,[37] should not appear more impatient of his own company, and he was vexed because of his inclination. It was impossible to regard her as a perfectly well-conducted young lady; she was wanting in a certain indispensable delicacy. It would therefore simplify matters greatly to be able to treat her as the object of one of those sentiments which are called by romancers "lawless passions." That she should seem to wish to get rid of him would help him to think more lightly of her, and to be able to think more lightly of her would make her much less perplexing. But Daisy, on this occasion, continued to present herself as an inscrutable combination of audacity and innocence.

She had been walking some quarter of an hour, attended by her two cavaliers, and responding in a tone of very childish gaiety, as it seemed to Winterbourne, to the pretty speeches of Mr. Giovanelli, when a carriage that had detached itself from the revolving train drew up beside the path. At the same moment Winterbourne perceived that his friend Mrs. Walker—the lady whose house he had lately left—was seated in the vehicle and was beckoning to him. Leaving Miss Miller's side, he hastened to obey her summons. Mrs. Walker was flushed; she wore an excited air. "It is really too dreadful," she said. "That girl must not do this sort of thing. She must not walk here with you two men. Fifty people have noticed her."

Winterbourne raised his eyebrows. "I think it's a pity to make too much fuss about it."

"It's a pity to let the girl ruin herself!"

"She is very innocent," said Winterbourne.

"She's very crazy!" cried Mrs. Walker. "Did you ever see anything so imbecile as her mother? After you had all left me, just now, I could not sit still for thinking of it. It seemed too pitiful, not even to attempt to save her. I ordered the carriage and put on my bonnet, and came here as quickly as possible. Thank heaven, I have found you!"

"What do you propose to do with us?" asked Winterbourne, smiling.

"To ask her to get in, to drive her about here for half-an-hour, so that the world may see she is not running absolutely wild, and then to take her safely home."

"I don't think it's a very happy thought," said Winterbourne; "but you can try."

[36]A hack writer who works for a penny a line. [37]Italian: suitor.

Mrs. Walker tried. The young man went in pursuit of Miss Miller, who had simply nodded and smiled at his interlocutor[38] in the carriage, and had gone her way with her companion. Daisy, on learning that Mrs. Walker wished to speak to her, retraced her steps with a perfect good grace and with Mr. Giovanelli at her side. She declared that she was delighted to have a chance to present this gentleman to Mrs. Walker. She immediately achieved the introduction, and declared that she had never in her life seen anything so lovely as Mrs. Walker's carriage-rug.

"I am glad you admire it," said this lady, smiling sweetly. "Will you get in and let me put it over you?"

"Oh, no, thank you," said Daisy. "I shall admire it much more as I see you driving round with it."

"Do get in and drive with me," said Mrs. Walker.

"That would be charming, but it's so enchanting just as I am!" and Daisy gave a brilliant glance at the gentlemen on either side of her.

"It may be enchanting, dear child, but it is not the custom here," urged Mrs. Walker, leaning forward in her victoria[39] with her hands devoutly clasped.

"Well, it ought to be, then!" said Daisy. "If I didn't walk I should expire."

"You should walk with your mother, dear," cried the lady from Geneva, losing patience.

"With my mother, dear!" exclaimed the young girl. Winterbourne saw that she scented interference. "My mother never walked ten steps in her life. And then, you know," she added with a laugh, "I am more than five years old."

"You are old enough to be more reasonable. You are old enough, dear Miss Miller, to be talked about."

Daisy looked at Mrs. Walker, smiling intensely. "Talked about? What do you mean?"

"Come into my carriage and I will tell you."

Daisy turned her quickened glance again from one of the gentlemen beside her to the other. Mr. Giovanelli was bowing to and fro, rubbing down his gloves and laughing very agreeably; Winterbourne thought it a most unpleasant scene. "I don't think I want to know what you mean," said Daisy presently. "I don't think I should like it."

Winterbourne wished that Mrs. Walker would tuck in her carriage-rug and drive away; but this lady did not enjoy being defied, as she afterwards told him. "Should you prefer being thought a very reckless girl?" she demanded.

"Gracious!" exclaimed Daisy. She looked again at Mr. Giovanelli, then she turned to Winterbourne. There was a little pink flush in her cheek; she was tremendously pretty. "Does Mr. Winterbourne think," she asked slowly, smiling, throwing back her head and glancing at him from head to foot, "that—to save my reputation—I ought to get into the carriage?"

Winterbourne coloured; for an instant he hesitated greatly. It seemed so strange to hear her speak that way of her "reputation." But he himself, in fact, must speak in accordance with gallantry. The finest gallantry, here, was simply to tell her the truth; and the truth, for Winterbourne, as the few indications I have been able to give have made him known to the reader, was that Daisy Miller should take Mrs. Walker's advice. He looked at her exquisite prettiness; and then he said very gently, "I think you should get into the carriage."

[38]In later editions James substituted "interlocutrix," a female questioner.

[39]Horse-drawn carriage.

Daisy gave a violent laugh. "I never heard anything so stiff! If this is improper, Mrs. Walker," she pursued, "then I am all improper, and you must give me up. Good-by; I hope you'll have a lovely ride!" and, with Mr. Giovanelli, who made a triumphantly obsequious salute, she turned away.

Mrs. Walker sat looking after her, and there were tears in Mrs. Walker's eyes. "Get in here, sir," she said to Winterbourne, indicating the place beside her. The young man answered that he felt bound to accompany Miss Miller; whereupon Mrs. Walker declared that if he refused her this favour she would never speak to him again. She was evidently in earnest. Winterbourne overtook Daisy and her companion and, offering the young girl his hand, told her that Mrs. Walker had made an imperious claim upon his society. He expected that in answer she would say something rather free, something to commit herself still further to that "recklessness" from which Mrs. Walker had so charitably endeavoured to dissuade her. But she only shook his hand, hardly looking at him; while Mr. Giovanelli bade him farewell with a too-emphatic flourish of the hat.

Winterbourne was not in the best possible humour as he took his seat in Mrs. Walker's victoria. "That was not clever of you," he said candidly, while the vehicle mingled again with the throng of carriages.

"In such a case," his companion answered, "I don't wish to be clever, I wish to be *earnest!*"

"Well, your earnestness has only offended her and put her off."

"It has happened very well," said Mrs. Walker. "If she is so perfectly determined to compromise herself, the sooner one knows it the better; one can act accordingly."

"I suspect she meant no harm," Winterbourne rejoined.

"So I thought a month ago. But she had been going too far."

"What has she been doing?"

"Everything that is not done here. Flirting with any man she could pick up; sitting in corners with mysterious Italians; dancing all the evening with the same partners; receiving visits at eleven o'clock at night. Her mother goes away when visitors come."

"But her brother," said Winterbourne, laughing, "sits up till midnight."

"He must be edified by what he sees. I'm told that at their hotel every one is talking about her, and that a smile goes round among all the servants when a gentleman comes and asks for Miss Miller."

"The servants be hanged!" said Winterbourne angrily. "The poor girl's fault," he presently added, "is that she is very uncultivated."

"She is naturally indelicate," Mrs. Walker declared. "Take that example this morning. How long had you known her at Vevey?"

"A couple of days."

"Fancy, then, her making it a personal matter that you should have left the place!"

Winterbourne was silent for some moments, then he said, "I suspect, Mrs. Walker, that you and I have lived too long at Geneva!" And he added a request that she should inform him with what particular design she had made him enter her carriage.

"I wished to beg you to cease your relations with Miss Miller—not to flirt with her—to give her no further opportunity to expose herself—to let her alone, in short."

"I'm afraid I can't do that," said Winterbourne. "I like her extremely."

"All the more reason that you shouldn't help her to make a scandal."

"There shall be nothing scandalous in my attentions to her."

"There certainly will be in the way she takes them. But I have said what I had on my conscience," Mrs. Walker pursued. "If you wish to rejoin the young lady I will put you down. Here, by-the-way, you have a chance."

The carriage was traversing that part of the Pincian Garden that overhangs the wall of Rome and overlooks the beautiful Villa Borghese.[40] It is bordered by a large parapet, near which there are several seats. One of the seats, at a distance, was occupied by a gentleman and a lady, towards whom Mrs. Walker gave a toss of her head. At the same moment these persons rose and walked towards the parapet. Winterbourne had asked the coachman to stop; he now descended from the carriage. His companion looked at him a moment in silence; then, while he raised his hat, she drove majestically away. Winterbourne stood there; he had turned his eyes towards Daisy and her cavalier. They evidently saw no one; they were too deeply occupied with each other. When they reached the low gardenwall they stood a moment looking off at the great flat-topped pine-clusters of the Villa Borghese; then Giovanelli seated himself, familiarly, upon the broad ledge of the wall. The western sun in the opposite sky sent out a brilliant shaft through a couple of cloud-bars, whereupon Daisy's companion took her parasol out of her hands and opened it. She came a little nearer and he held the parasol over her; then, still holding it, he let it rest upon her shoulder, so that both of their heads were hidden from Winterbourne. This young man lingered a moment, then he began to walk. But he walked—not towards the couple with the parasol; towards the residence of his aunt, Mrs. Costello.

He flattered himself on the following day that there was no smiling among the servants when he, at least, asked for Mrs. Miller at her hotel. This lady and her daughter, however, were not at home; and on the next day after, repeating his visit, Winterbourne again had the misfortune not to find them. Mrs. Walker's party took place on the evening of the third day, and in spite of the frigidity of his last interview with the hostess Winterbourne was among the guests. Mrs. Walker was one of those American ladies who, while residing abroad, make a point, in their own phrase, of studying European society; and she had on this occasion collected several specimens of her diversely-born fellow-mortals to serve, as it were, as text-books. When Winterbourne arrived Daisy Miller was not there, but in a few moments he saw her mother come in alone, very shyly and ruefully. Mrs. Miller's hair above her exposed-looking temples was more frizzled than ever. As she approached Mrs. Walker, Winterbourne also drew near.

"You see I've come all alone," said poor Mrs. Miller. "I'm so frightened; I don't know what to do; it's the first time I've ever been to a party alone—especially in this country. I wanted to bring Randolph or Eugenio, or someone, but Daisy just pushed me off by myself. I ain't used to going round alone."

"And does not your daughter intend to favour us with her society?" demanded Mrs. Walker, impressively.

"Well, Daisy's all dressed," said Mrs. Miller, with that accent of the dispassionate, if not of the philosophic, historian with which she always recorded the current incidents of her daughter's career. "She got dressed on purpose before dinner. But she's got a friend of hers there; that gentleman—the Italian—

[40]Originally the summer palace of the Borghese family, now an art museum and its grounds a public park.

that she wanted to bring. They've got going at the piano; it seems as if they couldn't leave off. Mr. Giovanelli sings splendidly. But I guess they'll come before very long," concluded Mrs. Miller hopefully.

"I'm sorry she should come—in that way," said Mrs. Walker.

"Well, I told her that there was no use in getting dressed before dinner if she was going to wait three hours," responded Daisy's mamma. "I didn't see the use of her putting on such a dress as that to sit round with Mr. Giovanelli."

"This is most horrible!" said Mrs. Walker, turning away and addressing herself to Winterbourne. *"Elle s'affiche.*[41] It's her revenge for my having ventured to remonstrate with her. When she comes I shall not speak to her."

Daisy came after eleven o'clock, but she was not, on such an occasion, a young lady to wait to be spoken to. She rustled forward in radiant loveliness, smiling and chattering, carrying a large bouquet and attended by Mr. Giovanelli. Everyone stopped talking, and turned and looked at her. She came straight to Mrs. Walker. "I'm afraid you thought I never was coming, so I sent mother off to tell you. I wanted to make Mr. Giovanelli practise some things before he came; you know he sings beautifully, and I want you to ask him to sing. This is Mr. Giovanelli; you know I introduced him to you; he's got the most lovely voice and he knows the most charming set of songs. I made him go over them this evening, on purpose; we had the greatest time at the hotel." Of all this Daisy delivered herself with the sweetest, brightest audibleness, looking now at her hostess and now round the room, while she gave a series of little pats, round her shoulders, to the edges of her dress. "Is there anyone I know?" she asked.

"I think everyone knows you!" said Mrs. Walker pregnantly, and she gave a very cursory greeting to Mr. Giovanelli. This gentleman bore himself gallantly. He smiled and bowed and showed his white teeth, he curled his moustaches and rolled his eyes, and performed all the proper functions of a handsome Italian at an evening party. He sang, very prettily, half-a-dozen songs, though Mrs. Walker afterwards declared that she had been quite unable to find out who asked him. It was apparently not Daisy who had given him his orders. Daisy sat at a distance from the piano, and though she had publicly, as it were, professed a high admiration for his singing, talked, not inaudibly, while it was going on.

"It's a pity these rooms are so small; we can't dance," she said to Winterbourne as if she had seen him five minutes before.

"I am not sorry we can't dance," Winterbourne answered; "I don't dance."

"Of course you don't dance; you're too stiff," said Miss Daisy. "I hope you enjoyed your drive with Mrs. Walker."

"No, I didn't enjoy it; I preferred walking with you."

"We paired off, that was much better," said Daisy. "But did you ever hear anything so cool as Mrs. Walker's wanting me to get into her carriage and drop poor Mr. Giovanelli, and under the pretext that it was proper? People have different ideas! It would have been most unkind; he had been talking about that walk for ten days."

"He should not have talked about it at all," said Winterbourne; "he would never have proposed to a young lady of this country to walk about the streets with him."

"About the streets?" cried Daisy, with her pretty stare. "Where then would he have proposed to her to walk? The Pincio is not the streets, either; and I, thank

[41]French: "She's making a spectacle of herself."

goodness, am not a young lady of this country. The young ladies of this country have a dreadfully poky time of it, so far as I can learn; I don't see why I should change my habits for *them.*"

"I am afraid your habits are those of a flirt," said Winterbourne gravely.

"Of course they are," she cried, giving him her little smiling stare again. "I'm a fearful, frightful flirt! Did you ever hear of a nice girl that was not? But I suppose you will tell me now that I am not a nice girl."

"You're a very nice girl, but I wish you would flirt with me and me only," said Winterbourne.

"Ah! thank you, thank you very much; you are the last man I should think of flirting with. As I have had the pleasure of informing you, you are too stiff."

"You say that too often," said Winterbourne.

Daisy gave a delighted laugh. "If I could have the sweet hope of making you angry, I should say it again."

"Don't do that; when I am angry I'm stiffer than ever. But if you won't flirt with me, do cease at least to flirt with your friend at the piano; they don't understand that sort of thing here."

"I thought they understood nothing else!" exclaimed Daisy.

"Not in young unmarried women."

"It seems to me much more proper in young unmarried women than in old married ones," Daisy declared.

"Well," said Winterbourne, "when you deal with natives you must go by the custom of the place. Flirting is a purely American custom; it doesn't exist here. So when you show yourself in public with Mr. Giovanelli and without your mother——"

"Gracious! poor mother!" interposed Daisy.

"Though you may be flirting, Mr. Giovanelli is not; he means something else."

"He isn't preaching, at any rate," said Daisy with vivacity. "And if you want very much to know, we are neither of us flirting, we are too good friends for that; we are very intimate friends."

"Ah!" rejoined Winterbourne, "if you are in love with each other it is another affair."

She had allowed him up to this point to talk so frankly that he had no expectation of shocking her by this ejaculation; but she immediately got up, blushing visibly, and leaving him to exclaim mentally that little American flirts were the queerest creatures in the world. "Mr. Giovanelli, at least," she said, giving her interlocutor a single glance, "never says such very disagreeable things to me."

Winterbourne was bewildered; he stood staring. Mr. Giovanelli had finished singing; he left the piano and came over to Daisy. "Won't you come into the other room and have some tea?" he asked, bending before her with his ornamental smile.

Daisy turned to Winterbourne, beginning to smile again. He was still more perplexed, for this inconsequent smile made nothing clear, though it seemed to prove, indeed, that she had a sweetness and softness that reverted instinctively to the pardon of offences. "It has never occurred to Mr. Winterbourne to offer me any tea," she said, with her little tormenting manner.

"I have offered advice," Winterbourne rejoined.

"I prefer weak tea!" cried Daisy, and she went off with the brilliant Giovanelli. She sat with him in the adjoining room, in the embrasure of the window, for the rest of the evening. There was an interesting performance at the piano, but neither of these young people gave heed to it. When Daisy came to take leave of Mrs. Walker, this lady conscientiously repaired the weakness of which she had been guilty at the moment of the young girl's arrival. She turned her back straight upon Miss Miller and left her to depart with what grace she might. Winterbourne was standing near the door; he saw it all. Daisy turned very pale and looked at her mother, but Mrs. Miller was humbly unconscious of any violation of the usual social forms. She appeared, indeed, to have felt an incongruous impulse to draw attention to her own striking observance of them. "Good-night, Mrs. Walker," she said; "we've had a beautiful evening. You see if I let Daisy come to parties without me, I don't want her to go away without me." Daisy turned away, looking with a pale, grave face at the circle near the door; Winterbourne saw that, for the first moment, she was too much shocked and puzzled even for indignation. He on his side was greatly touched.

"That was very cruel," he said to Mrs. Walker.

"She never enters my drawing-room again," replied his hostess.

Since Winterbourne was not to meet her in Mrs. Walker's drawing-room, he went as often as possible to Mrs. Miller's hotel. The ladies were rarely at home, but when he found them the devoted Giovanelli was always present. Very often the brilliant little Roman was in the drawing-room with Daisy alone. Mrs. Miller being apparently constantly of the opinion that discretion is the better part of surveillance. Winterbourne noted, at first with surprise, that Daisy on these occasions was never embarrassed or annoyed by his own entrance; but he very presently began to feel that she had no more surprises for him; the unexpected in her behavior was the only thing to expect. She showed no displeasure at her *tête-à-tête* with Giovanelli being interrupted; she could chatter as freshly and freely with two gentlemen as with one; there was always, in her conversation, the same odd mixture of audacity and puerility. Winterbourne remarked to himself that if she was seriously interested in Giovanelli it was very singular that she should not take more trouble to preserve the sanctity of their interviews, and he liked her the more for her innocent looking indifference and her apparently inexhaustible good humour. He could hardly have said why, but she seemed to him a girl who would never be jealous. At the risk of exciting a somewhat derisive smile on the reader's part, I may affirm that with regard to the women who had hitherto interested him, it very often seemed to Winterbourne among the possibilities that, given certain contingencies, he should be afraid—literally afraid—of these ladies; he had a pleasant sense that he should never be afraid of Daisy Miller. It must be added that this sentiment was not altogether flattering to Daisy; it was part of his conviction, or rather of his apprehension, that she would prove a very light young person.

But she was evidently very much interested in Giovanelli. She looked at him whenever he spoke; she was perpetually telling him to do this and to do that; she was constantly "chaffing" and abusing him. She appeared completely to have forgotten that Winterbourne had said anything to displease her at Mrs. Walker's little party. One Sunday afternoon, having gone to St. Peter's with his aunt, Winterbourne perceived Daisy strolling about the great church in company with the inevitable Giovanelli. Presently he pointed out the young girl and her cavalier to Mrs. Costello. This lady looked at them a moment through her eyeglass, and then she said:

"That's what makes you so pensive in these days, eh?"

"I had not the least idea I was pensive," said the young man.

"You are very much pre-occupied, you are thinking of something."

"And what is it," he asked, "that you accuse me of thinking of?"

"Of that young lady's—Miss Baker's, Miss Chandler's—what's her name? Miss Miller's intrigue with that little barber's block."[42]

"Do you call it an intrigue," Winterbourne asked—"an affair that goes on with such peculiar publicity?"

"That's their folly," said Mrs. Costello, "it's not their merit."

"No," rejoined Winterbourne, with something of that pensiveness to which his aunt had alluded. "I don't believe that there is anything to be called an intrigue."

"I have heard a dozen people speak of it; they say she is quite carried away by him."

"They are certainly very intimate," said Winterbourne.

Mrs. Costello inspected the young couple again with her optical instrument. "He is very handsome. One easily sees how it is. She thinks him the most elegant man in the world, the finest gentleman. She has never seen anything like him; he is better even than the courier. It was the courier probably who introduced him, and if he succeeds in marrying the young lady, the courier will come in for a magnificent commission."

"I don't believe she thinks of marrying him," said Winterbourne, "and I don't believe he hopes to marry her."

"You may be very sure she thinks of nothing. She goes on from day to day, from hour to hour, as they did in the Golden Age. I can imagine nothing more vulgar. And at the same time," added Mrs. Costello, "depend upon it that she may tell you any moment that she is 'engaged.'"

"I think that is more than Giovanelli expects," said Winterbourne.

"Who is Giovanelli?"

"The little Italian. I have asked questions about him and learned something. He is apparently a perfectly respectable little man. I believe he is in a small way a *cavaliere avvocato*.[43] But he doesn't move in what are called the first circles. I think it is really not absolutely impossible that the courier introduced him. He is evidently immensely charmed with Miss Miller. If she thinks him the finest gentleman in the world, he, on his side, has never found himself in personal contact with such splendor, such opulence, such expensiveness, as this young lady's. And then she must seem to him wonderfully pretty and interesting. I rather doubt that he dreams of marrying her. That must appear to him too impossible a piece of luck. He has nothing but his handsome face to offer, and there is a substantial Mr. Miller in that mysterious land of dollars. Giovanelli knows that he hasn't a title to offer. If he were only a count or a *marchese!*[44] He must wonder at his luck at the way they have taken him up."

"He accounts for it by his handsome face, and thinks Miss Miller a young lady *qui se passe ses fantaisies!*"[45] said Mrs. Costello.

"It is very true," Winterbourne pursued, "that Daisy and her mamma have not yet risen to that stage of—what shall I call it?—of culture, at which the idea of catching a count or a *marchese* begins. I believe that they are intellectually incapable of that conception."

"Ah! but the *avvocato* can't believe it," said Mrs. Costello.

[42]Dandy. [43]Italian: gentleman lawyer.
[44]An Italian rank of nobility, a marquis. [45]French: who gives in to her own whims.

Of the observation excited by Daisy's "intrigue," Winterbourne gathered that day at St. Peter's sufficient evidence. A dozen of the American colonists in Rome came to talk with Mrs. Costello, who sat on a little portable stool at the base of one of the great pilasters. The vesper service was going forward in splendid chants and organ-tones in the adjacent choir, and meanwhile, between Mrs. Costello and her friends, there was a great deal said about poor little Miss Miller's going really "too far." Winterbourne was not pleased with what he heard; but when, coming out upon the great steps of the church, he saw Daisy, who had emerged before him, get into an open cab with her accomplice and roll away through the cynical streets of Rome, he could not deny to himself that she was going very far indeed. He felt very sorry for her—not exactly that he believed that she had completely lost her head, but because it was painful to hear so much that was pretty, and undefended, and natural, assigned to a vulgar place among the categories of disorder. He made an attempt after this to give a hint to Mrs. Miller. He met one day in the Corso[46] a friend—a tourist like himself—who had just come out of the Doria Palace,[47] where he had been walking through the beautiful gallery. His friend talked for a moment about the superb portrait of Innocent X, by Velasquez,[48] which hangs in one of the cabinets of the palace, and then said, "And in the same cabinet, by-the-way, I had the pleasure of contemplating a picture of a different kind—that pretty American girl who you pointed out to me last week." In answer to Winterbourne's inquiries, his friend narrated that the pretty American girl—prettier than ever—was seated with a companion in the secluded nook in which the great papal portrait was enshrined.

"Who was her companion?" asked Winterbourne.

"A little Italian with a bouquet in his button hole. The girl is delightfully pretty, but I thought I understood from you the other day that she was a young lady *du meilleur monde.*"[49]

"So she is!" answered Winterbourne; and having assured himself that his informant had seen Daisy and her companion but five minutes before, he jumped into a cab and went to call on Mrs. Miller. She was at home; but she apologised to him for receiving him in Daisy's absence.

"She's gone out somewhere with Mr. Giovanelli," said Mrs. Miller. "She's always going round with Mr. Giovanelli."

"I have noticed that they are very intimate," Winterbourne observed.

"Oh! it seems as if they couldn't live without each other!" said Mrs. Miller. "Well, he's a real gentleman anyhow. I keep telling Daisy she's engaged!"

"And what does Daisy say?"

"Oh, she says she isn't engaged. But she might as well be!" this impartial parent resumed. "She goes on as if she was. But I've made Mr. Giovanelli promise to tell me, if *she* doesn't. I should want to write to Mr. Miller about it—shouldn't you?"

Winterbourne replied that he certainly should; and the state of mind of Daisy's mamma struck him as so unprecedented in the annals of parental vigilance that he gave up as utterly irrelevant the attempt to place her upon her guard.

[46]Roman street. [47]Roman baroque palace.

[48]Diego Rodriguez de Silva y Velásquez (1599–1660), Spanish painter whose portrait of Pope Innocent X (1649) is in the Doria Gallery in Rome.

[49]French: "of the best society."

After this Daisy was never at home, and Winterbourne ceased to meet her at the houses of their common acquaintance because, as he perceived, these shrewd people had quite made up their minds that she was going too far. They ceased to invite her, and they intimated that they desired to express to observant Europeans the great truth that, though Miss Daisy Miller was a young American lady, her behaviour was not representative—was regarded by her compatriots as abnormal. Winterbourne wondered how she felt about all the cold shoulders that were turned towards her, and sometimes it annoyed him to suspect that she did not feel at all. He said to himself that she was too light and childish, too uncultivated and unreasoning, too provincial, to have reflected upon her ostracism or even to have perceived it. Then at other moments he believed that she carried about in her elegant and irresponsible little organism a defiant, passionate, perfectly observant consciousness of the impression she produced. He asked himself whether Daisy's defiance came from the consciousness of innocence or from her being, essentially, a young person of the reckless class. It must be admitted that holding oneself to a belief in Daisy's "innocence" came to seem to Winterbourne more and more a matter of finespun gallantry. As I have already had occasion to relate, he was angry at finding himself reduced to chopping logic about this young lady; he was vexed at his want of instinctive certitude as to how far her eccentricities were generic, national, and how far they were personal. From either view of them he had somehow missed her, and now it was too late. She was "carried away" by Mr. Giovanelli.

A few days after his brief interview with her mother, he encountered her in that beautiful abode of flowering desolation known as the Palace of the Caesars.[50] The early Roman spring had filled the air with bloom and perfume, and the rugged surface of the Palatine was muffled with tender verdure. Daisy was strolling along the top of one of those great mounds of ruin that are embanked with mossy marble and paved with monumental inscriptions. It seemed to him that Rome had never been so lovely as just then. He stood looking off at the enchanting harmony of line and colour that remotely encircles the city, inhaling the softly humid odours and feeling the freshness of the year and the antiquity of the place reaffirm themselves in mysterious interfusion. It seemed to him also that Daisy had never looked so pretty; but this had been an observation of his whenever he met her. Giovanelli was at her side, and Giovanelli, too, wore an aspect of even unwonted brilliancy.

"Well," said Daisy, "I should think you would be lonesome!"

"Lonesome?" asked Winterbourne.

"You are always going round by yourself. Can't you get anyone to walk with you?"

"I am not so fortunate," said Winterbourne, "as your companion."

Giovanelli, from the first, had treated Winterbourne with distinguished politeness; he listened with a deferential air to his remarks; he laughed, punctiliously, at his pleasantries; he seemed disposed to testify to his belief that Winterbourne was a superior young man. He carried himself in no degree like a jealous wooer; he had obviously a great deal of tact; he had no objection to your expecting a little humility of him. It even seemed to Winterbourne at times that Giovanelli would find a certain mental relief in being able to have a private

[50]Ruins of palaces erected by the Caesars on the Palatine Hill, in Rome.

understanding with him—to say to him, as an intelligent man, that, bless you, *he* knew how extraordinary was this young lady, and didn't flatter himself with delusive—or at least *too* delusive—hopes of matrimony and dollars. On this occasion he strolled away from his companion to pluck a sprig of almond blossom, which he carefully arranged in his button hole.

"I know why you say that," said Daisy, watching Giovanelli. "Because you think I go round too much with *him!*" And she nodded at her attendant.

"Every one thinks so—if you care to know," said Winterbourne.

"Of course I care to know!" Daisy exclaimed seriously. "But I don't believe it. They are only pretending to be shocked. They don't really care a straw what I do. Besides, I don't go round so much."

"I think you will find they do care. They will show it—disagreeably."

Daisy looked at him a moment. "How—disagreeably?"

"Haven't you noticed anything?" Winterbourne asked.

"I have noticed you. But I noticed you were as stiff as an umbrella the first time I saw you."

"You will find I am not so stiff as several others," said Winterbourne, smiling.

"How shall I find it?"

"By going to see the others."

"What will they do to me?"

"They will give you the cold shoulder. Do you know what that means?"

Daisy was looking at him intently; she began to colour. "Do you mean as Mrs. Walker did the other night?"

"Exactly!" said Winterbourne.

She looked away at Giovanelli, who was decorating himself with his almond-blossom. Then looking back at Winterbourne—"I shouldn't think you would let people be so unkind!" she said.

"How can I help it?" he asked.

"I should think you would say something."

"I do say something," and he paused a moment. "I say that your mother tells me she believes you are engaged."

"Well, she does," said Daisy very simply.

Winterbourne began to laugh. "And does Randolph believe it?" he asked.

"I guess Randolph doesn't believe anything," said Daisy. Randolph's scepticism excited Winterbourne to further hilarity, and he observed that Giovanelli was coming back to them. Daisy, observing it too, addressed herself again to her countryman. "Since you have mentioned it," she said, "I *am* engaged." . . . Winterbourne looked at her; he had stopped laughing. "You don't believe it!" she added.

He was silent a moment; and then, "Yes, I believe it!" he said.

"Oh, no, you don't," she answered. "Well, then—I am not!"

The young girl and her cicerone[51] were on their way to the gate of the enclosure, so that Winterbourne, who had but lately entered, presently took leave of them. A week afterwards he went to dine at a beautiful villa on the Caelian Hill,[52] and, on arriving, dismissed his hired vehicle. The evening was charming, and he promised himself the satisfaction of walking home beneath the Arch of Constantine[53] and past the vaguely-lighted monuments of the Forum.[54] There

[51]Guide. [52]One of the hills of Rome.
[53]Memorial arch built to celebrate a Roman military victory in A.D. 312.
[54]Administrative and business center of ancient Rome.

was a waning moon in the sky, and her radiance was not brilliant, but she was veiled in a thin cloud-curtain which seemed to diffuse and equalise it. When, on his return from the villa (it was eleven o'clock), Winterbourne approached the dusky circle of the Colosseum, it recurred to him, as a lover of the picturesque, that the interior, in the pale moonshine, would be well worth a glance. He turned aside and walked to one of the empty arches, near which, as he observed, an open carriage—one of the little Roman streetcabs—was stationed. Then he passed in, among the cavernous shadows of the great structure, and emerged upon the clear and silent arena. The place had never seemed to him more impressive. One-half of the gigantic circus[55] was in deep shade; the other was sleeping in the luminous dusk. As he stood there he began to murmur Byron's famous lines, out of "Manfred;"[56] but before he had finished his quotation he remembered that if nocturnal meditations in the Colosseum are recommended by the poets, they are deprecated by the doctors. The historic atmosphere was there, certainly; but the historic atmosphere, scientifically considered, was no better than a villainous miasma. Winterbourne walked to the middle of the arena, to take a more general glance, intending thereafter to make a hasty retreat. The great cross in the centre was covered with shadow; it was only as he drew near it that he made it out distinctly. Then he saw that two persons were stationed upon the low steps which formed its base. One of these was a woman, seated; her companion was standing in front of her.

Presently the sound of the woman's voice came to him distinctly in the warm night-air. "Well, he looks at us as one of the old lions or tigers may have looked at the Christian martyrs!" These were the words he heard, in the familiar accent of Miss Daisy Miller.

"Let us hope he is not very hungry," responded the ingenious Giovanelli. "He will have to take me first; you will serve for dessert!"

Winterbourne stopped, with a sort of horror; and, it must be added, with a sort of relief. It was as if a sudden illumination had been flashed upon the ambiguity of Daisy's behaviour and the riddle had become easy to read. She was a young lady whom a gentleman need no longer be at pains to respect. He stood there looking at her—looking at her companion, and not reflecting that though he saw them vaguely, he himself must have been more brightly visible. He felt angry with himself that he had bothered so much about the right way of regarding Miss Daisy Miller. Then, as he was going to advance again, he checked himself; not from the fear that he was doing her injustice, but from a sense of the danger of appearing unbecomingly exhilarated by this sudden revulsion from cautious criticism. He turned away towards the entrance of the place; but as he did so he heard Daisy speak again.

"Why, it was Mr. Winterbourne! He saw me—and he cuts me!"

What a clever little reprobate she was, and how smartly she played at injured innocence! But he wouldn't cut her. Winterbourne came forward again, and went towards the great cross. Daisy had got up; Giovanelli lifted his hat. Winterbourne had not begun to think simply of the craziness, from a sanitary point of view, of a delicate young girl lounging away the evening in this nest

[55]Arena.

[56]"I do remember me, that in my youth,/When I was wandering,—upon such a night—/I stood within the Coliseum's wall,/Midst the chief relics of almighty Rome." From Byron's verse drama "Manfred" (1817), Act III, Scene iv, lines 8–11.

of malaria. What if she *were* a clever little reprobate? that was no reason for her dying of the *perniciosa*.[57] "How long have you been here?" he asked, almost brutally.

Daisy, lovely in the flattering moonlight, looked at him a moment. Then—"All the evening," she answered gently. . . . "I never saw anything so pretty."

"I am afraid," said Winterbourne, "that you will not think Roman fever very pretty. This is the way people catch it. I wonder," he added, turning to Giovanelli, "that you, a native Roman, should countenance such a terrible indiscretion."

"Ah," said the handsome native, "for myself, I am not afraid."

"Neither am I—for you! I am speaking for this young lady."

Giovanelli lifted his well-shaped eyebrows and showed his brilliant teeth. But he took Winterbourne's rebuke with docility. "I told the Signorina it was a grave indiscretion; but when was the Signorina ever prudent?"

"I never was sick, and I don't mean to be!" The Signorina declared. "I don't look like much, but I'm healthy! I was bound to see the Colosseum by moonlight; I shouldn't have wanted to go home without that; and we have had the most beautiful time, haven't we, Mr. Giovanelli? If there has been any danger, Eugenio can give me some pills. He has got some splendid pills."

"I should advise you," said Winterbourne, "to drive home as fast as possible and take one!"

"What you say is very wise," Giovanelli rejoined. "I will go and make sure the carriage is at hand." And he went forward rapidly.

Daisy followed with Winterbourne. He kept looking at her; she seemed not in the least embarrassed. Winterbourne said nothing; Daisy chattered about the beauty of the place. "Well, I *have* seen the Colosseum by moonlight!" she exclaimed. "That's one good thing." Then, noticing Winterbourne's silence, she asked him why he didn't speak. He made no answer; he only began to laugh. They passed under one of the dark archways; Giovanelli was in front with the carriage. Here Daisy stopped a moment, looking at the young American. "*Did* you believe I was engaged the other day?" she asked.

"It doesn't matter what I believed the other day," said Winterbourne, still laughing.

"Well, what do you believe now?"

"I believe that it makes very little difference whether you are engaged or not!"

He felt the young girl's pretty eyes fixed upon him through the thick gloom of the archway; she was apparently going to answer. But Giovanelli hurried her forward. "Quick, quick," he said; "if we get in by midnight we are quite safe."

Daisy took her seat in the carriage, and the fortunate Italian placed himself beside her. "Don't forget Eugenio's pills!" said Winterbourne, as he lifted his hat.

"I don't care," said Daisy, in a little strange tone, "Whether I have Roman fever or not!" Upon this the cab-driver cracked his whip, and they rolled away over the desultory patches of the antique pavement.

Winterbourne—to do him justice, as it were—mentioned to no one that he had encountered Miss Miller, at midnight, in the Colosseum with a gentleman; but nevertheless, a couple of days later, the fact of her having been there under these circumstances was known to every member of the little American circle,

[57]Italian: malaria, the Roman fever.

and commented accordingly. Winterbourne reflected that they had of course known it at the hotel, and that, after Daisy's return, there had been an exchange of remarks between the porter and the cabdriver. But the young man was conscious at the same moment that it had ceased to be a matter of serious regret to him that the little American flirt should be "talked about" by low-minded menials. These people, a day or two later, had serious information to give: the little American flirt was alarmingly ill. Winterbourne, when the rumor came to him, immediately went to the hotel for more news. He found that two or three charitable friends had preceded him, and that they were being entertained in Mrs. Miller's salon by Randolph.

"It's going round at night," said Randolph—"that's what made her sick. She's always going round at night. I shouldn't think she'd want to—it's so plaguey dark. You can't see anything here at night, except when there's a moon. In America there's always a moon!" Mrs. Miller was invisible; she was now, at least, giving her daughter the advantage of her society. It was evident that Daisy was dangerously ill.

Winterbourne went often to ask for news of her, and once he saw Mrs. Miller, who, though deeply alarmed, was—rather to his surprise—perfectly composed, and, as it appeared, a most efficient and judicious nurse. She talked a good deal about Dr. Davis, but Winterbourne paid her the compliment of saying to himself that she was not, after all, such a monstrous goose. "Daisy spoke of you the other day," she said to him. "Half the time she doesn't know what she's saying, but that time I think she did. She gave me a message; she told me to tell you. She told me to tell you that she never was engaged to that handsome Italian. I am sure I am very glad; Mr. Giovanelli hasn't been near us since she was taken ill. I thought he was so much a gentleman; but I don't call that very polite! A lady told me that he was afraid I was angry with him for taking Daisy round at night. Well, so I am; but I suppose he knows I'm a lady. I would scorn to scold him. Any way, she says, she's not engaged. I don't know why she wanted you to know; but she said to me three times—"Mind you tell Mr. Winterbourne.' And then she told me to ask if you remembered the time you went to that castle, in Switzerland. But I said I wouldn't give any such messages as that. Only, if she is not engaged, I'm sure I'm glad to know it."

But, as Winterbourne has said, it mattered very little. A week after this the poor girl died; it had been a terrible case of the fever. Daisy's grave was in the little Protestant cemetery, in an angle of the wall of imperial Rome, beneath the cypresses and the thick spring-flowers. Winterbourne stood there beside it, with a number of other mourners; a number larger than the scandal excited by the young lady's career would have led you to expect. Near him stood Giovanelli, who came nearer still before Winterbourne turned away. Giovanelli was very pale; on this occasion he had no flower in his buttonhole; he seemed to wish to say something. At last he said, "She was the most beautiful young lady I ever saw, and the most amiable." And then he added in a moment, "And she was the most innocent."

Winterbourne looked at him, and presently repeated his words, "And the most innocent?"

"The most innocent!"

Winterbourne felt sore and angry. "Why the devil," he asked, "did you take her to that fatal place?"

Mr. Giovanelli's urbanity was apparently imperturbable. He looked on the ground a moment, and then he said, "For myself, I had no fear; and she wanted to go."

"That was no reason!" Winterbourne declared.

The subtle Roman again dropped his eyes. "If she had lived, I should have got nothing. She would never have married me, I am sure."

"She would never have married you?"

"For a moment I hoped so. But no. I am sure."

Winterbourne listened to him; he stood staring at the raw protuberance among the April daisies. When he turned away again Mr. Giovanelli, with his light slow step, had retired.

Winterbourne almost immediately left Rome; but the following summer he again met his aunt, Mrs. Costello, at Vevey. Mrs. Costello was fond of Vevey. In the interval Winterbourne had often thought of Daisy Miller and her mystifying manners. One day he spoke of her to his aunt—said it was on his conscience he had done her injustice.

"I am sure I don't know," said Mrs. Costello. "How did your injustice affect her?"

"She sent me a message before her death which I didn't understand at the time. But I have understood it since. She would have appreciated one's esteem."

"Is that a modest way," asked Mrs. Costello, "of saying that she would have reciprocated one's affection?"

Winterbourne offered no answer to this question; but he presently said, "You were right in that remark that you made last summer. I was booked to make a mistake. I have lived too long in foreign parts."

Nevertheless, he went back to live at Geneva, whence there continue to come the most contradictory accounts of his motives of sojourn: a report that he is "studying" hard—an intimation that he is much interested in a very clever foreign lady.

1878 1878

THE REAL THING

I

When the porter's wife, who used to answer the house-bell, announced "A gentleman and a lady, sir," I had, as I often had in those days—the wish being father to the thought—an immediate vision of sitters. Sitters my visitors in this case proved to be; but not in the sense I should have preferred. There was nothing at first however to indicate that they might n't have come for a portrait. The gentleman, a man of fifty, very high and very straight, with a moustache slightly grizzled and a dark grey walking-coat admirably fitted, both of which I noted professionally—I don't mean as a barber or yet as a tailor—would have struck me as a celebrity if celebrities often were striking. It was a truth of which I had for some time been conscious that a figure with a good deal of frontage[1] was, as one

[1]I.e., imposing appearance.

might say, almost never a public institution. A glance at the lady helped to remind me of this paradoxical law: she also looked too distinguished to be a "personality." Moreover one would scarcely come across two variations together.

Neither of the pair immediately spoke—they only prolonged the preliminary gaze suggesting that each wished to give the other a chance. They were visibly shy; they stood there letting me take them in—which, as I afterwards perceived, was the most practical thing they could have done. In this way their embarrassment served their cause. I had seen people painfully reluctant to mention that they desired anything so gross as to be represented on canvas; but the scruples of my new friends appeared almost insurmountable. Yet the gentleman might have said "I should like a portrait of my wife," and the lady might have said "I should like a portrait of my husband." Perhaps they were n't husband and wife—this naturally would make the matter more delicate. Perhaps they wished to be done together—in which case they ought to have brought a third person to break the news.

"We come from Mr. Rivet," the lady finally said with a dim smile that had the effect of a moist sponge passed over a "sunk"[2] piece of painting, as well as of a vague allusion to vanished beauty. She was as tall and straight, in her degree, as her companion, and with ten years less to carry. She looked as sad as a woman could look whose face was not charged with expression; that is her tinted oval mask showed waste as an exposed surface shows friction. The hand of time had played over her freely, but to an effect of elimination. She was slim and stiff, and so well-dressed, in dark blue cloth, with lappets[3] and pockets and buttons, that it was clear she employed the same tailor as her husband. The couple had an indefinable air of prosperous thrift—they evidently got a good deal of luxury for their money. If I was to be one of their luxuries it would behove me to consider my terms.

"Ah Claude Rivet recommended me?" I echoed; and I added that it was very kind of him, though I could reflect that, as he only painted landscape, this was n't a sacrifice.

The lady looked very hard at the gentleman, and the gentleman looked round the room. Then staring at the floor a moment and stroking his moustache, he rested his pleasant eyes on me with the remark: "He said you were the right one."

"I try to be, when people want to sit."

"Yes, we should like to," said the lady anxiously.

"Do you mean together?"

My visitors exchanged a glance. "If you could do anything with *me* I suppose it would be double," the gentleman stammered.

"Oh yes, there's naturally a higher charge for two figures than for one."

"We should like to make it pay," the husband confessed.

"That's very good of you," I returned, appreciating so unwonted a sympathy—for I supposed he meant pay the artist.

A sense of strangeness seemed to dawn on the lady. "We mean for the illustrations—Mr. Rivet said you might put one in."

"Put in—an illustration?" I was equally confused.

"Sketch her off, you know," said the gentleman, colouring.

[2]Faded. [3]Folds, or flaps.

It was only then that I understood the service Claude Rivet had rendered me; he had told them how I worked in black-and-white, for magazines, for storybooks, for sketches of contemporary life, and consequently had copious employment for models. These things were true, but it was not less true—I may confess it now; whether because the aspiration was to lead to everything or to nothing I leave the reader to guess—that I could n't get the honours, to say nothing of the emoluments, of a great painter of portraits out of my head. My "illustrations" were my pot-boilers; I looked to a different branch of art—far and away the most interesting it had always seemed to me—to perpetuate my fame. There was no shame in looking to it also to make my fortune; but that fortune was by so much further from being made from the moment my visitors wished to be "done" for nothing. I was disappointed; for in the pictorial sense I had immediately *seen* them. I had seized their type—I had already settled what I would do with it. Something that wouldn't absolutely have pleased them, I afterwards reflected.

"Ah you're—you're—a—?" I began as soon as I had mastered my surprise. I could n't bring out the dingy word "models": it seemed so little to fit the case.

"We have n't had much practice," said the lady.

"We've got to *do* something, and we've thought that an artist in your line might perhaps make something of us," her husband threw off. He further mentioned that they did n't know many artists and that they had gone first, on the off-chance—he painted views of course, but sometimes put in figures; perhaps I remembered—to Mr. Rivet, whom they had met a few years before at a place in Norfolk where he was sketching.

"We used to sketch a little ourselves," the lady hinted.

"It's very awkward, but we absolutely *must* do something," her husband went on.

"Of course we're not so *very* young," she admitted with a wan smile.

With the remark that I might as well know something more about them the husband had handed me a card extracted from a neat new pocketbook—their appurtenances were all of the freshest—and inscribed with the words "Major Monarch." Impressive as these words were they did n't carry my knowledge much further; but my visitor presently added: "I've left the army and we've had the misfortune to lose our money. In fact our means are dreadfully small."

"It's awfully trying—a regular strain," said Mrs. Monarch.

They evidently wished to be discreet—to take care not to swagger because they were gentlefolk. I felt them willing to recognise this as something of a drawback, at the same time that I guessed at an underlying sense—their consolation in adversity—that they *had* their points. They certainly had; but these advantages struck me as preponderantly social; such for instance as would help to make a drawing-room look well. However, a drawing-room was always, or ought to be, a picture.

In consequence of his wife's allusion to their age Major Monarch observed: "Naturally it's more for the figure that we thought of going in. We can still hold ourselves up." On the instant I saw that the figure was indeed their strong point. His "naturally" did n't sound vain, but it lighted up the question. "*She* has the best one," he continued, nodding at his wife with a pleasant after-dinner absence of circumlocution. I could only reply, as if we were in fact sitting over our wine, that this did n't prevent his own from being very good; which led him in turn to make answer: "We thought that if you ever have to do people like us we might be something like it. *She* particularly—for a lady in a book, you know."

I was so amused by them that, to get more of it, I did my best to take their point of view; and though it was an embarrassment to find myself appraising physically, as if they were animals on hire or useful blacks, a pair of whom I should have expected to meet only in one of the relations in which criticism is tacit, I looked at Mrs. Monarch judicially enough to be able to exclaim after a moment with conviction: "Oh yes, a lady in a book!" She was singularly like a bad illustration.

"We'll stand up, if you like," said the Major; and he raised himself before me with a really grand air.

I could take his measure at a glance—he was six feet two and a perfect gentleman. It would have paid any club in process of formation and in want of a stamp to engage him at a salary to stand in the principal window. What struck me at once was that in coming to me they had rather missed their vocation; they could surely have been turned to better account for advertising purposes. I could n't of course see the thing in detail, but I could see them make somebody's fortune—I don't mean their own. There was something in them for a waistcoat-maker, an hotel-keeper or a soap-vendor. I could imagine "We always use it" pinned on their bosoms with the greatest effect; I had a vision of the brilliancy with which they would launch a table d'hôte.[4]

Mrs. Monarch sat still, not from pride but from shyness, and presently her husband said to her: "Get up, my dear, and show how smart you are." She obeyed, but she had no need to get up to show it. She walked to the end of the studio and then came back blushing, her fluttered eyes on the partner of her appeal. I was reminded of an incident I had accidentally had a glimpse of in Paris—being with a friend there, a dramatist about to produce a play, when an actress came to him to ask to be entrusted with a part. She went through her paces before him, walked up and down as Mrs. Monarch was doing. Mrs. Monarch did it quite as well, but I abstained from applauding. It was very odd to see such people apply for such poor pay. She looked as if she had ten thousand a year. Her husband had used the word that described her: she was in the London current jargon essentially and typically "smart." Her figure was, in the same order of ideas, conspicuously and irreproachably "good." For a woman of her age her waist was surprisingly small; her elbow moreover had the orthodox crook. She held her head at the conventional angle, but why did she come to *me?* She ought to have tried on jackets at a big shop. I feared my visitors were not only destitute but "artistic"—which would be a great complication. When she sat down again I thanked her, observing that what a draughtsman most valued in his model was the faculty of keeping quiet.

"Oh *she* can keep quiet," said Major Monarch. Then he added jocosely: "I've always kept her quiet."

"I'm not a nasty fidget, am I?" It was going to wring tears from me, I felt, the way she hid her head, ostrich-like, in the other broad bosom.

The owner of this expanse addressed his answer to me. "Perhaps it is n't out of place to mention—because we ought to be quite business-like, ought n't we?—that when I married her she was known as the Beautiful Statue."

"Oh dear!" said Mrs. Monarch ruefully.

"Of course I should want a certain amount of expression," I rejoined.

"Of *course!*"—and I had never heard such unanimity.

[4]I.e., a restaurant.

"And then I suppose you know that you'll get awfully tired."

"Oh, we *never* get tired!" they eagerly cried.

"Have you had any kind of practice?"

They hesitated—they looked at each other. "We've been photographed—*immensely,*" said Mrs. Monarch.

"She means the fellows have asked us themselves," added the Major.

"I see—because you're so good-looking."

"I don't know what they thought, but they were always after us."

"We always got our photographs for nothing," smiled Mrs. Monarch.

"We might have brought some, my dear," her husband remarked.

"I'm not sure we have any left. We've given quantities away," she explained to me.

"With our autographs and that sort of thing," said the Major.

"Are they to be got in the shops?" I enquired as a harmless pleasantry.

"Oh yes, *hers*—they used to be."

"Not now," said Mrs. Monarch with her eyes on the floor.

II

I could fancy the "sort of thing" they put on the presentation copies of their photographs, and I was sure they wrote a beautiful hand. It was odd how quickly I was sure of everything that concerned them. If they were now so poor as to have to earn shillings and pence they could never have had much of a margin. Their good looks had been their capital, and they had good-humouredly made the most of the career that this resource marked out for them. It was in their faces, the blankness, the deep intellectual repose of the twenty years of country-house visiting that had given them pleasant intonations. I could see the sunny drawing-rooms, sprinkled with periodicals she did n't read, in which Mrs. Monarch had continuously sat; I could see the wet shrubberies in which she had walked, equipped to admiration for either exercise. I could see the rich covers[5] the Major had helped to shoot and the wonderful garments in which, late at night, he repaired to the smoking-room to talk about them. I could imagine their leggings and waterproofs, their knowing tweeds and rugs, their rolls of sticks and cases of tackle and neat umbrellas; and I could evoke the exact appearance of their servants and the compact variety of their luggage on the platforms of country stations.

They gave small tips, but they were liked; they did n't do anything themselves, but they were welcome. They looked so well everywhere; they gratified the general relish for stature, complexion and "form." They knew it without fatuity or vulgarity, and they respected themselves in consequence. They were n't superficial; they were thorough and kept themselves up—it had been their line. People with such a taste for activity had to have some line. I could feel how even in a dull house they could have been counted on for the joy of life. At present something had happened—it didn't matter what, their little income had grown less, it had grown least—and they had to do something for pocket-money. Their friends could like them, I made out, without liking to support them. There was something about them that represented credit—their clothes,

[5]Woods and thickets from which game is driven for hunters.

their manners, their type; but if credit is a large empty pocket in which an occasional chink reverberates, the chink at least must be audible. What they wanted of me was to help to make it so. Fortunately they had no children—I soon divined that. They would also perhaps wish our relations to be kept secret: this was why it was "for the figure"—the reproduction of the face would betray them.

I liked them—I felt, quite as their friends must have done—they were so simple; and I had no objection to them if they would suit. But somehow with all their perfections I did n't easily believe in them. After all they were amateurs, and the ruling passion of my life was the detestation of the amateur. Combined with this was another perversity—an innate preference for the represented subject over the real one: the defect of the real one was so apt to be a lack of representation. I liked things that appeared; then one was sure. Whether they *were* or not was a subordinate and almost always a profitless question. There were other considerations, the first of which was that I already had two or three recruits in use, notably a young person with big feet, in alpaca, from Kilburn, who for a couple of years had come to me regularly for my illustrations and with whom I was still—perhaps ignobly—satisfied. I frankly explained to my visitors how the case stood, but they had taken more precautions than I supposed. They had reasoned out their opportunity, for Claude Rivet had told them of the projected *édition de luxe* of one of the writers of our day—the rarest of the novelists—who, long neglected by the multitudinous vulgar and dearly prized by the attentive (need I mention Philip Vincent?) had had the happy fortune of seeing, late in life, the dawn and then the full light of a higher criticism; an estimate in which on the part of the public there was something really of expiation. The edition preparing, planned by a publisher of taste, was practically an act of high reparation; the wood-cuts with which it was to be enriched were the homage of English art to one of the most independent representatives of English letters. Major and Mrs. Monarch confessed to me they had hoped I might be able to work *them* into my branch of the enterprise. They knew I was to do the first of the books, "Rutland Ramsay," but I had to make clear to them that my participation in the rest of the affair—this first book was to be a test—must depend on the satisfaction I should give. If this should be limited my employers would drop me with scarce common forms. It was therefore a crisis for me, and naturally I was making special preparations, looking about for new people, should they be necessary, and securing the best types. I admitted however that I should like to settle down to two or three good models who would do for everything.

"Should we have often to—a—put on special clothes?" Mrs. Monarch timidly demanded.

"Dear yes—that's half the business."

"And should we be expected to supply our own costumes?"

"Oh no; I've got a lot of things. A painter's models put on—or put off—anything he likes."

"And you mean—a—the same?"

"The same?"

Mrs. Monarch looked at her husband again.

"Oh she was just wondering," he explained, "if the costumes are in *general* use." I had to confess that they were, and I mentioned further that some of them—I had a lot of genuine greasy last-century things—had served their time, a hundred years ago, on living world-stained men and women; on figures not perhaps so far removed, in that vanished world, from *their* type, the Monarchs', *quoi!*[6] of a breeched and bewigged age. "We'll put on anything that *fits,*" said the Major.

"Oh I arrange that—they fit in the pictures."

"I'm afraid I should do better for the modern books. I'd come as you like," said Mrs. Monarch.

"She has got a lot of clothes at home: they might do for contemporary life," her husband continued.

"Oh I can fancy scenes in which you'd be quite natural." And indeed I could see the slipshod rearrangements of stale properties—the stories I tried to produce pictures for without the exasperation of reading them—whose sandy tracts the good lady might help to people. But I had to return to the fact that for this sort of work—the daily mechanical grind—I was already equipped: the people I was working with were fully adequate.

"We only thought we might be more like *some* characters," said Mrs. Monarch mildly, getting up.

Her husband also rose; he stood looking at me with a dim wistfulness that was touching in so fine a man. "Would n't it be rather a pull sometimes to have—a—to have—?" He hung fire; he wanted me to help him by phrasing what he meant. But I could n't—I did n't know. So he brought it out awkwardly: "The *real* thing; a gentleman, you know, or a lady." I was quite ready to give a general assent—I admitted that there was a great deal in that. This encouraged Major Monarch to say, following up his appeal with an unacted gulp: "It's awfully hard—we've tried everything." The gulp was communicative; it proved too much for his wife. Before I knew it Mrs. Monarch had dropped again upon a divan and burst into tears. Her husband sat down beside her, holding one of her hands; whereupon she quickly dried her eyes with the other, while I felt embarrassed as she looked up at me. "There is n't a confounded job I have n't applied for—waited for—prayed for. You can fancy we'd be pretty bad first. Secretaryships and that sort of thing? You might as well ask for a peerage. I'd be *anything*—I'm strong; a messenger or a coalheaver. I'd put on a gold-laced cap and open carriage-doors in front of the haberdasher's; I'd hang about a station to carry portmanteaux;[7] I'd be a postman. But they won't *look* at you; there are thousands as good as yourself already on the ground. *Gentlemen,* poor beggars, who've drunk their wine, who've kept their hunters!"

I was as reassuring as I knew how to be, and my visitors were presently on their feet again while, for the experiment, we agreed on an hour. We were discussing it when the door opened and Miss Churm came in with a wet umbrella. Miss Churm had to take the omnibus to Maida Vale and then walk half a mile. She looked a trifle blowsy and slightly splashed. I scarcely ever saw her come in without thinking afresh how odd it was that, being so little in herself, she should yet be so much in others. She was a meagre little Miss Churm, but was such an ample heroine of romance. She was only a freckled cockney,[8] but she could represent everything, from a fine lady to a shepherdess; she had the faculty as she might have had a fine voice or long hair. She could n't spell and she loved beer, but she had two or three "points," and practice, and a knack, and mother-wit, and a whimsical sensibility, and love of the theatre, and seven

[6]French: what! [7]Large suitcases.
[8]A slum dweller in London's East End, hence a member of the lower class.

sisters, and not an ounce of respect, especially for the *h.* The first thing my visitors saw was that her umbrella was wet, and in their spotless perfection they visibly winced at it. The rain had come on since their arrival.

"I'm all in a soak; there *was* a mess of people in the 'bus. I wish you lived near a stytion," said Miss Churm. I requested her to get ready as quickly as possible, and she passed into the room in which she always changed her dress. But before going out she asked me what she was to get into this time.

"It's the Russian princess, don't you know?" I answered; "the one with the 'golden eyes,' in black velvet, for the long thing in the *Cheapside*."[9]

"Golden eyes? I *say!*" cried Miss Churm, while my companions watched her with intensity as she withdrew. She always arranged herself, when she was late, before I could turn round; and I kept my visitors a little on purpose, so that they might get an idea, from seeing her, what would be expected of themselves. I mentioned that she was quite my notion of an excellent model—she was really very clever.

"Do you think she looks like a Russian princess?" Major Monarch asked with lurking alarm.

"When I make her, yes."

"Oh if you have to *make* her—!" he reasoned, not without point.

"That's the most you can ask. There are so many who are not makeable."

"Well now, *here's* a lady"—and with a persuasive smile he passed his arm into his wife's—"who's already made!"

"Oh I'm not a Russian princess," Mrs. Monarch protested a little coldly. I could see she had known some and did n't like them. There at once was a complication of a kind I never had to fear with Miss Churm.

This young lady came back in black velvet—the gown was rather rusty and very low on her lean shoulders—and with a Japanese fan in her red hands. I reminded her that in the scene I was doing she had to look over some one's head. "I forget whose it is; but it does n't matter. Just look over a head."

"I'd rather look over a stove," said Miss Churm; and she took her station near the fire. She fell into position, settled herself into a tall attitude, gave a certain backward inclination to her head and a certain forward droop to her fan, and looked, at least to my prejudiced sense, distinguished and charming, foreign and dangerous. We left her looking so while I went downstairs with Major and Mrs. Monarch.

"I believe I could come about as near as that," said Mrs. Monarch.

"Oh you think she's shabby, but you must allow for the alchemy of art."

However, they went off with an evident increase of comfort founded on their demonstrable advantage in being the real thing. I could fancy them shuddering over Miss Churm. She was very droll about them when I went back, for I told her what they wanted.

"Well, if *she* can sit I'll tyke to bookkeeping," said my model.

"She's very ladylike," I replied as an innocent form of aggravation.

"So much the worse for *you.* That means she can't turn round."

"She'll do for the fashionable novels."

"Oh yes, she'll *do* for them!" my model humorously declared. "Ain't they bad enough without her?" I had often sociably denounced them to Miss Churm.

[9]A magazine named for a commercial street in London.

III

It was for the elucidation of a mystery in one of these works that I first tried Mrs. Monarch. Her husband came with her, to be useful if necessary—it was sufficiently clear that as a general thing he would prefer to come with her. At first I wondered if this were for "propriety's" sake—if he were going to be jealous and meddling. The idea was too tiresome, and if it had been confirmed it would speedily have brought our acquaintance to a close. But I soon saw there was nothing in it and that if he accompanied Mrs. Monarch it was—in addition to the chance of being wanted—simply because he had nothing else to do. When they were separate his occupation was gone and they never *had* been separate. I judged rightly that in their awkward situation their close union was their main comfort and that this union had no weak spot. It was a real marriage, an encouragement to the hesitating, a nut for pessimists to crack. Their address was humble—I remember afterwards thinking it had been the only thing about them that was really professional—and I could fancy the lamentable lodgings in which the Major would have been left alone. He could sit there more or less grimly with his wife—he could n't sit there anyhow without her.

He had too much tact to try and make himself agreeable when he could n't be useful; so when I was too absorbed in my work to talk he simply sat and waited. But I liked to hear him talk—it made my work, when not interrupting it, less mechanical, less special. To listen to him was to combine the excitement of going out with the economy of staying at home. There was only one hindrance—that I seemed not to know any of the people this brilliant couple had known. I think he wondered extremely, during the term of our intercourse, whom the deuce I *did* know. He had n't a stray sixpence of an idea to fumble for, so we did n't spin it very fine; we confined ourselves to questions of leather and even of liquor—saddlers and breeches-makers and how to get excellent claret cheap—and matters like "good trains" and the habits of small game. His lore on these last subjects was astonishing—he managed to interweave the stationmaster with the ornithologist. When he could n't talk about greater things he could talk cheerfully about smaller, and since I could n't accompany him into reminiscences of the fashionable world he could lower the conversation without a visible effort to my level.

So earnest a desire to please was touching in a man who could so easily have knocked one down. He looked after the fire and had an opinion on the draught of the stove without my asking him, and I could see that he thought many of my arrangements not half knowing. I remember telling him that if I were only rich I'd offer him a salary to come and teach me how to live. Sometimes he gave a random sigh of which the essence might have been: "Give me even such a bare old barrack as *this,* and I'd do something with it!" When I wanted to use him he came alone; which was an illustration of the superior courage of women. His wife could bear her solitary second floor, and she was in general more discreet; showing by various small reserves that she was alive to the propriety of keeping our relations markedly professional—not letting them slide into sociability. She wished it to remain clear that she and the Major were employed, not cultivated, and if she approved of me as a superior, who could be kept in his place, she never thought me quite good enough for an equal.

She sat with great intensity, giving the whole of her mind to it, and was capable of remaining for an hour almost as motionless as before a photographer's lens. I could see she had been photographed often, but somehow the very habit that made her good for that purpose unfitted her for mine. At first I was extremely pleased with her ladylike air, and it was a satisfaction, on coming to follow her lines, to see how good they were and how far they could lead the pencil. But after a little skirmishing I began to find her too insurmountably stiff; do what I would with it my drawing looked like a photograph or a copy of a photograph. Her figure had no variety of expression—she herself had no sense of variety. You may say that this was my business and was only a question of placing her. Yet I placed her in every conceivable position and she managed to obliterate their differences. She was always a lady certainly, and into the bargain was always the same lady. She was the real thing, but always the same thing. There were moments when I rather writhed under the serenity of her confidence that she *was* the real thing. All her dealings with me and all her husband's were an implication that this was lucky for *me.* Meanwhile I found myself trying to invent types that approached her own, instead of making her own transform itself—in the clever way that was not impossible for instance to poor Miss Churm. Arrange as I would and take the precautions I would, she always came out, in my pictures, too tall—landing me in the dilemma of having represented a fascinating woman as seven feet high, which (out of respect perhaps to my own very much scantier inches) was far from my idea of such a personage.

The case was worse with the Major—nothing I could do would keep *him* down, so that he became useful only for the representation of brawny giants. I adored variety and range, I cherished human accidents, the illustrative note; I wanted to characterise closely, and the thing in the world I most hated was the danger of being ridden by a type. I had quarrelled with some of my friends about it; I had parted company with them for maintaining that one *had* to be, and that if the type was beautiful—witness Raphael and Leonardo[10]—the servitude was only a gain. I was neither Leonardo nor Raphael—I might only be a presumptuous young modern searcher; but I held that everything was to be sacrificed sooner than character. When they claimed that the obsessional form could easily *be* character I retorted, perhaps superficially, "Whose?" It could n't be everybody's—it might end in being nobody's.

After I had drawn Mrs. Monarch a dozen times I felt surer even than before that the value of such a model as Miss Churm resided precisely in the fact that she had no positive stamp, combined of course with the other fact that what she did have was a curious and inexplicable talent for imitation. Her usual appearance was like a curtain which she could draw up at request for a capital performance. This performance was simply suggestive; but it was a word to the wise—it was vivid and pretty. Sometimes even I thought it, though she was plain herself, too insipidly pretty; I made it a reproach to her that the figures drawn from her were monotonously (*bêtement,*[11] as we used to say) graceful. Nothing made her more angry: it was so much her pride to feel she could sit for characters that had nothing in common with each other. She would accuse me at such moments of taking away her "reputytion."

It suffered a certain shrinkage, this queer quantity, from the repeated visits of my new friends. Miss Churm was greatly in demand, never in want of employment, so I had no scruple in putting her off occasionally, to try them more

[10]Raphael Sanzio (1483–1520) and Leonardo da Vinci (1452–1519), Italian painters.
[11]French: stupidly.

at my ease. It was certainly amusing at first to do the real thing—it was amusing to do Major Monarch's trousers. They *were* the real thing, even if he did come out colossal. It was amusing to do his wife's back hair—it was so mathematically neat—and the particular "smart" tension of her tight stays. She lent herself especially to positions in which the face was somewhat averted or blurred; she abounded in ladylike back views and *profils perdus*.[12] When she stood erect she took naturally one of the attitudes in which court-painters represent queens and princesses; so that I found myself wondering whether, to draw out this accomplishment, I could n't get the editor of the *Cheapside* to publish a really royal romance, "A Tale of Buckingham Palace." Sometimes however the real thing and the make-believe came into contact; by which I mean that Miss Churm, keeping an appointment or coming to make one on days when I had much work in hand, encountered her invidious rivals. The encounter was not on their part, for they noticed her no more than if she had been the housemaid; not from intentional loftiness, but simply because as yet, professionally, they did n't know how to fraternise, as I could imagine they would have liked—or at least that the Major would. They could n't talk about the omnibus[13]—they always walked; and they did n't know what else to try—she was n't interested in good trains or cheap claret. Besides, they must have felt—in the air—that she was amused at them, secretly derisive of their ever knowing how. She wasn't a person to conceal the limits of her faith if she had had a chance to show them. On the other hand Mrs. Monarch did n't think her tidy; for why else did she take pains to say to me—it was going out of the way, for Mrs. Monarch—that she did n't like dirty women?

One day when my young lady happened to be present with my other sitters—she even dropped in, when it was convenient, for a chat—I asked her to be so good as to lend a hand in getting tea, a service with which she was familiar and which was one of a class that, living as I did in a small way, with slender domestic resources, I often appealed to my models to render. They liked to lay hands on my property, to break the sitting, and sometimes the china—it made them feel Bohemian. The next time I saw Miss Churm after this incident she surprised me greatly by making a scene about it—she accused me of having wished to humiliate her. She had n't resented the outrage at the time, but had seemed obliging and amused, enjoying the comedy of asking Mrs. Monarch, who sat vague and silent, whether she would have cream and sugar, and putting an exaggerated simper into the question. She had tried intonations—as if she too wished to pass for the real thing—till I was afraid my other visitors would take offence.

Oh they were determined not to do this, and their touching patience was the measure of their great need. They would sit by the hour, uncomplaining, till I was ready to use them; they would come back on the chance of being wanted and would walk away cheerfully if it failed. I used to go to the door with them to see in what magnificent order they retreated. I tried to find other employment for them—I introduced them to several artists. But they didn't "take," for reasons I could appreciate, and I became rather anxiously aware that after such disappointments they fell back upon me with a heavier weight. They did me the honour to think me most *their* form. They were n't romantic enough for the

[12]French: lost profiles, poses that show the back of the head more than the profile.
[13]Bus.

painters, and in those days there were few serious workers in black-and-white. Besides, they had an eye to the great job I had mentioned to them—they had secretly set their hearts on supplying the right essence for my pictorial vindication of our fine novelist. They knew that for this undertaking I should want no costume-effects, none of the frippery of past ages—that it was a case in which everything would be contemporary and satirical and presumably genteel. If I could work them into it their future would be assured, for the labour would of course be long and the occupation steady.

One day Mrs. Monarch came without her husband—she explained his absence by his having had to go to the City.[14] While she sat there in her usual relaxed majesty there came at the door a knock which I immediately recognised as the subdued appeal of a model out of work. It was followed by the entrance of a young man whom I at once saw to be a foreigner and who proved in fact an Italian acquainted with no English word but my name, which he uttered in a way that made it seem to include all others. I had n't then visited his country, nor was I proficient in his tongue; but as he was not so meanly constituted—what Italian is?—as to depend only on that member of expression he conveyed to me, in familiar but graceful mimicry, that he was in search of exactly the employment in which the lady before me was engaged. I was not struck with him at first, and while I continued to draw I dropped few signs of interest or encouragement. He stood his ground however—not importunately, but with a dumb dog-like fidelity in his eyes that amounted to innocent impudence, the manner of a devoted servant—he might have been in the house for years—unjustly suspected. Suddenly it struck me that this very attitude and expression made a picture; whereupon I told him to sit down and wait till I should be free. There was another picture in the way he obeyed me, and I observed as I worked that there were others still in the way he looked wonderingly, with his head thrown back, about the high studio. He might have been crossing himself in Saint Peter's. Before I finished I said to myself "The fellow's a bankrupt orange-monger, but a treasure."

When Mrs. Monarch withdrew he passed across the room like a flash to open the door for her, standing there with the rapt pure gaze of the young Dante spellbound by the young Beatrice.[15] As I never insisted, in such situations, on the blankness of the British domestic, I reflected that he had the making of a servant—and I needed one, but could n't pay him to be only that—as well as of a model; in short I resolved to adopt my bright adventurer if he would agree to officiate in the double capacity. He jumped at my offer, and in the event my rashness—for I had really known nothing about him—was-n't brought home to me. He proved a sympathetic though a desultory ministrant, and had in a wonderful degree the *sentiment de la pose.*[16] It was uncultivated, instinctive, a part of the happy instinct that had guided him to my door and helped him to spell out my name on the card nailed to it. He had had no other introduction to me than a guess, from the shape of my high north window, seen outside, that my place was a studio and that as a studio it would contain an artist. He had wandered to England in search of fortune, like

[14]London's financial and commercial center.

[15]Beatrice Portinari (1266–1290), Florentine woman said to be the ideal and the inspiration of the poet Dante, who first saw her when he was nine.

[16]French: instinct for posing.

other itinerants, and had embarked, with a partner and a small green handcart, on the sale of penny ices. The ices had melted away and the partner had dissolved in their train. My young man wore tight yellow trousers with reddish stripes and his name was Oronte. He was sallow but fair, and when I put him into some old clothes of my own he looked like an Englishman. He was as good as Miss Churm, who could look, when requested, like an Italian.

IV

I thought Mrs. Monarch's face slightly convulsed when, on her coming back with her husband, she found Oronte installed. It was strange to have to recognise in a scrap of a lazzarone[17] a competitor to her magnificent Major. It was she who scented danger first, for the Major was anecdotically unconscious. But Oronte gave us tea, with a hundred eager confusions—he had never been concerned in so queer a process—and I think she thought better of me for having at last an "establishment." They saw a couple of drawings that I had made of the establishment, and Mrs. Monarch hinted that it never would have struck her he had sat for them. "Now the drawings you make from *us*, they look exactly like us," she reminded me, smiling in triumph; and I recognised that this was indeed just their defect. When I drew the Monarchs I could n't anyhow get away from them—get into the character I wanted to represent; and I hadn't the least desire my model should be discoverable in my picture. Miss Churm never was, and Mrs. Monarch thought I hid her, very properly, because she was vulgar; whereas if she was lost it was only as the dead who go to heaven are lost—in the gain of an angel the more.

By this time I had got a certain start with "Rutland Ramsay," the first novel in the great projected series; that is I had produced a dozen drawings, several with the help of the Major and his wife, and I had sent them in for approval. My understanding with the publishers, as I have already hinted, had been that I was to be left to do my work, in this particular case, as I liked, with the whole book committed to me; but my connexion with the rest of the series was only contingent. There were moments when, frankly, it *was* a comfort to have the real thing under one's hand; for there were characters in "Rutland Ramsay" that were very much like it. There were people presumably as erect as the Major and women of as good a fashion as Mrs. Monarch. There was a great deal of countryhouse life—treated, it is true, in a fine fanciful ironical generalised way—and there was a considerable implication of knickerbockers[18] and kilts. There were certain things I had to settle at the outset; such things for instance as the exact appearance of the hero and the particular bloom and figure of the heroine. The author of course gave me a lead, but there was a margin for interpretation. I took the Monarchs into my confidence, I told them frankly what I was about, I mentioned my embarrassments and alternatives. "Oh take *him!*" Mrs. Monarch murmured sweetly, looking at her husband; and "What could you want better than my wife?" the Major enquired with the comfortable candour that now prevailed between us.

I was n't obliged to answer these remarks—I was only obliged to place my sitters. I was n't easy in mind, and I postponed a little timidly perhaps the solving

[17]Italian: beggar. [18]Trousers gathered at the knee, knickers.

of my question. The book was a large canvas, the other figures were numerous, and I worked off at first some of the episodes in which the hero and the heroine were not concerned. When once I had set *them* up I should have to stick to them—I could n't make my young man seven feet high in one place and five feet nine in another. I inclined on the whole to the latter measurement, though the Major more than once reminded me that *he* looked about as young as any one. It was indeed quite possible to arrange him, for the figure, so that it would have been difficult to detect his age. After the spontaneous Oronte had been with me a month, and after I had given him to understand several times over that his native exuberance would presently constitute an insurmountable barrier to our further intercourse, I waked to a sense of his heroic capacity. He was only five feet seven, but the remaining inches were latent. I tried him almost secretly at first, for I was really rather afraid of the judgment my other models would pass on such a choice. If they regarded Miss Churm as little better than a snare what would they think of the representation by a person so little the real thing as an Italian street-vendor of a protagonist formed by a public school?

If I went a little in fear of them it was n't because they bullied me, because they had got an oppressive foothold, but because in their really pathetic decorum and mysteriously permanent newness they counted on me so intensely. I was therefore very glad when Jack Hawley came home: he was always of such good counsel. He painted badly himself, but there was no one like him for putting his finger on the place. He had been absent from England for a year; he had been somewhere—I don't remember where—to get a fresh eye. I was in a good deal of dread of any such organ, but we were old friends; he had been away for months and a sense of emptiness was creeping into my life. I had n't dodged a missile for a year.

He came back with a fresh eye, but with the same old black velvet blouse, and the first evening he spent in my studio we smoked cigarettes till the small hours. He had done no work himself, he had only got the eye; so the field was clear for the production of my little things. He wanted to see what I had produced for the *Cheapside,* but he was disappointed in the exhibition. That at least seemed the meaning of two or three comprehensive groans which, as he lounged on my big divan, his leg folded under him, looking at my latest drawings, issued from his lips with the smoke of the cigarette.

"What's the matter with you?" I asked.

"What's the matter with *you?*"

"Nothing save that I'm mystified."

"You are indeed. You're quite off the hinge. What's the meaning of this new fad?" And he tossed me, with visible irreverence, a drawing in which I happened to have depicted both my elegant models. I asked if he did n't think it good, and he replied that it struck him as execrable, given the sort of thing I had always represented myself to him as wishing to arrive at; but I let that pass—I was so anxious to see exactly what he meant. The two figures in the picture looked colossal, but I supposed this was *not* what he meant, inasmuch as, for aught he knew to the contrary, I might have been trying for some such effect. I maintained that I was working exactly in the same way as when he last had done me the honour to tell me I might do something some day. "Well, there's a screw loose somewhere," he answered; "wait a bit and I'll discover it." I depended upon him to do so: where else was the fresh eye? But he produced at last nothing more luminous than "I don't know—I don't like your types." This was lame for a critic who had never consented to discuss with me anything but the question of execution, the direction of strokes and the mystery of values.

"In the drawings you've been looking at I think my types are very handsome."

"Oh, they won't do!"

"I've been working with new models."

"I see you have. *They* won't do."

"Are you very sure of that?"

"Absolutely—they're stupid."

"You mean *I* am—for I ought to get around that."

"You *can't*—with such people. Who are they?"

I told him, so far as was necessary, and he concluded heartlessly: *"Ce sont des gens qu'il faut mettre à la porte."*[19]

"You've never seen them; they're awfully good"—I flew to their defence.

"Not seen them? Why all this recent work of yours drops to pieces with them. It's all I want to see of them."

"No one else has said anything against it—the *Cheapside* people are pleased."

"Every one else is an ass, and the *Cheapside* people the biggest asses of all. Come, don't pretend at this time of day to have pretty illusions about the public, especially about publishers and editors. It's not for *such* animals you work—it's for those who know, *coloro che sanno,*"[20] so keep straight for *me* if you can't keep straight for yourself. There was a certain sort of thing you used to try for—and a very good thing is was. But this twaddle is n't *in* it." When I talked with Hawley later about "Rutland Ramsay" and its possible successors he declared that I must get back into my boat again or I should go to the bottom. His voice in short was the voice of warning.

I noted the warning, but I did n't turn my friends out of doors. They bored me a good deal; but the very fact that they bored me admonished me not to sacrifice them—if there was anything to be done with them—simply to irritation. As I look back at this phase they seem to me to have pervaded my life not a little. I have a vision of them as most of the time in my studio, seated against the wall on an old velvet bench to be out of the way, and resembling the while a pair of patient courtiers in a royal ante-chamber. I'm convinced that during the coldest weeks of the winter they held their ground because it saved them fire. Their newness was losing its gloss, and it was impossible not to feel them objects of charity. Whenever Miss Churm arrived they went away, and after I was fairly launched in "Rutland Ramsay" Miss Churm arrived pretty often. They managed to express to me tacitly that they supposed I wanted her for the low life of the book, and I let them suppose it, since they had attempted to study the work—it was lying about the studio—without discovering that it dealt only with the highest circles. They had dipped into the most brilliant of our novelists without deciphering many passages. I still took an hour from them, now and again, in spite of Jack Hawley's warning; it would be time enough to dismiss them, if dismissal should be necessary, when the rigour of the season was over. Hawley had made their acquaintance—he had met them at my fireside—and thought them a ridiculous pair. Learning that he was a painter they tried to approach him, to show him too that they were the real thing; but he looked at

[19]French: "They are people one must show to the door," i.e., get rid of.

[20]Italian: those who know, a quotation from Dante's *Inferno,* Canto IV, line 131.

them, across the big room, as if they were miles away; they were a compendium of everything he most objected to in the social system of his country. Such people as that, all convention and patent-leather, with ejaculations that stopped conversation, had no business in a studio. A studio was a place to learn to see, and how could you see through a pair of feather-beds?

The main inconvenience I suffered at their hands was that at first I was shy of letting it break upon them that my artful little servant had begun to sit to me for "Rutland Ramsay." They knew I had been odd enough—they were prepared by this time to allow oddity to an artist—to pick a foreign vagabond out of the streets when I might have had a person with whiskers and credentials; but it was some time before they learned how high I rated his accomplishments. They found him in an attitude more than once, but they never doubted I was doing him as an organ-grinder. There were several things they never guessed, and one of them was that for a striking scene in the novel, in which a footman briefly figured, it occurred to me to make use of Major Monarch as the menial. I kept putting this off, I did n't like to ask him to don the livery—beside the difficulty of finding a livery to fit him. At last, one day late in the winter, when I was at work on the despised Oronte, who caught one's idea on the wing, and was in the glow of feeling myself go very straight, they came in, the Major and his wife, with their society laugh about nothing (there was less and less to laugh at); came in like country-callers—they always reminded me of that—who have walked across the park after church and are presently persuaded to stay to luncheon. Luncheon was over, but they could stay to tea—I knew they wanted it. The fit was on me, however, and I could n't let my ardour cool and my work wait, with the fading daylight, while my model prepared it. So I asked Mrs. Monarch if she would mind laying it out—a request which for an instant brought all the blood to her face. Her eyes were on her husband's for a second, and some mute telegraphy passed between them. Their folly was over the next instant; his cheerful shrewdness put an end to it. So far from pitying their wounded pride, I must add, I was moved to give it as complete a lesson as I could. They bustled about together and got out the cups and saucers and made the kettle boil. I know they felt as if they were waiting on my servant, and when the tea was prepared I said: "He'll have a cup, please—he's tired." Mrs. Monarch brought him one where he stood, and he took it from her as if he had been a gentleman at a party squeezing a crush-hat with an elbow.

Then it came over me that she had made a great effort for me—made it with a kind of nobleness—and that I owed her a compensation. Each time I saw her after this I wondered what the compensation could be. I could n't go on doing the wrong thing to oblige them. Oh it *was* the wrong thing, the stamp of the work for which they sat—Hawley was not the only person to say it now. I sent in a large number of the drawings I had made for "Rutland Ramsay," and I received a warning that was more to the point than Hawley's. The artistic adviser of the house for which I was working was of opinion that many of my illustrations were not what had been looked for. Most of these illustrations were the subjects in which the Monarchs had figured. Without giving into the question of what *had* been looked for, I had to face the fact that at this rate I should n't get the other books to do. I hurled myself in despair on Miss Churm—I put her through all her paces. I not only adopted Oronte publicly as my hero, but one morning when the Major looked in to see if I did n't require him to finish a *Cheapside* figure for which he had begun to sit the week before, I told him I had changed my mind—I'd do the drawing from my man. At this my visitor turned pale and stood looking at me. "Is *he* your idea of an English gentleman?" he asked.

I was disappointed, I was nervous, I wanted to get on with my work; so I replied with irritation: "Oh my dear Major—I can't be ruined for *you!*"

It was a horrid speech, but he stood another moment—after which, without a word, he quitted the studio. I drew a long breath, for I said to myself that I should n't see him again. I had n't told him definitely that I was in danger of having my work rejected, but I was vexed at his not having felt the catastrophe in the air, read with me the moral of our fruitless collaboration, the lesson that in the deceptive atmosphere of art even the highest respectability may fail of being plastic.

I did n't owe my friends money, but I did see them again. They reappeared together three days later, and, given all the other facts, there was something tragic in that one. It was a clear proof they could find nothing else in life to do. They had threshed the matter out in a dismal conference—they had digested the bad news that they were not in for the series. If they were n't useful to me even for the *Cheapside* their function seemed difficult to determine, and I could only judge at first that they had come, forgivingly, decorously, to take a last leave. This made me rejoice in secret that I had little leisure for a scene; for I had placed both my other models in position together and I was pegging away at a drawing from which I hoped to derive glory. It had been suggested by the passage in which Rutland Ramsay, drawing up a chair to Artemisia's piano-stool, says extraordinary things to her while she ostensibly fingers out a difficult piece of music. I had done Miss Churm at the piano before—it was an attitude in which she knew how to take on an absolutely poetic grace. I wished the two figures to "compose" together with intensity, and my little Italian had entered perfectly into my conception. The pair were vividly before me, the piano had been pulled out; it was a charming show of blended youth and murmured love, which I had only to catch and keep. My visitors stood and looked at it, and I was friendly to them over my shoulder.

They made no response, but I was used to silent company and went on with my work, only a little disconcerted—even though exhilarated by the sense that *this* was at least the ideal thing—at not having got rid of them after all. Presently I heard Mrs. Monarch's sweet voice beside or rather above me: "I wish her hair were a little better done." I looked up and she was staring with a strange fixedness at Miss Churm, whose back was turned to her. "Do you mind my just touching it?" she went on—a question which made me spring up for an instant as with the instinctive fear that she might do the young lady a harm. But she quieted me with a glance I shall never forget—I confess I should like to have been able to paint *that*—and went for a moment to my model. She spoke to her softly, laying a hand on her shoulder and bending over her; and as the girl, understanding, gratefully assented, she disposed her rough curls, with a few quick passes, in such a way as to make Miss Churm's head twice as charming. It was one of the most heroic personal services I've ever seen rendered. Then Mrs. Monarch turned away with a low sigh and, looking about her as if for something to do, stooped to the floor with a noble humility and picked up a dirty rag that had dropped out of my paint-box.

The Major meanwhile had also been looking for something to do, and, wandering to the other end of the studio, saw before him my breakfast-things neglected, unremoved. "I say, can't I be useful here?" he called out to me with an irrepressible quaver. I assented with a laugh that I fear was awkward, and for the next ten minutes, while I worked, I heard the light clatter of china and the tinkle of spoons and glass. Mrs. Monarch assisted her husband—they washed up my crockery, they put it away. They wandered off into my little scullery, and I afterwards found that they had cleaned my knives and that my slender stock of plate had an unprecedented surface. When it came over me, the latent eloquence of what they were doing, I confess that my drawing was blurred for a moment—the picture swam. They had accepted their failure, but they could n't accept their fate. They had bowed their heads in bewilderment to the perverse and cruel law in virtue of which the real thing could be so much less precious than the unreal; but they did n't want to starve. If my servants were my models, then my models might be my servants. They would reverse the parts—the others would sit for the ladies and gentlemen and *they* would do the work. They would still be in the studio—it was an intense dumb appeal to me not to turn them out. "Take us on," they wanted to say—"we'll do *anything*."

My pencil dropped from my hand; my sitting was spoiled and I got rid of my sitters, who were also evidently rather mystified and awestruck. Then, alone with the Major and his wife I had a most uncomfortable moment. He put their prayer into a single sentence: "I say, you know—just let *us* do for you, can't you?" I could n't—it was dreadful to see them emptying my slops, but I pretended I could, to oblige them, for about a week. Then I gave them a sum of money to go away, and I never saw them again. I obtained the remaining books, but my friend Hawley repeats that Major and Mrs. Monarch did me a permanent harm, got me into false ways. If it be true I'm content to have paid the price—for the memory.

1892, 1909

THE BEAST IN THE JUNGLE

I

What determined the speech that startled him in the course of their encounter scarcely matters, being probably but some words spoken by himself quite without intention—spoken as they lingered and slowly moved together after their renewal of acquaintance. He had been conveyed by friends an hour or two before to the house at which she was staying; the party of visitors at the other house, of whom he was one, and thanks to whom it was his theory, as always, that he was lost in the crowd, had been invited over to luncheon. There had been after luncheon much dispersal, all in the interest of the original motive, a view of Weatherend itself and the fine things, intrinsic features, pictures, heirlooms, treasures of all the arts, that made the place almost famous; and the great rooms were so numerous that guests could wander at their will, hang back from the principal group and in cases where they took such matters with the last seriousness give themselves up to mysterious appreciations and measurements. There were persons to be observed, singly or in couples, bending toward objects in out-of-the-way corners with their hands on their knees and their heads nodding quite as with the emphasis of an excited sense of smell. When they were two they either mingled their sounds of ecstasy or melted into silences of even deeper import, so that there were aspects of the occasion that gave it for Marcher much the air of the "look round," previous to a sale highly advertised, that excites or quenches, as may be, the dream of acquisition. The dream of acquisition at Weatherend would have had to be wild indeed, and John Marcher found himself, among such suggestions, disconcerted almost equally by the presence of those who knew too much and by that of those who knew nothing. The great rooms caused so much poetry and history to press upon him that he needed some straying apart to feel in a proper relation with them, though this impulse was not, as happened, like the gloating of some of his companions, to be compared to the movements of a dog sniffing a cupboard. It had an issue promptly enough in a direction that was not to have been calculated.

It led, briefly, in the course of the October afternoon, to his closer meeting with May Bartram, whose face, a reminder, yet not quite a remembrance, as they sat much separated at a very long table, had begun merely by troubling him rather pleasantly. It affected him as the sequel of something of which he had lost the beginning. He knew it, and for the time quite welcomed it, as a continuation, but did n't know what it continued, which was an interest or an amusement the greater as he was also somehow aware—yet without a direct sign from her—that the young woman herself had n't lost the thread. She had n't lost it, but she would n't give it back to him, he saw, without some putting forth of his hand for it; and he not only saw that, but saw several things more, things odd enough in the light of the fact that at the moment some accident of grouping brought them face to face he was still merely fumbling with the idea that any contact between them in the past would have had no importance. If it had had no importance he scarcely knew why his actual impression of her should so seem to have so much; the answer to which, however, was that in such a life as they all appeared to be leading for the moment one could but take things as they came. He was satisfied, without in the least being able to say why, that this young lady might roughly have ranked in the house as a poor relation; satisfied also that she was not there on a brief visit, but was more or less a part of the establishment—almost a working, a remunerated part. Did n't she enjoy at periods a protection that she paid for by helping, among other services, to show the place and explain it, deal with the tiresome people, answer questions about the dates of the building, the styles of the furniture, the authorship of the pictures, the favourite haunts of the ghost? It was n't that she looked as if you could have given her shillings—it was impossible to look less so. Yet when she finally drifted toward him, distinctly handsome, though ever so much older—older than when he had seen her before—it might have been as an effect of her guessing that he had, within the couple of hours, devoted more imagination to her than to all the others put together, and had thereby penetrated to a kind of truth that the others were too stupid for. She *was* there on harder terms than any one; she was there as a consequence of things suffered, one way and another, in the interval of years; and she remembered him very much as she was remembered—only a good deal better.

By the time they at last thus came to speech they were alone in one of the rooms—remarkable for a fine portrait over the chimneyplace—out of which their friends had passed, and the charm of it was that even before they had spoken they had practically arranged with each other to stay behind for talk. The charm, happily, was in other things too—partly in there being scarce a spot at Weatherend without something to stay behind for. It was in the way the autumn day looked into the high windows as it waned; the way the red light, breaking at the close from under a low sombre sky, reached out in a long shaft and played over old wainscots, old tapestry, old gold, old colour. It was most of all perhaps in the way she came to him as if, since she had been turned on to deal with the simpler sort, he might, should he choose to keep the whole thing down, just take her mild attention for a part of her general business. As soon as he heard her voice, however, the gap was filled up and the missing link supplied; the slight irony he divined in her attitude lost its advantage. He almost jumped at it to get there before her. "I met you years and years ago in Rome. I remember all about it." She confessed to disappointment—she had been so sure he did n't; and to prove how well he did he began to pour the particular recollections that popped up as he called for them. Her face and her voice, all at his service now, worked the miracle—the impression operating like the torch of a lamplighter who touches into flame, one by one, a long row of gas-jets. Marcher flattered himself the illumination was brilliant, yet he was really still more pleased on her showing him, with amusement, that in his haste to make everything right he had got most things rather wrong. It had n't been at Rome—it had been at Naples; and it had n't been eight years before—it had been more nearly ten. She had n't been, either, with her uncle and aunt, but with her mother and her brother; in addition to which it was not with the Pembles *he* had been, but with the Boyers, coming down in their company from Rome—a point on which she insisted, a little to his confusion, and as to which she had her evidence in hand. The Boyers she had known, but did n't know the Pembles, though she had heard of them, and it was the people he was with who had made them acquainted. The incident of the thunderstorm that had raged round them with such violence as to drive them for refuge into an excavation—this incident had not occurred at the Palace of the Cæsars, but at Pompeii,[1] on an occasion when they had been present there at an important find.

He accepted her amendments, he enjoyed her corrections, though the moral of them was, she pointed out, that he *really* did n't remember the least thing about her; and he only felt it as a drawback that when all was made strictly historic there did n't appear much of anything left. They lingered together still, she neglecting her office—for from the moment he was so clever she had no proper right to him—and both neglecting the house, just waiting as to see if a memory or two more would n't again breathe on them. It had n't taken them many minutes, after all, to put down on the table, like the cards of a pack, those that constituted their respective hands; only what came out was that the pack was unfortunately not perfect—that the past, invoked, invited, encouraged, could give them, naturally, no more than it had. It had made them anciently meet—her at twenty, him at twenty-five; but nothing was so strange, they seemed to say to each other, as that, while so occupied, it had n't done a little more for them. They looked at each other as with the feeling of an occasion missed; the present would have been so much better if the other, in the far distance, in the

[1] I.e., not at Rome, the site of the Palace of the Caesars, but near Naples—at the ruined city of Pompeii, where archaeological excavations were taking place.

foreign land, had n't been so stupidly meagre. There were n't apparently, all counted, more than a dozen little old things that had succeeded in coming to pass between them; trivialities of youth, simplicities of freshness, stupidities of ignorance, small possible germs, but too deeply buried—too deeply (did n't it seem?) to sprout after so many years. Marcher could only feel he ought to have rendered her some service—saved her from a capsized boat in the Bay or at least recovered her dressing-bag, filched from her cab in the streets of Naples by a lazzarone with a stiletto. Or it would have been nice if he could have been taken with fever all alone at his hotel, and she could have come to look after him, to write to his people, to drive him out in convalescence. *Then* they would be in possession of the something or other that their actual show seemed to lack. It yet somehow presented itself, this show, as too good to be spoiled; so that they were reduced for a few minutes more to wondering a little helplessly why—since they seemed to know a certain number of the same people—their reunion had been so long averted. They did n't use that name for it, but their delay from minute to minute to join the others was a kind of confession that they did n't quite want it to be a failure. Their attempted supposition of reasons for their not having met but showed how little they knew of each other. There came in fact a moment when Marcher felt a positive pang. It was vain to pretend she was an old friend, for all the communities were wanting, in spite of which it was as an old friend that he saw she would have suited him. He had new ones enough—was surrounded with them for instance on the stage of the other house; as a new one he probably would n't have so much as noticed her. He would have liked to invent something, get her to make-believe with him that some passage of a romantic or critical kind *had* originally occurred. He was really almost reaching out in imagination—as against time—for something that would do, and saying to himself that if it did n't come this sketch of a fresh start would show for quite awkwardly bungled. They would separate, and now for no second or no third chance. They would have tried and not succeeded. Then it was, just at the turn, as he afterwards made it out to himself, that, everything else failing, she herself decided to take up the case and, as it were, save the situation. He felt as soon as she spoke that she had been consciously keeping back what she said and hoping to get on without it; a scruple in her that immensely touched him when, by the end of three or four minutes more, he was able to measure it. What she brought out, at any rate, quite cleared the air and supplied the link—the link it was so odd he should frivolously have managed to lose.

"You know you told me something I've never forgotten and that again and again has made me think of you since; it was that tremendously hot day when we went to Sorrento,[2] across the bay, for the breeze. What I allude to was what you said to me, on the way back, as we sat under the awning of the boat enjoying the cool. Have you forgotten?"

He had forgotten and was even more surprised than ashamed. But the great thing was that he saw in this no vulgar reminder of any "sweet" speech. The vanity of women had long memories, but she was making no claim on him of a compliment or a mistake. With another woman, a totally different one, he might have feared the recall possibly even of some imbecile "offer." So, in having to say that he had indeed forgotten, he was conscious rather of a loss than

[2]A resort town on the Bay of Naples.

of a gain; he already saw an interest in the manner of her mention. "I try to think—but I give it up. Yet I remember the Sorrento day."

"I'm not very sure you do," May Bartram after a moment said; "and I'm not very sure I ought to want you to. It's dreadful to bring a person back at any time to what he was ten years before. If you've lived away from it," she smiled, "so much the better."

"Ah, if *you* have n't why should I?" he asked.

"Lived away, you mean, from what I myself was?"

"From what *I* was. I was of course an ass," Marcher went on; "but I would rather know from you just the sort of ass I was than—from the moment you have something in your mind—not know anything."

Still, however, she hesitated. "But if you've completely ceased to be that sort—?"

"Why I can then all the more bear to know. Besides, perhaps I have n't."

"Perhaps. Yet if you have n't," she added, "I should suppose you'd remember. Not indeed that *I* in the least connect with my impression the invidious name you use. If I had only thought you foolish," she explained, "the thing I speak of would n't so have remained with me. It was about yourself." She waited as if it might come to him; but as, only meeting her eyes in wonder, he gave no sign, she burnt her ships.[3] "Has it ever happened?"

Then it was that, while he continued to stare, a light broke for him and the blood slowly came to his face, which began to burn with recognition. "Do you mean I told you—?" But he faltered, lest what came to him should n't be right, lest he should only give himself away.

"It was something about yourself that it was natural one should n't forget—that is if one remembered you at all. That's why I ask you," she smiled, "if the thing you then spoke of has ever come to pass?"

Oh then he saw, but he was lost in wonder and found himself embarrassed. This, he also saw, made her sorry for him, as if her allusion had been a mistake. It took him but a moment, however, to feel it had n't been, much as it had been a surprise. After the first little shock of it her knowledge on the contrary began, even if rather strangely, to taste sweet to him. She was the only other person in the world then who would have it, and she had had it all these years, while the fact of his having so breathed his secret had unaccountably faded from him. No wonder they could n't have met as if nothing had happened. "I judge," he finally said, "that I know what you mean. Only I had strangely enough lost any sense of having taken you so far into my confidence."

"Is it because you've taken so many others as well?"

"I've taken nobody. Not a creature since then."

"So that I'm the only person who knows?"

"The only person in the world."

"Well," she quickly replied, "I myself have never spoken. I've never, never repeated of you what you told me." She looked at him so that he perfectly believed her. Their eyes met over it in such a way that he was without a doubt. "And I never will."

She spoke with an earnestness that, as if almost excessive, put him at ease about her possible derision. Somehow the whole question was a new luxury to him—that is from the moment she was in possession. If she did n't take the

[3]I.e., she proceeded boldly, irreversibly.

sarcastic view she clearly took the sympathetic, and that was what he had had, in all the long time, from no one whomsoever. What he felt was that he could n't at present have begun to tell her, and yet could profit perhaps exquisitely by the accident of having done so of old. "Please don't then. We're just right as it is."

"Oh I am," she laughed, "if you are!" To which she added: "Then you do still feel in the same way?"

It was impossible he should n't take to himself that she was really interested, though it all kept coming as perfect surprise. He had thought of himself so long as abominably alone, and lo he was n't alone a bit. He had n't been, it appeared, for an hour—since those moments on the Sorrento boat. It was *she* who had been, he seemed to see as he looked at her—she who had been made so by the graceless fact of his lapse of fidelity. To tell her what he had told her—what had it been but to ask something of her? something that she had given, in her charity, without his having, by a remembrance, by a return of the spirit, failing another encounter, so much as thanked her. What he had asked of her had been simply at first not to laugh at him. She had beautifully not done so for ten years, and she was not doing so now. So he had endless gratitude to make up. Only for that he must see just how he had figured to her. "What, exactly, was the account I gave?"

"Of the way you did feel? Well, it was very simple. You said you had had from your earliest time, as the deepest thing within you, the sense of being kept for something rare and strange, possibly prodigious and terrible, that was soon or later to happen to you, that you had in your bones the foreboding and the conviction of, and that would perhaps overwhelm you."

"Do you call that very simple?" John Marcher asked.

She thought a moment. "It was perhaps because I seemed, as you spoke, to understand it."

"You do understand it?" he eagerly asked.

Again she kept her kind eyes on him. "You still have the belief?"

"Oh!" he exclaimed helplessly. There was too much to say.

"Whatever it's to be," she clearly made out, "it has n't yet come."

He shook his head in complete surrender now. "It has n't yet come. Only, you know, it is n't anything I'm to *do,* to achieve in the world, to be distinguished or admired for. I'm not such an ass as *that.* It would be much better, no doubt, if I were."

"It's to be something you're merely to suffer?"

"Well, say to wait for—to have to meet, to face, to see suddenly break out in my life; possibly destroying all further consciousness, possibly annihilating me; possibly, on the other hand, only altering everything, striking at the root of all my world and leaving me to the consequences, however they shape themselves."

She took this in, but the light in her eye continued for him not to be that of mockery. "Is n't what you describe perhaps but the expectation—or at any rate the sense of danger, familiar to so many people—of falling in love?"

John Marcher wondered. "Did you ask me that before?"

"No—I was n't so free-and-easy then. But it's what strikes me now."

"Of course," he said after a moment, "it strikes you. Of course it strikes *me.* Of course what's in store for me may be no more than that. The only thing is," he went on, "that I think if it had been that I should by this time know."

"Do you mean because you've *been* in love?" And then as he but looked at her in silence: "You've been in love, and it has n't meant such a cataclysm, has n't proved the great affair?"

"Here I am, you see. It has n't been overwhelming."

"Then it has n't been love," said May Bartram.

"Well, I at least thought it was. I took it for that—I've taken it till now. It was agreeable, it was delightful, it was miserable," he explained. "But it was n't strange. It was n't what *my* affair's to be."

"You want something all to yourself—something that nobody else knows or *has* known?"

"It is n't a question of what I 'want'—God knows I don't want anything. It's only a question of the apprehension that haunts me—that I live with day by day."

He said this so lucidly and consistently that he could see it further impose itself. If she had n't been interested before she'd have been interested now. "Is it a sense of coming violence?"

Evidently now too again he liked to talk of it. "I don't think of it as—when it does come—necessarily violent. I only think of it as natural and as of course above all unmistakeable. I think of it simply as *the* thing. *The* thing will of itself appear natural."

"Then how will it appear strange?"

Marcher bethought himself. "It won't—to *me.*"

"To whom then?"

"Well," he replied, smiling at last, "say to you."

"Oh then I'm to be present?"

"Why, you *are* present—since you know."

"I see." She turned it over. "But I mean at the catastrophe."[4]

At this, for a minute, their lightness gave way to their gravity; it was as if the long look they exchanged held them together. "It will only depend on yourself—if you'll watch with me."

"Are you afraid?" she asked.

"Don't leave me *now,*" he went on.

"Are you afraid?" she repeated.

"Do you think me simply out of my mind?" he pursued instead of answering. "Do I merely strike you as a harmless lunatic?"

"No," said May Bartram. "I understand you. I believe you."

"You mean you feel how my obsession—poor old thing!—may correspond to some possible reality?"

"To some possible reality."

"Then you *will* watch with me?"

She hesitated, then for the third time put her question. "Are you afraid?"

"Did I tell you I was—at Naples?"

"No, you said nothing about it."

"Then I don't know. And I should *like* to know," said John Marcher. "You'll tell me yourself whether you think so. If you'll watch with me you'll see."

"Very good then." They had been moving by this time across the room, and at the door, before passing out, they paused as for the full wind-up of their understanding. "I'll watch with you," said May Bartram.

[4]The final dramatic event in a play.

II

The fact that she "knew"—knew and yet neither chaffed him nor betrayed him—had in a short time begun to constitute between them a goodly bond, which became more marked when, within the year that followed their afternoon at Weatherend, the opportunities for meeting multiplied. The event that thus promoted these occasions was the death of the ancient lady her great-aunt, under whose wing, since losing her mother, she had to such an extent found shelter, and who, though but the widowed mother of the new successor to the property, had succeeded—thanks to a high tone and a high temper—in not forfeiting the supreme position at the great house. The deposition of this personage arrived but with her death, which, followed by many changes, made in particular a difference for the young woman in whom Marcher's expert attention had recognised from the first a dependent with a pride that might ache though it did n't bristle. Nothing for a long time had made him easier than the thought that the aching must have been much soothed by Miss Bartram's now finding herself able to set up a small home in London. She had acquired property, to an amount that made that luxury just possible, under her aunt's extremely complicated will, and when the whole matter began to be straightened out, which indeed took time, she let him know that the happy issue was at last in view. He had seen her again before that day, both because she had more than once accompanied the ancient lady to town and because he had paid another visit to the friends who so conveniently made of Weatherend one of the charms of their own hospitality. These friends had taken him back there; he had achieved there again with Miss Bartram some quiet detachment; and he had in London succeeded in persuading her to more than one brief absence from her aunt. They went together, on these latter occasions, to the National Gallery and the South Kensington Museum,[5] where, among vivid reminders, they talked of Italy at large—not now attempting to recover, as at first, the taste of their youth and their ignorance. That recovery, the first day at Weatherend, had served its purpose well, had given them quite enough; so that they were, to Marcher's sense, no longer hovering about the headwaters of their stream, but had felt their boat pushed sharply off and down the current.

They were literally afloat together; for our gentleman this was marked, quite as marked as that the fortunate cause of it was just the buried treasure of her knowledge. He had with his own hands dug up this little hoard, brought to light—that is to within reach of the dim day constituted by their discretions and privacies—the object of value the hiding-place of which he had, after putting it into the ground himself, so strangely, so long forgotten. The rare luck of his having again just stumbled on the spot made him indifferent to any other question; he would doubtless have devoted more time to the odd accident of his lapse of memory if he had n't been moved to devote so much to the sweetness, the comfort, as he felt, for the future, that this accident itself had helped to keep fresh. It had never entered into his plan that any one should "know," and mainly for the reason that it was n't in him to tell any one. That would have been impossible, for nothing but the amusement of a cold world would have waited on it. Since, however, a mysterious fate had opened his mouth betimes, in spite of him, he would count that a compensation and profit by it to the utmost. That

[5]The Victoria and Albert Museum in South Kensington, London.

the right person *should* know tempered the asperity of his secret more even than his shyness had permitted him to imagine; and May Bartram was clearly right, because—well, because there she was. Her knowledge simply settled it; he would have been sure enough by this time had she been wrong. There was that in his situation, no doubt, that disposed him too much to see her as a mere confidant, taking all her light for him from the fact—the fact only—of her interest in his predicament; from her mercy, sympathy, seriousness, her consent not to regard him as the funniest of the funny. Aware, in fine, that her price for him was just in her giving him this constant sense of his being admirably spared, he was careful to remember that she had also a life of her own, with things that might happen to *her,* things that in friendship one should likewise take account of. Something fairly remarkable came to pass with him, for that matter, in this connexion—something represented by a certain passage of his consciousness, in the suddenest way, from one extreme to the other.

He had thought himself, so long as nobody knew, the most disinterested person in the world, carrying his concentrated burden, his perpetual suspense, ever so quietly, holding his tongue about it, giving others no glimpse of it nor of its effect upon his life, asking of them no allowance and only making on his side all those that were asked. He had n't disturbed people with the queerness of their having to know a haunted man, though he had had moments of rather special temptation on hearing them say they were forsooth "unsettled." If they were as unsettled as he was—he who had never been settled for an hour in his life—they would know what it meant. Yet it was n't, all the same, for him to make them, and he listened to them civilly enough. This was why he had such good—though possibly such rather colourless—manners; this was why, above all, he could regard himself, in a greedy world, as decently—as in fact perhaps even a little sublimely—unselfish. Our point is accordingly that he valued this character quite sufficiently to measure his present danger of letting it lapse, against which he promised himself to be much on his guard. He was quite ready, none the less, to be selfish just a little, since surely no more charming occasion for it had come to him. "Just a little," in a word, was just as much as Miss Bartram, taking one day with another, would let him. He never would be in the least coercive, and would keep well before him the lines on which consideration for her—the very highest—ought to proceed. He would thoroughly establish the heads under which her affairs, her requirements, her peculiarities—he went so far as to give them the latitude of that name—would come into their intercourse. All this naturally was a sign of how much he took the intercourse itself for granted. There was nothing more to be done about *that.* It simply existed; had sprung into being with her first penetrating question to him in the autumn light there at Weatherend. The real form it should have taken on the basis that stood out large was the form of their marrying. But the devil in this was that the very basis itself put marrying out of the question. His conviction, his apprehension, his obsession, in short, was n't a privilege he could invite a woman to share; and that consequence of it was precisely what was the matter with him. Something or other lay in wait for him, amid the twists and the turns of the months and the years, like a crouching beast in the jungle. It signified little whether the crouching beast were destined to slay him or to be slain. The definite point was the inevitable spring of the creature; and the definite lesson from that was that a man of feeling did n't cause himself to be accompanied by a lady on a tiger-hunt. Such was the image under which he had ended by figuring his life.

They had at first, none the less, in the scattered hours spent together, made no allusion to that view of it; which was a sign he was handsomely alert to give that he did n't expect, that he in fact did n't care, always to be talking about it. Such a feature in one's outlook was really like a hump on one's back. The difference it made every minute of the day existed quite independently of discussion. One discussed of course *like* a hunchback, for there was always, if nothing else, the hunchback face. That remained, and she was watching him; but people watched best, as a general thing, in silence, so that such would be predominantly the manner of their vigil. Yet he did n't want, at the same time, to be tense and solemn; tense and solemn was what he imagined he too much showed for with other people. The thing to be, with the one person who knew, was easy and natural—to make the reference rather than be seeming to avoid it, to avoid it rather than be seeming to make it, and to keep it, in any case, familiar, facetious even, rather than pedantic and portentous. Some such consideration as the latter was doubtless in his mind for instance when he wrote pleasantly to Miss Bartram that perhaps the great thing he had so long felt as in the lap of the gods was no more than this circumstance, which touched him so nearly, of her acquiring a house in London. It was the first allusion they had yet again made, needing any other hitherto so little; but when she replied, after having given him the news, that she was by no means satisfied with such a trifle as the climax to so special a suspense, she almost set him wondering if she had n't even a larger conception of singularity for him than he had for himself. He was at all events destined to become aware little by little, as time went by, that she was all the while looking at his life, judging it, measuring it, in the light of the thing she knew, which grew to be at last, with the consecration of the years, never mentioned between them save as "the real truth" about him. That had always been his own form of reference to it, but she adopted the form so quietly that, looking back at the end of a period, he knew there was no moment at which it was traceable that she had, as he might say, got inside his idea, or exchanged the attitude of beautifully indulging for that of still more beautifully believing him.

It was always open to him to accuse her of seeing him but as the most harmless of maniacs, and this, in the long run—since it covered so much ground—was his easiest description of their friendship. He had a screw loose for her, but she liked him in spite of it and was practically, against the rest of the world, his kind wise keeper, unremunerated but fairly amused and, in the absence of other near ties, not disreputably occupied. The rest of the world of course thought him queer, but she, she only, knew how, and above all why, queer; which was precisely what enabled her to dispose the concealing veil in the right folds. She took his gaiety from him—since it had to pass with them for gaiety—as she took everything else; but she certainly so far justified by her unerring touch his finer sense of the degree to which he had ended by convincing her. *She* at least never spoke of the secret of his life except as "the real truth about you," and she had in fact a wonderful way of making it seem, as such, the secret of her own life too. That was in fine how he so constantly felt her as allowing for him; he could n't on the whole call it anything else. He allowed for himself, but she, exactly, allowed still more; partly because, better placed for a sight of the matter, she traced his unhappy perversion through reaches of its course into which he could scarce follow it. He knew how he felt, but, besides knowing that, she knew how he *looked* as well; he knew each of the things of importance he was insidiously kept from doing, but she could add up the amount they made, understand how much, with a lighter weight on his spirit, he might have done, and thereby establish how, clever as he was, he fell short. Above all she was in the secret of the difference between the forms he went through—those of his little office under Government, those of caring for his modest patrimony, for his library, for his garden in the country, for the people in London whose invitations he accepted and repaid—and the detachment that reigned beneath them and that made of all behaviour, all that could in the least be called behaviour, a long act of dissimulation. What it had come to was that he wore a mask painted with the social simper, out of the eyeholes of which there looked eyes of an expression not in the least matching the other features. This the stupid world, even after years, had never more than half-discovered. It was only May Bartram who had, and she achieved, by an art indescribable, the feat of at once—or perhaps it was only alternately—meeting the eyes from in front and mingling her own vision, as from over his shoulder, with their peep through the apertures.

So while they grew older together she did watch with him, and so she let this association give shape and colour to her own existence. Beneath *her* forms as well detachment had learned to sit, and behaviour had become for her, in the social sense, a false account of herself. There was but one account of her that would have been true all the while and that she could give straight to nobody, least of all to John Marcher. Her whole attitude was a virtual statement, but the perception of that only seemed called to take its place for him as one of the many things necessarily crowded out of his consciousness. If she had moreover, like himself, to make sacrifices to their real truth, it was to be granted that her compensation might have affected her as more prompt and more natural. They had long periods, in this London time, during which, when they were together, a stranger might have listened to them without in the least pricking up his ears; on the other hand the real truth was equally liable at any moment to rise to the surface, and the auditor would then have wondered indeed what they were talking about. They had from an early hour made up their mind that society was, luckily, unintelligent, and the margin allowed them by this had fairly become one of their commonplaces. Yet there were still moments when the situation turned almost fresh—usually under the effect of some expression drawn from herself. Her expressions doubtless repeated themselves, but her intervals were generous. "What saves us, you know, is that we answer so completely to so usual an appearance: that of the man and woman whose friendship has become such a daily habit—or almost—as to be at last indispensable." That for instance was a remark she had frequently enough had occasion to make, though she had given it at different times different developments. What we are especially concerned with is the turn it happened to take from her one afternoon when he had come to see her in honour of her birthday. This anniversary had fallen on a Sunday, at a season of thick fog and general outward gloom; but he had brought her his customary offering, having known her now long enough to have established a hundred small traditions. It was one of his proofs to himself, the present he made her on her birthday, that he had n't sunk into real selfishness. It was mostly nothing more than a small trinket, but it was always fine of its kind, and he was regularly careful to pay for it more than he thought he could afford. "Our habit saves you at least, don't you see? because it makes you, after all, for the vulgar, indistinguishable from other men. What's the most inveterate mark of men in general? Why the capacity to spend endless time with dull women—to spend it I won't say without being bored, but without minding that they are, without being driven off at a tangent by it; which comes to the same thing. I'm your dull woman, a part of the daily bread for which you pray at church. That covers your tracks more than anything."

"And what covers yours?" asked Marcher, whom his dull woman could mostly to this extent amuse. "I see of course what you mean by your saving me, in this way and that, so far as other people are concerned—I've seen it all along. Only what is it that saves *you?* I often think, you know, of that."

She looked as if she sometimes thought of that, too, but rather in a different way. "Where other people, you mean, are concerned?"

"Well, you're really so in with me, you know—as a sort of result of my being so in with yourself. I mean of my having such an immense regard for you, being so tremendously mindful of all you've done for me. I sometimes ask myself if it's quite fair. Fair I mean to have so involved and—since one may say it—interested you. I almost feel as if you had n't really had time to do anything else."

"Anything else but be interested?" she asked. "Ah, what else does one ever want to be? If I've been 'watching' with you, as we long ago agreed I was to do, watching's always in itself an absorption."

"Oh certainly," John Marcher said, "if you had n't had your curiosity—! Only does n't it sometimes come to you as time goes on that your curiosity is n't being particularly repaid?"

May Bartram had a pause. "Do you ask that, by any chance, because you feel at all that yours is n't? I mean because you have to wait so long."

Oh he understood what she meant! "For the thing to happen that never does happen? For the beast to jump out? No, I'm just where I was about it. It is n't a matter as to which I can *choose,* I can decide for a change. It is n't one as to which there *can* be a change. It's in the lap of the gods. One 's in the hands of one's law—there one is. As to the form the law will take, the way it will operate, that's its own affair."

"Yes," Miss Bartram replied; "of course one's fate's coming, of course it *has* come in its own form and its own way, all the while. Only, you know, the form and the way in your case were to have been—well, something so exceptional and, as one may say, so particularly *your* own."

Something in this made him look at her with suspicion. "You say 'were to *have* been,' as if in your heart you had begun to doubt."

"Oh!" she vaguely protested.

"As if you believed," he went on, "that nothing will now take place."

She shook her head slowly but rather inscrutably. "You're far from my thought."

He continued to look at her. "What then is the matter with you?"

"Well," she said after another wait, "the matter with me is simply that I'm more sure than ever my curiosity, as you call it, will be but too well repaid."

They were frankly grave now; he had got up from his seat, had turned once more about the little drawing-room to which, year after year, he brought his inevitable topic; in which he had, as he might have said, tasted their intimate community with every sauce, where every object was as familiar to him as the things of his own house and the very carpets were worn with his fitful walk very much as the desks in old counting-houses are worn by the elbows of generations of clerks. The generations of his nervous moods had been at work there, and the place was the written history of his whole middle life. Under the impression of what his friend had just said he knew himself, for some reason, more aware of these things; which made him, after a moment, stop again before her. "Is it possibly that you've grown afraid?"

"Afraid?" He thought, as she repeated the word, that his question had made her, a little, change colour; so that, lest he should have touched on a truth, he explained very kindly: "You remember that that was what you asked *me* long ago—that first day at Weatherend."

"Oh yes, and you told me you did n't know—that I was to see for myself. We've said little about it since, even in so long a time."

"Precisely," Marcher interposed—"quite as if it were too delicate a matter for us to make free with. Quite as if we might find, on pressure, that I *am* afraid. For then," he said, "we should n't, should we? quite know what to do."

She had for the time no answer to this question. "There have been days when I thought you were. Only, of course," she added, "there have been days when we have thought almost anything."

"Everything. Oh!" Marcher softly groaned as with a gasp, half-spent, at the face, more uncovered just then than it had been for a long while, of the imagination always with them. It had always had its incalculable moments of glaring out, quite as with the very eyes of the very Beast, and used as he was to them, they could still draw from him the tribute of a sigh that rose from the depths of his being. All they had thought, first and last, rolled over him; the past seemed to have been reduced to mere barren speculation. This in fact was what the place had just struck him as so full of—the simplification of everything but the state of suspense. That remained only by seeming to hang in the void surrounding it. Even his original fear, if fear it had been, had lost itself in the desert. "I judge, however," he continued, "that you see I'm not afraid now."

"What I see, as I make it out, is that you've achieved something almost unprecedented in the way of getting used to danger. Living with it so long and so closely you've lost your sense of it; you know it's there, but you're indifferent, and you cease even, as of old, to have to whistle in the dark. Considering what the danger is," May Bartram wound up, "I'm bound to say I don't think your attitude could well be surpassed."

John Marcher faintly smiled. "It's heroic?"

"Certainly—call it that."

It was what he would have liked indeed to call it. "I *am* then a man of courage?"

"That's what you were to show me."

He still, however, wondered. "But does n't the man of courage know what he's afraid of—or *not* afraid of? I don't know *that*, you see. I don't focus it. I can't name it. I only know I'm exposed."

"Yes, but exposed—how shall I say?—so directly. So intimately. That's surely enough."

"Enough to make you feel then—as what we may call the end and the upshot of our watch—that I'm not afraid?"

"You're not afraid. But it is n't," she said, "the end of our watch. That is it is n't the end of yours. You've everything still to see."

"Then why have n't *you*?" he asked. He had had, all along, today, the sense of her keeping something back, and he still had it. As this was his first impression of that it quite made a date. The case was the more marked as she did n't at first answer; which in turn made him go on. "You know something I don't."

Then his voice, for that of a man of courage, trembled a little. "You know what's to happen." Her silence, with the face she showed, was almost a confession—it made him sure. "You know, and you're afraid to tell me. It's so bad that you're afraid I'll find out."

All this might be true, for she did look as if, unexpectedly to her, he had crossed some mystic line that she had secretly drawn round her. Yet she might, after all, not have worried; and the real climax was that he himself, at all events, need n't. "You'll never find out."

III

It was all to have made, none the less, as I have said, a date; which came out in the fact that again and again, even after long intervals, other things that passed between them wore in relation to this hour but the character of recalls and results. Its immediate effect had been indeed rather to lighten insistence—almost to provoke a reaction; as if their topic had dropped by its own weight and as if moreover, for that matter, Marcher had been visited by one of his occasional warnings against egotism. He had kept up, he felt, and very decently on the whole, his consciousness of the importance of not being selfish, and it was true that he had never sinned in that direction without promptly enough trying to press the scales the other way. He often repaired his fault, the season permitting, by inviting his friend to accompany him to the opera; and it not infrequently thus happened that, to show he did n't wish her to have but one sort of food for her mind, he was the cause of her appearing there with him a dozen nights in the month. It even happened that, seeing her home at such times, he occasionally went in with her to finish, as he called it, the evening, and, the better to make his point, sat down to the frugal but always careful little supper that awaited his pleasure. His point was made, he thought, by his not eternally insisting with her on himself; made for instance, at such hours, when it befell that, her piano at hand and each of them familiar with it, they went over passages of the opera together. It chanced to be on one of these occasions, however, that he reminded her of her not having answered a certain question he had put to her during the talk that had taken place between them on her last birthday. "What is it that saves *you?*"—saved her, he meant, from that appearance of variation from the usual human type. If he had practically escaped remark, as she pretended, by doing, in the most important particular, what most men do—find the answer to life in patching up in alliance of a sort with a woman no better than himself—how had she escaped it, and how could the alliance, such as it was, since they must suppose it had been more or less noticed, have failed to make her rather positively talked about?

"I never said," May Bartram replied, "that it had n't made me a good deal talked about."

"Ah well then you're not 'saved.'"

"It has n't been a question for me. If you've had your woman I've had," she said, "my man."

"And you mean that makes you all right?"

Oh it was always as if there were so much to say! "I don't know why it should n't make me—humanly, which is what we're speaking of—as right as it makes you."

"I see," Marcher returned. "'Humanly,' no doubt, as showing that you're living for something. Not, that is, just for me and my secret."

May Bartram smiled. "I don't pretend it exactly shows that I'm not living for you. It's my intimacy with you that's in question."

He laughed as he saw what she meant. "Yes, but since, as you say, I'm only, so far as people make out, ordinary, you're—are n't you?—no more than ordinary either. You help me to pass for a man like another. So if I *am,* as I understand you, you're not compromised. Is that it?"

She had another of her waits, but she spoke clearly enough. "That's it. It's all that concerns me—to help you to pass for a man like another."

He was careful to acknowledge the remark handsomely. "How kind, how beautiful, you are to me! How shall I ever repay you?"

She had her last grave pause, as if there might be a choice of ways. But she chose. "By going on as you are."

It was into this going on as he was that they relapsed, and really for so long a time that the day inevitably came for a further sounding of their depths. These depths, constantly bridged over by a structure firm enough in spite of its lightness and of its occasional oscillation in the somewhat vertiginous air, invited on occasion, in the interest of their nerves, a dropping of the plummet and a measurement of the abyss. A difference had been made moreover, once for all, by the fact that she had all the while not appeared to feel the need of rebutting his charge of an idea within her that she did n't dare to express—a charge uttered just before one of the fullest of their later discussions ended. It had come up for him then that she "knew" something and that what she knew was bad—too bad to tell him. When he had spoken of it as visibly so bad that she was afraid he might find it out, her reply had left the matter too equivocal to be let alone and yet, for Marcher's special sensibility, almost too formidable again to touch. He circled about it at a distance that alternately narrowed and widened and that still was n't much affected by the consciousness in him that there was nothing she could "know," after all, any better than he did. She had no source of knowledge he had n't equally—except of course that she might have finer nerves. That was what women had where they were interested; they made out things, where people were concerned, that the people often could n't have made out for themselves. Their nerves, their sensibility, their imagination, were conductors and revealers, and the beauty of May Bartram was in particular that she had given herself so to his case. He felt in these days what, oddly enough, he had never felt before, the growth of a dread of losing her by some catastrophe—some catastrophe that yet would n't all be *the* catastrophe: partly because she had almost of a sudden begun to strike him as more useful to him than ever yet, and partly by reason of an appearance of uncertainty in her health, coincident and equally new. It was characteristic of the inner detachment he had hitherto so successfully cultivated and to which our whole account of him is a reference, it was characteristic that his complications, such as they were, had never yet seemed so as at this crisis to thicken about him, even to the point of making him ask himself if he were, by any chance, of a truth, within sight or sound, within touch or reach, within the immediate jurisdiction, of the thing that waited.

When the day came, as come it had to, that his friend confessed to him her fear of a deep disorder in her blood, he felt somehow the shadow of a change and the chill of a shock. He immediately began to imagine aggravations and disasters, and above all to think of her peril as the direct menace for himself of personal privation. This indeed gave him one of those partial recoveries of equanimity that were agreeable to him—it showed him that what was still first in his mind was the loss she herself might suffer. "What if she should have to die before knowing, before seeing—?" It would have been brutal, in the early stages of her trouble, to put that question to her; but it had immediately sounded for him to his own concern, and the possibility was what most made him sorry for her. If she did "know," moreover, in the sense of her having had some—what should he think?—mystical irresistible light, this would make the matter not better, but worse, inasmuch as her original adoption of his own curiosity had quite become the basis of her life. She had been living to see what would *be* to be seen, and it would quite lacerate her to have to give up before the accomplishment of the vision. These reflexions, as I say, quickened his generosity; yet, make them as he might, he saw himself, with the lapse of the period, more and more disconcerted. It lapsed for him with a strange steady sweep, and the oddest oddity was that it gave him, independently of the threat of much inconvenience, almost the only positive surprise his career, if career it could be called, had yet offered him. She kept the house as she had never done; he had to go to her to see her—she could meet him nowhere now, though there was scarce a corner of their loved old London in which she had n't in the past, at one time or another, done so; and he found her always seated by her fire in the deep old-fashioned chair she was less and less able to leave. He had been struck one day, after an absence exceeding his usual measure, with her suddenly looking much older to him than he had ever thought of her being; then he recognized that the suddenness was all on his side—he had just simply and suddenly noticed. She looked older because inevitably, after so many years, she *was* old, or almost; which was of course true in still greater measure of her companion. If she was old, or almost, John Marcher assuredly was, and yet it was her showing of the lesson, not his own, that brought the truth home to him. His surprises began here; when once they had begun they multiplied; they came rather with a rush; it was as if, in the oddest way in the world, they had all been kept back, sown in a thick cluster, for the late afternoon of life, the time at which for people in general the unexpected has died out.

One of them was that he should have caught himself—for he *had* so done—*really* wondering if the great accident would take form now as nothing more than his being condemned to see this charming woman, this admirable friend, pass away from him. He had never so unreservedly qualified her as while confronted in thought with such a possibility; in spite of which there was small doubt for him that as an answer to his long riddle the mere effacement of even so fine a feature of his situation would be an abject anticlimax. It would represent, as connected with his past attitude, a drop of dignity under the shadow of which his existence could only become the most grotesque of failures. He had been far from holding it a failure—long as he had waited for the appearance that was to make it a success. He had waited for quite another thing, not for such a thing as that. The breath of his good faith came short, however, as he recognised how long he had waited, or how long at least his companion had. That she, at all events, might be recorded as having waited in vain—this affected him sharply, and all the more because of his at first having done little more than amuse himself with the idea. It grew more grave as the gravity of her condition grew, and the state of mind it produced in him, which he himself ended by watching as if it had been some definite disfigurement of his outer person, may pass for another of his surprises. This conjoined itself still with another, the really stupefying consciousness of a question that he would have allowed to shape itself had he dared. What did everything mean—what, that is, did *she* mean, she and her vain waiting and her probable death and the soundless admonition of it all—unless that, at this time of day, it was simply, it was overwhelmingly too late? He had never at any stage of his queer consciousness admitted the whisper of such a correction; he had never till within these last few months been so false to his conviction as not to hold that what was to come to him had time, whether *he* struck himself as having it or not. That at last, at last, he certainly had n't it, to speak of, or had it but in the scantiest measure—such, soon enough, as things went with him, became the inference with which his old obsession had to reckon: and this it was not helped to do by the more and more confirmed appearance that the great vagueness casting the long shadow in which he had lived had, to attest itself, almost no margin left. Since it was in Time that he was to have met his fate, so it was in Time that his fate was to have acted; and as he waked up to the sense of no longer being young, which was exactly the sense of being stale, just as that, in turn, was the sense of being weak, he waked up to another matter beside. It all hung together; they were subject, he and the great vagueness, to an equal and indivisible law. When the possibilities themselves had accordingly turned stale, when the secret of the gods had grown faint, had perhaps even quite evaporated, that, and that only, was failure. It would n't have been failure to be bankrupt, dishonoured, pilloried, hanged; it was failure not to be anything. And so, in the dark valley into which his path had taken its unlooked-for twist, he wondered not a little as he groped. He did n't care what awful crash might overtake him, with what ignominy or what monstrosity he might yet be associated—since he was n't after all too utterly old to suffer—if it would only be decently proportionate to the posture he had kept, all his life, in the threatened presence of it. He had but one desire left—that he should n't have been "sold."

IV

Then it was that, one afternoon, while the spring of the year was young and new she met all in her own way his frankest betrayal of these alarms. He had gone in late to see her, but evening had n't settled and she was presented to him in that long fresh light of waning April days which affects us often with a sadness sharper than the greyest hours of autumn. The week had been warm, the spring was supposed to have begun early, and May Bartram sat, for the first time in the year, without a fire; a fact that, to Marcher's sense, gave the scene of which she formed part a smooth and ultimate look, an air of knowing, in its immaculate order and cold meaningless cheer, that it would never see a fire again. Her own aspect—he could scarce have said why—intensified this note. Almost as white as wax, with the marks and signs in her face as numerous and as fine as if they had been etched by a needle, with soft white draperies relieved by a faded green scarf on the delicate tone of which the years had further refined, she was the picture of a serene and exquisite but impenetrable sphinx, whose head, or indeed all whose person, might have been powdered with silver. She was a sphinx, yet with her white petals and green fronds she might have been a lily too—only an artificial lily, wonderfully imitated and constantly kept, without dust or stain, though not exempt from a slight droop and a complexity of faint creases, under some clear glass bell. The perfection of household care, of high polish and finish, always reigned in her rooms, but they now looked most as if everything had been wound up, tucked in, put away, so that she might sit with folded hands and with nothing more to do. She was "out of it," to Marcher's vision; her work was over; she communicated with him as across some gulf or from some island of rest that she had already reached, and it made him feel strangely abandoned. Was it—or rather was n't it—that if for so long she had been watching with him the answer to their question must have swum into her ken and taken on its name, so that her occupation was verily gone? He had as much as charged her with this in saying to her, many months before, that she even then knew something she was keeping from him. It was a point he had never since ventured to press, vaguely fearing as he did that it might become a difference, perhaps a disagreement, between them. He had in this later time turned nervous, which was what he in all the other years had never been; and the oddity was that his nervousness should have waited till he had begun to doubt, should have held off so long as he was sure. There was something, it seemed to him, that the wrong word would bring down on his head, something that would so at least ease off his tension. But he wanted not to speak the wrong word; that would make everything ugly. He wanted the knowledge he lacked to drop on him, if drop it could, by its own august weight. If she was to forsake him it was surely for her to take leave. This was why he did n't directly ask her again what she knew; but it was also why, approaching the matter from another side, he said to her in the course of his visit: "What do you regard as the very worst that at this time of day *can* happen to me?"

He had asked her that in the past often enough; they had, with the odd irregular rhythm of their intensities and avoidances, exchanged ideas about it and then had seen the ideas washed away by cool intervals, washed like figures traced in sea-sand. It had ever been the mark of their talk that the oldest allusions in it required but a little dismissal and reaction to come out again, sounding for the hour as new. She could thus at present meet his enquiry quite freshly and patiently. "Oh yes, I've repeatedly thought, only it always seemed to me of old that I could n't quite make up my mind. I thought of dreadful things, between which it was difficult to choose; and so must you have done."

"Rather! I feel now as if I had scarce done anything else. I appear to myself to have spent my life in thinking of nothing *but* dreadful things. A great many of them I've at different times named to you, but there were others I could n't name."

"They were too, too dreadful?"

"Too, too dreadful—some of them."

She looked at him a minute, and there came to him as he met it an inconsequent sense that her eyes, when one got their full clearness, were still as beautiful as they had been in youth, only beautiful with a strange cold light—a light that somehow was a part of the effect, if it was n't rather a part of the cause, of the pale hard sweetness of the season and the hour. "And yet," she said at last, "there are horrors we've mentioned."

It deepened the strangeness to see her, as such a figure in such a picture, talk of "horrors," but she was to do in a few minutes something stranger yet—though even of this he was to take the full measure but afterwards—and the note of it already trembled. It was, for the matter of that, one of the signs that her eyes were having again the high flicker of their prime. He had to admit, however, what she said. "Oh yes, there were times when we did go far." He caught himself in the act of speaking as if it all were over. Well, he wished it were; and the consummation depended for him clearly more and more on his friend.

But she had now a soft smile. "Oh far—!"

It was oddly ironic. "Do you mean you're prepared to go further?"

She was frail and ancient and charming as she continued to look at him, yet it was rather as if she had lost the thread. "Do you consider that we went far?"

"Why I thought it the point you were just making—that we *had* looked most things in the face."

"Including each other?" She still smiled. "But you're quite right. We've had together great imaginations, often great fears; but some of them have been unspoken.'

"Then the worst—we have n't faced that. I *could* face it, I believe, if I knew what you think it. I feel," he explained, "as if I had lost my power to conceive such things." And he wondered if he looked as blank as he sounded. "It's spent."

"Then why do you assume," she asked, "that mine is n't?"

"Because you've given me signs to the contrary. It is n't a question for you of conceiving, imagining, comparing. It is n't a question now of choosing." At last he came out with it." "You know something I don't. You've shown me that before."

These last words had affected her, he made out in a moment, exceedingly, and she spoke with firmness. "I've shown you, my dear, nothing."

He shook his head. "You can't hide it."

"Oh, oh!" May Bartram sounded over what she could n't hide. It was almost a smothered groan.

"You admitted it months ago, when I spoke of it to you as of something you were afraid I should find out. Your answer was that I could n't, that I would n't, and I don't pretend I have. But you had something therefore in mind, and I now see how it must have been, how it still is, the possibility that, of all possibilities, has settled itself for you as the worst. This," he went on, "is why I appeal to you. I'm only afraid of ignorance to-day—I'm not afraid of knowledge." And then as for a while she said nothing: "What makes me sure is that I see in your face and feel here, in the air and amid these appearances, that you're out of it. You've done. You've had your experience. You leave me to my fate."

Well, she listened, motionless and white in her chair, as on a decision to be made, so that her manner was fairly an avowal, though still, with a small fine inner stiffness, an imperfect surrender. "It *would* be the worst," she finally let herself say. "I mean the thing I've never said."

It hushed him a moment. "More monstrous than all the monstrosities we've named?"

"More monstrous. Is n't that what you sufficiently express," she asked, "in calling it the worst?"

Marcher thought. "Assuredly—if you mean, as I do, something that includes all the loss and all the shame that are thinkable."

"It would if it *should* happen," said May Bartram. "What we're speaking of, remember, is only my idea."

"It's your belief," Marcher returned. "That's enough for me. I feel your beliefs are right. Therefore if, having this one, you give me no more light on it, you abandon me."

"No, no!" she repeated. "I'm with you—don't you see?—still." And as to make it more vivid to him she rose from her chair—a movement she seldom risked in these days—and showed herself, all draped and all soft, in her fairness and slimness. "I have n't forsaken you."

It was really, in its effort against weakness, a generous assurance, and had the success of the impulse not, happily, been great, it would have touched him to pain more than to pleasure. But the cold charm in her eyes had spread, as she hovered before him, to all the rest of her person, so that it was for the minute almost a recovery of youth. He could n't pity her for that; he could only take her as she showed—as capable even yet of helping him. It was as if, at the same time, her light might at any instant go out; wherefore he must make the most of it. There passed before him with intensity the three or four things he wanted most to know; but the question that came of itself to his lips really covered the others. "Then tell me if I shall consciously suffer."

She promptly shook her head. "Never!"

It confirmed the authority he imputed to her, and it produced on him an extraordinary effect. "Well, what's better than that? Do you call that the worst?"

"You think nothing is better?" she asked.

She seemed to mean something so special that he again sharply wondered, though still with the dawn of a prospect of relief. "Why not, if one does n't *know?*" After which, as their eyes, over his question, met in a silence, the dawn deepened and something to his purpose came prodigiously out of her very face. His own, as he took it in, suddenly flushed to the forehead, and he gasped with the force of a perception to which, on the instant, everything fitted. The sound of his gasp filled the air; then he became articulate. "I see—if I don't suffer!"

In her own look, however, was doubt. "You see what?"

"Why what you mean—what you've always meant."

She again shook her head. "What I mean is n't what I've always meant. It's different."

"It's something new?"

She hung back from it a little. "Something new. It's not what you think. I see what you think."

His divination drew breath then; only her correction might be wrong. "It is n't that I *am* a blockhead?" he asked between faintness and grimness. "It is n't that it's all a mistake?"

"A mistake?" she pityingly echoed. *That* possibility, for her, he saw, would be monstrous; and if she guaranteed him the immunity from pain it would accordingly not be what she had in mind. "Oh no," she declared; "It's nothing of that sort. You've been right."

Yet he could n't help asking himself if she were n't, thus pressed, speaking but to save him. It seemed to him he should be most in a hole if his history should prove all a platitude. "Are you telling me the truth, so that I shan't have been a bigger idiot that I can bear to know? I *have n't* lived with a vain imagination, in the most besotted illusion? I have n't waited but to see the door shut in my face?"

She shook her head again. "However the case stands *that* is n't the truth. Whatever the reality, it *is* a reality. The door is n't shut. The door's open," said May Bartram.

"Then something's to come?"

She waited once again, always with her cold sweet eyes on him. "It's never too late." She had, with her gliding step, diminished the distance between them, and she stood nearer to him, close to him, a minute, as if still charged with the unspoken. Her movement might have been for some finer emphasis of what she was at once hesitating and deciding to say. He had been standing by the chimney-piece, fireless and sparely adorned, a small perfect old French clock and two morsels of rosy Dresden constituting all its furniture; and her hand grasped the shelf while she kept him waiting, grasped it a little as for support and encouragement. She only kept him waiting, however; that is he only waited. It had become suddenly, from her movement and attitude, beautiful and vivid to him that she had something more to give him; her wasted face delicately shone with it—it glittered almost as with the white lustre of silver in her expression. She was right, incontestably, for what he saw in her face was the truth, and strangely, without consequence, while their talk of it as dreadful was still in the air, she appeared to present it as inordinately soft. This, prompting bewilderment, made him but gape the more gratefully for her revelation, so that they continued for some minutes silent, her face shining at him, her contact imponderably pressing, and his stare all kind but all expectant. The end, none the less, was that what he had expected failed to come to him. Something else took place instead, which seemed to consist at first in the mere closing of her eyes. She gave way at the same instant to a slow fine shudder, and though he remained staring—though he stared in fact but the harder—turned off and regained her chair. It was the end of what she had been intending, but it left him thinking only of that.

"Well, you don't say—?"

She had touched in her passage a bell near the chimney and had sunk back strangely pale. "I'm afraid I'm too ill."

"Too ill to tell me?" It sprang up sharp to him, and almost to his lips, the fear she might die without giving him light. He checked himself in time from so expressing his question, but she answered as if she had heard the words.

"Don't you know—now?"

"'Now'—?" She had spoken as if some difference had been made within the moment. But her maid, quickly obedient to her bell, was already with them. "I know nothing." And he was afterwards to say to himself that he must have spoken with odious impatience, such an impatience as to show that, supremely disconcerted, he washed his hands of the whole question.

"Oh!" said May Bartram.

"Are you in pain?" he asked as the woman went to her.

"No," said May Bartram.

Her maid, who had put an arm round her as if to take her to her room, fixed on him eyes that appealingly contradicted her; in spite of which, however, he showed once more his mystification. "What then has happened?"

She was once more, with her companion's help, on her feet, and, feeling withdrawal imposed on him, he had blankly found his hat and gloves and had reached the door. Yet he waited for her answer. "What *was* to," she said.

V

He came back the next day, but she was then unable to see him, and as it was literally the first time this had occurred in the long stretch of their acquaintance he turned away, defeated and sore, almost angry—or feeling at least that such a break in their custom was really the beginning of the end—and wandered alone with his thoughts, especially with the one he was least able to keep down. She was dying and he would lose her; she was dying and his life would end. He stopped in the Park, into which he had passed, and stared before him at his recurrent doubt. Away from her the doubt pressed again; in her presence he had believed her, but as he felt his forlornness he threw himself into the explanation that, nearest at hand, had most of a miserable warmth for him and least of a cold torment. She had deceived him to save him—to put him off with something in which he should be able to rest. What could the thing that was to happen to him be, after all, but just this thing that had begun to happen? Her dying, her death, his consequent solitude—*that* was what he had figured as the Beast in the Jungle, that was what had been in the lap of the gods. He had had her word for it as he left her—what else on earth could she have meant? It was n't a thing of a monstrous order; not a fate rare and distinguished; not a stroke of fortune that overwhelmed and immortalised; it had only the stamp of the common doom. But poor Marcher at this hour judged the common doom sufficient. It would serve his turn, and even as the consummation of infinite waiting he would bend his pride to accept it. He sat down on a bench in the twilight. He had n't been a fool. Something had *been,* as she had said, to come. Before he rose indeed it had quite struck him that the final fact really matched with the long avenue through which he had had to reach it. As sharing his suspense and as giving herself all, giving her life, to bring it to an end, she had come with him every step of the way. He had lived by her aid, and to leave her behind would be cruelly, damnably to miss her. What could be more overwhelming than that?

Well, he was to know within the week, for though she kept him a while at bay, left him restless and wretched during a series of days on each of which he asked about her only again to have to turn away, she ended his trial by receiving him where she had always received him. Yet she had been brought out at some hazard into the presence of so many of the things that were, consciously, vainly, half their past, and there was scant service left in the gentleness of her mere desire, all too visible, to check his obsession and wind up his long trouble. That was clearly what she wanted, the one thing more for her own peace while she could still put out her hand. He was so affected by her state that, once seated by her chair, he was moved to let everything go; it was she herself therefore who brought him back, took up again, before she dismissed him, her last word of the other time. She showed how she wished to leave their business in order. "I'm not sure you understood. You've nothing to wait for more. It *has* come."

Oh how he looked at her! "Really?"

"Really."

"The thing that, as you said, *was* to?"

"The thing that we began in our youth to watch for."

Face to face with her once more he believed her; it was a claim to which he had so abjectly little to oppose. "You mean that it has come as a positive definite occurrence, with a name and a date?"

"Positive. Definite. I don't know about the 'name,' but oh with a date!"

He found himself again too helplessly at sea. "But come in the night—come and passed me by?"

May Bartram had her strange faint smile. "Oh no, it has n't passed you by!"

"But if I have n't been aware of it and it has n't touched me—?"

"Ah your not being aware of it"—and she seemed to hesitate an instant to deal with this—"your not being aware of it is the strangeness *in* the strangeness. It's the wonder *of* the wonder." She spoke as with the softness almost of a sick child, yet now at last, at the end of all, with the perfect straightness of a sibyl. She visibly knew that she knew, and the effect on him was of something coordinate, in its high character, with the law that had ruled him. It was the true voice of the law; so on her lips would the law itself have sounded. "It *has* touched you," she went on. "It has done its office. It has made you all its own."

"So utterly without my knowing it?"

"So utterly without your knowing it." His hand, as he leaned to her, was on the arm of her chair, and, dimly smiling always now, she placed her own on it. "It's enough if *I* know it."

"Oh!" he confusedly breathed, as she herself of late so often had done.

"What I long ago said is true. You'll never know now, and I think you ought to be content. You've *had* it," said May Bartram.

"But had what?"

"Why what was to have marked you out. The proof of your law. It has acted. I'm too glad," she then bravely added, "to have been able to see what it's *not."*

He continued to attach his eyes to her, and with the sense that it was all beyond him, and that *she* was too, he would still have sharply challenged her had n't he so felt it an abuse of her weakness to do more than take devoutly what she gave him, take it hushed as to a revelation. If he did speak, it was out of the foreknowledge of his loneliness to come. "If you're glad of what it's 'not' it might then have been worse?"

She turned her eyes away, she looked straight before her; with which after a moment: "Well, you know our fears."

He wondered. "It's something then we never feared?"

On this slowly she turned to him. "Did we ever dream, with all our dreams, that we should sit and talk of it thus?"

He tried for a little to make out that they had; but it was as if their dreams, numberless enough, were in solution in some thick cold mist through which thought lost itself. "It might have been that we could n't talk?"

"Well"—she did her best for him—"not from this side. This, you see," she said, "is the *other* side."

"I think," poor Marcher returned, "that all sides are the same to me." Then, however, as she gently shook her head in correction: "We might n't, as it were, have got across—?"

"To where we are—no. We're *here*"—she made her weak emphasis.

"And much good does it do us!" was her friend's frank comment.

"It does us the good it can. It does us the good that *it* is n't here. It's past. It's behind," said May Bartram. "Before—" but her voice dropped.

He had got up, not to tire her, but it was hard to combat his yearning. She after all told him nothing but that his light had failed—which he knew well enough without her. "Before—?" he blankly echoed.

"Before, you see, it was always to *come.* That kept it present."

"Oh I don't care what comes now! Besides," Marcher added, "it seems to me I liked it better present, as you say, than I can like it absent with *your* absence."

"Oh mine!"—and her pale hands made light of it.

"With the absence of everything." He had a dreadful sense of standing there before her for—so far as anything but this proved, this bottomless drop was concerned—the last time of their life. It rested on him with a weight he felt he could scarce bear, and this weight it apparently was that still pressed out what remained in him of speakable protest. "I believe you; but I can't begin to pretend I understand. *Nothing,* for me, is past; nothing *will* pass till I pass myself, which I pray my stars may be as soon as possible. Say, however," he added, "that I've eaten my cake, as you contend, to the last crumb—how can the thing I've never felt at all be the thing I was marked out to feel?"

She met him perhaps less directly, but she met him unperturbed. "You take your 'feelings' for granted. You were to suffer your fate. That was not necessarily to know it."

"How in the world—when what is such knowledge but suffering?"

She looked up at him a while in silence. "No—you don't understand."

"I suffer," said John Marcher.

"Don't, don't!"

"How can I help at least *that?"*

"Don't!" May Bartram repeated.

She spoke it in a tone so special, in spite of her weakness, that he stared an instant—stared as if some light, hitherto hidden, had shimmered across his vision. Darkness again closed over it, but the gleam had already become for him an idea. "Because I have n't the right—?"

"Don't *know*—when you need n't," she mercifully urged. "You need n't—for we should n't."

"Should n't?" If he could but know what she meant!

"No—it's too much."

"Too much?" he still asked but, with a mystification that was the next moment of a sudden to give way. Her words, if they meant something, affected him in this light—the light also of her wasted face—as meaning *all,* and the sense of what knowledge had been for herself came over him with a rush which broke through into a question. "Is it of that then you're dying?"

She but watched him, gravely at first, as to see, with this, where he was, and she might have seen something or feared something that moved her sympathy. "I would live for you still—if I could." Her eyes closed a little, as if, withdrawn into herself, she were for a last time trying. "But I can't!" she said as she raised them again to take leave of him.

She could n't indeed, as but too promptly and sharply appeared, and he had no vision of her after this that was anything but darkness and doom. They had parted for ever in that strange talk; access to her chamber of pain, rigidly guarded, was almost wholly forbidden him; he was feeling now moreover, in the face of doctors, nurses, the two or three relatives attracted doubtless by the presumption of what she had to "leave," how few were the rights, as they were called in such cases, that he had to put forward, and how odd it might even seem that their intimacy should n't have given him more of them. The stupidest fourth cousin had more, even though she had been nothing in such a person's life. She had been a feature of features in *his,* for what else was it to have been so indispensable? Strange beyond saying were the ways of existence, baffling for him the anomaly of his lack, as he felt it to be, of producible claim. A woman might have been, as it were, everything to him, and it might yet present him in no connexion that any one seemed held to recognise. If this was the case in these closing weeks it was the case more sharply on the occasion of the last offices rendered, in the great grey London cemetery, to what had been mortal, to what had been precious, in his friend. The concourse at her grave was not numerous, but he saw himself treated as scarce more nearly concerned with it than if there had been a thousand others. He was in short from this moment face to face with the fact that he was to profit extraordinarily little by the interest May Bartram had taken in him. He could n't quite have said what he expected, but he had n't surely expected this approach to a double privation. Not only had her interest failed him, but he seemed to feel himself unattended—and for a reason he could n't seize—by the distinction, the dignity, the propriety, if nothing else, of the man markedly bereaved. It was as if in the view of society he had not *been* markedly bereaved, as if there still failed some sign or proof of it, and as if none the less his character could never be affirmed nor the deficiency ever made up. There were moments as the weeks went by when he would have liked, by some almost aggressive act, to take his stand on the intimacy of his loss, in order that it *might* be questioned and his retort, to the relief of his spirit, so recorded; but the moments of an irritation more helpless followed fast on these, the moments during which, turning things over with a good conscience but with a bare horizon, he found himself wondering if he ought n't to have begun, so to speak, further back.

He found himself wondering indeed at many things, and this last speculation had others to keep it company. What could he have done, after all, in her lifetime, without giving them both, as it were, away? He could n't have made known she was watching him, for that would have published the superstition of the Beast. This was what closed his mouth now—now that the Jungle had been threshed to vacancy and that the Beast had stolen away. It sounded too foolish and too flat; the difference for him in this particular, the extinction in his life of the element of suspense, was such as in fact to surprise him. He could scarce have said what the effect resembled; the abrupt cessation, the positive prohibition, of music perhaps, more than anything else, in some place all adjusted and all accustomed to sonority and to attention. If he could at any rate have conceived lifting the veil from his image at some moment of the past (what had he done, after all, if not lift it to *her?*) so to do this to-day to talk to people at large of the Jungle cleared and confide to them that he now felt it as safe, would have been not only to see them listen as to a goodwife's tale, but really to hear himself tell one. What it presently came to in truth was that poor Marcher waded through his beaten grass, where no life stirred, where no breath sounded, where no evil eye seemed to gleam from a possible lair, very much as if vaguely looking for the Beast, and still more as if acutely missing it. He walked about in existence that had grown strangely more spacious, and, stopping fitfully in places where the undergrowth of life struck him as closer, asked himself yearningly, wondered secretly and sorely, if it would have lurked here or there. It would have at all events *sprung;* what was at least complete was his belief in the truth itself of the assurance given him. The change from his old sense to his new was absolute and final: what was to happen *had* so absolutely and finally happened that he was as little able to know a fear for his future as to know a hope; so absent in short was any question of anything still to come. He was to live entirely with the other question, that of his unidentified past, that of his having to see his fortune impenetrably muffled and masked.

The torment of this vision then his occupation, he could n't perhaps have consented to live but for the possibility of guessing. She had told him, his friend, not to guess; she had forbidden him, so far as he might, to know, and she had even in a sort denied the power in him to learn: which were so many things, precisely, to deprive him of rest. It was n't that he wanted, he argued for fairness, that anything past and done should repeat itself; it was only that he should n't as an anticlimax, have been taken sleeping so sound as not to be able to win back by an effort of thought the lost stuff of consciousness. He declared to himself at moments that he would either win it back or have done with consciousness for ever; he made this idea his one motive in fine, made it so much his passion that none other, to compare with it, seemed ever to have touched him. The lost stuff of consciousness became thus for him as a strayed or stolen child to an unappeasable father; he hunted it up and down very much as if he were knocking at doors and enquiring of the police. This was the spirit in which, inevitably, he set himself to travel; he started on a journey that was to be as long as he could make it; it danced before him that, as the other side of the globe could n't possibly have less to say to him, it might, by a possibility of suggestion, have more. Before he quitted London, however, he made a pilgrimage to May Bartram's grave, took his way to it through the endless avenues of the grim suburban metropolis, sought it out in the wilderness of tombs, and, though he had come but for the renewal of the act of farewell, found himself, when he had at last stood by it, beguiled into long intensities. He stood for an hour, powerless to turn away and yet powerless to penetrate the darkness of death; fixing with his eyes her inscribed name and date, beating his forehead against the fact of the secret they kept, drawing his breath, while he waited, as if some sense would in pity of him rise from the stones. He kneeled on the stones, however, in vain; they kept what they concealed; and if the face of the tomb did become a face for him it was because her two names became a pair of eyes that did n't know him. He gave them a last long look, but no palest light broke.

VI

He stayed away, after this, for a year; he visited the depths of Asia, spending himself on scenes of romantic interest, of superlative sanctity; but what was present to him everywhere was that for a man who had known what *he* had known the world was vulgar and vain. The state of mind in which he had lived for so many years shone out to him, in reflexion, as a light that coloured and refined, a light beside which the glow of the East was garish, cheap and thin. The terrible truth was that he had lost—with everything else—a distinction as well; the things he saw could n't help being common when he had become common to look at them. He was simply now one of them himself—he was in the dust, without a peg for the sense of difference; and there were hours when, before the temples of gods and the sepulchres of kings, his spirit turned for nobleness of association to the barely discriminated slab in the London suburb. That had become for him, and more intensely with time and distance, his one witness of a past glory. It was all that was left to him for proof or pride, yet the past glories of Pharaohs were nothing to him as he thought of it. Small wonder then that he came back to it on the morrow of his return. He was drawn there this time as irresistibly as the other, yet with a confidence, almost, that was doubtless the effect of the many months that had elapsed. He had lived, in spite of himself, into his change of feeling, and in wandering over the earth had wandered, as might be said, from the circumference to the centre of his desert. He had settled to his safety and accepted perforce his extinction; figuring to himself, with some colour, in the likeness of certain little old men he remembered to have seen, of whom, all meagre and wizened as they might look, it was related that they had in their time fought twenty duels or been loved by ten princesses. They indeed had been wondrous for others while he was but wondrous for himself; which, however, was exactly the cause of his haste to renew the wonder by getting back, as he might put it, into his own presence. That had quickened his steps and checked his delay. If his visit was prompt it was because he had been separated so long from the part of himself that alone he now valued.

It's accordingly not false to say that he reached his goal with a certain elation and stood there again with a certain assurance. The creature beneath the sod *knew* of his rare experience, so that, strangely now, the place had lost for him its mere blankness of expression. It met him in mildness—not, as before, in mockery; it wore for him the air of conscious greeting that we find, after absence, in things that have closely belonged to us and which seem to confess of themselves to the connexion. The plot of ground, the graven tablet, the tended flowers affected him so as belonging to him that he resembled for the hour a contented landlord reviewing a piece of property. Whatever had happened—well, had happened. He had not come back this time with the vanity of that question, his former worrying. "What, *what?*" now practically so spent. Yet he would none the less never again so cut himself off from the spot; he would come back to it every month, for if he did nothing else by its aid he at least held up his head. It thus grew for him, in the oddest way, a positive resource; he carried out his idea of periodical returns, which took their place at last among the most inveterate of his habits. What it all amounted to, oddly enough, was that in his finally so simplified world this garden of death gave him the few square feet of earth on which he could still most live. It was as if, being nothing anywhere else for any one, nothing even for himself, he were just everything here, and if not for a crowd of witnesses or indeed for any witness but John Marcher, then by clear right of the register that he could scan like an open page. The open page was the tomb of his friend, and *there* were the facts of the past, there the truth of his life, there the backward reaches in which he could lose himself. He did this from time to time with such effect that he seemed to wander through the old years with his hand in the arm of a companion who was, in the most extraordinary manner, his other, his younger self; and to wander, which was more extraordinary yet, round and round a third presence—not wandering she, but stationary, still whose eyes, turning with his revolution, never ceased to follow him, and whose seat was his point, so to speak, of orientation. Thus in short he settled to live—feeding all on the sense that he once *had* lived, and dependent on it not alone for a support but for an identity.

It sufficed him in its way for months and the year elapsed; it would doubtless even have carried him further but for an accident, superficially slight, which moved him, quite in another direction, with a force beyond any of his impressions of Egypt or of India. It was a thing of the merest chance—the turn, as he afterwards felt, of a hair, though he was indeed to live to believe that if light had n't come to him in this particular fashion it would still have come in another. He was to live to believe this, I say, though he was not to live, I may not less definitely mention, to do much else. We allow him at any rate the benefit of the conviction, struggling up for him at the end, that, whatever might have happened or not happened, he would have come round of himself to the light. The incident of an autumn day had put the match to the train laid from of old by his misery. With the light before him he knew that even of late his ache had only been smothered. It was strangely drugged, but it throbbed; at the touch it began to bleed. And the touch, in the event, was the face of a fellow mortal. This face, one grey afternoon when the leaves were thick in the alleys, looked into Marcher's own, at the cemetery, with an expression like the cut of a blade. He felt it, that is, so deep down that he winced at the steady thrust. The person who so mutely assaulted him was a figure he had noticed, on reaching his own goal, absorbed by a grave a short distance away, a grave apparently fresh, so that the emotion of the visitor would probably match it for frankness. This fact alone forbade further attention, though during the time he stayed he remained vaguely conscious of his neighbour, a middle-aged man apparently, in mourning whose bowed back, among the clustered monuments and mortuary yews, was constantly presented. Marcher's theory that these were elements in contact with which he himself revived, had suffered, on this occasion, it may be granted, a marked, an excessive check. The autumn day was dire for him as none had recently been, and he rested with a heaviness he had not yet known on the low stone table that bore May Bartram's name. He rested without power to move, as if some spring in him, some spell vouchsafed, had suddenly been broken for ever. If he could have done that moment as he wanted he would simply have stretched himself on the slab that was ready to take him, treating it as a place prepared to receive his last sleep. What in all the wide world had he now to keep awake for? He stared before him with the question, and it was then that, as one of the cemetery walks passed near him, he caught the shock of the face.

His neighbour at the other grave had withdrawn, as he himself, with force enough in him, would have done by now, and was advancing along the path on his way to one of the gates. This brought him close, and his pace was slow, so that—and all the more as there was a kind of hunger in his look—the two men were for a minute directly confronted. Marcher knew him at once for one of the deeply stricken—a perception so sharp that nothing else in the picture comparatively lived, neither his dress, his age, nor his presumable character and class; nothing lived but the deep ravage of the features he showed. He *showed* them—that was the point; he was moved, as he passed, by some impulse that was either a signal for sympathy or, more possibly, a challenge to an opposed sorrow. He might already have been aware of our friend, might at some previous hour have noticed in him the smooth habit of the scene, with which the state of his own senses so scantly consorted, and might thereby have been stirred as by an overt discord. What Marcher was at all events conscious of was in the first place that the image of scarred passion presented to him was conscious too—of something that profaned the air; and in the second that, roused, startled, shocked, he was yet the next moment looking after it, as it went, with envy. The most extraordinary thing that had happened to him—though he had given that name to other matters as well—took place, after his immediate vague stare, as a consequence of this impression. The stranger passed, but the raw glare of his grief remained, making our friend wonder in pity what wrong, what wound it expressed, that injury not to be healed. What had the man *had,* to make him by the loss of it so bleed and yet live?

Something—and this reached him with a pang—that *he,* John Marcher, had n't; the proof of which was precisely John Marcher's arid end. No passion had ever touched him, for this was what passion meant; he had survived and maundered and pined, but where had been *his* deep ravage? The extraordinary thing we speak of was the sudden rush of the result of this question. The sight that had just met his eyes named to him, as in letters of quick flame, something he had utterly, insanely missed, and what he had missed made these things a train of fire, made them mark themselves in an anguish of inward throbs. He had seen *outside* of his life, not learned it within, the way a woman was mourned when she had been loved for herself: such was the force of his conviction of the meaning of the stranger's face, which still flared for him as a smoky torch. It had n't come to him, the knowledge, on the wings of experience; it had brushed him, jostled him, upset him, with the disrespect of chance, the insolence of accident. Now that the illumination had begun, however, it blazed to the zenith, and what he presently stood there gazing at was the sounded void of his life. He gazed, he drew breath, in pain; he turned in his dismay, and, turning, he had before him in sharper incision than ever the open page of his story. The name on the table smote him as the passage of his neighbour had done, and what it said to him, full in the face, was that *she* was what he had missed. This was the awful thought, the answer to all the past, the vision at the dread clearness of which he grew as cold as the stone beneath him. Everything fell together, confessed, explained, overwhelmed; leaving him most of all stupefied at the blindness he had cherished. The fate he had been marked for he had met with a vengeance—he had emptied the cup to the lees; he had been the man of his time, *the* man, to whom nothing on earth was to have happened. That was the rare stroke—that was his visitation. So he saw it, as we say, in pale horror, while the pieces fitted and fitted. So *she* had seen it while he didn't, and so she served at this hour to drive the truth home. It was the truth, vivid and monstrous, that all the while he had waited the wait was itself his portion. This the companion of his vigil had at a given moment made out, and she had then offered him the chance to baffle his doom. One's doom, however, was never baffled, and on the day she told him his own had come down she had seen him but stupidly stare at the escape she offered him.

The escape would have been to love her; then, *then* he would have lived. *She* had lived—who could say now with what passion?—since she had loved him for himself; whereas he had never thought of her (ah how it hugely glared at him!) but in the chill of his egotism and the light of her use. Her spoken words came back to him—the chain stretched and stretched. The Beast had lurked indeed, and the Beast, at its hour, had sprung; it had sprung in that twilight of the cold April when, pale, ill, wasted, but all beautiful, and perhaps even then recoverable, she had risen from her chair to stand before him, and let him imaginably guess. It had sprung as he did n't guess; it had sprung as she hopelessly turned from him, and the mark, by the time he left her, had fallen where it *was* to fall. He had justified his fear and achieved his fate; he had failed, with the last exactitude, of all he was to fail of; and a moan now rose to his lips as he remembered she had prayed he might n't know. This horror of waking—*this* was knowledge, knowledge under the breath of which the very tears in his eyes seemed to freeze. Through them, none the less, he tried to fix it and hold it; he kept it there before him so that he might feel the pain. That at least, belated and bitter, had something of the taste of life. But the bitterness suddenly sickened him, and it was as if, horribly, he saw, in the truth, in the cruelty of his image, what had been appointed and done. He saw the Jungle of his life and saw the lurking Beast; then, while he looked, perceived it, as by a stir of the air, rise, huge and hideous, for the leap that was to settle him. His eyes darkened—it was close; and, instinctively turning, in his hallucination, to avoid it, he flung himself, face down, on the tomb.

1902 1903, 1909

Ambrose Bierce 1842–1914

In 1914, when he was seventy-one, Ambrose Bierce left the United States to report on the Mexican Revolution as an observer with the rebel army of Pancho Villa. One month after he arrived he wrote to a friend, "Pray for me—real hard." Shortly afterward Bierce disappeared, never to be seen again, and his mysterious fate has fascinated his biographers and his readers almost as much as the details of his misanthropic life. Bierce was born the child of poor farmers at Horse Cave Creek, Meigs County, in southeast Ohio. When he was four his family moved to a farm in Indiana, where he went to school. His parents' religious fervor left him with a lifelong hatred of faith and piety; his unhappy childhood is partially reflected in his stories filled with deaths, maimings, and the separations of parents, children, and families.

When Bierce was fifteen he went to work as a printer's devil (apprentice) on an antislavery newspaper in Indiana. Later he attended the Kentucky Military Institute for a year. And in 1861, with the outbreak of the Civil War, he enlisted in the Union Army. Bierce served with distinction throughout the war, rising from the rank of private to lieutenant and finally to the rank of brevet major. He re-enlisted twice and fought in some of the greatest and bloodiest battles of the war: Shiloh, Chickamauga, Lookout Mountain, Missionary Ridge.

Following the war, Bierce went west, first working in the San Francisco Mint but gradually establishing a career as a journalist, polemicist, and fiction writer. He spent the years from 1872 to 1876 in London, where his slashing brand of journalism won him fame and the title "Bitter Bierce." But he returned to California to write for William Randolph Hearst's San Francisco Examiner. *Bierce's writing, especially his fiction, was sardonic and obsessed with death. It has been said that "Death" was perhaps "his only character." In fact, the idea of death was not only central to Bierce's writing, it dominated his life. His early and crucial experiences in the Civil War had brought him face to face with a horrible and futile slaughter that had destroyed his youthful, romantic optimism. And in his later life Bierce was tortured by personal and professional disasters: friends and relatives fought bitterly with him, became estranged, committed suicide, died tragically. He grew increasingly cynical and malevolent, his writing vitriolic, filled with invective.*

Excerpts from his popular Devil's Dictionary *appeared from 1881 to 1906; it was a collection of waspish, witty epigrams and definitions that reflected the tone and flavor of much of his work. He defined "bride" as "a woman with a fine prospect of happiness behind her"; "Christian" as "one who believes that the New Testament is a divinely inspired book admirably suited to the spiritual needs of his neighbor"; "birth" as "The first and direst of all disasters." From 1867 until his disappearance, Bierce was a major figure in the development of American literary realism. He wrote essays, short stories, and major journalistic pieces. He was called a "West Coast Samuel Johnson," and his cynical and scathing newspaper articles were enormously popular. But his finest achievement is found in his short stories, tales about men trapped in the labyrinths of endless struggle, blinded by folly and romantic hope, abandoned to a cold and brutal providence.*

FURTHER READING: *Collected Works of Ambrose Bierce,* 12 vols., ed. W. Neale, 1909–1912; *Ambrose Bierce: Skepticism and Dissent,* ed. L. Berkove, 1980; *The Letters of Ambrose Bierce,* ed. B. Pope, 1922, 1967; V. Starrett, *Ambrose Bierce,* 1920; C. Grattan, *Bitter Bierce,* 1929; C. McWilliams, *Ambrose Bierce: A Biography,* 1929, 1967; P. Fatout, *Ambrose Bierce: The Devil's Lexicographer,* 1951; P. Fatout, *Ambrose Bierce and the Black Hills,* 1956; R. O'Conner, *Ambrose Bierce: A Biography,* 1967; M. Grenander, *Ambrose Bierce,* 1971; S. Woodruff, *The Short Stories of Ambrose Bierce,* 1964; *Critical Essays on Ambrose Bierce,* ed. C. Davidson, 1982; L. Berkove, *Ambrose Bierce: A Braver Man than Anybody Knew,* 1983; C. Davidson, *The Experimental Fictions of Ambrose Bierce,* 1984; R. Morris, *Ambrose Bierce: Alone in Bad Company,* 1995; L. Berkove, *The Moral Art of Ambrose Bierce,* 2002; D. Blume, *Ambrose Bierce's Civilians and Soldiers in Context,* 2004.

TEXT: *Tales of Soldiers and Civilians,* 1892.

AN OCCURRENCE AT OWL CREEK BRIDGE

I

A man stood upon a railroad bridge in northern Alabama, looking down into the swift water twenty feet below. The man's hands were behind his back, the wrists bound with a cord. A rope loosely encircled his neck. It was attached to a stout cross-timber above his head, and the slack fell to the level of his knees. Some loose boards laid upon the sleepers[1] supporting the metals of the railway supplied a footing for him and his executioners—two private soldiers of the Federal army, directed by a sergeant, who in civil life may have been a deputy sheriff. At a short remove upon the same temporary platform was an officer in the uniform of his rank, armed. He was a captain. A sentinel at each end of the bridge stood with his rifle in the position known as "support," that is to say, vertical in front of the left shoulder, the hammer resting on the forearm thrown straight across the chest—a formal and unnatural position, enforcing an erect carriage of the body. It did not appear to be the duty of these two men to know what was occurring at the center of the bridge; they merely blockaded the two ends of the foot plank which traversed it.

Beyond one of the sentinels, nobody was in sight; the railroad ran straight away into a forest for a hundred yards, then, curving, was lost to view. Doubtless there was an outpost farther along. The other bank of the stream was open ground—a gentle acclivity crowned with a stockade of vertical tree trunks, loopholed for rifles, with a single embrasure through which protruded the muzzle of a brass cannon commanding the bridge. Midway of the slope between bridge

[1]Ties, wooden beams to which railroad tracks are attached.

and fort were the spectators—a single company of infantry in line, at "parade rest," the butts of the rifles on the ground, the barrels inclining slightly backward against the right shoulder, the hands crossed upon the stock. A lieutenant stood at the right of the line, the point of his sword upon the ground, his left hand resting upon his right. Excepting the group of four at the center of the bridge, not a man moved. The company faced the bridge, staring stonily, motionless. The sentinels, facing the banks of the stream, might have been statues to adorn the bridge. The captain stood with folded arms, silent, observing the work of his subordinates, but making no sign. Death is a dignitary who when he comes announced is to be received with formal manifestations of respect, even by those most familiar with him. In the code of military etiquette silence and fixity are forms of deference.

The man who was engaged in being hanged was apparently about thirty-five years of age. He was a civilian, if one might judge from his dress, which was that of a planter. His features were good—a straight nose, firm mouth, broad forehead, from which his long, dark hair was combed straight back, falling behind his ears to the collar of his well-fitting frock coat. He wore a mustache and pointed beard, but no whiskers; his eyes were large and dark gray, and had a kindly expression which one would hardly have expected in one whose neck was in the hemp. Evidently this was no vulgar assassin. The liberal military code makes provision for hanging many kinds of people, and gentlemen are not excluded.

The preparations being complete, the two private soldiers stepped aside and each drew away the plank upon which he had been standing. The sergeant turned to the captain, saluted, and placed himself immediately behind that officer, who in turn moved apart one pace. These movements left the condemned man and the sergeant standing on the two ends of the same plank, which spanned three of the crossties of the bridge. The end upon which the civilian stood almost, but not quite reached a fourth. This plank had been held in place by the weight of the captain; it was now held by that of the sergeant. At a signal from the former, the latter would step aside, the plank would tilt, and the condemned man go down between two ties. The arrangement commended itself to his judgment as simple and effective. His face had not been covered nor his eyes bandaged. He looked a moment at his "unsteadfast footing," then let his gaze wander to the swirling water of the stream racing madly beneath his feet. A piece of dancing driftwood caught his attention and his eyes followed it down the current. How slowly it appeared to move! What a sluggish stream!

He closed his eyes in order to fix his last thoughts upon his wife and children. The water, touched to gold by the early sun, the brooding mists under the banks at some distance down the stream, the fort, the soldiers, the piece of drift—all had distracted him. And now he became conscious of a new disturbance. Striking through the thought of his dear ones was a sound which he could neither ignore nor understand, a sharp, distinct, metallic percussion like the stroke of a blacksmith's hammer upon the anvil; it had the same ringing quality. He wondered what it was, and whether immeasurably distant or near by—it seemed both. Its recurrence was regular, but as slow as the tolling of a death knell. He awaited each stroke with impatience and—he knew not why—apprehension. The intervals of silence grew progressively longer; the delays became maddening. With their greater infrequency the sounds increased in strength and sharpness. They hurt his ear like the thrust of a knife; he feared he would shriek. What he heard was the ticking of his watch.

He unclosed his eyes and saw again the water below him. "If I could free my hands," he thought, "I might throw off the noose and spring into the stream. By diving I could evade the bullets, and, swimming vigorously, reach the bank, take to the woods, and get away home. My home, thank God, is as yet outside their lines; my wife and little ones are still beyond the invader's farthest advance."

As these thoughts, which have here to be set down in words, were flashed into the doomed man's brain rather than evolved from it, the captain nodded to the sergeant. The sergeant stepped aside.

II

Peyton Farquhar was a well-to-do planter of an old and highly respected Alabama family. Being a slave owner and like other slave owners a politician, he was naturally an original secessionist and ardently devoted to the Southern cause. Circumstances of an imperious nature, which it is unnecessary to relate here, had prevented him from taking service with the gallant army which had fought the disastrous campaigns ending with the fall of Corinth,[2] and he chafed under the inglorious restraint, longing for the release of his energies, the larger life of the soldier, the opportunity for distinction. That opportunity, he felt, would come, as it comes to all in war time. Meanwhile he did what he could. No service was too humble for him to perform in aid of the South, no adventure too perilous for him to undertake if consistent with the character of a civilian who was at heart a soldier, and who in good faith and without too much qualification assented to at least a part of the frankly villainous dictum that all is fair in love and war.

One evening while Farquhar and his wife were sitting on a rustic bench near the entrance to his grounds, a gray-clad[3] soldier rode up to the gate and asked for a drink of water. Mrs. Farquhar was only too happy to serve him with her own white hands. While she was gone to fetch the water, her husband approached the dusty horseman and inquired eagerly for news from the front.

"The Yanks are repairing the railroads," said the man, "and are getting ready for another advance. They have reached the Owl Creek bridge, put it in order, and built a stockade on the north bank. The commandant has issued an order, which is posted everywhere, declaring that any civilian caught interfering with the railroad, its bridges, tunnels, or trains will be summarily hanged. I saw the order."

"How far is it to the Owl Creek bridge?" Farquhar asked.

"About thirty miles."

"Is there no force on this side the creek?"

"Only a picket post half a mile out, on the railroad, and a single sentinel at this end of the bridge."

"Suppose a man—a civilian and student of hanging—should elude the picket post and perhaps get the better of the sentinel," said Farquhar, smiling, "what could he accomplish?"

The soldier reflected. "I was there a month ago," he replied. "I observed that the flood of last winter had lodged a great quantity of driftwood against the wooden pier at this end of the bridge. It is now dry and would burn like tow."

[2]Corinth, Mississippi, occupied by Union forces in May, 1862.
[3]I.e., dressed in the gray uniform of a Confederate soldier.

The lady had now brought the water, which the soldier drank. He thanked her ceremoniously, bowed to her husband, and rode away. An hour later, after nightfall, he repassed the plantation, going northward in the direction from which he had come. He was a Federal scout.

III

As Peyton Farquhar fell straight downward through the bridge he lost consciousness and was as one already dead. From this state he was awakened—ages later, it seemed to him—by the pain of a sharp pressure upon his throat, followed by a sense of suffocation. Keen, poignant agonies seemed to shoot from his neck downward through every fiber of his body and limbs. These pains appeared to flash along well-defined lines of ramification and to beat with an inconceivably rapid periodicity. They seemed like streams of pulsating fire heating him to an intolerable temperature. As to his head, he was conscious of nothing but a feeling of fullness—of congestion. These sensations were unaccompanied by thought. The intellectual part of his nature was already effaced; he had power only to feel, and feeling was torment. He was conscious of motion. Encompassed in a luminous cloud, of which he was now merely the fiery heart, without material substance, he swung through unthinkable arcs of oscillation, like a vast pendulum. Then all at once, with terrible suddenness, the light about him shot upward with the noise of a loud plash; a frightful roaring was in his ears, and all was cold and dark. The power of thought was restored; he knew that the rope had broken and he had fallen into the stream. There was no additional strangulation; the noose about his neck was already suffocating him and kept the water from his lungs. To die of hanging at the bottom of a river!—the idea seemed to him ludicrous. He opened his eyes in the darkness and saw above him a gleam of light, but how distant, how inaccessible! He was still sinking, for the light became fainter and fainter until it was a mere glimmer. Then it began to grow and brighten, and he knew that he was rising toward the surface—knew it with reluctance, for he was now very comfortable. "To be hanged and drowned," he thought, "that is not so bad; but I do not wish to be shot." No, I will not be shot, that is not fair."

He was not conscious of an effort, but a sharp pain in his wrist apprised him that he was trying to free his hands. He gave the struggle his attention, as an idler might observe the feat of a juggler, without interest in the outcome. What splendid effort!—what magnificent, what super-human strength! Ah, that was a fine endeavor! Bravo! The cord fell away; his arms parted and floated upward, the hands dimly seen on each side in the growing light. He watched them with a new interest as first one and then the other pounced upon the noose at his neck. They tore it away and thrust it fiercely aside, its undulations resembling those of a water snake. "Put it back, put it back!" He thought he shouted these words to his hands, for the undoing of the noose had been succeeded by the direst pang that he had yet experienced. His neck ached horribly; his brain was on fire; his heart, which had been fluttering faintly, gave a great leap, trying to force itself out at his mouth. His whole body was racked and wrenched with an insupportable anguish! But his disobedient hands gave no heed to the command. They beat the water vigorously with quick, downward strokes, forcing him to the surface. He felt his head emerge; his eyes were blinded by the sunlight; his chest expanded convulsively, and with a supreme and crowning agony his lungs engulfed a great draught of air, which instantly he expelled in a shriek!

He was now in full possession of his physical senses. They were, indeed, preternaturally keen and alert. Something in the awful disturbance of his organic system had so exalted and refined them that they made record of things never before perceived. He felt the ripples upon his face and heard their separate sounds as they struck. He looked at the forest on the bank of the stream, saw the individual trees, the leaves and the veining of each leaf—saw the very insects upon them: the locusts, the brilliant-bodied flies, the gray spiders stretching their webs from twig to twig. He noted the prismatic colors in all the dewdrops upon a million blades of grass. The humming of the gnats that danced above the eddies of the stream, the beating of the dragonflies' wings, the strokes of the water spiders' legs, like oars which had lifted their boat—all these made audible music. A fish slid along beneath his eyes and he heard the rush of its body parting the water.

He had come to the surface facing down the stream; in a moment the visible world seemed to wheel slowly round, himself the pivotal point, and he saw the bridge, the fort, the soldiers upon the bridge, the captain, the sergeant, the two privates, his executioners. They were in silhouette against the blue sky. They shouted and gesticulated, pointing at him. The captain had drawn his pistol, but did not fire; the others were unarmed. Their movements were grotesque and horrible, their forms gigantic.

Suddenly he heard a sharp report and something struck the water smartly within a few inches of his head, spattering his face with spray. He heard the second report, and saw one of the sentinels with his rifle at his shoulder, a light cloud of blue smoke rising from the muzzle. The man in the water saw the eye of the man on the bridge gazing into his own through the sights of the rifle. He observed that it was a gray eye and remembered having read that gray eyes were keenest, and that all famous marksmen had them. Nevertheless, this one had missed.

A counterswirl had caught Farquhar and turned him half round; he was again looking into the forest on the bank opposite the fort. The sound of a clear, high voice in a monotonous singsong now rang out behind him and came across the water with distinctness that pierced and subdued all other sounds, even the beating of the ripples in his ears. Although no soldier, he had frequented camps enough to know the dread significance of that deliberate, drawling, aspirated chant; the lieutenant on shore was taking part in the morning's work. How coldly and pitilessly—with what an even, calm intonation, presaging and enforcing tranquillity in the men—with what accurately measured intervals fell those cruel words:

"Attention, company! . . . Shoulder arms! . . . Ready! . . . Aim! . . . Fire!"

Farquhar dived—dived as deeply as he could. The water roared in his ears like the voice of Niagara, yet he heard the dulled thunder of the volley and, rising again toward the surface, met shining bits of metal, singularly flattened, oscillating slowly downward. Some of them touched him on the face and hands, then fell away, continuing their descent. One lodged between his collar and his neck; it was uncomfortably warm and he snatched it out.

As he rose to the surface, gasping for breath, he saw that he had been a long time under water; he was perceptibly farther downstream—nearer to safety. The soldiers had almost finished reloading; the metal ramrods flashed all at once in the sunshine as they were drawn from the barrels, turned in the air, and thrust into their sockets. The two sentinels fired again, independently and ineffectually.

The hunted man saw all this over his shoulder; he was now swimming vigorously with the current. His brain was as energetic as his arms and legs; he thought with the rapidity of lightning.

"The officer," he reasoned, "will not make that martinet's error a second time. It is as easy to dodge a volley as a single shot. He has probably already given the command to fire at will. God help me, I cannot dodge them all!"

An appalling plash within two yards of him was followed by a loud, rushing sound, *diminuendo,*[4] which seemed to travel back through the air to the fort and died in an explosion which stirred the very river to its deeps! A rising sheet of water, which curved over him, fell down upon him, blinded him, strangled him! The cannon had taken a hand in the game. As he shook his head free from the commotion of the smitten water, he heard the deflected shot humming through the air ahead, and in an instant it was cracking and smashing the branches in the forest beyond.

"They will not do that again," he thought; "the next time they will use a charge of grape.[5] I must keep my eye upon the gun; the smoke will apprise me—the report arrives too late; it lags behind the missile. That is a good gun."

Suddenly he felt himself whirled round and round—spinning like a top. The water, the banks, the forests, the now distant bridge, fort, and men—all were commingled and blurred. Objects were represented by their colors only; circular horizontal streaks of color—that was all he saw. He had been caught in a vortex and was being whirled on with a velocity of advance and gyration which made him giddy and sick. In a few moments he was flung upon the gravel at the foot of the left bank of the stream—the southern bank—and behind a projecting point which concealed him from his enemies. The sudden arrest of his motion, the abrasion of one of his hands on the gravel, restored him, and he wept with delight. He dug his fingers into the sand, threw it over himself in handfuls, and audibly blessed it. It looked like gold, like diamonds, rubies, emeralds; he could think of nothing beautiful which it did not resemble. The trees upon the bank were giant garden plants; he noted a definite order in their arrangement, inhaled the fragrance of their blooms. A strange, roseate light shone through the spaces among their trunks and the wind made in their branches the music of aeolian harps.[6] He had no wish to perfect his escape—was content to remain in that enchanting spot until retaken.

A whiz and rattle of grapeshot among the branches high above his head roused him from his dream. The baffled cannoneer had fired him a random farewell. He sprang to his feet, rushed up the sloping bank, and plunged into the forest.

All that day he traveled, laying his course by the rounding sun. The forest seemed interminable; nowhere did he discover a break in it, not even a

[4]Italian: diminishing in volume.
[5]Grapeshot, a cluster of iron balls fired from a cannon.
[6]Stringed instruments that sound when exposed to the wind.

woodman's road. He had not known that he lived in so wild a region. There was something uncanny in the revelation.

By nightfall he was fatigued, footsore, famishing. The thought of his wife and children urged him on. At last he found a road which led him in what he knew to be the right direction. It was wide and straight as a city street, yet it seemed untraveled. No fields bordered it, no dwelling anywhere. Not so much as the barking of a dog suggested human habitation. The black bodies of the great trees formed a straight wall on both sides, terminating on the horizon in a point, like a diagram in a lesson in perspective. Overhead, as he looked up through this rift in the wood, shone great golden stars looking unfamiliar and grouped in strange constellations. He was sure they were arranged in some order which had a secret and malign significance. The wood on either side was full of singular noises, among which—once, twice, and again—he distinctly heard whispers in an unknown tongue.

His neck was in pain and lifting his hand to it he found it horribly swollen. He knew that it had a circle of black where the rope had bruised it. His eyes felt congested; he could no longer close them. His tongue was swollen with thirst; he relieved its fever by thrusting it forward from between his teeth into the cool air. How softly the turf had carpeted the untraveled avenue—he could no longer feel the roadway beneath his feet!

Doubtless, despite his suffering, he had fallen asleep while walking, for now he sees another scene—perhaps he has merely recovered from a delirium. He stands at the gate of his own home. All is as he left it, and all bright and beautiful in the morning sunshine. He must have traveled the entire night. As he pushes open the gate and passes up the wide white walk, he sees a flutter of female garments; his wife, looking fresh and cool and sweet, steps down from the veranda to meet him. At the bottom of the steps she stands waiting, with a smile of ineffable joy, an attitude of matchless grace and dignity. Ah, how beautiful she is! He springs forward with extended arms. As he is about to clasp her, he feels a stunning blow upon the back of the neck; a blinding white light blazes all about him with a sound like the shock of a cannon—then all is darkness and silence!

Peyton Farquhar was dead; his body, with a broken neck, swung gently from side to side beneath the timbers of the Owl Creek bridge.

1890, 1891

CHICKAMAUGA

One sunny autumn afternoon a child strayed away from its rude home in a small field and entered a forest unobserved. It was happy in a new sense of freedom from control, happy in the opportunity of exploration and adventure; for this child's spirit, in bodies of its ancestors, had for thousands of years been trained to memorable feats of discovery and conquest—victories in battles whose critical moments were centuries, whose victors' camps were cities of hewn stone. From the cradle of its race it had conquered its way through two continents and passing a great sea had penetrated a third, there to be born to war and dominion as a heritage.

The child was a boy aged about six years, the son of a poor planter. In his younger manhood the father had been a soldier, had fought against naked savages and followed the flag of his country into the capital of a civilized race to the far South. In the peaceful life of a planter the warrior-fire survived; once kindled, it is never extinguished. The man loved military books and pictures and the boy had understood enough to make himself a wooden sword, though even the eye of his father would hardly have known it for what it was. This weapon he now bore bravely, as became the son of an heroic race, and pausing now and again in the sunny space of the forest assumed, with some exaggeration, the postures of aggression and defense that he had been taught by the engraver's art. Made reckless by the ease with which he overcame invisible foes attempting to stay his advance, he committed the common enough military error of pushing the pursuit to a dangerous extreme, until he found himself upon the margin of a wide but shallow brook, whose rapid waters barred his direct advance against the flying foe that had crossed with illogical ease. But the intrepid victor was not to be baffled; the spirit of the race which had passed the great sea burned unconquerable in that small breast and would not be denied. Finding a place where some bowlders in the bed of the stream lay but a step or a leap apart, he made his way across and fell again upon the rear-guard of his imaginary foe, putting all to the sword.

Now that the battle had been won, prudence required that he withdraw to his base of operations. Alas; like many a mightier conqueror, and like one, the mightiest, he could not

curb the lust for war,
Nor learn that tempted Fate will leave the loftiest star.[1]

Advancing from the bank of the creek he suddenly found himself confronted with a new and more formidable enemy: in the path that he was following, sat, bolt upright, with ears erect and paws suspended before it, a rabbit! With a startled cry the child turned and fled, he knew not in what direction, calling with inarticulate cries for his mother, weeping, stumbling, his tender skin cruelly torn by brambles, his little heart beating hard with terror—breathless, blind with tears—lost in the forest! Then, for more than an hour, he wandered with erring feet through the tangled undergrowth, till at last, overcome by fatigue, he lay down in a narrow space between two rocks, within a few yards of the stream and still grasping his toy sword, no longer a weapon but a companion, sobbed himself to sleep. The wood birds sang merrily above his head; the squirrels, whisking their bravery of tail, ran barking from tree to tree, unconscious of the pity of it, and somewhere far away was a strange, muffled thunder, as if the partridges were drumming in celebration of nature's victory over the son of her immemorial enslavers. And back at the little plantation, where white men and black were hastily searching the fields and hedges in alarm, a mother's heart was breaking for her missing child.

Hours passed, and then the little sleeper rose to his feet. The chill of the evening was in his limbs, the fear of the gloom in his heart. But he had rested,

[1]Lines from *Childe Harold's Pilgrimage* (Canto 3, stanza 38), by the English poet George Gordon, Lord Byron (1788–1824).

and he no longer wept. With some blind instinct which impelled to action he struggled through the undergrowth about him and came to a more open ground—on his right the brook, to the left a gentle acclivity studded with infrequent trees; over all, the gathering gloom of twilight. A thin, ghostly mist rose along the water. It frightened and repelled him; instead of recrossing, in the direction whence he had come, he turned his back upon it, and went forward toward the dark inclosing wood. Suddenly he saw before him a strange moving object which he took to be some large animal—a dog, a pig—he could not name it; perhaps it was a bear. He had seen pictures of bears, but knew of nothing to their discredit and had vaguely wished to meet one. But something in form or movement of this object—something in the awkwardness of its approach—told him that it was not a bear, and curiosity was stayed by fear. He stood still and as it came slowly on gained courage every moment, for he saw that at least it had not the long, menacing ears of the rabbit. Possibly his impressionable mind was half conscious of something familiar in its shambling, awkward gait. Before it had approached near enough to resolve his doubts he saw that it was followed by another and another. To right and to left were many more; the whole open space about him was alive with them—all moving toward the brook.

They were men. They crept upon their hands and knees. They used their hands only, dragging their legs. They used their knees only, their arms hanging idle at their sides. They strove to rise to their feet, but fell prone in the attempt. They did nothing naturally, and nothing alike, save only to advance foot by foot in the same direction. Singly, in pairs and in little groups, they came on through the gloom, some halting now and again while others crept slowly past them, then resuming their movement. They came by dozens and by hundreds; as far on either hand as one could see in the deepening gloom they extended and the black wood behind them appeared to be inexhaustible. The very ground seemed in motion toward the creek. Occasionally one who had paused did not again go on, but lay motionless. He was dead. Some, pausing, made strange gestures with their hands, erected their arms and lowered them again, clasped their heads; spread their palms upward, as men are sometimes seen to do in public prayer.

Not all of this did the child note; it is what would have been noted by an elder observer; he saw little but that these were men, yet crept like babes. Being men, they were not terrible, though unfamiliarly clad. He moved among them freely, going from one to another and peering into their faces with childish curiosity. All their faces were singularly white and many were streaked and gouted with red. Something in this—something too, perhaps, in their grotesque attitudes and movements—reminded him of the painted clown whom he had seen last summer in the circus, and he laughed as he watched them. But on and ever on they crept, these maimed and bleeding men, as heedless as he of the dramatic contrast between his laughter and their own ghastly gravity. To him it was a merry spectacle. He had seen his father's negroes creep upon their hands and knees for his amusement—had ridden them so, "making believe" they were his horses. He now approached one of these crawling figures from behind and with an agile movement mounted it astride. The man sank upon his breast, recovered, flung the small boy fiercely to the ground as an unbroken colt might have done, then turned upon him a face that lacked a lower jaw—from the upper teeth to the throat was a great red gap fringed with hanging shreds of flesh and splinters of bone. The unnatural prominence of nose, the absence of chin, the fierce eyes, gave this man the appearance of a great bird of prey crimsoned in throat and breast by the blood of its quarry. The man rose to his knees, the child to his feet. The man shook his fist at the child; the child, terrified at last, ran to a tree near by, got upon the farther side of it and took a more serious view of the situation. And so the clumsy multitude dragged itself slowly and painfully along in hideous pantomime—moved forward down the slope like a swarm of great black beetles, with never a sound of going—in silence profound, absolute.

Instead of darkening, the haunted landscape began to brighten. Through the belt of trees beyond the brook shone a strange red light, the trunks and branches of the trees making a black lacework against it. It struck the creeping figures and gave them monstrous shadows, which caricatured their movements on the lit grass. It fell upon their faces, touching their whiteness with a ruddy tinge, accentuating the stains with which so many of them were freaked and maculated. It sparkled on buttons and bits of metal in their clothing. Instinctively the child turned toward the growing splendor and moved down the slope with his horrible companions; in a few moments had passed the foremost of the throng—not much of a feat, considering his advantages. He placed himself in the lead, his wooden sword still in hand, and solemnly directed the march, conforming his pace to theirs and occasionally turning as if to see that his forces did not straggle. Surely such a leader never before had such a following.

Scattered about upon the ground now slowly narrowing by the encroachment of this awful march to water, were certain articles to which, in the leader's mind, were coupled no significant associations: an occasional blanket, tightly rolled lengthwise, doubled and the ends bound together with a string; a heavy knapsack here, and there a broken rifle—such things, in short, as are found in the rear of retreating troops, the "spoor" of men flying from their hunters. Everywhere near the creek, which here had a margin of lowland, the earth was trodden into mud by the feet of men and horses. An observer of better experience in the use of his eyes would have noticed that these footprints pointed in both directions; the ground had been twice passed over—in advance and in retreat. A few hours before, these desperate, stricken men, with their more fortunate and now distant comrades, had penetrated the forest in thousands. Their successive battalions, breaking into swarms and re-forming in lines, had passed the child on every side—had almost trodden on him as he slept. The rustle and murmur of their march had not awakened him. Almost within a stone's throw of where he lay they had fought a battle; but all unheard by him were the roar of the musketry, the shock of the cannon, "the thunder of the captains and the shouting." He had slept through it all, grasping his little wooden sword with perhaps a tighter clutch in unconscious sympathy with his martial environment, but as heedless of the grandeur of the struggle as the dead who had died to make the glory.

The fire beyond the belt of woods on the farther side of the creek, reflected to earth from the canopy of its own smoke, was now suffusing the whole landscape. It transformed the sinuous line of mist to the vapor of gold. The water gleamed with dashes of red, and red, too, were many of the stones protruding above the surface. But that was blood; the less desperately wounded had stained them in crossing. On them, too, the child now crossed with eager steps; he was going to the fire. As he stood upon the farther bank he turned about to look at the companions of his march. The advance was arriving at the creek. The stronger had already drawn themselves to the brink and plunged their faces into the flood. Three or four who lay without motion appeared to have no heads. At this the child's eyes expanded with wonder; even his hospitable understanding could not accept a phenomenon implying such vitality as that. After slaking their thirst these men had not had the strength to back away from the water, nor to keep their heads above it. They were drowned. In rear of these, the open spaces of the forest showed the leader as many formless figures of his grim command as at first; but not nearly so many were in motion. He waved his cap for their encouragement and smilingly pointed with his weapon in the direction of the guiding light—a pillar of fire to this strange exodus.

Confident of the fidelity of his forces, he now entered the belt of woods, passed through it easily in the red illumination, climbed a fence, ran across a field, turning now and again to coquet with his responsive shadow, and so approached the blazing ruin of a dwelling. Desolation everywhere! In all the wide glare not a living thing was visible. He cared nothing for that; the spectacle pleased, and he danced with glee in imitation of the wavering flames. He ran about, collecting fuel, but every object that he found was too heavy for him to cast in from the distance to which the heat limited his approach. In despair he flung in his sword—a surrender to the superior forces of nature. His military career was at an end.

Shifting his position, his eyes fell upon some outbuildings which had an oddly familiar appearance, as if he had dreamed of them. He stood considering them with wonder, when suddenly the entire plantation, with its inclosing forest, seemed to turn as if upon a pivot. His little world swung half around; the points of the compass were reversed. He recognized the blazing building as his own home!

For a moment he stood stupefied by the power of the revelation, then ran with stumbling feet, making a half-circuit of the ruin. There, conspicuous in the light of the conflagration, lay the dead body of a woman—the white face turned upward, the hands thrown out and clutched full of grass, the clothing deranged, the long dark hair in tangles and full of clotted blood. The greater part of the forehead was torn away, and from the jagged hole the brain protruded, overflowing the temple, a frothy mass of gray, crowned with clusters of crimson bubbles—the work of a shell.

The child moved his little hands, making wild, uncertain gestures. He uttered a series of inarticulate and indescribable cries—something between the chattering of an ape and the gobbling of a turkey—a startling, soulless, unholy sound, the language of a devil. The child was a deaf mute.

Then he stood motionless, with quivering lips, looking down upon the wreck.

1892

Charlotte Perkins Gilman
1860–1935

Like the heroine of her short story "The Yellow Wall-Paper," Charlotte Perkins Gilman saw the world as a place where individual lives are often smothered by the power of convention and authority. Her own life was marred by an unhappy childhood, an ill-fated first marriage, recurring mental breakdowns, and public rejection of the social reforms for which she wrote and spoke. Yet, in the last half of the twentieth century, many of the ideals to which she devoted her life have become a part of the nation's fabric of beliefs, and she is now recognized as a vital force in the history of reform in the United States.

She was born Charlotte Perkins in Hartford, Connecticut. Among her ancestors were the renowned New England preacher Henry Ward Beecher and the most famous woman of nineteenth-century America, Harriet Beecher Stowe, the author of Uncle Tom's Cabin. *Charlotte Perkins seemed destined for a genteel and congenial New England upbringing, but shortly after her birth, her father abandoned his family, leaving his wife and children to lives strained by poverty and emotional deprivation.*

As a result, Charlotte Perkins received little formal education. But she was an avid reader of history and literature, and she had a natural talent for art. After a brief period of study at the Rhode Island School of Design, in Providence, she established herself as a designer of advertising cards for businesses. Later she worked as a children's tutor. And she began to write.

Her first publication, a poem, appeared in 1880. Three years later she published a short article in the Providence Journal. *In the following year she married a fellow artist, Charles Stetson, but the marriage was a failure almost from the start. Charlotte Perkins Stetson rejected the submissive role deemed proper for nineteenth-century married women. She refused to subside into a life solely devoted to the wifely duties of housekeeping, childrearing, and obedience to her husband. Instead, she focused her energies on painting and on writing poems, essays, and short stories.*

In 1884, the year of her marriage, her second poem was published. Entitled "In Duty Bound," it began, significantly enough, "In duty bound, a life hemmed in. . . ." And for the rest of her life, her writing reflected the belief that the patriarchal culture surrounding her was one that denigrated women, hemmed them in, thwarted their natural desires for intellectual growth and expression.

Oppressed by her unhappy marriage, she suffered periodic sieges of mental depression, and she was taken to the celebrated physician Silas Weir Mitchell, a neurologist known for his "rest-cure" for nervous disorders. The "rest-cure" prescribed for Charlotte Stetson required her isolation from just those modes of self-expression and intellectual growth that had sustained her sense of independence. She was told never again to write, never to paint, never to read for more than two hours a day.

It was the most advanced medical treatment of the age, and its ideal of the tranquilized mental patient anticipated much psychiatric therapy of the late twentieth century. But Charlotte Perkins Stetson saw that her sanity lay not in submission to her physician or her husband but in her freedom and independence. In 1888, to escape her "rest-cure" and her marriage, she moved to California, where she divorced her husband and helped support herself by running a boarding house.

Free of the constraints of marriage, she began to speak out boldly on political and social issues. She wrote and lectured on women's rights and argued for a utopian socialism that would end social injustice. Soon women's clubs and church groups began to seek her out as a lecturer. More and more magazines and newspapers published her essays and articles.

In 1900, she married George Gilman. It was a successful marriage—her new husband shared many of her social and political views—and she now wrote as Charlotte Perkins Gilman, but she continued her crusade for women's rights. From 1889 to 1891, she wrote for the Pacific Monthly, *a journal of social and political commentary published in Los Angeles. Later she edited* The Impress, *a journal of the Pacific Coast Women's Association, and from 1909 to 1916 she published and edited* The Forerunner, *a monthly magazine for which she wrote almost the entire contents—editorials, stories, articles, book reviews, poems, even the advertisements.*

For five years in the 1890s, Charlotte Perkins Gilman toured America as a lecturer, arguing that women were dominated by their fathers and husbands, that women were entrapped by their innocence and their upbringing. She insisted that home was more often a prison than a shelter, and she encouraged women to assert their rights and free themselves from unthinking devotion to cooking, cleaning, church, and children.

Censorious critics said that she "despised the home" more than any other American. They denounced her as a "man-hater" and argued that her feminism and her assaults on masculinity were revenge against the father who had abandoned her as a child. Later critics have pointed out that her sympathies were primarily for middle-class women and that she showed little concern for the destitute, for minorities, or for the millions of immigrants struggling to survive in late nineteenth-century America.

In part the criticism came because Charlotte Perkins Gilman was so effective and so untiring a worker for reform. In recent years she has been called one of the "ancestral mothers" of the modern feminist movement, but she wrote prolifically on a wide variety of political, social, and economic topics: poverty, health care, civil justice, the rights of labor. She published more than a thousand articles in addition to short stories, novels, and hundreds of poems. Her most significant book, Women and Economics *(1898), is a lengthy study of the ways in which male dominance was reinforced by the economic system of her society. A popular success, and widely influential in the 1890s, the book's arguments remain cogent today, nearly a century after its publication.*

Charlotte Perkins Gilman said that she wrote not to create literature but to improve the world, and she was most effective as an ideologue and a polemicist. One of the tools she used for this was utopian fiction, including Moving the Mountain *(1911),* Herland *(1915), and* With Her in Our Land *(1916)—all of which were published in* The Forerunner, *a feminist monthly journal that she founded in 1909, edited until 1916, and wrote most of the copy for. Her utopian novels offer a vision of a world governed by peaceful and rational principles and featuring full equality between men and women.*

In "The Yellow Wall-Paper" Gilman created a story of complex literary artistry. It has been called one of the best horror stories of the nineteenth century, and it has many of the elements of gothic horror tales: the female in distress, the isolated mansion, the locked room, the threat of masculine torment. In writing the story, Charlotte Perkins Gilman had drawn on her experience with mental illness. "The Yellow Wall-Paper" was, in part, her retaliation for the suffering she had experienced. Her own explanation was that she wrote the story to expose the mistakes made by medical science in treating the insane. But "The Yellow Wall-Paper" is more than a frightening tale, more than an effort to redress a grievance or correct therapeutic errors. It anticipates the psychological fiction of the twentieth century in its portrayal of alienation and of misunderstood suffering in a complacent society. It foreshadows the modern world's preoccupation with psychosis, distorted perceptions, receding distinctions between reality and hallucination. It is a surrealist picture of a tormented, isolated individual, and it is a call for understanding of a woman lost in a world without comprehension or memory, writhing in the tangles of madness and dead hope.

FURTHER READING: *The Charlotte Perkins Gilman Reader,* ed. A. Lane, 1980; *The Living of Charlotte Perkins Gilman: An Autobiography,* 1935; *The Diaries of Charlotte Perkins Gilman,* 2 vols., ed. D. Knight, 1993; *Charlotte Perkins Gilman: A Non-fiction Reader,* ed. L. Ceplair, 1991; *The Later Poetry of Charlotte Perkins Gilman,* ed. D. Knight, 1996; *Charlotte Perkins Gilman's Utopian Novels,* ed. M. Diskow, 1999; M. Hill, *Charlotte Perkins Gilman: The Making of a Radical Feminist,* 1980; B. Winkler, *Victorian Daughters,* 1980; G. Scharnhorst, *Charlotte Perkins Gilman,* 1985; P. Allen, *Building Domestic Liberty: Charlotte Perkins Gilman's Architectural Feminism,* 1988; *Charlotte Perkins Gilman: The Woman and Her Work,* ed. S. Meyering, 1991; A. Lane, *To Herland and Beyond: The Life and Work of Charlotte Perkins Gilman,* 1990; *Critical Essays on Charlotte Perkins Gilman,* ed. J. Karpinski, 1993; C. Kessler, *Charlotte Perkins Gilman: Her Progress Toward Utopia,* 1995; *Charlotte Perkins Gilman's Utopian Novels,* ed. M. Doskow, 1999; *Charlotte Perkins Gilman and Her Contemporaries,* ed. C. Davis and J. Knight, 2004.

TEXTS: "The Yellow Wall-Paper," *New England Magazine,* January 1892; other stories, *The Charlotte Perkins Gilman Reader,* ed. A. Lane, 1980.

THE YELLOW WALL-PAPER[1]

It is very seldom that mere ordinary people like John and myself secure ancestral halls for the summer.

A colonial mansion, a hereditary estate, I would say a haunted house, and reach the height of romantic felicity—but that would be asking too much of fate!

Still I will proudly declare that there is something queer about it.

Else, why should it be let so cheaply? And why have stood so long untenanted?

John laughs at me, of course, but one expects that in marriage.

John is practical in the extreme. He has no patience with faith, an intense horror of superstition, and he scoffs openly at any talk of things not to be felt and seen and put down in figures.

John is a physician, and *perhaps*—(I would not say it to a living soul, of course, but this is dead paper and a great relief to my mind—) *perhaps* that is one reason I do not get well faster.

You see he does not believe I am sick!

And what can one do?

If a physician of high standing, and one's own husband, assures friends and relatives that there is really nothing the matter with one but temporary nervous depression—a slight hysterical tendency—what is one to do?

My brother is also a physician, and also of high standing, and he says the same thing.

So I take phosphates or phosphites[2]—whichever it is, and tonics, and journeys, and air, and exercise, and am absolutely forbidden to "work" until I am well again.

[1]The variant spellings of "wall-paper" in the first, 1892, printing of the story are preserved here. Some typographical errors and misspellings have been silently corrected.

[2]Carbonated water and acid phosphate, flavored with a fruit syrup.

Personally, I disagree with their ideas.

Personally, I believe that congenial work, with excitement and change, would do me good.

But what is one to do?

I did write for a while in spite of them; but it *does* exhaust me a good deal—having to be so sly about it, or else meet with heavy opposition.

I sometimes fancy that in my condition if I had less opposition and more society and stimulus—but John says the very worst thing I can do is to think about my condition, and I confess it always makes me feel bad.

So I will let it alone and talk about the house.

The most beautiful place! It is quite alone, standing well back from the road, quite three miles from the village. It makes me think of English places that you read about, for there are hedges and walls and gates that lock, and lots of separate little houses for the gardeners and people.

There is a *delicious* garden! I never saw such a garden—large and shady, full of box-bordered[3] paths, and lined with long grape-covered arbors with seats under them.

There were greenhouses, too, but they are all broken now.

There was some legal trouble, I believe, something about the heirs and coheirs; anyhow, the place has been empty for years.

That spoils my ghostliness, I am afraid, but I don't care—there is something strange about the house—I can feel it.

I even said so to John one moonlight evening, but he said what I felt was a *draught*, and shut the window.

I get unreasonably angry with John sometimes. I'm sure I never used to be so sensitive. I think it is due to this nervous condition.

But John says if I feel so, I shall neglect proper self-control; so I take pains to control myself—before him, at least, and that makes me very tired.

I don't like our room a bit. I wanted one downstairs that opened on the piazza and had roses all over the window, and such pretty old-fashioned chintz hangings! but John would not hear of it.

He said there was only one window and not room for two beds, and no near room for him if he took another.

He is very careful and loving, and hardly lets me stir without special direction.

I have a schedule prescription for each hour in the day; he takes all care from me, and so I feel basely ungrateful not to value it more.

He said we came here solely on my account, that I was to have perfect rest and all the air I could get. "Your exercise depends on your strength, my dear," said he, "and your food somewhat on your appetite; but air you can absorb all the time." So we took the nursery at the top of the house.

It is a big, airy room, the whole floor nearly, with windows that look all ways, and air and sunshine galore. It was nursery first and then playroom and gymnasium, I should judge; for the windows are barred for little children, and there are rings and things in the walls.

The paint and paper look as if a boys' school had used it. It is stripped off—the paper—in great patches all around the head of my bed, about as far as I can reach, and in a great place on the other side of the room low down. I never saw a worse paper in my life.

[3]I.e., with borders of box, an evergreen shrub.

One of those sprawling flamboyant patterns committing every artistic sin.

It is dull enough to confuse the eye in following, pronounced enough to constantly irritate and provoke study, and when you follow the lame uncertain curves for a little distance they suddenly commit suicide—plunge off at outrageous angles, destroy themselves in unheard of contradictions.

The color is repellant, almost revolting; a smouldering unclean yellow, strangely faded by the slow-turning sunlight.

It is a dull yet lurid orange in some places, a sickly sulphur tint in others.

No wonder the children hated it! I should hate it myself if I had to live in this room long.

There comes John, and I must put this away,—he hates to have me write a word.

* * * * * *

We have been here two weeks, and I haven't felt like writing before, since that first day.

I am sitting by the window now, up in this atrocious nursery, and there is nothing to hinder my writing as much as I please, save lack of strength.

John is away all day, and even some nights when his cases are serious.

I am glad my case is not serious!

But these nervous troubles are dreadfully depressing.

John does not know how much I really suffer. He knows there is no *reason* to suffer, and that satisfies him.

Of course it is only nervousness. It does weigh on me so not to do my duty in any way!

I meant to be such a help to John, such a real rest and comfort, and here I am a comparative burden already!

Nobody would believe what an effort it is to do what little I am able,—to dress and entertain, and order things.

It is fortunate Mary is so good with the baby. Such a dear baby!

And yet I *cannot* be with him, it makes me so nervous.

I suppose John never was nervous in his life. He laughs at me so about this wall-paper!

At first he meant to repaper the room, but afterwards he said that I was letting it get the better of me, and that nothing was worse for a nervous patient than to give way to such fancies.

He said that after the wall-paper was changed it would be the heavy bedstead, and then the barred windows, and then that gate at the head of the stairs, and so on.

"You know the place is doing you good," he said, "and really, dear, I don't care to renovate the house just for a three months' rental."

"Then do let us go downstairs," I said, "there are such pretty rooms there."

Then he took me in his arms and called me a blessed little goose, and said he would go down cellar, if I wished, and have it whitewashed into the bargain.

But he is right enough about the beds and windows and things.

It is an airy and comfortable room as any one need wish, and, of course, I would not be so silly as to make him uncomfortable just for a whim.

I'm really getting quite fond of the big room, all but that horrid paper.

Out of one window I can see the garden, those mysterious deep-shaded arbors, the riotous old-fashioned flowers, and bushes and gnarly trees.

Out of another I get a lovely view of the bay and a little private wharf belonging to the estate. There is a beautiful shaded lane that runs down there from the house. I always fancy I see people walking in these numerous paths and arbors, but John has cautioned me not to give way to fancy in the least. He says that with my imaginative power and habit of story-making, a nervous weakness like mine is sure to lead to all manner of excited fancies, and that I ought to use my will and good sense to check the tendency. So I try.

I think sometimes that if I were only well enough to write a little it would relieve the press of ideas and rest me.

But I find I get pretty tired when I try.

It is so discouraging not to have any advice and companionship about my work. When I get really well, John says we will ask Cousin Henry and Julia down for a long visit; but he says he would as soon put fireworks in my pillowcase as to let me have those stimulating people about now.

I wish I could get well faster.

But I must not think about that. This paper looks to me as if it *knew* what a vicious influence it had!

There is a recurrent spot where the pattern lolls like a broken neck and two bulbous eyes stare at you upside down.

I get positively angry with the impertinence of it and the everlastingness. Up and down and sideways they crawl, and those absurd, unblinking eyes are everywhere. There is one place where two breadths didn't match, and the eyes go all up and down the line, one a little higher than the other.

I never saw so much expression in an inanimate thing before, and we all know how much expression they have! I used to lie awake as a child and get more entertainment and terror out of blank walls and plain furniture than most children could find in a toy-store.

I remember what a kindly wink the knobs of our big, old bureau used to have, and there was one chair that always seemed like a strong friend.

I used to feel that if any of the other things looked too fierce I could always hop into that chair and be safe.

The furniture in this room is no worse than inharmonious, however, for we had to bring it all from downstairs. I suppose when this was used as a playroom they had to take the nursery things out, and no wonder! I never saw such ravages as the children have made here.

The wall-paper, as I said before, is torn off in spots, and it sticketh closer than a brother[4]—they must have had perseverance as well as hatred.

Then the floor is scratched and gouged and splintered, the plaster itself is dug out here and there, and this great heavy bed which is all we found in the room, looks as if it had been through the wars.

But I don't mind it a bit—only the paper.

There comes John's sister. Such a dear girl as she is, and so careful of me! I must not let her find me writing.

She is a perfect and enthusiastic housekeeper, and hopes for no better profession. I verily believe she thinks it is the writing which made me sick!

But I can write when she is out, and see her a long way off from these windows.

[4]"There is a friend that sticketh closer than a brother" (Proverbs 18:24).

There is one that commands the road, a lovely shaded winding road, and one that just looks off over the country. A lovely country, too, full of great elms and velvet meadows.

This wallpaper has a kind of subpattern in a different shade, a particularly irritating one, for you can only see it in certain lights, and not clearly then.

But in the places where it isn't faded and where the sun is just so—I can see a strange, provoking, formless sort of figure, that seems to skulk about behind that silly and conspicuous front design.

There's sister on the stairs!

* * * * * *

Well, the Fourth of July is over! The people are all gone and I am tired out. John thought it might do me good to see a little company, so we just had mother and Nellie and the children down for a week.

Of course I didn't do a thing. Jennie sees to everything now.

But it tired me all the same.

John says if I don't pick up faster he shall send me to Weir Mitchell[5] in the fall.

But I don't want to go there at all. I had a friend who was in his hands once, and she says he is just like John and my brother, only more so!

Besides, it is such an undertaking to go so far.

I don't feel as if it was worth while to turn my hand over for anything, and I'm getting dreadfully fretful and querulous.

I cry at nothing, and cry most of the time.

Of course I don't when John is here, or anybody else, but when I am alone.

And I am alone a good deal just now. John is kept in town very often by serious cases, and Jennie is good and lets me alone when I want her to.

So I walk a little in the garden or down that lovely lane, sit on the porch under the roses, and lie down up here a good deal.

I'm getting really fond of the room in spite of the wallpaper. Perhaps *because* of the wallpaper.

It dwells in my mind so!

I lie here on this great immovable bed—it is nailed down, I believe—and follow that pattern about by the hour. It is as good as gymnastics, I assure you. I start, we'll say, at the bottom, down in the corner over there where it has not been touched, and I determine for the thousandth time that I *will* follow that pointless pattern to some sort of a conclusion.

I know a little of the principle of design, and I know this thing was not arranged on any laws of radiation, or alternation, or repetition, or symmetry, or anything else that I ever heard of.

It is repeated, of course, by the breadths, but not otherwise.

Looked at in one way each breadth stands alone, the bloated curves and flourishes—a kind of "debased Romanesque"[6] with *delirium tremens*[7]—go waddling up and down in isolated columns of fatuity.

[5]Silas Weir Mitchell (1829–1914), American physician known for his "rest-cure" treatment of "nervous disorders."

[6]Ornate style of architecture marked by curves and rounded arches.

[7]A violent mental disturbance accompanied by hallucinations, caused by alcoholism.

But, on the other hand, they connect diagonally, and the sprawling outlines run off in great slanting waves of optic horror, like a lot of wallowing seaweeds in full chase.

The whole thing goes horizontally, too, at least it seems so, and I exhaust myself in trying to distinguish the order of its going in that direction.

They have used a horizontal breadth for a frieze, and that adds wonderfully to the confusion.

There is one end of the room where it is almost intact, and there, when the crosslights fade and the low sun shines directly upon it, I can almost fancy radiation after all,—the interminable grotesque seems to form around a common center and rush off in headlong plunges of equal distraction.

It makes me tired to follow it. I will take a nap I guess.

* * * * * *

I don't know why I should write this.

I don't want to.

I don't feel able.

And I know John would think it absurd. But I *must* say what I feel and think in some way—it is such a relief!

But the effort is getting to be greater than the relief.

Half the time now I am awfully lazy, and lie down ever so much.

John says I mustn't lose my strength, and has me take cod liver oil and lots of tonics and things, to say nothing of ale and wine and rare meat.

Dear John! He loves me very dearly, and hates to have me sick. I tried to have a real earnest reasonable talk with him the other day, and tell him how I wish he would let me go and make a visit to Cousin Henry and Julia.

But he said I wasn't able to go, nor able to stand it after I got there; and I did not make out a very good case for myself, for I was crying before I had finished.

It is getting to be a great effort for me to think straight. Just this nervous weakness I suppose.

And dear John gathered me up in his arms, and just carried me upstairs and laid me on the bed, and sat by me and read to me till it tired my head.

He said I was his darling and his comfort and all he had, and that I must take care of myself for his sake, and keep well.

He says no one but myself can help me out of it, that I must use my will and self-control and not let any silly fancies run away with me.

There's one comfort, the baby is well and happy, and does not have to occupy this nursery with the horrid wallpaper.

If we had not used it, that blessed child would have! What a fortunate escape! Why, I wouldn't have a child of mine, an impressionable little thing, live in such a room for worlds.

I never thought of it before, but it is lucky that John kept me here after all, I can stand it so much easier than a baby, you see.

Of course I never mention it to them any more—I am too wise,—but I keep watch of it all the same.

There are things in that paper that nobody knows but me, or ever will.

Behind that outside pattern the dim shapes get clearer every day.

It is always the same shape, only very numerous.

And it is like a woman stooping down and creeping about behind that pattern. I don't like it a bit. I wonder—I begin to think—I wish John would take me away from here!

* * * * * *

It is so hard to talk with John about my case, because he is so wise, and because he loves me so.

But I tried it last night.

It was moonlight. The moon shines in all around just as the sun does.

I hate to see it sometimes, it creeps so slowly, and always comes in by one window or another.

John was asleep and I hated to waken him, so I kept still and watched the moonlight on that undulating wallpaper till I felt creepy.

The faint figure behind seemed to shake the pattern, just as if she wanted to get out.

I got up softly and went to feel and see if the paper *did* move, and when I came back John was awake.

"What is it, little girl?" he said. "Don't go walking about like that—you'll get cold."

I thought it was a good time to talk, so I told him that I really was not gaining here, and that I wished he would take me away.

"Why, darling!" said he, "our lease will be up in three weeks, and I can't see how to leave before.

"The repairs are not done at home, and I cannot possibly leave town just now. Of course if you were in any danger, I could and would, but you really are better, dear, whether you can see it or not. I am a doctor, dear, and I know. You are gaining flesh and color, your appetite is better, I feel really much easier about you."

"I don't weigh a bit more," said I, "nor as much; and my appetite may be better in the evening when you are here, but it is worse in the morning when you are away."

"Bless her little heart!" said he with a big hug, "she shall be as sick as she pleases! But now let's improve the shining hours[8] by going to sleep, and talk about it in the morning!"

"And you won't go away?" I asked gloomily.

"Why, how can I dear? It is only three weeks more and then we will take a nice little trip of a few days while Jennie is getting the house ready. Really dear you are better!"

"Better in body perhaps—" I began, and stopped short, for he sat up straight and looked at me with such a stern, reproachful look that I could not say another word.

"My darling," said he, "I beg of you, for my sake and for our child's sake, as well as for your own, that you will never for one instant let that idea enter your mind! There is nothing so dangerous, so fascinating, to a temperament like yours. It is a false and foolish fancy. Can you not trust me as a physician when I tell you so?"

So of course I said no more on that score, and we went to sleep before long. He thought I was asleep first, but I wasn't, and lay there for hours trying to decide

[8]An adaptation of "Song XX" from *The Divine Songs* of Isaac Watts (1674–1748), English hymnist:

How doth the little busy bee
  Improve each shining hour,
And gather honey all the day
  From every opening flower.

whether that front pattern and the back pattern really did move together or separately.

* * * * * *

On a pattern like this, by daylight, there is a lack of sequence, a defiance of law, that is a constant irritant to a normal mind.

The color is hideous enough, and unreliable enough, and infuriating enough, but the pattern is torturing.

You think you have mastered it, but just as you get well underway in following, it turns a back-somersault and there you are. It slaps you in the face, knocks you down, and tramples upon you. It is like a bad dream.

The outside pattern is a florid arabesque, reminding one of a fungus. If you can imagine a toadstool in joints, an interminable string of toadstools, budding and sprouting in endless convolutions—why, that is something like it.

That is, sometimes!

There is one marked peculiarity about this paper, a thing nobody seems to notice but myself, and that is that it changes as the light changes.

When the sun shoots in through the east window—I always watch for that first long, straight ray—it changes so quickly that I never can quite believe it.

That is why I watch it always.

By moonlight—the moon shines in all night when there is a moon—I wouldn't know it was the same paper.

At night in any kind of light, in twilight, candlelight, lamplight, and worst of all by moonlight, it becomes bars! The outside pattern I mean, and the woman behind it is as plain as can be.

I didn't realize for a long time what the thing was that showed behind, that dim sub-pattern, but now I am quite sure it is a woman.

By daylight she is subdued, quiet. I fancy it is the pattern that keeps her so still. It is so puzzling. It keeps me quiet by the hour.

I lie down ever so much now. John says it is good for me, and to sleep all I can.

Indeed he started the habit by making me lie down for an hour after each meal.

It is a very bad habit I am convinced, for you see I don't sleep.

And that cultivates deceit, for I don't tell them I'm awake—O no!

The fact is I am getting a little afraid of John.

He seems very queer sometimes, and even Jennie has an inexplicable look.

It strikes me occasionally, just as a scientific hypothesis,—that perhaps it is the paper!

I have watched John when he did not know I was looking, and come into the room suddenly on the most innocent excuses, and I've caught him several times *looking at the paper!* And Jennie too. I caught Jennie with her hand on it once.

She didn't know I was in the room, and when I asked her in a quiet, a very quiet voice, with the most restrained manner possible, what she was doing with the paper—she turned around as if she had been caught stealing, and looked quite angry—asked me why I should frighten her so!

Then she said that the paper stained everything it touched, that she had found yellow smooches[9] on all my clothes and John's, and she wished we would be more careful!

[9]Smudges, smears.

Did not that sound innocent? But I know she was studying that pattern, and I am determined that nobody shall find it out but myself.

* * * * * *

Life is very much more exciting now than it used to be. You see I have something more to expect, to look forward to, to watch. I really do eat better, and am more quiet than I was.

John is so pleased to see me improve! He laughed a little the other day, and said I seemed to be flourishing in spite of my wall-paper.

I turned it off with a laugh. I had no intention of telling him it was *because* of the wall-paper—he would make fun of me. He might even want to take me away.

I don't want to leave now until I have found it out. There is a week more, and I think that will be enough.

* * * * * *

I'm feeling ever so much better! I don't sleep much at night, for it is so interesting to watch developments; but I sleep a good deal in the daytime.

In the daytime it is tiresome and perplexing.

There are always new shoots on the fungus, and new shades of yellow all over it. I cannot keep count of them, though I have tried conscientiously.

It is the strangest yellow, that wall-paper! It makes me think of all the yellow things I every saw—not beautiful ones like buttercups, but old foul, bad yellow things.

But there is something else about that paper—the smell! I noticed it the moment we came into the room, but with so much air and sun it was not bad. Now we have had a week of fog and rain, and whether the windows are open or not, the smell is here.

It creeps all over the house.

I find it hovering in the dining-room, skulking in the parlor, hiding in the hall, lying in wait for me on the stairs.

It gets into my hair.

Even when I go to ride, if I turn my head suddenly and surprise it—there is that smell!

Such a peculiar odor, too! I have spent hours in trying to analyze it, to find what it smelled like.

It is not bad—at first, and very gentle, but quite the subtlest, most enduring odor I ever met.

In this damp weather it is awful, I wake up in the night and find it hanging over me.

It used to disturb me at first. I thought seriously of burning the house—to reach the smell.

But now I am used to it. The only thing I can think of that it is like is the *color* of the paper! A yellow smell.

There is a very funny mark on this wall, low down, near the mopboard. A streak that runs round the room. It goes behind every piece of furniture, except the bed, a long straight, even *smooch,* as if it had been rubbed over and over.

I wonder how it was done and who did it, and what they did it for. Round and round and round—round and round and round—it makes me dizzy!

* * * * * *

I really have discovered something at last.

Through watching so much at night, when it changes so, I have finally found out.

The front pattern *does* move—and no wonder! The woman behind shakes it!

Sometimes I think there are a great many women behind, and sometimes only one, and she crawls around fast, and her crawling shakes it all over.

Then in the very bright spots she keeps still, and in the very shady spots she just takes hold of the bars and shakes them hard.

And she is all the time trying to climb through. But nobody could climb through that pattern—it strangles so; I think that is why it has so many heads.

They get through, and then the pattern strangles them off and turns them upside down, and makes their eyes white!

If those heads were covered or taken off it would not be half so bad.

* * * * * *

I think that woman gets out in the daytime!

And I'll tell you why—privately—I've seen her!

I can see her out of every one of my windows!

It is the same woman, I know, for she is always creeping, and most women do not creep by daylight.

I see her in that long shaded lane, creeping up and down. I see her in those dark grape arbors, creeping all around the garden.

I see her on that long road under the trees creeping along, and when a carriage comes she hides under the blackberry vines.

I don't blame her a bit. It must be very humiliating to be caught creeping by daylight!

I always lock the door when I creep by daylight. I can't do it at night, for I know John would suspect something at once.

And John is so queer now, that I don't want to irritate him. I wish he would take another room! Besides, I don't want anybody to get that woman out at night but myself.

I often wonder if I could see her out of all the windows at once.

But, turn as fast as I can, I can only see out of one at one time.

And though I always see her, she *may* be able to creep faster than I can turn!

I have watched her sometimes away off in the open country, creeping as fast as a cloud shadow in a high wind.

* * * * * *

If only that top pattern could be gotten off from the under one! I mean to try it, little by little.

I have found out another funny thing, but I shan't tell it this time! It does not do to trust people too much.

There are only two more days to get this paper off, and I believe John is beginning to notice. I don't like the look in his eyes.

And I heard him ask Jennie a lot of professional questions about me. She had a very good report to give.

She said I slept a good deal in the daytime.

John knows I don't sleep very well at night, for all I'm so quiet!

He asked me all sorts of questions, too, and pretended to be very loving and kind.

As if I couldn't see through him!

Still, I don't wonder he acts so, sleeping under this paper for three months.

It only interests me, but I feel sure John and Jennie are secretly affected by it.

* * *

Hurrah! This is the last day, but it is enough. John to stay in town over night, and won't be out until this evening.

Jennie wanted to sleep with me—the sly thing! But I told her I should undoubtedly rest better for a night all alone.

That was clever, for really I wasn't alone a bit! As soon as it was moonlight and that poor thing began to crawl and shake the pattern, I got up and ran to help her.

I pulled and she shook, I shook and she pulled, and before morning we had peeled off yards of that paper.

A strip about as high as my head and half around the room.

And then when the sun came and that awful pattern began to laugh at me, I declared I would finish it to-day!

We go away to-morrow, and they are moving all my furniture down again to leave things as they were before.

Jennie looked at the wall in amazement, but I told her merrily that I did it out of pure spite at the vicious thing.

She laughed and said she wouldn't mind doing it herself, but I must not get tired.

How she betrayed herself that time!

But I am here, and no person touches this paper but me,—not *alive!*

She tried to get me out of the room—it was too patent! But I said it was so quiet and empty and clean now that I believed I would lie down again and sleep all I could; and not to wake me even for dinner—I would call when I woke.

So now she is gone, and the servants are gone, and the things are gone, and there is nothing left but that great bedstead nailed down, with the canvas mattress we found on it.

We shall sleep downstairs to-night, and take the boat home to-morrow.

I quite enjoy the room, now it is bare again.

How those children did tear about here!

This bedstead is fairly gnawed!

But I must get to work.

I have locked the door and thrown the key down into the front path.

I don't want to go out, and I don't want to have anybody come in, till John comes.

I want to astonish him.

I've got a rope up here that even Jennie did not find. If that woman does get out, and tries to get away, I can tie her!

But I forgot I could not reach far without anything to stand on!

This bed will *not* move!

I tried to lift and push it until I was lame, and then I got so angry I bit off a little piece at one corner—but it hurt my teeth.

Then I peeled off all the paper I could reach standing on the floor. It sticks horribly and the pattern just enjoys it! All those strangled heads and bulbous eyes and waddling fungus growths just shriek with derision!

I am getting angry enough to do something desperate. To jump out of the window would be admirable exercise, but the bars are too strong even to try.

Besides I wouldn't do it. Of course not. I know well enough that a step like that is improper and might be misconstrued.

I don't like to *look* out of the windows even—there are so many of those creeping women, and they creep so fast.

I wonder if they all come out of that wall-paper as I did?

But I am securely fastened now by my well-hidden rope—you don't get *me* out in the road there!

I suppose I shall have to get back behind the pattern when it comes night, and that is hard!

It is so pleasant to be out in this great room and creep around as I please!

I don't want to go outside. I won't, even if Jennie asks me to.

For outside you have to creep on the ground, and everything is green instead of yellow.

But here I can creep smoothly on the floor, and my shoulder just fits in that long smooch around the wall, so I cannot lose my way.

Why there's John at the door!

It is no use, young man, you can't open it!

How he does call and pound!

Now he's crying for an axe.

It would be a shame to break down that beautiful door!

"John dear!" said I in the gentlest voice, "the key is down by the front steps, under a plantain leaf!"

That silenced him for a few moments.

Then he said—very quietly indeed, "Open the door, my darling!"

"I can't," said I. "The key is down by the front door under a plantain leaf!

And then I said it again, several times, very gently and slowly, and said it so often that he had to go and see, and he got it of course, and came in. He stopped short by the door.

"What is the matter?" he cried. "For God's sake, what are you doing!"

I kept on creeping just the same, but I looked at him over my shoulder.

"I've got out at last," said I, "in spite of you and Jane. And I've pulled off most of the paper, so you can't put me back!"

Now why should that man have fainted? But he did, and right across my path by the wall, so that I had to creep over him every time!

1892

IF I WERE A MAN

"If I were a man, . . ." that was what pretty little Mollie Mathewson always said when Gerald would not do what she wanted him to—which was seldom.

That was what she said this bright morning, with a stamp of her little high-heeled slipper, just because he had made a fuss about that bill, the long one with the "account rendered," which she had forgotten to give him the first time and been afraid to the second—and now he had taken it from the postman himself.

Mollie was "true to type." She was a beautiful instance of what is reverentially called "a true woman." Little, of course—no true woman may be big. Pretty, of course—no true woman could possibly be plain. Whimsical, capricious, charming, changeable, devoted to pretty clothes and always "wearing them well," as the esoteric phrase has it. (This does not refer to the clothes—they do not wear well in the least—but to some special grace of putting them on and carrying them about, granted to but few, it appears.)

She was also a loving wife and a devoted mother possessed of "the social gift" and the love of "society" that goes with it, and, with all these was fond and proud of her home and managed it as capably as—well, as most women do.

If ever there was a true woman it was Mollie Mathewson, yet she was wishing heart and soul she was a man.

And all of a sudden she was!

She was Gerald, walking down the path so erect and square-shouldered, in a hurry for his morning train, as usual, and, it must be confessed, in something of a temper.

Her own words were ringing in her ears—not only the "last word," but several that had gone before, and she was holding her lips tight shut, not to say something she would be sorry for. But instead of acquiescence in the position taken by that angry little figure on the veranda, what she felt was a sort of superior pride, a sympathy as with weakness, a feeling that "I must be gentle with her," in spite of the temper.

A man! Really a man—with only enough subconscious memory of herself remaining to make her recognize the differences.

At first there was a funny sense of size and weight and extra thickness, the feet and hands seemed strangely large, and her long, straight, free legs swung forward at a gait that made her feel as if on stilts.

This presently passed, and in its place, growing all day, wherever she went, came a new and delightful feeling of being *the right size.*

Everything fitted now. Her back snugly against the seat-back, her feet comfortably on the floor. Her feet? . . . His feet! She studied them carefully. Never before, since her early school days, had she felt such freedom and comfort as to feet—they were firm and solid on the ground when she walked; quick, springy, safe—as when, moved by an unrecognizable impulse, she had run after, caught, and swung aboard the car.

Another impulse fished in a convenient pocket for change—instantly, automatically, bringing forth a nickel for the conductor and a penny for the newsboy.

These pockets came as a revelation. Of course she had known they were there, had counted them, made fun of them, mended them, even envied them; but she never had dreamed of how it *felt* to have pockets.

Behind her newspaper she let her consciousness, that odd mingled consciousness, rove from pocket to pocket, realizing the armored assurance of having all those things at hand, instantly get-at-able, ready to meet emergencies. The cigar case gave her a warm feeling of comfort—it was full; the firmly held fountain pen, safe unless she stood on her head; the keys, pencils, letters, documents, notebook, checkbook, bill folder—all at once, with a deep rushing sense of power and pride, she felt what she had never felt before in all her life—the possession of money, of her own earned money—hers to give or to withhold, not to beg for, tease for, wheedle for—hers.

That bill—why, if it had come to her—to him, that is—he would have paid it as a matter of course, and never mentioned it—to her.

Then, being he, sitting there so easily and firmly with his money in his pockets, she wakened to his life-long consciousness about money. Boyhood—its desires and dreams, ambitions. Young manhood—working tremendously for the wherewithal to make a home—for her. The present years with all their net of cares and hopes and dangers; the present moment, when he needed every cent for special plans of great importance, and this bill, long overdue and demanding payment, meant an amount of inconvenience wholly unnecessary if it had been given him when it first came; also, the man's keen dislike of that "account rendered."

"Women have no business sense!" she found herself saying. "And all that money just for hats—idiotic, useless, ugly things!"

With that she began to see the hats of the women in the car as she had never seen hats before. The men's seemed normal, dignified, becoming, with enough variety for personal taste, and with distinction in style and in age, such as she had never noticed before. But the women's—

With the eyes of a man and the brain of a man; with the memory of a whole lifetime of free action wherein the hat, close-fitting on cropped hair, had been no handicap; she now perceived the hats of women.

The massed fluffed hair was at once attractive and foolish, and on that hair, at every angle, in all colors, tipped, twisted, tortured into every crooked shape, made of any substance chance might offer, perched these formless objects. Then, on their formlessness the trimmings—these squirts of stiff feathers, these violent outstanding bows of glistening ribbon, these swaying, projecting masses of plumage which tormented the faces of bystanders.

Never in all her life had she imagined that this idolized millinery could look, to those who paid for it, like the decorations of an insane monkey.

And yet, when there came into the car a little woman, as foolish as any, but pretty and sweet-looking, up rose Gerald Mathewson and gave her his seat. And, later, when there came in a handsome red-cheeked girl, whose hat was wilder more violent in color and eccentric in shape than any other—when she stood nearby and her soft curling plumes swept his cheek once and again—he felt a sense of sudden pleasure at the intimate tickling touch—and she, deep down within, felt such a wave of shame as might well drown a thousand hats forever.

When he took his train, his seat in the smoking car, she had a new surprise. All about him were the other men, commuters too, and many of them friends of his.

To her, they would have been distinguished as "Mary Wade's husband," "the man Belle Grant is engaged to," "that rich Mr. Shopworth," or "that pleasant Mr. Beale." And they would all have lifted their hats to her, bowed, made polite conversation if near enough—especially Mr. Beale.

Now came the feeling of open-eyed acquaintance, of knowing men—as they were. The mere amount of this knowledge was a surprise to her—the whole background of talk from boyhood up, the gossip of barber-shop and club, the conversation of morning and evening hours on trains, the knowledge of political affiliation, of business standing and prospects, of character—in a light she had never known before.

They came and talked to Gerald, one and another. He seemed quite popular. And as they talked, with this new memory and new understanding, an understanding which seemed to include all these men's minds, there poured in on the submerged consciousness beneath a new, a startling knowledge—what men really think of women.

Good, average, American men were there; married men for the most part, and happy—as happiness goes in general. In the minds of each and all there seemed to be a two-story department, quite apart from the rest of their ideas, a separate place where they kept their thoughts and feelings about women.

In the upper half were the tenderest emotions, the most exquisite ideals, the sweetest memories, all lovely sentiments as to "home" and "mother," all delicate admiring adjectives, a sort of sanctuary, where a veiled statue, blindly adored, shared place with beloved yet commonplace experiences.

In the lower half—here that buried consciousness woke to keen distress—they kept quite another assortment of ideas. Here, even in this clean-minded husband of hers, was the memory of stories told at men's dinners, of worse ones overheard in street or car, of base traditions, coarse epithets, gross experiences—known, though not shared.

And all these in the department "woman," while in the rest of the mind—here was new knowledge indeed.

The world opened before her. Not the world she had been reared in—where Home had covered all the map, almost, and the rest had been "foreign," or "unexplored country," but the world as it was—man's world, as made, lived in, and seen, by men.

It was dizzying. To see the houses that fled so fast across the car window, in terms of builders' bills, or of some technical insight into materials and methods; to see a passing village with lamentable knowledge of who "owned it" and of how its Boss was rapidly aspiring in state power, or of how that kind of paving was a failure; to see shops, not as mere exhibitions of desirable objects, but as business ventures, many mere sinking ships, some promising a profitable voyage—this new world bewildered her.

She—as Gerald—had already forgotten about that bill, over which she—as Mollie—was still crying at home. Gerald was "talking business" with this man, "talking politics" with that, and now sympathizing with the carefully withheld troubles of a neighbor.

Mollie had always sympathized with the neighbor's wife before.

She began to struggle violently with this large dominant masculine consciousness. She remembered with sudden clearness things she had read, lectures she had heard, and resented with increasing intensity this serene masculine preoccupation with the male point of view.

Mr. Miles, the little fussy man who lived on the other side of the street, was talking now. He had a large complacent wife; Mollie had never liked her much, but had always thought him rather nice—he was so punctilious in small courtesies.

And here he was talking to Gerald—such talk!

"Had to come in here," he said. "Gave my seat to a dame who was bound to have it. There's nothing they won't get when they make up their minds to it—eh?"

"No fear!" said the big man in the next seat. "They haven't much mind to make up, you know—and if they do, they'll change it."

"The real danger," began the Rev. Alfred Smythe, the new Episcopal clergyman, a thin, nervous, tall man with a face several centuries behind the times, "is that they will overstep the limits of their God-appointed sphere."

"Their natural limits ought to hold 'em, I think," said cheerful Dr. Jones. "You can't get around physiology, I tell you."

"I've never seen any limits, myself, not to what they want, anyhow," said Mr. Miles. "Merely a rich husband and a fine house and no end of bonnets and dresses, and the latest thing in motors, and a few diamonds—and so on. Keeps us pretty busy."

There was a tired gray man across the aisle. He had a very nice wife, always beautifully dressed, and three unmarried daughters, also beautifully dressed—Mollie knew them. She knew he worked hard, too, and she looked at him now a little anxiously.

But he smiled cheerfully.

"Do you good, Miles," he said. "What else would a man work for? A good woman is about the best thing on earth."

"And a bad one's the worst, that's sure," responded Miles.

"She's a pretty weak sister, viewed professionally," Dr. Jones averred with solemnity, and the Rev. Alfred Smythe added, "She brought evil into the world."

Gerald Mathewson sat up straight. Something was stirring in him which he did not recognize—yet could not resist.

"Seems to me we all talk like Noah," he suggested drily. "Or the ancient Hindu scriptures. Women have their limitations, but so do we, God knows. Haven't we known girls in school and college just as smart as we were?"

"They cannot play our games," coldly replied the clergyman.

Gerald measured his meager proportions with a practiced eye.

"I never was particularly good at football myself," he modestly admitted, "but I've known women who could outlast a man in all-round endurance. Besides—life isn't spent in athletics!"

This was sadly true. They all looked down the aisle where a heavy ill-dressed man with a bad complexion sat alone. He had held the top of the columns once, with headlines and photographs. Now he earned less than any of them.

"It's time we woke up," pursued Gerald, still inwardly urged to unfamiliar speech. "Women are pretty much *people*, seems to me. I know they dress like fools—but who's to blame for that. We invent all those idiotic hats of theirs, and design their crazy fashions, and, what's more, if a woman is courageous enough to wear common-sense clothes—and shoes—which of us wants to dance with her?

"Yes, we blame them for grafting on us, but are we willing to let our wives work? We are not. It hurts our pride, that's all. We are always criticizing them for making mercenary marriages, but what do we call a girl who marries a chump with no money? Just a poor fool, that's all. And they know it.

"As for Mother Eve—I wasn't there and can't deny the story, but I will say this. If she brought evil into the world, we men have had the lion's share of keeping it going ever since—how about that?"

They drew into the city, and all day long in his business, Gerald was vaguely conscious of new views, strange feelings, and the submerged Mollie learned and learned.

1914

THE UNNATURAL MOTHER

"Don't tell me!" said old Mis' Briggs, with a forbidding shake of the head. "No mother that was a mother would desert her own child for anything on earth!"

"And leaving it a care on the town, too!" put in Susannah Jacobs. "As if we hadn't enough to do to take care of our own!"

Miss Jacobs was a well-to-do old maid, owning a comfortable farm and homestead, and living alone with an impoverished cousin acting as general servant, companion, and protégée. Mis' Briggs, on the contrary, had had thirteen children, five of whom remained to bless her, so that what maternal feeling Miss Jacobs might lack, Mis' Briggs could certainly supply.

"I should think," piped little Martha Ann Simmons, the village dressmaker, "that she might 'a saved her young one first and then tried what she could do for the town."

Martha had been married, had lost her husband, and had one sickly boy to care for.

The youngest Briggs girl, still unmarried at thirty-six, and in her mother's eyes a most tender infant, now ventured to make a remark.

"You don't any of you seem to think what she did for all of us—if she hadn't left hers we should all have lost ours, sure."

"You ain't no call to judge, Maria 'Melia," her mother hastened to reply. "You've no children of your own, and you can't judge of a mother's duty. No mother ought to leave her child, whatever happens. The Lord gave it to her to take care of—he never gave her other people's. You needn't tell me!"

"She was an unnatural mother," repeated Miss Jacobs harshly, "as I said to begin with!"

"What is the story?" asked the City Boarder. The City Boarder was interested in stories from a business point of view, but they did not know that. "What did this woman do?" she asked.

There was no difficulty in eliciting particulars. The difficulty was rather in discriminating amidst their profusion and contradictoriness. But when the City Boarder got it clear in her mind, it was somewhat as follows:

The name of the much-condemned heroine was Esther Greenwood, and she lived and died here in Toddsville.

Toddsville was a mill village. The Todds lived on a beautiful eminence overlooking the little town, as the castles of robber barons on the Rhine used to overlook their little towns.[1] The mills and the mill hands' houses were built close along the bed of the river. They had to be pretty close, because the valley was a narrow one, and the bordering hills were too steep for travel, but the water power was fine. Above the village was the reservoir, filling the entire valley save for a narrow road beside it, a fair blue smiling lake, edged with lilies and blue flag, rich in pickerel and perch. This lake gave them fish, it gave them ice, it gave the power that ran the mills that gave the town its bread. Blue Lake was both useful and ornamental.

[1]The term "robber barons" refers to German barons in the Middle Ages who forcibly extracted tolls from travelers passing through their realms; ships passing on the Rhine River were a favorite target. The term later came to refer to wealthy entrepreneurs like John D. Rockefeller (1839–1937), Andrew Carnegie (1835–1919), and Cornelius Vanderbilt (1794–1877), but that usage was not current in Gilman's time.

In this pretty and industrious village Esther had grown up, the somewhat neglected child of a heart-broken widower. He had lost a young wife, and three fair babies before her—this one was left him, and he said he meant that she should have all the chance there was.

"That was what ailed her in the first place!" they all eagerly explained to the City Boarder. "She never knew what 'twas to have a mother, and she grew up a regular tomboy! Why, she used to roam the country for miles around, in all weather like an Injun! And her father wouldn't take no advice!"

This topic lent itself to eager discussion. The recreant father, it appeared, was a doctor, not their accepted standby, the resident physician of the neighborhood, but an alien doctor, possessed of "views."

"You never heard such things as he advocated," Miss Jacobs explained. "He wouldn't give no medicines, hardly; said 'nature' did the curing—he couldn't."

"And he couldn't either—that was clear," Mrs. Briggs agreed. "Look at his wife and children dying on his hands, as it were! 'Physician, heal thyself,' I say."[2]

"But, Mother," Maria Amelia put in, "she was an invalid when he married her, they say; and those children died of polly—polly—what's that thing that nobody can help?"

"That may all be so," Miss Jacobs admitted, "but all the same, it's a doctor's business to give medicine. If 'nature' was all that was wanted, we needn't have any doctor at all!"

"I believe in medicine and plenty of it. I always gave my children a good clearance, spring and fall, whether anything ailed 'em or not, just to be on the safe side. And if there was anything the matter with 'em, they had plenty more. I never had anything to reproach myself with on that score," stated Mrs. Briggs, firmly. Then as a sort of concession to the family graveyard, she added piously, "The Lord giveth and the Lord taketh away."[3]

"You should have seen the way he dressed that child!" pursued Miss Jacobs. "It was a reproach to the town. Why, you couldn't tell at a distance whether it was a boy or a girl. And barefoot! He let that child go barefoot till she was so big we was actually mortified to see her."

It appeared that a wild, healthy childhood had made Esther very different in her early womanhood from the meek, well-behaved damsels of the little place. She was well enough liked by those who knew her at all, and the children of the place adored her, but the worthy matrons shook their heads and prophesied no good of a girl who was "queer."

She was described with rich detail in reminiscence, how she wore her hair short till she was fifteen—"just shingled like a boy's—it did seem a shame that girl had no mother to look after her—and her clo'se was almost a scandal, even when she did put on shoes and stockings. Just gingham—brown gingham—and *short!*"

"I think she was a real nice girl," said Maria Amelia. "I can remember her just as well! She was *so* nice to us children. She was five or six years older than I was, and most girls that age won't have anything to do with little ones. But she was kind and pleasant. She'd take us berrying and on all sorts of walks, and teach us new games and tell us things. I don't remember anyone that ever did us the good she did!"

[2]A reference to Luke 4:23.

[3]Job 1:21: "The Lord giveth, and the Lord taketh away; blessed be the name of the Lord."

Maria Amelia's thin chest heaved with emotion, and there were tears in her eyes; but her mother took her up somewhat sharply.

"That sounds well I must say—right before your own mother that's toiled and slaved for you! It's all very well for a young thing that's got nothing on earth to do to make herself agreeable to young ones. That poor blinded father of hers never taught her to do the work a girl should—naturally he couldn't."

"At least he might have married again and given her another mother," said Susannah Jacobs, with decision, with so much decision, in fact, that the City Boarder studied her expression for a moment and concluded that if this recreant father had not married again it was not for lack of opportunity.

Mrs. Simmons cast an understanding glance upon Miss Jacobs, and nodded wisely.

"Yes, he ought to have done that, of course. A man's not fit to bring up children, anyhow. How can they? Mothers have the instinct—that is, all natural mothers have. But, dear me! There's some as don't seem to *be* mothers—even when they have a child!"

"You're quite right, Mis' Simmons," agreed the mother of thirteen. "It's a divine instinct, I say. I'm sorry for the child that lacks it. Now this Esther. We always knew she wan't like other girls—she never seemed to care for dress and company and things girls naturally do, but was always philandering over the hills with a parcel of young ones. There wan't a child in town but would run after her. She made more trouble 'n a little in families, the young ones quotin' what Aunt Esther said, and tellin' what Aunt Esther did to their own mothers, and she only a young girl. Why, she actually seemed to care more for them children than she did for beaux or anything—it wasn't natural!"

"But she did marry?" pursued the City Boarder.

"Marry! Yes, she married finally. We all thought she never would, but she did. After the things her father taught her, it did seem as if he'd ruined *all* her chances. It's simply terrible the way that girl was trained."

"Him being a doctor," put in Mrs. Simmons, "made it different, I suppose."

"Doctor or no doctor," Miss Jacobs rigidly interposed, "it was a crying shame to have a young girl so instructed."

"Maria 'Melia," said her mother, "I want you should get me my smelling salts. They're up in the spare chamber, I believe. When your Aunt Marcia was here she had one of her spells—don't you remember?—and she asked for salts.[4] Look in the top bureau drawer—they must be there."

Maria Amelia, thirty-six but unmarried, withdrew dutifully, and the other ladies drew closer to the City Boarder.

"It's the most shocking thing I ever heard of," murmured Mrs. Briggs. "Do you know he—a father—actually taught his daughter how babies come!"

There was a breathless hush.

"He did," eagerly chimed in the little dressmaker. "All the particulars. It was perfectly awful!"

"He said," continued Mrs. Briggs, "that he expected her to be a mother and that she ought to understand what was before her!"

"He was waited on by a committee of ladies from the church, married ladies, all older than he was," explained Miss Jacobs severely. "They told him it was creating a scandal in the town—and what do you think he said?"

[4]Smelling salts.

There was another breathless silence.

Above, the steps of Maria Amelia were heard, approaching the stairs.

"It ain't there, Ma!"

"Well, you look in the highboy and in the top drawer; they're somewhere up there," her mother replied.

Then, in a sepulchral whisper:

"He told us—yes, ma'am, I was on that committee—he told us that until young women knew what was before them as mothers, they would not do their duty in choosing a father for their children! That was his expression—'choosing a father'! A nice thing for a young girl to be thinking of—a father for her children!"

"Yes, and more than that," inserted Miss Jacobs, who, though not on the committee, seemed familiar with its workings. "He told them—" But Mrs. Briggs waved her aside and continued swiftly—

"He taught that innocent girl about—the Bad Disease![5] Actually!"

"He did!" said the dressmaker. "It got out, too, all over town. There wasn't a man here would have married her after that."

Miss Jacobs insisted on taking up the tale. "I understand that he said it was 'to protect her'! Protect her, indeed! Against matrimony! As if any man alive would want to marry a young girl who knew all the evil of life! I was brought up differently, I assure you!"

"Young girls should be kept innocent!" Mrs. Briggs solemnly proclaimed. "Why, when I was married I knew no more what was before me than a babe unborn, and my girls were all brought up so, too!"

Then, as Maria Amelia returned with the salts, she continued more loudly. "But she did marry after all. And a mighty queer husband she got, too. He was an artist or something, made pictures for the magazines and such as that, and they do say she met him first out in the hills. That's the first 'twas known of it here, anyhow—them two traipsing about all over; him with his painting things! They married and just settled down to live with her father, for she vowed she wouldn't leave him; and he said it didn't make no difference where he lived, he took his business with him."

"They seemed very happy together," said Maria Amelia.

"Happy! Well, they might have been, I suppose. It was a pretty queer family, I think." And her mother shook her head in retrospection. "They got on all right for a while; but the old man died, and those two—well, I don't call it housekeeping—the way they lived!"

"No," said Miss Jacobs. "They spent more time out-of-doors than they did in the house. She followed him around everywhere. And for open lovemaking—"

They all showed deep disapproval at this memory. All but the City Boarder and Maria Amelia.

"She had one child, a girl," continued Mrs. Briggs, "and it was just shocking to see how she neglected that child from the beginnin'. She never seemed to have no maternal feelin' at all!"

"But I thought you said she was very fond of children," remonstrated the City Boarder.

"Oh, *children*, yes. She'd take up with any dirty-faced brat in town, even them Canucks.[6] I've seen her again and again with a whole swarm of the mill hands'

[5]Probably syphilis. [6]Canadians.

young ones round her, goin' on some picnic or other—'open air school,' she used to call it—*such* notions as she had. But when it come to her own child! Why—" Here the speaker's voice sank to a horrified hush. "She never had no baby clo'se for it! Not a single sock!"

The City Boarder was interested. "Why, what did she do with the little thing?"

"The Lord knows!" answered old Mis' Briggs. "She never would let us hardly see it when 'twas little. 'Shamed too, I don't doubt. But that's strange feelin's for a mother. Why, I was so proud of my babies! And I kept 'em lookin' so pretty! I'd 'a sat up all night and sewed and washed, but I'd 'a had my children look well!" And the poor old eyes filled with tears as she thought of the eight little graves in the churchyard, which she never failed to keep looking pretty, even now. "She just let that young one roll round in the grass like a puppy with hardly nothin' on! Why, a squaw does better. She does keep 'em done up for a spell! That child was treated worse 'n an Injun! We all done what we could, of course. We felt it no more 'n right. But she was real hateful about it, and we had to let her be."

"The child died?" asked the City Boarder.

"Died! Dear no! That's it you saw going by; a great strappin' girl she is, too, and promisin' to grow up well, thanks to Mrs. Stone's taking her. Mrs. Stone always thought a heap of Esther. It's a mercy to the child that she lost her mother, I do believe! How she ever survived that kind of treatment beats all! Why, that woman never seemed to have the first spark of maternal feeling to the end! She seemed just as fond of the other young ones after she had her own as she was before, and that's against nature. The way it happened was this. You see, they lived up the valley nearer to the lake than the village. He was away, and was coming home that night, it seems, driving from Drayton along the lake road. And she set out to meet him. She must 'a walked up to the dam to look for him; and we think maybe she saw the team clear across the lake. Maybe she thought he could get to the house and save little Esther in time—that's the only explanation we ever could put on it. But this is what she did; and you can judge for yourselves if any mother in her senses *could* 'a done such a thing! You see 'twas the time of that awful disaster, you've read of it, likely, that destroyed three villages. Well, she got to the dam and seen that 'twas givin' way—she was always great for knowin' all such things. And she just turned and ran. Jake Elder was up on the hill after a stray cow, and he seen her go. He was too far off to imagine what ailed her, but he said he never saw a woman run so in his life.

"And, if you'll believe it, she run right by her own house—never stopped—never looked at it. Just run for the village. Of course, she may have lost her head with the fright, but that wasn't like her. No, I think she had made up her mind to leave that innocent baby to die! She just ran down here and give warnin', and, of course, we sent word down valley on horseback, and there was no lives lost in all three villages. She started to run back as soon as we was 'roused, but 'twas too late then.

"Jake saw it all, though he was too far off to do a thing. He said he couldn't stir a foot, it was so awful. He seen the wagon drivin' along as nice as you please till it got close to the dam, and then Greenwood seemed to see the danger and shipped up like mad. He was the father, you know. But he wasn't quite in time—the dam give way and the water went over him like a tidal wave. She was almost to the gate when it struck the house and her—and we never found her body nor his for days and days. They was washed clear down river.

"Their house was strong, and it stood a little high and had some big trees between it and the lake, too. It was moved off the place and brought up against the side of the stone church down yonder, but 'twant wholly in pieces. And that child was found swimmin' round in its bed, most drowned, but not quite. The wonder is, it didn't die of a cold, but it's here yet—must have a strong constitution. Their folks never did nothing for it—so we had to keep it here."

"Well, now, Mother," said Maria Amelia Briggs. "It does seem to me that she did her duty. You know yourself that if she hadn't give warnin' all three of the villages would 'a been cleaned out—a matter of fifteen hundred people. And if she'd stopped to lug that child, she couldn't have got here in time. Don't you believe she was thinkin' of those mill hands' children?"

"Maria 'Melia, I'm ashamed of you!" said old Mis' Briggs. "But you ain't married and ain't a mother. A mother's duty is to her own child! She neglected her own to look after other folks'—the Lord never gave her them other children to care for!"

"Yes," said Miss Jacobs, "and here's her child, a burden on the town! She was an unnatural mother!"

1916

Kate Chopin 1851–1904

Although she became famous for her Louisiana dialect stories, Kate Chopin was born in St. Louis, Missouri and lived most of her life there. Her parents were Eliza and Thomas O'Flaherty. O'Flaherty was an Irish immigrant who became a rich merchant in St. Louis, and he arranged for his daughter Kate to be educated in a Roman Catholic convent school, learn fluent French, and become "one of the acknowledged belles" of society. At the age of nineteen she married Oscar Chopin (the name was pronounced in the French manner), and went to live in New Orleans, the picturesque and cosmopolitan city dominated by French Creole culture.

In 1879, after a decade in New Orleans, Oscar Chopin's business failed, and he moved his family to central Louisiana, where he managed plantations and ran a village store. In 1882, he died of swamp fever, and two years later Kate Chopin returned with her six children to St. Louis. Financially independent and bored with life as a society matron, she began to write poetry, sketches, and fiction dealing with Louisiana Creoles (descendants of early French and Spanish colonists), Cajuns (whose French ancestors had been exiled to Louisiana from Acadia in Canada in the eighteenth century), and the blacks and mixed-race Indians of the cities and back country. Her writing often considered subjects that challenged normative female scripts of the nineteenth century.

In 1889, she began At Fault *(1890), a novel that revolves around a strong female main character living on a Louisiana plantation and explores such themes as divorce and alcoholism. The novel was a failure, but soon Kate Chopin had begun to sell her local-color stories to newspapers and such national magazines as* Century *and* Vogue. *By 1898, she had written three novels (one of which she left unpublished and later destroyed) and nearly a hundred stories. Collections of her local-color tales of Creoles and Cajuns had been published in* Bayou Folk *(1894) and* A Night in Acadie *(1897).*

In 1899, she published her third novel, The Awakening, *later described as the story of "a sensuous woman who follows her inclinations." It was her masterpiece, but its theme of infidelity and the passions of its heroine brought condemnation from critics.* The Awakening *was judged "too strong drink for moral babes," a book that "should be labeled poison." Struck by the chorus of harsh criticism that followed the publication of her novel, Kate Chopin withdrew and ceased to write almost entirely. Five years later she died. Her shocking novel fell into obscurity; she was remembered only as one of the local-color writers who exploited the idioms and idiosyncrasies of the exotic provinces of America. Not until the 1950s did a critical reevaluation of Chopin begin. Reexamination of Chopin and her work has uncovered her attention to the works of other nineteenth-century writers, particularly Nathaniel Hawthorne and Henry James. Many critics now see Chopin's work as going beyond the conventions of popular fictions for women to portray the anguish of women and men who are bereft of hopeful illusions and impelled by forbidden desires.*

FURTHER READING: *The Complete Works of Kate Chopin,* 2 vols., ed. P. Seyersted, 1969; D. Rankin, *Kate Chopin and Her Creole Stories,* 1932; P. Seyersted, *Kate Chopin,* 1969, 1980; P. Skaggs, *Kate Chopin,* 1985; B. Ewell, *Kate Chopin,* 1986; E. Toth, *Kate Chopin,* 1990; *Perspectives on Kate Chopin,* ed. G. Ballenger, 1992; *Kate Chopin Reconsidered,* ed. L. Boren and S. Davis, 1992; J. Dyer, *The Awakening: A Novel of Beginnings,* 1993; *Critical Essays on Kate Chopin,* ed. A. Petry, 1996; E. Toth, *Unveiling Kate Chopin,* 1999; R. Evans, *Kate Chopin's Short Fiction,* 2001; N. Walker, *Kate Chopin, A Literary Life,* 2001; A. Stein, *Women and Autonomy in Kate Chopin's Short Fiction,* 2004.

TEXTS: *The Awakening,* 1899; *The Complete Works of Kate Chopin,* 2 vols., ed. P. Seyersted, 1969.

THE AWAKENING

I

A green and yellow parrot, which hung in a cage outside the door, kept repeating over and over:

"*Allez vous-en! Allez vous-en! Sapristi!*[1] That's all right!"

He could speak a little Spanish, and also a language which nobody understood, unless it was the mocking-bird that hung on the other side of the door, whistling his fluty notes out upon the breeze with maddening persistence.

Mr. Pontellier, unable to read his newspaper with any degree of comfort, arose with an expression and an exclamation of disgust. He walked down the gallery and across the narrow "bridges" which connected the Lebrun cottages one with the other. He had been seated before the door of the main house. The parrot and the mocking-bird were the property of Madame Lebrun, and they had the right to make all the noise they wished. Mr. Pontellier had the privilege of quitting their society when they ceased to be entertaining.

He stopped before the door of his own cottage, which was the fourth one from the main building and next to the last. Seating himself in a wicker rocker which was there, he once more applied himself to the task of reading the newspaper. The day was Sunday; the paper was a day old. The Sunday papers had not yet reached Grand Isle.[2] He was already acquainted with the market

[1]French: "Go away! Go away! For God's sake!"
[2]An island in the Gulf of Mexico, south of New Orleans.

reports, and he glanced restlessly over the editorials and bits of news which he had not had time to read before quitting New Orleans the day before.

Mr. Pontellier wore eye-glasses. He was a man of forty, of medium height and rather slender build; he stooped a little. His hair was brown and straight, parted on one side. His beard was neatly and closely trimmed.

Once in a while he withdrew his glance from the newspaper and looked about him. There was more noise than ever over at the house. The main building was called "the house," to distinguish it from the cottages. The chattering and whistling birds were still at it. Two young girls, the Farival twins, were playing a duet from "Zampa"[3] upon the piano. Madame Lebrun was bustling in and out, giving orders in a high key to a yard-boy whenever she got inside the house, and directions in an equally high voice to a dining-room servant whenever she got outside. She was a fresh, pretty woman, clad always in white with elbow sleeves. Her starched skirts crinkled as she came and went. Farther down, before one of the cottages, a lady in black was walking demurely up and down, telling her beads.[4] A good many persons of the *pension*[5] had gone over to the *Chênière Caminada*[6] in Beaudelet's lugger[7] to hear mass. Some young people were out under the water-oaks playing croquet. Mr. Pontellier's two children were there—sturdy little fellows of four and five. A quadroon[8] nurse followed them about with a far-away, meditative air.

Mr. Pontellier finally lit a cigar and began to smoke, letting the paper drag idly from his hand. He fixed his gaze upon a white sunshade[9] that was advancing at snail's pace from the beach. He could see it plainly between the gaunt trunks of the water-oaks and across the stretch of yellow camomile. The gulf looked far away, melting hazily into the blue of the horizon. The sunshade continued to approach slowly. Beneath its pink-lined shelter were his wife, Mrs. Pontellier, and young Robert Lebrun. When they reached the cottage, the two seated themselves with some appearance of fatigue upon the upper step of the porch, facing each other, each leaning against a supporting post.

"What folly! to bathe[10] at such an hour in such heat!" exclaimed Mr. Pontellier. He himself had taken a plunge at daylight. That was why the morning seemed long to him.

"You are burnt beyond recognition," he added, looking at his wife as one looks at a valuable piece of personal property which has suffered some damage. She held up her hands, strong, shapely hands, and surveyed them critically, drawing up her lawn[11] sleeves above the wrists. Looking at them reminded her of her rings, which she had given to her husband before leaving for the beach. She silently reached out to him, and he, understanding, took the rings from his vest pocket and dropped them into her open palm. She slipped them upon her fingers; then clasping her knees, she looked across at Robert and began to laugh. The rings sparkled upon her fingers. He sent back an answering smile.

"What is it?" asked Pontellier, looking lazily and amused from one to the other. It was some utter nonsense; some adventure out there in the water, and they both tried to relate it at once. It did not seem half so amusing when told.

[3]A romantic opera (1831) by the French composer Louis Hérold (1791–1833).
[4]I.e., using a string of beads to count prayers, such as those of the Rosary.
[5]French: boarding house. [6]An island in the Gulf of Mexico, near Grand Isle.
[7]Small vessel with a four-sided sail that hangs obliquely on the mast.
[8]A person with one-quarter black ancestry. [9]Parasol.
[10]Swim. [11]Fine linen or cotton cloth.

They realized this, and so did Mr. Pontellier. He yawned and stretched himself. Then he got up, saying he had half a mind to go over to Klein's hotel and play a game of billiards.

"Come go along, Lebrun," he proposed to Robert. But Robert admitted quite frankly that he preferred to stay where he was and talk to Mrs. Pontellier.

"Well, send him about his business when he bores you, Edna," instructed her husband as he prepared to leave.

"Here, take the umbrella," she exclaimed, holding it out to him. He accepted the sunshade, and lifting it over his head descended the steps and walked away.

"Coming back to dinner?" his wife called after him. He halted a moment and shrugged his shoulders. He felt in his vest pocket; there was a ten-dollar bill there. He did not know; perhaps he would return for the early dinner and perhaps he would not. It all depended upon the company which he found over at Klein's and the size of "the game." He did not say this, but she understood it, and laughed, nodding good-by to him.

Both children wanted to follow their father when they saw him starting out. He kissed them and promised to bring them back bonbons and peanuts.

II

Mrs. Pontellier's eyes were quick and bright; they were a yellowish brown, about the color of her hair. She had a way of turning them swiftly upon an object and holding them there as if lost in some inward maze of contemplation or thought.

Her eyebrows were a shade darker than her hair. They were thick and almost horizontal, emphasizing the depth of her eyes. She was rather handsome than beautiful. Her face was captivating by reason of a certain frankness of expression and a contradictory subtle play of features. Her manner was engaging.

Robert rolled a cigarette. He smoked cigarettes because he could not afford cigars, he said. He had a cigar in his pocket which Mr. Pontellier had presented him with, and he was saving it for his after-dinner smoke.

This seemed quite proper and natural on his part. In coloring he was not unlike his companion. A clean-shaved face made the resemblance more pronounced than it would otherwise have been. There rested no shadow of care upon his open countenance. His eyes gathered in and reflected the light and languor of the summer day.

Mrs. Pontellier reached over for a palm-leaf fan that lay on the porch and began to fan herself, while Robert sent between his lip light puffs from his cigarette. They chatted incessantly: about the things around them; their amusing adventure out in the water—it had again assumed its entertaining aspect; about the wind, the trees, the people who had gone to the *Chênière;* about the children playing croquet under the oaks, and the Farival twins, who were now performing the overture to "The Poet and the Peasant."[12]

Robert talked a good deal about himself. He was very young, and did not know any better. Mrs. Pontellier talked a little about herself for the same reason. Each was interested in what the other said. Robert spoke of his intention to go to Mexico in the autumn, where fortune awaited him. He was always intending to go to Mexico, but some way never got there. Meanwhile he held on

[12]A light opera (1846) by the Austrian composer Franz von Suppé (1819–1895).

to his modest position in a mercantile house in New Orleans, where an equal familiarity with English, French and Spanish gave him no small value as a clerk and correspondent.

He was spending his summer vacation, as he always did, with his mother at Grand Isle. In former times, before Robert could remember, "the house" had been a summer luxury of the Lebruns. Now, flanked by its dozen or more cottages, which were always filled with exclusive visitors from the "*Quartier Français,*"[13] it enabled Madame Lebrun to maintain the easy and comfortable existence which appeared to be her birthright.

Mrs. Pontellier talked about her father's Mississippi plantation and her girlhood home in the old Kentucky blue-grass country. She was an American woman, with a small infusion of French which seemed to have been lost in dilution. She read a letter from her sister, who was away in the East, and who had engaged herself to be married. Robert was interested, and wanted to know what manner of girls the sisters were, what the father was like, and how long the mother had been dead.

When Mrs. Pontellier folded the letter it was time for her to dress for the early dinner.

"I see Léonce isn't coming back," she said, with a glance in the direction whence her husband had disappeared. Robert supposed he was not, as there were a good many New Orleans club men over at Klein's.

When Mrs. Pontellier left him to enter her room, the young man descended the steps and strolled over toward the croquet players, where, during the half-hour before dinner, he amused himself with the little Pontellier children, who were very fond of him.

III

It was eleven o'clock that night when Mr. Pontellier returned from Klein's hotel. He was in an excellent humor, in high spirits, and very talkative. His entrance awoke his wife, who was in bed and fast asleep when he came in. He talked to her while he undressed, telling her anecdotes and bits of news and gossip that he had gathered during the day. From his trousers pockets he took a fistful of crumpled bank notes and a good deal of silver coin, which he piled on the bureau indiscriminately with keys, knife, handkerchief, and whatever else happened to be in his pockets. She was overcome with sleep, and answered him with little half utterances.

He thought it very discouraging that his wife, who was the sole object of his existence, evinced so little interest in things which concerned him, and valued so little his conversation.

Mr. Pontellier had forgotten the bonbons and peanuts for the boys. Notwithstanding he loved them very much, and went into the adjoining room where they slept to take a look at them and make sure that they were resting comfortably. The result of his investigation was far from satisfactory. He turned and shifted the youngsters about in bed. One of them began to kick and talk about a basket full of crabs.

[13]French: "French Quarter," the oldest part of New Orleans, where descendants of early French settlers lived in the nineteenth century.

Mr. Pontellier returned to his wife with the information that Raoul had a high fever and needed looking after. Then he lit a cigar and went and sat near the open door to smoke it.

Mrs. Pontellier was quite sure Raoul had no fever. He had gone to bed perfectly well, she said, and nothing had ailed him all day. Mr. Pontellier was too well acquainted with fever symptoms to be mistaken. He assured her the child was consuming[14] at that moment in the next room.

He reproached his wife with her inattention, her habitual neglect of the children. If it was not a mother's place to look after children, whose on earth was it? He himself had his hands full with his brokerage business. He could not be in two places at once; making a living for his family on the street, and staying at home to see that no harm befell them. He talked in a monotonous, insistent way.

Mrs. Pontellier sprang out of bed and went into the next room. She soon came back and sat on the edge of the bed, leaning her head down on the pillow. She said nothing, and refused to answer her husband when he questioned her. When his cigar was smoked out he went to bed, and in half a minute he was fast asleep.

Mrs. Pontellier was by that time thoroughly awake. She began to cry a little, and wiped her eyes on the sleeve of her *peignoir.*[15] Blowing out the candle, which her husband had left burning, she slipped her bare feet into a pair of satin *mules*[16] at the foot of the bed and went out on the porch, where she sat down in the wicker chair and began to rock gently to and fro.

It was then past midnight. The cottages were all dark. A single faint light gleamed out from the hallway of the house. There was no sound abroad except the hooting of an old owl in the top of a water-oak, and the everlasting voice of the sea, that was not uplifted at that soft hour. It broke like a mournful lullaby upon the night.

The tears came so fast to Mrs. Pontellier's eyes that the damp sleeve of her *peignoir* no longer served to dry them. She was holding the back of her chair with one hand; her loose sleeve had slipped almost to the shoulder of her uplifted arm. Turning, she thrust her face, steaming and wet, into the bend of her arm, and she went on crying there, not caring any longer to dry her face, her eyes, her arms. She could not have told why she was crying. Such experiences as the foregoing were not uncommon in her married life. They seemed never before to have weighed much against the abundance of her husband's kindness and a uniform devotion which had come to be tacit and self-understood.

An indescribable oppression, which seemed to generate in some unfamiliar part of her consciousness, filled her whole being with a vague anguish. It was like a shadow, like a mist passing across her soul's summer day. It was strange and unfamiliar; it was a mood. She did not sit there inwardly upbraiding her husband, lamenting at Fate, which had directed her footsteps to the path which they had taken. She was just having a good cry to herself. The mosquitoes made merry over her, biting her firm, round arms and nipping at her bare insteps.

The little stinging, buzzing imps succeeded in dispelling a mood which might have held her there in the darkness half a night longer.

[14]Running a temperature. [15]A loose dressing gown, a negligee. [16]Slippers.

The following morning Mr. Pontellier was up in good time to take the rockaway[17] which was to convey him to the steamer at the wharf. He was returning to the city to his business, and they would not see him again at the Island till the coming Saturday. He had regained his composure, which seemed to have been somewhat impaired the night before. He was eager to be gone, as he looked forward to a lively week in Carondelet Street.[18]

Mr. Pontellier gave his wife half of the money which he had brought away from Klein's hotel the evening before. She liked money as well as most women, and accepted it with no little satisfaction.

"It will buy a handsome wedding present for Sister Janet!" she exclaimed, smoothing out the bills as she counted them one by one.

"Oh! we'll treat Sister Janet better than that, my dear," he laughed, as he prepared to kiss her good-by.

The boys were tumbling about, clinging to his legs, imploring that numerous things be brought back to them. Mr. Pontellier was a great favorite, and ladies, men, children, even nurses, were always on hand to say good-by to him. His wife stood smiling and waving, the boys shouting, as he disappeared in the old rockaway down the sandy road.

A few days later a box arrived for Mrs. Pontellier from New Orleans. It was from her husband. It was filled with *friandises,*[19] with luscious and toothsome bits—the finest of fruits, *patés,*[20] a rare bottle or two, delicious syrups, and bonbons in abundance.

Mrs. Pontellier was always very generous with the contents of such a box; she was quite used to receiving them when away from home. The *patés,* and fruit were brought to the dining-room; the bonbons were passed around. And the ladies, selecting with dainty and discriminating fingers and a little greedily, all declared that Mr. Pontellier was the best husband in the world. Mrs. Pontellier was forced to admit that she knew of none better.

IV

It would have been a difficult matter for Mr. Pontellier to define to his own satisfaction or any one else's wherein his wife failed in her duty toward their children. It was something which he felt rather than perceived, and he never voiced the feeling without subsequent regret and ample atonement.

If one of the little Pontellier boys took a tumble whilst at play, he was not apt to rush crying to his mother's arms for comfort; he would more likely pick himself up, wipe the water out of his eyes and the sand out of his mouth, and go on playing. Tots as they were, they pulled together and stood their ground in childish battles with doubled fists and uplifted voices, which usually prevailed against the other brother-tots. The quadroon nurse was looked upon as a huge encumbrance, only good to button up waists and panties and to brush and part hair; since it seemed to be a law of society that hair must be parted and brushed.

In short, Mrs. Pontellier was not a mother-woman. The mother-women seemed to prevail that summer at Grand Isle. It was easy to know them, fluttering

[17]A light four-wheeled carriage, manufactured in Rockaway, New Jersey.

[18]Financial and commercial center of New Orleans.

[19]French: delicacies. [20]French: rich meat pastes.

about with extended, protecting wings when any harm, real or imaginary, threatened their precious brood. They were women who idolized their children, worshiped their husbands, and esteemed it a holy privilege to efface themselves as individuals and grow wings as ministering angels.

Many of them were delicious in the rôle; one of them was the embodiment of every womanly grace and charm. If her husband did not adore her, he was a brute, deserving of death by slow torture. Her name was Adèle Ratignolle. There are no words to describe her save the old ones that have served so often to picture the bygone heroine of romance and the fair lady of our dreams. There was nothing subtle or hidden about her charms; her beauty was all there, flaming and apparent: the spungold hair that comb nor confining pin could restrain; the blue eyes that were like nothing but sapphires; two lips that pouted, that were so red one could only think of cherries or some other delicious crimson fruit in looking at them. She was growing a little stout, but it did not seem to detract an iota from the grace of every step, pose, gesture. One would not have wanted her white neck[21] a mite less full or her beautiful arms more slender. Never were hands more exquisite than hers, and it was a joy to look at them when she threaded her needle or adjusted her gold thimble to her taper[22] middle finger as she sewed away on the little night-drawers or fashioned a bodice or a bib.

Madame Ratignolle was very fond of Mrs. Pontellier, and often she took her sewing and went over to sit with her in the afternoons. She was sitting there the afternoon of the day the box arrived from New Orleans. She had possession of the rocker, and she was busily engaged in sewing upon a diminutive pair of night-drawers.

She had brought the pattern of the drawers for Mrs. Pontellier to cut out—a marvel of construction, fashioned to enclose a baby's body so effectually that only two small eyes might look out from the garment, like an Eskimo's. They were designed for winter wear, when treacherous drafts came down chimneys and insidious currents of deadly cold found their way through key-holes.

Mrs. Pontellier's mind was quite at rest concerning the present material needs of her children, and she could not see the use of anticipating and making winter night garments the subject of her summer meditations. But she did not want to appear unamiable and uninterested, so she had brought forth newspapers, which she spread upon the floor of the gallery, and under Madame Ratignolle's directions she had cut a pattern of the impervious garment.

Robert was there, seated as he had been the Sunday before, and Mrs. Pontellier also occupied her former position on the upper step, leaning listlessly against the post. Beside her was a box of bonbons, which she held out at intervals to Madame Ratignolle.

That lady seemed at a loss to make a selection, but finally settled upon a stick of nougat, wondering if it were not too rich; whether it could possibly hurt her. Madame Ratignolle had been married seven years. About every two years she had a baby. At that time she had three babies, and was beginning to think of a fourth one. She was always talking about her "condition." Her "condition" was in no way apparent, and no one would have known a thing about it but for her persistence in making it the subject of conversation.

[21]A term used in the nineteenth century as a genteel synonym for "bosom" or "breast."
[22]Tapered.

Robert started to reassure her, asserting that he had known a lady who had subsisted upon nougat during the entire—but seeing the color mount into Mrs. Pontellier's face he checked himself and changed the subject.

Mrs. Pontellier, though she had married a Creole,[23] was not thoroughly at home in the society of Creoles; never before had she been thrown so intimately among them. There were only Creoles that summer at Lebrun's. They all knew each other, and felt like one large family, among whom existed the most amicable relations. A characteristic which distinguished them and which impressed Mrs. Pontellier most forcibly was their entire absence of prudery. Their freedom of expression was at first incomprehensible to her, though she had no difficulty in reconciling it with a lofty chastity which in the Creole woman seems to be inborn and unmistakable.

Never would Edna Pontellier forget the shock with which she heard Madame Ratignolle relating to old Monsieur Farival the harrowing story of one of her *accouchements,*[24] withholding no intimate detail. She was growing accustomed to like shocks, but she could not keep the mounting color back from her cheeks. Oftener than once her coming had interrupted the droll story with which Robert was entertaining some amused group of married women.

A book had gone the rounds of the *pension.* When it came her turn to read it, she did so with profound astonishment. She felt moved to read the book in secret and solitude, though none of the others had done so—to hide it from view at the sound of approaching footsteps. It was openly criticized and freely discussed at table. Mrs. Pontellier gave over being astonished, and concluded that wonders would never cease.

V

They formed a congenial group sitting there that summer afternoon—Madame Ratignolle sewing away, often stopping to relate a story or incident with much expressive gesture of her perfect hands; Robert and Mrs. Pontellier sitting idle, exchanging occasional words, glances or smiles which indicated a certain advanced stage of intimacy and *camaraderie.*[25]

He had lived in her shadow during the past month. No one thought anything of it. Many had predicted that Robert would devote himself to Mrs. Pontellier when he arrived. Since the age of fifteen, which was eleven years before, Robert each summer at Grand Isle had constituted himself the devoted attendant of some fair dame or damsel. Sometimes it was a young girl, again a widow; but as often as not it was some interesting married woman.

For two consecutive seasons he lived in the sunlight of Mademoiselle Duvigné's presence. But she died between summers; then Robert posed as an inconsolable; prostrating himself at the feet of Madame Ratignolle for whatever crumbs of sympathy and comfort she might be pleased to vouchsafe.

Mrs. Pontellier liked to sit and gaze at her fair companion as she might look upon a faultless Madonna.

[23]A term meaning "native," used in Louisiana to describe native-born descendants of early French and Spanish settlers.

[24]French: childbirths. [25]French: comradeship.

"Could any one fathom the cruelty beneath that fair exterior?" murmured Robert. "She knew that I adored her once, and she let me adore her. It was 'Robert, come; go; stand up; sit down; do this; do that; see if the baby sleeps; my thimble, please, that I left God knows where. Come and read Daudet[26] to me while I sew.'"

"*Par exemple!*[27] I never had to ask. You were always there under my feet, like a troublesome cat."

"You mean like an adoring dog. And just as soon as Ratignolle appeared on the scene, then it *was* like a dog. '*Passez! Adieu! Allez vous-en!*'"[28]

"Perhaps I feared to make Alphonse jealous," she interjoined, with excessive naïveté. That made them all laugh. The right hand jealous of the left! The heart jealous of the soul! But for that matter, the Creole husband is never jealous; with him the gangrene passion is one which has become dwarfed by disuse.

Meanwhile Robert, addressing Mrs. Pontellier, continued to tell of his one time hopeless passion for Madame Ratignolle; of sleepless nights, of consuming flames till the very sea sizzled when he took his daily plunge. While the lady at the needle kept up a little running, contemptuous comment:

"*Blagueur—farceur—gros bête, va!*"[29]

He never assumed this serio-comic tone when alone with Mrs. Pontellier. She never knew precisely what to make of it; at that moment it was impossible for her to guess how much of it was jest and what proportion was earnest. It was understood that he had often spoken words of love to Madame Ratignolle, without any thought of being taken seriously. Mrs. Pontellier was glad he had not assumed a similar rôle toward herself. It would have been unacceptable and annoying.

Mrs. Pontellier had brought her sketching materials, which she sometimes dabbled with in an unprofessional way. She liked the dabbling. She felt in it satisfaction of a kind which no other employment afforded her.

She had long wished to try herself on Madame Ratignolle. Never had that lady seemed a more tempting subject than at that moment, seated there like some sensuous Madonna, with the gleam of the fading day enriching her splendid color.

Robert crossed over and seated himself upon the step below Mrs. Pontellier, that he might watch her work. She handled her brushes with a certain ease and freedom which came, not from long and close acquaintance with them, but from a natural aptitude. Robert followed her work with close attention, giving forth little ejaculatory expressions of appreciation in French, which he addressed to Madame Ratignolle.

"*Mais ce n'est pas mal! Elle s'y connait, elle a de la force, oui.*"[30]

During his oblivious attention he once quietly rested his head against Mrs. Pontellier's arm. As gently she repulsed him. Once again he repeated the offense. She could not but believe it to be thoughtlessness on his part; yet that was no reason she should submit to it. She did not remonstrate, except again to repulse him quietly but firmly. He offered no apology.

The picture completed bore no resemblance to Madame Ratignolle. She was greatly disappointed to find that it did not look like her. But it was a fair enough piece of work, and in many respects satisfying.

[26]Alphonse Daudet (1840–1897), popular French novelist. [27]French: "For heaven's sake!"
[28]French: "Go on! Good-bye! Go away!" [29]French: "Joker—trickster—big fool, go!"
[30]French: "Not bad at all! She knows what she's doing, she has talent, yes."

Mrs. Pontellier evidently did not think so. After surveying the sketch critically she drew a broad smudge of paint across its surface, and crumpled the paper between her hands.

The youngsters came tumbling up the steps, the quadroon following at the respectful distance which they required her to observe. Mrs. Pontellier made them carry her paints and things into the house. She sought to detain them for a little talk and some pleasantry. But they were greatly in earnest. They had only come to investigate the contents of the bonbon box. They accepted without murmuring what she chose to give them, each holding out two chubby hands scoop-like, in the vain hope that they might be filled; and then away they went.

The sun was low in the west, and the breeze soft and languorous that came up from the south, charged with the seductive odor of the sea. Children, freshly befurbelowed,[31] were gathering for their games under the oaks. Their voices were high and penetrating.

Madame Ratignolle folded her sewing, placing thimble, scissors and thread all neatly together in the roll, which she pinned securely. She complained of faintness. Mrs. Pontellier flew for the cologne water and a fan. She bathed Madame Ratignolle's face with cologne, while Robert plied the fan with unnecessary vigor.

The spell was soon over, and Mrs. Pontellier could not help wondering if there were not a little imagination responsible for its origin, for the rose tint had never faded from her friend's face.

She stood watching the fair woman walk down the long line of galleries with the grace and majesty which queens are sometimes supposed to possess. Her little ones ran to meet her. Two of them clung about her white skirts, the third she took from its nurse and with a thousand endearments bore it along in her own fond, encircling arms. Though, as everybody well knew, the doctor had forbidden her to lift so much as a pin!

"Are you going bathing?" asked Robert of Mrs. Pontellier. It was not so much a question as a reminder.

"Oh, no," she answered, with a tone of indecision. "I'm tired; I think not." Her glance wandered from his face away toward the Gulf, whose sonorous murmur reached her like a loving but imperative entreaty.

"Oh, come!" he insisted. "You mustn't miss your bath. Come on. The water must be delicious; it will not hurt you. Come."

He reached up for her big, rough straw hat that hung on a peg outside the door, and put it on her head. They descended the steps, and walked away together toward the beach. The sun was low in the west and the breeze was soft and warm.

VI

Edna Pontellier could not have told why, wishing to go to the beach with Robert, she should in the first place have declined, and in the second place have followed in obedience to one of the two contradictory impulses which impelled her.

[31]I.e., dressed in fussy, elaborate clothes.

A certain light was beginning to dawn dimly within her,—the light which, showing the way, forbids it.

At that early period it served but to bewilder her. It moved her to dreams, to thoughtfulness, to the shadowy anguish which had overcome her the midnight when she had abandoned herself to tears.

In short, Mrs. Pontellier was beginning to realize her position in the universe as a human being, and to recognize her relations as an individual to the world within and about her. This may seem like a ponderous weight of wisdom to descend upon the soul of a young woman of twenty-eight—perhaps more wisdom than the Holy Ghost is usually pleased to vouchsafe to any woman.

But the beginning of things, of a world especially, is necessarily vague, tangled, chaotic, and exceedingly disturbing. How few of us ever emerge from such beginning! How many souls perish in its tumult!

The voice of the sea is seductive; never ceasing, whispering, clamoring, murmuring, inviting the soul to wander for a spell in abysses of solitude; to lose itself in mazes of inward contemplation.

The voice of the sea speaks to the soul. The touch of the sea is sensuous, enfolding the body in its soft, close embrace.

VII

Mrs. Pontellier was not a woman given to confidences, a characteristic hitherto contrary to her nature. Even as a child she had lived her own small life all within herself. At a very early period she had apprehended instinctively the dual life—that outward existence which conforms, the inward life which questions.

That summer at Grand Isle she began to loosen a little the mantle of reserve that had always enveloped her. There may have been—there must have been—influences, both subtle and apparent, working in their several ways to induce her to do this; but the most obvious was the influence of Adèle Ratignolle. The excessive physical charm of the Creole had first attracted her, for Edna had a sensuous susceptibility to beauty. Then the candor of the woman's whole existence, which every one might read, and which formed so striking a contrast to her own habitual reserve—this might have furnished a link. Who can tell what metals the gods use in forging the subtle bond which we call sympathy, which we might as well call love.

The two women went away one morning to the beach together, arm in arm, under the huge white sunshade. Edna had prevailed upon Madame Ratignolle to leave the children behind, though she could not induce her to relinquish a diminutive roll of needlework, which Adèle begged to be allowed to slip into the depths of her pocket. In some unaccountable way they had escaped from Robert.

The walk to the beach was no inconsiderable one, consisting as it did of a long, sandy path, upon which a sporadic and tangled growth that bordered it on either side made frequent and unexpected inroads. There were acres of yellow camomile[32] reaching out on either hand. Further away still, vegetable gardens abounded, with frequent small plantations of orange or lemon trees intervening. The dark green clusters glistened from afar in the sun.

[32]A strong-scented flower, a variety of aster.

The women were both of goodly height, Madame Ratignolle possessing the more feminine and matronly figure. The charm of Edna Pontellier's physique stole insensibly upon you. The lines of her body were long, clean and symmetrical; it was a body which occasionally fell into splendid poses; there was no suggestion of the trim, stereotyped fashion-plate about it. A casual and indiscriminating observer, in passing, might not cast a second glance upon the figure. But with more feeling and discernment he would have recognized the noble beauty of its modeling, and the graceful severity of poise and movement, which made Edna Pontellier different from the crowd.

She wore a cool muslin that morning—white, with a waving vertical line of brown running through it; also a white linen collar and the big straw hat which she had taken from the peg outside the door. The hat rested any way on her yellow-brown hair, that waved a little, was heavy, and clung close to her head.

Madame Ratignolle, more careful of her complexion, had twined a gauze veil about her head. She wore dogskin[33] gloves, with gauntlets that protected her wrists. She was dressed in pure white, with a fluffiness of ruffles that became her. The draperies and fluttering things which she wore suited her rich, luxuriant beauty as a greater severity of line could not have done.

There were a number of bath-houses along the beach, of rough but solid construction, built with small, protecting galleries facing the water. Each house consisted of two compartments, and each family at Lebrun's possessed a compartment for itself, fitted out with all the essential paraphernalia of the bath and whatever other conveniences the owners might desire. The two women had no intention of bathing; they had just strolled down to the beach for a walk and to be alone and near the water. The Pontellier and Ratignolle compartments adjoined one another under the same roof.

Mrs. Pontellier had brought down her key through force of habit. Unlocking the door of her bath-room she went inside, and soon emerged, bringing a rug, which she spread upon the floor of the gallery, and two huge hair pillows covered with crash,[34] which she placed against the front of the building.

The two seated themselves there in the shade of the porch, side by side, with their backs against the pillows and their feet extended. Madame Ratignolle removed her veil, wiped her face with a rather delicate handkerchief, and fanned herself with the fan which she always carried suspended somewhere about her person by a long, narrow ribbon. Edna removed her collar and opened her dress at the throat. She took the fan from Madame Ratignolle and began to fan both herself and her companion. It was very warm, and for a while they did nothing but exchange remarks about the heat, the sun, the glare. But there was a breeze blowing, a choppy, stiff wind that whipped the water into froth. It fluttered the skirts of the two women and kept them for a while engaged in adjusting, readjusting, tucking in, securing hair-pins and hat-pins. A few persons were sporting some distance away in the water. The beach was very still of human sound at that hour. The lady in black was reading her morning devotions on the porch of a neighboring bath-house. Two young lovers were exchanging their hearts' yearnings beneath the children's tent, which they had found unoccupied.

[33]Thick leather gloves made from the skins of dogs and sheep.
[34]Coarse, heavy linen cloth.

Edna Pontellier, casting her eyes about, had finally kept them at rest upon the sea. The day was clear and carried the gaze out as far as the blue sky went; there were a few white clouds suspended idly over the horizon. A lateen sail[35] was visible in the direction of Cat Island, and others to the south seemed almost motionless in the far distance.

"Of whom—of what are you thinking?" asked Adèle of her companion, whose countenance she had been watching with a little amused attention, arrested by the absorbed expression which seemed to have seized and fixed every feature into a statuesque repose.

"Nothing," returned Mrs. Pontellier, with a start, adding at once: "How stupid! But it seems to me it is the reply we make instinctively to such a question. Let me see," she went on, throwing back her head and narrowing her fine eyes till they shone like two vivid points of light. "Let me see. I was really not conscious of thinking of anything; but perhaps I can retrace my thoughts."

"Oh! never mind!" laughed Madame Ratignolle. "I am not quite so exacting. I will let you off this time. It is really too hot to think, especially to think about thinking."

"But for the fun of it," persisted Edna. "First of all, the sight of the water stretching so far away, those motionless sails against the blue sky, made a delicious picture that I just wanted to sit and look at. The hot wind beating in my face made me think—without any connection that I can trace—of a summer day in Kentucky, of a meadow that seemed as big as the ocean to the very little girl walking through the grass, which was higher than her waist. She threw out her arms as if swimming when she walked, beating the tall grass as one strikes out in the water. Oh, I see the connection now!"

"Where were you going that day in Kentucky, walking through the grass?"

"I don't remember now. I was just walking diagonally across a big field. My sun-bonnet obstructed the view. I could see only the stretch of green before me, and I felt as if I must walk on forever, without coming to the end of it. I don't remember whether I was frightened or pleased. I must have been entertained.

"Likely as not it was Sunday," she laughed; "and I was running away from prayers, from the Presbyterian service, read in a spirit of gloom by my father that chills me yet to think of."

"And have you been running away from prayers ever since, *ma chère?*"[36] asked Madame Ratignolle, amused.

"No! oh, no!" Edna hastened to say. "I was a little unthinking child in those days, just following a misleading impulse without question. On the contrary, during one period of my life religion took a firm hold upon me; after I was twelve and until—until—why, I suppose until now, though I never thought much about it—just driven along by habit. But do you know," she broke off, turning her quick eyes upon Madame Ratignolle and leaning forward a little so as to bring her face quite close to that of her companion, "sometimes I feel this summer as if I were walking through the green meadow again; idly, aimlessly, unthinking and unguided."

Madame Ratignolle laid her hand over that of Mrs. Pontellier, which was near her. Seeing that the hand was not withdrawn, she clasped it firmly and

[35]The oblique-hanging sail characteristic of a lugger.
[36]French: "My dear."

warmly. She even stroked it a little, fondly, with the other hand, murmuring in an undertone, "*Pauvre chèrie.*"[37]

The action was at first a little confusing to Edna, but she soon lent herself readily to the Creole's gentle caress. She was not accustomed to an outward and spoken expression of affection, either in herself or in others. She and her younger sister, Janet, had quarreled a good deal through force of unfortunate habit. Her older sister, Margaret, was matronly and dignified, probably from having assumed matronly and housewifely responsibilities too early in life, their mother having died when they were quite young. Margaret was not effusive: she was practical. Edna had had an occasional girl friend, but whether accidentally or not, they seemed to have been all of one type—the self-contained. She never realized that the reserve of her own character had much, perhaps everything, to do with this. Her most intimate friend at school had been one of rather exceptional intellectual gifts, who wrote finesounding essays, which Edna admired and strove to imitate; and with her she talked and glowed over the English classics, and sometimes held religious and political controversies.

Edna often wondered at one propensity which sometimes had inwardly disturbed her without causing any outward show or manifestation on her part. At a very early age—perhaps it was when she traversed the ocean of waving grass—she remembered that she had been passionately enamored of a dignified and sad-eyed cavalry officer who visited her father in Kentucky. She could not leave his presence when he was there, nor remove her eyes from his face, which was something like Napoleon's, with a lock of black hair falling across the forehead. But the cavalry officer melted imperceptibly out of her existence.

At another time her affections were deeply engaged by a young gentleman who visited a lady on a neighboring plantation. It was after they went to Mississippi to live. The young man was engaged to be married to the young lady, and they sometimes called upon Margaret, driving over of afternoons in a buggy. Edna was a little miss, just merging into her teens; and the realization that she herself was nothing, nothing, nothing to the engaged young man was a bitter affliction to her. But he, too, went the way of dreams.

She was a grown young woman when she was overtaken by what she supposed to be the climax of her fate. It was when the face and figure of a great tragedian began to haunt her imagination and stir her senses. The persistence of the infatuation lent it an aspect of genuineness. The hopelessness of it colored it with the lofty tunes of a great passion.

The picture of the tragedian stood enframed upon her desk. Any one may possess the portrait of a tragedian without exciting suspicion or comment. (This was a sinister reflection which she cherished.) In the presence of others she expressed admiration for his exalted gifts, as she handed the photograph around and dwelt upon the fidelity of the likeness. When alone she sometimes picked it up and kissed the cold glass passionately.

Her marriage to Léonce Pontellier was purely an accident, in this respect resembling many other marriages which masquerade as the decrees of Fate. It was in the midst of her secret great passion that she met him. He fell in love, as men are in the habit of doing, and pressed his suit with an earnestness and an ardor which left nothing to be desired. He pleased her; his absolute devotion flattered her. She fancied there was a sympathy of thought and taste between

[37]French: "Poor darling."

them, in which fancy she was mistaken. Add to this the violent opposition of her father and her sister Margaret to her marriage with a Catholic, and we need seek no further for the motives which led her to accept Monsieur Pontellier for her husband.

The acme of bliss, which would have been a marriage with the tragedian, was not for her in this world. As the devoted wife of a man who worshipped her, she felt she would take her place with a certain dignity in the world of reality, closing the portals forever behind her upon the realm of romance and dreams.

But it was not long before the tragedian had gone to join the cavalry officer and the engaged young man and a few others; and Edna found herself face to face with the realities. She grew fond of her husband, realizing with some unaccountable satisfaction that no trace of passion or excessive and fictitious warmth colored her affection, thereby threatening its dissolution.

She was fond of her children in an uneven, impulsive way. She would sometimes gather them passionately to her heart; she would sometimes forget them. The year before they had spent part of the summer with their grandmother Pontellier in Iberville. Feeling secure regarding their happiness and welfare, she did not miss them except with an occasional intense longing. Their absence was a sort of relief, though she did not admit this, even to herself. It seemed to free her of a responsibility which she had blindly assumed and for which Fate had not fitted her.

Edna did not reveal so much as all this to Madame Ratignolle that summer day when they sat with faces turned to the sea. But a good part of it escaped her. She had put her head down on Madame Ratignolle's shoulder. She was flushed and felt intoxicated with the sound of her own voice and the unaccustomed taste of candor. It muddled her like wine, or like a first breath of freedom.

There was the sound of approaching voices. It was Robert, surrounded by a troop of children, searching for them. The two little Pontelliers were with him, and he carried Madame Ratignolle's little girl in his arms. There were other children beside, and two nurse-maids followed, looking disagreeable and resigned.

The women at once rose and began to shake out their draperies and relax their muscles. Mrs. Pontellier threw the cushions and rug into the bathhouse. The children all scampered off to the awning, and they stood there in a line, gazing upon the intruding lovers, still exchanging their vows and sighs. The lovers got up, with only a silent protest, and walked slowly away somewhere else.

The children possessed themselves of the tent, and Mrs. Pontellier went over to join them.

Madame Ratignolle begged Robert to accompany her to the house; she complained of cramp in her limbs and stiffness of the joints. She leaned draggingly upon his arm as they walked.

VIII

"Do me a favor, Robert," spoke the pretty woman at his side, almost as soon as she and Robert had started on their slow, homeward way. She looked up in his face, leaning on his arm beneath the encircling shadow of the umbrella which he had lifted.

"Granted; as many as you like," he returned, glancing down into her eyes that were full of thoughtfulness and some speculation.

"I only ask for one; let Mrs. Pontellier alone."

"*Tiens!*" he exclaimed, with a sudden, boyish laugh. "*Voilà que Madame Ratignolle est jalouse!*"[38]

"Nonsense! I'm in earnest; I mean what I say. Let Mrs. Pontellier alone."

"Why?" he asked; himself growing serious at his companion's solicitation.

"She is not one of us; she is not like us. She might make the unfortunate blunder of taking you seriously."

His face flushed with annoyance, and taking off his soft hat he began to beat it impatiently against his leg as he walked. "Why shouldn't she take me seriously?" he demanded sharply. "Am I a comedian, a clown, a jack-in-the-box? Why shouldn't she? You Creoles! I have no patience with you! Am I always to be regarded as a feature of an amusing programme? I hope Mrs. Pontellier does take me seriously. I hope she had discernment enough to find in me something besides the *blagueur.* If I thought there was any doubt—"

"Oh, enough, Robert!" she broke into his heated outburst. "You are not thinking of what you are saying. You speak with about as little reflection as we might expect from one of those children down there playing in the sand. If your attentions to any married women here were ever offered with any intention of being convincing, you would not be the gentleman we all know you to be, and you would be unfit to associate with the wives and daughters of the people who trust you."

Madame Ratignolle had spoken what she believed to be the law and the gospel. The young man shrugged his shoulders impatiently.

"Oh! well! That isn't it," slamming his hat down vehemently upon his head. "You ought to feel that such things are not flattering to say to a fellow."

"Should our whole intercourse consist of an exchange of compliments? *Ma foi!*"[39]

"It isn't pleasant to have a woman tell you—" he went on, unheedingly, but breaking off suddenly: "Now if I were like Arobin—you remember Alcée Arobin and that story of the consul's wife at Biloxi?"[40] And he related the story of Alcée Arobin and the consul's wife; and another about the tenor of the French Opera,[41] who received letters which should never have been written; and still other stories, grave and gay, till Mrs. Pontellier and her possible propensity for taking young men seriously was apparently forgotten.

Madame Ratignolle, when they had regained her cottage, went in to take the hour's rest which she considered helpful. Before leaving her, Robert begged her pardon for the impatience—he called it rudeness—with which he had received her well-meant caution.

"You made one mistake, Adèle," he said, with a light smile; "there is no earthly possibility of Mrs. Pontellier ever taking me seriously. You should have warned me against taking myself seriously. Your advice might then have carried some weight and given me subject for some reflection. *Au revoir.*[42] But you look tired," he added, solicitously. "Would you like a cup of bouillon? Shall I stir you a toddy?[43] Let me mix you a toddy with a drop of Angostura."

[38]French: "Look! . . . Behold that Madame Ratignolle is jealous!"
[39]French: "Really!" [40]A resort town on the Gulf coast of Mississippi.
[41]An opera company in nineteenth-century New Orleans.
[42]French: "Good-bye." [43]A sweetened drink of spirits and hot water.

She acceded to the suggestion of bouillon, which was grateful and acceptable. He went himself to the kitchen, which was a building apart from the cottages and lying to the rear of the house. And he himself brought her the golden-brown bouillon, in a dainty Sèvres cup,[44] with a flaky cracker or two on the saucer.

She thrust a bare, white arm from the curtain which shielded her open door, and received the cup from his hands. She told him he was a *bon garçon,*[45] and she meant it. Robert thanked her and turned away toward "the house."

The lovers were just entering the grounds of the *pension.* They were leaning toward each other as the water-oaks bent from the sea. There was not a particle of earth beneath their feet. Their heads might have been turned upside-down, so absolutely did they tread upon blue ether. The lady in black, creeping behind them, looked a trifle paler and more jaded than usual. There was no sign of Mrs. Pontellier and the children. Robert scanned the distance for any such apparition. They would doubtless remain away till the dinner hour. The young man ascended to his mother's room. It was situated at the top of the house, made up of odd angles and a queer, sloping ceiling. Two broad dormer windows looked out toward the Gulf, and as far across it as a man's eye might reach. The furnishings of the room were light, cool, and practical.

Madame Lebrun was busily engaged at the sewing-machine. A little black girl sat on the floor, and with her hands worked the treadle of the machine. The Creole woman does not take any chances which may be avoided of imperiling her health.

Robert went over and seated himself on the broad sill of one of the dormer windows. He took a book from his pocket and began energetically to read it, judging by the precision and frequency with which he turned the leaves. The sewing-machine made a resounding clatter in the room; it was of a ponderous, by-gone make. In the lulls, Robert and his mother exchanged bits of desultory conversation.

"Where is Mrs. Pontellier?"

"Down at the beach with the children."

"I promised to lend her the Goncourt.[46] Don't forget to take it down when you go; it's there on the bookshelf over the small table." Clatter, clatter, clatter, bang! for the next five or eight minutes.

"Where is Victor going with the rockaway?"

"The rockaway? Victor?"

"Yes; down there in front. He seems to be getting ready to drive away somewhere."

"Call him." Clatter, clatter!

Robert uttered a shrill, piercing whistle which might have been heard back at the wharf.

"He won't look up."

Madame Lebrun flew to the window. She called "Victor!" She waved a handkerchief and called again. The young fellow below got into the vehicle and started the horse off at a gallop.

[44]A costly porcelain cup made in Sèvres, France.
[45]French: good boy.
[46]A novel by the French writers Edmond (1822–1896) and Jules (1839–1870) Goncourt.

Madame Lebrun went back to the machine, crimson with annoyance. Victor was the younger son and brother—a *tête montée,*[47] with a temper which invited violence and a will which no ax could break.

"Whenever you say the word I'm ready to thrash any amount of reason into him that he's able to hold."

"If your father had only lived!" Clatter, clatter, clatter, clatter, bang! It was a fixed belief with Madame Lebrun that the conduct of the universe and all things pertaining thereto would have been manifestly of a more intelligent and higher order had not Monsieur Lebrun been removed to other spheres during the early years of their married life.

"What do you hear from Montel?" Montel was a middle-aged gentleman whose vain ambition and desire for the past twenty years had been to fill the void which Monsieur Lebrun's taking off had left in the Lebrun household. Clatter, clatter, bang, clatter!

"I have a letter somewhere," looking in the machine drawer and finding the letter in the bottom of the work-basket. "He says to tell you he will be in Vera Cruz[48] the beginning of next month"—clatter, clatter!—"and if you still have the intention of joining him"—bang! clatter, clatter, bang!

"Why didn't you tell me so before, mother? You know I wanted—" Clatter, clatter, clatter!

"Do you see Mrs. Pontellier starting back with the children? She will be in late to luncheon again. She never starts to get ready for luncheon till the last minute." Clatter, clatter! "Where are you going?"

"Where did you say the Goncourt was?"

IX

Every light in the hall was ablaze; every lamp turned as high as it could be without smoking the chimney or threatening explosion. The lamps were fixed at intervals against the wall, encircling the whole room. Some one had gathered orange and lemon branches, and with these fashioned graceful festoons between. The dark green of the branches stood out and glistened against the white muslin curtains which draped the windows, and which puffed, floated, and flapped at the capricious will of a stiff breeze that swept up from the Gulf.

It was Saturday night a few weeks after the intimate conversation held between Robert and Madame Ratignolle on their way from the beach. An unusual number of husbands, fathers, and friends had come down to stay over Sunday; and they were being suitably entertained by their families, with the material help of Madame Lebrun. The dining tables had all been removed to one end of the hall, and the chairs ranged about in rows and in clusters. Each little family group had had its say and exchanged its domestic gossip earlier in the evening. There was now an apparent disposition to relax; to widen the circle of confidences and give a more general tone to the conversation.

Many of the children had been permitted to sit up beyond their usual bedtime. A small band of them were lying on their stomachs on the floor looking at the colored sheets of the comic papers which Mr. Pontellier had brought down. The little Pontellier boys were permitting them to do so, and making their authority felt.

[47]French: headstrong person. [48]Mexican city on the Gulf of Mexico.

Music, dancing, and a recitation or two were the entertainments furnished, or rather, offered. But there was nothing systematic about the programme, no appearance of prearrangement nor even premeditation.

At an early hour in the evening the Farival twins were prevailed upon to play the piano. They were girls of fourteen, always clad in the Virgin's colors, blue and white, having been dedicated to the Blessed Virgin at their baptism. They played a duet from "Zampa," and at the earnest solicitation of every one present followed it with the overture to "The Poet and the Peasant."

"*Allez vous-en! Sapristi!*" shrieked the parrot outside the door. He was the only being present who possessed sufficient candor to admit that he was not listening to these gracious performances for the first time that summer. Old Monsieur Farival, grandfather of the twins, grew indignant over the interruption, and insisted upon having the bird removed and consigned to regions of darkness. Victor Lebrun objected; and his decrees were as immutable as those of Fate. The parrot fortunately offered no further interruption to the entertainment, the whole venom of his nature apparently having been cherished up and hurled against the twins in that one impetuous outburst.

Later a young brother and sister gave recitations, which every one present had heard many times at winter evening entertainments in the city.

A little girl performed a skirt dance in the center of the floor. The mother played her accompaniments and at the same time watched her daughter with greedy admiration and nervous apprehension. She need have had no apprehension. The child was mistress of the situation. She had been properly dressed for the occasion in black tulle[49] and black silk tights. Her little neck and arms were bare, and her hair, artificially crimped, stood out like fluffy black plumes over her head. Her poses were full of grace, and her little black-shod toes twinkled as they shot out and upward with a rapidity and suddenness which were bewildering.

But there was no reason why every one should not dance. Madame Ratignolle could not, so it was she who gaily consented to play for the others. She played very well, keeping excellent waltz time and infusing an expression into the strains which was indeed inspiring. She was keeping up her music on account of the children, she said; because she and her husband both considered it a means of brightening the home and making it attractive.

Almost every one danced but the twins, who could not be induced to separate during the brief period when one or the other should be whirling around the room in the arms of a man. They might have danced together, but they did not think of it.

The children were sent to bed. Some went submissively; others with shrieks and protests as they were dragged away. They had been permitted to sit up till after the ice-cream, which naturally marked the limit of human indulgence.

The ice-cream was passed around with cake—gold and silver cake arranged on platters in alternate slices; it had been made and frozen during the afternoon back of the kitchen by two black women, under the supervision of Victor. It was pronounced a great success—excellent if it had only contained a little less vanilla or a little more sugar, if it had been frozen a degree harder, and if the salt might have been kept out of portions of it. Victor was proud of his achievement, and went about recommending it and urging every one to partake of it to excess.

[49]Thin, fine netting, usually of silk, used for veils and dresses.

After Mrs. Pontellier had danced twice with her husband, once with Robert, and once with Monsieur Ratignolle, who was thin and tall and swayed like a reed in the wind when he danced, she went out on the gallery and seated herself on the low window-sill, where she commanded a view of all that went on in the hall and could look out toward the Gulf. There was a soft effulgence in the east. The moon was coming up, and its mystic shimmer was casting a million lights across the distant, restless water.

"Would you like to hear Mademoiselle Reisz play?" asked Robert, coming out on the porch where she was. Of course Edna would like to hear Mademoiselle Reisz play; but she feared it would be useless to entreat her.

"I'll ask her," he said. "I'll tell her that you want to hear her. She likes you. She will come." He turned and hurried away to one of the far cottages, where Mademoiselle Reisz was shuffling away. She was dragging a chair in and out of her room, and at intervals objecting to the crying of a baby, which a nurse in the adjoining cottage was endeavoring to put to sleep. She was a disagreeable little woman, no longer young, who had quarreled with almost every one, owing to a temper which was self-assertive and a disposition to trample upon the rights of others. Robert prevailed upon her without any too great difficulty.

She entered the hall with him during a lull in the dance. She made an awkward, imperious little bow as she went in. She was a homely woman, with small weazened[50] face and body and eyes that glowed. She had absolutely no taste in dress, and wore a batch of rusty black lace with a bunch of artificial violets pinned to the side of her hair.

"Ask Mrs. Pontellier what she would like to hear me play," she requested of Robert. She sat perfectly still before the piano, not touching the keys, while Robert carried her message to Edna at the window. A general air of surprise and genuine satisfaction fell upon every one as they saw the pianist enter. There was a settling down, and a prevailing air of expectancy everywhere. Edna was a trifle embarrassed at being thus signaled out for the imperious little woman's favor. She would not dare to choose, and begged that Mademoiselle Reisz would please herself in her selections.

Edna was what she herself called very fond of music. Musical strains, well rendered, had a way of evoking pictures in her mind. She sometimes liked to sit in the room of mornings when Madame Ratignolle played or practiced. One piece which that lady played Edna had entitled "Solitude." It was a short, plaintive, minor strain. The name of the piece was something else, but she called it "Solitude." When she heard it there came before her imagination the figure of a man standing beside a desolate rock on the seashore. He was naked. His attitude was one of hopeless resignation as he looked toward a distant bird winging its flight away from him.

Another piece called to her mind a dainty young woman clad in an Empire gown,[51] taking mincing dancing steps as she came down a long avenue between tall hedges. Again, another reminded her of children at play, and still another of nothing on earth but a demure lady stroking a cat.

The very first chords which Mademoiselle Reisz struck upon the piano sent a keen tremor down Mrs. Pontellier's spinal column. It was not the first time she had heard an artist at the piano. Perhaps it was the first time she was

[50]Wizened: aged, wrinkled.
[51]A long gown with a high waist, fashionable during the Napoleonic era.

ready, perhaps the first time her being was tempered to take an impress of the abiding truth.

She waited for the material pictures which she thought would gather and blaze before her imagination. She waited in vain. She saw no pictures of solitude, of hope, of longing, or of despair. But the very passions themselves were aroused within her soul, swaying it, lashing it, as the waves daily beat upon her splendid body. She trembled, she was choking, and the tears blinded her.

Mademoiselle had finished. She arose, and bowing her stiff, lofty bow, she went away, stopping for neither thanks nor applause. As she passed along the gallery she patted Edna upon the shoulder.

"Well, how did you like my music?" she asked. The young woman was unable to answer; she pressed the hand of the pianist convulsively. Mademoiselle Reisz perceived her agitation and even her tears. She patted her again upon the shoulder as she said:

"You are the only one worth playing for. Those others? Bah!" and she went shuffling and sidling on down the gallery toward her room.

But she was mistaken about "those others." Her playing had aroused a fever of enthusiasm. "What passion!" "What an artist!" "I have always said no one could play Chopin[52] like Mademoiselle Reisz!" "That last prelude! Bon Dieu![53] It shakes a man!"

It was growing late, and there was a general disposition to disband. But some one, perhaps it was Robert, thought of a bath[54] at that mystic hour and under that mystic moon.

X

At all events Robert proposed it, and there was not a dissenting voice. There was not one but was ready to follow when he led the way. He did not lead the way, however, he directed the way; and he himself loitered behind with the lovers, who had betrayed a disposition to linger and hold themselves apart. He walked between them, whether with malicious or mischievous intent was not wholly clear, even to himself.

The Pontelliers and Ratignolles walked ahead; the women leaning upon the arms of their husbands. Edna could hear Robert's voice behind them, and could sometimes hear what he said. She wondered why he did not join them. It was unlike him not to. Of late he had sometimes held away from her for an entire day, redoubling his devotion upon the next and the next, as though to make up for hours that had been lost. She missed him the days when some pretext served to take him away from her, just as one misses the sun on a cloudy day without having thought much about the sun when it was shining.

The people walked in little groups toward the beach. They talked and laughed; some of them sang. There was a band playing down at Klein's hotel, and the strains reached them faintly, tempered by the distance. There were strange, rare odors abroad—a tangle of the sea smell and of weeds and damp, new-plowed earth, mingled with the heavy perfume of a field of white blossoms somewhere near. But the night sat lightly upon the sea and the land. There

[52]Frederic Chopin (1810–1849), Polish composer and pianist.
[53]French: "Good God!" [54]A swim.

was no weight of darkness; there were no shadows. The white light of the moon had fallen upon the world like the mystery and the softness of sleep.

Most of them walked into the water as though into a native element. The sea was quiet now, and swelled lazily in broad billows that melted into one another and did not break except upon the beach in little foamy crests that coiled back like slow, white serpents.

Edna had attempted all summer to learn to swim. She had received instructions from both the men and women; in some instances from the children. Robert had pursued a system of lessons almost daily; and he was nearly at the point of discouragement in realizing the futility of his efforts. A certain ungovernable dread hung about her when in the water, unless there was a hand near by that might reach out and reassure her.

But that night she was like the little tottering, stumbling, clutching child, who of a sudden realizes its powers, and walks for the first time alone, boldly and with over-confidence. She could have shouted for joy. She did shout for joy, as with a sweeping stroke or two she lifted her body to the surface of the water.

A feeling of exultation overtook her, as if some power of significant import had been given her to control the working of her body and her soul. She grew daring and reckless, overestimating her strength. She wanted to swim far out, where no woman had swum before.

Her unlooked-for achievement was the subject of wonder, applause, and admiration. Each one congratulated himself that his special teachings had accomplished this desired end.

"How easy it is!" she thought. "It is nothing," she said aloud; "why did I not discover before that it was nothing. Think of the time I have lost splashing about like a baby!" She would not join the groups in their sports and bouts, but intoxicated with her newly conquered power, she swam out alone.

She turned her face seaward to gather in an impression of space and solitude, which the vast expanse of water, meeting and melting with the moonlit sky, conveyed to her excited fancy. As she swam she seemed to be reaching out for the unlimited in which to lose herself.

Once she turned and looked toward the shore, toward the people she had left there. She had not gone any great distance—that is, what would have been a great distance for an experienced swimmer. But to her unaccustomed vision the stretch of water behind her assumed the aspect of a barrier which her unaided strength would never be able to overcome.

A quick vision of death smote her soul, and for a second of time appalled and enfeebled her senses. But by an effort she rallied her staggering faculties and managed to regain the land.

She made no mention of her encounter with death and her flash of terror, except to say to her husband, "I thought I should have perished out there alone."

"You were not so very far, my dear; I was watching you," he told her.

Edna went at once to the bath-house, and she had put on her dry clothes and was ready to return home before the others had left the water. She started to walk away alone. They all called to her and shouted to her. She waved a dissenting hand, and went on, paying no further heed to their renewed cries which sought to detain her.

"Sometimes I am tempted to think that Mrs. Pontellier is capricious," said Madame Lebrun, who was amusing herself immensely and feared that Edna's abrupt departure might put an end to the pleasure.

"I know she is," assented Mr. Pontellier; "sometimes, not often."

Edna had not traversed a quarter of the distance on her way home before she was overtaken by Robert.

"Did you think I was afraid?" she asked him, without a shade of annoyance.

"No; I knew you weren't afraid."

"Then why did you come? Why didn't you stay out there with the others?"

"I never thought of it."

"Thought of what?"

"Of anything. What difference does it make?"

"I'm very tired," she uttered, complainingly.

"I know you are."

"You don't know anything about it. Why should you know? I never was so exhausted in my life. But it isn't unpleasant. A thousand emotions have swept through me to-night. I don't comprehend half of them. Don't mind what I'm saying; I am just thinking aloud. I wonder if I shall ever be stirred again as Mademoiselle Reisz's playing moved me to-night. I wonder if any night on earth will ever again be like this one. It is like a night in a dream. The people about me are like some uncanny, half-human beings. There must be spirits abroad tonight."

"There are," whispered Robert. "Didn't you know this was the twenty-eighth of August?"

"The twenty-eighth of August?"

"Yes. On the twenty-eighth of August, at the hour of midnight, and if the moon is shining—the moon must be shining—a spirit that has haunted these shores for ages rises up from the Gulf. With its own penetrating vision the spirit seeks some one mortal worthy to hold him company, worthy of being exalted for a few hours into realms of the semi-celestials. His search has always hitherto been fruitless, and he has sunk back, disheartened, into the sea. But to-night he found Mrs. Pontellier. Perhaps he will never wholly release her from the spell. Perhaps she will never again suffer a poor, unworthy earthling to walk in the shadow of her divine presence."

"Don't banter me," she said, wounded at what appeared to be his flippancy. He did not mind the entreaty, but the tone with its delicate note of pathos was like a reproach. He could not explain; he could not tell her that he had penetrated her mood and understood. He said nothing except to offer her his arm, for, by her own admission, she was exhausted. She had been walking alone with her arms hanging limp, letting her white skirts trail along the dewy path. She took his arm, but she did not lean upon it. She let her hand lie listlessly, as though her thoughts were elsewhere—somewhere in advance of her body, and she was striving to overtake them.

Robert assisted her into the hammock which swung from the post before her door out to the trunk of a tree.

"Will you stay out here and wait for Mr. Pontellier?" he asked.

"I'll stay out here. Good-night."

"Shall I get you a pillow?"

"There's one here," she said, feeling about, for they were in the shadow.

"It must be soiled; the children have been tumbling it about."

"No matter." And having discovered the pillow, she adjusted it beneath her head. She extended herself in the hammock with a deep breath of relief. She was not a supercilious or an over-dainty woman. She was not much given to reclining in the hammock, and when she did so it was with no cat-like suggestion of voluptuous ease, but with a beneficent repose which seemed to invade her whole body.

"Shall I stay with you till Mr. Pontellier comes?" asked Robert, seating himself on the outer edge of one of the steps and taking hold of the hammock rope which was fastened to the post.

"If you wish. Don't swing the hammock. Will you get my white shawl which I left on the window-sill over at the house?"

"Are you chilly?"

"No; but I shall be presently."

"Presently?" he laughed. "Do you know what time it is? How long are you going to stay out here?"

"I don't know. Will you get the shawl?"

"Of course I will," he said, rising. He went over to the house, walking along the grass. She watched his figure pass in and out of the strips of moonlight. It was past midnight. It was very quiet.

When he returned with the shawl she took it and kept it in her hand. She did not put it around her.

"Did you say I should stay till Mr. Pontellier came back?"

"I said you might if you wished to."

He seated himself again and rolled a cigarette, which he smoked in silence. Neither did Mrs. Pontellier speak. No multitude of words could have been more significant than those moments of silence, or more pregnant with the first-felt throbbings of desire.

When the voices of the bathers were heard approaching, Robert said good-night. She did not answer him. He thought she was asleep. Again she watched his figure pass in and out of the strips of moonlight as he walked away.

XI

"What are you doing out here, Edna? I thought I should find you in bed," said her husband, when he discovered her lying there. He had walked up with Madame Lebrun and left her at the house. His wife did not reply.

"Are you asleep?" he asked, bending down close to look at her.

"No." Her eyes gleamed bright and intense, with no sleepy shadows, as they looked into his.

"Do you know it is past one o'clock? Come on," and he mounted the steps and went into their room.

"Edna!" called Mr. Pontellier from within, after a few moments had gone by.

"Don't wait for me," she answered. He thrust his head through the door.

"You will take cold out there," he said, irritably. "What folly is this? Why don't you come in?"

"It isn't cold; I have my shawl."

"The mosquitoes will devour you."

"There are no mosquitoes."

She heard him moving about the room; every sound indicating impatience and irritation. Another time she would have gone in at his request. She would, through habit, have yielded to his desire; not with any sense of submission or obedience to his compelling wishes, but unthinkingly, as we walk, move, sit, stand, go through the daily treadmill of the life which has been portioned out to us.

"Edna, dear, are you not coming in soon?" he asked again, this time fondly, with a note of entreaty.

"No; I am going to stay out here."

"This is more than folly," he blurted out. "I can't permit you to stay out there all night. You must come in the house instantly."

With a writhing motion she settled herself more securely in the hammock. She perceived that her will had blazed up, stubborn and resistant. She could not at that moment have done other than denied and resisted. She wondered if her husband had ever spoken to her like that before, and if she had submitted to his command. Of course she had; she remembered that she had. But she could not realize why or how she should have yielded, feeling as she then did.

"Léonce, go to bed," she said. "I mean to stay out here. I don't wish to go in, and I don't intend to. Don't speak to me like that again; I shall not answer you."

Mr. Pontellier had prepared for bed, but he slipped on an extra garment. He opened a bottle of wine, of which he kept a small and select supply in a buffet of his own. He drank a glass of the wine and went out on the gallery and offered a glass to his wife. She did not wish any. He drew up the rocker, hoisted his slippered feet on the rail, and proceeded to smoke a cigar. He smoked two cigars; then he went inside and drank another glass of wine. Mrs. Pontellier again declined to accept a glass when it was offered to her. Mr. Pontellier once more seated himself with elevated feet, and after a reasonable interval of time smoked some more cigars.

Edna began to feel like one who awakens gradually out of a dream, a delicious, grotesque, impossible dream, to feel again the realities pressing into her soul. The physical need for sleep began to overtake her; the exuberance which had sustained and exalted her spirit left her helpless and yielding to the conditions which crowded her in.

The stillest hour of the night had come, the hour before dawn, when the world seems to hold its breath. The moon hung low, and had turned from silver to copper in the sleeping sky. The old owl no longer hooted, and the water-oaks had ceased to moan as they bent their heads.

Edna arose, cramped from lying so long and still in the hammock. She tottered up the steps, clutching feebly at the post before passing into the house.

"Are you coming in, Léonce?" she asked, turning her face toward her husband.

"Yes, dear," he answered, with a glance following a misty puff of smoke. "Just as soon as I have finished my cigar."

XII

She slept but a few hours. They were troubled and feverish hours, disturbed with dreams that were intangible, that eluded her, leaving only an impression upon her half-awakened senses of something unattainable. She was up and dressed in the cool of the early morning. The air was invigorating and steadied somewhat her faculties. However, she was not seeking refreshment or help from any source, either external or from within. She was blindly following whatever impulse moved her, as if she had placed herself in alien hands for direction, and freed her soul of responsibility.

Most of the people at that early hour were still in bed and asleep. A few, who intended to go over to the *Chênière* for mass, were moving about. The lovers, who had laid their plans the night before, were already strolling toward the wharf. The lady in black, with her Sunday prayer-book, velvet and gold-clasped, and her Sunday silver beads, was following them at no great distance. Old Monsieur Farival was up, and was more than half inclined to do anything that suggested itself. He put on his big straw hat, and taking his umbrella from the stand in the hall, followed the lady in black, never overtaking her.

The little negro girl who worked Madame Lebrun's sewing-machine was sweeping the galleries with long, absent-minded strokes of the broom. Edna sent her up into the house to awaken Robert.

"Tell him I am going to the *Chênière.* The boat is ready; tell him to hurry."

He had soon joined her. She had never sent for him before. She had never asked for him. She had never seemed to want him before. She did not appear conscious that she had done anything unusual in commanding his presence. He was apparently equally unconscious of anything extraordinary in the situation. But his face was suffused with a quiet glow when he met her.

They went together back to the kitchen to drink coffee. There was no time to wait for any nicety of service. They stood outside the window and the cook passed them their coffee and a roll, which they drank and ate from the windowsill. Edna said it tasted good. She had not thought of coffee nor of anything. He told her he had often noticed that she lacked forethought.

"Wasn't it enough to think of going to the *Chênière* and waking you up?" she laughed. "Do I have to think of everything?—as Léonce says when he's in a bad humor. I don't blame him; he'd never be in a bad humor if it weren't for me."

They took a short cut across the sands. At a distance they could see the curious procession moving toward the wharf—the lovers, shoulder to shoulder, creeping; the lady in black, gaining steadily upon them; old Monsieur Farival, losing ground inch by inch, and a young barefooted Spanish girl, with a red kerchief on her head and a basket on her arm, bringing up the rear.

Robert knew the girl, and he talked to her a little in the boat. No one present understood what they said. Her name was Mariequita. She had a round, sly, piquant face and pretty black eyes. Her hands were small, and she kept them folded over the handle of her basket. Her feet were broad and coarse. She did not strive to hide them. Edna looked at her feet, and noticed the sand and slime between her brown toes.

Beaudelet grumbled because Mariequita was there, taking up so much room. In reality he was annoyed at having old Monsieur Farival, who considered himself the better sailor of the two. But he would not quarrel with so old a man as Monsieur Farival, so he quarreled with Mariequita. The girl was deprecatory at one moment, appealing to Robert. She was saucy the next, moving her head up and down, making "eyes" at Robert and making "mouths" at Beaudelet.

The lovers were all alone. They saw nothing, they heard nothing. The lady in black was counting her beads for the third time. Old Monsieur Farival talked incessantly of what he knew about handling a boat, and of what Beaudelet did not know on the same subject.

Edna liked it all. She looked Mariequita up and down, from her ugly brown toes to her pretty black eyes, and back again.

"Why does she look at me like that?" inquired the girl of Robert.

"Maybe she thinks you are pretty. Shall I ask her?"

"No. Is she your sweetheart?"

"She's a married lady, and has two children."

"Oh! well! Francisco ran away with Sylvano's wife, who had four children. They took all his money and one of the children and stole his boat."

"Shut up!"

"Does she understand?"

"Oh, hush!"

"Are those two married over there—leaning on each other?"

"Of course not," laughed Robert.

"Of course not," echoed Mariequita, with a serious, confirmatory bob of the head.

The sun was high up and beginning to bite. The swift breeze seemed to Edna to bury the sting of it into the pores of her face and hands. Robert held his umbrella over her.

As they went cutting sidewise through the water, the sails bellied taut, with the wind filling and overflowing them. Old Monsieur Farival laughed sardonically at something as he looked at the sails, and Beaudelet swore at the old man under his breath.

Sailing across the bay to the *Chênière Caminada,* Edna felt as if she were being borne away from some anchorage which had held her fast, whose chains had been loosening—had snapped the night before when the mystic spirit was abroad, leaving her free to drift withersoever she chose to set her sails. Robert spoke to her incessantly; he no longer noticed Mariequita. The girl had shrimps in her bamboo basket. They were covered with Spanish moss. She beat the moss down impatiently, and muttered to herself sullenly.

"Let us go to Grande Terre[55] to-morrow," said Robert in a low voice.

"What shall we do there?"

"Climb up the hill to the old fort and look at the little wriggling gold snakes, and watch the lizards sun themselves."

She gazed away toward Grande Terre and thought she would like to be alone there with Robert, in the sun, listening to the ocean's roar and watching the slimy lizards writhe in and out among the ruins of the old fort.

"And the next day or the next we can sail to the Bayou Brulow,"[56] he went on.

"What shall we do there?"

"Anything—cast bait for fish."

"No; we'll go back to Grande Terre. Let the fish alone."

"We'll go wherever you like," he said. "I'll have Tonie come over and help me patch and trim my boat. We shall not need Beaudelet nor any one. Are you afraid of the pirogue?"[57]

"Oh, no."

"Then I'll take you some night in the pirogue when the moon shines. Maybe your Gulf spirit will whisper to you in which of these islands the treasures are hidden—direct you to the very spot, perhaps."

"And in a day we should be rich!" she laughed. "I'd give it all to you, the pirate gold and every bit of treasure we could dig up. I think you would know how to spend it. Pirate gold isn't a thing to be hoarded or utilized. It is something to squander and throw to the four winds, for the fun of seeing the golden specks fly."

[55] An island near Grand Isle, in the Gulf of Mexico.

[56] A village, built on raised platforms, in the marshlands of the Gulf Coast.

[57] Dugout canoe.

"We'd share it, and scatter it together," he said. His face flushed.

They all went together up to the quaint little Gothic church of Our Lady of Lourdes, gleaming all brown and yellow with paint in the sun's glare.

Only Beaudelet remained behind, tinkering at his boat, and Mariequita walked away with her basket of shrimps, casting a look of childish ill-humor and reproach at Robert from the corner of her eye.

XIII

A feeling of oppression and drowsiness overcame Edna during the service. Her head began to ache, and the lights on the altar swayed before her eyes. Another time she might have made an effort to regain her composure; but her one thought was to quit the stifling atmosphere of the church and reach the open air. She arose, climbing over Robert's feet with a muttered apology. Old Monsieur Farival, flurried, curious, stood up, but upon seeing that Robert had followed Mrs. Pontellier, he sank back into his seat. He whispered an anxious inquiry of the lady in black, who did not notice him or reply, but kept her eyes fastened upon the pages of her velvet prayer-book.

"I felt giddy and almost overcome," Edna said, lifting her hands instinctively to her head and pushing her straw hat up from her forehead. "I couldn't have stayed through the service." They were outside in the shadow of the church. Robert was full of solicitude.

"It was folly to have thought of going in the first place, let alone staying. Come over to Madame Antoine's; you can rest there." He took her arm and led her away, looking anxiously and continuously down into her face.

How still it was, with only the voice of the sea whispering through the reeds that grew in the salt-water pools! The long line of little gray, weather-beaten houses nestled peacefully among the orange trees. It must always have been God's day on that low, drowsy island, Edna thought. They stopped, leaning over a jagged fence made of sea-drift, to ask for water. A youth, a mild-faced Acadian,[58] was drawing water from the cistern, which was nothing more than a rusty buoy, with an opening on one side, sunk in the ground. The water which the youth handed to them in a tin pail was not cold to taste, but it was cool to her heated face, and it greatly revived and refreshed her.

Madame Antoine's cot[59] was at the far end of the village. She welcomed them with all the native hospitality, as she would have opened her door to let the sunlight in. She was fat, and walked heavily and clumsily across the floor. She could speak no English, but when Robert made her understand that the lady who accompanied him was ill and desired to rest, she was all eagerness to make Edna feel at home and to dispose of her comfortably.

The whole place was immaculately clean, and the big, four-poster bed, snow-white, invited one to repose. It stood in a small side room which looked out across a narrow grass plot toward the shed, where there was a disabled boat lying keel upward.

[58]A descendant of the French Canadians who were expelled in 1755 from Acadia (Nova Scotia) and migrated to the Louisiana Gulf Coast.

[59]Cottage.

Madame Antoine had not gone to mass. Her son Tonie had, but she supposed he would soon be back, and she invited Robert to be seated and wait for him. But he went and sat outside the door and smoked. Madame Antoine busied herself in the large front room preparing dinner. She was boiling mullets[60] over a few red coals in the huge fireplace.

Edna, left alone in the little side room, loosened her clothes, removing the greater part of them. She bathed her face, her neck and arms in the basin that stood between the windows. She took off her shoes and stockings and stretched herself in the very center of the high, white bed. How luxurious it felt to rest thus in a strange, quaint bed, with its sweet country odor of laurel lingering about the sheets and mattress! She stretched her strong limbs that ached a little. She ran her fingers through her loosened hair for a while. She looked at her round arms as she held them straight up and rubbed them one after the other, observing closely, as if it were something she saw for the first time, the fine, firm quality and texture of her flesh. She clasped her hands easily above her head, and it was thus she fell asleep.

She slept lightly at first, half awake and drowsily attentive to the things about her. She could hear Madame Antoine's heavy, scraping tread as she walked back and forth on the sanded floor. Some chickens were clucking outside the windows, scratching for bits of gravel in the grass. Later she half heard the voices of Robert and Tonie talking under the shed. She did not stir. Even her eyelids rested numb and heavily over her sleepy eyes. The voices went on—Tonie's slow, Acadian drawl, Robert's quick, soft, smooth French. She understood French imperfectly unless directly addressed, and the voices were only part of the other drowsy, muffled sounds lulling her senses.

When Edna awoke it was with the conviction that she had slept long and soundly. The voices were hushed under the shed. Madame Antoine's step was no longer to be heard in the adjoining room. Even the chickens had gone elsewhere to scratch and cluck. The mosquito bar was drawn over her; the old woman had come in while she slept and let down the bar.[61] Edna arose quietly from the bed, and looking between the curtains of the window, she saw by the slanting rays of the sun that the afternoon was far advanced. Robert was out there under the shed, reclining in the shade against the sloping keel of the overturned boat. He was reading from a book. Tonie was no longer with him. She wondered what had become of the rest of the party. She peeped out at him two or three times as she stood washing herself in the little basin between the windows.

Madame Antoine had laid some coarse, clean towels upon a chair, and had placed a box of *poudre de riz*[62] within easy reach. Edna dabbed the powder upon her nose and cheeks as she looked at herself closely in the little distorted mirror which hung on the wall above the basin. Her eyes were bright and wide awake and her face glowed.

When she had completed her toilet she walked into the adjoining room. She was very hungry. No one was there. But there was a cloth spread upon the table that stood against the wall, and a cover was laid for one, with a crusty brown loaf and a bottle of wine beside the plate. Edna bit a piece from the brown loaf, tearing it with her strong, white teeth. She poured some of the

[60]Fish. [61]Mosquito barrier made of fine netting.
[62]French: face-powder.

wine into the glass and drank it down. Then she went softly out of doors, and plucking an orange from the low-hanging bough of a tree, threw it at Robert, who did not know she was awake and up.

An illumination broke over his whole face when he saw her and joined her under the orange tree.

"How many years have I slept?" she inquired. "The whole island seems changed. A new race of beings must have sprung up, leaving only you and me as past relics. How many ages ago did Madame Antoine and Tonie die? and when did our people from Grand Isle disappear from the earth?"

He familiarly adjusted a ruffle upon her shoulder.

"You have slept precisely one hundred years. I was left here to guard your slumbers; and for one hundred years I have been out under the shed reading a book. The only evil I couldn't prevent was to keep a broiled fowl from drying up."

"If it has turned to stone, still will I eat it," said Edna, moving with him into the house. "But really, what has become of Monsieur Farival and the others?"

"Gone hours ago. When they found that you were sleeping they thought it best not to awake you. Any way, I wouldn't have let them. What was I here for?"

"I wonder if Léonce will be uneasy!" she speculated, as she seated herself at table.

"Of course not; he knows you are with me," Robert replied, as he busied himself among sundry pans and covered dishes which had been left standing on the hearth.

"Where are Madame Antoine and her son?" asked Edna.

"Gone to Vespers,[63] and to visit some friends, I believe. I am to take you back in Tonie's boat whenever you are ready to go."

He stirred the smoldering ashes till the broiled fowl began to sizzle afresh. He served her with no mean repast, dripping[64] the coffee anew and sharing it with her. Madame Antoine had cooked little else than the mullets, but while Edna slept Robert had foraged the island. He was childishly gratified to discover her appetite, and to see the relish with which she ate the food which he had procured for her.

"Shall we go right away?" she asked, after draining her glass and brushing together the crumbs of the crusty loaf.

"The sun isn't as low as it will be in two hours," he answered.

"The sun will be gone in two hours."

"Well, let it go; who cares!"

They waited a good while under the orange trees, till Madame Antoine came back, panting, waddling, with a thousand apologies to explain her absence. Tonie did not dare to return. He was shy, and would not willingly face any woman except his mother.

It was very pleasant to stay there under the orange trees, while the sun dipped lower and lower, turning the western sky to flaming copper and gold. The shadows lengthened and crept out like stealthy, grotesque monsters across the grass.

Edna and Robert both sat upon the ground—that is, he lay upon the ground beside her, occasionally picking at the hem of her muslin gown.

Madame Antoine seated her fat body, broad and squat, upon a bench beside the door. She had been talking all the afternoon, and had wound herself up to the story-telling pitch.

[63]Evening church service. [64]Brewing.

And what stories she told them! But twice in her life she had left the *Chênière Caminada,* and then for the briefest span. All her years she had squatted and waddled there upon the island, gathering legends of the Baratarians[65] and the sea. The night came on, with the moon to lighten it. Edna could hear the whispering voices of dead men and the click of muffled gold.

When she and Robert stepped into Tonie's boat, with the red lateen sail, misty spirit forms were prowling in the shadows and among the reeds, and upon the water were phantom ships, speeding to cover.

XIV

The youngest boy, Etienne, had been very naughty, Madame Ratignolle said, as she delivered him into the hands of his mother. He had been unwilling to go to bed and had made a scene; whereupon she had taken charge of him and pacified him as well as she could. Raoul had been in bed and asleep for two hours.

The youngster was in his long white nightgown, that kept tripping him up as Madame Ratignolle led him along by the hand. With the other chubby fist he rubbed his eyes, which were heavy with sleep and ill humor. Edna took him in her arms, and seating herself in the rocker, began to coddle and caress him, calling him all manner of tender names, soothing him to sleep.

It was not more than nine o'clock. No one had yet gone to bed but the children.

Léonce had been very uneasy at first, Madame Ratignolle said, and had wanted to start at once for the *Chênière.* But Monsieur Farival had assured him that his wife was only overcome with sleep and fatigue, that Tonie would bring her safely back later in the day; and he had thus been dissuaded from crossing the bay. He had gone over to Klein's, looking up some cotton broker whom he wished to see in regard to securities, exchanges, stocks, bonds, or something of the sort, Madame Ratignolle did not remember what. He said he would not remain away late. She herself was suffering from heat and oppression, she said. She carried a bottle of salts and a large fan. She would not consent to remain with Edna, for Monsieur Ratignolle was alone, and he detested above all things to be left alone.

When Etienne had fallen asleep Edna bore him into the back room, and Robert went and lifted the mosquito bar that she might lay the child comfortably in his bed. The quadroon had vanished. When they emerged from the cottage Robert bade Edna good-night.

"Do you know we have been together the whole livelong day, Robert—since early this morning?" she said at parting.

"All but the hundred years when you were sleeping. Good-night."

He pressed her hand and went away in the direction of the beach. He did not join any of the others, but walked alone toward the Gulf.

Edna stayed outside, awaiting her husband's return. She had no desire to sleep or to retire; nor did she feel like going over to sit with the Ratignolles, or to join Madame Lebrun and a group whose animated voices reached here as they sat in conversation before the house. She let her mind wander back over

[65]Those who lived on Barataria Bay, an inlet of the Gulf of Mexico near the mouth of the Mississippi. In earlier days, it was a refuge for smugglers and pirates.

her stay at Grand Isle; and she tried to discover wherein this summer had been different from any and every other summer of her life. She could only realize that she herself—her present self—was in some way different from the other self. That she was seeing with different eyes and making the acquaintance of new conditions in herself that colored and changed her environment, she did not yet suspect.

She wondered why Robert had gone away and left her. It did not occur to her to think he might have grown tired of being with her the livelong day. She was not tired, and she felt that he was not. She regretted that he had gone. It was so much more natural to have him stay when he was not absolutely required to leave her.

As Edna waited for her husband she sang low a little song that Robert had sung as they crossed the bay. It began with "Ah! *Si tu savais,*"[66] and every verse ended with *"si tu savais."*

Robert's voice was not pretentious. It was musical and true. The voice, the notes, the whole refrain haunted her memory.

XV

When Edna entered the dining-room one evening a little late, as was her habit, an unusually animated conversation seemed to be going on. Several persons were talking at once, and Victor's voice was predominating, even over that of his mother. Edna had returned late from her bath, had dressed in some haste, and her face was flushed. Her head, set off by her dainty white gown, suggested a rich, rare blossom. She took her seat at table between old Monsieur Farival and Madame Ratignolle.

As she seated herself and was about to begin to eat her soup, which had been served when she entered the room, several persons informed her simultaneously that Robert was going to Mexico. She laid her spoon down and looked about her bewildered. He had been with her, reading to her all the morning, and had never even mentioned such a place as Mexico. She had not seen him during the afternoon; she had heard some one say he was at the house, upstairs with his mother. This she had thought nothing of, though she was surprised when he did not join her later in the afternoon, when she went down to the beach.

She looked across at him, where he sat beside Madame Lebrun, who presided. Edna's face was a blank picture of bewilderment, which she never thought of disguising. He lifted his eyebrows with the pretext of a smile as he returned her glance. He looked embarrassed and uneasy.

"When is he going?" she asked of everybody in general, as if Robert were not there to answer for himself.

"To-night!" "This very evening!" "Did you ever!" "What possesses him!" were some of the replies she gathered, uttered simultaneously in French and English.

"Impossible!" she exclaimed. "How can a person start off from Grand Isle to Mexico at a moment's notice, as if he were going over to Klein's or to the wharf or down to the beach?"

[66]French: "Couldst thou but know," the title of a song by the Irish composer Michael Balfe (1808–1870).

"I said all along I was going to Mexico; I've been saying so for years!" cried Robert, in an excited and irritable tone, with the air of a man defending himself against a swarm of stinging insects.

Madame Lebrun knocked on the table with her knife handle.

"Please let Robert explain why he is going, and why he is going to-night," she called out. "Really, this table is getting to be more and more like Bedlam[67] every day, with everybody talking at once. Sometimes—I hope God will forgive me—but positively, sometimes I wish Victor would lose the power of speech."

Victor laughed sardonically as he thanked his mother for her holy wish, of which he failed to see the benefit to anybody, except that it might afford her a more ample opportunity and license to talk herself.

Monsieur Farival thought that Victor should have been taken out in midocean in his earliest youth and drowned. Victor thought there would be more logic in thus disposing of old people with an established claim for making themselves universally obnoxious. Madame Lebrun grew a trifle hysterical; Robert called his brother some sharp, hard names.

"There's nothing much to explain, mother," he said; though he explained, nevertheless—looking chiefly at Edna—that he could only meet the gentleman whom he intended to join at Vera Cruz by taking such and such a steamer, which left New Orleans on such a day; that Beaudelet was going out with his lugger-load of vegetables that night, which gave him an opportunity of reaching the city and making his vessel in time.

"But when did you make up your mind to all this?" demanded Monsieur Farival.

"This afternoon," returned Robert, with a shade of annoyance.

"At what time this afternoon?" persisted the old gentleman, with nagging determination, as if he were cross-questioning a criminal in a court of justice.

"At four o'clock this afternoon, Monsieur Farival," Robert replied, in a high voice and with a lofty air, which reminded Edna of some gentleman on the stage.

She had forced herself to eat most of her soup, and now she was picking the flaky bits of a *court bouillon*[68] with her fork.

The lovers were profiting by the general conversation on Mexico to speak in whispers of matters which they rightly considered were interesting to no one but themselves. The lady in black had once received a pair of prayerbeads of curious workmanship from Mexico, with very special indulgence[69] attached to them, but she had never been able to ascertain whether the indulgence extended outside the Mexican border. Father Fochel of the Cathedral had attempted to explain it; but he had not done so to her satisfaction. And she begged that Robert would interest himself, and discover, if possible, whether she was entitled to the indulgence accompanying the remarkably curious Mexican prayer-beads.

Madame Ratignolle hoped that Robert would exercise extreme caution in dealing with the Mexicans, who, she considered, were a treacherous people, unscrupulous and revengeful. She trusted she did them no injustice in thus condemning them as a race. She had known personally but one Mexican, who made and sold excellent tamales, and whom she would have trusted implicitly, so soft-spoken was he. One day he was arrested for stabbing his wife. She never knew whether he had been hanged or not.

[67]A lunatic asylum. [68]Fish cooked in a highly seasoned sauce.
[69]Power to release one from the punishments due for sins.

Victor had grown hilarious, and was attempting to tell an anecdote about a Mexican girl who served chocolate one winter in a restaurant in Dauphine Street. No one would listen to him but old Monsieur Farival, who went into convulsions over the droll story.

Edna wondered if they had all gone mad, to be talking and clamoring at that rate. She herself could think of nothing to say about Mexico or the Mexicans.

"At what time do you leave?" she asked Robert.

"At ten," he told her. "Beaudelet wants to wait for the moon."

"Are you all ready to go?"

"Quite ready. I shall only take a hand-bag, and shall pack my trunk in the city."

He turned to answer some question put to him by his mother, and Edna, having finished her black coffee, left the table.

She went directly to her room. The little cottage was close and stuffy after leaving the outer air. But she did not mind; there appeared to be a hundred different things demanding her attention indoors. She began to set the toilet-stand to rights, grumbling at the negligence of the quadroon, who was in the adjoining room putting the children to bed. She gathered together stray garments that were hanging on the backs of chairs, and put each where it belonged in closet or bureau drawer. She changed her gown for a more comfortable and commodious wrapper. She rearranged her hair, combing and brushing it with unusual energy. Then she went in and assisted the quadroon in getting the boys to bed.

They were very playful and inclined to talk—to do anything but lie quiet and go to sleep. Edna sent the quadroon away to her supper and told her she need not return. Then she sat and told the children a story. Instead of soothing it excited them, and added to their wakefulness. She left them in heated argument, speculating about the conclusion of the tale which their mother promised to finish the following night.

The little black girl came in to say that Madame Lebrun would like to have Mrs. Pontellier go and sit with them over at the house till Mr. Robert went away. Edna returned answer that she had already undressed, that she did not feel quite well, but perhaps she would go over to the house later. She started to dress again, and got as far advanced as to remove her *peignoir.* But changing her mind once more she resumed the *peignoir,* and went outside and sat down before her door. She was over-heated and irritable, and fanned herself energetically for a while. Madame Ratignolle came down to discover what was the matter.

"All that noise and confusion at the table must have upset me," replied Edna, "and moreover, I hate shocks and surprises. The idea of Robert starting off in such a ridiculously sudden and dramatic way! As if it were a matter of life and death! Never saying a word about it all morning when he was with me."

"Yes," agreed Madame Ratignolle. "I think it was showing us all—you especially—very little consideration. It wouldn't have surprised me in any of the others; those Lebruns are all given to heroics. But I must say I should never have expected such a thing from Robert. Are you not coming down? Come on, dear; it doesn't look friendly."

"No," said Edna, a little sullenly. "I can't go to the trouble of dressing again; I don't feel like it."

"You needn't dress; you look all right; fasten a belt around your waist. Just look at me!"

"No," persisted Edna; "but you go on. Madame Lebrun might be offended if we both stayed away."

Madame Ratignolle kissed Edna good-night, and went away, being in truth rather desirous of joining in the general and animated conversation which was still in progress concerning Mexico and the Mexicans.

Somewhat later Robert came up, carrying his hand-bag.

"Aren't you feeling well?" he asked.

"Oh, well enough. Are you going right away?"

He lit a match and looked at his watch. "In twenty minutes," he said. The sudden and brief flare of the match emphasized the darkness for a while. He sat down upon a stool which the children had left out on the porch.

"Get a chair," said Edna.

"This will do," he replied. He put on his soft hat and nervously took it off again, and wiping his face with his handkerchief, complained of the heat.

"Take the fan," said Edna, offering it to him.

"Oh, no! Thank you. It does no good; you have to stop fanning some time, and feel all the more uncomfortable afterward."

"That's one of the ridiculous things which men always say. I have never known one to speak otherwise of fanning. How long will you be gone?"

"Forever, perhaps. I don't know. It depends upon a good many things."

"Well, in case it shouldn't be forever, how long will it be?"

"I don't know."

"This seems to me perfectly preposterous and uncalled for. I don't like it. I don't understand your motive for silence and mystery, never saying a word to me about it this morning." He remained silent, not offering to defend himself. He only said, after a moment:

"Don't part from me in an ill-humor. I never knew you to be out of patience with me before."

"I don't want to part in any ill-humor," she said. "But can't you understand? I've grown used to seeing you, to having you with me all the time, and your action seems unfriendly, even unkind. You don't even offer an excuse for it. Why, I was planning to be together, thinking of how pleasant it would be to see you in the city next winter."

"So was I," he blurted. "Perhaps that's the—" He stood up suddenly and held out his hand. "Good-by, my dear Mrs. Pontellier; good-by. You won't—I hope you won't completely forget me." She clung to his hand, striving to detain him.

"Write to me when you get there, won't you, Robert?" she entreated.

"I will, thank you. Good-by."

How unlike Robert! The merest acquaintance would have said something more emphatic than "I will, thank you; good-by," to such a request.

He had evidently already taken leave of the people over at the house, for he descended the steps and went to join Beaudelet, who was out there with an oar across his shoulder waiting for Robert. They walked away in the darkness. She could only hear Beaudelet's voice; Robert had apparently not even spoken a word of greeting to his companion.

Edna bit her handkerchief convulsively, striving to hold back and to hide, even from herself as she would have hidden from another, the emotion which was troubling—tearing—her. Her eyes were brimming with tears.

For the first time she recognized anew the symptoms of infatuation which she had felt incipiently as a child, as a girl in her earliest teens, and later as a young woman. The recognition did not lessen the reality, the poignancy of the revelation by any suggestion or promise of instability. The past was nothing to her;

offered no lesson which she was willing to heed. The future was a mystery which she never attempted to penetrate. The present alone was significant; was hers, to torture her as it was doing then with the biting conviction that she had lost that which she had held, that she had been denied that which her impassioned, newly awakened being demanded.

XVI

"Do you miss your friend greatly?" asked Mademoiselle Reisz one morning as she came creeping up behind Edna, who had just left her cottage on her way to the beach. She spent much of her time in the water since she had acquired finally the art of swimming. As their stay at Grand Isle drew near its close, she felt that she could not give too much time to a diversion which afforded her the only real pleasurable moments that she knew. When Mademoiselle Reisz came and touched her upon the shoulder and spoke to her, the woman seemed to echo the thought which was ever in Edna's mind; or better, the feeling which constantly possessed her.

Robert's going had some way taken the brightness, the color, the meaning out of everything. The conditions of her life were in no way changed, but her whole existence was dulled, like a faded garment which seems to be no longer worth wearing. She sought him everywhere—in others whom she induced to talk about him. She went up in the mornings to Madame Lebrun's room, braving the clatter of the old sewing-machine. She sat there and chatted at intervals as Robert had done. She gazed around the room at the pictures and photographs hanging upon the wall, and discovered in some corner an old family album, which she examined with the keenest interest, appealing to Madame Lebrun for enlightenment concerning the many figures and faces which she discovered between its pages.

There was a picture of Madame Lebrun with Robert as a baby, seated in her lap, a round-faced infant with a fist in his mouth. The eyes alone in the baby suggested the man. And that was he also in kilts, at the age of five, wearing long curls and holding a whip in his hand. It made Edna laugh, and she laughed, too, at the portrait in his first long trousers; while another interested her, taken when he left for college, looking thin, long-faced, with eyes full of fire, ambition and great intentions. But there was no recent picture, none which suggested the Robert who had gone away five days ago, leaving a void and wilderness behind him.

"Oh, Robert stopped having his pictures taken when he had to pay for them himself! He found wiser use for his money, he says," explained Madame Lebrun. She had a letter from him, written before he left New Orleans. Edna wished to see the letter, and Madame Lebrun told her to look for it either on the table or the dresser, or perhaps it was on the mantelpiece.

The letter was on the bookshelf. It possessed the greatest interest and attraction for Edna; the envelope, its size and shape, the post-mark, the handwriting. She examined every detail of the outside before opening it. There were only a few lines, setting forth that he would leave the city that afternoon, that he had packed his trunk in good shape, that he was well, and sent her his love and begged to be affectionately remembered to all. There was no special message to Edna except a postscript saying that if Mrs. Pontellier desired to finish the book which he had been reading to her, his mother would find it in his room, among other books there on the table. Edna experienced a pang of jealousy because he had written to his mother rather than to her.

Every one seemed to take for granted that she missed him. Even her husband, when he came down the Saturday following Robert's departure, expressed regret that he had gone.

"How do you get on without him, Edna?" he asked.

"It's very dull without him," she admitted. Mr. Pontellier had seen Robert in the city, and Edna asked him a dozen questions or more. Where had they met? On Carondelet Street, in the morning. They had gone "in" and had a drink and a cigar together. What had they talked about? Chiefly about his prospects in Mexico, which Mr. Pontellier thought were promising. How did he look? How did he seem—grave, or gay, or how? Quite cheerful, and wholly taken up with the idea of his trip, which Mr. Pontellier found altogether natural in a young fellow about to seek fortune and adventure in a strange, queer country.

Edna tapped her foot impatiently, and wondered why the children persisted in playing in the sun when they might be under the trees. She went down and led them out of the sun, scolding the quadroon for not being more attentive.

It did not strike her as in the least grotesque that she should be making of Robert the object of conversation and leading her husband to speak of him. The sentiment which she entertained for Robert in no way resembled that which she felt for her husband, or had ever felt, or ever expected to feel. She had all her life long been accustomed to harbor thoughts and emotions which never voiced themselves. They had never taken the form of struggles. They belonged to her and were her own, and she entertained the conviction that she had a right to them and that they concerned no one but herself. Edna had once told Madame Ratignolle that she would never sacrifice herself for her children, or for any one. Then had followed a rather heated argument; the two women did not appear to understand each other or to be talking the same language. Edna tried to appease her friend, to explain.

"I would give up the unessential; I would give my money, I would give my life for my children; but I wouldn't give myself. I can't make it more clear; it's only something which I am beginning to comprehend, which is revealing itself to me."

"I don't know what you would call the essential, or what you mean by the unessential," said Madame Ratignolle, cheerfully; "but a woman who would give her life for her children could do no more than that—your Bible tells you so. I'm sure I couldn't do more than that."

"Oh, yes you could!" laughed Edna.

She was not surprised at Mademoiselle Reisz's question the morning that lady, following her to the beach, tapped her on the shoulder and asked if she did not greatly miss her young friend.

"Oh, good morning, Mademoiselle; is it you? Why, of course I miss Robert. Are you going down to bathe?"

"Why should I go down to bathe at the very end of the season when I haven't been in the surf all summer," replied the woman, disagreeably.

"I beg your pardon," offered Edna, in some embarrassment, for she should have remembered that Mademoiselle Reisz's avoidance of the water had furnished a theme for much pleasantry. Some among them thought it was on account of her false hair, or the dread of getting the violets wet, while others attributed it to the natural aversion for water sometimes believed to accompany the artistic temperament. Mademoiselle offered Edna some chocolates in a paper bag, which she took from her pocket, by way of showing that she bore no ill feeling. She habitually ate chocolates for their sustaining quality; they contained much nutriment in small compass, she said. They saved her from starvation, as Madame Lebrun's table was utterly impossible; and no one save so impertinent a woman as Madame Lebrun could think of offering such food to people and requiring them to pay for it.

"She must feel very lonely without her son," said Edna, desiring to change the subject. "Her favorite son, too. It must have been quite hard to let him go."

Mademoiselle laughed maliciously.

"Her favorite son! Oh, dear! Who could have been imposing such a tale upon you? Aline Lebrun lives for Victor, and for Victor alone. She has spoiled him into the worthless creature he is. She worships him and the ground he walks on. Robert is very well in a way, to give up all the money he can earn to the family, and keep the barest pittance for himself. Favorite son, indeed! I miss the poor fellow myself, my dear. I liked to see him and to hear him about the place—the only Lebrun who is worth a pinch of salt. He comes to see me often in the city. I like to play to him. That Victor! hanging would be too good for him. It's a wonder Robert hasn't beaten him to death long ago."

"I thought he had great patience with his brother," offered Edna, glad to be talking about Robert, no matter what was said.

"Oh! he thrashed him well enough a year or two ago," said Mademoiselle. "It was about a Spanish girl whom Victor considered that he had some sort of claim upon. He met Robert one day talking to the girl, or walking with her, or bathing with her, or carrying her basket—I don't remember what;—and he became so insulting and abusive that Robert gave him a thrashing on the spot that has kept him comparatively in order for a good while. It's about time he was getting another."

"Was her name Mariequita?" asked Edna.

"Mariequita—yes, that was it; Mariequita. I had forgotten. Oh, she's a sly one, and a bad one, that Mariequita!"

Edna looked down at Mademoiselle Reisz and wondered how she could have listened to her venom so long. For some reason she felt depressed, almost unhappy. She had not intended to go into the water; but she donned her bathing suit, and left Mademoiselle alone, seated under the shade of the children's tent. The water was growing cooler as the season advanced. Edna plunged and swam about with an abandon that thrilled and invigorated her. She remained a long time in the water, half hoping that Mademoiselle Reisz would not wait for her.

But Mademoiselle waited. She was very amiable during the walk back, and raved much over Edna's appearance in her bathing suit. She talked about music. She hoped that Edna would go to see her in the city, and wrote her address with the stub of a pencil on a piece of card which she found in her pocket.

"When do you leave?" asked Edna.

"Next Monday; and you?"

"The following week," answered Edna, adding, "It has been a pleasant summer, hasn't it, Mademoiselle?"

"Well," agreed Mademoiselle Reisz, with a shrug, "rather pleasant, if it hadn't been for the mosquitoes and the Farival twins."

XVII

The Pontelliers possessed a very charming home on Esplanade Street[70] in New Orleans. It was a large, double cottage, with a broad front veranda, whose round, fluted columns supported the sloping roof. The house was painted a dazzling white; the outside shutters, or jalousies, were green. In the yard, which was kept scrupulously neat, were flowers and plants of every description which flourish in South Louisiana. Within doors the appointments were perfect after the conventional type. The softest carpets and rugs covered the floors; rich and tasteful draperies hung at doors and windows. There were paintings, selected with judgment and discrimination, upon the walls. The cut glass, the silver, the heavy damask which daily appeared upon the table were the envy of many women whose husbands were less generous than Mr. Pontellier.

Mr. Pontellier was very fond of walking about his house examining its various appointments and details, to see that nothing was amiss. He greatly valued his possessions, chiefly because they were his, and derived genuine pleasure from contemplating a painting, a statuette, a rare lace curtain—no matter what—after he had bought it and placed it among his household goods.

On Tuesday afternoons—Tuesday being Mrs. Pontellier's reception day[71]—there was a constant stream of callers—women who came in carriages or in the street cars, or walked when the air was soft and distance permitted. A light-colored mulatto boy, in dress coat and bearing a diminutive silver tray for the reception of cards, admitted them. A maid, in white fluted cap, offered the callers liqueur, coffee, or chocolate, as they might desire. Mrs. Pontellier, attired in a handsome reception gown, remained in the drawing-room the entire afternoon receiving her visitors. Men sometimes called in the evening with their wives.

This had been the programme which Mrs. Pontellier had religiously followed since her marriage, six years before. Certain evenings during the week she and her husband attended the opera or sometimes the play.

Mr. Pontellier left his home in the mornings between nine and ten o'clock, and rarely returned before half-past six or seven in the evening—dinner being served at half-past seven.

He and his wife seated themselves at table one Tuesday evening, a few weeks after their return from Grand Isle. They were alone together. The boys were being put to bed; the patter of their bare, escaping feet could be heard occasionally, as well as the pursuing voice of the quadroon, lifted in mild protest and entreaty. Mrs. Pontellier did not wear her usual Tuesday reception gown; she was in ordinary house dress. Mr. Pontellier, who was observant about such things, noticed it, as he served the soup and handled it to the boy in waiting.

"Tired out, Edna? Whom did you have? Many callers?" he asked. He tasted his soup and began to season it with pepper, salt, vinegar, mustard—everything within reach.

"There were a good many," replied Edna, who was eating her soup with evident satisfaction. "I found their cards when I got home; I was out."

[70]A fashionable street, lined with the elegant homes of the rich and socially prominent.

[71]That day, each week, when an upper-class woman received visitors in her home. To be "out" to a visitor calling on "reception day" was a great insult.

"Out!" exclaimed her husband, with something like genuine consternation in his voice as he laid down the vinegar cruet and looked at her through his glasses. "Why, what could have taken you out on Tuesday? What did you have to do?"

"Nothing. I simply felt like going out, and I went out."

"Well, I hope you left some suitable excuse," said her husband, somewhat appeased, as he added a dash of cayenne pepper to the soup.

"No, I left no excuse. I told Joe to say I was out, that was all."

"Why, my dear, I should think you'd understand by this time that people don't do such things; we've got to observe *les convenances*[72] if we ever expect to get on and keep up with the procession. If you felt that you had to leave home this afternoon, you should have left some suitable explanation for your absence.

"This soup is really impossible; it's strange that woman hasn't learned yet to make a decent soup. Any free-lunch stand in town serves a better one. Was Mrs. Belthrop here?"

"Bring the tray with the cards, Joe. I don't remember who was here."

The boy retired and returned after a moment, bringing the tiny silver tray, which was covered with ladies' visiting cards. He handed it to Mrs. Pontellier.

"Give it to Mr. Pontellier," she said.

Joe offered the tray to Mr. Pontellier, and removed the soup.

Mr. Pontellier scanned the names of his wife's callers, reading some of them aloud, with comments as he read.

"'The Misses Delasidas.' I worked a big deal in futures[73] for their father this morning; nice girls; it's time they were getting married. 'Mrs. Belthrop.' I tell you what it is, Edna; you can't afford to snub Mrs. Belthrop. Why, Belthrop could buy and sell us ten times over. His business is worth a good, round sum to me. You'd better write her a note. 'Mrs. James Highcamp.' Hugh! the less you have to do with Mrs. Highcamp, the better. 'Madame Laforcé.' Came all the way from Carrolton,[74] too, poor old soul. 'Miss Wiggs.' 'Mrs. Eleanor Boltons.'" He pushed the cards aside.

"Mercy!" exclaimed Edna, who had been fuming. "Why are you taking the thing so seriously and making such a fuss over it?"

"I'm not making any fuss over it. But it's just such seeming trifles that we've got to take seriously; such things count."

The fish was scorched. Mr. Pontellier would not touch it. Edna said she did not mind a little scorched taste. The roast was in some way not to his fancy, and he did not like the manner in which the vegetables were served.

"It seems to me," he said, "we spend money enough in this house to procure at least one meal a day which a man could eat and retain his self-respect."

"You used to think the cook was a treasure," returned Edna, indifferently.

"Perhaps she was when she first came; but cooks are only human. They need looking after, like any other class of persons that you employ. Suppose I didn't look after the clerks in my office, just let them run things their own way; they'd soon make a nice mess of me and my business."

[72]French: "the social conventions."

[73]Speculative purchase of stocks or other commodities, bought now for future delivery when, it is hoped, their value will have risen.

[74]A western section of New Orleans. Formerly a separate village, it was absorbed by the city in 1874.

"Where are you going?" asked Edna, seeing that her husband arose from table without having eaten a morsel except a taste of the highly-seasoned soup.

"I'm going to get my dinner at the club. Good night." He went into the hall, took his hat and stick from the stand, and left the house.

She was somewhat familiar with such scenes. They had often made her very unhappy. On a few previous occasions she had been completely deprived of any desire to finish her dinner. Sometimes she had gone into the kitchen to administer a tardy rebuke to the cook. Once she went to her room and studied the cookbook during an entire evening, finally writing out a menu for the week, which left her harassed with a feeling that, after all, she had accomplished no good that was worth the name.

But that evening Edna finished her dinner alone, with forced deliberation. Her face was flushed and her eyes flamed with some inward fire that lighted them. After finishing her dinner she went to her room, having instructed the boy to tell any other callers that she was indisposed.

It was a large, beautiful room, rich and picturesque in the soft, dim light which the maid had turned low. She went and stood at an open window and looked out upon the deep tangle of the garden below. All the mystery and witchery of the night seemed to have gathered there amid the perfumes and the dusky and tortuous outlines of flowers and foliage. She was seeking herself and finding herself in just such sweet, half-darkness which met her moods. But the voices were not soothing that came to her from the darkness and the sky above and the stars. They jeered and sounded mournful notes without promise, devoid even of hope. She turned back into the room and began to walk to and fro down its whole length, without stopping, without resting. She carried in her hands a thin handkerchief, which she tore into ribbons, rolled into a ball, and flung from her. Once she stopped, and taking off her wedding ring, flung it upon the carpet. When she saw it lying there, she stamped her heel upon it, striving to crush it. But her small boot heel did not make an indenture, not a mark upon the little glittering circlet.

In a sweeping passion she seized a glass vase from the table and flung it upon the tiles of the hearth. She wanted to destroy something. The crash and clatter were what she wanted to hear.

A maid, alarmed at the din of breaking glass, entered the room to discover what was the matter.

"A vase fell upon the hearth," said Edna. "Never mind; leave it till morning."

"Oh! you might get some of the glass in your feet, ma'am," insisted the young woman, picking up bits of the broken vase that were scattered upon the carpet. "And here's your ring, ma'am, under the chair."

Edna held out her hand, and taking the ring, slipped it upon her finger.

XVIII

The following morning Mr. Pontellier, upon leaving for his office, asked Edna if she would not meet him in town in order to look at some new fixtures for the library.

"I hardly think we need new fixtures, Léonce. Don't let us get anything new; you are too extravagant. I don't believe you ever think of saving or putting by."

"The way to become rich is to make money, my dear Edna, not to save it," he said. He regretted that she did not feel inclined to go with him and select new fixtures. He kissed her good-by, and told her she was not looking well and must take care of herself. She was unusually pale and very quiet.

She stood on the front veranda as he quitted the house, and absently picked a few sprays of jessamine[75] that grew upon a trellis near by. She inhaled the odor of the blossoms and thrust them into the bosom of her white morning gown. The boys were dragging along the banquette[76] a small "express wagon," which they had filled with blocks and sticks. The quadroon was following them with little quick steps, having assumed a fictitious animation and alacrity for the occasion. A fruit vender was crying his wares in the street.

Edna looked straight before her with a self-absorbed expression upon her face. She felt no interest in anything about her. The street, the children, the fruit vender, the flowers growing there under her eyes, were all part and parcel of an alien world which had suddenly become antagonistic.

She went back into the house. She had thought of speaking to the cook concerning her blunders of the previous night; but Mr. Pontellier had saved her that disagreeable mission, for which she was so poorly fitted. Mr. Pontellier's arguments were usually convincing with those whom he employed. He left home feeling quite sure that he and Edna would sit down that evening, and possibly a few subsequent evenings, to a dinner deserving of the name.

Edna spent an hour or two in looking over some of her old sketches. She could see their shortcomings and defects, which were glaring in her eyes. She tried to work a little, but found she was not in the humor. Finally she gathered together a few of the sketches—those which she considered the least discreditable; and she carried them with her when, a little later, she dressed and left the house. She looked handsome and distinguished in her street gown. The tan of the seashore had left her face, and her forehead was smooth, white, and polished beneath her heavy, yellow-brown hair. There were a few freckles on her face, and a small dark mole near the under lip and one on the temple, half-hidden in her hair.

As Edna walked along the street she was thinking of Robert. She was still under the spell of her infatuation. She had tried to forget him, realizing the inutility of remembering. But the thought of him was like an obsession, ever pressing itself upon her. It was not that she dwelt upon details of their acquaintance, or recalled in any special or peculiar way his personality; it was his being, his existence, which dominated her thought, fading sometimes as if it would melt into the mist of the forgotten, reviving again with an intensity which filled her with an incomprehensible longing.

Edna was on her way to Madame Ratignolle's. Their intimacy, begun at Grand Isle, had not declined, and they had seen each other with some frequency since their return to the city. The Ratignolles lived at no great distance from Edna's home, on the corner of a side street, where Monsieur Ratignolle owned and conducted a drug store which enjoyed a steady and prosperous trade. His father had been in the business before him, and Monsieur Ratignolle stood well in the community and bore an enviable reputation for integrity and clear-headedness. His family lived in commodious apartments over the store,

[75]Jasmine. [76]Sidewalk.

having an entrance on the side within the *porte cochère*.[77] There was something which Edna thought very French, very foreign, about their whole manner of living. In the large and pleasant salon which extended across the width of the house, the Ratignolles entertained their friends once a fortnight with a *soirée musicale*,[78] sometimes diversified by card-playing. There was a friend who played upon the 'cello. One brought his flute and another his violin, while there were some who sang and a number who performed upon the piano with various degrees of taste and agility. The Ratignolles' *soirées musicales* were widely known, and it was considered a privilege to be invited to them.

Edna found her friend engaged in assorting the clothes which had returned that morning from the laundry. She at once abandoned her occupation upon seeing Edna, who had been ushered without ceremony into her presence.

" 'Cité can do it as well as I; it is really her business," she explained to Edna, who apologized for interrupting her. And she summoned a young black woman, whom she instructed, in French, to be very careful in checking off the list which she handed her. She told her to notice particularly if a fine linen handkerchief of Monsieur Ratignolle's, which was missing last week, had been returned; and to be sure to set to one side such pieces as required mending and darning.

Then placing an arm around Edna's waist, she led her to the front of the house, to the salon, where it was cool and sweet with the odor of great roses that stood upon the hearth in jars.

Madame Ratignolle looked more beautiful than ever there at home, in a negligé which left her arms almost wholly bare and exposed the rich, melting curves of her white throat.

"Perhaps I shall be able to paint your picture some day," said Edna with a smile when they were seated. She produced the roll of sketches and started to unfold them. "I believe I ought to work again. I feel as if I wanted to be doing something. What do you think of them? Do you think it worth while to take it up again and study some more? I might study for a while with Laidpore."

She knew that Madame Ratignolle's opinion in such a matter would be next to valueless, that she herself had not alone decided, but determined; but she sought the words of praise and encouragement that would help her to put heart into her venture.

"Your talent is immense, dear!"

"Nonsense!" protested Edna, well pleased.

"Immense, I tell you," persisted Madame Ratignolle, surveying the sketches one by one, at close range, then holding them at arm's length, narrowing her eyes, and dropping her head on one side. "Surely, this Bavarian peasant is worthy of framing; and this basket of apples! never have I seen anything more lifelike. One might almost be tempted to reach out a hand and take one."

Edna could not control a feeling which bordered upon complacency at her friend's praise, even realizing, as she did, its true worth. She retained a few of the sketches, and gave all the rest to Madame Ratignolle, who appreciated the gift far beyond its value and proudly exhibited the pictures to her husband when he came up from the store a little later for his midday dinner.

[77]A carriage entrance with a porch roof to protect passengers from the weather.
[78]An evening musical party.

Mr. Ratignolle was one of those men who are called the salt of the earth. His cheerfulness was unbounded, and it was matched by his goodness of heart, his broad charity, and common sense. He and his wife spoke English with an accent which was only discernible through its un-English emphasis and a certain carefulness and deliberation. Edna's husband spoke English with no accent whatever. The Ratignolles understood each other perfectly. If ever the fusion of two human beings into one has been accomplished on this sphere it was surely in their union.

As Edna seated herself at table with them she thought, "Better a dinner of herbs,"[79] though it did not take her long to discover that [it] was no dinner of herbs, but a delicious repast, simple, choice, and in every way satisfying.

Monsieur Ratignolle was delighted to see her, though he found her looking not so well as at Grand Isle, and he advised a tonic. He talked a good deal on various topics, a little politics, some city news and neighborhood gossip. He spoke with an animation and earnestness that gave an exaggerated importance to every syllable he uttered. His wife was keenly interested in everything he said, laying down her fork the better to listen, chiming in, taking the words out of his mouth.

Edna felt depressed rather than soothed after leaving them. The little glimpse of domestic harmony which had been offered her, gave her no regret, no longing. It was not a condition of life which fitted her, and she could see in it but an appalling and hopeless ennui. She was moved by a kind of commiseration for Madame Ratignolle,—a pity for that colorless existence which never uplifted its possessor beyond the region of blind contentment, in which no moment of anguish ever visited her soul, in which she would never have the taste of life's delirium. Edna vaguely wondered what she meant by "life's delirium." It had crossed her thought like some unsought extraneous impression.

XIX

Edna could not help but think that it was very foolish, very childish, to have stamped upon her wedding ring and smashed the crystal vase upon the tiles. She was visited by no more outbursts, moving her to such futile expedients. She began to do as she liked and to feel as she liked. She completely abandoned her Tuesdays at home, and did not return the visits of those who had called upon her. She made no ineffectual efforts to conduct her household *en bonne ménagère,*[80] going and coming as it suited her fancy, and, so far as she was able, lending herself to any passing caprice.

Mr. Pontellier had been a rather courteous husband so long as he met a certain tacit submissiveness in his wife. But her new and unexpected line of conduct completely bewildered him. It shocked him. Then her absolute disregard for her duties as a wife angered him. When Mr. Pontellier became rude, Edna grew insolent. She had resolved never to take another step backward.

"It seems to me the utmost folly for a woman at the head of a household, and the mother of children, to spend in an atelier[81] days which would be better employed contriving for the comfort of her family."

[79]"Better is a dinner of herbs where love is, than a stalled ox and hatred therewith" (Proverbs 15:17).

[80]French: as a good housekeeper. [81]Art studio.

"I feel like painting," answered Edna. "Perhaps I shan't always feel like it."

"Then in God's name paint! but don't let the family go to the devil. There's Madame Ratignolle; because she keeps up her music, she doesn't let everything else go to chaos. And she's more of a musician than you are a painter."

"She isn't a musician, and I'm not a painter. It isn't on account of painting that I let things go."

"On account of what, then?"

"Oh! I don't know. Let me alone; you bother me."

It sometimes entered Mr. Pontellier's mind to wonder if his wife were not growing a little unbalanced mentally. He could see plainly that she was not herself. That is, he could not see that she was becoming herself and daily casting aside that fictitious self which we assume like a garment with which to appear before the world.

Her husband let her alone as she requested, and went away to his office. Edna went up to her atelier—a bright room in the top of the house. She was working with great energy and interest, without accomplishing anything, however, which satisfied her even in the smallest degree. For a time she had the whole household enrolled in the service of art. The boys posed for her. They thought it amusing at first, but the occupation soon lost its attractiveness when they discovered that it was not a game arranged especially for their entertainment. The quadroon sat for hours before Edna's palette, patient as a savage, while the house-maid took charge of the children, and the drawing-room went undusted. But the housemaid, too, served her term as model when Edna perceived that the young woman's back and shoulders were molded on classic lines, and that her hair, loosened from its confining cap, became an inspiration. While Edna worked she sometimes sang low the little air, "*Ah! si tu savais!*"

It moved her with recollections. She could hear again the ripple of the water, the flapping sail. She could see the glint of the moon upon the bay, and could feel the soft, gusty beating of the hot south wind. A subtle current of desire passed through her body, weakening her hold upon the brushes and making her eyes burn.

There were days when she was very happy without knowing why. She was happy to be alive and breathing, when her whole being seemed to be one with the sunlight, the color, the odors, the luxuriant warmth of some perfect Southern day. She liked then to wander alone in the strange and unfamiliar places. She discovered many a sunny, sleepy corner, fashioned to dream in. And she found it good to dream and to be alone and unmolested.

There were days when she was unhappy, she did not know why,—when it did not seem worth while to be glad or sorry, to be alive or dead; when life appeared to her like a grotesque pandemonium and humanity like worms struggling blindly toward inevitable annihilation. She would not work on such a day, nor weave fancies to stir her pulses and warm her blood.

XX

It was during such a mood that Edna hunted up Mademoiselle Reisz. She had not forgotten the rather disagreeable impression left upon her by their last interview; but she nevertheless felt a desire to see her—above all, to listen while she played upon the piano. Quite early in the afternoon she started upon her quest for the pianist. Unfortunately she had mislaid or lost Mademoiselle Reisz's card, and looking up her address in the city directory, she found that the woman lived on Bienville Street, some distance away. The directory which fell into her hands was a year or more old, however, and upon reaching the number indicated, Edna discovered that the house was occupied by a respectable family of mulattoes who had *chambres garnies*[82] to let. They had been living there for six months, and knew absolutely nothing of a Mademoiselle Reisz. In fact, they knew nothing of any of their neighbors; their lodgers were all people of the highest distinction, they assured Edna. She did not linger to discuss class distinctions with Madame Pouponne, but hastened to a neighboring grocery store, feeling sure that Mademoiselle would have left her address with the proprietor.

He knew Mademoiselle Reisz a good deal better than he wanted to know her, he informed his questioner. In truth, he did not want to know her at all, or anything concerning her—the most disagreeable and unpopular woman who ever lived in Bienville Street. He thanked heaven she had left the neighborhood, and was equally thankful that he did not know where she had gone.

Edna's desire to see Mademoiselle Reisz had increased tenfold since these unlooked-for obstacles had arisen to thwart it. She was wondering who could give her the information she sought, when it suddenly occurred to her that Madame Lebrun would be the one most likely to do so. She knew it was useless to ask Madame Ratignolle, who was on the most distant terms with the musician, and preferred to know nothing concerning her. She had once been almost as emphatic in expressing herself upon the subject as the corner grocer.

Edna knew that Madame Lebrun had returned to the city, for it was the middle of November. And she also knew where the Lebruns lived, on Chartres Street.

Their home from the outside looked like a prison, with iron bars before the door and lower windows. The iron bars were a relic of the old *régime*,[83] and no one had ever thought of dislodging them. At the side was a high fence enclosing the garden. A gate or door opening upon the street was locked. Edna rang the bell at this side garden gate, and stood upon the banquette, waiting to be admitted.

It was Victor who opened the gate for her. A black woman, wiping her hands upon her apron, was close at his heels. Before she saw them Edna could hear them in altercation, the woman—plainly an anomaly—claiming the right to be allowed to perform her duties, one of which was to answer the bell.

Victor was surprised and delighted to see Mrs. Pontellier, and he made no attempt to conceal either his astonishment or his delight. He was a darkbrowed, good-looking youngster of nineteen, greatly resembling his mother, but with ten times her impetuosity. He instructed the black woman to go at once and inform Madame Lebrun that Mrs. Pontellier desired to see her. The woman grumbled a refusal to do part of her duty when she had not been permitted to do it all, and started back to her interrupted task of weeding the garden. Whereupon Victor administered a rebuke in the form of a volley of abuse, which, owing to its rapidity and incoherence, was all but incomprehensible to Edna. Whatever it was, the rebuke was convincing, for the woman dropped her hoe and went mumbling into the house.

[82]French: furnished rooms.

[83]A term used to describe the period (1766–1803) when New Orleans was ruled by Spanish governors.

Edna did not wish to enter. It was very pleasant there on the side porch, where there were chairs, a wicker lounge, and a small table. She seated herself, for she was tired from her long tramp; and she began to rock gently and smooth out the folds of her silk parasol. Victor drew up his chair beside her. He at once explained that the black woman's offensive conduct was all due to imperfect training, as he was not there to take her in hand. He had only come up from the island the morning before, and expected to return next day. He stayed all winter at the island; he lived there, and kept the place in order and got things ready for the summer visitors.

But a man needed occasional relaxation, he informed Mrs. Pontellier, and every now and again he drummed up a pretext to bring him to the city. My! but he had had a time of it the evening before! He wouldn't want his mother to know, and he began to talk in a whisper. He was scintillant with recollections. Of course, he couldn't think of telling Mrs. Pontellier all about it, she being a woman and not comprehending such things. But it all began with a girl peeping and smiling at him through the shutters as he passed by. Oh! but she was a beauty! Certainly he smiled back, and went up and talked to her. Mrs. Pontellier did not know him if she supposed he was one to let an opportunity like that escape him. Despite herself, the youngster amused her. She must have betrayed in her look some degree of interest or entertainment. The boy grew more daring, and Mrs. Pontellier might have found herself, in a little while, listening to a highly colored story but for the timely appearance of Madame Lebrun.

That lady was still clad in white, according to her custom of the summer. Her eyes beamed an effusive welcome. Would not Mrs. Pontellier go inside? Would she partake of some refreshment? Why had she not been there before? How was that dear Mr. Pontellier and how were those sweet children? Had Mrs. Pontellier ever known such a warm November?

Victor went and reclined on the wicker lounge behind his mother's chair, where he commanded a view of Edna's face. He had taken her parasol from her hands while he spoke to her, and he now lifted it and twirled it above him as he lay on his back. When Madame Lebrun complained that it was *so* dull coming back to the city; that she saw *so* few people now; that even Victor, when he came up from the island for a day or two, had *so* much to occupy him and engage his time; then it was that the youth went into contortions on the lounge and winked mischievously at Edna. She somehow felt like a confederate in crime, and tried to look severe and disapproving.

There had been but two letters from Robert, with little in them, they told her. Victor said it was really not worth while to go inside for the letters, when his mother entreated him to go in search of them. He remembered the contents, which in truth he rattled off very glibly when put to the test.

One letter was written from Vera Cruz and the other from the City of Mexico. He had met Montel, who was doing everything toward his advancement. So far, the financial situation was no improvement over the one he had left in New Orleans, but of course the prospects were vastly better. He wrote of the City of Mexico, the buildings, the people and their habits, the conditions of life which he found there. He sent his love to the family. He inclosed a check to his mother, and hoped she would affectionately remember him to all his friends. That was about the substance of the two letters. Edna felt that if there had been a message for her, she would have received it. The despondent frame of mind in which she had left home began again to overtake her, and she remembered that she wished to find Mademoiselle Reisz.

Madame Lebrun knew where Mademoiselle Reisz lived. She gave Edna the address, regretting that she would not consent to stay and spend the remainder of the afternoon, and pay a visit to Mademoiselle Reisz some other day. The afternoon was already well advanced.

Victor escorted her out upon the banquette, lifted her parasol, and held it over her while he walked to the car[84] with her. He entreated her to bear in mind that the disclosures of the afternoon were strictly confidential. She laughed and bantered him a little, remembering too late that she should have been dignified and reserved.

"How handsome Mrs. Pontellier looked!" said Madame Lebrun to her son.

"Ravishing!" he admitted. "The city atmosphere has improved her. Some way she doesn't seem like the same woman."

XXI

Some people contended that the reason Mademoiselle Reisz always chose apartments up under the roof was to discourage the approach of beggars, peddlars and callers. There were plenty of windows in her little front room. They were for the most part dingy, but as they were nearly always open it did not make so much difference. They often admitted into the room a good deal of smoke and soot; but at the same time all the light and air that there was came through them. From her windows could be seen the crescent of the river, the masts of ships and the big chimneys of the Mississippi steamers. A magnificent piano crowded the apartment. In the next room she slept, and in the third and last she harbored a gasoline stove on which she cooked her meals when disinclined to descend to the neighboring restaurant. It was there also that she ate, keeping her belongings in a rare old buffet, dingy and battered from a hundred years of use.

When Edna knocked at Mademoiselle Reisz's front room door and entered, she discovered that person standing beside the window, engaged in mending or patching an old prunella gaiter.[85] The little musician laughed all over when she saw Edna. Her laugh consisted of a contortion of the face and all the muscles of the body. She seemed strikingly homely, standing there in the afternoon light. She still wore the shabby lace and the artificial bunch of violets on the side of her head.

"So you remembered me at last," said Mademoiselle. "I had said to myself, 'Ah, bah! she will never come.'"

"Did you want me to come?" asked Edna with a smile.

"I had not thought much about it," answered Mademoiselle. The two had seated themselves on a little bumpy sofa which stood against the wall. "I am glad, however, that you came. I have the water boiling back there, and was just about to make some coffee. You will drink a cup with me. And how is *la belle dame?*[86] Always handsome! always healthy! always contented!" She took Edna's hand between her strong wiry fingers, holding it loosely without warmth, and executing a sort of double theme upon the back and palm.

[84]Streetcar. [85]A high-button shoe with a cloth upper that covers the ankle.
[86]French: the beautiful lady.

"Yes," she went on; "I sometimes thought: 'She will never come. She promised as those women in society always do, without meaning it. She will not come.' For I really don't believe you like me, Mrs. Pontellier."

"I don't know whether I like you or not," replied Edna, gazing down at the little woman with a quizzical look.

The candor of Mrs. Pontellier's admission greatly pleased Mademoiselle Reisz. She expressed her gratification by repairing forthwith to the region of the gasoline stove and rewarding her guest with the promised cup of coffee. The coffee and the biscuit accompanying it proved very acceptable to Edna, who had declined refreshment at Madame Lebrun's and was now beginning to feel hungry. Mademoiselle set the tray which she brought in upon a small table near at hand, and seated herself once again on the lumpy sofa.

"I have had a letter from your friend," she remarked, as she poured a little cream into Edna's cup and handed it to her.

"My friend?"

"Yes, your friend Robert. He wrote to me from the City of Mexico."

"Wrote to *you?*" repeated Edna in amazement, stirring her coffee absently.

"Yes, to me. Why not? Don't stir all the warmth out of your coffee; drink it. Though the letter might as well have been sent to you; it was nothing but Mrs. Pontellier from beginning to end."

"Let me see it," requested the young woman, entreatingly.

"No; a letter concerns no one but the person who writes it and the one to whom it is written."

"Haven't you just said it concerned me from beginning to end?"

"It was written about you, not to you. 'Have you seen Mrs. Pontellier? How is she looking?' he asked. 'As Mrs. Pontellier says,' or 'as Mrs. Pontellier once said.' 'If Mrs. Pontellier should call upon you, play for her that Impromptu of Chopin's,[87] my favorite. I heard it here a day or two ago, but not as you play it. I should like to know how it affects her,' and so on, as if he supposed we were constantly in each other's society."

"Let me see the letter."

"Oh, no."

"Have you answered it?"

"No."

"Let me see the letter."

"No, and again, no."

"Then play the Impromptu for me."

"It is growing late; what time do you have to be home?"

"Time doesn't concern me. Your question seems a little rude. Play the Impromptu."

"But you have told me nothing of yourself. What are you doing?"

"Painting!" laughed Edna. "I am becoming an artist. Think of it!"

"Ah! an artist! You have pretensions, Madame."

"Why pretensions? Do you think I could not become an artist?"

"I do not know you well enough to say. I do not know your talent or your temperament. To be an artist includes much; one must possess many gifts—

[87]"Fantaisie-Impromptu in C-Sharp Minor," better known today in America as "I'm Always Chasing Rainbows."

absolute gifts—which have not been acquired by one's own effort. And, moreover, to succeed, the artist must possess the courageous soul."

"What do you mean by the courageous soul?"

"Courageous, *ma foi!*[88] The brave soul. The soul that dares and defies."

"Show me the letter and play for me the Impromptu. You see that I have persistence. Does that quality count for anything in art?"

"It counts with a foolish old woman whom you have captivated," replied Mademoiselle, with her wriggling laugh.

The letter was right there at hand in the drawer of the little table upon which Edna had just placed her coffee cup. Mademoiselle opened the drawer and drew forth the letter, the topmost one. She placed it in Edna's hands, and without further comment arose and went to the piano.

Mademoiselle played a soft interlude. It was an improvisation. She sat low at the instrument, and the lines of her body settled into ungraceful curves and angles that gave it an appearance of deformity. Gradually and imperceptibly the interlude melted into the soft opening minor chords of the Chopin Impromptu.

Edna did not know when the Impromptu began or ended. She sat in the sofa corner reading Robert's letter by the fading light. Mademoiselle had glided from the Chopin into the quivering love-notes of Isolde's song,[89] and back again to the Impromptu with its soulful and poignant longing.

The shadows deepened in the little room. The music grew strange and fantastic—turbulent, insistent, plaintive and soft with entreaty. The shadows grew deeper. The music filled the room. It floated out upon the night, over the housetops, the crescent of the river, losing itself in the silence of the upper air.

Edna was sobbing, just as she had wept one midnight at Grand Isle when strange, new voices awoke in her. She arose in some agitation to take her departure. "May I come again, Mademoiselle?" she asked at the threshold.

"Come whenever you feel like it. Be careful; the stairs and landings are dark; don't stumble."

Mademoiselle reëntered and lit a candle. Robert's letter was on the floor. She stooped and picked it up. It was crumpled and damp with tears. Mademoiselle smoothed the letter out, restored it to the envelope, and replaced it in the table drawer.

XXII

One morning on his way into town Mr. Pontellier stopped at the house of his old friend and family physician, Doctor Mandelet. The Doctor was a semi-retired physician, resting, as the saying is, upon his laurels. He bore a reputation for wisdom rather than skill—leaving the active practice of medicine to his assistants and younger contemporaries—and was much sought for in matters of consultation. A few families, united to him by bonds of friendship, he still attended when they required the services of a physician. The Pontelliers were among these.

[88]French: "to be sure!"

[89]A song sung by Isolde to her dead lover, Tristan, before she herself dies of grief, in the opera *Tristan and Isolde* (1857–1859), by Richard Wagner (1813–1883).

Mr. Pontellier found the Doctor reading at the open window of his study. His house stood rather far back from the street, in the center of a delightful garden, so that it was quiet and peaceful at the old gentleman's study window. He was a great reader. He stared up disapprovingly over his eye-glasses as Mr. Pontellier entered, wondering who had the temerity to disturb him at that hour of the morning.

"Ah, Pontellier! Not sick, I hope. Come and have a seat. What news do you bring this morning?" He was quite portly, with a profusion of gray hair, and small blue eyes which age had robbed of much of their brightness but none of their penetration.

"Oh! I'm never sick, Doctor. You know that I come of tough fiber—of that old Creole race of Pontelliers that dry up and finally blow away. I came to consult—no, not precisely to consult—to talk to you about Edna. I don't know what ails her."

"Madame Pontellier not well?" marveled the Doctor. "Why, I saw her—I think it was a week ago—walking along Canal Street, the picture of health, it seemed to me."

"Yes, yes; she seems quite well," said Mr. Pontellier, leaning forward and whirling his stick between his two hands; "but she doesn't act well. She's odd, she's not like herself. I can't make her out, and I thought perhaps you'd help me."

"How does she act?" inquired the doctor.

"Well, it isn't easy to explain," said Mr. Pontellier, throwing himself back in his chair. "She lets the housekeeping go to the dickens."

"Well, well; women are not all alike, my dear Pontellier. We've got to consider—"

"I know that; I told you I couldn't explain. Her whole attitude—toward me and everybody and everything—has changed. You know I have a quick temper, but I don't want to quarrel or be rude to a woman, especially my wife; yet I'm driven to it, and feel like ten thousand devils after I've made a fool of myself. She's making it devilishly uncomfortable for me," he went on nervously. "She's got some sort of notion in her head concerning the eternal rights of women; and—you understand—we meet in the morning at the breakfast table."

The old gentleman lifted his shaggy eyebrows, protruded his thick nether lip, and tapped the arms of his chair with his cushioned fingertips.

"What have you been doing to her, Pontellier?"

"Doing! *Parbleu!*"[90]

"Has she," asked the Doctor, with a smile, "has she been associating of late with a circle of pseudo-intellectual women—super-spiritual superior beings? My wife has been telling me about them."

"That's the trouble," broke in Mr. Pontellier, "she hasn't been associating with any one. She has abandoned her Tuesdays at home, has thrown over all her acquaintances, and goes tramping about by herself, moping in the streetcars, getting in after dark. I tell you she's peculiar. I don't like it; I feel a little worried over it."

This was a new aspect for the Doctor. "Nothing hereditary?" he asked, seriously. "Nothing peculiar about her family antecedents, is there?"

[90]French: "Good heavens!"

"Oh, no, indeed! She comes of sound old Presbyterian Kentucky stock. The old gentleman, her father, I have heard, used to atone for his weekday sins with his Sunday devotions. I know for a fact, that his race horses literally ran away with the prettiest bit of Kentucky farming land I ever laid eyes upon. Margaret—you know Margaret—she has all the Presbyterianism undiluted. And the youngest is something of a vixen. By the way, she gets married in a couple of weeks from now."

"Send your wife up to the wedding," exclaimed the Doctor, foreseeing a happy solution. "Let her stay among her own people for a while; it will do her good."

"That's what I want her to do. She won't go to the marriage. She says a wedding is one of the most lamentable spectacles on earth. Nice thing for a woman to say to her husband!" exclaimed Mr. Pontellier, fuming anew at the recollection.

"Pontellier," said the Doctor, after a moment's reflection, "let your wife alone for a while. Don't bother her, and don't let her bother you. Woman, my dear friend, is a very peculiar and delicate organism—a sensitive and highly organized woman, such as I know Mrs. Pontellier to be, is especially peculiar. It would require an inspired psychologist to deal successfully with them. And when ordinary fellows like you and me attempt to cope with their idiosyncrasies the result is bungling. Most women are moody and whimsical. This is some passing whim of your wife, due to some cause or causes which you and I needn't try to fathom. But it will pass happily over, especially if you let her alone. Send her around to see me."

"Oh! I couldn't do that; there'd be no reason for it," objected Mr. Pontellier.

"Then I'll go around and see her," said the Doctor. "I'll drop in to dinner some evening *en bon ami*."[91]

"Do! by all means," urged Mr. Pontellier. "What evening will you come? Say Thursday. Will you come Thursday?" he asked, rising to take his leave.

"Very well; Thursday. My wife may possibly have some engagement for me Thursday. In case she has, I shall let you know. Otherwise, you may expect me."

"I am going to New York on business very soon. I have a big scheme on hand, and want to be on the field proper to pull the ropes and handle the ribbons.[92] We'll let you in on the inside if you say so, Doctor," he laughed.

"No, I thank you, my dear sir," returned the Doctor. "I leave such ventures to you younger men with the fever of life still in your blood."

"What I wanted to say," continued Mr. Pontellier, with his hand on the knob; "I may have to be absent a good while. Would you advise me to take Edna along?"

"By all means, if she wishes to go. If not, leave her here. Don't contradict her. The mood will pass, I assure you. It may take a month, two, three months—possibly longer, but it will pass; have patience."

"Well, good-by, *à jeudi*,"[93] said Mr. Pontellier, as he let himself out.

The doctor would have liked during the course of conversation to ask, "Is there any man in the case?" but he knew his Creole too well to make such a blunder as that.

He did not resume his book immediately, but sat for a while meditatively looking out into the garden.

[91]French: "as a good friend." [92]Reins, i.e., to be in control. [93]French: "until Thursday."

XXIII

Edna's father was in the city, and had been with them several days. She was not very warmly or deeply attached to him, but they had certain tastes in common, and when together they were companionable. His coming was in the nature of a welcome disturbance; it seemed to furnish a new direction for her emotions.

He had come to purchase a wedding gift for his daughter, Janet, and an outfit for himself in which he might make a creditable appearance at her marriage. Mr. Pontellier had selected the bridal gift, as every one immediately connected with him always deferred to his taste in such matters. And his suggestions on the question of dress—which too often assumes the nature of a problem—were of inestimable value to his father-in-law. But for the past few days the old gentleman had been upon Edna's hands, and in his society she was becoming acquainted with a new set of sensations. He had been a colonel in the Confederate army, and still maintained, with the title, the military bearing which had always accompanied it. His hair and mustache were white and silky, emphasizing the rugged bronze of his face. He was tall and thin, and wore his coats padded, which gave a fictitious breadth and depth to his shoulders and chest. Edna and her father looked very distinguished together, and excited a good deal of notice during their perambulations. Upon his arrival she began by introducing him to her atelier and making a sketch of him. He took the whole matter very seriously. If her talent had been tenfold greater than it was, it would not have surprised him, convinced as he was that he had bequeathed to all of his daughters the germs of a masterful capability, which only depended upon their own efforts to be directed toward successful achievement.

Before her pencil he sat rigid and unflinching, as he had faced the cannon's mouth in days gone by. He resented the intrusion of the children, who gaped with wondering eyes at him, sitting so stiff up there in their mother's bright atelier. When they drew near he motioned them away with an expressive action of the foot, loath to disturb the fixed lines of his countenance, his arms, or his rigid shoulders.

Edna, anxious to entertain him, invited Mademoiselle Reisz to meet him, having promised him a treat in her piano playing; but Mademoiselle declined the invitation. So together they attended a *soirée musicale* at the Ratignolle's. Monsieur and Madame Ratignolle made much of the Colonel, installing him as the guest of honor and engaging him at once to dine with them the following Sunday, or any day which he might select. Madame coquetted with him in the most captivating and naïve manner, with eyes, gestures, and a profusion of compliments, till the Colonel's head felt thirty years younger on his padded shoulders. Edna marveled, not comprehending. She herself was almost devoid of coquetry.

There were one or two men whom she observed at the *soirée musicale;* but she would never have felt moved to any kittenish display to attract their notice—to any feline or feminine wiles to express herself toward them. Their personality attracted her in an agreeable way. Her fancy selected them, and she was glad when a lull in the music gave them an opportunity to meet her and talk with her. Often on the street the glance of strange eyes had lingered in her memory, and sometimes had disturbed her.

Mr. Pontellier did not attend these *soirées musicale*. He considered them *bourgeois*,[94] and found more diversion at the club. To Madame Ratignolle he said the music dispensed at her *soirées* was too "heavy," too far beyond his untrained comprehension. His excuse flattered her. But she disapproved of Mr. Pontellier's club, and she was frank enough to tell Edna so.

"It's a pity Mr. Pontellier doesn't stay home more in the evenings. I think you would be more—well, if you don't mind my saying it—more united, if he did."

"Oh! dear no!" said Edna, with a blank look in her eyes. "What should I do if he stayed home? We wouldn't have anything to say to each other."

She had not much of anything to say to her father, for that matter; but he did not antagonize her. She discovered that he interested her, though she realized that he might not interest her long; and for the first time in her life she felt as if she were thoroughly acquainted with him. He kept her busy serving him and ministering to his wants. It amused her to do so. She would not permit a servant or one of the children to do anything for him which she might do herself. Her husband noticed, and thought it was the expression of a deep filial attachment which he had never suspected.

The Colonel drank numerous "toddies" during the course of the day, which left him, however, imperturbed. He was an expert at concocting strong drinks. He had even invented some, to which he had given fantastic names, and for whose manufacture he required diverse ingredients that it devolved upon Edna to procure for him.

When Doctor Mandelet dined with the Pontelliers on Thursday he could discern in Mrs. Pontellier no trace of that morbid condition which her husband had reported to him. She was excited and in a manner radiant. She and her father had been to the race course, and their thoughts when they seated themselves at the table were still occupied with the events of the afternoon, and their talk was still of the track. The Doctor had not kept pace with turf affairs. He had certain recollections of racing in what he called "the good old times" when the Lecompte stables flourished, and he drew upon his fund of memories so that he might not be left out and seem wholly devoid of the modern spirit. But he failed to impose upon the Colonel, and was even far from impressing him with this trumped up knowledge of bygone days. Edna had staked her father on his last venture, with the most gratifying results to both of them. Besides, they had met some very charming people, according to the Colonel's impressions. Mrs. Mortimer Merriman and Mrs. James Highcamp, who were there with Alcée Arobin, had joined them and had enlivened the hours in a fashion that warmed him to think of.

Mr. Pontellier himself had no particular leaning toward horse-racing, and was even rather inclined to discourage it as a pastime, especially when he considered the fate of that blue-grass farm in Kentucky. He endeavored in a general way, to express a particular disapproval, and only succeeded in arousing the ire and opposition of his father-in-law. A pretty dispute followed, in which Edna warmly espoused her father's cause and the Doctor remained neutral.

He observed his hostess attentively from under his shaggy brows, and noted a subtle change which had transformed her from the listless woman he had known into a being who, for the moment, seemed palpitant with the forces of

[94]French: middle class.

life. Her speech was warm and energetic. There was no repression in her glance or gesture. She reminded him of some beautiful, sleek animal waking up in the sun.

The dinner was excellent. The claret was warm and the champagne was cold, and under their beneficent influence the threatened unpleasantness melted and vanished with the fumes of the wine.

Mr. Pontellier warmed up and grew reminiscent. He told some amusing plantation experiences, recollections of old Iberville and his youth, when he hunted 'possum in company with some friendly darky; thrashed the pecan trees, shot the grosbec,[95] and roamed the woods and fields in mischievous idleness.

The Colonel, with little sense of humor and the fitness of things, related a somber episode of those dark and bitter days, in which he had acted a conspicuous part and always formed a central figure. Nor was the Doctor happier in his selection, when he told the old, ever new and curious story of the waning of a woman's love, seeking strange, new channels, only to return to its legitimate source after days of fierce unrest. It was one of the many little human documents which had been unfolded to him during his long career as a physician. The story did not seem especially to impress Edna. She had one of her own to tell, of a woman who paddled away with her lover one night in a pirogue and never came back. They were lost amid the Baratarian Islands, and no one ever heard of them or found trace of them from that day to this. It was a pure invention. She said that Madame Antoine had related it to her. That, also, was an invention. Perhaps it was a dream she had had. But every glowing word seemed real to those who listened. They could feel the hot breath of the Southern night; they could hear the long sweep of the pirogue through the glistening moonlit water, the beating of birds' wings, rising startled from among the reeds in the salt-water pools; they could see the faces of the lovers, pale, close together, rapt in oblivious forgetfulness, drifting into the unknown.

The champagne was cold, and its subtle fumes played fantastic tricks with Edna's memory that night.

Outside, away from the glow of the fire and the soft lamplight, the night was chill and murky. The Doctor doubled his old-fashioned cloak across his breast as he strode home through the darkness. He knew his fellow-creatures better than most men; knew that inner life which so seldom unfolds itself to unanointed eyes. He was sorry he had accepted Pontellier's invitation. He was growing old, and beginning to need rest and an imperturbed spirit. He did not want the secrets of other lives thrust upon him.

"I hope it isn't Arobin," he muttered to himself as he walked. "I hope to heaven it isn't Alcée Arobin."

XXIV

Edna and her father had a warm, and almost violent dispute upon the subject of her refusal to attend her sister's wedding. Mr. Pontellier declined to interfere, to interpose either his influence or his authority. He was following Doctor Mandelet's advice, and letting her do as she liked. The Colonel reproached his daughter for her lack of filial kindness and respect, her want of

[95]French: gross beak, the night heron, a game bird with a large bill.

sisterly affection and womanly consideration. His arguments were labored and unconvincing. He doubted if Janet would accept any excuse—forgetting that Edna had offered none. He doubted if Janet would ever speak to her again, and he was sure Margaret would not.

Edna was glad to be rid of her father when he finally took himself off with his wedding garments and his bridal gifts, with his padded shoulders, his Bible reading, his "toddies" and ponderous oaths.

Mr. Pontellier followed him closely. He meant to stop at the wedding on his way to New York and endeavor by every means which money and love could devise to atone somewhat for Edna's incomprehensible action.

"You are too lenient, too lenient by far, Léonce," asserted the Colonel. "Authority, coercion are what is needed. Put your foot down good and hard; the only way to manage a wife. Take my word for it."

The Colonel was perhaps unaware that he had coerced his own wife into her grave. Mr. Pontellier had a vague suspicion of it which he thought it needless to mention at that late day.

Edna was not so consciously gratified at her husband's leaving home as she had been over the departure of her father. As the day approached when he was to leave her for a comparatively long stay, she grew melting and affectionate, remembering his many acts of consideration and his repeated expressions of an ardent attachment. She was solicitous about his health and his welfare. She bustled around, looking after his clothing, thinking about heavy underwear, quite as Madame Ratignolle would have done under similar circumstances. She cried when he went away, calling him her dear, good friend, and she was quite certain she would grow lonely before very long and go to join him in New York.

But after all, a radiant peace settled upon her when she at last found herself alone. Even the children were gone. Old Madame Pontellier had come herself and carried them off to Iberville with their quadroon. The old madame did not venture to say she was afraid they would be neglected during Léonce's absence; she hardly ventured to think so. She was hungry for them—even a little fierce in her attachment. She did not want them to be wholly "children of the pavement," she always said when begging to have them for a space. She wished them to know the country, with its streams, its fields, its woods, its freedom, so delicious to the young. She wished them to taste something of the life their father had lived and known and loved when he, too, was a little child.

When Edna was at last alone, she breathed a big, genuine sigh of relief. A feeling that was unfamiliar but very delicious came over her. She walked all through the house, from one room to another, as if inspecting it for the first time. She tried the various chairs and lounges, as if she had never sat and reclined upon them before. And she perambulated around the outside of the house, investigating, looking to see if windows and shutters were secure and in order. The flowers were like new acquaintances; she approached them in a familiar spirit, and made herself at home among them. The garden walks were damp, and Edna called to the maid to bring out her rubber sandals. And there she stayed, and stooped, digging around the plants, trimming, picking dead, dry leaves. The children's little dog came out, interfering, getting in her way. She scolded him, laughed at him, played with him. The garden smelled so good and looked so pretty in the afternoon sunlight. Edna plucked all the bright flowers she could find, and went into the house with them, she and the little dog.

Even the kitchen assumed a sudden interesting character which she had never before perceived. She went in to give directions to the cook, to say that the butcher would have to bring much less meat, that they would require only half their usual quantity of bread, of milk and groceries. She told the cook that she herself would be greatly occupied during Mr. Pontellier's absence, and she begged her to take all thought and responsibility of the larder upon her own shoulders.

That night Edna dined alone. The candelabra, with a few candles in the center of the table, gave all the light she needed. Outside the circle of light in which she sat, the large dining-room looked solemn and shadowy. The cook, placed upon her mettle, served a delicious repast—a luscious tenderloin broiled *à point*.[96] The wine tasted good; the *marron glacé*[97] seemed to be just what she wanted. It was so pleasant, too, to dine in a comfortable *peignoir*.

She thought a little sentimentally about Léonce and the children, and wondered what they were doing. As she gave a dainty scrap or two to the doggie, she talked intimately to him about Etienne and Raoul. He was beside himself with astonishment and delight over these companionable advances, and showed his appreciation by his little quick, snappy barks and a lively agitation.

Then Edna sat in the library after dinner and read Emerson[98] until she grew sleepy. She realized that she had neglected her reading, and determined to start anew upon a course of improving studies, now that her time was completely her own to do with as she liked.

After a refreshing bath, Edna went to bed. And as she snuggled comfortably beneath the eiderdown a sense of restfulness invaded her, such as she had not known before.

XXV

When the weather was dark and cloudy Edna could not work. She needed the sun to mellow and temper her mood to the sticking point. She had reached a stage when she seemed to be no longer feeling her way, working, when in the humor, with sureness and ease. And being devoid of ambition, and striving not toward accomplishment, she drew satisfaction from the work in itself.

On rainy or melancholy days Edna went out and sought the society of the friends she had made at Grand Isle. Or else she stayed indoors and nursed a mood with which she was becoming too familiar for her own comfort and peace of mind. It was not despair; but it seemed to her as if life were passing by, leaving its promise broken and unfulfilled. Yet there were other days when she listened, was led on and deceived by fresh promises which her youth held out to her.

She went again to the races, and again. Alcée Arobin and Mrs. Highcamp called for her one bright afternoon in Arobin's drag.[99] Mrs. Highcamp was a worldly but unaffected, intelligent, slim, tall blonde woman in the forties, with an indifferent manner and blue eyes that stared. She had a daughter who served her as a pretext for cultivating the society of young men of fashion. Alcée Arobin

[96]French: to perfection. [97]French: candied chestnuts.
[98]Ralph Waldo Emerson (1803–1882), whose essays emphasize the virtues of independence and individualism.
[99]A large coach with seats inside and on the roof.

was one of them. He was a familiar figure at the race course, the opera, the fashionable clubs. There was a perpetual smile in his eyes, which seldom failed to awaken a corresponding cheerfulness in any one who looked into them and listened to his good-humored voice. His manner was quiet, and at times a little insolent. He possessed a good figure, a pleasing face, not overburdened with depth of thought or feeling; and his dress was that of the conventional man of fashion.

He admired Edna extravagantly, after meeting her at the races with her father. He had met her before on other occasions, but she had seemed to him unapproachable until that day. It was at his instigation that Mrs. Highcamp called to ask her to go with them to the Jockey Club[100] to witness the turf event of the season.

There were possibly a few track men out there who knew the race horse as well as Edna, but there was certainly none who knew it better. She sat between her two companions as one having authority to speak. She laughed at Arobin's pretensions, and deplored Mrs. Highcamp's ignorance. The race horse was a friend and intimate associate of her childhood. The atmosphere of the stables and the breath of the blue grass paddock revived in her memory and lingered in her nostrils. She did not perceive that she was talking like her father as the sleek geldings ambled in review before them. She played for very high stakes, and fortune favored her. The fever of the game flamed in her cheeks and eyes, and it got into her blood and into her brain like an intoxicant. People turned their heads to look at her, and more than one lent an attentive ear to her utterances, hoping thereby to secure the elusive but everdesired "tip." Arobin caught the contagion of excitement which drew him to Edna like a magnet. Mrs. Highcamp remained, as usual, unmoved, with her indifferent stare and uplifted eyebrows.

Edna stayed and dined with Mrs. Highcamp upon being urged to do so. Arobin also remained and sent away his drag.

The dinner was quiet and uninteresting, save for the cheerful efforts of Arobin to enliven things. Mrs. Highcamp deplored the absence of her daughter from the races, and tried to convey to her what she had missed by going to the "Dante reading"[101] instead of joining them. The girl held a geranium leaf up to her nose and said nothing, but looked knowing and noncommittal. Mr. Highcamp was a plain, bald-headed man, who only talked under compulsion. He was unresponsive. Mrs. Highcamp was full of delicate courtesy and consideration toward her husband. She addressed most of her conversation to him at table. They sat in the library after dinner and read the evening papers together under the droplight;[102] while the younger people went into the drawing-room near by and talked. Miss Highcamp played some selections from Grieg[103] upon the piano. She seemed to have apprehended all of the composer's coldness and none of his poetry. While Edna listened she could not help wondering if she had lost her taste for music.

When the time came for her to go home, Mr. Highcamp grunted a lame offer to escort her, looking down at his slippered feet with tactless concern. It

[100]A social club for the rich and prominent.
[101]A group reading of works by Dante Alighieri (1265–1321), Italian author of *The Divine Comedy.*
[102]A lamp that can be lowered or raised to control the light.
[103]Edvard Grieg (1843–1907), Norwegian composer.

was Arobin who took her home. The car ride was long, and it was late when they reached Esplanade Street. Arobin asked permission to enter for a second to light his cigarette—his match safe[104] was empty. He filled his match safe, but did not light his cigarette until he left her, after she had expressed her willingness to go to the races with him again.

Edna was neither tired nor sleepy. She was hungry again, for the Highcamp dinner, though of excellent quality, had lacked abundance. She rummaged in the larder and brought forth a slice of Gruyère[105] and some crackers. She opened a bottle of beer which she found in the icebox. Edna felt extremely restless and excited. She vacantly hummed a fantastic tune as she poked at the wood embers on the hearth and munched a cracker.

She wanted something to happen—something, anything; she did not know what. She regretted that she had not made Arobin stay a half hour to talk over the horses with her. She counted the money she had won. But there was nothing else to do, so she went to bed, and tossed there for hours in a sort of monotonous agitation.

In the middle of the night she remembered that she had forgotten to write her regular letter to her husband; and she decided to do so next day and tell him about her afternoon at the Jockey Club. She lay wide awake composing a letter which was nothing like the one which she wrote next day. When the maid awoke her in the morning Edna was dreaming of Mr. Highcamp playing the piano at the entrance of a music store on Canal Street, while his wife was saying to Alcée Arobin, as they boarded an Esplanade Street car:

"What a pity that so much talent has been neglected! but I must go."

When, a few days later, Alcée Arobin again called for Edna in his drag, Mrs. Highcamp was not with him. He said they would pick her up. But as that lady had not been apprised of his intention of picking her up, she was not at home. The daughter was just leaving the house to attend the meeting of a branch Folk Lore Society, and regretted that she could not accompany them. Arobin appeared nonplused, and asked Edna if there were any one else she cared to ask.

She did not deem it worth while to go in search of any of the fashionable acquaintances from whom she had withdrawn herself. She thought of Madame Ratignolle, but knew that her fair friend did not leave the house, except to take a languid walk around the block with her husband after nightfall. Mademoiselle Reisz would have laughed at such a request from Edna. Madame Lebrun might have enjoyed the outing, but for some reason Edna did not want her. So they went alone, she and Arobin.

The afternoon was intensely interesting to her. The excitement came back upon her like a remittent fever. Her talk grew familiar and confidential. It was no labor to become intimate with Arobin. His manner invited easy confidence. The preliminary stage of becoming acquainted was one which he always endeavored to ignore when a pretty and engaging woman was concerned.

He stayed and dined with Edna. He stayed and sat beside the wood fire. They laughed and talked; and before it was time to go he was telling her how different life might have been if he had known her years before. With ingenuous frankness he spoke of what a wicked, ill-disciplined boy he had been, and impulsively drew up his cuff to exhibit upon his wrist the scar from a saber cut which he had received in a duel outside of Paris when he was nineteen. She

[104]Fireproof container for matches. [105]Cheese from Gruyère, Switzerland.

touched his hand as she scanned the red cicatrice[106] on the inside of his white wrist. A quick impulse that was somewhat spasmodic impelled her fingers to close in a sort of clutch upon his hand. He felt the pressure of her pointed nails in the flesh of his palm.

She arose hastily and walked toward the mantel.

"The sight of a wound or scar always agitates and sickens me," she said. "I shouldn't have looked at it."

"I beg your pardon," he entreated, following her; "it never occurred to me that it might be repulsive."

He stood close to her, and the effrontery in his eyes repelled the old, vanishing self in her, yet drew all her awakening sensuousness. He saw enough in her face to impel him to take her hand and hold it while he said his lingering good night.

"Will you go to the races again?" he asked.

"No," she said. "I've had enough of the races. I don't want to lose all the money I've won, and I've got to work when the weather is bright, instead of—"

"Yes; work; to be sure. You promised to show me your work. What morning may I come up to your atelier? To-morrow?"

"No!"

"Day after?"

"No, no."

"Oh, please don't refuse me! I know something of such things. I might help you with a stray suggestion or two."

"No, Good night. Why don't you go after you have said good night? I don't like you," she went on in a high, excited pitch, attempting to draw away her hand. She felt that her words lacked dignity and sincerity, and she knew that he felt it.

"I'm sorry you don't like me. I'm sorry I offended you. How have I offended you? What have I done? Can't you forgive me?" And he bent and pressed his lips upon her hand as if he wished never more to withdraw them.

"Mr. Arobin," she complained, "I'm greatly upset by the excitement of the afternoon; I'm not myself. My manner must have misled you in some way. I wish you to go, please." She spoke in a monotonous, dull tone. He took his hat from the table, and stood with eyes turned from her, looking into the dying fire. For a moment or two he kept an impressive silence.

"Your manner has not misled me, Mrs. Pontellier," he said finally. "My own emotions have done that. I couldn't help it. When I'm near you, how could I help it? Don't think anything of it, don't bother, please. You see, I go when you command me. If you wish me to stay away, I shall do so. If you let me come back, I—oh! you will let me come back?"

He cast one appealing glance at her, to which she made no response. Alcée Arobin's manner was so genuine that it often deceived even himself.

Edna did not care or think whether it were genuine or not. When she was alone she looked mechanically at the back of her hand which he had kissed so warmly. Then she leaned her head down on the mantelpiece. She felt somewhat like a woman who in a moment of passion is betrayed into an act of infidelity, and realizes the significance of the act without being wholly awakened from its glamour. The thought was passing vaguely through her mind, "What would he think?"

[106]Scar.

She did not mean her husband; she was thinking of Robert Lebrun. Her husband seemed to her now like a person whom she had married without love as an excuse.

She lit a candle and went up to her room. Alcée Arobin was absolutely nothing to her. Yet his presence, his manners, the warmth of his glances, and above all the touch of his lips upon her hand had acted like a narcotic upon her.

She slept a languorous sleep, interwoven with vanishing dreams.

XXVI

Alcée Arobin wrote Edna an elaborate note of apology, palpitant with sincerity. It embarrassed her; for in a cooler, quieter moment it appeared to her absurd that she should have taken his action so seriously, so dramatically. She felt sure that the significance of the whole occurrence had lain in her own self-consciousness. If she ignored his note it would give undue importance to a trivial affair. If she replied to it in a serious spirit it would still leave in his mind the impression that she had in a susceptible moment yielded to his influence. After all, it was no great matter to have one's hand kissed. She was provoked at his having written the apology. She answered in as light and bantering a spirit as she fancied it deserved, and she said would be glad to have him look in upon her at work whenever he felt the inclination and his business gave him the opportunity.

He responded at once by presenting himself at her home with all his disarming naïveté. And then there was scarcely a day which followed that she did not see him or was not reminded of him. He was prolific in pretexts. His attitude became one of good-humored subservience and tacit adoration. He was ready at all times to submit to her moods, which were as often kind as they were cold. She grew accustomed to him. They became intimate and friendly by imperceptible degrees, and then by leaps. He sometimes talked in a way that astonished her at first and brought the crimson into her face; in a way that pleased her at last, appealing to the animalism that stirred impatiently within her.

There was nothing which so quieted the turmoil of Edna's senses as a visit to Mademoiselle Reisz. It was then, in the presence of that personality which was offensive to her, that the woman, by her divine art, seemed to reach Edna's spirit and set it free.

It was misty, with heavy, lowering atmosphere, one afternoon, when Edna climbed the stairs to the pianist's apartments under the roof. Her clothes were dripping with moisture. She felt chilled and pinched as she entered the room. Mademoiselle was poking at a rusty stove that smoked a little and warmed the room indifferently. She was endeavoring to heat a pot of chocolate on the stove. The room looked cheerless and dingy to Edna as she entered. A bust of Beethoven, covered with a hood of dust, scowled at her from the mantelpiece.

"Ah! here comes the sunlight!" exclaimed Mademoiselle, rising from her knees before the stove. "Now it will be warm and bright enough; I can let the fire alone."

She closed the stove door with a bang, and approaching, assisted in removing Edna's dripping mackintosh.

"You are cold; you look miserable. The chocolate will soon be hot. But would you rather have a taste of brandy? I have scarcely touched the bottle which you brought me for my cold." A piece of red flannel was wrapped around Mademoiselle's throat; a stiff neck compelled her to hold her head on one side.

"I will take some brandy," said Edna, shivering as she removed her gloves and overshoes. She drank the liquor from the glass as a man would have done. Then flinging herself upon the uncomfortable sofa she said, "Mademoiselle, I am going to move away from my house on Esplanade Street."

"Ah!" ejaculated the musician, neither surprised nor especially interested. Nothing ever seemed to astonish her very much. She was endeavoring to adjust the bunch of violets which had become loose from its fastening in her hair. Edna drew her down upon the sofa, and taking a pin from her own hair, secured the shabby artificial flowers in their accustomed place.

"Aren't you astonished?"

"Passably. Where are you going? to New York? to Iberville? to your father in Mississippi? where?"

"Just two steps away," laughed Edna, "in a little four-room house around the corner. It looks so cozy, so inviting and restful, whenever I pass by; and it's for rent. I'm tired looking after that big house. It never seemed like mine, anyway—like home. It's too much trouble. I have to keep too many servants. I am tired bothering with them."

"That is not your true reason, *ma belle.*[107] There is no use in telling me lies. I don't know your reason, but you have not told me the truth." Edna did not protest or endeavor to justify herself.

"The house, the money that provides for it, are not mine. Isn't that enough reason?"

"They are your husband's," returned Mademoiselle, with a shrug and a malicious elevation of the eyebrows.

"Oh! I see there is no deceiving you. Then let me tell you: It is a caprice. I have a little money of my own from my mother's estate, which my father sends me by driblets. I won a large sum this winter on the races, and I am beginning to sell my sketches. Laidpore is more and more pleased with my work; he says it grows in force and individuality. I cannot judge that myself, but I feel that I have gained in ease and confidence. However, as I said, I have sold a good many through Laidpore. I can live in the tiny house for little or nothing, with one servant. Old Celestine, who works occasionally for me, says she will come stay with me and do my work. I know I shall like it, like the feeling of freedom and independence."

"What does your husband say?"

"I have not told him yet. I only thought of it this morning. He will think I am demented, no doubt. Perhaps you think so."

Mademoiselle shook her head slowly. "Your reason is not yet clear to me," she said.

Neither was it quite clear to Edna herself; but it unfolded itself as she sat for a while in silence. Instinct had prompted her to put away her husband's bounty in casting off her allegiance. She did not know how it would be when he returned. There would have to be an understanding, an explanation. Conditions would some way adjust themselves, she felt; but whatever came, she had resolved never again to belong to another than herself.

"I shall give a grand dinner before I leave the old house!" Edna exclaimed. "You will have to come to it, Mademoiselle. I will give you everything that you like to eat and drink. We shall sing and laugh and be merry for once." And she uttered a sigh that came from the very depths of her being.

[107]French: "my beauty."

If Mademoiselle happened to have received a letter from Robert during the interval of Edna's visits, she would give her the letter unsolicited. And she would seat herself at the piano and play as her humor prompted her while the young woman read the letter.

The little stove was roaring; it was red-hot, and the chocolate in the tin sizzled and sputtered. Edna went forward and opened the stove door, and Mademoiselle rising, took a letter from under the bust of Beethoven and handed it to Edna.

"Another! so soon!" she exclaimed, her eyes filled with delight. "Tell me, Mademoiselle, does he know that I see his letters?"

"Never in the world! He would be angry and would never write to me again if he thought so. Does he write to you? Never a line. Does he send you a message? Never a word. It is because he loves you, poor fool, and is trying to forget you, since you are not free to listen to him or to belong to him."

"Why do you show me his letters, then?"

"Haven't you begged for them? Can I refuse you anything? Oh! you cannot deceive me," and Mademoiselle approached her beloved instrument and began to play. Edna did not at once read the letter. She sat holding it in her hand, while the music penetrated her whole being like an effulgence, warming and frightening the dark places of her soul. It prepared her for joy and exultation.

"Oh!" she exclaimed, letting the letter fall to the floor. "Why did you not tell me?" She went and grasped Mademoiselle's hands up from the keys. "Oh! unkind! malicious! Why did you not tell me?"

"That he was coming back? No great news, *ma foi.*[108] I wonder he did not come long ago." "But when, when?" cried Edna, impatiently. "He does not say when."

"He says 'very soon.' You know as much about it as I do; it is all in the letter."

"But why? Why is he coming? Oh, if I thought—" and she snatched the letter from the floor and turned the pages this way and that way, looking for the reason, which was left untold.

"If I were young and in love with a man," said Mademoiselle, turning on the stool and pressing her wiry hands between her knees as she looked down at Edna, who sat on the floor holding the letter, "it seems to me he would have to be some *grand espirit;*[109] a man with lofty aims and ability to reach them; one who stood high enough to attract the notice of his fellow-men. It seems to me if I were young and in love I should never deem a man of ordinary caliber worthy of my devotion."

"Now it is you who are telling lies and seeking to deceive me, Mademoiselle; or else you have never been in love, and know nothing about it. Why," went on Edna, clasping her knees and looking up into Mademoiselle's twisted face, "do you suppose a woman knows why she loves? Does she select? Does she say to herself: 'Go to! Here is a distinguished statesman with presidential possibilities; I shall proceed to fall in love with him.' Or, 'I shall set my heart upon this musician, whose fame is on every tongue?' Or, 'This financier, who controls the world's money markets?' "

"You are purposely misunderstanding me, *ma reine.*[110] Are you in love with Robert?"

"Yes," said Edna. It was the first time she had admitted it, and a glow overspread her face, blotching it with red spots.

[108]French: "to be sure." [109]French: "great soul." [110]French: "my dear."

"Why?" asked her companion, "Why do you love him when you ought not to?"

Edna, with a motion or two, dragged herself on her knees before Mademoiselle Reisz, who took the glowing face between her two hands.

"Why? Because his hair is brown and grows away from his temples; because he opens and shuts his eyes, and his nose is a little out of drawing; because he has two lips and a square chin, and a little finger which he can't straighten from having played baseball too energetically in his youth. Because—"

"Because you do, in short," laughed Mademoiselle. "What will you do when he comes back?" she asked.

"Do? Nothing, except feel glad and happy to be alive."

She was already glad and happy to be alive at the mere thought of his return. The murky, lowering sky, which had depressed her a few hours before, seemed bracing and invigorating as she splashed through the streets on her way home.

She stopped at a confectioner's and ordered a huge box of bonbons for the children in Iberville. She slipped a card in the box, on which she scribbled a tender message and sent an abundance of kisses.

Before dinner in the evening Edna wrote a charming letter to her husband, telling him of her intention to move for a while into the little house around the block, and to give a farewell dinner before leaving, regretting that he was not there to share it, to help her out with the menu and assist her in entertaining the guests. Her letter was brilliant and brimming with cheerfulness.

XXVII

"What is the matter with you?" asked Arobin that evening. "I never found you in such a happy mood." Edna was tired by that time, and was reclining on the lounge before the fire.

"Don't you know the weather prophet has told us we shall see the sun pretty soon?"

"Well, that ought to be reason enough," he acquiesced. "You wouldn't give me another if I sat here all night imploring you." He sat close to her on a low tabouret,[111] and as he spoke his fingers lightly touched the hair that fell a little over her forehead. She liked the touch of his fingers through her hair, and closed her eyes sensitively.

"One of these days," she said, "I'm going to pull myself together for a while and think—try to determine what character of a woman I am; for, candidly, I don't know. By all the codes which I am acquainted with, I am a devilishly wicked specimen of the sex.[112] But some way I can't convince myself that I am. I must think about it."

"Don't. What's the use? Why should you bother thinking about it when I can tell you what manner of woman you are." His fingers strayed occasionally down to her warm, smooth cheeks and firm chin, which was growing a little full and double.

"Oh, yes! You will tell me that I am adorable; everything that is captivating. Spare yourself the effort."

"No; I shan't tell you anything of the sort, though I shouldn't be lying if I did."

"Do you know Mademoiselle Reisz?" she asked irrelevantly.

[111]A seat without arms or back. [112]I.e., the female sex.

"The pianist? I know her by sight. I've heard her play."

"She says queer things sometimes in a bantering way that you don't notice at the time and you find yourself thinking about afterward."

"For instance?"

"Well, for instance, when I left her to-day, she put her arms around me and felt my shoulder blades, to see if my wings were strong, she said. 'The bird that would soar above the level plain of tradition and prejudice must have strong wings. It is a sad spectacle to see the weaklings bruised, exhausted, fluttering back to earth.'"

"Whither would you soar?"

"I'm not thinking of any extraordinary flights. I only half comprehend her."

"I've heard she's partially demented," said Arobin.

"She seems to me wonderfully sane," Edna replied.

"I'm told she's extremely disagreeable and unpleasant. Why have you introduced her at a moment when I desired to talk of you?"

"Oh! talk of me if you like," cried Edna, clasping her hands beneath her head; "but let me think of something else while you do."

"I'm jealous of your thoughts to-night. They're making you a little kinder than usual; but some way I feel as if they were wandering, as if they were not here with me." She only looked at him and smiled. His eyes were very near. He leaned upon the lounge with an arm extended across her, while the other hand still rested upon her hair. They continued silently to look into each other's eyes. When he leaned forward and kissed her, she clasped his head, holding his lips to hers.

It was the first kiss of her life to which her nature had really responded. It was a flaming torch that kindled desire.

XXVIII

Edna cried a little that night after Arobin left her. It was only one phase of the multitudinous emotions which had assailed her. There was with her an overwhelming feeling of irresponsibility. There was the shock of the unexpected and the unaccustomed. There was her husband's reproach looking at her from the external things around her which he had provided for her external existence. There was Robert's reproach making itself felt by a quicker, fiercer, more overpowering love, which had awakened within her toward him. Above all, there was understanding. She felt as if a mist had been lifted from her eyes, enabling her to look upon and comprehend the significance of life, that monster made up of beauty and brutality. But among the conflicting sensations which assailed her, there was neither shame nor remorse. There was a dull pang of regret because it was not the kiss of love which had inflamed her, because it was not love which had held this cup of life to her lips.

XXIX

Without even waiting for an answer from her husband regarding his opinion or wishes in the matter, Edna hastened her preparations for quitting her home on Esplanade Street and moving into the little house around the block. A feverish anxiety attended her every action in that direction. There was no moment of deliberation, no interval of repose between the thought and its fulfillment.

Early upon the morning following those hours passed in Arobin's society, Edna set about securing her new abode and hurrying her arrangements for occupying it. Within the precincts of her home she felt like one who has entered and lingered within the portals of some forbidden temple in which a thousand muffled voices bade her begone.

Whatever was her own in this house, everything which she had acquired aside from her husband's bounty, she caused to be transported to the other house, supplying simple and meager deficiencies from her own resources.

Arobin found her with rolled sleeves, working in company with the housemaid when he looked in during the afternoon. She was splendid and robust, and had never appeared handsomer than in the old blue gown, with a red silk handkerchief knotted at random around her head to protect her hair from the dust. She was mounted upon a high step-ladder, unhooking a picture from the wall when he entered. He had found the front door open, and had followed his ring by walking in unceremoniously.

"Come down!" he said. "Do you want to kill yourself?" She greeted him with affected carelessness, and appeared absorbed in her occupation.

If he had expected to find her languishing, reproachful, or indulging in sentimental tears, he must have been greatly surprised.

He was no doubt prepared for any emergency, ready for any one of the foregoing attitudes, just as he bent himself easily and naturally to the situation which confronted him.

"No," she answered; "Ellen is afraid to mount the ladder. Joe is working over at the 'pigeon house'—that's the name Ellen gives it, because it's so small and looks like a pigeon house—and some one has to do this."

Arobin pulled off his coat, and expressed himself ready and willing to tempt fate in her place. Ellen brought him one of her dust-caps, and went into contortions of mirth, which she found it impossible to control, when she saw him put it on before the mirror as grotesquely as he could. Edna herself could not refrain from smiling when she fastened it at his request. So it was he who in turn mounted the ladder, unhooking pictures and curtains, and dislodging ornaments as Edna directed. When he had finished he took off his dust-cap and went out to wash his hands.

Edna was sitting on the tabouret, idly brushing the tips of a feather duster along the carpet when he came in again.

"Is there anything more you will let me do?" he asked.

"That is all," she answered. "Ellen can manage the rest." She kept the young woman occupied in the drawing-room, unwilling to be left alone with Arobin.

"What about the dinner?" he asked; "the grand event, the *coup d'état?*"[113]

"It will be day after to-morrow. Why do you call it the '*coup d'état?*' Oh! it will be very fine; all my best of everything—crystal, silver and gold, Sèvres, flowers, music, and champagne to swim in. I'll let Léonce pay the bills. I wonder what he'll say when he sees the bills."

"And you ask me why I call it a *coup d'état?*" Arobin had put on his coat, and he stood before her and asked if his cravat was plumb. She told him it was, looking no higher than the tip of his collar.

"When do you go to the 'pigeon house?'—with all due acknowledgement to Ellen."

[113]French: "sudden, decisive effort, a masterstroke."

"Day after to-morrow, after the dinner. I shall sleep there."

"Ellen, will you very kindly get me a glass of water?" asked Arobin. "The dust in the curtains, if you will pardon me for hinting such a thing, has parched my throat to a crisp."

"While Ellen gets the water," said Edna, rising, "I will say good-by and let you go. I must get rid of this grime, and I have a million things to do and think of."

"When shall I see you?" asked Arobin, seeking to detain her, the maid having left the room.

"At the dinner, of course. You are invited."

"Not before?—not to-night or to-morrow morning or to-morrow noon or night? Or the day after morning or noon? Can't you see yourself, without my telling you, what an eternity it is?"

He had followed her into the hall and to the foot of the stairway, looking up at her as she mounted with her face half turned to him.

"Not an instant sooner," she said. But she laughed and looked at him with eyes that at once gave him courage to wait and made it torture to wait.

XXX

Though Edna had spoken of the dinner as a very grand affair, it was in truth a very small affair and very select, in so much as the guests invited were few and were selected with discrimination. She had counted upon an even dozen seating themselves at her round mahogany board, forgetting for the moment that Madame Ratignolle was to the last degree *souffrante*[114] and unpresentable, and not foreseeing that Madame Lebrun would send a thousand regrets at the last moment. So there were only ten, after all, which made a cozy, comfortable number.

There were Mr. and Mrs. Merriman, a pretty, vivacious little woman in the thirties; her husband, a jovial fellow, something of a shallow-pate, who laughed a good deal at other people's witticisms, and had thereby made himself extremely popular. Mrs. Highcamp had accompanied them. Of course, there was Alcée Arobin; and Mademoiselle Reisz had consented to come. Edna had sent her a fresh bunch of violets with black lace trimmings for her hair. Monsieur Ratignolle brought himself and his wife's excuses. Victor Lebrun, who happened to be in the city, bent upon relaxation, had accepted with alacrity. There was a Miss Mayblunt, no longer in her teens, who looked at the world through lorgnettes and with the keenest interest. It was thought and said that she was intellectual; it was suspected of her that she wrote under a *nom de guerre.*[115] She had come with a gentleman by the name of Gouvernail, connected with one of the daily papers, of whom nothing special could be said, except that he was observant and seemed quiet and inoffensive. Edna herself made the tenth, and at half-past eight they seated themselves at table, Arobin and Monsieur Ratignolle on either side of their hostess.

Mrs. Highcamp sat between Arobin and Victor Lebrun. Then came Mrs. Merriman, Mr. Gouvernail, Miss Mayblunt, Mr. Merriman, and Mademoiselle Reisz next to Monsieur Ratignolle.

There was something extremely gorgeous about the appearance of the table, an effect of splendor conveyed by a cover of pale yellow satin under strips of

[114]French: ill. [115]French: fictitious name.

lace-work. There were wax candles in massive brass candelabra, burning softly under yellow silk shades; full, fragrant roses, yellow and red, abounded. There were silver and gold, as she had said there would be, and crystal which glittered like the gems which the women wore.

The ordinary stiff dining chairs had been discarded for the occasion and replaced by the most commodious and luxurious which could be collected throughout the house. Mademoiselle Reisz, being exceedingly diminutive, was elevated upon cushions, as small children are sometimes hoisted at table upon bulky volumes.

"Something new, Edna?" exclaimed Miss Mayblunt, with lorgnette directed toward a magnificent cluster of diamonds that sparkled, that almost sputtered, in Edna's hair, just over the center of her forehead.

"Quite new; 'brand' new, in fact; a present from my husband. It arrived this morning from New York. I may as well admit that this is my birthday, and that I am twenty-nine. In good time I expect you to drink my health. Meanwhile, I shall ask you to begin with this cocktail, composed—would you say 'composed?' " with an appeal to Miss Mayblunt—"composed by my father in honor of Sister Janet's wedding."

Before each guest stood a tiny glass that looked and sparkled like a garnet gem.

"Then, all things considered," spoke Arobin, "it might not be amiss to start out by drinking the Colonel's health in the cocktail which he composed, on the birthday of the most charming of women—the daughter whom he invented."

Mr. Merriman's laugh at this sally was such a genuine outburst and so contagious that it started the dinner with an agreeable swing that never slackened.

Miss Mayblunt begged to be allowed to keep her cocktail untouched before her, just to look at. The color was marvelous! She could compare it to nothing she had ever seen, and the garnet lights which it emitted were unspeakably rare. She pronounced the Colonel an artist, and stuck to it.

Monsieur Ratignolle was prepared to take things seriously: the *mets,* the *entremets,*[116] the service, the decorations, even the people. He looked up from his pompano[117] and inquired of Arobin if he were related to the gentleman of that name who formed one of the firm of Laitner and Arobin, lawyers. The young man admitted that Laitner was a warm personal friend, who permitted Arobin's name to decorate the firm's letterheads and to appear upon a shingle that graced Perdido Street.

"There are so many inquisitive people and institutions abounding," said Arobin, "that one is really forced as a matter of convenience these days to assume the virtue of an occupation if he has it not."

Monsieur Ratignolle stared a little, and turned to ask Mademoiselle Reisz if she considered the symphony concerts up to the standard which had been set the previous winter. Mademoiselle Reisz answered Monsieur Ratignolle in French, which Edna thought a little rude, under the circumstances, but characteristic. Mademoiselle had only disagreeable things to say of the symphony concerts, and insulting remarks to make of all the musicians of New Orleans, singly and collectively. All her interest seemed to be centered upon the delicacies placed before her.

[116] French: the main dish, the side dishes.
[117] A variety of fish found in the Gulf of Mexico, one of the most delicious of all food fishes.

Mr. Merriman said that Mr. Arobin's remark about inquisitive people reminded him of a man from Waco[118] the other day at the St. Charles Hotel—but as Mr. Merriman's stories were always lame and lacking point, his wife seldom permitted him to complete them. She interrupted him to ask if he remembered the name of the author whose book she had bought the week before to send to a friend in Geneva. She was talking "books" with Mr. Gouvernail and trying to draw from him his opinion upon current literary topics. Her husband told the story of the Waco man privately to Miss Mayblunt, who pretended to be greatly amused and to think it extremely clever.

Mrs. Highcamp hung with languid but unaffected interest upon the warm and impetuous volubility of her left-hand neighbor, Victor Lebrun. Her attention was never for a moment withdrawn from him after seating herself at table; and when he turned to Mrs. Merriman, who was prettier and more vivacious than Mrs. Highcamp, she waited with easy indifference for an opportunity to reclaim his attention. There was the occasional sound of music, of mandolins, sufficiently removed to be an agreeable accompaniment rather than an interruption to the conversation. Outside the soft, monotonous splash of a fountain could be heard; the sound penetrated into the room with the heavy odor of jessamine that came through the open windows.

The golden shimmer of Edna's satin gown spread in rich folds on either side of her. There was a soft fall of lace encircling her shoulders. It was the color of her skin, without the glow, the myriad living tints that one may sometimes discover in vibrant flesh. There was something in her attitude, in her whole appearance when she leaned her head against the high-backed chair and spread her arms, which suggested the regal woman, the one who rules, who looks on, who stands alone.

But as she sat there amid her guests, she felt the old ennui overtaking her; the hopelessness which so often assailed her, which came upon her like an obsession, like something extraneous, independent of volition. It was something which announced itself; a chill breath that seemed to issue from some vast cavern wherein discords wailed. There came over her the acute longing which always summoned into her spiritual vision the presence of the beloved one, overpowering her at once with a sense of the unattainable.

The moments glided on, while a feeling of good fellowship passed around the circle like a mystic cord, holding and binding these people together with jest and laughter. Monsieur Ratignolle was the first to break the pleasant charm. At ten o'clock he excused himself. Madame Ratignolle was waiting for him at home. She was *bien souffrante,*[119] and she was filled with vague dread, which only her husband's presence could allay.

Mademoiselle Reisz arose with Monsieur Ratignolle, who offered to escort her to the car. She had eaten well; she had tasted the good, rich wines, and they must have turned her head, for she bowed pleasantly to all as she withdrew from table. She kissed Edna upon the shoulder, and whispered: *"Bonne nuit, ma reine; soyez sage."*[120] She had been a little bewildered upon rising, or rather, descending from her cushions, and Monsieur Ratignolle gallantly took her arm and led her away.

Mrs. Highcamp was weaving a garland of roses, yellow and red. When she had finished the garland, she laid it lightly upon Victor's black curls. He

[118]Waco, Texas. [119]French: quite ill. [120]French: "Good night, my dear; be good."

was reclining far back in the luxurious chair, holding a glass of champagne to the light.

As if a magician's wand had touched him, the garland of roses transformed him into a vision of Oriental beauty. His cheeks were the color of crushed grapes, and his dusky eyes glowed with a languishing fire.

"Sapristi!" exclaimed Arobin.

But Mrs. Highcamp had one more touch to add to the picture. She took from the back of her chair a white silken scarf, with which she had covered her shoulders in the early part of the evening. She draped it across the boy in graceful folds, and in a way to conceal his black, conventional evening dress. He did not seem to mind what she did to him, only smiled showing a faint gleam of white teeth, while he continued to gaze with narrowing eyes at the light through his glass of champagne.

"Oh! to be able to paint in color rather than in words!" exclaimed Miss Mayblunt, losing herself in a rhapsodic dream as she looked at him.

"'There was a graven image of Desire
Painted with red blood on a ground of gold.'"[121]

murmured Gouvernail, under his breath.

The effect of the wine upon Victor was to change his accustomed volubility into silence. He seemed to have abandoned himself to a reverie, and to be seeing pleasing visions in the amber bead.

"Sing," entreated Mrs. Highcamp. "Won't you sing to us?"

"Let him alone," said Arobin.

"He's posing," offered Mr. Merriman; "let him have it out."

"I believe he's paralyzed," laughed Mrs. Merriman. And leaning over the youth's chair, she took the glass from his hand and held it to his lips. He sipped the wine slowly, and when he had drained the glass she laid it upon the table and wiped his lips with her little filmy handkerchief.

"Yes, I'll sing for you," he said, turning in his chair toward Mrs. Highcamp. He clasped his hands behind his head, and looking up at the ceiling began to hum a little, trying his voice like a musician tuning an instrument. Then, looking at Edna, he began to sing:

"Ah! si tu savais!"

"Stop!" she cried, "don't sing that. I don't want you to sing it," and she laid her glass so impetuously and blindly upon the table as to shatter it against a caraffee. The wine spilled over Arobin's legs and some of it trickled down upon Mrs. Highcamp's black gauze gown. Victor had lost all idea of courtesy, or else he thought his hostess was not in earnest, for he laughed and went on:

"Ah! si tu savais
Ce que tes yeux me disent"—[122]

[121]From the sonnet "A Cameo," by Algernon Charles Swinburne (1837–1909).
[122]French: "Ah! Couldst thou but know/What thine eyes tell me"—

"Oh! you mustn't! you mustn't," exclaimed Edna, and pushing back her chair she got up, and going behind him placed her hand over his mouth. He kissed the soft palm that pressed upon his lips.

"No, no, I won't, Mrs. Pontellier. I didn't know you meant it," looking up at her with caressing eyes. The touch of his lips was like a pleasing sting to her hand. She lifted the garland of roses from his head and flung it across the room.

"Come, Victor; you've posed long enough. Give Mrs. Highcamp her scarf."

Mrs. Highcamp undraped the scarf from about him with her own hands. Miss Mayblunt and Mr. Gouvernail suddenly conceived the notion that it was time to say good night. And Mr. and Mrs. Merriman wondered how it could be so late.

Before parting from Victor, Mrs. Highcamp invited him to call upon her daughter, who she knew would be charmed to meet him and talk French and sing French songs with him. Victor expressed his desire and intention to call upon Miss Highcamp at the first opportunity which presented itself. He asked if Arobin were going his way. Arobin was not.

The mandolin players had long since stolen away. A profound stillness had fallen upon the broad, beautiful street. The voices of Edna's disbanding guests jarred like a discordant note upon the quiet harmony of the night.

XXXI

"Well?" questioned Arobin, who had remained with Edna after the others had departed.

"Well," she reiterated, and stood up, stretching her arms, and feeling the need to relax her muscles after having been so long seated.

"What next?" he asked.

"The servants are all gone. They left when the musicians did. I have dismissed them. The house has to be closed and locked, and I shall trot around to the pigeon house, and shall send Celestine over in the morning to straighten things up."

He looked around, and began to turn out some of the lights.

"What about upstairs?" he inquired.

"I think it is all right; but there may be a window or two unlatched. We had better look; you might take a candle and see. And bring me my wrap and hat on the foot of the bed in the middle room."

He went up with the light, and Edna began closing doors and windows. She hated to shut in the smoke and the fumes of the wine. Arobin found her cape and hat, which he brought down and helped her to put on.

When everything was secured and the lights put out, they left through the front door, Arobin locking it and taking the key, which he carried for Edna. He helped her down the steps.

"Will you have a spray of jessamine?" he asked, breaking off a few blossoms as he passed.

"No; I don't want anything."

She seemed disheartened, and had nothing to say. She took his arm, which he offered her, holding up the weight of her satin train with the other hand. She looked down, noticing the black line of his leg moving in and out so close to her against the yellow shimmer of her gown. There was the whistle of a railway train somewhere in the distance, and the midnight bells were ringing. They met no one in their short walk.

The "pigeon-house" stood behind a locked gate, and a shallow *parterre*[123] that had been somewhat neglected. There was a small front porch, upon which a long window and the front door opened. The door opened directly into the parlor; there was no side entry. Back in the yard was a room for servants, in which old Celestine had been ensconced.

Edna had left a lamp burning low upon the table. She had succeeded in making the room look habitable and homelike. There were some books on the table and a lounge near at hand. On the floor was a fresh matting, covered with a rug or two; and on the walls hung a few tasteful pictures. But the room was filled with flowers. These were a surprise to her. Arobin had sent them, and had had Celestine distribute them during Edna's absence. Her bedroom was adjoining, and across a small passage were the dining-room and kitchen.

Edna seated herself with every appearance of discomfort.

"Are you tired?" he asked.

"Yes, and chilled, and miserable. I feel as if I had been wound up to a certain pitch—too tight—and something inside of me had snapped."

She rested her head against the table upon her bare arm.

"You want to rest," he said, "and to be quiet. I'll go; I'll leave you and let you rest."

"Yes," she replied.

He stood up beside her and smoothed her hair with his soft, magnetic hand. His touch conveyed to her a certain physical comfort. She could have fallen quietly asleep there if he had continued to pass his hand over her hair. He brushed the hair upward from the nape of her neck.

"I hope you will feel better and happier in the morning," he said. "You have tried to do too much in the past few days. The dinner was the last straw; you might have dispensed with it."

"Yes," she admitted; "it was stupid."

"No, it was delightful; but it has worn you out." His hand strayed to her beautiful shoulders, and he could feel the response of her flesh to his touch. He seated himself beside her and kissed her lightly upon the shoulder.

"I thought you were going away," she said, in an uneven voice.

"I am, after I have said good night."

"Good night," she murmured.

He did not answer, except to continue to caress her. He did not say good night until she had become supple to his gentle, seductive entreaties.

XXXII

When Mr. Pontellier learned of his wife's intention to abandon her home and take up her residence elsewhere he immediately wrote her a letter of unqualified disapproval and remonstrance. She had given reasons which he was unwilling to acknowledge as adequate. He hoped she had not acted upon her rash impulse; and he begged her to consider first, foremost, and above all else, what people would say. He was not dreaming of scandal when he uttered this

[123] French: garden.

warning; that was a thing which would never have entered into his mind to consider in connection with his wife's name or his own. He was simply thinking of his financial integrity. It might get noised about that the Pontelliers had met with reverses, and were forced to conduct their *ménage*[124] on a humbler scale than heretofore. It might do incalculable mischief to his business prospects.

But remembering Edna's whimsical turn of mind of late, and foreseeing that she had immediately acted upon her impetuous determination, he grasped the situation with his usual promptness and handled it with his well-known business tact and cleverness.

The same mail which brought to Edna his letter of disapproval carried instructions—the most minute instructions—to a well-known architect concerning the remodeling of his home, changes which he had long contemplated, and which he desired carried forward during his temporary absence.

Expert and reliable packers and movers were engaged to convey the furniture, carpets, pictures—everything movable, in short—to places of security. And in an incredibly short time the Pontellier house was turned over to the artisans. There was to be an addition—a small snuggery; there was to be frescoing, and hardwood flooring was to be put into such rooms as had not yet been subjected to this improvement.

Furthermore, in one of the daily papers appeared a brief notice to the effect that Mr. and Mrs. Pontellier were contemplating a summer sojourn abroad, and that their handsome residence on Esplanade Street was undergoing sumptuous alterations, and would not be ready for occupancy until their return. Mr. Pontellier had saved appearances!

Edna admired the skill of his maneuver, and avoided any occasion to balk his intentions. When the situation as set forth by Mr. Pontellier was accepted and taken for granted, she was apparently satisfied that it should be so.

The pigeon-house pleased her. It at once assumed the intimate character of a home, while she herself invested it with a charm which it reflected like a warm glow. There was with her a feeling of having descended in the social scale, with a corresponding sense of having risen in the spiritual. Every step which she took toward relieving herself from obligations added to her strength and expansion as an individual. She began to look with her own eyes; to see and to apprehend the deeper undercurrents of life. No longer was she content to "feed upon opinion" when her own soul had invited her.

After a little while, a few days, in fact, Edna went up and spent a week with her children in Iberville. They were delicious February days, with all the summer's promise hovering in the air.

How glad she was to see the children! She wept for very pleasure when she felt their little arms clasping her; their hard, ruddy cheeks pressed against her own glowing cheeks. She looked into their faces with hungry eyes that could not be satisfied with looking. And what stories they had to tell their mother! About the pigs, the cows, the mules! About riding to the mill behind Gluglu; fishing back in the lake with their Uncle Jasper; picking pecans with Lidie's little black brood, and hauling chips in their express wagon. It was a thousand times more fun to haul real chips for old lame Susie's real fire than to drag painted blocks along the banquette on Esplanade Street!

[124] French: household.

She went with them herself to see the pigs and the cows, to look at the darkies laying the cane, to thrash the pecan trees, and catch fish in the back lake. She lived with them a whole week long, giving them all of herself, and gathering and filling herself with their young existence. They listened, breathless, when she told them the house in Esplanade Street was crowded with workmen, hammering, nailing, sawing, and filling the place with clatter. They wanted to know where their bed was; what had been done with their rocking-horse; and where did Joe sleep, and where had Ellen gone, and the cook? But, above all, they were fired with a desire to see the little house around the block. Was there any place to play? Were there any boys next door? Raoul, with pessimistic foreboding, was convinced that there were only girls next door. Where would they sleep, and where would papa sleep? She told them the fairies would fix it all right.

The old Madame was charmed with Edna's visit, and showered all manner of delicate attentions upon her. She was delighted to know that the Esplanade Street house was in a dismantled condition. It gave her the promise and pretext to keep the children indefinitely.

It was with a wrench and a pang that Edna left her children. She carried away with her the sound of their voices and the touch of their cheeks. All along the journey homeward their presence lingered with her like the memory of a delicious song. But by the time she had regained the city the song no longer echoed in her soul. She was again alone.

XXXIII

It happened sometimes when Edna went to see Mademoiselle Reisz that the little musician was absent, giving a lesson or making some small necessary household purchase. The key was always left in a secret hiding-place in the entry, which Edna knew. If Mademoiselle happened to be away, Edna would usually enter and wait for her return.

When she knocked at Mademoiselle Reisz's door one afternoon there was no response; so unlocking the door, as usual, she entered and found the apartment deserted; as she had expected. Her day had been quite filled up, and it was for a rest, for a refuge, and to talk about Robert, that she sought out her friend.

She had worked at her canvas—a young Italian character study—all the morning, completing the work without the model; but there had been many interruptions, some incident to her modest housekeeping, and others of a social nature.

Madame Ratignolle had dragged herself over, avoiding the too public thoroughfares, she said. She complained that Edna had neglected her much of late. Besides, she was consumed with curiosity to see the little house and the manner in which it was conducted. She wanted to hear all about the dinner party; Monsieur Ratignolle had left *so* early. What had happened after she left? The champagne and grapes which Edna sent over were *too* delicious. She had so little appetite; they had refreshed and toned her stomach. Where on earth was she going to put Mr. Pontellier in that little house, and the boys? And then she made Edna promise to go to her when her hour of trial overtook her.

"At any time—any time of the day or night, dear," Edna assured her.

Before leaving Madame Ratignolle said:

"In some way you seem to me like a child, Edna. You seem to act without a certain amount of reflection which is necessary in this life. That is the reason I want to say you mustn't mind if I advise you to be a little careful while you are living alone. Why don't you have some one come and stay with you? Wouldn't Mademoiselle Reisz come?"

"No; she wouldn't wish to come, and I shouldn't want her always with me."

"Well, the reason—you know how evil-minded the world is—some one was talking of Alcée Arobin visiting you. Of course, it wouldn't matter if Mr. Arobin had not such a dreadful reputation. Monsieur Ratignolle was telling me that his attentions alone are considered enough to ruin a woman's name."

"Does he boast of his successes?" asked Edna, indifferently, squinting at her picture.

"No, I think not. I believe he is a decent fellow as far as that goes. But his character is so well known among the men. I shan't be able to come back and see you; it was very, very imprudent to-day."

"Mind the step!" cried Edna.

"Don't neglect me," entreated Madame Ratignolle; "and you don't mind what I said about Arobin, or having some one to stay with you."

"Of course not," Edna laughed. "You may say anything you like to me." They kissed each other good-by. Madame Ratignolle had not far to go, and Edna stood on the porch a while watching her walk down the street.

Then in the afternoon Mrs. Merriman and Mrs. Highcamp had made their "party call." Edna felt that they might have dispensed with the formality. They had also come to invite her to play *vingt-et-un*[125] one evening at Mrs. Merriman's. She was asked to go early, to dinner, and Mr. Merriman or Mr. Arobin would take her home. Edna accepted in a half-hearted way. She sometimes felt very tired of Mrs. Highcamp and Mrs. Merriman.

Late in the afternoon she sought refuge with Mademoiselle Reisz, and stayed there alone, waiting for her, feeling a kind of repose invade her with the very atmosphere of the shabby, unpretentious little room.

Edna sat at the window, which looked out over the house-tops and across the river. The window frame was filled with pots of flowers, and she sat and picked the dry leaves from a rose geranium. The day was warm, and the breeze which blew from the river was very pleasant. She removed her hat and laid it on the piano. She went on picking the leaves and digging around the plants with her hat pin. Once she thought she heard Mademoiselle Reisz approaching. But it was a young black girl, who came in, bringing a small bundle of laundry, which she deposited in the adjoining room, and went away.

Edna seated herself at the piano, and softly picked out with one hand the bars of a piece of music which lay open before her. A half-hour went by. There was the occasional sound of people going and coming in the lower hall. She was growing interested in her occupation of picking out the aria, when there was a second rap at the door. She vaguely wondered what these people did when they found Mademoiselle's door locked.

"Come in," she called, turning her face toward the door. And this time it was Robert Lebrun who presented himself. She attempted to rise; she could

[125]French: twenty-one, a card game.

not have done so without betraying the agitation which mastered her at sight of him, so she fell back upon the stool, only exclaiming, "Why, Robert!"

He came and clasped her hand, seemingly without knowing what he was saying or doing.

"Mrs. Pontellier! How do you happen—oh! how well you look! Is Mademoiselle Reisz not here? I never expected to see you."

"When did you come back?" asked Edna in an unsteady voice, wiping her face with her handkerchief. She seemed ill at ease on the piano stool, and he begged her to take the chair by the window. She did so, mechanically, while he seated himself on the stool.

"I returned day before yesterday," he answered, while he leaned his arm on the keys, bringing forth a crash of discordant sound.

"Day before yesterday!" she repeated, aloud; and went on thinking to herself, "day before yesterday," in a sort of an uncomprehending way. She had pictured him seeking her at the very first hour, and he had lived under the same sky since day before yesterday; while only by accident had he stumbled upon her. Mademoiselle must have lied when she said, "Poor fool, he loves you."

"Day before yesterday," she repeated, breaking off a spray of Mademoiselle's geranium; "then if you had not met me here to-day you wouldn't—when—that is, didn't you mean to come and see me?"

"Of course, I should have gone to see you. There have been so many things—" he turned the leaves of Mademoiselle's music nervously. "I started in at once yesterday with the old firm. After all there is as much chance for me here as there was there—that is, I might find it profitable some day. The Mexicans were not very congenial."

So he had come back because the Mexicans were not congenial; because business was as profitable here as there; because of reason, and not because he cared to be near her. She remembered the day she sat on the floor, turning the pages of his letter, seeking the reason which was left untold.

She had not noticed how he looked—only feeling his presence; but she turned deliberately and observed him. After all, he had been absent but a few months, and was not changed. His hair—the color of hers—waved back from his temples in the same way as before. His skin was not more burned than it had been at Grand Isle. She found in his eyes, when he looked at her for one silent moment, the same tender caress, with an added warmth and entreaty which had not been there before—the same glance which had penetrated to the sleeping places of her soul and awakened them.

A hundred times Edna had pictured Robert's return, and imagined their first meeting. It was usually at her home, whither he had sought her out at once. She always fancied him expressing or betraying in some way his love for her. And here, the reality was that they sat ten feet apart, she at the window, crushing geranium leaves in her hand and smelling them, he twirling around on the piano stool, saying:

"I was very much surprised to hear of Mr. Pontellier's absence; it's a wonder Mademoiselle Reisz did not tell me; and your moving—mother told me yesterday. I should think you would have gone to New York with him, or to Iberville with the children, rather than be bothered here with housekeeping. And you are going abroad, too, I hear. We shan't have you at Grand Isle next summer; it won't seem—do you see much of Mademoiselle Reisz? She often spoke of you in the few letters she wrote."

"Do you remember that you promised to write to me when you went away?" A flush overspread his whole face.

"I couldn't believe that my letters would be of any interest to you."

"That is an excuse; it isn't the truth." Edna reached for her hat on the piano. She adjusted it, sticking the hat pin through the heavy coil of hair with some deliberation.

"Are you not going to wait for Mademoiselle Reisz?" asked Robert.

"No; I have found when she is absent this long, she is liable not to come back till late." She drew on her gloves, and Robert picked up his hat.

"Won't you wait for her?" asked Edna.

"Not if you think she will not be back till late," adding, as if suddenly aware of some discourtesy in his speech, "and I should miss the pleasure of walking home with you." Edna locked the door and put the key back in its hiding-place.

They went together, picking their way across muddy streets and side-walks encumbered with the cheap display of small tradesmen. Part of the distance they rode in the car, and after disembarking, passed the Pontellier mansion, which looked broken and half torn asunder. Robert had never known the house, and looked at it with interest.

"I never knew you in your home," he remarked.

"I am glad you did not."

"Why?" She did not answer. They went on around the corner, and it seemed as if her dreams were coming true after all, when he followed her into the little house.

"You must stay and dine with me, Robert. You see I am all alone, and it is so long since I have seen you. There is so much I want to ask you."

She took off her hat and gloves. He stood irresolute, making some excuse about his mother who expected him; he even muttered something about an engagement. She struck a match and lit the lamp on the table; it was growing dusk. When he saw her face in the lamp-light, looking pained, with all the soft lines gone out of it, he threw his hat aside and seated himself.

"Oh! you know I want to stay if you will let me!" he exclaimed. All the softness came back. She laughed, and went and put her hand on his shoulder.

"This is the first moment you have seemed like the old Robert. I'll go tell Celestine." She hurried away to tell Celestine to set an extra place. She even sent her off in search of some added delicacy which she had not thought of for herself. And she recommended great care in dripping the coffee and having the omelet done to a proper turn.

When she reëntered, Robert was turning over magazines, sketches, and things that lay upon the table in great disorder. He picked up a photograph, and exclaimed:

"Alcée Arobin! What on earth is his picture doing here?"

"I tried to make a sketch of his head one day," answered Edna, "and he thought the photograph might help me. It was at the other house. I thought it had been left there. I must have packed it up with my drawing materials."

"I should think you would give it back to him if you have finished with it."

"Oh! I have a great many such photographs. I never think of returning them. They don't amount to anything." Robert kept on looking at the picture.

"It seems to me—do you think his head worth drawing? Is he a friend of Mr. Pontellier's? You never said you knew him."

"He isn't a friend of Mr. Pontellier's; he's a friend of mine. I always knew him—that is, it is only of late that I know him pretty well. But I'd rather talk about you, and know what you have been seeing and doing and feeling out there in Mexico." Robert threw aside the picture.

"I've been seeing the waves and the white beach of Grand Isle; the quiet, grassy street of the *Chênière;* the old fort at Grand Terre. I've been working like a machine, and feeling like a lost soul. There was nothing interesting."

She leaned her head upon her hand to shade her eyes from the light.

"And what have you been seeing and doing and feeling all these days?" he asked.

"I've been seeing the waves and the white beach of Grand Isle; the quiet, grassy street of the *Chênière Caminada;* the old sunny fort at Grande Terre. I've been working with a little more comprehension than a machine, and still feeling like a lost soul. There was nothing interesting."

"Mrs. Pontellier, you are cruel," he said, with feeling, closing his eyes and resting his head back in his chair. They remained in silence till old Celestine announced dinner.

XXXIV

The dining-room was very small. Edna's round mahogany would have almost filled it. As it was there was but a step or two from the little table to the kitchen, to the mantel, the small buffet, and the side door that opened out on the narrow brick-paved yard.

A certain degree of ceremony settled upon them with the announcement of dinner. There was no return to personalities. Robert related incidents of his sojourn in Mexico, and Edna talked of events likely to interest him, which had occurred during his absence. The dinner was of ordinary quality, except for the few delicacies which she had sent out to purchase. Old Celestine, with a bandana *tignon*[126] twisted about her head, hobbled in and out, taking a personal interest in everything; and she lingered occasionally to talk patois[127] with Robert, whom she had known as a boy.

He went out to a neighboring cigar stand to purchase cigarette papers, and when he came back he found that Celestine had served the black coffee in the parlor.

"Perhaps I shouldn't have come back," he said. "When you are tired of me, tell me to go."

"You never tire me. You must have forgotten the hours and hours at Grand Isle in which we grew accustomed to each other and used to being together."

"I have forgotten nothing at Grand Isle," he said, not looking at her, but rolling a cigarette. His tobacco pouch, which he laid upon the table, was a fantastic embroidered silk affair, evidently the handiwork of a woman.

"You used to carry your tobacco in a rubber pouch," said Edna, picking up the pouch and examining the needle work.

"Yes; it was lost."

"Where did you buy this one? In Mexico?"

[126]A turban made with a bright-colored kerchief.
[127]A local dialect of French, mixed with words from English, Spanish, etc.

"It was given to me by a Vera Cruz girl; they are very generous," he replied, striking a match and lighting his cigarette.

"They are very handsome, I suppose, those Mexican women; very picturesque, with their black eyes and their lace scarfs."

"Some are; others are hideous. Just as you find women everywhere."

"What was she like—the one who gave you the pouch? You must have known her very well."

"She was very ordinary. She wasn't of the slightest importance. I knew her well enough."

"Did you visit at her house? Was it interesting? I should like to know and hear about the people you met, and the impressions they made on you."

"There are some people who leave impressions not so lasting as the imprint of an oar upon the water."

"Was she such a one?"

"It would be ungenerous for me to admit that she was of that order and kind." He thrust the pouch back in his pocket, as if to put away the subject with the trifle which had brought it up.

Arobin dropped in with a message from Mrs. Merriman, to say that the card party was postponed on account of the illness of one of her children.

"How do you do, Arobin?" said Robert, rising from the obscurity.

"Oh! Lebrun. To be sure! I heard yesterday you were back. How did they treat you down in Mexique?"

"Fairly well."

"But not well enough to keep you there. Stunning girls, though, in Mexico. I thought I should never get away from Vera Cruz when I was down there a couple of years ago."

"Did they embroider slippers and tobacco pouches and hat-bands and things for you?" asked Edna.

"Oh! my! no! I didn't get so deep in their regard. I fear they made more impression on me than I made on them."

"You were less fortunate than Robert, then."

"I am always less fortunate than Robert. Has he been imparting tender confidences?"

"I've been imposing myself long enough," said Robert, rising, and shaking hands with Edna. "Please convey my regards to Mr. Pontellier when you write."

He shook hands with Arobin and went away.

"Fine fellow, that Lebrun," said Arobin when Robert had gone. "I never heard you speak of him."

"I knew him last summer at Grand Isle," she replied. "Here is that photograph of yours. Don't you want it?"

"What do I want with it? Throw it away." She threw it back on the table.

"I'm not going to Mrs. Merriman's," she said. "If you see her, tell her so. But perhaps I had better write. I think I shall write now, and say that I am sorry her child is sick, and tell her not to count on me."

"It would be a good scheme," acquiesced Arobin. "I don't blame you; stupid lot!"

Edna opened the blotter, and having procured paper and pen, began to write the note. Arobin lit a cigar and read the evening paper, which he had in his pocket.

"What is the date?" she asked. He told her.

"Will you mail this for me when you go out?"

"Certainly." He read to her little bits out of the newspaper, while she straightened things on the table.

"What do you want to do?" he asked, throwing aside the paper. "Do you want to go out for a walk or a drive or anything? It would be a fine night to drive."

"No; I don't want to do anything but just be quiet. You go away and amuse yourself. Don't stay."

"I'll go away if I must; but I shan't amuse myself. You know that I only live when I am near you."

He stood up to bid her good night.

"Is that one of the things you always say to women?"

"I have said it before, but I don't think I ever came so near meaning it," he answered with a smile. There were no warm lights in her eyes; only a dreamy, absent look.

"Good night. I adore you. Sleep well," he said, and he kissed her hand and went away.

She stayed alone in a kind of reverie—a sort of stupor. Step by step she lived over every instant of the time she had been with Robert after he had entered Mademoiselle Reisz's door. She recalled his words, his looks. How few and meager they had been for her hungry heart! A vision—a transcendently seductive vision of a Mexican girl arose before her. She writhed with a jealous pang. She wondered when he would come back. He had not said he would come back. She had been with him, had heard his voice and touched his hand. But some way he had seemed nearer to her off there in Mexico.

XXXV

The morning was full of sunlight and hope. Edna could see before her no denial—only the promise of excessive joy. She lay in bed awake, with bright eyes full of speculation. "He loves you, poor fool." If she could but get that conviction firmly fixed in her mind, what mattered about the rest? She felt she had been childish and unwise the night before in giving herself over to despondency. She recapitulated the motives which no doubt explained Robert's reserve. They were not insurmountable; they would not hold if he really loved her; they could not hold against her own passion, which he must come to realize in time. She pictured him going to his business that morning. She even saw how he was dressed; how he walked down one street, and turned the corner of another; saw him bending over his desk, talking to people who entered the office, going to his lunch, and perhaps watching for her on the street. He would come to her in the afternoon or evening, sit and roll his cigarette, talk a little, and go away as he had done the night before. But how delicious it would be to have him there with her! She would have no regrets, nor seek to penetrate his reserve if he still chose to wear it.

Edna ate her breakfast only half dressed. The maid brought her a delicious printed scrawl from Raoul, expressing his love, asking her to send him some bonbons, and telling her they had found that morning ten tiny white pigs all lying in a row beside Lidie's big white pig.

A letter also came from her husband, saying he hoped to be back early in March, and then they would get ready for that journey abroad which he had promised her so long, which he felt now fully able to afford; he felt able to travel as people should, without any thought of small economies—thanks to his recent speculations in Wall Street.

Much to her surprise she received a note from Arobin, written at midnight from the club. It was to say good morning to her, to hope she had slept well, to assure her of his devotion, which he trusted she in some faintest manner returned.

All these letters were pleasing to her. She answered the children in a cheerful frame of mind, promising them bonbons, and congratulating them upon their happy find of the little pigs.

She answered her husband with friendly evasiveness,—not with any fixed design to mislead him, only because all sense of reality had gone out of her life; she had abandoned herself to Fate, and awaited the consequences with indifference.

To Arobin's note she made no reply. She put it under Celestine's stove-lid.

Edna worked several hours with much spirit. She saw no one but a picture dealer, who asked her if it were true that she was going abroad to study in Paris.

She said possibly she might, and he negotiated with her for some Parisian studies to reach him in time for the holiday trade in December.

Robert did not come that day. She was keenly disappointed. He did not come the following day, nor the next. Each morning she awoke with hope, and each night she was a prey to despondency. She was tempted to seek him out. But far from yielding to the impulse, she avoided any occasion which might throw her in his way. She did not go to Mademoiselle Reisz's nor pass by Madame Lebrun's, as she might have done if he had still been in Mexico.

When Arobin, one night, urged her to drive with him, she went—out to the lake, on the Shell Road. His horses were full of mettle, and even a little unmanageable. She liked the rapid gait at which they spun along, and the quick, sharp sound of the horses' hoofs on the hard road. They did not stop anywhere to eat or to drink. Arobin was not needlessly imprudent. But they ate and they drank when they regained Edna's little dining-room—which was comparatively early in the evening.

It was late when he left her. It was getting to be more than a passing whim with Arobin to see her and be with her. He had detected the latent sensuality, which unfolded under his delicate sense of her nature's requirements like a torpid, torrid, sensitive blossom.

There was no despondency when she fell asleep that night; nor was there hope when she awoke in the morning.

XXXVI

There was a garden out in the suburbs; a small, leafy corner, with a few green tables under the orange trees. An old cat slept all day on the stone step in the sun, and an old *mulatresse*[128] slept her idle hours away in her chair at the open window, till some one happened to knock on one of the green tables. She had milk and cream cheese to sell, and bread and butter. There was no one who could make such excellent coffee or fry a chicken so golden brown as she.

[128]French: mulatto woman, one of mixed black and white ancestry.

The place was too modest to attract the attention of people of fashion, and so quiet as to have escaped the notice of those in search of pleasure and dissipation. Edna had discovered it accidentally one day when the high-board gate stood ajar. She caught sight of a little green table, blotched with the checkered sunlight that filtered through the quivering leaves overhead. Within she had found the slumbering *mulatresse,* the drowsy cat, and a glass of milk which reminded her of the milk she had tasted in Iberville.

She often stopped there during her perambulations; sometimes taking a book with her, and sitting an hour or two under the trees when she found the place deserted. Once or twice she took a quiet dinner there alone, having instructed Celestine beforehand to prepare no dinner at home. It was the last place in the city where she would have expected to meet any one she knew.

Still she was not astonished when, as she was partaking of a modest dinner late in the afternoon, looking into an open book, stroking the cat, which had made friends with her—she was not greatly astonished to see Robert come in at the tall garden gate.

"I am destined to see you only by accident," she said, shoving the cat off the chair beside her. He was surprised, ill at ease, almost embarrassed at meeting her thus so unexpectedly.

"Do you come here often?" he asked.

"I almost live here,' she said.

"I used to drop in very often for a cup of Catiche's good coffee. This is the first time since I came back."

"She'll bring you a plate, and you will share my dinner. There's always enough for two—even three." Edna had intended to be indifferent and as reserved as he when she met him; she had reached the determination by a laborious train of reasoning, incident to one of her despondent moods. But her resolve melted when she saw him before her, seated there beside her in the little garden, as if a designing Providence had led him into her path.

"Why have you kept away from me, Robert?" she asked, closing the book that lay open upon the table.

"Why are you so personal, Mrs. Pontellier? Why do you force me to idiotic subterfuges?" he exclaimed with sudden warmth. "I suppose there's no use telling you I've been very busy, or that I've been sick, or that I've been to see you and not found you at home. Please let me off with any one of these excuses."

"You are the embodiment of selfishness," she said. "You save yourself something—I don't know what—but there is some selfish motive, and in sparing yourself you never consider for a moment what I think, or how I feel your neglect and indifference. I suppose this is what you would call unwomanly; but I have got into a habit of expressing myself. It doesn't matter to me, and you may think me unwomanly if you like."

"No; I only think you cruel, as I said the other day. Maybe not intentionally cruel; but you seem to be forcing me into disclosures which can result in nothing; as if you would have me bare a wound for the pleasure of looking at it, without the intention or power of healing it."

"I'm spoiling your dinner, Robert; never mind what I say. You haven't eaten a morsel."

"I only came in for a cup of coffee." His sensitive face was all disfigured with excitement.

"Isn't this a delightful place?" she remarked. "I am so glad it has never actually been discovered. It is so quiet, so sweet, here. Do you notice there is scarcely a sound to be heard? It's so out of the way; and a good walk from the car. However, I don't mind walking. I always feel so sorry for women who don't like to walk; they miss so much—so many rare little glimpses of life; and we women learn so little of life on the whole.

"Catiche's coffee is always hot. I don't know how she manages it, here in open air. Celestine's coffee gets cold bringing it from the kitchen to the dining-room. Three lumps! How can you drink it so sweet? Take some of the cress with your chop; it's so biting and crisp. Then there's the advantage of being able to smoke with your coffee out here. Now, in the city—aren't you going to smoke?"

"After a while," he said, laying a cigar on the table.

"Who gave it to you?" she laughed.

"I bought it. I suppose I'm getting reckless; I bought a whole box." She was determined not to be personal again and make him uncomfortable.

The cat made friends with him, and climbed into his lap when he smoked his cigar. He stroked her silky fur, and talked a little about her. He looked at Edna's book, which he had read; and he told her the end, to save her the trouble of wading through it, he said.

Again he accompanied her back to her home; and it was after dusk when they reached the little "pigeon-house." She did not ask him to remain, which he was grateful for, as it permitted him to stay without the discomfort of blundering through an excuse which he had no intention of considering. He helped her to light the lamp; then she went into her room to take off her hat and to bathe her face and hands.

When she came back Robert was not examining the pictures and magazines as before; he sat off in the shadow, leaning his head back on the chair as if in a reverie. Edna lingered a moment beside the table, arranging the books there. Then she went across the room to where he sat. She bent over the arm of his chair and called his name.

"Robert," she said, "are you asleep?"

"No," he answered, looking up at her.

She leaned over and kissed him—a soft, cool, delicate kiss, whose voluptuous sting penetrated his whole being—then she moved away from him. He followed, and took her in his arms, just holding her close to him. She put her hand up to his face and pressed his cheek against her own. The action was full of love and tenderness. He sought her lips again. Then he drew her down upon the sofa beside him and held her hand in both of his.

"Now you know," he said, "now you know what I have been fighting against since last summer at Grand Isle; what drove me away and drove me back again."

"Why have you been fighting against it?" she asked. Her face glowed with soft lights.

"Why? Because you were not free; you were Léonce Pontellier's wife. I couldn't help loving you if you were ten times his wife; but so long as I went away from you and kept away I could help telling you so." She put her free hand up to his shoulder, and then against his cheek, rubbing it softly. He kissed her again. His face was warm and flushed.

"There in Mexico I was thinking of you all the time, and longing for you."

"But not writing to me," she interrupted.

"Something put into my head that you cared for me; and I lost my senses. I forgot everything but a wild dream of your some way becoming my wife."

"Your wife!"

"Religion, loyalty, everything would give way if only you cared."

"Then you must have forgotten that I was Léonce Pontellier's wife."

"Oh! I was demented, dreaming of wild, impossible things, recalling men who had set their wives free, we have heard of such things."

"Yes, we have heard of such things."

"I came back full of vague, mad intentions. And when I got here—"

"When you got here you never came near me!" She was still caressing his cheek.

"I realized what a cur I was to dream of such a thing, even if you had been willing."

She took his face between her hands and looked into it as if she would never withdraw her eyes more. She kissed him on the forehead, the eyes, the cheeks, and the lips.

"You have been a very, very foolish boy, wasting your time dreaming of impossible things when you speak of Mr. Pontellier setting me free! I am no longer one of Mr. Pontellier's possessions to dispose of or not. I give myself where I choose. If he were to say, 'Here, Robert, take her and be happy; she is yours,' I should laugh at you both."

His face grew a little white. "What do you mean?" he asked.

There was a knock at the door. Old Celestine came in to say that Madame Ratignolle's servant had come around the back way with a message that Madame had been taken sick and begged Mrs. Pontellier to go to her immediately.

"Yes, yes," said Edna, rising; "I promised. Tell her yes—to wait for me. I'll go back with her."

"Let me walk over with you," offered Robert.

"No," she said; "I will go with the servant." She went into her room to put on her hat, and when she came in again she sat once more upon the sofa beside him. He had not stirred. She put her arms about his neck.

"Good-by, my sweet Robert. Tell me good-by." He kissed her with a degree of passion which had not before entered into his caress, and strained her to him.

"I love you," she whispered, "only you; no one but you. It was you who woke me last summer out of a life-long, stupid dream. Oh! you have made me so unhappy with your indifference. Oh! I have suffered, suffered! Now you are here we shall love each other, my Robert. We shall be everything to each other. Nothing else in the world is of any consequence. I must go to my friend; but you will wait for me? No matter how late; you will wait for me, Robert?"

"Don't go; don't go! Oh! Edna, stay with me," he pleaded. "Why should you go? Stay with me, stay with me."

"I shall come back as soon as I can; I shall find you here." She buried her face in his neck, and said good-by again. Her seductive voice, together with his great love for her, had enthralled his senses, had deprived him of every impulse but the longing to hold her and keep her.

XXXVII

Edna looked in at the drug store. Monsieur Ratignolle was putting up a mixture himself, very carefully, dropping a red liquid into a tiny glass. He was grateful to Edna for having come; her presence would be a comfort to his wife. Madame Ratignolle's sister, who had always been with her at such trying times, had not been able to come up from the plantation, and Adèle had been inconsolable until Mrs. Pontellier so kindly promised to come to her. The nurse had been with them at night for the past week, as she lived a great distance away. And Dr. Mandelet had been coming and going all the afternoon. They were then looking for him any moment.

Edna hastened upstairs by a private stairway that led from the rear of the store to the apartments above. The children were all sleeping in a back room. Madame Ratignolle was in the salon, whither she had strayed in her suffering impatience. She sat on the sofa, clad in an ample white *peignoir,* holding a handkerchief tight in her hand with a nervous clutch. Her face was drawn and pinched, her sweet blue eyes haggard and unnatural. All her beautiful hair had been drawn back and plaited. It lay in a long braid on the sofa pillow, coiled like a golden serpent. The nurse, a comfortable looking *Griffe*[129] woman in white apron and cap, was urging her to return to her bedroom.

"There is no use, there is no use," she said at once to Edna. "We must get rid of Mandelet; he is getting too old and careless. He said he would be here at half-past seven; now it must be eight. See what time it is, Joséphine."

The woman was possessed of a cheerful nature, and refused to take any situation too seriously, especially a situation with which she was so familiar. She urged Madame to have courage and patience. But Madame only set her teeth hard into her under lip, and Edna saw the sweat gather in beads on her white forehead. After a moment or two she uttered a profound sigh and wiped her face with the handkerchief rolled in a ball. She appeared exhausted. The nurse gave her a fresh handkerchief, sprinkled with cologne water.

"This is too much!" she cried. "Mandelet ought to be killed! Where is Alphonse? Is it possible I am to be abandoned like this—neglected by every one?'"

"Neglected, indeed!" exclaimed the nurse. Wasn't she there? And here was Mrs. Pontellier leaving, no doubt, a pleasant evening at home to devote to her? And wasn't Monsieur Ratignolle coming that very instant through the hall? And Joséphine was quite sure she had heard Doctor Mandelet's coupé.[130] Yes, there it was, down at the door.

Adèle consented to go back to her room. She sat on the edge of a little low couch next to her bed.

Doctor Mandelet paid no attention to Madame Ratignolle's upbraidings. He was accustomed to them at such times, and was too well convinced of her loyalty to doubt it.

He was glad to see Edna, and wanted her to go with him into the salon and entertain him. But Madame Ratignolle would not consent that Edna should leave her for an instant. Between agonizing moments, she chatted a little, and said it took her mind off her sufferings.

Edna began to feel uneasy. She was seized with a vague dread. Her own like experiences seemed far away, unreal, and only half remembered. She recalled faintly an ecstasy of pain, the heavy odor of chloroform, a stupor which had deadened sensation, and an awakening to find a little new life to which she had given being, added to the great unnumbered multitude of souls that come and go.

She began to wish she had not come; her presence was not necessary. She might have invented a pretext for staying away; she might even invent a pretext

[129]French: the child of a mulatto and a black.
[130]A closed, horse-drawn carriage for two passengers.

now for going. But Edna did not go. With an inward agony, with a flaming outspoken revolt against the ways of Nature, she witnessed the scene [of] torture.

She was still stunned and speechless with emotion when later she leaned over her friend to kiss her and softly say good-by. Adèle, pressing her cheek, whispered in an exhausted voice: "Think of the children, Edna. Oh think of the children! Remember them!"

XXXVIII

Edna still felt dazed when she got outside in the open air. The Doctor's coupé had returned for him and stood before the *porte cochère*. She did not wish to enter the coupé, and told Doctor Mandelet she would walk; she was not afraid, and would go alone. He directed his carriage to meet him at Mrs. Pontellier's, and he started to walk home with her.

Up—away up, over the narrow street between the tall houses, the stars were blazing. The air was mild and caressing, but cool with the breath of spring and the night. They walked slowly, the Doctor with a heavy, measured tread and his hands behind him; Edna, in an absent-minded way, as she had walked one night at Grand Isle, as if her thoughts had gone ahead of her and she was striving to overtake them.

"You shouldn't have been there, Mrs. Pontellier," he said. "That was no place for you. Adéle is full of whims at such times. There were a dozen women she might have had with her, unimpressionable women. I felt that it was cruel, cruel. You shouldn't have gone."

"Oh, well!" she answered, indifferently. "I don't know that it matters after all. One has to think of the children some time or other; the sooner the better."

"When is Léonce coming back?"

"Quite soon. Some time in March."

"And you are going abroad?"

"Perhaps—no, I am not going. I'm not going to be forced into doing things. I don't want to go abroad. I want to be let alone. Nobody has any right—except children, perhaps—and even then, it seems to me—or it did seem—" She felt that her speech was voicing the incoherency of her thoughts, and stopped abruptly.

"The trouble is," sighed the Doctor, grasping her meaning intuitively, "that youth is given up to illusions. It seems to be a provision of Nature; a decoy to secure mothers for the race. And Nature takes no account of moral consequences, or arbitrary conditions which we create, and which we feel obliged to maintain at any cost."

"Yes," she said. "The years that are gone seem like dreams—if one might go on sleeping and dreaming—but to wake up and find—oh! well! perhaps it is better to wake up after all, even to suffer, rather than to remain a dupe to illusions all one's life."

"It seems to me, my dear child," said the Doctor at parting, holding her hand, "you seem to me to be in trouble. I am not going to ask for your confidence. I will only say that if ever you feel moved to give it to me, perhaps I might help you. I know I would understand, and I tell you there are not many who would—not many, my dear."

"Some way I don't feel moved to speak of things that trouble me. Don't think I am ungrateful or that I don't appreciate your sympathy. There are periods of despondency and suffering which take possession of me. But I don't want anything but my own way. That is wanting a good deal, of course, when you have to trample upon the lives, the hearts, the prejudices of others—but no matter—still, I shouldn't want to trample upon the little lives. Oh! I don't know what I'm saying, Doctor. Good night. Don't blame me for anything."

"Yes, I will blame you if you don't come and see me soon. We will talk of things you never have dreamt of talking about before. It will do us both good. I don't want you to blame yourself, whatever comes. Good night, my child."

She let herself in at the gate, but instead of entering she sat upon the step of the porch. The night was quiet and soothing. All the tearing emotion of the last few hours seemed to fall away from her like a somber, uncomfortable garment, which she had but to loosen to be rid of. She went back to that hour before Adèle had sent for her; and her senses kindled afresh in thinking of Robert's words, the pressure of his arms, and the feeling of his lips upon her own. She could picture at the moment no greater bliss on earth than possession of the beloved one. His expression of love had already given him to her in part. When she thought that he was there at hand, waiting for her, she grew numb with the intoxication of expectancy. It was so late; he would be asleep perhaps. She would awaken him with a kiss. She hoped he would be asleep that she might arouse him with her caresses.

Still, she remembered Adèle's voice whispering, "Think of the children; think of them." She meant to think of them; that determination had driven into her soul like a death wound—but not to-night. To-morrow would be time to think of everything.

Robert was not waiting for her in the little parlor. He was nowhere at hand. The house was empty. But he had scrawled on a piece of paper that lay in the lamplight:

"I love you. Good-by—because I love you."

Edna grew faint when she read the words. She went and sat on the sofa. Then she stretched herself out there, never uttering a sound. She did not sleep. She did not go to bed. The lamp sputtered and went out. She was still awake in the morning, when Celestine unlocked the kitchen door and came in to light the fire.

XXXIX

Victor, with hammer and nails and scraps of scantling,[131] was patching a corner of one of the galleries. Mariequita sat near by, dangling her legs, watching him work, and handing him nails from the tool-box. The sun was beating down upon them. The girl covered her head with her apron folded into a square pad. They had been talking for an hour or more. She was never tired of hearing Victor describe the dinner at Mrs. Pontellier's. He exaggerated every detail, making it appear a veritable Lucullean feast.[132] The flowers were in tubs, he said. The champagne was quaffed from huge golden goblets. Venus rising from the foam[133] could have presented no more entrancing a spectacle than Mrs.

[131]Timber.
[132]I.e., like those of Licinius Lucullus, a rich Roman who was famous for his banquets.
[133]In Roman myth, Venus, the goddess of love and beauty, was created out of sea foam.

Pontellier, blazing with beauty and diamonds at the head of the board, while the other women were all of them youthful houris,[134] possessed of incomparable charms.

She got it into her head that Victor was in love with Mrs. Pontellier, and he gave her evasive answers, framed so as to confirm her belief. She grew sullen and cried a little, threatening to go off and leave him to his fine ladies. There were a dozen men crazy about her at the *Chênière;* and since it was the fashion to be in love with married people, why, she could run away any time she liked to New Orleans with Célina's husband.

Célina's husband was a fool, a coward, and a pig, and to prove it to her, Victor intended to hammer his head into a jelly the next time he encountered him. This assurance was very consoling to Mariequita. She dried her eyes, and grew cheerful at the prospect.

They were still talking of the dinner and the allurements of city life when Mrs. Pontellier herself slipped around the corner of the house. The two youngsters stayed dumb with amazement before what they considered to be an apparition. But it was really she in flesh and blood, looking tired and a little travel-stained.

"I walked up from the wharf," she said, "and heard the hammering. I supposed it was you, mending the porch. It's a good thing. I was always tripping over those loose planks last summer. How dreary and deserted everything looks!"

It took Victor some time to comprehend that she had come in Beaudelet's lugger, that she had come alone, and for no purpose but to rest.

"There's nothing fixed up yet, you see. I'll give you my room; it's the only place."

"Any corner will do," she assured him.

"And if you can stand Philomel's cooking," he went on, "though I might try to get her mother while you are here. Do you think she would come?" turning to Mariequita.

Mariequita thought that perhaps Philomel's mother might come for a few days, and money enough.

Beholding Mrs. Pontellier make her appearance, the girl had at once suspected a lovers' rendezvous. But Victor's astonishment was so genuine, and Mrs. Pontellier's indifference so apparent, that the disturbing notion did not lodge long in her brain. She contemplated with the greatest interest this woman who gave the most sumptuous dinners in America, and who had all the men in New Orleans at her feet.

"What time will you have dinner?" asked Edna. "I'm very hungry; but don't get anything extra."

"I'll have it ready in little or no time," he said, bustling and packing away his tools. "You may go to my room to brush up and rest yourself. Mariequita will show you."

"Thank you," said Edna. "But, do you know, I have a notion to go down to the beach and take a good wash and even a little swim, before dinner?"

"The water is too cold!" they both exclaimed. "Don't think of it."

"Well, I might go down and try—dip my toes in. Why, it seems to me the sun is hot enough to have warmed the very depths of the ocean. Could you get me a couple of towels? I'd better go right away, so as to be back in time. It would be a little too chilly if I waited till this afternoon."

[134]Beautiful nymphs who dwell in the Moslem paradise.

Mariequita ran over to Victor's room, and returned with some towels, which she gave to Edna.

"I hope you have fish for dinner," said Edna, as she started to walk away; "but don't do anything extra if you haven't."

"Run and find Philomel's mother," Victor instructed the girl. "I'll go to the kitchen and see what I can do. By Gimminy! Women have no consideration! She might have sent me word."

Edna walked on down to the beach rather mechanically, not noticing anything special except that the sun was hot. She was not dwelling upon any particular train of thought. She had done all the thinking which was necessary after Robert went away, when she lay awake upon the sofa till morning.

She had said over and over to herself: "To-day it is Arobin; to-morrow it will be some one else. It makes no difference to me, it doesn't matter about Léonce Pontellier—but Raoul and Etienne!" She understood now clearly what she had meant long ago when she said to Adèle Ratignolle that she would give up the unessential, but she would never sacrifice herself for her children.

Despondency had come upon her there in the wakeful night, and had never lifted. There was no one thing in the world that she desired. There was no human being whom she wanted near her except Robert; and she even realized that the day would come when he, too, and the thought of him would melt out of her existence, leaving her alone. The children appeared before her like antagonists who had overcome her; who had overpowered and sought to drag her into the soul's slavery for the rest of her days. But she knew a way to elude them. She was not thinking of these things when she walked down to the beach.

The water of the Gulf stretched out before her, gleaming with the million lights of the sun. The voice of the sea is seductive, never ceasing, whispering, clamoring, murmuring, inviting the soul to wander in abysses of solitude. All along the white beach, up and down, there was no living thing in sight. A bird with a broken wing was beating the air above, reeling, fluttering, circling disabled down, down to the water.

Edna had found her old bathing suit still hanging, faded, upon its accustomed peg.

She put it on, leaving her clothing in the bath-house. But when she was there beside the sea, absolutely alone, she cast the unpleasant, pricking garments from her, and for the first time in her life she stood naked in the open air, at the mercy of the sun, the breeze that beat upon her, and the waves that invited her.

How strange and awful it seemed to stand naked under the sky! how delicious! She felt like some new-born creature, opening its eyes in a familiar world that it had never known.

The foamy wavelets curled up to her white feet, and coiled like serpents about her ankles. She walked out. The water was chill, but she walked on. The water was deep, but she lifted her white body and reached out with a long, sweeping stroke. The touch of the sea is sensuous, enfolding the body in its soft, close embrace.

She went on and on. She remembered the night she swam far out, and recalled the terror that seized her at the fear of being unable to regain the shore. She did not look back now, but went on and on, thinking of the blue-grass meadow that she had traversed when a little child, believing that it had no beginning and no end.

Her arms and legs were growing tired.

She thought of Léonce and the children. They were a part of her life. But they need not have thought that they could possess her, body and soul. How Mademoiselle Reisz would have laughed, perhaps sneered, if she knew! "And you call yourself an artist! What pretensions, Madame! The artist must possess the courageous soul that dares and defies."

Exhaustion was pressing upon and overpowering her.

"Good-by—because I love you." He did not know; he did not understand. He would never understand. Perhaps Doctor Mandelet would have understood if she had seen him—but it was too late; the shore was far behind her, and her strength was gone.

She looked into the distance, and the old terror flamed up for an instant, then sank again. Edna heard her father's voice and her sister Margaret's. She heard the barking of an old dog that was chained to the sycamore tree. The spurs of the cavalry officer clanged as he walked across the porch. There was the hum of bees, and the musky odor of pinks filled the air.

1897–1898 1899

THE STORM

I

The leaves were so still that even Bibi thought it was going to rain. Bobinôt, who was accustomed to converse on terms of perfect equality with his little son, called the child's attention to certain sombre clouds that were rolling with sinister intention from the west, accompanied by a sullen, threatening roar. They were at Friedheimer's store and decided to remain there till the storm had passed. They sat within the door on two empty kegs. Bibi was four years old and looked very wise.

"Mama'll be 'fraid, yes," he suggested with blinking eyes.

"She'll shut the house. Maybe she got Sylvie helpin' her this evenin'," Bobinôt responded reassuringly.

"No; she ent got Sylvie. Sylvie was helpin' her yistiday," piped Bibi.

Bobinôt arose and going across to the counter purchased a can of shrimps, of which Calixta was very fond. Then he returned to his perch on the keg and sat stolidly holding the can of shrimps while the storm burst. It shook the wooden store and seemed to be ripping great furrows in the distant field. Bibi laid his little hand on his father's knee and was not afraid.

II

Calixta, at home, felt no uneasiness for their safety. She sat at a side window sewing furiously on a sewing machine. She was greatly occupied and did not notice the approaching storm. But she felt very warm and often stopped to mop her face on which the perspiration gathered in beads. She unfastened her white sacque at the throat. It began to grow dark, and suddenly realizing the situation she got up hurriedly and went about closing windows and doors.

Out on the small front gallery she had hung Bobinôt's Sunday clothes to air and she hastened out to gather them before the rain fell. As she stepped outside, Alcée Laballière rode in at the gate. She had not seen him very often since her marriage, and never alone. She stood there with Bobinôt's coat in her hands, and the big rain drops began to fall. Alcée rode his horse under the shelter of a side projection where the chickens had huddled and there were plows and a harrow piled up in the corner.

"May I come and wait on your gallery till the storm is over, Calixta?" he asked.

"Come 'long in, M'sieur Alcée."

His voice and her own startled her as if from a trance, and she seized Bobinôt's vest. Alcée, mounting to the porch, grabbed the trousers and snatched Bibi's braided jacket that was about to be carried away by a sudden gust of wind. He expressed an intention to remain outside, but it was soon apparent that he might as well have been out in the open: the water beat in upon the boards in driving sheets, and he went inside, closing the door after him. It was even necessary to put something beneath the door to keep the water out.

"My! what a rain! It's good two years sence it rain' like that," exclaimed Calixta as she rolled up a piece of bagging and Alcée helped her to thrust it beneath the crack.

She was a little fuller of figure than five years before when she married; but she had lost nothing of her vivacity. Her blue eyes still retained their melting quality; and her yellow hair, dishevelled by the wind and rain, kinked more stubbornly than ever about her ears and temples.

The rain beat upon the low, shingled roof with a force and clatter that threatened to break an entrance and deluge them there. They were in the dining room—the sitting room—the general utility room. Adjoining was her bed room, with Bibi's couch along side her own. The door stood open, and the room with its white, monumental bed, its closed shutters, looked dim and mysterious.

Alcée flung himself into a rocker and Calixta nervously began to gather up from the floor the lengths of a cotton sheet which she had been sewing.

"If this keeps up, *Dieu sait*[1] if the levees goin' to stan' it!" she exclaimed.

"What have you got to do with the levees?"

"I got enough to do! An' there's Bobinôt with Bibi out in that storm—if he only didn' left Friedheimer's!"

"Let us hope, Calixta, that Bobinôt's got sense enough to come in out of a cyclone."

She went and stood at the window with a greatly disturbed look on her face. She wiped the frame that was clouded with moisture. It was stiflingly hot. Alcée got up and joined her at the window, looking over her shoulder. The rain was coming down in sheets obscuring the view of far-off cabins and enveloping the distant wood in a gray mist. The playing of the lightning was incessant. A bolt struck a tall chinaberry tree at the edge of the field. It filled all visible space with a blinding glare and the crash seemed to invade the very boards they stood upon.

Calixta put her hands to her eyes, and with a cry, staggered backward. Alcée's arm encircled her, and for an instant he drew her close and spasmodically to him.

[1]French: "God knows."

"Bonté!"[2] she cried, releasing herself from his encircling arm and retreating from the window, "the house'll go next! If I only knew w'ere Bibi was!" She would not compose herself; she would not be seated. Alcée clasped her shoulders and looked into her face. The contact of her warm, palpitating body when he had unthinkingly drawn her into his arms, had aroused all the old-time infatuation and desire for her flesh.

"Calixta," he said, "don't be frightened. Nothing can happen. The house is too low to be struck, with so many tall trees standing about. There! aren't you going to be quiet? say, aren't you?" He pushed her hair back from her face that was warm and steaming. Her lips were as red and moist as pomegranate seed. Her white neck and a glimpse of her full, firm bosom disturbed him powerfully. As she glanced up at him the fear in her liquid blue eyes had given place to a drowsy gleam that unconsciously betrayed a sensuous desire. He looked down into her eyes and there was nothing for him to do but to gather her lips in a kiss. It reminded him of Assumption.[3]

"Do you remember—in Assumption, Calixta?" he asked in a low voice broken by passion. Oh! she remembered; for in Assumption he had kissed her and kissed and kissed her; until his senses would well nigh fail, and to save her he would resort to a desperate flight. If she was not an immaculate dove in those days, she was still inviolate; a passionate creature whose very defenselessness had made her defense, against which his honor forbade him to prevail. Now—well, now—her lips seemed in a manner free to be tasted, as well as her round, white throat and her whiter breasts.

They did not heed the crashing torrents, and the roar of the elements made her laugh as she lay in his arms. She was a revelation in that dim, mysterious chamber; as white as the couch she lay upon. Her firm, elastic flesh that was knowing for the first time its birthright, was like a creamy lily that the sun invites to contribute its breath and perfume to the undying life of the world.

The generous abundance of her passion, without guile or trickery, was like a white flame which penetrated and found response in depths of his own sensuous nature that had never yet been reached.

When he touched her breasts they gave themselves up in quivering ecstasy, inviting his lips. Her mouth was a fountain of delight. And when he possessed her, they seemed to swoon together at the very borderland of life's mystery.

He stayed cushioned upon her, breathless, dazed, enervated, with his heart beating like a hammer upon her. With one hand she clasped his head, her lips lightly touching his forehead. The other hand stroked with a soothing rhythm his muscular shoulders.

The growl of the thunder was distant and passing away. The rain beat softly upon the shingles, inviting them to drowsiness and sleep. But they dared not yield.

The rain was over; and the sun was turning the glistening green world into a palace of gems. Calixta, on the gallery, watched Alcée ride away. He turned and smiled at her with a beaming face; and she lifted her pretty chin in the air and laughed aloud.

[2]French: "Kindness"—a cry of alarm.

[3]A Christian feast day (August 15) celebrating the ascension of the Virgin Mary into heaven.

III

Bobinôt and Bibi, trudging home, stopped without at the cistern to make themselves presentable.

"My! Bibi, w'at will yo' mama say! You ought to be ashame'. You oughtn' put on those good pants. Look at 'em! An' that mud on yo' collar! How you got that mud on yo' collar, Bibi? I never saw such a boy!" Bibi was the picture of pathetic resignation. Bobinôt was the embodiment of serious solicitude as he strove to remove from his own person and his son's the signs of their tramp over heavy roads and through wet fields. He scraped the mud off Bibi's bare legs and feet with a stick and carefully removed all traces from his heavy brogans. Then, prepared for the worst—the meeting with an over-scrupulous housewife, they entered cautiously at the back door.

Calixta was preparing supper. She had set the table and was dripping coffee at the hearth. She sprang up as they came in.

"Oh, Bobinôt! You back! My! but I was uneasy. W'ere you been during the rain? An' Bibi? he ain't wet? he ain't hurt?" She had clasped Bibi and was kissing him effusively. Bobinôt's explanations and apologies which he had been composing all along the way, died on his lips as Calixta felt him to see if he were dry, and seemed to express nothing but satisfaction at their safe return.

"I brought you some shrimps, Calixta," offered Bobinôt, hauling the can from his ample side pocket and laying it on the table.

"Shrimps! Oh, Bobinôt! you too good fo' anything! and she gave him a smacking kiss on the cheek that resounded. "*J'vous réponds,*[4] we'll have a feas' to night! umph-umph!"

Bobinôt and Bibi began to relax and enjoy themselves, and when the three seated themselves at table they laughed much and so loud that anyone might have heard them as far away as Laballière's.

IV

Alcée Laballière wrote to his wife, Clarisse, that night. It was a loving letter, full of tender solicitude. He told her not to hurry back, but if she and the babies liked it at Biloxi, to stay a month longer. He was getting on nicely; and though he missed them, he was willing to bear the separation a while longer—realizing that their health and pleasure were the first things to be considered.

V

As for Clarisse, she was charmed upon receiving her husband's letter. She and the babies were doing well. The society was agreeable; many of her old friends and acquaintances were at the bay. And the first free breath since her marriage seemed to restore the pleasant liberty of her maiden days. Devoted as she was to her husband, their intimate conjugal life was something which she was more than willing to forego for a while.

So the storm passed and every one was happy.

1898

[4]French: "I'll answer you."

Stephen Crane 1871–1900

Stephen Crane's father was a Methodist preacher in Newark, New Jersey, Crane's birthplace. His mother was a social leader and temperance crusader. Both parents exhibited a characteristic nineteenth-century faith in the benevolence of God, in the existence of free will, and in the significance of man in the universe—ideas that their son, in the course of his short and tempestuous life, would attack with humor and savage irony.

Crane had originally hoped to be a soldier, but in 1890, after two and a half years at a military prep school in New York, he entered Lafayette College to study mining-engineering. After one term he left Lafayette and transferred to Syracuse University. There he devoted most of his efforts to playing varsity baseball, working as a local correspondent for the New York Tribune, *and writing his first short stories. After less than a year at Syracuse, Crane withdrew and moved to New York City. There he mingled with Bohemian art students living in tenements, and he struggled to earn his way as a freelance journalist contributing items to New York newspapers.*

Crane's observation of life on New York's Bowery and his reading of exposés of New York slum life provided him with much of the background material for his first novel, Maggie, A Girl of the Streets *(1893). It was the first naturalistic novel written by an American, and its stark description of squalor and immorality was so shocking for its time that Crane, unable to find an interested publisher, was obliged to publish the novel at his own expense. In 1895, he published his first book of poems,* The Black Riders, *short, caustic, free-verse parables of the absurdity of the human condition. In the same year* The Red Badge of Courage *was published in book form, bringing Crane international acclaim.*

His travels as a reporter for a newspaper syndicate took him through the American West, to Mexico, and to Florida where he joined in the unsuccessful gun-running expedition to Cuba that led to his most famous short story, "The Open Boat." In 1897, Crane settled in England, became friends with Joseph Conrad and Henry James, and labored mightily at writing fiction and doing editorial hackwork in an effort to pay for his extravagant style of living. The next year, in spite of ill health, Crane went to Cuba as a war correspondent reporting on the Spanish-American War for the New York World. *When he returned to England early in 1899 he was suffering from tuberculosis, and in June 1900, after traveling to a German sanitarium to seek a cure, Crane died. He was twenty-eight.*

His early writing had been burlesques and satires, expressions of ironic detachment. Crane had announced that his ambition as a writer was to achieve personal honesty—to deflate romantic idealism, and portray men battered and alone in a hostile world. He has been viewed as an uncompromising determinist, a literary naturalist who saw human beings as wholly controlled by their environment and their heredity. At the same time he has been seen as a Christian symbolist expressing faith in the ultimate understanding and redemption of people. Crane was a pioneer of a new literary realism that was impressionistic in its vivid imagery, in its characterizations, and in its narrative style. And he was a master of irony, scrutinizing the persistent illusions of people and the disparity between their buoyant expectations and their doom.

FURTHER READING: *The Works of Stephen Crane,* 12 vols., ed. W. Follett, 1925–1927, 1963; *The Works of Stephen Crane,* 10 vols., ed. F. Bowers, 1969–1975; *The Correspondence of Stephen Crane,* 2 vols., ed. S. Wertheim and P. Sorrentino, 1988; J. Berryman, *Stephen Crane,* 1950, 1962, 1980; D. Hoffman, *The Poetry of Stephen Crane,* 1957; E. Cady, *Stephen Crane,* 1962, 1980; E. Solomon, *Stephen Crane: From Parody to Realism,* 1966; R. Stallman,

Stephen Crane, 1968; D. Gibson, *The Fiction of Stephen Crane,* 1968; M. LaFrance, *A Reading of Stephen Crane,* 1971; *Stephen Crane in Transition: Centenary Essays,* ed. J. Katz, 1972; *Stephen Crane's Career,* ed. T. Gullason, 1973; F. Bergon, *Stephen Crane's Artistry,* 1975; J. Nagel, *Stephen Crane and Literary Impressionism,* 1980; C. Wolford, *The Anger of Stephen Crane,* 1983; J. Colvert, *Stephen Crane,* 1984; M. Fried, *Realism, Writing, Disfiguration,* 1987; *Stephen Crane,* ed. H. Bloom, 1987; *Stephen Crane's The Red Badge of Courage,* ed. H. Bloom, 1987; B. Knapp, *Stephen Crane,* 1987; C. Wolford, *Stephen Crane: A Study of the Short Fiction,* 1989; D. Halliburton, *The Color of the Sky: A Study of Stephen Crane,* 1989; C. Benfey, *The Double Life of Stephen Crane,* 1992; S. Wertheim and P. Sorrentino, *The Crane Log: A Documentary Life of Stephen Crane,* 1993; P. Dooley, *The Pluralistic Philosophy of Stephen Crane,* 1993; *Recovering Crane: Essays on a Poet,* ed. R. Kelly and A. Lathrop, 1993; M. Robertson, *Stephen Crane: Journalism and the Making of Modern American Literature,* 1997; L. Davis, *Badge of Courage: The Life of Stephen Crane,* 1998; R. Morris, *Stephen Crane: A Biography,* 2005.

TEXTS: *The Poems of Stephen Crane,* ed. J. Katz, 1966; "The Open Boat," *The Works of Stephen Crane,* Vol. V, *Tales of Adventure,* ed. F. Bowers, 1970; "The Blue Hotel," *The Monster and Other Stories,* 1899.

BLACK RIDERS CAME FROM THE SEA[1]

Black riders came from the sea.
There was clang and clang of spear and shield,
And clash and clash of hoof and heel,
Wild shouts and the wave of hair
In the rush upon the wind:
Thus the ride of Sin.
1894 1895

IN THE DESERT

In the desert
I saw a creature, naked, bestial,
Who, squatting upon the ground,
Held his heart in his hands,
And ate of it.
I said: "Is it good, friend?"
"It is bitter—bitter," he answered;
"But I like it
Because it is bitter,
And because it is my heart."
1894 1895

[1]Crane's poems were published without titles. The titles used here were supplied by the editors.

A GOD IN WRATH

A god in wrath
Was beating a man;
He cuffed him loudly
With thunderous blows
That rang and rolled over the earth.
All people came running.
The man screamed and struggled,
And bit madly at the feet of the god.
The people cried:
"Ah, what a wicked man!"
And—
"Ah, what a redoubtable god!"
1894 1895

I SAW A MAN PURSUING THE HORIZON

I saw a man pursuing the horizon;
Round and round they sped.
I was disturbed at this;
I accosted the man.
"It is futile," I said,
"You can never—"

"You lie," he cried,
And ran on.
1894 1895

SUPPOSING THAT I SHOULD HAVE THE COURAGE

Supposing that I should have the courage
To let a red sword of virtue
Plunge into my heart,
Letting to the weeds of the ground
My sinful blood,
What can you offer me?
A gardened castle?
A flowery kingdom?

What? A hope?
Then hence with your red sword of virtue.
1894 1895

ON THE HORIZON THE PEAKS ASSEMBLED

On the horizon the peaks assembled;
And as I looked,
The march of the mountains began.
As they marched, they sang:
"Aye! We come! We come!"
1894 1895

A MAN FEARED THAT HE MIGHT FIND AN ASSASSIN

A man feared that he might find an assassin;
Another that he might find a victim.
One was more wise than the other.
1894 1895

DO NOT WEEP, MAIDEN, FOR WAR IS KIND

Do not weep, maiden, for war is kind.
Because your lover threw wild hands toward the sky
And the affrighted steed ran on alone,
Do not weep.
War is kind.

Hoarse, booming drums of the regiment,
Little souls who thirst for fight,
These men were born to drill and die.
The unexplained glory flies above them,
Great is the Battle-God, great, and his Kingdom—
A field where a thousand corpses lie.

Do not weep, babe, for war is kind.
Because your father tumbled in the yellow trenches,
Raged at his breast, gulped and died,
Do not weep.
War is kind.

Swift blazing flag of the regiment,
Eagle with crest of red and gold,
These men were born to drill and die.
Point for them the virtue of slaughter,
Make plain to them the excellence of killing
And a field where a thousand corpses lie.

Mother whose heart hung humble as a button
On the bright splendid shroud of your son,
Do not weep.
War is kind.
1895 1896, 1899

A MAN SAID TO THE UNIVERSE

A man said to the universe:
"Sir, I exist!"
"However," replied the universe,
"The fact has not created in me
A sense of obligation."
1894 1899

A MAN ADRIFT ON A SLIM SPAR

A man adrift on a slim spar
A horizon smaller than the rim of a bottle
Tented waves rearing lashy dark points
The near whine of froth in circles.
God is cold.

The incessant raise and swing of the sea
And growl after growl of crest
The sinkings, green, seething, endless
The upheaval half-completed.
God is cold.

The seas are in the hollow of The Hand;
Oceans may be turned to a spray
Raining down through the stars
Because of a gesture of pity toward a babe.
Oceans may become grey ashes,
Die with a long moan and a roar
Amid the tumult of the fishes
And the cries of the ships,
Because The Hand beckons the mice.

A horizon smaller than a doomed assassin's cap,
Inky, surging tumults
A reeling, drunken sky and no sky
A pale hand sliding from a polished spar.
God is cold.

The puff of a coat imprisoning air.
A face kissing the water-death
A weary slow sway of a lost hand
And the sea, the moving sea, the sea.
God is cold.
1897 1929

THE BLUE HOTEL

I

The Palace Hotel at Fort Romper was painted a light blue, a shade that is on the legs of a kind of heron, causing the bird to declare its position against any background. The Palace Hotel, then, was always screaming and howling in a way that made the dazzling winter landscape of Nebraska seem only a gray swampish hush. It stood alone on the prairie, and when the snow was falling the town two hundred yards away was not visible. But when the traveler alighted at the railway station he was obliged to pass the Palace Hotel before he could come upon the company of low clap-board houses which composed Fort Romper, and it was not to be thought that any traveler could pass the Palace Hotel without looking at it. Pat Scully, the proprietor, had proved himself a master of strategy when he chose his paints. It is true that on clear days, when the great trans-continental expresses, long lines of swaying Pullmans, swept through Fort Romper, passengers were overcome at the sight, and the cult that knows the brown-reds and the subdivisions of the dark greens of the East expressed shame, pity, horror, in a laugh. But to the citizens of this prairie town, and to the people who would naturally stop there, Pat Scully had performed a feat. With this opulence and splendor, these creeds, classes, egotisms, that streamed through Romper on the rails day after day, they had no color in common.

As if the displayed delights of such a blue hotel were not sufficiently enticing, it was Scully's habit to go every morning and evening to meet the leisurely trains that stopped at Romper and work his seductions upon any man that he might see wavering, gripsack in hand.

One morning, when a snow-crusted engine dragged its long string of freight cars and its one passenger coach to the station, Scully performed the marvel of catching three men. One was a shaky and quick-eyed Swede, with a great shining cheap valise; one was a tall bronzed cowboy, who was on his way to a ranch near the Dakota line; one was a little silent man from the East, who didn't look it, and didn't announce it. Scully practically made them prisoners. He was so nimble and merry and kindly that each probably felt it would be the height of brutality to try to escape. They trudged off over the creaking board sidewalks in the wake of the eager little Irishman. He wore a heavy fur cap squeezed tightly down on his head. It caused his two red ears to stick out stiffly, as if they were made of tin.

At last Scully, elaborately, with boisterous hospitality, conducted them through the portals of the blue hotel. The room which they entered was small. It seemed to be merely a proper temple for an enormous stove, which, in the center, was humming with godlike violence. At various points on its surface the iron had become luminous and glowed yellow from the heat. Beside the stove Scully's son Johnnie was playing High-Five[1] with an old farmer who had whiskers both gray and sandy. They were quarreling. Frequently the old farmer turned his face toward a box of sawdust—colored brown from tobacco juice—that was behind the stove, and spat with an air of great impatience and irritation. With a loud flourish of words Scully destroyed the game of cards, and bustled his son upstairs with part of the baggage of the new guests. He himself conducted them to three basins of the coldest water in the world. The cowboy and the Easterner burnished themselves fiery red with this water, until it seemed to be some kind of a metal polish. The Swede, however, merely dipped his fingers gingerly and with trepidation. It was notable that throughout this series of small ceremonies the three travelers were made to feel that Scully was very benevolent. He was conferring great favors upon them. He handed the towel from one to the other with an air of philanthropic impulse.

Afterward they went to the first room, and, sitting about the stove, listened to Scully's officious clamor at his daughters, who were preparing the midday meal. They reflected in the silence of experienced men who tread carefully amid new people. Nevertheless, the old farmer, stationary, invincible in his chair near the warmest part of the stove, turned his face from the sawdust box frequently and addressed a glowing commonplace to the strangers. Usually he was answered in short but adequate sentences by either the cowboy or the Easterner. The Swede said nothing. He seemed to be occupied in making furtive estimates of each man in the room. One might have thought that he had the sense of silly suspicion which comes to guilt. He resembled a badly frightened man.

Later, at dinner, he spoke a little, addressing his conversation entirely to Scully. He volunteered that he had come from New York, where for ten years he had worked as a tailor. These facts seemed to strike Scully as fascinating, and afterward he volunteered that he had lived at Romper for fourteen years. The Swede asked about the crops and the price of labor. He seemed barely to listen to Scully's extended replies. His eyes continued to rove from man to man.

Finally, with a laugh and a wink, he said that some of these Western communities were very dangerous; and after his statement he straightened his legs under the table, tilted his head, and laughed again, loudly. It was plain that the demonstration had no meaning to the others. They looked at him wondering and in silence.

II

As the men trooped heavily back into the front room, the two little windows presented views of a turmoiling sea of snow. The huge arms of the wind were making attempts—mighty, circular, futile—to embrace the flakes as they sped. A gate-post like a still man with a blanched face stood aghast amid this profligate fury. In a hearty voice Scully announced the presence of a blizzard. The guests of the blue hotel, lighting their pipes, assented with grunts of lazy masculine contentment. No island of the sea could be exempt in the degree of this little

[1]A card game.

room with its humming stove. Johnnie, son of Scully, in a tone which defined his opinion of his ability as a card-player, challenged the old farmer of both gray and sandy whiskers to a game of High-Five. The farmer agreed with a contemptuous and bitter scoff. They sat close to the stove, and squared their knees under a wide board. The cowboy and the Easterner watched the game with interest. The Swede remained near the window, aloof, but with a countenance that showed signs of an inexplicable excitement.

The play of Johnnie and the gray-beard was suddenly ended by another quarrel. The old man arose while casting a look of heated scorn at his adversary. He slowly buttoned his coat, and then stalked with fabulous dignity from the room. In the discreet silence of all the other men the Swede laughed. His laughter rang somehow childish. Men by this time had begun to look at him askance, as if they wished to inquire what ailed him.

A new game was formed jocosely. The cowboy volunteered to become the partner of Johnnie, and they all then turned to ask the Swede to throw in his lot with the little Easterner. He asked some questions about the game, and learning that it wore many names, and that he had played it when it was under an alias, he accepted the invitation. He strode toward the men nervously, as if he expected to be assaulted. Finally, seated, he gazed from face to face and laughed shrilly. This laugh was so strange that the Easterner looked up quickly, the cowboy sat intent and with his mouth open, and Johnnie paused, holding the cards with still fingers.

Afterward there was a short silence. Then Johnnie said: "Well, let's get at it. Come on now!" They pulled their chairs forward until their knees were bunched under the board. They began to play, and their interest in the game caused the others to forget the manner of the Swede.

The cowboy was a board-whacker. Each time that he held superior cards he whanged them, one by one, with exceeding force, down upon the improvised table, and took the tricks with a glowing air of prowess and pride that sent thrills of indignation into the hearts of his opponents. A game with a board-whacker in it is sure to become intense. The countenances of the Easterner and the Swede were miserable whenever the cowboy thundered down his aces and kings, while Johnnie, his eyes gleaming with joy, chuckled and chuckled.

Because of the absorbing play none considered the strange ways of the Swede. They paid strict heed to the game. Finally, during a lull caused by a new deal, the Swede suddenly addressed Johnnie: "I suppose there have been a good many men killed in this room." The jaws of the others dropped and they looked at him.

"What in hell are you talking about?" said Johnnie.

The Swede laughed again his blatant laugh, full of a kind of false courage and defiance. "Oh, you know what I mean all right," he answered.

"I'm a liar if I do!" Johnnie protested. The card was halted, and the men stared at the Swede. Johnnie evidently felt that as the son of the proprietor he should make a direct inquiry. "Now, what might you be drivin' at, mister?" he asked. The Swede winked at him. It was a wink full of cunning. His fingers shook on the edge of the board. "Oh, maybe you think I have been to nowheres. Maybe you think I'm a tenderfoot?"

"I don't know nothin' about you," answered Johnnie, "and I don't give a damn where you've been. All I got to say is that I don't know what you're driving at. There hain't never been nobody killed in this room."

The cowboy, who had been steadily gazing at the Swede, then spoke. "What's wrong with you, mister?"

Apparently it seemed to the Swede that he was formidably menaced. He shivered and turned white near the corners of his mouth. He sent an appealing glance in the direction of the little Easterner. During these moments he did not forget to wear his air of advanced pot-valor. "They say they don't know what I mean," he remarked mockingly to the Easterner.

The latter answered after prolonged and cautious reflection. "I don't understand you," he said, impassively.

The Swede made a movement then which announced that he thought he had encountered treachery from the only quarter where he had expected sympathy if not help. "Oh, I see you are all against me. I see."

The cowboy was in a state of deep stupefaction. "Say," he cried, as he tumbled the deck violently down upon the board. "Say, what are you gittin' at, hey?"

The Swede sprang up with the celerity[2] of a man escaping from a snake on the floor. "I don't want to fight!" he shouted. "I don't want to fight!"

The cowboy stretched his long legs indolently and deliberately. His hands were in his pockets. He spat into the sawdust box. "Well, who the hell thought you did?" he inquired.

The Swede backed rapidly toward a corner of the room. His hands were out protectingly in front of his chest, but he was making an obvious struggle to control his fright. "Gentlemen," he quavered, "I suppose I am going to be killed before I can leave this house! I suppose I am going to be killed before I can leave this house." In his eyes was the dying swan look. Through the windows could be seen the snow turning blue in the shadow of dusk. The wind tore at the house and some loose thing beat regularly against the clap-boards[3] like a spirit tapping.

A door opened, and Scully himself entered. He paused in surprise as he noted the tragic attitude of the Swede. Then he said: "What's the matter here?"

The Swede answered him swiftly and eagerly: "These men are going to kill me."

"Kill you!" ejaculated Scully. "Kill you! What are you talkin'?"

The Swede made the gesture of a martyr.

Scully wheeled sternly upon his son. "What is this, Johnnie?"

The lad had grown sullen. "Damned if I know," he answered. "I can't make no sense to it." He began to shuffle the cards, fluttering them together with an angry snap. "He says a good many men have been killed in this room, or something like that. And he says he's goin' to be killed here too. I don't know what ails him. He's crazy, I shouldn't wonder."

Scully then looked for explanation to the cowboy, but the cowboy simply shrugged his shoulders.

"Kill you?" said Scully again to the Swede. "Kill you? Man, you're off your nut."

"Oh, I know," burst out the Swede. "I know what will happen. Yes, I'm crazy—yes. Yes, of course, I'm crazy—yes. But I know one thing," There was a sort of sweat of misery and terror upon his face. "I know I won't get out of here alive."

The Swede held a huge fist in front of Johnnie's face.

The cowboy drew a deep breath, as if his mind was passing into the last stages of dissolution. "Well, I'm dog-goned," he whispered to himself.

[2]Quickness. [3]Narrow horizontal boards used as siding for the building.

Scully wheeled suddenly and faced his son. "You've been troublin' this man!"

Johnnie's voice was loud with its burden of grievance. "Why, good Gawd, I ain't done nothin' to 'im."

The Swede broke in. "Gentlemen, do not disturb yourselves. I will leave this house. I will go 'way because—" He accused them dramatically with his glance. "Because I do not want to be killed."

Scully was furious with his son. "Will you tell me what is the matter, you young divil? What's the matter, anyhow? Speak out!"

"Blame it," cried Johnnie in despair, "don't I tell you I don't know. He—he says we want to kill him, and that's all I know. I can't tell what ails him."

The Swede continued to repeat: "Never mind, Mr. Scully, never mind. I will leave this house. I will go away, because I do not wish to be killed. Yes, of course, I am crazy—yes. But I know one thing! I will go away. I will leave this house. Never mind, Mr. Scully, never mind. I will go away."

"You will not go 'way," said Scully. "You will not go 'way until I hear the reason of this business. If anybody has troubled you I will take care of him. This is my house. You are under my roof, and I will not allow any peaceable man to be troubled here. He cast a terrible eye upon Johnnie, the cowboy, and the Easterner.

"Never mind, Mr. Scully; never mind. I will go 'way. I do not wish to be killed." The Swede moved toward the door, which opened upon the stairs. It was evidently his intention to go at once for his baggage.

"No, no," shouted Scully peremptorily; but the white-faced man slid by him and disappeared. "Now," said Scully severely, "what does this mane?"

Johnnie and the cowboy cried together: "Why, we didn't do nothin' to 'im!"

Scully's eyes were cold. "No," he said, "you didn't?"

Johnnie swore a deep oath. "Why, this is the wildest loon I ever see. We didn't do nothin' at all. We were jest sittin' here playin' cards and he—"

The father suddenly spoke to the Easterner. "Mr. Blanc," he asked, "what has these boys been doin'?"

The Easterner reflected again. "I didn't see anything wrong at all," he said at last slowly.

Scully began to howl. "But what does it mane?" He stared ferociously at his son. "I have a mind to lather you for this, me boy."

Johnnie was frantic. "Well, what have I done?" he bawled at his father.

III

"I think you are tongue-tied," said Scully finally to his son, the cowboy and the Easterner, and at the end of this scornful sentence he left the room.

Upstairs the Swede was swiftly fastening the straps of his great valise. Once his back happened to be half-turned toward the door, and hearing a noise there, he wheeled and sprang up, uttering a loud cry. Scully's wrinkled visage showed grimly in the light of the small lamp he carried. This yellow effulgence,[4] streaming upward, colored only his prominent features, and left his eyes, for instance, in mysterious shadow. He resembled a murderer.

"Man, man!" he exclaimed, "have you gone daffy?"

[4]Radiance; brightness.

"Oh, no! Oh, no!" rejoined the other. "There are people in this world who know pretty nearly as much as you do—understand?"

For a moment they stood gazing at each other. Upon the Swede's deathly pale cheeks were two spots brightly crimson and sharply edged, as if they had been carefully painted. Scully placed the light on the table and sat himself on the edge of the bed. He spoke ruminatively. "By cracky, I never heard of such a thing in my life. It's a complete muddle. I can't for the soul of me think how you ever got this idea into your head." Presently he lifted his eyes and asked: "And did you sure think they were going to kill you?"

The Swede scanned the old man as if he wished to see into his mind. "I did," he said at last. He obviously suspected that this answer might precipitate an outbreak. As he pulled on a strap his whole arm shook, the elbow wavering like a bit of paper.

Scully banged his hand impressively on the foot-board of the bed. "Why, man, we're goin' to have a line of ilictric street-cars in this town next spring."

"'A line of electric street-cars,'" repeated the Swede stupidly.

"And," said Scully, "there's a new railroad goin' to be built down from Broken Arm[5] to here. Not to mintion the four churches and the smashin' big brick school-house. Then there's the big factory, too. Why, in two years Romper'll be a met-tro-pol-is."

Having finished the preparation of his baggage, the Swede straightened himself. "Mr. Scully," he said with sudden hardihood, "how much do I owe you?"

"You don't owe me anythin'," said the old man angrily.

"Yes, I do," retorted the Swede. He took seventy-five cents from his pocket and tendered it to Scully; but the latter snapped his fingers in disdainful refusal. However, it happened that they both stood gazing in a strange fashion at the three silver pieces on the Swede's open palm.

"I'll not take your money," said Scully at last. "Not after what's been goin' on here." Then a plan seemed to strike him. "Here," he cried, picking up his lamp and moving toward the door. "Here! Come with me a minute."

"No," said the Swede in overwhelming alarm.

"Yes," urged the old man. "Come on! I want you to come and see a picter—just across the hall—in my room."

The Swede must have concluded that his hour was come. His jaw dropped and his teeth showed like a dead man's. He ultimately followed Scully across the corridor, but he had the step of one hung in chains.

Scully flashed the light high on the wall of his own chamber. There was revealed a ridiculous photograph of a little girl. She was leaning against a balustrade[6] of gorgeous decoration, and the formidable bang to her hair was prominent. The figure was as graceful as an upright sled-stake, and, withal, it was of the hue of lead. "There," said Scully tenderly. "That's the picter of my little girl that died. Her name was Carrie. She had the purtiest hair you ever saw! I was that fond of her, she—"

Turning then he saw that the Swede was not contemplating the picture at all, but, instead, was keeping keen watch on the gloom in the rear.

"Look, man!" shouted Scully heartily. "That's the picter of my little gal that died. Her name was Carrie. And then here's the picter of my oldest boy, Michael. He's a lawyer in Lincoln an' doin' well. I gave that boy a grand eddycation, and

[5]Another town. [6]Railing.

I'm glad for it now. He's a fine boy. Look at 'im now. Ain't he bold as blazes, him there in Lincoln, an honored an' respicted gintleman. An honored an' respicted gintleman," concluded Scully with a flourish. And so saying, he smote the Swede jovially on the back.

The Swede faintly smiled.

"Now," said the old man, "there's only one more thing." He dropped suddenly to the floor and thrust his head beneath the bed. The Swede could hear his muffled voice. "I'd keep it under me piller if it wasn't for that boy Johnnie. Then there's the old woman—Where is it now? I never put it twice in the same place. Ah, now come out with you!"

Presently he backed clumsily from under the bed, dragging with him an old coat rolled into a bundle. "I've fetched him," he muttered. Kneeling on the floor he unrolled the coat and extracted from its heart a large yellow-brown whisky bottle.

His first maneuver was to hold the bottle up to the light. Reassured, apparently, that nobody had been tampering with it, he thrust it with a generous movement toward the Swede.

The weak-kneed Swede was about to eagerly clutch this element of strength, but he suddenly jerked his hand away and cast a look of horror upon Scully.

"Drink," said the old man affectionately. He had arisen to his feet, and now stood facing the Swede.

There was a silence. Then again Scully said: "Drink!"

The Swede laughed wildly. He grabbed the bottle, put it to his mouth, and as his lips curled absurdly around the opening and his throat worked, he kept his glance burning with hatred upon the old man's face.

IV

After the departure of Scully the three men, with the card-board still upon their knees, preserved for a long time an astounded silence. Then Johnnie said: "That's the dod-dangest Swede I ever see."

"He ain't no Swede," said the cowboy scornfully.

"Well, what is he then?" cried Johnnie. "What is he then?"

"It's my opinion," replied the cowboy deliberately, "he's some kind of a Dutchman." It was a venerable custom of the country to entitle as Swedes all light-haired men who spoke with a heavy tongue. In consequence the idea of the cowboy was not without its daring. "Yes, sir," he repeated. "It's my opinion this feller is some kind of a Dutchman."

"Well, he says he's a Swede, anyhow," muttered Johnnie sulkily. He turned to the Easterner. "What do you think, Mr. Blanc?"

"Oh, I don't know," replied the Easterner.

"Well, what do you think makes him act that way?" asked the cowboy.

"Why, he's frightened!" The Easterner knocked his pipe against a rim of the stove. "He's clear frightened out of his boots."

"What at?" cried Johnnie and cowboy together.

The Easterner reflected over his answer.

"What at?" cried the others again.

"Oh, I don't know, but it seems to me this man has been reading dime-novels, and he thinks he's right out in the middle of it—the shootin' and stabbin' and all."

"But," said the cowboy, deeply scandalized, "this ain't Wyoming, ner none of them places. This is Nebrasker."

"Yes," added Johnnie, "an' why don't he wait till he gits out West?"

The traveled Easterner laughed. "It isn't different there even—not in these days. But he thinks he's right in the middle of hell."

Johnnie and the cowboy mused long.

"It's awful funny," remarked Johnnie at last.

"Yes," said the cowboy. "This is a queer game. I hope we don't git snowed in, because then we'd have to stand this here man bein' around with us all the time. That wouldn't be no good."

"I wish pop would throw him out," said Johnnie.

Presently they heard a loud stamping on the stairs, accompanied by ringing jokes in the voice of old Scully, and laughter, evidently from the Swede. The men around the stove stared vacantly at each other. "Gosh," said the cowboy. The door flew open, and old Scully, flushed and anecdotal, came into the room. He was jabbering at the Swede, who followed him, laughing bravely. It was the entry of two roysterers[7] from a banquet hall.

"Come now," said Scully sharply to the three seated men, "move up and give us a chance at the stove." The cowboy and the Easterner obediently sidled their chairs to make room for the newcomers. Johnnie, however, simply arranged himself in a more indolent attitude, and then remained motionless.

"Come! Git over, there," said Scully.

"Plenty of room on the other side of the stove," said Johnnie.

"Do you think we want to sit in the draught?" roared the father.

But the Swede here interposed with a grandeur of confidence. "No, no. Let the boy sit where he likes," he cried in a bullying voice to the father.

"All right! All right!" said Scully deferentially. The cowboy and the Easterner exchanged glances of wonder.

The five chairs were formed in a crescent about one side of the stove. The Swede began to talk; he talked arrogantly, profanely, angrily. Johnnie, the cowboy and the Easterner maintained a morose silence, while old Scully appeared to be receptive and eager, breaking in constantly with sympathetic ejaculations.

Finally the Swede announced that he was thirsty. He moved in his chair, and said that he would go for a drink of water.

"I'll git it for you," cried Scully at once.

"No," said the Swede contemptuously. "I'll get it for myself." He arose and stalked with the air of an owner off into the executive parts of the hotel.

As soon as the Swede was out of hearing Scully sprang to his feet and whispered intensely to the others. "Upstairs he thought I was tryin' to poison 'im."

"Say," said Johnnie, "this makes me sick. Why don't you throw 'im out in the snow?"

"Why, he's all right now," declared Scully. "It was only that he was from the East and he thought this was a tough place. That's all. He's all right now."

The cowboy looked with admiration upon the Easterner. "You were straight," he said. "You were on to that there Dutchman."

"Well," said Johnnie to his father, "he may be all right now, but I don't see it. Other time he was scared, and now he's too fresh."

[7]Roisterers: revelers.

Scully's speech was always a combination of Irish brogue and idiom, Western twang and idiom, and scraps of curiously formal diction taken from the story-books and newspapers. He now hurled a strange mass of language at the head of his son. "What do I keep? What do I keep? What do I keep?" he demanded in a voice of thunder. He slapped his knee impressively, to indicate that he himself was going to make reply, and that all should heed. "I keep a hotel," he shouted. "A hotel, do you mind? A guest under my roof has sacred privileges. He is to be intimidated by none. Not one word shall he hear that would prijudice him in favor of goin' away. I'll not have it. There's no place in this here town where they can say they iver took in a guest of mine because he was afraid to stay here." He wheeled suddenly upon the cowboy and the Easterner. "Am I right?"

"Yes, Mr. Scully," said the cowboy, "I think you're right."

"Yes, Mr. Scully," said the Easterner, "I think you're right."

V

At six-o'clock supper, the Swede fizzed like a fire-wheel. He sometimes seemed on the point of bursting into riotous song, and in all his madness he was encouraged by old Scully. The Easterner was incased in reserve; the cowboy sat in wide-mouthed amazement, forgetting to eat, while Johnnie wrathily demolished great plates of food. The daughters of the house when they were obliged to replenish the biscuits approached as warily as Indians, and, having succeeded in their purposes, fled with ill-concealed trepidation. The Swede domineered the whole feast, and he gave it the appearance of a cruel bacchanal. He seemed to have grown suddenly taller; he gazed, brutally disdainful, into every face. His voice rang through the room. Once when he jabbed out harpoon-fashion with his fork to pinion a biscuit the weapon nearly impaled the hand of the Easterner which had been stretched quietly out for the same biscuit.

After supper, as the men filed toward the other room, the Swede smote Scully ruthlessly on the shoulder. "Well, old boy, that was a good square meal." Johnnie looked hopefully at his father; he knew that shoulder was tender from an old fall; and indeed it appeared for a moment as if Scully was going to flame out over the matter, but in the end he smiled a sickly smile and remained silent. The others understood from his manner that he was admitting his responsibility for the Swede's new viewpoint.

Johnnie, however, addressed his parent in an aside. "Why don't you license somebody to kick you downstairs?" Scully scowled darkly by way of reply.

When they were gathered about the stove, the Swede insisted on another game of High-Five. Scully gently deprecated the plan at first, but the Swede turned a wolfish glare upon him. The old man subsided, and the Swede canvassed the others. In his tone there was always a great threat. The cowboy and the Easterner both remarked indifferently that they would play. Scully said that he would presently have to go to meet the 6:58 train, and so the Swede turned menacingly upon Johnnie. For a moment their glances crossed like blades, and then Johnnie smiled and said: "Yes, I'll play."

They formed a square with the little board on their knees. The Easterner and the Swede were again partners. As the play went on, it was noticeable that the cowboy was not board-whacking as usual. Meanwhile, Scully, near the lamp, had put on his spectacles and, with an appearance curiously like an old priest, was reading a newspaper. In time he went out to meet the 6:58 train, and, despite his precautions, a gust of polar wind whirled into the room as he opened the door. Besides scattering the cards, it chilled the players to the marrow. The Swede cursed frightfully. When Scully returned, his entrance disturbed a cozy and friendly scene. The Swede again cursed. But presently they were once more intent, their heads bent forward and their hands moving swiftly. The Swede had adopted the fashion of board-whacking.

Scully took up his paper and for a long time remained immersed in matters which were extraordinarily remote from him. The lamp burned badly, and once he stopped to adjust the wick. The newspaper as he turned from page to page rustled with a slow and comfortable sound. Then suddenly he heard three terrible words: "You are cheatin'!"

Such scenes often prove that there can be little of dramatic import in environment. Any room can present a tragic front; any room can be comic. This little den was now hideous as a torture-chamber. The new faces of the men themselves had changed it upon the instant. The Swede held a huge fist in front of Johnnie's face, while the latter looked steadily over it into the blazing orbs of his accuser. The Easterner had grown pallid; the cowboy's jaw had dropped in that expression of bovine amazement which was one of his important mannerisms. After the three words, the first sound in the room was made by Scully's paper as it floated forgotten to his feet. His spectacles had also fallen from his nose, but by a clutch he had saved them in air. His hand, grasping the spectacles, now remained poised awkwardly and near his shoulder. He stared at the card-players.

Probably the silence was while a second elapsed. Then, if the floor had been suddenly twitched out from under the men they could not have moved quicker. The five had projected themselves headlong toward a common point. It happened that Johnnie in rising to hurl himself upon the Swede had stumbled slightly because of his curiously instinctive care for the cards and the board. The loss of the moment allowed time for the arrival of Scully, and also allowed the cowboy time to give the Swede a great push which sent him staggering back. The men found tongue together, and hoarse shouts of rage, appeal or fear burst from every throat. The cowboy pushed and jostled feverishly at the Swede, and the Easterner and Scully clung wildly to Johnnie; but, through the smoky air, above the swaying bodies of the peace-compellers, the eyes of the two warriors ever sought each other in glances of challenge that were at once hot and steely.

Of course the board had been overturned, and now the whole company of cards was scattered over the floor, where the boots of the men trampled the fat and painted kings and queens as they gazed with their silly eyes at the war that was waging above them.

Scully's voice was dominating the yells. "Stop now! Stop, I say! Stop, now—"

Johnnie, as he struggled to burst through the rank formed by Scully and the Easterner, was crying: "Well, he says I cheated! He says I cheated! I won't allow no man to say I cheated! If he says I cheated, he's a —— ——!"

The cowboy was telling the Swede: "Quit, now! Quit, d'ye hear—"

The screams of the Swede never ceased. "He did cheat! I saw him! I saw him—"

As for the Easterner, he was importuning in a voice that was not heeded. "Wait a moment, can't you? Oh, wait a moment. What's the good of a fight over a game of cards? Wait a moment—"

In this tumult no complete sentences were clear. "Cheat"—"Quit"—"He says"—These fragments pierced the uproar and rang out sharply. It was remarkable that whereas Scully undoubtedly made the most noise, he was the least heard of any of the riotous band.

Then suddenly there was a great cessation. It was as if each man had paused for breath, and although the room was still lighted with the anger of men, it could be seen that there was no danger of immediate conflict, and at once Johnnie, shouldering his way forward, almost succeeded in confronting the Swede. "What did you say I cheated for? What did you say I cheated for? I don't cheat and I won't let no man say I do!"

The Swede said: "I saw you! I saw you!"

"Well," cried Johnnie, "I'll fight any man what says I cheat!"

"No, you won't," said the cowboy. "Not here."

"Ah, be still, can't you?" said Scully, coming between them.

The quiet was sufficient to allow the Easterner's voice to be heard. He was repeating: "Oh, wait a moment, can't you? What's the good of a fight over a game of cards? Wait a moment."

Johnnie, his red face appearing above his father's shoulder, hailed the Swede again. "Did you say I cheated?"

The Swede showed his teeth. "Yes."

"Then," said Johnnie, "we must fight."

"Yes, fight," roared the Swede. He was like a demoniac.[8] "Yes, fight! I'll show you what kind of a man I am! I'll show you who you want to fight! Maybe you think I can't fight! Maybe you think I can't! I'll show you, you skin, you card-sharp![9] Yes, you cheated! You cheated! You cheated!"

"Well, let's git at it, then, mister," said Johnnie coolly.

The cowboy's brow was beaded with sweat from his efforts in intercepting all sorts of raids. He turned in despair to Scully. "What are you goin' to do now?"

A change had come over the Celtic visage[10] of the old man. He now seemed all eagerness; his eyes glowed.

"We'll let them fight," he answered stalwartly. "I can't put up with it any longer. I've stood this damned Swede till I'm sick. We'll let them fight."

VI

The men prepared to go out of doors. The Easterner was so nervous that he had great difficulty in getting his arms into the sleeves of his new leather-coat. As the cowboy drew his fur-cap down over his ears his hands trembled. In fact, Johnnie and old Scully were the only ones who displayed no agitation. These preliminaries were conducted without words.

Scully threw open the door. "Well, come on," he said. Instantly a terrific wind caused the flame of the lamp to struggle at its wick, while a puff of black smoke sprang from the chimney-top. The stove was in mid-current of the blast, and its

[8]A person possessed by a demon. [9]Cheater at cards.
[10]That is, his face was that of someone of Celtic descent, probably Irish.

voice swelled to equal the roar of the storm. Some of the scarred and bedabbled[11] cards were caught up from the floor and dashed helplessly against the further wall. The men lowered their heads and plunged into the tempest as into a sea.

No snow was falling, but great whirls and clouds of flakes, swept up from the ground by the frantic winds, were streaming southward with the speed of bullets. The covered land was blue with the sheen of an unearthly satin, and there was no other hue save where at the low black railway station—which seemed incredibly distant—one light gleamed like a tiny jewel. As the men floundered into a thigh-deep drift, it was known that the Swede was bawling out something. Scully went to him, put a hand on his shoulder and projected an ear. "What's that you say?" he shouted.

"I say," bawled the Swede again, "I won't stand much show against this gang. I know you'll all pitch on me."

Scully smote him reproachfully on the arm. "Tut, man," he yelled. The wind tore the words from Scully's lips and scattered them far a-lee.[12]

"You are all a gang of——" boomed the Swede, but the storm also seized the remainder of this sentence.

Immediately turning their backs upon the wind, the men had swung around a corner to the sheltered side of the hotel. It was the function of the little house to preserve here, amid this great devastation of snow, an irregular V-shape of heavily-incrusted grass, which crackled beneath the feet. One could imagine the great drifts piled against the windward side. When the party reached the comparative peace of this spot it was found that the Swede was still bellowing.

"Oh, I know what kind of a thing this is! I know you'll all pitch on me. I can't lick you all!"

Scully turned upon him panther-fashion. "You'll not have to whip all of us. You'll have to whip my son Johnnie. An' the man what troubles you durin' that time will have me to dale with."

The arrangements were swiftly made. The two men faced each other, obedient to the harsh commands of Scully, whose face, in the subtly luminous gloom, could be seen set in the austere impersonal lines that are pictured on the countenances of the Roman veterans. The Easterner's teeth were chattering, and he was hopping up and down like a mechanical toy. The cowboy stood rock-like.

The contestants had not stripped off any clothing. Each was in his ordinary attire. Their fists were up, and they eyed each other in a calm that had the elements of leonine[13] cruelty in it.

During this pause, the Easterner's mind, like a film, took lasting impressions of the three men—the iron-nerved master of the ceremony; the Swede, pale, motionless, terrible; and Johnnie, serene yet ferocious, brutish yet heroic. The entire prelude had in it a tragedy greater than the tragedy of action, and this aspect was accentuated by the long mellow cry of the blizzard, as it sped the tumbling and wailing flakes into the black abyss of the south.

"Now!" said Scully.

The two combatants leaped forward and crashed together like bullocks. There was heard the cushioned sound of blows, and of a curse squeezing out from between the tight teeth of one.

[11]Showing the results of being splattered with liquid. [12]Downwind. [13]Like lions.

As for the spectators, the Easterner's pent-up breath exploded from him with a pop of relief, absolute relief from the tension of the preliminaries. The cowboy bounded into the air with a yowl. Scully was immovable as from supreme amazement and fear at the fury of the fight which he himself had permitted and arranged.

For a time the encounter in the darkness was such a perplexity of flying arms that it presented no more detail than would a swiftly-revolving wheel. Occasionally a face, as if illumined by a flash of light, would shine out, ghastly and marked with pink spots. A moment later, the men might have been known as shadows, if it were not for the involuntary utterance of oaths that came from them in whispers.

Suddenly a holocaust of warlike desire caught the cowboy, and he bolted forward with the speed of a broncho. "Go it, Johnnie; go it! Kill him! Kill him!"

Scully confronted him. "Kape back," he said; and by his glance the cowboy could tell that this man was Johnnie's father.

To the Easterner there was a monotony of unchangeable fighting that was an abomination. This confused mingling was eternal to his sense, which was concentrated in a longing for the end, the priceless end. Once the fighters lurched near him, and as he scrambled hastily backward, he heard them breathe like men on the rack.

"Kill him, Johnnie! Kill him! Kill him! Kill him!" The cowboy's face was contorted like one of those agony masks in museums.

"Keep still," said Scully icily.

Then there was a sudden loud grunt, incomplete, cut short, and Johnnie's body swung away from the Swede and fell with sickening heaviness to the grass. The cowboy was barely in time to prevent the mad Swede from flinging himself upon his prone adversary. "No, you don't," said the cowboy, interposing an arm. "Wait a second."

Scully was at his son's side. "Johnnie! Johnnie, me boy?" His voice had a quality of melancholy tenderness. "Johnnie? Can you go on with it?" He looked anxiously down into the bloody pulpy face of his son.

There was a moment of silence, and then Johnnie answered in his ordinary voice: "Yes, I—it—yes."

Assisted by his father he struggled to his feet. "Wait a bit now till you git your wind," said the old man.

A few paces away the cowboy was lecturing the Swede. "No, you don't! Wait a second!"

The Easterner was plucking at Scully's sleeve. "Oh, this is enough," he pleaded. "This is enough! Let it go as it stands. This is enough!"

"Bill," said Scully, "git out of the road." The cowboy stepped aside. "Now." The combatants were actuated by a new caution as they advanced toward collision. They glared at each other, and then the Swede aimed a lightning blow that carried with it his entire weight. Johnnie was evidently half-stupid from weakness, but he miraculously dodged, and his fist sent the over-balanced Swede sprawling.

The cowboy, Scully and the Easterner burst into a cheer that was like a chorus of triumphant soldiery, but before its conclusion the Swede had scuffled agilely to his feet and come in berserk abandon at his foe. There was another perplexity of flying arms, and Johnnie's body again swung away and fell, even as a bundle might fall from a roof. The Swede instantly staggered to a little wind-waved tree and leaned upon it, breathing like an engine, while his savage and flame-lit eyes roamed from face to face as the men bent over Johnnie. There was a splendor of isolation in his situation at this time which the Easterner felt once when, lifting his eyes from the man on the ground, he beheld that mysterious and lonely figure, waiting.

"Are you any good yet, Johnnie?" asked Scully in a broken voice.

The son gasped and opened his eyes languidly. After a moment he answered: "No—I ain't—any good—any—more." Then, from shame and bodily ill, he began to weep, the tears furrowing down through the bloodstains on his face. "He was too—too—too heavy for me."

Scully straightened and addressed the waiting figure. "Stranger," he said, evenly, "it's all up with our side." Then his voice changed into that vibrant huskiness which is commonly the tone of the most simple and deadly announcements. "Johnnie is whipped."

Without replying, the victor moved off on the route to the front door of the hotel.

The cowboy was formulating new and unspellable blasphemies. The Easterner was startled to find that they were out in a wind that seemed to come direct from the shadowed arctic floes. He heard again the wail of the snow as it was flung to its grave in the south. He knew now that all this time the cold had been sinking into him deeper and deeper, and he wondered that he had not perished. He felt indifferent to the condition of the vanquished man.

"Johnnie, can you walk?" asked Scully.

"Did I hurt—hurt him any?" asked the son.

"Can you walk, boy? Can you walk?"

Johnnie's voice was suddenly strong. There was a robust impatience in it. "I asked you whether I hurt him any!"

"Yes, yes, Johnnie," answered the cowboy consolingly; "he's hurt a good deal."

They raised him from the ground, and as soon as he was on his feet he went tottering off, rebuffing all attempts at assistance. When the party rounded the corner they were fairly blinded by the pelting of the snow. It burned their faces like fire. The cowboy carried Johnnie through the drift to the door. As they entered some cards again rose from the floor and beat against the wall.

The Easterner rushed to the stove. He was so profoundly chilled that he almost dared to embrace the glowing iron. The Swede was not in the room. Johnnie sank into a chair, and folding his arms on his knees, buried his face in them. Scully, warming one foot and then the other at a rim of the stove, muttered to himself with Celtic mournfulness. The cowboy had removed his fur-cap, and with a dazed and rueful air he was now running one hand through his tousled locks. From overhead they could hear the creaking of boards, as the Swede tramped here and there in his room.

The sad quiet was broken by the sudden flinging open of a door that led toward the kitchen. It was instantly followed by an inrush of women. They precipitated themselves upon Johnnie amid a chorus of lamentation. Before they carried their prey off to the kitchen, there to be bathed and harangued with that mixture of sympathy and abuse which is a feat of their sex, the mother straightened herself and fixed old Scully with an eye of stern reproach. "Shame be upon you, Patrick Scully!" she cried. "Your own son, too. Shame be upon you!"

"There, now! Be quiet, now!" said the old man weakly.

"Shame be upon you, Patrick Scully!" The girls rallying to this slogan, sniffed disdainfully in the direction of those trembling accomplices, the cowboy and the Easterner. Presently they bore Johnnie away, and left the three men to dismal reflection.

VII

"I'd like to fight this here Dutchman myself," said the cowboy, breaking a long silence.

Scully wagged his head sadly. "No, that wouldn't do. It wouldn't be right. It wouldn't be right."

"Well, why wouldn't it?" argued the cowboy. "I don't see no harm in it."

"No," answered Scully with mournful heroism. "It wouldn't be right. It was Johnnie's fight, and now we mustn't whip the man just because he whipped Johnnie."

"Yes, that's true enough," said the cowboy; "but—he better not get fresh with me, because I couldn't stand no more of it."

"You'll not say a word to him," commanded Scully, and even then they heard the tread of the Swede on the stairs. His entrance was made theatric. He swept the door back with a bang and swaggered to the middle of the room. No one looked at him. "Well," he cried, insolently, at Scully, "I s'pose you'll tell me now how much I owe you?"

The old man remained stolid. "You don't owe me nothin'."

"Huh!" said the Swede, "huh! Don't owe 'im nothin'."

The cowboy addressed the Swede. "Stranger, I don't see how you come to be so gay around here."

Old Scully was instantly alert. "Stop!" he shouted, holding his hand forth, fingers upward. "Bill, you shut up!"

The cowboy spat carelessly into the sawdust box. "I didn't say a word, did I?" he asked.

"Mr. Scully," called the Swede, "how much do I owe you?" It was seen that he was attired for departure, and that he had his valise in his hand.

"You don't owe me nothin'," repeated Scully in his same imperturbable way.

"Huh!" said the Swede. "I guess you're right. I guess if it was any way at all, you'd owe me somethin'. That's what I guess." He turned to the cowboy. "'Kill him! Kill him! Kill him!'" he mimicked, and then guffawed victoriously. "Kill him!" He was convulsed with ironical humor.

But he might have been jeering the dead. The three men were immovable and silent, staring with glassy eyes at the stove.

The Swede opened the door and passed into the storm, giving one derisive glance backward at the still group.

As soon as the door was closed, Scully and the cowboy leaped to their feet and began to curse. They trampled to and fro, waving their arms and smashing into the air with their fists. "Oh, but that was a hard minute!" wailed Scully. "That was a hard minute! Him there leerin' and scoffin'! One bang at his nose was worth forty dollars to me that minute! How did you stand it, Bill?"

"How did I stand it?" cried the cowboy in a quivering voice. "How did I stand it? Oh!"

The old man burst into sudden brogue. "I'd loike to take that Swade," he wailed, "and hould 'im down on a shtone flure and bate 'im to a jelly wid a shtick!"

The cowboy groaned in sympathy. "I'd like to git him by the neck and ha-ammer him"—he brought his hand down on a chair with a noise like a pistol-shot—"hammer that there Dutchman until he couldn't tell himself from a dead coyote!"

"I'd bate 'im until he—"

"I'd show him some things—"

And then together they raised a yearning fanatic cry. "Oh-o-oh! if we only could—"

"Yes!"

"Yes!"

"And then I'd—"

"O-o-oh!"

VIII

The Swede, tightly gripping his valise, tacked across the face of the storm as if he carried sails. He was following a line of little naked gasping trees, which he knew must mark the way of the road. His face, fresh from the pounding of Johnnie's fists, felt more pleasure than pain in the wind and the driving snow. A number of square shapes loomed upon him finally, and he knew them as the houses of the main body of the town. He found a street and made travel along it, leaning heavily upon the wind whenever, at a corner, a terrific blast caught him.

He might have been in a deserted village. We picture the world as thick with conquering and elate humanity, but here, with the bugles of the tempest pealing, it was hard to imagine a peopled earth. One viewed the existence of man then as a marvel, and conceded a glamour of wonder to these lice which were caused to cling to a whirling, fire-smote, ice-locked, disease-stricken, space-lost bulb. The conceit of man was explained by this storm to be the very engine of life. One was a coxcomb[14] not to die in it. However, the Swede found a saloon.

In front of it an indomitable red light was burning, and the snow-flakes were made blood-color as they flew through the circumscribed territory of the lamp's shining. The Swede pushed open the door of the saloon and entered. A sanded expanse was before him, and at the end of it four men sat about a table drinking. Down one side of the room extended a radiant bar, and its guardian was leaning upon his elbows listening to the talk of the men at the table. The Swede dropped his valise upon the floor, and, smiling fraternally upon the barkeeper, said: "Gimme some whisky, will you?" The man placed a bottle, a whisky-glass, and glass of ice-thick water upon the bar. The Swede poured himself an abnormal portion of whisky and drank it in three gulps. "Pretty bad night," remarked the bartender indifferently. He was making the pretension of blindness, which is usually a distinction of his class; but it could have been seen that he was furtively studying the half-erased blood-stains on the face of the Swede. "Bad night," he said again.

"Oh, it's good enough for me," replied the Swede, hardily, as he poured himself some more whisky. The barkeeper took his coin and maneuvered it through its reception by the highly-nickeled cash-machine. A bell rang; a card labeled "20 cts." had appeared.

[14]A conceited person.

"No," continued the Swede, "this isn't too bad weather. It's good enough for me."

"So?" murmured the barkeeper languidly.

The copious drams made the Swede's eyes swim, and he breathed a trifle heavier. "Yes, I like this weather. I like it. It suits me." It was apparently his design to impart a deep significance to these words.

"So?" murmured the bartender again. He turned to gaze dreamily at the scroll-like birds and bird-like scrolls which had been drawn with soap upon the mirrors back of the bar.

"Well, I guess I'll take another drink," said the Swede presently. "Have something?"

"No, thanks; I'm not drinkin'," answered the bartender. Afterward he asked: "How did you hurt your face?"

The Swede immediately began to boast loudly. "Why, in a fight. I thumped the soul out of a man down here at Scully's hotel."

The interest of the four men at the table was at last aroused.

"Who was it?" said one.

"Johnnie Scully," blustered the Swede. "Son of the man what runs it. He will be pretty near dead for some weeks, I can tell you. I made a nice thing of him, I did. He couldn't get up. They carried him in the house. Have a drink?"

Instantly the men in some subtle way incased themselves in reserve. "No, thanks," said one. The group was of curious formation. Two were prominent local business men; one was the district-attorney; and one was a professional gambler of the kind known as "square." But a scrutiny of the group would not have enabled an observer to pick the gambler from the men of more reputable pursuits. He was, in fact, a man so delicate in manner, when among people of fair class, and so judicious in his choice of victims, that in the strictly masculine part of the town's life he had come to be explicitly trusted and admired. People called him a thoroughbred. The fear and contempt with which his craft was regarded was undoubtedly the reason that his quiet dignity shone conspicuous above the quiet dignity of men who might be merely hatters, billiard markers or grocery clerks. Beyond an occasional unwary traveler, who came by rail, this gambler was supposed to prey solely upon reckless and senile farmers, who, when flush with good crops, drove into town in all the pride and confidence of an absolutely invulnerable stupidity. Hearing at times in circuitous fashion of the despoilment of such a farmer, the important men of Romper invariably laughed in contempt of the victim, and if they thought of the wolf at all, it was with a kind of pride at the knowledge that he would never dare think of attacking their wisdom and courage. Besides, it was popular that this gambler had a real wife, and two real children in a neat cottage in a suburb, where he led an exemplary home life, and when any one even suggested a discrepancy in his character, the crowd immediately vociferated descriptions of this virtuous family circle. Then men who led exemplary home lives, and men who did not lead exemplary home lives, all subsided in a bunch, remarking that there was nothing more to be said.

However, when a restriction was placed upon him—as, for instance, when a strong clique of members of the new Pollywog Club refused to permit him, even as a spectator, to appear in the rooms of the organization—the candor and gentleness with which he accepted the judgment disarmed many of his foes and made his friends more desperately partisan. He invariably distinguished between himself and a respectable Romper man so quickly and frankly that his manner actually appeared to be a continual broadcast compliment.

And one must not forget to declare the fundamental fact of his entire position in Romper. It is irrefutable that in all affairs outside of his business, in all matters that occur eternally and commonly between man and man, this thieving card-player was so generous, so just, so moral, that, in a contest, he could have put to flight the consciences of nine-tenths of the citizens of Romper.

And so it happened that he was seated in this saloon with the two prominent local merchants and the district-attorney.

The Swede continued to drink raw whisky, meanwhile babbling at the barkeeper and trying to induce him to indulge in potations. "Come on. Have a drink. Come on. What—no? Well, have a little one then. By gawd, I've whipped a man to-night, and I want to celebrate. I whipped him good, too. Gentlemen," the Swede cried to the men at the table, "have a drink?"

"Ssh!" said the barkeeper.

The group at the table, although furtively attentive, had been pretending to be deep in talk, but now a man lifted his eyes toward the Swede and said shortly: "Thanks. We don't want any more."

At this reply the Swede ruffled out his chest like a rooster. "Well," he exploded, "it seems I can't get anybody to drink with me in this town. Seems so, don't it? Well!"

"Ssh!" said the barkeeper.

"Say," snarled the Swede, "don't you try to shut me up. I won't have it. I'm a gentleman, and I want people to drink with me. And I want 'em to drink with me now. Now—do you understand?" He rapped the bar with his knuckles.

Years of experience had calloused the bartender. He merely grew sulky. "I hear you," he answered.

"Well," cried the Swede, "listen hard then. See those men over there? Well, they're going to drink with me, and don't you forget it. Now you watch."

"Hi!" yelled the barkeeper, "this won't do!"

"Why won't it?" demanded the Swede. He stalked over to the table, and by chance laid his hand upon the shoulder of the gambler. "How about this?" he asked, wrathfully. "I asked you to drink with me."

The gambler simply twisted his head and spoke over his shoulder. "My friend, I don't know you."

"Oh, hell!" answered the Swede, "come and have a drink."

"Now, my boy," advised the gambler kindly, "take your hand off my shoulder and go 'way and mind your own business." He was a little slim man, and it seemed strange to hear him use this tone of heroic patronage to the burly Swede. The other men at the table said nothing.

"What? You won't drink with me, you little dude! I'll make you then! I'll make you!" The Swede had grasped the gambler frenziedly at the throat, and was dragging him from his chair. The other men sprang up. The barkeeper dashed around the corner of his bar. There was a great tumult, and then was seen a long blade in the hand of the gambler. It shot forward, and a human body, this citadel of virtue, wisdom, power, was pierced as easily as if it had been a melon. The Swede fell with a cry of supreme astonishment.

The prominent merchants and the district-attorney must have at once tumbled out of the place backward. The bartender found himself hanging limply to the arm of a chair and gazing into the eyes of a murderer.

"Henry," said the latter, as he wiped his knife on one of the towels that hung beneath the bar-rail, "you tell 'em where to find me. I'll be home, waiting for 'em." Then he vanished. A moment afterward the barkeeper was in the street dinning[15] through the storm for help, and, moreover, companionship.

The corpse of the Swede, alone in the saloon, had its eyes fixed upon a dreadful legend that dwelt a-top of the cash-machine. "This registers the amount of your purchase."

IX

Months later, the cowboy was frying pork over the stove of a little ranch near the Dakota line, when there was a quick thud of hoofs outside, and, presently, the Easterner entered with the letters and the papers.

"Well," said the Easterner at once, "the chap that killed the Swede has got three years. Wasn't much, was it?"

"He has? Three years?" The cowboy poised his pan of pork, while he ruminated upon the news. "Three years. That ain't much."

"No. It was a light sentence," replied the Easterner as he unbuckled his spurs. "Seems there was a good deal of sympathy for him in Romper."

"If the bartender had been any good," observed the cowboy thoughtfully, "he would have gone in and cracked that there Dutchman on the head with a bottle in the beginnin' of it and stopped all this here murderin'."

"Yes, a thousand things might have happened," said the Easterner tartly.

The cowboy returned his pan of pork to the fire, but his philosophy continued. "It's funny, ain't it? If he hadn't said Johnnie was cheatin' he'd be alive this minute. He was an awful fool. Game played for fun, too. Not for money. I believe he was crazy."

"I feel sorry for that gambler," said the Easterner.

"Oh, so do I," said the cowboy. "He don't deserve none of it for killin' who he did."

"The Swede might not have been killed if everything had been square."

"Might not have been killed?" exclaimed the cowboy. "Everythin' square? Why, when he said that Johnnie was cheatin' and acted like such a jackass? And then in the saloon he fairly walked up to git hurt?" With these arguments the cowboy browbeat the Easterner and reduced him to rage.

"You're a fool!" cried the Easterner viciously. "You're a bigger jackass than the Swede by a million majority. Now let me tell you one thing. Let me tell you something. Listen! Johnnie was cheating!"

"'Johnnie,'" said the cowboy blankly. There was a minute of silence, and then he said robustly: "Why, no. The game was only for fun."

"Fun or not," said the Easterner, "Johnnie was cheating. I saw him. I know it. I saw him. And I refused to stand up and be a man. I let the Swede fight it out alone. And you—you were simply puffing around the place and wanting to fight. And then old Scully himself! We are all in it! This poor gambler isn't even a noun. He is kind of an adverb. Every sin is the result of a collaboration. We, five of us, have collaborated in the murder of this Swede. Usually there are from a dozen to forty women really involved in every murder, but in this case

[15]Crying loudly.

it seems to be only five men—you, I, Johnnie, old Scully, and that fool of an unfortunate gambler came merely as a culmination, the apex of a human movement, and gets all the punishment."

The cowboy, injured and rebellious, cried out blindly into this fog of mysterious theory. "Well, I didn't do anythin', did I?"

1899

THE OPEN BOAT

A Tale Intended to Be After the Fact. Being the Experience of Four Men from the Sunk Steamer Commodore[1]

I

None of them knew the color of the sky. Their eyes glanced level, and were fastened upon the waves that swept toward them. These waves were of the hue of slate, save for the tops, which were of foaming white, and all of the men knew the colors of the sea. The horizon narrowed and widened, and dipped and rose, and at all times its edge was jagged with waves that seemed thrust up in points like rocks.

Many a man ought to have a bath-tub larger than the boat which here rode upon the sea. These waves were most wrongfully and barbarously abrupt and tall, and each froth-top was a problem in small boat navigation.

The cook squatted in the bottom and looked with both eyes at the six inches of gunwale[2] which separated him from the ocean. His sleeves were rolled over his fat forearms, and the two flaps of his unbuttoned vest dangled as he bent to bail out the boat. Often he said: "gawd! That was a narrow clip." As he remarked it he invariably gazed eastward over the broken sea.

The oiler,[3] steering with one of the two oars in the boat, sometimes raised himself suddenly to keep clear of water that swirled in over the stern. It was a thin little oar and it seemed often ready to snap.

The correspondent, pulling at the other oar, watched the waves and wondered why he was there.

The injured captain, lying in the bow, was at this time buried in that profound dejection and indifference which comes, temporarily at least, to even the bravest and most enduring when, willy nilly, the firm fails, the army loses, the ship goes down. The mind of the master of a vessel is rooted deep in the timbers of her, though he command for a day or a decade, and this captain had on him the stern impression of a scene in the grays of dawn of seven turned faces, and later a stump of a top-mast with a white ball on it that slashed to and

[1]On his way to report on the Cuban Revolution, Crane was aboard the tug *Commodore,* bound for Cuba with a cargo of arms for the revolutionaries, when it sank off the coast of Florida, January 2, 1897. After almost thirty hours at sea in a small dinghy, Crane landed at Daytona, Florida. Soon thereafter he shaped the details of his experience into a short story.

[2]The upper sides of a boat.

[3]crew member who oils machinery in a ship's engine room.

fro at the waves, went low and lower, and down. Thereafter there was something strange in his voice. Although steady, it was deep with mourning, and of a quality beyond oration or tears.

"Keep 'er a little more south, Billie," said he.

"'A little more south,' sir," said the oiler in the stern.

A seat in this boat was not unlike a seat upon a bucking broncho, and, by the same token, a broncho is not much smaller. The craft pranced and reared, and plunged like an animal. As each wave came, and she rose for it, she seemed like a horse making at a fence outrageously high. The manner of her scramble over these walls of water is a mystic thing, and, moreover, at the top of them were ordinarily these problems in white water, the foam racing down from the summit of each wave, requiring a new leap, and a leap from the air. Then, after scornfully bumping a crest, she would slide, and race, and splash down a long incline and arrive bobbing and nodding in front of the next menace.

A singular disadvantage of the sea lies in the fact that after successfully surmounting one wave you discover that there is another behind it just as important and just as nervously anxious to do something effective in the way of swamping boats. In a ten-foot dingey one can get an idea of the resources of the sea in the line of waves that is not probable to the average experience, which is never at sea in a dingey. As each salty wall of water approached, it shut all else from the view of the men in the boat, and it was the final outburst of the ocean, the last effort of the grim water. There was a terrible grace in the move of the waves, and they came in silence, save for the snarling of the crests.

In the wan light, the faces of the men must have been gray. Their eyes must have glinted in strange ways as they gazed steadily astern. Viewed from a balcony, the whole thing would doubtlessly have been weirdly picturesque. But the men in the boat had no time to see it, and if they had had leisure there were other things to occupy their minds. The sun swung steadily up the sky, and they knew it was broad day because the color of the sea changed from slate to emerald-green, streaked with amber lights, and the foam was like tumbling snow. The process of the breaking day was unknown to them. They were aware only of this effect upon the color of the waves that rolled toward them.

In disjointed sentences the cook and the correspondent argued as to the difference between a life-saving station and a house of refuge. The cook had said: "There's a house of refuge just north of the Mosquito Inlet Light, and as soon as they see us, they'll come off in their boat and pick us up."

"As soon as who see us?" said the correspondent.

"The crew," said the cook.

"Houses of refuge don't have crews," said the correspondent. "As I understand them, they are only places where clothes and grub are stored for the benefit of shipwrecked people. They don't carry crews."

"Oh, yes, they do," said the cook.

"No, they don't," said the correspondent.

"Well, we're not there yet, anyhow," said the oiler, in the stern.

"Well," said the cook, "perhaps it's not a house of refuge that I'm thinking of as being near Mosquito Inlet Light. Perhaps it's a life-saving station."

"We're not there yet," said the oiler, in the stern.

II

As the boat bounced from the top of each wave, the wind tore through the hair of the hatless men, and as the craft plopped her stern down again the spray slashed past them. The crest of each of these waves was a hill, from the top of which the men surveyed, for a moment, a broad tumultuous expanse, shining and wind-riven. It was probably splendid. It was probably glorious, this play of the free sea, wild with lights of emerald and white and amber.

"Bully good thing it's an on-shore wind," said the cook. "If not, where would we be? Wouldn't have a show."

"That's right," said the correspondent.

The busy oiler nodded his assent.

Then the captain, in the bow, chuckled in a way that expressed humor, contempt, tragedy, all in one. "Do you think we've got much of a show, now, boys?" said he.

Whereupon the three were silent, save for a trifle of hemming and hawing. To express any particular optimism at this time they felt to be childish and stupid, but they all doubtless possessed this sense of the situation in their mind. A young man thinks doggedly at such times. On the other hand, the ethics of their condition was decidedly against any open suggestion of hopelessness. So they were silent.

"Oh, well," said the captain, soothing his children, "we'll get ashore all right."

But there was that in his tone which made them think, so the oiler quoth: "Yes! If this wind holds!"

The cook was bailing. "Yes! If we don't catch hell in the surf."

Canton flannel[4] gulls flew near and far. Sometimes they sat down on the sea, near patches of brown sea-weed that rolled over the waves with a movement like carpets on a line in a gale. The birds sat comfortably in groups, and they were envied by some in the dingey, for the wrath of the sea was no more to them than it was to a covey of prairie chickens a thousand miles inland. Often they came very close and stared at the men with black bead-like eyes. At these times they were uncanny and sinister in their unblinking scrutiny, and the men hooted angrily at them, telling them to be gone. One came, and evidently decided to alight on the top of the captain's head. The bird flew parallel to the boat and did not circle, but made short sidelong jumps in the air in chicken-fashion. His black eyes were wistfully fixed upon the captain's head. "Ugly brute," said the oiler to the bird. "You look as if you were made with a jack-knife." The cook and the correspondent swore darkly at the creature. The captain naturally wished to knock it away with the end of the heavy painter,[5] but he did not dare do it, because anything resembling an emphatic gesture would have capsized this freighted boat, and so with his open hand, the captain gently and carefully waved the gull away. After it had been discouraged from the pursuit the captain breathed easier on account of his hair, and others breathed easier because the bird struck their minds at this time as being somehow gruesome and ominous.

In the meantime the oiler and the correspondent rowed. And also they rowed.

They sat together in the same seat, and each rowed an oar. Then the oiler took both oars; then the correspondent took both oars; then the oiler; then the

[4]Cotton flannel. [5]Rope for tying the boat to a wharf.

correspondent. They rowed and they rowed. The very ticklish part of the business was when the time came for the reclining one in the stern to take his turn at the oars. By the very last star of truth, it is easier to steal eggs from under a hen than it was to change seats in the dingey. First the man in the stern slid his hand along the thwart[6] and moved with care, as if he were of Sèvres.[7] Then the man in the rowing seat slid his hand along the other thwart. It was all done with the most extraordinary care. As the two sidled past each other, the whole party kept watchful eyes on the coming wave, and the captain cried: "Look out now! Steady there!"

The brown mats of sea-weed that appeared from time to time were like islands, bits of earth. They were travelling, apparently, neither one way nor the other. They were, to all intents, stationary. They informed the men in the boat that it was making progress slowly toward the land.

The captain, rearing cautiously in the bow, after the dingey soared on a great swell, said that he had seen the light-house at Mosquito Inlet. Presently the cook remarked that he had seen it. The correspondent was at the oars, then, and for some reason he too wished to look at the light-house, but his back was toward the far shore and the waves were important, and for some time he could not seize an opportunity to turn his head. But at last there came a wave more gentle than the others, and when at the crest of it he swiftly scoured the western horizon.

"See it?" said the captain.

"No," said the correspondent, slowly, "I didn't see anything."

"Look again," said the captain. He pointed. "It's exactly in that direction."

At the top of another wave, the correspondent did as he was bid, and this time his eyes chanced on a small still thing on the edge of the swaying horizon. It was precisely like the point of a pin. It took an anxious eye to find a light-house so tiny.

"Think we'll make it, Captain?"

"If this wind holds and the boat don't swamp, we can't do much else," said the captain.

The little boat, lifted by each towering sea, and splashed viciously by the crests, made progress that in the absence of sea-weed was not apparent to those in her. She seemed just a wee thing wallowing, miraculously, top-up, at the mercy of five oceans. Occasionally, a great spread of water, like white flames, swarmed into her.

"Bail her, cook," said the captain, serenely.

"All right, Captain," said the cheerful cook.

III

It would be difficult to describe the subtle brotherhood of men that was here established on the seas. No one said that it was so. No one mentioned it, but it dwelt in the boat, and each man felt it warm him. They were a captain, an oiler, a cook, and a correspondent, and they were friends, friends in a more curiously ironbound degree than may be common. The hurt captain, lying against

[6]A rower's seat built into the boat crosswise (athwart) to the keel.
[7]Delicate china made in Sèvres, France.

the water-jar in the bow, spoke always in a low voice and calmly but he could never command a more ready and swiftly obedient crew than the motley three of the dingey. It was more than a mere recognition of what was best for the common safety. There was surely in it a quality that was personal and heartfelt. And after this devotion to the commander of the boat there was this comradeship that the correspondent, for instance, who had been taught to be cynical of men, knew even at the time was the best experience of his life. But no one said that it was so. No one mentioned it.

"I wish we had a sail," remarked the captain. "We might try my overcoat on the end of an oar and give you two boys a chance to rest." So the cook and the correspondent held the mast and spread wide the overcoat, the oiler steered, and the little boat made good way with her new rig. Sometimes the oiler had to scull sharply to keep a sea from breaking into the boat, but otherwise sailing was a success.

Meanwhile the light-house had been growing slowly larger. It had now almost assumed color, and appeared like a little gray shadow on the sky. The man at the oars could not be prevented from turning his head rather often to try for a glimpse of this little gray shadow.

At last, from the top of each wave the men in the tossing boat could see land. Even as the light-house was an upright shadow on the sky, this land seemed but a long black shadow on the sea. It certainly was thinner than paper. "We must be about opposite New Smyrna," said the cook, who had coasted this shore often in schooners. "Captain, by the way, I believe they abandoned that life-saving station there about a year ago."

"Did they?" said the captain.

The wind slowly died away. The cook and the correspondent were not now obliged to slave in order to hold high the oar. But the waves continued their old impetuous swooping at the dingey, and the little craft, no longer under way, struggled woundily over them. The oiler or the correspondent took the oars again.

Shipwrecks are *apropos* of nothing. If men could only train for them and have them occur when the men had reached pink condition, there would be less drowning at sea. Of the four in the dingey none had slept any time worth mentioning for two days and two nights previous to embarking in the dingey, and in the excitement of clambering about the deck of a foundering ship they had also forgotten to eat heartily.

For these reasons, and for others, neither the oiler nor the correspondent was fond of rowing at this time. The correspondent wondered ingenuously how in the name of all that was sane could there be people who thought it amusing to row a boat. It was not an amusement; it was a diabolical punishment, and even a genius of mental aberrations could never conclude that it was anything but a horror to the muscles and a crime against the back. He mentioned to the boat in general how the amusement of rowing struck him, and the weary-faced oiler smiled in full sympathy. Previously to the foundering, by the way, the oiler had worked double-watch in the engine-room of the ship.

"Take her easy, now, boys," said the captain. "Don't spend yourselves. If we have to run a surf you'll need all your strength, because we'll sure have to swim for it. Take your time."

Slowly the land arose from the sea. From a black line it became a line of black and a line of white—trees and sand. Finally, the captain said that he could make out a house on the shore. "That's the house of refuge, sure," said the cook. "They'll see us before long, and come out after us."

The distant light-house reared high. "The keeper ought to be able to make us out now, if he's looking through a glass," said the captain. "He'll notify the life-saving people."

"None of those other boats could have got ashore to give word of the wreck," said the oiler, in a low voice. "Else the life-boat would be out hunting us."

Slowly and beautifully the land loomed out of the sea. The wind came again. It had veered from the northeast to the southeast. Finally, a new sound struck the ears of the men in the boat. It was the low thunder of the surf on the shore. "We'll never be able to make the light-house now," said the captain. "Swing her head a little more north, Billie."

"'A little more north,' sir," said the oiler.

Whereupon the little boat turned her nose once more down the wind, and all but the oarsman watched the shore grow. Under the influence of this expansion doubt and direful apprehension were leaving the minds of the men. The management of the boat was still most absorbing, but it could not prevent a quiet cheerfulness. In an hour, perhaps, they would be ashore.

Their back-bones had become thoroughly used to balancing in the boat and they now rode this wild colt of a dingey like circus men. The correspondent thought that he had been drenched to the skin, but happening to feel in the top pocket of his coat, he found therein eight cigars. Four of them were soaked with seawater; four were perfectly scatheless. After a search, somebody produced three dry matches, and thereupon the four waifs rode impudently in their little boat, and with an assurance of an impending rescue shining in their eyes, puffed at the big cigars and judged well and ill of all men. Everybody took a drink of water.

IV

"Cook," remarked the captain, "there don't seem to be any signs of life about your house of refuge."

"No," replied the cook. "Funny they don't see us!"

A broad stretch of lowly coast lay before the eyes of the men. It was dunes topped with dark vegetation. The roar of the surf was plain, and sometimes they could see the white lip of a wave as it spun up the beach. A tiny house was blocked out black upon the sky. Southward, the slim light-house lifted its little gray length.

Tide, wind, and waves were swinging the dingey northward. "Funny they don't see us," said the men.

The surf's roar was here dulled, but its tone was, nevertheless, thunderous and mighty. As the boat swam over the great rollers, the men sat listening to this roar. "We'll swamp sure," said everybody.

It is fair to say here that there was not a life-saving station within twenty miles in either direction, but the men did not know this fact and in consequence they made dark and opprobrious remarks concerning the eyesight of the nation's life-savers. Four scowling men sat in the dingey and surpassed records in the invention of epithets.

"Funny they don't see us."

The light-heartedness of a former time had completely faded. To their sharpened minds it was easy to conjure pictures of all kinds of incompetency and blindness and indeed, cowardice. There was the shore of the populous land, and it was bitter and bitter to them that from it came no sign.

"Well," said the captain, ultimately, "I suppose we'll have to make a try for ourselves. If we stay out here too long, we'll none of us have strength left to swim after the boat swamps."

And so the oiler, who was at the oars, turned the boat straight for the shore. There was a sudden tightening of muscles. There was some thinking.

"If we don't all get ashore—" said the captain. "If we don't all get ashore, I suppose you fellows know where to send news of my finish?"

They then briefly exchanged some addresses and admonitions. As for the reflections of the men, there was a great deal of rage in them. Perchance they might be formulated thus: "If I am going to be drowned—if I am going to be drowned—if I am going to be drowned, why, in the name of the seven mad gods who rule the sea, was I allowed to come thus far and contemplate sand and trees? Was I brought here merely to have my nose dragged away as I was about to nibble the sacred cheese of life? It is preposterous. If this old ninny-woman, Fate, cannot do better than this, she should be deprived of the management of men's fortunes. She is an old hen who knows not her intention. If she has decided to drown me, why did she not do it in the beginning and save me all this trouble. The whole affair is absurd. . . . But, no, she cannot mean to drown me. She dare not drown me. She cannot drown me. Not after all this work." Afterward the man might have had an impulse to shake his fist at the clouds. "Just you drown me, now, and then hear what I call you!"

The billows that came at this time were more formidable. They seemed always just about to break and roll over the little boat in a turmoil of foam. There was a preparatory and long growl in the speech of them. No mind unused to the sea would have concluded that the dingey could ascend these sheer heights in time. The shore was still afar. The oiler was a wily surfman. "Boys," he said, swiftly, "she won't live three minutes more and we're too far out to swim. Shall I take her to sea again, Captain?"

"Yes! Go ahead!" said the captain.

This oiler, by a series of quick miracles, and fast and steady oarsmanship, turned the boat in the middle of the surf and took her safely to sea again.

There was a considerable silence as the boat bumped over the furrowed sea to deeper water. Then somebody in gloom spoke. "Well, anyhow, they must have seen us from the shore by now."

The gulls went in slanting flight up the wind toward the gray desolate east. A squall, marked by dingy clouds, and clouds brick-red, like smoke from a burning building, appeared from the southeast.

"What do you think of those life-saving people? Ain't they peaches?"

"Funny they haven't seen us."

"Maybe they think we're out here for sport! Maybe they think we're fishin'. Maybe they think we're damned fools."

It was a long afternoon. A changed tide tried to force them southward, but wind and wave said northward. Far ahead, where coastline, sea, and sky formed their mighty angle, there were little dots which seemed to indicate a city on the shore.

"St. Augustine?"

The captain shook his head. "Too near Mosquito Inlet."

And the oiler rowed, and then the correspondent rowed. Then the oiler rowed. It was a weary business. The human back can become the seat of more aches and pains than are registered in books for the composite anatomy of a regiment. It is a limited area, but it can become the theatre of innumerable muscular conflicts, tangles, wrenches, knots, and other comforts.

"Did you ever like to row, Billie?" asked the correspondent.

"No," said the oiler. "Hang it."

When one exchanged the rowing-seat for a place in the bottom of the boat, he suffered a bodily depression that caused him to be careless of everything save an obligation to wiggle one finger. There was cold sea-water swashing to and fro in the boat, and he lay in it. His head, pillowed on a thwart, was within an inch of the swirl of a wave crest, and sometimes a particularly obstreperous sea came in-board and drenched him once more. But these matters did not annoy him. It is almost certain that if the boat had capsized he would have tumbled comfortably out upon the ocean as if he felt sure that it was a great soft mattress.

"Look! There's a man on the shore!"

"Where?"

"There! See 'im? See 'im?"

"Yes, sure! He's walking along."

"Now he's stopping. Look! He's facing us!"

"He's waving at us!"

"So he is! By thunder!"

"Ah, now, we're all right! Now we're all right! There'll be a boat out here for us in half an hour."

"He's going on. He's running. He's going up to that house there."

The remote beach seemed lower than the sea, and it required a searching glance to discern the little black figure. The captain saw a floating stick and they rowed to it. A bath-towel was by some weird chance in the boat, and, tying this on the stick, the captain waved it. The oarsman did not dare turn his head, so he was obliged to ask questions.

"What's he doing now?"

"He's standing still again. He's looking, I think. . . . There he goes again. Toward the house. . . . Now he's stopped again."

"Is he waving at us?"

"No, not now; he was, though."

"Look! There comes another man!"

"He's running."

"Look at him go, would you."

"Why, he's on a bicycle. Now he's met the other man. They're both waving at us. Look!"

"There comes something up the beach."

"What the devil is that thing?"

"Why, it looks like a boat."

"Why, certainly it's a boat."

"No, it's on wheels."

"Yes, so it is. Well, that must be the life-boat. They drag them along shore on a wagon."

"That's the life-boat, sure."

"No, by——, it's—it's an omnibus."

"I tell you it's a life-boat."

"It is not! It's an omnibus. I can see it plain. See? One of those big hotel omnibuses."

"By thunder, you're right. It's an omnibus, sure as fate. What do you suppose they are doing with an omnibus? Maybe they are going around collecting the life-crew, hey?"

"That's it, likely. Look! There's a fellow waving a little black flag. He's standing on the steps of the omnibus. There come those other two fellows. Now they're all talking together. Look at the fellow with the flag. Maybe he ain't waving it!"

"That ain't a flag, is it? That's his coat. Why, certainly, that's his coat."

"So it is. It's his coat. He's taken it off and is waving it around his head. But would you look at him swing it!"

"Oh, say, there isn't any life-saving station here. That's just a winter resort hotel omnibus that has brought over some of the boarders to see us drown."

"What's that idiot with the coat mean? What's he signaling, anyhow?"

"It looks as if he were trying to tell us to go north. There must be a life-saving station up there."

"No! He thinks we're fishing. Just giving us a merry hand. See? Ah, there, Willie."

"Well, I wish I could make something out of those signals. What do you suppose he means?"

"He don't mean anything. He's just playing."

"Well, if he'd just signal us to try the surf again, or to go to sea and wait, or go north, or go south, or go to hell—there would be some reason in it. But look at him. He just stands there and keeps his coat revolving like a wheel. The ass!"

"There come more people."

"Now there's quite a mob. Look! Isn't that a boat?"

"Where? Oh, I see where you mean. No, that's no boat."

"That fellow is still waving his coat."

"He must think we like to see him do that. Why don't he quit it. It don't mean anything."

"I don't know. I think he is trying to make us go north. It must be that there's a life-saving station there somewhere."

"Say, he ain't tired yet. Look at 'im wave."

"Wonder how long he can keep that up. He's been revolving his coat ever since he caught sight of us. He's an idiot. Why aren't they getting men to bring a boat out. A fishing boat—one of those big yawls—could come out here all right. Why don't he do something?"

"Oh, it's all right, now."

"They'll have a boat out here for us in less than no time, now that they've seen us."

A faint yellow tone came into the sky over the low land. The shadows on the sea slowly deepened. The wind bore coldness with it, and the men began to shiver.

"Holy smoke!" said one, allowing his voice to express his impious mood, "if we keep on monkeying out here! If we've got to flounder out here all night!"

"Oh, we'll never have to stay here all night! don't you worry. They've seen us now, and it won't be long before they'll come chasing out after us."

The shore grew dusky. The man waving a coat blended gradually into the gloom, and it swallowed in the same manner the omnibus and the group of people. The spray, when it dashed uproariously over the side, made the voyagers shrink and swear like men who were being branded.

"I'd like to catch the chump who waved the coat. I feel like soaking him one, just for luck."

"Why? What did he do?"

"Oh, nothing, but then he seemed so damned cheerful."

In the meantime the oiler rowed, and then the correspondent rowed, and then the oiler rowed. Gray-faced and bowed forward, they mechanically, turn by turn, plied the leaden oars. The form of the light-house had vanished from the southern horizon, but finally a pale star appeared, just lifting from the sea. The streaked saffron in the west passed before the all-merging darkness, and the sea to the east was black. The land had vanished, and was expressed only by the low and drear thunder of the surf.

"If I am going to be drowned—if I am going to be drowned—if I am going to be drowned, why, in the name of the seven mad gods who rule the sea, was I allowed to come thus far and contemplate sand and trees? Was I brought here merely to have my nose dragged away as I was about to nibble the sacred cheese of life?"

The patient captain, drooped over the water-jar, was sometimes obliged to speak to the oarsman.

"Keep her head up! Keep her head up!"

"'Keep her head up,' sir." The voices were weary and low.

This was surely a quiet evening. All save the oarsman lay heavily and listlessly in the boat's bottom. As for him, his eyes were just capable of noting the tall black waves that swept forward in a most sinister silence, save for an occasional subdued growl of a crest.

The cook's head was on a thwart, and he looked without interest at the water under his nose. He was deep in other scenes. Finally he spoke. "Billie," he murmured, dreamfully, "what kind of pie do you like best?"

V

"Pie," said the oiler and the correspondent, agitatedly. "Don't talk about those things, blast you!"

"Well," said the cook, "I was just thinking about ham sandwiches, and—"

A night on the sea in an open boat is a long night. As darkness settled finally, the shine of the light, lifting from the sea in the south, changed to full gold. On the northern horizon a new light appeared, a small bluish gleam on the edge of the waters. These two lights were the furniture of the world. Otherwise there was nothing but waves.

Two men huddled in the stern, and distances were so magnificent in the dingey that the rower was enabled to keep his feet partly warmed by thrusting them under his companions. Their legs indeed extended far under the rowing-seat until they touched the feet of the captain forward. Sometimes, despite the efforts of the tired oarsman, a wave came piling into the boat, an icy wave of the night, and the chilling water soaked them anew. They would twist their bodies for a moment and groan, and sleep the dead sleep once more, while the water in the boat gurgled about them as the craft rocked.

The plan of the oiler and the correspondent was for one to row until he lost the ability, and then arouse the other from his sea-water couch in the bottom of the boat.

The oiler plied the oars until his head drooped forward, and the overpowering sleep blinded him. And he rowed yet afterward. Then he touched a man in the bottom of the boat, and called his name. "Will you spell for me a little while?" he said, meekly.

"Sure, Billie," said the correspondent, awakening and dragging himself to a sitting position. They exchanged places carefully, and the oiler, cuddling down in the sea-water at the cook's side, seemed to go to sleep instantly.

The particular violence of the sea had ceased. The waves came without snarling. The obligation of the man at the oars was to keep the boat headed so that the tilt of the rollers would not capsize her, and to preserve her from filling when the crests rushed past. The black waves were silent and hard to be seen in the darkness. Often one was almost upon the boat before the oarsman was aware.

In a low voice the correspondent addressed the captain. He was not sure that the captain was awake, although this iron man seemed to be always awake. "Captain, shall I keep her making for that light north, sir?"

The same steady voice answered him. "Yes. Keep it about two points off the port bow."

The cook had tied a life-belt around himself in order to get even the warmth which this clumsy cork contrivance could donate, and he seemed almost stove-like when a rower, whose teeth invariably chattered wildly as soon as he ceased his labor, drooped down to sleep.

The correspondent, as he rowed, looked down at the two men sleeping under foot. The cook's arm was around the oiler's shoulders, and, with their fragmentary clothing and haggard faces, they were the babes of the sea, a grotesque rendering of the old babes in the wood.

Later he must have grown stupid at his work, for suddenly there was a growling of water, and a crest came with a roar and a swash into the boat, and it was a wonder that it did not set the cook afloat in his life-belt. The cook continued to sleep, but the oiler sat up, blinking his eyes and shaking with the new cold.

"Oh, I'm awful sorry, Billie," said the correspondent, contritely.

"That's all right, old boy," said the oiler, and lay down again and was asleep.

Presently it seemed that even the captain dozed, and the correspondent thought that he was the one man afloat on all the oceans. The wind had a voice as it came over the waves, and it was sadder than the end.

There was a long, loud swishing astern of the boat, and a gleaming trail of phosphorescence, like blue flame, was furrowed on the black waters. It might have been made by a monstrous knife.

Then there came a stillness, while the correspondent breathed with the open mouth and looked at the sea.

Suddenly there was another swish and another long flash of bluish light, and this time it was alongside the boat, and might almost have been reached with an oar. The correspondent saw an enormous fin speed like a shadow through the water, hurling the crystalline spray and leaving the long glowing trail.

The correspondent looked over his shoulder at the captain. His face was hidden, and he seemed to be asleep. He looked at the babes of the sea. They certainly were asleep. So, being bereft of sympathy, he leaned a little way to one side and swore softly into the sea.

But the thing did not then leave the vicinity of the boat. Ahead or astern, on one side or the other, at intervals long or short, fled the long sparkling streak, and there was to be heard the whiroo of the dark fin. The speed and power of the thing was greatly to be admired. It cut the water like a gigantic and keen projectile.

The presence of this biding thing did not affect the man with the same horror that it would if he had been a picknicker. He simply looked at the sea dully and swore in an undertone.

Nevertheless, it is true that he did not wish to be alone with the thing. He wished one of his companions to awaken by chance and keep him company with it. But the captain hung motionless over the water-jar and the oiler and the cook in the bottom of the boat were plunged in slumber.

VI

"If I am going to be drowned—if I am going to be drowned—if I am going to be drowned, why, in the name of the seven mad gods who rule the sea, was I allowed to come thus far and contemplate sand and trees?"

During this dismal night, it may be remarked that a man would conclude that it was really the intention of the seven mad gods to drown him, despite the abominable injustice of it. For it was certainly an abominable injustice to drown a man who had worked so hard, so hard. The man felt it would be a crime most unnatural. Other people had drowned at sea since galleys swarmed with painted sails, but still——

When it occurs to a man that nature does not regard him as important, and that she feels she would not maim the universe by disposing of him, he at first wishes to throw bricks at the temple, and he hates deeply the fact that there are no bricks and no temples. Any visible expression of nature would surely be pelleted with his jeers.

Then, if there be no tangible thing to hoot, he feels, perhaps, the desire to confront a personification and indulge in pleas, bowed to one knee, and with hands supplicant, saying: "Yes, but I love myself."

A high cold star on a winter's night is the word he feels that she says to him. Thereafter he knows the pathos of his situation.

The men in the dingey had not discussed these matters, but each had, no doubt, reflected upon them in silence and according to his mind. There was seldom any expression upon their faces save the general one of complete weariness. Speech was devoted to the business of the boat.

To chime the notes of his emotion, a verse mysteriously entered the correspondent's head. He had even forgotten that he had forgotten this verse, but it suddenly was in his mind.

> A soldier of the Legion lay dying in Algiers,
> There was lack of woman's nursing, there was dearth
>   of woman's tears;
> But a comrade stood beside him, and he took that
>   comrade's hand,
> And he said: "I never more shall see my own, my
>   native land."[8]

[8]A condensed version of the sentimental poem "Bingen on the Rhine" (1883) by Caroline E. S. Norton (1808–1877).

In his childhood, the correspondent had been made acquainted with the fact that a soldier of the legion lay dying in Algiers, but he had never regarded it as important. Myriads of his school-fellows had informed him of the soldier's plight, but the dinning had naturally ended by making him perfectly indifferent. He had never considered it his affair that a soldier of the Legion lay dying in Algiers, nor had it appeared to him as a matter for sorrow. It was less to him than the breaking of a pencil's point.

Now, however, it quaintly came to him as a human, living thing. It was no longer merely a picture of a few throes in the breast of a poet, meanwhile drinking tea and warming his feet at the grate; it was an actuality—stern, mournful, and fine.

The correspondent plainly saw the soldier. He lay on the sand with his feet out straight and still. While his pale left hand was upon his chest in an attempt to thwart the going of his life, the blood came between his fingers. In the far Algerian distance, a city of low square forms was set against a sky that was faint with the last sunset hues. The correspondent, plying the oars and dreaming of the slow and slower movements of the soldier, was moved by a profound and perfectly impersonal comprehension. He was sorry for the soldier of the Legion who lay dying in Algiers.

The thing which had followed the boat and waited had evidently grown bored at the delay. There was no longer to be heard the slash of the cutwater, and there was no longer the flame of the long trail. The light in the north still glimmered, but it was apparently no nearer to the boat. Sometimes the boom of the surf rang in the correspondent's ears, and he turned the craft seaward then and rowed harder. Southward, some one had evidently built a watch-fire on the beach. It was too low and too far to be seen, but it made a shimmering, roseate reflection upon the bluff back of it, and this could be discerned from the boat. The wind came stronger, and sometimes a wave suddenly raged out like a mountain-cat and there was to be seen the sheen and sparkle of a broken crest.

The captain, in the bow, moved on his water-jar and sat erect. "Pretty long night," he observed to the correspondent. He looked at the shore. "Those life-saving people take their time."

"Did you see that shark playing around?"

"Yes, I saw him. He was a big fellow, all right."

"Wish I had known you were awake."

Later the correspondent spoke into the bottom of the boat.

"Billie!" There was a slow and gradual disentanglement. "Billie, will you spell me?"

"Sure," said the oiler.

As soon as the correspondent touched the cold comfortable seawater in the bottom of the boat, and had huddled close to the cook's life-belt he was deep in sleep, despite the fact that his teeth played all the popular airs. This sleep was so good to him that it was but a moment before he heard a voice call his name in a tone that demonstrated the last stages of exhaustion. "Will you spell me?"

"Sure, Billie."

The light in the north had mysteriously vanished, but the correspondent took his course from the wide-awake captain.

Later in the night they took the boat farther out to sea, and the captain directed the cook to take one oar at the stern and keep the boat facing the seas.

He was to call out if he should hear the thunder of the surf. This plan enabled the oiler and the correspondent to get respite together. "We'll give those boys a chance to get into shape again," said the captain. They curled down and, after a few preliminary chatterings and trembles, slept once more the dead sleep. Neither knew they had bequeathed to the cook the company of another shark, or perhaps the same shark.

As the boat caroused on the waves, spray occasionally bumped over the side and gave them a fresh soaking, but this had no power to break their repose. The ominous slash of the wind and the water affected them as it would have affected mummies.

"Boys," said the cook, with the notes of every reluctance in his voice, "she's drifted in pretty close. I guess one of you had better take her to sea again." The correspondent, aroused, heard the crash of the toppled crests.

As he was rowing, the captain gave him some whiskey and water, and this steadied the chills out of him. "If I ever get ashore and anybody shows me even a photograph of an oar——"

At last there was a short conversation.

"Billie. . . . Billie, will you spell me?"

"Sure," said the oiler.

VII

When the correspondent again opened his eyes, the sea and the sky were each of the gray hue of the dawning. Later, carmine and gold was painted upon the waters. The morning appeared finally, in its splendor, with a sky of pure blue, and the sunlight flamed on the tips of the waves.

On the distant dunes were set many little black cottages, and a tall white wind-mill reared above them. No man, nor dog, nor bicycle appeared on the beach. The cottages might have formed a deserted village.

The voyagers scanned the shore. A conference was held in the boat. "Well," said the captain, "if no help is coming, we might better try a run through the surf right away. If we stay out here much longer we will be too weak to do anything for ourselves at all." The others silently acquiesced in this reasoning. The boat was headed for the beach. The correspondent wondered if none ever ascended the tall wind-tower, and if then they never looked seaward. This tower was a giant, standing with its back to the plight of the ants. It represented in a degree, to the correspondent, the serenity of nature amid the struggles of the individual—nature in the wind, and nature in the vision of men. She did not seem cruel to him then, nor beneficent, nor treacherous, nor wise. But she was indifferent, flatly indifferent. It is, perhaps, plausible that a man in this situation, impressed with the unconcern of the universe, should see the innumerable flaws of his life and have them taste wickedly in his mind and wish for another chance. A distinction between right and wrong seems absurdly clear to him, then, in this new ignorance of the grave-edge, and he understands that if he were given another opportunity he would mend his conduct and his words, and be better and brighter during an introduction, or a tea.

"Now, boys," said the captain, "she is going to swamp sure. All we can do is to work her in as far as possible, and then when she swamps, pile out and scramble for the beach. Keep cool now, and don't jump until she swamps sure."

The oiler took the oars. Over his shoulders he scanned the surf. "Captain," he said, "I think I'd better bring her about, and keep her head-on to the seas and back her in."

"All right Billie," said the captain. "Back her in." The oiler swung the boat then and, seated in the stern, the cook and the correspondent were obliged to look over their shoulders to contemplate the lonely and indifferent shore.

The monstrous inshore rollers heaved the boat high until the men were again enabled to see the white sheets of water scudding up the slanted beach. "We won't get in very close," said the captain. Each time a man could wrest his attention from the rollers, he turned his glance toward the shore, and in the expression of the eyes during this contemplation there was a singular quality. The correspondent, observing the others, knew that they were not afraid, but the full meaning of their glances was shrouded.

As for himself, he was too tired to grapple fundamentally with the fact. He tried to coerce his mind into thinking of it, but the mind was dominated at this time by the muscles, and the muscles said they did not care. It merely occurred to him that if he should drown it would be a shame.

There were no hurried words, no pallor, no plain agitation. The men simply looked at the shore. "Now, remember to get well clear of the boat when you jump," said the captain.

Seaward the crest of a roller suddenly fell with a thunderous crash, and the long white comber came roaring down upon the boat.

"Steady now," said the captain. The men were silent. They turned their eyes from the shore to the comber and waited. The boat slid up the incline, leaped at the furious top, bounced over it, and swung down the long back of the wave. Some water had been shipped and the cook bailed it out.

But the next crest crashed also. The tumbling boiling flood of white water caught the boat and whirled it almost perpendicular. Water swarmed in from all sides. The correspondent had his hands on the gunwale at this time, and when the water entered at that place he swiftly withdrew his fingers, as if he objected to wetting them.

The little boat, drunken with this weight of water, reeled and snuggled deeper into the sea.

"Bail her out, cook! Bail her out," said the captain.

"All right, Captain," said the cook.

"Now, boys, the next one will do for us, sure," said the oiler. "Mind to jump clear of the boat."

The third wave moved forward, huge, furious, implacable. It fairly swallowed the dingey, and almost simultaneously the men tumbled into the sea. A piece of life-belt had lain in the bottom of the boat, and as the correspondent went overboard he held this to his chest with his left hand.

The January water was icy, and he reflected immediately that it was colder than he had expected to find it off the coast of Florida. This appeared to his dazed mind as a fact important enough to be noted at the time. The coldness of the water was sad; it was tragic. This fact was somehow so mixed and confused with his opinion of his own situation that it seemed almost a proper reason for tears. The water was cold.

When he came to the surface he was conscious of little but the noisy water. Afterward he saw his companions in the sea. The oiler was ahead in the race. He was swimming strongly and rapidly. Off to the correspondent's left, the cook's great white and corked back bulged out of the water, and in the rear the captain was hanging with his one good hand to the keel of the overturned dingey.

There was a certain immovable quality to a shore, and the correspondent wondered at it amid the confusion of the sea.

It seemed also very attractive, but the correspondent knew that it was a long journey, and he paddled leisurely. The piece of life-preserver lay under him, and sometimes he whirled down the incline of a wave as if he were on a hand-sled.

But finally he arrived at a place in the sea where travel was beset with difficulty. He did not pause swimming to inquire what matter of current had caught him, but there his progress ceased. The shore was set before him like a bit of scenery on a stage, and he looked at it and understood with his eyes each detail of it.

As the cook passed, much farther to the left, the captain was calling to him. "Turn over on your back, cook! Turn over on your back and use the oar."

"All right, sir." The cook turned on his back, and, paddling with an oar, went ahead as if he were a canoe.

Presently the boat also passed to the left of the correspondent with the captain clinging with one hand to the keel. He would have appeared like a man raising himself to look over a board fence, if it were not for the extraordinary gymnastics of the boat. The correspondent marvelled that the captain could still hold to it.

They passed on, nearer to shore—the oiler, the cook, the captain—and following them went the water-jar, bouncing gayly over the seas.

The correspondent remained in the grip of this strange new enemy—a current. The shore, with its white slope of sand and its green bluff, topped with little silent cottages, was spread like a picture before him. It was very near to him then, but he was impressed as one who in a gallery looks at a scene from Brittany or Holland.

He thought: "Am I going to drown? Can it be possible? Can it be possible? Can it be possible?" Perhaps an individual must consider his own death to be the final phenomenon of nature.

But later a wave perhaps whirled him out of this small deadly current, for he found suddenly that he could again make progress toward the shore. Later still, he was aware that the captain, clinging with one hand to the keel of the dingey, had his face turned away from the shore and toward him, and was calling his name. "Come to the boat! Come to the boat!"

In his struggle to reach the captain and the boat, he reflected that when one gets properly wearied, drowning must really be a comfortable arrangement, a cessation of hostilities accompanied by a large degree of relief, and he was glad of it, for the main thing in his mind for some moments had been horror of the temporary agony. He did not wish to be hurt.

Presently he saw a man running along the shore. He was undressing with most remarkable speed. Coat, trousers, shirt, everything flew magically off him.

"Come to the boat," called the captain.

"All right, Captain." As the correspondent paddled, he saw the captain let himself down to bottom and leave the boat. Then the correspondent performed his one little marvel of the voyage. A large wave caught him and flung him with ease and supreme speed completely over the boat and far beyond it. It struck him even then as an event in gymnastics, and a true miracle of the sea. An overturned boat in the surf is not a plaything to a swimming man.

The correspondent arrived in water that reached only to his waist, but his condition did not enable him to stand for more than a moment. Each wave knocked him into a heap, and the under-tow pulled at him.

Then he saw the man who had been running and undressing, and undressing and running, come bounding into the water. He dragged ashore the cook, and then waded toward the captain, but the captain waved him away, and sent him to the correspondent. He was naked, naked as a tree in winter, but a halo was about his head, and he shone like a saint. He gave a strong pull, and a long drag, and a bully heave at the correspondent's hand. The correspondent, schooled in the minor formulae, said: "Thanks, old man." But suddenly the man cried: "What's that?" He pointed a swift finger. The correspondent said: "Go."

In the shallows, face downward, lay the oiler. His forehead touched sand that was periodically, between each wave, clear of the sea.

The correspondent did not know all that transpired afterward.

When he achieved safe ground he fell, striking the sand with each particular part of his body. It was as if he had dropped from a roof, but the thud was grateful to him.

It seems that instantly the beach was populated with men with blankets, clothes, and flasks, and women with coffee-pots and all the remedies sacred to their minds. The welcome of the land to the men from the sea was warm and generous, but a still and dripping shape was carried slowly up the beach, and the land's welcome for it could only be the different and sinister hospitality of the grave.

When it came night, the white waves paced to and fro in the moonlight, and the wind brought the sound of the great sea's voice to the men on shore, and they felt that they could then be interpreters.

1897 1897

Frank Norris 1870–1902

Perhaps as much as any other writer, Frank Norris, in his life and works, revealed the contradictions and paradoxes of America at the turn of the century. He was a confirmed realist who rejected the conventions of popular sentimental fiction, but, like one of his own characters, he was sometimes drawn to search for "True Romance," to "see everything through a rose-coloured mist—a mist that dulled all harsh outlines, all crude and violent colors." The principal influences on his ideas and writing came from Harvard College and from the French literary world, yet he felt that the "big American novel is going to come out of the West." His first published work, Yvernele, A Tale of Feudal France *(1891), was a lengthy romantic poem on a medieval theme, but in the work that followed he became the foremost exponent of literary naturalism in nineteenth-century America.*

Norris was born in Chicago and moved to San Francisco with his parents when he was fourteen. After prep school he studied art in London and Paris and attended the University of California, where he first read the work of Zola. He spent a year at Harvard, and there he began work on his novels McTeague *(1899) and* Vandover *and the* Brute *(1914). From Harvard, Norris went to South Africa to write travel sketches, but he got involved in the politics of the Boer War and was expelled from the country. Returning to San Francisco, he went to work for a magazine that published a number of his short stories, including "A Deal in Wheat," and serialized his first novel,* Moran of the Lady Letty *(1898), a wild tale of pirate adventures.*

In 1898, Norris went to Cuba to report on the Spanish-American War for McClure's *Magazine. He became an editor for the publishing firm of Doubleday, and in 1899 his novel,* McTeague, *was published, creating a literary scandal because of its sensational treatment of greed and degeneracy. In the same year Norris conceived his most ambitious work, three novels on the American West and the growth and distribution of wheat. The first book,* The Octopus, *dealing with the strangling greed of railroad owners and the growing of wheat, appeared in 1901 and was immediately successful. The second,* The Pit *(1903), dealt with the marketing of wheat. The third novel, which was to be named* The Wolf *and portray the consumption of the wheat in Europe, was never written. Norris had just completed the second volume of the trilogy when he died from a ruptured appendix in October 1902.*

Norris is often criticized for excessive sentiment in his realistic fiction, for his romantic reliance on the regenerative power of love, and for his philosophical inconsistencies. He was, in fact, less interested in literary or social theories than in achieving dramatic power in stories of individuals moved by forces of heredity and forces of history that they could not control and rarely understood. Norris believed that fiction can express the truth of life better than any other art, "better than painting, better than poetry, better than music." It was for him a means of getting at truth, of cutting through the "tissues and wrappings of flesh, down deep into the red, living heart of things."

FURTHER READING: *The Complete Edition of Frank Norris,* 10 vols., 1928 [1929]; *The Literary Criticism of Frank Norris,* ed. D. Pizer, 1962; *The Letters of Frank Norris,* ed. F. Walker, 1956; F. Walker, *Frank Norris: A Biography,* 1932; E. Marchand, *Frank Norris: A Study,* 1942; W. French, *Frank Norris,* 1962; D. Pizer, *The Novels of Frank Norris,* 1966; W. Dillingham, *Frank Norris: Instinct and Art,* 1969; D. Graham, *The Fiction of Frank Norris,* 1978; *Critical Essays on Frank Norris,* ed. D. Graham, 1980; *Frank Norris: The Critical Reception,* ed. J. McElrath, 1981; B. Hochman, *The Art of Frank Norris,* 1988; J. McElrath, *Frank Norris Revisited,* 1992.

TEXT: *The Complete Works of Frank Norris,* 7 vols., 1903.

A DEAL IN WHEAT

I

THE BEAR[1]—WHEAT AT SIXTY-TWO

As Sam Lewiston backed the horse into the shafts of his buckboard and began hitching the tugs to the whiffletree,[2] his wife came out from the kitchen door of the house and drew near, and stood for some time at the horse's head, her arms folded and her apron rolled around them. For a long moment neither spoke. They had talked over the situation so long and so comprehensively the night before that there seemed to be nothing more to say.

[1]In the jargon of stock exchanges, "bears" are traders who profit from a falling (bear) market; "bulls" profit from a rising (bull) market.

[2]Pivoted bar to which harness lines (tugs) are fastened.

The time was late in the summer, the place a ranch in southwestern Kansas, and Lewiston and his wife were two of a vast population of farmers, wheat growers, who at that moment were passing through a crisis—a crisis that at any moment might culminate in tragedy. Wheat was down to sixty-six.

At length Emma Lewiston spoke.

"Well," she hazarded, looking vaguely out across the ranch toward the horizon, leagues distant; "well, Sam, there's always that offer of brother Joe's. We can quit—and go to Chicago—if the worst comes."

"And give up!" exclaimed Lewiston, running the lines through the torets.[3] "Leave the ranch! Give up! After all these years!"

His wife made no reply for the moment. Lewiston climbed into the buckboard and gathered up the lines. "Well, here goes for the last try, Emmie," he said. "Good-by, girl. Maybe things will look better in town to-day."

"Maybe," she said gravely. She kissed her husband good-by and stood for some time looking after the buckboard traveling toward the town in a moving pillar of dust.

"I don't know," she murmured at length; "I don't know just how we're going to make out."

When he reached town, Lewiston tied the horse to the iron railing in front of the Odd Fellows' Hall, the ground floor of which was occupied by the post-office, and went across the street and up the stairway of a building of brick and granite—quite the most pretentious structure of the town—and knocked at a door upon the first landing. The door was furnished with a pane of frosted glass, on which in gold letters, was inscribed "Bridges & Co., Grain Dealers."

Bridges himself, a middle-aged man who wore a velvet skullcap and who was smoking a Pittsburg stogie, met the farmer at the counter and the two exchanged perfunctory greetings.

"Well," said Lewiston, tentatively, after a while.

"Well, Lewiston," said the other, "I can't take that wheat of yours at any better than sixty-two."

"Sixty-*two*."

"It's the Chicago price that does it, Lewiston. Truslow is bearing the stuff for all he's worth. It's Truslow and the bear clique that stick the knife to us. The price broke again this morning. We've just got a wire."

"Good heavens," murmured Lewiston, looking vaguely from side to side. "That—that ruins me. I *can't* carry my grain any longer—what with storage charges and—and—Bridges, I don't see just how I'm going to make out. Sixty-two cents a bushel! Why, man, what with this and with that it's cost me nearly a dollar a bushel to raise that wheat, and now Truslow——"

He turned away abruptly with a quick gesture of infinite discouragement.

He went down the stairs, and making his way to where his buckboard was hitched, got in, and, with eyes vacant, the reins slipping and sliding in his limp, half-open hands, drove slowly back to the ranch. His wife had seen him coming, and met him as he drew up before the barn.

"Well?" she demanded.

"Emmie," he said as he got out of the buckboard, laying his arm across her shoulder, "Emmie, I guess we'll take up with Joe's offer. We'll go to Chicago. We're cleaned out!"

[3]Harness rings.

II

THE BULL—WHEAT AT A DOLLAR-TEN

. . .——*and said Party of the Second Part further covenants and agrees to merchandise such wheat in foreign ports, it being understood and agreed between the Party of the First Part and the Party of the Second Part that the wheat hereinbefore mentioned is released and sold to the Party of the Second Part for export purposes only, and not for consumption or distribution within the boundaries of the United States of America or of Canada.*

"Now, Mr. Gates, if you will sign for Mr. Truslow, I guess that'll be all," remarked Hornung when he had finished reading.

Hornung affixed his signature to the two documents and passed them over to Gates, who signed for his principal client. Truslow—or, as he had been called ever since he had gone into the fight against Hornung's corner—the Great Bear. Hornung's secretary was called in and witnessed the signatures, and Gates thrust the contract into his Gladstone bag[4] and stood up, smoothing his hat.

"You will deliver the warehouse receipts for the grain," began Gates.

"I'll send a messenger to Truslow's office before noon," interrupted Hornung. "You can pay by certified check through the Illinois Trust people."

When the other had taken himself off, Hornung sat for some moments gazing abstractedly toward his office windows, thinking over the whole matter. He had just agreed to release to Truslow, at the rate of one dollar and ten cents per bushel, one hundred thousand out of the two million and odd bushels of wheat that he, Hornung, controlled, or actually owned. And for the moment he was wondering if, after all, he had done wisely in not goring the Great Bear to actual financial death. He had made him pay one hundred thousand dollars. Truslow was good for this amount. Would it not have been better to have put a prohibitive figure on the grain and forced the Bear into bankruptcy? True, Hornung would then be without his enemy's money, but Truslow would have been eliminated from the situation, and that—so Hornung told himself—was always a consummation most devoutly, strenuously and diligently to be striven for. Truslow once dead was dead, but the Bear was never more dangerous than when desperate.

"But so long as he can't get *wheat,*" muttered Hornung at the end of his reflections, "he can't hurt me. And he can't get it. That I *know.*"

For Hornung controlled the situation. So far back as the February of that year an "unknown bull" had been making his presence felt on the floor of the Board of Trade. By the middle of March the commercial reports of the daily press had begun to speak of "the powerful bull clique"; a few weeks later that legendary condition of affairs implied and epitomized in the magic words "Dollar Wheat" had been attained, and by the first of April, when the price had been boosted to one dollar and ten cents a bushel, Hornung had disclosed his hand, and in place of mere rumors, the definite and authoritative news that May wheat had been cornered in the Chicago Pit[5] went flashing around the world from Liverpool to Odessa and from Duluth to Buenos Ayres.

[4]A traveling bag with a rigid frame and flexible sides, named for William Gladstone (1809–1898), British statesman.

[5]Area in the exchange where actual trading is done. A speculator has "cornered" the market when he or she owns enough of a commodity to control the selling price.

It was—as the veteran operators were persuaded—Truslow himself who had made Hornung's corner possible. The Great Bear had for once overreached himself, and, believing himself all-powerful, had hammered the price just the fatal fraction too far down. Wheat had gone to sixty-two—for the time, and under the circumstances, an abnormal price. When the reaction came it was tremendous. Hornung saw his chance, seized it, and in a few months had turned the tables, had cornered the product, and virtually driven the bear clique out of the pit.

On the same day that the delivery of the hundred thousand bushels was made to Truslow, Hornung met his broker at his lunch club.

"Well," said the latter, "I see you let go that line of stuff to Truslow."

Hornung nodded; but the broker added:

"Remember, I was against it from the very beginning. I know we've cleared up over a hundred thou'. I would have fifty times preferred to have lost twice that and *smashed Truslow dead.* Bet you what you like he makes us pay for it somehow."

"Huh!" grunted his principal. "How about insurance and warehouse charges, and carrying expenses on that lot? Guess we'd have had to pay those, too, if we'd held on."

But the other put up his chin, unwilling to be persuaded. "I won't sleep easy," he declared, "till Truslow is busted."

III

The Pit

Just as Going mounted the steps on the edge of the pit the great gong struck, a roar of a hundred voices developed with the swiftness of successive explosions, the rush of a hundred men surging downward to the centre of the pit filled the air with the stamp and grind of feet, a hundred hands in eager strenuous gestures tossed upward from out the brown of the crowd, the official reporter in his cage on the margin of the pit leaned far forward with straining ear to catch the opening bid, and another day of battle was begun.

Since the sale of the hundred thousand bushels of wheat to Truslow the "Hornung crowd" had steadily shouldered the price higher until on this particular morning it stood at one dollar and a half. That was Hornung's price. No one else had any grain to sell.

But not ten minutes after the opening, Going was surprised out of all countenance to hear shouted from the other side of the pit these words:

"Sell May at one-fifty."

Going was for the moment touching elbows with Kimbark on one side and with Merriam on the other, all three belonging to the "Hornung crowd." Their answering challenge of *"Sold"* was as the voice of one man. They did not pause to reflect upon the strangeness of the circumstance. (That was for afterward.) Their response to the offer was as unconscious as reflex action and almost as rapid, and before the pit was well aware of what had happened the transaction of one thousand bushels was down upon Going's trading-card and fifteen hundred dollars had changed hands. But here was a marvel—the whole available supply of wheat cornered, Hornung master of the situation, invincible, unassailable; yet behold a man willing to sell, a Bear bold enough to raise his head.

"That was Kennedy, wasn't it, who made that offer?" asked Kimbark, as Going noted down the trade—"Kennedy, that new man?"

"Yes; who do you suppose he's selling for; who's willing to go short at this stage of the game?"

"Maybe he ain't short."

"Short! Great heavens, man; where'd he get the stuff?"

"Blamed if I know. We can account for every handful of May. Steady! Oh, there he goes again."

"Sell a thousand May at one-fifty," vociferated the bear-broker, throwing out his hand, one finger raised to indicate the number of "contracts" offered. This time it was evident that he was attacking the Hornung crowd deliberately, for, ignoring the jam of traders that swept toward him, he looked across the pit to where Going and Kimbark were shouting *"Sold! Sold!"* and nodded his head.

A second time Going made memoranda of the trade, and either the Hornung holdings were increased by two thousand bushels of May wheat or the Hornung bank account swelled by at least three thousand dollars of some unknown short's money.

Of late—so sure was the bull crowd of its position—no one had even thought of glancing at the inspection sheet on the bulletin board. But now one of Going's messengers hurried up to him with the announcement that this sheet showed receipts at Chicago for that morning of twenty-five thousand bushels, and not credited to Hornung. Some one had got hold of a line of wheat overlooked by the "clique" and was dumping it upon them.

"Wire the Chief," said Going over his shoulder to Merriam. This one struggled out of the crowd, and on a telegraph blank scribbled:

> "Strong bear movement—New man—Kennedy—Selling in lots of five contracts—Chicago receipts twenty-five thousand."

The message was despatched, and in a few moments the answer came back, laconic, of military terseness.

> "Support the market."

And Going obeyed, Merriam and Kimbark following, the new broker fairly throwing the wheat at them in thousand-bushel lots.

"Sell May at 'fifty; sell May; sell May." A moment's indecision, an instant's hesitation, the first faint suggestion of weakness, and the market would have broken under them. But for the better part of four hours they stood their ground, taking all that was offered, in constant communication with the Chief, and from time to time stimulated and steadied by his brief, unvarying command:

"Support the market."

At the close of the session they had bought in the twenty-five thousand bushels of May. Hornung's position was as stable as a rock, and the price closed even with the opening figure—one dollar and a half.

But the morning's work was the talk of all La Salle Street.[6] Who was back of the raid? What was the meaning of this unexpected selling? For weeks the Pit trading had been merely nominal. Truslow, the Great Bear, from whom the

[6] Location of the Chicago Board of Trade.

most serious attack might have been expected, had gone to his country seat at Geneva Lake, in Wisconsin, declaring himself to be out of the market entirely. He went bass fishing every day.

IV

The Belt Line

On a certain day toward the middle of the month, at a time when the mysterious Bear had unloaded some eighty thousand bushels upon Hornung, a conference was held in the library of Hornung's home. His broker attended it, and also a clean-faced, bright-eyed individual whose name of Cyrus Ryder might have been found upon the pay-roll of a rather well-known detective agency. For upward of half an hour after the conference began the detective spoke, the other two listening attentively, gravely.

"Then, last of all," concluded Ryder, "I made out I was a hobo, and began stealing rides on the Belt Line Railroad. Know the road? It just circles Chicago. Truslow owns it. Yes? Well, then I began to catch on. I noticed that cars of certain numbers—thirty-one naught thirty-four, thirty-two one ninety—well, the numbers don't matter, but anyhow, these cars were always switched on to the sidings by Mr. Truslow's main elevator D soon as they came in. The wheat was shunted in, and they were pulled out again. Well, I spotted one car and stole a ride on her. Say, look here, *that car went right around the city on the Belt, and came back to D again, and the same wheat in her all the time.* The grain was reinspected—it was raw, I tell you—and the warehouse receipts made out just as though the stuff had come in from Kansas or Iowa."

"The same wheat all the time!" interrupted Hornung.

"The same wheat—your wheat, that you sold to Truslow."

"Great snakes!" ejaculated Hornung's broker. "Truslow never took it abroad at all."

"Took it abroad! Say, he's just been running it around Chicago, like the supers in 'Shenandoah,'[7] round an' round, so you'd think it was a new lot, an' selling it back to you again."

"No wonder we couldn't account for so much wheat."

"Bought it from us at one-ten, and made us buy it back—our own wheat—at one-fifty."

Hornung and his broker looked at each other in silence for a moment. Then all at once Hornung struck the arm of his chair with his fist and exploded in a roar of laughter. The broker stared for one bewildered moment, then followed his example.

"Sold! Sold!" shouted Hornung almost gleefully. "Upon my soul it's as good as a Gilbert and Sullivan show. And we—Oh, Lord! Billy, shake on it, and hats off to my distinguished friend, Truslow. He'll be President some day. Hey! What? Prosecute him? Not I."

"He's done us out of a neat hatful of dollars for all that," observed the broker, suddenly grave.

[7]The supernumeraries, or "extras," in the cast of the Civil War play *Shenandoah* (1888) marched in a continuous circle across and behind the stage to give the impression of a vast army.

"Billy, it's worth the price."

"We've got to make it up somehow."

"Well, tell you what. We were going to boost the price to one seventy-five next week, and make that our settlement figure."

"Can't do it now. Can't afford it."

"No. Here; we'll let out a big link; we'll put wheat at two dollars, and let it go at that."

"Two it is, then," said the broker.

V

THE BREAD LINE

The street was very dark and absolutely deserted. It was a district on the "South Side," not far from the Chicago River, given up largely to wholesale stores, and after nightfall was empty of all life. The echoes slept but lightly hereabouts, and the slightest footfall, the faintest noise, woke them upon the instant and sent them clamoring up and down the length of the pavement between the iron-shuttered fronts. The only light visible came from the side door of a certain "Vienna" bakery, where at one o'clock in the morning loaves of bread were given away to any who should ask. Every evening about nine o'clock the outcasts began to gather about the side door. The stragglers came in rapidly, and the line—the "bread line," as it was called—began to form. By midnight it was usually some hundred yards in length, stretching almost the entire length of the block.

Toward ten in the evening, his coat collar turned up against the fine drizzle that pervaded the air, his hands in his pockets, his elbows gripping his sides, Sam Lewiston came up and silently took his place at the end of the line.

Unable to conduct his farm upon a paying basis at the time when Truslow, the "Great Bear," had sent the price of grain down to sixty-two cents a bushel, Lewiston had turned over his entire property to his creditors, and, leaving Kansas for good, had abandoned farming, and had left his wife at her sister's boarding-house in Topeka with the understanding that she was to join him in Chicago so soon as he had found a steady job. Then he had come to Chicago and had turned workman. His brother Joe conducted a small hat factory on Archer Avenue, and for a time he found there a meagre employment. But difficulties had occurred, times were bad, the hat factory was involved in debts, the repealing of a certain import duty on manufactured felt overcrowded the home market with cheap Belgian and French products, and in the end his brother had assigned[8] and gone to Milwaukee.

Thrown out of work, Lewiston drifted aimlessly about Chicago, from pillar to post, working a little, earning here a dollar, there a dime, but always sinking, sinking, till at last the ooze of the lowest bottom dragged at his feet and the rush of the great ebb went over him and engulfed him and shut him out from the light, and a park bench became his home and the "bread line" his chief makeshift of subsistence.

[8]Turned over his remaining property to his creditors.

He stood now in the infolding drizzle, sodden, stupefied with fatigue. Before and behind stretched the line. There was no talking. There was no sound. The street was empty. It was so still that the passing of a cable-car in the adjoining thoroughfare grated like prolonged rolling explosions, beginning and ending at immeasurable distances. The drizzle descended incessantly. After a long time midnight struck.

There was something ominous and gravely impressive in this interminable line of dark figures, close-pressed, soundless; a crowd, yet absolutely still; a close-packed, silent file, waiting, waiting in the vast deserted night-ridden street; waiting without a word, without a movement, there under the night and under the slow-moving mists of rain.

Few in the crowd were professional beggars. Most of them were workmen, long since out of work, forced into idleness by long-continued "hard times," by ill luck, by sickness. To them the "bread line" was a godsend. At least they could not starve. Between jobs here in the end was something to hold them up—a small platform, as it were, above the sweep of black water, where for a moment they might pause and take breath before the plunge.

The period of waiting on this night of rain seemed endless to those silent, hungry men; but at length there was a stir. The line moved. The side door opened. Ah, at last! They were going to hand out the bread.

But instead of the usual white-aproned under-cook with his crowded hampers there now appeared in the doorway a new man—a young fellow who looked like a bookkeeper's assistant. He bore in his hand a placard, which he tacked to the outside of the door. Then he disappeared within the bakery, locking the door after him.

A shudder of poignant despair, an unformed, inarticulate sense of calamity, seemed to run from end to end of the line. What had happened? Those in the rear, unable to read the placard, surged forward, a sense of bitter disappointment clutching at their hearts.

The line broke up, disintegrated into a shapeless throng—a throng that crowded forward and collected in front of the shut door whereon the placard was affixed. Lewiston, with the others, pushed forward. On the placard he read these words:

> "Owing to the fact that the price of grain has been increased to two dollars a bushel, there will be no distribution of bread from this bakery until further notice."

Lewiston turned away, dumb, bewildered. Till morning he walked the streets, going on without purpose, without direction. But now at last his luck had turned. Overnight the wheel of his fortunes had creaked and swung upon its axis, and before noon he had found a job in the street-cleaning brigade. In the course of time he rose to be first shift-boss, then deputy inspector, then inspector, promoted to the dignity of driving a red wagon with rubber tires and drawing a salary instead of mere wages. The wife was sent for and a new start made.

But Lewiston never forgot. Dimly he began to see the significance of things. Caught once in the cogs and wheels of a great and terrible engine, he had seen—none better—its workings. Of all the men who had vainly stood in the "bread line" on that rainy night in early summer, he, perhaps, had been the only one who had struggled up to the surface again. How many others had gone down in the great ebb? Grim question; he dared not think how many.

He had seen the two ends of a great wheat operation—a battle between Bear and Bull. The stories (subsequently published in the city's press) of Truslow's counter-move in selling Hornung his own wheat supplied the unseen section. The farmer—he who raised the wheat—was ruined upon one hand; the workingman—he who consumed it—was ruined upon the other. But between the two, the great operators, who never saw the wheat they traded in, bought and sold the world's food, gambled in the nourishment of entire nations, practiced their tricks, their chicanery and oblique shifty "deals," were reconciled in their differences, and went on through their appointed way, jovial, contented, enthroned, and unassailable.

1902

Jack London 1876–1916

Jack London was the illegitimate son of a father who was a wandering astrologer and a mother who was a spiritualist and medium. Born in San Francisco, London was raised in Oakland, where he roamed the waterfront and attended school only occasionally, but, as he reported in his autobiographical novel, Martin Eden *(1909), he read constantly, as much as nineteen hours a day. He "rode the rods" over the Sierras to the East, was jailed for vagrancy in Buffalo at eighteen, worked as an "oyster pirate" in San Francisco Bay, stealing from the oyster beds belonging to other fishermen. He sailed as a seaman on a sealing trip to Japan and in 1896 joined the gold rush to the Klondike, where he found no gold but gathered ample material for the brutal, vigorous life he portrayed in* The Call of the Wild *(1903) and* White Fang *(1906), novels of man and beast struggling against the tremendous forces of nature.*

From 1900 to 1916, London wrote more than fifty books, earning a million dollars, which he spent (as quickly as he earned it) in a frantic search for contentment. From social Darwinism London had absorbed the idea that to survive, people must adapt to irresistible natural forces and to "the stress and strain of life, its fevers and sweats and wild indulgences." Although his writing is often categorized simply as literary naturalism, the sources of his ideas were complex. London was most deeply influenced by the seemingly irreconcilable opposites of Nietzsche and Marx. From Nietzsche he borrowed the idea of the super human beings, evident in its most destructive form in Wolf Larsen, the predatory hero of London's The Sea Wolf *(1904). From Marx he took the idea of the need for social reform and of the power of economic determinism, concepts he embodied in his socialistic treatises,* The War of the Classes *(1905) and* The Human Drift *(1907), and in his terrifying vision of the coming of totalitarianism,* The Iron Heel *(1907).*

London was a storyteller of great emotional power and excitement, a master of tempo and pace whose adventure stories continue to fascinate a large reading public. As a writer, he was bold, sensational, tragic and, like his characters, a champion and a victim of the "wild indulgences" of life and nature.

FURTHER READING: *Letters from Jack London,* ed. K. Hendricks and I. Shepard, 1965; *The Letters of Jack London,* 3 vols., ed. E. Labor, R. Leitz, and M. Shepard, 1988; *Complete Short Stories of Jack London,* ed. E. Labor, R. Leitz, and I. Shepard, 1993; C. London, *The Book of Jack London,* 2 vols., 1921; J. London, *Jack London and His Times,* 1939, 1968; I. Stone, *Sailor on Horseback: The Biography of Jack London,* 1938; P. Foner, *Jack London: American Rebel,*

1947; R. O'Connor, *Jack London: A Biography,* 1964; F. Walker, *Jack London and the Klondike,* 1966; A. Sinclair, *Jack, A Biography of Jack London,* 1977, 1983; R. Kingman, *A Pictorial Life of Jack London,* 1981; J. Perry, *Jack London: An American Myth,* 1981; J. Hedrick, *Solitary Comrade: Jack London and His Work,* 1982; J. McClintock, *White Logic: Jack London's Short Stories,* 1975; C. Watson, *The Novels of Jack London,* 1983; *Critical Essays on Jack London,* ed. J. Tavernier-Courbin, 1983; J. Lundquist, *Jack London,* 1987; C. Stasz, *American Dreamers: Charmian and Jack London,* 1988; J. London, *Jack London and His Daughters,* 1991; R. Kingman, *Jack London: A Definitive Chronology,* 1992; T. Williams, *Jack London—The Movies: An Historical Survey,* 1992; *The Letters of Jack London,* ed. E. Labor, R. Leitz, and I. Shepard, 1988; *Complete Short Stories of Jack London,* ed. E. Labor, R. Leitz, and I. Shepard, 1993; E. Labor and J. Reesman, *Jack London,* 1994; J. Auerbach, *Male Call: Becoming Jack London,* 1996; *Rereading Jack London,* ed. L. Cassuto and J. Reesman, 1996; A. Kershaw, *Jack London: A Life,* 1997; J. Reesman, *Jack London: A Study of the Short Fiction,* 1999; R. Stefoff, *Jack London: An American Original,* 2002.

TEXTS: "The Law of Life," *Children of the Frost,* 1902; "To Build a Fire," *Lost Face,* 1910.

THE LAW OF LIFE

Old Koskoosh listened greedily. Though his sight had long since faded, his hearing was still acute, and the slightest sound penetrated to the glimmering intelligence which yet abode behind the withered forehead, but which no longer gazed forth upon the things of the world. Ah! That was Sit-cum-to-ha, shrilly anathematizing the dogs as she cuffed and beat them into the harnesses. Sit-cum-to-ha was his daughter's daughter, but she was too busy to waste a thought upon her broken grandfather, sitting alone there in the snow, forlorn and helpless. Camp must be broken. The long trail waited while the short day refused to linger. Life called her, and the duties of life, not death. And he was very close to death now.

The thought made the old man panicky for the moment, and he stretched forth a palsied hand which wandered tremblingly over the small heap of dry wood beside him. Reassured that it was indeed there, his hand returned to the shelter of his mangy furs, and he again fell to listening. The sulky crackling of half-frozen hides told him that the chief's moose-skin lodge had been struck, and even then was being rammed and jammed into portable compass. The chief was his son, stalwart and strong, headman of the tribesmen, and a mighty hunter. As the women toiled with the camp luggage, his voice rose, chiding them for their slowness. Old Koskoosh strained his ears. It was the last time he would hear that voice. There went Geehow's lodge! And Tusken's! Seven, eight, nine, only the shaman's[1] could be still standing. There! They were at work upon it now. He could hear the shaman grunt as he piled it on the sled. A child whimpered, and a woman soothed it with soft, crooning gutturals. Little Koo-tee, the old man thought, a fretful child, and not overstrong. It would die soon, perhaps, and they would burn a hole through the frozen tundra and pile rocks above to keep the wolverines away. Well, what did it matter? A few years at best, and as many an empty belly as a full one. And in the end, Death waited, ever-hungry and hungriest of them all.

[1]Medicine man's.

What was that? Oh, the men lashing the sleds and drawing tight the thongs. He listened, who would listen no more. The whiplashes snarled and bit among the dogs. Hear them whine! How they hated the work and the trail! They were off! Sled after sled churned slowly away into the silence. They were gone. They had passed out of his life, and he faced the last bitter hour alone. No. The snow crunched beneath a moccasin; a man stood beside him; upon his head a hand rested gently. His son was good to do this thing. He remembered other old men whose sons had not waited after the tribe. But his son had. He wandered away into the past, till the young man's voice brought him back.

"It is well with you?" he asked.

And the old man answered, "It is well."

"There be wood beside you," the younger man continued, "and the fire burns bright. The morning is gray, and the cold has broken. It will snow presently. Even now it is snowing."

"Aye, even now it is snowing."

"The tribesmen hurry. Their bales are heavy and their bellies flat with lack of feasting. The trail is long and they travel fast. I go now. It is well?"

"It is well. I am as a last year's leaf, clinging lightly to the stem. The first breath that blows, and I fall. My voice is become like an old woman's. My eyes no longer show me the way of my feet, and my feet are heavy, and I am tired. It is well."

He bowed his head in content till the last noise of the complaining snow had died away, and he knew his son was beyond recall. Then his hand crept out in haste to the wood. It alone stood between him and the eternity that yawned in upon him. At last the measure of his life was a handful of faggots. One by one they would go to feed the fire, and just so, step by step, death would creep upon him. When the last stick had surrendered up its heat, the frost would begin to gather strength. First his feet would yield, then his hands; and the numbness would travel, slowly, from the extremities to the body. His head would fall forward upon his knees, and he would rest. It was easy. All men must die.

He did not complain. It was the way of life, and it was just. He had been born close to the earth, close to the earth he had lived, and the law thereof was not new to him. It was the law of all flesh. Nature was not kindly to the flesh. She had no concern for that concrete thing called the individual. Her interest lay in the species, the race. This was the deepest abstraction old Koskoosh's barbaric mind was capable of, but he grasped it firmly. He saw it exemplified in all life. The rise of the sap, the bursting greenness of the willow bud, the fall of the yellow leaf—in this alone was told the whole history. But one task did Nature set the individual. Did he not perform it, he died. Did he perform it, it was all the same, he died. Nature did not care; there were plenty who were obedient, and it was only the obedience in this matter, not the obedient, which lived and lived always. The tribe of Koskoosh was very old. The old men he had known when a boy had known old men before them. Therefore it was true that the tribe lived, that it stood for the obedience of all its members, way down into the forgotten past, whose very resting places were unremembered. They did not count; they were episodes. They had passed away like clouds from a summer sky. He also was an episode and would pass away. Nature did not care. To life she set one task, gave one law. To perpetuate was the task of life, its law was death. A maiden was a good creature to look upon, full-breasted and strong, with spring to her step and light in her eyes. But her task was yet before her. The light in her eyes brightened, her step quickened, she was now bold with the young men, now timid, and she gave them of her own unrest. And ever she grew fairer and yet fairer to look upon, till some hunter, able no longer to withhold himself, took her to his lodge to cook and toil for him and to become the mother of his children. And with the coming of her offspring her looks left her. Her limbs dragged and shuffled, her eyes dimmed and bleared, and only the little children found joy against the withered cheek of the old squaw by the fire. Her task was done. But a little while, on the first pinch of famine or the first long trail, and she would be left, even as he had been left, in the snow, with a little pile of wood. Such was the law.

He placed a stick carefully upon the fire and resumed his meditations. It was the same everywhere, with all things. The mosquitoes vanished with the first frost. The little tree squirrel crawled away to die. When age settled upon the rabbit it became slow and heavy and could no longer outfoot its enemies. Even the big bald-face grew clumsy and blind and quarrelsome, in the end to be dragged down by a handful of yelping huskies. He remembered how he had abandoned his own father on an upper reach of the Klondike one winter, the winter before the missionary came with his talk books and his box of medicines. Many a time had Koskoosh smacked his lips over the recollection of that box, though now his mouth refused to moisten. The "painkiller" had been especially good. But the missionary was a bother after all, for he brought no meat into the camp, and he ate heartily, and the hunters grumbled. But he chilled his lungs on the divide by the Mayo, and the dogs afterward nosed the stones away and fought over his bones.

Koskoosh placed another stick on the fire and harked back deeper into the past. There was the time of the great famine, when the old men crouched empty-bellied to the fire, and let fall from their lips dim traditions of the ancient day when the Yukon ran wide open for three winters, and then lay frozen for three summers. He had lost his mother in that famine. In the summer the salmon run had failed, and the tribe looked forward to the winter and the coming of the caribou. Then the winter came, but with it there were no caribou. Never had the like been known, not even in the lives of the old men. But the caribou did not come, and it was the seventh year, and the rabbits had not replenished, and the dogs were naught but bundles of bones. And through the long darkness the children wailed and died, and the women, and the old men; and not one in ten of the tribe lived to meet the sun when it came back in the spring. That *was* a famine!

But he had seen times of plenty, too, when the meat spoiled on their hands, and the dogs were fat and worthless with overeating—times when they let the game go unkilled, and the women were fertile, and the lodges were cluttered with sprawling men-children and women-children. Then it was the men became high-stomached, and revived ancient quarrels, and crossed the divides to the south to kill the Pellys, and to the west that they might sit by the dead fires of the Tananas. He remembered, when a boy, during a time of plenty, when he saw a moose pulled down by the wolves. Zing-ha lay with him in the snow and watched—Zing-ha, who later became the craftiest of hunters, and who, in the end, fell through an air hole on the Yukon. They found him, a month afterward, just as he had crawled halfway out and frozen stiff to the ice.

But the moose. Zing-ha and he had gone out that day to play at hunting after the manner of their fathers. On the bed of the creek they struck the fresh track of a moose, and with it the tracks of many wolves. "An old one," Zing-ha, who was quicker at reading the sign, said, "an old one who cannot keep up with the herd. The wolves have cut him out from his brothers, and they will never leave him." And it was so. It was their way. By day and by night, never resting, snarling on his heels, snapping at his nose, they would stay by him to the end. How Zing-ha and he felt the blood lust quicken! The finish would be a sight to see!

Eager-footed, they took the trail, and even he, Koskoosh, slow of sight and an unversed tracker, could have followed it blind, it was so wide. Hot were they on the heels of the chase, reading the grim tragedy, fresh-written, at every step. Now they came to where the moose had made a stand. Thrice the length of a grown man's body, in every direction, had the snow been stamped about and uptossed. In the midst were the deep impressions of the splay-hoofed game, and all about, everywhere, were the lighter footmarks of the wolves. Some, while their brothers harried the kill, had lain to one side and rested. The full-stretched impress of their bodies in the snow was as perfect as though made the moment before. One wolf had been caught in a wild lunge of the maddened victim and trampled to death. A few bones, well picked, bore witness.

Again, they ceased the uplift of their snowshoes at a second stand. Here the great animal had fought desperately. Twice had he been dragged down, as the snow attested, and twice had he shaken his assailants clear and gained footing once more. He had done his task long since, but none the less was life dear to him. Zing-ha said it was a strange thing, a moose once down to get free again; but this one certainly had. The shaman would see signs and wonders in this when they told him.

And yet again, they came to where the moose had made to mount the bank and gain the timber. But his foes had laid on from behind, till he reared and fell back upon them, crushing two deep into the snow. It was plain the kill was at hand, for their brothers had left them untouched. Two more stands were hurried past, brief in time length and very close together. The trail was red now, and the clean stride of the great beast had grown short and slovenly. Then they heard the first sounds of the battle—not the full-throated chorus of the chase, but the short, snappy bark which spoke of close quarters and teeth to flesh. Crawling up the wind, Zing-ha bellied it through the snow, and with him crept he, Koskoosh, who was to be chief of the tribesmen in the years to come. Together they shoved aside the underbranches of a young spruce and peered forth. It was the end they saw.

The picture, like all of youth's impressions, was still strong with him, and his dim eyes watched the end played out as vividly as in that far-off time. Koskoosh marveled at this, for in the days which followed, when he was a leader of men and a head of councilors, he had done great deeds and made his name a curse in the mouths of the Pellys, to say naught of the strange white man he had killed, knife to knife, in open fight.

For long he pondered on the days of his youth, till the fire died down and the frost bit deeper. He replenished it with two sticks this time, and gauged his grip on life by what remained. If Sit-cum-to-ha had only remembered her grandfather, and gathered a larger armful, his hours would have been longer. It would have been easy. But she was ever a careless child, and honored not her ancestors from the time the Beaver, son of the son of Zing-ha, first cast eyes upon her. Well, what mattered it? Had he not done likewise in his own quick youth? For a while he listened to the silence. Perhaps the heart of his son might soften, and he would come back with the dogs to take his old father on with the tribe to where the caribou ran thick and the fat hung heavy upon them.

He strained his ears, his restless brain for the moment stilled. Not a stir, nothing. He alone took breath in the midst of the great silence. It was very lonely. Hark! What was that? A chill passed over his body. The familiar, long-drawn howl broke the void, and it was close at hand. Then on his darkened eyes was projected the vision of the moose—the old bull moose—the torn flanks and bloody sides, the riddled mane, and the great branching horns, down low and tossing to the last. He saw the flashing forms of gray, the gleaming eyes, the lolling tongues, the slavered fangs. And he saw the inexorable circle close in till it became a dark point in the midst of the stamped snow.

A cold muzzle thrust against his cheek, and at its touch his soul leaped back to the present. His hand shot into the fire and dragged out a burning faggot. Overcome for the nonce by his hereditary fear of men, the brute retreated, raising a prolonged call to his brothers; and greedily they answered, till a ring of crouching, jaw-slobbering gray was stretched round about. The old man listened to the drawing in of this circle. He waved his hand wildly, and sniffs turned to snarls; but the panting brutes refused to scatter. Now one wormed his chest forward, dragging his haunches after, now a second, now a third; but never a one drew back. Why should he cling to life? he asked, and dropped the blazing stick into the snow. It sizzled and went out. The circle grunted uneasily but held its own. Again he saw the last stand of the old bull moose, and Koskoosh dropped his head wearily upon his knees. What did it matter after all? Was it not the law of life?

1901, 1902

TO BUILD A FIRE

Day had broken cold and gray, exceedingly cold and gray, when the man turned aside from the main Yukon[1] trail and climbed the high earth-bank, where a dim and little-travelled trail led eastward through the fat spruce timberland. It was a steep bank, and he paused for breath at the top, excusing the act to himself by looking at his watch. It was nine o'clock. There was no sun nor hint of sun, though there was not a cloud in the sky. It was a clear day, and yet there seemed an intangible pall over the face of things, a subtle gloom that made the day dark, and that was due to the absence of sun. This fact did not worry the man. He was used to the lack of sun. It had been days since he had seen the sun, and he knew that a few more days must pass before that cheerful orb, due south, would just peep above the sky-line and dip immediately from view.

The man flung a look back along the way he had come. The Yukon lay a mile wide and hidden under three feet of ice. On top of this ice were as many feet of snow. It was all pure white, rolling in gentle undulations where the ice-jams of

[1]The story is set in the Yukon Territory, which is in the northwest corner of Canada, bordering Alaska. The Yukon River is a large stream that begins in the Yukon Territory and flows west through Canada to the Bering Sea.

the freeze-up had formed. North and south, as far as his eye could see, it was unbroken white, save for a dark hair-line that curved and twisted from around the spruce-covered island to the south, and that curved and twisted away into the north, where it disappeared behind another spruce-covered island. This dark hair-line was the trail—the main trail—that led south five hundred miles to the Chilcoot Pass, Dyea,[2] and salt water; and that led north seventy miles to Dawson,[3] and still on to the north a thousand miles to Nulato,[4] and finally to St. Michael[5] on the Bering Sea, a thousand miles and half a thousand more.

But all this—the mysterious, far-reaching hair-line trail, the absence of sun from the sky, the tremendous cold, and the strangeness and weirdness of it all—made no impression on the man. It was not because he was long used to it. He was a newcomer in the land, a *chechaquo,* and this was his first winter. The trouble with him was that he was without imagination. He was quick and alert in the things of life, but only in the things, and not in the significances. Fifty degrees below zero meant eighty-odd degrees of frost.[6] Such fact impressed him as being cold and uncomfortable, and that was all. It did not lead him to meditate upon his frailty as a creature of temperature, and upon man's frailty in general, able only to live within certain narrow limits of heat and cold; and from there on it did not lead him to the conjectural field of immortality and man's place in the universe. Fifty degrees below zero stood for a bite of frost that hurt and that must be guarded against by the use of mittens, ear-flaps, warm moccasins, and thick socks. Fifty degrees below zero was to him just precisely fifty degrees below zero. That there should be anything more to it than that was a thought that never entered his head.

As he turned to go on, he spat speculatively. There was a sharp, explosive crackle that startled him. He spat again. And again, in the air, before it could fall to the snow, the spittle crackled. He knew that at fifty below spittle crackled on the snow, but this spittle had crackled in the air. Undoubtedly it was colder than fifty below—how much colder he did not know. But the temperature did not matter. He was bound for the old claim on the left fork of Henderson Creek,[7] where the boys were already. They had come over across the divide from the Indian Creek country, while he had come the roundabout way to take a look at the possibilities of getting out logs in the spring from the islands in the Yukon. He would be in to camp by six o'clock; a bit after dark, it was true, but the boys would be there, a fire would be going, and a hot supper would be ready. As for lunch, he pressed his hand against the protruding bundle under his jacket. It was also under his shirt, wrapped up in a handkerchief and lying against the naked skin. It was the only way to keep the biscuits from freezing. He smiled agreeably to himself as he thought of those biscuits, each cut open and sopped in bacon grease, and each enclosing a generous slice of fried bacon.

[2]Chilcoot Pass is a break in the Coast Mountains in British Columbia and Alaska; also spelled Chilkoot. Dyea is a town in southern Alaska.

[3]Dawson City, a town in the Yukon Territory. [4]A town near the center of Alaska.

[5]A coastal town to the west of Nulato.

[6]That is, the temperature is more than 80 degrees below the freezing point of water (32° F).

[7]Henderson Creek, Indian Creek, and Sulphur Creek are streams in the Yukon Territory. Since the waterways are conspicuous and important features of the landscape, they are often used to identify locations.

He plunged in among the big spruce trees. The trail was faint. A foot of snow had fallen since the last sled had passed over, and he was glad he was without a sled, travelling light. In fact, he carried nothing but the lunch wrapped in the handkerchief. He was surprised, however, at the cold. It certainly was cold, he concluded, as he rubbed his numb nose and cheek-bones with his mittened hand. He was a warm-whiskered man, but the hair on his face did not protect the high cheek-bones and the eager nose that thrust itself aggressively into the frosty air.

At the man's heels trotted a dog, a big native husky, the proper wolf-dog, gray-coated and without any visible or temperamental difference from its brother, the wild wolf. The animal was depressed by the tremendous cold. It knew that it was no time for travelling. Its instinct told it a truer tale than was told to the man by the man's judgment. In reality, it was not merely colder than fifty below zero; it was colder than sixty below, than seventy below. It was seventy-five below zero. Since the freezing-point is thirty-two above zero, it meant that one hundred and seven degrees of frost obtained. The dog did not know anything about thermometers. Possibly in its brain there was no sharp consciousness of a condition of very cold such as was in the man's brain. But the brute had its instinct. It experienced a vague but menacing apprehension that subdued it and made it slink along at the man's heels, and that made it question eagerly every unwonted movement of the man as if expecting him to go into camp or to seek shelter somewhere and build a fire. The dog had learned fire, and it wanted fire, or else to burrow under the snow and cuddle its warmth away from the air.

The frozen moisture of its breathing had settled on its fur in a fine powder of frost, and especially were its jowls, muzzle, and eyelashes whitened by its crystalled breath. The man's red beard and mustache were likewise frosted, but more solidly, the deposit taking the form of ice and increasing with every warm, moist breath he exhaled. Also, the man was chewing tobacco, and the muzzle of ice held his lips so rigidly that he was unable to clear his chin when he expelled the juice. The result was that a crystal beard of the color and solidity of amber was increasing its length on his chin. If he fell down it would shatter itself, like glass, into brittle fragments. But he did not mind the appendage. It was the penalty all tobacco-chewers paid in that country, and he had been out before in two cold snaps. They had not been so cold as this, he knew, but by the spirit thermometer at Sixty Mile he knew they had been registered at fifty below and at fifty-five.

He held on through the level stretch of woods for several miles, crossed a wide flat of niggerheads,[8] and dropped down a bank to the frozen bed of a small stream. This was Henderson Creek, and he knew he was ten miles from the forks. He looked at his watch. It was ten o'clock. He was making four miles an hour, and he calculated that he would arrive at the forks at half-past twelve. He decided to celebrate that event by eating his lunch there.

The dog dropped in again at his heels, with a tail drooping discouragement, as the man swung along the creek-bed. The furrow of the old sled-trail was plainly visible, but a dozen inches of snow covered the marks of the last runners. In a month no man had come up or down that silent creek. The man held steadily on. He was not much given to thinking, and just then particularly he had nothing to think about save that he would eat lunch at the forks and that

[8]Clumps of grass.

at six o'clock he would be in camp with the boys. There was nobody to talk to; and, had there been, speech would have been impossible because of the ice-muzzle on his mouth. So he continued monotonously to chew tobacco and to increase the length of his amber beard.

Once in a while the thought reiterated itself that it was very cold and that he had never experienced such cold. As he walked along he rubbed his cheek-bones and nose with the back of his mittened hand. He did this automatically, now and again changing hands. But rub as he would, the instant he stopped his cheek-bones went numb, and the following instant the end of his nose went numb. He was sure to frost his cheeks; he knew that, and experienced a pang of regret that he had not devised a nose-strap of the sort Bud wore in cold snaps. Such a strap passed across the cheeks, as well, and saved them. But it didn't matter much, after all. What were frosted cheeks? A bit painful, that was all; they were never serious.

Empty as the man's mind was of thoughts, he was keenly observant, and he noticed the changes in the creek, the curves and bends and timber-jams, and always he sharply noted where he placed his feet. Once, coming around a bend, he shied abruptly, like a startled horse, curved away from the place where he had been walking, and retreated several paces back along the trail. The creek he knew was frozen clear to the bottom,—no creek could contain water in that arctic winter,—but he knew also that there were springs that bubbled out from the hillsides and ran along under the snow and on top of the ice of the creek. He knew that the coldest snaps never froze these springs, and he knew likewise their danger. They were traps. They hid pools of water under the snow that might be three inches deep, or three feet. Sometimes a skin of ice half an inch thick covered them, and in turn was covered by the snow. Sometimes there were alternate layers of water and ice-skin, so that when one broke through he kept on breaking through for a while, sometimes wetting himself to the waist.

That was why he had shied in such panic. He had felt the give under his feet and heard the crackle of a snow-hidden ice-skin. And to get his feet wet in such a temperature meant trouble and danger. At the very least it meant delay, for he would be forced to stop and build a fire, and under its protection to bare his feet while he dried his socks and moccasins. He stood and studied the creek-bed and its banks, and decided that the flow of water came from the right. He reflected awhile, rubbing his nose and cheeks, then skirted to the left, stepping gingerly and testing the footing for each step. Once clear of the danger, he took a fresh chew of tobacco and swung along at his four-mile gait. In the course of the next two hours he came upon several similar traps. Usually the snow above the hidden pools had a sunken, candied appearance that advertised the danger. Once again, however, he had a close call; and once, suspecting danger, he compelled the dog to go on in front. The dog did not want to go. It hung back until the man shoved it forward, and then it went quickly across the white, unbroken surface. Suddenly it broke through, floundered to one side, and got away to firmer footing. It had wet its forefeet and legs, and almost immediately the water that clung to it turned to ice. It made quick efforts to lick the ice off its legs, then dropped down in the snow and began to bite out the ice that had formed between the toes. This was a matter of instinct. To permit the ice to remain would mean sore feet. It did not know this. It merely obeyed the mysterious prompting that arose from the deep crypts of its being. But the man knew, having achieved a judgment on the subject, and he removed the mitten from his right hand and helped tear out the ice-particles. He did not expose his fingers more than a minute, and was astonished at the swift numbness that smote them. It certainly was cold. He pulled on the mitten hastily, and beat the hand savagely across his chest.

At twelve o'clock the day was at its brightest. Yet the sun was too far south on its winter journey to clear the horizon. The bulge of the earth intervened between it and Henderson Creek, where the man walked under a clear sky at noon and cast no shadow. At half-past twelve, to the minute, he arrived at the forks of the creek. He was pleased at the speed he had made. If he kept it up, he would certainly be with the boys by six. He unbuttoned his jacket and shirt and drew forth his lunch. The action consumed no more than a quarter of a minute, yet in that brief moment the numbness laid hold of the exposed fingers. He did not put the mitten on, but, instead, struck the fingers a dozen sharp smashes against his leg. Then he sat down on a snow-covered log to eat. The sting that followed upon the striking of his fingers against his leg ceased so quickly that he was startled. He had had no chance to take a bite of biscuit. He struck the fingers repeatedly and returned them to the mitten, baring the other hand for the purpose of eating. He tried to take a mouthful, but the ice-muzzle prevented. He had forgotten to build a fire and thaw out. He chuckled at his foolishness, and as he chuckled he noted the numbness creeping into the exposed fingers. Also, he noted that the stinging which had first come to his toes when he sat down was already passing away. He wondered whether the toes were warm or numb. He moved them inside the moccasins and decided that they were numb.

He pulled the mitten on hurriedly and stood up. He was a bit frightened. He stamped up and down until the stinging returned into the feet. It certainly was cold, was his thought. That man from Sulphur Creek had spoken the truth when telling how cold it sometimes got in the country. And he had laughed at him at the time! That showed one must not be too sure of things. There was no mistake about it, it *was* cold. He strode up and down, stamping his feet and threshing his arms, until reassured by the returning warmth. Then he got out matches and proceeded to make a fire. From the undergrowth, where high water of the previous spring had lodged a supply of seasoned twigs, he got his fire-wood. Working carefully from a small beginning, he soon had a roaring fire, over which he thawed the ice from his face and in the protection of which he ate his biscuits. For the moment the cold of space was outwitted. The dog took satisfaction in the fire, stretching out close enough for warmth and far enough away to escape being singed.

When the man had finished, he filled his pipe and took his comfortable time over a smoke. Then he pulled on his mittens, settled the ear-flaps of his cap firmly about his ears, and took the creek trail up the left fork. The dog was disappointed and yearned back toward the fire. This man did not know cold. Possibly all the generations of his ancestry had been ignorant of cold, of real cold, of cold one hundred and seven degrees below freezing-point. But the dog knew; all its ancestry knew, and it had inherited the knowledge. And it knew that it was not good to walk abroad in such fearful cold. It was the time to lie snug in a hole in the snow and wait for a curtain of cloud to be drawn across the face of outer space whence this cold came. On the other hand, there was no keen intimacy between the dog and the man. The one was the toil-slave of the other, and the only caresses it had ever received were the caresses of the whip-lash and of harsh and menacing throat-sounds that threatened the whip-lash. So the dog made no effort to communicate its apprehension to the man. It was not concerned in the welfare of the man; it was for its own sake that it yearned back toward the fire. But the man whistled, and spoke to it with the sound of whip-lashes, and the dog swung in at the man's heels and followed after.

The man took a chew of tobacco and proceeded to start a new amber beard. Also, his moist breath quickly powdered with white his mustache, eyebrows, and lashes. There did not seem to be so many springs on the left fork of the Henderson, and for half an hour the man saw no signs of any. And then it happened. At a place where there were no signs, where the soft, unbroken snow seemed to advertise solidity beneath, the man broke through. It was not deep. He wet himself halfway to the knees before he floundered out to the firm crust.

He was angry, and cursed his luck aloud. He had hoped to get into camp with the boys at six o'clock, and this would delay him an hour, for he would have to build a fire and dry out his foot-gear. This was imperative at that low temperature—he knew that much; and he turned aside to the bank, which he climbed. On top, tangled in the underbrush about the trunks of several small spruce trees, was a high-water deposit of dry fire-wood—sticks and twigs, principally, but also larger portions of seasoned branches and fine, dry, last-year's grasses. He threw down several large pieces on top of the snow. This served for a foundation and prevented the young flame from drowning itself in the snow it otherwise would melt. The flame he got by touching a match to a small shred of birch-bark that he took from his pocket. This burned even more readily than paper. Placing it on the foundation, he fed the young flame with wisps of dry grass and with the tiniest dry twigs.

He worked slowly and carefully, keenly aware of his danger. Gradually, as the flame grew stronger, he increased the size of the twigs with which he fed it. He squatted in the snow, pulling the twigs out from their entanglement in the brush and feeding directly to the flame. He knew there must be no failure. When it is seventy-five below zero, a man must not fail in his first attempt to build a fire—that is, if his feet are wet. If his feet are dry, and he fails, he can run along the trail for half a mile and restore his circulation. But the circulation of wet and freezing feet cannot be restored by running when it is seventy-five below. No matter how fast he runs, the wet feet will freeze the harder.

All this the man knew. The old-timer on Sulphur Creek had told him about it the previous fall, and now he was appreciating the advice. Already all sensation had gone out of his feet. To build the fire he had been forced to remove his mittens, and the fingers had quickly gone numb. His pace of four miles an hour had kept his heart pumping blood to the surface of his body and to all the extremities. But the instant he stopped, the action of the pump eased down. The cold of space smote the unprotected tip of the planet, and he, being on that unprotected tip, received the full force of the blow. The blood of his body recoiled before it. The blood was alive, like the dog, and like the dog it wanted to hide away and cover itself up from the fearful cold. So long as he walked four miles an hour, he pumped that blood, willy-nilly, to the surface; but now it ebbed away and sank down into the recesses of his body. The extremities were the first to feel its absence. His wet feet froze the faster, and his exposed fingers numbed the faster, though they had not yet begun to freeze. Nose and cheeks were already freezing, while the skin of all his body chilled as it lost its blood.

But he was safe. Toes and nose and cheeks would be only touched by the frost, for the fire was beginning to burn with strength. He was feeding it with twigs the size of his finger. In another minute he would be able to feed it with branches the size of his wrist, and then he could remove his wet foot-gear, and, while it dried, he could keep his naked feet warm by the fire, rubbing them at first, of course, with snow. The fire was a success. He was safe. He remembered the advice of the old-timer on Sulphur Creek, and smiled. The old-timer had been very serious in laying down the law that no man must travel alone in the Klondike[9] after fifty below. Well, here he was; he had had the accident; he was alone; and he had saved himself. Those old-timers were rather womanish, some of them, he thought. All a man had to do was to keep his head, and he was all right. Any man who was a man could travel alone. But it was surprising, the rapidity with which his cheeks and nose were freezing. And he had not thought his fingers could go lifeless in so short a time. Lifeless they were, for he could scarcely make them move together to grip a twig, and they seemed remote from his body and from him. When he touched a twig, he had to look and see whether or not he had hold of it. The wires were pretty well down between him and his finger-ends.

All of which counted for little. There was the fire, snapping and crackling and promising life with every dancing flame. He started to untie his moccasins. They were coated with ice; the thick German socks were like sheaths of iron halfway to the knees; and the moccasin strings were like rods of steel all twisted and knotted as by some conflagration. For a moment he tugged with his numb fingers, then, realizing the folly of it, he drew his sheath-knife.

But before he could cut the strings, it happened. It was his own fault or, rather, his mistake. He should not have built the fire under the spruce tree. He should have built it in the open. But it had been easier to pull the twigs from the brush and drop them directly on the fire. Now the tree under which he had done this carried a weight of snow on its boughs. No wind had blown for weeks, and each bough was fully freighted. Each time he had pulled a twig he had communicated a slight agitation to the tree—an imperceptible agitation, so far as he was concerned, but an agitation sufficient to bring about the disaster. High up in the tree one bough capsized its load of snow. This fell on the boughs beneath, capsizing them. This process continued, spreading out and involving the whole tree. It grew like an avalanche, and it descended without warning upon the man and the fire, and the fire was blotted out! Where it had burned was a mantle of fresh and disordered snow.

The man was shocked. It was as though he had just heard his own sentence of death. For a moment he sat and stared at the spot where the fire had been. Then he grew very calm. Perhaps the old-timer on Sulphur Creek was right. If he had only had a trail-mate he would have been in no danger now. The trail-mate could have built the fire. Well, it was up to him to build the fire over again, and this second time there must be no failure. Even if he succeeded, he would most likely lose some toes. His feet must be badly frozen by now, and there would be some time before the second fire was ready.

Such were his thoughts, but he did not sit and think them. He was busy all the time they were passing through his mind. He made a new foundation for a fire, this time in the open, where no treacherous tree could blot it out. Next,

[9]The region of the Yukon Territory in which the story tales place.

he gathered dry grasses and tiny twigs from the high-water flotsam.[10] He could not bring his fingers together to pull them out, but he was able to gather them by the handful. In this way he got many rotten twigs and bits of green moss that were undesirable, but it was the best he could do. He worked methodically, even collecting an armful of the larger branches to be used later when the fire gathered strength. And all the while the dog sat and watched him, a certain yearning wistfulness in its eyes, for it looked upon him as the fire-provider, and the fire was slow in coming.

When all was ready, the man reached in his pocket for a second piece of birch-bark. He knew the bark was there, and, though he could not feel it with his fingers, he could hear its crisp rustling as he fumbled for it. Try as he would, he could not clutch hold of it. And all the time, in his consciousness, was the knowledge that each instant his feet were freezing. This thought tended to put him in a panic, but he fought against it and kept calm. He pulled on his mittens with his teeth, and threshed his arms back and forth, beating his hands with all his might against his sides. He did this sitting down, and he stood up to do it; and all the while the dog sat in the snow, its wolf-brush of a tail curled around warmly over its forefeet, its sharp wolf-ears pricked forward intently as it watched the man. And the man, as he beat and threshed with his arms and hands, felt a great surge of envy as he regarded the creature that was warm and secure in its natural covering.

After a time he was aware of the first faraway signals of sensation in his beaten fingers. The faint tingling grew stronger till it evolved into a stinging ache that was excruciating, but which the man hailed with satisfaction. He stripped the mitten from his right hand and fetched forth the birch-bark. The exposed fingers were quickly going numb again. Next he brought out his bunch of sulphur matches. But the tremendous cold had already driven the life out of his fingers. In his effort to separate one match from the others, the whole bunch fell in the snow. He tried to pick it out of the snow, but failed. The dead fingers could neither touch nor clutch. He was very careful. He drove the thought of his freezing feet, and nose, and cheeks, out of his mind, devoting his whole soul to the matches. He watched, using the sense of vision in place of that of touch, and when he saw his fingers on each side the bunch, he closed them—that is, he willed to close them, for the wires were down, and the fingers did not obey. He pulled the mitten on the right hand, and beat it fiercely against his knee. Then, with both mittened hands, he scooped the bunch of matches, along with much snow, into his lap. Yet he was no better off.

After some manipulation he managed to get the bunch between the heels of his mittened hands. In this fashion he carried it to his mouth. The ice crackled and snapped when by a violent effort he opened his mouth. He drew the lower jaw in, curled the upper lip out of the way, and scraped the bunch with his upper teeth in order to separate a match. He succeeded in getting one, which he dropped on his lap. He was no better off. He could not pick it up. Then he devised a way. He picked it up in his teeth and scratched it on his leg. Twenty times he scratched before he succeeded in lighting it. As it flamed he held it with his teeth to the birch-bark. But the burning brimstone[11] went up his nostrils and into his lungs, causing him to cough spasmodically. The match fell into the snow and went out.

[10]Floating debris. [11]Sulfur.

The old-timer on Sulphur Creek was right, he thought in the moment of controlled despair that ensued: After fifty below, a man should travel with a partner. He beat his hands, but failed in exciting any sensation. Suddenly he bared both hands, removing the mittens with his teeth. He caught the whole bunch between the heels of his hands. His arm-muscles not being frozen enabled him to press the hand-heels tightly against the matches. Then he scratched the bunch along his leg. It flared into flame, seventy sulphur matches at once! There was no wind to blow them out. He kept his head to one side to escape the strangling fumes, and held the blazing bunch to the birch-bark. As he so held it, he became aware of sensation in his hand. His flesh was burning. He could smell it. Deep down below the surface he could feel it. The sensation developed into pain that grew acute. And still he endured it, holding the flame of the matches clumsily to the bark that would not light readily because his own burning hands were in the way, absorbing most of the flame.

At last, when he could endure no more, he jerked his hands apart. The blazing matches fell sizzling into the snow, but the birch-bark was alight. He began laying dry grasses and the tiniest twigs on the flame. He could not pick and choose, for he had to lift the fuel between the heels of his hands. Small pieces of rotten wood and green moss clung to the twigs, and he bit them off as well as he could with his teeth. He cherished the flame carefully and awkwardly. It meant life, and it must not perish. The withdrawal of blood from the surface of his body now made him begin to shiver, and he grew more awkward. A large piece of green moss fell squarely on the little fire. He tried to poke it out with his fingers, but his shivering frame made him poke too far, and he disrupted the nucleus of the little fire, the burning grasses and tiny twigs separating and scattering. He tried to poke them together again, but in spite of the tenseness of the effort, his shivering got away with him, and the twigs were hopelessly scattered. Each twig gushed a puff of smoke and went out. The fire-provider had failed. As he looked apathetically about him, his eyes chanced on the dog, sitting across the ruins of the fire from him, in the snow, making restless, hunching movements, slightly lifting one forefoot and then the other, shifting its weight back and forth on them with wistful eagerness.

The sight of the dog put a wild idea into his head. He remembered the tale of the man, caught in a blizzard, who killed a steer and crawled inside the carcass, and so was saved. He would kill the dog and bury his hands in the warm body until the numbness went out of them. Then he could build another fire. He spoke to the dog, calling it to him; but in his voice was a strange note of fear that frightened the animal, who had never known the man to speak in such way before. Something was the matter, and its suspicious nature sensed danger—it knew not what danger, but somewhere, somehow, in its brain arose an apprehension of the man. It flattened its ears down at the sound of the man's voice, and its restless, hunching movements and the liftings and shiftings of its forefeet became more pronounced; but it would not come to the man. He got on his hands and knees and crawled toward the dog. This unusual posture again excited suspicion, and the animal sidled mincingly[12] away.

The man sat up in the snow for a moment and struggled for calmness. Then he pulled on his mittens, by means of his teeth, and got upon his feet. He glanced down at first in order to assure himself that he was really standing up,

[12]Carefully, daintily.

for the absence of sensation in his feet left him unrelated to the earth. His erect position in itself started to drive the webs of suspicion from the dog's mind; and when he spoke peremptorily, with the sound of whip-lashes in his voice, the dog rendered its customary allegiance and came to him. As it came within reaching distance, the man lost his control. His arms flashed out to the dog, and he experienced genuine surprise when he discovered that his hands could not clutch, that there was neither bend nor feeling in the fingers. He had forgotten for the moment that they were frozen and that they were freezing more and more. All this happened quickly, and before the animal could get away, he encircled its body with his arms. He sat down in the snow, and in this fashion held the dog, while it snarled and whined and struggled.

But it was all he could do, hold its body encircled in his arms and sit there. He realized that he could not kill the dog. There was no way to do it. With his helpless hands he could neither draw nor hold his sheath-knife nor throttle the animal. He released it, and it plunged wildly away, with tail between its legs, and still snarling. It halted forty feet away and surveyed him curiously, with ears sharply pricked forward. The man looked down at his hands in order to locate them, and found them hanging on the ends of his arms. It struck him as curious that one should have to use his eyes in order to find out where his hands were. He began threshing his arms back and forth, beating the mittened hands against his sides. He did this for five minutes, violently, and his heart pumped enough blood up to the surface to put a stop to his shivering. But no sensation was aroused in the hands. He had an impression that they hung like weights on the ends of his arms, but when he tried to run the impression down, he could not find it.

A certain fear of death, dull and oppressive, came to him. This fear quickly became poignant as he realized that it was no longer a mere matter of freezing his fingers and toes, or of losing his hands and feet, but that it was a matter of life and death with the chances against him. This threw him into a panic, and he turned and ran up the creek-bed along the old, dim trail. The dog joined in behind and kept up with him. He ran blindly, without intention, in fear such as he had never known in his life. Slowly, as he ploughed and floundered through the snow, he began to see things again,—the banks of the creek, the old timber-jams, the leafless aspens, and the sky. The running made him feel better. He did not shiver. Maybe, if he ran on, his feet would thaw out; and, anyway, if he ran far enough, he would reach camp and the boys. Without doubt he would lose some fingers and toes and some of his face; but the boys would take care of him, and save the rest of him when he got there. And at the same time there was another thought in his mind that said he would never get to the camp and the boys; that it was too many miles away, that the freezing had too great a start on him, and that he would soon be stiff and dead. This thought he kept in the background and refused to consider. Sometimes it pushed itself forward and demanded to be heard, but he thrust it back and strove to think of other things.

It struck him as curious that he could run at all on feet so frozen that he could not feel them when they struck the earth and took the weight of his body. He seemed to himself to skim along above the surface, and to have no connection with the earth. Somewhere he had once seen a winged Mercury,[13] and he wondered if Mercury felt as he felt when skimming over the earth.

[13]The Roman version of the Greek god Hermes, who was notable for his swiftness and was often pictured with wings on his shoes and hat.

His theory of running until he reached camp and the boys had one flaw in it: He lacked the endurance. Several times he stumbled, and finally he tottered, crumpled up, and fell. When he tried to rise, he failed. He must sit and rest, he decided, and next time he would merely walk and keep on going. As he sat and regained his breath, he noted that he was feeling quite warm and comfortable. He was not shivering, and it even seemed that a warm glow had come to his chest and trunk. And yet, when he touched his nose or cheeks, there was no sensation. Running would not thaw them out. Nor would it thaw out his hands and feet. Then the thought came to him that the frozen portions of his body must be extending. He tried to keep this thought down, to forget it, to think of something else; he was aware of the panicky feeling that it caused, and he was afraid of the panic. But the thought asserted itself, and persisted, until it produced a vision of his body totally frozen. This was too much, and he made another wild run along the trail. Once he slowed down to a walk, but the thought of the freezing extending itself made him run again.

And all the time the dog ran with him, at his heels. When he fell down a second time, it curled its tail over its forefeet and sat in front of him, facing him, curiously eager and intent. The warmth and security of the animal angered him, and he cursed it till it flattened down its ears appeasingly. This time the shivering came more quickly upon the man. He was losing in his battle with the frost. It was creeping into his body from all sides. The thought of it drove him on, but he ran no more than a hundred feet, when he staggered and pitched headlong. It was his last panic. When he had recovered his breath and control, he sat up and entertained in his mind the conception of meeting death with dignity. However, the conception did not come to him in such terms. His idea of it was that he had been making a fool of himself, running around like a chicken with its head cut off—such was the simile that occurred to him. Well, he was bound to freeze anyway, and he might as well take it decently. With this newfound peace of mind came the first glimmerings of drowsiness. A good idea, he thought, to sleep off to death. It was like taking an anaesthetic. Freezing was not so bad as people thought. There were lots worse ways to die.

He pictured the boys finding his body next day. Suddenly he found himself with them, coming along the trail and looking for himself. And, still with them, he came around a turn in the trail and found himself lying in the snow. He did not belong with himself any more, for even then he was out of himself, standing with the boys and looking at himself in the snow. It certainly was cold, was his thought. When he got back to the States he could tell the folks what real cold was. He drifted on from this to a vision of the old-timer on Sulphur Creek. He could see him quite clearly, warm and comfortable, and smoking a pipe.

"You were right, old hoss; you were right," the man mumbled to the old-timer of Sulphur Creek.

Then the man drowsed off into what seemed to him the most comfortable and satisfying sleep he had ever known. The dog sat facing him and waiting. The brief day drew to a close in a long, slow twilight. There were no signs of a fire to be made, and, besides, never in the dog's experience had it known a man to sit like that in the snow and make no fire. As the twilight drew on, its eager yearning for the fire mastered it, and with a great lifting and shifting of forefeet, it whined softly, then flattened its ears down in anticipation of being chidden by the man. But the man remained silent. Later, the dog whined loudly. And still later it crept close to the man and caught the scent of death. This made the animal bristle and back away. A little longer it delayed, howling under the stars that leaped and danced and shone brightly in the cold sky. Then it turned and trotted up the trail in the direction of the camp it knew, where were the other food-providers and fire-providers.

1902 1910

Anna Julia Cooper c. 1858–1964

Anna Julia Cooper was born into slavery in North Carolina shortly before the start of the Civil War, the oldest daughter of a slave woman and her master. At the age of nine she received a scholarship to St. Augustine's Normal School, a teacher's college instituted to provide educators specifically for the African American community. Cooper remained at the school after graduating and joined the faculty. She married George Cooper, also a graduate of St. Augustine's, in 1877. She was widowed two years later, which left her free to pursue an academic career. In the 1880s she received both a Bachelor's and a Master's degree from Oberlin College and began her long and sometimes controversial tenure at Washington D.C.'s renowned M Street School.

Cooper published her best-known work, A Voice from the South, by a Black Woman of the South, *in 1892. A collection of essays touching on various cultural and social issues,* A Voice from the South *grew out of Cooper's long-standing political activism, particularly her deep commitment to fighting for the rights of black women. She continued to write in the first few decades of the twentieth century, publishing two more books. In 1925 she received a doctorate in French from the University of Paris. Anna Julia Cooper died in 1964.*

FURTHER READING: E. Alexander, "'We Must Be About Our Father's Business': Anna Julia Cooper and the Incorporation of the Nineteenth-Century African American Woman Intellectual," in *In Her Own Voice: Nineteenth-Century Woman Essayists,* ed. S. Lee Linkon, 1997; K. Baker-Fletcher, *A Singing Something: Womanist Reflections on Anna Julia Cooper,* 1994; K. Johnson, *Uplifting the Women and the Race: A Black Feminist Theoretical Critique of the Lives, Works and the Educational Philosophies of Anna Julia Cooper and Nannie Helen Burroughs,* 1997; *The Voice of Anna Julia Cooper, Including A Voice from the South and Other Important Essays, Papers, and Letters,* ed. C. Lambert and E. Bhan, 1998.

TEXT: *A Voice from the South,* 1892.

HAS AMERICA A RACE PROBLEM; IF SO, HOW CAN IT BEST BE SOLVED?

There are two kinds of peace in this world. The one produced by suppression, which is the passivity of death; the other brought about by a proper adjustment of living, acting forces. A nation or an individual may be at peace because all opponents have been killed or crushed; or, nation as well as individual may have found the secret of true harmony in the determination to live and let live.

A harmless looking man was once asked how many there were in his family.

"Ten," he replied grimly; "my wife's a one and I a zero." In that family there was harmony, to be sure, but it was the harmony of a despotism—it was the quiet of a muzzled mouth, the smoldering peace of a volcano crusted over.

Now I need not say that peace produced by suppression is neither natural nor desirable. Despotism is not one of the ideas that man has copied from nature. All through God's universe we see eternal harmony and symmetry as the unvarying result of the equilibrium of opposing forces. Fair play in an equal fight is the law written in Nature's book. And the solitary bully with his foot on the breast of his last antagonist has no warrant in any fact of God.

The beautiful curves described by planets and suns in their courses are the resultant of conflicting forces. Could the centrifugal force for one instant triumph, or should the centripetal grow weary and give up the struggle, immeasurable disaster would ensue—earth, moon, sun would go spinning off at a tangent or must fall helplessly into its master sphere. The acid counterbalances and keeps in order the alkali; the negative, the positive electrode. A proper equilibrium between a most inflammable explosive and the supporter of combustion, gives us water, the bland fluid that we cannot dispense with. Nay, the very air we breathe, which seems so calm, so peaceful, is rendered innocuous only by the constant conflict of opposing gases. Were the fiery, never-resting, all-corroding oxygen to gain the mastery we should be burnt to cinders in a trice. With the sluggish, inert nitrogen triumphant, we should die of inanition.[1]

These facts are only a suggestion of what must be patent to every student of history. Progressive peace in a nation is the result of conflict; and conflict, such as is healthy, stimulating, and progressive, is produced through the coexistence of radically opposing or racially different elements. Bellamy's ox-like men pictured in *Looking Backward,*[2] taking their daily modicum of provender from the grandmotherly government, with nothing to struggle for, no wrong to put down, no reform to push through, no rights to vindicate and uphold, are nice folks to read about; but they are not natural; they are not progressive. God's world is not governed that way. The child can never gain strength save by resistance, and there can be no resistance if all movement is in one direction and all opposition made forever an impossibility.

I confess I can see no deeper reason than this for the specializing of racial types in the world. Whatever our theory with reference to the origin of species and the unity of mankind, we cannot help admitting the fact that no sooner does a family of the human race take up its abode in some little nook between mountains, or on some plain walled in by their own hands, no sooner do they begin in earnest to live their own life, think their own thoughts, and trace out their own arts, than they begin also to crystallize some idea different from and generally opposed to that of other tribes or families.

Each race has its badge, its exponent, its message, branded in its forehead by the great Master's hand which is its own peculiar keynote, and its contribution to the harmony of nations.

Left entirely alone,—out of contact, that is with other races and their opposing ideas and conflicting tendencies, this cult is abnormally developed and there is unity without variety, a predominance of one tone at the expense of

[1]Exhaustion; emptiness.

[2]*Looking Backward* is a utopian novel published in 1888 by American writer Edward Bellamy (1850–1898).

moderation and harmony, and finally a sameness, a monotonous dullness which means stagnation,—death.

It is this of which M. Guizot[3] complains in Asiatic types of civilization; and in each case he mentions I note that there was but one race, one free force predominating.

In Lect. II. Hist. of Civ. he says:

"In Egypt the theocratic principle took possession of society and showed itself in its manners, its monuments and in all that has come down to us of Egyptian civilization. In India the same phenomenon occurs—a repetition of the almost exclusively prevailing influence of theocracy. In other regions the domination of a conquering caste; where such is the case the principle of force takes entire possession of society. In another place we discover society under the entire influence of the democratic principle. Such was the case in the commercial republics which covered the coasts of Asia Minor and Syria, in Ionia and Phœnicia. In a word whenever we contemplate the civilization of the ancients, we find them all impressed with *one ever prevailing character of unity,* visible in their institutions, their ideas and manners; *one sole influence seems to govern and determine all things.* . . . In one nation, as in Greece, the unity of the social principle led to a development of wonderful rapidity; no other people ever ran so brilliant a career in so short a time. But Greece had hardly become glorious before she appeared worn out. Her decline was as sudden as her rise had been rapid. It seems as if the principle which called Greek civilization into life was exhausted. No other came to invigorate it or supply its place. In India and Egypt where again only one principle of civilization prevailed (*one race predominant you see*) society became stationary. Simplicity produced monotony. Society continued to exist, but there was no progression. It remained torpid and inactive."

Now I beg you to note that in none of these systems was a RACE PROBLEM possible. The dominant race had settled that matter forever. Asiatic society was fixed in cast iron molds. Virtually there was but one race inspiring and molding the thought, the art, the literature, the government. It was against this shrivelling caste prejudice and intolerance that the zealous Buddha set his face like a flint. And I do not think it was all blasphemy in Renan[4] when he said Jesus Christ was first of democrats, i.e., a believer in the royalty of the individual, a preacher of the brotherhood of man through the fatherhood of God, a teacher who proved that the lines on which worlds are said to revolve are *imaginary,* that for all the distinctions of blue blood and black blood and red blood—*a man's a man for a' that.*[5] Buddha and the Christ, each in his own way, wrought to rend asunder the clamps and bands of caste, and to thaw out the ice of race tyranny and exclusiveness. The Brahmin, who was Aryan, spurned a suggestion even, from the Sudra, who belonged to the hated and proscribed Turanian race.[6] With a Pariah he could not eat or drink. They were to him outcasts and unclean. Association with them meant contamination; the hint of their social

[3]French historian François Pierre Guillaume Guizot (1787–1874).

[4]French scholar Ernest Renan (1823–1892), whose *Life of Jesus (Vie de Jésus)* attempted to demystify and demythologize the story of the life of Jesus of Nazareth.

[5]The title of a poem published in 1795 by Scottish poet Robert Burns (1759–1796).

[6]Brahmin and Sudra are the highest and lowest of the four castes in the traditional Indian caste system. Aryan and Turanian are subracial groups, Aryan being associated with European or Indian origin and Turanian with Middle Eastern origin.

equality was blasphemous. Respectful consideration for their rights and feelings was almost a physical no less than a moral impossibility.

No more could the Helots[7] among the Greeks have been said to contribute anything to the movement of their times. The dominant race had them effectually under its heel. It was the tyranny and exclusiveness of these nations, therefore, which brought about their immobility and resulted finally in the barrenness of their one idea. From this came the poverty and decay underlying their civilization, from this the transitory, ephemeral character of its brilliancy.

To quote Guizot again: "Society belonged to *one exclusive* power which could bear with no other. Every principle of a different tendency was proscribed. The governing principle would nowhere suffer by its side the manifestation and influence of a rival principle. This character of unity in their civilization is equally impressed upon their literature and intellectual productions. Those monuments of Hindoo literature lately introduced into Europe seem all struck from the same die. They all seem the result of one same fact, the expression of one idea. Religious and moral treatises, historical traditions, dramatic poetry, epics, all bear the same physiognomy. The same character of unity and monotony shines out in these works of mind and fancy, as we discover in their life and institutions." Not even Greece with all its classic treasures is made an exception from these limitations produced by exclusiveness.

But the course of empire moves one degree westward. Europe becomes the theater of the leading exponents of civilization, and here we have a *Race Problem,*—if, indeed, the confused jumble of races, the clash and conflict, the din and devastation of those stormy years can be referred to by so quiet and so dignified a term as "problem." Complex and appalling it surely was. Goths and Huns, Vandals and Danes, Angles, Saxons, Jutes[8]—could any prophet foresee that a vestige of law and order, of civilization and refinement would remain after this clumsy horde of wild barbarians had swept over Europe?

"Where is somebody'll give me some white for all this yellow?" cries one with his hands full of the gold from one of those magnificent monuments of antiquity which he and his tribe had just pillaged and demolished. Says the historian: "Their history is like a history of kites and crows." Tacitus[9] writes: "To shout, to drink, to caper about, to feel their veins heated and swollen with wine, to hear and see around them the riot of the orgy, this was the first need of the barbarians. The heavy human brute gluts himself with sensations and with noise."

Taine[10] describes them as follows:

"Huge white bodies, cool-blooded, with fierce blue eyes, reddish flaxen hair; ravenous stomachs, filled with meat and cheese, heated by strong drinks. Brutal drunken pirates and robbers, they dashed to sea in their two-sailed barks, landed anywhere, killed everything; and, having sacrificed in honor of their gods the tithe of all their prisoners, leaving behind the red light of their burning, went farther on to begin again."

A certain litany of the time reads: "From the fury of the Jutes, Good Lord deliver us." "Elgiva, the wife of one of their kings," says a chronicler of the time,

[7]The Helots were an ancient Greek people enslaved by the Spartans.

[8]Relatively barbaric German and Scandinavian groups who displaced Roman civilization in what would later become Italy, France, and Britain.

[9]Roman historian Publius Cornelius Tacitus (c. 56–117 B.C.).

[10]French historian Hippolyte Adolphe Taine (1828–1893).

"they hamstrung and subjected to the death she deserved;" and their heroes are frequently represented as tearing out the heart of their human victim and eating it while it still quivered with life.

A historian of the time, quoted by Taine, says it was the custom to buy men and women in all parts of England and to carry them to Ireland for sale. The buyers usually made the women pregnant and took them to market in that condition to ensure a better price. "You might have seen," continues the historian, "long files of young people of both sexes and of great beauty, bound with ropes and daily exposed for sale. They sold as slaves in this manner, their nearest relatives and even their own children."

What could civilization hope to do with such a swarm of sensuous, bloodthirsty vipers? Assimilation was horrible to contemplate. They will drag us to their level, quoth the culture of the times. Deportation was out of the question; and there was no need to talk of their emigrating. The fact is, the barbarians were in no hurry about moving. They didn't even care to colonize. They had come to stay. And Europe had to grapple with her race problem till time and God should solve it.

And how was it solved, and what kind of civilization resulted?

Once more let us go to Guizot. "Take ever so rapid a glance," says he, "at modern Europe and it strikes you at once as diversified, confused, and stormy. All the principles of social organization are found existing together within it; powers temporal, and powers spiritual, the theocratic, monarchic, aristocratic, and democratic elements, all classes of society *in a state of continual struggle* without any one having sufficient force to master the others and take sole possession of society." Then as to the result of this conflict of forces: "Incomparably more rich and diversified than the ancient, European civilization has within it the promise of *perpetual progress*. It has now endured more than fifteen centuries and in all that time has been in a state of progression, not so rapidly as the Greek nor yet so ephemeral. While in other civilizations the exclusive domination of a principle (*or race*) led to tyranny, in Europe the diversity of social elements (*growing out of the contact of different races*) the incapability of any one to exclude the rest, gave birth to the LIBERTY which now prevails. This inability of the various principles to exterminate one another compelled each to endure the others and made it necessary for them in order to live in common to enter into a sort of mutual understanding. Each consented to have only that part of civilization which equitably fell to its share. Thus, while everywhere else the predominance of one principle produced tyranny, the variety and warfare of the elements of European civilization gave birth to *reciprocity and liberty*."

There is no need to quote further. This is enough to show that the law holds good in sociology as in the world of matter, *that equilibrium, not repression among conflicting forces is the condition of natural harmony, of permanent progress, and of universal freedom.* That exclusiveness and selfishness in a family, in a community, or in a nation is suicidal to progress. Caste and prejudice mean immobility. One race predominance means death. The community that closes its gates against foreign talent can never hope to advance beyond a certain point. Resolve to keep out foreigners and you keep out progress. Home talent develops its one idea and then dies. Like the century plant it produces its one flower, brilliant and beautiful it may be, but it lasts only for a night. Its forces have exhausted themselves in that one effort. Nothing remains but to wither and to rot.

It was the Chinese wall that made China in 1800 A.D. the same as China in the days of Confucius.[11] Its women have not even yet learned that they need not bandage their feet if they do not relish it. The world has rolled on, but within that wall the thoughts, the fashions, the art, the tradition, and the beliefs are those of a thousand years ago. Until very recently, the Chinese were wholly out of the current of human progress. They were like gray headed infants—a man of eighty years with the concepts and imaginings of a babe of eight months. A civilization measured by thousands of years with a development that might be comprised within as many days—arrested development due to exclusive living.

But European civilization, rich as it was compared to Asiatic types, was still not the consummation of the ideal of human possibilities. One more degree westward the hand on the dial points. In Europe there was conflict, but the elements crystallized out in isolated nodules, so to speak. Italy has her dominant principle, Spain hers, France hers, England hers, and so on. The proximity is close enough for interaction and mutual restraint, though the acting forces are at different points. To preserve the balance of power, which is nothing more than the equilibrium of warring elements, England can be trusted to keep an eye on her beloved step-relation-in-law, Russia,—and Germany no doubt can be relied on to look after France and some others. It is not, however, till the scene changes and America is made the theater of action, that the interplay of forces narrowed down to a single platform.

Hither came Cavalier and Roundhead, Baptist and Papist, Quaker, Ritualist, Freethinker and Mormon, the conservative Tory, the liberal Whig, and the radical Independent,[12] the Spaniard, the Frenchman, the Englishman, the Italian, the Chinaman, the African, Swedes, Russians, Huns, Bohemians, Gypsies, Irish, Jews. Here surely was a seething caldron of conflicting elements. Religious intolerance and political hatred, race prejudice and caste pride—

> "Double, double, toil and trouble;
> Fire burn and cauldron bubble."[13]

Conflict, Conflict, Conflict.

America for Americans! This is the white man's country! The Chinese must go, shrieks the exclusionist. Exclude the Italians! Colonize the blacks in Mexico or deport them to Africa. Lynch, suppress, drive out, kill out! America for Americans!

"*Who are Americans?*" comes rolling back from ten million throats. Who are to do the packing and delivering of the goods? Who are the homefolks and who are the strangers? Who are the absolute and original tenants in fee-simple?

The red men used to be owners of the soil,—but they are about to be pushed over into the Pacific Ocean. They, perhaps, have the best right to call themselves "Americans" by law of primogeniture. They are at least the oldest inhabitants of whom we can at present identify any traces. If early settlers from abroad merely are meant and it is only a question of squatters' rights—why,

[11] Chinese philosopher (551–479 B.C.); author of *Analects.*

[12] A list of groups who disagreed, sometimes violently (as in the case of the Cavaliers and Roundheads, who fought against each other in the seventeenth-century English Civil War), on matters of religion and politics.

[13] A witches' chant in Shakespeare's *Macbeth* (Act IV, scene i).

the May flower, a pretty venerable institution, landed in the year of Grace 1620,[14] and the first delegation from Africa just one year ahead of that,—in 1619. The first settlers seem to have been almost as much mixed as we are on this point; and it does not seem at all easy to decide just what individuals we mean when we yell "America for the Americans." At least the cleavage cannot be made by hues and noses if we are to seek for the genuine F.F. V.'s[15] as the inhabitants best entitled to the honor of that name.

The fact is this nation was foreordained to conflict from its incipiency. Its elements were predestined from their birth to an irrepressible clash followed by the stable equilibrium of opposition. Exclusive possession belongs to none. There never was a point in its history when it did. There was never a time since America became a nation when there were not more than one race, more than one party, more than one belief contending for supremacy. Hence no one is or can be supreme. All interests must be consulted, all claims conciliated. Where a hundred free forces are lustily clamoring for recognition and each wrestling mightily for the mastery, individual tyrannies must inevitably be chiselled down, individual bigotries worn smooth and malleable, individual prejudices either obliterated or concealed. America is not from choice more than of necessity republic in form and democratic in administration. The will of the majority must rule simply because no class, no family, no individual has ever been able to prove sufficient political legitimacy to impose their yoke on the country. All attempts at establishing oligarchy must be made by wheedling and cajoling, pretending that not supremacy but service is sought. The nearest approach to outspoken self-assertion is in the conciliatory tones of candid compromise. "I will let you enjoy that if you will not hinder me in the pursuit of this" has been the American sovereign's home policy since his first Declaration of Independence was inscribed as his policy abroad. Compromise and concession, liberality and toleration were the conditions of the nation's birth and are the *sine qua non*[16] of its continued existence. A general amnesty and universal reciprocity are the only *modus vivendi*[17] in a nation whose every citizen is his own king, his own priest and his own pope.

De Tocqueville,[18] years ago, predicted that republicanism must fail in America. But if republicanism fails, America fails, and somehow I can not think this colossal stage was erected for a tragedy. I must confess to being an optimist on the subject of my country. It is true we are too busy making history, and have been for some years past, to be able to write history yet, or to understand and interpret it. Our range of vision is too short for us to focus and image our conflicts. Indeed Von Holtz, the clearest headed of calm spectators, says he doubts if the history of American conflict can be written yet even by a disinterested foreigner. The clashing of arms and the din of battle, the smoke of cannon and the heat of combat, are not yet cleared away sufficiently for us to have the judicial vision of historians. Our jottings are like newspaper reports written in the saddle, mid prancing steeds and roaring artillery.

[14]That is, 1620 A.D. (*Anno Domini,* Year of the Lord).

[15]First Families of Virginia: those who trace their ancestry from the original English settlers who arrived at Jamestown in 1607.

[16]Something that is necessary; literally: without which not.

[17]Lifestyle; literally: mode of living.

[18]French historian Alexis de Tocqueville (1805–1859), author of *Democracy in America* (1835–1840).

But of one thing we may be sure: The God of battles is in the conflicts of history. The evolution of civilization is His care, eternal progress His delight. As the European was higher and grander than the Asiatic, so will American civilization be broader and deeper and closer to the purposes of the Eternal than any the world has yet seen. This the last page is to mark the climax of history, the bright consummate flower unfolding *charity toward all and malice toward none,*[19] the final triumph of universal reciprocity born of universal conflict with forces that cannot be exterminated. Here at last is an arena in which every agony has a voice and free speech. Not a spot where no wrong can exist, but where each feeblest interest can cry with Themistocles,[20] "*Strike, but hear me!*" Here you will not see as in Germany women hitched to a cart with donkeys; not perhaps because men are more chivalrous here than there, but because woman can speak. Here labor will not be starved and ground to powder, because the laboring man can make himself heard. Here races that are weakest can, *if they so elect,* make themselves felt.

The supremacy of one race,—the despotism of a class or the tyranny of an individual can not ultimately prevail on a continent held in equilibrium by such conflicting forces and by so many and such strong fibred races as there are struggling on this soil. Never in America shall one man dare to say as Germany's somewhat bumptious emperor[21] is fond of proclaiming: "There is only one master in the country and I am he. I shall suffer no other beside me. Only to God and my conscience am I accountable." The strength of the opposition tones down and polishes off all such ugly excrescencies as that. "I am the State," will never be proclaimed above a whisper on a platform where there is within arm's length another just as strong, possibly stronger, who holds, or would like to hold that identical proposition with reference to himself. In this arena then is to be the last death struggle of political tyranny, of religious bigotry, and intellectual intolerance, of caste illiberality and class exclusiveness. And the last monster that shall be throttled forever methinks is race prejudice. Men will here learn that a race, as a family, may be true to itself without seeking to exterminate all others. That for the note of the feeblest there is room, nay a positive need, in the harmonies of God. That the principles of true democracy are founded in universal reciprocity, and that "A man's a man" was written when God first stamped His own image and superscription on His child and breathed into his nostrils the breath of life. And I confess I can pray for no nobler destiny for my country than that it may be the stage, however far distant in the future, whereon these ideas and principles shall ultimately mature; and culminating here at whatever cost of production shall go forth hence to dominate the world.

Methought I saw a mighty conflagration, plunging and heaving, surging and seething, smoking and rolling over this American continent. Strong men and wise men stand helpless in mute consternation. Empty headed babblers add the din of their bray to the crashing and crackling of the flames. But the hungry flood rolls on. The air is black with smoke and cinders. The sky is red with

[19]A reference to the text of the second inaugural address (1865) of Abraham Lincoln (1809–1865).

[20]Themistocles (c. 527–460 B.C.) was a leader in the Athenian defense against the invading Persians; victor in the Battle of Salamis (480 B.C.).

[21]German Emperor Wilhelm II (1859–1941), who reigned from 1888 until the end of World War I (1918).

lurid light. Forked tongues of fiery flame dart up and lick the pale stars, and seem to laugh at men's feebleness and frenzy. As I look on I think of Schiller's[22] sublime characterization of fire: "Frightful becomes this God-power, when it snatches itself free from fetters and stalks majestically forth on its own career—the free daughter of Nature." Ingenuity is busy with newly patented snuffers all warranted to extinguish the flame. The street gamin with a hooked wire pulls out a few nuggets that chanced to be lying on the outskirts where they were cooked by the heat; and gleefully cries "What a nice fire to roast my chestnuts," and like little Jack Horner, "what a nice boy am I!"

Meantime this expedient, that expedient, the other expedient is suggested by thinkers and theorizers hoping to stifle the angry, roaring, devouring demon and allay the mad destruction.

"Wehe wenn sie losgelassen,
Wachsend ohne Widerstand,
Durch die volkbelebten Gassen
Walzt den ungeheuren Brand!"[23]

But the strength of the Omnipotent is in it. The hand of God is leading it on. It matters not whether you and I in mad desperation cast our quivering bodies into it as our funeral pyre; or whether, like the street urchins, we pull wires to secure the advantage of the passing moment. We can neither help it nor hinder; only

"Let thy gold be cast in the furnace,
Thy red gold, precious and bright.
Do not fear the hungry fire
With its caverns of burning light."[24]

If it takes the dearest idol, the pet theory or the darling 'ism', the pride, the selfishness, the prejudices, the exclusiveness, the bigotry and intolerance, the conceit of self, of race, or of family superiority,—nay, if it singe from thee thy personal gratifications in thy distinction by birth, by blood, by sex—everything,—and leave thee nothing but thy naked manhood, solitary and unadorned,—let them go—let them go!

"And thy gold shall return more precious,
Free from every spot and stain,
For gold must be tried by fire."[25]

And the heart of nations must be tried by pain; and their polish, their true culture must be wrought in through conflict.

Has America a Race Problem?

Yes.

[22]German Romantic poet and playwright Johann Christoph Friedrich von Schiller (1759–1805).

[23]A quotation from Schiller's poem "The Song of the Bell" ("*Das Lied von der Glocke*"), which describes the destruction caused by fire: "Beware when it is unleashed / Growing without hindrance / Through the people-crowded streets / Rolls the monstrous fire!"

[24]Lines from the poem "Gold," by Adelaide Anne Procter (1825–1864).

[25]A continuation of Procter's poem.

What are you going to do about it?

Let it alone and mind my own business. It is God's problem and He will solve it in time. It is deeper than Gehenna.[26] What can you or I do!

Are there then no duties and special lines of thought growing out of the present conditions of this problem?

Certainly there are. *Imprimis,*[27] let every element of the conflict see that it represent a positive force so as to preserve a proper equipoise in the conflict. No shirking, no skulking, no masquerading in another's uniform. Stand by your guns. And be ready for the charge. The day is coming, and now is, when America must ask each citizen not "who was your grandfather and what the color of his cuticle," but "*What can you do?*" Be ready each individual element,—each race, each class, each family, each man to reply "*I engage to undertake an honest man's share.*"

God and time will work the problem. You and I are only to stand for the quantities *at their best,* which he means us to represent.

Above all, for the love of humanity stop the mouth of those learned theorizers, the expedient mongers, who come out annually with their new and improved method of getting the answer and clearing the slate: amalgamation, deportation, colonization and all the other ations that were ever devised or dreampt of. If Alexander[28] wants to be a god, let him; but don't have Alexander hawking his patent plan for universal deification. If all could or would follow Alexander's plan, just the niche in the divine cosmos meant for man would be vacant. And we think that men have a part to play in this great drama no less than gods, and so if a few are determined to be white—amen, so be it; but don't let them argue as if there were no part to be played in life by black men and black women, and as if to become white were the sole specific and panacea for all the ills that flesh is heir to—the universal solvent for all America's irritations. And again, if an American family of whatever condition or hue takes a notion to reside in Africa or in Mexico, or in the isles of the sea, it is most un-American for any power on this continent to seek to gainsay or obstruct their departure; but on the other hand, no power or element of power on this continent, least of all a self-constituted tribunal of "recent arrivals," possesses the right to begin figuring beforehand to calculate what it would require *to send* ten millions of citizens, whose ancestors have wrought here from the planting of the nation, to the same places at so much per head—at least till some one has consulted those heads.

We would not deprecate the fact, then, that America has a Race Problem. It is guaranty of the perpetuity and progress of her institutions, and insures the breadth of her culture and the symmetry of her development. More than all, let us not disparage the factor which the Negro is appointed to contribute to that problem. America needs the Negro for ballast if for nothing else. His tropical warmth and spontaneous emotionalism may form no unseemly counterpart to the cold and calculating Anglo-Saxon. And then his instinct for law and order, his inborn respect for authority, his inaptitude for rioting and anarchy, his gentleness and cheerfulness as a laborer, and his deep-rooted faith in God will prove indispensable and invaluable elements in a nation menaced as America is by anarchy, socialism, communism, and skepticism poured in with all the

[26]Hell. [27]First.

[28]Macedonian ruler and conqueror Alexander the Great (356–323 B.C.).

jail birds from the continents of Europe and Asia. I believe with our own Dr. Crummell[29] that "the Almighty does not preserve, rescue, and build up a lowly people merely for ignoble ends." And the historian of American civilization will yet congratulate this country that she has had a Race Problem and that descendants of the black race furnished one of its largest factors.

1892

from WOMAN VERSUS THE INDIAN

The American woman of to-day not only gives tone directly to her immediate world, but her tiniest pulsation ripples out and out, down and down, till the outermost circles and the deepest layers of society feel the vibrations. It is preeminently an age of organizations. The "leading woman," the preacher, the reformer, the organizer "enthuses" her lieutenants and captains, the literary women, the thinking women, the strong, earnest, irresistible women; these in turn touch their myriads of church clubs, social clubs, culture clubs, pleasure clubs and charitable clubs, till the same lecture has been duly administered to every married man in the land (not to speak of sons and brothers) from the President in the White House to the stone-splitter of the ditches. And so woman's lightest whisper is heard as in Dionysius'[1] ear, by quick relays and endless reproductions, through every recess and cavern as well as on every hilltop and mountain in her vast domain. And her mandates are obeyed. When she says "thumbs up," woe to the luckless thumb that falters in its rising. They may be little things, the amenities of life, the little nothings which cost nothing and come to nothing, and yet can make a sentient being so comfortable or so miserable in this life, the oil of social machinery, which we call the courtesies of life, all are under the magic key of woman's permit.

The American woman then is responsible for American manners. Not merely the right ascension and declination of the satellites of her own drawing room; but the rising and the setting of the pestilential or life-giving orbs which seem to wander afar in space, all are governed almost wholly through her magnetic polarity. The atmosphere of street cars and parks and boulevards, of cafes and hotels and steamboats is charged and surcharged with her sentiments and restrictions. Shop girls and serving maids, cashiers and accountant clerks, scribblers and drummers, whether wage earner, salaried toiler, or proprietress, whether laboring to instruct minds, to save souls, to delight fancies, or to win bread,—the working women of America in whatever station or calling they may be found, are subjects, officers, or rulers of a strong centralized government, and bound together by a system of codes and countersigns, which, though unwritten, forms a network of perfect subordination and unquestioning obedience as marvelous as that of the Jesuits.[2] At the head and center in this regime stands the Leading Woman in the principality. The one talismanic word that plays

[29]Alexander Crummell (1819–1898), clergyman in the African American Episcopal church and crusader for the abolition of slavery.

[1]Dionysius the Elder (c. 430–367 B.C.) and Dionysius the Younger (c. 395–343 B.C.) were rulers of Syracuse.

[2]A Roman Catholic order noted for its discipline and intellectual rigor.

along the wires from palace to cook-shop, from imperial Congress to the distant plain, is *Caste.*[3] With all her vaunted independence, the American woman of to-day is as fearful of losing caste as a Brahmin in India. That is the law under which she lives, the precepts which she binds as frontlets between her eyes and writes on the door-posts of her homes, the lesson which she instils into her children with their first baby breakfasts, the injunction she lays upon husband and lover with direst penalties attached.

The queen of the drawing room is absolute ruler under this law. Her pose gives the cue. The microscopic angle at which her pencilled brows are elevated, signifies who may be recognized and who are beyond the pale. The delicate intimation is, quick as electricity, telegraphed down. Like the wonderful transformation in the House that Jack Built[4] (or regions thereabouts) when the rat began to gnaw the rope, the rope to hang the butcher, the butcher to kill the ox, the ox to drink the water, the water to quench the fire, the fire to burn the stick, the stick to beat the dog, and the dog to worry the cat, and on, and on, and on,—when milady causes the inner arch over her matchless orbs to ascend the merest trifle, *presto!* the Miss at the notions counter grows curt and pert, the dress goods clerk becomes indifferent and taciturn, hotel waiters and ticket dispensers look the other way, the Irish street laborer snarls and scowls, conductors, policemen and park superintendents jostle and push and threaten, and society suddenly seems transformed into a band of organized adders, snapping, and striking and hissing just because they like it on general principles. The tune set by the head singer, sung through all keys and registers, with all qualities of tone,—the smooth, flowing, and gentle, the creaking, whizzing, grating, screeching, growling—according to ability, taste, and temperament of the singers. Another application of like master, like man. In this case, like mistress, like nation.

It was the good fortune of the Black Woman of the South to spend some weeks, not long since, in a land over which floated the Union Jack.[5] The Stars and Stripes were not the only familiar experiences missed. A uniform, matter-of-fact courtesy, a genial kindliness, quick perception of opportunities for rendering any little manly assistance, a readiness to give information to strangers,—a hospitable, thawing-out atmosphere everywhere—in shops and waiting rooms, on cars and in the streets, actually seemed to her chilled little soul to transform the commonest boor in the service of the public into one of nature's noblemen, and when the old whipped-cur feeling was taken up and analyzed she could hardly tell whether it consisted mostly of self pity for her own wounded sensibilities, or of shame for her country and mortification that her countrymen offered such an unfavorable contrast.

Some American girls, I noticed recently, in search of novelty and adventure, were taking an extended trip through our country unattended by gentleman friends; their wish was to write up for a periodical or lecture the ease and facility, the comfort and safety of American travel, even for the weak and unprotected, under our well-nigh perfect railroad systems and our gentlemanly and efficient corps of officials and public servants. I have some material I could furnish these young ladies, though possibly it might not be just on the side they wish to have illuminated. The Black Woman of the South has to do considerable travelling in this country, often unattended. She thinks she is quiet and unobtrusive in her

[3]The hierarchical ordering of society. [4]A nursery rhyme. [5]The British flag.

manner, simple and inconspicuous in her dress, and can see no reason why in any chance assemblage of *ladies,* or even a promiscuous gathering of ordinarily well-bred and dignified individuals, she should be signaled out for any marked consideration. And yet she has seen these same "gentlemanly and efficient" railroad conductors, when their cars had stopped at stations having no raised platforms, making it necessary for passengers to take the long and trying leap from the car step to the ground or step on the narrow little stool placed under by the conductor, after standing at their posts and handing woman after woman from the steps to the stool, thence to the ground, or else relieving her of satchels and bags and enabling her to make the descent easily, deliberately fold their arms and turn round when the Black Woman's turn came to alight—bearing her satchel, and bearing besides another unnamable burden inside the heaving bosom and tightly compressed lips. The feeling of slighted womanhood is unlike every other emotion of the soul. Happily for the human family, it is unknown to many and indescribable to all. Its poignancy, compared with which even Juno's *spretae injuria formae*[6] is earthly and vulgar, is holier than that of jealousy, deeper than indignation, tenderer than rage. Its first impulse of wrathful protest and proud self vindication is checked and shamed by the consciousness that self assertion would outrage still further the same delicate instinct. Were there a brutal attitude of hate or of ferocious attack, the feminine response of fear or repulsion is simple and spontaneous. But when the keen sting comes through the finer sensibilities, from a hand which, by all known traditions and ideals of propriety, should have been trained to reverence and respect them, the condemnation of man's inhumanity to woman is increased and embittered by the knowledge of personal identity with a race of beings so fallen.

I purposely forbear to mention instances of personal violence to colored women travelling in less civilized sections of our country, where women have been forcibly ejected from cars, thrown out of seats, their garments rudely torn, their person wantonly and cruelly injured. America is large and must for some time yet endure its out-of-the-way jungles of barbarism as Africa its uncultivated tracts of marsh and malaria. There are murderers and thieves and villains in both London and Paris. Humanity from the first has had its vultures and sharks, and representatives of the fraternity who prey upon mankind may be expected no less in America than elsewhere. That this virulence breaks out most readily and commonly against colored persons in this country, is due of course to the fact that they are, generally speaking, weak and can be imposed upon with impunity. Bullies are always cowards at heart and may be credited with a pretty safe instinct in scenting their prey. Besides, society, where it has not exactly said to its dogs "s-s-sik him!" has at least engaged to be looking in another direction or studying the rivers on Mars. It is not of the dogs and their doings, but of society holding the leash that I shall speak. It is those subtile exhalations of atmospheric odors for which woman is accountable, the indefinable, unplaceable aroma which seems to exude from the very pores in her finger tips like the delicate sachet so dexterously hidden and concealed in her linens; the essence of her teaching, guessed rather than read, so adroitly is the lettering and wording manipulated; it is the undertones of the picture laid finely on by woman's own practiced hand, the reflection of the lights and shadows on her own brow; it is, in a

[6]In Greek mythology, the insult to the goddess Juno when the mortal Paris chose the goddess Aphrodite as more beautiful than she.

word, the reputation of our nation for general politeness and good manners and of our fellow citizens to be somewhat more than cads or snobs that shall engage our present study. There can be no true test of national courtesy without travel. Impressions and conclusions based on provincial traits and characteristics can thus be modified and generalized. Moreover, the weaker and less influential the experimenter, the more exact and scientific the deductions. Courtesy "for revenue only" is not politeness, but diplomacy. Any rough can assume civility toward those of "his set," and does not hesitate to carry it even to servility toward those in whom he recognizes a possible patron or his master in power, wealth, rank, or influence. But, as the chemist prefers distilled H_2O[7] in testing solutions to avoid complications and unwarranted reactions, so the Black Woman holds that her femininity linked with the impossibility of popular affinity or unexpected attraction through position and influence in her case makes her a touchstone of American courtesy exceptionally pure and singularly free from extraneous modifiers. The man who is courteous to her is so, not because of anything he hopes or fears or sees, but because *he is a gentleman.*

I would eliminate also from the discussion all uncharitable reflections upon the orderly execution of laws existing in certain states of this Union, requiring persons known to be colored to ride in one car, and persons supposed to be white in another. A good citizen may use his influence to have existing laws and statutes changed or modified, but a public servant must not be blamed for obeying orders. A railroad conductor is not asked to dictate measures, nor to make and pass laws. His bread and butter are conditioned on his managing his part of the machinery as he is told to do. If, therefore, I found myself in that compartment of a train designated by the sovereign law of the state for presumable Caucasians, and for colored persons only when traveling in the capacity of nurses and maids, should a conductor inform me, as a gentleman might, that I had made a mistake, and offer to show me the proper car for black ladies; I might wonder at the expensive arrangements of the company and of the state in providing special and separate accommodations for the transportation of the various hues of humanity, but I certainly could not take it as a want of courtesy on the conductor's part that he gave the information. It is true, public sentiment precedes and begets all laws, good or bad; and on the ground I have taken, our women are to be credited largely as teachers and moulders of public sentiment. But when a law has passed and received the sanction of the land, there is nothing for our officials to do but enforce it till repealed; and I for one, as a loyal American citizen, will give those officials cheerful support and ready sympathy in the discharge of their duty. But when a great burly six feet of masculinity with sloping shoulders and unkempt beard swaggers in, and, throwing a roll of tobacco into one corner of his jaw, growls out at me over the paper I am reading, "Here gurl," (I am past thirty) "you better git out 'n dis kyar 'f yer don't, I'll put yer out,"—my mental annotation is *Here's an American citizen who has been badly trained. He is sadly lacking in both 'sweetness' and 'light';* and when in the same section of our enlightened and progressive country, I see from the car window, working on private estates, convicts from the state penitentiary, among them squads of boys from fourteen to eighteen years of age in a chain-gang, their feet chained together and heavy blocks attached—not in 1850, but in 1890, '91 and '92, I make a note on the flyleaf of

[7]Water.

my memorandum, *The women in this section should organize a Society for the Prevention of Cruelty to Human Beings, and disseminate civilizing tracts, and send throughout the region apostles of anti-barbarism for the propagation of humane and enlightened ideas.* And when farther on in the same section our train stops at a dilapidated station, rendered yet more unsightly by dozens of loafers with their hands in their pockets while a productive soil and inviting climate beckon in vain to industry; and when, looking a little more closely, I see two dingy little rooms with "FOR LADIES" swinging over one and "FOR COLORED PEOPLE" over the other; while wondering under which head I come, I notice a little way off the only hotel proprietor of the place whittling a pine stick as he sits with one leg thrown across an empty goods box; and as my eye falls on a sample room next door which seems to be driving the only wide-awake and popular business of the commonwealth, I cannot help ejaculating under my breath, "What a field for the missionary woman." I know that if by any fatality I should be obliged to lie over at that station, and, driven by hunger, should be compelled to seek refreshments or the bare necessaries of life at the only public accommodation in the town, that same stick-whittler would coolly inform me, without looking up from his pine splinter, "We doan uccommodate no niggers hyur." And yet we are so scandalized at Russia's barbarity and cruelty to the Jews! We pay a man a thousand dollars a night just to make us weep, by a recital of such heathenish inhumanity as is practiced on Sclavonic soil.[8]

1892

Abraham Cahan 1860–1951

Writer, journalist, editor, and commentator, Abraham Cahan was arguably the most influential Jewish American, culturally and artistically, in the first half of the twentieth century. Born in 1860 in Vilna, Lithuania, the son of Jewish teachers, Cahan received a fairly broad education during his adolescent years. He graduated from the Vilna Teachers Institute in 1881 and began teaching in the town of Velizh. Over the next several months he became involved in the radical revolutionary movement. After the assassination of Czar Alexander of Russia, he and other socialists were forced to flee the region. Cahan emigrated to the United States in 1882 as a result, eventually settling in New York. Over the next several years he established a reputation within socialist and labor circles as an articulate and persuasive journalistic advocate. In 1890 he assumed the editorship of a Hebrew Trades newspaper, to which he also contributed columns that combined Jewish cultural materials with Marxist ideology.

By the mid-1890s Cahan began writing fiction. His first success came in 1896 with the publication of his novella Yekl: A Tale of the New York Ghetto. *Praised by leading critics such as William Dean Howells,* Yekl *established Cahan as a keen observer of the seemingly oppressive social forces bearing down on the immigrant classes at the turn of the twentieth century. In 1898 his* The Imported Bridegroom and Other Stories of the New York Ghetto *appeared, and over the next decade he published numerous additional short stories in national magazines. Cahan also wrote several important*

[8]Slavonic; Slavic.

novels in the early decades of the twentieth century, including The White Terror and the Red: A Novel of Revolutionary Russia *(1905) and* The Rise of David Levinsky *(1917). In addition to publishing fiction, he served for more than forty years as editor of the Jewish* Daily Forward, *a socialist Yiddish newspaper with a reputation for addressing the everyday struggles faced by its massive immigrant readership. In the final years of his life, he was hampered by illness. Abraham Cahan died at the age of 91 in 1951.*

FURTHER READING: J. Chametzky, *From the Ghetto: The Fiction of Abraham Cahan,* 1977; M. Rischin, *Grandma Never Lived in America: The New Journalism of Abraham Cahan,* 1985; S. Marovitz, *Abraham Cahan,* 1996.

TEXT: *The Imported Bridegroom and Other Stories of the New York Ghetto,* 1898.

THE IMPORTED BRIDEGROOM

I

Flora was alone in the back parlor, which she had appropriated for a sort of boudoir. She sat in her rocker, in front of the parlor stove, absorbed in *Little Dorrit.*[1] Her well-groomed girlish form was enveloped in a kindly warmth whose tender embrace tinged her interest in the narrative with a triumphant consciousness of the snowstorm outside.

Little by little the rigid afternoon light began to fade into a melancholy gray. Dusk was creeping into the room in almost visible waves. Flora let the book rest on her lap and fixed her gaze on the twinkling scarlet of the stove-glass. The thickening twilight, the warmth of the apartment, and the atmosphere of the novel blended together, and for some moments Flora felt far away from herself.

She was the only girl of her circle who would read Dickens, Scott, or Thackeray in addition to the *Family Story Paper* and the *Fireside Companion,*[2] which were the exclusive literary purveyors to her former classmates at the Chrystie Street Grammar School. There were a piano and a neat little library in her room.

She was rather tall and well formed. Her oblong ivory face, accentuated by a mass of unruly hair of a lusterless black, was never deserted by a faint glimmer of a smile, at once pensive and arch. When she broke into one of her hearty, good-natured laughs, her deep, dark, appealing eyes would seem filled with grief. Her nose, a trifle too precipitous, gave an unexpected tone to the extreme picturesqueness of the whole effect, and, when she walked, partook of the dignity of her gait.

A month or two before we make Flora's acquaintance she had celebrated her twentieth birthday, having been born in this little private house on Mott Street,[3] which was her father's property.

A matchmaker[4] had recently called, and he had launched into a eulogy of a young Jewish physician; but old Stroon had cut him short, in his blunt way: His only child was to marry a God-fearing business man, and no fellow deep in

[1]A novel by the English novelist Charles Dickens (1812–1870).
[2]Periodicals that published low-grade popular fiction.
[3]A street in Manhattan. [4]A person who arranges marriages.

Gentile lore and shaving his beard need apply.[5] As to Flora, she was burning to be a doctor's wife. A rising young merchant, a few years in the country, was the staple matrimonial commodity in her set. Most of her married girl friends, American-born themselves, like Flora, had husbands of this class—queer fellows, whose broken English had kept their own sweethearts chuckling. Flora hated the notion of marrying as the other Mott or Bayard Street[6] girls did. She was accustomed to use her surroundings for a background, throwing her own personality into high relief. But apart from this, she craved a more refined atmosphere than her own, and the vague ideal she had was an educated American gentleman, like those who lived uptown.[7]

Accordingly, when the word "doctor" had left the matchmaker's lips, she seized upon it as a great discovery. In those days—the early eighties—a match of this kind was an uncommon occurrence in the New York Ghetto.

Flora pictured a clean-shaven, high-hatted, spectacled gentleman jumping out of a buggy, and the image became a fixture in her mind. "I won't marry anybody except a doctor," she would declare, with conscious avoidance of bad grammar, as it behooved a doctor's wife.

But what was to be done with father's opposition? Asriel Stroon had never been the man to yield, and now that he grew more devout every day, her case seemed hopeless. But then Flora was her father's daughter, and when she took a resolve she could not imagine herself otherwise than carrying it out, sooner or later.

Flora's thoughts were flowing in this direction when her father's gruff voice made itself heard from the dining room below. It was the anniversary of his father's death. In former years he would have contented himself with obit services, at the synagogue; this time, however, he had passed the day in fasting and chanting psalms at home, in addition to lighting his own candle in front of the cantor's[8] desk and reciting *Kaddish*[9] for the departed soul, at the house of prayer. It touched Flora's heart to think of him fasting and praying all day, and, with her book in her hand, she ran down to meet him.

"Just comin' from the synagogue, papa?" she greeted him affectionately, in English. "This settles your fast, don't it?"

"It is not so easy to settle with Him, my daughter," he returned, in Yiddish, pointing to the ceiling. "You can never be through serving the Uppermost. Hurry up, Tamara!" he added, in the direction of the adjoining kitchen.

"You ain' goin' to say more Thilim[10] tonight, are you, pa?"

"Why, does it cost you too much?" he snarled good-humoredly.

"Yes it does—your health. I won't let you sing again. You are weak and you got enough."

"Hush! It is not potato soup; you can never have enough of it." He fell to tugging nervously at his white beard, which grew in a pair of tiny imperials. "Tamara! It's time to break the fast, isn't it?"

[5]"Gentile lore" is the body of knowledge that non-Jews, or Jews too well assimilated into non-Jewish culture, would have. Asriel Stroon's opposition to shaving beards indicates that he is an Orthodox Jew.

[6]Another street in Manhattan. The references to Mott Street and Bayard Street are references to the Jewish community in Manhattan.

[7]A more prosperous and socially higher part of Manhattan.

[8]The leader of songs, chants, and prayer in a Jewish synagogue.

[9]A prayer for a deceased loved one. [10]Psalms.

"You can wash your hands. Supper is ready," came the housekeeper's pleasant voice.

He took off his brown derby, and covered his steel-gray hair with a velvet skullcap; and as he carried his robust, middle-sized body into the kitchen, to perform his ablutions,[11] his ruddy, gnarled face took on an air of piety.

When supper was over and Asriel and Tamara were about to say grace, Flora resumed the reading of her novel.

"Off with that lump of Gentile nastiness while holy words are being said!" the old man growled.

Flora obeyed, in amazement. Only a few months before she had seldom seen him intone grace at all. She was getting used to his new habits, but such rigor as he now displayed was unintelligible to her, and she thought it unbearable.

"You can read your book a little after. The wisdom of it will not run away," chimed in Tamara, with good-natured irony. She was a poor widow of forty. Asriel had engaged her for her piety and for the rabbinical learning of her late husband, as much as for her culinary fame in the Ghetto.

Asriel intoned grace in indistinct droning accents. By degrees, however, as he warmed up to the Hebrew prayer, whose words were a conglomeration of incomprehensible sounds to him, he fell to swaying to and fro, and his voice broke into an exalted, heart-rending singsong, Tamara accompanying him in whispers, and dolefully nodding her bewigged head all the while.

Flora was moved. The scene was novel to her, and she looked on with the sympathetic reverence of a Christian visiting a Jewish synagogue on the Day of Atonement.[12]

At last the fervent tones died away in a solemn murmur. Silence fell over the cozy little room. Asriel sat tugging at his scanty beard as if in an effort to draw it into a more venerable growth.

"Flora!" he presently growled. "I am going to Europe."

When Asriel Stroon thought he spoke, and when he spoke he acted.

"Goin' to Europe! Are you crazy, papa? What are you talkin' about?"

"Just what you hear. After Passover I am going to Europe. I must take a look at Pravly."[13]

"But you ain't been there over thirty-five years. You don't remember not'in' at all."

"I don't remember Pravly? Better than Mott Street; better than my nose. I was born there, my daughter," he added, as he drew closer to her and began to stroke her glossless black hair. This he did so seldom that the girl felt her heart swelling in her throat. She was yearning after him in advance.

Tamara stared in beaming amazement at the grandeur of the enterprise. "Are you really going?" she queried, with a touch of envy.

"What will you do there?—It's so far away!" Flora resumed, for want of a weightier argument at hand.

"Never mind, my child; I won't have to walk all the way."

"But the Russian police will arrest you for stayin' away so long. Didn't you say they would?"

[11]Washing oneself as an act of religious observance. Like the skullcap, it is a sign of Asriel's piety.
[12]Yom Kippur—a day of religious observance through fasting and prayer.
[13]The Russian town from which he had emigrated to America.

"The kernel of a hollow nut!" he replied, extemporizing an equivalent of "fiddlesticks!" Flora was used to his metaphors, although they were at times rather vague, and set one wondering how they came into his head at all. "The kernel of a hollow nut! Show a *treif*[14] gendarme a *kosher*[15] coin, and he will be shivering with ague. Long live the American dollar!"

She gave him a prolonged, far-away look, and said, peremptorily: "Mister, you am' goin' nowheres."

"Tamara, hand me my Psalter,[16] will you?" the old man grumbled.

When the girl was gone, the housekeeper inquired: "And Flora—will you take her along?"

"What for? That she might make fun of our ways there, or that the pious people should point their fingers at her and call her Gentile girl, hey? She will stay with you and collect rent. I did not have her in Pravly, and I want to be there as I used to. I feel like taking a peep at the graves of my folks. It is pulling me by the heart, Tamara," he added, in a grave undertone, as he fell to turning over the leaves of his Psalter.

II

When Asriel Stroon had retired from business, he suddenly grew fearful of death. Previously he had had no time for that. What with his flour store, two bakeries, and some real estate, he had been too busy to live, much less to think of death. He had never been seen at the synagogue on weekdays; and on the Sabbath, when, enveloped in his praying-shawl, he occupied a seat at the East Wall, he would pass the time drowsing serenely and nodding unconscious approval of the cantor's florid improvisations, or struggling to keep flour out of his mind, where it clung as pertinaciously[17] as it did to his long Sabbath coat.

The first sermon that failed to lull him to sleep was delivered by a newly landed preacher, just after Asriel had found it more profitable to convert his entire property into real estate. The newcomer dwelt, among other things, upon the fate of the wicked after death and upon their forfeited share in the World to Come. As Asriel listened to the fiery exhortation it suddenly burst upon him that he was very old and very wicked. "I am as full of sins as a watermelon is of seeds," he said to himself, on coming out of the synagogue. "You may receive notice to move at any time, Asriel. And where is your baggage? Got anything to take along to the other world, as the preacher said, hey?"

Alas! he had been so taken up with earthly title deeds that he had given but little thought to such deeds as would entitle him to a "share in the World-to-Come"; and while his valuable papers lay secure between the fireproof walls of his iron safe, his soul was left utterly exposed to the flames of Sheol.

Then it was that he grew a pair of bushy sidelocks,[18] ceased trimming his twin goatees, and, with his heart divided between yearning after the business he had sold and worrying over his sins, spent a considerable part of his unlimited leisure reading psalms.

[14]Unclean or impure; non-kosher. [15]Proper; in accordance with Jewish law.
[16]Psalm book. [17]Persistently. [18]Long hair at the side of the face.

What a delight it was to wind off chapter after chapter! And how smoothly it now came off, in his father's (peace upon him!) singsong, of which he had not even thought for more than thirty years, but which suddenly came pouring out of his throat, together with the first verse he chanted! Not that Asriel Stroon could have told you the meaning of what he was so zestfully intoning, for in his boyhood he had scarcely gone through the Pentateuch[19] when he was set to work by his father's side, at flax heckling. But then the very sounds of the words and the hereditary intonation, added to the consciousness that it was psalms he was reciting, "made every line melt like sugar in his mouth," as he once described it to the devout housekeeper.

He grew more pious and exalted every day, and by degrees fell prey to a feeling to which he had been a stranger for more than three decades.

Asriel Stroon grew homesick.

It was thirty-five years since he had left his birthplace; thirty years or more since, in the whirl of his American successes, he had lost all interest in it. Yet now, in the fifty-eighth year of his life, he suddenly began to yearn and pine for it.

Was it the fervor of his religious awakening which resoldered the long-broken link? At all events, numerous as were the examples of piety within the range of his American acquaintance, his notion of genuine Judaism was somehow inseparably associated with Pravly. During all the years of his life in New York he had retained a vague but deep-rooted feeling that American piety was as tasteless an article as American cucumbers and American fish—the only things in which his ecstasy over the adopted country admitted its hopeless inferiority to his native town.

III

On a serene afternoon in May, Asriel drove up to Pravly in a peasant's wagon. He sat listlessly gazing at the unbroken line of wattle-fences and running an imaginary stick along the endless zigzag of their tops. The activity of his senses seemed suspended.

Presently a whiff of May aroma awakened his eye to a many-colored waving expanse, and his ear to the languorous whisper of birds. He recognized the plushy clover knobs in the vast array of placid magnificence, and the dandelions and the golden buttercups, although his poor mother tongue could not afford a special name for each flower, and he now addressed them collectively as *tzatzkes*[20]—a word he had not used for thirty-five years. He looked at the tzatzkes, as they were swaying thoughtfully hither and thither, and it somehow seemed to him that it was not the birds but the clover blossoms which did the chirping. The whole scene appealed to his soul as a nodding, murmuring congregation engrossed in the solemnity of worship. He felt as though there were no such flowers in America, and that he had not seen any since he had left his native place.

Echoes of many, many years ago called to Asriel from amid the whispering host. His soul burst into song. He felt like shutting his eyes and trusting himself to the caressing breath of the air, that it might waft him whithersoever it

[19]The first five books of the Hebrew and Christian scriptures. [20]Playthings; toys.

chose. His senses were in confusion: he beheld a sea of fragrance; he inhaled heavenly music; he listened to a symphony of hues.

"What a treat to breathe! What a paradise!" he exclaimed in his heart. "The cholera take it, how delicious! Do you deserve it, old sinner you? Ten plagues you do! But hush! the field is praying—"

With a wistful babyish look he became absorbed in a gigantic well-sweep[21] suspended from the clear sky, and then in the landscape it overhung. The woody mass darkling in the distance was at once racing about and standing still. Fleecy clouds crawled over a hazy hilltop. And yonder—behold! a long, broad streak of silver gleaming on the horizon! Is it a lake? Asriel's eyes are riveted and memories stir in his breast. He recalls not the place itself, but he can remember his reminiscences of it. During his first years in America, at times when he would surrender himself to the sweet pangs of homesickness and dwell, among other things, on the view that had seen him off to the unknown land, his mind would conjure up something like the effect now before his eyes. As a dream does it comes back to him now. The very shadows of thirty-five years ago are veiled.

Asriel gazes before him in deep reverence. The sky is letting itself down with benign solemnity, its measureless trough filled with melody, the peasant's wagon creaking an accompaniment to it all—to every speck of color, as well as to every sound of the scene.

At one moment he felt as though he had strayed into the other world; at another, he was seized with doubt as to his own identity. "Who are you?" he almost asked himself, closing and reopening his hand experimentally. "Who or what is that business which you call life? Are you alive, Asriel? Whereupon he somehow remembered Flora's photograph, and, taking it out of his bosom pocket, fell to contemplating it.

The wagon turned into a side road, and the Polish peasant, leaning forward, cursed and whipped the animal into a peevish trot. Presently something gray hove in sight. Far away, below, hazy blotches came creeping from behind the sky. The wagon rolls downhill. Asriel is in a flurry. He feels like one on the eve of a great event, he knows not exactly what.

The wagon dashes on. Asriel's heart is all of a flutter. Suddenly—O Lord of the Universe! Why, there glistens the brook—what do you call it? "'Repka?'" he asks the driver.

"Repka!" the other replies, without facing about.

"Repka, a disease into her heart! Repka, dear, may she live long! Who could beat Asriel in swimming?" Over there, on the other side, it was where Asriel's father once chased him for bathing during Nine Days. He bumped his head against the angle of a rock, did the little scamp, and got up with a deep, streaming gash in his lower lip. The mark is still there, and Asriel delights to feel it with his finger now. As he does so the faces of some of his playmates rise before him. Pshaw! he could whip every one of them! Was he not a daredevil of a loafer! But how many of those fellow truants of his will he find alive? he asks himself, and the question wrings his heart.

Asriel strains his eyes at the far distance till, behold! smoke is spinning upward against the blue sky. He can make out the chimney pots. His soul overflows. Sobs choke his breath. "Say!" he begins, addressing himself to the driver. But "say" is English. "*Sloukhai!*" he shouts, with delight in the Polish word. He utters

[21]A spring or fountain.

the names of the surrounding places, and the dull peasant's nods of assent thrill him to the core. He turns this way and that, and in his paroxysm of impatience all but leaps out of the wagon.

The rambling groups of houses define their outlines. Asriel recognizes the Catholic church. His heart bounds with joy. "Hush, wicked thing! It's a church of Gentiles." But the wicked thing surreptitiously resumes its greeting. And over there, whitening at some distance from the other dwellings—what is it? "The nobleman's palace, as sure as I am a Jew!" He had forgotten all about it, as sure as he was a Jew! But what is the nobleman s name? Is he alive?—And there is the mill—the same mill! "I'll swoon away!" he says to himself audibly.

Asriel regains some composure.

Half an hour later he made his entry into his native town. Here he had expected his agitation to pass the bounds of his physical strength; but it did not. At this moment he was solemnly serene.

The town had changed little, and he recognized it at once. Every spot greeted him, and his return of the salutation was a speechless devotional pathos. He found several things which had faded out of his enshrined picture of the place, and the sight of these moved his soul even more powerfully than those he had looked forward to. Only in one instance was he taken aback. Sure enough, this is Synagogue Lane, as full of puddles as ever; but what has come over him? He well remembers that little alley in the rear; and yet it runs quite the other way. Length has turned into width.

And here is Leizer Poisner's inn. "But how rickety it has become!" Asriel's heart exclaims with a pang, as though at sight of a friend prematurely aged and run to seed. He can almost smell the stable occupying the entire length of the little building, and he remembers every room Hello! The same market place, the same church with the bailiff's office by its side! The sparse row of huts on the river bank, the raft bridge, the tannery—everything was the same as he had left it; and yet it all had an odd, mysterious, far-away air—like things seen in a cyclorama. It was Pravly and at the same time it was not; or, rather, it certainly was the same dear old Pravly, but added to it was something else, through which it now gazed at Asriel. Thirty-five years lay wrapped about the town.

Still, Stroon feels like Asrielke[22] Thirteen Hairs, as his nickname had been here. Then he relapses into the Mott Street landlord, and for a moment he is an utter stranger in his birthplace. Why, he could buy it all up now! He could discount all the rich men in town put together; and yet there was a time when he was of the meanest hereabout. An overpowering sense of triumph surged into his breast. Hey, there! Where are your bigbugs—Zorach Latozky, Reb[23] Lippe, Reb Nochum? Are they alive? Thirty-five years ago Asrielke considered it an honor to shake their palm branch on the Feast of Tabernacles,[24] while now out with your purses, you proud magnates, measure fortunes with Asrielke the heckler, if you dare! His heart swells with exultation. And yet—the black year take it!—it yearns and aches, does Asriel's heart. He looks at Pravly, and his soul is pining for Pravly—for the one of thirty-five years ago, of which this is only

[22]The "ke" is a diminutive; that is, the addition converts Asriel to more of a youthful name, like "Billy" instead of "Bill."

[23]Rabbi, or Mister.

[24]A harvest festival in memory of the time when the Israelites were wandering in the wilderness.

a reflection—for the one in which he was known as a crack-brained rowdy of a mechanic, a poor devil living on oatmeal and herring.

With the townspeople of his time Asriel's experience was somewhat different from what he felt in the case of inanimate Pravly. As he confronted them some faces lighted up with their identity at once; and there were even some younger people in whom he instantly recognized the transcribed images of their deceased parents. But many a countenance was slow to catch the reflection of the past which shone out of his eyes; and in a few instances it was not until the name was revealed to Asriel that the retrospective likeness would begin to struggle through the unfamiliar features before him.

"Shmulke!" he shrieked, the moment he caught sight of an old crony, as though they had been parted for no more than a month. Shmulke is not the blooming, sprightly young fellow of yore. He has a white beard and looks somewhat decrepit. Asriel, however, feels as if the beard were only glued to the smooth face he had known. But how Asriel's heart does shrink in his bosom! The fever of activity in which he had passed the thirty-five years had kept him deaf to the departing footsteps of Time. Not until recently had he realized that the words "old man" applied to him; but even then the fact never came home to him with such convincing, with such terrible force, as it did now that he stood face to face with Shmulke. Shmulke was his mirror.

"Shmulke, Angel of Death, an inflammation into your bones!" he shouted, as he suddenly remembered his playmate's byname and fell on his shoulder.

Shmulke feels awkward. He is ashamed of the long-forgotten nickname, and is struggling to free himself from the unwelcome embrace; but Asriel is much the stronger of the two, and he continues to squeeze him and pat him, grunting and puffing for emotion as he does so.

Aunt Sarah-Rachel, whom Asriel had left an elderly but exceedingly active and clever tradeswoman, he found a bag of bones and in her dotage.

"Don't you know me, auntie?" he implored her. She made no reply, and went on munching her lips. "Can it be that you don't know Asrielke, who used to steal raisins from your grocery?"

"She does not understand anything!" Asriel whispered, in consternation.

IV

Asriel's first Sabbath in the native place he was revisiting was destined to be a memorable day in the annals of that peaceful little town.

At the synagogue, during the morning service, he was not the only object of interest. So far as the furtive glances that came through the peepholes of the women's compartment were concerned, a much younger guest, from a hamlet near by, had even greater magnetism than he. Reb Lippe, for forty years the "finest householder" of the community, expected to marry his youngest daughter to an *Illoui,*[25] and he now came to flaunt him, and the five-thousand ruble[26] dowry he represented, before the congregation.

[25]An exceptionally smart person, especially one knowledgeable of the Jewish traditions (i.e., the Talmud).

[26]Rouble: the Russian equivalent of the American dollar.

Only nineteen and a poor orphan, the fame of the prospective bridegroom, as a marvel of acumen and memory, reached far and wide. Few of the subtlest rabbinical minds in the district were accounted his match in debate, and he was said to have some two thousand Talmudical folios literally at his finger's ends. This means that if you had placed the tip of your finger on some word of a volume, he could have told you the word which came under your pressure on any other page you might name. As we shall have to cultivate the young man's acquaintance, let it be added that he was quite boyish of figure, and that had it not been for an excess of smiling frankness, his pale, blue-eyed face would have formed the nearest Semitic approach to the current portraits of Lord Byron. His admirers deplored his lack of staidness. While visiting at Pravly, in a manner, as the guest of the town, he was detected giving snuff to a pig, and then participating with much younger boys in a race over the bridge.

His betrothment to Reb Lippe's daughter was still the subject of negotiation, and there were said to be serious obstacles in the way. The prodigy's relatives were pleased with Reb Lippe's pedigree and social rank, but thought that the boy could marry into a wealthier family and get a prettier girl into the bargain. Nevertheless Reb Lippe's manner at the synagogue was as though the engagement were an accomplished fact, and he kept the young man by his side, his own seat being next the rabbi's, which was by the Holy Ark.[27]

Asriel, as a newcomer, and out of respect for his fabulous wealth, was also accorded a seat of honor on the other side of the Ark. Before he had expatriated himself his place used to be near the door—a circumstance which was fresh in the mind of Reb Lippe, who chafed to see him divert attention from the prodigy and his purchaser. Now Reb Lippe was a proud old gentleman, too jealous of the memory of his rabbinical ancestry and of his own time-honored dignity to give way to a mere boor of a heckler, no matter how much American gold he had to atone for his antecedents. Accordingly, when his fellow trustee suggested that the American ought to be summoned to the reading of the Third Section in the week's portion of the Pentateuch—the highest honor connected with the reading of the Law, and one for which the visiting nabob was sure to pay a liberal donation—the venerable countenance turned crimson.

"Let the sections be auctioned off!" he jerked out.

The proceeding was seldom practiced on an ordinary Sabbath; but Rep Lippe's will was law, as peremptory and irresistible as the Law of Moses, with which it was now concerned. And so the worshippers presently found themselves converted into so many eyewitnesses of a battle of purses.

"Five gildens[28] for the Third!" called out the weazen-faced little sexton from the reading platform, in the traditional sing-song that became his draggling black beard so well. As a bona-fide business transaction is not allowed on the holy day, even though the house of God be the sole gainer by it, the sexton's figures were fictitious—in so far, at least, as they were understood to represent double the actual amount to be paid to the synagogue by the purchaser of the good deed.

"Six gildens for the Third!" he went on in interpretation of a frowning nod from Reb Lippe.

[27]A wooden chest, often containing sacred texts, symbolic of the presence of God.
[28]A unit of money.

A contemptuous toss of Asriel's head threw another gilden on top of the sum. Two other members signaled to the auctioneer, and, warming up to his task, he sang out with gusto, "Eight gildens for the Third!"

Then came in rapid succession: "Nine gildens for the Third! Ten gildens for the Third! Eleven gildens, twelve, thirteen, fourteen gildens for the Third!"

The other bidders, one by one, dropped out of the race, and when the sum reached sixty gildens the field was left to Reb Lippe and Asriel.

The congregation was spellbound. Some with gaping mouths, others with absorbed simpers on their faces, but all with sportsman-like fire in their eyes, the worshipers craned their necks in the direction of the two contestants alternately.

The prodigy had edged away from his seat to a coign of vantage. He was repeatedly called back by winks from his uncle, but was too deeply interested in the progress of the auction to heed them.

"Seventy gildens for the Third! Seventy-one, seventy-two, three, four, five, seventy-six, seventy-seven, eight, nine, eighty gildens for the Third!"

The skirmish waxed so hot, shots flew so thick and so fast, that the perspiring sexton, and with him some of the spectators, was swiveling his head from right to left and from left to right with the swift regularity of gymnastic exercise.

It must be owned that so far as mute partisanship was concerned, Asriel had the advantage of his adversary, for even some of Reb Lippe's staunchest friends and admirers had a lurking relish for seeing it brought home to their leading citizen that there were wealthier people than he in the world.

The women, too, shared in the excitement of the morning. Their windows were glistening with eyes, and the reports of their lucky occupants to the anxious knots in the rear evoked hubbubs of conflicting interjections which came near involving the matronly assemblage in civil war.

The Third Section brought some twenty-eight rubles, net. Asriel was certain that the last bid had been made by him, and that the honor and the good deed were accordingly his. When it came to the reading, however, and the Third Section was reached, the reader called out Reb Lippe's name.

Asriel was stupefied.

"Hold on! That won't do!" he thundered, suddenly feeling himself an American citizen. "I have bought it and I mean to have it." His face was fire; his eyes looked havoc.

A wave of deprecation swept over the room. Dozens of reading desks were slapped for order. Reb Lippe strode up to the platform, pompous, devout, resplendent in the gold lace of his praying-shawl and the flowing silver of his beard, as though the outburst of indignation against Asriel were only an ovation to himself. He had the cunning of a fox, the vanity of a peacock, and the sentimentality of a woman during the Ten Days of Penance. There were many skeptics as to the fairness of the transaction, but these were too deeply impressed by the grandeur of his triumphal march to whisper an opinion. The prodigy alone spoke his mind.

"Why, I do think the other man was the last to nod—may I be ill if he was not," the *enfant terrible* said quite audibly, and was hushed by his uncle.

"Is he really going to get it?" Asriel resumed, drowning all opposition with his voice. "Milk a billy goat! You can't play that trick on me! Mine was the last bid. Twenty-eight scurvy rubles! Pshaw! I am willing to pay a hundred, two hundred, five hundred. I can buy up all Pravly, Reb Lippe, his gold lace and all, and sell him at a loss, too!" He made a dash at the reading platform, as if to take the Third Section by force, but the bedlam which his sally called forth checked him.

"Is this a market place?" cried the second trustee, with conscious indignation.

"Shut the mouth of that boor!" screamed a member, in sincere disgust.

"Put him out!" yelled another, with relish in the scene.

"If he can't behave in a holy place let him go back to his America!" exclaimed a third, merely to be in the running. But his words had the best effect: They reminded Asriel that he was a stranger and that the noise might attract the police.

At the same moment he saw the peaked face of the aged rabbi by his side. Taking him by the arm, the old man begged him not to disturb the Sabbath.

Whether the mistake was on Asriel's side or on the sexton's, or whether there was any foul play in the matter, is not known; but Asriel relented and settled down at his desk to follow the remainder of the reading in his Pentateuch, although the storm of revenge which was raging in his breast soon carried off his attention, and he lost track.

The easy success of his first exhortation brought the rabbi to Asriel's side once again.

"I knew your father—peace upon him! He was a righteous Jew," he addressed him in a voice trembling and funereal with old age. "Obey me, my son, ascend the platform, and offer the congregation a public apology. The Holy One—blessed be He will help you."

The rabbi's appeal moved Asriel to tears, and tingling with devout humility he was presently on the platform, speaking in his blunt, gruff way.

"Do not take it hard, my rabbis! I meant no offense to any one, though there was a trick—as big as a fat bull. Still, I donate two hundred rubles, and let the cantor recite 'God full of Mercy' for the souls of my father and mother—peace upon them."

It was quite a novel way of announcing one's contribution, and the manner of his apology, too, had at once an amusing and a scandalizing effect upon the worshipers, but the sum took their breath away and silenced all hostile sentiment.

The reading over, and the scrolls restored, amid a tumultuous acclaim, to the Holy Ark, the cantor resumed his place at the Omud, chanting a hurried *Half-Kaddish*. "And say ye Amen!" he concluded abruptly, as if startled, together with his listeners, into sudden silence.

Nodding or shaking their heads, or swaying their forms to and fro, some, perhaps mechanically, others with composed reverence, still others in a convulsion of religious fervor, the two or three hundred men were joined in whispering chorus, offering the solemn prayer of *Mussaff*.[29] Here and there a sigh made itself heard amid the monotony of speechless, gesticulating ardor; a pair of fingers snapped in an outburst of ecstasy, a sob broke from some corner, or a lugubrious murmur from the women s room. The prodigy, his eyes shut, and his countenance stern with unfeigned rapture, was violently working his lips as if to make up for the sounds of the words which they dared not utter. Asriel was shaking and tossing about. His face was distorted with the piteous, reproachful mien of a neglected child about to burst into tears, his twin imperials dancing plaintively to his whispered intonations. He knew not what his lips said, but he did know that his soul was pouring itself forth before Heaven, and that his heart might break unless he gave way to his restrained sobs.

[29]A prayer service for the Sabbath and special holiday observances.

At last the silent devotions were at an end. One after another the worshipers retreated, each three paces from his post. Only three men were still absorbed in the sanctity of the great prayer: the rabbi, for whom the cantor was respectfully waiting with the next chant, Reb Lippe, who would not "retreat" sooner than the rabbi, and Asriel, who, in his frenzy of zeal, was repeating the same benediction for the fifth time.

When Asriel issued forth from the synagogue he found Pravly completely changed. It was as if, while he was praying and battling, the little town had undergone a trivializing process. All the poetry of thirty-five years' separation had fled from it, leaving a heap of beggarly squalor. He felt as though he had never been away from the place, and were tired to death of it, and at the same time his heart was contracted with homesickness for America. The only interest the town now had for him was that of a medium to be filled with the rays of his financial triumph. "I'll show them who they are and who Asriel is," he comforted himself.

The afternoon service was preceded by a sermon. The "town preacher" took his text, as usual, from the passage in the "Five Books"[30] which had been read in the morning. But he contrived to make it the basis of an allusion to the all-absorbing topic of gossip. Citing the Talmud and the commentaries with ostentatious profuseness, he laid particular stress on the good deed of procuring a scholar of sacred lore for one's son-in-law.

"It is a well-known saying in tractate[31] *Psohim,*" he said, "that one should be ready to sell his all in order to marry his daughter to a scholar.' On the other hand, 'to give your daughter in marriage to a boor is like giving her to a lion.' Again, in tractate *Berochath* we learn that 'to give shelter to a scholar bent upon sacred studies, and to sustain him from your estates, is like offering sacrifices to God'; and 'to give wine to such a student' is, according to a passage in tractate *Sota,* 'tantamount to pouring it out on an altar.'"

Glances converged on Reb Lippe and the prodigy by his side.

Proceeding with his argument, the learned preacher, by an ingenious chain of quotations and arithmetical operations upon the numerical value of letters, arrived at the inference that compliance with the above teachings was one of the necessary conditions of securing a place in the Garden of Eden.

All of which filled Asriel's heart with a new dread of the world to come and with a rankling grudge against Reb Lippe. He came away from the synagogue utterly crushed, and when he reached his inn the prodigy was the prevailing subject of his chat with the landlord.

V

In the evening of the same day, at the conclusion of the Sabbath, the auction of another good deed took place, and once more the purses of Reb Lippe and Asriel clashed in desperate combat.

This time the good deed assumed the form of a prodigy of Talmudic learning in the character of a prospective son-in-law.

[30]The Pentateuch.

[31]A tractate is a tract, or treatise. *Psohim, Berochath,* and *Sota* are specific tractates that the "town preacher" cites.

The room (at the residence of one of the young man's uncles) was full of bearded Jews, tobacco smoke, and noise. There were Shaya, the prodigy himself, his two uncles, Reb Lippe, his eldest son, and two of his lieutenants, Asriel, his landlord, and a matchmaker. A live broad-shouldered samovar, its air-holes like so many glowing eyes, stood in the center of the table. Near it lay Flora's photograph, representing her in all the splendor of Grand Street millinery.[32]

The youthful hero of the day eyed the portrait with undisguised, open-mouthed curiosity, till, looked out of countenance by the young lady's doleful, penetrating eyes, he turned from it, but went on viewing it with furtive interest.

His own formula of a bride was a hatless image. The notion, therefore, of this princess becoming his wife both awed him and staggered his sense of decorum. Then the smiling melancholy of the Semitic face upset his image of himself in his mind and set it afloat in a haze of phantasy. "I say you need not look at me like that," he seemed to say to the picture. "Pshaw! you are a Jewish girl after all, and I am not afraid of you a bit. But what makes you so sad? Can I do anything for you? Why don't you answer? Do take off that hat, will you?"

Reb Lippe's daughter did not wear a hat, but she was not to his liking, and he now became aware of it. On the other hand, the word "America" had a fascinating ring, and the picture it conjured was a blend of Talmudic and modern glory.

Reb Lippe's venerable beard was rippled with a nervous smile.

"Yes, I am only a boor!" roared Asriel, with a touch of Bounderby[33] ostentation. "But you know it is not myself I want the boy to marry. Twenty thousand rubles, spot cash, then, and when the old boor takes himself off, Shaya will inherit ten times as much. She is my only child, and when I die—may I be choked if I take any of my houses into the grave. Worms don't eat houses, you know."

The quality of his unhackneyed phrase vexed the sedate old talmudists, and one of them remarked, as he pointed a sarcastic finger at the photograph: "Your girl looks like the daughter of some titled Gentile. Shaya is a Jewish boy."

"You don't like my girl, don't you?" Asriel darted back. "And why, pray? Is it because she is not a lump of ugliness and wears a hat? The grand rabbi of Wilna is as pious as any of you, isn't he? Well, when I was there, on my way here, I saw his daughter, and she also wore a hat and was also pretty. Twenty thousand rubles!"

By this time the prodigy was so absorbed in the proceedings that he forgot the American photograph, as well as the bearing which the auction in progress had upon himself. Leaning over the table as far as the samovar would allow, and propping up his face with both arms, he watched the scene with thrilling but absolutely disinterested relish.

After a great deal of whispering and suppressed excitement in the camp of Asriel's foe, Reb Lippe's son announced: "Ten thousand rubles and five years' board." This, added to Reb Lippe's advantages over his opponent by virtue of his birth, social station, and learning, as well as of his residing in Russia, was supposed to exceed the figure named by Asriel. In point of fact, everybody in the room knew that the old talmudist's bid was much beyond his depth; but the assemblage had no time to be surprised by his sum, for no sooner had it

[32]The making and selling of hats.

[33]Josiah Bounderby is an aggressive, blustery character in *Hard Times* (1854), a novel by the English novelist Charles Dickens (1812–1870).

been uttered than Asriel yelled out, with impatient sarcasm: "Thirty thousand rubles, and life-long board, and lodging, and bath money, and stocking darning, and cigarettes, and matches, and mustard, and soap—and what else?"

The prodigy burst into a chuckle, and was forthwith pulled down to his chair. He took a liking to the rough-and-ready straightforwardness of the American.

There was a pause. Shaya and his uncles were obviously leaning toward the "boor." Asriel was clearly the master of the situation.

At last Reb Lippe and his suite rose from their seats.

"You can keep the bargain!" he said to Asriel, with a sardonic smile.

"And be choked with it!" added his son.

"What is your hurry, Reb Lippe?" said one of the uncles, rushing to the old man's side with obsequious solicitude. "Why, the thing is not settled yet. We don't know whether—"

"You don't, but I do. I won't take that boy if *he* brings twenty thousand rubles to *his* marriage portion. Good-night!"

"Good-night and good-year!" Asriel returned. "Why does the cat hate the cream? Because it is locked up."

An hour afterward the remainder of the gathering were touching glasses and interchanging *mazol-tovs*[34] upon the engagement of Flora Stroon to Shaya Golub.

"And now receive my *mazol-tov!*" said Asriel, pouncing upon the prodigy and nearly crushing him in his mighty embrace. "*Mazol-tov* to you, Flora's bridegroom! *Mazol-tov* to you, Flora's predestinated one! My child's dear little bridegroom!" he went on, hiding his face on the young man's shoulder. "I am only a boor, but you shall be my son-in-law. I'll dine you and wine you, as the preacher commanded, pearls will I strew on your righteous path, a crown will I place on your head—I am only a boor!"

Sobs rang in the old man s voice. The bystanders looked on in smiling, pathetic silence.

"A boor, but an honest man," some one whispered to the uncles.

"A heart of gold!" put in the innkeeper.

"And what will Flora say?" something whispered to Asriel, from a corner of his overflowing heart. "Do you mean to tell me that the American young lady will marry this old-fashioned, pious fellow?" "Hold your tongue, fool you!" Asriel snarled inwardly. "She will have to marry him, and that settles it, and don't you disturb my joy. It's for her good as well as for mine."

With a sudden movement he disengaged his arms, and, taking off his enormous gold watch and chain, he put it on Shaya, saying: "Wear it in good health, my child. This is your first present from your sweetheart. But wait till we come to America!"

The next morning Asriel visited the cemetery, and was overawed by its size. While living Pravly had increased by scarcely a dozen houses, the number of dwellings in silent Pravly had nearly doubled.

The headstones, mostly of humble size and weatherworn, were a solemn minority in a forest of plain wooden monuments, from which hung, for identification, all sorts of unceremonious tokens, such as old tin cans, bottomless pots, cast-off hats, shoes, and what not. But all this, far from marring the impressiveness of the place, accentuated and heightened the inarticulate tragedy of

[34]Congratulations; wishes of good luck.

its aspect. The discarded utensils or wearing apparel seemed to be brooding upon the days of their own prime, when they had participated in the activities of the living town yonder. They had an effect of mysterious muteness, as of erstwhile animated beings—comrades of the inmates of the overgrown little mounds underneath, come to join them in the eternal rest of the city of death.

"Father! Father!" Asriel began, in a loud synagogue intonation, as he prostrated himself upon an old grave, immediately after the cantor had concluded his prayer and withdrawn from his side. "It is I, Asriel, your son—do you remember? I have come all the way from America to ask you to pray for me and my child. She is a good girl, father, and I am trying to lead her on the path of righteousness. She is about to marry the greatest scholar of God's Law hereabouts. Do pray that the boy may find favor in her eyes, father! You know, father dear, that I am only a boor, and woe is me! I am stuffed full of sins. But now I am trying to make up and to be a good Jew. Will you pray the Uppermost to accept my penance?" he besought, with growing pathos in his voice. "You are near Him, father, so do take pity upon your son and see to it that his sins are forgiven. Will you pray for me? Will you? But, anyhow, I care more for Flora—Bloome, her Yiddish name is. What am I? A rusty lump of nothing. But Flora—she is a flower. Do stand forth before the High Tribunal and pray that no ill wind blow her away from me, that no evil eye injure my treasure. She lost her mother when she was a baby, poor child, and she is the only consolation I have in the world. But you are her grandfather—do pray for her!"

Asriel's face shone, his heavy voice rang in a dismal, rapturous, devotional singsong. His eyes were dry, but his soul was full of tears and poetry, and he poured it forth in passionate, heart-breaking cadences.

"What is the difference between this grass blade and myself?" he asked, a little after. "Why should you give yourself airs, Asriel? Don't kick, be good, be pious, carry God in your heart, and make no fuss! Be as quiet as this grass, for hark! the hearse is coming after you, the contribution boxes are jingling, the Angel of Death stands ready with his knife—Oh, do pray for your son, father!" he shrieked, in terror.

He paused. A bee, droning near by, seemed to be praying like himself, and its company stirred Asriel's heart.

"Oh, father! I have not seen you for thirty-five years. Thirty-five years!" he repeated in deliberate tones and listening to his own voice.

"We are the thirty-five?" some distant tombstones responded, and Asriel could not help pausing to look about, and then he again repeated, "Thirty-five years! Can I never see you again, father? Can't I see your dear face and talk to you, as of old, and throw myself into fire or water for you? Can't I? Can't I? Do you remember how you used to keep me on your knees or say prayers with me at the synagogue, and box my ears so that the black year took me when you caught me skipping in the prayer book? Has it all flown away? Has it really?"

He paused as though for an answer, and then resumed, with a bitter, malicious laugh at his own expense: "Your father is silent, Asriel! Not a word, even if you tear yourself to pieces. All is gone, Asrielke! All, all, all is lost forever!"

His harsh voice collapsed. His speech died away in a convulsion of subdued sobbing. His soul went on beseeching his father to admit him to the restful sanctity of his company.

When Asriel rose to his feet and his eye fell upon a tombstone precisely like his father's, he frowned upon it, with a sense of jealousy. On his way to his mother's grave, in the older part of the cemetery, he ever and anon turned to look back. His father's tombstone was rapidly becoming merged in a forest of other monuments. His dead father, his poor father, was losing his individuality, till he was a mere speck in this piebald medley of mounds, stones, boards, and all sorts of waste. Asriel felt deeply hurt. He retraced his steps till his father's resting place once more became the center of the world.

Then he went to pay his respects and tears to the graves of his mother, sisters, brothers, uncles. At last, completely exhausted, he took to walking among the other headstones. As he stopped to make out their Hebrew inscriptions, he would now hang his head, in heart-wringing reminiscence, now heave a sigh, or clap his hands, in grievous surprise.

The tombstones and tomb-boards were bathed in the reddish gold of the late afternoon sun. Asriel had not yet broken his fast, but although shattered in body and spirit he felt no hunger and was reluctant to leave the graveyard. He found here more of his contemporaries that he well remembered, more of the Pravly of his time, than in the town a verst[35] or two away. The place asserted a stronger claim upon him and held him by the force of its unearthly fascination.

When he reached town at last, he felt newborn. Pravly was again dear to his heart, although Flora and America drew him to them with more magnetism than ever. He strove to speak in soft accents, and went about the houses of his relatives and the poor of the town, distributing various sums and begging the recipients of his gifts "to have pity and not to thank him," lest it should detract from the value of his good deed.

Then he went to make peace with Reb Lippe.

"You are going to stay here, so you can get another prodigy," he pleaded humbly. "But one cannot get such goods in America. Besides, you can read Talmud yourself, while I am only a boor, and what have I done to make sure of my share in the world to come? Here are three hundred rubles for charity. Do forgive me, Reb Lippe, will you? What will you lose by it?"

There were others in the room, and the unique pathos of the plea touched and amused them at once. Reb Lippe was moved to the point of tears. Moreover, the present situation took the venom out of his defeat.

"I forgive you with all my heart," he said impulsively, patting "the boor" as he would a child. "Be seated. May the Uppermost bring you home in peace and bless the union. There is another young man who is worthy of my daughter; and Shaya—may the Holy One—blessed be He—grant him the will and the power to spread His Law in America. The Jews there want a young man like him, and I am glad he is going with you. You are taking a precious stone with you, Reb Asriel. Hold it dear."

"You bet I will," Asriel replied gleefully.

VI

The nearer Asriel, with the prodigy in tow, came to New York, the deeper did Pravly sink into the golden mist of romance, and the more real did the great American city grow in his mind. Every mile added detail to the picture, and every new bit of detail made it dearer to his heart.

[35]A Russian measure of distance; slightly more than a kilometer.

He was going home. He felt it more keenly, more thrillingly every day, every hour, every minute.

Sandy Hook[36] hove in sight.

Can there be anything more beautiful, more sublime, and more uplifting than the view, on a clear summer morning, of New York harbor from an approaching ship? Shaya saw in the enchanting effect of sea, verdure, and sky a new version of his visions of paradise, where, ensconced behind luxuriant foliage, the righteous—venerable old men with silvery beards—were nodding and swaying over gold-bound tomes of the Talmud. Yet, overborne with its looming grandeur, his heart grew heavy with suspense, and he clung close to Asriel.

All was bustle and expectation on board. The little deck engines never ceased rumbling, and the passengers, spruced up as if for church, were busy about their baggage, or promenading with a festive, nervous air.

Asriel twitched and bit his lip in rapture.

"Oh, how blue the water is!" said Shaya wistfully.

"America is a fine country, is it not?" the old man rejoined. "But it can't hold a candle to Flora. Wait till you see her. You just try to be a good boy," he kept murmuring; "stick to your Talmud, and don't give a *peper*[37] for anything else, and all God has given me shall be yours. I have no son to say *Kaddish* for my soul when I am dead. Will you be my Kaddish, Shaya? Will you observe the anniversary of my death?" he queried, in a beseeching tone which the young man had never heard from him.

"Of course I will," Shaya returned, like a dutiful child.

"Will you? May you live long for it. In palaces will I house you, like the eye in my head will I cherish you. I am only a boor, but she is my daughter, my only child, and my whole life in this world."

Asriel kept Flora unadvised as to the name of the steamer or the date of his arrival. Upon landing he did not go directly to his residence, but first took his importation into a large "clothing and gents' furnishing store" on Broadway, from which the *illoui* emerged completely transformed. Instead of his uncouth cap and the draggling coat which had hidden his top boots from view, he was now arrayed in the costliest "Prince Albert,"[38] the finest summer derby, and the most elegant button shoes the store contained. This and a starched shirt-front, a turned-down collar, and a gaudy puff-tie set into higher relief the Byronic[39] effect of his intellectual, winsome face.

Asriel snapped his fingers for delight. He thought him easily the handsomest and best-dressed man on Broadway. "It is the Divine Presence shining upon him!" he murmured to himself, dragging the young man by the hand, as if he were a truant schoolboy. Barring the prodigy's sidelocks (badges of divine learning and piety), which were tightly curled into two little cushions in front of his ears, he now thought him thoroughly Americanized.

The prodigy, however, felt tied and fettered in the garb of Gentile civilization, and as he trudged along by his convoy's side, he viewed his transformed self in the store windows, or stared, rabbit-like, at the lumbering stagecoaches and the hurrying noblemen.

[36]A projection of the New Jersey coast. [37]The Dutch word for *pepper.*

[38]A long, double-breasted coat like that often worn by Prince Albert (1819–1861), Prince Consort during the reign of England's Queen Victoria.

[39]That is, like George Gordon, Lord Byron, the flamboyant English poet (1788–1824).

Asriel let himself and his charge in noiselessly with the latch-key, which had accompanied him, together with a bunch of other keys, on his tour. They entered the hallway on tiptoe.

The little house rang with the voluminous tones of Flora's piano, through which trickled the doleful tremolo of her subdued contralto. Since her father had left her pining for his return, "Home, Sweet Home" had become her favorite tune.

Flora was alone in the house, and her unconscious welcome was all the sweeter to Asriel's soul for the grieving note which ran through it. His heart throbbed with violence. Shaya's sank in awe. He had never heard a piano except through the window of some nobleman's house.

"Hush! Do you hear?" the old man whispered. "That's your predestined bride." With that he led the way downstairs. There they paused to kiss the divine name on the *Mezuzah*[40] of the doorpost.

"Tamara!" Asriel called, under his breath, looking for the pious housekeeper in the dining room and in the kitchen. "She is not in. Must be out marketing or about her good deeds. A dear soul she! Oh, it's her fast day; she fasts Mondays and Thursdays."

Then he stepped up in front of a tin box that was nailed to one of the kitchen doors and took out his pocketbook. It was one of the contribution-boxes of the "Meyer-the-Wonder-worker Fund," which is devoted to the support of pious old European Jews who go to end their days in the Land of Israel. Every orthodox Jew in the world keeps a similar box in his house and drops a coin into it whenever he escapes some danger. Asriel had safely crossed the wide ocean, and his offering was a handful of silver.

"Well, you stay here, Shaya, and don't budge till you are called," he said; and leaving the young man to his perplexity he betook himself upstairs, to surprise his daughter.

Flora burst into tears of joy, and hugged him again and again, while he stroked her black hair or stood scowling and grinning for admiration.

"Ah, you dear, cranky papa!" she burst out, for the fourth time realizing that he was actually come back to her, and for the fourth time attacking him.

At last he thought they had had enough. He was dying to protract the scene, but there was that troublesome job to get rid of, and Asriel was not the man to put such things off. Whenever he felt somewhat timid he would grow facetious. This was the case at the present juncture.

"Well, Flora, guess what sort of present your papa has brought you," he said, reddening to his ears. "I'll bet you you won't hit if you keep on guessing till tomorrow. No girl has ever got such a present as long as America is America."

Flora's eyes danced with joyous anticipation. Her mind was ablaze with diamonds, rubies, emeralds, sapphires, pearls.

"I have got a bridegroom for you—a fifteen-thousand-dollar one. Handsomest and smartest fellow on earth. He is an *illoui*."

"A what?" she asked, in amazement.

"Oh, a wonderful chap, you know, deep in the Talmud and the other holy books. He could knock all the rabbis of Europe to smithereens. The biggest bug in Pravly was after him, but I beat him clean out of his boots. Shaya! Come right up!"

[40]A small box containing a parchment with sacred scripture.

The girl gazed at her father in bewilderment. Was he joking or was he in dead, terrific earnest?

Shaya made his appearance, with his eyes on the floor, and wringing the index finger of his right hand, as he was wont to do whenever he felt ill at ease, which was seldom, however.

Flora's brain was in a whirl.

"This is your predestined bridegroom, my daughter. A fine present, is it not? Did you ever expect such a raisin of a sweetheart, hey? Well, children, I must go around to see about the baggage. Have a chat and be acquainted." With that he advanced to the door.

"Papa! Papa!" Flora frantically called to him. But he never turned his head and went his way.

In her despair she rushed at the young stranger, who was still wringing his finger, as he stood in the middle of the parlor, eyeing the carpet, and snapped out:—

"Mister, you had better go. If you think you are going to be my bridegroom, you are sadly mistaken."

She spoke in Yiddish, but her pronunciation, particularly of the letter "r," was so decidedly American that to Shaya it sounded at once like his native tongue and the language of Gentiles. However, it was Yiddish enough, and the fact of this imposing young lady speaking it gave him the feeling of being in the presence of a Jewish princess of biblical times.

"Where shall I go? I don't know anybody here." He said it with an air of naïve desperation which touched the girl's heart. "Where is my fault?" he added pleadingly.

She gave him a close look, and, taking him by his clean-cut beardless chin, opened her eyes wide at him, and broke into a hearty laugh.

"My father has really brought you over to marry me?" she questioned, for the first time awakening to the humorous side of the situation, and again she burst out laughing.

Shaya blushed and took hold of his finger, but he forthwith released it and also broke into a giggle. Her merriment set him at his ease, and her labored Yiddish struck him as the prattle of a child.

Flora was amused and charmed as with a baby. Shaya felt as if he were playing with another boy.

Of all the immigrants who had married or were engaged to marry some of her girlfriends, none had, just after landing, been so presentable, so sweet-faced, and so droll as this scholarly looking fellow. There would have been nothing odd in her marrying him a year or two later, after he had picked up some broken English and some of the customs of the country. But then her mind was firmly made up, and she had boasted to her friends that she was bound to marry a doctor, and here this boy was not even going to be a business man, but an orthodox rabbi or something of the sort. The word "rabbi" was associated in her mind with the image of an unkempt, long-skirted man who knew nothing of the world, took snuff, and made life a nuisance to himself and to others. Is she going to be a *rabbitzen*[41]? No! No! No! Come what may, none but a refined American gentleman shall lead her under the nuptial canopy! And in her rage she fled from the parlor and went to nurse her misery on the dining room lounge.

[41]A rabbi's wife.

Presently, as she lay with her hands clasped under her head, abandoned to her despair and fury, and yet unable to realize that it was all in real earnest, a fretting sensation settled somewhere in her heart. At first it was only like a grain of sand, but it kept growing till it lay a heavy, unbearable lump. She could not stand the idea of that poor, funny dear being left alone and scared out of his wits. Still, she would not stir. Let papa take him away or she will leave the house and go to work in a factory.

"Tamara!" she suddenly raised herself to say, the moment the housekeeper came into the room. "There is a man upstairs. He must be hungry."

"Then why don't you give him something to eat?" Tamara responded tartly. "You know it is Monday and I am faint. But who is he and what is he doing upstairs? Let him come down."

"Go and see him for yourself," snapped Flora. "You will find him one of your set—a Talmudical scholar, a pious soul," she added, with a venomous laugh.

Tamara bent upon her a look full of resentment as well as of devout reproach, and betook herself upstairs.

When Asriel came he explained that Shaya was not going to be a rabbi, nor dress otherwise than as an American gentleman, but that he would lead a life of piety and spend his time studying the Talmud, partly at home and partly at some synagogue. "What, then, have I worked all my life for?" he pleaded. "I am only a boor, my daughter, and how long does a fellow live? Don't darken my days, Flora."

Tamara kept nodding pious assent. "In the old country a girl like you would be glad to marry such a child of the Law," she expostulated with the girl. "It is only here that we are sinners and girls marry none but worldly men. May every daughter of Israel be blessed with such a match."

"Mind your own business!" Flora exploded. She understood her father's explanation but vaguely, and it had the opposite of the desired effect upon her.

"Leave her alone. The storm will blow over," Asriel whispered.

When Asriel's baggage arrived it proved to include a huge box full of Hebrew books. They were of various sizes, but twenty-five of them were large, uniform, leather-bound folio volumes, portly and resplendent in a superabundance of gilding and varnish. Of these, twenty contained the whole of the Babylonian Talmud together with the various commentaries, the remaining five comprising the Alphos. After a little a walnut bookcase made its appearance. It was accorded a place of honor in the front parlor, and Asriel, Tamara, and Shaya busied themselves with arranging the sacred books on its shelves.

Flora sat eyeing them sarcastically, till, sobs rising to her throat, she retired to the seclusion of her bedroom, on the top floor, and burst out crying as if her heart would break. The contents of all those books, which her father had imported as accessories of her would-be bridegroom, were Chinese to her. She had never seen so many of them nor given a moment's attention to the occasional talks which she had chanced to overhear concerning such books and the men who spent their lives reading them. They now frightened her, as if they were filled with weird incantations and Shaya were the master of some uncanny art.

The prodigy was busy arranging his library, now and then opening a book to examine its print. Presently, as he was squatting down before a chair upon which he was turning over the leaves of a bulky volume, his attention was arrested by a celebrated passage. Without changing his posture, he proceeded to glance it over, until, completely absorbed, he fell to humming the words, in that peculiar singsong, accompanied by indescribable controversial gesticulations, which seem to be as indispensable in reading Talmud as a pair of eyes.

"Look, look!" Tamara nudged Asriel, whom she was helping to transfer the remaining books to the marble table. Asriel turned his head toward the prodigy, and for a few moments the two stood staring at the odd, inspiring spectacle with gaping admiration. Then the housekeeper and her employer exchanged a glance of intelligence, she nodding her bewigged head piously, as much as to say: "What a find Heaven has placed in your way!"

"The Uppermost has blessed you," she added in whispers.

"May he enjoy long life with us!" Asriel returned, with a sigh.

"Flora does not know what a treasure the Lord of the Universe has sent her."

"She will," he rejoined curtly.

VII

It was at the head of a dozen venerable Talmudists, including the rabbi of the congregation, that Asriel returned from the synagogue next Saturday morning. The learned company was entertained with wine, cold fish, and some of the lemon pie and genuine Yiddish pastry for which Tamara was famous.

"Here is life, Mr. Stroon! Here is life, Shaya!" each of the guests said, raising his glass.

"Life and peace! Life and peace!" was the uniform response. "God bless the union and let them live a hundred and twenty years," pursued Reb Mendele, a little man with luxuriant red sidelocks, as he reached for a piece of Sabbath cake.

"And grant that they give birth to children and bring them up to the Law, the Bridal Canopy, and deeds of righteousness," chimed in another, whose earlocks were two sorry corkscrew-like appendages, as he held up a slice of fish on the points of his fork.

"And Shaya continue a child of the Law and study it with never-failing zeal," came from between a dangling pair of tubes.

"That's the point!" emphasized a chorus of munching mouths.

"But where is the bride?" somebody demanded. "She must show herself! she must show herself!"

"That's right," Reb Mendele seconded heartily. "Out with the bride! 'And the daughters of Jerusalem come out dancing,'" he quoted; "and what do they say? 'Lift thine eyes, young man, and behold the maiden thou choosest. Do not set thine eye on beauty——.'" He broke off abruptly, reddening. The remainder of the quoted passage runs as follows: "Set thine eye (the maidens say to the young man) on good family connections, as is written in Proverbs: 'False is grace and vain is beauty: a woman that feareth the Lord shall indeed be praised.'" It would have been anything but appropriate to the occasion, and while the Chaldaic and the Hebrew of the citation were Greek to Asriel, there was the prodigy to resent it.

Another hoary-headed[42] child of the Law interposed: "'Go forth and look, O ye daughters of Zion, on King Solomon, with the crown wherewith his mother hath crowned him on the day of the joy of his espousals, and on the day of

[42]White-haired.

the joy of his heart.' Saith the Talmud: 'By "the day of his espousals" is meant the day of the Giving of the Law.' Accordingly, when Shaya's wedding takes place, if God be pleased, it will be an espousal in the literal as well as in the Talmudic sense, for is he not full of Law? It will therefore be the Giving of the Law in marriage to Reb Asriel's daughter, will it not?"

"Never mind blushing, Shaya," said the rabbi, although the prodigy, engrossed with the "paradise taste" of the lemon pie—a viand he had never dreamed of—and keeping a sharp eye on the dwindling contents of the tart-dish, was too busy to blush.

Flora was in her bedroom, the place of her voluntary exile most of the time that her compulsory sweetheart was in the house. Her father was kind and attentive to her, as usual, and never mentioned Shaya's name to her. But she knew that he was irrevocably bent upon the marriage, and her mood often verged on suicide. Could it really be that after all her cherished dreams of afternoon drives in Central Park, in a doctor's buggy and with the doctor himself by her side, she was doomed to be the wife of that clumsy rustic, who did not even know how to shake hands or to bow to a lady, and who could not say a word without performing some grotesque gesture or curling his horrid sidelocks? Oh, what would the girls say! She had twitted them on the broken English of their otherwise worldly and comparatively well-mannered sweethearts, and now she herself was matched with that wretch of a holy soul!

And yet Shaya was never in her mind invested in the image of a "clumsy rustic" nor of a "holy soul." Whenever she saw him she would screw up a frown, but on one occasion, when their eyes met across the supper table, they could not help smiling to each other, like children at church.

"Flora dear, I want to speak to you," Asriel said, knocking at the locked door of her hiding-place.

"Leave me alone, papa, will you? I've got a headache," she responded.

"That's all right, but unlock the door. I won't eat you up."

She was burning to have her father broach the painful subject, so that she might have it out with him. With that end in view, she set her teeth and turned the key. But Asriel came in so unaggressive, so meek, in a pleading attitude so utterly unlike him, that he took her by surprise, as it were, and she stood completely disarmed.

"I beg you, my daughter, do not shorten my days, and come downstairs," he entreated with heartfelt ardor. "I have so little to live, and the Uppermost has sent me a piece of comfort so that I may die a righteous Jew—will you take it away from me? Will you put me to shame before God and man?"

The words and the pathos with which they were delivered so oddly contrasted with all she knew of her father that she felt as if he were really praying for his life. She was deeply touched and dazed, and before she knew what she was about, found herself in the crowded little dining room below.

"Good Sabbath, Flora, good Sabbath!" the venerable assemblage greeted her.

"Good Sabbath!" she returned, bowing gracefully, and blushing.

"May your guest be pleasing to you," one of the company went on in time-honored phrase; "and, if God be pleased, we shall live to make merry at your wedding."

Flora's face turned a deeper red.

Several of the Talmudists were itching for some banter at the expense of the young pair, but the American girl's dignified bearing and her commanding figure and dress bore down every tendency in that direction, so that the scholarly old gentlemen turned their overflowing spirits in other channels.

"Give us some Law, Shaya!" said Reb Mendele, with a Talmudic wave of both hands.

"That's right," the others concurred. "Your prospective father-in-law is feasting us upon fare of the earth, and it is meet that you should regale us with Words of Law."

Shaya, his face as red as Flora's, was eyeing the tablecloth as he murmured, "'No conversing during repast.'"

"Words of Law are no converse," Reb Mendele retorted. "The Commentary adds: 'Not so much as to quote the precept about silence during repast,'" Shaya rejoined reluctantly, without raising his eyes. "Now the precept is Words of the Law, is it not? Which means that the prohibition does extend to Words of Law."

Apart from his embarrassment, the prodigy was somehow loath to engage in a spiritual discussion in the presence of the stylish young lady.

"Why did you quote it then?" Reb Mendele pursued aggressively. He referred to two other passages, in support of his position; and Shaya, with his eyes still on the tablecloth, and refraining from all gesticulation, could not help showing the irrelevance of both. It was a "knock-out blow," but his red-bearded opponent cleverly extricated himself from the ignominy of his defeat by assuming an amused air, as if it had all been mere bait to decoy the prodigy to a display of his erudition and mental powers; and retaining his smile against further emergency, Reb Mendele hazarded another assault. Some of the other Talmudists took a hand. The battle waxed hot, though Shaya, fighting single-handed against half a dozen elders, remained calm, and parried their blows with a shamefaced but contemptuous look, never raising a finger nor his eyes from the tablecloth. Once in the fray, he would not have Flora see him get the worst of it.

She, on her part, could not help a growing interest in the debate, and finally accepted the chair which Tamara had tenderly placed by her side five minutes before. To be sure, she understood not a word of the controversy. To her it was something like a boxing-match, with every exciting element of the sport, but without any of its violence (which alone kept Flora from attending pugilistic performances), though the arms and fingers of our venerable combatants were even more active than are the arms and fists of two athletes in a modern ring. As she watched the progress of the discussion she became conscious of a decided partisan feeling in favor of the younger man. "It ain't fair a bit!" she said to herself. "Six old-timers against one boy—I declare!"

Asriel and Tamara, to both of whom the contest was as unintelligible as it was to Flora, were so abandoned to their admiration of the youthful disputant that they omitted to notice the girl's undisguised interest in the scene and to congratulate themselves upon it. The host followed the controversy with a sheepish look of reverence, as if the company were an assemblage of kings. The housekeeper looked on with a beaming face, and every time one of the patriarchs made a bold attack, she would nod her head as if she understood it all, and conceded the strength of his contention.

Egged on by Flora's presence as well as by the onslaughts of his adversaries, Shaya gradually warmed up to the debate, until, having listened, with sardonic patience, to a lengthy and heated argument by a fleshy child of the Law, he suddenly leaped upon his man.

"Is this the way you understand the passage?" he shouted, with a vicious chuckle. Then, thrusting his curly head in his opponent's face, and savagely gesticulating, he poured forth a veritable cataract of the most intricate syllogisms and quotations.

It was quite a new Shaya. His blue eyes flashed fire, his whole countenance gleamed, his singsong rang with tuneful ferocity.

"But it seems to me that Rabbi Yohanon does not say that," the portly Talmudist objected. "I am afraid you have misquoted him."

It was the drowning man's straw. Even Flora, who understood the Yiddish of the retort, could see that; and her heart bounded with cruel delight.

"Have I? You are sure, are you?" Shaya demanded, with boyish virulence. "All right. We shall see!" With which he darted out of the room and upstairs.

"The boy is a *gaon*,"[43] the corpulent old man remarked humbly. "What a head! What a memory, what a *chariff!*"[44]

"Yes, and what a *bokki!*"[45] chimed in the rabbi. "One cannot help wondering when he had time to study up so much."

"He'll just take a peep at a book and then he knows it all by heart," put in Asriel. "He licked all the rabbis around Pravly."

The boorish remark disposed some of the listeners to laugh, but they did not.

"You have got a treasure, Mr. Stroon," said Reb Mendele.

"You bet!" the host answered with a blissful simper, as he took to stroking his daughter's hair.

"You know what the Talmud says, Mr. Stroon?" resumed the rabbi. "That he who supports a scholar of the Law is like unto him who offers sacrifices."

"I know," Asriel returned exultingly. At the Pravly synagogue the preacher had applied the same quotation to Reb Lippe.

Presently Shaya returned with a pile of huge volumes in his arms. His citation proved correct, and meeting with no further opposition, but too far carried away by the subject to quit it so soon, he volunteered an extemporaneous discourse. His face was now wrapped in genial, infantile ecstasy and his intonation was a soft, impassioned melody. The old man followed him with paternal admiration.

When he concluded and leaned back in his chair, he gave Flora a triumphant smile. The color mounted to her cheeks and she dropped her gaze. At the same moment Asriel flung himself upon the young hero.

"Oh, you dear little sparrow!" he exclaimed, lifting Shaya in his arms like a baby, and passionately kissing him.

Tamara wiped her eyes with her apron. Flora had a mind to flee for safety, but she forthwith saw herself out of danger, for her father seemed unmindful of her presence, and the first thing he did as he let the prodigy down was to invite his guests upstairs to show them the newly imported library.

As the patriarchal company was filing out of the dining room, Shaya, passing by Flora, said to her gleefully: "I gave it to them, didn't I?"

"Tell me now," said Tamara, when the two women found themselves alone in the room; "ought you not to thank God for such a treasure of a sweetheart?"

"He is nothing of the kind to me," Flora burst out, "and he never will be, either. I don't care how long papa is going to keep him in the house."

[43]A genius. [44]Extraordinary intelligence. [45]Learned man.

VIII

"Oh, papa!" sobbed Flora; "will you ever put an end to it? You know I'll never marry him."

"Do I compel you to?" he replied. "What do you care if he is in the house? He does not take away your dinner, does he? Imagine that he is your brother and don't bother your head about him. The boy has become so dear to me that I feel as if he were my own son. Will *you* recite Kaddish for my soul? Will you play for me at the anniversary of my death? God thought I was not good enough to have a son, but he sent me this holy child to take the place of one. As I hear him read his holy books," he went on, with mounting pathos, "it melts like ice cream in my heart. It pleased the Uppermost to make a boor of your papa. Well, I suppose He knows his business, and I am not going to poke my nose in, and ask questions; but He seems to have taken pity on me after all, and in my old age he has sent me an angel, so that I may get the credit of supporting him. Did you hear what the wise men said? That to support a man who does nothing but study sacred books is as good as offering sacrifices. Yes, my daughter, God has put this boy in my hands; He sent me all the way to Pravly for him—all to give me a chance to make up for my sins. Do you want me to kick him out? Not if New York turned upside down."

"But, father—"

"Hold on! Let me talk the heart out of myself. It's no use asking me to send him away. He is God's gift. He is as holy as a Purity.[46] You are my daughter, and he is my son. I don't chase you under the bridal canopy with a strap, do I? If God does not wish the match, it won't come off, that's all."

The conversation took place about a fortnight after the great debate. Asriel lived in the hope that when Shaya had learned some English and the ways of Flora's circle, she would get to like him. He could not see how it was possible to withstand the charms of the young man whom he sincerely thought the handsomest fellow in the Jewish colony. He provided him with a teacher, and trusted the rest to time and God.

"Just fix him up in English and a little figuring, and that's all," he instructed the teacher. "But mind you, don't take him too far into those Gentile books of yours. He does not want any of the monkey tricks they teach the children at college. Do you understand?"

Flora was getting used to Shaya's presence in the house, as if he actually were a newly discovered brother of hers, brought up in a queer way which she could not understand, and it was only occasionally and at growing intervals that the situation would burst upon her, and she would plead with her father as she had done.

The two young people frequently found themselves alone. The door between the front parlor, which was now Shaya's study, and Flora's boudoir[47] was most of the time open. They often talked together, and she quizzed him about his manners, and once or twice even went over his English lessons with him, laughing at his mispronunciations, and correcting them in the imposing manner of her former schoolteachers.

"Why do you work your fingers like that?" she once said, with a pained look. "Can't you try and read without them?"

[46]The scrolls of the Law. [47]Bedroom or dressing room.

"I am used to it from the Talmud—he—he—he!" he tittered, as if acknowledging a compliment.

Her piano did not disturb him in his studies, for in the synagogues, where he had grown up, he had been used to reading in a turmoil of other voices; but he loved the instrument, and he would often pause to listen to Flora's energetic strokes through the door. When the tune was a melancholy one its first accords would make him start, with a thrill; and as he proceeded to listen his heart would contract with a sharp feeling of homesickness, and at the same time he would be longing for still more familiarity in the performer's manner toward him. Sometimes he would cross over to her room and quietly stand behind her while she was playing.

"Ah, it is so nice!" he once said, feeling himself in a paradise on earth.

"What are you doing here?" she exclaimed, facing about toward him, in affected surprise. "Music ain't for a 'holy child' like yourself." She mocked a favorite expression of her father's.

"Don't say that," he reproached her. "You always like to tease me. Why don't I tease you?"

Upon the whole, Shaya took the situation quite recklessly. He studied his Talmud and his English, let Tamara cloy him with all sorts of tidbits, and roamed about the streets and public buildings. In less than six months he knew the city and its suburbs much better than Flora, and could tell the meaning of thousands of printed English words, although he neither knew how to use them himself nor recognized them in the speech of others. Flora was amazed by his rapid progress, and the facility with which he mastered his Arithmetic and English Grammar in neither of which she had been strong at school—even piqued her ambition. It was as if she had been beaten by the "holy soul" on her own ground.

The novelty of studying things so utterly out of his rut was like a newly discovered delicacy to his mental palate. He knew by heart a considerable part of the English translation in his Hebrew prayer book and Old Testament, and his greatest pleasure, when Asriel was not about, was to do arithmetical problems. But the problems were all child's play to him, and he craved some higher grade of intellectual food in the same Gentile line. This he knew from his Talmud to be contained in the "Wisdom of Measuring," which he had learned of his teacher to call Geometry.

"Bring me a Geometry, please," he whispered to his instructor.

"I will, but don't say a word to Mr. Stroon about it."

The forbidden fruit was furnished, and the prodigy of sacred lore applied himself to it with voracity.

"How cunning!" he said to the teacher, in a transport of enthusiasm. "Of course, it is not as deep as Talmud, but I never dreamed there were such subtle things in the Gentile books at all—may I be ill if I did."

"This is only the beginning of it," the other returned, in whispered exultation. "Wait till you get deeper into it. And then there are other books, far more interesting."

"Say, young fellow!" Asriel said to Shaya's teacher a week or so later; "you need not trouble your righteous legs to bring you here any more. You are getting too thick with the boy."

Shaya now found no difficulty in plodding through the theorems and problems unaided. But he yearned after his teacher and friend, and for several days could relish neither his Talmud nor his contraband Geometry. He grew restless. His soul was languishing with thirst.

"Guess where I have been," he confidentially said to Flora, coming from the street one afternoon. He spoke in Yiddish, and she answered in English, interspersed with the same dialect.

"Not in the synagogue, studying?" she queried.

"No—at the Astor Library," he whispered. "They have such a lot of books there, Flora! Upstairs and downstairs—large rooms like rich synagogues, with shelves all over the walls, and all full of books. Have you ever been there, Flora?"

"N—no!" she owned, with reluctance. The "holy soul" was clearly forging ahead of her in a world which she considered all her own; and she hated the idea of it, and liked it at the same time. "What did you do there?"

"I just looked at the books—oh, what a lot!—and then I found out how to get a Geometry—they have everything in the world, I tell you—and I did some problems. Don't tell your father I was there."

"Of course I won't," she said intimately. "Can ladies come in?"

"Certainly; they have a separate place for them, though; will you go there with me?"

"Some day," she rejoined evasively.

"Will you? Oh, it's so nice to be sitting and reading there! Only you must sit still. I forgot myself, and as I was figuring out some nice point, I began to reason aloud, so a fine old gentleman stepped up to my side and touched me on the shoulder. Oh, I got so scared, Flora! But he did not do me anything—may I be ill if he did. He only told me to be quiet."

Flora burst out laughing.

"I'll bet you, you was singing in that funny way you have when you are studying the Talmud."

"Yes," he admitted joyfully.

"And working your hands and shaking the life out of yourself," she pursued, mimicking his gestures.

"No, I was not—may I not live till tomorrow if I was," he protested vehemently, with a touch of resentment. "Oh, it is so nice to be there! I never knew there were so many Gentile books in the world at all. I wonder what they are all about. Only I am so troubled about my English." He interrupted himself, with a distressed air. "When I asked them for the book, and how to get it, they could not understand me."

"I can understand everything you say when you speak English. You're all right," she comforted him. His troubled, childlike smile and his shining clear blue eyes, as he spoke, went to her heart.

"You can, but other people can't. I so wish I could speak it like you, Flora. Do read a page or two with me, will you? I'll get my Reader—shall I?"

"What's your hurry? Can't you wait?

He could not wait. He was in a fever of impatience to inhale the whole of the Gentile language—definitions, spelling, pronunciation, and all—with one desperate effort. It was the one great impediment that seemed to stand between him and the enchanted new world that had revealed itself to him.

"Oh, do hear me read—may you live long, Flora! It somehow draws me as with a kind of impure force. Will you?"

"All right," she yielded, with kindly curiosity at the fervor of his request, and feeling flattered.

He had been reading perhaps a quarter of an hour when he grew absent-minded.

"You must have skipped a line again," she said, in an awkward undertone.

"Oh, yes!"

They were seated at a respectful distance, with the corner of the marble table between them, her full, well-modeled bust erect and stately against the pier-glass. She wore a waist of dark-blue silk, trimmed with red, and there was a red ribbon in her shock of inky hair. Presently she leaned forward to see a mispronounced word for herself. Their heads found themselves close together. Her ivory cheek almost touched his.

"Where is it?" she questioned, under her breath.

He made no reply. His glance was riveted to her raven eyelashes. A dash of scarlet lurking under her chin dazed his brain. After a slight pause he said, as he timidly stroked her burning cheek: "It is so smooth!"

She had an impulse to withdraw her face, but felt benumbed. He went on patting her, until, meeting with no resistance, his lips touched her cheek, in a gingerly kiss. Both lowered their eyes. They were silent, but their hearts, each conscious of the other's beatings, throbbed wildly.

"Bad boy!" she then whispered, without raising her head.

After another silence, as their eyes met, they burst into a subdued nervous titter.

"You must not do that again," she said. "Is this the kind of pious man you are?"

"Don't say that, Flora—pray don't. You know it hurts my feelings when you speak like that," he implored her. And impelled by the embarrassed, affectionate sadness of her mien, he seized her hand and fell to kissing first her fingers and then her eyes, as though beseeching them to reveal the meaning of their somber look. Their lips met and clung together in a trance of passion. When they parted Shaya felt ten years older, and as his eye fell upon the bookcase, he wondered what those glittering, massive tomes were doing there.

"Will you tell your father that you want to be my sweetheart?" he asked after a while.

His voice and his features appeared to her in a novel aspect.

"How do you know I do?" she said, with playful defiance, hiding a burst of admiration which was lost upon the unworldly young man.

"Why—don't you?" he demanded solicitously.

Then, a sudden light of inspiration coming in her eyes, Flora said, "Hol' on! How would you like to be a doctor, Shayie?"

"But your father would turn me out if I began to study for it."

She grew thoughtful. "But suppose he had no objection?" she queried, her bashfulness suddenly returning to her face.

"Oh, then I should be dying to study doctor books—any kind of Gentile books you wanted me to, Flora. But Reb Asriel won't let me."

"Listen! Can you keep a secret?" she asked like a conspiring little schoolgirl.

"You mean about your being my sweetheart?"

"No!" she rejoined impatiently. "I mean the other thing—your studyin'. Papa needn't get wind of it till it's too late—you understand? If you are smart, we can fix that."

"That's all right. I am awful clever at keeping a secret," he boasted.

"Well, I want you to be a doctor, Shayie," she resumed, with matronly tenderness. "If you are, I'll care for you, and you'll be my birdie boy, an' all; if not, you won't. Oh, won't it be lovely when everybody knows that you go to college and study together with nice, educated uptown fellows! We would go to theaters together and read different books. You'll make a daisy of a college boy, too—you bet. Would you like to wear a high hat, and spec's, and ride in a buggy with a driver? Would you, would you, bad boy, you? Hello, Doctor Golub! How are you?"

She presented her lips, and they kissed again and again.

"You know what, Shayie?[48] When papa comes I'll go out somewheres, so you can tell him—you know what I mean. It'll make it so much easier to fool him. Will you tell him?"

"I am ashamed."

"I won't tell him."

"Don't be angry—I will. I shall always do everything you tell me, Flora," he said, looking into her black gleaming eyes—"always, always!" And in the exuberance of his delight he once again felt himself a little boy, and broke out into a masterly imitation of the crow of a cock, jumping up and flapping his arms for a pair of wings.

When Asriel and Shaya were alone in the parlor, the young man said, as he fell to wringing his index finger, "Flora wants me to tell you that she is satisfied."

"Satisfied with what?" the old man demanded, leaping to his feet.

"To be my sweetheart."

"Is she? Did she say so? When? Tamara!" he yelled, rushing downstairs and dragging the prodigy along, "Tamara! May you live long! The Uppermost has taken pity upon me after all. Floraly has come around—blessed be the Uppermost."

"Blessed be the Uppermost!" Tamara echoed, her pleasant, swarthy face beaming with heartfelt delight. "When He wills, walls of iron must give way. It is a divine match—any one can see it is. May they live a hundred and twenty years together. Mazol-tov!"

"Mazol-tov to you and to all of us," Asriel responded. "But where is Flora? Fetch some drink, Tamara."

He stepped up to the "Wonder-worker box," and deposited a silver coin for the support of the pilgrims at Palestine, saying as he did so: "I thank and praise thee, O Lord of the Universe, for thy mercy toward me. Mayest Thou grant the children long years, and keep up in Shaya his love for thy sacred Law. You know the match is all of your own making, and you must take care of it. I am only your slave, that's all."

IX

"Is Shayaly in?" inquired old Asriel on entering Flora's room one morning in midsummer. It was four months after his daughter's betrothment to the Talmudist had been celebrated by a solemn ceremony and a sumptuous feast, the wedding having been set for a later date. The crowning glory of his achievement Stroon postponed, like a rare bottle of wine, for some future day. He dreaded to indulge himself in such a rapid succession of This World joys lest he might draw upon his Share in the World-to-come. Will the Uppermost let him live to

[48]Shayie, like Floraly below, is an affectionate nickname.

see his daughter and the "holy child," standing side by side under the Canopy? Asriel was now confident that He would. "Is Shayaly in?"

"Of course he is—papa," Flora answered, raising her face from her book. Her "papa" was added aloud, and as if upon afterthought.

The parlor door stood ajar. Asriel stationed himself near by and listened to the young man's habitual singsong. The old man's face gradually became radiant with bliss.

"My crown, my Messiah, my Kaddish! My Share in the World-to-come!" he muttered.

"Did you have breakfast, papa?" Flora demanded, speaking still louder than before.

At this moment Shaya's singsong broke out with fresh enthusiasm and his Hebrew words became distinct. Asriel waved her away fiercely. After a little he remarked in a subdued voice, as he pointed to the front parlor,—

"*This* is my breakfast. This is for the soul, my child; the worms of the grave cannot touch it, and you take it along to the other world. Everything else is a lot of rubbish."

He made to leave, but could not help pausing, in fresh admiration, and then, softly opening the parlor door he entered the sanctum, on tiptoe, in order to feast his eye as well as his ear on the thrilling scene. He found Shaya rapturously swaying and singing over a Talmud volume. Flora watched her father with roguish delight.

"I am afraid I must not be gloating over him like this," Asriel rebuked himself in his heart. "I may give him the evil eye." When he regained the back parlor he said, under his breath: "Floraly, I am afraid your company may disturb him sometimes. A pretty sweetheart is apt to stir a fellow's brains, you know, and take him away from the Law. He had better study more at the synagogues."

The girl blushed to her charcoal hair and dropped her glance. But her father had scarcely gained his room, on the floor above, when she flew into the front parlor with a ringing giggle.

"Now you can go right on, dearie," she said, encircling Shaya's neck with one arm, and producing with the other an English textbook on Natural Philosophy, which had lain open under the huge Hebrew volume.

"You heard me holler, didn't you?"

"Of course I did," Shaya answered beamingly. "He interrupted me in the middle of such a cunning explanation!"

"Did he? What was it about? All about sounds—the same as before?"

"Yes, but it is even more brainy than what I told you."

He proceeded to expound, in Yiddish, what he had been reading on Acoustics, she listening to his enthusiastic popularization with docile, loving inattention.

The young man made a pretense of spending his afternoons, and sometimes also mornings, at the various synagogues of the Jewish quarter. His proud guardian encouraged this habit, in order that his "daughter's bridegroom" might disseminate his sacred knowledge among other congregations than his own. "Your learning is the gift of God, Shayaly," he would say, "and you needn't be ashamed to peddle it around. Reb Lippe said America wanted a man like you to spread the holy Law here. Go and do it, my son, and the Uppermost will help us all for your sake."

The prodigy and his importer were the talk of the orthodox colony, and nothing was more pleasing to Asriel than to hear the praises of his daughter's fiancé sounded by the Talmudists. There came a time, however, when, in his own synagogue, at least, these encomiums ceased. Asriel missed them keenly and pestered the learned men of the congregation with incessant talks about Shaya, for the purpose of worrying out some acknowledgment of his phenomenal talents. But the concession was mostly made in a half-hearted way, and poor Asriel would be left hungrier than ever. Particularly was his heart longing for the warm eulogies of Reb Tzalel, a poor, sickly old peddler, who was considered one of the most pious and learned men in the neighborhood. Asriel liked the man for his nervous sincerity and uncompromising self-respect. He often asked him to his house, but the tattered, underfed peddler invariably declined the invitation.

"What will I do there, Reb Asriel?" he would say, with the pained sort of smile which would light up his ghastly old face whenever he spoke. "Look at your costly carpet and furniture, and bear in mind that you are a landlord and I a poor peddler! At the synagogue I like you better, for here we are equals. Saith the verse in the Book of Job: 'Whereas He is one that shows no favor to chieftains, and distinguishes not the rich before the indigent, for all of them are the work of his hands.'" Reb Tzalel translated the verse into Yiddish for the benefit of his listener, whereupon Asriel felt a much wealthier man than he was, and at the same time he had a sense of humiliation, as though his money were something to be ashamed of.

This man's unusual reticence on the point of Shaya's merits chagrined Asriel sorely, and his mind even began to be troubled by some vague misgivings on that score.

One evening Asriel sat by Reb Tzalel's side in the study rooms of his synagogue. It was in the latter part of November, and Shaya's wedding was to take place during the Feast of Hanuccah,[49] some few weeks later. The evening services, which on week days were held in these rooms, were over, and the "learners" could now give themselves to their divine studies undisturbed, save for the possible and unwelcome advent of some belated Ten Worshipers. The two spacious, dingy rooms, their connecting doors wide open, were dimly lighted with candles placed upon the plain long deal tables ranged against their discolored walls. The open bookcases were filled with dilapidated old volumes, many more being in use or strewn about, in chaotic heaps, on the tables, benches, or window sills.

In one room, around one of the long tables, were gathered the members of the daily Mishnah[50] class. There were about a dozen of them, mostly poor peddlers or artisans—a humble, seedy, pitiable lot, come after a hard day's work or freezing, to "take a holy word into their mouths." Hardly one of these was up to the Gemarah[51] part of the Talmud, and even the Mishnah only few could brave single-handed. They sat at their open books following their voluntary teacher, a large, heavy, middle-aged man—a mass of unkempt beard, flesh, and rags, ablaze with the intellectual fury of his enormous black eyes. He was reading aloud, with ferocious appetite, swaying and jerking his disheveled bulk, as he ever and anon tossed up his head to interpret the Mishnah to his pupils, and

[49]Hanukkah: an eight-day festival that falls in December, commemorating the Temple in Jerusalem.

[50]The first section of the Talmud.

[51]A section of the Talmud featuring rabbinical commentaries.

every little while breaking off in the middle of a sentence, or even a word, to let his class shout the other half as a guaranty of proficiency. Some of his listeners plodded along the lines of their books, in humble silence, with their index fingers for fescues; the brighter ones boldly interrupted the ponderous man, joyously anticipating his explanations or pointing out some discrepancy; one old dissembler repeated unintelligible half-sentences with well-acted gusto; another little old fellow betrayed the fog in his mind by timid nods of assent, while still another was bravely kept from dozing off on his holy book by frequent neighborly nudges from the man next him. Standing behind the members of the class were some envying "boors," like our poor Asriel, to whom even the Mishnah was a luxury beyond their intellectual means.

One of the long tables in the adjoining room was covered with the open folios of the daily Gemarah class—some fifteen men of all ages and economical conditions from the doddering apple-vender, to whom the holy books are the only source of pleasure in this life as well as in the other, to the well-fed, overdressed young furniture-dealer, with whom the Talmud is a second nature, contracted in the darker days of his existence in Russia. There were several "keen brains" in the group, and a former "prodigy" or two, like Shaya. The class needed no guide, but one old man with a boyish face framed in snow-white hair, and wearing a sea of unstarched linen collar about his emaciated neck, was their chosen reader. He also left many sentences unuttered, but he did it merely because he thought them too well-known to need repetition. Whenever he had something to add to the text, he would address himself to the man by his side, snapping his fingers at him genially, and at times all but pinching him for ecstasy. The others participated now by a twirl of a finger, now by the swift repetition of a whole syllogism, now by an indescribable system of gestures, enacting, in dumb show, the whole logical process involved in a nice point. All at once the whole class would burst into a bedlam of voices and gesticulations. When the whirlwind of enthusiasm subsided, it might be followed by a bit of pleasantry from the exuberance of good spirits at having got the better of a difficult point—and upon the whole the motley company looked like a happy family at the Sabbath table.

The other long tables in both rooms were occupied by *lomdim,*[52] each intent upon the good deed of studying "for study's sake" by himself: some humming to their musty folios melodiously; others smiling and murmuring to them, like a fond mother to her babe; still others wailing or grumbling or expostulating with their books, or slapping them and yelling for delight, or roaring like a lion in a cage. A patriarch teaching his ten-year-old grandson and both shouting at the top of their voices, in an entanglement of pantomime; a swarthy little grammar-school boy going it on his own hook over a volume bigger than himself; a "fine householder" in reduced circumstances dignifiedly swinging his form and twirling his sidelock as if he were confiding a secret to his immense golden beard; one or two of the hollow-voiced *prooshim,* who had come to America in search of fortune, but who were now supported by the congregation for giving all their time to "the law and the service"; a knot of men engaged in a mixed discussion of "words of laws and "words of every-day life"—all these voices and murmurs mingled in one effervescence of the sublime and the ridiculous, with tragedy for a keynote—twenty centuries thrown pellmell in a chaos of sound and motion.

[52]Learned men.

Asriel could have lived on the spectacle, and although unable to participate in it himself, he now, since the advent of the prodigy, looked upon it as a world in which he was not without a voice. He was seated in a remote corner of the Gemarah room, now watching the noisy scenes with open-mouthed reverence, now turning to admire Reb Tzalel by his side. The cadaverous face and burning eyes of the peddler were sneering at the drab-colored page before him, while his voice sounded melancholy, like a subdued bugle call.

Presently Reb Tzalel paused, and the two engaged in converse. As Asriel was boasting of Shaya's genius and kindliness of disposition, vainly courting his friend for a word of assent, the peddler, suddenly reddening in the face, interrupted him:

"What's the use of playing cat and rat, Mr. Stroon?" he burst out with his ghastly smile. "I may as well tell you what lies like a heavy stone on my heart. Your Shaya is going to the bad. He is an *appikoros*."[53]

"An appikoros!" Asriel demanded, as if the word had suddenly acquired a new meaning.

"Yes, an appikoros, and a Jeroboam[54] the son of Nebat—he sins, and leads others to sin," the Talmudist declared tartly. "I hated to cause you the pain, Mr. Stroon, but he has gone too far in Gentile books, and when he is here and you are not about he talks to everybody he can get hold of concerning the way the world swings around the sun, how rain and thunder, day and night—everything—can be explained as a matter of common sense, and that there is no God in heaven, and all that sort of vile stuff that you hear from every appikoros—may they all be hurled from one end of the world to the other! Everything can be explained—may the Angel of Death explain it to them, may they—"

"Hold on, Reb Tzalel!" Asriel shouted: "You need not curse him: you don't feed him, do you? And what you say is a lie!—as big a lie as Og[55] the King of Bashan!" he concluded with calm ferocity, raising his burly figure from the bench.

"A lie, is it? Very well, then—you shall know all. Little Mendele saw your imported decoration smoking a cigarette last Sabbath."

"Shaya smoke on the Sabbath!" Asriel echoed. The practical, concrete nature of this sin came home to him with a more forceful blow than all the peddler had said about Shaya's ungodly theories. "Begone!" the surrounding chaos seemed to say to the "boor." "From now on you have nothing to do here!"

"Shaya smoke a cigarette on the Sabbath!" he repeated. "Well, and I have this to say, that Mendele, and yourself, and the whole lot of you are nothing but a set of first-class liars and begrudging gossip-mongers. It must give him a belly-ache to think that he could not afford such a bridegroom for his girl and that I could. Well, I have got a prodigy for my daughter and he has licked the whole lot of you learned fellows to ground coffee. I have got him—see?—and let all my enemies and the boy's enemies burst for envy." He clicked his tongue and snapped his fingers, and for a moment stood glaring witheringly at his interlocutor.

"Well, I am not going to argue with a boor," said Reb Tzalel, in utter disgust.

His words were drowned in the noise, but the "boor" reached Asriel's ear and touched him on the raw. "Shut up, Reb Tzalel!" he said, paling.

[53]Apostate; atheist. [54]A king of Israel. His story is told in Book of Kings I.
[55]A king of the Amorites, defeated and killed by Moses and his followers.

"Why should I? This is not your house. It is God's dwelling. Here I am richer than you. I only wanted to say that it is not you I pity. You have been a boor, and that's what you are and will be. But the boy was about to become a great man in Israel, and you have brought him over here for bedeviled America to turn him into an appikoros. Woe! woe! woe!"

"Keep still, Reb Tzalel; take pity," Asriel implored, in a squeaking voice. "Don't spill any salt over my wounds. Forgive me—you know I am a boor. Do take pity and say no more; but all you have said—they have said—is a lie—the cholera choke me if it is not." And gasping for breath, he ran out of the synagogue.

When he found himself in the street he was conscious of some terrific blow having just been dealt him, but did not clearly realize its full meaning; and what had transpired a minute before, between him and Reb Tzalel, seemed to have occurred in the remote past. The clamor of the street peddlers, and the whole maze of squalor and noise through which he was now scurrying, he appeared to hear and to view at a great distance, as if it all were on the other side of a broad river, he hurrying on his lonely way along the deserted bank opposite.

"An appikoros! an appikoros!" he said to himself, vainly trying to grasp the meaning of the word which he knew but too well. "An appikoros, smoking on the Sabbath!" The spectacle smote him in cold blood. "Shaya smoke on the holy Sabbath! It's a lie!"

He started in the direction of Mendele's residence, bent upon thrashing the red-haired talebearer to death. Soon, however, he halted and turned homeward. The courage failed Asriel Stroon to face the man who had seen his daughter's fiancé smoke a cigarette on a Saturday. Then Shaya appeared to his mind as something polluted, sacrilegious, and although this something had nothing in common with his beloved prodigy, save the name, and the young man whitened in the distance, pure and lovely as ever, Asriel's rage surged in the direction of his home, and he mended pace to storm the house as soon as he could get there.

When he collected his wits he decided to wait till he found out everything for himself. For the first time, perhaps, he felt himself a coward. He quailed before the thought that what he had heard from the learned peddler might prove true, and he cringingly begged his own mind to put off the culminating agony of believing it.

Nevertheless, when he saw Shaya, at the supper table, his heart whispered to him, in dismay: "An appikoros!" and the unuttered word enveloped the prodigy in a forbidding, sinister atmosphere.

He now hated Shaya; he felt as though he feared him.

"Where have you been so late, papa?" Flora inquired.

"Deep in the earth. You care much where your papa is, do you?" he snarled.

"Papa!" she said deprecatingly; "are you mad?"

He made no response.

"Have you been to the Mariv service?" Shaya intervened. "I studied at the Souvalk Synagogue today."

Asriel remained grimly uncommunicative.

The young people, reinforced by Tamara, made several other attempts at conversation, but the dogged taciturnity of the head of the family cast a spell of misery over them all, and the meal passed in unsupportable silence.

"See if papa ain't getting on to what you are doing, Shayie," Flora said, when the two were alone.

"Pshaw! is it the first time you see him out of humor? He must have had some trouble with a tenant or janitor."

"He must have," she assented gloomily. "But what if he gets wind? I'm worrying the life out of myself about it."

"So am I. I love your father just the same as if he were my own papa. I wish the wedding were over, don't you?" he asked in his childish way.

X

On the following morning Asriel repaired to the Souvalk Synagogue to attend the service (his usual place of worship he had not the heart to visit), and, incidentally, to ascertain how Shaya had spent his time there the day before.

To his consternation he learned that his "daughter's bridegroom" had not been seen there for weeks.

Asriel held his counsel, and took to shadowing the young man.

He now had no doubt as to the accuracy of Reb Tzalel's story. But it gave him no pain. It was Shaya no longer; it was not his daughter's bridegroom; it was not the prodigy he had imported—it was an appikoros. But then Asriel's heart withered at the notion of being the victim of systematic deception. Shaya was an appikoros and a secret, sneaking enemy.

"That youngster trick Asriel Stroon!" He panted with hatred and thrilled with a detective-like passion to catch Shaya in the act of some grave violation of the Mosaic Law.

He went about the various synagogues where the young man was supposed to study the Talmud, with a keen foretaste of his vicious joy at finding that he had been playing truant. Yet each time his fervent expectations were realized he would, instead of triumph, experience an overpowering sense of defeat.

"You have been cheated out of your boots by a stripling, Asrielke—woe to your foolish head!" he tortured himself, reveling in an agony of fury. "Ah, a cholera into him! I'll show him how to fool Asriel Stroon!"

He discovered that Shaya's frequent companion was his former teacher of English, whom he often visited in his attic room on Clinton Street, and he impatiently awaited the next Saturday to raid the atheistic resort and to overtake Shaya smoking or writing on the holy day. But the climax came a day or two sooner.

After tracing Shaya to the Clinton Street house Asriel stood waiting around a corner, at a vantage point from which he could see the windows of the two garret rooms one of which was the supposed scene of the young man's ungodly pursuits. He had no definite purpose in view, for it was not Sabbath, and he would not spoil his game by apprehending his man in the mere act of reading Gentile books. Yet he was rooted to the place, and remained aimlessly waiting, with his eyes riveted to the windows which they could not penetrate. Tired at last, and overcome with a sense of having been engaged in a fool's errand, he returned home, and, reaching his bedroom, sank on the bed in a prostration of hurt pride and impotent rage.

On the following morning he returned to his post. The attic windows drew him like the evil one, as he put it to himself.

He had been keeping watch for some minutes when, to his fierce joy, Shaya and his accomplice sallied forth into the street. He dogged their steps to Grand

Street, and thence, through the Bowery, to Lafayette Place, where they disappeared behind the massive doors of an imposing structure, apparently neither a dwelling place nor an office building.

"Dis a choych?" Asriel asked a passerby.

"A church? No, it's a library—the Astor Library," the stranger explained.

"Ah, a lot of Gentile books!" he exclaimed to himself, disappointed in one way and triumphant in another. The accustomed neighborhood and the novelty of his impressions increased the power of the "evil one" over him. He took up a position whence he could observe without being observed, and waited for the two young men to come out. What he would gain by tracing them back to the Jewish quarter he never asked himself. He waited because the "evil one" would not let him stir from the spot.

An hour passed. He was growing faint with hunger; yet he never moved. "He has not had his lunch, either," he thought. "Still, he can stand it. It's the witchcraft of the Gentile books—may he be burned to death!—keeping up his strength. They'll come out in a minute or two."

Many more minutes elapsed, and still Asriel waited. At last "Here, they are, the convert Jews! Look at them—how jolly! It's the Black Year shining out of their faces—may they shine on their death-beds! That beggar of a teacher I shall have arrested."

He followed them through Fourth Street back to the Bowery and down the rumbling thoroughfare, till—"a lamentation!" they entered a Christian restaurant!

A terrific pang smote Asriel's heart. It was as if he saw his temple, the embodiment of many years of labor, the object of his fondest cares, just completed and ready to be dedicated, suddenly enveloped in flames. The prodigy, *his* prodigy, his Kaddish, his glory in this and the other world, plunged into the very thick of impurity!

He made to rush after them, but checked himself to wait till the treife [unclean] food was served them. A few minutes later he made his entry, cool and collected as a regular customer.

Each of the two young men was bent on a veal cutlet. The collegian was dispatching his with the nonchalant appetite and ease of manner of an habitué,[56] whereas poor Shaya looked like one affecting to relish his first plate of raw oysters. The smells proceeding from the kitchen made him dizzy, and the cutlet itself, partly because he was accustomed to meat of a better quality, but mainly through the consciousness of eating treife, inclined him to nausea.

Asriel took a vacant chair at the same table.

"Bless the sitter,[57] Shaya!" he said.

The two young men were petrified.

"How is the pork—does it taste well?" Asriel pursued.

"It is not pork. It is veal cutlet," the teacher found tongue to retort.

"I am not speaking to you, am I?" Asriel hissed out. Murder was swelling in his heart. But at this point the waiter came up to his side.

"Vot'll ye have?"

"Notink!" Asriel replied, suddenly rising from his seat and rushing out, as if this were the most terrible sort of violence he could conceive.

[56]Someone accustomed to the place. [57]A traditional greeting to the host at his table.

XI

Asriel found his daughter playing.

"Stop that or I'll smash your Gentile piano to pieces!" he commanded her, feeling as though the instrument had all along been in the conspiracy and were now bidding him defiance.

"Why, what's the matter?" she questioned, getting up from her stool in stupefaction.

"Matter? Bluff a dead rooster, not me—my head is still on my shoulders. Here it is, you see?" he added, taking himself by the head. "It's all up, Flora."

"What do you mean?" she made out to inquire.

"I mean that if Shayke[58] ever enters this house I'll murder both of you. You thought your papa was a fool, didn't you? Well, you are a poor hand at figuring, Flora. I knew everything, but I wanted some particulars. I have got them all now here, in my pocket, and a minute ago I took the pleasure of bidding him 'bless the sitter' in a Gentile restaurant—may he be choked with his treife gorge!"

"You've got no business to curse him like that!" she flamed out, coloring violently.

"*I* have no business? And who is to stop me, pray?"

"*I* am. It ain't my fault. You know I did not care at first."

The implication that he had only himself to blame threw him into a new frenzy. But he restrained himself, and said with ghastly deliberation: "Flora, you are not going to marry him."

"I *am*. I can't live without him," she declared with quiet emphasis.

Asriel left her room.

"It's all gone, Tamara! My candle is blown out," he said, making his way from the dining room to the kitchen. "There is no Shaya any longer."

"A weeping, a darkness to me! Has an accident—mercy and peace!—befallen the child?"

"Yes, he is 'dead and buried, and gone from the market place.' Worse than that: a convert Jew is worse than a dead one. It's all gone, Tamara!" he repeated gravely. "I have just seen him eating treife in a Gentile restaurant. America has robbed me of my glory."

"Woe is me!" the housekeeper gasped, clutching at her wig. "Treife! Does he not get enough to eat here?" She then burst out, "Don't I serve him the best food there is in the world? Any king would be glad to get such dinners."

"Well, it seems treife tastes better," Asriel rejoined bitterly. "A calamity upon my sinful head! We must have evil-eyed the child; we have devoured him with our admiring looks."

While Asriel was answering her volley of questions, Flora stealthily left the house.

When Stroon missed her he hurried off to Clinton Street. There he learned of the landlady that her lodger had left a short while before, in the company of his friend and a young lady whom the two young men had found waiting in her parlor. In his despair Asriel betook himself to the Astor Library, to some of Flora's friends, and even to the Bowery restaurant.

[58]A contemptuous form of Shaya's name.

When he reached home, exhausted with fatigue and rage, he found his daughter in her room.

"Where have you been?" he demanded, sternly.

"I'll tell you where, but don't aggravate yourself, papaly," she replied in beseeching, tearful accents.

"Where have you been?"

"I am going to tell you, but don't blame Shaya. He is awful fond of you. It's all my fault. He didn't want to go, but I couldn't help it, papaly. We've been to the city court and got married by a judge. Shaya didn't want to.

"You married!"

"Yes, but don't be angry, papaly darlin'. We'll do everything to please you. If you don't want him to be a doctor, he won't."

"A doctor!" he resumed, still speaking like one in a daze. "Is that what you have been up to? I see—you have got the best of me, after all. You married, Flora?" he repeated, unable to apply the meaning of the word to his daughter. "In court—without Canopy and Dedication—like Gentiles? What have you done, Flora?" He sank into a chair, gnashing his teeth and tearing at his sidelocks.

"Papaly, papaly, don't!" she sobbed, hugging and kissing him. "You know I ain't to blame for it all."

It dawned upon him that no serious wrong had been committed, after all, and that it could all be mended by a Jewish marriage ceremony; and so great was his relief at the thought that it took away all his anger, and he even felt as if he were grateful to his daughter for not being guilty of a graver transgression than she was.

"I know you are not to blame," he said, tragic in his calmness. "America has done it all. But what is the use talking! It's gone, and I am not going to take another sin upon my soul. I won't let you be his wife without Canopy and Dedication. Let the Jewish wedding come off at once—this week—tomorrow. You have got the best of me and I don't kick, do I? It seems God does not want Asrielke the boor to have some joy in his old age, nor a Kaddish for his soul, when the worms will be feasting upon his silly bones—"

"Oh, don't say that, papa. It'll break my heart if you do. You know Shaya is as good as a son to you."

"An appikoros my son? An appikoros my Kaddish? No," he rejoined, shaking his head pensively.

As he said it he felt as if Flora, too, were a stranger to him. He descended to the basement in a state of mortal indifference. "I have lost everything, Tamara," he said. "I have no daughter, either. I am all alone in the world—alone as a stone."

He had no sooner closed the kitchen door behind him, than Flora was out and away to Clinton Street to surprise her bridegroom with the glad news of her father's surrender.

The housekeeper was in the kitchen, sewing upon some silk vestments for the scrolls of her synagogue. Asriel stood by her side, leaning against the cupboard door, in front of the Palestine box. Speaking in a bleak, resigned undertone, he told her of Flora's escapade and of his determination to make the best of it by precipitating the Jewish ceremony. A gorgeous celebration was now, of course, out of the question. The proposed fête which was to have been the talk of the synagogues and which had been the center of his sweetest dreams had suddenly turned in his imagination to something like a funeral feast. Tamara bade him be of good cheer, and cited Rabbi Nochum And-This-Too, who would hail the severest blows of fate with the words: "And this, too, is for the best." But Asriel would not be comforted.

"Yes, Tamara, it is gone, all gone," he murmured forlornly. "It was all a dream—a last year's lemon pie. It has flown away and you can't catch it. Gone, and that's all. You know how I feel? As if some fellow had played a joke on me."

The pious woman was moved.

"But it is a sin to take things so close to heart," she said impetuously. "You must take care of your health. Bear up under your affliction like a righteous Jew, Reb Asriel. Trust to the Uppermost, and you will live to rejoice in your child and in her children, if God be pleased."

Asriel heaved a sigh and fell silent. He stood with his eyes upon the pilgrim box, listening to the whisper of her needle.

"You know what; let us go to the Land of Israel," he presently said, as though continuing an interrupted sentence. "They have got the best of me. I cannot change the world. Let them live as they please and be responsible to the Uppermost for themselves. I don't care the kernel of a hollow nut. I shall give Flora half my property and the rest I'll sell. You are a righteous woman, Tamara. Why not marry and end our days serving God in the Holy Land together?"

Tamara plied her needle with redoubled zeal. He could see only her glossy black wig and the flaming dusk of her cheek.

"We'll have a comfortable living and plenty of money for deeds of charity," he pursued. "I know I am only a boor. Do I say I am not? But is a boor no human being at all? Can't I die a righteous Jew?" he pleaded piteously.

The glossy wig bent lower and the silk rustled busily.

"You know that I have on my tongue what I have on my lung, Tamara. I mean what I say, and we want no matchmakers. America is now treife to me. I can't show my head. The world is dark and empty to me. All is gone, gone, gone. I am a little baby, Tamara. Come, take pity. I shall see Flora married according to the laws of Moses and Israel, and then let us put up a canopy and set out on our journey. I want to be born again. Well?"

There was no response.

"Well, Tamara?"

"Since it is the will of God," she returned resignedly, without raising her head from the vestments.

XII

Flora was all of a flutter with impatience to share her joy with Shaya, and yearning for his presence. She had not seen him since he had become her legal husband, and the two or three hours seemed a week.

When the German landlady of the little Clinton Street house told her that neither her lodger nor his friend were in the attic room the young woman's heart sank within her. Her message seemed to be bubbling over and her overwrought mind too weak to bear it another minute. She mentally berated her absent bridegroom, and not knowing whither to bend her steps in quest of him she repaired to some girl friends to while away the time and to deliver herself of part of her burden to them.

"When he comes tell him he da's[59] not leave for one second till I come back. Tell him I've got some grand news for him," she instructed the landlady, struggling hard against a wild temptation to unbosom herself to the stranger.

It was about eight o'clock when she returned. Shaya met her in the hallway. "Well?" he inquired anxiously.

"Well?" she mocked him. "You are a daisy! Why didn't you wait? Couldn't you guess I'd come?"

"How should I? But tell me what your father says. Why should you torment me?"

"He says he don't want you," she replied. But her look told even a more encouraging tale than the one she had to deliver, and they flew into mutual embrace in an outburst of happiness which seemed to both of them unlike any they had ever experienced before.

"A life into your little eyes! A health into your little hands and feet!" he muttered, stroking her arm sheepishly. "You shall see how fine it will all come out. You don't know me yet. I tell you you don't begin to know me," he kept repeating with some braggadocio and without distinctly knowing what he meant.

They were to return home at once and to try to pacify Asriel as best they could. When Flora pressed him to take his hat and overcoat, however, he looked reluctant and then said:

"Floraly, you know what; come upstairs for just one minute. We are reading the nicest book you ever saw, and there is a lot of such nice gentlemen there!—several genuine Americans—Christians. Do come, Floraly." He drew her up the two flights of stairs almost by force. "Don't be afraid: the landlady knows all about it," he whispered. "You'll see what nice people. I tell you they are so educated, and they love Jews so much! A Jew is the same as a Gentile to them—even better."

Flora felt a lump growing in her heart. The notion of Shaya being at this minute interested in anything outside of herself and their mutual happiness literally dazed her, and before she had time to recover from her shock she was in the over-crowded attic.

There were some ten or twelve men in the room, some seated—two on chairs, two on the host's trunk, and three on his bed—the others standing by the window or propping the sloping wall with their heads. They were clustered about a round table, littered with books, papers, and cigarette stumps. A tin can was hissing on the flat top of a little parlor stove, and some of the company were sipping Russian tea from tumblers, each with a slice of lemon floating in it. The group was made up of a middle-aged man with a handsome and intensely intellectual Scotch face, who was a laborer by day and a philosopher by night; a Swedish tailor with the face of a Catholic priest; a Zurich Ph.D. in blue eyeglasses; a young Hindoo who eked out a wretched existence by selling first-rate articles to second-rate weeklies, and several Russian Jews, all of them insatiable debaters and most of them with university or gymnasium diplomas. The group met every Thursday to read and discuss Harriet Martineau's "Auguste Comte,"[60] under the guidance of the Scotchman, who was a leading spirit in positivist circles.

[59]Dares.

[60]A very highly regarded English translation (1853) by Harriet Martineau (1802–1876) of the work of French philosopher Auguste Comte (1798–1857).

The philosopher surrendered his chair to the lady, in a flurry of chivalry, but a seat was made for him on the trunk, and he forthwith resumed his reading with well-bred impetuosity, the kerosene lamp in the center of the table casting a halo upon his frank, pleasant face.

His auditors were now listening with conscious attention, some of the younger men affecting an absorbed mien or interrupting the reader with unnecessary questions. Shaya's eyes were traveling between Flora and the Scotchman's audience. "Did you ever see such a beautiful and stylish young lady?" he seemed to be saying. "She is my bride—mine and nobody else's in the world," and, "Look at these great men, Flora—I am their chum." Presently, however, he became engrossed in the reading; and only half-conscious of Flora's presence, he sat leaning forward, his mouth wide open, his face rapt, and his fingers quietly reproducing the mental gymnastics of Comte's system in the air.

The young woman gazed about her in perplexity. The Scotchman and his reading inspired her with respect, but the rest of the company and the *tout ensemble*[61] of the scene impressed her as the haunt of queer individuals, meeting for some sinister purpose. It was anything but the world of intellectual and physical elegance into which she had dreamed to be introduced by marriage to a doctor. Any society of "custom peddlers" was better dressed than these men, who appeared to her more like some of the grotesque and uncouth characters in Dickens's novels than an assemblage of educated people. For a moment even Shaya seemed a stranger and an enemy. Overcome by the stuffy, overheated atmosphere of the misshapen apartment, she had a sense of having been kidnapped into the den of some terrible creatures, and felt like crying for help. Next she was wondering what her Shaya could have in common with these shabby beings and what it all had to do with becoming a doctor and riding in a buggy.

"Shaya!" she whispered, tugging him by the coat-sleeve.

"Just one moment, Floraly," he begged her. "Ah, it's so deep!"

A discussion engaged itself. The Russians fell to greedily. One of them, in particular, a young man with a dignified bass, was hateful to Flora. She could not have told you why, but his voice, coupled with the red embroidery of his Little-Russian shirt front, cut her to the quick.

The room was full of smoke and broken English.

Shaya was brimful of arguments and questions which he had not the courage to advance; and so he sat, now making a vehement gesture of despair at somebody else's absurdities, now nodding violent approval, and altogether fidgeting about in a St. Vitus's dance[62] of impotent pugnacity.[63]

"Shaya, it is getting late, and papa—"

"One second, do please, Floraly, may you live long," he implored her, with some irritation; and taking the book from the Scotchman's hand, he fell to turning over its leaves in a feverish search of what struck him as a misinterpreted passage.

Flora was going to protest and to threaten to leave without him, but she could neither speak nor stir from her seat. A nightmare of desolation and jealousy choked her—jealousy of the Scotchman's book, of the Little-Russian shirt, of the empty tea-glasses with the slices of lemon on their bottoms, of the whole excited crowd, and of Shaya's entire future, from which she seemed excluded.

1898

[61]Totality. [62]A disease characterized by involuntary jerking movements.
[63]Quarrelsomeness.

Edith Wharton 1862–1937

Henry James, a close friend of her later years, called Edith Wharton "an angel of devastation"; a more respectful public has come to regard her as the grande dame *of American letters. She was, like Henry James, born into a wealthy and privileged society whose character she unflinchingly recorded in her fiction. The daughter of one of New York's oldest families, she was christened Edith Newbold Jones and raised in a manner suited to her elevated class. She was educated at home by tutors and taken for extended tours abroad, where she acquired her lifelong admiration for European art and culture. From her family and their friends she absorbed the social ideals and the prejudices that characterized the genteel society into which she was born and in which she was destined to move throughout her life.*

In 1885, after her formal "coming out," Edith Jones married Edward Wharton, a decorous gentleman from a wealthy Boston family. Although Edward Wharton was thirteen years older, he was congenial and from a family as socially distinguished as her own. At first their life together appeared to be one of gratifying ease and riches. Living off generous allowances granted by their families, and Edith Wharton's inheritances, the two traveled frequently between Europe and America. They purchased homes in New York City and in fashionable Newport, Rhode Island. They visited relatives and friends in city mansions and country estates, often accompanied by a retinue of their own servants. But the marriage soon came to be described as "unfortunate." Their relationship was passionless. They had little in common beyond their upper-class backgrounds. Edith Wharton's interests were intellectual and artistic, none of which her husband shared. She became distant. He became more and more erratic, disruptive, irascible. Their separations grew more and more extended.

Edith Wharton had been fascinated by books and storytelling since her childhood. In her teens she had worked at writing a novel that she named Fast and Loose, *and in 1878, her mother paid for the private publication of* Verses, *a volume of her precocious daughter's poetry. Now faced with a disintegrating marriage and hoping to escape what she saw as a stultifying life as a society matron, Edith Wharton returned to writing. Drawing first on her interest in the decorative arts, she collaborated on a popular guide to interior decorating,* The Decoration of Houses *(1897), and she began writing short fiction for the genteel magazines of the day. In 1899, she published her first collection of stories,* The Greater Inclination. *It was a surprising success, and, as she later wrote, it "broke the chains that had held me so long in a kind of torpor."*

In her writing Edith Wharton disdained the mawkish sentiment so common to the popular fiction of her time. She had a talent for irony and satire and an acute knowledge of the American society of the rich, the pieties they preached, the intolerance they embraced, the conventions they obeyed and evaded. She worked diligently, learning the discipline and craftsmanship required for serious fiction. More stories and novels followed, and in 1905, she published The House of Mirth, *which firmly established her reputation as a writer. The book also revealed her major strengths—an intimate knowledge of upper-class society and an ability to dramatize the plight of men and women who were bound by rigid social conventions.*

In the first years of the new century, the behavior of Edith Wharton's husband had become increasingly neurotic—even violent—and in 1911 she published Ethan Frome, *a novel of spiritual isolation and despair that seemed to be inspired by her own troubled marriage and her pessimism about life and love. It was her sixteenth book in thirteen years, and it has often been judged her finest work. In 1912, she published* The Reef, *a novel that critics have described as "Jamesian" because of its similarity to the penetrating psychological analysis found in the novels of her friend Henry James. In 1913, she published* The Custom of the Country, *and in that same year she finally gained a divorce from her husband of twenty-eight years.*

Free of the burdens of marriage, Edith Wharton settled permanently in Paris, where she continued to write, now with even greater intensity. During World War I (1914–1918), she worked for the Allied cause, establishing hostels for refugees, writing stories, essays, and books about the war in France, earning the gratitude of the French government, which made her a Chevalier of the French Legion of Honor. Two years after the war she published The Age of Innocence *(1920), for which she became, in 1921, the first woman to receive a Pulitzer Prize.*

In her remaining years, Edith Wharton wrote continuously, averaging a volume a year until her death in 1937 at the age of seventy-five. In all she published more than forty books of fiction, literary criticism, poetry, autobiography, architecture and interior design, travel, and gardening. But The Age of Innocence *(1920) has remained her most popular novel and is in many ways her most characteristic work. Its setting is the world she knew well: upper-class New York in the 1870s. The novel's theme is the conflict between society's demands for social conformity and the individual's needs for personal fulfillment. Her descriptions of late-nineteenth-century upper-class life and manners are acutely perceptive and rich with implications. But she was at her best in portraying the interior lives of women, the self-delusions that imprison them, and the dilemmas that torment them in a society unyielding in its attitudes toward fidelity and sexual liberty.*

The best-known works of Edith Wharton's last years were nonfiction: a study of her craft, entitled The Writing of Fiction *(1925), and her autobiographical* A Backward Glance *(1934). With the passing of the genteel era that she had depicted so well, her fiction seemed increasingly old-fashioned, a record of a bygone and artificial world. She wrote to F. Scott Fitzgerald, "I must represent the literary equivalent of tufted furniture and chandeliers." American critics now judged her to be only a lesser Henry James, a novelist of manners who described the same social world but whose writing lacked the rich psychological insights that James had achieved in his finest works. Edith Wharton, in turn, judged twentieth-century America to be ever more crass and materialistic, marred by cultural changes that she could not admire and to which she would not adjust. In her final years she preferred to remain in Europe where she could preserve an older way of life, associate with the literati and the well-born, and view American vulgarity from afar. After her death she was buried, as her will directed, in France.*

In the first decades after her death, Wharton was sometimes criticized as a literary elitist, disdaining ordinary men and women whose birth and ill-formed lives left them unschooled in the graces of her narrow world and unworthy as subjects for her writing. And it is true that her satire of the newly risen, her mockery of their undistinguished lineage and social blunders, often seemed to suggest that she saw the misdeeds of the upper class as somehow more becoming than those of social upstarts and the lowly.

But, a half century after her death readers have rediscovered Edith Wharton. A new generation has been attracted to her emphasis on the perceptions and experiences of women, their ruthless conflicts with one another, their struggles against social coercion, and their yearning for a life richer than one dominated by polite society and matrimonial duty. Collections of Wharton's short stories and a dozen of her novels, including her masterpieces, The House of Mirth, Ethan Frome, *and* The Age of Innocence, *have been republished. Her life and her ideas have recently been analyzed in elaborate biographies and numerous critical studies. Her stories have been made into richly evocative films and television movies that appeal to vast audiences. And she has, in the last decade, come to be praised as one of the most important American writers of the last hundred years.*

FURTHER READING: *The Collected Short Stories of Edith Wharton,* 2 vols., ed. R. Lewis, 1968; *The Letters of Edith Wharton,* ed. R. Lewis and N. Lewis, 1988; *Edith Wharton: The Uncollected Critical Writings,* ed. F. Wegener, 1996; B. Nevius, *Edith Wharton: A Study of Her Fiction,* 1953; M. Lyde, *Edith Wharton,* 1959; O. Coolidge, *Edith Wharton, 1862–1937,* 1964; G. Kellogg, *The Two Lives of Edith Wharton,* 1965; M. Bell, *Edith Wharton and Henry James,* 1965; *Edith Wharton: A Collection of Critical Essays,* ed. I. Howe, 1962; G. Walton, *Edith Wharton: A Critical Interpretation,* 1970, 1983; L. Auchincloss, *Edith Wharton: A Woman in Her Time,* 1971; G. Lindberg, *Edith Wharton and the Novel of Manners,* 1975; R. Lewis, *Edith Wharton,* 1975; M. McDowell, *Edith Wharton,* 1975, 1991; C. Wolff, *A Feast of Words: The Triumph of Edith Wharton,* 1977; E. Ammons, *Edith Wharton's Argument with America,* 1980; C. Rae, *Edith Wharton's New York Quartet,* 1984; J. Fryer, *The Imaginative Structures of Edith Wharton and Willa Cather,* 1986; *Edith Wharton,* ed. H. Bloom, 1986; P. Vita-Finzi, *Edith Wharton and the Art of Fiction,* 1990; L. Raphael, *Edith Wharton's Prisoners of Shame,* 1991; B. White, *Edith Wharton: A Study of the Short Fiction,* 1991; C. Waid, *Edith Wharton's Letters from the Underground,* 1991; G. Erlich, *The Sexual Education of Edith Wharton,* 1992; *Edith Wharton: New Critical Essays,* ed. A. Bendixxen and A. Zilversmit, 1992; K. Hadley, *Interstices of the Tale: Edith Wharton's Narrative Strategies,* 1993; S. Benstock, *No Gifts from Chance: A Biography of Edith Wharton,* 1994; E. Dwight, *Edith Wharton: An Extraordinary Life,* 1994; S. Goodman, *Edith Wharton's Inner Circle,* 1994; C. Singley, *Edith Wharton: Matters of Mind and Spirit,* 1995; *The Cambridge Companion to Edith Wharton,* ed. M. Bell, 1995; A. Price, *The End of The Age of Innocence,* 1996; H. Killoran, *Edith Wharton: Art and Illusion,* 1996; S. Wright, *Edith Wharton A to Z.* 1998; M. Montgomery, *Displaying Women,* 1998; A. Tintner, *Edith Wharton in Context,* 1999; C. Preston, *Edith Wharton's Social Register,* 2000; J. Geer, *Edith Wharton,* 2002; J. Kassanoff, *Edith Wharton and the Politics of Race,* 2004.

TEXT: *The Descent of Man,* 1904.

THE OTHER TWO

I

Waythorn, on the drawing-room hearth, waited for his wife to come down to dinner.

It was their first night under his own roof, and he was surprised at his thrill of boyish agitation. He was not so old, to be sure—his glass[1] gave him little more than the five-and-thirty years to which his wife confessed—but he had fancied himself already in the temperate zone; yet here he was listening for her step with a tender sense of all it symbolised, with some old trail of verse about the garlanded nuptial door-posts floating through his enjoyment of the pleasant room and the good dinner just beyond it.

They had been hastily recalled from their honeymoon by the illness of Lily Haskett, the child of Mrs. Waythorn's first marriage. The little girl, at Waythorn's desire, had been transferred to his house on the day of her mother's wedding, and the doctor, on their arrival, broke the news that she was ill with typhoid, but declared that all the symptoms were favourable. Lily could

[1]Mirror.

show twelve years of unblemished health, and the case promised to be a light one. The nurse spoke as reassuringly, and after a moment of alarm Mrs. Waythorn had adjusted herself to the situation. She was very fond of Lily—her affection for the child had perhaps been her decisive charm in Waythorn's eyes—but she had the perfectly balanced nerves which her little girl had inherited, and no woman ever wasted less tissue in unproductive worry. Waythorn was therefore quite prepared to see her come in presently, a little late because of a last look at Lily, but as serene and well-appointed as if her good-night kiss had been laid on the brow of health. Her composure was restful to him; it acted as ballast to his somewhat unstable sensibilities. As he pictured her bending over the child's bed he thought how soothing her presence must be in illness: her very step would prognosticate recovery.

His own life had been a gray one, from temperament rather than circumstance, and he had been drawn to her by the unperturbed gaiety which kept her fresh and elastic at an age when most women's activities are growing either slack or febrile. He knew what was said about her; for, popular as she was, there had always been a faint undercurrent of detraction. When she had appeared in New York, nine or ten years earlier, as the pretty Mrs. Haskett whom Gus Varick had unearthed somewhere—was it in Pittsburg or Utica?—society, while promptly accepting her, had reserved the right to cast a doubt on its own indiscrimination. Enquiry, however, established her undoubted connection with a socially reigning family, and explained her recent divorce as the natural result of a runaway match at seventeen; and as nothing was known of Mr. Haskett it was easy to believe the worst of him.

Alice Haskett's remarriage with Gus Varick was a passport to the set whose recognition she coveted, and for a few years the Varicks were the most popular couple in town. Unfortunately the alliance was brief and stormy, and this time the husband had his champions. Still, even Varick's staunchest supporters admitted that he was not meant for matrimony, and Mrs. Varick's grievances were of a nature to bear the inspection of the New York courts. A New York divorce is in itself a diploma of virtue,[2] and in the semiwidowhood of this second separation Mrs. Varick took on an air of sanctity, and was allowed to confide her wrongs to some of the most scrupulous ears in town. But when it was known that she was to marry Waythorn there was a momentary reaction. Her best friends would have preferred to see her remain in the rôle of the injured wife, which was as becoming to her as crape to a rosy complexion. True, a decent time had elapsed, and it was not even suggested that Waythorn had supplanted his predecessor. People shook their heads over him, however, and one grudging friend, to whom he affirmed that he took the step with his eyes open, replied oracularly: "Yes—and with your ears shut."

Waythorn could afford to smile at these innuendoes. In the Wall Street phrase, he had "discounted" them. He knew that society has not yet adapted itself to the consequences of divorce, and that till the adaptation takes place every woman who uses the freedom the law accords her must be her own social justification. Waythorn had an amused confidence in his wife's ability to justify herself. His expectations were fulfilled, and before the wedding took place Alice Varick's group had rallied openly to her support. She took it all imperturbably: she had a way of surmounting obstacles without seeming to be aware

[2] In the early 1900s in New York State, adultery was the only legal basis for divorce.

of them, and Waythorn looked back with wonder at the trivialities over which he had worn his nerves thin. He had the sense of having found refuge in a richer, warmer nature than his own, and his satisfaction, at the moment, was humourously summed up in the thought that his wife, when she had done all she could for Lily, would not be ashamed to come down and enjoy a good dinner.

The anticipation of such enjoyment was not, however, the sentiment expressed by Mrs. Waythorn's charming face when she presently joined him. Though she had put on her most engaging teagown she had neglected to assume the smile that went with it, and Waythorn thought he had never seen her look so nearly worried.

"What is it?" he asked. "Is anything wrong with Lily?"

"No; I've just been in and she's still sleeping." Mrs. Waythorn hesitated. "But something tiresome has happened."

He had taken her two hands, and now perceived that he was crushing a paper between them.

"This letter?"

"Yes—Mr. Haskett has written—I mean his lawyer has written."

Waythorn felt himself flush uncomfortably. He dropped his wife's hands.

"What about?"

"About seeing Lily. You know the courts——"

"Yes, yes," he interrupted nervously.

Nothing was known about Haskett in New York. He was vaguely supposed to have remained in the outer darkness from which his wife had been rescued, and Waythorn was one of the few who were aware that he had given up his business in Utica and followed her to New York in order to be near his little girl. In the days of his wooing, Waythorn had often met Lily on the doorstep, rosy and smiling, on her way "to see papa."

"I am so sorry," Mrs. Waythorn murmured.

He roused himself. "What does he want?"

"He wants to see her. You know she goes to him once a week."

"Well—he doesn't expect her to go to him now, does he?"

"No—he has heard of her illness; but he expects to come here."

"Here?"

Mrs. Waythorn reddened under his gaze. They looked away from each other.

"I'm afraid he has the right. . . . You'll see. . . ." She made a proffer of the letter.

Waythorn moved away with a gesture of refusal. He stood staring about the softly lighted room, which a moment before had seemed so full of bridal intimacy.

"I'm so sorry," she repeated. "If Lily could have been moved——"

"That's out of the question," he returned impatiently.

"I suppose so."

Her lip was beginning to tremble, and he felt himself a brute.

"He must come, of course," he said. "What is—his day?"

"I'm afraid—to-morrow."

"Very well. Send a note in the morning."

The butler entered to announce dinner.

Waythorn turned to his wife. "Come—you must be tired. It's beastly, but try to forget about it," he said, drawing her hand through his arm.

"You're so good, dear. I'll try," she whispered back.

Her face cleared at once, and as she looked at him across the flowers, between the rosy candle-shades, he saw her lips waver back into a smile.

"How pretty everything is!" she sighed luxuriously.

He turned to the butler. "The champagne at once, please. Mrs. Waythorn is tired."

In a moment or two their eyes met above the sparkling glasses. Her own were quite clear and untroubled: he saw that she had obeyed his injunction and forgotten.

II

Waythorn, the next morning, went down town earlier than usual. Haskett was not likely to come till the afternoon, but the instinct of flight drove him forth. He meant to stay away all day—he had thoughts of dining at his club. As his door closed behind him he reflected that before he opened it again it would have admitted another man who had as much right to enter it as himself, and the thought filled him with a physical repugnance.

He caught the "elevated" at the employés' hour, and found himself crushed between two layers of pendulous humanity. At Eighth Street the man facing him wriggled out, and another took his place. Waythorn glanced up and saw that it was Gus Varick. The men were so close together that it was impossible to ignore the smile of recognition on Varick's handsome overblown face. And after all—why not? They had always been on good terms, and Varick had been divorced before Waythorn's attentions to his wife began. The two exchanged a word on the perennial grievance of the congested trains, and when a seat at their side was miraculously left empty the instinct of self-preservation made Waythorn slip into it after Varick.

The latter drew the stout man's breath of relief. "Lord—I was beginning to feel like a pressed flower." He leaned back, looking unconcernedly at Waythorn. "Sorry to hear that Sellers is knocked out again."

"Sellers?" echoed Waythorn, starting at his partner's name.

Varick looked surprised. "You didn't know he was laid up with the gout?"

"No. I've been away—I only got back last night." Waythorn felt himself reddening in anticipation of the other's smile.

"Ah—yes; to be sure. And Sellers's attack came on two days ago. I'm afraid he's pretty bad. Very awkward for me, as it happens, because he was just putting through a rather important thing for me."

"Ah?" Waythorn wondered vaguely since when Varick had been dealing in "important things." Hitherto he had dabbled only in the shallow pools of speculation, with which Waythorn's office did not usually concern itself.

It occurred to him that Varick might be talking at random, to relieve the strain of their propinquity. That strain was becoming momentarily more apparent to Waythorn, and when, at Cortlandt Street, he caught sight of an acquaintance and had a sudden vision of the picture he and Varick must present to an initiated eye, he jumped up with a muttered excuse.

"I hope you'll find Sellers better," said Varick civilly, and he stammered back: "If I can be of any use to you——" and let the departing crowd sweep him to the platform.

At his office he heard that Sellers was in fact ill with the gout, and would probably not be able to leave the house for some weeks.

"I'm sorry it should have happened so, Mr. Waythorn," the senior clerk said with affable significance. "Mr. Sellers was very much upset at the idea of giving you such a lot of extra work just now."

"Oh, that's no matter," said Waythorn hastily. He secretly welcomed the pressure of additional business, and was glad to think that, when the day's work was over, he would have to call at his partner's on the way home.

He was late for luncheon, and turned in at the nearest restaurant instead of going to his club. The place was full, and the waiter hurried him to the back of the room to capture the only vacant table. In the cloud of cigar-smoke Waythorn did not at once distinguish his neighbours: but presently, looking about him, he saw Varick seated a few feet off. This time, luckily, they were too far apart for conversation, and Varick, who faced another way, had probably not even seen him; but there was an irony in their renewed nearness.

Varick was said to be fond of good living, and as Waythorn sat despatching his hurried luncheon he looked across half enviously at the other's leisurely degustation of his meal. When Waythorn first saw him he had been helping himself with critical deliberation to a bit of Camembert at the ideal point of liquefaction, and now, the cheese removed, he was just pouring his *café double* from its little two-storied earthen pot. He poured slowly, his ruddy profile bent above the task, and one beringed white hand steadying the lid of the coffee-pot; then he stretched his other hand to the decanter of cognac at his elbow, filled a liqueur-glass, took a tentative sip, and poured the brandy into his coffee-cup.

Waythorn watched him in a kind of fascination. What was he thinking of—only of the flavour of the coffee and the liqueur? Had the morning's meeting left no more trace in his thoughts than on his face? Had his wife so completely passed out of his life that even this odd encounter with her present husband, within a week after her remarriage, was no more than an incident in his day? And as Waythorn mused, another idea struck him: had Haskett ever met Varick as Varick and he had just met? The recollection of Haskett perturbed him, and he rose and left the restaurant, taking a circuitous way out to escape the placid irony of Varick's nod.

It was after seven when Waythorn reached home. He thought the footman who opened the door looked at him oddly.

"How is Miss Lily?" he asked in haste.

"Doing very well, sir. A gentleman——"

"Tell Barlow to put off dinner for half an hour," Waythorn cut him off, hurrying upstairs.

He went straight to his room and dressed without seeing his wife. When he reached the drawing-room she was there, fresh and radiant. Lily's day had been good; the doctor was not coming back that evening.

At dinner Waythorn told her of Sellers's illness and of the resulting complications. She listened sympathetically, adjuring him not to let himself be overworked, and asking vague feminine questions about the routine of the office. Then she gave him the chronicle of Lily's day; quoted the nurse and doctor, and told him who had called to inquire. He had never seen her more serene and unruffled. It struck him, with a curious pang, that she was very happy in being with him, so happy that she found a childish pleasure in rehearsing the trivial incidents of her day.

After dinner they went to the library, and the servant put the coffee and liqueurs on a low table before her and left the room. She looked singularly soft and girlish in her rosy pale dress, against the dark leather of one of his bachelor armchairs. A day earlier the contrast would have charmed him.

He turned away now, choosing a cigar with affected deliberation.

"Did Haskett come?" he asked, with his back to her.

"Oh yes—he came."

"You didn't see him, of course?"

She hesitated a moment. "I let the nurse see him."

That was all. There was nothing more to ask. He swung round toward her, applying a match to his cigar. Well, the thing was over for a week, at any rate. He would try not to think of it. She looked up at him, a trifle rosier than usual, with a smile in her eyes.

"Ready for your coffee, dear?"

He leaned against the mantelpiece, watching her as she lifted the coffee-pot. The lamplight struck a gleam from her bracelets and tipped her soft hair with brightness. How light and slender she was, and how each gesture flowed into the next! She seemed a creature all compact of harmonies. As the thought of Haskett receded, Waythorn felt himself yielding again to the joy of possessorship. They were his, those white hands with their flitting motions, his the light haze of hair, the lips and eyes. . . .

She set down the coffee-pot, and reached for the decanter of cognac, measured off a liqueur-glass and poured it into his cup.

Waythorn uttered a sudden exclamation.

"What is the matter?" she said, startled.

"Nothing; only—I don't take cognac in my coffee."

"Oh, how stupid of me," she cried.

Their eyes met, and she blushed a sudden agonised red.

III

Ten days later, Mr. Sellers, still house-bound, asked Waythorn to call on his way down town.

The senior partner, with his swaddled foot propped up by the fire, greeted his associate with an air of embarrassment.

"I'm sorry, my dear fellow; I've got to ask you to do an awkward thing for me."

Waythorn waited, and the other went on, after a pause apparently given to the arrangement of his phrases: "The fact is, when I was knocked out I had just gone into a rather complicated piece of business for—Gus Varick."

"Well?" said Waythorn, with an attempt to put him at his ease.

"Well—it's this way; Varick came to me the day before my attack. He had evidently had an inside tip from somebody, and had made about a hundred thousand. He came to me for advice, and I suggested his going in with Vanderlyn."

"Oh, the deuce!" Waythorn exclaimed. He saw in a flash what had happened. The investment was an alluring one, but required negotiation. He listened quietly while Sellers put the case before him, and, the statement ended, he said: "You think I ought to see Varick?"

"I'm afraid I can't as yet. The doctor is obdurate. And this thing can't wait. I hate to ask you, but no one else in the office knows the ins and outs of it."

Waythorn stood silent. He did not care a farthing for the success of Varick's venture, but the honour of the office was to be considered, and he could hardly refuse to oblige his partner.

"Very well," he said, "I'll do it."

That afternoon, apprised by telephone, Varick called at the office. Waythorn, waiting in his private room, wondered what the others thought of it. The newspapers, at the time of Mrs. Waythorn's marriage, had acquainted their readers with every detail of her previous matrimonial ventures, and Waythorn could fancy the clerks smiling behind Varick's back as he was ushered in.

Varick bore himself admirably. He was easy without being undignified, and Waythorn was conscious of cutting a much less impressive figure. Varick had no experience of business, and the talk prolonged itself for nearly an hour while Waythorn set forth with scrupulous precision the details of the proposed transaction.

"I'm awfully obliged to you," Varick said as he rose. "The fact is I'm not used to having much money to look after, and I don't want to make an ass of myself—" He smiled, and Waythorn could not help noticing that there was something pleasant about his smile. "It feels uncommonly queer to have enough cash to pay one's bills. I'd have sold my soul for it a few years ago!"

Waythorn winced at the allusion. He had heard it rumoured that a lack of funds had been one of the determining causes of the Varick separation, but it did not occur to him that Varick's words were intentional. It seemed more likely that the desire to keep clear of embarrassing topics had fatally drawn him into one. Waythorn did not wish to be outdone in civility.

"We'll do the best we can for you," he said. "I think this is a good thing you're in."

"Oh, I'm sure it's immense. It's awfully good of you——" Varick broke off, embarrassed. "I suppose the thing's settled now—but if——"

"If anything happens before Sellers is about, I'll see you again," said Waythorn quietly. He was glad, in the end, to appear the more self-possessed of the two.

. . . . . .

The course of Lily's illness ran smooth, and as the days passed Waythorn grew used to the idea of Haskett's weekly visit. The first time the day came round, he stayed out late, and questioned his wife as to the visit on his return. She replied at once that Haskett had merely seen the nurse downstairs, as the doctor did not wish any one in the child's sick-room till after the crisis.

The following week Waythorn was again conscious of the recurrence of the day, but had forgotten it by the time he came home to dinner. The crisis of the disease came a few days later, with a rapid decline of fever, and the little girl was pronounced out of danger. In the rejoicing which ensued the thought of Haskett passed out of Waythorn's mind, and one afternoon, letting himself into the house with a latch-key, he went straight to his library without noticing a shabby hat and umbrella in the hall.

In the library he found a small effaced-looking man with a thinnish gray beard sitting on the edge of a chair. The stranger might have been a piano-tuner, or one of those mysteriously efficient persons who are summoned in emergencies to adjust some detail of the domestic machinery. He blinked at Waythorn through a pair of gold-rimmed spectacles and said mildly: "Mr. Waythorn, I presume? I am Lily's father."

Waythorn flushed. "Oh——" he stammered uncomfortably. He broke off, disliking to appear rude. Inwardly he was trying to adjust the actual Haskett to the image of him projected by his wife's reminiscences. Waythorn had been allowed to infer that Alice's first husband was a brute.

"I am sorry to intrude," said Haskett, with his over-the-counter politeness.

"Don't mention it," returned Waythorn, collecting himself. "I suppose the nurse has been told?"

"I presume so. I can wait," said Haskett. He had a resigned way of speaking, as though life had worn down his natural powers of resistance.

Waythorn stood on the threshold, nervously pulling off his gloves.

"I'm sorry you've been detained. I will send for the nurse," he said; and as he opened the door he added with an effort: "I'm glad we can give you a good report of Lily." He winced as the *we* slipped out, but Haskett seemed not to notice it.

"Thank you, Mr. Waythorn. It's been an anxious time for me."

"Ah, well, that's past. Soon she'll be able to go to you." Waythorn nodded and passed out. In his own room he flung himself down with a groan. He hated the womanish sensibility which made him suffer so acutely from the grotesque chances of life. He had known when he married that his wife's former husbands were both living, and that amid the multiplied contacts of modern existence there were a thousand chances to one that he would run against one or the other, yet he found himself as much disturbed by his brief encounter with Haskett as though the law had not obligingly removed all difficulties in the way of their meeting.

Waythorn sprang up and began to pace the room nervously. He had not suffered half as much from his two meetings with Varick. It was Haskett's presence in his own house that made the situation so intolerable. He stood still, hearing steps in the passage.

"This way, please," he heard the nurse say. Haskett was being taken upstairs, then: not a corner of the house but was open to him. Waythorn dropped into another chair, staring vaguely ahead of him. On his dressing-table stood a photograph of Alice, taken when he had first known her. She was Alice Varick then—how fine and exquisite he had thought her! Those were Varick's pearls about her neck. At Waythorn's instance they had been returned before her marriage. Had Haskett ever given her any trinkets—and what had become of them, Waythorn wondered? He realised suddenly that he knew very little of Haskett's past or present situation; but from the man's appearance and manner of speech he could reconstruct with curious precision the surroundings of Alice's first marriage. And it startled him to think that she had, in the background of her life, a phase of existence so different from anything with which he had connected her. Varick, whatever his faults, was a gentleman, in the conventional, traditional sense of the term: the sense which at that moment seemed, oddly enough, to have most meaning to Waythorn. He and Varick had the same social habits, spoke the same language, understood the same allusions. But this other man . . . it was grotesquely uppermost in Waythorn's mind that Haskett had worn a made-up tie attached with an elastic. Why should that ridiculous detail symbolise the whole man? Waythorn was exasperated by his own paltriness, but the fact of the tie expanded, forced itself on him, became as it were the key to Alice's past. He could see her, as

Mrs. Haskett, sitting in a "front parlour" furnished in plush, with a pianola,[3] and a copy of "Ben Hur"[4] on the centre-table. He could see her going to the theatre with Haskett—or perhaps even to a "Church Sociable"—she in a "picture hat" and Haskett in a black frock-coat, a little creased, with the made-up tie on an elastic. On the way home they would stop and look at the illuminated shop-windows, lingering over the photographs of New York actresses. On Sunday afternoons Haskett would take her for a walk, pushing Lily ahead of them in a white enamelled perambulator, and Waythorn had a vision of the people they would stop and talk to. He could fancy how pretty Alice must have looked, in a dress adroitly constructed from the hints of a New York fashion-paper, and how she must have looked down on the other women, chafing at her life, and secretly feeling that she belonged in a bigger place.

For the moment his foremost thought was one of wonder at the way in which she had shed the phase of existence which her marriage with Haskett implied. It was as if her whole aspect, every gesture, every inflection, every allusion, were a studied negation of that period of her life. If she had denied being married to Haskett she could hardly have stood more convicted of duplicity than in this obliteration of the self which had been his wife.

Waythorn started up, checking himself in the analysis of her motives. What right had he to create a fantastic effigy of her and then pass judgment on it? She had spoken vaguely of her first marriage as unhappy, had hinted, with becoming reticence, that Haskett had wrought havoc among her young illusions. . . . It was a pity for Waythorn's peace of mind that Haskett's very inoffensiveness shed a new light on the nature of those illusions. A man would rather think that his wife has been brutalised by her first husband than that the process has been reversed.

IV

"Mr. Waythorn, I don't like that French governess of Lily's."

Haskett, subdued and apologetic, stood before Waythorn in the library, revolving his shabby hat in his hand.

Waythorn, surprised in his armchair over the evening paper, stared back perplexedly at his visitor.

"You'll excuse my asking to see you," Haskett continued. "But this is my last visit, and I thought if I could have a word with you it would be a better way than writing to Mrs. Waythorn's lawyer."

Waythorn rose uneasily. He did not like the French governess either; but that was irrelevant.

"I am not so sure of that," he returned stiffly; "but since you wish it I will give your message to—my wife." He always hesitated over the possessive pronoun in addressing Haskett.

The latter sighed. "I don't know as that will help much. She didn't like it when I spoke to her."

[3]A player piano.
[4]*Ben Hur, A Tale of the Christ* (1880), a bestselling novel by Lew Wallace (1827–1905).

Waythorn turned red. "When did you see her?" he asked.

"Not since the first day I came to see Lily—right after she was taken sick. I remarked to her then that I didn't like the governess."

Waythorn made no answer. He remembered distinctly that, after that first visit, he had asked his wife if she had seen Haskett. She had lied to him then, but she had respected his wishes since; and the incident cast a curious light on her character. He was sure she would not have seen Haskett that first day if she had divined that Waythorn would object, and the fact that she did not divine it was almost as disagreeable to the latter as the discovery that she had lied to him.

"I don't like the woman," Haskett was repeating with mild persistency. "She ain't straight, Mr. Waythorn—she'll teach the child to be underhand. I've noticed a change in Lily—she's too anxious to please—and she don't always tell the truth. She used to be the straightest child, Mr. Waythorn——" He broke off, his voice a little thick. "Not but what I want her to have a stylish education," he ended.

Waythorn was touched. "I'm sorry, Mr. Haskett; but frankly, I don't quite see what I can do."

Haskett hesitated. Then he laid his hat on the table, and advanced to the hearth-rug, on which Waythorn was standing. There was nothing aggressive in his manner, but he had the solemnity of a timid man resolved on a decisive measure.

"There's just one thing you can do, Mr. Waythorn," he said. "You can remind Mrs. Waythorn that, by the decree of the courts, I am entitled to have a voice in Lily's bringing up." He paused, and went on more deprecatingly: "I'm not the kind to talk about enforcing my rights, Mr. Waythorn. I don't know as I think a man is entitled to rights he hasn't known how to hold on to; but this business of the child is different. I've never let go there—and I never mean to."

. . . . . .

The scene left Waythorn deeply shaken. Shamefacedly, in indirect ways, he had been finding out about Haskett; and all that he had learned was favourable. The little man, in order to be near his daughter, had sold out his share in a profitable business in Utica, and accepted a modest clerkship in a New York manufacturing house. He boarded in a shabby street and had few acquaintances. His passion for Lily filled his life. Waythorn felt that this exploration of Haskett was like groping about with a dark-lantern in his wife's past; but he saw now that there were recesses his lantern had not explored. He had never enquired into the exact circumstances of his wife's first matrimonial rupture. On the surface all had been fair. It was she who had obtained the divorce, and the court had given her the child. But Waythorn knew how many ambiguities such a verdict might cover. The mere fact that Haskett retained a right over his daughter implied an unsuspected compromise. Waythorn was an idealist. He always refused to recognise unpleasant contingencies till he found himself confronted with them, and then he saw them followed by a special train of consequences. His next days were thus haunted, and he determined to try to lay the ghosts by conjuring them up in his wife's presence.

When he repeated Haskett's request a flame of anger passed over her face; but she subdued it instantly and spoke with a slight quiver of outraged motherhood.

"It is very ungentlemanly of him," she said.

The word grated on Waythorn. "That is neither here nor there. It's a bare question of rights."

She murmured: "It is not as if he could ever be a help to Lily——"

Waythorn flushed. This was even less to his taste. "The question is," he repeated, "what authority has he over her?"

She looked downward, twisting herself a little in her seat. "I am willing to see him—I thought you objected," she faltered.

In a flash he understood that she knew the extent of Haskett's claims. Perhaps it was not the first time she had resisted them.

"My objecting has nothing to do with it," he said coldly; "if Haskett has a right to be consulted you must consult him."

She burst into tears, and he saw that she expected him to regard her as a victim.

Haskett did not abuse his rights. Waythorn had felt miserably sure that he would not. But the governess was dismissed, and from time to time the little man demanded an interview with Alice. After the first outburst she accepted the situation with her usual adaptability. Haskett had once reminded Waythorn of the piano-tuner, and Mrs. Waythorn, after a month or two, appeared to class him with that domestic familiar. Waythorn could not but respect the father's tenacity. At first he had tried to cultivate the suspicion that Haskett might be "up to" something, that he had an object in securing a foothold in the house. But in his heart Waythorn was sure of Haskett's single-mindedness; he even guessed in the latter a mild contempt for such advantages as his relation with the Waythorns might offer. Haskett's sincerity of purpose made him invulnerable, and his successor had to accept him as a lien on the property.

. . . . . .

Mr. Sellers was sent to Europe to recover from his gout, and Varick's affairs hung on Waythorn's hands. The negotiations were prolonged and complicated; they necessitated frequent conferences between the two men, and the interests of the firm forbade Waythorn's suggesting that his client should transfer his business to another office.

Varick appeared well in the transaction. In moments of relaxation his coarse streak appeared, and Waythorn dreaded his geniality; but in the office he was concise and clear-headed, with a flattering deference to Waythorn's judgment. Their business relations being so affably established, it would have been absurd for the two men to ignore each other in society. The first time they met in a drawing-room, Varick took up their intercourse in the same easy key, and his hostess's grateful glance obliged Waythorn to respond to it. After that they ran across each other frequently, and one evening at a ball Waythorn, wandering through the remoter rooms, came upon Varick seated beside his wife. She coloured a little, and faltered in what she was saying; but Varick nodded to Waythorn without rising, and the latter strolled on.

In the carriage, on the way home, he broke out nervously: "I didn't know you spoke to Varick."

Her voice trembled a little. "It's the first time—he happened to be standing near me; I didn't know what to do. It's so awkward, meeting everywhere—and he said you had been very kind about some business."

"That's different," said Waythorn.

She paused a moment. "I'll do just as you wish," she returned pliantly. "I thought it would be less awkward to speak to him when we meet."

Her pliancy was beginning to sicken him. Had she really no will of her own—no theory about her relation to these men? She had accepted Haskett—did she mean to accept Varick? It was "less awkward," as she had said, and her instinct was to evade difficulties or to circumvent them. With sudden vividness Waythorn saw how the instinct had developed. She was "as easy as an old shoe"—a shoe that too many feet had worn. Her elasticity was the result of tension in too many different directions. Alice Haskett—Alice Varick—Alice Waythorn—she had been each in turn, and had left hanging to each name a little of her privacy, a little of her personality, a little of the inmost self where the unknown god abides.

"Yes—it's better to speak to Varick," said Waythorn wearily.

V

The winter wore on, and society took advantage of the Waythorns' acceptance of Varick. Harassed hostesses were grateful to them for bridging over a social difficulty, and Mrs. Waythorn was held up as a miracle of good taste. Some experimental spirits could not resist the diversion of throwing Varick and his former wife together, and there were those who thought he found a zest in the propinquity. But Mrs. Waythorn's conduct remained irreproachable. She neither avoided Varick nor sought him out. Even Waythorn could not but admit that she had discovered the solution of the newest social problem.

He had married her without giving much thought to that problem. He had fancied that a woman can shed her past like a man. But now he saw that Alice was bound to hers both by the circumstances which forced her into continued relation with it, and by the traces it had left on her nature. With grim irony Waythorn compared himself to a member of a syndicate. He held so many shares in his wife's personality and his predecessors were his partners in the business. If there had been any element of passion in the transaction he would have felt less deteriorated by it. The fact that Alice took her change of husbands like a change of weather reduced the situation to mediocrity. He could have forgiven her for blunders, for excesses; for resisting Haskett, for yielding to Varick; for anything but her acquiescence and her tact. She reminded him of a juggler tossing knives; but the knives were blunt and he knew they would never cut her.

And then, gradually, habit formed a protecting surface for his sensibilities. If he paid for each day's comfort with the small change of his illusions, he grew daily to value the comfort more and set less store upon the coin. He had drifted into a dulling propinquity with Haskett and Varick and he took refuge in the cheap revenge of satirising the situation. He even began to reckon up the advantages which accrued from it, to ask himself if it were not better to own a third of a wife who knew how to make a man happy than a whole one who had lacked opportunity to acquire the art. For it *was* an art, and made up, like all others, of concessions, eliminations and embellishments; of lights judiciously thrown and shadows skilfully softened. His wife knew exactly how to manage the lights, and he knew exactly to what training she owed her skill. He even tried to trace the source of his obligations, to discriminate between the influences which had combined to produce his domestic happiness: he perceived that Haskett's commonness had made Alice worship good breeding, while Varick's liberal construction of the marriage bond had taught her to value the conjugal virtues; so that he was directly indebted to his predecessors for the devotion which made his life easy if not inspiring.

From this phase he passed into that of complete acceptance. He ceased to satirise himself because time dulled the irony of the situation and the joke lost its humour with its sting. Even the sight of Haskett's hat on the hall table had ceased to touch the springs of epigram. The hat was often seen there now, for it had been decided that it was better for Lily's father to visit her than for the little girl to go to his boarding-house. Waythorn, having acquiesced in this arrangement, had been surprised to find how little difference it made. Haskett was never obtrusive, and the few visitors who met him on the stairs were unaware of his identity. Waythorn did not know how often he saw Alice, but with himself Haskett was seldom in contact.

One afternoon, however, he learned on entering that Lily's father was waiting to see him. In the library he found Haskett occupying a chair in his usual provisional way. Waythorn always felt grateful to him for not leaning back.

"I hope you'll excuse me, Mr. Waythorn," he said rising. "I wanted to see Mrs. Waythorn about Lily, and your man asked me to wait here till she came in."

"Of course," said Waythorn, remembering that a sudden leak had that morning given over the drawing-room to the plumbers.

He opened his cigar-case and held it out to his visitor, and Haskett's acceptance seemed to mark a fresh stage in their intercourse. The spring evening was chilly, and Waythorn invited his guest to draw up his chair to the fire. He meant to find an excuse to leave Haskett in a moment; but he was tired and cold, and after all the little man no longer jarred on him.

The two were enclosed in the intimacy of their blended cigar-smoke when the door opened and Varick walked into the room. Waythorn rose abruptly. It was the first time that Varick had come to the house, and the surprise of seeing him, combined with the singular inopportuneness of his arrival, gave a new edge to Waythorn's blunted sensibilities. He stared at his visitor without speaking.

Varick seemed too preoccupied to notice his host's embarrassment.

"My dear fellow," he exclaimed in his most expansive tone, "I must apologise for tumbling in on you in this way, but I was too late to catch you down town, and so I thought——"

He stopped short, catching sight of Haskett, and his sanguine colour deepened to a flush which spread vividly under his scant blond hair. But in a moment he recovered himself and nodded slightly. Haskett returned the bow in silence, and Waythorn was still groping for speech when the footman came in carrying a tea-table.

The intrusion offered a welcome vent to Waythorn's nerves. "What the deuce are you bringing this here for?" he said sharply.

"I beg your pardon, sir, but the plumbers are still in the drawing-room, and Mrs. Waythorn said she would have tea in the library." The footman's perfectly respectful tone implied a reflection on Waythorn's reasonableness.

"Oh, very well," said the latter resignedly, and the footman proceeded to open the folding tea-table and set out its complicated appointments. While this interminable process continued the three men stood motionless, watching it with a fascinated stare, till Waythorn, to break the silence, said to Varick: "Won't you have a cigar?"

He held out the case he had just tendered to Haskett, and Varick helped himself with a smile. Waythorn looked about for a match, and finding none, proffered a light from his own cigar. Haskett, in the background, held his ground mildly, examining his cigar-tip now and then, and stepping forward at the right moment to knock its ashes into the fire.

The footman at last withdrew, and Varick immediately began: "If I could just say half a word to you about this business——"

"Certainly," stammered Waythorn; "in the dining-room——"

But as he placed his hand on the door it opened from without, and his wife appeared on the threshold.

She came in fresh and smiling, in her street dress and hat, shedding a fragrance from the boa[5] which she loosened in advancing.

"Shall we have tea in here, dear?" she began; and then she caught sight of Varick. Her smile deepened, veiling a slight tremor of surprise.

"Why, how do you do?" she said with a distinct note of pleasure.

As she shook hands with Varick she saw Haskett standing behind him. Her smile faded for a moment, but she recalled it quickly, with a scarcely perceptible side-glance at Waythorn.

"How do you do, Mr. Haskett?" she said, and shook hands with him a shade less cordially.

The three men stood awkwardly before her, till Varick, always the most self-possessed, dashed into an explanatory phrase.

"We—I had to see Waythorn a moment on business," he stammered, brick-red from chin to nape.

Haskett stepped forward with his air of mild obstinacy. "I am sorry to intrude; but you appointed five o'clock—" he directed his resigned glance to the timepiece on the mantel.

She swept aside their embarrassment with a charming gesture of hospitality. "I'm so sorry—I'm always late; but the afternoon was so lovely." She stood drawing off her gloves, propitiatory and graceful, diffusing about her a sense of ease and familiarity in which the situation lost its grotesqueness. "But before talking business," she added brightly, "I'm sure every one wants a cup of tea."

She dropped into her low chair by the tea-table, and the two visitors, as if drawn by her smile, advanced to receive the cups she held out.

She glanced about for Waythorn, and he took the third cup with a laugh.

1904

[5]A long, fluffy scarf.

Paul Laurence Dunbar (1872–1906)

Paul Laurence Dunbar stands among the most accomplished and acclaimed African American literary artists of the nineteenth century. Born in Dayton, Ohio, in 1872 to ex-slaves, he was raised by his mother after his parents divorced when he was four. Early on he exhibited a keen intellect and excelled as a student. He was also well-liked by his peers. Despite being the only African American attending his high school, Dunbar was elected class president and was selected to deliver the poem at his commencement ceremony. Shortly after graduating, however, he began to experience the acute discrimination that African Americans at the turn of the century often encountered. Even with his impressive academic credentials, Dunbar, because he was black, was unable to find professional employment in Dayton and was forced to settle for a job as an elevator operator.

In 1893 Dunbar partly financed the publication of his first book of poetry, Oak and Ivy. *A mix of sentimental and serious verse, with some pieces written in standard English and others in more experimental vernacular,* Oak and Ivy *immediately demonstrated Dunbar's impressive range and established him as an emerging literary talent. Writers such as James Whitcomb Riley and Frederick Douglass praised him as a promising young poet. At the same time, popular audiences increasingly demanded more of his dialect poems. In 1895 he continued to add to his reputation with the publication of his second collection,* Majors and Minors. *It received accolades from nearly all quarters, including influential critic William Dean Howells, who would write an introduction for Dunbar's 1896 book* Lyrics of Lowly Life. *By the end of the decade his status as an internationally celebrated poet seemed secure.*

In 1898 Dunbar married teacher and poet Alice Ruth Moore. That same year he began to distinguish himself in prose. Though his essays, short stories, and novels such as The Uncalled *(1898) and* The Sport of the Gods *(1902) continued to address issues of racial injustice, Dunbar's journalism and fiction never received as much critical attention as his poetry. In the last few years of his life, his health declined precipitously due to the effects of heavy drinking and tuberculosis. Paul Laurence Dunbar died in 1906 at the age of 33.*

FURTHER READING: A. Gayle, *Oak and Ivy: A Biography of Paul Laurence Dunbar,* 1971; P. Revell, *Paul Laurence Dunbar,* 1979; *The Collected Poetry of Paul Laurence Dunbar,* ed., J. Braxton, 1993; E. Alexander, *Lyrics of Sunshine and Shadow: The Tragic Courtship and Marriage of Paul Laurence Dunbar and Alice Ruth Moore: A History of Love and Violence among the African American Elite,* 2001.

TEXTS: *The Strength of Gideon and Other Stories,* 1900; *The Complete Poems of Paul Laurence Dunbar,* 1913; "The Race Question Discussed," *Toledo* (Ohio) *Journal,* December 18, 1898; "The Fourth of July and Race Outrages," *New York Times,* July 10, 1903.

THE INGRATE

I

Mr. Leckler was a man of high principle. Indeed, he himself had admitted it at times to Mrs. Leckler. She was often called into counsel with him. He was one of those large souled creatures with a hunger for unlimited advice, upon which he never acted. Mrs. Leckler knew this, but like the good, patient little wife that she was, she went on paying her poor tribute of advice and admiration. To-day her husband's mind was particularly troubled,—as usual, too, over a matter of principle. Mrs. Leckler came at his call."

Mrs. Leckler," he said, "I am troubled in my mind. I—in fact, I am puzzled over a matter that involves either the maintaining or relinquishing of a principle."

"Well, Mr. Leckler?" said his wife, interrogatively.

"If I had been a scheming, calculating Yankee, I should have been rich now; but all my life I have been too generous and confiding. I have always let principle stand between me and my interests." Mr. Leckler took himself all too seriously to be conscious of his pun, and went on: "Now this is a matter in which my duty and my principles seem to conflict. It stands thus: Josh has been doing a piece of plastering for Mr. Eckley over in Lexington, and from what he says, I think that city rascal has misrepresented the amount of work to me and so cut down the pay for it. Now, of course, I should not care, the matter of a dollar or two being nothing to me; but it is a very different matter when we consider poor Josh." There was deep pathos in Mr. Leckler's tone. "You know Josh is anxious to buy his freedom, and I allow him a part of whatever he makes; so you see it's he that's affected. Every dollar that he is cheated out of cuts off just so much from his earnings, and puts further away his hope of emancipation."

If the thought occurred to Mrs. Leckler that, since Josh received only about one-tenth of what he earned, the advantage of just wages would be quite as much her husband's as the slave's, she did not betray it, but met the naïve reasoning with the question, "But where does the conflict come in, Mr. Leckler?"

"Just here. If Josh knew how to read and write and cipher—"

"Mr. Leckler, are you crazy!"

"Listen to me, my dear, and give me the benefit of your judgment. This is a very momentous question. As I was about to say, if Josh knew these things, he could protect himself from cheating when his work is at too great a distance for me to look after it for him."

"But teaching a slave—"

"Yes, that's just what is against my principles. I know how public opinion and the law look at it. But my conscience rises up in rebellion every time I think of that poor black man being cheated out of his earnings. Really, Mrs. Leckler, I think I may trust to Josh's discretion, and secretly give him such instructions as will permit him to protect himself."

"Well, of course, it's just as you think best," said his wife.

"I knew you would agree with me," he returned. "It's such a comfort to take counsel with you, my dear!" And the generous man walked out on to the veranda, very well satisfied with himself and his wife, and prospectively pleased with Josh. Once he murmured to himself, "I'll lay for Eckley next time."

Josh, the subject of Mr. Leckler's charitable solicitations, was the plantation plasterer. His master had given him his trade, in order that he might do whatever such work was needed about the place; but he became so proficient in his duties, having also no competition among the poor whites, that he had grown to be in great demand in the country thereabout. So Mr. Leckler found it profitable, instead of letting him do chores and field work in his idle time, to hire him out to neighboring farms and planters. Josh was a man of more than ordinary intelligence; and when he asked to be allowed to pay for himself by working overtime, his master readily agreed,—for it promised more work to be done, for which he could allow the slave just what he pleased. Of course, he knew now that when the black man began to cipher this state of affairs would be changed; but it would mean such an increase of profit from the outside, that he could afford to give up his own little peculations. Anyway, it would be many years before the slave could pay the two thousand dollars, which price he had set upon him. Should he approach that figure, Mr. Leckler felt it just possible that the market in slaves would take a sudden rise.

When Josh was told of his master's intention, his eyes gleamed with pleasure, and he went to his work with the zest of long hunger. He proved a remarkably apt pupil. He was indefatigable in doing the tasks assigned him. Even Mr. Leckler, who had great faith in his plasterer's ability, marveled at the speed at which he had acquired the three R's. He did not know that on one of his many trips a free negro had given Josh the rudimentary tools of learning, and that since the slave had been adding to his store of learning by poring over signs and every bit of print that he could spell out. Neither was Josh so indiscreet as to intimate to his benefactor that he had been anticipated in his good intentions.

It was in this way, working and learning, that a year passed away, and Mr. Leckler thought that his object had been accomplished. He could safely trust Josh to protect his own interests, and so he thought that it was quite time that his servant's education should cease.

"You know, Josh," he said, "I have already gone against my principles and against the law for your sake, and of course a man can't stretch his conscience too far, even to help another who's being cheated; but I reckon you can take care of yourself now."

"Oh, yes, suh, I reckon I kin," said Josh.

"And it wouldn't do for you to be seen with any books about you now."

"Oh, no, suh, su't'n'y not." He didn't intend to be seen with any books about him.

It was just now that Mr. Leckler saw the good results of all he had done, and his heart was full of a great joy, for Eckley had been building some additions to his house, and sent for Josh to do the plastering for him. The owner admonished his slave, took him over a few examples to freshen his memory, and sent him forth with glee. When the job was done, there was a discrepancy of two dollars in what Mr. Eckley offered for it and the price which accrued from Josh's measurements. To the employer's surprise, the black man went over the figures with him and convinced him of the incorrectness of the payment,—and the additional two dollars were turned over.

"Some o' Leckler's work," said Eckley, "teaching a nigger to cipher! Close-fisted old reprobate,[1]—I've a mind to have the law on him." Mr. Leckler heard the story with great glee. "I laid for him that time—the old fox." But to Mrs. Leckler he said: "You see, my dear wife, my rashness in teaching Josh to figure for himself is vindicated. See what he has saved for himself."

"What did he save?" asked the little woman indiscreetly.

Her husband blushed and stammered for a moment, and then replied, "Well, of course, it was only twenty cents saved to him, but to a man buying his freedom every cent counts; and after all, it is not the amount, Mrs. Leckler, it's the principle of the thing."

"Yes," said the lady meekly.

[1]An immoral person.

II

Unto the body it is easy for the master to say, "Thus far shalt thou go, and no farther." Gyves, chains and fetters[2] will enforce that command. But what master shall say unto the mind, "Here do I set the limit of your acquisition. Pass it not"? Who shall put gyves upon the intellect, or fetter the movement of thought? Joshua Leckler, as custom denominated him, had tasted of the forbidden fruit, and his appetite had grown by what it fed on. Night after night he crouched in his lonely cabin, by the blaze of a fat pine brand, poring over the few books that he had been able to secure and smuggle in. His fellow-servants alternately laughed at him and wondered why he did not take a wife. But Joshua went on his way. He had no time for marrying or for love; other thoughts had taken possession of him. He was being swayed by ambitions other than the mere fathering of slaves for his master. To him his slavery was deep night. What wonder, then, that he should dream, and that through the ivory gate[3] should come to him the forbidden vision of freedom? To own himself, to be master of his hands, feet, of his whole body—something would clutch at his heart as he thought of it; and the breath would come hard between his lips. But he met his master with an impassive face, always silent, always docile; and Mr. Leckler congratulated himself that so valuable and intelligent a slave should be at the same time so tractable. Usually intelligence in a slave meant discontent; but not so with Josh. Who more content than he? He remarked to his wife: "You see, my dear, this is what comes of treating even a nigger right."

Meanwhile the white hills of the North were beckoning to the chattel,[4] and the north winds were whispering to him to be a chattel no longer. Often the eyes that looked away to where freedom lay were filled with a wistful longing that was tragic in its intensity, for they saw the hardships and the difficulties between the slave and his goal and, worst of all, an iniquitous law,—liberty's compromise with bondage, that rose like a stone wall between him and hope,—a law that degraded every free-thinking man to the level of a slave-catcher. There it loomed up before him, formidable, impregnable, insurmountable. He measured it in all its terribleness, and paused. But on the other side there was liberty; and one day when he was away at work, a voice came out of the woods and whispered to him "Courage!"—and on that night the shadows beckoned him as the white hills had done, and the forest called to him, "Follow."

"It seems to me that Josh might have been able to get home to-night," said Mr. Leckler, walking up and down his veranda; "but I reckon it's just possible that he got through too late to catch a train." In the morning he said: "Well, he's not here yet; he must have had to do some extra work. If he doesn't get here by evening, I'll run up there."

In the evening, he did take the train for Joshua's place of employment, where he learned that his slave had left the night before. But where could he have gone? That no one knew, and for the first time it dawned upon his master that Josh had run away. He raged; he fumed; but nothing could be done until morning, and all the time Leckler knew that the most valuable slave on his plantation

[2]Gyves, chains, and fetters are terms for devices used to shackle prisoners.
[3]In Greek mythology, the gate through which the gods send false dreams to mortals.
[4]Personal property, which is Josh's legal status as a slave.

was working his way toward the North and freedom. He did not go back home, but paced the floor all night long. In the early dawn he hurried out, and the hounds were put on the fugitive's track. After some nosing around they set off toward a stretch of woods. In a few minutes they came yelping back, pawing their noses and rubbing their heads against the ground. They had found the trail, but Josh had played the old slave trick of filling his tracks with cayenne pepper. The dogs were soothed, and taken deeper into the wood to find the trail. They soon took it up again, and dashed away with low bays. The scent led them directly to a little wayside station about six miles distant. Here it stopped. Burning with the chase, Mr. Leckler hastened to the station agent. Had he seen such a negro? Yes, he had taken the northbound train two nights before.

"But why did you let him go without a pass?" almost screamed the owner.

"I didn't," replied the agent. "He had a written pass, signed James Leckler, and I let him go on it."

"Forged, forged!" yelled the master. "He wrote it himself."

"Humph!" said the agent, "how was I to know that? Our niggers round here don't know how to write."

Mr. Leckler suddenly bethought him to hold his peace. Josh was probably now in the arms of some northern abolitionist, and there was nothing to be done now but advertise; and the disgusted master spread his notices broadcast before starting for home. As soon as he arrived at his house, he sought his wife and poured out his griefs to her.

"You see, Mrs. Leckler, this is what comes of my goodness of heart. I taught that nigger to read and write, so that he could protect himself,—and look how he uses his knowledge. Oh, the ingrate, the ingrate! The very weapon which I give him to defend himself against others he turns upon me. Oh, it's awful,—awful! I've always been too confiding. Here's the most valuable nigger on my plantation gone,—gone, I tell you,—and through my own kindness. It isn't his value, though, I'm thinking so much about. I could stand his loss, if it wasn't for the principle of the thing, the base ingratitude he has shown me. Oh, if I ever lay hands on him again!" Mr. Leckler closed his lips and clenched his fist with an eloquence that laughed at words.

Just at this time, in one of the underground railway stations,[5] six miles north of the Ohio, an old Quaker was saying to Josh: "Lie still,—thee'll be perfectly safe there. Here comes John Trader, our local slave catcher, but I will parley with him and send him away. Thee need not fear. None of thy brethren who have come to us have ever been taken back to bondage.—Good-evening, Friend Trader!" and Josh heard the old Quaker's smooth voice roll on, while he lay back half smothering in a bag, among other bags of corn and potatoes.

It was after ten o'clock that night when he was thrown carelessly into a wagon and driven away to the next station, twenty-five miles to the northward. And by such stages, hiding by day and traveling by night, helped by a few of his own people who were blessed with freedom, and always by the good Quakers wherever found, he made his way into Canada. And on one never-to-be-forgotten morning he stood up, straightened himself, breathed God's blessed air, and knew himself free!

[5]The underground railway was a system of routes and stops by which residents of free stat[e]s helped escaped slaves travel through those states to safety in Canada.

III

To Joshua Leckler this life in Canada was all new and strange. It was a new thing for him to feel himself a man and to have his manhood recognized by the whites with whom he came into free contact. It was new, too, this receiving the full measure of his worth in work. He went to his labor with a zest that he had never known before, and he took a pleasure in the very weariness it brought him. Ever and anon there came to his ears the cries of his brethren in the South. Frequently he met fugitives who, like himself, had escaped from bondage; and the harrowing tales that they told him made him burn to do something for those whom he had left behind him. But these fugitives and the papers he read told him other things. They said that the spirit of freedom was working in the United States, and already men were speaking out boldly in behalf of the manumission of the slaves; already there was a growing army behind that noble vanguard, Sumner, Phillips, Douglass, Garrison. He heard the names of Lucretia Mott and Harriet Beecher Stowe,[6] and his heart swelled, for on the dim horizon he saw the first faint streaks of dawn.

So the years passed. Then from the surcharged clouds a flash of lightning broke, and there was the thunder of cannon and the rain of lead over the land. From his home in the North he watched the storm as it raged and wavered, now threatening the North with its awful power, now hanging dire and dreadful over the South. Then suddenly from out the fray came a voice like the trumpet tone of God to him: "Thou and thy brothers are free!" Free, free, with the freedom not cherished by the few alone, but for all that had been bound. Free, with the freedom not torn from the secret night, but open to the light of heaven.

When the first call for colored soldiers came, Joshua Leckler hastened down to Boston, and enrolled himself among those who were willing to fight to maintain their freedom. On account of his ability to read and write and his general intelligence, he was soon made an orderly sergeant. His regiment had already taken part in an engagement before the public roster of this band of Uncle Sam's niggers, as they were called, fell into Mr. Leckler's hands. He ran his eye down the column of names. It stopped at that of Joshua Leckler, Sergeant, Company F. He handed the paper to Mrs. Leckler with his finger on the place:

"Mrs. Leckler," he said, "this is nothing less than a judgment on me for teaching a nigger to read and write. I disobeyed the law of my state and, as a result, not only lost my nigger, but furnished the Yankees with a smart officer to help them fight the South. Mrs. Leckler, I have sinned—and been punished. But I am content, Mrs. Leckler; it all came through my kindness of heart,—and your mistaken advice. But, oh, that ingrate, that ingrate!"

1900

[6]Charles Sumner, Wendell Phillips, Frederick Douglass, William Lloyd Garrison, Lucretia Mott, and Harriet Beecher Stowe were major figures in the anti-slavery movement.

WE WEAR THE MASK

We wear the mask that grins and lies,
It hides our cheeks and shades our eyes,—
This debt we pay to human guile;
With torn and bleeding hearts we smile,
And mouth with myriad subtleties.

Why should the world be overwise,
In counting all our tears and sighs?
Nay, let them only see us, while
    We wear the mask.

We smile, but O great Christ, our cries
To thee from tortured souls arise.
We sing, but oh the clay is vile
Beneath our feet, and long the mile;
But let the world dream otherwise,
    We wear the mask!

1896

AN ANTE-BELLUM SERMON

We is gathahed hyeah, my brothahs,
    In dis howlin' wildaness,
Fu' to speak some words of comfo't
    To each othah in distress.
An' we chooses fu' ouah subjic'
    Dis—we'll 'splain it by an' by;
    "An' de Lawd said, 'Moses, Moses,'
    An' de man said, 'Hyeah am I.'"

Now ole Pher'oh, down in Egypt,
    Was de wuss man evah bo'n,
An' he had de Hebrew chillun
    Down dah wukin' in his co'n;
'Twell de Lawd got tiahed o' his foolin',
    An' sez he: "I'll let him know—
Look hyeah, Moses, go tell Pher'oh
    Fu' to let dem chillun go."

"An' ef he refuse to do it,
    I will make him rue de houah,
Fu' I'll empty down on Egypt
    All de vials of my powah."

Yes, he did—an' Pher'oh's ahmy
Wasn't wuth a ha'f a dime;
Fu' de Lawd will he'p his chillun,
You kin trust him evah time.

An' yo' enemies may 'sail[1] you
In de back an' in de front;
But de Lawd is all aroun' you,
Fu' to ba' de battle's brunt.
Dey kin fo'ge yo' chains an' shackles
F'om de mountains to de sea;
But de Lawd will sen' some Moses
Fu' to set his chillun free.

An' de lan' shall hyeah his thundah,
Lak a blas' f'om Gab'el's ho'n,[2]
Fu' de Lawd of hosts is mighty
When he girds his ahmor on.
But fu' feah some one mistakes me,
I will pause right hyeah to say,
Dat I'm still a-preachin' ancient,
I ain't talkin' 'bout to-day.

But I tell you, fellah christuns,
Things'll happen mighty strange;
Now, de Lawd done dis fu' Isrul,
An' his ways don't nevah change,
An' de love he showed to Isrul
Wasn't all on Isrul spent;
Now don't run an' tell yo' mastahs
Dat I's preachin' discontent.

Cause I isn't; I'se a-judgin'
Bible people by deir ac's;
I'se a-givin' you de Scriptuah,
I'se a-handin' you de fac's.
Cose ole Pher'oh b'lieved in slav'ry,
But de Lawd he let him see,
Dat de people he put bref in,—
Evah mothah's son was free.

An' dah's othahs thinks lak Pher'oh,
But dey calls de Scriptuah liar,
Fu' de Bible says "a servant
Is a-worthy of his hire."[3]

[1]Assail. [2]The angel Gabriel's horn. [3]Luke 10:17: "the laborer is worthy of his hire."

An' you cain't git roun' nor thoo dat,
An' you cain't git ovah it,
Fu' whatevah place you git in,
Dis hyeah Bible too'll fit.

So you see de Lawd's intention,
Evah sence de worl' began,
Was dat His almighty freedom
Should belong to evah man,
But I think it would be bettah,
Ef I'd pause agin to say,
Dat I'm talkin' 'bout ouah freedom
In a Bibleistic way.

But de Moses is a-comin',
An' he's comin', suah and fas'
We kin hyeah his feet a-trompin',
We kin hyeah his trumpit blas'.
But I want to wa'n you people,
Don't you git too brigity;[4]
An' don't you git to braggin'
'Bout dese things, you wait an' see.

But when Moses wif his powah
Comes an' sets us chillun free,
We will praise de gracious Mastah
Dat has gin us liberty;
An' we'll shout ouah halleluyahs,
On dat mighty reck'nin' day,
When we'se reco'nised ez citiz'—[5]
Huh uh! Chillun, let us pray!

1896

WHEN MALINDY SINGS

G'way an' quit dat noise, Miss Lucy—
Put dat music book away;
What's de use to keep on tryin'?
Ef you practise twell you're gray,
You cain't sta't no notes a-flyin'
Lak de ones dat rants and rings
F'om de kitchen to de big woods
When Malindy sings.

[4]Perhaps "biggity"—that is, "uppity." [5]Citizens.

You ain't got de nachel o'gans
Fu' to make de soun' come right,
You ain't got de tu'ns an' twistin's
Fu' to make it sweet an' light.
Tell you one thing now, Miss Lucy,
An' I'm tellin' you fu' true,
When hit comes to raal right singin',
'T ain't no easy thing to do.

Easy 'nough fu' folks to hollah,
Lookin' at de lines an' dots,
When dey ain't no one kin sence it,
An' de chune comes in, in spots;
But fu' real melojous music,
Dat jes' strikes you' hea't and clings,
Jes' you stan' an' listen wif me
When Malindy sings.

Ain't you nevah hyeahd Malindy?
Blessed soul, tek up de cross!
Look hyeah, ain't you jokin', honey?
Well, you don't know whut you los'.
Y' ought to hyeah dat gal a-wa'blin',
Robins, la'ks, an' all dem things,
Heish dey moufs an' hides dey faces
When Malindy sings.

Fiddlin' man jes' stop his fiddlin',
Lay his fiddle on de she'f;
Mockin'-bird quit tryin' to whistle,
'Cause he jes' so shamed hisse'f.
Folks a-playin' on de banjo
Draps dey fingahs on de strings—
Bless yo' soul—fu'gits to move 'em,
When Malindy sings.

She jes' spreads huh mouf and hollahs,
"Come to Jesus,"[1] twell you hyeah
Sinnahs' tremblin' steps and voices,
Timid-lak a-drawin' neah;
Den she tu'ns to "Rock of Ages,"
Simply to de cross she clings,
An' you fin' yo' teahs a-drappin'
When Malindy sings.

Who dat says dat humble praises
Wif de Master nevah counts?

[1]"Come to Jesus," "Rock of Ages," and "Swing Low, Sweet Chariot" are Christian hymns.

Heish yo' mouf, I hyeah dat music,
Ez hit rises up an' mounts—
Floatin' by de hills an' valleys,
Way above dis buryin' sod,
Ez hit makes its way in glory
To de very gates of God!

Oh, hit's sweetah dan de music
Of an edicated band;
An' hit's dearah dan de battle's
Song o' triumph in de lan'.
It seems holier dan evenin'
When de solemn chu'ch bell rings,
Ez I sit an' ca'mly listen
While Malindy sings.

Towsah, stop dat ba'kin', hyeah me!
Mandy, mek dat chile keep still;
Don't you hyeah de echoes callin'
F'om de valley to de hill?
Let me listen, I can hyeah it,
Th'oo de bresh of angels' wings,
Sof' an' sweet, "Swing Low, Sweet Chariot,"
Ez Malindy sings.

1896

THE COLORED SOLDIERS

If the muse were mine to tempt it
And my feeble voice were strong,
If my tongue were trained to measures,
I would sing a stirring song.
I would sing a song heroic
Of those noble sons of Ham,
Of the gallant colored soldiers
Who fought for Uncle Sam!

In the early days you scorned them,
And with many a flip and flout
Said "These battles are the white man's,
And the whites will fight them out."
Up the hills you fought and faltered,
In the vales you strove and bled,
While your ears still heard the thunder
Of the foes' advancing tread.

Then distress fell on the nation,
And the flag was drooping low;
Should the dust pollute your banner?
No! the nation shouted, No!
So when War, in savage triumph,
Spread abroad his funeral pall—
Then you called the colored soldiers,
And they answered to your call.

And like hounds unleashed and eager
For the life blood of the prey,
Sprung they forth and bore them bravely
In the thickest of the fray.
And where'er the fight was hottest,
Where the bullets fastest fell,
There they pressed unblanched and fearless
At the very mouth of hell.

Ah, they rallied to the standard
To uphold it by their might;
None were stronger in the labors,
None were braver in the fight.
From the blazing breach of Wagner
To the plains of Olustee,[1]
They were foremost in the fight
Of the battles of the free.

And at Pillow![2] God have mercy
On the deeds committed there,
And the souls of those poor victims
Sent to Thee without a prayer.
Let the fulness of Thy pity
O'er the hot wrought spirits sway
Of the gallant colored soldiers
Who fell fighting on that day!

Yes, the Blacks enjoy their freedom,
And they won it dearly, too;
For the life blood of their thousands
Did the southern fields bedew.
In the darkness of their bondage,
In the depths of slavery's night,
Their muskets flashed the dawning,
And they fought their way to light.

[1]The Battle of Fort Wagner (1863, near Charleston, South Carolina) and the Battle of Olustee (1864, near Lake City, Florida) were Civil War battles in which African Americans fought for the North.

[2]The Battle of Fort Pillow (1864, at Henning, Tennessee). "The deeds" included a massacre of surrendered African American troops by the Confederates.

They were comrades then and brothers,
  Are they more or less to-day?
They were good to stop a bullet
  And to front the fearful fray.
They were citizens and soldiers,
  When rebellion raised its head;
And the traits that made them worthy,—
  Ah! those virtues are not dead.

They have shared your nightly vigils,
  They have shared your daily toil;
And their blood with yours commingling
  Has enriched the Southern soil.
They have slept and marched and suffered
  'Neath the same dark skies as you,
They have met as fierce a foeman,
  And have been as brave and true.

And their deeds shall find a record
  In the registry of Fame;
For their blood has cleansed completely
  Every blot of Slavery's shame.
So all honor and all glory
  To those noble sons of Ham—[3]
The gallant colored soldiers
  Who fought for Uncle Sam!

1896

WHEN DEY 'LISTED COLORED SOLDIERS

Dey was talkin' in de cabin, dey was talkin' in de hall;
But I listened kin' o' keerless, not a-t'inkin' 'bout it all;
An' on Sunday, too, I noticed, dey was whisp'rin' mighty much,
Stan'in' all erroun' de roadside w'en dey let us out o' chu'ch.
But I didn't t'ink erbout it 'twell de middle of de week,
An' my 'Lias come to see me, an' somehow he couldn't speak.
Den I seed all in a minute whut he'd come to see me for;—
Dey had 'listed colo'ed sojers an' my 'Lias gwine to wah.

Oh, I hugged him, an' I kissed him, an' I baiged him not to go;
But he tol' me dat his conscience, hit was callin' to him so,
An' he couldn't baih to lingah w'en he had a chanst to fight
For de freedom dey had gin him an' de glory of de right.

[3] Africans and African Americans were sometimes called "sons of Ham" because in Genesis 9:18–29 Ham, one of Moses's sons, commits a misdeed that causes Moses to say that he and his descendants will be the servants of Ham's brothers and their descendants.

So he kissed me, an' he lef' me, w'en I'd p'omised to be true;
An' dey put a knapsack on him, an' a coat all colo'ed blue.
So I gin him pap's ol' Bible f'om de bottom of de draw',—
W'en dey 'listed colo'ed sojers an' my 'Lias went to wah.

But I t'ought of all de weary miles dat he would have to tramp,
An' I couldn't be contented w'en dey tuk him to de camp.
W'y my hea't nigh broke wid grievin' 'twell I seed him on de street;
Den I felt lak I could go an' th'ow my body at his feet.
For his buttons was a-shinin', an' his face was shinin', too,
An' he looked so strong an' mighty in his coat o' sojer blue,
Dat I hollahed, "Step up, manny," dough my th'oat was so' an' raw,—
W'en dey 'listed colo'ed sojers an' my 'Lias went to wah.

Ol' Mis' cried w'en mastah lef' huh, young Miss mou'ned huh brothah Ned,
An' I didn't know dey feelin's is de ve'y wo'ds dey said
W'en I tol' 'em I was so'y. Dey had done gin up dey all;
But dey only seemed mo' proudah dat dey men had hyeahed de call.
Bofe my mastahs went in gray suits, an' I loved de Yankee blue,
But I t'ought dat I could sorrer for de losin' of 'em too;
But I couldn't, for I didn't know de ha'f o' whut I saw,
'Twell dey 'listed colo'ed sojers an' my 'Lias went to wah.

Mastah Jack come home all sickly; he was broke for life, dey said;
An' dey lef' my po' young mastah some'r's on de roadside,—dead.
W'en de women cried an' mou'ned 'em, I could feel it thoo an' thoo,
For I had a loved un fightin' in de way o' dangah, too.
Den dey tol' me dey had laid him some'r's way down souf to res',
Wid de flag dat he had fit for shinin' daih acrost his breas'.
Well, I cried, but den I reckon dat's whut Gawd had called him for,
W'en dey 'listed colo'ed sojers an' my 'Lias went to wah.

1903

SYMPATHY

I know what the caged bird feels, alas!
  When the sun is bright on the upland slopes;
When the wind stirs soft through the springing grass,
And the river flows like a stream of glass;
  When the first bird sings and the first bud opes,
And the faint perfume from its chalice steals—
I know what the caged bird feels!

I know why the caged bird beats his wing
  Till its blood is red on the cruel bars;

For he must fly back to his perch and cling
When he fain would be on the bough a-swing;
And a pain still throbs in the old, old scars
And they pulse again with a keener sting—
I know why he beats his wing!

I know why the caged bird sings, ah me,
When his wing is bruised and his bosom sore,—
When he beats his bars and he would be free;
It is not a carol of joy or glee,
But a prayer that he sends from his heart's deep core,
But a plea, that upward to Heaven he flings—
I know why the caged bird sings!

1896

THE RACE QUESTION DISCUSSED

NEGRO AND WHITE MAN

(SUGGESTED BY THE WILMINGTON, N.C. RIOTS)

Loud, from the South, Damascan cries
Fall on our ears, unheeded still.
No helping powers stir or rise.
Hate's opiate numbs the nation's will.
Slumbers the north. (While honor dies!)
Soothed by th' insidious breath of lies!

It would seem that the man who sits at his desk in the North and writes about the troubles in the South is very apt to be like a doctor who prescribes for a case he has no chance to diagnose. It would be true in this instance, also, if it were not that what has happened in Georgia has happened in Ohio and Illinois. The race riots in North Carolina were of a piece with the same proceedings in the state of Lincoln. The men who shoot the Negro in Hogansville are blood brothers to those who hang him in Urbana, and the deed is neither better nor worse because it happens in one section of the country or other. The race spirit in the United States is not local but general.

To the outsider, unacquainted with the vagaries of our national prejudice, the recent and sudden change of attitude of the American toward the Negro would appear inconsistent, to say the least. We are presented with the spectacle of a people gushing, through glowing headlines, over the bravery of its black heroes. In an incredibly short space of time—almost too brief, it would seem, for the mental transition of the individual, much less the nation—we find the mouthpieces of this same people chronicling the armed resistance of the community to the Negroes in the exercise of those powers and privileges which are the glory of the country for which the colored men fought. The drama of this sudden change of heart is incongruous to the point of ghastly humor.

The new attitude may be interpreted as saying: "Negroes, you may fight for us, but you may not vote for us. You may prove a strong bulwark when the bullets are flying, but you must stand from the line when the ballots are in the air. You may be heroes in war, but you must be cravens in peace."

It is true, as has been insistently urged, that it would be expedient for the Negro to forego his suffrage and climb to worth and to the world's respect by other means. By other means! That is the cry of the miners when they ask him out of the mines. It is the word of the whole commercial world when they ask him out of everything—the American shibboleth.[1] Relinquish! Relinquish! And from the dust of the very lowest places, the places that grind men's souls and kill ambition, the Negroes seek to climb to places of worth and respect.

In order to cool the passions and allay the prejudices of the superior race the entire self-effacement of the Negro would be expedient—as expedient as it would be cowardly; and, say what you will of the American people, their respect is not to be won by cowardice. Let those suffering people relinquish one single right that has been given them and the rapacity of the other race, encouraged by yielding, will ravage them from every privilege that they possess. Passion and prejudice are not sated by concession, but grow by what they feed on.

The Vaudois,[2] hiding like wild beasts in their mountain fastnesses, shot like goats upon their own hills, purpling with their blood the streams of their own valleys, France could hate, but dared not despise. The Indian himself, ground to dust under the heel of civilization, driven to death by the greed of a stronger people, will not be remembered with a sneer. But for the Negro honor is dangerous; only cowardice is safe.

The African is told that he is not yet ready to participate in government, because he has not yet learned to govern himself, and the race which preaches this proves its own right to political domination by the rioting, the rapine and the slaughter, with which for weeks past the civilized world has been scandalized. Since when was ever a psychological published with a musket?

After all, the question is not one of the Negro's fitness to rule or to vote, but of the right of the whites to murder him for the sake of instruction. Not a groan that the Romans wrung from the hearts of the conquered Britons, but echoed and re-echoed in the sound of her own fall. Every drop of blood that France drew from her own suffering Huguenots on St. Bartholomew's Day[3] but called its brother to the hungry sod on that awful 14th day of July.[4] Rome sated her thirst for blood and called it civilization. France indulged her barbaric fancy and named it religion. America strides through the ashes of burning homes, over the bodies of murdered men, women and children, holding aloft the banner of progress.

Progress! Necessity! Expedience!

But why is it necessary to excuse these acts of sophistry? Is not murder murder? Is not rapine rapine? Is not outrage outrage?

[1]A slogan meaningful to those who use it, but empty to others.

[2]Inhabitants of the Vaud region of Switzerland.

[3]The Huguenots were French Protestants. In the St. Bartholomew's Day massacre of 1572, which actually went on for nearly a month, many thousands of Huguenots were killed by Catholics.

[4]July 14, 1789, was the date of the fall of the Bastille, a prison in Paris. The capture of the Bastille by the revolutionaries was one of the principal symbolic events of the French Revolution.

The whites are stronger than the blacks. Why not then say to them openly: "We don't like you; we do not want you in certain places. Therefore when we please we will kill you. We are strong people; you are weak. What we choose to do we will do; right or no right. There is no one to wage with us a holy war in the cause of humanity."

Even the church has attempted to explain and palliate and we are told from the pulpit that the Negroes have been taught a salutary lesson: that the whites must prevail. The murderers of Wilmington[5] are congratulated upon the effort they have made toward civilization and purer government. And some of this within a stone's throw of the nation's capitol: When the reckoning shall come, what shall such ministers say? They have not stoned martyrs but they have burned their shoulders with the coats of those who did; and every such is an accomplice dyed with the same blood of the men who stood redhanded over the murdered blacks. And yet, what else could we expect from the pulpit, when we remember that less than forty years ago with the same smug complacency, it was finding excuses for slavery in tracing out the divine intention?

The passions of the people often need a spiritual backing, and shame to say, we have a clergy always ready and willing to furnish it, whether it be when man restrains his fellow men from the exercise of his national rights or murders him for pursuing his political dues. It is a disgrace to the honor of their calling, a reflection upon the intelligences of their heroes, and an insult to the God they profess to serve.

The text for better and for different sermons might be found for those divines in Paul's first epistle to the Corinthians. It is as apt to-day as it was then, and it applies to the American people with no less strength than it did to the older race. "Take heed," said the apostle, "lest by any means this liberty of yours become a stumbling block to them that are weak."[6]

We are comforted with the statement that the sudden enfranchisement of the Negro was a mistake. Perhaps it was, but the whites made it. The mistakes of life are not corrected in that way. Their effects are eternal. You cannot turn back the years and put ten millions of people into the condition that four millions were thirty years ago. You cannot ignore the effects that have ensued, the changes that have followed, and make the problem of today the problem of 1865. It is a different one. The whole aspect of the case has changed. The Negro has changed. Public opinion has shifted. Try as you will, though it has grown away, you cannot put the plant back into the seed. Of course you can root it up entirely; but beware of its juices.

Thirty years ago the American people told the Negro that he was a man with a man's full powers. They deemed it that important they did what they have done few times in the history of the country—they wrote it down in their constitution. And now they come with the shot gun in the South and sophistry in the North to prove to him that it was all wrong.

For so long a time has the black man believed that he is an American citizen that he will not be easily convinced to the contrary. It will take more than the

[5]Wilmington, North Carolina, was the scene of major racial violence in November 1898. Dunbar's essay was published in the following month.

[6]I Corinthians 8:9.

hangings, the burnings and the lynchings, both North and South, to prove it to his satisfaction. He is not so credulous as he was. He is a different man. The American people cannot turn back the tide of years and make him what he was. And so it was an entirely new people with whom they have to deal. It is an entirely new problem which is presented to them for solution. Why then should it not be met with calmness, justice, breadth and manliness which should characterize a great nation?

If the problem is as much the Negro's as the white man's—and I do not say that it is not—he is doing his best to settle it. He is acquiring property. Yes he even builds churches to the religion whose servants preach his damnation. He is going forward. Such catastrophes as the Southern riots, terrible though they be, are but incidents in his growth, which is inevitable. The principle of manhood is springing to life within him. Every year men are being educated to live for it. Every year to some—to many, it seems—God gives the better grace to die for it.

1898

THE FOURTH OF JULY AND RACE OUTRAGES

Belleville, Wilmington, Evansville, the Fourth of July, and Kishineff,[1] a curious combination and yet one replete with a ghastly humor. Sitting with closed lips over our own bloody deeds we accomplish the fine irony of a protest to Russia. Contemplating with placid eyes the destruction of all the Declaration of Independence and the Constitution stood for, we celebrate the thing which our own action proclaims we do not believe in.

But it is over and done. The Fourth is come and gone. The din has ceased and the smoke has cleared away. Nothing remains but the litter of all and a few reflections. The sky-rocket has ascended, the firecrackers have burst, the roman candles have sputtered, the "nigger chasers"—a pertinent American name—have run their courses, and we have celebrated the nation's birthday. Yes, and we black folks have celebrated.

Dearborn Street and Armour Avenue[2] have been all life and light. Not even the Jews and the Chinaman have been able to outdo us in the display of loyalty. And we have done it all because we have not stopped to think just how little it means to us.

The papers are full of the reports of peonage in Alabama.[3] A new and more dastardly slavery there has arisen to replace the old. For the sake of reenslaving the Negro, the Constitution has been trampled under feet, the rights of man have been laughed out of court, and the justice of God has been made a jest and we celebrate.

[1]Belleville, Wilmington, and Evansville were the sites of racial violence against African Americans; Kishineff was the site of Russian violence against its Jewish population.

[2]Streets in Chicago, Illinois.

[3]A kind of legally imposed servitude based on debt.

Every wire, no longer in the South alone, brings us news of a new hanging or a new burning, some recent outrage against a helpless people, some fresh degradation of an already degraded race. One man sins and a whole nation suffers, and we celebrate.

Like a dark cloud, pregnant with terror and destruction, disenfranchisement has spread its wings over our brethren of the South. Like the same dark cloud, industrial prejudice glooms above us in the North. We may not work save when the new-come foreigner refuses to, and then they, high prized above our sacrificial lives, may shoot us down with impunity. And yet we celebrate.

With citizenship discredited and scored, with violated homes and long unheeded prayers, with bleeding hands uplifted, still sore and smarting from long beating at the door of opportunity, we raise our voices and sing, "My Country, 'Tis of Thee";[4] we shout and sing while from the four points of the compass comes our brothers' unavailing cry, and so we celebrate.

With a preacher, one who a few centuries ago would have sold indulgences to the murderers on St. Bartholomew's Day,[5] with such a preacher in a Chicago pulpit, jingling his thirty pieces of silver,[6] distorting the number and nature of our crimes, excusing anarchy, apologizing for murder, and tearing to tatters the teachings of Jesus Christ while he cries, "Release unto us Barabbas,"[7] we celebrate.

But there are some who sit silent within their closed rooms and hear as from afar the din of joy come muffled to their ears as on some later day their children and their children's sons shall hear a nation's cry for succor in her need. Aye, there be some who on this festal day kneel in their private closets and with hands upraised and bleeding hearts cry out to God, if there still lives a God, "How long, O God, How long?"[8]

1903

Theodore Dreiser 1871–1945

Theodore Dreiser was America's greatest literary naturalist. One of thirteen children, he was raised in Terre Haute, Indiana, in misery and bruising poverty. His penniless German immigrant father was fiercely pious, obsessed by religion. His mother was gentle, helpless, and illiterate—Dreiser himself taught her to read and write. His wandering and shiftless brothers and sisters, with their public drunkenness, illegitimate babies, and jail terms brought him despair and constant humiliation.

[4]The first line of the patriotic song "America."

[5]A reference to the 1572 massacre of French Protestants by Roman Catholics.

[6]The payment to Judas Iscariot for betraying Jesus (Matthew 26: 14–16).

[7]Barabbas was a criminal released by Pontius Pilate, at the request of the attending mob, instead of the innocent Jesus, who was then crucified.

[8]A reference to the refrains of various Psalms, especially 13 and 35.

At fifteen Dreiser fled from home and went to Chicago, where he washed dishes in a cheap restaurant, clerked in a store, and painted advertising signs. He read constantly and, like one of his own helpless characters, he dreamt of wealth and social success in the great metropolis. When he was eighteen, a sympathetic teacher helped him enter the University of Indiana, but Dreiser quit after a year and returned to Chicago, where he embarked on another series of menial jobs and wandered the city streets at night, storing up impressions of drunks, thieves, prostitutes, and beggars.

Finally he got a job at a newspaper and began a career that took him to St. Louis, Cleveland, Pittsburgh, and eventually New York City, where he became a freelance journalist and a magazine editor. He read widely the evolutionary theorizing of such philosophers as Thomas Huxley and Herbert Spencer, and as the last remnants of Dreiser's religious faith drained away he was left with the deterministic belief that a human being is merely a mechanism moved by chemical and physical forces beyond his or her control.

In 1899, he began writing Sister Carrie. *When he submitted the manuscript to a publisher it was rejected because it was thought likely to offend "the feminine readers who control the destinies of so many novels. . . ." In 1900, when the novel was finally accepted and published, only 456 copies were sold, and Dreiser earned so little in royalties ($68.40) that he came to believe the novel had been "suppressed" by censorious prudes. Not until 1907, when it was reissued, did* Sister Carrie *finally reach a sizable reading public and begin to shape the development of American literature.*

In 1911, Dreiser published Jennie Gerhardt, *whose heroine, misled and victimized by fate, was modeled after Dreiser's own sisters. In 1912, he published* The Financier, *the first of a trilogy on the ruthlessness of American capitalism that included* The Titan *(1914) and* The Stoic *(published posthumously in 1947). In 1925, he published* An American Tragedy, *his greatest work and a critical and financial success.*

Dreiser's works, like the man himself, are ponderous and sprawling. His prose is fumbling, inexact, cliché-ridden; yet its piling up of details can produce striking portrayals of human experience. Dreiser's powerful frankness widened the social and sexual range possible for literature in America. He struck at the American myth that success and fame are to be achieved by work and virtue. He was seized by a dark, chaotic view of life, yet his determinism was softened by a romantic sensibility and by a powerful sympathy for people at radical odds with society, characters Dreiser saw as "haunted by poverty," filled with "gallant dreams," but "helpless in the clutch of relentless fate."

FURTHER READING: *Letters of Theodore Dreiser,* 3 vols., R. Elias, 1959; D. Dudley, *Dreiser and the Land of the Free,* 1932, 1946; R. Elias, *Theodore Dreiser: Apostle of Nature,* 1949; F. Matthiessen, *Theodore Dreiser,* 1951; *The Stature of Theodore Dreiser,* ed. A. Kazin and C. Shapiro, 1955; P. Gerber, *Theodore Dreiser,* 1964; W. Swanberg, *Dreiser,* 1965; C. Shapiro, *Theodore Dreiser: Our Bitter Patriot,* 1962; Y. Hakutani, *Young Dreiser,* 1980; R. Lingeman, *Theodore Dreiser,* 2 vols., 1986, 1990; J. McAleer, *Theodore Dreiser: An Introduction and Interpretation,* 1968; R. Lehan, *Theodore Dreiser: His World and His Novels,* 1969; E. Moers, *Two Dreisers: The Man and the Novelist,* 1970; R. Warren, *Homage to Theodore Dreiser,* 1971; D. Pizer, *The Novels of Theodore Dreiser,* 1976; *Critical Essays on Theodore Dreiser,* ed. D. Pizer, 1981; L. Hussman, *Dreiser and His Fiction,* 1983; J. Griffin, *The Small Canvas: An Introduction to Dreiser's Short Stories,* 1985; R. Lingeman, *Theodore Dreiser: At the Gates of the City, 1871–1907,* 1986; R. Lingeman, *Theodore Dreiser: An American Journey, 1908–1945,* 1990; L. Zanine, *Mechanism and Mysticism: The Influence of Science on the Thought and Work of Theodore Dreiser,* 1993; *Theodore Dreiser: Beyond Naturalism,* ed. M. Gogol, 1995; D. Pizer, *Literary Masters: Theodore Dreiser,* 2000; *A Theodore Dreiser Encyclopedia,* ed. K. Newlin, 2003; *The Cambridge Companion to Theodore Dreiser,* ed. L. Cassuto and C. Eby, 2004; J. Loving, *The Last Titan: A Life of Theodore Dreiser,* 2005.

TEXTS: *Sister Carrie,* 1917; *Free and Other Stories,* 1918.

FREE

The large and rather comfortable apartment of Rufus Haymaker, architect, in Central Park West,[1] was very silent. It was scarcely dawn yet, and at the edge of the park, over the way, looking out from the front windows which graced this abode and gave it its charm, a stately line of poplars was still shrouded in a gray morning mist. From his bedroom at one end of the hall, where, also, a glimpse of the park was to be had, came Mr. Haymaker at this early hour to sit by one of these broader windows and contemplate these trees and a small lake beyond. He was very fond of Nature in its manifold art forms—quite poetic, in fact.

He was a tall and spare man of about sixty, not ungraceful, though slightly stoop-shouldered, with heavy overhanging eyebrows and hair, and a short, professionally cut gray mustache and beard, which gave him a severe and yet agreeable presence. For the present he was clad in a light-blue dressing gown with silver cords, which enveloped him completely. He had thin, pale, long-fingered hands, wrinkled at the back and slightly knotted at the joints, which bespoke the artist, in mood at least, and his eyes had a weary and yet restless look in them.

For only yesterday Doctor Storm, the family physician, who was in attendance on his wife, ill now for these three weeks past with a combination of heart lesion, kidney poisoning and neuritis, had taken him aside and said very softly and affectionately, as though he were trying to spare his feelings: "To-morrow, Mr. Haymaker, if your wife is no better I will call in my friend, Doctor Grainger, whom you know, for a consultation. He is more of an expert in these matters of the heart"—the heart, Mr. Haymaker had time to note ironically—"than I am. Together we will make a thorough examination, and then I hope we will be better able to say what the possibilities of her recovery really are. It's been a very trying case, a very stubborn one, I might say. Still, she has a great deal of vitality and is doing as well as could be expected, all things considered. At the same time, though I don't wish to alarm you unnecessarily—and there is no occasion for great alarm yet—still I feel it my duty to warn you that her condition is very serious indeed. Not that I wish you to feel that she is certain to die. I don't think she is. Not at all. Just the contrary. She may get well, and probably will, and live all of twenty years more." (Mentally Mr. Haymaker sighed a purely spiritual sigh.) "She has fine recuperative powers, so far as I can judge, but she has a bad heart, and this kidney trouble has not helped it any. Just now, when her heart should have the least strain, it has the most.

"She is just at that point where, as I may say, things are in the balance. A day or two, or three or four at the most, ought to show which way things will go. But, as I have said before, I do not wish to alarm you unnecessarily. We are not nearly at the end of our tether. We haven't tried blood transfusion yet, and there are several arrows to that bow. Besides, at any moment she may respond more vigorously to medication than she has heretofore—especially in connection with her kidneys. In that case the situation would be greatly relieved at once.

"However, as I say, I feel it my duty to speak to you in this way in order that you may be mentally prepared for any event, because in such an odd combination as this the worst may happen at any time. We never can tell. As an old

[1]Fashionable street in New York City.

friend of yours and Mrs. Haymaker's, and knowing how much you two mean to each other"—Mr. Haymaker merely stared at him vacantly—"I feel it my duty to prepare you in this way. We all of us have to face these things. Only last year I lost my dear Matilda, my youngest child, as you know. Just the same, as I say, I have the feeling that Mrs. Haymaker is not really likely to die soon, and that we—Doctor Grainger and myself—will still be able to pull her through. I really do."

Doctor Storm looked at Mr. Haymaker as though he were very sorry for him—an old man long accustomed to his wife's ways and likely to be made very unhappy by her untimely end; whereas Mr. Haymaker, though staring in an almost sculptural way, was really thinking what a farce it all was, what a dull mixture of error and illusion on the part of all. Here he was, sixty years of age, weary of all this, of life really—a man who had never been really happy in all the time that he had been married; and yet here was his wife, who from conventional reasons believed that he was or should be, and who on account of this was serenely happy herself, or nearly so. And this doctor, who imagined that he was old and weak and therefore in need of this loving woman's care and sympathy and understanding! Unconsciously he raised a deprecating hand.

Also his children, who thought him dependent on her and happy with her; his servants and her and his friends thinking the same thing, and yet he really was not. It was all a lie. He was unhappy. Always he had been unhappy, it seemed, ever since he had been married—for over thirty-one years now. Never in all that time, for even so much as a single day, had he ever done anything but long, long, long, in a pale, constrained way—for what, he scarcely dared think—not to be married any more—to be free—to be as he was before ever he saw Mrs. Haymaker.

And yet being conventional in mood and training and utterly domesticated by time and conditions over which he seemed not to have much control—nature, custom, public opinion, and the like, coming into play as forces—he had drifted, had not taken any drastic action. No, he had merely drifted, wondering if time, accident or something might not interfere and straighten out his life for him, but it never had. Now weary, old, or rapidly becoming so, he condemned himself for his inaction. Why hadn't he done something about it years before? Why hadn't he broken it up before it was too late, and saved his own soul, his longing for life, color? But no, he had not. Why complain so bitterly now?

All the time the doctor had talked this way before he had wanted to smile a wry, dry, cynical smile, for in reality he did not want Mrs. Haymaker to live—or at least at the moment he thought so. He was too miserably tired of it all. And so now, after nearly twenty-four hours of the same unhappy thought, sitting by this window looking at a not distant building which shone faintly in the haze, he ran his fingers through his hair as he gazed, and sighed.

How often in these weary months, and even years, past—ever since he and his wife had been living here, and before—had he come to these or similar windows while she was still asleep, to sit and dream! For some years now they had not even roomed together, so indifferent had the whole state become; though she did not seem to consider that significant, either. Life had become more or less of a practical problem to her, one of position, place, prestige. And yet how often, viewing his life in retrospect, had he wished that his life had been as sweet as his dreams—that his dreams had come true.

After a time on this early morning, for it was still gray, with the faintest touch of pink in the east, he shook his head solemnly and sadly, then rose and returned along the hall to his wife's bedroom, at the door of which he paused to look where she lay seriously ill, and beside her in an armchair, fast asleep, a trained nurse who was supposedly keeping the night vigil ordered by the doctor, but who no doubt was now very weary. His wife was sleeping also—very pale, very thin now, and very weak. He felt sorry for her at times, in spite of his own weariness; now, for instance. Why need he have made so great a mistake so long ago? Perhaps it was his own fault for not having been wiser in his youth. Then he went quietly on to his own room, to lie down and think.

Always these days, now that she was so very ill and the problem of her living was so very acute, the creeping dawn thus roused him—to think. It seemed as though he could not really sleep soundly any more, so stirred and distrait was he. He was not so much tired or physically worn as mentally bored or disappointed. Life had treated him so badly, he kept thinking to himself over and over. He had never had the woman he really wanted, though he had been married so long, had been faithful, respectable and loved by her, in her way. "In her way," he half quoted to himself as he lay there.

Presently he would get up, dress and go down to his office as usual if his wife were not worse. But—but, he asked himself—would she be? Would that slim and yet so durable organism of hers—quite as old as his own, or nearly so—break under the strain of this really severe illness? That would set him free again, and nicely, without blame or comment on him. He could then go where he chose once more, do as he pleased—think of that—without let or hindrance. For she was ill at last, so very ill, the first and really great illness she had endured since their marriage. For weeks now she had been lying so, hovering, as it were, between life and death, one day better, the next day worse, and yet not dying, and with no certainty that she would, and yet not getting better either. Doctor Storm insisted that it was a leak in her heart which had suddenly manifested itself which was causing all the real trouble. He was apparently greatly troubled as to how to control it.

During all this period Mr. Haymaker had been, as usual, most sympathetic. His manner toward her was always soft, kindly, apparently tender. He had never really begrudged her anything—nothing certainly that he could afford. He was always glad to see her and the children humanly happy—though they, too, largely on account of her, he thought, had proved a disappointment to him—because he had always sympathized with her somewhat unhappy youth, narrow and stinted; and yet he had never been happy himself, either, never in all the time that he had been married. If she had endured much, he kept telling himself when he was most unhappy, so had he, only it was harder perhaps for women to endure things than men—he was always willing to admit that—only also she had had his love, or thought she had, an actual spiritual peace, which he had never had. She knew she had a faithful husband. He felt that he had never really had a wife at all, not one that he could love as he knew a wife should be loved. His dreams as to that!

Going to his office later the same day—it was in one of those tall buildings that face Madison Square—he had looked first, in passing, at the trees that line Central Park West, and then at the bright wall of apartment houses facing it, and meditated sadly, heavily. Here the sidewalks were crowded with nursemaids and children at play, and in between them, of course, the occasional citizen loitering or going about his errands. The day was so fine, so youthful, as spring days will seem at times. As he looked, especially at the children, and the young men bustling office-ward, mostly in new spring suits, he sighed and wished that he were young once more. Think how brisk and hopeful they were! Everything was before them. They could still pick and choose—no age or established conditions to stay them. Were any of them, he asked himself for the thousandth time, it seemed to him, as wearily connected as he had been at their age? Did they each have a charming young wife to love—one of whom they were passionately fond—such a one as he had never had; or did they not?

Wondering, he reached his office on one of the top-most floors of one of those highest buildings commanding a wide view of the city, and surveyed it wearily. Here were visible the two great rivers of the city, its towers and spires and far-flung walls. From these sometimes, even yet, he seemed to gain a patience to live, to hope. How in his youth all this had inspired him—or that other city that was then. Even now he was always at peace here, so much more so than in his own home, pleasant as it was. Here he could look out over this great scene and dream or he could lose the memory in his work that his love-life had been a failure. The great city, the buildings he could plan or supervise, the efficient help that always surrounded him—his help, not hers—aided to take his mind off himself and that deep-seated inner ache or loss.

The care of Mr. Haymaker's apartment during his wife's illness and his present absence throughout the day, devolved upon a middle-aged woman of great seriousness, Mrs. Elfridge by name, whom Mrs. Haymaker had employed years before; and under her a maid of all work, Hester, who waited on table, opened the door, and the like; and also at present two trained nurses, one for night and one for day service, who were in charge of Mrs. Haymaker. The nurses were both bright, healthy, blue-eyed girls, who attracted Mr. Haymaker and suggested all the youth he had never had—without really disturbing his poise. It would seem as though that could never be any more.

In addition, of course, there was the loving interest of his son Wesley and his daughter Ethelberta—whom his wife had named so in spite of him—both of whom had long since married and had children of their own and were living in different parts of the great city. In this crisis both of them came daily to learn how things were, and occasionally to stay for the entire afternoon or evening, or both. Ethelberta had wanted to come and take charge of the apartment entirely during her mother's illness, only Mrs. Haymaker, who was still able to direct, and fond of doing so, would not hear of it. She was not so ill but that she could still speak, and in this way could inquire and direct. Besides, Mrs. Elfridge was as good as Mrs. Haymaker in all things that related to Mr. Haymaker's physical comfort, or so she thought.

If the truth will come out—as it will in so many pathetic cases—it was never his physical so much as his spiritual or affectional comfort that Mr. Haymaker craved. As said before, he had never loved Mrs. Haymaker, or certainly not since that now long-distant period back in Muskegon, Michigan, where both had been born and where they had lived and met at the ages, she of fifteen, he of seventeen. It had been, strange as it might seem now, a love match at first sight with them. She had seemed so sweet, a girl of his own age or a little younger, the daughter of a local chemist. Later, when he had been forced by poverty to go out into the world to make his own way, he had written her much, and imagined her to be all that she had seemed at fifteen, and more—a dream among fair women. But Fortune, slow in coming to his aid and fickle in fulfilling his dreams, had brought it about that for several years more he had been compelled to stay away nearly all of the time, unable to marry her; during which period, unknown to himself really, his own point of view had altered. How it had happened he could never tell really, but so it was. The great city, larger experiences—while she was still enduring the smaller ones—other faces, dreams of larger things, had all combined to destroy it or her, only he had not quite realized it then. He was always so slow in realizing the full import of the immediate thing, he thought.

That was the time, as he had afterward told himself—how often!—that he should have discovered his mistake and stopped. Later it always seemed to become more and more impossible. Then, in spite of some heartache to her and some distress to himself, no doubt, all would be well for him now. But no; he had been too inexperienced, too ignorant, too bound by all the conventions and punctilio of his simple Western world. He thought an engagement, however unsatisfactory it might come to seem afterward, was an engagement, and binding. An honorable man would not break one—or so his country moralists argued.

Yes, at that time he might have written her, he might have told her, then. But he had been too sensitive and kindly to speak of it. Afterward it was too late. He feared to wound her, to undo her, to undo her life. But now—now—look at his! He had gone back on several occasions before marriage, and might have seen and done and been free if he had had but courage and wisdom—but no; duty, order, the beliefs of the region in which he had been reared, and of America—what it expected and what she expected and was entitled to—had done for him completely. He had not spoken. Instead, he had gone on and married her without speaking of the change in himself, without letting her know how worse than ashes it had all become. God, what a fool he had been! how often since he had told himself over and over.

Well, having made a mistake it was his duty perhaps, at least according to current beliefs, to stick by it and make the best of it;—a bargain was a bargain in marriage, if no where else—but still that had never prevented him from being unhappy. He could not prevent that himself. During all these long years, therefore, owing to these same conventions—what people would think and say—he had been compelled to live with her, to cherish her, to pretend to be happy with her—"another perfect union," as he sometimes said to himself. In reality he had been unhappy, horribly so. Even her face wearied him at times, and her presence, her mannerisms. Only this other morning Doctor Storm, by his manner indicating that he thought him lonely, in danger of being left all alone and desperately sad and neglected in case she died had irritated him greatly. Who would take care of him? his eyes had seemed to say—and yet he himself wanted nothing so much as to be alone for a time, at least, in this life, to think for himself, to do for himself, to forget this long, dreary period in which he had pretended to be something that he was not.

Was he never to be rid of the dull round of it, he asked himself now, never before he himself died? And yet shortly afterward he would reproach himself for these very thoughts, as being wrong, hard, unkind—thoughts that would certainly condemn him in the eyes of the general public, that public which made reputations and one's general standing before the world.

During all this time he had never even let her know—no, not once—of the tremendous and soul-crushing sacrifice he had made. Like the Spartan boy, he had concealed the fox gnawing at his vitals.[2] He had not complained. He had been, indeed, the model husband, as such things go in conventional walks. If you doubted it look at his position, or that of his children; or his wife—her mental and physical comfort, even in her illness, her unfailing belief that he was all he should be! Never once apparently, during all these years, had she doubted his love or felt him to be unduly unhappy—or, if not that exactly, if not fully accepting his love as something that was still at a fever heat, the thing it once was—still believing that he found pleasure and happiness in being with her, a part of the home which together they had built up, these children they had reared, comfort in knowing that it would endure to the end! To the end! During all these years she had gone on molding his and her lives—as much as that was possible in his case—and those of their children, to suit herself; and thinking all the time that she was doing what he wanted or at least what was best for him and them.

How she adored convention! What did she not think she knew in regard to how things ought to be—mainly what her old home surroundings had taught her, the American idea of this, that and the other. Her theories in regard to friends, education of the children, and so on, had in the main prevailed, even when he did not quite agree with her; her desires for certain types of pleasure and amusement, of companionship, and so on, were conventional types always and had also prevailed. There had been little quarrels, of course, always had been—what happy home is free of them?—but still he had always given in, or nearly always, and had acted as though he were satisfied in so doing.

But why, therefore, should he complain now, or she ever imagine, or ever have imagined, that he was unhappy? She did not, had not. Like all their relatives and friends of the region from which they sprang, and here also—and she had been most careful to regulate that, courting whom she pleased and ignoring all others—she still believed most firmly, more so than ever, that she knew what was best for him, what he really thought and wanted. It made him smile most wearily at times.

For in her eyes—in regard to him, at least, not always so with others, he had found—marriage was a sacrament, sacrosanct, never to be dissolved. One life, one love. Once a man had accepted the yoke or even asked a girl to marry him it was his duty to abide by it. To break an engagement, to be unfaithful to a wife, even unkind to her—what a crime, in her eyes! Such people ought to be drummed out of the world. They were really not fit to live—dogs, brutes!

And yet, look at himself—what of him? What of one who had made a mistake in regard to all this? Where was his compensation to come from, his peace and happiness? Here on earth or only in some mythical heaven—that odd, angelic heaven that she still believed in? What a farce! And all her friends and his would think he would be so miserable now if she died, or at least ought to be. So far had asinine convention and belief in custom carried the world. Think of it!

But even that was not the worst. No; that was not the worst, either. It had been the gradual realization coming along through the years that he had married an essentially small, narrow woman who could never really grasp his point of view—

[2]In an ancient fable, a Spartan boy stole a fox and hid it in his clothing. When the fox began to gnaw the boy's flesh he stoically endured the pain rather than reveal that he was a thief.

or, rather, the significance of his dreams or emotions—and yet with whom, nevertheless, because of this original promise or mistake, he was compelled to live. Grant her every quality of goodness, energy, industry, intent—as he did freely—still there was this; and it could never be adjusted, never. Essentially, as he had long since discovered, she was narrow, ultraconventional, whereas he was an artist by nature, brooding and dreaming strange dreams and thinking of far-off things which she did not or could not understand or did not sympathize with, save in a general and very remote way. The nuances of his craft, the wonders and subtleties of forms and angles—had she ever realized how significant these were to him, let alone to herself? No, never. She had not the least true appreciation of them—never had had. Architecture? Art? What could they really mean to her, desire as she might to appreciate them? And he could not now go elsewhere to discover that sympathy. No. He had never really wanted to, since the public and she would object, and he thinking it half evil himself.

Still, how was it, he often asked himself, that Nature could thus allow one conditioned or equipped with emotions and seekings such as his, not of an utterly conventional order, to seek out and pursue one like Ernestine, who was not fitted to understand him or to care what his personal moods might be? Was love truly blind, as the old saw insisted, or did Nature really plan, and cleverly, to torture the artist mind—as it did the pearl-bearing oyster with a grain of sand—with something seemingly inimical, in order that it might produce beauty? Sometimes he thought so. Perhaps the many interesting and beautiful buildings he had planned—the world called them so, at least—had been due to the loving care he lavished on them, being shut out from love and beauty elsewhere. Cruel Nature, that cared so little for the dreams of man—the individual man or woman!

At the time he had married Ernestine he was really too young to know exactly what it was he wanted to do or how it was he was going to feel in the years to come; and yet there was no one to guide him, to stop him. The custom of the time was all in favor of this dread disaster. Nature herself seemed to desire it—mere children being the be-all and the end-all of everything everywhere. Think of that as a theory! Later, when it became so clear to him what he had done, and in spite of all the conventional thoughts and conditions that seemed to bind him to this fixed condition, he had grown restless and weary, but never really irritable. No, he had never become that.

Instead he had concealed it all from her, persistently, in all kindness; only this hankering after beauty of mind and body in ways not represented by her had hurt so—grown finally almost too painful to bear. He had dreamed and dreamed of something different until it had become almost an obsession. Was it never to be, that something different, never, anywhere, in all time? What a tragedy! Soon he would be dead and then it would never be anywhere—anymore! Ernestine was charming, he would admit, or had been at first, though time had proved that she was not charming to him either mentally or physically in any compelling way; but how did that help him now? How could it? He had actually found himself bored by her for more than twenty-seven years now, and this other dream growing, growing, growing—until——

But now he was old, and she was dying, or might be, and it could not make so much difference what happened to him or to her; only it could, too, because he wanted to be free for a little while, just for a little while, before he died.

To be free! free!

One of the things that had always irritated him about Mrs. Haymaker was this, that in spite of his determination never to offend the social code in any way—he had felt for so many reasons, emotional as well as practical, that he could not afford so to do—and also in spite of the fact that he had been tortured by this show of beauty in the eyes and bodies of others, his wife, fearing perhaps in some strange psychic way that he might change, had always tried to make him feel or believe—premeditatedly and of a purpose, he thought—that he was not the kind of man who would be attractive to women; that he lacked some physical fitness, some charm that other men had, which would cause all young and really charming women to turn away from him. Think of it! He to whom so many women had turned with questioning eyes!

Also that she had married him largely because she had felt sorry for him! He chose to let her believe that, because he was sorry for her. Because other women had seemed to draw near to him at times in some appealing or seductive way she had insisted that he was not even a cavalier, let alone a Lothario;[3] that he was ungainly, slow, uninteresting—to all women but her!

Persistently, he thought, and without any real need, she had harped on this, fighting chimeras,[4] a chance danger in the future; though he had never given her any real reason, and had never even planned to sin against her in any way—never. She had thus tried to poison his own mind in regard to himself and his art—and yet—and yet——Ah, those eyes of other women, their haunting beauty, the flitting something they said to him of infinite, inexpressible delight. Why had his life been so very hard?

One of the disturbing things about all this was the iron truth which it had driven home, namely, that Nature, unless it were expressed or represented by some fierce determination within, which drove one to do, be, cared no whit for him or any other man or woman. Unless one acted for oneself, upon some stern conclusion nurtured within, one might rot and die spiritually. Nature did not care. "Blessed be the meek"—yes. Blessed be the strong, rather, for they made their own happiness. All these years in which he had dwelt and worked in this knowledge, hoping for something but not acting, nothing had happened, except to him, and that in an unsatisfactory way. All along he had seen what was happening to him; and yet held by convention he had refused to act always, because somehow he was not hard enough to act. He was not strong enough, that was the real truth—had not been. Almost like a bird in a cage, an animal peeping out from behind bars, he had viewed the world of free thought and freer action. In many a drawing-room, on the street, or in his own home even, had he not looked into an eye, the face of someone who seemed to offer understanding, to know, to sympathize, though she might not have, of course; and yet religiously and moralistically, like an anchorite,[5] because of duty and current belief and what people would say and think, Ernestine's position and faith in him, her comfort, his career and that of the children—he had put them all aside, out of his mind, forgotten them almost, as best he might. It had been hard at times, and sad, but so it had been.

And look at him now, old, not exactly feeble yet—no, not that yet, not quite!—but life weary and almost indifferent. All these years he had wanted, wanted—wanted—an understanding mind, a tender heart, the some one

[3]A ladies' man, a seducer. [4]Imaginary monsters, illusions.
[5]One who lives a solitary life, a recluse.

woman—she must exist somewhere—who would have sympathized with all the delicate shades and meanings of his own character, his art, his spiritual as well as his material dreams——And yet look at him! Mrs. Haymaker had always been with him, present in the flesh or the spirit, and—so——

Though he could not ever say that she was disagreeable to him in a material way—he could not say that she had ever been that exactly—still she did not correspond to his idea of what he needed, and so——Form had meant so much to him, color; the glorious perfectness of a glorious woman's body, for instance, the color of her thoughts, moods—exquisite they must be, like his own at times; but no, he had never had the opportunity to know one intimately. No, not one, though he had dreamed of her so long. He had never even dared whisper this to any one, scarcely to himself. It was not wise, not socially fit. Thoughts like this would tend to social ostracism in his circle, or rather hers—for had she not made the circle?

And here was the rub with Mr. Haymaker, at least, that he could not make up his mind whether in his restlessness and private mental complaints he were not even now guilty of a great moral crime in so thinking. Was it not true that men and women should be faithful in marriage whether they were happy or not? Was there not some psychic law governing this matter of union—one life, one love—which made the thoughts and the pains and the subsequent sufferings and hardships of the individual, whatever they might be, seem unimportant? The churches said so. Public opinion and the law seemed to accept this. There were so many problems, so much order to be disrupted, so much pain caused, many insoluble problems where children were concerned—if people did not stick. Was it not best, more blessed—socially, morally, and in every other way important—for him to stand by a bad bargain rather than to cause so much disorder and pain, even though he lost his own soul emotionally? He had thought so—or at least he had acted as though he thought so—and yet——How often had he wondered over this!

Take, now, some other phases. Granting first that Mrs. Haymaker had, according to the current code, measured up to the requirements of a wife, good and true, and that at first after marriage there had been just enough of physical and social charm about her to keep his state from becoming intolerable, still there was this old ache; and then newer things which came with the birth of the several children: First Elwell—named after a cousin of hers, not his—who had died only two years after he was born; and then Wesley; and then Ethelberta. How he had always disliked that name!—largely because he had hoped to call her Ottilie, a favorite name of his; or Janet, after his mother.

Curiously the arrival of these children and the death of poor little Elwell at two had somehow, in spite of his unrest, bound him to this matrimonial state and filled him with a sense of duty, and pleasure even—almost entirely apart from her, he was sorry to say—in these young lives; though if there had not been children, as he sometimes told himself, he surely would have broken away from her; he could not have stood it. They were so odd in their infancy, those little ones, so troublesome and yet so amusing—little Elwell, for instance, whose nose used to crinkle with delight when he would pretend to bite his neck, and whose gurgle of pleasure was so sweet and heart-filling that it positively thrilled and lured him. In spite of his thoughts concerning Ernestine—and always in those days they were rigidly put down as unmoral and even evil, a certain unsocial streak in him perhaps which was against law and order and social well-being—he came to have a deep and abiding feeling for Elwell. The latter, in some chemic,[6] almost unconscious way, seemed to have arrived as a balm to his misery, a bandage for his growing wound—sent by whom, by what, how? Elwell had seized upon his imagination, and so his heartstrings—had come, indeed, to make him feel understanding and sympathy there in that little child; to supply, or seem to at least, what he lacked in the way of love and affection from one whom he could truly love. Elwell was never so happy apparently as when snuggling in his arms, not Ernestine's, or lying against his neck. And when he went for a walk or elsewhere there was Elwell always ready, arms up, to cling to his neck. He seemed, strangely enough, inordinately fond of his father, rather than his mother, and never happy without him. On his part, Haymaker came to be wildly fond of him—that queer little lump of a face, suggesting a little of himself and of his own mother, not so much of Ernestine, or so he thought, though he would not have objected to that. Not at all. He was not so small as that. Toward the end of the second year, when Elwell was just beginning to be able to utter a word or two, he had taught him that silly old rhyme which ran "There were three kittens," and when it came to "and they shall have no——" he would stop and say to Elwell, "What now?" and the latter would gurgle "puh!"—meaning, of course, pie.

Ah, those happy days with little Elwell, those walks with him over his shoulder or on his arm, those hours in which of an evening he would rock him to sleep in his arms! Always Ernestine was there, and happy in the thought of his love for little Elwell and her, her more than anything else perhaps; but it was an illusion—that latter part. He did not care for her even then as she thought he did. All his fondness was for Elwell, only she took it as evidence of his growing or enduring affection for her—another evidence of the peculiar working of her mind. Women were like that, he supposed—some women.

And then came that dreadful fever, due to some invading microbe which the doctors could not diagnose or isolate, infantile paralysis perhaps; and little Elwell had finally ceased to be as flesh and was eventually carried forth to the lorn, disagreeable graveyard near Woodlawn. How he had groaned internally, indulged in sad, despondent thoughts concerning the futility of all things human, when this had happened! It seemed for the time being as if all color and beauty had really gone out of his life for good.

"Man born of woman is of few days and full of troubles,"[7] the preacher whom Mrs. Haymaker had insisted upon having into the house at the time of the funeral had read. "He fleeth also as a shadow and continueth not."[8]

Yes; so little Elwell had fled, as a shadow, and in his own deep sorrow at the time he had come to feel the first and only sad, deep sympathy for Ernestine that he had ever felt since marriage; and that because she had suffered so much—had lain in his arms after the funeral and cried so bitterly. It was terrible, her sorrow. Terrible—a mother grieving for her first-born! Why was it, he had thought at the time, that he had never been able to think or make her all she ought to be to him? Ernestine at this time had seemed better, softer, kinder, wiser, sweeter than she had ever seemed; more worthy, more interesting than ever he had thought her before. She had slaved so during the child's illness, stayed awake night after night, watched over him with such loving care—done everything, in short, that a loving human heart could do to rescue her young

[6]Chemical. [7]Job 14:1. [8]Job 14:2.

from the depths; and yet even then he had not really been able to love her. No, sad and unkind as it might seem, he had not. He had just pitied her and thought her better, worthier! What cursed stars disordered the minds and moods of people so? Why was it that these virtues of people, their good qualities, did not make you love them, did not really bind them to you, as against the things you could not like? Why? He had resolved to do better in his thoughts, but somehow, in spite of himself, he had never been able so to do.

Nevertheless, at that time he seemed to realize more keenly than ever her order, industry, frugality, a sense of beauty within limits, a certain laudable ambition to do something and be somebody—only, only he could not sympathize with her ambitions, could not see that she had anything but a hopelessly commonplace and always unimportant point of view. There was never any flare to her, never any true distinction of mind or soul. She seemed always, in spite of anything he might say or do, hopelessly to identify doing and being with money and current opinion—neighborhood public opinion, almost—and local social position, whereas he knew that distinguished doing might as well be connected with poverty and shame and disgrace as with these other things—wealth and station, for instance; a thing which she could never quite understand apparently, though he often tried to tell her, much against her mood always.

Look at the cases of the great artists! Some of the greatest architects right here in the city, or in history, were of peculiar, almost disagreeable, history. But no, Mrs. Haymaker could not understand anything like that, anything connected with history, indeed—she hardly believed in history, its dark, sad pages, and would never read it, or at least did not care to. And as for art and artists—she would never have believed that wisdom and art understanding and true distinction might take their rise out of things necessarily low and evil—never.

Take now, the case of young Zingara. Zingara was an architect like himself, whom he had met more than thirty years before, here in New York, when he had first arrived, a young man struggling to become an architect of significance, only he was very poor and rather unkempt and disreputable-looking. Haymaker had found him several years before his marriage to Ernestine in the dark offices of Pyne & Starboard, Architects, and had been drawn to him definitely; but because he smoked all the time and was shabby as to his clothes and had no money—why, Mrs. Haymaker, after he had married her, and though he had known Zingara nearly four years, would have none of him. To her he was low, and a failure, one who would never succeed. Once she had seen him in some cheap restaurant that she chanced to be passing, in company with a drabby-looking maid, and that was the end.

"I wish you wouldn't bring him here any more, dear," she had insisted; and to have peace he had complied—only, now look. Zingara had since become a great architect, but now of course, owing to Mrs. Haymaker, he was definitely alienated. He was the man who had since designed the Æsculapian Club; and Symphony Hall with its delicate façade; as well as the tower of the Wells Building, sending its sweet lines so high, like a poetic thought or dream. But Zingara was now a dreamy recluse like himself, very exclusive, as Haymaker had long since come to know, and indifferent as to what people thought or said.

But perhaps it was not just obtuseness to certain of the finer shades and meanings of life, but an irritating aggressiveness at times, backed only by her limited understanding, which caused her to seek and wish to be here, there and the other place; wherever, in her mind, the truly successful—which meant nearly always the materially successful of a second or third rate character—were, which irritated him most of all. How often had he tried to point out the difference between true and shoddy distinction—the former rarely connected with great wealth.

But no. So often she seemed to imagine such queer people to be truly successful, when they were really not—usually people with just money, or a very little more.

And in the matter of rearing and educating and marrying their two children, Wesley and Ethelberta, who had come after Elwell—what peculiar pains and feelings had not been involved in all this for him. In infancy both of these had seemed sweet enough, and so close to him, though never quite so wonderful as Elwell. But, as they grew, it seemed somehow as though Ernestine had come between him and them. First, it was the way she had raised them, the very stiff and formal manner in which they were supposed to move and be, copied from the few new-rich whom she had chanced to meet through him—and admired in spite of his warnings. That was the irony of architecture as a profession—it was always bringing such queer people close to one, and for the sake of one's profession, sometimes, particularly in the case of the young architect, one had to be nice to them. Later, it was the kind of school they should attend. He had half imagined at first that it would be the public school, because they both had begun as simple people; but no, since they were prospering it had to be a private school for each, and not one of his selection, either—or hers, really—but one to which the Barlows and the Westervelts, two families of means with whom Ernestine had become intimate, sent their children and therefore thought excellent!

The Barlows! Wealthy, but, to him, gross and mediocre people who had made a great deal of money in the manufacture of patent medicines out West, and who had then come to New York to splurge, and had been attracted to Ernestine—not him particularly, he imagined—because Haymaker had built a town house for them, and also because he was gaining a fine reputation. They were dreadful really, so *gauche,*[9] so truly dull; and yet somehow they seemed to suit Ernestine's sense of fitness and worth at the time, because, as she said, they were good and kind—like her Western home folks; only they were not really. She just imagined so. They were worthy enough people in their way, though with no taste. Young Fred Barlow had been sent to the expensive Gaillard School for Boys, near Morristown,[10] where they were taught manners and airs, and little else, as Haymaker always thought, though Ernestine insisted that they were given a religious training as well. And so Wesley had to go there—for a time, anyhow. It was the best school.

And similarly, because Mercedes Westervelt, senseless, vain little thing, was sent to Briarcliff School, near White Plains,[11] Ethelberta had to go there. Think of it! It was all so silly, so pushing. How well he remembered the long, delicate campaign which preceded this, the logic and tactics employed, the importance of it socially to Ethelberta, the tears and cajolery. Mrs. Haymaker could always cry so easily, or seem to be on the verge of it, when she wanted anything; and somehow, in spite of the fact that he knew her tears were unimportant, or timed and for a purpose, he could never stand out against them,

[9]Crude, lacking social grace. [10]In New Jersey, near New York City.
[11]Suburb of New York City.

and she knew it. Always he felt moved or weakened in spite of himself. He had no weapon wherewith to fight them, though he resented them as a part of the argument. Positively Mrs. Haymaker could be as sly and as ruthless as Machiavelli[12] himself at times, and yet believe all the while that she was tender, loving, self-sacrificing, generous, moral and a dozen other things, all of which led to the final achievement of her own aims. Perhaps this was admirable from one point of view, but it irritated him always. But if one were unable to see him- or herself, their actual disturbing inconsistencies, what were you to do?

And again, he had by then been married so long that it was almost impossible to think of throwing her over, or so it seemed at the time. They had reached the place then where they had supposedly achieved position together, though in reality it was all his—and not such position as he was entitled to, at that. Ernestine—and he was thinking this in all kindness—could never attract the ideal sort. And anyhow, the mere breath of a scandal between them, separation or unfaithfulness, which he never really contemplated, would have led to endless bickering and social and commercial injury, or so he thought. All her strong friends—and his, in a way—those who had originally been his clients, would have deserted him. Their wives, their own social fears, would have compelled them to ostracize him! He would have been a scandal-marked architect, a brute for objecting to so kind and faithful and loving a wife. And perhaps he would have been, at that. He could never quite tell, it was all so mixed and tangled.

Take, again, the marriage of his son Wesley into the De Gaud family—George de Gaud *père*[13] being nothing more than a retired real-estate speculator and promoter who had money, but nothing more; and Irma de Gaud, the daughter, being a gross, coarse, sensuous girl, physically attractive no doubt, and financially reasonably secure, or so she had seemed; but what else? Nothing, literally nothing; and his son had seemed to have at least some spiritual ideals at first. Ernestine had taken up with Mrs. George de Gaud—a miserable, narrow creature, so Haymaker thought—largely for Wesley's sake, he presumed. Anyhow, everything had been done to encourage Wesley in his suit and Irma in her toleration, and now look at them! De Gaud *père* had since failed and left his daughter practically nothing. Irma had been interested in anything but Wesley's career, had followed what she considered the smart among the new-rich—a smarter, wilder, newer new-rich than ever Ernestine had fancied, or could. To-day she was without a thought for anything besides teas and country clubs and theaters—and what else?

And long since Wesley had begun to realize it himself. He was an engineer now, in the employ of one of the great construction companies, a moderately successful man. But even Ernestine, who had engineered the match and thought it wonderful, was now down on her. She had begun to see through her some years ago, when Irma had begun to ignore her; only before it was always the De Gauds here, and the De Gauds there. Good gracious, what more could any one want than the De Gauds—Irma de Gaud, for instance? Then came the concealed dissension between Irma and Wesley, and now Mrs. Haymaker insisted that Irma had held, and was holding Wesley back. She was not the right woman for him. Almost—against all her prejudices—she was willing

[12]Renaissance Italian statesman (1469–1527) renowned as cunning and amoral.
[13]French: father, senior.

that he should leave her. Only, if Haymaker had broached anything like that in connection with himself!

And yet Mrs. Haymaker had been determined, because of what she considered the position of the De Gauds at that time, that Wesley should marry Irma. Wesley now had to slave at mediocre tasks in order to have enough to allow Irma to run in so-called fast society of a second or third rate. And even at that she was not faithful to him—or so Haymaker believed. There were so many strange evidences. And yet Haymaker felt that he did not care to interfere now. How could he? Irma was tired of Wesley, and that was all there was to it. She was looking elsewhere, he was sure.

Take but one more case, that of Ethelberta. What a name! In spite of all Ernestine's determination to make her so successful and thereby reflect some credit on her had she really succeeded in so doing? To be sure, Ethelberta's marriage was somewhat more successful financially than Wesley's had proved to be, but was she any better placed in other ways? John Kelso—"Jack," as she always called him—with his light ways and lighter mind, was he really any one!—anything more than a waster? His parents stood by him no doubt, but that was all; and so much the worse for him. According to Mrs. Haymaker at the time, he, too, was an ideal boy, admirable, just the man for Ethelberta, because the Kelsos, *père* and *mère,*[14] had money. Horner Kelso had made a kind of fortune in Chicago in the banknote business, and had settled in New York, about the time that Ethelberta was fifteen, to spend it. Ethelberta had met Grace Kelso at school.

And now see! She was not unattractive, and had some pleasant, albeit highly affected, social ways; she had money, and a comfortable apartment in Park Avenue; but what had it all come to? John Kelso had never done anything really, nothing. His parents' money and indulgence and his early training for a better social state had ruined him if he had ever had a mind that amounted to anything. He was idle, pleasure-loving, mentally indolent, like Irma de Gaud. Those two should have met and married, only they could never have endured each other. But how Mrs. Haymaker had courted the Kelsos in her eager and yet diplomatic way, giving teas and receptions and theater parties; and yet he had never been able to exchange ten significant words with either of them, or the younger Kelsos either. Think of it!

And somehow in the process Ethelberta, for all his early affection and tenderness and his still kindly feeling for her, had been weaned away from him and had proved a limited and conventional girl, somewhat like her mother, and more inclined to listen to her than to him—though he had not minded that really. It had been the same with Wesley before her. Perhaps, however, a child was entitled to its likes and dislikes, regardless.

But why had he stood for it all, he now kept asking himself. Why? What grand results, if any, had been achieved? Were their children so wonderful?—their lives? Would he not have been better off without her—his children better, even, by a different woman?—hers by a different man? Wouldn't it have been better if he had destroyed it all, broken away? There would have been pain, of course, terrible consequences, but even so he would have been free to go, to do, to reorganize his life on another basis. Zingara had avoided marriage entirely—wise man. But no, no; always convention, that long list of reasons and terrors he was

[14]French: mother.

always reciting to himself. He had allowed himself to be pulled round by the nose, God only knows why, and that was all there was to it. Weakness, if you will, perhaps; fear of convention; fear of what people would think and say.

Always now he found himself brooding over the dire results to him of all this respect on his part for convention, moral order, the duty of keeping society on an even keel, of not bringing disgrace to his children and himself and her, and yet ruining his own life emotionally by so doing. To be respectable had been so important that it had resulted in spiritual failure for him. But now all that was over with him, and Mrs. Haymaker was ill, near to death, and he was expected to wish her to get well, and be happy with her for a long time yet! Be happy! In spite of anything he might wish or think he ought to do, he couldn't. He couldn't even wish her to get well.

It was too much to ask. There was actually a haunting satisfaction in the thought that she might die now. It wouldn't be much, but it would be something—a few years of freedom. That was something. He was not utterly old yet, and he might have a few years of peace and comfort to himself still—and—and——That dream—that dream—though it might never come true now—it couldn't really—still—still——He wanted to be free to go his own way once more, to do as he pleased, to walk, to think, to brood over what he had not had—to brood over what he had not had! Only, only, whenever he looked into her pale sick face and felt her damp limp hands he could not quite wish that, either; not quite, not even now. It seemed too hard, too brutal—only—only——So he wavered.

No; in spite of her long-past struggle over foolish things and in spite of himself and all he had endured or thought he had, he was still willing that she should live; only he couldn't wish it exactly. Yes, let her live if she could. What matter to him now whether she lived or died? Whenever he looked at her he could not help thinking how helpless she would be without him, what a failure at her age, and so on. And all along, as he wryly repeated to himself, she had been thinking and feeling that she was doing the very best for him and her and the children!—that she was really the ideal wife for him, making every dollar go as far as it would, every enjoyment yield the last drop for them all, every move seeming to have been made to their general advantage! Yes, that was true. There was a pathos about it, wasn't there? But as for the actual results——!

The next morning, the second after his talk with Doctor Storm, found him sitting once more beside his front window in the early dawn, and so much of all this, and much more, was coming back to him, as before. For the thousandth or the ten-thousandth time, as it seemed to him, in all the years that had gone, he was concluding again that his life was a failure. If only he were free for a little while just to be alone and think, perhaps to discover what life might bring him yet; only on this occasion his thoughts were colored by a new turn in the situation. Yesterday afternoon, because Mrs. Haymaker's condition had grown worse, the consultation between Grainger and Storm was held, and to-day sometime transfusion was to be tried, that last grim stand taken by physicians in distress over a case; blood taken from a strong ex-cavalryman out of a position, in this case, and the best to be hoped for, but not assured. In this instance his thoughts were as before wavering. Now supposing she really died, in spite of this? What would he think of himself then? He went back after a time and looked in on her where she was still sleeping. Now she was not so strong as before, or so she seemed; her pulse was not so good, the nurse said. And now as before his mood changed in her favor, but only for a little while. For later, waking, she seemed to look and feel better.

Later he came up to the dining room, where the nurse was taking her breakfast, and seating himself beside her, as was his custom these days, asked: "How do you think she is to-day?"

He and the night nurse had thus had their breakfasts together for days. This nurse, Miss Filson, was such a smooth, pink, graceful creature, with light hair and blue eyes, the kind of eyes and color that of late, and in earlier years, had suggested to him the love time or youth that he had missed.

The latter looked grave, as though she really feared the worst but was concealing it.

"No worse, I think, and possibly a little better," she replied, eyeing him sympathetically. He could see that she too felt that he was old and in danger of being neglected. "Her pulse is a little stronger, nearly normal now, and she is resting easily. Doctor Storm and Doctor Grainger are coming, though, at ten. Then they'll decide what's to be done. I think if she's worse that they are going to try transfusion. The man has been engaged.[15] Doctor Storm said that when she woke to-day she was to be given strong beef tea. Mrs. Elfridge is making it now. The fact that she is not much worse, though, is a good sign in itself, I think."

Haymaker merely stared at her from under his heavy gray eyebrows. He was so tired and gloomy, not only because he had not slept much of late himself but because of this sawing to and fro between his varying moods. Was he never to be able to decide for himself what he really wished? Was he never to be done with this interminable moral or spiritual problem? Why could he not make up his mind on the side of moral order, sympathy, and be at peace? Miss Filson pattered on about other heart cases, how so many people lived years and years after they were supposed to die of heart lesion; and he meditated as to the grayness and strangeness of it all, the worthlessness of his own life, the variability of his own moods. Why was he so? How queer—how almost evil, sinister—he had become at times; how weak at others. Last night as he had looked at Ernestine lying in bed, and this morning before he had seen her, he had thought if she only would die—if he were only really free once more, even at this late date. But then when he had seen her again this morning and now when Miss Filson spoke of transfusion, he felt sorry again. What good would it do him now? Why should he want to kill her? Could such evil ideas go unpunished either in this world or the next? Supposing his children could guess! Supposing she did die now—and he wished it so fervently only this morning—how would he feel? After all, Ernestine had not been so bad. She had tried, hadn't she—only she had not been able to make a success of things, as he saw it, and he had not been able to love her, that was all. He reproached himself once more now with the hardness and the cruelty of his thoughts.

The opinion of the two physicians was that Mrs. Haymaker was not much better and that this first form of blood transfusion must be resorted to—injected straight via a pump—which should restore her greatly provided her heart did not bleed it out too freely. Before doing so, however, both men once more spoke to Haymaker, who in an excess of self-condemnation insisted that no expense must be spared. If her life was in danger, save it by any means—all. It

[15] I.e., the blood donor has been hired.

was precious to her, to him and to her children. So he spoke. Thus he felt that he was lending every force which could be expected of him, aside from fervently wishing for her recovery, which even now, in spite of himself, he could not do. He was too weary of it all, the conventional round of duties and obligations. But if she recovered, as her physicians seemed to think she might if transfusion were tried, if she gained even, it would mean that he would have to take her away for the summer to some quiet mountain resort—to be with her hourly during the long period in which she would be recovering. Well, he would not complain now. That was all right. He would do it. He would be bored of course, as usual, but it would be too bad to have her die when she could be saved. Yes, that was true. And yet—

He went down to his office again and in the meantime this first form of transfusion was tried, and proved a great success, apparently. She was much better, so the day nurse phoned at three; very much better. At five-thirty Mr. Haymaker returned, no unsatisfactory word having come in the interim, and there she was, resting on a raised pillow, if you please, and looking so cheerful, more like her old self than he had seen her in some time.

At once then his mood changed again. They were amazing, these variations in his own thoughts, almost chemic, not volitional, decidedly peculiar for a man who was supposed to know his own mind—only did one, ever? Now she would not die. Now the whole thing would go on as before. He was sure of it. Well, he might as well resign himself to the old sense of failure. He would never be free now. Everything would go on as before, the next and the next day the same. Terrible! Though he seemed glad—really grateful, in a way, seeing her cheerful and hopeful once more—still the obsession of failure and being once more bound forever returned now. In his own bed at midnight he said to himself: "Now she will really get well. All will be as before. I will never be free. I will never have a day—a day! Never!"

But the next morning, to his surprise and fear or comfort, as his moods varied, she was worse again; and then once more he reproached himself for his black thoughts. Was he not really killing her by what he thought? he asked himself—these constant changes in his mood? Did not his dark wishes have power? Was he not as good as a murderer in his way? Think, if he had always to feel from now on that he had killed her by wishing so! Would not that be dreadful—an awful thing really? Why was he this way? Could he not be human, kind?

When Doctor Storm came at nine-thirty, after a telephone call from the nurse, and looked grave and spoke of horses' blood as being better, thicker than human blood—not so easily bled out of the heart when injected as a serum—Haymaker was beside himself with self-reproaches and sad, disturbing fear. His dark, evil thoughts of last night and all these days had done this, he was sure. Was he really a murderer at heart, a dark criminal, plotting her death?—and for what? Why had he wished last night that she would die? Her case must be very desperate.

"You must do your best," he now said to Doctor Storm. "Whatever is needful—she must not die if you can help it."

"No, Mr. Haymaker," returned the latter sympathetically. "All that can be done will be done. You need not fear. I have an idea that we didn't inject enough yesterday, and anyhow human blood is not thick enough in this case. She responded, but not enough. We will see what we can do to-day."

Haymaker, pressed with duties, went away, subdued and sad. Now once more he decided that he must not tolerate these dark ideas any more, must rid himself of these black wishes, whatever he might feel. It was evil. They would eventually come back to him in some dark way, he might be sure. They might be influencing her. She must be allowed to recover if she could without any opposition on his part. He must now make a further sacrifice of his own life, whatever it cost. It was only decent, only human. Why should he complain now, anyhow, after all these years! What difference would a few more years make? He returned at evening, consoled by his own good thoughts and a telephone message at three to the effect that his wife was much better. This second injection had proved much more effective. Horses' blood was plainly better for her. She was stronger, and sitting up again. He entered at five, and found her lying there pale and weak, but still with a better light in her eye, a touch of color in her cheeks—or so he thought—more force, and a very faint smile for him, so marked had been the change. How great and kind Doctor Storm really was! How resourceful! If she would only get well now! If this dread siege would only abate! Doctor Storm was coming again at eight.

"Well, how are you, dear?" she asked, looking at him sweetly and lovingly, and taking his hand in hers.

He bent and kissed her forehead—a Judas kiss, he had thought up to now, but not so to-night. To-night he was kind, generous—anxious, even, for her to live.

"All right, dearest; very good indeed. And how are you? It's such a fine evening out. You ought to get well soon so as to enjoy these spring days."

"I'm going to," she replied softly. "I feel so much better. And how have you been? Has your work gone all right?"

He nodded and smiled and told her bits of news. Ethelberta had phoned that she was coming, bringing violets. Wesley had said he would be here at six, with Irma! Such-and-such people had asked after her. How could he have been so evil, he now asked himself, as to wish her to die? She was not so bad—really quite charming in her way, an ideal wife for some one, if not him. She was as much entitled to live and enjoy her life as he was to enjoy his; and after all she was the mother of his children, had been with him all these years. Besides, the day had been so fine—it was now—a wondrous May evening. The air and sky were simply delicious. A lavender haze was in the air. The telephone bell now ringing brought still another of a long series of inquiries as to her condition. There had been so many of these during the last few days, the maid said, and especially to-day—and she gave Mr. Haymaker a list of names. See, he thought, she had even more friends than he, being so good, faithful, worthy. Why should he wish her ill?

He sat down to dinner with Ethelberta and Wesley when they arrived, and chatted quite gayly—more hopefully than he had in weeks. His own varying thoughts no longer depressing him, for the moment he was happy. How were they? What were the children all doing? At eight-thirty Doctor Storm came again, and announced that he thought Mrs. Haymaker was doing very well indeed, all things considered.

"Her condition is fairly promising, I must say," he said. "If she gets through another night or two comfortably without falling back I think she'll do very well from now on. Her strength seems to be increasing a fraction. However, we must not be too optimistic. Cases of this kind are very treacherous. Tomorrow we'll see how she feels, whether she needs any more blood."

He went away, and at ten Ethelberta and Wesley left for the night, asking to be called if she grew worse, thus leaving him alone once more. He sat and meditated. At eleven, after a few moments at his wife's bedside—absolute quiet had been the doctors' instructions these many days—he himself went to bed. He was very tired. His varying thoughts had afflicted him so much that he was always tired, it seemed—his evil conscience, he called it—but to-night he was sure he would sleep. He felt better about himself, about life. He had done better, to-day. He should never have tolerated such dark thoughts. And yet—and yet—and yet——

He lay on his bed near a window which commanded a view of a small angle of the park, and looked out. There were the spring trees, as usual, silvered now by the light, a bit of lake showing at one end. Here in the city a bit of sylvan scenery such as this was so rare and so expensive. In his youth he had been so fond of water, any small lake or stream or pond. In his youth, also, he had loved the moon, and to walk in the dark. It had all, always, been so suggestive of love and happiness, and he had so craved love and happiness and never had it. Once he had designed a yacht club, the base of which suggested waves. Once, years ago, he had thought of designing a lovely cottage or country house for himself and some new love—that wonderful one—if ever she came and he were free. How wonderful it would all have been. Now—now—the thought at such an hour and especially when it was too late, seemed sacrilegious, hard, cold, unmoral, evil. He turned his face away from the moonlight and sighed, deciding to sleep and shut out these older and darker and sweeter thoughts if he could, and did.

Presently he dreamed, and it was as if some lovely spirit of beauty—that wondrous thing he had always been seeking—came and took him by the hand and led him out, out by dimpling streams and clear rippling lakes and a great, noble highway where were temples and towers and figures in white marble. And it seemed as he walked as if something had been, or were, promised him—a lovely fruition to something which he craved—only the world toward which he walked was still dark or shadowy, with something sad and repressing about it, a haunting sense of a still darker distance. He was going toward beauty apparently, but he was still seeking, seeking, and it was dark there when——

"Mr. Haymaker! Mr. Haymaker!" came a voice—soft, almost mystical at first, and then clearer and more disturbing, as a hand was laid on him. "Will you come at once? It's Mrs. Haymaker!"

On the instant he was on his feet seizing the blue silk dressing gown hanging at his bed's head, and adjusting it as he hurried. Mrs. Elfridge and the nurse were behind him, very pale and distrait, wringing their hands. He could tell by that that the worst was at hand. When he reached the bedroom—her bedroom—there she lay as in life—still, peaceful, already limp, as though she were sleeping. Her thin, and as he sometimes thought, cold, lips were now parted in a faint, gracious smile, or trace of one. He had seen her look that way, too, at times; a really gracious smile, and wise, wiser than she was. The long, thin, graceful hands were open, the fingers spread slightly apart as though she were tired, very tired. The eyelids, too, rested wearily on tired eyes. Her form, spare as always, was outlined clearly under the thin coverlets. Miss Filson, the night nurse, was saying something about having fallen asleep for a moment, and waking only to find her so. She was terribly depressed and disturbed, possibly because of Doctor Storm.

Haymaker paused, greatly shocked and moved by the sight—more so than by anything since the death of little Elwell. After all, she had tried, according to her light. But now she was dead—and they had been together so long! He came forward, tears of sympathy springing to his eyes, then sank down beside the bed on his knees so as not to disturb her right hand where it lay.

"Ernie, dear," he said gently. "Ernie—are you really gone?" His voice was full of sorrow; but to himself it sounded false, traitorous.

He lifted the hand and put it to his lips sadly, then leaned his head against her, thinking of his long, mixed thoughts these many days, while both Mrs. Elfridge and the nurse began wiping their eyes. They were so sorry for him, he was so old now!

After a while he got up—they came forward to persuade him at last—looking tremendously sad and distrait, and asked Mrs. Elfridge and the nurse not to disturb his children. They could not aid her now. Let them rest until morning. Then he went back to his own room and sat down on the bed for a moment, gazing out on the same silvery scene that had attracted him before. It was dreadful. So then his dark wishing had come true at last? Possibly his black thoughts had killed her after all. Was that possible? Had his voiceless prayers been answered in this grim way? And did she know now what he had really thought? Dark thought. Where was she now? What was she thinking now if she knew? Would she hate him—haunt him? It was not dawn yet, only two or three in the morning, and the moon was still bright. And in the next room she was lying, pale and cool, gone forever now out of his life.

He got up after a time and went forward into that pleasant front room where he had so often loved to sit, then back into her room to view the body again. Now that she was gone, here more than elsewhere, in her dead presence, he seemed better able to collect his scattered thoughts. She might see or she might not—might know or not. It was all over now. Only he could not help but feel a little evil. She had been so faithful, if nothing more, so earnest in behalf of him and of his children. He might have spared her these last dark thoughts of these last few days. His feelings were so jumbled that he could not place them half the time. But at the same time the ethics of the past, of his own irritated feelings and moods in regard to her, had to be adjusted somehow before he could have peace. They must be adjusted, only how—how? He and Mrs. Elfridge had agreed not to disturb Doctor Storm any more to-night. They were all agreed to get what rest they could against the morning.

After a time he came forward once more to the front room to sit and gaze at the park. Here, perhaps, he could solve these mysteries for himself, think them out, find out what he did feel. He was evil for having wished all he had, that he knew and felt. And yet there was his own story, too—his life. The dawn was breaking by now; a faint grayness shaded the east and dimly lightened this room. A tall pier mirror between two windows now revealed him to himself—spare, angular, disheveled, his beard and hair astray and his eyes weary. The figure he made here as against his dreams of a happier life, once he were free, now struck him forcibly. What a farce! What a failure! Why should he, of all people, think of further happiness in love, even if he were free? Look at his reflection here in this mirror. What a picture—old, grizzled, done for! Had he not known that for so long? Was it not too ridiculous? Why should he have tolerated such vain thoughts? What could he of all people hope for now? No thing of beauty would have him now. Of course not. That glorious dream of his youth was gone forever. It was a mirage, an ignis fatuus.[16] His wife might just as well have lived as died, for all the difference it would or could make to him. Only, he was really free just the same, almost as it were in spite of his varying moods. But he was old, weary, done for, a recluse and ungainly.

Now the innate cruelty of life, its blazing ironic indifference to him and so many grew rapidly upon him. What had he had? What all had he not missed? Dismally he stared first at his dark wrinkled skin; the crow's-feet at the sides of his eyes; the wrinkles across his forehead and between the eyes; his long, dark, wrinkled hands—handsome hands they once were, he thought; his angular, stiff body. Once he had been very much of a personage, he thought, striking, forceful, dynamic—but now! He turned and looked out over the park where the young trees were, and the lake, to the pinking dawn—just a trace now—a significant thing in itself at this hour surely—the new dawn, so wondrously new for younger people—then back at himself. What could he wish for now—what hope for?

As he did so his dream came back to him—that strange dream of seeking and being led and promised and yet always being led forward into a dimmer, darker land. What did that mean? Had it any real significance? Was it all to be dimmer, darker still? Was it typical of his life? He pondered.

"Free!" he said after a time. "Free! I know now how that is. I am free now, at last! Free! . . . Free! . . . Yes—free . . . to die!"

So he stood there ruminating and smoothing his hair and his beard.

1918

from *SISTER CARRIE*

CHAPTER I

THE MAGNET ATTRACTING—A WAIF AMID FORCES

When Caroline Meeber boarded the afternoon train for Chicago, her total outfit consisted of a small trunk, a cheap imitation alligator-skin satchel, a small lunch in a paper box, and yellow leather snap purse, containing her ticket, a scrap of paper with her sister's address in Van Buren Street, and four dollars in money. It was in August, 1889. She was eighteen years of age, bright, timid, and full of the illusions of ignorance and youth. Whatever touch of regret at parting characterized her thoughts, it was certainly not for advantages now being given up. A gush of tears at her mother's farewell kiss, a touch in her throat when the cars clacked by the flour mill where her father worked by the day, a pathetic sigh as the familiar green environs of the village passed in review, and the threads which bound her so lightly to girlhood and home were irretrievably broken.

To be sure there was always the next station, where one might descend and return. There was the great city, bound more closely by these very trains which

[16]A misleading light, a deceptive hope.

came up daily. Columbia City[1] was not so very far away, even once she was in Chicago. What, pray, is a few hours—a few hundred miles? She looked at the little slip bearing her sister's address and wondered. She gazed at the green landscape, now passing in swift review, until her swifter thoughts replaced its impression with vague conjectures of what Chicago might be.

When a girl leaves her home at eighteen, she does one of two things. Either she falls into saving hands and becomes better, or she rapidly assumes the cosmopolitan standard of virtue and becomes worse. Of an intermediate balance, under the circumstances, there is no possibility. The city has its cunning wiles, no less than the infinitely smaller and more human tempter. There are large forces which allure with all the soulfulness of expression possible in the most cultured human.

The gleam of a thousand lights is often as effective as the persuasive light in a wooing and fascinating eye. Half the undoing of the unsophisticated and natural mind is accomplished by forces wholly superhuman. A blare of sound, a roar of life, vast array of human hives, appeal to the astonished senses in equivocal terms. Without a counsellor at hand to whisper cautious interpretations, what falsehoods may not these things breathe into the unguarded ear! Unrecognized for what they are, their beauty, like music, too often relaxes, then weakens, then perverts the simpler human perceptions.

Caroline, or Sister Carrie, as she had been half affectionately termed by the family, was possessed of a mind rudimentary in its power of observation and analysis. Self-interest with her was high, but not strong. It was, nevertheless, her guiding characteristic. Warm with the fancies of youth, pretty with the insipid prettiness of the formative period, possessed of a figure promising eventual shapeliness and an eye alight with certain native intelligence, she was a fair example of the middle American class—two generations removed from the emigrant. Books were beyond her interest—knowledge a sealed book. In the intuitive graces she was still crude. She could scarcely toss her head gracefully. Her hands were almost ineffectual. The feet, though small, were set flatly. And yet she was interested in her charms, quick to understand the keener pleasures of life, ambitious to gain in material things. A half-equipped little knight she was, venturing to reconnoitre the mysterious city and dreaming wild dreams of some vague, far-off supremacy, which should make it prey and subject—the proper penitent, grovelling at a woman's slipper.

"That," said a voice in her ear, "is one of the prettiest little resorts in Wisconsin."

"Is it?" she answered nervously.

The train was just pulling out of Waukesha.[2] For some time she had been conscious of a man behind. She felt him observing her mass of hair. He had been fidgetting, and with natural intuition she felt a certain interest growing in that quarter. Her maidenly reserve, and a certain sense of what was conventional under the circumstances, called her to forestall and deny this familiarity, but the daring and magnetism of the individual, born of past experiences and triumphs, prevailed. She answered.

He leaned forward to put his elbows upon the back of her seat and proceeded to make himself volubly agreeable.

"Yes, that is a great resort for Chicago people. The hotels are swell. You are not familiar with this part of the country, are you?"

[1]A small town in northern Indiana. [2]A city in southeastern Wisconsin.

"Oh, yes, I am," answered Carrie. "That is, I live at Columbia City. I have never been through here, though."

"And so this is your first visit to Chicago," he observed.

All the time she was conscious of certain features out of the side of her eye. Flush, colorful cheeks, a light moustache, grey fedora hat.[3] She now turned and looked upon him in full, the instincts of self-protection and coquetry[4] mingling confusedly in her brain.

"I didn't say that," she said.

"Oh," he answered, in a very pleasing way and with an assumed air of mistake, "I thought you did."

Here was a type of the travelling canvasser[5] for a manufacturing house—a class which at that time was first being dubbed by the slang of the day "drummers." He came within the meaning of a still newer term, which had sprung into general use among Americans in 1880, and which concisely expressed the thought of one whose dress or manners are calculated to elicit the admiration of susceptible young women—a "masher."[6] His suit was of a striped and crossed pattern of brown wool, new at that time, but since become familiar as a business suit. The low crotch of the vest revealed a stiff shirt bosom of white and pink stripes. From his coat sleeves protruded a pair of linen cuffs of the same pattern, fastened with large, gold plate buttons, set with the common yellow agates known as "cat's-eyes." His fingers bore several rings—one, the ever-enduring heavy seal—and from his vest dangled a neat gold watch chain, from which was suspended the secret insignia of the Order of Elks. The whole suit was rather tight-fitting, and was finished off with heavy-soled tan shoes, highly polished, and the grey fedora hat. He was, for the order of intellect represented, attractive, and whatever he had to recommend him, you may be sure was not lost upon Carrie, in this, her first glance.

Lest this order of individual should permanently pass, let me put down some of the most striking characteristics of his most successful manner and method. Good clothes, of course, were the first essential, the things without which he was nothing. Strong physical nature, actuated by a keen desire for the feminine, was the next. A mind free of any consideration of the problems or forces of the world and actuated not by greed, but an insatiable love of variable pleasure. His method was always simple. Its principal element was daring, backed, of course, by an intense desire and admiration for the sex. Let him meet with a young woman once and he would approach her with an air of kindly familiarity, not unmixed with pleading, which would result in most cases in a tolerant acceptance. If she showed any tendency to coquetry he would be apt to straighten her tie, or if she "took up" with him at all, to call her by her first name. If he visited a department store it was to lounge familiarly over the counter and ask some leading questions. In more exclusive circles, on the train or in waiting stations, he went slower. If some seemingly vulnerable object appeared he was all attention—to pass the compliments of the day, to lead the way to the parlor car, carrying her grip, or, failing that, to take a seat next her with the hope of being able to court her to her destination. Pillows, books, a footstool, the shade lowered all these figured in the things which he could do. If, when she reached her

[3]A men's style of soft felt hat with the top creased front-to-back.
[4]Flirtatiousness. [5]Traveling salesman.
[6]A man who tries to establish connections with women he encounters casually.

destination he did not alight and attend her baggage for her, it was because, in his own estimation, he had signally failed.

A woman should some day write the complete philosophy of clothes. No matter how young, it is one of the things she wholly comprehends. There is an indescribably faint line in the matter of man's apparel which somehow divides for her those who are worth glancing at and those who are not. Once an individual has passed this faint line on the way downward he will get no glance from her. There is another line at which the dress of a man will cause her to study her own. This line the individual at her elbow now marked for Carrie. She became conscious of an inequality. Her own plain blue dress, with its black cotton tape trimmings, now seemed to her shabby. She felt the worn state of her shoes.

"Let's see," he went on, "I know quite a number of people in your town. Morgenroth the clothier and Gibson the dry goods man."

"Oh, do you?" she interrupted, aroused by memories of longings their show windows had cost her.

At last he had a clew to her interest, and followed it deftly. In a few minutes he had come about into her seat. He talked of sales of clothing, his travels, Chicago, and the amusements of that city.

"If you are going there, you will enjoy it immensely. Have you relatives?"

"I am going to visit my sister," she explained.

"You want to see Lincoln Park,"[7] he said, "and Michigan Boulevard.[8] They are putting up great buildings there. It's a second New York—great. So much to see—theatres, crowds, fine houses—oh, you'll like that."

There was a little ache in her fancy of all he described. Her insignificance in the presence of so much magnificence faintly affected her. She realized that hers was not to be a round of pleasure, and yet there was something promising in all the material prospect he set forth. There was something satisfactory in the attention of this individual with his good clothes. She could not help smiling as he told her of some popular actress of whom she reminded him. She was not silly, and yet attention of this sort had its weight.

"You will be in Chicago some little time, won't you?" he observed at one turn of the now easy conversation.

"I don't know," said Carrie vaguely—a flash vision of the possibility of her not securing employment rising in her mind.

"Several weeks, anyhow," he said, looking steadily into her eyes.

There was much more passing now than the mere words indicated. He recognized the indescribable thing that made up for fascination and beauty in her. She realized that she was of interest to him from the one standpoint which a woman both delights in and fears. Her manner was simple, though for the very reason that she had not yet learned the many little affectations with which women conceal their true feelings. Some things she did appeared bold. A clever companion—had she ever had one—would have warned her never to look a man in the eyes so steadily.

"Why do you ask?" she said.

"Well, I'm going to be there several weeks. I'm going to study stock at our place and get new samples. I might show you 'round."

[7]The name for both a neighborhood in the northern part of Chicago and a large public park located in that neighborhood.

[8]Michigan Avenue: a major north-south street in Chicago.

"I don't know whether you can or not. I mean I don't know whether I can. I shall be living with my sister, and——"

"Well, if she minds, we'll fix that." He took out his pencil and a little pocket note-book as if it were all settled. "What is your address there?"

She fumbled her purse which contained the address slip.

He reached down in his hip pocket and took out a fat purse. It was filled with slips of paper, some mileage books, a roll of greenbacks. It impressed her deeply. Such a purse had never been carried by anyone attentive to her. Indeed, an experienced traveller, a brisk man of the world, had never come within such close range before. The purse, the shiny tan shoes, the smart new suit, and the air with which he did things, built up for her a dim world of fortune, of which he was the centre. It disposed her pleasantly toward all he might do.

He took out a neat business card, on which was engraved Bartlett, Caryoe & Company, and down in the left-hand corner, Chas. H. Drouet.

"That's me," he said, putting the card in her hand and touching his name. "It's pronounced Drew-eh. Our family was French, on my father's side."

She looked at it while he put up his purse. Then he got out a letter from a bunch in his coat pocket. "This is the house I travel for," he went on, pointing to a picture on it, "corner of State and Lake." There was pride in his voice. He felt that it was something to be connected with such a place, and he made her feel that way.

"What is your address?" he began again, fixing his pencil to write.

She looked at his hand.

"Carrie Meeber," she said slowly. "Three hundred and fifty-four West Van Buren Street, care S. C. Hanson."

He wrote it carefully down and got out the purse again. "You'll be at home if I come around Monday night?" he said.

"I think so," she answered.

How true it is that words are but the vague shadows of the volumes we mean. Little audible links, they are, chaining together great inaudible feelings and purposes. Here were these two, bandying little phrases, drawing purses, looking at cards, and both unconscious of how inarticulate all their real feelings were. Neither was wise enough to be sure of the working of the mind of the other. He could not tell how his luring succeeded. She could not realize that she was drifting, until he secured her address. Now she felt that she had yielded something—he, that he had gained a victory. Already they felt that they were somehow associated. Already he took control in directing the conversation. His words were easy. Her manner was relaxed.

They were nearing Chicago. Signs were everywhere numerous. Trains flashed by them. Across wide stretches of flat, open prairie they could see lines of telegraph poles stalking across the fields toward the great city. Far away were indications of suburban towns, some big smokestacks towering high in the air.

Frequently there were two-story frame houses standing out in the open fields, without fence or trees, lone outposts of the approaching army of homes.

To the child, the genius with imagination, or the wholly untravelled, the approach to a great city for the first time is wonderful thing. Particularly if it be evening—that mystic period between the glare and gloom of the world when life is changing from one sphere or condition to another. Ah, the promise of the night. What does it not hold for the weary! What old illusion of hope is not here forever repeated! Says the soul of the toiler to itself, "I shall soon be free. I shall be in the ways and the hosts of the merry. The streets, the lamps, the lighted chamber set for dining, are for me. The theatre, the halls, the parties, the ways of rest and the paths of song—these are mine in the night." Though all humanity be still enclosed in the shops, the thrill runs abroad. It is in the air. The dullest feel something which they may not always express or describe. It is the lifting of the burden of toil.

Sister Carrie gazed out of the window. Her companion, affected by her wonder, so contagious are all things, felt anew some interest in the city and pointed out its marvels.

"This is Northwest Chicago," said Drouet. "This is the Chicago River," and he pointed to a little muddy creek, crowded with the huge masted wanderers from far-off waters nosing the black-posted banks. With a puff, a clang, and a clatter of rails it was gone. "Chicago is getting to be a great town," he went on. "It's a wonder. You'll find lots to see here."

She did not hear this very well. Her heart was troubled by a kind of terror. The fact that she was alone, away from home, rushing into a great sea of life and endeavor, began to tell. She could not help but feel a little choked for breath—a little sick as her heart beat so fast. She half closed her eyes and tried to think it was nothing, that Columbia City was only little way off.

"Chicago! Chicago!" called the brakeman, slamming open the door. They were rushing into a more crowded yard, alive with the clatter and clang of life. She began to gather up her poor little grip and closed her hand firmly upon her purse. Drouet arose, kicked his legs to straighten his trousers, and seized his clean yellow grip.

"I suppose your people will be here to meet you?" he said. "Let me carry your grip."

"Oh, no," she said. "I'd rather you wouldn't. I'd rather you wouldn't be with me when I meet my sister."

"All right," he said in all kindness. "I'll be near, though, in case she isn't here, and take you out there safely."

"You're so kind," said Carrie, feeling the goodness of such attention in her strange situation.

"Chicago!" called the brakeman, drawing the word out long. They were under a great shadowy train shed, where the lamps were already beginning to shine out, with passenger cars all about and the train moving at a snail's pace. The people in the car were all up and crowding about the door.

"Well, here we are," said Drouet, leading the way to the door. "Good-bye, till I see you Monday."

"Good-bye," she answered, taking his proffered hand.

"Remember, I'll be looking till you find your sister."

She smiled into his eyes.

They filed out, and he affected to take no notice of her. A lean-faced, rather commonplace woman recognized Carrie on the platform and hurried forward.

"Why, Sister Carrie!" she began, and there was embrace of welcome.

Carrie realized the change of affectional atmosphere at once. Amid all the maze, uproar, and novelty she felt cold reality taking her by the hand. No world of light and merriment. No round of amusement. Her sister carried with her most of the grimness of shift and toil.

"Why, how are all the folks at home?" she began "how is father, and mother?"

Carrie answered, but was looking away. Down the aisle, toward the gate leading into the waiting-room and the street, stood Drouet. He was looking back. When he saw that she saw him and was safe with her sister he turned to go, sending back the shadow of a smile. Only Carrie saw it. She felt something lost to her when he moved away. When he disappeared she felt his absence thoroughly. With her sister she was much alone, a lone figure in a tossing, thoughtless sea.

CHAPTER II

WHAT POVERTY THREATENED—OF GRANITE AND BRASS

Minnie's flat, as the one-floor resident apartments were then being called, was in a part of West Van Buren Street inhabited by families of laborers and clerks, men who had come, and were still coming, with the rush of population pouring in at the rate of 50,000 a year. It was on the third floor, the front windows looking down into the street, where, at night, the lights of grocery stores were shining and children were playing. To Carrie, the sound of the little bells upon the horse-cars, as they tinkled in and out of hearing, was as pleasing as it was novel. She gazed into the lighted street when Minnie brought her into the front room, and wondered at the sounds, the movement, the murmur of the vast city which stretched for miles and miles in every direction.

Mrs. Hanson, after the first greetings were over, gave Carrie the baby and proceeded to get supper. Her husband asked a few questions and sat down to read the evening paper. He was a silent man, American born, of a Swede father, and now employed as a cleaner of refrigerator cars at the stock-yards. To him the presence or absence of his wife's sister was a matter of indifference. Her personal appearance did not affect him one way or the other. His one observation to the point was concerning the chances of work in Chicago.

"It's a big place," he said. "You can get in somewhere in a few days. Everybody does."

It had been tacitly understood beforehand that she was to get work and pay her board. He was of a clean, saving disposition, and had already paid a number of monthly installments on two lots far out on the West Side. His ambition was some day to build a house on them.

In the interval which marked the preparation of the meal Carrie found time to study the flat. She had some slight gift of observation and that sense, so rich in every woman—intuition.

She felt the drag of a lean and narrow life. The walls of the rooms were discordantly papered. The floors were covered with matting and the hall laid with a thin rag carpet. One could see that the furniture was of that poor, hurriedly patched together quality sold by the installment houses.[9]

She sat with Minnie, in the kitchen, holding the baby until it began to cry. Then she walked and sang to it, until Hanson, disturbed in his reading, came and took it. A pleasant side to his nature came out here. He was patient. One could see that he was very much wrapped up in his offspring.

[9]Stores that sell on installment plans (for customers who cannot afford to pay the full price at once).

"Now, now," he said, walking. "There, there," and there was a certain Swedish accent noticeable in his voice.

"You'll want to see the city first, won't you?" said Minnie, when they were eating. "Well, we'll go out Sunday and see Lincoln Park.

Carrie noticed that Hanson had said nothing to this. He seemed to be thinking of something else.

"Well," she said, "I think I'll look around tomorrow. I've got Friday and Saturday, and it won't be any trouble. Which way is the business part?"

Minnie began to explain, but her husband took this part of the conversation to himself.

"It's that way," he said, pointing east. "That's east." Then he went off into the longest speech he had yet indulged in, concerning the lay of Chicago. "You'd better look in those big manufacturing houses along Franklin Street and just the other side of the river," he concluded. "Lots of girls work there. You could get home easy, too. It isn't very far."

Carrie nodded and asked her sister about the neighborhood. The latter talked in a subdued tone, telling the little she knew about it, while Hanson concerned himself with the baby. Finally he jumped up and handed the child to his wife.

"I've got to get up early in the morning, so I'll go to bed," and off he went, disappearing into the dark little bedroom off the hall, for the night.

"He works way down at the stock-yards," explained Minnie, "so he's got to get up at half-past five."

"What time do you get up to get breakfast?" asked Carrie.

"At about twenty minutes of five."

Together they finished the labor of the day, Carrie washing the dishes while Minnie undressed the baby and put it to bed. Minnie's manner was one of trained industry, and Carrie could see that it was a steady round of toil with her.

She began to see that her relations with Drouet would have to be abandoned. He could not come here. She read from the manner of Hanson, in the subdued air of Minnie, and, indeed, the whole atmosphere of the flat, a settled opposition to anything save a conservative round of toil. If Hanson sat every evening in the front room and read his paper, if he went to bed at nine, and Minnie a little later, what would they expect of her? She saw that she would first need to get work and establish herself on a paying basis before she could think of having company of any sort. Her little flirtation with Drouet seemed now an extraordinary thing.

"No," she said to herself, "he can't come here."

She asked Minnie for ink and paper, which were upon the mantel in the dining-room, and when the latter had gone to bed at ten, got out Drouet's card and wrote him.

"I cannot have you call on me here. You will have to wait until you hear from me again. My sister's place is so small."

She troubled herself over what else to put in the letter. She wanted to make some reference to their relations upon the train, but was too timid. She concluded by thanking him for his kindness in a crude way, then puzzled over the formality of signing her name, and finally decided upon the severe, winding up with a "Very truly," which she subsequently changed to "Sincerely." She sealed and addressed the letter, and going in the front room, the alcove of which contained her bed, drew the one small rocking-chair up to the open window, and sat looking out upon the night and streets in silent wonder. Finally, wearied by her own reflections, she began to grow dull in her chair, and feeling the need of sleep, arranged her clothing for the night and went to bed.

When she awoke at eight the next morning, Hanson had gone. Her sister was busy in the dining-room, which was also the sitting-room, sewing. She worked, after dressing, to arrange a little breakfast for herself, and then advised with Minnie as to which way to look. The latter had changed considerably since Carrie had seen her. She was now a thin, though rugged, woman of twenty-seven, with ideas of life colored by her husband's, and fast hardening into narrower conceptions of pleasure and duty than had ever been hers in a thoroughly circumscribed youth. She had invited Carrie, not because she longed for her presence, but because the latter was dissatisfied at home, and could probably get work and pay her board here. She was pleased to see her in a way but reflected her husband's point of view in the matter of work. Anything was good enough so long as it paid—say, five dollars a week to begin with. A shop girl was the destiny prefigured for the newcomer. She would get in one of the great shops and do well enough until—well, until something happened. Neither of them knew exactly what. They did not figure on promotion. They did not exactly count on marriage. Things would go on, though, in a dim kind of way until the better thing would eventuate, and Carrie would be rewarded for coming and toiling in the city. It was under such auspicious circumstances that she started out this morning to look for work.

Before following her in her round of seeking, let us look at the sphere in which her future was to lie. In 1889 Chicago had the peculiar qualifications of growth which made such adventuresome pilgrimages even on the part of young girls plausible. Its many and growing commercial opportunities gave it widespread fame, which made of it a giant magnet, drawing to itself, from all quarters, the hopeful and the hopeless—those who had their fortune yet to make and those whose fortunes and affairs had reached a disastrous climax elsewhere. It was a city of over 500,000, with the ambition, the daring, the activity of a metropolis of a million. Its streets and houses were already scattered over an area of seventy-five square miles. Its population was not so much thriving upon established commerce as upon the industries which prepared for the arrival of others. The sound of the hammer engaged upon the erection of new structures was everywhere heard. Great industries were moving in. The huge railroad corporations which had long before recognized the prospects of the place had seized upon vast tracts of land for transfer and shipping purposes. Street-car lines had been extended far out into the open country in anticipation of rapid growth. The city had laid miles and miles of streets and sewers through regions where, perhaps, one solitary house stood out alone—a pioneer of the populous ways to be. There were regions open to the sweeping winds and rain, which were yet lighted throughout the night with long, blinking lines of gas-lamps, fluttering in the wind. Narrow board walks extended out, passing here a house, and there a store, at far intervals, eventually ending on the open prairie.

In the central portion was the vast wholesale and shopping district, to which the uninformed seeker for work usually drifted. It was a characteristic of Chicago then, and one not generally shared by other cities, that individual firms of any pretension occupied individual buildings. The presence of ample ground made this possible. It gave an imposing appearance to most of the wholesale houses, whose offices were upon the ground floor and in plain view of the street. The large plates of window glass, now so common, were then rapidly coming into use, and gave to the ground floor offices a distinguished and prosperous look. The casual wanderer could see as he passed a polished array of office fixtures, much frosted glass, clerks hard at work, and genteel businessmen in "nobby"[10] suits and clean linen lounging about or sitting in groups. Polished brass or nickel signs at the square stone entrances announced the firm and the nature of the business in rather neat and reserved terms. The entire metropolitan centre possessed a high and mighty air calculated to overawe and abash the common applicant, and to make the gulf between poverty and success seem both wide and deep.

Into this important commercial region the timid Carrie went. She walked east along Van Buren Street through a region of lessening importance, until it deteriorated into a mass of shanties and coal-yards, and finally verged upon the river. She walked bravely forward, led by an honest desire to find employment and delayed at every step by the interest of the unfolding scene, and a sense of helplessness amid so much evidence of power and force which she did not understand. These vast buildings, what were they? These strange energies and huge interests, for what purposes were they there? She could have understood the meaning of a little stone-cutter's yard at Columbia City, carving little pieces of marble for individual use, but when the yards of some huge stone corporation came into view, filled with spur tracks and flat cars, transpierced by docks from the river and traversed overhead by immense trundling cranes of wood and steel, it lost all significance in her little world.

It was so with the vast railroad yards, with the crowded array of vessels she saw at the river, and the huge factories over the way, lining the water's edge. Through the open windows she could see the figures of men and women in working aprons, moving busily about. The great streets were wall-lined mysteries to her; the vast offices, strange mazes which concerned far-off individuals of importance. She could only think of people connected with them as counting money, dressing magnificently, and riding in carriages. What they dealt in, how they labored, to what end it all came, she had only the vaguest conception. It was all wonderful, all vast, all far removed, and she sank in spirit inwardly and fluttered feebly at the heart as she thought of entering any one of these mighty concerns and asking for something to do—something that she could do—anything.

CHAPTER III

A Wee Question of Fortune—Four-Fifty a Week

Once across the river and into the wholesale district, she glanced about her for some likely door at which to apply. As she contemplated the wide windows and imposing signs, she became conscious of being gazed upon and understood for what she was—a wage-seeker. She had never done this thing before, and lacked courage. To avoid a certain indefinable shame she felt at being

[10]Stylish.

caught spying about for a position, she quickened her steps and assumed an air of indifference supposedly common to one upon an errand. In this way she passed many manufacturing and wholesale houses without once glancing in. At last, after several blocks of walking, she felt that this would not do, and began to look about again, though without relaxing her pace. A little way on she saw a great door which, for some reason, attracted her attention. It was ornamented by a small brass sign, and seemed to be the entrance to a vast hive of six or seven floors.

"Perhaps," she thought, "they may want some one," and crossed over to enter. When she came within a score of feet of the desired goal, she saw through the window a young man in a grey checked suit. That he had anything to do with the concern, she could not tell, but because he happened to be looking in her direction her weakening heart misgave her[11] and she hurried by, too overcome with shame to enter. Over the way stood a great six-story structure, labelled Storm and King, which she viewed with rising hope. It was a wholesale dry goods concern and employed women. She could see them moving about now and then upon the upper floors. This place she decided to enter, no matter what. She crossed over and walked directly toward the entrance. As she did so, two men came out and paused in the door. A telegraph messenger in blue dashed past her and up the few steps that led to the entrance and disappeared. Several pedestrians out of the hurrying throng which filled the sidewalks passed about her as she paused, hesitating. She looked helplessly around, and then, seeing herself observed, retreated. It was too difficult a task. She could not go past them.

So severe a defeat told sadly upon her nerves. Her feet carried her mechanically forward, every foot of her progress being a satisfactory portion of a flight which she gladly made. Block after block passed by. Upon streetlamps at the various corners she read names such as Madison, Monroe, La Salle, Clark, Dearborn, State, and still she went, her feet beginning to tire upon the broad stone flagging. She was pleased in part that the streets were bright and clean. The morning sun, shining down with steadily increasing warmth, made the shady side of the streets pleasantly cool. She looked at the blue sky overhead with more realisation of its charm than had ever come to her before.

Her cowardice began to trouble her in a way. She turned back, resolving to hunt up Storm and King and enter. On the way, she encountered a great wholesale shoe company, through the broad plate windows of which she saw an enclosed executive department, hidden by frosted glass. Without this enclosure, but just within the street entrance, sat a grey-haired gentleman at a small table, with a large open ledger before him. She walked by this institution several times hesitating, but, finding herself unobserved, faltered past the screen door and stood humble waiting.

"Well, young lady," observed the old gentleman, looking at her somewhat kindly, "what is it you wish?"

"I am, that is, do you—I mean, do you need any help?" she stammered.

"Not just at present," he answered smiling. "Not just at present. Come in some time next week. Occasionally we need some one."

She received the answer in silence and backed awkwardly out. The pleasant nature of her reception rather astonished her. She had expected that it would

[11]That is, she had misgivings.

be more difficult, that something cold and harsh would be said—she knew not what. That she had not been put to shame and made to feel her unfortunate position, seemed remarkable.

Somewhat encouraged, she ventured into another large structure. It was a clothing company, and more people were in evidence—well-dressed men of forty and more, surrounded by brass railings.

An office boy approached her.

"Who is it you wish to see?" he asked.

"I want to see the manager," she said. He ran away and spoke to one of a group of three men who were conferring together. One of these came towards her.

"Well?" he said coldly. The greeting drove all courage from her at once.

"Do you need any help?" she stammered.

"No," he replied abruptly, and turned upon his heel.

She went foolishly out, the office boy deferentially swinging the door for her, and gladly sank into the obscuring crowd. It was a severe setback to her recently pleased mental state.

Now she walked quite aimlessly for a time, turning here and there, seeing one great company after another, but finding no courage to prosecute her single inquiry. High noon came, and with it hunger. She hunted out an unassuming restaurant and entered, but was disturbed to find that the prices were exorbitant for the size of her purse. A bowl of soup was all that she could afford, and, with this quickly eaten, she went out again. It restored her strength somewhat and made her moderately bold to pursue the search.

In walking a few blocks to fix upon some probable place, she again encountered the firm of Storm and King, and this time managed to get in. Some gentlemen were conferring close at hand, but took no notice of her. She was left standing, gazing nervously upon the floor. When the limit of her distress had been nearly reached, she was beckoned to by a man at one of the many desks within the near-by railing.

"Who is it you wish to see?" he required.

"Why, anyone, if you please," she answered. "I am looking for something to do."

"Oh, you want to see Mr. McManus," he returned. "Sit down," and he pointed to a chair against the neighboring wall. He went on leisurely writing, until after a time a short, stout gentleman came in from the street.

"Mr. McManus," called the man at the desk, "this young woman wants to see you."

The short gentleman turned about towards Carrie, and she arose and came forward.

"What can I do for you, miss?" he inquired, surveying her curiously.

"I want to know if I can get a position," she inquired.

"As what?" he asked.

"Not as anything in particular," she faltered.

"Have you ever had any experience in the wholesale dry goods business?" he questioned.

"No, sir," she replied.

"Are you a stenographer or typewriter?"

"No, sir."

"Well, we haven't anything here," he said. "We employ only experienced help."

She began to step backward toward the door, when something about her plaintive face attracted him.

"Have you ever worked at anything before?" he inquired.

"No, sir," she said.

"Well, now, it's hardly possible that you would get anything to do in a wholesale house of this kind. Have you tried the department stores?"

She acknowledged that she had not.

"Well, if I were you," he said, looking at her rather genially, "I would try the department stores. They often need young women as clerks."

"Thank you," she said, her whole nature relieved by this spark of friendly interest.

"Yes," he said, as she moved toward the door, "you try the department stores," and off he went.

At that time the department store was in its earliest form of successful operation, and there were not many. The first three in the United States, established about 1884, were in Chicago. Carrie was familiar with the names of several through the advertisements in the "Daily News,"[12] and now proceeded to seek them. The words of Mr. McManus had somehow managed to restore her courage, which had fallen low, and she dared to hope that this new line would offer her something. Some time she spent in wandering up and down, thinking to encounter the buildings by chance, so readily is the mind, bent upon prosecuting a hard but needful errand, eased by that self-deception which the semblance of search, without the reality, gives. At last she inquired of a police officer, and was directed to proceed "two blocks up," where she would find "The Fair."

The nature of these vast retail combinations, should they ever permanently disappear, will form an interesting chapter in the commercial history of our nation. Such a flowering out of a modest trade principle the world had never witnessed up to that time. They were along the line of the most effective retail organization, with hundreds of stores coordinated into one and laid out upon the most imposing and economic basis. They were handsome, bustling, successful affairs, with a host of clerks and a swarm of patrons. Carrie passed along the busy aisles, much affected by the remarkable displays of trinkets, dress goods, stationery, and jewelry. Each separate counter was a show place of dazzling interest and attraction. She could not help feeling the claim of each trinket and valuable upon her personally, and yet she did not stop. There was nothing there which she could not have used—nothing which she did not long to own. The dainty slippers and stockings, the delicately frilled skirts and petticoats, the laces, ribbons, hair-combs, purses, all touched her with individual desire, and she felt keenly the fact that not any of these things were in the range of her purchase. She was a work-seeker, an outcast without employment, one whom the average employee could tell at a glance was poor and in need of a situation.

It must not be thought that anyone could have mistaken her for a nervous, sensitive, high-strung nature, cast unduly upon a cold, calculating, and unpoetic world. Such certainly she was not. But women are peculiarly sensitive to their adornment.

Not only did Carrie feel the drag of desire for all which was new and pleasing in apparel for women, but she noticed too, with a touch at the heart, the

[12]An afternoon daily newspaper.

fine ladies who elbowed and ignored her, brushing past in utter disregard of her presence, themselves eagerly enlisted in the materials which the store contained. Carrie was not familiar with the appearance of her more fortunate sisters of the city. Neither had she before known the nature and appearance of the shop girls with whom she now compared poorly. They were pretty in the main, some even handsome, with an air of independence and indifference which added, in the case of the more favored, a certain piquancy. Their clothes were neat, in many instances fine, and wherever she encountered the eye of one it was only to recognize in it a keen analysis of her own position—her individual shortcomings of dress and that shadow of manner which she thought must hang about her and make clear to all who and what she was. A flame of envy lighted in her heart. She realized in a dim way how much the city held—wealth, fashion, ease—every adornment for women, and she longed for dress and beauty with a whole heart.

On the second floor were the managerial offices, to which, after some inquiry, she was now directed. There she found other girls ahead of her, applicants like herself, but with more of that self-satisfied and independent air which experience of the city lends; girls who scrutinized her in a painful manner. After a wait of perhaps three-quarters of an hour, she was called in turn.

"Now," said a sharp, quick-mannered Jew, who was sitting at a roll-top desk near the window, "have you ever worked in any other store?"

"No, sir," said Carrie.

"Oh, you haven't," he said, eyeing her keenly.

"No, sir," she replied.

"Well, we prefer young women just now with some experience. I guess we can't use you."

Carrie stood waiting a moment, hardly certain whether the interview had terminated.

"Don't wait!" he exclaimed. "Remember we are very busy here."

Carrie began to move quickly to the door.

"Hold on," he said, calling her back. "Give me your name and address. We want girls occasionally."

When she had gotten safely into the street, she could scarcely restrain the tears. It was not so much the particular rebuff which she had just experienced, but the whole abashing trend of the day. She was tired and nervous. She abandoned the thought of appealing to the other department stores and now wandered on, feeling a certain safety and relief in mingling with the crowd.

In her indifferent wandering she turned into Jackson Street, not far from the river, and was keeping her way along the south side of that imposing thoroughfare, when a piece of wrapping paper, written on with marking ink and tacked up on the door, attracted her attention. It read, "Girls wanted—wrappers & stitchers." She hesitated a moment, then entered.

The firm of Speigelheim & Co., makers of boys' caps, occupied one floor of the building, fifty feet in width and some eighty feet in depth. It was a place rather dingily lighted, the darkest portions having incandescent lights, filled with machines and work benches. At the latter labored quite a company of girls and some men. The former were drabby-looking[13] creatures, stained in face with oil and dust, clad in thin, shapeless, cotton dresses and shod with more or

[13]Plain, unattractive, with perhaps a suggestion of looking like prostitutes.

less worn shoes. Many of them had their sleeves rolled up, revealing bare arms, and in some cases, owing to the heat, their dresses were open at the neck. They were a fair type of nearly the lowest order of shop-girls—careless, slouchy, and more or less pale from confinement. They were not timid, however; were rich in curiosity, and strong in daring and slang.

Carrie looked about her, very much disturbed and quite sure that she did not want to work here. Aside from making her uncomfortable by sidelong glances, no one paid her the least attention. She waited until the whole department was aware of her presence. Then some word was sent around, and a foreman, in an apron and shirt sleeves, the latter rolled up to his shoulders, approached.

"Do you want to see me?" he asked.

"Do you need any help?" said Carrie, already learning directness of address.

"Do you know how to stitch caps?" he returned.

"No, sir," she replied.

"Have you ever had any experience at this kind of work?" he inquired.

She answered that she had not.

"Well," said the foreman, scratching his ear meditatively, "we do need a stitcher. We like experienced help, though. We've hardly got time to break people in." He paused and looked away out of the window. "We might, though, put you at finishing," he concluded reflectively.

"How much do you pay a week?" ventured Carrie, emboldened by a certain softness in the man's manner and his simplicity of address.

"Three and a half," he answered.

"Oh," she was about to exclaim, but checked herself and allowed her thoughts to die without expression.

"We're not exactly in need of anybody," he went on vaguely, looking her over as one would a package. "You can come on Monday morning, though," he added, "and I'll put you to work."

"Thank you," said Carrie weakly.

"If you come, bring an apron," he added.

He walked away and left her standing by the elevator, never so much as inquiring her name.

While the appearance of the shop and the announcement of the price paid per week operated very much as a blow to Carrie's fancy, the fact that work of any kind was offered after so rude a round of experience was gratifying. She could not begin to believe that she would take the place, modest as her aspirations were. She had been used to better than that. Her mere experience and the free out-of-door life of the country caused her nature to revolt at such confinement. Dirt had never been her share. Her sister's flat was clean. This place was grimy and low, the girls were careless and hardened. They must be bad-minded and hearted, she imagined. Still, a place had been offered her. Surely Chicago was not so bad if she could find one place in one day. She might find another and better later.

Her subsequent experiences were not of a reassuring nature, however. From all the more pleasing or imposing places she was turned away abruptly with the most chilling formality. In others where she applied only the experienced were required. She met with painful rebuffs, the most trying of which had been in a manufacturing cloak house, where she had gone to the fourth floor to inquire.

"No, no," said the foreman, a rough, heavily built individual, who looked after a miserably lighted workshop, "we don't want anyone. Don't come here."

With the wane of the afternoon went her hopes, her courage, and her strength. She had been astonishingly persistent. So earnest an effort was well deserving of a better reward. On every hand, to her fatigued senses, the great business portion grew larger, harder, more stolid in its indifference. It seemed as if it was all closed to her, that the struggle was too fierce for her to hope to do anything at all. Men and women hurried by in long, shifting lines. She felt the flow of the tide of effort and interest—felt her own helplessness without quite realizing the wisp on the tide that she was. She cast about vainly for some possible place to apply, but found no door which she had the courage to enter. It would be the same thing all over. The old humiliation of her plea, rewarded by curt denial. Sick at heart and in body, she turned to the west, the direction of Minnie's flat, which she had now fixed in mind, and began that wearisome, baffled retreat which the seeker for employment at nightfall too often makes. In passing through Fifth Avenue, south towards Van Buren Street, where she intended to take a car, she passed the door of a large wholesale shoe house, through the plate-glass windows of which she could see a middle-aged gentleman sitting at a small desk. One of those forlorn impulses which often grow out of a fixed sense of defeat, the last sprouting of a baffled and uprooted growth of ideas, seized upon her. She walked deliberately through the door and up to the gentleman, who looked at her weary face with partially awakened interest.

"What is it?" he said.

"Can you give me something to do?" said Carrie.

"Now, I really don't know," he said kindly. "What kind of work is it you want—you're not a typewriter, are you?"

"Oh, no," answered Carrie.

"Well, we only employ book-keepers and typewriters here. You might go around to the side and inquire upstairs. They did want some help upstairs a few days ago. Ask for Mr. Brown."

She hastened around to the side entrance and was taken up by the elevator to the fourth floor.

"Call Mr. Brown, Willie," said the elevator man to a boy near by.

Willie went off and presently returned with the information that Mr. Brown said she should sit down and that he would be around in a little while.

It was a portion of the stock room which gave no idea of the general character of the place, and Carrie could form no opinion of the nature of the work.

"So you want something to do," said Mr. Brown, after he inquired concerning the nature of her errand. "Have you ever been employed in a shoe factory before?"

"No, sir," said Carrie.

"What is your name?" he inquired, and being informed, "Well, I don't know as I have anything for you. Would you work for four and a half a week?"

Carrie was too worn by defeat not to feel that it was considerable. She had not expected that he would offer her less than six. She acquiesced, however, and he took her name and address.

"Well," he said, finally, "you report here at eight o'clock Monday morning. I think I can find something for you to do."

He left her revived by the possibilities, sure that she had found something at last. Instantly the blood crept warmly over her body. Her nervous tension relaxed. She walked out into the busy street and discovered a new atmosphere. Behold, the throng was moving with a lightsome step. She noticed that men and women were smiling. Scraps of conversation and notes of laughter floated to her. The air was light. People were already pouring out of the buildings, their labor ended for the day. She noticed that they were pleased, and thoughts of her sister's home and the meal that would be awaiting her quickened her steps. She hurried on, tired perhaps, but no longer weary of foot. What would not Minnie say! Ah, the long winter in Chicago—the lights, the crowd, the amusement! This was a great, pleasing metropolis after all. Her new firm was a goodly institution. Its windows were of huge plate glass. She could probably do well there. Thoughts of Drouet returned—of the things he had told her. She now felt that life was better, that it was livelier, sprightlier. She boarded a car in the best of spirits, feeling her blood still flowing pleasantly. She would live in Chicago, her mind kept saying to itself. She would have a better time than she had ever had before—she would be happy.

CHAPTER IV

The Spendings of Fancy—Facts Answer with Sneers

For the next two days Carrie indulged in the most high-flown speculations.

Her fancy plunged recklessly into privileges and amusements which would have been much more becoming had she been cradled a child of fortune. With ready will and quick mental selection she scattered her meagre four-fifty per week with a swift and graceful hand. Indeed, as she sat in her rocking-chair these several evenings before going to bed and looked out upon the pleasantly lighted street, this money cleared for its prospective possessor the way to every joy and every bauble which the heart of woman may desire. "I will have a fine time," she thought.

Her sister Minnie knew nothing of these rather wild cerebrations, though they exhausted the markets of delight. She was too busy scrubbing the kitchen woodwork and calculating the purchasing power of eighty cents for Sunday's dinner. When Carrie had returned home, flushed with her first success and ready, for all her weariness, to discuss the now interesting events which led up to her achievement, the former had merely smiled approvingly and inquired whether she would have to spend any of it for car fare. This consideration had not entered in before, and it did not now for long affect the glow of Carrie's enthusiasm. Disposed as she then was to calculate upon that vague basis which allows the subtraction of one sum from another without any perceptible diminution, she was happy.

When Hanson came home at seven o'clock, he was inclined to be a little crusty—his usual demeanor before supper. This never showed so much in anything he said as in a certain solemnity of countenance and the silent manner in which he slopped about. He had a pair of yellow carpet slippers which he enjoyed wearing, and these he would immediately substitute for his solid pair of shoes. This, and washing his face with the aid of common washing soap until it glowed a shiny red, constituted his only preparation for his evening meal. He would then get his evening paper and read in silence.

For a young man, this was rather a morbid turn of character, and so affected Carrie. Indeed, it affected the entire atmosphere of the flat, as such things are inclined to do, and gave to his wife's mind its subdued and tactful turn, anxious to avoid taciturn replies. Under the influence of Carrie's announcement he brightened up somewhat.

"You didn't lose any time, did you?" he remarked, smiling a little.

"No," returned Carrie with a touch of pride.

He asked her one or two more questions and then turned to play with the baby, leaving the subject until it was brought up again by Minnie at the table.

Carrie, however, was not to be reduced to the common level of observation which prevailed in the flat.

"It seems to be such a large company," she said, at one place.

"Great big plate-glass windows and lots of clerks. The man I saw said they hired ever so many people."

"It's not very hard to get work now," put in Hanson, "if you look right."

Minnie, under the warming influence of Carrie's good spirits and her husband's somewhat conversational mood, began to tell Carrie of some of the well-known things to see—things the enjoyment of which cost nothing.

"You'd like to see Michigan Avenue. There are such fine houses. It is such a fine street."

"Where is H. R. Jacob's?" interrupted Carrie, mentioning one of the theatres devoted to melodrama which went by that name at the time.

"Oh, it's not very far from here," answered Minnie. "It's in Halstead Street, right up here."

"How I'd like to go there. I crossed Halstead Street today, didn't I?"

At this there was a slight halt in the natural reply. Thoughts are a strangely permeating factor. At her suggestion of going to the theatre, the unspoken shade of disapproval to the doing of those things which involved the expenditure of money—shades of feeling which arose in the mind of Hanson and then in Minnie—slightly affected the atmosphere of the table. Minnie answered "yes," but Carrie could feel that going to the theatre was poorly advocated here. The subject was put off for a little while until Hanson, through with his meal, took his paper and went into the front room.

When they were alone, the two sisters began a somewhat freer conversation, Carrie interrupting it to hum a little, as they worked at the dishes.

"I should like to walk up and see Halstead Street, if it isn't too far," said Carrie, after a time. "Why don't we go to the theatre tonight?"

"Oh, I don't think Sven would want to go tonight," returned Minnie. "He has to get up so early."

"He wouldn't mind—he'd enjoy it," said Carrie.

"No, he doesn't go very often," returned Minnie.

"Well, I'd like to go," rejoined Carrie. "Let's you and me go."

Minnie pondered a while, not upon whether she could or would go—for that point was already negatively settled with her—but upon some means of diverting the thoughts of her sister to some other topic.

"We'll go some other time," she said at last, finding no ready means of escape.

Carrie sensed the root of the opposition at once.

"I have some money," she said. "You go with me." Minnie shook her head.

"He could go along," said Carrie.

"No," returned Minnie softly, and rattling the dishes to drown the conversation. "He wouldn't."

It had been several years since Minnie had seen Carrie, and in that time the latter's character had developed a few shades. Naturally timid in all things that related to her own advancement, and especially so when without power or resource, her craving for pleasure was so strong that it was the one stay of her nature. She would speak for that when silent on all else.

"Ask him," she pleaded softly.

Minnie was thinking of the resource which Carrie's board would add. It would pay the rent and would make the subject of expenditure a little less difficult to talk about with her husband. But if Carrie was going to think of running around in the beginning there would be a hitch somewhere. Unless Carrie submitted to a solemn round of industry and saw the need of hard work without longing for play, how was her coming to the city to profit them? These thoughts were not those of a cold, hard nature at all. They were the serious reflections of a mind which invariably adjusted itself, without much complaining, to such surroundings as its industry could make for it.

At last she yielded enough to ask Hanson. It was a half-hearted procedure without a shade of desire on her part.

"Carrie wants us to go to the theatre," she said, looking in upon her husband. Hanson looked up from his paper, and they exchanged a mild look, which said as plainly as anything: "This isn't what we expected."

"I don't care to go," he returned. "What does she want to see?"

"H. R. Jacob's," said Minnie.

He looked down at his paper and shook his head negatively.

When Carrie saw how they looked upon her proposition, she gained a still clearer feeling of their way of life. It weighed on her, but took no definite form of opposition.

"I think I'll go down and stand at the foot of the stairs," she said, after a time.

Minnie made no objection to this, and Carrie put on her hat and went below.

"Where has Carrie gone?" asked Hanson, coming back into the dining-room when he heard the door close.

"She said she was going down to the foot of the stairs," answered Minnie. "I guess she just wants to look out a while."

"She oughtn't to be thinking about spending her money on theatres already, do you think?" he said.

"She just feels a little curious, I guess," ventured Minnie. "Everything is so new."

"I don't know," said Hanson, and went over to the baby, his forehead slightly wrinkled.

He was thinking of a full career of vanity and wastefulness which a young girl might indulge in, and wondering how Carrie could contemplate such a course when she had so little, as yet, with which to do.

On Saturday Carrie went out by herself—first toward the river, which interested her, and then back along Jackson Street, which was then lined by the pretty houses and fine lawns which subsequently caused it to be made into a boulevard. She was struck with the evidences of wealth, although there was, perhaps, not a person on the street worth more than a hundred thousand dollars. She was glad to be out of the flat, because already she felt that it was a narrow, humdrum place, and that interest and joy lay elsewhere. Her thoughts now were of a more liberal character, and she punctuated them with speculations as to the whereabouts of Drouet. She was not sure but that he might call anyhow Monday night, and, while she felt a little disturbed at the possibility, there was, nevertheless, just the shade of a wish that he would.

On Monday she arose early and prepared to go to work. She dressed herself in a worn shirt-waist of dotted blue percale, a skirt of light-brown serge rather faded, and a small straw hat which she had worn all summer at Columbia City. Her shoes were old, and her necktie was in that crumpled, flattened state which time and much wearing impart. She made a very average looking shop-girl with the exception of her features. These were slightly more even than common, and gave her a sweet, reserved, and pleasing appearance.

It is no easy thing to get up early in the morning when one is used to sleeping until seven and eight, as Carrie had been at home. She gained some inkling of the character of Hanson's life when, half asleep, she looked out into the dining-room at six o'clock and saw him silently finishing his breakfast. By the time she was dressed he was gone, and she, Minnie, and the baby ate together, the latter being just old enough to sit in a high chair and disturb the dishes with a spoon. Her spirits were greatly subdued now when the fact of entering upon strange and untried duties confronted her. Only the ashes of all her fine fancies were remaining—ashes still concealing, nevertheless, a few red embers of hope. So subdued was she by her weakening nerves, that she ate quite in silence going over imaginary conceptions of the character of the shoe company, the nature of the work, her employer's attitude. She was vaguely feeling that she would come in contact with the great owners, that her work would be where grave, stylishly dressed men occasionally look on.

"Well, good luck," said Minnie, when she was ready to go. They had agreed it was best to walk, that morning at least, to see if she could do it every day—sixty cents a week for car fare being quite an item under the circumstances.

"I'll tell you how it goes tonight," said Carrie.

Once in the sunlit street, with laborers tramping by in either direction, the horse-cars passing crowded to the rails with the small clerks and floor help in the great wholesale houses, and men and women generally coming out of doors and passing about the neighborhood, Carrie felt slightly reassured. In the sunshine of the morning, beneath the wide, blue heavens, with a fresh wind astir, what fears, except the most desperate, can find a harborage? In the night, or the gloomy chambers of the day, fears and misgivings wax strong, but out in the sunlight there is, for a time, cessation even of the terror of death.

Carrie went straight forward until she crossed the river, and then turned into Fifth Avenue. The thoroughfare, in this part, was like a walled canon of brown stone and dark red brick. The big windows looked shiny and clean. Trucks were rumbling in increasing numbers; men and women, girls and boys were moving onward in all directions. She met girls of her own age, who looked at her as if with contempt for her diffidence. She wondered at the magnitude of this life and at the importance of knowing much in order to do anything in it at all. Dread at her own inefficiency crept upon her. She would not know how, she would not be quick enough. Had not all the other places refused her because she did not know something or other? She would be scolded, abused, ignominiously discharged.

It was with weak knees and a slight catch in her breathing that she came up to the great shoe company at Adams and Fifth Avenue and entered the elevator. When she stepped out on the fourth floor there was no one at hand, only great aisles of boxes piled to the ceiling. She stood, very much frightened, awaiting some one.

Presently Mr. Brown came up. He did not seem to recognize her.

"What is it you want?" he inquired.

Carrie's heart sank.

"You said I should come this morning to see about work—"

"Oh," he interrupted. "Um—yes. What is your name?"

"Carrie Meeber."

"Yes," said he. "You come with me."

He led the way through dark, box-lined aisles which had the smell of new shoes, until they came to an iron door which opened into the factory proper. There was a large, low-ceiled room, with clacking, rattling machines at which men in white shirt sleeves and blue gingham aprons were working. She followed him diffidently through the clattering automatons,[14] keeping her eyes straight before her, and flushing slightly. They crossed to a far corner and took an elevator to the sixth floor. Out of the array of machines and benches, Mr. Brown signalled a foreman.

"This is the girl," he said, and turning to Carrie, "You go with him." He then returned, and Carrie followed her new superior to a little desk in a corner, which he used as a kind of official centre.

"You've never worked at anything like this before, have you?" he questioned, rather sternly.

"No, sir," she answered.

He seemed rather annoyed at having to bother with such help, but put down her name and then led her across to where a line of girls occupied stools in front of clacking machines. On the shoulder of one of the girls who was punching eye-holes in one piece of the upper, by the aid of the machine, he put his hand.

"You," he said, "show this girl how to do what you're doing. When you get through, come to me."

The girl so addressed rose promptly and gave Carrie her place.

"It isn't hard to do," she said, bending over. "You just take this so, fasten it with this clamp, and start the machine."

She suited action to word, fastened the piece of leather, which was eventually to form the right half of the upper of a man's shoe, by little adjustable clamps, and pushed a small steel rod at the side of the machine. The latter jumped to the task of punching, with sharp, snapping clicks, cutting circular bits of leather out of the side of the upper, leaving the holes which were to hold the laces. After observing a few times, the girl let her work at it alone. Seeing that it was fairly well done, she went away.

The pieces of leather came from the girl at the machine to her right, and were passed on to the girl at her left. Carrie saw at once that an average speed was necessary or the work would pile up on her and all those below would be delayed. She had no time to look about, and bent anxiously to her task. The girls at her left and right realized her predicament and feelings, and, in a way, tried to aid her, as much as they dared, by working slower.

At this task she labored incessantly for some time, finding relief from her own nervous fears and imaginings in the humdrum, mechanical movement of the machine. She felt, as the minutes passed, that the room was not very light. It had

[14]Machines.

a thick odor of fresh leather, but that did not worry her. She felt the eyes of the other help upon her, and troubled lest she was not working fast enough.

Once, when she was fumbling at the little clamp, having made a slight error in setting in the leather, a great hand appeared before her eyes and fastened the clamp for her. It was the foreman. Her heart thumped so that she could scarcely see to go on.

"Start your machine," he said, "start your machine. Don't keep the line waiting."

This recovered her sufficiently and she went excitedly on, hardly breathing until the shadow moved away from behind her. Then she heaved a great breath.

As the morning wore on the room became hotter. She felt the need of a breath of fresh air and a drink of water, but did not venture to stir. The stool she sat on was without a back or foot-rest, and she began to feel uncomfortable. She found, after a time, that her back was beginning to ache. She twisted and turned from one position to another slightly different, but it did not ease her for long. She was beginning to weary.

"Stand up, why don't you?" said the girl at her right, without any form of introduction. "They won't care."

Carrie looked at her gratefully. "I guess I will," she said.

She stood up from her stool and worked that way for a while, but it was a more difficult position. Her neck and shoulders ached in bending over.

The spirit of the place impressed itself on her in a rough way. She did not venture to look around, but above the clack of the machine she could hear an occasional remark. She could also note a thing or two out of the side of her eye.

"Did you see Harry last night?" said the girl at her left, addressing her neighbor.

"No."

"You ought to have seen the tie he had on. Gee, but he was a mark."

"S-s-t," said the other girl, bending over her work. The first, silenced, instantly assumed a solemn face. The foreman passed slowly along, eyeing each worker distinctly. The moment he was gone, the conversation was resumed again.

"Say," began the girl at her left, "what jeh think he said?"

"I don't know."

"He said he saw us with Eddie Harris at Martin's last night." "No!" They both giggled.

A youth with tan-colored hair, that needed clipping very badly, came shuffling along between the machines, bearing a basket of leather bindings under his left arm, and pressed against his stomach. When near Carrie, he stretched out his right hand and gripped one girl under the arm.

"Aw, let me go," she exclaimed angrily. "Duffer."[15]

He only grinned broadly in return.

"Rubber!" he called back as she looked after him. There was nothing of the gallant in him.

Carrie at last could scarcely sit still. Her legs began to tire and she wanted to get up and stretch. Would noon never come? It seemed as if she had worked an entire day. She was not hungry at all, but weak, and her eyes were tired, straining at the one point where the eye-punch came down. The girl at the

[15]A clumsy or stupid person.

right noticed her squirmings and felt sorry for her. She was concentrating herself too thoroughly—what she did really required less mental and physical strain. There was nothing to be done, however. The halves of the uppers came piling steadily down. Her hands began to ache at the wrists and then in the fingers, and towards the last she seemed one mass of dull, complaining muscles, fixed in an eternal position and performing a single mechanical movement which became more and more distasteful, until as last it was absolutely nauseating. When she was wondering whether the strain would ever cease, a dull-sounding bell clanged somewhere down an elevator shaft, and the end came. In an instant there was a buzz of action and conversation. All the girls instantly left their stools and hurried away in an adjoining room, men passed through, coming from some department which opened on the right. The whirling wheels began to sing in a steadily modifying key, until at last they died away in a low buzz. There was an audible stillness, in which the common voice sounded strange.

Carrie got up and sought her lunch box. She was stiff, a little dizzy, and very thirsty. On the way to the small space portioned off by wood, where all the wraps and lunches were kept, she encountered the foreman, who stared at her hard.

"Well," he said, "did you get along all right?"

"I think so," she replied, very respectfully.

"Um," he replied, for want of something better, and walked on.

Under better material conditions, this kind of work would not have been so bad, but the new socialism which involves pleasant working conditions for employees had not then taken hold upon manufacturing companies.

The place smelled of the oil of the machines and the new leather—a combination which, added to the stale odors of the building, was not pleasant even in cold weather. The floor, though regularly swept every evening, presented a littered surface. Not the slightest provision had been made for the comfort of the employees, the idea being that something was gained by giving them as little and making the work as hard and unremunerative as possible. What we know of foot-rests, swivel-back chairs, dining-rooms for the girls, clean aprons and curling irons supplied free, and a decent cloak room, were unthought of. The washrooms were disagreeable, crude, if not foul places, and the whole atmosphere was sordid.

Carrie looked about her, after she had drunk a tinful of water from a bucket in one corner, for a place to sit and eat. The other girls had ranged themselves about the windows or the work-benches of those of the men who had gone out. She saw no place which did not hold a couple or a group of girls, and being too timid to think of intruding herself, she sought out her machine and, seated upon her stool, opened her lunch on her lap. There she sat listening to the chatter and comment about her. It was, for the most part, silly and graced by the current slang. Several of the men in the room exchanged compliments with the girls at long range.

"Say, Kitty," called one to a girl who was doing a waltz step in a few feet of space near one of the windows, "are you going to the ball with me?"

"Look out, Kitty," called another, "you'll jar your back hair."

"Go on, Rubber," was her only comment.

As Carrie listened to this and much more of similar familiar badinage among the men and girls, she instinctively withdrew into herself. She was not used to this type, and felt that there was something hard and low about it all. She feared that the young boys about would address such remarks to her—boys who, beside Drouet, seemed uncouth and ridiculous. She made the average feminine distinction between clothes, putting worth, goodness, and distinction in a dress suit, and leaving all the unlovely qualities and those beneath notice in overalls and jumper.

She was glad when the short half hour was over and the wheels began to whirr again. Though wearied, she would be inconspicuous. This illusion ended when another young man passed along the aisle and poked her indifferently in the ribs with his thumb. She turned about, indignation leaping to her eyes, but he had gone on and only once turned to grin. She found it difficult to conquer an inclination to cry.

The girl next her noticed her state of mind. "Don't you mind," she said. "He's too fresh."

Carrie said nothing, but bent over her work. She felt as though she could hardly endure such a life. Her idea of work had been so entirely different. All during the long afternoon she thought of the city outside and its imposing show, crowds, and fine buildings. Columbia City and the better side of her home life came back. By three o'clock she was sure it must be six, and by four it seemed as if they had forgotten to note the hour and were letting all work overtime. The foreman became a true ogre, prowling constantly about, keeping her tied down to her miserable task. What she heard of the conversation about her only made her feel sure that she did not want to make friends with any of these. When six o'clock came she hurried eagerly away, her arms aching and her limbs stiff from sitting in one position.

As she passed out along the hall after getting her hat, a young machine hand, attracted by her looks, made bold to jest with her.

"Say, Maggie," he called, "if you wait, I'll walk with you."

It was thrown so straight in her direction that she knew who was meant, but never turned to look.

In the crowded elevator, another dusty, toil-stained youth tried to make an impression on her by leering in her face.

One young man, waiting on the walk outside for the appearance of another, grinned at her as she passed.

"Ain't going my way, are you?" he called jocosely.[16]

Carrie turned her face to the west with a subdued heart. As she turned the corner, she saw through the great shiny window the small desk at which she had applied. There were the crowds, hurrying with the same buzz and energy-yielding enthusiasm. She felt a slight relief, but it was only at her escape. She felt ashamed in the face of better dressed girls who went by. She felt as though she should be better served, and her heart revolted.

[In the intervening chapters, Carrie has formed liaisons first with Drouet and then with a married man named Hurstwood, who was prosperous at the time but has ruined himself by impetuously stealing money, leaving his family, and running away with Carrie. Carrie has begun to earn money as an actress, but Hurstwood is sinking deeper and deeper into incapacity and despair.]

[16]Playfully.

CHAPTER XL

A Public Dissension—A Final Appeal

There was no after-theatre lark, however, so far as Carrie was concerned. She made her way homeward, thinking about her absence. Hurstwood was asleep, but roused up to look as she passed through to her own bed.

"Is that you?" he said.

"Yes," she answered.

The next morning at breakfast she felt like apologizing.

"I couldn't get home last evening," she said.

"Ah, Carrie," he answered, "what's the use saying that? I don't care. You needn't tell me that, though."

"I couldn't," said Carrie, her color rising. Then, seeing that he looked as if he said "I know," she exclaimed: "Oh, all right. I don't care."

From now on, her indifference to the flat was even greater. There seemed no common ground on which they could talk to one another. She let herself be asked for expenses. It became so with him that he hated to do it. He preferred standing off the butcher and baker. He ran up a grocery bill of sixteen dollars with Oeslogge, laying in a supply of staple articles, so that they would not have to buy any of those things for some time to come. Then he changed his grocery. It was the same with the butcher and several others. Carrie never heard anything of this directly from him. He asked for such as he could expect, drifting farther and farther into a situation which could have but one ending.

In this fashion, September went by.

"Isn't Mr. Drake going to open his hotel?" Carrie asked several times.

"Yes. He won't do it before October, though, now."

Carrie became disgusted. "Such a man," she said to herself frequently. More and more she visited. She put most of her spare money in clothes, which, after all, was not an astonishing amount. At last the opera she was with announced its departure within four weeks. "Last two weeks of the Great Comic Opera success——The———," etc., was upon all billboards and in the newspapers, before she acted.

"I'm not going out on the road," said Miss Osborne.

Carrie went with her to apply to another manager.

"Ever had any experience?" was one of his questions.

"I'm with the company at the Casino now."

"Oh, you are?" he said.

The end of this was another engagement at twenty per week.

Carrie was delighted. She began to feel that she had a place in the world. People recognized ability.

So changed was her state that the home atmosphere became intolerable. It was all poverty and trouble there, or seemed to be, because it was a load to bear. It became a place to keep away from. Still she slept there, and did a fair amount of work, keeping it in order. It was a sitting place for Hurstwood. He sat and rocked, rocked and read, enveloped in the gloom of his own fate. October went by, and November. It was the dead of winter almost before he knew it, and there he sat.

Carrie was doing better, that he knew. Her clothes were improved now, even fine. He saw her coming and going, sometimes picturing to himself her rise. Little eating had thinned him somewhat. He had no appetite. His clothes, too, were a poor man's clothes. Talk about getting something had become even too threadbare and ridiculous for him. So he folded his hands and waited—for what, he could not anticipate.

At last, however, troubles became too thick. The hounding of creditors, the indifference of Carrie, the silence of the flat, and presence of winter, all joined to produce a climax. It was effected by the arrival of Oeslogge, personally, when Carrie was there.

"I call about my bill," said Mr. Oeslogge.

Carrie was only faintly surprised.

"How much is it?" she asked.

"Sixteen dollars," he replied.

"Oh, that much?" said Carrie. "Is this right?" she asked, turning to Hurstwood.

"Yes," he said.

"Well, I never heard anything about it."

She looked as if she thought he had been contracting some needless expense.

"Well, we had it all right," he answered. Then he went to the door. "I can't pay you anything on that today," he said, mildly.

"Well, when can you?" said the grocer.

"Not before Saturday, anyhow," said Hurstwood.

"Huh!" returned the grocer. "This is fine. I must have that. I need the money."

Carrie was standing farther back in the room, hearing it all. She was greatly distressed. It was so bad and commonplace. Hurstwood was annoyed also.

"Well," he said, "there's no use talking about it now. If you'll come in Saturday, I'll pay you something on it."

The grocery man went away.

"How are we going to pay it?" asked Carrie, astonished by the bill. "I can't do it."

"Well, you don't have to," he said. "He can't get what he can't get. He'll have to wait."

"I don't see how we ran up such a bill as that," said Carrie.

"Well, we ate it," said Hurstwood.

"It's funny," she replied, still doubting.

"What's the use of your standing there and talking like that, now?" he asked. "Do you think I've had it alone? You talk as if I'd taken something."

"Well, it's too much, anyhow," said Carrie. "I oughtn't to be made to pay for it. I've got more than I can pay for now."

"All right," replied Hurstwood, sitting down in silence. He was sick of the grind of this thing.

Carrie went out and there he sat, determining to do something.

There had been appearing in the papers about this time rumors and notices of an approaching strike on the trolley lines in Brooklyn. There was general dissatisfaction as to the hours of labor required and the wages paid. As usual—and for some inexplicable reason—the men chose the winter for the forcing of the hand of their employers and the settlement of their difficulties.

Hurstwood had been reading of this thing, and wondering concerning the huge tie-up which would follow. A day or two before this trouble with Carrie, it came. On a cold afternoon, when everything was grey and it threatened to snow, the papers announced that the men had been called out on all the lines. Being so utterly idle, and his mind filled with the numerous predictions which had been made concerning the scarcity of labor this winter and the panicky state of the financial market, Hurstwood read this with interest. He noted the claims of the striking motormen and conductors, who said that they had been wont to receive two dollars a day in times past, but that for a year or more "trippers" had been introduced, which cut down their chance of livelihood one-half, and increased their hours of servitude from ten to twelve, and even fourteen. These "trippers" were men put on during the busy and rush hours, to take a car out for one trip. The compensation paid for such a trip was only twenty-five cents. When the rush or busy hours were over, they were laid off. Worst of all, no man might know when he was going to get a car. He must come to the barns in the morning and wait around in fair and foul weather until such time as he was needed. Two trips were an average reward for so much waiting—a little over three hours' work for fifty cents. The work of waiting was not counted.

The men complained that this system was extending, and that the time was not far off when but a few out of 7,000 employees would have regular two-dollar-a-day work at all. They demanded that the system be abolished, and that ten hours be considered a day's work, barring unavoidable delays, with $2.25 pay. They demanded immediate acceptance of these terms, which the various trolley companies refused.

Hurstwood at first sympathized with the demands of these men—indeed, it is a question whether he did not always sympathize with them to the end, belie him as his actions might. Reading nearly all the news, he was attracted first by the scare-heads with which the trouble was noted in the "World."[17] He read it fully—the names of the seven companies involved, the number of men.

"They're foolish to strike in this sort of weather," he thought to himself. "Let 'em win if they can, though."

The next day there was even a larger notice of it. "Brooklynites Walk," said the "World." "Knights of Labor[18] Tie up the Trolley Lines Across the Bridge." "About Seven Thousand Men Out."

Hurstwood read this, formulating to himself his own idea of what would be the outcome. He was a great believer in the strength of corporations.

"They can't win," he said, concerning the men. "They haven't any money. The police will protect the companies. They've got to. The public has to have its cars."

He didn't sympathise with the corporations, but strength was with them. So was property and public utility.

"Those fellows can't win," he thought.

[17]The New York *World,* a newspaper owned by Joseph Pulitzer (1847–1911), a publisher noted for sensationalism.

[18]A major labor union.

Among other things, he noticed a circular issued by one of the companies, which read:

"ATLANTIC AVENUE RAILROAD.

"SPECIAL NOTICE.

"The motormen and conductors and other employees of this company having abruptly left its service, an opportunity is now given to all loyal men who have struck against their will to be reinstated, providing they will make their applications by twelve o'clock noon on Wednesday, January 16th. Such men will be given employment (with guaranteed protection) in the order in which such applications are received, and runs and positions assigned them accordingly. Otherwise, they will be considered discharged, and every vacancy will be filled by a new man as soon as his services can be secured.

"(Signed)
"Benjamin Norton,
"President."

He also noted among the want ads, one of which read:

"WANTED.—50 skilled motormen, accustomed to Westinghouse system, to run U.S. mail cars only, in the City of Brooklyn; protection guaranteed."

He noted particularly in each the "protection guaranteed." It signified to him the unassailable power of the companies.

"They've got the militia on their side," he thought. "There isn't anything those men can do."

While this was still in his mind, the incident with Oeslogge and Carrie occurred. There had been a good deal to irritate him, but this seemed much the worst. Never before had she accused him of stealing—or very near that. She doubted the naturalness of so large a bill. And he had worked so hard to make expenses seem light. He had been "doing" butcher and baker in order not to call on her. He had eaten very little—almost nothing.

"Damn it all!" he said. "I can get something. I'm not down yet."

He thought that he really must do something now. It was too cheap to sit around after such an insinuation as this. Why, after a little, he would be standing anything.

He got up and looked out the window into the chilly street. It came gradually into his mind, as he stood there, to go to Brooklyn.

"Why not?" his mind said. "Anyone can get work over there. You'll get two a day."

"How about accidents?" said a voice. "You might get hurt."

"Oh, there won't be much of that," he answered. "They've called out the police. Anyone who wants to run a car will be protected all right."

"You don't know how to run a car," rejoined the voice.

"I won't apply as a motorman," he answered. "I can ring up fares all right."

"They'll want motormen, mostly."

"They'll take anybody; that I know."

For several hours he argued pro and con with this mental counsellor, feeling no need to act at once in a matter so sure of profit.

In the morning he put on his best clothes, which were poor enough, and began stirring about, putting some bread and meat into a page of a newspaper. Carrie watched him, interested in this new move.

"Where are you going?" she asked.

"Over to Brooklyn," he answered. Then, seeing her still inquisitive, he added: "I think I can get on over there."

"On the trolley lines?" said Carrie, astonished.

"Yes," he rejoined.

"Aren't you afraid?" she asked.

"What of?" he answered. "The police are protecting them."

"The paper said four men were hurt yesterday."

"Yes," he returned; "but you can't go by what the papers say. They'll run the cars all right."

He looked rather determined now, in a desolate sort of way, and Carrie felt very sorry. Something of the old Hurstwood was here—the least shadow of what was once shrewd and pleasant strength. Outside, it was cloudy and blowing a few flakes of snow.

"What a day to go over there," thought Carrie.

Now he left before she did, which was a remarkable thing, and tramped eastward to Fourteenth Street and Sixth Avenue, where he took the car. He had read that scores of applicants were applying at the office of the Brooklyn City Railroad building and were being received. He made his way there by horse-car and ferry—a dark, silent man—to the offices in question. It was a long way, for no cars were running, and the day was cold; but he trudged along grimly. Once in Brooklyn, he could clearly see and feel that a strike was on. People showed it in their manner. Along the routes of certain tracks not a car was running. About certain corners and nearby saloons small groups of men were lounging. Several spring wagons passed him, equipped with plain wooden chairs, and labelled "Flatbush" or "Prospect Park. Fare, Ten Cents." He noticed cold and even gloomy faces. Labor was having its little war.

When he came near the office in question, he saw a few men standing about, and some policemen. On the far corners were other men—whom he took to be strikers—watching. All the houses were small and wooden, the streets poorly paved. After New York, Brooklyn looked actually poor and hard-up.

He made his way into the heart of the small group, eyed by policemen and the men already there. One of the officers addressed him.

"What are you looking for?"

"I want to see if I can get a place."

"The offices are up those steps," said the bluecoat. His face was a very neutral thing to contemplate. In his heart of hearts, he sympathized with the strikers and hated this "scab."[19] In his heart of hearts, also, he felt the dignity and use of the police force, which commanded order. Of its true social significance, he never once dreamed. His was not the mind for that. The two feelings blended in him—neutralized one another and him. He would have fought for this man as determinedly as for himself, and yet only so far as commanded. Strip him of his uniform, and he would have soon picked his side.

Hurstwood ascended a dusty flight of steps and entered a small, dust-colored office, in which were a railing, a long desk, and several clerks.

[19]A person who thwarts a strike by working while the strikers refuse to work.

"Well, sir?" said a middle-aged man, looking up at him from the long desk.

"Do you want to hire any men?" inquired Hurstwood.

"What are you—a motorman?"

"No; I'm not anything," said Hurstwood.

He was not at all abashed by his position. He knew these people needed men. If one didn't take him, another would. This man could take him or leave him, just as he chose.

"Well, we prefer experienced men, of course," said the man. He paused, while Hurstwood smiled indifferently. Then he added: "Still, I guess you can learn. What is your name?"

"Wheeler," said Hurstwood.

The man wrote an order on a small card. "Take that to our barns," he said, "and give it to the foreman. He'll show you what to do."

Hurstwood went down and out. He walked straight away in the direction indicated, while the policemen looked after.

"There's another wants to try it," said Officer Kiely to Officer Macey.

"I have my mind he'll get his fill," returned the latter, quietly. They had been in strikes before.

CHAPTER XLI

The Strike

The barn at which Hurstwood applied was exceedingly short-handed, and was being operated practically by three men as directors. There were a lot of green hands around—queer, hungry-looking men, who looked as if want had driven them to desperate means. They tried to be lively and willing, but there was an air of hang-dog[20] diffidence about the place.

Hurstwood went back through the barns and out into a large, enclosed lot, where were a series of tracks and loops. A half-dozen cars were there, manned by instructors, each with a pupil at the lever. More pupils were waiting at one of the rear doors of the barn.

In silence Hurstwood viewed this scene, and waited. His companions took his eye for a while, though they did not interest him much more than the cars. They were an uncomfortable-looking gang, however. One or two were very thin and lean. Several were quite stout. Several others were rawboned and sallow, as if they had been beaten upon by all sorts of rough weather.

"Did you see by the paper they are going to call out the militia?" Hurstwood heard one of them remark.

"Oh, they'll do that," returned the other. "They always do."

"Think we're liable to have much trouble?" said another, whom Hurstwood did not see.

"Not very."

"That Scotchman that went out on the last car," put in a voice, "told me that they hit him in the ear with a cinder."

A small, nervous laugh accompanied this.

[20]Ashamed, lacking confidence.

"One of those fellows on the Fifth Avenue line must have had a hell of a time, according to the papers," drawled another. "They broke his car windows and pulled him off into the street 'fore the police could stop 'em."

"Yes; but there are more police around today," was added by another.

Hurstwood hearkened without much mental comment. These talkers seemed scared to him. Their gabbling was feverish—things said to quiet their own minds. He looked out into the yard and waited.

Two of the men got around quite near him, but behind his back. They were rather social, and he listened to what they said.

"Are you a railroad man?" said one.

"Me? No. I've always worked in a paper factory."

"I had a job in Newark[21] until last October," returned the other, with reciprocal feeling.

There were some words which passed too low to hear. Then the conversation became strong again.

"I don't blame these fellers for striking," said one. "They've got the right of it, all right, but I had to get something to do."

"Same here," said the other. "If I had any job in Newark I wouldn't be over here takin' chances like these."

"It's hell these days, ain't it?" said the man. "A poor man ain't nowhere. You could starve, by God, right in the streets, and there ain't most no one would help you."

"Right you are," said the other. "The job I had I lost 'cause they shut down. They run all summer and lay up a big stock, and then shut down."

Hurstwood paid some little attention to this. Somehow, he felt a little superior to these two—a little better off. To him these were ignorant and commonplace, poor sheep in a driver's hand.

"Poor devils," he thought, speaking out of the thoughts and feelings of a bygone period of success. "Next," said one of the instructors.

"You're next," said a neighbor, touching him.

He went out and climbed on the platform. The instructor took it for granted that no preliminaries were needed.

"You see this handle," he said, reaching up to an electric cut-off, which was fastened to the roof. "This throws the current off or on. If you want to reverse the car you turn it over here. If you want to send it forward, you put it over here. If you want to cut off the power, you keep it in the middle."

Hurstwood smiled at the simple information.

"Now, this handle here regulates your speed. To here," he said, pointing with his finger, "gives you about four miles an hour. This is eight. When it's full on, you make about fourteen miles an hour."

Hurstwood watched him calmly. He had seen motormen work before. He knew just about how they did it, and was sure he could do as well, with a very little practice.

The instructor explained a few more details, and then said:

"Now, we'll back her up."

Hurstwood stood placidly by, while the car rolled back into the yard.

"One thing you want to be careful about, and that is to start easy. Give one degree time to act before you start another. The one fault of most men is that

[21]Newark, New Jersey.

they always want to throw her wide open. That's bad. It's dangerous, too. Wears out the motor. You don't want to do that."

"I see," said Hurstwood.

He waited and waited, while the man talked on.

"Now you take it," he said, finally.

The ex-manager laid hand to the lever and pushed it gently, as he thought. It worked much easier than he imagined, however, with the result that the car jerked quickly forward, throwing him back against the door. He straightened up sheepishly, while the instructor stopped the car with the brake.

"You want to be careful about that," was all he said.

Hurstwood found, however, that handling a brake and regulating speed were not so instantly mastered as he had imagined. Once or twice he would have ploughed through the rear fence if it had not been for the hand and word of his companion. The latter was rather patient with him, but he never smiled.

"You've got to get the knack of working both arms at once," he said. "It takes a little practice."

One o'clock came while he was still on the car practicing, and he began to feel hungry. The day set in snowing, and he was cold. He grew weary of running to and fro on the short track.

They ran the car to the end and both got off. Hurstwood went into the barn and sought a car step, pulling out his paper-wrapped lunch from his pocket. There was no water and the bread was dry, but he enjoyed it. There was no ceremony about dining. He swallowed and looked about, contemplating the dull, homely labor of the thing. It was disagreeable—miserably disagreeable—in all its phases. Not because it was bitter, but because it was hard. It would be hard to anyone, he thought.

After eating, he stood about as before, waiting until his turn came.

The intention was to give him an afternoon of practice, but the greater part of the time was spent in waiting about.

At last evening came, and with it hunger and a debate with himself as to how he should spend the night. It was half-past five. He must soon eat. If he tried to go home, it would take him two hours and a half of cold walking and riding. Besides he had orders to report at seven the next morning, and going home would necessitate his rising at an unholy and disagreeable hour. He had only something like a dollar and fifteen cents of Carrie's money, with which he had intended to pay the two weeks' coal bill before the present idea struck him.

"They must have some place around here," he thought. "Where does that fellow from Newark stay?"

Finally he decided to ask. There was a young fellow standing near one of the doors in the cold, waiting a last turn. He was a mere boy in years—twenty-one about—but with a body lank and long, because of privation. A little good living would have made this youth plump and swaggering.

"How do they arrange this, if a man hasn't any money?" inquired Hurstwood, discreetly.

The fellow turned a keen, watchful face on the inquirer.

"You mean eat?" he replied.

"Yes, and sleep. I can't go back to New York tonight."

"The foreman 'll fix that if you ask him, I guess. He did me."

"That so?"

"Yes. I just told him I didn't have anything. Gee, I couldn't go home. I live way over in Hoboken."[22]

Hurstwood only cleared his throat by way of acknowledgment.

"They've got a place upstairs here, I understand. I don't know what sort of a thing it is. Purty tough, I guess. He gave me a meal ticket this noon. I know that wasn't much."

Hurstwood smiled grimly, and the boy laughed.

"It ain't no fun, is it?" he inquired, wishing vainly for a cheery reply.

"Not much," answered Hurstwood.

"I'd tackle him now," volunteered the youth. "He may go 'way."

Hurstwood did so.

"Isn't there some place I can stay around here tonight?" he inquired. "If I have to go back to New York, I'm afraid I won't"

"There're some cots upstairs," interrupted the man, "if you want one of them."

"That'll do," he assented.

He meant to ask for a meal ticket, but the seemingly proper moment never came, and he decided to pay himself that night.

"I'll ask him in the morning."

He ate in a cheap restaurant in the vicinity, and, being cold and lonely, went straight off to seek the loft in question. The company was not attempting to run cars after nightfall. It was so advised by the police.

The room seemed to have been a lounging place for night workers. There were some nine cots in the place, two or three wooden chairs, a soap box, and a small, round-bellied stove, in which a fire was blazing. Early as he was, another man was there before him. The latter was sitting beside the stove warming his hands.

Hurstwood approached and held out his own toward the fire. He was sick of the bareness and privation of all things connected with his venture, but was steeling himself to hold out. He fancied he could for a while.

"Cold, isn't it?" said the early guest.

"Rather."

A long silence.

"Not much of a place to sleep in, is it?" said the man.

"Better than nothing," replied Hurstwood.

Another silence.

"I believe I'll turn in," said the man.

Rising, he went to one of the cots and stretched himself, removing only his shoes, and pulling the one blanket and dirty old comforter over him in a sort of bundle. The sight disgusted Hurstwood, but he did not dwell on it, choosing to gaze into the stove and think of something else. Presently he decided to retire, and picked a cot, also removing his shoes.

While he was doing so, the youth who had advised him to come here entered, and, seeing Hurstwood, tried to be genial.

"Better'n nothin'," he observed, looking around.

Hurstwood did not take this to himself. He thought it to be an expression of individual satisfaction, and so did not answer. The youth imagined he was out

[22]Hoboken, New Jersey.

of sorts, and set to whistling softly. Seeing another man asleep, he quit that and lapsed into silence.

Hurstwood made the best of a bad lot by keeping on his clothes and pushing away the dirty covering from his head, but at last he dozed in sheer weariness. The covering became more and more comfortable, its character was forgotten, and he pulled it about his neck and slept. In the morning he was aroused out of a pleasant dream by several men stirring about in the cold, cheerless room. He had been back in Chicago in fancy, in his own comfortable home. Jessica had been arranging to go somewhere, and he had been talking with her about it. This was so clear in his mind, that he was startled now by the contrast of this room. He raised his head, and the cold, bitter reality jarred him into wakefulness.

"Guess I'd better get up," he said.

There was no water on this floor. He put on his shoes in the cold and stood up, shaking himself in his stiffness. His clothes felt disagreeable, his hair bad.

"Hell!" he muttered, as he put on his hat.

Downstairs things were stirring again.

He found a hydrant, with a trough which had once been used for horses, but there was no towel here, and his handkerchief was soiled from yesterday. He contented himself with wetting his eyes with the ice-cold water. Then he sought the foreman, who was already on the ground.

"Had your breakfast yet?" inquired that worthy.

"No," said Hurstwood.

"Better get it, then; your car won't be ready for a little while."

Hurstwood hesitated.

"Could you let me have a meal ticket?" he asked with an effort.

"Here you are," said the man, handing him one.

He breakfasted as poorly as the night before on some fried steak and bad coffee. Then he went back.

"Here," said the foreman, motioning him, when he came in. "You take this car out in a few minutes."

Hurstwood climbed up on the platform in the gloomy barn and waited for a signal. He was nervous, and yet the thing was a relief. Anything was better than the barn.

On this the fourth day of the strike, the situation had taken a turn for the worse. The strikers, following the counsel of their leaders and the newspapers, had struggled peaceably enough. There had been no great violence done. Cars had been stopped, it is true, and the men argued with. Some crews had been won over and led away, some windows broken, some jeering and yelling done; but in no more than five or six instances had men been seriously injured. These by crowds whose acts the leaders disclaimed.

Idleness, however, and the sight of the company, backed by the police, triumphing, angered the men. They saw that each day more cars were going on, each day more declarations were being made by the company officials that the effective opposition of the strikers was broken. This put desperate thoughts in the minds of the men. Peaceful methods meant, they saw, that the companies would soon run all their cars and those who had complained would be forgotten. There was nothing so helpful to the companies as peaceful methods. All at once they blazed forth, and for a week there was storm and stress. Cars were assailed, men attacked, policemen struggled with, tracks torn up, and shots fired, until at last street fights and mob movements became frequent, and the city was invested with militia.

Hurstwood knew nothing of the change of temper.

"Run your car out," called the foreman, waving a vigorous hand at him. A green conductor jumped up behind and rang the bell twice as a signal to start. Hurstwood turned the lever and ran the car out through the door into the street in front of the barn. Here two brawny policemen got up beside him on the platform—one on either hand.

At the sound of a gong near the barn door, two bells were given by the conductor and Hurstwood opened his lever.

The two policemen looked about them calmly.

"'Tis cold, all right, this morning," said the one on the left, who possessed a rich brogue.

"I had enough of it yesterday," said the other. "I wouldn't want a steady job of this."

"Nor I."

Neither paid the slightest attention to Hurstwood, who stood facing the cold wind, which was chilling him completely, and thinking of his orders.

"Keep a steady gait," the foreman had said. "Don't stop for anyone who doesn't look like a real passenger. Whatever you do, don't stop for a crowd."

The two officers kept silent for a few moments.

"The last man must have gone through all right," said the officer on the left. "I don't see his car anywhere."

"Who's on there?" asked the second officer, referring, of course, to its complement of policemen.

"Schaeffer and Ryan."

There was another silence, in which the car ran smoothly along. There were not so many houses along this part of the way. Hurstwood did not see many people either. The situation was not wholly disagreeable to him. If he were not so cold, he thought he would do well enough.

He was brought out of this feeling by the sudden appearance of a curve ahead, which he had not expected. He shut off the current and did an energetic turn at the brake, but not in time to avoid an unnaturally quick turn. It shook him up and made him feel like making some apologetic remarks, but he refrained.

"You want to look out for them things," said the officer on the left, condescendingly.

"That's right," agreed Hurstwood, shamefacedly.

"There's lots of them on this line," said the officer on the right. Around the corner a more populated way appeared. One or two pedestrians were in view ahead. A boy coming out of a gate with a tin milk bucket gave Hurstwood his first objectionable greeting.

"Scab!" he yelled. "Scab!"

Hurstwood heard it, but tried to make no comment, even to himself. He knew he would get that, and much more of the same sort, probably.

At a corner farther up a man stood by the track and signalled the car to stop.

"Never mind him," said one of the officers. "He's up to some game."

Hurstwood obeyed. At the corner he saw the wisdom of it. No sooner did the man perceive the intention to ignore him, than he shook his fist.

"Ah, you bloody coward!" he yelled.

Some half dozen men, standing on the corner, flung taunts and jeers after the speeding car.

Hurstwood winced the least bit. The real thing was slightly worse than the thoughts of it had been.

Now came in sight, three or four blocks farther on, a heap of something on the track.

"They've been at work, here, all right," said one of the policemen.

"We'll have an argument, maybe," said the other.

Hurstwood ran the car close and stopped. He had not done so wholly, however, before a crowd gathered about. It was composed of ex-motormen and conductors in part, with a sprinkling of friends and sympathizers.

"Come off the car, pardner," said one of the men in a voice meant to be conciliatory. "You don't want to take the bread out of another man's mouth, do you?"

Hurstwood held to his brake and lever, pale and very uncertain what to do.

"Stand back," yelled one of the officers, leaning over the platform railing. "Clear out of this, now. Give the man a chance to do his work."

"Listen, pardner," said the leader, ignoring the policeman and addressing Hurstwood. "We're all working men, like yourself. If you were a regular motorman, and had been treated as we've been, you wouldn't want anyone to come in and take your place, would you? You wouldn't want anyone to do you out of your chance to get your rights, would you?"

"Shut her off! shut her off!" urged the other of the policemen, roughly. "Get out of this, now," and he jumped the railing and landed before the crowd and began shoving. Instantly the other officer was down beside him.

"Stand back, now," they yelled. "Get out of this. What the hell do you mean? Out, now."

It was like a small swarm of bees.

"Don't shove me," said one of the strikers, determinedly. "I'm not doing anything."

"Get out of this!" cried the officer, swinging his club. "I'll give ye a bat on the sconce. Back, now."

"What the hell!" cried another of the strikers, pushing the other way, adding at the same time some lusty oaths.

Crack came an officer's club on his forehead. He blinked his eyes blindly a few times, wabbled[23] on his legs, threw up his hands, and staggered back. In return, a swift fist landed on the officer's neck.

Infuriated by this, the latter plunged left and right, laying about madly with his club. He was ably assisted by his brother of the blue, who poured ponderous oaths upon the troubled waters. No severe damage was done, owing to the agility of the strikers in keeping out of reach. They stood about the sidewalk now and jeered.

"Where is the conductor?" yelled one of the officers, getting his eye on that individual, who had come nervously forward to stand by Hurstwood. The latter had stood gazing upon the scene with more astonishment than fear.

"Why don't you come down here and get these stones off the track?" inquired the officer. "What you standing there for? Do you want to stay here all day? Get down."

[23]Wobbled.

Hurstwood breathed heavily in excitement and jumped down with the nervous conductor as if he had been called.

"Hurry up, now," said the other policeman.

Cold as it was, these officers were hot and mad. Hurstwood worked with the conductor, lifting stone after stone and warming himself by the work.

"Ah, you scab, you!" yelled the crowd. "You coward! Steal a man's job, will you? Rob the poor, will you, you thief? We'll get you yet, now. Wait."

Not all of this was delivered by one man. It came from here and there, incorporated with much more of the same sort and curses.

"Work, you blackguards," yelled a voice. "Do the dirty work. You're the suckers that keep the poor people down!"

"May God starve ye yet," yelled an old Irish woman, who now threw open a nearby window and stuck out her head.

"Yes, and you," she added, catching the eye of one of the policemen. "You bloody, murtherin' thafe! Crack my son over the head, will you, you hard-hearted, murtherin' divil? Ah, ye——"

But the officer turned a deaf ear.

"Go to the devil, you old hag," he half muttered as he stared round upon the scattered company.

Now the stones were off, and Hurstwood took his place again amid a continued chorus of epithets. Both officers got up beside him and the conductor rang the bell, when, bang! bang! through window and door came rocks and stones. One narrowly grazed Hurstwood's head. Another shattered the window behind.

"Throw open your lever," yelled one of the officers, grabbing at the handle himself.

Hurstwood complied and the car shot away, followed by a rattle of stones and a rain of curses.

"That——hit me in the neck," said one of the officers. "I gave him a good crack for it, though."

"I think I must have left spots on some of them," said the other.

"I know that big guy that called us a——" said the first. "I'll get him yet for that."

"I thought we were in for it sure, once there," said the second.

Hurstwood, warmed and excited, gazed steadily ahead. It was an astonishing experience for him. He had read of these things, but the reality seemed something altogether new. He was no coward in spirit. The fact that he had suffered this much now rather operated to arouse a stolid determination to stick it out. He did not recur in thought to New York or the flat. This one trip seemed a consuming thing.

They now ran into the business heart of Brooklyn uninterrupted. People gazed at the broken windows of the car and at Hurstwood in his plain clothes. Voices called "scab" now and then, as well as other epithets, but no crowd attacked the car. At the downtown end of the line, one of the officers went to call up his station and report the trouble.

"There's a gang out there," he said, "laying for us yet. Better send some one over there and clean them out."

The car ran back more quietly—hooted, watched, flung at, but not attacked. Hurstwood breathed freely when he saw the barns.

"Well," he observed to himself, "I came out of that all right."

The car was turned in and he was allowed to loaf a while, but later he was again called. This time a new team of officers was aboard. Slightly more confident, he sped the car along the commonplace streets and felt somewhat less fearful. On one side, however, he suffered intensely. The day was raw, with a sprinkling of snow and a gusty wind, made all the more intolerable by the speed of the car. His clothing was not intended for this sort of work. He shivered, stamped his feet, and beat his arms as he had seen other motormen do in the past, but said nothing. The novelty and danger of the situation modified in a way his disgust and distress at being compelled to be here, but not enough to prevent him from feeling grim and sour. This was a dog's life, he thought. It was a tough thing to have to come to.

The one thought that strengthened him was the insult offered by Carrie. He was not down so low as to take all that, he thought. He could do something—this, even—for a while. It would get better. He would save a little.

A boy threw a clod of mud while he was thus reflecting and hit him upon the arm. It hurt sharply and angered him more than he had been any time since morning.

"The little cur!" he muttered.

"Hurt you?" asked one of the policemen.

"No," he answered.

At one of the corners, where the car slowed up because of a turn, an ex-motorman, standing on the sidewalk, called to him:

"Won't you come out, pardner, and be a man? Remember we're fighting for a decent day's wages, that's all. We've got families to support." The man seemed most peaceably inclined.

Hurstwood pretended not to see him. He kept his eyes straight on before and opened the lever wide. The voice had something appealing in it.

All morning this went on and long into the afternoon. He made three such trips. The dinner he had was no stay for such work and the cold was telling on him. At each end of the line he stopped to thaw out, but he could have groaned at the anguish of it. One of the barnmen, out of pity, loaned him a heavy cap and a pair of sheepskin gloves, and for once he was extremely thankful.

On the second trip of the afternoon he ran into a crowd about half way along the line, that had blocked the car's progress with an old telegraph pole.

"Get that thing off the track," shouted the two policemen.

"Yah, yah, yah!" yelled the crowd. "Get it off yourself."

The two policemen got down and Hurstwood started to follow.

"You stay there," one called. "Some one will run away with your car."

Amid the babel[24] of voices, Hurstwood heard one close beside him.

"Come down, pardner, and be a man. Don't fight the poor. Leave that to the corporations."

He saw the same fellow who had called to him from the corner. Now, as before, he pretended not to hear him.

[24]Confused noise, named after the Tower of Babel, built by prideful men who wanted to reach up to Heaven. They were prevented by God from accomplishing the task when he gave them separate languages so that they could no longer communicate with one another. The story is told in Genesis 11.

"Come down," the man repeated gently. "You don't want to fight poor men. Don't fight at all." It was a most philosophic and jesuitical[25] motorman.

A third policeman joined the other two from somewhere and some one ran to telephone for more officers. Hurstwood gazed about, determined but fearful.

A man grabbed him by the coat.

"Come off of that," he exclaimed, jerking at him and trying to pull him over the railing.

"Let go," said Hurstwood, savagely.

"I'll show you—you scab!" cried a young Irishman, jumping up on the car and aiming a blow at Hurstwood. The latter ducked and caught it on the shoulder instead of the jaw.

"Away from here," shouted an officer, hastening to the rescue, and adding, of course, the usual oaths.

Hurstwood recovered himself, pale and trembling. It was becoming serious with him now. People were looking up and jeering at him. One girl was making faces.

He began to waver in his resolution, when a patrol wagon rolled up and more officers dismounted. Now the track was quickly cleared and the release effected.

"Let her go now, quick," said the officer, and again he was off.

The end came with a real mob, which met the car on its return trip a mile or two from the barns. It was an exceedingly poor-looking neighborhood. He wanted to run fast through it, but again the track was blocked. He saw men carrying something out to it when he was yet a half-dozen blocks away.

"There they are again!" exclaimed one policeman.

"I'll give them something this time," said the second officer, whose patience was becoming worn. Hurstwood suffered a qualm of body as the car rolled up. As before, the crowd began hooting, but now, rather than come near, they threw things. One or two windows were smashed and Hurstwood dodged a stone.

Both policemen ran out toward the crowd, but the latter replied by running toward the car. A woman—a mere girl in appearance—was among these, bearing a rough stick. She was exceedingly wrathful and struck at Hurstwood, who dodged. Thereupon, her companions, duly encouraged, jumped on the car and pulled Hurstwood over. He had hardly time to speak or shout before he fell.

"Let go of me," he said, falling on his side.

"Ah, you sucker," he heard some one say. Kicks and blows rained on him. He seemed to be suffocating. Then two men seemed to be dragging him off and he wrestled for freedom.

"Let up," said a voice, "you're all right. Stand up."

He was let loose and recovered himself. Now he recognized two officers. He felt as if he would faint from exhaustion. Something was wet on his chin. He put up his hand and felt, then looked. It was red.

"They cut me," he said, foolishly, fishing for his handkerchief.

"Now, now," said one of the officers. "It's only a scratch."

His senses became cleared now and he looked around. He was standing in a little store, where they left him for the moment. Outside, he could see, as he

[25]Good at making logical arguments.

stood wiping his chin, the car and the excited crowd. A patrol wagon was there, and another.

He walked over and looked out. It was an ambulance, backing in.

He saw some energetic charging by the police and arrests being made.

"Come on, now, if you want to take your car," said an officer, opening the door and looking in. He walked out, feeling rather uncertain of himself. He was very cold and frightened.

"Where's the conductor?" he asked.

"Oh, he's not here now," said the policeman.

Hurstwood went toward the car and stepped nervously on. As he did so there was a pistol shot. Something stung his shoulder.

"Who fired that?" he heard an officer exclaim. "By God! who did that?" Both left him, running toward a certain building. He paused a moment and then got down.

"George!" exclaimed Hurstwood, weakly, "this is too much for me."

He walked nervously to the corner and hurried down a side street.

"Whew!" he said, drawing in his breath.

A half block away, a small girl gazed at him.

"You'd better sneak," she called.

He walked homeward in a blinding snowstorm, reaching the ferry by dusk. The cabins were filled with comfortable souls, who studied him curiously. His head was still in such a whirl that he felt confused. All the wonder of the twinkling lights of the river in a white storm passed for nothing. He trudged doggedly on until he reached the flat. There he entered and found the room warm. Carrie was gone. A couple of evening papers were lying on the table where she left them. He lit the gas and sat down. Then he got up and stripped to examine his shoulder. It was a mere scratch. He washed his hands and face, still in a brown study, apparently, and combed his hair. Then he looked for something to eat, and finally, his hunger gone, sat down in his comfortable rocking-chair. It was a wonderful relief.

He put his hand to his chin, forgetting, for the moment, the papers.

"Well," he said, after a time, his nature recovering itself, "that's a pretty tough game over there."

Then he turned and saw the papers. With half a sigh he picked up the "World."

"Strike Spreading in Brooklyn," he read. "Rioting Breaks Out in all Parts of the City."

He adjusted his paper very comfortably and continued. It was the one thing he read with absorbing interest.

CHAPTER XLV

Curious Shifts of the Poor

The gloomy Hurstwood, sitting in his cheap hotel, where he had taken refuge with seventy dollars—the price of his furniture—between him and nothing, saw a hot summer out and a cool fall in, reading. He was not wholly indifferent to the fact that his money was slipping away. As fifty cents after fifty cents were paid out for a day's lodging he became uneasy, and finally took a cheaper room—thirty-five cents a day—to make his money last longer. Frequently he saw notices of Carrie. Her picture was in the "World" once or twice, and an old "Herald"[26] he found in a chair informed him that she had recently appeared with some others at a benefit for something or other. He read these things with mingled feelings. Each one seemed to put her farther and farther away into a realm which became more imposing as it receded from him. On the billboards, too, he saw a pretty poster, showing her as the Quaker Maid, demure and dainty. More than once he stopped and looked at these, gazing at the pretty face in a sullen sort of way. His clothes were shabby, and he presented a marked contrast to all that she now seemed to be.

Somehow, so long as he knew she was at the Casino, though he had never any intention of going near her, there was a subconscious comfort for him—he was not quite alone. The show seemed such a fixture that, after a month or two, he began to take it for granted that it was still running. In September it went on the road and he did not notice it. When all but twenty dollars of his money was gone, he moved to a fifteen-cent lodging-house in the Bowery, where there was a bare lounging-room filled with tables and benches as well as some chairs. Here his preference was to close his eyes and dream of other days, a habit which grew upon him. It was not sleep at first, but a mental hearkening back to scenes and incidents in his Chicago life. As the present became darker, the past grew brighter, and all that concerned it stood in relief.

He was unconscious of just how much this habit had hold of him until one day he found his lips repeating an old answer he had made to one of his friends. They were in Fitzgerald and Moy's.[27] It was as if he stood in the door of his elegant little office, comfortably dressed, talking to Sagar Morrison about the value of South Chicago real estate in which the latter was about to invest.

"How would you like to come in on that with me?" he heard Morrison say.

"Not me," he answered, just as he had years before. "I have my hands full now."

The movement of his lips aroused him. He wondered whether he had really spoken. The next time he noticed anything of the sort he really did talk.

"Why don't you jump, you bloody fool?" he was saying. "Jump!"

It was a funny English story he was telling to a company of actors. Even as his voice recalled him, he was smiling. A crusty old codger, sitting near by, seemed disturbed; at least, he stared in a most pointed way. Hurstwood straightened up. The humor of the memory fled in an instant and he felt ashamed. For relief, he left his chair and strolled out into the streets.

One day, looking down the ad columns of the "Evening World,"[28] he saw where a new play was at the Casino. Instantly, he came to a mental halt. Carrie had gone! He remembered seeing a poster of her only yesterday, but no doubt it was one left uncovered by the new signs. Curiously, this fact shook him up. He had almost to admit that somehow he was depending upon her being in the city. Now she was gone. He wondered how this important fact had skipped him. Goodness knows when she would be back now. Impelled by a nervous fear, he

[26]A New York City newspaper.
[27]A prosperous saloon in Chicago of which Hurstwood was the manager before his fall.
[28]The afternoon edition of the New York *World*.

rose and went into the dingy hall, where he counted his remaining money, unseen. There were but ten dollars in all.

He wondered how all these other lodging-house people around him got along. They didn't seem to do anything. Perhaps they begged—unquestionably they did. Many was the dime he had given to such as they in his day. He had seen other men asking for money on the streets. Maybe he could get some that way. There was horror in this thought.

Sitting in the lodging-house room, he came to his last fifty cents. He had saved and counted until his health was affected. His stoutness had gone. With it, even the semblance of a fit in his clothes. Now he decided he must do something, and, walking about, saw another day go by, bringing him down to his last twenty cents—not enough to eat for the morrow.

Summoning all his courage, he crossed to Broadway and up to the Broadway Central hotel. Within a block he halted, undecided. A big, heavy-faced porter was standing at one of the side entrances, looking out. Hurstwood purposed to appeal to him. Walking straight up, he was upon him before he could turn away.

"My friend," he said, recognizing even in his plight the man's inferiority, "is there anything about this hotel that I could get to do?"

The porter stared at him the while he continued to talk.

"I'm out of work and out of money and I've got to get something,—it doesn't matter what. I don't care to talk about what I've been, but if you'd tell me how to get something to do, I'd be much obliged to you. It wouldn't matter if it only lasted a few days just now. I've got to have something."

The porter still gazed, trying to look indifferent. Then, seeing that Hurstwood was about to go on, he said:

"I've nothing to do with it. You'll have to ask inside."

Curiously, this stirred Hurstwood to further effort.

"I thought you might tell me."

The fellow shook his head irritably.

Inside went the ex-manager and straight to an office off the clerk's desk. One of the managers of the hotel happened to be there. Hurstwood looked him straight in the eye.

"Could you give me something to do for a few days?" he said. "I'm in a position where I have to get something at once."

The comfortable manager looked at him, as much as to say: "Well, I should judge so."

"I came here," explained Hurstwood, nervously, "because I've been a manager myself in my day. I've had bad luck in a way but I'm not here to tell you that. I want something to do, if only for a week."

The man imagined he saw a feverish gleam in the applicant's eye.

"What hotel did you manage?" he inquired.

"It wasn't a hotel," said Hurstwood. "I was manager of Fitzgerald and Moy's place in Chicago for fifteen years."

"Is that so?" said the hotel man. "How did you come to get out of that?"

The figure of Hurstwood was rather surprising in contrast to the fact.

"Well, by foolishness of my own. It isn't anything to talk about now. You could find out if you wanted to. I'm 'broke' now and, if you will believe me, I haven't eaten anything today."

The hotel man was slightly interested in this story. He could hardly tell what to do with such a figure, and yet Hurstwood's earnestness made him wish to do something.

"Call Olsen," he said, turning to the clerk.

In reply to a bell and a disappearing hall-boy, Olsen, the head porter, appeared.

"Olsen," said the manager, "is there anything downstairs you could find for this man to do? I'd like to give him something."

"I don't know, sir," said Olsen. "We have about all the help we need. I think I could find something, sir, though, if you like."

"Do. Take him to the kitchen and tell Wilson to give him something to eat."

"All right, sir," said Olsen.

Hurstwood followed. Out of the manager's sight, the head porter's manner changed.

"I don't know what the devil there is to do," he observed.

Hurstwood said nothing. To him the big trunk hustler was a subject for private contempt.

"You're to give this man something to eat," he observed to the cook.

The latter looked Hurstwood over, and seeing something keen and intellectual in his eyes, said:

"Well, sit down over there."

Thus was Hurstwood installed in the Broadway Central, but not for long. He was in no shape or mood to do the scrub work that exists about the foundation of every hotel. Nothing better offering, he was set to aid the fireman, to work about the basement, to do anything and everything that might offer. Porters, cooks, firemen, clerks—all were over him. Moreover his appearance did not please these individuals—his temper was too lonely—and they made it disagreeable for him.

With the stolidity and indifference of despair, however, he endured it all, sleeping in an attic at the roof of the house, eating what the cook gave him, accepting a few dollars a week, which he tried to save. His constitution was in no shape to endure.

One day the following February he was sent on an errand to a large coal company's office. It had been snowing and thawing and the streets were sloppy. He soaked his shoes in his progress and came back feeling dull and weary. All the next day he felt unusually depressed and sat about as much as possible, to the irritation of those who admired energy in others.

In the afternoon some boxes were to be moved to make room for new culinary supplies. He was ordered to handle a truck. Encountering a big box, he could not lift it.

"What's the matter there?" said the head porter. "Can't you handle it?"

He was straining to lift it, but now he quit.

"No," he said, weakly.

The man looked at him and saw that he was deathly pale.

"Not sick, are you?" he asked. "I think I am," returned Hurstwood.

"Well, you'd better go sit down, then."

This he did, but soon grew rapidly worse. It seemed all he could do to crawl to his room, where he remained for a day.

"That man Wheeler's sick," reported one of the lackeys to the night clerk.

"What's the matter with him?"

"I don't know. He's got a high fever."

The hotel physician looked at him.

"Better send him to Bellevue," he recommended. "He's got pneumonia."

Accordingly, he was carted away.

In three weeks the worst was over, but it was nearly the first of May before his strength permitted him to be turned out. Then he was discharged.

No more weakly looking object ever strolled out into the spring sunshine than the once hale, lusty manager. All his corpulency had fled. His face was thin and pale, his hands white, his body flabby. Clothes and all, he weighed but one hundred and thirty-five pounds. Some old garments had been given him—a cheap brown coat and misfit pair of trousers. Also some change and advice. He was told to apply to the charities.

Again he resorted to the Bowery lodging-house, brooding over where to look. From this it was but a step to beggary.

"What can a man do?" he said. "I can't starve."

His first application was in sunny Second Avenue. A well-dressed man came leisurely strolling toward him out of Stuyvesant Park. Hurstwood nerved himself and sidled near.

"Would you mind giving me ten cents?" he said, directly. "I'm in a position where I must ask some one."

The man scarcely looked at him, fished in his vest pocket and took out a dime.

"There you are," he said.

"Much obliged," said Hurstwood, softly, but the other paid no more attention to him.

Satisfied with his success and yet ashamed of his situation, he decided that he would only ask for twenty-five cents more, since that would be sufficient. He strolled about sizing up people, but it was long before just the right face and situation arrived. When he asked, he was refused. Shocked by this result, he took an hour to recover and then asked again. This time a nickel was given him. By the most watchful effort he did get twenty cents more, but it was painful.

The next day he resorted to the same effort, experiencing a variety of rebuffs and one or two generous receptions. At last it crossed his mind that there was a science of faces, and that a man could pick the liberal countenance if he tried.

It was no pleasure to him, however, this stopping of passers-by. He saw one man taken up for it and now troubled lest he should be arrested. Nevertheless, he went on, vaguely anticipating that indefinite something which is always better.

It was with a sense of satisfaction, then, that he saw announced one morning the return of the Casino Company, "with Miss Carrie Madenda." He had thought of her often enough in days past. How successful she was—how much money she must have! Even now, however, it took a severe run of ill luck to decide him to appeal to her. He was truly hungry before he said:

"I'll ask her. She won't refuse me a few dollars."

Accordingly, he headed for the Casino one afternoon, passing it several times in an effort to locate the stage entrance. Then he sat in Bryant Park, a block away, waiting. "She can't refuse to help me a little," he kept saying to himself.

Beginning with half-past six, he hovered like a shadow about the Thirty-ninth Street entrance, pretending always to be a hurrying pedestrian and yet fearful lest he should miss his object. He was slightly nervous, too, now that the eventful hour had arrived; but being weak and hungry, his ability to suffer was modified. At last he saw that the actors were beginning to arrive, and his nervous tension increased, until it seemed as if he could not stand much more.

Once he thought he saw Carrie coming and moved forward, only to see that he was mistaken.

"She can't be long, now," he said to himself, half fearing to encounter her and equally depressed at the thought that she might have gone in by another way. His stomach was so empty that it ached.

Individual after individual passed him, nearly all well dressed, almost all indifferent. He saw coaches rolling by, gentlemen passing with ladies—the evening's merriment was beginning in this region of theatres and hotels.

Suddenly a coach rolled up and the driver jumped down to open the door. Before Hurstwood could act, two ladies flounced across the broad walk and disappeared in the stage door. He thought he saw Carrie, but it was so unexpected, so elegant and far away, he could hardly tell. He waited a while longer, growing feverish with want, and then seeing that the stage door no longer opened, and that a merry audience was arriving, he concluded it must have been Carrie and turned away.

"Lord," he said, hastening out of the street into which the more fortunate were pouring, "I've got to get something."

At that hour, when Broadway is wont to assume its most interesting aspect, a peculiar individual invariably took his stand at the corner of Twenty-sixth Street and Broadway—a spot which is also intersected by Fifth Avenue. This was the hour when the theatres were just beginning to receive their patrons. Fire signs announcing the night's amusements blazed on every hand. Cabs and carriages, their lamps gleaming like yellow eyes, pattered by. Couples and parties of three and four freely mingled in the common crowd, which poured by in a thick stream, laughing and jesting. On Fifth Avenue were loungers—a few wealthy strollers, a gentleman in evening dress with his lady on his arm, some club-men passing from one smoking-room to another. Across the way the great hotels showed a hundred gleaming windows, their cafes and billiard-rooms filled with a comfortable, well-dressed, and pleasure-loving throng. All about was the night, pulsating with the thoughts of pleasure and exhilaration—the curious enthusiasm of a great city bent upon finding joy in a thousand different ways.

This unique individual was no less than an ex-soldier turned religionist, who, having suffered the whips and privations of our peculiar social system, had concluded that his duty to the God which he conceived lay in aiding his fellowman. The form of aid which he chose to administer was entirely original with himself. It consisted of securing a bed for all such homeless wayfarers as should apply to him at this particular spot, though he had scarcely the wherewithal to provide a comfortable habitation for himself. Taking his place amid this lightsome atmosphere, he would stand, his stocky figure cloaked in a great cape overcoat, his head protected by a broad slouch hat, awaiting the applicants who had in various ways learned the nature of his charity. For a while he would stand alone, gazing like any idler upon an ever-fascinating scene. On the evening in question, a policeman passing saluted him as "captain," in a friendly way. An urchin who had frequently seen him before, stopped to gaze. All others took him for nothing out of the ordinary, save in the matter of dress, and conceived of him as a stranger whistling and idling for his own amusement.

As the first half-hour waned, certain characters appeared. Here and there in the passing crowds one might see, now and then, a loiterer edging interestedly near. A slouchy figure crossed the opposite corner and glanced furtively in his direction. Another came down Fifth Avenue to the corner of Twenty-sixth Street, took a general survey, and hobbled off again. Two or three noticeable Bowery types[29] edged along the Fifth Avenue side of Madison Square, but did not venture over. The soldier, in his cape overcoat, walked a short line of ten feet at his corner, to and fro, indifferently whistling.

As nine o'clock approached, some of the hubbub of the earlier hour passed. The atmosphere of the hotels was not so youthful. The air, too, was colder. On every hand curious figures were moving—watchers and peepers, without an imaginary circle, which they seemed afraid to enter—a dozen in all. Presently, with the arrival of a keener sense of cold, one figure came forward. It crossed Broadway from out the shadow of Twenty-sixth Street, and, in a halting, circuitous way, arrived close to the waiting figure. There was something shamefaced or diffident about the movement, as if the intention were to conceal any idea of stopping until the very last moment. Then suddenly, close to the soldier, came the halt.

The captain looked in recognition, but there was no especial greeting. The newcomer nodded slightly and murmured something like one who waits for gifts. The other simply motioned toward the edge of the walk.

"Stand over there," he said.

By this the spell was broken. Even while the soldier resumed his short, solemn walk, other figures shuffled forward. They did not so much as greet the leader, but joined the one, sniffling and hitching and scraping their feet.

"Cold, ain't it?"

"I'm glad winter's over."

"Looks as though it might rain."

The motley company had increased to ten. One or two knew each other and conversed. Others stood off a few feet, not wishing to be in the crowd and yet not counted out. They were peevish, crusty, silent, eying nothing in particular and moving their feet.

There would have been talking soon, but the soldier gave them no chance. Counting sufficient to begin, he came forward.

"Beds, eh, all of you?"

There was a general shuffle and murmur of approval.

"Well, line up here. I'll see what I can do. I haven't a cent myself."

They fell into a sort of broken, ragged line. One might see, now, some of the chief characteristics by contrast. There was a wooden leg in the line. Hats were all drooping, a group that would ill become a second-hand Hester Street basement collection. Trousers were all warped and frayed at the bottom and coats

[29]People who are clearly not affluent. The Bowery is a poor section of New York.

worn and faded. In the glare of the store lights, some of the faces looked dry and chalky; others were red with blotches and puffed in the cheeks and under the eyes; one or two were rawboned and reminded one of railroad hands. A few spectators came near, drawn by the seemingly conferring group, then more and more, and quickly there was a pushing, gaping crowd. Some one in the line began to talk.

"Silence!" exclaimed the captain. "Now, then, gentlemen, these men are without beds. They have to have some place to sleep tonight. They can't lie out in the streets. I need twelve cents to put one of them to bed. Who will give it to me?"

No reply.

"Well, we'll have to wait here, boys, until some one does. Twelve cents isn't so very much for one man."

"Here's fifteen," exclaimed a young man, peering forward with strained eyes. "It's all I can afford."

"All right. Now I have fifteen. Step out of the line," and seizing one by the shoulder, the captain marched him off a little way and stood him up alone.

Coming back, he resumed his place and began again.

"I have three cents left. These men must be put to bed somehow. There are"—counting—"one, two, three, four, five, six, seven, eight, nine, ten, eleven, twelve men. Nine cents more will put the next man to bed; give him a good, comfortable bed for the night. I go right along and look after that myself. Who will give me nine cents?"

One of the watchers, this time a middle-aged man, handed him a five-cent piece.

"Now, I have eight cents. Four more will give this man a bed. Come, gentlemen. We are going very slow this evening. You all have good beds. How about these?"

"Here you are," remarked a bystander, putting a coin into his hand.

"That," said the captain, looking at the coin, "pays for two beds for two men and gives me five on the next one. Who will give me seven cents more?"

"I will," said a voice.

Coming down Sixth Avenue this evening, Hurstwood chanced to cross east through Twenty-sixth Street toward Third Avenue. He was wholly disconsolate in spirit, hungry to what he deemed an almost mortal extent, weary, and defeated. How should he get at Carrie now? It would be eleven before the show was over. If she came in a coach, she would go away in one. He would need to interrupt under most trying circumstances. Worst of all, he was hungry and weary, and at best a whole day must intervene, for he had not heart to try again tonight. He had no food and no bed.

When he neared Broadway, he noticed the captain's gathering of wanderers, but thinking it to be the result of a street preacher or some patent medicine fakir, was about to pass on. However, in crossing the street toward Madison Square Park, he noticed the line of men whose beds were already secured, stretching out from the main body of the crowd. In the glare of the neighboring electric light he recognized a type of his own kind—the figures whom he saw about the streets and in the lodging-houses, drifting in mind and body like himself. He wondered what it could be and turned back.

There was the captain curtly pleading as before. He heard with astonishment and a sense of relief the oft-repeated words: "These men must have a bed." Before him was the line of unfortunates whose beds were yet to be had, and seeing a newcomer quietly edge up and take a position at the end of the line, he decided to do likewise. What use to contend? He was weary tonight. It was a simple way out of one difficulty, at least. To-morrow, maybe, he would do better.

Back of him, where some of those were whose beds were safe, a relaxed air was apparent. The strain of uncertainty being removed, he heard them talking with moderate freedom and some leaning toward sociability. Politics, religion, the state of the government, some newspaper sensations, and the more notorious facts the world over, found mouthpieces and auditors there. Cracked and husky voices pronounced forcibly upon odd matters. Vague and rambling observations were made in reply.

There were squints, and leers, and some dull, ox-like stares from those who were too dull or too weary to converse.

Standing tells. Hurstwood became more weary waiting. He thought he should drop soon and shifted restlessly from one foot to the other. At last his turn came. The man ahead had been paid for and gone to the blessed line of success. He was now first, and already the captain was talking for him.

"Twelve cents, gentlemen—twelve cents puts this man to bed. He wouldn't stand here in the cold if he had any place to go."

Hurstwood swallowed something that rose to his throat. Hunger and weakness had made a coward of him.

"Here you are," said a stranger, handing money to the captain.

Now the latter put a kindly hand on the ex-manager's shoulder. "Line up over there," he said.

Once there, Hurstwood breathed easier. He felt as if the world were not quite so bad with such a good man in it. Others seemed to feel like himself about this.

"Captain's a great feller, ain't he?" said the man ahead—a little, woebegone, helpless-looking sort of individual, who looked as though he had ever been the sport and care of fortune.

"Yes," said Hurstwood, indifferently.

"Huh! there's a lot back there yet," said a man farther up, leaning out and looking back at the applicants for whom the captain was pleading.

"Yes. Must be over a hundred tonight," said another.

"Look at the guy in the cab," observed a third.

A cab had stopped. Some gentleman in evening dress reached out a bill to the captain, who took it with simple thanks and turned away to his line. There was a general craning of necks as the jewel in the white shirt front sparkled and the cab moved off. Even the crowd gaped in awe.

"That fixes up nine men for the night," said the captain, counting out as many of the line near him. "Line up over there. Now, then, there are only seven. I need twelve cents."

Money came slowly. In the course of time the crowd thinned out to a meagre handful. Fifth Avenue, save for an occasional cab or foot passenger, was bare. Broadway was thinly peopled with pedestrians. Only now and then a stranger passing noticed the small group, handed out a coin, and went away, unheeding.

The captain remained stolid and determined. He talked on, very slowly, uttering the fewest words and with a certain assurance, as though he could not fail.

"Come; I can't stay out here all night. These men are getting tired and cold. Some one give me four cents."

There came a time when he said nothing at all. Money was handed him, and for each twelve cents he singled out a man and put him in the other line. Then he walked up and down as before, looking at the ground.

The theatres let out. Fire signs disappeared. A clock struck eleven. Another half-hour and he was down to the last two men.

"Come, now," he exclaimed to several curious observers; "eighteen cents will fix us all up for the night. Eighteen cents. I have six. Somebody give me the money. Remember, I have to go over to Brooklyn yet tonight. Before that I have to take these men down and put them to bed. Eighteen cents."

No one responded. He walked to and fro, looking down for several minutes, occasionally saying softly: "Eighteen cents." It seemed as if this paltry sum would delay the desired culmination longer than all the rest had. Hurstwood, buoyed up slightly by the long line of which he was a part, refrained with an effort from groaning, he was so weak.

At last a lady in opera cape and rustling skirts came down Fifth Avenue, accompanied by her escort. Hurstwood gazed wearily, reminded by her both of Carrie in her new world and of the time when he had escorted his own wife in like manner.

While he was gazing, she turned and, looking at the remarkable company, sent her escort over. He came, holding a bill in his fingers, all elegant and graceful.

"Here you are," he said.

"Thanks," said the captain, turning to the two remaining applicants. "Now we have some for to-morrow night," he added.

Therewith he lined up the last two and proceeded to the head, counting as he went.

"One hundred and thirty-seven," he announced. "Now, boys, line up. Right dress there. We won't be much longer about this. Steady, now."

He placed himself at the head and called out "Forward." Hurstwood moved with the line. Across Fifth Avenue, through Madison Square by the winding paths, east on Twenty-third Street, and down Third Avenue wound the long, serpentine company. Midnight pedestrians and loiterers stopped and stared as the company passed. Chatting policemen, at various corners, stared indifferently or nodded to the leader, whom they had seen before. On Third Avenue they marched, a seemingly weary way, to Eighth Street, where there was a lodginghouse, closed, apparently, for the night. They were expected, however.

Outside in the gloom they stood, while the leader parleyed within. Then doors swung open and they were invited in with a "Steady, now."

Some one was at the head showing rooms, so that there was no delay for keys. Toiling up the creaky stairs, Hurstwood looked back and saw the captain, watching; the last one of the line being included in his broad solicitude. Then he gathered his cloak about him and strolled out into the night.

"I can't stand much of this," said Hurstwood, whose legs ached him painfully, as he sat down upon the miserable bunk in the small, lightless chamber allotted to him. "I've got to eat, or I'll die."

1900 1917

The Literature of the Twentieth Century (1900 to 1945)

The United States began the twentieth century with a population of less than 76,000,000, almost two-thirds of it living on farms and in rural villages. Motor vehicles—dominant symbols of mobility and industrialism that would soon transform American life—had just begun to appear. In all the land there were only 8,000 automobiles and a mere 150 miles of paved country roads. On the other hand, the American arts at this time were poised on the brink of a turbulent modernity. In little more than two decades, American painters, architects, composers, and writers would adopt a variety of avant-garde doctrines so revolutionary as to exhaust the traditional vocabulary of the arts and require the introduction of new descriptive terms such as futurism, expressionism, post-impressionism, dadaism, imagism, and surrealism.

The Armory Show of 1913

The coming changes could be seen in the visual arts early in the century. The first exhibit of modern European art in the United States took place in 1908. Five years later a vast art show, held in a National Guard armory in New York City, marked a turning point in American cultural history and introduced large numbers of Americans to modern art for the first time. Many of the 1,600 works in the Armory Show departed radically from past tradition: Urban slums and people at the neglected end of the socio-economic spectrum were portrayed with harsh realism by American artists of what the newspapers derisively called the "Ash Can School"; paintings by European artists were filled with the visual gymnastics of neo-impressionism or with the geometric fragments and shifting viewpoints of the new cubism that seemed to defy all logic.[1] Such "artistic anarchism" stunned the public and made the Armory Show a scandalous success. Bewildered critics scoffed at the show's "freak art"; students of traditional art hanged radical new artists in effigy; former President Theodore Roosevelt dismissed the startling paintings and sculpture as work of "the lunatic fringe." But the Armory Show of 1913 signaled the rise of artistic techniques and ideologies that would persist in American art throughout the twentieth century and help to spur analogous changes in American poetry, drama, and fiction.

[1]Neo-impressionism was a term used to describe the work of French painter Georges-Pierre Seurat (1859–1891) and others who followed his example. Seurat avoided the smooth blending of colors that had been the usual practice in painting, instead developing techniques that used small fragments of pure color and depended on the eye of the viewer to blend them. Cubism was a style of painting developed in the early twentieth century, principally by Spanish painter Pablo Picasso (1881–1973) and French painter Georges Braques (1882–1963), that rejected three-dimensional perspective, attempting instead to represent visual experience by showing various two-dimensional views of the subject combined on the same canvas.

Literary Trends

Although the form and direction of modern American writing had clearly begun to emerge in the first decades of the century, World War I (1914–1918) stands as a dividing line between the nineteenth century and contemporary America. In the years preceding the war, nineteenth-century realism and naturalism remained vital forces in American literature. Henry James, then living in England, published novels, such as *The Ambassadors* (1903) and *The Golden Bowl* (1904), that stretched the boundaries of realism and pointed toward literary modernism. The literary naturalists Stephen Crane and Frank Norris died at the beginning of the century, but Theodore Dreiser's *Sister Carrie,* a commercial and critical failure when first published in 1900, was reissued in 1907 and won high praise for its grim, naturalistic portrayal of American society. A few years later, Ezra Pound, T. S. Eliot, and others began publishing works that would change the character of American poetry.

But these were not the texts that dominated the nation's literary tastes. In 1900, the best-selling novel in the United States was *To Have and To Hold,* a now mostly forgotten historical romance by Mary Johnston. In 1902, the bestseller was Owen Wister's *The Virginian,* a western that established a pattern for hundreds of cowboy adventure stories and movies that have followed—and was itself revived as a television series in the 1960s. The most popular single work of fiction of the entire period (by the 1990s its sales had exceeded 6,000,000 copies) was *The Wonderful Wizard of Oz* (1900), by L. Frank Baum. The growth of mass-circulation periodicals also created a rich marketplace for popular writers. By the 1920s, general-audience magazines that had circulations in the millions were paying as much as $6,000 for a short story and $60,000 for a serial (the equivalent of about $300,000 in modern purchasing power).

On the other hand, a rising number of "little magazines" offered fare of a more substantial sort, bringing numerous avant-garde writers to the attention of a limited elite audience. One of the most influential was *Poetry: A Magazine of Verse,* founded in Chicago by Harriet Monroe in 1912. Its first issue contained two poems by Ezra Pound, and in 1915 it printed both T. S. Eliot's "The Love Song of J. Alfred Prufrock" and Wallace Stevens's "Sunday Morning." Within a few years it had also published works by Edwin Arlington Robinson, Carl Sandburg, and Robert Frost, followed soon after by Robinson Jeffers and Hart Crane. The works of these poets forced changes in the traditional relationships between poets and their audiences, requiring readers with modernist sympathies. The "modernism" they practiced was, like the visual art that had shocked those attending the 1913 Armory Show, more "abstract," less "representational" than the literary works readers had been accustomed to. Poems like Eliot's *The Waste Land,* Stevens's "Thirteen Ways of Looking at a Blackbird," and many of Pound's poems fragmented the reader's view of the subject in ways that bore comparison to the cubist paintings of Pablo Picasso, Georges Braque, and Marcel DuChamp.

Reform Movements

World War I had its origins in the political turmoil of the early 1900s and in the rivalries of European imperial powers. America's leaders claimed that the war was necessary as a crusade to "Keep the Free in Freedom" and make the world safe for democracy. At the war's end, President Woodrow Wilson proclaimed that Americans had gained everything for which they had fought. But it soon became clear that out of the war's catastrophes and appalling waste had come little more than a sense of the failure of political leadership. No abiding solutions to the world's problems were found, and the years following the war saw a resurgence of radical nationalism and the rise of a new totalitarianism that would bring on World War II in less than a quarter of a century.

During World War I, some national attention had been drawn away from movements for political and social reform. But with the onset of peace, reform efforts founded in the nineteenth century gathered new strength, especially movements for women's rights and for temperance. Both women and men began working with renewed vigor to obtain for women the right to vote. They held protest marches, picketed government offices, purposely got themselves arrested, and went on hunger strikes while in jail—all to dramatize the need for equal rights in the polling booths. Their campaign was so successful that less than a year after the end of the war Congress had passed, and one year later the states had ratified, the Nineteenth Amendment, which declared that the right to vote could no longer be denied "on account of sex."

Meanwhile, the Women's Christian Temperance Union and the Anti-Saloon League had been raising funds for speakers and propaganda pamphleteers to denounce "Demon Rum" and "John Barleycorn." "Drys" debated "Wets" at town meetings, churches, and schools. Crusading temperance groups held parades and rallies and made campaign contributions to political candidates who would "vote right on the liquor issue." Victory for the temperance movement came in 1919 when the Eighteenth Amendment to the Constitution was ratified, prohibiting the sale of alcoholic beverages in the United States. But the triumph of temperance was only a seeming victory. America refused to go dry. The manufacture and sale of illegal alcohol flourished, and during the "Roaring Twenties" the drinking of alcohol by many Americans even increased. Prohibition had failed to purify America. Instead it brought many of the excesses—including the rise of organized crime and widespread disrespect for the law—that have continued to plague America since the 1920s. At the same time, racial and other sorts of bigotry were on the rise, even including the reemergence of the Ku Klux Klan, a sinister movement from the nineteenth-century Reconstruction era, this time as a viable political force in the North as well as the South. After fourteen years under Prohibition, the nation in 1933 finally acknowledged its failure to legislate virtue and sobriety. With the ratification of the Twenty-First Amendment, prohibition was repealed.

Literary Modernism

Reform victories at the end of "The Great War" had seemed to indicate the beginning of a better age, but many were not so optimistic. Many of the writers of the postwar era self-consciously declared that they were a "Lost Generation," devoid of faith and alienated from a civilization they felt no longer made any sense. The fiction of F. Scott Fitzgerald and Ernest Hemingway was especially effective in capturing the feeling of shellshock that characterized "lost generation" writing. Yet despite the grim tone of much of the creative output of the 1920s, American literature achieved a new diversity and reached great heights. The publication in 1922 of Eliot's *The Waste Land,* one of the most influential American poems of the twentieth century, helped to establish a modern tradition of highly intellectual poetry full of elite references and symbolism. In 1920 Sinclair Lewis published his denunciation of American small-town provincialism in *Main Street,* and in the same year Dreiser began writing the widely praised naturalist work *An American Tragedy* (1925). Fitzgerald summarized the experiences and attitudes of upper-class whites in his short stories and in his novel *The Great Gatsby* (1926). Hemingway wrote *The Sun Also Rises* (1926) and *A Farewell to Arms* (1929), and William Faulkner published *The Sound and the Fury* (1929).

After the First World War new American dramatists emerged as well, and for the first time in its history the American theater ceased to be dependent on the dramatic traditions of Europe. Experimental playwrights, hostile to outworn and timid theatrical convention, created works of tragedy, realism, and social protest. In the new American theater, plots, dialogue, staging, and acting differed radically from the bland drama of the past. Plays by "advanced" dramatists won large audiences and drew widespread critical acclaim. Early in the 1920s the most prominent of the new American playwrights, Eugene O'Neill, established an international reputation with such plays as *The Emperor Jones* (1920), *Anna Christie* (1921), and *The Hairy Ape* (1922).

Visual Arts, Architecture, and Music

The years between the two world wars were a time of new directions and achievements in all the arts. Museums and galleries were established in large and small cities throughout the United States. New York's Museum of Modern Art was founded in 1929, and New York City became the center of modern art in America, attracting artists from all over America and Europe to the visual richness of towering buildings and scenes of massed humanity. The term *modern art* had been used as early as the 1890s to describe the works of artists who deliberately chose to depart from the traditional forms, techniques, and subjects of familiar European art history. By the 1920s *modernism* and *modernistic* were part of the everyday vocabulary of millions of Americans who confronted the experimentalism of twentieth-century painting and sculpture. New theories of art appeared, justifying flat abstractions or surrealism with nightmarish representations of the unconscious. Art came to be accepted as diverse, unusual, and indecipherable. Artists attempted to present meanings without depicting conventional forms or familiar things, just as modernist literature often seemed to consist of poetry and prose that was unfamiliar and scarcely explicable.

It was a time for radical experiments in other arts, too. The American skyscraper became the preeminent achievement of twentieth-century architecture. The American motion picture industry rose to world dominance. And with the establishment of such music schools as Eastman and Julliard after World War I, American-trained musicians began to challenge the graduates of famous European music conservatories. But more notable still was the birth of jazz. African American jazz is an art form that grew out of nineteenth- and early twentieth-century African American musical forms—including the blues, spirituals, and ragtime. The jazz music of American-black musicians—

arguably the most influential art form ever to originate in the United States—spread throughout the world. And in 1938, when Benny Goodman led a racially mixed jazz orchestra in a concert at prestigious Carnegie Hall in New York City, it was clear that jazz had been fully accepted in mainstream American society as well.

The rise of jazz was closely associated with "The Harlem Renaissance"—a period of artistic eruption extending from approximately 1900 to 1940 (the most pronounced years being 1923–1929) during which African Americans depicted their experiences and celebrated their unique cultural heritage through the musical, visual, and literary arts. The primary socioeconomic factor in the development of the Harlem Renaissance was the "Great Migration." In this huge relocation, millions of African Americans moved northward, fleeing the enforcement in Southern states of post-Reconstruction segregation through the terrorism of lynching and through the pervasive, debilitating effects of systematic exclusion from economic opportunity and social equality. African Americans were drawn to the Northeast and Midwest by the growing number of industrial jobs in cities like Chicago, St. Louis, New York, and Philadelphia. The "Harlem Renaissance" actually stretched well beyond Harlem and encompassed a wide range of ideological efforts (from W. E. B. Du Bois and the NAACP to Marcus Garvey and the United Negro Improvement Association) to create social justice for African Americans. Some of the most important writers of the Harlem Renaissance were Langston Hughes, Zora Neale Hurston, Claude McKay, Nella Larsen, James Weldon Johnson, and Countee Cullen—a diverse grouping who, despite their cultural cohesiveness, produced works treating a variety of subjects in a variety of styles and genres. Their works, and others such as Jean Toomer's novel *Cane* (1923), showed that modernism was not a strictly Anglo-American phenomenon.

A Crash, a Depression, and Another War

In 1929, the stock market crashed and set off the Great Depression, a cataclysmic event that shattered public complacency and transformed American society in the 1930s. The abrupt end of what had seemed to be permanent prosperity further weakened the nation's confidence in its government, its political leaders, and its fundamental democratic ideals. Social activism became the order of the day. American artists of all kinds began to produce works of political and social criticism. Painters created harsh visions of American life on farms and in cities. Photographers recorded the miseries of poverty. American writers also made significant contributions. John Steinbeck described the lives of factory workers and migrant farmers in journalistic reports, short stories, and such novels as *Of Mice and Men* (1937) and *The Grapes of Wrath* (1939). Writers such as Joseph Kalar, Langston Hughes, and Tillie Lerner Olsen wrote important oppositional political poetry, their poetic form often calling into question or ignoring the widely accepted principles of modernism. And modernist poets like Wallace Stevens and William Carlos Williams attempted to produce literature that was more socially relevant than their previous works and to meditate more deeply on the necessary relation between art and reality. The Great Depression, with its associated economic and social concerns, lasted through the entire decade of the 1930s, making them, in American memory, a sobering counterpoint to the manic delirium of the 1920s. It ended only with the arrival of a still more monstrous disaster: World War II.

The first half of the twentieth century in the United States was a time of tremendous social, political, and technological change. Anglo-American modernism, and its responses to that change, was certainly the dominant literary mode of the time, but literary production (and, indeed, modernism itself) was much more varied than the terrain described in studies that focus only on writers like Pound, Eliot, Faulkner, and Hemingway. The different voices and perspectives that emerged between the turn of the century and World War II proliferated in a way that set the stage for the rich diversity, but some would also say the cacophony, of postmodern America.

You can find more general resources about this period on our Companion Website™ at <www.prenhall.com/mcmichael>.

International Affairs, Exploration, Settlement, and Science

1900 Hawaii granted territorial status, National census: population 75,994,575

1901 United States Steel Corporation founded

1903 U.S. acquires Panama Canal Zone
1903 Ford Motor Company founded
1903 Wright brothers make first airplane flight
1904–1914 Panama Canal built

1907 Electric washing machine invented

1910 Ford Model T first produced

1912 First neon sign created

1913 First assembly line begins to operate at Ford
1913 Niels Bohr develops theory of atomic structure

Politics and Government

1900 Socialist Party formed

1901 Anti-saloon leader Carrie Nation makes first raid on a saloon, Wichita, Kansas
1901 President McKinley assassinated. Theodore Roosevelt becomes president
1901 Socialist Party of America formed

1904 Theodore Roosevelt elected president
1906 Federal Pure Food and Drug Act passed
1907–1909 Georgia, Oklahoma, Mississippi, North Carolina, Tennessee, Alabama enact "dry" laws

1912–1946 Progressive party established
1912 Woodrow Wilson elected president. Reelected 1916
1913 Federal Reserve Bank and Department of Labor established

Society and Culture

1900 Theodore Dreiser publishes *Sister Carrie*
1900–1920 Most American workers have sixty-hour, six-day work week
1901 Connecticut passes first law regulating auto speed

1902 First Rose Bowl football game
1903 *The Great Train Robbery* exhibited, first film telling a story
1903 Henry James publishes *The Ambassadors*

1907 First Mother's Day celebration
1907 Henry Adams publishes *The Education of Henry Adams*
1908 Works by American Ash Can School of painters exhibited
1909 National Association for the Advancement of Colored People founded
1910 Boy Scouts of America founded
1911 Irving Berlin publishes "Alexander's Ragtime Band"

1913 Armory Show opens in New York. First large exhibit of modern art in America
1913 Mack Sennett begins making movie comedies

International Affairs, Exploration, Settlement, and Science	Politics and Government	Society and Culture
1914 Robert Goddard gets first U.S. patent for multistage rockets **1914–1918** World War I		
1917 U.S. buys Virgin Islands from Denmark	**1917** U.S. declares war on Germany. First U.S. troops land in France	**1917** Pulitzer Prize awards inaugurated. First jazz band recording made **1918** Theatre Guild established
1918 Armistice, World War I ends **1918–1919** World-wide influenza epidemic kills millions; 500,000 die in U.S.		
1919–1921 Civil war in Russia	**1919** U.S. Senate fails to approve the Versailles Treaty ending World War I **1919** Communist party, American Legion, and RCA established in U.S.	**1919–1926** Jack Dempsey heavy-weight boxing champion of the world
1920 National census: population 105,710,620. Urban population exceeds rural population for the first time **1920** League of Nations organized. U.S. Senate refuses to vote for membership	**1920** Prohibition (18th) Amendment goes into effect **1920** Transcontinental airmail begins. 19th Amendment gives women the vote **1920** Warren G. Harding elected President **1920–1933** Sale of intoxicating beverages prohibited in U.S.	**1920** Sinclair Lewis publishes *Main Street.* F. Scott Fitzgerald publishes his first novel, *This Side of Paradise* **1920** KDKA, Cincinnati transmits first regular radio broadcasts in U.S.
1921 Albert Einstein wins Nobel Prize for physics **1922** Mussolini forms Fascist government in Italy **1922** Union of Soviet Socialist Republics established		**1922** Lincoln Memorial dedicated in Washington, D.C. **1922** T. S. Eliot publishes *The Waste Land* **1922** *Reader's Digest* founded **1922** First radio commercial broadcast
	1923–1924 Teapot Dome scandal, corrupt Harding administration exposed **1923** Harding dies. Calvin Coolidge becomes president	**1923** Five-day, forty-hour work week introduced by steel industry
1924 Adolf Hitler writes *Mein Kampf*	**1924** Calvin Coolidge elected president	**1924** Premiere of "Rhapsody in Blue" by George Gershwin **1925** Publication of *The New Negro,* ed. Alain Locke. **1925** F. Scott Fitzgerald publishes *The Great Gatsby*

International Affairs, Exploration, Settlement, and Science

1926 Hirohito becomes emperor of Japan
1927 Charles Lindbergh flies the Atlantic alone
1928 Television tube developed
1929 First auto radios installed
1930 Jet propulsion engine developed
1931 Japanese invade Manchuria
1933 Hitler voted into power in Germany
1934 SS *Normandie,* French ocean liner, crosses Atlantic in 107 hours
1935 Anti-Semitic laws passed in Germany
1935–1936 Italy invades Ethiopia
1936 King Edward VIII of Great Britain abdicates
1936–1939 Spanish Civil War
1938 Germany absorbs Austria
1939 Scientists inform President Roosevelt of the possibility of making an atomic bomb
1939 Russia invades Finland
1939 Germany invades Poland in September. World War II begins

Politics and Government

1927–1933 U.S. Marines occupy Nicaragua
1928 Congress appropriates $32,000,000 to enforce Prohibition laws
1928 Herbert Hoover defeats Al Smith for the presidency
1929 Stock market crash. The Great Depression begins
1932 Franklin Roosevelt elected president. Reelected 1936, 1940, 1944
1933–1936 Severe drought. Plains states become "Dust Bowl"
1933 Twenty-first Amendment repeals Prohibition
1935 W.P.A. established
1939–1945 World War II brings economic boom to U.S.

Society and Culture

1926 Ernest Hemingway publishes *The Sun Also Rises*
1927 *The Jazz Singer,* first full-length sound movie
1928 First Mickey Mouse cartoon
1929 William Faulkner publishes *The Sound and the Fury*
1930 Sinclair Lewis first American to win the Nobel Prize for literature
1933 Film *King Kong* released
1935 Premiere of George Gershwin's *Porgy and Bess*
1936 Eugene O'Neill receives Nobel Prize for literature
1936 Margaret Mitchell publishes *Gone with the Wind*
1936 Sprinter Jesse Owens wins four gold medals at the Berlin Olympics
1939 John Steinbeck publishes *The Grapes of Wrath*

International Affairs, Exploration, Settlement, and Science	Politics and Government	Society and Culture
1940 German "blitzkrieg" conquers Norway, Denmark, Low Countries, and France	**1940** Alien Registration Act	**1940** Ernest Hemingway publishes *For Whom the Bell Tolls* **1940** Color television first shown
1941 December, Japan bombs Pearl Harbor. U.S. declares war on Japan, Germany, and Italy	**1941** Selective Service System extends draftees' service to 18 months	**1941** Orson Wells directs and stars in the film *Citizen Kane* **1941** First television commercial shown
1942 Atomic Age begins with first self-sustaining nuclear chain reaction		
		1943 Jitterbug dancing becomes popular **1943** Rogers and Hammerstein's *Oklahoma!* opens
1944 June, D-Day; Allies invade France	**1944** FDR reelected President for fourth term	

Mark Twain	1835–1910
Bret Harte	1836–1902
William Dean Howells	1837–1920
Henry Adams	1838–1918
Ambrose Bierce	1842–1914
Henry James	1843–1916
George Washington Cable	1844–1925
Joel Chandler Harris	1848–1908
Sarah Orne Jewett	1849–1909
Kate Chopin	1851–1904
Mary E. Wilkins Freeman	1852–1930
Charles Waddell Chesnutt	1858–1932
Charlotte Perkins Gilman	1860–1935
Owen Wister	1860–1938
O. Henry (William Sydney Porter)	1862–1910
Edith Wharton	1862–1937
W. E. B. Du Bois	1868–1963
Edwin Arlington Robinson	1869–1935
Frank Norris	1870–1902
James Weldon Johnson	1871–1938
Willa Cather	1873–1947
Ellen Glasgow	1873–1945
Robert Frost	1874–1963
Gertrude Stein	1874–1946
Sherwood Anderson	1876–1941
Gertrude Simmons Bonnin (Zitkala Sa)	1876–1938
Susan Glaspell	1876–1948
Wallace Stevens	1879–1955
William Carlos Williams	1883–1963
Sinclair Lewis	1885–1951
Ezra Pound	1885–1972
Alain Locke	1886–1954
Robinson Jeffers	1887–1962
Marianne Moore	1887–1972
T. S. Eliot	1888–1965
Eugene O'Neill	1888–1953
Katherine Anne Porter	1890–1980
Zora Neale Hurston	1891–1960
E. E. Cummings	1894–1962
Jean Toomer	1894–1967
John Dos Passos	1896–1970
Scott Fitzgerald	1896–1940
William Faulkner	1897–1962
Hart Crane	1899–1932
Ernest Hemingway	1899–1961
Thomas Wolfe	1900–1938
Langston Hughes	1902–1967
John Steinbeck	1902–1968
Countée Cullen	1903–1946

Reading the Historical Context

Henry Adams 1838–1918

Henry Adams was born into the most distinguished family in America. His great-grandfather (John Adams) and grandfather (John Quincy Adams) were U.S. presidents; his father, Charles Francis Adams, was a congressman, diplomat, and public servant of great talent and merit. Henry Adams himself was educated at Harvard; he traveled and studied abroad, and he enjoyed the company and friendship of America's greatest politicians, artists, and intellectuals. He was a novelist, a professor at Harvard, a historian of great stature and significance. He was rich, worldly, cultivated. And he was also a self-professed "failure."

In the 1890s, while traveling in the north of France, he became fascinated by the cathedrals of Normandy. He saw them as symbols of unity in a chaotic, meaningless world, and he wrote of them in one of his most important books, Mont-Saint-Michel and Chartres *(1904). Adams had lived in a world of ceaseless change. He believed it was a distempered world that honored not thought but energy, not service to humankind but material success. And as the twentieth century unfolded, he grew more and more pessimistic about American civilization and his own achievements. Yet his sense of the decline of culture and his sense of personal failure inspired his greatest work,* The Education of Henry Adams *(1907, 1918).*

The Education *was a memoir in which Adams, describing himself in the third person, recorded his efforts to extract reason and purpose from the discordant experience of America. His "education" was his eventual discovery that all humankind's science and knowledge had not resolved the basic mysteries of life or revealed whether the universe is controlled by divine unity or by the movement of chaotic force. This dichotomy eventually resolved in* The Education of Henry Adams *into the pairing of "The Virgin," representing the force of religion, especially organized religion, and "The Dynamo," the power of human energy and resourcefulness culminating in the technological achievements of the nineteenth century and leading into the technologically charged present of the early twentieth. His meditation on these oppositional forces, Chapter XXV of* The Education of Henry Adams, *is presented here.*

TEXT: *The Education of Henry Adams,* 1918.

from *THE EDUCATION OF HENRY ADAMS*

CHAPTER XXV

THE DYNAMO AND THE VIRGIN[1] (1900)

Until the Great Exposition of 1900[2] closed its doors in November, Adams haunted it, aching to absorb knowledge, and helpless to find it. He would have liked to know how much of it could have been grasped by the best-informed man in

[1]Michael Faraday (1791–1867) developed the first dynamo (electrical generator) in 1831. Here Adams compares the dynamo, the symbol of modern technology, to the Virgin Mary, the symbol of medieval Christianity.

[2]The Paris Exposition of April–November 1900.

the world. While he was thus meditating chaos, Langley[3] came by, and showed it to him. At Langley's behest, the Exhibition dropped its superfluous rags and stripped itself to the skin, for Langley knew what to study, and why, and how; while Adams might as well have stood outside in the night, staring at the Milky Way. Yet Langley said nothing new, and taught nothing that one might not have learned from Lord Bacon,[4] three hundred years before; but though one should have known the "Advancement of Science" as well as one knew the "Comedy of Errors,"[5] the literary knowledge counted for nothing until some teacher should show how to apply it. Bacon took a vast deal of trouble in teaching King James I[6] and his subjects, American or other, towards the year 1620, that true science was the development or economy of forces; yet an elderly American in 1900 knew neither the formula nor the forces; or even so much as to say to himself that his historical business in the Exposition concerned only the economies or developments of force since 1893, when he began the study at Chicago.[7]

Nothing in education is so astonishing as the amount of ignorance it accumulates in the form of inert facts. Adams had looked at most of the accumulations of art in the storehouses called Art Museums; yet he did not know how to look at the art exhibits of 1900. He had studied Karl Marx and his doctrines of history[8] with profound attention, yet he could not apply them at Paris. Langley, with the ease of a great master of experiment, threw out of the field every exhibit that did not reveal a new application of force, and naturally threw out, to begin with, almost the whole art exhibit. Equally, he ignored almost the whole industrial exhibit. He led his pupil directly to the forces. His chief interest was in new motors to make his airship feasible, and he taught Adams the astonishing complexities of the new Daimler motor,[9] and of the automobile, which, since 1893, had become a nightmare at a hundred kilometres an hour, almost as destructive as the electric tram which was only ten years older; and threatening to become as terrible as the locomotive steam-engine itself, which was almost exactly Adams's own age.

Then he showed his scholar the great hall of dynamos, and explained how little he knew about electricity or force of any kind, even of his own special sun, which spouted heat in inconceivable volume, but which, as far as he knew, might spout less or more, at any time, for all the certainty he felt in it. To him, the dynamo itself was but an ingenious channel for conveying somewhere the heat latent in a few tons of poor coal hidden in a dirty engine-house carefully kept out of sight; but to Adams the dynamo became a symbol of infinity. As he grew accustomed to the great gallery of machines, he began to feel the forty-foot dynamos as a moral force, much as the early Christians felt the Cross. The planet itself seemed less impressive, in its old-fashioned, deliberate, annual or daily revolution, than this huge wheel, revolving within arm's-length at some vertiginous speed, and barely murmuring—scarcely humming an audible warning to stand a hair's-breadth further for respect of power—while it would not wake the baby lying close against its frame. Before the end, one began to pray to it;

[3]Samuel Langley (1834–1906), American scientist.
[4]Francis Bacon (1561–1626), English philosopher and scientist, author of *The Advancement of Learning* (1605).
[5]Shakespeare's play, 1594. [6]King of England (1603–1625).
[7]Adams saw similar technological exhibits at the Columbian Exposition in Chicago in 1893.
[8]Karl Marx (1818–1883) set forth his theories of history in *Das Kapital* (1867).
[9]Gottlieb Daimler (1834–1900), German developer of the internal-combustion engine.

inherited instinct taught the natural expression of man before silent and infinite force. Among the thousand symbols of ultimate energy, the dynamo was not so human as some, but it was the most expressive.

Yet the dynamo, next to the steam-engine, was the most familiar of exhibits. For Adams's objects its value lay chiefly in its occult mechanism. Between the dynamo in the gallery of machines and the engine-house outside, the break of continuity amounted to abysmal fracture for a historian's objects. No more relation could he discover between the steam and the electric current than between the Cross and the cathedral. The forces were interchangeable if not reversible, but he could see only an absolute *fiat* in electricity as in faith. Langley could not help him. Indeed, Langley seemed to be worried by the same trouble, for he constantly repeated that the new forces were anarchical, and specially that he was not responsible for the new rays, that were little short of parricidal in their wicked spirit towards science. His own rays, with which he had doubled the solar spectrum, were altogether harmless and beneficent; but Radium denied its God—or, what was to Langley the same thing, denied the truths of his Science. The force was wholly new.[10]

A historian who asked only to learn enough to be as futile as Langley or Kelvin,[11] made rapid progress under this teaching, and mixed himself up in the tangle of ideas until he achieved a sort of Paradise of ignorance vastly consoling to his fatigued senses. He wrapped himself in vibrations and rays which were new, and he would have hugged Marconi and Branly[12] had he met them, as he hugged the dynamo; while he lost his arithmetic in trying to figure out the equation between the discoveries and the economies of force. The economies, like the discoveries, were absolute, supersensual, occult; incapable of expression in horse-power. What mathematical equivalent could he suggest as the value of a Branly coherer? Frozen air, or the electric furnace, had some scale or measurement, no doubt, if somebody could invent a thermometer adequate to the purpose; but X-rays[13] had played no part whatever in man's consciousness, and the atom itself had figured only as a fiction of thought. In these seven years man had translated himself into a new universe which had no common scale of measurement with the old. He had entered a supersensual world, in which he could measure nothing except by chance collisions of movements imperceptible to his senses, perhaps even imperceptible to his instruments, but perceptible to each other, and so to some known ray at the end of the scale. Langley seemed prepared for anything, even for an indeterminable number of universes interfused—physics stark mad in metaphysics.

Historians undertake to arrange sequences,—called stories, or histories—assuming in silence a relation of cause and effect. These assumptions, hidden in the depths of dusty libraries, have been astounding, but commonly unconscious and childlike; so much so, that if any captious critic were to drag them

[10]In 1881, Langley had measured the sun's radiation and demonstrated that the solar spectrum is far greater than had previously been thought. The subsequent discovery of radium revealed a different kind of radiation, caused by the disintegration of the atom, the further study of which led to revolutionary discoveries in atomic and nuclear physics.

[11]William Thomson, Baron Kelvin (1824–1907), British scientist.

[12]Guglielmo Marconi (1874–1937), Italian inventor of the radio telegraph. Edouard Branly (1846–1940), French inventor of a coherer (detector) of radio waves.

[13]Discovered in 1895 by William Roentgen (1845–1923).

to light, historians would probably reply, with one voice, that they had never supposed themselves required to know what they were talking about. Adams, for one, had toiled in vain to find out what he meant. He had even published a dozen volumes of American history for no other purpose than to satisfy himself whether, by the severest process of stating, with the least possible comment, such facts as seemed sure, in such order as seemed rigorously consequent, he could fix for a familiar moment a necessary sequence of human movement. The result had satisfied him as little as at Harvard College. Where he saw sequence, other men saw something quite different, and no one saw the same unit of measure. He cared little about his experiments and less about his statesmen, who seemed to him quite as ignorant as himself and, as a rule, no more honest; but he insisted on a relation of sequence, and if he could not reach it by one method, he would try as many methods as science knew. Satisfied that the sequence of men led to nothing and that the sequence of their society could lead no further, while the mere sequence of time was artificial, and the sequence of thought was chaos, he turned at last to the sequence of force; and thus it happened that, after ten years' pursuit, he found himself lying in the Gallery of Machines at the Great Exposition of 1900, his historical neck broken by the sudden irruption of forces totally new.

Since no one else showed much concern, an elderly person without other cares had no need to betray alarm. The year 1900 was not the first to upset schoolmasters. Copernicus and Galileo[14] had broken many professorial necks about 1600; Columbus had stood the world on its head towards 1500; but the nearest approach to the revolution of 1900 was that of 310, when Constantine set up the Cross.[15] The rays that Langley disowned, as well as those which he fathered, were occult, supersensual, irrational; they were a revelation of mysterious energy like that of the Cross; they were what, in terms of mediæval science, were called immediate modes of the divine substance.

The historian was thus reduced to his last resources. Clearly if he was bound to reduce all these forces to a common value, this common value could have no measure but that of their attraction on his own mind. He must treat them as they had been felt; as convertible, reversible, interchangeable attractions on thought. He made up his mind to venture it; he would risk translating rays into faith. Such a reversible process would vastly amuse a chemist, but the chemist could not deny that he, or some of his fellow physicists, could feel the force of both. When Adams was a boy in Boston, the best chemist[16] in the place had probably never heard of Venus except by way of scandal,[17] or of the Virgin except as idolatry;[18] neither had he heard of dynamos or automobiles or radium; yet his mind was ready to feel the force of all, though the rays were unborn and the women were dead.

Here opened another totally new education, which promised to be by far the most hazardous of all. The knife-edge along which he must crawl, like Sir

[14]Copernicus (1473–1543) asserted and Galileo (1564–1642) affirmed that the earth moves around the sun.

[15]The Emperor Constantine I (288?–337) legalized Christianity in the Roman Empire in 313.

[16]A pharmacist, druggist.

[17]I.e., druggists knew of Venus (Roman goddess of love) only because they dispensed medicines for the disease of Venus—venereal disease.

[18]Protestants reject the worship of the Virgin Mary as a form of idolatry or false worship.

Lancelot in the twelfth century,[19] divided two kingdoms of force which had nothing in common but attraction. They were as different as a magnet is from gravitation, supposing one knew what a magnet was, or gravitation, or love. The force of the Virgin was still felt at Lourdes,[20] and seemed to be as potent as X-rays; but in America neither Venus nor Virgin ever had value as force—at most as sentiment. No American had ever been truly afraid of either.

This problem in dynamics gravely perplexed an American historian. The Woman had once been supreme; in France she still seemed potent, not merely as a sentiment, but as a force. Why was she unknown in America? For evidently America was ashamed of her, and she was ashamed of herself, otherwise they would not have strewn fig-leaves[21] so profusely all over her. When she was a true force, she was ignorant of fig-leaves, but the monthly-magazine-made American female had not a feature that would have been recognized by Adam. The trait was notorious, and often humorous, but any one brought up among Puritans knew that sex was sin. In any previous age, sex was strength. Neither art nor beauty was needed. Every one, even among Puritans, knew that neither Diana of the Ephesians[22] nor any of the Oriental goddesses was worshipped for her beauty. She was goddess because of her force; she was the animated dynamo; she was reproduction—the greatest and most mysterious of all energies; all she needed was to be fecund. Singularly enough, not one of Adams's many schools of education had ever drawn his attention to the opening lines of Lucretius, though they were perhaps the finest in all Latin literature, where the poet invoked Venus exactly as Dante invoked the Virgin:—

> "Quae quoniam rerum naturam *sola* gubernas."[23]

The Venus of Epicurean philosophy survived in the Virgin of the Schools:[24]—

> "Donna, sei tanto grande, e tanto vali,
> Che qual vuol grazia, e a te non ricorre,
> Sua disianza vuol volar senz' ali."[25]

All this was to American thought as though it had never existed. The true American knew something of the facts, but nothing of the feelings; he read the letter, but he never felt the law. Before this historical chasm, a mind like that of Adams felt itself helpless; he turned from the Virgin to the Dynamo as though he were a Branly coherer. On one side, at the Louvre and at Chartres, as he knew by the record of work actually done and still before his eyes, was the highest energy ever known to man, the creator of four-fifths of his noblest art, exercising vastly more attraction over the human mind than

[19] A reference to a test of valor undergone by Sir Lancelot in a medieval chivalric story.

[20] French shrine dedicated to the Virgin Mary.

[21] Used to cover the sexual organs of human figures in paintings and statues.

[22] Fertility goddess of the ancient Near East.

[23] Latin: "Since thou alone dost govern the nature of things." From *De Rerum Natura (On the Nature of Things)*, I, 21, by the Roman poet Lucretius (99?–55? B.C.).

[24] I.e., the Virgin as described by scholastic philosophers of the Middle Ages.

[25] Italian: "Lady [Virgin Mary], thou art so great and so much worth,/That he who wishes grace and seeks not thee,/Would have his wish fly upward without wings." Dante, *Paradiso*, Canto XXXIII, lines 13–15.

all the steam-engines and dynamos ever dreamed of; and yet this energy was unknown to the American mind. An American Virgin would never dare command; an American Venus would never dare exist.

The question, which to any plain American of the nineteenth century seemed as remote as it did to Adams, drew him almost violently to study, once it was posed; and on this point Langleys were as useless as though they were Herbert Spencers[26] or dynamos. The idea survived only as art. There one turned as naturally as though the artist were himself a woman. Adams began to ponder, asking himself whether he knew of any American artist who had ever insisted on the power of sex, as every classic had always done; but he could think only of Walt Whitman; Bret Harte, as far as the magazines would let him venture; and one or two painters, for the flesh-tones. All the rest had used sex for sentiment, never for force; to them, Eve was a tender flower, and Herodias[27] an unfeminine horror. American art, like the American language and American education, was as far as possible sexless. Society regarded this victory over sex as its greatest triumph, and the historian readily admitted it, since the moral issue, for the moment, did not concern one who was studying the relations of unmoral force. He cared nothing for the sex of the dynamo until he could measure its energy.

Vaguely seeking a clue, he wandered through the art exhibit, and, in his stroll, stopped almost every day before St. Gaudens's General Sherman,[28] which had been given the central post of honor. St. Gaudens himself was in Paris, putting on the work his usual interminable last touches, and listening to the usual contradictory suggestions of brother sculptors. Of all the American artists who gave to American art whatever life it breathed in the seventies, St. Gaudens was perhaps the most sympathetic, but certainly the most inarticulate. General Grant or Don Cameron[29] had scarcely less instinct of rhetoric than he. All the others—the Hunts, Richardson, John La Farge, Stanford White[30]—were exuberant; only St. Gaudens could never discuss or dilate on an emotion, or suggest artistic arguments for giving to his work the forms that he felt. He never laid down the law, or affected the despot, or became brutalized like Whistler[31] by the brutalities of his world. He required no incense; he was no egoist; his simplicity of thought was excessive; he could not imitate, or give any form but his own to the creations of his hand. No one felt more strongly than he the strength of other men, but the idea that they could affect him never stirred an image in his mind.

This summer his health was poor and his spirits were low. For such a temper, Adams was not the best companion, since his own gaiety was not *folle*;[32] but he risked going now and then to the studio on Mont Parnasse[33] to draw him out

[26]English philosopher and social Darwinist (1820–1903).

[27]Wife of King Herod. She caused the death of John the Baptist (Mark 6:17–28).

[28]Statue of American Civil War General William T. Sherman by Augustus Saint-Gaudens (1848–1907), Irish American sculptor. Then on display in Paris, the statue is now in Central Park in New York City.

[29]James Donald Cameron (1833–1918), senator from Pennsylvania, secretary of war under President Ulysses S. Grant, and a friend of Adams. Both Grant and Cameron were known to be spare with words.

[30]William Morris Hunt (1824–1879), painter; Richard Morris Hunt (1828–1895), architect; Henry Richardson (1838–1886), architect; John La Farge (1835–1910), artist; Stanford White (1853–1906), architect.

[31]James McNeill Whistler (1834–1903), acid-tongued American painter.

[32]French: extravagant, excessive. [33]Artists' quarter in Paris.

for a stroll in the Bois de Boulogne,[34] or dinner as pleased his moods, and in return St. Gaudens sometimes let Adams go about in his company.

Once St. Gaudens took him down to Amiens,[35] with a party of Frenchmen, to see the cathedral. Not until they found themselves actually studying the sculpture of the western portal, did it dawn on Adams's mind that, for his purposes, St. Gaudens on that spot had more interest to him than the cathedral itself. Great men before great monuments express great truths, provided they are not taken too solemnly. Adams never tired of quoting the supreme phrase of his idol Gibbon,[36] before the Gothic cathedrals: "I darted a contemptuous look on the stately monuments of superstition." Even in the footnotes of his history, Gibbon had never inserted a bit of humor more human than this, and one would have paid largely for a photograph of the fat little historian, on the background of Notre Dame of Amiens, trying to persuade his readers—perhaps himself—that he was darting a contemptuous look on the stately monument, for which he felt in fact the respect which every man of his vast study and active mind always feels before objects worthy of it; but besides the humor, one felt also the relation. Gibbon ignored the Virgin, because in 1789 religious monuments were out of fashion. In 1900 his remark sounded fresh and simple as the green fields to ears that had heard a hundred years of other remarks, mostly no more fresh and certainly less simple. Without malice, one might find it more instructive than a whole lecture of Ruskin.[37] One sees what one brings, and at that moment Gibbon brought the French Revolution. Ruskin brought reaction against the Revolution. St. Gaudens had passed beyond all. He liked the stately monuments much more than he liked Gibbon or Ruskin; he loved their dignity; their unity; their scale; their lines; their lights and shadows; their decorative sculpture; but he was even less conscious than they of the force that created it all—the Virgin, the Woman—by whose genius "the stately monuments of superstition" were built, through which she was expressed. He would have seen more meaning in Isis with the cow's horns, at Edfoo,[38] who expressed the same thought. The art remained, but the energy was lost even upon the artist.

Yet in mind and person St. Gaudens was a survival of the 1500s; he bore the stamp of the Renaissance, and should have carried an image of the Virgin round his neck, or stuck in his hat, like Louis XI.[39] In mere time he was a lost soul that had strayed by chance into the twentieth century, and forgotten where it came from. He writhed and cursed at his ignorance, much as Adams did at his own, but in the opposite sense. St. Gaudens was a child of Benvenuto Cellini,[40] smothered in an American cradle. Adams was a quintessence of Boston, devoured by curiosity to think like Benvenuto. St. Gaudens's art was starved

[34]Park in Paris.

[35]City north of Paris. Its Gothic cathedral, dedicated to the Virgin Mary, is the largest in France.

[36]Edward Gibbon (1737–1794), English author of *The Decline and Fall of the Roman Empire* (1776–1788). Here Adams paraphrases an entry from Gibbon's *French Journal* for February 21, 1763.

[37]John Ruskin (1819–1900), English critic of art and architecture.

[38]Egyptian fertility goddess whose statue Adams had seen at Edfu on the Nile River. She was often portrayed with a cow's horns.

[39]King of France (1423–1483). Extremely pious, he traditionally wore religious emblems on his clothing.

[40]Italian goldsmith and sculptor (1500–1571).

from birth, and Adams's instinct was blighted from babyhood. Each had but half of a nature, and when they came together before the Virgin of Amiens they ought both to have felt in her the force that made them one; but it was not so. To Adams she became more than ever a channel of force; to St. Gaudens she remained as before a channel of taste.

For a symbol of power, St. Gaudens instinctively preferred the horse, as was plain in his horse and Victory of the Sherman monument. Doubtless Sherman also felt it so. The attitude was so American that, for at least forty years, Adams had never realized that any other could be in sound taste. How many years had he taken to admit a notion of what Michael Angelo and Rubens[41] were driving at? He could not say; but he knew that only since 1895 had he begun to feel the Virgin or Venus as force, and not everywhere even so. At Chartres—perhaps at Lourdes—possibly at Cnidos[42] if one could still find there the divinely naked Aphrodite of Praxiteles[43]—but otherwise one must look for force to the goddesses of Indian mythology. The idea died out long ago in the German and English stock. St. Gaudens at Amiens was hardly less sensitive to the force of the female energy than Matthew Arnold at the Grande Chartreuse.[44] Neither of them felt goddesses as power—only as reflected emotion, human expression, beauty, purity, taste, scarcely even as sympathy. They felt a railway train as power; yet they, and all other artists, constantly complained that the power embodied in a railway train could never be embodied in art. All the steam in the world could not, like the Virgin, build Chartres.

Yet in mechanics, whatever the mechanicians might think, both energies acted as interchangeable forces on man, and by action on man all known force may be measured. Indeed, few men of science measured force in any other way. After once admitting that a straight line was the shortest distance between two points, no serious mathematician cared to deny anything that suited his convenience, and rejected no symbol, unproved or unproveable, that helped him to accomplish work. The symbol was force, as a compass needle or a triangle was force, as the mechanist might prove by losing it, and nothing could be gained by ignoring their value. Symbol or energy, the Virgin had acted as the greatest force the Western world ever felt, and had drawn man's activities to herself more strongly than any other power, natural or supernatural, had ever done; the historian's business was to follow the track of the energy; to find where it came from and where it went to; its complex source and shifting channels; its values, equivalents, conversions. It could scarcely be more complex than radium; it could hardly be deflected, diverted, polarized, absorbed more perplexingly than other radiant matter. Adams knew nothing about any of them, but as a mathematical problem of influence on human progress, though all were occult, all reacted on his mind, and he rather inclined to think the Virgin easiest to handle.

The pursuit turned out to be long and tortuous, leading at last into the vast forest of scholastic science. From Zeno to Descartes, hand in hand with Thomas

[41]Michelangelo (1475–1564), Italian artist; Peter Paul Rubens (1577–1640), Flemish painter.

[42]Ancient Greek city in Asia Minor (present-day Turkey), site of the "Aphrodite" by Praxiteles, one of the most famous statues of the ancient world.

[43]Greek sculptor (4th century B.C.)

[44]In "Stanzas from the Grande Chartreuse" (1855), the English poet Matthew Arnold (1822–1888) laments the loss of the faith that inspired earlier Christians.

Aquinas, Montaigne, and Pascal,[45] one stumbled as stupidly as though one were still a German student of 1860.[46] Only with the instinct of despair could one force one's self into this old thicket of ignorance after having been repulsed at a score of entrances more promising and more popular. Thus far, no path had led anywhere, unless perhaps to an exceedingly modest living. Forty-five years of study had proved to be quite futile for the pursuit of power; one controlled no more force in 1900 than in 1850, although the amount of force controlled by society had enormously increased. The secret of education still hid itself somewhere behind ignorance, and one fumbled over it as feebly as ever. In such labyrinths, the staff is a force almost more necessary than the legs; the pen becomes a sort of blind-man's dog, to keep him from falling into the gutters. The pen works for itself, and acts like a hand, modelling the plastic material over and over again to the form that suits it best. The form is never arbitrary, but is a sort of growth like crystallization, as any artist knows too well; for often the pencil or pen runs into side-paths and shapelessness, loses its relations, stops or is bogged. Then it has to return on its trail, and recover, if it can, its line of force. The result of a year's work depends more on what is struck out than on what is left in; on the sequence of the main lines of thought, than on their play or variety. Compelled once more to lean heavily on this support, Adams covered more thousands of pages with figures as formal as though they were algebra, laboriously striking out, altering, burning, experimenting, until the year had expired, the Exposition had long been closed, and winter drawing to its end, before he sailed from Cherbourg, on January 19, 1901, for home.

1907 1918

Reading the Critical Context

The "modernism" practiced by the new breed of poets, fiction writers, and dramatists who increasingly dominated the American literary landscape in the early to middle twentieth century emphasized literature as a variety of art, comparable in all important respects to music, painting, sculpture, and architecture—all of which were enjoying thriving modernist phases of their own. Writing was seen not as self-expression or storytelling, but as the crafting of an object for aesthetic contemplation. T. S. Eliot wrote that "The emotion of art is impersonal"; Archibald MacLeish, in his poem "Ars Poetica," declared paradoxically that "A poem should be palpable and mute / As a globed fruit." Literature was symbolization, not conversation. And the value of the artwork was not in its faithful

[45]Zeno of Citium (334?–262? B.C.), Greek philosopher; René Descartes (1596–1650), French philosopher and mathematician; St. Thomas Aquinas (1225?–1274), Roman Catholic philosopher; Michel Eyquem de Montaigne (1533–1592), French essayist; Blaise Pascal (1623–1662), French mathematician and moralist.

[46]After his graduation from Harvard, Henry Adams continued his studies, in Germany (1858–1860).

copying of the original but in its use of the materials of art to render psychological reality or to explore technical possibilities—in the use of color, line, and form in visual art, or language and form in literary art. Fiction writers like William Faulkner and Gertrude Stein experimented with narrative techniques that thwarted conventional chronology and narrative flow, challenging readers and giving them a new experience of fictionality. Poets like Eliot, Ezra Pound, and Wallace Stevens and dramatists like Eugene O'Neill likewise produced works that defied easy comprehension, as they attempted to achieve a literary equivalent to the non-representational abstractness of cubist and post-impressionist paintings. Major American literary figures of the period expressed their conceptions of the nature of their art in terms such as the following:

> Wallace Stevens: *Beauty is momentary in the mind/The fitful tracing of a portal / But in the flesh it is immortal.*
>
> T. S. Eliot: *Poetry is not a turning loose of emotion, but an escape from emotion; it is not the expression of personality, but an escape from personality.*
>
> Gertrude Stein: *I have always noticed that in portraits of really great writers the mouth is always firmly closed.*
>
> Archibald MacLeish: *A poem should not mean/But be.*
>
> William Carlos Williams: *No ideas but in things.*
>
> F. Scott Fitzgerald: *Character* is *action.*
>
> Ernest Hemingway: *All good books have one thing in common—they are truer than if they had really happened.*
>
> William Faulkner: *Facts and truth really don't have much to do with each other.*
>
> John Steinbeck: *We spend all our life trying to be less lonesome. One of our ancient methods is to tell a story begging the listener to say—and to feel—"Yes, that's the way it is, or at least that's the way I feel it. You're not as alone as you thought."*
>
> Robert Frost: *Writing free verse is like playing tennis with the net down.*

T. S. Eliot 1888–1965

Besides being one of the most important American poets of the early twentieth century, T. S. Eliot was one of the era's most notable critical theorists. The following essay by Eliot is a major early statement of modernist literary theory. It is drawn from his highly influential essay collection, The Sacred Wood *(1920).*

TEXT: *The Sacred Wood,* 1920.

TRADITION AND THE INDIVIDUAL TALENT

I

In English writing we seldom speak of tradition, though we occasionally apply its name in deploring its absence. We cannot refer to "the tradition" or to "a tradition"; at most, we employ the adjective in saying that the poetry of So-and-so is "traditional" or even "too traditional." Seldom, perhaps, does the word appear except in a phrase of censure. If otherwise, it is vaguely approbative, with the implication, as to the work approved, of some pleasing archaeological reconstruction. You can hardly make the word agreeable to English ears without this comfortable reference to the reassuring science of archaeology.

Certainly the word is not likely to appear in our appreciations of living or dead writers. Every nation, every race, has not only its own creative, but its own critical turn of mind; and is even more oblivious of the shortcomings and limitations of its critical habits than of those of its creative genius. We know, or think we know, from the enormous mass of critical writing that has appeared in the French language the critical method or habit of the French; we only conclude (we are such unconscious people) that the French are "more critical" than we, and sometimes even plume ourselves a little with the fact, as if the French were the less spontaneous. Perhaps they are; but we might remind ourselves that criticism is as inevitable as breathing, and that we should be none the worse for articulating what passes in our minds when we read a book and feel an emotion about it, for criticizing our own minds in their work of criticism. One of the facts that might come to light in this process is our tendency to insist, when we praise a poet, upon those aspects of his work in which he least resembles any one else. In these aspects or parts of his work we pretend to find what is individual, what is the peculiar essence of the man. We dwell with satisfaction upon the poet's difference from his predecessors, especially his immediate predecessors; we endeavour to find something that can be isolated in order to be enjoyed. Whereas if we approach a poet without this prejudice we shall often find that not only the best, but the most individual parts of his work may be those in which the dead poets, his ancestors, assert their immortality most vigorously. And I do not mean the impressionable period of adolescence, but the period of full maturity.

Yet if the only form of tradition, of handing down, consisted in following the ways of the immediate generation before us in a blind or timid adherence to its successes, "tradition" should positively be discouraged. We have seen many such simple currents soon lost in the sand; and novelty is better than repetition. Tradition is a matter of much wider significance. It cannot be inherited, and if you want it you must obtain it by great labour. It involves, in the first place, the historical sense, which we may call nearly indispensable to any one who would continue to be a poet beyond his twenty-fifth year; and the historical sense involves a perception, not only of the pastness of the past, but of its presence; the historical sense compels a man to write not merely with his own generation in his bones, but with a feeling that the whole of the literature of Europe from Homer and within it the whole of the literature of his own country has a simultaneous existence and composes a simultaneous order. This historical sense, which is a sense of the timeless as well as of the temporal and of the timeless and of the temporal together, is what makes a writer traditional. And it is at the same time what makes a writer most acutely conscious of his place in time, of his own contemporaneity.

No poet, no artist of any art, has his complete meaning alone. His significance, his appreciation is the appreciation of his relation to the dead poets and artists. You cannot value him alone; you must set him, for contrast and comparison, among the dead. I mean this as a principle of aesthetic, not merely historical, criticism. The necessity that he shall conform, that he shall cohere, is not onesided; what happens when a new work of art is created is something that happens simultaneously to all the works of art which preceded it. The existing monuments form an ideal order among themselves, which is modified by the introduction of the new (the really new) work of art among them. The existing order is complete before the new work arrives; for order to persist after the supervention of novelty, the whole *existing* order must be, if ever so slightly, altered; and so the relations, proportions, values of each work of art toward the whole are readjusted; and this is conformity between the old and the new. Whoever has approved this idea of order, of the form of European, of English literature will not find it preposterous that the past should be altered by the present as much as the present is directed by the past. And the poet who is aware of this will be aware of great difficulties and responsibilities.

In a peculiar sense he will be aware also that he must inevitably be judged by the standards of the past. I say judged, not amputated, by them; not judged to be as good as, or worse or better than, the dead; and certainly not judged by the canons of dead critics. It is a judgment, a comparison, in which two things are measured by each other. To conform merely would be for the new work not really to conform at all; it would not be new, and would therefore not be a work of art. And we do not quite say that the new is more valuable because it fits in; but its fitting in is a test of its value—a test, it is true, which can only be slowly and cautiously applied, for we are none of us infallible judges of conformity. We say: it appears to conform, and is perhaps individual, or it appears individual, and may conform; but we are hardly likely to find that it is one and not the other.

To proceed to a more intelligible exposition of the relation of the poet to the past: he can neither take the past as a lump, an indiscriminate bolus,[1] nor can he form himself wholly on one or two private admirations, nor can he form himself wholly upon one preferred period. The first course is inadmissible, the second is an important experience of youth, and the third is a pleasant and highly desirable supplement. The poet must be very conscious of the main current, which does not at all flow invariably through the most distinguished reputations. He must be quite aware of the obvious fact that art never improves, but that the material of art is never quite the same. He must be aware that the mind of Europe—the mind of his own country—a mind which he learns in time to be much more important than his own private mind—is a mind which changes, and that this change is a development which abandons nothing *en route,* which does not superannuate either Shakespeare, or Homer, or the rock drawing of the Magdalenian[2]—draughtsmen. That this development, refinement perhaps, complication certainly, is not, from the point of view of the artist, any improvement. Perhaps not even an improvement from the point of view of the psychologist or not to the extent which we imagine; perhaps only in the end based upon a complication in economics and machinery. But the difference between the present and the past is that the conscious present is an awareness of the past in a way and to an extent which the past's awareness of itself cannot show.

Some one said: "The dead writers are remote from us because we *know* so much more than they did." Precisely, and they are that which we know.

[1]A large pill. [2]Paleolithic.

I am alive to a usual objection to what is clearly part of my programme for the *métier*[3] of poetry. The objection is that the doctrine requires a ridiculous amount of erudition (pedantry), a claim which can be rejected by appeal to the lives of poets in any pantheon. It will even be affirmed that much learning deadens or perverts poetic sensibility. While, however, we persist in believing that a poet ought to know as much as will not encroach upon his necessary receptivity and necessary laziness, it is not desirable to confine knowledge to whatever can be put into a useful shape for examinations, drawing-rooms, or the still more pretentious modes of publicity. Some can absorb knowledge, the more tardy must sweat for it. Shakespeare acquired more essential history from Plutarch[4] than most men could from the whole British Museum. What is to be insisted upon is that the poet must develop or procure the consciousness of the past and that he should continue to develop this consciousness throughout his career.

What happens is a continual surrender of himself as he is at the moment to something which is more valuable. The progress of an artist is a continual self-sacrifice, a continual extinction of personality.

There remains to define this process of depersonalization and its relation to the sense of tradition. It is in this depersonalization that art may be said to approach the condition of science. I, therefore, invite you to consider, as a suggestive analogy, the action which takes place when a bit of finely filiated platinum is introduced into a chamber containing oxygen and sulphur dioxide.

II

Honest criticism and sensitive appreciation are directed not upon the poet but upon the poetry. If we attend to the confused cries of the newspaper critics and the *susurrus*[5] of popular repetition that follows, we shall hear the names of poets in great numbers; if we seek not Blue-book[6] knowledge but the enjoyment of poetry, and ask for a poem, we shall seldom find it. I have tried to point out the importance of the relation of the poem to other poems by other authors, and suggested the conception of poetry as a living whole of all the poetry that has been written. The other aspect of this Impersonal theory of poetry is the relation of the poem to its author. And I hinted, by an analogy, that the mind of the mature poet differs from that of the immature one not precisely in any valuation of "personality," not being necessarily more interesting, or having "more to say," but rather by being a more finely perfected medium in which special, or very varied, feelings are at liberty to enter into new combinations.

The analogy was that of the catalyst. When the two gases previously mentioned are mixed in the presence of a filament of platinum, they form sulphurous acid. This combination takes place only if the platinum is present; nevertheless the newly formed acid contains no trace of platinum, and the

[3]French: craft.

[4]Greek biographer and philosopher. (A.D. 46?–120?). An English translation of his *Parallel Lives* (biographies of notable Greeks and Romans) provided much of the material used by Shakespeare in writing his Roman plays.

[5]Latin: whispering, murmuring.

[6]A book listing persons who are socially important.

platinum itself is apparently unaffected; has remained inert, neutral, and unchanged. The mind of the poet is the shred of platinum. It may partly or exclusively operate upon the experience of the man himself; but, the more perfect the artist, the more completely separate in him will be the man who suffers and the mind which creates; the more perfectly will the mind digest and transmute the passions which are its material.

The experience, you will notice, the elements which enter the presence of the transforming catalyst, are of two kinds: emotions and feelings. The effect of a work of art upon the person who enjoys it is an experience different in kind from any experience not of art. It may be formed out of one emotion, or may be a combination of several; and various feelings, inhering for the writer in particular words or phrases or images, may be added to compose the final result. Or great poetry may be made without the direct use of any emotion whatever: composed out of feelings solely. Canto XV of the *Inferno* (Brunetto Latini)[7] is a working up of the emotion evident in the situation; but the effect, though single as that of any work of art, is obtained by considerable complexity of detail. The last quatrain gives an image, a feeling attaching to an image, which "came," which did not develop simply out of what precedes, but which was probably in suspension in the poet's mind until the proper combination arrived for it to add itself to. The poet's mind is in fact a receptacle for seizing and storing up numberless feelings, phrases, images, which remain there until all the particles which can unite to form a new compound are present together.

If you compare several representative passages of the greatest poetry you see how great is the variety of types of combination, and also how completely any semi-ethical criterion of "sublimity" misses the mark. For it is not the "greatness," the intensity, of the emotions, the components, but the intensity of the artistic process, the pressure, so to speak, under which the fusion takes place, that counts. The episode of Paolo and Francesca[8] employs a definite emotion, but the intensity of the poetry is something quite different from whatever intensity in the supposed experience it may give the impression of. It is no more intense, furthermore, than Canto XXVI, the voyage of Ulysses,[9] which has not the direct dependence upon an emotion. Great variety is possible in the process of transmutation of motion: the murder of Agamemnon,[10] or the agony of Othello,[11] gives an artistic effect apparently closer to a possible original than the scenes from Dante. In the *Agamemnon,* the artistic emotion approximates to the emotion of an actual spectator; in *Othello* to the emotion of the protagonist himself. But the difference between art and the event is always absolute; the combination which is the murder of Agamemnon is probably as complex as that which is the voyage of Ulysses. In either case there has

[7]Italian philosopher (1212–1294) whose works and teachings influenced Dante. In Canto XV of the *Inferno* Dante portrays Latini as tormented in Hell for having scoffed at God. The last quatrain of the canto suggests that Latini is triumphant because of his worldly wisdom and his art even though he must suffer in Hell because of his worldly sins.

[8]Illicit lovers whose torments are described by Dante in the *Inferno,* Canto V.

[9]In Canto XXVI of the *Inferno,* Ulysses, who is portrayed as confined to Hell for giving "false counseling," speaks of his last voyage.

[10]The murder of Agamemnon by his wife, Clytemnestra, and her lover, Aegisthus, is portrayed in *Agamemnon,* by the Greek dramatist Aeschylus (525–456 B.C.).

[11]Othello's agony, after he has murdered his wife for infidelity only to discover that she was innocent, is portrayed in Shakespeare's *Othello* (1607).

been a fusion of elements. The ode of Keats[12] contains a number of feelings which have nothing particular to do with the nightingale, but which the nightingale, partly, perhaps, because of its attractive name, and partly because of its reputation, served to bring together.

The point of view which I am struggling to attack is perhaps related to the metaphysical theory of the substantial unity of the soul: for my meaning is, that the poet has, not a "personality" to express, but a particular medium, which is only a medium and not a personality, in which impressions and experiences combine in peculiar and unexpected ways. Impressions and experiences which are important for the man may take no place in the poetry, and those which become important in the poetry may play quite a negligible part in the man, the personality.

I will quote a passage which is unfamiliar enough to be regarded with fresh attention in the light—or darkness—of these observations:

And now methinks I could e'en chide myself
For doating on her beauty, though her death
Shall be revenged after no common action.
Does the silkworm expend her yellow labours
For thee? For thee does she undo herself?
Are lordships sold to maintain ladyships
For the poor benefit of a bewildering minute?
Why does yon fellow falsify highways,
And put his life between the judge's lips,
To refine such a thing—keeps horse and men
To beat their valours for her?...[13]

In this passage (as is evident if it is taken in its context) there is a combination of positive and negative emotions: an intensely strong attraction toward beauty and an equally intense fascination by the ugliness which is contrasted with it and which destroys it. This balance of contrasted emotion is in the dramatic situation to which the speech is pertinent, but that situation alone is inadequate to it. This is, so to speak, the structural emotion, provided by the drama. But the whole effect, the dominant tone, is due to the fact that a number of floating feelings, having an affinity to this emotion by no means superficially evident, have combined with it to give us a new art emotion.

It is not in his personal emotions, the emotions provoked by particular events in his life, that the poet is in any way remarkable or interesting. His particular emotions may be simple, or crude, or flat. The emotion in his poetry will be a very complex thing, but not with the complexity of the emotions of people who have very complex or unusual emotions in life. One error, in fact, of eccentricity in poetry is to seek for new human emotions to express; and in this search

[12]"Ode to a Nightingale" (1819) by the English poet John Keats (1795–1821).

[13]From *The Revenger's Tragedy* (Act III, Scene v, lines 68–78) by Cyril Tourneur (1575?–1626?), English dramatist.

for novelty in the wrong place it discovers the perverse. The business of the poet is not to find new emotions, but to use the ordinary ones and, in working them up into poetry, to express feelings which are not in actual emotions at all. And emotions which he has never experienced will serve his turn as well as those familiar to him. Consequently, we must believe that "emotion recollected in tranquillity"[14] is an inexact formula. For it is neither emotion, nor recollection, nor, without distortion of meaning, tranquillity. It is a concentration, and a new thing resulting from the concentration, of a very great number of experiences which to the practical and active person would not seem to be experiences at all; it is a concentration which does not happen consciously or of deliberation. These experiences are not "recollected," and they finally unite in an atmosphere which is "tranquil" only in that it is a passive attending upon the event. Of course this is not quite the whole story. There is a great deal, in the writing of poetry, which must be conscious and deliberate. In fact, the bad poet is usually unconscious where he ought to be conscious, and conscious where he ought to be unconscious. Both errors tend to make him "personal." Poetry is not a turning loose of emotion, but an escape from emotion; it is not the expression of personality, but an escape from personality. But, of course, only those who have personality and emotions know what it means to want to escape from these things.

III

ὁ δὲ νοῦς ἴσως θειότερόν τι χαί ἀπθές ἐστιν.[15]

This essay proposes to halt at the frontier of metaphysics or mysticism, and confine itself to such practical conclusions as can be applied by the responsible person interested in poetry. To divert interest from the poet to the poetry is a laudable aim; for it would conduce to a juster estimation of actual poetry, good and bad. There are many people who appreciate the expression of sincere emotion in verse, and there is a smaller number of people who can appreciate technical excellence. But very few know when there is an expression of *significant* emotion, emotion which has its life in the poem and not in the history of the poet. The emotion of art is impersonal. And the poet cannot reach this impersonality without surrendering himself wholly to the work to be done. And he is not likely to know what is to be done unless he lives in what is not merely the present, but the present moment of the past, unless he is conscious, not of what is dead, but of what is already living.

1919, 1920

[14]From the Preface to William Wordsworth's *Lyrical Ballads* (1800). In the Preface Wordsworth asserts that poetry arises out of "emotion recollected in tranquillity."

[15]A quotation from *De Anima* (Book I, Chapter iv, 408 b 29), in which Aristotle asserts that the intellect (as part of the soul) is indestructible: Memory, loving, and hating all die with the body, "while the intellect is doubtless a thing more divine and is unaffected."

Literature of the Twentieth Century

O. Henry (William Sydney Porter)
1862–1910

William Sydney Porter, who wrote under the pseudonym "O. Henry," is generally regarded as the modern master of the popular short story. Born in Greensboro, North Carolina, in 1862, Porter was raised by relatives who provided him with an excellent education. At the age of nineteen poor health forced him to move to Texas. Once there, he took a variety of jobs, including ranch-hand, editor, newspaper columnist, and bank teller. When the First National Bank of Austin accused him of embezzlement, he fled to Honduras to avoid prosecution. He returned to the United States two years later after word reached him that his wife was gravely ill. He was quickly tried and convicted of the crime and served a short prison sentence in Ohio, where he began to write and publish fiction under several pen names.

Porter moved to New York City in 1902 after his parole and began his career as a professional writer. Though he published the novel Cabbages and Kings *in 1904 and a smattering of poems, he devoted his energies almost entirely to writing short fiction. In 1904 and 1905, for example, he wrote and published nearly 115 stories as a contract writer for the New York weekly* Sunday World. *His first collection of tales,* The Four Million *appeared in 1906 and sold very well. Over the next four years he would publish another thirteen volumes of fiction. William Sydney Porter died in 1910 at the age of 47.*

FURTHER READING: *The Complete Works of O. Henry,* 1953; R. O'Connor, *O. Henry: The Legendary Life of William Sydney Porter,* 1970; R. Harris, *O. Henry: A Reference Guide,* 1980; D. Stuart, *O. Henry: A Biography of William Sydney Porter,* 1990; E. Current-Garcia, *O. Henry: A Study of the Short Fiction,* 1993; *O. Henry,* ed. H. Bloom, 1999.

TEXT: *Strictly Business,* 1910.

A MUNICIPAL REPORT

The cities are full of pride,
Challenging each to each—
This from her mountainside,
That from her burthened beach.
—R. KIPLING[1]

[1]Joseph Rudyard Kipling (1865–1936), British poet and author of short fiction.

Fancy a novel about Chicago or Buffalo, let us say, or Nashville, Tennessee! There are just three big cities in the United States that are "story cities"—New York, of course, New Orleans, and, best of the lot, San Francisco.

—FRANK NORRIS[2]

East is East, and West is San Francisco, according to Californians. Californians are a race of people; they are not merely inhabitants of a State. They are the Southerners of the West. Now, Chicagoans are no less loyal to their city; but when you ask them why, they stammer and speak of lake fish and the new Odd Fellows Building. But Californians go into detail.

Of course they have, in the climate, an argument that is good for half an hour while you are thinking of your coal bills and heavy underwear. But as soon as they come to mistake your silence for conviction, madness comes upon them, and they picture the city of the Golden Gate as the Bagdad[3] of the New World. So far, as a matter of opinion, no refutation is necessary. But, dear cousins all (from Adam and Eve descended), it is a rash one who will lay his finger on the map and say: "In this town there can be no romance—what could happen here?" Yes, it is a bold and a rash deed to challenge in one sentence history, romance, and Rand and McNally.[4]

NASHVILLE.—A city, port of delivery, and the capital of the State of Tennessee, is on the Cumberland River and on the N. C. & St. L. and the L. & N. railroads.[5] This city is regarded as the most important educational centre in the South.

I stepped off the train at 8 P.M. Having searched the thesaurus in vain for adjectives, I must, as a substitution, hie me to comparison in the form of a recipe.

Take of London fog 30 parts; malaria 10 parts; gas leaks 20 parts; dewdrops gathered in a brick yard at sunrise, 25 parts; odor of honeysuckle 15 parts. Mix.

The mixture will give you an approximate conception of a Nashville drizzle. It is not so fragrant as a moth-ball nor as thick as pea-soup; but 'tis enough—'twill serve.

I went to a hotel in a tumbril.[6] It required strong self-suppression for me to keep from climbing to the top of it and giving an imitation of Sidney Carton.[7] The vehicle was drawn by beasts of a bygone era and driven by something dark and emancipated.

I was sleepy and tired, so when I got to the hotel I hurriedly paid it the fifty cents it demanded (with approximate lagniappe, I assure you). I knew its habits; and I did not want to hear it prate about its old "marster" or anything that happened "befo' de wah."

The hotel was one of the kind described as "renovated." That means $20,000 worth of new marble pillars, tiling, electric lights and brass cuspidors in the

[2]Benjamin Franklin Norris (1870–1902), American novelist and short story writer.
[3]Baghdad, a Middle Eastern city, the capital of modern Iraq, mentioned here as an exotic location.
[4]A major producer of maps of various sorts.
[5]The Nashville, Chattanooga, and St. Louis Railroad and the Louisville and Nashville Railroad.
[6]An open cart.
[7]Sydney Carton is the hero of *A Tale of Two Cities,* by the British novelist Charles Dickens (1812–1870). In Dickens's novel, set in the French Revolution, prisoners, including Sydney Carton, are transported in tumbrils to the scaffolds where they are to die by guillotine.

lobby, and a new L. & N. time table and a lithograph of Lookout Mountain[8] in each one of the great rooms above. The management was without reproach, the attention full of exquisite Southern courtesy, the service as slow as the progress of a snail and as good-humored as Rip Van Winkle.[9] The food was worth traveling a thousand miles for. There is no other hotel in the world where you can get such chicken livers *en brochette*.[10]

At dinner I asked a Negro waiter if there was anything doing in town. He pondered gravely for a minute, and then replied: "Well, boss, I don't really reckon there's anything at all doin' after sundown."

Sundown had been accomplished; it had been drowned in the drizzle long before. So that spectacle was denied me. But I went forth upon the streets in the drizzle to see what might be there.

> It is built on undulating grounds; and the streets are lighted by electricity at a cost of $32,470 per annum.

As I left the hotel there was a race riot. Down upon me charged a company of freedmen, or Arabs, or Zulus, armed with—no, I saw with relief that they were not rifles, but whips. And I saw dimly a caravan of black, clumsy vehicles; and at the reassuring shouts, "Kyar you anywhere in the town, boss, fuh fifty cents," I reasoned that I was merely a "fare" instead of a victim.

I walked through long streets, all leading uphill. I wondered how those streets ever came down again. Perhaps they didn't until they were "graded." On a few of the "main streets" I saw lights in stores here and there; saw street cars go by conveying worthy burghers hither and yon; saw people pass engaged in the art of conversation, and heard a burst of semi-lively laughter issuing from a soda-water and ice-cream parlor. The streets other than "main" seemed to have enticed upon their borders houses consecrated to peace and domesticity. In many of them lights shone behind discreetly drawn window shades; in a few pianos tinkled orderly and irreproachable music. There was, indeed, little "doing." I wished I had come before sundown. So I returned to my hotel.

> In November, 1864, the Confederate General Hood advanced against Nashville, where he shut up a National force under General Thomas. The latter then sallied forth and defeated the Confederates in a terrible conflict.

All my life I have heard of, admired, and witnessed the fine marksmanship of the South in its peaceful conflicts in the tobacco-chewing regions. But in my hotel a surprise awaited me. There were twelve bright, new, imposing, capacious brass cuspidors in the great lobby, tall enough to be called urns and so wide-mouthed that the crack pitcher of a lady baseball team should have been able to throw a ball into one of them at five paces distant. But, although a terrible battle had raged and was still raging, the enemy had not suffered. Bright, new, imposing, capacious, untouched, they stood. But, shades of Jefferson Brick! the tile floor—the beautiful tile floor! I could not avoid thinking of the battle

[8]A scenic mountain near Chattanooga, Tennessee.

[9]The protagonist of the story "Rip Van Winkle," by American writer Washington Irving (1783–1859).

[10]On a skewer.

of Nashville, and trying to draw, as is my foolish habit, some deductions about hereditary marksmanship.

Here I first saw Major (by misplaced courtesy) Wentworth Caswell. I knew him for a type the moment my eyes suffered from the sight of him. A rat has no geographical habitat. My old friend, A. Tennyson,[11] said, as he so well said almost everything:

> Prophet, curse me the blabbing lip,
> And curse me the British vermin, the rat.

Let us regard the word "British" as interchangeable *ad lib*. A rat is a rat.

This man was hunting about the hotel lobby like a starved dog that had forgotten where he had buried a bone. He had a face of great acreage, red, pulpy, and with a kind of sleepy massiveness like that of Buddha. He possessed one single virtue—he was very smoothly shaven. The mark of the beast is not indelible upon a man until he goes about with a stubble. I think that if he had not used his razor that day I would have repulsed his advances, and the criminal calendar of the world would have been spared the addition of one murder.

I happened to be standing within five feet of a cuspidor when Major Caswell opened fire upon it. I had been observant enough to perceive that the attacking force was using Gatlings instead of squirrel rifles; so I sidestepped so promptly that the major seized the opportunity to apologize to a noncombatant. He had the blabbing lip. In four minutes he had become my friend and had dragged me to the bar.

I desire to interpolate here that I am a Southerner. But I am not one by profession or trade. I eschew the string tie, the slouch hat, the Prince Albert,[12] the number of bales of cotton destroyed by Sherman,[13] and plug chewing. When the orchestra plays Dixie I do not cheer. I slide a little lower on the leather-cornered seat and, well, order another Würzburger and wish that Longstreet[14] had—but what's the use?

Major Caswell banged the bar with his fist, and the first gun at Fort Sumter[15] re-echoed. When he fired the last one at Appomattox I began to hope. But then he began on family trees, and demonstrated that Adam was only a third cousin of a collateral branch of the Caswell family. Genealogy disposed of, he took up, to my distaste, his private family matters. He spoke of his wife, traced her descent back to Eve, and profanely denied any possible rumor that she may have had relations in the land of Nod.

By this time I began to suspect that he was trying to obscure by noise the fact that he had ordered the drinks, on the chance that I would be bewildered into paying for them. But when they were down he crashed a silver dollar loudly upon the bar. Then, of course, another serving was obligatory. And when I had paid for that I took leave of him brusquely; for I wanted no more of him. But before I had obtained my release he had prated loudly of an income that his wife received, and showed a handful of silver money.

[11]British poet Alfred, Lord Tennyson (1809–1892).

[12]A double-breasted coat of the type worn by Albert (1819–1861), the Prince Consort of Britain's Queen Victoria.

[13]Union General William Tecumseh Sherman (1820–1891).

[14]Confederate General James Longstreet (1821–1904).

[15]The fort near Charleston, South Carolina, where the Civil War began.

When I got my key at the desk the clerk said to me courteously: "If that man Caswell has annoyed you, and if you would like to make a complaint, we will have him ejected. He is a nuisance, a loafer, and without any known means of support, although he seems to have some money most the time. But we don't seem to be able to hit upon any means of throwing him out legally."

"Why, no," said I, after some reflection; "I don't see my way clear to making a complaint. But I would like to place myself on record as asserting that I do not care for his company. Your town," I continued, "seems to be a quiet one. What manner of entertainment, adventure, or excitement have you to offer to the stranger within your gates?"

"Well, sir," said the clerk, "there will be a show here next Thursday. It is—I'll look it up and have the announcement sent up to your room with the ice water. Good night."

After I went up to my room I looked out the window. It was only about ten o'clock, but I looked upon a silent town. The drizzle continued, spangled with dim lights, as far apart as currants in a cake sold at the Ladies' Exchange.

"A quiet place," I said to myself, as my first shoe struck the ceiling of the occupant of the room beneath mine. "Nothing of the life here that gives color and variety to the cities in the East and West. Just a good, ordinary, humdrum, business town."

> Nashville occupies a foremost place among the manufacturing centres of the country. It is the fifth boot and shoe market in the United States, the largest candy and cracker manufacturing city in the South, and does an enormous wholesale dry-goods, grocery, and drug business.

I must tell you how I came to be in Nashville, and I assure you the digression brings as much tedium to me as it does to you. I was traveling elsewhere on my own business, but I had a commission from a Northern literary magazine to stop over there and establish a personal connection between the publication and one of its contributors, Azalea Adair.

Adair (there was no clue to the personality except the handwriting) had sent in some essays (lost art!) and poems that had made the editors swear approvingly over their one o'clock luncheon. So they had commissioned me to round up said Adair and corner by contract his or her output at two cents a word before some other publisher offered her ten or twenty.

At nine o'clock the next morning, after my chicken livers *en brochette* (try them if you can find that hotel), I strayed out into the drizzle, which was still on for an unlimited run. At the first corner I came upon Uncle Cæsar. He was a stalwart Negro, older than the pyramids, with gray wool and a face that reminded me of Brutus,[16] and a second afterwards of the late King Cettiwayo. He wore the most remarkable coat that I ever had seen or expect to see. It reached to his ankles and had once been a Confederate gray in colors. But rain and sun and age had so variegated it that Joseph's coat,[17] beside it, would have faded to a pale monochrome. I must linger with that coat, for it has to do with the story—the story that is so long in coming, because you can hardly expect anything to happen in Nashville.

[16]One of the conspirators who assassinated Julius Caesar in 44 B.C.

[17]A fine coat of many colors given to Joseph by his father Jacob in Genesis, Chapter 37.

Once it must have been the military coat of an officer. The cape of it had vanished, but all adown its front it had been frogged and tasseled magnificently. But now the frogs and tassels were gone. In their stead had been patiently stitched (I surmised by some surviving "black mammy") new frogs made of cunningly twisted common hempen twine. This twine was frayed and disheveled. It must have been added to the coat as a substitute for vanished splendors, with tasteless but painstaking devotion, for it followed faithfully the curves of the long-missing frogs. And, to complete the comedy and pathos of the garment, all its buttons were gone save one. The second button from the top alone remained. The coat was fastened by other twine strings tied through the buttonholes and other holes rudely pierced in the opposite side. There was never such a weird garment so fantastically bedecked and of so many mottled hues. The lone button was the size of a half-dollar, made of yellow horn and sewed on with coarse twine.

This Negro stood by a carriage so old that Ham[18] himself might have started a hack line with it after he left the ark with the two animals hitched to it. As I approached he threw open the door, drew out a feather duster, waved it without using it, and said in deep, rumbling tones:

"Step right in, suh; ain't a speck of dust in it—jus' got back from a funeral, suh."

I inferred that on such gala occasions carriages were given an extra cleaning. I looked up and down the street and perceived that there was little choice among the vehicles for hire that lined the curb. I looked in my memorandum book for the address of Azalea Adair.

"I want to go to 861 Jessamine Street," I said, and was about to step into the hack. But for an instant the thick, long, gorilla-like arm of the old Negro barred me. On his massive and saturnine face a look of sudden suspicion and enmity flashed for a moment. Then, with quickly returning conviction, he asked blandishingly: "What are you gwine there for, boss?"

"What is that to you?" I asked, a little sharply.

"Nothin', suh, jus' nothin'. Only it's a lonesome kind of part of town and few folks ever has business out there. Step right in. The seats is clean—jes' got back from a funeral, suh."

A mile and a half it must have been to our journey's end. I could hear nothing but the fearful rattle of the ancient hack over the uneven brick paving; I could smell nothing but the drizzle, now further flavored with coal smoke and something like a mixture of tar and oleander blossoms. All I could see through the streaming windows were two rows of dim houses.

> The city has an area of 10 square miles; 181 miles of streets, of which 137 miles are paved; a system of waterworks that cost $2,000,000, with 77 miles of mains.

Eight-sixty-one Jessamine Street was a decayed mansion. Thirty yards back from the street it stood, outmerged in a splendid grove of trees and untrimmed shrubbery. A row of box bushes overflowed and almost hid the paling fence from sight; the gate was kept closed by a rope noose that encircled the gate

[18]A son of Noah who is cursed by his father and made the servant of his brothers (Genesis, Chapter 7). In the pro-slavery and post-slavery South, he is often identified as the beginning of the "Negro" race.

post and the first paling of the gate. But when you got inside you saw that 861 was a shell, a shadow, a ghost of former grandeur and excellence. But in the story, I have not yet got inside.

When the hack had ceased from rattling and the weary quadrupeds came to a rest I handed my jehu his fifty cents with an additional quarter, feeling a glow of conscious generosity, as I did so. He refused it.

"It's two dollars, suh," he said.

"How's that?" I asked. "I plainly heard you call out at the hotel: 'Fifty cents to any part of the town.'"

"It's two dollars, suh," he repeated obstinately. "It's a long ways from the hotel."

"It is within the city limits and well within them," I argued. "Don't think that you have picked up a greenhorn Yankee. Do you see those hills over there?" I went on, pointing toward the east (I could not see them, myself, for the drizzle); "well, I was born and raised on their other side. You old fool nigger, can't you tell people from other people when you see 'em?"

The grim face of King Cettiwayo softened. "Is you from the South, suh? I reckon it was them shoes of yourn fooled me. They is somethin' sharp in the toes for a Southern gen'l'man to wear."

"Then the charge is fifty cents, I suppose?" said I inexorably.

His former expression, a mingling of cupidity and hostility, returned, remained ten seconds, and vanished.

"Boss," he said, "fifty cents is right; but I *needs* two dollars, suh; I'm *obleeged* to have two dollars. I ain't *demandin'* it now, suh; after I knows whar you's from; I'm jus' sayin' that I *has* to have two dollars to-night, and business is mighty po'."

Peace and confidence settled upon his heavy features. He had been luckier than he had hoped. Instead of having picked up a greenhorn, ignorant of rates, he had come upon an inheritance.

"You confounded old rascal," I said, reaching down into my pocket, "you ought to be turned over to the police."

For the first time I saw him smile. He knew; *he knew;* HE KNEW.

I gave him two one-dollar bills. As I handed them over I noticed that one of them had seen parlous times. Its upper right-hand corner was missing, and it had been torn through in the middle, but joined again. A strip of blue tissue paper, pasted over the split, preserved its negotiability.

Enough of the African bandit for the present: I left him happy, lifted the rope and opened the creaky gate.

The house, as I said, was a shell. A paint brush had not touched it in twenty years. I could not see why a strong wind should not have bowled it over like a house of cards until I looked again at the trees that hugged it close—the trees that saw the battle of Nashville and still drew their protecting branches around it against storm and enemy and cold.

Azalea Adair, fifty years old, white-haired, a descendant of the cavaliers, as thin and frail as the house she lived in, robed in the cheapest and cleanest dress I ever saw, with an air as simple as a queen's, received me.

The reception room seemed a mile square, because there was nothing in it except some rows of books, on unpainted white-pine bookshelves, a cracked marble-top table, a rag rug, a hairless horsehair sofa and two or three chairs. Yes, there was a picture on the wall, a colored crayon drawing of a cluster of pansies. I looked around for the portrait of Andrew Jackson[19] and the pinecone hanging basket but they were not there.

Azalea Adair and I had conversation, a little of which will be repeated to you. She was a product of the old South, gently nurtured in the sheltered life. Her learning was not broad, but was deep and of splendid originality in its somewhat narrow scope. She had been educated at home, and her knowledge of the world was derived from inference and by inspiration. Of such is the precious, small group of essayists made. While she talked to me I kept brushing my fingers, trying, unconsciously, to rid them guiltily of the absent dust from the half-calf backs of Lamb, Chaucer, Hazlitt, Marcus Aurelius, Montaigne and Hood.[20] She was exquisite, she was a valuable discovery. Nearly everybody nowadays knows too much—oh, so much too much—of real life.

I could perceive clearly that Azalea Adair was very poor.

A house and a dress she had, not much else, I fancied. So, divided between my duty to the magazine and my loyalty to the poets and essayists who fought Thomas in the valley of the Cumberland, I listened to her voice, which was like a harpsichord's, and found that I could not speak of contracts. In the presence of the nine Muses and the three Graces one hesitated to lower the topic to two cents. There would have to be another colloquy after I had regained my commercialism. But I spoke of my mission, and three o'clock of the next afternoon was set for the discussion of the business proposition.

"Your town," I said, as I began to make ready to depart (which is the time for smooth generalities), "seems to be a quiet, sedate place. A home town, I should say, where few things out of the ordinary ever happen."

> It carries on an extensive trade in stoves and hollow ware with the West and South, and its flouring mills have a daily capacity of more than 2,000 barrels.

Azalea Adair seemed to reflect.

"I have never thought of it that way," she said, with a kind of sincere intensity that seemed to belong to her. "Isn't it in the still, quiet places that things do happen? I fancy that when God began to create the earth on the first Monday morning one could have leaned out one's window and heard the drops of mud splashing from His trowel as He built up the everlasting hills. What did the noisiest project in the world—I mean the building of the tower of Babel—result in finally? A page and a half of Esperanto[21] in the *North American Review*."[22]

"Of course," said I platitudinously, "human nature is the same everywhere; but there is more color—er—more drama and movement and—er—romance in some cities than in others."

"On the surface," said Azalea Adair. "I have traveled many times around the world in a golden airship wafted on two wings—print and dreams. I have seen (on one of my imaginary tours) the Sultan of Turkey bowstring with his own hands one of his wives who had uncovered her face in public. I have seen a

[19]Andrew Jackson (1767–1845), seventh president of the United States, made his home in Nashville.

[20]A genteel assortment of literary and philosophical writers.

[21]An artificial language created out of other languages in an attempt to craft a universal medium for communication.

[22]A prestigious literary magazine.

man in Nashville tear up his theatre tickets because his wife was going out with her face covered—with rice powder. In San Francisco's Chinatown I saw the slave girl Sing Yee dipped slowly, inch by inch, in boiling almond oil to make her swear she would never see her American lover again. She gave in when the boiling oil had reached three inches above her knee. At a euchre party in East Nashville the other night I saw Kitty Morgan cut dead by seven of her schoolmates and lifelong friends because she had married a house painter. The boiling oil was sizzling as high as her heart; but I wish you could have seen the fine little smile that she carried from table to table. Oh, yes, it is a humdrum town. Just a few miles of red brick houses and mud and stores and lumber yards."

Some one knocked hollowly at the back of the house. Azalea Adair breathed a soft apology and went to investigate the sound. She came back in three minutes with brightened eyes, a faint flush on her cheeks, and ten years lifted from her shoulders.

"You must have a cup of tea before you go," she said, "and a sugar cake."

She reached and shook a little iron bell. In shuffled a small Negro girl about twelve, barefoot, not very tidy, glowering at me with thumb in mouth and bulging eyes.

Azalea Adair opened a tiny, worn purse and drew out a dollar bill, a dollar bill with the upper right-hand corner missing, torn in two pieces and pasted together again with a strip of blue tissue paper. It was one of the bills I had given the piratical Negro—there was no doubt of it.

"Go up to Mr. Baker's store on the corner, Impy," she said, handing the girl the dollar bill, "and get a quarter of a pound of tea—the kind he always sends me—and ten cents worth of sugar cakes. Now, hurry. The supply of tea in the house happens to be exhausted," she explained to me.

Impy left by the back way. Before the scrape of her hard, bare feet had died away on the back porch, a wild shriek—I was sure it was hers—filled the hollow house. Then the deep, gruff tones of an angry man's voice mingled with the girl's further squeals and unintelligible words.

Azalea Adair rose without surprise or emotion and disappeared. For two minutes I heard the hoarse rumble of the man's voice; then something like an oath and a slight scuffle, and she returned calmly to her chair.

"This is a roomy house," she said, "and I have a tenant for part of it. I am sorry to have to rescind my invitation to tea. It was impossible to get the kind I always use at the store. Perhaps to-morrow Mr. Baker will be able to supply me."

I was sure that Impy had not had time to leave the house. I inquired concerning street-car lines and took my leave. After I was well on my way I remembered that I had not learned Azalea Adair's name. But to-morrow would do.

That same day I started in on the course of iniquity that this uneventful city forced upon me. I was in the town only two days, but in that time I managed to lie shamelessly by telegraph, and to be an accomplice—after the fact, if that is the correct legal term—to a murder.

As I rounded the corner nearest my hotel the Afrite coachman of the polychromatic, nonpareil[23] coat seized me, swung open the dungeony door of his peripatetic sarcophagus, flirted his feather duster and began his ritual: "Step right in, boss. Carriage is clean—jus' got back from a funeral. Fifty cents to any——"

[23]Polychromatic: many-colored; nonpareil: matchless.

And then he knew me and grinned broadly. "'Scuse me, boss; you is de gen'l' man what rid out with me dis mawnin'. Thank you kindly, suh."

"I am going out to 861 again to-morrow afternoon at three," said I, "and if you will be here, I'll let you drive me. So you know Miss Adair?" I concluded, thinking of my dollar bill.

"I belonged to her father, Judge Adair, suh," he replied.

"I judge that she is pretty poor," I said. "She hasn't much money to speak of, has she?"

For an instant I looked again at the fierce countenance of King Cettiwayo, and then he changed back to an extortionate old Negro hack driver.

"She ain't gwine to starve, suh," he said slowly. "She has reso'ces, suh; she has reso'ces."

"I shall pay you fifty cents for the trip," said I.

"Dat is puffeckly correct, suh," he answered humbly. "I jus' *had* to have dat two dollars dis mawnin', boss."

I went to the hotel and lied by electricity. I wired the magazine: "A. Adair holds out for eight cents a word."

The answer that came back was: "Give it to her quick, you duffer."

Just before dinner "Major" Wentworth Caswell bore down upon me with the greetings of a long-lost friend. I have seen few men whom I have so instantaneously hated, and of whom it was so difficult to be rid. I was standing at the bar when he invaded me; therefore I could not wave the white ribbon in his face. I would have paid gladly for the drinks, hoping, thereby, to escape another; but he was one of those despicable, roaring, advertising bibbers who must have brass bands and fireworks attend upon every cent that they waste in their follies.

With an air of producing millions he drew two one-dollar bills from a pocket and dashed one of them upon the bar. I looked once more at the dollar bill with the upper right-hand corner missing, torn through the middle, and patched with a strip of blue tissue paper. It was my dollar bill again. It could have been no other.

I went up to my room. The drizzle and the monotony of a dreary, eventless Southern town had made me tired and listless. I remember that just before I went to bed I mentally disposed of the mysterious dollar bill (which might have formed the clew to a tremendously fine detective story of San Francisco) by saying to myself sleepily: "Seems as if a lot of people here own stock in the Hack-Driver's Trust. Pays dividends promptly, too. Wonder if—" Then I fell asleep.

King Cettiwayo was at his post the next day, and rattled my bones over the stones out to 861. He was to wait and rattle me back again when I was ready.

Azalea Adair looked paler and cleaner and frailer than she had looked on the day before. After she had signed the contract at eight cents per word she grew still paler and began to slip out of her chair. Without much trouble I managed to get her up on the antediluvian[24] horsehair sofa and then I ran out to the sidewalk and yelled to the coffee-colored Pirate to bring a doctor. With a wisdom that I had not suspected in him, he abandoned his team and struck off up the street afoot, realizing the value of speed. In ten minutes he returned with a grave, gray-haired and capable man of medicine. In a few words (worth much less than eight cents each) I explained to him my presence in the hollow house of mystery. He bowed with stately understanding, and turned to the old Negro.

[24]"Before the flood"—i.e., Noah's flood.

"Uncle Cæsar," he said calmly, "run up to my house and ask Miss Lucy to give you a cream pitcher full of fresh milk and half a tumbler of port wine. And hurry back. Don't drive—run. I want you to get back sometime this week."

It occurred to me that Dr. Merriman also felt a distrust as to the speeding powers of the land-pirate's steeds. After Uncle Cæsar was gone, lumberingly, but swiftly, up the street, the doctor looked me over with great politeness and as much careful calculation until he had decided that I might do.

"It is only a case of insufficient nutrition," he said. "In other words, the result of poverty, pride, and starvation. Mrs. Caswell has many devoted friends who would be glad to aid her, but she will accept nothing except from that old Negro, Uncle Cæsar, who was once owned by her family."

"Mrs. Caswell!" said I, in surprise. And then I looked at the contract and saw that she had signed it "Azalea Adair Caswell."

"I thought she was Miss Adair," I said.

"Married to a drunken, worthless loafer, sir," said the doctor. "It is said that he robs her even of the small sums that her old servant contributes toward her support."

When the milk and wine had been brought the doctor soon revived Azalea Adair. She sat up and talked of the beauty of the autumn leaves that were then in season, and their height of color. She referred lightly to her fainting seizure as the outcome of an old palpitation of the heart. Impy fanned her as she lay on the sofa. The doctor was due elsewhere, and I followed him to the door. I told him that it was within my power and intentions to make a reasonable advance of money to Azalea Adair on future contributions to the magazine, and he seemed pleased.

"By the way," he said, "perhaps you would like to know that you have had royalty for a coachman. Old Cæsar's grandfather was a king in Congo. Cæsar himself has royal ways, as you may have observed."

As the doctor was moving off I heard Uncle Cæsar's voice inside: "Did he git bofe of dem two dollars from you, Mis' Zalea?"

"Yes, Cæsar," I heard Azalea Adair answer weakly. And then I went in and concluded business negotiations with our contributor. I assumed the responsibility of advancing fifty dollars, putting it as a necessary formality in binding our bargain. And then Uncle Cæsar drove me back to the hotel.

Here ends all of the story as far as I can testify as a witness. The rest must be only bare statements of facts.

At about six o'clock I went out for a stroll. Uncle Cæsar was at his corner. He threw open the door of his carriage, flourished his duster and began his depressing formula: "Step right in, suh. Fifty cents to anywhere in the city—hack's puffickly clean, suh—jus' got back from a funeral——"

And then he recognized me. I think his eyesight was getting bad. His coat had taken on a few more faded shades of color, the twine strings were more frayed and ragged, the last remaining button—the button of yellow horn—was gone. A motley descendant of kings was Uncle Cæsar!

About two hours later I saw an excited crowd besieging the front of a drug store. In a desert where nothing happens this was manna; so I edged my way inside. On an extemporized couch of empty boxes and chairs was stretched the mortal corporeality of Major Wentworth Caswell. A doctor was testing him for the immortal ingredient. His decision was that it was conspicuous by its absence.

The erstwhile Major had been found dead on a dark street and brought by curious and ennuied citizens to the drug store. The late human being had been engaged in terrific battle—the details showed that. Loafer and reprobate though he had been, he had been also a warrior. But he had lost. His hands were yet clinched so tightly that his fingers would not be opened. The gentle citizens who had known him stood about and searched their vocabularies to find some good words, if it were possible, to speak of him. One kind-looking man said, after much thought: "When 'Cas' was about fo'teen he was one of the best spellers in school."

While I stood there the fingers of the right hand of "the man that was," which hung down the side of a white pine box, relaxed, and dropped something at my feet. I covered it with one foot quietly, and a little later on I picked it up and pocketed it. I reasoned that in his last struggle his hand must have seized that object unwittingly and held it in a death grip.

At the hotel that night the main topic of conversation, with the possible exceptions of politics and prohibition, was the demise of Major Caswell. I heard one man say to a group of listeners:

"In my opinion, gentlemen, Caswell was murdered by some of these no-account niggers for his money. He had fifty dollars this afternoon which he showed to several gentlemen in the hotel. When he was found the money was not on his person."

I left the city the next morning at nine, and as the train was crossing the bridge over the Cumberland River I took out of my pocket a yellow horn overcoat button the size of a fifty-cent piece, with frayed ends of coarse twine hanging from it, and cast it out of the window into the slow, muddy waters below.

I wonder what's doing in Buffalo!

1910

Owen Wister 1860–1938

Though Owen Wister was a prolific writer of fiction and social commentary, his claim to literary distinction rests almost entirely on the publication of a single book, his 1902 bestseller The Virginian: A Horseman of the Plains, *universally regarded as the first American Western novel. Wister was born into an affluent Philadelphia family in 1860, his mother a writer and daughter of a celebrated American actress, his father a prosperous physician. As a boy he traveled abroad extensively and attended schools in Switzerland and England. After graduating from Harvard University in 1882, he studied music in France briefly. In 1885 he returned to Harvard and three years later graduated from its law school. Soon after Wister took a position in a prestigious Philadelphia firm and embarked on a career in the law.*

During the 1880s Wister, because of poor health, began spending long periods of time in the Western territories of the United States. In 1892, after receiving encouragement from former classmate and friend Theodore Roosevelt, he began writing stories based on those experiences and publishing them in Harper's *magazine. Within a few years he left his law practice to devote his energies to writing full-time. Gradually over the next decade he developed something of a national reputation. In 1898 he published his first novel,* Lin Mclean, *which sold modestly. Four year later, however,* The Virginian *made him the most celebrated writer in America. It remained the country's best-selling book for nearly two years after it appeared. Despite his success as a writer of Western fiction, Wister never wrote another novel in the genre he pioneered. He would go on to write aristocratic novels such as* Philosophy *4 (1904) and* Lady Baltimore *(1906), numerous children's books, collections of polemical essays, and an acclaimed memoir of Theodore Roosevelt. Owen Wister died in 1938.*

FURTHER READING: *My Dear Wister: The Frederic Remington-Owen Wister Letters,* ed. B. Vorpahl, 1972; G. Fenin and W. Everson, *The Western,* 1973; J. Cobbs, *Owen Wister: Chronicler of the West, Gentleman of the East,* 1984; D. Payne, *Owen Wister,* 1985.

TEXT: *The Virginian,* 1902.

from *THE VIRGINIAN*

CHAPTER 4

DEEP INTO CATTLE LAND

Morning had been for some while astir in Medicine Bow[1] before I left my quilts. The new day and its doings began around me in the store, chiefly at the grocery counter. Dry-goods were not in great request. The early rising cowboys were off again to their work; and those to whom their night's holiday had left any dollars were spending these for tobacco, or cartridges, or canned provisions for the journey to their distant camps. Sardines were called for, and potted chicken, and devilled ham: a sophisticated nourishment, at first sight, for these sons of the sage-brush. But portable ready-made food plays of necessity a great part in the opening of a new country. These picnic pots and cans were the first of her trophies that Civilization dropped upon Wyoming's virgin soil. The cowboy is now gone to worlds invisible; the wind has blown away the white ashes of his camp-fires; but the empty sardine box lies rusting over the face of the Western earth.

So through my eyes half closed I watched the sale of these tins, and grew familiar with the ham's inevitable trade-mark—that label with the devil and his horns and hoofs and tail very pronounced, all colored a sultry prodigious scarlet. And when each horseman had made his purchase, he would trail his spurs over the floor, and presently the sound of his horse's hoofs would be the last of him. Through my dozing attention came various fragments of talk, and sometimes useful bits of knowledge. For instance, I learned the true value of tomatoes in this country. One fellow was buying two cans of them.

"Meadow Creek dry already?" commented the proprietor.

"Been dry ten days," the young cowboy informed him. And it appeared that along the road he was going, water would not be reached much before

[1]A small town in southeastern Wyoming.

sundown, because this Meadow Creek had ceased to run. His tomatoes were for drink. And thus they have refreshed me many times since.

"No beer?" suggested the proprietor.

The boy made a shuddering face. "Don't say its name to me!" he exclaimed. "I couldn't hold my breakfast down." He rang his silver money upon the counter. "I've swore off for three months," he stated. "I'm going to be as pure as the snow!" And away he went jingling out of the door, to ride seventy-five miles. Three more months of hard, unsheltered work, and he would ride into town again, with his adolescent blood crying aloud for its own.

"I'm obliged," said a new voice, rousing me from a new doze. "She's easier this morning, since the medicine." This was the engineer, whose sick wife had brought a hush over Medicine Bow's rioting. "I'll give her them flowers soon as she wakes," he added.

"Flowers?" repeated the proprietor.

"You didn't leave that bunch at our door?"

"Wish I'd thought to do it."

"She likes to see flowers," said the engineer. And he walked out slowly, with his thanks unachieved. He returned at once with the Virginian; for in the band of the Virginian's hat were two or three blossoms.

"It don't need mentioning," the Southerner was saying, embarrassed by any expression of thanks. "If we had knowed last night—"

"You didn't disturb her any," broke in the engineer. "She's easier this morning. I'll tell her about them flowers."

"Why, it don't need mentioning," the Virginian again protested, almost crossly. "The little things looked kind o' fresh, and I just picked them." His eye now fell upon me, where I lay upon the counter. "I reckon breakfast will be getting through," he remarked.

I was soon at the wash trough. It was only half-past six, but many had been before me,—one glance at the roller-towel told me that. I was afraid to ask the landlady for a clean one, and so I found a fresh handkerchief, and accomplished a sparing toilet. In the midst of this the drummers joined me, one by one, and they used the degraded towel without hesitation. In a way they had the best of me; filth was nothing to them.

The latest risers in Medicine Bow, we sat at breakfast together; and they essayed some light familiarities with the landlady. But these experiments were failures. Her eyes did not see, nor did her ears hear them. She brought the coffee and the bacon with a sedateness that propriety itself could scarce have surpassed. Yet impropriety lurked noiselessly all over her. You could not have specified how; it was interblended with her sum total. Silence was her apparent habit and her weapon; but the American drummer found that she could speak to the point when need came for this. During the meal he had praised her golden hair. It was golden indeed, and worth a high compliment; but his kind displeased her. She had let it pass, however, with no more than a cool stare. But on taking his leave, when he came to pay for the meal, he pushed it too far.

"Pity this must be our last," he said; and as it brought no answer, "Ever travel?" he inquired. "Where I go, there's room for a pair of us."

"Then you'd better find another jackass," she replied quietly.

I was glad that I had not asked for a clean towel.

From the commercial travellers I now separated myself, and wandered alone in pleasurable aimlessness. It was seven o'clock. Medicine Bow stood voiceless and unpeopled. The cowboys had melted away. The inhabitants were indoors, pursuing the business or the idleness of the forenoon. Visible motion there was none. No shell upon the dry sands could lie more lifeless than Medicine Bow. Looking in at the store, I saw the proprietor sitting with his pipe extinct. Looking in at the saloon, I saw the dealer dealing dumbly to himself. Up in the sky there was not a cloud nor a bird, and on the earth the lightest straw lay becalmed. Once I saw the Virginian at an open door, where the golden-haired landlady stood talking with him. Sometimes I strolled in the town, and sometimes out on the plain I lay down with my day dreams in the sagebrush. Pale herds of antelope were in the distance, and near by the demure prairie-dogs sat up and scrutinized me. Steve, Trampas, the riot of horsemen, my lost trunk, Uncle Hughey, with his abortive brides—all things merged in my thoughts in a huge, delicious indifference. It was like swimming slowly at random in an ocean that was smooth, and neither too cool nor too warm. And before I knew it, five lazy imperceptible hours had gone thus. There was the Union Pacific train, coming as if from shores forgotten.

Its approach was silent and long drawn out. I easily reached town and the platform before it had finished watering at the tank. It moved up, made a short halt, I saw my trunk come out of it, and then it moved away silently as it had come, smoking and dwindling into distance unknown.

Beside my trunk was one other, tied extravagantly with white ribbon. The fluttering bows caught my attention, and now I suddenly saw a perfectly new sight. The Virginian was further down the platform, doubled up with laughing. It was good to know that with sufficient cause he could laugh like this; a smile had thus far been his limit of external mirth. Rice now flew against my hat, and hissing gusts of rice spouted on the platform. All the men left in Medicine Bow appeared like magic, and more rice choked the atmosphere. Through the general clamor a cracked voice said, "Don't hit her in the eye, boys!" and Uncle Hughey rushed proudly by me with an actual wife on his arm. She could easily have been his granddaughter. They got at once into a vehicle. The trunk was lifted in behind. And amid cheers, rice, shoes, and broad felicitations, the pair drove out of town, Uncle Hughey shrieking to the horses and the bride waving unabashed adieus.

The word had come over the wires from Laramie:[2] "Uncle Hughey has made it this time. Expect him on to-day's number two." And Medicine Bow had expected him.

Many words arose on the departure of the new-married couple.

"Who's she?"

"What's he got for her?"

"Got a gold mine up Bear Creek."

And after comment and prophecy, Medicine Bow returned to its dinner.

This meal was my last here for a long while. The Virginian's responsibility now returned; duty drove the Judge's trustworthy man to take care of me again. He had not once sought my society of his own accord; his distaste for what he supposed me to be (I don't exactly know what this was) remained unshaken. I have thought that matters of dress and speech should not carry with them so much mistrust in our democracy; thieves are presumed innocent until proved guilty, but a starched collar is condemned at once. Perfect civility and obligingness I

[2]Another town, much larger than Medicine Bow, in Wyoming.

certainly did receive from the Virginian, only not a word of fellowship. He harnessed the horses, got my trunk, and gave me some advice about taking provisions for our journey, something more palatable than what food we should find along the road. It was well thought of, and I bought quite a parcel of dainties, feeling that he would despise both them and me. And thus I took my seat beside him, wondering what we should manage to talk about for two hundred and sixty-three miles.

Farewell in those days was not said in Cattle Land. Acquaintances watched our departure with a nod or with nothing, and the nearest approach to "Good-by" was the proprietor's "So-long." But I caught sight of one farewell given without words.

As we drove by the eating-house, the shade of a side window was raised, and the landlady looked her last upon the Virginian. Her lips were faintly parted, and no woman's eyes ever said more plainly, "I am one of your possessions." She had forgotten that it might be seen. Her glance caught mine, and she backed into the dimness of the room. What look she may have received from him, if he gave her any at this too public moment, I could not tell. His eyes seemed to be upon the horses, and he drove with the same mastering ease that had roped the wild pony yesterday. We passed the ramparts of Medicine Bow,—thick heaps and fringes of tin cans, and shelving mounds of bottles cast out of the saloons. The sun struck these at a hundred glittering points. And in a moment we were in the clean plains, with the prairie-dogs and the pale herds of antelope. The great, still air bathed us, pure as water and strong as wine; the sunlight flooded the world; and shining upon the breast of the Virginian's flannel shirt lay a long gold thread of hair! The noisy American drummer had met defeat, but this silent free lance had been easily victorious.

It must have been five miles that we travelled in silence, losing and seeing the horizon among the ceaseless waves of the earth. Then I looked back, and there was Medicine Bow, seemingly a stone's throw behind us. It was a full half-hour before I looked back again, and there sure enough was always Medicine Bow. A size or two smaller, I will admit, but visible in every feature, like something seen through the wrong end of a field glass. The East-bound express was approaching the town, and I noticed the white steam from its whistle; but when the sound reached us, the train had almost stopped. And in reply to my comment upon this, the Virginian deigned to remark that it was more so in Arizona.

"A man come to Arizona," he said, "with one of them telescopes to study the heavenly bodies. He was a Yankee, seh, and a right smart one, too. And one night we was watchin' for some little old fallin' stars that he said was due, and I saw some lights movin' along across the mesa pretty lively, an' I sang out. But he told me it was just the train. And I told him I didn't know yu' could see the cyars that plain from his place. 'Yu' can see them,' he said to me, 'but it is las' night's cyars you're lookin' at.'" At this point the Virginian spoke severely to one of the horses. "Of course," he then resumed to me, "that Yankee man did not mean quite all he said.—You, Buck!" he again broke off suddenly to the horse. "But Arizona, seh," he continued, "it cert'nly has a mos' deceivin' atmospheah. Another man told me he had seen a lady close one eye at him when he was two minutes hard run from her." This time the Virginian gave Buck the whip.

"What effect," I inquired with a gravity equal to his own, "does this extraordinary foreshortening have upon a quart of whiskey?"

"When it's outside yu', seh, no distance looks too far to go to it."

He glanced at me with an eye that held more confidence than hitherto he had been able to feel in me. I had made one step in his approval. But I had many yet to go. This day he preferred his own thoughts to my conversation, and so he did all the days of this first journey; while I should have greatly preferred his conversation to my thoughts. He dismissed some attempts that I made upon the subject of Uncle Hughey so that I had not the courage to touch upon Trampas, and that chill brief collision which might have struck the spark of death. Trampas! I had forgotten him till this silent drive I was beginning. I wondered if I should ever see him, or Steve, or any of those people again. And this wonder I expressed aloud.

"There's no tellin' in this country," said the Virginian. "Folks come easy, and they go easy. In settled places, like back in the States, even a poor man mostly has a home. Don't care if it's only a barrel on a lot, the fello' will keep frequentin' that lot, and if yu' want him yu' can find him. But out hyeh in the sage-brush, a man's home is apt to be his saddle blanket. First thing yu' know, he has moved it to Texas."

"You have done some moving yourself," I suggested.

But this word closed his mouth. "I have had a look at the country," he said, and we were silent again. Let me, however, tell you here that he had set out for a "look at the country" at the age of fourteen; and that by his present age of twenty-four he had seen Arkansas, Texas, New Mexico, Arizona, California, Oregon, Idaho, Montana, and Wyoming. Everywhere he had taken care of himself, and survived; nor had his strong heart yet waked up to any hunger for a home. Let me also tell you that he was one of thousands drifting and living thus, but (as you shall learn) one in a thousand.

Medicine Bow did not forever remain in sight. When next I thought of it and looked behind, nothing was there but the road we had come; it lay like a ship's wake across the huge ground swell of the earth. We were swallowed in a vast solitude. A little while before sunset, a cabin came in view; and here we passed our first night. Two young men lived here, tending their cattle. They were fond of animals. By the stable a chained coyote rushed nervously in a circle, or sat on its haunches and snapped at gifts of food ungraciously. A tame young elk walked in and out of the cabin door, and during supper it tried to push me off my chair. A half-tame mountain sheep practiced jumping from the ground to the roof. The cabin was papered with posters of a circus, and skins of bear and silver fox lay upon the floor. Until nine o'clock one man talked to the Virginian, and one played gayly upon a concertina; and then we all went to bed. The air was like December, but in my blankets and a buffalo robe I kept warm, and luxuriated in the Rocky Mountain silence. Going to wash before breakfast at sunrise, I found needles of ice in a pail. Yet it was hard to remember that this quiet, open, splendid wilderness (with not a peak in sight just here) was six thousand feet high. And when breakfast was over there was no December left; and by the time the Virginian and I were ten miles upon our way, it was June. But always every breath that I breathed was pure as water and strong as wine.

We never passed a human being this day. Some wild cattle rushed up to us and away from us; antelope stared at us from a hundred yards; coyotes ran skulking through the sage-brush to watch us from a hill; at our noon meal we killed a rattlesnake and shot some young sage chickens, which were good at supper, roasted at our campfire.

By half-past eight we were asleep beneath the stars, and by half-past four I was drinking coffee and shivering. The horse, Buck, was hard to catch this second morning. Whether some hills that we were now in had excited him, or whether the better water up here had caused an effervescence in his spirits, I cannot say. But I was as hot as July by the time we had him safe in harness, or, rather, unsafe in harness. For Buck, in the mysterious language of horses, now taught wickedness to his side partner, and about eleven o'clock they laid their evil heads together and decided to break our necks.

We were passing, I have said, through a range of demi-mountains.[3] It was a little country where trees grew, water ran, and the plains were shut out for a while. The road had steep places in it, and places here and there where you could fall off and go bounding to the bottom among stones. But Buck, for some reason, did not think these opportunities good enough for him. He selected a more theatrical moment. We emerged from a narrow canyon suddenly upon five hundred cattle and some cowboys branding calves by a fire in a corral. It was a sight that Buck knew by heart. He instantly treated it like an appalling phenomenon. I saw him kick seven ways; I saw Muggins kick five ways; our furious motion snapped my spine like a whip. I grasped the seat. Something gave a forlorn jingle. It was the brake.

"Don't jump!" commanded the trustworthy man.

"No," I said, as my hat flew off.

Help was too far away to do anything for us. We passed scathless[4] through a part of the cattle, I saw their horns and backs go by. Some earth crumbled, and we plunged downward into water rocking among stones, and upward again through some more crumbling earth. I heard a crash, and saw my trunk landing in the stream.

"She's safer there," said the trustworthy man.

"True," I said.

"We'll go back for her," said he, with his eye on the horses and his foot on the crippled brake. A dry gully was coming, and no room to turn. The farther side of it was terraced with rock. We should simply fall backward, if we did not fall forward first. He steered the horses straight over, and just at the bottom swung them, with astonishing skill, to the right along the hard-baked mud. They took us along the bed up to the head of the gully, and through a thicket of quaking asps. The light trees bent beneath our charge and bastinadoed the wagon as it went over them. But their branches enmeshed the horses' legs, and we came to a harmless standstill among a bower of leaves.

I looked at the trustworthy man, and smiled vaguely. He considered me for a moment.

"I reckon," said he, "you're feelin' about halfway between 'Oh, Lord!' and 'Thank God!'"

"That's quite it," said I, as he got down on the ground.

"Nothing's broke," said he, after a searching examination. And he indulged in a true Virginian expletive. "Gentlemen, hush!" he murmured gently, looking at me with his grave eyes; "one time I got pretty near scared. You, Buck," he continued, "some folks would beat you now till yu'd be uncertain whether yu' was a hawss or a railroad accident. I'd do it myself, only it wouldn't cure yu'."

[3]Half-mountains—that is, small ones. [4]Unscathed; unharmed.

I now told him that I supposed he had saved both our lives. But he detested words of direct praise. He made some grumbling rejoinder, and led the horses out of the thicket. Buck, he explained to me, was a good horse, and so was Muggins. Both of them generally meant well, and that was the Judge's reason for sending them to meet me. But these broncos had their off days. Off days might not come very often; but when the humor seized a bronco, he had to have his spree. Buck would now behave himself as a horse should for probably two months. "They are just like humans," the Virginian concluded.

Several cowboys arrived on a gallop to find how many pieces of us were left. We returned down the hill; and when we reached my trunk, it was surprising to see the distance that our runaway had covered. My hat was also found, and we continued on our way.

Buck and Muggins were patterns of discretion through the rest of the mountains. I thought when we camped this night that it was strange Buck should be again allowed to graze at large, instead of being tied to a rope while we slept. But this was my ignorance. With the hard work that he was gallantly doing, the horse needed more pasture than a rope's length would permit him to find. Therefore he went free, and in the morning gave us but little trouble in catching him.

We crossed a river in the forenoon, and far to the north of us we saw the Bow Leg Mountains, pale in the bright sun. Sunk Creek flowed from their western side, and our two hundred and sixty-three miles began to grow a small thing in my eyes. Buck and Muggins, I think, knew perfectly that to-morrow would see them home. They recognized this region; and once they turned off at a fork in the road. The Virginian pulled them back rather sharply.

"Want to go back to Balaam's?" he inquired of them. "I thought you had more sense."

I asked, "Who was Balaam?"

"A maltreater of hawsses," replied the cowpuncher. "His ranch is on Butte Creek oveh yondeh." And he pointed to where the diverging road melted into space. "The Judge bought Buck and Muggins from him in the spring."

"So he maltreats horses?" I repeated.

"That's the word all through this country. A man that will do what they claim Balaam does to a hawss when he's mad, ain't fit to be called human." The Virginian told me some particulars.

"Oh!" I almost screamed at the horror of it, and again, "Oh!"

"He'd have prob'ly done that to Buck as soon as he stopped runnin' away. If I caught a man doin' that—"

We were interrupted by a sedate-looking traveller riding upon an equally sober horse.

"Mawnin', Taylor," said the Virginian, pulling up for gossip. "Ain't you strayed off your range pretty far?"

"You're a nice one!" replied Mr. Taylor, stopping his horse and smiling amiably.

"Tell me something I don't know," retorted the Virginian.

"Hold up a man at cards and rob him," pursued Mr. Taylor. "Oh, the news has got ahead of you!"

"Trampas has been hyeh explainin', has he?" said the Virginian with a grin.

"Was that your victim's name?" said Mr. Taylor, facetiously. "No, it wasn't him that brought the news. Say, what did you do, anyway?"

"So that thing has got around," murmured the Virginian. "Well, it wasn't worth such wide repawtin'." And he gave the simple facts to Taylor, while I sat wondering at the contagious powers of Rumor. Here, through this voiceless land, this desert, this vacuum, it had spread like a change of weather. "Any news up your way?" the Virginian concluded.

Importance came into Mr. Taylor's countenance. "Bear Creek is going to build a schoolhouse," said he.

"Goodness gracious!" drawled the Virginian. "What's that for?"

Now Mr. Taylor had been married for some years. "To educate the offspring of Bear Creek," he answered with pride.

"Offspring of Bear Creek," the Virginian meditatively repeated. "I don't remember noticin' much offspring. There was some white tail deer, and a right smart o'jack rabbits."

"The Swintons have moved up from Drybone," said Mr. Taylor, always seriously. "They found it no place for young children. And there's Uncle Carmody with six, and Ben Dow. And Westfall has become a family man, and—"

"Jim Westfall!" exclaimed the Virginian. "Him a fam'ly man! Well, if this hyeh Territory is goin' to get full o'fam'ly men and empty o'game, I believe I'll—"

"Get married yourself," suggested Mr. Taylor.

"Me! I ain't near reached the marriageable age. No, seh! But Uncle Hughey has got there at last, yu' know."

"Uncle Hughey!" shouted Mr. Taylor. He had not heard this. Rumor is very capricious. Therefore the Virginian told him, and the family man rocked in his saddle.

"Build your schoolhouse," said the Virginian. "Uncle Hughey has qualified himself to subscribe to all such propositions. Got your eye on a schoolmarm?"

CHAPTER 5

ENTER THE WOMAN

"We are taking steps," said Mr. Taylor. "Bear Creek ain't going to be hasty about a schoolmarm."

"Sure," assented the Virginian. "The children wouldn't want yu' to hurry."

But Mr. Taylor was, as I have indicated, a serious family man. The problem of educating his children could appear to him in no light except a sober one. "Bear Creek," he said, "don't want the experience they had over at Calef. We must not hire an ignoramus."

"Sure!" assented the Virginian again.

"Nor we don't want no gad-a-way flirt," said Mr. Taylor.

"She must keep her eyes on the blackboa'd," said the Virginian, gently.

"Well, we can wait till we get a guaranteed article," said Mr. Taylor. "And that's what we're going to do. It can't be this year, and it needn't to be. None of the kids is very old, and the schoolhouse has got to be built." He now drew a letter from his pocket, and looked at me. "Are you acquainted with Miss Mary Stark Wood of Bennington, Vermont?" he inquired.

I was not acquainted with her at this time.

"She's one we are thinking of. She's a correspondent with Mrs. Balaam." Taylor handed me the letter. "She wrote that to Mrs. Balaam, and Mrs. Balaam said the best thing was for to let me see it and judge for myself. I'm taking it back to Mrs. Balaam. Maybe you can give me your opinion how it sizes up with the letters they write back East?"

The communication was mainly of a business kind, but also personal, and freely written. I do not think that its writer expected it to be exhibited as a document. The writer wished very much that she could see the West. But she could not gratify this desire merely for pleasure, or she would long ago have accepted the kind invitation to visit Mrs. Balaam's ranch. Teaching school was something she would like to do, if she were fitted for it. "Since the mills failed" (the writer said) "we have all gone to work and done a lot of things so that mother might keep on living in the old house. Yes, the salary would be a temptation. But, my dear, isn't Wyoming bad for the complexion? And could I sue them if mine got damaged? It is still admired. I could bring one male witness AT LEAST to prove that!" Then the writer became businesslike again. Even if she came to feel that she could leave home, she did not at all know that she could teach school. Nor did she think it right to accept a position in which one had had no experience. "I do love children, boys especially," she went on. "My small nephew and I get on famously. But imagine if a whole benchful of boys began asking me questions that I couldn't answer! What should I do? For one could not spank them all, you know! And mother says that I ought not to teach anybody spelling, because I leave the U out of HONOR."

Altogether it was a letter which I could assure Mr. Taylor "sized up" very well with the letters written in my part of the United States. And it was signed, "Your very sincere spinster, Molly Stark Wood."

"I never seen HONOR spelled with a U," said Mr. Taylor, over whose not highly civilized head certain portions of the letter had lightly passed.

I told him that some old-fashioned people still wrote the word so.

"Either way would satisfy Bear Creek," said Mr. Taylor, "if she's otherwise up to requirements."

The Virginian was now looking over the letter musingly, and with awakened attention.

"'Your very sincere spinster,'" he read aloud slowly.

"I guess that means she's forty," said Taylor.

"I reckon she is about twenty," said the Virginian. And again he fell to musing over the paper that he held.

"Her handwriting ain't like any I've saw," pursued Mr. Taylor. "But Bear Creek would not object to that, provided she knows 'rithmetic and George Washington, and them kind of things."

"I expect she is not an awful sincere spinster," surmised the Virginian, still looking at the letter, still holding it as if it were some token.

Has any botanist set down what the seed of love is? Has it anywhere been set down in how many ways this seed may be sown? In what various vessels of gossamer it can float across wide spaces? Or upon what different soils it can fall, and live unknown, and bide its time for blooming?

The Virginian handed back to Taylor the sheet of note paper where a girl had talked as the women he had known did not talk. If his eyes had ever seen such maidens, there had been no meeting of eyes; and if such maidens had ever spoken to him, the speech was from an established distance. But here was a free language, altogether new to him. It proved, however, not alien to his understanding, as it was alien to Mr. Taylor's.

We drove onward, a mile perhaps, and then two. He had lately been full of words, but now he barely answered me, so that a silence fell upon both of us. It must have been all of ten miles that we had driven when he spoke of his own accord.

"Your real spinster don't speak of her lot that easy," he remarked. And presently he quoted a phrase about the complexion, "'Could I sue them if mine got damaged?'" and he smiled over this to himself, shaking his head. "What would she be doing on Bear Creek?" he next said. And finally: "I reckon that witness will detain her in Vermont. And her mother'll keep livin' at the old house."

Thus did the cow-puncher deliver himself, not knowing at all that the seed had floated across wide spaces, and was biding its time in his heart.

On the morrow we reached Sunk Creek. Judge Henry's welcome and his wife's would have obliterated any hardships that I had endured, and I had endured none at all.

For a while I saw little of the Virginian. He lapsed into his native way of addressing me occasionally as "seh"—a habit entirely repudiated by this land of equality. I was sorry. Our common peril during the runaway of Buck and Muggins had brought us to a familiarity that I hoped was destined to last. But I think that it would not have gone farther, save for a certain personage—I must call her a personage. And as I am indebted to her for gaining me a friend whose prejudice against me might never have been otherwise overcome, I shall tell you her little story, and how her misadventures and her fate came to bring the Virginian and me to an appreciation of one another. Without her, it is likely I should also not have heard so much of the story of the schoolmarm, and how that lady at last came to Bear Creek.

CHAPTER 6

EM'LY

My personage was a hen, and she lived at the Sunk Creek Ranch.

Judge Henry's ranch was notable for several luxuries. He had milk, for example. In those days his brother ranchmen had thousands of cattle very often, but not a drop of milk, save the condensed variety. Therefore they had no butter. The Judge had plenty. Next rarest to butter and milk in the cattle country were eggs. But my host had chickens. Whether this was because he had followed cockfighting in his early days, or whether it was due to Mrs. Henry, I cannot say. I only know that when I took a meal elsewhere, I was likely to find nothing but the eternal "sowbelly,"[5] beans, and coffee; while at Sunk Creek the omelet and the custard were frequent. The passing traveller was glad to tie his horse to the fence here, and sit down to the Judge's table. For its fame was as wide as Wyoming. It was an oasis in the Territory's desolate bill-of-fare.

[5]Salt pork.

The long fences of Judge Henry's home ranch began upon Sunk Creek soon after that stream emerged from its canyon through the Bow Leg. It was a place always well cared for by the owner, even in the days of his bachelorhood. The placid regiments of cattle lay in the cool of the cottonwoods by the water, or slowly moved among the sagebrush, feeding upon the grass that in those forever departed years was plentiful and tall. The steers came fat off his unenclosed range and fattened still more in his large pasture; while his small pasture, a field some eight miles square, was for several seasons given to the Judge's horses, and over this ample space there played and prospered the good colts which he raised from Paladin, his imported stallion. After he married, I have been assured that his wife's influence became visible in and about the house at once. Shade trees were planted, flowers attempted, and to the chickens was added the much more troublesome turkey. I, the visitor, was pressed into service when I arrived, green from the East. I took hold of the farmyard and began building a better chicken house, while the Judge was off creating meadow land in his gray and yellow wilderness. When any cowboy was unoccupied, he would lounge over to my neighborhood, and silently regard my carpentering.

Those cowpunchers bore names of various denominations. There was Honey Wiggin; there was Nebrasky, and Dollar Bill, and Chalkeye. And they came from farms and cities, from Maine and from California. But the romance of American adventure had drawn them all alike to this great playground of young men, and in their courage, their generosity, and their amusement at me they bore a close resemblance to each other. Each one would silently observe my achievements with the hammer and the chisel. Then he would retire to the bunkhouse, and presently I would overhear laughter. But this was only in the morning. In the afternoon on many days of the summer which I spent at the Sunk Creek Ranch I would go shooting, or ride up toward the entrance of the canyon and watch the men working on the irrigation ditches. Pleasant systems of water running in channels were being led through the soil, and there was a sound of rippling here and there among the yellow grain; the green thick alfalfa grass waved almost, it seemed, of its own accord, for the wind never blew; and when at evening the sun lay against the plain, the rift of the canyon was filled with a violet light, and the Bow Leg Mountains became transfigured with hues of floating and unimaginable color. The sun shone in a sky where never a cloud came, and noon was not too warm nor the dark too cool. And so for two months I went through these pleasant uneventful days, improving the chickens, an object of mirth, living in the open air, and basking in the perfection of content.

I was justly styled a tenderfoot.[6] Mrs. Henry had in the beginning endeavored to shield me from this humiliation; but when she found that I was inveterate in laying my inexperience of Western matters bare to all the world, begging to be enlightened upon rattlesnakes, prairie-dogs, owls, blue and willow grouse, sagehens, how to rope a horse or tighten the front cinch of my saddle, and that my spirit soared into enthusiasm at the mere sight of so ordinary an animal as a white-tailed deer, she let me rush about with my firearms and made no further effort to stave off the ridicule that my blunders perpetually earned from the ranch hands, her own humorous husband, and any chance visitor who stopped for a meal or stayed the night.

[6]An inexperienced newcomer.

I was not called by my name after the first feeble etiquette due to a stranger in his first few hours had died away. I was known simply as "the tenderfoot." I was introduced to the neighborhood (a circle of eighty miles) as "the tenderfoot." It was thus that Balaam, the maltreater of horses, learned to address me when he came a two days' journey to pay a visit. And it was this name and my notorious helplessness that bid fair to end what relations I had with the Virginian. For when Judge Henry ascertained that nothing could prevent me from losing myself, that it was not uncommon for me to saunter out after breakfast with a gun and in thirty minutes cease to know north from south, he arranged for my protection. He detailed an escort for me; and the escort was once more the trustworthy man! The poor Virginian was taken from his work and his comrades and set to playing nurse for me. And for a while this humiliation ate into his untamed soul. It was his lugubrious lot to accompany me in my rambles, preside over my blunders, and save me from calamitously passing into the next world. He bore it in courteous silence, except when sneaking was necessary. He would show me the lower ford, which I could never find for myself, generally mistaking a quicksand for it. He would tie my horse properly. He would recommend me not to shoot my rifle at a white-tailed deer in the particular moment that the outfit wagon was passing behind the animal on the further side of the brush. There was seldom a day that he was not obliged to hasten and save me from sudden death or from ridicule, which is worse. Yet never once did he lose his patience and his gentle, slow voice, and apparently lazy manner remained the same, whether we were sitting at lunch together, or up in the mountain during a hunt, or whether he was bringing me back my horse, which had run away because I had again forgotten to throw the reins over his head and let them trail.

"He'll always stand if yu' do that," the Virginian would say. "See how my hawss stays right quiet yondeh."

After such admonition he would say no more to me. But this tame nursery business was assuredly gall to him. For though utterly a man in countenance and in his self-possession and incapacity to be put at a loss, he was still boyishly, proud of his wild calling, and wore his leathers straps and jingled his spurs with obvious pleasure. His tiger limberness and his beauty were rich with unabated youth; and that force which lurked beneath his surface must often have curbed his intolerance of me. In spite of what I knew must be his opinion of me, the tenderfoot, my liking for him grew, and I found his silent company more and more agreeable. That he had spells of talking, I had already learned at Medicine Bow. But his present taciturnity might almost have effaced this impression, had I not happened to pass by the bunkhouse one evening after dark, when Honey Wiggin and the rest of the cowboys were gathered inside it.

That afternoon the Virginian and I had gone duck shooting. We had found several in a beaver dam, and I had killed two as they sat close together; but they floated against the breastwork of sticks out in the water some four feet deep, where the escaping current might carry them down the stream. The Judge's red setter had not accompanied us, because she was expecting a family.

"We don't want her along anyways," the cowpuncher had explained to me. "She runs around mighty irresponsible, and she'll stand a prairie-dog 'bout as often as she'll stand a bird. She's a triflin' animal."

My anxiety to own the ducks caused me to pitch into the water with all my clothes on, and subsequently crawl out a slippery, triumphant, weltering heap.

The Virginian's serious eyes had rested upon this spectacle of mud; but he expressed nothing, as usual.

"They ain't overly good eatin'," he observed, tying the birds to his saddle. "They're divers."

"Divers!" I exclaimed. "Why didn't they dive?"

"I reckon they was young ones and hadn't experience."

"Well," I said, crestfallen, but attempting to be humorous, "I did the diving myself."

But the Virginian made no comment. He handed me my double-barrelled English gun, which I was about to leave deserted on the ground behind me, and we rode home in our usual silence, the mean little white-breasted, sharp-billed divers dangling from his saddle.

It was in the bunkhouse that he took his revenge. As I passed I heard his gentle voice silently achieving some narrative to an attentive audience, and just as I came by the open window where he sat on his bed in shirt and drawers, his back to me, I heard his concluding words, "And the hat on his haid was the one mark showed yu' he weren't a snappin'-turtle."

The anecdote met with instantaneous success, and I hurried away into the dark. The next morning I was occupied with the chickens. Two hens were fighting to sit on some eggs that a third was daily laying, and which I did not want hatched, and for the third time I had kicked Em'ly off seven potatoes she had rolled together and was determined to raise I know not what sort of family from. She was shrieking about the henhouse as the Virginian came in to observe (I suspect) what I might be doing now that could be useful for him to mention in the bunkhouse.

He stood awhile, and at length said, "We lost our best rooster when Mrs. Henry came to live hyeh."

I paid no attention.

"He was a right elegant Dominicker,"[7] he continued.

I felt a little ruffled about the snapping-turtle, and showed no interest in what he was saying, but continued my functions among the hens. This unusual silence of mine seemed to elicit unusual speech from him.

"Yu' see, that rooster he'd always lived round hyeh when the Judge was a bachelor, and he never seen no ladies or any persons wearing female gyarments. You ain't got rheumatism, seh?"

"Me? No."

"I reckoned maybe them little odd divers yu' got damp goin' afteh—" He paused.

"Oh, no, not in the least, thank you."

"Yu' seemed sort o' grave this mawnin', and I'm cert'nly glad it ain't them divers."

"Well, the rooster?" I inquired finally.

"Oh, him! He weren't raised where he could see petticoats. Mrs. Henry she come hyeh from the railroad with the Judge afteh dark. Next mawnin' early she walked out to view her new home, and the rooster was a-feedin' by the door, and he seen her. Well, seh, he screeched that awful I run out of the bunkhouse; and he jus' went over the fence and took down Sunk Creek shoutin' fire, right along. He has never come back."

[7]A Dominique, or Dominick, chicken—a variety marked with gray, barred plumage.

"There's a hen over there now that has no judgment," I said, indicating Em'ly. She had got herself outside the house, and was on the bars of a corral, her vociferations[8] reduced to an occasional squawk. I told him about the potatoes.

"I never knowed her name before," said he. "That runaway rooster, he hated her. And she hated him same as she hates 'em all."

"I named her myself," said I, "after I came to notice her particularly. There's an old maid at home who's charitable, and belongs to the Cruelty to Animals,[9] and she never knows whether she had better cross in front of a street car or wait. I named the hen after her. Does she ever lay eggs?"

The Virginian had not "troubled his haid" over the poultry.

"Well, I don't believe she knows how. I think she came near being a rooster."

"She's sure manly-lookin'," said the Virginian. We had walked toward the corral, and he was now scrutinizing Em'ly with interest.

She was an egregious fowl. She was huge and gaunt, with great yellow beak, and she stood straight and alert in the manner of responsible people. There was something wrong with her tail. It slanted far to one side, one feather in it twice as long as the rest. Feathers on her breast there were none. These had been worn entirely off by her habit of sitting upon potatoes and other rough abnormal objects. And this lent to her appearance an air of being decollete,[10] singularly at variance with her otherwise prudish ensemble. Her eye was remarkably bright, but somehow it had an outraged expression. It was as if she went about the world perpetually scandalized over the doings that fell beneath her notice. Her legs were blue, long, and remarkably stout.

"She'd ought to wear knickerbockers," murmured the Virginian. "She'd look a heap better 'n some o' them college students. And she'll set on potatoes, yu' say?"

"She thinks she can hatch out anything. I've found her with onions, and last Tuesday I caught her on two balls of soap."

In the afternoon the tall cowpuncher and I rode out to get an antelope.

After an hour, during which he was completely taciturn, he said: "I reckon maybe this hyeh lonesome country ain't been healthy for Em'ly to live in. It ain't for some humans. Them old trappers in the mountains gets skewed in the haid mighty often, an' talks out loud when nobody's nigher 'n a hundred miles."

"Em'ly has not been solitary," I replied. "There are forty chickens here."

"That's so," said he. "It don't explain her."

He fell silent again, riding beside me, easy and indolent in the saddle. His long figure looked so loose and inert that the swift, light spring he made to the ground seemed an impossible feat. He had seen an antelope where I saw none.

"Take a shot yourself," I urged him, as he motioned me to be quick. "You never shoot when I'm with you."

"I ain't hyeh for that," he answered. "Now you've let him get away on yu'!"

The antelope had in truth departed.

"Why," he said to my protest, "I can hit them things any day. What's your notion as to Em'ly?"

"I can't account for her," I replied.

[8]Noisy cries.
[9]American Society for the Prevention of Cruelty to Animals (ASPCA), founded in 1866.
[10]Wearing a low-cut garment that exposes part of the breast.

"Well," he said musingly, and then his mind took one of those particular turns that made me love him, "Taylor ought to see her. She'd be just the school-marm for Bear Creek!"

"She's not much like the eating-house lady at Medicine Bow," I said.

He gave a hilarious chuckle. "No, Em'ly knows nothing o' them joys. So yu' have no notion about her? Well, I've got one. I reckon maybe she was hatched after a big thunderstorm."

"In a big thunderstorm!" I exclaimed.

"Yes. Don't yu' know about them, and what they'll do to aiggs? A big case o' lightnin' and thunder will addle aiggs and keep 'em from hatchin'. And I expect one came along, and all the other aiggs of Em'ly's set didn't hatch out, but got plumb addled, and she happened not to get addled that far, and so she just managed to make it through. But she cert'nly ain't got a strong haid. "I fear she has not," said I.

"Mighty hon'ble intentions," he observed. "If she can't make out to lay anything, she wants to hatch somethin', and be a mother anyways."

"I wonder what relation the law considers that a hen is to the chicken she hatched but did not lay?" I inquired.

The Virginian made no reply to this frivolous suggestion. He was gazing over the wide landscape gravely and with apparent inattention. He invariably saw game before I did, and was off his horse and crouched among the sage while I was still getting my left foot clear of the stirrup. I succeeded in killing an antelope, and we rode home with the head and hindquarters.

"No." said he. "It's sure the thunder, and not the lonesomeness. How do yu' like the lonesomeness yourself?"

I told him that I liked it.

"I could not live without it now," he said. "This has got into my system." He swept his hand out at the vast space of world. "I went back home to see my folks onced. Mother was dyin' slow, and she wanted me. I stayed a year. But them Virginia mountains could please me no more. Afteh she was gone, I told my brothers and sisters good-by. We like each other well enough, but I reckon I'll not go back."

We found Em'ly seated upon a collection of green California peaches, which the Judge had brought from the railroad.

"I don't mind her any more," I said; "I'm sorry for her."

"I've been sorry for her right along," said the Virginian. "She does hate the roosters so." And he said that he was making a collection of every class of object which he found her treating as eggs.

But Em'ly's egg-industry was terminated abruptly one morning, and her unquestioned energies diverted to a new channel. A turkey which had been sitting in the root-house appeared with twelve children, and a family of bantams occurred almost simultaneously. Em'ly was importantly scratching the soil inside Paladin's corral when the bantam tribe of newly born came by down the lane, and she caught sight of them through the bars. She crossed the corral at a run, and intercepted two of the chicks that were trailing somewhat behind their real mamma. These she undertook to appropriate, and assumed a high tone with the bantam, who was the smaller, and hence obliged to retreat with her still numerous family. I interfered, and put matters straight; but the adjustment was only temporary. In an hour I saw Em'ly immensely busy with two more bantams, leading them about and taking a care of them which I must admit seemed perfectly efficient.

And now came the first incident that made me suspect her to be demented. She had proceeded with her changelings[11] behind the kitchen, where one of the irrigation ditches ran under the fence from the hayfield to supply the house with water. Some distance along this ditch inside the field were the twelve turkeys in the short, recently cut stubble. Again Em'ly set off instantly like a deer. She left the dismayed bantams behind her. She crossed the ditch with one jump of her stout blue legs, flew over the grass, and was at once among the turkeys, where, with an instinct of maternity as undiscriminating as it was reckless, she attempted to huddle some of them away. But this other mamma was not a bantam, and in a few moments Em'ly was entirely routed in her attempt to acquire a new variety of family.

This spectacle was witnessed by the Virginian and myself, and it overcame him. He went speechless across to the bunkhouse, by himself, and sat on his bed, while I took the abandoned bantams back to their own circle.

I have often wondered what the other fowls thought of all this. Some impression it certainly did make upon them. The notion may seem out of reason to those who have never closely attended to other animals than man; but I am convinced that any community which shares some of our instincts will share some of the resulting feelings, and that birds and beasts have conventions, the breach of which startles them. If there be anything in evolution, this would seem inevitable; At all events, the chickenhouse was upset during the following several days. Em'ly disturbed now the bantams and now the turkeys, and several of these latter had died, though I will not go so far as to say that this was the result of her misplaced attentions. Nevertheless, I was seriously thinking of locking her up till the broods should be a little older, when another event happened, and all was suddenly at peace.

The Judge's setter came in one morning, wagging her tail. She had had her puppies, and she now took us to where they were housed, in between the floor of a building and the hollow ground. Em'ly was seated on the whole litter.

"No," I said to the Judge, "I am not surprised. She is capable of anything."

In her new choice of offspring, this hen had at length encountered an unworthy parent. The setter was bored by her own puppies. She found the hole under the house an obscure and monotonous residence compared with the dining room, and our company more stimulating and sympathetic than that of her children. A much-petted contact with our superior race had developed her dog intelligence above its natural level, and turned her into an unnatural, neglectful mother, who was constantly forgetting her nursery for worldly pleasures.

At certain periods of the day she repaired to the puppies and fed them, but came away when this perfunctory ceremony was accomplished; and she was glad enough to have a governess bring them up. She made no quarrel with Em'ly, and the two understood each other perfectly. I have never seen among animals any arrangement so civilized and so perverted. It made Em'ly perfectly happy. To see her sitting all day jealously spreading her wings over some blind puppies was sufficiently curious; but when they became large enough to come out from under the house and toddle about in the proud hen's wake, I longed for some distinguished naturalist. I felt that our ignorance made us inappropriate spectators of such a phenomenon. Em'ly scratched and clucked, and

[11]Changeling: a child switched at birth for the parent's real child.

the puppies ran to her, pawed her with their fat limp little legs, and retreated beneath her feathers in their games of hide and seek. Conceive, if you can, what confusion must have reigned in their infant minds as to who the setter was!

"I reckon they think she's the wet-nurse," said the Virginian.

When the puppies grew to be boisterous, I perceived that Em'ly's mission was approaching its end. They were too heavy for her, and their increasing scope of playfulness was not in her line. Once or twice they knocked her over, upon which she arose and pecked them severely, and they retired to a safe distance, and sitting in a circle, yapped at her. I think they began to suspect that she was only a hen after all. So Em'ly resigned with an indifference which surprised me, until I remembered that if it had been chickens, she would have ceased to look after them by this time.

But here she was again "out of a job," as the Virginian said.

"She's raised them puppies for that triflin' setter, and now she'll be huntin' around for something else useful to do that ain't in her business.

Now there were other broods of chickens to arrive in the henhouse, and I did not desire any more bantam and turkey performances. So, to avoid confusion, I played a trick upon Em'ly. I went down to Sunk Creek and fetched some smooth, oval stones. She was quite satisfied with these, and passed a quiet day with them in a box. This was not fair, the Virginian asserted.

"You ain't going to jus' leave her fooled that a-way?"

I did not see why not.

"Why, she raised them puppies all right. Ain't she showed she knows how to be a mother anyways? Em'ly ain't going to get her time took up for nothing while I'm round hyeh," said the cowpuncher.

He laid a gentle hold of Em'ly and tossed her to the ground. She, of course, rushed out among the corrals in a great state of nerves.

"I don't see what good you do meddling," I protested.

To this he deigned no reply, but removed the unresponsive stones from the straw.

"Why, if they ain't right warm!" he exclaimed plaintively. "The poor, deluded son-of-a-gun!" And with this unusual description of a lady, he sent the stones sailing like a line of birds. "I'm regular getting stuck on Em'ly," continued the Virginian. "Yu' needn't to laugh. Don't yu' see she's got sort o' human feelin's and desires? I always knowed hawsses was like people, and my collie, of course. It is kind of foolish, I expect, but that hen's goin' to have a real aigg di-rectly, right now, to set on." With this he removed one from beneath another hen. "We'll have Em'ly raise this hyeh," said he, "so she can put in her time profitable."

It was not accomplished at once; for Em'ly, singularly enough, would not consent to stay in the box whence she had been routed. At length we found another retreat for her, and in these new surroundings, with a new piece of work for her to do, Em'ly sat on the one egg which the Virginian had so carefully provided for her.

Thus, as in all genuine tragedies, was the stroke of Fate wrought by chance and the best intentions.

Em'ly began sitting on Friday afternoon near sundown. Early next morning my sleep was gradually dispersed by a sound unearthly and continuous. Now it dwindled, receding to a distance; again it came near, took a turn, drifted to the other side of the house; then, evidently, whatever it was, passed my door close, and I jumped upright in my bed. The high, tense strain of vibration, nearly, but not quite, a musical note, was like the threatening scream of machinery, though weaker, and I bounded out of the house in my pajamas.

There was Em'ly, dishevelled, walking wildly about, her one egg miraculously hatched within ten hours. The little lonely yellow ball of down went cheeping along behind, following its mother as best it could. What, then, had happened to the established period of incubation? For an instant the thing was like a portent, and I was near joining Em'ly in her horrid surprise, when I saw how it all was. The Virginian had taken an egg from a hen which had already been sitting for three weeks.

I dressed in haste, hearing Em'ly's distracted outcry. It steadily sounded, without perceptible pause for breath, and marked her erratic journey back and forth through stables, lanes, and corrals. The shrill disturbance brought all of us out to see her, and in the henhouse I discovered the new brood making its appearance punctually.

But this natural explanation could not be made to the crazed hen. She continued to scour the premises, her slant tail and its one preposterous feather waving as she aimlessly went, her stout legs stepping high with an unnatural motion, her head lifted nearly off her neck, and in her brilliant yellow eye an expression of more than outrage at this overturning of a natural law. Behind her, entirely ignored and neglected, trailed the little progeny. She never looked at it. We went about our various affairs, and all through the clear, sunny day that unending metallic scream pervaded the premises. The Virginian put out food and water for her, but she tasted nothing. I am glad to say that the little chicken did. I do not think that the hen's eyes could see, except in the way that sleepwalkers' do.

The heat went out of the air, and in the canyon the violet light began to show. Many hours had gone, but Em'ly never ceased. Now she suddenly flew up in a tree and sat there with her noise still going; but it had risen lately several notes into a slim, acute level of terror, and was not like machinery any more, nor like any sound I ever heard before or since. Below the tree stood the bewildered little chicken, cheeping, and making tiny jumps to reach its mother.

"Yes," said the Virginian, "it's comical. Even her aigg acted different from anybody else's." He paused, and looked across the wide, mellowing plain with the expression of easygoing gravity so common with him. Then he looked at Em'ly in the tree and the yellow chicken.

"It ain't so damned funny," said he.

We went in to supper, and I came out to find the hen lying on the ground, dead. I took the chicken to the family in the henhouse.

No, it was not altogether funny any more. And I did not think less of the Virginian when I came upon him surreptitiously digging a little hole in the field for her.

"I have buried some citizens here and there, said he, "that I have respected less."

And when the time came for me to leave Sunk Creek, my last word to the Virginian was, "Don't forget Em'ly."

"I ain't likely to," responded the cowpuncher. "She is just one o'them parables."

Save when he fell into his native idioms (which, they told me, his wanderings had well-nigh obliterated until that year's visit to his home again revived them in his speech), he had now for a long while dropped the "seh," and all other barriers between us. We were thorough friends, and had exchanged many confidences both of the flesh and of the spirit. He even went the length of saying that he would write me the Sunk Creek news if I would send him a line now and then. I have many letters from him now. Their spelling came to be faultless, and in the beginning was little worse than George Washington's.

The Judge himself drove me to the railroad by another way—across the Bow Leg Mountains, and south through Balaam's Ranch and Drybone to Rock Creek.

"I'll be very homesick," I told him.

"Come and pull the latch-string whenever you please," he bade me. I wished that I might! No lotus land ever cast its spell upon man's heart more than Wyoming had enchanted mine.

1902

James Weldon Johnson (1871–1938)

Arguably among the three or four most accomplished African Americans of the early twentieth century, James Weldon Johnson achieved distinction in his own lifetime as a novelist, poet, autobiographer, editor, lyricist, educator, ambassador, political organizer, and cultural leader. Born in 1871 to middle-class parents in Jacksonville, Florida, Johnson was groomed from an early age to flourish in American mainstream white culture. His mother, a teacher, passed on to her eldest son her appreciation for literature and music; his father imparted a sense of professional acumen. As a young man he received a classical college education at Atlanta University. After graduating in 1894, Johnson came home to Jacksonville, accepting a principal's position at Stanton School. A few years later he left for New York to pursue a career as a songwriter. His success was almost immediate; he became one of the best-known lyricists on Broadway at the turn of the century. In 1906 Johnson left New York to serve as a government diplomat, first in Venezuela, then later in Nicaragua. At the same time, he continued to contribute poetry to prestigious periodicals such as Century Magazine.

Johnson's first book, a collection of poetry titled Sence You Went Away, *appeared in 1900. But it would be his second book, a novel, that would establish for him a permanent place in American literary history. Published anonymously in 1912,* The Autobiography of an Ex-Colored Man *initially received little critical or popular attention. Increasingly, however, the leading intellectuals and artists of the Harlem Renaissance responded to the psychological dramas enacted by Johnson's protagonist, a black man who wrestles with myriad issues of racial identity in American culture.* The Autobiography of an Ex-Colored Man *is now credited with providing a literary template for much of the most significant work of the Harlem Renaissance. A decade later, Johnson edited the profoundly influential anthology,* The Book of American Negro Poetry *(1922). The year 1927 proved to be his most productive as a writer, as it saw the republication under Johnson's name of* The Autobiography of an Ex-Coloured Man *(spelling now slightly altered), his book of verse* God's Trombones, *and his acclaimed autobiography* Along the Way.

In 1930, after serving in national leadership positions in the NAACP for more than a decade and a half, Johnson was offered a teaching position at Fisk University in Nashville. He accepted the Adam K. Spence Chair of Creative Literature, which he held until his death in 1938. James Weldon Johnson died in an automobile accident at the age of 67.

FURTHER READING: *Along This Way: The Autobiography of James Weldon Johnson,* 1969; *The Selected Writings of James Weldon Johnson,* ed. S. Wilson, 1995; E. Levy, *James Weldon Johnson: Black Leader, Black Voice,* 1973; *James Weldon Johnson and Arna Wendell Bontemps: A Reference Guide,* ed. R. Fleming, 1978; R. Fleming, *James Weldon Johnson,* 1987; *Critical Essays on James Weldon Johnson,* ed. M. Price and L. Oliver, 1997.

TEXTS: *Saint Peter Relates an Incident,* 1935; *The Autobiography of an Ex-Colored Man,* 1912.

LIFT EVERY VOICE AND SING[1]

Lift every voice and sing
Till earth and heaven ring,
Ring with the harmonies of Liberty;
Let our rejoicing rise
High as the listening skies,
Let it resound loud as the rolling sea.
Sing a song full of the faith that the dark past has taught us,
Sing a song full of the hope that the present has brought us.
Facing the rising sun of our new day begun,
Let us march on till victory is won.

Stony the road we trod,
Bitter the chastening rod,
Felt in the days when hope unborn had died;
Yet with a steady beat,
Have not our weary feet
Come to the place for which our fathers sighed?
We have come over a way that with tears has been watered,
We have come, treading our path through the blood of the
    slaughtered,
Out from the gloomy past,
Till now we stand at last
Where the white gleam of our bright star is cast.

God of our weary years,
God of our silent tears,
Thou who hast brought us thus far on the way;

[1]This song, often referred to as "The Negro National Anthem" and as the "official song of the N.A.A.C.P.," was composed collaboratively by James Weldon Johnson (lyrics) and his brother John Rosamond Johnson (music).

Thou who hast by Thy might
Led us into the light,
Keep us forever in the path, we pray.
Lest our feet stray from the places, our God, where we met Thee,
Lest, our hearts drunk with the wine of the world, we forget Thee;
Shadowed beneath Thy hand,
May we forever stand.
True to our God,
True to our native land.

1900

from *THE AUTOBIOGRAPHY OF AN EX-COLORED MAN*

CHAPTER 1

I know that in writing the following pages I am divulging the great secret of my life, the secret which for some years I have guarded far more carefully than any of my earthly possessions; and it is a curious study to me to analyze the motives which prompt me to do it. I feel that I am led by the same impulse which forces the unfound-out criminal to take somebody into his confidence, although he knows that the act is liable, even almost certain, to lead to his undoing. I know that I am playing with fire, and I feel the thrill which accompanies that most fascinating pastime; and, back of it all, I think I find a sort of savage and diabolical desire to gather up all the little tragedies of my life, and turn them into a practical joke on society.

And, too, I suffer a vague feeling of unsatisfaction, of regret, of almost remorse from which I am seeking relief, and of which I shall speak in the last paragraph of this account.

I was born in a little town of Georgia a few years after the close of the Civil War. I shall not mention the name of the town, because there are people still living there who could be connected with this narrative. I have only a faint recollection of the place of my birth. At times I can close my eyes, and call up in a dream-like way things that seem to have happened ages ago in some other world. I can see in this half vision a little house,—I am quite sure it was not a large one;—I can remember that flowers grew in the front yard, and that around each bed of flowers was a hedge of vari-colored glass bottles stuck in the ground neck down. I remember that once, while playing around in the sand, I became curious to know whether or not the bottles grew as the flowers did, and I proceeded to dig them up to find out; the investigation brought me a terrific spanking which indelibly fixed the incident in my mind. I can remember, too, that behind the house was a shed under which stood two or three wooden washtubs. These tubs were the earliest aversion of my life, for regularly on certain evenings I was plunged into one of them, and scrubbed until my skin ached. I can remember to this day the pain caused by the strong, rank soap getting into my eyes.

Back from the house a vegetable garden ran, perhaps, seventy-five or one hundred feet; but to my childish fancy it was an endless territory. I can still recall the thrill of joy, excitement and wonder it gave me to go on an exploring expedition through it, to find the blackberries, both ripe and green, that grew along the edge of the fence.

I remember with what pleasure I used to arrive at, and stand before, a little enclosure in which stood a patient cow chewing her cud, how I would occasionally offer her through the bars a piece of my bread and molasses, and how I would jerk back my hand in half fright if she made any motion to accept my offer.

I have a dim recollection of several people who moved in and about this little house, but I have a distinct mental image of only two; one, my mother, and the other, a tall man with a small, dark mustache. I remember that his shoes or boots were always shiny, and that he wore a gold chain and a great gold watch with which he was always willing to let me play. My admiration was almost equally divided between the watch and chain and the shoes. He used to come to the house evenings, perhaps two or three times a week; and it became my appointed duty whenever he came to bring him a pair of slippers, and to put the shiny shoes in a particular corner; he often gave me in return for this service a bright coin which my mother taught me to promptly drop in a little tin bank. I remember distinctly the last time this tall man came to the little house in Georgia; that evening before I went to bed he took me up in his arms, and squeezed me very tightly; my mother stood behind his chair wiping tears from her eyes. I remember how I sat upon his knee, and watched him laboriously drill a hole through a ten-dollar gold piece, and then tie the coin around my neck with a string. I have worn that gold piece around my neck the greater part of my life, and still possess it, but more than once I have wished that some other way had been found of attaching it to me besides putting a hole through it.

On the day after the coin was put around my neck my mother and I started on what seemed to me an endless journey. I knelt on the seat and watched through the train window the corn and cotton fields pass swiftly by until I fell asleep. When I fully awoke we were being driven through the streets of a large city—Savannah. I sat up and blinked at the bright lights. At Savannah we boarded a steamer which finally landed us in New York. From New York we went to a town in Connecticut, which became the home of my boyhood.

My mother and I lived together in a little cottage which seemed to me to be fitted up almost luxuriously; there were horse-hair covered chairs in the parlor, and a little square piano; there was a stairway with red carpet on it leading to a half second story; there were pictures on the walls, and a few books in a glass-doored case. My mother dressed me very neatly, and I developed that pride which well-dressed boys generally have. She was careful about my associates, and I myself was quite particular. As I look back now I can see that I was a perfect little aristocrat. My mother rarely went to anyone's house, but she did sewing, and there were a great many ladies coming to our cottage. If I were around they would generally call me, and ask me my name and age and tell my mother what a pretty boy I was. Some of them would pat me on the head and kiss me.

My mother was kept very busy with her sewing; sometimes she would have another woman helping her. I think she must have derived a fair income from her work. I know, too, that at least once each month she received a letter; I used to watch for the postman, get the letter, and run to her with it; whether she was busy or not she would take it and instantly thrust it into her bosom. I never saw her read one of them. I knew later that these letters contained money and, what was to her, more than money. As busy as she generally was she, however, found time to teach me my letters and figures and how to spell a number of easy words. Always on Sunday evenings she opened the little square piano, and picked out hymns. I can recall now that whenever she played hymns from the book her tempos were always decidedly largo. Sometimes on other evenings when she was not sewing she would play simple accompaniments to some old southern songs which she sang. In these songs she was freer, because she played them by ear. Those evenings on which she opened the little piano were the happiest hours of my childhood. Whenever she started toward the instrument I used to follow her with all the interest and irrepressible joy that a pampered pet dog shows when a package is opened in which he knows there is a sweet bit for him. I used to stand by her side, and often interrupt and annoy her by chiming in with strange harmonies which I found either on the high keys of the treble or low keys of the bass. I remember that I had a particular fondness for the black keys. Always on such evenings, when the music was over, my mother would sit with me in her arms often for a very long time. She would hold me close, softly crooning some old melody without words, all the while gently stroking her face against my head; many and many a night I thus fell asleep. I can see her now, her great dark eyes looking into the fire, to where? No one knew but she. The memory of that picture has more than once kept me from straying too far from the place of purity and safety in which her arms held me.

At a very early age I began to thump on the piano alone, and it was not long before I was able to pick out a few tunes. When I was seven years old I could play by ear all of the hymns and songs that my mother knew. I had also learned the names of the notes in both clefs, but I preferred not to be hampered by notes. About this time several ladies for whom my mother sewed heard me play, and they persuaded her that I should at once be put under a teacher; so arrangements were made for me to study the piano with a lady who was a fairly good musician; at the same time arrangements were made for me to study my books with this lady's daughter. My music teacher had no small difficulty at first in pinning me down to the notes. If she played my lesson over for me I invariably attempted to reproduce the required sounds without the slightest recourse to the written characters. Her daughter, my other teacher, also had her worries. She found that, in reading, whenever I came to words that were difficult or unfamiliar I was prone to bring my imagination to the rescue and read from the picture. She has laughingly told me, since then, that I would sometimes substitute whole sentences and even paragraphs from what meaning I thought the illustrations conveyed. She said she sometimes was not only amused at the fresh treatment I would give an author's subject, but that when I gave some new and sudden turn to the plot of the story she often grew interested and even excited in listening to hear what kind of a denouement I would bring about. But I am sure this was not due to dullness, for I made rapid progress in both my music and my books.

And so, for a couple of years my life was divided between my music and my school books. Music took up the greater part of my time. I had no playmates, but amused myself with games—some of them my own invention—which could be played alone. I knew a few boys whom I had met at the church which I attended with my mother, but I had formed no close friendships with any of them. Then, when I was nine years old, my mother decided to enter me in the public school, so all at once I found myself thrown among a crowd of boys of all sizes and kinds; some of them seemed to me like savages. I shall never forget the bewilderment, the pain, the heart-sickness of that first day at school. I seemed to be the only stranger in the place; every other boy seemed to know every other boy. I was fortunate enough, however, to be assigned to a teacher who knew me; my mother made her dresses. She was one of the ladies who used to pat me on the head and kiss me. She had the tact to address a few words directly to me; this gave me a certain sort of standing in the class, and put me somewhat at ease.

Within a few days I had made one staunch friend, and was on fairly good terms with most of the boys. I was shy of the girls, and remained so; even now, a word or look from a pretty woman sets me all a-tremble. This friend I bound to me with hooks of steel in a very simple way. He was a big awkward boy with a face full of freckles and a head full of very red hair. He was perhaps fourteen years of age; that is, four or five years older than any other boy in the class. This seniority was due to the fact that he had spent twice the required amount of time in several of the preceding classes. I had not been at school many hours before I felt that "Red Head"—as I involuntarily called him—and I were to be friends. I do not doubt that this feeling was strengthened by the fact that I had been quick enough to see that a big, strong boy was a friend to be desired at a public school; and, perhaps, in spite of his dullness, "Red Head" had been able to discern that I could be of service to him. At any rate there was a simultaneous mutual attraction.

The teacher had strung the class promiscuously round the walls of the room for a sort of trial heat for places of rank; when the line was straightened out I found that by skillful maneuvering I had placed myself third, and had piloted "Red Head" to the place next to me. The teacher began by giving us to spell the words corresponding to our order in the line. "Spell first." "Spell second." "Spell third." I rattled off, "t-h-i-r-d, third," in a way which said, "Why don't you give us something hard?" As the words went down the line I could see how lucky I had been to get a good place together with an easy word. As young as I was I felt impressed with the unfairness of the whole proceeding when I saw the tailenders going down before "twelfth" and "twentieth," and I felt sorry for those who had to spell such words in order to hold a low position. "Spell fourth." "Red Head," with his hands clutched tightly behind his back, began bravely, "f-o-r-t-h." Like a flash a score of hands went up, and the teacher began saying, "No snapping of fingers, no snapping of fingers." This was the first word missed, and it seemed to me that some of the scholars were about to lose their senses; some were dancing up and down on one foot with a hand above their heads, the fingers working furiously, and joy beaming all over their faces; others stood still, their hands raised not so high, their fingers working less rapidly, and their faces expressing not quite so much happiness; there were still others who did not move nor raise their hands, but stood with great wrinkles on their foreheads, looking very thoughtful.

The whole thing was new to me, and I did not raise my hand, but slyly whispered the letter "u" to "Red Head" several times. "Second chance," said the teacher. The hands went down and the class became quiet. "Red Head," his face now red, after looking beseechingly at the ceiling, then pitiably at the floor, began very haltingly, "f-u-." Immediately an impulse to raise hands went through the class, but the teacher checked it, and poor "Red Head," though he knew that each letter he added only took him farther out of the way, went doggedly on and finished, "r-t-h." The hand raising was now repeated with more hubbub and excitement than at first. Those who before had not moved a finger were now waving their hands above their heads. "Red Head" felt that he was lost. He looked very big and foolish, and some of the scholars began to snicker. His helpless condition went straight to my heart, and gripped my sympathies. I felt that if he failed it would in some way be my failure. I raised my hand, and under cover of the excitement and the teacher's attempts to regain order, I hurriedly shot up into his ear twice, quite distinctly, "f-o-u-r-t-h," "f-o-u-r-t-h." The teacher tapped on her desk and said, "Third and last chance." The hands came down, the silence became oppressive. "Red Head" began, "f"—Since that day I have waited anxiously for many a turn of the wheel of fortune, but never under greater tension than I watched for the order in which those letters would fall from "Red's" lips—"o-u-r-t-h." A sigh of relief and disappointment went up from the class. Afterwards, through all our school days, "Red Head" shared my wit and quickness and I benefited by his strength and dogged faithfulness.

There were some black and brown boys and girls in the school, and several of them were in my class. One of the boys strongly attracted my attention from the first day I saw him. His face was as black as night, but shone as though it was polished; he had sparkling eyes, and when he opened his mouth he displayed glistening white teeth. It struck me at once as appropriate to call him "Shiny face," or "Shiny eyes," or "Shiny teeth," and I spoke of him often by one of these names to the other boys. These terms were finally merged into "Shiny," and to that name he answered good-naturedly during the balance of his public school days.

"Shiny" was considered without question to be the best speller, the best reader, the best penman, in a word, the best scholar, in the class. He was very quick to catch anything; but, nevertheless, studied hard; thus he possessed two powers very rarely combined in one boy. I saw him year after year, on up into the high school, win the majority of the prizes for punctuality, deportment, essay writing and declamation. Yet it did not take me long to discover that, in spite of his standing as a scholar, he was in some way looked down upon.

The other black boys and girls were still more looked down upon. Some of the boys often spoke of them as "niggers." Sometimes on the way home from school a crowd would walk behind them repeating:

"Nigger, nigger, never die,
Black face and shiny eye."

On one such afternoon one of the black boys turned suddenly on his tormentors, and hurled a slate; it struck one of the white boys in the mouth, cutting a slight gash in his lip. At sight of the blood the boy who had thrown the slate ran, and his companions quickly followed. We ran after them pelting them with stones until they separated in several directions. I was very much wrought up over the affair, and went home and told my mother how one of the "niggers" had struck a boy with a slate. I shall never forget how she turned on me. "Don't you ever use that word again," she said, "and don't you ever bother the colored children at school. You ought to be ashamed of yourself." I did hang my head in shame, but not because she had convinced me that I had done wrong, but because I was hurt by the first sharp word she had ever given me.

My school days ran along very pleasantly. I stood well in my studies, not always so well with regard to my behavior. I was never guilty of any serious misconduct, but my love of fun sometimes got me into trouble. I remember, however, that my sense of humor was so sly that most of the trouble usually fell on the head of the other fellow. My ability to play on the piano at school exercises was looked upon as little short of marvelous in a boy of my age. I was not chummy with many of my mates, but, on the whole, was about as popular as it is good for a boy to be.

One day near the end of my second term at school the principal came into our room, and after talking to the teacher, for some reason said, "I wish all of the white scholars to stand for a moment." I rose with the others. The teacher looked at me, and calling my name said, "You sit down for the present, and rise with the others." I did not quite understand her, and questioned, "Ma'm?" She repeated with a softer tone in her voice, "You sit down now, and rise with the others." I sat down dazed. I saw and heard nothing. When the others were asked to rise I did not know it. When school was dismissed I went out in a kind of stupor. A few of the white boys jeered me, saying, "Oh, you're a nigger too." I heard some black children say, "We knew he was colored." "Shiny" said to them, "Come along, don't tease him," and thereby won my undying gratitude.

I hurried on as fast as I could, and had gone some distance before I perceived that "Red Head" was walking by my side. After a while he said to me, "Le' me carry your books." I gave him my strap without being able to answer. When we got to my gate he said as he handed me my books, "Say, you know my big red agate? I can't shoot with it any more. I'm going to bring it to school for you to-morrow." I took my books and ran into the house. As I passed through the hallway I saw that my mother was busy with one of her customers; I rushed up into my own little room, shut the door, and went quickly to where my looking-glass hung on the wall. For an instant I was afraid to look, but when I did I looked long and earnestly. I had often heard people say to my mother, "What a pretty boy you have." I was accustomed to hear remarks about my beauty; but, now, for the first time, I became conscious of it, and recognized it. I noticed the ivory whiteness of my skin, the beauty of my mouth, the size and liquid darkness of my eyes, and how the long black lashes that fringed and shaded them produced an effect that was strangely fascinating even to me. I noticed the softness and glossiness of my dark hair that fell in waves over my temples, making my forehead appear whiter than it really was. How long I stood there gazing at my image I do not know. When I came out and reached the head of the stairs, I heard the lady who had been with my mother going out. I ran downstairs, and rushed to where my mother was sitting with a piece of work in her hands. I buried my head in her lap and blurted out, "Mother, mother, tell me, am I a nigger?" I could not see her face, but I knew the piece of work dropped to the floor, and I felt her hands on my head. I looked up into her face and repeated, "Tell me, mother, am I a nigger?" There were tears in her eyes, and I could see that she was suffering for me. And then it was that I looked at her critically for the first time. I had thought of her in a childish way only as the most beautiful woman in the world; now I looked at her searching for defects. I could see that her skin was almost brown, that her hair was not so soft as mine, and that she did differ in some way from the other ladies who came to the house; yet, even so, I could see that she was very beautiful, more beautiful than any of them. She must have felt that I was examining her, for she hid her face in my hair, and said with difficulty, "No, my darling, you are not a nigger." She went on, "You are as good as anybody; if anyone calls you a nigger don't notice them." But the more she talked the less was I reassured, and I stopped her by asking, "Well, mother, am I white? Are you white?" She answered tremblingly, "No, I am not white, but you—your father is one of the greatest men in the country—the best blood of the South is in you—" This suddenly opened up in my heart a fresh chasm of misgiving and fear, and I almost fiercely demanded, "Who is my father? Where is he?" She stroked my hair and said, "I'll tell you about him some day." I sobbed, "I want to know now." She answered, "No, not now."

Perhaps it had to he done, but I have never forgiven the woman who did it so cruelly. It may be that she never knew that she gave me a sword-thrust that day in school which was years in healing.

CHAPTER V

The next morning I got out of the car at Jacksonville[1] with a stiff and aching body. I determined to ask no more porters, not even my benefactor, about stopping places; so I found myself on the street not knowing where to go. I walked along listlessly until I met a colored man who had the appearance of a preacher. I asked him if he could direct me to a respectable boarding-house for colored people. He said that if I walked along with him in the direction he was going he would show me such a place. I turned and walked at his side. He proved to be a minister, and asked me a great many direct questions about myself. I answered as many as I saw fit to answer; the others I evaded or ignored. At length, we stopped in front of a frame house, and my guide informed me that it was the place. A woman was standing in the doorway, and he called to her saying that he had brought her a new boarder. I thanked him for his trouble, and after he had urged upon me to attend his church while I was in the city, he went on his way.

I went in and found the house neat and not uncomfortable. The parlor was furnished with cane-bottomed chairs, each of which was adorned with a white crocheted tidy.[2] The mantel over the fireplace had a white crocheted cover; a marble-topped center table held a lamp, a photograph album and several trinkets, each of which was set upon a white crocheted mat. There was a cottage organ in a corner of the room, and I noted that the lamp-racks upon it were covered with white crocheted mats. There was a matting on the floor, but a white crocheted carpet would not have been out of keeping. I made arrangements with the landlady for my hoard and lodging; the amount was, I think, three dollars and a half a week. She was a rather fine looking, stout, brown-skinned woman of about forty years of age. Her husband was a light colored Cuban, a man about one half her size, and one whose age could not be guessed from his appearance. He was small in size, but a handsome black mustache and typical Spanish eyes redeemed him from insignificance.

I was in time for breakfast, and at the table I had the opportunity to see my fellow-boarders. There were eight or ten of them. Two, as I afterwards learned, were colored Americans. All of them were cigar makers and worked in one of

[1]Jacksonville, Florida. [2]A decorative covering.

the large factories—cigar making is the one trade in which the color-line is not drawn. The conversation was carried on entirely in Spanish, and my ignorance of the language subjected me more to alarm than embarrassment. I had never heard such uproarious conversation; everybody talked at once, loud exclamations, rolling "*carambas,*"[3] menacing gesticulations with knives, forks, and spoons. I looked every moment for the clash of blows. One man was emphasizing his remarks by flourishing a cup in his hand, seemingly forgetful of the fact that it was nearly full of hot coffee. He ended by emptying it over what was, relatively, the only quiet man at the table excepting myself, bringing from him a volley of language which made the others appear dumb by comparison. I soon learned that in all of this clatter of voices and table utensils they were discussing purely ordinary affairs and arguing about mere trifles, and that not the least ill-feeling was aroused. It was not long before I enjoyed the spirited chatter and badinage at the table as much as I did my meals,—and the meals were not bad.

I spent the afternoon in looking around the town. The streets were sandy, but were well shaded by fine oak trees, and far preferable to the clay roads of Atlanta. One or two public squares with green grass and trees gave the city a touch of freshness. That night after supper I spoke to my landlady and her husband about my intentions. They told me that the big winter hotels would not open within two months. It can easily be imagined what effect this news had on me. I spoke to them frankly about my financial condition and related the main fact of my misfortune in Atlanta. I modestly mentioned my ability to teach music and asked if there was any likelihood of my being able to get some scholars. My landlady suggested that I speak to the preacher who had shown me her house; she felt sure that through his influence I should be able to get up a class in piano. She added, however, that the colored people were poor, and that the general price for music lessons was only twenty-five cents. I noticed that the thought of my teaching white pupils did not even remotely enter her mind. None of this information made my prospects look much brighter.

The husband, who up to this time had allowed the woman to do most of the talking, gave me the first bit of tangible hope; he said that he could get me a job as a "stripper" in the factory where he worked, and that if I succeeded in getting some music pupils I could teach a couple of them every night, and so make a living until something better turned up. He went on to say that it would not be a bad thing for me to stay at the factory and learn my trade as a cigar maker, and impressed on me that, for a young man knocking about the country, a trade was a handy thing to have. I determined to accept his offer and thanked him heartily. In fact, I became enthusiastic, not only because I saw a way out of my financial troubles, but also because I was eager and curious over the new experience I was about to enter. I wanted to know all about the cigar making business. This narrowed the conversation down to the husband and myself, so the wife went in and left us talking.

He was what is called a *regalía*[4] workman, and earned from thirty-five to forty dollars a week. He generally worked a sixty dollar job; that is, he made cigars for which he was paid at the rate of sixty dollars per thousand. It was impossible for him to make a thousand in a week because he had to work very carefully and slowly. Each cigar was made entirely by hand. Each piece of filler and each

[3]*Caramba:* a Spanish word expressing surprise or strong feeling.
[4]He was paid for the volume of his production rather than for the number of hours he worked.

wrapper had to be selected with care. He was able to make a bundle of one hundred cigars in a day, not one of which could be told from the others by any difference in size or shape, or even by any appreciable difference in weight. This was the acme of artistic skill in cigar making. Workmen of this class were rare, never more than three or four of them in one factory, and it was never necessary for them to remain out of work. There were men who made two, three, and four hundred cigars of the cheaper grades in a day; they had to be very fast in order to make decent week's wages. Cigar making was a rather independent trade; the men went to work when they pleased and knocked off when they felt like doing so. As a class the workmen were careless and improvident; some very rapid makers would not work more than three or four days out of the week, and there were others who never showed up at the factory on Mondays. "Strippers" were the boys who pulled the long stems from the tobacco leaves. After they had served at that work for a certain time they were given tables as apprentices.

All of this was interesting to me; and we drifted along in conversation until my companion struck the subject nearest his heart, the independence of Cuba. He was an exile from the island, and a prominent member of the Jacksonville *Junta*.[5] Every week sums of money were collected from *juntas* all over the country. This money went to buy arms and ammunition for the insurgents. As the man sat there nervously smoking his long, "green" cigar, and telling me of the Gomezes, both the white one and the black one, of Macco and Bandera, he grew positively eloquent. He also showed that he was a man of considerable education and reading. He spoke English excellently, and frequently surprised me by using words one would hardly expect from a foreigner. The first one of this class of words he employed almost shocked me, and I never forgot it,'twas "ramify."[6] We sat on the piazza until after ten o'clock. When he arose to go in to bed it was with the understanding that I should start in the factory on the next day.

I began work the next morning seated at a barrel with another boy, who showed me how to strip the stems from the leaves, to smooth out each half leaf, and to put the "rights" together in one pile, and the "lefts" together in another pile on the edge of the barrel. My fingers, strong and sensitive from their long training, were well adapted to this kind of work; and within two weeks I was accounted the fastest "stripper" in the factory. At first the heavy odor of the tobacco almost sickened me; but when I became accustomed to it I liked the smell. I was now earning four dollars a week, and was soon able to pick up a couple more by teaching a few scholars at night, whom I had secured through the good offices of the preacher I had met on my first morning in Jacksonville.

At the end of about three months, through my skill as a "stripper" and the influence of my landlord, I was advanced to a table, and began to learn my trade; in fact, more than my trade; for I learned not only to make cigars, but also to smoke, to swear, and to speak Spanish. I discovered that I had a talent for languages as well as for music. The rapidity and ease with which I acquired Spanish astonished my associates. In a short time I was able not only to understand most of what was said at the table during meals, but to join in the conversation. I bought a method for learning the Spanish language, and with the aid of my landlord as a teacher, by constant practice with my fellow workmen,

[5]An interest group. In this case, the cause is Cuban independence.
[6]To result in complications.

and by regularly reading the Cuban newspapers, and finally some books of standard Spanish literature which were at the house, I was able in less than a year to speak like a native. In fact, it was my pride that I spoke better Spanish than many of the Cuban workmen at the factory.

After I had been in the factory a little over a year, I was repaid for all the effort I had put forth to learn Spanish by being selected as "reader." The "reader" is quite an institution in all cigar factories which employ Spanish-speaking workmen. He sits in the center of the large room in which the cigar makers work and reads to them for a certain number of hours each day all the important news from the papers and whatever else he may consider would be interesting. He often selects an exciting novel, and reads it in daily installments. He must, of course, have a good voice, but he must also have a reputation among the men for intelligence, for being well posted and having in his head a stock of varied information. He is generally the final authority on all arguments which arise; and, in a cigar factory, these arguments are many and frequent, ranging from discussions on the respective and relative merits of rival baseball clubs to the duration of the sun's light and energy—cigar-making is a trade in which talk does not interfere with work. My position as "reader" not only released me from the rather monotonous work of rolling cigars, and gave me something more in accord with my tastes, but also added considerably to my income. I was now earning about twenty-five dollars a week, and was able to give up my peripatetic method of giving music lessons. I hired a piano and taught only those who could arrange to take their lessons where I lived. I finally gave up teaching entirely; as what I made scarcely paid for my time and trouble. I kept the piano, however, in order to keep up my own studies, and occasionally I played at some church concert or other charitable entertainment.

Through my music teaching and my not absolutely irregular attendance at church I became acquainted with the best class of colored people in Jacksonville. This was really my entrance into the race. It was my initiation into what I have termed the freemasonry of the race. I had formulated a theory of what it was to be colored, now I was getting the practice. The novelty of my position caused me to observe and consider things which, I think, entirely escaped the young men I associated with; or, at least, were so commonplace to them as not to attract their attention. And of many of the impressions which came to me then I have realized the full import only within the past few years, since I have had a broader knowledge of men and history, and a fuller comprehension of the tremendous struggle which is going on between the races in the South.

It is a struggle; for though the black man fights passively he nevertheless fights; and his passive resistance is more effective at present than active resistance could possibly be. He bears the fury of the storm as does the willow tree.

It is a struggle; for though the white man of the South may be too proud to admit it, he is, nevertheless, using in the contest his best energies; he is devoting to it the greater part of his thought and much of his endeavor. The South to-day stands panting and almost breathless from its exertions.

And how the scene of the struggle has shifted! The battle was first waged over the right of the Negro to be classed as a human being with a soul; later, as to whether he had sufficient intellect to master even the rudiments of learning; and to-day it is being fought out over his social recognition.

I said somewhere in the early part of this narrative that because the colored man looked at everything through the prism of his relationship to society as a *colored* man, and because most of his mental efforts ran through the narrow channel bounded by his rights and his wrongs, it was to be wondered at that he has progressed so broadly as he has. The same thing may be said of the white man of the South; most of his mental efforts run through one narrow channel; his life as a man and a citizen, many of his financial activities and all of his political activities are impassably limited by the ever present "Negro question." I am sure it would be safe to wager that no group of Southern white men could get together and talk for sixty minutes without bringing up the "race question." If a Northern white man happened to be in the group the time could be safely cut to thirty minutes. In this respect I consider the condition of the whites more to be deplored than that of the blacks. Here, a truly great people, a people that produced a majority of the great historic Americans from Washington to Lincoln now forced to use up its energies in a conflict as lamentable as it is violent.

I shall give the observations I made in Jacksonville as seen through the light of after years; and they apply generally to every Southern community. The colored people may be said to be roughly divided into three classes, not so much in respect to themselves as in respect to their relations with the whites. There are those constituting what might be called the desperate class,—the men who work in the lumber and turpentine camps, the ex-convicts, the bar-room loafers are all in this class. These men conform to the requirements of civilization much as a trained lion with low muttered growls goes through his stunts under the crack of the trainer's whip. They cherish a sullen hatred for all white men, and they value life as cheap. I have heard more than one of them say, "I'll go to hell for the first white man that bothers me." Many who have expressed that sentiment have kept their word; and it is that fact which gives such prominence to this class; for in numbers it is but a small proportion of the colored people, but it often dominates public opinion concerning the whole race. Happily, this class represents the black people of the South far below their normal physical and moral condition, but in its increase lies the possibility of grave dangers. I am sure there is no more urgent work before the white South, not only for its present happiness, but its future safety, than the decreasing of this class of blacks. And it is not at all a hopeless class; for these men are but the creatures of conditions, as much so as the slum and criminal elements of all the great cities of the world are creatures of conditions. Decreasing their number by shooting and burning them off will not be successful; for these men are truly desperate, and thoughts of death, however terrible, have little effect in deterring them from acts the result of hatred or degeneracy. This class of blacks hate everything covered by a white skin, and in return they are loathed by the whites. The whites regard them just about as a man would a vicious mule, a thing to be worked, driven and beaten, and killed for kicking.

The second class, as regards the relation between blacks and whites, comprises the servants, the washer-women, the waiters, the cooks, the coachmen, and all who are connected with the whites by domestic service. These may be generally characterized as simple, kindhearted and faithful; not over fine in their moral deductions, but intensely religious, and relatively,—such matters can be judged only relatively,—about as honest and wholesome in their lives as any other grade of society. Any white person is "good" who treats them kindly, and they love them for that kindness. In return, the white people with whom they have to do regard them with indulgent affection. They come into close daily contact with the whites, and may be called the connecting link between whites and blacks; in fact, it is through them that the whites know the rest of their colored neighbors. Between this class of the blacks and the whites there is little or no friction.

The third class is composed of the independent workmen and tradesmen, and of the well-to-do and educated colored people; and, strange to say, for a directly opposite reason they are as far removed from the whites as the members of the first class I mentioned. These people live in a little world of their own; in fact, I concluded that if a colored man wanted to separate himself from his white neighbors he had but to acquire some money, education and culture, and to live in accordance. For example, the proudest and fairest lady in the South could with propriety—and it is what she would most likely do—go to the cabin of Aunt Mary her cook, if Aunt Mary were sick, and minister to comfort with her own hands; but if Mary's daughter, Eliza, a girl who used to run around my lady's kitchen, but who has received an education and married a prosperous young colored man, were at death's door, my lady would no more think of crossing the threshold of Eliza's cottage than she would of going into a barroom for a drink.

I was walking down the street one day with a young man who was born in Jacksonville, but had been away to prepare himself for a professional life. We passed a young white man, and my companion said to me, "You see that young man? We grew up together, we have played, hunted, and fished together, we have even eaten and slept together, and now since I have come back home he barely speaks to me." The fact that the whites of the South despise and ill-treat the desperate class of blacks is not only explainable according to the ancient laws of human nature, but it is not nearly so serious or important as the fact that as the progressive colored people advance they constantly widen the gulf between themselves and their white neighbors. I think that the white people somehow feel that colored people who have education and money, who wear good clothes and live in comfortable houses, are "putting on airs," that they do these things for the sole purpose of "spiting the white folks," or are, at best, going through a sort of monkey-like imitation. Of course, such feelings can only cause irritation or breed disgust. It seems that the whites have not yet been able to realize and understand that these people in striving to better their physical and social surroundings in accordance with their financial and intellectual progress are simply obeying an impulse which is common to human nature the world over. I am in grave doubt as to whether the greater part of the friction in the South is caused by the whites having a natural antipathy to Negroes as a race, or an acquired antipathy to Negroes in certain relations to themselves. However that may be, there is to my mind no more pathetic side of this many sided question than the isolated position into which are forced the very colored people who most need and who could best appreciate sympathetic coöperation; and their position grows tragic when the effort is made to couple them, whether or no, with the Negroes of the first class I mentioned.

This latter class of colored people are well disposed towards the whites, and always willing to meet them more than half way. They, however, feel keenly any injustice or gross discrimination, and generally show their resentment. The effort is sometimes made to convey the impression that the better class of colored people fight against riding in "Jim Crow" cars[7] because they want to ride with white people or object to being with humbler members of their own race. The truth is they object to the humiliation of being forced to ride in a *particular* car, aside from the fact that that car is distinctly inferior, and that they are required to pay full first-class fare. To say that the whites are forced to ride in the superior car is less than a joke. And, too, odd as it may sound, refined colored people get no more pleasure out of riding with offensive Negroes than anybody else would get.

I can realize more fully than I could years ago that the position of the advanced element of the colored race is often very trying. They are the ones among the blacks who carry the entire weight of the race question; it worries the others very little, and I believe the only thing which at times sustains them is that they know that they are in the right. On the other hand, this class of colored people get a good deal of pleasure out of life; their existence is far from being one long groan about their condition. Out of a chaos of ignorance and poverty they have evolved a social life of which they need not be ashamed. In cities where the professional and well-to-do class is large, they have formed society,—society as discriminating as the actual conditions will allow it to be; I should say, perhaps, society possessing discriminating tendencies which become rules as fast as actual conditions allow. This statement will, I know, sound preposterous, even ridiculous, to some persons; but as this class of colored people is the least known of the race it is not surprising. These social circles are connected throughout the country, and a person in good standing in one city is readily accepted in another. One who is on the outside will often find it a difficult matter to get in. I know of one case personally in which money to the extent of thirty or forty thousand dollars and a fine house, not backed up by a good reputation, after several years of repeated effort, failed to gain entry for the possessor. These people have their dances and dinners and card parties, their musicals and their literary societies. The women attend social affairs dressed in good taste, and the men in evening dress-suits which they own; and the reader will make a mistake to confound these entertainments with the "Bellman's Balls" and "Whitewashers' Picnics" and "Lime Kiln Clubs" with which the humorous press of the country illustrates "Cullud Sassiety."

Jacksonville, when I was there, was a small town, and the number of educated and well-to-do colored people was few; so this society phase of life did not equal what I have since seen in Boston, Washington, Richmond, and Nashville; and it is upon what I have more recently seen in these cities that I have made the observations just above. However, there were many comfortable and pleasant homes in Jacksonville to which I was often invited. I belonged to the literary society—at which we generally discussed the race question—and attended all of the church festivals and other charitable entertainments. In this way I passed three years which were not at all the least enjoyable of my life. In fact, my joy took such an exuberant turn that I fell in love with a young school teacher and began to have dreams of matrimonial bliss; but another turn in the course of my life brought these dreams to an end.

[7]"Jim Crow" is a name for laws and customs that enforced racial segregation; "Jim Crow" cars were railroad cars in which black passengers were required to ride.

I do not wish to mislead my readers into thinking that I led a life in Jacksonville which would make copy as the hero of a Sunday School library book. I was a hale fellow well met with all of the workmen at the factory, most of whom knew little and cared less about social distinctions. From their example I learned to be careless about money; and for that reason I constantly postponed and finally abandoned returning to Atlanta University. It seemed impossible for me to save as much as two hundred dollars. Several of the men at the factory were my intimate friends, and I frequently joined them in their pleasures. During the summer months we went almost every Monday on an excursion to a seaside resort called Pablo Beach. These excursions were always crowded. There was a dancing pavilion, a great deal of drinking and generally a fight or two to add to the excitement. I also contracted the cigar-maker's habit of riding around in a hack on Sunday afternoons. I sometimes went with my cigar-maker friends to public balls that were given at a large hall on one of the main streets. I learned to take a drink occasionally and paid for quite a number that my friends took; but strong liquors never appealed to my appetite. I drank them only when the company I was in required it, and suffered for it afterwards. On the whole, though I was a bit wild, I can't remember that I ever did anything disgraceful, or, as the usual standard for young men goes, anything to forfeit my claim to respectability.

At one of the first public balls I attended I saw the Pullman car porter who had so kindly assisted me in getting to Jacksonville. I went immediately to one of my factory friends and borrowed fifteen dollars with which to repay the loan my benefactor had made me. After I had given him the money, and was thanking him, I noticed that he wore what was, at least, an exact duplicate of my lamented black and gray tie. It was somewhat worn, but distinct enough for me to trace the same odd design which had first attracted my eye. This was enough to arouse my strongest suspicions, but whether it was sufficient for the law to take cognizance of I did not consider. My astonishment and the ironical humor of the situation drove everything else out of my mind.

These balls were attended by a great variety of people. They were generally given by the waiters of some one of the big hotels, and were often patronized by a number of hotel guests who came to "see the sights." The crowd was always noisy, but good-natured; there was much quadrille[8] dancing, and a strong-lunged man called figures in a voice which did not confine itself to the limits of the hall. It is not worth the while for me to describe in detail how these people acted; they conducted themselves in about the same manner as I have seen other people at similar balls conduct themselves. When one has seen something of the world and human nature he must conclude, after all, that between people in like stations of life there is very little difference the world over.

However, it was at one of these balls that I first saw the cake-walk. There was a contest for a gold watch, to be awarded to the hotel head-waiter receiving the greatest number of votes. There was some dancing while the votes were being counted. Then the floor was cleared for the cake-walk. A half-dozen guests from some of the hotels took seats on the stage to act as judges, and twelve or fourteen couples began to walk for a "sure enough" highly decorated cake, which was in plain evidence. The spectators crowded about the space reserved for the

[8]A type of formal square dance.

contestants and watched them with interest and excitement. The couples did not walk around in a circle, but in a square, with the men on the inside. The fine points to be considered were the bearing of the men, the precision with which they turned the corners, the grace of the women, and the ease with which they swung around the pivots. The men walked with stately and soldierly step, and the women with considerable grace. The judges arrived at their decision by a process of elimination. The music and the walk continued for some minutes; then both were stopped while the judges conferred, when the walk began again several couples were left out. In this way the contest was finally narrowed down to three or four couples. Then the excitement became intense; there was much partisan cheering as one couple or another would execute a turn in extra elegant style. When the cake was finally awarded the spectators were about evenly divided between those who cheered the winners and those who muttered about the unfairness of the judges. This was the cake-walk in its original form, and it is what the colored performers on the theatrical stage developed into the prancing movements now known all over the world, and which some Parisian critics pronounced the acme of poetic motion.

There are a great many colored people who are ashamed of the cake-walk, but I think they ought to be proud of it. It is my opinion that the colored people of this country have done four things which refute the oft advanced theory that they are an absolutely inferior race, which demonstrate that they have originality and artistic conception; and, what is more, the power of creating that which can influence and appeal universally. The first two of these are the Uncle Remus stories, collected by Joel Chandler Harris,[9] and the Jubilee songs, to which the Fisk singers made the public and the skilled musicians of both America and Europe listen. The other two are ragtime music and the cake-walk. No one who has traveled can question the world-conquering influence of ragtime; and I do not think it would be an exaggeration to say that in Europe the United States is popularly known better by ragtime than by anything else it has produced in a generation. In Paris they call it American music. The newspapers have already told how the practice of intricate cake walk steps has taken up the time of European royalty and nobility. These are lower forms of art, but they give evidence of a power that will some day be applied to the higher forms. In this measure, at least, and aside from the number of prominent individuals the colored people of the United States have produced, the race has been a world influence; and all of the Indians between Alaska and Patagonia[10] haven't done as much.

Just when I was beginning to look upon Jacksonville as my permanent home, and was beginning to plan about marrying the young school teacher, raising a family, and working in a cigar factory the rest of my life, for some reason, which I do not now remember, the factory at which I worked was indefinitely shut down. Some of the men got work in other factories in town, some decided to go to Key West and Tampa, others made up their minds to go to New York for work. All at once a desire like a fever seized me to see the North again, and I cast my lot with those bound for New York.

[9]American journalist and fiction-writer (1848–1908).
[10]Located at the southern tip of South America.

CHAPTER XI

I have now reached that part of my narrative where I must be brief, and touch only lightly on important facts; therefore, the reader must make up his mind to pardon skips and jumps and meager details.

When I reached New York I was completely lost. I could not have felt more a stranger had I been suddenly dropped into Constantinople.[11] I knew not where to turn or how to strike out. I was so oppressed by a feeling of loneliness that the temptation to visit my old home in Connecticut was well nigh irresistible. I reasoned, however, that unless I found my old music teacher, I should be, after so many years of absence, as much of a stranger there as in New York; and, furthermore, that in view of the step which I had decided to take, such a visit would be injudicious. I remembered, too, that I had some property there in the shape of a piano and a few books, but decided that it would not be worth what it might cost me to take possession.

By reason of the fact that my living expenses in the South had been very small, I still had nearly four hundred dollars of my capital left. In contemplation of this, my natural and acquired Bohemian tastes asserted themselves, and I decided to have a couple of weeks' good time before worrying seriously about the future. I went to Coney Island and the other resorts; took in the pre-season shows along Broadway, and ate at first class restaurants; but I shunned the old Sixth Avenue district as though it were pest infected. My few days of pleasure made appalling inroads upon what cash I had, and caused me to see that it required a good deal of money to live in New York as I wished to live, and that I should have to find, very soon, some more or less profitable employment. I was sure that unknown, without friends or prestige, it would be useless to try to establish myself as a teacher of music; so I gave that means of earning a livelihood scarcely any consideration. And even had I considered it possible to secure pupils, as I then felt, I should have hesitated about taking up a work in which the chances for any considerable financial success are necessarily so small. I had made up my mind that since I was not going to be a Negro, I would avail myself of every possible opportunity to make a white man's success; and that, if it can be summed up in any one word, means "money."

I watched the "want" columns in the newspapers and answered a number of advertisements; but in each case found the positions were such as I could not fill or did not want. I also spent several dollars for "ads" which brought me no replies. In this way I came to know the hopes and disappointments of a large and pitiable class of humanity in this great city, the people who look for work through the newspapers. After some days of this sort of experience, I concluded that the main difficulty with me was that I was not prepared for what I wanted to do. I then decided upon a course which, for an artist, showed an uncommon amount of practical sense and judgment. I made up my mind to enter a business college. I took a small room, ate at lunch counters, in order to economize, and pursued my studies with the zeal that I have always been able to put into any work upon which I set my heart. Yet, in spite of all my economy, when

[11] Istanbul, Turkey. As Constantinople it was capital of the Eastern Roman Empire and then the Byzantine Empire.

I had been at the school for several months, my funds gave out completely. I reached the point where I could not afford sufficient food for each day. In this plight, I was glad to get, through one of the teachers, a job as an ordinary clerk in a downtown wholesale house. I did my work faithfully, and received a raise of salary before I expected it. I even managed to save a little money out of my modest earnings. In fact, I began then to contract the money fever, which later took strong possession of me. I kept my eyes open, watching for a chance to better my condition. It finally came in the form of a position with a house which was at the time establishing a South American department. My knowledge of Spanish was, of course, the principal cause of my good luck; and it did more for me; it placed me where the other clerks were practically put out of competition with me. I was not slow in taking advantage of the opportunity to make myself indispensable to the firm.

What an interesting and absorbing game is money making! After each deposit at my savings-bank, I used to sit and figure out, all over again, my principal and interest, and make calculations on what the increase would be in such and such time. Out of this I derived a great deal of pleasure. I denied myself as much as possible in order to swell my savings. Even so much as I enjoyed smoking, I limited myself to an occasional cigar, and that was generally of a variety which in my old days at the "Club" was known as a "Henry Mud."[12] Drinking I cut out altogether, but that was no great sacrifice.

The day on which I was able to figure up $1,000.00 marked an epoch in my life. And this was not because I had never before had money. In my gambling days and while I was with my "millionaire" I handled sums running high up into the hundreds; but they had come to me like fairy god-mother's gifts, and at a time when my conception of money was that it was made only to spend. Here, on the other hand, was a thousand dollars which I had earned by days of honest and patient work, a thousand dollars which I had carefully watched grow from the first dollar; and I experienced, in owning them, a pride and satisfaction which to me was an entirely new sensation. As my capital went over the thousand dollar mark, I was puzzled to know what to do with it, how to put it to the most advantageous use. I turned down first one scheme and then another, as though they had been devised for the sole purpose of gobbling up my money. I finally listened to a friend who advised me to put all I had in New York real estate; and under his guidance I took equity in a piece of property on which stood a rickety old tenement-house. I did not regret following this friend's advice, for in something like six months I disposed of my equity for more than double my investment. From that time on I devoted myself to the study of New York real estate, and watched for opportunities to make similar investments. In spite of two or three speculations which did not turn out well, I have been remarkably successful. To-day I am the owner and part-owner of several flat-houses. I have changed my place of employment four times since returning to New York, and each change has been a decided advancement. Concerning the position which I now hold, I shall say nothing except that it pays extremely well.

As my outlook on the world grew brighter, I began to mingle in the social circles of the men with whom I came in contact; and gradually, by a process of elimination, I reached a grade of society of no small degree of culture. My

[12]An inexpensive cigar.

appearance was always good and my ability to play on the piano, especially ragtime, which was then at the height of its vogue, made me a welcome guest. The anomaly of my social position often appealed strongly to my sense of humor. I frequently smiled inwardly at some remark not altogether complimentary to people of color; and more than once I felt like declaiming, "I am a colored man. Do I not disprove the theory that one drop of Negro blood renders a man unfit?" Many a night when I returned to my room after an enjoyable evening, I laughed heartily over what struck me as the capital joke I was playing.

Then I met her, and what I had regarded as a joke was gradually changed into the most serious question of my life. I first saw her at a musical which was given one evening at a house to which I was frequently invited. I did not notice her among the other guests before she came forward and sang two sad little songs. When she began I was out in the hallway where many of the men were gathered; but with the first few notes I crowded with others into the doorway to see who the singer was. When I saw the girl, the surprise which I had felt at the first sound of her voice was heightened; she was almost tall and quite slender, with lustrous yellow hair and eyes so blue as to appear almost black. She was as white as a lily, and she was dressed in white. Indeed, she seemed to me the most dazzlingly white thing I had ever seen. But it was not her delicate beauty which attracted me most; it was her voice, a voice which made one wonder how tones of such passionate color could come from so fragile a body.

I determined that when the program was over I would seek an introduction to her; but at the moment, instead of being the easy man of the world, I became again the bashful boy of fourteen, and my courage failed me. I contented myself with hovering as near her as politeness would permit; near enough to hear her voice, which in conversation was low, yet thrilling, like the deeper middle tones of a flute. I watched the men gather around her talking and laughing in an easy manner, and wondered how it was possible for them to do it. But destiny, my special destiny, was at work. I was standing near, talking with affected gayety to several young ladies, who, however, must have remarked my preoccupation; for my second sense of hearing was alert to what was being said by the group of which the girl in white was the center, when I heard her say, "I think his playing of Chopin[13] is exquisite." And one of my friends in the group replied, "You haven't met him? Allow me—" then turning to me, "Old man, when you have a moment I wish you to meet Miss——." I don't know what she said to me or what I said to her. I can remember that I tried to be clever, and experienced a growing conviction that I was making myself appear more and more idiotic. I am certain, too, that, in spite of my Italian-like complexion, I was as red as a beet.

Instead of taking the car I walked home. I needed the air and exercise as a sort of sedative. I am not sure whether my troubled condition of mind was due to the fact that I had been struck by love or to the feeling that I had made a bad impression upon her.

As the weeks went by, and when I had met her several more times, I came to know that I was seriously in love; and then began for me days of worry, for I had more than the usual doubts and fears of a young man in love to contend with.

[13]Polish composer Frédéric Chopin (1810–1849), who is especially known for his compositions for the piano.

Up to this time I had assumed and played my rôle as a white man with a certain degree of nonchalance, a carelessness as to the outcome, which made the whole thing more amusing to me than serious; but now I ceased to regard "being a white man" as a sort of practical joke. My acting had called for mere external effects. Now I began to doubt my ability to play the part. I watched her to see if she was scrutinizing me, to see if she was looking for anything in me which made me differ from the other men she knew. In place of an old inward feeling of superiority over many of my friends, I began to doubt myself. I began even to wonder if I really was like the men I associated with; if there was not, after all, an indefinable something which marked a difference.

But, in spite of my doubts and timidity, my affair progressed; and I finally felt sufficiently encouraged to decide to ask her to marry me. Then began the hardest struggle of my life, whether to ask her to marry me under false colors or to tell her the whole truth. My sense of what was exigent made me feel there was no necessity of saying anything; but my inborn sense of honor rebelled at even indirect deception in this case. But however much I moralized on the question, I found it more and more difficult to reach the point of confession. The dread that I might lose her took possession of me each time I sought to speak, and rendered it impossible for me to do so. That moral courage requires more than physical courage is no mere poetic fancy. I am sure I would have found it easier to take the place of a gladiator, no matter how fierce the Numidian lion,[14] than to tell that slender girl that I had Negro blood in my veins. The fact which I had at times wished to cry out, I now wished to hide forever.

During this time we were drawn together a great deal by the mutual bond of music. She loved to hear me play Chopin, and was herself far from being a poor performer of his compositions. I think I carried her every new song that was published which I thought suitable to her voice, and played the accompaniment for her. Over these songs we were like two innocent children with new toys. She had never been anything but innocent; but my innocence was a transformation wrought by my love for her, love which melted away my cynicism and whitened my sullied soul and gave me back the wholesome dreams of my boyhood. There is nothing better in all the world that a man can do for his moral welfare than to love a good woman.

My artistic temperament also underwent an awakening. I spent many hours at my piano, playing over old and new composers. I also wrote several little pieces in a more or less Chopinesque style, which I dedicated to her. And so the weeks and months went by. Often words of love trembled on my lips, but I dared not utter them, because I knew they would have to be followed by other words which I had not the courage to frame. There might have been some other woman in my set with whom I could have fallen in love and asked to marry me without a word of explanation; but the more I knew this girl, the less could I find it in my heart to deceive her. And yet, in spite of this specter that was constantly looming up before me, I could never have believed that life held such happiness as was contained in those dream days of love.

One Saturday afternoon, in early June, I was coming up Fifth Avenue, and at the corner of Twenty-third Street I met her. She had been shopping. We

[14]Numidia was an ancient African kingdom that was conquered by Rome. Lions from Numidia were used in gladiatorial entertainments.

stopped to chat for a moment, and I suggested that we spend half an hour at the Eden Musée.[15] We were standing leaning on the rail in front of a group of figures, more interested in what we had to say to each other than in the group, when my attention became fixed upon a man who stood at my side studying his catalogue. It took me only an instant to recognize in him my old friend "Shiny." My first impulse was to change my position at once. As quick as a flash I considered all the risks I might run in speaking to him, and most especially the delicate question of introducing him to her. I must confess that in my embarrassment and confusion I felt small and mean. But before I could decide what to do he looked around at me and, after an instant, said, "Pardon me; but isn't this——?" The nobler part in me responded to the sound of his voice, and I took his hand in a hearty clasp. Whatever fears I had felt were quickly banished, for he seemed, at a glance, to divine my situation, and let drop no word that would have aroused suspicion as to the truth. With a slight misgiving I presented him to her, and was again relieved of fear. She received the introduction in her usual gracious manner, and without the least hesitancy or embarrassment joined in the conversation. An amusing part about the introduction was that I was upon the point of introducing him as "Shiny," and stammered a second or two before I could recall his name. We chatted for some fifteen minutes. He was spending his vacation North, with the intention of doing four or six weeks' work in one of the summer schools; he was also going to take a bride back with him in the fall. He asked me about myself, but in so diplomatic a way that I found no difficulty in answering him. The polish of his language and the unpedantic manner in which he revealed his culture greatly impressed her; and after we had left the Musée she showed it by questioning me about him. I was surprised at the amount of interest a refined black man could arouse. Even after changes in the conversation she reverted several times to the subject of "Shiny." Whether it was more than mere curiosity I could not tell; but I was convinced that she herself knew very little about prejudice.

Just why it should have done so I do not know; but somehow the "Shiny" incident gave me encouragement and confidence to cast the die of my fate; but I reasoned that since I wanted to marry her only, and since it concerned her alone, I would divulge my secret to no one else, not even her parents.

One evening, a few days afterwards, at her home, we were going over some new songs and compositions, when she asked me, as she often did, to play the "13th Nocturne."[16] When I began she drew a chair near to my right, and sat leaning with her elbow on the end of the piano, her chin resting on her hand, and her eyes reflecting the emotions which the music awoke in her. An impulse which I could not control rushed over me, a wave of exaltation, the music under my fingers sank almost to a whisper, and calling her for the first time by her Christian name, but without daring to look at her, I said, "I love you, I love you, I love you." My fingers were trembling, so that I ceased playing. I felt her hand creep to mine, and when I looked at her her eyes were glistening with tears. I understood, and could scarcely resist the longing to take her in my arms; but I remembered, remembered that which has been the sacrificial altar of so much happiness—Duty; and bending over her hand in mine, I said, "Yes, I love you;

[15] A wax museum in New York City.
[16] A composition by Chopin. A nocturne is a soft, dreamy piece for the piano.

but there is something more, too, that I must tell you." Then I told her, in what words I do not know, the truth. I felt her hand grow cold, and when I looked up she was gazing at me with a wild, fixed stare as though I was some object she had never seen. Under the strange light in her eyes I felt that I was growing black and thick-featured and crimp-haired. She appeared not to have comprehended what I had said. Her lips trembled and she attempted to say something to me; but the words stuck in her throat. Then dropping her head on the piano she began to weep with great sobs that shook her frail body. I tried to console her, and blurted out incoherent words of love; but this seemed only to increase her distress, and when I left her she was still weeping.

When I got into the street I felt very much as I did the night after meeting my father and sister at the opera in Paris, even a similar desperate inclination to get drunk; but my self-control was stronger. This was the only time in my life that I ever felt absolute regret at being colored, that I cursed the drops of African blood in my veins, and wished that I were really white. When I reached my rooms I sat and smoked several cigars while I tried to think out the significance of what had occurred. I reviewed the whole history of our acquaintance, recalled each smile she had given me, each word she had said to me that nourished my hope. I went over the scene we had just gone through, trying to draw from it what was in my favor and what was against me. I was rewarded by feeling confident that she loved me, but I could not estimate what was the effect upon her of my confession. At last, nervous and unhappy, I wrote her a letter, which I dropped into the mail-box before going to bed, in which I said:

> I understand, understand even better than you, and so I suffer even more than you. But why should either of us suffer for what neither of us is to blame? If there is any blame, it belongs to me, and I can only make the old, yet strongest plea that can be offered, I love you; and I know that my love, my great love, infinitely overbalances that blame, and blots it out. What is it that stands in the way of our happiness? It is not what you feel or what I feel; it is not what you are or what I am. It is what others feel and are. But, oh! is that a fair price? In all the endeavors and struggles of life, in all our strivings and longings there is only one thing worth seeking, only one thing worth winning, and that is love. It is not always found; but when it is, there is nothing in all the world for which it can be profitably exchanged.

The second morning after, I received a note from her which stated briefly that she was going up in New Hampshire to spend the summer with relatives there. She made no reference to what had passed between us; nor did she say exactly when she would leave the city. The note contained no single word that gave me any clue to her feelings. I could only gather hope from the fact that she had written at all. On the same evening, with a degree of trepidation which rendered me almost frightened, I went to her house.

I met her mother, who told me that she had left for the country that very afternoon. Her mother treated me in her usual pleasant manner, which fact greatly reassured me; and I left the house with a vague sense of hope stirring in my breast, which sprang from the conviction that she had not yet divulged my secret. But that hope did not remain with me long. I waited one, two, three weeks, nervously examining my mail every day, looking for some word from her. All of the letters received by me seemed so insignificant, so worthless, because there was none from her. The slight buoyancy of spirit which I had felt gradually dissolved into gloomy heartsickness. I became preoccupied, I lost appetite, lost sleep, and lost ambition. Several of my friends intimated to me that perhaps I was working too hard.

She stayed away the whole summer. I did not go to the house, but saw her father at various times, and he was as friendly as ever. Even after I knew that she was back in town I did not go to see her. I determined to wait for some word or sign. I had finally taken refuge and comfort in my pride, pride which, I suppose, I came by naturally enough.

The first time I saw her after her return was one night at the theater. She and her mother sat in company with a young man whom I knew slightly, not many seats away from me. Never did she appear more beautiful; and yet, it may have been my fancy, she seemed a trifle paler and there was a suggestion of haggardness in her countenance. But that only heightened her beauty; the very delicacy of her charm melted down the strength of my pride. My situation made me feel weak and powerless, like a man trying with his bare hands to break the iron bars of his prison cell. When the performance was over I hurried out and placed myself where, unobserved, I could see her as she passed out. The haughtiness of spirit in which I had sought relief was all gone, and I was willing and ready to undergo any humiliation.

Shortly afterward we met at a progressive card party, and during the evening we were thrown together at one of the tables as partners. This was really our first meeting since the eventful night at her house. Strangely enough, in spite of our mutual nervousness, we won every trick of the game, and one of our opponents jokingly quoted the old saw, "Lucky at cards, unlucky in love." Our eyes met, and I am sure that in the momentary glance my whole soul went out to her in one great plea. She lowered her eyes and uttered a nervous little laugh. During the rest of the game I fully merited the unexpressed and expressed abuse of my various partners; for my eyes followed her wherever she was, and I played whatever card my fingers happened to touch.

Later in the evening she went to the piano and began to play very softly, as to herself, the opening bars of the 13th Nocturne. I felt that the psychic moment of my life had come, a moment which if lost could never be called back; and, in as careless a manner as I could assume, I sauntered over to the piano and stood almost bending over her. She continued playing; but, in a voice that was almost a whisper, she called me by my Christian name and said, "I love you, I love you, I love you." I took her place at the piano and played the Nocturne in a manner that silenced the chatter of the company both in and out of the room; involuntarily closing it with the major triad.

We were married the following spring, and went to Europe for several months. It was a double joy for me to be in France again under such conditions.

First there came to us a little girl, with hair and eyes dark like mine, but who is growing to have ways like her mother. Two years later there came a boy, who has my temperament, but is fair like his mother, a little golden-headed god, a face and head that would have delighted the heart of an old Italian master. And this boy, with his mother's eyes and features, occupies an inner sanctuary of my heart; for it was for him that she gave all; and that is the second sacred sorrow of my life.

The few years of our married life were supremely happy, and, perhaps she was even happier than I; for after our marriage, in spite of all the wealth of her love which she lavished upon me, there came a new dread to haunt me, a dread which I cannot explain and which was unfounded, but one that never left me. I was in constant fear that she would discover in me some shortcoming which she would unconsciously attribute to my blood rather than to a failing of human nature. But no cloud ever came to mar our life together; her loss to me is irreparable. My children need a mother's care, but I shall never marry again. It is to my children that I have devoted my life. I no longer have the same fear for myself of my secret being found out; for since my wife's death I have gradually dropped out of social life; but there is nothing I would not suffer to keep the "brand" from being placed upon them.

It is difficult for me to analyze my feelings concerning my present position in the world. Sometimes it seems to me that I have never really been a Negro, that I have been only a privileged spectator of their inner life; at other times I feel that I have been a coward, a deserter, and I am possessed by a strange longing for my mother's people.

Several years ago I attended a great meeting in the interest of Hampton Institute[17] at Carnegie Hall.[18] The Hampton students sang the old songs and awoke memories that left me sad. Among the speakers were R. C. Ogden, Ex-Ambassador Choate, and Mark Twain;[19] but the greatest interest of the audience was centered in Booker T. Washington;[20] and not because he so much surpassed the others in eloquence, but because of what he represented with so much earnestness and faith. And it is this that all of that small but gallant band of colored men who are publicly fighting the cause of their race have behind them. Even those who oppose them know that these men have the eternal principles of right on their side, and they will be victors even though they should go down in defeat. Beside them I feel small and selfish. I am an ordinarily successful white man who has made a little money. They are men who are making history and a race. I, too, might have taken part in a work so glorious.

My love for my children makes me glad that I am what I am, and keeps me from desiring to be otherwise; and yet, when I sometimes open a little box in which I still keep my fast yellowing manuscripts, the only tangible remnants of a vanished dream, a dead ambition, a sacrificed talent, I cannot repress the thought, that, after all, I have chosen the lesser part, that I have sold my birthright for a mess of pottage.[21]

1912

[17]A historically black college in Hampton, Virginia.

[18]A renowned concert hall in New York City.

[19]Robert Curtis Ogden (1836–1913), a Philadelphia businessman and promoter of education; Joseph Hodges Chaote (1832–1917), ambassador to Great Britain from 1899 to 1905; Mark Twain (1835–1910), American writer.

[20]African American educator and man of letters (1856–1915); an alumnus of Hampton Institute.

[21]An allusion to Esau, who sold to his brother Jacob, in return for something to eat, his rights and privileges as the eldest son of their father Isaac (Genesis 25).

W. E. B. Du Bois 1868–1963

In 1997, the July issue of The Crisis was dedicated to a man it praised as "the premier crusading voice of civil rights"—a man who also made an indelible mark on the nineteenth and twentieth centuries as a philosopher, author, teacher, and editor. Although William Edward Burghardt Du Bois (pronounced du-boys*) died on the eve of the Rev. Martin Luther King's famous "I Have a Dream" speech and, therefore, did not live to witness the landmark civil rights legislation that followed, he did much to help realize King's dream. During his lifetime, Du Bois authored nineteen books, edited eighteen books, and contributed hundreds of essays and columns to leading publications throughout the world. Moreover, he was a professor of sociology, history, Latin, Greek, English, and German, as well as a co-founder and leader of the Niagara Movement, the National Negro Academy, the Pan-African Congress, and the National Association for the Advancement of Colored People (NAACP), where he worked for nearly thirty years.*

Du Bois was born in Great Barrington, Massachusetts, on February 23, 1868, five years after Lincoln signed the Emancipation Proclamation outlawing American slavery. Since blacks in Great Barrington faced relatively little discrimination, young Du Bois was able to matriculate in the city's public schools, where he managed, early on, to outdistance his peers. In 1884, he graduated at the top of his high school class and was selected to deliver the class oration, speaking on Wendell Phillips—a famed abolitionist and Massachusetts senator whose leadership qualities Du Bois greatly admired and hoped to emulate. About the speech, Du Bois recalled, "This was my first sweet taste of the world's applause. There were flowers and upturned faces, music and marching, and there was my mother's smile." Unfortunately, a year later his mother and closest friend died, leaving him an orphan. Du Bois had planned to attend Harvard, but without adequate financial support he had little hope of getting there. Knowing his conundrum and recognizing his superior intellect, his community gave him a modest scholarship, which he used to attend Fisk University in Nashville, Tennessee.

The influence of Fisk on Du Bois proved deep and abiding. During his three years on the campus, he enjoyed warm, mutually beneficial relationships with his fellow students, gained a lifelong appreciation of the strength and resiliency of southern black culture, and excelled in his classes. On the surface all seemed well but, in reality, it was not. Du Bois had arrived in Tennessee in 1885, eight years after Reconstruction had ended and federal troops began withdrawing from the South, essentially giving free rein to the Ku Klux Klan (KKK) and other former slaveholders. Having been enraged by their defeat in the Civil War, the KKK began reconstituting white supremacy. Consequently, Nashville was a city still deeply divided by race. There, Du Bois met for the first time large numbers of impoverished, southern blacks and became aware of the realities of their lives. He would later write, "No one but a Negro going into the South without previous experience of color caste can have any conception of its barbarism." Determined to combat the overwhelming racial inequities, the young student spent his summers teaching at a one-room school in rural Tennessee, an experience he recounts in The Souls of Black Folk. *Notes one scholar, "Without the experience of an education at a southern black college, it is questionable whether Du Bois would ever have written* The Souls of Black Folk, *his histories of the slave trade and Reconstruction, or any number of works in which the several regions and societies of the black diaspora are linked and grounded in the black South."*

Shortly after celebrating his twentieth birthday, Du Bois received his bachelor's degree from Fisk and set off for Massachusetts to realize his dream of studying at Harvard College. Seven years later, having graduated cum laude in philosophy and completed further study at the University of Berlin, he received his Ph.D. from Harvard, becoming the first African American to do so. His doctoral thesis, The Suppression of the African Slave Trade to the United States of America *(1896), established him as a historian and became the first volume published in the prestigious Harvard Historical Monograph series. So as the new century was coming into full swing, the self-described "Fisk and Harvard man" was clearly among the nation's most well-trained intellectuals and scholars.*

Academic degrees in hand, Du Bois confidently set out, as he penned in his journal, "to make a name in science, to make a name in art and thus to raise my race." He taught at universities and wrote his own work, and by 1910 he had published his favorite book, the biography John Brown, *and his monumental sociological work,* The Philadelphia Negro: A Social Study. *During this time he had also written his most celebrated work,* The Souls of Black Folk, *a montage of philosophy, history, autobiography, fiction, theory, and music, which Harlem Renaissance novelist Jesse Fauset praised, calling it "a personal favor," and which social scientist Max Weber called a "splendid work" that he wished to translate to German.*

The Souls of Black Folk *remains the most popular and influential of Du Bois's books. It consists of fourteen essays, varying in theme from a history of the Freedmen's Bureau and Reconstruction, to a mournful lament of the author's deceased infant son, Burghardt, to a celebration of Negro spirituals or "sorrow songs," to a critique of Booker T. Washington's politics of racial accommodation. Lyrical and aphoristic, its notions of "the veil," "double consciousness," and "the problem of the color-line" in the twentieth century have become both prophetic and staples of African American literary theory. The book's overarching goal, as Du Bois makes clear throughout, is to theorize about black life in America and, in so doing, to promote the idea of "human brotherhood."*

W. E. B. Du Bois died at the age of ninety-five in Accra, Ghana, having touched countless lives. As editor of the NAACP's official organ, The Crisis, *he helped launch the career of many of America's most talented writers: Zora Neale Hurston, Sterling Brown, Countee Cullen, Jesse Fauset, and Langston Hughes, who once expressed his "gratitude and continued admiration" in a handwritten letter to Du Bois. Appreciative of Du Bois's long fight against injustices on both sides of the Atlantic, the Liberian government awarded him its highest medal, the Liberian Order of African Redemption, in 1941. In the spring of 2003, the University of Wisconsin convened an international conference to commemorate the 100th anniversary of* The Souls of Black Folk, *and in so doing celebrated, as Donald Gibson put it, "one of the most well-regarded, most versatile intellectuals ever to emerge from the American cultural soil."*

FURTHER READING: *The Complete Published Works of W. E. B. Du Bois,* ed. Herbert Aptheker, 1973–1986; *The Correspondence of W. E. B. Du Bois,* 3 vols., ed. H. Aptheker, 1997; *Against Racism: Unpublished Essays, Papers, Addresses 1887–1961,* ed. H. Aptheker, 1988; *Newspaper Columns 1883–1944, 1945–1961,* ed. H. Aptheker, 1986; *W. E. B. Du Bois Speaks: Speeches and Addresses, 1890–1919, 1920–1963,* 2 vols., ed. Philip Foner, 1988; F. Broderick, *W. E. B. Du Bois: A Negro Leader in Time of Crisis,* 1959; *Black Titan: W. E. B. Du Bois,* ed. J. H. Clarke, 1970; S. G. Du Bois, *His Day Is Marching On: A Memoir of W. E. B. Du Bois,* 1971; R. Logan, *W. E. B. Du Bois: A Profile,* 1971; A. Rampersad, *The Art and Imagination of W. E. B. Du Bois,* 1976; J. Moore, *W. E. B. Du Bois,* 1981; J. DeMarco, *The Social Thought of W. E. B. Du Bois,* 1983; *Critical Essays on W. E. B. Du Bois,* ed. W. Andrews, 1985; M. Marable, *W. E. B. Du Bois: Black Radical Democrat,* 1986; G. Horne, *Black and Red: W. E. B. Du Bois and the Afro-American Response to the Cold War, 1944–1963,* 1986; C. West, *The American Evasion of Philosophy: A Genealogy of Pragmatism,* 1989; D. Lewis, *W. E. B. Du Bois: Biography of a Race, 1886–1919,* 1993; E. Sundquist, *To Wake the Nations: Race in the Making of American Literature,* 1993; K. Byerman, *Seizing the Word: History, Art, and Self in the Works of W. E. B. Du Bois,* 1994; K. Pobi-Asamani, *W. E. B. Du Bois: His*

Contribution to Pan-Africanism, 1994; S. Zamir, *Dark Voices: W. E. B. Du Bois and American Thought,* 1995; *W. E. B. Du Bois on Race and Culture: Philosophy, Politics, and Poetics,* ed. B. Bell, E. Grosholz, and J. Stewart, 1996; A. Reed, *W. E. B. Du Bois and American Political Thought,* 1997; D. Lewis, *W. E. B. Du Bois: The Fight for Equality and the American Century, 1919–1963,* 2000; *W. E. B. Du Bois: An Encyclopedia,* ed. G. Horne and M. Young, 2001; *W. E. B. Du Bois and Race: Essays Celebrating the Centennial Publication of The Souls of Black Folk,* ed. C. Fontenot and M. Morgan, 2002.

TEXTS: *The Souls of Black Folk,* 1903; "A Mild Suggestion," *The Crisis,* January 1912; "On Being Crazy," *The Crisis,* June 1923; "The Comet" and "A Litany in Atlanta," *Darkwater,* 1920.

from *THE SOULS OF BLACK FOLK*

THE FORETHOUGHT

Herein lie buried many things which if read with patience may show the strange meaning of being black here in the dawning of the Twentieth Century. This meaning is not without interest to you, Gentle Reader; for the problem of the Twentieth Century is the problem of the color-line.

I pray you, then, receive my little book in all charity, studying my words with me, forgiving mistake and foible for sake of the faith and passion that is in me, and seeking the grain of truth hidden there.

I have sought here to sketch, in vague, uncertain outline, the spiritual world in which ten thousand thousand Americans live and strive. First, in two chapters I have tried to show what Emancipation meant to them, and what was its aftermath. In a third chapter I have pointed out the slow rise of personal leadership, and criticised candidly the leader who bears the chief burden of his race to-day. Then, in two other chapters I have sketched in swift outline the two worlds within and without the Veil, and thus have come to the central problem of training men for life. Venturing now into deeper detail, I have in two chapters studied the struggles of the massed millions of the black peasantry, and in another have sought to make clear the present relations of the sons of master and man.

Leaving, then, the world of the white man, I have stepped within the Veil, raising it that you may view faintly its deeper recesses,—the meaning of its religion, the passion of its human sorrow, and the struggle of its greater souls. All this I have ended with a tale twice told but seldom written.

Some of these thoughts of mine have seen the light before in other guise. For kindly consenting to their republication here, in altered and extended form, I must thank the publishers of *The Atlantic Monthly, The World's Work, The Dial, The New World,* and the *Annals of the American Academy of Political and Social Science.*

Before each chapter, as now printed, stands a bar of the Sorrow Songs,—some echo of haunting melody from the only American music which welled up from black souls in the dark past. And, finally, need I add that I who speak here am bone of the bone and flesh of the flesh of them that live within the Veil?

W. E. B. DU B.

ATLANTA, GA., FEB. 1, 1903.

VII

Of the Black Belt

I am black but comely, O ye daughters of Jerusalem,
As the tents of Kedar, as the curtains of Solomon.
Look not upon me, because I am black,
Because the sun hath looked upon me:
My mother's children were angry with me;
They made me the keeper of the vineyards;
But mine own vineyard have I not kept.

—The Song of Solomon

Out of the North the train thundered, and we woke to see the crimson soil of Georgia stretching away bare and monotonous right and left. Here and there lay straggling, unlovely villages, and lean men loafed leisurely at the depots; then again came the stretch of pines and clay. Yet we did not nod, nor weary of the scene; for this is historic ground. Right across our track, three hundred and sixty years ago, wandered the cavalcade of Hernando de Soto, looking for gold and the Great Sea; and he and his foot-sore captives disappeared yonder in the grim forests to the west. Here sits Atlanta, the city of a hundred hills, with something Western, something Southern, and something quite its own, in its busy life. And a little past Atlanta, to the southwest, is the land of the Cherokees, and there, not far from where Sam Hose was crucified, you may stand on a spot which is to-day the centre of the Negro problem,—the centre of those nine million men who are America's dark heritage from slavery and the slave-trade.

Not only is Georgia thus the geographical focus of our Negro population, but in many other respects, both now and yesterday, the Negro problems have seemed to be centered in this State. No other State in the Union can count a million Negroes among its citizens,—a population as large as the slave population of the whole Union in 1800; no other State fought so long and strenuously to gather this host of Africans. Oglethorpe thought slavery against law and gospel; but the circumstances which gave Georgia its first inhabitants were not calculated to furnish citizens over-nice in their ideas about rum and slaves. Despite the prohibitions of the trustees, these Georgians, like some of their descendants, proceeded to take the law into their own hands; and so pliant were the judges, and so flagrant the smuggling, and so earnest were the prayers of Whitefield, that by the middle of the eighteenth century all restrictions were swept away, and the slave-trade went merrily on for fifty years and more.

Down in Darien, where the Delegal riots took place some summers ago, there used to come a strong protest against slavery from the Scotch Highlanders; and the Moravians of Ebenezer did not like the system. But not till the Haytian Terror of Toussaint was the trade in men even checked; while the national statute of 1808 did not suffice to stop it. How the Africans poured in!—fifty thousand between 1790 and 1810, and then, from Virginia and from smugglers, two thousand a year for many years more. So the thirty thousand Negroes of Georgia in 1790 were doubled in a decade,—were over a hundred thousand in 1810, had reached two hundred thousand in 1820, and half a million at the time of the war. Thus like a snake the black population writhed upward.

But we must hasten on our journey. This that we pass as we leave Atlanta is the ancient land of the Cherokees,—that brave Indian nation which strove so long for its fatherland, until Fate and the United States Government drove them beyond the Mississippi. If you wish to ride with me you must come into the "Jim Crow Car." There will be no objection,—already four other white men, and a little white girl with her nurse, are in there. Usually the races are mixed in there; but the white coach is all white. Of course this car is not so good as the other, but it is fairly clean and comfortable. The discomfort lies chiefly in the hearts of those four black men yonder—and in mine.

We rumble south in quite a business-like way. The bare red clay and pines of Northern Georgia begin to disappear, and in their place appears a rich rolling land, luxuriant, and here and there well tilled. This is the land of the Creek Indians; and a hard time the Georgians had to seize it. The towns grow more frequent and more interesting, and brand-new cotton mills rise on every side. Below Macon the world grows darker; for now we approach the Black Belt,—that strange land of shadows, at which even slaves paled in the past, and whence come now only faint and half-intelligible murmurs to the world beyond. The "Jim Crow Car" grows larger and a shade better; three rough field-hands and two or three white loafers accompany us, and the newsboy still spreads his wares at one end. The sun is setting, but we can see the great cotton country as we enter it,—the soil now dark and fertile, now thin and gray, with fruit-trees and dilapidated buildings,—all the way to Albany.

At Albany, in the heart of the Black Belt, we stop. Two hundred miles south of Atlanta, two hundred miles west of the Atlantic, and one hundred miles north of the Great Gulf lies Dougherty County, with ten thousand Negroes and two thousand whites. The Flint River winds down from Andersonville, and, turning suddenly at Albany, the county-seat, hurries on to join the Chattahoochee and the sea. Andrew Jackson knew the Flint well, and marched across it once to avenge the Indian Massacre at Fort Mims. That was in 1814, not long before the battle of New Orleans; and by the Creek treaty that followed this campaign, all Dougherty County, and much other rich land, was ceded to Georgia. Still, settlers fought shy of this land, for the Indians were all about, and they were unpleasant neighbors in those days. The panic of 1837, which Jackson bequeathed to Van Buren, turned the planters from the impoverished lands of Virginia, the Carolinas, and east Georgia, toward the West. The Indians were removed to Indian Territory, and settlers poured into these coveted lands to retrieve their broken fortunes. For a radius of a hundred miles about Albany, stretched a great fertile land, luxuriant with forests of pine, oak, ash, hickory, and poplar; hot with the sun and damp with the rich black swamp-land; and here the corner-stone of the Cotton Kingdom was laid.

Albany is to-day a wide-streeted, placid, Southern town, with a broad sweep of stores and saloons, and flanking rows of homes,—whites usually to the north, and blacks to the south. Six days in the week the town looks decidedly too small for itself, and takes frequent and prolonged naps. But on Saturday suddenly the whole county disgorges itself upon the place, and a perfect flood of black peasantry pours through the streets, fills the stores, blocks the sidewalks, chokes the thoroughfares, and takes full possession of the town. They are black, sturdy, uncouth country folk, good-natured and simple, talkative to a degree, and yet far more silent and brooding than the crowds of the Rhine-pfalz, or Naples, or Cracow. They drink considerable quantities of whiskey, but do not get very drunk; they talk and laugh loudly at times, but seldom quarrel or fight. They walk up and down the streets, meet and gossip with friends, stare at the shop windows, buy coffee, cheap candy, and clothes, and at dusk drive home—happy? well no, not exactly happy, but much happier than as though they had not come.

Thus Albany is a real capital,—a typical Southern county town, the centre of the life of ten thousand souls; their point of contact with the outer world, their centre of news and gossip, their market for buying and selling, borrowing and lending, their fountain of justice and law. Once upon a time we knew country life so well and city life so little, that we illustrated city life as that of a closely crowded country district. Now the world has well-nigh forgotten what the country is, and we must imagine a little city of black people scattered far and wide over three hundred lonesome square miles of land, without train or trolley, in the midst of cotton and corn, and wide patches of sand and gloomy soil.

It gets pretty hot in Southern Georgia in July,—a sort of dull, determined heat that seems quite independent of the sun; so it took us some days to muster courage enough to leave the porch and venture out on the long country roads, that we might see this unknown world. Finally we started. It was about ten in the morning, bright with a faint breeze, and we jogged leisurely southward in the valley of the Flint. We passed the scattered box-like cabins of the brick-yard hands, and the long tenement-row facetiously called "The Ark," and were soon in the open country, and on the confines of the great plantations, of other days. There is the "Joe Fields place"; a rough old fellow was he, and had killed many a "nigger" in his day. Twelve miles his plantation used to run,—a regular barony. It is nearly all gone now; only straggling bits belong to the family, and the rest has passed to Jews and Negroes. Even the bits which are left are heavily mortgaged, and, like the rest of the land, tilled by tenants. Here is one of them now,—a tall brown man, a hard worker and a hard drinker, illiterate, but versed in farm-lore, as his nodding crops declare. This distressingly new board house is his, and he has just moved out of yonder moss-grown cabin with its one square room.

From the curtains in Benton's house, down the road, a dark comely face is staring at the strangers; for passing carriages are not every-day occurrences here. Benton is an intelligent yellow man with a good-sized family, and manages a plantation blasted by the war and now the broken staff of the widow. He might be well-to-do, they say; but he carouses too much in Albany. And the half-desolate spirit of neglect born of the very soil seems to have settled on these acres. In times past there were cotton-gins and machinery here; but they have rotted away.

The whole land seems forlorn and forsaken. Here are the remnants of the vast plantations of the Sheldons, the Pellots, and the Rensons; but the souls of them are passed. The houses lie in half ruin, or have wholly disappeared; the fences have flown, and the families are wandering in the world. Strange vicissitudes have met these whilom masters. Yonder stretch the wide acres of Bildad Reasor; he died in war-time, but the upstart overseer hastened to wed the widow. Then he went, and his neighbors too, and now only the black tenant remains; but the shadow-hand of the master's grand-nephew or cousin or creditor stretches out of the gray distance to connect the rack-rent remorselessly, and so the land is uncared-for and poor. Only black tenants can stand such a system, and they only because they must. Ten miles we have ridden to-day and have seen no white face.

A resistless feeling of depression falls slowly upon us, despite the gaudy sunshine and the green cotton-fields. This, then, is the Cotton Kingdom,—the shadow of a marvellous dream. And where is the King? Perhaps this is he,—the sweating ploughman, tilling his eighty acres with two lean mules, and fighting a hard battle with debt. So we sit musing, until, as we turn a corner on the sandy road, there comes a fairer scene suddenly in view,—a neat cottage snugly ensconced by the road, and near it a little store. A tall bronzed man rises from the porch as we hail him, and comes out to our carriage. He is six feet in height, with a sober face that smiles gravely. He walks too straight to be a tenant,—yes, he owns, two hundred and forty acres. "The land is run down since the boom-days of eighteen hundred and fifty," he explains, and cotton is low. Three black tenants live on his place, and in his little store he keeps a small stock of tobacco, snuff, soap, and soda, for the neighborhood. Here is his gin-house with new machinery just installed. Three hundred bales of cotton went through it last year. Two children he has sent away to school. Yes, he says sadly, he is getting on, but cotton is down to four cents; I know how Debt sits staring at him.

Wherever the King may be, the parks and palaces of the Cotton Kingdom have not wholly disappeared. We plunge even now into great groves of oak and towering pine, with an undergrowth of myrtle and shrubbery. This was the "home-house" of the Thompsons,—slave-barons who drove their coach and four in the merry past. All is silence now, and ashes, and tangled weeds. The owner put his whole fortune into the rising cotton industry of the fifties, and with the falling prices of the eighties he packed up and stole away. Yonder is another grove, with unkempt lawn, great magnolias, and grass-grown paths. The Big House stands in half-ruin, its great front door staring blankly at the street, and the back part grotesquely restored for its black tenant. A shabby, well-built Negro he is, unlucky and irresolute. He digs hard to pay rent to the white girl who owns the remnant of the place. She married a policeman, and lives in Savannah.

Now and again we come to churches. Here is one now,—Shepherd's, they call it,—a great whitewashed barn of a thing, perched on stilts of stone, and looking for all the world as though it were just resting here a moment and might be expected to waddle off down the road at almost any time. And yet it is the centre of a hundred cabin homes; and sometimes, of a Sunday, five hundred persons from far and near gather here and talk and eat and sing. There is a school-house near,—a very airy, empty shed; but even this is an improvement, for usually the school is held in the church. The churches vary from log-huts to those like Shepherd's, and the schools from nothing to this little house that sits demurely on the county line. It is a tiny plank-house, perhaps ten by twenty, and has within a double row of rough unplaned benches, resting mostly on legs, sometimes on boxes. Opposite the door is a square home-made desk. In one corner are the ruins of a stove, and in the other a dim blackboard. It is the cheerfulest schoolhouse I have seen in Dougherty, save in town. Back of the schoolhouse is a lodge-house two stories high and not quite finished. Societies meet there, societies "to care for the sick and bury the dead"; and these societies grow and flourish.

We had come to the boundaries of Dougherty, and were about to turn west along the county-line, when all these sights were pointed out to us by a kindly old man, black, white-haired, and seventy. Forty-five years he had lived here, and now supports himself and his old wife by the help of the steer tethered yonder and the charity of his black neighbors. He shows us the farm of the Hills just across the county line in Baker,—a widow and two strapping sons, who raised ten bales (one need not add "cotton" down here) last year. There are fences and pigs and cows, and the soft-voiced, velvet-skinned young Memnon, who sauntered half-bashfully over to greet the strangers, is proud of his home. We turn now to the west along the county line. Great dismantled trunks of pines tower above the green cotton-fields, cracking their naked gnarled fingers toward the border of living forest beyond. There is little beauty in this region, only a sort of crude abandon that suggests power,—a naked grandeur, as it were. The houses are bare and straight; there are no hammocks or easy-chairs, and few flowers. So when, as here at Rawdon's, one sees a vine clinging to a little porch, and home-like windows peeping over the fences, one takes a long breath. I think I never before quite realized the place of the Fence in civilization. This is the Land of the Unfenced, where crouch on either hand scores of ugly one-room cabins, cheerless and dirty. Here lies the Negro problem in its naked dirt and penury. And here are no fences. But now and then the criss-cross rails or straight palings break into view, and then we know a touch of culture is near. Of course Harrison Gohagen,—a quiet yellow man, young, smooth-faced, and diligent,—of course he is lord of some hundred acres, and we expect to see a vision of well-kept rooms and fat beds and laughing children. For has he not fine fences? And those over yonder, why should they build fences on the rack-rented land? It will only increase their rent.

On we wind, through sand and pines and glimpses of old plantations, till there creeps into sight a cluster of buildings,—wood and brick, mills and houses, and scattered cabins. It seemed quite a village. As it came nearer and nearer, however, the aspect changed: the buildings were rotten, the bricks were falling out, the mills were silent, and the store was closed. Only in the cabins appeared now and then a bit of lazy life. I could imagine the place under some weird spell, and was half-minded to search out the princess. An old ragged black man, honest, simple, and improvident, told us the tale. The Wizard of the North—the Capitalist—had rushed down in the seventies to woo this coy dark soil. He bought a square mile or more, and for a time the field-hands sang, the gins groaned, and the mills buzzed. Then came a change. The agent's son embezzled the funds and ran off with them. Then the agent himself disappeared.

Finally the new agent stole even the books, and the company in wrath closed its business and its houses, refused to sell, and let houses and furniture and machinery rust and rot. So the Waters-Loring plantation was stilled by the spell of dishonesty, and stands like some gaunt rebuke to a scarred land.

Somehow that plantation ended our day's journey; for I could not shake off the influence of that silent scene. Back toward town we glided, past the straight and thread-like pines, past a dark tree-dotted pond where the air was heavy with a dead sweet perfume. White slender-legged curlews flitted by us, and the garnet blooms of the cotton looked gay against the green and purple stalks. A peasant girl was hoeing in the field, white-turbaned and black-limbed. All this we saw, but the spell still lay upon us.

How curious a land is this,—how full of untold story, of tragedy and laughter, and the rich legacy of human life; shadowed with a tragic past, and big with future promise! This is the Black Belt of Georgia. Dougherty County is the west end of the Black Belt, and men once called it the Egypt of the Confederacy. It is full of historic interest. First there is the Swamp, to the west, where the Chickasawhatchee flows sullenly southward. The shadow of an old plantation lies at its edge, forlorn and dark. Then comes the pool; pendent gray moss and brackish waters appear, and forests filled with wild-fowl. In one place the wood is on fire, smouldering in dull red anger; but nobody minds. Then the swamp grows beautiful; a raised road, built by chained Negro convicts, dips down into it, and forms a way walled and almost covered in living green. Spreading trees spring from a prodigal luxuriance of undergrowth; great dark green shadows fade into the black background, until all is one mass of tangled semi-tropical foliage, marvellous in its weird savage splendor. Once we crossed a black silent stream, where the sad trees and writhing creepers, all glinting fiery yellow and green, seemed like some vast cathedral,—some green Milan builded of wildwood. And as I crossed, I seemed to see again that fierce tragedy of seventy years ago. Osceola, the Indian-Negro chieftain, had risen in the swamps of Florida, vowing vengeance. His war-cry reached the red Creeks of Dougherty, and their war-cry rang from the Chattahoochee to the sea. Men and women and children fled and fell before them as they swept into Dougherty. In yonder shadows a dark and hideously painted warrior glided stealthily on,—another and another, until three hundred had crept into the treacherous swamp. Then the false slime closing about them called the white men from the east. Waist-deep, they fought beneath the tall trees, until the war-cry was hushed and the Indians glided back into the west. Small wonder the wood is red.

Then came the black slaves. Day after day the clank of chained feet marching from Virginia and Carolina to Georgia was heard in these rich swamp lands. Day after day the songs of the callous, the wail of the motherless, and the muttered curses of the wretched echoed from the Flint to the Chickasawhatchee, until by 1860 there had risen in West Dougherty perhaps the richest slave kingdom the modern world ever knew. A hundred and fifty barons commanded the labor of nearly six thousand Negroes, held sway over farms with ninety thousand acres of tilled land, valued even in times of cheap soil at three millions of dollars. Twenty thousand bales of ginned cotton went yearly to England, New and Old; and men that came there bankrupt made money and grew rich. In a single decade the cotton output increased fourfold and the value of lands was tripled. It was the heyday of the *nouveau riche,* and a life of careless extravagance reigned among the masters. Four and six bob-tailed thoroughbreds rolled their coaches to town; open hospitality and gay entertainment were the rule. Parks and groves were laid out, rich with flower and vine, and in the midst stood the low wide-halled "big house," with its porch and columns and great fireplaces.

And yet with all this there was something sordid, something forced,—a certain feverish unrest and recklessness; for was not all this show and tinsel built upon a groan? "This land was a little Hell," said a ragged, brown, and grave-faced man to me. We were seated near a roadside blacksmith-shop, and behind was the bare ruin of some master's home. "I've seen niggers drop dead in the furrow, but they were kicked aside, and the plough never stopped. And down in the guard-house, there's where the blood ran."

With such foundations a kingdom must in time sway and fall. The masters moved to Macon and Augusta, and left only the irresponsible overseers on the land. And the result is such ruin as this, the Lloyd "home-place":—great waving oaks, a spread of lawn, myrtles and chestnuts, all ragged and wild; a solitary gate-post standing where once was a castle entrance; an old rusty anvil lying amid rotting bellows and wood in the ruins of a blacksmith shop; a wide rambling old mansion, brown and dingy, filled now with the grandchildren of the slaves who once waited on its tables; while the family of the master has dwindled to two lone women, who live in Macon and feed hungrily off the remnants of an earldom. So we ride on, past phantom gates and falling homes,—past the once flourishing farms of the Smiths, the Gandys, and the Lagores,—and find all dilapidated and half ruined, even there where a solitary white woman, a relic of other days, sits alone in state among miles of Negroes and rides to town in her ancient coach each day.

This was indeed the Egypt of the Confederacy,—the rich granary whence potatoes and corn and cotton poured out to the famished and ragged Confederate troops as they battled for a cause lost long before 1861. Sheltered and secure, it became the place of refuge for families, wealth, and slaves. Yet even then the hard ruthless rape of the land began to tell. The red-clay subsoil already had begun to peer above the loam. The harder the slaves were driven the more careless and fatal was their farming. Then came the revolution of war and Emancipation, the bewilderment of Reconstruction,—and now, what is the Egypt of the Confederacy, and what meaning has it for the nation's weal or woe?

It is a land of rapid contrasts and of curiously mingled hope and pain. Here sits a pretty blue-eyed quadroon hiding her bare feet; she was married only last week, and yonder in the field is her dark young husband, hoeing to support her, at thirty cents a day without board. Across the way is Gatesby, brown and tall, lord of two thousand acres shrewdly won and held. There is a store conducted by his black son, a blacksmith shop, and a ginnery. Five miles below here is a town owned and controlled by one white New Englander. He owns almost a Rhode Island county, with thousands of acres and hundreds of black laborers. Their cabins look better than most, and the farm, with machinery and fertilizers, is much more business-like than any in the county, although the manager drives hard bargains in wages. When now we turn and look five miles above, there on the edge of town are five houses of prostitutes,—two of blacks and three of whites; and in one of the houses of the whites a worthless black boy was harbored too openly two years ago; so he was hanged for rape. And here, too, is the high whitewashed fence of the "stockade," as the county prison is called; the white folks say it is ever full of black criminals,—the black folks say that only colored boys are sent to jail, and they not because they are guilty, but because the State needs criminals to eke out its income by their forced labor.

The Jew is the heir of the slave-baron in Dougherty; and as we ride westward, by wide stretching cornfields and stubby orchards of peach and pear, we see on all sides within the circle of dark forest a Land of Canaan. Here and there are tales of projects for money-getting, born in the swift days of Reconstruction,—"improvement" companies, wine companies, mills and factories; nearly all failed, and the Jew fell heir. It is a beautiful land, this Dougherty, west of the Flint. The forests are wonderful, the solemn pines have disappeared, and this is the "Oakey Woods," with its wealth of hickories, beeches, oaks, and palmettos. But a pall of debt hangs over the beautiful land; the merchants are in debt to the wholesalers, the planters are in debt to the merchants, the tenants owe the planters, and laborers bow and bend beneath the burden of it all. Here and there a man has raised his head above these murky waters. We passed one fenced stock-farm, with grass and grazing cattle, that looked very homelike after endless corn and cotton. Here and there are black freeholders: there is the gaunt dull-black Jackson, with his hundred acres. "I says, 'Look up! If you don't look up you can't get up,'" remarks Jackson, philosophically. And he's gotten up. Dark Carter's neat barns would do credit to New England. His master helped him to get a start, but when the black man died last fall the master's sons immediately laid claim to the estate. "And them white folks will get it, too," said my yellow gossip.

I turn from these well-tended acres with a comfortable feeling that the Negro is rising. Even then, however, the fields, as we proceed, begin to redden and the trees disappear. Rows of old cabins appear filled with renters and laborers,—cheerless, bare, and dirty, for the most part, although here and there the very age and decay makes the scene picturesque. A young black fellow greets us. He is twenty-two, and just married. Until last year he had good luck renting; then cotton fell, and the sheriff seized and sold all he had. So he moved here, where the rent is higher, the land poorer, and the owner inflexible; he rents a forty-dollar mule for twenty dollars a year. Poor lad!—a slave at twenty-two. This plantation, owned now by a Russian Jew, was a part of the famous Bolton estate. After the war it was for many years worked by gangs of Negro convicts,—and black convicts then were even more plentiful than now; it was a way of making Negroes work, and the question of guilt was a minor one. Hard tales of cruelty and mistreatment of the chained freemen are told but the county authorities were deaf until the free-labor market was nearly ruined by wholesale migration. Then they took the convicts from the plantations, but not until one of the fairest regions of the "Oakey Woods" had been ruined and ravished into a red waste, out of which only a Yankee or a Jew could squeeze more blood from debt-cursed tenants.

No wonder that Luke Black, slow, dull, and discouraged, shuffles to our carriage and talks hopelessly. Why should he strive? Every year finds him deeper in debt. How strange that Georgia, the world-heralded refuge of poor debtors, should bind her own to sloth and misfortune as ruthlessly as ever England did! The poor land groans with its birth-pains, and brings forth scarcely a hundred pounds of cotton to the acre, where fifty years ago it yielded eight times as much. Of this meagre yield the tenant pays from a quarter to a third in rent, and most of the rest in interest on food and supplies bought on credit. Twenty years yonder sunken-cheeked, old black man has labored under that system, and now, turned day-laborer, is supporting his wife and boarding himself on his wages of a dollar and a half a week, received only part of the year.

The Bolton convict farm formerly included the neighboring plantation. Here it was that the convicts were lodged in the great log prison still standing. A dismal place it still remains, with rows of ugly huts filled with surly ignorant tenants. "What rent do you pay here?" I inquired. "I don't know,—what is it, Sam?" "All we make," answered Sam. It is a depressing place,—bare, unshaded, with no charm of past association, only a memory of forced human toil,—now, then, and before the war. They are not happy, these black men whom we meet throughout this region. There is little of the joyous abandon and playfulness which we are wont to associate with the plantation Negro. At best, the natural good-nature is edged with complaint or has changed into sullenness and gloom. And now and then it blazes forth in veiled but hot anger. I remember one big red-eyed black whom we met by the roadside. Forty-five years he had labored on this farm, beginning with nothing, and still having nothing. To be sure, he had given four children a common-school training, and perhaps if the new fence-law had not allowed unfenced crops in West Dougherty he might have raised a little stock and kept ahead. As it is, he is hopelessly in debt, disappointed, and embittered. He stopped us to inquire after the black boy in Albany, whom it was said a policeman had shot and killed for loud talking on the sidewalk. And then he said slowly: "Let a white man touch me, and he dies; I don't boast this,—I don't say it around loud, or before the children,—but I mean it. I've seen them whip my father and my old mother in them cotton-rows till the blood ran; by—" and we, passed on.

Now Scars, whom we met next lolling under the chubby oak-trees, was of quite different fibre. Happy?—Well, yes; he laughed and flipped pebbles, and thought the world was as it was. He had worked here twelve years and has nothing but a mortgaged mule. Children? Yes, seven; but they hadn't been to school this year;—couldn't afford books and clothes, and couldn't spare their work. There go part of them to the fields now,—three big boys astride mules, and a strapping girl with bare brown legs. Careless ignorance and laziness here, fierce hate and vindictiveness there,—these are the extremes of the Negro problem which we met that day, and we scarce knew which we preferred.

Here and there we meet distinct characters quite out of the ordinary. One came out of a piece of newly cleared ground, making a wide detour to avoid the snakes. He was an old, hollow-cheeked man, with a drawn and characterful brown face. He had a sort of self-contained quaintness and rough humor impossible to describe; a certain cynical earnestness that puzzled one. "The niggers were jealous of me over on the other place," he said, "and so me and the old woman begged this piece of woods, and I cleared it up myself. Made nothing for two years, but I reckon I've got a crop now." The cotton looked tall and rich, and we praised it. He curtsied low, and then bowed almost to the ground, with an imperturbable gravity that seemed almost suspicious. Then he continued, "My mule died last week,"—a calamity in this land equal to a devastating fire in town,—"but a white man loaned me another." Then he added, eyeing us, "Oh, I gets along with white folks." We turned the conversation. "Bears? deer?" he answered, "well, I should say there were," and he let fly a string of brave oaths, as he told hunting-tales of the swamp. We left him standing still in the middle of the road looking after us, and yet apparently not noticing us.

The Whistle place, which includes his bit of land, was bought soon after the war by an English syndicate, the "Dixie Cotton and Corn Company." A marvellous deal of style their factor put on, with his servants and coach-and-six; so much so that the concern soon landed in inextricable bankruptcy. Nobody lives in the old house now, but a man comes each winter out of the North and collects his high rents. I know not which are the more touching,—such old empty houses, or the homes of the masters' sons. Sad and bitter tales lie hidden back of those white doors,—tales of poverty, of struggle, of disappointment. A revolution such as that of '63 is a terrible thing; they that rose rich in the morning often slept in paupers' beds. Beggars and vulgar speculators rose to rule over them, and their children went astray. See yonder sad-colored house, with its cabins and fences and glad crops? It is not glad within; last month the prodigal son of the struggling father wrote home from the city for money. Money! Where was it to come from? And so the son rose in the night and killed his baby, and killed his wife, and shot himself dead. And the world passed on.

I remember wheeling around a bend in the road beside a graceful bit of forest and a singing brook. A long low house faced us, with porch and flying pillars, great oaken door, and a broad lawn shining in the evening sun. But the window-panes were gone, the pillars were worm-eaten, and the moss-grown roof was falling in. Half curiously I peered through the unhinged door, and saw where, on the wall across the hall, was written in once gay letters a faded "Welcome."

Quite a contrast to the southwestern part of Dougherty County is the northwest. Soberly timbered in oak and pine, it has none of that half-tropical luxuriance of the southwest. Then, too, there are fewer signs of a romantic past, and more of systematic modern land-grabbing and money-getting. White people are more in evidence here, and farmer and hired labor replace to some extent the absentee landlord and rack-rented tenant. The crops have neither the luxuriance of the richer land nor the signs of neglect so often seen, and there were fences and meadows here and there. More of this land was poor, and beneath the notice of the slave-baron, before the war. Since then his nephews and the poor whites and the Jews have seized it. The returns of the farmer are too small to allow much for wages, and yet he will not sell off small farms. There is the Negro Sanford; he has worked fourteen years as overseer on the Ladson place, and "paid out enough for fertilizers to have bought a farm," but the owner will not sell off a few acres.

Two children—a boy and a girl—are hoeing sturdily in the fields on the farm where Corliss works. He is smooth-faced and brown, and is fencing up his pigs. He used to run a successful cotton-gin, but the Cotton Seed Oil Trust has forced the price of ginning so low that he says it hardly pays him. He points out a stately old house over the way as the home of "Pa Willis." We eagerly ride over, for "Pa Willis" was the tall and powerful black Moses who led the Negroes for a generation, and led them well. He was a Baptist preacher, and when he died two thousand black people followed him to the grave; and now they preach his funeral sermon each year. His widow lives here,—a weazened, sharp-featured little woman, who curtsied quaintly as we greeted her. Further on lives Jack Delson, the most prosperous Negro farmer in the county. It is a joy to meet him,—a great broad-shouldered, handsome black man, intelligent and jovial. Six hundred and fifty acres he owns, and has eleven black tenants. A neat and tidy home nestled in a flower-garden, and a little store stands beside it.

We pass the Munson place, where a plucky white widow is renting and struggling; and the eleven hundred acres of the Sennet plantation, with its Negro overseer. Then the character of the farms begins to change. Nearly all the lands belong to Russian Jews; the overseers are white, and the cabins are bare board-houses scattered here and there. The rents are high, and day-laborers and "contract" hands abound. It is a keen, hard struggle for living here, and few have time to talk. Tired with the long ride, we gladly drive into Gillonsville. It is a silent cluster of farm-houses standing on the cross-roads, with one of its stores closed and the other kept by a Negro preacher. They tell great tales of busy times at Gillonsville before all the railroads came to Albany; now it is chiefly a memory. Riding down the street, we stop at the preacher's and seat ourselves before the door. It was one of those scenes one cannot soon forget:—a wide, low, little house, whose motherly roof reached over and sheltered a snug little porch. There we sat, after the long hot drive, drinking cool water,—the talkative little storekeeper who is my daily companion; the silent old black woman patching pantaloons and saying never a word; the ragged picture of helpless misfortune who called in just to see the preacher; and finally the neat matronly preacher's wife, plump, yellow, and intelligent. "Own land?" said the wife; "well, only this house." Then she added quietly, "We did buy seven hundred acres up yonder, and paid for it; but they cheated us out of it. Sells was the owner." "Sells!" echoed the ragged misfortune, who was leaning against the balustrade and listening, "he's a regular cheat. I worked for him thirty-seven days this spring, and he paid me in cardboard checks which were to be cashed at the end of the month. But he never cashed them,—kept putting me off. Then the sheriff came and took my mule and corn and furniture—" "Furniture?" I asked; "but furniture is exempt from seizure by law." "Well, he took it just the same," said the hard-faced man.

XI

OF THE PASSING OF THE FIRST-BORN

O sister, sister, thy first-begotten,
The hands that cling and the feet that follow,
The voice of the child's blood crying yet,
Who hath remembered me? who hath forgotten?
Thou has forgotten, O summer swallow,
But the world shall end when I forget.

—SWINBURNE

"Unto you a child is born," sang the bit of yellow paper that fluttered into my room one brown October morning. Then the fear of fatherhood mingled wildly with the job of creation; I wondered how it looked and how it felt,—what were its eyes, and how its hair curled and crumpled itself. And I thought in awe of her, she who had slept with Death to tear a man-child from underneath her heart, while I was unconsciously wandering. I fled to my wife and child, repeating the while to myself half wonderingly, "Wife and child? Wife and child?"—fled fast and faster than boat and steam-car, and yet must ever impatiently await them; away from the hard-voiced city, away from the flickering sea into my own Berkshire Hills that sit all sadly guarding the gates of Massachusetts.

Up the stairs I ran to the wan mother and whimpering babe, to the sanctuary on whose altar a life at my bidding had offered itself to win a life, and won. What is this tiny formless thing, this new-born wail from an unknown world,—all head and voice? I handle it curiously, and watch perplexed its winking, breathing, and sneezing. I did not love it then; it seemed a ludicrous thing to love; but her I loved, my girl-mother, she whom now I saw unfolding like the glory of the morning—the transfigured woman.

Through her I came to love the wee thing, as it grew and waxed strong; as its little soul unfolded itself in twitter and cry and half-formed word, and as its eyes caught the gleam and flash of life. How beautiful he was, with his olive-tinted flesh and dark gold ringlets, his eyes of mingled blue and brown, his perfect little limbs, and the soft voluptuous roll which the blood of Africa had moulded into his features! I held him in my arms, after we had sped far away to our Southern home,—held him, and glanced at the hot red soil of Georgia and the breathless city of a hundred hills, and felt a vague unrest. Why was his hair tinted with gold? An evil omen was golden hair in my life. Why had not the brown of his eyes crushed out and killed the blue?—for brown were his father's eyes, and his father's father's. And thus in the Land of the Color-line I saw, as it fell across my baby, the shadow of the Veil.

Within the Veil was he born, said I; and there within shall he live,—a Negro and a Negro's son. Holding in that little head—ah, bitterly!—the unbowed pride of a hunted race, clinging with that tiny dimpled hand—ah, wearily!—to a hope not hopeless but unhopeful, and seeing with those bright wondering eyes that peer into my soul a land whose freedom is to us a mockery and whose liberty a lie. I saw the shadow of the Veil as it passed over my baby, I saw the cold city towering above the blood-red land. I held my face beside his little cheek, showed him the star-children and the twinkling lights as they began to flash, and stilled with an even-song the unvoiced terror of my life.

So sturdy and masterful he grew, so filled with bubbling life, so tremulous with the unspoken wisdom of a life but eighteen months distant from the All-life,—we were not far from worshipping this revelation of the divine, my wife and I. Her own life builded and moulded itself upon the child; he tinged her every dream and idealized her every effort. No hands but hers must touch and garnish those little limbs; no dress or frill must touch them that had not wearied her fingers; no voice but hers could coax him off to Dreamland, and she and he together spoke some soft and unknown tongue and in it held communion. I too mused above his little white bed; saw the strength of my own arm stretched onward through the ages through the newer strength of his; saw the dream of my black fathers stagger a step onward in the wild phantasm of the world; heard in his baby voice the voice of the Prophet that was to rise within the Veil.

And so we dreamed and loved and planned by fall and winter, and the full flush of the long Southern spring, till the hot winds rolled from the fetid Gulf, till the roses shivered and the still stern sun quivered its awful light over the hills of Atlanta. And then one night the little feet pattered wearily to the wee white bed, and the tiny hands trembled; and a warm flushed face tossed on the pillow, and we knew baby was sick. Ten days he lay there,—a swift week and three endless days, wasting, wasting away. Cheerily the mother nursed him the first days, and laughed into the little eyes that smiled again. Tenderly then she hovered round him, till the smile fled away and Fear crouched beside the little bed.

Then the day ended not, and night was a dreamless terror, and joy and sleep slipped away. I hear now that Voice at midnight calling me from dull and dreamless trance,—crying, "The Shadow of Death! The Shadow of Death!" Out into the starlight I crept, to rouse the gray physician,—the Shadow of Death, the Shadow of Death. The hours trembled on; the night listened; the ghastly dawn glided like a tired thing across the lamplight. Then we two alone looked upon the child as he turned toward us with great eyes, and stretched his string-like hands,—the Shadow of Death! And we spoke no word, and turned away.

He died at eventide, when the sun lay like a brooding sorrow above the western hills, veiling its face; when the winds spoke not, and the trees, the great green trees he loved, stood motionless. I saw his breath beat quicker and quicker, pause, and then his little soul leapt like a star that travels in the night and left a world of darkness in its train. The day changed not; the same tall trees peeped in at the windows, the same green grass glinted in the setting sun. Only in the chamber of death writhed the world's most piteous thing—a childless mother.

I shirk not. I long for work. I pant for a life full of striving. I am no coward, to shrink before the rugged rush of the storm, nor even quail before the awful shadow of the Veil. But hearken, O Death! Is not this my life hard enough,—is not that dull land that stretches its sneering web about me cold enough,—is not all the world beyond these four little walls pitiless enough, but that thou must needs enter here,—thou, O Death? About my head the thundering storm beat like a heartless voice, and the crazy forest pulsed with the curses of the weak; but what cared I, within my home beside my wife and baby boy? Was thou so jealous of one little coign of happiness that thou must needs enter there,—thou, O Death?

A perfect life was his, all joy and love, with tears to make it brighter,—sweet as a summer's day beside the Housatonic. The world loved him; the women kissed his curls, the men looked gravely into his wonderful eyes, and the children hovered and fluttered about him. I can see him now, changing like the sky from sparkling laughter to darkening frowns, and then to wondering thoughtfulness as he watched the world. He knew no color-line, poor dear,—and the Veil, though it shadowed him, had not yet darkened half his sun. He loved the white matron, he loved his black nurse; and in his little world walked souls alone, uncolored and unclothed. I—yea, all men—are larger and purer by the infinite breath of that one little life. She who in simple clearness of vision sees beyond the stars said when he had flown, "He will be happy There; he ever loved beautiful things." And I, far more ignorant, and blind by the web of mine own weaving, sit alone winding words and muttering, "If still he be, and he be There, and there be a There, let him be happy, O Fate!"

Blithe was the morning of his burial, with bird and song and sweet-smelling flowers. The trees whispered to the grass, but the children sat with hushed faces. And yet it seemed a ghostly unreal day,—the wraith of Life. We seemed to rumble down an unknown street behind a little white bundle of posies, with the shadow of a song in our ears. The busy city dinned about us; they did not say much, those pale-faced hurrying men and women; they did not say much,—they only glanced and said, "Niggers!"

We could not lay him in the ground there in Georgia, for the earth there is strangely red; so we bore him away to the northward, with his flowers and his little folded hands. In vain, in vain!—for where, O God! beneath thy broad blue sky shall my dark baby rest in peace,—where Reverence dwells, and Goodness, and a Freedom that is free?

All that day and all that night there sat an awful gladness in my heart,—nay, blame me not if I see the world thus darkly through the Veil,—and my soul whispers ever to me, saying, "Not dead, not dead, but escaped; not bond, but free." No bitter meanness now shall sicken his baby heart till it die a living death, no taunt shall madden his happy boyhood. Fool that I was to think or wish that this little soul should grow choked and deformed within the Veil! I might have known that yonder deep unworldly look that ever and anon floated past his eyes was peering far beyond this narrow Now. In the poise of his little curl-crowned head did there not sit all that wild pride of being which his father had hardly crushed in his own heart? For what, forsooth, shall a Negro want with pride amid the studied humiliations of fifty million fellows? Well sped, my boy, before the world had dubbed your ambition insolence, had held your ideals unattainable, and taught you to cringe and bow. Better far this nameless void that stops my life than a sea of sorrow for you.

Idle words; he might have borne his burden more bravely than we,—aye, and found it lighter too, some day; for surely, surely this is not the end. Surely there shall yet dawn some mighty morning to lift the Veil and set the prisoned free. Not for me,—I shall die in my bonds,—but for fresh young souls who have not known the night and waken to the morning; a morning when men ask of the workman, not "Is he white?" but "Can he work?" When men ask artists, not "Are they black?" but "Do they know?" Some morning this may be, long, long years to come. But now there wails, on that dark shore within the Veil, the same deep voice, *Thou shalt forego!* And all have I foregone at that command, and with small complaint,—all save that fair young form that lies so coldly wed with death in the nest I had builded.

If one must have gone, why not I? Why may I not rest me from this restlessness and sleep from this wide waking? Was not the world's alembic, Time, in his young hands, and is not my time waning? Are there so many workers in the vineyard that the fair promise of this little body could lightly be tossed away? The wretched of my race that line the alleys of the nation sit fatherless and unmothered; but Love sat beside his cradle, and in his ear Wisdom waited to speak. Perhaps now he knows the All-love, and needs not to be wise. Sleep, then, child,—sleep till I sleep and waken to a baby voice and the ceaseless patter of little feet—above the Veil.

THE AFTERTHOUGHT

Hear my cry, O God the Reader; vouchsafe that this my book fall not stillborn into the world-wilderness. Let there spring, Gentle One, from out its leaves vigor of thought and thoughtful deed to reap the harvest wonderful. (Let the ears of a guilty people tingle with truth, and seventy millions sigh for the righteousness which exalteth nations, in this drear day when human brotherhood is mockery and a snare.) Thus in Thy good time may infinite reason turn the tangle straight, and these crooked marks on a fragile leaf be not indeed

THE END

1903

from *THE CRISIS*

A MILD SUGGESTION

They were sitting on the leeward deck of the vessel and the colored man was there with his usual look of unconcern. Before the seasickness his presence aboard had caused some upheaval. The Woman, for instance, glancing at the Southerner, had refused point blank to sit beside him at meals, so she had changed places with the Little Old Lady. The Westerner, who sat opposite, said he did not care a——, then he looked at the Little Old Lady, and added in a lower voice to the New Yorker that there was no accounting for tastes. The Southerner from the other table broadened his back and tried to express with his shoulders both ancestors and hauteur. All this, however, was half forgotten during the seasickness, and the Woman sat beside the colored man for a full half hour before she noticed it, and then was glad to realize that the Southerner was too sick to see. Now again with sunshine and smiling weather, they all quite naturally reverted (did the Southerner suggest it?) to the Negro problem. The usual solutions had been suggested: education, work, emigration, etc.

They had not noticed the back of the colored man, until the thoughtless Westerner turned toward him and said breezily: “Well, now, what do you say? I guess you are rather interested.” The colored man was leaning over the rail and about to light his cigarette—he had several such bad habits, as the Little Old Lady noticed. The Southerner simply stared. Over the face of the colored man went the shadow of several expressions; some the New Yorker could interpret, others he could not.

“I have,” said the colored man, with deliberation, “a perfect solution.” The Southerner selected a look of disdain from his repertoire, and assumed it. The Woman moved nearer, but partly turned her back. The Westerner and the Little Old Lady sat down. “Yes,” repeated the colored man, “I have a perfect solution. The trouble with most of the solutions which are generally suggested is that they aggravate the disease.” The Southerner could not help looking interested. “For instance,” proceeded the colored man, airily waving his hand, “take education; education means ambition, dissatisfaction and revolt. You cannot both educate people and hold them down.”

“Then stop educating them,” growled the Southerner aside.

"Or," continued the colored man, "if the black man works, he must come into competition with whites———"

"He sure will, and it ought to be stopped," returned the Westerner. "It brings down wages."

"Precisely," said the speaker, "and if by underselling the labor market he develops a few millionaires, how now would you protect your residential districts or your select social circles or—your daughters?"

The Southerner started angrily, but the colored man was continuing placidly with a far-off look in his eyes. "Now, migration is both costly and inhuman; the transportation would be the smallest matter. You must buy up perhaps a thousand millions' worth of Negro property; you must furnish some capital for the masses of poor; you must get some place for them to go; you must protect them there, and here you must pay not only higher wages to white men, but still higher on account of the labor scarcity. Meantime, the Negroes suddenly removed from one climate and social system to another climate and utterly new conditions would die in droves—it would be simply prolonged murder at enormous cost.

"Very well," continued the colored man, seating himself and throwing away his cigarette, "listen to my plan," looking almost quizzically at the Little Old Lady; "you must not be alarmed at its severity—it may seem radical, but really it is—it is—well, it is quite the only practical thing and it has surely one advantage: it settles the problem once, suddenly, and forever. My plan is this: You now outnumber us nearly ten to one. I propose that on a certain date, shall we say next Christmas, or possibly Easter, 1912? No, come to think of it, the first of January, 1913, would, for historical reasons, probably be best. Well, then, on the first of January, 1913, let each person who has a colored friend invite him to dinner. This would take care of a few; among such friends might be included the black mammies and faithful old servants of the South; in this way we could get together quite a number. Then those who have not the pleasure of black friends might arrange for meetings, especially in "white" churches and Young Men's and Young Women's Christian Associations, where Negroes are not expected. At such meetings, contrary to custom, the black people should not be seated by themselves, but distributed very carefully among the whites. The remaining Negroes who could not be flattered or attracted by these invitations should be induced to assemble among themselves at their own churches or at little parties and house warmings.

"The few stragglers, vagrants and wanderers could be put under careful watch and ward. Now, then, we have the thing in shape. First, the hosts of those invited to dine should provide themselves with a sufficient quantity of cyanide of potassium, placing it carefully in the proper cups, and being careful not to mix the cups. Those at church and prayer meeting could choose between long sharp stilettoes and pistols—I should recommend the former as less noisy. Those who guard the colored assemblies and the stragglers without should carefully surround the groups and use Winchesters.[1] Then, at a given signal, let the colored folk of the United States be quietly dispatched; the signal might be a church bell or the singing of the national hymn; probably the bell would be best, for the diners would be eating."

[1]Rifles manufactured by the Winchester Repeating Rifle Company.

By this time the auditors of the colored man were staring; the Southerner had forgotten to pose; the Woman had forgotten to watch the Southerner; the Westerner was staring with admiration; there were tears in the eyes of the Little Old Lady, while the New Yorker was smiling; but the colored man held up a deprecating hand: "Now don't prejudge my plan," he urged. "The next morning there would be ten million funerals, and therefore no Negro problem. Think how quietly the thing would be settled; no more bother, no more argument; the whole country united and happy. Even the Negroes would be a great deal happier than they are at present. Instead of being made heirs to hope by education, or ambitious by wealth, or exiled invalids on the fever coast, they would all be happily ensconced in Heaven. Of course, I admit that at first the plan may seem a little abrupt and cruel, and yet is it more cruel than present conditions, and would it not be well to be a little more abrupt in our social solutions? At any rate think it over," and the colored man dropped lazily into his steamer chair and felt for another cigarette.

The crowd slowly dispersed; the Southerner chose the Woman, but was heard to say something about fools. The Westerner turned to the New Yorker and said: "Now, what in hell do you suppose that darky meant?" But the Little Old Lady went silently to her cabin.

1912

ON BEING CRAZY[1]

It was one o'clock and I was hungry. I walked into a restaurant, seated myself and reached for the bill-of-fare. My table companion rose.

"Sir," said he, "do you wish to force your company on those who do not want you?"

No, said I, I wish to eat.

"Are you aware, Sir, that this is social equality?"

Nothing of the sort, Sir, it is hunger—and I ate.

The day's work done, I sought the theatre. As I sank into my seat, the lady shrank and squirmed.

I beg pardon, I said.

"Do you enjoy being where you are not wanted?" she asked coldly.

Oh no, I said.

"Well you are not wanted here."

I was surprised. I fear you are mistaken, I said. I certainly want the music and I like to think the music wants me to listen to it.

"Usher," said the lady, "this is social equality."

No, madame, said the usher, it is the second movement of Beethoven's Fifth Symphony.

[1]From *The Crisis,* June 1923.

After the theatre, I sought the hotel where I had sent my baggage. The clerk scowled.

"What do you want?" he asked.

Rest, I said.

"This is a white hotel," he said.

I looked around. Such a color scheme requires a great deal of cleaning, I said, but I don't know that I object.

"We object," said he.

Then why—I began, but he interrupted.

"We don't keep 'niggers'," he said, "we don't want social equality."

Neither do I. I replied gently, I want a bed.

I walked thoughtfully to the train. I'll take a sleeper through Texas. I'm a bit dissatisfied with this town.

"Can't sell you one."

I only want to hire it, said I, for a couple of nights.

"Can't sell you a sleeper in Texas," he maintained. "They consider that social equality."

I consider it barbarism, I said, and I think I'll walk.

Walking, I met a wayfarer who immediately walked to the other side of the road where it was muddy. I asked his reasons.

"'Niggers' is dirty," he said.

So is mud, said I. Moreover I added, I am not as dirty as you—at least, not yet.

"But you're a 'nigger', ain't you?" he asked.

My grandfather was so-called.

"Well then!" he answered triumphantly.

Do you live in the South? I persisted, pleasantly.

"Sure," he growled, "and starve there."

I should think you and the Negroes might get together and vote out starvation.

"We don't let them vote."

We? Why not? I said in surprise.

"'Niggers' is too ignorant to vote."

But, I said, I am not so ignorant as you.

"But you're a 'nigger'."

Yes, I'm certainly what you mean by that.

"Well then!" he returned, with that curiously inconsequential note of triumph. "Moreover," he said, "I don't want my sister to marry a nigger."

I had not seen his sister, so I merely murmured, let her say, no.

"By God you shan't marry her, even if she said yes."

But—but I don't want to marry her, I answered a little perturbed at the personal turn.

"Why not!" he yelled, angrier than ever.

Because I'm already married and I rather like my wife.

"Is she a 'nigger'?" he asked suspiciously.

Well, I said again, her grandmother—was called that.

"*Well then!*" he shouted in that oddly illogical way.

I gave up. Go on, I said, either you are crazy or I am.

"We both are," he said as he trotted along in the mud.

1923

A LITANY OF ATLANTA[1]

O Silent God, Thou whose voice afar in mist and mystery hath left our ears a-hungered in these fearful days—

Hear us, good Lord!

Listen to us, Thy children: our faces dark with doubt are made a mockery in Thy Sanctuary. With uplifted hands we front Thy Heaven, O God, crying:

We beseech Thee to hear us, good Lord!

We are not better than our fellows, Lord; we are but weak and human men. When our devils do deviltry, curse Thou the doer and the deed,—curse them as we curse them, do to them all and more than ever they have done to innocence and weakness, to womanhood and home.

Have mercy upon us, miserable sinners!

And yet, whose is the deeper guilt? Who made these devils? Who nursed them in crime and fed them on injustice? Who ravished and debauched their mothers and their grandmothers? Who bought and sold their crime and waxed fat and rich on public iniquity?

Thou knowest, good God!

Is this Thy Justice, O Father, that guile be easier than innocence and the innocent be crucified for the guilt of the untouched guilty?

Justice, O Judge of men!

Wherefore do we pray? Is not the God of the Fathers dead? Have not seers seen in Heaven's halls Thine hearsed and lifeless form stark amidst the black and rolling smoke of sin, where all along bow bitter forms of endless dead?

Awake, Thou that sleepest!

Thou art not dead, but flown afar, up hills of endless light, through blazing corridors of suns, where worlds do swing of good and gentle men, of women strong and free—far from the cozenage, black hypocrisy, and chaste prostitution of this shameful speck of dust!

Turn again, O Lord; leave us not to perish in our sin!

From lust of body and lust of blood,—

Great God, deliver us!

From lust of power and lust of gold,—

Great God, deliver us!

From the leagued lying of despot and of brute,—

Great God, deliver us!

[1]This poem, published in the *The Independent* in October 1906, responds to recent acts of racial violence in Atlanta.

A city lay in travail, God our Lord, and from her loins sprang twin Murder and Black Hate. Red was the midnight; clang, crack, and cry of death and fury filled the air and trembled underneath the stars where church spires pointed silently to Thee. And all this was to sate the greed of greedy men who hide behind the veil of vengeance!

Bend us Thine ear, O Lord!

In the pale, still morning we looked upon the deed. We stopped our ears and held our leaping hands, but they—did they not wag their heads and leer and cry with bloody jaws: *Cease from Crime!* The word was mockery, for thus they train a hundred crimes while we do cure one.

Turn again our captivity, O Lord!

Behold this maimed and broken thing, dear God; it was an humble black man, who toiled and sweat to save a bit from the pittance paid him. They told him: *Work and Rise!* He worked. Did this man sin? Nay, but someone told how someone said another did—one whom he had never seen nor known. Yet for that man's crime this man lieth maimed and murdered, his wife naked to shame, his children to poverty and evil.

Hear us, O heavenly Father!

Doth not this justice of hell stink in Thy nostrils, O God? How long shall the mounting flood of innocent blood roar in Thine ears and pound in our hearts for vengeance? Pile the pale frenzy of blood-crazed brutes, who do such deeds, high on Thine Altar, Jehovah Jireh,[2] and burn it in hell forever and forever!

Forgive us, good Lord; we know not what we say![3]

Bewildered we are and passion-tossed, mad with the madness of a mobbed and mocked and murdered people; straining at the armposts of Thy throne, we raise our shackled hands and charge Thee, God, by the bones of our stolen fathers, by the tears of our dead mothers, by the very blood of Thy crucified Christ: What meaneth this? Tell us the plan; give us the sign!

Keep not Thou silent, O God!

Sit not longer blind, Lord God, deaf to our prayer and dumb to our dumb suffering. Surely Thou, too, art not white, O Lord, a pale, bloodless, heartless thing!

Ah! Christ of all the Pities!

Forgive the thought! Forgive these wild, blasphemous words! Thou art still the God of our black fathers and in Thy Soul's Soul sit some soft darkenings of the evening, some shadowings of the velvet night.

[2]Jehovah Jireh is the name given by Abraham to the place where he went to sacrifice his son Isaac before being spared that ordeal by God (Genesis 22). As a name for God, it implies that God will provide us with what we need.

[3]An allusion to Christ's words while being crucified: "Father, forgive them, for they know not what they do" (Luke 23:34).

But whisper—speak—call, great God, for Thy silence is white terror to our hearts! The way, O God, show us the way and point us the path!

Whither? North is greed and South is blood; within, the coward, and without, the liar. Whither? To death?
Amen! Welcome, dark sleep!

Whither? To life? But not this life, dear God, not this. Let the cup pass from us, tempt us not beyond our strength, for there is that clamoring and clawing within, to whose voice we would not listen, yet shudder lest we must,—and it is red. Ah! God! It is a red and awful shape.
Selah![4]

In yonder East trembles a star.
Vengeance is Mine; I will repay, saith the Lord![5]

Thy Will, O Lord, be done![6]
Kyrie Eleison![7]

Lord, we have done these pleading, wavering words.
We beseech Thee to hear us, good Lord!

We bow our heads and hearken soft to the sobbing of women and little children.
We beseech Thee to hear us, good Lord!

Our voices sink in silence and in night.
Hear us, good Lord!

In night, O God of a godless land!
Amen!

In silence, O Silent God.
Selah!

1906 1920

THE COMET

He stood a moment on the steps of the bank, watching the human river that swirled down Broadway.[1] Few noticed him. Few ever noticed him save in a way that stung. He was outside the world—"nothing!" as he said bitterly. Bits of the words of the walkers came to him.

"The comet?"

[4]A Hebrew word used as a concluding interjection in psalms.
[5]A quotation from Romans 12:19.
[6]An allusion to The Lord's Prayer, which can be found in Matthew 6 and Luke 11.
[7]A prayer used in Roman Catholic mass, which can be translated "Lord have mercy."
[1]The story is set in New York City.

"The comet——"

Everybody was talking of it. Even the president, as he entered, smiled patronizingly at him, and asked:

"Well, Jim, are you scared?"

"No," said the messenger shortly. "I thought we'd journeyed through the comet's tail once," broke in the junior clerk affably.

"Oh, that was Halley's,"[2] said the president; "this is a new comet, quite a stranger, they say—wonderful, wonderful! I saw it last night. Oh, by the way, Jim," turning again to the messenger, "I want you to go down into the lower vaults today."

The messenger followed the president silently. Of course, they wanted *him* to go down to the lower vaults. It was too dangerous for more valuable men. He smiled grimly and listened.

"Everything of value has been moved out since the water began to seep in," said the president; "but we miss two volumes of old records. Suppose you nose around down there,—it isn't very pleasant, I suppose."

"Not very," said the messenger, as he walked out.

"Well, Jim, the tail of the new comet hits us at noon this time," said the vault clerk, as he passed over the keys; but the messenger passed silently down the stairs. Down he went beneath Broadway, where the dim light filtered through the feet of hurrying men; down to the dark basement beneath; down into the blackness and silence beneath that lowest cavern. Here with his dark lantern he groped in the bowels of the earth, under the world.

He drew a long breath as he threw back the last great iron door and stepped into the fetid slime within. Here at last was peace, and he groped moodily forward. A great rat leaped past him and cobwebs crept across his face. He felt carefully around the room, shelf by shelf, on the muddied floor, and in crevice and corner. Nothing. Then he went back to the far end, where somehow the wall felt different. He sounded and pushed and pried. Nothing. He started away. Then something brought him back. He was sounding and working again when suddenly the whole black wall swung as on mighty hinges, and blackness yawned beyond. He peered in; it was evidently a secret vault—some hiding place of the old bank unknown in newer times. He entered hesitatingly. It was a long, narrow room with shelves, and at the far end, an old iron chest. On a high shelf lay the two missing volumes of records, and others. He put them carefully aside and stepped to the chest. It was old, strong, and rusty. He looked at the vast and old-fashioned lock and flashed his light on the hinges. They were deeply incrusted with rust. Looking about, he found a bit of iron and began to pry. The rust had eaten a hundred years, and it had gone deep. Slowly, wearily, the old lid lifted, and with a last, low groan lay bare its treasure—and he saw the dull sheen of gold!

"Boom!"

A low, grinding, reverberating crash struck upon his ear. He started up and looked about. All was black and Still. He groped for his light and swung it about him. Then he knew! The great stone door had swung to. He forgot the gold and looked death squarely in the face. Then with a sigh he went methodically to work. The cold sweat stood on his forehead; but he searched, pounded, pushed,

[2]Halley's Comet, whose orbit brings it close to Earth every 75 years. The story refers to its appearance in 1910.

and worked until after what seemed endless hours his hand struck a cold bit of metal and the great door swung again harshly on its hinges, and then, striking against something soft and heavy, stopped. He had just room to squeeze through. There lay the body of the vault clerk, cold and stiff. He stared at it, and then felt sick and nauseated. The air seemed unaccountably foul, with a strong, peculiar odor. He stepped forward, clutched at the air, and fell fainting across the corpse.

He awoke with a sense of horror, leaped from the body, and groped up the stairs, calling to the guard. The watchman sat as if asleep, with the gate swinging free. With one glance at him the messenger hurried up to the sub-vault. In vain he called to the guards. His voice echoed and re-echoed weirdly. Up into the great basement he rushed. Here another guard lay prostrate on his face, cold and still. A fear arose in the messenger's heart. He dashed up to the cellar floor, up into the bank. The stillness of death lay everywhere and everywhere bowed, bent, and stretched the silent forms of men. The messenger paused and glanced about. He was not a man easily moved; but the sight was appalling! "Robbery and murder," he whispered slowly to himself as he saw the twisted, oozing mouth of the president where he lay half-buried on his desk. Then a new thought seized him: If they found him here alone—with all this money and all these dead men—what would his life be worth? He glanced about, tiptoed cautiously to a side door, and again looked behind. Quietly he turned the latch and stepped out into Wall Street.

How silent the street was! Not a soul was stirring, and yet it was high-noon—Wall Street? Broadway? He glanced almost wildly up and down, then across the street, and as he looked, a sickening horror froze in his limbs. With a choking cry of utter fright he lunged, leaned giddily against the cold building, and stared helplessly at the sight.

In the great stone doorway a hundred men and women and children lay crushed and twisted and jammed, forced into that great, gaping doorway like refuse in a can—as if in one wild, frantic rush to safety, they had rushed and ground themselves to death. Slowly the messenger crept along the walls, wetting his parched mouth and trying to comprehend, stilling the tremor in his limbs and the rising terror in his heart. He met a business man, silk-hatted and frock-coated, who had crept, too, along that smooth wall and stood now stone dead with wonder written on his lips. The messenger turned his eyes hastily away and sought the curb. A woman leaned wearily against the signpost, her head bowed motionless on her lace and silken bosom. Before her stood a street car, silent, and within—but the messenger but glanced and hurried on. A grimy newsboy sat in the gutter with the "last edition" in his uplifted hand: "Danger!" screamed its black headlines. "Warnings wired around the world. The Comet's tail sweeps past us at noon. Deadly gases expected. Close doors and windows. Seek the cellar." The messenger read and staggered on. Far out from a window above, a girl lay with gasping face and sleevelets[3] on her arms. On a store step sat a little, sweet-faced girl looking upward toward the skies, and in the carriage by her lay—but the messenger looked no longer. The cords gave way—the terror burst in his veins, and with one great, gasping cry he sprang desperately forward and ran,—ran as only the frightened run, shrieking and fighting the

[3]Protective coverings worn over the sleeves of a garment.

air until with one last wail of pain he sank on the grass of Madison Square[4] and lay prone and still.

When he rose, he gave no glance at the still and silent forms on the benches, but, going to a fountain, bathed his face; then hiding himself in a corner away from the drama of death, he quietly gripped himself and thought the thing through: The comet had swept the earth and this was the end. Was everybody dead? He must search and see.

He knew that he must steady himself and keep calm, or he would go insane. First he must go to a restaurant. He walked up Fifth Avenue to a famous hostelry and entered its gorgeous, ghost-haunted halls. He beat back the nausea, and, seizing a tray from dead hands, hurried into the street and ate ravenously, hiding to keep out the sights.

"Yesterday, they would not have served me," he whispered, as he forced the food down.

Then he started up the street,—looking, peering, telephoning, ringing alarms; silent, silent all. Was nobody—nobody—he dared not think the thought and hurried on.

Suddenly he stopped still. He had forgotten. My God! How could he have forgotten? He must rush to the subway—then he almost laughed. No—a car; if he could find a Ford. He saw one. Gently he lifted off its burden, and took his place on the seat. He tested the throttle. There was gas. He glided off, shivering, and drove up the street. Everywhere stood, leaned, lounged, and lay the dead, in grim and awful silence. On he ran past an automobile, wrecked and overturned; past another, filled with a gay party whose smiles yet lingered on their death-struck lips; on past crowds and groups of cars, pausing by dead policemen; at 42nd Street he had to detour to Park Avenue to avoid the dead congestion. He came back on Fifth Avenue at 57th and flew past the Plaza and by the park with its hushed babies and silent throng, until as he was rushing past 72nd Street he heard a sharp cry, and saw a living form leaning wildly out an upper window. He gasped. The human voice sounded in his ears like the voice of God.

"Hello—hello—help, in God's name!" wailed the woman. "There's a dead girl in here and a man and—and see yonder dead men lying in the street and dead horses—for the love of God go and bring the officers——" And the words trailed off into hysterical tears.

He wheeled the car in a sudden circle, running over the still body of a child and leaping on the curb. Then he rushed up the steps and tried the door and rang violently. There was a long pause, but at last the heavy door swung back. They stared a moment in silence. She had not noticed before that he was a Negro. He had not thought of her as white. She was a woman of perhaps twenty-five—rarely beautiful and richly gowned, with darkly-golden hair, and jewels. Yesterday, he thought with bitterness, she would scarcely have looked at him twice. He would have been dirt beneath her silken feet. She stared at him. Of all the sorts of men she had pictured as coming to her rescue she had not dreamed of one like him. Not that he was not human, but he dwelt in a world so far from hers, so infinitely far, that he seldom even entered her thought. Yet as she looked at him curiously he seemed quite commonplace and usual. He

[4] A city park bordered on one side by Broadway.

was a tall, dark workingman of the better class, with a sensitive face trained to stolidity and a poor man's clothes and hands. His face was soft and slow and his manner at once cold and nervous, like fires long banked, but not out.

So a moment each paused and gauged the other; then the thought of the dead world without rushed in and they started toward each other.

"What has happened?" she cried. "Tell me! Nothing stirs. All is silence! I see the dead strewn before my window as winnowed by the breath of God,—and see——" She dragged him through great, silken hangings to where, beneath the sheen of mahogany and silver, a little French maid lay stretched in quiet, everlasting sleep, and near her a butler lay prone in his livery.

The tears streamed down the woman's cheeks and she clung to his arm until the perfume of her breath swept his face and he felt the tremors racing through her body.

"I had been shut up in my dark room developing pictures of the comet which I took last night; when I came out—I saw the dead!

"What has happened?" she cried again.

He answered slowly:

"Something—comet or devil—swept across the earth this morning and—many are dead!"

"Many? Very many?"

"I have searched and I have seen no other living soul but you."

She gasped and they stared at each other.

"My—father!" she whispered.

"Where is he?"

"He started for the office."

"Where is it?"

"In the Metropolitan Tower."

"Leave a note for him here and come."

Then he stopped.

"No," he said firmly—"first, we must go—to Harlem."

"Harlem!" she cried. Then she understood. She tapped her foot at first impatiently. She looked back and shuddered. Then she came resolutely down the steps.

"There's a swifter car in the garage in the court," she said.

"I don't know how to drive it," he said.

"I do," she answered.

In ten minutes they were flying to Harlem on the wind. The Stutz rose and raced like an airplane. They took the turn at 110th Street on two wheels and slipped with a shriek into 135th.

He was gone but a moment. Then he returned, and his face was gray. She did not look, but said:

"You have lost—somebody?"

"I have lost—everybody," he said, simply—"unless——"

He ran back and was gone several minutes—hours they seemed to her.

"Everybody," he said, and he walked slowly back with something film-like in his hand which he stuffed into his pocket.

"I'm afraid I was selfish," he said. But already the car was moving toward the park among the dark and lined dead of Harlem—the brown, still faces, the knotted hands, the homely garments, and the silence—the wild and haunting silence. Out of the park, and down Fifth Avenue they whirled. In and out among the dead they slipped and quivered, needing no sound of bell or horn, until the great, square Metropolitan Tower hove in sight. Gently he laid the dead elevator boy aside; the car shot upward. The door of the office stood open. On the threshold lay the stenographer, and, staring at her, sat the dead clerk. The inner office was empty, but a note lay on the desk, folded and addressed but unsent:

Dear Daughter:

I've gone for a hundred mile spin in Fred's new Mercedes. Shall not be back before dinner. I'll bring Fred with me.

J.B.H.

"Come," she cried nervously. "We must search the city."

Up and down, over and across, back again—on went that ghostly search. Everywhere was silence and death—death and silence! They hunted from Madison Square to Spuyten Duyvel; they rushed across the Williamsburg Bridge; they swept over Brooklyn; from the Battery and Morningside Heights they scanned the river. Silence, silence everywhere, and no human sign. Haggard and bedraggled they puffed a third time slowly down Broadway, under the broiling sun, and at last stopped. He sniffed the air. An odor—a smell—and with the shifting breeze a sickening stench filled their nostrils and brought its awful warning. The girl settled back helplessly in her seat.

"What can we do?" she cried.

It was his turn now to take the lead, and he did it quickly.

"The long distance telephone—the telegraph and the cable—night rockets and then—flight!"

She looked at him now with strength and confidence. He did not look like men, as she had always pictured men; but he acted like one and she was content. In fifteen minutes they were at the central telephone exchange. As they came to the door he stepped quickly before her and pressed her gently back as he closed it. She heard him moving to and fro, and knew his burdens—the poor, little burdens he bore. When she entered, he was alone in the room. The grim switchboard flashed its metallic face in cryptic, sphinx-like immobility. She seated herself on a stool and donned the bright earpiece. She looked at the mouthpiece. She had never looked at one so closely before. It was wide and black, pimpled with usage; inert; dead; almost sarcastic in its unfeeling curves. It looked—she beat back the thought—but it looked,—it persisted in looking like—she turned her head and found herself alone. One moment she was terrified; then she thanked him silently for his delicacy and turned resolutely, with a quick intaking of breath.

"Hello!" she called in low tones. She was calling to the world. The world *must* answer. Would the world *answer?* Was the world——

Silence!

She had spoken too low.

"Hello!" she cried, full-voiced.

She listened. Silence! Her heart beat quickly. She cried in clear, distinct, loud tones: "Hello—hello—hello!"

What was that whirring? Surely—no—was it the click of a receiver?

She bent close, she moved the pegs in the holes, and called and called, until her voice rose almost to a shriek, and her heart hammered. It was as if she had heard the last flicker of creation, and the evil was silence. Her voice dropped to a sob. She sat stupidly staring into the black and sarcastic mouthpiece, and the thought came again. Hope lay dead within her. Yes, the cable and the rockets remained; but the world—she could not frame the thought or say the word. It was too mighty—too terrible! She turned toward the door with a new fear in her heart. For the first time she seemed to realize that she was alone in the world with a stranger, with something more than a stranger,—with a man alien in blood and culture—unknown, perhaps unknowable. It was awful! She must escape—she must fly; he must not see her again. Who knew what awful thoughts—

She gathered her silken skirts deftly about her young, smooth limbs—listened, and glided into a sidehall. A moment she shrank back: the hall lay filled with dead women; then she leaped to the door and tore at it, with bleeding fingers, until it swung wide. She looked out. He was standing at the top of the alley,—silhouetted, tall and black, motionless. Was he looking at her or away? She did not know—she did not care. She simply leaped and ran—ran until she found herself alone amid the dead and the tall ramparts of towering buildings.

She stopped. She was alone. Alone! Alone on the streets—alone in the city—perhaps alone in the world! There crept in upon her the sense of deception—of creeping hands behind her back—of silent, moving things she could not see,—of voices hushed in fearsome conspiracy. She looked behind and sideways, started at strange sounds and heard still stranger, until every nerve within her stood sharp and quivering, stretched to scream at the barest touch. She whirled and flew back, whimpering like a child, until she found that narrow alley again and the dark, silent figure silhouetted at the top. She stopped and rested; then she walked silently toward him, looked at him timidly; but he said nothing as he handed her into the car. Her voice caught as she whispered:

"Not—that."

And he answered slowly: "No—not that!"

They climbed into the car. She bent forward on the wheel and sobbed, with great, dry, quivering sobs, as they flew toward the cable office on the east side, leaving the world of wealth and prosperity for the world of poverty and work. In the world behind them were death and silence, grave and grim, almost cynical, but always decent; here it was hideous. It clothed itself in every ghastly form of terror, struggle, hate, and suffering. It lay wreathed in crime and squalor, greed and lust. Only in its dread and awful silence was it like to death everywhere.

Yet as the two, flying and alone, looked upon the horror of the world, slowly, gradually, the sense of all-enveloping death deserted them. They seemed to move in a world silent and asleep,—not dead. They moved in quiet reverence, lest somehow they wake these sleeping forms who had, at last, found peace. They moved in some solemn, world-wide *Friedhof*,[5] above which some mighty arm had waved its magic wand. All nature slept until—until, and quick with the same startling thought, they looked into each other's eyes—he, ashen, and she, crimson, with unspoken thought. To both, the vision of a mighty beauty—of vast, unspoken things, swelled in their souls; but they put it away.

[5]A cemetery.

Great, dark coils of wire came up from the earth and down from the sun and entered this low lair of witchery. The gathered lightnings of the world centered here, binding with beams of light the ends of the earth. The doors gaped on the gloom within. He paused on the threshold.

"Do you know the code?" she asked.

"I know the call for help—we used it formerly at the bank."

She hardly heard. She heard the lapping of the waters far below,—the dark and restless waters—the cold and luring waters, as they called. He stepped within. Slowly she walked to the wall, where the water called below, and stood and waited. Long she waited, and he did not come. Then with a start she saw him, too, standing beside the black waters. Slowly he removed his coat and stood there silently. She walked quickly to him and laid her hand on his arm. He did not start or look. The waters lapped on in luring, deadly rhythm. He pointed down to the waters, and said quietly:

"The world lies beneath the waters now—may I go?"

She looked into his stricken, tired face, and a great pity surged within her heart. She answered in a voice clear and calm, "No."

Upward they turned toward life again, and he seized the wheel. The world was darkening to twilight, and a great, gray pall was falling mercifully and gently on the sleeping dead. The ghastly glare of reality seemed replaced with the dream of some vast romance. The girl lay silently back, as the motor whizzed along, and looked half-consciously for the elf-queen to wave life into this dead world again. She forgot to wonder at the quickness with which he had learned to drive her car. It seemed natural. And then as they whirled and swung into Madison Square and at the door of the Metropolitan Tower she gave a low cry, and her eyes were great! Perhaps she had seen the elf-queen?

The man led her to the elevator of the tower and deftly they ascended. In her father's office they gathered rugs and chairs, and he wrote a note and laid it on the desk; then they ascended to the roof and he made her comfortable. For a while she rested and sank to dreamy somnolence, watching the worlds above and wondering. Below lay the dark shadows of the city and afar was the shining of the sea. She glanced at him timidly as he set food before her and took a shawl and wound her in it, touching her reverently, yet tenderly. She looked up at him with thankfulness in her eyes, eating what he served. He watched the city. She watched him. He seemed very human,—very near now.

"Have you had to work hard?" she asked softly.

"Always," he said.

"I have always been idle," she said. "I was rich."

"I was poor," he almost echoed.

"The rich and the poor are met together," she began, and he finished: "The Lord is the Maker of them all."

"Yes," she said slowly; "and how foolish our human distinctions seem—now," looking down to the great dead city stretched below, swimming in unlightened shadows.

"Yes—I was not—human, yesterday," he said.

She looked at him. "And your people were not my people," she said; "but today——" She paused. He was a man,—no more; but he was in some larger sense a gentleman,—sensitive, kindly, chivalrous, everything save his hands and—his face. Yet yesterday——

"Death, the leveler!" he muttered.

"And the revealer," she whispered gently, rising to her feet with great eyes. He turned away, and after fumbling a moment sent a rocket into the darkening air. It arose, shrieked, and flew up, a slim path of light, and scattering its stars abroad, dropped on the city below. She scarcely noticed it. A vision of the world had risen before her. Slowly the mighty prophecy of her destiny overwhelmed her. Above the dead past hovered the Angel of Annunciation.[6] She was no mere woman. She was neither high nor low, white nor black, rich nor poor. She was primal woman; mighty mother of all men to come and Bride of Life. She looked upon the man beside her and forgot all else but his manhood, his strong, vigorous manhood—his sorrow and sacrifice. She saw him glorified. He was no longer a thing apart, a creature below, a strange outcast of another clime and blood, but her Brother Humanity incarnate, Son of God and great All-Father of the race to be.

He did not glimpse the glory in her eyes, but stood looking outward toward the sea and sending rocket after rocket into the unanswering darkness. Dark-purple clouds lay banked and billowed in the west. Behind them and all around, the heavens glowed in dim, weird radiance that suffused the darkening world and made almost a minor music. Suddenly, as though gathered back in some vast hand, the great cloud-curtain fell away. Low on the horizon lay a long, white star—mystic, wonderful! And from it fled upward to the pole, like some wan bridal veil, a pale, wide sheet of flame that lighted all the world and dimmed the stars.

In fascinated silence the man gazed at the heavens and dropped his rockets to the floor. Memories of memories stirred to life in the dead recesses of his mind. The shackles seemed to rattle and fall from his soul. Up from the crass and crushing and cringing of his caste leaped the lone majesty of kings long dead. He arose within the shadows, tall, straight, and stern, with power in his eyes and ghostly scepters hovering to his grasp. It was as though some mighty Pharaoh lived again, or curled Assyrian lord. He turned and looked upon the lady, and found her gazing straight at him.

Silently, immovably, they saw each other face to face—eye to eye. Their souls lay naked to the night. It was not lust; it was not love—it was some vaster, mightier thing that needed neither touch of body nor thrill of soul. It was a thought divine, splendid.

Slowly, noiselessly, they moved toward each other—the heavens above, the seas around, the city grim and dead below. He loomed from out the velvet shadows vast and dark. Pearl-white and slender, she shone beneath the stars. She stretched her jeweled hands abroad. He lifted up his mighty arms, and they cried each to the other, almost with one voice, "The world is dead."

"Long live the——"

"Honk! Honk!" Hoarse and sharp the cry of a motor drifted clearly up from the silence below. They started backward with a cry and gazed upon each other with eyes that faltered and fell, with blood that boiled.

"Honk! Honk! Honk! Honk!" came the mad cry again, and almost from their feet a rocket blazed into the air and scattered its stars upon them. She covered her eyes with her hands, and her shoulders heaved. He dropped and

[6]An allusion to the Christian Annunciation, in which Mary was told that she would be the mother of God's son.

bowed, groped blindly on his knees about the floor. A blue flame spluttered lazily after an age, and she heard the scream of an answering rocket as it flew.

Then they stood still as death, looking to opposite ends of the earth.

"Clang—crash—clang!"

The roar and ring of swift elevators shooting upward from below made the great tower tremble. A murmur and babel of voices[7] swept in upon the night. All over the once dead city the lights blinked, flickered, and flamed; and then with a sudden clanging of doors the entrance to the platform was filled with men, and one with white and flying hair rushed to the girl and lifted her to his breast. "My daughter!" he sobbed.

Behind him hurried a younger, comelier man, carefully clad in motor costume, who bent above the girl with passionate solicitude and gazed into her staring eyes until they narrowed and dropped and her face flushed deeper and deeper crimson.

"Julia," he whispered; "my darling, I thought you were gone forever."

She looked up at him with strange, searching eyes.

"Fred," she murmured, almost vaguely, "is the world—gone?"

"Only New York," he answered; "it is terrible—awful! You know,—but you, how did you escape—how have you endured this horror? Are you well? Unharmed?"

"Unharmed!" she said.

"And this man here?" he asked, encircling her drooping form with one arm and turning toward the Negro. Suddenly he stiffened and his hand flew to his hip. "Why!" he snarled. "It's—a—nigger—Julia! Has he—has he dared——"

She lifted her head and looked at her late companion curiously and then dropped her eyes with a sigh.

"He has dared—all, to rescue me," she said quietly, "and I—thank him—much." But she did not look at him again. As the couple turned away, the father drew a roll of bills from his pockets.

"Here, my good fellow," he said, thrusting the money into the man's hands, "take that,—what's your name?"

"Jim Davis," came the answer, hollow-voiced.

"Well, Jim, I thank you. I've always liked your people. If you ever want a job, call on me." And they were gone.

The crowd poured up and out of the elevators, talking and whispering.

"Who was it?"

"Are they alive?"

"How many?"

"Two!"

"Who was saved?"

"A white girl and a nigger—there she goes."

"A nigger? Where is he? Let's lynch the damned——"

"Shut up—he's all right—he saved her."

"Saved hell! He had no business——"

"Here he comes."

Into the glare of the electric lights the colored man moved slowly, with the eyes of those that walk and sleep.

[7]An incomprehensible confusion, like that at the Tower of Babel (Genesis 11).

"Well, what do you think of that?" cried a bystander; "of all New York, just a white girl and a nigger!"

The colored man heard nothing. He stood silently beneath the glare of the light, gazing at the money in his hand and shrinking as he gazed; slowly he put his other hand into his pocket and brought out a baby's filmy cap, and gazed again. A woman mounted to the platform and looked about, shading her eyes. She was brown, small, and toil-worn, and in one arm lay the corpse of a dark baby. The crowd parted and her eyes fell on the colored man; with a cry she tottered toward him.

"Jim!"

He whirled and, with a sob of joy, caught her in his arms.

1920

Edwin Arlington Robinson

1869–1935

The first major poet of twentieth-century America, E. A. Robinson fit the romantic stereotype of the poet as a lonely, struggling genius. Through much of his life he experienced personal tragedy, poverty, and public disregard—all of which were reflected in his somber, often stoical poetry. He was the third son of a small-town Maine businessman and of a mother whose New England ancestors included the early colonial poet Anne Bradstreet. Except for some juvenile poems, Robinson showed little aptitude as a youth. He was an indifferent student, and after his graduation from high school, his father refused the expense of his further education. Eventually, when he was almost twenty-two, Robinson managed to enroll as a special student at Harvard, but after two years he left Harvard and returned home to Gardiner, Maine.

During the next few years he completed two books of poetry, the first of which, The Torrent and the Night Before *(1896), he published at his own expense. With the appearance of his second book,* The Children of the Night *(1897), he left home and moved to New York. Gardiner, which appeared as Tilbury Town in Robinson's poems, provided him with a colorful array of New England character types—drunkards, dreamers, and misfits with names like Richard Cory, Bewick Finzer, and Eben Flood. They embodied the spiritual drought and moral failure that Robinson made the thematic center of much of his work.*

In New York, Robinson tried his hand at journalism and later worked as a time-keeper during the construction of the New York subway system. Following the publication in 1902 of Captain Craig, *he received, with the help of President Theodore Roosevelt, a job at the New York Customs House, and in 1910 he published his fourth book of poems,* The Town Down the River. *The following year Robinson spent his first summer at the MacDowell Colony for artists in the New Hampshire countryside, where he was to return every summer for the rest of his life. There, with freedom to concentrate on his writing, he began his most productive years. The appearance of* The Man Against the Sky *(1916) marked the beginning of his reputation. The next decade saw the publication of* The Three Taverns *(1920),* Avon's Harvest *(1921), and* Dionysus in Doubt *(1925). His* Collected

Poems *(1921) brought him the first of three Pulitzer Prizes, and his long narrative poem* Tristram *(1927) became a bestseller.*

Robinson was a transitional figure between the nineteenth and twentieth centuries. His life spanned the waning years of the genteel era and the rebellious period of disillusionment that followed World War I. An older generation found his poetry dangerously radical, marred by formlessness; the modernists found it tamely conservative. His deepest roots were in the Puritan ethic of his forebears. His fascination with the interior drama of human defeat earned him a reputation for pessimism, but it was a pessimism qualified by the positive values of a New England conscience—endurance, moral courage, and the conviction that, as he once put it, "There's a good deal to live for, but a man has to go through hell really to find it out."

FURTHER READING: *Selected Letters of Edwin Arlington Robinson,* ed. R. Torrence, 1940; E. Fussell, *Edwin Arlington Robinson: The Literary Background of a Traditional Poet,* 1954; *Selected Poems of Edwin Arlington Robinson,* ed. M. Zabel, 1965, 1966; W. Anderson, *Edwin Arlington Robinson,* 1967; W. Robinson, *Edwin Arlington Robinson: A Poetry of the Act,* 1967; H. Franchere, *Edwin Arlington Robinson,* 1968; L. Coxe, *Edwin Arlington Robinson: The Life of Poetry,* 1968; *Edwin Arlington Robinson: Centenary Essays,* ed. E. Barnard, 1973; R. Cary, *Early Reception of Edwin Arlington Robinson,* 1974; *Uncollected Poems and Prose of Edwin Arlington Robinson,* ed. R. Cary, 1975; C. Joyner, *Edwin Arlington Robinson: A Reference Guide,* 1978; *Edwin Arlington Robinson,* ed. H. Bloom, 1988; R. Hoffpauir, *The Contemplative Poetry of Edwin Arlington Robinson, Robert Frost, and Yvor Winters,* 2002.

TEXT: *The Collected Poems of Edwin Arlington Robinson,* 1921.

LUKE HAVERGAL

Go to the western gate, Luke Havergal,
There where the vines cling crimson on the wall,
And in the twilight wait for what will come.
The leaves will whisper there of her, and some,
Like flying words, will strike you as they fall;
But go, and if you listen she will call.
Go to the western gate, Luke Havergal—
Luke Havergal.

No, there is not a dawn in eastern skies
To rift the fiery night that's in your eyes;
But there, where western glooms are gathering,
The dark will end the dark, if anything:
God slays Himself with every leaf that flies,
And hell is more than half of paradise.
No, there is not a dawn in eastern skies—
In eastern skies.

Out of a grave I come to tell you this,
Out of a grave I come to quench the kiss
That flames upon your forehead with a glow
That blinds you to the way that you must go.

Yes, there is yet one way to where she is,
Bitter, but one that faith may never miss.
Out of a grave I come to tell you this—
To tell you this.

There is the western gate, Luke Havergal,
There are the crimson leaves upon the wall.
Go, for the winds are tearing them away,—
Nor think to riddle[1] the dead words they say,
Nor any more to feel them as they fall;
But go, and if you trust her she will call.
There is the western gate, Luke Havergal—
Luke Havergal.

1896

ZOLA

Because he puts the compromising chart
Of hell before your eyes, you are afraid;
Because he counts the price that you have paid
For innocence, and counts it from the start,
You loathe him. But he sees the human heart
Of God meanwhile, and in His hand was weighed
Your squeamish and emasculate crusade
Against the grim dominion of his art.

Never until we conquer the uncouth
Connivings of our shamed indifference
(We call it Christian faith) are we to scan
The racked and shrieking hideousness of Truth
To find, in hate's polluted self-defence
Throbbing, the pulse, the divine heart of man.

1896

RICHARD CORY

Whenever Richard Cory went down town,
We people on the pavement looked at him:
He was a gentleman from sole to crown,
Clean favored, and imperially slim.

And he was always quietly arrayed,
And he was always human when he talked;

[1]Interpret.

But still he fluttered pulses when he said
"Good-morning," and he glittered when he walked.

And he was rich—yes, richer than a king—
And admirably schooled in every grace:
In fine, we thought that he was everything
To make us wish that we were in his place.

So on we worked, and waited for the light,
And went without the meat, and cursed the bread;
And Richard Cory, one calm summer night,
Went home and put a bullet through his head.

1897

CLIFF KLINGENHAGEN

Cliff Klingenhagen had me in to dine
With him one day; and after soup and meat,
And all the other things there were to eat,
Cliff took two glasses and filled one with wine
And one with wormwood.[1] Then without a sign
For me to choose at all, he took the draught
Of bitterness himself, and lightly quaffed
It off, and said the other one was mine.

And when I asked him what the deuce he meant
By doing that, he only looked at me
And smiled, and said it was a way of his.
And though I know the fellow, I have spent
Long time a-wondering when I shall be
As happy as Cliff Klingenhagen is.

1897

MINIVER CHEEVY

Miniver Cheevy, child of scorn,
    Grew lean while he assailed the seasons;
He wept that he was ever born,
    And he had reasons.

Miniver loved the days of old
    When swords were bright and steeds were prancing;
The vision of a warrior bold
    Would set him dancing.

[1]The bitter oil extracted from the wormwood plant.

Miniver sighed for what was not,
And dreamed, and rested from his labors;
He dreamed of Thebes and Camelot,[1]
And Priam's[2] neighbors.

Miniver mourned the ripe renown
That made so many a name so fragrant;
He mourned Romance, now on the town,
And Art, a vagrant.

Miniver loved the Medici,[3]
Albeit he had never seen one;
He would have sinned incessantly
Could he have been one.

Miniver cursed the commonplace
And eyed a khaki suit with loathing;
He missed the mediæval grace
Of iron clothing.

Miniver scorned the gold he sought,
But sore annoyed was he without it;
Miniver thought, and thought, and thought,
And thought about it.

Miniver Cheevy, born too late,
Scratched his head and kept on thinking;
Miniver coughed, and called it fate,
And kept on drinking.

1907

HOW ANNANDALE WENT OUT

"They called it Annandale—and I was there
To flourish, to find words, and to attend:
Liar, physician, hypocrite, and friend,
I watched him; and the sight was not so fair
As one or two that I have seen elsewhere:
An apparatus not for me to mend—
A wreck, with hell between him and the end,
Remained of Annandale; and I was there.

[1]Thebes: name of cities in ancient Egypt and Greece; Camelot: legendary site of King Arthur's palace.
[2]Mythological king of Troy during the Trojan War.
[3]Powerful family of Renaissance Florence, Italy, with a reputation for predatory ruthlessness and sinfulness.

"I knew the ruin as I knew the man;
So put the two together, if you can,
Remembering the worst you know of me.
Now view yourself as I was, on the spot—
With a slight kind of engine. Do you see?
Like this . . . You wouldn't hang me? I thought not."

1910

EROS TURANNOS[1]

She fears him, and will always ask
  What fated her to choose him;
She meets in his engaging mask
  All reasons to refuse him;
But what she meets and what she fears
  Are less than are the downward years;
Drawn slowly to the foamless weirs[2]
  Of age, were she to lose him.

Between a blurred sagacity
  That once had power to sound him,
And Love, that will not let him be
  The Judas[3] that she found him,
Her pride assuages her almost,
As if it were alone the cost.—
He sees that he will not be lost,
  And waits and looks around him.

A sense of ocean and old trees
  Envelops and allures him;
Tradition, touching all he sees,
  Beguiles and reassures him;
And all her doubts of what he says
Are dimmed with what she knows of days—
Till even prejudice delays
  And fades, and she secures him.

The falling leaf inaugurates
  The reign of her confusion;
The pounding wave reverberates
  The dirge of her illusion;
And home, where passion lived and died,
Becomes a place where she can hide,
While all the town and harbor side
  Vibrate with her seclusion.

[1]Greek: Love, the Tyrant. [2]A dam in a stream, used to regulate or measure water flow.
[3]Christ's disciple who betrayed Him.

We tell you, tapping on our brows,
The story as it should be,—
As if the story of a house
Were told, or ever could be;
We'll have no kindly veil between
Her visions and those we have seen—
As if we guessed what hers have been,
Or what they are or would be.

Meanwhile we do no harm; for they
That with a god have striven,
Not hearing much of what we say,
Take what the god has given;
Though like waves breaking it may be
Or like a changed familiar tree,
Or like a stairway to the sea
Where down the blind are driven.

1914

MR. FLOOD'S PARTY

Old Eben Flood, climbing alone one night
Over the hill between the town below
And the forsaken upland hermitage
That held as much as he should ever know
On earth again of home, paused warily.
The road was his with not a native near;
And Eben, having leisure, said aloud,
For no man else in Tilbury Town to hear:

"Well, Mr. Flood, we have the harvest moon
Again, and we may not have many more;
The bird is on the wing,[1] the poet says,
And you and I have said it here before.
Drink to the bird." He raised up to the light
The jug that he had gone so far to fill,
And answered huskily: "Well, Mr. Flood,
Since you propose it, I believe I will."

Alone, as if enduring to the end
A valiant armor of scarred hopes outworn,

[1]An allusion to a quatrain in Edward FitzGerald's *The Rubáiyát of Omar Khayyám* (1859): "Come, fill the Cup, and in the fire of Spring / Your Winter-garment of Repentance fling: / The Bird of Time has but a little way / To flutter—and the Bird is on the Wing."

He stood there in the middle of the road
Like Roland's ghost winding a silent horn.[2]
Below him, in the town among the trees,
Where friends of other days had honored him,
A phantom salutation of the dead
Rang thinly till old Eben's eyes were dim.

Then, as a mother lays her sleeping child
Down tenderly, fearing it may awake,
He set the jug down slowly at his feet
With trembling care, knowing that most things break;
And only when assured that on firm earth
It stood, as the uncertain lives of men
Assuredly did not, he paced away,
And with his hand extended paused again:

"Well, Mr. Flood, we have not met like this
In a long time; and many a change has come
To both of us, I fear, since last it was
We had a drop together. Welcome home!"
Convivially returning with himself,
Again he raised the jug up to the light;
And with an acquiescent quaver said:
"Well, Mr. Flood, if you insist, I might.

"Only a very little, Mr. Flood—
For auld lang syne. No more, sir; that will do."
So, for the time, apparently it did,
And Eben evidently thought so too;
For soon amid the silver loneliness
Of night he lifted up his voice and sang,
Secure, with only two moons listening,
Until the whole harmonious landscape rang—

"For auld lang syne." The weary throat gave out,
The last word wavered, and the song was done.
He raised again the jug regretfully
And shook his head, and was again alone.
There was not much that was ahead of him,
And there was nothing in the town below
Where strangers would have shut the many doors
That many friends had opened long ago.

1920

[2]Roland, the embattled hero of the medieval French romance *Chanson de Roland,* proudly waited until he was overwhelmed before sounding his horn to summon help.

Robert Frost 1874–1963

To his rural New England neighbors, Robert Frost was an unlikely farmer who wrote poetry into the late hours and milked his cows at midnight. To much of the American public, he was a white-thatched, rustic sage, a poet of rural simplicity and public virtue. To intimate friends, he was a man frequently driven by a cantankerous desire to carry on what he called his "lover's quarrel with the world."

Although he came to be known as a poet of New England, Frost was born in San Francisco and spent his early childhood in the Far West. At the death of his father, when Frost was eleven, the family moved to Salem, New Hampshire. After graduating from high school as valedictorian and class poet in 1892, Frost entered Dartmouth College but soon left to work at odd jobs and write poetry. In 1897 he tried college again, Harvard, but he left after two years, having acquired an enduring dislike for academic convention.

For the next twelve years Frost eked out a minimal living by teaching and farming while continuing to write his poems. In 1912 he decided to venture everything on a literary career. Leaving New Hampshire, he sailed for England, where he hoped "to write poetry without further scandal to friends or family." In London, he soon found a publisher, and his first book, A Boy's Will *(1913), brought him to the attention of influential critics, among them the American expatriate Ezra Pound, who praised Frost as an authentic poet, "vurry Amur'k'n."*

Following the publication of a second volume of poems, North of Boston *(1914), Frost returned home, determined to win recognition in his native land. To support himself he taught in colleges and gave poetry readings throughout much of the United States. His fame grew with the appearance of a succession of books:* Mountain Interval *(1916),* New Hampshire *(1923),* West-Running Brook *(1928),* A Further Range *(1936),* A Witness Tree *(1942),* Steeple Bush *(1947), and* In the Clearing *(1962). By the end of his life he had become a national bard: He received honorary degrees from forty-four colleges and universities and won four Pulitzer Prizes, the U.S. Senate passed resolutions honoring his birthdays, and when he was eighty-seven he read his poetry at the inauguration of President John F. Kennedy.*

Frost had rejected the revolutionary poetic principles of his contemporaries, choosing instead "the old-fashioned way to be new." He employed the plain speech of rural New Englanders and preferred the short, traditional forms of lyric and narrative. As a poet of nature he had obvious affinities with romantic writers, notably Wordsworth and Emerson. He saw nature as a storehouse of analogy and symbol, announcing, "I'm always saying something that's just the edge of something more," but he had little faith in religious dogma or speculative thought. His concern with nature reflected deep moral uncertainties, and his poetry, for all its apparent simplicity, often probes mysteries of darkness and irrationality in the bleak and chaotic landscapes of an indifferent universe where men and women stand alone, forsaken and perplexed.

FURTHER READING: *Selected Letters of Robert Frost,* ed. L. Thompson, 1964; *Selected Prose of Robert Frost,* ed. H. Cox and E. Lathem, 1966; L. Thompson, *Robert Frost: The Early Years,* 1966; L. Thompson, *Robert Frost: The Years of Triumph,* 1970; *Robert Frost: Centennial Essays,* 3 vols., ed. J. Thorpe, 1974–1978; L. Thompson and R. Winnick, *Robert Frost: The Later Years,* 1976; J. Kemp, *Robert Frost and New England,* 1979; J. Potter, *Robert Frost Handbook,* 1980; T. Sharma, *Robert Frost's Poetic Style,* 1981; W. Pritchard, *Frost: A Literary Life Reconsidered,* 1984, 1993; R. Wakefield, *Robert Frost and the Opposing Lights of the Hour,* 1985; J. Walsh, *Into My Own: The English Years of Robert Frost,* 1912–1915, 1988; M. Marcus, *The Poems of Robert Frost,* 1991; J. Meyer, *Robert Frost: A Biography,* 1996; M. Richardson, *The*

Ordeal of Robert Frost, 1997; *Elected Friends: Robert Frost & Edward Thomas to One Another,* ed. M. Spencer, 2003; R. Pack, *Belief and Uncertainty in the Poetry of Robert Frost,* 2003.

TEXTS: *North of Boston,* 1915; *Mountain Interval,* 1921; *Harper's Magazine,* 1920; *The Poetry of Robert Frost,* ed. E. Lathem, 1969.

MENDING WALL

Something there is that doesn't love a wall,
That sends the frozen-ground-swell under it
And spills the upper boulders in the sun,
And makes gaps even two can pass abreast.
The work of hunters is another thing:
I have come after them and made repair
Where they have left not one stone on a stone,
But they would have the rabbit out of hiding,
To please the yelping dogs. The gaps I mean,
No one has seen them made or heard them made,
But at spring mending-time we find them there.
I let my neighbor know beyond the hill;
And on a day we meet to walk the line
And set the wall between us once again.
We keep the wall between us as we go.
To each the boulders that have fallen to each.
And some are loaves and some so nearly balls
We have to use a spell to make them balance:
"Stay where you are until our backs are turned!"
We wear our fingers rough with handling them.
Oh, just another kind of outdoor game,
One on a side. It comes to little more:
There where it is we do not need the wall:
He is all pine and I am apple orchard.
My apple trees will never get across
And eat the cones under his pines, I tell him.
He only says, "Good fences make good neighbors."
Spring is the mischief in me, and I wonder
If I could put a notion in his head:
"*Why* do they make good neighbors? Isn't it
Where there are cows? But here there are no cows.
Before I built a wall I'd ask to know
What I was walling in or walling out,
And to whom I was like to give offense.
Something there is that doesn't love a wall,
That wants it down." I could say "Elves" to him,
But it's not elves exactly, and I'd rather
He said it for himself. I see him there,

Bringing a stone grasped firmly by the top
In each hand, like an old-stone savage armed.
He moves in darkness as it seems to me,
Not of woods only and the shade of trees.
He will not go behind his father's saying,
And he likes having thought of it so well
He says again, "Good fences make good neighbors."

1914

HOME BURIAL

He saw her from the bottom of the stairs
Before she saw him. She was starting down,
Looking back over her shoulder at some fear.
She took a doubtful step and then undid it
To raise herself and look again. He spoke
Advancing toward her: "What is it you see
From up there always?—for I want to know."
She turned and sank upon her skirts at that,
And her face changed from terrified to dull.
He said to gain time: "What is it you see?"
Mounting until she cowered under him.
"I will find out now—you must tell me, dear."
She, in her place, refused him any help,
With the least stiffening of her neck and silence.
She let him look, sure that he couldn't see,
Blind creature; and awhile he didn't see.
But at last he murmured, "Oh," and again, "Oh."

"What is it—what?" she said.

"Just that I see."

"You don't," she challenged. "Tell me what it is."

"The wonder is I didn't see at once.
I never noticed it from here before.
I must be wonted[1]
to it—that's the reason.
The little graveyard where my people are!
So small the window frames the whole of it.
Not so much larger than a bedroom, is it?
There are three stones of slate and one of marble,
Broad-shouldered little slabs there in the sunlight
On the sidehill. We haven't to mind *those.*

[1]Accustomed.

But I understand: it is not the stones,
But the child's mound——"

"Don't, don't, don't,
don't," she cried.

She withdrew, shrinking from beneath his arm
That rested on the banister, and slid downstairs;
And turned on him with such a daunting look,
He said twice over before he knew himself:
"Can't a man speak of his own child he's lost?"

"Not you!—Oh, where's my hat? Oh, I don't need it!
I must get out of here. I must get air.—
I don't know rightly whether any man can."

"Amy! Don't go to someone else this time.
Listen to me. I won't come down the stairs."
He sat and fixed his chin between his fists.
"There's something I should like to ask you, dear."

"You don't know how to ask it."

"Help me, then."

Her fingers moved the latch for all reply.

"My words are nearly always an offense.
I don't know how to speak of anything
So as to please you. But I might be taught,
I should suppose. I can't say I see how.
A man must partly give up being a man
With womenfolk. We could have some arrangement
By which I'd bind myself to keep hands off
Anything special you're a-mind to name.
Though I don't like such things 'twixt those that love.
Two that don't love can't live together without them,
But two that do can't live together with them."
She moved the latch a little. "Don't—don't go.
Don't carry it to someone else this time.
Tell me about it if it's something human.
Let me into your grief. I'm not so much
Unlike other folks as your standing there
Apart would make me out. Give me my chance.
I do think, though, you overdo it a little.
What was it brought you up to think it the thing
To take your mother-loss of a first child
So inconsolably—in the face of love.
You'd think his memory might be satisfied——"

"There you go sneering now!"

"I'm not, I'm not!
You make me angry. I'll come down to you.
God, what a woman! And it's come to this,
A man can't speak of his own child that's dead."
"You can't because you don't know how to speak.
If you had any feelings, you that dug
With your own hand—how could you?—his little grave;
I saw you from that very window there,
Making the gravel leap and leap in air,
Leap up, like that, like that, and land so lightly
And roll back down the mound beside the hole.
I thought, Who is that man? I didn't know you.
And I crept down the stairs and up the stairs
To look again, and still your spade kept lifting.
Then you came in. I heard your rumbling voice
Out in the kitchen, and I don't know why,
But I went near to see with my own eyes.
You could sit there with the stains on your shoes
Of the fresh earth from your own baby's grave
And talk about your everyday concerns.
You had stood the spade up against the wall
Outside there in the entry, for I saw it."

"I shall laugh the worst laugh I ever laughed.
I'm cursed. God, if I don't believe I'm cursed."

"I can repeat the very words you were saying:
'Three foggy mornings and one rainy day
Will rot the best birch fence a man can build.'
Think of it, talk like that at such a time!
What had how long it takes a birch to rot
To do with what was in the darkened parlor?
You *couldn't* care! The nearest friends can go
With anyone to death, comes so far short
They might as well not try to go at all.
No, from the time when one is sick to death,
One is alone, and he dies more alone.
Friends make pretense of following to the grave,
But before one is in it, their minds are turned
And making the best of their way back to life
And living people, and things they understand.
But the world's evil. I won't have grief so
If I can change it. Oh, I won't, I won't!"

"There, you have said it all and you feel better.
You won't go now. You're crying. Close the door.
The heart's gone out of it: why keep it up?
Amy! There's someone coming down the road!"

"*You*—oh, you think the talk is all. I must go—
Somewhere out of this house, How can I make you——"

"If—you—do!" She was opening the door wider.
"Where do you mean to go? First tell me that.
I'll follow and bring you back by force. I *will!*——"

1914

AFTER APPLE-PICKING

My long two-pointed ladder's sticking through a tree
Toward heaven still,
And there's a barrel that I didn't fill
Beside it, and there may be two or three
Apples I didn't pick upon some bough.
But I am done with apple-picking now.
Essence of winter sleep is on the night,
The scent of apples: I am drowsing off.
I cannot rub the strangeness from my sight
I got from looking through a pane of glass
I skimmed this morning from the drinking trough
And held against the world of hoary grass.
It melted, and I let it fall and break.
But I was well
Upon my way to sleep before it fell,
And I could tell
What form my dreaming was about to take.
Magnified apples appear and disappear,
Stem end and blossom end,
And every fleck of russet showing clear.
My instep arch not only keeps the ache,
It keeps the pressure of a ladder-round.
I feel the ladder sway as the boughs bend
And I keep hearing from the cellar bin
The rumbling sound
Of load on load of apples coming in.
For I have had too much
Of apple-picking: I am overtired
Of the great harvest I myself desired.
There were ten thousand thousand fruit to touch,
Cherish in hand, lift down, and not let fall.
For all
That struck the earth,
No matter if not bruised or spiked with stubble,
Went surely to the cider-apple heap
As of no worth.

One can see what will trouble
This sleep of mine, whatever sleep it is.
Were he not gone,
The woodchuck could say whether it's like his
Long sleep, as I describe its coming on,
Or just some human sleep.
1914

THE ROAD NOT TAKEN

Two roads diverged in a yellow wood,
And sorry I could not travel both
And be one traveler, long I stood
And looked down one as far as I could
To where it bent in the undergrowth;

Then took the other, as just as fair,
And having perhaps the better claim,
Because it was grassy and wanted wear;
Though as for that, the passing there
Had worn them really about the same,

And both that morning equally lay
In leaves no step had trodden black.
Oh, I kept the first for another day!
Yet knowing how way leads on to way,
I doubted if I should ever come back.

I shall be telling this with a sigh
Somewhere ages and ages hence:
Two roads diverged in a wood, and I—
I took the one less traveled by,
And that has made all the difference.
1914–1915 1915, 1916

AN OLD MAN'S WINTER NIGHT

All out-of-doors looked darkly in at him
Through the thin frost, almost in separate stars,
That gathers on the pane in empty rooms.
What kept his eyes from giving back the gaze
Was the lamp tilted near them in his hand.
What kept him from remembering what it was
That brought him to that creaking room was age.

He stood with barrels round him—at a loss.
And having scared the cellar under him
In clomping here, he scared it once again
In clomping off—and scared the outer night,
Which has its sounds, familiar, like the roar
Of trees and crack of branches, common things,
But nothing so like beating on a box.
A light he was to no one but himself
Where now he sat, concerned with he knew what,
A quiet light, and then not even that.
He consigned to the moon—such as she was,
So late-arising—to the broken moon,
As better than the sun in any case
For such a charge, his snow upon the roof,
His icicles along the wall to keep;
And slept. The log that shifted with a jolt
Once in the stove, disturbed him and he shifted,
And eased his heavy breathing, but still slept.
One aged man—one man—can't keep a house,
A farm, a countryside, or if he can,
It's thus he does it of a winter night.
1906 1916

BIRCHES

When I see birches bend to left and right
Across the lines of straighter darker trees,
I like to think some boy's been swinging them.
But swinging doesn't bend them down to stay
As ice storms do. Often you must have seen them.
Loaded with ice a sunny winter morning
After a rain. They click upon themselves
As the breeze rises, and turn many-colored
As the stir cracks and crazes their enamel.
Soon the sun's warmth makes them shed crystal shells
Shattering and avalanching on the snow crust—
Such heaps of broken glass to sweep away
You'd think the inner dome of heaven had fallen.
They are dragged to the withered bracken by the load,
And they seem not to break; though once they are bowed
So low for long, they never right themselves:
You may see their trunks arching in the woods
Years afterwards, trailing their leaves on the ground
Like girls on hands and knees that throw their hair
Before them over their heads to dry in the sun.
But I was going to say when Truth broke in
With all her matter of fact about the ice storm,

I should prefer to have some boy bend them
As he went out and in to fetch the cows—
Some boy too far from town to learn baseball,
Whose only play was what he found himself,
Summer or winter, and could play alone.
One by one he subdued his father's trees
By riding them down over and over again
Until he took the stiffness out of them,
And not one but hung limp, not one was left
For him to conquer. He learned all there was
To learn about not launching out too soon
And so not carrying the tree away
Clear to the ground. He always kept his poise
To the top branches, climbing carefully
With the same pains you use to fill a cup
Up to the brim, and even above the brim.
Then he flung outward, feet first, with a swish,
Kicking his way down through the air to the ground.
So was I once myself a swinger of birches.
And so I dream of going back to be.
It's when I'm weary of considerations,
And life is too much like a pathless wood
Where your face burns and tickles with the cobwebs
Broken across it, and one eye is weeping
From a twig's having lashed across it open.
I'd like to get away from earth awhile
And then come back to it and begin over.
May no fate willfully misunderstand me
And half grant what I wish and snatch me away
Not to return. Earth's the right place for love:
I don't know where it's likely to go better.
I'd like to go by climbing a birch tree,
And climb black branches up a snow-white trunk
Toward heaven, till the tree could bear no more,
But dipped its top and set me down again.
That would be good both going and coming back.
One could do worse than be a swinger of birches.
1913–1914 1915

THE OVEN BIRD[1]

There is a singer everyone has heard,
Loud, a mid-summer and a mid-wood bird,
Who makes the solid tree trunks sound again.

[1]An American warbler that builds a dome-shaped nest.

He says that leaves are old and that for flowers
Mid-summer is to spring as one to ten.
He says the early petal-fall is past,
When pear and cherry bloom went down in showers
On sunny days a moment overcast;
And comes that other fall we name the fall.
He says the highway dust is over all.
The bird would cease and be as other birds
But that he knows in singing not to sing.
The question that he frames in all but words
Is what to make of a diminished thing.
1906–1907 1916

FOR ONCE, THEN, SOMETHING

Others taunt me with having knelt at well-curbs
Always wrong to the light, so never seeing
Deeper down in the well than where the water
Gives me back in a shining surface picture
Me myself in the summer heaven, godlike,
Looking out of a wreath of fern and cloud puffs.
Once, when trying with chin against a well-curb,
I discerned, as I thought, beyond the picture,
Through the picture, a something white, uncertain,
Something more of the depths—and then I lost it.
Water came to rebuke the too clear water.
One drop fell from a fern, and lo, a ripple
Shook whatever it was lay there at bottom,
Blurred it, blotted it out. What was that whiteness?
Truth? A pebble of quartz? For once, then, something.
1920

FIRE AND ICE

Some say the world will end in fire,
Some say in ice.
From what I've tasted of desire
I hold with those who favor fire.
But if it had to perish twice,
I think I know enough of hate
To say that for destruction ice
Is also great
And would suffice.
1920

DESIGN

I found a dimpled spider, fat and white,
On a white heal-all,[1] holding up a moth
Like a white piece of rigid satin cloth—
Assorted characters of death and blight
Mixed ready to begin the morning right,
Like the ingredients of a witches' broth—
A snow-drop spider, a flower like a froth,
And dead wings carried like a paper kite.

What had that flower to do with being white,
The wayside blue and innocent heal-all?
What brought the kindred spider to that height,
Then steered the white moth thither in the night?
What but design of darkness to appall?—
If design govern in a thing so small.

1922

NOTHING GOLD CAN STAY

Nature's first green is gold,
Her hardest hue to hold.
Her early leaf's a flower;
But only so an hour.
Then leaf subsides to leaf.
So Eden sank to grief,
So dawn goes down to day.
Nothing gold can stay.

1923

STOPPING BY WOODS ON A SNOWY EVENING

Whose woods these are I think I know.
His house is in the village, though;
He will not see me stopping here
To watch his woods fill up with snow.

My little horse must think it queer
To stop without a farmhouse near
Between the woods and frozen lake
The darkest evening of the year.

[1]A plant, normally with blue blossoms, reputed to have healing powers.

He gives his harness bells a shake
To ask if there is some mistake.
The only other sound's the sweep
Of easy wind and downy flake.

The woods are lovely, dark and deep,
But I have promises to keep,
And miles to go before I sleep,
And miles to go before I sleep.

1923

ACQUAINTED WITH THE NIGHT

I have been one acquainted with the night.
I have walked out in rain—and back in rain.
I have outwalked the furthest city light.

I have looked down the saddest city lane.
I have passed by the watchman on his beat
And dropped my eyes, unwilling to explain.

I have stood still and stopped the sound of feet
When far away an interrupted cry
Came over houses from another street,

But not to call me back or say good-by;
And further still at an unearthly height
One luminary clock against the sky

Proclaimed the time was neither wrong nor right.
I have been one acquainted with the night.

1928

WEST-RUNNING BROOK

"Fred, where is north?"

"North? North is there, my love.
The brook runs west."

"West-Running Brook then call it."
(West-Running Brook men call it to this day.)
"What does it think it's doing running west
When all the other country brooks flow east
To reach the ocean? It must be the brook
Can trust itself to go by contraries

The way I can with you—and you with me—
Because we're—we're—I don't know what we are.
What are we?"

"Young or new?"

"We must be something
We've said we two. Let's change that to we three.
As you and I are married to each other,
We'll both be married to the brook. We'll build
Our bridge across it, and the bridge shall be
Our arm thrown over it asleep beside it.
Look, look, it's waving to us with a wave
To let us know it hears me."

"Why, my dear,
That wave's been standing off this jut of shore—
(The black stream, catching on a sunken rock,
Flung backward on itself in one white wave,
And the white water rode the black forever,
Not gaining but not losing, like a bird
White feathers from the struggle of whose breast
Flecked the dark stream and flecked the darker pool
Below the point, and were at last driven wrinkled
In a white scarf against the far-shore alders.)
"That wave's been standing off this jut of shore
Ever since rivers, I was going to say,
Were made in heaven. It wasn't waved to us."

"It wasn't, yet it was. If not to you,
It was to me—in an annunciation."[1]

"Oh, if you take it off to lady-land,
As't were the country of the Amazons[2]
We men must see you to the confines of
And leave you there, ourselves forbid to enter—
It is your brook! I have no more to say."

"Yes, you have, too. Go on. You thought of something."

"Speaking of contraries, see how the brook
In that white wave runs counter to itself.

[1]An important announcement, such as the annunciation (revelation) to the Virgin Mary that she was to be the mother of Christ.

[2]In classical myth the tribe of female warriors who lived in Asia Minor in a society where women dominated and men were subjugated.

It is from that in water we were from
Long, long before we were from any creature.
Here we, in our impatience of the steps,
Get back to the beginning of beginnings,
The stream of everything that runs away.
Some say existence like a Pirouot
And Pirouette,[3] forever in one place,
Stands still and dances, but it runs away;
It seriously, sadly, runs away
To fill the abyss's void with emptiness.
It flows beside us in this water brook,
But it flows over us. It flows between us
To separate us for a panic moment.
It flows between us, over us, and *with* us.
And it is time, strength, tone, light, life, and love—
And even substance lapsing unsubstantial;
The universal cataract of death
That spends to nothingness—and unresisted,
Save by some strange resistance in itself,
Not just a swerving, but a throwing back,
As if regret were in it and were sacred.
It has this throwing backward on itself
So that the fall of most of it is always
Raising a little, sending up a little.
Our life runs down in sending up the clock.
The brook runs down in sending up our life.
The sun runs down in sending up the brook.
And there is something sending up the sun.
It is this backward motion toward the source,
Against the stream, that most we see ourselves in,
The tribute of the current to the source.
It is from this in nature we are from.
It is most us."

"Today will be the day
You said so."

"No, today will be the day
You said the brook was called West-Running Brook."

"Today will be the day of what we both said."

1928

[3]Frost refers to traditional characters in French pantomime.

DESERT PLACES

Snow falling and night falling fast, oh, fast
In a field I looked into going past,
And the ground almost covered smooth in snow,
But a few weeds and stubble showing last.

The woods around it have it—it is theirs.
All animals are smothered in their lairs.
I am too absent-spirited to count;
The loneliness includes me unawares.

And lonely as it is, that loneliness
Will be more lonely ere it will be less—
A blanker whiteness of benighted[1] snow
With no expression, nothing to express.

They cannot scare me with their empty spaces
Between stars—on stars where no human race is.
I have it in me so much nearer home
To scare myself with my own desert places.

1934

NEITHER OUT FAR NOR IN DEEP

The people along the sand
All turn and look one way.
They turn their back on the land.
They look at the sea all day.

As long as it takes to pass
A ship keeps raising its hull;
The wetter ground like glass
Reflects a standing gull.

The land may vary more;
But wherever the truth may be—
The water comes ashore,
And the people look at the sea.

They cannot look out far.
They cannot look in deep.
But when was that ever a bar
To any watch they keep?

1934

[1]Darkened by the night or by ignorance.

DIRECTIVE

Back out of all this now too much for us,
Back in a time made simple by the loss
Of detail, burned, dissolved, and broken off
Like graveyard marble sculpture in the weather,
There is a house that is no more a house
Upon a farm that is no more a farm
And in a town that is no more a town.
The road there, if you'll let a guide direct you
Who only has at heart your getting lost,
May seem as if it should have been a quarry—
Great monolithic knees the former town
Long since gave up pretense of keeping covered.
And there's a story in a book about it:
Besides the wear of iron wagon wheels
The ledges show lines ruled southeast-northwest,
The chisel work of an enormous Glacier
That braced his feet against the Arctic Pole.
You must not mind a certain coolness from him
Still said to haunt this side of Panther Mountain.
Nor need you mind the serial ordeal
Of being watched from forty cellar holes
As if by eye pairs out of forty firkins.[1]
As for the woods' excitement over you
That sends light rustle rushes to their leaves,
Charge that to upstart inexperience.
Where were they all not twenty years ago?
They think too much of having shaded out
A few old pecker-fretted[2] apple trees.
Make yourself up a cheering song of how
Someone's road home from work this once was,
Who may be just ahead of you on foot
Or creaking with a buggy load of grain.
The height of the adventure is the height
Of country where two village cultures faded
Into each other. Both of them are lost.
And if you're lost enough to find yourself
By now, pull in your ladder road behind you
And put a sign up closed to all but me.
Then make yourself at home. The only field
Now left's no bigger than a harness gall.[3]
First there's the children's house of make-believe,
Some shattered dishes underneath a pine,
The playthings in the playhouse of the children.
Weep for what little things could make them glad.

[1]Small barrels. [2]I.e., marked by woodpeckers. [3]A sore, caused by a chafing harness.

Then for the house that is no more a house,
But only a belilaced cellar hole,
Now slowly closing like a dent in dough.
This was no playhouse but a house in earnest.
Your destination and your destiny's
A brook that was the water of the house,
Cold as a spring as yet so near its source,
Too lofty and original to rage.
(We know the valley streams that when aroused
Will leave their tatters hung on barb and thorn.)
I have kept hidden in the instep arch
Of an old cedar at the waterside
A broken drinking goblet like the Grail[4]
Under a spell so the wrong ones can't find it,
So can't get saved, as Saint Mark says they mustn't[5]
(I stole the goblet from the children's playhouse.)
Here are your waters and your watering place.
Drink and be whole again beyond confusion.
1946 1946, 1947

IN WINTER IN THE WOODS ALONE[1]

In winter in the woods alone
Against the trees I go.
I mark a maple for my own
And lay the maple low.

At four o'clock I shoulder ax,
And in the afterglow
I link a line of shadowy tracks
Across the tinted snow.

I see for Nature no defeat
In one tree's overthrow
Or for myself in my retreat
For yet another blow.
1963

[4]The Holy Grail, the cup said to have been used by Jesus at the Last Supper.

[5]"And he said unto them, unto you it is given to know the mystery of the kingdom of God; but unto them that are without, all these things are done in parables: That seeing they may see, and not perceive; and hearing they may hear, and not understand; lest at any time they should be converted and their sins should be forgiven them." (Mark 4:11–12).

[1]Frost left the poem untitled. The present title has been supplied by the editor.

Gertrude Simmons Bonnin (Zitkala Sa) 1876–1938

Gertrude Simmons Bonnin was born in 1876 at the Pine Ridge River Reservation in South Dakota to a full-blooded Yankton-Nakota Sioux mother and a white father. Soon after, her father deserted the family and her mother remarried. In 1884, at the age of eight, Bonnin left her reservation to attend White's Manual Labor Institute in Wabash, Indiana, a Quaker missionary school for Native Americans. After several years she left White's and came home to South Dakota, but she returned four years later, in 1891, and graduated at the age of nineteen after completing her studies. She enrolled as a scholarship student at Earlham College in Richmond, Indiana, another Quaker institution, where she excelled as an orator and a musician. Her talent as a violinist earned her a second scholarship, this one to the acclaimed New England Conservatory of Music in Boston.

In 1898 Bonnin accepted a position at Carlisle Indian School, in Carlisle, Pennsylvania, teaching music. At about this time, she began to write autobiographical essays that eventually found publication in such prestigious national magazines as Harper's *and* Atlantic Monthly. *She was fired from Carlisle when her writings started appearing in print, in large part because they questioned the pedagogical vision of schools like Carlisle that sought to make the Native American population more like the European American. In 1901 Bonnin published* Old Indian Legends, *a collection of stories written in English based on the oral tales she listened to as a girl growing up on the Pine Ridge Reservation. She signed the book as Zitkala Sa, the Sioux name she began to use after college, which means Red Bird. The next year she married fellow Yankton-Nakota Sioux Raymond Talesfase Bonnin, an employee of the Indian Service.*

Over the next decade and a half the two were transferred from reservation to reservation around the country until 1916, when they settled permanently in Washington, D.C. after Bonnin's husband secured a position there as a law clerk. For a while after, she edited American Indian Magazine, *but increasingly her attention was focused on political causes promoting Native American rights. In 1921 she published* American Indian Stories, *a collection that combined her earlier autobiographical essays with the accounts of other Native Americans who had suffered similar injustices. Gertrude Simmons Bonnin died in 1938 and is buried at Arlington National Cemetery.*

FURTHER READING: A. Wiget, *Native American Literature,* 1985; P. Allen, *The Sacred Hoop: Recovering the Feminine in American Indian Traditions,* 1986; A. Krupat, *For Those Who Came After: A Study of Native American Autobiography,* 1989.

TEXT: *American Indian Stories,* 1921.

from THE SCHOOL DAYS OF AN INDIAN GIRL

I

THE LAND OF RED APPLES

There were eight in our party of bronzed children who were going East with the missionaries. Among us were three young braves, two tall girls, and we three little ones, Judéwin, Thowin, and I.

We had been very impatient to start on our journey to the Red Apple Country, which, we were told, lay a little beyond the great circular horizon of the Western prairie. Under a sky of rosy apples we dreamt of roaming as freely and happily as we had chased the cloud shadows on the Dakota plains. We had anticipated much pleasure from a ride on the iron horse, but the throngs of staring palefaces disturbed and troubled us.

On the train, fair women, with tottering babies on each arm, stopped their haste and scrutinized the children of absent mothers. Large men, with heavy bundles in their hands, halted near by, and riveted their glassy blue eyes upon us.

I sank deep into the corner of my seat, for I resented being watched. Directly in front of me, children who were no larger than I hung themselves upon the backs of their seats, with their bold white faces toward me. Sometimes they took their forefingers out of their mouths and pointed at my moccasined feet. Their mothers, instead of reproving such rude curiosity, looked closely at me, and attracted their children's further notice to my blanket. This embarrassed me, and kept me constantly on the verge of tears.

I sat perfectly still, with my eyes downcast, daring only now and then to shoot long glances around me. Chancing to turn to the window at my side, I was quite breathless upon seeing one familiar object. It was the telegraph pole which strode by at short paces. Very near my mother's dwelling, along the edge of a road thickly bordered with wild sunflowers, some poles like these had been planted by white men. Often I had stopped, on my way down the road, to hold my ear against the pole, and, hearing its low moaning, I used to wonder what the paleface had done to hurt it. Now I sat watching for each pole that glided by to be the last one.

In this way I had forgotten my uncomfortable surroundings, when I heard one of my comrades call out my name. I saw the missionary standing very near, tossing candies and gums into our midst. This amused us all, and we tried to see who could catch the most of the sweetmeats.

Though we rode several days inside of the iron horse, I do not recall a single thing about our luncheons.

It was night when we reached the school grounds. The lights from the windows of the large buildings fell upon some of the icicled trees that stood beneath them. We were led toward an open door, where the brightness of the lights within flooded out over the heads of the excited palefaces who blocked our way. My body trembled more from fear than from the snow I trod upon.

Entering the house, I stood close against the wall. The strong glaring light in the large whitewashed room dazzled my eyes. The noisy hurrying of hard shoes upon a bare wooden floor increased the whirring in my ears. My only safety seemed to be in keeping next to the wall. As I was wondering in which direction to escape from all this confusion, two warm hands grasped me firmly, and in the same moment I was tossed high in midair. A rosy-cheeked paleface woman caught me in her arms. I was both frightened and insulted by such trifling. I stared into her eyes, wishing her to let me stand on my own feet, but she jumped me up and down with increasing enthusiasm. My mother had never made a plaything of her wee daughter. Remembering this I began to cry aloud.

They misunderstood the cause of my tears, and placed me at a white table loaded with food. There our party were united again. As I did not hush my crying, one of the older ones whispered to me, "Wait until you are alone in the night."

It was very little I could swallow besides my sobs, that evening.

"Oh, I want my mother and my brother Dawée! I want to go to my aunt!" I pleaded; but the ears of the palefaces could not hear me.

From the table we were taken along an upward incline of wooden boxes, which I learned afterward to call a stairway. At the top was a quiet hall, dimly lighted. Many narrow beds were in one straight line down the entire length of the wall. In them lay sleeping brown faces, which peeped just out of the coverings. I was tucked into bed with one of the tall girls, because she talked to me in my mother tongue and seemed to soothe me.

I had arrived in the wonderful land of rosy skies, but I was not happy, as I had thought I should be. My long travel and the bewildering sights had exhausted me. I fell asleep, heaving deep, tired sobs. My tears were left to dry themselves in streaks, because neither my aunt nor my mother was near to wipe them away.

II

THE CUTTING OF MY LONG HAIR

The first day in the land of apples was a bitter-cold one; for the snow still covered the ground, and the trees were bare. A large bell rang for breakfast, its loud metallic voice crashing through the belfry overhead and into our sensitive ears. The annoying clatter of shoes on bare floors gave us no peace. The constant clash of harsh noises, with an undercurrent of many voices murmuring an unknown tongue, made a bedlam within which I was securely tied. And though my spirit tore itself in struggling for its lost freedom, all was useless.

A paleface woman, with white hair, came up after us. We were placed in a line of girls who were marching into the dining room. These were Indian girls, in stiff shoes and closely clinging dresses. The small girls wore sleeved aprons and shingled hair. As I walked noiselessly in my soft moccasins, I felt like sinking to the floor, for my blanket had been stripped from my shoulders. I looked hard at the Indian girls, who seemed not to care that they were even more immodestly dressed than I, in their tightly fitting clothes. While we marched in, the boys entered at an opposite door. I watched for the three young braves who came in our party. I spied them in the rear ranks, looking as uncomfortable as I felt.

A small bell was tapped, and each of the pupils drew a chair from under the table. Supposing this act meant they were to be seated, I pulled out mine and at once slipped into it from one side. But when I turned my head, I saw that I was the only one seated, and all the rest at our table remained standing. Just as I began to rise, looking shyly around to see how chairs were to be used, a second bell was sounded. All were seated at last, and I had to crawl back into my chair again. I heard a man's voice at one end of the hall, and I looked around to see him. But all the others hung their heads over their plates. As I glanced at the long chain of tables, I caught the eyes of a paleface woman upon me. Immediately I dropped my eyes, wondering why I was so keenly watched by the strange woman. The man ceased his mutterings, and then a third bell was tapped. Every one picked up his knife and fork and began eating. I began crying instead, for by this time I was afraid to venture anything more.

But this eating by formula was not the hardest trial in that first day. Late in the morning, my friend Judéwin gave me a terrible warning. Judéwin knew a few words of English; and she had overheard the paleface woman talk about cutting our long, heavy hair. Our mothers had taught us that only unskilled warriors who were captured had their hair shingled[1] by the enemy. Among our people, short hair was worn by mourners, and shingled hair by cowards!

We discussed our fate some moments, and when Judéwin said, "We have to submit, because they are strong," I rebelled.

"No, I will not submit!" I will struggle first!" I answered.

I watched my chance, and when no one noticed I disappeared. I crept up the stairs as quietly as I could in my squeaking shoes,—my moccasins had been exchanged for shoes. Along the hall I passed, without knowing whither I was going. Turning aside to an open door, I found a large room with three white beds in it. The windows were covered with dark green curtains, which made the room very dim. Thankful that no one was there, I directed my steps toward the corner farthest from the door. On my hands and knees I crawled under the bed, and cuddled myself in the dark corner.

From my hiding place I peered out, shuddering with fear whenever I heard footsteps near by. Though in the hall loud voices were calling my name, and I knew that even Judéwin was searching for me, I did not open my mouth to answer. Then the steps were quickened and the voices became excited. The sounds came nearer and nearer. Women and girls entered the room. I held my breath and watched them open closet doors and peep behind large trunks. Some one threw up the curtains, and the room was filled with sudden light. What caused them to stoop and look under the bed I do not know. I remember being dragged out, though I resisted by kicking and scratching wildly. In spite of myself, I was carried downstairs and tied fast in a chair.

I cried aloud, shaking my head all the while until I felt the cold blades of the scissors against my neck, and heard them gnaw off one of my thick braids. Then I lost my spirit. Since the day I was taken from my mother I had suffered extreme indignities. People had stared at me. I had been tossed about in the air like a wooden puppet. And now my long hair was shingled like a coward's! In my anguish I moaned for my mother, but no one came to comfort me. Not a soul reasoned quietly with me, as my own mother used to do; for now I was only one of many little animals driven by a herder.

III

The Snow Episode

A short time after our arrival we three Dakotas were playing in the snowdrift. We were all still deaf to the English language, excepting Judéwin, who always heard such puzzling things. One morning we learned through her ears that we were forbidden to fall lengthwise in the snow, as we had been doing, to see our own impressions. However, before many hours we had forgotten the order, and were having great sport in the snow, when a shrill voice called us. Looking

[1]Cut short.

up, we saw an imperative hand beckoning us into the house. We shook the snow off ourselves, and started toward the woman as slowly as we dared.

Judéwin said: "Now the paleface is angry with us. She is going to punish us for falling into the snow. If she looks straight into your eyes and talks loudly, you must wait until she stops. Then, after a tiny pause, say, 'No.'" The rest of the way we practiced upon the little word "no."

As it happened, Thowin was summoned to judgment first. The door shut behind her with a click.

Judéwin and I stood silently listening at the keyhole. The paleface woman talked in very severe tones. Her words fell from her lips like crackling embers, and her inflection ran up like the small end of a switch. I understood her voice better than the things she was saying. I was certain we had made her very impatient with us. Judéwin heard enough of the words to realize all too late that she had taught us the wrong reply.

"Oh, poor Thowin!" she gasped, as she put both hands over her ears.

Just then I heard Thowin's tremulous answer, "No."

With an angry exclamation, the woman gave her a hard spanking. Then she stopped to say something. Judéwin said it was this: "Are you going to obey my word the next time?"

Thowin answered again with the only word at her command, "No."

This time the woman meant her blows to smart, for the poor frightened girl shrieked at the top of her voice. In the midst of the whipping the blows ceased abruptly, and the woman asked another question: "Are you going to fall in the snow again?"

Thowin gave her bad password another trial. We heard her say feebly, "No! No!"

With this the woman hid away her half-worn slipper, and led the child out, stroking her black shorn head. Perhaps it occurred to her that brute force is not the solution for such a problem. She did nothing to Judéwin nor to me. She only returned to us our unhappy comrade, and left us alone in the room.

During the first two or three seasons misunderstandings as ridiculous as this one of the snow episode frequently took place, bringing unjustifiable frights and punishments into our little lives.

Within a year I was able to express myself somewhat in broken English. As soon as I comprehended a part of what was said and done, a mischievous spirit of revenge possessed me. One day I was called in from my play for some misconduct. I had disregarded a rule which seemed to me very needlessly binding. I was sent into the kitchen to mash the turnips for dinner. It was noon, and steaming dishes were hastily carried into the dining-room. I hated turnips, and their odor which came from the brown jar was offensive to me. With fire in my heart, I took the wooden tool that the paleface woman held out to me. I stood upon a step, and, grasping the handle with both hands, I bent in hot rage over the turnips. I worked my vengeance upon them. All were so busily occupied that no one noticed me. I saw that the turnips were in a pulp, and that further beating could not improve them; but the order was, "Mash these turnips," and mash them I would! I renewed my energy; and as I sent the masher into the bottom of the jar, I felt a satisfying sensation that the weight of my body had gone into it.

Just here a paleface woman came up to my table. As she looked into the jar, she shoved my hands roughly aside. I stood fearless and angry. She placed her red hands upon the rim of the jar. Then she gave one lift and stride away from the table. But lo! the pulpy contents fell through the crumbled bottom to the floor! She spared me no scolding phrases that I had earned. I did not heed them. I felt triumphant in my revenge, though deep within me I was a wee bit sorry to have broken the jar.

As I sat eating my dinner, and saw that no turnips were served, I whooped in my heart for having once asserted the rebellion within me.

IV

The Devil

Among the legends the old warriors used to tell me were many stories of evil spirits. But I was taught to fear them no more than those who stalked about in material guise. I never knew there was an insolent chieftain among the bad spirits, who dared to array his forces against the Great Spirit, until I heard this white man's legend from a paleface woman.

Out of a large book she showed me a picture of the white man's devil. I looked in horror upon the strong claws that grew out of his fur-covered fingers. His feet were like his hands. Trailing at his heels was a scaly tail tipped with a serpent's open jaws. His face was a patchwork: he had bearded cheeks, like some I had seen palefaces wear; his nose was an eagle's bill, and his sharp-pointed ears were pricked up like those of a sly fox. Above them a pair of cow's horns curved upward. I trembled with awe, and my heart throbbed in my throat, as I looked at the king of evil spirits. Then I heard the paleface woman say that this terrible creature roamed loose in the world, and that little girls who disobeyed school regulations were to be tortured by him.

That night I dreamt about this evil divinity. Once again I seemed to be in my mother's cottage. An Indian woman had come to visit my mother. On opposite sides of the kitchen stove, which stood in the center of the small house, my mother and her guest were seated in straight-backed chairs. I played with a train of empty spools hitched together on a string. It was night, and the wick burned feebly. Suddenly I heard some one turn our door-knob from without.

My mother and the woman hushed their talk, and both looked toward the door. It opened gradually. I waited behind the stove. The hinges squeaked as the door was slowly, very slowly pushed inward.

Then in rushed the devil! He was tall! He looked exactly like the picture I had seen of him in the white man's papers. He did not speak to my mother, because he did not know the Indian language, but his glittering yellow eyes were fastened upon me. He took long strides: around the stove, passing behind the woman's chair. I threw down my spools, and ran to my mother. He did not fear her, but followed closely after me. Then I ran round and round the stove, crying aloud for help. But my mother and the woman seemed not to know my danger. They sat still, looking quietly upon the devil's chase after me. At last I grew dizzy. My head revolved as on a hidden pivot. My knees became numb, and doubled under my weight like a pair of knife blades without a spring. Beside my mother's chair I fell in a heap. Just as the devil stooped over me with outstretched claws my mother awoke from her quiet indifference, and lifted me on her lap. Whereupon the devil vanished, and I was awake.

On the following morning I took my revenge upon the devil. Stealing into the room where a wall of shelves was filled with books, I drew forth The Stories of the Bible. With a broken slate pencil I carried in my apron pocket, I began by scratching out his wicked eyes. A few moments later, when I was ready to leave the room, there was a ragged hole in the page where the picture of the devil had once been.

V

IRON ROUTINE

A loud-clamoring bell awakened us at half-past six in the cold winter mornings. From happy dreams of Western rolling lands and unlassoed freedom we tumbled out upon chilly bare floors back again into a paleface day. We had short time to jump into our shoes and clothes, and wet our eyes with icy water, before a small hand bell was vigorously rung for roll call.

There were too many drowsy children and too numerous orders for the day to waste a moment in any apology to nature for giving her children such a shock in the early morning. We rushed downstairs, bounding over two high steps at a time, to land in the assembly room.

A paleface woman, with a yellow-covered roll book open on her arm and a gnawed pencil in her hand, appeared at the door. Her small, tired face was coldly lighted with a pair of large gray eyes.

She stood still in a halo of authority, while over the rim of her spectacles her eyes pried nervously about the room. Having glanced at her long list of names and called out the first one, she tossed up her chin and peered through the crystals of her spectacles to make sure of the answer "Here."

Relentlessly her pencil black-marked our daily records if we were not present to respond to our names, and no chum of ours had done it successfully for us. No matter if a dull headache or the painful cough of slow consumption[2] had delayed the absentee, there was only time enough to mark the tardiness. It was next to impossible to leave the iron routine after the civilizing machine had once begun its day's buzzing; and as it was inbred in me to suffer in silence rather than to appeal to the ears of one whose open eyes could not see my pain, I have many times trudged in the day's harness heavy-footed, like a dumb sick brute.

Once I lost a dear classmate. I remember well how she used to mope along at my side, until one morning she could not raise her head from her pillow. At her deathbed I stood weeping, as the paleface woman sat near her moistening the dry lips. Among the folds of the bedclothes I saw the open pages of the white man's Bible. The dying Indian girl talked disconnectedly of Jesus the Christ and the paleface who was cooling her swollen hands and feet.

I grew bitter, and censured the woman for cruel neglect of our physical ills. I despised the pencils that moved automatically, and the one teaspoon which dealt out, from a large bottle, healing to a row of variously ailing Indian children. I blamed the hard-working, well-meaning, ignorant woman who was

[2]An old-fashioned name for tuberculosis.

inculcating[3] in our hearts her superstitious ideas. Though I was sullen in all my little troubles, as soon as I felt better I was ready again to smile upon the cruel woman. Within a week I was again actively testing the chains which tightly bound my individuality like a mummy for burial.

The melancholy of those black days has left so long a shadow that it darkens the path of years that have since gone by. These sad memories rise above those of smoothly grinding school days. Perhaps my Indian nature is the moaning wind which stirs them now for their present record. But, however tempestuous this is within me, it comes out as the low voice of a curiously colored seashell, which is only for those ears that are bent with compassion to hear it.

1921

Carl Sandburg 1878–1967

Like his contemporary, Robert Frost, Carl Sandburg lived to enjoy enormous popular acclaim; by the end of his life he had become a familiar figure to national television audiences who listened to him read his poems, sing folk ballads, and tell anecdotes about Abraham Lincoln. But unlike Frost, Sandburg never gained the broad approval of the literary establishment, the critics whom Sandburg in turn accused of taking snobbish pride in the fact that "the average truck driver . . . can't understand them."

Sandburg longed, as had his literary forebear Walt Whitman, to be a poet of the people, to be read by "farmers, thieves, and deacons—and not by little cliques." His poetic exaltation of the ordinary man and the commonplace world was largely the result of a deeply imbedded Populism, absorbed during his youth. Born in Illinois, the son of Swedish immigrants, he left public school when he was thirteen, took on odd jobs, and became a housepainter's apprentice. Although he later attended college, his formal education had less impact on him than did the people he came to know while he wandered throughout America, working as a milkman, porter, stagehand, brickmaker, dishwasher, housepainter, carpenter, salesman, and newspaper reporter.

In 1912 Sandburg moved to Chicago, where he eventually joined the staff of the Chicago Daily News. *His colloquial poetry, with its apparently spontaneous freeverse unorthodoxies, appeared in such volumes as* Chicago Poems *(1916),* Cornhuskers *(1918),* Smoke and Steel *(1920),* Slabs of the Sunburnt West *(1922), and* The People, Yes *(1936). Sandburg's poems reflected the folklore and history of the land and his faith in a vital America of the masses. In Abraham Lincoln, Sandburg saw the supreme justification for a faith in the wisdom of the common man, and it was a mythic Lincoln, the hero of the people, who emerged from the six-volume Lincoln biography,* The Prairie Years *and* The War Years *(1926–1939), that earned Sandburg a Pulitzer Prize for history, in 1940.*

Sandburg's writing is an expression of Whitmanian optimism and democratic sentiment shaped by the rhythms of midwestern speech. His poetry ranges from the abbreviated imagism of "Fog" to such free-verse effusions as "Chicago" and The People, Yes,

[3]Implanting.

unrestrained portrayals of America's rich diversity, descriptions of the virtues of the ordinary people, the mob, that Sandburg saw as the vindication of democratic life.

FURTHER READING: *The Complete Poems of Carl Sandburg,* 1970; *The Letters of Carl Sandburg,* ed. H. Mitgang, 1968; B. Weirick, *From Whitman to Sandburg,* 1924; K. Detzer, *Carl Sandburg,* 1941; R. Crowder, *Carl Sandburg,* 1964; H. Durnell, *The America of Carl Sandburg,* 1965; J. Haas, *Carl Sandburg,* 1967; N. Callahan, *Carl Sandburg: Lincoln of Our Literature,* 1969; G. Allen, *Carl Sandburg,* 1972; N. Callahan, *Carl Sandburg: His Life and Works,* 1988; D. Salwak, *Carl Sandburg: A Reference Guide,* 1988; P. Niven, *Carl Sandburg: A Biography,* 1991; P. Yannella, *The Other Carl Sandburg,* 1996.

TEXTS: *Chicago Poems,* 1916; *Cornhuskers,* 1918; *Smoke and Steel,* 1920.

CHICAGO

Hog Butcher for the World,
Tool Maker, Stacker of Wheat,
Player with Railroads and the Nation's Freight Handler;
Stormy, husky, brawling,
City of the Big Shoulders:

They tell me you are wicked and I believe them, for I have seen your painted women under the gas lamps luring the farm boys.
And they tell me you are crooked and I answer: Yes, it is true I have seen the gunman kill and go free to kill again.
And they tell me you are brutal and my reply is: On the faces of women and children I have seen the marks of wanton hunger.
And having answered so I turn once more to those who sneer at this my city, and I give them back the sneer and say to them:
Come and show me another city with lifted head singing so proud to be alive and coarse and strong and cunning.
Flinging magnetic curses amid the toil of piling job on job, here is a tall bold slugger set vivid against the little soft cities;
Fierce as a dog with tongue lapping for action, cunning as a savage pitted against the wilderness,
Bareheaded,
Shoveling,
Wrecking,
Planning,
Building, breaking, rebuilding,
Under the smoke, dust all over his mouth, laughing with white teeth,
Under the terrible burden of destiny laughing as a young man laughs,
Laughing even as an ignorant fighter laughs who has never lost a battle,
Bragging and laughing that under his wrist is the pulse, and under his ribs the heart of the people,
Laughing!
Laughing the stormy, husky, brawling laughter of Youth, half-naked, sweating, proud to be Hog Butcher, Tool Maker, Stacker of Wheat, Player with Railroads and Freight Handler to the Nation.

1914

LOST

Desolate and lone
All night long on the lake
Where fog trails and mist creeps,
The whistle of a boat
Calls and cries unendingly,
Like some lost child
In tears and trouble
Hunting the harbor's breast
And the harbor's eyes.

1916

GRACELAND

Tomb of a millionaire,
A multi-millionaire, ladies and gentlemen,
Place of the dead where they spend every year
The usury of twenty-five thousand dollars
For upkeep and flowers
To keep fresh the memory of the dead.
The merchant prince gone to dust
Commanded in his written will
Over the signed name of his last testament
Twenty-five thousand dollars be set aside
For roses, lilacs, hydrangeas, tulips,
For perfume and color, sweetness of remembrance
Around his last long home.
(A hundred cash[1] girls want nickels to go to the movies tonight.
In the back stalls of a hundred saloons, women are at tables
Drinking with men or waiting for men jingling loose silver dollars in their pockets.
In a hundred furnished rooms is a girl who sells silk or dress goods or leather stuff for six dollars a week wages
And when she pulls on her stockings in the morning she is reckless about God and the newspapers and the police, the talk of her home town or the name people call her.)

1916

[1]Cashier.

FOG

The fog comes
on little cat feet.

It sits looking
over harbor and city
on silent haunches
and then moves on.

1916

PSALM OF THOSE WHO GO FORTH BEFORE DAYLIGHT

The policeman buys shoes slow and careful; the teamster buys gloves slow and careful; they take care of their feet and hands; they live on their feet and hands.

The milkman never argues; he works alone and no one speaks to him; the city is asleep when he is on the job; he puts a bottle on six hundred porches and calls it a day's work; he climbs two hundred wooden stairways; two horses are company for him; he never argues.

The rolling-mill men[1] and the sheet-steel men are brothers of cinders; they empty cinders out of their shoes after the day's work; they ask their wives to fix burnt holes in the knees of their trousers; their necks and ears are covered with a smut; they scour their necks and ears; they are brothers of cinders.

1918

FOUR PRELUDES ON PLAYTHINGS OF THE WIND

"The past is a bucket of ashes."

1

The woman named To-morrow
sits with a hairpin in her teeth
and takes her time

[1]Men who work in a factory where metal is rolled into sheets, bars, etc.

and does her hair the way she wants it
and fastens at last the last braid and coil
and puts the hairpin where it belongs
and turns and drawls: Well, what of it?
My grandmother, Yesterday, is gone.
What of it? Let the dead be dead.

2

The doors were cedar
and the panels strips of gold
and the girls were golden girls
and the panels read and the girls chanted:
We are the greatest city,
the greatest nation:
nothing like us ever was.

The doors are twisted on broken hinges.
Sheets of rain swish through on the wind where the golden girls
ran and the panels read:
We are the greatest city,
the greatest nation,
nothing like us ever was.

3

It has happened before.
Strong men put up a city and got a nation together,
And paid singers to sing and women to warble:
We are the greatest city,
the greatest nation,
nothing like us ever was.

And while the singers sang
and the strong men listened
and paid the singers well
and felt good about it all,
there were rats and lizards who listened
. . . and the only listeners left now
. . . are . . . the rats . . . and the lizards.

And there are black crows
crying, "Caw, caw,"
bringing mud and sticks
building a nest
over the words carved
on the doors where the panels were cedar
and the strips on the panels were gold
and the golden girls came singing:
    We are the greatest city,
    the greatest nation:
    nothing like us ever was.

The only singers now are crows crying, "Caw, caw,"
And the sheets of rain whine in the wind and doorways.
And the only listeners now are . . . the rats . . . and the lizards.

4

The feet of the rats
scribble on the door sills;
the hieroglyphs of the rat footprints
chatter the pedigrees of the rats
and babble of the blood
and gabble[1] of the breed
of the grandfathers and the great-grandfathers of the rats.

And the wind shifts
and the dust on a door sill shifts
and even the writing of the rat footprints
tells us nothing, nothing at all
about the greatest city, the greatest nation
where the strong men listened
and the women warbled: Nothing like us ever was.

1920

[1]Rapid, incoherent speech.

Willa Cather 1873–1947

In 1883, when she was nine, Willa Cather's family migrated westward from her birthplace in Virginia to the prairie lands of Nebraska. There she grew up among the pioneering European immigrants whose qualities of courage, sensitivity, and perseverance she was later to portray in her novels and short stories of rural and small-town America.

Challenging normative gender roles, a teenaged Cather wore her hair short, dressed in boys' clothes, and signed her name "William Cather." Following high school, she attended the newly formed University of Nebraska, and on graduation returned east to Pennsylvania, where she worked on a Pittsburgh newspaper and taught high-school English. All the while, like novelist Kate Chopin, she read works by Nathaniel Hawthorne and Henry James, both of whom would influence the work she went on to write.

In 1900 Cather began publishing poems and short stories. Her first book of poetry, April Twilights, *appeared in 1903. Following the publication of a collection of her short stories,* The Troll Garden *(1905), she moved to New York City, where she worked for six years on the editorial staff of* McClure's *magazine. Her first novel,* Alexander's Bridge *(1912), was set in England, but she soon returned to the frontier world of the prairies with* O Pioneers! *(1913). Next came* The Song of the Lark *(1915),* My Antonia *(1918), and collections of short stories:* Youth and the Bright Medusa *(1920) and* Obscure Destinies *(1932). In her later years she came to perceive the sprawling cities of the East and the joyless materialism of the twentieth century as symbolic expressions of a decline in order and meaning, and she turned to depictions of the more distant past. She wrote of the struggles of early Roman Catholic missionaries among the Indians of New Mexico in* Death Comes for the Archbishop *(1927), and of the lives of settlers in seventeenth-century Québec in* Shadows on the Rock *(1931). Cather's artistry is marked by her vivid portrayals of ordinary men and women who struggle to find meaningful lives in the midst of adversity. Her success can be credited, at least in part, to what she called "the gift of sympathy."*

FURTHER READING: *The Novels and Stories of Willa Cather,* 13 vols., 1937–1941; *Willa Cather's Collected Short Fiction,* ed. V. Faulkner, 1965, 1970; M. Bennett, *The World of Willa Cather,* 1951, 1961, 1995; P. Gerber, *Willa Cather,* 1975, 1995; P. Robinson, *Willa: The Life of Willa Cather,* 1983; *Critical Essays on Willa Cather,* ed. J. Murphy, 1984; *Willa Cather,* ed. H. Bloom, 1985; S. Rosowski, *The Voyage Perilous: Willa Cather's Romanticism,* 1986; S. O'Brien, *Willa Cather: The Emerging Voice,* 1987; J. Woodress, *Willa Cather: A Literary Life,* 1987; M. Maguire, *After the World Broke in Two: The Later Novels of Willa Cather,* 1990; J. Middleton, *Willa Cather's Modernism: A Study of Style and Technique,* 1990; L. Wasserman, *Willa Cather: A Study of the Short Fiction,* 1991; D. Carlin, *Cather, Canon, and the Politics of Reading,* 1992; *A Reader's Companion to the Fiction of Willa Cather,* ed. J. March, M. Arnold, and D. Lynn, 1993; E. Wagenknecht, *Willa Cather,* 1993; F. Kaye, *Isolation and Masquerade: Willa Cather's Women,* 1993; J. Urgo, *Willa Cather and the Myths of American Migration,* 1995; G. Reynolds, *Willa Cather in Context,* 1996; J. Stout, *Willa Cather: The Writer and Her World,* 2000; J. Goldberg, *Willa Cather and Others,* 2001; *Willa Cather: The Contemporary Reviews,* ed. M. O'Connor, 2001; *The Cambridge Companion to Willa Cather,* ed. M. Lindemann, 2004; *Willa Cather and Material Culture: Real-World Writing, Writing the Real World,* ed. J. Stout, 2005.

TEXT: *Youth and the Bright Medusa,* 1920.

A WAGNER MATINÉE

I received one morning a letter, written in pale ink on glassy, blue-lined notepaper, and bearing the postmark of a little Nebraska town. This communication, worn and rubbed, looking as if it had been carried for some days in a coat pocket that was none too clean, was from my Uncle Howard, and informed me that his wife had been left a small legacy by a bachelor relative, and that it would be necessary for her to go to Boston to attend to the settling of the estate. He requested me to meet her at the station and render her whatever services might be necessary. On examining the date indicated as that of her arrival, I found it to be no later than to-morrow. He had characteristically delayed writing until, had I been away from home for a day, I must have missed my aunt altogether.

The name of my Aunt Georgiana opened before me a gulf of recollection so wide and deep that, as the letter dropped from my hand, I felt suddenly a stranger to all the present conditions of my existence, wholly ill at ease and out of place amid the familiar surroundings of my study. I became, in short, the gangling farmer-boy my aunt had known, scourged with chilblains[1] and bashfulness, my hands cracked and sore from the corn-husking. I sat again before her parlour organ, fumbling the scales with my stiff, red fingers, while she, beside me, made canvas mittens for the huskers.

The next morning, after preparing my landlady for a visitor, I set out for the station. When the train arrived, I had some difficulty in finding my aunt. She was the last of the passengers to alight, and it was not until I got her into the carriage that she seemed really to recognize me. She had come all the way in a day coach; her linen duster had become black with soot and her black bonnet grey with dust during the journey. When we arrived at my boarding-house, the landlady put her to bed at once and I did not see her again until the next morning.

Whatever shock Mrs. Springer experienced at my aunt's appearance, she considerately concealed. As for myself, I saw my aunt's battered figure with that feeling of awe and respect with which we behold explorers who have left their ears and fingers north of Franz-Josef Land,[2] or their health somewhere along the Upper Congo.[3]

My Aunt Georgiana had been a music-teacher at the Boston Conservatory, somewhere back in the late sixties. One summer, while visiting in the little village among the Green Mountains[4] where her ancestors had dwelt for generations, she had kindled the callow fancy of my uncle, Howard Carpenter, then an idle, shiftless boy of twenty-one. When she returned to her duties in Boston, Howard followed her, and the upshot of this infatuation was that she eloped with him, eluding the reproaches of her family and the criticism of her friends by going with him to the Nebraska frontier. Carpenter, who, of course, had no money, took up a homestead[5] in Red Willow County, fifty miles from the railroad. There they had measured off their land themselves, driving across the prairie in a wagon, to the wheel of which they had tied a red cotton handkerchief, and counting its revolutions. They built a dugout in the red hillside,

[1]Inflammation caused by exposure to the cold.
[2]Archipelago in the Arctic Ocean, near the North Pole.
[3]The Congo River in equatorial Africa. [4]In Vermont.
[5]Free land offered by the U.S. government to encourage settlement of the frontier.

one of those cave dwellings whose inmates so often reverted to primitive conditions. Their water they got from the lagoons where the buffalo drank, and their slender stock of provisions was always at the mercy of bands of roving Indians. For thirty years my aunt had not been farther than fifty miles from the homestead.

I owed to this woman most of the good that ever came my way in my boyhood, and had a reverential affection for her. During the years when I was riding herd for my uncle, my aunt, after cooking the three meals—the first of which was ready at six o'clock in the morning—and putting the six children to bed, would often stand until midnight at her ironing-board, with me at the kitchen table beside her, hearing me recite Latin declensions and conjugations, gently shaking me when my drowsy head sank down over a page of irregular verbs. It was to her, at her ironing or mending, that I read my first Shakespeare, and her old textbook on mythology was the first that ever came into my empty hands. She taught me my scales and exercises on the little parlour organ which her husband had bought her after fifteen years during which she had not so much as seen a musical instrument. She would sit beside me by the hour, darning and counting, while I struggled with the "Joyous Farmer."[6] She seldom talked to me about music, and I understood why. Once when I had been doggedly beating out some easy passages from an old score of "Euryanthe"[7] I had found among her music-books, she came up to me and, putting her hands over my eyes, gently drew my head back upon her shoulder, saying tremulously, "Don't love it so well, Clark, or it may be taken from you."

When my aunt appeared on the morning after her arrival in Boston, she was still in a semi-somnambulant state. She seemed not to realize that she was in the city where she had spent her youth, the place longed for hungrily half a lifetime. She had been so wretchedly train-sick throughout the journey that she had no recollection of anything but her discomfort, and, to all intents and purposes, there were but a few hours of nightmare between the farm in Red Willow County and my study on Newbury Street. I had planned a little pleasure for her that afternoon, to repay her for some of the glorious moments she had given me when we used to milk together in the straw-thatched cow-shed and she, because I was more than usually tired, or because her husband had spoken sharply to me, would tell me of the splendid performance of the "Huguenots"[8] she had seen in Paris, in her youth.

At two o'clock the Symphony Orchestra was to give a Wagner[9] program, and I intended to take my aunt; though, as I conversed with her, I grew doubtful about her enjoyment of it. I suggested our visiting the Conservatory and the Common[10] before lunch, but she seemed altogether too timid to wish to venture out. She questioned me absently about various changes in the city, but she was chiefly concerned that she had forgotten to leave instructions about feeding half-skimmed milk to a certain weakling calf, "old Maggie's calf, you know, Clark," she explained, evidently having forgotten how long I had been away. She was further troubled because she had neglected to tell her daughter about

[6]Short piano piece (1848) for beginning students, by Robert Schumann (1810–1856), German composer.
[7]Opera (1823) by Carl Maria von Weber (1786–1826), German composer.
[8]Opera (1836) by Giacomo Meyerbeer (1791–1864), German-French composer.
[9]Richard Wagner (1813–1883), German composer. [10]The Boston Common, a public park.

the freshly opened kit[11] of mackerel in the cellar, which would spoil if it were not used directly.

I asked her whether she had ever heard any of the Wagnerian operas, and found that she had not, though she was perfectly familiar with their respective situations, and had once possessed the piano score of "The Flying Dutchman."[12] I began to think it would be best to get her back to Red Willow County without waking her, and regretted having suggested the concert.

From the time we entered the concert hall, however, she was a trifle less passive and inert, and for the first time seemed to perceive her surroundings. I had felt some trepidation lest she might become aware of her queer, country clothes, or might experience some painful embarrassment at stepping suddenly into the world to which she had been dead for more than a quarter of a century. But, again, I found how superficially I had judged her. She sat looking about her with eyes as impersonal, almost as stony, as those with which the granite Rameses[13] in a museum watches the froth and fret that ebbs and flows about his pedestal. I have seen this same aloofness in old miners who drift into the Brown Palace Hotel at Denver, their pockets full of bullion, their linen soiled, their haggard faces unshaven; standing in the thronged corridors as solitary as though they were still in a frozen camp on the Yukon.

The matinée audience was made up chiefly of women. One lost the contour of faces and figures, indeed any effect of line whatever, and there was only the colour of bodices past counting, the shimmer of fabrics soft and firm, silky and sheer; red, mauve, pink, blue, lilac, purple, écru, rose, yellow, cream, and white, all the colours that an impressionist finds in a sunlit landscape, with here and there the dead shadow of a frock coat. My Aunt Georgiana regarded them as though they had been so many daubs of tube-paint on a palette.

When the musicians came out and took their places, she gave a little stir of anticipation, and looked with quickening interest down over the rail at that invariable grouping, perhaps the first wholly familiar thing that had greeted her eye since she had left old Maggie and her weakling calf. I could feel how all those details sank into her soul, for I had not forgotten how they had sunk into mine when I came fresh from ploughing forever and forever between green aisles of corn, where, as in a treadmill, one might walk from daybreak to dusk without perceiving a shadow of change. The clean profiles of the musicians, the gloss of their linen, the dull black of their coats, the beloved shapes of the instruments, the patches of yellow light on the smooth, varnished bellies of the 'cellos and the bass viols in the rear, the restless, wind-tossed forest of fiddle necks and bows—I recalled how, in the first orchestra I ever heard, those long bow-strokes seemed to draw the heart out of me, as a conjurer's stick reels out yards of paper ribbon from a hat.

The first number was the "Tannhäuser"[14] overture. When the horns drew out the first strain of the Pilgrims' Chorus, Aunt Georgiana clutched my coat-sleeve. Then it was I first realized that for her this broke a silence of thirty years. I saw again the tall, naked house on the prairie, black and grim as a wooden fortress; the black pond where I had learned to swim, its margin pitted with

[11]A wooden tub. [12]Opera (1843) by Richard Wagner.

[13]Ancient statue of an Egyptian pharaoh (king).

[14]Opera (1845) by Richard Wagner in which the hero meets a group of pilgrims journeying to Rome.

sun-dried cattle tracks; the rain-gullied clay banks about the naked house, the four dwarf ash seedlings where the dish-cloths were always hung to dry before the kitchen door. The world there was the flat world of the ancients; to the east, a cornfield that stretched to daybreak; to the west, a corral that reached to sunset; between, the conquests of peace, dearer-bought than those of war.

The overture closed, my aunt released my coat-sleeve, but she said nothing. She sat quietly looking at the orchestra. What, I wondered, did she get from it? She had been a good pianist in her day, I knew, and her musical education had been broader than that of most music-teachers of a quarter of a century ago. She had often told me of Mozart's[15] operas and Meyerbeer's, and I could remember hearing her sing, years ago, certain melodies of Verdi.[16] When I had fallen ill with a fever in her house, she used to sit by my cot in the evening—when the cool night wind blew in through the faded mosquito netting tacked over the window and I lay watching a certain bright star that burned red above the cornfield—and sing "Home to our mountains, O, let us return!"[17] in a way fit to break the heart of a Vermont boy near dead of homesickness already.

I watched her closely through the prelude to "Tristan and Isolde,"[18] trying vainly to conjecture what that seething turmoil of strings and winds might mean to her, but she sat mutely staring at the violin bows that drove obliquely downward, like the streaks of rain in a summer shower. Had this music any message for her? Had she enough left to at all comprehend this power which had kindled the world since she had left it? I was in a fever of curiosity, but Aunt Georgiana preserved her utter immobility throughout the number from "The Flying Dutchman," though her fingers worked mechanically upon her black dress, as if, of themselves, they were recalling the piano score they had once played. Poor hands! They had been stretched and twisted into mere tentacles to hold and lift and knead with; on one of them a thin, worn band that had once been a wedding ring. As I pressed and gently quieted one of those groping hands, I remembered their services for me in other days.

Soon after the tenor began the "Prize Song,"[19] I heard a quick-drawn breath and turned to my aunt. Her eyes were closed, but the tears were glistening on her cheeks, and I think, in a moment more, they were in my eyes as well. It never really died, then—the soul which can suffer so excruciatingly and so interminably; it withers to the outward eye only; like that strange moss which can lie on a dusty shelf half a century and yet, if placed in water, grows green again.

During the intermission before the second half, I questioned my aunt and found that the "Prize Song" was not new to her. Some years before there had drifted to the farm in Red Willow County a young German, a tramp cowpuncher, who had sung in the chorus at Bayreuth[20] when he was a boy, along with the other peasant boys and girls. Of a Sunday morning he used to sit on his gingham-sheeted bed in the hands' bedroom which opened off the kitchen, cleaning the leather of his boots and saddle, singing the "Prize Song," while my

[15]Wolfgang Amadeus Mozart (1756–1791), Austrian composer.

[16]Giuseppe Verdi (1813–1901), Italian composer.

[17]Words sung by an imprisoned gypsy in Act IV of the opera *Il Trovatore* (1853), by Giuseppe Verdi.

[18]Opera (1865) by Richard Wagner.

[19]From *Die Meistersinger von Nürnberg* (1867), by Richard Wagner.

[20]City in Germany, home of an annual music festival devoted to the performance of operas composed by Richard Wagner.

aunt went about her work in the kitchen. She had hovered over him until she had prevailed upon him to join the country church, though his sole fitness for this step, in so far as I could gather, lay in his boyish face and his possession of this divine melody. Shortly afterward, he had gone to town on the Fourth of July, been drunk for several days, lost his money at a faro[21] table, ridden a saddled Texas steer on a bet, and disappeared with a fractured collar-bone. All this my aunt told me huskily, wanderingly, during the intermission.

"Well, we have come to better things than the old 'Trovatore'[22] at any rate, Aunt Georgie?" I asked, with a well-meant effort at jocularity.

Her lip quivered and she hastily put her handkerchief up to her mouth. From behind it she murmured, "And you have been hearing this ever since you left me, Clark?" Her question was the gentlest and saddest of reproaches.

The second half of the programme consisted of four numbers from the "Ring"[23] and closed with Siegfried's funeral march.[24] Throughout these I felt that my aunt had drifted quite away from me. From time to time her eyes looked up at the lights, burning softly under their dull glass globes.

The deluge of sound poured on and on; I never knew what she found in the shining current of it; I never knew how far it bore her, or past what happy islands. From the trembling of her face I could well believe that before the last number she had been carried out where the myriad graves are, into the grey, nameless burying grounds of the sea; or into some world of death vaster yet, where, from the beginning of the world, hope has lain down with hope and dream with dream and, renouncing, slept.

The concert was over; the people filed out of the hall chattering and laughing, glad to relax and find the living level again, but my kinswoman made no effort to rise. The harpist slipped the green felt cover over his instrument; the flute-players shook the water from their mouthpieces; the men of the orchestra went out one by one, leaving the stage to the chairs and music-stands, empty as a winter cornfield.

I spoke to my aunt. She turned to me with a sad little smile. "I don't want to go, Clark. I suppose we must."

I understood. For her, just outside the concert hall, lay the black pond with the cattle-tracked bluffs; the tall, unpainted house, with weather-curled boards, naked as a tower, the crook-backed ash seedlings where the dishcloths hung to dry; the gaunt, moulting turkeys picking up refuse about the kitchen door.

1904, 1920

PAUL'S CASE

It was Paul's afternoon to appear before the faculty of the Pittsburgh High School to account for his various misdemeanors. He had been suspended a week ago, and his father had called at the Principal's office and confessed his

[21]Popular card game for gamblers in nineteenth-century America.

[22]*Il Trovatore,* by Giuseppe Verdi.

[23]*Der Ring des Nibelungen,* a cycle of four related operas (1869–1876) by Richard Wagner.

[24]From *Götterdämmerung* (1876), the final opera of Wagner's Ring Cycle.

perplexity about his son. Paul entered the faculty room suave and smiling. His clothes were a trifle outgrown, and the tan velvet on the collar of his open overcoat was frayed and worn; but for all that there was something of a dandy about him, and he wore an opal pin in his neatly knotted black four-in-hand, and a red carnation in his buttonhole. This latter adornment the faculty somehow felt was not properly significant of the contrite spirit befitting a boy under the ban of suspension.

Paul was tall for his age and very thin, with high, cramped shoulders and a narrow chest. His eyes were remarkable for a certain hysterical brilliancy, and he continually used them in a conscious, theatrical sort of way, peculiarly offensive in a boy. The pupils were abnormally large, as though he were addicted to belladonna, but there was a glassy glitter about them which that drug does not produce.

When questioned by the Principal as to why he was there, Paul stated, politely enough, that he wanted to come back to school. This was a lie, but Paul was quite accustomed to lying; found it, indeed, indispensable for overcoming friction. His teachers were asked to state their respective charges against him, which they did with such a rancor and aggrievedness as evinced that this was not a usual case. Disorder and impertinence were among the offenses named, yet each of his instructors felt that it was scarcely possible to put into words the real cause of the trouble, which lay in a sort of hysterically defiant manner of the boy's; in the contempt which they all knew he felt for them, and which he seemingly made not the least effort to conceal. Once, when he had been making a synopsis of a paragraph at the blackboard, his English teacher had stepped to his side and attempted to guide his hand. Paul had started back with a shudder and thrust his hands violently behind him. The astonished woman could scarcely have been more hurt and embarrassed had he struck at her. The insult was so involuntary and definitely personal as to be unforgettable. In one way and another, he had made all his teachers, men and women alike, conscious of the same feeling of physical aversion. In one class he habitually sat with his hand shading his eyes; in another he always looked out of the window during the recitation; in another had made a running commentary on the lecture, with humorous intent.

His teachers felt this afternoon that his whole attitude was symbolized by his shrug and his flippantly red carnation flower, and they fell upon him without mercy, his English teacher leading the pack. He stood through it smiling, his pale lips parted over his white teeth. (His lips were continually twitching, and he had a habit of raising his eyebrows that was contemptuous and irritating to the last degree.) Older boys than Paul had broken down and shed tears under that ordeal, but his set smile did not once desert him, and his only sign of discomfort was the nervous trembling of the fingers that toyed with the buttons of his overcoat, and an occasional jerking of the other hand which held his hat. Paul was also smiling, always glancing about him, seeming to feel that people might be watching him and trying to detect something. This conscious expression, since it was as far as possible from boyish mirthfulness, was usually attributed to insolence or "smartness."

As the inquisition proceeded, one of his instructors repeated an impertinent remark of the boy's, and the Principal asked him whether he thought that a courteous speech to make to a woman. Paul shrugged his shoulders slightly and his eyebrows twitched.

"I don't know," he replied. "I didn't mean to be polite or impolite, either. I guess it's a sort of way I have, of saying things regardless."

The Principal asked him whether he didn't think that a way it would be well to get rid of. Paul grinned and said he guessed so. When he was told that he could go, he bowed gracefully and went out. His bow was like a repetition of the scandalous red carnation.

His teachers were in despair, and his drawing-master voiced the feeling of them all when he declared there was something about the boy which none of them understood. He added: "I don't really believe that smile of his comes altogether from insolence; there's something sort of haunted about it. The boy is not strong for one thing. There is something wrong about the fellow."

The drawing-master had come to realize that, in looking at Paul, one saw only his white teeth and the forced animation of his eyes. One warm afternoon the boy had gone to sleep at his drawing-board, and his master had noted with amazement what a white, blue-veined face it was; drawn and wrinkled like an old man's about the eyes, the lips twitching even in his sleep.

His teachers left the building dissatisfied and unhappy; humiliated to have felt so vindictive toward a mere boy, to have uttered this feeling in cutting terms, and to have set each other on, as it were, in the gruesome game of intemperate reproach. One of them remembered having seen a miserable street cat set at bay by a ring of tormentors.

As for Paul, he ran down the hill whistling the Soldiers' Chorus from *Faust,* looking behind him now and then to see whether some of his teachers were not there to witness his light-heartedness. As it was now late in the afternoon and Paul was on duty that evening as usher at Carnegie Hall, he decided that he would not go home to supper.

When he reached the concert hall, the doors were not yet open. It was chilly outside, and he decided to go up into the picture gallery—always deserted at this hour—where there were some of Raffelli's gay studies of Paris streets and an airy blue Venetian scene or two that always exhilarated him. He was delighted to find no one in the gallery but the old guard, who sat in the corner, a newspaper on his knee, a black patch over one eye and the other closed. Paul possessed himself of the place and walked confidently up and down, whistling under his breath. After a while he sat down before a blue Rico and lost himself. When he bethought him to look at his watch, it was after seven o'clock, and he rose with a start and ran downstairs, making a face at Augustus Caesar, peering out from the cast-room, and an evil gesture at the Venus of Milo as he passed her on the stairway.

When Paul reached the ushers' dressing-room, half a dozen boys were there already, and he began excitedly to tumble into his uniform. It was one of the few that at all approached fitting, and Paul thought it very becoming—though he knew the tight, straight coat accentuated his narrow chest, about which he was exceedingly sensitive. He was always excited while he dressed, twanging all over to the tuning of the strings and the preliminary flourishes of the horns in the music-room; but tonight he seemed quite beside himself, and he teased and plagued the boys until, telling him that he was crazy, they put him down on the floor and sat on him.

Somewhat calmed by his suppression, Paul dashed out to the front of the house to seat the early comers. He was a model usher. Gracious and smiling he ran up and down the aisles. Nothing was too much trouble for him; he carried messages and brought programs as though it were his greatest pleasure in life, and all the people in his section thought him a charming boy, feeling that he remembered and admired them. As the house filled, he grew more and more vivacious and animated, and the color came to his cheeks and lips. It was very much as though this were a great reception and Paul were the host. Just as the musicians came out to take their places, his English teacher arrived with checks for the seats which a prominent manufacturer had taken for the season. She betrayed some embarrassment when she handed Paul the tickets, and a *hauteur* which subsequently made her feel very foolish. Paul was startled for a moment, and had the feeling of wanting to put her out; what business had she here among all these fine people and gay colors? He looked her over and decided that she was not appropriately dressed and must be a fool to sit downstairs in such togs. The tickets had probably been sent her out of kindness, he reflected, as he put down a seat for her, and she had about as much right to sit there as he had.

When the symphony began, Paul sank into one of the rear seats with a long sigh of relief, and lost himself as he had done before the Rico. It was not that symphonies, as such, meant anything in particular to Paul, but the first sight of the instruments seemed to free some hilarious spirit within him; something that struggled there like the genie in the bottle found by the Arab fisherman. He felt a sudden zest of life; the lights danced before his eyes and the concert hall blazed into unimaginable splendor. When the soprano soloist came on, Paul forgot even the nastiness of his teacher's being there, and gave himself up to the peculiar intoxication such personages always had for him. The soloist chanced to be a German woman, by no means in her first youth, and the mother of many children; but she wore a satin gown and a tiara, and she had that indefinable air of achievement, that world-shine upon her, which always blinded Paul to any possible defects.

After a concert was over, Paul was often irritable and wretched until he got to sleep—and tonight he was even more than usually restless. He had the feeling of not being able to let down; of its being impossible to give up his delicious excitement which was the only thing that could be called living at all. During the last number he withdrew and, after hastily changing his clothes in the dressing-room, slipped out to the side door where the singer's carriage stood. Here he began pacing rapidly up and down the walk, waiting to see her come out.

Over yonder the Schenley, in its vacant stretch, loomed big and square through the fine rain, the windows of its twelve stories glowing like those of a lighted cardboard house under a Christmas tree. All the actors and singers of any importance stayed there when they were in Pittsburgh, and a number of the big manufacturers of the place lived there in the winter. Paul had often hung about the hotel, watching the people go in and out, longing to enter and leave schoolmasters and dull care behind him forever.

At last the singer came out, accompanied by the conductor, who helped her into her carriage and closed the door with a cordial *auf wiedersehen*[1]—which set Paul to wondering whether she were not an old sweetheart of his. Paul followed the carriage over to the hotel, walking so rapidly as not to be far from the entrance when the singer alighted and disappeared behind the swinging glass

[1]German: Goodbye.

doors which were opened by a Negro in a tall hat and a long coat. In the moment that the door was ajar, it seemed to Paul that he, too, entered. He seemed to feel himself go after her up the steps, into the warm, lighted building, into an exotic, tropical world of shiny, glistening surfaces and basking ease. He reflected upon the mysterious dishes that were brought into the dining-room, the green bottles in buckets of ice, as he had seen them in the supper-party pictures of the Sunday supplement. A quick gust of wind brought the rain down with sudden vehemence, and Paul was startled to find that he was still outside in the slush of the gravel driveway; that his boots were letting in the water and his scanty overcoat was clinging wet about him; that the lights in front of the concert hall were out, and that the rain was driving in sheets between him and the orange glow of the windows above him. There it was, what he wanted—tangibly before him, like the fairy world of a Christmas pantomime; as the rain beat in his face, Paul wondered whether he were destined always to shiver in the black night outside, looking up at it.

He turned and walked reluctantly toward the car tracks. The end had to come sometime; his father in his night-clothes at the top of the stairs, explanations that did not explain, hastily improvised fictions that were forever tripping him up, his upstairs room and its horrible yellow wallpaper, the creaking bureau with the greasy plush collar-box, and over his painted wooden bed the pictures of George Washington and John Calvin, and the framed motto. "Feed my Lambs," which had been worked in red worsted by his mother, whom Paul could not remember.

Half an hour later, Paul alighted from the Negley Avenue car and went slowly down one of the side streets off the main thoroughfare. It was a highly respectable street, where all the houses were exactly alike, and where business men of moderate means begot and reared large families of children, all of whom went to Sabbath School and learned the shorter catechism, and were interested in arithmetic; all of whom were as exactly alike as their homes, and of a piece of the monotony in which they lived. Paul never went up Cordelia Street without a shudder of loathing. His home was next to the house of the Cumberland minister. He approached it tonight with the nerveless sense of defeat, the hopeless feeling of sinking back forever into ugliness and commonness that he had always had when he came home. The moment he turned into Cordelia Street he felt the waters close above his head. After each of these orgies of living, he experienced all the physical depression which follows a debauch; the loathing of respectable beds, of common food, of a house permeated by kitchen odors; a shuddering repulsion for the flavorless, colorless mass of every-day existence; a morbid desire for cool things and soft lights and fresh flowers.

The nearer he approached the house, the more absolutely unequal Paul felt to the sight of it all: his ugly sleeping chamber; the old bathroom with the grimy zinc tub, the cracked mirror, the dripping spigots; his father, at the top of the stairs, his hairy legs sticking out from his nightshirt, his feet thrust into carpet slippers. He was so much later than usual that there would certainly be enquiries and reproaches. Paul stopped short before the door. He felt that he could not be accosted by his father tonight; that he could not toss again on that miserable bed. He would not go in. He would tell his father that he had no carfare, and it was raining so hard he had gone home with one of the boys and stayed all night.

Meanwhile, he was wet and cold. He went around to the back of the house and tried one of the basement windows, found it open, and raised it cautiously, and scrambled down the cellar wall to the floor. There he stood, holding his breath, terrified by the noise he had made; but the floor above him was silent, and there was no creak on the stairs. He found a soap-box, and carried it over to the soft ring of light that streamed from the furnace door, and sat down. He was horribly afraid of rats, so he did not try to sleep, but sat looking distrustfully at the dark, still terrified lest he might have awakened his father. In such reactions, after one of the experiences which made days and nights out of the dreary blanks of the calendar, when his senses were deadened, Paul's head was always singularly clear. Suppose his father had heard him getting in at the window and had come down and shot him for a burglar? Then, again, suppose his father had come down, pistol in hand, and he had cried out in time to save himself, and his father had been horrified to think how nearly he had killed him? Then again, suppose a day should come when his father would remember that night, and wish there had been no warning cry to stay his hand? With this last supposition Paul entertained himself until daybreak.

The following Sunday was fine; the sodden November chill was broken by the last flash of autumnal summer. In the morning Paul had to go to church and Sabbath School, as always. On seasonable Sunday afternoons the burghers of Cordelia Street usually sat out on their front "stoops," and talked to their neighbors on the next stoop, or called to those across the street in neighborly fashion. The men sat placidly on gay cushions placed upon the steps that led down to the sidewalk, while the women, in their Sunday "waists,"[2] sat in rockers on the cramped porches, pretending to be greatly at their ease. The children played in the streets; there were so many of them that the place resembled the recreation grounds of a kindergarten. The men on the steps, all in their shirt-sleeves, their vests unbuttoned, sat with their legs well apart, their stomachs comfortably protruding, and talked of the prices of things, or told anecdotes of the sagacity of their various chiefs and overlords. They occasionally looked over the multitude of squabbling children, listened affectionately to their high-pitched, nasal voices, smiling to see their own proclivities reproduced in their offspring, and interspersed their legends of the iron kings with remarks about their sons' progress at school, their grades in arithmetic, and the amounts they had saved in their toy banks.

On this last Sunday of November, Paul sat all afternoon on the lowest step of his "stoop," staring into the street, while his sisters, in their rockers, were talking to the minister's daughters next door about how many shirtwaists they had made in the last week, and how many waffles someone had eaten at the last church supper. When the weather was warm, and his father was in a particularly jovial frame of mind, the girls made lemonade, which was always brought out in a red-glass pitcher, ornamented with forget-me-nots in blue enamel. This the girls thought very fine, and the neighbors joked about the suspicious color of the pitcher.

Today Paul's father, on the top step, was talking to a young man who shifted a restless baby from knee to knee. He happened to be the young man who was daily held up to Paul as a model, and after whom it was his father's dearest hope that he would pattern. This young man was of a ruddy complexion, with

[2]A stiff, formal blouse.

a compressed, red mouth, and faded, nearsighted eyes, over which he wore thick spectacles, with gold bows that curved about his ears. He was clerk to one of the magnates of a great steel corporation, and was looked upon in Cordelia Street as a young man with a future. There was a story that, some five years ago—he was now barely twenty-six—he had been a trifle "dissipated," but in order to curb his appetites and save the loss of time and strength that a sowing of wild oats might have entailed, he had taken his chief's advice, oft reiterated to his employees, and at twenty-one had married the first woman whom he could persuade to share his fortunes. She happened to be an angular schoolmistress, much older than he, who also wore thick glasses, and who had now borne him four children, all nearsighted like herself.

The young man was relating how his chief, now cruising in the Mediterranean, kept in touch with all the details of the business, arranging his office hours on his yacht just as though he were at home, and "knocking off work enough to keep two stenographers busy." His father told, in turn, the plan his corporation was considering, of putting in an electric railway plant at Cairo.[3] Paul snapped his teeth; he had an awful apprehension that they might spoil it all before he got there. Yet he rather liked to hear these legends of the iron kings, that were told and retold on Sundays and holidays; these stories of palaces in Venice, yachts on the Mediterranean, and high play at Monte Carlo appealed to his fancy, and he was interested in the triumphs of cash-boys who had become famous, though he had no mind for the cash-boy stage.

After supper was over, and he had helped to dry the dishes, Paul nervously asked his father whether he could go to George's to get some help in his geometry, and still more nervously asked for carfare. This latter request he had to repeat, as his father, on principle, did not like to hear requests for money, whether much or little. He asked Paul whether he could not go to some boy who lived nearer, and told him that he ought not to leave his school work until Sunday; but he gave him the dime. He was not a poor man, but he had a worthy ambition to come up in the world. His only reason for allowing Paul to usher was that he thought a boy ought to be earning a little.

Paul bounded upstairs, scrubbed the greasy odor of the dishwater from his hands with the ill-smelling soap he hated, and then shook over his fingers a few drops of violet water from the bottle he kept hidden in his drawer. He left the house with his geometry conspicuously under his arm, and the moment he got out of Cordelia Street and boarded a downtown car, he shook off the lethargy of two deadening days, and began to live again.

The leading juvenile of the permanent stock company which played at one of the downtown theaters was an acquaintance of Paul's, and the boy had been invited to drop in at the Sunday-night rehearsals whenever he could. For more than a year Paul had spent every available moment loitering about Charley Edward's dressing-room. He had won a place among Edward's following not only because the young actor, who could not afford to employ a dresser, often found him useful, but because he recognized in Paul something akin to what churchmen term "vocation."

It was at the theater and at Carnegie Hall[4] that Paul really lived; the rest was but a sleep and a forgetting. This was Paul's fairy tale, and it had for him all the

[3]Cairo, Illinois, on the Mississippi River, where it meets the Ohio.
[4]Concert Hall.

allurement of a secret love. The moment he inhaled the gassy, painty, dusty odor behind the scenes, he breathed like a prisoner set free, and felt within him the possibility of doing or saying splendid, brilliant things. The moment the cracked orchestra beat out the overture from *Martha,* or jerked at the serenade from *Rigoletto,*[5] all stupid and ugly things slid from him, and his senses were deliciously, yet delicately fired.

Perhaps it was because, in Paul's world, the natural nearly always wore the guise of ugliness, that a certain element of artificiality seemed to him necessary in beauty. Perhaps it was because his experience of life elsewhere was so full of Sabbath-School picnics, petty economies, wholesome advice as to how to succeed in life, and the unescapable odors of cooking, that he found this existence so alluring, these smartly clad men and women so attractive, that he was so moved by these starry apple orchards that bloomed perennially under the limelight.

It would be difficult to put it strongly enough how convincingly the stage entrance of the theater was for Paul the actual portal of Romance. Certainly none of the company ever suspected it, least of all Charley Edwards. It was very like the old stories that used to float about London of fabulously rich Jews, who had subterranean halls, with palms, and fountains, and soft lamps and richly appareled women who never saw the disenchanting light of London day. So, in the midst of that smoke-palled city, enamored of figures and grimy oil, Paul had his secret temple, his wishing-carpet, his bit of blue-and-white Mediterranean shore bathed in perpetual sunshine.

Several of Paul's teachers had a theory that his imagination had been perverted by garish fiction; but the truth was he scarcely ever read at all. The books at home were not such as would either tempt or corrupt a youthful mind, and as for reading the novels that some of his friends urged upon him—well, he got what he wanted much more quickly from music; any sort of music, from an orchestra to a barrel-organ. He needed only the spark, the indescribable thrill that made his imagination master of his senses, and he could make plots and pictures enough of his own. It was equally true that he was not stage-struck—not, at any rate, in the usual acceptation of the expression. He had no desire to become an actor, any more than he had to become a musician. He felt no necessity to do any of these things; what he wanted was to see, to be in the atmosphere, float on the wave of it, to be carried out, blue league after league, away from everything.

After a night behind the scenes, Paul found the schoolroom more than ever repulsive; the bare floors and naked walls; the prosy men who never wore frock coats, or violets in their buttonholes; the women with their dull gowns, shrill voices, and pitiful seriousness about prepositions that govern the dative. He could not bear to have the other pupils think, for a moment, that he took these people seriously; he must convey to them that he considered it all trivial, and was there only by way of a joke, anyway. He had autographed pictures of all the members of the stock company which he showed his classmates, telling them the most incredible stories of his familiarity with these people, of his acquaintance with the soloists who came to Carnegie Hall, his suppers with them and the flowers he sent them. When these stories lost their effect, and his audience

[5]*Martha* (1847), opera by the German composer Friedrich von Flotow (1812–1883); *Rigoletto* (1851), opera by the Italian composer Giuseppe Verdi (1873–1901).

grew listless, he would bid all the boys goodbye, announcing that he was going to travel for a while; going to Naples, to California, to Egypt. Then, next Monday, he would slip back, conscious and nervously smiling; his sister was ill, and he would have to defer his voyage until spring.

Matters went steadily worse with Paul at school. In the itch to let his instructors know how heartily he despised them, and how thoroughly he was appreciated elsewhere, he mentioned once or twice that he had no time to fool with theorems, adding—with a twitch of the eyebrows and a touch of that nervous bravado which so perplexed them—that he was helping the people down at the stock company; they were old friends of his.

The upshot of the matter was that the Principal went to Paul's father, and Paul was taken out of school and put to work. The manager at Carnegie Hall was told to get another usher in his stead; the doorkeeper at the theater was warned not to admit him to the house; and Charley Edwards remorsefully promised the boy's father not to see him again.

The members of the stock company were vastly amused when some of Paul's stories reached them—especially the women. They were hard-working women, most of them supporting indolent husbands or brothers, and they laughed rather bitterly at having stirred the boy to such fervid and florid inventions. They agreed with the faculty and with his father, that Paul's was a bad case.

The east-bound train was plowing through a January snowstorm; the dull dawn was beginning to show grey when the engine whistled a mile out of Newark. Paul started up from the seat where he had lain curled in uneasy slumber, rubbed the breath-misted window-glass with his hand, and peered out. The snow was whirling in curling eddies above the white bottom lands, and the drifts lay already deep in the fields and along the fences, while here and there the tall dead grass and dried weed stalks protruded black above it. Lights shone from the scattered houses, and a gang of laborers who stood beside the track waved their lanterns.

Paul had slept very little, and he felt grimy and uncomfortable. He had made the all-night journey in a day coach because he was afraid if he took a Pullman he might be seen by some Pittsburgh business man who had noticed him in Denny and Carson's office. When the whistle woke him, he clutched quickly at his breast pocket, glancing about him with an uncertain smile. But the little, clay-bespattered Italians were still sleeping, the slatternly women across the aisle were in open-mouthed oblivion, and even the crumby, crying babies were for the time stilled. Paul settled back to struggle with his impatience as best he could.

When he arrived at the Jersey City station, he hurried through his breakfast, manifestly ill at ease and keeping a sharp eye about him. After he reached the Twenty-Third Street station, he consulted a cabman, and had himself driven to a men's furnishing establishment which was just opening for the day. He spent upward of two hours there, buying with endless reconsidering and great care. His new street suit he put on in the fitting-room; the frock coat and dress clothes clothes he had bundled into the cab with his new shirts. Then he drove to a hatter's and a shoe house. His next errand was at Tiffany's, where he selected silver-mounted brushes and a scarfpin. He would not wait to have his silver marked, he said. Lastly, he stopped at a trunk shop on Broadway, and had his purchases packed into various traveling-bags.

It was a little after one o'clock when he drove up to the Waldorf,[6] and, after settling with the cabman, went into the office. He registered from Washington; said his mother and father had been abroad, and that he had come down to await the arrival of their steamer. He told his story plausibly and had no trouble, since he offered to pay for them in advance, in engaging his rooms; a sleeping-room, sitting-room, and bath.

Not once, but a hundred times Paul had planned his entry into New York. He had gone over every detail of it with Charley Edwards, and in his scrapbook at home there were pages of description about New York hotels, cut from the Sunday papers.

When he was shown to his sitting-room on the eighth floor, he saw at a glance that everything was as it should be; there was but one detail in his mental picture that the place did not realize, so he rang for the bell-boy and sent him down for flowers. He moved about nervously until the boy returned, putting away his new linen and fingering it delightedly as he did so. When the flowers came, he put them hastily into water, and then tumbled into a hot bath. Presently he came out of his white bathroom, resplendent in his new silk underwear, and playing with the tassels of his red robe. The snow was whirling so fiercely outside his windows that he could scarcely see across the street; but within, the air was deliciously soft and fragrant. He put the violets and jonquils on the taboret beside the couch, and threw himself down with a long sigh, covering himself with a Roman blanket. He was thoroughly tired; he had been in such haste, he had stood up to such a strain, covered so much ground in the last twenty-four hours, that he wanted to think how it had all come about. Lulled by the sound of the wind, the warm air, and the cool fragrance of the flowers, he sank into deep, drowsy retrospection.

It had been wonderfully simple; when they had shut him out of the theater and concert hall, when they had taken away his bone, the whole thing was virtually determined. The rest was a mere matter of opportunity. The only thing that at all surprised him was his own courage—for he realized well enough that he had always been tormented by fear, a sort of apprehensive dread which, of late years, as the meshes of the lies he had told closed about him, had been pulling the muscles of his body tighter and tighter. Until now, he could not remember a time when he had not been dreading something. Even when he was a little boy, it was always there—behind him, or before, or on either side. There had always been the shadowed corner, the dark place into which he dared not look, but from which something seemed always to be watching him—and Paul had done things that were not pretty to watch, he knew.

But now he had a curious sense of relief, as though he had at last thrown down the gauntlet to the thing in the corner.

Yet it was but a day since he had been sulking in the traces; but yesterday afternoon that he had been sent to the bank with Denny and Carson's deposit, as usual—but this time he was instructed to leave the book to be balanced. There was above two thousand dollars in checks, and nearly a thousand in the banknotes which he had taken from the book and quietly transferred to his pocket. At the bank he had made out a new deposit slip. His nerves had been steady enough to permit of his returning to the office, where he had finished his work and asked for a full day's holiday tomorrow, Saturday, giving a perfectly

[6]Famous New York City hotel.

reasonable pretext. The bank book, he knew, would not be returned before Monday or Tuesday, and his father would be out of town for the next week. From the time he slipped the banknotes into his pocket until he boarded the night train for New York, he had not known a moment's hesitation.

How astonishingly easy it had all been; here he was, the thing done; and this time there would be no awakening, no figure at the top of the stairs. He watched the snowflakes whirling by his window until he fell asleep.

When he awoke, it was four o'clock in the afternoon. He bounded up with a start; one of his precious days gone already! He spent nearly an hour in dressing, watching every stage of his toilet carefully in the mirror. Everything was quite perfect; he was exactly the kind of boy he had always wanted to be.

When he went downstairs, Paul took a carriage and drove up Fifth Avenue toward the Park. The snow had somewhat abated; carriages and tradesmen's wagons were hurrying soundlessly to and fro in the winter twilight; boys in woolen mufflers were shoveling off the doorsteps; the Avenue stages made fine spots of color against the white street. Here and there on the corners whole flower gardens blooming behind glass windows, against which the snowflakes stuck and melted; violets, roses, carnations, lilies-of-the-valley—somehow vastly more lovely and alluring that they blossomed thus unnaturally in the snow. The Park itself was a wonderful stage winter-piece.

When he returned, the pause of the twilight had ceased, and the tune of the streets had changed. The snow was falling faster, lights streamed from the hotels that reared their many stories fearlessly up into the storm, defying the raging Atlantic winds. A long, black stream of carriages poured down the Avenue, intersected here and there by other streams, tending horizontally. There were a score of cabs about the entrance of his hotel, and his driver had to wait. Boys in livery were running in and out of the awning stretched across the sidewalk, up and down the red velvet carpet laid from the door to the street. Above, about, within it all, was the rumble and roar, the hurry and toss of thousands of human beings as hot for pleasure as himself, and on every side of him towered the glaring affirmation of the omnipotence of wealth.

The boy set his teeth and drew his shoulders together in a spasm of realization; the plot of all dramas, the text of all romances, the nerve-stuff of all sensations was whirling about him like the snowflakes. He burnt like a fagot in a tempest.

When Paul came down to dinner, the music of the orchestra floated up the elevator shaft to greet him. As he stepped into the thronged corridor, he sank back into one of the chairs against the wall to get his breath. The lights, the chatter, the perfumes, the bewildering medley of color—he had, for a moment, the feeling of not being able to stand it. But only for a moment; these were his own people, he told himself. He went slowly about the corridors, through the writing-rooms, smoking-rooms, reception-rooms, as though he were exploring the chambers of an enchanted palace, built and peopled for him alone.

When he reached the dining-room he sat down at a table near a window. The flowers, the white linen, the many-colored wine-glasses, the gay toilettes of the women, the low popping of corks, the undulating repetitions of the *Blue Danube* from the orchestra, all flooded Paul's dream with bewildering radiance. When the roseate tinge of his champagne was added—that cold, precious, bubbling stuff that creamed and foamed in his glass—Paul wondered that there were honest men in the world at all. This was what all the world was fighting for, he reflected; this was what all the struggle was about. He doubted the reality of his past. Had he ever known a place called Cordelia Street, a place where fagged-looking business men boarded the early car? Mere rivets in a machine they seemed to Paul—sickening men, with combings of children's hair always hanging to their coats, and the smell of cooking in their clothes. Cordelia Street—Ah, that belonged to another time and country! Had he not always been thus, had he not sat here night after night, from as far back as he could remember, looking pensively over just such shimmering textures, and slowly twirling the stem of a glass like this one between his thumb and middle finger? He rather thought he had.

He was not in the least abashed or lonely. He had no especial desire to meet or to know any of these people; all he demanded was the right to look on and conjecture, to watch the pageant. The mere stage properties were all he contended for. Nor was he lonely later in the evening, in his loge at the Opera. He was entirely rid of his nervous misgivings, of his forced aggressiveness, of the imperative desire to show himself different from his surroundings. He felt now that his surroundings explained him. Nobody questioned the purple; he had only to wear it passively. He had only to glance down at his dress coat to reassure himself that here it would be impossible for anyone to humiliate him.

He found it hard to leave his beautiful sitting-room to go to bed that night, and sat long watching the raging storm from his turret window. When he went to sleep, it was with the lights turned on in his bedroom; partly because of his old timidity, and partly so that, if he should wake in the night, there would be no wretched moment of doubt, no horrible suspicion of yellow wallpaper, or of Washington and Calvin above his bed.

On Sunday morning the city was practically snowbound. Paul breakfasted late, and in the afternoon he fell in with a wild San Francisco boy, a freshman at Yale, who said he had run down for a "little flyer" over Sunday. The young man offered to show Paul the night side of the town, and the two boys went off together after dinner, not returning to the hotel until seven o'clock the next morning. They had started out in the confiding warmth of a champagne friendship, but their parting in the elevator was singularly cool. The freshman pulled himself together to make his train, and Paul went to bed. He awoke at two o'clock in the afternoon, very thirsty and dizzy, and rang for ice-water, coffee, and the Pittsburgh papers.

On the part of the hotel management, Paul excited no suspicion. There was this to be said for him, that he wore his spoils with dignity and in no way made himself conspicuous. His chief greediness lay in his ears and eyes, and his excesses were not offensive ones. His dearest pleasures were the grey winter twilights in his sitting-room; his quiet enjoyment of his flowers, his clothes, his wide divan, his cigarette, and his sense of power. He could not remember a time when he had felt so at peace with himself. The mere release from the necessity of petty lying, lying every day and every day, restored his self-respect. He had never lied for pleasure, even at school; but to make himself noticed and admired, to assert his difference from other Cordelia Street boys; and he felt a good deal more manly, more honest, even, now that he had no need for boastful pretensions, now that he could, as his actor friends used to say, "dress the part." It was characteristic that remorse did not occur to him. His golden days went by without a shadow, and he made each as perfect as he could.

On the eighth day after his arrival in New York, he found the whole affair exploited in the Pittsburgh papers, exploited with a wealth of detail which indicated that local news of a sensational nature was at a low ebb. The firm of Denny and Carson announced that the boy's father had refunded the full amount of his theft, and that they had no intention of prosecuting. The Cumberland minister had been interviewed, and expressed his hope of yet reclaiming the motherless lad, and Paul's Sabbath-School teacher declared that she would spare no effort to that end. The rumor had reached Pittsburgh that the boy had been seen in a New York hotel, and his father had gone East to find him and bring him home.

Paul had just come in to dress for dinner; he sank into the chair, weak in the knees, and clasped his head in his hands. It was to be worse than jail, even; the tepid waters of Cordelia Street were to close over him finally and forever. The grey monotony stretched before him in hopeless, unrelieved years—Sabbath School, Young People's Meeting, the yellow-papered room, the damp dish-towels; it all rushed back upon him with sickening vividness. He had the old feeling that the orchestra had suddenly stopped, the sinking sensation that the play was over. The sweat broke out on his face, and he sprang to his feet, looked about him with his white, conscious smile, and winked at himself in the mirror. With something of the childish belief in miracles with which he had so often gone to class, all his lessons unlearned, Paul dressed and dashed whistling down the corridor to the elevator.

He had no sooner entered the dining-room and caught the measure of the music than his remembrance was lightened by his old elastic power of claiming the moment, mounting with it, and finding it all-sufficient. The glare and glitter about him, the mere scenic accessories had again, and for the last time, their old potency. He would show himself that he was game, he would finish the thing splendidly. He doubted, more than ever, the existence of Cordelia Street, and for the first time he drank his wine recklessly. Was he not, after all, one of these fortunate beings? Was he not still himself, and in his own place? He drummed a nervous accompaniment to the music and looked about him, telling himself over and over that it had paid.

He reflected drowsily, to the swell of the violin and the chill sweetness of his wine, that he might have done it more wisely. He might have caught an outbound steamer and been well out of their clutches before now. But the other side of the world had seemed too far away and too uncertain then; he could not have waited for it; his need had been too sharp. If he had to choose over again, he would do the same thing tomorrow. He looked affectionately about the dining-room, now gilded with a soft mist. Ah, it had paid indeed!

Paul was awakened next morning by a painful throbbing in his head and feet. He had thrown himself across the bed without undressing, and had slept with his shoes on. His limbs and hands were lead-heavy, and his tongue and throat were parched. There came upon him one of those fateful attacks of clear-headedness that never occurred except when he was physically exhausted and his nerves hung loose. He lay still and closed his eyes and let the tide of realities wash over him.

His father was in New York, "stopping at some joint or other," he told himself. The memory of successive summers on the front stoop fell upon him like a weight of black water. He had not a hundred dollars left; and he knew now, more than ever, that money was everything, the wall that stood between all he loathed and all he wanted. The thing was winding itself up; he had thought of that on his first glorious day in New York, and had even provided a way to snap the thread. It lay on his dressing-table now; he had got it out last night when he came blindly up from dinner—but the shiny metal hurt his eyes, and he disliked the look of it, anyway.

He rose and moved about with a painful effort, succumbing now and again to attacks of nausea. It was the old depression exaggerated; all the world had become Cordelia Street. Yet somehow he was not afraid of anything, was absolutely calm; perhaps because he had looked into the dark corner at last, and knew. It was bad enough, what he saw there; but somehow not so bad as his long fear of it had been. He saw everything clearly now. He had a feeling that he had made the best of it, that he had lived the sort of life he was meant to live, and for half an hour he sat staring at the revolver. But he told himself that was not the way, so he went downstairs and took a cab to the ferry.

When Paul arrived at Newark, he got off the train and took another cab, directing the driver to follow the Pennsylvania tracks out of town. The snow lay heavy on the roadways and had drifted deep in the open fields. Only here and there the dead grass or dried weed stalks projected, singularly black, above it. Once well into the country, Paul dismissed the carriage and walked, floundering along the tracks, his mind a medley of irrelevant things. He seemed to hold in his brain an actual picture of everything he had seen that morning. He remembered every feature of both his drivers, the toothless old woman from whom he had bought the red flowers in his coat, the agent from whom he had got his ticket, and all of his fellow-passengers on the ferry. His mind, unable to cope with vital matters near at hand, worked feverishly and deftly at sorting and grouping these images. They made for him a part of the ugliness of the world, of the ache in his head, and the bitter burning on his tongue. He stooped and put a handful of snow into his mouth as he walked, but that, too, seemed hot. When he reached a little hillside, where the tracks ran through a cut some twenty feet below him, he stopped and sat down.

The carnations in his coat were drooping with cold, he noticed; their red glory over. It occurred to him that all the flowers he had seen in the show windows that first night must have gone the same way, long before this. It was only one splendid breath they had, in spite of their brave mockery at the winter outside the glass. It was a losing game in the end, it seemed, this revolt against the homilies by which the world is run. Paul took one of the blossoms carefully from his coat and scooped a little hole in the snow, where he covered it up. Then he dozed awhile, from his weak condition, seeming insensible to the cold.

The sound of an approaching train woke him and he started to his feet, remembering only his resolution, and afraid lest he should be too late. He stood watching the approaching locomotive, his teeth chattering, his lips drawn away from them in a frightened smile; once or twice he glanced nervously sidewise, as though he were being watched. When the right moment came, he jumped. As he fell, the folly of his haste occurred to him with merciless clearness, the vastness of what he had left undone. There flashed through his brain, clearer than ever before, the blue of Adriatic water, the yellow of Algerian sands.

He felt something strike his chest—his body being thrown swiftly through the air, on and on, immeasurably far and fast, while his limbs gently relaxed. Then, because the picture-making mechanism was crushed, the disturbing visions flashed into black, and Paul dropped back into the immense design of things.

1905, 1920

Ellen Glasgow 1873–1945

Ellen Glasgow believed that she was "born a novelist." At the age of seven she wrote her first short story. At sixteen, she began work on a novel that she named Sharp Realities *because it was meant to serve as an antidote to the mawkish, sentimental fiction of the day. When the manuscript was rejected by an editor, she impulsively burned it and vowed never to write another. But within a few months she began work on a second novel,* The Descendant, *which she completed when she was twenty-two. Published in 1897,* The Descendant *was a surprising success; three reprintings were required to meet the public demand. The novel's realistic treatment of contemporary life brought Ellen Glasgow to the attention of the American literary establishment. And it shocked her family and friends when they discovered that so genteel and well-bred a young lady had written an "amoral" and "indelicate" novel of Bohemian life in New York City.*

In the next decade, Ellen Glasgow won national renown as a sardonic novelist and pessimistic critic of American culture. Her dark view of life derived in part from a childhood that was lonely and unhappy. She was born shortly after the end of the American Civil War and lived most of her life in Richmond, Virginia. Her family was well-to-do and socially distinguished. But she was a frail and sickly child, too delicate to attend school. Recurring illness, which plagued her through life, and her lack of schooling isolated her from other children—even from her own brothers and sisters, causing her to turn to an inward life of the imagination.

From her childhood and adolescence, Ellen Glasgow accepted few illusions about the delights of marriage and family life. Her mother was a gentle but neurotic invalid who agitated her family with hysterical eruptions and "nervous breakdowns." Ellen Glasgow's father was stern and domineering, fired with a religious zeal that he sought to instill in his children. His harsh and unsettling piety inspired in his daughter Ellen, she later wrote, the feeling that she was "damned all day."

As she grew up, Ellen Glasgow became fiercely independent. She rejected her father's religion and refused to attend his church. Her stand was inspired by her own truculent nature and by the ideas she found in the writing of scientists such as Charles Darwin. Her father once offered to pay her if she would stop reading Darwin's "atheistical blasphemies," but she refused. Like many other nineteenth-century people, she found in Darwin's On the Origin of Species *(1859) and in the deterministic idea of "natural selection" a logical explanation for the unsympathetic world she knew and portrayed in her books.*

She wrote, in all, twenty novels plus volumes of short stories, poetry, literary criticism, and autobiography. Her work was praised as "bruising realism" that dealt bravely with actual life, and it was disdained as morbid, dreary, harmful to the innocent minds of the young. Hamlin Garland praised her work as "bold, fearless, and unconventional" and expressed surprise that so refined a gentlewoman could exhibit such "alarming candor" and be so filled with the "bitterness of age."

Ellen Glasgow's novels have been praised as a social history of the American South as it developed after the Civil War. She wrote of a society in transition, of the "New South" in conflict with the obsolete ideals of the "Old South." She wrote of the decay of a social elite, of the rise of the new rich and the fall of a plantation aristocracy. She treated subjects thought to be forbidden to novelists: adultery, miscegenation, bastardy, the commonplace cruelties in American marriages. She lashed out at follies she saw in religion, in politics, in the ideals of romantic love. She attacked what she called the "evasive idealism" of American life, the refusal to face hard facts, the shallow-minded craving for happy endings and easy solutions to intractable human problems.

She was a rigorous writer who would not yield to the romantic appetites of the reading public, yet her work was popular and widely honored. Five of her novels were bestsellers; two were made into motion pictures. A dozen colleges and universities offered her honorary degrees, most of which she refused. And in 1942 she was awarded the Pulitzer Prize for Fiction. Her writing was described as "the turning-point in the literary history of the South," for it marked a beginning of the Southern literary renaissance and prepared the way for the realism of writers such as William Faulkner, Flannery O'Connor, and Eudora Welty.

In 1955, The New York Times *named her "the wittiest novelist in our history," and she is best remembered for three comedies of manners,* The Romantic Comedians *(1926),* They Stooped to Folly *(1929), and* The Sheltered Life *(1932). The novels dissected the relationships between men and women with a caustic irony. Ellen Glasgow believed that women are morally superior to men and denounced the ideal of self-sacrificing womanhood. She wrote of the disillusionments inevitable in love, asserting that women are happiest when they can enjoy "the tranquil immunity of a mind" that "has finished with love."*

Like many satirists, Ellen Glasgow saw life as difficult and cruel, and she once remarked that she had never in her life been happy. Yet she found a bitter pleasure in describing the stern realities of existence—because she knew them and because she believed that writers, above all others, must describe life as it is, rich in ungratified desires and ruled by the tyrannic force of environment and heredity.

FURTHER READING: *The Collected Stories of Ellen Glasgow,* ed. R. Meeker, 1963; *Ellen Glasgow's Reasonable Doubts: A Collection of Her Writings,* ed. J. Raper, 1988; *Letters of Ellen Glasgow,* ed. B. Rouse, 1958; S. Godbold, *Ellen Glasgow and the Woman Within,* 1972; L. Rubin, *No Place on Earth: Ellen Glasgow, James Banch Cabell, and Richmond-in-Virginia,* 1959; F. McDowell, *Ellen Glasgow and the Ironic Art of Fiction,* 1960; B. Rouse, *Ellen Glasgow,* 1962; J. Santas, *Ellen Glasgow's American Dream,* 1965; J. Raper, *Without Shelter: The Early Career of Ellen Glasgow,* 1971; M. Richards, *Ellen Glasgow's Development as a Novelist,* 1971; *Ellen Glasgow: Centennial Essays,* ed. T. Inge, 1976; J. Raper, *From the Sunken Garden: The Fiction of Ellen Glasgow, 1916–1945,* 1980; M. Thiebaux, *Ellen Glasgow,* 1982; L. Wagner, *Ellen Glasgow: Beyond Convention,* 1982; C. Sanders, *Writing the Margins,* 1987; P. Matthews, *Ellen Glasgow and a Woman's Traditions,* 1994.

TEXT: *The Shadowy Third and Other Stories,* 1923.

THE DIFFERENCE

Outside, in the autumn rain, the leaves were falling.

For twenty years, every autumn since her marriage, Margaret Fleming had watched the leaves from this window; and always it had seemed to her that they were a part of her life which she held precious. As they fell she had known that they carried away something she could never recover—youth, beauty, pleasure, or only memories that she wanted to keep. Something gracious, desirable and fleeting; but never until this afternoon had she felt that the wind was sweeping away the illusion of happiness by which she lived. Beyond the panes, against which the rain was beating in gray sheets, she looked out on the naked outlines of the city: bleak houses, drenched grass in squares, and boughs of trees where a few brown or yellow leaves were clinging.

On the hearth rug the letter lay where it had fallen a few minutes—or was it a few hours ago? The flames from the wood fire cast a glow on the white pages; and she imagined that the ugly words leaped out to sting her like scorpions as she moved by them. Not for worlds, she told herself, would she stoop and touch them again. Yet what need had she to touch them when each slanting black line was etched in her memory with acid? Never, though she lived a hundred years, could she forget the way the letters fell on the white paper!

Once, twice, three times, she walked from window to door and back again from door to window. The wood fire burned cheerfully with a whispering sound. As the lights and shadows stirred over the familiar objects she had once loved, her gaze followed them hungrily. She had called this upstairs library George's room, and she realized now that every piece of furniture, every book it contained, had been chosen to please him. He liked the golden brown of the walls, the warm colours in the Persian rugs, the soft depth of the cushioned chairs. He liked, too, the flamboyant red lilies beneath the little Chippendale mirror.

After twenty years of happiness, of comradeship, of mutual independence, after all that marriage could mean to two equal spirits, was there nothing left except ashes? Could twenty years of happiness be destroyed in an afternoon, in an hour? Stopping abruptly, with a jerk which ran like a spasm through her slender figure, she gazed with hard searching eyes over the red lilies into the mirror. The grave beauty of her face, a beauty less of flesh than of spirit, floated there in the shadows like a flower in a pond.

"I am younger than he is by a year," she thought, "and yet he can begin over again to love, while a new love for me would be desecration."

There was the sound of his step on the stair. An instant later his hand fell on the door, and he entered the room.

Stooping swiftly, she picked up the letter from the rug and hid it in her bosom. Then turning toward him, she received his kiss with a smile. "I didn't wait lunch for you," she said.

"I got it at the club." After kissing her cheek, he moved to the fire and stood warming his hands. "Beastly day. No chance of golf, so I've arranged to see that man from Washington. You won't get out, I suppose?"

She shook her head. "No, I sha'n't get out."

Did he know, she wondered, that this woman had written to her? Did he suspect that the letter lay now in her bosom? He had brought the smell of rain, the taste of dampness, with him into the room; and this air of the outer world enveloped him while he stood there, genial, robust, superbly vital, clothed in his sanguine temperament as in the healthy red and white of his flesh. Still boyish at forty-five, he had that look of perennial innocence which some men carry untarnished through the most enlightening experiences. Even his moustache and his sharply jutting chin could not disguise the softness that hovered always about his mouth, where she noticed now, with her piercing scrutiny, the muscles were growing lax. Strange that she had never seen this until she discovered that George loved another woman! The thought flashed into her mind that she knew him in reality no better than if she had lived with a stranger for twenty years. Yet, until a few hours ago, she would have said, had any one asked her, that their marriage was as perfect as any mating between a man and a woman could be in this imperfect world.

"You're wise. The wind's still in the east, and there is no chance, I'm afraid, of a change." He hesitated an instant, stared approvingly at the red lilies, and remarked abruptly, "Nice colour."

"You always liked red." Her mouth lost its softness. "And I was pale even as a girl."

His genial gaze swept her face. "Oh, well, there's red and red, you know. Some cheeks look best pale."

Without replying to his words, she sat looking up at him while her thoughts, escaping her control, flew from the warm room out into the rough autumn weather. It was as if she felt the beating of the rain in her soul, as if she were torn from her security and whirled downward and onward in the violence of the storm. On the surface of her life nothing had changed. The fire still burned; the lights and shadows still flickered over the Persian rugs; her husband still stood there, looking down on her through the cloudless blue of his eyes. But the real Margaret, the vital part of her, was hidden far away in that deep place where the seeds of mysterious impulses and formless desires lie buried. She knew that there were secrets within herself which she had never acknowledged in her own thoughts; that there were unexpressed longings which had never taken shape even in her imagination. Somewhere beneath the civilization of the ages there was the skeleton of the savage.

The letter in her bosom scorched her as if it were fire. "That was why you used to call me magnolia blossom," she said in a colourless voice, and knew it was only the superficial self that was speaking.

His face softened; yet so perfectly had the note of sentiment come to be understood rather than expressed in their lives that she could feel his embarrassment. The glow lingered in his eyes, but he answered only, "Yes, you were always like that."

An irrepressible laugh broke from her. Oh, the irony, the bitterness! "Perhaps you like them pale!" she tossed back mockingly, and wondered if this Rose Morrison who had written to her was coloured like her name?

He looked puzzled but solicitous. "I'm afraid I must be off. If you are not tired, could you manage to go over these galleys this afternoon? I'd like to read the last chapter aloud to you after the corrections are made." He had written a book on the history of law; and while he drew the roll of proof sheets from his pocket, she remembered, with a pang as sharp as the stab of a knife, all the work of last summer when they had gathered material together. He needed her for his work, she realized, if not for his pleasure. She stood, as she had always done, for the serious things of his life. This book could not have been written without her. Even his success in his profession had been the result of her efforts as well as his own.

"I'm never too tired for that," she responded, and though she smiled up at him, it was a smile that hurt her with its irony.

"Well, my time's up," he said. "By the way, I'll need my heavier golf things if it is fine to-morrow." To-morrow was Sunday, and he played golf with a group of men at the Country Club every Sunday morning.

"They are in the cedar closet. I'll get them out."

"The medium ones, you know. That English tweed."

"Yes, I know. I'll have them ready." Did Rose Morrison play golf, she wondered.

"I'll try to get back early to dinner. There was a button loose on the waistcoat I wore last evening. I forgot to mention it this morning."

"Oh, I'm sorry. I left it to the servants, but I'll look after it myself." Again this perverse humour seized her. Had he ever asked Rose Morrison to sew on a button?

At the door he turned back. "And I forgot to ask you this morning to order flowers for Morton's funeral. It is to be Monday."

The expression on her face felt as stiff as a wax mask, and though she struggled to relax her muscles, they persisted in that smile of inane cheerfulness. "I'll order them at once, before I begin the galleys," she answered.

Rising from the couch on which she had thrown herself at his entrance, she began again her restless pacing from door to window. The library was quiet except for the whispering flames. Outside in the rain the leaves were falling thickly, driven hither and thither by the wind which rocked the dappled boughs of the sycamores. In the gloom of the room the red lilies blazed.

The terror, which had clutched her like a living thing, had its fangs in her heart. Terror of loss, of futility. Terror of the past because it tortured her. Terror of the future because it might be empty even of torture. "He is mine, and I will never give him up," she thought wildly. "I will fight to the end for what is mine."

There was a sound at the door and Winters, the butler, entered. "Mrs. Chambers, Madam. She was quite sure you would be at home."

"Yes, I am at home." She was always at home, even in illness, to Dorothy Chambers. Though they were so different in temperament, they had been friends from girlhood; and much of the gaiety of Margaret's life had been supplied by Dorothy. Now, as her friend entered, she held out her arms. "You come whenever it rains, dear," she said. "It is so good of you." Yet her welcome was hollow, and at the very instant when she returned her friend's kiss she was wishing that she could send her away. That was one of the worst things about suffering; it made one indifferent and insincere.

Dorothy drew off her gloves, unfastened her furs, and after raising her veil over the tip of her small inquisitive nose, held out her hand with a beseeching gesture.

"I've come straight from a committee luncheon. Give me a cigarette."

Reaching for the Florentine box on the desk, Margaret handed it to her. A minute later, while the thin blue flame shot up between them, she asked herself if Dorothy could look into her face and not see the difference?

Small, plain, vivacious, with hair of ashen gold, thin intelligent features, and a smile of mocking brilliance, Dorothy was the kind of woman whom men admire without loving and women love without admiring. As a girl she had been a social success without possessing a single one of the qualities upon which social success is supposed to depend.

Sinking back in her chair, she blew several rings of smoke from her lips and watched them float slowly upward.

"We have decided to give a bridge party. There's simply no other way to raise money. Will you take a table?"

Margaret nodded. "Of course." Suffering outside of herself made no difference to her. Her throbbing wound was the only reality.

"Janet is going to lend us her house." A new note had come into Dorothy's voice. "I haven't seen her since last spring. She had on a new hat, and was looking awfully well. You know Herbert has come back."

Margaret started. At last her wandering attention was fixed on her visitor. "Herbert? And she let him?" There was deep disgust in her tone.

Dorothy paused to inhale placidly before she answered. "Well, what else could she do? He tried to make her get a divorce, and she wouldn't."

A flush stained Margaret's delicate features. "I never understood why she didn't. He made no secret of what he wanted. He showed her plainly that he loved the other woman."

Dorothy's only reply was a shrug; but after a moment, in which she smoked with a luxurious air, she commented briefly, "But man's love isn't one of the eternal verities."

"Well, indifference is, and he proved that he was indifferent to Janet. Yet she has let him come back to her. I can't see what she is to get out of it."

Dorothy laughed cynically. "Oh, she enjoys immensely the attitude of forgiveness, and at last he has permitted her to forgive him. There is a spiritual vanity as well as a physical one, you know, and Janet's weakness is spiritual."

"But to live with a man who doesn't love her? To remember every minute of the day and night that it is another woman he loves?"

"And every time that she remembers it she has the luxury of forgiving again." Keenness flickered like a blade in Dorothy's gray eyes. "You are very lovely, Margaret," she said abruptly. "The years seem only to leave you rarer and finer, but you know nothing about life."

A smile quivered and died on Margaret's lips. "I might retort that you know nothing about love."

With an impatient birdlike gesture Dorothy tossed her burned-out cigarette into the fire. "Whose love?" she inquired as she opened the Florentine box, "Herbert's or yours?"

"It's all the same, isn't it?"

By the flame of the match she had struck, Dorothy's expression appeared almost malign. "There, my dear, is where you are wrong," she replied. "When a man and a woman talk of love they speak two different languages. They can never understand each other because women love with their imagination and men with their senses. To you love is a thing in itself, a kind of abstract power like religion; to Herbert it is simply the way he feels."

"But if he loves the other woman, he doesn't love Janet; and yet he wants to return to her."

Leaning back in her chair, Dorothy surveyed her with a look which was at once sympathetic and mocking. Her gaze swept the pure grave features; the shining dusk of the hair; the narrow nose with its slight arch in the middle; the straight red lips with their resolute pressure; the skin so like a fading rose-leaf. Yes, there was beauty in Margaret's face if one were only artist or saint enough to perceive it.

"There is so much more in marriage than either love or indifference," she remarked casually. "There is, for instance, comfort."

"Comfort?" repeated Margaret scornfully. She rose, in her clinging draperies of chiffon, to place a fresh log on the fire. "If he really loves the other woman, Janet ought to give him up," she said.

At this Dorothy turned on her. "Would you, if it were George?" she demanded.

For an instant, while she stood there in front of the fire, it seemed to Margaret that the room whirled before her gaze like the changing colours in a kaleidoscope. Then a gray cloud fell over the brightness, and out of this cloud there emerged only the blaze of the red lilies. A pain struck her in the breast, and she remembered the letter she had hidden there.

"Yes," she answered presently. "I should do it if it were George."

A minute afterward she became conscious that while she spoke, a miracle occurred within her soul.

The tumult of sorrow, of anger, of bitterness, of despair, was drifting farther and farther away. Even the terror, which was worse than any tumult, had vanished. In that instant of renunciation she had reached some spiritual haven. What she had found, she understood presently, was the knowledge that there is no support so strong as the strength that enables one to stand alone.

"I should do it if it were George," she said again, very slowly.

"Well, I think you would be very foolish." Dorothy had risen and was lowering her veil. "For when George ceases to be desirable for sentimental reasons, he will still have his value as a good provider." Her mocking laugh grated on Margaret's ears. "Now, I must run away. I only looked in for an instant. I've a tea on hand, and I must go home and dress."

When she had gone, Margaret stood for a minute, thinking deeply. For a minute only, but in that space of time her decision was made. Crossing to the desk, she telephoned for the flowers. Then she left the library and went into the cedar closet at the end of the hall. When she had found the golf clothes George wanted, she looked over them carefully and hung them in his dressing room. Her next task was to lay out his dinner clothes and to sew the loose button on the waistcoat he had worn last evening. She did these things deliberately, automatically, repeating as if it were a formula, "I must forget nothing"; and when at last she had finished, she stood upright, with a sigh of relief, as if a burden had rolled from her shoulders. Now that she had attended to the details of existence, she would have time for the problem of living.

Slipping out of her gray dress, she changed into a walking suit of blue homespun. Then, searching among the shoes in her closet, she selected a pair of heavy boots she had worn in Maine last summer. As she put on a close[1] little hat and tied a veil of blue chiffon over her face, she reflected, with bitter mirth, that only in novels could one hide one's identity behind a veil.

In the hall downstairs she met Winters, who stared at her discreetly but disapprovingly.

"Shall I order the car, madam?"

She shook her head, reading his thoughts as plainly as if he had uttered them. "No, it has stopped raining. I want to walk."

The door closed sharply on her life of happiness, and she passed out into the rain-soaked world where the mist caught her like damp smoke. So this was what it meant to be deserted, to be alone on the earth! The smell of rain, the smell that George had brought with him into the warm room upstairs, oppressed her as if it were the odour of melancholy.

As the chill pierced her coat, she drew her furs closely about her neck, and walked briskly in the direction of the street car. The address on the letter she carried was burned into her memory not in numbers, but in the thought that it was a villa George owned in an unfashionable suburb named Locust Park. Though she had never been there, she knew that, with the uncertain trolley service she must expect, it would take at least two hours to make the trip and return. Half an hour for Rose Morrison; and even then it would be night, and

[1]Tight-fitting.

Winters at least would be anxious, before she reached home. Well, that was the best she could do.

The street car came, and she got in and found a seat behind a man who had been shooting and carried a string of partridges. All the other seats were filled with the usual afternoon crowd for the suburbs—women holding bundles or baskets and workmen returning from the factories. A sense of isolation like spiritual darkness descended upon her; and she closed her eyes and tried to bring back the serenity she had felt in the thought of relinquishment. But she could remember only a phrase of Dorothy's which floated like a wisp of thistledown through her thoughts, "Spiritual vanity. With some women it is stronger than physical vanity." Was that her weakness, vanity, not of the body, but of the spirit?

Thoughts blew in and out of her mind like dead leaves, now whirling, now drifting, now stirring faintly in her consciousness with a moaning sound. Twenty years. Nothing but that. Love and nothing else in her whole life. . . . The summer of their engagement. A rose garden in bloom. The way he looked. The smell of roses. Or was it only the smell of dead leaves rotting to earth? . . . All the long, long years of their marriage. Little things that one never forgot. The way he laughed. The way he smiled. The look of his hair when it was damp on his forehead. The smell of cigars in his clothes. The three lumps of sugar in his coffee. The sleepy look in his face when he stood ready to put out the lights while she went up the stairs. Oh, the little things that tore at one's heart!

The street car stopped with a jerk, and she got out and walked through the drenched grass in the direction one of the women had pointed out to her.

"The Laurels? That low yellow house at the end of this lane, farther on where the piles of dead leaves are. You can't see the house now, the lane turns, but it's just a stone's throw farther on."

Thanking her, Margaret walked on steadily toward the turn in the lane. Outside of the city the wind blew stronger, and the coloured leaves, bronze, yellow, crimson, lay in a thick carpet over the muddy road. In the west a thin line of gold shone beneath a range of heavy, smoke-coloured clouds. From the trees rain still dripped slowly; and between the road and the line of gold in the west there stretched the desolate autumn landscape.

"Oh, the little things!" her heart cried in despair. "The little things that make happiness!"

Entering the sagging gate of The Laurels, she passed among mounds of sodden leaves which reminded her of graves, and followed the neglected walk between rows of leafless shrubs which must have looked gay in summer. The house was one of many cheap suburban villas (George had bought it, she remembered, at an auction) and she surmised that, until this newest tenant came, it must have stood long unoccupied. The whole place wore, she reflected as she rang the loosened bell, a furtive and insecure appearance.

After the third ring the door was hurriedly opened by a dishevelled maid, who replied that her mistress was not at home.

"Then I shall wait," said Margaret firmly. "Tell your mistress, when she comes in, that Mrs. Fleming is waiting to see her." With a step as resolute as her words, she entered the house and crossed the hall to the living room where a bright coal fire was burning.

The room was empty, but a canary in a gilded cage at the window broke into song as she entered. On a table stood a tray containing the remains of tea; and beside it there was a half-burned cigarette in a bronze Turkish bowl. A book—she saw instantly that it was a volume of the newest plays—lay face downward beneath a pair of eyeglasses, and a rug, which had fallen from the couch, was in a crumpled pile on the floor.

"So she isn't out," Margaret reflected; and turning at a sound, she confronted Rose Morrison.

For an instant it seemed to the older woman that beauty like a lamp blinded her eyes. Then, as the cloud passed, she realized that it was only a blaze, that it was the loveliness of dead leaves when they are burning.

"So you came?" said Rose Morrison, while she gazed at her with the clear and competent eyes of youth. Her voice, though it was low and clear, had no softness; it rang like a bell. Yes, she had youth, she had her flamboyant loveliness; but stronger than youth and loveliness, it seemed to Margaret, surveying her over the reserves and discriminations of the centuries, was the security of one who had never doubted her own judgment. Her power lay where power usually lies in an infallible self-esteem.

"I came to talk it over with you," began Margaret quietly; and though she tried to make her voice insolent, the deep instinct of good manners was greater than her effort. "You tell me that my husband loves you."

The glow, the flame, in Rose Morrison's face made Margaret think again of leaves burning. There was no embarrassment, there was no evasion even, in the girl's look. Candid and unashamed, she appeared to glory in this infatuation, which Margaret regarded as worse than sinful, since it was vulgar.

"Oh, I am so glad that you did," Rose Morrison's sincerity was disarming. "I hated to hurt you. You can never know what it cost me to write that letter; but I felt that I owed it to you to tell you the truth. I believe that we always owe people the truth."

"And did George feel this way also?"

"George?" The flame mounted until it enveloped her. "Oh, he doesn't know. I tried to spare him. He would rather do anything than hurt you, and I thought it would be so much better if we could talk it over and find a solution just between ourselves. I knew if you cared for George, you would feel as I do about sparing him."

About sparing him! As if she had done anything for the last twenty years, Margaret reflected, except think out new and different ways of sparing George!

"I don't know," she answered, as she sat down in obedience to the other's persuasive gesture. "I shall have to think a minute. You see this has been—well, rather—sudden."

"I know, I know." The girl looked as if she did. "May I give you a cup of tea? You must be chilled."

"No, thank you. I am quite comfortable."

"Not even a cigarette? Oh, I wonder what you Victorian women did for a solace when you weren't allowed even a cigarette!"

You Victorian women! In spite of her tragic mood, a smile hovered on Margaret's lips. So that was how this girl classified her. Yet Rose Morrison had fallen in love with a Victorian man.

"Then I may?" said the younger woman with her full-throated laugh. From her bright red hair, which was brushed straight back from her forehead, to her splendid figure, where her hips swung free like a boy's, she was a picture of barbaric beauty. There was a glittering hardness about her, as if she had been washed in some indestructible glaze; but it was the glaze of youth, not of experience. She reminded Margaret of a gilded statue she had seen once in a museum; and the girl's eyes, like the eyes of the statue, were gleaming, remote and impassive—eyes that had never looked on reality. The dress she wore was made of some strange "art cloth," dyed in brilliant hues, fashioned like a kimono, and girdled at the hips with what Margaret mistook for a queer piece of rope. Nothing, not even her crude and confident youth, revealed Rose Morrison to her visitor so completely as this end of rope.

"You are an artist?" she asked, for she was sure of her ground. Only an artist, she decided, could be at once so arrogant with destiny and so ignorant of life.

"How did you know? Has George spoken of me?"

Margaret shook her head. "Oh, I knew without any one's telling me."

"I have a studio in Greenwich Village,[2] but George and I met last summer at Ogunquit.[3] I go there every summer to paint."

"I didn't know." How easily, how possessively, this other woman spoke her husband's name.

"It began at once." To Margaret, with her inherited delicacy and reticence, there was something repellent in this barbaric simplicity of emotion.

"But you must have known that he was married," she observed coldly.

"Yes, I knew, but I could see, of course, that you did not understand him."

"And you think that you do?" If it were not tragic, how amusing it would be to think of her simple George as a problem!

"Oh, I realize that it appears very sudden to you; but in the emotions time counts for so little. Just living with a person for twenty years doesn't enable one to understand him, do you think?"

"I suppose not. But do you really imagine," she asked in what struck her as a singularly impersonal tone for so intimate a question, "that George is complex?"

The flame, which was revealed now as the illumination of some secret happiness, flooded Rose Morrison's features. As she leaned forward, with clasped hands, Margaret noticed that the girl was careless about those feminine details by which George declared so often that he judged a woman. Her hair was carelessly arranged; her finger nails needed attention; and beneath the kimono-like garment, a frayed place showed at the back of her stocking. Even her red morocco slippers were run down at the heels; and it seemed to Margaret that this physical negligence had extended to the girl's habit of thought.

"He is so big, so strong and silent, that it would take an artist to understand him," answered Rose Morrison passionately. Was this really, Margaret wondered, the way George appeared to the romantic vision?

"Yes, he is not a great talker," she admitted. "Perhaps if he talked more, you might find him less difficult." Then before the other could reply, she inquired sharply, "Did George tell you that he was misunderstood?"

"How you misjudge him!" The girl had flown to his defense; and though Margaret had been, as she would have said, "a devoted wife," she felt that all this vehemence was wasted. After all, George, with his easy, prosaic temperament, was only made uncomfortable by vehemence. "He never speaks of you except in the most beautiful way," Rose Morrison was insisting. "He realizes perfectly

[2]District of New York City, renowned as the home of artists and freethinking Bohemians.
[3]Summer resort on the coast of Maine.

what you have been to him, and he would rather suffer in silence all his life than make you unhappy."

"Then what is all this about?" Though she felt that it was unfair, Margaret could not help putting the question.

Actually there were tears in Rose Morrison's eyes. "I could not bear to see his life ruined," she answered. "I hated to write to you; but how else could I make you realize that you were standing in the way of his happiness? If it were just myself, I could have borne it in silence. I would never have hurt you just for my own sake; but, the subterfuge, the dishonesty, is spoiling his life. He does not say so, but, oh, I see it every day because I love him!" As she bent over, the firelight caught her hair, and it blazed out triumphantly like the red lilies in Margaret's library.

"What is it that you want me to do?" asked Margaret in her dispassionate voice.

"I felt that we owed you the truth," responded the girl, "and I hoped that you would take what I wrote you in the right spirit."

"You are sure that my husband loves you?"

"Shall I show you his letters?" The girl smiled as she answered, and her full red lips reminded Margaret suddenly of raw flesh. Was raw flesh, after all, what men wanted?

"No!" The single word was spoken indignantly.

"I thought perhaps they would make you see what it means," explained Rose Morrison simply. "Oh, I wish I could do this without causing you pain!"

"Pain doesn't matter. I can stand pain."

"Well, I'm glad you aren't resentful. After all, why should we be enemies? George's happiness means more than anything else to us both."

"And you are sure you know best what is for George's happiness?"

"I know that subterfuge and lies and dishonesty cannot bring happiness." Rose Morrison flung out her arms with a superb gesture. "Oh, I realize that it is a big thing, a great thing, I am asking of you. But in your place, if I stood in his way, I should so gladly sacrifice myself for his sake I should give him his freedom. I should acknowledge his right to happiness, to self-development."

A bitter laugh broke from Margaret's lips. What a jumble of sounds these catchwords of the new freedom made! What was this self-development which could develop only through the sacrifice of others? How would these immature theories survive the compromises and concessions and adjustments which made marriage permanent?

"I cannot feel that our marriage has interfered with his development," she rejoined presently.

"You may be right," Rose Morrison conceded the point. "But to-day he needs new inspiration, new opportunities. He needs the companionship of a modern mind."

"Yes, he has kept young at my cost," thought the older woman. "I have helped by a thousand little sacrifices, by a thousand little cares and worries, to preserve this unnatural youth which is destroying me. I have taken over the burden of details in order that he might be free for the larger interests of life. If he is young to-day, it is at the cost of my youth."

For the second time that day, as she sat there in silence, with her eyes on the blooming face of Rose Morrison, a wave of peace, the peace of one who has been shipwrecked and then swept far off into some serene haven, enveloped her. Something to hold by, that at least she had found. The law of sacrifice, the ideal of self-surrender, which she had learned in the past. For twenty years she had given freely, abundantly, of her best; and to-day she could still prove to him that she was not beggared. She could still give the supreme gift of her happiness. "How he must love you!" she exclaimed. "How he must love you to have hurt me so much for your sake! Nothing but a great love could make him so cruel."

"He does love me," answered Rose Morrison, and her voice was like the song of a bird.

"He must." Margaret's eyes were burning, but no tears came. Her lips felt cracked with the effort she made to keep them from trembling. "I think if he had done this thing with any other motive than a great love, I should hate him until I died." Then she rose and held out her hand. "I shall not stand in your way," she added.

Joy flashed into the girl's eyes. "You are very noble," she answered. "I am sorry if I have hurt you. I am sorry, too, that I called you old-fashioned."

Margaret laughed. "Oh, I am old-fashioned. I am so old-fashioned that I should have died rather than ruin the happiness of another woman."

The joy faded from Rose Morrison's face. "It was not I," she answered. "It was life. We cannot stand in the way of life."

"Life to-day, God yesterday, what does it matter? It is a generation that has grasped everything except personal responsibility." Oh, if one could only keep the humour! A thought struck her, and she asked abruptly, "When your turn comes, if it ever does, will you give way as I do?"

"That will be understood. We shall not hold each other back."

"But you are young. You will tire first. Then he must give way?" Why, in twenty years George would be sixty-five and Rose Morrison still a young woman!

Calm, resolute, uncompromising, Rose Morrison held open the door. "Whatever happens, he would never wish to hold me back."

Then Margaret passed out, the door closed behind her, and she stood breathing deep draughts of the chill, invigorating air. Well, that was over.

The lawn, with its grave-like mounds of leaves, looked as mournful as a cemetery. Beyond the bare shrubs the road glimmered; the wind still blew in gusts, now rising, now dying away with a plaintive sound; in the west the thread of gold had faded to a pale greenish light. Veiled in the monotonous fall of the leaves, it seemed to Margaret that the desolate evening awaited her.

"How he must love her," she thought, not resentfully, but with tragic resignation. "How he must love her to have sacrificed me as he has done."

This idea, she found as she walked on presently in the direction of the street car, had taken complete possession of her point of view. Through its crystal lucidity she was able to attain some sympathy with her husband's suffering. What agony of mind he must have endured in these past months, these months when they had worked so quietly side by side on his book! What days of gnawing remorse! What nights of devastating anguish! How this newer love must have rent his heart asunder before he could stoop to the baseness of such a betrayal! Tears, which had not come for her own pain, stung her eyelids. She knew that he must have fought it hour by hour, day by day, night by night. Conventional as he was, how violent this emotion must have been to have conquered him so completely. "Terrible as an army with banners," she repeated softly, while a pang of jealousy shot through her heart. Was there in George, she asked now, profounder depths of feeling than she had ever reached; was there some secret garden of romance where she had never entered? Was George larger, wilder, more adventurous in imagination, than she had dreamed? Had the perfect lover lain hidden in his nature, awaiting only the call of youth?

The street car returned almost empty; and she found restfulness in the monotonous jolting, as if it were swinging her into some world beyond space and time, where mental pain yielded to the sense of physical discomfort. After the agony of mind, the aching of body was strangely soothing.

Here and there, the lights of a house flashed among the trees, and she thought, with an impersonal interest, of the neglected villa, surrounded by mounds of rotting leaves, where that girl waited alone for happiness. Other standards. This was how the newer generation appeared to Margaret—other standards, other morals. Facing life stripped bare of every safeguard, of every restraining tradition, with only the courage of ignorance, of defiant inexperience, to protect one. That girl was not wilfully cruel. She was simply greedy for emotion; she was gasping at the pretense of happiness like all the rest of her undisciplined generation. She was caught by life because she had never learned to give up, to do without, to stand alone.

Her corner had come, and she stepped with a sensation of relief on the wet pavement. The rain was dripping steadily in a monotonous drizzle. While she walked the few blocks to her door, she forced herself by an effort of will to go on, step by step, not to drop down in the street and lose consciousness.

The tinkle of the bell and the sight of Winters's face restored her to her senses.

"Shall I bring you tea, madam?"

"No, it is too late."

Going upstairs to her bedroom, she took off her wet clothes and slipped into her prettiest tea gown, a trailing thing of blue satin and chiffon. While she ran the comb through her damp hair and touched her pale lips with colour, she reflected that even renunciation was easier when one looked desirable. "But it is like painting the cheeks of the dead," she thought, as she turned away from the mirror and walked with a dragging step to the library. Never, she realized suddenly, had she loved George so much as in this hour when she had discovered him only to lose him.

As she entered, George hurried to meet her with an anxious air. "I didn't hear you come in, Margaret. I have been very uneasy. Has anything happened?"

By artificial light he looked younger even than he had seemed in the afternoon; and this boyishness of aspect struck her as strangely pathetic. It was all a part, she told herself, of that fulfilment which had come too late, of that perilous second blooming, not of youth, but of Indian Summer. The longing to spare him, to save him from the suffering she had endured, pervaded her heart.

"Yes, something has happened," she answered gently. "I have been to see Rose Morrison."

As she spoke the name, she turned away from him, and walking with unsteady steps across the room, stood looking down into the fire. The knowledge of all that she must see when she turned, of the humiliation, the anguish, the remorse in his eyes, oppressed her heart with a passion of shame and pity. How could she turn and look on his wounded soul which she had stripped bare?

"Rose Morrison?" he repeated in an expressionless voice. "What do you know of Rose Morrison?"

At his question she turned quickly, and faced not anguish, not humiliation, but emptiness. There was nothing in his look except the blankness of complete surprise. For an instant the shock made her dizzy; and in the midst of the dizziness there flashed through her mind the memory of an evening in her childhood, when she had run bravely into a dark room where they told her an ogre was hiding, and had found that it was empty.

"She wrote to me." Her legs gave way as she replied, and, sinking into the nearest chair, she sat gazing up at him with an immobile face.

A frown gathered his eyebrows, and a purplish flush (he flushed so easily of late) mounted slowly to the smooth line of his hair. She watched the quiver that ran through his under lip (strange that she had not noticed how it had thickened) while his teeth pressed it sharply. Everything about him was acutely vivid to her, as if she were looking at him closely for the first time. She saw the furrow between his eyebrows, the bloodshot stain on one eyeball, the folds of flesh beneath his jutting chin, the crease in his black tie, the place where his shirt gave a little because it had grown too tight—all these insignificant details would exist indelibly in her brain.

"She wrote to you?" His voice sounded strained and husky, and he coughed abruptly as if he were trying to hide his embarrassment. "What the devil! But you don't know her."

"I saw her this afternoon. She told me everything."

"Everything?" Never had she imagined that he could appear so helpless, so lacking in the support of any conventional theory. A hysterical laugh broke from her, a laugh as utterly beyond her control as a spasm, and at the sound he flushed as if she had struck him. While she sat there she realized that she had no part or place in the scene before her. Never could she speak the words that she longed to utter. Never could she make him understand the real self behind the marionette at which he was looking. She longed with all her heart to say: "There were possibilities in me that you never suspected. I also am capable of a great love. In my heart I also am a creature of romance, of adventure. If you had only known it, you might have found in marriage all that you have sought elsewhere . . ." This was what she longed to cry out, but instead she said merely,

"She told me of your love. She asked me to give you up."

"She asked you to give me up?" His mouth fell open as he finished, and while he stared at her he forgot to shut it. It occurred to her that he had lost the power of inventing a phrase, that he could only echo the ones she had spoken. How like a foolish boy he looked as he stood there, in front of the sinking fire, trying to hide behind that hollow echo!

"She said that I stood in your way." The phrase sounded so grotesque as she uttered it that she found herself laughing again. She had not wished to speak these ugly things. Her heart was filled with noble words, with beautiful sentiments, but she could not make her lips pronounce them in spite of all the efforts she made. And she recalled suddenly the princess in the fairy tale who, when she opened her mouth, found that toads and lizards escaped from it instead of pearls and rubies.

At first he did not reply, and it seemed to her that only mechanical force could jerk his jaw back into place and close the eyelids over his vacant blue eyes. When at last he made a sound, it was only the empty echo again, "stood in my way!"

"She is desperately in earnest." Justice wrung this admission from her. "She feels that this subterfuge is unfair to us all. Your happiness, she thinks, is what we should consider first, and she is convinced that I should be sacrificed to your future. She was perfectly frank. She suppressed nothing."

For the first time George Fleming uttered an original sound. "O Lord!" he exclaimed devoutly.

"I told her that I did not wish to stand in your way," resumed Margaret, as if the exclamation had not interrupted the flow of her thoughts. "I told her I would give you up."

Suddenly, without warning, he exploded. "What, in the name of heaven, has it got to do with you?" he demanded.

"To do with me?" It was her turn to echo. "But isn't that girl—" she corrected herself painfully—"isn't she living in your house at this minute?"

He cast about helplessly for an argument. When at last he discovered one, he advanced it with a sheepish air, as if he recognized its weakness. "Well, nobody else would take it, would they?"

"She says that you love her."

He shifted his ground nervously. "I can't help what she says, can I?"

"She offered to show me your letters."

"Compliments, nothing more."

"But you must love her, or you couldn't—you wouldn't——" A burning flush scorched Margaret's body.

"I never said that I . . ." Even with her he had always treated the word love as if it were a dangerous explosive, and he avoided touching it now, "that I cared for her in that way."

"Then you do in another way?"

He glanced about like a trapped animal. "I am not a fool, am I? Why, I am old enough to be her father! Besides, I am not the only one anyway. She was living with a man when I met her, and he wasn't the first. She isn't bad, you know. It's a kind of philosophy with her. She calls it self . . ."

"I know." Margaret cut the phrase short. "I have heard what she calls it." So it was all wasted! Nothing that she could do could lift the situation above the level of the commonplace, the merely vulgar. She was defrauded not only of happiness, but even of the opportunity to be generous. Her sacrifice was as futile as that girl's passion. "But she is in love with you now," she said.

"I suppose she is." His tone had grown stubborn. "But how long would it last? In six months she would be leaving me for somebody else. Of course, I won't see her again," he added, with the manner of one who is conceding a reasonable point. Then, after a pause in which she made no response, his stubbornness changed into resentment. "Anybody would think that you are angry because I am not in love with her!" he exclaimed. "Anybody would think—but I don't understand women!"

"Then you will not—you do not mean to leave me?" she asked; and her manner was as impersonal, she was aware, as if Winters had just given her notice.

"Leave you?" He glanced appreciatively round the room. "Where on earth could I go?"

For an instant Margaret looked at him in silence. Then she insisted coldly, "To her, perhaps. She thinks that you are in love with her."

"Well, I suppose I've been a fool," he confessed, after a struggle, "but you are making too much of it."

Yes, she was making too much of it; she realized this more poignantly than he would ever be able to do. She felt like an actress who has endowed a comic part with the gesture of high tragedy. It was not, she saw clearly now, that she had misunderstood George, but that she had overplayed life.

"We met last summer at Ogunquit." She became aware presently that he was still making excuses and explanations about nothing. "You couldn't go about much, you know, and we went swimming and played golf together. I liked her, and I could see that she liked me. When we came away I thought we'd break it off, but somehow we didn't. I saw her several times in New York. Then she came here unexpectedly, and I offered her that old villa nobody would rent. You don't understand such things, Margaret. It hadn't any more to do with you than—than——" He hesitated, fished in the stagnant waters of his mind, and flung out abruptly, "than golf has. It was just a sort of—well, sort of—recreation."

Recreation! The memory of Rose Morrison's extravagant passion smote her sharply. How glorified the incident had appeared in the girl's imagination, how cheap and tawdry it was in reality. A continual compromise with the second best, an inevitable surrender to the average, was this the history of all romantic emotion? For an instant, such is the perversity of fate, it seemed to the wife that she and this strange girl were united by some secret bond which George could not share—by the bond of woman's immemorial disillusionment.

"I wouldn't have had you hurt for worlds, Margaret," said George, bending over her. The old gentle voice, the old possessive and complacent look in his sleepy blue eyes, recalled her wandering senses. "If I could only make you see that there wasn't anything in it."

She gazed up at him wearily. The excitement of discovery, the exaltation, the anguish, had ebbed away, leaving only gray emptiness. She had lost more than love, more than happiness, for she had lost her belief in life.

"If there had been anything in it, I might be able to understand," she replied.

He surveyed her with gloomy severity. "Hang it all! You act as if you wanted me to be in love with her." Then his face cleared as if by magic. "You're tired out, Margaret and you're nervous. There's Winters now. You must try to eat a good dinner."

Anxious, caressing, impatient to have the discussion end and dinner begin, he stooped and lifted her in his arms. For an instant she lay there without moving, and in that instant her gaze passed from his face to the red lilies and the uncurtained window beyond.

Outside the leaves were falling.

1923

Gertrude Stein 1874–1946

To the world at large, Gertrude Stein and the life she led have been even more fascinating than the books she wrote or the literary theories she devised. She lived most of her life in France, where she was the confidante of celebrated artists and writers. She was a patron of Pablo Picasso and the subject of one of his most famous paintings. Writers such as Thornton Wilder, Sherwood Anderson, F. Scott Fitzgerald, and Ernest Hemingway came to her apartment in Paris to listen to her ideas on modern literature. Her association with avant-grade art and her own eccentric literary works made her a familiar symbol of modernism. Even those who have never read her books know her famous line, "A rose is a rose is a rose is a rose."

Stein was born in Allegheny, Pennsylvania, and for much of her childhood she lived in Oakland, California. Her family was well-to-do, and she enjoyed a privileged life, indulged by servants, governesses, and tutors. At eighteen she entered Radcliffe College, where she developed her interest in writing. Later, critics and biographers would find it significant that her professor of composition praised her "unusual power of abstract thought" but complained "Your vehemence runs away with your syntax" and gave her a C.

She also attended classes taught by the famous psychologist William James, a Harvard professor and brother of the novelist Henry James. In 1897, with James's encouragement, she entered Johns Hopkins University to study medicine and prepare for research in the psychology of perception and understanding. But she found medical school tedious and constricting. She was bored by her teachers and her fellow students, and they, in turn, had little patience with her imperious self-assurance. In 1901, in her last term, she made little effort to study, failed most of her courses, and left the university without an M.D. degree.

Stein then decided to move to Europe, where she could live comfortably on the inheritance she had received after the death of her father. In 1904 she settled in Paris, and with her brother Leo, a student of modern art, began collecting the paintings of Cézanne, Renoir, Matisse, and Picasso. Soon the Stein apartment became a gathering place, a salon, for avant-garde artists and writers from Europe and America. One of the regular visitors was Picasso, who in 1905 began to paint his famous portrait of her.

In the same year she began writing her first book, Three Lives *(1909), stories of three women, one of them "The Gentle Lena," who submit to their fate in a world they cannot control.* Three Lives *has been called a masterpiece of realism, and it remains one of her most successful and least obscure works. Her next important book,* Tender Buttons *(1914), a collection of observations on objects and forms, departed radically from convention, stressing "the value of the individual word" so that the reader might see actual objects rather than the mere printed text that described them. In 1922 she published* Geography and Plays, *a collection of poems, plays, and descriptions of people and places that is rich with puns, rhythmic phrases, and the word repetitions that had become characteristic of her style.* The Making of Americans, *her long and sprawling novel of an American family, was, she believed, her literary masterwork. It appeared in 1925, and that same year she was invited to lecture on her literary theories at Cambridge and Oxford Universities in England.*

In her writing Stein often departed from conventional word order and coherence. She submerged her meaning in cryptic language and puzzling abstractions in an attempt to go beneath the surface of language to essential reality. She believed that repetition of words and phrases could erase their superficial meaning and reveal their true sense. William Carlos Williams said she was "smashing every connotation that words have ever had, in order to get them back clean." Her psychological studies had taught her that experience in life is jumbled and disorganized, and she insisted that literature should recreate that jumbled experience. Therefore, traditional fiction, with clearly understandable characters and with events organized in sequential time, was false because it presented an artificial world that had never existed.

Stein's theories of literary language, grammar, vocabulary, and prose form were published in 1931 in How to Write. *One of her most obscure and difficult works, it had a narrow audience. But she soon began work on a book that would bring her, for the first time, to the attention of a large reading public. It was* The Autobiography of Alice B. Toklas *(1933). Supposedly written by her longtime companion and lover, Alice B. Toklas, it was in fact Gertrude Stein's own memoirs. Her descriptions of life in Paris and the famous people she had known made the book widely popular in Europe and in the United States. The following year her opera* Four Saints in Three Acts, *set to music by the American composer Virgil Thomson, was produced on Broadway. It battered operatic conventions with an exuberant vigor that left audiences noisily cheering or stunned into puzzled silence.*

Capitalizing on her new fame and notoriety, Stein returned to America in 1934 for a lecture tour. She became a national celebrity, pictured in newspapers and quoted on the radio. American editors and book publishers who had once rejected her writing as too obscure, too exotic for their readers, now urged her to send them her essay and book manuscripts. She was at the peak of her fame, and in the remaining years of the 1930s and the 1940s more than twenty volumes of her work was published. In all she wrote more than fifty books and was renowned both as a famous writer and as "The Matron Saint of Paris Art," "The Sibyl of Montparnasse." When she died in 1946, it seemed as though a cultural monument in Paris had fallen.

FURTHER READING: J. Mellow, *Charmed Circle: Gertrude Stein and Company,* 1974; J. Hobhouse, *Everybody Who Was Anybody: A Biography of Gertrude Stein,* 1975; R. Dubnick, *The Structure of Obscurity,* 1984; J. Walker, *The Making of a Modernist,* 1984; *Critical Essays on Gertrude Stein,* ed. M. Hoffman, 1986; *Gertrude Stein,* ed. H. Bloom, 1986; *Gertrude Stein and the Making of Literature,* ed. S. Neuman and I. Nadel, 1988; *A Gertrude Stein Companion,* ed. B. Kellner, 1988; L. Ruddick, *Reading Gertrude Stein,* 1990; J. Bowers, *They Watch Me as They Watch This,* 1991; E. Fifer, *Rescued Readings: A Reconstruction of Gertrude Stein's Difficult Texts,* 1992; E. Berry, *Curved Thought and Textual Wandering: Gertrude Stein's Postmodernism,* 1992; L. Wagner-Martin, *"Favored Strangers": Gertrude Stein and Her Family,* 1995; M. Dickie, *Stein, Bishop, & Rich: Lyrics of Love, War, & Place,* 1997; M. Weiss, *Gertrude Stein and Richard Wright: The Poetics and Politics of Modernism,* 1998; *The Critical Response to Gertrude Stein,* ed. K. Curnutt, 2000; J. Gill, *Detecting Gertrude Stein, and Other Suspects on the Shadow Side of Modernism,* 2003; A. Blizzard, *Portraits of the 20th Century Self: An Interartistic Study of Gertrude Stein's Literary Portraits and Early Modernist Portraits by Paul Cézanne, Henri Matisse, and Pablo Picasso,* 2004.

TEXTS: "The Gentle Lena," *Three Lives,* 1909; "Susie Asado," *Geography and Plays,* 1922; "Picasso," *Portraits and Prayers,* 1934; "A Movie," *Operas and Plays,* 1987.

from *THREE LIVES*

THE GENTLE LENA

Lena was patient, gentle, sweet and german. She had been a servant for four years and had liked it very well.

Lena had been brought from Germany to Bridgepoint by a cousin and had been in the same place there for four years.

This place Lena had found very good. There was a pleasant, unexacting mistress and her children, and they all liked Lena very well.

There was a cook there who scolded Lena a great deal but Lena's german patience held no suffering and the good incessant woman really only scolded so for Lena's good.

Lena's german voice when she knocked and called the family in the morning was as awakening, as soothing, and as appealing, as a delicate soft breeze in midday, summer. She stood in the hallway every morning a long time in her unexpectant and unsuffering german patience calling to the young ones to get up. She would call and wait a long time and then call again, always even, gentle, patient, while the young ones fell back often into that precious, tense, last bit of sleeping that gives a strength of joyous vigor in the young, over them that have come to the readiness of middle age, in their awakening.

Lena had good hard work all morning, and on the pleasant, sunny afternoons she was sent out into the park to sit and watch the little two year old girl baby of the family.

The other girls, all them that make the pleasant, lazy crowd, that watch the children in the sunny afternoons out in the park, all liked the simple, gentle, german Lena very well. They all, too, liked very well to tease her, for it was so easy to make her mixed and troubled, and all helpless, for she could never learn to know just what the other quicker girls meant by the queer things they said.

The two or three of these girls, the ones that Lena always sat with, always worked together to confuse her. Still it was pleasant, all this life for Lena.

The little girl fell down sometimes and cried, and then Lena had to soothe her. When the little girl would drop her hat, Lena had to pick it up and hold it. When the little girl was bad and threw away her playthings, Lena told her she could not have them and took them from her to hold until the little girl should need them.

It was all a peaceful life for Lena, almost as peaceful as a pleasant leisure. The other girls, of course, did tease her, but then that only made a gentle stir within her.

Lena was a brown and pleasant creature, brown as blonde races often have them brown, brown, not with the yellow or the red or the chocolate brown of sun burned countries, but brown with the clear color laid flat on the light toned skin beneath, the plain, spare brown that makes it right to have been made with hazel eyes, and not too abundant straight, brown hair, hair that only later deepens itself into brown from the straw yellow of a german childhood.

Lena had the flat chest, straight back and forward falling shoulders of the patient and enduring working woman, though her body was now still in its milder girlhood and work had not yet made these lines too clear.

The rarer feeling that there was with Lena, showed in all the even quiet of her body movements, but in all it was the strongest in the patient, old-world ignorance, and earth made pureness of her brown, flat, soft featured face. Lena had eyebrows that were a wondrous thickness. They were black, and spread, and very cool, with their dark color and their beauty, and beneath them were her hazel eyes, simple and human, with the earth patience of the working, gentle, german woman.

Yes it was all a peaceful life for Lena. The other girls, of course, did tease her, but then that only made a gentle stir within her.

"What you got on your finger Lena," Mary, one of the girls she always sat with, one day asked her. Mary was good natured, quick, intelligent and Irish.

Lena had just picked up the fancy paper made accordion that the little girl had dropped beside her, and was making it squeak sadly as she pulled it with her brown, strong, awkward finger.

"Why, what is it, Mary, paint?" said Lena, putting her finger to her mouth to taste the dirt spot.

"That's awful poison Lena, don't you know?" said Mary, "that green paint that you just tasted."

Lena had sucked a good deal of the green paint from her finger. She stopped and looked hard at the finger. She did not know just how much Mary meant by what she said.

"Ain't it poison, Nellie, that green paint, that Lena sucked just now," said Mary. "Sure it is Lena, it's real poison, I ain't foolin' this time anyhow."

Lena was a little troubled. She looked hard at her finger where the paint was, and she wondered if she had really sucked it.

It was still a little wet on the edges and she rubbed it off a long time on the inside of her dress, and in between she wondered and looked at the finger and thought, was it really poison that she had just tasted.

"Ain't it too bad, Nellie, Lena should have sucked that," Mary said.

Nellie smiled and did not answer. Nellie was dark and thin, and looked Italian. She had a big mass of black hair that she wore high up on her head, and that made her face look very fine.

Nellie always smiled and did not say much, and then she would look at Lena to perplex her.

And so they all three sat with their little charges in the pleasant sunshine a long time. And Lena would often look at her finger and wonder if it was really poison that she had just tasted and then she would rub her finger on her dress a little harder.

Mary laughed at her and teased her and Nellie smiled a little and looked queerly at her.

Then it came time, for it was growing cooler, for them to drag together the little ones, who had begun to wander, and to take each one back to its own mother. And Lena never knew for certain whether it was really poison, that green stuff that she had tasted.

During these four years of service, Lena always spent her Sundays out at the house of her aunt, who had brought her four years before to Bridgepoint.

This aunt, who had brought Lena, four years before, to Bridgepoint, was a hard, ambitious, well meaning, german woman. Her husband was a grocer in the town, and they were very well to do. Mrs. Haydon, Lena's aunt, had two daughters who were just beginning as young ladies, and she had a little boy who was not honest and who was very hard to manage.

Mrs. Haydon was a short, stout, hard built, german woman. She always hit the ground very firmly and compactly as she walked. Mrs. Haydon was all a compact and well hardened mass, even to her face, reddish and darkened from its early blonde, with its hearty, shiny cheeks, and doubled chin well covered over with the uproll from her short, square neck.

The two daughters, who were fourteen and fifteen, looked like unkneaded, unformed mounds of flesh beside her.

The elder girl, Mathilda, was blonde, and slow, and simple, and quite fat. The younger, Bertha, who was almost as tall as her sister, was dark, and quicker, and she was heavy, too, but not really fat.

These two girls the mother had brought up very firmly. They were well taught for their position. They were always both well dressed, in the same kinds of hats and dresses, as is becoming in two german sisters. The mother liked to have them dressed in red. Their best clothes were red dresses, made of good heavy cloth, and strongly trimmed with braid of a glistening black. They had stiff, red felt hats, trimmed with black velvet ribbon, and a bird. The mother dressed matronly, in a bonnet and in black, always sat between her two big daughters, firm, directing, and repressed.

The only weak spot in this good woman's conduct was the way she spoiled her boy, who was not honest and who was very hard to manage.

The father of this family was a decent, quiet, heavy, and uninterfering german man. He tried to cure the boy of his bad ways, and make him honest, but the mother could not make herself let the father manage, and so the boy was brought up very badly.

Mrs. Haydon's girls were now only just beginning as young ladies, and so to get her niece, Lena, married, was just then the most important thing that Mrs. Haydon had to do.

Mrs. Haydon had four years before gone to Germany to see her parents, and had taken the girls with her. This visit had been for Mrs. Haydon most successful, though her children had not liked it very well.

Mrs. Haydon was a good and generous woman, and she patronized her parents grandly, and all the cousins who came from all about to see her. Mrs. Haydon's people were of the middling class of farmers. They were not peasants, and they lived in a town of some pretension, but it all seemed very poor and smelly to Mrs. Haydon's american born daughters.

Mrs. Haydon liked it all. It was familiar, and then here she was so wealthy and important. She listened and decided, and advised all of her relations how to do things better. She arranged their present and their future for them, and showed them how in the past they had been wrong in all their methods.

Mrs. Haydon's only trouble was with her two daughters, whom she could not make behave well to her parents. The two girls were very nasty to all their numerous relations. Their mother could hardly make them kiss their grandparents, and every day the girls would get a scolding. But then Mrs. Haydon was so very busy that she did not have time to really manage her stubborn daughters.

These hard working, earth-rough german cousins were to these american born children, ugly and dirty and as far below them as were Italian or negro workmen, and they could not see how their mother could ever bear to touch them, and then all the women dressed so funny, and were worked all rough and different.

The two girls stuck up their noses at them all, and always talked in English to each other about how they hated all these people and how they wished their mother would not do so. The girls could talk some German, but they never chose to use it.

It was her eldest brother's family that most interested Mrs. Haydon. Here there were eight children, and out of the eight, five of them were girls.

Mrs. Haydon thought it would be a fine thing to take one of these girls back with her to Bridgepoint and get her well started. Everybody liked that she should do so, and they were all willing that it should be Lena.

Lena was the second girl in her large family. She was at this time just seventeen years old. Lena was not an important daughter in the family. She was always sort of dreamy and not there. She worked hard and went very regularly at it, but even good work never seemed to bring her near.

Lena's age just suited Mrs. Haydon's purpose. Lena could first go out to service, and learn how to do things, and then, when she was a little older, Mrs. Haydon could get her a good husband. And then Lena was so still and docile, she would never want to do things her own way. And then, too, Mrs. Haydon, with all her hardness had wisdom, and she could feel the rarer strain there was in Lena.

Lena was willing to go with Mrs. Haydon. Lena did not like her german life very well. It was not the hard work but the roughness that disturbed her. The people were not gentle, and the men when they were glad were very boisterous, and would lay hold of her and roughly tease her. They were good people enough around her, but it was all harsh and dreary for her.

Lena did not really know that she did not like it. She did not know that she was always dreamy and not there. She did not think whether it would be different for her away off there in Bridgepoint. Mrs. Haydon took her and got her different kinds of dresses, and then took her with them to the steamer. Lena did not really know what it was that had happened to her.

Mrs. Haydon, and her daughters, and Lena traveled second class on the steamer. Mrs. Haydon's daughters hated that their mother should take Lena. They hated to have a cousin, who was to them, little better than a nigger, and then everybody on the steamer there would see her. Mrs. Haydon's daughters said things like this to their mother, but she never stopped to hear them, and the girls did not dare to make their meaning very clear. And so they could only go on hating Lena hard, together. They could not stop her from going back with them to Bridgepoint.

Lena was very sick on the voyage. She thought, surely before it was over that she would die. She was so sick she could not even wish that she had not started. She could not eat, she could not moan, she was just blank and scared, and sure that every minute she would die. She could not hold herself in, nor help herself in her trouble. She just staid where she had been put, pale, and scared, and weak, and sick, and sure that she was going to die.

Mathilda and Bertha Haydon had no trouble from having Lena for a cousin on the voyage, until the last day that they were on the ship, and by that time they had made their friends and could explain.

Mrs. Haydon went down every day to Lena, gave her things to make her better, held her head when it was needful, and generally was good and did her duty by her.

Poor Lena had no power to be strong in such trouble. She did not know how to yield to her sickness nor endure. She lost all her little sense of being in her suffering. She was so scared, and then at her best, Lena, who was patient, sweet, and quiet, had not self-control, nor any active courage.

Poor Lena was so scared and weak, and every minute she was sure that she would die.

After Lena was on land again a little while, she forgot all her bad suffering. Mrs. Haydon got her the good place, with the pleasant unexacting mistress, and her children, and Lena began to learn some English and soon was very happy and content.

All her Sundays out Lena spent at Mrs. Haydon's house. Lena would have liked much better to spend her Sundays with the girls she always sat with, and who often asked her, and who teased her and made a gentle stir within her, but it never came to Lena's unexpectant and unsuffering german nature to do something different from what was expected of her, just because she would like it that way better. Mrs. Haydon had said that Lena was to come to her house every other Sunday, and so Lena always went there.

Mrs. Haydon was the only one of her family who took any interest in Lena. Mr. Haydon did not think much of her. She was his wife's cousin and he was good to her, but she was for him stupid, and a little simple, and very dull, and sure some day to need help and to be in trouble. All young poor relations, who were brought from Germany to Bridgepoint were sure, before long, to need help and to be in trouble.

The little Haydon boy was always very nasty to her. He was a hard child for any one to manage, and his mother spoiled him very badly. Mrs. Haydon's daughters as they grew older did not learn to like Lena any better. Lena never knew that she did not like them either. She did not know that she was only happy with the other quicker girls, she always sat with in the park, and who laughed at her and always teased her.

Mathilda Haydon, the simple, fat, blonde, older daughter felt very badly that she had to say that this was her cousin Lena, this Lena who was little better for her than a nigger. Mathilda was an overgrown, slow, flabby, blonde, stupid, fat girl, just beginning as a woman; thick in her speech and dull and simple in her mind, and very jealous of all her family and of other girls, and proud that she could have good dresses and new hats and learn music, and hating very badly to have a cousin who was a common servant. And then Mathilda remembered very strongly that dirty nasty place that Lena came from and that Mathilda had so turned up her nose at, and where she had been made so angry because her mother scolded her and liked all those rough, cow-smelly people.

Then, too, Mathilda would get very mad when her mother had Lena at their parties, and when she talked about how good Lena was, to certain german mothers in whose sons, perhaps, Mrs. Haydon might find Lena a good husband. All this would make the dull, blonde, fat Mathilda very angry. Sometimes she would get so angry that she would, in her thick, slow way, and with jealous anger blazing in her light blue eyes, tell her mother that she did not see how she could like that nasty Lena; and then her mother would scold Mathilda, and tell her that she knew her cousin Lena was poor and Mathilda must be good to poor people.

Mathilda Haydon did not like relations to be poor. She told all her girl friends what she thought of Lena, and so the girls would never talk to Lena at Mrs. Haydon's parties. But Lena in her unsuffering and unexpectant patience never really knew that she was slighted. When Mathilda was with her girls in the street or in the park and would see Lena, she always turned up her nose and barely nodded to her, and then she would tell her friends how funny her mother was to take care of people like that Lena, and how, back in Germany, all Lena's people lived just like pigs.

The younger daughter, the dark, large, but not fat, Bertha Haydon, who was very quick in her mind, and in her ways, and who was the favorite with her father, did not like Lena, either. She did not like her because for her Lena was a fool and so stupid, and she would let those Irish and Italian girls laugh at her and tease her, and everybody always made fun of Lena, and Lena never got mad, or even had sense enough to know that they were all making an awful fool of her.

Bertha Haydon hated people to be fools. Her father, too, thought Lena was a fool, and so neither the father nor the daughter ever paid any attention to Lena, although she came to their house every other Sunday.

Lena did not know how all the Haydons felt. She came to her aunt's house all her Sunday afternoons that she had out, because Mrs. Haydon had told her she must do so. In the same way Lena always saved all of her wages. She never thought of any way to spend it. The german cook, the good woman who always scolded Lena, helped her to put it in the bank each month, as soon as she got it. Sometimes before it got into the bank to be taken care of, somebody would ask Lena for it. The little Haydon boy sometimes asked and would get it, and sometimes some of the girls, the ones Lena always sat with, needed some more money; but the german cook, who always scolded Lena, saw to it that this did not happen very often. When it did happen she would scold Lena very sharply, and for the next few months she would not let Lena touch her wages, but put it in the bank for her on the same day that Lena got it.

So Lena always saved her wages, for she never thought to spend them, and she always went to her aunt's house for her Sundays because she did not know that she could do anything different.

Mrs. Haydon felt more and more every year that she had done right to bring Lena back with her, for it was all coming out just as she had expected. Lena was good and never wanted her own way, she was learning English, and saving all her wages, and soon Mrs. Haydon would get her a good husband.

All these four years Mrs. Haydon was busy looking around among all the german people that she knew for the right man to be Lena's husband, and now at last she was quite decided.

The man Mrs. Haydon wanted for Lena was a young german-american tailor, who worked with his father. He was good and all the family were very saving, and Mrs. Haydon was sure that this would be just right for Lena, and then too, this young tailor always did whatever his father and his mother wanted.

This old german tailor and his wife, the father and the mother of Herman Kreder, who was to marry Lena Mainz, were very thrifty, careful people. Herman was the only child they had left with them, and he always did everything they wanted. Herman was now twenty-eight years old, but he had never stopped being scolded and directed by his father and his mother. And now they wanted to see him married.

Herman Kreder did not care much to get married. He was a gentle soul and a little fearful. He had a sullen temper, too. He was obedient to his father and his mother. He always did his work well. He often went out on Saturday nights and on Sundays, with other men. He liked it with them but he never became really joyous. He liked to be with men and he hated to have women with them. He was obedient to his mother, but he did not care much to get married.

Mrs. Haydon and the elder Kreders had often talked the marriage over. They all three liked it very well. Lena would do anything that Mrs. Haydon wanted, and Herman was always obedient in everything to his father and his mother. Both Lena and Herman were saving and good workers and neither of them ever wanted their own way.

The elder Kreders, everybody knew, had saved up all their money, and they were hard, good german people, and Mrs. Haydon was sure that with these people Lena would never be in any trouble. Mr. Haydon would not say anything about it. He knew old Kreder had a lot of money and owned some good houses, and he did not care what his wife did with that simple, stupid Lena, so long as she would be sure never to need help or to be in trouble.

Lena did not care much to get married. She liked her life very well where she was working. She did not think much about Herman Kreder. She thought he was a good man and she always found him very quiet. Neither of them ever spoke much to the other. Lena did not care much just then about getting married.

Mrs. Haydon spoke to Lena about it very often. Lena never answered anything at all. Mrs. Haydon thought, perhaps Lena did not like Herman Kreder. Mrs. Haydon could not believe that any girl not even Lena, really had no feeling about getting married.

Mrs. Haydon spoke to Lena very often about Herman. Mrs. Haydon sometimes got very angry with Lena. She was afraid that Lena, for once, was going to be stubborn, now when it was all fixed right for her to be married.

"Why you stand there so stupid, why don't you answer, Lena," said Mrs. Haydon one Sunday, at the end of a long talking that she was giving Lena about Herman Kreder, and about Lena's getting married to him.

"Yes ma'am," said Lena, and then Mrs. Haydon was furious with this stupid Lena. "Why don't you answer with some sense, Lena, when I ask you if you don't like Herman Kreder. You stand there so stupid and don't answer just like you ain't heard a word what I been saying to you. I never see anybody like you, Lena. If you going to burst out at all, why don't you burst out sudden instead of standing there so silly and don't answer. And here I am so good to you, and find you a good husband so you can have a place to live in all your own. Answer me, Lena, don't you like Herman Kreder? He is a fine young fellow, almost too good for you, Lena, when you stand there so stupid and don't make no answer. There ain't many poor girls that get the chance you got now to get married."

"Why, I do anything you say, Aunt Mathilda. Yes, I like him. He don't say much to me, but I guess he is a good man, and I do anything you say for me to do."

"Well then Lena, why you stand there so silly all the time and not answer when I asked you."

"I didn't hear you say you wanted I should say anything to you. I didn't know you wanted me to say nothing. I do whatever you tell me it's right for me to do. I marry Herman Kreder, if you want me."

And so for Lena Mainz the match was made.

Old Mrs. Kreder did not discuss the matter with her Herman. She never thought that she needed to talk such things over with him. She just told him about getting married to Lena Mainz who was a good worker and very saving and never wanted her own way, and Herman made his usual little grunt in answer to her.

Mrs. Kreder and Mrs. Haydon fixed the day and made all the arrangements for the wedding and invited everybody who ought to be there to see them married.

In three months Lena Mainz and Herman Kreder were to be married.

Mrs. Haydon attended to Lena's getting all the things that she needed. Lena had to help a good deal with the sewing. Lena did not sew very well. Mrs. Haydon scolded because Lena did not do it better, but then she was very good to

Lena, and she hired a girl to come and help her. Lena still stayed on with her pleasant mistress, but she spent all her evenings and her Sundays with her aunt and all the sewing.

Mrs. Haydon got Lena some nice dresses. Lena liked that very well. Lena liked having new hats even better, and Mrs. Haydon had some made for her by a real milliner who made them very pretty.

Lena was nervous these days, but she did not think much about getting married. She did not know really what it was, that, which was always coming nearer.

Lena liked the place where she was with the pleasant mistress and the good cook, who always scolded, and she liked the girls she always sat with. She did not ask if she would like being married any better. She always did whatever her aunt said and expected, but she was always nervous when she saw the Kreders with their Herman. She was excited and she liked her new hats, and everybody teased her and every day her marrying was coming nearer, and yet she did not really know what it was, this that was about to happen to her.

Herman Kreder knew more what it meant to be married and he did not like it very well. He did not like to see girls and he did not want to have to have one always near him. Herman always did everything that his father and his mother wanted and now they wanted that he should be married.

Herman had a sullen temper; he was gentle and he never said much. He liked to go out with other men, but he never wanted that there should be any women with them. The men all teased him about getting married. Herman did not mind the teasing but he did not like very well the getting married and having a girl always with him.

Three days before the wedding day, Herman went away to the country to be gone over Sunday. He and Lena were to be married Tuesday afternoon. When the day came Herman had not been seen or heard from.

The old Kreder couple had not worried much about it. Herman always did everything they wanted and he would surely come back in time to get married. But when Monday night came, and there was no Herman, they went to Mrs. Haydon to tell her what had happened.

Mrs. Haydon got very much excited. It was hard enough to work so as to get everything all ready, and then to have that silly Herman go off that way, so no one could tell what was going to happen. Here was Lena and everything all ready, and now they would have to make the wedding later so that they would know that Herman would be sure to be there.

Mrs. Haydon was very much excited, and then she could not say much to the old Kreder couple. She did not want to make them angry, for she wanted very badly now that Lena should be married to their Herman.

At last it was decided that the wedding should be put off a week longer. Old Mr. Kreder would go to New York to find Herman, for it was very likely that Herman had gone there to his married sister.

Mrs. Haydon sent word around, about waiting until a week from that Tuesday, to everybody that had been invited, and then Tuesday morning she sent for Lena to come down to see her.

Mrs. Haydon was very angry with poor Lena when she saw her. She scolded her hard because she was so foolish, and now Herman had gone off and nobody could tell where he had gone to, and all because Lena always was so dumb and silly. And Mrs. Haydon was just like a mother to her, and Lena always stood there so stupid and did not answer what anybody asked her, and Herman was so silly too, and now his father had to go and find him. Mrs. Haydon did not think that any old people should be good to their children. Their children always were so thankless, and never paid any attention, and older people were always doing things for their good. Did Lena think it gave Mrs. Haydon any pleasure, to work so hard to make Lena happy, and get her a good husband, and then Lena was so thankless and never did anything that anybody wanted. It was a lesson to poor Mrs. Haydon not to do things any more for anybody. Let everybody take care of themselves and never come to her with any troubles; she knew better now than to meddle to make other people happy. It just made trouble for her and her husband did not like it. He always said she was too good, and nobody ever thanked her for it, and there Lena was always standing stupid and not answering anything anybody wanted. Lena could always talk enough to those silly girls she liked so much, and always sat with, but who never did anything for her except to take away her money, and here was her aunt who tried so hard and was so good to her and treated her just like one of her own children and Lena stood there, and never made any answer and never tried to please her aunt, or to do anything that her aunt wanted. "No, it ain't no use your standin' there and cryin', now, Lena. It's too late now to care about that Herman. You should have cared some before, and then you wouldn't have to stand and cry now, and be a disappointment to me, and then I get scolded by my husband for taking care of everybody, and nobody ever thankful. I am glad you got the sense to feel sorry now, Lena, anyway, and I try to do what I can to help you out in your trouble, only you don't deserve to have anybody take any trouble for you. But perhaps you know better next time. You go home now and take care you don't spoil your clothes and that new hat, you had no business to be wearin' that this morning, but you ain't got no sense at all, Lena. I never in my life see anybody be so stupid."

Mrs. Haydon stopped and poor Lena stood there in her hat, all trimmed with pretty flowers, and the tears coming out of her eyes, and Lena did not know what it was that she had done, only she was not going to be married and it was a disgrace for a girl to be left by a man on the very day she was to be married.

Lena went home all alone, and cried in the street car.

Poor Lena cried very hard all alone in the street car. She almost spoiled her new hat with her hitting it against the window in her crying. Then she remembered that she must not do so.

The conductor was a kind man and he was very sorry when he saw her crying. "Don't feel so bad, you get another feller, you are such a nice girl," he said to make her cheerful. "But Aunt Mathilda said now, I never get married," poor Lena sobbed out for her answer. "Why you really got trouble like that," said the conductor, "I just said that now to josh you. I didn't ever think you really was left by a feller. He must be a stupid feller. But don't you worry, he wasn't much good if he could go away and leave you, lookin' to be such a nice girl. You just tell all your trouble to me, and I help you." The car was empty and the conductor sat down beside her to put his arm around her, and to be a comfort to her. Lena suddenly remembered where she was, and if she did things like that her aunt would scold her. She moved away from the man into the corner. He laughed, "Don't be scared," he said, "I wasn't going to hurt you. But you just keep up your spirit. You are a real nice girl, and you'll be sure to get a real good husband. Don't you let nobody fool you. You're all right and I don't want to scare you."

The conductor went back to his platform to help a passenger get on the car. All the time Lena stayed in the street car, he would come in every little while and reassure her, about her not to feel so bad about a man who hadn't no more sense than to go away and leave her. She'd be sure yet to get a good man, she needn't be so worried, he frequently assured her.

He chatted with the other passenger who had just come in, a very well dressed old man, and then with another who came in later, a good sort of a working man, and then another who came in, a nice lady, and he told them all about Lena's having trouble, and it was too bad there were men who treated a poor girl so badly. And everybody in the car was sorry for poor Lena and the workman tried to cheer her, and the old man looked sharply at her, and said she looked like a good girl, but she ought to be more careful and not to be so careless, and things like that would not happen to her, and the nice lady went and sat beside her and Lena liked it, though she shrank away from being near her.

So Lena was feeling a little better when she got off the car, and the conductor helped her, and he called out to her, "You be sure you keep up a good heart now. He wasn't no good that feller and you were lucky for to lose him. You'll get a real man yet, one that will be better for you. Don't you be worried, you're a real nice girl as I ever see in such trouble," and the conductor shook his head and went back into his car to talk it over with the other passengers he had there.

The german cook, who always scolded Lena, was very angry when she heard the story. She never did think Mrs. Haydon would do so much for Lena, though she was always talking so grand about what she could do for everybody. The good german cook always had been a little distrustful of her. People who always thought they were so much never did really do things right for anybody. Not that Mrs. Haydon wasn't a good woman. Mrs. Haydon was a real, good, german woman, and she did really mean to do well by her niece Lena. The cook knew that very well, and she had always said so, and she always had liked and respected Mrs. Haydon, who always acted very proper to her, and Lena was so backward, when there was a man to talk to, Mrs. Haydon did have hard work when she tried to marry Lena. Mrs. Haydon was a good woman, only she did talk sometimes too grand. Perhaps this trouble would make her see it wasn't always so easy to do, to make everybody do everything just like she wanted. The cook was very sorry now for Mrs. Haydon. All this must be such a disappointment, and such a worry to her, and she really had always been very good to Lena. But Lena had better go and put on her other clothes and stop with all that crying. That wouldn't do nothing now to help her, and if Lena would be a good girl, and just be real patient, her aunt would make it all come out right yet for her. "I just tell Mrs. Aldrich, Lena, you stay here yet a little longer. You know she is always so good to you, Lena, and I know she let you, and I tell her all about that stupid Herman Kreder. I got no patience, Lena, with anybody who can be so stupid. You just stop now with your crying, Lena, and take off them good clothes and put them away so you don't spoil them when you need them, and you can help me with the dishes and everything will come off better for you. You see if I ain't right by what I tell you. You just stop crying now Lena quick, or else I scold you."

Lena still choked a little and was very miserable inside her but she did everything just as the cook told her.

The girls Lena always sat with were very sorry to see her look so sad with her trouble. Mary the Irish girl sometimes got very angry with her. Mary was always very hot when she talked of Lena's aunt Mathilda, who thought she was so grand, and had such stupid, stuck up daughters. Mary wouldn't be a fat fool like that ugly tempered Mathilda Haydon, not for anything anybody could ever give her. How Lena could keep on going there so much when they all always acted as if she was just dirt to them, Mary never could see. But Lena never had any sense of how she should make people stand round for her, and that was always all the trouble with her. And poor Lena, she was so stupid to be sorry for losing that gawky fool who didn't ever know what he wanted and just said "ja" to his mamma and his papa, like a baby, and was scared to look at a girl straight, and then sneaked away the last day like as if somebody was going to do something to him. Disgrace, Lena talking about disgrace! It was a disgrace for a girl to be seen with the likes of him, let alone to be married to him. But that poor Lena, she never did know how to show herself off for what she was really. Disgrace to have him go away and leave her. Mary would just like to get a chance to show him. If Lena wasn't worth fifteen like Herman Kreder, Mary would just eat her own head all up. It was a good riddance Lena had of that Herman Kreder and his stingy, dirty parents, and if Lena didn't stop crying about it,—Mary would just naturally despise her.

Poor Lena, she knew very well how Mary meant it all, this she was always saying to her. But Lena was very miserable inside her. She felt the disgrace it was for a decent german girl that a man should go away and leave her. Lena knew very well that her aunt was right when she said the way Herman had acted to her was a disgrace to everyone that knew her. Mary and Nellie and the other girls she always sat with were always very good to Lena but that did not make her trouble any better. It was a disgrace the way Lena had been left, to any decent family, and that could never be made any different to her.

And so the slow days wore on, and Lena never saw her Aunt Mathilda. At last on Sunday she got word by a boy to go and see her aunt Mathilda. Lena's heart beat quick for she was very nervous now with all this that had happened to her. She went just as quickly as she could to see her Aunt Mathilda.

Mrs. Haydon quick, as soon as she saw Lena, began to scold her for keeping her aunt waiting so long for her, and for not coming in all the week to see her, to see if her aunt should need her, and so her aunt had to send a boy to tell her. But it was easy, even for Lena, to see that her aunt was not really angry with her. It wasn't Lena's fault, went on Mrs. Haydon, that everything was going to happen all right for her. Mrs. Haydon was very tired taking all this trouble for her, and when Lena couldn't even take trouble to come and see her aunt, to see if she needed anything to tell her. But Mrs. Haydon really never minded things like that when she could do things for anybody. She was tired now, all the trouble she had been taking to make things right for Lena, but perhaps now Lena heard it she would learn a little to be thankful to her. "You get all ready to be married Tuesday. Lena, you hear me." said Mrs. Haydon to her. "You come here Tuesday morning and I have everything all ready for you. You wear your new dress I got you, and your hat with all them flowers on it, and you be very careful coming you don't get your things all dirty, you so careless all the time, Lena, and not thinking, and you act sometimes you never got no head at all on you. You go home now, and you tell your Mrs. Aldrich that you leave her Tuesday. Don't you go forgetting now, Lena, anything I ever told you what you should do to be careful. You be a good girl, now Lena. You get married Tuesday to Herman Kreder." And that was all Lena ever knew of what had happened all this week to Herman Kreder. Lena forgot there was anything to know about it. She was really to be married Tuesday, and her Aunt Mathilda said she was a good girl, and now there was no disgrace left upon her.

Lena now fell back into the way she always had of being always dreamy and not here, the way she always had been, except for the few days she was so excited, because she had been left by a man the very day she was to have been married. Lena was a little nervous all these last days, but she did not think much about what it meant for her to be married.

Herman Kreder was not so content about it. He was quiet and was sullen and he knew he could not help it. He knew now he just had to let himself get married. It was not that Herman did not like Lena Mainz. She was as good as any other girl could be for him. She was a little better perhaps than other girls he saw, she was so very quiet, but Herman did not like to always have to have a girl around him. Herman had always done everything that his mother and his father wanted. His father had found him in New York, where Herman had gone to be with his married sister.

Herman's father when he had found him coaxed Herman a long time and went on whole days with his complaining to him, always troubled but gentle and quite patient with him, and always he was worrying to Herman about what was the right way his boy Herman should always do, always whatever it was his mother ever wanted from him, and always Herman never made him any answer.

Old Mr. Kreder kept on saying to him, he did not see how Herman could think now, it could be any different. When you make a bargain you just got to stick right to it, that was the only way old Mr. Kreder could ever see it, and saying you would get married to a girl and she got everything all ready, that was a bargain just like one you make in business and Herman he had made it, and now Herman he would just have to do it, old Mr. Kreder didn't see there was any other way a good boy like his Herman had, to do it. And then too that Lena Mainz was such a nice girl and Herman hadn't ought to really give his father so much trouble and make him pay out all that money, to come all the way to New York just to find him, and they both lose all that time from their working, when all Herman had to do was just to stand up, for an hour, and then he would be all right married, and it would be all over for him, and then everything at home would never be any different to him.

And his father went on; there was his poor mother saying always how her Herman always did everything before she ever wanted, and now just because he got notions in him, and wanted to show people how he could be stubborn, he was making all this trouble for her, and making them pay all that money just to run around and find him. "You got no idea Herman, how bad mama is feeling about the way you been acting Herman," said old Mr. Kreder to him. "She says she never can understand how you can be so thankless Herman. It hurts her very much you been so stubborn, and she find you such a nice girl for you, like Lena Mainz who is always just so quiet and always saves up all her wages, and she never wanting her own way at all like some girls are always all the time to have it, and your mama trying so hard, just so you could be comfortable Herman to be married, and then you act so stubborn Herman. You like all young people Herman, you think only about yourself, and what you are just wanting, and your mama she is thinking only what is good for you to have, for you in the future. Do you think your mama wants to have a girl around to be a bother, for herself, Herman. Its just for you Herman she is always thinking, and she talks always about how happy she will be, when she sees her Herman married to a nice girl, and then when she fixed it all up so good for you, so it never would be any bother to you, just the way she wanted you should like it, and you say yes all right, I do it, and then you go away like this and act stubborn, and make all this trouble everybody to take for you, and we spend money, and I got to travel all round to find you. You come home now with me Herman and get married, and I tell your mama she better not say anything to you about how much it cost me to come all the way to look for you—Hey Herman," said his father coaxing, "Hey, you come home now and get married. All you got to do Herman is just to stand up for an hour Herman, and then you don't never to have any more bother to it—Hey Herman!—you come home with me tomorrow and get married. Hey Herman."

Herman's married sister liked her brother Herman, and she had always tried to help him, when there was anything she knew he wanted. She liked it that he was so good and always did everything that their father and their mother wanted, but still she wished it could be that he could have more his own way, if there was anything he ever wanted.

But now she thought Herman with his girl was very funny. She wanted that Herman should be married. She thought it would do him lots of good to get married. She laughed at Herman when she heard the story. Until his father came to find him, she did not know why it was Herman had come just then to New York to see her. When she heard the story she laughed a good deal at her brother Herman and teased him a good deal about his running away, because he didn't want to have a girl to be all the time around him.

Herman's married sister liked her brother Herman, and she did not want him not to like to be with women. He was good, her brother Herman, and it would surely do him good to get married. It would make him stand up for himself stronger. Herman's sister always laughed at him and always she would try to reassure him. "Such a nice man as my brother Herman acting like as if he was afraid of women. Why the girls all like a man like you Herman, if you didn't always run away when you saw them. It do you good really Herman to get married, and then you got somebody you can boss around when you want to. It do you good Herman to get married, you see if you don't like it, when you really done it. You go along home now with papa, Herman and get married to that Lena. You don't know how nice you like it Herman when you try once how you can do it. You just don't be afraid of nothing, Herman. You good enough for any girl to marry, Herman. Any girl be glad to have a man like you to be always with them Herman. You just go along home with papa and try it what I say, Herman. Oh you so funny Herman, when you sit there, and then run away and leave your girl behind you. I know she is crying like anything Herman for to lose you. Don't be bad to her Herman. You go along home with papa now and get married Herman. I'd be awful ashamed Herman, to really have a brother didn't have spirit enough to get married, when a girl is just dying for to have him. You always like me to be with you Herman. I don't see why you say you don't want a girl to be all the time around you. You always been good to me Herman, and I know you always be good to that Lena, and you soon feel just like as if she had always been there with you. Don't act like as if you wasn't a nice strong man, Herman. Really I laugh at you Herman, but you know I like awful well to see you real happy.

You go home and get married to that Lena, Herman. She is a real pretty girl and real nice and good and quiet and she make my brother Herman very happy. You just stop your fussing now with Herman, papa. He go with you to-morrow papa, and you see he like it so much to be married, he make everybody laugh just to see him be so happy. Really truly, that's the way it will be with you Herman. You just listen to me what I tell you Herman." And so his sister laughed at him and reassured him, and his father kept on telling what the mother always said about her Herman, and he coaxed him and Herman never said anything in answer, and his sister packed his things up and was very cheerful with him, and she kissed him, and then she laughed and then she kissed him, and his father went and bought the tickets for the train, and at last late on Sunday he brought Herman back to Bridgepoint with him.

It was always very hard to keep Mrs. Kreder from saying what she thought, to her Herman, but her daughter had written her a letter, so as to warn her not to say anything about what he had been doing, to him, and her husband came in with Herman and said, "Here we are come home mama, Herman and me, and we are very tired it was so crowded coming," and then he whispered to her. "You be good to Herman, mama, he didn't mean to make us so much trouble," and so old Mrs. Kreder, held in what she felt was so strong in her to say to her Herman. She just said very stiffly to him, "I'm glad to see you come home to-day, Herman." Then she went to arrange it all with Mrs. Haydon.

Herman was now again just like he always had been, sullen and very good, and very quiet, and always ready to do whatever his mother and his father wanted. Tuesday morning came, Herman got his new clothes on and went with his father and his mother to stand up for an hour and get married. Lena was there in her new dress, and her hat with all the pretty flowers, and she was very nervous for now she knew she was really very soon to be married. Mrs. Haydon had everything all ready. Everybody was there just as they should be and very soon Herman Kreder and Lena Mainz were married.

When everything was really over, they went back to the Kreder house together. They were all now to live together, Lena and Herman and the old father and the old mother, in the house where Mr. Kreder had worked so many years as a tailor, with his son Herman always there to help him.

Irish Mary had often said to Lena she never did see how Lena could ever want to have anything to do with Herman Kreder and his dirty stingy parents. The old Kreders were to an Irish nature, a stingy, dirty couple. They had not the freehearted, thoughtless, fighting, mud bespattered, ragged, peat-smoked cabin dirt that Irish Mary knew and could forgive and love. Theirs was the german dirt of saving, of being dowdy and loose and foul in your clothes so as to save them and yourself in washing, having your hair greasy to save it in the soap and drying, having your clothes dirty, not in freedom, but because so it was cheaper, keeping the house close and smelly because so it cost less to get it heated, living so poorly not only so as to save money but so they should never even know themselves that they had it, working all the time not only because from their nature they just had to and because it made them money but also that they never could be put in any way to make them spend their money.

This was the place Lena now had for her home and to her it was very different than it could be for an Irish Mary. She too was german and was thrifty, though she was always so dreamy and not there. Lena was always careful with things and she always saved her money, for that was the only way she knew how to do it. She never had taken care of her own money and she never had thought how to use it.

Lena Mainz had been, before she was Mrs. Herman Kreder, always clean and decent in her clothes and in her person, but it was not because she ever thought about it or really needed so to have it, it was the way her people did in the german country where she came from, and her Aunt Mathilda and the good german cook who always scolded, had kept her on and made her, with their scoldings, always more careful to keep clean and to wash real often. But there was no deep need in all this for Lena and so, though Lena did not like the old Kreders, though she really did not know that, she did not think about their being stingy dirty people.

Herman Kreder was cleaner than the old people, just because it was his nature to keep cleaner, but he was used to his mother and his father, and he never thought that they should keep things cleaner. And Herman too always saved all his money, except for that little beer he drank when he went out with other men of an evening the way he always liked to do it, and he never thought of any other way to spend it. His father had always kept all the money for them and he always was doing business with it. And then too Herman really had no money, for he always had worked for his father, and his father had never thought to pay him.

And so they began all four to live in the Kreder house together, and Lena began soon with it to look careless and a little dirty, and to be more lifeless with it, and nobody ever noticed much what Lena wanted, and she never really knew herself what she needed.

The only real trouble that came to Lena with their living all four there together, was the way old Mrs. Kreder scolded. Lena had always been used to being scolded, but this scolding of old Mrs. Kreder was very different from the way she ever before had had to endure it.

Herman, now he was married to her, really liked Lena very well. He did not care very much about her but she never was a bother to him being there around him, only when his mother worried and was nasty to them because Lena was so careless, and did not know how to save things right for them with their eating, and all the other ways with money, that the old woman had to save it.

Herman Kreder had always done everything his mother and his father wanted but he did not really love his parents very deeply. With Herman it was always only that he hated to have any struggle. It was all always all right with him when he could just go along and do the same thing over every day with his working, and not to hear things, and not to have people make him listen to their anger. And now his marriage, and he just knew it would, was making trouble for him. It made him hear more what his mother was always saying, with her scolding. He had to really hear it now because Lena was there, and she was so scared and dull always when she heard it. Herman knew very well with his mother, it was all right if one ate very little and worked hard all day and did not hear her when she scolded, the way Herman always had done before they were so foolish about his getting married and having a girl there to be all the time around him, and now he had to help her so the girl could learn too, not to hear it when his mother scolded, and not to look so scared, and not to eat much, and always to be sure to save it.

Herman really did not know very well what he could do to help Lena to understand it. He could never answer his mother back to help Lena, that never would make things any better for her, and he never could feel in himself any way to comfort Lena, to make her strong not to hear his mother, in all the awful ways she always scolded. It just worried Herman to have it like that all the time around him. Herman did not know much about how a man could make a struggle with a mother, to do much to keep her quiet, and indeed Herman never knew much how to make a struggle against anyone who really wanted to have anything very badly. Herman all his life never wanted anything so badly, that he would really make a struggle against any one to get it. Herman all his life only wanted to live regular and quiet, and not talk much and to do the same way every day like every other with his working. And now his mother had made him get married to this Lena and now with his mother making all that scolding, he had all this trouble and this worry always on him.

Mrs. Haydon did not see Lena now very often. She had not lost her interest in her niece Lena, but Lena could not come much to her house to see her, it would not be right, now Lena was a married woman. And then too Mrs. Haydon had her hands full just then with her two daughters, for she was getting them ready to find them good husbands, and then too her own husband now worried her very often about her always spoiling that boy of hers, so he would be sure to turn out no good and be a disgrace to a german family, and all because his mother always spoiled him. All these things were very worrying now to Mrs. Haydon, but still she wanted to be good to Lena, though she could not see her very often. She only saw her when Mrs. Haydon went to call on Mrs. Kreder or when Mrs. Kreder came to see Mrs. Haydon, and that never could be very often. Then too these days Mrs. Haydon could not scold Lena, Mrs. Kreder was always there with her, and it would not be right to scold Lena when Mrs. Kreder was there, who had now the real right to do it. And so her aunt always said nice things now to Lena, and though Mrs. Haydon sometimes was a little worried when she saw Lena looking sad and not careful, she did not have time just then to really worry much about it.

Lena now never any more saw the girls she always used to sit with. She had no way now to see them and it was not in Lena's nature to search out ways to see them, nor did she now ever think much of the days when she had been used to see them. They never any of them had come to the Kreder house to see her. Not even Irish Mary had ever thought to come to see her. Lena had been soon forgotten by them. They had soon passed away from Lena and now Lena never thought any more that she had ever known them.

The only one of her old friends who tried to know what Lena liked and what she needed, and who always made Lena come to see her, was the good german cook who had always scolded. She now scolded Lena hard for letting herself go so, and going out when she was looking so untidy. "I know you going to have a baby Lena, but that's no way for you to be looking. I am ashamed most to see you come and sit here in my kitchen, looking so sloppy and like you never used to Lena. I never see anybody like you Lena. Herman is very good to you, you always say so, and he don't treat you bad ever though you don't deserve to have anybody good to you, you so careless all the time, Lena, letting yourself go like you never had anybody tell you what was the right way you should know how to be looking. No, Lena, I don't see no reason you should let yourself go so and look so untidy Lena, so I am ashamed to see you sit there looking so ugly, Lena. No Lena that ain't no way ever I see a woman make things come out better, letting herself go so every way and crying all the time like as if you had real trouble. I never wanted to see you marry Herman Kreder, Lena, I knew what you got to stand with that old woman always, and that old man, he is so stingy too and he don't say things out but he ain't any better in his heart than his wife with her bad ways, I know that Lena, I know they don't hardly give you enough to eat, Lena, I am real sorry for you, Lena, you know that Lena, but that ain't any way to be going round so untidy Lena, even if you have got all that trouble. You never see me do like that Lena, though sometimes I got a headache so I can't see to stand to be working hardly, and nothing comes right with all my cooking, but I always see Lena, I look decent. That's the only way a german girl can make things come out right Lena. You hear me what I am saying to you Lena. Now you eat something nice Lena, I got it all ready for you, and you wash up and be careful Lena and the baby will come all right to you, and then I make your Aunt Mathilda see that you live in a house soon all alone with Herman and your baby, and then everything go better for you. You hear me what I say to you Lena. Now don't let me ever see you come looking like this any more Lena, and you just stop with that always crying. You ain't got no reason to be sitting there now with all that crying, I never see anybody have trouble it did them any good to do the way you are doing, Lena. You hear me Lena. You go home now and you be good the way I tell you Lena, and I see what I can do. I make your Aunt Mathilda make old Mrs. Kreder let you be till you get your baby all right. Now don't you be scared and so silly Lena. I don't like to see you act so silly Lena when really you got a nice man and so many things really any girl should be grateful to be having. Now you go home Lena to-day and you do the way I say, to you, and I see what I can do to help you."

"Yes Mrs. Aldrich" said the good german woman to her mistress later, "Yes Mrs. Aldrich that's the way it is with them girls when they want so to get married. They dont know when they got it good Mrs. Aldrich. They never know what it is they're really wanting when they got it, Mrs. Aldrich. There's that poor Lena, she just been here crying and looking so careless so I scold her, but that was no good that marrying for that poor Lena, Mrs. Aldrich. She do look so pale and sad now Mrs. Aldrich, it just break my heart to see her. She was a good girl was Lena, Mrs. Aldrich, and I never had no trouble with her like I got with so many young girls nowadays, Mrs. Aldrich, and I never see any girl any better to work right than our Lena, and now she got to stand it all the time with that old woman Mrs. Kreder. My! Mrs. Aldrich, she is a bad old woman to her. I never see Mrs. Aldrich how old people can be so bad to young girls and not have no kind of patience with them. If Lena could only live with her Herman, he ain't so bad the way men are, Mrs. Aldrich, but he is just the way always his mother wants him, he ain't got no spirit in him, and so I don't really see no help for that poor Lena. I know her aunt, Mrs. Haydon, meant it all right for her Mrs. Aldrich, but poor Lena, it would be better for her if her Herman had stayed there in New York that time he went away to leave her. I don't like it the way Lena is looking now, Mrs. Aldrich. She looks like as if she don't have no life left in her hardly, Mrs. Aldrich, she just drags around and looks so dirty and after all the pains I always took to teach her and to keep her nice in her ways and looking. It don't do no good to them, for them girls to get married Mrs. Aldrich, they are much better when they only know it, to stay in a good place when they got it, and keep on regular with their working. I don't like it the way Lena looks now Mrs. Aldrich. I wish I knew some way to help that poor Lena, Mrs. Aldrich, but she is a bad old woman, that old Mrs. Kreder, Herman's mother. I speak to

Mrs. Haydon real soon, Mrs. Aldrich, I see what we can do now to help that poor Lena."

These were really bad days for poor Lena. Herman always was real good to her and now he even sometimes tried to stop his mother from scolding Lena. "She ain't well now mama, you let her be now you hear me. You tell me what it is you want she should be doing, I tell her. I see she does it right just the way you want it mama. You let be, I say now mama, with that always scolding Lena. You let be, I say now, you wait till she is feeling better." Herman was getting really strong to struggle, for he could see that Lena with that baby working hard inside her, really could not stand it any longer with his mother and the awful ways she always scolded.

It was a new feeling Herman now had inside him that made him feel he was strong to make a struggle. It was new for Herman Kreder really to be wanting something, but Herman wanted strongly now to be a father, and he wanted badly that his baby should be a boy and healthy. Herman never had cared really very much about his father and his mother, though always, all his life, he had done everything just as they wanted, and he had never really cared much about his wife, Lena, though he always had been very good to her, and had always tried to keep his mother off her, with the awful way she always scolded, but to be really a father of a little baby, that feeling took hold of Herman very deeply. He was almost ready, so as to save his baby from all trouble, to really make a strong struggle with his mother and with his father, too, if he would not help him to control his mother.

Sometimes Herman even went to Mrs. Haydon to talk all this trouble over. They decided then together, it was better to wait there all four together for the baby, and Herman could make Mrs. Kreder stop a little with her scolding, and then when Lena was a little stronger, Herman should have his own house for her, next door to his father, so he could always be there to help him in his working, but so they could eat and sleep in a house where the old woman could not control them and they could not hear her awful scolding.

And so things went on, the same way, a little longer. Poor Lena was not feeling any joy to have a baby. She was scared the way she had been when she was so sick on the water. She was scared now every time when anything would hurt her. She was scared and still and lifeless, and sure that every minute she would die. Lena had no power to be strong in this kind of trouble, she could only sit still and be scared, and dull, and lifeless, and sure that every minute she would die.

Before very long, Lena had her baby. He was a good, healthy little boy, the baby. Herman cared very much to have the baby. When Lena was a little stronger he took a house next door to the old couple, so he and his own family could eat and sleep and do the way they wanted. This did not seem to make much change now for Lena. She was just the same as when she was waiting with her baby. She just dragged around and was careless with her clothes and all lifeless, and she acted always and lived on just as if she had no feeling. She always did everything regular with the work, the way she always had had to do it, but she never got back any spirit in her. Herman was always good and kind, and always helped her with her working. He did everything he knew to help her. He always did all the active new things in the house and for the baby. Lena did what she had to do the way she always had been taught it. She always just kept going now with her working, and she was always careless, and dirty, and a little dazed, and lifeless. Lena never got any better in herself of this way of being that she had had ever since she had been married.

Mrs. Haydon never saw any more of her niece, Lena. Mrs. Haydon had now so much trouble with her own house, and her daughters getting married, and her boy, who was growing up, and who always was getting so much worse to manage. She knew she had done right by Lena. Herman Kreder was a good man, she would be glad to get one so good, sometimes, for her own daughters, and now they had a home to live in together, separate from the old people, who had made their trouble for them. Mrs. Haydon felt she had done very well by her niece, Lena, and she never thought now she needed any more to go and see her. Lena would do very well now without her aunt to trouble herself any more about her.

The good german cook who had always scolded, still tried to do her duty like a mother to poor Lena. It was very hard now to do right by Lena. Lena never seemed to hear now what anyone was saying to her. Herman was always doing everything he could to help her. Herman always, when he was home, took good care of the baby. Herman loved to take care of his baby. Lena never thought to take him out or to do anything she didn't have to.

The good cook sometimes made Lena come to see her. Lena would come with her baby and sit there in the kitchen, and watch the good woman cooking, and listen to her sometimes a little, the way she used to, while the good german woman scolded her for going around looking so careless when now she had no trouble, and sitting there so dull, and always being just so thankless. Sometimes Lena would wake up a little and get back into her face her old, gentle, patient, and unsuffering sweetness, but mostly Lena did not seem to hear much when the good german woman scolded. Lena always liked it when Mrs. Aldrich her good mistress spoke to her kindly, and then Lena would seem to go back and feel herself to be like she was when she had been in service. But mostly Lena just lived along and was careless in her clothes, and dull, and lifeless.

By and by Lena had two more little babies. Lena was not so much scared now when she had the babies. She did not seem to notice very much when they hurt her, and she never seemed to feel very much now about anything that happened to her.

They were very nice babies, all these three that Lena had, and Herman took good care of them always. Herman never really cared much about his wife, Lena. The only things Herman ever really cared for were his babies. Herman always was very good to his children. He always had a gentle, tender way when he held them. He learned to be very handy with them. He spent all the time he was not working, with them. By and by he began to work all day in his own home so that he could have his children always in the same room with him.

Lena always was more and more lifeless and Herman now mostly never thought about her. He more and more took all the care of their three children. He saw to their eating right and their washing, and he dressed them every morning, and he taught them the right way to do things, and he put them to their sleeping, and he was now always every minute with them. Then there was to come to them, a fourth baby. Lena went to the hospital near by to have the baby. Lena seemed to be going to have much trouble with it. When the baby was come out at last, it was like its mother, lifeless. While it was coming, Lena had grown very pale and sicker. When it was all over Lena had died, too, and nobody knew just how it had happened to her.

The good german cook who had always scolded Lena, and had always to the last day tried to help her, was the only one who ever missed her. She remembered how nice Lena had looked all the time she was in service with her, and how her voice had been so gentle and sweet-sounding, and how she always was a good girl, and how she never had to have any trouble with her, the way she always had with all the other girls who had been taken into the house to help her. The good cook sometimes spoke so of Lena when she had time to have a talk with Mrs. Aldrich, and this was all the remembering there now ever was of Lena.

Herman Kreder now always lived very happy, very gentle, very quiet, very well content alone with his three children. He never had a woman any more to be all the time around him. He always did all his own work in his house, when he was through every day with the work he was always doing for his father. Herman always was alone, and he always worked alone, until his little ones were big enough to help him. Herman Kreder was very well content now and he always lived very regular and peaceful, and with every day just like the next one, always alone now with his three good, gentle children.

1909

SUSIE ASADO

Sweet sweet sweet sweet sweet tea.
Susie Asado.
Sweet sweet sweet sweet sweet tea.
Susie Asado.
Susie Asado which is a told tray sure.
A lean on the shoe this means slips slips hers.
When the ancient light grey is clean it is yellow, it
is a silver seller.
This is a please this is a please there are the saids
to jelly. These are the wets these say the sets to leave
a crown to Incy.
Incy is short for incubus.
A pot. A pot is a beginning of a rare bit of trees.
Trees tremble, the old vats are in bobbles, bobbles which
shade and shove and render clean, render clean must.
Drink pups.
Drink pups drink pups lease a sash hold, see it shine
and a bobolink has pins. It shows a nail.
What is a nail. A nail is unison.
Sweet sweet sweet sweet sweet tea.

1922

PICASSO

One whom some were certainly following was one who was completely charming. One whom some were certainly following was one who was charming. One whom some were following was one who was completely charming. One whom some were following was one who was certainly completely charming.

Some were certainly following and were certain that the one they were then following was one working and was one bringing out of himself then something. Some were certainly following and were certain that the one they were then following was one bringing out of himself then something that was coming to be a heavy thing, a solid thing and a complete thing.

One whom some were certainly following was one working and certainly was one bringing something out of himself then and was one who had been all his living had been one having something coming out of him.

Something had been coming out of him, certainly it had been coming out of him, certainly it was something, certainly it had been coming out of him and it had meaning, a charming meaning, a solid meaning, a struggling meaning, a clear meaning.

One whom some were certainly following and some were certainly following him, one whom some were certainly following was one certainly working.

One whom some were certainly following was one having something coming out of him something having meaning and this one was certainly working then.

This one was working and something was coming then, something was coming out of this one then. This one was one and always there was something coming out of this one and always there had been something coming out of this one. This one had never been one not having something coming out of this one. This one was one having something coming out of this one. This one had been one whom some were following. This one was one whom some were following. This one was being one whom some were following. This one was one who was working.

This one was one who was working. This one was one being one having something being coming out of him. This one was one going on having something come out of him. This one was one going on working. This one was one whom some were following. This one was one who was working.

This one always had something being coming out of this one. This one was working. This one always had been working. This one was always having something that was coming out of this one that was a solid thing, a charming thing, a lovely thing, a perplexing thing, a disconcerting thing, a simple thing, a clear thing, a complicated thing, an interesting thing, a disturbing thing, a repellant thing, a very pretty thing. This one was one certainly being one having something coming out of him. This one was one whom some were following. This one was one who was working.

This one was one who was working and certainly this one was needing to be working so as to be one being working. This one was one having something coming out of him. This one would be one all his living having something coming out of him. This one was working and then this one was working and this one was needing to be working, not to be one having something coming out of him something having meaning, but was needing to be working so as to be one working.

This one was certainly working and working was something this one was certain this one would be doing and this one was doing that thing, this one was working. This one was not one completely working. This one was not ever completely working. This one certainly was not completely working.

This one was one having always something being coming out of him, something having completely a real meaning. This one was one whom some were following. This one was one who was working. This one was one who was working and he was one needing this thing needing to be working so as to be one having some way of being one having some way of working. This one was one who was working. This one was one having something come out of him something having meaning. This one was one always having something come out of him and this thing the thing coming out of him always had real meaning. This one was one who was working. This one was one who was almost always working. This one was not one completely working. This one was one not ever completely working. This one was not one working to have anything come out of him. This one did have something having meaning that did come out of him. He always did have something come out of him. He was working, he was not ever completely working. He did have some following. They were always following him. Some were certainly following him. He was one who was working. He was one having something coming out of him something having meaning. He was not ever completely working.

1934

A MOVIE

Eyes are a surprise
Printzess a dream
Buzz is spelled with z
Fuss is spelled with s
So is business.
The UNITED STATES is comical.

Now I want to tell you about the Monroe doctrine. We think very nicely we think very well of the Monroe doctrine.

American painter painting in French country near railroad track. Mobilisation locomotive passes with notification for villages.

Where are American tourists to buy my pictures sacre nom d'un pipe says the american painter.

American painter sits in cafe and contemplates empty pocket book as taxi cabs file through Paris carrying French soldiers to battle of the Marne. I guess I'll be a taxi driver here in gay Paree says the american painter.

Painter sits in studio trying to learn names of streets with help of Bretonne peasant femme de menage. He becomes taxi driver. Ordinary street scene in war time Paris.

Being lazy about getting up in the mornings he spends some of his dark nights in teaching Bretonne femme de menage peasant girl how to drive the taxi so she can replace him when he wants to sleep.

America comes into the war american painter wants to be american soldier. Personnel officer interviews him. What have you been doing, taxiing. You know Paris, Secret Service for you go on taxiing.

He goes on taxiing and he teaches Bretonne f. m. english so she can take his place if need be.

One night he reads his paper under the light. Policeman tells him to move up, don't want to wants to read.

Man comes up wants to go to the station.

Painter has to take him. Gets back, reading again.

Another man comes wants to go to the station. Painter takes him.

Comes back to read again. Two american officers come up. Want to go to the station.

Painter says Tired of the station take you to Berlin if you like. No station.

Officers say give you a lot if you take us outside town on way to the south, first big town.

He says alright got to stop at home first to get his coat.

Stops at home calls out to Bretonne f. m. Get busy telegraph to all your relations, you have them all over, ask have you any american officers staying forever. Be back to-morrow.

Back to-morrow. Called up by chief secret service. Goes to see him. Money has been disappearing out of quartermaster's department in chunks. You've got a free hand. Find out something.

Goes home. Finds f. m. Bretonne surrounded with telegrams and letters from relatives. Americans everywhere but everywhere. She groans. Funny Americans everywhere but everywhere they all said. Many funny Americans everywhere. Two Americans not so funny here my fifth cousin says, she is helping in the hospital in Avignon. Such a sweet american soldier. So young so tall so tender. Not very badly hurt but will stay a long long time. He has been visited by american officers who live in a villa. Two such nice ladies live there too and they spend and they spend, they buy all the good sweet food in Avignon. "Is that something William Sir," says the Bretonne f. m.

Its snowing but no matter we will get there in the taxi. Take us two days and two nights you inside and me out. Hurry. They start, the funny little taxi goes over the mountains with and without assistance, all tired out he is inside, she driving when they turn down the hill into Avignon. Just then two Americans on motor cycles come on and Bretonne f. m. losing her head grand smash. American painter wakes up burned, he sees the two and says by God and makes believe he is dead. The two are very helpful. A team comes along and takes american painter and all to hospital. Two Americans ride off on motor cycles direction of Nimes and Pont du Gard.

Arrival at hospital, interview with the wounded American who described two american officers who had been like brothers to him, didn't think any officers could be so chummy with a soldier. Took me out treated me, cigarettes everything fine.

Where have they gone on to, to Nimes.

Yes Pont du Gard.

American painter in bed in charge of french nursing nun but manages to escape and leave for Pont du Gard in mended taxi. There under the shadow of that imperishable monument of the might and industry of ancient Rome exciting duel. French gendarme american painter, taxi, f. m. Bretonne, two american crooks with motor cycles on which they try to escape over the top of the Pont du Gard, great stunt, they are finally captured. They have been the receivers of the stolen money.

After many other adventures so famous has become the american painter, Bretonne femme de menage and taxi that in the march under the arch at the final triumph of the allies the taxi at the special request of General Pershing brings up the rear of the procession after the tanks, the Bretonne driving and the american painter inside waving the american flag Old Glory and the tricolor.

CURTAIN

1987

Sherwood Anderson 1876–1941

In his stories of rural and small-town life, Sherwood Anderson sought to portray what he called "the ugliness of life, the strange beauty of life. . . ." His sketches and tales drew upon his own experiences in the American Midwest at the end of the nineteenth century. He had grown up in the small town of Clyde, Ohio, the basis for fictional Winesburg, Ohio, which was the setting of his most notable work. When he was twenty, he left home, drawn to the metropolis of Chicago, where he took a job as a laborer. When the Spanish-American War (1898) gave him the chance to escape the dull routine of day-labor, he enlisted, serving in the army for a year. After the war he returned to Chicago, where he worked as an advertising salesman and began to write his first tales and sketches. In 1907, he moved to Elyria, Ohio, to establish a paint firm, but his literary ambitions soon came into conflict with his duties as a small-town businessman. In 1913 he abandoned his business, returned once again to Chicago, and at the age of thirty-seven began his life as a writer, asserting, "I will be a servant to words alone."

He wrote Windy McPherson's Son *(1916) and* Marching Men *(1917), novels about successful men who abandoned their own selfish aims to become populist heroes, helping the "little people." In 1919 he published* Winesburg, Ohio, *his masterpiece, a collection of tales of the "grotesque" characters he had known during his youth in Ohio. Anderson's successful volumes of short stories,* The Triumph of the Egg *(1921),* Horses and Men *(1923), and* Death in the Woods *(1933), contained work of great merit, but his later novels, among them* Many Marriages *(1923),* Dark Laughter *(1925), and* Kit Brandon *(1936), were failures and showed only flashes of the finer qualities of his earlier writing.*

Anderson was preoccupied by a desire to describe the agonies and the failures of the unsuccessful, the deprived, and the inarticulate. His range was narrow, and his idealized perceptions of innocence were sometimes shallow. Yet his sensitive depictions of poverty and eccentricity and his deceptively simple style, with its matter-of-fact midwestern sentences, opened new perspectives for twentieth-century literature. He influenced a wide range of

American writers, including Hart Crane, John Steinbeck, Thomas Wolfe, Ernest Hemingway, and William Faulkner, who, in 1956, acknowledged Anderson as "the father of my generation of American writers and the tradition of American writing which our successors will carry on."

FURTHER READING: J. Schevill, *Sherwood Anderson: His Life and Work,* 1951; I. Howe, *Sherwood Anderson,* 1951, 1966; *Letters of Sherwood Anderson,* ed. H. Jones and W. Rideout, 1953; R. Burbank, *Sherwood Anderson,* 1964; *The Achievement of Sherwood Anderson: Essays in Criticism,* ed. R. White, 1966; D. Anderson, *Sherwood Anderson: An Introduction and Interpretation,* 1967; *Sherwood Anderson's Memoirs,* ed. R. White, 1969; *Sherwood Anderson: A Collection of Critical Essays,* ed. W. Rideout, 1974; *Critical Essays on Sherwood Anderson,* ed. D. Anderson, 1981; *Sherwood Anderson: Collected Letters,* ed. C. Modlin, 1983; K. Townsend, *Sherwood Anderson,* 1987; R. Papinchak, *Sherwood Anderson: A Study of the Short Stories,* 1992; J. Small, *A Reader's Guide to the Short Stories of Sherwood Anderson,* 1994; *Sherwood Anderson,* ed. H. Bloom, 2003; R. Dunne, *A New Book of the Grotesques Contemporary Approaches to Sherwood Anderson's Early Fiction,* 2005.

TEXTS: *The Triumph of the Egg,* 1921; *Winesburg, Ohio,* 1919.

I WANT TO KNOW WHY

We got up at four in the morning, that first day in the east. On the evening before we had climbed off a freight train at the edge of town, and with the true instinct of Kentucky boys had found our way across town and to the racetrack and the stables at once. Then we knew we were all right. Hanley Turner right away found a nigger we knew. It was Bildad Johnson who in the winter works at Ed Becker's livery barn in our home town, Beckersville. Bildad is a good cook as almost all our niggers are and of course he, like everyone in our part of Kentucky who is anyone at all, likes the horses. In the spring Bildad begins to scratch around. A nigger from our country can flatter and wheedle anyone into letting him do most anything he wants. Bildad wheedles the stable men and the trainers from the horse farms in our country around Lexington. The trainers come into town in the evening to stand around and talk and maybe get into a poker game. Bildad gets in with them. He is always doing little favors and telling about things to eat, chicken browned in a pan, and how is the best way to cook sweet potatoes and corn bread. It makes your mouth water to hear him.

When the racing season comes on and the horses go to the races and there is all the talk on the streets in the evenings about the new colts, and everyone says when they are going over to Lexington or to the spring meeting at Churchill Downs or to Latonia,[1] and the horsemen that have been down to New Orleans or maybe at the winter meeting at Havana in Cuba come home to spend a week before they start out again, at such a time when everything talked about in Beckersville is just horses and nothing else and the outfits start out and horse racing is in every breath of air you breathe, Bildad shows up with a job as cook for some outfit. Often when I think about it, his always going all season to the races and working in the livery barn in the winter

[1]Famous race tracks in Louisville and Covington, Kentucky.

where horses are and where men like to come and talk about horses, I wish I was a nigger. It's a foolish thing to say, but that's the way I am about being around horses, just crazy. I can't help it.

Well, I must tell you about what we did and let you in on what I'm talking about. Four of us boys from Beckersville, all whites and sons of men who live in Beckersville regular, made up our minds we were going to the races, not just to Lexington or Louisville, I don't mean, but to the big eastern track we were always hearing our Beckersville men talk about, to Saratoga.[2] We were all pretty young then. I was just turned fifteen and I was the oldest of the four. It was my scheme. I admit that and I talked the others into trying it. There was Hanley Turner and Henry Rieback and Tom Tumberton and myself. I had thirty-seven dollars I had earned during the winter working nights and Saturdays in Enoch Myer's grocery. Henry Rieback had eleven dollars and the others, Hanley and Tom, had only a dollar or two each. We fixed it all up and laid low until the Kentucky spring meetings were over and some of our men, the sportiest ones, the ones we envied the most, had cut out—then we cut out too.

I won't tell you the trouble we had beating our way on freights and all. We went through Cleveland and Buffalo and other cities and saw Niagara Falls. We bought things there, souvenirs and spoons and cards and shells with pictures of the Falls on them for our sisters and mothers, but thought we had better not send any of the things home. We didn't want to put the folks on our trail and maybe be nabbed.

We got into Saratoga as I said at night and went to the track. Bildad fed us up. He showed us a place to sleep in hay over a shed and promised to keep still. Niggers are all right about things like that. They won't squeal on you. Often a white man you might meet, when you had run away from home like that, might appear to be all right and give you a quarter or a half dollar or something, and then go right and give you away. White men will do that, but not a nigger. You can trust them. They are squarer with kids. I don't know why.

At the Saratoga meeting that year there were a lot of men from home. Dave Williams and Arthur Mulford and Jerry Myers and others. Then there was a lot from Louisville and Lexington Henry Rieback knew but I didn't. They were professional gamblers and Henry Rieback's father is one too. He is what is called a sheet[3] writer and goes away most of the year to tracks. In the winter when he is home in Beckersville he don't stay there much but goes away to cities and deals faro.[4] He is a nice man and generous, is always sending Henry presents, a bicycle and a gold watch and a Boy Scout suit of clothes and things like that.

My own father is a lawyer. He's all right, but don't make much money and can't buy me things and anyway I'm getting so old now I don't expect it. He never said nothing to me against Henry, but Hanley Turner and Tom Tumberton's fathers did. They said to their boys that money so come by is no good and they didn't want their boys brought up to hear gamblers' talk and be thinking about such things and maybe embrace them.

That's all right and I guess the men know what they are talking about, but I don't see what it's got to do with Henry or horses either. That's what I'm

[2]Race track at Saratoga Springs, New York.
[3]A racing form, printed information on horses, jockeys, and races.
[4]A card game popular with gamblers in the nineteenth and early twentieth century.

writing this story about. I'm puzzled. I'm getting to be a man and want to think straight and be O.K, and there's something I saw at the race meeting at the eastern track I can't figure out.

I can't help it, I'm crazy about thoroughbred horses. I've always been that way. When I was ten years old and saw I was growing to be big and couldn't be a rider I was so sorry I nearly died. Harry Hellinfinger in Beckersville, whose father is Postmaster, is grown up and too lazy to work, but likes to stand around in the street and get up jokes on boys like sending them to a hardware store for a gimlet[5] to bore square holes and other jokes like that. He played one on me. He told me that if I would eat a half a cigar I would be stunted and not grow any more and maybe could be a rider. I did it. When father wasn't looking I took a cigar out of his pocket and gagged it down some way. It made me awful sick and the doctor had to be sent for, and then it did no good. I kept right on growing. It was a joke. When I told what I had done and why most fathers would have whipped me but mine didn't.

Well, I didn't get stunted and didn't die. It serves Harry Hellinfinger right. Then I made up my mind I would like to be a stable boy, but had to give that up too. Mostly niggers do that work and I knew father wouldn't let me go into it. No use to ask him.

If you've never been crazy about thorough breds it's because you've never been around where they are much and don't know any better. They're beautiful. There isn't anything so lovely and clean and full of spunk and honest and everything as some race horses. On the big horse farms that are all around our town Beckersville there are tracks and the horses run in the early morning. More than a thousand times I've got out of bed before daylight and walked two or three miles to the tracks. Mother wouldn't of let me go but father always says, "Let him alone." So I got some bread out of the bread box and some butter and jam, gobbled it and lit out.

At the tracks you sit on the fence with men, whites and niggers, and they chew tobacco and talk, and then the colts are brought out. It's early and the grass is covered with shiny dew and in another field a man is plowing and they are frying things in a shed where the track niggers sleep, and you know how a nigger can giggle and laugh and say things that make you laugh. A white man can't do it and some niggers can't but a track nigger can every time.

And so the colts are brought out and some are just galloped by stable boys, but almost every morning on a big track owned by a rich man who lives maybe in New York, there are always, nearly every morning, a few colts and some of the old race horses and geldings[6] and mares that are cut loose.

It brings a lump up into my throat when a horse runs. I don't mean all horses but some. I can pick them nearly every time. It's in my blood like in the blood of race-track niggers and trainers. Even when they just go slop-jogging along with a little nigger on their backs I can tell a winner. If my throat hurts and it's hard for me to swallow, that's him. He'll run like Sam Hill when you let him out. If he don't win every time it'll be a wonder and because they've got him in a pocket behind another[7] or he was pulled or got off bad at the post or something. If I wanted to be a gambler like Henry Rieback's father I could get

[5]Small hand tool with a spiral point, used for boring round holes.

[6]A male horse, castrated to make him gentle.

[7]I.e., blocked by other horses, front and sides.

rich. I know I could and Henry says so too. All I would have to do is to wait 'til that hurt comes when I see a horse and then bet every cent. That's what I would do if I wanted to be a gambler, but I don't.

When you're at the tracks in the morning—not the race tracks but the training tracks around Beckersville—you don't see a horse, the kind I've been talking about, very often, but it's nice anyway. Any thoroughbred, that is sired right and out of a good mare and trained by a man that knows how, can run. If he couldn't what would he be there for and not pulling a plow?

Well, out of the stables they come and the boys are on their backs and it's lovely to be there. You hunch down on top of the fence and itch inside you. Over in the sheds the niggers giggle and sing. Bacon is being fried and coffee made. Everything smells lovely. Nothing smells better than coffee and manure and horses and niggers and bacon frying and pipes being smoked out of doors on a morning like that. It just gets you, that's what it does.

But about Saratoga. We was there six days and not a soul from home seen us and everything came off just as we wanted it to, fine weather and horses and races and all. We beat our way home and Bildad gave us a basket with fried chicken and bread and other eatables in, and I had eighteen dollars when we got back to Beckersville. Mother jawed and cried but Pop didn't say much. I told everything we done except one thing. I did and saw that alone. That's what I'm writing about. It got me upset. I think about it at night. Here it is.

At Saratoga we laid up nights in the hay in the shed Bildad had showed us and ate with the niggers early and at night when the race people had all gone away. The men from home stayed mostly in the grandstand and betting field, and didn't come out around the places where the horses are kept except to the paddocks[8] just before a race when the horses are saddled. At Saratoga they don't have paddocks under an open shed as at Lexington and Churchill Downs and other tracks down in our country, but saddle the horses right out in an open place under trees on a lawn as smooth and nice as Banker Bohon's front yard here in Beckersville. It's lovely. The horses are sweaty and nervous and shine and the men come out and smoke cigars and look at them and the trainers are there and the owners, and your heart thumps so you can hardly breathe.

Then the bugle blows for post[9] and the boys that ride come running out with their silk clothes on and you run to get a place by the fence with the niggers.

I always am wanting to be a trainer or owner, and at the risk of being seen and caught and sent home I went to the paddocks before every race. The other boys didn't but I did.

We got to Saratoga on a Friday and on Wednesday the next week the big Mullford Handicap[10] was to be run. Middlestride was in it and Sunstreak. The weather was fine and the track fast. I couldn't sleep the night before.

What had happened was that both these horses are the kind it makes my throat hurt to see. Middlestride is long and looks awkward and is a gelding. He belongs to Joe Thompson, a little owner from home who only has a half-dozen horses. The Mullford Handicap is for a mile and Middlestride can't untrack[11]

[8]Area where horses are saddled and paraded before a race.

[9]A signal to assemble horses and riders at the starting point of the race.

[10]A race in which swifter horses and riders are assigned extra weight to carry—to equalize chances of winning.

[11]Start.

fast. He goes away slow and is always way back at the half, then he begins to run and if the race is a mile and a quarter he'll just eat up everything and get there.

Sunstreak is different. He is a stallion and nervous and belongs on the biggest farm we've got in our country, the Van Riddle place that belongs to Mr. Van Riddle of New York. Sunstreak is like a girl you think about sometimes but never see. He is hard all over and lovely too. When you look at his head you want to kiss him. He is trained by Jerry Tillford who knows me and has been good to me lots of times, lets me walk into a horse's stall to look at him close and other things. There isn't anything as sweet as that horse. He stands at the post quiet and not letting on, but he is just burning up inside. Then when the barrier goes up he is off like his name, Sunstreak. It makes you ache to see him. It hurts you. He just lays down and runs like a bird dog. There can't be anything I ever see run like him except Middlestride when he gets untracked and stretches himself.

Gee! I ached to see that race and those two horses run, ached and dreaded it too. I didn't want to see either of our horses beaten. We had never sent a pair like that to the races before. Old men in Beckersville said so and the niggers said so. It was a fact.

Before the race I went over to the paddocks to see. I looked a last look at Middlestride, who isn't such a much standing in a paddock that way, then I went to see Sunstreak.

It was his day. I knew when I seen him. I forgot all about being seen myself and walked right up. All the men from Beckersville were there and no one noticed me except Jerry Tillford. He saw me and something happened. I'll tell you about that.

I was standing looking at that horse and aching. In some way, I can't tell how, I knew just how Sunstreak felt inside. He was quiet and letting the niggers rub his legs and Mr. Van Riddle himself put the saddle on, but he was just a raging torrent inside. He was like the water in the river at Niagara Falls just before it goes plunk down. That horse wasn't thinking about running. He don't have to think about that. He was just thinking about holding himself back 'til the time for the running came. I knew that. I could just in a way see right inside him. He was going to do some awful running and I knew it. He wasn't bragging or letting on much or prancing or making a fuss, but just waiting. I knew it and Jerry Tillford his trainer knew. I looked up and then that man and I looked into each other's eyes. Something happened to me. I guess I loved the man as much as I did the horse because he knew what I knew. Seemed to me there wasn't anything in the world but that man and the horse and me. I cried and Jerry Tillford had a shine in his eyes. Then I came away to the fence to wait for the race. The horse was better than me, more steadier, and now I know better than Jerry. He was the quietest and he had to do the running.

Sunstreak ran first of course and he busted the world's record for a mile. I've seen that if I never see anything more. Everything came out just as I expected. Middlestride got left at the post and was way back and closed up to be second, just as I knew he would. He'll get a world's record too some day. They can't skin the Beckersville country on horses.

I watched the race calm because I knew what would happen. I was sure. Hanley Turner and Henry Rieback and Tom Tumberton were all more excited than me.

A funny thing had happened to me. I was thinking about Jerry Tillford the trainer and how happy he was all through the race. I liked him that afternoon even more than I ever liked my own father. I almost forgot the horses thinking that way about him. It was because of what I had seen in his eyes as he stood in the paddocks beside Sunstreak before the race started. I knew he had been watching and working with Sunstreak since the horse was a baby colt, had taught him to run and be patient and when to let himself out and not to quit, never. I knew that for him it was like a mother seeing her child do something brave or wonderful. It was the first time I ever felt for a man like that.

After the race that night I cut out from Tom and Hanley and Henry. I wanted to be by myself and I wanted to be near Jerry Tillford if I could work it. Here is what happened.

The track in Saratoga is near the edge of town. It is all polished up and trees around, the evergreen kind, and grass and everything painted and nice. If you go past the track you get to a hard road made of asphalt for automobiles, and if you go along this for a few miles there is a road turns off to a little rummy-looking farmhouse set in a yard.

That night after the race I went along that road because I had seen Jerry and some other men go that way in an automobile. I didn't expect to find them. I walked for a ways and then sat down by a fence to think. It was the direction they went in. I wanted to be as near Jerry as I could. I felt close to him. Pretty soon I went up the side road—I don't know why—and came to the rummy farmhouse. I was just lonesome to see Jerry, like wanting to see your father at night when you are a young kid. Just then an automobile came along and turned in. Jerry was in it and Henry Rieback's father, and Arthur Bedford from home, and Dave Williams and two other men I didn't know. They got out of the car and went into the house, all but Henry Rieback's father who quarreled with them and said he wouldn't go. It was only about nine o'clock, but they were all drunk and the rummy-looking farmhouse was a place for bad women to stay in. That's what it was. I crept up along a fence and looked through a window and saw.

It's what give me the fantods.[12] I can't make it out. The women in the house were all ugly mean-looking women, not nice to look at or be near. They were homely too, except one who was tall and looked a little like the gelding Middlestride, but not clean like him, but with a hard ugly mouth. She had red hair. I saw everything plain. I got up by an old rosebush by an open window and looked. The women had on loose dresses and sat around in chairs. The men came in and some sat on the women's laps. The place smelled rotten and there was rotten talk, the kind a kid hears around a livery stable in a town like Beckersville in the winter but don't ever expect to hear talked when there are women around. it was rotten. A nigger wouldn't go into such a place.

I looked at Jerry Tillford. I've told you how I had been feeling about him on account of his knowing what was going on inside of Sunstreak in the minute before he went to the post for the race in which he made a world's record.

Jerry bragged in that bad-woman house as I know Sunstreak wouldn't never have bragged. He said that he made that horse, that it was him that won the race and made the record. He lied and bragged like a fool. I never heard such silly talk.

[12]High nervous tension, a fit.

And then, what do you suppose he did! He looked at the woman in there, the one that was lean and hard-mouthed and looked a little like the gelding Middlestride, but not clean like him, and his eyes began to shine just as they did when he looked at me and at Sunstreak in the paddocks at the track in the afternoon. I stood there by the window—gee!—but I wished I hadn't gone away from the tracks, but had stayed with the boys and the niggers and the horses. The tall rotten-looking woman was between us just as Sunstreak was in the paddocks in the afternoon.

Then, all of a sudden, I began to hate that man. I wanted to scream and rush in the room and kill him. I never had such a feeling before. I was so mad clean through that I cried and my fists were doubled up so my fingernails cut my hands.

And Jerry's eyes kept shining and he waved back and forth, and then he went and kissed that woman and I crept away and went back to the tracks and to bed and didn't sleep hardly any, and then next day I got the other kids to start home with me and never told them anything I seen.

I been thinking about it ever since. I can't make it out. Spring has come again and I'm nearly sixteen and go to the tracks mornings same as always, and I see Sunstreak and Middlestride and a new colt named Strident I'll bet will lay them all out, but no one thinks so but me and two or three niggers.

But things are different. At the tracks the air don't taste as good or smell as good. It's because a man like Jerry Tillford, who knows what he does, could see a horse like Sunstreak run, and kiss a woman like that the same day. I can't make it out. Darn him, what did he want to do like that for? I keep thinking about it and it spoils looking at horses and smelling things and hearing niggers laugh and everything. Sometimes I'm so mad about it I want to fight someone. It gives me the fantods. What did he do it for? I want to know why.

1921

from *WINESBURG, OHIO*

THE BOOK OF THE GROTESQUE

The writer, an old man with a white mustache, had some difficulty in getting into bed. The windows of the house in which he lived were high and he wanted to look at the trees when he awoke in the morning. A carpenter came to fix the bed so that it would be on a level with the window.

Quite a fuss was made about the matter. The carpenter, who had been a soldier in the Civil War, came into the writer's room and sat down to talk of building a platform for the purpose of raising the bed. The writer had cigars lying about and the carpenter smoked.

For a time the two men talked of the raising of the bed and then they talked of other things. The soldier got on the subject of the war. The writer, in fact, led him to that subject. The carpenter had once been a prisoner in Andersonville prison[1] and had lost a brother. The brother had died of starvation, and

[1]A Confederate prison, located in Andersonville, Georgia, notorious for the extreme hardships that the Union prisoners endured.

whenever the carpenter got upon that subject he cried. He, like the old writer, had a white mustache, and when he cried he puckered up his lips and the mustache bobbed up and down. The weeping old man with the cigar in his mouth was ludicrous. The plan the writer had for the raising of his bed was forgotten and later the carpenter did it in his own way and the writer, who was past sixty, had to help himself with a chair when he went to bed at night.

In his bed the writer rolled over on his side and lay quite still. For years he had been beset with notions concerning his heart. He was a hard smoker and his heart fluttered. The idea had got into his mind that he would some time die unexpectedly and always when he got into bed he thought of that. It did not alarm him. The effect in fact was quite a special thing and not easily explained. It made him more alive, there in bed, than at any other time. Perfectly still he lay and his body was old and not of much use any more, but something inside him was altogether young. He was like a pregnant woman, only that the thing inside him was not a baby but a youth. No, it wasn't a youth, it was a woman, young, and wearing a coat of mail like a knight. It is absurd, you see, to try to tell what was inside the old writer as he lay on his high bed and listened to the fluttering of his heart. The thing to get at is what the writer, or the young thing within the writer, was thinking about.

The old writer, like all of the people in the world, had got, during his long life, a great many notions in his head. He had once been quite handsome and a number of women had been in love with him. And then, of course, he had known people, many people, known them in a peculiarly intimate way that was different from the way in which you and I know people. At least that is what the writer thought and the thought pleased him. Why quarrel with an old man concerning his thoughts?

In the bed the writer had a dream that was not a dream. As he grew somewhat sleepy but was still conscious, figures began to appear before his eyes. He imagined the young indescribable thing within himself was driving a long procession of figures before his eyes.

You see the interest in all this lies in the figures that went before the eyes of the writer. They were all grotesques. All of the men and women the writer had ever known had become grotesques.

The grotesques were not all horrible. Some were amusing, some almost beautiful, and one, a woman all drawn out of shape, hurt the old man by her grotesqueness. When she passed he made a noise like a small dog whimpering. Had you come into the room you might have supposed the old man had unpleasant dreams or perhaps indigestion.

For an hour the procession of grotesques passed before the eyes of the old man, and then, although it was a painful thing to do, he crept out of bed and began to write. Some one of the grotesques had made a deep impression on his mind and he wanted to describe it.

At his desk the writer worked for an hour. In the end he wrote a book which he called "The Book of the Grotesque." It was never published, but I saw it once and it made an indelible impression on my mind. The book had one central thought that is very strange and has always remained with me. By remembering it I have been able to understand many people and things that I was never able to understand before. The thought was involved but a simple statement of it would be something like this:

That in the beginning when the world was young there were a great many thoughts but no such thing as a truth. Man made the truths himself and each truth was a composite of a great many vague thoughts. All about in the world were the truths and they were all beautiful.

The old man had listed hundreds of the truths in his book. I will not try to tell you of all of them. There was the truth of virginity and the truth of passion, the truth of wealth and of poverty, of thrift and of profligacy, of carelessness and abandon. Hundreds and hundreds were the truths and they were all beautiful.

And then the people came along. Each as he appeared snatched up one of the truths and some who were quite strong snatched up a dozen of them.

It was the truths that made the people grotesques. The old man had quite an elaborate theory concerning the matter. It was his notion that the moment one of the people took one of the truths to himself, called it his truth, and tried to live his life by it, he became a grotesque and the truth he embraced became a falsehood.

You can see for yourself how the old man, who had spent all of his life writing and was filled with words, would write hundreds of pages concerning this matter. The subject would become so big in his mind that he himself would be in danger of becoming a grotesque. He didn't, I suppose, for the same reason that he never published the book. It was the young thing inside him that saved the old man.

Concerning the old carpenter who fixed the bed for the writer, I only mentioned him because he, like many of what are called very common people, became the nearest thing to what is understandable and lovable of all the grotesques in the writer's book.

1919

HANDS

Upon the half decayed veranda of a small frame house that stood near the edge of a ravine near the town of Winesburg, Ohio, a fat little old man walked nervously up and down. Across a long field that had been seeded for clover but that had produced only a dense crop of yellow mustard weeds, he could see the public highway along which went a wagon filled with berry pickers returning from the fields. The berry pickers, youths and maidens, laughed and shouted boisterously. A boy clad in a blue shirt leaped from the wagon and attempted to drag after him one of the maidens, who screamed and protested shrilly. The feet of the boy in the road kicked up a cloud of dust that floated across the face of the departing sun. Over the long field came a thin girlish voice. "Oh, you Wing Biddlebaum, comb your hair, it's falling into your eyes," commanded the voice to the man, who was bald and whose nervous little hands fiddled about the bare white forehead as though arranging a mass of tangled locks.

Wing Biddlebaum, forever frightened and beset by a ghostly band of doubts, did not think of himself as in any way a part of the life of the town where he had lived for twenty years. Among all the people of Winesburg but one had come close to him. With George Willard, son of Tom Willard, the proprietor of the

New Willard House, he had formed something like a friendship. George Willard was the reporter on the *Winesburg Eagle* and sometimes in the evenings he walked out along the highway to Wing Biddlebaum's house. Now as the old man walked up and down on the veranda, his hands moving nervously about, he was hoping that George Willard would come and spend the evening with him. After the wagon containing the berry pickers had passed, he went across the field through the tall mustard weeds and climbing a rail fence peered anxiously along the road to the town. For a moment he stood thus, rubbing his hands together and looking up and down the road, and then, fear overcoming him, ran back to walk again upon the porch on his own house.

In the presence of George Willard, Wing Biddlebaum, who for twenty years had been the town mystery, lost something of his timidity, and his shadowy personality, submerged in a sea of doubts, came forth to look at the world. With the young reporter at his side, he ventured in the light of day into Main Street or strode up and down on the rickety front porch of his own house, talking excitedly. The voice that had been low and trembling became shrill and loud. The bent figure straightened. With a kind of wriggle, like a fish returned to the brook by the fisherman, Biddlebaum the silent began to talk, striving to put into words the ideas that had been accumulated by his mind during long years of silence.

Wing Biddlebaum talked much with his hands. The slender expressive fingers, forever active, forever striving to conceal themselves in his pockets or behind his back, came forth and became the piston rods of his machinery of any expression.

The story of Wing Biddlebaum is a story of hands. Their restless activity, like unto the beating of the wings of an imprisoned bird, had given him his name. Some obscure poet of the town had thought of it. The hands alarmed their owner. He wanted to keep them hidden away and looked with amazement at the quiet inexpressive hands of other men who worked beside him in the fields, or passed, driving sleepy teams on country roads.

When he talked to George Willard, Wing Biddlebaum closed his fists and beat with them upon a table or on the walls of his house. The action made him more comfortable. If the desire to talk came to him when the two were walking in the fields, he sought out a stump or the top board of a fence and with his hands pounding busily talked with renewed ease.

The story of Wing Biddlebaum's hands is worth a book in itself. Sympathetically set forth it would tap many strange, beautiful qualities in obscure men. It is a job for a poet. In Winesburg the hands had attracted attention merely because of their activity. With them Wing Biddlebaum had picked as high as a hundred and forty quarts of strawberries in a day. They became his distinguishing feature, the source of his fame. Also they made more grotesque an already grotesque and elusive individuality. Winesburg was proud of the hands of Wing Biddlebaum in the same spirit in which it was proud of Banker White's new stone house and Wesley Moyer's bay stallion, Tony Tip, that had won the two-fifteen trot at the fall races in Cleveland.

As for George Willard, he had many times wanted to ask about the hands. At times an almost overwhelming curiosity had taken hold of him. He felt that there must be a reason for their strange activity and their inclination to keep hidden away and only a growing respect for Wing Biddlebaum kept him from blurting out the questions that were often in his mind.

Once he had been on the point of asking. The two were walking in the fields on a summer afternoon and had stopped to sit upon a grassy bank. All afternoon Wing Biddlebaum had talked as one inspired. By a fence he had stopped and beating like a giant woodpecker upon the top board had shouted at George Willard, condemning his tendency to be too much influenced by the people about him, "You are destroying yourself," he cried. "You have the inclination to be alone and to dream and you are afraid of dreams. You want to be like others in town here. You hear them talk and you try to imitate them."

On the grassy bank Wing Biddlebaum had tried again to drive his point home. His voice became soft and reminiscent, and with a sigh of contentment he launched into a long rambling talk, speaking as one lost in a dream.

Out of the dream Wing Biddlebaum made a picture for George Willard. In the picture men lived again in a kind of pastoral golden age. Across a green open country came clean-limbed young men, some afoot, some mounted upon horses. In crowds the young men came to gather about the feet of an old man who sat beneath a tree in a tiny garden and who talked to them.

Wing Biddlebaum became wholly inspired. For once he forgot the hands. Slowly they stole forth and lay upon George Willard's shoulders. Something new and bold came into the voice that talked. "You must try to forget all you have learned," said the old man. "You must begin to dream. From this time on you must shut your ears to the roaring of the voices."

Pausing in his speech, Wing Biddlebaum looked long and earnestly at George Willard. His eyes glowed. Again he raised the hands to caress the boy and then a look of horror swept over his face.

With a convulsive movement of his body, Wing Biddlebaum sprang to his feet and thrust his hands deep into his trousers pockets. Tears came to his eyes. "I must be getting along home. I can talk no more with you," he said nervously.

Without looking back, the old man had hurried down the hillside and across a meadow, leaving George Willard perplexed and frightened upon the grassy slope. With a shiver of dread the boy arose and went along the road toward town. "I'll not ask him about his hands," he thought, touched by the memory of the terror he had seen in the man's eyes. "There's something wrong, but I don't want to know what it is. His hands have something to do with his fear of me and of everyone."

And George Willard was right. Let us look briefly into the story of the hands. Perhaps our talking of them will arouse the poet who will tell the hidden wonder story of the influence for which the hands were but fluttering pennants of promise.

In his youth Wing Biddlebaum had been a school teacher in a town in Pennsylvania. He was not then known as Wing Biddlebaum, but went by the less euphonic name of Adolph Myers. As Adolph Myers he was much loved by the boys of his school.

Adolph Myers was meant by nature to be a teacher of youth. He was one of those rare, little-understood men who rule by a power so gentle that it passes as a lovable weakness. In their feeling for the boys under their charge such men are not unlike the finer sort of women in their love of men.

And yet that is but crudely stated. It needs the poet there. With the boys of his school, Adolph Myers had walked in the evening or had sat talking until dusk upon the schoolhouse steps lost in a kind of dream. Here and there went his hands, caressing the shoulders of the boys, playing about the tousled heads.

As he talked his voice became soft and musical. There was a caress in that also. In a way the voice and the hands, the stroking of the shoulders and the touching of the hair were a part of the schoolmaster's effort to carry a dream into the young minds. By the caress that was in his fingers he expressed himself. He was one of those men in whom the force that creates life is diffused, not centralized. Under the caress of his hands doubt and disbelief went out of the minds of the boys and they began also to dream.

And then the tragedy. A half-witted boy of the school became enamored of the young master. In his bed at night he imagined unspeakable things and in the morning went forth to tell his dreams as facts. Strange, hideous accusations fell from his loose-hung lips. Through the Pennsylvania town went a shiver. Hidden, shadowy doubts that had been in men's minds concerning Adolph Myers were galvanized into beliefs.

The tragedy did not linger. Trembling lads were jerked out of bed and questioned. "He put his arms about me," said one. "His fingers were always playing in my hair," said another.

One afternoon a man of the town, Henry Bradford, who kept a saloon, came to the schoolhouse door. Calling Adolph Myers into the school yard he began to beat him with his fists. As his hard knuckles beat down into the frightened face of the school-master, his wrath became more and more terrible. Screaming with dismay, the children ran here and there like disturbed insects. "I'll teach you to put your hands on my boy, you beast," roared the saloon keeper, who, tired of beating the master, had begun to kick him about the yard.

Adolph Myers was driven from the Pennsylvania town in the night. With lanterns in their hands a dozen men came to the door of the house where he lived alone and commanded that he dress and come forth. It was raining and one of the men had a rope in his hands. They had intended to hang the schoolmaster, but something in his figure, so small, white, and pitiful, touched their hearts and they let him escape. As he ran away into the darkness they repented of their weakness and ran after him, swearing and throwing sticks and great balls of soft mud at the figure that screamed and ran faster and faster into the darkness.

For twenty years Adolph Myers had lived alone in Winesburg. He was but forty but looked sixty-five. The name of Biddlebaum he got from a box of goods seen at a freight station as he hurried through an eastern Ohio town. He had an aunt in Winesburg, a black-toothed old woman who raised chickens, and with her he lived until she died. He had been ill for a year after the experience in Pennsylvania, and after his recovery worked as a day laborer in the fields, going timidly about and striving to conceal his hands. Although he did not understand what had happened he felt that the hands must be to blame. Again and again the fathers of the boys had talked of the hands. "Keep your hands to yourself," the saloon keeper had roared, dancing, with fury in the schoolhouse yard.

Upon the veranda of his house by the ravine, Wing Biddlebaum continued to walk up and down until the sun had disappeared and the road beyond the field was lost in the grey shadows. Going into his house he cut slices of bread and spread honey upon them. When the rumble of the evening train that took away the express cars loaded with the day's harvest of berries had passed and restored the silence of the summer night, he went again to walk upon the veranda. In the darkness he could not see the hands and they became quiet.

Although he still hungered for the presence of the boy, who was the medium through which he expressed his love of man, the hunger became again a part of his loneliness and his waiting. Lighting a lamp, Wing Biddlebaum washed the few dishes soiled by his simple meal and, setting up a folding cot by the screen door that led to the porch, prepared to undress for the night. A few stray white bread crumbs lay on the cleanly washed floor by the table; putting the lamp upon a low stool he began to pick up the crumbs, carrying them to his mouth one by one with unbelievable rapidity. In the dense blotch of light beneath the table, the kneeling figure looked like a priest engaged in some service of his church. The nervous expressive fingers, flashing in and out of the light, might well have been mistaken for the fingers of the devotee going swiftly through decade after decade of his rosary.

1919

MOTHER

Elizabeth Willard, the mother of George Willard, was tall and gaunt and her face was marked with smallpox scars. Although she was but forty-five, some obscure disease had taken the fire out of her figure. Listlessly she went about the disorderly old hotel looking at the faded wall-paper and the ragged carpets and, when she was able to be about, doing the work of a chambermaid among beds soiled by the slumbers of fat traveling men. Her husband, Tom Willard, a slender, graceful man with square shoulders, a quick military step, and a black mustache trained to turn sharply up at the ends, tried to put the wife out of his mind. The presence of the tall ghostly figure, moving slowly through the halls, he took as a reproach to himself. When he thought of her he grew angry and swore. The hotel was unprofitable and forever on the edge of failure and he wished himself out of it. He thought of the old house and the woman who lived there with him as things defeated and done for. The hotel in which he had begun life so hopefully was now a mere ghost of what a hotel should be. As he went spruce and business-like through the streets of Winesburg, he sometimes stopped and turned quickly about as though fearing that the spirit of the hotel and of the woman would follow him even into the streets. "Damn such a life, damn it!" he sputtered aimlessly.

Tom Willard had a passion for village politics and for years had been the leading Democrat in a strongly Republican community. Some day, he told himself, the tide of things political will turn in my favor and the years of ineffectual service count big in the bestowal of rewards. He dreamed of going to Congress and even of becoming governor. Once when a younger member of the party arose at a political conference and began to boast of his faithful service, Tom Willard grew white with fury. "Shut up, you," he roared, glaring about. "What do you know of service? What are you but a boy? Look at what I've done here! I was a Democrat here in Winesburg when it was a crime to be a Democrat. In the old days they fairly hunted us with guns."

Between Elizabeth and her one son George there was a deep unexpressed bond of sympathy, based on a girlhood dream that had long ago died. In the son's presence she was timid and reserved, but sometimes while he hurried about town intent upon his duties as a reporter, she went into his room and closing the door knelt by a little desk, made of a kitchen table, that sat near a window. In the room by the desk she went through a ceremony that was half a prayer, half a demand, addressed to the skies. In the boyish figure she yearned to see something half forgotten that had once been a part of herself recreated. The prayer concerned that. "Even though I die, I will in some way keep defeat from you," she cried, and so deep was her determination that her whole body shook. Her eyes glowed and she clenched her fists. "If I am dead and see him becoming a meaningless drab figure like myself, I will come back," she declared. "I ask God now to give me that privilege. I demand it. I will pay for it. God may beat me with his fists. I will take any blow that may befall if but this my boy be allowed to express something for us both." Pausing uncertainly, the woman stared about the boy's room. "And do not let him become smart and successful either," she added vaguely.

The communion between George Willard and his mother was outwardly a formal thing without meaning. When she was ill and sat by the window in her room he sometimes went in the evening to make her a visit. They sat by a window that looked over the roof of a small frame building into Main Street. By turning their heads they could see through another window, along an alleyway that ran behind the Main Street stores and into the back door of Abner Groff's bakery. Sometimes as they sat thus a picture of village life presented itself to them. At the back door of his shop appeared Abner Groff with a stick or an empty milk bottle in his hand. For a long time there was a feud between the baker and a grey cat that belonged to Sylvester West, the druggist. The boy and his mother saw the cat creep into the door of the bakery and presently emerge followed by the baker, who swore and waved his arms about. The baker's eyes were small and red and his black hair and beard were filled with flour dust. Sometimes he was so angry that, although the cat had disappeared, he hurled sticks, bits of broken glass, and even some of the tools of his trade about. Once he broke a window at the back of Sinning's Hardware Store. In the alley the grey cat crouched behind barrels filled with torn paper and broken bottles above which flew a black swarm of flies. Once when she was alone, and after watching a prolonged and ineffectual outburst on the part of the baker, Elizabeth Willard put her head down on her long white hands and wept. After that she did not look along the alleyway any more, but tried to forget the contest between the bearded man and the cat. It seemed like a rehearsal of her own life, terrible in its vividness.

In the evening when the son sat in the room with his mother, the silence made them both feel awkward. Darkness came on and the evening train came in at the station. In the street below feet tramped up and down upon a board sidewalk. In the station yard, after the evening train had gone, there was a heavy silence. Perhaps Skinner Leason, the express agent, moved a truck the length of the station platform. Over on Main Street sounded a man's voice, laughing. The door of the express office banged. George Willard arose and crossing the room fumbled for the doorknob. Sometimes he knocked against a chair, making it scrape along the floor. By the window sat the sick woman, perfectly still, listless. Her long hands, white and bloodless, could be seen drooping over the ends of the arms of the chair. "I think you had better be out among the boys. You are too much indoors," she said, striving to relieve the embarrassment of the departure. "I thought I would take a walk," replied George Willard, who felt awkward and confused.

One evening in July, when the transient guests who made the New Willard House their temporary home had become scarce, and the hallways, lighted only by kerosene lamps turned low, were plunged in gloom, Elizabeth Willard had an adventure. She had been ill in bed for several days and her son had not come to visit her. She was alarmed. The feeble blaze of life that remained in her body was blown into a flame by her anxiety and she crept out of bed, dressed and hurried along the hallway toward her son's room, shaking with exaggerated fears. As she went along she steadied herself with her hand, slipped along the papered walls of the hall and breathed with difficulty. The air whistled through her teeth. As she hurried forward she thought how foolish she was. "He is concerned with boyish affairs," she told herself. "Perhaps he has now begun to walk about in the evening with girls."

Elizabeth Willard had a dread of being seen by guests in the hotel that had once belonged to her father and the ownership of which still stood recorded in her name in the county courthouse. The hotel was continually losing patronage because of its shabbiness and she thought of herself as also shabby. Her own room was in an obscure corner and when she felt able to work she voluntarily worked among the beds, preferring the labor that could be done when the guests were abroad seeking trade among the merchants of Winesburg.

By the door of her son's room the mother knelt upon the floor and listened for some sound from within. When she heard the boy moving about and talking in low tones a smile came to her lips. George Willard had a habit of talking aloud to himself and to hear him doing so had always given his mother a peculiar pleasure. The habit in him, she felt, strengthened the secret bond that existed between them. A thousand times she had whispered to herself of the matter. "He is groping about, trying to find himself," she thought. "He is not a dull clod, all words and smartness. Within him there is a secret something that is striving to grow. It is the thing I let be killed in myself."

In the darkness in the hallway by the door the sick woman arose and started again toward her own room. She was afraid that the door would open and the boy come upon her. When she had reached a safe distance and was about to turn a corner into a second hallway she stopped and bracing herself with her hands waited, thinking to shake off a trembling fit of weakness that had come upon her. The presence of the boy in the room had made her happy. In her bed, during the long hours alone, the little fears that had visited her had become giants. Now they were all gone. "When I get back to my room I shall sleep," she murmured gratefully.

But Elizabeth Willard was not to return to her bed and to sleep. As she stood trembling in the darkness the door of her son's room opened and the boy's father, Tom Willard, stepped out. In the light that steamed out at the door he stood with the knob in his hand and talked. What he said infuriated the woman.

Tom Willard was ambitious for his son. He had always thought of himself as a successful man, although nothing he had ever done had turned out successfully. However, when he was out of sight of the New Willard House and had no fear of coming upon his wife, he swaggered and began to dramatize himself as one of the chief men of the town. He wanted his son to succeed. He it was who had secured for the boy the position on the *Winesburg Eagle*. Now, with a ring of earnestness in his voice, he was advising concerning some course of conduct. "I tell you what, George, you've got to wake up," he said sharply. "Will Henderson has spoken to me three times concerning the matter. He says you go along for hours not hearing when you are spoken to and acting like a gawky girl. What ails you?" Tom Willard laughed good-naturedly. "Well, I guess you'll get over it," he said. "I told Will that. You're not a fool and you're not a woman. You're Tom Willard's son and you'll wake up. I'm not afraid. What you say clears things up. If being a newspaper man had put the notion of becoming a writer into your mind that's all right. Only I guess you'll have to wake up to do that too, eh?"

Tom Willard went briskly along the hallway and down a flight of stairs to the office. The woman in the darkness could hear him laughing and talking with a guest who was striving to wear away a dull evening by dozing in a chair by the office door. She returned to the door of her son's room. The weakness had passed from her body as by a miracle and she stepped boldly along. A thousand ideas raced through her head. When she heard the scraping of a chair and the sound of a pen scratching upon paper, she again turned and went back along the hallway to her own room.

A definite determination had come into the mind of the defeated wife of the Winesburg hotel keeper. The determination was the result of long years of quiet and rather ineffectual thinking. "Now," she told herself, "I will act. There is something threatening my boy and I will ward it off." The fact that the conversation between Tom Willard and his son had been rather quiet and natural, as though an understanding existed between them, maddened her. Although for years she had hated her husband, her hatred had always before been a quite impersonal thing. He had been merely a part of something else that she hated. Now, and by the few words at the door, he had become the thing personified. In the darkness of her own room she clenched her fists and glared about. Going to a cloth bag that hung on a nail by the wall she took out a long pair of sewing scissors and held them in her hand like a dagger. "I will stab him," she said aloud. "He has chosen to be the voice of evil and I will kill him. When I have killed him something will snap within myself and I will die also. I will be a release for all of us."

In her girlhood and before her marriage with Tom Willard, Elizabeth had borne a somewhat shaky reputation in Winesburg. For years she had been what is called "stage-struck" and had paraded through the streets with traveling men guests at her father's hotel, wearing loud clothes and urging them to tell her of life in the cities out of which they had come. Once she startled the town by putting on men's clothes and riding a bicycle down Main Street.

In her own mind the tall dark girl had been in those days much confused. A great restlessness was in her and it expressed itself in two ways. First there was an uneasy desire for change, for some big definite movement to her life. It was this feeling that had turned her mind to the stage. She dreamed of joining some company and wandering over the world, seeing always new faces and giving something out of herself to all people. Sometimes at night she was quite beside herself with the thought, but when she tried to talk of the matter to the members of the theatrical companies that came to Winesburg and stopped at her father's hotel, she got nowhere. They did not seem to know what she meant, or if she did get something of her passion expressed, they only laughed. "It's not like that," they said. "It's as dull and uninteresting as this here. Nothing comes of it."

With the traveling men when she walked about with them, and later with Tom Willard, it was quite different. Always they seemed to understand and sympathize with her. On the side streets of the village, in the darkness under the trees, they took hold of her hand and she thought that something unexpressed in herself came forth and became a part of an unexpressed something in them.

And then there was the second expression of her restlessness. When that came she felt for a time released and happy. She did not blame the men who walked with her and later she did not blame Tom Willard. It was always the same, beginning with kisses and ending, after strange wild emotions, with peace and then sobbing repentance. When she sobbed she put her hand upon the face of the man and had always the same thought. Even though he were large and bearded she thought he had become suddenly a little boy. She wondered why he did not sob also.

In her room, tucked away in a corner of the old Willard House, Elizabeth Willard lighted a lamp and put it on a dressing table that stood by the door. A thought had come into her mind and she went to a closet and brought out a small square box and set it on the table. The box contained material for make-up and had been left with other things by a theatrical company that had once been stranded in Winesburg. Elizabeth Willard had decided that she would be beautiful. Her hair was still black and there was a great mass of it braided and coiled about her head. The scene that was to take place in the office below began to grow in her mind. No ghostly worn-out figure should confront Tom Willard, but something quite unexpected and startling. Tall and with dusky cheeks and hair that fell in a mass from her shoulders, a figure should come striding down the stairway before the startled loungers in the hotel office. The figure it would be silent—it would be swift and terrible. As a tigress whose cub had been threatened would she appear, coming out of the shadows, stealing noiselessly along and holding the long wicked scissors in her hand.

With a little broken sob in her throat, Elizabeth Willard blew out the light that stood upon the table and stood weak and trembling in the darkness. The strength that had been as a miracle in her body left and she half reeled across the floor, clutching at the back of the chair in which she had spent so many long days staring out over the tin roofs into the main street of Winesburg. In the hallway there was the sound of footsteps and George Willard came in at the door. Sitting in a chair beside his mother he began to talk. "I'm going to get out of here," he said. "I don't know where I shall go or what I shall do but I am going away."

The woman in the chair waited and trembled. An impulse came to her. "I suppose you had better wake up," she said. "You think that? You will go to the city and make money, eh? It will be better for you, you think, to be a business man, to be brisk and smart and alive?" She waited and trembled.

The son shook his head. "I suppose I can't make you understand, but oh, I wish I could," he said earnestly. "I can't even talk to father about it. I don't try. There isn't any use. I don't know what I shall do. I just want to go away and look at people and think."

Silence fell upon the room where the boy and woman sat together. Again, as on the other evenings, they were embarrassed. After a time the boy tried again to talk. "I suppose it won't be for a year or two but I've been thinking about it," he said, rising and going toward the door. "Something father said makes it sure that I shall have to go away." He fumbled with the doorknob. In the room the silence became unbearable to the woman. She wanted to cry out with joy because of the words that had come from the lips of her son, but the expression of joy had become impossible to her. "I think you had better go out among the boys. You are too much indoors," she said. "I thought I would go for a little walk," replied the son stepping awkwardly out of the room and closing the door.

1919

TANDY

Until she was seven years old she lived in an old unpainted house on an unused road that led off Trunion Pike. Her father gave her but little attention and her mother was dead. The father spent his time talking and thinking of religion. He proclaimed himself an agnostic and was so absorbed in destroying the ideas of God that had crept into the minds of his neighbors that he never saw God manifesting himself in the little child that, half forgotten, lived here and there on the bounty of her dead mother's relatives.

A stranger came to Winesburg and saw in the child what the father did not see. He was a tall, redhaired young man who was almost always drunk. Sometimes he sat in a chair before the New Willard House with Tom Hard, the father. As Tom talked, declaring there could be no God, the stranger smiled and winked at the bystanders. He and Tom became friends and were much together.

The stranger was the son of a rich merchant of Cleveland and had come to Winesburg on a mission. He wanted to cure himself of the habit of drink, and thought that by escaping from his city associates and living in a rural community he would have a better chance in the struggle with the appetite that was destroying him.

His sojourn in Winesburg was not a success. The dullness of the passing hours led to his drinking harder than ever. But he did succeed in doing something. He gave a name rich with meaning to Tom Hard's daughter.

One evening when he was recovering from a long debauch the stranger came reeling along the main street of the town. Tom Hard sat in a chair before the New Willard House with his daughter, then a child of five, on his knees. Beside him on the board sidewalk sat young George Willard. The stranger dropped into a chair beside them. His body shook and when he tried to talk his voice trembled.

It was late evening and darkness lay over the town and over the railroad that ran along the foot of a little incline before the hotel. Somewhere in the distance, off to the west, there was a prolonged blast from the whistle of a passenger engine. A dog that had been sleeping in the roadway arose and barked. The stranger began to babble and made a prophecy concerning the child that lay in the arms of the agnostic.

"I came here to quit drinking," he said, and tears began to run down his cheeks. He did not look at Tom Hard, but leaned forward and stared into the darkness as though seeing a vision. "I ran away to the country to be cured, but

I am not cured. There is a reason." He turned to look at the child who sat up very straight on her father's knee and returned the look.

The stranger touched Tom Hard on the arm. "Drink is not the only thing to which I am addicted," he said. "There is something else. I am a lover and have not found my thing to love. That is a big point if you know enough to realize what I mean. It makes my destruction inevitable, you see. There are few who understand that."

The stranger became silent and seemed overcome with sadness, but another blast from the whistle of the passenger engine aroused him. "I have not lost faith. I proclaim that. I have only been brought to the place where I know my faith will not be realized," he declared hoarsely. He looked hard at the child and began to address her, paying no more attention to the father. "There is a woman coming," he said, and his voice was now sharp and earnest. "I have missed her, you see. She did not come in my time. You may be the woman. It would be like fate to let me stand in her presence once, on such an evening as this, when I have destroyed myself with drink and she is as yet only a child."

The shoulders of the stranger shook violently, and when he tried to roll a cigarette the paper fell from his trembling fingers. He grew angry and scolded. "They think it's easy to be a woman, to be loved, but I know better," he declared. Again he turned to the child. "I understand," he cried. "Perhaps of all men I alone understand."

His glance again wandered away to the darkened street. "I know about her, although she has never crossed my path," he said softly. "I know about her struggles and her defeats. It is because of her defeats that she is to me the lovely one. Out of her defeats has been born a new quality in woman. I have a name for it. I call it Tandy. I made up the name when I was a true dreamer and before my body became vile. It is the quality of being strong to be loved. It is something men need from women and that they do not get."

The stranger arose and stood before Tom Hard. His body rocked back and forth and he seemed about to fall, but instead he dropped to his knees on the sidewalk and raised the hands of the little girl to his drunken lips. He kissed them ecstatically. "Be Tandy, little one," he pleaded. "Dare to be strong and courageous. That is the road. Venture anything. Be brave enough to dare to be loved. Be something more than man or woman. Be Tandy."

The stranger arose and staggered off down the street. A day or two later he got aboard a train and returned to his home in Cleveland. On the summer evening, after the talk before the hotel, Tom Hard took the girl child to the house of a relative where she had been invited to spend the night. As he went along in the darkness under the trees he forgot the babbling voice of the stranger and his mind returned to the making of arguments by which he might destroy men's faith in God. He spoke his daughter's name and she began to weep.

"I don't want to be called that," she declared. "I want to be called Tandy—Tandy Hard." The child wept so bitterly that Tom Hard was touched and tried to comfort her. He stopped beneath a tree and, taking her into his arms, began to caress her. "Be good, now," he said sharply; but she would not be quieted. With childish abandon she gave herself over to grief, her voice breaking the evening stillness of the street. "I want to be Tandy. I want to be Tandy. I want to be Tandy Hard," she cried, shaking her head and sobbing as though her young strength were not enough to bear the vision the words of the drunkard had brought to her.

1919

John Dos Passos 1896–1970

In 1917, John Dos Passos called himself "red, radical and revolutionary." Over the next decades he wrote novels, plays, and news stories that attacked capitalism, big business, and big government. Editors of popular journals considered his work too radical to be published in their magazines. He wrote instead for the communist journal New Masses*—but he did so, he later said, not to support communism but because he wanted to give voice to his own "pacifist radical tendency."*

Dos Passos consistently spoke out for the underdog, for the laboring men and women of America, the oppressed, the impoverished. He saw the United States as divided into two nations: those who are well-to-do and those who do without. But by the early 1930s Dos Passos's political views had begun to shift. By 1937, he could write that the Communist Party was "fundamentally opposed to our democracy" and that Marxism was a "reactionary force and an impediment to progress."

As the years passed, Dos Passos seemed to move ever more to the right. He became a contributor to publications in the United States that espoused the conservative cause. His former hatred of business turned to admiration; his defense of organized labor changed to sharp attack. In his last years he supported American involvement in Vietnam and spoke out against the "hysteria" of those who objected to the war. Dos Passos seemed to be a classic example of the young radical who becomes more and more conservative as he grows older and richer. But from another perspective, his entire career may be seen not as a shift from political left to right but as an obstinate defense of the individual against whatever giant impersonal system Dos Passos believed at the time to be most threatening.

Few American writers have attempted to create such a broad picture of the social and political nature of the United States. Dos Passos depicts the nation in its passage through extraordinary events: wars, depressions, political upheavals. And through these events he maintains the same focus: that of a man with a deep concern for his native land. Dos Passos was born in Chicago in 1896, the grandson of an impoverished Portuguese immigrant. His father, a successful corporation lawyer, could provide his son with European travel, send him to fashionable prep schools and then to Harvard. In 1916, after graduating from college, Dos Passos went to Spain to study art and architecture. The next year he left his studies to serve as a volunteer ambulance driver for the Red Cross in France and Italy during the First World War.

When the war ended Dos Passos set out to make his way as a journalist. He became deeply involved with the crucial political and social issues of the day: He reported on the Sacco and Vanzetti case and the Great Depression of the 1930s; he wrote articles on the suffering of exploited peasants in Mexico and described labor battles between large corporations and striking coal miners in Kentucky. For fifty years, from 1920 to 1970, Dos Passos continually wrote on the social and political events that profoundly shaped modern-day America. He was the author of histories, travel books, essays, and a dozen noteworthy novels, beginning with One Man's Initiation *(1917),* Three Soldiers *(1921), and* Manhattan Transfer *(1925).*

His greatest achievement was writing three novels that make up the trilogy U.S.A.: The 42nd Parallel *(1930),* 1919 *(1932), and* The Big Money *(1936). They were a penetrating depiction of the disillusionment that followed the First World War. Called "collective novels" because they showed men and women in the mass, they presented a vast panorama of American society. Dos Passos portrayed the rapidly shifting scenes and the endless variety of life in America. He used new narrative techniques derived from impressionistic art, from experimental cinema, and from "stream of consciousness" novels that presented the flow of thought in the human mind. He interrupted the narratives with insertions of capsule biographies, "Camera Eyes," and "Newsreels," using "quick-flash" techniques—blending pieces of news stories, song lyrics, and newspaper headlines.*

From his writing a central image emerges: the individual dwarfed by the size and power of society—the common man, the solitary figure battling against what Dos Passos called "the Leviathan State." Dos Passos defined himself as an observer. He attempted to report accurately what he saw, not what ought to be. His view of life was harsh, unsentimental, and critics have called his writing a "fiction of despair." He created a portrait of the nation by describing its ordinary citizens, but he did not assume an inevitable triumph for the common man. He believed that in a world of materialism and conflict no final triumph is possible, that at best a tolerable equilibrium might be maintained, but only with unceasing resistance to all ideas and all powers that would promise to improve the lot of men and women at the cost of their liberties.

FURTHER READING: J. Wrenn, *John Dos Passos,* 1961; R. Davis, *John Dos Passos,* 1962; J. Brantley, *The Fiction of John Dos Passos,* 1968; *Dos Passos: The Critics, and the Writer's Intention,* ed. A. Belkind, 1971; M. Landsberg, *Dos Passos' Path to U.S.A.: A Political Biography, 1912–1936,* 1972; *Dos Passos: A Collection of Critical Essays,* ed. A Hook, 1974; G. Becker, *John Dos Passos,* 1974; I. Colley, *Dos Passos and the Fiction of Despair,* 1978; L. Wagner, *Dos Passos: Artist as American,* 1979; T. Ludington, *John Dos Passos: A Twentieth-Century Odyssey,* 1980; R. Rosen, *John Dos Passos: Politics and the Writer,* 1981; V. Carr, *Dos Passos: A Life,* 1984; M. Clark, *Dos Passos's Early Fiction,* 1987; D. Pizer, *Dos Passos' U.S.A.: A Critical Study,* 1988; *Dos Passos: The Critical Heritage,* ed. B. Maine, 1988; M. Clark, *Dos Passos's Early Fiction, 1912–1938,* 1990; J. Casey, *Dos Passos and the Ideology of the Feminine,* 1998; L. Nanney, *John Dos Passos,* 1998; *John Dos Passos' U.S.A.: A Documentary Volume,* ed. D. Pizer, 2003.

TEXT: *U.S.A.*, 1938.

from *U.S.A.*

PREFACE[1]

The young man walks fast by himself through the crowd that thins into the night streets; feet are tired from hours of walking; eyes greedy for warm curve of faces, answering flicker of eyes, the set of a head, the lift of a shoulder, the way hands spread and clench; blood tingles with wants; mind is a beehive of hopes buzzing and stinging; muscles ache for the knowledge of jobs, for the roadmender's pick and shovel work, the fisherman's knack with a hook when he hauls on the slithery net from the rail of the lurching trawler, the swing of the bridgeman's arm as he slings down the whitehot rivet, the engineer's slow grip wise on the throttle, the dirtfarmer's use of his whole body when, whoaing the mules, he yanks the plow from the furrow. The young man walks by himself searching through the crowd with greedy eyes, greedy ears taut to hear, by himself, alone.

The streets are empty. People have packed into subways, climbed into streetcars and buses; in the stations they've scampered for suburban trains; they've

[1]Published in 1938 as a preface to the three novels, *The 42nd Parallel, 1919,* and *The Big Money,* collected in the trilogy *U.S.A.*

filtered into lodgings and tenements, gone up in elevators into apartment-houses. In a show-window two sallow window-dressers in their shirtsleeves are bringing out a dummy girl in a red evening dress, at a corner welders in masks lean into sheets of blue flame repairing a cartrack, a few drunk bums shamble along, a sad streetwalker fidgets under an arclight. From the river comes the deep rumbling whistle of a steamboat leaving dock. A tug hoots far away.

The young man walks by himself, fast but not fast enough, far but not far enough (faces slide out of sight, talk trails into tattered scraps, footsteps tap fainter in alleys); he must catch the last subway, the streetcar, the bus, run up the gangplanks of all the steamboats, register at all the hotels, work in the cities, answer the want-ads, learn the trades, take up the jobs, live in all the boardinghouses, sleep in all the beds. One bed is not enough, one job is not enough, one life is not enough. At night, head swimming with wants, he walks by himself alone.

No job, no woman, no house, no city.

Only the ears busy to catch the speech are not alone; the ears are caught tight, linked tight by the tendrils of phrased words, the turn of a joke, the singsong fade of a story, the gruff fall of a sentence; linking tendrils of speech twine through the city blocks, spread over pavements, grow out along broad parked avenues, speed with the trucks leaving on their long night runs over roaring highways, whisper down sandy byroads past wornout farms, joining up cities and fillingstations, roundhouses, steamboats, planes groping along airways; words call out on mountain pastures, drift slow down rivers widening to the sea and the hushed beaches.

It was not in the long walks through jostling crowds at night that he was less alone, or in the training camp at Allentown, or in the day on the docks at Seattle, or in the empty reek of Washington City hot boyhood summer nights, or in the meal on Market Street,[2] or in the swim off the red rocks at San Diego, or in the bed full of fleas in New Orleans, or in the cold razor-wind off the lake, or in the gray faces trembling in the grind of gears in the street under Michigan Avenue,[3] or in the smokers of limited expresstrains, or walking across country, or riding up the dry mountain canyons, or the night without a sleepingbag among frozen bear-tracks in the Yellowstone, or canoeing Sundays in the Quinnipiac;[4]

but in his mother's words telling about long ago, in his father's telling about when I was a boy, in the kidding stories of uncles, in the lies the kids told at school, the hired man's yarns, the tall tales the doughboys told after taps;

it was the speech that clung to the ears, the link that tingled in the blood; U.S.A.

U.S.A. is the slice of a continent. U.S.A. is a group of holding companies, some aggregations of trade unions, a set of laws bound in calf, a radio network, a chain of moving picture theatres, a column of stock-quotations rubbed out and written in by a Western Union boy on a blackboard, a public-library full of old newspapers and dogeared historybooks with protests scrawled on the margins in pencil. U.S.A. is the world's greatest rivervalley fringed with mountains and hills, U.S.A. is a set of bigmouthed officials with too many bank accounts. U.S.A. is a lot of men buried in their uniforms in Arlington Cemetery.[5] U.S.A. is the

[2]In San Francisco. [3]In Chicago.
[4]River in Connecticut. [5]The National Cemetery, Arlington, Virginia.

letters at the end of an address when you are away from home. But mostly U.S.A. is the speech of the people.

1938

from *THE 42ND PARALLEL*

PROTEUS[1]

Steinmetz[2] was a hunchback, son of a hunchback lithographer.

He was born in Breslau in eighteen sixtyfive, graduated with highest honors at seventeen from the Breslau Gymnasium,[3] went to the University of Breslau to study mathematics;

mathematics to Steinmetz was muscular strength and long walks over the hills and the kiss of a girl in love and big evenings spent swilling beer with your friends;

on his broken back he felt the topheavy weight of society the way working-men felt it on their straight backs, the way poor students felt it, was a member of a socialist club, editor of a paper called *The People's Voice.*

Bismarck[4] was sitting in Berlin like a big paper-weight to keep the new Germany feudal, to hold down the empire for his bosses the Hohenzollerns.[5]

Steinmetz had to run off to Zurich[6] for fear of going to jail; at Zurich his mathematics woke up all the professors at the Polytechnic;

but Europe in the eighties was no place for a penniless German student with a broken back and a big head filled with symbolic calculus and wonder about electricity that is mathematics made power and a socialist at that.

With a Danish friend he sailed for America steerage on an old French line boat *La Champagne,*

lived in Brooklyn at first and commuted to Yonkers[7] where he had a twelvedollar a week job with Rudolph Eichemeyer[8] who was a German exile from fortyeight an inventor and electrician and owner of a factory where he made hatmaking machinery and electrical generators.

In Yonkers he [Steinmetz] worked out the theory of the Third Harmonics and the law of hysteresis which states in a formula the hundredfold relations between the metallic heat, density, frequency when the poles change places in the core of a magnet under an alternating current.

[1]In Greek myth, Proteus, an old man of the sea, could alter his shape at will, to escape his enemies.

[2]Karl August Steinmetz (1865–1923), a German engineer and inventor. Forced to flee Germany because of his political views, he came to the United States in 1889 and changed his name to Charles Proteus Steinmetz.

[3]A secondary school that prepares students for entrance into a university.

[4]Otto von Bismarck (1815–1898), German statesman known as the "Iron Chancellor." From 1871 to 1890 he served as the first chancellor of the newly united Germany.

[5]The royal family that ruled Germany from 1871 to 1918. [6]In Switzerland.

[7]Near New York City.

[8]Rudolf Eickemeyer (1831–1895), German inventor who came to the United States in 1850, after the failure of the liberal revolution of 1848 in Germany.

It is Steinmetz's law of hysteresis that makes possible all the transformers that crouch in little boxes and gableroofed houses in all the hightension lines all over everywhere. The mathematical symbols of Steinmetz's law are the patterns of all transformers everywhere.

In eighteen ninetytwo when Eichemeyer sold out to the corporation that was to form General Electric, Steinmetz was entered in the contract along with other valuable apparatus. All his life Steinmetz was a piece of apparatus belonging to General Electric.

First his laboratory was at Lynn, then it was moved and the little hunchback with it to Schenectady, the electric city.

General Electric humored him, let him be a socialist, let him keep a greenhouseful of cactuses lit up by mercury lights, let him have alligators, talking crows and a gila monster for pets and the publicity department talked up the wizard, the medicine man who knew the symbols that opened up the doors of Ali Baba's cave.[9]

Steinmetz jotted a formula on his cuff and next morning a thousand new powerplants had sprung up and the dynamos sang dollars and the silence of the transformers was all dollars,

and the publicity department poured oily stories into the ears of the American public every Sunday and Steinmetz became the little parlor magician,

who made a toy thunderstorm in his laboratory and made all the toy trains run on time and the meat stay cold in the icebox and the lamp in the parlor and the great lighthouses and the searchlights and the revolving beams of light that guide airplanes at night towards Chicago, New York, St. Louis, Los Angeles,

and they let him be a socialist and believe that human society could be improved the way you can improve a dynamo and they let him be pro-German and write a letter offering his services to Lenin[10] because mathematicians are so impractical who make up formulas by which you can build powerplants, factories, subway systems, light, heat, air, sunshine but not human relations that affect the stockholders' money and the directors' salaries.

Steinmetz was a famous magician and he talked to Edison[11] tapping with the Morse code on Edison's knee.

because Edison was so very deaf
and he went out West
to make speeches that nobody understood
and he talked to Bryan[12] about God on a railroad train
and all the reporters stood round while he and Einstein
met face to face,
but they couldn't catch what they said

[9]Ali Baba, in the *Arabian Nights*, used the magic words "open sesame" to open the doors to the treasure cave of the Forty Thieves.

[10]Vladimir Ilych Lenin (1870–1924), Russian revolutionary and founder of Bolshevism.

[11]Thomas Alva Edison (1847–1931), American inventor.

[12]William Jennings Bryan (1860–1925), American political leader and defender of religious fundamentalism.

and Steinmetz was the most valuable piece of apparatus General Electric had until he wore out and died.

1930

from *1919*

NEWSREEL XLIII

the placards borne by the radicals were taken away from them, their clothing torn and eyes blackened before the service and ex-service men had finished with them

34 Die After Drinking Wood Alcohol—Trains in France May Soon Stop

Gerard Throws His Hat into the Ring[1]

SUPREME COURT DASHES LAST HOPE OF MOIST MOUTH[2]

LIFE BOAT CALLED BY ROCKET SIGNALS SEARCHES IN VAIN FOR SIXTEEN HOURS

America I love you
You're like a sweetheart of mine

LES GENS SAGES FUIENT LES REUNIONS POLITIQUES[3]

WALLSTREET CLOSES WEAK: FEARS TIGHT MONEY

From ocean to ocean
For you my devotion
Is touching each boundary line

LITTLE CARUSO EXPECTED[4]

his mother, Mrs. W. D. McGillicudy, said: "My first husband was killed while crossing tracks in front of a train, my second husband was killed in the same way and now it is my son

[1]James Watson Gerard (1867–1951), American lawyer and ambassador to Germany, 1913–1917. In 1919 Gerard declared his intention to seek nomination as the Democratic presidential candidate in the national elections of 1920. The Democratic convention chose instead James M. Cox, who was in turn defeated by the Republican candidate, Warren G. Harding.

[2]A reference to the U.S. Supreme Court decision that upheld the legality of the Volstead Act and the Eighteenth Amendment establishing Prohibition in the United States.

[3]French: Wise people shun political gatherings.

[4]A reference to Gloria Caruso (born December 18, 1919), daughter of Enrico Caruso (1873–1921), Italian operatic tenor.

Just like a little baby
Climbing its mother's knee

MACHINEGUNS MOW DOWN MOBS IN KNOXVILLE[5]

America I love you

Aviators Lived for Six Days on Shellfish

the police compelled the demonstrators to lower these flags and ordered the convention not to exhibit any red emblems save the red in the starry banner of the United States; it may not be indiscreet to state, however, in any case it cannot dim his glory, that General Pershing was confined to his stateroom through seasickness when the message arrived. Old Fellow of 89 Treasures Chewinggum as Precious Souvenir Couldn't Maintain His Serenity In Closing League Debates

And there's a hundred million others like me

1932

THE BODY OF AN AMERICAN[1]

Whereas theCongressoftheunitedstates byaconcurrentresolutionadoptedon the4thdayofmarch lastauthorizedthe Secretaryofwar to cause to be brought to theunitedstates the body of an Americanwhowasamemberoftheamericanexpeditionaryforcesineurope wholosthislifeduringtheworldwarandwhoseidentityhas notbeenestablished for burial inthememorialamphitheatreofthe nationalcemeteryat arlingtonvirginia

In the tarpaper morgue at Chalons-sur-Marne[2] in the reek of chloride of lime[3] and the dead, they picked out the pine box that held all that was left of

enie menie minie moe plenty other pine boxes stacked up there containing what they'd scraped up of Richard Roe

and other person or persons unknown. Only one can go. How did they pick John Doe?

Make sure he ain't a dinge,[4] boys,
make sure he ain't a guinea or a kike,[5]

[5]A reference to the suppression of race riots that occurred in Knoxville, Tennessee, August 31–September 1, 1919.

[1]On March 4, 1921, the U.S. Congress authorized the burial, in the Arlington National Cemetery, of an unknown American soldier killed in France in the First World War. The burial ceremony took place on Armistice Day, November 11, 1921.

[2]In October, 1921, the bodies of four unknown American soldiers were exhumed from a military cemetery in France and taken to Chalons-sur-Marne, a village east of Paris. There one of the four bodies was selected for burial at Arlington National Cemetery as the Unknown Soldier.

[3]A disinfectant powder. [4]Slang for Negro. [5]Slang for an Italian or a Jew.

how can you tell a guy's a hundredpercent when all you've got's a gunnysack full of bones, bronze buttons stamped with the screaming eagle and a pair of roll puttees?

. . . and the gagging chloride and the puky dirt-stench of the yearold dead . . .

> The day withal was too meaningful and tragic for applause. Silence, tears, songs and prayer, muffled drums and soft music were the instrumentalities today of national approbation.

John Doe was born (thudding din of blood in love into the shuddering soar of a man and a woman alone indeed together lurching into

and ninemonths sick drowse waking into scared agony and the pain and blood and mess of birth). John Doe was born

and raised in Brooklyn, in Memphis, near the lakefront in Cleveland, Ohio, in the stench of the stockyards in Chi, on Beacon Hill, in an old brick house in Alexandria Virginia, on Telegraph Hill, in a halftimbered Tudor cottage in Portland the city of roses,

in the Lying-In Hospital old Morgan endowed[6] on Stuyvesant Square,

across the railroad tracks, out near the country club, in a shack cabin tenement apartmenthouse exclusive residential suburb;

scion of one of the best families in the social register, won first prize in the baby parade at Coronado Beach, was marbles champion of the Little Rock grammarschools, crack basketball player at the Booneville High, quarterback at the State Reformatory, having saved the sheriff's kid from drowning in the Little Missouri River was invited to Washington to be photographed shaking hands with the President on the White House steps;—

> though this was a time of mourning, such an assemblage necessarily has about it a touch of color. In the boxes are seen the court uniforms of foreign diplomats, the gold braid of our own and foreign fleets and armies, the black of the conventional morning dress of American statesmen, the varicolored furs and outdoor wrapping garments of mothers and sisters come to mourn, the drab and blue of soldiers and sailors, the glitter of musical instruments and the white and black of a vested choir

—busboy harveststiff hogcaller boyscout champeen cornshucker of Western Kansas bellhop at the United States Hotel at Saratoga Springs office boy callboy fruiter telephone lineman longshoreman lumberjack plumber's helper,

worked for an exterminating company in Union City, filled pipes in an opium joint in Trenton, N.J.

Y.M.C.A. secretary, express agent, truckdriver, fordmechanic, sold books in Denver Colorado: Madam would you be willing to help a young man work his way through college?

President Harding,[7] with a reverence seemingly more significant because of his high temporal station, concluded his speech:

[6]In 1897 John Pierpont Morgan (1837–1913), American banking magnate, donated $1 million for the building of a lying-in (maternity) hospital in New York City.

[7]Warren Gamaliel Harding (1865–1923), 29th president of the United States. He spoke at the services for the Unknown Soldier held at Arlington Cemetery, November 11, 1921.

We are met today to pay the impersonal tribute;
the name of him whose body lies before us took flight with his imperishable soul . . .
as a typical soldier of this representative democracy he fought and died believing in the indisputable justice of his country's cause . . .

by raising his right hand and asking the thousands within the sound of his voice to join in the prayer:

Our Father which art in heaven hallowed be thy name . . .

Naked he went into the army;

they weighed you, measured you, looked for flat feet, squeezed your penis to see if you had clap, looked up your anus to see if you had piles, counted your teeth, made you cough, listened to your heart and lungs, made you read the letters on the card, charted your urine and your intelligence,

gave you a service record for a future (imperishable soul)

and an identification tag stamped with your serial number to hang around your neck, issued O D[8] regulation equipment, a condiment can and a copy of the articles of war.

Atten'SHUN suck in your gut you c——r wipe that smile off your face eyes right wattja tink dis is a choirch-social? For-war-D'ARCH.

John Doe.

and Richard Roe and other person or persons unknown

drilled hiked, manual of arms, ate slum,[9] learned to salute, to soldier, to loaf in the latrines, forbidden to smoke on deck, overseas guard duty, forty men and eight horses,[10] shortarm inspection[11] and the ping of shrapnel and the shrill bullets combing the air and the sorehead woodpeckers the machineguns mud cooties[12] gasmasks and the itch.

Say feller tell me how I can get back to my outfit.

John Doe had a head

for twentyodd years intensely the nerves of the eyes the ears the palate the tongue the fingers the toes the armpits, the nerves warmfeeling under the skin charged the coiled brain with hurt sweet warm cold mine must dont sayings print headlines:

Thou shalt not the multiplication table long division, Now is the time for all good men knocks but once at a young man's door, It's a great life if Ish gebibbel,[13] The first five year'll be the Safety First, Suppose a hun tried to rape you my country right or wrong, Catch 'em young, What he dont know wont treat 'em rough, Tell 'em nothing, He got what was coming to him he got his, This is a white man's country, Kick the bucket, Gone west, If you dont like it you can croaked him

[8]Olive drab, the color used for military uniforms and equipment.
[9]Slumgullion; a slang term for stew.
[10]To show carrying capacity, French railway cars used for transporting troops in World War I were marked "40 hommes, 8 chevaux"—40 men, 8 horses.
[11]Slang term for inspection of genitals for signs of venereal disease.
[12]Lice. [13]Yiddish: I don't worry.

Say buddy cant you tell me how I can get back to my outfit?

Cant help jumpin when them things go off, give me the trots them things do. I lost my identification tag swimmin in the Marne, roughhousin with a guy while we was waitin to be deloused, in bed with a girl named Jeanne (Love moving picture wet French postcard dream began with saltpeter[14] in the coffee and ended at the propho station[15]);—

Say soldier for chrissake cant you tell me how I can get back to my outfit?

John Doe's
heart pumped blood:
alive thudding silence of blood in your ears
down in the clearing in the Oregon forest where the punkins were punkincolor pouring into the blood through the eyes and the fallcolored trees and the bronze hoopers were hopping through the dry grass, where tiny striped snails hung on the underside of the blades and the flies hummed, wasps droned, bumblebees buzzed, and the woods smelt of wine and mushrooms and apples, homey smell of fall pouring into the blood,
and I dropped the tin hat[16] and the sweaty pack and lay flat with the dogday sun licking my throat and adamsapple and the tight skin over the breastbone.

The shell had his number on it.

The blood ran into the ground.

The service record dropped out of the filing cabinet when the quartermaster sergeant got blotto that time they had to pack up and leave the billets in a hurry.
The identification tag was in the bottom of the Marne.

The blood ran into the ground, the brains oozed out of the cracked skull and were licked up by the trenchrats, the belly swelled and raised a generation of bluebottle flies,
and the incorruptible skeleton,
and the scraps of dried viscera and skin bundled in khaki

they took to Chalons-sur-Marne
and laid it out in a pine coffin
and took it home to God's Country on a battleship
and buried it in a sarcophagus in the Memorial Amphitheatre in the Arlington National Cemetery
and draped the Old Glory over it
and the bugler played taps

[14]Potassium nitrate, thought to be capable of depressing sexual appetite.
[15]Short for "prophylactic station," a medical dispensary for treatment and prevention of venereal disease.
[16]Military steel helmet.

and Mr. Harding prayed to God and the diplomats and the generals and the admirals and the brasshats and the politicians and the handsomely dressed ladies out of the society column of the *Washington Post* stood up solemn
and thought how beautiful sad Old Glory God's Country it was to have the bugler play taps and the three volleys made their ears ring.

Where his chest ought to have been they pinned
the Congressional Medal, the D.S.C.,[17] the Medaille Militaire, the Belgian Croix de Guerre, the Italian gold medal, the Vitutea Militara sent by Queen Marie of Rumania, the Czechoslovak war cross, the Virtuti Militari of the Poles, a wreath sent by Hamilton Fish, Jr., of New York,[18] and a little wampum presented by a deputation of Arizona redskins in warpaint and feathers. All the Washingtonians brought flowers.

Woodrow Wilson brought a bouquet of poppies.[19]

1932

from *THE BIG MONEY*

NEWSREEL LXVI[1]

HOLMES DENIES STAY[2]

A better world's in birth[3]

Tiny Wasps Imported From Korea In Battle To Death
With Asiatic Beetle

[17]The Congressional Medal of Honor and the Distinguished Service Cross, American military awards for valor.

[18]Hamilton Fish, Sr. (1888–1981) was a U.S. congressman and author of the congressional resolution that established the memorial to the Unknown Soldier.

[19]Woodrow Wilson (1856–1924), 28th president of the United States. In ill health, Wilson rode in a carriage for only a short distance in the funeral procession. In honor of the American war dead, he wore an American Legion memorial poppy in his lapel. He did not attend the ceremonies at Arlington Cemetery.

[1]"Newsreel LXVI" and "The Camera Eye (50)" refer to the celebrated trial and execution of Nicola Sacco and Bartolomeo Vanzetti, who had been charged with a murder committed in Massachusetts in 1920. Liberal supporters of Sacco and Vanzetti insisted that the two men were innocent of the crime and had been convicted solely because of their unpopular, radical political views.

[2]On August 20, 1927, three days before the execution of Sacco and Vanzetti, Justice Oliver Wendell Holmes of the U.S. Supreme Court refused to order a "stay" or "halt" to the scheduled execution.

[3]This quotation and the six italicized lines interspersed below it are from "The Internationale," the revolutionary song of Communism.

BOY CARRIED MILE DOWN SEWER; SHOT OUT ALIVE

CHICAGO BARS MEETINGS[4]

For justice thunders condemnation

Washington Keeps Eye On Radicals

Arise rejected of the earth

PARIS BRUSSELS MOSCOW GENEVA ADD THEIR VOICES

It is the final conflict
Let each stand in his place

Geologist Lost In Cave Six Days

The International Party

SACCO AND VANZETTI MUST DIE

Shall be the human race.

Much I thought of you when I was lying in the death house—the singing, the kind tender voices of the children from the playground where there was all the life and the joy of liberty—just one step from the wall that contains the buried agony of three buried souls.[5] *It would remind me so often of you and of your sister and I wish I could see you every moment, but I feel better that you will not come to the death house so that you could not see the horrible picture of three living in agony waiting to be electrocuted.*[6]

1936

THE CAMERA EYE (50)[1]

they have clubbed us off the streets they are stronger they are rich they hire and fire the politicians the newspapereditors the old judges the small men with reputations the collegepresidents the wardheelers (listen businessmen

[4]As the execution date approached, protest meetings were held throughout the United States and Europe.

[5]Imprisoned with Sacco and Vanzetti and also awaiting execution was Celestino F. Madeiros, a convicted murderer.

[6]A passage taken from a letter written by Nicola Sacco to his son, Dante, August 18, 1927.

[1]In the following passages Dos Passos draws upon his experiences while working for the Sacco and Vanzetti Defense Committee in Boston during the 1920s.

collegepresidents judges America will not forget her betrayers) they hire the men with guns the uniforms the policecars the patrolwagons

all right you have won you will kill the brave men our friends tonight

there is nothing left to do we are beaten we the beaten crowd together in these old dingy schoolrooms on Salem Street shuffle up and down the gritty creaking stairs sit hunched with bowed heads on benches and hear the old words of the haters of oppression made new in sweat and agony tonight

our work is over the scribbled phrases the nights typing releases the smell of the printshop the sharp reek of newprinted leaflets the rush for Western Union stringing words into wires the search for stinging words to make you feel who are your oppressors America

America our nation has been beaten by strangers who have turned our language inside out who have taken the clean words our fathers spoke and made them slimy and foul

their hired men sit on the judge's bench they sit back with their feet on the tables under the dome of the State House they are ignorant of our beliefs they have the dollars the guns the armed forces the powerplants

they have built the electricchair and hired the executioner to throw the switch

all right we are two nations

America our nation has been beaten by strangers who have bought the laws and fenced off the meadows and cut down the woods for pulp and turned our pleasant cities into slums and sweated the wealth out of our people and when they want to they hire the executioner to throw the switch

but do they know that the old words of the immigrants are being renewed in blood and agony tonight do they know that the old American speech of the haters of oppression is new tonight in the mouth of an old woman from Pittsburgh of a husky boilermaker from Frisco who hopped freights clear from the Coast to come here in the mouth of a Back Bay[2] socialworker in the mouth of an Italian printer of a hobo from Arkansas the language of the beaten nation is not forgotten in our ears tonight

the men in the deathhouse made the old words new before they died

If it had not been for these things, I might have lived out my life talking at streetcorners to scorning men. I might have died unknown, unmarked, a failure. This is our career and our triumph. Never in our full life can we hope to do such work for tolerance, for justice, for man's understanding of man as now we do by an accident.[3]

now their work is over the immigrants haters of oppression lie quiet in black suits in the little undertaking parlor in the North End the city is quiet the men of the conquering nation are not to be seen on the streets

[2]A fashionable residential section of Boston.

[3]A passage from a statement made by Vanzetti after he was sentenced, April 9, 1927.

they have won why are they scared to be seen on the streets? on the streets you see only the downcast faces of the beaten the streets belong to the beaten nation all the way to the cemetery where the bodies of the immigrants are to be burned we line the curbs in the drizzling rain we crowd the wet sidewalks elbow to elbow silent pale looking with scared eyes at the coffins

we stand defeated America

1936

from *U.S.A.*

VAG[1]

The young man waits at the edge of the concrete, with one hand he grips a rubbed suitcase of phony leather, the other hand almost making a fist, thumb up

that moves in ever so slight an arc when a car slithers past, a truck roars clatters; the wind of cars passing ruffles his hair, slaps grit in his face.

Head swims, hunger has twisted the belly tight,

he has skinned a heel through the torn sock, feet ache in the broken shoes, under the threadbare suit carefully brushed off with the hand, the torn drawers have a crummy feel, the feel of having slept in your clothes; in the nostrils lingers the staleness of discouraged carcasses crowded into a transient camp, the carbolic stench of the jail, on the taut cheeks the shamed flush from the boring eyes of cops and deputies, railroadbulls (they eat three squares a day, they are buttoned into wellmade clothes, they have wives to sleep with, kids to play with after supper, they work for the big men who buy their way, they stick their chests out with the sureness of power behind their backs). Git the hell out, scram. Know what's good for you, you'll make yourself scarce. Gittin' tough, eh? Think you kin take it, eh?

The punch in the jaw, the slam on the head with the nightstick, the wrist grabbed and twisted behind the back, the big knee brought up sharp into the crotch,

the walk out of town with sore feet to stand and wait at the edge of the hissing speeding string of cars where the reek of ether and lead and gas melts into the silent grassy smell of the earth.

[1]Slang for vagrant, vagabond. This section is the conclusion of *U.S.A.*

Eyes black with want seek out the eyes of the drivers, a hitch, a hundred miles down the road.

Overhead in the blue a plane drones. Eyes follow the silver Douglas that flashes once in the sun and bores its smooth way out of sight into the blue.

(The transcontinental passengers sit pretty, big men with bankaccounts, highlypaid jobs, who are saluted by doormen; telephonegirls say goodmorning to them. Last night after a fine dinner, drinks with friends, they left Newark. Roar of climbing motors slanting up into the inky haze. Lights drop away. An hour staring along a silvery wing at a big lonesome moon hurrying west through curdling scum. Beacons flash in a line across Ohio.

At Cleveland the plane drops banking in a smooth spiral, the string of lights along the lake swings in a circle. Climbing roar of the motors again; slumped in the soft seat drowsing through the flat moonlight night.

Chi. A glimpse of the dipper. Another spiral swoop from cool into hot air thick with dust and the reek of burnt prairies.

Beyond the Mississippi dawn creeps up behind through the murk over the great plains. Puddles of mist go white in the Iowa hills, farms, fences, silos, steel glint from a river. The blinking eyes of the beacons reddening into day. Watercourses vein the eroded hills.

Omaha. Great cumulus clouds, from coppery churning to creamy to silvery white, trail brown skirts of rain over the hot plains. Red and yellow badlands, tiny horned shapes of cattle.

Cheyenne. The cool high air smells of sweetgrass.

The tightbaled clouds to westward burst and scatter in tatters over the straw-colored hills. Indigo mountains jut rimrock. The plane breasts a huge crumbling cloudbank and toboggans over bumpy air across green and crimson slopes into the sunny dazzle of Salt Lake.

The transcontinental passenger thinks contracts, profits, vacationtrips, mighty continent between Atlantic and Pacific, power, wires humming dollars, cities jammed, hills empty, the indiantrail leading into the wagonroad, the macadamed pike, the concrete skyway; trains, planes; history the billion-dollar speedup,

and in the bumpy air over the desert ranges towards Las Vegas

sickens and vomits into the carton container the steak and mushrooms he ate in New York. No matter, silver in the pocket, greenbacks in the wallet, drafts, certified checks, plenty restaurants in L.A.)

The young man waits on the side of the road; the plane has gone; thumb moves in a small arc when a car tears hissing past. Eyes seek the driver's eyes. A hundred miles down the road. Head swims, belly tightens, wants crawl over his skin like ants:

went to school, books said opportunity, ads promised speed, own your home, shine bigger than your neighbor, the radiocrooner whispered girls, ghosts of platinum girls coaxed from the screen, millions in winnings were chalked up on the boards in the offices, paychecks were for hands willing to work, the cleared desk of an executive with three telephones on it;

waits with swimming head, needs knot the belly, idle hands numb, beside the speeding traffic.

A hundred miles down the road.

1936, 1938

Eugene O'Neill 1888–1953

Eugene O'Neill was born in a Broadway hotel and raised in the world of the American theater. His father was a famous actor, and in early childhood Eugene toured with his parents in theatrical road companies traveling throughout the United States. At the age of eighteen he entered Princeton, but at the end of his freshman year he was expelled for a drunken prank and "general hell-raising." He went to New York City, where he took a secretarial job in a business firm. When he was twenty, he sailed to Central America to prospect for gold and then signed on as an ordinary seaman on ships sailing to South America, Africa, and Europe.

After three years of wandering, he returned to New York, where he supported himself with odd jobs and lived in waterfront dives among outcasts like those he later depicted in his plays. When he was twenty-four, an attack of tuberculosis, worsened by his own rebellious dissipations, sent him to a sanitarium. During his illness he decided to become a playwright, and after his convalescence he enrolled at Harvard to study drama. In 1914 he published Thirst and Other One-Act Plays. *Two years later* Bound East for Cardiff *was staged, followed in 1917 by* The Long Voyage Home.

During the 1920s and early 1930s, O'Neill achieved a series of theatrical triumphs with the production of such plays as Beyond the Horizon *(1920)—for which he was awarded the first of four Pulitzer Prizes*—The Emperor Jones *(1920),* Anna Christie *(1921),* The Hairy Ape *(1922),* Desire Under the Elms *(1924), and* Strange Interlude *(1928). In 1931 his* Mourning Becomes Electra *was widely proclaimed a dramatic masterpiece, and in 1936 he became the second American, after Sinclair Lewis, to win a Nobel Prize for Literature. O'Neill had won wealth and international renown, but in the late 1930s he withdrew into retirement and seclusion. His critical reputation declined, and his works vanished from the popular stage. In 1946 he returned to the theater with* The Iceman Cometh, *a long and notable tragedy portraying a haunted man struggling to break free of his illusions. But not until the production of* Long Day's Journey into Night *in 1956, three years after O'Neill's death, was there a lasting revival of interest in his works.*

O'Neill was a restless theatrical experimenter. His writing was shaped by European expressionistic drama and by literary naturalists such as Jack London, who portrayed people caught by overwhelming forces in a world indifferent to suffering and hope. O'Neill's plays were frequently autobiographical, pessimistic expressions of the agonies of his own life and of the degeneration he saw around him. He viewed humanity as moved by destructive passions, living in disharmony with nature, and dehumanized by a materialistic society.

O'Neill's plays are sometimes disparaged for their social pleading, their nihilism, and their occasional lapses into "overheated rhetoric." Yet his psychological probing of alienation and his depiction of the suffering of ordinary mortals made him America's most influential playwright. In little more than a decade, he transformed the American theater, changing it "utterly," in the words of Sinclair Lewis, "from a false world of neat and competent trickery into a world of splendor and fear and greatness."

FURTHER READING: S. Winther, *Eugene O'Neill: A Critical Study,* 1934, 1961; R. Skinner, *Eugene O'Neill: A Poet's Quest,* 1935, 1964; E. Engel, *The Haunted Heroes of Eugene O'Neill,* 1953; D. Falk, *Eugene O'Neill and the Tragic Tension,* 1958; *O'Neill and His Plays,* ed. O. Cargill, N. Fagin, and W. Fischer, 1961; D. Alexander, *The Tempering of Eugene O'Neill,* 1962; J. Miller, *Eugene O'Neill and the American Critic,* 1962; A. and B. Gelb, *O'Neill,* 1962,

1973; F. Carpenter, *Eugene O'Neill,* 1964, 1979; J. Raleigh, *The Plays of Eugene O'Neill,* 1965; L. Schaeffer, *O'Neill: Son and Playwright,* 1968; T. Bogard, *Contour in Time: The Plays of Eugene O'Neill,* 1972, 1988; L. Chabrowe, *Ritual and Pathos: The Theater of O'Neill,* 1976; *Eugene O'Neill: A Collection of Criticism,* ed. E. Griffin, 1976; J. Chothia, *Forging a Language: A Study of the Plays of Eugene O'Neill,* 1980; V. Floyd, *Eugene O'Neill: A World View,* 1980; C. Sinha, *Eugene O'Neill's Tragic Vision,* 1981; N. Berlin, *Eugene O'Neill,* 1982; *Eugene O'Neill's Critics,* ed. H. Frenz and S. Tuck, 1984; *Critical Essays on Eugene O'Neill,* ed. J. Martine, 1984; M. Renald, *The Eugene O'Neill Companion,* 1984; J. Barlow, *Final Acts,* 1985; V. Floyd, *The Plays of Eugene O'Neill,* 1985; *Critical Approaches to O'Neill,* ed. J. Stoupe, 1987; *Eugene O'Neill's Century,* ed. R. Moorton, 1991; K. Eisen, *The Inner Strength of Opposites: O'Neill's Novelistic Drama,* 1993; J. Pfister, *Staging Depth,* 1995; *The Cambridge Companion to Eugene O'Neill,* ed. M. Manheim, 1998; B. Voglino, *Perverse Mind: Eugene O'Neill's Struggle with Closure,* 1999; M. Miliora, *Narcissism, the Family, and Madness: A Self-Psychological Study of Eugene O'Neill and His Plays,* 2000; E. Tornqvist, *Eugene O'Neill: A Playwright's Theatre,* 2004; D. Alexander, *Eugene O'Neill's Last Plays: Separating Art from Autobiography,* 2005.

TEXT: *Three Plays: The Hairy Ape, Anna Christie, The First Man,* 1922.

THE HAIRY APE

CHARACTERS

ROBERT SMITH, "YANK"
PADDY
LONG
MILDRED DOUGLAS
HER AUNT
SECOND ENGINEER
A GUARD
A SECRETARY OF AN ORGANIZATION
Stokers, Ladies, Gentlemen, etc.

SCENE ONE

The firemen's forecastle of a transatlantic liner an hour after sailing from New York for the voyage across. Tiers of narrow, steel bunks, three deep, on all sides. An entrance in rear. Benches on the floor before the bunks. The room is crowded with men, shouting, cursing, laughing, singing—a confused, inchoate uproar swelling into a sort of unity, a meaning—the bewildered, furious, baffled defiance of a beast in a cage. Nearly all of the men are drunk. Many bottles are passed from hand to hand. All are dressed in dungaree pants, heavy ugly shoes. Some wear singlets, but the majority are stripped to the waist.

The treatment of this scene, or any other scene in the play, should by no means be naturalistic. The effect sought after is a cramped space in the bowels of a ship, imprisoned by white steel. The lines of bunks, the uprights supporting them, cross each other like the steel framework of a cage. The ceiling crushes down upon the men's heads. They cannot stand upright. This accentuates the natural stooping posture which shoveling coal and the resultant overdevelopment of back and shoulder muscles have given them. The men themselves should resemble those pictures in which the appearance of Neanderthal Man is guessed at. All are hairy-chested, with long arms of tremendous power, and low, receding brows above their small, fierce, resentful eyes. All the civilized white races are represented, but except for the slight differentiation in color of hair, skin, eyes, all these men are alike.

The curtain rises on a tumult of sound. YANK *is seated in the foreground. He seems broader, fiercer, more truculent, more powerful, more sure of himself than the rest. They respect his superior strength—the grudging respect of fear. Then, too, he represents to them a self-expression, the very last word in what they are, their most highly developed individual.*

VOICES. Gif me trink dere, you!
'Ave a wet!
Salute!
Gesundheit!
Skoal!
Drunk as a lord, God stiffen you!
Here's how!
Luck!
Pass back that bottle, damn you!
Pourin' it down his neck!
Ho, Froggy! Where the devil have you been?
La Touraine,[1]
I hit him smash in yaw, py Gott!
Jenkins—the First—he's a rotten swine—
And the coppers nabbed him—and I run—
I like peer better. It don't pig head gif you.
A slut, I'm saying'! She robbed me aslape—
To hell with 'em all!
You're a bloody liar!
Say dot again! (*Commotion. Two men about to fight are pulled apart.*)
No scrappin' now!
Tonight—
See who's the best man!
Bloody Dutchman!
Tonight on the for'ard square.
I'll bet on Dutchy.
He packa da wallop. I tella you!
Shut up, Wop!
No fightin' maties. We're all chums, ain't we!
(*A voice starts bawling a song.*)

"Beer, beer, glorious beer!
Fill yourselves right up to here."

[1]French ocean liner.

YANK. (*for the first time seeming to take notice of the uproar about him, turns around threateningly—in a tone of contemptuous authority*) Choke off dat noise! Where d'yuh get dat beer stuff? Beer, hell! Beer's for goils—and Dutchmen. Me for somep'n with a kick to it. Gimmie a drink, one of youse guys. (*Several bottles are eagerly offered. He takes a tremendous gulp at one of them; then, keeping the bottle in his hand, glares belligerently at the owner, who hastens to acquiesce in this robbery by saying*) All righto, Yank. Keep it and have another. (YANK *contemptuously turns his back on the crowd again. For a second there is an embarrassed silence. Then—*)

VOICES. We must be passing the Hook.[2]
She's beginning to roll to it.
Six days in hell—and then Southampton.[3]
Py Yesus, I vish somepody take my first vatch for me!
Gittin' seasick, Square-head?
Drink up and forget it!
What's in your bottle?
Gin.
Dot's nigger trink.
Absinthe? It's doped. You'll go off your chump, Froggy!
Cochon![4]
Whisky, that's the ticket!
Where's Paddy?
Going asleep
Sing up that whisky song Paddy. (*They all turn to an old, wizened Irishman who is dozing, very drunk, on the benches forward. His face is extremely monkey-like with all the sad, patient pathos of that animal in his small eyes.*)
Singa da song, Caruso Pat!
He's gettin' old. The drink is too much for him.
He's too drunk.

PADDY. (*blinking about him, starts to his feet resentfully, swaying, holding on to the edge of a bunk*) I'm never too drunk to sing. 'Tis only when I'm dead to the world I'd be wishful to sing at all. (*with a sort of sad contempt*) "Whisky Johnny," ye want? A chanty, ye want? Now that's a queer wish from the ugly like of you, God help you. But no matther. (*He starts to sing in a thin, nasal, doleful tone:*)

"Oh, whisky is the life of man!
Whisky! O Johnny! (They all join in on this.)
Oh, whisky is the life of man!
Whisky for my Johnny! (Again chorus.)
"Oh, whisky drove my old man mad!
Whisky! O Johnny!
Oh, whisky drove my old man mad!
Whisky for my Johnny!"

YANK. (*again turning around scornfully*) Aw hell! Nix on dat old sailing ship stuff! All dat bull's dead, see? And you're dead, too, yuh damned old Harp,[5] on'y

[2]Sandy Hook, a peninsula at the mouth of New York Bay, leading to the open sea.
[3]In England. [4]French: Pig! [5]Slang term for Irishman.

yuh don't know it. Take it easy, see. Give us a rest. Nix on de loud noise. (*with a cynical grin*) Can't youse see I'm tryin' to t'ink?

ALL. (*repeating the word after him as one with the same cynical amused mockery*) Think! (*The chorused word has a brazen metallic quality as if their throats were phonograph horns. It is followed by a general uproar of hard, barking laughter.*)

VOICES. Don't be cracking your head wit ut, Yank.
You gat headache, py yingo!
One thing about it—it rhymes with drink!
Ha, ha, ha!
Drink, don't think!
Drink, don't think!
Drink, don't think! (*A whole chorus of voices has taken up this refrain, stamping on the floor, pounding on the benches with fists.*)

YANK. (*taking a gulp from his bottle—good-naturedly*) Aw right. Can de noise. I got yuh de foist time. (*The uproar subsides. A very drunken sentimental tenor begins to sing*):

"Far away in Canada,
Far across the sea,
There's a lass who fondly waits
Making a home for me—"

YANK. (*fiercely contemptuous*) Shut up, yuh lousy boob! Where d'yuh get dat tripe? Home? Home, hell! I'll make a home for yuh! I'll knock yuh dead. Home! T'hell wit home! Where d'yu get dat tripe? Dis is home, see? What d'yuh want with home? (*proudly*) I runned away from mine when I was a kid. On'y too glad to beat it, dat was me. Home was lickings for me, dat's all. But yuh can bet your shoit no one ain't never licked me since! Wanter try it, any of youse? Huh! I guess not. (*in a more placated but still contemptuous tone*) Goils waitin' for yuh, huh? Aw, hell! Dat's all tripe. Dey don't wait for no one. Dey'd double-cross yuh for a nickel. Dey're all tarts, get me? Treat 'em rough, dat's me. To hell wit 'em. Tarts, dat's what, de whole bunch of 'em.

LONG. (*very drunk, jumps on a bench excitedly, gesticulating with a bottle in his hand*) Listen 'ere, Comrade! Yank 'ere is right. 'E says this 'ere stinkin' ship is our 'ome. And 'e says as 'ome is 'ell. An 'e's right! This is 'ell. We lives in 'ell, Comrades—and right enough we'll die in it. (*raging*) and who's ter blame, I arsk yer? We ain't. We wasn't born this rotten way. All men is born free and ekal. That's in the bleedin' Bible, maties. But what d'they care for the Bible—them lazy, bloated swine what travels first cabin? Them's the ones. They dragged us down 'til we're on'y wage slaves in the bowels of a bloody ship, sweatin, burnin' up, eatin' coal dust! Hit's them's ter blame—the damned Capitalist class! (*There had been a gradual murmur of contemptuous resentment rising among the men until now he is interrupted by a storm of catcalls, hisses, boos, hard laughter.*)

VOICES. Turn it off!
Shut up!
Sit down!
Closa da face!
Tamn fool! (*Etc.*)

YANK. (*standing up and glaring at* LONG) Sit down before I knock yuh down! (LONG *makes haste to efface himself.* YANK *goes on contemptuously*) De Bible, huh? De

Cap'tlist class, huh? Aw nix on dat Salvation Army-Socialist bull, Git a soapbox! Hire a hall! Come and be saved, huh? Jerk us to Jesus, huh? Aw g'wan! I've listened to lots of guys like you, see. Yuh're all wrong. Wanter know what I t'ink? Yuh ain't no good for no one. Yuh're de bunk. Yuh ain't go no noive, get me? Yuh're yellow, dat's what. Yellow, dat's you. Say! What's dem slobs in de foist cabin got to do wit us? We're better men dan dey are, ain't we? Sure! One of us guys could clean up de whole mob with one mit. Put one of 'em down here for one watch in de stokehole, what'd happen? Dey'd carry him off on a stretcher. Dem boids don't amount to nothin'. Dey're just baggage. Who makes dis old tub run? Ain't it us guys? Well den, we belong, don't we? We belong and dey don't. Dat's all. (*A loud chorus of approval.* YANK *goes on*) As for dis bein' hell—aw, nuts! Yuh lost your noive, dat's what. Dis is a man's job, get me? It belongs. It runs dis tub. No stiffs need apply. But yuh're a stiff, see? Yuh're yellow, dat's you.

VOICES. (*with a great hard pride in them*)

Righto!
A man's job!
Talk is cheap, Long.
He never could hold up his end.
Divil take him!
Yank's right. We make it go.
Py Gott, Yank say right ting!
We don't need no one cryin' over us.
Makin' speeches.
Throw him out!
Yellow!
Chuck him overboard!
I'll break his jaw for him!
(*They crowd around* LONG *threateningly.*)

YANK. (*half good-natured again—contemptuously*) Aw, take it easy. Leave him alone. He ain't woith a punch. Drink up. Here's how, whoever owns dis. (*He takes a long swallow from his bottle. All drink with him. In a flash all is hilarious amiability again, back-slapping, loud talk, etc.*)

PADDY. (*who has been sitting in a blinking, melancholy daze—suddenly cries out in a voice full of sorrow*) We belong to this, you're saying? We make the ship to go, you're saying? Yerra[6] then, that Almighty God have pity on us! (*His voice runs into the wail of a keen,[7] he rocks back and forth on his bench. The men stare at him, startled and impressed in spite of themselves*) Oh, to be back in the fine days of my youth, ochone![8] Oh, there was fine beautiful ships them days—clippers wid tall masts touching the sky—fine strong men in them—men that was sons of the sea as if 'twas the mother that bore them. Oh, the clean skins of them, and the clear eyes, the straight backs and full chests of them! Brave men they was, and bold men surely! We'd be sailing out, bound down round the Horn[9] maybe. We'd be making sail in the dawn, with a fair breeze, singing a chanty song wid no care to it. And astern the land would be sinking low and dying out, but we'd give it no heed but a laugh, and never a look behind. For the day that was, was enough, for we was free men—and I'm thinking 'tis only slaves do be giving heed to the day that's gone or the day to come—until they're old like me. (*with*

[6]Irish: Truly. [7]A lamentation for the dead.
[8]Irish: alas! [9]Cape Horn, at the southern tip of South America.

a sort of religious exaltation) Oh, to be scudding south again wid the power of the Trade Wind driving her on steady through the nights and the days! Full sail on her! Nights and days! Nights when the foam of the wake would be flaming wid fire, when the sky'd be blazing and winking wid stars. Or the full of the moon maybe. Then you'd see her driving through the gray night, her sails stretching aloft all silver and white, not a sound on the deck, the lot of us dreaming dreams, till you'd believe 'twas no real ship at all you was on but a ghost ship like the *Flying Dutchman* they say does be roaming the seas forevermore without touching a port. And there was the days, too. A warm sun on the clean decks. Sun warming the blood of you, and wind over the miles of shiny green ocean like strong drink to your lungs. Work—aye, hard work—but who'd mind that at all? Sure, you worked under the sky and 'twas work wid skill and daring to it. And wid the day done, in the dog watch, smoking me pipe at ease, the lookout would be raising land maybe, and we'd see the mountains of South Americy wid the red fire of the setting sun painting their white tops and clouds floating by them! (*His tone of exaltation ceases. He goes on mournfully*) Yerra, what's the use of talking? 'Tis a dead man's whisper. (*To* YANK *resentfully*) 'Twas them days men belonged to ships, not now. 'Twas them days a ship was part of the sea, and a man was part of a ship, and the sea joined all together and made it one. (*scornfully*) Is it one wid this you'd be, Yank—black smoke from the funnels smudging the sea, smudging the decks—the bloody engines pounding and throbbing and shaking—wid divil a sight of sun or a breath of clean air—choking our lungs wid coal dust—breaking our backs and hearts in the hell of the stokehole—feeding the bloody furnace—feeding our lives along wid the coal, I'm thinking—caged in by steel from a sight of the sky like bloody apes in the Zoo! (*with a harsh laugh*) Ho-ho, divil mend you! Is it to belong to that you're wishing? Is it a flesh and blood wheel of the engines you'd be?

YANK. (*who has been listening with a contemptuous sneer, barks out the answer*) Sure ting! Dat's me. What about it?

PADDY. (*as if to himself—with great sorrow*) Me time is past due. That a great wave wid sun in the heart of it may sweep over the side sometime I'd be dreaming of the days that's gone!

YANK. Aw, yuh crazy Mick![10] (*He springs to his feet and advances on* PADDY *threateningly—then stops, fighting some queer struggle within himself—lets his hands fall to his sides—contemptuously*) Aw, take it easy. Yuh're aw right, at dat. Yuh're bugs, dat's all—nutty as a cuckoo. All dat tripe yuh been pullin'—Aw, dat's all right. On'y it's dead, get me? Yuh don't belong no more, see. Yuh don't get de stuff. Yuh're too old. (*disgustedly*) But aw say, come up for air oncet in a while, can't yuh? See what's happened since yuh croaked. (*He suddenly bursts forth vehemently, growing more and more excited*) Say! Sure! Sure I meant it! What de hell—Say, lemme talk! Hey! Hey, you old Harp! Hey, youse guys! Say, listen to me—wait a moment—I gotter talk, see. I belong and he don't. He's dead but I'm livin'. Listen to me! Sure I'm part of de engines! Why de hell not! Dey move, don't dey? Dey're speed, ain't day? Dey smash trou, don't dey? Twenty-five knots a hour! Dat's goin' some! Dat's new stuff! Dat belongs! But him, he's too old. He gets dizzy. Say, listen. All dat crazy tripe about suns and winds, fresh air and de rest of it—Aw hell, dat's all a dope dream! Hittin' de pipe of de past, dat's what he's doin'. He's old and don't belong no more. But me, I'm young! I'm in de pink!

[10]Slang term for Irishman.

I move wit it. It, get me! I mean de ting dat's de guts of all dis. It ploughs trou all de tripe he's been saying'. It blows dat up! It knocks dat dead! It slams dat offen de face of de oith! It, get me! De engines and de coal and de smoke and all de rest of it! He can't breathe and swallow coal dust, but I kin, see? Dat's fresh air for me! Dat's food for me! I'm new, get me? Hell in de stokehole? Sure! It takes a man to work in hell. Hell, sure, dat's my fav'rite climate. I eat it up! I git fat on it! It's me makes it hot! It's me makes it roar! It's me makes it move! Sure, on'y for me everything stops. It all goes dead, get me? De noise and smoke and all de engines movin' de woild, dey stop. Dere ain't nothin' no more! Dat's what I'm sayin'. Everything else dat makes de woild move, somep'n makes it move. It can't move witout somep'n else, see? Den yuh get down to me. I'm at de bottom, get me! Dere ain't nothin' foither. I'm de end! I'm de start! I start somep'n and de woild moves! It—dat's me—de new dat's moiderin' de old! I'm de ting in coal dat makes it boin; I'm steam and oil for de engines; I'm de ting in noise dat makes yuh hear it; I'm smoke and express trains and steamers and factory whistles; I'm de ting in gold dat makes it money! And I'm what makes iron into steel! Steel, dat stands for de whole ting! And I'm steel—steel—steel! I'm de muscles in steel, de punch behind it. (*As he says this he pounds with his fist against the steel bunks. All the men, roused to a pitch of frenzied self-glorification by his speech, do likewise. There is a deafening metallic roar, through which* YANK'S *voice can be heard bellowing*) Slaves, hell! We run de whole woiks. All de rich guys dat tink dey're somep'n, dey ain't nothin'! Dey don't belong. But us guys, we're in de move, we're at de bottom, de whole ting is us! (PADDY *from the start of* YANK'S *speech has been taking one gulp after another from his bottle, at first frightenedly, as if he were afraid to listen, then desperately, as if to drown his senses, but finally has achieved complete indifferent, even amused, drunkenness.* YANK *sees his lips moving. He quells the uproar with a shout*) Hey, youse guys, take it easy! Wait a moment! De nutty Harp is sayin' somep'n.

PADDY. (*is heard now—throws his head back with a mocking burst of laughter*) Ho-ho-ho-ho-ho—

YANK. (*drawing back his fist, with a snarl*) Aw! Look out who yuh're givin' the bark!

PADDY. (*begins to sing the "Miller of Dee" with enormous good nature*)

"I care for nobody, no, not I,
And nobody cares for me."

YANK. (*good-natured himself in a flash, interrupts* PADDY *with a slap on the bare back like a report*) Dat's de stuff! Now you're gettin' wise to somep'n. Care for nobody, dat's de dope! To hell with 'em all! And nix on nobody else carin'. I kin care for myself, get me! (*Eight bells sound, muffled, vibrating through the steel walls as if some enormous brazen gong were imbedded in the heart of the ship. All the men jump up mechanically, file through the door silently close upon each other's heels in what is very like a prisoner's lockstep.* YANK *slaps* PADDY *on the back*) Our watch, yuh old Harp! (*mockingly*) Come on down in hell. Eat up de coal dust. Drink in de heat. It's it, see! Act like yuh liked it, yuh better—or croak yuhself.

PADDY. (*with jovial defiance*) To the devil wid it; I'll not report this watch. Let thim log[11] me and be damned. I'm no slave the like of you. I'll be sittin' here at me ease, and drinking, and thinking, and dreaming dreams.

[11]Enter charges of disobedience into the ship's log (record).

YANK. (*contemptuously*) Tinkin' and dreamin', what'll that get yuh? What's tinkin' got to do wit it? We move, don't we? Speed, ain't it? Fog, dat's all you stand for. But we drive trou dat, don't we? We split dat up and smash trou—twenty-five knots an hour! (*Turns his back on* PADDY *scornfully*) Aw, yuh make me sick! Yuh don't belong! (*He strides out the door in rear.* PADDY *hums to himself, blinking drowsily.*)

CURTAIN

SCENE TWO

Two days out. A section of the promenade deck. MILDRED DOUGLAS *and her aunt are discovered reclining in deck chairs. The former is a girl of twenty, slender, delicate, with a pale, pretty face marred by a self-conscious expression of disdainful superiority. She looks fretful, nervous and discontented, bored by her own anemia. Her aunt is a pompous and proud—and fat—old lady. She is a type even to the point of a double chin and lorgnettes.*[12] *She is dressed pretentiously, as if afraid her face alone would never indicate her position in life.* MILDRED *is dressed all in white.*

The impression to be conveyed by this scene is one of the beautiful, vivid life of the sea all about—sunshine on the deck in a great flood, the fresh sea wind blowing across it. In the midst of this, these two incongruous, artificial figures, inert and disharmonious, the elder like a gray lump of dough touched up with rouge, the younger looking as if the vitality of her stock had been sapped before she was conceived, so that she is the expression not of its life energy but merely of the artificialities that energy had won for itself in the spending.

MILDRED. (*looking up with affected dreaminess*) How the black smoke swirls back against the sky! Is it not beautiful?

AUNT. (*without looking up*) I dislike smoke of any kind.

MILDRED. My great-grandmother smoked a pipe—a clay pipe.

AUNT. (*ruffling*) Vulgar!

MILDRED. She was too distant a relative to be vulgar. Time mellows pipes.

AUNT. (*pretending boredom but irritated*) Did the sociology you took up at college teach you that—to play the ghoul on every possible occasion, excavating old bones? Why not let your great-grandmother rest in her grave?

MILDRED. (*dreamily*) With her pipe beside her—puffing in Paradise.

AUNT. (*with spite*) Yes, you are a natural born ghoul. You are even getting to look like one, my dear.

MILDRED. (*in a passionless tone*) I detest you, Aunt. (*looking at her critically*) Do you know what you remind me of? Of a cold pork pudding against a background of linoleum tablecloth in the kitchen of a—but the possibilities are wearisome. (*She closes her eyes*)

AUNT. (*with a bitter laugh*) *Merci*[13] for your candor. But since I am and must be your chaperon—in appearance, at least—let us patch up some sort of armed truce. For my part you are quite free to indulge any pose of eccentricity that beguiles you—as long as you observe the amenities—

MILDRED. (*drawling*) The inanities?

[12]Eyeglasses with a handle. [13]French: Thanks.

AUNT. (*going on as if she hadn't heard*) After exhausting the morbid thrills of social service work on New York's East Side[14]—how they must have hated you, by the way, the poor that you made so much poorer in their own eyes?—you are now bent on making your slumming international. Well, I hope Whitechapel will provide the needed nerve tonic. Do not ask me to chaperon you there, however. I told your father I would not. I loathe deformity. We will hire an army of detectives and you may investigate everything—they allow you to see.

MILDRED. (*protesting with a trace of genuine earnestness*) Please do not mock my attempts to discover how the other half lives. Give me credit for some sort of groping sincerity in that at least. I would like to help them. I would like to be some use in the world. Is it my fault I don't know how? I would like to be sincere, to touch life somewhere. (*with weary bitterness*) But I'm afraid I have neither the vitality nor integrity. All that was burnt out in our stock before I was born. Grandfather's blast furnaces, flaming to the sky, melting steel, making millions—then father keeping those home fires burning, making more millions—and little me at the tail-end of it all. I'm a waste product in the Bessemer process[15]—like the millions. Or rather, I inherit the acquired trait of the by-product, wealth, but none of the energy, none of the strength of the steel that made it. I am sired by gold and damned by it, as they say at the race track—damned in more ways than one. (*She laughs mirthlessly*).

AUNT. (*unimpressed—superciliously*) You seem to be going in for sincerity today. It isn't becoming to you, really—except as an obvious pose. Be as artificial as you are, I advise. There's a sort of sincerity in that, you know. And, after all, you must confess you like that better.

MILDRED. (*again affected and bored*) Yes, I suppose I do. Pardon me for my outburst. When a leopard complains of its spots, it must sound rather grotesque. (*in a mocking tone*) Purr, little Leopard. Purr, scratch, tear, kill, gorge yourself and be happy—only stay in the jungle where your spots are camouflaged. In a cage they make you conspicuous.

AUNT. I don't know what you are talking about.

MILDRED. It would be rude to talk about anything to you. Let's just talk. (*She looks at her wrist watch*) Well, thank goodness, it's about time for them to come for me. That ought to give me a new thrill, Aunt.

AUNT. (*affectedly troubled*) You don't mean to say you're really going? The dirt—the heat must be frightful—

MILDRED. Grandfather started as a puddler.[16] I should have inherited an immunity to heat that would make a salamander[17] shiver. It will be fun to put it to the test.

AUNT. But don't you have to have the captain's—or someone's—permission to visit the stokehole?

MILDRED. (*with a triumphant smile*) I have it—both his and the chief engineer's. Oh, they didn't want to at first, in spite of my social service credentials. They didn't seem a bit anxious that I should investigate how the other half lives and works on a ship. So I had to tell them that my father, the president of Nazareth Steel, chairman of the board of directors of this line, had told me it would be all right.

AUNT. He didn't.

[14]A district of tenements and slums, as is London's Whitechapel, following.
[15]A process for making steel. [16]A steelworker.
[17]Mythical animal thought to endure fire without harm.

MILDRED. How naïve age makes one! But I said he did, Aunt. I even said he had given me a letter to them—which I had lost. And they were afraid to take the chance that I might be lying. (*excitedly*) So it's ho! for the stokehole. The second engineer is to escort me. (*looking at her watch again*) It's time. And here he comes, I think. (*The* SECOND ENGINEER *enters. He is a husky, fine-looking man of thirty-five or so. He stops before the two and tips his cap, visibly embarrassed and ill-at-ease.*)

SECOND ENGINEER. Miss Douglas?

MILDRED. (*throwing off her rugs and getting to her feet*) Are we all ready to start?

SECOND ENGINEER. In just a second, ma'am. I'm waiting for the Fourth.[18] He's coming along.

MILDRED. (*with a scornful smile*) You don't care to shoulder this responsibility alone, is that it?

SECOND ENGINEER. (*forcing a smile*) Two are better than one. (*disturbed by her eyes, glances out to sea—blurts out*) A fine day we're having.

MILDRED. Is it?

SECOND ENGINEER. A nice warm breeze—

MILDRED. It feels cold to me.

SECOND ENGINEER. But it's hot enough in the sun—

MILDRED. Not hot enough for me. I don't like Nature. I was never athletic.

SECOND ENGINEER. (*forcing a smile*) Well you'll find it hot enough where you're going.

MILDRED. Do you mean hell?

SECOND ENGINEER. (*flabbergasted, decides to laugh*) Ho-ho! No, I mean the stokehole.

MILDRED. My grandfather was a puddler. He played with boiling steel.

SECOND ENGINEER. (*all at sea—uneasy*) Is that so? Hum, you'll excuse me, ma'am, but are you intending to wear that dress?

MILDRED. Why not?

SECOND ENGINEER. You'll likely rub against oil and dirt. It can't be helped.

MILDRED. It doesn't matter. I have lots of white dresses.

SECOND ENGINEER. I have an old coat you might throw over—

MILDRED. I have fifty dresses like this. I will throw this one into the sea when I come back. That ought to wash it clean, don't you think?

SECOND ENGINEER. (*doggedly*) There's ladders to climb down that are none too clean—and dark alleyways—

MILDRED. I will wear this very dress and none other.

SECOND ENGINEER. No offense meant. It's none of my business. I was only warning you—

MILDRED. Warning? That sounds thrilling.

SECOND ENGINEER. (*looking down the deck—with a sigh of relief*) There's the Fourth now. He's waiting for us. If you'll come—

MILDRED. Go on. I'll follow you. (*He goes.* MILDRED *turns a mocking smile on her aunt*) An oaf—but a handsome, virile oaf.

AUNT. (*scornfully*) Poser!

MILDRED. Take care. He said there were dark alleyways—

AUNT. (*in the same tone*) Poser!

MILDRED. (*biting her lips angrily*) You are right. But would that my millions were not so anemically chaste!

[18]I.e., the fourth-ranking Engineering Officer.

AUNT. Yes, for a fresh pose I have no doubt you would drag the name of Douglas in the gutter!

MILDRED. From which it sprang. Good-by, Aunt. Don't pray too hard that I may fall into the fiery furnace.

AUNT. Poser!

MILDRED. (*viciously*) Old hag! (*She slaps her aunt insultingly across the face and walks off, laughing gaily.*)

AUNT. (*screams after her*) I said poser!

CURTAIN

SCENE THREE

The stokehole. In the rear, the dimly-outlined bulks of the furnaces and boilers. High overhead one hanging electric bulb sheds just enough light through the murky air laden with coal dust to pile up masses of shadows everywhere. A line of men, stripped to the waist, is before the furnace doors. They bend over, looking neither to right nor left, handling their shovels as if they were part of their bodies, with a strange, awkward, swinging rhythm. They use the shovels to throw open the furnace doors. Then from these fiery round holes in the black a flood of terrific light and heat pours full upon the men who are outlined in silhouette in the crouching, inhuman attitudes of chained gorillas. The men shovel with a rhythmic motion, swinging as on a pivot from the coal which lies in heaps on the floor behind to hurl it into the flaming mouths before them. There is a tumult of noise—the brazen clang of the furnace doors as they are flung open or slammed shut, the grating, teeth-gritting grind of steel against steel, of crunching coal. This clash of sounds stuns one's ears with its rending dissonance. But there is order in it, rhythm, a mechanical regulated recurrence, a tempo. And rising above all, making the air hum with the quiver of liberated energy, the roar of leaping flames in the furnaces, the monotonous throbbing beat of the engines.

As the curtain rises, the furnace doors are shut. The men are taking a breathing spell. One or two are arranging the coal behind them, pulling it into more accessible heaps. The others can be dimly made out leaning on their shovels in relaxed attitudes of exhaustion.

PADDY. (*from somewhere in the line—plaintively*) Yerra, will this divil's own watch nivir end? Me back is broke. I'm destroyed entirely.

YANK. (*from the center of the line—with exuberant scorn*) Aw, yuh make me sick! Lie down and croak, why don't yuh? Always beefin', dat's you! Say, dis is a cinch! Dis was made for me! It's my meat, get me! (*A whistle is blown—a thin, shrill note from somewhere overhead in the darkness.* YANK *curses without resentment*) Dere's de damn engineer crackin' de whip. He tinks we're loafin'.

PADDY. (*vindictively*) God stiffen him!

YANK. (*in an exultant tone of command*) Come on, youse guys! Git into de game! She's gittin' hungry! Pile some grub in her. Trow it into her belly! Come on now, all of youse! Open her up! (*At this last all the men, who have followed his movements of getting into position, throw open their furnace doors with a deafening clang. The fiery light floods over their shoulders as they bend round for the coal. Rivulets of sooty sweat have traced maps on their backs. The enlarged muscles form bunches of high light and shadow.*)

YANK. (*chatting a count as he shovels without seeming effort*) One—two—tree—(*His voice rising exultantly in the joy of battle*) Dat's de stuff! Let her have it! All togedder now! Sling it into her! Let her ride! Shoot de piece now! Call de toin on her! Drive her into it! Feel her move! Watch her smoke! Speed, dat's her middle name! Give her coal, youse guys! Coal, dat's her booze! Drink it up, baby! Let's see yuh sprint! Dig in and gain a lap! Dere she go-o-es. (*This last in the chanting formula of the gallery gods at the six-day bike race. He slams his furnace door shut. The others do likewise with as much unison as their wearied bodies will permit. The effect is one of one fiery eye after another being blotted out with a series of accompanying bangs.*)

PADDY. (*groaning*) Me back is broke. I'm bate out—bate—(*There is a pause. Then the inexorable whistle sounds again from the dim regions above the electric light. There is a growl of cursing rage from all sides.*)

YANK. (*shaking his fist upward—contemptuously*) Take it easy dere, you! Who d'yuh tink's runnin' dis game, me or you? When I get ready, we move. Not before! When I get ready, get me!

VOICES. (*approvingly*) That's the stuff!
Yank tal him, py golly!
Yank ain't affeerd.
Goot poy, Yank!
Give him hell!
Tell 'im 'e's a bloody swine!
Bloody slave-driver!

YANK. (*contemptuously*) He ain't got no noive. He's yellow, get me? All de engineers is yellow. Dey got streaks a mile wide. Aw, to hell wit him! Let's move, youse guys. We had a rest. Come on, she needs it! Give her pep! It ain't for him. Him and his whistle, dey don't belong. But we belong, see! We gotter feed de baby! Come on! (*He turns and flings his furnace door open. They all follow his lead. At this instant the* SECOND *and* FOURTH ENGINEER *enter from darkness on the left with* MILDRED *between them. She starts, turns paler, her pose is crumbling, she shivers with fright in spite of the blazing heat, but forces herself to leave the* ENGINEERS *and take a few steps nearer the men. She is right behind* YANK . *All this happens quickly while the men have their backs turned.*)

YANK. Come on, youse guys! (*He is turning to get coal when the whistle sounds again in a peremptory, irritating note. This drives* YANK *into a sudden fury. While the other men have turned full around and stopped dumbfoundedly by the spectacle of* MILDRED *standing there in her white dress,* YANK *does not turn far enough to see her. Besides, his head is thrown back, he blinks upward through the murk trying to find the owner of the whistle, he brandishes his shovel murderously over his head in one hand, pounding on his chest, gorilla-like, with the other, shouting*) Toin off dat whistle! Come down outa dere, yuh yellow, brass-buttoned, Belfast bum, yuh! Come down and I'll knock yer brains out! Yuh lousy, stinkin', yellow mut of a Catholic-moiderin' bastard! Come down and I'll moider yuh! Pullin dat whistle on me, huh? I'll show yuh! I'll crash yer skull in! I'll drive yer teet-down yer troat! I'll slam yer nose trou de back of yer head! I'll cut yer guts out for a nickel, yuh lousy boob, yuh dirty, crummy, muck-eatin' son of a—(*Suddenly he becomes conscious of all the other men staring at something directly behind his back. He whirls defensively with a snarling, murderous growl, crouching to spring, his lips drawn back over his teeth, his small eyes gleaming ferociously. He sees* MILDRED, *like a white apparition in the full light from the open furnace doors. He glares into her eyes, turned to stone. As for her, during his speech she has listened, paralyzed with horror, terror, her whole personality crushed, beaten in, collapsed, by the terrific impact of this unknown, abysmal brutality, naked and shameless. As she looks at his gorilla face, as his eyes bore into hers, she utters a low, choking cry and shrinks away from him, putting both hands up before her eyes to shut out the sight of his face, to protect her own. This startles* YANK *to a reaction. His mouth falls open, his eyes grow bewildered.*)

MILDRED. (*about to faint—to the* ENGINEERS, *who now have her one by each arm—whimperingly*) Take me away! Oh, the filthy beast! (*She faints. They carry her quickly back, disappearing in the darkness at the left, rear. An iron door clangs shut. Rage and bewildered fury rush back on* YANK. *He feels himself insulted in some unknown fashion in the very heart of his pride. He roars* "God damn yuh!" *and hurls his shovel after them at the door which has just closed. It hits the steel bulkhead with a clang and falls clattering on the steel floor. From overhead the whistle sounds again in a long, angry, insistent command.*)

CURTAIN

SCENE FOUR

The firemen's forecastle. YANK'S *watch has just come off duty and had dinner. Their faces and bodies shine from a soap-and-water scrubbing but around their eyes, where a hasty dousing does not touch, the coal dust sticks like black make-up, giving them a queer, sinister expression.* YANK *has not washed either face or body. He stands out in contrast to them, a blackened, brooding figure. He is seated forward on a bench in the exact attitude of Rodin's "The Thinker."*[19] *The others, most of them smoking pipes, are staring at* YANK *half-apprehensively, as if fearing an outburst; half-amusedly, as if they saw a joke somewhere that tickled them.*

VOICES. He ain't ate nothin'.
Py golly, a fallar gat to gat grub in him.
Divil a lie.
Yank feeda da fire, no feeda da face.
Ha-ha.
He ain't even washed hisself.
He's forgot.
Hey, Yank, you forgot to wash.

YANK. (*sullenly*) Forgot nothin! To hell with washin'.

VOICES. It'll stick to you.
It'll get under your skin.
Give yer the bleedin' itch, that's wot.

VOICES. It'll stick to you.
It makes spots on you—like a leopard.
Like a piebald nigger, you mean.
Better wash up, Yank.
You sleep better.
Wash up, Yank!
Wash up! Wash up!

[19] Statue of a man sitting, with his chin on his fist, deep in thought, by Auguste Rodin (1840–1917), French sculptor.

YANK. (*resentfully*) Aw say, youse guys. Lemme alone. Can't youse see I'm tryin' to tink?

ALL. (*repeating the word after him as one with cynical mockery*) Think! (*The word has a brazen, metallic quality as if their throats were phonograph horns. It is followed by a chorus of hard, barking laughter.*)

YANK. (*springing to his feet and glaring at them belligerently*) Yes, tink! Tink, dat's what I said! What about it? (*They are silent, puzzled by his sudden resentment at what used to be one of his jokes.* YANK *sits down again in the same attitude of "The Thinker."*)

VOICES. Leave him alone.
He's got a grouch on.
Why wouldn't he?

PADDY. (*with a wink at the others*) Sure I know what's the matther. 'Tis aisy to see. He's fallen in love. I'm telling you.

ALL. (*repeating the word after him as one with cynical mockery*) Love! (*The word has a brazen, metallic quality as if their throats were phonograph horns. It is followed by a chorus of hard, barking laughter.*)

YANK. (*with a contemptuous snort*) Love, Hell! Hate, dat's what. I've fallen in hate, get me?

PADDY. (*philosophically*) 'Twould take a wise man to tell one from the other. (*with a bitter, ironical scorn, increasing as he goes on*) But I'm telling you it's love that's in it. Sure what else but love for us poor bastes in the stokehole would be bringing a fine lady, dressed like a white quane, down a mile of ladders and steps to be havin' a look at us (*A growl of anger goes up from all sides.*)

LONG. (*jumping on a bench—hectically*) Hinsultin' us! Hinsultin' us, the bloody cow! And them bloody engineers! What right 'as they got to be exhibitin' us 's if we was bleedin' monkeys in a menagerie? Did we sign for hinsults to our dignity as 'onest workers? Is that in the ship's articles?[20] You kin bloody well bet it ain't! But I knows why they done it. I arsked a deck steward 'o she was and 'e told me. 'Er old man's a bleedin' millionaire, a bloody Capitalist! 'E's got enuf bloody gold to sink this bleedin' ship! 'E makes arf the bloody steel in the world! 'E owns this bloody boat! And you and me, Comrades, we're 'is slaves! and the skipper and mates and engineers, they're 'is slaves! And she's 'is bloody daughter and we're all 'er slaves, too! And she gives 'er orders as 'ow she wants to see the bloody animals below decks and down they takes 'er! (*There is a roar of rage from all sides.*)

YANK. (*blinking at him bewilderedly*) Say! Wait a moment! Is all dat straight goods?

LONG. Straight as string! The bleedin' steward as waits on 'em, 'e told me about 'er. And what're we goin' ter do, I arsks yer? 'Ave we got ter swaller 'er hinsults like dogs? It ain't in the ship's articles. I tell yer we got a case. We kin go to law—

YANK. (*with abysmal contempt*) Hell! Law!

ALL. (*repeating the word after him as one with cynical mockery*) Law! (*The word has a brazen metallic quality as if their throats were phonograph horns. It is followed by a chorus of hard, barking laughter.*)

LONG. (*feeling the ground slipping from under his feet—desperately*) As voters and citizens we kin force the bloody governments—

YANK. (*with abysmal contempt*) Hell! Governments!

[20]Employment contract.

ALL. (*repeating the word after him as one with cynical mockery*) Governments! (*The word has a brazen metallic quality as if their throats were phonograph horns. It is followed by a chorus of hard, barking laughter.*)

LONG. (*hysterically*) We're free and equal in the sight of God—

YANK. (*with abysmal contempt*) Hell! God!

ALL. (*repeating the word after him as one with cynical mockery.*) God! (*The word has a brazen metallic quality as if their throats were phonograph horns. It is followed by a chorus of hard, barking laughter.*)

YANK. (*witheringly*) Aw, join de Salvation Army!

ALL. Sit down! Shut up! Damn fool! Sea-lawyer![21] (LONG *slinks back out of sight.*)

PADDY. (*continuing the trend of his thoughts as if he had never been interrupted—bitterly*) And there she was standing behind us, and the Second pointing at us like a man you'd hear in a circus would be saying: In this cage is a queerer kind of baboon than ever you'd find in darkest Africa. We roast them in their own sweat—and be damned if you won't hear some of them saying they like it! (*He glances scornfully at* YANK.)

YANK. (*with a bewildered uncertain growl*) Aw!

PADDY. And there was Yank roarin' curses and turning round wid his shovel to brain her—and she looked at him, and him at her—

YANK. (*slowly*) She was all white. I tought she was a ghost. Sure.

PADDY. (*with heavy, biting sarcasm*) 'Twas love at first sight, divil a doubt of it! If you'd seen the endearin' look on her pale mug when she shriviled away with her hands over her eyes to shut out the sight of him! Sure, 'twas as if she'd seen a great hairy ape escaped from the Zoo!

YANK. (*stung—with a growl of rage*) Aw!

PADDY. And the loving way Yank heaved his shovel at the skull of her, only she was out the door! (*A grin breaking over his face*) 'Twas touching, I'm telling you! It put the touch of home, swate home in the stokehole. (*There is a roar of laughter from all.*)

YANK. (*glaring at* PADDY *menacingly*) Aw, choke dat off, see!

PADDY. (*not heeding him—to the others*) And her grabbin' at the Second's arm for protection. (*With a grotesque imitation of a woman's voice*) Kiss me, Engineer dear, for it's dark down here and me old man's in Wall Street making money! Hug me tight, darlin', for I'm afeered in the dark and me mother's on deck makin' eyes at the skipper! (*another roar of laughter*)

YANK. (*threateningly*) Say! What yuh tryin' to do, kid me, yuh old Harp!

PADDY. Divil a bit! Ain't I wishin' myself you'd brained her?

YANK. (*fiercely*) I'll brain her! I'll brain her yet, wait 'n' see! (*Coming over to* PADDY *slowly*) Say, is dat what she called me—a hairy ape?

PADDY. She looked it at you if she didn't say the word itself.

YANK. (*grinning horribly*) Hairy ape, huh? Sure! Dat's de way she looked at me aw right. Hairy ape! So dat's me, huh? (*bursting into rage—as if she were still in front of him*) Yuh skinny tart! Yuh white-faced bum, yuh! I'll show you who's a ape! (*turning to the others, bewilderment seizing him again*) Say, youse guys. I was bawlin' him out for pullin' de whistle on us. You heard me. And den I seen youse lookin' at somep'n and I tought he'd sneaked down to come up in back of me, and I hopped round to knock him dead wit de shovel. And dere she was wit de light on her! Christ, yuh coulda pushed me over with a finger! I was scared, get me? Sure I tought she was a ghost, see? She was all in white like dey

[21]A complainer, troublemaker.

wrap around stiffs. You seen her. Kin yuh blame me? She didn't belong, dat's what. And den when I come to and seen it was a real skoit and seen de way she was lookin' at me—like Paddy said—Christ, I was sore, get me? I don't stand for dat stuff from nobody. And I flung de shovel—on'y she'd beat it. (*furiously*) I wished it'd banged her! I wished it'd knocked her block off!

LONG. And be 'anged for murder or 'lectrocuted? She ain't bleedin' well worth it.

YANK. I don't give a damn what! I'd be square wit her, wouldn't I? Tink I wanter let her put somep'n over on me? Tink I'm goin' to let her git away wit dat stuff? Yuh don't know me! No one ain't never put nothin' over on me and got away wit it, see!—not dat kind of stuff—no guy and no skoit neither! I'll fix her! Maybe she'll come down again—

VOICE. No chance, Yank. You scared her out of a year's growth.

YANK. I scared her? Why de hell should I scare her? Who de hell is she? Ain't she de same as me? Hairy ape, huh? (*with his old confident bravado*) I'll show her I'm better'n her, if she on'y knew it. I belong and she don't, see! I move and she's dead! Twenty-five knots a hour, dat's me! Dat carries her but I make dat. She's on'y baggage. Sure! (*again bewilderedly*) But, Christ, she was funny lookin'! Did yuh pipe her hands? White and skinny. Yuh could see de bones through 'em. And her mush, dat was dead white, too. And her eyes, dey was like dey'd seen a ghost. Me, dat was! Sure! Hairy ape! Ghost, huh? Look at dat arm! (*He extends his right arm, swelling out of the great muscles*) I coulda took her wit dat, wit just my little finger even, and broke her in two. (*Again bewilderedly*) Say, who is dat skoit, huh? What is she? What's she come from? Who made her? Who give her de noive to look at me like dat? Dis ting's got my goat right. I don't get her. She's new to me. What does a skoit like her mean, huh? She don't belong, get me! I can't see her. (*with growing anger*) But one ting I'm wise to, aw right, aw right! Youse all kin bet your shoits I'll git even wit her. I'll show her if she tinks she—She grinds de organ and I'm on de string, huh? I'll fix her! Let her come down again and I'll fling her in de furnace! She'll move den! She won't shiver at nothin', den! Speed, dat'll be her! She'll belong den! (*He grins horribly*)

PADDY. She'll never come. She's had her belly-full, I'm telling you. She'll be in bed now, I'm thinking, wid ten doctors and nurses feedin' her salts[22] to clean the fear out of her.

YANK. (*enraged*) Yuh think I made her sick, too, do yuh? Just lookin' at me, huh? Hairy ape, huh? (*in a frenzy of rage*) I'll fix her! I'll tell her where to git off! She'll get down on her knees and take it back or I'll bust de face offen her! (*shaking one fist upward and beating on his chest with the other*) I'll find yuh! I'm comin', d'yuh hear? I'll fix yuh, God damn you! (*He makes a rush for the door.*)

VOICES. Stop him!
He'll get shot!
He'll murder her!
Trip him up!
Hold him!
Gott, he's strong!
Hold him down!
Look out for a kick!
Pin his arms!

[22]A laxative, such as Epsom salts.

(They have all piled on him and, after a fierce struggle, by sheer weight of numbers have borne him to the floor just inside the door.)

PADDY. (*who has remained detached*) Kape him down till he's cooled off. (*Scornfully*) Yerra, Yank, you're a great fool. Is it payin' attention at all you are to the like of that skinny sow widout one drop of rale blood in her?

YANK. (*frenziedly, from the bottom of the heap*) She done me doit! She done me doit, didn't she? I'll git square wit her! I'll get her some way! Git offen me, youse guys! Lemme up! I'll show her who's a ape!

CURTAIN

SCENE FIVE

Three weeks later. A corner of Fifth Avenue in the Fifties on a fine Sunday morning. A general atmosphere of clean, well-tidied, wide street; a flood of mellow, tempered sunshine; gentle, genteel breezes. In the rear, the show windows of two shops, a jewelry establishment on the corner, a furrier's next to it. Here the adornments of extreme wealth are tantalizingly displayed. The jeweler's window is gaudy with glittering diamonds, emeralds, rubies, pearls, etc., fashioned in ornate tiaras, crowns, necklaces, collars, etc. From each piece hangs an enormous tag from which a dollar sign and numerals in intermittent electric lights wink out the incredible prices. The same in the furrier's. Rich furs of all varieties hang there bathed in a downpour of artificial light. The general effect is of a background of magnificence cheapened and made grotesque by commercialism, a background in tawdry disharmony with the clear light and sunshine on the street itself.

Up the side street YANK *and* LONG *come swaggering.* LONG *is dressed in shore clothes, wears a black Windsor tie, cloth cap.* YANK *is in his dirty dungarees. A fireman's cap with black peak is cocked defiantly on the side of his head. He has not shaved for days and around his fierce, resentful eyes—as around those of* LONG *to a lesser degree—the black smudge of coal dust still sticks like make-up. They hesitate and stand together at the corner, swaggering, looking around them with a forced, defiant contempt.*

LONG. (*indicating it all with an oratorical gesture*) Well, 'ere we are. Fif' Avenoo. This 'ere's their bleedin' private lane, as yer might say. (*bitterly*) We're trespassers 'ere. Proletarians keep orf the grass!

YANK. (*dully*) I don't see no grass, yuh boob. (*staring at the sidewalk*) Clean, ain't it? Yuh could eat a fried egg offen it. The white wings[23] got some job sweepin' dis up. (*Looking up and down the avenue—surlily*) Where's all de white-collar stiffs yuh said was here—and de skoits—*her* kind?

LONG. In church, blarst 'em! Arskin' Jesus to give 'em more money.

YANK. Choich, huh? I useter go to church onct—sure—when I was a kid. Me old man and woman, dey made me. Dey never went demselves, dough. Always got too big a head on Sunday mornin', dat was dem. (*with a grin*) Dey was scrappers for fair, bot' of dem. On Satiday nights when dey bot' got a skinful dey could put up a bout oughter been staged at de Garden.[24] When dey got trough dere wasn't a chair or table with a leg under it. Or else dey bot' jumped on me

[23]White-uniformed street cleaners.

[24]Madison Square Garden in New York City, an arena sometimes used for boxing matches.

for somep'n. Dat was where I loined to take punishment. (*with a grin and a swagger*) I'm a chip offen de old block, get me?

LONG. Did yer old man follow the sea?

YANK. Naw. Worked along shore. I runned away when me old lady croaked wit de tremens.[25] I helped at truckin' and in de market. Den I shipped in de stokehole. Sure. Dat belongs. De rest was nothin'. (*looking around him*) I ain't never seen dis before. De Brooklyn waterfront, dat was where I was dragged up. (*taking a deep breath*) Dis ain't so bad at dat, huh?

LONG. Not bad? Well, we pays for it wiv our bloody sweat, if yer wants to know!

YANK. (*with sudden angry disgust*) Aw, hell! I don't see no one, see—like her. All dis gives me a pain. It don't belong. Say, ain't dere a back room around dis dump? Let's go shoot a ball.[26] All dis is too clean and quiet and dolled-up, get me! It gives me a pain.

LONG. Wait and yer'll bloody well see—

YANK. I don't wait for no one. I keep on de move. Say, what yuh drag me up here for, anyway? Tryin' to kid me, yuh simp, yuh?

LONG. Yer wants to get back at 'er, don't yer? That's what yer been sayin' every bloomin' hour since she hinsulted yer.

YANK. (*vehemently*) Sure ting I do! Didn't I try to get even wit her in Southhampton? Didn't I sneak on de dock and wait for her by de gangplank? I was goin' to spit in her pale mug. Sure, right in her pop-eyes! Dat woulda made me even, see? But no chanct. Dere was a whole army of plainclothes bulls around. Dey spotted me and gimme de bum's rush. I never seen her. But I'll git square wit her yet, you watch. (*Furiously*) De lousy tart! She tinks she kin get away wit moider—but not wit me! I'll fix her! I'll tink of a way!

LONG. (*as disgusted as he dares to be*) Ain't that why I brought yer up 'ere—to show yer? Yer been lookin' at this 'ere 'ole affair wrong. Yer been actin' an' talkin' 's if it was all a bleedin' personal matter between yer and that bloody cow. I wants to convince yer she was on'y a representative of 'er clarss. I wants to awaken yer bloody clarss consciousness. Then yer'll see it's 'er clarss yer've got to fight, not 'er alone. There's a ole mob of 'em like 'er, Gawd blind 'em!

YANK. (*spitting on his hands—belligerently*) De more de merrier when I gits started. Bring on de gang!

LONG. Yer'll see 'em in arf a mo', when that church lets out. (*He turns and sees the window display in the two stores for the first time*) Blimey![27] Look at that, will yer? (*They both walk back and stand looking in the jeweler's.* LONG *flies into a fury*) Just look at this 'ere bloomin' mess! Just look at it! Look at the bleedin' prices on 'em—more'n our 'ole bloody stokehole makes in ten voyages sweatin' in 'ell! And they—'er and 'er bloody clarss—buys 'em for toys to dangle on 'em! One of these 'ere would buy scoff[28] for a starvin' family for a year!

YANK. Aw, cut de sob stuff! T' hell wit de starvin' family! Yuh'll be passin' de hat to me next. (*with naïve admiration*) Say, dem tings is pretty huh? Bet yuh dey'd hock for a piece of change aw right. (*then turning away, bored*) But, aw hell, what good are dey? Let her have 'em. Dey don't belong no more'n she does. (*with a gesture of sweeping the jewelers into oblivion*) All dat don't count, get me?

[25]Delirium tremens, a violent mental disturbance caused by alcoholism. [26]I.e., shoot pool.
[27]A slang contraction of "God blind me!" At the time, a strong oath. [28]Slang: food.

LONG. (*who has moved to the furrier's—indignantly*) And I s'pose this 'ere don't count neither—skins of poor, 'armless animals slaughtered so as 'er and 'ers can keep their bleedin' noses warm!

YANK. (*who has been staring at something inside—with queer excitement*) Take a slant at dat! Git it de once-over! Monkey fur—two t'ousand bucks! (*bewilderedly*) Is dat straight goods—monkey fur! What de hell—?

LONG. (*bitterly*) It's straight enuf. (*with grim humor*) They wouldn't bloody well pay that for a 'airy ape's skin—no, nor for the 'ole livin' ape with all 'is 'ead, and a body, and soul thrown in!

YANK. (*clenching his fists, his face growing pale with rage as if the skin in the window were a personal insult*) Trowin' it up in my face! Christ! I'll fix her!

LONG. (*excitedly*) Church is out. 'Ere they come, the bleedin' swine. (*after a glance at* YANK'S *lowering face—uneasily*) Easy goes, Comrade. Keep yer bloomin' temper. Remember force defeats itself. It ain't our weapon. We must impress our demands through peaceful means—the votes of the on-marching proletarians of the bloody world!

YANK. (*with abysmal contempt*) Votes, hell! votes is a joke, see. Votes for women! Let dem do it!

LONG. (*still more uneasily*) Calm, now. Treat 'em wiv the proper contempt. Observe the bleedin' parasites but 'old yer 'orses.

YANK. (*angrily*) Git away from me! Yuh're yellow, dat's what. Force, dat's me! De punch, dat's me every time, see! (*The crowd from church enter from the right, sauntering slowly and affectedly, their heads held stiffly up, looking neither to right nor left, talking in toneless, simpering voices. The women are rouged, calcimined, dyed, overdressed to the nth degree. The men are in Prince Alberts,*[29] *high hats, spats, canes, etc. A procession of gaudy marionettes, yet with something of the relentless horror of Frankensteins in their detached, mechanical unawareness.*)

VOICES. Dear Doctor Caiphas! He is so sincere!
What was the sermon?
I dozed off.
About the radicals, my dear—and the false doctrines that are being preached.
We must organize a hundred per cent American bazaar.
And let everyone contribute one one-hundredth per cent of their income tax.
What an original idea!
We can devote the proceeds to rehabilitating the veil of the temple.[30]
But that has been done so many times.

YANK. (*glaring from one to the other of them—with an insulting snort of scorn*) Huh! Huh! (*Without seeming to see him, they make wide detours to avoid the spot where he stands in the middle of the sidewalk.*)

LONG. (*frightenedly*) Keep yer bloomin' mouth shut, I tells yer.

YANK. (*viciously*) G'wan! Tell it to Sweeney! (*He swaggers away and deliberately lurches into a top-hatted gentleman, then glares at him pugnaciously*) Say, who d'yuh tink yuh're bumpin'? Tink yuh own de oith?

GENTLEMAN. (*coldly and affectedly*) I beg your pardon. (*He has not looked at* YANK *and passes on without a glance, leaving him bewildered.*)

[29]Elegant, long-tailed suit coats.
[30]The curtain hung before a church sanctuary, usually during Lent.

LONG. (*rushing up and grabbing* YANK'S *arm*) 'Ere! Come away! This wasn't what I meant. Yer'll 'ave the bloody coppers down on us.

YANK. (*savagely—giving him a push that sends him sprawling*) G'wan!

LONG. (*picks himself up—hysterically*) I'll pop orf then. This ain't what I meant. And whatever 'appens, yer can't blame me. (*He slinks off left.*)

YANK. T' hell wit youse! (*He approaches a lady—with a vicious grin and a smirking wink*) Hello, Kiddo. How's every little ting? Got anything on for tonight? I know an old boiler down to de docks we kin crawl into. (*The lady stalks by without a look, without a change of pace.* YANK *turns to others—insultingly*) Holy smokes, what a mug! Go hide yuhself before de horses shy at yuh. Gee, pipe de heine[31] on dat one! Say, youse, yuh look like de stoin[32] of a ferryboat. Paint and powder! All dolled up to kill! Yuh look like stiffs laid out for de boneyard! Aw, g'wan, de lot of youse! Yuh give me an eyeache. Yuh don't belong, get me! Look at me, why don't youse dare? I belong, dat's me! (*pointing to skyscraper across the street which is in process of construction—with bravado*) See dat building goin' up dere? See de steel work? Steel, dat's me! Youse guys live on it and tink yuh're somep'n. But I'm *in* it, see! I'm de hoistin' engine dat makes it go up! I'm it—de inside and bottom of it! Sure! I'm steel and steam and smoke and de rest of it! It moves—speed—twenty-five stories up—and me at de top and bottom—movin'! Youse simps don't move. Yuh're on'y dolls I winds up to see 'm spin. Yuh're de garbage, get me—de leavin's—de ashes we dump over de side! Now, what 'a' yuh gotta say? (*But as they seem neither to see nor hear him, he flies into a fury.*) Bums! Pigs! Tarts! Bitches! (*He turns in a rage on the men, bumping viciously into them but not jarring them the least bit. Rather it is he who recoils after each collision. He keeps growling.*) Git off de oith! G'wan, yuh bum! Look where yuh're goin', can't yuh? Git out here! Fight, why don't yuh? Put up yer mits! Don't be a dog! Fight or I'll knock yuh dead! (*But, without seeming to see him, they all answer with mechanical affected politeness* "I beg your pardon." *Then at a cry from one of the women, they all scurry to the furrier's window.*)

THE WOMAN. (*ecstatically, with a gasp of delight*) Monkey fur! (*The whole crowd of men and women chorus after her in the same tone of affected delight.* "Monkey fur!")

YANK. (*with a jerk of his head back on his shoulders, as if he had received a punch full in the face—raging*) I see yuh, all in white! I see yuh, yuh white-faced tart, yuh! Hairy ape, huh? I'll hairy ape yuh! (*He bends down and grips at the street curbing as if to pluck it out and hurl it. Foiled in this, snarling with passion, he leaps to the lamppost on the corner and tries to pull it up for a club. Just at that moment a bus is heard rumbling up. A fat, high-hatted, spatted gentleman runs out from the side street. He calls out plaintively* "Bus! Bus! Stop here!" *and runs full tilt into the bending, straining* YANK, *who is bowled off his balance.*)

YANK. (*seeing a fight—with a roar of joy as he springs to his feet*) At last! Bus, huh? I'll bust yuh! (*He lets drive a terrific swing, his fist landing full on the fat gentleman's face. But the gentleman stands unmoved as if nothing had happened.*)

GENTLEMAN. I beg your pardon. (*then irritably*) You have made me lose my bus. (*He claps his hands and begins to scream*) Officer! officer! (*Many police whistles shrill out on the instant and a whole platoon of policemen rush in on* YANK *from all sides. He tries to fight but is clubbed to the pavement and fallen upon. The crowd at the window have not moved or noticed this disturbance. The clanging gong of the patrol wagon approaches with a clamoring din.*)

CURTAIN

[31]I.e., look at the rump. [32]The stern, the rear end.

SCENE SIX

Night of the following day. A row of cells in the prison on Blackwell's Island.[33] *The cells extend back diagonally from right front to left rear. They do not stop, but disappear in the dark background as if they ran on, numberless, into infinity. One electric bulb from the low ceiling of the narrow corridor sheds its light through the heavy steel bars of the cell at the extreme front and reveals part of the interior.* YANK *can be seen within, crouched on the edge of his cot in the attitude of Rodin's "The Thinker." His face is spotted with black and blue bruises. A blood-stained bandage is wrapped around his head.*

YANK. (*suddenly starting as if awakening from a dream, reaches out and shakes the bars—aloud to himself, wonderingly*) Steel. Dis is de Zoo, huh? (*A burst of hard, barking laughter comes from the unseen occupants of the cells, runs back down the tier, and abruptly ceases.*)

VOICES. (*mockingly*) The Zoo? That's a new name for this coop—a damn good name!
Steel, eh? You said a mouthful. This is the old iron house.
Who is that boob talkin'?
He's the bloke they brung in out of his head. The bulls had beat him up fierce.

YANK. (*dully*) I musta been dreamin'. I thought I was in a cage at de Zoo—but de apes don't talk, do dey?

VOICES. (*with mocking laughter*) You're in a cage aw right.
A coop!
A pen!
A sty!
A kennel! (*hard laughter—a pause*)
Say, guy! Who are you? No, never mind lying. What are you?
Yes, tell us your sad story. What's your game?
What did they jug yuh for?

YANK. (*dully*) I was a fireman—stokin' on de liners. (*then with sudden rage, rattling his cell bars*) I'm a hairy ape, get me? And I'll bust youse all in de jaw if yuh don't lay off kiddin' me.

VOICES. Huh! You're a hard boiled duck, ain't you!
When you spit, it bounces! (*laughter*)
Aw, can it. He's a regular guy. Ain't you?
What did he say he was—a ape?

YANK. (*defiantly*) Sure ting! Ain't dat what youse all are—apes? (*a silence, then a furious rattling of bars down the corridor*).

A VOICE. (*thick with rage*) I'll show yuh who's a ape, yuh bum!

VOICES. Ssshh! Nix!
Can de noise!
Piano!
You'll have the guard down on us!

YANK. (*scornfully*) De guard? Yuh mean de keeper, don't yuh? (*angry exclamations from all the cells*)

[33]Island in the East River in New York City, now called Roosevelt Island.

VOICE. (*placatingly*) Aw, don't pay no attention to him. He's off his nut from the beatin'-up he got. Say, you guy! We're waitin' to hear what they landed you for—or ain't yuh tellin'?

YANK. Sure, I'll tell youse. Sure! Why de hell not? On'y—youse won't get me. Nobody gets me but me, see? I started to tell de Judge and all he says was: "Toity days to tink it over."—Tink it over! Christ, dat's all I been doin' for weeks! (*after a pause*) I was tryin' to git even wit someone, see?—someone dat done me doit.

VOICES. (*cynically*) De old stuff, I bet. Your goil, huh?
Give yuh the double-cross, huh?
That's them ever time!
Did yuh beat up de odder guy?

YANK. (*disgustedly*) Aw, yuh're all wrong! Sure dere was a skoit in it—but not what youse mean, not dat old tripe. Dis was a new kind of skoit. She was dolled up all in white—in de stokehole. I tought she was a ghost. Sure. (*A pause.*)

VOICES. (*whispering*) Gee, he's still nutty.
Let him rave. It's fun listenin'.

YANK. (*unheeding—groping in his thoughts*) Her hands—dey was skinny and white like dey wasn't real but painted on somep'n. Dere was a million miles from me to her—twenty-five knots a hour. She was like some dead ting de cat brung in. Sure, dat's what. She didn't belong. She belonged in de window of a toy store, or on de top of a garbage can, see! Sure! (*He breaks out angrily.*) But would yuh believe it, she had de noive to do me doit. She lamped[34] me like she was seein' somep'n broke loose from de menagerie. Christ, yuh'd oughter seen her eyes! (*He rattles the bars of his cell furiously.*) But I'll get back at her yet, you watch! And if I can't find her I'll take it out on de gang she runs wit. I'm wise to where dey hangs out now. I'll show her who belongs! I'll show her who's in de move and who ain't. You watch my smoke!

VOICES. (*serious and joking*) Dat's de talkin'!
Take her for all she's got!
What was this dame, anyway? Who was she, eh?

YANK. I dunno. First cabin stiff. Her old man's a millionaire, dey says—name of Douglas.

VOICES. Douglas? That's the president of the Steel Trust, I bet.
Sure. I seen his mug in de papers.
He's filthy with dough.

VOICE. Hey, feller, take a tip from me. If you want to get back at that dame, you better join the Wobblies. You'll get some action then.

YANK. Wobblies? What de hell's dat?

VOICE. Ain't you ever heard of the I. W. W.?[35]

YANK. Naw. What is it?

VOICE. A gang of blokes—a tough gang. I been readin' about 'em today in the paper. The guard give me the *Sunday Times*. There's a long spiel about 'em. It's from a speech made in the Senate by a guy named Senator Queen. (*He is in the cell next to* YANK'S. *There is a rustling of paper*) Wait'll I see if I got light enough and I'll read you. Listen (*He reads.*) "There is a menace existing in this country today which threatens the vitals of our fair Republic—as foul a

[34] I.e., looked at.

[35] Industrial Workers of the World, a radical labor organization founded in 1905. Its members were nicknamed "Wobblies."

menace against the very life-blood of the American Eagle as was the foul conspiracy of Catiline[36] against the eagles of ancient Rome!"

VOICE. (*disgustedly*) Aw, hell! Tell him to salt de tail of dat eagle!

VOICE. (*reading*) "I refer to that devil's brew of rescals, jailbirds, murderers, and cutthroats who libel all honest working men by calling themselves the Industrial Workers of the World; but in the light of their nefarious plots, I call them the Industrial *Wreckers* of the World!"

YANK. (*with vengeful satisfaction*) Wreckers, dat's right dope! Dat belongs! Me for dem!

VOICE. Ssshh! (*reading*) "This fiendish organization is a foul ulcer on the fair body of our Democracy—"

VOICE. Democracy, hell! Give him the boid, fellers—the raspberry! (*They do.*)

VOICE. Ssshh! (*reading*) "Like Cato[37] I say to this Senate, the I. W. W. must be destroyed! For they represent an ever-present dagger pointed at the heart of the greatest nation the world has ever known, where all men are born free and equal, with equal opportunities to all, where the Founding Fathers have guaranteed to each one happiness, where Truth, Honor, Liberty, Justice, and the Brotherhood of Man are a religion absorbed with one's mother's milk, taught at our father's knee, sealed, signed, and stamped upon the glorious Constitution of these United States!" (*a perfect storm of hisses, catcalls, boos, and hard laughter*)

VOICES. (*scornfully*) Hurrah for de Fort' of July!
Pass de hat!
Liberty!
Justice!
Honor!
Opportunity!
Brotherhood!

ALL. (*with abysmal scorn*) Aw, hell!

VOICE. Give that Queen Senator guy the bark! All togedder now—one—two—tree—(*a terrific chorus of barking and yapping*)

GUARD. (*from a distance*) Quiet there, youse—or I'll git the hose. (*The noise subsides.*)

YANK. (*with growling rage*) I'd like to catch dat senator guy alone for a second. I'd loin him some trute!

VOICE. Ssshh! Here's where he gits down to cases on the Wobblies. (*reads*) "They plot with fire in one hand and dynamite in the other. They stop not before murder to gain their ends, nor at the outraging of defenseless womanhood. They would tear down society, put the lowest scum in the seats of the mighty, turn Almighty God's revealed plan for the world topsy-turvy, and make of our sweet and lovely civilization a shambles, a desolation where man, God's masterpiece, would soon degenerate back to the ape!"

VOICE. (*to* YANK) Hey, you guy. There's your ape stuff again.

YANK. (*with a growl of fury*) I got him. So dey blow up tings, do dey? Dey turn tings around, do dey? Hey, lend me dat paper, will yuh?

VOICE. Sure. Give it to him. On'y keep it to yourself, see. We don't wanter listen to no more of that slop.

VOICE. Here you are. Hide it under your mattress.

[36]Lucius Sergius Catilina (108?–62 B.C.), Roman revolutionary conspirator.
[37]Marcus Porcius Cato (234–149 B.C.), Roman senator who urged the destruction of Carthage.

YANK. (*reaching out*) Tanks. I can't read much but I kin manage. (*He sits, the paper in the hand at his side, in the attitude of Rodin's "The Thinker." A pause. Several snores from down the corridor. Suddenly* YANK *jumps to his feet with a furious groan as if some appalling thought had crashed on him—bewilderedly*) Sure—her old man—president of de Steel Trust—makes half de steel in de world—steel—where I tought I belonged—drivin' trou—movin'—in dat—to make *her*—and cage me in for her to spit on! Christ! (*He shakes the bars of his cell door till the whole tier trembles. Irritated, protesting exclamations from those awakened or trying to get to sleep*) He made dis—dis cage! Steel! *It* don't belong, dat's what! Cages, cells, locks, bolts, bars—dat's what it means!—holdin' me down with him at de top! But I'll drive trou! Fire, dat melts it! I'll be fire—under de heap—fire dat never goes out—hot as hell—breakin' out in de night—(*While he has been saying this last he has shaken his cell door to a clanging accompaniment. As he comes to the "breakin' out" he seizes one bar with both hands and, putting his two feet up against the others so that his position is parallel to the floor like a monkey's, he gives a great wrench backwards. The bar bends like a licorice stick under his tremendous strength. Just at this moment the* PRISON GUARD *rushes in, dragging a hose behind him.*)

GUARD. (*angrily*) I'll loin youse bums to wake me up! (*sees* YANK) Hello, it's you, huh? Got the D. T.'s[38] hey? Well, I'll cure 'em. I'll drown your snakes for yuh! (*noticing the bar*) Hell, look at dat bar bended! On'y a bug is strong enough for dat!

YANK. (*glaring at him*) Or a hairy ape, yuh big yellow bum! Look out! Here I come! (*He grabs another bar.*)

GUARD. (*scared now—yelling off left*) Toin de hose on, Ben!—full pressure! And call de others—and a straitjacket! (*The curtain is falling. As it hides* YANK *from view, there is a splattering smash as the stream of water hits the steel of* YANK'S *cell.*)

CURTAIN

SCENE SEVEN

Nearly a month later. An I. W. W. local near the waterfront, showing the interior of a front room on the ground floor, and the street outside. Moonlight on the narrow street, buildings massed in black shadow. The interior of the room, which is general assembly room, office, and reading room, resembles some dingy settlement boys' club. A desk and high stool are in one corner. A table with papers, stacks of pamphlets, chairs about it, is at center. The whole is decidedly cheap, banal, commonplace and unmysterious as a room could be. The SECRETARY *is perched on the stool making entries in a large ledger. An eye shade casts his face into shadows. Eight or ten men, longshoremen, iron workers, and the like, are grouped about the table. Two are playing checkers. One is writing a letter. Most of them are smoking pipes. A big signboard is on the wall at the rear, "Industrial Workers of the World—Local No. 57."*

YANK *comes down the street outside. He is dressed as in Scene Five. He moves cautiously, mysteriously. He comes to a point opposite the door; tiptoes softly up to it, listens, is impressed by the silence within, knocks carefully, as if he were guessing at the password to some secret rite. Listens. No answer. Knocks again a bit louder. No answer. Knocks impatiently, much louder.*

[38]Delirium tremens.

SECRETARY. (*turning around on his stool*) What the hell is that—someone knocking? (*shouts*) Come in, why don't you? (*All the men in the room look up.* YANK *opens the door slowly, gingerly, as if afraid of an ambush. He looks around for secret doors, mystery, is taken aback by the commonplaceness of the room and the men in it, thinks he may have gotten in the wrong place, then sees the signboard on the wall and is reassured.*)

YANK. (*blurts out*) Hello.

MEN. (*reservedly*) Hello.

YANK. (*more easily*) I thought I'd bumped into de wrong dump.

SECRETARY. (*scrutinizing him carefully*) Maybe you have. Are you a member?

YANK. Naw, not yet. Dat's what I come for—to join.

SECRETARY. That's easy. What's your job—longshore?

YANK. Naw, Fireman—stoker on de liners.

SECRETARY. (*with satisfaction*) Welcome to our city. Glad to know you people are waking up at last. We haven't got many members in your line.

YANK. Naw. Dey're all dead to de woild.

SECRETARY. Well, you can help to wake 'em. What's your name? I'll make out your card.

YANK. (*confused*) Name? Lemme tink.

SECRETARY. (*sharply*) Don't you know your own name?

YANK. Sure; but I been just Yank for so long—Bob, dat's it—Bob Smith.

SECRETARY. (*writing*) Robert Smith. (*fills out the rest of the card*) Here you are. Cost you half a dollar.

YANK. Is dat all—four bits? Dat's easy. (*gives the* SECRETARY *the money*)

SECRETARY. (*throwing it in drawer*) Thanks. Well, make yourself at home. No introductions needed. There's literature on the table. Take some of those pamphlets with you to distribute aboard ship. They may bring results. Sow the seed, only go about it right. Don't get caught and fired. We got plenty out of work. What we need is men who can hold their jobs—and work for us at the same time.

YANK. Sure. (*But he still stands, embarrassed and uneasy.*)

SECRETARY. (*looking at him—curiously*) What did you knock for? Think we had a coon in uniform to open doors?

YANK. Naw. I tought it was locked—and dat yuh'd wanter give me the once-over trou a peep-hole or somep'n to see if I was right.

SECRETARY. (*alert and suspicious but with an easy laugh*) Think we were running a crap game? That door is never locked. What put that in your nut?

YANK. (*with a knowing grin, convinced that this is all camouflage, a part of the secrecy*) Dis burg is full of bulls, ain't it?

SECRETARY. (*sharply*) What have the cops got to do with us? We're breaking no laws.

YANK. (*with a knowing wink*) Sure. Youse wouldn't for woilds. Sure. I'm wise to dat.

SECRETARY. You seem to be wise to a lot of stuff none of us knows about.

YANK. (*with another wink*) Aw, dat's aw right, see. (*then made a bit resentful by the suspicious glances from all sides*) Aw, can it! Youse needn't put me trou de toid degree. Can't youse see I belong? Sure! I'm reg'lar. I'll stick, get me? I'll shoot de woiks for youse. Dat's why I wanted to join in.

SECRETARY. (*breezily, feeling him out*) That's the right spirit. Only are you sure you understand what you've joined? It's all plain and above board; still, some guys get a wrong slant on us. (*sharply*) What's your notion of the purpose of the I. W. W.?

YANK. Aw, I know all about it.

SECRETARY. (*sarcastically*) Well, give us some of your valuable information.

YANK. (*cunningly*) I know enough not to speak outa my toin. (*then resentfully again*) Aw, say! I'm reg'lar. I'm wise to de game. I know yuh got to watch your step with a stranger. For all youse know, I might be a plain-clothes dick, or somep'n, dat's what yuh're tinkin', huh? Aw, forget it! I belong, see? Ask any guy down to de docks if I don't.

SECRETARY. Who said you didn't?

YANK. After I'm 'nitiated, I'll show yuh.

SECRETARY. (*astounded*) Initiated? There's no initiation.

YANK. (*disappointed*) Ain't there no password—no grip or nothin'?

SECRETARY. What'd you think this is—the Elks—or the Black Hand?[39]

YANK. De Elks, hell! De Black Hand, dey're a lot of yellow back-stickin' Ginees.[40] Dis is a man's gang, ain't it?

SECRETARY. You said it! That's why we stand on our two feet in the open. We got no secrets.

YANK. (*surprised but admiringly*) Yuh mean to say yuh always run wide open—like dis?

SECRETARY. Exactly.

YANK. Den yuh sure got your noive wit youse!

SECRETARY. (*sharply*) Just what was it made you want to join us? Come out with that straight.

YANK. Yuh call me? Well, I got noive, too! Here's my hand. Yuh wanter blow tings up, don't yuh? Well, dat's me! I belong!

SECRETARY. (*with pretended carelessness*) You mean change the unequal conditions of society by legitimate direct action—or with dynamite?

YANK. Dynamite! Blow it offen de oith—steel—all de cages—all de factories, steamers, buildings, jails—de Steel Trust and all dat makes it go.

SECRETARY. So—that's your idea, eh? And did you have any special job in that line you wanted to propose to us? (*He makes a sign to the men, who get up cautiously one by one and group behind* YANK.)

YANK. (*boldly*) Sure, I'll come out wit it. I'll show youse I'm one of de gang. Dere's dat millionaire guy, Douglas—

SECRETARY. President of the Steel Trust, you mean? Do you want to assassinate him?

YANK. Naw, dat don't get yuh nothin'. I mean blow up de factory, de woiks, where he makes de steel. Dat's what I'm after—to blow up de steel, knock all de steel in de woild up to de moon. Dat'll fix things! (*eagerly, with a touch of bravado*) I'll do it by me lonesome! I'll show yuh! Tell me where his woiks is, how to git there, all de dope. Gimme de stuff, de old butter—and watch me do de rest! Watch de smoke and see it move! I don't give a damn if dey nab me—long as it's done! I'll soive life for it—and give 'em de laugh! (*half to himself*) And I'll write her a letter and tell her de hairy ape done it. Dat'll square tings.

SECRETARY. (*stepping away from* YANK) Very interesting. (*He gives a signal. The men, huskies all, throw themselves on* YANK *and before he knows it they have his legs and arms pinioned. But he is too flabbergasted to make a struggle, anyway. They feel him over for weapons.*)

MAN. No gat, no knife. Shall we give him what's what and put the boots to him?

[39]Elks: an American fraternal organization. Black Hand: Italian underworld organization of the mid-nineteenth century.

[40]"Guineas," slang term for Italians.

SECRETARY. No. He isn't worth the trouble we'd get into. He's too stupid. (*He comes closer and laughs mockingly in* YANK'S *face*) Ho-ho! By God, this is the biggest joke they've put up on us yet. Hey, you Joke! Who sent you—Burns or Pinkerton?[41] No, by God, you're such a bonehead I'll bet you're in the Secret Service! Well, you dirty spy, you rotten agent provocator, you can go back and tell whatever skunk is paying you blood-money for betraying your brothers that he's wasting his coin. You couldn't catch a cold. And tell him that all he'll ever get on us, or ever has got, is just his own sneaking plots that he's framed up to put us in jail. We are what our manifesto says we are, neither more or less—and we'll give him a copy of that any time he calls. And as for you—(*He glares scornfully at* YANK, *who is sunk in an oblivious stupor*) Oh, hell, what's the use of talking? You're a brainless ape.

YANK. (*aroused by the word to fierce but futile struggles*) What's dat, you Sheeny[42] bum, yuh!

SECRETARY. Throw him out, boys. (*In spite of his struggles, this is done with gusto and éclat. Propelled by several parting kicks,* YANK *lands sprawling in the middle of the narrow cobbled street. With a growl he starts to get up and storm the closed door, but stops bewildered by the confusion in his brain, pathetically impotent. He sits there, brooding, in as near to the attitude of Rodin's "The Thinker" as he can get in his position.*)

YANK. (*bitterly*) So dem boids don't tink I belong, neider. Aw, to hell wit 'em! Dey're in de wrong pew—de same old bull—soap-boxes and Salvation Army—no guts! Cut out an hour offen de job a day and make me happy! Gimme a dollar more a day and make me happy! Tree square a day, and cauliflowers in de front yard—ekal rights—a woman and kids—a lousy vote—and I'm all fixed for Jesus, huh? Aw, hell! What does dat get yuh? Dis ting's in your inside, but it ain't your belly. Feedin' your face—sinkers and coffee—dat don't touch it. It's way down—at de bottom. Yuh can't grab it, and yuh can't stop it. It moves, and everything moves. It stops and de whole woild stops. Dat's me now—I don't tick, see?—I'm a busted Ingersoll,[43] dat's what. Steel was me, and I owned de woild. Now I ain't steel, and de woild owns me. Aw, hell! I can't see—it's all dark, get me? It's all wrong! (*He turns a bitter mocking face up like an ape gibbering at the moon*) Say, youse up dere, Man in de Moon, yuh look so wise, gimme de answer, huh? Slip me de inside dope, de information right from de stable—where do I get off at, huh?

A POLICEMAN. (*who has come up the street in time to hear this last—with grim humor*) You'll get off at the station, you boob, if you don't get up out of that and keep movin'.

YANK. (*looking up at him—with a hard, bitter laugh*) Sure! Lock me up! Put me in a cage! Dat's de on'y answer yuh know. G'wan lock me up!

POLICEMAN. What you been doin'?

YANK. Enuf to gimme life for! I was born, see? Sure, dat's de charge. Write it in de blotter. I was born, get me!

POLICEMAN. (*jocosely*) God pity your old woman! (*then matter-of-factly*) But I've no time for kidding. You're soused. I'd run you in but it's too long a walk to the station. Come on now, get up, or I'll fan your ears with this club. Beat it now! (*He hauls* YANK *to his feet.*)

YANK. (*in a vague mocking tone*) Say, where do I go from here?

POLICEMAN. (*giving him a push—with a grin, indifferently*) Go to hell.

CURTAIN

[41]Detective agencies. [42]Slang term for Jewish. [43]An brand of inexpensive watch.

SCENE EIGHT

Twilight of the next day. The monkey house at the Zoo. One spot of clear gray light falls on the front of one cage so that the interior can be seen. The other cages are vague, shrouded in shadow from which chatterings pitched in a conversational tone can be heard. On the one cage a sign from which the word "gorilla" stands out. The gigantic animal himself is seen squatting on his haunches on a bench in much the same attitude of Rodin's "The Thinker." YANK *enters from the left. Immediately a chorus of angry chattering and screeching breaks out. The gorilla turns his eyes but makes no sound or move.*

YANK. (*with a hard, bitter laugh*) Welcome to your city, huh? Hail, hail, de gang's all here! (*At the sound of his voice the chattering dies away into an attentive silence.* YANK *walks up to the gorilla's cage and, leaning over the railing, stares in at its occupant, who stares back at him, silent and motionless. There is a pause of dead stillness. Then* YANK *begins to talk in a friendly confidential tone, half mockingly, but with a deep undercurrent of sympathy*) Say, yuh're some hard-lookin' guy, ain't yuh? I seen lots of tough nuts dat de gang called gorillas, but yuh're the foist real one I ever seen. Some chest yuh got, and shoulders, and dem arms and mits! I bet yuh got a punch in eider fist dat'd knock 'em all silly! (*This with genuine admiration. The gorilla, as if he understood, stands upright, swelling out his chest and pounding on it with his fist.* YANK *grins sympathetically*) Sure, I get yuh. Yuh challenge de whole woild, huh? Yuh got what I was sayin' even if yuh muffed de woids. (*then bitterness creeping in*) And why wouldn't yuh get me? Ain't we both members of de same club—de Hairy Apes? (*They stare at each other—a pause—then* YANK *goes on slowly and bitterly*) So yuh're what she seen when she looked at me, de white-faced tart! I was you to her, get me? On'y outa de cage—broke out—free to moider her, see? Sure! Dat's what she tought. She wasn't wise dat I was in a cage, too—worser'n yours—sure—a damn sight—'cause you got some chanct to bust loose—but me—(*He grows confused.*) Aw, hell! It's all wrong, ain't it? (*A pause*) I s'pose yuh wanter know what I'm doin' here, huh? I been warmin' a bench down to de Battery[44]—ever since last night. Sure. I seen de sun come up. Dat was pretty, too—all red and pink and green. I was lookin' at de skyscrapers—steel—and all de ships comin' in, sailin' out, all over de oith—and dey was steel, too. De sun was warm, dey wasn't no clouds, and dere was a breeze blowin'. Sure, it was great stuff. I got it aw right—what Paddy said about dat bein' de right dope—on'y I couldn't get *in* it, see? I couldn't belong in dat. It was over my head. And I kept tinkin'—and den I beat it up here to see what youse was like. And I waited till dey was all gone to git yuh alone. Say, how d'yuh feel sittin' in dat pen all de time, havin' to stand for 'em comin' and starin' at yuh—de white-faced, skinny tarts and de boobs what marry 'em—makin' fun of yuh, laughin' at yuh, gittin' scared of yuh—damn 'em! (*He pounds on the rail with his fist. The gorilla rattles the bars of his cage and snarls. All the other monkeys set up an angry chattering in the darkness.* YANK *goes on excitedly*) Sure! Dat's de way it hits me, too. On'y yuh're lucky, see? You don't belong wit 'em and yuh know it. But me, I belong wit 'em—but I don't, see? Dey don't belong wit me, dat's what. Get me? Tinkin' is hard—(*He passes one hand across his forehead with a painful gesture. The gorilla growls impatiently.* YANK *goes on gropingly*) It's dis way, what I'm drivin' at. Youse can sit and dope dream in de past,

[44]A park at the southern end of Manhattan Island.

green woods, de jungle and de rest of it. Den yuh belong and dey don't. Den yuh kin laugh at 'em, see? Yuh're de champ of de world. But me—I ain't got no past to tink in, nor nothin' dat's comin', on'y what's now—and dat don't belong. Sure, you're de best off! You can't tink, can yuh? Yuh can't talk neider. But I kin make a bluff at talkin' and tinkin'—a'most git away wit it—a'most!—and dat's where de joker comes in. (*He laughs.*) I ain't on oith and I ain't in heaven, get me? I'm in de middle tryin' to separate 'em, takin' all de woist punches from bot' of 'em. Maybe dat's what dey call hell, huh? But you, yuh're at de bottom. You belong? Sure! Yuh're de on'y one in de woild dat does, yuh lucky stiff! (*The gorilla growls proudly.*) And dat's why dey gotter put yuh in a cage, see? (*The gorilla roars angrily.*) Sure! Yuh get me. It beats it when you try to tink it or talk it—it's way down—deep—behind—you 'n' me we feel it. Sure! Bot' members of dis club! (*he laughs—then in a savage tone*) What de hell! T'hell wit it! A little action, dat's our meat! Dat belongs! Knock 'em down and keep bustin' 'em till dey croaks yuh with a gat—wit a steel! Sure! are yuh game? Dey've looked at youse, ain't dey—in a cage? Wanter get even? Wanter wind up like a sport 'stead of croaken' slow in dere? (*The gorilla roars an emphatic affirmative.* YANK *goes on with a sort of furious exaltation.*) Sure! Yuh're reg'lar! Yuh'll stick to de finish! Me 'n' you, huh?—bot' members of dis club! We'll put up one last start bout dat'll knock 'em offen deir seats! Dey'll have to make de cages stronger after we're trou! (*The gorilla is straining at his bars, growling, hopping from one foot to the other.* YANK *takes a jimmy from under his coat and forces the lock on the cage door. He throws this open.*) Pardon from de governor! Step out and shake hands. I'll take yuh for a walk down Fif' Avenoo. We'll knock 'em offen de oith and croak with de band playin'. Come on, Brother. (*The gorilla scrambles gingerly out of his cage. Goes to* YANK *and stands looking at him.* YANK *keeps his mocking tone—holds out his hand*) Shake—de secret grip of our order. (*Something, the tone of mockery, perhaps, suddenly enrages the animal. With a spring he wraps his huge arms around* YANK *in a murderous hug. There is a cracking snap of crushed ribs—a gasping cry, still mocking, from* YANK.) Hey, I didn't say kiss me! (*The gorilla lets the crushed body slip to the floor; stands over it uncertainly, considering; then picks it up, throws it in the cage, shuts the door, and shuffles off menacingly into the darkness at left. A great uproar of frightened chattering and whimpering comes from the other cages. Then* YANK *moves, groaning, opening his eyes, and there is silence. He mutters painfully*) Say—dey oughter match him—with Zybszko.[45] He got me, aw right! I'm trou. Even him didn't tink I belonged. (*then, with sudden passionate despair*) Christ, where do I get off at? Where do I fit in? (*checking himself as suddenly*) Aw, what de hell! No squawkin', see! No quittin', get me! Croak wit your boots on! (*He grabs hold of the bars of the cage and hauls himself painfully to his feet—looks around him bewilderedly—forces a mocking laugh.*) In de cage, huh? (*in the strident tones of a circus barker*) Ladies and gents, step forward and take a slant at de one and only—(*his voice weakening*) one and original—Hairy Ape from de wilds of—(*He slips in a heap on the floor and dies. The monkeys set up a chattering, whimpering wail. And, perhaps, the Hairy Ape at last belongs.*)

CURTAIN

1922

[45]Stanislaus Zbyszko, a famous wrestler of the 1920s.

Susan Glaspell 1876–1948

In an era when most male playwrights confined female characters to stereotypes or silence, Susan Keating Glaspell put real women front and center on her stage and insisted that the truth about their lives and their struggle for identity, equality, and power be seen and heard. But this radical contribution to American theater was barely acknowledged by theater critics and scholars until feminist readers and researchers rediscovered this writer and her work in the 1970s–1980s. Now Glaspell is mentioned side by side with playwright Eugene O'Neill as a major voice not only in the founding of the theater company known as the Provincetown Players, but also in the creation of an authentic American drama.

Glaspell's middle-class upbringing in the conservative world of Davenport, Iowa, informed much of the material that filled her early stories and novels about traditional young women seeking marriage and happiness. As she matured as a writer, however, she became increasingly aware of the political reality of a world where women were denied voting rights, property rights, and many other rights now considered unquestionably theirs. These themes eventually became central to the plots of her later, occasionally controversial, writings, including her most famous play, Trifles, *based on an actual murder case she had covered while working as a young reporter in Des Moines, Iowa.*

Like other educated women at the turn of the century, Glaspell grew restless with the numerous restrictions on women and became inspired by the avant-garde social, political, and cultural movements happening in the United States and Europe. Like other artists of the time, including renowned literary stylist Gertrude Stein and Imagist poet Hilda Doolittle, Glaspell traveled abroad to explore new personal and professional possibilities. When she returned to America, she settled on the east coast, dividing her time between the sea town of Provincetown, Massachusetts, and the thriving artistic community of Greenwich Village in New York City. By this time, she had married George Cook, a socialist, intellectual, and writer, who, with Glaspell and a small group of artistic friends, had grown dissatisfied with the sentimental and commercial drama that dominated the American stage. Eager to revitalize drama as a living art engaged with real human issues and problems relevant to an ordinary individual's life, Glaspell and Cook founded the Provincetown Players in 1915 and began to write, produce, and perform the first serious modern American drama. Eugene O'Neill, poet Edna St. Vincent Millay, and journalist John Reed were just a few of the literary and visual artists associated with this exciting new experiment in theater.

Revolution and rebellion were in the air in this time of war and social upheaval. Glaspell became involved with the early feminist and socialist movements, joining such activists as Jane Addams, Helen Hull, and Emma Goldman in conversations about "the New Woman" of the twentieth century. A member of the radical feminist club Heterodoxy—a group of twenty-five women, including writer Charlotte Perkins Gilman, who began meeting in 1912 to discuss ways to promote economic, sexual, political, and professional freedom for women—Glaspell once said, "I am interested in all progressive movements, whether feminist, social, or economic. . . ." Her writing demonstrated that consciousness in increasingly powerful ways.

First performed at the Wharf theater in Provincetown in 1916, Glaspell's one-act play Trifles *boldly illustrates her literary and feminist activism. On a stage set with the most ordinary of domestic scenes, the kitchen of a farmer's wife who never actually appears in the play, Glaspell exposed not just the harshness of a rural world that remained largely invisible to her urban audience, but, more importantly, such brutal oppression of a woman's spirit that the consequence was murder. This revelation unfolds quietly, as two women, Mrs. Hale and Mrs. Peters, gather together the "trifles" of Minnie Wright's life—her apron, a bottle of preserves, her sewing—and in the process uncover the motive for the crime committed before the play opens. The depth of psychological insight into, and the resulting empathy with, Minnie's violent action has gained this play the critical admiration of feminist critics and modern audiences since it was reclaimed for study and performance in the late twentieth century. Even today,* Trifles *raises complex and controversial questions about gender differences, social roles, and individual responsibilities to the claims of justice versus the law.*

After several years of exciting and productive investment in their growing theater company (Glaspell wrote eleven of the ninety-three plays performed in New York and Provincetown) she and her husband parted ways with the Provincetown Players in 1922. The couple traveled to Greece, where George Cook died two years later and where Glaspell continued to write works that explored the tensions women face in marriage and society. In 1927, while still in Europe, she remarried, and in 1930 she wrote Alison's House, *a play loosely based on Emily Dickinson's life, for which she won the Pulitzer Prize (only the second woman to do so).*

Glaspell died in Provincetown in the summer of 1948, leaving behind a literary legacy that includes thirteen plays, fourteen novels, and fifty short stories, articles, and essays. It is her drama more than her fiction, however, that will ensure her a lasting place in modern American literature. Like novelist Kate Chopin and other courageous women writers of that era, she wrote honestly and searingly of women's resistance to oppression at a time when radical female voices were rarely heard and even more rarely heeded.

FURTHER READING: C. W. E. Bigsby, *A Critical Introduction to Twentieth-Century American Drama,* 1982; *Plays by Susan Glaspell,* ed. C. W. E. Bigsby, 1987; *Modern American Drama: The Female Canon,* ed. J. Schlueter, 1990; V. Makowsky, *Susan Glaspell's Century of American Women: A Critical Interpretation of Her Work,* 1993; *Susan Glaspell: Essays on Her Theater and Fiction,* ed. L. Ben-Zvi, 1995; S. Burke, *American Feminist Playwrights,* 1996; B. O. Rajkowska, *Susan Glaspell: A Critical Biography,* 2000. *Susan Glaspell: Essays on Her Theater and Fiction,* ed. L. Ben-Zvi, 2002; L. Ben-Zvi, *Susan Glaspell: Her Life and Times,* 2005; K. Hinz-Bode, *Susan Glaspell and the Anxiety of Expression, Language, and Isolation in the Plays,* 2006.

TEXT: *Trifles,* 1916.

TRIFLES

CHARACTERS

GEORGE HENDERSON, *County Attorney*
HENRY PETERS, *Sheriff*
LEWIS HALE, *A Neighboring Farmer*
MRS. PETERS
MRS. HALE

SCENE: *The kitchen in the now abandoned farmhouse of John Wright, a gloomy kitchen, and left without having been put in order—unwashed pans under the sink, a loaf of bread outside the breadbox, a dish towel on the table—other signs of incompleted work. At the rear the outer door opens and the* SHERIFF *comes in followed by the* COUNTY ATTORNEY *and*

HALE. *The* SHERIFF *and* HALE *are men in middle life, the* COUNTY ATTORNEY *is a young man; all are much bundled up and go at once to the stove. They are followed by two women—the* SHERIFF'S WIFE *first; she is a slight wiry woman, a thin nervous face.* MRS. HALE *is larger and would ordinarily be called more comfortable looking, but she is disturbed now and looks fearfully about as she enters. The women have come in slowly, and stand close together near the door.*

COUNTY ATTORNEY (*Rubbing his hands*): This feels good. Come up to the fire, ladies.

MRS. PETERS (*After taking a step forward*): I'm not—cold.

SHERIFF (*Unbuttoning his overcoat and stepping away from the stove as if to mark the beginning of official business*): Now, Mr. Hale, before we move things about, you explain to Mr. Henderson just what you saw when you came here yesterday morning.

COUNTY ATTORNEY: By the way, has anything been moved? Are things just as you left them yesterday?

SHERIFF (*Looking about*): It's just the same. When it dropped below zero last night, I thought I'd better send Frank out this morning to make a fire for us—no use getting pneumonia with a big case on, but I told him not to touch anything except the stove—and you know Frank.

COUNTY ATTORNEY: Somebody should have been left here yesterday.

SHERIFF: Oh—yesterday. When I had to send Frank to Morris Center for that man who went crazy—I want you to know I had my hands full yesterday, I knew you could get back from Omaha by today and as long as I went over everything here myself—

COUNTY ATTORNEY: Well, Mr. Hale, tell just what happened when you came here yesterday morning.

HALE: Harry and I had started to town with a load of potatoes. We came along the road from my place and as I got here I said, "I'm going to see if I can't get John Wright to go in with me on a party telephone." I spoke to Wright about it once before and he put me off, saying folks talked too much anyway, and all he asked was peace and quiet—I guess you know about how much he talked himself; but I thought maybe if I went to the house and talked about it before his wife, though I said to Harry that I didn't know as what his wife wanted made much difference to John—

COUNTY ATTORNEY: Let's talk about that later, Mr. Hale. I do want to talk about that, but tell now just what happened when you got to the house.

HALE: I didn't hear or see anything; I knocked at the door, and still it was all quiet inside. I knew they must be up, it was past eight o'clock. So I knocked again, and I thought I heard somebody say, "Come in." I wasn't sure, I'm not sure yet, but I opened the door—this door (*Indicating the door by which the two women are still standing*) and there in that rocker—(*Pointing to it*) sat Mrs. Wright.

(*They all look at the rocker.*)

COUNTY ATTORNEY: What—what was she doing?

HALE: She was rockin' back and forth. She had her apron in her hand and was kind of—pleating it.

COUNTY ATTORNEY: And how did she—look?

HALE: Well, she looked queer.

COUNTY ATTORNEY: How do you mean—queer?

HALE: Well, as if she didn't know what she was going to do next. And kind of done up.

COUNTY ATTORNEY: How did she seem to feel about your coming?

HALE: Why, I don't think she minded—one way or other. She didn't pay much attention. I said, "How do, Mrs. Wright, it's cold, ain't it?" And she said, "Is it?"—and went on kind of pleating at her apron. Well, I was surprised; she didn't ask me to come up to the stove, or to set down, but just sat there, not even looking at me, so I said, "I want to see John." And then she—laughed. I guess you would call it a laugh. I thought of Harry and the team outside, so I said a little sharp: "Can't I see John?" "No," she says, kind o' dull like. "Ain't he home?" says I. "Yes," says she, "he's home." "Then why can't I see him?" I asked her, out of patience. "'Cause he's dead," says she. "*Dead?*" says I. She just nodded her head, not getting a bit excited, but rockin' back and forth. "Why—where is he?" says I, not knowing what to say. She just pointed upstairs—like that. (*Himself pointing to the room above*) I got up, with the idea of going up there. I walked from there to here—then I says, "Why, what did he die of?" "He died of a rope round his neck," says she, and just went on pleatin' at her apron. Well, I went out and called Harry. I thought I might—need help. We went upstairs and there he was lyin'—

COUNTY ATTORNEY: I think I'd rather have you go into that upstairs, where you can point it all out. Just go on now with the rest of the story.

HALE: Well, my first thought was to get that rope off. It looked . . . (*Stops, his face twitches*) . . . but Harry, he went up to him, and he said, "No, he's dead all right, and we'd better not touch anything." So we went back down stairs. She was still sitting that same way. "Has anybody been notified?" I asked. "No," says she, unconcerned. "Who did this, Mrs. Wright?" said Harry. He said it businesslike—and she stopped pleatin' of her apron. "I don't know," she says. "You don't *know?*" says Harry. "No," says she. "Weren't you sleepin' in the bed with him?" says Harry. "Yes," says she, "but I was on the inside." "Somebody slipped a rope round his neck and strangled him and you didn't wake up?" says Harry. "I didn't wake up," she said after him. We must 'a looked as if we didn't see how that could be, for after a minute she said, "I sleep sound." Harry was going to ask her more questions but I said maybe we ought to let her tell her story first to the coroner, or the sheriff, so Harry went fast as he could to Rivers' place, where there's a telephone.

COUNTY ATTORNEY: And what did Mrs. Wright do when she knew that you had gone for the coroner?

HALE: She moved from that chair to this one over here (*Pointing to a small chair in the corner*) and just sat there with her hands held together and looking down. I got a feeling that I ought to make some conversation, so I said I had come in to see if John wanted to put in a telephone, and at that she started to laugh, and then she stopped and looked at me—scared. (*The* COUNTY ATTORNEY, *who has had his notebook out, makes a note.*) I dunno, maybe it wasn't scared. I wouldn't like to say it was. Soon Harry got back, and then Dr. Lloyd came, and you, Mr. Peters, and so I guess that's all I know that you don't.

COUNTY ATTORNEY (*Looking around*): I guess we'll go upstairs first—and then out to the barn and around there. (*To the* SHERIFF) You're convinced that there was nothing important here—nothing that would point to any motive.

SHERIFF: Nothing here but kitchen things.

(The COUNTY ATTORNEY, *after again looking around the kitchen, opens the door of a cupboard closet. He gets up on a chair and looks on a shelf. Pulls his hand away, sticky.)*

COUNTY ATTORNEY: Here's a nice mess.

(The women draw nearer.)

MRS. PETERS (*To the other woman*): Oh, her fruit; it did freeze. (*To the* COUNTY ATTORNEY) She worried about that when it turned so cold. She said the fire'd go out and her jars would break.

SHERIFF: Well, can you beat the women! Held for murder and worryin' about her preserves.

COUNTY ATTORNEY: I guess before we're through she may have something more serious than preserves to worry about.

HALE: Well, women are used to worrying over trifles.

(The two women move a little closer together.)

COUNTY ATTORNEY (*With the gallantry of a young politician*): And yet, for all their worries, what would we do without the ladies? (*The women do not unbend. He goes to the sink, takes a dipperful of water from the pail and pouring it into a basin, washes his hands. Starts to wipe them on the roller towel, turns it for a cleaner place.*) Dirty towels! (*Kicks his foot against the pans under the sink*) Not much of a housekeeper, would you say, ladies?

MRS. HALE (*Stiffly*): There's a great deal of work to be done on a farm.

COUNTY ATTORNEY: To be sure. And yet (*With a little bow to her*) I know there are some Dickson county farmhouses which do not have such roller towels.

(He gives it a pull to expose its full length again.)

MRS. HALE: Those towels get dirty awful quick. Men's hands aren't always as clean as they might be.

COUNTY ATTORNEY: Ah, loyal to your sex, I see. But you and Mrs. Wright were neighbors. I suppose you were friends, too.

MRS. HALE (*Shaking her head*): I've not seen much of her of late years. I've not been in this house—it's more than a year.

COUNTY ATTORNEY: And why was that? You didn't like her?

MRS. HALE: I liked her all well enough. Farmers' wives have their hands full, Mr. Henderson. And then—

COUNTY ATTORNEY: Yes—?

MRS. HALE (*Looking about*): It never seemed a very cheerful place.

COUNTY ATTORNEY: No—it's not cheerful. I shouldn't say she had the homemaking instinct.

MRS. HALE: Well, I don't know as Wright had, either.

COUNTY ATTORNEY: You mean that they didn't get on very well?

MRS. HALE: No, I don't mean anything. But I don't think a place'd be any cheer-fuller for John Wright's being in it.

COUNTY ATTORNEY: I'd like to talk more of that a little later. I want to get the lay of things upstairs now.

(He goes to the left, where three steps lead to a stair door.)

SHERIFF: I suppose anything Mrs. Peters does'll be all right. She was to take in some clothes for her, you know, and a few little things. We left in such a hurry yesterday.

COUNTY ATTORNEY: Yes, but I would like to see what you take, Mrs. Peters, and keep an eye out for anything that might be of use to us.

MRS. PETERS: Yes, Mr. Henderson.

(The women listen to the men's steps on the stairs, then look about the kitchen.)

MRS. HALE: I'd hate to have men coming into my kitchen, snooping around and criticizing.

(She arranges the pans under sink which the COUNTY ATTORNEY *had shoved out of place.)*

MRS. PETERS: Of course it's no more than their duty.

MRS. HALE: Duty's all right, but I guess that deputy sheriff that came out to make the fire might have got a little of this on. (*Gives the roller towel a pull*) Wish I'd thought of that sooner. Seems mean to talk about her for not having things slicked up when she had to come away in such a hurry.

MRS. PETERS (*Who has gone to a small table in the left rear corner of the room, and lifted one end of a towel that covers a pan*): She had a bread set.

(Stands still)

MRS. HALE (*Eyes fixed on a loaf of bread beside the breadbox, which is on a low shelf at the other side of the room. Moves slowly toward it*): She was going to put this in there. (*Picks up loaf, then abruptly drops it. In a manner of returning to familiar things*) It's a shame about her fruit. I wonder if it's all gone. (*Gets up on the chair and looks*) I think there's some here that's all right, Mrs. Peters. Yes—here; (*Holding it toward the window*) this is cherries, too. (*Looking again*) I declare I believe that's the only one. (*Gets down, jar in her hand. Goes to the sink and wipes it off on the outside*) She'll feel awful bad after all her hard work in the hot weather. I remember the afternoon I put up my cherries last summer.

(She puts the jar on the big kitchen table, center of the room. With a sigh, is about to sit down in the rocking-chair. Before she is seated realizes what chair it is; with a slow look at it, steps back. The chair which she has touched rocks back and forth.)

MRS. PETERS: Well, I must get those things from the front room closet. (*She goes to the door at the right, but after looking into the other room, steps back.*) You coming with me, Mrs. Hale? You could help me carry them.

(They go in the other room; reappear, MRS. PETERS *carrying a dress and skirt,* MRS. HALE *following with a pair of shoes.)*

MRS. PETERS: My, it's cold in there.

(She puts the clothes on the big table, and hurries to the stove.)

MRS. HALE (*Examining her skirt*): Wright was close. I think maybe that's why she kept so much to herself. She didn't even belong to the Ladies Aid. I suppose she felt she couldn't do her part, and then you don't enjoy things when you feel shabby. She used to wear pretty clothes and be lively, when she was Minnie Foster, one of the town girls singing in the choir. But that—oh, that was thirty years ago. This all you was to take in?

MRS. PETERS: She said she wanted an apron. Funny thing to want, for there isn't much to get you dirty in jail, goodness knows. But I suppose just to make her feel more natural. She said they was in the top drawer in this cupboard. Yes, here. And then her little shawl that always hung behind the door. (*Opens stair door and looks*) Yes, here it is.

(Quickly shuts door leading upstairs)

MRS. HALE (*Abruptly moving toward her*): Mrs. Peters?

MRS. PETERS: Yes, Mrs. Hale?

MRS. HALE: Do you think she did it?

MRS. PETERS (*In a frightened voice*): Oh, I don't know.

MRS. HALE: Well, I don't think she did. Asking for an apron and her little shawl. Worrying about her fruit.

MRS. PETERS (*Starts to speak, glances up, where footsteps are heard in the room above. In a low voice*): Mr. Peters says it looks bad for her. Mr. Henderson is awful sarcastic in a speech and he'll make fun of her sayin' she didn't wake up.

MRS. HALE: Well, I guess John Wright didn't wake when they was slipping that rope under his neck.

MRS. PETERS (*Crossing slowly to table and placing shawl and apron on table with other clothing*): No, it's strange. It must have been done awful crafty and still. They say it was such a—funny way to kill a man, rigging it all up like that.

MRS. HALE (*Crossing to left of* MRS. PETERS *at table*): That's just what Mr. Hale said. There was a gun in the house. He says that's what he can't understand.

MRS. PETERS: Mr. Henderson said coming out that what was needed for the case was a motive; something to show anger, or—sudden feeling.

MRS. HALE (*Who is standing by the table*): Well, I don't see any signs of anger around here. (*She puts her hand on the dish towel which lies on the table, stands looking down at table, one-half of which is clean, the other half messy.*) It's wiped to here. (*Makes a move as if to finish work, then turns and looks at loaf of bread outside the breadbox. Drops towel. In that voice of coming back to familiar things*) Wonder how they are finding things upstairs. (*Crossing below table to down right*) I hope she had it a little more red-up up there. You know, it seems kind of *sneaking*. Locking her up in town and then coming out here and trying to get her own house to turn against her!

MRS. PETERS: But, Mrs. Hale, the law is the law.

MRS. HALE: I s'pose 'tis. (*Unbuttoning her coat.*) Better loosen up your things, Mrs. Peters. You won't feel them when you go out. (MRS. PETERS *takes off her fur tippet, goes to hang it on chair back left of table, stands looking at the work basket on floor near down left window.*)

MRS. PETERS: She was piecing a quilt. (*She brings the large sewing basket to the center table and they look at the bright pieces,* MRS. HALE *above the table and* MRS. PETERS *left of it.*)

MRS. HALE: It's a log cabin pattern. Pretty, isn't it? I wonder if she was goin' to quilt it or just knot it? (*Footsteps have been heard coming down the stairs. The* SHERIFF *enters followed by* HALE *and the* COUNTY ATTORNEY.)

SHERIFF: They wonder if she was going to quilt it or just knot it! (*The men laugh, the women look abashed.*)

COUNTY ATTORNEY (*Rubbing his hands over the stove*): Frank's fire didn't do much up there, did it? Well, let's go out to the barn and get that cleared up.

(The men go outside by up left door.)

MRS. HALE (*Resentfully*): I don't know as there's anything so strange, our takin' up our time with little things while we're waiting for them to get the evidence. (*She sits in chair right of table smoothing out a block with decision.*) I don't see as it's anything to laugh about.

MRS. PETERS (*Apologetically*): Of course they've got awful important things on their minds.

(Pulls up a chair and joins MRS. HALE *at the table)*

MRS. HALE (*Examining another block*): Mrs. Peters, look at this one. Here, this is the one she was working on, and look at the sewing! All the rest of it has been so nice and even. And look at this! It's all over the place! Why, it looks as if she didn't know what she was about!

(After she has said this they look at each other, then start to glance back at the door. After an instant MRS. HALE *has pulled at a knot and ripped the sewing.)*

MRS. PETERS: Oh, what are you doing, Mrs. Hale?

MRS. HALE (*Mildly*): Just pulling out a stitch or two that's not sewed very good. (*Threading a needle*) Bad sewing always made me fidgety.

MRS. PETERS (*Nervously*): I don't think we ought to touch things.

MRS. HALE: I'll just finish up this end. (*Suddenly stopping and leaning forward*) Mrs. Peters?

MRS. PETERS: Yes, Mrs. Hale?

MRS. HALE: What do you suppose she was so nervous about?

MRS. PETERS: Oh—I don't know. I don't know as she was nervous. I sometimes sew awful queer when I'm just tired. (MRS. HALE *starts to say something, looks at* MRS. PETERS, *then goes on sewing.*) Well, I must get these things wrapped up. They may be through sooner than we think. (*Putting apron and other things together*) I wonder where I can find a piece of paper, and string.

MRS. HALE: In that cupboard, maybe.

MRS. PETERS (*Looking in cupboard*): Why, here's a birdcage. (*Holds it up*) Did she have a bird, Mrs. Hale?

MRS. HALE: Why, I don't know whether she did or not—I've not been here for so long. There was a man around last year selling canaries cheap, but I don't know as she took one; maybe she did. She used to sing real pretty herself.

MRS. PETERS (*Glancing around*): Seems funny to think of a bird here. But she must have had one, or why would she have a cage? I wonder what happened to it.

MRS. HALE: I s'pose maybe the cat got it.

MRS. PETERS: No, she didn't have a cat. She's got that feeling some people have about cats—being afraid of them. My cat got in her room and she was real upset and asked me to take it out.

MRS. HALE: My sister Bessie was like that. Queer, ain't it?

MRS. PETERS (*Examining the cage*): Why, look at this door. It's broke. One hinge is pulled apart.

MRS. HALE (*Looking too*): Looks as if someone must have been rough with it.

MRS. PETERS: Why, yes.

(She brings the cage forward and puts it on the table.)

MRS. HALE: I wish if they're going to find any evidence they'd be about it. I don't like this place.

MRS. PETERS: But I'm awful glad you came with me, Mrs. Hale. It would be lonesome for me sitting here alone.

MRS. HALE: It would, wouldn't it? (*Dropping her sewing*) But I tell you what I do wish, Mrs. Peters. I wish I had come over sometimes when she was here. I—(*Looking around the room*)—wish I had.

MRS. PETERS: But of course you were awful busy, Mrs. Hale—your house and your children.

MRS. HALE: I could've come. I stayed away because it weren't cheerful—and that's why I ought to have come. I—I've never liked this place. Maybe because it's down in a hollow and you don't see the road. I dunno what it is but it's a lonesome place and always was. I wish I had come over to see Minnie Foster sometimes. I can see now—

(Shakes her head)

MRS. PETERS: Well, you mustn't reproach yourself, Mrs. Hale. Somehow we just don't see how it is with other folks until—something comes up.

MRS. HALE: Not having children makes less work—but it makes a quiet house, and Wright out to work all day, and no company when he did come in. Did you know John Wright, Mrs. Peters?

MRS. PETERS: Not to know him; I've seen him to town. They say he was a good man.

MRS. HALE: Yes—good; he didn't drink, and kept his word as well as most, I guess, and paid his debts. But he was a hard man, Mrs. Peters. Just to pass the time of day with him—(*Shivers*) Like a raw wind that gets to the bone. (*Pauses, her eye falling on the cage*) I should think she would'a wanted a bird. But what do you suppose went wrong with it?

MRS. PETERS: I don't know, unless it got sick and died.

(She reaches over and swings the broken door, swings it again. Both women watch it.)

MRS. HALE: You weren't raised round here, were you? (MRS. PETERS *shakes her head.*) You didn't know—her?

MRS. PETERS: Not till they brought her yesterday.

MRS. HALE: She—come to think of it, she was kind of like a bird herself—real sweet and pretty, but kind of timid and—fluttery. How—she—did—change. (*Silence, then as if struck by a happy thought and relieved to get back to every day things*) Tell you what, Mrs. Peters, why don't you take the quilt in with you? It might take up her mind.

MRS. PETERS: Why, I think that's a real nice idea, Mrs. Hale. There couldn't possibly be any objection to it, could there? Now, just what would I take? I wonder if her patches are in here—and her things.

(They look in the sewing basket.)

MRS. HALE: Here's some red. I expect this has got sewing things in it. (*Brings out a fancy box*) What a pretty box. Looks like something somebody would give you. Maybe her scissors are in here. (*Opens box. Suddenly puts her hand to her nose*) Why—(MRS. PETERS *bends nearer, then turns her face away.*) There's something wrapped up in this piece of silk.

MRS. PETERS: Why, this isn't her scissors.

MRS. HALE (*Lifting the silk*): Oh, Mrs. Peters—it's—

(MRS. PETERS bends closer.)

MRS. PETERS: It's the bird.

MRS. HALE (*Jumping up*): But, Mrs. Peters—look at it! Its neck! Look at its neck! It's all—other side to.

MRS. PETERS: Somebody—wrung—its—neck.

(Their eyes meet. A look of growing comprehension, of horror. Steps are heard outside. MRS. HALE *slips box under quilt pieces, and sinks into her chair. Enter* SHERIFF *and* COUNTY ATTORNEY. MRS. PETERS *rises.)*

COUNTY ATTORNEY (*As one turning from serious things to little pleasantries*): Well, ladies, have you decided whether she was going to quilt it or knot it?

MRS. PETERS: We think she was going to—knot it.

COUNTY ATTORNEY: Well, that's interesting, I'm sure. (*Seeing the birdcage*) Has the bird flown?

MRS. HALE (*Putting more quilt pieces over the box*): We think the—cat got it.

COUNTY ATTORNEY (*Preoccupied*): Is there a cat?

(MRS. HALE *glances in a quick covert way at* MRS. PETERS.)

MRS. PETERS: Well, not now. They're superstitious, you know. They leave.

COUNTY ATTORNEY (*To* SHERIFF PETERS, *continuing an interrupted conversation*): No sign at all of anyone having come from the outside. Their own rope. Now let's go up again and go over it piece by piece. (*They start upstairs.*) It would have to have been someone who knew just the—

(MRS. PETERS *sits down. The two women sit there not looking at one another, but as if peering into something and at the same time holding back. When they talk now it is in the manner of feeling their way over strange ground, as if afraid of what they are saying, but as if they can not help saying it.*)

MRS. HALE: She liked the bird. She was going to bury it in that pretty box.

MRS. PETERS (*In a whisper*): When I was a girl—my kitten—there was a boy took a hatchet, and before my eyes—and before I could get there—(*Covers her face an instant*) If they hadn't held me back I would have—(*Catches herself, looks upstairs where steps are heard, falters weakly*)—hurt him.

MRS. HALE (*With a slow look around her*): I wonder how it would seem never to have had any children around. (*Pause*) No, Wright wouldn't like the bird—a thing that sang. She used to sing. He killed that too.

MRS. PETERS (*Moving uneasily*): We don't know who killed the bird.

MRS. HALE: I knew John Wright.

MRS. PETERS: It was an awful thing was done in this house that night, Mrs. Hale. Killing a man while he slept, slipping a rope around his neck that choked the life out of him.

MRS. HALE: His neck. Choked the life out of him.

(*Her hand goes out and rests on the birdcage.*)

MRS. PETERS (*With rising voice*): We don't know who killed him. We don't know.

MRS. HALE (*Her own feeling not interrupted*): If there'd been years and years of nothing, then a bird to sing to you, it would be awful—still, after the bird was still.

MRS. PETERS (*Something within her speaking*): I know what stillness is. When we homesteaded in Dakota, and my first baby died—after he was two years old, and me with no other then—

MRS. HALE (*Moving*): How soon do you suppose they'll be through, looking for the evidence?

MRS. PETERS: I know what stillness is. (*Pulling herself back*) The law has got to punish crime, Mrs. Hale.

MRS. HALE (*Not as if answering that*): I wish you'd seen Minnie Foster when she wore a white dress with blue ribbons and stood up there in the choir and sang.

(*A look around the room*) Oh, I wish I'd come over here once in a while! That was a crime! That was a crime! Who's going to punish that?

MRS. PETERS (*Looking upstairs*): We mustn't—take on.

MRS. HALE: I might have known she needed help! I know how things can be—for women. I tell you, it's queer, Mrs. Peters. We live close together and we live far apart. We all go through the same things—it's all just a different kind of the same thing. (*Brushes her eyes; noticing the jar of fruit, reaches out for it*) If I was you I wouldn't tell her her fruit was gone. Tell her it ain't. Tell her it's all right. Take this in to prove it to her. She—she may never know whether it was broke or not.

MRS. PETERS (*Takes the jar, looks about for something to wrap it in; takes petticoat from the clothes brought from the other room, very nervously begins winding this around the jar. In a false voice*): My, it's a good thing the men couldn't hear us. Wouldn't they just laugh! Getting all stirred up over a little thing like a—dead canary. As if that could have anything to do with—with—wouldn't they laugh!

(The men are heard coming down stairs.)

MRS. HALE (*Under her breath*): Maybe they would—maybe they wouldn't.

COUNTY ATTORNEY: No, Peters, it's all perfectly clear except a reason for doing it. But you know juries when it comes to women. If there was some definite thing. Something to show—something to make a story about—a thing that would connect up with this strange way of doing it—

(The women's eyes meet for an instant. Enter HALE *from outer door.)*

HALE: Well, I've got the team around. Pretty cold out there.

COUNTY ATTORNEY: I'm going to stay here a while by myself. (*To the* SHERIFF.) You can send Frank out for me, can't you? I want to go over everything. I'm not satisfied that we can't do better.

SHERIFF: Do you want to see what Mrs. Peters is going to take in?

(The COUNTY ATTORNEY *goes to the table, picks up the apron, laughs.)*

COUNTY ATTORNEY: Oh I guess they're not very dangerous things the ladies have picked out. (*Moves a few things about, disturbing the quilt pieces which cover the box. Steps back*) No, Mrs. Peters doesn't need supervising. For that matter, a sheriff's wife is married to the law. Ever think of it that way, Mrs. Peters?

MRS. PETERS: Not—just that way.

SHERIFF (*Chuckling*): Married to the law. (*Moves toward the other room*) I just want you to come in here a minute, George. We ought to take a look at these windows.

COUNTY ATTORNEY (*Scoffingly*): Oh, windows!

SHERIFF: We'll be right out, Mr. Hale.

(HALE *goes outside. The* SHERIFF *follows the* COUNTY ATTORNEY *into the other room. Then* MRS. HALE *rises, hands tight together, looking intensely at* MRS. PETERS, *whose eyes make a slow turn, finally meeting* MRS. HALE'S. *A moment* MRS. HALE *holds her, then her own eyes point the way to where the box is concealed. Suddenly* MRS. PETERS *throws back quilt pieces and tries to put the box in the bag she is carrying. It is too big. She opens box, starts to take bird out, cannot touch it, goes to pieces, stands there helpless. Sound of a knob turning in the other room.* MRS. HALE *snatches her box and puts it in the pocket of her big coat. Enter* COUNTY ATTORNEY *and* SHERIFF.*)*

COUNTY ATTORNEY (*Facetiously*): Well, Henry, at least we found out that she was not going to quilt it. She was going to—what is it you call it, ladies?

MRS. HALE (*Her hand against her pocket*): We call it—knot it, Mr. Henderson.

CURTAIN

1916

Sinclair Lewis 1885–1951

The first American to win the Nobel prize for literature, Sinclair Lewis is remembered for his literary achievement as a novelist and for introducing into the American popular consciousness a cast of unforgettable character types. He was born Harry Sinclair Lewis, the son of a doctor in the small town of Sauk Centre, Minnesota, in 1885. Aside from losing his mother at an early age, his childhood was relatively uneventful. After finishing high school, he attended Yale, where he began writing for the university's student publication, Literary Magazine and Courant. *Upon graduating in 1908, Lewis traveled west, stopping first in Iowa for a brief stint to work as a newspaper reporter and then in California, where he wrote and sold story outlines to Jack London. By 1910 he returned east to take a job in a New York publishing house.*

Over the next decade Lewis wrote several apprentice novels, including Our Mr. Wrenn *(1914),* The Job *(1917), and* Free Air *(1919). They attracted a modest readership and the attention of a small group of admiring critics. With the publication of* Main Street *in 1920, however, his literary fame skyrocketed. The novel sold in the hundreds of thousands and established Lewis as a major literary figure. Its satirical treatment of small-town America resonated mightily with the public. In 1922, Lewis followed up* Main Street*'s success with* Babbitt, *another best-selling attack on middle-class pretension. The 1920s saw the publication of two more major novels by Lewis,* Arrowsmith *in 1925 and* Elmer Gantry *in 1927. He was awarded the Pulitzer prize for* Arrowsmith *but turned it down for a variety of personal and philosophical reasons. In 1930 he received and accepted the Nobel prize.*

Lewis continued to publish in the last two decades of his life, but none of these later works seemed to possess the power of the writing from his major period of the 1920s. Increasingly, he fell out of favor with readers and critics in the decade leading up to World War II. In the early 1940s he taught briefly at the University of Wisconsin and the University of Minnesota. After the war Lewis relocated to Italy, where he died in 1951.

FURTHER READING: M. Schorer, *Sinclair Lewis: An American Life,* 1961; V. Sheean, *Dorothy and Red,* 1963; D. Dooley, *The Art of Sinclair Lewis,* 1967; H. Smith, *Sinclair Lewis,* 1973; V. Parrington, *Sinclair Lewis: Our Own Diogenes,* 1973; M. Light, *The Quixotic Vision of Sinclair Lewis,* 1975; *Sinclair Lewis at 100: Papers Presented at a Centennial Conference,* 1985; *Critical Essays on Sinclair Lewis,* ed. M. Bucco, 1986; J. Hutchisson, *The Rise of Sinclair Lewis,* 1996; R. Lingeman, *Sinclair Lewis: Rebel from Main Street,* 2002.

TEXT *Babbitt,* 1922.

from *BABBITT*

CHAPTER 1

I

The towers of Zenith[1] aspired above the morning mist; austere towers of steel and cement and limestone, sturdy as cliffs and delicate as silver rods. They were neither citadels nor churches, but frankly and beautifully office-buildings.

The mist took pity on the fretted structures of earlier generations: the Post Office with its shingle-tortured mansard, the red brick minarets of hulking old houses, factories with stingy and sooted windows, wooden tenements colored like mud. The city was full of such grotesqueries, but the clean towers were thrusting them from the business center, and on the farther hills were shining new houses, homes—they seemed—for laughter and tranquillity.

Over a concrete bridge fled a limousine of long sleek hood and noiseless engine. These people in evening clothes were returning from an all-night rehearsal of a Little Theater play, an artistic adventure considerably illuminated by champagne. Below the bridge curved a railroad, a maze of green and crimson lights. The New York Flyer boomed past, and twenty lines of polished steel leaped into the glare.

In one of the skyscrapers the wires of the Associated Press were closing down. The telegraph operators wearily raised their celluloid eye-shades after a night of talking with Paris and Peking. Through the building crawled the scrubwomen, yawning, their old shoes slapping. The dawn mist spun away. Cues of men with lunch-boxes clumped toward the immensity of new factories, sheets of glass and hollow tile, glittering shops where five thousand men worked beneath one roof, pouring out the honest wares that would be sold up the Euphrates[2] and across the veldt.[3] The whistles rolled out in greeting a chorus cheerful as the April dawn; the song of labor in a city built—it seemed—for giants.

II

There was nothing of the giant in the aspect of the man who was beginning to awaken on the sleeping-porch of a Dutch Colonial[4] house in that residential district of Zenith known as Floral Heights.

His name was George F. Babbitt. He was forty-six years old now, in April, 1920, and he made nothing in particular, neither butter nor shoes nor poetry, but he was nimble in the calling of selling houses for more than people could afford to pay.

His large head was pink, his brown hair thin and dry. His face was babyish in slumber, despite his wrinkles and the red spectacle-dents on the slopes of his nose. He was not fat but he was exceedingly well fed; his cheeks were pads, and the unroughened hand which lay helpless upon the khaki-colored blanket was

[1] The fictional mid-size, Midwestern city that is the setting for *Babbitt*.
[2] A river that flows through Turkey, Syria, and Iraq. [3] The grassy plains of southern Africa.
[4] An architectural style featuring an asymmetrical roof, steeper on one side than on the other (called a gambrel roof).

slightly puffy. He seemed prosperous, extremely married and unromantic; and altogether unromantic appeared this sleeping-porch, which looked on one sizable elm, two respectable grass-plots, a cement driveway, and a corrugated iron garage. Yet Babbitt was again dreaming of the fairy child, a dream more romantic than scarlet pagodas by a silver sea.

For years the fairy child had come to him. Where others saw but Georgie Babbitt, she discerned gallant youth. She waited for him, in the darkness beyond mysterious groves. When at last he could slip away from the crowded house he darted to her. His wife, his clamoring friends, sought to follow, but he escaped, the girl fleet beside him, and they crouched together on a shadowy hillside. She was so slim, so white, so eager! She cried that he was gay and valiant, that she would wait for him, that they would sail—

Rumble and bang of the milk-truck.

Babbitt moaned; turned over; struggled back toward his dream. He could see only her face now, beyond misty waters. The furnace-man slammed the basement door. A dog barked in the next yard. As Babbitt sank blissfully into a dim warm tide, the paper-carrier went by whistling, and the rolled-up *Advocate* thumped the front door. Babbitt roused, his stomach constricted with alarm. As he relaxed, he was pierced by the familiar and irritating rattle of some one cranking a Ford: snap-ah-ah, snap-ah-ah, snap-ah-ah. Himself a pious motorist, Babbitt cranked with the unseen driver, with him waited through taut hours for the roar of the starting engine, with him agonized as the roar ceased and again began the infernal patient snap-ah-ah—a round, flat sound, a shivering cold-morning sound, a sound infuriating and inescapable. Not till the rising voice of the motor told him that the Ford was moving was he released from the panting tension. He glanced once at his favorite tree, elm twigs against the gold patina of sky, and fumbled for sleep as for a drug. He who had been a boy very credulous of life was no longer greatly interested in the possible and improbable adventures of each new day.

He escaped from reality till the alarm-clock rang, at seven-twenty.

III

It was the best of nationally advertised and quantitatively produced alarm-clocks, with all modern attachments, including cathedral chime, intermittent alarm, and a phosphorescent dial. Babbitt was proud of being awakened by such a rich device. Socially it was almost as creditable as buying expensive cord tires.

He sulkily admitted now that there was no more escape, but he lay and detested the grind of the real-estate business, and disliked his family, and disliked himself for disliking them. The evening before, he had played poker at Vergil Gunch's till midnight, and after such holidays he was irritable before breakfast. It may have been the tremendous home-brewed beer of the prohibition-era and the cigars to which that beer enticed him; it may have been resentment of return from this fine, bold man-world to a restricted region of wives and stenographers, and of suggestions not to smoke so much.

From the bedroom beside the sleeping-porch, his wife's detestably cheerful "Time to get up, Georgie boy," and the itchy sound, the brisk and scratchy sound, of combing hairs out of a stiff brush.

He grunted; he dragged his thick legs, in faded baby-blue pajamas, from under the khaki blanket; he sat on the edge of the cot, running his fingers through his wild hair, while his plump feet mechanically felt for his slippers. He looked regretfully at the blanket—forever a suggestion to him of freedom and heroism. He had bought it for a camping trip which had never come off. It symbolized gorgeous loafing, gorgeous cursing, virile flannel shirts.

He creaked to his feet, groaning at the waves of pain which passed behind his eyeballs. Though he waited for their scorching recurrence, he looked blurrily out at the yard. It delighted him, as always; it was the neat yard of a successful business man of Zenith, that is, it was perfection, and made him also perfect. He regarded the corrugated iron garage. For the three-hundred-and-sixty-fifth time in a year he reflected, "No class to that tin shack. Have to build me a frame garage. But by golly it's the only thing on the place that isn't up-to-date!" While he stared he thought of a community garage for his acreage development, Glen Oriole. He stopped puffing and jiggling. His arms were akimbo. His petulant, sleep-swollen face was set in harder lines. He suddenly seemed capable, an official, a man to contrive, to direct, to get things done.

On the vigor of his idea he was carried down the hard, clean, unused-looking hall into the bathroom.

Though the house was not large it had, like all houses on Floral Heights, an altogether royal bathroom of porcelain and glazed tile and metal sleek as silver. The towel-rack was a rod of clear glass set in nickel. The tub was long enough for a Prussian Guard, and above the set bowl was a sensational exhibit of tooth-brush holder, shaving-brush holder, soap-dish, sponge-dish, and medicine-cabinet, so glittering and so ingenious that they resembled an electrical instrument-board. But the Babbitt whose god was Modern Appliances was not pleased. The air of the bathroom was thick with the smell of a heathen toothpaste. "Verona been at it again! 'Stead of sticking to Lilidol, like I've re-peat-ed-ly asked her, she's gone and gotten some confounded stinkum stuff that makes you sick!"

The bath-mat was wrinkled and the floor was wet. (His daughter Verona eccentrically took baths in the morning, now and then.) He slipped on the mat, and slid against the tub. He said "Damn!" Furiously he snatched up his tube of shaving-cream, furiously he lathered, with a belligerent slapping of the unctuous brush, furiously he raked his plump cheeks with a safety-razor. It pulled. The blade was dull. He said, "Damn—oh—oh—damn it!"

He hunted through the medicine-cabinet for a packet of new razor-blades (reflecting, as invariably, "Be cheaper to buy one of these dinguses and strop your own blades,") and when he discovered the packet, behind the round box of bicarbonate of soda, he thought ill of his wife for putting it there and very well of himself for not saying "Damn." But he did say it, immediately afterward, when with wet and soap-slippery fingers he tried to remove the horrible little envelope and crisp clinging oiled paper from the new blade. Then there was the problem, oft-pondered, never solved, of what to do with the old blade, which might imperil the fingers of his young. As usual, he tossed it on top of the medicine-cabinet, with a mental note that some day he must remove the fifty or sixty other blades that were also, temporarily, piled up there. He finished his shaving in a growing testiness increased by his spinning headache and by the emptiness in his stomach. When he was done, his round face smooth and streamy and his eyes stinging from soapy water, he reached for a towel. The family towels were wet, wet and clammy and vile, all of them wet, he found, as he blindly snatched them—his own face-towel, his wife's, Verona's, Ted's,

Tinka's, and the lone bath-towel with the huge welt of initial. Then George F. Babbitt did a dismaying thing. He wiped his face on the guest-towel! It was a pansy-embroidered trifle which always hung there to indicate that the Babbitts were in the best Floral Heights society. No one had ever used it. No guest had ever dared to. Guests secretively took a corner of the nearest regular towel.

He was raging, "By golly, here they go and use up all the towels, every doggone one of 'em, and they use 'em and get 'em all wet and sopping, and never put out a dry one for me—of course, I'm the goat!—and then I want one and—I'm the only person in the doggone house that's got the slightest doggone bit of consideration for other people and thoughtfulness and consider there may be others that may want to use the doggone bathroom after me and consider—"

He was pitching the chill abominations into the bath-tub, pleased by the vindictiveness of that desolate flapping sound; and in the midst his wife serenely trotted in, observed serenely, "Why Georgie dear, what are you doing? Are you going to wash out the towels? Why, you needn't wash out the towels. Oh, Georgie, you didn't go and use the guest-towel, did you?"

It is not recorded that he was able to answer.

For the first time in weeks he was sufficiently roused by his wife to look at her.

IV

Myra Babbitt—Mrs. George F. Babbitt—was definitely mature. She had creases from the corners of her mouth to the bottom of her chin, and her plump neck bagged. But the thing that marked her as having passed the line was that she no longer had reticences before her husband, and no longer worried about not having reticences. She was in a petticoat now, and corsets which bulged, and unaware of being seen in bulgy corsets. She had become so dully habituated to married life that in her full matronliness she was as sexless as an anemic nun. She was a good woman, a kind woman, a diligent woman, but no one, save perhaps Tinka her ten-year-old, was at all interested in her or entirely aware that she was alive.

After a rather thorough discussion of all the domestic and social aspects of towels she apologized to Babbitt for his having an alcoholic headache; and he recovered enough to endure the search for a B.V.D.[5] undershirt which had, he pointed out, malevolently been concealed among his clean pajamas.

He was fairly amiable in the conference on the brown suit.

"What do you think, Myra?" He pawed at the clothes hunched on a chair in their bedroom, while she moved about mysteriously adjusting and patting her petticoat and, to his jaundiced eye, never seeming to get on with her dressing. "How about it? Shall I wear the brown suit another day?"

"Well, it looks awfully nice on you."

"I know, but gosh, it needs pressing."

"That's so. Perhaps it does."

"It certainly could stand being pressed, all right."

"Yes, perhaps it wouldn't hurt it to be pressed."

"But gee, the coat doesn't need pressing. No sense in having the whole darn suit pressed, when the coat doesn't need it."

[5]A brand name; abbreviation for the company name: Bradley, Voorhees, and Day.

"That's so." "But the pants certainly need it, all right. Look at them—look at those wrinkles—the pants certainly do need pressing."

"That's so. Oh, Georgie, why couldn't you wear the brown coat with the blue trousers we were wondering what we'd do with them?"

"Good Lord! Did you ever in all my life know me to wear the coat of one suit and the pants of another? What do you think I am? A busted bookkeeper?"

"Well, why don't you put on the dark gray suit to-day, and stop in at the tailor and leave the brown trousers?"

"Well, they certainly need—Now where the devil is that gray suit? Oh, yes, here we are."

He was able to get through the other crises of dressing with comparative resoluteness and calm.

His first adornment was the sleeveless dimity[6] B.V.D. undershirt, in which he resembled a small boy humorlessly wearing a cheesecloth tabard at a civic pageant. He never put on B.V.D.'s without thanking the God of Progress that he didn't wear tight, long, old-fashioned undergarments, like his father-in-law and partner, Henry Thompson. His second embellishment was combing and slicking back his hair. It gave him a tremendous forehead, arching up two inches beyond the former hair-line. But most wonder-working of all was the donning of his spectacles.

There is character in spectacles—the pretentious tortoiseshell, the meek pince-nez of the school teacher, the twisted silver-framed glasses of the old villager. Babbitt's spectacles had huge, circular, frameless lenses of the very best glass; the ear-pieces were thin bars of gold. In them he was the modern business man; one who gave orders to clerks and drove a car and played occasional golf and was scholarly in regard to Salesmanship. His head suddenly appeared not babyish but weighty, and you noted his heavy, blunt nose, his straight mouth and thick, long upper lip, his chin overfleshy but strong; with respect you beheld him put on the rest of his uniform as a Solid Citizen.

The gray suit was well cut, well made, and completely undistinguished. It was a standard suit. White piping on the V of the vest added a flavor of law and learning. His shoes were black laced boots, good boots, honest boots, standard boots, extraordinarily uninteresting boots. The only frivolity was in his purple knitted scarf. With considerable comment on the matter to Mrs. Babbitt (who, acrobatically fastening the back of her blouse to her skirt with a safety-pin, did not hear a word he said), he chose between the purple scarf and a tapestry effect with stringless brown harps among blown palms, and into it he thrust a snake-head pin with opal eyes.

A sensational event was changing from the brown suit to the gray the contents of his pockets. He was earnest about these objects. They were of eternal importance, like baseball or the Republican Party. They included a fountain pen and a silver pencil (always lacking a supply of new leads) which belonged in the righthand upper vest pocket. Without them he would have felt naked. On his watch-chain were a gold penknife, silver cigar-cutter, seven keys (the use of two of which he had forgotten), and incidentally a good watch. Depending from the chain was a large, yellowish elk's-tooth-proclamation of his membership in the Brotherly and Protective Order of Elks.[7] Most significant of all was his loose-leaf pocket note-book, that modern and efficient note-book which

[6]A lightweight cotton fabric. [7]A men's club.

contained the addresses of people whom he had forgotten, prudent memoranda of postal money-orders which had reached their destinations months ago, stamps which had lost their mucilage, clippings of verses by T. Cholmondeley Frink and of the newspaper editorials from which Babbitt got his opinions and his polysyllables, notes to be sure and do things which he did not intend to do, and one curious inscription—D.S.S. D.M.Y.P.D.F.

But he had no cigarette-case. No one had ever happened to give him one, so he hadn't the habit, and people who carried cigarette-cases he regarded as effeminate.

Last, he stuck in his lapel the Boosters' Club button. With the conciseness of great art the button displayed two words: "Boosters-Pep!" It made Babbitt feel loyal and important. It associated him with Good Fellows, with men who were nice and human, and important in business circles. It was his V.C., his Legion of Honor ribbon, his Phi Beta Kappa key.[8]

With the subtleties of dressing ran other complex worries. "I feel kind of punk this morning," he said. "I think I had too much dinner last evening. You oughtn't to serve those heavy banana fritters."

"But you asked me to have some."

"I know, but—I tell you, when a fellow gets past forty he has to look after his digestion. There's a lot of fellows that don't take proper care of themselves. I tell you at forty a man's a fool or his doctor—I mean, his own doctor. Folks don't give enough attention to this matter of dieting. Now I think—Course a man ought to have a good meal after the day's work, but it would be a good thing for both of us if we took lighter lunches."

"But Georgie, here at home I always do have a light lunch."

"Mean to imply I make a hog of myself, eating down-town? Yes, sure! You'd have a swell time if you had to eat the truck that new steward hands out to us at the Athletic Club! But I certainly do feel out of sorts, this morning. Funny, got a pain down here on the left side—but no, that wouldn't be appendicitis, would it? Last night, when I was driving over to Verg Gunch's, I felt a pain in my stomach, too. Right here it was—kind of a sharp shooting pain. I—Where'd that dime go to? Why don't you serve more prunes at breakfast? Of course I eat an apple every evening—an apple a day keeps the doctor away—but still, you ought to have more prunes, and not all these fancy doodads."

"The last time I had prunes you didn't eat them."

"Well, I didn't feel like eating 'em, I suppose. Matter of fact, I think I did eat some of 'em. Anyway—I tell you it's mighty important to—I was saying to Verg Gunch, just last evening, most people don't take sufficient care of their diges—"

"Shall we have the Gunches for our dinner, next week?"

"Why sure; you bet."

"Now see here, George: I want you to put on your nice dinner-jacket that evening."

"Rats! The rest of 'em won't want to dress."

"Of course they will. You remember when you didn't dress for the Littlefields' supper-party, and all the rest did, and how embarrassed you were."

"Embarrassed, hell! I wasn't embarrassed. Everybody knows I can put on as expensive a Tux. as anybody else, and I should worry if I don't happen to have

[8]The Victoria Cross (V.C.) and Legion of Honor ribbon are high honors bestowed by the British and French governments, respectively. Phi Beta Kappa is an exclusive academic honor society.

it on sometimes. All a darn nuisance, anyway. All right for a woman, that stays around the house all the time, but when a fellow's worked like the dickens all day, he doesn't want to go and hustle his head off getting into the soup-and-fish for a lot of folks that he's seen in just reg'lar ordinary clothes that same day."

"You know you enjoy being seen in one. The other evening you admitted you were glad I'd insisted on your dressing. You said you felt a lot better for it. And oh, Georgie, I do wish you wouldn't say 'Tux.' It's 'dinner-jacket.'"

"Rats, what's the odds?"

"Well, it's what all the nice folks say. Suppose Lucile McKelvey heard you calling it a 'Tux.'"

"Well, that's all right now! Lucile McKelvey can't pull anything on me! Her folks are common as mud, even if her husband and her dad are millionaires! I suppose you're trying to rub in your exalted social position! Well, let me tell you that your revered paternal ancestor, Henry T., doesn't even call it a 'Tux'! He calls it a 'bobtail jacket for a ringtail monkey,' and you couldn't get him into one unless you chloroformed him!"

"Now don't be horrid, George."

"Well, I don't want to be horrid, but Lord! you're getting as fussy as Verona. Ever since she got out of college she's been too rambunctious to live with—doesn't know what she wants—well, I know what she wants!—all she wants is to marry a millionaire, and live in Europe, and hold some preacher's hand, and simultaneously at the same time stay right here in Zenith and be some blooming kind of a socialist agitator or boss charity-worker or some damn thing! Lord, and Ted is just as bad! He wants to go to college, and he doesn't want to go to college. Only one of the three that knows her own mind is Tinka. Simply can't understand how I ever came to have a pair of shillyshallying children like Rone and Ted. I may not be any Rockefeller or James J. Shakespeare, but I certainly do know my own mind, and I do keep right on plugging along in the office and—Do you know the latest? Far as I can figure out, Ted's new bee is he'd like to be a movie actor and—And here I've told him a hundred times, if he'll go to college and law-school and make good, I'll set him up in business and—Verona just exactly as bad. Doesn't know what she wants. Well, well, come on! Aren't you ready yet? The girl rang the bell three minutes ago."

V

Before he followed his wife, Babbitt stood at the westernmost window of their room. This residential settlement, Floral Heights, was on a rise; and though the center of the city was three miles away—Zenith had between three and four hundred thousand inhabitants now—he could see the top of the Second National Tower, an Indiana limestone building of thirty-five stories.

Its shining walls rose against April sky to a simple cornice like a streak of white fire. Integrity was in the tower, and decision. It bore its strength lightly as a tall soldier. As Babbitt stared, the nervousness was soothed from his face, his slack chin lifted in reverence. All he articulated was "That's one lovely sight!" but he was inspired by the rhythm of the city; his love of it renewed. He beheld the tower as a temple-spire of the religion of business, a faith passionate, exalted, surpassing common men; and as he clumped down to breakfast he whistled the ballad "Oh, by gee, by gosh, by jingo" as though it were a hymn melancholy and noble.

CHAPTER 2

I

Relieved of Babbitt's bumbling and the soft grunts with which his wife expressed the sympathy she was too experienced to feel and much too experienced not to show, their bedroom settled instantly into impersonality.

It gave on the sleeping-porch. It served both of them as dressing-room, and on the coldest nights Babbitt luxuriously gave up the duty of being manly and retreated to the bed inside, to curl his toes in the warmth and laugh at the January gale.

The room displayed a modest and pleasant color-scheme, after one of the best standard designs of the decorator who "did the interiors" for most of the speculative-builders' houses in Zenith. The walls were gray, the woodwork white, the rug a serene blue; and very much like mahogany was the furniture—the bureau with its great clear mirror, Mrs. Babbitt's dressing-table with toilet-articles of almost solid silver, the plain twin beds, between them a small table holding a standard electric bedside lamp, a glass for water, and a standard bedside book with colored illustrations—what particular book it was cannot be ascertained, since no one had ever opened it. The mattresses were firm but not hard, triumphant modern mattresses which had cost a great deal of money; the hot-water radiator was of exactly the proper scientific surface for the cubic contents of the room. The windows were large and easily opened, with the best catches and cords, and Holland roller-shades guaranteed not to crack. It was a masterpiece among bedrooms, right out of Cheerful Modern Houses for Medium Incomes. Only it had nothing to do with the Babbitts, nor with any one else. If people had ever lived and loved here, read thrillers at midnight and lain in beautiful indolence on a Sunday morning, there were no signs of it. It had the air of being a very good room in a very good hotel. One expected the chambermaid to come in and make it ready for people who would stay but one night, go without looking back, and never think of it again.

Every second house in Floral Heights had a bedroom precisely like this.

The Babbitts' house was five years old. It was all as competent and glossy as this bedroom. It had the best of taste, the best of inexpensive rugs, a simple and laudable architecture, and the latest conveniences. Throughout, electricity took the place of candles and slatternly hearth-fires. Along the bedroom baseboard were three plugs for electric lamps, concealed by little brass doors. In the halls were plugs for the vacuum cleaner, and in the living-room plugs for the piano lamp, for the electric fan. The trim dining-room (with its admirable oak buffet, its leaded-glass cupboard, its creamy plaster walls, its modest scene of a salmon expiring upon a pile of oysters) had plugs which supplied the electric percolator and the electric toaster.

In fact there was but one thing wrong with the Babbitt house: It was not a home.

II

Often of a morning Babbitt came bouncing and jesting in to breakfast. But things were mysteriously awry to-day. As he pontifically tread the upper hall he looked into Verona's bedroom and protested, "What's the use of giving the family a high-class house when they don't appreciate it and tend to business and get down to brass tacks?"

He marched upon them: Verona, a dumpy brown-haired girl of twenty-two, just out of Bryn Mawr, given to solicitudes about duty and sex and God and the unconquerable bagginess of the gray sports-suit she was now wearing. Ted—Theodore Roosevelt Babbitt—a decorative boy of seventeen. Tinka—Katherine—still a baby at ten, with radiant red hair and a thin skin which hinted of too much candy and too many ice cream sodas. Babbitt did not show his vague irritation as he tramped in. He really disliked being a family tyrant, and his nagging was as meaningless as it was frequent. He shouted at Tinka, "Well, kittiedoolie!" It was the only pet name in his vocabulary, except the "dear" and "hon." with which he recognized his wife, and he flung it at Tinka every morning.

He gulped a cup of coffee in the hope of pacifying his stomach and his soul. His stomach ceased to feel as though it did not belong to him, but Verona began to be conscientious and annoying, and abruptly there returned to Babbitt the doubts regarding life and families and business which had clawed at him when his dream-life and the slim fairy girl had fled.

Verona had for six months been filing-clerk at the Gruensberg Leather Company offices, with a prospect of becoming secretary to Mr. Gruensberg and thus, as Babbitt defined it, "getting some good out of your expensive college education till you're ready to marry and settle down."

But now said Verona: "Father! I was talking to a classmate of mine that's working for the Associated Charities—oh, Dad, there's the sweetest little babies that come to the milk-station there!—and I feel as though I ought to be doing something worth while like that."

"What do you mean 'worth while'? If you get to be Gruensberg's secretary—and maybe you would, if you kept up your shorthand and didn't go sneaking off to concerts and talkfests every evening—I guess you'll find thirty-five or forty bones a week worth while!"

"I know, but—oh, I want to—contribute—I wish I were working in a settlement-house. I wonder if I could get one of the department-stores to let me put in a welfare-department with a nice rest-room and chintzes and wicker chairs and so on and so forth. Or I could—"

"Now you look here! The first thing you got to understand is that all this uplift and flipflop and settlement-work and recreation is nothing in God's world but the entering wedge for socialism. The sooner a man learns he isn't going to be coddled, and he needn't expect a lot of free grub and, uh, all these free classes and flipflop and doodads for his kids unless he earns 'em, why, the sooner he'll get on the job and produce—produce—produce! That's what the country needs, and not all this fancy stuff that just enfeebles the will-power of the working man and gives his kids a lot of notions above their class. And you—if you'd tend to business instead of fooling and fussing—All the time! When I was a young man I made up my mind what I wanted to do, and stuck to it through thick and thin, and that's why I'm where I am to-day, and—Myra! What do you let the girl chop the toast up into these dinky little chunks for? Can't get your fist onto 'em. Half cold, anyway!"

Ted Babbitt, junior in the great East Side High School, had been making hiccup-like sounds of interruption. He blurted now, "Say, Rone, you going to—" Verona whirled. "Ted! Will you kindly not interrupt us when we're talking about serious matters!"

"Aw punk," said Ted judicially. "Ever since somebody slipped up and let you out of college, Ammonia, you been pulling these nut conversations about what-nots and so-on-and-so-forths. Are you going to—I want to use the car tonight."

Babbitt snorted, "Oh, you do! May want it myself!" Verona protested, "Oh, you do, Mr. Smarty! I'm going to take it myself!" Tinka wailed, "Oh, papa, you said maybe you'd drive us down to Rosedale!" and Mrs. Babbitt, "Careful, Tinka, your sleeve is in the butter." They glared, and Verona hurled, "Ted, you're a perfect pig about the car!"

"Course you're not! Not a-tall!" Ted could be maddeningly bland. "You just want to grab it off, right after dinner, and leave it in front of some skirt's house all evening while you sit and gas about lite'ature and the highbrows you're going to marry—if they only propose!"

"Well, Dad oughtn't to EVER let you have it! You and those beastly Jones boys drive like maniacs. The idea of your taking the turn on Chautauqua Place at forty miles an hour!"

"Aw, where do you get that stuff! You're so darn scared of the car that you drive up-hill with the emergency brake on!"

"I do not! And you—Always talking about how much you know about motors, and Eunice Littlefield told me you said the battery fed the generator!"

"You—why, my good woman, you don't know a generator from a differential." Not unreasonably was Ted lofty with her. He was a natural mechanic, a maker and tinkerer of machines; he lisped in blueprints for the blueprints came.

"That'll do now!" Babbitt flung in mechanically, as he lighted the gloriously satisfying first cigar of the day and tasted the exhilarating drug of the *Advocate-Times* headlines.

Ted negotiated: "Gee, honest, Rone, I don't want to take the old boat, but I promised couple o' girls in my class I'd drive 'em down to the rehearsal of the school chorus, and, gee, I don't want to, but a gentleman's got to keep his social engagements."

"Well, upon my word! You and your social engagements! In high school!"

"Oh, ain't we select since we went to that hen college! Let me tell you there isn't a private school in the state that's got as swell a bunch as we got in Gamma Digamma this year. There's two fellows that their dads are millionaires. Say, gee, I ought to have a car of my own, like lots of the fellows." Babbitt almost rose. "A car of your own! Don't you want a yacht, and a house and lot? That pretty nearly takes the cake! A boy that can't pass his Latin examinations, like any other boy ought to, and he expects me to give him a motor-car, and I suppose a chauffeur, and an areoplane maybe, as a reward for the hard work he puts in going to the movies with Eunice Littlefield! Well, when you see me giving you—"

Somewhat later, after diplomacies, Ted persuaded Verona to admit that she was merely going to the Armory, that evening, to see the dog and cat show. She was then, Ted planned, to park the car in front of the candy-store across from the Armory and he would pick it up. There were masterly arrangements regarding leaving the key, and having the gasoline tank filled; and passionately, devotees of the Great God Motor, they hymned the patch on the spare inner-tube, and the lost jack-handle.

Their truce dissolving, Ted observed that her friends were "a scream of a bunch-stuck-up gabby four-flushers." His friends, she indicated, were "disgusting imitation sports, and horrid little shrieking ignorant girls." Further: "It's disgusting of you to smoke cigarettes, and so on and so forth, and those clothes you've got on this morning, they're too utterly ridiculous—honestly, simply disgusting."

Ted glanced over to the low beveled mirror in the buffet, regarded his charms, and smirked. His suit, the latest thing in Old Eli Togs, was skin-tight, with skimpy trousers to the tops of his glaring tan boots, a chorus-man waistline, pattern of an agitated check, and across the back a belt which belted nothing. His scarf was an enormous black silk wad. His flaxen hair was ice-smooth, pasted back without parting. When he went to school he would add a cap with a long vizor like a shovel-blade. Proudest of all was his waistcoat, saved for, begged for, plotted for; a real Fancy Vest of fawn with polka dots of a decayed red, the points astoundingly long. On the lower edge of it he wore a high-school button, a class button, and a fraternity pin.

And none of it mattered. He was supple and swift and flushed; his eyes (which he believed to be cynical) were candidly eager. But he was not over-gentle. He waved his hand at poor dumpy Verona and drawled: "Yes, I guess we're pretty ridiculous and disgusticulus, and I rather guess our new necktie is some smear!"

Babbitt barked: "It is! And while you're admiring yourself, let me tell you it might add to your manly beauty if you wiped some of that egg off your mouth!"

Verona giggled, momentary victor in the greatest of Great Wars, which is the family war. Ted looked at her hopelessly, then shrieked at Tinka: "For the love o'Pete, quit pouring the whole sugar bowl on your corn flakes!"

When Verona and Ted were gone and Tinka upstairs, Babbitt groaned to his wife: "Nice family, I must say! I don't pretend to be any baa-lamb, and maybe I'm a little cross-grained at breakfast sometimes, but the way they go on jab-jab-jabbering, I simply can't stand it. I swear, I feel like going off some place where I can get a little peace. I do think after a man's spent his lifetime trying to give his kids a chance and a decent education, it's pretty discouraging to hear them all the time scrapping like a bunch of hyenas and never—and never—Curious; here in the paper it says—Never silent for one mom—Seen the morning paper yet?"

"No, dear." In twenty-three years of married life, Mrs. Babbitt had seen the paper before her husband just sixty-seven times.

"Lots of news. Terrible big tornado in the South. Hard luck, all right. But this, say, this is corking! Beginning of the end for those fellows! New York Assembly has passed some bills that ought to completely outlaw the socialists! And there's an elevator-runners' strike in New York and a lot of college boys are taking their places. That's the stuff! And a mass-meeting in Birmingham's demanded that this Mick[9] agitator, this fellow De Valera, be deported. Dead right, by golly! All these agitators paid with German gold anyway. And we got no business interfering with the Irish or any other foreign government. Keep our hands strictly off. And there's another well-authenticated rumor from Russia that Lenin is dead. That's fine. It's beyond me why we don't just step in there and kick those Bolshevik cusses out."

"That's so," said Mrs. Babbitt.

"And it says here a fellow was inaugurated mayor in overalls—a preacher, too! What do you think of that!"

"Humph! Well!"

[9]An offensive colloquialism meaning Irish.

He searched for an attitude, but neither as a Republican, a Presbyterian, an Elk, nor a real-estate broker did he have any doctrine about preacher-mayors laid down for him, so he grunted and went on. She looked sympathetic and did not hear a word. Later she would read the headlines, the society columns, and the department-store advertisements.

"What do you know about this! Charley McKelvey still doing the sassiety stunt as heavy as ever. Here's what that gushy woman reporter says about last night:

> *Never is Society with the big, big S more flattered than when they are bidden to partake of good cheer at the distinguished and hospitable residence of Mr. and Mrs. Charles L. McKelvey as they were last night. Set in its spacious lawns and landscaping, one of the notable sights crowning Royal Ridge, but merry and homelike despite its mighty stone walls and its vast rooms famed for their decoration, their home was thrown open last night for a dance in honor of Mrs. McKelvey's notable guest. Miss J. Sneeth of Washington. The wide hall is so generous in its proportions that it made a perfect ballroom, its hardwood floor reflecting the charming pageant above its polished surface. Even the delights of dancing paled before the alluring opportunities for tête-à-têtes*[10] *that invited the soul to loaf in the long library before the baronial fireplace, or in the drawing-room with its deep comfy armchairs, its shaded lamps just made for a sly whisper of pretty nothings all à deux,*[11] *or even in the billiard room where one could take a cue and show a prowess at still another game than that sponsored by Cupid and Terpsichore.*[12]

There was more, a great deal more, in the best urban journalistic style of Miss Elnora Pearl Bates, the popular society editor of the *Advocate-Times.* But Babbitt could not abide it. He grunted. He wrinkled the newspaper. He protested: "Can you beat it! I'm willing to hand a lot of credit to Charley McKelvey. When we were in college together, he was just as hard up as any of us, and he's made a million good bucks out of contracting and hasn't been any dishonester or bought any more city councils than was necessary. And that's a good house of his—though it ain't any 'mighty stone walls' and it ain't worth the ninety thousand it cost him. But when it comes to talking as though Charley McKelvey and all that booze-hoisting set of his are any blooming bunch of of, of Vanderbilts, why, it makes me tired!"

Timidly from Mrs. Babbitt: "I would like to see the inside of their house though. It must be lovely. I've never been inside."

"Well, I have! Lots of—couple of times. To see Chaz about business deals, in the evening. It's not so much. I wouldn't *want* to go there to dinner with that gang of, of high-binders. And I'll bet I make a whole lot more money than some of those tin-horns that spend all they got on dress-suits and haven't got a decent suit of underwear to their name! Hey! What do you think of this!"

Mrs. Babbitt was strangely unmoved by the tidings from the Real Estate and Building column of the *Advocate-Times:*

> Ashtabula Street, 496—J. K. Dawson to
> Thomas Mullally, April 17, 15.7 × 112.2,
> mtg. $4000 . . . . Nom.

And this morning Babbitt was too disquieted to entertain her with items from Mechanics' Liens, Mortgages Recorded, and Contracts Awarded.[13] He rose. As he looked at her his eyebrows seemed shaggier than usual. Suddenly:

[10]One-on-one conversation. [11]For two.
[12]The god of romantic love and the muse of dance.
[13]Additional features of the "Real Estate" section of the newspaper.

"Yes, maybe—Kind of shame to not keep in touch with folks like the McKelveys. We might try inviting them to dinner, some evening. Oh, thunder, let's not waste our good time thinking about 'em! Our little bunch has a lot liver times than all those plutes.[14] Just compare a real human like you with these neurotic birds like Lucile McKelvey—all highbrow talk and dressed up like a plush horse! You're a great old girl, hon.!"

He covered his betrayal of softness with a complaining: "Say, don't let Tinka go and eat any more of that poison nutfudge. For Heaven's sake, try to keep her from ruining her digestion. I tell you, most folks don't appreciate how important it is to have a good digestion and regular habits. Be back 'bout usual time, I guess."

He kissed her—he didn't quite kiss her—he laid unmoving lips against her unflushing cheek. He hurried out to the garage, muttering: "Lord, what a family! And now Myra is going to get pathetic on me because we don't train with this millionaire outfit. Oh, Lord, sometimes I'd like to quit the whole game. And the office worry and detail just as bad. And I act cranky and—I don't mean to, but I get—So darn tired!"

1922

Ezra Pound 1885–1972

"E.P."—for two generations the mere initials have identified one of the founders of Anglo-American modernism, the first and the last of a band of revolutionists who changed the course of twentieth-century poetry. Yeats, Eliot, D. H. Lawrence, Joyce, Frost, and Williams are only a few of those who acknowledged their debt to Pound. He survived them all, and not until his death at the age of eighty-seven in Venice did it seem that a remarkable literary era had finally ended.

Pound was born in Hailey, Idaho, and raised in Pennsylvania. At fifteen he entered college already proficient in Latin, and resolved that by the age of thirty he "would know more about poetry than any man living." He attended Hamilton College and the University of Pennsylvania, where he majored in romance philology while reading his way through a large portion of classical and European literatures. At Pennsylvania, from which he received his M.A. in 1906, he associated with two other young poets—and future imagists—William Carlos Williams and Hilda Doolittle. His academic teaching career lasted four months; he was fired from his first job, at Wabash College, for having a woman in his room. The following year he sailed as a deckhand on a cattle boat for Europe and remained there for most of his life.

From Venice, where he published (and then reviewed) his first book of poems, A Lume Spento *(1908), Pound settled in London and set about to reform English letters and "To resuscitate the dead art / of poetry." The London years, between 1908 and 1920, were those in which his dictum "Make it new!" became the rallying cry of modernism, and, as London became the center of literary activity, Pound became the center of the center—discovering, coaching, promoting, and serving as a tireless gadfly to whatever new talent came his way.*

[14]Plutocrats; the wealthy and powerful.

With T. E. Hulme, he started imagism, the writing of short, free-verse poems each presenting a single image; with Wyndham Lewis, he promoted vorticism, a literary version of cubism that argued for poetry of "vigorous impact" with a single image at its "vortex." He published translations of Chinese poetry and Japanese Noh drama, initiating the techniques borrowed and derived from Asian literary traditions that became a modernist vogue. As overseas editor for Harriet Monroe's Poetry Magazine, *he used its pages, along with those of other little magazines, to explain his principles of reform and to introduce such poets as Eliot and Frost to American audiences. During these years he was also writing some of his best poetry.* Personae, *which has been praised as his most important collection, first appeared in 1909 and was often reprinted with additions from subsequent major books—*Ripostes *(1912) and* Lustra *(1916). At the same time he was at work on the early sections of the* Cantos, *the projected epic poem that was to be his life's work.*

After World War I, Pound summarized his disillusionment with the war and with England in Hugh Selwyn Mauberley *(1920). He then moved to Paris for the next four years, mixing with the British and American expatriates of the "Lost Generation." During this time Pound collaborated with T. S. Eliot on the editing of Eliot's epic poem* The Waste Land. *Without Pound's contribution,* The Waste Land *would be a very different poem from the one so thoroughly canonized today.*

In 1924 Pound moved to Italy. Under the spell of Benito Mussolini and Italian fascism he became preoccupied with economic theory, issuing increasingly violent diatribes against American capitalism, usury, and Jews. His views are reflected in the Cantos *and in such prose works as* Jefferson and/or Mussolini *(1935). With the outbreak of World War II, he began broadcasting pro-Fascist propaganda to England and America. When the war ended, he was arrested, charged with treason, and held in an outdoor cage at an American prison camp near Pisa, Italy. He was returned to the United States for trial, but after psychiatric examination was declared insane and interned at St. Elizabeths Hospital, a mental institution near Washington, D.C. In 1948, the* Pisan Cantos, *written by Pound during his imprisonment near Pisa, was awarded the Bollingen Prize by a group of distinguished literary judges. The furor that resulted from the awarding of a prize to a "traitor" divided the literary world. Eventually, through the intervention of Frost, Eliot, Hemingway, and others, Pound was released and allowed to return to Italy. The* Cantos, *now numbering over a hundred, ended in 1960, and Pound retired to silence.*

Pound's central position in the canon of modernism was established primarily on the basis of assessments (by Eliot and the many critics who followed his lead) of his formal achievements. But Pound himself would probably have been wary of such narrow evaluations. From the beginning of his work on the Cantos *in the 1910s, Pound was committed to a social and political poetry, a "poem including history." Although past critical efforts judged his poetry separately from his politics, more recent efforts assert that the two should be judged together. But the various tensions and contradictions embodied in Ezra Pound's life and work have not diminished his towering influence over twentieth-century American poetry. At the end of his life Pound acknowledged his failure as a social theorist and as a poet. He had become the lost leader for the failed ideas of a departed age. Few literary figures had stirred such hatred, but fewer still had labored so prodigiously for poetry and aroused such gratitude and admiration.*

FURTHER READING: *The Letters of Ezra Pound, 1907–1941,* ed. D. Paige, 1950; J. Cornell, *The Trial of Ezra Pound,* 1966; N. Stock, *The Life of Ezra Pound,* 1970, 1982; P. Ackroyd, *Ezra Pound and His World,* 1981; P. Nichols, *Ezra Pound: Politics, Economics, and Writing,* 1984; J. Wilhelm, *The American Roots of Ezra Pound,* 1985; K. Oderman, *Ezra Pound and the Erotic Medium,* 1986; M. Kayman, *The Modernism of Ezra Pound,* 1986; J. Tyell, *Ezra Pound,*

1987; J. Tytell, *Ezra Pound: The Solitary Volcano,* 1987; K. Lindberg, *Reading Pound Reading,* 1987; H. Carpenter, *A Serious Character: The Life of Ezra Pound,* 1988; R. Casillo, *The Genealogy of Demons: Anti-Semitism, Fascism, and the Myths of Ezra Pound,* 1988; W. Flory, *The American Ezra Pound,* 1989; J. Wilhelm, *Ezra Pound in London and Paris,* 1990; S. Rainey, *Ezra Pound and the Monument of Culture,* 1991; S. Hamilton, *Ezra Pound and the Symbolist Inheritance,* 1992; D. Davie, *Studies in Ezra Pound,* 1992; *Pound in Multiple Perspective: A Collection of Critical Essays,* ed. A. Gibson, 1993; T. Joseph, *Ezra Pound's Epic Variations: The Cantos and Major Long Poems,* 1995; M. Perloff, *The Dance of the Intellect: Studies in the Poetry of the Pound Tradition,* 1996; T. Grieve, *Ezra Pound's Early Poetry and Poetics,* 1997; *Ezra and Dorothy Pound: Letters in Captivity,* ed. O. Pound and R. Spoo, 1999; W. Baumann, *Roses from the Steel Dust: Collected Essays on Ezra Pound,* 2000; *Ezra Pound: Nature and Myth,* ed. W. Pratt, 2002; I. Nadel, *Ezra Pound: A Literary Life,* 2004.

TEXTS: *Personae,* 1926; *The Cantos,* 1934; *The Literary Essays of Ezra Pound,* 1935.

PORTRAIT D'UNE FEMME[1]

Your mind and you are our Sargasso Sea,[2]
London has swept about you this score[3] years
And bright ships left you this or that in fee.[4]
Ideas, old gossip, oddments of all things,
Strange spars of knowledge and dimmed wares of price.
Great minds have sought you—lacking someone else.
You have been second always. Tragical?
No. You preferred it to the usual thing:
One dull man, dulling and uxorious,[5]
One average mind—with one thought less, each year.
Oh, you are patient, I have seen you sit
Hours, where something might have floated up.
And now you pay one. Yes, you richly pay.
You are a person of some interest, one comes to you
And takes strange gain away:
Trophies fished up; some curious suggestion;
Fact that leads nowhere; and a tale or two,
Pregnant with mandrakes,[6] or with something else
That might prove useful and yet never proves,
That never fits a corner or shows use,
Or finds its hour upon the loom of days:
The tarnished, gaudy, wonderful old work;
Idols and ambergris[7] and rare inlays,
These are your riches, your great store; and yet
For all this sea-hoard of deciduous[8] things,
Strange woods half sodden, and new brighter stuff:

[1]French: Portrait of a Lady.
[2]An area of the North Atlantic Ocean, known for its entangling, floating seaweed.
[3]Twenty. [4]Payment.
[5]Submissive to one's wife.
[6]An herb. Its roots were thought to have magical properties, among them the power to promote conception in women.
[7]Waxy substance, from whales, used in making perfume. [8]Passing, impermanent.

In the slow float of differing light and deep,
No! there is nothing! In the whole and all,
Nothing that's quite your own.
Yet this is you.

1912, 1926

SALUTATION

O generation of the thoroughly smug
    and thoroughly uncomfortable,
I have seen fishermen picnicking in the sun,
I have seen them with untidy families,
I have seen their smiles full of teeth
    and heard ungainly laughter.
And I am happier than you are,
And they were happier than I am;
And the fish swim in the lake
    and do not even own clothing.

1913, 1916

A PACT

I make a pact with you, Walt Whitman—
I have detested you long enough.
I come to you as a grown child
Who has had a pig-headed father;
I am old enough now to make friends
It was you that broke the new wood,
Now is a time for carving.
We have one sap and one root—
Let there be commerce between us.

1913, 1916

IN A STATION OF THE METRO[1]

The apparition of these faces in the crowd;
Petals on a wet, black bough.

1913, 1916

[1] The Paris subway.

THE RIVER-MERCHANT'S WIFE: A LETTER[1]

While my hair was still cut straight across my forehead
I played about the front gate, pulling flowers.
You came by on bamboo stilts, playing horse,
You walked about my seat, playing with blue plums.
And we went on living in the village of Chokan:[2]
Two small people, without dislike or suspicion.

At fourteen I married My Lord you.
I never laughed, being bashful.
Lowering my head, I looked at the wall.
Called to, a thousand times, I never looked back.

At fifteen I stopped scowling,
I desired my dust to be mingled with yours
Forever and forever and forever.
Why should I climb the look out?

At sixteen you departed,
You went into far Ku-to-yen,[3] by the river of swirling eddies,
And you have been gone five months.
The monkeys make sorrowful noise overhead.

You dragged your feet when you went out.
By the gate now, the moss is grown, the different mosses,
Too deep to clear them away!
The leaves fall early this autumn, in wind.
The paired butterflies are already yellow with August
Over the grass in the West garden;
They hurt me. I grow older.
If you are coming down through the narrows of the river Kiang,[4]
Please let me know beforehand,
And I will come out to meet you
As far as Chō-fū-Sa.[5]

By Rihaku[6]

1915

[1]Pound's translation of a poem by the Chinese poet Li Po (701–762).
[2]Near Nanjing (formerly Nanking), on the lower Yangtse River, in eastern China.
[3]Dangerous gorge and reef, on the upper Yangtse River.
[4]The Yangtse River. [5]A port, upstream on the Yangtse.
[6]Japanese name for the poet Li Po. In making his translation, Pound drew upon documents using Japanese versions of Chinese names and locations.

from *HUGH SELWYN MAUBERLEY*

(LIFE AND CONTACTS)

I

E. P. Ode Pour L'Election De Son Sepulchre[1]

For three years, out of key with his time,
He strove to resuscitate the dead art
Of poetry; to maintain "the sublime"
In the old sense. Wrong from the start—

No, hardly, but seeing he had been born
In a half savage country, out of date;
Bent resolutely on wringing lilies from the acorn;
Capaneus;[2] trout for factitious bait;

Ιδμεν γάρ τοι πάνθ', όσ' ἐνί Τροίη[3]
Caught in the unstopped ear;
Giving the rocks small lee-way
The chopped seas held him, therefore, that year.

His true Penelope[4] was Flaubert,[5]
He fished by obstinate isles;
Observed the elegance of Circe's[6] hair
Rather than the mottoes on sun-dials.[7]

Unaffected by "the march of events,"
He passed from men's memory in *l'an trentiesme*
De son eage;[8] the case presents
No adjunct to the Muses' diadem.

[1]French: E. P. [Ezra Pound] Ode on the Choice of His Tomb. The title is taken from "De l'élection de son sépulchre," an ode by the French poet Pierre de Ronsard (1524–1585).

[2]One of seven heroes who attacked Thebes. For his defiance of Zeus he was struck dead by a thunderbolt.

[3]Greek: For we know everything that is in Troy, from the alluring song of the Sirens (*Odyssey,* Book XII, line 189). Odysseus ordered his sailors' ears to be sealed with wax so they would not hear the Sirens' song and destroy themselves, while he had himself tied to the ship's mast so that he might listen safely with "unstopped ear."

[4]Odysseus's wife. [5]Gustave Flaubert (1821–1880), French novelist.

[6]The enchantress who turned Odysseus's crew into swine.

[7]Commonplace sayings, often "Time Flies."

[8]French: the thirtieth year of his life, a quotation adapted from *Le Testament* by the French poet François Villon (1431–1463?).

II

The age demanded an image
Of its accelerated grimace,
Something for the modern stage,
Not, at any rate, an Attic[9] grace;

Not, not certainly, the obscure reveries
Of the inward gaze;
Better mendacities
Than the classics in paraphrase!

The "age demanded" chiefly a mould in plaster,
Made with no loss of time,
A prose kinema,[10] not, not assuredly, alabaster
Or the "sculpture" of rhyme.

III

The tea-rose tea-gown, etc.
Supplants the mousseline of Cos,[11]
The pianola[12] "replaces"
Sappho's barbitos.[13]

Christ follows Dionysus,[14]
Phallic and ambrosial
Made way for macerations;[15]
Caliban casts out Ariel.[16]

All things are a flowing,
Sage Heracleitus[17] says;
But a tawdry cheapness
Shall outlast our days.

Even the Christian beauty
Defects—after Samothrace;[18]
We see τὸ καλὸν[19]
Decreed in the market place.

[9]Characteristic of ancient Attica or Athens, hence elegant.
[10]Greek: motion, whence "cinema" for "moving picture."
[11]Fine cloth from the Greek island of Cos. [12]Player piano.
[13]Sappho: sixth-century B.C. Greek poetess; barbitos: a lyre.
[14]Greek god of fertility and of wine. [15]Extreme religious fasting that emaciates the body.
[16]Two characters in Shakespeare's *The Tempest*—Caliban: gross and bestial; Ariel: beautiful and ethereal.
[17]Greek philosopher (sixth century B.C.) who emphasized the principle of change.
[18]I.e., in the manner of Samothrace, Greek island where the statue "Winged Victory" was found and the home of a Dionysian religious cult.
[19]Greek: the beautiful.

Faun's flesh is not to us,
Nor the saint's vision.
We have the press for wafer;[20]
Franchise for circumcision.

All men, in law, are equals.
Free of Pisistratus,[21]
We choose a knave or an eunuch
To rule over us.

O bright Apollo,
τιν' ἀνδρα, τίν' ἥρωα, τίνα Θεὸν[22]
What god, man, or hero
Shall I place a tin wreath upon!

IV

These fought in any case,
and some believing,
pro domo,[23] in any case . . .[24]

Some quick to arm,
some for adventure,
some from fear of weakness,
some from fear of censure,
some for love of slaughter, in imagination,
learning later . . .
some in fear, learning love of slaughter;

Died some, pro patria,
non "dulce" non "et decor"[25] . . .
walked eye-deep in hell
believing in old men's lies, then unbelieving
came home, home to a lie,
home to many deceits,
home to old lies and new infamy;
usury age-old and age-thick
and liars in public places.

[20]Of the Christian communion service. [21]Athenian tyrant (sixth century B.C.).

[22]Greek: what man, what hero, what god, Pound's adaptation from one of the *Olympian Odes* by the Greek lyric poet Pindar (c. 522–442 B.C.).

[23]Latin: for home, Pound's adaptation from *De Domo Sua* by the Roman statesman and orator Cicero (106–43 B.C.).

[24]Marks of ellipsis in poetry, here and below, are Pound's.

[25]Latin: for country, neither "sweet" nor "fitting." Pound ironically adapts Horace's "Dulce et decorum est pro patria mori," "It is sweet and fitting to die for one's country." (*Odes*, Book III, Ode ii, line 13).

Daring as never before, wastage as never before.
Young blood and high blood,
fair cheeks, and fine bodies;

fortitude as never before

frankness as never before,
disillusions as never told in the old days,
hysterias, trench confessions,
laughter out of dead bellies.

V

There died a myriad,
And of the best, among them,
For an old bitch gone in the teeth,
For a botched civilization,

Charm, smiling at the good mouth,
Quick eyes gone under earth's lid,

For two gross of broken statues,
For a few thousand battered books.

1920, 1926, 1949

from *THE CANTOS*

I[1]

And then went down to the ship,
Set keel to breakers, forth on the godly sea, and
We[2] set up mast and sail on that swart ship,
Bore sheep aboard her, and our bodies also
Heavy with weeping, and winds from sternward
Bore us out onward with bellying canvas,
Circe's[3] this craft, the trim-coifed goddess,
Then sat we amidships, wind jamming the tiller,
Thus with stretched sail, we went over sea till day's end.
Sun to his slumber, shadows o'er all the ocean,

[1]Canto I is based on Homer's *Odyssey* (Book XI) and describes the visit of Odysseus to Hades (the underworld).
[2]Odysseus and his companions.
[3]The enchantress Circe instructed Odysseus how to sail to Hades, where he could learn from Theban prophet Tiresias how to return home to Ithaca.

Came we then to the bounds of deepest water,
To the Kimmerian lands,[4] and peopled cities
Covered with close-webbed mist, unpierced ever
With glitter of sun-rays
Nor with stars stretched, nor looking back from heaven
Swartest night stretched over wretched men there,
The ocean flowing backward, came we then to the place
Aforesaid by Circe.
Here did they rites, Perimedes and Eurylochus,[5]
And drawing sword from my hip
I dug the ell-square pitkin;[6]
Poured we libations unto each the dead,
First mead and then sweet wine, water mixed with white flour.
Then prayed I many a prayer to the sickly death's-heads;
As set in Ithaca, sterile bulls of the best
For sacrifice, heaping the pyre with goods,
A sheep to Tiresias only, black and a bell-sheep.[7]
Dark blood flowed in the fosse,[8]
Souls out of Erebus,[9] cadaverous dead, of brides
Of youths and of the old who had borne much;
Souls stained with recent tears, girls tender,
Men many, mauled with bronze lance heads,
Battle spoil, bearing yet dreory[10] arms,
These many crowded about me; with shouting,
Pallor upon me, cried to my men for more beasts;
Slaughtered the herds, sheep slain of bronze;
Poured ointment, cried to the gods,
To Pluto[11] the strong, and praised Proserpine;
Unsheathed the narrow sword,
I sat to keep off the impetuous impotent dead,
Till I should hear Tiresias.
But first Elpenor[12] came, our friend Elpenor,
Unburied, cast on the wide earth,
Limbs that we left in the house of Circe,
Unwept, unwrapped in sepulchre, since toils urged other.
Pitiful spirit. And I cried in hurried speech:
"Elpenor, how art thou come to this dark coast?
"Cam'st thou afoot, outstripping seamen?"
And he in heavy speech:
"Ill fate and abundant wine. I slept in Circe's ingle.[13]

[4]Cimmeria, a mist-shrouded land at the edge of the world, near the entrance to Hades, where Odysseus met the spirits of the dead.
[5]Two of Odysseus's companions. [6]A small pit, an arm's-length (one ell) square.
[7]The sheep, wearing a bell, that leads the flock. [8]Ditch.
[9]Place of darkness where the souls of the dead passed on their way to Hades.
[10]Anglo-Saxon: bloody.
[11]Greek god who ruled the underworld with his queen Persephone (Proserpine).
[12]One of Odysseus's companions who had died. His spirit speaks, following.
[13]Chimney-corner, hence house.

"Going down the long ladder unguarded,
"I fell against the buttress,
"Shattered the nape-nerve,[14] the soul sought Avernus.[15]
"But thou, O King, I bid remember me, unwept, unburied,
"Heap up mine arms, be tomb by sea-bord, and inscribed:
"*A man of no fortune, and with a name to come.*
"And set my oar up, that I swung mid fellows."

And Anticlea[16] came, whom I beat off, and then Tiresias Theban,
Holding his golden wand, knew me, and spoke first:
"A second time?[17] why? man of ill star,
"Facing the sunless dead and this joyless region?
"Stand from the fosse, leave me my bloody bever[18]
"For soothsay,"[19]
          And I stepped back,
And he strong with the blood, said then: "Odysseus
"Shalt return through spiteful Neptune,[20] over dark seas,
"Lose all companions." And then Anticlea came.
Lie quiet Divus. I mean, that is Andreas Divus,[21]
In officina Wecheli, 1538,[22] out of Homer.
And he[23] sailed, by Sirens and thence outward and away
And unto Circe.
          Venerandam,[24]
In the Cretan's[25] phrase, with the golden crown, Aphrodite,
Cypri munimenta sortita est,[26] mirthful, oricalchi,[27] with golden
Girdles and breast bands, thou with dark eyelids
Bearing the golden bough of Argicida.[28] So that:

1917, 1919, 1925

[14]Neck-nerve.
[15]Italian lake that is, according to Virgil, the entrance to the underworld.
[16]The mother of Odysseus. She had died during his absence from Ithaca. Odysseus had been instructed by Circe to spurn his mother's spirit until Tiresias had spoken.
[17]This was their second meeting. [18]Drink.
[19]Before prophesying, Tiresias had to drink of the sacrificial blood.
[20]Roman god of the sea.
[21]Pound intrudes to address Andreas Divus, author of a Latin translation of the *Odyssey,* published in Paris in 1538, a copy of which Pound owned.
[22]Latin: at the workshop of Wechel, a phrase taken from the imprint in Pound's copy of Divus.
[23]Odysseus.
[24]Latin: Compelling admiration, a reference to Aphrodite, Greek goddess of love.
[25]The Cretan, Georgius Dartona, whose Latin translations of the Homeric hymns (including a hymn to Aphrodite) were included in the book by Divus.
[26]Latin: The fortifications of Cyprus were her chosen realm. A quotation from Dartona's hymn to Aphrodite. According to legend Aphrodite first appeared in Cyprus.
[27]Pound's spelling of Latin *orichalci,* of copper. Dartona described Aphrodite wearing copper earrings.
[28]Latin: slayer of Argos. In classical myth, Hermes slew the 100-eyed Argos. One of the 12 Olympian gods, Hermes carried a golden staff with which he conducted the souls of the dead to Hades.

II

Hang it all, Robert Browning,[1]
there can be but the one "Sordello."
But Sordello, and my Sordello?
Lo Sordels si fo di Mantovana.[2]
So-shu[3] churned in the sea.
Seal sports in the spray-whited circles of cliff-wash,
Sleek head, daughter of Lir,[4]
        eyes of Picasso[5]
Under black fur-hood, lithe daughter of Ocean;
And the wave runs in the beach-groove:
"Eleanor, ἑλένανς and ελέπτολις!"[6]
        And poor old Homer blind, blind as a bat,
Ear, ear for the sea-surge, murmur of old men's voices:
"Let her go back to the ships,[7]
Back among Grecian faces, lest evil come on our own,
Evil and further evil, and a curse cursed on our children,
Moves, yes she moves like a goddess
And has the face of a god
        and the voice of Schoeney's[8] daughters,
And doom goes with her in walking,
Let her go back to the ships,
        back among Grecian voices."
And by the beach-run, Tyro,[9]
        Twisted arms of the sea-god,
Lithe sinews of water, gripping her, cross-hold,
And the blue-gray glass of the wave tents them,
Glare azure of water, cold-welter, close cover,
Quiet sun-tawny sand-stretch,
The gulls broad out their wings,
        nipping between the splay feathers;

[1]English poet (1812–1889), author of the poem *Sordello* (1840). Here, Sordello refers to the title character of Browning's poem and to an actual man, a thirteenth-century Italian poet, who appeared in Dante's *Purgatorio* (VI).

[2]Provençal: Sordello was from the region around Mantua.

[3]The Japanese name for the Chinese philosopher Chuang Tzu. "Churned in the sea" is perhaps meant to echo a Chinese pronunciation of "Chuang Tzu" and to suggest "churned in the sea of experience."

[4]Celtic sea god.

[5]Pablo Picasso (1881–1973), Spanish Cubist painter. Pound suggests that the eyes of the figures in Picasso's paintings are dark, like those of the seal described here.

[6]Greek: "ship-destroying" and "town-destroying." An adaptation of a quotation from the *Agamemnon* (lines 689–690), by Aeschylus, which describes Helen of Troy as "ship-destroying, man-destroying, and town-destroying." Pound substitutes "Eleanor" for "man-destroying" (Greek "elandros"), and thereby alludes both to Helen of Troy and to Eleanor of Aquitaine (1122?–1204), who likewise brought discord among men.

[7]The quotation beginning here is from *The Iliad* (Book III, lines 158–160). The old men of Troy speak of Helen as they see Menelaus and Paris fight.

[8]Atlanta, the daughter of Schoeneus, challenged her suitors to a footrace. Those she defeated were put to death.

[9]A mortal raped by the sea-god Poseidon, who caused a great wave to curl over them for concealment.

Snipe come for their bath,
        bend out their wing-joints,
Spread wet wings to the sun-film,
And by Scios,[10]
        to left of the Naxos[11] passage,
Naviform[12] rock overgrown,
        algae cling to its edge,
There is a wine-red glow in the shallows,
        a tin flash in the sun-dazzle.

The ship landed in Scios,
        men wanting spring-water,
And by the rock-pool a young boy loggy with vine-must,[13]
        "To Naxos? Yes, we'll take you to Naxos,
Cum' along lad." "Not that way!"
"Aye that way is Naxos."
        And I said: "It's a straight ship."
And an ex-convict out of Italy[14]
        knocked me into the fore-stays,
(He was wanted for manslaughter in Tuscany)
        And the whole twenty against me,
Mad for a little slave money.
        And they took her out of Scios
And off her course . . .
        And the boy came to, again, with the racket,
And looked out over the bows,
        and to eastward, and to the Naxos passage.
God-sleight then, god-sleight:
        Ship stock fast in sea-swirl,
Ivy upon the oars, King Pentheus,[15]
        grapes with no seed but sea-foam,
Ivy in scupper-hole.
Aye, I, Actes, stood there,
        and the god stood by me,
Water cutting under the keel,
Sea-break from stern forrards,
        wake running off from the bow,
And where was gunwale, there now was vine-trunk,
And tenthril were cordage had been,
        grape-leaves on the rowlocks,

[10]Chios, Greek island near Naxos, in the Aegean Sea.

[11]Greek island known for its wine and as a center for the worship of Dionysus (Bacchus).

[12]Having the shape of a ship.

[13]Fermenting grape juice. The boy is Dionysus to whom the grape wine and ivy are sacred.

[14]In Greek myth, Dionysus, hoping to go to Naxos, took passage on a ship manned by Italian pirates. Only one member of the crew, the steersman, recognized him as a god. The others resolved to change course to Asia where they could sell their passenger as a slave. Dionysus then caused the ship to halt; ivy entangled the masts and sails, wine flowed over the deck, and wild beasts appeared to guard him. The pirates, frightened by the magic, the "god-sleight," leaped into the sea and were changed into dolphins. Only the steersman was spared.

[15]The steersman, Acoetes, is reciting the story to Pentheus of Thebes to warn him of the power of Dionysus.

Heavy vine on the oarshafts,
And, out of nothing, a breathing,
hot breath on my ankles,
Beasts like shadows in glass,
a furred tail upon nothingness.
Lynx-purr, and heathery smell of beasts,
where tar smell had been,
Sniff and pad-foot of beasts,
eye-glitter out of black air.
The sky overshot, dry, with no tempest,
Sniff and pad-foot of beasts,
fur brushing my knee-skin,
Rustle of airy sheaths,
dry forms in the œ*ther.*[16]
And the ship like a keel in ship-yard,
slung like an ox in smith's sling,
Ribs stuck fast in the ways,
grape-cluster over pin-rack,
void air taking pelt.
Lifeless air become sinewed,
feline leisure of panthers,
Leopards sniffing the grape shoots by scupper-hole,
Crouched panthers by fore-hatch,
And the sea blue-deep about us,
green-ruddy in shadows,
And Lyæus:[17] "From now, Actes, my altars,
Fearing no bondage,
fearing no cat of the wood,
Safe with my lynxes,
feeding grapes to my leopards,
Olibanum[18] is my incense,
the vines grow in my homage."

The back-swell now smooth in the rudder-chains,
Black snout of a porpoise
where Lycabs[19] had been,
Fish-scales on the oarsmen.
And I worship.
I have seen what I have seen.
When they brought the boy I said:
"He has a god in him,
though I do not know which god."
And they kicked me into the fore-stays.
I have seen what I have seen:
Medon's[20] face like the face of a dory,[21]

[16]Latin: air. [17]Another name for Dionysus.
[18]Frankincense. [19]One of the sailors who had tried to abduct Dionysus.
[20]Another sailor. [21]A fish.

Arms shrunk into fins. And you, Pentheus,
Had as well listen to Tiresias, and to Cadmus,[22]
        or your luck will go out of you.
Fish-scales over groin muscles,
        lynx-purr amid sea . . .
And of a later year,
        pale in the wine-red algæ,
If you will lean over the rock,
        the coral face under wave-tinge,
Rose-paleness under water-shift,
        Ileuthyeria,[23] fair Dafne[24] of sea-bords,
The swimmer's arms turned to branches,
Who will say in what year,
        fleeing what band of tritons,
The smooth brows, seen, and half seen,
        now ivory stillness.

And So-shu churned in the sea, So-shu also,
        using the long moon for a churn-stick . . .
Lithe turning of water,
        sinews of Poseidon,
Black azure and hyaline,[25]
        glass wave over Tyro,
Close cover, unstillness,
        bright welter of wave-cords,
Then quiet water,
        quiet in the buff sands,
Sea-fowl stretching wing-joints,
        splashing in rock-hollows and sand-hollows
In the wave-runs by the half-dune;
Glass-glint of wave in the tide-rips against sunlight,
        pallor of Hesperus,[26]
Grey peak of the wave,
        wave, colour of grape's pulp,

Olive grey in the near,
        far, smoke grey of the rock-slide,
Salmon-pink wings of the fish-hawk
        cast grey shadows in water,
The tower like a one-eyed great goose
        cranes up out of the olive-grove,
And we have heard the fauns chiding Proteus[27]
        in the smell of hay under the olive-trees,

[22]Grandfather of Pentheus and founder of Thebes. With Tiresias he had urged Pentheus not to forbid the worship of Dionysus.
[23]A nymph.
[24]Daphne, a nymph who was turned into a tree to save her from her pursuer, Apollo.
[25]Clear, transparent. [26]The evening star (the planet Venus).
[27]Greek sea god who could assume different shapes.

And the frogs singing against the fauns
        in the half-light.
And . . .

1917, 1925

XLV

With *Usura*[1]
With usura hath no man a house of good stone
each block cut smooth and well fitting
that design might cover their face,
with usura
hath no man a painted paradise on his church wall
harpes et luz[2]
or where virgin receiveth message[3]
and halo projects from incision,
with usura
seeth no man Gonzaga his heirs and his concubines[4]
no picture is made to endure nor to live with
but it is made to sell and sell quickly
with usura, sin against nature,
is thy bread ever more of stale rags
is thy bread dry as paper,
with no mountain wheat, no strong flour
with usura the line grows thick[5]
with usura is no clear demarcation
and no man can find site for his dwelling.
Stone cutter is kept from his stone
weaver is kept from his loom
WITH USURA
wool comes not to market
sheep bringeth no gain with usura
Usura is a murrain,[6] usura
blunteth the needle in the maid's hand
and stoppeth the spinner's cunning. Pietro Lombardo[7]
came not by usura

[1]Latin: usury, interest paid for money borrowed. Pound uses the term to refer generally to greed for money.

[2]French: harps and lutes. Quoted from François Villon's *Le Testament* (line 896): "In my parish church I see a painted paradise where there are harps and lutes."

[3]I.e., paintings of the Annunciation, the announcement to Mary, by the angel Gabriel, that she will be the mother of Jesus (Luke 1:26–38).

[4]The portraits, by Andrea Mantegna (1431–1506), of Ludovico Gonzaga (1414–1478), with members of his family and court, on the walls of the ducal palace in Mantua, Italy.

[5]Pound believed that the lines in Italian painting grew thick and coarse after the rise of usury.

[6]Plague. [7]Italian sculptor (1435–1515).

Duccio[8] came not by usura
nor Pier della Francesca; Zuan Bellin'[9] not by usura
nor was 'La Calunnia'[10] painted.
Came not by usura Angelico; came not Ambrogio Praedis,[11]
Came no church of cut stone signed: *Adamo me fecit.*[12]
Not by usura St Trophime;[13]
Not by usura Saint Hilaire,[14]
Usura rusteth the chisel
It rusteth the craft and the craftsman
It gnaweth the thread in the loom
None learneth to weave gold in her pattern;
Azure hath a canker by usura; cramoisi[15] is unbroidered
Emerald findeth no Memling[16]
Usura slayeth the child in the womb
It stayeth the young man's courting
It hath brought palsey[17] to bed, lyeth
between the young bride and her bridegroom
        CONTRA NATURAM[18]
They have brought whores for Eleusis[19]
Corpses are set to banquet
at behest of usura.

1936, 1937

LXXXI

What thou lovest well remains,
                    the rest is dross
What thou lov'st well shall not be reft from thee
What thou lov'st well is thy true heritage
Whose world, or mine or theirs
                    or is it of none?
First came the seen, then thus the palpable
Elysium, though it were in the halls of hell,
What thou lovest well is thy true heritage
What thou lov'st well shall not be reft from thee.

[8]Duccio de Buoninsegna (1260?–1318?), the first great Sienese painter.
[9]Piero della Francesca (1420?–1492?) and Giovanni Bellini (1430?–1516), Italian painters.
[10]*La Calumnia,* a painting by the Italian Sandro Botticelli (1445?–1510).
[11]Fra Angelico (1387?–1455) and Ambrogio de Predis (1455?–1506?), Italian painters.
[12]Latin: Adam made me, Pound's recollection of an inscription carved on a stone column in the Church of San Zeno Maggiore in Verona, Italy.
[13]Church in Arles, France.
[14]Church in Poitiers, France.
[15]French: crimson cloth.
[16]Hans Memling (1430?–1495), Flemish painter.
[17]I.e., the aged, the infirm.
[18]Latin: contrary to nature.
[19]Ancient religious sanctuary near Athens, Greece.

The ant's a centaur in his dragon world.
Pull down thy vanity, it is not man
Made courage, or made order, or made grace,
        Pull down thy vanity, I say pull down.
Learn of the green world what can be thy place
In scaled invention or true artistry,
Pull down thy vanity,
                    Paquin[1] pull down!
The green casque has outdone your elegance.[2]

"Master thyself, then others shall thee beare"[3]
        Pull down thy vanity,
Thou art a beaten dog beneath the hail,
A swollen magpie in a fitful sun,
Half black half white
Nor knowst'ou wing from tail
Pull down thy vanity
            How mean thy hates
Fostered in falsity,
            Pull down thy vanity,
Rathe[4] to destroy, niggard[5] in charity,
Pull down thy vanity,
            I say pull down.

But to have done instead of not doing
        this is not vanity
To have, with decency, knocked
That a Blunt should open[6]
        To have gathered from the air a live tradition
or from a fine old eye the unconquered flame
This is not vanity.
        Here error is all in the not done,
all in the diffidence that faltered . . .[7]

1947, 1948

A RETROSPECT

There has been so much scribbling about a new fashion in poetry, that I may perhaps be pardoned this brief recapitulation and retrospect.

In the spring or early summer of 1912, 'H.D.', Richard Aldington[1] and myself decided that we were agreed upon the three principles following:

[1]A Parisian dress designer.
[2]I.e., the green forms of insects outdo the artificial designs of Paquin.
[3]A paraphrase of Chaucer's *Ballade of Good Counsel,* line 13.
[4]Hasty, quick. [5]Stingy.
[6]A reference to Matthew 7:7, "knock, and it shall be opened unto you." Wilfred Blunt (1840–1922), English poet and political essayist whose independent ways were much admired by Pound.
[7]Pound's ellipsis.

[1]'H. D.,' Hilda Doolittle (1886–1961), American poet; Richard Aldington (1892–1962), English American poet and novelist; with Pound, H. D., and Amy Lowell, Aldington was a founder of imagism.

1. Direct treatment of the 'thing' whether subjective or objective.
2. To use absolutely no word that does not contribute to the presentation.
3. As regarding rhythm: to compose in the sequence of the musical phrase, not in sequence of a metronome.

Upon many points of taste and predilection we differed, but agreeing upon these three positions we thought we had as much right to a group name, at least as much right, as a number of French 'schools' proclaimed by Mr. Flint in the August number of Harold Monro's magazine for 1911.[2]

This school has since been 'joined' or 'followed' by numerous people who, whatever their merits, do not show any signs of agreeing with the second specification. Indeed *vers libre*[3] has become as prolix and as verbose as any of the flaccid varieties that preceded it. It has brought faults of its own. The actual language and phrasing is often as bad as that of our elders without even the excuse that the words are shovelled in to fill a metric pattern or to complete the noise of a rhyme-sound. Whether or not the phrases followed by the followers are musical must be left to the reader's decision. At times I can find a marked metre in 'vers libres,' as stale and hackneyed as any pseudo-Swinburnian,[4] at times the writers seem to follow no musical structure whatever. But it is, on the whole, good that the field should be ploughed. Perhaps a few good poems have come from the new method, and if so it is justified.

Criticism is not a circumscription or a set of prohibitions. It provides fixed points of departure. It may startle a dull reader into alertness. That little of it which is good is mostly in stray phrases; or if it be an older artist helping a younger it is in great measure but rules of thumb, cautions gained by experience.

I set together a few phrases on practical working about the time the first remarks on imagisme were published. The first use of the word 'Imagiste' was in my note to T. E. Hulme's[5] five poems, printed at the end of my 'Ripostes' in the autumn of 1912. I reprint my cautions from *Poetry*[6] for March, 1913.

A FEW DON'TS

An 'Image' is that which presents an intellectual and emotional complex in an instant of time. I use the term 'complex' rather in the technical sense employed by the newer psychologists, such as Hart,[7] though we might not agree absolutely in our application.

It is the presentation of such a 'complex' instantaneously which gives that sense of sudden liberation; that sense of freedom from time limits and space limits; that sense of sudden growth, which we experience in the presence of the greatest works of art.

[2]Frank Stewart Flint (1885–1960), English poet and translator whose essay "Imagisme" appeared in *Poetry Review,* published by Harold Monro (1879–1932).

[3]Free verse that follows no regular rhythmic, stanzaic, or rhyme pattern.

[4]Modeled after the melodic poetry of Algernon Charles Swinburne (1837–1909), English poet.

[5]English writer (1883–1917), called the "father of imagism."

[6]A "Magazine of Verse" founded in Chicago in 1912 by Harriet Monroe (1861–1936).

[7]Bernard Hart (1879–1966), English psychiatrist.

It is better to present one Image in a lifetime than to produce voluminous works.

All this, however, some may consider open to debate. The immediate necessity is to tabulate A LIST OF DON'TS for those beginning to write verses. I can not put all of them into Mosaic negative.

To begin with, consider the three propositions (demanding direct treatment, economy of words, and the sequence of the musical phrase), not as dogma—never consider anything as dogma—but as the result of long contemplation, which, even if it is some one else's contemplation, may be worth consideration.

Pay no attention to the criticism of men who have never themselves written a notable work. Consider the discrepancies between the actual writing of the Greek poets and dramatists, and the theories of the Graeco-Roman grammarians, concocted to explain their metres.

LANGUAGE

Use no superfluous word, no adjective which does not reveal something.

Don't use such an expression as 'dim lands *of peace*'. It dulls the image. It mixes an abstraction with the concrete. It comes from the writer's not realizing that the natural object is always the adequate symbol.

Go in fear of abstractions. Do not retell in mediocre verse what has already been done in good prose. Don't think any intelligent person is going to be deceived when you try to shirk all the difficulties of the unspeakably difficult art of good prose by chopping your composition into line lengths.

What the expert is tired of today the public will be tired of tomorrow.

Don't imagine that the art of poetry is any simpler than the art of music, or that you can please the expert before you have spent at least as much effort on the art of verse as the average piano teacher spends on the art of music.

Be influenced by as many great artists as you can, but have the decency either to acknowledge the debt outright, or to try to conceal it.

Don't allow 'influence' to mean merely that you mop up the particular decorative vocabulary of some one or two poets whom you happen to admire. A Turkish war correspondent was recently caught red-handed babbling in his despatches of 'dove-grey' hills, or else it was 'pearl-pale', I can not remember.

Use either no ornament or good ornament.

RHYTHM AND RHYME

Let the candidate fill his mind with the finest cadences he can discover, preferably in a foreign language,[8] so that the meaning of the words may be less likely to divert his attention from the movement; e.g., Saxon charms, Hebridean Folk Songs, the verse of Dante, and the lyrics of Shakespeare—if he can dissociate the vocabulary from the cadence. Let him dissect the lyrics of Goethe

[8]"This is for rhythm, his vocabulary must of course be found in his native tongue."—Pound's note.

coldly into their component sound values, syllables long and short, stressed and unstressed, into vowels and consonants.

It is not necessary that a poem should rely on its music, but if it does rely on its music that music must be such as will delight the expert.

Let the neophyte know assonance and alliteration, rhyme immediate and delayed, simple and polyphonic, as a musician would expect to know harmony and counterpoint and all the minutiae of his craft. No time is too great to give to these matters or to any one of them, even if the artist seldom have need of them.

Don't imagine that a thing will 'go' in verse just because it's too dull to go in prose.

Don't be 'viewy'—leave that to the writers of pretty little philosophic essays. Don't be descriptive; remember that the painter can describe a landscape much better than you can, and that he has to know a deal more about it.

When Shakespeare talks of the 'Dawn in russet mantle clad' he presents something which the painter does not present. There is in this line of his nothing that one can call description; he presents.

Consider the way of the scientists rather than the way of an advertising agent for a new soap.

The scientist does not expect to be acclaimed as a great scientist until he has *discovered* something. He begins by learning what has been discovered already. He goes from that point onward. He does not bank on being a charming fellow personally. He does not expect his friends to applaud the results of his freshman class work. Freshmen in poetry are unfortunately not confined to a definite and recognizable class room. They are 'all over the shop'. Is it any wonder 'the public is indifferent to poetry?'

Don't chop your stuff into separate *iambs.* Don't make each line stop dead at the end, and then begin every next line with a heave. Let the beginning of the next line catch the rise of the rhythm wave, unless you want a definite longish pause.

In short, behave as a musician, a good musician, when dealing with that phase of your art which has exact parallels in music. The same laws govern, and you are bound by no others.

Naturally, your rhythmic structure should not destroy the shape of your words, or their natural sound, or their meaning. It is improbable that, at the start, you will be able to get a rhythm-structure strong enough to affect them very much, though you may fall a victim to all sorts of false stopping due to line ends and cæsurae.

The Musician can rely on pitch and the volume of the orchestra. You can not. The term harmony is misapplied in poetry; it refers to simultaneous sounds of different pitch. There is, however, in the best verse a sort of residue of sound which remains in the ear of the hearer and acts more or less as an organ-base.

A rhyme must have in it some slight element of surprise if it is to give pleasure; it need not be bizarre or curious, but it must be well used if used at all.

Vide further Vildrac and Duhamel's[9] notes on rhyme in *'Technique Poetique'.*

That part of your poetry which strikes upon the imaginative *eye* of the reader will lose nothing by translation into a foreign tongue; that which appeals to the ear can reach only those who take it in the original.

[9]Charles Vildrac (1882–1971) and Georges Duhamel (1884–1966), French poets, authors of *Notes sur la Technique Poétique,* 1925.

Consider the definiteness of Dante's presentation, as compared with Milton's rhetoric. Read as much of Wordsworth as does not seem too unutterably dull.

If you want the gist of the matter go to Sappho, Catullus, Villon, Heine[10] when he is in the vein, Gautier when he is not too frigid; or, if you have not the tongues, seek out the leisurely Chaucer. Good prose will do you no harm, and there is good discipline to be had by trying to write it.

Translation is likewise good training, if you find that your original matter 'wobbles' when you try to rewrite it. The meaning of the poem to be translated can not 'wobble'.

If you are using a symmetrical form, don't put in what you want to say and then fill up the remaining vacuums with slush.

Don't mess up the perception of one sense by trying to define it in terms of another. This is usually only the result of being too lazy to find the exact word. To this clause there are possibly exceptions.

The first three simple prescriptions will throw out nine-tenths of all the bad poetry now accepted as standard and classic; and will prevent you from many a crime of production.

'. . . *Mais d'abord il faut être un poéte*',[11] as MM. Duhamel and Vildrac have said at the end of their little book, *'Notes sur la Technique Poétique.'*

CREDO

Rhythm.—I believe in an 'absolute rhythm', a rhythm, that is, in poetry which corresponds exactly to the emotion or shade of emotion to be expressed. A man's rhythm must be interpretative, it will be, therefore, in the end, his own, uncounterfeiting, uncounterfeitable.

Symbols.—I believe that the proper and perfect symbol is the natural object, that if a man use 'symbols' he must so use them that their symbolic function does not obtrude; so that *a* sense, and the poetic quality of the passage, is not lost to those who do not understand the symbol as such, to whom, for instance, a hawk is a hawk.

Technique.—I believe in technique as the test of a man's sincerity; in law when it is ascertainable; in the trampling down of every convention that impedes or obscures the determination of the law, or the precise rendering of the impulse.

Form.—I think there is a 'fluid' as well as a 'solid' content, that some poems may have form as a tree has form, some as water poured into a vase. That most symmetrical forms have certain uses. That a vast number of subjects cannot be precisely, and therefore not properly rendered in symmetrical forms.

'Thinking that alone worthy wherein the whole art is employed'.[12] I think the artist should master all known forms and systems of metric, and I have with some persistence set about doing this, searching particularly into those periods wherein the systems came to birth or attained their maturity. It has

[10]Sappho, Greek poet (sixth century B.C.); Catullus (84?–54? B.C.), Roman poet; François Villon (1431–1463), French poet; Heinrich Heine (1797–1856), German poet.

[11]French: "But, to begin with, one must be a poet."

[12]"Dante, *De Volgari Eloquio*,"—Pound's note.

been complained, with some justice, that I dump my note-books on the public. I think that only after a long struggle will poetry attain such a degree of development, or, if you will, modernity, that it will vitally concern people who are accustomed, in prose, to Henry James and Anatole France, in music to Debussy.[13] I am constantly contending that it took two centuries of Provence and one of Tuscany to develop the media of Dante's masterwork, that it took the latinists of the Renaissance, and the Pleiade,[14] and his own age of painted speech to prepare Shakespeare his tools. It is tremendously important that great poetry be written, it makes no jot of difference who writes it. The experimental demonstrations of one man may save the time of many—hence my furore over Arnaut Daniel[15]—if a man's experiments try out one new rime, or dispense conclusively with one iota of currently accepted nonsense, he is merely playing fair with his colleagues when he chalks up his result.

No man ever writes very much poetry that 'matters'. In bulk, that is, no one produces much that is final, and when a man is not doing this highest thing, thus saying the thing once for all and perfectly; when he is not matching Ποικιλόθρου', αθάνατ'' Αφρόδιτα,[16] or 'Hist—said Kate the Queen', he had much better be making the sorts of experiment which may be of use to him in his later work, or to his successors.

'The lyf so short, the craft so long to lerne.' It is a foolish thing for a man to begin his work on a too narrow foundation, it is a disgraceful thing for a man's work not to show steady growth and increasing fineness from first to last.

As for 'adaptations'; one finds that all the old masters of painting recommend to their pupils that they begin by copying masterwork, and proceed to their own composition.

As for 'Every man his own poet', the more every man knows about poetry the better. I believe in every one writing poetry who wants to; most do. I believe in every man knowing enough of music to play 'God bless our home' on the harmonium, but I do not believe in every man giving concerts and printing his sin.

The mastery of any art is the work of a lifetime. I should not discriminate between the 'amateur' and the 'professional'. Or rather I should discriminate quite often in favour of the amateur, but I should discriminate between the amateur and the expert. It is certain that the present chaos will endure until the Art of poetry has been preached down the amateur gullet, until there is such a general understanding of the fact that poetry is an art and not a pastime; such a knowledge of technique; of technique of surface and technique of content, that the amateurs will cease to try to drown out the masters.

If a certain thing was said once for all in Atlantis or Arcadia, in 450 Before Christ or in 1290 after, it is not for us moderns to go saying it over, or to go obscuring the memory of the dead by saying the same thing with less skill and less conviction.

[13]Franois Anatole Thibault (1844–1924), French writer; Claude Achille Debussy (1862–1918), French composer.

[14]A group of sixteenth-century French poets who celebrated the writers of antiquity. Their name came from the legendary Pleiades, daughters of Atlas, who were transformed into stars.

[15]Provençal troubador (twelfth century). In Dante's *Purgatorio* (XXVI, line 117), he is described as the "miglior fabbro," the "better craftsman." He invented the sestina form (six six-line stanzas) used by Dante and Petrarch.

[16]Greek: Shimmering-throned, immortal Aphrodite, a quotation from Sappho.

My pawing over the ancients and semi-ancients has been one struggle to find out what has been done, once for all, better than it can ever be done again, and to find out what remains for us to do, and plenty does remain, for if we still feel the same emotions as those which launched the thousand ships, it is quite certain that we come on these feelings differently, through different nuances, by different intellectual gradations. Each age has its own abounding gifts yet only some ages transmute them into matter of duration. No good poetry is ever written in a manner twenty years old, for to write in such a manner shows conclusively that the writer thinks from books, convention and *cliché,* and not from life, yet a man feeling the divorce of life and his art may naturally try to resurrect a forgotten mode if he finds in that mode some leaven, or if he think he sees in it some element lacking in contemporary art which might unite that art again to its sustenance, life.

In the art of Daniel and Cavalcanti,[17] I have seen that precision which I miss in the Victorians, that explicit rendering, be it of external nature, or of emotion. Their testimony is of the eyewitness, their symptoms are first hand.

As for the nineteenth century, with all respect to its achievements, I think we shall look back upon it as a rather blurry, messy sort of period, a rather sentimentalistic, mannerish sort of a period. I say this without any self-righteousness, with no self-satisfaction.

As for there being a 'movement' or my being of it, the conception of poetry as a 'pure art' in the sense in which I use the term, revived with Swinburne. From the puritanical revolt to Swinburne, poetry had been merely the vehicle—yes, definitely, Arthur Symons'[18] scruples and feelings about the word not withholding—the ox-cart and post-chaise for transmitting thoughts poetic or otherwise. And perhaps the 'great Victorians', though it is doubtful, and assuredly the 'nineties' continued the development of the art, confining their improvements, however, chiefly to sound and to refinements of manner.

Mr Yeats[19] has once and for all stripped English poetry of its perdamnable rhetoric. He has boiled away all that is not poetic—and a good deal that is. He has become a classic in his own lifetime and *nel mezzo del cammin.*[20] He has made our poetic idiom a thing pliable, a speech without inversions.

Robert Bridges, Maurice Hewlett and Frederic Manning are[21] in their different ways seriously concerned with overhauling the metric, in testing the language and its adaptability to certain modes. Ford Hueffer[22] is making some sort of experiments in modernity. The Provost of Oriel[23] continues his translation of the *Divina Commedia.*

As to Twentieth century poetry, and the poetry which I expect to see written during the next decade or so, it will, I think, move against poppy-cock, it will be harder and saner, it will be what Mr Hewlett calls 'nearer the bone'. It will

[17]Guido Cavalcanti (1255?–1300), Italian lyric poet.

[18]Arthur Symons (1865–1945), English poet and critic.

[19]William Butler Yeats (1865–1939), Anglo-Irish poet.

[20]"Midway in the journey," a quotation from the first line of Dante's *Inferno.*

[21]"(Dec. 1911)."—Pound's note. He cites Robert Bridges (1844–1930), Poet Laureate of England (1913–1930); Maurice Hewlett (1861–1923), English novelist and poet; Frederic Manning (1887–1935), Australian poet who lived in England.

[22]Ford Madox Ford (1873–1939), English novelist.

[23]Charles Lancelot Shadwell (1840–1919), provost of Oriel College, Oxford (1905–1914), whose translations of Dante had begun to appear in the 1880s.

be as much like granite as it can be, its force will lie in its truth, its interpretative power (of course, poetic force does always rest there); I mean it will not try to seem forcible by rhetorical din, and luxurious riot. We will have fewer painted adjectives impeding the shock and stroke of it. At least for myself, I want it so, austere, direct, free from emotional slither.

What is there now, in 1917, to be added?

. . .

1918

T. S. Eliot 1888–1965

In the period between the two world wars, poetry and criticism were largely dominated by a single figure, T. S. Eliot. Even more than Ezra Pound, he shaped the tastes and critical vocabulary of a generation. The Waste Land, *the most startling and innovative of Eliot's poems, had the effect, as William Carlos Williams remarked, of "an atom bomb"; and in the decades that followed, Eliot became the major poet writing in English and the authoritative voice of modern criticism—esteemed, imitated, and quoted on both sides of the Atlantic.*

Eliot was a descendant of a prominent New England family dating from the seventeenth century. He was born in St. Louis, Missouri. In his youth he attended a Boston preparatory school and then entered Harvard, where he studied literature and philosophy. He served as editor of the Harvard Advocate, *and he developed, from reading the poetry of the French symbolists, his early poetic style. From Harvard, Eliot went to Europe to complete a doctoral dissertation on F. H. Bradley, an English philosopher from whom Eliot derived one of his pervasive themes, the "isolated consciousness."*

When World War I began, Eliot settled in London, where he worked as a bank clerk. In 1917, in the wake of a fateful meeting with Ezra Pound, Eliot published his first book of poems, Prufrock and Other Observations. *He became an editor of the* Egoist *and then founding editor of the* Criterion, *for which he wrote some of his early reviews and criticism. Then in 1922,* The Waste Land *(dedicated to its editor, Pound) became the poem that set the tone of the postwar era. Emphasizing the decay of Western culture, Eliot's poem was heralded as the major document of modern despair. Its ranging meters and fragmented style—an interweaving of reminiscences, vignettes, literary allusions, and anthropological lore—became models of modernist techniques.*

Loosely patterned on medieval Grail legend, The Waste Land *reflects the theme and direction of Eliot's own life: the quest for salvation. In the years that followed, Eliot's writing expressed a deepening conservatism in religion and politics. In 1927 he startled many admirers by announcing his adoption of British citizenship and his conversion to the Church of England. The change was paralleled by the movement of his poetry from the secular to the ascetic—from the pessimism of "Gerontion" (1919), to the religious faith of "Ash Wednesday" (1930), the "conversion" poem drawn from the Anglican service and the disciplines of Christian asceticism. Eliot's poetry culminated in the religious meditations of* Four Quartets *(1936–1943), in which the theme of spiritual quest becomes both personal and universal, presenting man's effort to transcend the force of time and to achieve the "still moment" of the eternal.*

In his later years Eliot devoted himself mainly to verse drama, a genre he had long wanted to restore to the modern stage. His first play, based upon the martyrdom of Saint Thomas Becket, Murder in the Cathedral *(1935), met with some success. The later plays, in contemporary settings, include* The Family Reunion *(1939),* The Cocktail Party *(1950),* The Confidential Clerk *(1954), and* The Elder Statesman *(1958). Although Eliot's plays are often impressive in their poetry, in general, their sophisticated moral and religious arguments have kept them from achieving wide popular appreciation.*

The antiromantic tendency of Eliot's literary criticism was evident with his first book of essays, The Sacred Wood *(1920). His focus on the English writers of the sixteenth and seventeenth centuries led to a general reassessment of poetic tradition. Most notable was his "discovery" of the Metaphysical poets, in an essay that made John Donne and his followers a contemporary vogue. In 1948 Eliot's achievements were recognized by awards of the British Order of Merit and the Nobel Prize for Literature. In the years that followed, Eliot's reputation declined, yet he continued to the end to exercise authority in the world of letters, just as his masterpiece,* The Waste Land, *has remained one of the most influential poems of the twentieth century.*

FURTHER READING: *Collected Plays,* 1962; *The Waste Land: A Facsimile and Transcript of the Original Drafts,* ed. V. Eliot, 1971; L. Gordon, *Eliot's Early Years,* Vol. I, 1977, *Eliot's New Life,* Vol. II, 1988; C. Behr, *T. S. Eliot: A Chronology of His Life and Works,* 1982; P. Ackroyd, *T. S. Eliot: A Life,* 1984; *The Letters of T. S. Eliot,* Vols. I and II, ed. V. Eliot, 1988, 1991; F. Pinion, *A T. S. Eliot Companion,* 1988; M. Scofield, *T. S. Eliot: The Poems,* 1988; C. Ricks, *Eliot and Prejudice,* 1989; E. Sigg, *The American T. S. Eliot,* 1989; J. Brooker and J. Bentley, *Reading the Waste Land,* 1990; T. Sharpe, *T. S. Eliot: A Literary Life,* 1992; *The Cambridge Companion to T. S. Eliot,* ed. A. Moody, 1994; D. Chinitz, *T. S. Eliot and the Cultural Divide,* 2003; J. Miller, *T. S. Eliot: The Making of an American Poet,* 2005; R. Badenhausen, *T. S. Eliot and the Art of Collaboration,* 2005; L. Rainey, *Revisiting the Waste Land,* 2005.

TEXT: *Collected Poems, 1909–1962,* 1963, with corrections supplied by the editor.

THE LOVE SONG OF J. ALFRED PRUFROCK

S'io credessi che mia risposta fosse
a persona che mai tornasse al mondo,
questa fiamma staria senza più scosse.
Ma per ciò giammai di questo fondo
non tornò vivo alcun, s'i'odo il vero,
senza tema d'infamia ti rispondo.[1]

Let us go then, you and I,
When the evening is spread out against the sky
Like a patient etherised upon a table;
Let us go through certain half-deserted streets,
The muttering retreats

[1]"If I thought my reply were to one who could ever return to the world, this flame would shake no more; but since, if what I hear is true, none ever did return alive from this depth, I answer you without fear of infamy." The flame (or spirit) of Guido de Montefeltro, suffering in Hades for his sins, confesses to the poet Dante (*Inferno,* Canto XXVII, lines 61–66).

Of restless nights in one-night cheap hotels
And sawdust restaurants with oyster-shells:
Streets that follow like a tedious argument
Of insidious intent
To lead you to an overwhelming question . . .[2]
Oh, do not ask, "What is it?"
Let us go and make our visit.

In the room the women come and go
Talking of Michelangelo.
The yellow fog that rubs its back upon the window-panes,
The yellow smoke that rubs its muzzle on the window-panes,
Licked its tongue into the corners of the evening,
Lingered upon the pools that stand in drains,
Let fall upon its back the soot that falls from chimneys,
Slipped by the terrace, made a sudden leap,
And seeing that it was a soft October night,
Curled once about the house, and fell asleep.

And indeed there will be time
For the yellow smoke that slides along the street
Rubbing its back upon the window-panes;
There will be time, there will be time
To prepare a face to meet the faces that you meet;
There will be time to murder and create,
And time for all the works and days[3] of hands
That lift and drop a question on your plate;
Time for you and time for me,
And time yet for a hundred indecisions,
And for a hundred visions and revisions,
Before the taking of a toast and tea.

In the room the women come and go
Talking of Michelangelo.

And indeed there will be time
To wonder, "Do I dare?" and, "Do I dare?"
Time to turn back and descend the stair,
With a bald spot in the middle of my hair—
(They will say: "How his hair is growing thin!")
My morning coat, my collar mounting firmly to the chin,
My necktie rich and modest, but asserted by a simple pin—
(They will say: "But how his arms and legs are thin!")
Do I dare
Disturb the universe?

[2]Here, and throughout, the ellipsis points are Eliot's and do not indicate omissions by the editor.

[3]A reference to *Works and Days*, a poem, by the ancient Greek poet Hesiod, on the rural life and labors of a peasant.

In a minute there is time
For decisions and revisions which a minute will reverse.

For I have known them all already, known them all—
Have known the evenings, mornings, afternoons,
I have measured out my life with coffee spoons;
I know the voices dying with a dying fall
Beneath the music from a farther room.
So how should I presume?

And I have known the eyes already, known them all—
The eyes that fix you in a formulated phrase,
And when I am formulated, sprawling on a pin,
When I am pinned and wriggling on the wall,
Then how should I begin
To spit out all the butt-ends of my days and ways?
And how should I presume?

And I have known the arms already, known them all—
Arms that are braceleted and white and bare
(But in the lamplight, downed with light brown hair!)
Is it perfume from a dress
That makes me so digress?
Arms that lie along a table, or wrap about a shawl.
And should I then presume?
And how should I begin?

. . . . .

Shall I say, I have gone at dusk through narrow streets
And watched the smoke that rises from the pipes
Of lonely men in shirt-sleeves, leaning out of windows? . . .
I should have been a pair of ragged claws
Scuttling across the floors of silent seas.

. . . . .

And the afternoon, the evening, sleeps so peacefully!
Smoothed by long fingers,
Asleep . . . tired . . . or it malingers,
Stretched on the floor, here beside you and me.
Should I, after tea and cakes and ices,
Have the strength to force the moment to its crisis?

But though I have wept and fasted, wept and prayed,
Though I have seen my head (grown slightly bald) brought in upon
a platter,[4]

[4]The prophet John the Baptist was beheaded and his head brought on a platter to Salome, the daughter of Herodias (Matthew 14:1–11).

I am no prophet—and here's no great matter;
I have seen the moment of my greatness flicker,
And I have seen the eternal Footman hold my coat, and snicker,
And in short, I was afraid.

And would it have been worth it, after all,
After the cups, the marmalade, the tea,
Among the porcelain, among some talk of you and me,
Would it have been worth while,
To have bitten off the matter with a smile,
To have squeezed the universe into a ball[5]
To roll it towards some overwhelming question,
To say: "I am Lazarus, come from the dead,[6]
Come back to tell you all, I shall tell you all"—
If one, settling a pillow by her head,
Should say: "That is not what I meant at all.
That is not it, at all."

And would it have been worth it, after all,
Would it have been worth while,
After the sunsets and the dooryards and the sprinkled streets,
After the novels, after the teacups, after the skirts that trail along
the floor—
And this, and so much more?—
It is impossible to say just what I mean!
But as if a magic lantern threw the nerves in patterns on a screen:
Would it have been worth while
If one, settling a pillow or throwing off a shawl,
And turning toward the window, should say:
"That is not it at all,
That is not what I meant, at all."

. . . . .

No! I am not Prince Hamlet, nor was meant to be;
Am an attendant lord, one that will do
To swell a progress,[7] start a scene or two,
Advise the prince: no doubt, an easy tool,
Deferential, glad to be of use,
Politic, cautious, and meticulous;
Full of high sentence,[8] but a bit obtuse;
At times, indeed, almost ridiculous—
Almost, at times, the Fool.

[5]An allusion to the poem "To His Coy Mistress," by the English poet Andrew Marvell (1621–1678): "Let us roll all our strength and all/Our sweetness up into one ball. . . ."

[6]The rich man Dives, suffering in Hell, begged that Lazarus be returned from heaven to earth to warn sinners of the torments that await them (Luke 16:19–31).

[7]To be part of a royal procession. [8]Judgment, pronouncement.

I grow old . . . I grow old . . .
I shall wear the bottoms of my trousers rolled.[9]
Shall I part my hair behind? Do I dare to eat a peach?
I shall wear white flannel trousers, and walk upon the beach.
I have heard the mermaids[10] singing, each to each.

I do not think that they will sing to me.

I have seen them riding seaward on the waves
Combing the white hair of the waves blown back
When the wind blows the water white and black.

We have lingered in the chambers of the sea
By sea-girls wreathed with seaweed red and brown
Till human voices wake us, and we drown.
1910–1911 1915, 1917

PRELUDES

I

The winter evening settles down
With smell of steaks in passageways.
Six o'clock.
The burnt-out ends of smoky days
And now a gusty shower wraps
The grimy scraps
Of withered leaves about your feet
And newspapers from vacant lots;
The showers beat
On broken blinds and chimney-pots,
And at the corner of the street
A lonely cab-horse steams and stamps.
And then the lighting of the lamps.

II

The morning comes to consciousness
Of faint stale smells of beer
From the sawdust-trampled street
With all its muddy feet that press
To early coffee-stands.

[9]To form fashionable cuffs. [10]Mythical alluring creatures, half woman and half fish.

With the other masquerades
That times resumes,
One thinks of all the hands
That are raising dingy shades
In a thousand furnished rooms.

III

You tossed a blanket from the bed,
You lay upon your back, and waited;
You dozed, and watched the night revealing
The thousand sordid images
Of which your soul was constituted;
They flickered against the ceiling.
And when all the world came back
And the light crept up between the shutters
And you heard the sparrows in the gutters,
You had such a vision of the street
As the street hardly understands;
Sitting along the bed's edge, where
You curled the papers from your hair,
Or clasped the yellow soles of feet
In the palms of both soiled hands.

IV

His soul stretched tight across the skies
That fade behind a city block,
Or trampled by insistent feet
At four and five and six o'clock;
And short square fingers stuffing pipes,
And evening newspapers, and eyes
Assured of certain certainties,
The conscience of a blackened street
Impatient to assume the world.

I am moved by fancies that are curled
Around these images, and cling:
The notion of some infinitely gentle
Infinitely suffering thing.
Wipe your hand across your mouth, and laugh;
The worlds revolve like ancient women
Gathering fuel in vacant lots.
1910–1911 1915, 1917

GERONTION[1]

Thou has nor youth nor age
But as it were an after-dinner's sleep
Dreaming on both.[2]

Here I am, an old man in a dry month
Being read to by a boy, waiting for rain.
I was neither at the hot gates[3]
Nor fought in the warm rain
Nor knee deep in the salt marsh, heaving a cutlass,
Bitten by flies, fought.
My house is a decayed house,
And the Jew squats on the window sill, the owner,
Spawned in some estaminet[4] of Antwerp,
Blistered in Brussels, patched and peeled[5] in London.
The goat coughs at night in the field overhead;
Rocks, moss, stonecrop,[6] iron, merds.[7]
The woman keeps the kitchen, makes tea,
Sneezes at evening, poking the peevish gutter.
                                        I an old man,
A dull head among windy spaces.

Signs are taken for wonders. "We would see a sign!"[8]
The word within a word, unable to speak a word,
Swaddled with darkness. In the juvescence[9] of the year
Came Christ the tiger

In depraved May, dogwood and chestnut, flowering judas,[10]
To be eaten, to be divided, to be drunk
Among whispers; by Mr. Silvero[11]
With caressing hands, at Limoges[12]
Who walked all night in the next room;
By Hakagawa, bowing among the Titians;[13]
By Madame de Tornquist, in the dark room
Shifting the candles; Fräulein von Kulp
Who turned in the hall, one hand on the door.
        Vacant shuttles
Weave the wind. I have no ghosts,

[1]A name derived from Greek "geron," "an old man."
[2]Shakespeare, *Measure for Measure* (Act III, Scene i, lines 32–34).
[3]At Thermopylae (Greek: hot gates) the Greeks battled the Persian invaders under Xerxes (480 B.C.).
[4]A cheap café.
[5]Medical procedures that, with blistering, were used to treat inflammation and venereal disease.
[6]A scrubby plant. [7]French: excrement.
[8]Jesus rebuked the doubting Pharisees when they said, "Master we would see a sign from thee" (Matthew 12:38–39).
[9]Juvenescence, youth. [10]The tree on which Judas was said to have hanged himself.
[11]An acquaintance (like Hakagawa, line 26) recalled by the aged Gerontion.
[12]French city noted for fine porcelain. [13]Paintings by the Italian artist Titian (1477–1576).

An old man in a draughty house
Under a windy knob.

After such knowledge, what forgiveness? Think now
History has many cunning passages, contrived corridors
And issues; deceives with whispering ambitions,
Guides us by vanities. Think now
She gives when our attention is distracted,
And what she gives, gives with such supple confusions
That the giving famishes the craving. Gives too late
What's not believed in, or if still believed,
In memory only, reconsidered passion. Gives too soon
Into weak hands, what's thought can be dispensed with
Till the refusal propagates a fear. Think
Neither fear nor courage saves us. Unnatural-vices
Are fathered by our heroism. Virtues
Are forced upon us by our impudent crimes.
These tears are shaken from the wrath-bearing tree.[14]

The tiger springs in the new year. Us he devours. Think at last
We have not reached conclusion, when I
Stiffen in a rented house. Think at last
I have not made this show purposelessly
And it is not by any concitation[15]
Of the backward devils.
I would meet you upon this honestly.
I that was near your heart was removed therefrom
To lose beauty in terror, terror in inquisition.
I have lost my passion: why should I need to keep it
Since what is kept must be adulterated?
I have lost my sight, smell, hearing, taste and touch:
How should I use them for your closer contact?

These with a thousand small deliberations
Protract the profit of their chilled delirium,
Excite the membrane, when the sense has cooled,
With pungent sauces, multiply variety
In a wilderness of mirrors. What will the spider do,
Suspend its operations, will the weevil
Delay? De Bailhache, Fresca, Mrs. Cammel,[16] whirled
Beyond the circuit of the shuddering Bear[17]
In fractured atoms. Gull against the wind, in the windy straits
Of Belle Isle,[18] or running on the Horn.[19]
White feathers in the snow, the Gulf claims,

[14]The tree from which Adam and Eve ate the forbidden fruit (Genesis 2:16–17; 3:16–19).
[15]Agitation, excitement. [16]Other names recollected by Gerontion.
[17]One of constellations Ursa, the Big or Little Dipper.
[18]Straits between Labrador and Newfoundland, Canada.
[19]Cape Horn, at the southern tip of South America.

And an old man driven by the Trades[20]
To a sleepy corner.
Tenants of the house.
Thoughts of a dry brain in a dry season.
1919 1920

THE WASTE LAND[1]

"Nam Sibyllam quidem Cumis ego ipse oculis meis vidi in ampulla pendere, et cum illi pueri dicerent: Σίβυλλα τί θέλεις; *respondebat illa:* ἀποθανεῖν θέλω. "[2]

For Ezra Pound
il miglior fabbro.[3]

I. THE BURIAL OF THE DEAD[4]

April is the cruellest month, breeding
Lilacs out of the dead land, mixing
Memory and desire, stirring
Dull roots with spring rain.
Winter kept us warm, covering
Earth in forgetful snow, feeding
A little life with dried tubers.
Summer surprised us, coming over the Starnbergersee[5]
With a shower of rain; we stopped in the colonnade,
And went on in sunlight, into the Hofgarten,[6]
And drank coffee, and talked for an hour.
Bin gar keine Russin, stamm' aus Litauen, echt deutsch.[7]
And when we were children, staying at the archduke's,
My cousin's, he took me out on a sled,
And I was frightened. He said, Marie,
Marie, hold on tight. And down we went.
In the mountains, there you feel free.
I read, much of the night, and go south in the winter.

[20]Trade winds.

[1]Footnotes to this poem and to Eliot's "Notes on 'The Waste Land'" are supplied by the editor.

[2]"For I myself saw with my own eyes the Sibyl of Cumae [in Italy] hanging in a bottle; and when the boys cried to her, 'Sibyl, what do you want?' she used to reply, 'I want to die.'" (Petronius, *Satyricon,* Chapter XLVIII). The Sibyl, a prophetess, had been given long life by Apollo, but she had failed to ask for eternal youth and health.

[3]"The better craftsman," a quotation from Dante's *Purgatorio* (Canto XXVI, line 117). Pound had assisted Eliot in writing "The Waste Land."

[4]The title of the services for the dead in *The Book of Common Prayer* of the Church of England.

[5]Lake near Munich, Germany. [6]Public park in Munich.

[7]German: I'm not Russian; I come from Lithuania, pure German.

What are the roots that clutch, what branches grow
Out of this stony rubbish? Son of man,
You cannot say, or guess, for you know only
A heap of broken images, where the sun beats,
And the dead tree gives no shelter, the cricket no relief,
And the dry stone no sound of water. Only
There is shadow under this red rock,
(Come in under the shadow of this red rock),
And I will show you something different from either
Your shadow at morning striding behind you
Or your shadow at evening rising to meet you;
I will show you fear in a handful of dust.
Frisch weht der Wind
Der Heimat zu.
Mein Irisch Kind,
Wo weilest du?[8]
"You gave me hyacinths[9] first a year ago;
"They called me the hyacinth girl."
—Yet when we came back, late, from the hyacinth garden,
Your arms full, and your hair wet, I could not
Speak, and my eyes failed, I was neither
Living nor dead, and I knew nothing,
Looking into the heart of light, the silence.
Oed' und leer das Meer.[10]

Madame Sosostris, famous clairvoyante,
Had a bad cold, nevertheless
Is known to be the wisest woman in Europe,
With a wicked pack of cards.[11] Here, said she,
Is your card, the drowned Phoenician Sailor,
(Those are pearls that were his eyes.[12] Look!)
Here is Belladonna, the Lady of the Rocks,
The lady of situations.
Here is the man with three staves, and here the Wheel,
And here is the one-eyed merchant, and this card,
Which is blank, is something he carries on his back,
Which I am forbidden to see. I do not find
The Hanged Man. Fear death by water.
I see crowds of people, walking round in a ring.
Thank you. If you see dear Mrs. Equitone,
Tell her I bring the horoscope myself:
One must be so careful these days.

[8]"Fresh blows the wind / To the homeland / My Irish child; / Where are you waiting?" See Eliot's note, I, line 31 (page 1328).

[9]A flower named for Hyacinthus, ancient Greek fertility god. The Hyacinthia, a resurrection festival in his honor, was celebrated in July to commemorate the seasonal rebirth and growth of vegetation.

[10]"Desolate and empty the sea." See Eliot's note, I, line 42.

[11]Tarot cards, used in fortune-telling. See Eliot's note, I, line 46.

[12]From Shakespeare's *The Tempest* (Act I, Scene ii, line 398).

Unreal City,
Under the brown fog of a winter dawn,
A crowd flowed over London Bridge, so many,
I had not thought death had undone so many.[13]
Sighs, short and infrequent, were exhaled,
And each man fixed his eyes before his feet.
Flowed up the hill and down King William Street,
To where Saint Mary Woolnoth[14] kept the hours
With a dead sound on the final stroke of nine.
There I saw one I knew, and stopped him, crying: "Stetson!
"You who were with me in the ships at Mylae![15]
"That corpse you planted last year in your garden,
"Has it begun to sprout? Will it bloom this year?
"Or has the sudden frost disturbed its bed?
"O keep the Dog far hence, that's friend to men,
"Or with his nails he'll dig it up again![16]
"You! hypocrite lecteur!—mon semblable,—mon frère!"[17]

II. A GAME OF CHESS

The Chair she sat in, like a burnished throne,
Glowed on the marble,[18] where the glass
Held up by standards wrought with fruited vines
From which a golden Cupidon[19] peeped out
(Another hid his eyes behind his wing)
Doubled the flames of sevenbranched candelabra
Reflecting light upon the table as
The glitter of her jewels rose to meet it,
From satin cases poured in rich profusion.
In vials of ivory and coloured glass
Unstoppered, lurked her strange synthetic perfumes,
Unguent, powdered, or liquid—troubled, confused
And drowned the sense in odours; stirred by the air
That freshened from the window, these ascended
In fattening the prolonged candle-flames,
Flung their smoke into the laquearia,[20]
Stirring the pattern on the coffered ceiling.
Huge sea-wood fed with copper
Burned green and orange, framed by the coloured stone,
In which sad light a carvèd dolphin swam.

[13]A quotation from Dante's *Inferno*. See Eliot's note, I, line 63. [14]London church.

[15]Site of a Roman naval victory over the Carthaginians (260 B.C.).

[16]An adaptation from John Webster's *The White Devil* (1612): "But keep the wolf far thence, that's foe to men, / For with his nails he'll dig them up again." (Act V, Scene iv, lines 97–98).

[17]French: "hypocrite reader!—my likeness,—my brother!" See Eliot's note, I, line 76.

[18]An adaptation of the description of Cleopatra's barge in Shakespeare's *Antony and Cleopatra:* "The barge she sat in, like a burnish'd throne, / Burn'd on the water." (Act II, Scene ii, lines 196–197).

[19]A statue of Cupid, Roman god of love. [20]Fretted ceiling. See Eliot's note, II, line 92.

Above the antique mantel was displayed
As though a window gave upon the sylvan scene[21]
The change of Philomel,[22] by the barbarous king
So rudely forced; yet there the nightingale
Filled all the desert with inviolable voice
And still she cries, and still the world pursues,
"Jug Jug"[23] to dirty ears.
And other withered stumps of time
Were told upon the walls; staring forms
Leaned out, leaning, hushing the room enclosed.
Footsteps shuffled on the stair.
Under the firelight, under the brush, her hair
Spread out in fiery points
Glowed into words, then would be savagely still.

"My nerves are bad to-night. Yes, bad. Stay with me.
"Speak to me. Why do you never speak? Speak.
"What are you thinking of? What thinking? What?
"I never know what you are thinking. Think."

I think we are in rats' alley
Where the dead men lost their bones.

"What is that noise?"
The wind under the door.
"What is that noise now? What is the wind doing?"
Nothing again nothing.
"Do

"You know nothing? Do you see nothing? Do you remember
Nothing?"
I remember
Those are pearls that were his eyes.
"Are you alive, or not? Is there nothing in your head?"
But

O O O O that Shakespeherian Rag—
It's so elegant
So intelligent[24]

"What shall I do now? What shall I do?
"I shall rush out as I am, and walk the street
"With my hair down, so. What shall we do tomorrow?
"What shall we ever do?"
The hot water at ten.

[21]A reference to *Paradise Lost* (Book IV, line 140) where Milton describes the Garden of Eden.
[22]In classical legend Philomel was raped by Tereus, King of Thrace. The gods then turned her into a nightingale. The story is told in Ovid's *Metamorphoses*. See Eliot's note, II, line 99.
[23]Words traditionally used in English poetry to represent the song of the nightingale.
[24]Lines adapted from the lyrics of *That Shakespearian Rag*, a popular song of 1912.

And if it rains, a closed car at four.
And we shall play a game of chess,
Pressing lidless eyes and waiting for a knock upon the door.
When Lil's husband got demobbed,[25] I said—
I didn't mince my words, I said to her myself,
HURRY UP PLEASE IT'S TIME[26]
Now Albert's coming back, make yourself a bit smart.
He'll want to know what you done with that money he gave you
To get yourself some teeth. He did, I was there.
You have them all out, Lil, and get a nice set,
He said, I swear, I can't bear to look at you.
And no more can't I, I said, and think of poor Albert,
He's been in the army four years, he wants a good time,
And if you don't give it him, there's others will, I said.
Oh is there, she said. Something o' that, I said.
Then I'll know who to thank, she said, and give me a straight look.
HURRY UP PLEASE IT'S TIME
If you don't like it you can get on with it, I said,
Others can pick and choose if you can't.
But if Albert makes off, it won't be for lack of telling.
You ought to be ashamed, I said, to look so antique.
(And her only thirty-one.)
I can't help it, she said, pulling a long face,
It's them pills I took, to bring it off, she said
(She's had five already, and nearly died of young George.)
The chemist[27] said it would be all right, but I've never been the same.
You *are* a proper fool, I said.
Well, if Albert won't leave you alone, there it is, I said,
What you get married for if you don't want children?
HURRY UP PLEASE IT'S TIME
Well, that Sunday Albert was home, they had a hot gammon,[28]
And they asked me in to dinner, to get the beauty of it hot—
HURRY UP PLEASE IT'S TIME
HURRY UP PLEASE IT'S TIME
Goonight Bill. Goonight Lou. Goonight May. Goonight.
Ta ta. Goonight. Goonight.
Good night, ladies, good night, sweet ladies, good night, good night.[29]

III. THE FIRE SERMON

The river's tent is broken; the last fingers of leaf
Clutch and sink into the wet bank. The wind
Crosses the brown land, unheard. The nymphs are departed.

[25]Demobilized from the army. [26]English pubkeeper's call to announce closing time.
[27]English pharmacist. [28]Smoked ham.
[29]From the speech by Ophelia, after she has gone mad. Shakespeare, *Hamlet* (Act IV, Scene v, lines 72–74).

Sweet Thames, run softly, till I end my song.[30]
The river bears no empty bottles, sandwich papers,
Silk handkerchiefs, cardboard boxes, cigarette ends
Or other testimony of summer nights. The nymphs are departed.
And their friends, the loitering heirs of City directors;[31]
Departed, have left no addresses.
By the waters of Leman I sat down and wept[32] . . .
Sweet Thames, run softly till I end my song,
Sweet Thames, run softly, for I speak not loud or long.
But at my back in a cold blast I hear[33]
The rattle of the bones, and chuckle spread from ear to ear.
A rat crept softly through the vegetation
Dragging its slimy belly on the bank
While I was fishing in the dull canal
On a winter evening round behind the gashouse
Musing upon the king my brother's wreck
And on the king my father's death before him.[34]
White bodies naked on the low damp ground
And bones cast in a little low garret,
Rattled by the rat's foot only, year to year.
But at my back from time to time I hear
The sound of horns and motors, which shall bring
Sweeney to Mrs. Porter[35] in the spring.
O the moon shone bright on Mrs. Porter
And on her daughter
They wash their feet in soda water
Et, O ces voix d'enfants chantant dans la coupole.[36]

Twit twit twit
Jug jug jug jug jug jug
So rudely forc'd.
Tereu[37]

[30]A quotation from Edmund Spenser's "Prothalamion" (1596), which describes an elegant procession of nymphs down the river Thames.

[31]Directors of business firms in the City, the financial district of London.

[32]From the lamentations of the Jews exiled from Palestine: "By the rivers of Babylon, there we sat down, yea, we wept, when we remembered Zion" (Psalm 137). Eliot substitutes "Leman," the French name for Lake Geneva, Switzerland.

[33]Adapted from "To His Coy Mistress," by Andrew Marvell (1621–1678): "But at my back I always hear / Time's wingèd chariot hurrying near" (lines 21–22).

[34]Adapted from the words of Ferdinand, son of the King of Naples, in Shakespeare's *The Tempest* (Act I, Scene ii, lines 389–391): "Sitting on a bank, / Weeping against the King my father's wreck, / This music crept by me upon the waters."

[35]Here, as elsewhere in Eliot's poetry, Sweeney represents crude humankind. Mrs. Porter and her daughter were whores described in a bawdy song popular with British troops in World War I. See Eliot's note, III, line 199.

[36]French: And, O those voices of children [choirboys] singing in the dome. From "Parsifal," a sonnet by Paul Verlaine (1844–1896).

[37]A conventional representation, with "jug, jug," of the nightingale's song and an allusion to King Tereus, the despoiler of Philomela.

Unreal City
Under the brown fog of a winter noon
Mr. Eugenides,[38] the Smyrna[39] merchant
Unshaven, with a pocket full of currants
C.i.f. London: documents at sight,[40]
Asked me in demotic[41] French
To luncheon at the Cannon Street Hotel
Followed by a weekend at the Metropole.
At the violet hour, when eyes and back
Turn upward from the desk, when the human engine waits
Like a taxi throbbing waiting
I Tiresias, though blind, throbbing between two lives,[42]
Old man with wrinkled female breasts, can see
At the violet hour, the evening hour that strives
Homeward, and brings the sailor home from sea,[43]
The typist home at teatime, clears her breakfast, lights
Her stove, and lays out food in tins.
Out of the window perilously spread
Her drying combinations[44] touched by the sun's last rays,
On the divan are piled (at night her bed)
Stockings, slippers, camisoles, and stays.[45]
I Tiresias, old man with wrinkled dugs[46]
Perceived the scene, and foretold the rest—
I too awaited the expected guest.
He, the young man carbuncular,[47] arrives,
A small house agent's clerk, with one bold stare,
One of the low on whom assurance sits
As a silk hat on a Bradford millionaire.[48]
The time is now propitious, as he guesses,
The meal is ended, she is bored and tired,
Endeavours to engage her in caresses
Which still are unreproved, if undesired.
Flushed and decided, he assaults at once;
Exploring hands encounter no defence;
His vanity requires no response,
And makes a welcome of indifference.
(And I Tiresias have foresuffered all
Enacted on this same divan or bed;

[38]Greek for *wellborn*. [39]Seaport in Turkey.

[40]Business terms used in the buying and selling of commodities. See Eliot's note, III, line 210.

[41]Vulgar.

[42]Tiresias, a blind prophet in Greek myth, had been transformed into a woman for seven years. See Eliot's note, III, line 218.

[43]Eliot refers (see his note) to "Sappho's lines," probably a reference to her poem to Hesperus, the Evening Star that brings "home all things the bright morning dispersed." Eliot may also have had in mind the lines from "Requiem" by Robert Louis Stevenson (1850–1894): "Home is the sailor, home from the sea."

[44]One-piece underwear.

[45]Camisoles: short, sleeveless underwear. Stays: corset with bone stiffeners.

[46]Breasts. [47]Afflicted with carbuncles, boils.

[48]One of the newly rich from the English industrial city of Bradford.

I who have sat by Thebes below the wall
And walked among the lowest of the dead.)[49]
Bestows one final patronising kiss,
And gropes his way, finding the stairs unlit . . .
She turns and looks a moment in the glass,
Hardly aware of her departed lover;
Her brain allows one half-formed thought to pass:
"Well now that's done: and I'm glad it's over."
When lovely woman stoops to folly and
Paces about her room again, alone,
She smoothes her hair with automatic hand,
And puts a record on the gramophone.[50]

"This music crept by me upon the waters"[51]
And along the Strand,[52] up Queen Victoria Street.
O City, City, I can sometimes hear
Beside a public bar in Lower Thames Street,
The pleasant whining of a mandoline
And a clatter and a chatter from within
Where fishmen lounge at noon: where the walls
Of Magnus Martyr[53] hold
Inexplicable splendour of Ionian white and gold.

The river sweats
Oil and tar
The barges drift
With the turning tide
Red sails
Wide
To leeward, swing on the heavy spar.
The barges wash
Drifting logs
Down Greenwich Reach[54]
Past the Isle of Dogs.[55]
        Weialala leia
        Wallala leialala[56]
Elizabeth and Leicester[57]
Beating oars
The stern was formed

[49]Tiresias made his prophecies in Thebes, where he lived, and in Hades, the underworld, after his death.

[50]An ironic adaptation from Oliver Goldsmith's *The Vicar of Wakefield* (Chapter 24): "When lovely woman stoops to folly, / And finds too late that men betray; / What charm can soothe her melancholy? / What art can wash her guilt away?"

[51]From *The Tempest.*

[52]A London street.

[53]A London church built by Sir Christopher Wren (1632–1723). See Eliot's note, III, line 264.

[54]The Thames River at Greenwich.

[55]A peninsula in the Thames.

[56]The refrain in the song of the Rhine-maidens from the opera *Die Götterdämmerung,* by Richard Wagner (1813–1883).

[57]Queen Elizabeth I of England and Robert Dudley, the Earl of Leicester. Their boat-ride on the Thames (see Eliot's note, III, line 279) is contrasted to the three sordid love affairs that follow (lines 292–308).

A gilded shell
Red and gold
The brisk swell
Rippled both shores
Southwest wind
Carried down stream
The peal of bells
White towers
Weialala leia
Wallala leialala

"Trams[58] and dusty trees.
Highbury bore me. Richmond and Kew
Undid me.[59] By Richmond I raised my knees
Supine on the floor of a narrow canoe."

"My feet are at Moorgate,[60] and my heart
Under my feet. After the event
He wept. He promised 'a new start.'
I made no comment. What should I resent?"

"On Margate Sands.[61]
I can connect
Nothing with nothing.
The broken fingernails of dirty hands.
My people humble people who expect
Nothing."
la la

To Carthage then I came[62]

Burning burning burning burning[63]
O Lord Thou pluckest me out[64]
O Lord Thou pluckest

burning

[58]Streetcars.

[59]Highbury: London suburb; Richmond and Kew: park and resort areas near London. Eliot echoes the lines from Dante, "Siena bore me; Maremma undid me," used also by Ezra Pound in one of his "Hugh Selwyn Mauberley" poems.

[60]Slum area of London. [61]A seaside resort on the Thames.

[62]From St. Augustine's *Confessions* (Book III, Chapter i). See Eliot's note, III, line 307.

[63]From the Fire Sermon of Buddha, which calls for a life free of fiery passion. See Eliot's note, III, line 308.

[64]In his *Confessions,* St. Augustine thanks the Lord for plucking him from his broiling, unholy loves. See Eliot's note, III, line 309.

IV. DEATH BY WATER

Phlebas the Phoenician, a fortnight dead,
Forgot the cry of gulls, and the deep sea swell
And the profit and loss.
                    A current under sea
Picked his bones in whispers. As he rose and fell
He passed the stages of his age and youth
Entering the whirlpool.
                    Gentile or jew
O you who turn the wheel[65] and look to windward,
Consider Phlebas, who was once handsome and tall as you.

V. WHAT THE THUNDER SAID[66]

After the torch light red on sweaty faces
After the frosty silence in the gardens
After the agony in stony places
The shouting and the crying
Prison and palace and reverberation
Of thunder of spring over distant mountains
He who was living is now dead[67]
We who were living are now dying
With a little patience

Here is no water but only rock
Rock and no water and the sandy road
The road winding above among the mountains
Which are mountains of rock without water
If there were water we should stop and drink
Amongst the rock one cannot stop or think
Sweat is dry and feet are in the sand
If there were only water amongst the rock
Dead mountain mouth of carious[68] teeth that cannot spit
Here one can neither stand nor lie nor sit
There is not even silence in the mountains
But dry sterile thunder without rain
There is not even solitude in the mountains
But red sullen faces sneer and snarl
From doors of mudcracked houses
                    If there were water

[65]The wheel of fortune or (more likely) a ship's steersman's wheel.
[66]In the Indian *Upanishads,* the Lord speaks through the thunder.
[67]Lines 322–328 refer to Christ's ordeal after The Last Supper and His martyrdom.
[68]Decayed.

And no rock
If there were rock
And also water
And water
A spring
A pool among the rock
If there were the sound of water only
Not the cicada
And dry grass singing
But sound of water over a rock
Where the hermit-thrush sings in the pine trees
Drip drop drip drop drop drop drop
But there is no water

Who is the third, who walks always beside you?[69]
When I count, there are only you and I together
But when I look ahead up the white road
There is always another one walking beside you
Gliding wrapt in a brown mantle, hooded
I do not know whether a man or a woman
—But who is that on the other side of you?
What is that sound high in the air[70]
Murmur of maternal lamentation
Who are those hooded hordes swarming
Over endless plains, stumbling in cracked earth
Ringed by the flat horizon only
What is the city over the mountains
Cracks and reforms and bursts in the violet air
Falling towers
Jerusalem Athens Alexandria
Vienna London
Unreal
A woman drew her long black hair out tight
And fiddled whisper music on those strings
And bats with baby faces in the violet light
Whistled, and beat their wings
And crawled head downward down a blackened wall
And upside down in air were towers
Tolling reminiscent bells, that kept the hours
And voices singing out of empty cisterns and exhausted wells.

In this decayed hole among the mountains
In the faint moonlight, the grass is singing
Over the tumbled graves, about the chapel
There is the empty chapel,[71] only the wind's home.

[69]After His crucifixion, Christ appeared before two travelers to Emmaus (Luke 24:13–31). See also Eliot's note, V, line 360.

[70]Lines 367–377 allude to the upheavals resulting from the Russian Revolution that threatened the centers of civilization: Jerusalem, Athens, Alexandria, etc. See Eliot's note, V, lines 366–377.

[71]The Chapel Perilous wherein the knight was prepared for his quest for the Holy Grail.

It has no windows, and the door swings,
Dry bones can harm no one.
Only a cock stood on the rooftree
Co co rico co co rico[72]
In a flash of lightning. Then a damp gust
Bringing rain

Ganga[73] was sunken, and the limp leaves
Waited for rain, while the black clouds
Gathered far distant, over Himavant.[74]
The jungle crouched, humped in silence.
Then spoke the thunder
DA
Datta:[75] what have we given?
My friend, blood shaking my heart
The awful daring of a moment's surrender
Which an age of prudence can never retract
By this, and this only, we have existed
Which is not to be found in our obituaries
Or in memories draped by the beneficent spider
Or under seals broken by the lean solicitor
In our empty rooms
DA
Dayadhvam:[76] I have heard the key
Turn in the door once and turn once only
We think of the key, each in his prison
Thinking of the key, each confirms a prison
Only at nightfall, aethereal rumours
Revive for a moment a broken Coriolanus[77]
DA
Damyata:[78] The boat responded
Gaily, to the hand expert with sail and oar
The sea was calm, your heart would have responded
Gaily, when invited, beating obedient
To controlling hands

I sat upon the shore
Fishing,[79] with the arid plain behind me
Shall I at least set my lands in order?[80]
London Bridge is falling down falling down falling down

[72]The sound of the cock's crow (French version), indicating the coming of dawn and renewal.
[73]The Ganges River. [74]The Himalaya Mountains.
[75]Sanskrit: Give. From the words of the thunder in the *Upanishads.* [76]Sanskrit: Sympathize.
[77]Roman general and title character of Shakespeare's *Coriolanus.* He was ruined by his pride and the ingratitude of the masses.
[78]Sanskrit: Control yourselves.
[79]The Fisher King, to whom Eliot alludes, is, like Christ, a symbol of resurrection. See Eliot's note, V, line 425.
[80]"Thus saith the Lord, Set thine house in order: for thou shalt die, and not live" (Isaiah 38:1).

Poi s'ascose nel foco che gli affina[81]
Quando fiam uti chelidon[82]—O swallow swallow
Le Prince d'Aquitàine à la tour abolie[83]
These fragments I have shored against my ruins
Why then Ile fit you.[84] Hieronymo's mad againe.[85]
Datta. Dayadhvam. Damyata.

Shantih shantih shantih[86]

1914?–1922 1922

NOTES ON "THE WASTE LAND"[1]

Not only the title, but the plan and a good deal of the incidental symbolism of the poem were suggested by Miss Jessie L. Weston's book on the Grail legend: *From Ritual to Romance* (Cambridge). Indeed, so deeply am I indebted, Miss Weston's book will elucidate the difficulties of the poem much better than my notes can do; and I recommend it (apart from the great interest of the book itself) to any who think such elucidation of the poem worth the trouble. To another work of anthropology I am indebted in general, one which has influenced our generation profoundly; I mean *The Golden Bough*;[2] I have used especially the two volumes *Adonis, Attis, Osiris.* Anyone who is acquainted with these works will immediately recognise in the poem certain references to vegetation ceremonies.

I. The Burial of the Dead

Line 20. Cf. Ezekiel II, i.

23. Cf. Ecclesiastes XII, v.

31. V. *Tristan und Isolde,* I, verses 5–8.

42. Id. III, verse 24.

46. I am not familiar with the exact constitution of the Tarot pack of cards, from which I have obviously departed to suit my own convenience. The Hanged Man, a member of the traditional pack, fits my purpose in two ways: because he

[81]Italian: Then he hid himself in the flame that purifies them, i.e., the flame that destroys lust. Dante, *Purgatorio* (Canto XXVI, *line* 148).

[82]"When shall I be like the swallow?" From the anonymous Latin poem (fourth century?) "Pervigilium Veneris" ("The Vigil of Venus"), celebrating love and the return of spring. See Eliot's note, V, line 429.

[83]French: The Prince of Aquitaine at the ruined tower. From the sonnet "El Desdichado" by Gérard de Nerval (1808–1855).

[84]From *The Spanish Tragedy* by Thomas Kyd (1557?–1595?). The words are spoken by Hieronymo, who seeks revenge for the murder of his son.

[85]The subtitle of *The Spanish Tragedy.*

[86]Sanskrit: The Peace which passeth understanding. See Eliot's note, V, line 434.

[1]In *The Frontiers of Criticism* (1956) Eliot wrote, "When it came to print *The Waste Land* as a little book [1922]—for the poem on its first appearance in *The Dial* [1922] and in *The Criterion* [1922] had no notes whatever—it was discovered that the poem was inconveniently short, so I set to work to expand the notes, in order to provide a few more pages of printed matter. . . ."

[2]Anthropological study (1890) of myth and religion, by Sir James Frazer (1854–1941).

is associated in my mind with the Hanged God of Frazer, and because I associate him with the hooded figure in the passage of the disciples to Emmaus in Part V. The Phoenician Sailor and the Merchant appear later; also the "crowds of people," and Death by Water is executed in Part IV. The Man with Three Staves (an authentic member of the Tarot pack) I associate, quite arbitrarily, with the Fisher King himself.

60. Cf. Baudelaire:

> "Fourmillante cité, cité pleine de rêves,
> Où le spectre en plein jour raccroche le passant."[3]

63. Cf. *Inferno,* III, 55–57:

> "si lunga tratta
> di gente, ch'io non avrei mai creduto
> che morte tanta n'avesse disfatta."[4]

64. Cf. *Inferno,* IV, 25–27:

> "Quivi, secondo che per ascoltare,
> "non avea pianto, ma' che di sospiri,
> "che l'aura eterna facevan tremare."[5]

68. A phenomenon which I have often noticed.
74. Cf. the Dirge in Webster's *White Devil.*
76. V. Baudelaire, Preface to *Fleurs du mal.*

II. A GAME OF CHESS

77. Cf. *Antony and Cleopatra,* II, ii, l. 190.
92. Laquearia. V. *Aeneid,* I, 726:

> dependent lychni laquearibus aureis incensi, et noctem flammis funalia vincunt.[6]

98. Sylvan scene. V. Milton, *Paradise Lost,* IV, 140.
99. V. Ovid, *Metamorphoses,* VI, Philomela.
100. Cf. Part III, l. 204.
115. Cf. Part III, l. 195.
118. Cf. Webster: "Is the wind in that door still?"[7]
126. Cf. Part I, l. 37, 48.
138. Cf. the game of chess in Middleton's *Women Beware Women.*[8]

III. THE FIRE SERMON

176. V. Spenser, *Prothalamion.*
192. Cf. *The Tempest,* I, ii.
196. Cf. Marvell, *To His Coy Mistress.*
197. Cf. Day, *Parliament of Bees:*

> "When of the sudden, listening, you shall hear,
> "A noise of horns and hunting, which shall bring

[3]"Swarming city, city full of dreams, / Where the ghost in broad daylight accosts the passerby." From the opening lines of the poem "Les Sept Vieillards" ("The Seven Old Men"), by the French poet Charles Baudelaire (1821–1867).

[4]"So long a train of people, I should never have believed death had undone so many."

[5]"Here was no complaint, that could be heard, except of sighs, which caused the eternal air to tremble."

[6]Lighted lamps hang from the gold, fretted ceiling, and flaming torches drive out the night.

[7]I.e., "Is he breathing still?" Spoken of a dying man in John Webster's *The Devil's Law-Case* (1623).

[8]In Thomas Middleton's play (1657), a young wife is seduced while her guardian is occupied with a game of chess.

"Actaeon to Diana in the spring,
"Where all shall see her naked skin[9]. . ."

199. I do not know the origin of the ballad from which these lines are taken: it was reported to me from Sydney, Australia.

202. V. Verlaine, *Parsifal.*

210. The currants were quoted at a price "cost insurance and freight to London"; and the Bill of Lading, etc., were to be handed to the buyer upon payment of the sight draft.

218. Tiresias, although a mere spectator and not indeed a "character," is yet the most important personage in the poem, uniting all the rest. Just as the one-eyed merchant, seller of currants, melts into the Phoenician Sailor, and the latter is not wholly distinct from Ferdinand Prince of Naples,[10] so all the women are one woman, and the two sexes meet in Tiresias. What Tiresias *sees,* in fact, is the substance of the poem. The whole passage from Ovid is of great anthropological interest:

". . .Cum Iunone iocos et maior vestra profecto est
Quam, quae contingit maribus," dixisse, "voluptas."
Illa negat; placuit quae sit sententia docti
Quaerere Tiresiae: venus huic erat utraque nota.
Nam duo magnorum viridi coeuntia silva
Corpora serpentum baculi violaverat ictu
Deque viro factus, mirabile, femina septem
Egerat autumnos; octavo rursus eosdem
Vidit et "est vestrae si tanta potentia plagae,"
Dixit "ut auctoris sortem in contraria mutet,
Nunc quoque vos feriam!" percussis anguibus isdem
Forma prior rediit genetivaque venit imago.
Arbiter hic igitur sumptus de lite iocosa
Dicta Iovis firmat; gravius Saturnia iusto
Nec pro materia fertur doluisse suique
Iudicis aeterna damnavit lumina nocte,
At pater omnipotens (neque enim licet inrita cuiquam
Facta dei fecisse deo) pro lumine adempto
Scire futura dedit poenamque levavit honore.[11]

221. This may not appear as exact as Sappho's lines, but I had in mind the "longshore" or "dory" fisherman, who returns at nightfall.

253. V. Goldsmith, the song in *The Vicar of Wakefield.*

257. V. *The Tempest,* as above.

264. The interior of St. Magnus Martyr is to my mind one of the finest among Wren's interiors. See *The Proposed Demolition of Nineteen City Churches:* (P.S. King & Son, Ltd.).

[9]From "Character 3" of John Day's Elizabethan verse dialogues, *The Parliament of Bees* (1641).

[10]In Shakespeare's *The Tempest.*

[11]The Latin quotation, from Ovid's *Metamorphoses* (Book III, lines 320–338), may be summarized as: Jove and Juno once argued whether women or men received more pleasure in lovemaking. To settle the argument they agreed to ask Tiresias, who had once been transformed into a woman. Tiresias, agreeing with Jove, said that women received more pleasure. The answer so angered Juno that she blinded Tiresias. Whereupon, as compensation, Jove gave the blind Tiresias the power to know the future.

266. The Song of the (three) Thames-daughters begins here. From line 292 to 306 inclusive they speak in turn. V. *Götterdämmerung,* III, i: the Rhine-daughters.[12]

279. V. Froude, *Elizabeth,* Vol. I, ch. iv, letter of De Quadra to Philip of Spain: "In the afternoon we were in a barge, watching the games on the river. (The queen) was alone with Lord Robert and myself on the poop, when they began to talk nonsense, and went so far that Lord Robert at last said, as I was on the spot there was no reason why they should not be married if the queen pleased."[13]

293. Cf. *Purgatorio,* V. 133:

> "Ricorditi di me, che son la Pia;
> "Siena mi fe', disfecemi Maremma."[14]

307. V. St. Augustine's *Confessions:* "to Carthage then I came, where a cauldron of unholy loves sang all about mine ears."

308. The complete text of the Buddha's Fire Sermon (which corresponds in importance to the Sermon on the Mount) from which these words are taken, will be found translated in the late Henry Clarke Warren's *Buddhism in Translation* (Harvard Oriental Series). Mr. Warren was one of the great pioneers of Buddhist studies in the Occident.

309. From St. Augustine's *Confessions* again. The collocation of these two representatives of eastern and western asceticism, as the culmination of this part of the poem, is not an accident.

V. What the Thunder Said

In the first part of Part V three themes are employed: the journey to Emmaus, the approach to the Chapel Perilous (see Miss Weston's book) and the present decay of eastern Europe.

357. This is *Turdus aonalaschkae pallasii,* the hermit-thrush which I have heard in Quebec Province. Chapman says (*Handbook of Birds of Eastern North America*) "it is most at home in secluded woodland and thickety retreats. . . . Its notes are not remarkable for variety or volume, but in purity and sweetness of tone and exquisite modulation they are unequalled." Its "water-dripping song" is justly celebrated.

360. The following lines were stimulated by the account of one of the Antarctic expeditions (I forget which, but I think one of Shackleton's): it was related that the party of explorers, at the extremity of their strength, had the constant delusion that there was *one more member* than could actually be counted.

366–77. Cf. Hermann Hesse, *Blick ins Chaos:* "Schon ist halb Europa, schon ist zumindest der halbe Osten Europas auf dem Wege zum Chaos, fährt betrunken im heiligen Wahn am Abgrund entlang und singt dazu, singt betrunken

[12]Eliot compares the three modern daughters of the Thames with the three legendary Rhine-maidens in *Die Götterdämmerung,* one of the four operas in Richard Wagner's *Der Ring des Nibelungen* (1853–1870).

[13]The quotation, taken from a letter from the Spanish Ambassador (Bishop de Quadra) to his king, appeared in a biography of Queen Elizabeth I by the English historian James Anthony Froude (1818–1894).

[14]Italian: "Remember me, who am La Pia; Siena bore me, Maremma undid me." Spoken by a Sienese woman, La Pia, who was killed in Maremma.

und hymnisch wie Dmitri Karamasoff sang. Ueber diese Lieder lacht der Bürger beleidigt, der Heilige und Seher hört sie mit Tränen."[15]

402. "Datta, dayadhvam, damyata" (Give, sympathise, control). The fable of the meaning of the Thunder is found in the *Brihadaranyaka—Upanishad,* 5, 1. A translation is found in Deussen's *Sechzig Upanishads des Veda,* p. 489.

408. Cf. Webster, *The White Devil,* V, vi:

"... they'll remarry
Ere the worm pierce your winding-sheet, ere the spider
Make a thin curtain for your epithaphs."

412. Cf. *Inferno,* XXXIII, 46:

"ed io sentii chiavar l'uscio di sotto
all'orrible torre."[16]

Also F. H. Bradley, *Appearance and Reality,* p. 346.

"My external sensations are no less private to myself than are my thoughts or my feelings. In either case my experience falls within my own circle, a circle closed on the outside; and, with all its elements alike, every sphere is opaque to the others which surround it. . . . In brief, regarded as an existence which appears in a soul, the whole world for each is peculiar and private to that soul."

425. V. Weston: *From Ritual to Romance;* chapter on the Fisher King.

428. V. *Purgatorio,* XXVI, 48.

"'Ara vos prec er aquella valor
'que vos condus al som de l'escalina,
'sovegna vos a temps de ma dolor.'
Poi s'ascose nel foco che gli affina."[17]

429. V. *Pervigilium Veneris.* Cf. Philomela in Parts II and III.

430. V. Gerard de Nerval, Sonnet *El Desdichado.*

432. V. Kyd's *Spanish Tragedy.*

434. Shantih. Repeated as here, a formal ending to an Upanishad. "The Peace which passeth understanding" is our equivalent to this word.

1922

JOURNEY OF THE MAGI[1]

'A cold coming we had of it,
Just the worst time of the year
For a journey, and such a long journey:
The ways deep and the weather sharp,

[15]"Already half of Europe, already at least half of Eastern Europe, is on the way to chaos, going drunk, in spiritual madness, along the edge of the abyss, while singing drunkenly and rapturously, as did Dimitri Karamazov [in Dostoyevsky's *The Brothers Karamazov*]. The shocked bourgeois laughs at these songs; the saint and the prophet hear them with tears." From *A Glimpse into Chaos* by Herman Hesse (1877–1962), German poet and novelist.

[16]"And below I heard the door of the horrible tower being locked."

[17]"'Now I pray you, by the goodness that guides you to the top of this stairway [i.e., to paradise], be mindful in due season of my pain.' Then he hid himself in the flame that purifies." The words are spoken to Dante by the poet Arnaut Daniel, who is suffering for his sins of lust.

[1]One of a series of lyrics, the "Ariel Poems," on the theme of death and rebirth. The speaker is one of the three wise men whose journey to Bethlehem, to the birth of Christ, is described in Matthew 2:1–11.

The very dead of winter.'[2]
And the camels galled,[3] sore-footed, refractory,
Lying down in the melting snow.
There were times we regretted
The summer palaces on slopes, the terraces,
And the silken girls bringing sherbet.
Then the camel men cursing and grumbling
And running away, and wanting their liquor and women,
And the night-fires going out, and the lack of shelters,
And the cities hostile and the towns unfriendly
And the villages dirty and charging high prices:
A hard time we had of it.
At the end we preferred to travel all night,
Sleeping in snatches,
With the voices singing in our ears, saying
That this was all folly.

Then at dawn we came down to a temperate valley,
Wet, below the snow line, smelling of vegetation,
With a running stream and a water-mill beating the darkness,
And three trees on the low sky.[4]
And an old white horse[5] galloped away in the meadow.
Then we came to a tavern with vine-leaves over the lintel,[6]
Six hands at an open door dicing for pieces of silver,[7]
And feet kicking the empty wine-skins.
But there was no information, and so we continued
And arrived at evening, not a moment too soon
Finding the place; it was (you may say) satisfactory.

All this was a long time ago, I remember,
And I would do it again, but set down
This set down
This: were we led all that way for
Birth or Death? There was a Birth, certainly,
We had evidence and no doubt. I had seen birth and death,
But had thought they were different; this Birth was
Hard and bitter agony for us, like Death, our death.
We returned to our places, these Kingdoms,
But no longer at ease here, in the old dispensation,
With an alien people clutching their gods.
I should be glad of another death.

1927

[2]The first five lines are taken from a nativity sermon by Lancelot Andrewes (1555–1626), Bishop of Winchester.

[3]Rubbed raw by their harness.

[4]A suggestion of the three crosses on Calvary and the "darkness over all the land" (Matthew 27:38, 45).

[5]"Behold a white horse; and he that sat upon him was Faithful and True" (Revelation 19:11).

[6]The Israelites marked their door lintels with sacrificial blood so that the Lord would pass over them when he smote the Egyptians. (Exodus 12:7–13). Here, the vine leaves on the tavern door suggest instead the vegetation sacred to such pagan fertility gods as Dionysus, god of wine.

[7]A suggestion of the silver paid Judas for the betrayal of Christ.

E. E. Cummings 1894–1962

From the time he left college in 1916 until his death in 1962, E. E. Cummings held only one formal job: For three months he answered letters for a mail-order firm. Later he compared those three months to his time spent in a French concentration camp during the First World War. For Cummings, life was too important to spend in pursuit of the material success desired by "most people." Instead he chose to be a dedicated, full-time artist: a painter, a novelist, a playwright, a "nonlecturer"—but most of all a poet.

Edward Estlin Cummings was born in Cambridge, Massachusetts. His father was a Harvard professor who later served as a Unitarian minister in Boston. Cummings went to Harvard, and at his graduation gave the commencement address, speaking on "The New Art." In 1917, after taking his M.A. at Harvard and suffering his brief ordeal as a mail-order letter writer, Cummings went to France to serve as a volunteer ambulance driver with the Red Cross in World War I.

Shortly after arriving in France, Cummings was imprisoned for three months in a concentration camp, partly because of the stupidity of the French military authorities and partly because of Cummings's own stubbornness (he refused to say he hated the Germans; he would only admit that he loved the French). After influential friends secured his release, Cummings was encouraged to write about his experiences. The result was The Enormous Room *(1922), a novel that was the first significant statement of his lifelong dedication to individual freedom and his opposition to the dehumanizing forces he saw in the modern world.*

After World War I, Cummings returned to Europe to study painting. He joined the artistic expatriates who flourished in Paris in the 1920s, and whose experimentation in the visual arts profoundly influenced his literary development. In 1923 his first volume of poetry, Tulips and Chimneys, *was published. The following year he returned to America, and in 1925 he published XLI Poems. During the remainder of his life he traveled widely and wrote expansively: plays; a book describing a journey to Russia,* Eimi *(1933); and the poems that made him famous.*

Cummings's poetry is noted for its eccentric and playful style: its unusual typography, odd spellings, and deliberate grammatical tricks. But beneath the surface of trickery and apparent formlessness, his poetry is curiously conventional. He was a love poet in the romantic tradition; he celebrated families, parents, children, fun, and old-fashioned virtues. He admired youth, spring, and all things natural. He hated automatic patriotism and deplored intellectualism—the rationality that, he believed, stifles humankind's ability to feel deeply. He fiercely condemned the inhumanity of science and technology, writing, "Never will mankind become human . . . until it rises up and smashes its machines." He found modern conveniences contemptible; he shunned electricity in his home, hated radio and television, and called packaged food "Battle Creek seaweed." Above all he loved poetry. Reading to an indifferent audience in 1950, he finally grew angry and stormed out, shouting at his apathetic listeners, "Well, write poetry, for God's sake; it's the only thing that matters."

FURTHER READING: N. Friedman, *E. E. Cummings: The Growth of a Writer,* 1964, 1980; *Selected Letters of E. E. Cummings,* ed. F. Dupee and G. Stade, 1969; *E. E. Cummings: The Critical Reception,* ed. L. Dendinger, 1979; R. Kennedy, *Dreams in the Mirror: A Biography of E. E. Cummings,* 1980; *Critical Essays on E. E. Cummings,* ed. G. Rotella, 1984; M. Cohen, *Poet and Painter: The Aesthetic of E. E. Cummings' Early Work,* 1987; R. Kennedy, *E. E. Cummings Revisited,* 1993; N. Friedman, *(Re)Valuing Cummings,* 1996; M. Heusser, *I Am My Writing: The Poetry of E. E. Cummings,* 1997; *E. E. Cummings,* ed. H. Bloom, 2003; C. Sawyer-Laucanno, *E. E. Cummings: A Biography,* 2004.

TEXTS: *The Dial,* January, May 1920; *The Complete Poems, 1904–1962,* 1999.

[in Just-][1]

in Just-
spring   when the world is mud-
luscious the little
lame balloonman

whistles   far   and wee

and eddieandbill come
running from marbles and
piracies and it's
spring

when the world is puddle-wonderful

the queer
old balloonman whistles
far   and   wee
and bettyandisbel come dancing

from hopscotch and jump-rope and

it's
spring
and
      the

                  goat-footed

balloonMan   whistles
far
and
wee

1920

[O sweet spontaneous]

O sweet spontaneous
earth how often have
the
doting

[1]Titles in brackets are supplied by the editors.

fingers of
prurient philosophers pinched
and
poked

thee
has the naughty thumb
of science prodded
thy

beauty how
often have religions taken
thee upon their scraggy knees
squeezing and

buffeting thee that thou mightest conceive
gods
but
true

to the incomparable
couch of death thy
rhythmic
lover
thou answerest

them only with

spring

1920

[Buffalo Bill's[1] defunct]

Buffalo Bill's
defunct
who used to
ride a watersmooth-silver
stallion
and break onetwothreefourfive pigeonsjustlikethat
Jesus

he was a handsome man
and what i want to know is
how do you like your blueeyed boy
Mister Death

1920

[1]William F. Cody (1846–1917), American frontiersman and later a star performer in "Buffalo Bill's Wild West Show," which toured America and Europe in the 1880s and 1890s.

[the Cambridge ladies who live in furnished souls]

the Cambridge ladies who live in furnished souls
are unbeautiful and have comfortable minds
(also, with the church's protestant blessings
daughters, unscented shapeless spirited)
they believe in Christ and Longfellow, both dead,
are invariably interested in so many things—
at the present writing one still finds
delighted fingers knitting for the is it Poles?
perhaps. While permanent faces coyly bandy
scandal of Mrs. N and Professor D
. . . . the Cambridge ladies do not care, above
Cambridge if sometimes in its box of
sky lavender and cornerless, the
moon rattles like a fragment of angry candy

1922, 1923

["next to of course god america i"]

"next to of course god america i
love you land of the pilgrims' and so forth oh
say can you see by the dawn's early my
country 'tis of centuries come and go
and are no more what of it we should worry
in every language even deafanddumb
thy sons acclaim your glorious name by gorry
by jingo by gee by gosh by gum
why talk of beauty what could be more beauti-
ful than these heroic happy dead
who rushed like lions to the roaring slaughter
they did not stop to think they died instead
then shall the voice of liberty be mute?"

He spoke. And drank rapidly a glass of water

1925, 1926

[my sweet old etcetera]

my sweet old etcetera
aunt lucy during the recent

war could and what
is more did tell you just
what everybody was fighting

for,
my sister

isabel created hundreds
(and
hundreds) of socks not to
mention shirts fleaproof earwarmers

etcetera wristers etcetera, my
mother hoped that

i would die etcetera
bravely of course my father used
to become hoarse talking about how it was
a privilege and if only he
could meanwhile my

self etcetera lay quietly
in the deep mud et
cetera
(dreaming,
et
    cetera, of
Your smile
eyes knees and of your Etcetera)

1926

[somewhere i have never travelled,gladly beyond]

somewhere i have never travelled,gladly beyond
any experience,your eyes have their silence:
in your most frail gesture are things which enclose me,
or which i cannot touch because they are too near

your slightest look easily will unclose me
though i have closed myself as fingers,
you open always petal by petal myself as Spring opens
(touching skillfully,mysteriously) her first rose

or if your wish be to close me,i and
my life will shut very beautifully,suddenly,
as when the heart of this flower imagines
the snow carefully everywhere descending;

nothing which we are to perceive in this world equals
the power of your intense fragility:whose texture
compels me with the colour of its countries,
rendering death and forever with each breathing

(i do not know what it is about you that closes
and opens;only something in me understands
the voice of your eyes is deeper than all roses)
nobody,not even the rain,has such small hands

1931

[r-p-o-p-h-e-s-s-a-g-r]

r-p-o-p-h-e-s-s-a-g-r
who
a)s w(e loo)k
upnowgath
PPEGORHRASS
eringint(o-
aThe):l
eA
!p:
S a
(r
rIvInG.gRrEaPsPhOs)
to
rea(be)rran(com)gi(e)ngly
,grasshopper;

1932, 1935

[anyone lived in a pretty how town]

anyone lived in a pretty how town
(with up so floating many bells down)
spring summer autumn winter
he sang his didn't he danced his did.

Women and men (both little and small)
cared for anyone not at all
they sowed their isn't they reaped their same
sun moon stars rain

children guessed(but only a few
and down they forgot as up they grew
autumn winter spring summer)
that noone loved him more by more

when by now and tree by leaf
she laughed his joy she cried his grief

bird by snow and stir by still
anyone's any was all to her

someones married their everyones
laughed their cryings and did their dance
(sleep wake hope and then)they
said their nevers they slept their dream

stars rain sun moon
(and only the snow can begin to explain
how children are apt to forget to remember
with up so floating many bells down)

one day anyone died i guess
(and noone stooped to kiss his face)
busy folk buried them side by side
little by little and was by was

all by all and deep by deep
and more by more they dream their sleep
noone and anyone earth by april
wish by spirit and if by yes.

Women and men(both dong and ding)
summer autumn winter spring
reaped their sowing and went their came
sun moon stars rain

1940

[pity this busy monster,manunkind]

pity this busy monster,manunkind,

not. Progress is a comfortable disease:
your victim(death and life safely beyond)

plays with the bigness of his littleness
—electrons deify one razorblade
into a mountainrange;lenses extend

unwish through curving wherewhen till unwish
returns on its unself.
A world of made
is not a world of born—pity poor flesh

and trees,poor stars and stones,but never this
fine specimen of hypermagical

ultraomnipotence. We doctors know

a hopeless case if—listen:there's a hell
of a good universe next door;let's go

1943, 1944

[when serpents bargain for the right to squirm]

when serpents bargain for the right to squirm
and the sun strikes to gain a living wage—
when thorns regard their roses with alarm
and rainbows are insured against old age

when every thrush may sing no new moon in
if all screech-owls have not okayed his voice
—and any wave signs on the dotted line
or else an ocean is compelled to close

when the oak begs permission of the birch
to make an acorn—valleys accuse their
mountains of having altitude—and march
denounces april as a saboteur

then we'll believe in that incredible
unanimal mankind(and not until)

1948, 1950

[l(a]

l(a
le
af
fa
ll
s)
one
l
iness

1958

Hart Crane 1899–1932

Although the quantity of his work was small (he published only two volumes of poetry in his lifetime), Hart Crane has achieved a position in the first rank of American poets. His fame rests primarily on his extraordinary and controversial poems, yet his life was so turbulent, so much the model for popular, exaggerated notions of the poet, that it, too, has been partly responsible for his renown.

Crane, an avowed homosexual, was a neurotic, self-destructive alcoholic whose life was a chaotic jumble of emotional confusion and despair. Born in Ohio in 1899, he spent much of his early life with his grandparents in refuge from the fierce wrangling of his strong-willed mother and father. His father, a successful manufacturer of candy (he invented Life Savers), tried unsuccessfully to make his son into a businessman; his mother, a domineering woman of artistic pretensions, imposed her religious enthusiasms on her son's consciousness.

Crane began to write poetry as a schoolboy. He published his first poem when he was seventeen, and in the same year he dropped out of school to begin a life of wandering and frantic excess, interrupted by periods of intense creativity. In his early twenties, he finally managed to break with his family, an event that coincided with the writing of his first major poems. He then left Ohio for New York City, where he unknowingly moved into a room once occupied by Washington Roebling, the builder of the Brooklyn Bridge. There Crane began work on the loosely unified series of poems out of which he eventually created his masterpiece, The Bridge.

In 1926, his first volume of poetry, White Buildings, *was published. But the book received mixed reviews, and Crane's life turned sour once more. After a final, bitter argument with his mother, he fled to Europe. Seven months later he returned to New York, and there, late in 1929, he finished* The Bridge. *In 1930 he went to Mexico, planning to write an epic poem on Mexican history and hoping to create a stable emotional life, but in April 1932, while returning from Mexico to New York by sea, Crane walked to the stern of his ship, leaped into the sea, and drowned. He was thirty-two.*

The Bridge *was Crane's endeavor to write a national epic, a "mythical synthesis of America" such as Walt Whitman had attempted in* Leaves of Grass. *Written partly in refutation of T. S. Eliot's* The Waste Land, *which Crane felt was too pessimistic and ignored "spiritual events and possibilities,"* The Bridge *reflected his desire to find unity in an age of disharmony and disbelief. He wanted to unite, literally and figuratively, the old and the new, east and west, human and divine. That he failed is conceded by many. He achieved poetic intensity at the expense of clarity and reason; his poetry is flawed by vague meanings and jumbled images and symbols. Nevertheless, the force of his poetic imagination and his extraordinary power to portray the human quest for unity, love, and beauty have brought him recognition as one of the finest poets of twentieth-century America, despite his tormented, brief life and the ravaging emotions that led to his destruction.*

FURTHER READING: B. Weber, *Hart Crane: A Biographical and Critical Study,* 1948, 1970; *The Letters of Hart Crane, 1916–1932,* ed. B. Weber, 1952, 1965; *Critical Essays on Hart Crane,* ed. D. Clark, 1982; *Hart Crane: A Reference Guide,* ed. J. Schwartz, 1983; E. Brunner, *Splendid Failure: Hart Crane and the Making of "The Bridge,"* 1985; *Hart Crane,* ed. H. Bloom, 1986; P. Giles, *Hart Crane: The Contexts of "The Bridge,"* 1986; M. Bennett, *Unfractioned Idiom: Hart Crane and Modernism,* 1987; W. Berthoff, *Hart Crane: A Re-Introduction,* 1989; P. Mariani, *The Broken Tower: A Life of Hart Crane,* 1999; R. Lewis, *The Poetry of Hart Crane,* 2000; C. Fisher, *Hart Crane: A Life* 2002.

TEXT: *The Complete Poems and Selected Letters and Prose of Hart Crane,* ed. B. Weber, 1966.

CHAPLINESQUE[1]

We make our meek adjustments,
Contented with such random consolations
As the wind deposits
In slithered and too ample pockets.

For we can still love the world, who find
A famished kitten on the step, and know
Recesses for it from the fury of the street,
Or warm torn elbow coverts.

We will sidestep, and to the final smirk
Dally the doom of that inevitable thumb
That slowly chafes its puckered index toward us,
Facing the dull squint with what innocence
And what surprise!

And yet these fine collapses are not lies
More than the pirouettes of any pliant cane;
Our obsequies are, in a way, no enterprise.
We can evade you, and all else but the heart:
What blame to us if the heart live on.

The game enforces smirks; but we have seen
The moon in lonely alleys make
A grail of laughter of an empty ash can,
And through all sound of gaiety and quest
Have heard a kitten in the wilderness.

1921, 1926

AT MELVILLE'S[1] TOMB

Often beneath the wave, wide from this ledge
The dice of drowned men's bones he saw bequeath
An embassy. Their numbers as he watched,
Beat on the dusty shore and were obscured.

And wrecks passed without sound of bells,
The calyx[2] of death's bounty giving back
A scattered chapter, livid hieroglyph,
The portent wound in corridors of shells.

[1]Inspired by the comedian Charlie Chaplin, whom Crane saw in the movie *The Kid,* in 1921.
[1]Herman Melville (1819–1891). He is buried at Woodlawn Cemetery in New York City.
[2]"This calyx refers in a double ironic sense both to cornucopia and vortex made by a sinking vessel."—Crane.

Then in the circuit calm of one vast coil,
Its lashings charmed and malice reconciled,
Frosted eyes there were that lifted altars;
And silent answers crept across the stars.

Compass, quadrant and sextant contrive
No farther tides . . .[3] High in the azure steeps
Monody shall not wake the mariner.
This fabulous shadow only the sea keeps.
1926

VOYAGES

I

Above the fresh ruffles of the surf
Bright striped urchins flay each other with sand.
They have contrived a conquest for shell shucks,
And their fingers crumble fragments of baked weed
Gaily digging and scattering.

And in answer to their treble interjections
The sun beats lightning on the waves,
The waves fold thunder on the sand;
And could they hear me I would tell them:

O brilliant kids, frisk with your dog,
Fondle your shells and sticks, bleached
By time and the elements; but there is a line
You must not cross nor ever trust beyond it
Spry cordage of your bodies to caresses
To lichen-faithful from too wide a breast.
The bottom of the sea is cruel.
1921–1923 1923, 1926

II

—And yet this great wink of eternity,
Of rimless floods, unfettered leewardings,
Samite[1] sheeted and processioned where
Her undinal[2] vast belly moonward bends,
Laughing the wrapt inflections of our love;

[3]Here, and throughout, the ellipsis points are Crane's and do not indicate omissions by the editor.
[1]Heavy silk, threaded with silver and gold, used in medieval ecclesiastical robes.
[2]From Undine, a water goddess—hence, "oceanic."

Take this Sea, whose diapason[3] knells
On scrolls of silver snowy sentences,
The sceptred terror of whose sessions rends
As her demeanors motion well or ill,
All but the pieties of lovers' hands.

And onward, as bells of San Salvador[4]
Salute the crocus lustres of the stars,
In these poinsettia meadows of her tides,—
Adagios of islands, O my Prodigal,
Complete the dark confessions her veins spell.

Mark how her turning shoulders wind the hours,
And hasten while her penniless rich palms
Pass superscription of bent foam and wave,—
Hasten, while they are true,—sleep, death, desire,
Close round one instant in one floating flower.

Bind us in time, O Seasons clear, and awe.
O minstrel galleons of Carib fire,
Bequeath us to no earthly shore until
Is answered in the vortex of our grave
The seal's wide spindrift[5] gaze toward paradise.
1924 1926

III

Infinite consanguinity[6] it bears—
This tendered theme of you that light
Retrieves from sea plains where the sky
Resigns a breast that every wave enthrones;
While ribboned water lanes I wind
Are laved and scattered with no stroke
Wide from your side, whereto this hour
The sea lifts, also, reliquary hands.

And so, admitted through black swollen gates
That must arrest all distance otherwise,—
Past whirling pillars and lithe pediments,
Light wrestling there incessantly with light,
Star kissing star through wave on wave unto
Your body rocking!
and where death, if shed,

[3]Musical notes or harmony.
[4]A reference to the legendary tolling bells of a sunken city off San Salvador.
[5]Sea foam. [6]Blood relationship.

Presumes no carnage, but this single change,—
Upon the steep floor flung from dawn to dawn
The silken skilled transmemberment of song;

Permit me voyage, love, into your hands . . .
1924 1926

from *THE BRIDGE*

TO BROOKLYN BRIDGE

How many dawns, chill from his rippling rest
The seagull's wings shall dip and pivot him,
Shedding white rings of tumult, building high
Over the chained bay waters Liberty—

Then, with inviolate curve, forsake our eyes
As apparitional as sails that cross
Some page of figures to be filed away;
—Till elevators drop us from our day . . .

I think of cinemas, panoramic sleights
With multitudes bent toward some flashing scene
Never disclosed, but hastened to again,
Foretold to other eyes on the same screen;

And Thee,[1] across the harbor, silver-paced
As though the sun took step of thee, yet left
Some motion ever unspent in thy stride,—
Implicitly thy freedom staying thee!

Out of some subway scuttle, cell or loft
A bedlamite[2] speeds to thy parapets,
Tilting there momently, shrill shirt ballooning,
A jest falls from the speechless caravan.

Down Wall,[3] from girder into street noon leaks,
A rip-tooth of the sky's acetylene;
All afternoon the cloud-flown derricks turn . . .
Thy cables breathe the North Atlantic still.

And obscure as that heaven of the Jews,
Thy guerdon[4] . . . Accolade thou dost bestow
Of anonymity time cannot raise:
Vibrant reprieve and pardon thou dost show.

[1]I.e., Brooklyn Bridge. [2]Lunatic.
[3]Wall Street in New York City. [4]Reward.

O harp and altar, of the fury fused,
(How could mere toil align thy choiring strings!)
Terrific threshold of the prophet's pledge,
Prayer of pariah, and the lover's cry,—

Again the traffic lights that skim thy swift
Unfractioned idiom, immaculate sigh of stars,
Beading thy path—condense eternity:
And we have seen night lifted in thine arms.

Under thy shadow by the piers I waited;
Only in darkness is thy shadow clear.
The City's fiery parcels all undone,
Already snow submerges an iron year . . .

O Sleepless as the river under thee,
Vaulting the sea, the prairies' dreaming sod,
Unto us lowliest sometime sweep, descend
And of the curveship lend a myth to God.
1926 1927, 1930

POWHATAN'S DAUGHTER

"*—Pocahuntus, a well-featured but wanton yong girle . . . of the age of eleven or twelve years, get the boyes forth with her into the market place, and make them wheele, falling on their hands, turning their heels upwards, whom she would followe, and wheele so herself, naked as she was, all the fort over.*"[1]

THE HARBOR DAWN

400 years and more . . . or is it from the soundless shore of sleep that time

Insistently through sleep—a tide of voices—
They meet you listening midway in your dream,
The long, tired sounds, fog-insulated noises:
Gongs in white surplices, beshrouded wails,
Far strum of fog horns . . . signals dispersed in veils.

And then a truck will lumber past the wharves
As winch engines begin throbbing on some deck;
Or a drunken stevedore's howl and thud below
Comes echoing alley-upward through dim snow.

[1]From William Strachey, *Historie of Travell into Virginia Britania,* written 1609–1612, first published 1849.

And if they take your sleep away sometimes
They give it back again. Soft sleeves of sound
Attend the darkling harbor, the pillowed bay;
Somewhere out there in blankness steam

Spills into steam, and wanders, washed away
—Flurried by keen fifings, eddied
Among distant chiming buoys—adrift. The sky,
Cool feathery fold, suspends, distills
This wavering slumber. . . . Slowly—
Immemorially the window, the half-covered chair
Ask nothing but this sheath of pallid air.

recalls you to your love, there in a waking dream to merge your seed

And you beside me, blessèd now while sirens
Sing to us, stealthily weave us into day—
Serenely now, before day claims our eyes
Your cool arms murmurously about me lay.

While myriad snowy hands are clustering at the panes—

your hands within my hands are deeds;
my tongue upon your throat—singing
arms close; eyes wide, undoubtful
dark
drink the dawn—
a forest shudders in your hair!

—with whom?

The window goes blond slowly. Frostily clears.
From Cyclopean[2] towers across Manhattan waters
—Two—three bright window-eyes aglitter, disk
The sun, released—aloft with cold gulls hither.

Who is the woman with us in the dawn? . . . whose is the flesh our feet have moved upon

The fog leans one last moment on the sill.
Under the mistletoe of dreams, a star—
As though to join us at some distant hill—
Turns in the waking west and goes to sleep.
1926 1927, 1930

VAN WINKLE

Streets spread past store and factory—sped by sunlight and her smile . . .

Macadam, gun-grey as the tunny's[1] belt,
Leaps from Far Rockaway to Golden Gate:[2]
Listen! the miles a hurdy-gurdy grinds—
Down gold arpeggios mile on mile unwinds.

[2]Gigantic—as though built by giants.
[1]A tuna. [2]I.e., from the Atlantic to the Pacific.

Times earlier, when you hurried off to school,
—It is the same hour though a later day—
You walked with Pizarro in a copybook,
And Cortes rode up, reining tautly in—
Firmly as coffee grips the taste,—and away!

Like Memory, she is time's truant, shall take you by the hand . . .

There was Priscilla's[3] cheek close in the wind.
And Captain Smith,[4] all beard and certainty,
And Rip Van Winkle bowing by the way,—
"Is this Sleepy Hollow,[5] friend—?" And he—

And Rip forgot the office hours,
and he forgot the pay;
Van Winkle sweeps a tenement
way down on Avenue A,—

The grind-organ says . . . Remember, remember
The cinder pile at the end of the backyard
Where we stoned the family of young
Garter snakes under . . . And the monoplanes
We launched—with paper wings and twisted
Rubber bands . . . Recall—recall

the rapid tongues
That flittered from under the ash heap day
After day whenever your stick discovered
Some sunning inch of unsuspecting fibre—
It flashed back at your thrust, as clean as fire.

And Rip was slowly made aware
that he, Van Winkle, was not here
nor there. He woke and swore he'd seen Broadway
a Catskill daisy chain in May—

So memory, that strikes a rhyme out of a box,
Or splits a random smell of flowers through glass—
Is it the whip stripped from the lilac tree
One day in spring my father took to me,
Or is it the Sabbatical, unconscious smile
My mother almost brought me once from church
And once only, as I recall—?

It flickered through the snow screen, blindly
It forsook her at the doorway, it was gone
Before I had left the window. It
Did not return with the kiss in the hall.

[3]Priscilla Alden of the Pilgrim Colony at Plymouth.
[4]John Smith, English explorer said to have been rescued by Pocahontas.
[5]The setting of "The Legend of Sleepy Hollow" (1819), by Washington Irving.

Macadam, gun-grey as the tunny's belt,
Leaps from Far Rockaway to Golden Gate. . . .
Keep hold of that nickel for car-change, Rip,—
Have you got your "*Times*"[6]—?
And hurry along, Van Winkle—it's getting late!
1927, 1930

THE RIVER

. . . and past the din and slogans of the year—

Stick your patent name on a signboard
brother—all over—going west—young man[1]
Tintex—Japalac[2]—Certain-teed[3] Overalls ads
and lands sakes! under the new playbill ripped
in the guaranteed corner—see Bert Williams[4] what?
Minstrels when you steal a chicken just
save me the wing for if it isn't
Erie it ain't for miles around a
Mazda[5]—and the telegraphic night coming on Thomas

a Ediford[6]—and whistling down the tracks
a headlight rushing with the sound—can you
imagine—while an EXPRESS makes time like
SCIENCE—COMMERCE AND THE HOLYGHOST
RADIO ROARS IN EVERY HOME WE HAVE THE NORTHPOLE
WALLSTREET AND VIRGINBIRTH WITHOUT STONES OR
WIRES OR EVEN RUNning brooks connecting ears
and no more sermons windows flashing roar
breathtaking—as you like it . . . eh?

So the 20th Century—so
whizzed the Limited[7]—roared by and left
three men, still hungry on the tracks, ploddingly
watching the tail lights wizen and converge, slipping
gimleted and neatly out of sight

* * *

[6]The *New York Times.*

[1]"Go west, young man," a saying often attributed (incorrectly) to Horace Greeley, nineteenth-century newspaper publisher.

[2]Brand names for widely sold cloth dye and household paint products.

[3]Brand name for home maintenance products. [4]Black vaudeville comedian (1877–1922).

[5]A fusion of advertisement slogans for the Erie Railroad, for Eastman cameras ("If it isn't an Eastman, it isn't a Kodak"), and for Mazda light bulbs.

[6]A pun that combines the names of the inventor Thomas A. Edison (1847–1931), the automaker Henry Ford (1863–1947), and the Archbishop of Canterbury and saint, Thomas à Becket (1118?–1170).

[7]Twentieth-Century Limited: luxurious, high-speed, passenger train.

The last bear, shot drinking in the Dakotas
Loped under wires[8] that span the mountain stream.
Keen instruments, strung to a vast precision
Bind town to town and dream to ticking dream.
But some men take their liquor slow—and count
—Though they'll confess no rosary nor clue—
The river's minute by the far brook's year.
Under a world of whistles, wires and steam
Caboose-like they go ruminating through
Ohio, Indiana—blind baggage—
To Cheyenne tagging . . . Maybe Kalamazoo.

to those whose addresses are never near

Time's rendings, time's blendings they construe
As final reckonings of fire and snow;
Strange bird-wit, like the elemental gist
Of unwalled winds they offer, singing low
My Old Kentucky Home and *Casey Jones,*
Some Sunny Day. I heard a road-gang chanting so.
And afterwards, who had a colt's eyes—one said,
"Jesus! Oh I remember watermelon days!" And sped
High in a cloud of merriment, recalled
"—And when my Aunt Sally Simpson smiled," he drawled—
"It was almost Louisiana, long ago."
"There's no place like Booneville though, Buddy,"
One said, excising a last burr from his vest,
"—For early trouting." Then peering in the can,
"—But I kept on the tracks." Possessed, resigned.
He trod the fire down pensively and grinned,
Spreading dry shingles of a beard. . . .

Behind
My father's cannery works I used to see
Rail-squatters ranged in nomad raillery,
The ancient men—wifeless or runaway
Hobo-trekkers that forever search
An empire wilderness of freight and rails.
Each seemed a child, like me, on a loose perch,
Holding to childhood like some termless play.
John, Jake or Charley, hopping the slow freight
—Memphis to Tallahassee—riding the rods,
Blind fists of nothing, humpty-dumpty clods.

Yet they touch something like a key perhaps.
From pole to pole across the hills, the states
—They know a body under the wide rain;

[8]Telegraph and telephone wires.

but who have touched her, knowing her without name

Youngsters with eyes like fjords, old reprobates
With racetrack jargon,—dotting immensity
They lurk across her, knowing her yonder breast
Snow-silvered, sumac-stained or smoky blue—
Is past the valley-sleepers, south or west.
—As I have trod the rumorous midnights, too,

And past the circuit of the lamp's thin flame
(O Nights that brought me to her body bare!)
Have dreamed beyond the print that bound her name.
Trains sounding the long blizzards out—I heard
Wail into distances I knew were hers.
Papooses crying on the wind's long mane
Screamed redskin dynasties that fled the brain,
—Dead echoes! But I knew her body there,
Time like a serpent down her shoulder, dark,
And space, an eaglet's wing, laid on her hair.

Under the Ozarks, domed by Iron Mountain,[9]
The old gods of the rain lie wrapped in pools
Where eyeless fish[10] curvet[11] a sunken fountain
nor the myths of her fathers . . .
And re-descend with corn from querulous crows.
Such pilferings make up their timeless eatage,
Propitiate them for their timber torn
By iron, iron—always the iron dealt cleavage!
They doze, now, below axe and powder horn.

And Pullman breakfasters glide glistening steel.
From tunnel into field—iron strides the dew—
Straddles the hill, a dance of wheel on wheel.
You have a half-hour's wait at Siskiyou,[12]
Or stay the night and take the next train through.
Southward, near Cairo[13] passing, you can see

The Ohio merging,—borne down Tennessee;
And if it's summer and the sun's in dusk
Maybe the breeze will lift the River's musk
—As though the waters breathed that you might know
Memphis Johnny, Steamboat Bill, Missouri Joe.
Oh, lean from the window, if the train slows down,
As though you touched hands with some ancient clown,
—A little while gaze absently below
And hum *Deep River* with them while they go.

[9]In southeast Missouri. [10]Blind fish that dwell in underground waters.
[11]Curve or leap about. [12]In northern California. [13]In southern Illinois.

Yes, turn again and sniff once more—look see,
O Sheriff, Brakeman and Authority—
Hitch up your pants and crunch another quid,[14]
For you, too, feed the River timelessly.
And few evade full measure of their fate;
Always they smile out eerily what they seem.
I could believe he joked at heaven's gate—
Dan Midland[15]—jolted from the cold brake-beam.
Down, down—born pioneers in time's despite,
Grimed tributaries to an ancient flow—
They win no frontier by their wayward plight,
But drift in stillness, as from Jordan's brow.[16]

You will not hear it as the sea; even stone
Is not more hushed by gravity . . . But slow,
As loth to take more tribute—sliding prone
Like one whose eyes were buried long ago

The River, spreading, flows—and spends your dream.
What are you, lost within this tideless spell?
You are your father's father, and the stream—
A liquid theme that floating niggers swell.

Damp tonnage and alluvial march of days—
Nights turbid, vascular with silted shale
And roots surrendered down of moraine clays:
The Mississippi drinks the farthest dale.

O quarrying passion, undertowed sunlight!
The basalt surface drags a jungle grace
Ochreous and lynx-barred in lengthening might;
Patience! and you shall reach the biding place!

Over De Soto's bones[17] the freighted floors
Throb past the City storied of three thrones.[18]
Down two more turns the Mississippi pours
(Anon tall ironsides up from salt lagoons)

And flows within itself, heaps itself free.
All fades but one thin skyline 'round . . . Ahead
No embrace opens but the stinging sea;
The River lifts itself from its long bed,

[14]Wad of chewing tobacco. [15]A legendary hobo killed while "riding the rods."
[16]The bank of the Jordan River in Palestine.
[17]The Spanish explorer Hernando de Soto (1500–1542) was buried in the Mississippi River near present-day New Orleans.
[18]New Orleans was governed alternately by the monarchies of France, Spain, and England.

Poised wholly on its dream, a mustard glow
Tortured with history, its one will—flow!
—The Passion spreads in wide tongues, choked and slow,
Meeting the Gulf, hosannas silently below.
1926 1928, 1930

THE TUNNEL

To Find the
Western path
Right thro' the
Gates of Wrath.
—BLAKE[1]

Performances, assortments, résumés—
Up Times Square to Columbus Circle[2] lights
Channel the congresses, nightly sessions,
Refractions of the thousand theatres, faces—
Mysterious kitchens. . . . You shall search them all.
Someday by heart you'll learn each famous sight
And watch the curtain lift in hell's despite;
You'll find the garden in the third act dead,
Finger your knees—and wish yourself in bed
With tabloid crime-sheets perched in easy sight.

Then let you reach your hat and go.
As usual, let you—also
walking down—exclaim
to twelve upward leaving
a subscription praise
for what time slays.

Or can't you quite make up your mind to ride;
A walk is better underneath the L[3] a brisk
Ten blocks or so before? But you find yourself
Preparing penguin flexions of the arms,—
As usual you will meet the scuttle yawn:
The subway yawns the quickest promise home.

Be minimum, then, to swim the hiving swarms
Out of the Square, the Circle burning bright—
Avoid the glass doors gyring[4] at your right,
Where boxed alone a second, eyes take fright
—Quite unprepared rush naked back to light:

[1]From "Morning" (lines 1–2), by William Blake (1757–1827), English poet.
[2]Along Broadway, in New York City. [3]The elevated railway. [4]Spinning.

And down beside the turnstile press the coin
Into the slot. The gongs already rattle.

And so
of cities you bespeak
subways, rivered under streets
and rivers. . . . In the car
the overtone of motion
underground, the monotone
of motion is the sound
of other faces, also underground—

"Let's have a pencil Jimmy—living now
at Floral Park
Flatbush[5]—on the fourth of July—
like a pigeon's muddy dream—potatoes
to dig in the field—travlin the town—too—
night after night—the Culver line[6]—the
girls all shaping up—it used to be—"
Our tongues recant like beaten weather vanes.
This answer lives like verdigris,[7] like hair
Beyond extinction, surcease of the bone;
And repetition freezes—"What

"what do you want? getting weak on the links?
fandaddle daddy don't ask for change—IS THIS
FOURTEENTH? it's half past six she said—if
you don't like my gate why did you
swing on it, why *didja*
swing on it
anyhow—"

And somehow anyhow swing—

The phonographs of hades in the brain
Are tunnels that re-wind themselves, and love
A burnt match skating in a urinal—
Somewhere above Fourteenth TAKE THE EXPRESS
To brush some new presentiment of pain—

"But I want service in this office service
I said—after
the show she cried a little afterwards but—"

Whose head is swinging from the swollen strap?
Whose body smokes along the bitten rails,

[5]Section of New York City in the borough of Brooklyn.
[6]A former branch of the Brooklyn Rapid Transit system; originally elevated, later converted to a subway.
[7]A greenish-blue substance.

Bursts from a smoldering bundle far behind
In back forks of the chasms of the brain,—
Puffs from a river stump far out behind
In interborough fissures of the mind . . .?

And why do I often meet your visage[8] here,
Your eyes like agate lanterns—on and on
Below the toothpaste and the dandruff ads?
—And did their riding eyes right through your side,
And did their eyes like unwashed platters ride?
And Death, aloft,—gigantically down
Probing through you—toward me, O evermore!
And when they dragged your retching flesh,
Your trembling hands that night through Baltimore—
That last night on the ballot rounds,[9] did you
Shaking, did you deny the ticket, Poe?

For Gravesend Manor change at Chambers Street.[10]
The platform hurries along to a dead stop.
The intent escalator lifts a serenade
Stilly
Of shoes, umbrellas, each eye attending its shoe, then
Bolting outright somewhere above where streets
Burst suddenly in rain. . . . The gongs recur:
Elbows and levers, guard and hissing door.
Thunder is galvothermic[11] here below. . . . The car
Wheels off. The train rounds, bending to a scream,
Taking the final level for the dive
Under the river—
And somewhat emptier than before,
Demented, for a hitching second, humps; then
Lets go. . . . Toward corners of the floor
Newspapers wing, revolve and wing.
Blank windows gargle signals through the roar.

And does the Dæmon take you home, also,
Wop washerwoman, with the bandaged hair?
After the corridors are swept, the cuspidors—
The gaunt sky-barracks cleanly now, and bare,
O Genoese,[12] do you bring mother eyes and hands
Back home to children and to golden hair?

Dæmon, demurring and eventful yawn!
Whose hideous laughter is a bellows mirth
—Or the muffled slaughter of a day in birth—

[8]The poet addresses Edgar Allan Poe.
[9]A reference to the death of Poe in Baltimore, on Election Day, October 7, 1849.
[10]Near the southern tip of Manhattan Island.
[11]Galvanothermic; i.e., produces heat by electricity.
[12]Christopher Columbus.

O cruelly to inoculate the brinking dawn
With antennæ toward worlds that glow and sink;—
To spoon us out more liquid than the dim
Locution of the eldest star, and pack
The conscience navelled in the plunging wind,
Umbilical to call—and straightway die!

O caught like pennies beneath soot and steam,
Kiss of our agony thou gatherest;
Condensed, thou takest all—shrill ganglia
Impassioned with some song we fail to keep.
And yet, like Lazarus,[13] to feel the slope,
The sod and billow breaking,—lifting ground,

—A sound of waters bending astride the sky
Unceasing with some Word that will not die . . .!

* * *

A tugboat, wheezing wreaths of steam,
Lunged past, with one galvanic blare stove up the River.
I counted the echoes assembling, one after one,
Searching, thumbing and midnight on the piers.
Lights, coasting, left the oily tympanum of waters;
The blackness somewhere gouged glass on a sky.
And this thy harbor, O my City, I have driven under,
Tossed from the coil of ticking towers. . . . Tomorrow,
And to be. . . . Here by the River that is East—
Here at the waters' edge the hands drop memory;
Shadowless in that abyss they unaccounting lie.
How far away the star has pooled the sea—
Or shall the hands be drawn away, to die?

Kiss of our agony Thou gatherest,
O Hand of Fire
gatherest—

1926 1927, 1930

ATLANTIS

Music is then the knowledge of that which relates to love in harmony and system.

PLATO[1]

Through the bound cable strands, the arching path
Upward, veering with light, the flight of strings—
Taut miles of shuttling moonlight syncopate
The whispered rush, telepathy of wires.

[13]Jesus raised Lazarus from the dead (John 11:43–44).
[1]From the *Symposium*, III, 403.

Up the index of night, granite and steel—
Transparent meshes—fleckless and gleaming staves—
Sibylline voices[2] flicker, waveringly stream
As though a god were issue of the strings. . . .

And through that cordage, threading with its call
One arc synoptic of all tides below—
Their labyrinthine mouths of history
Pouring reply as though all ships at sea
Complighted in one vibrant breath made cry,—
"Make thy love sure—to weave whose song we ply!"
—From black embankments, moveless soundings hailed,
So seven oceans answer from their dream.

And on, obliquely up bright carrier bars
New octaves trestle the twin monoliths
Beyond whose frosted capes the moon bequeaths
Two worlds of sleep (O arching strands of song!)—
Onward and up the crystal-flooded aisle
White tempest nets file upward, upward ring
With silver terraces the humming spars,
The loft of vision, palladium helm of stars.

Sheerly the eyes, like seagulls stung with rime[3]—
Slit and propelled by glistening fins of light—
Pick biting way up towering looms that press
Sidelong with flight of blade on tendon blade
—Tomorrows into yesteryear—and link
What cipher-script of time no traveller reads
But who, through smoking pyres of love and death,
Searches the timeless laugh of mythic spears.

Like hails, farewells—up planet-sequined heights
Some trillion whispering hammers glimmer Tyre:[4]
Serenely, sharply up the long anvil cry
Of inchling aeons silence rivets Troy.[5]
And you, aloft there—Jason![6] hesting[7] shout!
Still wrapping harness to the swarming air!
Silvery the rushing wake, surpassing call,
Beams yelling Æolus![8] splintered in the straights!

From gulfs unfolding, terrible of drums,
Tall Vision-of-the-Voyage, tensely spare—
Bridge, lifting night to cycloramic crest
Of deepest day—O Choir, translating time

[2]Voices of the Sibyls, female oracles and prophets of the ancient world. [3]White frost.
[4]Ancient Phoenician city. [5]Scene of the Trojan War described by Homer.
[6]Greek leader in the quest for the Golden Fleece. [7]Commanding.
[8]Keeper of the winds in classical myth.

Into what multitudinous Verb the suns
And synergy of waters ever fuse, recast
In myriad syllables,—Psalm of Cathay![9]
O Love, thy white, pervasive Paradigm . . . !

We left the haven hanging in the night—
Sheened harbor lanterns backward fled the keel.
Pacific here at time's end, bearing corn,—
Eyes stammer through the pangs of dust and steel.
And still the circular, indubitable frieze
Of heaven's meditations, yoking wave
To kneeling wave, one song devoutly binds—
The vernal strophe chimes from deathless strings!

O Thou steeled Cognizance whose leap commits
The agile precincts of the lark's return;
Within whose lariat sweep encinctured sing
In single chrysalis the many twain,
Of stars Thou art the stitch and stallion glow
And like an organ, Thou, with sound of doom—
Sight, sound and flesh Thou leadest from time's realm
As love strikes clear direction for the helm.

Swift peal of secular light, intrinsic Myth
Whose fell unshadow is death's utter wound,—
O River-throated—iridescently upborne
Through the bright drench and fabric of our veins;
With white escarpments swinging into light,
Sustained in tears the cities are endowed
And justified conclamant with ripe fields
Revolving through their harvests in sweet torment.

Forever Deity's glittering Pledge, O Thou
Whose canticle fresh chemistry assigns
To wrapt inception and beatitude,—
Always through blinding cables, to our joy,
Of thy white seizure springs the prophecy:
Always through spiring cordage, pyramids
Of silver sequel, Deity's young name
Kinetic of white choiring wings . . . ascends.

Migrations that must needs void memory,
Inventions that cobblestone the heart,—
Unspeakable Thou Bridge to Thee, O Love.
Thy pardon for this history, whitest Flower,
O Answerer of all,—Anemone,—
Now while thy petals spend the suns about us, hold—
(O Thou whose radiance doth inherit me)
Atlantis,—hold thy floating singer late!

[9]Ancient name for China.

So to thine Everpresence, beyond time,
Like spears ensanguined[10] of one tolling star
That bleeds infinity—the orphic[11] strings,
Sidereal phalanxes, leap and converge:
—One Song, one Bridge of Fire! Is it Cathay,
Now pity steeps the grass and rainbows ring
The serpent with the eagle in the leaves . . .?
Whispers antiphonal[12] in azure swing.
1926 1930

Edgar Lee Masters 1868–1950

Edgar Lee Masters wrote prolifically, but is best remembered as the author of Spoon River Anthology *(1915), one of the incontestable masterpieces of twentieth-century American poetry. He was born in Garnett, Kansas, located just southwest of Kansas City, in 1868. During his childhood his family relocated to the farm country of western Illinois. After high school, Masters worked briefly for a newspaper while he made preparations to enroll at Knox College in Galesburg, Illinois. Ultimately he decided against attending the university and instead studied law under his father. In 1893 he established a law partnership in Chicago. A decade later he joined Clarence Darrow's law firm, where he remained until 1911, when he left and started practicing law on his own.*

Masters started writing essays, poems, and plays under a pseudonym, Dexter Wallace, in the 1890s. Much of his work from this period is unremarkable. In 1914, however, he began to write a series of poems based on his boyhood experiences in western Illinois. They were first published, under another pseudonym, Webster Ford, in issues of a St. Louis periodical, Reedy's Mirror, *in 1914. A year later he collected the poems and published, this time under his own name, the first edition of* Spoon River Anthology. *Its impact was immediate. Established writers such as Theodore Dreiser, Carl Sandburg, Ezra Pound, and Amy Lowell recognized the volume as an American classic and heralded Masters as a genuine American literary talent. He would release an expanded edition of* Spoon River Anthology *in 1916 and publish a follow-up titled* The New Spoon River *in 1924. His other volumes of poetry include* Songs and Satires *(1916),* The Great Valley *(1916),* Starved Rock *(1919), and* Domesday Book *(1920), which Masters always believed was his best. All possess moments of intensity and power, but none manage to match the overall artistic feat of* Spoon River Anthology. *In the 1930s and 1940s, Masters experimented with fiction and biography, including studies of Abraham Lincoln, Walt Whitman, and Mark Twain. Edgar Lee Masters died in 1950.*

FURTHER READING: *Across Spoon River: An Autobiography,* 1991; *The Harmony of Deeper Music: Posthumous Poems of Edgar Lee Masters,* ed. F. Robinson, 1976; J. Flanagan, *Edgar Lee Masters: The Spoon River Poet and His Critics,* 1974; *The Vision of This Land: Studies of Vachel Lindsay, Edgar Lee Masters, and Carl Sandburg,* ed. J. Hallwas and D. Reader, 1976;

[10] Made bloody.
[11] Mystic, oracular. In Greek myth the musician Orpheus could charm animals and even the gods.
[12] Like a psalm or an anthem sung in response during church service.

H. Masters, *Edgar Lee Masters: A Biographical Sketchbook About a Famous American Author,* 1978; R. Primeau, *Beyond Spoon River: The Legacy of Edgar Lee Masters,* 1981; J. Wrenn and M. Wrenn, *Edgar Lee Masters,* 1983; *The Enduring River: Edgar Lee Masters' Uncollected Spoon River Poems,* ed. H. Russell, 1991: H. Russell, *Edgar Lee Masters: A Biography,* 2001.

TEXT: *Spoon River Anthology, New Edition, with New Poems,* 1916.

from *SPOON RIVER ANTHOLOGY*

KNOWLT HOHEIMER

I was the first fruits of the battle of Missionary Ridge.[1]
When I felt the bullet enter my heart
I wished I had staid at home and gone to jail
For stealing the hogs of Curl Trenary,
Instead of running away and joining the army.
Rather a thousand times the county jail
Than to lie under this marble figure with wings,
And this granite pedestal
Bearing the words, "*Pro Patria.*"[2]
What do they mean, anyway?

1915

NELLIE CLARK

I was only eight years old;
And before I grew up and knew what it meant
I had no words for it, except
That I was frightened and told my Mother;
And that my Father got a pistol
And would have killed Charlie, who was a big boy,
Fifteen years old, except for his Mother.
Nevertheless the story clung to me.
But the man who married me, a widower of thirty-five,
Was a newcomer and never heard it
Till two years after we were married.
Then he considered himself cheated,
And the village agreed that I was not really a virgin.
Well, he deserted me, and I died
The following winter.

1915

[1]Site of the Civil-War Battle of Missionary Ridge, near Chattanooga, Tennesee, in November 1863.

[2]"For country"—meaning that he died for his country.

PETIT, THE POET

Seeds in a dry pod, tick, tick, tick,
Tick, tick, tick, like mites in a quarrel—
Faint iambics[1] that the full breeze wakens—
But the pine tree makes a symphony thereof.
Triolets, villanelles, rondels, rondeaus,[2]
Ballades by the score with the same old thought:
The snows and the roses of yesterday are vanished;
And what is love but a rose that fades?
Life all around me here in the village:
Tragedy, comedy, valor and truth,
Courage, constancy, heroism, failure—
All in the loom, and oh what patterns!
Woodlands, meadows, streams and rivers—
Blind to all of it all my life long.
Triolets, villanelles, rondels, rondeaus,
Seeds in a dry pod, tick, tick, tick,
Tick, tick, tick, what little iambics,
While Homer and Whitman roared in the pines?

1915

ANNE RUTLEDGE[1]

Out of me unworthy and unknown
The vibrations of deathless music;
"With malice toward none, with charity for all."[2]
Out of me the forgiveness of millions toward millions,
And the beneficent face of a nation
Shining with justice and truth.
I am Anne Rutledge who sleep beneath these weeds,
Beloved in life of Abraham Lincoln,
Wedded to him, not through union,
But through separation.
Bloom forever, O Republic,
From the dust of my bosom!

1915

[1]A type of metrical foot in poetry. [2]A list of poetic forms.

[1]Anne Rutledge (1813–1835) was a woman to whom the young Abraham Lincoln may have been engaged, but she died of typhoid at the age of 22.

[2]A famous passage from Abraham Lincoln's Second Inaugural Address.

LUCINDA MATLOCK

I went to the dances at Chandlerville,
And played snap-out at Winchester.[1]
One time we changed partners,
Driving home in the moonlight of middle June,
And then I found Davis.
We were married and lived together for seventy years,
Enjoying, working, raising the twelve children,
Eight of whom we lost
Ere I had reached the age of sixty.
I spun, I wove, I kept the house, I nursed the sick,
I made the garden, and for holiday
Rambled over the fields where sang the larks,
And by Spoon River[2] gathering many a shell,
And many a flower and medicinal weed—
Shouting to the wooded hills, singing to the green valleys.
At ninety-six I had lived enough, that is all,
And passed to a sweet repose.
What is this I hear of sorrow and weariness,
Anger, discontent and drooping hopes?
Degenerate sons and daughters,
Life is too strong for you—
It takes life to love Life.

1915

Anzia Yezierska 1880(?)–1970

Anzia Yezierska was born to Jewish parents on the Russian-Polish border in the early 1880s. In 1900 she emigrated to the United States with her parents and nine siblings, settling in one of the impoverished immigrant neighborhoods on the Lower East Side of New York City. As a teenager Yezierska worked in sweatshops during the day and took classes at night. Within a few years she managed to secure a scholarship to Columbia University and studied to be a domestic-science teacher. She also ceased using the name Hattie Mayer, that she had been given upon arrival in the United States, returning instead to her European name Anzia Yezierska. In 1910, at the age of twenty-five, Yezierska married Jacob Gordon, a New York attorney, but the marriage was annulled within a few months. In 1911 she married Arnold Levitas, a teacher, and a year later gave birth to a daughter. The couple separated within a few years after Yezierska decided to devote her life to her writing, and in 1917–1918 she formed a romantic attachment with philosopher John Dewey, a professor at Columbia University.

[1]Chandlerville and Winchester are small towns in Illinois.
[2]A river that flows past Lewiston, Illinois, where Masters lived as a teenager.

Yezierska's first published story, "The Free Vacation House," appeared in 1915. In 1919 her "The Fat of the Land" received honors as the best of The Best Short Stories of 1919. *The following year she brought out her first collection of short fiction,* Hungry Hearts, *and it established her as an emergent voice in Jewish American literature. She was particularly praised for her effectiveness in capturing the Yiddish-influenced speech patterns of New York's Jewish Ghetto and for her portrayals of strong, independent women. Yezierska attracted the attention of Hollywood studios as a script writer after the appearance of her second short-story collection,* Children of Loneliness, *and her first novel,* Salome of the Tenements, *both published in 1923. During the 1930s, she participated in the Works Progress Administration's Writers' Project. After World War II she continued to write fiction and contributed regularly to the* New York Times Book Review. *Anzia Yezierska died in California in 1970.*

FURTHER READING: *The Open Cage: An Anzia Yezierska Collection,* ed. A. Kessler-Harris, 1979; C. Schoen, *Anzia Yezierska,* 1982; L. Henriksen, *Anzia Yezierska: A Writer's Life,* 1988; *How I Found America: Collected Stories of Anzia Yezierska,* ed. V. Gornick, 1991; N. Rosen, *John and Anzia: An American Romance,* 1997; D. Konzett, *Ethnic Modernisms: Anzia Yezierska, Zora Neale Hurston, Jean Rhys, and the Aesthetics of Dislocation,* 2002; *Middlebrow Moderns: Popular American Women Writers of the 1920s,* ed. L Botshon and M. Goldsmith, 2003.

TEXT: *Hungry Hearts,* 1920.

THE FAT OF THE LAND

In an air-shaft so narrow that you could touch the next wall with your bare hands, Hanneh Breineh leaned out and knocked on her neighbor's window.

"Can you loan me your wash-boiler for the clothes?" she called.

Mrs. Pelz threw up the sash.

"The boiler? What's the matter with yours again? Didn't you tell me you had it fixed already last week?"

"A black year on him, the robber, the way he fixed it! If you have no luck in this world, then it's better not to live. There I spent out fifteen cents to stop up one hole, and it runs out another. How I ate out my gall bargaining with him he should let it down to fifteen cents! He wanted yet a quarter, the swindler. Gottuniu! My bitter heart on him for every penny he took from me for nothing!"

"You got to watch all those swindlers, or they'll steal the whites out of your eyes," admonished Mrs. Pelz. "You should have tried out your boiler before you paid him. Wait a minute till I empty out my dirty clothes in a pillow-case; then I'll hand it to you."

Mrs. Pelz returned with the boiler and tried to hand it across to Hanneh Breineh, but the soap-box refrigerator on the window-sill was in the way.

"You got to come in for the boiler yourself," said Mrs. Pelz.

"Wait only till I tie my Sammy on to the high-chair he shouldn't fall on me again. He's so wild that ropes won't hold him."

Hanneh Breineh tied the child in the chair, stuck a pacifier in his mouth, and went in to her neighbor. As she took the boiler Mrs. Pelz said:

"Do you know Mrs. Melker ordered fifty pounds of chicken for her daughter's wedding? And such grand chickens! Shining like gold! My heart melted in me just looking at the flowing fatness of those chickens."

Hanneh Breineh smacked her thin, dry lips, a hungry gleam in her sunken eyes.

"Fifty pounds!" she gasped. "It ain't possible. How do you know?"

"I heard her with my own ears. I saw them with my own eyes. And she said she will chop up the chicken livers with onions and eggs for an appetizer, and then she will buy twenty-five pounds of fish, and cook it sweet and sour with raisins, and she said she will bake all her shtrudels on pure chicken fat."

"Some people work themselves up in the world," sighed Hanneh Breineh. "For them is America flowing with milk and honey. In Savel Mrs. Melker used to get shriveled up from hunger. She and her children used to live on potato-peelings and crusts of dry bread picked out from the barrels; and in America she lives to eat chicken, and apple shtrudels[1] soaking in fat."

"The world is a wheel always turning," philosophized Mrs. Pelz. "Those who were high go down low, and those who've been low go up higher. Who will believe me here in America that in Poland I was a cook in a banker's house? I handled ducks and geese every day. I used to bake coffee-cake with cream so thick you could cut it with a knife."

"And do you think I was a nobody in Poland?" broke in Hanneh Breineh, tears welling in her eyes as the memories of her past rushed over her. "But what's the use of talking? In America money is everything. Who cares who my father or grandfather was in Poland? Without money I'm a living dead one. My head dries out worrying how to get for the children the eating a penny cheaper."

Mrs. Pelz wagged her head, a gnawing envy contracting her features.

"Mrs. Melker had it good from the day she came," she said, begrudgingly. "Right away she sent all her children to the factory, and she began to cook meat for dinner every day. She and her children have eggs and buttered rolls for breakfast each morning like millionaires."

A sudden fall and a baby's scream, and the boiler dropped from Hanneh Breineh's hands as she rushed into her kitchen, Mrs. Pelz after her. They found the high-chair turned on top of the baby.

"Gewalt! Save me! Run for a doctor!" cried Hanneh Breineh, as she dragged the child from under the high-chair. "He's killed! He's killed! My only child! My precious lamb!" she shrieked as she ran back and forth with the screaming infant.

Mrs. Pelz snatched little Sammy from the mother's hands.

"Meshugneh![2] What are you running around like a crazy, frightening the child? Let me see. Let me tend to him. He ain't killed. Yet." She hastened to the sink to wash the child's face, and discovered a swelling lump on his forehead. "Have you a quarter in your house?" she asked.

"Yes, I got one," replied Hanneh Breineh, climbing on a chair. "I got to keep it on a high shelf where the children can't get it."

Mrs. Pelz seized the quarter Hanneh Breineh handed down to her.

"Now pull your left eyelid three times while I'm pressing the quarter, and you'll see the swelling go down."

Hanneh Breineh took the child again in her arms, shaking and cooing over it and caressing it.

"Ah-ah-ah, Sammy! Ah-ah-ah-ah, little lamb! Ah-ah-ah, little bird! Ah-ah-ah-ah, precious heart! Oh, you saved my life; I thought he was killed," gasped

[1]Strudel(s): a kind of fruit-filled or cheese-filled pastry. [2]Meshuggeneh: idiot; crazy fool.

Hanneh Breineh, turning to Mrs. Pelz. "Oi-i!"[3] she sighed, "a mother's heart! Always in fear over her children. The minute anything happens to them all life goes out of me. I lose my head and I don't know where I am any more."

"No wonder the child fell," admonished Mrs. Pelz. "You should have a red ribbon or red beads on his neck to keep away the evil eye. Wait. I got something in my machine-drawer."

Mrs. Pelz returned, bringing the boiler and a red string, which she tied about the child's neck while the mother proceeded to fill the boiler.

A little later Hanneh Breineh again came into Mrs. Pelz's kitchen, holding Sammy in one arm and in the other an apronful of potatoes. Putting the child down on the floor, she seated herself on the unmade kitchen-bed and began to peel the potatoes in her apron.

"Woe to me!" sobbed Hanneh Breineh. "To my bitter luck there ain't no end. With all my other troubles, the stove got broke. I lighted the fire to boil the clothes, and it's to get choked with smoke. I paid rent only a week ago, and the agent don't want to fix it. A thunder should strike him! He only comes for the rent, and if anything has to be fixed, then he don't want to hear nothing.

"Why comes it to me so hard?" went on Hanneh Breineh, the tears streaming down her cheeks. "I can't stand it no more. I came into you for a minute to run away from my troubles. It's only when I sit myself down to peel potatoes or nurse the baby that I take time to draw a breath, and beg only for death."

Mrs. Pelz, accustomed to Hanneh Breineh's bitter outbursts, continued her scrubbing.

"Ut!"[4] exclaimed Hanneh Breineh, irritated at her neighbor's silence, "what are you tearing up the world with your cleaning? What's the use to clean up when everything only gets dirty again?"

"I got to shine up my house for the holidays."

"You've got it so good nothing lays on your mind but to clean your house. Look on this little blood-sucker," said Hanneh Breineh, pointing to the wizened child, made prematurely solemn from starvation and neglect. "Could anybody keep that brat clean? I wash him one minute, and he is dirty the minute after." Little Sammy grew frightened and began to cry. "Shut up!" ordered the mother, picking up the child to nurse it again. "Can't you see me take a rest for a minute?"

The hungry child began to cry at the top of its weakened lungs.

"Na, na, you glutton." Hanneh Breineh took out a dirty pacifier from her pocket and stuffed it into the baby's mouth. The grave, pasty-faced infant shrank into a panic of fear, and chewed the nipple nervously, clinging to it with both his thin little hands.

"For what did I need yet the sixth one?" groaned Hanneh Breineh, turning to Mrs. Pelz. "Wasn't it enough five mouths to feed? If I didn't have this child on my neck, I could turn myself around and earn a few cents." She wrung her hands in a passion of despair. "Gottuniu! The earth should only take it before it grows up!"

"Shah! Shah!"[5] reproved Mrs. Pelz. "Pity yourself on the child. Let it grow up already so long as it is here. See how frightened it looks on you." Mrs. Pelz took the child in her arms and petted it. "The poor little lamb! What did it done you should hate it so?"

[3]Oy: an exclamation of dismay or exasperation. [4]A meaningless interjection, like "oh!"
[5]Hush!

Hanneh Breineh pushed Mrs. Pelz away from her.

"To whom can I open the wounds of my heart?" she moaned. "Nobody has pity on me. You don't believe me, nobody believes me until I'll fall down like a horse in the middle of the street. Oi weh![6] Mine life is so black for my eyes! Some mothers got luck. A child gets run over by a car, some fall from a window, some burn themselves up with a match, some get choked with diphtheria; but no death takes mine away."

"God from the world, stop cursing!" admonished Mrs. Pelz. "What do you want from the poor children? Is it their fault that their father makes small wages? Why do you let it all out on them?" Mrs. Pelz sat down beside Hanneh Breineh. "Wait only till your children get old enough to go to the shop and earn money," she consoled. "Push only through those few years while they are yet small; your sun will begin to shine; you will live on the fat of the land, when they begin to bring you in the wages each week."

Hanneh Breineh refused to be comforted.

"Till they are old enough to go to the shop and earn money they'll eat the head off my bones," she wailed. "If you only knew the fights I got by each meal. Maybe I gave Abe a bigger piece of bread than Fanny. Maybe Fanny got a little more soup in her plate than Jake. Eating is dearer than diamonds. Potatoes went up a cent on a pound, and milk is only for millionaires. And once a week, when I buy a little meat for the Sabbath, the butcher weighs it for me like gold, with all the bones in it. When I come to lay the meat out on a plate and divide it up, there ain't nothing to it but bones. Before, he used to throw me in a piece of fat extra or a piece of lung, but now you got to pay for everything, even for a bone to the soup."

"Never mind; you'll yet come out from all your troubles. Just as soon as your children get old enough to get their working papers the more children you got, the more money you'll have."

"Why should I fool myself with the false shine of hope? Don't I know it's already my black luck not to have it good in this world? Do you think American children will right away give everything they earn to their mother?"

"I know what is with you the matter," said Mrs. Pelz. "You didn't eat yet today. When it is empty in the stomach, the whole world looks black. Come, only let me give you something good to taste in the mouth; that will freshen you up." Mrs. Pelz went to the cupboard and brought out the saucepan of gefülte fish[7] that she had cooked for dinner and placed it on the table in front of Hanneh Breineh. "Give a taste my fish," she said, taking one slice on a spoon, and handing it to Hanneh Breineh with a piece of bread. "I wouldn't give it to you on a plate because I just cleaned up my house, and I don't want to dirty up more dishes."

"What, am I a stranger you should have to serve me on a plate yet!" cried Hanneh Breineh, snatching the fish in her trembling fingers.

"Oi weh! How it melts through all the bones!" she exclaimed, brightening as she ate. "May it be for good luck to us all!" she exulted, waving aloft the last precious bite.

Mrs. Pelz was so flattered that she even ladled up a spoonful of gravy.

"There is a bit of onion and carrot in it," she said, as she handed it to her neighbor.

[6]A variation on "oy" or "oi." [7]Gefilte fish: a kind of cooked fish balls.

Hanneh Breineh sipped the gravy drop by drop, like a connoisseur sipping wine.

"Ah-h-h! A taste of that gravy lifts me up to heaven!" As she disposed leisurely of the slice of onion and carrot she relaxed and expanded and even grew jovial. "Let us wish all our troubles on the Russian Czar! Let him burst with our worries for rent! Let him get shriveled with our hunger for bread! Let his eyes dry out of his head looking for work!

"Shah! I'm forgetting from everything," she exclaimed, jumping up. "It must be eleven or soon twelve, and my children will be right away out of school and fall on me like a pack of wild wolves. I better quick run to the market and see what cheaper I can get for a quarter."

Because of the lateness of her coming, the stale bread at the nearest bakeshop was sold out, and Hanneh Breineh had to trudge from shop to shop in search of the usual bargain, and spent nearly an hour to save two cents.

In the meantime the children returned from school, and, finding the door locked, climbed through the fire-escape, and entered the house through the window. Seeing nothing on the table, they rushed to the stove. Abe pulled a steaming potato out of the boiling pot, and so scalded his fingers that the potato fell to the floor; where upon the three others pounced on it.

"It was my potato," cried Abe, blowing his burned fingers, while with the other hand and his foot he cuffed and kicked the three who were struggling on the floor. A wild fight ensued, and the potato was smashed under Abe's foot amid shouts and screams. Hanneh Breineh, on the stairs, heard the noise of her famished brood, and topped their cries with curses and invectives.

"They are here already, the savages! They are here already to shorten my life! They heard you all over the hall, in all the houses around!"

The children, disregarding her words, pounced on her market-basket, shouting ravenously: "Mamma, I'm hungry! What more do you got to eat?"

They tore the bread and herring out of Hanneh Breineh's basket and devoured it in starved savagery, clamoring for more.

"Murderers!" screamed Hanneh Breineh, goaded beyond endurance. "What are you tearing from me my flesh? From where should I steal to give you more? Here I had already a pot of potatoes and a whole loaf of bread and two herrings, and you swallowed it down in the wink of an eye. I have to have Rockefeller's millions to fill your stomachs."

All at once Hanneh Breineh became aware that Benny was missing. "Oi weh!" she burst out, wringing her hands in a new wave of woe, "where is Benny? Didn't he come home yet from school?"

She ran out into the hall, opened the grime-coated window, and looked up and down the street; but Benny was nowhere in sight.

"Abe, Jake, Fanny, quick, find Benny!" entreated Hanneh Breineh, as she rushed back into the kitchen. But the children, anxious to snatch a few minutes' play before the school-call, dodged past her and hurried out.

With the baby on her arm, Hanneh Breineh hastened to the kindergarten.

"Why are you keeping Benny here so long?" she shouted at the teacher as she flung open the door.

If you had my bitter heart, you would send him home long ago and not wait till I got to come for him."

The teacher turned calmly and consulted her record-cards.

"Benny Safron? He wasn't present this morning."

"Not here?" shrieked Hanneh Breineh. "I pushed him out myself he should go. The children didn't want to take him, and I had no time. Woe is me! Where is my child?" She began pulling her hair and beating her breast as she ran into the street.

Mrs. Pelz was busy at a pushcart, picking over some spotted apples, when she heard the clamor of an approaching crowd. A block off she recognized Hanneh Breineh, her hair disheveled, her clothes awry, running toward her with her yelling baby in her arms, the crowd following.

"Friend mine," cried Hanneh Breineh, falling on Mrs. Pelz's neck, "I lost my Benny, the best child of all my children." Tears streamed down her red, swollen eyes as she sobbed. "Benny! mine heart, mine life! Oi-i-i!"

Mrs. Pelz took the frightened baby out of the mother's arms.

"Still yourself a little! See how you're frightening your child."

"Woe to me! Where is my Benny? Maybe he's killed already by a car. Maybe he fainted away from hunger. He didn't eat nothing all day long. Gottuniu! Pity yourself on me!"

She lifted her hands full of tragic entreaty.

"People, my child! Get me my child! I'll go crazy out of my head! Get me my child, or I'll take poison before your eyes!"

"Still yourself a little!" pleaded Mrs. Pelz.

"Talk not to me!" cried Hanneh Breineh, wringing her hands. "You're having all your children. I lost mine. Every good luck comes to other people. But I didn't live yet to see a good day in my life. Mine only joy, mine Benny, is lost away from me."

The crowd followed Hanneh Breineh as she wailed through the streets, leaning on Mrs. Pelz. By the time she returned to her house the children were back from school; but seeing that Benny was not there, she chased them out in the street, crying:

"Out of here, you robbers, gluttons! Go find Benny!" Hanneh Breineh crumpled into a chair in utter prostration. "Oi weh! he's lost! Mine life; my little bird; mine only joy! How many nights I spent nursing him when he had the measles! And all that I suffered for weeks and months when he had the whooping-cough! How the eyes went out of my head till I learned him how to walk, till I learned him how to talk! And such a smart child! If I lost all the others, it wouldn't tear me so by the heart."

She worked herself up into such a hysteria, crying, and tearing her hair, and hitting her head with her knuckles, that at last she fell into a faint. It took some time before Mrs. Pelz, with the aid of neighbors, revived her.

"Benny, mine angel!" she moaned as she opened her eyes.

Just then a policeman came in with the lost Benny.

"Na, na, here you got him already!" said Mrs. Pelz. "Why did you carry on so for nothing? Why did you tear up the world like a crazy?"

The child's face was streaked with tears as he cowered, frightened and forlorn. Hanneh Breineh sprang toward him, slapping his cheeks, boxing his ears, before the neighbors could rescue him from her.

"Woe on your head!" cried the mother. "Where did you lost yourself? Ain't I got enough worries on my head than to go around looking for you? I didn't have yet a minute's peace from that child since he was born!"

"See a crazy mother!" remonstrated Mrs. Pelz, rescuing Benny from another beating. "Such a mouth! With one breath she blesses him when he is lost, and with the other breath she curses him when he is found."

Hanneh Breineh took from the window-sill a piece of herring covered with swarming flies, and putting it on a slice of dry bread, she filled a cup of tea that had been stewing all day, and dragged Benny over to the table to eat.

But the child, choking with tears, was unable to touch the food.

"Go eat!" commanded Hanneh Breineh. "Eat and choke yourself eating!"

"Maybe she won't remember me no more. Maybe the servant won't let me in," thought Mrs. Pelz, as she walked by the brownstone house on Eighty-Fourth Street where she had been told Hanneh Breineh now lived. At last she summoned up enough courage to climb the steps. She was all out of breath as she rang the bell with trembling fingers. "Oi weh! even the outside smells riches and plenty! Such curtains! And shades on all windows like by millionaires! Twenty years ago she used to eat from the pot to the hand, and now she lives in such a palace."

A whiff of steam-heated warmth swept over Mrs. Pelz as the door opened, and she saw her old friend of the tenements dressed in silk and diamonds like a being from another world.

"Mrs. Pelz, is it you!" cried Hanneh Breineh, overjoyed at the sight of her former neighbor. "Come right in. Since when are you back in New York?"

"We came last week," mumbled Mrs. Pelz, as she was led into a richly carpeted reception-room.

"Make yourself comfortable. Take off your shawl," urged Hanneh Breineh.

But Mrs. Pelz only drew her shawl more tightly around her, a keen sense of her poverty gripping her as she gazed, abashed by the luxurious wealth that shone from every corner.

"This shawl covers up my rags," she said, trying to hide her shabby sweater.

"I'll tell you what; come right into the kitchen," suggested Hanneh Breineh. "The servant is away for this afternoon, and we can feel more comfortable there. I can breathe like a free person in my kitchen when the girl has her day out."

Mrs. Pelz glanced about her in an excited daze. Never in her life had she seen anything so wonderful as a white-tiled kitchen, with its glistening porcelain sink and the aluminum pots and pans that shone like silver.

"Where are you staying now?" asked Hanneh Breineh, as she pinned an apron over her silk dress.

"I moved back to Delancey Street, where we used to live," replied Mrs. Pelz, as she seated herself cautiously in a white enameled chair.

"Oi weh! What grand times we had in that old house when we were neighbors!" sighed Hanneh Breineh, looking at her old friend with misty eyes.

"You still think on Delancey Street? Haven't you more high-class neighbors uptown here?"

"A good neighbor is not to be found every day," deplored Hanneh Breineh. "Uptown here, where each lives in his own house, nobody cares if the person next door is dying or going crazy from loneliness. It ain't anything like we used to have it in Delancey Street, when we could walk into one another's rooms without knocking, and borrow a pinch of salt or a pot to cook in."

Hanneh Breineh went over to the pantry-shelf.

"We are going to have a bite right here on the kitchen-table like on Delancey Street. So long there's no servant to watch us we can eat what we please."

"Oi! How it waters my mouth with appetite, the smell of the herring and onion!" chuckled Mrs. Pelz, sniffing the welcome odors with greedy pleasure.

Hanneh Breineh pulled a dish-towel from the rack and threw one end of it to Mrs. Pelz.

"So long there's no servant around, we can use it together for a napkin. It's dirty, anyhow. How it freshens up my heart to see you!" she rejoiced as she poured out her tea into a saucer. "If you would only know how I used to beg my daughter to write for me a letter to you; but these American children, what is to them a mother's feelings?"

"What are you talking!" cried Mrs. Pelz. "The whole world rings with you and your children. Everybody is envying you. Tell me how began your luck?"

"You heard how my husband died with consumption," replied Hanneh Breineh. "The five hundred dollars lodge money gave me the first lift in life, and I opened a little grocery store. Then my son Abe married himself to a girl with a thousand dollars. That started him in business, and now he has the biggest shirt-waist factory on West Twenty-Ninth Street."

"Yes, I heard your son had a factory." Mrs. Pelz hesitated and stammered; "I'll tell you the truth. What I came to ask you—I thought maybe you would beg your son Abe if he would give my husband a job."

"Why not?" said Hanneh Breineh. "He keeps more than five hundred hands. I'll ask him if he should take in Mr. Pelz."

"Long years on you, Hanneh Breineh! You'll save my life if you could only help my husband get work."

"Of course my son will help him. All my children like to do good. My daughter Fanny is a milliner on Fifth Avenue, and she takes in the poorest girls in her shop and even pays them sometimes while they learn the trade." Hanneh Breineh's face lit up, and her chest filled with pride as she enumerated the successes of her children. "And my son Benny he wrote a play on Broadway and he gave away more than a hundred free tickets for the first night."

"Benny? The one who used to get lost from home all the time? You always did love that child more than all the rest. And what is Sammy your baby doing?"

"He ain't a baby no longer. He goes to college and quarterbacks the football team. They can't get along without him.

"And my son Jake, I nearly forgot him. He began collecting rent in Delancey Street, and now he is boss of renting the swellest apartment-houses on Riverside Drive."

"What did I tell you? In America children are like money in the bank," purred Mrs. Pelz, as she pinched and patted Hanneh Breineh's silk sleeve. "Oi weh! How it shines from you! You ought to kiss the air and dance for joy and happiness. It is such a bitter frost outside; a pail of coal is so dear, and you got it so warm with steam heat. I had to pawn my feather bed to have enough for the rent, and you are rolling in money."

"Yes, I got it good in some ways, but money ain't everything," sighed Hanneh Breineh.

"You ain't yet satisfied?"

"But here I got no friends," complained Hanneh Breineh.

"Friends?" queried Mrs. Pelz. "What greater friend is there on earth than the dollar?"

"Oi! Mrs. Pelz; if you could only look into my heart! I'm so choked up! You know they say a cow has a long tongue, but can't talk." Hanneh Breineh shook her head wistfully, and her eyes filmed with inward brooding. "My children give me everything from the best. When I was sick, they got me a nurse by day and one by night. They bought me the best wine. If I asked for dove's milk, they would buy it for me; but—but—I can't talk myself out in their language. They want to make me over for an American lady, and I'm different." Tears cut their way under her eyelids with a pricking pain as she went on: "When I was poor, I was free, and could holler and do what I like in my own house. Here I got to lie still like a mouse under a broom. Between living up to my Fifth-Avenue daughter and keeping up with the servants, I am like a sinner in the next world that is thrown from one hell to another." The doorbell rang, and Hanneh Breineh jumped up with a start.

"Oi weh! It must be the servant back already!" she exclaimed, as she tore off her apron. "Oi weh! Let's quickly put the dishes together in a dish-pan. If she sees I eat on the kitchen table, she will look on me like the dirt under her feet."

Mrs. Pelz seized her shawl in haste.

"I better run home quick in my rags before your servant sees me."

"I'll speak to Abe about the job," said Hanneh Breineh, as she pushed a bill into the hand of Mrs. Pelz, who edged out as the servant entered.

"I'm having fried potato lotkes special for you, Benny," said Hanneh Breineh, as the children gathered about the table for the family dinner given in honor of Benny's success with his new play. "Do you remember how you used to lick the fingers from them?"

"Oh, mother!" reproved Fanny. "Any one hearing you would think we were still in the pushcart district."

"Stop your nagging, sis, and let ma alone," commanded Benny, patting his mother's arm affectionately. "I'm home only once a month. Let her feed me what she pleases. My stomach is bomb-proof."

"Do I hear that the President is coming to your play?" said Abe, as he stuffed a napkin over his diamond-studded shirt-front.

"Why shouldn't he come?" returned Benny. "The critics say it's the greatest antidote for the race hatred created by the war. If you want to know, he is coming to-night; and what's more, our box is next to the President's."

"Nu, mammeh," sallied Jake, "did you ever dream in Delancey Street that we should rub sleeves with the President?"

"I always said that Benny had more head than the rest of you," replied the mother.

As the laughter died away, Jake went on:

"Honor you are getting plenty; but how much mezummen does this play bring you? Can I invest any of it in real estate for you?"

"I'm getting ten per cent royalties of the gross receipts," replied the youthful playwright.

"How much is that?" queried Hanneh Breineh.

"Enough to buy up all your fish-markets in Delancey Street," laughed Abe in good-natured raillery at his mother.

Her son's jest cut like a knife-thrust in her heart. She felt her heart ache with the pain that she was shut out from their successes. Each added triumph only widened the gulf. And when she tried to bridge this gulf by asking questions, they only thrust her back upon herself.

"Your fame has even helped me get my hat trade solid with the Four Hundred," put in Fanny. "You bet I let Mrs. Van Suyden know that our box is next to the President's. She said she would drop in to meet you. Of course she let on to me that she hadn't seen the play yet, though my designer said she saw her there on the opening night."

"Oh, Gosh, the toadies!" sneered Benny. "Nothing so sickens you with success as the way people who once shoved you off the sidewalk come crawling to you on their stomachs begging you to dine with them."

"Say, that leading man of yours he's some class!" cried Fanny. "That's the man I'm looking for. Will you invite him to supper after the theater?"

The playwright turned to his mother.

"Say, ma," he said, laughingly, "how would you like a real actor for a son-in-law?"

"She should worry," mocked Sam. "She'll be discussing with him the future of the Greek drama. Too bad it doesn't happen to be Warfield, or mother could give him tips on the 'Auctioneer.'"[8]

Jake turned to his mother with a covert grin.

"I guess you'd have no objection if Fanny got next to Benny's leading man. He makes at least fifteen hundred a week. That wouldn't be such a bad addition to the family, would it?"

Again the bantering tone stabbed Hanneh Breineh. Everything in her began to tremble and break loose.

"Why do you ask me?" she cried, throwing her napkin into her plate. "Do I count for a person in this house? If I'll say something, will you even listen to me? What is to me the grandest man that my daughter could pick out? Another enemy in my house! Another person to shame himself from me!" She swept in her children in one glance of despairing anguish as she rose from the table. "What worth is an old mother to American children? The President is coming tonight to the theater, and none of you asked me to go." Unable to check the rising tears, she fled toward the kitchen and banged the door.

They all looked at one another guiltily.

"Say, sis," Benny called out sharply, "what sort of frame-up is this? Haven't you told mother that she was to go with us to-night?"

"Yes—I—" Fanny bit her lips as she fumbled evasively for words. "I asked her if she wouldn't mind my taking her some other time."

"Now you have made a mess of it!" fumed Benny. "Mother'll be too hurt to go now."

"Well, I don't care," snapped Fanny. "I can't appear with mother in a box at the theater. Can I introduce her to Mrs. Van Suyden? And suppose your leading man should ask to meet me?"

"Take your time, sis. He hasn't asked yet," scoffed Benny.

"The more reason I shouldn't spoil my chances. You know mother. She'll spill the beans that we come from Delancey Street the minute we introduce her anywhere. Must I always have the black shadow of my past trailing after me?"

"But have you no feelings for mother?" admonished Abe.

"I've tried harder than all of you to do my duty. I've lived with her." She turned angrily upon them. "I've borne the shame of mother while you bought

[8]A reference to the play "The Auctioneer," written by Charles Klein and Lee Arthur. David Warfield was the actor who played the leading role in the play.

her off with a present and a treat here and there. God knows how hard I tried to civilize her so as not to have to blush with shame when I take her anywhere. I dressed her in the most stylish Paris models, but Delancey Street sticks out from every inch of her. Whenever she opens her mouth, I'm done for. You fellows had your chance to rise in the world because a man is free to go up as high as he can reach up to; but I, with all my style and pep, can't get a man my equal because a girl is always judged by her mother."

They were silenced by her vehemence, and unconsciously turned to Benny.

"I guess we all tried to do our best for mother," said Benny, thoughtfully. "But wherever there is growth, there is pain and heartbreak. The trouble with us is that the ghetto of the Middle Ages and the children of the twentieth century have to live under one roof, and—"

A sound of crashing dishes came from the kitchen, and the voice of Hanneh Breineh resounded through the dining-room as she wreaked her pent-up fury on the helpless servant.

"Oh, my nerves! I can't stand it any more! There will be no girl again for another week!" cried Fanny.

"Oh, let up on the old lady," protested Abe. "Since she can't take it out on us any more, what harm is it if she cusses the servants?"

"If you fellows had to chase around employment agencies, you wouldn't see anything funny about it. Why can't we move into a hotel that will do away with the need of servants altogether?"

"I got it better," said Jake, consulting a notebook from his pocket. "I have on my list an apartment on Riverside Drive where there's only a small kitchenette; but we can do away with the cooking, for there is a dining service in the building."

The new Riverside apartment to which Hanneh Breineh was removed by her socially ambitious children was for the habitually active mother an empty desert of enforced idleness. Deprived of her kitchen, Hanneh Breineh felt robbed of the last reason for her existence. Cooking and marketing and puttering busily with pots and pans gave her an excuse for living and struggling and bearing up with her children. The lonely idleness of Riverside Drive stunned all her senses and arrested all her thoughts. It gave her that choked sense of being cut off from air, from life, from everything warm and human. The cold indifference, the each-for-himself look in the eyes of the people about her were like stinging slaps in the face. Even the children had nothing real or human in them. They were starched and stiff miniatures of their elders.

But the most unendurable part of the stifling life on Riverside Drive was being forced to eat in the public dining-room. No matter how hard she tried to learn polite table manners, she always found people staring at her, and her daughter rebuking her for eating with the wrong fork or guzzling the soup or staining the cloth.

In a fit of rebellion Hanneh Breineh resolved never to go down to the public dining-room again, but to make use of the gas-stove in the kitchenette to cook her own meals. That very day she rode down to Delancey Street and purchased a new market-basket. For some time she walked among the haggling pushcart venders, relaxing and swimming in the warm waves of her old familiar past.

A fish-peddler held up a large carp in his black, hairy hand and waved it dramatically:

"Women! Women! Fourteen cents a pound!"

He ceased his raucous shouting as he saw Hanneh Breineh in her rich attire approach his cart.

"How much?" she asked, pointing to the fattest carp.

"Fifteen cents, lady," said the peddler, smirking as he raised his price.

"Swindler! Didn't I hear you call fourteen cents?" shrieked Hanneh Breineh, exultingly, the spirit of the penny chase surging in her blood. Diplomatically, Hanneh Breineh turned as if to go, and the fisherman seized her basket in frantic fear.

"I should live; I'm losing money on the fish, lady," whined the peddler. "I'll let it down to thirteen cents for you only."

"Two pounds for a quarter, and not a penny more," said Hanneh Breineh, thrilling again with the rare sport of bargaining, which had been her chief joy in the good old days of poverty.

"No, I want to make the first sale for good luck." The peddler threw the fish on the scale.

As he wrapped up the fish, Hanneh Breineh saw the driven look of worry in his haggard eyes, and when he counted out the change from her dollar, she waved it aside. "Keep it for your luck," she said, and hurried off to strike a new bargain at a pushcart of onions.

Hanneh Breineh returned triumphantly with her purchases. The basket under her arm gave forth the old, home-like odors of herring and garlic, while the scaly tail of a four-pound carp protruded from its newspaper wrapping. A gilded placard on the door of the apartment-house proclaimed that all merchandise must be delivered through the trade entrance in the rear; but Hanneh Breineh with her basket strode proudly through the marble-paneled hall and rang nonchalantly for the elevator.

The uniformed hall-man, erect, expressionless, frigid with dignity, stepped forward:

"Just a minute, madam. I'll call a boy to take up your basket for you."

Hanneh Breineh, glaring at him, jerked the basket savagely from his hands. "Mind your own business!" she retorted. "I'll take it up myself. Do you think you're a Russian policeman to boss me in my own house?"

Angry lines appeared on the countenance of the representative of social decorum.

"It is against the rules, madam," he said, stiffly.

"You should sink into the earth with all your rules and brass buttons. Ain't this America? Ain't this a free country? Can't I take up in my own house what I buy with my own money?" cried Hanneh Breineh, reveling in the opportunity to shower forth the volley of invectives that had been suppressed in her for the weeks of deadly dignity of Riverside Drive.

In the midst of this uproar Fanny came in with Mrs. Van Suyden. Hanneh Breineh rushed over to her, crying:

"This bossy policeman won't let me take up my basket in the elevator."

The daughter, unnerved with shame and confusion, took the basket in her white-gloved hand and ordered the hall-boy to take it around to the regular delivery entrance.

Hanneh Breineh was so hurt by her daughter's apparent defense of the hall-man's rules that she utterly ignored Mrs. Van Suyden's greeting and walked up the seven flights of stairs out of sheer spite.

"You see the tragedy of my life?" broke out Fanny, turning to Mrs. Van Suyden.

"You poor child! You go right up to your dear, old lady mother, and I'll come some other time."

Instantly Fanny regretted her words. Mrs. Van Suyden's pity only roused her wrath the more against her mother.

Breathless from climbing the stairs, Hanneh Breineh entered the apartment just as Fanny tore the faultless millinery creation from her head and threw it on the floor in a rage.

"Mother, you are the ruination of my life! You have driven away Mrs. Van Suyden, as you have driven away all my best friends. What do you think we got this apartment for but to get rid of your fish smells and your brawls with the servants? And here you come with a basket on your arm as if you just landed from steerage! And this afternoon, of all times, when Benny is bringing his leading man to tea. When will you ever stop disgracing us?"

"When I'm dead," said Hanneh Breineh, grimly. "When the earth will cover me up, then you'll be free to go your American way. I'm not going to make myself over for a lady on Riverside Drive. I hate you and all your swell friends. I'll not let myself be choked up here by you or by that hall-boss policeman that is higher in your eyes than your own mother."

"So that's your thanks for all we've done for you?" cried the daughter.

"All you've done for me!" shouted Hanneh Breineh. "What have you done for me? You hold me like a dog on a chain! It stands in the Talmud; some children give their mothers dry bread and water and go to heaven for it, and some give their mother roast duck and go to Gehenna[9] because it's not given with love."

"You want me to love you yet?" raged the daughter. "You knocked every bit of love out of me when I was yet a kid. All the memories of childhood I have is your everlasting cursing and yelling that we were gluttons."

The bell rang sharply, and Hanneh Breineh flung open the door.

"Your groceries, ma'am," said the boy.

Hanneh Breineh seized the basket from him, and with a vicious fling sent it rolling across the room, strewing its contents over the Persian rugs and inlaid floor. Then seizing her hat and coat, she stormed out of the apartment and down the stairs.

Mr. and Mrs. Pelz sat crouched and shivering over their meager supper when the door opened, and Hanneh Breineh in fur coat and plumed hat charged into the room.

"I come to cry out to you my bitter heart," she sobbed. "Woe is me! It is so black for my eyes!"

"What is the matter with you, Hanneh Breineh?" cried Mrs. Pelz in bewildered alarm.

"I am turned out of my own house by the brass-buttoned policeman that bosses the elevator. Oi-i-i-i! Weh-h-h-h! What have I from my life? The whole world rings with my son's play. Even the President came to see it, and I, his mother, have not seen it yet. My heart is dying in me like in a prison," she went on wailing. "I am starved out for a piece of real eating. In that swell restaurant is nothing but napkins and forks and lettuce-leaves. There are a dozen plates

[9] Hell.

to every bite of food. And it looks so fancy on the plate, but it's nothing but straw in the mouth. I'm starving, but I can't swallow down their American eating."

"Hanneh Breineh," said Mrs. Pelz, "you are sinning before God. Look on your fur coat; it alone would feed a whole family for a year. I never had yet a piece of fur trimming on a coat, and you are in fur from the neck to the feet. I never had yet a piece of feather on a hat, and your hat is all feathers."

"What are you envying me?" protested Hanneh Breineh. "What have I from all my fine furs and feathers when my children are strangers to me? All the fur coats in the world can't warm up the loneliness inside my heart. All the grandest feathers can't hide the bitter shame in my face that my children shame themselves from me."

Hanneh Breineh suddenly loomed over them like some ancient, heroic figure of the Bible condemning unrighteousness.

"Why should my children shame themselves from me? From where did they get the stuff to work themselves up in the world? Did they get it from the air? How did they get all their smartness to rise over the people around them? Why don't the children of born American mothers write my Benny's plays? It is I, who never had a chance to be a person, who gave him the fire in his head. If I would have had a chance to go to school and learn the language, what couldn't I have been? It is I and my mother and my mother's mother and my father and father's father who had such a black life in Poland; it is our choked thoughts and feelings that are flaming up in my children and making them great in America. And yet they shame themselves from me!"

For a moment Mr. and Mrs. Pelz were hypnotized by the sweep of her words. Then Hanneh Breineh sank into a chair in utter exhaustion. She began to weep bitterly, her body shaking with sobs.

"Woe is me! For what did I suffer and hope on my children? A bitter old age—my end. I'm so lonely!"

All the dramatic fire seemed to have left her. The spell was broken. They saw the Hanneh Breineh of old, ever discontented, ever complaining even in the midst of riches and plenty.

"Hanneh Breineh," said Mrs. Pelz, "the only trouble with you is that you got it too good. People will tear the eyes out of your head because you're complaining yet. If I only had your fur coat! If I only had your diamonds! I have nothing. You have everything. You are living on the fat of the land. You go right back home and thank God that you don't have my bitter lot."

"You got to let me stay here with you," insisted Hanneh Breineh. "I'll not go back to my children except when they bury me. When they will see my dead face, they will understand how they killed me."

Mrs. Pelz glanced nervously at her husband. They barely had enough covering for their one bed; how could they possibly lodge a visitor?

"I don't want to take up your bed," said Hanneh Breineh. "I don't care if I have to sleep on the floor or on the chairs, but I'll stay here for the night."

Seeing that she was bent on staying, Mr. Pelz prepared to sleep by putting a few chairs next to the trunk, and Hanneh Breineh was invited to share the rickety bed with Mrs. Pelz.

The mattress was full of lumps and hollows. Hanneh Breineh lay cramped and miserable, unable to stretch out her limbs. For years she had been accustomed to hair mattresses and ample woolen blankets, so that though she covered herself with her fur coat, she was too cold to sleep. But worse than the cold were the creeping things on the wall. And as the lights were turned low, the mice came through the broken plaster and raced across the floor. The foul odors of the kitchen-sink added to the night of horrors.

"Are you going back home?" asked Mrs. Pelz, as Hanneh Breineh put on her hat and coat the next morning.

"I don't know where I'm going," she replied, as she put a bill into Mrs. Pelz's hand.

For hours Hanneh Breineh walked through the crowded ghetto streets. She realized that she no longer could endure the sordid ugliness of her past, and yet she could not go home to her children. She only felt that she must go on and on.

In the afternoon a cold, drizzling rain set in. She was worn out from the sleepless night and hours of tramping. With a piercing pain in her heart she at last turned back and boarded the subway for Riverside Drive. She had fled from the marble sepulcher of the Riverside apartment to her old home in the ghetto; but now she knew that she could not live there again. She had outgrown her past by the habits of years of physical comforts, and these material comforts that she could no longer do without choked and crushed the life within her.

A cold shudder went through Hanneh Breineh as she approached the apartment-house. Peering through the plate glass of the door she saw the face of the uniformed hall-man. For a hesitating moment she remained standing in the drizzling rain, unable to enter, and yet knowing full well that she would have to enter.

Then suddenly Hanneh Breineh began to laugh. She realized that it was the first time she had laughed since her children had become rich. But it was the hard laugh of bitter sorrow. Tears streamed down her furrowed cheeks as she walked slowly up the granite steps.

"The fat of the land!" muttered Hanneh Breineh, with a choking sob as the hall-man with immobile face deferentially swung open the door—"the fat of the land!"

1920

Edna St. Vincent Millay 1892–1950

Edna St. Vincent Millay was born in Rockland, Maine, a small town on the Atlantic coast, in 1892. She and her two sisters were raised by their mother, Cora Buzzelle Millay, a practical nurse who had divorced her husband Harry in 1900, and who instilled into her daughters a passion for literature and music. With her mother's encouragement, Millay began to write poetry while in high school. One poem in particular, "Renascence," published in 1912 in The Lyric Year, *attracted the attention of New York literati. As a result, a sponsor materialized and helped her attend college briefly at Barnard and then, with the aid of a scholarship, Vassar. She published* Renascence and Other Poems, *her first collection of verse, in 1917. After graduating from Vassar in 1918, Millay settled in Greenwich Village, where she lived a stimulating, if often financially strapped, life among New York's artistic avant-grade. She continued to write and briefly pursued acting, joining the Provincetown Players as both a playwright and performer.*

During the years immediately following World War I, Millay wrote short fiction, lectured, and served as a foreign correspondent for Vanity Fair. *She published her second book of poetry,* A Few Figs from Thistles, *in 1920 and her third,* Second April, *in 1921. These were critically well-received, and a broader acclaim came with her fourth volume,* The Harp-Weaver and Other Poems *(1923), which won the Pulitzer Prize, distinguishing her as the first woman to receive that award. She published two more significant collections of verse over the next eight years,* The Buck in the Snow *(1928) and* Fatal Interview *(1931). Critics agree that in these two books Millay continued at the height of her poetic powers. In the 1930s and 1940s, her art became increasingly political, and she seemed to fall out of favor with readers and critics alike. Edna St. Vincent Millay died in 1950 at the age of 58.*

FURTHER READING: J. Gould, *The Poet and Her Book: A Biography of Edna St. Vincent Millay,* 1969; J. Nierman, *Edna St. Vincent Millay: A Reference Guide,* 1977; N. Brittin, *Edna St. Vincent Millay,* 1982; J. Veatch, *The Short Stories of Edna St. Vincent Millay,* 1990; H. Scott, *Edna St. Vincent Millay: The Rebirth (1892–1950), An Appreciation,* ed. M. Myers, 1992; *Critical Essays on Edna St. Vincent Millay,* ed. W. Thesing, 1993; *Millay at 100: A Critical Reappraisal,* ed. D. Freedman, 1995; D. Epstein, *What Lips My Lips Have Kissed: The Loves And Love Poems of Edna St. Vincent Millay,* 2001; N. Milford, *Savage Beauty: The Life of Edna St. Vincent Millay,* 2001.

TEXTS: *Second April,* 1921; *A Few Figs from Thistles: Poems and Sonnets,* 1922; *The Harp-Weaver and Other Poems,* 1923; *Collected Poems,* 1956.

SPRING

To what purpose, April, do you return again?
Beauty is not enough.
You can no longer quiet me with the redness
Of little leaves opening stickily.
I know what I know.
The sun is hot on my neck as I observe
The spikes of the crocus.
The smell of the earth is good.
It is apparent that there is no death.
But what does that signify?
Not only under ground are the brains of men
Eaten by maggots.
Life in itself
Is nothing,
An empty cup, a flight of uncarpeted stairs.
It is not enough that yearly, down this hill,
April
Comes like an idiot, babbling and strewing flowers.

1921

FIRST FIG

My candle burns at both ends;
It will not last the night;
But ah, my foes, and oh, my friends—
It gives a lovely light!

1922

[I SHALL FORGET YOU PRESENTLY, MY DEAR]

I shall forget you presently, my dear,
So make the most of this, your little day,
Your little month, your little half a year,
Ere I forget, or die, or move away,
And we are done forever; by and by
I shall forget you, as I said, but now,
If you entreat me with your loveliest lie
I will protest you with my favourite vow.
I would indeed that love were longer-lived,
And oaths were not so brittle as they are,
But so it is, and nature has contrived
To struggle on without a break thus far,—
Whether or not we find what we are seeking
Is idle, biologically speaking.

1922

[EUCLID ALONE HAS LOOKED ON BEAUTY BARE]

Euclid[1] alone has looked on Beauty bare.
Let all who prate of Beauty hold their peace,
And lay them prone upon the earth and cease
To ponder on themselves, the while they stare
At nothing, intricately drawn nowhere
In shapes of shifting lineage; let geese
Gabble and hiss, but heroes seek release
From dusty bondage into luminous air.
O blinding hour, O holy, terrible day,
When first the shaft into his vision shone
Of light anatomized! Euclid alone
Has looked on Beauty bare. Fortunate they
Who, though once only and then but far away,
Have heard her massive sandal set on stone.

1923

[1]Euclid (c. 325–265) was an ancient Greek mathematician who established many of the basic principles of geometry.

Wallace Stevens 1879–1955

Wallace Stevens—are we for him?
Brother, he's our father!

Theodore Roethke was speaking for the next generation when he thus paid tribute to the man who, in his final years, became one of the most noted of American poets. A reticent man who placed unusual value upon his privacy, Stevens remained during his lifetime something of a mystery. He successfully pursued two seemingly incompatible careers: business and art. His business, he said, was "insurance," and unlike his most distinguished contemporaries, Pound, Eliot, and Williams, he was rarely comfortable in the role of professional poet. He lived a quiet, secluded life, disliked giving public readings, and in his last years refused a Harvard lectureship on the grounds that acceptance would force his retirement from "the office." Yet for over forty years he was deeply dedicated to poetry, and many younger poets agreed with Roethke's assertion that they had been influenced by a master.

Stevens spent his boyhood in his birthplace, Reading, Pennsylvania, where his father was a prosperous attorney. Stevens's earliest ambition was to be a writer, and after three years at Harvard, where he published poems in the Harvard Advocate, *he went to New York in 1900 for a try at journalism. But the following year, on his father's advice, he entered New York Law School. Admitted to the bar in 1904, he worked for several law firms before marrying and moving to Connecticut, where he eventually rose to the position of vice-president of the Hartford Accident and Indemnity Company.*

During his years in New York, with the modernist movement gaining momentum, Stevens became acquainted with a number of young writers, among them the poets William Carlos Williams and Marianne Moore. He also began submitting his own poems to the little magazines and, for a time, tried writing for the experimental theater. It was not until 1923, however, that Stevens, at the age of forty-four, was finally persuaded to publish a book of poems, Harmonium. *The book's poor reception (fewer than one hundred copies were sold) and its author's growing business responsibilities almost led him to abandon poetry. For over a decade he published little, but with the reprinting of* Harmonium *(1931) and the resulting increase in critical attention, he began his years of steady publication.*

In 1935 Stevens published Ideas of Order. *Then followed* The Man with the Blue Guitar *(1937),* Parts of a World *(1942),* Transport to Summer *(1947), and* The Auroras of Autumn *(1950). These, along with a collection of his occasional lectures on poetry,* The Necessary Angel *(1951), established him as a major American poet. For the publication of his* Collected Poems *(1954) he received his second National Book Award and a Pulitzer Prize. After his death, his previously uncollected work appeared in* Opus Posthumous *(1957), and his* Letters *were published in 1966.*

From the beginning it was evident that Harmonium *was part of a revolution in American poetry. Although some of its best poems, including "Sunday Morning," are relatively traditional in form, the book baffled even the most sophisticated. Stevens had rebelled against the "stale intelligence" of the past. Setting out "to make a new intelligence prevail," he invoked the comic, the strange, the bizarre. He adopted a variety of experimental styles, creating poetic surfaces of Frenchified elegance, exotic imagery, odd sounds, curious analogies, and inscrutable titles.*

For many readers it seemed that Stevens had carried originality to the point of mere eccentricity, and he was called a "dandy," a "virtuoso of the inane," a writer of "near nonsense." But beneath his gaudiest surfaces, Stevens's abiding concerns were clearly present. He confronted the contemporary abandonment of traditional values and sought to come to terms with the confusions of his time. The problem of the relation between the ideal and the real became a constant theme in his later poetry, and he elaborated a series of oppositions between inner and outer worlds—between subject and object, perceiver and perceived, fiction and fact, or as he most often phrased it, between "imagination and reality." These contraries meet ultimately in his concept of a "supreme fiction," a modern mythology that might serve as a replacement for the mythologies of the past, a new vision with "which men could propose to themselves a fulfilment." Although he constantly dealt with the nature of poetry, in his later work Stevens became increasingly meditative and philosophical, an intellectual elitist, at times difficult and obscure, who wrote, as he admitted, "for a gallery of one's own."

FURTHER READINGS: H. Stevens, *Souvenirs and Prophecies: The Young Wallace Stevens,* 1977; P. Brazeau, *Parts of a World: Wallace Stevens Remembered,* 1983; H. Vendler, *Wallace Stevens: Words Chosen out of Desire,* 1984; M. Bates, *Wallace Stevens: A Mythology of Self,* 1985; J. Richardson, *Wallace Stevens: The Early Years,* 1986; J. Carroll, *Wallace Stevens' Supreme Fiction: A New Romanticism,* 1987; J. Leonard and C. Wharton, *The Fluent Mundo: Wallace Stevens and the Structure of Reality,* 1988; J. Richardson, *Wallace Stevens: The Later Years,* 1988; E. Cook, *Poetry, Word-Play, and Word-War in Wallace Stevens,* 1988; B. Fisher, *Wallace Stevens: The Intensest Rendezvous,* 1990; M. Halliday, *Stevens and the Interpersonal,* 1991; J. Longenbach, *Wallace Stevens: The Plain Sense of Things,* 1991; A. Filreis, *Wallace Stevens and the Actual World,* 1991; G. Lensing, *Wallace Stevens: A Poet's Growth,* 1991; T. Grey, *The Wallace Stevens Case,* 1991; B. Leggett, *Early Stevens: The Nietzschean Intertext,* 1992; D. Schwarz, *Narrative and Representation in the Poetry of Wallace Stevens,* 1993; G. MacLeod, *Wallace Stevens and Modern Art,* 1993; J. McCann, *Wallace Stevens Revisited,* 1995; A. Whiting, *The Never-Resting Mind,* 1996; G. Lensing, *Wallace Stevens and the Seasons,* 2001; B. Eeckhout, *Wallace Stevens and the Limits of Reading and Writing,* 2002; *Wallace Stevens,* ed. H. Bloom, 2003; B. Leggett, *Late Stevens: The Final Fiction,* 2005; M. Woodland, *Wallace Stevens and the Apocalyptic Mode,* 2005.

TEXTS: *The Collected Poems of Wallace Stevens,* 1954; *Opus Posthumous,* 1957.

PETER QUINCE AT THE CLAVIER[1]

I

Just as my fingers on these keys
Make music, so the selfsame sounds
On my spirit make a music, too.

Music is feeling, then, not sound;
And thus it is that what I feel,
Here in this room, desiring you,

[1]In Shakespeare's *A Midsummer Night's Dream,* Peter Quince (a carpenter) attempts, with little success, to direct a group in putting on a play. Clavier: the keyboard of a musical instrument, such as a harmonium (reed organ) or harpsichord.

Thinking of your blue-shadowed silk,
Is music. It is like the strain
Waked in the elders by Susanna.[2]

Of a green evening, clear and warm,
She bathed in her still garden, while
The red-eyed elders watching, felt

The basses of their beings throb
In witching chords, and their thin blood
Pulse pizzicati[3] of Hosanna.[4]

II

In the green water, clear and warm,
Susanna lay.
She searched
The touch of springs,
And found
Concealed imaginings.
She sighed,
For so much melody.

Upon the bank, she stood
In the cool
Of spent emotions.
She felt, among the leaves,
The dew
Of old devotions.

She walked upon the grass,
Still quavering.
The winds were like her maids,
On timid feet,
Fetching her woven scarves,
Yet wavering.

A breath upon her hand
Muted the night.
She turned—
A cymbal crashed,
And roaring horns.

[2]A reference to the story of Daniel and Susanna in the Apocrypha of the Bible. Two elders were obsessed with lust for Susanna. When rejected by her they falsely charged her with fornication. When they were questioned by Daniel their lies were exposed, and they were put to death.
[3]Musical notes made when the strings of an instrument such as a harpsichord are plucked.
[4]A cry of adoration or praise.

III

Soon, with a noise like tambourines,
Came her attendant Byzantines.[5]

They wondered why Susanna cried
Against the elders by her side;

And as they whispered, the refrain
Was like a willow swept by rain.

Anon, their lamps' uplifted flame
Revealed Susanna and her shame.

And then, the simpering Byzantines
Fled, with a noise like tambourines.

IV

Beauty is momentary in the mind—
The fitful tracing of a portal;
But in the flesh it is immortal.
The body dies; the body's beauty lives.
So evenings die, in their green going,
A wave, interminably flowing.
So gardens die, their meek breath scenting
The cowl of winter, done repenting.
So maidens die, to the auroral
Celebration of a maiden's choral.
Susanna's music touched the bawdy strings
Of those white elders; but, escaping,
Left only Death's ironic scraping.
Now, in its immortality, it plays
On the clear viol of her memory,
And makes a constant sacrament of praise.

1915, 1923

DISILLUSIONMENT OF TEN O'CLOCK

The houses are haunted
By white night-gowns.
None are green,
Or purple with green rings,

[5]Natives of the ancient city of Byzantium (present-day Istanbul, Turkey).

Or green with yellow rings,
Or yellow with blue rings.
None of them are strange,
With socks of lace
And beaded ceintures.[1]
People are not going
To dream of baboons and periwinkles.[2]
Only, here and there, an old sailor,
Drunk and asleep in his boots,
Catches tigers
In red weather.

1915, 1923

SUNDAY MORNING

I

Complacencies of the peignoir,[1] and late
Coffee and oranges in a sunny chair,
And the green freedom of a cockatoo
Upon a rug mingle to dissipate
The holy hush of ancient sacrifice.
She dreams a little, and she feels the dark
Encroachment of that old catastrophe,
As a calm darkens among water-lights.
The pungent oranges and bright, green wings
Seem things in some procession of the dead,
Winding across wide water, without sound.
The day is like wide water, without sound,
Stilled for the passing of her dreaming feet
Over the seas, to silent Palestine,
Dominion of the blood and sepulchre.

II

Why should she give her bounty to the dead?
What is divinity if it can come
Only in silent shadows and in dreams?
Shall she not find in comforts of the sun,
In pungent fruit and bright, green wings, or else
In any balm or beauty of the earth,
Things to be cherished like the thought of heaven?

[1]Belts, sashes. [2]A plant with blue and white flowers.
[1]A woman's negligee, a dressing gown.

Divinity must live within herself:
Passions of rain, or moods in falling snow;
Grievings in loneliness, or unsubdued
Elations when the forest blooms; gusty
Emotions on wet roads on autumn nights;
All pleasures and all pains, remembering
The bough of summer and the winter branch.
These are the measures destined for her soul.

III

Jove[2] in the clouds had his inhuman birth.
No mother suckled him, no sweet land gave
Large-mannered motions to his mythy mind.
He moved among us, as a muttering king,
Magnificent, would move among his hinds,[3]
Until our blood, commingling, virginal,
With heaven, brought such requital to desire
The very hinds discerned it, in a star.
Shall our blood fail? Or shall it come to be
The blood of paradise? And shall the earth
Seem all of paradise that we shall know?
The sky will be much friendlier then than now,
A part of labor and a part of pain,
And next in glory to enduring love,
Not this dividing and indifferent blue.

IV

She says, "I am content when wakened birds,
Before they fly, test the reality
Of misty fields, by their sweet questionings;
But when the birds are gone, and their warm fields
Return no more, where, then, is paradise?"
There is not any haunt of prophecy,
Nor any old chimera[4] of the grave,
Neither the golden underground, nor isle
Melodious, where spirits gat them home,
Nor visionary south, nor cloudy palm
Remote on heaven's hill, that has endured
As April's green endures; or will endure
Like her remembrance of awakened birds,
Or her desire for June and evening, tipped
By the consummation of the swallow's wings.

[2]Jupiter, god of the sky and chief Roman deity.
[3]Servants, farm hands. [4]Illusion, unattainable ideal.

V

She says, "But in contentment I still feel
The need of some imperishable bliss."
Death is the mother of beauty; hence from her,
Alone, shall come fulfilment to our dreams
And our desires. Although she strews the leaves
Of sure obliteration on our paths,
The path sick sorrow took, the many paths
Where triumph rang its brassy phrase, or love
Whispered a little out of tenderness,
She makes the willow shiver in the sun
For maidens who were wont to sit and gaze
Upon the grass, relinquished to their feet.
She causes boys to pile new plums and pears
On disregarded plate. The maidens taste
And stray impassioned in the littering leaves.

VI

Is there no change of death in paradise?
Does ripe fruit never fall? Or do the boughs
Hang always heavy in that perfect sky,
Unchanging, yet so like our perishing earth,
With rivers like our own that seek for seas
They never find, the same receding shores
That never touch with inarticulate pang?
Why set the pear upon those river-banks
Or spice the shores with odors of the plum?
Alas, that they should wear our colors there,
The silken weavings of our afternoons,
And pick the strings of our insipid lutes!
Death is the mother of beauty, mystical,
Within whose burning bosom we devise
Our earthly mothers waiting, sleeplessly.

VII

Supple and turbulent, a ring of men
Shall chant in orgy on a summer morn
Their boisterous devotion to the sun,
Not as a god, but as a god might be,
Naked among them, like a savage source.
Their chant shall be a chant of paradise,
Out of their blood, returning to the sky;
And in their chant shall enter, voice by voice,
The windy lake wherein their lord delights,

The trees, like serafin,[5] and echoing hills,
That choir among themselves long afterward.
They shall know well the heavenly fellowship
Of men that perish and of summer morn.
And whence they came and whither they shall go
The dew upon their feet shall manifest.

VIII

She hears, upon that water without sound,
A voice that cries, "The tomb in Palestine
Is not the porch of spirits lingering.
It is the grave of Jesus, where he lay."
We live in an old chaos of the sun,
Or old dependency of day and night,
Or island solitude, unsponsored, free,
Of that wide water, inescapable.
Deer walk upon our mountains, and the quail
Whistle about us their spontaneous cries;
Sweet berries ripen in the wilderness;
And, in the isolation of the sky,
At evening, casual flocks of pigeons make
Ambiguous undulations as they sink,
Downward to darkness, on extended wings.

1915, 1923

DOMINATION OF BLACK

At night, by the fire,
The colors of the bushes
And of the fallen leaves,
Repeating themselves,
Turned in the room,
Like the leaves themselves
Turning in the wind.
Yes: but the color of the heavy hemlocks
Came striding.
And I remembered the cry of the peacocks.

The colors of their tails
Were like the leaves themselves

[5]Seraphim, heavenly beings.

Turning in the wind,
In the twilight wind.
They swept over the room,
Just as they flew from the boughs of the hemlocks
Down to the ground.
I heard them cry—the peacocks.
Was it a cry against the twilight
Or against the leaves themselves
Turning in the wind,
Turning as the flames
Turned in the fire,
Turning as the tails of the peacocks
Turned in the loud fire,
Loud as the hemlocks
Full of the cry of the peacocks?
Or was it a cry against the hemlocks?

Out of the window,
I saw how the planets gathered
Like the leaves themselves
Turning in the wind.
I saw how the night came,
Came striding like the color of the heavy hemlocks
I felt afraid.
And I remembered the cry of the peacocks.

1916, 1923

THE DEATH OF A SOLDIER

Life contracts and death is expected,
As in a season of autumn.
The soldier falls.

He does not become a three-days personage,
Imposing his separation,
Calling for pomp.

Death is absolute and without memorial,
As in a season of autumn,
When the wind stops,

When the wind stops and, over the heavens,
The clouds go, nevertheless,
In their direction.

1918, 1931

ANECDOTE OF THE JAR

I placed a jar in Tennessee,
And round it was, upon a hill.
It made the slovenly wilderness
Surround that hill.

The wilderness rose up to it,
And sprawled around, no longer wild.
The jar was round upon the ground
And tall and of a port in air.

It took dominion everywhere.
The jar was gray and bare.
It did not give of bird or bush,
Like nothing else in Tennessee.

1919, 1923

A HIGH-TONED OLD CHRISTIAN WOMAN

Poetry is the supreme fiction, madame.
Take the moral law and make a nave[1] of it
And from the nave build haunted heaven. Thus,
The conscience is converted into palms,
Like windy citherns[2] hankering for hymns.
We agree in principle. That's clear. But take
The opposing law and make a peristyle,[3]
And from the peristyle project a masque[4]
Beyond the planets. Thus, our bawdiness,
Unpurged by epitaph, indulged at last,
Is equally converted into palms,
Squiggling like saxophones. And palm for palm,
Madame, we are where we began. Allow,
Therefore, that in the planetary scene
Your disaffected flagellants,[5] well-stuffed,
Smacking their muzzy[6] bellies in parade,
Proud of such novelties of the sublime,
Such tink and tank and tunk-a-tunk-tunk,

[1]The main body of a rectangular church building.
[2]A medieval musical instrument of the guitar family, a zither.
[3]A series of columns around a building or a courtyard.
[4]A festive dance or drama in which the actors wore masks.
[5]Those who flagellate, or whip, themselves in religious ceremonies. Hence those who undergo self-punishment.
[6]Dull-spirited, or befuddled by drink.

May, merely may, madame, whip from themselves
A jovial hullabaloo among the spheres.
This will make widows wince. But fictive things
Wink as they will. Wink most when widows wince.

1922, 1923

THE EMPEROR OF ICE-CREAM

Call the roller of big cigars,
The muscular one, and bid him whip
In kitchen cups concupiscent curds.
Let the wenches dawdle in such dress
As they are used to wear, and let the boys
Bring flowers in last month's newspapers.
Let be be finale of seem.
The only emperor is the emperor of ice-cream.

Take from the dresser of deal,[1]
Lacking the three glass knobs, that sheet
On which she embroidered fantails[2] once
And spread it so as to cover her face.
If her horny feet protrude, they come
To show how cold she is, and dumb.
Let the lamp affix its beam.
The only emperor is the emperor of ice-cream.

1922, 1923

THE IDEA OF ORDER AT KEY WEST

She sang beyond the genius of the sea.
The water never formed to mind or voice,
Like a body wholly body, fluttering
Its empty sleeves; and yet its mimic motion
Made constant cry, caused constantly a cry,
That was not ours although we understood,
Inhuman, of the veritable ocean.

The sea was not a mask. No more was she.
The song and water were not medleyed sound
Even if what she sang was what she heard,
Since what she sang was uttered word by word.
It may be that in all her phrases stirred
The grinding water and the gasping wind;
But it was she and not the sea we heard.

[1] Made of cheap pine or fir planks.   [2] Fan-shaped designs, like the tails of birds.

For she was the maker of the song she sang.
The ever-hooded, tragic-gestured sea
Was merely a place by which she walked to sing.
Whose spirit is this? we said, because we knew
It was the spirit that we sought and knew
That we should ask this often as she sang.

If it was only the dark voice of the sea
That rose, or even colored by many waves;
If it was only the outer voice of sky
And cloud, of the sunken coral water-walled,
However clear, it would have been deep air,
The heaving speech of air, a summer sound
Repeated in a summer without end
And sound alone. But it was more than that,
More even than her voice, and ours, among
The meaningless plungings of water and the wind,
Theatrical distances, bronze shadows heaped
On high horizons, mountainous atmospheres
Of sky and sea.
It was her voice that made
The sky acutest at its vanishing.
She measured to the hour its solitude.
She was the single artificer of the world
In which she sang. And when she sang, the sea,
Whatever self it had, became the self
That was her song, for she was the maker. Then we,
As we beheld her striding there alone,
Knew that there never was a world for her
Except the one she sang and, singing, made.

Ramon Fernandez,[1] tell me, if you know,
Why, when the singing ended and we turned
Toward the town, tell why the glassy lights,
The lights in the fishing boats at anchor there,
As the night descended, tilting the air,
Mastered the night and portioned out the sea,
Fixing emblazoned zones and fiery poles,
Arranging, deepening, enchanting night.

Oh! Blessed rage for order, pale Ramon,
The maker's rage to order words of the sea,
Words of the fragrant portals, dimly-starred,
And of ourselves and of our origins,
In ghostlier demarcations, keener sounds.
1934, 1935

[1]Stevens reported that he chose this name at random: "Ramon Fernandez was not intended to be anyone at all."

OF MODERN POETRY

The poem of the mind in the act of finding
What will suffice. It has not always had
To find: the scene was set; it repeated what
Was in the script.
Then the theatre was changed
To something else. Its past was a souvenir.
It has to be living, to learn the speech of the place.
It has to face the men of the time and to meet
The women of the time. It has to think about war
And it has to find what will suffice. It has
To construct a new stage. It has to be on that stage
And, like an insatiable actor, slowly and
With meditation, speak words that in the ear,
In the delicatest ear of the mind, repeat,
Exactly, that which it wants to hear, at the sound
Of which, an invisible audience listens,
Not to the play, but to itself, expressed
In an emotion as of two people, as of two
Emotions becoming one. The actor is
A metaphysician in the dark, twanging
An instrument, twanging a wiry string that gives
Sounds passing through sudden rightnesses, wholly
Containing the mind, below which it cannot descend,
Beyond which it has no will to rise.
It must
Be the finding of a satisfaction, and may
Be of a man skating, a woman dancing, a woman
Combing. The poem of the act of the mind.

1940, 1942

FINAL SOLILOQUY OF THE INTERIOR PARAMOUR

Light the first light of evening, as in a room
In which we rest and, for small reason, think
The world imagined is the ultimate good.

This is, therefore, the intensest rendezvous.
It is in that thought that we collect ourselves,
Out of all the indifferences, into one thing:

Within a single thing, a single shawl
Wrapped tightly round us, since we are poor, a warmth,
A light, a power, the miraculous influence.

Here, now, we forget each other and ourselves.
We feel the obscurity of an order, a whole,
A knowledge, that which arranged the rendezvous.

Within its vital boundary, in the mind.
We say God and the imagination are one . . .
How high that highest candle lights the dark.

Out of this same light, out of the central mind,
We make a dwelling in the evening air,
In which being there together is enough.

1951, 1953

THE PLAIN SENSE OF THINGS

After the leaves have fallen, we return
To a plain sense of things. It is as if
We had come to an end of the imagination,
Inanimate in an inert savoir.

It is difficult even to choose the adjective
For this blank cold, this sadness without cause.
The great structure has become a minor house.
No turban walks across the lessened floors.

The greenhouse never so badly needed paint.
The chimney is fifty years old and slants to one side.
A fantastic effort has failed, a repetition
In a repetitiousness of men and flies.

Yet the absence of the imagination had
Itself to be imagined. The great pond,
The plain sense of it, without reflections, leaves,
Mud, water like dirty glass, expressing silence

Of a sort, silence of a rat come out to see,
The great pond and its waste of the lilies, all this
Had to be imagined as an inevitable knowledge,
Required, as a necessity requires.

1952, 1954

OF MERE BEING[1]

The palm at the end of the mind,
Beyond the last thought, rises
In the bronze decor,

[1]This is sometimes referred to as "the last poem Stevens wrote," Actually, it is one of several unpublished poems that were found after his death in 1955 and published in *Opus Posthumous* in 1957.

A gold-feathered bird
Sings in the palm, without human meaning,
Without human feeling, a foreign song.

You know then that it is not the reason
That makes us happy or unhappy.
The bird sings. Its feathers shine.

The palm stands on the edge of space.
The wind moves slowly in the branches.
The bird's fire-fangled feathers dangle down.

1957

William Carlos Williams
1883–1963

Along with nineteenth-century Russian playwright Anton Chekhov, William Carlos Williams is one of the two most famous doctors in modern literary history. He was also perhaps the most influential source for U.S. poetry of the second half of the twentieth century. Williams was born in Rutherford, New Jersey, in 1883 and died there in 1963. Throughout his career he often emphasized things American and working class, belying his international and privileged background. His father was British and his mother was the product of Basque and European Jewish descent by way of Puerto Rico. As a child, Williams was schooled in Geneva and Paris, and he attended high school in New York City. In 1902 he was admitted to medical school at the University of Pennsylvania. He did his internship in New York City, studied pediatrics for a year in Leipzig, and then returned to Rutherford, where he practiced medicine for the rest of his career.

By the time he got to the University of Pennsylvania, Williams had developed an interest in writing poetry and was writing a lot of it, mostly in imitation of the English Romantics. While at Penn, he met the poets Ezra Pound and Hilda Doolittle (also known as H.D.). Williams's relationship with Pound was intense, lifelong, and often antagonistic; he often spoke of his life as being divided into "Before Pound" and "After Pound." After graduating from medical school, Williams continued to write poems in the moments between patients, and he published his first volume of poetry, Poems *(1909), at his own expense (at a cost of fifty dollars). It was a thin volume of imitative verse that sold only "about four copies" at thirty-five cents each, but it was the first of the more than forty volumes of stories, novels, plays, essays, and poetry that were to come. In 1913 he published a second volume of verse,* The Tempers, *followed by* Al Que Quiere! *(1917),* Kora in Hell *(1920), and* Sour Grapes *(1921). In 1923 he published* Spring and All, *which contained some of his most anthologized poems, including "Spring and All" and "The Red Wheelbarrow," poems whose spare images exemplified Williams's famous dictum, "No ideas but in things." Collected editions of his poems appeared in 1934 and 1938. His most ambitious work,* Paterson, *was an epic poem, a montage of images and themes mixed with the details of American history, published in installments: the first book in 1946, the sixth, posthumously, in 1963.*

Williams famously disagreed with some of his most famous contemporaries. He disparaged T. S. Eliot and Ezra Pound for their expatriation, their elitist allusiveness, and their preference for dead European literature rather than the material world, calling Eliot's The Waste Land *(1922) "the great catastrophe." Like the nineteenth-century U.S. poet Walt Whitman, Williams was committed to celebrating a multicultural America, and like his older contemporary Robert Frost, he remained convinced that the universal could only be found in the local. But Williams also had many things in common with the high modernists. Like Pound and Eliot, he demanded hard, clear, concrete images, and he echoed Pound when he wrote in the preface to* Kora in Hell: *"Nothing is good save the new." Like Pound and Eliot, and unlike Frost, Williams spent his poetic career trying to create a sinewy free verse. He found traditional forms to be flaccid and no longer useful, writing in "The Poem as a Field of Action": "I propose sweeping changes from top to bottom of the poetic structure. . . . I say we are through with the iambic pentameter as presently conceived . . . through with the measured quatrain, the staid concatenations of sounds in the usual stanza, the sonnet." Williams's most famous contributions to the development of twentieth-century free verse are "the variable foot," and a flexible use of three-line stanzas, both of which he uses extensively in his important late poem "Asphodel, That Greeny Flower."*

The differences between Pound and Eliot on the one side and Williams on the other have been emphasized by the many later poets who claim Williams as their dominant influence. Black Mountain poets like Charles Olson and Robert Creeley and Beat poets like Allen Ginsberg explicitly reject the dominating early twentieth-century influence of Pound and Eliot and embrace Williams as a neglected giant. They tend to emphasize Williams's localism, his concrete language, and his supple forms. These later poets' specific opposition of Williams to Pound and Eliot has tended to exaggerate their poetic differences, and has sometimes confused the literary and the political. Postwar poets may have found in Williams a poet with modernist techniques whose democratic tendencies and working class affinities were much more palatable than Pound's and Eliot's frequent facism. Many of the literary differences among Williams and Pound and Eliot are divergences of degree rather than kind, and Williams's egalitarian outlook has often been overstated. Parts of Paterson *and a poem like "To Elsie" show the same kind of elitism that characterized most Anglo-American modernism.*

Due primarily to the critical dominance of Pound and Eliot in the first half of the twentieth century, Williams, until the last decade of his life, often saw himself as the great neglected American poet. Common readers had shunned him and erudite critics had scorned him. But since the 1950s, Williams's influence has been tremendous, and his work has drawn the serious poetic and scholarly attention that eluded him for most of his life.

FURTHER READING: *The Autobiography of William Carlos Williams,* 1951; *The Selected Letters of William Carlos Williams,* ed. J. Thirwall, 1957, 1985; A. Ostrom, *The Poetic World of William Carlos Williams,* 1966; T. Whitaker, *William Carlos Williams,* 1968; J. Guimond, *The Art of William Carlos Williams,* 1968; J. Breslin, *William Carlos Williams: An American Artist,* 1970; M. Weaver, *William Carlos Williams: The American Background,* 1971; J. Mazzaro, *William Carlos Williams: The Later-Poems,* 1973; R. Coles, *William Carlos Williams: The Knack of Survival in America,* 1975; R. Doyle, *William Carlos Williams and the American Poem,* 1982; H. Sayre, *The Visual Art of William Carlos Williams,* 1983; S. Cushman, *William Carlos Williams and the Meanings of Measure,* 1985; *William Carlos Williams,* ed. H. Bloom, 1986; C. MacGowan, *William Carlos Williams's Early Poetry: The Visual Arts,* 1987; P. Schmidt, *William Carlos Williams, the Arts, and Literary Tradition,* 1988; A. Fisher-Wirth, *William Carlos Williams and Autobiography,* 1989; J. Riddell, *The Inverted Bell: Modernism and the Counter-Poetics of*

William Carlos Williams, 1991; D. Markos, *Ideas in Things: The Poems of William Carlos Williams,* 1994; D. Morris, *The Writings of William Carlos Williams: Publicity for the Self,* 1995; S. Koehler, *Countries of the Mind: The Poetry of William Carlos Williams,* 1998; *William Carlos Williams and the Language of Poetry,* ed. B. Hatlen and D. Tryphonopoulos, 2002.

TEXTS: *The Collected Poems of William Carlos Williams,* Vol. I, ed. A. Litz and C. MacGowan, 1986; *The Collected Poems of William Carlos Williams,* Vol. II, ed. C. MacGowan, 1988.

CON BRIO[1]

Miserly, is the best description of that poor fool
Who holds Lancelot to have been a morose fellow,
Dolefully brooding over the events which had naturally to follow
The high time of his deed with Guinevere.[2]
He has a sick historical sight, if I judge rightly,
To believe any such thing as that ever occurred.
But, by the god of blood, what else is it that has deterred
Us all from an out and out defiance of fear
But this same perdamnable miserliness,
Which cries about our necks how we shall have less and less
Than we have now if we spend too wantonly?
Bah, this sort of slither is below contempt!
In the same vein we should have apple trees exempt
From bearing anything but pink blossoms all the year,
Fixed permanent lest their bellies wax unseemly, and the dear
Innocent days of them be wasted quite.
How can we have less? Have we not the deed?
Lancelot thought little, spent his gold and rode to fight
Mounted, if God was willing, on a good steed.

1913

THE YOUNG HOUSEWIFE

At ten A.M. the young housewife
moves about in negligee behind
the wooden walls of her husband's house.
I pass solitary in my car.

Then again she comes to the curb
to call the ice-man, fish-man, and stands
shy, uncorseted, tucking in
stray ends of hair, and I compare her
to a fallen leaf.

[1]Italian: With Vigor. [2]The wife of King Arthur; she committed adultery with Sir Lancelot.

The noiseless wheels of my car
rush with a crackling sound over
dried leaves as I bow and pass smiling.

1916

PASTORAL

When I was younger
it was plain to me
I must make something of myself.
Older now
I walk back streets
admiring the houses
of the very poor:
roof out of line with sides
the yards cluttered
with old chicken wire, ashes,
furniture gone wrong;
the fences and outhouses
built of barrel-staves
and parts of boxes, all,
if I am fortunate,
smeared a bluish green
that properly weathered
pleases me best
of all colors.
No one

will believe this
of vast import to the nation.

1917

TRACT

I will teach you my townspeople
how to perform a funeral—
for you have it over a troop
of artists—
unless one should scour the world—
you have the ground sense necessary.

See! the hearse leads.
I begin with a design for a hearse.
For Christ's sake not black—
nor white either—and not polished!

Let it be weathered—like a farm wagon—
with gilt wheels (this could be
applied fresh at small expense)
or no wheels at all:
a rough dray[1] to drag over the ground.

Knock the glass out!
My God—glass, my townspeople!
For what purpose? Is it for the dead
to look out or for us to see
how well he is housed or to see
the flowers or the lack of them—
or what?
To keep the rain and snow from him?
He will have a heavier rain soon:
pebbles and dirt and what not.
Let there be no glass—
and no upholstery, phew!
and no little brass rollers
and small easy wheels on the bottom—
my townspeople what are you thinking of?

A rough plain hearse then
with gilt wheels and no top at all.
On this the coffin lies
by its own weight.

No wreaths please—
especially no hot house flowers.
Some common memento is better,
something he prized and is known by:
his old clothes—a few books perhaps—
God knows what! You realize
how we are about these things
my townspeople—
something will be found—anything
even flowers if he had come to that.
So much for the hearse.

For heaven's sake though see to the driver!
Take off the silk hat; In fact
that's no place at all for him—
up there unceremoniously
dragging our friend out to his own dignity!
Bring him down—bring him down!
Low and inconspicuous! I'd not have him ride
on the wagon at all—damn him—
the undertaker's understrapper!

[1]A low cart, without sides or wheels, a sledge.

Let him hold the reins
and walk at the side
and inconspicuously too!

Then briefly as to yourselves:
Walk behind—as they do in France,
seventh class, or if you ride
Hell take curtains! Go with some show
of inconvenience; sit openly—
to the weather as to grief.
Or do you think you can shut grief in?
What—from us? We who have perhaps
nothing to lose? Share with us
share with us—it will be money
in your pockets.
Go now
I think you are ready.

1916, 1917

DANSE RUSSE[1]

If when my wife is sleeping
and the baby and Kathleen[2]
are sleeping
and the sun is a flame-white disc
in silken mists
above shining trees,—
if I in my north room
dance naked, grotesquely
before my mirror
waving my shirt round my head
and singing softly to myself:
"I am lonely, lonely.
I was born to be lonely,
I am best so!"
If I admire my arms, my face,
my shoulders, flanks, buttocks
against the yellow drawn shades,—

Who shall say I am not
the happy genius[3] of my household?

1916, 1917

[1]French: Russian Dance. [2]Kathleen McBride, nursemaid for the Williams children.
[3]Distinctive local spirit.

QUEEN-ANNE'S-LACE[1]

Her body is not so white as
anemone petals nor so smooth—nor
so remote a thing. It is a field
of the wild carrot taking
the field by force; the grass
does not raise above it.
Here is no question of whiteness,
white as can be, with a purple mole
at the center of each flower.
Each flower is a hand's span
of her whiteness. Wherever
his hand has lain there is
a tiny purple blemish. Each part
is a blossom under his touch
to which the fibres of her being
stem one by one, each to its end,
until the whole field is a
white desire, empty, a single stem,
a cluster, flower by flower,
a pious wish to whiteness gone over—
or nothing.

1920, 1921

SPRING AND ALL

By the road to the contagious hospital
under the surge of the blue
mottled clouds driven from the
northeast—a cold wind. Beyond, the
waste of broad, muddy fields
brown with dried weeds, standing and fallen

patches of standing water
the scattering of tall trees

All along the road the reddish
purplish, forked, upstanding, twiggy
stuff of bushes and small trees
with dead, brown leaves under them
leafless vines—

Lifeless in appearance, sluggish
dazed spring approaches—

[1]A wild carrot, which has clusters of white flowers often with a purple blossom in the center.

They enter the new world naked,
cold, uncertain of all
save that they enter. All about them
the cold, familiar wind—

Now the grass, tomorrow
the stiff curl of wildcarrot leaf

One by one objects are defined—
It quickens: clarity, outline of leaf

But now the stark dignity of
entrance—Still, the profound change
has come upon them: rooted, they
grip down and begin to awaken
1923

TO ELSIE

The pure products of America
go crazy—
mountain folk from Kentucky

or the ribbed north end of
Jersey
with its isolate lakes and

valleys, its deaf-mutes, thieves
old names
and promiscuity between

devil-may-care men who have taken
to railroading
out of sheer lust of adventure—

and young slatterns, bathed
in filth
from Monday to Saturday

to be tricked out that night
with gauds
from imaginations which have no

peasant traditions to give them
character
but flutter and flaunt

sheer rags—succumbing without
emotion
save numbed terror

under some hedge of choke-cherry
or viburnum—
which they cannot express—

Unless it be that marriage
perhaps
with a dash of Indian blood

will throw up a girl so desolate
so hemmed round
with disease or murder

that she'll be rescued by an
agent—
reared by the state and
sent out at fifteen to work in
some hard-pressed
house in the suburbs—

some doctor's family, some Elsie—
voluptuous water
expressing with broken

brain the truth about us—
her great
ungainly hips and flopping breasts

addressed to cheap
jewelry
and rich young men with fine eyes

as if the earth under our feet
were
an excrement of some sky

and we degraded prisoners
destined
to hunger until we eat filth

while the imagination strains
after deer
going by fields of goldenrod in

the stifling heat of September
Somehow
it seems to destroy us

It is only in isolate flecks that
something
is given off

No one
to witness
and adjust, no one to drive the car
1923

THE RED WHEELBARROW

so much depends
upon

a red wheel
barrow

glazed with rain
water

beside the white
chickens
1923

AT THE BALL GAME

The crowd at the ball game
is moved uniformly

by a spirit of uselessness
which delights them—

all the exciting detail
of the chase

and the escape, the error
the flash of genius—

all to no end save beauty
the eternal—

So in detail they, the crowd,
are beautiful

for this
to be warned against

saluted and defied—
It is alive, venomous

it smiles grimly
its words cut—

The flashy female with her
mother, gets it—

The Jew gets it straight—it
is deadly, terrifying—

It is the Inquisition, the
Revolution

It is beauty itself
that lives

day by day in them
idly—

This is
the power of their faces

It is summer, it is the solstice[1]
the crowd is

cheering, the crowd is laughing
in detail

permanently, seriously
without thought

1923

BETWEEN WALLS

the back wings
of the

hospital where
nothing

will grow lie
cinders

[1]The beginning of summer, around June 22.

in which shine
the broken

pieces of a green
bottle

1934

THIS IS JUST TO SAY

I have eaten
the plums
that were in
the icebox

and which
you were probably
saving
for breakfast

Forgive me
they were delicious
so sweet
and so cold

1934

THE YACHTS

contend in a sea which the land partly encloses
shielding them from the too-heavy blows
of an ungoverned ocean which when it chooses

tortures the biggest hulls, the best man knows
to pit against its beatings, and sinks them pitilessly.
Mothlike in mists, scintillant in the minute

brilliance of cloudless days, with broad bellying sails
they glide to the wind tossing green water
from their sharp prows while over them the crew crawls

ant-like, solicitously grooming them, releasing,
making fast as they turn, lean far over and having
caught the wind again, side by side, head for the mark.

In a well guarded arena of open water surrounded by
lesser and greater craft which, sycophant, lumbering
and flittering follow them, they appear youthful, rare

as the light of a happy eye, live with the grace
of all that in the mind is fleckless, free and
naturally to be desired. Now the sea which holds them

is moody, lapping their glossy sides, as if feeling
for some slightest flaw but fails completely.
Today no race. Then the wind comes again. The yachts

move, jockeying for a start, the signal is set and they
are off. Now the waves strike at them but they are too
well made, they slip through, though they take in canvas.

Arms with hands grasping seek to clutch at the prows.
Bodies thrown recklessly in the way are cut aside.
It is a sea of faces about them in agony, in despair

until the horror of the race dawns staggering the mind,
the whole sea become an entanglement of watery bodies
lost to the world bearing what they cannot hold. Broken,

beaten, desolate, reaching from the dead to be taken up
they cry out, failing, failing! their cries rising
in waves still as the skillful yachts pass over.

1935

THESE

are the desolate, dark weeks
when nature in its barrenness
equals the stupidity of man.

The year plunges into night
and the heart plunges
lower than night

to an empty, windswept place
without sun, stars or moon
but a peculiar light as of thought

that spins a dark fire—
whirling upon itself until,
in the cold, it kindles

to make a man aware of nothing
that he knows, not loneliness
itself—Not a ghost but

would be embraced—emptiness,
despair—(They
whine and whistle) among

the flashes and booms of war;
houses of whose rooms
the cold is greater than can be thought,

the people gone that we loved,
the beds lying empty, the couches
damp, the chairs unused—

Hide it away somewhere
out of the mind, let it get roots
and grow, unrelated to jealous
ears and eyes—for itself
In this mine they come to dig—all.
Is this the counterfoil to sweetest

music? The source of poetry that
seeing the clock stopped, says,
The clock has stopped

that ticked yesterday so well?
and hears the sound of lakewater
splashing—that is now stone.

1938

SEAFARER

The sea will wash in
but the rocks—jagged ribs
riding the cloth of foam
or a knob or pinnacles
with gannets[1]—
are the stubborn man.

He invites the storm, he
lives by it! instinct
with fears that are not fears
but prickles of ecstasy,
a secret liquor, a fire

[1]Large seabirds.

that inflames his blood to
coldness so that the rocks
seem rather to leap
at the sea than the sea
to envelop them. They strain
forward to grasp ships
or even the sky itself that
bends down to be torn
upon them. To which he says,
It is I! who am the rocks!
Without me nothing laughs.
1948

LANDSCAPE WITH THE FALL OF ICARUS

According to Brueghel[1]
when Icarus fell
it was spring
a farmer was ploughing
his field
the whole pageantry

of the year was
awake tingling
near

the edge of the sea
concerned
with itself

sweating in the sun
that melted
the wings' wax

unsignificantly
off the coast
there was

a splash quite unnoticed
this was
Icarus drowning
1960, 1962

[1]Pieter Brueghel (1525?–1569), Flemish artist whose painting "Landscape with the Fall of Icarus" (1555?) displays just such a pastoral scene as Williams describes.

Robinson Jeffers 1887–1962

Robinson Jeffers's disturbing narrations of the decay of modern culture have marked him as one of the misanthropes of American literature, a "poet of inhumanism." He saw humankind as fatally detached from nature and morbidly pursuing material goods and sensual pleasure. Little in Jeffers's early life foreshadowed his pessimistic vision of people and society. He was born to a comfortably prosperous family in Pittsburgh, Pennsylvania. His father, a Presbyterian preacher and theologian, tutored him in languages, the classics, and the Bible and sent him to school in Switzerland and Germany. After his graduation from college, Jeffers briefly studied for an M.A. in literature, attended medical school for three years, and then studied forestry and the law. When a modest inheritance freed him from the necessity of earning a living, he settled near Monterey, California, on what he called the "future-ridden coast," a land "pregnant with dreams." There he built a stone house and tower overlooking the Pacific and withdrew from the world to write poetry.

Jeffers's early work, Flagons and Apples *(1912) and* Californians *(1916), was conventional and undistinguished. In 1924, he published* Tamar, and Other Poems, *a volume whose desolate reflections on the futility of human aspirations brought Jeffers his first recognition. In volumes that soon followed,* The Woman at Point Sur *(1927),* Cawdor *(1928),* Dear Judas *(1929), and through such later works as* The Double Axe *(1948),* Hungerfield *(1952), and* The Beginning of the End *(1963), he reiterated his denunciation of modern life.*

The long, melodic lines of his free-verse and blank-verse poems were Whitmanesque, yet Jeffers's poetic aim was not "to open up new fields for poetry, but only to reclaim old freedom." His ideas were formed by the tragic vision of life he had absorbed from classical literature and by the deterministic doctrines of late nineteenth-century science. Ultimately he came to foresee with pleasure the eventual destruction of humankind, a species that, to Jeffers, had long since cast off its divinity and had become merely "the animals Christ was rumored to have died for."

FURTHER READING: *The Collected Poetry of Robinson Jeffers,* ed. T. Hunt, Vol. I, 1988, Vol. II, 1990, Vol. III, 1991; *The Selected Letters of Robinson Jeffers, 1897–1962,* ed. A. Ridgeway, 1968; L. Powell, *Robinson Jeffers: The Man and His Work,* 1932, 1934, 1940; R. Gilbert, *Shine, Perishing Republic: Robinson Jeffers and the Tragic Sense in Modern Poetry,* 1936; R. Squires, *The Loyalties of Robinson Jeffers,* 1956, 1963; M. Monjian, *Robinson Jeffers: A Study in Inhumanism,* 1958; F. Carpenter, *Robinson Jeffers,* 1962; M. Bennet, *The Stone Mason of Tor House,* 1966; Brother Antoninus (W. Everson), *Robinson Jeffers: Fragments of an Older Fury,* 1968; A. Coffin, *Robinson Jeffers: Poet of Inhumanism,* 1970; R. Brophy, *Robinson Jeffers: Myth, Ritual, and Symbol in His Narrative Poems,* 1973; J. Shebl, *In This Wild Water,* 1976; W. Nolte, *Rock and Hawk: Robinson Jeffers and the Romantic Agony,* 1978; R. Zaller, *The Cliffs of Solitude: A Reading of Robinson Jeffers,* 1983; J. Karman, *Robinson Jeffers: Poet of California,* 1987; W. Everson, *The Excesses of God,* 1988; *Critical Essays on Robinson Jeffers,* ed. J. Karman, 1990; *Centennial Essays for Robinson Jeffers,* ed. R. Zaller, 1991; *Robinson Jeffers: Dimensions of a Poet,* ed. R. Brophy, 1995; T. Hunt, *Robinson Jeffers and a Galaxy of Writers,* 1995; T. Beers, ". . . *a thousand graceful subtleties,*" 1995; J. Cusatis, *The Life I Could Write: The Personal and Artistic Integrity of Robinson Jeffers,* 2003.

TEXT: *The Selected Poetry of Robinson Jeffers,* 1959.

BOATS IN A FOG

Sports and gallantries, the stage, the arts, the antics of dancers,
The exuberant voices of music,
Have charm for children but lack nobility; it is bitter earnestness
That makes beauty; the mind
Knows, grown adult.
A sudden fog-drift muffled the ocean,
A throbbing of engines moved in it,
At length, a stone's throw out, between the rocks and the vapor,
One by one moved shadows
Out of the mystery, shadows, fishing-boats, trailing each other
Following the cliff for guidance,
Holding a difficult path between the peril of the sea-fog
And the foam on the shore granite.
One by one, trailing their leader, six crept by me,
Out of the vapor and into it,
The throb of their engines subdued by the fog, patient and cautious,
Coasting all round the peninsula
Back to the buoys in Monterey[1] harbor. A flight of pelicans
Is nothing lovelier to look at;
The flight of the planets is nothing nobler; all the arts lose virtue
Against the essential reality
Of creatures going about their business among the equally
Earnest elements of nature.

1925

HURT HAWKS

I

The broken pillar of the wing jags from the clotted shoulder,
The wing trails like a banner in defeat,
No more to use the sky forever but live with famine
And pain a few days: cat nor coyote
Will shorten the week of waiting for death, there is game without talons.
He stands under the oak-bush and waits
The lame feet of salvation; at night he remembers freedom
And flies in a dream, the dawns ruin it.
He is strong and pain is worse to the strong, incapacity is worse.
The curs of the day come and torment him
At distance, no one but death the redeemer will humble that head,
The intrepid readiness, the terrible eyes.

[1]In California.

The wild God of the world is sometimes merciful to those
That ask mercy, not often to the arrogant.
You do not know him, you communal people, or you have forgotten him;
Intemperate and savage, the hawk remembers him;
Beautiful and wild, the hawks, and men that are dying, remember him.

II

I'd sooner, except the penalties, kill a man than a hawk; but the great
  redtail
Had nothing left but unable misery
From the bones too shattered for mending, the wing that trailed under his
  talons when he moved.
We had fed him six weeks, I gave him freedom,
He wandered over the foreland hill and returned in the evening, asking
  for death,
Not like a beggar, still eyed with the old
Implacable arrogance. I gave him the lead gift in the twilight. What fell was
  relaxed,
Owl-downy, soft feminine feathers; but what
Soared: the fierce rush: the night-herons by the flooded river cried fear at
  its rising
Before it was quite unsheathed from reality.

1928

SHINE, PERISHING REPUBLIC

While this America settles in the mould of its vulgarity, heavily thickening to
  empire,
And protest, only a bubble in the molten mass, pops and sighs out, and the
  mass hardens,

I sadly smiling remember that the flower fades to make fruit, the fruit rots to
  make earth.
Out of the mother; and through the spring exultances, ripeness and
  decadence; and home to the mother.

You making haste haste on decay: not blameworthy; life is good, be it
  stubbornly long or suddenly
A mortal splendor: meteors are not needed less than mountains: shine,
  perishing republic.

But for my children, I would have them keep their distance from the
  thickening center; corruption
Never has been compulsory, when the cities lie at the monster's feet there
  are left the mountains.

And boys, be in nothing so moderate as in love of man, a clever servant, insufferable master.
There is the trap that catches noblest spirits, that caught—they say—God, when he walked on earth.

1930

Marianne Moore 1887–1972

By the end of her life, Marianne Moore was well-known as one of America's most devoted baseball fans and as one of its premier poets. Her devotion to baseball won her the honor of throwing out the first ball at the opening of the 1968 season at Yankee Stadium in New York. Her poetic descriptions of exotic animals and plants, and things as varied as steamrollers and quartz crystal clocks won her numerous awards and the distinction of being described as "The World's Greatest Living Observer."

She spent her childhood near St. Louis, Missouri, and in Carlisle, Pennsylvania. After graduating from Bryn Mawr College in 1909, she returned to Carlisle, where she taught for four years in a U.S. government school for American Indians. In 1916, having already begun to distinguish herself as one of the nation's innovative "new poets," she moved east, eventually settling in New York City. She worked in the New York Public Library and then became editor of a literary magazine, The Dial, *all the while developing her meticulous and subtle poetic craft. Her first book, Poems (1921), was published in England by her friends and without her knowledge. In 1924 her prize-winning volume* Observations *appeared, followed by* The Pangolin *(1936),* What Are Years *(1941), and* Nevertheless *(1944). Her* Collected Poems *were published in 1951, and in a single year (1952), she received a Bollingen Prize, a Pulitzer Prize, and a National Book Award for Poetry.*

Marianne Moore was a book reviewer, translator, and essayist, as well as poet, and her sprightly and eccentric ways were, to many, as engaging as her fresh and compact writing. She had an acute eye for detail, and her poetry is marked by movements from "imagistic" portrayals of visible objects to metaphysical reflections. She sprinkled her poetry with quotations, which she compared to "collections of flies in amber." She used near or approximate rhyme and light rhyme—in which the rhyming syllables of words are unaccented. Much of her verse was syllabic, relying on the number of syllables in a poetic line, rather than on a conventional pattern of stress accents, to produce a subdued metrical cadence. As a result, some of her poems display the rhetorical qualities of succinct prose, yet with their carefully controlled forms, their glittering surfaces, and their intellectual complexities they are expressions of an authentic poetic imagination and "lit with piercing glances into the life of things."

FURTHER READING: *The Complete Prose of Marianne Moore,* ed. P. Willis, 1986; J. Slatin, *The Savage's Romance: The Poetry of Marianne Moore,* 1986; G. Schulman, *Marianne Moore: The Poetry of Engagement,* 1986; *Marianne Moore: The Art of a Modernist,* ed. J. Parisi, 1990; C. Molesworth, *Marianne Moore: A Literary Life,* 1990; C. Miller, *Marianne Moore: Questions of Authority,* 1995; L. Leavell, *Marianne Moore and the Visual Arts,* 1995; *The Selected Letters of Marianne Moore,* ed. B. Costello, 1997; E. Joyce, *Cultural Critique and Abstraction: Marianne Moore and the Avant Garde,* 1998; *The Critical Response to Marianne Moore,* ed. E. Gregory, 2003; *Marianne Moore,* ed. H. Bloom, 2004.

TEXTS: The text of "Poetry" is from *Collected Poems,* 1951; all other poems are from *The Complete Poems of Marianne Moore,* 1980.

TO A STEAM ROLLER

The illustration
is nothing to you without the application.
You lack half wit. You crush all the particles down
into close conformity, and then walk back and forth on them.

Sparkling chips of rock
are crushed down to the level of the parent block.
Were not "impersonal judgment in aesthetic
matters, a metaphysical impossibility," you

might fairly achieve
it. As for butterflies, I can hardly conceive
of one's attending upon you, but to question
the congruence of the complement is vain, if it exists.

1915, 1921

THE FISH

wade
through black jade.
Of the crow-blue mussel shells, one keeps
adjusting the ash heaps;
opening and shutting itself like

an
injured fan.
The barnacles which encrust the side
of the wave, cannot hide
there for the submerged shafts of the

sun,
split like spun
glass, move themselves with spotlight swiftness
into the crevices—
in and out, illuminating

the
turquoise sea
of bodies. The water drives a wedge
of iron through the iron edge
of the cliff; whereupon the stars,

pink
rice-grains, ink-
bespattered jellyfish, crabs like green
lilies, and submarine
toadstools, slide each on the other.

All
external
marks of abuse are present on this
defiant edifice—
all the physical features of

ac-
cident—lack
of cornice, dynamite grooves, burns, and
hatchet strokes, these things stand
out on it; the chasm side is
dead.

Repeated
evidence has proved that it can live
on what can not revive
its youth. The sea grows old in it.
1918, 1921

POETRY[1]

I, too, dislike it: there are things that are important beyond
all this fiddle.
Reading it, however, with a perfect contempt for it, one
discovers in
it after all, a place for the genuine.
Hands that can grasp, eyes
that can dilate, hair that can rise
if it must, these things are important not because a

high-sounding interpretation can be put upon them but
because they are
useful. When they become so derivative as to become
unintelligible,
the same thing may be said for all of us, that we
do not admire what
we cannot understand: the bat
holding on upside down or in quest of something to

[1]The text reprinted here is from *Collected Poems* (1951). In a revised version, published in *The Complete Poems* (1967), the poem was reduced to three lines: "I, too, dislike it. / Reading it, however, with a perfect contempt for it, one discovers in / it, after all, a place for the genuine."

eat, elephants pushing, a wild horse taking a roll, a tireless
wolf under
a tree, the immovable critic twitching his skin like a horse
that feels a flea, the baseball
fan, the statistician—
nor is it valid
to discriminate against "business documents and
school-books";[2] all these phenomena are important. One
must make a distinction
however: when dragged into prominence by half poets,
the result is not poetry,
nor till the poets among us can be
"literalists of
the imagination"[3]—above
insolence and triviality and can present

for inspection, "imaginary gardens with real toads in them,"
shall we have
it. In the meantime, if you demand on the one hand,
the raw material of poetry in
all its rawness and
that which is on the other hand
genuine, you are interested in poetry.

1919, 1935

NO SWAN SO FINE

"No water so still as the
dead fountains of Versailles,"[1] No swan,
with swart blind look askance
and gondoliering legs, so fine
as the chintz china one with fawn-
brown eyes and toothed gold
collar on to show whose bird it was.

[2]"Diary of Tolstoy, p. 84: 'Where the boundary between prose and poetry lies, I shall never be able to understand. The question is raised in manuals of style, yet the answer to it lies beyond me. Poetry is verse: prose is not verse. Or else poetry is everything with the exception of business documents and school books.'"—Moore's note. The quotation is from *The Diaries of Leo Tolstoy* (1917).

[3]"Yeats, *Ideas of Good and Evil* (A. H. Bullen, 1903), p. 182. 'The limitation of his view was from the very intensity of his vision; he was a too literal realist of imagination, as others are of nature; and because he believed that the figures seen by the mind's eye, when exalted by inspiration, were "eternal existences," symbols of divine essences, he hated every grace of style that might obscure their lineaments'"—Moore's note. The quotation is from an essay, "William Blake and His Illustrations to the *Divine Comedy*," by William Butler Yeats.

[1]"'There is no water so still as in the dead fountains of Versailles.' Percy Phillip, *New York Times Magazine,* May 10, 1931."—Moore's note.

Lodged in the Louis Fifteenth
candelabrum[2]-tree of cockscomb-
tinted buttons, dahlias, 10 sea urchins, and everlastings,
it perches on the branching foam
of polished sculptured
flowers—at ease and tall. The king is dead.
1932, 1935

THE MIND IS AN ENCHANTING THING

is an enchanted thing
like the glaze on a
katydid-wing
subdivided by sun
till the nettings are legion.
Like Gieseking playing Scarlatti;[1]

like the apteryx-awl[2]
as a beak, or the
kiwi's rain shawl
of haired feathers, the mind
feeling its way as though blind,
walks along with its eyes on the ground.

It has memory's ear
that can hear without
having to hear.
Like the gyroscope's fall,
truly unequivocal
because trued by regnant certainty,

it is a power of
strong enchantment. It
is like the dove-
neck animated by
sun; it is memory's eye;
it's conscientious inconsistency.

It tears off the veil; tears
the temptation, the
mist the heart wears,
from its eyes—if the heart
has a face; it takes apart
dejection. It's fire in the dove-neck's

[2]"A pair of Louis XV candelabra with Dresden figures of swans belonging to Lord Balfour."—Moore's note. The age of Louis XV, King of France (1715–1774), was one of ornate and delicate art.
[1]Walter Gieseking (1895–1956), German pianist; Alessandro Scarlatti (1659–1725), Italian composer.
[2]A flightless bird with a long bill like an awl and hairlike plumage, a kiwi.

iridescence; in the
inconsistencies
of Scarlatti.
Unconfusion submits
its confusion to proof; it's
not a Herod's oath[3] that cannot change.
1943, 1944

IN DISTRUST OF MERITS

Strengthened to live, strengthened to die for
medals and positioned victories?
They're fighting, fighting, fighting the blind
man who thinks he sees,—
who cannot see that the enslaver is
enslaved; the hater, harmed. O shining O
firm star, O tumultuous
ocean lashed till small things go
as they will, the mountainous
wave makes us who look, know

depth. Lost at sea before they fought! O
star of David, star of Bethlehem,
O black imperial lion
of the Lord—emblem
of a risen world—be joined at last, be
joined. There is hate's crown beneath which all is
death; there's love's without which none
is king; the blessed deeds bless
the halo. As contagion
of sickness makes sickness,

contagion of trust can make trust. They're
fighting in deserts and caves, one by
one, in battalions and squadrons;
they're fighting that I
may yet recover from the disease, My
Self; some have it lightly; some will die. "Man's
wolf to man" and we devour
ourselves. The enemy could not
have made a greater breach in our
defenses. One pilot-

[3]King Herod, delighted with Salome's dance, swore to grant her any reward. When she asked for the head of John the Baptist, Herod, out of regard for his oath, had John beheaded. Matthew 14:3–11.

ing a blind man can escape him, but
Job disheartened by false comfort knew
that nothing can be so defeating
as a blind man who
can see. O alive who are dead, who are
proud not to see, O small dust of the earth
that walks so arrogantly,
trust begets power and faith is
an affectionate thing. We
vow, we make this promise

to the fighting—it's a promise—"We'll
never hate black, white, red, yellow, Jew,
Gentile, Untouchable." We are
not competent to
make our vows. With set jaw they are fighting,
fighting, fighting,—some we love whom we know,
some we love but know not—that
hearts may feel and not be numb.
It cures me; or am I what
I can't believe in? Some

in snow, some on crags, some in quicksands,
little by little, much by much, they
are fighting fighting fighting that where
there was death there may
be life. "When a man is prey to anger,
he is moved by outside things; when he holds
his ground in patience patience
patience, that is action or
beauty," the soldier's defense
and hardest armor for

the fight. The world's an orphans' home. Shall
we never have peace without sorrow?
without pleas of the dying for
help that won't come? O
quiet form upon the dust, I cannot
look and yet I must. If these great patient
dyings—all these agonies
and wound bearings and bloodshed—
can teach us how to live, these
dyings were not wasted.

Hate-hardened heart, O heart of iron,
iron is iron till it is rust.
There never was a war that was
not inward; I must
fight till I have conquered in myself what
causes war, but I would not believe it.

I inwardly did nothing.
O Iscariot-like crime!
Beauty is everlasting
and dust is for a time.

1943 1943, 1944

The New Negro 1925

Published in 1925, The New Negro *sought, in the words of its editor Alain Locke, to "document the New Negro culturally and socially,—to register the transformations of the inner and outer life of the Negro in America." In pursuing that mission,* The New Negro *presented the works of many black writers who were living and working in Harlem. By crystallizing their efforts in a single collection, the anthology became the core of the Harlem Renaissance. A selection of works from this pivotal volume are here presented together, rather than in sections devoted to separate authors, in the interest of presenting the Harlem Renaissance writers as they appeared to the literary public of their own time.*

TEXT: *The New Negro, An Interpretation,* 1925.

from *THE NEW NEGRO*

FOREWORD

Alain Locke, Editor[1]

This volume aims to document the New Negro culturally and socially,—to register the transformations of the inner and outer life of the Negro in America that have so significantly taken place in the last few years. There is ample evidence of a New Negro in the latest phases of social change and progress, but still more in the internal world of the Negro mind and spirit. Here in the very heart of the folk-spirit are the essential forces, and folk interpretation is truly vital and representative only in terms of these. Of all the voluminous literature on the Negro, so much is mere external view and commentary that we may warrantably say that nine-tenths of it is *about* the Negro rather than of him, so that it is the Negro problem rather than the Negro that is known and mooted in the general mind. We turn therefore in the other direction to the elements of truest social portraiture, and discover in the artistic self-expression of the Negro to-day a new figure on the national canvas and a new force in the foreground of affairs. Whoever wishes to see the Negro in his essential traits, in the

[1]Alain Locke (1886–1954), best known as editor of *The New Negro,* also published numerous other works on African American art and culture.

full perspective of his achievement and possibilities, must seek the enlightenment of that self-portraiture which the present developments of Negro culture are offering. In these pages, without ignoring either the fact that there are important interactions between the national and the race life, or that the attitude of America toward the Negro is as important a factor as the attitude of the Negro toward America, we have nevertheless concentrated upon self-expression and the forces and motives of self-determination. So far as he is culturally articulate, we shall let the Negro speak for himself.

Yet the New Negro must be seen in the perspective of a New World, and especially of a New America. Europe seething in a dozen centers with emergent nationalities, Palestine full of a renascent Judaism—these are no more alive with the progressive forces of our era than the quickened centers of the lives of black folk. America seeking a new spiritual expansion and artistic maturity, trying to found an American literature, a national art, and national music implies a Negro-American culture seeking the same satisfactions and objectives. Separate as it may be in color and substance, the culture of the Negro is of a pattern integral with the times and with its cultural setting. The achievements of the present generation have eventually made this apparent. Liberal minds to-day cannot be asked to peer with sympathetic curiosity into the darkened Ghetto of a segregated race life. That was yesterday. Nor must they expect to find a mind and soul bizarre and alien as the mind of a savage, or even as naive and refreshing as the mind of the peasant or the child. That too was yesterday, and the day before. Now that there is cultural adolescence and the approach to maturity,—there has come a development that makes these phases of Negro life only an interesting and significant segment of the general American scene.

Until recently, except for occasional discoveries of isolated talent here and there, the main stream of this development has run in the special channels of "race literature" and "race journalism." Particularly as a literary movement, it has gradually gathered momentum in the effort and output of such progressive race periodicals as the *Crisis*[2] under the editorship of Dr. Du Bois and more lately, through the quickening encouragement of Charles Johnson, in the brilliant pages of *Opportunity,* a Journal of Negro Life.[3] But more and more the creative talents of the race have been taken up into the general journalistic, literary and artistic agencies, as the wide range of the acknowledgments of the material here collected will in itself be sufficient to demonstrate. Recently in a project of *The Survey Graphic,*[4] whose Harlem Number of March, 1925, has been taken by kind permission as the nucleus of this book, the whole movement was presented as it is epitomized in the progressive Negro community of the American metropolis. Enlarging this stage we are now presenting the New Negro in a national and even international scope. Although there are few centers that can be pointed out approximating Harlem's significance, the full significance of that even is a racial awakening on a national and perhaps even a world scale.

That is why our comparison is taken with those nascent movements of folk-expression and self-determination which are playing a creative part in the world

[2]The official magazine of the National Association for the Advancement of Colored People, founded, and edited for many years, by W. E. B. Du Bois (1868–1963).

[3]The magazine of the National Urban League, edited by Charles Spurgeon Johnson (1893–1956).

[4]A magazine, founded in 1912, that focused on sociological and political issues and research. The Special issue to which Locke refers was titled "Harlem: Mecca of the New Negro."

to-day. The galvanizing shocks and reactions of the last few years are making by subtle processes of internal reorganization a race out of its own disunited and apathetic elements. A race experience penetrated in this way invariably flowers. As in India, in China, in Egypt, Ireland, Russia, Bohemia, Palestine and Mexico, we are witnessing the resurgence of a people: it has aptly been said,—"For all who read the signs aright, such a dramatic flowering of a new race-spirit is taking place close at home—among American Negroes."

Negro life is not only establishing new contacts and founding new centers, it is finding a new soul. There is a fresh spiritual and cultural focusing. We have, as the heralding sign, an unusual outburst of creative expression. There is a renewed race-spirit that consciously and proudly sets itself apart. Justifiably then, we speak of the offerings of this book embodying these ripening forces as culled from the first fruits of the Negro Renaissance.

1925

VESTIGES

Harlem Sketches

Rudolph Fisher[1]

I

Shepherd! Lead Us

Ezekiel Taylor, preacher of the gospel of Jesus Christ, walked slowly along One Hundred and Thirty-third Street, conspicuously alien. He was little and old and bent. A short, bushy white beard framed his shiny black face and his tieless celluloid collar. A long, greasy, green-black Prince Albert,[2] with lapels frayed and buttons worn through to their metal hung loosely from his shoulders. His trousers were big and baggy and limp, yet not enough so to hide the dejected bend of his knees.

A little boy noted the beard and gibed, "Hey, Santa Claus! 'Tain't Chris'mas yet!" And the little boy's playmates chorused, "Haw, haw! Lookit the colored Santa Claus!"

"For of such is the kingdom of heaven," mused Ezekiel Taylor. No. The kingdom of Harlem. Children turned into mockers. Satan in the hearts of infants. Harlem—city of the devil—outpost of hell.

Darkness settled, like the gloom in the old preacher's heart; darkness an hour late, for these sinners even tinkered with God's time, substituting their "daylight-saving." Wicked, yes. But sad too, as though they were desperately

[1]Rudolph Fisher (1897–1934) was a writer and musician, who also was trained as a physician (in radiology).

[2]A double-breasted coat of the type worn by Albert (1819–1861), the Prince Consort of Britain's Queen Victoria.

warding off the inescapable night of sorrow in which they must suffer for their sins. Harlem. What a field! What numberless souls to save!—These very taunting children who knew not even the simplest of the commandments—

But he was old and alone and defeated. The world had called to his best. It had offered money, and they had gone; first the young men whom he had fathered, whom he had brought up from infancy in his little Southern church; then their wives and children, whom they eventually sent for; and finally their parents, loath to leave their shepherd and their dear, decrepit shacks, but dependent and without choice.

"Whyn't y' come to New York?" old Deacon Gassoway had insisted. "Martin and Eli and Jim Lee and his fambly's all up da' now an' doin' fine. We'll all git together an' start a chu'ch of our own, an' you'll still be pastor an' it'll be jes' same as 'twas hyeh." Full of that hope, he had come. But where were they? He had captained his little ship till it sank; he had clung to a splint and been tossed ashore; but the shore was cold, gray, hard and rock-strewn.

He had been in barren places before but God had been there too. Was Harlem then past hope? Was the connection between this place and heaven broken, so that the servant of God went hungry while little children ridiculed? Into his mind, like a reply, crept an old familiar hymn, and he found himself humming it softly:

The Lord will provide,
The Lord will provide,
In some way or 'nother,
The Lord will provide.
It may not be in your way,
It may not be in mine,
But yet in His own way
The Lord will provide.

Then suddenly, astonished, he stopped, listening. He had not been singing alone—a chorus of voices somewhere near had caught up his hymn. Its volume was gradually increasing. He looked about for a church. There was none. He covered his deaf ear so that it might not handicap his good one. The song seemed to issue from one of the private houses a little way down the street.

He approached with eager apprehension and stood wonderingly before a long flight of brownstone steps leading to an open entrance. The high first floor of the house, that to which the steps led, was brightly lighted, and the three front windows had their panes covered with colored tissue-paper designed to resemble church windows. Strongly, cheeringly the song came out to the listener:

The Lord will provide,
The Lord will provide,
In some way or 'nother,
The Lord will provide.

Ezekiel Taylor hesitated an incredulous moment, then smiling, he mounted the steps and went in.

The Reverend Shackleton Ealey had been inspired to preach the gospel by the draft laws of 1917.[3] He remained in the profession not out of gratitude to its having kept him out of war, but because he found it a far less precarious mode of living than that devoted to poker, black-jack and dice. He was stocky and flat-faced and yellow, with many black freckles and the eyes of a dogfish. And he was clever enough not to conceal his origin, but to make capital out of his conversion from gambler to preacher and to confine himself to those less enlightened groups that thoroughly believed in the possibility of so sudden and complete a transformation.

The inflow of rural folk from the South was therefore fortune, and Reverend Shackleton Ealey spent hours in Pennsylvania station[4] greeting newly arrived migrants, urging them to visit his meeting-place and promising them the satisfaction of "that old-time religion." Many had come—and contributed.

This was prayer-meeting night. Reverend Ealey had his seat on a low platform at the distant end of the double room originally designed for a "parlor." From behind a pulpit-stand improvised out of soap-boxes and covered with calico, he counted his congregation and estimated his profit.

A stranger entered uncertainly, looked about a moment, and took a seat near the door. Reverend Shackleton Ealey appraised him: a little bent-over old man with a bushy white beard and a long Prince Albert coat. Perfect type—fertile soil. He must greet this stranger at the close of the meeting and effusively make him welcome.

But Sister Gassoway was already by the stranger's side, shaking his hand vigorously and with unmistakable joy; and during the next hymn she came over to old man Gassoway and whispered in his ear, whereupon he jumped up wide-eyed, looked around, and made broadly smiling toward the newcomer. Others turned to see, and many, on seeing, began to whisper excitedly into their neighbor's ear and turned to see again. The stranger was occasioning altogether too great a stir. Reverend Ealey decided to pray.

His prayer was a masterpiece. It besought of God protection for His people in a strange and wicked land; it called down His damnation upon those dens of iniquity, the dance halls, the theaters, the cabarets; it berated the poker-sharp, the blackjack player, the dice-roller; it denounced the drunkard, the bootlegger, the dope-peddler; and it ended in a sweeping tirade against the wolf-in-sheep's clothing, whatever his motive might be.

Another hymn and the meeting came to a close.

The stranger was surrounded before Reverend Ealey could reach him. When finally he approached the old preacher with extended hand and hollow-hearted smile, old man Gassoway was saying:

"Yas, suh, Rev'n Taylor, dass jes' whut we goin' do. Start makin' 'rangements tomorrer. Martin an' Jim Lee's over to Ebeneezer, but dey doan like it 'tall. Says hit's too hifalutin for 'em, de way dese Harlem cullud folks wushup; Ain't got no Holy Ghos' in 'em, dass whut. Jes' come in an' set down an' git up an' go out. Never moans, never shouts, never even says 'amen.' Most of us is hyeh, an' we gonna git together an' start us a ch'ch of our own, wid you f' pastor, like we said. Yas, suh. Hyeh's Brother Ealey now. Brother Ealey, dis hyeh's our old preacher Rev'n Taylor. We was jes' tellin' him—"

[3]That is, he became a minister in order to receive an exemption from military service.
[4]A major railway station in New York City.

The Reverend Shackleton Ealey had at last a genuine revelation—that the better-yielding half of his flock was on the wing. An old oath of frustration leaped to his lips—"God—" but he managed to bite it in the middle—"bless you, my brother," he growled.

II

MAJUTAH

It was eleven o'clock at night. Majutah knew that Harry would be waiting on the doorstep downstairs. He knew better than to ring the bell so late—she had warned him. And there was no telephone. Grandmother wouldn't consent to having a telephone in the flat—she thought it would draw lightning. As if every other flat in the house didn't have one, as if lightning would strike all the others and leave theirs unharmed! Grandmother was such a nuisance with her old fogeyisms. If if weren't for her down-home ideas there'd be no trouble getting out now to go to the cabaret with Harry. As it was, Majutah would have to steal down the hall past Grandmother's room in the hope that she would be asleep.

Majutah looked to her attire. The bright red sandals and scarlet stockings, she fancied, made her feet look smaller and her legs bigger. This was desirable, since her black crepe dress, losing in width what style had added to its length, would not permit her to sit comfortably and cross her knees without occasioning ample display of everything below them. Her vanity-case mirror revealed how exactly the long pendant earrings matched her red coral beads and how perfectly becoming the new close bob was, and assured her for the tenth time that Egyptian rouge made her skin look lighter. She was ready.

Into the narrow hallway she tipped, steadying herself against the walls, and slowly approached the outside door at the end. Grandmother's room was the last off the hallway. Majutah reached it, slipped successfully past, and started silently to open the door to freedom.

"Jutie?"

How she hated to be called Jutie! Why couldn't the meddlesome old thing say Madge like everyone else?

"Ma'am?"

"Wha' you goin' dis time o' night?"

"Just downstairs to mail a letter."

"You easin' out mighty quiet, if dat's all you goin' do. Come 'eh. Lemme look at you."

Majutah slipped off her pendants and beads and laid them on the floor. She entered her grandmother's room, standing where the foot of the bed would hide her gay shoes and stockings. Useless precautions. The shrewd old woman inspected her granddaughter a minute in disapproving silence, then asked:

"Well, wha's de letter?"

"Hello, Madge," said Harry. "What held you up? You look mad enough to bite bricks."

"I am. Grandmother, of course. She's a pest. Always nosing and meddling. I'm grown, and the money I make supports both of us, and I'm sick of acting like a kid just to please her."

"How'd you manage?"

"I didn't manage. I just gave her a piece of my mind and came on out."

"Mustn't hurt the old lady's feelings. It's just her way of looking out for you."

"I don't need any looking out for—or advice either!"

"Excuse me. Which way—Happy's or Edmonds'?"

"Edmonds'—darn it!"

"Right."

It was two o'clock in the morning. Majutah's grandmother closed her Bible and turned down the oil lamp by which she preferred to read it. For a long time she sat thinking of Jutie—and of Harlem, this city of Satan. It was Harlem that had changed Jutie—this great, noisy, heartless, crowded place where you lived under the same roof with a hundred people you never knew; where night was alive and morning dead. It was Harlem—those brazen women with whom Jutie sewed, who swore and shimmied and laughed at the suggestion of going to church. Jutie wore red stockings. Jutie wore dresses that looked like night-gowns. Jutie painted her face and straightened her hair, instead of leaving it as God intended. Jutie—lied—often.

And while Madge laughed at a wanton song, her grandmother knelt by her bed and through the sinful babel of the airshaft, through her own silent tears, prayed to God in heaven for Jutie's lost soul.

III

Learnin'

"Too much learnin' ain' good f' nobody. When I was her age I couldn't write my own name."

"You can't write much mo' 'n that now. Too much learnin'! Whoever heard o' sich a thing!"

Anna's father, disregarding experience in arguing with his wife, pressed his point. "Sho they's sich a thing as too much learnin'! 'At gal's gittin' so she don't b'lieve nuthin'!"

"Hmph! Didn't she jes' tell me las' night she didn'b'lieve they ever was any Adam an' Eve?"

"Well, I ain' so sho they ever was any myself! An' one thing is certain: If that gal o' mine wants to keep on studyin' an' go up there to that City College[5] an' learn how to teach school an' be somebody, I'll work my fingers to the bone to help her do it! Now!"

"That ain' what I'm talkin' 'bout. You ain' worked no harder 'n I is to help her git this far. Hyeh she is ready to graduate from high school. Think of it—high school! When we come along they didn' even *have* no high schools. Fus' thing y' know she be so far above us we can't reach her with a fence-rail. Then you'll wish you'd a listened to me. What I says is, she done gone far enough."

"Ain' no sich thing as far enough when you wants to go farther. 'Tain' as if it was gonna cost a whole lot. That's the trouble with you cullud folks now. Git so far an' stop—set down—through—don't want no mo'." Her disgust was boundless. "Y' got too much cotton field in you, that's what!"

[5]Now a part of City University of New York (CUNY).

The father grinned. "They sho' ain' no cotton field in yo' mouth, honey."

"No, they ain't. An' they ain' no need o' all this arguin' either, 'cause all that gal's got to do is come in hyeh right now an' put her arms 'roun' y' neck, an' you'd send her to Europe if she wanted to go!"

"Well, all I says is, when dey gits to denyin' de Bible hit's time to stop 'em."

"Well all *I* says is, if Cousin Sukie an' yo' no 'count brother, Jonathan, can send their gal all the way from Athens to them Howard's[6] an' pay car-fare an' boa'd an' ev'ything, we can send our gal—"

She broke off as a door slammed. There was a rush, a delightful squeal, and both parents were being smothered in a cyclone of embraces by a wildly jubilant daughter.

"Mummy! Daddy! I won it! I won it!"

"What under the sun—?"

"The scholarship, Mummy! The scholarship!"

"No!"

"Yes, I did! I can go to Columbia! I can go to Teachers College![7] Isn't it great?"

Anna's mother turned triumphantly to her husband; but he was beaming at his daughter.

"You sho' is yo' daddy's chile. Teachers College! Why, that's wha' I been wantin' you to go all along!"

IV

REVIVAL

Rare sight in a close-built, top-heavy city—space. A wide open lot, extending along One Hundred and Thirty-eighth Street almost from Lenox to Seventh Avenue; baring the mangy backs of a long row of One Hundred and Thirty-ninth Street houses; disclosing their gaping, gasping windows, their shameless strings of half-laundered rags, which gulp up what little air the windows seek to inhale. Occupying the Lenox Avenue end of the lot, the so-called Garvey tabernacle, wide, low, squat, with its stingy little entrance; occupying the other, the church tent where summer camp meetings are held.

Pete and his buddy, Lucky, left their head-to-head game of coon-can as darkness came on. Time to go out—had to save gas. Pete went to the window and looked down at the tent across the street.

"Looks like the side show of a circus. Ever been in?"

"Not me. I'm a preacher's son—got enough o' that stuff when I was a kid and couldn't protect myself."

"Ought to be a pretty good show when some o' them old-time sisters get happy. Too early for the cabarets; let's go in a while, just for the hell of it."

"You sure are hard up for somethin' to do."

"Aw, come on. Somethin' funny's bound to happen. You might even get religion, you dam' bootlegger."

[6]Probably a reference to Howard University, a historically black university, founded in 1867 as a part of Reconstruction, located in Washington, D.C.

[7]Teachers College of Columbia University, in New York City.

Lucky grinned. "Might meet some o' my customers, you mean."

Through the thick, musty heat imprisoned by the canvas shelter a man's voice rose, leading a spiritual. Other voices chimed eagerly in, some high, clear, sweet; some low, mellow, full,—all swelling, rounding out the refrain till it filled the place, so that it seemed the flimsy walls and roof must soon be torn from their moorings and swept aloft with the song:

Where you running, sinner?
Where you running, I say?
Running from the fire—
You can't cross here!

The preacher stood waiting for the song to melt away. There was a moment of abysmal silence, into which the thousand blasphemies filtering in from outside dropped unheeded.

The preacher was talking in deep, impressive tones. One old patriarch was already supplementing each statement with a matter-of-fact "amen!" of approval.

The preacher was describing hell. He was enumerating without exception the horrors that befall the damned: maddening thirst for the drunkard; for the gambler, insatiable flame, his own greed devouring his soul. The preacher's voice no longer talked—it sang; mournfully at first, monotonously up and down, up and down—a chant in minor mode; then more intensely, more excitedly; now fairly strident.

The amens of approval were no longer matter-of-fact, perfunctory. They were quick, spontaneous, escaping the lips of their own accord; they were frequent and loud and began to come from the edges of the assembly instead of just the front rows. The old men cried, "Help him, Lord!" "Preach the word!" "Glory!" taking no apparent heed of the awfulness of the description, and the old women continuously moaned aloud, nodding their bonneted heads, or swaying rhythmically forward and back in their seats.

Suddenly the preacher stopped, leaving the old men and old women still noisy with spiritual momentum. He stood motionless till the last echo of approbation subsided, then repeated the text from which his discourse had taken origin; repeated it in a whisper, lugubrious, hoarse, almost inaudible: "'In—hell—'" paused, then without warning, wildly shrieked, "'In hell—'" stopped—returned to his hoarse whisper—"'he lifted up his eyes. . . .'"

"What the hell you want to leave for?" Pete complained when he and Lucky reached the sidewalk. "That old bird would 'a' coughed up his gizzard in two more minutes. What's the idea?"

"Aw hell—I don't know.—You think that stuff's funny. You laugh at it. I don't, that's all." Lucky hesitated. The urge to speak outweighed the fear of being ridiculed. "Dam"f I know what it is—maybe because it makes me think of the old folks or somethin'—but—hell—it just sorter—gets me—"

Lucky turned abruptly away and started off. Pete watched him for a moment with a look that should have been astonished, outraged, incredulous—but wasn't. He overtook him, put an arm about his shoulders, and because he had to say something as they walked on, muttered reassuringly:

"Well—if you ain't the damndest fool—"

1925

FOG[1]

John Matheus[2]

The stir of life echoed. On the bridge between Ohio and West Virginia was the rumble of heavy trucks, the purr of high power engines in Cadillacs and Paiges, the rattle of Fords. A string of loaded freight cars pounded along on the C. & P. tracks, making a thunderous, if tedious way to Mingo.[3] A steamboat's hoarse whistle boomed forth between the swish, swish, chug, chug of a mammoth stern paddle wheel with the asthmatic poppings of the pistons. The raucous shouts of smutty speaking street boys, the noises of a steam laundry, the clank and clatter of a pottery, the godless voices of women from Water Street houses of ill fame, all these blended in a sort of modern babel, common to all the towers of destruction erected by modern civilization.

These sounds were stirring when the clock sounded six on top of the Court House, that citadel of Law and Order, with the statue of Justice looming out of an alcove above the imposing stone entrance, blindfolded and in her right hand the scales of Judgment. Even so early in the evening the centers from which issued these inharmonious notes were scarcely visible. This sinister cloak of a late November twilight Ohio Valley fog had stealthily spread from somewhere beneath the somber river bed, down from somewhere in the lowering West Virginia hills. The fog extended its tentacles over city and river, gradually obliterating traces of familiar landscapes. At five-thirty the old Panhandle bridge,[4] supported by massive sandstone pillars, stalwart as when erected fifty years before to serve a generation now passed behind the portals of life, had become a spectral outline against the sky as the toll keepers of the New bridge looked northward up the Ohio River.

Now at six o'clock the fog no longer distorted; it blotted out, annihilated. One by one the street lights came on, giving an uncertain glare in spots, enabling peeved citizens to tread their way homeward without recognizing their neighbor ten feet ahead, whether he might be Jew or Gentile, Negro or Pole, Slav, Croatian, Italian or one hundred per cent American.

An impatient crowd of tired workers peered vainly through the gloom to see if the headlights of the interurban car were visible through the thickening haze. The car was due at Sixth and Market at six-ten and was scheduled to leave at six-fifteen for many little towns on the West Virginia side.

At the same time as these uneasy toilers were waiting, on the opposite side of the river the car had stopped to permit some passengers to descend and disappear in the fog. The motorman, fagged and jaded by the monotony of many stoppings and startings, waited mechanically for the conductor's bell to signal, "Go ahead."

The fog was thicker, more impenetrable. It smothered the headlight. Inside the car in the smoker, that part of the seats nearest the motorman's box, partitioned from the rest, the lights were struggling bravely against a fog of tobacco smoke, almost as opaque as the dull gray blanket of mist outside.

[1]Awarded first prize *Opportunity* contest, 1925 [note in original text].

[2]American writer and professor of romance languages (1887–1983).

[3]This could be Mingo, Ohio, or Mingo, West Virginia.

[4]A reference to the Northern Panhandle, the northernmost extension of West Virginia.

A group of red, rough men, sprawled along the two opposite bench-formed seats, parallel to the sides of the car, were talking to one another in the thin, flat colorless English of their mountain state, embellished with the homely idioms of the coal mine, the oil field, the gas well.

"When does this here meetin' start, Bill?"

"That 'air notice read half after seven."

"What's time now?"

"Damned 'f I know. Hey, Lee, what time's that pocket clock of yourn's got?"

"Two past six."

There was the sound of a match scratching against the sole of a rough shoe.

"Gimme a light, Lafe."

In attempting to reach for the burning match before its flame was extinguished, the man stepped forward and stumbled over a cheap suitcase of imitation leather. A vile-looking stogie fell in the aisle.

"God! Your feet're bigger'n Bills's."

The crowd laughed uproariously. The butt of this joke grinned and showed a set of dirty nicotine-stained teeth. He recovered his balance in time to save the flaring match. He was a tremendous man, slightly stooped, with taffy-colored, straggling hair and little pig eyes.

Between initial puffs he drawled: "Now you're barkin' up the wrong tree. I only wear elevens."

"Git off'n me, Lee Cromarty," growled Bill. "You hadn't ought to be rumlin' of *my* feathers the wrong way—and you a-plannin' to ride the goat."

Lake, a consumptive appearing, undersized, bovine-eyed individual, spat out the remark: "Naow, there! You had better be kereful. Men have been nailed to the cross for less than that."

"Ha! ha!—ho! ho! ho!"

There was a joke to arouse the temper of the crowd.

A baby began to cry lustily in the rear and more commodious end of the car reserved for nonsmokers. His infantine wailing smote in sharp contrast upon the ears of the hilarious joshers, filling the silence that followed the subsidence of the laughter.

"Taci, bimba. Non aver paura!"[5]

Nobody understood the musical words of the patient, Madonna-eyed Italian mother, not even the baby, for it continued its yelling. She opened her gay-colored shirt waist and pressed the child to her bosom. He was quieted.

"She can't speak United States, but I bet her Tony Spaghetti votes the same as you an' me. The young 'un 'll have more to say about the future of these United States than your children an' mine unless we carry forward the work such as we are going to accomplish to-night."

"Yeh, you're damned right," answered the scowling companion of the lynx-eyed citizen in khaki clothes, who had thus commented upon the foreign woman's offspring.

"They breed like cats. They'll outnumber us, unless——"

A smell of garlic stifled his speech. Nich and Mike Axa-minter, late for the night shift at the La Belle, bent over the irate American, deluging him with the odor of garlic and voluble, guttural explosions of a Slovak tongue.

[5]Italian: "Hush, baby. Don't be afraid!"

"What t' hell! Git them buckets out o' my face, you hunkies,[6] you!"

Confused and apologetic the two men moved forward.

"Isn't this an awful fog, Barney," piped a gay, girlish voice.

"I'll tell the world it is," replied her red-haired companion, flinging a half-smoked cigarette away in the darkness as he assisted the girl to the platform.

They made their way to a vacant seat in the end of the car opposite the smoker, pausing for a moment respectfully to make the sign of the cross before two Sisters of Charity,[7] whose flowing black robes and ebon headdress contrasted strikingly with the pale whiteness of their faces. The nuns raised their eyes, slightly smiled and continued their orisons[8] on dark decades of rosaries with pendant crosses of ivory.

"Let's sit here," whispered the girl. "I don't want to be by those niggers."

In a few seconds they were settled. There were cooings of sweet words, limpid-eyed soul glances. They forgot all others. The car was theirs alone.

"Say, boy, ain't this some fog. Yuh can't see the old berg."

"'Sthat so. I hadn't noticed."

Two Negro youths thus exchanged words. They were well dressed and sporty.

"Well, it don't matter, as long as it don't interfere with the dance."

"I hope Daisy will be there. She's some stunnin' high-brown an' I don't mean maybe."

"O boy!"

Thereupon one began to hum "Daddy, O Daddy" and the other whistled softly the popular air from "Shuffle Along" entitled "Old-Fashioned Love."

"Oi, oi! Ven I say vill dis car shtart. Ve must mek dot train fur Pittsburgh."

"Ach, Ish ka bibble.[9] They can't do a thing without us, Laban."

They settled down in their seats to finish the discussion in Yiddish, emphasizing the conversation with shrugs of the shoulder and throaty interjections.

In a seat apart to themselves, for two seats in front and behind were unoccupied, sat an old Negro man and a Negro woman, evidently his wife. Crowded between them was a girl of fourteen or fifteen.

"This heah is suah cu'us weather," complained the old man.

"We all nevah had no sich fog in Oklahoma."

The girl's hair was bobbed and had been straightened by "Poro" treatment, giving her an Egyptian cast of features.

"Gran'pappy," said the girl, "yo' cain't see ovah yander."

"Ain't it de troot, chile."

"Ne' min', sugah," assured the old woman. "Ah done paid dat 'ployment man an' he sayed yo' bound tuh lak de place. Dis here lady what's hirin' yo' is no po' trash an' she wants a likely gal lak yo' tuh ten' huh baby."

Now these series of conversations did not transpire in chronological order. They were uttered more or less simultaneously during the interval that the little conductor stood on tiptoe in an effort to keep one hand on the signal rope, craning his neck in a vain and dissatisfied endeavor to pierce the miasma of the

[6]Immigrants from central or eastern Europe. [7]Nuns.
[8]Prayers. [9]Yiddish: "I should worry."

fog. The motorman chafed in his box, thinking of the drudging lot of the laboring man. He registered discontent.

The garrulous group in the smoker were smoldering cauldrons of discontent. In truth their dissatisfaction ran the gamut of hate. It was stretching out to join hands with an unknown and clandestine host to plot, preserve, defend their dwarfed and twisted ideals.

The two foreign intruders in the smoker squirmed under the merciless, half articulate antipathy. They asked nothing but a job to make some money. In exchange for that magic English word job, they endured the terror that walked by day, the boss. They grinned stupidly at profanity, dirt, disease, disaster. Yet they were helping to make America.

Three groups in the car on this foggy evening were united under the sacred mantle of a common religion. Within its folds they sensed vaguely a something of happiness. The Italian mother radiated the joy of her child. Perhaps in honor of her and in reverence the two nuns with downcast eyes, trying so hard to forget the world, were counting off the rosary of the blessed Virgin—"Ave, Maria," "Hail, Mary, full of grace, the Lord is with thee; blessed art thou among women."

The youth and his girl in their tiny circle of mutual attraction and affection could not as in Edwin Markham's poem[10] widen the circle to include all, or even embrace that small circumscribed area of humanity within the car.

And the Negroes? Surely there was no hate in their minds. The gay youths were rather indifferent. The trio from the South, journeying far for a greater freedom philosophically accepted the inevitable "slings and arrows of outrageous fortune."

The Jews were certainly enveloped in a racial consciousness, unerringly fixed on control and domination of money, America's most potent factor in respectability.

The purplish haze of fog contracted. Its damp presence slipped into the car and every passenger shivered and peered forth to see. Their eyes were as the eyes of the blind!

At last the signal bell rang out staccato. The car suddenly lurched forward, shaking from side to side the passengers in their seats. The wheels scraped and began to turn. Almost at once a more chilling wetness filtered in from the river. In the invisibility of the fog it seemed that one was travelling through space, in an aeroplane perhaps, going nobody knew where.

The murmur of voices buzzed in the smoker, interrupted by the boisterous outbursts of laughter. A red glare tinted the fog for a second and disappeared. La Belle was "shooting" the furnaces. Then a denser darkness and the fog.

The car lurched, scintillating sparks flashed from the trolley wire, a terrific crash—silence. The lights went out. Before anybody could think or scream, there came a falling sensation, such as one experiences when dropped unexpectedly in an elevator or when diving through the scenic railways of the city amusements parks, or more exactly when one has nightmare and dreams of falling, falling, falling.

"The bridge has given way. God! The muddy water! The fog! Darkness. Death."

[10]Perhaps a reference to "The Man with a Hoe," the most famous poem of American poet Edwin Markham (1852–1940).

These thoughts flashed spontaneously in the consciousness of the rough ignorant fellows, choking in the fumes of their strong tobacco, came to the garlic scented "hunkies," to the Italian Madonna, to the Sisters of Charity, to the lover boy and his lover girl, to the Negro youths, to the Jews thinking in Yiddish idioms, to the old Negro man and his wife and the Egyptian-faced girl, with the straightened African hair, even to the bored motorman and the weary conductor.

To drown, to strangle, to suffocate, to die! In the dread silence the words screamed like exploding shells within the beating temples of terror-stricken passengers and crew.

Then protest, wild, mad, tumultuous, frantic protest. Life at bay and bellowing furiously against its ancient arch-enemy and antithesis—Death. An oath, screams—dull, paralyzing, vomit-stirring nausea. Holy, unexpressed intimacies, deeply rooted prejudices were roughly shaken from their smug moorings. The Known to be changed for an Unknown, the ever expected, yet unexpected, Death. No! No! Not that.

Lee Cromarty saw things in that darkness. A plain, one-story frame house, a slattern woman on the porch, an overgrown, large-hipped girl with his face. Then the woman's whining, scolding voice and the girl's bashful confidences. What was dimming that picture? What cataract was blurring his vision? Was it the fog?

To Lafe, leader of the crowd, crouched in his seat, his fingers clawing the air for a grasping place, came a vision of a hill-side grave—his wife's—and he saw again how she looked in her coffin—then the fog.

"I'll not report at the mine," thought Bill. "Wonder what old Bunner will say to that."

The mine foreman's grizzled face dangled for a second before him and was swallowed in the fog.

Hoarse, gasping exhalations. Men, old men, young men, sobbing. "Pietà! Madre mia![11]—Mercy, Virgin Mary! My child!"

No thoughts of fear or pain on the threshold of death, that shadow from whence all children flow, but all the Mother Love focused to save the child.

"*Memorare,* remember, O most gracious Virgin Mary, that never was it known that any one who fled to thy protection, implored thy help and sought thy intercession was left unaided."

The fingers sped over the beads of the rosary. But looming up, unerasable, shuttled the kaleidoscope of youth, love, betrayal, renunciation, the vows. *Miserere, Jesu!*[12]

Life is ever lord of Death
And Love can never lose its own.

The girl was hysterical, weeping, screaming, laughing. Did the poet dream an idle dream, a false mirage? Death is master. Death is stealing Love away. How could a silly girl believe or know the calm of poesy?

The boy crumbled. His swagger and bravado melted. The passionate call of sex became a blur. He was not himself, yet he was looking at himself, a confusion in space, in night, in Fog. And who was she hanging limp upon his arm?

[11]Italian: "Pity! My mother!" [12]Latin: "Have pity, Jesus!"

That dance? The jazz dance? Ah, the dance! The dance of Life was ending. The orchestra was playing a dirge and Death was leading the Grand March. Fog! Impenetrable fog!

All the unheeded, forgotten warnings of ranting preachers, all the prayers of simple black mothers, the Mercy-Seat,[13] the Revival, too late. Terror could give no articulate expression to these muffled feelings. They came to the surface of a blunted consciousness, incoherent.

Was there a God in Israel? Laban remembered Russia and the pogrom.[14] He had looked into the eyes of Fate that day and watched God die with his mother and sisters. Here he was facing Fate again. There was no answer. He was silent.

His companion sputtered, fumed, screeched. He clung to Laban in pieces.

Laban remembered the pogrom. The old Negro couple remembered another horror. They had been through the riots in Tulsa. There they had lost their son and his wife, the Egyptian-faced girl's father and mother. They had heard the whine of bullets, the hiss of flame, the howling of human wolves, killing in the most excruciating manner. The water was silent. The water was merciful.

The old woman began to sing in a high quavering minor key:

> Lawdy, won't yo' ketch mah groan,
> O Lawdy, Lawdy, won't yo' ketch mah groan.

The old man cried out: "Judgment! Judgment!"

The Egyptian-faced girl wept. She was sore afraid, sore afraid. And the fog was round about them.

Time is a relative term. The philosophers are right for once. What happened inside the heads of these men and women seemed to them to have consumed hours instead of seconds. The conductor mechanically grabbed for the trolley rope, the motorman threw on the brakes.

The reaction came. Fear may become inarticulate and paralyzed. Then again it may become belligerent and self-protective, striking blindly in the maze. Darkness did not destroy completely the sense of direction.

"The door! The exit!"

A mad rush to get out, not to be trapped without a chance, like rats in a trap.

"Out of my way! Damn you—out of my way!"

Somebody yelled: "Sit still!"

Somebody hissed: "Brutes! Beasts!"

Another concussion, accompanied by the grinding of steel. The car stopped, lurched backward, swayed, and again stood still. Excited shouts re-echoed from the ends of the bridge. Automobile horns tooted. An age seemed to pass, but the great splash did not come. There was still time—maybe. The car was emptied.

"Run for the Ohio end!" someone screamed.

The fog shut off every man from his neighbor. The sound of scurrying feet reverberated, of the Italian woman and her baby, of the boy carrying his girl, of the Negro youths, of the old man and his wife, half dragging the Egyptian-faced

[13]A covering on the Ark of the Covenant representing the throne of God.
[14]One of a series of violent attacks on Russia's Jewish population.

girl, of the Sisters of Charity, of the miners. Flitting like wraiths in Homer's Hades, seeking life.[15]

In a few minutes all were safe on Ohio soil. The bridge still stood. A street light gave a ghastly glare through the fog. The whore houses on Water Street brooded evilly in the shadows. Dogs barked, the Egyptian-faced girl had fainted. The old Negro woman panted, "Mah Jesus! Mah Jesus!"

The occupants of the deserted car looked at one another. The icy touch of the Grave began to thaw. There was a generous intermingling. Everybody talked at once, inquiring, congratulating.

"Look after the girl," shouted Lee Cromarty. "Help the old woman, boys."

Bells began to ring. People came running. The ambulance arrived. The colored girl had recovered. Then everybody shouted again. Profane miners, used to catastrophe, were strangely moved. The white boy and girl held hands.

"Sing us a song, old woman," drawled Lafe.

"He's heard mah groan. He done heard it," burst forth the old woman in a song flood of triumph.

> Yes, he conquered Death and Hell,
> An' He never said a mumblin' word,
> Not a word, not a word.

"How you feelin', Mike," said Bill to the garlic eater.

"Me fine. Me fine."

The news of the event spread like wildfire. The street was now crowded. The police arrived. A bridge official appeared, announcing the probable cause of the accident, a slipping of certain supports. The girders fortunately had held. A terrible tragedy had been prevented.

"I'm a wash-foot Baptist[16] an' I don't believe in Popery,"[17] said Lake, "but, fellers, let's ask them ladies in them air mournin' robes to say a prayer of thanksgiving for the bunch."

The Sisters of Charity did say a prayer, not an audible petition for the ears of men, but a whispered prayer for the ears of God, the Benediction of Thanksgiving, uttered by the Catholic Church through many years, in many tongues and places.

"De profundis," added the silently moving lips of the white-faced nuns. "Out of the depths have we cried unto Thee, O Lord. And Thou hast heard our cries."

The motorman was no longer dissatisfied. The conductor's strength had been renewed like the eagle's.

"Boys," drawled Lake, "I'll be damned if I'm goin' to that meetin' to-night."

"Nor me," affirmed Lee Cromarty.

"Nor me," repeated all the others.

The fog still crept from under the bed of the river and down from the lowering hills of West Virginia—dense, tenacious, stealthy, chilling, but from about the hearts and minds of some rough, unlettered men another fog had begun to lift.

1925

[15]An allusion to Odysseus's visit to Hades in the central books of Homer's *Odyssey*.

[16]A Baptist sub-denomination that, following the example of Jesus's humbling himself as told in John 13, has members of the congregation wash the feet of others.

[17]Roman Catholicism.

FERN[1]

Jean Toomer

Face flowed into her eyes. Flowed in soft cream foam and plaintive ripples, in such a way that wherever your glance may momentarily have rested, it immediately thereafter wavered in the direction of her eyes. The soft suggestion of down slightly darkened, like the shadow of a bird's wing might, the creamy brown color of her upper lip. Why, after noticing it, you sought her eyes, I cannot tell you. Her nose was aquiline,[2] Semitic. If you have heard a Jewish cantor sing, if he has touched you and made your own sorrow seem trivial when compared with his, you will know my feeling when I follow the curves of her profile, like mobile rivers, to their common delta. They were strange eyes. In this, that they sought nothing—that is, nothing that was obvious and tangible and that one could see, and they gave the impression that nothing was to be denied. When a woman seeks, you will have observed, her eyes deny. Fern's eyes desired nothing that you could give her; there was no reason why they should withhold. Men saw her eyes and fooled themselves. Fern's eyes said to them that she was easy. When she was young, a few men took her, but got no joy from it. And then, once done, they felt bound to her (quite unlike their hit and run with other girls), felt as though it would take them a lifetime to fulfill an obligation which they could find no name for. They became attached to her, and hungered after finding the barest trace of what she might desire. As she grew up, new men who came to town felt as almost everyone did who ever saw her: that they would not be denied. Men were everlastingly bringing her their bodies. Something inside of her got tired of them, I guess, for I am certain that for the life of her she could not tell why or how she began to turn them off. A man in fever is no trifling thing to send away. They began to leave her, baffled and ashamed, yet vowing to themselves that some day they would do some fine thing for her: send her candy every week and not let her know whom it came from, watch out for her wedding-day and give her a magnificent something with no name on it, buy a house and deed it to her, rescue her from some unworthy fellow who had tricked her into marrying him. As you know, men are apt to idolize or fear that which they cannot understand, especially if it be a woman. She did not deny them, yet the fact was that they were denied. A sort of superstition crept into their consciousness of her being somehow above them. Being above them meant that she was not to be approached by anyone. She became a virgin. Now a virgin in a small southern town is by no means the usual thing, if you will believe me. That the sexes were made to mate is the practice of the South. Particularly, black folks were made to mate. And it is black folks whom I have been talking about thus far. What white men thought of Fern I can arrive at only by analogy. They let her alone.

Anyone, of course, could see her, could see her eyes. If you walked up the Dixie Pike most any time of day, you'd be most like to see her resting listless-like on the railing of her porch, back propped against a post, head tilted a

[1]From Jean Toomer's *Cane*. Additional selections from *Cane* are included in the individual author section for Jean Toomer.

[2]Shaped like an eagle's beak.

little forward because there was a nail in the porch post just where her head came which for some reason or other she never took the trouble to pull out. Her eyes, if it were sunset, rested idly where the sun, molten and glorious, was pouring down between the fringe of pines. Or maybe they gazed at the gray cabin on the knoll from which an evening folk-song was coming. Perhaps they followed a cow that had been turned loose to roam and feed on cotton-stalks and corn leaves. Like as not they'd settle on some vague spot above the horizon, though hardly a trace of wistfulness would come to them. If it were dusk, then they'd wait for the search-light of the evening train which you could see miles up the track before it flared across the Dixie Pike, close to her home. Wherever they looked, you'd follow them and then waver back. Like her face, the whole countryside seemed to flow into her eyes. Flowed into them with the soft listless cadence of Georgia's South. A young Negro, once, was looking at her, spellbound, from the road. A white man passing in a buggy had to flick him with his whip if he was to get by without running him over. I first saw her on her porch. I was passing with a fellow whose crusty numbness (I was from the North and suspected of being prejudiced and stuck-up) was melting as he found me warm. I asked him who she was. "That's Fern," was all that I could get from him. Some folks already thought that I was given to nosing around; I let it go at that, so far as questions were concerned. But at first sight of her I felt as if I heard a Jewish cantor sing. As if his singing rose above the unheard chorus of a folk-song. And I felt bound to her. I too had my dreams: something I would do for her. I have knocked about from town to town too much not to know the futility of mere change of place. Besides, picture if you can, this cream-colored solitary girl sitting at a tenement window looking down on the indifferent throngs of Harlem. Better that she listen to folk-songs at dusk in Georgia, you would say, and so would I. Or, suppose she came up North and married. Even a doctor or a lawyer, say, one who would be sure to get along—that is, make money. You and I know, who have had experience in such things, that love is not a thing like prejudice which can be bettered by changes of town. Could men in Washington, Chicago, or New York, more than the men of Georgia, bring her something left vacant by the bestowal of their bodies? You and I who know men in these cities will have to say, they could not. See her out and out a prostitute along State Street in Chicago. See her move into a southern town where white men are more aggressive. See her become a white man's concubine. . . . Something I must do for her. There was myself. What could I do for her? Talk, of course. Push back the fringe of pines upon new horizons. To what purpose? and what for? Her? Myself? Men in her case seem to lose their selfishness. I lost mine before I touched her. I ask you, friend (it makes no difference if you sit in the Pullman or the Jim Crow[3] as the train crosses her road), what thoughts would come to you—that is, after you'd finished with the thoughts that leap into men's minds at the sight of a pretty woman who will not deny them; what thoughts would come to you, had you seen her in a quick flash, keen and intuitively, as she sat there on her porch when your train thundered by? Would you have got off at the next station and

[3]A Pullman car was a high-priced railway accommodation that included a berth for sleeping. Jim Crow cars were less desirable accommodations in which African American passengers were forced to ride.

come back for her to take her where? Would you have completely forgotten her as soon as you reached Macon, Atlanta, Augusta, Pasadena, Madison, Chicago, Boston, or New Orleans? Would you tell your wife or sweetheart about a girl you saw? Your thoughts can help me, and I would like to know. Something I would do for her. . . .

One evening I walked up the Pike on purpose, and stopped to say hello. Some of her family were about, but they moved away to make room for me. Damn if I knew how to begin. Would you? Mr. and Miss So-and-So, people, the weather, the crops, the new preacher, the frolic, the church benefit, rabbit and possum hunting, the new soft drink they had at old Pap's store, the schedule of the trains, what kind of town Macon was, Negro's migration north, boll-weevils, syrup, the Bible—to all these things she gave a yassur or nassur, without further comment. I began to wonder if perhaps my own emotional sensibility had played one of its tricks on me. "Let's take a walk," I at last ventured. The suggestion, coming after so long an isolation, was novel enough, I guess, to surprise. But it wasn't that. Something told me that men before me had said just that as a prelude to the offering of their bodies. I tried to tell her with my eyes. I think she understood. The thing from her that made my throat catch, vanished. Its passing left her visible in a way I'd thought, but never seen. We walked down the Pike with people on all the porches gaping at us. "Doesn't it make you mad?" She meant the row of petty gossiping people. She meant the world. Through a canebrake that was ripe for cutting, the branch was reached. Under a sweet-gum tree, and where reddish leaves had dammed the creek a little, we sat down. Dusk, suggesting the almost imperceptible procession of giant trees, settled with a purple haze about the cane. I felt strange, as I always do in Georgia, particularly at dusk. I felt that things unseen to men were tangibly immediate. It would not have surprised me had I had vision. People have them in Georgia more often than you would suppose. A black woman once saw the mother of Christ and drew her in charcoal on the courthouse wall. . . . When one is on the soil of one's ancestors, most anything can come to one. . . . From force of habit, I suppose, I held Fern in my arms—that is, without at first noticing it. Then my mind came back to her. Her eyes, unusually weird and open, held me. Held God. He flowed in as I've seen the countryside flow in. Seen men. I must have done something—what, I don't know, in the confusion of my emotion. She sprang up. Rushed some distance from me. Fell to her knees, and began swaying, swaying. Her body was tortured with something it could not let out. Like boiling sap it flooded arms and fingers till she shook them as if they burned her. It found her throat, and spattered inarticulately in plaintive, convulsive sounds, mingled with calls to Christ Jesus. And then she sang, brokenly. A Jewish cantor singing with a broken voice. A child's voice, uncertain, or an old man's. Dusk hid her; I could hear only her song. It seemed to me as though she were pounding her head in anguish upon the ground. I rushed to her. She fainted in my arms.

There was talk about her fainting with me in the canefield. And I got one or two ugly looks from town men who'd set themselves up to protect her. In fact, there was talk of making me leave town. But they never did. They kept a watch-out for me, though. Shortly after, I came back North. From the train window I saw her as I crossed her road. Saw her on her porch, head tilted a little forward where the nail was, eyes vaguely focused on the sunset. Saw her face flow into them, the countryside and something that I call God, flowing into them. . . . Nothing ever really happened. Nothing ever came to Fern, not even I. Something I would do for her. Some fine unnamed thing. . . . And, friend, you? She is still living, I have reason to know. Her name, against the chance that you might happen down that way, is Fernie May Rosen.

1923

SPUNK[1]

Zora Neale Hurston

I

A giant of a brown-skinned man sauntered up the one street of the Village and out into the palmetto thickets with a small pretty woman clinging lovingly to his arm.

"Looka theah, folkses!" cried Elijah Mosley, slapping his leg gleefully. "Theah they go, big as life an' brassy as tacks."

All the loungers in the store tried to walk to the door with an air of nonchalance but with small success.

"Now pee-eople!" Walter Thomas gasped. "Will you look at 'em!"

"But that's one thing Ah likes about Spunk Banks—he ain't skeered of nothin' on God's green footstool—*nothin'!* He rides that log down at saw-mill jus' like he struts 'round wid another man's wife—jus' don't give a kitty. When Tes' Miller got cut to giblets on that circle-saw, Spunk steps right up and starts ridin'. The rest of us was skeered to go near it."

A round-shouldered figure in overalls much too large, came nervously in the door and the talking ceased. The men looked at each other and winked.

"Gimme some soda-water. Sass'prilla[2] Ah reckon," the newcomer ordered, and stood far down the counter near the open pickled pig-feet tub to drink it.

Elijah nudged Walter and turned with mock gravity to the new-comer.

"Say, Joe, how's everything up yo' way? How's yo' wife?"

Joe started and all but dropped the bottle he held in his hands. He swallowed several times painfully and his lips trembled.

"Aw 'Lige, you oughtn't to do nothin' like that," Walter grumbled. Elijah ignored him.

"She jus' passed heah a few minutes ago goin' thata way," with a wave of his hand in the direction of the woods.

Now Joe knew his wife had passed that way. He knew that the men lounging in the general store had seen her, moreover, he knew that the men knew *he* knew. He stood there silent for a long moment staring blankly, with his Adam's apple twitching nervously up and down his throat. One could actually *see* the pain he was suffering, his eyes, his face, his hands and even the dejected slump

[1]Awarded second prize, *Opportunity* contest, 1925 [note in original text].
[2]Sarsaparilla: a non-alcoholic drink akin to root beer.

of his shoulders. He set the bottle down upon the counter. He didn't bang it, just eased it out of his hand silently and fiddled with his suspender buckle.

"Well, Ah'm goin' after her to-day. Ah'm goin' an' fetch her back. Spunk's done gone too fur."

He reached deep down into his trouser pocket and drew out a hollow ground razor, large and shiny, and passed his moistened thumb back and forth over the edge.

"Talkin' like a man, Joe. Course that's *yo'* fambly affairs, but Ah like to see grit in anybody."

Joe Kanty laid down a nickel and stumbled out into the street.

Dusk crept in from the woods. Ike Clarke lit the swinging oil lamp that was almost immediately surrounded by candle-flies. The men laughed boisterously behind Joe's back as they watched him shamble woodward.

"You oughtn't to said whut you did to him, Lige—look how it worked him up," Walter chided.

"And Ah hope it did work him up. 'Tain't even decent for a man to take and take like he do."

"Spunk will sho' kill him."

"Aw, Ah doan't know. You never kin tell. He might turn him up an' spank him fur gettin' in the way, but Spunk wouldn't shoot no unarmed man. Dat razor he carried outa heah ain't gonna run Spunk down an' cut him, an' Joe ain't got the nerve to go up to Spunk with it knowing he totes that Army .45. He makes that break outa heah to bluff us. He's gonna hide that razor behind the first likely palmetto root an' sneak back home to bed. Don't tell me nothin' 'bout that rabbit-foot colored man. Didn't he meet Spunk an' Lena face to face one day las' week an' mumble sumthin' to Spunk 'bout lettin' his wife alone?"

"What did Spunk say?" Walter broke in—"Ah like him fine but 'tain't right the way he carries on wid Lena Kanty, jus' cause Joe's timid 'bout fightin'."

"You wrong theah, Walter. 'Tain't cause Joe's timid at all, it's cause Spunk wants Lena. If Joe was a passle of wile cats Spunk would tackle the job just the same. He'd go after *anything* he wanted the same way. As Ah wuz sayin' a minute ago, he tole Joe right to his face that Lena was his. 'Call her,' he says to Joe. 'Call her and see if she'll come. A woman knows her boss an' she answers when he calls.' 'Lena, ain't I yo' husband?' Joe sorter whines out. Lena looked at him real disgusted but she don't answer and she don't move outa her tracks. Then Spunk reaches out an' takes hold of her arm an' says: 'Lena, youse mine. From now on Ah works for you an' fights for you an' Ah never wants you to look to nobody for a crumb of bread, a stitch of close or a shingle to go over yo' head, but *me* long as Ah live. Ah'll git the lumber foh owah house to-morrow. Go home an' git yo' things together!'

"'Thass mah house,' Lena speaks up. 'Papa gimme that.'

"'Well,' says Spunk, 'doan give up whut's yours, but when youse inside don't forgit youse mine, an' let no other man git outa his place wid you!'

"Lena looked up at him with her eyes so full of love that they wuz runnin' over, an' Spunk seen it an' Joe seen it too, and his lip started to tremblin' and his Adam's apple was galloping up and down his neck like a race horse. Ah bet he's wore out half a dozen Adam's apples since Spunk's been on the job with Lena. That's all he'll do. He'll be back heah after while swallowin' an' workin' his lips like he wants to say somethin' an' can't."

"But didn't he do *nothin'* to stop 'em?"

"Nope, not a frazzlin' thing—jus' stood there. Spunk took Lena's arm and walked off jus' like nothin' ain't happened and he stood there gazin' after them till they was outa sight. Now you know a woman don't want no man like that. I'm jus' waitin' to see whut he's goin' to say when he gits back."

II

But Joe Kanty never came back, never. The men in the store heard the sharp report of a pistol somewhere distant in the palmetto thicket and soon Spunk came walking leisurely, with his big black Stetson set at the same rakish angle and Lena clinging to his arm, came walking right into the general store. Lena wept in a frightened manner.

"Well," Spunk announced calmly, "Joe come out there wid a meatax an' made me kill him."

He sent Lena home and led the men back to Joe—Joe crumpled and limp with his right hand still clutching his razor.

"See mah back? Mah cloes cut clear through. He sneaked up an' tried to kill me from the back, but Ah got him, an' got him good, first shot," Spunk said.

The men glared at Elijah, accusingly.

"Take him up an' plant him in 'Stoney lonesome,'" Spunk said in a careless voice. "Ah didn't wanna shoot him but he made me do it. He's a dirty coward, jumpin' on a man from behind."

Spunk turned on his heel and sauntered away to where he knew his love wept in fear for him and no man stopped him. At the general store later on, they all talked of locking him up until the sheriff should come from Orlando, but no one did anything but talk.

A clear case of self-defense, the trial was a short one, and Spunk walked out of the court house to freedom again. He could work again, ride the dangerous log-carriage that fed the singing, snarling, biting, circle-saw; he could stroll the soft dark lanes with his guitar. He was free to roam the woods again; he was free to return to Lena. He did all of these things.

III

"Whut you reckon, Walt?" Elijah asked one night later. "Spunk's gittin' ready to marry Lena!"

"Naw! Why, Joe ain't had time to git cold yit. Nohow Ah didn't figger Spunk was the marryin' kind."

"Well, he is," rejoined Elijah. "He done moved most of Lena's things—and her along wid 'em—over to the Bradley house. He's buying it. Jus' like Ah told yo' all right in heah the night Joe wuz kilt. Spunk's crazy 'bout Lena. He don't want folks to keep on talkin' 'bout her—thass reason he's rushin' so. Funny thing 'bout that bob-cat, wan't it?"

"What bob-cat, 'Lige? Ah ain't heered 'bout none."

"Ain't cher? Well, night befo' las' was the fust night Spunk an' Lena moved together an' jus' as they was goin' to bed, a big black bob-cat, black all over, you hear me, *black,* walked round and round that house and howled like forty, an' when Spunk got his gun an' went to the winder to shoot it, he says it stood right still an' looked him in the eye, an' howled right at him. The thing got Spunk so nervoused up he couldn't shoot. But Spunk says twan't no bob-cat nohow. He says it was Joe done sneaked back from Hell!"

"Humph!" sniffed Walter, "he oughter be nervous after what he done. Ah reckon Joe come back to dare him to marry Lena, or to come out an' fight. Ah bet he'll be back time and agin, too. Know what Ah think? Joe wuz a braver man than Spunk."

There was a general shout of derision from the group.

"Thass a fact," went on Walter. "Lookit whut he done; took a razor an' went out to fight a man he knowed toted a gun an' wuz a crack shot, too; 'nother thing Joe wuz skeered of Spunk, skeered plumb stiff! But he went jes' the same. It took him a long time to get his nerve up. 'Tain't nothin' for Spunk to fight when he ain't skeered of nothin'. Now, Joe's done come back to have it out wid the man that's got all he ever had. Y'll know Joe ain't never had nothin' nor wanted nothin' besides Lena. It musta been a h'ant cause ain' nobody never seen no black bob-cat."

"'Nother thing," cut in one of the men, "Spunk wuz cussin' a blue streak to-day 'cause he 'lowed dat saw wuz wobblin'—almos' got 'im once. The machinist come, looked it over an' said it wuz alright. Spunk musta been leanin' t'wards it some. Den he claimed somebody pushed 'im but 'twant nobody close to 'im. Ah wuz glad when knockin' off time come. I'm skeered of dat man when he gits hot. He'd beat you full of button holes as quick as he's look atcher."

IV

The men gathered the next evening in a different mood, no laughter. No badinage this time.

"Look, 'Lige, you goin' to set up wid Spunk?"

"Naw, Ah reckon not, Walter. Tell yuh the truth, Ah'm a lil bit skittish. Spunk died too wicket—died cussin' he did. You know he thought he wuz done outa life."

"Good Lawd, who'd he think done it?"

"Joe."

"Joe Kanty? How come?"

"Walter, Ah b'leeve Ah will walk up thata way an' set. Lena would like it Ah reckon."

"But whut did he say, 'Lige?"

Elijah did not answer until they had left the lighted store and were strolling down the dark street.

"Ah wuz loadin' a wagon wid scantlin' right near the saw when Spunk fell on the carriage but 'fore Ah could git to him the saw got him in the body—awful sight. Me an' Skint Miller got him off but it was too late. Anybody could see that. The fust thing he said wuz: 'He pushed me, 'Lige—the dirty hound pushed me in the back!'—He was spittin' blood at ev'ry breath. We laid him on the sawdust pile with his face to the East so's he could die easy. He helt mah han' till the last, Walter, and said: 'It was Joe, 'Lige—the dirty sneak shoved me . . . he didn't dare come to mah face . . . but Ah'll git the son-of-a-wood louse soon's Ah get there an' make hell too hot for him. . . . Ah felt him shove me. . .!' Thass how he died."

"If spirits kin fight, there's a powerful tussle goin' on somewhere ovah Jordan 'cause Ah b'leeve Joe's ready for Spunk an' ain't skeered any more—yas, Ah b'leeve Joe pushed 'im mahself."

They had arrived at the house. Lena's lamentations were deep and loud. She had filled the room with magnolia blossoms that gave off a heavy sweet odor. The keepers of the wake tipped about whispering in frightened tones. Everyone in the village was there, even old Jeff Kanty, Joe's father, who a few hours before would have been afraid to come within ten feet of him, stood leering triumphantly down upon the fallen giant as if his fingers had been the teeth of steel that laid him low.

The cooling board consisted of three sixteen-inch boards on saw horses, a dingy sheet was his shroud.

The women ate heartily of the funeral baked meats and wondered who would be Lena's next. The men whispered coarse conjectures between guzzles of whiskey.

1925

HARLEM WINE

Countée Cullen

This is not water running here,
These thick rebellious streams
That hurtle flesh and bone past fear
Down alleyways of dreams.

This is a wine that must flow on
Not caring how or where,
So it has ways to flow upon
Where song is in the air.

So it can woo an artful flute
With loose, elastic lips,
Its measurement of joy compute
With blithe, ecstatic hips.

1925

WHITE HOUSES

Claude McKay

Your door is shut against my tightened face,
And I am sharp as steel with discontent;
But I possess the courage and the grace
To bear my anger proudly and unbent.

The pavement slabs burn loose beneath my feet,
A chafing savage, down the decent street,
And passion rends my vitals as I pass,
Where boldly shines your shuttered door of glass.
Oh I must search for wisdom every hour,
Deep in my wrathful bosom sore and raw,
And find in it the superhuman power
To hold me to the letter of your law!
Oh I must keep my heart inviolate
Against the potent poison of your hate.

1925

I TOO

Langston Hughes

I, too, sing America.

I am the darker brother.
They send me to eat in the kitchen
When company comes.
But I laugh,
And eat well,
And grow strong.

To-morrow
I'll sit at the table
When company comes
Nobody 'll dare
Say to me,
"Eat in the kitchen"
Then.

Besides, they'll see how beautiful I am
And be ashamed,—

I, too, am America.

1925

THE BLACK FINGER

Angelina Grimke

I have just seen a most beautiful thing
Slim and still,
Against a gold, gold sky,

A straight black cypress,
Sensitive,
Exquisite,
A black finger
Pointing upwards.
Why, beautiful still finger, are you black?
And why are you pointing upwards?

1925

THE ROAD

Helene Johnson

Ah, little road all whirry in the breeze,
A leaping clay hill lost among the trees,
The bleeding note of rapture streaming thrush
Caught in a drowsy hush
And stretched out in a single singing line of dusky song.
Ah little road, brown as my race is brown,
Your trodden beauty like our trodden pride,
Dust of the dust, they must not bruise you down.
Rise to one brimming golden, spilling cry!

1925

Countée Cullen 1903–1946

He was born Countée Porter and raised in Baltimore and in New York City. When he was fifteen he was adopted by the Reverend Frederick Cullen, a Methodist minister in Harlem, who took his foster son on a tour of the Holy Land and to the literary shrines of Europe and strongly encouraged his academic interests. Cullen went to New York University, where he was elected to Phi Beta Kappa and won awards for his poetry. In 1925, Color, *his first book of poems, was published. By the time he was twenty-six, he had published three more volumes:* Copper Sun *(1927),* The Ballad of the Brown Girl *(1927), and* The Black Christ *(1929). He wrote a Harlem novel,* One Way to Heaven *(1932), translated Euripides's* Medea *(1935), and served as an editor for two important African American magazines of the day:* Opportunity, Journal of Negro Life, *and The* Crisis, *an official periodical of the NAACP. But after his early, prolific years, Cullen's productivity declined, and he supported himself mainly by teaching French in the New York public schools, although he continued to write verse and in 1946 collaborated in writing a Broadway musical,* St. Louis Woman. *In 1947 his collected poems were published posthumously under the title* On These I Stand.

Cullen, a conscientious, dedicated craftsman, was one of the most notable writers of the Harlem Renaissance, a period of remarkable literary achievement by black writers in

New York City during the 1920s. Cullen's techniques were conventional; his models were the romantic poets, not black poets, and he often insisted that his poems in particular and poetry in general should be free from political or racial matters. At other times he could not escape the fact of his race. His finest poem, "Heritage," is an assertion of the black American's relationship with Africa, and he came to acknowledge that "in spite of myself, I find that I am actuated by a strong sense of race consciousness. This grows upon me." Cullen was caught between his conflicting allegiances to his art, his country, and his race, but, like other black writers after him, he managed to create a body of memorable writing out of disparate loyalties and ideologies and out of his struggles in a world that made "a poet black, and bid him sing."

FURTHER READING: B. Ferguson, *Countée Cullen and the Negro Renaissance,* 1966; M. Perry, *A Bio-Biography of Countée Cullen, 1903–1946,* 1971; A. Shucard, *Countée Cullen,* 1984; *My Soul's High Song: The Collected Writings of Countée Cullen,* ed. G. Early, 1991; S. Onyeberechi, *Critical Essays: Achebe, Baldwin, Cullen, Ngugi, and Tutuola,* 1999.

TEXT: *On These I Stand,* 1947.

YET DO I MARVEL

I doubt not God is good, well-meaning, kind,
And did He stoop to quibble could tell why
The little buried mole continues blind,
Why flesh that mirrors Him must some day die,
Make plain the reason tortured Tantalus[1]
Is baited by the fickle fruit, declare
If merely brute caprice dooms Sisyphus[2]
To struggle up a never-ending stair.
Inscrutable His ways are, and immune
To catechism by a mind too strewn
With petty cares to slightly understand
What awful brain compels His awful hand.
Yet do I marvel at this curious thing:
To make a poet black, and bid him sing!

1924, 1925

FOR A LADY I KNOW

She even thinks that up in heaven
Her class lies late and snores,
While poor black cherubs rise at seven
To do celestial chores.

1924, 1925

[1]In Greek myth, Tantalus, for his defiance of the gods, was condemned forever to stand, "tantalized," with food and drink just beyond his grasp.

[2]A crafty deceiver in Greek myth who was condemned eternally to push a huge stone up the slope of a hill.

INCIDENT

(For Eric Walrond)[1]

Once riding in old Baltimore,
Heart-filled, head-filled with glee,
I saw a Baltimorean
Keep looking straight at me.

Now I was eight and very small,
And he was no whit bigger,
And so I smiled, but he poked out
His tongue, and called me, "Nigger."

I saw the whole of Baltimore
From May until December;
Of all the things the happened there
That's all that I remember.

1924, 1924

FROM THE DARK TOWER

(To Charles S. Johnson)[1]

We shall not always plant while others reap
The golden increment of bursting fruit,
Not always countenance, abject and mute,
That lesser men should hold their brothers cheap;
Not everlastingly while others sleep
Shall we beguile their limbs with mellow flute,
Not always bend to some more subtle brute;
We were not made eternally to weep.

The night whose sable breast relieves the stark
White stars is no less lovely being dark
And there are buds that cannot bloom at all
In light, but crumple, piteous, and fall;
So in the dark we hide the heart that bleeds,
And wait, and tend our agonizing seeds.

1924, 1927

[1]Eric Walrond (1898–1966) was a writer of short stories and, like Countée Cullen, a part of the Harlem Renaissance.

[1]Charles Spurgeon Johnson (1893–1956) was editor of *Opportunity,* the magazine of the National Urban League.

A BROWN GIRL DEAD

With two white roses on her breasts,
White candles at head and feet,
Dark Madonna of the grave she rests;
Lord Death has found her sweet.

Her mother pawned her wedding ring
To lay her out in white;
She'd be so proud she'd dance and sing
To see herself tonight.

1925

HERITAGE

(For Harold Jackman)[1]

What is Africa to me:
Copper sun or scarlet sea,
Jungle star or jungle track,
Strong bronzed me, or regal black
Women from whose loins I sprang
When the birds of Eden sang?
One three centuries removed
From the scenes his fathers loved,
Spicy grove, cinnamon tree,
What is Africa to me?

So I lie, who all day long
Want no sound except the song
Sung by wild barbaric birds
Goading massive jungle herds,
Juggernauts of flesh that pass
Trampling tall defiant grass
Where young forest lovers lie,
Plighting troth beneath the sky.
So I lie, who always hear,
Though I cram against my ear
Both my thumbs, and keep them there,
Great drums throbbing through the air.
So I die, whose fount of pride,
Dear distress, and joy allied,
Is my somber flesh and skin,
With the dark blood dammed within

[1]Harold Jackman (1901–1961) was a playwright, director, and editor associated with the Harlem Renaissance.

Like great pulsing tides of wine
That, I fear, must burst the fine
Channels of the chafing net
Where they surge and foam and fret.

Africa? A book one thumbs
Listlessly, till slumber comes.
Unremembered are her bats
Circling through the night, her cats
Crouching in the river reeds,
Stalking gentle flesh that feeds
By the river brink; no more
Does the bugle-throated roar
Cry that monarch claws have leapt
From the scabbards where they slept.
Silver snakes that once a year
Doff the lovely coats you wear,
Seek no covert in your fear
Lest a mortal eye should see;
What's your nakedness to me?
Here no leprous flowers rear
Fierce corollas[2] in the air;
Here no bodies sleek and wet,
Dripping mingled rain and sweat,
Tread the savage measures of
Jungle boys and girls in love.
What is last year's snow to me,
Last year's anything? The tree
Budding yearly must forget
How its past arose or set—
Bough and blossom, flower, fruit,
Even what shy bird with mute
Wonder at her travail there,
Meekly labored in its hair.
One three centuries removed
From the scenes his fathers loved,
Spicy grove, cinnamon tree,
What is Africa to me?

So I lie, who finds no peace
Night or day, no slight release
From the unremittant beat
Made by cruel padded feet
Walking through my body's street.
Up and down they go, and back,
Treading out a jungle track.
So I lie, who never quite
Safely sleep from rain at night—

[2]Petals.

I can never rest at all
When the rain begins to fall;
Like a soul gone mad with pain
I must match its weird refrain;
Ever must I twist and squirm,
Writhing like a baited worm,
While its primal measures drip
Through my body, crying, "Strip!
Doff this new exuberance.
Come and dance the Lover's Dance!"
In an old remembered way
Rain works on me night and day.
Quaint, outlandish heathen gods
Black men fashion out of rods,
Clay, and brittle bits of stone,
In a likeness like their own
My conversion came high-priced;
I belong to Jesus Christ,
Preacher of humility;
Heathen gods are naught to me.

Father, Son, and Holy Ghost,
So I make an idle boast;
Jesus of the twice-turned cheek,[3]
Lamb of God, although I speak
With my mouth thus, in my heart
Do I play a double part.
Ever at Thy glowing altar
Must my heart grow sick and falter,
Wishing He I served were black,
Thinking then it would not lack
Precedent of pain to guide it,
Let who would or might deride it;
Surely then this flesh would know
Yours had borne a kindred woe.
Lord, I fashion dark gods, too,
Daring even to give You
Dark despairing features where,
Crowned with dark rebellious hair,
Patience wavers just so much as
Mortal grief compels, while touches
Quick and hot, of anger, rise
To smitten cheek and weary eyes.
Lord, forgive me if my need
Sometimes shapes all human creed.

[3]". . . whosoever shall smite thee on thy right cheek, turn to him the other also." (Matthew 5:39).

All day long and all night through,
One thing only must I do:
Quench my pride and cool my blood,
Lest I perish in the flood.
Lest a hidden ember set
Timber that I thought was wet
Burning like the dryest flax,
Melting like the merest wax,
Lest the grave restore its dead.
Not yet has my heart or head
In the least way realized
They and I are civilized.

1925

SCOTTSBORO[1], TOO, IS WORTH ITS SONG

(A poem to American poets)

I said:
Now will the poets sing,—
Their cries go thundering
Like blood and tears
Into the nation's ears,
Like lightning dart
Into the nation's heart.
Against disease and death and all things fell,
And war,
Their strophes rise and swell
To jar
The foe smug in his citadel.

Remembering their sharp and pretty
Tunes for Sacco and Vanzetti,[2]
I said:
Here too's a cause divinely spun
For those whose eyes are on the sun,

[1]In 1931, nine black youths were indicted at Scottsboro, Alabama, for the rape of two white girls. The dubious testimony of the accusers and the blatant disregard for proper legal procedures during the subsequent trials provoked numerous protests by those who believed the defendants were innocent victims of racism.

[2]In 1920, Nicola Sacco and Bartolomeo Vanzetti were arrested in Massachusetts for robbery and murder. Their case stirred worldwide demonstrations by those supporters who charged that their arrest, conviction, and subsequent execution (1927) occurred only because the two men were foreigners and had unpopular, radical political views.

Here in epitome
Is all disgrace
And epic wrong,
Like wine to brace
The minstrel heart, and blare it into song.

Surely, I said,
Now will the poets sing.
But they have raised no cry.
I wonder why.

1934, 1940

Jean Toomer 1894–1967

From beginning to end, Jean Toomer's life vacillated between the white and black worlds. His father deserted his family after a year of marriage, and Toomer grew up unhappily in the home of his maternal grandfather, who had once been acting governor of Louisiana during the Reconstruction period after the Civil War. Following high school, Toomer restlessly shifted from one city and from one college to another. He studied agriculture at the University of Wisconsin and in Massachusetts; he entered a physical training program in Chicago; he studied sociology and history at colleges in New York City, sold cars in Chicago, taught physical education in Milwaukee, worked in a shipyard in New Jersey.

After several years of wandering, Toomer returned to his grandfather's home in Washington, D.C. There he began to write and quickly succeeded, placing poems in several avant-garde magazines. In 1921, still restless, he went to Georgia, as superintendent of a rural black school. Although he was there but four months, his stay deeply influenced him, and provided him with the material for his novel Cane *(1923).*

The book, with its mixture of poems, quasi-dramas, and short fiction, was widely acclaimed as a notable contribution to the experimental fiction of the time and as a major work in the history of black literature. Toomer became one of the leaders, along with Langston Hughes and Countée Cullen, of the Harlem Literary Renaissance of the 1920s. Following the publication of Cane, *Toomer went to France, and there he fell under the influence of Georges Gurdjieff, a Russian philosopher whose mystical system "Unitism" helped turn Toomer away from the world of daily experience and into a private world of introspection. For a time Toomer continued to write, but his work became increasingly abstract, and he published little. In his last years he became a Quaker and lectured occasionally at Quaker meetings. By the end of his life he had retreated almost completely into literary obscurity, yet in* Cane *he had created a literary monument, a testament to his perception of the distressed and uprooted lives of black men and women living in white America.*

FURTHER READING: *The Wayward and the Seeking: A Collection of the Writings of Jean Toomer,* ed. D. Turner, 1981; *The Collected Poems of Jean Toomer,* ed. R. Jones and M. Latimer, 1988; *A Jean Toomer Reader: Selected Unpublished Writings,* ed. F. Rusch, 1993; *Anger and Beyond: The Negro Writer in the United States,* ed. H. Hill, 1966; *Studies in Cane,* ed. F. Durham,

1971; B. Benson and M. Dillard, *Jean Toomer,* 1980; N. McKay, *Jean Toomer: A Study of His Literary Life and Work,* 1984; C. Kerman, *The Lives of Jean Toomer,* 1987; *Jean Toomer: A Critical Evaluation,* ed. T. O'Daniel, 1988; R. Byrd, *Jean Toomer's Years with Gurdjieff,* 1990; C. Larson, *Invisible Darkness,* 1993. J. Woodson, *To Make a New Race: Gurdjieff, Toomer, and the Harlem Renaissance,* 1999.

TEXT: *Cane,* 1923.

from *CANE*

BLOOD-BURNING MOON

I

Up from the skeleton stone walls, up from the rotting floor boards and the solid hand-hewn beams of oak of the pre-war cotton factory, dusk came. Up from the dusk the full moon came. Glowing like a fired pine-knot, it illumined the great door and soft showered the Negro shanties aligned along the single street of factory town. The full moon in the great door was an omen. Negro women improvised songs against its spell.

Louisa sang as she came over the crest of the hill from the white folks' kitchen. Her skin was the color of oak leaves on young trees in fall. Her breasts, firm and up-pointed like ripe acorns. And her singing had the low murmur of winds in fig trees. Bob Stone, younger son of the people she worked for, loved her. By the way the world reckons things, he had won her. By measure of that warm glow which came into her mind at thought of him, he had won her. Tom Burwell, whom the whole town called Big Boy, also loved her. But working in the fields all day, and far away from her, gave him no chance to show it. Though often enough of evenings he had tried to. Somehow, he never got along. Strong as he was with hands upon the ax or plow, he found it difficult to hold her. Or so he thought. But the fact was that he held her to factory town more firmly than he thought for. His black balanced, and pulled against, the white of Stone, when she thought of them. And her mind was vaguely upon them as she came over the crest of the hill, coming from the white folks' kitchen. As she sang softly at the evil face of the full moon.

A strange stir was in her. Indolently, she tried to fix upon Bob or Tom as the cause of it. To meet Bob in the canebrake, as she was going to do an hour or so later, was nothing new. And Tom's proposal which she felt on its way to her could be indefinitely put off. Separately, there was no unusual significance to either one. But for some reason, they jumbled when her eyes gazed vacantly at the rising moon. And from the jumble came the stir that was strangely within her. Her lips trembled. The slow rhythm of her song grew agitant and restless. Rusty black and tan spotted hounds, lying in the dark corners of porches or prowling around back yards, put their noses in the air and caught its tremor. They began plaintively to yelp and howl. Chickens woke up and cackled. Intermittently, all over the countryside dogs barked and roosters crowed as if heralding a weird dawn or some ungodly awakening. The women sang lustily.

Their songs were cotton-wads to stop their ears. Louisa came down into factory town and sank wearily upon the step before her home. The moon was rising towards a thick cloud-bank which soon would hide it.

> Red nigger moon. Sinner!
> Blood-burning moon. Sinner!
> Come out that fact'ry door.

II

Up from the deep dusk of a cleared spot on the edge of the forest a mellow glow arose and spread fan-wise into the low-hanging heavens. And all around the air was heavy with the scent of boiling cane. A large pile of cane-stalks lay like ribboned shadows upon the ground. A mule, harnessed to a pole, trudged lazily round and round the pivot of the grinder. Beneath a swaying oil lamp, a Negro alternately whipped out at the mule, and fed cane-stalks to the grinder. A fat boy waddled pails of fresh ground juice between the grinder and the boiling stove. Steam came from the copper boiling pan. The scent of cane came from the copper pan and drenched the forest and the hill that sloped to factory town, beneath its fragrance. It drenched the men in circle seated around the stove. Some of them chewed at the white pulp of stalks, but there was no need for them to, if all they wanted was to taste the cane. One tasted it in factory town. And from factory town one could see the soft haze thrown by the glowing stove upon the low-hanging heavens.

Old David Georgia stirred the thickening syrup with a long ladle, and every so often drew it off. Old David Georgia tended his stove and told tales about the white folk, about moonshining and cotton picking, and about sweet nigger gals, to the men who sat there about his stove to listen to him. Tom Burwell chewed cane-stalk and laughed with the others till someone mentioned Louisa. Till some one said something about Louisa and Bob Stone, about the silk stockings she must have gotten from him. Blood ran up Tom's neck hotter than the glow that flooded from the stove. He sprang up. Glared at the men and said, "She's my gal." Will Manning laughed. Tom strode over to him. Yanked him up and knocked him to the ground. Several of Manning's friends got up to fight for him. Tom whipped out a long knife and would have cut them to shreds if they hadnt ducked into the woods. Tom had had enough. He nodded to Old David Georgia and swung down the path to factory town. Just then, the dogs started barking and the roosters began to crow. Tom felt funny. Away from the fight, away from the stove, chill got to him. He shivered. He shuddered when he saw the full moon rising towards the cloud-bank. He who didnt give a godam for the fears of old women. He forced his mind to fasten on Louisa. Bob Stone. Better not be. He turned into the street and saw Louisa sitting before her home. He went towards her, ambling, touched the brim of a marvelously shaped, spotted, felt hat, said he wanted to say something to her, and then found that he didnt know what he had to say, or if he did, that he couldnt say it. He shoved his big fists in his overalls, grinned, and started to move off.

"Youall want me, Tom?"

"Thats what us wants, sho, Louisa."

"Well, here I am—"

"An here I is, but that aint ahelpin none, all th same."

"You wanted to say something? . . ."

"I did that, sho. But words is like th spots on dice: no matter how y fumbles em, there's times when they jes wont come. I dunno why. Seems like th love I feels fo yo done stole m tongue. I got it now. Whee! Louisa, honey, I oughtnt tell y, I feel I oughtnt cause yo is young and goes t church an I has had other gals, but Louisa I sho do love y. Lil gal, Ise watched y from them first days when youall sat right here befo yo door befo th well an sang sometimes in a way that like t broke m heart. Ise carried y with me into th fields, day after day, an after that, an I sho can plow when yo is there, an I can pick cotton. Yassur! Come near beatin Barlo yesterday. I sho did. Yassur! An next year if old Stone'll trust me, I'll have a farm. My own. My bales will buy you what y gets from white folks now. Silk stockings an purple dresses—course I dont believe what some folks been whisperin as t how y gets them things now. White folks always did do for niggers what they likes. An they jes cant help alikin yo, Louisa. Bob Stone likes y. Course he does. But not th way folks is awhisperin. Does he, hon?"

"I dont know what you mean, Tom"

"Course y dont. Ise already cut two niggers. Had t hon, t tell em so. Niggers always tryin t make somethin out a nothin. And then besides, white folks aint up t them tricks so much nowadays. Godam better not be. Leastawise not with yo. Cause I wouldnt stand f it. Nassur."

"What would you do, Tom?"

"Cut him jes like I cut a nigger."

"No, Tom—"

"I said I would an there aint no mo to it. But that aint th talk f now. Sing, honey Louisa, an while I'm listenin t y I'll be makin love."

Tom took her hand in his. Against the tough thickness of his own, hers felt soft and small. His huge body slipped down to the step beside her. The full moon sank upward into the deep purple of the cloud-bank. An old woman brought a lighted lamp and hung it on the common well whose bulky shadow squatted in the middle of the road, opposite Tom and Louisa. The old woman lifted the well-lid, took hold the chain, and began drawing up the heavy bucket. As she did so, she sang. Figures shifted, restless-like, between lamp and window in the front rooms of the shanties. Shadows of the figures fought each other on the gray dust of the road. Figures raised the windows and joined the old woman in song. Louisa and Tom, the whole street, singing:

Red nigger moon. Sinner!
Blood-burning moon. Sinner!
Come out that fact'ry door.

III

Bob Stone sauntered from his veranda out into the gloom of fir trees and magnolias. The clear white of his skin paled, and the flush of his cheeks turned purple. As if to balance this outer change, his mind became consciously a white man's. He passed the house with its huge open hearth which, in the days of slavery, was the plantation cookery. He saw Louisa bent over that hearth. He went in as a master should and took her. Direct, honest, bold. None of this sneaking that he had to go through now. The contrast was repulsive to him. His family had lost ground. Hell no, his family still owned the niggers, practically. Damned if they did, or he wouldnt have to duck around so. What would they think if they knew? His mother? His sister? He shouldnt mention them, shouldnt think of them in this connection. There in the dusk he blushed at doing so. Fellows about town were all right, but how about his friends up North? He could see them incredible, repulsed. They didnt know. The thought first made him laugh. Then, with their eyes still upon him, he began to feel embarrassed. He felt the need of explaining things to them. Explain hell. They wouldnt understand, and moreover, who ever heard of a Southerner getting on his knees to any Yankee, or anyone. No sir. He was going to see Louisa to-night, and love her. She was lovely—in her way. Nigger way. What way was that? Damned if he knew. Must know. He'd known her long enough to know. Was there something about niggers that you couldnt know? Listening to them at church didnt tell you anything. Looking at them didnt tell you anything. Talking to them didnt tell you anything—unless it was gossip, unless they wanted to talk. Of course, about farming, and licker, and craps—but those werent nigger. Nigger was something more. How much more? Something to be afraid of, more? Hell no. Who ever heard of being afraid of a nigger? Tom Burwell. Cartwell had told him that Tom went with Louisa after she reached home. No sir. No nigger had ever been with his girl. He'd like to see one try. Some position for him to be in. Him, Bob Stone, of the old Stone family, in a scrap with a nigger over a nigger girl. In the good old days . . . Ha! Those were the days. His family had lost ground. Not so much, though. Enough for him to have cut through old Lemon's canefield by way of the woods, that he might meet her. She was worth it. Beautiful nigger gal. Why nigger? Why not, just gal? No, it was because she was a nigger that he went to her. Sweet . . . The scent of boiling cane came to him. Then he saw the rich glow of the stove. He heard the voices of the men circled around it. He was about to skirt the clearing when he heard his own name mentioned. He stopped. Quivering. Leaning against a tree, he listened.

"Bad nigger. Yassur, he sho is one bad nigger when he gets started."

"Tom Burwell's been on th gang[1] three times fo cuttin men."

"What y think he's agwine t do t Bob Stone?"

"Dunno yet. He aint found out. When he does—Baby!"

"Aint no tellin."

"Young Stone aint no quitter an I ken tell y that. Blood of th old uns in his veins."

"Thats right. He'll scrap, sho."

"Be gettin too hot f niggers round this away."

"Shut up, nigger. Y dont know what y talkin bout."

Bob Stone's ears burned as though he had been holding them over the stove. Sizzling heat welled up within him. His feet felt as if they rested on red-hot

[1]I.e., sentenced to a prison chain gang.

coals. They stung him to quick movement. He circled the fringe of the glowing. Not a twig cracked beneath his feet. He reached the path that led to factory town. Plunged furiously down it. Halfway along, a blindness within him veered him aside. He crashed into the bordering canebrake. Cane leaves cut his face and lips. He tasted blood. He threw himself down and dug his fingers in the ground. The earth was cool. Cane-roots took the fever from his hands. After a long while, or so it seemed to him, the thought came to him that it must be time to see Louisa. He got to his feet and walked calmly to their meeting place. No Louisa. Tom Burwell had her. Veins in his forehead bulged and distended. Saliva moistened the dried blood on his lips. He bit down on his lips. He tasted blood. Not his own blood; Tom Burwell's blood. Bob drove through the cane and out again upon the road. A hound swung down the path before him towards factory town. Bob couldnt see it. The dog loped aside to let him pass. Bob's blind rushing made him stumble over it. He fell with a thud that dazed him. The hound yelped. Answering yelps came from all over the countryside. Chickens cackled. Roosters crowed, heralding the bloodshot eyes of southern awakening. Singers in the town were silenced. They shut their windows down. Palpitant between the rooster crows, a chill hush settled upon the huddled forms of Tom and Louisa. A figure rushed from the shadow and stood before them. Tom popped to his feet.

"Whats y want?"

"I'm Bob Stone."

"Yassur—an I'm Tom Burwell. Whats y want?"

Bob lunged at him. Tom side-stepped, caught him by the shoulder, and flung him to the ground. Straddled him.

"Let me up."

"Yassur—but watch yo doins, Bob Stone."

A few dark figures, drawn by the sound of scuffle, stood about them. Bob sprang to his feet.

"Fight like a man, Tom Burwell, an I'll lick y."

Again he lunged. Tom side-stepped and flung him to the ground. Straddled him.

"Get off me, you godam nigger you."

"Yo sho has started somethin now. Get up."

Tom yanked him up and began hammering at him. Each blow sounded as if it smashed into a precious, irreplaceable soft something. Beneath them, Bob staggered back. He reached in his pocket and whipped out a knife.

"Thats my game, sho."

Blue flash, a steel blade slashed across Bob Stone's throat. He had a sweetish sick feeling. Blood began to flow. Then he felt a sharp twitch of pain. He let his knife drop. He slapped one hand against his neck. He pressed the other on top of his head as if to hold it down. He groaned. He turned, and staggered towards the crest of the hill in the direction of white town. Negroes who had seen the fight slunk into their homes and blew the lamps out. Louisa, dazed, hysterical, refused to go indoors. She slipped, crumbled, her body loosely propped against the woodwork of the well. Tom Burwell leaned against it. He seemed rooted there.

Bob reached Broad Street. White men rushed up to him. He collapsed in their arms.

"Tom Burwell. . . ."

White men like ants upon a forage rushed about. Except for the taut hum of their moving, all was silent. Shotguns, revolvers, rope, kerosene, torches. Two high-powered cars with glaring search-lights. They came together. The taut hum rose to a low roar. Then nothing could be heard but the flop of their feet in the thick dust of the road. The moving body of their silence preceded over the crest of the hill into factory town. It flattened the Negroes beneath it. It rolled to the wall of the factory, where it stopped. Tom knew that they were coming. He couldnt move. And then he saw the search lights of the two cars glaring down on him. A quick shot went through him. He stiffened. He started to run. A yell went up from the mob. Tom wheeled about and faced them. They poured down on him. They swarmed. A large man with dead-white face and flabby cheeks came to him and almost jabbed a gun-barrel through his guts.

"Hands behind y, nigger."

Tom's wrists were bound. The big man shoved him to the well. Burn him over it, and when the woodwork caved in, his body would drop to the bottom. Two deaths for a godam nigger. Louisa was driven back. The mob pushed in. Its pressure, its momentum was too great. Drag him to the factory. Wood and stakes already there. Tom moved in the direction indicated. But they had to drag him. They reached the great door. Too many to get in there. The mob divided and flowed around the walls to either sides. The big man shoved him through the door. The mob pressed in from the sides. Taut humming. No words. A stake was sunk into the ground. Rotting floor boards piled around it. Kerosene poured on the rotting floor boards. Tom bound to the stake. His breast was bare. Nail scratches let little lines of blood trickle down and mat into the hair. His face, his eyes were wet and stony. Except for irregular breathing, one would have thought him already dead. Torches were flung onto the pile. A great flare muffled in black smoke shot upward. The mob yelled. The mob was silent. Now Tom could be seen within the flames. Only his head, erect, lean, like a blackened stone. Stench of burning flesh soaked the air. Tom's eyes popped. His head settled downward. The mob yelled. Its yell echoed against the skeleton stone walls and sounded like a hundred yells. Like a hundred mobs yelling. Its yell thudded against the thick front wall and fell back. Ghost of a yell slipped through the flames and out the great door of the factory. It fluttered like a dying thing down the single street of factory town. Louisa, upon the step before her home, did not hear it, but her eyes opened slowly. They saw the full moon glowing in the great door. The full moon, an evil thing, an omen, soft showering the homes of folks she knew. Where were they, these people? She'd sing, and perhaps they'd come out and join her. Perhaps Tom Burwell would come. At any rate, the full moon in the great door was an omen which she must sing to:

Red nigger moon. Sinner!
Blood-burning moon. Sinner!
Come out that fact'ry door.

1923

COTTON SONG

Come, brother, come. Lets lift it;
Come now, hewit! roll away!
Shackles fall upon the Judgment Day
But lets not wait for it.

God's body's got a soul,
Bodies like to roll the soul,
Cant blame God if we dont roll,
Come, brother, roll, roll!

Cotton bales are the fleecy way
Weary sinner's bare feet trod,
Softly, softly to the throne of God,
"We aint agwine t wait until th Judgment Day!

Nassur; nassur,
Hump.
Eoho, eoho, roll away!
We aint agwine t wait until th Judgment Day!"

God's body's got a soul,
Bodies like to roll the soul,
Cant blame God if we dont roll,
Come, brother, roll, roll!

1923

CARMA

Wind is in the cane. Come along.
Cane leaves swaying, rusty with talk,
Scratching choruses above the guinea's squawk,
Wind is in the cane. Come along.

Carma, in overalls, and strong as any man, stands behind the old brown mule, driving the wagon home. It bumps, and groans, and shakes as it crosses the railroad track. She, riding it easy. I leave the men around the stove to follow her with my eyes down the red dust road. Nigger woman driving a Georgia chariot down an old dust road. Dixie Pike is what they call it. Maybe she feels my gaze, perhaps she expects it. Anyway, she turns. The sun, which has been slanting over her shoulder, shoots primitive rockets into her mangrove-gloomed, yellow flower face. Hi! Yip! God has left the Moses-people for the nigger. "Gedap." Using reins to slap the mule, she disappears in a cloudy rumble at some indefinite point along the road.

(The sun is hammered to a band of gold. Pine-needles, like mazda, are brilliantly aglow. No rain has come to take the rustle from the falling sweet-gum leaves. Over in the forest, across the swamp, a sawmill blows its closing whistle. Smoke curls up. Marvelous web spun by the spider sawdust pile. Curls up and spreads itself pine-high above the branch, a single silver band along the eastern valley. A black boy . . . you are the most sleepiest man I ever seed, Sleeping Beauty . . . cradled on a gray mule, guided by the hollow sound of cowbells, heads for them through a rusty cotton field. From down the railroad track, the chug-chug of a gas engine announces that the repair gang is coming home. A girl in the yard of a whitewashed shack not much larger than the stack of worn ties piled before it, sings. Her voice is loud. Echoes, like rain, sweep the valley. Dusk takes the polish from the rails. Lights twinkle in scattered houses. From far away, a sad strong song. Pungent and composite, the smell of farmyards is the fragrance of the woman. She does not sing; her body is a song. She is in the forest, dancing. Torches flare . . . juju men, greegree, witch-doctors . . . torches go out . . . . The Dixie Pike has grown from a goat path in Africa.

Night.

Foxie, the bitch, slicks back her ears and barks at the rising moon.)

Wind is in the corn. Come along.
Corn leaves swaying, rusty with talk,
Scratching choruses above the guinea's squawk,
Wind is in the corn. Come along.

Carma's tale is the crudest melodrama. Her husband's in the gang.[1] And its her fault he got there. Working with a contractor, he was away most of the time. She had others. No one blames her for that. He returned one day and hung around the town where he picked up week-old boasts and rumors . . . . Bane accused her. She denied. He couldn't see that she was becoming hysterical. He would have liked to take his fists and beat her. Who was strong as a man. Stronger. Words, like corkscrews, wormed to her strength. It fizzled out. Grabbing a gun, she rushed from the house and plunged across the road into a cane-brake . . . . There, in quarter heaven, shone the crescent moon . . . . Bane was afraid to follow till he heard the gun go off. Then he wasted half an hour gathering the neighbor men. They met in the road where lamp-light showed tracks dissolving in the loose earth about the cane. The search began. Moths flickered the lamps. They put them out. Really, because she still might be live enough to shoot. Time and space have no meaning in a canefield. No more than the interminable stalks . . . . Some one stumbled over her. A cry went up. From the road, one would have thought that they were cornering a rabbit or a skunk . . . . It is difficult carrying dead weight through cane. They placed her on the sofa. A curious, nosey somebody looked for the wound. This fussing with her clothes aroused her. Her eyes

[1]That is, he is in prison, and has to work as part of a chain-gang.

were weak and pitiable for so strong a woman. Slowly, then like a flash, Bane came to know that the shot she fired, with averted head, was aimed to whistle like a dying hornet through the cane. Twice deceived, and one deception proved the other. His head went off. Slashed one of the men who'd helped, the man who'd stumbled over her. Now he's in the gang. Who was her husband. Should she not take others, this Carma, strong as a man, whose tale as I have told it is the crudest melodrama?

Wind is in the cane. Come along.
Cane leaves swaying, rusty with talk,
Scratching choruses above the guinea's squawk,
Wind is in the cane. Come along.

1923

SONG OF THE SON

Pour O pour that parting soul in song,
O pour it in the sawdust glow of night,
Into the velvet pine-smoke air to-night,
And let the valley carry it along.
And let the valley carry it along.

O land and soil, red soil and sweet-gum tree,
So scant of grass, so profligate of pines,
Now just before an epoch's sun declines
Thy son, in time, I have returned to thee,
Thy son, I have in time returned to thee.

In time, for though the sun is setting on
A song-lit race of slaves, it has not set;
Though late, O soil, it is not too late yet
To catch thy plaintive soul, leaving, soon gone,
Leaving, to catch thy plaintive soul soon gone.

O Negro slaves, dark purple ripened plums,
Squeezed, and bursting in the pine-wood air,
Passing, before they stripped the old tree bare
One plum was saved for me, one seed becomes

An everlasting song, a singing tree,
Caroling softly souls of slavery,
What they were, and what they are to me,
Caroling softly souls of slavery.

1923

Zora Neale Hurston 1891?–1960

Zora Neale Hurston was born in the small town of Notasulga, Alabama, probably in the year 1891. The date is uncertain—in later life she frequently reported her birth year as 1901 or 1903. When she was about three years old her family moved to Eatonville, Florida, the first completely black town to be incorporated in the United States. Her father was a carpenter and a Baptist preacher. He became an important figure in Eatonville and served as mayor. But it was her mother who most influenced Zora Neale Hurston's life. Her mother had been a schoolteacher before her marriage, and she encouraged her daughter to reach out in life, to "jump at the sun."

When Hurston was thirteen, her mother died. Hurston's father, unwilling or unable to care for his daughter, sent her away to live with relatives, passed her "around the family like a bad penny." Life in all-black Eatonville had been idyllic. Now, far from Eatonville, she confronted for the first time the difficulty of growing up black among whites. She attended school and did household chores for her relatives, but when her father suffered financial reverses and could no longer contribute to her care, she was returned home and left to fend for herself.

She found jobs working as a maid. Later she ran off to work as a wardrobe girl with a theatrical group touring Florida and the South. For a time she lived in Baltimore, where she supported herself by working as a waitress while she took high school classes. In 1918, hoping to prepare herself to be a writer, she moved to Washington, D.C. and entered Howard University. She enrolled in literature courses, joined the campus literary club, and published her first short story, "John Redding Goes to Sea," in the Howard University literary journal.

When another of her short stories was published in a New York City magazine, she left Washington, D.C. and moved to New York. She was a woman of high spirits, a born storyteller, and she immediately found a wide circle of friends. With their help she got a job as secretary to the best-selling novelist Fannie Hurst and won a scholarship to Barnard College, of Columbia University, graduating in 1928 with a bachelor's degree in anthropology.

Her class papers had attracted the attention of her anthropology professors, and after graduation she was awarded a fellowship to go back to the South to collect folklore. When she completed her research, she returned to New York City and began writing dramatic sketches based on the material she had collected. In 1932 she produced her own stage review, The Great Day. *The show was a critical success, but it failed to draw audiences large enough to pay its way and soon closed.*

In 1934 her first novel, Jonah's Gourd Vine, *was published. The novel, based on her experiences in Eatonville and on the folklore material she had collected, was a critical and financial success, selected as one of the offerings of the Book of the Month Club. The following year, her publishers, encouraged by the success of* Jonah's Gourd Vine, *brought out a collection of her short writings,* Mules and Men.

In 1936, now a successful writer with a growing reputation as a folklorist, Hurston received a fellowship from the Guggenheim Foundation to support her research. She went to the Caribbean to collect more black folklore, and while there she wrote her second novel, Their Eyes Were Watching God *(1937). Set in Eatonville, the novel told of a young black woman determined to find self-realization and love. It was Zora Neale Hurston's finest novel and brought her wide critical acclaim.*

At the urging of her publishers, she next wrote an autobiography, Dust Tracks on a Road *(1942). It was an award-winning success. But not all reviews were approving.*

Black activist critics charged that she had neglected the burning issues of racism, that she had failed to deal realistically with minority life in America, that she presented only a "white-washed" picture of American blacks. It is true that her writing did not emphasize the plight of black Americans and the bitterness of their struggle. But her aim was not to report racial tempests or to cry out for social change. She wanted to portray the culture and people of the American South that she knew, to write about human beings not about race: "My interest lies in what makes a man or woman do such-and-so regardless of his color."

For a brief time during World War II she taught at a black college in Florida while continuing to write fiction. But the tastes of the book-reading public had begun to change, and when she submitted her next novel to her publishers it was rejected. She then changed publishers and submitted the manuscript of a different novel that was published in 1948 as Seraph on the Suwanee. *It received favorable reviews, but to the surprise of Hurston's readers, and to the dismay of her critics, the book was not about blacks but about whites.*

Her career now began its decline. Her best work and her greatest public success had come in the 1930s. Now her manuscripts were increasingly rejected by publishers, and her personal life was shattered when she became the victim of charges (later disproved) that she had molested children. Her "crime" was widely reported in lurid newspaper stories, and Zora Neale Hurston, feeling betrayed by her friends and by the system of legal justice, disappeared, later to be discovered working as a housemaid in Florida.

She continued to write magazine articles on the lives of black men and women in America, and over the years she worked on a novel of the Jews and the biblical Herod, but the manuscript was rejected by every publishing house she sent it to. In her last years she scraped out a living by working as a librarian, as a substitute teacher, and by writing articles for a local weekly newspaper. In 1960 she died, penniless, in a welfare home in Florida.

By the time of her death, Hurston's work had been forgotten; her books had long since gone out of print and could only be found on the back shelves of used book stores. But then in the late 1970s she was rediscovered. Her finest novel, Their Eyes Were Watching God, *was republished. New critical studies of her fiction and biographies appeared that praised her writing and probed the meaning of her stories and the events of her life. Her achievement had been remarkable. She had published more books than any other American black woman, receiving critical and popular acclaim from black and white readers alike. And in recording the lives and the language of black men and women in the American South, she had preserved a part of the black tradition in America that would otherwise have been lost.*

Now, in the twenty-first century, Hurston's popularity is even greater. Her work is widely studied in schools and colleges. Her novels and stories continue to be reprinted in new editions. Even the unpublished manuscripts of her writing have been searched out and printed. And her play, Polk County, *has recently been staged with great success, winning tributes as a dramatic triumph and, from one critic, praise as a playgoer's joyous feast, decorated with "more voodoo, sass, and authentic blues than a fruitcake has chewy bits."*

FURTHER READING: D. Turner, *In a Minor Chord,* 1971; R. Hemenway, *Zora Neale Hurston: A Literary Biography,* 1977; *I Love Myself When I Am Laughing, and Then Again When I Am Looking Mean and Impressive: A Zora Neale Hurston Reader,* ed. A. Walker, 1979; L. Howard, *Zora Neale Hurston,* 1980; K. Holloway, *The Character of the Word: The Texts of Zora Neale Hurston,* 1987; M. Awkward, *Inspiriting Influences: Tradition, Revision, and Afro-American Women's Novels,* 1989; M. Lyons, *Sorrow's Kitchen: The Life and Folklore of Zora Neale Hurston,* 1990; *Zora! Zora Neale Hurston: The Woman and Her Country,* ed. N. Nathiri, 1991; P. Witcover, *Zora Neale Hurston,* 1991; J. Yates, *Zora Neale Hurston: A Story Teller's Life,* 1991; D.

Plant, *Every Tub Must Sit on Its Own Bottom: The Philosophy and Politics of Zora Neale Hurston,* 1995; C. Wall, *Women of the Harlem Renaissance,* 1995; T. Harris, *The Power of the Porch: The Story Teller's Craft in Zora Neale Hurston,* 1996; L. Hill, *Social Rituals and the Verbal Art of Zora Neale Hurston,* 1996; *Critical Essays on Zora Neale Hurston,* ed. G. Cronin, 1998; *Zora Neale Hurston's Their Eyes Were Watching God: A Casebook,* ed. C. Wall, 2000; *Zora Neale Hurston: Every Tongue Got to Confess: Negro Folk-Tales from the Gulf States,* ed. C. Kaplan, 2001; *Zora Neale Hurston: A Life in Letters,* ed. C. Kaplan, 2001; V. Boyd, *Wrapped in Rainbows: The Life of Zora Neale Hurston,* 2002; M. West, *Zora Neale Hurston and American Literary Culture,* 2005; T. Patterson, *Zora Neale Hurston and a History of Southern Life,* 2005.

TEXTS: *World Tomorrow,* May 1928; *Story Magazine,* August 1933.

HOW IT FEELS TO BE COLORED ME

I am colored but I offer nothing in the way of extenuating circumstances except the fact that I am the only Negro in the United States whose grandfather on the mother's side was *not* an Indian chief.

I remember the very day that I became colored. Up to my thirteenth year I lived in the little Negro town of Eatonville, Florida. It is exclusively a colored town. The only white people I knew passed through the town going to or coming from Orlando. The native whites rode dusty horses, the Northern tourists chugged down the sandy village road in automobiles. The town knew the Southerners and never stopped cane chewing when they passed. But the Northerners were something else again. They were peered at cautiously from behind curtains by the timid. The more venturesome would come out on the porch to watch them go past and got just as much pleasure out of the tourists as the tourists got out of the village.

The front porch might seem a daring place for the rest of the town, but it was a gallery seat to me. My favorite place was atop the gate-post. Proscenium box[1] for a born first-nighter.[2] Not only did I enjoy the show, but I didn't mind the actors knowing that I liked it. I usually spoke to them in passing. I'd wave at them and when they returned my salute, I would say something like this: "Howdy-do-well-I-thank-you-where-you-goin'?" Usually the automobile or the horse paused at this, and after a queer exchange of compliments, I would probably "go a piece of the way" with them, as we say in farthest Florida. If one of my family happened to come to the front in time to see me, of course negotiations would be rudely broken off. But even so, it is clear that I was the first "welcome-to-our-state" Floridian, and I hope the Miami Chamber of Commerce will please take notice.

During this period, white people differed from colored to me only in that they rode through town and never lived there. They liked to hear me "speak pieces" and sing and wanted to see me dance the parse-me-la, and gave me generously of their small silver for doing these things, which seemed strange to me for I wanted to do them so much that I needed bribing to stop. Only they didn't know it. The colored people gave no dimes. They deplored any

[1]The proscenium is the front portion of the stage, so the proscenium box is the "best seat in the house."

[2]A person who attends the first performance in the run of a play—thus, an avid theatergoer.

joyful tendencies in me, but I was their Zora nevertheless. I belonged to them, to the nearby hotels, to the county—everybody's Zora.

But changes came in the family when I was thirteen, and I was sent to school in Jacksonville. I left Eatonville, the town of the oleanders, as Zora. When I disembarked from the river-boat at Jacksonville, she was no more. It seemed that I had suffered a sea change. I was not Zora of Orange County any more, I was now a little colored girl. I found it out in certain ways. In my heart as well as in the mirror, I became a fast brown—warranted not to rub nor run.

But I am not tragically colored. There is no great sorrow dammed up in my soul, nor lurking behind my eyes. I do not mind at all. I do not belong to the sobbing school of Negrohood who hold that nature somehow has given them a lowdown dirty deal and whose feelings are all hurt about it. Even in the helter-skelter skirmish that is my life, I have seen that the world is to the strong regardless of a little pigmentation more or less. No, I do not weep at the world—I am too busy sharpening my oyster knife.

Someone is always at my elbow reminding me that I am the granddaughter of slaves. It fails to register depression with me. Slavery is sixty years in the past. The operation was successful and the patient is doing well, thank you. The terrible struggle that made me an American out of a potential slave said "On the line!" The Reconstruction[3] said "Get set!"; and the generation before said "Go!" I am off to a flying start and I must not halt in the stretch to look behind and weep. Slavery is the price I paid for civilization, and the choice was not with me. It is a bully adventure and worth all that I have paid through my ancestors for it. No one on earth ever had a greater chance for glory. The world to be won and nothing to be lost. It is thrilling to think—to know that for any act of mine, I shall get twice as much praise or twice as much blame. It is quite exciting to hold the center of the national stage, with the spectators not knowing whether to laugh or to weep.

The position of my white neighbor is much more difficult. No brown specter pulls up a chair beside me when I sit down to eat. No dark ghost thrusts its leg against mine in bed. The game of keeping what one has is never so exciting as the game of getting.

I do not always feel colored. Even now I often achieve the unconscious Zora of Eatonville before the Hegira.[4] I feel most colored when I am thrown against a sharp white background.

For instance at Barnard.[5] "Beside the waters of the Hudson" I feel my race. Among the thousand white persons, I am a dark rock surged upon, overswept by a creamy sea. I am surged upon and overswept, but through it all, I remain myself. When covered by the waters, I am; and the ebb but reveals me again.

Sometimes it is the other way around. A white person is set down in our midst, but the contrast is just as sharp for me. For instance, when I sit in the drafty basement that is The New World Cabaret with a white person, my color comes. We

[3]The post–Civil War Reconstruction of the South (1865–1876), in which increased opportunity for African Americans was a major goal.

[4]The Hegira was the relocation of Muhammud and his followers from Mecca to Medina; here it means Hurston's ironically analogous relocation from Eatonville to Jacksonville and then to the North.

[5]Barnard College, the women's college in Manhattan that Hurston attended.

enter chatting about any little nothing that we have in common and are seated by the jazz waiters. In the abrupt way that jazz orchestras have, this one plunges into a number. It loses no time in circumlocutions, but gets right down to business. It constricts the thorax and splits the heart with its tempo and narcotic harmonies. This orchestra grows rambunctious, rears on its hind legs and attacks the tonal veil with primitive fury, rending it, clawing it until it breaks through the jungle beyond. I follow those heathen—follow them exultingly. I dance wildly inside myself; I yell within, I whoop; I shake my assegai[6] above my head, I hurl it true to the mark *yeeeooww!* I am in the jungle and living in the jungle way. My face is painted red and yellow and my body is painted blue. My pulse is throbbing like a war drum. I want to slaughter something—give pain, give death to what, I do not know. But the piece ends. The men of the orchestra wipe their lips and rest their fingers. I creep back slowly to the veneer we call civilization with the last tone and find the white friend sitting motionless in his seat, smoking calmly.

"Good music they have here," he remarks, drumming the table with his fingertips.

Music! The great blobs of purple and red emotion have not touched him. He has only heard what I felt. He is far away and I see him but dimly across the ocean and the continent that have fallen between us. He is so pale with his whiteness then and I am *so* colored.

At certain times I have no race, I am *me.* When I set my hat at a certain angle and saunter down Seventh Avenue, Harlem City, feeling as snooty as the lions in front of the Forty-Second Street Library, for instance. So far as my feelings are concerned, Peggy Hopkins Joyce[7] on the Boule Mich[8] with her gorgeous raiment, stately carriage, knees knocking together in a most aristocratic manner, has nothing on me. The cosmic Zora emerges. I belong to no race nor time. I am the eternal feminine with its string of beads.

I have no separate feeling about being an American citizen and colored. It merely astonishes me. How can any deny themselves the pleasure of my company! It's beyond me.

But in the main, I feel like a brown bag of miscellany propped against a wall. Against a wall in company with other bags, white, red and yellow. Pour out the contents, and there is discovered a jumble of small things priceless and worthless. A first-water diamond, an empty spool, bits of broken glass, lengths of string, a key to a door long since crumbled away, a rusty knifeblade, old shoes saved for a road that never was and never will be, a nail bent under the weight of things too heavy for any nail, a dried flower or two, still a little fragrant. In your hand is the brown bag. On the ground before you is the jumble it held—so much like the jumble in the bags, could they be emptied, that all might be dumped in a single heap and the bags refilled without altering the content of any greatly. A bit of colored glass more or less would not matter. Perhaps that is how the Great Stuffer of Bags filled them in the first place—who knows?

1928

[6]A light wooden spear, usually with a metal blade, used by the Bantu tribe of Africa.

[7]Peggy Hopkins Joyce (1893–1957) was an actress and socialite who was socially conspicuous in the 1920s.

[8]"Boule Mich" is a colloquial rendering of the Boulevard Saint-Michel, a Parisian street whose cafes were popular haunts for Americans in Paris in the 1920s.

THE GILDED SIX-BITS

It was a Negro yard around a Negro house in a Negro settlement that looked to the payroll of the G and G Fertilizer works for its support.

But there was something happy about the place. The front yard was parted in the middle by a sidewalk from gate to door-step, a sidewalk edged on either side by quart bottles driven neck down into the ground on a slant. A mess of homey flowers planted without a plan but blooming cheerily from their helter-skelter places. The fence and house were whitewashed. The porch and steps scrubbed white.

The front door stood open to the sunshine so that the floor of the front room could finish drying after its weekly scouring. It was Saturday. Everything clean from the front gate to the privy house. Yard raked so that the strokes of the rake would make a pattern. Fresh newspaper cut in fancy edge on the kitchen shelves.

Missie May was bathing herself in the galvanized washtub in the bedroom. Her dark-brown skin glistened under the soapsuds that skittered down from her wash rag. Her stiff young breasts thrust forward aggressively like broad-based cones with the tips lacquered in black.

She heard men's voices in the distance and glanced at the dollar clock on the dresser.

"Humph! Ah'm way behind time t'day! Joe gointer be heah 'fore Ah git mah clothes on if Ah don't make haste."

She grabbed the clean meal sack at hand and dried herself hurriedly and began to dress. But before she could tie her slippers, there came the ring of singing metal on wood. Nine times.

Missie May grinned with delight. She had not seen the big tall man come stealing in the gate and creep up the walk grinning happily at the joyful mischief he was about to commit. But she knew that it was her husband throwing silver dollars in the door for her to pick up and pile beside her plate at dinner. It was this way every Saturday afternoon. The nine dollars hurled into the open door, he scurried to a hiding place behind the cape jasmine bush and waited.

Missie May promptly appeared at the door in mock alarm.

"Who dat chunkin' money in mah do'way?" She demanded. No answer from the yard. She leaped off the porch and began to search the shrubbery. She peeped under the porch and hung over the gate to look up and down the road. While she did this, the man behind the jasmine darted to the china berry tree. She spied him and gave chase.

"Nobody ain't gointer be chunkin' money at me and Ah not do 'em nothin'," she shouted in mock anger. He ran around the house with Missie May at his heels. She overtook him at the kitchen door. He ran inside but could not close it after him before she crowded in and locked with him in a rough and tumble. For several minutes the two were a furious mass of male and female energy. Shouting, laughing, twisting, turning, tussling, tickling each other in the ribs; Missie May clutching onto Joe and Joe trying, but not too hard, to get away.

"Missie May, take yo' hand out mah pocket!" Joe shouted out between laughs.

"Ah ain't, Joe, not lessen you gwine gimme whateve' it is good you got in yo' pocket. Turn it go, Joe, do Ah'll tear yo' clothes."

"Go on tear 'em. You de one dat pushes de needles round heah. Move yo' hand Missie May."

"Lemme git dat paper sack out yo' pocket. Ah bet its candy kisses."

"Tain't. Move yo' hand. Woman ain't go no business in a man's clothes nohow. Go way."

Missie May gouged way down and gave an upward jerk and triumphed.

"Unhhunh! Ah got it. It 'tis so candy kisses. Ah knowed you had somethin' for me in yo' clothes. Now Ah got to see whut's in every pocket you got."

Joe smiled indulgently and let his wife go through all of his pockets and take out the things that he had hidden there for her to find. She bore off the chewing gum, the cake of sweet soap, the pocket handkerchief as if she had wrested them from him, as if they had not been bought for the sake of this friendly battle.

"Whew! dat play-fight done got me all warmed up." Joe exclaimed. "Got me some water in de kittle?"

"Yo' water is on de fire and yo' clean things is cross de bed. Hurry up and wash yo'self and git changed so we kin eat. Ah'm hongry." As Missie said this, she bore the steaming kettle into the bedroom.

"You ain't hongry, sugar," Joe contradicted her. "Youse jes' a little empty. Ah'm de one whut's hongry. Ah could eat up camp meetin', back off 'ssociation, and drink Jurdan dry. Have it on de table when Ah git out de tub."

"Don't you mess wid mah business, man. You git in yo' clothes. Ah'm a real wife, not no dress and breath. Ah might not look lak one, but if you burn me, you won't git a thing but wife ashes."

Joe splashed in the bedroom and Missie May fanned around in the kitchen. A fresh red and white checked cloth on the table. Big pitcher of buttermilk beaded with pale drops of butter from the churn. Hot fried mullet, crackling bread, ham hock atop a mound of string beans and new potatoes, and perched on the window-sill a pone of spicy potato pudding.

Very little talk during the meal but that little consisted of banter that pretended to deny affection but in reality flaunted it. Like when Missie May reached for a second helping of the tater pone. Joe snatched it out of her reach.

After Missie May had made two or three unsuccessful grabs at the pan, she begged, "Aw, Joe gimme some mo' dat tater pone."

"Nope, sweetenin' is for us men-folks. Y'all pritty lil frail eels don't need nothin' lak dis. You too sweet already."

"Please, Joe."

"Naw, naw. Ah don't want you to git no sweeter than whut you is already. We goin' down de road a lil piece t'night so you go put on yo' Sunday-go-to-meetin' things."

Missie May looked at her husband to see if he was playing some prank. "Sho nuff, Joe?"

"Yeah. We goin' to de ice cream parlor."

"Where de ice cream parlor at, Joe?"

"A new man done come heah from Chicago and he done got a place and took and opened it up for a ice cream parlor, and bein' as it's real swell, Ah wants you to be one de first ladies to walk in dere and have some set down."

"Do Jesus, Ah ain't knowed nothin' 'bout it. Who de man done it?"

"Mister Otis D. Slemmons, of spots and places—Memphis, Chicago, Jacksonville, Philadelphia and so on."

"Dat heavy-set man wid his mouth full of gold teeths?"

"Yeah, Where did you see 'im at?"

"Ah went down to de sto' tuh git a box of lye and Ah seen 'im standin' on de corner talkin' to some of de mens, and Ah come on back and went to scrubbin' de floor, and he passed and tipped his hat whilst Ah was scourin' de steps. Ah thought Ah never seen *him* befo'."

Joe smiled pleasantly. "Yeah, he's up to date. He got de finest clothes Ah ever seen on a colored man's back."

"Aw, he don't look no better in his clothes than you do in yourn. He got a puzzlegut on 'im and he so chuckle-headed, he got a pone behind his neck."

Joe looked down at his own abdomen and said wistfully, "Wisht Ah had a build on me lak he got. He ain't puzzle-gutted, honey. He jes' got a corperation. Dat make 'im look lak a rich white man. All rich mens is got some belly on 'em."

"Ah seen de pitchers of Henry Ford and he's a spare-built man and Rockefeller look lak he ain't got but one gut. But Ford and Rockefeller and dis Slemmons and all de rest kin be as many-gutted as dey please, Ah'm satisfed wid you jes' lak you is, baby. God took pattern after a pine tree and built you noble. Youse a pritty man, and if Ah knowed any way to make you mo' pritty still Ah'd take and do it."

Joe reached over gently and toyed with Missie May's ear. "You jes' say dat cause you love me, but Ah know Ah can't hold no light to Otis D. Slemmons. Ah ain't never been nowhere and Ah ain't got nothin' but you."

Missie May got on his lap and kissed him and he kissed back in kind. Then he went on. "All de womens is crazy 'bout 'im everywhere he go."

"How you know dat, Joe?"

"He tole us so hisself."

"Dat don't make it so. His mouf is cut cross-ways, ain't it? Well, he kin lie jes' lak anybody else."

"Good Lawd, Missie! You womens sho is hard to sense into things. He's got a five-dollar gold piece for a stick-pin and he got a ten-dollar gold piece on his watch chain and his mouf is jes' crammed full of gold teethes. Sho wisht it wuz mine. And whut make it so cool, he got money 'cumulated. And womens give it all to 'im."

"Ah don't see whut de womens see on 'im. Ah wouldn't give 'im a wink if de sheriff wuz after 'im."

"Well, he tole us how de white womens in Chicago give 'im all dat gold money. So he don't 'low nobody to touch it at all. Not even put dey finger on it. Dey tole 'im not to. You kin make 'miration at it, but don't tetch it."

"Whyn't he stay up dere where dey so crazy 'bout 'im?"

"Ah reckon dey done made 'im vast-rich and he wants to travel some. He say dey wouldn't leave 'im hit a lick of work. He got mo' lady people crazy 'bout him than he kin shake a stick at."

"Joe, Ah hates to see you so dumb. Dat stray nigger jes' tell y'all anything and y'all b'lieve it."

"Go 'head on now, honey and put on yo' clothes. He talkin' 'bout his pritty womens—Ah want 'im to see *mine.*"

Missie May went off to dress and Joe spent the time trying to make his stomach punch out like Slemmons' middle. He tried the rolling swagger of the stranger, but found that his tall bone-and-muscle stride fitted ill with it. He just had time to drop back into his seat before Missie May came in dressed to go.

On the way home that night Joe was exultant. "Didn't Ah say ole Otis was swell? Can't he talk Chicago talk? Wuzn't dat funny whut he said when great big fat ole Ida Armstrong come in? He asted me, 'Who is dat broad wid de forte shake?' Dat's a new word. Us always thought forty was a set of figgers but he showed us where it means a whole heap of things. Sometimes he don't say forty, he jes' say thirty-eight and two and dat mean de same thing. Know whut he tole me when Ah wuz payin' for our ice cream? He say, 'Ah have to hand it to you, Joe. Dat wife of yours is jes' thirty-eight and two. Yessuh, she's forte!' Ain't he killin'?"

"He'll do in case of a rush. But he sho is got uh heap uh gold on 'im. Dat's de first time Ah ever seed gold money. It lookted good on him sho nuff, but it'd look a whole heap better on you."

"Who, me? Missie May youse crazy! Where would a po' man lak me git gold money from?"

Missie May was silent for a minute, then she said, "Us might find some goin' long de road some time. Us could."

"Who would be losin' gold money round heah? We ain't even seen none dese white folks wearin' no gold money on dey watch chain. You must be figgerin' Mister Packard or Mister Cadillac goin' pass through heah."

"You don't know whut been lost 'round heah. Maybe somebody way back in memorial times lost they gold money and went on off and it ain't never been found. And then if we wuz to find it, you could wear some 'thout havin' no gang of womens lak dat Slemmons say he got."

Joe laughed and hugged her. "Don't be so wishful 'bout me. Ah'm satisfied de way Ah is. So long as Ah be yo' husband, Ah don't keer 'bout nothin' else. Ah'd ruther all de other womens in de world to be dead than for you to have de toothache. Less we go to bed and git our night rest."

It was Saturday night once more before Joe could parade his wife in Slemmons' ice cream parlor again. He worked the night shift and Saturday was his only night off. Every other evening around six o'clock he left home, and dying dawn saw him hustling home around the lake where the challenging sun flung a flaming sword from east to west across the trembling water.

That was the best part of life—going home to Missie May. Their whitewashed house, the mock battle on Saturday, the dinner and ice cream parlor afterwards, church on Sunday nights when Missie outdressed any woman in town—all, everything was right.

One night around eleven the acid ran out at the G. and G. The foreman knocked off the crew and let the steam die down. As Joe rounded the lake on his way home, a lean moon rode the lake in a silver boat. If anybody had asked Joe about the moon on the lake, he would have said he hadn't paid it any attention. But he saw it with his feelings. It made him yearn painfully for Missie, Creation obsessed him. He thought about children. They had been married for more than a year now. They had money put away. They ought to be making little feet for shoes. A little boy child would be about right.

He saw a dim light in the bedroom and decided to come in through the kitchen door. He could wash the fertilizer dust off himself before presenting himself to Missie May. It would be nice for her not to know that he was there until he slipped into his place in bed and hugged her back. She always liked that.

He eased the kitchen door open slowly and silently, but when he went to set his dinner bucket on the table he bumped it into a pile of dishes, and something crashed to the floor. He heard his wife gasp in fright and hurried to reassure her.

"Iss me, honey. Don't get skeered."

There was a quick, large movement in the bedroom. A rustle, a thud, and a stealthy silence. The light went out.

What? Robbers? Murderers? Some varmint attacking his helpless wife, perhaps. He struck a match, threw himself on guard and stepped over the doorsill into the bedroom.

The great belt on the wheel of Time slipped and eternity stood still. By the match light he could see the man's legs fighting with his breeches in his frantic desire to get them on. He had both chance and time to kill the intruder in his helpless condition—half in and half out of his pants—but he was too weak to take action. The shapeless enemies of humanity that live in the hours of Time had waylaid Joe. He was assaulted in his weakness. Like Samson awakening after his haircut. So he just opened his mouth and laughed.

The match went out and he struck another and lit the lamp. A howling wind raced across his heart, but underneath its fury he heard his wife sobbing and Slemmons pleading for his life. Offering to buy it with all that he had. "Please, suh, don't kill me. Sixty-two dollars at de sto'. Gold money."

Joe just stood. Slemmons looked at the window, but it was screened. Joe stood out like a rough-backed mountain between him and the door. Barring him from escape, from sunrise, from life.

He considered a surprise attack upon the big clown that stood there laughing like a chessy cat. But before his fist could travel an inch, Joe's own rushed out to crush him like a battering ram. Then Joe stood over him.

"Git into yo' damn rags, Slemmons, and dat quick."

Slemmons scrambled to his feet and into his vest and coat. As he grabbed his hat, Joe's fury overrode his intentions and he grabbed at Slemmons with his left hand and struck at him with his right. The right landed. The left grazed the front of his vest. Slemmons was knocked a somersault into the kitchen and fled through the open door. Joe found himself alone with Missie May, with the golden watch charm clutched in his left fist. A short bit of broken chain dangled between his fingers.

Missie May was sobbing. Wails of weeping without words. Joe stood, and after awhile he found out that he had something in his hand. And then he stood and felt without thinking and without seeing with his natural eyes. Missie May kept on crying and Joe kept on feeling so much and not knowing what to do with all his feelings, he put Slemmons' watch charm in his pants pocket and took a good laugh and went to bed.

"Missie May, whut you cryin' for?"

"Cause Ah love you so hard and Ah know you don't love *me* no mo'."

Joe sank his face into the pillow for a spell then he said huskily, "You don't know de feelings of dat yet, Missie May."

"Oh Joe, honey, he said he wuz gointer give me dat gold money and he jes' kept on after me—"

Joe was very still and silent for a long time. Then he said, "Well, don't cry no mo', Missie May. Ah got yo' gold piece for you."

The hours went past on their rusty ankles. Joe still and quiet on one bedrail and Missie May wrung dry of sobs on the other. Finally the sun's tide crept upon the shore of night and drowned all its hours. Missie May with her face stiff and streaked towards the window saw the dawn come into her yard. It was day. Nothing more. Joe wouldn't be coming home as usual. No need to fling open the front door and sweep off the porch, making it nice for Joe. Never no more breakfast to cook; no more washing and starching of Joe's jumper-jackets and pants. No more nothing. So why get up?

With this strange man in her bed, she felt embarrassed to get up and dress. She decided to wait till he had dressed and gone. Then she would get up, dress quickly and be gone forever beyond reach of Joe's looks and laughs. But he never moved. Red light turned to yellow, then white.

From beyond the no-man's land between them came a voice. A strange voice that yesterday had been Joe's.

"Missie May, ain't you gonna fix me no breakfus'?"

She sprang out of bed. "Yeah, Joe. Ah didn't reckon you wuz hongry."

No need to die today. Joe needed her for a few more minutes anyhow.

Soon there was a roaring fire in the cook stove. Water bucket full and two chickens killed. Joe loved fried chicken and rice. She didn't deserve a thing and good Joe was letting her cook him some breakfast. She rushed hot biscuits to the table as Joe took his seat.

He ate with his eyes in his plate. No laughter, no banter.

"Missie May, you ain't eatin' yo' breakfus'."

"Ah don't choose none, Ah thank yuh."

His coffee cup was empty. She sprang to refill it. When she turned from the stove and bent to set the cup beside Joe's plate, she saw the yellow coin on the table between them.

She slumped into her seat and wept into her arms.

Presently Joe said calmly, "Missie May, you cry too much. Don't look back lak Lot's wife and turn to salt."

The sun, the hero of every day, the impersonal old man that beams as brightly on death as on birth, came up every morning and raced across the blue dome and dipped into the sea of fire every evening. Water ran down hill and birds nested.

Missie knew why she didn't leave Joe. She couldn't. She loved him too much, but she could not understand why Joe didn't leave her. He was polite, even kind at times, but aloof.

There were no more Saturday romps. No ringing silver dollars to stack beside her plate. No pockets to rifle. In fact the yellow coin in his trousers was like a monster hiding in the cave of his pockets to destroy her.

She often wondered if he still had it, but nothing could have induced her to ask nor yet to explore his pockets to see for herself. Its shadow was in the house whether or no.

One night Joe came home around midnight and complained of pains in the back. He asked Missie to rub him down with liniment. It had been three months since Missie had touched his body and it all seemed strange. But she rubbed him. Grateful for the chance. Before morning, youth triumphed and Missie exulted. But the next day, as she joyfully made up their bed, beneath her pillow she found the piece of money with the bit of chain attached.

Alone to herself, she looked at the thing with loathing, but look she must. She took it into her hands with trembling and saw first thing that it was no gold piece. It was a gilded half dollar. Then she knew why Slemmons had forbidden anyone to touch his gold. He trusted village eyes at a distance not to recognize his stick-pin as a gilded quarter, and his watch charm as a four-bit piece.

She was glad at first that Joe had left it there. Perhaps he was through with her punishment. They were man and wife again. Then another thought came clawing at her. He had come home to buy from her as if she were any woman in the long house. Fifty cents for her love. As if to say that he could pay as well as Slemmons. She slid the coin into his Sunday pants pocket and dressed herself and left his house.

Halfway between her house and the quarters she met her husband's mother, and after a short talk she turned and went back home. Never would she admit defeat to that woman who prayed for it nightly. If she had not the substance of marriage she had the outside show. Joe must leave *her*. She let him see she didn't want his old gold four-bits too.

She saw no more of the coin for some time though she knew that Joe could not help finding it in his pocket. But his health kept poor, and he came home at least every ten days to be rubbed.

The sun swept around the horizon, trailing its robes of weeks and days. One morning as Joe came in from work, he found Missie May chopping wood. Without a word he took the ax and chopped a huge pile before he stopped.

"You ain' got no business choppin' wood, and you know it."

"How come? Ah been choppin' it for de last longest."

"Ah ain't blind. You makin' feet for shoes."

"Won't you be glad to have a lil baby chile, Joe?"

"You know dat 'thout astin' me."

"Iss gointer be a boy chile and de very spit of you."

"You reckon, Missie May?"

"Who else could it look lak?"

Joe said nothing, but he thrust his hand deep into his pocket and fingered something there.

It was almost six months later Missie May took to bed and Joe went and got his mother to come wait on the house.

Missie May delivered a fine boy. Her travail was over when Joe came in from work one morning. His mother and the old women were drinking great bowls of coffee around the fire in the kitchen.

The minute Joe came into the room his mother called him aside.

"How did Missie May make out?" he asked quickly.

"Who, dat gal? She strong as a ox. She gointer have plenty mo'. We done fixed her wid de sugar and lard to sweeten her for de nex' one."

Joe stood silent awhile.

"You ain't ast 'bout de baby, Joe. You oughter be mighty proud cause he sho is de spittin' image of yuh, son. Dat's yourn all right, if you never git another one, dat un is yourn. And you know Ah'm mighty proud too, son, cause Ah never thought well of you marryin' Missie May cause her ma used tuh fan her foot round right smart and Ah been mighty skeered dat Missie May wuz gointer git misput on her road."

Joe said nothing. He fooled around the house till late in the day then just before he went to work, he went and stood at the foot of the bed and asked his wife how she felt. He did this every day during the week.

On Saturday he went to Orlando to make his market. It had been a long time since he had done that.

Meat and lard, meal and flour, soap and starch. Cans of corn and tomatoes. All the staples. He fooled around town for awhile and bought bananas and apples. Way after while he went around to the candy store.

"Hellow, Joe," the clerk greeted him. "Ain't seen you in a long time."

"Nope, Ah ain't been heah. Been round in spots and places."

"Want some of them molasses kisses you always buy?"

"Yessuh." He threw the gilded half dollar on the counter. "Will dat spend?"

"Whut is it, Joe? Well, I'll be doggone! A gold-plated four-bit piece. Where'd you git it, Joe?"

"Offen a stray nigger dat come through Eatonville. He had it on his watch chain for a charm—goin' round making out iss gold money. Ha ha! He had a quarter on his tie pin and it wuz all golded up too. Tryin' to fool people. Makin' out he so rich and everything. Ha! Ha! Tryin' to tole off folkses wives from home."

"How did you git it, Joe? Did he fool you, too?"

"Who, me? Naw suh! He ain't fooled me none. Know whut Ah done? He come round me wid his smart talk. Ah hauled off and knocked 'im down and took his old four-bits way from 'im. Gointer buy my wife some good ole lasses kisses wid it. Gimme fifty cents worth of dem candy kisses."

"Fifty cents buys a mightly lot of candy kisses, Joe. Why don't you split it up and take some chocolate bars, too. They eat good, too."

"Yessuh, dey do, but Ah wants all dat in kisses. Ah got a lil boy chile home now. Tain't a week old yet, but he kin suck a sugar tit and maybe eat one them kisses hisself."

Joe got his candy and left the store. The clerk turned to the next customer. "Wisht I could be like these darkies. Laughin' all the time. Nothin' worries 'em."

Back in Eatonville, Joe reached his own front door. There was the ring of singing metal on wood. Fifteen times. Missie May couldn't run to the door, but she crept there as quickly as she could.

"Joe Banks, Ah hear you chunkin' money in mah do'way. You wait till Ah got mah strength back and Ah'm gointer fix you for dat."

1933

Thomas Wolfe 1900–1938

Thomas Wolfe was born in Asheville, North Carolina, the youngest of eight children. His father was a stonecutter, fond of Shakespeare and rhetoric, and he saw to it that his precocious son, Tom, unlike the other poor children of that rural region, was educated in a private school, where his writing talent was first recognized and encouraged. Thomas Wolfe went on to the University of North Carolina and, after graduation, to Harvard, where he developed his literary talents by studying playwriting, and after two years at Harvard, received an M.A. degree.

From Harvard, Wolfe moved to New York, where he taught at New York University. But a trip to Europe begun in the fall of 1924 interrupted his teaching career and led to crucial events in his development as a writer: After a memorable year in Europe, he met on the return voyage Aline Bernstein, a married woman eighteen years older than Wolfe. She became Wolfe's confidante, editor, and inspiration. With her emotional and financial support he completed Look Homeward, Angel, *his first novel. It was submitted to*

Scribner's in 1929, where it was read by Maxwell Perkins, who was also the editor of Fitzgerald and Hemingway. Working closely with Perkins, Wolfe revised the manuscript, and it was published in October 1929.

The novel, which corresponds closely to the experiences of Wolfe's first twenty years, was a critical success, and it was singled out for particular praise in 1930 by Sinclair Lewis in his Nobel Prize acceptance speech. The only people who did not like the book, it seemed, were the inhabitants of Wolfe's hometown who felt insulted by their portraits in a novel drawn so clearly from Wolfe's own background. In 1935, again with substantial help from Perkins, Wolfe published Of Time and the River, *which is in effect a sequel to his first book. It continued the story of Eugene Gant, Wolfe's own fictional equivalent. But the book met with less critical favor than* Look Homeward, Angel. *Reviewers objected to the biographical basis and the formlessness of the novel. Barnard De Voto, a noted critic of American literature, was concise: Wolfe may be a genius, but "genius is not enough." Perhaps more significant for Wolfe than the mixed reviews was the fact that he broke with his editor, Perkins, and his publisher, Scribner's.*

Fortunately for Wolfe, he soon established a similar relationship with Edward Aswell, an editor at Harper and Brothers, and in 1938 he delivered an enormous manuscript of nearly a million words. While Aswell was editing the manuscript, Wolfe went on a tour of the western United States. There he contracted pneumonia. Subsequently it was discovered that he was suffering from tuberculosis of the brain. He returned to the East, to Baltimore, where he died on September 15, 1938. He was thirty-seven.

From the mass of material Wolfe had left behind, his editor fashioned three posthumously published books: the novels The Web and the Rock *(1939) and* You Can't Go Home Again *(1940), and a compilation of sketches, fiction, and drama,* The Hills Beyond *(1941). Like the earlier novels they reveal Wolfe's strengths and weaknesses. His creative energy made his writing rich with vitality and human sensations; at the same time, this energy was so uncontrolled and excessive as to overwhelm his novels with undigested experiences and ill-defined ideas. In places his work shines with passion, excitement, the joys of life. In others it is dulled by insistent emotional pleading, by intensity without respite.*

He attempted a great task: He wished to discover "an entire universe" and "a complete language"; he wanted to portray the wide range of the American experience, and to that end he planned an elaborate, structured, myth-laden series of works spanning the history of America. But death came too soon, and today Thomas Wolfe is best remembered as the author of a few formless but powerful novels. Yet his work also includes essays, plays, and short stories, and it is paradoxical that in such shorter works, where the limitations of space and time impose a need for restraint and control, Wolfe achieves some of his best work, marked by vitality and power, and with clear insight into the turbulence and the breadth of American life.

FURTHER READING: *The Letters of Thomas Wolfe,* ed. E. Nowell, 1956; *The World of Thomas Wolfe,* ed. C. Holman, 1962; *The Letters of Thomas Wolfe to His Mother,* ed. C. Holman and S. Ross, 1968; *Thomas Wolfe: Three Decades of Criticism,* ed. L. Field, 1968; *The Notebooks of Thomas Wolfe,* 2 vols., ed. R. Kennedy and P. Reeves, 1970; *Thomas Wolfe: The Critical Reception,* ed. P. Reeves, 1974; *The Loneliness at the Core: Studies in Thomas Wolfe,* ed. C. Holman, 1975; L. Gurko, *Thomas Wolfe: Beyond the Romantic Ego,* 1975; E. Evans, *Thomas Wolfe,* 1984; *Critical Essays on Thomas Wolfe,* ed. S. Phillipson, 1985; D. Donald, *Look Homeward: A Life of Thomas Wolfe,* 1987; J. Idol, *A Thomas Wolfe Companion,* 1987; L. Field, *Thomas Wolfe and His Editors,* 1987; C. Johnston, *Of Time and the Artist,* 1996; S. Holliday, *Thomas Wolfe and the Politics of Modernism,* 2001; R. Ensign, *Lean Down Your Ear upon the Earth, and Listen: Thomas Wolfe's Greener Modernism,* 2003.

TEXT: *From Death to Morning,* 1935.

ONLY THE DEAD KNOW BROOKLYN

Dere's no guy livin' dat known Brooklyn t'roo an' t'roo, because it'd take a guy a lifetime just to find his way aroun' duh f——town.

So like I say, I'm waitin' for my train t' come when I sees dis big guy standin' deh—dis is duh foist I eveh see of him. Well, he's lookin' wild, y' know, an' I can see dat he's had plenty, but still he's holdin' it; he talks good an' is walkin' straight enough. So den, dis big guy steps up to a little guy dat's standin' deh, an' says, "How d'yuh get t' eighteent' Avenoo an' Sixty-sevent' Street?" he says.

"Jesus! Yuh got me, chief," duh little guy says to him. "I ain't been heah long myself. Where is duh place?" he says. "Out in duh Flatbush section somewhere?"

"Nah," duh big guy says. "It's out in Bensonhoist. But I was neveh deh befoeh. How d'yuh get deh?"

"Jesus," duh little guy says, scratchin' his head, y'know—yuh could see duh little guy didn't know his way about—"yuh got me, chief. I neveh hoid of it. Do any of youse guys know where it is?" he says to me.

"Sure," I says. "It's out in Bensonhoist. Yuh take duh Fourt' Avenoo express, get off at Fifty-nint' Street, change to a Sea Beach local deh, get off at Eighteent' Avenoo an' Sixty-toid, an' den walk down foeh blocks. Dat's all yuh got to do," I says.

"G'wan!" some wise guy dat I neveh seen befoeh pipes up. "Whatcha talkin' about?" he says—oh, he was wise, y'know. "Duh guy is crazy! I tell yuh what yuh do," he says to duh big guy. "Yuh change to duh West End line at Toity-sixt'," he tells him. "Get off at Noo Utrecht an' Sixteent' Avenoo," he says. "Walk two blocks oveh, foeh blocks up," he says, "an' you'll be right deh." Oh, a *wise* guy, y'know.

"Oh, yeah?" I says. "Who told *you* so much?" He got me sore because he was so wise about it. "How long you been livin' heah?" I says.

"All my life," he says. "I was bawn in Williamsboig," he says. "An' I can tell you t'ings about dis town you neveh hoid of," he says.

"Yeah?" I says.

"Yeah," he says.

"Well, den, you can tell me t'ings about dis town dat nobody else has eveh hoid of, either. Maybe you make it all up yoehself at night," I says, "befoeh you go to sleep—like cuttin' out papeh dolls, or somp'n."

"Oh, yeah?" he says. "You're pretty wise, ain't yuh?"

"Oh, I don't know," I says. "Duh boids ain't usin my head for Lincoln's statue yet," I says. "But I'm wise enough to know a phony when I see one."

"Yeah?" he says. "A wise guy, huh? Well, you're so wise dat some one's goin' t'bust yuh one right on duh snoot some day," he says. "Dat's how wise *you* are."

Well, my train was comin', or I'da smacked him den and dere, but when I seen duh train was comin', all I said was, "All right, mugg! I'm sorry I can't stay to take keh of you, but I'll be seein' yuh sometime, I hope, out in duh cemetery." So den I says to duh big guy, who'd been standin' deh all duh time, "You come wit me," I says. So when we gets onto duh train I says to him, "Where yuh goin' out in Bensonhoist?" I says. "What numbeh are yuh lookin' for?" I says. *You* know—I t'ought if he told me duh address I might be able to help him out.

"Oh," he says, "I'm not lookin' for no one. I don't know no one out deh."

"Then whatcha goin' out deh for?" I says.

"Oh," duh guy says, "I'm just goin' out to see duh place," he says. "I like duh sound of duh name—Bensonhoist, y'know—so I t'ought I'd go out an' have a look at it."

"Whatcha tryin' t'hand me?" I says. "Whatcha tryin' t'do—kid me?" *You* know, I t'ought duh guy was bein' wise wit me.

"No," he says, "I'm tellin' yuh duh troot. I like to go out an' take a look at places wit nice names like dat. I like to go out an' look at all kinds of places," he says.

"How'd yuh know deh was such a place," I says, "if yuh neveh been deh befoeh?"

"Oh," he says, "I got a map."

"A *map?*" I says.

"Sure," he says, "I got a map dat ells me about all dese places. I take it wit me every time I come out heah," he says.

And Jesus! Wit dat, he pulls it out of his pocket, an' so help me, but he's *got* it—he's tellin' duh troot—a big map of duh whole f——place with all duh different pahts mahked out. You know—Canarsie an' East Noo Yawk an' Flatbush, Bensonhoist, Sout' Brooklyn, duh Heights, Bay Ridge, Greenpernt—duh whole goddam layout, he's got it right deh on duh map.

"You been to any of dose places?" I says.

"Sure," he says, "I been to most of 'em. I was down in Red Hook just last night," he says.

"Jesus! Red Hook!" I says. "Whatcha do down deh?"

"Oh," he says, "nuttin' much. I just walked aroun'. I went into a coupla places an' had a drink," he says, "but most of the time I just walked aroun'."

"Just walked aroun'?" I says.

"Sure," he says, "just lookin' at t'ings, y'know."

"Oh," he says, "I don't know duh name of duh place, but I could find it on my map," he says. "One time I was walkin' across some big fields where deh ain't no houses," he says, "but I could see ships oveh deh all lighted up. Dey was loadin'. So I walks across duh fields," he says, "to where duh ships are."

"Sure," I says, "I know where you was. You was down to duh Erie Basin."

"Yeah," he says, "I guess dat was it. Dey had some of dose big elevators an' cranes an' dey was loadin' ships, an' I could see some ships in drydock all lighted up, so I walks across duh fields to where dey are," he says.

"Den what did yuh do?" I says.

"Oh," he says, "nuttin' much. I came on back across duh fields after a while an' went into a coupla places an' had a drink."

"Didn't nuttin' happen while yuh was in dere?" I says.

"No," he says. "Nuttin' much. A coupla guys was drunk in one of duh places an' started a fight, but dey bounced 'em out," he says, "an' den one of duh guys stahted to come back again, but duh bartender gets his baseball bat out from under duh counteh, so duh guy goes on."

"Jesus!" I said, "Red Hook!"

"Sure," he says. "Dat's where it was, all right."

"Well, you keep outa deh," I says. "You stay away from deh."

"Why?" he says. "What's wrong wit it?"

"Oh," I says, "it's a good place to stay away from, dat's all. It's a good place to keep out of."

"Why?" he says. "Why is it?"

Jesus! Whatcha gonna do wit a guy as dumb as dat? I saw it wasn't no use to try to tell him nuttin', he wouldn't know what I was talkin' about, so I just says to him, "Oh, nuttin'. Yuh might get lost down deh, dat's all."

"Lost?" he says. "No, *I* wouldn't get lost. I got a map," he says.

A map! Red Hook! Jesus!

So den duh guy begins to ast me all kinds of nutty questions: how big was Brooklyn an' could I find my way aroun' in it, an' how long would it take a guy to know duh place.

"Listen!" I says. "You get dat idea outa yoeh head right now," I says. "You ain't neveh gonna get to know Brooklyn," I says. "Not in a hunderd yeahs. I been livin' heah all my life," I says, "an' I don't even know all deh is to know about it, so how do you expect to know duh town," I says, "when you don't even live heah?"

"Yes," he says, "but I got a map to help me find my way about."

"Map or no map," I says, "yuh ain't gonna get to know Brooklyn wit no map," I says.

"Can you swim?" he says, just like dat. Jesus! By dat time, y'know, I begun to see dat guy was some kind of nut. He'd had plenty to drink, of course, but he had dat crazy look in his eye I didn't like. "Can you swim?" he says.

"Sure," I says. "Can't you?"

"No," he says. "Not more'n a stroke or two. I neveh loined good."

"Well, it's easy," I says. "All yuh need is a little confidence. Duh way I loined, me older bruddeh pitched me off duh dock one day when I was eight yeahs old, cloes an' all. 'You'll swim,' he says. 'You'll swim all right—or drown.' An', believe me, I *swam!* When yuh know yuh got to, you'll do it. Duh only t'ing yuh need is confidence. An' once you've loined," I says, "you've got nuttin' else to worry about. You'll neveh forget it. It's somp'n dat stays wit yuh as long as yuh live."

"Can you swim good?" he says.

"Like a fish," I tells him. "I'm a regulah fish in duh wateh," I says. "I loined to swim right off duh docks wit all duh oddeh kids," I says.

"What would you do if yuh saw a man drownin'?" duh guy says.

"Do? Why, I'd jump in an' pull him out," I says. "Dat's what I'd do."

"Did yuh eveh see a man drown?" he says.

"Sure," I says. "I see two guys—bot' times at Coney Island. Dey got out too far, an' neider one could swim. Dey drowned befoeh any one could get to 'em."

"What becomes of people after dey've drowned out heah?" he says.

"Drowned out where?" I says.

"Out heah in Brooklyn."

"I don't know whatcha mean," I says. "Neveh hoid of no one drownin' heah in Brooklyn, unless you mean a swimmin' pool. Yuh can't drown in Brooklyn," I says. "Yuh gotta drown somewhere else—in duh ocean, where dere's wateh."

"Drownin'," duh guy says, lookin' at his map. "Drownin'." Jesus! I could see by den he was some kind of nut, he had dat crazy expression in his eyes when he looked at you, an' I didn't know what he might do. So we was comin' to a station, an' it wasn't my stop, but I got off anyway, an' waited for duh next train.

"Drownin'," duh guy says, lookin' at his map. "Drownin'."

Jesus! I've t'ought about dat guy a t'ousand times since den an' wondered what eveh happened to 'm goin' out to look at Bensonhoist because he liked duh name! Walkin' aroun' t'roo Red Hook by himself at night an' lookin' at his map! How many people did I see get drowned out heah in Brooklyn! How long would it take a guy with a good map to know all deh was to know about Brooklyn!

Jesus! What a nut *he* was! I wondeh what eveh happened to 'im, anyway! I wondeh if some one knocked him on duh head, or if he's still wanderin' aroun' in duh subway in duh middle of duh night wit his little map! Duh poor guy! Say, I've got to laugh, at dat, when I t'ink about him! Maybe he's found out by now dat he'll neveh live long enough to know duh whole of Brooklyn. It'd take a guy a lifetime to know Brooklyn t'roo an' t'roo. An' even den, yuh wouldn't know it all.

1935

THE FAR AND THE NEAR

On the outskirts of a little town upon a rise of land that swept back from the railway there was a tidy little cottage of white boards, trimmed vividly with green blinds. To one side of the house there was a garden neatly patterned with plots of growing vegetables, and an arbor for the grapes which ripened late in August. Before the house there were three mighty oaks which sheltered it in their clean and massive shade in summer, and to the other side there was a border of gay flowers. The whole place had an air of tidiness, thrift, and modest comfort.

Every day, a few minutes after two o'clock in the afternoon, the limited express between two cities passed this spot. At that moment the great train, having halted for a breathing-space at the town near by, was beginning to lengthen evenly into its stroke, but it had not yet reached the full drive of its terrific speed. It swung into view deliberately, swept past with a powerful swaying motion of the engine, a low smooth rumble of its heavy cars upon pressed steel, and then it vanished in the cut. For a moment the progress of the engine could be marked by heavy bellowing puffs of smoke that burst at spaced intervals above the edges of the meadow grass, and finally nothing could be heard but the solid clacking tempo of the wheels receding into the drowsy stillness of the afternoon.

Every day for more than twenty years, as the train had approached this house, the engineer had blown on the whistle, and every day, as soon as she heard this signal, a woman had appeared on the back porch of the little house and waved to him. At first she had a small child clinging to her skirts, and now this child had grown to full womanhood, and every day she, too, came with her mother to the porch and waved.

The engineer had grown old and gray in service. He had driven his great train, loaded with its weight of lives, across the land ten thousand times. His own children had grown up and married, and four times he had seen before him on the tracks the ghastly dot of tragedy converging like a cannon ball to its eclipse of horror at the boiler head—a light spring wagon filled with children, with its clustered row of small stunned faces; a cheap automobile stalled upon the tracks, set with wooden figures of people paralyzed with fear; a battered hobo walking by the rail, too deaf to hear the whistle's warning; and a form flung past his window with a scream—all this the man had seen and known. He had known all the grief, the joy, the peril and the labor such a man could know; he had grown seamed and weathered in his loyal service, and now, schooled by the qualities of faith and courage and humbleness that attended his labor, he had grown old, and had the grandeur and the wisdom these men have.

But no matter what peril or tragedy he had known, the vision of the little house and the women waving to him with a brave free motion of the arm had become fixed in the mind of the engineer as something beautiful and enduring, something beyond all change and ruin, and something that would always be the same, no matter what mishap, grief or error might break the iron schedule of his days.

The sight of the little house and of these two women gave him the most extraordinary happiness he had ever known. He had seen them in a thousand lights, a hundred weathers. He had seen them through the harsh bare light of wintry gray across the brown and frosted stubble of earth, and he had seen them again in the green luring sorcery of April.

He felt for them and for the little house in which they lived such tenderness as a man might feel for his own children, and at length the picture of their lives was carved so sharply in his heart that he felt that he knew their lives completely, to every hour and moment of the day, and he resolved that one day, when his years of service should be ended, he would go and find these people and speak at last with them whose lives had been so wrought into his own.

That day came. At last the engineer stepped from a train onto the station platform of the town where these two women lived. His years upon the rail had ended. He was a pensioned servant of his company, with no more work to do. The engineer walked slowly through the station and out into the streets of the town. Everything was as strange to him as if he had never seen this town before. As he walked on, his sense of bewilderment and confusion grew. Could this be the town he had passed ten thousand times? Were these the same houses he had seen so often from the high windows of his cab? It was all as unfamiliar, as disquieting as a city in a dream, and the perplexity of his spirit increased as he went on.

Presently the houses thinned into the straggling outposts of the town, and the street faded into a country road—the one on which the women lived. And the man plodded on slowly in the heat and dust. At length he stood before the house he sought. He knew at once that he had found the proper place. He saw the lordly oaks before the house, the flower beds, the garden and the arbor, and farther off, the glint of rails.

Yes, this was the house he sought, the place he had passed so many times, the destination he had longed for with such happiness. But now that he had found it, now that he was here, why did his hand falter on the gate; why had the town, the road, the earth, the very entrance to this place he loved turned unfamiliar as the landscape of some ugly dream? Why did he now feel this sense of confusion, doubt and hopelessness?

At length he entered the gate, walked slowly up the path and in a moment more had mounted three short steps that led up to the porch, and was knocking at the door. Presently he heard steps in the hall, the door was opened, and a woman stood facing him.

And instantly, with a sense of bitter loss and grief, he was sorry he had come. He knew at once that the woman who stood there looking at him with a mistrustful eye was the same woman who had waved to him so many thousand times. But her face was harsh and pinched and meager; the flesh sagged wearily in sallow folds, and the small eyes peered at him with timid suspicion and uneasy doubt. All the brave freedom, the warmth and the affection that he had read into her gesture, vanished in the moment that he saw her and heard her unfriendly tongue.

And now his own voice sounded unreal and ghastly to him as he tried to explain his presence, to tell her who he was and the reason he had come. But he faltered on, fighting stubbornly against the horror of regret, confusion, disbelief that surged up in his spirit, drowning all his former joy and making his act of hope and tenderness seem shameful to him.

At length the woman invited him almost unwillingly into the house, and called her daughter in a harsh shrill voice. Then, for a brief agony of time, the man sat in an ugly little parlor, and he tried to talk while the two women stared at him with a dull, bewildered hostility, a sullen, timorous restraint.

And finally, stammering a crude farewell, he departed. He walked away down the path and then along the road toward town, and suddenly he knew that he was an old man. His heart, which had been brave and confident when it looked along the familiar vista of the rails, was now sick with doubt and horror as it saw the strange and unsuspected visage of an earth which had always been within a stone's throw of him, and which he had never seen or known. And he knew that all the magic of that bright lost way, the vista of that shining line, the imagined corner of that small good universe of hope's desire, was gone forever, could never be got back again.

1935

F. Scott Fitzgerald 1896–1940

In 1925 T. S. Eliot described The Great Gatsby, *written by F. Scott Fitzgerald, as "the first step that American fiction has taken since Henry James." Fitzgerald seemed destined for almost unlimited success as one of America's great writers, but only a few years later, John Dos Passos began a letter to him by calling him a "poor miserable bastard" who was spilling his talent out "in little pieces." In the early 1920s, Fitzgerald was the embodiment as well as the chronicler of the Jazz Age (a term for which he was largely responsible). He was handsome, uninhibited, and successful. He not only wrote some of the best prose, but he also drank the best wines, knew the best people, went to the best parties, and lived as though the money supply would never dry up. Even in 1931, two years after the stock market crash and well into the Great Depression, Fitzgerald's writing earned nearly $40,000. But the money supply did dry up. And the acclaim. In 1939 his royalties totaled only $33; by the following year not a single one of his books was in print. His life, which had represented the fulfillment of the American dream of wealth and achievement, seemed to end in a nightmare of squandered talent and despair.*

He was born Francis Scott Key Fitzgerald (among his forebears was the author of The Star Spangled Banner*). In his hometown of St. Paul, Minnesota, his family was considered socially prominent and genteelly poor. With the financial aid of relatives he was sent to prep school and to Princeton. In college he compiled a record of social triumphs and* *academic failures, and in 1917, his senior year, he left Princeton to serve in World War I. In Alabama, where he was sent for military training, he fell hopelessly in love with Zelda Sayre. She was the embodiment of all his romantic notions of a Southern belle, and when Fitzgerald was discharged from the army in 1919, he was determined to win success, fame, and Zelda. He took a job with an advertising agency and worked on short stories and a novel at night. Eventually his first novel,* This Side of Paradise, *was accepted for publication. The book appeared in March 1920. A week later Fitzgerald and Zelda were married.*

This Side of Paradise, *with its portrayal of the casual dissipations of "flaming youth," was an immediate commercial success, and Zelda and Scott Fitzgerald attempted to live up to—or even beyond—his fictional portraits of scandalous young men and women. They swam in public fountains in New York, rode to parties on the hoods of taxis, fought with waiters, and danced on dining tables. Life had become a long cocktail party, yet Fitzgerald managed somehow to continue writing. In 1922, he published his second novel,* The Beautiful and Damned, *and a collection of short stories,* Tales of the Jazz Age. *In 1923, he wrote a satirical play,* The Vegetable, Or from Postman to President. *It was a critical and financial failure, and to maintain his extravagant lifestyle, Fitzgerald ground out short stories rapidly for money, which he squandered just as rapidly. In 1925 Fitzgerald managed to complete* The Great Gatsby. *It was a critical success but a commercial disappointment; it sold only about half as many copies as either of his first two novels, and it earned little more than enough to repay debts to his publishers.*

Over the next two years Fitzgerald wrote little; it was, in his own words, a time of "1,000 parties and no work." In desperation he went to Hollywood, in 1927, for his first period of screenwriting, an occupation that was to sustain him for much of his remaining life. In 1934, Tender is the Night *was published. The year of its publication, it sold only 13,000 copies, and although it is a precise indictment of irresponsible social values of the 1930s, the critics harshly accused Fitzgerald of ignoring the Depression while writing a frivolous novel about neurotic Americans who preferred Europe over their native land.*

Battered by the illness of his wife (in the 1930s, Zelda began to suffer a series of mental breakdowns), by his own alcoholism, and by the failures of his writing, Fitzgerald now worked mainly in Hollywood. He continued to engage in periodic drinking bouts and grew seriously ill. In November 1940 he suffered a heart attack and a second one a month later. On December 21, 1940, he died. He was forty-four. His last novel, The Last Tycoon, *remained unfinished.*

At the time of his death Fitzgerald was considered (when considered at all) a failed literary hope, a writer victimized by his own indulgences. But since the 1940s his literary reputation has steadily risen. Today he is judged to be one of the major American prose writers of the twentieth century, and more copies of his works are now sold each year than were sold during his entire lifetime. In a number of his short stories, and in his finest novels, The Great Gatsby *and* Tender is the Night, *Fitzgerald had revealed, as no other American writer had, the stridency of an age of glittering innocence. In vivid and graceful prose he had, at the same time, portrayed the hollowness of the American worship of riches and the American dreams of love and splendor and gratified desire.*

FURTHER READING: A. Mizener, *The Far Side of Paradise: A Biography,* 1951, 1967; *The Letters of F. Scott Fitzgerald,* ed. A. Turnbull, 1963; A. Latham, *Crazy Sundays: F. Scott Fitzgerald in Hollywood,* 1971; S. Mayfield, *Exiles from Paradise: Zelda and Scott Fitzgerald,* 1972; *The Notebooks of F. Scott Fitzgerald,* ed. M. Bruccoli, 1980; *Correspondence of F. Scott Fitzgerald,* ed. M. Bruccoli and M. Duggan, 1980; M. Bruccoli, *Some Sort of Epic Grandeur: The Life of F.*

Scott Fitzgerald, 1983; S. Donaldson, *Fool for Love: F. Scott Fitzgerald,* 1983; W. Dixon, *The Cinematic Vision of F. Scott Fitzgerald,* 1986; A. Petry, *Fitzgerald's Craft of Short Fiction: The Collected Stories 1920–1935,* 1989; J. Kuehl, *F. Scott Fitzgerald: A Study of the Short Fiction,* 1991; J. Meyers, *Scott Fitzgerald: A Biography,* 1993; *F. Scott Fitzgerald: A Life in Letters,* ed. M. Bruccoli, 1994; R. Roulston and H. Roulston, *The Winding Road to West Egg,* 1995; *New Essays on F. Scott Fitzgerald's Neglected Stories,* ed. J. Bryer, 1996; J. Baughman, *F. Scott Fitzgerald,* 2000; L. Pelzer, *Student Companion to F. Scott Fitzgerald,* 2000; M. Bruccoli, *Classes on F. Scott Fitzgerald,* 2001; *F. Scott Fitzgerald,* ed. H. Bloom, 2002; *A Historical Guide to F. Scott Fitzgerald,* ed. K. Curnutt, 2004.

TEXTS: *Flappers and Philosophers,* 1920; *Metropolitan Magazine,* December 1922.

BERNICE BOBS HER HAIR[1]

After dark on Saturday night one could stand on the first tee of the golf-course and see the country-club windows as a yellow expanse over a very black and wavy ocean. The waves of this ocean, so to speak, were the heads of many curious caddies, a few of the more ingenious chauffeurs, the golf professional's deaf sister—and there were usually several stray, diffident waves who might have rolled inside had they so desired. This was the gallery.

The balcony was inside. It consisted of the circle of wicker chairs that lined the wall of the combination clubroom and ballroom. At these Saturday-night dances it was largely feminine; a great babel[2] of middle-aged ladies with sharp eyes and icy hearts behind lorgnettes and large bosoms. The main function of the balcony was critical. It occasionally showed grudging admiration, but never approval, for it is well known among ladies over thirty-five that when the younger set dance in the summer-time it is with the very worst intentions in the world, and if they are not bombarded with stony eyes stray couples will dance weird barbaric interludes in the corners, and the more popular, more dangerous, girls will sometimes be kissed in the parked limousines of unsuspecting dowagers.[3]

But, after all, this critical circle is not close enough to the stage to see the actors' faces and catch the subtler byplay. It can only frown and lean, ask questions and make satisfactory deductions from its set of postulates, such as the one which states that every young man with a large income leads the life of a hunted partridge. It never really appreciates the drama of the shifting, semicruel world of adolescence. No; boxes, orchestra-circle, principals, and chorus are represented by the medley of faces and voices that sway to the plaintive African rhythm of Dyer's dance orchestra.

From sixteen-year-old Otis Ormonde, who has two more years at Hill School, to G. Reece Stoddard, over whose bureau at home hangs a Harvard law diploma; from little Madeleine Hogue, whose hair still feels strange and uncomfortable on top of her head, to Bessie MacRae, who has been the life of the

[1]Cuts her hair short.

[2]Confused noise, named after the Tower of Babel, built by prideful men who wanted to reach up to Heaven. They were prevented by God from accomplishing the task when he gave them separate languages so that they could no longer communicate with one another. The story is told in Genesis 11.

[3]Elderly women of high rank, or widows with property.

party a little too long—more than ten years—the medley is not only the centre of the stage but contains the only people capable of getting an un-obstructed view of it.

With a flourish and a bang the music stops. The couples exchange artificial, effortless smiles, facetiously repeat "la-de-da-da dum-dum," and then the clatter of young feminine voices soars over the burst of clapping.

A few disappointed stags caught in midfloor as they had been about to cut in subsided listlessly back to the walls, because this was not like the riotous Christmas dances—these summer hops were considered just pleasantly warm and exciting, where even the younger marrieds rose and performed ancient waltzes and terrifying fox trots to the tolerant amusement of their younger brothers and sisters.

Warren McIntyre, who casually attended Yale, being one of the unfortunate stags, felt in his dinner-coat pocket for a cigarette and strolled out onto the wide, semidark veranda, where couples were scattered at tables, filling the lantern-hung night with vague words and hazy laughter. He nodded here and there at the less absorbed and as he passed each couple some half-forgotten fragment of a story played in his mind, for it was not a large city and every one was Who's Who to every one else's past. There, for example, were Jim Strain and Ethel Demorest, who had been privately engaged for three years. Every one knew that as soon as Jim managed to hold a job for more than two months she would marry him. Yet how bored they both looked, and how wearily Ethel regarded Jim sometimes, as if she wondered why she had trained the vines of her affection on such a wind-shaken poplar.

Warren was nineteen and rather pitying with those of his friends who hadn't gone East to college. But, like most boys, he bragged tremendously about the girls of his city when he was away from it. There was Genevieve Ormonde, who regularly made the rounds of dances, house-parties, and football games at Princeton, Yale, Williams, and Cornell; there was black-eyed Roberta Dillon, who was quite as famous to her own generation as Hiram Johnson or Ty Cobb;[4] and, of course, there was Marjorie Harvey, who besides having a fairylike face and a dazzling, bewildering tongue was already justly celebrated for having turned five cart-wheels in succession during the last pump-and-slipper dance at New Haven.

Warren, who had grown up across the street from Marjorie, had long been "crazy about her." Sometimes she seemed to reciprocate his feeling with a faint gratitude, but she had tried him by her infallible test and informed him gravely that she did not love him. Her test was that when she was away from him she forgot him and had affairs with other boys. Warren found this discouraging, especially as Marjorie had been making little trips all summer, and for the first two or three days after each arrival home he saw great heaps of mail on the Harveys' hall table addressed to her in various masculine handwritings. To make matters worse, all during the month of August she had been visited by her cousin Bernice from Eau Claire, and it seemed impossible to see her alone. It was always necessary to hunt round and find some one to take care of Bernice. As August waned this was becoming more and more difficult.

[4]Hiram Warren Johnson (1866–1945) was governor of California and later a U.S. senator. Tyrus Raymond Cobb (1886–1961) was a star baseball player for the Detroit Tigers.

Much as Warren worshipped Marjorie, he had to admit that Cousin Bernice was sorta dopeless.[5] She was pretty, with dark hair and high color, but she was no fun on a party. Every Saturday night he danced a long arduous duty dance with her to please Marjorie, but he had never been anything but bored in her company.

"Warren"—a soft voice at his elbow broke in upon his thoughts, and he turned to see Marjorie, flushed and radiant as usual. She laid a hand on his shoulder and a glow settled almost imperceptibly over him.

"Warren," she whispered, "do something for me—dance with Bernice. She's been stuck with little Otis Ormonde for almost an hour."

Warren's glow faded.

"Why—sure," he answered half-heartedly.

"You don't mind, do you? I'll see that you don't get stuck."

"'Sall right."

Marjorie smiled—that smile that was thanks enough.

"You're an angel, and I'm obliged loads."

With a sigh the angel glanced round the veranda, but Bernice and Otis were not in sight. He wandered back inside, and there in front of the women's dressing-room he found Otis in the centre of a group of young men who were convulsed with laughter. Otis was brandishing a piece of timber he had picked up, and discoursing volubly.

"She's gone in to fix her hair," he announced wildly. "I'm waiting to dance another hour with her."

Their laughter was renewed.

"Why don't some of you cut in?" cried Otis resentfully. "She likes more variety."

"Why, Otis," suggested a friend, "you've just barely got used to her."

"Why the two-by-four, Otis?" inquired Warren, smiling.

"The two-by-four? Oh, this? This is a club. When she comes out I'll hit her on the head and knock her in again."

Warren collapsed on a settee and howled with glee.

"Never mind, Otis," he articulated finally. "I'm relieving you this time."

Otis simulated a sudden fainting attack and handed the stick to Warren.

"If you need it, old man," he said hoarsely.

No matter how beautiful or brilliant a girl may be, the reputation of not being frequently cut in on makes her position at a dance unfortunate. Perhaps boys prefer her company to that of the butterflies with whom they dance a dozen times an evening, but youth in this jazz-nourished generation is temperamentally restless, and the idea of fox-trotting more than one full fox trot with the same girl is distasteful, not to say odious. When it comes to several dances and the intermissions between she can be quite sure that a young man, once relieved, will never tread on her wayward toes again.

Warren danced the next full dance with Bernice, and finally, thankful for the intermission, he led her to a table on the veranda. There was a moment's silence while she did unimpressive things with her fan.

"It's hotter here than in Eau Claire," she said.

Warren stifled a sigh and nodded. It might be for all he knew or cared. He wondered idly whether she was a poor conversationalist because she got no attention or got no attention because she was a poor conversationalist.

[5]Uninteresting.

"You going to be here much longer?" he asked, and then turned rather red. She might suspect his reasons for asking.

"Another week," she answered, and stared at him as if to lunge at his next remark when it left his lips.

Warren fidgeted. Then with a sudden charitable impulse he decided to try part of his line on her. He turned and looked at her eyes.

"You've got an awfully kissable mouth," he began quietly.

This was a remark that he sometimes made to girls at college proms when they were talking in just such half dark as this. Bernice distinctly jumped. She turned an ungraceful red and became clumsy with her fan. No one had ever made such a remark to her before.

"Fresh!"—the word had slipped out before she realized it, and she bit her lip. Too late she decided to be amused, and offered him a flustered smile.

Warren was annoyed. Though not accustomed to have that remark taken seriously, still it usually provoked a laugh or a paragraph of sentimental banter. And he hated to be called fresh, except in a joking way. His charitable impulse died and he switched the topic.

"Jim Strain and Ethel Demorest sitting out as usual," he commented.

This was more in Bernice's line, but a faint regret mingled with her relief as the subject changed. Men did not talk to her about kissable mouths, but she knew that they talked in some such way to other girls.

"Oh, yes," she said, and laughed. "I hear they've been mooning round for years without a red penny. Isn't it silly?"

Warren's disgust increased. Jim Strain was a close friend of his brother's, and anyway he considered it bad form to sneer at people for not having money. But Bernice had had no intention of sneering. She was merely nervous.

II

When Marjorie and Bernice reached home at half after midnight they said good night at the top of the stairs. Though cousins, they were not intimates. As a matter of fact Marjorie had no female intimates—she considered girls stupid. Bernice on the contrary all through this parent-arranged visit had rather longed to exchange those confidences flavored with giggles and tears that she considered an indispensable factor in all feminine intercourse. But in this respect she found Marjorie rather cold; felt somehow the same difficulty in talking to her that she had in talking to men. Marjorie never giggled, was never frightened, seldom embarrassed, and in fact had very few of the qualities which Bernice considered appropriately and blessedly feminine.

As Bernice busied herself with tooth-brush and paste this night she wondered for the hundredth time why she never had any attention when she was away from home. That her family were the wealthiest in Eau Claire; that her mother entertained tremendously, gave little dinners for her daughter before all dances and bought her a car of her own to drive round in, never occurred to her as factors in her home-town social success. Like most girls she had been brought up on the warm milk prepared by Annie Fellows Johnston and on novels in which the female was beloved because of certain mysterious womanly qualities always mentioned but never displayed.

Bernice felt a vague pain that she was not at present engaged in being popular. She did not know that had it not been for Marjorie's campaigning she would have danced the entire evening with one man; but she knew that even in Eau Claire other girls with less position and less pulchritude were given a much bigger rush. She attributed this to something subtly unscrupulous in those girls. It had never worried her, and if it had her mother would have assured her that the other girls cheapened themselves and that men really respected girls like Bernice.

She turned out the light in her bathroom, and on an impulse decided to go in and chat for a moment with her aunt Josephine, whose light was still on. Her soft slippers bore her noiselessly down the carpeted hall, but hearing voices inside she stopped near the partly opened door. Then she caught her own name, and without any definite intention of eavesdropping lingered—and the thread of the conversation going on inside pierced her consciousness sharply as if it had been drawn through with a needle.

"She's absolutely hopeless!" It was Marjorie's voice. "Oh, I know what you're going to say! So many people have told you how pretty and sweet she is, and how she can cook! What of it? She has a bum time. Men don't like her."

"What's a little cheap popularity?"

Mrs. Harvey sounded annoyed.

"It's everything when you're eighteen," said Marjorie emphatically. "I've done my best. I've been polite and I've made men dance with her, but they just won't stand being bored. When I think of that gorgeous coloring wasted on such a ninny, and think what Martha Carey could do with it—oh!"

"There's no courtesy these days."

Mrs. Harvey's voice implied that modern situations were too much for her. When she was a girl all young ladies who belonged to nice families had glorious times.

"Well," said Marjorie, "no girl can permanently bolster up a lame-duck visitor, because these days it's every girl for herself. I've even tried to drop her hints about clothes and things, and she's been furious—given me the funniest looks. She's sensitive enough to know she's not getting away with much, but I'll bet she consoles herself by thinking that she's very virtuous and that I'm too gay and fickle and will come to a bad end. All unpopular girls think that way. Sour grapes! Sarah Hopkins refers to Genevieve and Roberta and me as gardenia girls! I'll bet she'd give ten years of her life and her European education to be a gardenia girl and have three or four men in love with her and be cut in on every few feet at dances."

"It seems to me," interrupted Mrs. Harvey rather wearily, "that you ought to be able to do something for Bernice. I know she's not very vivacious."

Marjorie groaned.

"Vivacious! Good grief! I've never heard her say anything to a boy except that it's hot or the floor's crowded or that she's going to school in New York next year. Sometimes she asks them what kind of car they have and tells them the kind she has. Thrilling!"

There was a short silence, and then Mrs. Harvey took up her refrain:

"All I know is that other girls not half so sweet and attractive get partners. Martha Carey, for instance, is stout and loud, and her mother is distinctly common. Roberta Dillon is so thin this year that she looks as though Arizona were the place for her. She's dancing herself to death."

"But, mother," objected Marjorie impatiently, "Martha is cheerful and awfully witty and an awfully slick girl, and Roberta's a marvellous dancer. She's been popular for ages!"

Mrs. Harvey yawned.

"I think it's that crazy Indian blood in Bernice," continued Marjorie. "Maybe she's a reversion to type. Indian women all just sat round and never said anything."

"Go to bed, you silly child," laughed Mrs. Harvey. "I wouldn't have told you that if I'd thought you were going to remember it. And I think most of your ideas are perfectly idiotic," she finished sleepily.

There was another silence, while Marjorie considered whether or not convincing her mother was worth the trouble. People over forty can seldom be permanently convinced of anything. At eighteen our convictions are hills from which we look; at forty-five they are caves in which we hide.

Having decided this, Marjorie said good night. When she came out into the hall it was quite empty.

III

While Marjorie was breakfasting late next day Bernice came into the room with a rather formal good morning, sat down opposite, stared intently over and slightly moistened her lips.

"What's on your mind?" inquired Marjorie, rather puzzled.

Bernice paused before she threw her hand-grenade.

"I heard what you said about me to your mother last night."

Marjorie was startled, but she showed only a faintly heightened color and her voice was quite even when she spoke.

"Where were you?"

"In the hall. I didn't mean to listen—at first."

After an involuntary look of contempt Marjorie dropped her eyes and became very interested in balancing a stray corn-flake on her finger.

"I guess I'd better go back to Eau Claire—if I'm such a nuisance." Bernice's lower lip was trembling violently and she continued on a wavering note: "I've tried to be nice, and—and I've been first neglected and then insulted. No one ever visited me and got such treatment."

Marjorie was silent.

"But I'm in the way, I see. I'm a drag on you. Your friends don't like me." She paused, and then remembered another one of her grievances. "Of course I was furious last week when you tried to hint to me that that dress was unbecoming. Don't you think I know how to dress myself?"

"No," murmured Marjorie less than half-aloud.

"What?"

"I didn't hint anything," said Marjorie succinctly. "I said, as I remember, that it was better to wear a becoming dress three times straight than to alternate it with two frights."

"Do you think that was a very nice thing to say?"

"I wasn't trying to be nice." Then after a pause: "When do you want to go?"

Bernice drew in her breath sharply.

"Oh!" It was a little half-cry.

Marjorie looked up in surprise.

"Didn't you say you were going?"

"Yes, but——"

"Oh, you were only bluffing!"

They stared at each other across the breakfast-table for a moment. Misty waves were passing before Bernice's eyes, while Marjorie's face wore that rather hard expression that she used when slightly intoxicated undergraduates were making love to her.

"So you were bluffing," she repeated as if it were what she might have expected.

Bernice admitted it by bursting into tears. Marjorie's eyes showed boredom.

"You're my cousin," sobbed Bernice. "I'm v-v-visiting you. I was to stay a month, and if I go home my mother will know and she'll wah-wonder——"

Marjorie waited until the shower of broken words collapsed into little sniffles.

"I'll give you my month's allowance," she said coldly, "and you can spend this last week anywhere you want. There's a very nice hotel——"

Bernice's sobs rose to a flute note, and rising of a sudden she fled from the room.

An hour later, while Marjorie was in the library absorbed in composing one of those non-committal, marvellously elusive letters that only a young girl can write, Bernice reappeared, very red-eyed and consciously calm. She cast no glance at Marjorie but took a book at random from the shelf and sat down as if to read. Marjorie seemed absorbed in her letter and continued writing. When the clock showed noon Bernice closed her book with a snap.

"I suppose I'd better get my railroad ticket."

This was not the beginning of the speech she had rehearsed up-stairs, but as Marjorie was not getting her cues—wasn't urging her to be reasonable; it's all a mistake—it was the best opening she could muster.

"Just wait till I finish this letter," said Marjorie without looking round. "I want to get it off in the next mail."

After another minute, during which her pen scratched busily, she turned round and relaxed with an air of "at your service." Again Bernice had to speak.

"Do you want me to go home?"

"Well," said Marjorie, considering, "I suppose if you're not having a good time you'd better go. No use being miserable."

"Don't you think common kindness——"

"Oh, please don't quote *Little Women*!"[6] cried Marjorie impatiently. "That's out of style."

"You think so?"

"Heavens, yes! What modern girl could live like those inane females?"

"They were the models for our mothers."

Marjorie laughed.

"Yes, they were—not! Besides, our mothers were all very well in their way, but they know very little about their daughters' problems."

Bernice drew herself up.

"Please don't talk about my mother."

Marjorie laughed.

"I don't think I mentioned her."

Bernice felt that she was being led away from her subject.

[6]A very popular novel by Louisa May Alcott (1832–1888).

"Do you think you've treated me very well?"

"I've done my best. You're rather hard material to work with."

The lids of Bernice's eyes reddened.

"I think you're hard and selfish, and you haven't a feminine quality in you."

"Oh, my Lord!" cried Marjorie in desperation. "You little nut! Girls like you are responsible for all the tiresome colorless marriages; all those ghastly inefficiencies that pass as feminine qualities. What a blow it must be when a man with imagination marries the beautiful bundle of clothes that he's been building ideals round, and finds that she's just a weak, whining, cowardly mass of affectations!"

Bernice's mouth had slipped half open.

"The womanly woman!" continued Marjorie. "Her whole early life is occupied in whining criticisms of girls like me who really do have a good time."

Bernice's jaw descended farther as Marjorie's voice rose.

"There's some excuse for an ugly girl whining. If I'd been irretrievably ugly I'd never have forgiven my parents for bringing me into the world. But you're starting life without any handicap—" Marjorie's little fist clinched. "If you expect me to weep with you you'll be disappointed. Go or stay, just as you like." And picking up her letters she left the room.

Bernice claimed a headache and failed to appear at luncheon. They had a matinée date for the afternoon, but the headache persisting, Marjorie made explanation to a not very downcast boy. But when she returned late in the afternoon she found Bernice with a strangely set face waiting for her in her bedroom.

"I've decided," began Bernice without preliminaries, "that maybe you're right about things—possibly not. But if you'll tell me why your friends aren't—aren't interested in me I'll see if I can do what you want me to."

Marjorie was at the mirror shaking down her hair.

"Do you mean it?"

"Yes."

"Without reservations? Will you do exactly what I say?"

"Well, I——"

"Well nothing! Will you do exactly as I say?"

"If they're sensible things."

"They're not! You're no case for sensible things."

"Are you going to make—to recommend——"

"Yes, everything. If I tell you to take boxing-lessons you'll have to do it. Write home and tell your mother you're going to stay another two weeks."

"If you'll tell me——"

"All right—I'll just give you a few examples now. First, you have no ease of manner. Why? Because you're never sure about your personal appearance. When a girl feels that she's perfectly groomed and dressed she can forget that part of her. That's charm. The more parts of yourself you can afford to forget the more charm you have."

"Don't I look all right?"

"No; for instance, you never take care of your eyebrows. They're black and lustrous, but by leaving them straggly they're a blemish. They'd be beautiful if you'd take care of them in one-tenth the time you take doing nothing. You're going to brush them so that they'll grow straight."

Bernice raised the brows in question.

"Do you mean to say that men notice eyebrows?"

"Yes—subconsciously. And when you go home you ought to have your teeth straightened a little. It's almost imperceptible, still——"

"But I thought," interrupted Bernice in bewilderment, "that you despised little dainty feminine things like that."

"I hate dainty minds," answered Marjorie. "But a girl has to be dainty in person. If she looks like a million dollars she can talk about Russia, ping-pong, or the League of Nations and get away with it."

"What else?"

"Oh, I'm just beginning! There's your dancing."

"Don't I dance all right?"

"No, you don't—you lean on a man; yes, you do—ever so slightly. I noticed it when we were dancing together yesterday. And you dance standing up straight instead of bending over a little. Probably some old lady on the side-line once told you that you looked so dignified that way. But except with a very small girl it's much harder on the man, and he's the one that counts."

"Go on." Bernice's brain was reeling.

"Well, you've got to learn to be nice to men who are sad birds. You look as if you'd been insulted whenever you're thrown with any except the most popular boys. Why, Bernice, I'm cut in on every few feet—and who does most of it? Why, those very sad birds. No girl can afford to neglect them. They're the big part of any crowd. Young boys too shy to talk are the very best conversational practice. Clumsy boys are the best dancing practice. If you can follow them and yet look graceful you can follow a baby tank across a barb-wire sky-scraper."

Bernice sighed profoundly, but Marjorie was not through.

"If you go to a dance and really amuse, say, three sad birds that dance with you; if you talk so well to them that they forget they're stuck with you, you've done something. They'll come back next time, and gradually so many sad birds will dance with you that the attractive boys will see there's no danger of being stuck—then they'll dance with you."

"Yes," agreed Bernice faintly. "I think I begin to see."

"And finally," concluded Marjorie, "poise and charm will just come. You'll wake up some morning knowing you've attained it, and men will know it too."

Bernice rose.

"It's been awfully kind of you—but nobody's ever talked to me like this before, and I feel sort of startled."

Marjorie made no answer but gazed pensively at her own image in the mirror.

"You're a peach to help me," continued Bernice.

Still Marjorie did not answer, and Bernice thought she had seemed too grateful.

"I know you don't like sentiment," she said timidly.

Marjorie turned to her quickly.

"Oh, I wasn't thinking about that. I was considering whether we hadn't better bob your hair."

Bernice collapsed backward upon the bed.

IV

On the following Wednesday evening there was a dinner-dance at the country club. When the guests strolled in Bernice found her place-card with a slight feeling of irritation. Though at her right sat G. Reece Stoddard, a most desirable and distinguished young bachelor, the all-important left held only Charley Paulson. Charley lacked height, beauty, and social shrewdness, and in her new enlightenment Bernice decided that his only qualification to be her partner was that he had never been stuck with her. But this feeling of irritation left with the last of the soup-plates, and Marjorie's specific instruction came to her. Swallowing her pride she turned to Charley Paulson and plunged.

"Do you think I ought to bob my hair, Mr. Charley Paulson?"

Charley looked up in surprise.

"Why?"

"Because I'm considering it. It's such a sure and easy way of attracting attention."

Charley smiled pleasantly. He could not know this had been rehearsed. He replied that he didn't know much about bobbed hair. But Bernice was there to tell him.

"I want to be a society vampire, you see," she announced coolly, and went on to inform him that bobbed hair was the necessary prelude. She added that she wanted to ask his advice, because she had heard he was so critical about girls.

Charley, who knew as much about the psychology of women as he did of the mental states of Buddhist contemplatives, felt vaguely flattered.

"So I've decided," she continued, her voice rising slightly, "that early next week I'm going down to the Sevier Hotel barber-shop, sit in the first chair, and get my hair bobbed." She faltered, noticing that the people near her had paused in their conversation and were listening; but after a confused second Marjorie's coaching told, and she finished her paragraph to the vicinity at large. "Of course I'm charging admission, but if you'll all come down and encourage me I'll issue passes for the inside seats."

There was a ripple of appreciative laughter, and under cover of it G. Reece Stoddard leaned over quickly and said close to her ear: "I'll take a box right now."

She met his eyes and smiled as if he had said something surpassingly brilliant.

"Do you believe in bobbed hair?" asked G. Reece in the same undertone.

"I think it's unmoral," affirmed Bernice gravely. "But, of course, you've either got to amuse people or feed 'em or shock 'em." Marjorie had culled this from Oscar Wilde. It was greeted with a ripple of laughter from the men and a series of quick, intent looks from the girls. And then as though she had said nothing of wit or moment Bernice turned again to Charley and spoke confidentially in his ear.

"I want to ask you your opinion of several people. I imagine you're a wonderful judge of character."

Charley thrilled faintly—paid her a subtle compliment by overturning her water.

Two hours later, while Warren McIntyre was standing passively in the stag line abstractedly watching the dancers and wondering whither and with whom Marjorie had disappeared, an unrelated perception began to creep slowly upon him—a perception that Bernice, cousin to Marjorie, had been cut in on several times in the past five minutes. He closed his eyes, opened them and looked again. Several minutes back she had been dancing with a visiting boy, a matter easily accounted for; a visiting boy would know no better. But now she was dancing with some one else, and there was Charley Paulson headed for her with enthusiastic determination in his eye. Funny—Charley seldom danced with more than three girls an evening.

Warren was distinctly surprised when—the exchange having been effected—the man relieved proved to be none other than G. Reece Stoddard himself. And

G. Reece seemed not at all jubilant at being relieved. Next time Bernice danced near, Warren regarded her intently. Yes, she was pretty, distinctly pretty; and to-night her face seemed really vivacious. She had that look that no woman, however histrionically proficient, can successfully counterfeit—she looked as if she were having a good time. He liked the way she had her hair arranged, wondered if it was brilliantine that made it glisten so. And that dress was becoming—a dark red that set off her shadowy eyes and high coloring. He remembered that he had thought her pretty when she first came to town, before he had realized that she was dull. Too bad she was dull—dull girls unbearable—certainly pretty though.

His thoughts zigzagged back to Marjorie. This disappearance would be like other disappearances. When she reappeared he would demand where she had been—would be told emphatically that it was none of his business. What a pity she was so sure of him! She basked in the knowledge that no other girl in town interested him; she defied him to fall in love with Genevieve or Roberta.

Warren sighed. The way to Marjorie's affections was a labyrinth indeed. He looked up. Bernice was again dancing with the visiting boy. Half unconsciously he took a step out from the stag line in her direction, and hesitated. Then he said to himself that it was charity. He walked toward her—collided suddenly with G. Reece Stoddard.

"Pardon me," said Warren.

But G. Reece had not stopped to apologize. He had again cut in on Bernice.

That night at one o'clock Marjorie, with one hand on the electric-light switch in the hall, turned to take a last look at Bernice's sparkling eyes.

"So it worked?"

"Oh, Marjorie, yes!" cried Bernice.

"I saw you were having a gay time."

"I did! The only trouble was that about midnight I ran short of talk. I had to repeat myself—with different men of course. I hope they won't compare notes."

"Men don't," said Marjorie, yawning, "and it wouldn't matter if they did—they'd think you were even trickier."

She snapped out the light, and as they started up the stairs Bernice grasped the banister thankfully. For the first time in her life she had been danced tired.

"You see," said Marjorie at the top of the stairs, "one man sees another man cut in and he thinks there must be something there. Well, we'll fix up some new stuff to-morrow. Good night."

"Good night."

As Bernice took down her hair she passed the evening before her in review. She had followed instructions exactly. Even when Charley Paulson cut in for the eighth time she had simulated delight and had apparently been both interested and flattered. She had not talked about the weather or Eau Claire or automobiles or her school, but had confined her conversation to me, you, and us.

But a few minutes before she fell asleep a rebellious thought was churning drowsily in her brain—after all, it was she who had done it. Marjorie, to be sure, had given her her conversation, but then Marjorie got much of her conversation out of things she read. Bernice had bought the red dress, though she had never valued it highly before Marjorie dug it out of her trunk—and her own voice had said the words, her own lips had smiled, her own feet had danced. Marjorie nice girl—vain, though—nice evening—nice boys—like Warren—Warren—Warren—what's-his-name—Warren——

She fell asleep.

V

To Bernice the next week was a revelation. With the feeling that people really enjoyed looking at her and listening to her came the foundation of self-confidence. Of course there were numerous mistakes at first. She did not know, for instance, that Draycott Deyo was studying for the ministry; she was unaware that he had cut in on her because he thought she was a quiet, reserved girl. Had she known these things she would not have treated him to the line which began "Hello, Shell Shock!" and continued with the bathtub story—"It takes a frightful lot of energy to fix my hair in the summer—there's so much of it—so I always fix it first and powder my face and put on my hat; then I get into the bathtub, and dress afterward. Don't you think that's the best plan?"

Though Draycott Deyo was in the throes of difficulties concerning baptism by immersion and might possibly have seen a connection, it must be admitted that he did not. He considered feminine bathing an immoral subject, and gave her some of his ideas on the depravity of modern society.

But to offset that unfortunate occurrence Bernice had several signal successes to her credit. Little Otis Ormonde pleaded off from a trip East and elected instead to follow her with a puppy-like devotion, to the amusement of his crowd and to the irritation of G. Reece Stoddard, several of whose afternoon calls Otis completely ruined by the disgusting tenderness of the glances he bent on Bernice. He even told her the story of the two-by-four and the dressing-room to show her how frightfully mistaken he and every one else had been in their first judgment of her. Bernice laughed off that incident with a slight sinking sensation.

Of all Bernice's conversation perhaps the best known and most universally approved was the line about the bobbing of her hair.

"Oh, Bernice, when you goin' to get the hair bobbed?"

"Day after to-morrow maybe," she would reply, laughing. "Will you come and see me? Because I'm counting on you, you know."

"Will we? You know! But you better hurry up."

Bernice, whose tonsorial intentions were strictly dishonorable, would laugh again.

"Pretty soon now. You'd be surprised."

But perhaps the most significant symbol of her success was the gray car of the hypercritical Warren McIntyre, parked daily in front of the Harvey house. At first the parlor-maid was distinctly startled when he asked for Bernice instead of Marjorie; after a week of it she told the cook that Miss Bernice had gotta hold a Miss Marjorie's best fella.

And Miss Bernice had. Perhaps it began with Warren's desire to rouse jealousy in Marjorie; perhaps it was the familiar though unrecognized strain of Marjorie in Bernice's conversation; perhaps it was both of these and something of sincere attraction besides. But somehow the collective mind of the younger set knew within a week that Marjorie's most reliable beau had made an amazing face-about and was giving an indisputable rush to Marjorie's guest. The question of the moment was how Marjorie would take it. Warren called Bernice on the 'phone twice a day, sent her notes, and they were frequently seen together in his roadster, obviously engrossed in one of those tense, significant conversations as to whether or not he was sincere.

Marjorie on being twitted only laughed. She said she was mighty glad that Warren had at last found some one who appreciated him. So the younger set laughed, too, and guessed that Marjorie didn't care and let it go at that.

One afternoon when there were only three days left of her visit Bernice was waiting in the hall for Warren, with whom she was going to a bridge party. She was in rather a blissful mood, and when Marjorie—also bound for the party—appeared beside her and began casually to adjust her hat in the mirror, Bernice was utterly unprepared for anything in the nature of a clash. Marjorie did her work very coldly and succinctly in three sentences.

"You may as well get Warren out of your head," she said coldly.

"What?" Bernice was utterly astounded.

"You may as well stop making a fool of yourself over Warren McIntyre. He doesn't care a snap of his fingers about you."

For a tense moment they regarded each other—Marjorie scornful, aloof; Bernice astounded, half-angry, half-afraid. Then two cars drove up in front of the house and there was a riotous honking. Both of them gasped faintly, turned, and side by side hurried out.

All through the bridge party Bernice strove in vain to master a rising uneasiness. She had offended Marjorie, the sphinx of sphinxes. With the most wholesome and innocent intentions in the world she had stolen Marjorie's property. She felt suddenly and horribly guilty. After the bridge game, when they sat in an informal circle and the conversation became general, the storm gradually broke. Little Otis Ormonde inadvertently precipitated it.

"When you going back to kindergarten, Otis?" some one had asked.

"Me? Day Bernice gets her hair bobbed."

"Then your education's over," said Marjorie quickly. "That's only a bluff of hers. I should think you'd have realized."

"That a fact?" demanded Otis, giving Bernice a reproachful glance.

Bernice's ears burned as she tried to think up an effectual come-back. In the face of this direct attack her imagination was paralyzed.

"There's a lot of bluffs in the world," continued Marjorie quite pleasantly. "I should think you'd be young enough to know that, Otis."

"Well," said Otis, "maybe so. But gee! With a line like Bernice's—"

"Really?" yawned Marjorie. "What's her latest bon mot?"

No one seemed to know. In fact, Bernice, having trifled with her muse's beau, had said nothing memorable of late.

"Was that really all a line?" asked Roberta curiously.

Bernice hesitated. She felt that wit in some form was demanded of her, but under her cousin's suddenly frigid eyes she was completely incapacitated.

"I don't know," she stalled.

"Splush!" said Marjorie. "Admit it!"

Bernice saw that Warren's eyes had left a ukulele he had been tinkering with and were fixed on her questioningly.

"Oh, I don't know!" she repeated steadily. Her cheeks were glowing.

"Splush!" remarked Marjorie again.

"Come through, Bernice," urged Otis. "Tell her where to get off."

Bernice looked round again—she seemed unable to get away from Warren's eyes.

"I like bobbed hair," she said hurriedly, as if he had asked her a question, "and I intend to bob mine."

"When?" demanded Marjorie.

"Any time."

"No time like the present," suggested Roberta.

Otis jumped to his feet.

"Good stuff!" he cried. "We'll have a summer bobbing party. Sevier Hotel barber-shop, I think you said."

In an instant all were on their feet. Bernice's heart throbbed violently.

"What?" she gasped.

Out of the group came Marjorie's voice, very clear and contemptuous.

"Don't worry—she'll back out!"

"Come on, Bernice!" cried Otis, starting toward the door.

Four eyes—Warren's and Marjorie's—stared at her, challenged her, defied her. For another second she wavered wildly.

"All right," she said swiftly, "I don't care if I do."

An eternity of minutes later, riding down-town through the late afternoon beside Warren, the others following in Roberta's car close behind, Bernice had all the sensations of Marie Antoinette bound for the guillotine in a tumbrel. Vaguely she wondered why she did not cry out that it was all a mistake. It was all she could do to keep from clutching her hair with both hands to protect it from the suddenly hostile world. Yet she did neither. Even the thought of her mother was no deterrent now. This was the test supreme of her sportsmanship; her right to walk unchallenged in the starry heaven of popular girls.

Warren was moodily silent, and when they came to the hotel he drew up at the curb and nodded to Bernice to precede him out. Roberta's car emptied a laughing crowd into the shop, which presented two bold plate-glass windows to the street.

Bernice stood on the curb and looked at the sign, Sevier Barber-Shop. It was a guillotine indeed, and the hangman was the first barber, who, attired in a white coat and smoking a cigarette, leaned nonchalantly against the first chair. He must have heard of her; he must have been waiting all week, smoking eternal cigarettes beside that portentous, too-often-mentioned first chair. Would they blindfold her? No, but they would tie a white cloth round her neck lest any of her blood—nonsense—hair—should get on her clothes.

"All right, Bernice," said Warren quickly.

With her chin in the air she crossed the sidewalk, pushed open the swinging screen-door, and giving not a glance to the uproarious, riotous row that occupied the waiting bench, went up to the first barber.

"I want you to bob my hair."

The first barber's mouth slid somewhat open. His cigarette dropped to the floor.

"Huh?"

"My hair—bob it!"

Refusing further preliminaries, Bernice took her seat on high. A man in the chair next to her turned on his side and gave her a glance, half lather, half amazement. One barber started and spoiled little Willy Schuneman's monthly haircut. Mr. O'Reilly in the last chair grunted and swore musically in ancient Gaelic as a razor bit into his cheek. Two bootblacks became wide-eyed and rushed for her feet. No, Bernice didn't care for a shine.

Outside a passer-by stopped and stared; a couple joined him; half a dozen small boys' noses sprang into life, flattened against the glass; and snatches of conversation borne on the summer breeze drifted in through the screen-door.

"Lookada long hair on a kid!"

"Where'd yuh get 'at stuff? 'At's a bearded lady he just finished shavin'."

But Bernice saw nothing, heard nothing. Her only living sense told her that this man in the white coat had removed one tortoise-shell comb and then another; that his fingers were fumbling clumsily with unfamiliar hairpins; that this hair, this wonderful hair of hers, was going—she would never again feel its long voluptuous pull as it hung in a dark-brown glory down her back. For a second she was near breaking down, and then the picture before her swam mechanically into her vision—Marjorie's mouth curling in a faint ironic smile as if to say:

"Give up and get down! You tried to buck me and I called your bluff. You see you haven't got a prayer."

And some last energy rose up in Bernice, for she clinched her hands under the white cloth, and there was a curious narrowing of her eyes that Marjorie remarked on to some one long afterward.

Twenty minutes later the barber swung her round to face the mirror, and she flinched at the full extent of the damage that had been wrought. Her hair was not curly, and now it lay in lank lifeless blocks on both sides of her suddenly pale face. It was ugly as sin—she had known it would be ugly as sin. Her face's chief charm had been a Madonna-like simplicity. Now that was gone and she was—well, frightfully mediocre—not stagy; only ridiculous, like a Greenwich Villager who had left her spectacles at home.

As she climbed down from the chair she tried to smile—failed miserably. She saw two of the girls exchange glances; noticed Marjorie's mouth curved in attenuated mockery—and that Warren's eyes were suddenly very cold.

"You see"—her words fell into an awkward pause—"I've done it."

"Yes, you've—done it," admitted Warren.

"Do you like it?"

There was a half-hearted "Sure" from two or three voices, another awkward pause, and then Marjorie turned swiftly and with serpentlike intensity to Warren.

"Would you mind running me down to the cleaners?" she asked. "I've simply got to get a dress there before supper. Roberta's driving right home and she can take the others."

Warren stared abstractedly at some infinite speck out the window. Then for an instant his eyes rested coldly on Bernice before they turned to Marjorie.

"Be glad to," he said slowly.

VI

Bernice did not fully realize the outrageous trap that had been set for her until she met her aunt's amazed glance just before dinner.

"Why, Bernice!"

"I've bobbed it, Aunt Josephine."

"Why, child!"

"Do you like it?"

"Why, Ber-nice!"

"I suppose I've shocked you."

"No, but what'll Mrs. Deyo think tomorrow night? Bernice, you should have waited until after the Deyos' dance—you should have waited if you wanted to do that."

"It was sudden, Aunt Josephine. Anyway, why does it matter to Mrs. Deyo particularly?"

"Why, child," cried Mrs. Harvey, "in her paper on 'The Foibles of the Younger Generation' that she read at the last meeting of the Thursday Club she devoted fifteen minutes to bobbed hair. It's her pet abomination. And the dance is for you and Marjorie!"

"I'm sorry."

"Oh, Bernice, what'll your mother say? She'll think I let you do it."

"I'm sorry."

Dinner was an agony. She had made a hasty attempt with a curling-iron, and burned her finger and much hair. She could see that her aunt was both worried and grieved, and her uncle kept saying, "Well, I'll be darned!" over and over in a hurt and faintly hostile tone. And Marjorie sat very quietly, intrenched behind a faint smile, a faintly mocking smile.

Somehow she got through the evening. Three boys called; Marjorie disappeared with one of them, and Bernice made a listless unsuccessful attempt to entertain the two others—sighed thankfully as she climbed the stairs to her room at half past ten. What a day!

When she had undressed for the night the door opened and Marjorie came in.

"Bernice," she said, "I'm awfully sorry about the Deyo dance. I'll give you my word of honor I'd forgotten all about it."

"'Sall right," said Bernice shortly. Standing before the mirror she passed her comb slowly through her short hair.

"I'll take you down-town to-morrow," continued Marjorie, "and the hairdresser'll fix it so you'll look slick. I didn't imagine you'd go through with it. I'm really mighty sorry."

"Oh, 'sall right!"

"Still it's your last night, so I suppose it won't matter much."

Then Bernice winced as Marjorie tossed her own hair over her shoulders and began to twist it slowly into two long blond braids until in her cream-colored negligée she looked like a delicate painting of some Saxon princess. Fascinated, Bernice watched the braids grow. Heavy and luxurious they were, moving under the supple fingers like restive snakes—and to Bernice remained this relic and the curling-iron and a to-morrow full of eyes. She could see G. Reece Stoddard, who liked her, assuming his Harvard manner and telling his dinner partner that Bernice shouldn't have been allowed to go to the movies so much; she could see Draycott Deyo exchanging glances with his mother and then being conscientiously charitable to her. But then perhaps by to-morrow Mrs. Deyo would have heard the news; would send round an icy little note requesting that she fail to appear—and behind her back they would all laugh and know that Marjorie had made a fool of her; that her chance at beauty had been sacrificed to the jealous whim of a selfish girl. She sat down suddenly before the mirror, biting the inside of her cheek.

"I like it," she said with an effort. "I think it'll be becoming."

Marjorie smiled.

"It looks all right. For heaven's sake, don't let it worry you!"

"I won't."

"Good night, Bernice."

But as the door closed something snapped within Bernice. She sprang dynamically to her feet, clinching her hands, then swiftly and noiselessly crossed over to her bed and from underneath it dragged out her suitcase. Into it she tossed toilet articles and a change of clothing. Then she turned to her trunk and quickly dumped in two drawerfuls of lingerie and summer dresses. She moved quietly, but with deadly efficiency, and in three-quarters of an hour her trunk was locked and strapped and she was fully dressed in a becoming new travelling suit that Marjorie had helped her pick out.

Sitting down at her desk she wrote a short note to Mrs. Harvey, in which she briefly outlined her reasons for going. She sealed it, addressed it, and laid it on her pillow. She glanced at her watch. The train left at one, and she knew that if she walked down to the Marborough Hotel two blocks away she could easily get a taxicab.

Suddenly she drew in her breath sharply and an expression flashed into her eyes that a practised character reader might have connected vaguely with the set look she had worn in the barber's chair—somehow a development of it. It was quite a new look for Bernice and it carried consequences.

She went stealthily to the bureau, picked up an article that lay there, and turning out all the lights stood quietly until her eyes became accustomed to the darkness. Softly she pushed open the door to Marjorie's room. She heard the quiet, even breathing of an untroubled conscience asleep.

She was by the bedside now, very deliberate and calm. She acted swiftly. Bending over she found one of the braids of Marjorie's hair, followed it up with her hand to the point nearest the head, and then holding it a little slack so that the sleeper would feel no pull, she reached down with the shears and severed it. With the pigtail in her hand she held her breath. Marjorie had muttered something in her sleep. Bernice deftly amputated the other braid, paused for an instant, and then flitted swiftly and silently back to her own room.

Down-stairs she opened the big front door, closed it carefully behind her, and feeling oddly happy and exuberant stepped off the porch into the moonlight, swinging her heavy grip like a shopping-bag. After a minute's brisk walk she discovered that her left hand still held the two blond braids. She laughed unexpectedly—had to shut her mouth hard to keep from emitting an absolute peal. She was passing Warren's house now, and on the impulse she set down her baggage, and swinging the braids like pieces of rope flung them at the wooden porch, where they landed with a slight thud. She laughed again, no longer restraining herself.

"Huh!" she giggled wildly. "Scalp the selfish thing!"

Then picking up her suitcase she set off at a half-run down the moonlit street.

1920

WINTER DREAMS[1]

Some of the caddies were poor as sin and lived in one-room houses with a neurasthenic cow in the front yard, but Dexter Green's father owned the second best grocery store in Dillard—the best one was "The Hub," patronized by the wealthy people from Lake Erminie—and Dexter caddied only for pocket-money.

[1]The first published version of the story. Though now considered the best version and "aesthetically superior," the text was altered and shortened soon after it appeared, by editors and perhaps by Fitzgerald himself, for republication in an English magazine (1923) and in *All the Sad Young Men* (1926). Some spelling and punctuation errors have been corrected by the present editor for this edition.

In the fall when the days became crisp and grey and the long Minnesota winter shut down like the white lid of a box, Dexter's skis moved over the snow that hid the fairways of the golf course. At these times the country gave him a feeling of profound melancholy—it offended him that the links should lie in enforced fallowness, haunted by ragged sparrows for the long season. It was dreary, too, that on the tees where the gay colors fluttered in summer there were now only the desolate sand-boxes[2] knee-deep in crusted ice. When he crossed the hills the wind blew cold as misery, and if the sun was out he tramped with his eyes squinted up against the hard dimensionless glare.

In April the winter ceased abruptly. The snow ran down into Lake Erminie scarcely tarrying for the early golfers to brave the season with red and black balls.[3] Without elation, without an interval of moist glory the cold was gone.

Dexter knew that there was something dismal about this northern spring, just as he knew there was something gorgeous about the fall. Fall made him clench his hands and tremble and repeat idiotic sentences to himself and make brisk abrupt gestures of command to imaginary audiences and armies. October filled him with hope which November raised to a sort of ecstatic triumph, and in this wood the fleeting brilliant impressions of the summer at Lake Erminie were ready grist to his will. He became a golf champion and defeated Mr. T. A. Hedrick in a marvelous match played over a hundred times in the fairways of his imagination, a match each detail of which he changed about untiringly—sometimes winning with almost laughable ease, sometimes coming up magnificently from behind. Again, stepping from a Pierce-Arrow[4] automobile, like Mr. Mortimer Jones, he strolled frigidly into the lounge of the Erminie Golf Club—or perhaps, surrounded by an admiring crowd, he gave an exhibition of fancy diving from the springboard of the Erminie Club raft . . . Among those most impressed was Mr. Mortimer Jones.

And one day it came to pass that Mr. Jones, himself and not his ghost, came up to Dexter, almost with tears in his eyes and said that Dexter was the —— best caddy in the club and wouldn't he decide not to quit if Mr. Jones made it worth his while, because every other —— caddy in the club lost one ball a hole for him—regularly——

"No, sir," said Dexter, decisively, "I don't want to caddy anymore." Then, after a pause, "I'm too old."

"You're—why, you're not more than fourteen. Why did you decide just this morning that you wanted to quit? You promised that next week you'd go over to the state tournament with me."

"I decided I was too old."

Dexter handed in his "A Class" badge,[5] collected what money was due him from the caddy master and caught the train for Dillard.

"The best——caddy I ever saw," shouted Mr. Mortimer Jones over a drink that afternoon, "Never lost a ball! Willing! Intelligent! Quiet! Honest! Grateful!——"

The little girl who had done this was eleven—beautifully ugly as little girls are apt to be who are destined after a few years to be inexpressibly lovely and bring

[2]Receptacles for the sand formerly used to tee a golf ball.
[3]For play on snow covered ground.
[4]Elegant and costly American automobile produced from 1901 to 1938.
[5]Indication that he was a caddy of the highest rank.

no end of misery to a great number of men. The spark, however, was perceptible. There was a general ungodliness in the way her lips twisted down at the corners when she smiled and in the—Heaven help us!—in the almost passionate quality of her eyes. Vitality is born early in such women. It was utterly in evidence now, shining through her thin frame in a sort of glow.

She had come eagerly out on to the course at nine o'clock with a white linen nurse and five small new golf clubs in a white canvas bag which the nurse was carrying. When Dexter first saw her she was standing by the caddy house, rather ill-at-ease and trying to conceal the fact by engaging her nurse in an obviously unnatural conversation illumined by startling and irrevelant smiles from herself.

"Well, it's certainly a nice day, Hilda," Dexter heard her say, then she drew down the corners of her mouth, smiled and glanced furtively around, her eyes in transit falling for an instant on Dexter.

Then to the nurse:

"Well, I guess there aren't very many people out here this morning, are there?"

The smile again radiant, blatantly artificial—convincing.

"I don't know what we're supposed to do now," said the nurse, looking nowhere in particular.

"Oh, that's all right"—the smile—"I'll fix it up."

Dexter stood perfectly still, his mouth faintly ajar. He knew that if he moved forward a step his stare would be in her line of vision—if he moved backward he would lose his full view of her face—For a moment he had not realized how young she was. Now he remembered having seen her several times the year before—in bloomers.

Suddenly, involuntarily, he laughed, a short abrupt laugh—then, startled by himself, he turned and began to walk quickly away.

"Boy!"

Dexter stopped.

"Boy——"

Beyond question he was addressed. Not only that, but he was treated to that absurd smile, that preposterous smile—the memory of which at least half a dozen men were to carry to the grave.

"Boy, do you know where the golf teacher is?"

"He's giving a lesson."

"Well, do you know where the caddy-master is?"

"He's not here yet this morning."

"Oh." For a moment this baffled her. She stood alternately on her right and left foot.

"We'd like to get a caddy," said the nurse, "Mrs. Mortimer Jones sent us out to play golf and we don't know how without we get a caddy."

Here she was stopped by an ominous glance from Miss Jones, followed immediately by the smile.

"There aren't any caddies here except me," said Dexter to the nurse, "And I got to stay here in charge until the caddy-master gets here."

"Oh."

Miss Jones and her retinue now withdrew and at a proper distance from Dexter became involved in a heated conversation. The conversation was concluded by Miss Jones taking one of the clubs and hitting it on the ground with violence. For further emphasis she raised it again and was about to bring it down smartly upon the nurse's bosom, when the nurse seized the club and twisted it from her hands.

"You darn *fool!*" cried Miss Jones wildly.

Another argument ensued. Realizing that the elements of the comedy were implied in the scene, Dexter several times began to smile but each time slew the smile before it reached maturity. He could not resist the monstrous conviction that the little girl was justified in beating the nurse.

The situation was resolved by the fortuitous appearance of the caddy-master who was appealed to immediately by the nurse.

"Miss Jones is to have a little caddy and this one says he can't go."

"Mr. McKenna said I was to wait here till you came," said Dexter quickly.

"Well, he's here now." Miss Jones smiled cheerfully at the caddy-master. Then she dropped her bag and set off at a haughty mince toward the first tee.

"Well?" The caddy-master turned to Dexter, "What you standing there like a dummy for? Go pick up the young lady's clubs."

"I don't think I'll go out today," said Dexter.

"You don't——"

"I think I'll quit."

The enormity of his decision frightened him. He was a favorite caddy and the thirty dollars a month he earned through the summer were not to be made elsewhere in Dillard. But he had received a strong, emotional shock and his perturbation required a violent and immediate outlet.

It is not so simple as that, either. As so frequently would be the case in the future, Dexter was unconsciously dictated to by his winter dreams.

Now, of course, the quality and the seasonability of these winter dreams varied, but the stuff of them remained. They persuaded Dexter several years later to pass up a business course at the State University—his father, prospering now, would have paid his way—for the precarious advantage of attending an older and more famous university in the East, where he was bothered by his scanty funds. But do not get the impression, because his winter dreams happened to be concerned at first with musings on the rich, that there was anything shoddy in the boy. He wanted not association with glittering things and glittering people—he wanted the glittering things themselves. Often he reached out for the best without knowing why he wanted it—and sometimes he ran up against the mysterious denials and prohibitions in which life indulges. It is with one of those denials and not with his career as a whole that this story deals.

He made money. It was rather amazing. After college he went to the city from which Lake Erminie draws its wealthy patrons. When he was only twenty-three and had been there not quite two years, there were already people who liked to say, "Now *there's* a boy—" All about him rich men's sons were peddling bonds precariously, or investing patrimonies precariously, or plodding through the two dozen volumes of canned rubbish in the "George Washington Commercial Course," but Dexter borrowed a thousand dollars on his college degree and his steady eyes, and bought a partnership in a *laundry*.

It was a small laundry when he went into it. Dexter made a specialty of learning how the English washed fine woolen golf stockings without shrinking them. Inside of a year he was catering to the trade who wore knickerbockers. Men were insisting that their Shetland hose and sweaters go to his laundry just as they had insisted on a caddy who could find golf balls. A little later he was doing their wives' lingerie as well—and running five branches in different parts of the city. Before he was twenty-seven he owned the largest string of laundries in his section of the country. It was then that he sold out and went to New York. But the part of his story that concerns us here goes back to when he was making his first big success.

When he was twenty-three Mr. W. L. Hart, one of the grey-haired men who like to say "Now there's a boy"—gave him a guest card to the Lake Erminie Club for over a week-end. So he signed his name one day on the register, and that afternoon played golf in a foursome with Mr. Hart and Mr. Sandwood and Mr. T. A. Hedrick. He did not consider it necessary to remark that he had once carried Mr. Hart's bag over this same links and that he knew every trap and gully with his eyes shut—but he found himself glancing at the four caddies who trailed them, trying to catch a gleam or gesture that would remind him of himself, that would lessen the gap which lay between his past and his future.

It was a curious day, slashed abruptly with fleeting, familiar impressions. One minute he had the sense of being a trespasser—in the next he was impressed by the tremendous superiority he felt toward Mr. T. A. Hedrick, who was a bore and not even a good golfer any more.

Then, because of a ball Mr. Hart lost near the fifteenth green an enormous thing happened. While they were searching the stiff grasses of the rough there was a clear call of "Fore!" from behind a hill in their rear. And as they all turned abruptly from their search a bright new ball sliced abruptly over the hill and caught Mr. T. A. Hedrick rather neatly in the stomach.

Mr. T. A. Hedrick grunted and cursed.

"By Gad!" cried Mr. Hedrick, "they ought to put some of these crazy women off the course. It's getting to be outrageous."

A head and a voice came up together over the hill:

"Do you mind if we go through?"

"You hit me in the stomach!" thundered Mr. Hedrick.

"Did I?" The girl approached the group of men. "I'm sorry. I yelled 'Fore!'"

Her glance fell casually on each of the men. She nodded to Sandwood and then scanned the fairway for her ball.

"Did I bounce off into the rough?"

It was impossible to determine whether this question was ingenuous or malicious. In a moment, however, she left no doubt, for as her partner came up over the hill she called cheerfully.

"Here I am! I'd have gone on the green except that I hit something."

As she took her stance for a short mashie[6] shot, Dexter looked at her closely. She wore a blue gingham dress, rimmed at throat and shoulders with a white edging that accentuated her tan. The quality of exaggeration, of thinness that had made her passionate eyes and down turning mouth absurd at eleven was gone now. She was arrestingly beautiful. The color in her cheeks was centered like the color in a picture—it was not a "high" color, but a sort of fluctuating and feverish warmth, so shaded that it seemed at any moment it would recede and disappear. This color and the mobility of her mouth gave a continual impression of flux, of intense life, of passionate vitality—balanced only partially by the sad luxury of her eyes.

[6]Former name of the modern five iron.

She swung her mashie impatiently and without interest, pitching the ball into a sandpit on the other side of the green. With a quick insincere smile and a careless "Thank you!" she went on after it.

"That Judy Jones!" remarked Mr. Hedrick on the next tee, as they waited—some moments—for her to play on ahead, "All she needs is to be turned up and spanked for six months and then to be married off to an old-fashioned cavalry captain."

"Gosh, she's good looking!" said Mr. Sandwood, who was just over thirty.

"Good-looking!" cried Mr. Hedrick contemptuously, "she always looks as if she wanted to be kissed! Turning those big cow-eyes on every young calf in town!"

It is doubtful if Mr. Hedrick intended a reference to the maternal instinct.

"She'd play pretty good golf if she'd try," said Mr. Sandwood.

"She has no form," said Mr. Hedrick solemnly.

"She has a nice figure," said Mr. Sandwood.

"Better thank the Lord she doesn't drive a swifter ball," said Mr. Hart, winking at Dexter. "Come on. Let's go."

Later in the afternoon the sun went down with a riotous swirl of gold and varying blues and scarlets, and left the dry rustling night of western summer. Dexter watched from the verandah of the Erminie Club, watched the even overlap of the waters in the little wind, silver molasses under the harvest moon. Then the moon held a finger to her lips and the lake became a clear pool, pale and quiet. Dexter put on his bathing suit and swam out to the farthest raft, where he stretched dripping on the wet canvas of the spring board.

There was a fish jumping and a star shining and the lights around the lake were gleaming. Over on a dark peninsula a piano was playing the songs of last summer and of summers before that—songs from "The Pink Lady" and "The Chocolate Soldier" and "Mlle. Modiste"[7]—and because the sound of a piano over a stretch of water had always seemed beautiful to Dexter he lay perfectly quiet and listened.

The tune the piano was playing at that moment had been gay and new five years before when Dexter was a sophomore at college. They had played it at a prom once and because he could not afford the luxury of proms in those days he had stood outside the gymnasium and listened. The sound of the tune and the splash of the fish jumping precipitated in him a sort of ecstasy and it was with that ecstasy he viewed what happened to him now. The ecstasy was a gorgeous appreciation. It was his sense that, for once, he was magnificently atune to life and that everything about him was radiating a brightness and a glamour he might never know again.

A low pale oblong detached itself suddenly from the darkness of the peninsula, spitting forth the reverberate sound of a racing motorboat. Two white streamers of cleft water rolled themselves out behind it and almost immediately the boat was beside him, drowning out the hot tinkle of the piano in the drone of its spray. Dexter raising himself on his arms was aware of a figure standing at the wheel, of two dark eyes regarding him over the lengthening space of water—then the boat had gone by and was sweeping in an immense and purposeless circle of spray round and round in the middle of the lake. With equal eccentricity one of the circles flattened out and headed back toward the raft.

[7]Popular stage musicals of the first decades of the twentieth century.

"Who's that?" she called, shutting off her motor. She was so near now that Dexter could see her bathing suit, which consisted apparently of pink rompers. "Oh—you're one of the men I hit in the stomach."

The nose of the boat bumped the raft. After an inexpert struggle, Dexter managed to twist the line around a two-by-four. Then the raft tilted rakishly as she sprang on.

"Well, kiddo," she said huskily, "do you"—she broke off. She had sat herself upon the springboard, found it damp and jumped up quickly,—"do you want to go surf-board riding?"

He indicated that he would be delighted.

"The name is Judy Jones. Ghastly reputation but enormously popular." She favored him with an absurd smirk—rather, what tried to be a smirk, for, twist her mouth as she might, it was not grotesque, it was merely beautiful. "See that house over on the peninsula?"

"No."

"Well, there's a house there that I live in only you can't see it because it's too dark. And in that house there is a fella waiting for me. When he drove up by the door I drove out by the dock because he has watery eyes and asks me if I have an ideal."

There was a fish jumping and a star shining and the lights around the lake were gleaming. Dexter sat beside Judy Jones and she explained how her boat was driven. Then she was in the water, swimming to the floating surf-board with an exquisite crawl. Watching her was as without effort to the eye as watching a branch waving or a sea-gull flying. Her arms, burned to butternut, moved sinuously among the dull platinum ripples, elbow appearing first, casting the forearm back with a cadence of falling water, then reaching out and down stabbing a path ahead.

They moved out into the lake and, turning, Dexter saw that she was kneeling on the low rear of the now up-tilted surf-board.

"Go faster," she called, "fast as it'll go."

Obediently he jammed the lever forward and the white spray mounted at the bow. When he looked around again the girl was standing up on the rushing board, her arms spread ecstatically, her eyes lifted toward the moon.

"It's awful cold, kiddo," she shouted, "What's your name anyways."

"The name is Dexter Green. Would it amuse you to know how good you look back there?"

"Yes," she shouted, "It would amuse me. Except that I'm too cold. Come to dinner tomorrow night."

He kept thinking how glad he was that he had never caddied for this girl. The damp gingham clinging made her like a statue and turned her intense mobility to immobility at last.

"—At seven o'clock," she shouted, "Judy Jones, Girl, who hit man in stomach. Better write it down"—and then, "Faster—oh, faster!"

Had he been as calm inwardly as he was in appearance, Dexter would have had time to examine his surroundings in detail. He received, however, an enduring impression that the house was the most elaborate he had ever seen. He had known for a long time that it was the finest on Lake Erminie, with a Pompeiian swimming pool and twelve acres of lawn and garden. But what gave it an air of breathless intensity was the sense that it was inhabited by Judy Jones—that it was as casual a thing to her as the little house in the village had once been to

Dexter. There was a feeling of mystery in it, of bedrooms upstairs more beautiful and strange than other bedrooms, of gay and radiant activities taking place through these deep corridors and of romances that were not musty and laid already in lavender, but were fresh and breathing and set forth in rich motor cars and in great dances whose flowers were scarcely withered. They were more real because he could feel them all about him, pervading the air with the shades and echoes of still vibrant emotion.

And so while he waited for her to appear he peopled the soft deep summer room and the sun porch that opened from it with the men who had already loved Judy Jones. He knew the sort of men they were—the men who when he first went to college had entered from the great prep schools with graceful clothes and the deep tan of healthy summer, who did nothing or anything with the same debonair ease.

Dexter had seen that, in one sense, he was better than these men. He was newer and stronger. Yet in acknowledging to himself that he wished his children to be like them he was admitting that he was but the rough, strong stuff from which this graceful aristocracy eternally sprang.

When, a year before, the time had come when he could wear good clothes, he had known who were the best tailors in America, and the best tailor in America had made him the suit he wore this evening. He had acquired that particular reserve peculiar to his university, that set it off from other universities. He recognized the value to him of such a mannerism and he had adopted it; he knew that to be careless in dress and manner required more confidence than to be careful. But carelessness was for his children. His mother's name had been Krimslich. She was a Bohemian of the peasant class and she had talked broken English to the end of her days. Her son must keep to the set patterns.

He waited for Judy Jones in her house, and he saw these other young men around him. It excited him that many men had loved her. It increased her value in his eyes.

At a little after seven Judy Jones came downstairs. She wore a blue silk afternoon dress. He was disappointed at first that she had not put on something more elaborate, and this feeling was accentuated when, after a brief greeting, she went to the door of a butler's pantry and pushing it open called: "You can serve dinner, Martha." He had rather expected that a butler would announce dinner, that there would be a cocktail perhaps. It even offended him that she should know the maid's name.

Then he put these thoughts behind him as they sat down together on a chintz-covered lounge.

"Father and mother won't be here," she said.

"Ought I to be sorry?"

"They're really quite nice," she confessed, as if it had just occurred to her. "I think my father's the best looking man of his age I've ever seen. And mother looks about thirty."

He remembered the last time he had seen her father, and found he was glad the parents were not to be here tonight. They would wonder who he was. He had been born in Keeble, a Minnesota village fifty miles father north and he always gave Keeble as his home instead of Dillard. Country towns were well enough to come from if they weren't inconveniently in sight and used as footstools by fashionable lakes.

Before dinner he found the conversation unsatisfactory. The beautiful Judy seemed faintly irritable—as much so as it was possible to be with a comparative stranger. They discussed Lake Erminie and its golf course, the surfboard riding of the night before and the cold she had caught, which made her voice more husky and charming than ever. They talked of his university which she had visited frequently during the past two years, and of the nearby city which supplied Lake Erminie with its patrons and whither Dexter would return next day to his prospering laundries.

During dinner she slipped into a moody depression which gave Dexter a feeling of guilt. Whatever petulance she uttered in her throaty voice worried him. Whatever she smiled at—at him, at a silver fork, at nothing—, it disturbed him that her smile could have no root in mirth, or even in amusement. When the red corners of her lips curved down, it was less a smile than an invitation to a kiss.

Then, after dinner, she led him out on the dark sun-porch and deliberately changed the atmosphere.

"Do I seem gloomy?" she demanded.

"No, but I'm afraid I'm boring you," he answered quickly.

"You're not. I like you. But I've just had an unpleasant afternoon. There was a—man I cared about. He told me out of a clear sky that he was poor as a church-mouse. He'd never even hinted it before. Does this sound horribly mundane?"

"Perhaps he was afraid to tell you."

"I suppose he was," she answered thoughtfully. "He didn't start right. You see, if I'd thought of him as poor—well, I've been mad about loads of poor men, and fully intended to marry them all. But in this case, I hadn't thought of him that way and my interest in him wasn't strong enough to survive the shock."

"I know. As if a girl calmly informed her financé that she was a widow. He might not object to widows, but——"

"Let's start right," she suggested suddenly. "Who are you, anyhow?"

For a moment Dexter hesitated. There were two versions of his life that he could tell. There was Dillard and his caddying and his struggle through college, or——

"I'm nobody," he announced. "My career is largely a matter of futures."

"Are you poor?"

"No," he said frankly. "I'm probably making more money than any man my age in the northwest. I know that's an obnoxious remark, but you advised me to start right."

There was a pause. She smiled, and with a touch of amusement.

"You sound like a man in a play."

"It's your fault. You tempted me into being assertive."

Suddenly she turned her dark eyes directly upon him and the corners of her mouth drooped until her face seemed to open like a flower. He dared scarcely to breathe, he had the sense that she was exerting some force upon him; making him overwhelmingly conscious of the youth and mystery that wealth imprisons and preserves, the freshness of many clothes, of cool rooms and gleaming things, safe and proud above the hot struggles of the poor.

The porch was bright with the bought luxury of starshine. The wicker of the settee squeaked fashionably when he put his arm around her, commanded by her eyes. He kissed her curious and lovely mouth and committed himself to the following of a grail.

It began like that—and continued, with varying shades of intensity, on such a note right up to the dénoument. Dexter surrendered a part of himself to the most direct and unprincipled personality with which he had ever come in contact. Whatever the beautiful Judy Jones desired, she went after with the full pressure of her charm. There was no divergence of method, no jockeying for position or premeditation of effects—there was very little mental quality in any of her affairs. She simply made men conscious to the highest degree of her physical loveliness.

Dexter had no desire to change her. Her deficiencies were knit up with a passionate energy that transcended and justified them.

When, as Judy's head lay against his shoulder that first night, she whispered:

"I don't know what's the matter with me. Last night I thought I was in love with a man and tonight I think I'm in love with you——"

It seemed to him a beautiful and romantic thing to say. It was the exquisite excitability that for the moment he controlled and owned. But a week later he was compelled to view this same quality in a different light. She took him in her roadster to a picnic supper and after supper she disappeared, likewise in her roadster, with another man. Dexter became enormously upset and was scarcely able to be decently civil to the other people present. When she assured him that she had not kissed the other man he knew she was lying—yet he was glad that she had taken the trouble to lie to him.

He was, as he found before the summer ended, one of a dozen, a varying dozen, who circulated about her. Each of them had at one time been favored above all others—about half of them still basked in the solace of occasional sentimental revivals. Whenever one showed signs of dropping out through long neglect she granted him a brief honeyed hour which encouraged him to tag along for a year or so longer. Judy made these forays upon the helpless and defeated without malice, indeed half unconscious that there was anything mischievous in what she did.

When a new man came to town everyone dropped out—dates were automatically cancelled.

The helpless part of trying to do anything about it was that she did it all herself. She was not a girl who could be "won" in the kinetic sense—she was proof against cleverness, she was proof against charm, if any of these assailed her too strongly she would immediately resolve the affair to a physical basis and under the magic of her physical splendor the strong as well as the brilliant played her game and not their own. She was entertained only by the gratification of her desires and by the direct exercise of her own charm. Perhaps from so much youthful love, so many youthful lovers she had come, in self defense, to nourish herself wholly from within.

Succeeding Dexter's first exhilaration came restlessness and dissatisfaction. The helpless ecstasy of losing himself in her charm was a powerful opiate rather than a tonic. It was fortunate for his work during the winter that those moments of ecstasy came infrequently. Early in their acquaintance it had seemed for a while that there was a deep and mutual attraction—that first August for example—three days of long evenings on her dusky verandah, of strange wan kisses through the late afternoon, in shadowy alcoves or behind the protecting trellises of the garden arbors, of mornings when she was fresh as a dream and almost shy at meeting him in the clarity of the rising day. There was all the ecstasty of an engagement about it, sharpened by his realization that there was no engagement. It was during those three days that, for the first time, he had asked her to marry him. She said, "maybe some day," she said, "kiss me," she said, "I'd like to marry you," she said, "I love you,"—she said—nothing.

The three days were interrupted by the arrival of a New York man who visited the Jones's for half September. To Dexter's agony, rumor engaged them. The man was the son of the president of a great trust company. But at the end of a month it was reported that Judy was yawning. At a dance one night she sat all evening in a motor boat with an old beau, while the New Yorker searched the club for her frantically. She told the old beau that she was bored with her visitor and two days later he left. She was seen with him at the station and it was reported that he looked very mournful indeed.

On this note the summer ended. Dexter was twenty-four and he found himself increasingly in a position to do as he wished. He joined two clubs in the city and lived at one of them. Though he was by no means an integral part of the staglines at these clubs he managed to be on hand at dances where Judy Jones was likely to appear. He could have gone out socially as much as he liked—he was an eligible young man, now, and popular with downtown fathers. His confessed devotion to Judy Jones had rather solidified his position. But he had no social aspirations and rather despised the dancing men who were always on tap for the Thursday and Saturday parties and who filled in at dinners with the younger married set. Already he was playing with the idea of going East to New York. He wanted to take Judy Jones with him. No disillusion as to the world in which she had grown up could cure his illusion as to her desirability.

Remember that—for only in the light of it can what he did for her be understood.

Eighteen months after he first met Judy Jones, he became engaged to another girl. Her name was Irene Scheerer and her father was one of the men who had always believed in Dexter. Irene was light haired and sweet and honorable and a little stout and she had two beaus whom she pleasantly relinquished when Dexter formally asked her to marry him.

Summer, fall, winter, spring, another summer, another fall—so much he had given of his active life to the curved lips of Judy Jones. She had treated him with interest, with encouragement, with malice, with indifference, with contempt. She had inflicted on him the innumerable little slights and indignities possible in such a case—as if in revenge for having ever cared for him at all. She had beckoned him and yawned at him and beckoned him again and he had responded often with bitterness and narrowed eyes. She had brought him ecstatic happiness and intolerable agony of spirit. She had caused him untold inconvenience and not a little trouble. She had insulted him and she had ridden over him and she had played his interest in her against his interest in his work—for fun. She had done everything to him except to criticize him—this she had not done—it seemed to him only because it might have sullied the utter indifference she manifested and sincerely felt toward him.

When autumn had come and gone again it occurred to him that he could not have Judy Jones. He had to beat this into his mind but he convinced himself at last. He lay awake at night for a while and argued it over. He told himself the trouble and the pain she had caused him, he enumerated her glaring deficiencies as a wife. Then he said to himself that he loved her and after a while he fell asleep. For a week, lest he imagine her husky voice over the telephone or her eyes opposite him at lunch, he worked hard and late and at night he went to his office and plotted out his years.

At the end of a week he went to a dance and cut in on her once. For almost the first time since they had met he did not ask her to sit out with him or tell her that she was lovely. It hurt him that she did not miss these things—that was all. He was not jealous when he saw that there was a new man tonight. He had been hardened against jealousy long before.

He stayed late at the dance. He sat for an hour with Irene Scheerer and talked about books and about music. He knew very little about either. But he was beginning to be master of his own time now and he had a rather priggish notion that he—the young and already fabulously successful Dexter Green—should know more about such things.

That was in October when he was twenty-five. In January Dexter and Irene became engaged. It was to be announced in June and they were to be married three months later.

The Minnesota winter prolonged itself interminably and it was almost May when the winds came soft and the snow ran down into Lake Erminie at last. For the first time in over a year Dexter was enjoying a certain tranquility of spirit. Judy Jones had been in Florida and afterwards in Hot Springs[8] and somewhere she had been engaged and somewhere she had broken it off. At first, when Dexter had definitely given her up, it had made him sad that people still linked them together and asked for news of her, but when he began to be placed at dinner next to Irene Scheerer people didn't ask him about her any more—they told him about her. He ceased to be an authority on her.

May at last. Dexter walked the streets at night when the darkness was damp as rain, wondering that so soon, with so little done, so much of ecstacy had gone from him. May, one year back had been marked by Judy's poignant, unforgivable, yet forgiven turbulence—it had been one of those rare times when he fancied she had grown to care for him. That old penny's worth of happiness he had spent for this bushel of content. He knew that Irene would be no more than a curtain spread behind him, a hand moving among gleaming tea cups, a voice calling to children . . . fire and loveliness were gone, magic of night and the hushed wonder of the hours and seasons . . . slender lips, down turning, dropping to his lips like poppy petals, bearing him up into a heaven of eyes . . . a haunting gesture, light of a warm lamp on her hair. The thing was deep in him. He was too strong, to alive for it to die lightly.

In the middle of May when the weather balanced for a few days on the thin bridge that led to deep summer he turned in one night at Irene's house. Their engagement was to be announced in a week now—no one would be surprised at it. And tonight they would sit together on the lounge at the College Club and look on for an hour at the dancers. It gave him a sense of solidity to go with her——She was so sturdily popular, so intensely a "good egg."

He mounted the steps of the brown stone house and stepped inside.

"Irene," he called.

[8]Fashionable health spa and resort in Virginia.

Mrs. Scheerer came out of the living room to meet him.

"Dexter," she said, "Irene's gone upstairs with a splitting headache. She wanted to go with you but I made her go to bed."

"Nothing serious I——"

"Oh, no. She's going to play golf with you in the morning. You can spare her for just one night, can't you, Dexter?"

Her smile was kind. She and Dexter liked each other. In the living room he talked for a moment before he said goodnight.

Returning to the College Club, where he had rooms, he stood in the doorway for a moment and watched the dancers. He leaned against the door post, nodded at a man or two—yawned.

"Hello, kiddo."

The familiar voice at his elbow startled him. Judy Jones had left a man and crossed the room to him—Judy Jones, a slender enameled doll in cloth of gold, gold in a band at her head, gold in two slipper points at her dress's hem. The fragile glow of her face seemed to blossom as she smiled at him. A breeze of warmth and light blew through the room. His hands in the pockets of his dinner jacket tightened spasmodically. He was filled with a sudden excitement.

"When did you get back?" he asked casually.

"Come here and I'll tell you about it."

She turned and he followed her. She had been away—he could have wept at the wonder of her return. She had passed through enchanted streets, doing young things that were like plaintive music. All mysterious happenings, all fresh and quickening hopes, had gone away with her, come back with her now.

She turned in the doorway.

"Have you a car here? If you haven't I have."

"I have a coupé."

In then, with a rustle of golden cloth.

He slammed the door. Into so many cars she had stepped—like this—like that—her back against the leather, so—her elbow resting on the door—waiting. She would have been soiled long since had there been anything to soil her,—except herself—but these things were all her own outpouring.

With an effort he forced himself to start the car and avoiding her surprised glance backed into the street. This was nothing, he must remember. She had done this before and he had put her behind him, as he would have slashed a bad account from his books.

He drove slowly downtown and affecting a disinterested abstraction traversed the deserted streets of the business section, peopled here and there, where a movie was giving out its crowd or where consumptive or pugilistic youth lounged in front of pool halls. The clink of glasses and the slap of hands on the bars issued from saloons, cloisters of glazed glass and dirty yellow light.

She was watching him closely and the silence was embarrassing yet in this crisis he could find no casual word with which to profane the hour. At a convenient turning he began to zig-zag back toward the College Club.

"Have you missed me?" she asked suddenly.

"Everybody missed you."

He wondered if she knew of Irene Scheerer. She had been back only a day—her absence had been almost contemporaneous with his engagement.

"What a remark!" Judy laughed sadly—without sadness. She looked at him searchingly. He became absorbed for a moment in the dashboard.

"You're handsomer than you used to be," she said thoughtfully. "Dexter, you have the most rememberable eyes."

He could have laughed at this, but he did not laugh. It was the sort of thing that was said to sophomores. Yet it stabbed at him.

"I'm awfully tired of everything, kiddo." She called everyone kiddo, endowing the obsolete slang with careless, individual comradery. "I wish you'd marry me."

The directness of this confused him. He should have told her now that he was going to marry another girl but he could not tell her. He could as easily have sworn that he had never loved her.

"I think we'd get along," she continued, on the same note, "unless probably you've forgotten me and fallen love with another girl."

Her confidence was obviously enormous. She had said, in effect, that she found such a thing impossible to believe, that if it were true he had merely committed a childish indiscretion—and probably to show off. She would forgive him, because it was not a matter of any moment but rather something to be brushed aside lightly.

"Of course you could never love anybody but me," she continued, "I like the way you love me. Oh, Dexter, have you forgotten last year?"

"No, I haven't forgotten."

"Neither have I!"

Was she sincerely moved—or was she carried along by the wave of her own acting?

"I wish we could be like that again," she said, and he forced himself to answer:

"I don't think we can."

"I suppose not . . . I hear you're giving Irene Scheerer a violent rush."

There was not the faintest emphasis on the name, yet Dexter was suddenly ashamed.

"Oh, take me home," cried Judy suddenly, "I don't want to go back to that idiotic dance—with those children."

Then, as he turned up the street that led to the residence district, Judy began to cry quietly to herself. He had never seen her cry before.

The dark street lightened, the dwellings of the rich loomed up around them, he stopped his coupé in front of the great white bulk of the Mortimer Jones's house, somnolent, gorgeous, drenched with the splendor of the damp moonlight. Its solidity startled him. The strong walls, the fine steel of the girders, the breadth and beam and pomp of it were there only to bring out the contrast with the young beauty beside him.

It was sturdy to accentuate her slightness—as if to show what a breeze could be generated by a butterfly's wing.

He sat perfectly quiet, his nerves in wild clamor, afraid that if he moved he would find her irresistibly in his arms. Two tears had rolled down her wet face and trembled on her upper lip.

"I'm more beautiful than anybody else," she said brokenly, "why can't I be happy?" Her moist eyes tore at his stability—mouth turned slowly downward with an exquisite sadness. "I'd like to marry you if you'll have me, Dexter. I suppose you think I'm not worth having but I'll be so beautiful for you, Dexter."

A million phrases of anger, of pride, of passion, of hatred, of tenderness fought on his lips. Then a perfect wave of emotion washed over him, carrying off with it a sediment of wisdom, of convention, of doubt, of honor. This was his girl who was speaking, his own, his beautiful, his pride.

"Won't you come in?" he heard her draw in her breath sharply.

Waiting.

"All right," his voice was trembling, "I'll come in."

It seems strange to say that neither when it was over nor a long time afterward did he regret that night. Looking at it from the perspective of ten years, the fact that Judy's flare for him endured just one month seemed of little importance. Nor did it matter that by his yielding he subjected himself to a deeper agony in the end and gave serious hurt to Irene Scheerer and to Irene's parents who had befriended him. There was nothing sufficiently pictorial about Irene's grief to stamp itself on his mind.

Dexter was at bottom hard-minded. The attitude of the city on his action was of no importance to him, not because he was going to leave the city, but because any outside attitude on the situation seemed superficial. He was completely indifferent to popular opinion. Nor, when he had seen that it was no use, that he did not possess in himself the power to move fundamentally or to hold Judy Jones, did he bear any malice toward her. He loved her and he would love her until the day he was too old for loving—but he could not have her. So he tasted the deep pain that is reserved only for the strong, just as he had tasted for a little while the deep happiness.

Even the ultimate falsity of the grounds upon which Judy terminated the engagement—that she did not want to "take him away" from Irene, that it was on her conscience—did not revolt him. He was beyond any revulsion or any amusement.

He went east in February with the intention of selling out his laundries and settling in New York—but the war came to America in March and changed his plans. He returned to the west, handed over the management of the business to his partner and went into the first officers' training camp in late April. He was one of those young thousands who greeted the war with a certain amount of relief, welcoming the liberation from webs of tangled emotion.

This story is not his biography, remember, although things creep into it which have nothing to do with those dreams he had when he was young. We are almost done with them and with him now. There is only one more incident to be related here and it happens seven years farther on.

It took place in New York, where he had done well—so well that there were no barriers too high for him now. He was thirty-two years old, and, except for one flying trip immediately after the war, he had not been west in seven years. A man named Devlin from Detroit came into his office to see him in a business way, and then and there this incident occurred, and closed out, so to speak, this particular side of his life.

"So, you're from the middle west," said the man Devlin with careless curiosity. "That's funny—I thought men like you were probably born and raised on Wall Street. You know—wife of one of my best friends in Detroit came from your city. I was an usher at the wedding."

Dexter waited with no apprehension of what was coming. There was a magic that his city would never lose for him. Just as Judy's house had always seemed to him more mysterious and gay than other houses, so his dream of the city itself, now that he had gone from it, was pervaded with a melancholy beauty.

"Judy Simms," said Devlin with no particular interest, "Judy Jones she was once."

"Yes, I knew her." A dull impatience spread over him. He had heard, of course, that she was married,—perhaps deliberately he had heard no more.

"Awfully nice girl," brooded Devlin, meaninglessly, "I'm sort of sorry for her."

"Why?" Something in Dexter was alert, receptive, at once.

"Oh, Joe Simms has gone to pieces in a way. I don't mean he beats her, you understand, or anything like that. But he drinks and runs around——"

"Doesn't she run around?"

"No. Stays at home with her kids."

"Oh."

"She's a little too old for him," said Devlin.

"Too old!" cried Dexter, "why man, she's only twenty-seven."

He was possessed with a wild notion of rushing out into the streets and taking a train to Detroit. He rose to his feet, spasmodically, involuntarily.

"I guess you're busy," Devlin apologized quickly. "I didn't realize——"

"No, I'm not busy," said Dexter, steadying his voice, "I'm not busy at all. Not busy at all. Did you say she was—twenty-seven? No, I said she was twenty-seven."

"Yes, you did," agreed Devlin drily.

"Go on, then. Go on."

"What do you mean?"

"About Judy Jones."

Devlin looked at him helplessly.

"Well, that's—I told you all there is to it. He treats her like the devil. Oh, they're not going to get divorced or anything. When he's particularly outrageous she forgives him. In fact, I'm inclined to think she loves him. She was a pretty girl when she first came to Detroit."

A pretty girl! The phrase struck Dexter as ludicrous.

"Isn't she—a pretty girl any more?"

"Oh, she's all right."

"Look here," said Dexter, sitting down suddenly, "I don't understand. You say she was a 'pretty girl' and now you say she's 'all right.' I don't understand what you mean—Judy Jones wasn't a pretty girl, at all. She was a great beauty. Why, I knew her, I knew her. She was——"

Devlin laughed pleasantly.

"I'm not trying to start a row," he said. "I think Judy's a nice girl and I like her. I can't understand how a man like Joe Simms could fall madly in love with her, but he did." Then he added, "Most of the women like her."

Dexter looked closely at Devlin, thinking wildly that there must be a reason for this, some insensitivity in the man or some private malice.

"Lots of women fade just-like-*that*," Devlin snapped his fingers. "You must have seen it happen. Perhaps I've forgotten how pretty she was at her wedding. I've seen her so much since then, you see. She has nice eyes."

A sort of dullness settled down upon Dexter. For the first time in his life he felt like getting very drunk. He knew that he was laughing loudly at something Devlin had said but he did not know what it was or why it was funny. When Devlin went, in a few minutes, he lay down on his lounge and looked out the window at the New York skyline into which the sun was sinking in dull lovely shades of pink and gold.

He had thought that having nothing else to lose he was invulnerable at last—but he knew that he had just lost something more, as surely as if he had married Judy Jones and seen her fade away before his eyes.

The dream was gone. Something had been taken from him. In a sort of panic he pushed the palms of his hands into his eyes and tried to bring up a picture of the waters lapping at Lake Erminie and the moonlit verandah, and gingham on the golf links and the dry sun and the gold color of her neck's soft down. And her mouth damp to his kisses and her eyes plaintive with melancholy and her freshness like new fine linen in the morning. Why these things were no longer in the world. They had existed and they existed no more.

For the first time in years the tears were streaming down his face. But they were for himself now. He did not care about mouth and eyes and moving hands. He wanted to care and he could not care. For he had gone away and he could never go back any more. The gates were closed, the sun was gone down and there was no beauty but the grey beauty of steel that withstands all time. Even the grief he could have borne was left behind in the country of illusion, of youth, of the richness of life, where his winter dreams had flourished.

"Long ago," he said, "long ago, there was something in me, but now that thing is gone. I cannot cry. I cannot care. That thing will come back no more."

1922

Ernest Hemingway 1899–1961

Ernest Hemingway was born in Oak Park, Illinois, a suburb of Chicago. His father, a well-to-do physician, initiated his son into the rituals of hunting and fishing and bequeathed to him a way of life, and of death. In 1917, after graduation from high school, Hemingway went to work as a reporter for the Kansas City Star. *Rejected for army service in World War I because of poor vision, he volunteered to serve as a driver for an American ambulance unit in France. He then transferred to duty on the Italian front, where he was seriously wounded in the explosion of a mortar shell. He was the first American to be wounded and survive during World War I on the Italian front. After his recovery, and with decorations for valor which he believed he did not deserve, Hemingway returned home. He worked for the Toronto* Star, *covered the Greco-Turkish War as a foreign correspondent, and then returned to Paris, which, after World War I, was a city full of intellectual life, creativity, and genius.*

In Paris, Hemingway—along with Gertrude Stein, Ezra Pound, T. S. Eliot, and James Joyce—helped create a revolution in literary style and language. He developed a spare, tight, reportorial prose based on deceptively simple sentence structure. He used a restricted vocabulary, precise imagery, and an impersonal, dramatic tone. His first book, Three Stories and Ten Poems, *appeared in 1923. Three years later, with the publication of* The Sun Also Rises, *Hemingway became the spokesman for the men and women that Gertrude Stein had called "a lost generation."*

His works have sometimes been read as an essentially negative commentary on a modern world filled with sterility, failure, and death. Yet that nihilistic vision is repeatedly *modified by Hemingway's affirmative assertion of the possibility of living with style and courage. His primary concern was an individual's "moment of truth" (a notion derived from bullfighting), and he was fascinated by the threat of physical, emotional, or psychic death, a fascination reflected in his lifelong preoccupation with stories of war (*A Farewell to Arms, *1929, and* For Whom the Bell Tolls, *1940), the bullfight (*Death in the Afternoon, *1932), and the hunt (*Green Hills of Africa, *1935). To Hemingway, a person's greatest achievement is to show "grace under pressure," or what he described in* The Sun Also Rises *as holding the "purity of line through the maximum of exposure."*

Hemingway's stature as a writer was confirmed with the publication of A Farewell to Arms *in 1929. The novel portrays a farewell both to war and to love. Hemingway had rejected the romantic ideal of the ultimate union of lovers. He suggested instead that all relationships must end in destruction and in death.*

In 1937 he became a foreign correspondent covering the Spanish Civil War. Three years later he published For Whom the Bell Tolls. *Set in Spain during the Civil War, the novel restates his view of love found and lost and describes the indomitable spirit of the common people. In 1952 the same judgment was reflected in his portrayal of the old fisherman, Santiago, triumphant even in defeat, in* The Old Man and the Sea.

Hemingway received wide acclaim for his novels and for his short stories, which include some of the finest in the English language. In 1954 he was awarded a Nobel Prize for his "mastery of the art of modern narration." He became a public figure whose pronouncements and adventures were publicized and scrutinized throughout the world. Numerous parallels exist between the events of Hemingway's life and those of his characters, but few were closer than those of Richard Cantwell, the hero of Across the River and into the Trees *(1950), whose attempts at stoic control of physical and mental illness foreshadow the struggles and defeats of Hemingway's final years, which ended when he, as his father had done some thirty years before, took his own life on July 2, 1961.*

FURTHER READING: C. Baker, *Ernest Hemingway: The Writer as Artist,* 1952, 1956, 1963, 1972; C. Baker, *Ernest Hemingway: A Life Story,* 1969; *The Short Stories of Ernest Hemingway: Critical Essays,* ed. J. Benson, 1975; S. Donaldson, *By Force of Will: The Life and Art of Ernest Hemingway,* 1977; *Ernest Hemingway: The Papers of a Writer,* ed. B. Oldsey, 1981; *Ernest Hemingway: Selected Letters,* ed. C. Baker, 1981; P. Griffin, *Along with Youth: Hemingway, The Early Years,* 1985; M. Reynolds, *The Young Hemingway,* 1986; K. Lynn, *Hemingway: The Life and the Work,* 1987; P. Smith, *A Reader's Guide to the Short Stories of Ernest Hemingway,* 1989; M. Reynolds, *Hemingway: The Paris Years,* 1989; *New Critical Approaches to the Short Stories of Ernest Hemingway,* ed. J. Benson, 1990; *Hemingway: Essays of Reassessment,* ed. F. Scafella, 1991; M. Reynolds, *Hemingway: The American Homecoming,* 1992; J. Mellow, *Hemingway: A Life Without Consequences,* 1994; M. Mandel, *Reading Hemingway,* 1995; *The Cambridge Companion to Hemingway,* ed. S. Donaldson, 1996; D. Moddelmog, *Reading Desire: In Pursuit of Ernest Hemingway,* 1999; M. Bruccoli, *Classes on Ernest Hemingway,* 2002.

TEXT: *The Complete Short Stories of Ernest Hemingway,* 1987.

BIG TWO-HEARTED RIVER

PART I

The train went on up the track out of sight, around one of the hills of burnt timber. Nick sat down on the bundle of canvas and bedding the baggage man had pitched out of the door of the baggage car. There was no town, nothing but the rails and the burned-over country. The thirteen saloons that had lined the one street of Seney had not left a trace. The foundations of the Mansion House hotel stuck up above the ground. The stone was chipped and split by the fire. It was all that was left of the town of Seney. Even the surface had been burned off the ground.

Nick looked at the burned-over stretch of hillside, where he had expected to find the scattered houses of the town and then walked down the railroad track to the bridge over the river. The river was there. It swirled against the log spiles[1] of the bridge. Nick looked down into the clear, brown water, colored from the pebbly bottom, and watched the trout keeping themselves steady in the current with wavering fins. As he watched them they changed their positions by quick angles, only to hold steady in the fast water again. Nick watched them a long time.

He watched them holding themselves with their noses into the current, many trout in deep, fast moving water, slightly distorted as he watched far down through the glassy convex surface of the pool, its surface pushing and swelling smooth against the resistance of the log-driven piles of the bridge. At the bottom of the pool were the big trout. Nick did not see them at first. Then he saw them at the bottom of the pool, big trout looking to hold themselves on the gravel bottom in a varying mist of gravel and sand, raised in spurts by the current.

Nick looked down into the pool from the bridge. It was a hot day. A kingfisher flew up the stream. It was a long time since Nick had looked into a stream and seen trout. They were very satisfactory. As the shadow of the kingfisher moved up the stream, a big trout shot upstream in a long angle, only his shadow marking the angle, then lost his shadow as he came through the surface of the water, caught the sun, and then, as he went back into the stream under the surface, his shadow seemed to float down the stream with the current, unresisting, to his post under the bridge where he tightened facing up into the current.

Nick's heart tightened as the trout moved. He felt all the old feeling.

He turned and looked down the stream. It stretched away, pebbly-bottomed with shallows and big boulders and a deep pool as it curved away around the foot of a bluff.

Nick walked back up the ties to where his pack lay in the cinders beside the railway track. He was happy. He adjusted the pack harness around the bundle, pulling straps tight, slung the pack on his back, got his arms through the shoulder straps and took some of the pull off his shoulders by leaning his forehead against the wide band of the tump-line.[2] Still, it was too heavy. It was much too heavy. He had his leather rod-case in his hand and leaning forward to keep the weight of the pack high on his shoulders he walked along the road that paralleled the railway track, leaving the burned town behind in the heat, and then turned off around a hill with a high, fire-scarred hill on either side onto a road that went back into the country. He walked along the road feeling the ache from the pull of the heavy pack. The road climbed steadily. It was hard work walking up-hill. His muscles ached and the day was hot, but Nick felt happy. He felt he had left everything behind, the need for thinking, the need to write, other needs. It was all back of him.

[1]Heavy support timbers, piles.
[2]A strap passed across the forehead to help support a backpack.

From the time he had gotten down off the train and the baggage man had thrown his pack out of the open car door things had been different. Seney was burned, the country was burned over and changed, but it did not matter. It could not all be burned. He knew that. He hiked along the road, sweating in the sun, climbing to cross the range of hills that separated the railway from the pine plains.

The road ran on, dipping occasionally, but always climbing. Nick went on up. Finally the road after going parallel to the burnt hillside reached the top. Nick leaned back against a stump and slipped out of the pack harness. Ahead of him, as far as he could see, was the pine plain. The burned country stopped off at the left with the range of hills. On ahead islands of dark pine trees rose out of the plain. Far off to the left was the line of the river. Nick followed it with his eye and caught glints of the water in the sun.

There was nothing but the pine plain ahead of him, until the far blue hills that marked the Lake Superior height of land. He could hardly see them, faint and far away in the heat-light over the plain. If he looked too steadily they were gone. But if he only half-looked they were there, the far-off hills of the height of land.

Nick sat down against the charred stump and smoked a cigarette. His pack balanced on the top of the stump, harness holding ready, a hollow molded in it from his back. Nick sat smoking, looking out over the country. He did not need to get his map out. He knew where he was from the position of the river.

As he smoked, his legs stretched out in front of him, he noticed a grasshopper walk along the ground and up onto his woolen sock. The grasshopper was black. As he had walked along the road, climbing, he had started many grasshoppers from the dust. They were all black. They were not the big grasshoppers with yellow and black or red and black wings whirring out from their black wing sheathing as they fly up. These were just ordinary hoppers, but all sooty black in color. Nick had wondered about them as he walked, without really thinking about them. Now, as he watched the black hopper that was nibbling at the wool of his sock with its fourway lip, he realized that they had all turned black from living in the burned-over land. He realized that the fire must have come the year before, but the grasshoppers were all black now. He wondered how long they would stay that way.

Carefully he reached his hand down and took hold of the hopper by the wings. He turned him up, all his legs walking in the air, and looked at his jointed belly. Yes, it was black too, iridescent where the black and head were dusty.

"Go on, hopper," Nick said, speaking out loud for the first time. "Fly away somewhere."

He tossed the grasshopper up into the air and watched him sail away to a charcoal stump across the road.

Nick stood up. He leaned his back against the weight of his pack where it rested upright on the stump and got his arms through the shoulder straps. He stood with the pack on his back on the brow of the hill looking out across the country, toward the distant river and then struck down the hillside away from the road. Underfoot the ground was good walking. Two hundred yards down the hillside the fire line stopped. Then it was sweet fern, growing ankle high, to walk through, and clumps of jack pines; a long undulating country with frequent rises and descents, sandy underfoot and the country alive again.

Nick kept his direction by the sun. He knew where he wanted to strike the river and he kept on through the pine plain, mounting small rises to see other rises ahead of him and sometimes from the top of a rise a great solid island of pines off to his right or his left. He broke off some sprigs of the heathery sweet fern, and put them under his pack straps. The chafing crushed it and he smelled it as he walked.

He was tired and very hot, walking across the uneven, shadeless pine plain. At any time he knew he could strike the river by turning off to his left. It could not be more than a mile away. But he kept on toward the north to hit the river as far upstream as he could go in one day's walking.

For some time as he walked Nick had been in sight of one of the big islands of pine standing out above the rolling high ground he was crossing. He dipped down and then as he came slowly up to the crest of the bridge he turned and made toward the pine trees.

There was no underbrush in the island of pine trees. The trunks of the trees went straight up or slanted toward each other. The trunks were straight and brown without branches. The branches were high above. Some interlocked to make a solid shadow on the brown forest floor. Around the grove of trees was a bare space. It was brown and soft underfoot as Nick walked on it. This was the over-lapping of the pine needle floor, extending out beyond the width of the high branches. The trees had grown tall and the branches moved high, leaving in the sun this bare space they had once covered with shadow. Sharp at the edge of this extension of the forest floor commenced the sweet fern.

Nick slipped off his pack and lay down in the shade. He lay on his back and looked up into the pine trees. His neck and back and the small of his back rested as he stretched. The earth felt good against his back. He looked up at the sky, through the branches, and then shut his eyes. He opened them and looked up again. There was a wind high up in the branches. He shut his eyes again and went to sleep.

Nick woke stiff and cramped. The sun was nearly down. His pack was heavy and the straps painful as he lifted it on. He leaned over with the pack on and picked up the leather rod-case and started out from the pine trees across the sweet fern swale, toward the river. He knew it could not be more than a mile.

He came down a hillside covered with stumps into a meadow. At the edge of the meadow flowed the river. Nick was glad to get to the river. He walked upstream through the meadow. His trousers were soaked with the dew as he walked. After the hot day, the dew had come quickly and heavily. The river made no sound. It was too fast and smooth. At the edge of the meadow, before he mounted to a piece of high ground to make camp, Nick looked down the river at the trout rising. They were rising to insects come from the swamp on the other side of the stream when the sun went down. The trout jumped out of water to take them. While Nick walked through the little stretch of meadow alongside the stream, trout had jumped high out of water. Now as he looked down the river, the insects must be settling on the surface, for the trout were feeding steadily all down the stream. As far down the long stretch as he could see, the trout were rising, making circles all down the surface of the water, as though it were starting to rain.

The ground rose, wooded and sandy, to overlook the meadow, the stretch of river and the swamp. Nick dropped his pack and rod-case and looked for a level piece of ground. He was very hungry and he wanted to make his camp before he cooked. Between two jack pines, the ground was quite level. He took the ax out of the pack and chopped out two projecting roots. That leveled a piece of ground large enough to sleep on. He smoothed out the sandy soil with his hand and pulled all the sweet fern bushes by their roots. His hands smelled good from the sweet fern. He smoothed the uprooted earth. He did not want anything making lumps under the blankets. When he had the ground smooth, he spread his three blankets. One he folded double, next to the ground. The other two he spread on top.

With the ax he slit off a bright slab of pine from one of the stumps and split it into pegs for the tent. He wanted them long and solid to hold in the ground. With the tent unpacked and spread on the ground, the pack, leaning against a jackpine, looked much smaller. Nick tied the rope that served the tent for a ridge-pole to the trunk of one of the pine trees and pulled the tent up off the ground with the other end of the rope and tied it to the other pine. The tent hung on the rope like a canvas on a clothesline. Nick poked a pole he had cut up under the back peak of the canvas and then made it a tent by pegging out the sides. He pegged the sides out taut and drove the pegs deep, hitting them down into the ground with the flat of the ax until the rope loops were buried and the canvas was drum tight.

Across the open mouth of the tent Nick fixed cheesecloth to keep out mosquitoes. He crawled inside under the mosquito bar with various things from the pack to put at the head of the bed under the slant of the canvas. Inside the tent the light came through the brown canvas. It smelled pleasantly of canvas. Already there was something mysterious and homelike. Nick was happy as he crawled inside the tent. He had not been unhappy all day. This was different though. Now things were done. There had been this to do. Now it was done. It had been a hard trip. He was very tired. That was done. He had made his camp. He was settled. Nothing could touch him. It was a good place to camp. He was there, in the good place. He was in his home where he had made it. Now he was hungry.

He came out, crawling under the cheesecloth. It was quite dark outside. It was lighter in the tent.

Nick went over to the pack and found, with his fingers, a long nail in a paper sack of nails, in the bottom of the pack. He drove it into the pine tree, holding it close and hitting it gently with the flat of the ax. He hung the pack up on the nail. All his supplies were in the pack. They were off the ground and sheltered now.

Nick was hungry. He did not believe he had ever been hungrier. He opened and emptied a can of pork and beans and a can of spaghetti into the frying pan.

"I've got a right to eat this kind of stuff, if I'm willing to carry it," Nick said. His voice sounded strange in the darkening woods. He did not speak again.

He started a fire with some chunks of pine he got with the ax from a stump. Over the fire he stuck a wire grill, pushing the four legs down into the ground with his boot. Nick put the frying pan on the grill over the flames. He was hungrier. The beans and spaghetti warmed. Nick stirred them and mixed them together. They began to bubble, making little bubbles that rose with difficulty to the surface. There was a good smell. Nick got out a bottle of tomato catchup and cut four slices of bread. The little bubbles were coming faster now. Nick sat down beside the fire and lifted the frying pan off. He poured about half the contents out into the tin plate. It spread slowly on the plate. Nick knew it was too hot. He poured on some tomato catchup. He knew the beans and spaghetti were still too hot. He looked at the fire, then at the tent, he was not going to spoil it all by burning his tongue. For years he had never enjoyed fried bananas because he had never been able to wait for them to cool. His tongue was very sensitive. He was very hungry. Across the river in the swamp, in the almost dark, he saw a mist rising. He looked at the tent once more. All right. He took a full spoonful from the plate.

"Chrise," Nick said, "Geezus Chrise," he said happily.

He ate the whole plateful before he remembered the bread. Nick finished the second plateful with the bread, mopping the plate shiny. He had not eaten since a cup of coffee and a ham sandwich in the station restaurant at St. Ignace. It had been a very fine experience. He had been that hungry before, but had not been able to satisfy it. He could have made camp hours before if he had wanted to. There were plenty of good places to camp on the river. But this was good.

Nick tucked two big chips of pine under the grill. The fire flared up. He had forgotten to get water for the coffee. Out of the pack he got a folding canvas bucket and walked down the hill, across the edge of the meadow, to the stream. The other bank was in the white mist. The grass was wet and cold as he knelt on the bank and dipped the canvas bucket into the stream. It bellied and pulled hard in the current. The water was ice cold. Nick rinsed the bucket and carried it full up to the camp. Up away from the stream it was not so cold.

Nick drove another big nail and hung up the bucket full of water. He dipped the coffee pot half full, put some more chips under the grill onto the fire and put the pot on. He could not remember which way he made coffee. He could remember an argument about it with Hopkins, but not which side he had taken. He decided to bring it to a boil. He remembered now that was Hopkins' way. He had once argued about everything with Hopkins. While he waited for the coffee to boil, he opened a small can of apricots. He liked to open cans. He emptied the can of apricots out into a tin cup. While he watched the coffee on the fire, he drank the juice syrup of the apricots, carefully at first to keep from spilling, then meditatively, sucking the apricots down. They were better than fresh apricots.

The coffee boiled as he watched. The lid came up and coffee and grounds ran down the side of the pot. Nick took it off the grill. It was a triumph for Hopkins. He put sugar in the empty apricot cup and poured some of the coffee out to cool. It was too hot to pour and he used his hat to hold the handle of the coffee pot. He would not let it steep in the pot at all. Not the first cup. It should be straight Hopkins all the way. Hop deserved that. He was a very serious coffee drinker. He was the most serious man Nick had ever known. Not heavy, serious. That was a long time ago. Hopkins spoke without moving his lips. He had played polo. He made millions of dollars in Texas. He had borrowed carfare to go to Chicago, when the wire came that his first big well had come in. He could have wired for money. That would have been too slow. They called Hop's girl the Blonde Venus. Hop did not mind because she was not his real girl. Hopkins said very confidently that none of them would make fun of his real girl. He was right. Hopkins went away when the telegram came. That was on the Black River. It took eight days for the telegram to reach him. Hopkins gave away his .22 caliber Colt automatic pistol to Nick. He gave his camera to Bill.

It was to remember him always by. They were all going fishing again next summer. The Hop Head was rich. He would get a yacht and they would all cruise along the north shore of Lake Superior. He was excited but serious. They said good-bye and all felt bad. It broke up the trip. They never saw Hopkins again. That was a long time ago on the Black River.

Nick drank the coffee, the coffee according to Hopkins. The coffee was bitter. Nick laughed. It made a good ending to the story. His mind was starting to work. He knew he could choke it because he was tired enough. He spilled the coffee out of the pot and shook the grounds loose into the fire. He lit a cigarette and went inside the tent. He took off his shoes and trousers, sitting on the blankets, rolled the shoes up inside the trousers for a pillow and got in between the blankets.

Out through the front of the tent he watched the flow of the fire, when the night wind blew on it. It was a quiet night. The swamp was perfectly quiet. Nick stretched under the blanket comfortably. A mosquito hummed close to his ear. Nick sat up and lit a match. The mosquito was on the canvas, over his head. Nick moved the match quickly up to it. The mosquito made a satisfactory hiss in the flame. The match went out. Nick lay down again under the blanket. He turned on his side and shut his eyes. He was sleepy. He felt sleep coming. He curled up under the blanket and went to sleep.

PART II

In the morning the sun was up and the tent was starting to get hot. Nick crawled out under the mosquito netting stretched across the mouth of the tent, to look at the morning. The grass was wet on his hands as he came out. He held his trousers and his shoes in his hands. The sun was just up over the hill. There was the meadow, the river and the swamp. There were birch trees in the green of the swamp on the other side of the river.

The river was clear and smoothly fast in the early morning. Down about two hundred yards were three logs all the way across the stream. They made the water smooth and deep above them. As Nick watched, a mink crossed the river on the logs and went into the swamp. Nick was excited. He was excited by the early morning and the river. He was really too hurried to eat breakfast, but he knew he must. He built a little fire and put on the coffee pot.

While the water was heating in the pot he took an empty bottle and went down over the edge of the high ground to the meadow. The meadow was wet with dew and Nick wanted to catch grasshoppers for bait before the sun dried the grass. He found plenty of good grasshoppers. They were at the base of the grass stems. Sometimes they clung to a grass stem. They were cold and wet with dew, and could not jump until the sun warmed them. Nick picked them up, taking only the medium-sized brown ones, and put them into the bottle. He turned over a log and just under the shelter of the edge were several hundred hoppers. It was a grasshopper lodging house. Nick put about fifty of the medium browns into the bottle. While he was picking up the hoppers the others warmed in the sun and commenced to hop away. They flew when they hopped. At first they made one flight and stayed stiff when they landed, as though they were dead.

Nick knew that by the time he was through with breakfast they would be as lively as ever. Without dew in the grass it would take him all day to catch a bottle full of good grasshoppers and he would have to crush many of them, slamming at them with his hat. He washed his hands at the stream. He was excited to be near it. Then he walked up to the tent. The hoppers were already jumping stiffly in the grass. In the bottle, warmed by the sun, they were jumping in a mass. Nick put in a pine stick as a cork. It plugged the mouth of the bottle enough, so the hoppers could not get out and left plenty of air passage.

He had rolled the log back and knew he could get grasshoppers there every morning.

Nick laid the bottle full of jumping grasshoppers against a pine trunk. Rapidly he mixed some buckwheat flour with water and stirred it smooth, one cup of flour, one cup of water. He put a handful of coffee in the pot and dipped a lump of grease out of a can and slid it sputtering across the hot skillet. On the smoking skillet he poured smoothly the buckwheat batter. It spread like lava, the grease spitting sharply. Around the edges the buckwheat cake began to firm, then brown, then crisp. The surface was bubbling slowly to porousness. Nick pushed under the browned under surface with a fresh pine chip. He shook the skillet sideways and the cake was loose on the surface. I won't try and flop it, he thought. He slid the chip of clean wood all the way under the cake, and flopped it over onto its face. It sputtered in the pan.

When it was cooked Nick regreased the skillet. He used all the batter. It made another big flapjack and one smaller one.

Nick ate a big flapjack and a smaller one, covered with apple butter. He put apple butter on the third cake, folded it over twice, wrapped it in oiled paper and put it in his shirt pocket. He put the apple butter jar back in the pack and cut bread for two sandwiches.

In the pack he found a big onion. He sliced it in two and peeled the silky outer skin. Then he cut one half into slices and made onion sandwiches. He wrapped them in oiled paper and buttoned them in the other pocket of his khaki shirt. He turned the skillet upside down on the grill, drank the coffee, sweetened and yellow brown with the condensed milk in it, and tidied up the camp. It was a good camp.

Nick took his fly rod out of the leather rod-case, jointed it, and shoved the rod-case back into the tent. He put on the reel and threaded the line through the guides. He had to hold it from hand to hand, as he threaded it, or it would slip back through its own weight. It was heavy, double tapered fly line. Nick had paid eight dollars for it a long time ago. It was made heavy to lift back in the air and come forward flat and heavy and straight to make it possible to cast a fly which has no weight. Nick opened the aluminum leader box. The leaders were coiled between the damp flannel pads. Nick had wet the pads at the water cooler on the train up to St. Ignace. In the damp pads the gut leaders had softened and Nick unrolled one and tied it by a loop at the end to the heavy fly line. He fastened a hook on the end of the leader. It was a small hook; very thin and springy.

Nick took it from his hook book, sitting with the rod across his lap. He tested the knot and the spring of the rod by pulling the line taut. It was a good feeling. He was careful not to let the hook bite into his finger.

He started down to the stream, holding his rod, the bottle of grasshoppers hung from his neck by a thong tied in half hitches around the neck of the bottle. His landing net hung by a hook from his belt. Over his shoulder was a long flour sack tied at each corner into an ear. The cord went over his shoulder. The sack flapped against his legs.

Nick felt awkward and professionally happy with all his equipment hanging from him. The grasshopper bottle swung against his chest. In his shirt the breast pockets bulged against him with the lunch and his fly book.

He stepped into the stream. It was a shock. His trousers clung tight to his legs. His shoes felt the gravel. The water was a rising cold shock.

Rushing, the current sucked against his legs. Where he stepped in, the water was over his knees. He waded with the current. The gravel slid under his shoes. He looked down at the swirl of water below each leg and tipped up the bottle to get a grasshopper.

The first grasshopper gave a jump in the neck of the bottle and went out into the water. He was sucked under in a whirl by Nick's right leg and came to the surface a little way down stream. He floated rapidly, kicking. In a quick circle, breaking the smooth surface of the water, he disappeared. A trout had taken him.

Another hopper poked his face out of the bottle. His antennæ wavered. He was getting his front legs out of the bottle to jump. Nick took him by the head and held him while he threaded the slim hook under his chin, down through his thorax and into the last segments of his abdomen. The grasshopper took hold of the hook with his front feet, spitting tobacco juice on it. Nick dropped him into the water.

Holding the rod in his right hand he let out line against the pull of the grasshopper in the current. He stripped off line from the reel with his left hand and let it run free. He could see the hopper in the waves of the current. It went out of sight.

There was a tug on the line. Nick pulled against the taut line. It was his first strike. Holding the now living rod across the current, he brought in the line with his left hand. The rod bent in jerks, the trout pumping against the current. Nick knew it was a small one. He lifted the rod straight up in the air. It bowed in the pull.

He saw the trout in the water jerking with his head and body against the shifting tangent of the line in the stream.

Nick took the line in his left hand and pulled the trout, thumping tiredly against the current, to the surface. His back was mottled the clear, water-over-gravel color, his side flashing in the sun. The rod under his right arm, Nick stooped, dipping his right hand into the current. He held the trout, never still, with his moist right hand, while he unhooked the barb from his mouth, then dropped him back into the stream.

He hung unsteadily in the current, then settled to the bottom beside a stone. Nick reached down his hand to touch him, his arm to the elbow under water. The trout was steady in the moving stream, resting on the gravel, beside a stone. As Nick's fingers touched him, touched his smooth, cool, underwater feeling he was gone, gone in a shadow across the bottom of the stream.

He's all right, Nick thought. He was only tired.

He had wet his hand before he touched the trout, so he would not disturb the delicate mucus that covered him. If a trout was touched with a dry hand, a white fungus attacked the unprotected spot. Years before when he had fished crowded streams, with fly fishermen ahead of him, Nick had again and again come on dead trout, furry with white fungus, drifted against a rock, or floating belly up in some pool. Nick did not like to fish with other men on the river. Unless they were of your party, they spoiled it.

He wallowed down the stream, above his knees in the current, through the fifty yards of shallow water above the pile of logs that crossed the stream. He did not rebait his hook and held it in his hand as he waded. He was certain he could catch small trout in the shallows, but he did not want them. There would be no big trout in the shallows this time of the day.

Now the water deepened to his thighs sharply and coldly. Ahead was the smooth dammed-back flood of water above the logs. The water was smooth and dark; on the left, the lower edge of the meadow; on the right the swamp.

Nick leaned back against the current and took a hopper from the bottle. He threaded the hopper on the hook and spat on him for good luck. Then he pulled several yards of line from the reel and tossed the hopper out ahead onto the fast, dark water. It floated down toward the logs, then the weight of the line pulled the bait under the surface. Nick held the rod in his right hand, letting the line run out through his fingers.

There was a long tug. Nick struck and the rod came alive and dangerous, bent double, the line tightening, coming out of the water, tightening, all in a heavy, dangerous, steady pull. Nick felt the moment when the leader would break if the strain increased and let the line go.

The reel ratcheted into a mechanical shriek as the line went out in a rush. Too fast. Nick could not check it, the line rushing out, the reel note rising as the line ran out.

With the core of the reel showing, his heart feeling stopped with the excitement, leaning back against the current that mounted icily his thighs, Nick thumbed the reel hard with his left hand. It was awkward getting his thumb inside the fly reel frame.

As he put on pressure the line tightened into sudden hardness and beyond the logs a huge trout went high out of water. As he jumped, Nick lowered the tip of the rod. But he felt, as he dropped the tip to ease the strain, the moment when the strain was too great; the hardness too tight. Of course, the leader had broken. There was no mistaking the feeling when all spring left the line and it became dry and hard. Then it went slack.

His mouth dry, his heart down, Nick reeled in. He had never seen so big a trout. There was a heaviness, a power not to be held, and then the bulk of him, as he jumped. He looked as broad as a salmon.

Nick's hand was shaky. He reeled in slowly. The thrill had been too much. He felt, vaguely, a little sick, as though it would be better to sit down.

The leader had broken where the hook was tied to it. Nick took it in his hand. He thought of the trout somewhere on the bottom, holding himself steady over the gravel, far down below the light, under the logs, with the hook in his jaw. Nick knew the trout's teeth would cut through the snell of the hook. The hook would imbed itself in his jaw. He'd bet the trout was angry. Anything that size would be angry. That was a trout. He had been solidly hooked. Solid as a rock. He felt like a rock, too, before he started off. By God, he was a big one. By God, he was the biggest one I ever heard of.

Nick climbed out onto the meadow and stood, water running down his trousers and out of his shoes, his shoes squelchy. He went over and sat on the logs. He did not want to rush his sensations any.

He wriggled his toes in the water, in his shoes, and got out a cigarette from his breast pocket. He lit it and tossed the match into the fast water below the logs. A tiny trout rose at the match, as it swung around in the fast current. Nick laughed. He would finish the cigarette.

He sat on the logs, smoking, drying in the sun, the sun warm on his back, the river shallow ahead entering the woods, curving into the woods, shallows, light glittering, big water-smooth rocks, cedars along the bank and white birches, the logs warm in the sun, smooth to sit on, without bark, gray to the touch; slowly the feeling of disappointment left him. It went away slowly, the feeling of disappointment that came sharply after the thrill that made his shoulders ache. It was all right now. His rod lying out on the logs, Nick tied a new hook on the leader, pulling the gut tight until it grimped into itself a hard knot.

He baited up, then picked up the rod and walked to the far end of the logs to get into the water, where it was not too deep. Under and beyond the logs was a deep pool. Nick walked around the shallow shelf near the swamp shore until he came out on the shallow bed of the stream.

On the left, where the meadow ended and the woods began, a great elm tree was uprooted. Gone over in a storm, it lay back into the woods, its roots clotted with dirt, grass growing in them, rising a solid bank beside the stream. The river cut to the edge of the uprooted tree. From where Nick stood he could see deep channels, like ruts, cut in the shallow bed of the stream by the flow of the current. Pebbly where he stood and pebbly and full of boulders beyond; where it curved near the tree roots, the bed of the stream was marly and between the ruts of deep water green weed fronds swung in the current.

Nick swung the rod back over his shoulder and forward, and the line, curving forward, laid the grasshopper down on one of the deep channels in the weeds. A trout struck and Nick hooked him.

Holding the rod far out toward the uprooted tree and sloshing backward in the current, Nick worked the trout, plunging, the rod bending alive, out of danger of the weeds into the open river. Holding the rod, pumping alive against the current, Nick brought the trout in. He rushed, but always came, the spring of the rod yielding to the rushes, sometimes jerking under water, but always bringing him in. Nick eased downstream with the rushes. The rod above his head he led the trout over the net, then lifted.

The trout hung heavy in the net, mottled trout back and silver sides in the meshes. Nick unhooked him; heavy sides, good to hold, big undershot jaw, and slipped him, heaving and big sliding, into the long sack that hung from his shoulders in the water.

Nick spread the mouth of the sack against the current and it filled, heavy with water. He held it up, the bottom in the stream, and the water poured out through the sides. Inside at the bottom was the big trout, alive in the water.

Nick moved downstream. The sack out ahead of him sunk heavy in the water, pulling from his shoulders.

It was getting hot, the sun hot on the back of his neck.

Nick had one good trout. He did not care about getting many trout. Now the stream was shallow and wide. There were trees along both banks. The trees of the left bank made short shadows on the current in the forenoon sun. Nick knew there were trout in each shadow. In the afternoon, after the sun had crossed toward the hills, the trout would be in the cool shadows on the other side of the stream.

The very biggest ones would lie up close to the bank. You could always pick them up there on the Black. When the sun was down they all moved out into the current. Just when the sun made the water blinding in the glare before it went down, you were liable to strike a big trout anywhere in the current. It was almost impossible to fish then, the surface of the water was blinding as a mirror in the sun. Of course, you could fish upstream, but in a stream like the Black, or this, you had to wallow against the current and in a deep place, the water piled up on you. It was no fun to fish upstream with this much current.

Nick moved along through the shallow stretch watching the banks for deep holes. A beech tree grew close beside the river, so that the branches hung down into the water. The stream went back in under the leaves. There were always trout in a place like that.

Nick did not care about fishing that hole. He was sure he would get hooked in the branches.

It looked deep though. He dropped the grasshopper so the current took it under water, back in under the overhanging branch. The line pulled hard and Nick struck. The trout threshed heavily, half out of water in the leaves and branches. The line was caught. Nick pulled hard and the trout was off. He reeled in and holding the hook in his hand, walked down the stream.

Ahead, close to the left bank, was a big log. Nick saw it was hollow; pointing up river the current entered it smoothly, only a little ripple spread each side of the log. The water was deepening. The top of the hollow log was gray and dry. It was partly in shadow.

Nick took the cork out of the grasshopper bottle and a hopper clung to it. He picked him off, hooked him and tossed him out. He held the rod far out so that the hopper on the water moved into the current flowing into the hollow log. Nick lowered the rod and the hopper floated in. There was a heavy strike. Nick swung the rod against the pull. It felt as though he were hooked into the log itself, except for the live feeling.

He tried to force the fish out into the current. It came, heavily.

The line went slack and Nick thought the trout was gone. Then he saw him, very near, in the current shaking his head, trying to get the hook out. His mouth was clamped shut. He was fighting the hook in the clear flowing current.

Looping in the line with his left hand, Nick swung the rod to make the line taut and tried to lead the trout toward the net, but he was gone, out of sight, the line pumping. Nick fought him against the current, letting him thump in the water against the spring of the rod. He shifted the rod to his left hand, worked the trout upstream, holding his weight, fighting on the rod, and then let him down into the net. He lifted him clear of the water, a heavy half circle in the net, the net dripping, unhooked him and slid him into the sack.

He spread the mouth of the sack and looked down in at the two big trout alive in the water.

Through the deepening water, Nick waded over to the hollow log. He took the sack off, over his head, the trout flopping as it came out of the water, and hung it so the trout were deep in the water. Then he pulled himself up on the log and sat, the water from his trouser and boots running down into the stream. He laid his rod down, moved along to the shady end of the log and took the sandwiches out of his pocket. He dipped the sandwiches in the cold water. The current carried away the crumbs. He ate the sandwiches and dipped his hat full of water to drink, the water running through his hat just ahead of his drinking.

It was cool in the shade, sitting on the log. He took a cigarette out and struck a match to light it. The match sunk into the gray wood, making a tiny furrow. Nick leaned over the side of the log, found a hard place and lit the match. He sat smoking and watching the river.

Ahead the river narrowed and went into a swamp. The river became smooth and deep and the swamp looked solid with cedar trees, their trunks close together, their branches solid. It would not be possible to walk through a swamp like that. The branches grew so low. You would have to keep almost level with the ground to move at all. You could not crash through the branches. That must be why the animals that lived in swamps were built the way they were, Nick thought.

He wished he had brought something to read. He felt like reading. He did not feel like going on into the swamp. He looked down the river. A big cedar slanted all the way across the stream. Beyond that the river went into the swamp.

Nick did not want to go in there now. He felt a reaction against deep wading with the water deepening up under his armpits, to hook big trout in places impossible to land them. In the swamp the banks were bare, the big cedars came together overhead, the sun did not come through, except in patches; in the fast deep water, in the half light, the fishing would be tragic. In the swamp fishing was a tragic adventure. Nick did not want it. He did not want to go down the stream any further today.

He took out his knife, opened it and stuck it in the log. Then he pulled up the sack, reached into it and brought out one of the trout. Holding him near the tail, hard to hold, alive, in his hand, he wacked him against the log. The trout quivered, rigid. Nick laid him on the log in the shade and broke the neck of the other fish the same way. He laid them side by side on the log. They were fine trout.

Nick cleaned them, slitting them from the vent to the tip of the jaw. All the insides and the gills and tongue came out in one piece. They were both males; long gray-white strips of milt, smooth and clean. All the insides clean and compact, coming out all together. Nick tossed the offal ashore for the minks to find.

He washed the trout in the stream. When he held them back up in the water they looked like live fish. Their color was not gone yet. He washed his hands and dried them on the log. Then he laid the trout on the sack spread out on the log, rolled them up in it, tied the bundle and put it in the landing net. His knife was still standing, blade stuck in the log. He cleaned it on the wood and put it in his pocket.

Nick stood up on the log, holding his rod, the landing net hanging heavy, then stepped into the water and splashed ashore. He climbed the bank and cut up into the woods, toward the high ground. He was going back to camp. He looked back. The river just showed through the trees. There were plenty of days coming when he could fish the swamp.

1924 1925, 1938

William Faulkner 1897–1962

After he received a Nobel Prize for Literature in 1949, William Faulkner's reputation and influence spread throughout the world. But, ironically, the Nobel Prize was awarded largely for works that he had written years before and were so little recognized at the time of their publication that most of them were out of print by the 1940s. The only Faulkner novel that had come close to being a bestseller in its day was Sanctuary, *a book more famous for its shock value than for its literary quality.*

Faulkner was born William Cuthbert Falkner (the "u" he added to his last name when he began to publish) in New Albany, Mississippi. When he was four or five years old, the family moved to Oxford, Mississippi, where he resided for the rest of his life. Oxford was, with some fictional modifications, a prototype of Jefferson, in the mythical county of Yoknapatawpha, the setting of Sartoris *and most of his subsequent works. His central theme, however, was not Oxford, or Mississippi, or even America. It was, as he put it, the universal theme of "the problems of the human heart in conflict with itself."*

Faulkner began his literary career as a poet rather than a fiction writer, but his poetry was undistinguished and commercially unsuccessful. He turned to the writing of prose in 1925 after meeting Sherwood Anderson in New Orleans. With Faulkner's third published novel, Sartoris, *which he completed in 1927 and which was printed in 1929, he "discovered," as he said later, "that my own little postage stamp of native soil was worth writing about and that I would never live long enough to exhaust it, and that by sublimating the actual into the apocryphal I would have complete liberty to use whatever talent I might have to its absolute top. It opened up a gold mine of other people, so I created a cosmos of my own." Using his own cosmos to express his universal theme of "the problems of the human heart," Faulkner created the novels for which he is now best known:* The Sound and the Fury *(1929),* As I Lay Dying *(1930),* The Hamlet *(1940), and* Go Down, Moses *(1942).*

In 1948, after six years in which he published only a few short stories, he resumed his career with Intruder in the Dust. *Three years later* Requiem for a Nun, *a kind of sequel to* Sanctuary, *appeared. His most ambitious single effort was, perhaps,* A Fable *(1954), an allegorical novel, which took him at least nine years to write and which has so far proved baffling to readers and critics alike.* The Town *(1957) and* The Mansion *(1959) complete the trilogy on the Snopes family, which began with* The Hamlet. *Faulkner's last novel,* The Reivers, *was published on June 4, 1962. A month later he died.*

Faulkner also published about seventy short stories, some of which were later incorporated into novels, such as "Wash" in Absalom, Absalom!, *"Spotted Horses" in* The Hamlet, *and "The Bear" (with a long section added) in* Go Down, Moses. *Collections of short stories appeared in* These 13 *(1931),* Doctor Martino and Other Stories *(1934),* Knight's Gambit *(1949),* Collected Stories of William Faulkner *(1950), and* Big Woods *(1955).*

Although his home was always Mississippi, Faulkner traveled extensively. He trained as a pilot for the Royal Canadian Flying Corps during 1918, worked in New York City in 1920 and 1921, spent most of 1925 in New Orleans and Europe, and labored off and on for several years as a script writer in Hollywood. Like many other American writers, he never graduated from college, but he read omnivorously a wide variety of literature: the Bible, Greek and Roman classics, Shakespeare, the standard English and American poets and novelists, and such modern writers as the French symbolist poets and Conrad, Joyce, and Eliot. Through the late 1920s and the 1930s, his bold experiments in the dislocation of narrative time and his use of stream-of-consciousness techniques placed him in the forefront of the avant-garde. Faulkner's verbal innovations and the labyrinthine organization of his novels make him difficult to read, but his popularity continues to grow, and today he is considered by many to have been the greatest writer of fiction that the United States has yet produced.

FURTHER READING: *Faulkner in the University,* ed. F. Gwynn and J. Blotner, 1959; J. Faulkner, *My Brother Bill,* 1963; *Essays, Speeches and Public Letters by William Faulkner,* ed. J. Meriwether, 1966; J. Blotner, *Faulkner: A Biography,* 2 vols., 1974, 1 vol., 1982; *Selected Letters of William Faulkner,* ed. J. Blotner, 1977; *Uncollected Short Stories of William Faulkner,* ed. J. Blotner, 1979; D. Minter, *William Faulkner: His Life and Work,* 1980, 1997; M. Kreisworth, *William Faulkner: The Making of a Novelist,* 1983; C. Brooks, *William Faulkner: First Encounters,* 1983; M. Putzel, *Genius of Place: William Faulkner's Triumphant Beginnings,* 1985; J. Sensibar, *The Origins of Faulkner's Art,* 1985; S. Oates, *William Faulkner: The Man and Artist,* 1987; T. Connolly, *Faulkner's World: A Directory of His People and Synopses of Actions in His Published Works,* 1988; F. Karl, *William Faulkner: American Writer,* 1989; M. Millgate, *The Achievement of William Faulkner,* 1989; Andre Bleikasten, *The Ink of Melancholy: Faulkner's Novels from 'The Sound and the Fury' to 'Light in August,'* 1991; J. Ferguson, *Faulkner's Short Fiction,* 1991; J. Williamson, *William Faulkner and Southern History,* 1993; D. Jones, *A Reader's Guide to the Short Stories of William Faulkner,* 1994; D. Roberts, *Faulkner and Southern Womanhood,* 1994; R. Gray, *The Life of William Faulkner,* 1995; *The Cambridge Companion to William Faulkner,* ed. P. Weinstein, 1995; M. Millgate, *Faulkner's Place,* 1997; D. Singal, *William Faulkner: The Making of a Modernist,* 1997; *Readings on William Faulkner,* ed. C. Swisher, 1998; J. Watson, *William Faulkner: Self-Presentation and Performance,* 2000; *William Faulkner: Six Decades of Criticism,* ed. L. Wagner-Martin, 2002; E. Welty, *On William Faulkner,* 2003.

TEXTS: *Collected Stories of William Faulkner,* 1950; *Intruder in the Dust,* 1948.

THAT EVENING SUN

I

Monday is no different from any other weekday in Jefferson now. The streets are paved now, and the telephone and electric companies are cutting down more and more of the shade trees—the water oaks, the maples and locusts and elms—to make room for iron poles bearing clusters of bloated and ghostly and bloodless grapes, and we have a city laundry which makes the rounds on Monday morning, gathering the bundles of clothes into bright-colored, specially-made motor cars: the soiled wearing of a whole week now flees apparition-like behind alert and irritable electric horns, with a long diminishing noise of rubber and asphalt like tearing silk, and even the Negro women who still take in white people's washing after the old custom, fetch and deliver it in automobiles.

But fifteen years ago, on Monday morning the quiet, dusty, shady streets would be full of Negro women with, balanced on their steady, turbaned heads, bundles of clothes tied up in sheets, almost as large as cotton bales, carried so without touch of hand between the kitchen door of the white house and the blackened washpot beside a cabin door in Negro Hollow.

Nancy would set her bundle on top of her head, then upon the bundle in turn she would set the black straw sailor hat which she wore winter and summer. She was tall, with a high, sad face sunken a little where her teeth were missing. Sometimes we would go a part of the way down the lane across the pasture with her, to watch the balanced bundle and the hat that never bobbed nor wavered, even when she walked down into the ditch and up the other side and stooped through the fence. She would go down on her hands and knees and crawl through the gap, her head rigid, uptilted, the bundle steady as a rock or a balloon, and rise to her feet again and go on.

Sometimes the husbands of the washing women would fetch and deliver the clothes, but Jesus never did that for Nancy, even before father told him to stay away from our house, even when Dilsey was sick and Nancy would come to cook for us.

And then about half the time we'd have to go down the lane to Nancy's cabin and tell her to come on and cook breakfast. We would stop at the ditch, because father told us to not have anything to do with Jesus—he was a short black man, with a razor scar down his face—and we would throw rocks at Nancy's house until she came to the door, leaning her head around it without any clothes on.

"What yawl mean, chunking my house?" Nancy said. "What you little devils mean?"

"Father says for you to come on and get breakfast," Caddy said. "Father says it's over a half an hour now, and you've got to come this minute."

"I ain't studying no breakfast," Nancy said. "I going to get my sleep out."

"I bet you're drunk," Jason said. "Father says you're drunk. Are you drunk, Nancy?"

"Who says I is?" Nancy said. "I got to get my sleep out. I ain't studying no breakfast."

So after a while we quit chunking the cabin and went back home. When she finally came, it was too late for me to go to school. So we thought it was whisky until that day they arrested her again and they were taking her to jail and they passed Mr Stovall. He was the cashier in the bank and a deacon in the Baptist church, and Nancy began to say:

"When you going to pay me, white man? When are you going to pay me, white man? It's been three times now since you paid me a cent—" Mr Stovall knocked her down, but she kept saying, "When you going to pay me, white man? It's been three times now since—" until Mr Stovall kicked her in the mouth with his heel and the marshall caught Mr Stovall back, and Nancy lying in the street, laughing. She turned her head and spat out some blood and teeth and said, "It's been three times now since he paid me a cent."

That was how she lost her teeth, and all that day they told about Nancy and Mr Stovall, and all that night the ones that passed the jail could hear Nancy singing and yelling. They could see her hands holding to the window bars, and a lot of them stopped along the fence, listening to her and to the jailer trying to make her stop. She didn't shut up until almost daylight, when the jailer began to hear a bumping and scraping upstairs and he went up there and found Nancy hanging from the window bar. He said that it was cocaine and not whisky, because no nigger would try to commit suicide unless he was full of cocaine, because a nigger full of cocaine wasn't a nigger any longer.

The jailer cut her down and revived her; then he beat her, whipped her. She had hung herself with her dress. She had fixed it all right, but when they arrested her she didn't have on anything except a dress and so she didn't have anything to tie her hands with and she couldn't make her hands let go of the window ledge. So the jailer heard the noise and ran up there and found Nancy hanging from the window, stark naked, her belly already swelling out a little, like a little balloon.

When Dilsey was sick in her cabin and Nancy was cooking for us, we could see her apron swelling out; that was before father told Jesus to stay away from the house. Jesus was in the kitchen, sitting behind the stove, with his razor scar on his black face like a piece of dirty string. He said it was a watermelon that Nancy had under her dress.

"It never come off your vine, though," Nancy said.

"Off of what vine?" Caddy said.

"I can cut down the vine it did come off of," Jesus said.

"What makes you want to talk like that before these children?" Nancy said. "Whyn't you go on to work? You done et. You want Mr Jason to catch you hanging around his kitchen, talking that way before these children?"

"Talking what way?" Caddy said. "What vine?"

"I can't hang around white man's kitchen," Jesus said. "But white man can hang around mine. White man can come in my house, but I can't stop him. When white man want to come in my house, I ain't got no house. I can't stop him, but he can't kick me outen it. He can't do that."

Dilsey was still sick in her cabin. Father told Jesus to stay off our place. Dilsey was still sick. It was a long time. We were in the library after supper.

"Isn't Nancy through in the kitchen yet?" mother said. "It seems to me that she has had plenty of time to have finished the dishes."

"Let Quentin go and see," father said. "Go and see if Nancy is through, Quentin. Tell her she can go on home."

I went to the kitchen. Nancy was through. The dishes were put away and the fire was out. Nancy was sitting in a chair, close to the cold stove. She looked at me.

"Mother wants to know if you are through," I said.

"Yes," Nancy said. She looked at me. "I done finished." She looked at me.

"What is it?" I said. "What is it?"

"I ain't nothing but a nigger," Nancy said. "It ain't none of my fault."

She looked at me, sitting in the chair before the cold stove, the sailor hat on her head. I went back to the library. It was the cold stove and all, when you think of a kitchen being warm and busy and cheerful. And with a cold stove and the dishes all put away, and nobody wanting to eat at that hour.

"Is she through?" mother said.

"Yessum," I said.

"What is she doing?" mother said.

"She's not doing anything. She's through."

"I'll go and see," father said.

"Maybe she's waiting for Jesus to come and take her home." Caddy said.

"Jesus is gone," I said. Nancy told us how one morning she woke up and Jesus was gone.

"He quit me," Nancy said. "Done gone to Memphis, I reckon. Dodging them city *po*-lice for a while, I reckon."

"And a good riddance," father said. "I hope he stays there."

"Nancy's scaired of the dark," Jason said.

"So are you," Caddy said.

"I'm not," Jason said.

"Scairy cat," Caddy said.

"I'm not," Jason said.

"You, Candace!" mother said. Father came back.

"I am going to walk down the lane with Nancy," he said. "She says that Jesus is back."

"Has she seen him?" mother said.

"No. Some Negro sent her word that he was back in town. I won't be long."

"You'll leave me alone, to take Nancy home?" mother said. "Is her safety more precious to you than mine?"

"I won't be long," father said.

"You'll leave these children unprotected, with that Negro about?"

"I'm going too," Caddy said. "Let me go, Father."

"What would he do with them, if he were unfortunate enough to have them?" father said.

"I want go to, too," Jason said.

"Jason!" mother said. She was speaking to father. You could tell that by the way she said the name. Like she believed that all day father had been trying to think of doing the thing she wouldn't like the most, and that she knew all the time that after a while he would think of it. I stayed quiet, because father and I both knew that mother would want him to make me stay with her if she just thought of it in time. So father didn't look at me. I was the oldest. I was nine and Caddy was seven and Jason was five.

"Nonsense," father said. "We won't be long."

Nancy had her hat on. We came to the lane. "Jesus always been good to me." Nancy said. "Whenever he had two dollars, one of them was mine." We walked in the lane. "If I just get through the lane," Nancy said. "I be all right then."

The lane was always dark. "This is where Jason got scared on Hallowe'en," Caddy said.

"I didn't," Jason said.

"Can't Aunt Rachel do anything with him?" father said. Aunt Rachel was old. She lived in a cabin beyond Nancy's, by herself. She had white hair and she smoked a pipe in the door, all day long; she didn't work any more. They said she was Jesus' mother. Sometimes she said she was and sometimes she said she wasn't any kin to Jesus.

"Yes, you did," Caddy said. "You were scairder than Frony. You were scairder than T.P. even. Scairder than niggers."

"Can't nobody do nothing with him," Nancy said. "He say I done woke up the devil in him and ain't but one thing going to lay it down again."

"Well, he's gone now," father said. "There's nothing for you to be afraid of now. And if you'd just let white men alone."

"Let what white men alone?" Caddy said. "How let them alone?"

"He ain't gone nowhere," Nancy said. "I can feel him. I can feel him now, in this lane. He hearing us talk, every word, hid somewhere, waiting. I ain't seen him, and I ain't going to see him again but once more, with that razor in his mouth. That razor on that string down his back, inside his shirt. And then I ain't going to be even surprised."

"I wasn't scaird," Jason said.

"If you'd behave yourself, you'd have kept out of this," father said. "But it's all right now. He's probably in St. Louis now. Probably got another wife by now and forgot all about you."

"If he has, I better not find out about it," Nancy said. "I'd stand there right over them, and every time he wropped her, I'd cut that arm off. I'd cut his head off and I'd slit her belly and I'd shove—"

"Hush," father said.

"Slit whose belly, Nancy?" Caddy said.

"I wasn't scaired," Jason said. "I'd walk right down this lane by myself."

"Yah," Caddy said. "You wouldn't dare to put your foot down in it if we were not here too."

II

Dilsey was still sick, so we took Nancy home every night until mother said, "How much longer is this going on? I to be left alone in this big house while you take home a frightened Negro?"

We fixed a pallet in the kitchen for Nancy. One night we waked up, hearing the sound. It was not singing and it was not crying, coming up the dark stairs. There was a light in mother's room and we heard father going down the hall, down the back stairs, and Caddy and I went into the hall. The floor was cold. Our toes curled away from it while we listened to the sound. It was like singing and it wasn't like singing, like the sounds that Negroes make.

Then it stopped and we heard father going down the back stairs, and we went to the head of the stairs. Then the sound began again, in the stairway, not loud, and we could see Nancy's eyes halfway up the stairs, against the wall. They looked like cat's eyes do, like a big cat against the wall, watching us. When we came down the steps to where she was, she quit making the sound again, and we stood there until father came back up from the kitchen, with his pistol in his hand. He went back down with Nancy and they came back with Nancy's pallet.

We spread the pallet in our room. After the light in mother's room went off, we could see Nancy's eyes again. "Nancy," Caddy whispered, "are you asleep, Nancy?"

Nancy whispered something. It was oh or no, I don't know which. Like nobody had made it, like it came from nowhere and went nowhere, until it was like Nancy was not there at all; that I had looked so hard at her eyes on the stairs that they had got printed on my eyeballs, like the sun does when you have closed your eyes and there is no sun. "Jesus," Nancy whispered. "Jesus."

"Was it Jesus?" Caddy said. "Did he try to come into the kitchen?"

"Jesus," Nancy said. Like this: Jeeeeeeeeeeeeeeesus, until the sound went out, like a match or a candle does.

"It's the other Jesus she means," I said.

"Can you see us, Nancy?" Caddy whispered. "Can you see our eyes too?"

"I ain't nothing but a nigger," Nancy said. "God knows. God knows."

"What did you see down there in the kitchen?" Caddy whispered. "What tried to get in?"

"God knows," Nancy said. We could see her eyes. "God knows."

Dilsey got well. She cooked dinner. "You'd better stay in bed a day or two longer," father said.

"What for?" Dilsey said. "If I had been a day later, this place would be to rack and ruin. Get on out of here now, and let me get my kitchen straight again."

Dilsey cooked supper too. And that night, just before dark, Nancy came into the kitchen.

"How do you know he's back?" Dilsey said. "You ain't seen him."

"Jesus is a nigger," Jason said.

"I can feel him," Nancy said. "I can feel him laying yonder in the ditch."

"Tonight?" Dilsey said. "Is he there tonight?"

"Dilsey's a nigger too," Jason said.

"You try to eat something," Dilsey said.

"I don't want nothing," Nancy said.

"I ain't a nigger," Jason said.

"Drink some coffee." Dilsey said. She poured a cup of coffee for Nancy. "Do you know he's out there tonight? How come you know it's tonight?"

"I know," Nancy said. "He's there, waiting. I know. I done lived with him too long. I know what he is fixing to do fore he know it himself."

"Drink some coffee," Dilsey said. Nancy held the cup to her mouth and blew into the cup. Her mouth pursed out like a spreading adder's, like a rubber mouth, like she had blown all the color out of her lips with blowing the coffee.

"I ain't a nigger," Jason said. "Are you a nigger, Nancy?"

"I hellborn, child," Nancy said. "I won't be nothing soon. I going back where I come from soon."

III

She began to drink the coffee. While she was drinking, holding the cup in both hands, she began to make the sound again. She made the sound into the cup and the coffee sploshed out onto her hands and her dress. Her eyes looked at us and she sat there, her elbows on her knees, holding the cup in both hands, looking at us across the wet cup, making the sound. "Look at Nancy," Jason said. "Nancy can't cook for us now. Dilsey's got well now."

"You hush up," Dilsey said. Nancy held the cup in both hands, looking at us, making the sound, like there were two of them: one looking at us and the other making the sound. "Whyn't you let Mr Jason telefoam the marshal?" Dilsey said. Nancy stopped then, holding the cup in her long brown hands. She tried to drink some coffee again, but it sploshed out of the cup, onto her hands and her dress, and she put the cup down. Jason watched her.

"I can't swallow it," Nancy said. "I swallows but it won't go down me."

"You go down to the cabin," Dilsey said. "Frony will fix you a pallet and I'll be there soon."

"Won't no nigger stop him," Nancy said.

"I ain't a nigger," Jason said. "Am I, Dilsey?"

"I reckon not," Dilsey said. She looked at Nancy. "I don't reckon so. What you going to do, then?"

Nancy looked at us. Her eyes went fast, like she was afraid there wasn't time to look, without hardly moving at all. She looked at us, at all three of us at one time. "You member that night I stayed in yawls' room?" she said. She told about how we waked up early the next morning, and played. We had to play quiet, on her pallet, until father woke up and it was time to get breakfast. "Go and ask your maw to let me stay here tonight," Nancy said. "I won't need no pallet. We can play some more."

Caddy asked mother. Jason went too. "I can't have Negroes sleeping in the bedrooms," mother said. Jason cried. He cried until mother said he couldn't have any dessert for three days if he didn't stop. Then Jason said he would stop if Dilsey would make a chocolate cake. Father was there.

"Why don't you do something about it?" mother said. "What do we have officers for?"

"Why is Nancy afraid of Jesus?" Caddy said. "Are you afraid of father, mother?"

"What could the officers do?" father said. "If Nancy hasn't seen him, how could the officers find him?"

"Then why is she afraid?" mother said.

"She says he is there. She says she knows he is there tonight."

"Yet we pay taxes," mother said. "I must wait here alone in this big house while you take a Negro woman home."

"You know that I am not lying outside with a razor," father said.

"I'll stop if Dilsey will make a chocolate cake," Jason said. Mother told us to go out and father said he didn't know if Jason would get a chocolate cake or not, but he knew what Jason was going to get in about a minute. We went back to the kitchen and told Nancy.

"Father said for you to go home and lock the door, and you'll be all right," Caddy said. "All right from what, Nancy? Is Jesus mad at you?" Nancy was holding the coffee cup in her hands again, her elbows on her knees and her hands holding the cup between her knees. She was looking into the cup. "What have you done that made Jesus mad?" Caddy said. Nancy let the cup go. It didn't break on the floor, but the coffee spilled out, and Nancy sat there with her hands still making the shape of the cup. She began to make that sound again, not loud. Not singing and not unsinging. We watched her.

"Here," Dilsey said. "You quit that, now. You get aholt of yourself. You wait here. I going to get Versh to walk home with you." Dilsey went out.

We looked at Nancy. Her shoulders kept shaking, but she quit making the sound. We watched her. "What's Jesus going to do to you?" Caddy said. "He went away."

Nancy looked at us. "We had fun that night I stayed in yawls' room, didn't we?"

"I didn't," Jason said. "I didn't have any fun."

"You were asleep in mother's room," Caddy said. "You were not there."

"Let's go down to my house and have some more fun," Nancy said.

"Mother won't let us," I said. "It's too late now."

"Don't bother her," Nancy said. "We can tell her in the morning. She won't mind."

"She wouldn't let us," I said.

"Don't ask her now," Nancy said. "Don't bother her now."

"She didn't say we couldn't go," Caddy said.

"We didn't ask," I said.

"If you go, I'll tell," Jason said.

"We'll have fun," Nancy said. "They won't mind, just to my house. I been working for yawl a long time. They won't mind."

"I'm not afraid to go." Caddy said. "Jason is the one that's afraid. He'll tell."

"I'm not," Jason said.

"Yes, you are," Caddy said. "You'll tell."

"I won't tell," Jason said. "I'm not afraid."

"Jason ain't afraid to go with me," Nancy said. "Is you, Jason?"

"Jason is going to tell," Caddy said. The lane was dark. We passed the pasture gate. "I bet if something was to jump out from behind that gate, Jason would holler."

"I wouldn't," Jason said. We walked down the lane. Nancy was talking loud.

"What are you talking so loud for, Nancy?" Caddy said.

"Who; me?" Nancy said. "Listen at Quentin and Caddy and Jason saying I'm talking loud."

"You talk like there was five of us here," Caddy said. "You talk like father was here too."

"Who; me talking loud, Mr. Jason?" Nancy said.

"Nancy called Jason 'Mister,'" Caddy said.

"Listen how Caddy and Quentin and Jason talk," Nancy said.

"We're not talking loud," Caddy said. "You're the one that's talking like father—"

"Hush," Nancy said; "hush, Mr. Jason."

"Nancy called Jason 'Mister' aguh—"

"Hush," Nancy said. She was talking loud when we crossed the ditch and stooped through the fence where she used to stoop through with the clothes on her head. Then we came to her house. We were going fast then. She opened the door. The smell of the house was like the lamp and the smell of Nancy was like the wick, like they were waiting for one another to begin to smell. She lit the lamp and closed the door and put the bar up. Then she quit talking loud, looking at us.

"What're we going to do?" Caddy said.

"What do yawl want to do?" Nancy said.

"You said we would have some fun," Caddy said.

There was something about Nancy's house; something you could smell besides Nancy and the house. Jason smelled it, even. "I don't want to stay here." he said. "I want to go home."

"Go home, then," Caddy said.

"I don't want to go by myself," Jason said.

"We're going to have some fun," Nancy said.

"How?" Caddy said.

Nancy stood by the door. She was looking at us, only it was like she had emptied her eyes, like she had quit using them. "What do you want to do?" she said.

"Tell us a story," Caddy said. "Can you tell a story?"

"Yes," Nancy said.

"Tell it," Caddy said. We looked at Nancy. "You don't know any stories."

"Yes," Nancy said. "Yes I do."

She came and sat in a chair before the hearth. There was a little fire there. Nancy built it up, when it was already hot inside. She built a good blaze. She told a story. She talked like her eyes looked, like her eyes watching us and her voice talking to us did not belong to her. Like she was living somewhere else, waiting somewhere else. She was outside the cabin. Her voice was inside and the shape of her, the Nancy that could stoop under a barbed wire fence with a bundle of clothes balanced on her head as though without weight, like a balloon, was there. But that was all. "And so this here queen come walking up to the ditch, where that bad man was hiding. She was walking up to the ditch, and she say, 'If I can just get past this here ditch,' was what she say . . ."

"What ditch?" Caddy said. "A ditch like that one there? Why did a queen want to go into a ditch?"

"To get to her house," Nancy said. She looked at us. "She had to cross the ditch to get into her house quick and bar the door."

"Why did she want to go home and bar the door?" Caddy said.

IV

Nancy looked at us. She quit talking. She looked at us. Jason's legs stuck straight out of his pants where he sat on Nancy's lap. "I don't think that's a good story," he said. "I want to go home."

"Maybe we had better," Caddy said. She got up from the floor. "I bet they are looking for us right now." She went toward the door.

"No," Nancy said. "Don't open it." She got up quick and passed Caddy. She didn't touch the door, the wooden bar.

"Why not?" Caddy said.

"Come back to the lamp," Nancy said. "We'll have fun. You don't have to go."

"We ought to go," Caddy said. "Unless we have a lot of fun." She and Nancy came back to the fire, the lamp.

"I want to go home," Jason said. "I'm going to tell."

"I know another story," Nancy said. She stood close to the lamp. She looked at Caddy, like when your eyes look up at a stick balanced on your nose. She had to look down to see Caddy, but her eyes looked like that, like when you are balancing a stick.

"I won't listen to it," Jason said. "I'll bang on the floor."

"It's a good one," Nancy said. "It's better than the other one."

"What's it about?" Caddy said. Nancy was standing by the lamp. Her hand was on the lamp, against the light, long and brown.

"Your hand is on that hot globe," Caddy said. "Don't it feel hot to your hand?"

Nancy looked at her hand on the lamp chimney. She took her hand away, slow. She stood there, looking at Caddy, wringing her long hand as though it were tied to her wrist with a string.

"Let's do something else," Caddy said.

"I want to go home," Jason said.

"I got some popcorn," Nancy said. She looked at Caddy and then at Jason and then at me and then at Caddy again. "I got some popcorn."

"I don't like popcorn," Jason said. "I'd rather have candy."

Nancy looked at Jason. "You can hold the popper." She was still wringing her hand; it was long and limp and brown.

"All right," Jason said. "I'll stay a while if I can do that. Caddy can't hold it. I'll want to go home if Caddy holds the popper."

Nancy built up the fire. "Look at Nancy putting her hands in the fire," Caddy said. "What's the matter with you, Nancy?"

"I got popcorn," Nancy said. "I got some." She took the popper from under the bed. It was broken. Jason began to cry.

"Now we can't have any popcorn," he said.

"We ought to go home, anyway," Caddy said. "Come on, Quentin."

"Wait," Nancy said; "wait. I can fix it. Don't you want to help me fix it?"

"I don't think I want any," Caddy said. "It's too late now."

"You help me, Jason," Nancy said. "Don't you want to help me?"

"No," Jason said. "I want to go home."

"Hush," Nancy said; "hush. Watch. Watch me. I can fix it so Jason can hold it and pop the corn." She got a piece of wire and fixed the popper.

"It won't hold good," Caddy said.

"Yes, it will," Nancy said. "Yawl watch. Yawl help me shell some corn."

The popcorn was under the bed too. We shelled it into the popper and Nancy helped Jason hold the popper over the fire.

"It's not popping," Jason said. "I want to go home."

"You wait," Nancy said. "It'll begin to pop. We'll have fun then." She was sitting close to the fire. The lamp was turned up so high it was beginning to smoke. "Why don't you turn it down some?" I said.

"It's all right," Nancy said. "I'll clean it. Yawl wait. The popcorn will start in a minute."

"I don't believe it's going to start," Caddy said. "We ought to start home, anyway. They'll be worried."

"No," Nancy said. "It's going to pop. Dilsey will tell um yawl with me. I been working for yawl long time. They won't mind if yawl at my house. You wait, now. It'll start popping any minute now."

Then Jason got some smoke in his eyes and he began to cry. He dropped the popper into the fire. Nancy got a wet rag and wiped Jason's face, but he didn't stop crying.

"Hush," she said. "Hush." But he didn't hush. Caddy took the popper out of the fire.

"It's burned up," she said. "You'll have to get some more popcorn, Nancy."

"Did you put all of it in?" Nancy said.

"Yes," Caddy said. Nancy looked at Caddy. Then she took the popper and opened it and poured the cinders into her apron and began to sort the grains, her hands long and brown, and we watching her.

"Haven't you got any more?" Caddy said.

"Yes," Nancy said; "yes. Look. This here ain't burnt. All we need to do is—"

"I want to go home," Jason said. "I'm going to tell."

"Hush," Caddy said. We all listened. Nancy's head was already turned toward the barred door, her eyes filled with red lamplight. "Somebody is coming," Caddy said.

Then Nancy began to make that sound again, not loud, sitting there above the fire, her long hands dangling between her knees; all of a sudden water began to come out on her face in big drops, running down her face, carrying in each one a little turning ball of firelight like a spark until it dropped off her chin. "She's not crying," I said.

"I ain't crying," Nancy said. Her eyes were closed. "I ain't crying. Who is it?"

"I don't know," Caddy said. She went to the door and looked out. "We've got to go now," she said. "Here comes father."

"I'm going to tell," Jason said. "Yawl made me come."

The water still ran down Nancy's face. She turned in her chair. "Listen. Tell him. Tell him we going to have fun. Tell him I take good care of yawl until in the morning. Tell him to let me come home with yawl and sleep on the floor.

Tell him I won't need no pallet. We'll have fun. You member last time how we had so much fun?"

"I didn't have fun," Jason said. "You hurt me. You put smoke in my eyes. I'm going to tell."

V

Father came in. He looked at us. Nancy did not get up.

"Tell him," she said.

"Caddy made us come down here," Jason said. "I didn't want to."

Father came to the fire. Nancy looked up at him. "Can't you go to Aunt Rachel's and stay?" he said. Nancy looked up at father, her hands between her knees. "He's not here," father said. "I would have seen him. There's not a soul in sight."

"He in the ditch," Nancy said. "He waiting in the ditch yonder."

"Nonsense," father said. He looked at Nancy. "Do you know he's there?"

"I got the sign," Nancy said.

"What sign?"

"I got it. It was on the table when I come in. It was a hogbone, with blood meat still on it, laying by the lamp. He's out there. When yawl walk out that door, I gone."

"Gone where, Nancy?" Caddy said.

"I'm not a tattletale," Jason said.

"Nonsense," father said.

"He out there," Nancy said. "He looking through that window this minute, waiting for yawl to go. Then I gone."

"Nonsense," father said. "Lock up your house and we'll take you on to Aunt Rachel's."

"'Twon't do no good," Nancy said. She didn't look at father now, but he looked down at her, at her long, limp, moving hands. "Putting it off won't do no good."

"Then what do you want to do?" father said.

"I don't know," Nancy said. "I can't do nothing. Just put it off. And that don't do no good. I reckon it belong to me. I reckon what I going to get ain't no more than mine."

"Get what?" Caddy said. "What's yours?"

"Nothing," father said. "You all must get to bed."

"Caddy made me come," Jason said.

"Go on to Aunt Rachel's," father said.

"It won't do no good," Nancy said. She sat before the fire, her elbows on her knees, her long hands between her knees. "When even your own kitchen wouldn't do no good. When even if I was sleeping on the floor in the room with your children, and the next morning there I am, and blood—"

"Hush," father said. "Lock the door and put out the lamp and go to bed."

"I scared of the dark," Nancy said. "I scared for it to happen in the dark."

"You mean you're going to sit right here with the lamp lighted?" father said. Then Nancy began to make the sound again, sitting before the fire, her long hands between her knees. "Ah, damnation," father said. "Come along, chillen. It's past bedtime."

"When yawl go home, I gone," Nancy said. She talked quieter now, and her face looked quiet, like her hands. "Anyway, I got my coffin money saved up with Mr. Lovelady." Mr. Lovelady was a short, dirty man who collected the Negro insurance, coming around the cabins or the kitchens every Saturday morning, to collect fifteen cents. He and his wife lived at the hotel. One morning his wife committed suicide. They had a child, a little girl. He and the child went away. After a week or two he came back alone. We would see him going along the lanes and the back streets on Saturday mornings.

"Nonsense," father said. "You'll be the first thing I'll see in the kitchen tomorrow morning."

"You'll see what you'll see, I reckon," Nancy said. "But it will take the Lord to say what that will be."

VI

We left her sitting before the fire.

"Come and put the bar up," father said. But she didn't move. She didn't look at us again, sitting quietly there between the lamp and the fire. From some distance down the lane we could look back and see her through the open door.

"What, Father?" Caddy said. "What's going to happen?"

"Nothing," father said. Jason was on father's back, so Jason was the tallest of all of us. We went down in to the ditch. I looked at it, quiet. I couldn't see much where the moonlight and the shadows tangled.

"If Jesus is hid here, he can see us, can't he?" Caddy said.

"He's not there," father said. "He went away a long time ago."

"You made me come," Jason said, high; against the sky it looked like father had two heads, a little one and a big one. "I didn't want to."

We went up out of the ditch. We could still see Nancy's house and the open door, but we couldn't see Nancy now, sitting before the fire with the door open, because she was tired. "I just done got tired," she said. "I just a nigger. It ain't no fault of mine."

But we could hear her, because she began just after we came up out of the ditch, the sound that was not singing and not unsinging. "Who will do our washing now, Father?" I said.

"I'm not a nigger," Jason said, high and close to father's head.

"You're worse," Caddy said, "you are a tattletale. If something was to jump out, you'd be scairder than a nigger."

"I wouldn't," Jason said.

"You'd cry," Caddy said.

"Caddy," father said.

"I wouldn't!" Jason said.

"Scairy cat," Caddy said.

"Candace!" father said.

1928? 1931

from *INTRUDER IN THE DUST*

CHAPTER ONE

It was just noon that Sunday morning when the sheriff reached the jail with Lucas Beauchamp though the whole town (the whole county too for that matter) had known since the night before that Lucas had killed a white man.

He was there, waiting. He was the first one, standing lounging trying to look occupied or at least innocent, under the shed in front of the closed blacksmith's shop across the street from the jail where his uncle would be less likely to see him if or rather when he crossed the Square toward the postoffice for the eleven oclock mail.

Because he knew Lucas Beauchamp too—as well that is as any white person knew him. Better than any maybe unless it was Carothers Edmonds on whose place Lucas lived seventeen miles from town, because he had eaten a meal in Lucas' house. It was in the early winter four years ago; he had been only twelve then and it had happened this way: Edmonds was a friend of his uncle; they had been in school at the same time at the State University, where his uncle had gone after he came back from Harvard and Heidelberg[1] to learn enough law to get himself chosen County Attorney, and the day before Edmonds had come in to town to see his uncle on some county business and had stayed the night with them and at supper that evening Edmonds had said to him:

'Come out home with me tomorrow and go rabbit hunting:' and then to his mother: 'I'll send him back in tomorrow afternoon. I'll send a boy along with him while he's out with his gun:' and then to him again: 'He's got a good dog.'

'He's got a boy,' his uncle said and Edmonds said:

'Does his boy run rabbits too?' and his uncle said:

'We'll promise he wont interfere with yours.'

So the next morning he and Aleck Sander went home with Edmonds. It was cold that morning, the first winter cold-snap; the hedgerows were rimed and stiff with frost and the standing water in the roadside drainage ditches was skimmed with ice and even the edges of the running water in the Nine Mile branch glinted fragile and scintillant like fairy glass and from the first farmyard they passed and then again and again and again came the windless tang of woodsmoke and they could see in the back yards the black iron pots already steaming while women in the sunbonnets still of summer or men's old felt hats and long men's overcoats stoked wood under them and the men with crokersack aprons tied with wire over their overalls whetted knives or already moved about the pens where hogs grunted and squealed, not quite startled, not alarmed but just alerted as though sensing already even though only dimly their rich and immanent destiny; by nightfall the whole land would be hung with their spectral intact tallowcolored empty carcasses immobilised by the heels in attitudes of frantic running as though full tilt at the center of the earth.

And he didn't know how it happened. The boy, one of Edmonds' tenant's sons, older and larger than Aleck Sander who in his turn was larger than he although they were the same age, was waiting at the house with the dog—a true rabbit dog, some hound, a good deal of hound, maybe mostly hound, redbone

[1]Harvard University, in Cambridge, Massachusetts, and the University of Heidelberg (Universität Heidelberg), in Heidelberg, Germany.

and black-and-tan with maybe a little pointer somewhere once, a potlicker,[2] a nigger dog which it took but one glance to see had an affinity a rapport with rabbits such as people said Negroes had with mules—and Aleck Sander already had his tapstick—one of the heavy nuts which bolt railroad rails together, driven onto a short length of broom-handle—which Aleck Sander could throw whirling end over end at a running rabbit pretty near as accurately as he could shoot the shotgun—and Aleck Sander and Edmonds' boy with tapsticks and he with the gun they went down through the park and across a pasture to the creek where Edmonds' boy knew the footlog was and he didn't know how it happened, something a girl might have been expected and even excused for doing but nobody else, halfway over the footlog and not even thinking about it who had walked the top rail of a fence many a time twice that far when all of a sudden the known familiar sunny winter earth was upside down and flat on his face and still holding the gun he was rushing not away from the earth but away from the bright sky and he could remember still the thin bright tinkle of the breaking ice and how he didn't even feel the shock of the water but only of the air when he came up again. He had dropped the gun too so he had to dive, submerge again to find it, back out of the icy air into the water which as yet felt neither, neither cold or not and where even his sodden garments—boots and thick pants and sweater and hunting coat—didn't even feel heavy but just slow, and found the gun and tried again for bottom then thrashed one-handed to the bank and treading water and clinging to a willow-branch he reached the gun up until someone took it; Edmonds' boy obviously since at that moment Aleck Sander rammed down at him the end of a long pole, almost a log whose first pass struck his feet out from under him and sent his head under again and almost broke his hold on the willow until a voice said:

'Get the pole out of his way so he can get out'—just a voice, not because it couldn't be anybody else but either Aleck Sander or Edmonds' boy but because it didn't matter whose: climbing out now with both hands among the willows, the skim ice crinkling and tinkling against his chest, his clothes like soft cold lead which he didn't move in but seemed rather to mount into like a poncho or a tarpaulin: up the bank until he saw two feet in gum boots which were neither Edmonds' boy's nor Aleck Sander's and then the legs, the overalls rising out of them and he climbed on and stood up and saw a Negro man with an axe on his shoulder, in a heavy sheeplined coat and a broad pale felt hat such as his grandfather had used to wear, looking at him and that was when he saw Lucas Beauchamp for the first time that he remembered or rather for the first time because you didn't forget Lucas Beauchamp; gasping, shaking and only now feeling the shock of the cold water, he looked up at the face which was just watching him without pity commiseration or anything else, not even surprise: just watching him, whose owner had made no effort whatever to help him up out of the creek, had in fact ordered Aleck Sander to desist with the pole which had been the one token toward help that anybody had made—a face which in his estimation might have been under fifty or even forty except for the hat and the eyes, and inside a Negro's skin but that was all even to a boy of twelve shaking with cold and still panting from shock and exertion because what looked out of it had no pigment at all, not even the white man's lack of it, not arrogant, not even scornful: just intractable and composed. Then Edmonds' boy said

[2]A worthless dog.

something to the man, speaking a name: something Mister Lucas: and then he knew who the man was, remembering the rest of the story which was a piece, a fragment of the country's chronicle which few if any knew better than his uncle: how the man was son of one of old Carothers McCaslin's, Edmonds' great grandfather's, slaves who had been not just old Carothers' slave but his son too: standing and shaking steadily now for what seemed to him another whole minute while the man stood looking at him with nothing whatever in his face. Then the man turned, speaking not even back over his shoulder, already walking, not even waiting to see if they heard, let alone were going to obey:

'Come on to my house.'

'I'll go back to Mr Edmonds',' he said. The man didn't look back. He didn't even answer.

'Tote his gun, Joe,' he said.

So he followed, with Edmonds' boy and Aleck Sander following him, in single file along the creek toward the bridge and the road. Soon he had stopped shaking; he was just cold and wet now and most of that would go if he just kept moving. They crossed the bridge. Ahead now was the gate where the drive went up through the park to Edmonds' house. It was almost a mile; he would probably be dry and warm both by the time he got there and he still believed he was going to turn in at the gate and even after he knew that he wasn't or anyway hadn't, already beyond it now, he was still telling himself the reason was that, although Edmonds was a bachelor and there were no women in the house, Edmonds himself might refuse to let him out of the house again until he could be returned to his mother, still telling himself this even after he knew that the true reason was that he could no more imagine himself contradicting the man striding on ahead of him than he could his grandfather, not from any fear of nor even the threat of reprisal but because like his grandfather the man striding ahead of him was simply incapable of conceiving himself by a child contradicted and defied.

So he didn't even check when they passed the gate, he didn't even look at it and now they were in no well-used tended lane leading to tenant or servant quarters and marked by walking feet but a savage gash half gully and half road mounting a hill with an air solitary independent and intractable too and then he saw the house, the cabin and remembered the rest of the story, the legend: how Edmonds' father had deeded to his Negro first cousin and his heirs in perpetuity the house and the ten acres of land it sat in—an oblong of earth set forever in the middle of the two-thousand-acre plantation like a postage stamp in the center of an envelope—the paintless wooden house, the paintless picket fence whose paintless latchless gate the man kneed open still without stopping or once looking back and, he following and Aleck Sander and Edmonds' boy following him, strode on into the yard. It would have been grassless even in summer; he could imagine it, completely bare, no weed no sprig of anything, the dust each morning swept by some of Lucas' womenfolks with a broom made of willow switches bound together, into an intricate series of whorls and overlapping loops which as the day advanced would be gradually and slowly defaced by the droppings and the cryptic three-toed prints of chickens like (remembering it now at sixteen) a terrain in miniature out of the age of the great lizards, the four of them walking in what was less than walk because its surface was dirt too yet more than path, the footpacked strip running plumbline straight between two borders of tin cans and empty bottles and shards of china and earthenware set into the ground, up to the paintless steps and the paintless gallery along whose edge sat more cans but larger—empty gallon buckets which had once contained molasses or perhaps paint and wornout water or milk pails and one five-gallon can for kerosene with its top cut off and half of what had once been somebody's (Edmonds' without doubt) kitchen hot water tank sliced longways like a banana—out of which flowers had grown last summer and from which the dead stalks and the dried and brittle tendrils still leaned and drooped, and beyond this the house itself, gray and weathered and not so much paintless as independent of and intractable to paint so that the house was not only the one possible continuation of the stern untended road but was its crown too as the carven ailanthus[3] leaves are the Greek column's capital.

Nor did the man pause yet, up the steps and across the gallery and opened the door and entered and he and then Edmonds' boy and Aleck Sander followed: a hall dim even almost dark after the bright outdoors and already he could smell that smell which he had accepted without question all his life as being the smell always of the places where people with any trace of Negro blood live as he had that all people named Mallison are Methodists, then a bedroom: a bare worn quite clean paintless rugless floor, in one corner and spread with a bright patchwork quilt a vast shadowy tester bed which had probably come out of old Carothers McCaslin's house, and a battered cheap Grand Rapids dresser and then for the moment no more or at least little more; only later would he notice—or remember that he had seen—the cluttered mantel on which sat a kerosene lamp hand-painted with flowers and a vase filled with spills of twisted newspaper and above the mantel the colored lithograph of a three-year-old calendar in which Pocahontas in the quilled fringed buckskins of a Sioux or Chippewa chief stood against a balustrade[4] of Italian marble above a garden of formal cypresses and shadowy in the corner opposite the bed a chromo portrait[5] of two people framed heavily in gold-painted wood on a gold-painted easel. But he hadn't seen that at all yet because that was behind him and all he now saw was the fire—the clay-daubed fieldstone chimney in which a halfburned backlog glowed and smoldered in the gray ashes and beside it in a rocking chair something which he thought was a child until he saw the face, and then he did pause long enough to look at her because he was about to remember something else his uncle had told him about or at least in regard to Lucas Beauchamp, and looking at her he realised for the first time how old the man actually was, must be—a tiny old almost doll-sized woman much darker than the man, in a shawl and an apron, her head bound in an immaculate white cloth on top of which sat a painted straw hat bearing some kind of ornament. But he couldn't think what it was his uncle had said or told him and then he forgot that he had remembered even the having been told, sitting in the chair himself now squarely before the hearth where Edmonds' boy was building up the fire with split logs and pine slivers and Aleck Sander squatting tugged off the wet boots and then his trousers and standing he got out of the coat and sweater and his shirt, both of them having to dodge around and past and under the man who stood straddled on the hearth, his back to the fire in the gum boots and the hat and only the sheepskin coat removed and then the old woman was beside him again less tall than he and Aleck Sander even at twelve, with another of the bright patchwork quilts on her arm.

[3]Ailanthus is a kind of deciduous Asian tree. [4]Railing. [5]A colored print.

'Strip off,' the man said.

'No I——' he said.

'Strip off,' the man said. So he stripped off the wet unionsuit too and then he was in the chair again in front of the now bright and swirling fire, enveloped in the quilt like a cocoon, enclosed completely now in that unmistakable odor of Negroes—that smell which if it were not for something that was going to happen to him within a space of time measurable now in minutes he would have gone to his grave never once pondering speculating if perhaps that smell were really not the odor of a race nor even actually of poverty but perhaps of a condition: an idea: a belief: an acceptance, a passive acceptance by them themselves of the idea that being Negroes they were not supposed to have facilities to wash properly or often or even to wash bathe often even without the facilities to do it with; that in fact it was a little to be preferred that they did not. But the smell meant nothing now or yet; it was still an hour yet before the thing would happen and it would be four years more before he would realise the extent of its ramifications and what it had done to him and he would be a man grown before he would realise, admit that he had accepted it. So he just smelled it and then dismissed it because he was used to it, he had smelled it off and on all his life and would continue to: who had spent a good part of that life in Paralee's, Aleck Sander's mother's cabin in their back yard where he and Aleck Sander played in the bad weather when they were little and Paralee would cook whole meals for them halfway between two meals at the house and he and Aleck Sander would eat them together, the food tasting the same to each; he could not even imagine an existence from which the odor would be missing to return no more. He had smelled it forever, he would smell it always; it was a part of his inescapable past, it was a rich part of his heritage as a Southerner; he didn't even have to dismiss it, he just no longer smelled it at all as the pipe smoker long since never did smell at all the cold pipereek which is as much a part of his clothing as their buttons and buttonholes, sitting drowsing a little even in the warm huddled rankness of the quilt, rousing a little when he heard Edmonds' boy and Aleck Sander get up from where they had been squatting against the wall and leave the room, but not much, sinking again into the quilt's warm reek while there stood over him still, back to the fire and hands clasped behind him and except for the clasped hands and the missing axe and the sheeplined coat exactly as when he had looked up out of the creek and seen him first, the man in the gum boots and the faded overalls of a Negro but with a heavy gold watchchain looping across the bib of the overalls and shortly after they entered the room he had been conscious of the man turning and taking something from the cluttered mantel and putting it into his mouth and later he had seen what it was: a gold toothpick such as his own grandfather had used: and the hat was a worn handmade beaver such as his grandfather had paid thirty and forty dollars apiece for, not set but raked slightly above the face pigmented like a Negro's but with a nose high in the bridge and even hooked a little and what looked out through it or from behind it not black nor white either, not arrogant at all and not even scornful: just intolerant inflexible and composed.

Then Aleck Sander came back with his clothes, dried now and still almost hot from the stove and he dressed, stamping into his stiffened boots; Edmonds' boy squatting again against the wall was still eating something from his hand and he said: 'I'll have my dinner at Mr Edmonds'.'

The man neither protested nor acquiesced. He didn't stir; he was not even looking at him. He just said, inflexible and calm: 'She done already dished it up now:' and he went on past the old woman who stood aside from the door to let him pass, into the kitchen: an oilcloth-covered table set in the bright sunny square of a southern window where—he didn't know how he knew it since there were no signs, traces, soiled plates to show it—Edmonds' boy and Aleck Sander had already eaten, and sat down and ate in his turn of what obviously was to be Lucas' dinner—collard greens, a slice of sidemeat fried in flour, big flat pale heavy half-cooked biscuits, a glass of buttermilk: nigger food too, accepted and then dismissed also because it was exactly what he had expected, it was what Negroes ate, obviously because it was what they liked, what they chose; not (at twelve: he would be a man grown before he experienced his first amazed dubiety[6] at this) that out of their long chronicle this was all they had had a chance to learn to like except the ones who ate out of white folks' kitchens but that they had elected this out of all eating because this was their palates and their metabolism; afterward, ten minutes later and then for the next four years he would be trying to tell himself that it was the food which had thrown him off. But he would know better; his initial error, misjudgment had been there all the time, not even needing to be abetted by the smell of the house and the quilt in order to survive what had looked out (and not even at him: just looked out) from the man's face; rising at last and with the coin, the half-dollar already in his hand going back into the other room: when he saw for the first time because he happened to be facing it now the gold-framed portrait-group on its gold easel and he went to it, stooping to peer at it in its shadowy corner where only the gold leaf gleamed, before he knew he was going to do it. It had been retouched obviously; from behind the round faintly prismatic glass dome as out of a seer's crystal ball there looked back at him again the calm intolerant face beneath the swaggering rake of the hat, a tieless starched collar clipped to a white starched shirt with a collarbutton shaped like a snake's head and almost as large, the watch-chain looped now across a broadcloth vest inside a broadcloth coat and only the toothpick missing, and beside him the tiny doll-like woman in another painted straw hat and a shawl; that is it must have been the woman though it looked like nobody he had ever seen before and then he realised it was more than that: there was something ghastly, almost intolerably wrong about it or her: when she spoke and he looked up, the man still standing straddled before the fire and the woman sitting again in the rocking chair in its old place almost in the corner and she was not looking at him now and he knew she had never looked at him since he re-entered yet she said:

'That's some more of Lucas' doings:' and he said,

'What?' and the man said,

'Molly dont like it because the man that made it took her headrag off:' and that was it, she had hair; it was like looking at an embalmed corpse through the hermetic glass lid of a coffin and he thought *Molly. Of course* because he remembered now what it was his uncle had told him about Lucas or about them. He said:

'Why did he take it off?'

'I told him to,' the man said. 'I didn't want no field nigger picture in the house:' and he walked toward them now, putting the fist holding the half-dollar

[6]Doubt; uncertainty.

back into his pocket and scooping the dime and the two nickels—all he had—into the palm with it, saying,

'You came from town. My uncle knows you—Lawyer Gavin Stevens.'

'I remember your mama too,' she said. 'She use to be Miss Maggie Dandridge.'

'That was my grandmother,' he said. 'My mother's name was Stevens too:' and extended the coins: and in the same second in which he knew she would have taken them he knew that only by that one irrevocable second was he forever now too late, forever beyond recall, standing with the slow hot blood as slow as minutes themselves up his neck and face, forever with his dumb hand open and on it the four shameful fragments of milled and minted dross, until at last the man had something that at least did the office of pity.

'What's that for?' the man said, not even moving, not even tilting his face downward to look at what was on his palm: for another eternity and only the hot dead moveless blood until at last it ran to rage so that at least he could bear the shame: and watched his palm turn over not flinging the coins but spurning them downward ringing onto the bare floor, bouncing and one of the nickels even rolling away in a long swooping curve with a dry minute sound like the scurry of a small mouse: and then his voice:

'Pick it up!'

And still nothing, the man didn't move, hands clasped behind him, looking at nothing; only the rush of the hot dead heavy blood out of which the voice spoke, addressing nobody: 'Pick up his money:' and he heard and saw Aleck Sander and Edmonds' boy reach and scurry among the shadows near the floor. 'Give it to him,' the voice said: and saw Edmonds' boy drop his two coins into Aleck Sander's palm and felt Aleck Sander's hand fumble the four of them at his own dropped hand and then into it. 'Now go on and shoot your rabbit,' the voice said. 'And stay out of that creek.'

CHAPTER TWO

And they walked again in the bright cold (even though it was noon now and about as warm as it would ever get today probably), back across the creek bridge and (suddenly: looking around, they had gone almost a half-mile along the creek and he didn't even remember it) the dog put a rabbit into a brier patch beside a cottonfield and yapping hysterically hoicked[7] it out again, the small frantic tawny-colored blob looking one instant spherical and close-coupled as a croquet ball and the next one long as a snake, bursting out of the thicket ahead of the dog, the small white flare of its scut zigzagging across the skeletoned cottonrows like the sail of a toy boat on a windy pond while across the thicket Aleck Sander yelled:

'Shoot him! Shoot him!' then 'Whyn't you shoot him?' and then he turned without haste and walked steadily to the creek and drew the four coins from his pocket and threw them out into the water: and sleepless in bed that night he knew that the food had been not just the best Lucas had to offer but all he had to offer; he had gone out there this morning as the guest not of Edmonds but of old Carothers McCaslin's plantation and Lucas knew it when he didn't and so Lucas had beat him, stood straddled in front of the hearth and without even

[7]Jerked.

moving his clasped hands from behind his back had taken his own seventy cents and beat him with them, and writhing with impotent fury he was already thinking of the man whom he had never seen but once and that only twelve hours ago, as within the next year he was to learn every white man in that whole section of the country had been thinking about him for years: *We got to make him be a nigger first. He's got to admit he's a nigger. Then maybe we will accept him as he seems to intend to be accepted.* Because he began at once to learn a good deal more about Lucas. He didn't hear it: he learned it, all that anyone who knew that part of the country could tell him about the Negro who said 'ma'am' to women just as any white man did and who said 'sir' and 'mister' to you if you were white but who you knew was thinking neither and he knew you knew it but who was not even waiting, daring you to make the next move, because he didn't even care. For instance, this.

It was a Saturday afternoon three years ago at the crossroads store four miles from Edmonds' place where at some time during Saturday afternoon every tenant and renter and freeholder white or black in the neighborhood would at least pass and usually stop, quite often even to buy something, the saddled trace-galled mules and horses tied among the willows and birches and sycamores in the trampled mud below the spring and their riders overflowing the store itself out onto the dusty banquette in front, standing or squatting on their heels drinking bottled sodapop and spitting tobacco and rolling without hurry cigarettes and striking deliberate matches to smoked-out pipes; this day there were three youngish white men from the crew of a nearby sawmill, all a little drunk, one of whom had a reputation for brawling and violence, and Lucas came in in the worn black broadcloth suit which he wore to town and on Sundays and the worn fine hat and the heavy watch-chain and the toothpick, and something happened, the story didn't say or perhaps didn't even know what, perhaps the way Lucas walked, entered speaking to no one and went to the counter and made his purchase (it was a five-cent carton of gingersnaps) and turned and tore the end from the carton and removed the toothpick and put it into his breast pocket and shook one of the gingersnaps into his palm and put it into his mouth, or perhaps just nothing was enough, the white man on his feet suddenly saying something to Lucas, saying 'You goddamn biggity stiff-necked stinking burrheaded Edmonds sonofabitch:' and Lucas chewed the gingersnap and swallowed and the carton already tilted again over his other hand, turned his head quite slowly and looked at the white man a moment and then said:

'I aint a Edmonds. I dont belong to these new folks. I belongs to the old lot. I'm a McCaslin.'

'Keep on walking around here with that look on your face and what you'll be is crowbait,' the white man said. For another moment or at least a half one Lucas looked at the white man with a calm speculative detachment; slowly the carton in one of his hands tilted further until another gingersnap dropped into his other palm, then lifting the corner of his lip he sucked an upper tooth, quite loud in the abrupt silence but with no implication whatever of either derision or rebuttal or even disagreement, with no implication of anything at all but almost abstractedly, as a man eating gingersnaps in the middle of a hundred-mile solitude would—if he did—suck a tooth, and said:

'Yes, I heard that idea before, And I notices that the folks that brings it up aint even Edmondses:' whereupon the white man even as he sprang up reached blindly back where on the counter behind him lay a half-dozen plow singletrees and snatched one of them up and had already started the downswing when the son of the store's proprietor, himself a youngish active man, came either around or over the counter and grasped the other so that the singletree merely flew harmlessly across the aisle and crashed against the cold stove; then another man was holding the man too.

'Get out of here, Lucas!' the proprietor's son said over his shoulder. But still Lucas didn't move, quite calm, not even scornful, not even contemptuous, not even very alert, the gaudy carton still poised in his left hand and the small cake in the right, just watching while the proprietor's son and his companion held the foaming and cursing white man. 'Get to hell out of here, you damn fool!' the proprietor's son shouted: and only then did Lucas move, without haste, turning without haste and going on toward the door, raising his right hand to his mouth so that as he went out the door they could see the steady thrust of his chewing.

Because there was the half-dollar. The actual sum was seventy cents of course and in four coins but he had long since during that first few fractions of a second transposed translated them into the one coin one integer in mass and weight out of all proportion to its mere convertible value; there were times in fact when, the capacity of his spirit for regret or perhaps just simple writhing or whatever it was at last spent for a moment and even quiescent, he would tell himself *At least I have the half-dollar, at least I have something* because now not only his mistake and its shame but its protagonist too—the man, the Negro, the room, the moment, the day itself—had annealed vanished into the round hard symbol of the coin and he would seem to see himself lying watching regretless and even peaceful as day by day the coin swelled to its gigantic maximum, to hang fixed at last forever in the black vault of his anguish like the last dead and waneless moon and himself, his own puny shadow gesticulant and tiny against it in frantic and vain eclipse: frantic and vain yet indefatigable too because he would never stop, he could never give up now who had debased not merely his manhood but his whole race too; each afternoon after school and all day Saturday, unless there was a ball game or he went hunting or there was something else he wanted or needed to do, he would go to his uncle's office where he would answer the telephone or run errands, all with some similitude of responsibility even if not actually of necessity; at least it was an intimation of his willingness to carry some of his own weight. He had begun it when he was a child, when he could scarcely remember, out of that blind and absolute attachment to his mother's only brother which he had never tried to reason about, and he had done it ever since; later, at fifteen and sixteen and seventeen he would think of the story of the boy and his pet calf which he lifted over the pasture fence each day; years passed and they were a grown man and a bull still being lifted over the pasture fence each day.

He deserted his calf. It was less than three weeks to Christmas; every afternoon after school and all day Saturday he was either in the Square or where he could see it, watch it. It was cold for another day or two, then it got warm, the wind softened then the bright sun hazed over and it rained yet he still walked or stood about the street where the store windows were already filling with toys and Christmas goods and fireworks and colored lights and evergreen and tinsel or behind the steamy window of the drugstore or barbershop watched the country faces, the two packages—the four two-for-a-quarter cigars for Lucas and the tumbler of snuff for his wife—in their bright Christmas paper in his pocket, until at last he saw Edmonds and gave them to him to deliver Christmas morning. But that merely discharged (with doubled interest) the seventy cents; there still remained the dead monstrous heatless disc which hung nightly in the black abyss of the rage and impotence: *If he would just be a nigger first, just for one second, one little infinitesimal second:* so in February he began to save his money—the twenty-five cents his father gave him each week as allowance and the twenty-five cents his uncle paid him as office salary—until in May he had enough and with his mother helping him chose the flowered imitation silk dress and sent it by mail to Molly Beauchamp, care of Carothers Edmonds R.F.D.[8] and at last he had something like ease because the rage was gone and all he could not forget was the grief and the shame; the disc still hung in the black vault but it was almost a year old now and so the vault itself was not so black with the disc paling and he could even sleep under it as even the insomniac dozes at last under his waning and glareless moon. Then it was September; school would begin in another week. He came home one afternoon and his mother was waiting for him.

'Here's something for you,' she said. It was a gallon bucket of fresh homemade sorghum molasses and he knew the answer at once long before she finished speaking: 'Somebody from Mr Edmonds' place sent it to you.'

'Lucas Beauchamp,' he said, cried almost. 'How long has he been gone? Why didn't he wait for me?'

'No,' his mother said. 'He didn't bring it himself. He sent it in. A white boy brought it on a mule.'

And that was all. They were right back where they had started; it was all to do over again; it was even worse this time because this time Lucas had commanded a white hand to pick up his money and give it back to him. Then he realised that he couldn't even start over again because to take the can of molasses back and fling it into Lucas' front door would only be the coins again for Lucas again to command somebody to pick up and return, not to mention the fact that he would have to ride a Shetland pony which he had outgrown and was ashamed of except that his mother wouldn't agree yet to let him have a fullsized horse or at least the kind of fullsized horse he wanted and that his uncle had promised him, seventeen miles in order to reach the door to fling it through. This would have to be all; whatever would or could set him free was beyond not merely his reach but even his ken; he could only wait for it if it came and do without it if it didn't.

And four years later he had been free almost eighteen months and he thought it was all: old Molly dead and her and Lucas' married daughter moved with her husband to Detroit and he heard now at last by chance remote and belated hearsay that Lucas was living alone in the house, solitary kinless and intractable, apparently not only without friends even in his own race but proud of it. He had seen him three times more, on the Square in town and not always on Saturday—in fact it would be a year from the last time before he would realise that he had never seen him in town on Saturday when all the other Negroes and most of the whites too from the country came in, nor even that the occasions when he did see him were almost exactly a year apart and that the reason he saw him then was not that Lucas' presence had happened to coincide with his own chance passage through the Square but that he had coincided with

[8]R.F.D.: rural free delivery.

Lucas' annual and necessary visits—but on weekdays like the white men who were not farmers but planters, who wore neckties and vests like the merchants and doctors and lawyers themselves, as if he refused, declined to accept even that little of the pattern not only of Negro but of country Negro behavior, and always in the worn brushed obviously once-expensive black broadcloth suit of the portrait-photograph on the gold easel and the raked fine hat and the boiled white shirt of his own grandfather's time and the tieless collar and the heavy watch-chain and the gold toothpick like the one his own grandfather had carried in his upper vest pocket: the first time in the second winter; he had spoken first though Lucas had remembered him at once; he thanked him for the molasses and Lucas had answered exactly as his grandfather himself might, only the words, the grammar any different:

'They turned out good this year. When I was making um I remembered how a boy's always got a sweet tooth for good molasses:' and went on, saying over his shoulder: 'Dont fall in no more creeks this winter:' and saw him twice more after that—the black suit, the hat, the watch-chain but the next time he didn't have the toothpick and this time Lucas looked straight at him, straight into his eyes from five feet away and passed him and he thought *He has forgotten me. He doesn't even remember me anymore* until almost the next year when his uncle told him that Molly, the old wife, had died a year ago. Nor did he bother, take time to wonder then how his uncle (obviously Edmonds had told him) happened to know about it because he was already counting rapidly backward; he said thought with a sense of vindication, easement, triumph almost: *She had just died then. That was why he didn't see me. That was why he didn't have the toothpick:* thinking with a kind of amazement: *He was grieving. You dont have to not be a nigger in order to grieve* and then he found that he was waiting, haunting the Square almost as he had done two years ago when he was watching for Edmonds to give him the two Christmas presents to deliver, through the next two then three then four months before it occurred to him that when he had seen Lucas in town it had always been only once each year in January or February and then for the first time he realised why: he had come in to pay the yearly taxes on his land. So it was late January, a bright cold afternoon. He stood on the bank corner in the thin sun and saw Lucas come out of the courthouse and cross the Square directly toward him, in the black suit and the tieless shirt and the fine old hat at its swaggering rake, walking so erect that the coat touched him only across the shoulders from which it hung and he could already see the cocked slanted glint of the gold toothpick and he could feel the muscles of his face, waiting and then Lucas looked up and once more looked straight into his eyes for perhaps a quarter of a minute and then away and came straight on and then even side-stepped a little in order to pass him and passed him and went on; nor did he look back either, standing at the curb-edge in the thin cold sun thinking *He didn't even fail to remember me this time. He didn't even know me. He hasn't even bothered to forget me:* thinking in a sort of peace even: *It's over. That was all* because he was free, the man who for three years had obsessed his life waking and sleeping too had walked out of it. He would see him again of course; without doubt they would pass on the street in town like this once each year for the rest of Lucas' life but that would be all: the one no longer the man but only the ghost of him who had ordered the two Negro boys to pick up his money and give it back to him; the other only the memory of the child who had offered it and then flung it down, carrying into manhood only the fading tagend of that old once-frantic shame and anguish and need not for revenge, vengeance but simply for reequalization, reaffirmation of his masculinity and his white blood. And someday the one would not even be any longer the ghost of the man who had ordered the coins picked up and to the other the shame and anguish would no longer be a thing remembered and recallable but merely a breath a whisper like the bitter-sweet-sour taste of the sheep sorrel eaten by the boy in his dead childhood, remembered only in the instant of tasting and forgotten before it could be placed and remembered; he could imagine them as old men meeting, quite old, at some point in that agony of naked inanesthetisable nerve-ends which for lack of a better word men call being alive at which not only their elapsed years but the half-century of discrepancy between them would be as indistinguishable and uncountable as that many sand grains in a coal pile and he saying to Lucas: *I was the boy who when you gave me half of your dinner tried to pay you with some things which people in those days called seventy cents' worth of money and so all I could think of to save my face was to fling it on the floor? Dont you remember?* and Lucas: *Was that me?* or vice versa, turned around and it was Lucas saying *I was the man when you throwed your money on the floor and wouldn't pick it up I had to have two niggers pick it up and hand it back to you? Dont you remember?* and he this time: *Was that me?* Because it was over now. He had turned the other cheek and it had been accepted. He was free.

Then he came back through the Square late that Saturday afternoon (there had been a ball game on the High School field) and he heard that Lucas had killed Vinson Gowrie out at Fraser's store; word had come for the sheriff about three oclock and had been relayed on by another party-line telephone down into the opposite corner of the county where the sheriff had gone this morning on business and where a messenger might quite possibly find him some time between now and tomorrow's sunup: which would make little difference since even if the sheriff had been in his office he would probably be too late since Fraser's store was in Beat Four and if Yoknapatawpha County was the wrong place for a nigger to shoot a white man in the back then Beat Four was the last place even in Yoknapatawpha County a nigger with any judgment—or any other stranger of any color—would have chosen to shoot anybody least of all one named Gowrie before or behind either; already the last car full of the young men and some not so young whose business addresses not only on Saturday afternoons but all week too were the poolhall and the barbershop and some of whom even had some vague connection with cotton or automobiles or land- and stock-sales, who bet on prizefights and punchboards and national ballgames, had long since left the Square to hurry the fifteen miles to park along the highway in front of the constable's house where the constable had taken Lucas and the story said had handcuffed him to a bedpost and was now sitting over him with a shotgun (and Edmonds too of course by now; even a fool country constable would have had sense enough to send for Edmonds only four miles away even before hollering for the sheriff) in case the Gowries and their connections decided not to wait until they had buried Vinson first; of course Edmonds would be there; if Edmonds had been in town today he would certainly have seen him at some time during the morning and before he went to the ballpark and since he had not obviously Edmonds had been at home, only four miles away; a messenger could have reached him and Edmonds himself could have been at the constable's house almost before the other messenger had memorised the sheriff's telephone and the message to give him and then rode to the nearest telephone where he could use either: which—Edmonds (again something nagged for a second's flash at his attention) and the constable—would be two while the Lord Himself would have to stop to count the Gowries and Ingrums and Workitts and if Edmonds was busy eating supper or reading the paper or counting his money or something the constable would be just one even with the shotgun: but then he was free, hardly even pausing really, walking on to the corner where he would turn for home and not until he saw how much of sun, how much was left of afternoon still in the street then turned back retracing his steps for several yards before he remembered why in the world he didn't cut straight across the now almost empty Square to the outside stairs leading up to the office.

Though of course there was really no reason to expect his uncle to be in the office this late on Saturday afternoon but once on the stairs he could at least throw that away, happening to be wearing rubber soles today though even then the wooden stairs creaked and rumbled unless you trod the inside edge close to the wall: thinking how he had never really appreciated rubber soles before, how nothing could match them for giving you time to make up your mind what you really wanted to do and then he could see the office door closed now although it was still too early for his uncle to have had the lights on but besides the door itself had that look which only locked doors have so even hard soles wouldn't have mattered, unlocking the door with his key then locking it with the thumb-latch behind him and crossed to the heavy swivel roller chair which had been his grandfather's before his uncle's and sat down behind the littered table which his uncle used in place of the rolltop desk of his grandfather's old time and across which the county's legal business had passed longer than he could remember, since in fact his memory was memory or anyway his, and so battered table and dogeared faded papers and the needs and passions they represented and the measured and bounded county too were all coeval and one, the last of the sun coming through the mulberry tree then the window behind him onto the table the stacked untidy papers the inkwell the tray of paperclips and fouled rusted penpoints and pipecleaners and the overturned corncob pipe in its spill of ash beside the stained unwashed coffeecup and saucer and the colored mug from the Heidelberg *stübe*[9] filled with twisted spills of newspaper to light the pipes with like the vase sitting on Lucas' mantel that day and before he even knew he had thought of it he rose taking up the cup and saucer and crossed the room picking up the coffeepot and the kettle too in passing and in the lavatory emptied the grounds and rinsed the pot and cup and filled the kettle and set it and the pot the cup and saucer back on the shelf and returned to the chair and sat down again after really no absence at all, still in plenty of time to watch the table and all its familiar untidy clutter all fading toward one anonymity of night as the sunlight died: thinking remembering how his uncle had said that all man had was time, all that stood between him and the death he feared and abhorred was time yet he spent half of it inventing ways of getting the other half past: and suddenly he remembered from nowhere what it was that had been nagging at his attention: Edmonds was not at home nor even in Mississippi; he was in a hospital in New Orleans being operated on for gallstones, the heavy chair making a rumbling clatter on the wooden floor almost as loud as a wagon on a wooden bridge as he rose and then stood beside the table until the echo died away

[9]Parlor; living room.

and there was only the sound of his breathing: because he was free: and then he moved: because his mother would know what time baseball games finished even if she couldn't have heard the yelling from across the edge of town and she would know that even he could use up only so much of twilight getting home, locking the door behind him then down the stairs again, the Square filled with dusk now and the first lights coming on in the drugstore (they had never been off in the barbershop and the poolhall since the bootblack and the porter unlocked the doors and swept out the hair and cigarette stubs at six oclock this morning) and the mercantile ones too so that the rest of the county except Beat Four would have somewhere to wait until word could come in from Fraser's store that all was okeydoke again and they could unpark the trucks and cars and wagons and mules from the back streets and alleys and go home and go to bed: turning the corner this time and now the jail, looming, lightless except for the one crossbarred rectangle in the upper front wall where on ordinary nights the nigger crapshooters and whiskey-peddlers and razor-throwers would be yelling down to their girls and women on the street below and where Lucas would have been these three hours now (very likely banging on the steel door for somebody to bring him his supper or perhaps having already had it and now merely to complain about its quality since without doubt he would consider that his right too along with the rest of his lodging and keep) except that people seemed to hold that the one sole end of the entire establishment of public office was to elect one man like Sheriff Hampton big enough or at least with sense and character enough to run the county and then fill the rest of the jobs with cousins and inlaws who had failed to make a living at everything else they ever tried. But then he was free and besides it was probably all over by now and even if it wasn't he knew what he was going to do and there was plenty of time yet for that, tomorrow would be time enough for that; all he would need to do tonight was to give Highboy about two extra cups of oats against tomorrow and at first he believed he was or at least in a moment was going to be ravenously hungry himself, sitting down at the familiar table in the familiar room among the bright linen and silver and the water glasses and the bowl of narcissus and gladioli and a few roses in it too and his uncle said,

'Your friend Beauchamp seems to have done it this time.'

'Yes,' he said. 'They're going to make a nigger out of him once in his life anyway.'

'Charles!' his mother said.—eating rapidly, eating quite a lot and talking rapidly and quite a lot too about the ball game and waiting to get hungry any minute any second now until suddenly he knew that even the last bite had been too much, still chewing at it to get it down to where it would swallow, already getting up.

'I'm going to the picture show,' he said.

'You haven't finished,' his mother said: then she said, 'The show doesn't begin for almost an hour yet:' and then not even just to his father and uncle but to all time all A.D. of Our Lord one thousand and nine hundred and thirty and forty and fifty: 'I dont want him to go to town tonight. I dont want—and then at last one wail one cry to the supreme: his father himself: out of that nightraddled dragonregion of fears and terrors in which women—mothers anyway—seemed from choice almost to dwell: 'Charlie—' until his uncle put his napkin down and rose too and said:

'Then here's your chance to wean him. I want him to do an errand for me anyway:' and out: on the front gallery in the dark cool and after a while his uncle said: 'Well? Go on.'

'Aint you coming?' he said. Then he said, 'But why? Why?'

'Does that matter?' his uncle said, and then said what he had already heard when he passed the barbershop going on two hours ago now: 'Not now. Not to Lucas nor anybody else of his color out there.' But he had already thought of that himself not just before his uncle said it but even before whoever it had been in front of the barbershop two hours ago did, and for that matter the rest of it too: 'In fact the true why is not what crisis he faced beyond which life would be no longer bearable until he shot a white man in the back but why of all white men he must pick a Gowrie to shoot and out of all possible places Beat Four to do it in. —Go on. But don't be late. After all a man ought to be kind even to his parents now and then.'

And sure enough one of the cars and for all he knew maybe all of them had got back to the barbershop and the poolhall so apparently Lucas was still chained and peaceful to the bedpost and the constable sitting over him (it was probably a rocking chair) with the cold shotgun and probably the constable's wife had served their supper there and Lucas with a good appetite, sharp set for his since he not only wouldn't have to pay for it but you dont shoot somebody every day in the week: and at last it seemed to be more or less authentic that the sheriff had finally got the word and sent word back that he would return to town late tonight and would fetch Lucas in early tomorrow morning and he would have to do something, pass the time somehow until the picture show was out so he might as well go to it and he crossed the Square to the courthouse yard and sat down on a bench in the dark cool empty solitude among the bitten shadows the restless unwindy vernal leaves against the starry smore of heaven where he could watch the lighted marquee in front of the picture show and perhaps the sheriff was right; he seemed able to establish enough contact with Gowries and Ingrums and Workitts and McCallums to persuade them to vote for him every eight years so maybe he knew approximately what they would do under given situations or perhaps the people in the barbershop were right and the Ingrums and Gowries and Workitts were waiting not until they had buried Vinson tomorrow but simply because it would be Sunday in three hours now and they didn't want to have to hurry, bolt through the business in order to finish it by midnight and not violate the Sabbath: then the first of the crowd dribbled then flowed beneath the marquee blinking into the light and even fumbling a little for a second or even a minute or two yet, bringing back into the shabby earth a fading remnant of the heart's celluloid and derring dream so he could go home now, in fact he would have to: who knew by simple instinct when picture shows were over just as she did when ball games were and though she would never really forgive him for being able to button his own buttons and wash behind his ears at least she accepted it and would not come after him herself but merely send his father and by starting now ahead of the picture show's dispersal he would have the empty street until he got home, until he reached the corner of the yard in fact and his uncle stepped out from beside the hedge, hatless, smoking one of the cob pipes.

'Listen,' his uncle said. 'I talked to Hampton down at Peddlers Field Old Town and he had already telephoned Squire Fraser and Fraser himself went to Skipworth's house and saw Lucas handcuffed to the bedpost and it's all right, everything's quiet out there tonight and tomorrow morning Hampton will have Lucas locked up in the jail—'

'I know,' he said. 'They wont lynch him until after midnight tomorrow night, after they have buried Vinson and got rid of Sunday:' walking on: 'It's all right with me. Lucas didn't have to work this hard not to be a nigger just on my account.' Because he was free: in bed: in the cool familiar room in the cool familiar dark because he knew what he was going to do and he had forgotten after all to tell Aleck Sander to give Highboy the extra feed against tomorrow but in the morning would do just as well because he was going to sleep tonight because he had something about ten thousand times quicker than just sheep to count; in fact he was going to go to sleep so fast he probably wouldn't have time to count more than about ten of them: with rage, an almost unbearable excruciation of outrage and fury: any white man to shoot in the back but this one of all white men at all: youngest of a family of six brothers one of whom had already served a year in federal penitentiary for armed resistance as an army deserter and another term at the state penal farm for making whiskey, and a ramification of cousins and inlaws covering a whole corner of the county and whose total number probably even the old grandmothers and maiden aunts couldn't have stated offhand—a connection of brawlers and farmers and fox-hunters and stock- and timber-traders who would not even be the last anywhere to let one of its number be killed by anyone but only among the last since it in its turn was integrated and interlocked and intermarried with other brawlers and fox-hunters and whiskeymakers not even into a simple clan or tribe but a race a species which before now had made their hill stronghold good against the county and the federal government too, which did not even simply inhabit nor had merely corrupted but had translated and transmogrified that whole region of lonely pine hills dotted meagrely with small tilted farms and peripatetic sawmills and contraband whiskey-kettles where peace officers from town didn't even go unless they were sent for and strange white men didn't wander far from the highway after dark and no Negro at any time—where as a local wit said once the only stranger ever to enter with impunity was God and He only by daylight and on Sunday—into a synonym for independence and violence: an idea with physical boundaries like a quarantine for plague so that solitary unique and alone out of all the county it was known to the rest of the county by the number of its survey co-ordinate—Beat Four—as in the middle twenties people knew where Cicero Illinois was and who lived there and what they did who neither knew nor cared what state Chicago was in: and since this was not enough choosing the one moment when the one man white or black—Edmonds—out of all Yoknapatawpha County or Mississippi or America or the world too for that matter who would have had any inclination let alone power and ability (and here he had to laugh even though he was just about to go to sleep, remembering how he had even thought at first that if Edmonds had been at home it would have made any difference anywhere, remembering the face the angle of the hat the figure straddled baronial as a duke or a squire or a congressman before the fire hands clasped behind it and not even looking down at them but just commanding two nigger boys to pick up the coins and give them back to him, not even needing to remember his uncle reminding him ever since he had got big enough to understand the words that no man could come between another man and his destiny because even his uncle for all Harvard and Heidelberg couldn't have pointed out the man with enough temerity and delusion just to come between Lucas and merely what he wanted to do) to try to stand between Lucas and the violent fate he had courted was lying flat on his back in a New Orleans operating room: yet that was what Lucas had had to pick, that time that victim and that place: another Saturday afternoon and the same store where he had already had trouble with a white man at least once before: chose the first suitable convenient Saturday afternoon and with an old single action Colt pistol of a calibre and type not even made anymore which was exactly the sort of pistol Lucas would own exactly as no other still alive man in the county owned a gold toothpick lay in wait at the store—the one sure place where sooner or later on Saturday afternoon that whole end of the county would pass—until the victim appeared and shot him and nobody knew why yet and as far as he had discovered that afternoon or even when he finally left the Square that night nobody had even wondered yet since why didn't matter least of all to Lucas since he had apparently he had been working for twenty or twenty-five years with indefatigable and unflagging concentration toward this one crowning moment; followed him into the woods about one good spit from the store and shot him in the back within hearing distance of the crowd around it and was still standing over the body the fired pistol put neatly away into his hip pocket again when the first ones reached the scene where he would without doubt have been lynched immediately out of hand except for the same Doyle Fraser who had saved him from the singletree seven years ago and old Skipworth, the constable—a little driedup wizened stonedeaf old man not much larger than a half-grown boy with a big nickelplated pistol loose in one coat pocket and in the other a guttapercha eartrumpet on a rawhide thong around his neck like a foxhorn, who on this occasion anyway revealed an almost gratuitous hardihood and courage, getting Lucas (who made no resistance whatever, merely watching this too with that same calm detached not even scornful interest) out of the crowd and took him to his home and chained him to the bedpost until the sheriff could come and get him and bring him in to town and keep him while the Gowries and Workitts and Ingrums and the rest of their guests and connections could get Vinson buried and Sunday passed and so be fresh and untrammelled for the new week and its duties and believe it or not even the night passed, the tentative roosters at false dawn then the interval then the loud fairy clangor of the birds and through the east window he could see the trees against gray light and then the sun itself high and furious above the trees glaring at him and it was already late, this of course must happen to him too: but then he was free and he would feel better after breakfast and he could always say he was going to Sunday school but then he wouldn't have to say anything by going out the back, strolling: across the back yard and into the lot and across it and through the woods to the railroad to the depot and then back to the Square then he thought of a simpler way than that and then quit thinking about it at all, through the front hall and across the front gallery and down the walk to the street and it was here he would remember later having first noticed that he had seen no Negro except Paralee when she brought his breakfast; by ordinary at this hour on Sunday morning he would have seen on almost every gallery housemaids or cooks in their fresh Sunday aprons with brooms or perhaps talking from gallery to gallery across the contiguous yardspaces and the children too fresh and scrubbed for Sunday school with clutched palmsweaty nickels though perhaps it was a little too early for that or perhaps by mutual consent or even interdiction there would be no Sunday school today, only church and so at some mutual concorded moment say about halfpast eleven all the air over Yoknapatawpha County would reverberate soundlessly like heatshimmer with one concerted adjuration calm the hearts of these bereaved and angry men vengeance is mine saith the lord thou shalt not kill except that this was a little late too, they should have mentioned this to Lucas yesterday, past the jail the barred second storey window whose interstices on an ordinary Sunday would have been thick with dark hands and beyond them even a glint now and then of eyewhites in the shadows and the mellow voices calling and laughing down to the Negro girls and women passing or stopping along the street and this was when he realised that except for Paralee he had seen no Negro since yesterday afternoon though it would be tomorrow before he would learn that the ones who lived in the Hollow and Freedmantown hadn't come to work at all since Saturday night: nor on the Square either, not even in the barbershop where Sunday morning was the bootblack's best day shining shoes and brushing clothes and running errands and drawing baths for the bachelor truck-drivers and garage hands who lived in rented rooms and the young men and the ones not so young who worked hard all week in the poolhall and the sheriff really had finally got back to town and had even torn himself away from his Sunday to go for Lucas: listening: hearing the talk: a dozen of them who had hurried out to Fraser's store yesterday afternoon and returned empty-handed (and he gathered one car full had even gone back last night, yawning and lounging now and complaining of lack of sleep: and that to be added to Lucas' account too) and he had heard all this before too and had even thought of it himself before that:

'I wonder if Hampton took a shovel with him. That's all he's going to need.'

'They'll lend him a shovel out there.'

'Yes—if there's anything to bury. They have gasoline even in Beat Four.'

'I thought old Skipworth was going to take care of that.'

'Sure. But that's Beat Four. They'll do what Skipworth tells them as long as he's got the nigger. But he's going to turn him over to Hampton. That's when it'll happen. Hope Hampton might be sheriff in Yoknapatawpha County but he's just another man in Beat Four.'

'No. They wont do nothing today. They're burying Vinson this afternoon and to burn a nigger right while the funeral's going on wouldn't be respectful to Vinson.'

'That's so. It'll probably be tonight.'

'On Sunday night?'

'Is that the Gowries' fault? Lucas ought to thought of that before he picked out Saturday to kill Vinson on.'

'I don't know about that. Hope Hampton's going to be a hard man to take a prisoner away from too.'

'A nigger murderer? Who in this county or state either is going to help him protect a nigger that shoots white men in the back?'

'Or the South either.'

'Yes. Or the South either.' He had heard it all before: outside again now: only his uncle might decide to come to town before time to go for the noon mail at the postoffice and if his uncle didn't see him then he really could tell his mother he didn't know where he was and of course he thought first of the empty office but if he went there that's exactly where his uncle would come too: because—and he remembered again that he had forgot to give Highboy the extra feed this morning too but it was too late now and besides he was going to carry feed with him anyway—he knew exactly what he was going to do: the sheriff had left town about nine oclock; the constable's house was fifteen miles away on a gravel road not too good but the sheriff should certainly go there and be back with Lucas by noon even if he stopped to make a few votes while there; long before that time he would go home and saddle Highboy and tie a sack of feed behind the saddle and turn him in a straight line in the opposite direction from Fraser's store and ride in that one undeviable direction for twelve hours which would be about midnight tonight and feed Highboy and rest him until daylight or even longer if he decided to and then ride the twelve hours back which would be eighteen actually or maybe even twenty-four or even thirty-six but at least all over finished done, no more fury and outrage to have to lie in bed with like trying to put yourself to sleep counting sheep and he turned the corner and went along the opposite side of the street and under the shed in front of the closed blacksmith shop, the heavy double wooden doors not locked with a hasp or latch but with a padlocked chain passed through an augerhole in each one so that the slack of the chain created an insag almost like an alcove; standing in it nobody could have seen him from either up the street or down it nor even passing along it (which would not be his mother anyway today) unless they stopped to look and now the bells began ringing in mellow unhurried discordant strophe and antistrophe from steeple to pigeonswirled steeple across the town, streets and Square one sudden decorous flow of men in their dark suits and women in silks and parasols and girls and young men two and two, flowing and decorous beneath that mellow uproar into that musical clamor: gone, Square and street empty again though still the bells rang on for a while yet, skydwellers, groundless denizens of the topless air too high too far insentient to the crawling earth then ceasing stroke by hasteless stroke from the subterrene shudder of organs and the cool frantic monotone of the settled pigeons. Two years ago his uncle had told him that there was nothing wrong with cursing; on the contrary it was not only useful but substituteless but like everything else valuable it was precious only because the supply was limited and if you wasted it on nothing on its urgent need you might find yourself bankrupt so he said *What the hell am I doing here* then answered himself the obvious answer: not to see Lucas, he had seen Lucas but so that Lucas could see him again if he so wished, to look back at him not just from the edge of mere uniqueless death but from the gasoline-roar of apotheosis. Because he was free. Lucas was no longer his responsibility, he was no longer Lucas' keeper; Lucas himself had discharged him.

Then suddenly the empty street was full of men. Yet there were not many of them, not two dozen, some suddenly and quietly from nowhere. Yet they seemed to fill it, block it, render it suddenly interdict as though not that nobody could pass them, pass through it, use it as a street but that nobody would dare, would even approach near enough to essay the gambit as people stay well away from a sign saying High Voltage or Explosive. He knew, recognised them all; some of them he had even seen and listened to in the barbershop two hours ago—the young men or men under forty, bachelors, the homeless who had the Saturday and Sunday baths in the barbershop—truckdrivers and garagehands, the oiler from the cotton gin, a sodajerker from the drugstore and the ones who could be seen all week long in or around the poolhall who did nothing at all that anyone knew, who owned automobiles and spent money nobody really knew exactly how they earned on weekends in Memphis or New Orleans brothels—the men who his uncle said were in every little Southern town, who never really led mobs nor even instigated them but were always the nucleus of them because of their mass availability. Then he saw the car; he recognised it too even in the distance without knowing or for that matter stopping to wonder how, himself moving out of his concealing doorway into the street and then across it to the edge of the crowd which made no sound but just stood there blocking the sidewalk beside the jail fence and overflowing into the street while the car came up not fast but quite deliberately, almost decorously as a car should move on Sunday morning, and drew in to the curb in front of the jail and stopped. A deputy was driving it. He made no move to get out. Then the rear door opened and the sheriff emerged—a big, a tremendous man with no fat and little hard pale eyes in a cold almost bland pleasant face who without even glancing at them turned and held the door open. Then Lucas got out, slowly and stiffly, exactly like a man who has spent the night chained to a bedpost, fumbling a little and bumping or at least raking his head against the top of the door so that as he emerged his crushed hat tumbled from his head onto the pavement almost under his feet. And that was the first time he had ever seen Lucas without the hat on and in the same second he realised that with the possible exception of Edmonds they there in the street watching him were probably the only white people in the county who had ever seen him uncovered: watching as, still bent over as he had emerged from the car, Lucas began to reach stiffly for the hat. But already in one vast yet astonishingly supple stoop the sheriff had picked it up and handed it back to Lucas who still bent over seemed to fumble at the hat too. Yet almost at once the hat was creased back into its old shape and now Lucas was standing up, erect except for his head, his face as he brushed the hat back and forth against the sleeve of his forearm rapid and light and deft as you stroke a razor. Then his head, his face went back and up too and in a motion not quite sweeping he set the hat back on his head at the old angle which the hat itself seemed to assume as if he had flung it up, and erect now in the black suit crumpled too from whatever night he had spent (there was a long grimed smear down one entire side from shoulder to ankle as if he had been lying on an unswept floor a long time in one position without being able to change it) Lucas looked at them for the first time and he thought *Now. He will see me now* and then he thought *He saw me. And that's all* and then he thought *He hasn't seen anybody* because the face was not even looking at them but just toward them, arrogant and calm and with no more defiance in it than fear: detached, impersonal, almost musing, intractable and composed, the eyes blinking a little in the sunlight even after the sound, an indraw of breath went up from somewhere in the crowd and a single voice said:

'Knock it off again, Hope. Take his head too this time.'

'You boys get out of here,' the sheriff said. 'Go back to the barbershop:' turning, saying to Lucas: 'All right. Come on.' And that was all, the face for another moment looking not at them but just toward them, the sheriff already walking toward the jail door when Lucas turned at last to follow him and by hurrying a little he could even get Highboy saddled and be out of the lot before his mother began to send Aleck Sander to look for him to come and eat dinner. Then he saw Lucas stop and turn and he was wrong because Lucas even knew where he was in the crowd before he turned, looking straight at him before he got turned around even, speaking to him:

'You, young man,' Lucas said. 'Tell your uncle I wants to see him:' then turned again and walked on after the sheriff, still a little stiffly in the smeared black suit, the hat arrogant and pale in the sunlight, the voice in the crowd saying:

'Lawyer hell. He wont even need an undertaker when them Gowries get through with him tonight:' walking on past the sheriff who himself had stopped now and was looking back at them, saying in his mild cold bland heatless voice:

'I told you folks once to get out of here. I aint going to tell you again.'

1948

Langston Hughes 1902–1967

Although Langston Hughes became the leader of the Harlem writers who created the Black Literary Renaissance of the 1920s, he was born in Joplin, Missouri, and spent most of his youth in the American Midwest. He first came to New York in 1921 to attend Columbia University. A year later he shipped out as a seaman and cook's helper on a tramp steamer to Africa and Europe. He lived and worked in Paris and Italy and then returned to the United States, where he took a job as a busboy in a Washington, D.C., hotel. There, in 1925, he was "discovered" by the poet Vachel Lindsay, who praised Hughes's poems and advised him to devote himself to literature and to "hide and write and study and think."

But Hughes had begun writing long before. In grammar school he had been chosen class poet, and while still in high school he published two poems in national magazines. His first books, The Weary Blues *(1926) and* Fine Clothes to the Jew *(1927), won poetry prizes and brought him wide acclaim. His first novel,* Not Without Laughter, *appeared in 1930. Hughes had a wide-ranging talent. He was a successful humorist and a historian of the lives of blacks. He wrote novels, short stories, poems, children's books, song lyrics, and operas. He translated foreign writers and wrote numerous plays, three of which were produced on Broadway.*

Much of his best writing was journalistic. In 1937 he served as a foreign correspondent covering the Spanish Civil War for the Baltimore Afro-American *newspaper. His most popular works were newspaper sketches written for the* Chicago Defender *in the 1940s. The sketches recounted the adventures and opinions of an innocent, downtrodden Negro, "Simple," whose penetrating views of blacks and whites provided Hughes with the means for making broad satirical and critical commentary on society and government.*

Hughes was a worldly cosmopolite who lived an almost nomadic life. He traveled to Mexico, Cuba, and the Caribbean, to Africa, Western Europe, the Soviet Union, China, and Japan. But he was most influenced by his American experience, by his black heritage, and by the vivid life of New York City's Harlem with its blues and jazz music that so influenced the structure and rhythm of such poems as "The Weary Blues."

Langston Hughes was the first black American to support himself as a professional writer. In all, he produced more than sixty books. He was also one of the first American writers to receive extended and serious critical attention for realistic portrayals of black Americans. Through his poetry, fiction, and essays, he became one of the dominant voices speaking out for the significance of black culture at the core of life in twentieth-century America. In the twenty-first century his work still proclaims, "I, too, am America."

FURTHER READING: *I Wonder as I Wander: An Autobiographical Journey,* 1956; *The Langston Hughes Reader,* 1958; J. Emanuel, *Langston Hughes,* 1967; M. Meltzer, *Langston Hughes: A Biography,* 1968; C. Rollins, *Black Troubadour,* 1970; F. Berry, *Langston Hughes: Before and Beyond Harlem,* 1983; A. Rampersad, *The Life of Langston Hughes,* 2 vols., 1986; S. Tracy, *Langston Hughes and the Blues,* 1988; R. Miller, *The Art and Imagination of Langston Hughes,* 1989; H. Ostrom, *Langston Hughes,* 1993; *Short Stories of Langston Hughes,* ed. A. Harper, 1997; *Langston Hughes: The Contemporary Reviews,* ed. T. Dace, 1997; *Langston Hughes,* ed. H. Bloom, 2002; *The Collected Works of Langston Hughes,* 16 vols., ed. A. Rampersad and others, 2001–2003.

TEXTS: "Dream Boogie," "Harlem," and "Theme for English B" from *Montage of a Dream Deferred,* 1951. All other poems from *Selected Poems of Langston Hughes,* 1973. "On the Road" from *Laughing to Keep from Crying,* 1952.

THE NEGRO SPEAKS OF RIVERS

To W. E. B. Du Bois[1]

I've known rivers:
I've known rivers ancient as the world and older than the flow
of human blood in human veins.

My soul has grown deep like the rivers.

I bathed in the Euphrates[2] when dawns were young.
I built my hut near the Congo and it lulled me to sleep.
I looked upon the Nile and raised the pyramids above it.
I heard the singing of the Mississippi when Abe Lincoln
went down to New Orleans, and I've seen its muddy
bosom turn all golden in the sunset.

I've known rivers:
Ancient, dusky rivers.

My soul has grown deep like the rivers.
1920 1921, 1926

THE WEARY BLUES

Droning a drowsy syncopated tune,
Rocking back and forth to a mellow croon,
I heard a Negro play.

[1]William Edward Burghardt Du Bois (1868–1963), black American writer and civil rights leader.
[2]Euphrates: river flowing through Turkey, Syria, and Iraq into the Persian Gulf. Congo: river flowing through west central Africa into the Atlantic. Nile: river flowing through Egypt into the Mediterranean. Each passes through lands where ancient civilizations once flourished.

Down on Lenox Avenue[1] the other night
By the pale dull pallor of an old gas light
He did a lazy sway. . . .
He did a lazy sway. . . .
To the tune o' those Weary Blues.
With his ebony hands on each ivory key
He made that poor piano moan with melody.
O Blues!
Swaying to and fro on his rickety stool
He played that sad raggy tune like a musical fool.
Sweet Blues!
Coming from a black man's soul.
O Blues!
In a deep song voice with a melancholy tone
I heard that Negro sing, that old piano moan—
"Ain't got nobody in all this world,
Ain't got nobody but ma self.
I's gwine to quit ma frownin'
And put ma troubles on the shelf."
Thump, thump, thump, went his foot on the floor.
He played a few chords then he sang some more—
"I got the Weary Blues
And I can't be satisfied.
Got the Weary Blues
And can't be satisfied—
I ain't happy no mo'
And I wish that I had died."
And far into the night he crooned that tune.
The stars went out and so did the moon.
The singer stopped playing and went to bed
While the Weary Blues echoed through his head.
He slept like a rock or a man that's dead.

1926

YOUNG GAL'S BLUES

I'm gonna walk to the graveyard
'Hind ma friend Miss Cora Lee.
Gonna walk to the graveyard
'Hind ma dear friend Cora Lee.
Cause when I'm dead some
Body'll have to walk behind me.

I'm goin' to the po' house
To see ma old Aunt Clew.

[1]Street in New York City's Harlem.

Goin' to the po' house
To see ma old Aunt Clew.
When I'm old an' ugly
I'll want to see somebody, too.

The po' house is lonely
An' the grave is cold.
O, the po' house is lonely,
The graveyard grave is cold.
But I'd rather be dead than
To be ugly an' old.

When love is gone what
Can a young gal do?
When love is gone, O,
What can a young gal do?
Keep on a-lovin' me, daddy,
Cause I don't want to be blue.

1927

NOTE ON COMMERCIAL THEATRE

You've taken my blues and gone—
You sing 'em on Broadway
And you sing 'em in Hollywood Bowl,
And you mixed 'em up with symphonies
And you fixed 'em
So they don't sound like me.
Yep, you done taken my blues and gone.

You also took my spirituals and gone.
You put me in *Macbeth* and *Carmen Jones*
And all kinds of *Swing Mikados*[1]
And in everything but what's about me—
But someday somebody'll
Stand up and talk about me,
And write about me—
Black and beautiful—
And sing about me,
And put on plays about me!
I reckon it'll be
Me myself!

Yes, it'll be me.

1949

[1]Hughes refers to three Broadway shows produced with black casts.

DREAM BOOGIE

Good morning, daddy!
Ain't you heard
The boogie-woogie rumble
Of a dream deferred?

Listen closely:
You'll hear their feet
Beating out and beating out a——

You think
It's a happy beat?

Listen to it closely:
Ain't you heard
something underneath
like a——

What did I say?

Sure,
I'm happy!
Take it away!

Hey, pop!
Re-bop!
Mop!

Y-e-a-h!

1951

HARLEM

What happens to a dream deferred?

Does it dry up
like a raisin in the sun?
Or fester like a sore——
And then run?
Does it stink like rotten meat?
Or crust and sugar over——
like a syrupy sweet?

Maybe it just sags
like a heavy load.

Or does it explode?

1951

THEME FOR ENGLISH B

The instructor said,
Go home and write
a page tonight.
And let that page come out of you—
Then, it will be true.

I wonder if it's that simple?
I am twenty-one, colored, born in Winston-Salem.[1]
I went to school there, then Durham, then here
to this college[2] on the hill above Harlem.
I am the only colored student in my class.
The steps from the hill lead down into Harlem,
through a park, then I cross St. Nicholas,[3]
Eighth Avenue, Seventh, and I come to the Y,
the Harlem Branch Y, where I take the elevator
up to my room, sit down, and write this page:
It's not easy to know what is true for you or me
at twenty-two, my age. But I guess I'm what
I feel and see and hear, Harlem, I hear you:
hear you, hear me—we two—you, me, talk on this page.
(I hear New York, too.) Me—who?
Well, I like to eat, sleep, drink, and be in love.
I like to work, read, learn, and understand life.
I like a pipe for a Christmas present,
or records—Bessie,[4] bop, or Bach.
I guess being colored doesn't make me *not* like
the same things other folks like who are other races.
So will my page be colored that I write?
Being me, it will not be white.
But it will be
a part of you, instructor.
You are white—
yet a part of me, as I am a part of you.
That's American.
Sometimes perhaps you don't want to be a part of me.
Nor do I often want to be a part of you.
But we are, that's true!
As I learn from you,
I guess you learn from me—
although you're older—and white—
and somewhat more free.

This is my page for English B.

1951

[1]Winston-Salem, North Carolina; Durham, North Carolina.
[2]Columbia University in New York City [3]Street near Columbia University.
[4]Bessie Smith (c. 1898–1937), famous American blues singer.

ON THE ROAD

He was not interested in the snow. When he got off the freight, one early evening during the depression, Sargeant never even noticed the snow. But he must have felt it seeping down his neck, cold, wet, sopping in his shoes. But if you had asked him, he wouldn't have known it was snowing. Sargeant didn't see the snow, not even under the bright lights of the main street, falling white and flaky against the night. He was too hungry, too sleepy, too tired.

The Reverend Mr. Dorset, however, saw the snow when he switched on his porch light, opened the front door of his parsonage, and found standing there before him a big black man with snow on his face, a human piece of night with snow on his face—obviously unemployed.

Said the Reverend Mr. Dorset before Sargeant even realized he'd opened his mouth: "I'm sorry. No! Go right on down this street four blocks and turn to your left, walk up seven and you'll see the Relief Shelter. I'm sorry, No!" He shut the door.

Sargeant wanted to tell the holy man that he had already been to the Relief Shelter, been to hundreds of relief shelters during the depression years, the beds were always gone and supper was over, the place was full, and they drew the color line anyhow. But the minister said, "No," and shut the door. Evidently he didn't want to hear about it. And he *had* a door to shut.

The big black man turned away. And even yet he didn't see the snow, walking right into it. Maybe he sensed it, cold, wet, sticking to his jaws, wet on his black hands, sopping in his shoes. He stopped and stood on the sidewalk hunched over—hungry, sleepy, cold—looking up and down. Then he looked right where he was—in front of a church. Of course! A church! Sure, right next to a parsonage, certainly a church.

It had *two* doors.

Broad white steps in the night all snowy white. Two high arched doors with slender stone pillars on either side. And way up, a round lacy window with a stone crucifix in the middle and Christ on the crucifix in stone. All this was pale in the street lights, solid and stony pale in the snow.

Sargeant blinked. When he looked up the snow fell into his eyes. For the first time that night he *saw* the snow. He shook his head. He shook the snow from his coat sleeves, felt hungry, felt lost, felt not lost, felt cold. He walked up the steps of the church. He knocked at the door. No answer. He tried the handle. Locked. He put his shoulder against the door and his long black body slanted like a ramrod. He pushed. With loud rhythmic grunts, like the grunts in a chain-gang song, he pushed against the door.

"I'm tired . . . Huh! . . . Hongry . . . Uh! . . . I'm sleepy . . . Huh! I'm cold . . . I got to sleep somewheres," Sargeant said. "This here is a church, ain't it? Well, uh!"

He pushed against the door.

Suddenly, with an undue cracking and screaking, the door began to give way to the tall black Negro who pushed ferociously against the door.

By now two or three white people had stopped in the street, and Sargeant was vaguely aware of some of them yelling at him concerning the door. Three or four more came running, yelling at him.

"Hey!" they said. "Hey!"

"Uh-huh," answered the big tall Negro, "I know it's a white folks' church, but I got to sleep somewhere." He gave another lunge at the door. "Huh!"

And the door broke open.

But just when the door gave way, two white cops arrived in a car, ran up the steps with their clubs and grabbed Sargeant. But Sargeant for once had no intention of being pulled or pushed away from the door.

Sargeant grabbed, but not for anything so weak as a broken door. He grabbed for one of the tall stone pillars beside the door, grabbed at and caught it. And held it. The cops pulled and Sargeant pulled. Most of the people in the street got behind the cops and helped them pull.

"A big black unemployed Negro holding onto our church!" thought the people. "The idea!"

The cops began to beat Sargeant over the head, and nobody protested. But he held on.

And then the church fell down.

Gradually, the big stone front of the church fell down, the walls and the rafters, the crucifix and the Christ. Then the whole thing fell down, covering the cops and the people with bricks and stones and debris. The whole church fell down in the snow.

Sargeant got out from under the church and went walking on up the street with the stone pillar on his shoulder. He was under the impression that he had buried the parsonage and the Reverend Mr. Dorset who said, "No!" So he laughed, and threw the pillar six blocks up the street and went on.

Sargeant thought he was alone, but listening to the crunch, crunch, crunch on the snow of his own footsteps, he heard other footsteps, too, doubling his own. He looked around and there was Christ walking beside him, the same Christ that had been on the cross on the church—still stone with a rough stone surface, walking along beside him just like he was broken off the cross when the church fell down.

"Well, I'll be dogged," said Sargeant. "This here's the first time I ever seed you off the cross."

"Yes," said Christ, crunching his feet in the snow. "You had to pull the church down to get me off the cross."

"You glad?" said Sargeant.

"I sure am," said Christ.

They both laughed.

"I'm a hell of a fellow, ain't I?" said Sargeant. "Done pulled the church down!"

"You did a good job," said Christ. "They have kept me nailed on a cross for nearly two thousand years."

"Whee-ee-e!" said Sargeant. "I know you are glad to get off."

"I sure am," said Christ.

They walked on in the snow. Sargeant looked at the man of stone.

"And you been up there two thousand years?"

"I sure have," Christ said.

"Well, if I had a little cash," said Sargeant, "I'd show you around a bit."

"I been around," said Christ.

"Yeah, but that was a long time ago."

"All the same," said Christ, "I've been around."

They walked on in the snow until they came to the railroad yards. Sargeant was tired, sweating and tired.

"Where you goin'?" Sargeant said, stopping by the tracks. He looked at Christ. Sargeant said, "I'm just a bum on the road. How about you? Where you goin'?"

"God knows," Christ said, "but I'm leavin' here."

They saw the red and green lights of the railroad yard half veiled by the snow that fell out of the night. Away down the track they saw a fire in a hobo jungle.

"I can go there and sleep," Sargeant said.

"You can?"

"Sure," said Sargeant. "That place ain't got no doors."

Outside the town, along the tracks, there were barren trees and bushes below the embankment, snow-gray in the dark. And down among the trees and bushes there were makeshift houses made out of boxes and tin and old pieces of wood and canvas. You couldn't see them in the dark, but you knew they were there if you'd ever been on the road, if you had ever lived with the homeless and hungry in a depression.

"I'm side-tracking," Sargeant said. "I'm tired."

"I'm gonna make it on to Kansas City," said Christ.

"O.K.," Sargeant said. "So long!"

He went down into the hobo jungle and found himself a place to sleep. He never did see Christ no more. About six A.M. a freight came by. Sargeant scrambled out of the jungle with a dozen or so more hoboes and ran along the track, grabbing at the freight. It was dawn, early dawn, cold and gray.

"Wonder where Christ is by now?" Sargeant thought. "He must-a gone on way on down the road. He didn't sleep in this jungle."

Sargeant grabbed the train and started to pull himself up into a moving coal car, over the edge of a wheeling coal car. But strangely enough, the car was full of cops. The nearest cop rapped Sargeant soundly across the knuckles with his night stick. Wham! Rapped his big black hands for clinging to the top of the car. Wham! But Sargeant did not turn loose. He clung on and tried to pull himself into the car. He hollered at the top of his voice, "Damn it, lemme in this car!"

"Shut up," barked the cop. "You crazy coon!" He rapped Sargeant across the knuckles and punched him in the stomach. "You ain't out in no jungle now. This ain't no train. You in jail."

Wham! across his bare black fingers clinging to the bars of his cell. Wham! between the steel bars low down against his shins.

Suddenly Sargeant realized that he really was in jail. He wasn't on no train. The blood of the night before had dried on his face, his head hurt terribly, and a cop outside in the corridor was hitting him across the knuckles for holding onto the door, yelling and shaking the cell door.

"They must-a took me to jail for breaking down the door last night," Sargeant thought, "that church door."

Sargeant went over and sat on a wooden bench against the cold stone wall. He was emptier than ever. His clothes were wet, clammy cold wet, and shoes sloppy with snow water. It was just about dawn. There he was, locked up behind a cell door, nursing his bruised fingers.

The bruised fingers were his, but not the *door*.

Not the *club*, but the fingers.

"You wait," mumbled Sargeant, black against the jail wall. "I'm gonna break down this door, too."

"Shut up—or I'll paste you one," said the cop.

"I'm gonna break down this door," yelled Sargeant as he stood up in his cell.

Then he must have been talking to himself because he said, "I wonder where Christ's gone? I wonder if he's gone to Kansas City?"

1934 1935

John Steinbeck 1902–1968

John Steinbeck was the foremost novelist of the American Depression of the 1930s. He was born in Salinas, California, the locale of much of his finest fiction. His sympathy for the migrant workers and the downtrodden, so evident in his writing, was the result of first-hand knowledge of their struggles. From his boyhood he was self-supporting; he worked as a laborer, a seaman on a cattle-boat (where he hoped and failed to become a writer), newspaper reporter, bricklayer, chemist's assistant, surveyor, and migratory fruit picker. His writing reflected his concern with the rituals of manual labor, people "doing" rather than "being," and he believed that the writer's first duty was to "set down his time as nearly as he can understand it" and serve as "the watch-dog of society . . . to satirize its silliness, to attack its injustices, to stigmatize its faults."

The publication of Tortilla Flat *(1935), the tender, sentimental portrait of the indestructibility of the California* paisanos, *brought him sudden fame. In the following year* In Dubious Battle *appeared. It was Steinbeck's most clearly "proletarian" novel of class struggle, depicting the lives of migrant workers and their resistance to exploitation by the entrenched forces of society. In* Of Mice and Men *(1937) he portrayed the friendship of two itinerant workers who yearn for a permanent home they will never find. In* The Long Valley *(1938) he described the fate of the lowly whose instinctive responses to life led only to destruction.* The Grapes of Wrath *(1939), generally regarded as his masterpiece, showed the migration of the "Okies" from the "Dust Bowls" to California, a migration that ended in broken dreams and misery but at the same time affirmed the ability of the common people to endure and prevail.*

Steinbeck's treatment of the social problems of his time, particularly the plight of the dispossessed farmer, earned him a Pulitzer Prize in 1940 and, in 1962, a Nobel Prize for Literature. At its best, Steinbeck's lyric prose vividly caught the qualities of speech, the character, the legends, and the humor of his native region. He was a superb storyteller whose reforming vision led him to contrast the conflicting moral codes of people in search of permanent ideals: "What we have always wanted," he wrote in The Sea of Cortez *(1941), "is an* unchangeable, *and we have found that only a compass point, a thought, an individual ideal, does not change."*

FURTHER READING: *Steinbeck: A Life in Letters,* ed. E. Steinbeck and R. Wallsten, 1975; N. Valjean, *John Steinbeck,* 1975; J. Benson, *The True Adventures of John Steinbeck, Writer,* 1984; L. Owens, *John Steinbeck's Re-Vision of America,* 1985; J. Timmerman, *John Steinbeck's Fiction,* 1986; J. Hughes, *John Steinbeck: A Study of the Short Fiction,* 1989; J. Timmerman, *The Domestic Landscape of John Steinbeck's Short Stories,* 1990; *The Steinbeck Question: New Essays in Criticism,* ed. D. Noble, 1993; W. French, *John Steinbeck's Fiction Revisited,* 1994; J. Parini, *John Steinbeck: A Biography,* 1994; R. Simmond, *John Steinbeck: The War Years,* 1996; *Beyond Boundaries: Rereading John Steinbeck,* ed. S. Shillinglaw and K. Hearle, 2002; *John Steinbeck,* ed. H. Bloom, 2003; S. George, *The Moral Philosophy of John Steinbeck,* 2005; J. Schulz, *John Steinbeck A to Z,* 2005.

TEXT: *The Long Valley,* 1938.

from *THE LONG VALLEY*

THE SNAKE

It was almost dark when young Dr. Phillips swung his sack to his shoulder and left the tide pool. He climbed up over the rocks and squashed along the street in his rubber boots. The street lights were on by the time he arrived at his little commercial laboratory on the cannery street of Monterey. It was a tight little building, standing partly on piers over the bay water and partly on the land. On both sides the big corrugated-iron sardine canneries crowded in on it.

Dr. Phillips climbed the wooden steps and opened the door. The white rats in their cages scampered up and down the wire, and the captive cats in their pens miewed for milk. Dr. Phillips turned on the glaring light over the dissection table and dumped his clammy sack on the floor. He walked to the glass cages by the window where the rattlesnakes lived, leaned over and looked in.

The snakes were bunched and resting in the corners of the cage, but every head was clear; the dusty eyes seemed to look at nothing, but as the young man leaned over the cage the forked tongues, black on the ends and pink behind, twittered out and waved slowly up and down. Then the snakes recognized the man and pulled in their tongues.

Dr. Phillips threw off his leather coat and built a fire in the tin stove; he set a kettle of water on the stove and dropped a can of beans into the water. Then he stood staring down at the sack on the floor. He was a slight young man with the mild, preoccupied eyes of one who looks through a microscope a great deal. He wore a short blond beard.

The draft ran breathily up the chimney and a glow of warmth came from the stove. The little waves washed quietly about the piles under the building. Arranged on shelves about the room were tier above tier of museum jars containing the mounted marine specimens the laboratory dealt in.

Dr. Phillips opened a side door and went into his bedroom, a book-lined cell containing an army cot, a reading light and an uncomfortable wooden chair. He pulled off his rubber boots and put on a pair of sheepskin slippers. When he went back to the other room the water in the kettle was already beginning to hum.

He lifted his sack to the table under the white light and emptied out two dozen common starfish. These he laid out side by side on the table. His preoccupied eyes turned to the busy rats in the wire cages. Taking grain from a paper sack, he poured it into the feeding troughs. Instantly the rats scrambled down from the wire and fell upon the food. A bottle of milk stood on a glass shelf between a small mounted octopus and a jellyfish. Dr. Phillips lifted down the milk and walked to the cat cage, but before he filled the containers he reached in the cage and gently picked out a big rangy alley tabby. He stroked her for a moment and then dropped her in a small black painted box, closed the lid and bolted it and then turned on a petcock which admitted gas into the killing chamber. While the short soft struggle went on in the black box he filled the saucers with milk. One of the cats arched against his hand and he smiled and petted her neck.

The box was quiet now. He turned off the petcock, for the airtight box would be full of gas.

On the stove the pan of water was bubbling furiously about the can of beans. Dr. Phillips lifted out the can with a big pair of forceps, opened it, and emptied the beans into a glass dish. While he ate he watched the starfish on the table. From between the rays little drops of milky fluid were exuding. He bolted his beans and when they were gone he put the dish in the sink and stepped to the equipment cupboard. From this he took a microscope and a pile of little glass dishes. He filled the dishes one by one with sea water from a tap and arranged them in a line beside the starfish. He took out his watch and laid it on the table under the pouring white light. The waves washed with little sighs against the piles under the floor. He took an eyedropper from a drawer and bent over the starfish.

At that moment there were quick soft steps on the wooden stairs and a strong knocking at the door. A slight grimace of annoyance crossed the young man's face as he went to open. A tall, lean woman stood in the doorway. She was dressed in a severe dark suit—her straight black hair, growing low on a flat forehead, was mussed as though the wind had been blowing it. Her black eyes glittered in the strong light.

She spoke in a soft throaty voice, "May I come in? I want to talk to you."

"I'm very busy just now," he said half-heartedly. "I have to do things at times." But he stood away from the door. The tall woman slipped in.

"I'll be quiet until you can talk to me."

He closed the door and brought the uncomfortable chair from the bedroom. "You see," he apologized, "the process is started and I must get to it." So many people wandered in and asked questions. He had little routines of explanations for the commoner processes. He could say them without thinking. "Sit here. In a few minutes I'll be able to listen to you."

The tall woman leaned over the table. With the eyedropper the young man gathered fluid from between the rays of the starfish and squirted it into a bowl of water, and then he drew some milky fluid and squirted it in the same bowl and stirred the water gently with the eyedropper. He began his little patter of explanation.

"When starfish are sexually mature they release sperm and ova when they are exposed at low tide. By choosing mature specimens and taking them out of the water, I give them a condition of low tide. Now I've mixed the sperm and eggs. Now I put some of the mixture in each one of these ten watch glasses. In ten minutes I will kill those in the first glass with menthol, twenty minutes later I will kill the second group and then a new group every twenty minutes. Then I will have arrested the process in stages, and I will mount the series on microscope slides for biologic study." He paused. "Would you like to look at this first group under the microscope?"

"No, thank you."

He turned quickly to her. People always wanted to look through the glass. She was not looking at the table at all, but at him. Her black eyes were on him, but they did not seem to see him. He realized why—the irises were as dark as the pupils, there was no color line between the two. Dr. Phillips was piqued at her answer. Although answering questions bored him, a lack of interest in what he was doing irritated him. A desire to arouse her grew in him.

"While I'm waiting the first ten minutes I have something to do. Some people don't like to see it. Maybe you'd better step into that room until I finish."

"No," she said in her soft flat tone. "Do what you wish. I will wait until you can talk to me." Her hands rested side by side on her lap. She was completely at rest. Her eyes were bright but the rest of her was almost in a state of suspended animation. He thought, "Low metabolic rate, almost as low as a frog's, from the looks." The desire to shock her out of her inanition possessed him again.

He brought a little wooden cradle to the table, laid out scalpels and scissors and rigged a big hollow needle to a pressure tube. Then from the killing chamber he brought the limp dead cat and laid it in the cradle and tied its legs to hooks in the sides. He glanced sidewise at the woman. She had not moved. She was still at rest.

The cat grinned up into the light, its pink tongue stuck out between its needle teeth. Dr. Phillips deftly snipped open the skin at the throat; with a scalpel he slit through and found an artery. With flawless technique he put the needle in the vessel and tied it in with gut. "Embalming fluid," he explained. "Later I'll inject yellow mass into the veinous system and red mass into the arterial system—for bloodstream dissection—biology classes."

He looked around at her again. Her dark eyes seemed veiled with dust. She looked without expression at the cat's open throat. Not a drop of blood had escaped. The incision was clean. Dr. Phillips looked at his watch. "Time for the first group." He shook a few crystals of menthol into the first watch-glass.

The woman was making him nervous. The rats climbed about on the wire of their cage again and squeaked softly. The waves under the building beat with little shocks on the piles.

The young man shivered. He put a few lumps of coal in the stove and sat down. "Now," he said. "I haven't anything to do for twenty minutes." He noticed how short her chin was between lower lip and point. She seemed to awaken slowly, to come up out of some deep pool of consciousness. Her head raised and her dark dusty eyes moved about the room and then came back to him.

"I was waiting," she said. Her hands remained side by side on her lap. "You have snakes?"

"Why, yes," he said rather loudly. "I have about two dozen rattlesnakes. I milk out the venom and send it to the anti-venom laboratories."

She continued to look at him but her eyes did not center on him, rather they covered him and seemed to see in a big circle all around him. "Have you a male snake, a male rattlesnake?"

"Well, it just happens I know I have. I came in one morning and found a big snake in—in coition with a smaller one. That's very rare in captivity. You see, I do know I have a male snake."

"Where is he?"

"Why, right in the glass cage by the window there."

Her head swung slowly around but her two quiet hands did not move. She turned back toward him. "May I see?"

He got up and walked to the case by the window. On the sand bottom the knot of rattlesnakes lay entwined, but their heads were clear. The tongues came out and flickered a moment and then waved up and down feeling the air for vibrations. Dr. Phillips nervously turned his head. The woman was standing beside him. He had not heard her get up from the chair. He had heard only the splash of water among the piles and the scampering of the rats on the wire screen.

She said softly, "Which is the male you spoke of?"

He pointed to a thick, dusty grey snake lying by itself in one corner of the cage. "That one. He's nearly five feet long. He comes from Texas. Our Pacific coast snakes are usually smaller. He's been taking all the rats, too. When I want the others to eat I have to take him out."

The woman stared down at the blunt dry head. The forked tongue slipped out and hung quivering for a long moment. "And you're sure he's a male."

"Rattlesnakes are funny," he said glibly. "Nearly every generalization proves wrong. I don't like to say anything definite about rattlesnakes, but—yes—I can assure you he's a male."

Her eyes did not move from the flat head. "Will you sell him to me?"

"Sell him?" he cried. "Sell him to you?"

"You do sell specimens, don't you?"

"Oh—yes. Of course I do. Of course I do."

"How much? Five dollars? Ten?"

"Oh! Not more than five. But—do you know anything about rattlesnakes? You might be bitten."

She looked at him for a moment. "I don't intend to take him. I want to leave him here, but—I want him to be mine. I want to come here and look at him and feed him and to know he's mine." She opened a little purse and took out a five-dollar bill. "Here! Now he is mine."

Dr. Phillips began to be afraid. "You could come to look at him without owning him."

"I want him to be mine."

"Oh, Lord!" he cried. "I've forgotten the time." He ran to the table. "Three minutes over. It won't matter much." He shook menthol crystals into the second watch-glass. And then he was drawn back to the cage where the woman still stared at the snake.

She asked, "What does he eat?"

"I feed them white rats, rats from the cage over there."

"Will you put him in the other cage? I want to feed him."

"But he doesn't need food. He's had a rat already this week. Sometimes they don't eat for three or four months. I had one that didn't eat for over a year."

In her low monotone she asked, "Will you sell me a rat?"

He shrugged his shoulders. "I see. You want to watch how rattlesnakes eat. All right. I'll show you. The rat will cost twenty-five cents. It's better than a bullfight if you look at it one way, and it's simply a snake eating his dinner if you look at it another." His tone had become acid. He hated people who made sport of natural processes. He was not a sportsman but a biologist. He could kill a thousand animals for knowledge, but not an insect for pleasure. He'd been over this in his mind before.

She turned her head slowly toward him and the beginning of a smile formed on her thin lips. "I want to feed my snake," she said. "I'll put him in the other cage." She had opened the top of the cage and dipped her hand in before he knew what she was doing. He leaped forward and pulled her back. The lid banged shut.

"Haven't you any sense," he asked fiercely. "Maybe he wouldn't kill you, but he'd make you damned sick in spite of what I could do for you."

"You put him in the other cage then," she said quietly.

Dr. Phillips was shaken. He found that he was avoiding the dark eyes that didn't seem to look at anything. He felt that it was profoundly wrong to put a rat into the cage, deeply sinful; and he didn't know why. Often he had put rats in the cage when someone or other had wanted to see it, but this desire tonight sickened him. He tried to explain himself out of it.

"It's a good thing to see," he said. "It shows you how a snake can work. It makes you have a respect for a rattlesnake. Then, too, lots of people have dreams about the terror of snakes making the kill. I think because it is a subjective rat. The person is the rat. Once you see it the whole matter is objective. The rat is only a rat and the terror is removed."

He took a long stick equipped with a leather noose from the wall. Opening the trap he dropped the noose over the big snake's head and tightened the thong. A piercing dry rattle filled the room. The thick body writhed and slashed about the handle of the stick as he lifted the snake out and dropped it in the feeding cage. It stood ready to strike for a time, but the buzzing gradually ceased. The snake crawled into a corner, made a big figure eight with its body and lay still.

"You see," the young man explained, "these snakes are quite tame. I've had them a long time. I suppose I could handle them if I wanted to, but everyone who does handle rattlesnakes gets bitten sooner or later. I just don't want to take the chance." He glanced at the woman. He hated to put in the rat. She had moved over in front of the new cage; her black eyes were on the stony head of the snake again.

She said, "Put in a rat."

Reluctantly he went to the rat cage. For some reason he was sorry for the rat, and such a feeling had never come to him before. His eyes went over the mass of swarming white bodies climbing up the screen toward him. "Which one?" he thought. "Which one shall it be?" Suddenly he turned angrily to the woman. "Wouldn't you rather I put in a cat? Then you'd see a real fight. The cat might even win, but if it did it might kill the snake. I'll sell you a cat if you like."

She didn't look at him. "Put in a rat," she said. "I want him to eat."

He opened the rat cage and thrust his hand in. His fingers found a tail and he lifted a plump, red-eyed rat out of the cage. It struggled up to try to bite his fingers and, failing, hung spread out and motionless from its tail. He walked quickly across the room, opened the feeding cage and dropped the rat in on the sand floor. "Now, watch it," he cried.

The woman did not answer him. Her eyes were on the snake where it lay still. Its tongue flicking in and out rapidly, tasted the air of the cage.

The rat landed on its feet, turned around and sniffed at its pink naked tail and then unconcernedly trotted across the sand, smelling as it went. The room was silent. Dr. Phillips did not know whether the water sighed among the piles or whether the woman sighed. Out of the corner of his eye he saw her body crouch and stiffen.

The snake moved out smoothly, slowly. The tongue flicked in and out. The motion was so gradual, so smooth that it didn't seem to be motion at all. In the other end of the cage the rat perked up in a sitting position and began to lick down the fine white hair on its chest. The snake moved on, keeping always a deep S curve in its neck.

The silence beat on the young man. He felt the blood drifting up in his body. He said loudly, "See! He keeps the striking curve ready. Rattlesnakes are cautious, almost cowardly animals. The mechanism is so delicate. The snake's dinner is to be got by an operation as deft as a surgeon's job. He takes no chances with his instruments."

The snake had flowed to the middle of the cage by now. The rat looked up, saw the snake and then unconcernedly went back to licking its chest.

"It's the most beautiful thing in the world," the young man said. His veins were throbbing. "It's the most terrible thing in the world."

The snake was close now. Its head lifted a few inches from the sand. The head weaved slowly back and forth, aiming, getting distance, aiming. Dr. Phillips glanced again at the woman. He turned sick. She was weaving too, not much, just a suggestion.

The rat looked up and saw the snake. It dropped to four feet and back up, and then—the stroke. It was impossible to see, simply a flash. The rat jarred as though under an invisible blow. The snake backed hurriedly into the corner from which it had come, and settled down, its tongue working constantly.

"Perfect!" Dr. Phillips cried. "Right between the shoulder blades. The fangs must almost have reached the heart."

The rat stood still, breathing like a little white bellows. Suddenly it leaped in the air and landed on its side. Its legs kicked spasmodically for a second and it was dead.

The woman relaxed, relaxed sleepily.

"Well," the young man demanded, "it was an emotional bath, wasn't it?"

She turned her misty eyes to him. "Will he eat it now?" she asked.

"Of course he'll eat it. He didn't kill it for a thrill. He killed it because he was hungry."

The corners of the woman's mouth turned up a trifle again. She looked back at the snake. "I want to see him eat it."

Now the snake came out of its corner again. There was no striking curve in its neck, but it approached the rat gingerly, ready to jump back in case it attacked. It nudged the body gently with its blunt nose, and drew away. Satisfied that it was dead, the snake touched the body all over with its chin, from head to tail. It seemed to measure the body and to kiss it. Finally it opened its mouth and unhinged its jaws at the corners.

Dr. Phillips put his will against his head to keep it from turning toward the woman. He thought, "If she's opening her mouth, I'll be sick. I'll be afraid." He succeeded in keeping his eyes away.

The snake fitted its jaws over the rat's head and then with a slow peristaltic pulsing, began to engulf the rat. The jaws gripped and the whole throat crawled up, and the jaws gripped again.

Dr. Phillips turned away and went to his work table. "You've made me miss one of the series," he said bitterly. "The set won't be complete." He put one of the watch glasses under a low-power microscope and looked at it, and then angrily he poured the contents of all the dishes into the sink. The waves had fallen so that only a wet whisper came up through the floor. The young man lifted a trapdoor at his feet and dropped the starfish down into the black water. He paused at the cat, crucified in the cradle and grinning comically into the light. Its body was puffed with embalming fluid. He shut off the pressure, withdrew the needle and tied the vein.

"Would you like some coffee?" he asked.

"No, thank you. I shall be going pretty soon."

He walked to her where she stood in front of the snake cage. The rat was swallowed, all except an inch of pink tail that stuck out of the snake's mouth like a sardonic tongue. The throat heaved again and the tail disappeared. The jaws snapped back into their sockets, and the big snake crawled heavily to the corner, made a big eight and dropped its head on the sand.

"He's asleep now," the woman said. "I'm going now. But I'll come back and feed my snake every little while. I'll pay for the rats. I want him to have plenty. And sometime—I'll take him away with me." Her eyes came out of their dusty dream for a moment. "Remember, he's mine. Don't take his poison. I want him to have it. Goodnight." She walked swiftly to the door and went out. He heard her footsteps on the stairs, but he could not hear her walk away on the pavement.

Dr. Phillips turned a chair around and sat down in front of the snake cage. He tried to comb out his thought as he looked at the torpid snake. "I've read so much about psychological sex symbols," he thought. "It doesn't seem to explain. Maybe I'm too much alone. Maybe I should kill the snake. If I knew—no, I can't pray to anything."

For weeks he expected her to return. "I will go out and leave her alone here when she comes," he decided. "I won't see the damned thing again."

She never came again. For months he looked for her when he walked about in the town. Several times he ran after some tall woman thinking it might be she. But he never saw her again—ever.

1938

THE VIGILANTE

The great surge of emotion, the milling and shouting of the people fell gradually to silence in the town park. A crowd of people still stood under the elm trees, vaguely lighted by a blue street light two blocks away. A tired quiet settled on the people; some members of the mob began to sneak away into the darkness. The park lawn was cut to pieces by the feet of the crowd.

Mike knew it was all over. He could feel the let-down in himself. He was as heavily weary as though he had gone without sleep for several nights, but it was a dreamlike weariness, a grey comfortable weariness. He pulled his cap down over his eyes and moved away, but before leaving the park he turned for one last look.

In the center of the mob someone had lighted a twisted newspaper and was holding it up. Mike could see how the flame curled about the feet of the grey naked body hanging from the elm tree. It seemed curious to him that negroes turn a bluish grey when they are dead. The burning newspaper lighted the heads of the uplooking men, silent men and fixed; they didn't move their eyes from the hanged man.

Mike felt a little irritation at whoever it was who was trying to burn the body. He turned to a man who stood beside him in the near-darkness. "That don't do no good," he said.

The man moved away without replying.

The newspaper torch went out, leaving the park almost black by contrast. But immediately another twisted paper was lighted and held up against the feet. Mike moved to another watching man. "That don't do no good," he repeated. "He's dead now. They can't hurt him none."

The second man grunted but did not look away from the flaming paper. "It's a good job," he said. "This'll save the county a lot of money and no sneaky lawyers getting in."

"That's what I say," Mike agreed. "No sneaky lawyers. But it don't do no good to try to burn him."

The man continued staring toward the flame. "Well, it can't do much harm, either."

Mike filled his eyes with the scene. He felt that he was dull. He wasn't seeing enough of it. Here was a thing he would want to remember later so he could tell about it, but the dull tiredness seemed to cut the sharpness off the picture. His brain told him this was a terrible and important affair, but his eyes and his feelings didn't agree. It was just ordinary. Half an hour before, when he had been howling with the mob and fighting for a chance to help pull on the rope, then his chest had been so full that he had found he was crying. But now everything was dead, everything unreal; the dark mob was made up of stiff lay-figures. In the flamelight the faces were as expressionless as wood. Mike felt the stiffness, the unreality in himself, too. He turned away at last and walked out of the park.

The moment he left the outskirts of the mob a cold loneliness fell upon him. He walked quickly along the street wishing that some other man might be walking beside him. The wide street was deserted, empty, as unreal as the park had been. The two steel lines of the car tracks stretched glimmering away down the street under the electroliers, and the dark store windows reflected the midnight globes.

A gentle pain began to make itself felt in Mike's chest. He felt with his fingers; the muscles were sore. Then he remembered. He was in the front line of the mob when it rushed the closed jail door. A driving line forty men deep had crashed Mike against the door like the head of a ram. He had hardly felt it then, and even now the pain seemed to have the dull quality of loneliness.

Two blocks ahead the burning neon word BEER hung over the sidewalk. Mike hurried toward it. He hoped there would be people there, and talk, to remove this silence; and he hoped the men wouldn't have been to the lynching.

The bartender was alone in his little bar, a small, middle-aged man with a melancholy moustache and an expression like an aged mouse, wise and unkempt and fearful.

He nodded quickly as Mike came in. "You look like you been walking in your sleep," he said.

Mike regarded him with wonder. "That's just how I feel, too, like I been walking in my sleep."

"Well, I can give you a shot if you want."

Mike hesitated. "No—I'm kind of thirsty. I'll take a beer. . . . Was you there?"

The little man nodded his mouse-like head again. "Right at the last, after he was all up and it was all over. I figured a lot of the fellas would be thirsty, so I came back and opened up. Nobody but you so far. Maybe I was wrong."

"They might be along later," said Mike. "There's a lot of them still in the park. They cooled off, though. Some of them trying to burn him with newspapers. That don't do no good."

"Not a bit of good," said the little bartender. He twitched his thin moustache.

Mike knocked a few grains of celery salt into his beer and took a long drink. "That's good," he said. "I'm kind of dragged out."

The bartender leaned close to him over the bar, his eyes were bright. "Was you there all the time—to the jail and everything?"

Mike drank again and then looked through his beer and watched the beads of bubbles rising from the grains of salt in the bottom of the glass. "Everything," he said. "I was one of the first in the jail, and I helped pull on the rope. There's times when citizens got to take the law in their own hands. Sneaky lawyer comes along and gets some fiend out of it."

The mousy head jerked up and down. "You God-dam' right," he said. "Lawyers can get them out of anything. I guess the nigger was guilty all right."

"Oh, sure! Somebody said he even confessed."

The head came close over the bar again. "How did it start, mister? I was only there after it was all over, and then I only stayed a minute and then came back to open up in case any of the fellas might want a glass of beer."

Mike drained his glass and pushed it out to be filled. "Well, of course everybody knew it was going to happen. I was in a bar across from the jail. Been there all afternoon. A guy came in and says, 'What are we waiting for?' So we went across the street, and a lot more guys was there and a lot more come. We all stood there and yelled. Then the sheriff come out and made a speech, but we yelled him down. A guy with a twenty-two rifle went along the street and shot out the street lights. Well, then we rushed the jail doors and bust them. The sheriff wasn't going to do nothing. It wouldn't do him no good to shoot a lot of honest men to save a nigger fiend."

"And election coming on, too," the bartender put in.

"Well, the sheriff started yelling, 'Get the right man, boys, for Christ's sake get the right man. He's in the fourth cell down.'

"It was kind of pitiful," Mike said slowly. "The other prisoners was so scared. We could see them through the bars. I never seen such faces."

The bartender excitedly poured himself a small glass of whiskey and poured it down. "Can't blame 'em much. Suppose you was in for thirty days and a lynch mob came through. You'd be scared they'd get the wrong man."

"That's what I say. It was kind of pitiful. Well, we got to the nigger's cell. He just stood stiff with his eyes closed like he was dead drunk. One of the guys slugged him down and he got up, and then somebody else socked him and he went over and hit his head on the cement floor." Mike leaned over the bar and tapped the polished wood with his forefinger. "'Course this is only my idea, but I think that killed him. Because I helped get his clothes off, and he never made a wiggle, and when we strung him up he didn't jerk around none. No, sir. I think he was dead all the time, after that second guy smacked him."

"Well, it's all the same in the end."

"No, it ain't. You like to do the thing right. He had it coming to him, and he should have got it." Mike reached into his trousers pocket and brought out a piece of torn blue denim. "That's a piece of the pants he had on."

The bartender bent close and inspected the cloth. He jerked his head up at Mike. "I'll give you a buck for it."

"Oh no, you won't!"

"All right. I'll give you two bucks for half of it."

Mike looked suspiciously at him. "What you want it for?"

"Here! Give me your glass! Have a beer on me. I'll pin it up on the wall with a little card under it. The fellas that come in will like to look at it."

Mike haggled the piece of cloth in two with his pocket knife and accepted two silver dollars from the bartender.

"I know a show card writer," the little man said. "Comes in every day. He'll print me up a nice little card to go under it." He looked wary. "Think the sheriff will arrest anybody?"

"'Course not. What's he want to start any trouble for? There was a lot of votes in that crowd tonight. Soon as they all go away, the sheriff will come and cut the nigger down and clean up some."

The bartender looked toward the door. "I guess I was wrong about the fellas wanting a drink. It's getting late."

"I guess I'll get along home. I feel tired."

"If you go south, I'll close up and walk a ways with you. I live on south Eighth."

"Why, that's only two blocks from my house. I live on south Sixth. You must go right past my house. Funny I never saw you around."

The bartender washed Mike's glass and took off the long apron. He put on his hat and coat, walked to the door and switched off the red neon sign and the house lights. For a moment the two men stood on the sidewalk looking back toward the park. The city was silent. There was no sound from the park. A policeman walked along a block away, turning his flash into the store windows.

"You see?" said Mike. "Just like nothing happened."

"Well, if the fellas wanted a glass of beer they must have gone someplace else."

"That's what I told you," said Mike.

They swung along the empty street and turned south, out of the business district. "My name's Welch," the bartender said. "I only been in this town about two years."

The loneliness had fallen on Mike again. "It's funny—" he said, and then, "I was born right in this town, right in the house I live in now. I got a wife but no kids. Both of us born right in this town. Everybody knows us."

They walked on for a few blocks. The stores dropped behind and the nice houses with bushy gardens and cut lawns lined the street. The tall shade trees were shadowed on the sidewalk by the street lights. Two night dogs went slowly by, smelling at each other.

Welch said softly—"I wonder what kind of a fella he was—the nigger, I mean."

Mike answered out of his loneliness. "The papers all said he was a fiend. I read all the papers. That's what they all said."

"Yes, I read them, too. But it makes you wonder about him. I've known some pretty nice niggers."

Mike turned his head and spoke protestingly. "Well, I've knew some dam' fine niggers myself. I've worked right 'longside some niggers and they was as nice as any white man you could want to meet. —But not no fiends."

His vehemence silenced little Welch for a moment. Then he said, "You couldn't tell, I guess, what kind of a fella he was?"

"No—he just stood there stiff, with his mouth shut and his eyes tight closed and his hands right down at his sides. And then one of the guys smacked him. It's my idea he was dead when we took him out."

Welch sidled close on the walk. "Nice gardens along here. Must take a lot of money to keep them up." He walked even closer, so that his shoulder touched Mike's arm. "I never been to a lynching. How's it make you feel—afterwards?"

Mike shied away from the contact. "It don't make you feel nothing." He put down his head and increased his pace. The little bartender had nearly to trot to keep up. The street lights were fewer. It was darker and safer. Mike burst out, "Makes you feel kind of cut off and tired, but kind of satisfied, too. Like you done a good job—but tired and kind of sleepy." He slowed his steps. "Look, there's a light in the kitchen. That's where I live. My old lady's waiting up for me." He stopped in front of his little house.

Welch stood nervously beside him. "Come into my place when you want a glass of beer—or a shot. Open till midnight. I treat my friends right." He scampered away like an aged mouse.

Mike called, "Good night."

He walked around the side of his house and went in the back door. His thin, petulant wife was sitting by the open gas oven warming herself. She turned complaining eyes on Mike where he stood in the doorway.

Then her eyes widened and hung on his face. "You been with a woman," she said hoarsely. "What woman you been with?"

Mike laughed. "You think you're pretty slick, don't you? You're a slick one, ain't you? What makes you think I been with a woman?"

She said fiercely, "You think I can't tell by the look on your face that you been with a woman?"

"All right," said Mike. "If you're so slick and know-it-all, I won't tell you nothing. You can just wait for the morning paper."

He saw doubt come into the dissatisfied eyes. "Was it the nigger?" she asked. "Did they get the nigger? Everybody said they was going to."

"Find out for yourself if you're so slick. I ain't going to tell you nothing."

He walked through the kitchen and went into the bathroom. A little mirror hung on the wall. Mike took off his cap and looked at his face. "By God, she was right," he thought. "That's just exactly how I do feel."

1938

Katherine Anne Porter 1890–1980

Katherine Anne Porter published only one novel and few short stories, but she enjoyed a reputation as one of America's finest stylists. Her writing is "disciplined" (one of her own terms), ironic, concentrated, and precise. Working within a narrow range and with limited subject matter, she produced short stories of high distinction, an achievement that she suggested was the result of her dedication to art, "the substance of faith and the only reality."

Although she wrote prose of great clarity, Porter kept the details of her life obscure. She hid her poverty-stricken origins by suggesting that she came from a family of plantation aristocrats, but she was actually born in a small log house in Indian Creek, Texas, which later in life she described as a "god-forsaken wilderness." She adopted her grandmother's name and called herself Katherine Anne Porter, but she had been christened Callie Russell Porter, a name that lacked, she believed, suitable elegance. Her mother was sickly and died when Porter was two. Her father, a ne'er-do-well, failed to provide his children with a stable family life or an education.

Porter told of being educated in Catholic convents as a child, and critics have concluded that her intellectual background was Roman Catholic. In fact, as her biographer has pointed out, she had only a single year of formal education—in a school for young ladies in a small Texas town, where she was taught dancing, elocution, drama, and good manners, and was exposed to "fine" literature. At sixteen she married, hoping to escape her drab life, but the marriage was a failure.

To support herself she taught drama and elocution in small Texas towns. Having great natural beauty and a talent for theatricals, she got a job in Chicago as an extra in early motion pictures. Soon she had worked her way up from bit player to director of publicity for a movie studio. She had published some essays in regional journals, and in 1920 she was sent to Mexico to write magazine articles about the land, the people, and their customs. In Mexico she became involved in revolutionary political movements and absorbed the impressions and met the characters that were to appear in some of her best short stories. A journey from Mexico to Europe in 1931 provided the background for her long and famous novel, Ship of Fools.

Porter did her finest literary work in the 1920s and 1930s. Her first published story appeared in 1922 and her first book, Flowering Judas and Other Stories, *in 1930. A second collection of earlier stories,* Pale Horse, Pale Rider, *was published in 1939; a third collection,* The Leaning Tower and Other Stories, *appeared in 1944. In explaining why she had not written more during the twenties and thirties, Katherine Anne Porter was typically vague and cryptic: "I was not one of those who could flourish in the conditions of the past two decades." In her final years the quantity of her writing remained small. A book of her critical essays,* The Days Before, *was published in 1952;* Ship of Fools *appeared in 1962 and was later made into an award winning motion picture. Her last work,* The Never Ending Wrong *(1977), is a memoir of events surrounding the trial and execution of Sacco and Vanzetti in the 1920s. After 1940, she spent much time lecturing and teaching at colleges and universities in the United States, taking great pleasure in being a professor at institutions she had once been unqualified to attend.*

Katherine Anne Porter has been called "a maker of darkish parables" because of her portrayal of the impoverished spirit of humankind in the modern world and because of her repeated use of the themes of isolation, guilt, and spiritual denial. Many of her most highly regarded stories are set in the South, the Southwest, or in Mexico (she called Mexico "my familiar country"). They frequently turn on the conflicts between the regions' fixed social orders and movements for change. Her works are rich (some critics say over-rich) in symbolism, and she was often a harsh moralist, giving cruelly severe portrayals of the weaknesses of men and women. Yet she is now judged to have been one of the best American writers of short fiction in the twentieth century, and her finest stories, such as "María Concepción," are praised as "completely original works," for in the world of the modern short story "there is simply nothing like them."

FURTHER READING: H. Mooney, *The Fiction and Criticism of Katherine Anne Porter,* 1957, 1962; R. West, *Katherine Anne Porter,* 1963; W. Nance, *Katherine Anne Porter and the Art of Rejection,* 1964; G. Hendrick, *Katherine Anne Porter,* 1965; W. Emmons, *Katherine Anne Porter: The Regional Stories,* 1967; *Katherine Anne Porter: A Critical Symposium,* ed. L. Hartley and G. Core, 1969; *The Collected Essays and Occasional Writings of Katherine Anne Porter,* 1970; M. Liberman, *Katherine Anne Porter's Fiction,* 1971; J. Hardy, *Katherine Anne Porter,* 1973; *Katherine Anne Porter: A Collection of Critical Essays,* ed. R. Warren, 1979; E. Lopez, *Conversations with Katherine Anne Porter,* 1981; J. Givner, *Katherine Anne Porter,* 1982, 1990; D. Unrue, *Truth and Vision in Katherine Anne Porter's Fiction,* 1985; *Katherine Anne Porter: Conversations,* ed. J. Givner, 1987; D. Unrue, *Understanding Katherine Anne*

Porter, 1988; *The Letters of Katherine Anne Porter,* ed. I. Bayley, 1990; R. Binkmeyer, *Katherine Anne Porter's Artistic Development,* 1993; Stout, *Katherine Anne Porter: A Sense of the Times,* 1995; *Critical Essays on Katharine Anne Porter,* ed. D. Harbour, 1997; *Katherine Anne Porter,* ed. H. Bloom, 2001; *From Texas to the World and Back,* ed. M. Busby and D. Heaberlin, 2001; D. Unrue, *Katherine Anne Porter: The Life of an Artist,* 2005.

TEXT: *The Collected Stories of Katherine Anne Porter,* 1965.

FLOWERING JUDAS

Braggioni sits heaped upon the edge of a straight-backed chair much too small for him, and sings to Laura in a furry, mournful voice. Laura has begun to find reasons for avoiding her own house until the latest possible moment, for Braggioni is there almost every night. No matter how late she is, he will be sitting there with a surly, waiting expression, pulling at his kinky yellow hair, thumbing the strings of his guitar, snarling a tune under his breath. Lupe the Indian maid meets Laura at the door, and says with a flicker of a glance towards the upper room, "He waits."

Laura wishes to lie down, she is tired of her hairpins and the feel of her long tight sleeves, but she says to him, "Have you a new song for me this evening?" If he says yes, she asks him to sing it. If he says no, she remembers his favorite one, and asks him to sing it again. Lupe brings her a cup of chocolate and a plate of rice, and Laura eats at the small table under the lamp, first inviting Braggioni, whose answer is always the same: "I have eaten, and besides, chocolate thickens the voice."

Laura says, "Sing, then," and Braggioni heaves himself into song. He scratches the guitar familiarly as though it were a pet animal, and sings passionately off key, taking the high notes in a prolonged painful squeal. Laura, who haunts the markets listening to the ballad singers, and stops every day to hear the blind boy playing his reed-flute in Sixteenth of September Street,[1] listens to Braggioni with pitiless courtesy, because she dares not smile at his miserable performance. Nobody dares to smile at him. Braggioni is cruel to everyone, with a kind of specialized insolence, but he is so vain of his talents, and so sensitive to slights, it would require a cruelty and vanity greater than his own to lay a finger on the vast cureless wound of his self-esteem. It would require courage, too, for it is dangerous to offend him, and nobody has this courage.

Braggioni loves himself with such tenderness and amplitude and eternal charity that his followers—for he is a leader of men, a skilled revolutionist, and his skin has been punctured in horrible warfare—warm themselves in the reflected glow, and say to each other: "He has a real nobility, a love of humanity raised above mere personal affections." The excess of this self-love has flowed out, inconveniently for her, over Laura, who, with so many others, owes her comfortable situation and her salary to him. When he is in a very good humor, he tells her, "I am tempted to forgive you for being a *gringa.*

[1]Street in Mexico City, named for the first day of the revolution for independence in 1810.

Gringita!"[2] and Laura, burning, imagines herself leaning forward suddenly, and with a sound back-handed slap wiping the suety smile from his face. If he notices her eyes at these moments he gives no sign.

She knows what Braggioni would offer her, and she must resist tenaciously without appearing to resist, and if she could avoid it she would not admit even to herself the slow drift of his intention. During these long evenings which have spoiled a long month for her, she sits in her deep chair with an open book on her knees, resting her eyes on the consoling rigidity of the printed page when the sight and sound of Braggioni singing threaten to identify themselves with all her remembered afflictions and to add their weight to her uneasy premonitions of the future. The gluttonous bulk of Braggioni has become a symbol of her many disillusions, for a revolutionist should be lean, animated by heroic faith, a vessel of abstract virtues. This is nonsense, she knows it now and is ashamed of it. Revolution must have leaders, and leadership is a career for energetic men. She is, her comrades tell her, full of romantic error, for what she defines as cynicism in them is merely "a developed sense of reality." She is almost too willing to say, "I am wrong, I suppose I don't really understand the principles," and afterward she makes a secret truce with herself, determined not to surrender her will to such expedient logic. But she cannot help feeling that she has been betrayed irreparably by the disunion between her way of living and her feeling of what life should be, and at times she is almost contented to rest in this sense of grievance as a private source of consolation. Sometimes she wishes to run away, but she stays. Now she longs to fly out of this room, down the narrow stairs, and into the street where the houses lean together like conspirators under a single mottled lamp, and leave Braggioni singing to himself.

Instead she looks at Braggioni, frankly and clearly, like a good child who understands the rules of behavior. Her knees cling together under sound blue serge, and her round white collar is not purposely nun-like. She wears the uniform of an idea, and has renounced vanities. She was born Roman Catholic, and in spite of her fear of being seen by someone who might make a scandal of it, she slips now and again into some crumbling little church, kneels on the chilly stone, and says a Hail Mary on the gold rosary she bought in Tehuantepec.[3] It is no good and she ends by examining the altar with its tinsel flowers and ragged brocades, and feels tender about the battered doll-shape of some male saint whose white, lace-trimmed drawers hang limply around his ankles below the hieratic dignity of his velvet robe. She has encased herself in a set of principles derived from her early training, leaving no detail of gesture or of personal taste untouched, and for this reason she will not wear lace made on machines. This is her private heresy, for in her special group the machine is sacred, and will be the salvation of the workers. She loves fine lace, and there is a tiny edge of fluted cobweb on this collar, which is one of twenty precisely alike, folded in blue tissue paper in the upper drawer of her clothes chest.

Braggioni catches her glance solidly as if he had been waiting for it, leans forward, balancing his paunch between his spread knees, and sings with tremendous emphasis, weighing his words. He has, the song relates, no father

[2]Spanish (contemptuous): foreign girl. Little foreign girl! [3]Town in southern Mexico.

and no mother, nor even a friend to console him; lonely as a wave of the sea he comes and goes, lonely as a wave. His mouth opens round and yearns sideways, his balloon cheeks grow oily with the labor of song. He bulges marvelously in his expensive garments. Over his lavender collar, crushed upon a purple necktie, held by a diamond hoop: over his ammunition belt of tooled leather worked in silver, buckled cruelly around his gasping middle: over the tops of his glossy yellow shoes Braggioni swells with ominous ripeness, his mauve silk hose stretched taut, his ankles bound with the stout leather thongs of his shoes.

When he stretches his eyelids at Laura she notes again that his eyes are the true tawny yellow cat's eyes. He is rich, not in money, he tells her, but in power, and this power brings with it the blameless ownership of things, and the right to indulge his love of small luxuries. "I have a taste for the elegant refinements," he said once, flourishing a yellow silk handkerchief before her nose. "Smell that? It is Jockey Club, imported from New York." Nonetheless he is wounded by life. He will say so presently. "It is true everything turns to dust in the hand, to gall on the tongue." He sighs and his leather belt creaks like a saddle girth. "I am disappointed in everything as it comes. Everything." He shakes his head. "You, poor thing, you will be disappointed too. You are born for it. We are more alike than you realize in some things. Wait and see. Some day you will remember what I have told you, you will know that Braggioni was your friend."

Laura feels a slow chill, a purely physical sense of danger, a warning in her blood that violence, mutilation, a shocking death, wait for her with lessening patience. She has translated this fear into something homely, immediate, and sometimes hesitates before crossing the street. "My personal fate is nothing, except as testimony of a mental attitude," she reminds herself, quoting from some forgotten philosophic primer, and is sensible enough to add, "Anyhow, I shall not be killed by an automobile if I can help it."

"It may be true I am as corrupt, in another way, as Braggioni," she thinks in spite of herself, "as callous, as incomplete," and if this is so, any kind of death seems preferable. Still she sits quietly, she does not run. Where could she go? Uninvited she has promised herself to this place; she can no longer imagine herself as living in another country, and there is no pleasure in remembering her life before she came here.

Precisely what is the nature of this devotion, its true motives, and what are its obligations? Laura cannot say. She spends part of her days in Xochimilco,[4] near by, teaching Indian children to say in English, "The cat is on the mat." When she appears in the classroom they crowd about her with smiles on their wise, innocent, clay-colored faces, crying, "Good morning my ticher!" in immaculate voices, and they make of her desk a fresh garden of flowers every day.

During her leisure she goes to union meetings and listens to busy important voices quarreling over tactics, methods, internal politics. She visits the prisoners of her own political faith in their cells, where they entertain themselves with counting cockroaches, repenting of their indiscretions, composing their memoirs, writing out manifestoes and plans for their comrades who are still walking about free, hands in pockets, sniffing fresh air. Laura brings

[4]Town near Mexico City.

them food and cigarettes and a little money, and she brings messages disguised in equivocal phrases from the men outside who dare not set foot in the prison for fear of disappearing into the cells kept empty for them. If the prisoners confuse night and day, and complain, "Dear little Laura, time doesn't pass in this infernal hole, and I won't know when it is time to sleep unless I have a reminder," she brings them their favorite narcotics, and says in a tone that does not wound them with pity, "Tonight will really be night for you," and though her Spanish amuses them, they find her comforting, useful. If they lose patience and all faith, and curse the slowness of their friends in coming to their rescue with money and influence, they trust her not to repeat everything, and if she inquires, "Where do you think we can find money, or influence?" they are certain to answer, "Well, there is Braggioni, why doesn't he do something?"

She smuggles letters from headquarters to men hiding from firing squads in back streets in mildewed houses, where they sit in tumbled beds and talk bitterly as if all Mexico were at their heels, when Laura knows positively they might appear at the band concert in the Alameda[5] on Sunday morning, and no one would notice them. But Braggioni says, "Let them sweat a little. The next time they may be careful. It is very restful to have them out of the way for a while." She is not afraid to knock on any door in any street after midnight, and enter in the darkness, and say to one of these men who is really in danger: "They will be looking for you—seriously—tomorrow morning after six. Here is some money from Vincente. Go to Vera Cruz[6] and wait."

She borrows money from the Roumanian agitator to give to his bitter enemy the Polish agitator. The favor of Braggioni is their disputed territory, and Braggioni holds the balance nicely, for he can use them both. The Polish agitator talks love to her over café tables, hoping to exploit what he believes is her secret sentimental preference for him, and he gives her misinformation which he begs her to repeat as the solemn truth to certain persons. The Roumanian is more adroit. He is generous with his money in all good causes, and lies to her with an air of ingenuous candor, as if he were her good friend and confidant. She never repeats anything they may say. Braggioni never asks questions. He has other ways to discover all that he wishes to know about them.

Nobody touches her, but all praise her gray eyes, and the soft, round under lip which promises gayety, yet is always grave, nearly always firmly closed: and they cannot understand why she is in Mexico. She walks back and forth on her errands, with puzzled eyebrows, carrying her little folder of drawings and music and school papers. No dancer dances more beautifully than Laura walks, and she inspires some amusing, unexpected ardors, which cause little gossip, because nothing comes of them. A young captain who had been a soldier in Zapata's[7] army attempted, during a horseback ride near Cuernavaca,[8] to express his desire for her with the noble simplicity befitting a rude folk-hero: but gently, because he was gentle. This gentleness was his defeat, for when he alighted, and removed her foot from the stirrup, and essayed to

[5]A park in central Mexico City. [6]On the Gulf of Mexico.
[7]Emiliano Zapata (1877?–1919), Mexican revolutionary leader.
[8]City south of Mexico City.

draw her down into his arms, her horse, ordinarily a tame one, shied fiercely, reared and plunged away. The young hero's horse careered blindly after his stable-mate, and the hero did not return to the hotel until rather late that evening. At breakfast he came to her table in full charro dress, gray buckskin jacket and trousers with strings of silver buttons down the leg, and he was in a humorous, careless mood. "May I sit with you?" and "You are a wonderful rider. I was terrified that you might be thrown and dragged. I should never have forgiven myself. But I cannot admire you enough for your riding!"

"I learned to ride in Arizona," said Laura.

"If you will ride with me again this morning, I promise you a horse that will not shy with you," he said. But Laura remembered that she must return to Mexico City at noon.

Next morning the children made a celebration and spent their playtime writing on the blackboard, "We lov ar ticher," and with tinted chalks they drew wreaths of flowers around the words. The young hero wrote her a letter: "I am a very foolish, wasteful, impulsive man. I should have first said I love you, and then you would not have run away. But you shall see me again." Laura thought, "I must send him a box of colored crayons," but she was trying to forgive herself for having spurred her horse at the wrong moment.

A brown, shock-haired youth came and stood in her patio one night and sang like a lost soul for two hours, but Laura could think of nothing to do about it. The moonlight spread a wash of gauzy silver over the clear spaces of the garden, and the shadows were cobalt blue. The scarlet blossoms of the Judas tree were dull purple, and the names of the colors repeated themselves automatically in her mind, while she watched not the boy, but his shadow, fallen like a dark garment across the fountain rim, trailing in the water. Lupe came silently and whispered expert counsel in her ear: "If you will throw him one little flower, he will sing another song or two and go away." Laura threw the flower, and he sang a last song and went away with the flower tucked in the band of his hat. Lupe said, "He is one of the organizers of the Typographers Union, and before that he sold corridos[9] in the Merced market,[10] and before that, he came from Guanajuato, where I was born. I would not trust any man, but I trust least those from Guanajuato."

She did not tell Laura that he would be back again the next night and the next, or that he would follow her at a certain fixed distance around the Merced market, through the Zócalo,[11] up Francisco I. Madero Avenue,[12] and so along the Paseo de la Reforma to Chapultepec Park, and into the Philosopher's Footpath, still with that flower withering in his hat, and an indivisible attention in his eyes.

Now Laura is accustomed to him, it means nothing except that he is nineteen years old and is observing a convention with all propriety, as though it were founded on a law of nature, which in the end it might well prove to be. He is beginning to write poems which he prints on a wooden press, and he leaves them stuck like handbills in her door. She is pleasantly disturbed by

[9]Spanish: ballads. [10]Open air market in Mexico City.
[11]The popular name for Constitution Square in central Mexico City.
[12]Named for the revolutionary leader (1873–1913) who served as president of Mexico, 1911–1913.

the abstract, unhurried watchfulness of his black eyes which will in time turn easily towards another object. She tells herself that throwing the flower was a mistake, for she is twenty-two years old and knows better; but she refuses to regret it, and persuades herself that her negation of all external events as they occur is a sign that she is gradually perfecting herself in the stoicism she strives to cultivate against that disaster she fears, though she cannot name it.

She is not at home in the world. Every day she teaches children who remain strangers to her, though she loves their tender round hands and their charming opportunist savagery. She knocks at unfamiliar doors not knowing whether a friend or a stranger shall answer, and even if a known face emerges from the sour gloom of that unknown interior, still it is the face of a stranger. No matter what this stranger says to her, nor what her message to him, the very cells of her flesh reject knowledge and kinship in one monotonous word. No. No. No. She draws her strength from this one holy talismanic word which does not suffer her to be led into evil. Denying everything, she may walk anywhere in safety, she looks at everything without amazement.

No, repeats this firm unchanging voice of her blood; and she looks at Braggioni without amazement. He is a great man, he wishes to impress this simple girl who covers her great round breasts with thick dark cloth, and who hides long, invaluably beautiful legs under a heavy skirt. She is almost thin except for the incomprehensible fullness of her breasts, like a nursing mother's, and Braggioni, who considers himself a judge of women, speculates again on the puzzle of her notorious virginity, and takes the liberty of speech which she permits without a sign of modesty, indeed, without any sort of sign, which is disconcerting.

"You think you are so cold, Wait and see. You will surprise yourself some day! May I be there to advise you!" He stretches his eyelids at her, and his ill-humored cat's eyes waver in a separate glance for the two points of light marking the opposite ends of a smoothly drawn path between the swollen curve of her breasts. He is not put off by that blue serge, nor by her resolutely fixed gaze. There is all the time in the world. His cheeks are bellying with the wind of song. "O girl with the dark eyes," he sings, and reconsiders. "But yours are not dark. I can change all that. O girl with the green eyes, you have stolen my heart away!" then his mind wanders to the song, and Laura feels the weight of his attention being shifted elsewhere. Singing thus, he seems harmless, he is quite harmless, there is nothing to do but sit patiently and say "No," when the moment comes. She draws a full breath, and her mind wanders also, but not far. She dares not wander too far.

Not for nothing has Braggioni taken pains to be a good revolutionist and a professional lover of humanity. He will never die of it. He has the malice, the cleverness, the wickedness, the sharpness of wit, the hardness of heart, stipulated for loving the world profitably. *He will never die of it.* He will live to see himself kicked out from his feeding trough by other hungry world-saviors. Traditionally he must sing in spite of his life which drives him to bloodshed, he tells Laura, for his father was a Tuscany peasant who drifted to Yucatan and married a Maya woman: a woman of race, an aristocrat. They gave him the love and knowledge of music, thus: and under the rip of his thumbnail, the strings of the instrument complain like exposed nerves.

Once he was called Delgadito[13] by all the girls and married women who ran after him; he was so scrawny all his bones showed under his thin cotton clothing, and he could squeeze his emptiness to the very backbone with his two hands. He was a poet and the revolution was only a dream then; too many women loved him and sapped away his youth, and he could never find enough to eat anywhere, anywhere! Now he is a leader of men, crafty men who whisper in his ear, hungry men who wait for hours outside his office for a word with him, emaciated men with wild faces who waylay him at the street gate with a timid, "Comrade, let me tell you . . ." and they blow the foul breath from their empty stomachs in his face.

He is always sympathetic. He gives them handfuls of small coins from his own pocket, he promises them work, there will be demonstrations, they must join the unions and attend the meetings, above all they must be on the watch for spies. They are closer to him than his own brothers, without them he can do nothing—until tomorrow, comrade!

Until tomorrow. "They are stupid, they are lazy, they are treacherous, they would cut my throat for nothing," he says to Laura. He has good food and abundant drink, he hires an automobile and drives in the Paseo on Sunday morning, and enjoys plenty of sleep in a soft bed beside a wife who dares not disturb him; and he sits pampering his bones in easy billows of fat, singing to Laura, who knows and thinks these things about him. When he was fifteen, he tried to drown himself because he loved a girl, his first love, and she laughed at him. "A thousand women have paid for that," and his tight little mouth turns down at the corners. Now he perfumes his hair with Jockey Club, and confides to Laura: "One woman is really as good as another for me, in the dark. I prefer them all."

His wife organizes unions among the girls in the cigarette factories, and walks in picket lines, and even speaks at meetings in the evenings. But she cannot be brought to acknowledge the benefits of true liberty. "I tell her I must have my freedom, net. She does not understand my point of view." Laura has heard this many times. Braggioni scratches the guitar and meditates. "She is an instinctively virtuous woman, pure gold, no doubt of that. If she were not, I should lock her up, and she knows it."

His wife, who works so hard for the good of the factory girls, employs part of her leisure lying on the floor weeping because there are so many women in the world, and only one husband for her, and she never knows where nor when to look for him. He told her: "Unless you can learn to cry when I am not here, I must go away for good." That day he went away and took a room at the Hotel Madrid.

It is this month of separation for the sake of higher principles that has been spoiled not only for Mrs. Braggioni, whose sense of reality is beyond criticism, but for Laura, who feels herself bogged in a nightmare. Tonight Laura envies Mrs. Braggioni, who is alone, and free to weep as much as she pleases about a concrete wrong. Laura has just come from a visit to the prison, and she is waiting for tomorrow with a bitter anxiety as if tomorrow may not come, but time may be caught immovably in this hour, with herself

[13]Spanish: Skinny.

transfixed, Braggioni singing on forever, and Eugenio's body not yet discovered by the guard.

Braggioni says: "Are you going to sleep?" Almost before she can shake her head, he begins telling her about the May-day disturbances coming on in Morelia,[14] for the Catholics hold a festival in honor of the Blessed Virgin, and the Socialists celebrate their martyrs on that day. "There will be two independent processions, starting from either end of town, and they will march until they meet, and the rest depends . . ." He asks her to oil and load his pistols. Standing up, he unbuckles his ammunition belt, and spreads it laden across her knees. Laura sits with the shells slipping through the cleaning cloth dipped in oil, and he says again he cannot understand why she works so hard for the revolutionary idea unless she loves some man who is in it. "Are you not in love with someone?" "No," says Laura. "And no one is in love with you?" "No." "Then it is your own fault. No woman need go begging. Why, what is the matter with you? The legless beggar woman in the Alameda has a perfectly faithful lover. Did you know that?"

Laura peers down the pistol barrel and says nothing, but a long, slow faintness rises and subsides in her; Braggioni curves his swollen fingers around the throat of the guitar and softly smothers the music out of it, and when she hears him again he seems to have forgotten her, and is speaking in the hypnotic voice he uses when talking in small rooms to a listening, close-gathered crowd. Some day this world, now seemingly so composed and eternal, to the edges of every sea shall be merely a tangle of gaping trenches, of crashing walls and broken bodies. Everything must be torn from its accustomed place where it has rotted for centuries, hurled skyward and distributed, cast down again clean as rain, without separate identity. Nothing shall survive that the stiffened hands of poverty have created for the rich and no one shall be left alive except the elect spirits destined to procreate a new world cleansed of cruelty and injustice, ruled by benevolent anarchy: "Pistols are good, I love them, cannon are even better, but in the end I pin my faith to good dynamite," he concludes, and strokes the pistol lying in her hands. "Once I dreamed of destroying this city, in case it offered resistance to General Ortíz,[15] but it fell into his hands like an overripe pear."

He is made restless by his own words, rises and stands waiting. Laura holds up the belt to him: "Put that on, and go kill somebody in Morelia, and you will be happier," she says softly. The presence of death in the room makes her bold. "Today, I found Eugenio going into a stupor. He refused to allow me to call the prison doctor. He had taken all the tablets I brought him yesterday. He said he took them because he was bored."

"He is a fool, and his death is his own business," says Braggioni, fastening his belt carefully.

"I told him if he had waited only a little while longer, you would have got him set free," says Laura. "He said he did not want to wait."

"He is a fool and we are rid of him," says Braggioni, reaching for his hat.

[14]City west of Mexico City.

[15]Pascual Ortiz Rubio (1877–1963), revolutionary leader of the 1920s and president of Mexico (1930–1932).

He goes away. Laura knows his mood has changed, she will not see him any more for a while. He will send word when he needs her to go on errands into strange streets, to speak to the strange faces that will appear, like clay masks with the power of human speech, to mutter their thanks to Braggioni for his help. Now she is free, and she thinks, I must run while there is time. But she does not go.

Braggioni enters his own house where for a month his wife has spent many hours every night weeping and tangling her hair upon her pillow. She is weeping now, and she weeps more at the sight of him, the cause of all her sorrows. He looks about the room. Nothing is changed, the smells are good and familiar, he is well acquainted with the woman who comes toward him with no reproach except grief on her face. He says to her tenderly: "You are so good, please don't cry any more, you dear good creature." She says, "Are you tired, my angel? Sit here and I will wash your feet." She brings a bowl of water, and kneeling, unlaces his shoes, and when from her knees she raises her sad eyes under her blackened lids, he is sorry for everything, and bursts into tears. "Ah, yes, I am hungry, I am tired, let us eat something together," he says, between sobs. His wife leans her head on his arm and says, "Forgive me!" and this time he is refreshed by the solemn, endless rain of her tears.

Laura takes off her serge dress and puts on a white linen nightgown and goes to bed. She turns her head a little to one side, and lying still, reminds herself that it is time to sleep. Numbers tick in her brain like little clocks, soundless doors close of themselves around her. If you would sleep, you must not remember anything, the children will say tomorrow, good morning, my teacher, the poor prisoners who come every day bringing flowers to their jailor. 1-2-3-4-5—it is monstrous to confuse love with revolution, night with day, life with death—ah, Eugenio!

The tolling of the midnight bell is a signal, but what does it mean? Get up, Laura, and follow me: come out of your sleep, out of your bed, out of this strange house. What are you doing in this house? Without a word, without fear she rose and reached for Eugenio's hand, but he eluded her with a sharp, sly smile and drifted away. This is not all, you shall see—Murderer, he said, follow me, I will show you a new country, but it is far away and we must hurry. No, said Laura, not unless you take my hand, no; and she clung first to the stair rail, and then to the topmost branch of the Judas tree that bent down slowly and set her upon the earth, and then to the rocky ledge of a cliff, and then to the jagged wave of a sea that was not water but a desert of crumbling stone. Where are you taking me, she asked in wonder but without fear. To death, and it is a long way off, and we must hurry, said Eugenio. No, said Laura, not unless you take my hand. Then eat these flowers, poor prisoner, said Eugenio in a voice of pity, take and eat: and from the Judas tree he stripped the warm bleeding flowers, and held them to her lips. She saw that his hand was fleshless, a cluster of small white petrified branches, and his eye sockets were without light, but she ate the flowers greedily for they satisfied both hunger and thirst. Murderer! said Eugenio, and Cannibal! This is my body and my blood. Laura cried No! and at the sound of her own voice, she awoke trembling, and was afraid to sleep again.

1930

The Literature of the Twentieth Century (1945 to Present)

The United States emerged from World War II as the wealthiest and most powerful nation in the world, and was on its way to such technological achievements as the conquest of space, the harnessing of nuclear energy, a leading role in computer technology, and participation in the mapping of human genetic structures. It would emerge from the twentieth century as the lone dominant military and economic power on the planet. But along the way, it would also fight two unsuccessful wars in small Asian countries and suffer major challenges to its democratic principles—in the Congressional anti-Communism hearings of the 1950s, the Civil Rights and anti-war movements of the 1960s, the impeachment and resignation of a president in the 1970s, the Iran-Contra debacle of the 1980s, the impeachment of another president (in an alleged-sex-and-perjury scandal) in the 1990s, and a highly controversial outcome to the presidential election of 2000. Equally serious, by the turn of the century, the gap between rich and poor in the United States would have grown wider than ever, and the percentage of the American population held in prisons would be among the highest in the world.

Conformity and Dissent

In many ways, World War II was the catalyst for social and economic change that would take place in the decades following it. After the war, the United States found itself with a tremendously expanded industrial production capacity and newly opened markets around the world. Its workforce was changing dramatically due to the GI Bill and due to the fact that women and African Americans experienced increased economic mobility in wartime industry and the military. The U.S. government, supported for the most part by mass culture, moved to refocus American energy toward what came to be known as the Cold War. Indeed, the 1950s are often remembered as a time of conformity, corporatism, and vigilant resistance to Soviet (and also Chinese) Communism—with President Dwight Eisenhower, who had been the commander of Allied forces during World War II, as emblem of the military might, material prosperity, and homogeneity of the era. On the other hand, there were indications, such as Senator Joseph McCarthy's zealous anti-Communist campaign in the early 1950s, that revealed the uneasiness that lurked just beneath the surface. The 1950s were a time of bomb shelters, suburbs, and the "man in the gray flannel suit" (from the title of a best-selling 1955 novel by Sloan Wilson and successful 1956 movie starring Gregory Peck)—that is, the individual caught up in the drive for material success, but unsure that the hoped-for success is really worth the price. And President Eisenhower himself, in a farewell speech at the end of his second four-year term, warned, "In the councils of government, we must guard against the acquisition of unwarranted influence, whether sought or unsought, by the military-industrial complex. The potential for the disastrous rise of misplaced power exists and will persist." But the 1950s were also the decade of Beat poetry and of the desegregation movement that led to the Supreme Court's *Brown v. Board of Education* decision, the Montgomery bus boycott, and the other civil rights landmarks that were to follow.

Very little was muted about the social and political upheaval of the 1960s, a period when civil rights, black power, women's rights, the anti-war movement, and gay rights all became part of the national consciousness. The list of landmark events of the 1960s is long and deeply inscribed on the national consciousness, and it marks both tremendous hope and tremendous despair. The decade that began with students "sitting in" (that is, nonviolently protesting racial segregation) at a Woolworth's lunch counter in Greensboro, North Carolina, ended with astronauts walking on the moon. The Cold War that had begun in the 1950s was escalated in the 1960s with the Bay of Pigs (an unsuccessful invasion of Cuba sponsored by the United States), the Cuban Missile Crisis (a nearly catastrophic showdown between the United States and the Soviet Union), and the Vietnam War. The promise of the 1963 march on Washington that culminated in Martin Luther King's "I Have a Dream" speech was offset by the assassinations of Medgar Evers, John Kennedy, Robert Kennedy, Malcolm X, and King himself. Civil rights metamorphosed into black power, and American cities like Detroit, Chicago, Newark, and Los Angeles burned in rebellion. Radical groups like the Black Panthers and the Weather Underground emphasized self-determination, but their efforts were marred by violent acts that inspired retaliatory violence in return. The National Organization for Women was founded in 1966, and the Stonewall riots in New York City brought the gay rights movement into the open in 1969. Environmentalism, protests against the Vietnam War, and the various liberation movements current at the time brought huge numbers of young people to protest marches that made the more conservative elements in American society increasingly nervous. The energy and spirit that coalesced around the various social protest movements accelerated events at a pace that led inevitably to backlash—culminating in the national trauma experienced when Ohio National Guardsmen shot to death four students participating in an anti-war protest and wounded thirteen others at Kent State University in May 1970.

The culture and rhetoric of the 1960s still inform many segments of U.S. society today, but in the aftermath it seemed that the 1960s idealism had met with more failure than success. President Richard Nixon's resignation and the spluttering end of the Vietnam War were symbolic victories for liberalizing forces that by the mid-1970s had otherwise been tamed or suppressed. Leaders of 1960s liberation movements became mainstream politicians, academics, or even stockbrokers, and the radical political energy that created academic programs like Women's Studies or Ethnic Studies proved less disruptive once it was safely confined within the walls of U.S. universities. The Watergate scandal that ended the Nixon presidency is often described as a defining moment of the 1970s. But a still more significant event, in the longer term, was the de-industrialization that began in the United States in the 1970s, leading to a globalization of economic arrangements and an increased concentration of wealth in the upper regions of society that would characterize the rest of the century.

Literature in the Postmodern Era

Writers in the years following World War II, like those of the "Lost Generation" following World War I, were conscious of standing at the beginning of a new era. The rumblings beneath the surface of social conformity were clearly reflected in the new literature of the 1950s. While the stories and poems that filled the pages between ads for Maytags and Fords in the *New Yorker* or *Saturday Evening Post* often underscored the idea of a uniform upper-middle-class America, works that expressed the tension between the mass culture and individual experience were also emerging. In the 1940s, modernist writers had published some of their most important work (Eliot's *Four Quartets,* Pound's *Pisan Cantos,* Stevens's *Notes Toward a Supreme Fiction,* and the first two books of Williams's *Paterson*), which in some sense signaled the end of a literary era but also helped provide inspiration for the writers of the 1950s. J. D. Salinger's *The Catcher in the Rye,* Saul Bellow's *The Adventures of Augie March,* and Ralph Ellison's *Invisible Man* all showed modernist strains, but at the same time bore distinctive markings as products of post-war America. In 1955 an epoch-defining poetry event in San Francisco, billed as *6 Poets at 6 Gallery,* brought together Beat poet Allen Ginsberg (giving the first public reading of his poem "Howl"), the then little-known Gary Snyder, and four other new-generation poets, with their friend novelist Jack Kerouac in the audience, to read and celebrate a sort of poetry that departed as radically from modernism as modernism itself had departed decades earlier from pre-WWI poetry. This event and Ginsberg's other wide-ranging public recitations of the contradictions and vulgarities of America irrevocably changed the poetic landscape, influencing a whole generation of writers—even contributing to a loosening of the verse and sharpening of the political consciousness of a more established writer like Robert Lowell. Meanwhile, Kerouac celebrated unconventional existence in *On the Road* (1957) and other novels, and Snyder helped set the stage for the 1960s youth rebellion with his treatments of Native American culture (as in "The Berry Feast," the poem he read in *6 Poets at 6 Gallery*), Oriental philosophy, and environmental themes.

The Beat writers were deeply influenced by jazz and often appropriated African American idioms in their work. African American literature flourished in the 1950s, with Ellison's *Invisible Man,* James Baldwin's *Go Tell It on the Mountain* and *Giovanni's Room,* and Gwendolyn Brooks's influential *Maud Martha.* These works continued in the strong tradition of African American literature of the Harlem Renaissance and Richard Wright's novels such as *Native Son* (1940). They also continued the tradition of social protest already present in those previous works, but now made more dramatically visible.

The literature of the 1960s was as varied as the events. Many American prose writers turned to experimental techniques, absurd humor, and mocking examination of the irrational and disordered. The stories of writers like John Cheever and Donald Barthelme reinvigorated the short story form and did much to establish the norms for short fiction of the following decades. Tom Wolfe helped to define a "New Journalism." African American writers made as big an impact on mainstream American culture as they had during the Harlem Renaissance. Particularly notable as a landmark in the post-WWII development of African American literature was the publication of *Black Fire: An Anthology of Afro-American Writing,* edited by LeRoi Jones (later known as Amiri Baraka) and

Larry Neal and representative of the Black Arts Movement (BAM). The works of Baldwin, Baraka, and Nikki Giovanni, among many others, were instrumental in defining and representing the civil rights and black power movements. Baldwin's *The Fire Next Time* brought a clear-eyed and uncompromising vision of what he called "the racial nightmare" to white America. And white female writers like Betty Friedan, Sylvia Plath, Mary McCarthy, and Anne Sexton laid much of the groundwork for the directions that white, middle-class feminism would take in the 1970s and 1980s.

Popular culture, especially popular music, took on new significance in the 1960s. The music of Motown, the Beatles, Bob Dylan, Joan Baez, the Rolling Stones, Janis Joplin, and San Francisco bands like the Grateful Dead, along with specific performances at places like Newport, Woodstock, and Altamont, helped define and support alternative culture. At the same time, the mass commercial packaging of forms like rhythm-and-blues and rock-and-roll, forms that had their roots in African American traditions, showed how readily popular culture could be appropriated into big business. As for popular literature, romance novels and other mass-consumption literature continued to thrive despite the rise of television and the strong competition of motion pictures as rival forms of popular entertainment. During the Depression of the 1930s the profitable mass market for literature had temporarily declined, but after World War II it expanded enormously with the growth of the population, the increase of wealth and education, the expansion of mass-distribution book clubs, and the technical advances in printing that made possible the publication of vast numbers of inexpensive paperbacks.

Reconfiguring the Literary Canon

The literary response to this time of political, economic, and literary-critical retrenchment was wide-ranging. Alongside the importation of European deconstructive and post-structuralist literary theory, a substantial postmodern American literature emerged. John Barth, Thomas Pynchon (whose massive *Gravity's Rainbow* quickly became a cult phenomenon), and Don DeLillo wrote novels grounded in linguistic games, the absurd, and the surreal. Authors like Kurt Vonnegut (*Slaughterhouse-Five*) and Joseph Heller (*Catch-22*) created diffident, alienated "anti-heroes" trapped in situations that were deeply traumatic yet seemed utterly meaningless. Meanwhile, the institutionalization of gender and ethnic politics in universities opened up literary canons to additional groups of writers that had previously been neglected or excluded. Black women writers like Alice Walker, Gloria Naylor, Paule Marshall, Toni Morrison, and Toni Cade Bambara brought vitality and cultural richness to mainstream publishing, and broadened an African American literary tradition that had previously been dominated by men. The Latino literature that emerged out of political movements, like Luis Valdez's *El Teatro Campesino,* found nourishment in both the university and small presses like *Quinto Sol.* The 1970s saw the publication of many important Latino works—to which in the succeeding decades an increasingly rich fund of Latina literature (that is, literature written by women from Spanish-speaking countries) was added.

Native tribes in the United States termed the 1950s "the termination era," a period when the federal government seemed to be moving in the direction of terminating all funding to tribes. The termination era resulted in increased tribal poverty, relocation of Indians from reservations to cities, and increases in Native infant mortality rates. This experience, along with longstanding tribal traditions and cultures, helped to shape the Native American literature that flourished in the late twentieth century. Among many others, N. Scott Momaday, James Welch, Louise Erdrich, Leslie Marmon Silko, Sherman Alexie, Simon Ortiz, Gerald Vizenor, and Joy Harjo established a new cultural prominence for Native American literature and an interest in their contemporary cultures.

U.S. writers of the 1970s, 1980s, and 1990s had more and more commerce with popular culture, and the breakneck speed of late-twentieth-century technological innovation helped to blur the lines between the high and the low, the popular and the serious, the literary and the nonliterary. What had previously been considered "nonliterary" cultural products challenged the traditional dominance of print literature as bearer of the era's cultural legacy. Television, film, the Internet, and digital technology, which enable the creation of a previously unimagined range of representational or abstract images, began to rearrange ideas about poetry, narrative, and the nature of art. As the twentieth century became the twenty-first, the battle for production, control, and distribution of images was increasingly recognized as a powerful social and political determinant.

As a result, "literature," as it has traditionally been defined, now shares the stage with a growing variety of textual productions. Some critics condemn what they view as a "decentering" of literature—as students of literature now pursue curricula that include studies in "poststructuralist" literary theory, less-known works by writers of color, and the products of filmmakers like Spike Lee alongside more traditional fare like Shakespeare's *Hamlet* and Melville's *Moby-Dick.* Other critics view studying and considering literature in conjunction with many different kinds of texts an exciting development. They contend that writers have always been exposed to and influenced by a range of textual productions, including historical accounts, legends, music, and illustrations, and that to study literary texts while also studying other forms of cultural textual production is to draw closer to, not farther from, the writers and concerns of the past.

The Study of Literature in the Twenty-First Century

Literature, regardless of its form, offers urgent messages from the past. By studying a broad cross-section of American literature and literary forms, both past and present, we discover links among the concerns of different time periods and gain new perspectives on how American women and men of the past have struggled with the same issues that we struggle with today. For instance, recurrent concerns with alienation and seeming meaninglessness—which troubled the naturalists of the late nineteenth century and then resurfaced with the "Lost Generation" after World War I, again with the Beats in the 1950s, and yet again with the postmodernists of the late 1960s and early 1970s—seem still a fresh topic in a twenty-first-century world troubled by runaway technology and a seemingly never-ending stream of crises of values. In the other direction, the reliance on natural harmony by Emerson and Thoreau in the early nineteenth century resonates again in the environmental concerns voiced in poetry produced in the late twentieth century by poets like Gary Snyder. Also, long before contemporary poets were self-publishing, nineteenth-century poet Emily Dickinson was engaged in home-based literary production so that she could avoid editors who wanted to alter the artistic integrity of her poems. Likewise, more than a century before musicians began recording on independent labels to escape corporate control of their work, escaped slave Frederick Douglass began his own newspaper so that no one else could control what writing subjects he chose and how he chose to write about them. And in the late nineteenth and early twentieth centuries, activist Charlotte Perkins Gilman began to publish her own literary journal so that she, too, would have artistic and political control of her work.

By the year 2006, the population of the United States had risen to approximately 300,000,000. Three out of every four Americans now live in large urban centers. They own more than 200,000,000 motor vehicles, enough to hold the entire population of Europe—in the front seats. They travel on more than 4,000,000 miles of roads and streets; more land in the United States is now paved than remains in virgin wilderness. The United States remains one of the most socially diverse countries in the world—a land where more than 27 million foreign-born men and women now live. In America, more than 300 identifiable dialects and languages are spoken, and 250 different religious denominations coexist. At the same time, the nation continues to struggle with unresolved issues related to environmental threats, questions of economic and social justice, and the need to find effective means to live in harmony with other cultures around the world. Within the context of such societal challenges, American writers continue to explore their own lives and their own visions of the land and its people, confronting the questions of American civilization and forming their experiences into new literature.

You can find more general resources about this period on our Companion Website™ at <www.prenhall.com/mcmichael>.

International Affairs, Exploration, Settlement, and Science	Politics and Government	Society and Culture
1945 May, Germany surrenders **1945** August, Atomic bombs dropped on Hiroshima and Nagasaki. Japan surrenders	**1945** FDR dies. Harry S. Truman becomes president **1945** Rationing of shoes, butter, and tires ends	**1945** Tennessee Williams's *The Glass Menagerie* opens in New York City
	1946 Inflation rate rises to 18.2 percent	
		1947 Jackie Robinson joins the Brooklyn Dodgers, breaking baseball's color line
1948 Transistor invented **1948** Israel gains independence	**1948** President Truman ends segregation in the U.S. armed services	**1948** Kinsey report *Sexual Behavior in the Human Male* published **1948** T.S. Eliot wins Nobel Prize for literature. Ezra Pound publishes the*Pisan Cantos*
1949 Chinese communists proclaim People's Republic of China **1949** Apartheid established in South Africa		**1949** William Faulkner wins Nobel Prize for literature
1950 National Census: population 150,697,361 **1950–1953** Korean War	**1950** Senator Joseph McCarthy begins his attacks on Communism in government	**1950** Gwendolyn Brooks, first African American awarded a Pulitzer for book of poetry, *Annie Allen* **1951** Carson McCullers publishes *Ballad of the Sad Café*
	1952 Eisenhower elected president. Reelected 1956	
1953 Mount Everest climbed **1953** Francis Crich and James Watson discover DNA's structure, the double helix	**1953** Department of Health, Education, and Welfare established	
	1954 U.S. Supreme Court rules school segregation unconstitutional	**1954** Elvis Presley releases first record on Sun label. Rock music begins **1954** Ernest Hemingway wins Nobel Prize for literature
1955 First microwave oven for consumer public produced		
1956 First contraceptive pill marketed **1956–1959** Cuban civil war. Victory for Castro forces		**1956** Rev. Martin Luther King, Jr., leads Montgomery, Alabama, bus boycott **1956** Grace Metalious publishes *Peyton Place*

International Affairs, Exploration, Settlement, and Science

1957 Russia successfully launches "Sputnik," first man-made satellite

1961 Berlin Wall seals Iron Curtain

1961 Soviet cosmonaut first man to orbit earth

1962 Russian missiles withdrawn from Cuba after America threatens action

1962 Second Vatican council meets in Rome's St. Peter's Basilica

1967 Six-Day War between Israel and Arab nations

1967 Christian Bernard performs first human heart transplant

1968 *Apollo 8* orbits the moon

1969 World population estimated at 3.5 billion

1969 U.S. astronauts land on the moon

1970 U.S. population 203,211,926

1971 *Mariner 9* photographs Mars

1971 First computer microchips developed by Intel scientists

Politics and Government

1957 Civil Rights Act

1958–1959 Alaska and Hawaii become states

1960 John F. Kennedy elected president

1963 John F. Kennedy assassinated. Lyndon B. Johnson becomes president

1965–1979 Annual inflation rate rises from 2% to 13%

1967 Thurgood Marshall, U.S. solicitor general, appointed to the Supreme Court by President Johnson

1968 Robert Kennedy and Rev. Martin Luther King, Jr., assassinated

1968 Richard M. Nixon elected 37th president. Reelected 1972

1969 First U.S. troops withdrawn from Vietnam. Anti–Vietnam War demonstrations increase

1969–1979 Average annual household income rises from $8,000 to $16,000

1971 26th Amendment gives 18-year-olds the vote

1971–1979 Price of gold rises from $40 to $340 per ounce

Society and Culture

1960 Presidential debates appear on TV

1962 John Steinbeck wins Nobel Prize for literature

1964 Beatles and Rolling Stones release their first albums

1965 Hippie phenomenon begins in San Francisco

1968 78 million TV sets in the U.S.

1969 Pants suits become stylish for women

1969 The Woodstock Festival

1969 Stonewall riots in Greenwich Village, New York City

1971 *Fiddler on the Roof* becomes longest-running musical in Broadway history

International Affairs, Exploration, Settlement, and Science	Politics and Government	Society and Culture
	1971 Supreme Court upholds decision requiring the busing of schoolchildren for racial balance	
	1972 Watergate scandal emerges **1972** U.S. military conscription ends	**1972** First issue of *Ms.* magazine published
1973 Gene-splicing first achieved **1973** OPEC quintuples oil prices	**1973** Spiro Agnew resigns as vice president **1973** *Roe v. Wade* legalizes abortion **1974** July, U.S. House of Representatives recommends impeachment of President Nixon. August, Nixon resigns	
1975 Last U.S. forces withdraw from Vietnam **1975** World population exceeds 4 billion **1976** Supersonic jet transport between U.S. and Europe—4 hours **1976** Mao Tse-tung, Chairman of Chinese Communist party, dies	**1976** Jimmy Carter elected president	**1976** Saul Bellow wins Nobel Prize for literature **1976** U.S. celebrates Bicentennial
	1977 President Carter pardons draft resisters	**1977** *Star Wars* becomes biggest box office draw to date
1978 Three American balloonists make first successful Atlantic crossing **1978** Over 900 die in mass suicide in Guyana religious commune **1979** Mob seizes U.S. Embassy in Iran	**1978** Panama Canal Treaty gives control of canal to Panama in 1999 **1979** U.S. and China establish full diplomatic relations **1979** OPEC nations continue to raise oil prices. Gas shortage and inflation strike U.S.	**1978** Isaac Bashevi Singer wins Nobel Prize for literature **1978** Life expectancy in U.S. reaches 69.6 years for men, 77.2 years for women
1980 National Census: population 226,545,805 **1980** Mt. St. Helens volcano eruption kills thirty-four	**1980** Ronald Reagan elected president. Reelected 1984	**1980** TV show *Dallas* claims 300,000,000 viewers worldwide
1981 Iran releases U.S. hostages **1981** AIDS virus first diagnosed	**1981** Sandra Day O'Connor made first woman Justice of U.S. Supreme Court	**1981** Median U.S. family income $22,388

International Affairs, Exploration, Settlement, and Science	Politics and Government	Society and Culture
1982 Britain defeats Argentina in 74-day Falklands war **1982** First successful artificial heart implant		**1982–1983** U.S. households average 6 hours 55 minutes TV-watching per day **1982** Michael Jackson's *Thriller* becomes best-selling music album in history
1983 U.S. invades island of Grenada	**1983** U.S. Supreme Court declares anti-abortion laws unconstitutional	**1983** Last episode of *M*A*S*H* on CBS draws 121,624,000 viewers **1983** Tennessee Williams dies
	1984 President Reagan proposes budget with record deficit of $180 billion **1984** Geraldine Ferraro nominated by Democrats to run for vice presidency	
1985 Mikhail Gorbachev named leader of U.S.S.R.; proclaims "glasnost"	**1985** U.S. becomes debtor nation	**1985** The *New Yorker* magazine sold for $142 million **1985** Crack cocaine first appears in U.S.
1986 Light plane *Voyager* flies nonstop around the world **1986** U.S. warplanes attack Libya **1986** Nuclear accident at Chernobyl power plant in the Soviet Union	**1986** Ivan Boesky fined $100 million for insider trading on Wall Street	
	1987 U.S. celebrates 200-year anniversary of the Constitution **1987** President Reagan submits first U.S. trillion-dollar budget **1988** George H. W. Bush elected president **1988** U.S. Supreme Court rules censorship of student publications by school officials is legal	**1987** TV evangelists' sex and money scandals exposed
1989 Chinese army crushes student rally in Beijing's Tiananmen Square **1989** Popular uprisings overthrow iron-curtain governments; Cold War ends **1989** U.S. invades Panama		**1989** *E.T.*, all-time top money-making movie, earns $228,618,939 **1989–1990** Honda Accord is best-selling car in U.S.

International Affairs, Exploration, Settlement, and Science

1990 U.S. population 249,632,692
1990 Nelson Mandela freed from prison after 27 years
1991 U.S.S.R. collapses into Commonwealth of Independent States
1991 UN forces attack Iraq, liberate Kuwait
1991 World Wide Web launched by British scientist Tim Berners-Lee
1992 Earth Summit, environmental conference, meets in Rio de Janeiro, Brazil
1992 U.S. sends peace-keeping troops to Somalia
1993 Medical research identifies genes linked to lethal diseases
1993 U.S. and Russia sign treaty to reduce nuclear arms
1995–1996 U.S. sends peacekeeping troops to Yugoslavia
1997 British Colony of Hong Kong returned to Chinese rule
1997 First mammal (Dolly, a sheep) successfully cloned
1998 Emission limits set at Global Warming summit
1998 FDA approves virility drug, Viagra
1999 U.S. transfers full control of Panama Canal to Panama
1999 Estimated world population 6 billion

Politics and Government

1990 U.S. Supreme Court upholds right to burn U.S. flag
1991 $78 billion for S&L bailout approved
1992 U.S. National debt exceeds $3 trillion
1993 Federal forces besiege Branch Davidian religious cult in Texas. 72 die
1995 Republicans gain control of Congress, promise to "downsize" government
1995 Federal budget bill fails to pass. U.S. government temporarily shut down
1996 President signs into law sweeping new telecommunications bill
1998 U.S. House of Representatives impeaches President Clinton for "high crimes and misdemeanors"
1999 Following trial by U.S. Senate, President Clinton is acquitted

Society and Culture

1990 *Chorus Line,* longest-running Broadway show, closes after 6,317 performances
1992 U.S. households with TVs, 98.2%; with refrigerators, 97.2%
1992 Riots in Los Angeles, 52 dead, damage exceeds $1 billion
1993 Toni Morrison wins Nobel Prize for literature
1993 Average salary for major-league baseball player rises to $1,076,089
1995 O.J. Simpson found not guilty in news media "Trial of the Century"
1995 Terrorists blow up Federal Building in Oklahoma City. 169 killed
1995 Million Man March in Washington, D.C.
1998 Median age of Americans rises to 35 years, highest ever
1998 Baseball star Mark McGuire hits a record 70 homeruns
1999 Mexican drug traffic declared worst criminal threat to U.S. in last half century

International Affairs, Exploration, Settlement, and Science	Politics and Government	Society and Culture
1999 Global anxieties about "Y2K" technology collapse		**1999** Stock market reaches all-time high. Dow Jones average exceeds 11,000 **1999** High school shooting in Columbine, Colorado leaves 15 dead **1999** Harry Potter becomes the most popular children's literature series and a marketing phenomenon **1999** Ralph Ellison's long awaited second novel, *Juneteenth,* published posthumously
2000 Genome project unlocks the mystery of the human blueprint **2000** Dot.com companies collapse and stock market tumbles **2001** Slobodan Milosevic, former Yugoslav president, becomes first head of state tried as war criminal in international court **2001** Terrorist attack on NYC's World Trade Center. U.S. attacks Afghanistan in its war on terrorism	**2000** Supreme Court, in a 5–4 ruling, puts George W. Bush in the White House	**2000** Third wave feminism redefines feminist activism and identity **2000** Tiger Woods is youngest ever Grand Slam golf winner **2001** V. S. Naipaul, from Trinidad, wins the Nobel Prize
2002 Euro banknote becomes official currency of 12 European Union nations	**2002** Enron scandal exposes corporate corruption	**2002** Denzel Washington and Halle Berry win best actor and best actress Oscars—the first time two African Americans win in the same year **2002** New Jersey legislators call for the resignation of Amiri Baraka as poet laureate of New Jersey following his poem "They Blew Up America" in response to the events of September 11, 2001
2003 U.S. Shuttle disaster kills all crew members **2003** U.S. invades Iraq without United Nations approval. Largest ever international peace movement protests war		

W. E. B. Du Bois	1868–1963
Willa Cather	1873–1947
Robert Frost	1874–1963
Gertrude Stein	1874–1946
Susan Glaspell	1876–1948
Wallace Stevens	1879–1955
William Carlos Williams	1883–1963
Ezra Pound	1885–1972
Robinson Jeffers	1887–1962
Marianne Moore	1887–1972
T. S. Eliot	1888–1965
Eugene O'Neill	1888–1953
Katherine Anne Porter	1890–1980
Zora Neale Hurston	1891–1960
E. E. Cummings	1894–1962
Jean Toomer	1894–1967
John Dos Passos	1896–1970
William Faulkner	1897–1962
Ernest Hemingway	1899–1961
Langston Hughes	1902–1967
John Steinbeck	1902–1968
Countée Cullen	1903–1946
Ann Petry	1908–1997
Theodore Roethke	1908–1963
Richard Wright	1908–1960
Eudora Welty	1909–2001
Elizabeth Bishop	1911–1979
Tennessee Williams	1911–1983
Tillie Olsen	1913–
Ralph Ellison	1914–1994
Randall Jarrell	1914–1965
Bernard Malamud	1914–1986
Saul Bellow	1915–2005
Shirley Jackson	1916–1965
Robert Lowell	1917–1977
Richard Wilbur	1921–
Kurt Vonnegut	1922–
James Dickey	1923–1997
Joseph Heller	1923–1999
Denise Levertov	1923–1997
James Baldwin	1924–1987
Flannery O'Connor	1925–1964
William Styron	1925–
A. R. Ammons	1926–2001
Allen Ginsberg	1926–1997
W. S. Merwin	1927–
Edward Albee	1928–
Anne Sexton	1928–1974
Martin Luther King, Jr.	1929–1968
Adrienne Rich	1929–

Gary Synder	1930–
Toni Morrison	1931–
Sylvia Plath	1932–1963
John Updike	1932–
Philip Roth	1933–
Amiri Baraka	1934–
N. Scott Momaday	1934–
Sonia Sanchez	1934–
Tomás Rivera	1935–1984
Don DeLillo	1936–
June Jordan	1936–2002
Tina Howe	1937–
Thomas Pynchon	1937–
Raymond Carver	1938–1988
Joyce Carol Oates	1938–
Toni Cade Bambara	1939–1995
Maxine Hong Kingston	1940–
Bobbie Ann Mason	1940–
James Welch	1940–2003
Frederick Busch	1941–2006
Billy Collins	1941–
Simon Ortiz	1941–
Gloria Anzaldúa	1942–2004
James Alan McPherson	1943–
Alice Walker	1944–
August Wilson	1945–2005
Tim O'Brien	1946–
Leslie Marmon Silko	1948–
Jamaica Kincaid	1949–
David Bradley	1950–
Gloria Naylor	1950–
Rita Dove	1952–
Amy Tan	1952–
Louise Erdrich	1954–
Sherman Alexie	1966–

Reading the Historical Context

With its *Brown vs. Board of Education* decision in 1954, the Supreme Court reversed the United States' long history of legalized racial discrimination. Declaring that public schools could no longer legally be segregated on the basis of race, the decision set in motion a period of turbulent change as the Southern states, and, to a lesser but nonetheless often traumatic degree, the Northern states as well, had to come to terms with their responsibilities to their African American citizenry as equal partners in American democracy. The civil rights movement of the 1950s and 1960s saw both peaceful protests and violent confrontations as black leaders like Martin Luther King pressed hard against the status quo that was so comfortable for the empowered and so demoralizing to the disenfranchised.

On the heels of the civil rights movement came an equally powerful and disruptive social ferment in the form of the anti-war movement as protesters, especially young people, spoke out against what they saw as the injustice and even irrationality of the Vietnam War. And joining in the general rise of social protest were a new energizing of the movement for women's rights, a new level of interest in the rights of Native Americans, and a newly visible push for equal treatment of homosexual Americans. The following are three documents of very different sorts—a speech, a chapter from a novel, and a transcription of a myth from an oral culture—that relate to these foci of interest in sectors of the American population that saw themselves as somehow excluded from the power structure of the late-twentieth-century United States.

Martin Luther King, Jr. 1929–1968

As the Civil Rights Movement gained momentum in the late 1950s, the need for an effective spokesman and symbol for the movement's principles was satisfied by the emergence of Dr. Martin Luther King, Jr., a Baptist preacher who advocated a nonviolent resistance much like that practiced by Mohandas Gandhi (1869–1948) in his leadership of the movement for Indian independence directed against Great Britain in the 1930s and 1940s. King rose to prominence as leader of the Montgomery, Alabama Bus Boycott in 1956. That boycott was soon validated by a Supreme Court decision outlawing forced segregation of public transportation—a decision that, following so soon after Brown vs. Board of Education, *made it clear that the days of Jim Crow laws were numbered. Perhaps the highest moment of the civil rights movement occurred in August 1963 with the* March on Washington for Jobs and Freedom, *in which King played a major role. On August 28 King, from the steps of the Lincoln Memorial, delivered what has come to be known as the "I Have a Dream" speech, a masterpiece of oratory that galvanized the 200,000 plus participants in the* March on Washington *and perhaps contributed to the passage of the landmark Civil Rights Act of 1964, which not only brought the era of "Jim Crow" officially to an end but also included prohibitions against discrimination on the basis of sex and thus was important in the long run for women's rights as well as the rights of racial minorities. King himself continued to campaign for the rights of African Americans and for the downtrodden in general until he was assassinated by a white racist in Memphis, Tennessee, on April 4, 1968.*

TEXT: *The Peaceful Warrior,* 1968.

I HAVE A DREAM

Five score years ago, a great American, in whose symbolic shadow we stand, signed the Emancipation Proclamation.[1] This momentous decree came as a great beacon light of hope to millions of Negro slaves who had been seared in the flames of withering injustice. It came as a joyous daybreak to end the long night of captivity.[2] But one hundred years later, we must face the tragic fact that the Negro is still not free.

One hundred years later, the life of the Negro is still sadly crippled by the manacles of segregation and the chains of discrimination. One hundred years later, the Negro lives on a lonely island of poverty in the midst of a vast ocean of material prosperity. One hundred years later, the Negro is still languishing in the corners of American society and finds himself an exile in his own land.

So we have come here today to dramatize an appalling condition. In a sense we have come to our nation's capital to cash a check. When the architects of our republic wrote the magnificent words of the Constitution and the Declaration of Independence, they were signing a promissory note to which every American was to fall heir.

This note was a promise that all men would be guaranteed the inalienable rights of life, liberty, and the pursuit of happiness. It is obvious today that America has defaulted on this promissory note insofar as her citizens of color are concerned. Instead of honoring this sacred obligation, America has given the Negro people a bad check which has come back marked "insufficient funds." But we refuse to believe that the bank of justice is bankrupt. We refuse to believe that there are insufficient funds in the great vaults of opportunity of this nation.

So we have come to cash this check—a check that will give us upon demand the riches of freedom and the security of justice. We have also come to this hallowed spot to remind America of the fierce urgency of now. This is no time to engage in the luxury of cooling off or to take the tranquilizing drug of gradualism. Now is the time to rise from the dark and desolate valley of segregation to the sunlit path of racial justice.[3] Now is the time to open the doors of opportunity to all of God's children. Now is the time to lift our nation from the quicksands of racial injustice to the solid rock of brotherhood.[4]

[1]Abraham Lincoln (1809–1865), who issued the Emancipation Proclamation, freeing slaves in the seceding states, on January 1, 1863. King's opening echoes the beginning of Lincoln's Gettysburg Address (November 19, 1863): "Four score and seven years ago . . ."

[2]Cf. Psalm 30:5: "For his anger endureth but a moment; in his favor is life: weeping may endure for a night, but joy cometh in the morning."

[3]Cf. Psalms 23:4: "Yea, though I walk through the valley of the shadow of death, I will fear no evil."

[4]An allusion to Christ's parable comparing a house built on sand to a house built on rock (Luke 6:46–49 and Matthew 7:24–27).

It would be fatal for the nation to overlook the urgency of the moment and to underestimate the determination of the Negro. This sweltering summer of the Negro's legitimate discontent[5] will not pass until there is an invigorating autumn of freedom and equality. Nineteen sixty-three is not an end, but a beginning. Those who hope that the Negro needed to blow off steam and will now be content will have a rude awakening if the nation returns to business as usual. There will be neither rest nor tranquility in America until the Negro is granted his citizenship rights.

The whirlwinds of revolt will continue to shake the foundations of our nation until the bright day of justice emerges. But there is something that I must say to my people who stand on the warm threshold which leads into the palace of justice. In the process of gaining our rightful place we must not be guilty of wrongful deeds. Let us not seek to satisfy our thirst for freedom by drinking from the cup of bitterness and hatred.

We must forever conduct our struggle on the high plane of dignity and discipline. We must not allow our creative protest to degenerate into physical violence. Again and again we must rise to the majestic heights of meeting physical force with soul force.

The marvelous new militancy which has engulfed the Negro community must not lead us to distrust of all white people, for many of our white brothers, as evidenced by their presence here today, have come to realize that their destiny is tied up with our destiny and their freedom is inextricably bound to our freedom.

We cannot walk alone. And as we walk, we must make the pledge that we shall march ahead. We cannot turn back. There are those who are asking the devotees of civil rights, "When will you be satisfied?" We can never be satisfied as long as our bodies, heavy with the fatigue of travel, cannot gain lodging in the motels of the highways and the hotels of the cities. We cannot be satisfied as long as the Negro's basic mobility is from a smaller ghetto to a larger one. We can never be satisfied as long as a Negro in Mississippi cannot vote and a Negro in New York believes he has nothing for which to vote. No, no, we are not satisfied, and we will not be satisfied until justice rolls down like waters and righteousness like a mighty stream.[6]

I am not unmindful that some of you have come here out of great trials and tribulations. Some of you have come fresh from narrow cells. Some of you have come from areas where your quest for freedom left you battered by the storms of persecution and staggered by the winds of police brutality. You have been the veterans of creative suffering. Continue to work with the faith that unearned suffering is redemptive.[7]

Go back to Mississippi, go back to Alabama, go back to Georgia, go back to Louisiana, go back to the slums and ghettos of our northern cities, knowing that somehow this situation can and will be changed. Let us not wallow

[5]An allusion to the opening words of Shakespeare's *Richard III:* "Now is the winter of our discontent/Made glorious summer . . ."

[6]Cf. Amos 5:24: "But let judgment run down as waters, and righteousness as a mighty stream."

[7]Cf. Exodus 6:6: "Wherefore say unto the children of Israel, I *am* the LORD, and I will bring you out from under the burdens of the Egyptians, and I will rid you out of their bondage, and I will redeem you with a stretched out arm, and with great judgments."

in the valley of despair.[8] I say to you today, my friends, that in spite of the difficulties and frustrations of the moment, I still have a dream. It is a dream deeply rooted in the American dream.

I have a dream that one day this nation will rise up and live out the true meaning of its creed: "We hold these truths to be self-evident: that all men are created equal."[9] I have a dream that one day on the red hills of Georgia the sons of former slaves and the sons of former slaveowners will be able to sit down together at a table of brotherhood. I have a dream that one day even the state of Mississippi, a desert state, sweltering with the heat of injustice and oppression, will be transformed into an oasis of freedom and justice. I have a dream that my four children will one day live in a nation where they will not be judged by the color of their skin but by the content of their character. I have a dream today.

I have a dream that one day the state of Alabama, whose governor's lips are presently dripping with the words of interposition and nullification,[10] will be transformed into a situation where little black boys and black girls will be able to join hands with little white boys and white girls and walk together as sisters and brothers. I have a dream today. I have a dream that one day every valley shall be exalted, every hill and mountain shall be made low, the rough places will be made plain, and the crooked places will be made straight, and the glory of the Lord shall be revealed, and all flesh shall see it together.[11] This is our hope. This is the faith with which I return to the South. With this faith we will be able to hew out of the mountain of despair a stone of hope. With this faith we will be able to transform the jangling discords of our nation into a beautiful symphony of brotherhood. With this faith we will be able to work together, to pray together, to struggle together, to go to jail together, to stand up for freedom together, knowing that we will be free one day.

This will be the day when all of God's children will be able to sing with a new meaning, "My country, 'tis of thee, sweet land of liberty, of thee I sing. Land where my fathers died, land of the pilgrim's pride, from every mountainside, let freedom ring."[12] And if America is to be a great nation, this must become true. So let freedom ring from the prodigious hilltops of New Hampshire. Let freedom ring from the mighty mountains of New York. Let freedom ring from the heightening Alleghenies of Pennsylvania! Let freedom ring from the snowcapped Rockies of Colorado! Let freedom ring from the curvaceous peaks of California! But not only that; let freedom ring from Stone Mountain of Georgia! Let freedom ring from Lookout Mountain of Tennessee! Let freedom ring from every hill and every molehill of Mississippi. From every mountainside, let freedom ring.

[8]Cf. Psalms 23:4: "Yea, though I walk through the valley of the shadow of death, I will fear no evil . . ."

[9]A passage from the Declaration of Independence.

[10]Governor George Wallace, who strongly asserted that the State of Alabama had the right to maintain segregated facilities. Interposition is an attempt to interpose the state's sovereignty over its citizens ahead of the sovereignty of the federal government. Nullification is an attempt by the state to prevent the enforcement of federal laws within its boundaries.

[11]Isaiah 40:4–5: "Every valley shall be exalted, and every mountain and hill shall be made low: and the crooked shall be made straight, and the rough places plain: and the glory of the LORD shall be revealed, and all flesh shall see *it* together."

[12]From the patriotic hymn "America," by Samuel F. Smith (1808–1895)."

When we let freedom ring, when we let it ring from every village and every hamlet, from every state and every city, we will be able to speed up that day when all of God's children, black men and white men, Jews and Gentiles, Protestants and Catholics, will be able to join hands and sing in the words of the old Negro spiritual, "Free at last! free at last! thank God Almighty, we are free at last!"

1963

Tim O'Brien 1946–

Tim O'Brien is a novelist especially known for his accounts of service in the Vietnam War. His novels include If I Die in a Combat Zone, Box Me Up and Send Me Home *(1973),* Going After Cacciato *(1978),* The Things They Carried *(1990), and* In the Lake of the Woods *(1994). O'Brien, born in Austin, Minnesota, in 1946, attended Macalester College in St. Paul, Minnesota, and, upon graduation in 1968, was immediately drafted into the U.S. Army. He served in Vietnam in 1969–1970. After the expiration of his two-year term in the army, O'Brien returned home to resume normal life as a graduate student at Harvard and later as a teacher of creative writing. The selection from* The Things They Carried *presented here deals with O'Brien's protagonist's experience of being drafted to serve in a war he did not believe in and the difficult decision as to whether he would accept the conscription or resist.*

TEXT: *The Things They Carried,* 1991.

from *THE THINGS THEY CARRIED*

ON THE RAINY RIVER

This is one story I've never told before. Not to anyone. Not to my parents, not to my brother or sister, not even to my wife. To go into it, I've always thought, would only cause embarrassment for all of us, a sudden need to be elsewhere, which is the natural response to a confession. Even now, I'll admit, the story makes me squirm. For more than twenty years I've had to live with it, feeling the shame, trying to push it away, and so by this act of remembrance, by putting the facts down on paper, I'm hoping to relieve at least some of the pressure on my dreams. Still, it's a hard story to tell. All of us, I suppose, like to believe that in a moral emergency we will behave like the heroes of our youth, bravely and forthrightly, without thought of personal loss or discredit. Certainly that was my conviction back in the summer of 1968. Tim O'Brien: a secret hero. The Lone Ranger.[1] If the stakes ever became high enough—if the evil were evil

[1]The perfectly virtuous, invariably successful hero of the popular radio, television, comic book, and movie series *The Lone Ranger.*

enough, if the good were good enough—I would simply tap a secret reservoir of courage that had been accumulating inside me over the years. Courage, I seemed to think, comes to us in finite quantities, like an inheritance, and by being frugal and stashing it away and letting it earn interest, we steadily increase our moral capital in preparation for that day when the account must be drawn down. It was a comforting theory. It dispensed with all those bothersome little acts of daily courage; it offered hope and grace to the repetitive coward; it justified the past while amortizing the future.

In June of 1968, a month after graduating from Macalester College,[2] I was drafted to fight a war I hated. I was twenty-one years old. Young, yes, and politically naive, but even so the American war in Vietnam seemed to me wrong. Certain blood was being shed for uncertain reasons. I saw no unity of purpose, no consensus on matters of philosophy or history or law. The very facts were shrouded in uncertainty: Was it a civil war? A war of national liberation or simple aggression? Who started it, and when, and why? What really happened to the USS *Maddox* on that dark night in the Gulf of Tonkin?[3] Was Ho Chi Minh a Communist stooge, or a nationalist savior, or both, or neither? What about the Geneva Accords? What about SEATO and the Cold War?[4] What about dominoes? America was divided on these and a thousand other issues, and the debate had spilled out across the floor of the United States Senate and into the streets, and smart men in pinstripes could not agree on even the most fundamental matters of public policy. The only certainty that summer was moral confusion. It was my view then, and still is, that you don't make war without knowing why. Knowledge, of course, is always imperfect, but it seemed to me that when a nation goes to war it must have reasonable confidence in the justice and imperative of its cause. You can't fix your mistakes. Once people are dead, you can't make them undead.

In any case those were my convictions, and back in college I had taken a modest stand against the war. Nothing radical, no hothead stuff, just ringing a few doorbells for Gene McCarthy,[5] composing a few tedious, uninspired editorials for the campus newspaper. Oddly, though, it was almost entirely an intellectual activity. I brought some energy to it, of course, but it was the energy that accompanies almost any abstract endeavor; I felt no personal danger; I felt no sense of an impending crisis in my life. Stupidly, with a kind of smug removal that I can't begin to fathom, I assumed that the problems of killing and dying did not fall within my special province.

The draft notice arrived on June 17, 1968. It was a humid afternoon, I remember, cloudy and very quiet, and I'd just come in from a round of golf. My mother and father were having lunch out in the kitchen. I remember opening

[2]A private undergraduate liberal arts college in St. Paul, Minnesota.

[3]A reference to an alleged, though not clearly confirmed, North Vietnamese attack on U.S. ships in 1964 that was used to justify Congressional action authorizing the U.S. presence in Vietnam. Ho Chi Minh was the head of the government of North Vietnam.

[4]Geneva Accords: standards for humanitarian behavior in international conflict that originated in various conventions held in Geneva, Switzerland, in the nineteenth and twentieth centuries. SEATO: the Southeast Asia Treaty Organization, an alliance whose member nations, led by the United States, were responsible for the intervention that became the Vietnam War.

[5]Eugene McCarthy (1916–2005) was a U.S. senator from Minnesota whose anti-war stance as a candidate for the presidency in 1968 became a rallying point for young people opposed to the Vietnam War.

up the letter, scanning the first few lines, feeling the blood go thick behind my eyes. I remember a sound in my head. It wasn't thinking, just a silent howl. A million things all at once—I was too *good* for this war. Too smart, too compassionate, too everything. It couldn't happen. I was above it. I had the world dicked—Phi Beta Kappa and summa cum laude and president of the student body and a full-ride scholarship for grad studies at Harvard. A mistake, maybe—a foul-up in the paperwork. I was no soldier. I hated Boy Scouts. I hated camping out. I hated dirt and tents and mosquitoes. The sight of blood made me queasy, and I couldn't tolerate authority, and I didn't know a rifle from a slingshot. I was a *liberal,* for Christ sake: If they needed fresh bodies, why not draft some back-to-the-stone-age hawk? Or some dumb jingo[6] in his hard hat and Bomb Hanoi button, or one of LBJ's[7] pretty daughters, or Westmoreland's[8] whole handsome family—nephews and nieces and baby grandson. There should be a law, I thought. If you support a war, if you think it's worth the price, that's fine, but you have to put your own precious fluids on the line. You have to head for the front and hook up with an infantry unit and help spill the blood. And you have to bring along your wife, or your kids, or your lover. A *law,* I thought.

I remember the rage in my stomach. Later it burned down to a smoldering self-pity, then to numbness. At dinner that night my father asked what my plans were.

"Nothing," I said. "Wait."

I spent the summer of 1968 working in an Armour meat-packing plant in my hometown of Worthington, Minnesota. The plant specialized in pork products, and for eight hours a day I stood on a quarter-mile assembly line—more properly, a disassembly line—removing blood clots from the necks of dead pigs. My job title, I believe, was Declotter. After slaughter, the hogs were decapitated, split down the length of the belly, pried open, eviscerated[9] and strung up by the hind hocks on a high conveyer belt. Then gravity took over. By the time a carcass reached my spot on the line, the fluids had mostly drained out, everything except for thick clots of blood in the neck and upper chest cavity. To remove the stuff, I used a kind of water gun. The machine was heavy, maybe eighty pounds, and was suspended from the ceiling by a heavy rubber cord. There was some bounce to it, an elastic up-and-down give, and the trick was to maneuver the gun with your whole body, not lifting with the arms, just letting the rubber cord do the work for you. At one end was a trigger; at the muzzle end was a small nozzle and a steel roller brush. As a carcass passed by, you'd lean forward and swing the gun up against the clots and squeeze the trigger, all in one motion, and the brush would whirl and water would come shooting out and you'd hear a quick splattering sound as the clots dissolved into a fine red mist. It was not pleasant work. Goggles were a necessity, and a rubber apron, but even so it was like standing for eight hours a day under a lukewarm blood-shower. At night I'd go home smelling of pig. It wouldn't go away. Even after a hot bath, scrubbing hard, the stink was always there—like old bacon, or sausage, a

[6]A person who advocates military action, especially of an imperialistic nature.
[7]LBJ: President Lyndon Baines Johnson (1908–1973).
[8]General William Westmoreland (1914–2005), commander of U.S. forces in Vietnam (1964–1968) and then U.S. Army Chief of Staff (1968–1972).
[9]Disemboweled.

dense greasy pig-stink that soaked deep into my skin and hair. Among other things, I remember, it was tough getting dates that summer. I felt isolated; I spent a lot of time alone. And there was also that draft notice tucked away in my wallet.

In the evenings I'd sometimes borrow my father's car and drive aimlessly around town, feeling sorry for myself, thinking about the war and the pig factory and how my life seemed to be collapsing toward slaughter. I felt paralyzed. All around me the options seemed to be narrowing, as if I were hurtling down a huge black funnel, the whole world squeezing in tight. There was no happy way out. The government had ended most graduate school deferments; the waiting lists for the National Guard and Reserves were impossibly long; my health was solid; I didn't qualify for CO[10] status—no religious grounds, no history as a pacifist. Moreover, I could not claim to be opposed to war as a matter of general principle. There were occasions, I believed, when a nation was justified in using military force to achieve its ends, to stop a Hitler or some comparable evil, and I told myself that in such circumstances I would've willingly marched off to the battle. The problem, though, was that a draft board did not let you choose your war.

Beyond all this, or at the very center, was the raw fact of terror. I did not want to die. Not ever. But certainly not then, not there, not in a wrong war. Driving up Main Street, past the courthouse and the Ben Franklin[11] store, I sometimes felt the fear spreading inside me like weeds. I imagined myself dead. I imagined myself doing things I could not do—charging an enemy position, taking aim at another human being.

At some point in mid-July I began thinking seriously about Canada. The border lay a few hundred miles north, an eight-hour drive. Both my conscience and my instincts were telling me to make a break for it, just take off and run like hell and never stop. In the beginning the idea seemed purely abstract, the word Canada printing itself out in my head; but after a time I could see particular shapes and images, the sorry details of my own future—a hotel room in Winnipeg, a battered old suitcase, my father's eyes as I tried to explain myself over the telephone. I could almost hear his voice, and my mother's. Run, I'd think. Then I'd think, Impossible. Then a second later I'd think, *Run.*

It was a kind of schizophrenia. A moral split. I couldn't make up my mind. I feared the war, yes, but I also feared exile. I was afraid of walking away from my own life, my friends and my family, my whole history, everything that mattered to me. I feared losing the respect of my parents. I feared the law. I feared ridicule and censure. My hometown was a conservative little spot on the prairie, a place where tradition counted, and it was easy to imagine people sitting around a table down at the old Gobbler Café on Main Street, coffee cups poised, the conversation slowly zeroing in on the young O'Brien kid, how the damned sissy had taken off for Canada. At night, when I couldn't sleep, I'd sometimes carry on fierce arguments with those people. I'd be screaming at them, telling them how much I detested their blind, thoughtless, automatic acquiescence to it all, their simple-minded patriotism, their prideful ignorance, their love-it-or-leave-it platitudes, how they were sending me off to fight a war

[10] Conscientious Objector, meaning that he objected to war as a matter of deeply held principle.
[11] A chain of low-price variety stores.

they didn't understand and didn't want to understand. I held them responsible. By God, yes, I *did.* All of them—I held them personally and individually responsible—the polyestered Kiwanis boys, the merchants and farmers, the pious churchgoers, the chatty housewives, the PTA and the Lions club and the Veterans of Foreign Wars[12] and the fine upstanding gentry out at the country club. They didn't know Bao Dai[13] from the man in the moon. They didn't know history. They didn't know the first thing about Diem's[14] tyranny, or the nature of Vietnamese nationalism, or the long colonialism of the French—this was all too damned complicated, it required some reading—but no matter, it was a war to stop the Communists, plain and simple, which was how they liked things, and you were a treasonous pussy if you had second thoughts about killing or dying for plain and simple reasons.

I was bitter, sure. But it was so much more than that. The emotions went from outrage to terror to bewilderment to guilt to sorrow and then back again to outrage. I felt a sickness inside me. Real disease.

Most of this I've told before, or at least hinted at, but what I have never told is the full truth. How I cracked. How at work one morning, standing on the pig line, I felt something break open in my chest. I don't know what it was. I'll never know. But it was real, I know that much, it was a physical rupture—a cracking-leaking-popping feeling. I remember dropping my water gun. Quickly, almost without thought, I took off my apron and walked out of the plant and drove home. It was midmorning, I remember, and the house was empty. Down in my chest there was still that leaking sensation, something very warm and precious spilling out, and I was covered with blood and hog-stink, and for a long while I just concentrated on holding myself together. I remember taking a hot shower. I remember packing a suitcase and carrying it out to the kitchen, standing very still for a few minutes, looking carefully at the familiar objects all around me. The old chrome toaster, the telephone, the pink and white Formica on the kitchen counters. The room was full of bright sunshine. Everything sparkled. My house, I thought. My life. I'm not sure how long I stood there, but later I scribbled out a short note to my parents.

What it said, exactly, I don't recall now. Something vague. Taking off, will call, love Tim.

I drove north.

It's a blur now, as it was then, and all I remember is a sense of high velocity and the feel of the steering wheel in my hands. I was riding on adrenaline. A giddy feeling, in a way, except there was the dreamy edge of impossibility to it—like running a dead-end maze—no way out—it couldn't come to a happy conclusion and yet I was doing it anyway because it was all I could think of to

[12]The Kiwanis Club, PTA (Parent-Teacher Association), Lions Club, and Veterans of Foreign Wars are civic organizations that would be likely to advocate conservative values.

[13]Bao Dai (1913–1997) was Emperor of Vietnam, a hereditary title. He was the titular head of government under French colonial rule, but was removed from that position in 1955 when Vietnam was divided into North and South and South Vietnam declared itself a republic.

[14]Ngo Dinh Diem (1901–1963) was president of the South Vietnamese republic from 1955 to 1963, when he was assassinated, apparently with the approval of the U.S. government. His assassination was a crucial event in the growth of the conflict, and the enmeshment of the United States, in Vietnam.

do. It was pure flight, fast and mindless. I had no plan. Just hit the border at high speed and crash through and keep on running. Near dusk I passed through Bemidji, then turned northeast toward International Falls. I spent the night in the car behind a closed-down gas station a half mile from the border. In the morning, after gassing up, I headed straight west along the Rainy River, which separates Minnesota from Canada, and which for me separated one life from another. The land was mostly wilderness. Here and there I passed a motel or bait shop, but otherwise the country unfolded in great sweeps of pine and birch and sumac. Though it was still August, the air already had the smell of October, football season, piles of yellow-red leaves, everything crisp and clean. I remember a huge blue sky. Off to my right was the Rainy River, wide as a lake in places, and beyond the Rainy River was Canada.

For a while I just drove, not aiming at anything, then in the late morning I began looking for a place to lie low for a day or two. I was exhausted, and scared sick, and around noon I pulled into an old fishing resort called the Tip Top Lodge. Actually it was not a lodge at all, just eight or nine tiny yellow cabins clustered on a peninsula that jutted northward into the Rainy River. The place was in sorry shape. There was a dangerous wooden dock, an old minnow tank, a flimsy tar paper boathouse along the shore. The main building, which stood in a cluster of pines on high ground, seemed to lean heavily to one side, like a cripple, the roof sagging toward Canada. Briefly, I thought about turning around, just giving up, but then I got out of the car and walked up to the front porch.

The man who opened the door that day is the hero of my life. How do I say this without sounding sappy? Blurt it out—the man saved me. He offered exactly what I needed, without questions, without any words at all. He took me in. He was there at the critical time—a silent, watchful presence. Six days later, when it ended, I was unable to find a proper way to thank him, and I never have, and so, if nothing else, this story represents a small gesture of gratitude twenty years overdue.

Even after two decades I can close my eyes and return to that porch at the Tip Top Lodge. I can see the old guy staring at me. Elroy Berdahl: eighty-one years old, skinny and shrunken and mostly bald. He wore a flannel shirt and brown work pants. In one hand, I remember, he carried a green apple, a small paring knife in the other. His eyes had the bluish gray color of a razor blade, the same polished shine, and as he peered up at me I felt a strange sharpness, almost painful, a cutting sensation, as if his gaze were somehow slicing me open. In part, no doubt, it was my own sense of guilt, but even so I'm absolutely certain that the old man took one look and went right to the heart of things—a kid in trouble. When I asked for a room, Elroy made a little clicking sound with his tongue. He nodded, led me out to one of the cabins, and dropped a key in my hand. I remember smiling at him. I also remember wishing I hadn't. The old man shook his head as if to tell me it wasn't worth the bother.

"Dinner at five-thirty," he said. "You eat fish?"

"Anything," I said.

Elroy grunted and said, "I'll bet."

We spent six days together at the Tip Top Lodge. Just the two of us. Tourist season was over, and there were no boats on the river, and the wilderness seemed to withdraw into a great permanent stillness. Over those six days Elroy Berdahl and I took most of our meals together. In the mornings we sometimes went out on long hikes into the woods, and at night we played Scrabble or listened to records or sat reading in front of his big stone fireplace. At times I felt the awkwardness of an intruder, but Elroy accepted me into his quiet routine without fuss or ceremony. He took my presence for granted, the same way he might've sheltered a stray cat—no wasted sighs or pity—and there was never any talk about it. Just the opposite. What I remember more than anything is the man's willful, almost ferocious silence. In all that time together, all those hours, he never asked the obvious questions: Why was I there? Why alone? Why so preoccupied? If Elroy was curious about any of this, he was careful never to put it into words.

My hunch, though, is that he already knew. At least the basics. After all, it was 1968, and guys were burning draft cards, and Canada was just a boat ride away. Elroy Berdahl was no hick. His bedroom, I remember, was cluttered with books and newspapers. He killed me at the Scrabble board, barely concentrating, and on those occasions when speech was necessary he had a way of compressing large thoughts into small, cryptic packets of language. One evening, just at sunset, he pointed up at an owl circling over the violet-lighted forest to the west.

"Hey, O'Brien," he said. "There's Jesus."

The man was sharp—he didn't miss much. Those razor eyes. Now and then he'd catch me staring out at the river, at the far shore, and I could almost hear the tumblers clicking in his head. Maybe I'm wrong, but I doubt it.

One thing for certain, he knew I was in desperate trouble. And he knew I couldn't talk about it. The wrong word—or even the right word—and I would've disappeared. I was wired and jittery. My skin felt too tight. After supper one evening I vomited and went back to my cabin and lay down for a few moments and then vomited again; another time, in the middle of the afternoon, I began sweating and couldn't shut it off. I went through whole days feeling dizzy with sorrow. I couldn't sleep; I couldn't lie still. At night I'd toss around in bed, half awake, half dreaming, imagining how I'd sneak down to the beach and quietly push one of the old man's boats out into the river and start paddling my way toward Canada. There were times when I thought I'd gone off the psychic edge. I couldn't tell up from down, I was just falling, and late in the night I'd lie there watching weird pictures spin through my head. Getting chased by the Border Patrol—helicopters and searchlights and barking dogs—I'd be crashing through the woods, I'd be down on my hands and knees—people shouting out my name—the law closing in on all sides—my hometown draft board and the FBI and the Royal Canadian Mounted Police. It all seemed crazy and impossible. Twenty-one years old, an ordinary kid with all the ordinary dreams and ambitions, and all I wanted was to live the life I was born to—a mainstream life—I loved baseball and hamburgers and cherry Cokes—and now I was off on the margins of exile, leaving my country forever, and it seemed so impossible and terrible and sad.

I'm not sure how I made it through those six days. Most of it I can't remember. On two or three afternoons, to pass some time, I helped Elroy get the place ready for winter, sweeping down the cabins and hauling in the boats, little chores that kept my body moving. The days were cool and bright. The nights were very dark. One morning the old man showed me how to split and stack firewood, and for several hours we just worked in silence out behind his house.

At one point, I remember, Elroy put down his maul[15] and looked at me for a long time, his lips drawn as if framing a difficult question, but then he shook his head and went back to work. The man's self-control was amazing. He never pried. He never put me in a position that required lies or denials. To an extent, I suppose, his reticence was typical of that part of Minnesota, where privacy still held value, and even if I'd been walking around with some horrible deformity—four arms and three heads—I'm sure the old man would've talked about everything except those extra arms and heads. Simple politeness was part of it. But even more than that, I think, the man understood that words were insufficient. The problem had gone beyond discussion. During that long summer I'd been over and over the various arguments, all the pros and cons, and it was no longer a question that could be decided by an act of pure reason. Intellect had come up against emotion. My conscience told me to run, but some irrational and powerful force was resisting, like a weight pushing me toward the war. What it came down to, stupidly, was a sense of shame. Hot, stupid shame. I did not want people to think badly of me. Not my parents, not my brother and sister, not even the folks down at the Gobbler Café. I was ashamed to be there at the Tip Top Lodge. I was ashamed of my conscience, ashamed to be doing the right thing.

Some of this Elroy must've understood. Not the details, of course, but the plain fact of crisis.

Although the old man never confronted me about it, there was one occasion when he came close to forcing the whole thing out into the open. It was early evening, and we'd just finished supper, and over coffee and dessert I asked him about my bill, how much I owed so far. For a long while the old man squinted down at the tablecloth.

"Well, the basic rate," he said, "is fifty bucks a night. Not counting meals. This makes four nights, right?"

I nodded. I had three hundred and twelve dollars in my wallet.

Elroy kept his eyes on the tablecloth. "Now that's an onseason price. To be fair, I suppose we should knock it down a peg or two." He leaned back in his chair. "What's a reasonable number, you figure?"

"I don't know," I said. "Forty?"

"Forty's good. Forty a night. Then we tack on food—say another hundred? Two hundred sixty total?"

"I guess."

He raised his eyebrows. "Too much?"

"No, that's fair. It's fine. Tomorrow, though . . . I think I'd better take off tomorrow."

Elroy shrugged and began clearing the table. For a time he fussed with the dishes, whistling to himself as if the subject had been settled. After a second he slapped his hands together.

"You know what we forgot?" he said. "We forgot wages. Those odd jobs you done. What we have to do, we have to figure out what your time's worth. Your last job—how much did you pull in an hour?"

"Not enough," I said.

[15]A heavy hammer for driving stakes or wedges or splitting wood.

"A bad one?"

"Yes. Pretty bad."

Slowly then, without intending any long sermon, I told him about my days at the pig plant. It began as a straight recitation of the facts, but before I could stop myself I was talking about the blood clots and the water gun and how the smell had soaked into my skin and how I couldn't wash it away. I went on for a long time. I told him about wild hogs squealing in my dreams, the sounds of butchery, slaughterhouse sounds, and how I'd sometimes wake up with that greasy pig-stink in my throat.

When I was finished, Elroy nodded at me.

"Well, to be honest," he said, "when you first showed up here, I wondered about all that. The aroma, I mean. Smelled like you was awful damned fond of pork chops." The old man almost smiled. He made a snuffling sound, then sat down with a pencil and a piece of paper. "So what'd this crud job pay? Ten bucks an hour? Fifteen?"

"Less."

Elroy shook his head. "Let's make it fifteen. You put in twenty-five hours here, easy. That's three hundred seventy-five bucks total wages. We subtract the two hundred sixty for food and lodging, I still owe you a hundred and fifteen."

He took four fifties out of his shirt pocket and laid them on the table.

"Call it even," he said.

"No."

"Pick it up. Get yourself a haircut."

The money lay on the table for the rest of the evening. It was still there when I went back to my cabin. In the morning, though, I found an envelope tacked to my door. Inside were the four fifties and a two-word note that said EMERGENCY FUND.

The man knew.

Looking back after twenty years, I sometimes wonder if the events of that summer didn't happen in some other dimension, a place where your life exists before you've lived it, and where it goes afterward. None of it ever seemed real. During my time at the Tip Top Lodge I had the feeling that I'd slipped out of my own skin, hovering a few feet away while some poor yo-yo with my name and face tried to make his way toward a future he didn't understand and didn't want. Even now I can see myself as I was then. It's like watching an old home movie: I'm young and tan and fit. I've got hair—lots of it. I don't smoke or drink. I'm wearing faded blue jeans and a white polo shirt. I can see myself sitting on Elroy Berdahl's dock near dusk one evening, the sky a bright shimmering pink, and I'm finishing up a letter to my parents that tells what I'm about to do and why I'm doing it and how sorry I am that I'd never found the courage to talk to them about it. I ask them not to be angry. I try to explain some of my feelings, but there aren't enough words, and so I just say that it's a thing that has to be done. At the end of the letter I talk about the vacations we used to take up in this north country, at a place called Whitefish Lake, and how the scenery here reminds me of those good times. I tell them I'm fine. I tell them I'll write again from Winnipeg or Montreal or wherever I end up.

On my last full day, the sixth day, the old man took me out fishing on the Rainy River. The afternoon was sunny and cold. A stiff breeze came in from the north, and I remember how the little fourteen-foot boat made sharp rocking motions as we pushed off from the dock. The current was fast. All around us, I remember, there was a vastness to the world, an unpeopled rawness, just the trees and the sky and the water reaching out toward nowhere. The air had the brittle scent of October.

For ten or fifteen minutes Elroy held a course upstream, the river choppy and silver-gray, then he turned straight north and put the engine on full throttle. I felt the bow lift beneath me. I remember the wind in my ears, the sound of the old outboard Evinrude.[16] For a time I didn't pay attention to anything, just feeling the cold spray against my face, but then it occurred to me that at some point we must've passed into Canadian waters, across that dotted line between two different worlds, and I remember a sudden tightness in my chest as I looked up and watched the far shore come at me. This wasn't a daydream. It was tangible and real. As we came in toward land, Elroy cut the engine, letting the boat fishtail lightly about twenty yards off shore. The old man didn't look at me or speak. Bending down, he opened up his tackle box and busied himself with a bobber and a piece of wire leader, humming to himself, his eyes down.

It struck me then that he must've planned it. I'll never be certain, of course, but I think he meant to bring me up against the realities, to guide me across the river and to take me to the edge and to stand a kind of vigil as I chose a life for myself.

I remember staring at the old man, then at my hands, then at Canada. The shoreline was dense with brush and timber. I could see tiny red berries on the bushes. I could see a squirrel up in one of the birch trees, a big crow looking at me from a boulder along the river. That close—twenty yards—and I could see the delicate latticework of the leaves, the texture of the soil, the browned needles beneath the pines, the configurations of geology and human history. Twenty yards. I could've done it. I could've jumped and started swimming for my life. Inside me, in my chest, I felt a terrible squeezing pressure. Even now, as I write this, I can still feel that tightness. And I want you to feel it—the wind coming off the river, the waves, the silence, the wooded frontier. You're at the bow of a boat on the Rainy River. You're twenty-one years old, you're scared, and there's a hard squeezing pressure in your chest.

What would you do?

Would you jump? Would you feel pity for yourself? Would you think about your family and your childhood and your dreams and all you're leaving behind? Would it hurt? Would it feel like dying? Would you cry, as I did?

I tried to swallow it back. I tried to smile, except I was crying.

Now, perhaps, you can understand why I've never told this story before. It's not just the embarrassment of tears. That's part of it, no doubt, but what embarrasses me much more, and always will, is the paralysis that took my heart. A moral freeze: I couldn't decide, I couldn't act, I couldn't comport myself with even a pretense of modest human dignity.

All I could do was cry. Quietly, not bawling, just the chest-chokes.

[16]A brand of boat motors.

At the rear of the boat Elroy Berdahl pretended not to notice. He held a fishing rod in his hands, his head bowed to hide his eyes. He kept humming a soft, monotonous little tune. Everywhere, it seemed, in the trees and water and sky, a great worldwide sadness came pressing down on me, a crushing sorrow, sorrow like I had never known it before. And what was so sad, I realized, was that Canada had become a pitiful fantasy. Silly and hopeless. It was no longer a possibility. Right then, with the shore so close, I understood that I would not do what I should do. I would not swim away from my hometown and my country and my life. I would not be brave. That old image of myself as a hero, as a man of conscience and courage, all that was just a threadbare pipe dream. Bobbing there on the Rainy River, looking back at the Minnesota shore, I felt a sudden swell of helplessness come over me, a drowning sensation, as if I had toppled overboard and was being swept away by the silver waves. Chunks of my own history flashed by. I saw a seven-year-old boy in a white cowboy hat and a Lone Ranger mask and a pair of holstered six-shooters; I saw a twelve-year-old Little League shortstop pivoting to turn a double play; I saw a sixteen-year-old kid decked out for his first prom, looking spiffy in a white tux and a black bow tie, his hair cut short and flat, his shoes freshly polished. My whole life seemed to spill out into the river, swirling away from me, everything. I had ever been or ever wanted to be. I couldn't get my breath; I couldn't stay afloat; I couldn't tell which way to swim. A hallucination, I suppose, but it was as real as anything I would ever feel. I saw my parents calling to me from the far shoreline. I saw my brother and sister, all the townsfolk, the mayor and the entire Chamber of Commerce and all my old teachers and girlfriends and high school buddies. Like some weird sporting event: everybody screaming from the sidelines, rooting me on—a loud stadium roar. Hotdogs and popcorn—stadium smells, stadium heat. A squad of cheerleaders did cartwheels along the banks of the Rainy River; they had megaphones and pompoms and smooth brown thighs. The crowd swayed left and right. A marching band played fight songs. All my aunts and uncles were there, and Abraham Lincoln, and Saint George, and a nine-year-old girl named Linda who had died of a brain tumor back in fifth grade, and several members of the United States Senate, and a blind poet scribbling notes, and LBJ, and Huck Finn, and Abbie Hoffman,[17] and all the dead soldiers back from the grave, and the many thousands who were later to die—villagers with terrible burns, little kids without arms or legs—yes, and the Joint Chiefs of Staff were there, and a couple of popes, and a first lieutenant named Jimmy Cross, and the last surviving veteran of the American Civil War, and Jane Fonda dressed up as Barbarella,[18] and an old man sprawled beside a pigpen, and my grandfather, and Gary Cooper, and a kind-faced woman carrying an umbrella and a copy of Plato's *Republic,* and a million ferocious citizens waving flags of all shapes and colors—people in hard hats, people in headbands—they were all whooping and chanting and urging me toward one shore or the other. I saw faces from my distant past and distant future. My wife was there. My unborn daughter waved at me, and my two sons hopped up and

[17]Abbie Hoffman (1936–1989) was a leader of the anti-war movement.

[18]*Barbarella* was a 1968 movie starring actress Jane Fonda (1937–), who later became a prominent anti-war activist.

down, and a drill sergeant named Blyton sneered and shot up a finger and shook his head. There was a choir in bright purple robes. There was a cabbie from the Bronx. There was a slim young man I would one day kill with a hand grenade along a red clay trail outside the village of My Khe.

The little aluminum boat rocked softly beneath me. There was the wind and the sky.

I tried to will myself overboard.

I gripped the edge of the boat and leaned forward and thought, *Now*.

I did try. It just wasn't possible.

All those eyes on me—the town, the whole universe—and I couldn't risk the embarrassment. It was as if there were an audience to my life, that swirl of faces along the river, and in my head I could hear people screaming at me. Traitor! they yelled. Turncoat! Pussy! I felt myself blush. I couldn't tolerate it. I couldn't endure the mockery, or the disgrace, or the patriotic ridicule. Even in my imagination, the shore just twenty yards away, I couldn't make myself be brave. It had nothing to do with morality. Embarrassment, that's all it was.

And right then I submitted.

I would go to the war—I would kill and maybe die—because I was embarrassed not to.

That was the sad thing. And so I sat in the bow of the boat and cried.

It was loud now. Loud, hard crying.

Elroy Berdahl remained quiet. He kept fishing. He worked his line with the tips of his fingers, patiently, squinting out at his red and white bobber on the Rainy River. His eyes were flat and impassive. He didn't speak. He was simply there, like the river and the late-summer sun. And yet by his presence, his mute watchfulness, he made it real. He was the true audience. He was a witness, like God, or like the gods, who look on in absolute silence as we live our lives, as we make our choices or fail to make them.

"Ain't biting," he said.

Then after a time the old man pulled in his line and turned the boat back toward Minnesota.

I don't remember saying goodbye. That last night we had dinner together, and I went to bed early, and in the morning Elroy fixed breakfast for me. When I told him I'd be leaving, the old man nodded as if he already knew. He looked down at the table and smiled.

At some point later in the morning it's possible that we shook hands—I just don't remember—but I do know that by the time I'd finished packing the old man had disappeared. Around noon, when I took my suitcase out to the car, I noticed that his old black pickup truck was no longer parked in front of the house. I went inside and waited for a while, but I felt a bone certainty that he wouldn't be back. In a way, I thought, it was appropriate. I washed up the breakfast dishes, left his two hundred dollars on the kitchen counter, got into the car, and drove south toward home.

The day was cloudy. I passed through towns with familiar names, through the pine forests and down to the prairie, and then to Vietnam, where I was a soldier, and then home again. I survived, but it's not a happy ending. I was a coward. I went to the war.

1990

Diné bahane': *The Navajo Creation Story*

The earliest Americans arrived from Asia as early as 30,000 B.C., *perhaps even earlier. They came across a land bridge that reached from the Old World to the New, across the Bering Sea between present-day Siberia and Alaska. They were immigrants, the first of a succession of peoples who came to America bringing with them their languages, customs, beliefs, and visions.*

By the time Columbus arrived in 1492, Native Americans had developed hundreds of different cultures and languages. Theirs were oral cultures, their traditions and religions preserved in oral tales and myths. Spoken literature was handed down from generation to generation, to speakers and talkers, who memorized the stories, shaping and adapting them to meet the changes they experienced. Like the people of all cultures, they developed myths and legends that explained their origins and the origin of the worlds they lived in. Stories, poems, and orations were part of their daily lives, essential to the cohesiveness of their cultures and as guides to life—and to death.

Until the twentieth century the literature of Native Americans in the United States was overshadowed by the culture and the literature of the European settlers who had come to the New Eden across the Atlantic. But the last half of the twentieth century saw a rebirth of interest in the culture, the art, the literature of Native Americans. Just as many Americans have come more fully to understand and to emulate the Native Americans' profound interest in preserving the land and its animals, so modern-day Americans of all cultural varieties are beginning to understand and to value more fully the oral and written art of America's first immigrants.

Like many creation stories and epic narratives, the Diné bahane', *or "history of the people," is not originally a single, unified literary work; rather, it is a story cycle intended to be recited orally as a means of passing on values and traditions from one generation to the next. An integral part of the Navajo's culture and art, the* Diné bahane' *embraces features of myth, parable, and allegory laced with detailed observation and a deeply poetic awareness of what it means to be human. To this day, the story cycle of the* Diné bahane' *remains vital as a dynamic account of tribal origins in which a mythic past merges with material history to create a persisting Navajo identity, even as the contemporary world encroaches steadily on tribal life. Children first encounter it before reaching school age when they learn their place in an elaborate clan system. They are likely to hear parts of it recited by parents or grandparents on one occasion or another as they grow up, and more and more frequently today, may be asked to read portions of it during their formal education. Elders who know it well from having heard it again and again in a number of settings declare that it requires a lifetime of listening before it can be fully understood.*

Never composed in writing by those who created it, never recited in its entirety, and never intended to be confined to a printed volume, the narrative cycle varies depending on the performer, the occasion of its telling, and the audience at hand. Its chameleon-like quality makes capturing it, shaping it into a coherent whole, and converting it to written text a highly challenging endeavor. The portion of the cycle printed here is part of a comprehensive compilation and translation of the myth cycle by Paul G. Zolbrod in the early 1980s—the result of a long-term process of text retrieval and assembly intended both to preserve the essential qualities of the oral story cycle and to demonstrate the degree to which Native American oral tradition can be seen as a wellspring of an indigenous American literature.

TEXT: *Diné bahane': The Navajo Creation Story,* ed. P. Zolbrod, 1984.

[THE QUARREL BETWEEN FIRST MAN AND FIRST WOMAN]

Áltsé hastiin the First Man became a great hunter in the fourth world.[1] So he was able to provide his wife *Áltsé asdzáá* the First Woman with plenty to eat.

As a result, she grew very fat.

Now one day he brought home a fine, fleshy deer.

His wife boiled some of it, and together they had themselves a hearty meal.

When she had finished eating, *Áltsé asdzáá* the First Woman wiped her greasy hands on her sheath.

She belched deeply. And she had this to say:

"Thank you *shijóózh* my vagina," she said.

"Thank you for that delicious dinner."

To which *Áltsé hastiin* the First Man replied this way:

"Why do you say that?" he replied.

"Why not thank me?

"Was it not I who killed the deer whose flesh you have just feasted on?

"Was it not I who carried it here for you to eat?

"Was it not I who skinned it?

"Who made it ready for you to boil?

"Is *shijóózh* your vagina the great hunter, that you should thank it and not me?"

To which *Áltsé asdzáá* offered this answer:

"As a matter of fact, she is," offered she.

"In a manner of speaking it is *jóósh* the vagina who hunts.

"Were it not for *jóósh* you would not have killed that deer.

"Were it not for her you would not have carried it here.

"You would not have skinned it.

"You lazy men would do nothing around here were it not for *jóósh.*

"In truth, *Jóósh* the vagina does all the work around here."

To which *Áltsé hastiin* the First Man had this to say:

"Then perhaps you women think you can live without us men," he said.

"Maybe you need only *nihijóózh* your vaginas.

"*Nihijóózh* your great huntresses.

"*Nihijóózh* your tireless workers."

Quickly came this reply from *Áltsé asdzáá* the First Woman:

"All things do not exist thanks alone to you," she replied quickly. "We could live alone if we wanted to.

"We are the ones who till the fields, after all.

"We are the ones who gather the food, after all.

[1]Thanks to cataclysmic floods related to their own misbehavior, the people have had to flee from three previous worlds.

"We can live on the crops that we grow. We can live on the seeds that we gather. We can live on the berries that we find and on the fruits that we bring.

Things exist thanks as much to us as to you. We have no need of you men."

On and on they argued that way, *Áltsé hastiin* the First Man permitting himself to grow angrier and angrier with each reply his wife made; *Áltsé asdzáa* the First Woman permitting herself to grow more and more vexing with each reply she offered.

Until at length he stalked out of the shelter where they had lived together as man and wife. Out he stalked and jumped across the fire in front of their home, where he remained all that night with only his anger to keep him company.

. . .

Early next morning he walked to the center of the village and called loudly so that everyone could hear:

"All you men!" he called.

"Gather round me.

"I wish to speak to you.

"I wish to instruct you.

"As for the women, let them stay where they are.

"Not one woman do I wish to see.

"I have nothing to say to any woman around here."

Soon all the males were assembled around *Áltsé hastiin* the First Man. And he repeated to them what his wife had said the previous night. Then he told the men this:

"The women think they can live without us," he told the men. "They think that things can continue to exist thanks as much to them as to us.

"Well, let us see if all that is true.

"Let us see if they can hunt and till the fields, with only *jóósh* the vagina to help them. Let us see what sort of living they can make, with only *jóósh* to assist them.

"We will cross the stream and live apart from them. And from *jóósh.*

"We will keep the raft with us on our side of the water, so that even when they long for us they may not have us.

"If they seek companionship, let them seek it with *jóósh* the vagina.

"And if *jóósh* wishes to shout, let her shout to herself.

"Let us see what *jóósh* the vagina brings forth when she hears the sound of her own voice. We will see what happens when they try to sustain life without help from us."

. . .

So it was that all the men gathered at the river.

Áltsé hastiin even summoned the twins *nádleeh,* who were neither entirely male nor entirely female. They were covered with meal when they arrived, for they had been grinding corn.

This is what *Áltsé hastiin* the First Man asked them:

"What do you have that you have made all by yourselves?" he asked them.

"What is there that you have made without the help of any woman?"

Answered the twins *nádleeh,* who were no more female than they were male:

"We each have a set of grinding stones that we have made," they answered.

"We have cups and bowls. We have baskets and other utensils.

"We have made those things by ourselves with the help of no woman."

To which *Áltsé hastiin* the First Man had this to say:

"Go fetch those things and bring them here; for you must come with us," he said.

"You are as much men as you are women. And you have made those things with no woman's help.

"Let the women learn what it means to live without the help of any man.

"Let them learn to live without anything that has been made by someone who is even part of a man."

. . .

So the men ferried across the river, taking the nonchildbearing twins *nádleeh* with them. They crossed over to the north bank. And with them they carried their stone axes, their wooden scythes, their hoes of bone, and the utensils that the twins had invented. In fact, they took anything that they had made themselves.

After they had crossed, they sent the raft-downstream, inviting the men of the *Kiis'áanii* to join them, from whom six clans did join. They too had allowed their women to anger them.

As some of the young men rode across the stream they wept at having to part with their wives. They had not been angered by anything the women had said. But they had become used to doing whatever *Áltsé hastiin* had told them to do.

The men left behind everything the women had made by themselves. And they left behind everything the women had helped them to make or to raise. They took only what they had produced without the help of any woman.

. . .

Once they reached the north bank of the river, some of the men set out to hunt. For the young boys needed food. Others set to work cutting willows for huts. For the young boys also needed shelter.

It seems that they managed very well. Within four days they had plenty of food, and, they built strong homes for themselves and the boys. Within four days they were sure that they could get along without women.

They were sure they would thrive without women to make them angry. And their spirits were high, at least at first, it is said.

. . .

It is also said that the women, too, were in high spirits at first.

That winter they had plenty of food. They worked and they ate. They sang songs and they told stories. Often they came down to the bank of the river where the men could hear them and see them. And there they taunted them.

One of them would pull her sheath over her head and shake her bare body. Another would do likewise; then she would turn her back toward the men, and bend forward, and wiggle her buttocks.

"Hey you men," called yet another meanwhile. "Look over here. Look at that!"

"Don't you see what you're missing?" shouted still another.

Others would then similarly bare themselves to the men. All together they would laugh and cry out. Thus they teased the men, alternately calling them obscene names and coaxing them suggestively. They used their bodies to tempt the men until they were sure that the men longed for them as much as they longed for the men.

. . .

In the spring the men prepared a few small fields and managed to raise a little bit of corn. Still, they did not have much of it to eat, and they had to depend on hunting for most of their food.

Meanwhile, the women cultivated their entire farm. But without hoes they could not work the soil properly. And without scythes they were unable to harvest well. So that during their second winter alone they were forced to live on a smaller crop. They did not sing as much or tell as many stories as they had done the previous winter.

The women planted less the second spring while the men cleared more land than they had cleared the year before. So the crops of the men increased while those of the women decreased. And during the winter that followed, the women began to suffer for want of food. Some of them had to gather the seeds of wild plants to get enough to eat.

During the autumn of the third year of the separation many women jumped into the river and tried to swim over to the north shore where the men lived. But they were carried away by the current and were never seen again.

By the end of the fourth year the men had more food than they could eat. Corn and pumpkins lay untouched in the fields while the women starved.

But the separation was still having a bad effect on the men, even if they had raised enough crops for themselves. For during the entire time that they lived apart, the men longed for the women just as badly as the women longed for them. That longing grew, in fact, on both sides of the stream.

So strong did it become that members of both sexes indulged in the practice of masturbation. The women sought to satisfy themselves with long stones and thick quills. They attempted intercourse with cactus or with bone. The men, meanwhile, tried to relieve their longing with mud, or else they used the flesh of freshly slain game.

There was one in particular called *K'íídeesdizi,* whose name means Man With Wrappings On in the White Man's language. One morning he went out hunting alone and found a place far from the village where nobody would see him. Once out there he killed a deer just as the light of day began to wane.

He then made a brush circle and lit a fire therein, according to the manner of doing such things in those times. Into the fire he placed a piece of venison from his quarry, meaning to eat a little of it and then to spend the night there, satisfying his longing for the companionship of his wife. He would return the next morning with the rest of his game and share it with the others.

As darkness fell, he ate the meat. And while he watched the sky darken, he began thinking about his wife on the opposite bank of the river.

The more he thought of her, the more he longed for her. The greater his longing, the more he desired her, especially as the sky in the west darkened and gave way to black night.

"It was not I who was angered by a woman," thought he. "It was not my wife who said she could get along without us men."

And as he reflected on such things, he found himself longing all the more. In the darkness he pictured the women standing on the far shore of the river beckoning to the men. He pictured them cupping their hands under their breasts suggestively. He pictured them as they shook their naked bodies to tease the men. He imagined he could see them wiggling their buttocks at them.

Surely his own wife was among the women who desired the company of their husbands.

Full of such thoughts, and longing so for her, he took the liver from the body of the slain deer and cut a slit into it. Then he placed it by the fire to warm.

"So be it," said he when the liver felt as warm as his wife had felt whenever he and she would lie close together. "I have no quarrel with my wife or any woman.

"No quarrel whatsoever."

Upon saying which, he placed the liver carefully below himself where his legs joined.

But just then *Né'éshjaa'* the Owl cried out. He had come unseen upon Man With Wrappings On.

"Wu'hu'hu'hu'," cried he from somewhere just outside the brush circle.

"Wu'hu'hu'hu'," he was heard to cry.

"Stop, *K'íídeesdizi!* Stop that.

"Do nothing with that liver if you do not intend eating it!"

Startled, Man With Wrappings On returned the liver to the fire. Then he stepped outside the brush circle and walked around, looking in vain for whomever had just spoken.

Finding no one, he came back to the fireside, lay down, and tried to sleep, attempting at first to put his wife out of his mind and to forget his longing.

Well into the night he lay there unable to sleep. Try as he might, he could not stop thinking of her, and the more he thought of her the more he missed her. The more he missed her the more he desired her. Until he finally reached for the liver again, which still lay warm by the fire. Taking it into his hands again, he listened carefully for the cry he had heard earlier. But he could hear nothing.

"Ah," thought he. "Now's the time."

"Come, wife-liver.

"Come to me now!"

Upon thinking which, he again positioned the liver below himself.

But hardly had he done so when again he heard the cry of *Né'éshjaa'* the Owl.

"Wu'hu'hu'hu'," he heard him cry.

"Stop, *K'íídeesdizi!* Stop that.

"Eat that liver; do not have intercourse with it!"

Startled again, Man With Wrappings On quickly returned the liver. Then he curled up and tried again to sleep, doing what he could to forget that he missed his wife. But he was unable to do so. On into the night he lay there, missing her. The more he missed her, the more he desired her. The more he desired her, the more easily he imagined that she lay there close to him. Thus he waited, listening for any sound that might break the silence and stop him. Hearing nothing, however, he once more longed for the warm liver.

"Now perhaps that meddling fool is gone," he thought as he took it in his hands and once again placed it against himself.

"Now," he whispered hoarsely.

"Let it be now, no matter who's out there."

His having hardly said so, the voice again broke the silence.

"Wu'hu'hu'hu'," cried the voice.

"*K'íídeesdizi,* stop! Stop that.

"If you do not intend to eat that liver, keep it away from yourself."

With a start, *K'íídeesdizi* replaced the liver by the fire. Again he tried to rid himself of his desire and sleep. Unable to do that, though, he lay there until the eastern sky began to show the gray light of the oncoming dawn. He lay there desiring his wife, longing for her all the more as he thought of her, all the more anxiously imagining that she lay close beside him, nestling her warmth against the full length of his great longing. He lay there in the silence until he could contain himself no longer, and until he cried out, scarcely in control of himself.

"I don't care," he gasped.

"I don't care who's out there. I don't care where he may be. It's got to be now. It must be now." And he grabbed the liver and thrust it against his penis.

No sooner than which the voice of *Né'éshjaa'* the Owl rang out.

"*K'íídeesdizi* you must stop that. Stop!

"Do not have intercourse with that liver; leave it alone."

Man With Wrappings On then threw the liver back to the fire and sprang to his feet. "Who are you, anyway?" he demanded. He faced one way, then another. He stalked to the outer edge of the brush circle and paced around it, first one way, then the next twice around, then back again the way he originally went. "Where are you?" he asked.

"Can't you leave a person alone?

"Or can't you at least face a man and explain yourself as someone ought to do?"

Whereupon *Né'éshjaa'* the Owl suddenly appeared. And he softly spoke these words.

"I really mean you no harm, grandchild," spoke he.

"But I also insist on what I am telling you.

"What you are trying to do is altogether out of place. You cannot make things normal by treating the liver of a slain deer as if it were your wife."

K'íídeesdizi took a moment to consider.

Indeed, the liver was not his wife.

Nothing he might do with it would bring her to him. Nothing he did with it would take him to her.

"Wait right there, granduncle," he said to *Né'éshjaa'* after a short pause. Then he returned to the center of the brush circle and built a fresh fire. From the carcass of the slain deer he cut a choice tenderloin. He sliced it thin and cooked it together with the liver. Taking that for himself to eat, he offered the steak to Owl.

"Here, granduncle," he said, handing it to *Né'éshjaa'*.

"You eat this while I eat the liver."

"Thank you, my grandchild," said he. "But turn your back to me. I do not eat in anyone's plain sight."

Thus he ate behind the back of *K'íídeesdizi* the Man With Wrappings On, promising that after he finished he would explain himself, which indeed is as much as anyone ought to do.

. . .

"It has been nearly four years, now," explained *Né'éshjaa'* the Owl, "since you men left the women over there on the other shore, as you yourself certainly know.

"Whether the women are to blame or the men, no good can come of the separation.

"Fewer of the women now remain than you menfolk left behind. Many of them have plunged into the water and disappeared. As for those who remain, they are abusing themselves any way they can in the absence of you men. They have intercourse with long stones. They seek to satisfy themselves with thick quills. Some insert cactus into themselves. Some handle the bones of animals as if they were their husbands.

"What is more, they grow hungry for want of food.

"Suppose that those who remain eventually threw themselves into the water because they are in such misery? That will leave only you men living on the surface of this world. Do you think you can sustain life by yourselves? Will the liver of a slain deer bear your children?

"I do not know how long they can endure over there, meanwhile. Just yesterday I overheard *Áltsé asdzáá* the First Woman lament to her followers. She grieved for those who had disappeared into the water, and she pitied those who have survived only to long for their husbands on empty stomachs. She even confessed that she wished to hear the voice of her husband *Áltsé hastiin* the First Man once more.

"I mention all of that for your sake, grandson. And for the sake of the others.

"Somehow you must contrive to have the women brought across the river so that they can rejoin the men. Otherwise this disorder will continue until the world we now know comes to an end. Even the sky will disappear, and with it all the work that has been done so far. Life can go on only if the women and the men reunite.

"Now I must go, grandson," concluded *Né'éshjaa'* the Owl to *K'íídeesdizi* the Man With Wrappings On. "I have nothing more to say.

"Except that I leave it to you to devise a way to bring the men and the women together again."

· · ·

K'íídeesdizi thought carefully about what he had been told, and then he returned to the village. Once there he started straight toward *Áltsé hastiin* the First Man to repeat outright what *Né'éshjaa'* had said. But he thought the better of that, remembering how angry he had been after his quarrel with *Áltsé asdzáá* the First Woman.

Instead, he assembled several of the older men and began to reason with them.

"Think about it," he reasoned, after he had explained what he had heard. "Over there our women are starving. What good is our food over here if they have little to eat?

"One by one they plunge into the water. Or else they abuse themselves with long stones and thick quills, or with cactus and the bones of animals. Suppose that they were all to perish while we survived? Could we possibly sustain life without them? Can mud bear our children? Can the livers of slain deer nurture our offspring?

"If life is to go on, we and the women must rejoin each other. Otherwise this disorder will continue until the world as we know it disappears.

"Who knows?

"Even the sky could come to an end, together with all the work that has so far been done."

Thus he spoke to various men, getting them all to agree. And together they decided to induce *Áltsé hastiin* the First Man to change his mind and initiate a reunion.

One by one they managed to get him to reconsider.

"Did you hear plaintive voices over there on the other shore last night?" someone would ask him early one morning.

"Unless I'm mistaken I believe that yet another woman jumped into the river," someone else might say. "Over there across the water. Where they struggle to survive."

"How terrible it must be on the opposite bank," said still another. "No food to eat. No men for companionship."

Said yet another: "Perhaps I was dreaming, but all night long I thought I heard a woman pleading. I cannot be sure—after all, I have not heard her voice up close for four years now—but it sounded like *Áltsé asdzáá* the First Woman. But then why should that matter to me? She insisted that the women can get along just fine without us men, after all."

. . .

By the end of the fourth year of the separation, *Áltsé hastiin* the First Man did indeed wonder whether he had acted wisely. So he called the men together and asked them what they thought. And this is what one of them said:

"Over there our women are starving," he said.

Added another:

"What good is our food on this side of the river if our women starve on the other side?" he added.

And another spoke these words:

"One by one they leap into the water. Meanwhile, those who remain abuse themselves with long stones and thick quills, or with cactus and the bones of animals," were his words.

And asked still another:

"Suppose we survived while they all perished?" he asked. "Could we possibly sustain life without them? Can mud bear our children? Can the livers of slain deer raise our offspring?

"If this present disorder continues, the world as we know it will come to an end.

"Who knows?

"Even the sky would disappear, along with everything else that has so far been created."

. . .

Áltsé hastiin the First Man thought carefully about what the men were saying. And he finally sent one of them down to the river. He instructed him to call across the stream and ask if *Áltsé asdzáá* the First Woman was still there. If so, would she be willing to come to the water's edge and hear something her husband had to say?

When she received that message she gladly came to the river. Whereupon *Áltsé hastiin* asked her this question:

"Do you still think you can live alone?" he asked her.

To which she gave this response:

"I no longer believe that I can," she responded.

"I do not think that any woman here can live alone.

"And I now regret the things I said to you."

That is what she told him.

And this is what he replied to her:

"And I am sorry that I let the things you said make me angry," he replied.

. . .

So it was that the men and the women put their quarrel to an end. *Áltsé asdzáá* the First Woman instructed her followers to gather at the bank of the river on their side. And *Áltsé hastiin* the First Man instructed his to gather at the bank on their side.

He then sent the raft over to the women's side, where they were ferried across to the opposite shore. There they were told to bathe and to dry their bodies with meal. The two sexes would remain separated until nightfall. Then they would rejoin each other and resume their lives together, it is said.

1984

Literature of the Twentieth Century

Eudora Welty 1909–2001

Eudora Welty was born and raised in Jackson, Mississippi. She attended Mississippi State College for Women for two years and then transferred to the University of Wisconsin, graduating in 1929. The following year she entered Columbia University in New York to study advertising. Two years later she returned to Jackson, where she worked for a local radio station and wrote society news for a Memphis newspaper. She also wrote publicity for the WPA and worked for a state commission to attract tourists to Mississippi.

Welty began her first serious attempts at writing after her return to Mississippi from New York in 1931. In June of 1936 her first short story, "Death of a Traveling Salesman," was published. She wrote several novels, the last of those being Losing Battles *(1970) and* The Optimist's Daughter *(1972), and numerous short stories that have been widely anthologized, translated into various foreign languages, and dramatized on Broadway and on television.*

Welty's writing displays a strong sense of place. She insisted that successful fiction depends in large measure on the appropriate location of the appropriate action. "It seems plain," she observed, "that the art that speaks most clearly, explicitly, directly, and passionately from its place of origin will remain the longest understood." Welty evinced a strong sense of her southern heritage, yet she was capable of a sustained detachment when writing about the South. Her fiction is largely concerned with the inner life, the mysteries of human beings confronting each other. Her writing reveals the sharp eye of a painter or photographer, displaying an acute sense of light, color, and atmosphere.

As a Southerner, Eudora Welty has often been compared to William Faulkner, a fellow Mississippian, but although her writing resembles Faulkner's in its attention to metaphor and symbol and in its concern for the South and its landscape, her writing does not exhibit the tragic vision of Faulkner and his concern with the dissolution of a moribund society. And she is at her best in short stories—even her novels have the qualities of extended short tales—which present her ironic view of human beings struggling amid the follies of life and the menace of death.

FURTHER READING: *Selected Stories of Eudora Welty,* 1954; R. Vande Kieft, *Eudora Welty,* 1962, 1987; A. Appel, *A Season of Dreams: The Fiction of Eudora Welty,* 1965; J. Bryant, *Eudora Welty,* 1968; *The Eye of the Story: Selected Essays and Reviews,* 1978; *Eudora Welty: Critical Essays,* ed. P. Prenshaw, 1979; *The Collected Stories of Eudora Welty,* 1980; M. Kreyling, *Eudora Welty's Achievement of Order,* 1980; E. Evans, *Eudora Welty,* 1981; A. Devlin, *Eudora Welty's Chronicle,* 1983; *One Writer's Beginnings,* 1984; C. Manning, *Ears Opening Like Morning Glories: Eudora Welty and the Love of Story Telling,* 1985; *Eudora Welty,* ed. H. Bloom, 1986; *Welty: A Life in Literature,* ed. A. Devlin, 1987; L. Westling, *Eudora Welty,* 1989; *Critical Essays on Eudora Welty,* ed. W. Turner and L. Harding, 1989; R. MacNeil, *Seeing Black and White,* 1990; P. Schmidt, *The Heart of the Story: Eudora Welty's Fiction,* 1991; G. Mortimer, *Daughter of the Swan: Love and Knowledge in Eudora Welty's Fiction,* 1993; R. Weston, *Gothic Traditions and Narrative Techniques in the Fiction of Eudora Welty,* 1994; J. Gretlund, *Eudora Welty's Aesthetics of Place,* 1994; *More Conversations with Eudora Welty,* ed. P. Prenshaw, 1996; C. Johnston, *Eudora Welty: A Study of the Short Fiction,* 1997; A. Waldron, *Eudora: A Writer's Life,* 1998; M. Kreyling, *Understanding Eudora Welty,* 1999; S. Marrs, *One Writer's Imagination: The Fiction of Eudora Welty,* 2002.

TEXT: *A Curtain of Green,* 1941.

POWERHOUSE

Powerhouse is playing!

He's here on tour from the city—"Powerhouse and His Keyboard"—"Powerhouse and His Tasmanians"—think of the things he calls himself! There's no one in the world like him. You can't tell what he is. "Nigger man"?—he looks more Asiatic, monkey, Jewish, Babylonian, Peruvian, fanatic, devil. He has pale gray eyes, heavy lids, maybe horny like a lizard's, but big glowing eyes when they're open. He has African feet of the greatest size, stomping, both together, on each side of the pedals. He's not coal black—beverage colored—looks like a preacher when his mouth is shut, but then it opens—vast and obscene. And his mouth is going every minute: like a monkey's when it looks for something. Improvising, coming on a light and childish melody—*smooch*—he loves it with his mouth.

Is it possible that he could be this! When you have him there performing for you, that's what you feel. You know people on a stage—and people of a darker race—so likely to be marvelous, frightening.

This is a white dance. Powerhouse is not a show-off like the Harlem boys, not drunk, not crazy—he's in a trance; he's a person of joy, a fanatic. He listens as much as he performs, a look of hideous, powerful rapture on his face. Big arched eyebrows that never stop traveling, like a Jew's—wandering-Jew eyebrows. When he plays he beats down piano and seat and wears them away. He is in motion every moment—what could be more obscene? There he is with his great head, fat stomach, and little round piston legs, and long yellow-sectioned strong big fingers, at rest about the size of bananas. Of course you know how he sounds—you've heard him on records—but still you need to see him. He's going all the time, like skating around the skating rink or rowing a boat. It makes everybody crowd around, here in this shadowless steel-trussed hall with the rose-like posters of Nelson Eddy[1] and the testimonial for the mind-reading horse in handwriting magnified five hundred times. Then all quietly he lays his finger on a key with the promise and serenity of a sibyl touching the book.

Powerhouse is so monstrous he sends everybody into oblivion. When any group, any performers, come to town, don't people always come out and hover near, leaning inward about them, to learn what it is? What is it? Listen. Remember how it was with the acrobats Watch them carefully, hear the least word, especially what they say to one another, in another language—don't let them escape you; it's the only time for hallucination the last time. They can't stay. They'll be somewhere else this time tomorrow.

Powerhouse has as much as possible done by signals. Everybody, laughing as if to hide a weakness, will sooner or later hand him up a written request. Powerhouse reads each one, studying with a secret face: that is the face which looks like a mask—anybody's; there is a moment when he makes a decision. Then a light slides under his eyelids, and he says, "92!" or some combination of figures—never a name. Before a number the band is all frantic, misbehaving, pushing, like children in a schoolroom, and he is the teacher getting silence. His hands over the keys, he says sternly, "You-all ready? You-all ready to do some serious walking?"—waits—then, STAMP. Quiet. STAMP, for the second time. This is absolute. Then a set of rhythmic kicks against the floor to communicate the tempo. Then, O Lord! say the distended-eyes from beyond the boundary of the trumpets, Hello and good-by, and they are all down the first note like a waterfall.

This note marks the end of any known discipline. Powerhouse seems to abandon them all—he himself seems lost—down in the song, yelling up like somebody in a whirlpool—not guiding them—hailing them only. But he knows, really. He cries out, but he must know exactly. "Mercy! . . . What I say! . . . Yeah!" And then drifting, listening—"Where that skin beater?"—wanting drums, and starting up and pouring it out in the greatest delight and brutality. On the sweet pieces such a leer for everybody! He looks down so benevolently upon all our faces and whispers the lyrics to us. And if you could hear him at this moment

[1]Nelson Eddy (1901–1967) was a singer and movie actor who starred in a number of popular musicals in the 1930s and 1940s.

on "Marie, the Dawn is Breaking"![2] He's going up the keyboard with a few fingers in some very derogatory triplet-routine, he gets higher and higher, and then he looks over the end of the piano, as if over a cliff. But not in a show-off way—the song makes him do it.

He loves the way they all play, too—all those next to him. The far section of the band is all studious, wearing glasses, every one—they don't count. Only those playing around Powerhouse are the real ones. He has a bass fiddler from Vicksburg, black as pitch, named Valentine, who plays with his eyes shut and talking to himself, very young: Powerhouse has to keep encouraging him. "Go on, go on, give it up, bring it on out there!" When you heard him like that on records, did you know he was really pleading?

He calls Valentine out to take a solo.

"What you going to play?" Powerhouse looks out kindly from behind the piano; he opens his mouth and shows his tongue, listening.

Valentine looks down, drawing against his instrument, and says without a lip movement, "'Honeysuckle Rose.'"[3]

He has a clarinet player named Little Brother, and loves to listen to anything he does. He'll smile and say, "Beautiful!" Little Brother takes a step forward when he plays and stands at the very front, with the whites of his eyes like fishes swimming. Once when he played a low note, Powerhouse muttered in dirty praise, "He went clear downstairs to get that one!"

After a long time, he holds up the number of fingers to tell the band how many choruses still to go—usually five. He keeps his directions down to signals.

It's a bad night outside. It's a white dance, and nobody dances, except a few straggling jitterbugs and two elderly couples. Everybody just stands around the band and watches Powerhouse. Sometimes they steal glances at one another, as if to say, Of course, you know how it is with *them*—Negroes—band leaders—they would play the same way, giving all they've got, for an audience of one. . . . When somebody, no matter who, gives everything, it makes people feel ashamed for him.

Late at night they play the one waltz they will ever consent to play—by request, "Pagan Love Song."[4] Powerhouse's head rolls and sinks like a weight between his waving shoulders. He groans, and his fingers drag into the keys heavily, holding on to the notes, retrieving. It is a sad song.

"You know what happened to me?" says Powerhouse.

Valentine hums a response, dreaming at the bass.

"I got a telegram my wife is dead," says Powerhouse, with wandering fingers.

"Uh-huh?"

His mouth gathers and forms a barbarous O while his fingers walk up straight, unwillingly, three octaves.

"Gypsy? Why how come her to die, didn't you just phone her up in the night last night long distance?"

[2]A song by American songwriter Irving Berlin (1888–1989).

[3]A jazz number written by Thomas "Fats" Waller (1904–1943) and Andy Razaf (1895–1973).

[4]A song by Arthur Freed (1894–1973) and Nacio Herb Brown (1896–1964); it was the theme song for a 1929 movie, *The Pagan*.

"Telegram say—here the words: Your wife is dead." He puts 4/4 over the 3/4.

"Not but four words?" This is the drummer, an unpopular boy named Scoot, a disbelieving maniac.

Powerhouse is shaking his vast cheeks. "What the hell was she trying to do? What was she up to?"

"What name has it got signed, if you got a telegram?" Scoot is spitting away with those wire brushes.

Little Brother, the clarinet player, who cannot now speak, glares and tilts back.

"Uranus Knockwood is the name signed." Powerhouse lifts his eyes open. "Ever heard of him?" A bubble shoots out on his lip like a plate on a counter.

Valentine is beating slowly on with his palm and scratching the strings with his long blue nails. He is fond of a waltz, Powerhouse interrupts him.

"I don't know him. Don't know who he is." Valentine shakes his head with the closed eyes.

"Say it agin."

"Uranus Knockwood."

"That ain't Lenox Avenue."

"It ain't Broadway."

"Ain't ever seen it wrote out in any print, even for horse racing."

"Hell, that's on a star, boy, ain't it?" Crash of the cymbals.

"What the hell was she up to?" Powerhouse shudders. "Tell me, tell me, tell me." He makes triplets, and begins a new chorus. He holds three fingers up.

"You say you got a telegram." This is Valentine, patient and sleepy, beginning again.

Powerhouse is elaborate. "Yas, the time I go out, go way downstairs along a long cor-ri-dor to where they puts us: coming back along the cor-ri-dor: steps out and hands me a telegram: Your wife is dead."

"Gypsy?" The drummer like a spider over his drums.

"Aaaaaaaaa!" shouts Powerhouse, flinging out both powerful arms for three whole beats to flex his muscles, then kneading a dough of bass notes. His eyes glitter. He plays the piano like a drum sometimes—why not?

"Gypsy? Such a dancer?"

"Why you don't hear it straight from your agent? Why it ain't come from headquarters? What you been doing, getting telegrams in the *corridor,* signed nobody?"

They all laugh. End of that chorus.

"What time is it?" Powerhouse calls. "What the hell place is this? Where is my watch and chain?"

"I hang it on you," whimpers Valentine. "It still there."

There it rides on Powerhouse's great stomach, down where he can never see it.

"Sure did hear some clock striking twelve while ago. Must be *midnight.*"

"It going to be intermission," Powerhouse declares, lifting up his finger with the signet ring.

He draws the chorus to an end. He pulls a big Northern hotel towel out of the deep pocket in his vast, special-cut tux pants and pushes his forehead into it.

"If she went and killed herself!" he says with a hidden face. "If she up and jumped out that window!" He gets to his feet, turning vaguely, wearing the towel on his head.

"Ha, ha!"

"Sheik, sheik!"

"She wouldn't do that." Little Brother sets down his clarinet like a precious vase, and speaks. He still looks like an East Indian queen, implacable, divine, and full of snakes. "You ain't going to expect people doing what they says over long distance."

"Come on!" roars Powerhouse. He is already at the back door, he has pulled it wide open, and with a wild, gathered-up face is smelling the terrible night.

Powerhouse, Valentine, Scoot and Little Brother step outside into the drenching rain.

"Well, they emptying buckets," says Powerhouse in a mollified voice. On the street he holds his hands out and turns up the blanched palms like sieves.

A hundred dark, ragged, silent, delighted Negroes have come around from under the eaves of the hall, and follow wherever they go.

"Watch out Little Brother don't shrink," says Powerhouse. "You just the right size now, clarinet don't suck you in. You got a dry throat, Little Brother, you in the desert?" He reaches into the pocket and pulls out a paper of mints. "Now hold 'em in your mouth—don't chew 'em. I don't carry around nothing without limit."

"Go in that joint and have beer," says Scoot, who walks ahead.

"Beer? Beer? You know what beer is? What do they say is beer? What's beer? Where I been?"

"Down yonder where it say World Café—that do? They are in Negrotown now.

Valentine patters over and holds open a screen door warped like a sea shell, bitter in the wet, and they walk in, stained darker with the rain and leaving footprints. Inside, sheltered dry smells stand like screens around a table covered with a red-checkered cloth, in the center of which flies hang onto an obelisk-shaped ketchup bottle. The midnight walls are checkered again with admonishing "Not Responsible" signs and black-figured, smoky calendars. It is a waiting, silent, limp room. There is a burned-out-looking nickelodeon and right beside it a long-necked wall instrument labeled "Business Phone, Don't Keep Talking." Circled phone numbers are written up everywhere. There is a worn-out peacock feather hanging by a thread to an old, thin, pink, exposed light bulb, where it slowly turns around and around, whoever breathes.

A waitress watches.

"Come here, living statue, and get all this big order of beer we fixing to give."

"Never seen you before anywhere." The waitress moves and comes forward and slowly shows little gold leaves and tendrils over her teeth. She shoves up her shoulders and breasts. "How I going to know who you might be? Robbers? Coming in out of the black of night right at midnight, setting down so big at my table?"

"Boogers," says Powerhouse, his eyes opening lazily as in a cave.

The girl screams delicately with pleasure. O Lord, she likes talk and scares.

"Where you going to find enough beer to put out on this here table?"

She runs to the kitchen with bent elbows and sliding steps.

"Here's a million nickels," says Powerhouse, pulling his hand out of his pocket and sprinkling coins out, all but the last one, which he makes vanish like a magician.

Valentine and Scoot take the money over to the nickelodeon, which looks as battered as a slot machine, and read all the names of the records out loud.

"Whose 'Tuxedo Junction'?"[5] asks Powerhouse.

"You know whose."

"Nickelodeon, I request you please to play 'Empty Bed Blues'[6] and let Bessie Smith sing."

Silence: they hold it like a measure.

"Bring me all those nickels on back here," says Powerhouse. "Look at that! What you tell me the name of this place?"

"White dance, week night, raining, Alligator, Mississippi, long ways from home."

"Uh-huh."

"Sent for You Yesterday and Here You Come Today"[7] plays.

The waitress, setting the tray of beer down on a back table, comes up taut and apprehensive as a hen. "Says in the kitchen, back there putting their eyes to little hole peeping out, that you is Mr Powerhouse. . . . They knows from a picture they seen."

"They seeing right tonight, that is him," says Little Brother.

"You him?"

"That is him in the flesh," says Scoot.

"Does you wish to touch him?" asks Valentine. "Because he don't bite."

"You passing through?"

"Now you got everything right."

She waits like a drop, hands languishing together in front.

"Little-Bit, ain't you going to bring the beer?"

She brings it, and goes behind the cash register and smiles, turning different ways. The little fillet of gold in her mouth is gleaming.

"The Mississippi River's here," she says once.

Now all the watching Negroes press in gently and bright-eyed through the door, as many as can get in. One is a little boy in a straw sombrero which has been coated with aluminum paint all over.

Powerhouse, Valentine, Scoot and Little Brother drink beer, and their eyelids come together like curtains. The wall and the rain and the humble beautiful waitress waiting on them and the other Negroes watching enclose them.

"Listen!" whispers Powerhouse, looking into the ketchup bottle and slowly spreading his performer's hands over the damp, wrinkling cloth with the red squares. "Listen how it is. My wife gets missing me. Gypsy. She goes to the window. She looks out and sees you know what. Street. Sign saying Hotel. People walking. Somebody looks up. Old man. She looks down, out the window. Well? . . . *Ssssst! Plooey!* What she do? Jump out and bust her brains all over the world."

He opens his eyes.

[5]A jazz number composed by Erskine Hawkins (1914–1993).

[6]A song composed and sung by legendary jazz singer Bessie Smith (1898–1937).

[7]A song by Johnny Mercer (1909–1976).

"That's it," agrees Valentine. "You gets a telegram."

"Sure she misses you," Little Brother adds.

"No, it's night time." How softly he tells them! "Sure. It's the night time. She say, What do I hear? Footsteps walking up the hall? That him? Footsteps go on off. It's not me. I'm in Alligator, Mississippi, she's crazy. Shaking all over. Listens till her ears and all grow out like old music-box horns but still she can't hear a thing. She says, All right! I'll jump out the window then. Got on her nightgown. I know that nightgown, and her thinking there. Says, Ho hum, all right, and jumps out the window. Is she mad at me! Is she crazy! She don't leave *nothing* behind her!"

"Ya! Ha!"

"Brains and insides everywhere, Lord, Lord."

All the watching Negroes stir in their delight, and to their higher delight he says affectionately, "Listen! Rats in here."

"That must be the way, boss."

"Only, naw, Powerhouse, that ain't true. That sound too *bad*."

"Does? I even know who finds her," cries Powerhouse. "That no-good pussy-footed crooning creeper, that creeper that follow around after me, coming up like weeds behind me, following around after me everything I do and messing around on the trail I leave. Bets my numbers, sings my songs, gets close to my agent like a Betsy-bug; when I going out he just coming in. I got him now! I got my eye on him."

"Know who he is?"

"Why it's that old Uranus Knockwood!"

"Ya! Ha!"

"Yeah, and he coming now, he going to find Gypsy. There he is, coming around that corner, and Gypsy kadoodling down, oh-oh, watch out! *Sssst! Plooey!* See, there she is in her little old nightgown, and her insides and brains all scattered round."

A sigh fills the room.

"Hush about her brains. Hush about her insides."

"Ya! Ha! You talking about her brains and insides—old Uranus Knockwood," says Powerhouse, "look down and say Jesus! He say, Look here what I'm walking round in!"

They all burst into halloos of laughter. Powerhouse's face looks like a big hot iron stove.

"Why, he picks her up and carries her off!" he says.

"Ya! Ha!"

"Carries her *back* around the corner. . . ."

"Oh, Powerhouse!"

"You know him."

"Uranus Knockwood!"

"Yeahhh!"

"He take our wives when we gone!"

"He come in when we goes out!"

"Uh-huh!"

"He go out when we comes in!"

"Yeahhh!"

"He standing behind the door!"

"Old Uranus Knockwood."

"You know him."

"Middle-size man."

"Wears a hat."

"That's him."

Everybody in the room moans with pleasure. The little boy in the fine silver hat opens a paper and divides out a jelly roll among his followers.

And out of the breathless ring somebody moves forward like a slave, leading a great logy Negro with bursting eyes, and says, "This here is Sugar-Stick Thompson, that dove down to the bottom of July Creek and pulled up all those drownded white people fall out of a boat. Last summer, pulled up fourteen."

"Hello," says Powerhouse, turning and looking around at them all with his great daring face until they nearly suffocate.

Sugar-Stick, their instrument, cannot speak; he can only look back at the others.

"Can't even swim. Done it by holding his breath," says the fellow with the hero.

Powerhouse looks at him seekingly.

"I his half brother," the fellow puts in.

They step back.

"Gypsy say," Powerhouse rumbles gently again, looking at *them,* "'What is the use? I'm gonna jump out so far—so far. . . .' *Sssst—!*"

"Don't, boss, don't do it again," says Little Brother.

"It's awful," says the waitress. "I hates that Mr Knockwoods. All that the truth?"

"Want to see the telegram I got from him?" Powerhouse's hand goes to the vast pocket.

"Now wait, now wait, boss." They all watch him.

"It must be the real truth," says the waitress, sucking in her lower lip, her luminous eyes turning sadly, seeking the windows.

"No, babe, it ain't the truth." His eyebrows fly up, and he begins to whisper to her out of his vast oven mouth. His hand stays in his pocket. "Truth is something worse, I ain't said what, yet. It's something hasn't come to me, but I ain't saying it won't. And when it does, then want me to tell you?" He sniffs all at once, his eyes come open and turn up, almost too far. He is dreamily smiling.

"Don't, boss, don't, Powerhouse!"

"Oh!" the waitress screams.

"Go on git out of here!" bellows Powerhouse, taking his hand out of his pocket and clapping after her red dress.

The ring of watchers breaks and falls away.

"*Look* at that! Intermission is up," says Powerhouse.

He folds money under a glass, and after they go out, Valentine leans back in and drops a nickel in the nickelodeon behind them, and it lights up and begins to play "The Goona Goo."[8] The feather dangles still.

"Take a telegram!" Powerhouse shouts suddenly up into the rain over the street. "Take a answer. Now what was that name?"

They get a little tired.

"Uranus Knockwood."

[8]A popular jazz tune of the time.

"You ought to know."

"Yas? Spell it to me."

They spell it all the ways it could be spelled. It puts them in a wonderful humor.

"Here's the answer. I got it right here. 'What in the hell you talking about? Don't make any difference: I gotcha.' Name signed: Powerhouse."

"That going to reach him, Powerhouse?" Valentine speaks in a maternal voice.

"Yas, yas."

All hushing, following him up the dark street at a distance, like old rained-on black ghosts, the Negroes are afraid they will die laughing.

Powerhouse throws back his vast head into the steaming rain, and a look of hopeful desire seems to blow somehow like a vapor from his own dilated nostrils over his face and bring a mist to his eyes.

"Reach him and come out the other side."

"That's it, Powerhouse, that's it. You got him now."

Powerhouse lets out a long sigh.

"But ain't you going back there to call up Gypsy long distance, the way you did last night in that other place? I seen a telephone. . . . Just to see if she there at home?"

There is a measure of silence. That is one crazy drummer that's going to get his neck broken some day.

"No," growls Powerhouse. "No! How many thousand times tonight I got to say No?"

He holds up his arm in the rain.

"You sure-enough unroll your voice some night, it about reach up yonder to her," says Little Brother, dismayed.

They go on up the street, shaking the rain off and on them like birds.

Back in the dance hall, they play "San." The jitterbugs start up like windmills stationed over the floor, and in their orbits—one circle, another, a long stretch and a zigzag—dance the elderly couples with old smoothness, undisturbed and stately.

When Powerhouse first came back from intermission, no doubt full of beer, they said, he got the band tuned up again in his own way. He didn't strike the piano keys for pitch—he simply opened his mouth and gave falsetto howls—in A, D and so on—they tuned by him. Then he took hold of the piano, as if he saw it for the first time in his life, and tested it for strength, hit it down in the bass, played an octave with his elbow, lifted the top, looked inside, and leaned against it with all his might. He sat down and played it for a few minutes with outrageous force and got it under his power—a bass deep and coarse as a sea net—then produced something glimmering and fragile, and smiled. And who could ever remember any of the things he says? They are just inspired remarks that roll out of his mouth like smoke.

They've requested "Somebody Loves Me,"[9] and he's already done twelve or fourteen choruses, piling them up nobody knows how, and it will be a wonder if he ever gets through. Now and then he calls and shouts, "'Somebody loves

[9]A popular song by George Gershwin (1898–1937).

me! Somebody loves me, I wonder who!'" His mouth gets to be nothing but a volcano. "I wonder who!"

"Maybe . . ." He uses all his right hand on a trill.

"Maybe . . ." He pulls back his spread fingers, and looks out upon the place where he is. A vast, impersonal and yet furious grimace transfigures his wet face.

". . . Maybe it's you!"

1941

Richard Wright 1908–1960

Richard Wright experienced a troubled and frightening Southern boyhood. His father deserted his family and left his son to be raised in an oppressive environment by his fundamentalist grandmother and stern mother. Although hindered by limited educational opportunities for blacks in the South in the 1920s, he distinguished himself in the classroom, graduating as valedictorian and having a story published while still in high school. But his talents could not find recognition in his segregated society, and, like thousands of other blacks of the time, he fled north, first to Memphis, Tennessee, and then to Chicago.

In Chicago, Wright had several menial jobs. During the Depression he became involved with the Federal Negro Theatre (a WPA project) and with the Illinois Writers' Project. At this time, he began to attend meetings of the John Reed Club, a group supported by the Communist Party. Throughout the 1930s, under the sponsorship of the John Reed Club, Wright wrote and published stories and essays. Although leaders of the Communist Party complained of his failure to follow the party line in his writing, he continued to work within the party (an affiliation that lasted until 1944), and in 1937 he moved to New York to become Harlem editor of the Daily Worker. *His first book,* Uncle Tom's Children: Four Novellas, *was published in 1938, and he subsequently won a Guggenheim Fellowship that enabled him to complete and publish* Native Son *in 1940.*

Native Son, *his dramatic and gripping story of a black man's struggle with poverty, racism, and the justice system in the 1930s, won immediate acclaim and sold a quarter of a million copies in its first month of publication. Rewritten for the stage, it was produced in 1941 and became one of the first plays by an African American playwright to be presented on Broadway. In 1945,* Black Boy, *an autobiographical account of his youth in the South, was published, and Wright again received great popular acclaim. During this time he was also an important supporter of younger black writers, including Margaret Walker, Ralph Ellison, and James Baldwin. He had become the first black American whose work appeared on national bestseller lists, but in 1947, embittered by the racial prejudice he had encountered, he emigrated to Europe, where he was to live until his death.*

Wright published more novels, essays, and stories, but his later work never received the popular or critical acclaim of Native Son *and* Black Boy. *The work that he did after leaving the United States has generally been neglected.* American Hunger, *Wright's autobiographical sequel to* Black Boy, *never received favorable attention. And although the essays collected in* White Man, Listen! *are significant contributions to twentieth-century racial history and* The Outsider *is notable as an existentialist novel, Richard*

Wright's most defining work remains Native Son. *He was at work on a novel when he died of a heart attack in France on November 28, 1960.*

FURTHER READING: *Richard Wright: Letters to Joe C. Brown,* ed. T. Knipp, 1968; C. Webb, *Richard Wright: A Biography,* 1968; D. McCall, *The Example of Richard Wright,* 1969; E. Margolies, *The Art of Richard Wright,* 1969; R. Bone, *Richard Wright,* 1969; J. Williams, *The Most Native of Sons: A Biography of Richard Wright,* 1970; R. Brignano, *Richard Wright: An Introduction to the Man and His Works,* 1970; R. Abcarian, *Richard Wright's "Native Son": A Critical Handbook,* 1970; *Richard Wright: Impressions and Perspectives,* ed. D. Ray and R. Farnsworth, 1973; K. Kinnamon, *The Emergence of Richard Wright,* 1973; *Richard Wright Reader,* ed. E. Wright and M. Fabre, 1978; M. Fabre, *The Unfinished Quest of Richard Wright,* 1979; A. Gayle, *Richard Wright: Ordeal of a Native Son,* 1980; R. Felgar, *Richard Wright,* 1980; *Critical Essays on Richard Wright,* ed. Y. Hakutani, 1982; M. Fabre, *The World of Richard Wright,* 1985; J. Joyce, *Richard Wright's Art of Tragedy,* 1986; *Richard Wright,* ed. H. Bloom, 1987; M. Walker, *Richard Wright: Daemonic Genius,* 1988; J. Trotman, *Richard Wright: Myth and Realities,* 1989; M. Fabre, *Richard Wright: Books and Writers,* 1990; *Conversations with Richard Wright,* ed. K. Kinnamon and M. Fabre, 1993; *Richard Wright: Critical Perspectives Past and Present,* ed. H. Gates and K. Appiah, 1993; Y. Hakutani, *Richard Wright and Racial Discourse,* 1996; T. Caron, *Struggles over the World: Race and Religion in O'Connor, Faulkner, Hurston, and Wright,* 2000; R. Felgar, *Student Companion to Richard Wright,* 2000; A. Janmohamed, *The Death-Bound-Subject: Richard Wright's Archaeology of Death,* 2005.

TEXT: *Native Son,* 1998.

from *NATIVE SON*

[Bigger Thomas, the main character in *Native Son,* is a twenty-year-old African American living in poverty in a Chicago ghetto with his mother and a younger brother, Buddy, and sister, Vera, in the 1930s. At the beginning of the following episode, he is scheduled to meet with a wealthy white man named Dalton to discuss a possible job as chauffeur for the Dalton family.]

Outside his window he saw the sun dying over the roof-tops in the western sky and watched the first shade of dusk fall. Now and then a street car ran past. The rusty radiator hissed at the far end of the room. All day long it had been spring-like; but now dark clouds were slowly swallowing the sun. All at once the street lamps came on and the sky was black and close to the house-tops.

Inside his shirt he felt the cold metal of the gun resting against his naked skin; he ought to put it back between the mattresses. No! He would keep it. He would take it with him to the Dalton place. He felt that he would be safer if he took it. He was not planning to use it and there was nothing in particular that he was afraid of, but there was in him an uneasiness and distrust that made him feel that he ought to have it along. He was going among white people, so he would take his knife and his gun; it would make him feel that he was the equal of them, give him a sense of completeness. Then he thought of a good reason why he should take it; in order to get to the Dalton place, he had to go through a white neighborhood. He had not heard of any Negroes being molested recently, but he felt that it was always possible.

Far away a clock boomed five times. He sighed and got up and yawned and stretched his arms high above his head to loosen the muscles of his body. He got his overcoat, for it was growing cold outdoors; then got his cap. He tiptoed to the door, wanting to slip out without his mother hearing him. Just as he was about to open it, she called,

"Bigger!"

He stopped and frowned.

"Yeah, Ma."

"You going to see about that job?"

"Yeah."

"Ain't you going to eat?"

"I ain't got time now."

She came to the door, wiping her soapy hands upon an apron.

"Here; take this quarter and buy you something."

"O.K."

"And be careful, son."

He went out and walked south to Forty-sixth Street, then eastward. Well, he would see in a few moments if the Daltons for whom he was to work were the ones he had seen and heard about in the movie. But while walking through this quiet and spacious white neighborhood, he did not feel the pull and mystery of the thing as strongly as he had in the movie. The houses he passed were huge; lights glowed softly in windows. The streets were empty, save for an occasional car that zoomed past on swift rubber tires. This was a cold and distant world; a world of white secrets carefully guarded. He could feel a pride, a certainty, and a confidence in these streets and houses. He came to Drexel Boulevard and began to look for 4605. When he came to it, he stopped and stood before a high, black, iron picket fence, feeling constricted inside. All he had felt in the movie was gone; only fear and emptiness filled him now.

Would they expect him to come in the front way or back? It was queer that he had not thought of that. Goddamn! He walked the length of the picket fence in front of the house, seeking for a walk leading to the rear. But there was none. Other than the front gate, there was only a driveway, the entrance to which was securely locked. Suppose a police saw him wandering in a white neighborhood like this? It would be thought that he was trying to rob or rape somebody. He grew angry. Why had he come to take this goddamn job? He could have stayed among his own people and escaped feeling this fear and hate. This was not his world; he had been foolish in thinking that he would have liked it. He stood in the middle of the sidewalk with his jaws clamped tight; he wanted to strike something with his fist. Well. . . . Goddamn! There was nothing to do but go in the front way. If he were doing wrong, they could not kill him, at least; all they could do was to tell him that he could not get the job.

Timidly, he lifted the latch on the gate and walked to the steps. He paused, waiting for someone to challenge him. Nothing happened. Maybe nobody was home? He went to the door and saw a dim light burning in a shaded niche above a doorbell. He pushed it and was startled to hear a soft gong sound within. Maybe he had pushed it too hard? Aw, what the hell! He had to do better than this; he relaxed his taut muscles and stood at ease, waiting. The doorknob turned. The door opened. He saw a white face. It was a woman.

"Hello!"

"Yessum," he said.

"You want to see somebody?"

"Er. . . . Er. . . . I want to see Mr. Dalton."

"Are you the Thomas boy?"

"Yessum."

"Come in."

He edged through the door slowly, then stopped halfway. The woman was so close to him that he could see a tiny mole at the corner of her mouth. He held his breath. It seemed that there was not room enough for him to pass without actually touching her.

"Come on in," the woman said.

"Yessum," he whispered.

He squeezed through and stood uncertainly in a softly lighted hallway.

"Follow me," she said.

With cap in hand and shoulders sloped, he followed, walking over a rug so soft and deep that it seemed he was going to fall at each step he took. He went into a dimly lit room.

"Take a seat," she said. "I'll tell Mr. Dalton that you're here and he'll be out in a moment."

"Yessum."

He sat and looked up at the woman; she was staring at him and he looked away in confusion. He was glad when she left. That old bastard! What's so damn funny about me? I'm just like she is. . . . He felt that the position in which he was sitting was too awkward and found that he was on the very edge of the chair. He rose slightly to sit farther back; but when he sat he sank down so suddenly and deeply that he thought the chair had collapsed under him. He bounded halfway up, in fear; then, realizing what had happened, he sank distrustfully down again. He looked round the room; it was lit by dim lights glowing from a hidden source. He tried to find them by roving his eyes, but could not. He had not expected anything like this; he had not thought that this world would be so utterly different from his own that it would intimidate him. On the smooth walls were several paintings whose nature he tried to make out, but failed. He would have liked to examine them, but dared not. Then he listened; a faint sound of piano music floated to him from somewhere. He was sitting in a white home; dim lights burned round him; strange objects challenged him; and he was feeling angry and uncomfortable.

"All right. Come this way."

He started at the sound of a man's voice.

"Suh?"

"Come this way."

Misjudging how far back he was sitting in the chair, his first attempt to rise failed and he slipped back, resting on his side. Grabbing the arms of the chair, he pulled himself upright and found a tall, lean, white-haired man holding a piece of paper in his hand. The man was gazing at him with an amused smile that made him conscious of every square inch of skin on his black body.

"Thomas?" the man asked. "Bigger Thomas?"

"Yessuh," he whispered; not speaking, really; but hearing his words roll involuntarily from his lips.

"Come this way."

"Yessuh."

He followed the man out of the room and down a hall. The man stopped abruptly. Bigger paused, bewildered; then he saw coming slowly toward him a tall, thin, white woman, walking silently, her hands lifted delicately in the air and touching the walls to either side of her. Bigger stepped back to let her pass. Her face and hair were completely white; she seemed to him like a ghost. The man took her arm gently and held her for a moment. Bigger saw that she was old and her grey eyes looked stony.

"Are you all right?" the man asked.

"Yes," she answered.

"Where's Peggy?"

"She's preparing dinner. I'm quite all right, Henry."

The man let go of the woman and she walked on slowly, the long white fingers of her hands just barely touching the walls. Behind the woman, following at the hem of her dress, was a big white cat, pacing without sound. She's blind! Bigger thought in amazement.

"Come on; this way," the man said.

"Yessuh."

He wondered if the man had seen him staring at the woman. He would have to be careful here. There were so many strange things. He followed the man into a room.

"Sit down."

"Yessuh," he said, sitting.

"That was Mrs. Dalton," the man said. "She's blind."

"Yessuh."

"She has a very deep interest in colored people."

"Yessuh," Bigger whispered. He was conscious of the effort to breathe; he licked his lips and fumbled nervously with his cap.

"Well, I'm Mr. Dalton."

"Yessuh."

"Do you think you'd like driving a car?"

"Oh, yessuh."

"Did you bring the paper?"

"Suh?"

"Didn't the relief give you a note to me?"

"Oh, yessuh!"

He had completely forgotten about the paper. He stood to reach into his vest pocket and, in doing so, dropped his cap. For a moment his impulses were deadlocked; he did not know if he should pick up his cap and then find the paper, or find the paper and then pick up his cap. He decided to pick up his cap.

"Put your cap here," said Mr. Dalton, indicating a place on his desk.

"Yessuh."

Then he was stone-still; the white cat bounded past him and leaped upon the desk; it sat looking at him with large placid eyes and mewed plaintively.

"What's the matter, Kate?" Mr. Dalton asked, stroking the cat's fur and smiling. Mr. Dalton turned back to Bigger. "Did you find it?"

"Nawsuh. But I got it here, somewhere."

He hated himself at that moment. Why was he acting and feeling this way? He wanted to wave his hand and blot out the white man who was making him feel this. If not that, he wanted to blot himself out. He had not raised his eyes to the level of Mr. Dalton's face once since he had been in the house. He stood with his knees slightly bent, his lips partly open, his shoulders stooped; and his eyes held a look that went only to the surface of things. There was an organic conviction in him that this was the way white folks wanted him to be when in their presence; none had ever told him that in so many words, but their manner had made him feel that they did. He laid the cap down, noticing that Mr. Dalton was watching him closely. Maybe he was not acting right? Goddamn! Clumsily, he searched for the paper. He could not find it at first and he felt called upon to say something for taking so long.

"I had it right here in my vest pocket," he mumbled.

"Take your time."

"Oh, here it is."

He drew the paper forth. It was crumpled and soiled. Nervously, he straightened it out and handed it to Mr. Dalton, holding it by its very tip end.

"All right, now," said Mr. Dalton. "Let's see what you've got here. You live at 3721 Indiana Avenue?"

"Yessuh."

Mr. Dalton paused, frowned, and looked up at the ceiling.

"What kind of a building is that over there?"

"You mean where I live, suh?"

"Yes."

"Oh, it's just an old building."

"Where do you pay rent?"

"Down on Thirty-first Street."

"To the South Side Real Estate Company?"

"Yessuh."

Bigger wondered what all these questions could mean; he had heard that Mr. Dalton owned the South Side Real Estate Company, but he was not sure.

"How much rent do you pay?"

"Eight dollars a week."

"For how many rooms?"

"We just got one, suh."

"I see. . . . Now, Bigger, tell me, how old are you?"

"I'm twenty, suh."

"Married?"

"Nawsuh."

"Sit down. You needn't stand. And I won't be long."

"Yessuh."

He sat. The white cat still contemplated him with large, moist eyes.

"Now, you have a mother, a brother, and a sister?"

"Yessuh."

"There are four of you?"

"Yessuh, there's four of us," he stammered, trying to show that he was not as stupid as he might appear. He felt a need to speak more, for he felt that maybe Mr. Dalton expected it. And he suddenly remembered the many times his mother had told him not to look at the floor when talking with white folks or asking for a job. He lifted his eyes and saw Mr. Dalton watching him closely. He dropped his eyes again.

"They call you Bigger?"

"Yessuh."

"Now, Bigger, I'd like to talk with you a little. . . ."

Yes, Goddammit! He knew what was coming. He would be asked about that time he had been accused of stealing auto tires and had been sent to the reform school. He felt guilty, condemned. He should not have come here.

"The relief people said some funny things about you. I'd like to talk to you about them. Now, you needn't feel ashamed with me," said Mr. Dalton, smiling. "I was a boy myself once and I think I know how things are. So just be yourself. . . ." Mr. Dalton pulled out a package of cigarettes. "Here; have one."

"Nawsuh; thank you, suh."

"You don't smoke?"

"Yessuh. But I just don't want one now."

"Now, Bigger, the relief people said you were a very good worker when you were interested in what you were doing. Is that true?"

"Well, I do my work, suh."

"But they said you were always in trouble. How do you explain that?"

"I don't know, suh."

"Why did they send you to the reform school?"

His eyes glared at the floor.

"They said I was stealing!" he blurted defensively. "But I wasn't."

"Are you sure?"

"Yessuh."

"Well, how did you get mixed up in it?"

"I was with some boys and the police picked us up."

Mr. Dalton said nothing. Bigger heard a clock ticking somewhere behind him and he had a foolish impulse to look at it. But he restrained himself.

"Well, Bigger, how do you feel about it now?"

"Suh? 'Bout what?"

"If you had a job, would you steal now?"

"Oh, nawsuh. I don't steal."

"Well," said Mr. Dalton, "they say you can drive a car and I'm going to give you a job."

He said nothing.

"You think you can handle it?"

"Oh, yessuh."

"The pay calls for $20 a week, but I'm going to give you $25. The extra $5 is for yourself, for you to spend as you like. You will get the clothes you need and your meals. You're to sleep in the back room, above the kitchen. You can give the $20 to your mother to keep your brother and sister in school. How does that sound?"

"It sounds all right. Yessuh."

"I think we'll get along."

"Yessuh."

"I don't think we'll have any trouble."

"Nawsuh."

"Now, Bigger," said Mr. Dalton, "since that's settled, let's see what you'll have to do every day. I leave every morning for my office at nine. It's a twenty-minute drive. You are to be back at ten and take Miss Dalton to school. At twelve, you call for Miss Dalton at the University. From then until night you are more or less free. If either Miss Dalton or I go out at night, of course, you do the driving. You work every day, but we don't get up till noon on Sundays. So you will have Sunday mornings to yourself, unless something unexpected happens. You get one full day off every two weeks."

"Yessuh."

"You think you can handle that?"

"Oh, yessuh."

"And any time you're bothered about anything, come and see me. Let's talk it over."

"Yessuh."

"Oh, Father!" a girl's voice sang out.

"Yes, Mary," said Mr. Dalton.

Bigger turned and saw a white girl walk into the room. She was very slender.

"Oh, I didn't know you were busy."

"That's all right, Mary. What is it?"

Bigger saw that the girl was looking at him. Yes; she was the same girl he had seen in the movie.

"Is this the new chauffeur, Father?"

"What do you want, Mary?"

"Will you get the tickets for the Thursday concert?"

"At Orchestra Hall?"

"Yes."

"Yes. I'll get them."

"Is this the new chauffeur?"

"Yes," said Mr. Dalton. "This is Bigger Thomas."

"Hello, Bigger," the girl said.

Bigger swallowed. He looked at Mr. Dalton, then felt that he should not have looked.

"Good evening, mam."

The girl came close to him and stopped just opposite his chair.

"Bigger, do you belong to a union?" she asked.

"Now, Mary!" said Mr. Dalton, frowning.

"Well, Father, he should," the girl said, turning to him, then back to Bigger. "Do you?"

"Mary. . . ." said Mr. Dalton.

"I'm just asking him a question, Father!"

Bigger hesitated. He hated the girl then. Why did she have to do this when he was trying to get a job?

"No'm," he mumbled, his head down and his eyes glowering.

"And why not?" the girl asked.

Bigger heard Mr. Dalton mumble something. He wished Mr. Dalton would speak and end this thing. He looked up and saw Mr. Dalton staring at the girl. She's making me lose my job! he thought. Goddamn! He knew nothing about unions, except that they were considered bad. And what did she mean by talking to him this way in front of Mr. Dalton, who, surely, didn't like unions?

"We can settle about the union later, Mary," said Mr. Dalton.

"But you wouldn't mind belonging to a union, would you?" the girl asked.

"I don't know, mam," Bigger said.

"Now, Mary, you can see that the boy is new," said Mr. Dalton. "Leave him alone."

The girl turned and poked out a red tongue at him.

"All right, Mr. Capitalist!" She turned again to Bigger. "Isn't he a capitalist, Bigger?"

Bigger looked at the floor and did not answer. He did not know what a capitalist was.

The girl started to leave, but stopped.

"Oh, Father, if he hasn't anything else to do, let him drive me to my lecture at the University tonight."

"I'm talking to him now, Mary. He'll be through in a moment."

The girl picked up the cat and walked from the room. There was a short interval of silence. Bigger wished the girl had not said anything about unions. Maybe he would not be hired now? Or, if hired, maybe he would be fired soon if she kept acting like that. He had never seen anyone like her before. She was not a bit the way he had imagined she would be.

"Oh, Mary!" Mr. Dalton called.

"Yes, Father," Bigger heard her answer from the hallway.

Mr. Dalton rose and left the room. He sat still, listening. Once or twice he thought he heard the girl laugh, but he was not sure. The best thing he could do was to leave that crazy girl alone. No wonder they called her a Communist in the movies. She was crazy, all right. He had heard about unions; in his mind unions and Communists were linked. He relaxed a little, then stiffened when he heard Mr. Dalton walk back into the room. Wordlessly, the white man sat behind the desk and picked up the paper and looked at it in a long silence. Bigger watched him with lowered eyes; he knew that Mr. Dalton was thinking of something other than that paper. In his heart he cursed the crazy girl. Maybe Mr. Dalton was deciding not to hire him? Goddamn! Maybe he would not get the extra five dollars a week now? *Goddamn that woman!* She spoiled everything! Maybe Mr. Dalton would feel that he could not trust him.

"Oh, Bigger," said Mr. Dalton.

"Yessuh."

"I want you to know why I'm hiring you."

"Yessuh."

"You see, Bigger, I'm a supporter of the National Association for the Advancement of Colored People. Did you ever hear of that organization?"

"Nawsuh."

"Well, it doesn't matter," said Mr. Dalton. "Have you had your dinner?"

"Nawsuh."

"Well, I think you'll do."

Mr. Dalton pushed a button. There was silence. The woman who had answered the front door came in.

"Yes, Mr. Dalton."

"Peggy, this is Bigger. He's going to drive for us. Give him something to eat, and show him where he's to sleep and where the car is."

"Yes, Mr. Dalton."

"And, Bigger, at eight-thirty, drive Miss Dalton out to the University and wait for her," said Mr. Dalton.

"Yessuh."

"That's all now."

"Yessuh."

"Come with me," Peggy said.

Bigger rose and got his cap and followed the woman through the house to the kitchen. The air was full of the scent of food cooking and pots bubbled on the stove.

"Sit here," Peggy said, clearing a place for him at a white-topped table. He sat and rested his cap on his knees. He felt a little better now that he was out of the front part of the house, but still not quite comfortable.

"Dinner isn't quite ready yet," Peggy said. "You like bacon and eggs?"

"Yessum."

"Coffee?"

"Yessum."

He sat looking at the white walls of the kitchen and heard the woman stir about behind him.

"Did Mr. Dalton tell you about the furnace?"

"No'm."

"Well, he must have forgotten it. You're supposed to attend to that, too. I'll show you where it is before you go."

"You mean I got to keep the fire going, mam?"

"Yes. But it's easy. Did you ever fire before?"

"No'm."

"You can learn. There's nothing to it."

"Yessum."

Peggy seemed kind enough, but maybe she was being kind in order to shove her part of the work on him. Well, he would wait and see. If she got nasty, he would talk to Mr. Dalton about her. He smelt the odor of frying bacon and realized that he was very hungry. He had forgotten to buy a sandwich with the quarter his mother had given him, and he had not eaten since morning. Peggy placed a plate, knife, fork, spoon, sugar, cream, and bread before him; then she dished up the bacon and eggs.

"You can get more if you want it."

The food was good. This was not going to be a bad job. The only thing bad so far was that crazy girl. He chewed his bacon and eggs while some remote part of his mind considered in amazement how different the girl had seemed in the movie. On the screen she was not dangerous and his mind could do with her as it liked. But here in her home she walked over everything, put herself in the way. He had quite forgotten that Peggy was in the kitchen and when his plate was empty he took a soft piece of bread and began to sop it clean, carrying the bread to his mouth in huge chunks.

"You want some more?"

He stopped chewing and laid the bread aside. He had not wanted to let her see him do that; he did that only at home.

"No'm," he said. "I got a plenty."

"You reckon you'll like it here?" Peggy asked.

"Yessum. I hope so."

"This is a swell place," Peggy said. "About as good as you'll find anywhere. The last colored man who worked for us stayed ten years."

Bigger wondered why she said "us." She must stand in with the old man and old woman pretty good, he thought.

"Ten years?" he said.

"Yes; ten years. His name was Green. He was a good man, too."

"How come he to leave?"

"Oh, he was smart, that Green was. He took a job with the government. Mrs. Dalton made him go to night school. Mrs. Dalton's always trying to help somebody."

Yes; Bigger knew that. But he was not going to any night school. He looked at Peggy; she was bent over the sink, washing dishes. Her words had challenged him and he felt he had to say something.

"Yessum, he was smart," he said. "And ten years is a long time."

"Oh, it wasn't so long," Peggy said. "I've been here twenty years myself. I always was one for sticking to a job. I always say when you get a good place, then stick there. A rolling stone gathers no moss, and it's true."

Bigger said nothing.

"Everything's simple and nice around here," Peggy said. "They've got millions, but they live like human beings. They don't put on airs and strut. Mrs. Dalton believes that people should be that way."

"Yessum."

"They're Christian people and believe in everybody working hard. And living a clean life. Some people think we ought to have more servants than we do, but we get along. It's just like one big family."

"Yessum."

"Mr. Dalton's a fine man," Peggy said.

"Oh, yessum. He is."

"You know, he does a lot for your people."

"My people?" asked Bigger, puzzled.

"Yes, the colored people. He gave over five million dollars to colored schools."

"Oh!"

"But Mrs. Dalton's the one who's really nice. If it wasn't for her, he would not be doing what he does. She made him rich. She had millions when he married her. Of course, he made a lot of money himself afterwards out of real estate. But most of the money's hers. She's blind, poor thing. She lost her sight ten years ago. Did you see her yet?"

"Yessum."

"Was she alone?"

"Yessum."

"Poor thing! Mrs. Patterson, who takes care of her, is away for the week-end and she's all alone. Isn't it too bad, about her?"

"Oh, yessum," he said, trying to get into his voice some of the pity for Mrs. Dalton that he thought Peggy expected him to feel.

"It's really more than a job you've got here," Peggy went on. "It's just like home. I'm always telling Mrs. Dalton that this is the only home I'll ever know. I wasn't in this country but two years before I started working here. . . ."

"Oh," said Bigger, looking at her.

"I'm Irish, you know," she said. "My folks in the old country feel about England like the colored folks feel about this country. So I know something about colored people. Oh, these are fine people, fine as silk. Even the girl. Did you meet her yet?"

"Yessum."

"Tonight?"

"Yessum."

Peggy turned and looked at him sharply.

"She's a sweet thing," she said. "I've known her since she was two years old. But she's kind of wild, she is. Always in hot water. Keeps her folks worried. The Lord only knows where she got her wild ways. But she's got 'em. If you stay around here long, you'll get to know her."

Bigger wanted to ask about the girl, but thought that he had better not do that now.

"If you're through, I'll show you the furnace and the car, and where your room is," she said and turned the fire low under the pots on the stove.

"Yessum."

He rose and followed her out of the kitchen, down a narrow stairway at the end of which was the basement. It was dark; Bigger heard a sharp click and the light came on.

"This way. . . . What did you say your name was?"

"Bigger, mam."

"What?"

"Bigger."

He smelt the scent of coal and ashes and heard fire roaring. He saw a red bed of embers glowing in the furnace.

"This is the furnace," she said.

"Yessum."

"Every morning you'll find the garbage here; you burn it and put the bucket on the dumb-waiter."

"Yessum."

"You never have to use a shovel for coal. It's a self-feeder. Look, see?"

Peggy pulled a lever and there came a loud rattle of fine lumps of coal sliding down a metal chute. Bigger stooped and saw, through the cracks of the furnace, the coal spreading out fanwise over the red bed of fire.

"That's fine," he mumbled in admiration.

"And you don't have to worry about water, either. It fills itself."

Bigger liked that; it was easy; it would be fun, almost.

"Your biggest trouble will be taking out the ashes and sweeping. And keep track of how the coal runs; when it's low, tell me or Mr. Dalton and we'll order some more."

"Yessum. I can handle it."

"Now, to get to your room all you have to do is go up these back stairs. Come on."

He followed up a stretch of stairs. She opened a door and switched on a light and Bigger saw a large room whose walls were covered with pictures of girls' faces and prize fighters.

"This was Green's room. He was always one for pictures. But he kept things neat and nice. It's plenty warm here. Oh, yes; before I forget. Here are the keys to the room and the garage and the car. Now, I'll show you the garage. You have to get to it from the outside."

He followed her down the steps and outside into the driveway. It was much warmer.

"Looks like snow," Peggy said.

"Yessum."

"This is the garage," she said, unlocking and pushing open a door which, as it swung in, made lights come on automatically. "You always bring the car out and wait at the side door for the folks. Let's see. You say you're driving Miss Dalton tonight?"

"Yessum."

"Well, she leaves at eight-thirty. So you're free until then. You can look over your room if you want to."

"Yessum. I reckon I will."

Bigger went behind Peggy down the stairs and back into the basement. She went to the kitchen and he went to his room. He stood in the middle of the floor, looking at the walls. There were pictures of Jack Johnson, Joe Louis, Jack Dempsey, and Henry Armstrong; there were others of Ginger Rogers, Jean Harlow, and Janet Gaynor.[1] The room was large and had two radiators. He felt the bed; it was soft. Gee! He would bring Bessie here some night. Not right at once; he would wait until he had learned the ropes of the place. A room all to himself! He could bring a pint of liquor up here and drink it in peace. He would not have to slip around any more. He would not have to sleep with Buddy and stand Buddy's kicking all night long. He lit a cigarette and stretched himself full length upon the bed. Ohhhh. . . . This was not going to be bad at all. He looked at his dollar watch; it was seven. In a little while he would go down and examine the car. And he would buy himself another watch, too. A dollar watch was not good enough for a job like this; he would buy a gold one. There were a lot of new things he would get. Oh, boy! This would be an easy life. Everything was all right, except that girl. She worried him. She might cause him to lose his job if she kept talking about unions. She was a funny girl, all right. Never in his life had he met anyone like her. She puzzled him. She was rich, but she didn't act like she was rich. She acted like. . . . Well, he didn't know exactly what she did act like. In all of the white women he had met, mostly on jobs and at relief stations, there was always a certain coldness and reserve; they stood their distance and spoke to him from afar. But this girl waded right in and hit him between the eyes with her words and ways. Aw, hell! What good was there in thinking about her like this? Maybe she was all right. Maybe he would just have to get used to her; that was all. I bet she spends a plenty of dough, he thought. And the old man had given five million dollars to colored people. If a man could give five million dollars away, then millions must be as common to him as nickels. He rose up and sat on the edge of the bed.

What make of car was he to drive? He had not thought to look when Peggy had opened the garage door. He hoped it would be a Packard, or a Lincoln, or a Rolls Royce. Boy! Would he drive! Just wait! Of course, he would be careful when he was driving Miss or Mr. Dalton. But when he was alone he would burn up the pavement; he would make those tires smoke!

He licked his lips; he was thirsty. He looked at his watch; it was ten past eight. He would go to the kitchen and get a drink of water and then drive the car out of the garage. He went down the steps, through the basement to the stairs leading to the kitchen door. Though he did not know it, he walked on tiptoe. He eased the door open and peeped in. What he saw made him suck his breath in; Mrs. Dalton in flowing white clothes was standing stone-still in the middle of the kitchen floor. There was silence, save for the slow ticking of a large clock on a

[1]Four boxing champions, of whom all but Dempsey were black, and three female movie stars, all white.

white wall. For a moment he did not know if he should go in or go back down the steps; his thirst was gone. Mrs. Dalton's face was held in an attitude of intense listening and her hands were hanging loosely at her sides. To Bigger her face seemed to be capable of hearing in every pore of the skin and listening always to some low voice speaking. Sitting quietly on the floor beside her was the white cat, its large black eyes fastened upon him. It made him uneasy just to look at her and that white cat; he was about to close the door and tiptoe softly back down the stairs when she spoke.

"Are you the new boy?"

"Yessum."

"Did you want something?"

"I didn't mean to disturb you, mam. I—I. . . . I just wanted a drink of water."

"Well, come on in. I think you'll find a glass somewhere."

He went to the sink, watching her as he walked, feeling that she could see him even though he knew that she was blind. His skin tingled. He took a glass from a narrow shelf and filled it from a faucet. As he drank he stole a glance at her over the rim of the glass. Her face was still, tilted, waiting. It reminded him of a dead man's face he had once seen. Then he realized that Mrs. Dalton had turned and listened to the sound of his feet as he had walked. She knows exactly where I'm standing, he thought.

"You like your room?" she asked; and as she spoke he realized that she had been standing there waiting to hear the sound of his glass as it had clinked on the sink.

"Oh, yessum."

"I hope you're a careful driver."

"Oh, yessum. I'll be careful."

"Did you ever drive before?"

"Yessum. But it was a grocery truck."

He had the feeling that talking to a blind person was like talking to someone whom he himself could scarcely see.

"How far did you go in school, Bigger?"

"To the eighth grade, mam."

"Do you ever think of going back?"

"Well, I gotta work now, mam."

"Suppose you had the chance to go back?"

"Well, I don't know, mam."

"The last man who worked here went to night school and got an education."

"Yessum."

"What would you want to be if you had an education?"

"I don't know, mam."

"Did you ever think about it?"

"No'm."

"You would rather work?"

"I reckon I would, mam."

"Well, we'll talk about that some other time. I think you'd better get the car for Miss Dalton now."

"Yessum."

He left her standing in the middle of the kitchen floor, exactly as he had found her. He did not know just how to take her; she made him feel that she would judge all he did harshly but kindly. He had a feeling toward her that was akin to that which he held toward his mother. The difference in his feelings toward Mrs. Dalton and his mother was that he felt that his mother wanted him to do the things *she* wanted him to do, and he felt that Mrs. Dalton wanted him to do the things she felt that *he* should have wanted to do. But he did not want to go to night school. Night school was all right; but he had other plans. Well, he didn't know just what they were right now, but he was working them out.

The night air had grown warmer. A wind had risen. He lit a cigarette and unlocked the garage; the door swung in and again he was surprised and pleased to see the lights spring on automatically. These people's got everything, he mused. He examined the car; it was a dark blue Buick, with steel spoke wheels and of a new make. He stepped back from it and looked it over; then he opened the door and looked at the dashboard. He was a little disappointed that the car was not so expensive as he had hoped, but what it lacked in price was more than made up for in color and style. "It's all right," he said half-aloud. He got in and backed it into the driveway and turned it round and pulled it up to the side door.

"Is that you, Bigger?"

The girl stood on the steps.

"Yessum."

He got out and held the rear door open for her.

"Thank you."

He touched his cap and wondered if it were the right thing to do.

"Is it that university-school out there on the Midway, mam?"

Through the rear mirror above him he saw her hesitate before answering.

"Yes; that's the one."

He pulled the car into the street and headed south, driving about thirty-five miles an hour. He handled the car expertly, picking up speed at the beginning of each block and slowing slightly as he approached each street intersection.

"You drive well," she said.

"Yessum," he said proudly.

He watched her through the rear mirror as he drove; she was kind of pretty, but very little. She looked like a doll in a show window: black eyes, white face, red lips. And she was not acting at all now as she had acted when he first saw her. In fact, she had a remote look in her eyes. He stopped the car at Forty-seventh Street for a red light; he did not have to stop again until he reached Fifty-first Street where a long line of cars formed in front of him and a long line in back. He held the steering wheel lightly, waiting for the line to move forward. He had a keen sense of power when driving; the feel of a car added something to him. He loved to press his foot against a pedal and sail along, watching others stand still, seeing the asphalt road unwind under him. The lights flashed from red to green and he nosed the car forward.

"Bigger!"

"Yessum."

"Turn at this corner and pull up on a side street."

"Here, mam?"

"Yes; here."

Now, what on earth did this mean? He pulled the car off Cottage Grove Avenue and drew to a curb. He turned to look at her and was startled to see that she was sitting on the sheer edge of the back seat, her face some six inches from his.

"I scare you?" she asked softly, smiling.

"Oh, no'm," he mumbled, bewildered.

He watched her through the mirror. Her tiny white hands dangled over the back of the front seat and her eyes looked out vacantly.

"I don't know how to say what I'm going to say," she said.

He said nothing. There was a long silence. What in all hell did this girl want? A street car rumbled by. Behind him, reflected in the rear mirror, he saw the traffic lights flash from green to red, and back again. Well, whatever she was going to say, he wished she would say it and get it over. This girl was strange. She did the unexpected every minute. He waited for her to speak. She took her hands from the back of the front seat and fumbled in her purse.

"Gotta match?"

"Yessum."

He dug a match from his vest pocket.

"Strike it," she said.

He blinked. He struck the match and held the flame for her. She smoked awhile in silence.

"You're not a tattle-tale, are you?" she asked with a smile.

He opened his mouth to reply, but no words came. What she had asked and the tone of voice in which she had asked it made him feel that he ought to have answered in some way; but what?

"I'm not going to the University," she said at last. "But you can forget that. I want you to drive me to the Loop. But if anyone should ask you, then I went to the University, see, Bigger?"

"Yessum; it's all right with me," he mumbled.

"I think I can trust you."

"Yessum."

"After all, I'm on your side."

Now, what did *that* mean? She was on *his* side. What side was he on? Did she mean that she liked colored people? Well, he had heard that about her whole family. Was she really crazy? How much did her folks know of how she acted? But if she were really crazy, why did Mr. Dalton let him drive her out?

"I'm going to meet a friend of mine who's also a friend of yours," she said.

"Friend of mine!" he could not help exclaiming.

"Oh, you don't know him yet," she said, laughing.

"Oh."

"Go to the Outer Drive and then to 16 Lake Street."

"Yessum."

Maybe she was talking about the Reds? *That* was it! But none of his friends were Reds. What was all this? If Mr. Dalton should ask him if he had taken her to the University, he would have to say yes and depend upon her to back him up. But suppose Mr. Dalton had someone watching, someone who would tell where he had really taken her? He had heard that many rich people had detectives working for them. If only he knew what this was all about he would feel much better. And she had said that she was going to meet someone who was a friend of his. He didn't want to meet any Communists. They didn't have any money. He felt that it was all right for a man to go to jail for robbery, but to go to jail for fooling around with Reds was bunk. Well, he would drive her; that was what he had been hired for. But he was going to watch his step in this business. The only thing he hoped was that she would not make him lose his job. He pulled the car off the Outer Drive at Seventh Street, drove north on Michigan Boulevard to Lake Street, then headed west for two blocks, looking for number 16.

"It's right here, Bigger."

"Yessum."

He pulled to a stop in front of a dark building.

"Wait," she said, getting out of the car.

He saw her smiling broadly at him, almost laughing. He felt that she knew every feeling and thought he had at that moment and he turned his head away in confusion. Goddamn that woman!

"I won't be long," she said.

She started off, then turned back.

"Take it easy, Bigger. You'll understand it better bye and bye."

"Yessum," he said, trying to smile; but couldn't.

"Isn't there a song like that, a song your people sing?"

"Like what, mam?"

"We'll understand it better bye and bye?"

"Oh, yessum."

She was an odd girl, all right. He felt something in her over and above the fear she inspired in him. She responded to him as if he were human, as if he lived in the same world as she. And he had never felt that before in a white person. But why? Was this some kind of game? The guarded feeling of freedom he had while listening to her was tangled with the hard fact that she was white and rich, a part of the world of people who told him what he could and could not do.

He looked at the building into which she had gone; it was old and unpainted; there were no lights in the windows or doorway. Maybe she was meeting her sweetheart? If that was all, then things would straighten out. But if she had gone to meet those Communists? And what were Communists like, anyway? Was *she* one? What made people Communists? He remembered seeing many cartoons of Communists in newspapers and always they had flaming torches in their hands and wore beards and were trying to commit murder or set things on fire. People who acted that way were crazy. All he could recall having heard about Communists was associated in his mind with darkness, old houses, people speaking in whispers, and trade unions on strike. And this was something like it.

He stiffened; the door into which she had gone opened. She came out, followed by a young white man. They walked to the car; but, instead of getting into the back seat, they came to the side of the car and stood, facing him. At once Bigger recognized the man as the one he had seen in the newsreel in the movie.

"Oh, Bigger, this is Jan. And Jan, this is Bigger Thomas."

Jan smiled broadly, then extended an open palm toward him. Bigger's entire body tightened with suspense and dread.

"How are you, Bigger?"

Bigger's right hand gripped the steering wheel and he wondered if he ought to shake hands with this white man.

"I'm fine," he mumbled.

Jan's hand was still extended. Bigger's right hand raised itself about three inches, then stopped in mid-air.

"Come on and shake," Jan said.

Bigger extended a limp palm, his mouth open in astonishment. He felt Jan's fingers tighten about his own. He tried to pull his hand away, ever so gently, but Jan held on, firmly, smiling.

"We may as well get to know each other," Jan said. "I'm a friend of Mary's."

"Yessuh," he mumbled.

"First of all," Jan continued, putting his foot upon the running board, "don't say *sir* to me. I'll call you Bigger and you'll call me Jan. That's the way it'll be between us. How's that?"

Bigger did not answer. Mary was smiling. Jan still gripped his hand and Bigger held his head at an oblique angle, so that he could, by merely shifting his eyes, look at Jan and then out into the street whenever he did not wish to meet Jan's gaze. He heard Mary laughing softly.

"It's all right, Bigger," she said. "Jan *means* it."

He flushed warm with anger. Goddamn her soul to hell! Was she laughing at him? Were they making fun of him? What was it that they wanted? Why didn't they leave him alone? He was not bothering them. Yes, anything could happen with people like these. His entire mind and body were painfully concentrated into a single sharp point of attention. He was trying desperately to understand. He felt foolish sitting behind the steering wheel like this and letting a white man hold his hand. What would people passing along the street think? He was very conscious of his black skin and there was in him a prodding conviction that Jan and men like him had made it so that he would be conscious of that black skin. Did not white people despise a black skin? Then why was Jan doing this? Why was Mary standing there so eagerly, with shining eyes? What could they get out of this? Maybe they did not despise him? But they made him feel his black skin by just standing there looking at him, one holding his hand and the other smiling. He felt he had no physical existence at all right then; he was something he hated, the badge of shame which he knew was attached to a black skin. It was a shadowy region, a No Man's Land, the ground that separated the white world from the black that he stood upon. He felt naked, transparent; he felt that this white man, having helped to put him down, having helped to deform him, held him up now to look at him and be amused. At that moment he felt toward Mary and Jan a dumb, cold, and inarticulate hate.

"Let me drive awhile," Jan said, letting go of his hand and opening the door.

Bigger looked at Mary. She came forward and touched his arm.

"It's all right, Bigger," she said.

He turned in the seat to get out, but Jan stopped him.

"No; stay in and move over."

He slid over and Jan took his place at the wheel. He was still feeling his hand strangely; it seemed that the pressure of Jan's fingers had left an indelible imprint. Mary was getting into the front seat, too.

"Move over, Bigger," she said.

He moved closer to Jan. Mary pushed herself in, wedging tightly between him and the outer door of the car. There were white people to either side of him; he was sitting between two vast white looming walls. Never in his life had he been so close to a white woman. He smelt the odor of her hair and felt the soft pressure of her thigh against his own. Jan headed the car back to the Outer Drive, weaving in and out of the line of traffic. Soon they were speeding along the lake front, past a huge flat sheet of dully gleaming water. The sky was heavy with snow clouds and the wind was blowing strong.

"Isn't it glorious tonight?" she asked.

"God, yes!" Jan said.

Bigger listened to the tone of their voices, to their strange accents, to the exuberant phrases that flowed so freely from their lips.

"That sky!"

"And that water!"

"It's so beautiful it makes you ache just to look at it," said Mary.

"This is a beautiful world, Bigger," Jan said, turning to him. "Look at that skyline!"

Bigger looked without turning his head; he just rolled his eyes. Stretching to one side of him was a vast sweep of tall buildings flecked with tiny squares of yellow light.

"We'll own all that some day, Bigger," Jan said with a wave of his hand. "After the revolution it'll be ours. But we'll have to fight for it. What a world to win, Bigger! And when that day comes, things'll be different. There'll be no white and no black; there'll be no rich and no poor."

Bigger said nothing. The car whirred along.

"We seem strange to you, don't we, Bigger?" Mary asked.

"Oh, no'm," he breathed softly, knowing that she did not believe him, but finding it impossible to answer her in any other way.

His arms and legs were aching from being cramped into so small a space, but he dared not move. He knew that they would not have cared if he had made himself more comfortable, but his moving would have called attention to himself and his black body. And he did not want that. These people made him feel things he did not want to feel. If he were white, if he were like them, it would have been different. But he was black. So he sat still, his arms and legs aching.

"Say, Bigger," asked Jan, "where can we get a good meal on the South Side?"

"Well," Bigger said, reflectively.

"We want to go to a *real* place," Mary said, turning to him gayly.

"You want to go to a night club?" Bigger asked in a tone that indicated that he was simply mentioning names and not recommending places to go.

"No; we want to eat."

"Look, Bigger. We want one of those places where colored people eat, not one of those show places."

What *did* these people want? When he answered his voice was neutral and toneless.

"Well, there's Ernie's Kitchen Shack. . . ."

"That sounds good!"

"Let's go there, Jan," Mary said.

"O.K.," Jan said. "Where is it?"

"It's at Forty-seventh Street and Indiana," Bigger told them.

Jan swung the car off the Outer Drive at Thirty-first Street and drove westward to Indiana Avenue. Bigger wanted Jan to drive faster, so that they could reach Ernie's Kitchen Shack in the shortest possible time. That would allow him a chance to sit in the car and stretch out his cramped and aching legs while they ate. Jan turned onto Indiana Avenue and headed south. Bigger wondered what Jack and Gus and G. H. would say if they saw him sitting between two white people in a car like this. They would tease him about such a thing as long as they could remember it. He felt Mary turn in her seat. She placed her hand on his arm.

"You know, Bigger, I've long wanted to go into these houses," she said, pointing to the tall, dark apartment buildings looming to either side of them, "and just *see* how your people live. You know what I mean? I've been to England, France and Mexico, but I don't know how people live ten blocks from me. We know so *little* about each other. I just want to *see.* I want to *know* these people. Never in my life have I been inside of a Negro home. Yet they *must* live like we live. They're *human.* . . . There are twelve million of them. . . . They live in our country. . . . In the same city with us. . . ." her voice trailed off wistfully.

There was silence. The car sped through the Black Belt, past tall buildings holding black life. Bigger knew that they were thinking of his life and the life of his people. Suddenly he wanted to seize some heavy object in his hand and grip it with all the strength of his body and in some strange way rise up and stand in naked space above the speeding car and with one final blow blot it out—with himself and them in it. His heart was beating fast and he struggled to control his breath. This thing was getting the better of him; he felt that he should not give way to his feelings like this. But he could not help it. Why didn't they leave him alone? What had he done to them? What good could they get out of sitting here making him feel so miserable?

"Tell me where it is, Bigger," Jan said.

"Yessuh."

Bigger looked out and saw that they were at Forty-sixth Street.

"It's at the end of the next block, suh."

"Can I park along here somewhere?"

"Oh; yessuh."

"Bigger, *please!* Don't say *sir* to me. . . . I don't *like* it. You're a man just like I am; I'm no better than you. Maybe other white men like it. But I don't. Look, Bigger. . . ."

"Yes. . . ." Bigger paused, swallowed, and looked down at his black hands. "O.K.," he mumbled, hoping that they did not hear the choke in his voice.

"You see, Bigger. . . ." Jan began.

Mary reached her hand round back of Bigger and touched Jan's shoulder. "Let's get out," she said hurriedly.

Jan pulled the car to the curb and opened the door and stepped out. Bigger slipped behind the steering wheel again, glad to have room at last for his arms and legs. Mary got out of the other door. Now, he could get some rest. So intensely taken up was he with his own immediate sensations, that he did not look up until he felt something strange in the long silence. When he did look he saw, in a split second of time, Mary turn her eyes away from his face. She was looking at Jan and Jan was looking at her. There was no mistaking the meaning of the look in their eyes. To Bigger it was plainly a bewildered and questioning look, a look that asked: What on earth is wrong with him? Bigger's teeth clamped tight and he stared straight before him.

"Aren't you coming with us, Bigger?" Mary asked in a sweet tone that made him want to leap at her.

The people in Ernie's Kitchen Shack knew him and he did not want them to see him with these white people. He knew that if he went in they would ask one another: *Who're them white folks Bigger's hanging around with?*

"I—I. . . . I don't want to go in. . . ." he whispered breathlessly.

"Aren't you hungry?" Jan asked.

"Naw; I ain't hungry."

Jan and Mary came close to the car.

"Come and sit with us anyhow," Jan said.

"I. . . . I. . . ." Bigger stammered.

"It'll be all right," Mary said.

"I can stay here. Somebody has to watch the car," he said.

"Oh, to hell with the car!" Mary said. "Come on in."

"I don't want to eat," Bigger said stubbornly.

"Well," Jan sighed. "If that's the way you feel about it, we won't go in."

Bigger felt trapped. Oh, Goddamn! He saw in a flash that he could have made all of this very easy if he had simply acted from the beginning as if they were doing nothing unusual. But he did not understand them; he distrusted them, really hated them. He was puzzled as to why they were treating him this way. But, after all, this was his job and it was just as painful to sit here and let them stare at him as it was to go in.

"O.K.," he mumbled angrily.

He got out and slammed the door. Mary came close to him and caught his arm. He stared at her in a long silence; it was the first time he had ever looked directly at her, and he was able to do so only because he was angry.

"Bigger," she said, "you don't have to come in unless you really want to. Please, don't think. . . . Oh, Bigger. . . . We're not trying to make you feel badly. . . ."

Her voice stopped. In the dim light of the street lamp Bigger saw her eyes cloud and her lips tremble. She swayed against the car. He stepped backward, as though she were contaminated with an invisible contagion. Jan slipped his arm about her waist, supporting her. Bigger heard her sob softly. Good God! He had a wild impulse to turn around and walk away. He felt ensnared in a tangle of deep shadows, shadows as black as the night that stretched above his head. The way he had acted had made her cry, and yet the way she had acted had made him feel that he had to act as he had toward her. In his relations with her he felt that he was riding a seesaw; never were they on a common level; either he or she was up in the air. Mary dried her eyes and Jan whispered something to her. Bigger wondered what he could say to his mother, or the relief, or Mr. Dalton, if he left them. They would be sure to ask why he had walked off his job, and he would not be able to tell.

"I'm all right, now, Jan," he heard Mary say. "I'm sorry. I'm just a fool, I suppose. . . . I acted a ninny." She lifted her eyes to Bigger. "Don't mind me, Bigger. I'm just silly, I guess. . . ."

He said nothing.

"Come on, Bigger," Jan said in a voice that sought to cover up everything. "Let's eat."

Jan caught his arm and tried to pull him forward, but Bigger hung back. Jan and Mary walked toward the entrance of the café and Bigger followed, confused and resentful. Jan went to a small table near a wall.

"Sit down, Bigger."

Bigger sat. Jan and Mary sat in front of him.

"You like fried chicken?" Jan asked.

"Yessuh," he whispered.

He scratched his head. How on earth could he learn not to say *yessuh* and *yessum* to white people in one night when he had been saying it all his life long? He looked before him in such a way that his eyes would not meet theirs. The waitress came and Jan ordered three beers and three portions of fried chicken.

"Hi, Bigger!"

He turned and saw Jack waving at him, but staring at Jan and Mary. He waved a stiff palm in return. Goddamn! Jack walked away hurriedly. Cautiously, Bigger looked round; the waitresses and several people at other tables were staring at him. They all knew him and he knew that they were wondering as he would have wondered if he had been in their places. Mary touched his arm.

"Have you ever been here before, Bigger?"

He groped for neutral words, words that would convey information but not indicate any shade of his own feelings.

"A few times."

"It's very nice," Mary said.

Somebody put a nickel in an automatic phonograph and they listened to the music. Then Bigger felt a hand grab his shoulder.

"Hi, Bigger! Where you been?"

He looked up and saw Bessie laughing in his face.

"Hi," he said gruffly.

"Oh, 'scuse me. I didn't know you had company," she said, walking away with her eyes upon Jan and Mary.

"Tell her to come over, Bigger," Mary said.

Bessie had gone to a far table and was sitting with another girl.

"She's over there now," Bigger said.

The waitress brought the beer and chicken.

"This is simply grand!" Mary exclaimed.

"You got something there," Jan said, looking at Bigger. "Did I say that right, Bigger?"

Bigger hesitated.

"That's the way they say it," he spoke flatly.

Jan and Mary were eating. Bigger picked up a piece of chicken and bit it. When he tried to chew he found his mouth dry. It seemed that the very organic functions of his body had altered; and when he realized why, when he understood the cause, he could not chew the food. After two or three bites, he stopped and sipped his beer.

"Eat your chicken," Mary said. "It's good!"

"I ain't hungry," he mumbled.

"Want some more beer?" Jan asked after a long silence.

Maybe if he got a little drunk it would help him.

"I don't mind," he said.

Jan ordered another round.

"Do they keep anything stronger than beer here?" Jan asked.

"They got anything you want," Bigger said.

Jan ordered a fifth of rum and poured a round. Bigger felt the liquor warming him. After a second drink Jan began to talk.

"Where were you born, Bigger?"

"In the South."

"Whereabouts?"

"Mississippi."

"How far did you go in school?"

"To the eighth grade."

"Why did you stop?"

"No money."

"Did you go to school in the North or South?"

"Mostly in the South. I went two years up here."

"How long have you been in Chicago?"

"Oh, about five years."

"You like it here?"

"It'll do."

"You live with your people?"

"My mother, brother, and sister."

"Where's your father?"

"Dead."

"How long ago was that?"

"He got killed in a riot when I was a kid—in the South."

There was silence. The rum was helping Bigger.

"And what was done about it?" Jan asked.

"Nothing, far as I know."

"How do you feel about it?"

"I don't know."

"Listen, Bigger, that's what we want to *stop*. That's what we Communists are fighting. We want to stop people from treating others that way. I'm a member of the Party. Mary sympathizes. Don't you think if we got together we could stop things like that?"

"I don't know," Bigger said; he was feeling the rum rising to his head. "There's a lot of white people in the world."

"You've read about the Scottsboro boys?"[2]

"I heard about 'em."

"Don't you think we did a good job in helping to keep 'em from killing those boys?"

"It was all right."

"You know, Bigger," said Mary, "we'd like to be friends of yours."

He said nothing. He drained his glass and Jan poured another round. He was getting drunk enough to look straight at them now. Mary was smiling at him.

"You'll get used to us," she said.

Jan stoppered the bottle of rum.

"We'd better go," he said.

"Yes," Mary said. "Oh, Bigger, I'm going to Detroit at nine in the morning and I want you to take my small trunk down to the station. Tell father and he'll let you make up your time. You better come for the trunk at eight-thirty."

"I'll take it down."

[2]Nine young black men who were falsely accused of raping two white women. The trial, at Scottsboro, Alabama, resulting in convictions, most of which were later overturned, was an extreme instance of racial prejudice.

Jan paid the bill and they went back to the car. Bigger got behind the steering wheel. He was feeling good. Jan and Mary got into the back seat. As Bigger drove he saw her resting in Jan's arms.

"Drive around in the park awhile, will you, Bigger?"

"O.K."

He turned into Washington Park and pulled the car slowly round and round the long gradual curves. Now and then he watched Jan kiss Mary in the reflection of the rear mirror above his head.

"You got a girl, Bigger?" Mary asked.

"I got a girl," he said.

"I'd like to meet her some time."

He did not answer. Mary's eyes stared dreamily before her, as if she were planning future things to do. Then she turned to Jan and laid her hand tenderly upon his arm.

"How was the demonstration?"

"Pretty good. But the cops arrested three comrades."

"Who were they?"

"A Y. C. L.-er[3] and two Negro women. Oh, by the way, Mary. We need money for bail badly."

"How much?"

"Three thousand."

"I'll mail you a check."

"Swell."

"Did you work hard today?"

"Yeah. I was at a meeting until three this morning. Max and I've been trying to raise bail money all day today."

"Max is a darling, isn't he?"

"He's one of the best lawyers we've got."

Bigger listened; he knew that they were talking Communism and he tried to understand. But he couldn't.

"Jan."

"Yes, honey."

"I'm coming out of school this spring and I'm going to join the Party."

"*Gee,* you're a brick!"

"But I'll have to be careful."

"Say, how's about your working with me, in the office?"

"No, I want to work among Negroes. That's where people are needed. It seems as though they've been pushed out of everything."

"That's true."

"When I see what they've done to those people, it makes me *so* mad. . . ."

"Yes; it's awful."

"And I feel so helpless and useless. I want to *do* something."

"I knew all along you'd come through."

"Say, Jan, do you know many Negroes? I want to meet some."

"I don't know any very well. But you'll meet them when you're in the Party."

"They have so much *emo*tion! What a people! If we could ever get them going. . . ."

[3]A member of the Young Communist League.

"We can't have a revolution without 'em," Jan said. "They've got to be organized. They've got spirit. They'll give the Party something it needs."

"And their songs—the spirituals! Aren't they marvelous?" Bigger saw her turn to him. "Say, Bigger, can you sing?"

"I can't sing," he said.

"Aw, Bigger," she said, pouting. She tilted her head, closed her eyes and opened her mouth.

> *"Swing low, sweet chariot,*
> *Coming fer to carry me home. . . ."*[4]

Jan joined in and Bigger smiled derisively. Hell, that ain't the tune, he thought.

"Come on, Bigger, and help us sing it," Jan said.

"I can't sing," he said again.

They were silent. The car purred along. Then he heard Jan speaking in low tones.

"Where's the bottle?"

"Right here."

"I want a sip."

"I'll take one, too, honey."

"Going heavy tonight, ain't you?"

"About as heavy as you."

They laughed. Bigger drove in silence. He heard the faint, musical gurgle of liquor.

"Jan!"

"What?"

"That was a *big* sip!"

"Here; you get even."

Through the rear mirror he saw her tilt the bottle and drink.

"Maybe Bigger wants another one, Jan. Ask him."

"Oh, say, Bigger! Here; take a swig!"

He slowed the car and reached back for the bottle; he tilted it twice, taking two huge swallows.

"Woooow!" Mary laughed.

"You took a *swig,* all right," Jan said.

Bigger wiped his mouth with the back of his hand and continued driving slowly through the dark park. Now and then he heard the half-empty bottle of rum gurgling. They getting plastered, he thought, feeling the effect of the rum creeping outward to his fingers and upward to his lips. Presently, he heard Mary giggle. Hell, she's plastered already! The car rolled slowly round and round the sloping curves. The rum's soft heat was spreading fanwise out from his stomach, engulfing his whole body. He was not driving; he was simply sitting and floating along smoothly through darkness. His hands rested lightly on the steering wheel and his body slouched lazily down in the seat. He looked

[4]The first lines of a hymn composed by Wallis Willis, an African American slave owned by a member of the Choctaw Indian tribe. It was later popularized as part of the repertoire of the Jubilee Singers of Fisk University.

at the mirror; Mary was lying flat on her back in the rear seat and Jan was bent over her. He saw a faint sweep of white thigh. They plastered, all right, he thought. He pulled the car softly round the curves, looking at the road before him one second and up at the mirror the next. He heard Jan whispering; then he heard them both sigh. Filled with a sense of them, his muscles grew gradually taut. He sighed and sat up straight, fighting off the stiffening feeling in his loins. But soon he was slouched again. His lips were numb. I'm almost drunk, he thought. His sense of the city and park fell away; he was floating in the car and Jan and Mary were in back, kissing, spooning. A long time passed. Jan sat up and pulled Mary with him.

"It's one o'clock, honey," Mary said. "I better go in."

"O.K. But let's drive a little more. It's great here."

"Father says I'm a bad girl."

"I'm sorry, darling."

"I'll call you in the morning before I go."

"Sure. What time?"

"About eight-thirty."

"Gee, but I hate to see you go to Detroit."

"I hate to go too. But I got to. You see, honey, I got to make up for being bad with you down in Florida. I got to do what Mother and Father say for awhile."

"I hate to see you go just the same."

"I'll be back in a couple of days."

"A couple of days is a long time."

"You're silly, but you're sweet," she said, laughing and kissing him.

"You better drive on, Bigger," Jan called.

He swung the car out of the park and headed for Forty-sixth Street.

"I'll get out here, Bigger!"

He stopped the car. Bigger heard them speak in whispers.

"Good-bye, Jan."

"Good-bye, honey."

"I'll call you tomorrow?"

"Sure."

Jan stood at the front door of the car and held out his palm. Bigger shook timidly.

"It's been great meeting you, Bigger," Jan said.

"O.K.," Bigger mumbled.

"I'm damn glad I know you. Look. Have another drink."

Bigger took a big swallow.

"You better give me one, too, Jan. It'll make me sleep," Mary said.

"You're sure you haven't had enough?"

"Aw, come on, honey."

She got out of the car and stood on the curb. Jan gave her the bottle and she tilted it.

"Whoa!" Jan said.

"What's the matter?"

"I don't want you to pass out."

"I can hold it."

Jan tilted the bottle and emptied it, then laid it in the gutter. He fumbled clumsily in his pockets for something. He swayed; he was drunk.

"You lose something, honey?" Mary lisped; she, too, was drunk.

"Naw; I got some stuff here I want Bigger to read. Listen, Bigger, I got some pamphlets here. I want you to read 'em, see?"

Bigger held out his hand and received a small batch of booklets.

"O.K."

"I really want you to read 'em, now. We'll have a talk 'bout 'em in a coupla days. . . ." His speech was thick.

"I'll read 'em," Bigger said, stifling a yawn and stuffing the booklets into his pocket.

"I'll see that he reads 'em," Mary said.

Jan kissed her again. Bigger heard a Loop-bound car rumbling far down the avenue.

"Well, good-bye," he said.

"Goo'-bye, honey," Mary said. "I'm gonna ride up front with Bigger."

She got into the front seat. The street car clanged to a stop. Jan swung onto it and it started north. Bigger drove toward Drexel Boulevard. Mary slumped down in the seat and sighed. Her legs sprawled wide apart. The car rolled along. Bigger's head was spinning.

"You're very nice, Bigger," she said.

He looked at her. Her face was pasty white. Her eyes were glassy. She was very drunk.

"I don't know," he said.

"My! But you say the *funniest* things," she giggled.

"Maybe," he said.

She leaned her head on his shoulder.

"You don't mind, do you?"

"I don't mind."

"You know, for three hours you haven't said *yes* or *no*."

She doubled up with laughter. He tightened with hate. Again she was looking inside of him and he did not like it. She sat up and dabbed at her eyes with a handkerchief. He kept his eyes straight in front of him and swung the car into the driveway and brought it to a stop. He got out and opened the door. She did not move. Her eyes were closed.

"We're here," he said.

She tried to get up and slipped back into the seat.

"Aw, shucks!"

She's drunk, *really* drunk, Bigger thought. She stretched out her hand.

"Here; gimme a lift. I'm wobbly. . . ."

She was resting on the small of her back and her dress was pulled up so far that he could see where her stockings ended on her thighs. He stood looking at her for a moment; she raised her eyes and looked at him. She laughed.

"Help me, Bigger. I'm stuck."

He helped her and his hands felt the softness of her body as she stepped to the ground. Her dark eyes looked at him feverishly from deep sockets. Her hair was in his face, filling him with its scent. He gritted his teeth, feeling a little dizzy.

"Where's my hat? I dropped it somewhere. . . ."

She swayed as she spoke and he tightened his arms about her, holding her up. He looked round; her hat was lying on the running board.

"Here it is," he said.

As he picked it up he wondered what a white man would think seeing him here with her like this. Suppose old man Dalton saw him now? Apprehensively, he looked up at the big house. It was dark and silent.

"Well," Mary sighed. "I suppose I better go to bed. . . ."

He turned her loose, but had to catch her again to keep her off the pavement. He led her to the steps.

"Can you make it?"

She looked at him as though she had been challenged.

"Sure. Turn me loose. . . ."

He took his arm from her and she mounted the steps firmly and then stumbled loudly on the wooden porch. Bigger made a move toward her, but stopped, his hands outstretched, frozen with fear. Good God, she'll wake up everybody! She was half-bent over, resting on one knee and one hand, looking back at him in amused astonishment. That girl's crazy! She pulled up and walked slowly back down the steps, holding onto the railing. She swayed before him, smiling.

"I sure am drunk. . . ."

He watched her with a mingled feeling of helplessness, admiration, and hate. If her father saw him here with her now, his job would be over. But she was beautiful, slender, with an air that made him feel that she did not hate him with the hate of other white people. But, for all of that, she was white and he hated her. She closed her eyes slowly, then opened them; she was trying desperately to take hold of herself. Since she was not able to get to her room alone, ought he to call Mr. Dalton or Peggy? Naw. . . . That would betray her. And, too, in spite of his hate for her, he was excited standing here watching her like this. Her eyes closed again and she swayed toward him. He caught her.

"I'd better help you," he said.

"Let's go the back way, Bigger. I'll stumble sure as hell . . . and wake up everybody . . . if we go up the front. . . ."

Her feet dragged on the concrete as he led her to the basement. He switched on the light, supporting her with his free hand.

"I didn't know I was sho drunk," she mumbled.

He led her slowly up the narrow stairs to the kitchen door, his hand circling her waist and the tips of his fingers feeling the soft swelling of her breasts. Each second she was leaning more heavily against him.

"Try to stand up," he whispered fiercely as they reached the kitchen door.

He was thinking that perhaps Mrs. Dalton was standing in flowing white and staring with stony blind eyes in the middle of the floor, as she had been when he had come for the glass of water. He eased the door back and looked. The kitchen was empty and dark, save for a faint blue hazy light that seeped through a window from the winter sky.

"Come on."

She pulled heavily on him, her arm about his neck. He pushed the door in and took a step inside and stopped, waiting, listening. He felt her hair brush his lips. His skin glowed warm and his muscles flexed; he looked at her face in the dim light, his senses drunk with the odor of her hair and skin. He stood for a moment, then whispered in excitement and fear:

"Come on; you got to get to your room."

He led her out of the kitchen into the hallway; he had to walk her a step at a time. The hall was empty and dark; slowly he half-walked and half-dragged her to the back stairs. Again he hated her; he shook her.

"Come on; wake up!"

She did not move or open her eyes; finally she mumbled something and swayed limply. His fingers felt the soft curves of her body and he was still, looking at her, enveloped in a sense of physical elation. This little bitch! he thought. Her face was touching his. He turned her round and began to mount the steps, one by one. He heard a slight creaking and stopped. He looked, straining his eyes in the gloom. But there was no one. When he got to the top of the steps she was completely limp and was still trying to mumble something. Goddamn! He could move her only by lifting her bodily. He caught her in his arms and carried her down the hall, then paused. Which was her door? Goddamn!

"Where's your room?" he whispered.

She did not answer. Was she completely out? He could not leave her here; if he took his hands from her she would sink to the floor and lie there all night. He shook her hard, speaking as loudly as he dared.

"Where's your room?"

Momentarily, she roused herself and looked at him with blank eyes.

"Where's your room?" he asked again.

She rolled her eyes toward a door. He got her as far as the door and stopped. Was this really her room? Was she too drunk to know? Suppose he opened the door to Mr. and Mrs. Dalton's room? Well, all they could do was fire him. It wasn't his fault that she was drunk. He felt strange, possessed, or as if he were acting upon a stage in front of a crowd of people. Carefully, he freed one hand and turned the knob of the door. He waited; nothing happened. He pushed the door in quietly; the room was dark and silent. He felt along the wall with his fingers for the electric switch and could not find it. He stood, holding her in his arms, fearful, in doubt. His eyes were growing used to the darkness and a little light seeped into the room from the winter sky through a window. At the far end of the room he made out the shadowy form of a white bed. He lifted her and brought her into the room and closed the door softly.

"Here; wake up, now."

He tried to stand her on her feet and found her weak as jelly. He held her in his arms again, listening in the darkness. His senses reeled from the scent of her hair and skin. She was much smaller than Bessie, his girl, but much softer. Her face was buried in his shoulder; his arms tightened about her. Her face turned slowly and he held his face still, waiting for her face to come round, in front of his. Then her head leaned backward, slowly, gently; it was as though she had given up. Her lips, faintly moist in the hazy blue light, were parted and he saw the furtive glints of her white teeth. Her eyes were closed. He stared at her dim face, the forehead capped with curly black hair. He eased his hand, the fingers spread wide, up the center of her back and her face came toward him and her lips touched his, like something he had imagined. He stood her on her feet and she swayed against him. He tightened his arms as his lips pressed tightly against hers and he felt her body moving strongly. The thought and conviction that Jan had had her a lot flashed through his mind. He kissed her again and felt the sharp bones of her hips move in a hard and veritable grind. Her mouth was open and her breath came slow and deep.

He lifted her and laid her on the bed. Something urged him to leave at once, but he leaned over her, excited, looking at her face in the dim light, not wanting to take his hands from her breasts. She tossed and mumbled sleepily. He tightened his fingers on her breasts, kissing her again, feeling her move toward him. He was aware only of her body now; his lips trembled. Then he stiffened. The door behind him had creaked.

He turned and a hysterical terror seized him, as though he were falling from a great height in a dream. A white blur was standing by the door, silent, ghostlike. It filled his eyes and gripped his body. It was Mrs. Dalton. He wanted to knock her out of his way and bolt from the room.

"Mary!" she spoke softly, questioningly.

Bigger held his breath. Mary mumbled again; he bent over her, his fists clenched in fear. He knew that Mrs. Dalton could not see him; but he knew that if Mary spoke she would come to the side of the bed and discover him, touch him. He waited tensely, afraid to move for fear of bumping into something in the dark and betraying his presence.

"Mary!"

He felt Mary trying to rise and quickly he pushed her head back to the pillow.

"She must be asleep," Mrs. Dalton mumbled.

He wanted to move from the bed, but was afraid he would stumble over something and Mrs. Dalton would hear him, would know that someone besides Mary was in the room. Frenzy dominated him. He held his hand over her mouth and his head was cocked at an angle that enabled him to see Mary and Mrs. Dalton by merely shifting his eyes. Mary mumbled and tried to rise again. Frantically, he caught a corner of the pillow and brought it to her lips. He had to stop her from mumbling, or he would be caught. Mrs. Dalton was moving slowly toward him and he grew tight and full, as though about to explode. Mary's fingernails tore at his hands and he caught the pillow and covered her entire face with it, firmly. Mary's body surged upward and he pushed downward upon the pillow with all of his weight, determined that she must not move or make any sound that would betray him. His eyes were filled with the white blur moving toward him in the shadows of the room. Again Mary's body heaved and he held the pillow in a grip that took all of his strength. For a long time he felt the sharp pain of her fingernails biting into his wrists. The white blur was still.

"Mary? Is that *you?*"

He clenched his teeth and held his breath, intimidated to the core by the awesome white blur floating toward him. His muscles flexed taut as steel and he pressed the pillow, feeling the bed give slowly, evenly, but silently. Then suddenly her fingernails did not bite into his wrists. Mary's fingers loosened. He did not feel her surging and heaving against him. Her body was still.

"Mary! Is that *you?*"

He could see Mrs. Dalton plainly now. As he took his hands from the pillow he heard a long slow sigh go up from the bed into the air of the darkened room, a sigh which afterwards, when he remembered it, seemed final, irrevocable.

"Mary! Are you ill?"

He stood up. With each of her movements toward the bed his body made a movement to match hers, away from her, his feet not lifting themselves from the floor, but sliding softly and silently over the smooth deep rug, his muscles flexed so taut they ached. Mrs. Dalton now stood over the bed. Her hands reached out and touched Mary.

"Mary! Are you asleep? I heard you moving about. . . ."

Mrs. Dalton straightened suddenly and took a quick step back.

"You're dead drunk! You *stink* with whiskey!"

She stood silently in the hazy blue light, then she knelt at the side of the bed. Bigger heard her whispering. She's praying, he thought in amazement and the words echoed in his mind as though someone had spoken them aloud. Finally, Mrs. Dalton stood up and her face tilted to that upward angle at which she always held it. He waited, his teeth clamped, his fists clenched. She moved slowly toward the door; he could scarcely see her now. The door creaked; then silence.

He relaxed and sank to the floor, his breath going in a long gasp. He was weak and wet with sweat. He stayed crouched and bent, hearing the sound of his breathing filling the darkness. Gradually, the intensity of his sensations subsided and he was aware of the room. He felt that he had been in the grip of a weird spell and was now free. The fingertips of his right hand were pressed deeply into the soft fibers of the rug and his whole body vibrated from the wild pounding of his heart. He had to get out of the room, and quickly. Suppose that had been *Mr.* Dalton? His escape had been narrow enough, as it was.

He stood and listened. Mrs. Dalton might be out there in the hallway. How could he get out of the room? He all but shuddered with the intensity of his loathing for this house and all it had made him feel since he had first come into it. He reached his hand behind him and touched the wall; he was glad to have something solid at his back. He looked at the shadowy bed and remembered Mary as some person he had not seen in a long time. She was still there. Had he hurt her? He went to the bed and stood over her; her face lay sideways on the pillow. His hand moved toward her, but stopped in mid-air. He blinked his eyes and stared at Mary's face; it was darker than when he had first bent over her. Her mouth was open and her eyes bulged glassily. Her bosom, her bosom, her—her bosom was not moving! He could not hear her breath coming and going now as he had when he had first brought her into the room! He bent and moved her head with his hand and found that she was relaxed and limp. He snatched his hand away. Thought and feeling were balked in him; there was something he was trying to tell himself, desperately, but could not. Then, convulsively, he sucked his breath in and huge words formed slowly, ringing in his ears: *She's dead. . . .*

The reality of the room fell from him; the vast city of white people that sprawled outside took its place. She was dead and he had killed her. He was a murderer, a Negro murderer, a black murderer. He had killed a white woman. He had to get away from here.

1940

Ralph Ellison 1914–1994

Ralph Ellison became one of the most important U.S. writers of the twentieth century when he published Invisible Man*—a novel that turns the odyssey of its young African American protagonist into a deft and incisive commentary on the Western literary tradition and American history.*

Named after Ralph Waldo Emerson, the nineteenth-century essayist and poet, Ralph Waldo Ellison was born in Oklahoma in 1914. He did well in school and won a scholarship to the Tuskegee Institute in 1933, where he studied music. Before graduating he went north to Harlem to study sculpture. In New York, where he was befriended and encouraged by Richard Wright, Ellison began to write. Like many other intellectuals of the time, he became involved with the left-wing political movements of the Depression period, but Ellison's flirtation with communism was brief, and the party is bitingly satirized in Invisible Man. *In 1942, Ellison became the editor of* Negro Quarterly *and, after serving time in the Merchant Marine during World War II, he seriously began work on his novel. After the completion of* Invisible Man, *Ellison held various academic positions while he continued to work on his promised second novel. A collection of his essays,* Shadow and Act, *was published in 1964.*

Despite all the acclaim that it received, Invisible Man *has been criticized as insufficiently militant. In a sense, the criticism is just, for the novel is both so subtle and so complex that it lacks the immediate emotional impact of, for example, Richard Wright's novel* Native Son. *Ellison's* Invisible Man *is based on a set of symbols, on the conscious use of myth, and on historical allusions. It presents the traditional theme of the development of youth into maturity and is concerned, in Ellison's words, with "the American theme," the search for identity.* Invisible Man *is not, therefore, merely a racial protest novel. Ellison's intellect and his artistic imagination were too complex to stop at the presentation merely of anger and militancy, no matter how justified. His aim was broader. Early in life he gained, he said, "a passion to link together all I loved within the Negro community and all those things I felt in the world which lay beyond."* Invisible Man *achieves such a linking. It equates the social maturation of a young black boy with the archetypal theme of self-realization; it portrays the black man as the symbol of all men and their aspirations and frustrations, and it achieves Ellison's self-professed goal in art, the "universal."*

FURTHER READING: *Invisible Man: A Collection of Critical Essays,* ed. J. Reilly, 1970; R. O'Meally, *The Craft of Ralph Ellison,* 1980; R. List, *Dedalus in Harlem: The Joyce-Ellison Connection,* 1982; *Ralph Ellison,* ed. H. Bloom, 1986; A. Nadel, *Invisible Criticism: Ralph Ellison and the American Canon,* 1988; J. Watts, *Heroism and the Black Intellectual,* 1994; *Conversations with Ralph Ellison,* ed. M. Graham and A. Singh, 1995; *Cultural Contexts for Ralph Ellison's Invisible Man,* ed. E. Sundquist, 1995; *Trading Twelves: The Selected Letters of Ralph Ellison and Albert Murray,* ed. A. Murray and J. Callahan, 2000; *The Critical Response to Ralph Ellison,* ed. R. Butler, 2000; *Living with Music: Ralph Ellison's Jazz Writings,* ed. R. O'Meally, 2001; K. Warren, *So Black and Blue: Ralph Ellison and the Occasion of Criticism,* 2003; *A Historical Guide to Ralph Ellison,* ed. S. Tracy, 2004.

TEXT: *Invisible Man,* 1952.

from *INVISIBLE MAN*

CHAPTER I

It goes a long way back, some twenty years. All my life I had been looking for something, and everywhere I turned someone tried to tell me what it was. I accepted their answers too, though they were often in contradiction and even self-contradictory. I was naïve. I was looking for myself and asking everyone except myself questions which I, and only I, could answer. It took me a long time and much painful boomeranging of my expectations to achieve a realization everyone else appears to have been born with: That I am nobody but myself. But first I had to discover that I am an invisible man!

And yet I am no freak of nature, nor of history. I was in the cards, other things having been equal (or unequal) eighty-five years ago. I am not ashamed of my grandparents for having been slaves. I am only ashamed of myself for having at one time been ashamed. About eighty-five years ago they were told that they were free, united with others of our country in everything pertaining to the common good, and, in everything social, separate like the fingers of the hand. And they believed it. They exulted in it. They stayed in their place, worked hard, and brought up my father to do the same. But my grandfather is the one. He was an odd old guy, my grandfather, and I am told I take after him. It was he who caused the trouble. On his deathbed he called my father to him and said, "Son, after I'm gone I want you to keep up the good fight. I never told you, but our life is a war and I have been a traitor all my born days, a spy in the enemy's country ever since I give up my gun back in the Reconstruction. Live with your head in the lion's mouth. I want you to overcome 'em with yeses, undermine 'em with grins, agree 'em to death and destruction, let 'em swoller you till they vomit or bust wide open." They thought the old man had gone out of his mind. He had been the meekest of men. The younger children were rushed from the room, the shades drawn and the flame of the lamp turned so low that it sputtered on the wick like the old man's breathing. "Learn it to the younguns," he whispered fiercely; then he died.

But my folks were more alarmed over his last words than over his dying. It was as though he had not died at all, his words caused so much anxiety. I was warned emphatically to forget what he had said and, indeed, this is the first time it has been mentioned outside the family circle. It had a tremendous effect upon me, however. I could never be sure of what he meant. Grandfather had been a quiet old man who never made any trouble, yet on his deathbed he had called himself a traitor and a spy, and he had spoken of his meekness as a dangerous activity. It became a constant puzzle which lay unanswered in the back of my mind. And whenever things went well for me I remembered my grandfather and felt guilty and uncomfortable. It was as though I was carrying out his advice in spite of myself. And to make it worse, everyone loved me for it. I was praised by the most lily-white men of the town. I was considered an example of desirable conduct—just as my grandfather had been. And what puzzled me was that the old man had defined it as *treachery.* When I was praised for my conduct I felt a guilt that in some way I was doing something that was really against the wishes of the white folks, that if they had understood they would have desired me to act just the opposite, that I should have been sulky and mean, and that that really would have been what they wanted, even though they were fooled and thought they wanted me to act as I did. It made me afraid that some day they would look upon me as a traitor and I would be lost. Still I was more afraid to act any other way because they didn't like that at all. The old man's words were like a curse. On my graduation day I delivered an oration in which I showed that humility was the secret, indeed, the very essence of progress. (Not that I believed this—how could I, remembering my grandfather?—I only believed that it worked.) It was a great success. Everyone praised me and I was invited to give the speech at a gathering of the town's leading white citizens. It was a triumph for our whole community.

It was in the main ballroom of the leading hotel. When I got there I discovered that it was on the occasion of a smoker, and I was told that since I was to be there anyway I might as well take part in the battle royal to be fought by some of my schoolmates as part of the entertainment. The battle royal came first.

All of the town's big shots were there in their tuxedoes, wolfing down the buffet foods, drinking beer and whiskey and smoking black cigars. It was a large room with a high ceiling. Chairs were arranged in neat rows around three sides of a portable boxing ring. The fourth side was clear, revealing a gleaming space of polished floor. I had some misgivings over the battle royal, by the way. Not from a distaste for fighting, but because I didn't care too much for the other fellows who were to take part. They were tough guys who seemed to have no grandfather's curse worrying their minds. No one could mistake their toughness. And besides, I suspected that fighting a battle royal might detract from the dignity of my speech. In those pre-invisible days I visualized myself as a potential Booker T. Washington.[1] But the other fellows didn't care too much for me either, and there were nine of them. I felt superior to them in my way, and I didn't like the manner in which we were all crowded together into the servants' elevator. Nor did they like my being there. In fact, as the warmly lighted floors flashed past the elevator we had words over the fact that I, by taking part in the fight, had knocked one of their friends out of a night's work.

We were led out of the elevator through a rococo hall into an anteroom and told to get into our fighting togs. Each of us was issued a pair of boxing gloves and ushered out into the big mirrored hall, which we entered looking cautiously about us and whispering, lest we might accidentally be heard above the noise of the room. It was foggy with cigar smoke. And already the whiskey was taking effect. I was shocked to see some of the most important men of the town quite tipsy. They were all there—bankers, lawyers, judges, doctors, fire chiefs, teachers, merchants. Even one of the more fashionable pastors. Something we could not see was going on up front. A clarinet was vibrating sensuously and the men were standing up and moving eagerly forward. We were a small tight group, clustered together, our bare upper bodies touching and shining with anticipatory sweat; while up front the big shots were becoming increasingly excited over something we still could not see. Suddenly I heard the school superintendent, who had told me to come, yell, "Bring up the shines, gentlemen! Bring up the little shines!"

[1]African American educator (1856–1915), author of *Up from Slavery* (1901).

We were rushed up to the front of the ballroom, where it smelled even more strongly of tobacco and whiskey. Then we were pushed into place. I almost wet my pants. A sea of faces, some hostile, some amused, ringed around us, and in the center, facing us, stood a magnificent blonde—stark naked. There was dead silence. I felt a blast of cold air chill me. I tried to back away, but they were behind me and around me. Some of the boys stood with lowered heads, trembling. I felt a wave of irrational guilt and fear. My teeth chattered, my skin turned to goose flesh, my knees knocked. Yet I was strongly attracted and looked in spite of myself. Had the price of looking been blindness, I would have looked. The hair was yellow like that of a circus kewpie doll, the face heavily powdered and rouged, as though to form an abstract mask, the eyes hollow and smeared a cool blue, the color of a baboon's butt. I felt a desire to spit upon her as my eyes brushed slowly over her body. Her breasts were firm and round as the domes of East Indian temples, and I stood so close as to see the fine skin texture and beads of pearly perspiration glistening like dew around the pink and erected buds of her nipples. I wanted at one and the same time to run from the room, to sink through the floor, or go to her and cover her from my eyes and the eyes of the others with my body; to feel the soft thighs, to caress her and destroy her, to love her and murder her, to hide from her, and yet to stroke where below the small American flag tattooed upon her belly her thighs formed a capital V. I had a notion that of all in the room she saw only me with her impersonal eyes.

And then she began to dance, a slow sensuous movement; the smoke of a hundred cigars clinging to her like the thinnest of veils. She seemed like a fair bird-girl girdled in veils calling to me from the angry surface of some gray and threatening sea. I was transported. Then I became aware of the clarinet playing and the big shots yelling at us. Some threatened us if we looked and others if we did not. On my right I saw one boy faint. And now a man grabbed a silver pitcher from a table and stepped close as he dashed ice water upon him and stood him up and forced two of us to support him as his head hung and moans issued from his thick bluish lips. Another boy began to plead to go home. He was the largest of the group, wearing dark red fighting trunks much too small to conceal the erection which projected from him as though in answer to the insinuating low-registered moaning of the clarinet. He tried to hide himself with his boxing gloves.

And all the while the blonde continued dancing, smiling faintly at the big shots who watched her with fascination, and faintly smiling at our fear. I noticed a certain merchant who followed her hungrily, his lips loose and drooling. He was a large man who wore diamond studs in a shirtfront which swelled with the ample paunch underneath, and each time the blonde swayed her undulating hips he ran his hand through the thin hair of his bald head and, with his arms upheld, his posture clumsy like that of an intoxicated panda, wound his belly in a slow and obscene grind. This creature was completely hypnotized. The music had quickened. As the dancer flung herself about with a detached expression on her face, the men began reaching out to touch her. I could see their beefy fingers sink into the soft flesh. Some of the others tried to stop them and she began to move around the floor in graceful circles, as they gave chase, slipping and sliding over the polished floor. It was mad. Chairs went crashing, drinks were spilt, as they ran laughing and howling after her. They caught her just as she reached a door, raised her from the floor, and tossed her as college boys are tossed at a hazing, and above her red, fixed-smiling lips I saw the terror and disgust in her eyes, almost like my own terror and that which I saw in some of the other boys. As I watched, they tossed her twice and her soft breasts seemed to flatten against the air and her legs flung wildly as she spun. Some of the sober ones helped her to escape. And I started off the floor, heading for the anteroom with the rest of the boys.

Some were still crying and in hysteria. But as we tried to leave we were stopped and ordered to get into the ring. There was nothing to do but what we were told. All ten of us climbed under the ropes and allowed ourselves to be blindfolded with broad bands of white cloth. One of the men seemed to feel a bit sympathetic and tried to cheer us up as we stood with our backs against the ropes. Some of us tried to grin. "See that boy over there?" one of the men said. "I want you to run across at the bell and give it to him right in the belly. If you don't get him, I'm going to get you. I don't like his looks." Each of us was told the same. The blindfolds were put on. Yet even then I had been going over my speech. In my mind each word was as bright as flame. I felt the cloth pressed into place, and frowned so that it would be loosened when I relaxed.

But now I felt a sudden fit of blind terror. I was unused to darkness. It was as though I had suddenly found myself in a dark room filled with poisonous cottonmouths. I could hear the bleary voices yelling insistently for the battle royal to begin.

"Get going in there!"

"Let me at that big nigger!"

I strained to pick up the school superintendent's voice, as though to squeeze some security out of that slightly more familiar sound.

"Let me at those black sonsabitches!" someone yelled.

"No, Jackson, no!" another voice yelled. "Here, somebody, help me hold Jack."

"I want to get at that ginger-colored nigger. Tear him limb from limb," the first voice yelled.

I stood against the ropes trembling. For in those days I was what they called ginger-colored, and he sounded as though he might crunch me between his teeth like a crisp ginger cookie.

Quite a struggle was going on. Chairs were being kicked about and I could hear voices grunting as with a terrific effort. I wanted to see, to see more desperately than ever before. But the blindfold was tight as a thick skin-puckering scab and when I raised my gloved hands to push the layers of white aside a voice yelled, "Oh, no you don't, black bastard! Leave that alone!"

"Ring the bell before Jackson kills him a coon!" someone boomed in the sudden silence. And I heard the bell clang and the sound of the feet scuffling forward.

A glove smacked against my head. I pivoted, striking out stiffly as someone went past, and felt the jar ripple along the length of my arm to my shoulder. Then it seemed as though all nine boys had turned upon me at once. Blows pounded me from all sides while I struck out as best I could. So many blows landed upon me that I wondered if I were not the only blind-folded fighter in the ring, or if the man called Jackson hadn't succeeded in getting me after all.

Blindfolded, I could no longer control my motions. I had no dignity. I stumbled about like a baby or a drunken man. The smoke had become thicker and with each new blow it seemed to sear and further restrict my lungs. My saliva became like hot bitter glue. A glove connected with my head, filling my mouth with warm blood. It was everywhere. I could not tell if the moisture I felt upon my body was sweat or blood. A blow landed hard against the nape of my neck. I felt myself going over, my head hitting the floor. Streaks of blue light filled the black world behind the blindfold. I lay prone, pretending that I was knocked out, but felt myself seized by hands and yanked to my feet. "Get going, black boy! Mix it up!" My arms were like lead, my head smarting from blows. I managed to feel my way to the ropes and held on, trying to catch my breath. A glove landed in my mid-section and I went over again, feeling as though the smoke had become a knife jabbed into my guts. Pushed this way and that by the legs milling around me, I finally pulled erect and discovered that I could see the black, sweat-washed forms weaving in the smoky-blue atmosphere like drunken dancers weaving to the rapid drum-like thuds of blows.

Everyone fought hysterically. It was complete anarchy. Everybody fought everybody else. No group fought together for long. Two, three, four, fought one, then turned to fight each other, were themselves attacked. Blows landed below the belt and in the kidney, with the gloves open as well as closed, and with my eye partly opened now there was not so much terror. I moved carefully, avoiding blows, although not too many to attract attention, fighting from group to group. The boys groped about like blind, cautious crabs crouching to protect their mid-sections, their heads pulled in short against their shoulders, their arms stretched nervously before them, with their fists testing the smoke-filled air like the knobbed feelers of hypersensitive snails. In one corner I glimpsed a boy violently punching the air and heard him scream in pain as he smashed his hand against a ring post. For a second I saw him bent over holding his hand, then going down as a blow caught his unprotected head. I played one group against the other, slipping in and throwing a punch then stepping out of range while pushing the others into the melee to take the blows blindly aimed at me. The smoke was agonizing and there were no rounds, no bells at three minute intervals to relieve our exhaustion. The room spun round me, a swirl of lights, smoke, sweating bodies surrounded by tense white faces. I bled from both nose and mouth, the blood spattering upon my chest.

The men kept yelling, "Slug him, black boy! Knock his guts out!"

"Uppercut him! Kill him! Kill that big boy!"

Taking a fake fall, I saw a boy going down heavily beside me as though we were felled by a single blow, saw a sneaker-clad foot shoot into his groin as the two who had knocked him down stumbled upon him. I rolled out of range, feeling a twinge of nausea.

The harder we fought the more threatening the men became. And yet, I had begun to worry about my speech again. How would it go? Would they recognize my ability? What would they give me?

I was fighting automatically when suddenly I noticed that one after another of the boys was leaving the ring. I was surprised, filled with panic, as though I had been left alone with an unknown danger. Then I understood. The boys had arranged it among themselves. It was the custom for the two men left in the ring to slug it out for the winner's prize. I discovered this too late. When the bell sounded two men in tuxedoes leaped into the ring and removed the blindfold. I found myself facing Tatlock, the biggest of the gang. I felt sick at my stomach. Hardly had the bell stopped ringing in my ears than it clanged again and I saw him moving swiftly toward me. Thinking of nothing else to do I hit him smash on the nose. He kept coming, bringing the rank sharp violence of stale sweat. His face was a black blank of a face, only his eyes alive—with hate of me and aglow with a feverish terror from what had happened to us all. I became anxious. I wanted to deliver my speech and he came at me as though he meant to beat it out of me. I smashed him again and again, taking his blows as they came. Then on a sudden impulse I struck him lightly and as we clinched, I whispered, "Fake like I knocked you out, you can have the prize."

"I'll break your behind," he whispered hoarsely.

"For *them?*"

"For *me,* sonofabitch!"

They were yelling for us to break it up and Tatlock spun me half around with a blow, and as a joggled camera sweeps in a reeling scene, I saw the howling red faces crouching tense beneath the cloud of blue-gray smoke. For a moment the world wavered, unraveled, flowed, then my head cleared and Tatlock bounced before me. The fluttering shadow before my eyes was his jabbing left hand. Then falling forward, my head against his damp shoulder, I whispered, "I'll make it five dollars more."

"Go to hell!"

But his muscles relaxed a trifle beneath my pressure and I breathed, "Seven?"

"Give it to your ma," he said, ripping me beneath the heart.

And while I still held him I butted him and moved away. I felt myself bombarded with punches. I fought back with hopeless desperation. I wanted to deliver my speech more than anything else in the world, because I felt that only these men could judge truly my ability, and now this stupid clown was ruining my chances. I began fighting carefully now, moving in to punch him and out again with my greater speed. A lucky blow to his chin and I had him going too—until I heard a loud voice yell, "I got my money on the big boy."

Hearing this, I almost dropped my guard. I was confused: Should I try to win against the voice out there? Would not this go against my speech, and was not this a moment for humility, for nonresistance? A blow to my head as I danced about sent my right eye popping like a jack-in-the-box and settled my dilemma. The room went red as I fell. It was a dream fall, my body languid and fastidious as to where to land, until the floor became impatient and smashed up to meet me. A moment later I came to. An hypnotic vice said FIVE emphatically. And I lay there, hazily watching a dark red spot of my own blood shaping itself into a butterfly, glistening and soaking into the soiled gray world of the canvas.

When the voice drawled TEN I was lifted up and dragged to a chair. I sat dazed. My eye pained and swelled with each throb of my pounding heart and I wondered if now I would be allowed to speak. I was wringing wet, my mouth still bleeding. We were grouped along the wall now. The other boys ignored me as they congratulated Tatlock and speculated as to how much they would be paid. One boy whimpered over his smashed hand. Looking up front, I saw attendants in white jackets rolling the portable ring away and placing a small square rug in the vacant space surrounded by chairs. Perhaps, I thought, I will stand on the rug to deliver my speech.

Then the M.C. called to us, "Come on up here boys and get your money."

We ran forward to where the men laughed and talked in their chairs, waiting. Everyone seemed friendly now.

"There it is on the rug," the man said. I saw the rug covered with coins of all dimensions and a few crumpled bills. But what excited me, scattered here and there, were the gold pieces.

"Boys, it's all yours," the man said. "You get all you grab."

"That's right, Sambo," a blond man said, winking at me confidentially.

I trembled with excitement, forgetting my pain. I would get the gold and the bills, I thought. I would use both hands. I would throw my body against the boys nearest me to block them from the gold.

"Get down on the rug now," the man commanded, "and don't anyone touch it until I give the signal."

"This ought to be good," I heard.

As told, we got around the square rug on our knees. Slowly the man raised his freckled hand as we followed it upward with our eyes.

I heard, "These niggers look like they're about to pray!"

Then, "Ready," the man said, "Go!"

I lunged for a yellow coin lying on the blue design of the carpet, touching it and sending a surprised shriek to join those rising around me. I tried frantically to remove my hand but could not let go. A hot, violent force tore through my body, shaking me like a wet rat. The rug was electrified. The hair bristled up on my head as I shook myself free. My muscles jumped, my nerves jangled, writhed. But I saw that this was not stopping the other boys. Laughing in fear and embarrassment, some were holding back and scooping up the coins knocked off by the painful contortions of the others. The men roared above us as we struggled.

"Pick it up, goddamnit, pick it up!" someone called like a bass-voiced parrot. "Go on, get it!"

I crawled rapidly around the floor, picking up the coins, trying to avoid the coppers and to get greenbacks and the gold. Ignoring the shock by laughing, as I brushed the coins off quickly, I discovered that I could contain the electricity—a contradiction, but it works. Then the men began to push us onto the rug. Laughing embarrassedly, we struggled out of their hands and kept after the coins. We were all wet and slippery and hard to hold. Suddenly I saw a boy lifted into the air, glistening with sweat like a circus seal, and dropped, his wet back landing flush upon the charged rug, heard him yell and saw him literally dance upon his back, his elbows beating a frenzied tattoo upon the floor, his muscles twitching like the flesh of a horse stung by many flies. When he finally rolled off, his face was gray and no one stopped him when he ran from the floor amid booming laughter.

"Get the money," the M.C. called. "That's good hard American cash!"

And we snatched and grabbed, snatched and grabbed. I was careful not to come too close to the rug now, and when I felt the hot whiskey breath descend upon me like a cloud of foul air I reached out and grabbed the leg of a chair. It was occupied and I held on desperately.

"Leggo, nigger! Leggo!"

The huge face wavered down to mine as he tried to push me free. But my body was slippery and he was too drunk. It was Mr. Colcord, who owned a chain of movie houses and "entertainment palaces." Each time he grabbed me I slipped out of his hands. It became a real struggle. I feared the rug more than I did the drunk, so I held on, surprising myself for a moment by trying to topple *him* upon the rug. It was such an enormous idea that I found myself actually carrying it out. I tried not to be obvious, yet when I grabbed his leg, trying to tumble him out of the chair, he raised up roaring with laughter, and, looking at me with soberness dead in the eye, kicked me viciously in the chest. The chair leg flew out of my hand and I felt myself going and rolled. It was as though I had rolled through a bed of hot coals. It seemed a whole century would pass before I would roll free, a century in which I was seared through the deepest levels of my body to the fearful breath within me and the breath seared and heated to the point of explosion. It'll all be over in a flash, I thought as I rolled clear. It'll all be over in a flash.

But not yet, the men on the other side were waiting, red faces swollen as though from apoplexy as they bent forward in their chairs. Seeing their fingers coming toward me, I rolled away as a fumbled football rolls off the receiver's fingertips, back into the coals. That time I luckily sent the rug sliding out of place and heard the coins ringing against the floor and the boys scuffling to pick them up and the M.C. calling, "All right, boys that's all. Go get dressed and get your money."

I was limp as a dish rag. My back felt as though it had been beaten with wires.

When we had dressed the M.C. came in and gave us each five dollars, except Tatlock, who got ten for being last in the ring. Then he told us to leave. I was not to get a chance to deliver my speech, I thought. I was going out into the dim alley in despair when I was stopped and told to go back. I returned to the ballroom, where the men were pushing back their chairs and gathering in groups to talk.

The M.C. knocked on a table for quiet. "Gentlemen," he said, "we almost forgot about an important part of the program. A most serious part, gentlemen. This boy was brought here to deliver a speech which he made at his graduation yesterday . . ."

"Bravo!"

"I'm told that he is the smartest boy we've got out there in Greenwood. I'm told that he knows more big words than a pocket-sized dictionary."

Much applause and laughter.

"So now, gentlemen, I want you to give him your attention."

There was still laughter as I faced them, my mouth dry, my eye throbbing. I began slowly, but evidently my throat was tense, because they began shouting, "Louder! Louder!"

"We of the younger generation extol the wisdom of that great leader and educator," I shouted, "who first spoke these flaming words of wisdom: 'A ship lost at sea for many days suddenly sighted a friendly vessel. From the mast of the unfortunate vessel was seen a signal: "Water, water; we die of thirst!" The answer from the friendly vessel came back: "Cast down your bucket where you are." The captain of the distressed vessel, at last heeding the injunction, cast down his bucket, and it came up full of fresh sparkling water from the mouth of the Amazon River.' And like him I say, and in his words, 'To those of my race who depend upon bettering their condition in a foreign land, or who underestimate the importance of cultivating friendly relations with the Southern white man, who is his next-door neighbor, I would say: "Cast down your bucket where you are"—cast it down in making friends in every manly way of the people of all races by whom we are surrounded . . .'"

I spoke automatically and with such fervor that I did not realize that the men were still talking and laughing until my dry mouth, filling up with blood from the cut, almost strangled me. I coughed, wanting to stop and go to one of the tall brass, sand-filled spittoons to relieve myself, but a few of the men, especially the superintendent, were listening and I was afraid. So I gulped it down, blood, saliva and all, and continued. (What powers of endurance I had during those days! What enthusiasm! What a belief in the rightness of things!) I spoke even louder in spite of the pain. But still they talked and still they laughed, as though deaf with cotton in dirty ears. So I spoke with greater emotional emphasis. I closed my ears and swallowed blood until I was nauseated. The speech seemed a hundred times as long as before, but I could not leave out a single word. All had to be said, each memorized nuance considered, rendered. Nor was that all. Whenever I uttered a word of three syllables a group of voices would yell for me to repeat it. I used the phrase "social responsibility" and they yelled:

"What's that word you say, boy?"

"Social responsibility," I said.

"What?"

"Social . . ."

"Louder."

". . . responsibility."

"More!"

"Respon—"

"Repeat!"

"—sibility."

The room filled with the uproar of laughter until, no doubt, distracted by having to gulp down my blood, I made a mistake and yelled a phrase I had often seen denounced in newspaper editorials, heard debated in private.

"Social . . ."

"What?" they yelled.

". . . equality—"

The laughter hung smokelike in the sudden stillness. I opened my eyes, puzzled. Sounds of displeasure filled the room. The M.C. rushed forward. They shouted hostile phrases at me. But I did not understand.

A small dry mustached man in the front row blared out, "Say that slowly, son!"

"What, sir?"

"What you just said!"

"Social responsibility, sir," I said.

"You weren't being smart, were you, boy?" he said, not unkindly.

"No, sir!"

"You sure that about 'equality' was a mistake?"

"Oh, yes, sir," I said. "I was swallowing blood."

"Well, you had better speak more slowly so we can understand. We mean to do right by you, but you've got to know your place at all times. All right, now, go on with your speech."

I was afraid. I wanted to leave but I wanted also to speak and I was afraid they'd snatch me down.

"Thank you, sir," I said, beginning where I had left off, and having them ignore me as before.

Yet when I finished there was a thunderous applause. I was surprised to see the superintendent come forth with a package wrapped in white tissue paper, and, gesturing for quiet, address the men.

"Gentlemen, you see that I did not overpraise this boy. He makes a good speech and some day he'll lead his people in the proper paths. And I don't have to tell you that that is important in these days and times. This is a good, smart boy, and so to encourage him in the right direction, in the name of the Board of Education I wish to present him a prize in the form of this . . ."

He paused, removing the tissue paper and revealing a gleaming calfskin brief case.

". . . in the form of this first-class article from Shad Whitmore's shop."

"Boy," he said, addressing me, "take this prize and keep it well. Consider it a badge of office. Prize it. Keep developing as you are and some day it will be filled with important papers that will help shape the destiny of your people."

I was so moved that I could hardly express my thanks. A rope of bloody saliva forming a shape like an undiscovered continent drooled upon the leather and I wiped it quickly away. I felt an importance that I had never dreamed.

"Open it and see what's inside," I was told.

My fingers a-tremble, I complied, smelling the fresh leather and finding an official-looking document inside. It was a scholarship to the state college for Negroes. My eyes filled with tears and I ran awkwardly off the floor.

I was overjoyed; I did not even mind when I discovered that the gold pieces I had scrambled for were brass pocket tokens advertising a certain make of automobile.

When I reached home everyone was excited. Next day the neighbors came to congratulate me. I even felt safe from grandfather, whose deathbed curse usually spoiled my triumphs. I stood beneath his photograph with my brief case in hand and smiled triumphantly into his stolid black peasant's face. It was a face that fascinated me. The eyes seemed to follow everywhere I went.

That night I dreamed I was at a circus with him and that he refused to laugh at the clowns no matter what they did. Then later he told me to open my brief case and read what was inside and I did, finding an official envelope stamped with the state seal; and inside the envelope, I found another and another, endlessly, and I thought I would fall of weariness. "Them's years," he said. "Now open that one." And I did and in it I found an engraved document containing a short message in letters of gold. "Read it," my grandfather said. "Out loud!"

"To Whom It May Concern," I intoned. "Keep This Nigger-Boy Running."

I awoke with the old man's laughter ringing in my ears.

(It was a dream I was to remember and dream again for many years after. But at that time I had no insight into its meaning. First I had to attend college.)

1952

Tennessee Williams 1911–1983

Tennessee Williams achieved his first great stage success with The Glass Menagerie. *Produced in New York City in 1945, it won the New York Drama Critics' Circle Prize as the best play of the year. It portrays an American family struggling to survive physically and spiritually in the late 1930s. In writing the play, Williams drew heavily upon his own family experiences, describing the lives of his mother, his sister, and himself. He was born Thomas Lanier Williams in Columbus, Mississippi. His father, a traveling shoe-salesman, spent little time at home, and for the first years of his life, Williams and his mother lived with his mother's father, an Episcopal clergyman. In 1918, when Williams was seven, his father became a sales manager for a shoe company in St. Louis, Missouri, and seven-year-old Tom and his sister were uprooted and moved to the city. Timid and sickly, the boy found St. Louis a painful change from the happy life he had led while living in his grandfather's rectory in Mississippi. He found few friends; his mother and father quarreled incessantly; and his father, who believed that his indulgent wife had "sissified" their son, taunted him with the name "Miss Nancy." Enveloped in an unhappy world, Williams, like his counterpart Tom Wingfield in* The Glass Menagerie, *found escape and adventure in the movies, which affected him so intensely, he later recalled, that he "used to want to climb into the screen and join the action."*

At fourteen he won first prize ($25) in an essay contest sponsored by a national magazine, The Smart Set. *When he was seventeen his first published story, a gothic tale named "The Vengeance of Nitrocris," appeared in an issue of* Weird Tales. *The next year he entered the University of Missouri, but in 1932, at his father's insistence, he withdrew from the university and took a job in the shoe factory where his father was a sales manager. After three years working in the company warehouse, a period that Williams later described as a "living death," he had a nervous breakdown. Following a year's recuperation with his grandparents in Memphis, Tennessee, he returned to college, eventually graduating from the University of Iowa with a B.A. in 1938.*

Williams had begun writing plays at the University of Missouri, and after his graduation he continued to write while supporting himself with a variety of menial jobs. By 1939, he was calling himself "Tennessee"—plain "Tom Williams" being, he thought, "rather dull." In that same year he won a national drama award for a group of plays called American Blues. *The next year his first play to be produced by a major company,* Battle of Angels, *opened in Boston and failed, closing after only one performance. Two years later he was hired as a screenwriter for Metro-Goldwyn-Mayer in Hollywood. None of his scripts was accepted, and after a few months he lost his job, but one of his rejected scripts,* The Gentleman Caller, *he later rewrote as* The Glass Menagerie.

In the decades that followed, Williams averaged a play every two years. Of his most memorable dramas, A Streetcar Named Desire *(1947) and* Cat on a Hot Tin Roof *(1955) each won a Pulitzer Prize for drama. In 1956, his controversial film* Baby Doll *was produced, and it was followed by such Broadway and motion-picture successes as* Suddenly Last Summer *(1958),* Sweet Bird of Youth *(1959), and* Night of the Iguana *(1961). In all, fifteen movies have been made from Williams's works. In addition to plays he wrote a novel,* The Roman Spring of Mrs. Stone *(1950), two volumes of poetry, and six volumes of prose, including three collections of short stories.*

Williams's plays have shocked audiences by confronting them with an array of behaviors never presented before on the American stage: murder, rape, castration, drug addiction, homosexuality, alcoholism, fetishism, nymphomania, even cannibalism. By dealing with such subjects Williams helped break taboos long imposed on the American theater, preparing the way for dramatists who would follow with even harsher depictions of violence and sexuality. In spite of, or perhaps because of, his subject matter, Williams's popularity has soared in the decades following his death. Productions of his plays are repeatedly brought back to Broadway—in 2005, two of his plays, A Streetcar Named Desire *and* The Glass Menagerie, *ran on Broadway at the same time. And yearly, more than 900 productions of his plays are staged throughout the world.*

Williams's writing has sometimes been dismissed as willful pandering to the prurient interests of theatergoers. Yet the popular and critical acclaim that his work continues to receive has come not simply because he writes of the bizarre and fantastic but also because his plays are filled with fascinating characters and compelling dialogue. They are illuminated, even gilded, by verbal, visual, and sound symbolism that is intended to convey meanings beyond those possible in what Williams has termed "the exhausted theater of realism." He employs an array of expressionistic literary and theatrical devices: special settings, musical themes, unusual sound and lighting effects—all as a means of leading his audience to see the truths that lurk beneath life's surface.

Williams's characters and their actions are often exaggerated. They are made to resemble the characters and events of ancient myths. Certain character types recur frequently: the outsider, a man or woman who differs from the mass of humankind by seeing clearly the frightening horror of life; the physically and emotionally deformed; the neurotic and the insane; real or would-be artists; victims and victimizers; and foreigners—strangers like the gentleman caller in The Glass Menagerie—*who intrude on and disrupt the lives of others. His characters are commonly overwhelmed by one another and by a growing awareness that the universe is indifferent to their suffering.*

In Williams's view, "Whether or not we admit it to ourselves, we are all haunted by a truly awful sense of impermanence." To dramatize his dark and narrow vision of life, he wrote of faded men and women, consumed by time and decay. They attempt to escape by moving, by fleeing; they can resist time but never overcome it—for life in Williams's plays can only be attenuated, never triumphant. Yet he shows that for those who come to see clearly the frightening chaos of the world there is a kind of victory, for their vision brings release from guilt and from pointless despair. They can then achieve the kind of dignity Williams believed to be possible if one lives "steadfastly, as if he, too, like a character in a play, were immured against the corrupting rush of time."

FURTHER READING: N. Benjamin, *Tennessee Williams: The Man and His Work,* 1961; F. Donahue, *The Dramatic World of Tennessee Williams,* 1964; E. Jackson, *The Broken World of Tennessee Williams,* 1965; M. Gilbert, *Tennessee Williams and Friends,* 1965; M. Steen, *A Look at Tennessee Williams,* 1969; *The Theatre of Tennessee Williams,* 5 vols. 1972–1976; *Memoirs,* 1975; *Tennessee Williams: A Tribute,* ed. J. Tharpe, 1977; M. Yacowar, *Tennessee Williams and Film,* 1977; *The World of Tennessee Williams,* ed. R. Leavitt, 1978; *Twentieth-Century Interpretations of the Glass Menagerie,* 1983; H. Rasky, *Tennessee Williams,* 1986; *Tennessee Williams,* ed. H. Bloom, 1987; R. Bloxill, *Tennessee Williams,* 1987; *Tennessee Williams' The Glass Menagerie,* ed. H. Bloom, 1988; J. Thompson, *Tennessee Williams' Plays,* 1988; R. Hayman, *Tennessee Williams: Everyone Else Is an Audience,* 1993; L. Leverich, *Tom: The Unknown Tennessee Williams,* 1995; *The Cambridge Companion to Tennessee Williams,* ed. M. Roudané, 1997; N. Tischler, *Student Companion to Tennessee Williams,* 2000; *The Selected Letters of Tennessee Williams,* 2 vols., ed. A. Devlin, 2002, 2004; J. Thompson, *Tennessee Williams's Plays: Memory, Myth, and Symbol,* 2002; G. Heintzelmann and A. Howard, *Tennessee Williams A to Z,* 2005.

TEXT: *The Glass Menagerie,* 1945.

THE GLASS MENAGERIE

Nobody, not even the rain, has such small hands.[1]

—E. E. CUMMINGS

THE CHARACTERS

AMANDA WINGFIELD (*the mother*): A little woman of great but confused vitality clinging frantically to another time and place. Her characterization must be carefully created, not copied from type. She is not paranoiac, but her life is paranoia. There is much to admire in Amanda, and as much to love and pity as there is to laugh at. Certainly she has endurance and a kind of heroism, and though her foolishness makes her unwittingly cruel at times, there is tenderness in her slight person.

LAURA WINGFIELD (*her daughter*): Amanda, having failed to establish contact with reality, continues to live vitally in her illusions, but Laura's situation is even graver. A childhood illness has left her crippled, one leg slightly shorter than the other, and held in a brace. This defect need not be more than suggested on the stage. Stemming from this, Laura's separation increases till she is like a piece of her own glass collection, too exquisitely fragile to move from the shelf.

TOM WINGFIELD (*her son*): And the narrator of the play. A poet with a job in a warehouse. His nature is not remorseless, but to escape from a trap he has to act without pity.

JIM O'CONNOR (*the gentleman caller*): A nice, ordinary young man.

SCENE ONE

The Wingfield apartment is in the rear of the building, one of those vast hive-like conglomerations of cellular living-units that flower as warty growths in overcrowded urban centers of lower middle-class population and are symptomatic of the impulse of this largest and fundamentally enslaved section of American society to avoid fluidity and differentiation and to exist and function as one interfused mass of automatism.

The apartment faces an alley and is entered by a fire escape, a structure whose name is a touch of accidental poetic truth, for all of these huge buildings are always burning with the slow and implacable fires of human desperation. The fire escape is part of what we see—that is, the landing of it and steps descending from it.

The scene is memory and is therefore nonrealistic. Memory takes a lot of poetic license. It omits some details; others are exaggerated, according to the emotional value of the articles it touches, for memory is seated predominantly in the heart. The interior is therefore rather dim and poetic.

[1]From "[somewhere i have never travelled, gladly beyond]."

At the rise of the curtain, the audience is faced with the dark, grim rear wall of the Wingfield tenement. This building is flanked on both sides by dark, narrow alleys which run into murky canyons of tangled clotheslines, garbage cans, and the sinister latticework of neighboring fire escapes. It is up and down these side alleys that exterior entrances and exits are made during the play. At the end of Tom's opening commentary, the dark tenement wall slowly becomes transparent and reveals the interior of the ground-floor Wingfield apartment.

Nearest the audience is the living room, which also serves as a sleeping room for Laura, the sofa unfolding to make her bed. Just beyond, separated from the living room by a wide arch or second proscenium with transparent faded portieres (or second curtain), is the dining room. In an old-fashioned whatnot in the living room are seen scores of transparent glass animals. A blown-up photograph of the father hangs on the wall of the living room, to the left of the archway. It is the face of a very handsome young man in a doughboy's First World War cap. He is gallantly smiling, ineluctably smiling, as if to say "I will be smiling forever."

Also hanging on the wall, near the photograph, are a typewriter keyboard chart and a Gregg shorthand diagram. An upright typewriter on a small table stands beneath the charts.

The audience hears and sees the opening scene in the dining room through both the transparent fourth wall of the building and the transparent gauze portiers of the dining-room arch. It is during this revealing scene that the fourth wall slowly ascends, out of sight. This transparent exterior wall is not brought down again until the very end of the play, during Tom's final speech.

The narrator is an undisguised convention of the play. He takes whatever license with dramatic convention is convenient to his purposes.

Tom enters, dressed as a merchant sailor, and strolls across to the fire escape. There he stops and lights a cigarette. He addresses the audience.

TOM: Yes, I have tricks in my pocket, I have things up my sleeve. But I am the opposite of a stage magician. He gives you illusion the appearance of truth. I give you truth in the pleasant disguise of illusion.

To begin with, I turn back time. I reverse it to that quaint period, the thirties, when the huge middle class of America was matriculating in a school for the blind. Their eyes had failed them, or they had failed their eyes, and so they were having their fingers pressed forcibly down on the fiery Braille alphabet of a dissolving economy.

In Spain there was a revolution. Here there was only shouting and confusion. In Spain there was Guernica.[2] Here there were disturbances of labor, sometimes pretty violent, in otherwise peaceful cities such as Chicago, Cleveland, Saint Louis . . .

This is the social background of the play.

[Music begins to play]

The play is memory. Being a memory play, it is dimly lighted, it is sentimental, it is not realistic. In memory everything seems to happen to music. That explains the fiddle in the wings.

[2]Town in northern Spain, bombed in April 1937 by German planes flying for the Fascists during the Spanish Civil War.

I am the narrator of the play, and also a character in it. The other characters are my mother, Amanda, my sister, Laura, and a gentleman caller who appears in the final scenes. He is the most realistic character in the play, being an emissary from a world of reality that we were somehow set apart from. But since I have a poet's weakness for symbols, I am using this character also as a symbol; he is the long-delayed but always expected something that we live for.

There is a fifth character in the play who doesn't appear except in this larger-than-life-size photograph over the mantel. This is our father who left us a long time ago. He was a telephone man who fell in love with long distances; he gave up his job with the telephone company and skipped the light fantastic out of town . . .

The last we heard of him was a picture postcard from Mazatlan, on the Pacific coast of Mexico, containing a message of two words: "Hello—Goodbye!" and no address.

I think the rest of the play will explain itself. . . .

[Amanda's voice becomes audible through the portieres.]

[Legend on screen: "Ou sont les neiges d'antan?"[3]]

[Tom divides the portieres and enters the dining room. Amanda and Laura are seated at a drop-leaf table. Eating is indicated by gestures without food or utensils. Amanda faces the audience. Tom and Laura are seated in Profile. The interior is lit up softly and through the scrim we see Amanda and Laura seated at the table.]

AMANDA [*calling*]: Tom?

TOM: Yes, Mother.

AMANDA: We can't say grace until you come to the table!

TOM: Coming, Mother. [*He bows slightly and withdraws, reappearing a few moments later in his place at the table.*]

AMANDA [*to her son*]: Honey, don't *push* with your *fingers.* If you have to push with something, the thing to push with is a crust of bread. And chew—chew! Animals have secretions in their stomachs which enable them to digest food without mastication, but human beings are supposed to chew their food before they swallow it down. Eat food leisurely, son, and really enjoy it. A well-cooked meal has lots of delicate flavors that have to be held in the mouth for appreciation. So chew your food and give your salivary glands a chance to function!

[Tom deliberately lays his imaginary fork down and pushes his chair back from the table.]

TOM: I haven't enjoyed one bite of this dinner because of your constant directions on how to eat it. It's you that make me rush through meals with your hawklike attention to every bite I take. Sickening—spoils my appetite—all this discussion of—animals' secretion—salivary glands—mastication!

AMANDA [*lightly*]: Temperament like a Metropolitan star!

[Tom rises and walks toward the living room.]

You're not excused from the table.

TOM: I'm getting a cigarette.

AMANDA: You smoke too much.

[Laura rises.]

[3]French: "Where are the snows of bygone years?" A refrain from "Ballade of the Ladies of Bygone Times" by François Villon (1431–1463?).

LAURA: I'll bring in the blanc mange.

[Tom remains standing with his cigarette by the portieres.]

AMANDA [*rising*]: No, sister, no, sister—you be the lady this time and I'll be the darky.

LAURA: I'm already up.

AMANDA: Resume your seat, little sister—I want you to stay fresh and pretty—for gentlemen callers!

LAURA [*sitting down*]: I'm not expecting any gentlemen callers.

AMANDA [*crossing out to the kitchenette, airily*]: Sometimes they come when they are least expected! Why, I remember one Sunday afternoon in Blue Mountain—

[She enters the kitchenette.]

TOM: I know what's coming!

LAURA: Yes. But let her tell it.

TOM: Again?

LAURA: She loves to tell it.

[Amanda returns with a bowl of dessert.]

AMANDA: One Sunday afternoon in Blue Mountain—your mother received—*seventeen!*—gentlemen callers! Why, sometimes there weren't chairs enough to accommodate them all. We had to send the nigger over to bring in folding chairs from the parish house.

TOM [*remaining at the portieres*]: How did you entertain those gentlemen callers?

AMANDA: I understood the art of conversation!

TOM: I bet you could talk.

AMANDA: Girls in those days *knew* how to talk, I can tell you.

TOM: Yes?

[Image on screen: Amanda as a girl on a porch, greeting callers.]

AMANDA: They knew how to entertain their gentlemen callers. It wasn't enough for a girl to be possessed of a pretty face and a graceful figure—although I wasn't slighted in either respect. She also needed to have nimble wit and a tongue to meet all occasions.

TOM: What did you talk about?

AMANDA: Things of importance going on in the world! Never anything coarse or common or vulgar.

[She addresses Tom as though he were seated in the vacant chair at the table though he remains by the portieres. He plays this scene as though reading from a script.]

My callers were gentlemen—all! Among my callers were some of the most prominent young planters of the Mississippi Delta—planters and sons of planters!

[Tom motions for music and a spot of light on Amanda. Her eyes lift, her face glows, her voice becomes rich and elegiac.]

[Screen legend: "Ou sont les neiges d'antan?"]

There was young Champ Laughlin who later became vice-president of the Delta Planters Bank. Hadley Stevenson who was drowned in Moon Lake and left his widow one hundred and fifty thousand in Government bonds. There were the Cutrere brothers, Wesley and Bates. Bates was one of my bright particular beaux! He got in a quarrel with that wild Wainwright boy. They shot it out on the floor of Moon Lake Casino. Bates was shot through the stomach. Died in the ambulance on his way to Memphis. His widow was also well provided-for, came into eight or ten thousand acres, that's all. She married him on the rebound—never loved her—carried my picture on him the night he died! And there was that boy that every girl in the Delta had set her cap for! That beautiful, brilliant young Fitzhugh boy from Greene County!

TOM: What did he leave his widow?

AMANDA: He never married! Gracious, you talk as though all of my old admirers had turned up their toes to the daisies!

TOM: Isn't this the first you've mentioned that still survives?

AMANDA: That Fitzhugh boy went North and made a fortune—came to be known as the Wolf of Wall Street! He had the Midas touch, whatever he touched turned to gold! And I could have been Mrs. Duncan J. Fitzhugh, mind you! But—I picked your *father!*

LAURA [*rising*]: Mother, let me clear the table.

AMANDA: No, dear, you go in front and study your typewriter chart. Or practice your shorthand a little. Stay fresh and pretty!—It's almost time for our gentlemen callers to start arriving. [*She flounces girlishly toward the kitchenette*] How many do you suppose we're going to entertain this afternoon?

[Tom throws down the paper and jumps up with a groan.]

LAURA [*alone in the dining room*]: I don't believe we're going to receive any, Mother.

AMANDA [*reappearing, airily*]: What? No one—not one? You must be joking!

[Laura nervously echoes her laugh. She slips in a fugitive manner through the half-open portieres and draws them gently behind her. A shaft of very clear light is thrown on her face against the faded tapestry of the curtains. Faintly the music of "The Glass Menagerie" is heard as she continues, lightly:]

Not one gentleman caller? It can't be true! There must be a flood, there must have been a tornado!

LAURA: It isn't a flood, it's not a tornado, Mother. I'm just not popular like you were in Blue Mountain. . . .

[Tom utters another groan. Laura glances at him with a faint, apologetic smile. Her voice catches a little:]

Mother's afraid I'm going to be an old maid.

[The scene dims out with the "Glass Menagerie" music.]

SCENE TWO

On the dark stage the screen is lighted with the image of blue roses. Gradually Laura's figure becomes apparent and the screen goes out. The music subsides.

Laura is seated in the delicate ivory chair at the small claw-foot table. She wears a dress of soft violet material for a kimono—her hair is tied back from her forehead with a ribbon. She is washing and polishing her collection of glass. Amanda appears on the fire escape steps. At the sound of her ascent, Laura catches her breath, thrusts the bowl of ornaments away, and sets herself stiffly before the diagram of the typewriter keyboard as though it held her spellbound. Something has happened to Amanda. It is written in her face as she climbs to the landing: a look that is grim and hopeless and a little absurd. She has on one of those cheap or imitation velvety-looking cloth coats with imitation fur collar. Her hat is five or six years old, one of those dreadful cloche hats that were worn in the late Twenties, and she is clutching an enormous black patent-leather pocketbook with nickel clasps and initials. This is her full-dress outfit, the one she usually wears to the D.A.R.[4] *Before entering she looks through the door. She purses her lips, opens her eyes very wide, rolls them upward and shakes her head. Then she slowly lets herself in the door. Seeing her mother's expression Laura touches her lips with a nervous gesture.*

LAURA: Hello, Mother, I was—[*She makes a nervous gesture toward the chart on the wall. Amanda leans against the shut door and stares at Laura with a martyred look.*]

AMANDA: Deception? Deception? [*She slowly removes her hat and gloves, continuing the sweet suffering stare. She lets the hat and gloves fall on the floor—a bit of acting.*]

LAURA [*shakily*]: How was the D.A.R. meeting?

[*Amanda slowly opens her purse and removes a dainty white handkerchief which she shakes out delicately and delicately touches to her lips and nostrils.*]

Didn't you go to the D.A.R. meeting, Mother?

AMANDA [*faintly, almost inaudibly*]:—No.—No. [*then more forcibly:*] I did not have the strength—to go to the D.A.R. In fact, I did not have the courage! I wanted to find a hole in the ground and hide myself in it forever! [*She crosses slowly to the wall and removes the diagram of the typewriter keyboard. She holds it in front of her for a second, staring at it sweetly and sorrowfully—then bites her lips and tears it in two pieces.*]

LAURA [*faintly*]: Why did you do that, Mother?

[*Amanda repeats the same procedure with the chart of the Gregg Alphabet.*]

Why are you—

AMANDA: Why? Why? How old are you, Laura?

LAURA: Mother, you know my age.

AMANDA: I thought that you were an adult; it seems that I was mistaken.

[*She crosses slowly to the sofa and sinks down and stares at Laura.*]

LAURA: Please don't stare at me, Mother.

[*Amanda closes her eyes and lowers her head. There is a ten-second pause.*]

AMANDA: What are we going to do, what is going to become of us, what is the future?

[*There is another pause.*]

LAURA: Has something happened, Mother?

[*Amanda draws a long breath, takes out the handkerchief again, goes through the dabbing process.*]

Mother, has—something happened?

AMANDA: I'll be all right in a minute, I'm just bewildered—[*She hesitates.*]—by life. . . .

LAURA: Mother, I wish that you would tell me what's happened!

AMANDA: As you know, I was supposed to be inducted into my office at the D.A.R. this afternoon.

[*Screen image: A swarm of typewriters.*]

But I stopped off at Rubicam's Business College to speak to your teachers about your having a cold and ask them what progress they thought you were making down there.

LAURA: Oh. . . .

[4]I.e., to a meeting of the Daughters of the American Revolution, a patriotic society dedicated to celebration of the participants of the American Revolution.

AMANDA: I went to the typing instructor and introduced myself as your mother. She didn't know who you were. "Wingfield," she said, "We don't have any such student enrolled at the school!"

I assured her she did, that you had been going to classes since early in January. "I wonder," she said, "If you could be talking about that terribly shy little girl who dropped out of school after only a few days' attendance?"

"No," I said, "Laura, my daughter, has been going to school every day for the past six weeks!"

"Excuse me," she said. She took the attendance book out and there was your name, unmistakably printed, and all the dates you were absent until they decided you had dropped out of school.

I still said, "No, there must have been some mistake! There must have been some mix-up in the records!"

And she said, "No—I remember her perfectly now. Her hands shook so that she couldn't hit the right keys! The first time we gave a speed test, she broke down completely—was sick at the stomach and almost had to be carried into the wash room! After that morning she never showed up any more. We phoned the house but never got any answer"—While I was working at Famous-Barr, I suppose, demonstrating those—

[She indicates a brassiere with her hands.]

Oh! I felt so weak I could barely keep on my feet! I had to sit down while they got me a glass of water! Fifty dollars' tuition, all of our plans—my hopes and ambitions for you—just gone up the spout, just gone up the spout like that.

[Laura draws a long breath and gets awkwardly to her feet. She crosses to the Victrola and winds it up.]

What are you doing?

LAURA: Oh! [*She releases the handle and returns to her seat.*]

AMANDA: Laura, where have you been going when you've gone out pretending that you were going to business college?

LAURA: I've just been going out walking.

AMANDA: That's not true.

LAURA: It is. I just went walking.

AMANDA: Walking? Walking? In winter? Deliberately courting pneumonia in that light coat? Where did you walk to, Laura?

LAURA: All sorts of places—mostly in the park.

AMANDA: Even after you'd started catching that cold?

LAURA: It was the lesser of two evils, Mother.

[Screen image: Winter scene in a park.]

I couldn't go back there. I—threw up—on the floor!

AMANDA: From half past seven till after five every day you mean to tell me you walked around in the park, because you wanted to make me think that you were still going to Rubicam's Business College?

LAURA: It wasn't as bad as it sounds. I went inside places to get warmed up.

AMANDA: Inside where?

LAURA: I went in the art museum and the bird houses at the Zoo. I visited the penguins every day! Sometimes I did without lunch and went to the movies. Lately I've been spending most of my afternoons in the Jewel Box, that big glass house where they raise tropical flowers.

AMANDA: You did all this to deceive me, just for deception?

[Laura looks down.] Why?

LAURA: Mother, when you're disappointed, you get that awful suffering look on your face, like the picture of Jesus' mother in the museum!

AMANDA: Hush!

LAURA: I couldn't face it.

[There is a pause. A whisper of strings is heard. Legend on screen: "The Crust of Humility."]

AMANDA [*hopelessly fingering the huge pocketbook*]: So what are we going to do the rest of our lives? Stay home and watch the parades go by? Amuse ourselves with the glass menagerie, darling? Eternally play those worn-out phonograph records your father left as a painful reminder of him? We won't have a business career—we've given that up because it gave us nervous indigestion! [*She laughs wearily.*] What is there left but dependency all our lives? I know so well what becomes of unmarried women who aren't prepared to occupy a position. I've seen such pitiful cases in the South—barely tolerated spinsters living upon the grudging patronage of sister's husband or brother's wife!—stuck away in some little mousetrap of a room—encouraged by one in-law to visit another—little birdlike women without any nest—eating the crust of humility all their life! Is that the future that we've mapped out for ourselves? I swear it's the only alternative I can think of! [*She pauses.*] It isn't a very pleasant alternative, is it? [*She pauses again.*] Of course—some girls *do marry.*

[Laura twists her hands nervously.]

Haven't you ever liked some boy?

LAURA: Yes. I liked one once. [*She rises.*] I came across his picture a while ago.

AMANDA [*with some interest*]: He gave you his picture?

LAURA: No, it's in the yearbook.

AMANDA [*disappointed*]: Oh—a high school boy.

[Screen image: Jim as the high school hero bearing a silver cup.]

LAURA: Yes. His name was Jim. [*She lifts the heavy annual from the claw-foot table.*] Here he is in *The Pirates of Penzance.*

AMANDA [*absently*]: The what?

LAURA: The operetta the senior class put on. He had a wonderful voice and we sat across the aisle from each other Mondays, Wednesdays and Fridays in the Aud. Here he is with the silver cup for debating! See his grin?

AMANDA [*absently*]: He must have had a jolly disposition.

LAURA: He used to call me—Blue Roses.

[Screen image: Blue roses.]

AMANDA: Why did he call you such a name as that?

LAURA: When I had that attack of pleurosis—he asked me what was the matter when I came back. I said pleurosis—he thought I said Blue Roses! So that's what he always called me after that. Whenever he saw me, he'd holler, "Hello, Blue Roses!" I didn't care for the girl that he went out with. Emily Meisenbach. Emily was the best-dressed girl at Soldan. She never struck me, though, as being sincere . . . It says in the Personal Section—they're engaged. That's—six years ago! They must be married by now.

AMANDA: Girls that aren't cut out for business careers usually wind up married to some nice man. [*She gets up with a spark of revival.*] Sister, that's what you'll do!

[Laura utters a startled, doubtful laugh. She reaches quickly for a piece of glass.]

LAURA: But, Mother—

AMANDA: Yes? [*She goes over to the phonograph.*]

LAURA [*in a tone of frightened apology*]: I'm—crippled!

AMANDA: Nonsense! Laura, I've told you never, never to use that word. Why, you're not crippled, you just have a little defect—hardly noticeable, even! When people have some slight disadvantage like that, they cultivate other things to make up for it—develop charm—and vivacity—and—*charm!* That's all you have to do! [*She turns again to the phonograph.*] One thing your father had *plenty of*—was *charm!*

[The scene fades out with music.]

SCENE THREE

Legend on screen: "After the fiasco—"

Tom speaks from the fire escape landing.

TOM: After the fiasco at Rubicam's Business College, the idea of getting a gentleman caller for Laura began to play a more and more important part in Mother's calculations. It became an obsession. Like some archetype of the universal unconscious, the image of the gentleman caller haunted our small apartment. . . .

[Screen image: A young man at the door of a house with flowers.]

An evening at home rarely passed without some allusion to this image, this specter, this hope. . . . Even when he wasn't mentioned, his presence hung in Mother's preoccupied look and in my sister's frightened, apologetic manner—hung like a sentence passed upon the Wingfields!

Mother was a woman of action as well as words. She began to take logical steps in the planned direction. Late that winter and in the early spring—realizing that extra money would be needed to properly feather the nest and plume the bird—she conducted a vigorous campaign on the telephone, roping in subscribers to one of those magazines for matrons called *The Homemaker's Companion,* the type of journal that features the serialized sublimations of ladies of letters who think in terms of delicate cuplike breasts, slim, tapering waists, rich, creamy thighs, eyes like wood smoke in autumn, fingers that soothe and caress like strains of music, bodies as powerful as Etruscan sculpture.

[Screen image: The cover of a glamor magazine.]

[Amanda enters with the telephone on a long extension cord. She is spotlighted in the dim stage.]

AMANDA: Ida Scott? This is Amanda Wingfield! We *missed* you at the D.A.R. last Monday! I said to myself: She's probably suffering with that sinus condition! How is that sinus condition?

Horrors! Heaven have mercy!—You're a Christian martyr, yes, that's what you are, a Christian martyr!

Well, I just now happened to notice that your subscription to the *Companion's* about to expire! Yes, it expires with the next issue, honey!—just when that wonderful new serial by Bessie Mae Hopper is getting off to such an exciting start. Oh, honey, it's something that you can't miss! You remember how *Gone with the Wind* took everybody by storm? You simply couldn't go out if you hadn't read it. All everybody *talked* was Scarlett O'Hara. Well, this is a book that critics already compare to *Gone with the Wind*. It's the *Gone with the Wind* of the post–World-War generation!—What?—Burning?—Oh, honey, don't let them burn, go take a look in the oven and I'll hold the wire! Heavens—I think she's hung up!

[The scene dims out.]

[Legend on screen: "You think I'm in love with Continental Shoemakers?]"

[Before the lights come up again, the violent voices of Tom and Amanda are heard. They are quarrelling behind the portieres. In front of them stands Laura with clenched hands and panicky expression. A clear pool of light is on her figure throughout this scene.]

TOM: What in Christ's name am I—

AMANDA [*shrilly*]: Don't you use that—

TOM: —supposed to do!

AMANDA: —expression! Not in my—

TOM: Ohhh!

AMANDA: —presence! Have you gone out of your senses?

TOM: I have, that's true, *driven* out!

AMANDA: What is the matter with you, you—big—big—IDIOT!

TOM: Look!—I've got *no thing*, no single thing—

AMANDA: Lower your voice!

TOM: —in my life here that I can call my own! Everything is—

AMANDA: Stop that shouting!

TOM: Yesterday you confiscated my books! You had the nerve to—

AMANDA: I took that horrible novel back to the library—yes! That hideous book by that insane Mr. Lawrence.

[Tom laughs wildly,]

I cannot control the output of diseased minds or people who cater to them—

[Tom laughs still more wildly.]

BUT I WON'T ALLOW SUCH FILTH BROUGHT INTO MY HOUSE! No, no, no, no, no!

TOM: House, house! Who pays rent on it, who makes a slave of himself to—

AMANDA [*fairly screeching*]: Don't you DARE to—

TOM: No, no, *I* mustn't say things! *I've* got to just—

AMANDA: Let me tell you—

TOM: I don't want to hear any more!

[He tears the portieres open. The dining-room area is lit with a turgid smoky red glow. Now we see Amanda; her hair is in metal curlers and she is wearing a very old bathrobe, much too large for her slight figure, a relic of the faithless Mr. Wingfield. The upright typewriter now stands on the drop-leaf table, along with a wild disarray of manuscripts. The quarrel was probably precipitated by Amanda's interruption of Tom's creative labor. A chair lies overthrown on the floor. Their gesticulating shadows are cast on the ceiling by the fiery glow.]

AMANDA: You *will* hear more, you—

TOM: No, I won't hear more, I'm going out!

AMANDA: You come right back in—

TOM: Out, out, out! Because I'm—

AMANDA: Come back here, Tom Wingfield! I'm not through talking to you!

TOM: Oh, go—

LAURA [*desperately*]:—Tom!

AMANDA: You're going to listen, and no more insolence from you! I'm at the end of my patience!

[He comes back toward her.]

TOM: What do you think I'm at? Aren't I supposed to have any patience to reach the end of, Mother? I know, I know. It seems unimportant to you, what I'm *doing*—what I *want* to do—having a little *difference* between them! You don't think that—

AMANDA: I think you've been doing things that you're ashamed of. That's why you act like this. I don't believe that you go every night to the movies. Nobody goes to the movies night after night. Nobody in their right minds goes to the movies as often as you pretend to. People don't go to the movies at nearly midnight, and movies don't let out at two A.M.: Come in stumbling. Muttering to yourself like a maniac! You get three hours' sleep and then go to work. Oh, I can picture the way you're doing down there. Moping, doping, because you're in no condition.

TOM [*wildly*]: No, I'm in no condition!

AMANDA: What right have you got to jeopardize your job? Jeopardize the security of us all? How do you think we'd manage if you were—

TOM: Listen! You think I'm crazy about the *warehouse?* [*He bends fiercely toward her slight figure.*] You think I'm in love with the Continental Shoemakers? You think I want to spend fifty-five *years* down there in that—*celotex interior!* with—*fluorescent—tubes!* I'd rather somebody picked up a crowbar and battered out my brains—than go back mornings! I *go!* Every time you come in yelling that Goddamn "*Rise and Shine!*" "*Rise and Shine!*" I say to myself. "How *lucky dead* people are!" But I get up. I *go!* For sixty-five dollars a month I give up all that I dream of doing and being *ever!* And you say self—*self's* all I ever think of. Why, listen, if self is what I thought of, Mother, I'd be where he is—GONE! [*He points to his father's picture.*] As far as the system of transportation reaches! [*He starts past her. She grabs his arm.*] Don't grab at me, Mother!

AMANDA: Where are you going?

TOM: I'm going to the *movies!*

AMANDA: I don't believe that lie!

[Tom crouches toward her, overtowering her tiny figure. She backs away, gasping.]

TOM: I'm going to opium dens! Yes, opium dens, dens of vice and criminals' hangouts, Mother. I've joined the Hogan Gang, I'm a hired assassin, I carry a tommy gun in a violin case! I run a string of cat houses in the Valley! They call me Killer, Killer Wingfield, I'm leading a double-life, a simple, honest warehouse worker by day, by night a dynamic *czar* of the *underworld, Mother.* I go to gambling casinos, I spin away fortunes on the roulette table! I wear a patch over one eye and a false mustache, sometimes I put on green whiskers. On those occasions they call me—*El Diablo!*[5] Oh, I could tell you many things to make you sleepless! My enemies plan to dynamite this place. They're going to blow us all sky-high some night! I'll be glad, very happy, and so will you! You'll go up, up on a broomstick, over Blue Mountain with seventeen gentlemen callers! You ugly—babbling old—*witch. . . .*

[He goes through a series of violent, clumsy movements, seizing his overcoat, lunging to the door, pulling it fiercely open. The women watch him, aghast. His arm catches in the sleeve of the coat as he struggles to pull it on. For a moment he is pinioned by the bulky garment. With an outraged groan he tears the coat off again,

[5]Spanish: The Devil!

splitting the shoulder of it, and hurls it across the room. It strikes against the shelf of Laura's glass collection, and there is a tinkle of shattering glass. Laura cries out as if wounded.]

[Music.]

[Screen legend: "The Glass Menagerie."]

LAURA [*shrilly*]: *My glass!*—menagerie. . . . [*She covers her face and turns away.*]

[But Amanda is still stunned and stupefied by the "ugly witch" so that she barely notices this occurrence. Now she recovers her speech.]

AMANDA [*in an awful voice*]: I won't speak to you—until you apologize!

[She crosses through the portieres and draws them together behind her. Tom is left with Laura. Laura clings weakly to the mantel with her face averted. Tom stares at her stupidly for a moment. Then he crosses to the shelf. He drops awkwardly on his knees to collect the fallen glass, glancing at Laura as if he would speak but couldn't.]

["The Glass Menagerie" music steals in as the scene dims out.]

SCENE FOUR

The interior of the apartment is dark. There is a faint light in the alley. A deep-voiced bell in a church is tolling the hour of five.

Tom appears at the top of the alley. After each solemn boom of the bell in the tower, he shakes a little noisemaker or rattle as if to express the tiny spasm of man in contrast to the sustained power and dignity of the Almighty. This and the unsteadiness of his advance make it evident that he has been drinking. As he climbs the few steps to the fire escape landing light steals up inside. Laura appears in the front room in a nightdress. She notices that Tom's bed is empty. Tom fishes in his pockets for his door key, removing a motley assortment of articles in his search, including a shower of movie ticket stubs and an empty bottle. At last he finds the key, but just as he is about to insert it, it slips from his fingers. He strikes a match and crouches below the door.

TOM [*bitterly*]: One crack—and it falls through!

[Laura opens the door.]

LAURA: Tom! Tom, what are you doing?

TOM: Looking for a door key.

LAURA: Where have you been all this time?

TOM: I have been to the movies.

LAURA: All this time at the movies?

TOM: There was a very long program. There was a Garbo picture and a Mickey Mouse and a travelogue and a newsreel and a preview of coming attractions. And there was an organ solo and a collection for the Milk Fund—simultaneously—which ended up in a terrible fight between a fat lady and an usher!

LAURA [*innocently*]: Did you have to stay through everything?

TOM: Of course! And, oh, I forgot! There was a big stage show! The headliner on this stage show was Malvolio the Magician. He performed wonderful tricks, many of them, such as pouring water back and forth between pitchers. First it turned to wine and then it turned to beer and then it turned to whisky. I know it was whisky it finally turned into because he needed somebody to come up out of the audience to help him, and I came up—both shows! It was Kentucky Straight Bourbon. A very generous fellow, he gave souvenirs. [*He pulls from his back pocket a shimmering rainbow-colored scarf.*] He gave me this. This is his magic scarf. You can have it, Laura. You wave it over a canary cage and you get a bowl of goldfish. You wave it over the goldfish bowl and they fly away canaries. . . . But the wonderfullest trick of all was the coffin trick. We nailed him into a coffin and he got out of the coffin without removing one nail. [*He has come inside.*] There is a trick that would come in handy for me—get me out of this two-by-four situation! [*He flops on the bed and starts removing his shoes.*]

LAURA: Tom—shhh!

TOM: What're you shushing me for?

LAURA: You'll wake up Mother.

TOM: Goody, goody! Pay'er back for all those "Rise an' Shines." [*He lies down, groaning.*] You know it don't take much intelligence to get yourself into a nailed-up coffin, Laura. But who the hell ever got himself out of one without removing one nail?

[As if in answer, the father's grinning photograph lights up. The scene dims out.]

[Immediately following, the church bell is heard striking six. At the sixth stroke the alarm clock goes off in Amanda's room, and after a few moments we hear her calling: "Rise and Shine! Rise and Shine! Laura, go tell your brother to rise and shine!"]

TOM [*sitting up slowly*]: I'll rise—but I won't shine.

[The light increases.]

AMANDA: Laura, tell your brother his coffee is ready.

[Laura slips into the front room.]

LAURA: Tom!—It's nearly seven. Don't make Mother nervous.

[He stares at her stupidly.]

[beseechingly:] Tom, speak to Mother this morning. Make up with her, apologize, speak to her!

TOM: She won't to me. It's her that started not speaking.

LAURA: If you just say you're sorry she'll start speaking.

TOM: Her not speaking—is that such a tragedy?

LAURA: Please—please!

AMANDA [*calling from the kitchenette*]: Laura, are you going to do what I asked you to do, or do I have to get dressed and go out myself?

LAURA: Going, going—soon as I get on my coat!

[She pulls on a shapeless felt hat with a nervous, jerky movement, pleadingly glancing at Tom. She rushes awkwardly for her coat. The coat is one of Amanda's inaccurately made-over, the sleeves too short for Laura.]

Butter and what else?

AMANDA [*entering from the kitchenette*]: Just butter. Tell them to charge it.

LAURA: Mother, they make such faces when I do that.

AMANDA: Sticks and stones can break our bones, but the expression on Mr. Garfinkel's face won't harm us! Tell your brother his coffee is getting cold.

LAURA [*at the door*]: Do what I asked you, will you, will you, Tom?

[He looks sullenly away.]

AMANDA: Laura, go now or just don't go at all!

LAURA [*rushing out*]: Going—going!

[A second later she cries out. Tom springs up and crosses to the door. Tom opens the door.]

TOM: Laura?

LAURA: I'm all right. I slipped, but I'm all right.

AMANDA [*peering anxiously after her*]: If anyone breaks a leg on those fire-escape steps, the landlord ought to be sued for every cent he possesses! [*She shuts the door. Now she remembers she isn't speaking to Tom and returns to the other room.*]

[As Tom comes listlessly for his coffee, she turns her back to him and stands rigidly facing the window on the gloomy gray vault of the area-way. Its light on her face with its aged but childish features is cruelly sharp, satirical as a Daumier[6] print.]

[The music of "Ave Maria" is heard softly.]

[Tom glances sheepishly but sullenly at her averted figure and slumps at the table. The coffee is scalding hot; he sips it and gasps and spits it back in the cup. At his gasp, Amanda catches her breath and half turns. Then she catches herself and turns back to the window. Tom blows on his coffee, glancing sidewise at his mother. She clears her throat. Tom clears his. He starts to rise, sinks back down again, scratches his head, clears his throat again. Amanda coughs. Tom raises his cup in both hands to blow on it, his eyes staring over the rim of it at his mother for several moments. Then he slowly sets the cup down and awkwardly and hesitantly rises from the chair.]

TOM [*hoarsely*]: Mother. I—I apologize, Mother.

[Amanda draws a quick, shuddering breath. Her face works grotesquely. She breaks into childlike tears.]

I'm sorry for what I said, for everything that I said, I didn't mean it.

AMANDA [*sobbingly*]: My devotion has made me a witch and so I make myself hateful to my children!

TOM: No, you *don't*.

AMANDA: I worry so much, don't sleep, it makes me nervous!

TOM [*gently*]: I understand that.

AMANDA: I've had to put up a solitary battle all these years. But you're my right-hand bower! Don't fall down, don't fail!

TOM [*gently*]: I try, Mother.

AMANDA [*with great enthusiasm*]: Try and you will *succeed!* [*The notion makes her breathless.*] Why, you—you're just *full* of natural endowments! Both of my children—they're *unusual* children! Don't you think I know it? I'm so—*proud!* Happy and—feel I've—so much to be thankful for but—promise me one thing, son!

TOM: What, Mother?

AMANDA: Promise, son, you'll—never be a drunkard!

TOM [*turns to her grinning*]: I will never be a drunkard, Mother.

AMANDA: That's what frightened me so, that you'd be drinking! Eat a bowl of Purina!

TOM: Just coffee, Mother.

AMANDA: Shredded wheat biscuit?

TOM: No. No, Mother, just coffee.

AMANDA: You can't put in a day's work on an empty stomach. You've got ten minutes—don't gulp! Drinking too-hot liquids makes cancer of the stomach. . . . Put cream in.

TOM: No, thank you.

AMANDA: To cool it.

TOM: No! No, thank you, I want it black.

[6]Honoré Daumier (1808–1879), French caricaturist and painter.

AMANDA: I know, but it's not good for you. We have to do all that we can to build ourselves up. In these trying times we live in, all that we have to cling to is—each other. . . . That's why it's important to—Tom, I—I sent out your sister so I could discuss something with you. If you hadn't spoken I would have spoken to you. [*She sits down.*]

TOM [*gently*]: What is it, Mother, that you want to discuss?

AMANDA: *Laura!*

[Tom puts his cup down slowly.]

[Legend on screen: "Laura." Music: "The Glass Menagerie."]

TOM: —Oh.—Laura . . .

AMANDA [*touching his sleeve*]: You know how Laura is. So quiet but—still water runs deep! She notices things and I think she—broods about them.

[Tom looks up.]

A few days ago I came in and she was crying.

TOM: What about?

AMANDA: You.

TOM: Me?

AMANDA: She has an idea that you're not happy here.

TOM: What gave her that idea?

AMANDA: What gives her any idea? However, you do act strangely. I—I'm not criticizing, understand *that!* I know your ambitions do not lie in the warehouse, that like everybody in the whole wide world—you've had to—make sacrifices, but—Tom—Tom—life's not easy, it calls for—Spartan endurance! There's so many things in my heart that I cannot describe to you! I've never told you but I—*loved* your father. . . .

TOM [*gently*]: I know that, Mother.

AMANDA: And you—when I see you taking after his ways! Staying out late—and—well, you *had* been drinking the night you were in that—terrifying condition! Laura says that you hate the apartment and that you go out nights to get away from it! Is that true, Tom?

TOM: No. You say there's so much in your heart that you can't describe to me. That's true of me, too. There's so much in my heart that I can't describe to *you!* So let's respect each other's—

AMANDA: But, why—*why,* Tom—are you always so *restless?* Where do you *go* to, nights?

TOM: I—go to the movies.

AMANDA: Why do you go to the movies so much, Tom?

TOM: I go to the movies because—I like adventure. Adventure is something I don't have much of at work, so I go to the movies.

AMANDA: But, Tom, you go to the movies *entirely* too *much!*

TOM: I like a lot of adventure.

[Amanda looks baffled, then hurt. As the familiar inquisition resumes, Tom becomes hard and impatient again. Amanda slips back into her querulous attitude toward him.]

[Image on screen: A sailing vessel with Jolly Roger.]

AMANDA: Most young men find adventure in their careers.

TOM: Then most young men are not employed in a warehouse.

AMANDA: The world is full of young men employed in warehouses and offices and factories.

TOM: Do all of them find adventure in their careers?

AMANDA: They do or they do without it! Not everybody has a craze for adventure.

TOM: Man is by instinct a lover, a hunter, a fighter, and none of those instincts are given much play at the warehouse!

AMANDA: Man is by instinct! Don't quote instinct to me! Instinct is something that people have got away from! It belongs to animals! Christian adults don't want it!

TOM: What do Christian adults want, then, Mother?

AMANDA: Superior things! Things of the mind and the spirit! Only animals have to satisfy instincts! Surely your aims are somewhat higher than theirs! Than monkeys—pigs—

TOM: I reckon they're not.

AMANDA: You're joking. However, that isn't what I wanted to discuss.

TOM [*rising*]: I haven't much time.

AMANDA [*pushing his shoulders*]: Sit down.

TOM: You want me to punch in red at the warehouse, Mother?

AMANDA: You have five minutes. I want to talk about Laura.

[Screen legend: "Plans and Provisions."]

TOM: All right! What about Laura?

AMANDA: We have to be making some plans and provisions for her. She's older than you, two years, and nothing has happened. She just drifts along doing nothing. It frightens me terribly how she just drifts along.

TOM: I guess she's the type that people call home girls.

AMANDA: There's no such type, and if there is, it's a pity! That is unless the home is hers, with a husband!

TOM: What?

AMANDA: Oh, I can see the handwriting on the wall as plain as I see the nose in front of my face! It's terrifying! More and more you remind me of your father! He was out all hours without explanation!—Then *left! Goodbye!* And me with the bag to hold. I saw that letter you got from the Merchant Marine. I know what you're dreaming of. I'm not standing here blindfolded. [*She pauses.*] Very well, then. Then *do* it! But not till there's somebody to take your place.

TOM: What do you mean?

AMANDA: I mean that as soon as Laura has got somebody to take care of her, married, a home of her own, independent—why, then you'll be free to go wherever you please, on land, on sea, whichever way the wind blows you! But until that time you've got to look out for your sister. I don't say me because I'm old and don't matter! I say for your sister because she's young and dependent.

I put her in business college—a dismal failure! Frightened her so it made her stick at the stomach. I took her over to the Young People's League at the church. Another fiasco. She spoke to nobody, nobody spoke to her. Now all she does is fool with those pieces of glass and play those worn-out records. What kind of a life is that for a girl to lead?

TOM: What can I do about it?

AMANDA: Overcome selfishness! Self, self, self is all that you ever think of!

[Tom springs up and crosses to get his coat. It is ugly and bulky. He pulls on a cap with earmuffs.]

Where is your muffler? Put your wool muffler on!

[He snatches it angrily from the closet, tosses it around his neck and pulls both ends tight.]

Tom! I haven't said what I had in mind to ask you.

TOM: I'm too late to—

AMANDA [*catching his arm—very importunately; then shyly*]: Down at the warehouse, aren't there some—nice young men?

TOM: No!

AMANDA: There *must* be—*some* . . .

TOM: Mother—[*He gestures.*]

AMANDA: Find out one that's clean-living—doesn't drink and ask him out for sister!

TOM: What?

AMANDA: For *sister!* To *meet!* Get *acquainted!*

TOM [*stamping to the door*]: Oh, my *go-osh!*

AMANDA: Will you?

[He opens the door. She says, imploringly:]

Will you?

[He starts down the fire escape.]

Will you? *Will* you, dear?

TOM [*calling back*]: Yes!

[Amanda closes the door hesitantly and with a troubled but faintly hopeful expression.]

[Screen image: The cover of a glamor magazine.]

[The spotlight picks up Amanda at the phone.]

AMANDA: Ella Cartwright? This is Amanda Wingfield!

How are you, honey?

How is that kidney condition?

[There is a five-second pause.]

Horrors!

[There is another pause.]

You're a Christian martyr, yes, honey, that's what you are, a Christian martyr! Well, I just now happened to notice in my little red book that your subscription to the *Companion* has just run out! I knew that you wouldn't want to miss out on the wonderful serial starting in this new issue. It's by Bessie Mae Hopper, the first thing she's written since *Honeymoon for Three.* Wasn't that a strange and interesting story? Well, this one is even lovelier, I believe. It has a sophisticated, society background. It's all about the horsey set on Long Island!

[The light fades out.]

SCENE FIVE

Legend on the screen: "Annunciation."

Music is heard as the light slowly comes on.

It is early dusk of a spring evening. Supper has just been finished in the Wingfield apartment. Amanda and Laura, in light-colored dresses, are removing dishes from the table in the dining room, which is shadowy, their movements formalized almost as a dance or ritual, their moving forms as pale and silent as moths. Tom, in white shirt and trousers, rises from the table and crosses toward the fire escape.

AMANDA [*as he passes her*]: Son, will you do me a favor?

TOM: What?

AMANDA: Comb your hair! You look so pretty when your hair is combed!

[Tom slouches on the sofa with the evening paper. Its enormous headline reads: "Franco Triumphs."][7]

There is only one respect in which I would like you to emulate your father.

TOM: What respect is that?

AMANDA: The care he always took of his appearance. He never allowed himself to look untidy.

[He throws down the paper and crosses to the fire escape.]

Where are you going?

TOM: I'm going out to smoke.

AMANDA: You smoke too much. A pack a day at fifteen cents a pack. How much would that amount to in a month? Thirty times fifteen is how much Tom? Figure it out and you will be astounded at what you could save. Enough to give you a night-school course in accounting at Washington U.! Just think what a wonderful thing that would be for you, son!

[Tom is unmoved by the thought.]

TOM: I'd rather smoke. [*He steps out on the landing, letting the screen door slam.*]

AMANDA [*sharply*]: I know! That's the tragedy of it. . . . [*Alone, she turns to look at her husband's picture.*]

[Dance music: "The World Is Waiting for the Sunrise!"]

TOM [*to the audience*]: Across the alley from us was the Paradise Dance Hall. On evenings in spring the windows and doors were open and the music came outdoors. Sometimes the lights were turned out except for a large glass sphere that hung from the ceiling. It would turn slowly about and filter the dusk with delicate rainbow colors. Then the orchestra played a waltz or a tango, something that had a slow and sensuous rhythm. Couples would come outside, to the relative privacy of the alley. You could see them kissing behind ash pits and telephone poles. This was the compensation for lives that passed like mine, without any change or adventure. Adventure and change were imminent in this year. They were waiting around the corner for all these kids. Suspended in the mist over Berchtesgaden, caught in the folds of Chamberlain's umbrella.[8] In Spain there was Guernica! But here there was only hot swing music and liquor, dance halls, bars, and movies, and sex that hung in the gloom like a chandelier and flooded the world with brief, deceptive rainbows. . . . All the world was waiting for bombardments!

[Amanda turns from the picture and comes outside.]

AMANDA [*sighing*]: A fire escape landing's a poor excuse for a porch. [*She spreads a newspaper on a step and sits down, gracefully and demurely as if she were settling into a swing on a Mississippi veranda.*] What are you looking at?

TOM: The moon.

[7]A reference to a military victory of Francisco Franco, leader of the Fascist forces in the Spanish Civil War.

[8]Near Berchtesgaden, Germany, Neville Chamberlain, the Prime Minister of Great Britain (1937–1940), met with Adolf Hitler in a futile effort to avoid World War II. On his return to England, he declared that he had arranged for "peace in our time." Because of his folly, Chamberlain and the umbrella that he carried subsequently became symbols of the foolish appeasement of evil.

AMANDA: Is there a moon this evening?

TOM: It's rising over Garfinkel's Delicatessen.

AMANDA: So it is! A little silver slipper of a moon. Have you made a wish on it yet?

TOM: Um-hum.

AMANDA: What did you wish for?

TOM: That's a secret.

AMANDA: A secret, huh? Well, I won't tell mine either. I will be just as mysterious as you.

TOM: I bet I can guess what yours is.

AMANDA: Is my head so transparent?

TOM: You're not a sphinx.

AMANDA: No, I don't have secrets. I'll tell you what I wished for on the moon. Success and happiness for my precious children! I wish for that whenever there's a moon, and when there isn't a moon, I wish for it, too.

TOM: I thought perhaps you wished for a gentleman caller.

AMANDA: Why do you say that?

TOM: Don't you remember asking me to fetch one?

AMANDA: I remember suggesting that it would be nice for your sister if you brought home some nice young man from the warehouse. I think that I've made that suggestion more than once.

TOM: Yes, you have made it repeatedly.

AMANDA: Well?

TOM: We are going to have one.

AMANDA: *What?*

TOM: A gentleman caller!

[The annunciation is celebrated with music.]

[Amanda rises.]

[Image on screen: A caller with a bouquet.]

AMANDA: You mean you have asked some nice young man to come over?

TOM: Yep. I've asked him to dinner.

AMANDA: You really did?

TOM: I did!

AMANDA: You did, and did he—*accept?*

TOM: He did!

AMANDA: Well, well—well, well! That's—lovely!

TOM: I thought that you would be pleased.

AMANDA: It's definite then?

TOM: Very definite.

AMANDA: Soon?

TOM: Very soon.

AMANDA: For heaven's sake, stop putting on and tell me some things, will you?

TOM: What things do you want me to tell you?

AMANDA: *Naturally* I would like to know when he's *coming!*

TOM: He's coming tomorrow.

AMANDA: *Tomorrow?*

TOM: Yep. Tomorrow.

AMANDA: But, Tom!

TOM: Yes, Mother?

AMANDA: Tomorrow gives me no time!

TOM: Time for what?

AMANDA: Preparations! Why didn't you phone me at once, as soon as you asked him, the minute that he accepted? Then, don't you see, I could have been getting ready!

TOM: You don't have to make any fuss.

AMANDA: Oh, Tom, Tom, Tom, of course I have to make a fuss! I want things nice, not sloppy! Not thrown together. I'll certainly have to do some fast thinking, won't I?

TOM: I don't see why you have to think at all.

AMANDA: You just don't know. We can't have a gentleman caller in a pigsty! All my wedding silver has to be polished, the monogrammed table linen ought to be laundered! The windows have to be washed and fresh curtains put up. And how about clothes? We have to *wear* something, don't we?

TOM: Mother, this boy is no one to make a fuss over!

AMANDA: Do you realize he's the first young man we've introduced to your sister? It's terrible, dreadful, disgraceful that poor little sister has never received a single gentleman caller! Tom, come inside!

[She opens the screen door.]

TOM: What for?

AMANDA: I want to ask you some things.

TOM: If you're going to make such a fuss, I'll call it off, I'll tell him not to come!

AMANDA: You certainly won't do anything of the kind. Nothing offends people worse than broken engagements. It simply means I'll have to work like a Turk! We won't be brilliant, but we will pass inspection. Come on inside.

[Tom follows her inside, groaning.]

Sit down.

TOM: Any particular place you would like me to sit?

AMANDA: Thank heavens I've got that new sofa! I'm also making payments on a floor lamp I'll have sent out! And put the chintz covers on, they'll brighten things up! Of course I'd hoped to have these walls re-papered. . . . What is the young man's name?

TOM: His name is O'Connor.

AMANDA: That, of course, means fish—tomorrow is Friday! I'll have that salmon loaf—with Durkee's dressing! What does he do? He works at the warehouse?

TOM: Of course! How else would I—

AMANDA: Tom, he—doesn't drink?

TOM: Why do you ask me that?

AMANDA: Your father *did!*

TOM: Don't get started on that!

AMANDA: He *does* drink, then?

TOM: Not that I know of!

AMANDA: Make sure, be certain! The last thing I want for my daughter's a boy who drinks!

TOM: Aren't you being a little bit premature? Mr. O'Connor has not yet appeared on the scene!

AMANDA: But will tomorrow. To meet your sister, and what do I know about his character? Nothing! Old maids are better off than wives of drunkards!

TOM: Oh, my God!

AMANDA: Be still!

TOM [*leaning forward to whisper*]: Lots of fellows meet girls whom they don't marry!

AMANDA: Oh, talk sensibly, Tom—and don't be sarcastic! [*She has gotten a hairbrush.*]

TOM: What are you doing?

AMANDA: I'm brushing that cowlick down! [*She attacks his hair with the brush.*] What is this young man's position at the warehouse?

TOM [*submitting grimly to the brush and the interrogation*]: This young man's position is that of a shipping clerk, Mother.

AMANDA: Sounds to me like a fairly responsible job, the sort of a job *you* would be in if you just had more *get-up*. What is his salary? Have you any idea?

TOM: I would judge it to be approximately eighty-five dollars a month.

AMANDA: Well—not princely, but—

TOM: Twenty more than I make.

AMANDA: Yes, how well I know! But for a family man, eighty-five dollars a month is not much more than you can just get by on. . . .

TOM: Yes, but Mr. O'Connor is not a family man.

AMANDA: He might be, mightn't he? Some time in the future?

TOM: I see. Plans and provisions.

AMANDA: You are the only young man that I know of who ignores the fact that the future becomes the present, the present the past, and the past turns into everlasting regret if you don't plan for it!

TOM: I will think that over and see what I can make of it.

AMANDA: Don't be supercilious with your mother! Tell me some more about this—what do you call him?

TOM: James D. O'Connor. The D. is for Delaney.

AMANDA: Irish on *both* sides! *Gracious!* And doesn't drink?

TOM: Shall I call him up and ask him right this minute?

AMANDA: The only way to find out about those things is to make discreet inquiries at the proper moment. When I was a girl in Blue Mountain and it was suspected that a young man drank, the girl whose attentions he had been receiving, if any girl *was,* would sometimes speak to the minister of his church, or rather her father would if her father was living, and sort of feel him out on the young man's character. That is the way such things are discreetly handled to keep a young woman from making a tragic mistake!

TOM: Then how did you happen to make a tragic mistake?

AMANDA: That innocent look of your father's had everyone fooled! He *smiled*—the world was *enchanted!* No girl can do worse than put herself at the mercy of a handsome appearance! I hope that Mr. O'Connor is not too good-looking.

TOM: No, he's not too good-looking. He's covered with freckles and hasn't too much of a nose.

AMANDA: He's not right-down homely, though?

TOM: Not right-down homely. Just medium homely, I'd say.

AMANDA: Character's what to look for in a man.

TOM: That's what I've always said, Mother.

AMANDA: You've never said anything of the kind and I suspect you would never give it a thought.

TOM: Don't be so suspicious of me.

AMANDA: At least I hope he's the type that's up and coming.

TOM: I think he really goes in for self-improvement.

AMANDA: What reason have you to think so?

TOM: He goes to night school.

AMANDA [*beaming*]: Splendid! What does he do, I mean study?

TOM: Radio engineering and public speaking!

AMANDA: Then he has visions of being advanced in the world! Any young man who studies public speaking is aiming to have an executive job some day! And radio engineering! A thing for the future! Both of these facts are very illuminating. Those are the sort of things that a mother should know concerning any young man who comes to call on her daughter. Seriously or—not.

TOM: One little warning. He doesn't know about Laura. I didn't let on that we had dark ulterior motives. I just said, why don't you come and have dinner with us? He said okay and that was the whole conversation.

AMANDA: I bet it was! You're eloquent as an oyster. However, he'll know about Laura when he gets here. When he sees how lovely and sweet and pretty she is, he'll thank his lucky stars he was asked to dinner.

TOM: Mother, you mustn't expect too much of Laura.

AMANDA: What do you mean?

TOM: Laura seems all those things to you and me because she's ours and we love her. We don't even notice she's crippled any more.

AMANDA: Don't say crippled! You know that I never allow that word to be used!

TOM: But face facts, Mother. She is and—that's not all—

AMANDA: What do you mean "not all"?

TOM: Laura is very different from other girls.

AMANDA: I think the difference is to her advantage.

TOM: Not quite all—in the eyes of others—strangers—she's terribly shy and lives in a world of her own and those things make her seem a little peculiar to people outside the house.

AMANDA: Don't say peculiar.

TOM: Face the facts. She is.

[The dance hall music changes to a tango that has a minor and somewhat ominous tone.]

AMANDA: In what way is she peculiar—may I ask?

TOM [*gently*]: She lives in a world of her own—a world of little glass ornaments, Mother. . . .

[He gets up. Amanda remains holding the brush, looking at him, troubled.]

She plays old phonograph records and—that's about all—[*He glances at himself in the mirror and crosses to the door.*]

AMANDA [*sharply*]: Where are you going?

TOM: I'm going to the movies. [*He goes out the screen door.*]

AMANDA: Not to the movies, every night to the movies! [*She follows quickly to the screen door.*] I don't believe you always go to the movies!

[He is gone. Amanda looks worriedly after him for a moment. Then vitality and optimism return and she turns from the door, crossing the portieres.]

Laura! Laura!

[Laura answers from the kitchenette.]

LAURA: Yes, Mother.

AMANDA: Let those dishes go and come in front!

[Laura appears with a dish towel. Amanda speaks to her gaily.]

Laura, come here and make a wish on the moon!

[Screen image: The Moon.]

LAURA [*entering*]: Moon—moon?

AMANDA: A little silver slipper of a moon. Look over your left shoulder, Laura, and make a wish!

[Laura looks faintly puzzled as if called out of sleep. Amanda seizes her shoulders and turns her at an angle by the door.]

Now! Now, darling, *wish!*

LAURA: What shall I wish for, Mother?

AMANDA [*her voice trembling and her eyes suddenly filling with tears*]: Happiness! Good fortune!

[The sound of the violin rises and the stage dims out.]

SCENE SIX

The light comes up on the fire escape landing. Tom is leaning against the grill, smoking.

[Screen image: The high school hero.]

TOM: And so the following evening I brought Jim home to dinner. I had known Jim slightly in high school. In high school Jim was a hero. He had tremendous Irish good nature and vitality with the scrubbed and polished look of white chinaware. He seemed to move in a continual spotlight. He was a star in basketball, captain of the debating club, president of the senior class and the glee club and he sang the lead in the annual light operas. He was always running or bounding, never just walking. He seemed always at the point of defeating the law of gravity. He was shooting with such velocity through his adolescence that you would logically expect him to arrive at nothing short of the White House by the time he was thirty. But Jim apparently ran into more interference after his graduation from Soldan. His speed had definitely slowed. Six years after he left high school he was holding a job that wasn't much better than mine.

[Screen image: The Clerk.]

He was the only one at the warehouse with whom I was on friendly terms. I was valuable to him as someone who could remember his former glory, who had seen him win basketball games and the silver cup in debating. He knew of my secret practice of retiring to a cabinet of the washroom to work on poems when business was slack in the warehouse. He called me Shakespeare. And while the other boys in the warehouse regarded me with suspicious hostility, Jim took a humorous attitude toward me. Gradually his attitude affected the others, their hostility wore off and they also began to smile at me as people smile at an oddly fashioned dog who trots across their path at some distance.

I knew that Jim and Laura had known each other at Soldan, and I had heard Laura speak admiringly of his voice. I didn't know if Jim remembered her or not. In high school Laura had been as unobtrusive as Jim had been astonishing. If he did remember Laura, it was not as my sister, for when I asked him to dinner, he grinned and said, "You know, Shakespeare, I never thought of you as having folks!"

He was about to discover that I did. . . .

[Legend on screen: "The accent of a coming foot."]

[The light dims out on Tom and comes up in the Wingfield living room—a delicate lemony light. It is about five on a Friday evening of late spring which comes "scattering poems in the sky."]

[Amanda has worked like a Turk in preparation for the gentleman caller. The results are astonishing. The new floor lamp with its rose silk shade is in place, a colored paper lantern conceals the broken light fixture in the ceiling, new billowing white curtains are at the windows, chintz covers are on the chairs and sofa, a pair of new sofa pillows make their initial appearance. Open boxes and tissue paper are scattered on the floor.]

[Laura stands in the middle of the room with lifted arms while Amanda crouches before her, adjusting the hem of a new dress, devout and ritualistic. The dress is colored and designed by memory. The arrangement of Laura's hair is changed; it is softer and more becoming. A fragile, unearthly prettiness has come out in Laura: she is like a piece of translucent glass touched by light, given a momentary radiance, not actual, not lasting.]

AMANDA [*impatiently*]: Why are you trembling?

LAURA: Mother, you've made me so nervous!

AMANDA: How have I made you nervous?

LAURA: By all this fuss! You make it seem so important!

AMANDA: I don't understand you, Laura. You couldn't be satisfied with just sitting home, and yet whenever I try to arrange something for you, you seem to resist it. [*She gets up.*] Now take a look at yourself. No, wait! Wait just a moment—I have an idea!

LAURA: What is it now?

[Amanda produces two powder puffs which she wraps in handkerchiefs and stuffs in Laura's bosom.]

LAURA: Mother, what are you doing?

AMANDA: They call them "Gay Deceivers"!

LAURA: I won't wear them!

AMANDA: You will!

LAURA: Why should I?

AMANDA: Because, to be painfully honest, your chest is flat.

LAURA: You make it seem like we were setting a trap.

AMANDA: All pretty girls are a trap, a pretty trap, and men expect them to be.

[Legend on screen: "A pretty trap."]

Now look at yourself, young lady. This is the prettiest you will ever be! [*She stands back to admire Laura.*] I've got to fix myself now! You're going to be surprised by your mother's appearance!

[Amanda crosses through the portieres, humming gaily. Laura moves slowly to the long mirror and stares solemnly at herself. A wind blows the white curtains inward in a slow, graceful motion and with a faint, sorrowful sighing.]

AMANDA [*from somewhere behind the portieres*]: It isn't dark enough yet.

[Laura turns slowly before the mirror with a troubled look.]

[Legend on screen: "This is my sister: Celebrate her with strings!" Music plays.]

AMANDA [*laughing, still not visible*]: I'm going to show you something. I'm going to make a spectacular appearance!

LAURA: What is it, Mother?

AMANDA: Possess your soul in patience—you will see! Something I've resurrected from that old trunk! Styles haven't changed so terribly much after all. . . . [*She parts the portieres.*] Now just look at your mother! [*She wears a girlish frock of yellowed voile with a blue silk sash. She carries a bunch of jonquils—the legend of her youth is nearly revived. Now she speaks feverishly:*] This is the dress in which I led the cotillion. Won the cakewalk twice at Sunset Hill, wore one Spring to the Governor's Ball in Jackson! See how I sashayed around the ballroom, Laura? [*She raises her skirt and does a mincing step around the room.*] I wore it on Sundays for my gentlemen callers! I had it on the day I met your father. . . . I had malaria fever all that Spring. The change of climate from East Tennessee to the Delta—weakened resistance. I had a little temperature all the time—not enough to be serious—just enough to make me restless and giddy! Invitations poured in—parties all over the Delta! "Stay in bed," said Mother, "you have a fever!"—but I just wouldn't. I took quinine but kept on going, going! Evenings, dances! Afternoons, long, long rides! Picnics—lovely! So lovely, that country in May—all lacy with dogwood, literally flooded with jonquils! That was the spring I had the craze for jonquils. Jonquils became an absolute obsession. Mother said, "Honey, there's no more room for jonquils." And still I kept on bringing in more jonquils. Whenever, wherever I saw them, I'd say, "Stop! Stop! I see jonquils!" I made the young men help me gather the jonquils! It was a joke, Amanda and her jonquils. Finally there were no more vases to hold them, every available space was filled with jonquils. No vases to hold them? All right, I'll hold them myself! And then I—[*She stops in front of the picture. Music plays.*] met your father! Malaria fever and jonquils and then—this—boy. . . . [*She switches on the rose-colored lamp.*] I hope they get here before it starts to rain. [*She crosses the room and places the jonquils in a bowl on the table.*] I gave your brother a little extra change so he and Mr. O'Connor could take the service car home.

LAURA [*with an altered look*]: What did you say his name was?

AMANDA: O'Connor.

LAURA: What is his first name?

AMANDA: I don't remember. Oh, yes, I do. It was—Jim!

[Laura sways slightly and catches hold of a chair.]

[Legend on screen: "Not, Jim!"]

LAURA [*faintly*]: Not—Jim!

AMANDA: Yes, that was it, it was Jim! I've never known a Jim that wasn't nice! [*The music becomes ominous.*]

LAURA: Are you sure his name is Jim O'Connor?

AMANDA: Yes. Why?

LAURA: Is he the one that Tom used to know in high school?

AMANDA: He didn't say so. I think he just got to know him at the warehouse.

LAURA: There was a Jim O'Connor we both knew in high school—[*then, with effort*] If that is the one that Tom is bringing to dinner—you'll have to excuse me, I won't come to the table.

AMANDA: What sort of nonsense is this?

LAURA: You asked me once if I'd ever liked a boy. Don't you remember I showed you this boy's picture?

AMANDA: You mean the boy you showed me in the year-book?

LAURA: Yes, that boy.

AMANDA: Laura, Laura, were you in love with that boy?

LAURA: I don't know, Mother. All I know is I couldn't sit at the table if it was him!

AMANDA: It won't be him! It isn't the least bit likely. But whether it is or not, you will come to the table. You will not be excused.

LAURA: I'll have to be, Mother.

AMANDA: I don't intend to humor your silliness, Laura. I've had too much from you and your brother, both! So just sit down and compose yourself till they come. Tom has forgotten his key so you'll have to let them in, when they arrive.

LAURA [*panicky*]: Oh, Mother—*you* answer the door!

AMANDA [*lightly*]: I'll be in the kitchen—busy!

LAURA: Oh, Mother, please answer the door, don't make me do it!

AMANDA [*crossing into the kitchenette*]: I've got to fix the dressing for the salmon. Fuss, fuss—silliness!—over a gentleman caller!

[The door swings shut. Laura is left alone.]

[Legend on screen: "Terror!"]

[She utters a low moan and turns off the lamp—sits stiffly on the edge of the sofa, knotting her fingers together.]

[Legend on screen: "The Opening of a Door!"]

[Tom and Jim appear on the fire escape steps and climb to the landing. Hearing their approach, Laura rises with a panicky gesture. She retreats to the portieres. The doorbell rings. Laura catches her breath and touches her throat. Low drums sound.]

AMANDA [*calling*]: Laura, sweetheart! The door!

[Laura stares at it without moving.]

JIM: I think we just beat the rain.

TOM: Uh-huh. [*He rings again, nervously. Jim whistles and fishes for a cigarette.*]

AMANDA [*very, very gaily*]: Laura, that is your brother and Mr. O'Connor! Will you let them in, darling!

[Laura crosses toward the kitchenette door.]

LAURA [*breathlessly*]: Mother—you go to the door!

[Amanda steps out of the kitchenette and stares furiously at Laura. She points imperiously at the door.]

LAURA: Please, please!

AMANDA [*in fierce whisper*]: What is the matter with you, you silly thing?

LAURA [*desperately*]: Please, you answer it, *please!*

AMANDA: I told you I wasn't going to humor you, Laura. Why have you chosen this moment to lose your mind?

LAURA: Please, please, please, you go!

AMANDA: You'll have to go to the door because I can't!

LAURA [*despairingly*]: I can't either!

AMANDA: *Why?*

LAURA: I'm *sick!*

AMANDA: I'm sick, too—of your nonsense! Why can't you and your brother be normal people? Fantastic whims and behavior!

[Tom gives a long ring.]

Preposterous goings on! Can you give me one reason—[*She calls out lyrically.*] *Coming! Just one second!*—why should you be afraid to open a door? Now you answer it, Laura!

LAURA: Oh, oh, oh . . . [*She returns through the portieres, darts to the Victrola, winds it frantically and turns it on.*]

AMANDA: Laura Wingfield, you march right to that door!

LAURA: *Yes—yes, Mother!*

[A faraway, scratchy rendition of "Dardanella" softens the air and gives her strength to move through it. She slips to the door and draws it cautiously open. Tom enters with the caller, Jim O'Connor.]

TOM: Laura, this is Jim. Jim, this is my sister, Laura.

JIM [*stepping inside*]: I didn't know that Shakespeare had a sister!

LAURA [*retreating, stiff and trembling, from the door*]: How—how do you do?

JIM [*heartily, extending his hand*]: Okay!

[Laura touches it hesitantly with hers.]

JIM: Your hand's *cold,* Laura!

LAURA: Yes, well—I've been playing the Victrola. . . .

JIM: Must have been playing classical music on it! You ought to play a little hot swing music to warm you up!

LAURA: Excuse me—I haven't finished playing the Victrola. . . . [*She awkwardly hurries into the front room. She pauses a second by the Victrola. Then she catches her breath and darts through the portieres like a frightened deer.*]

JIM [*grinning*]: What was the matter?

TOM: Oh—with Laura? Laura is—terribly shy.

JIM: Shy, huh? It's unusual to meet a shy girl nowadays. I don't believe you ever mentioned you had a sister.

TOM: Well, now you know. I have one. Here is the *Post Dispatch.* You want a piece of it?

JIM: Uh-huh.

TOM: What piece? The comics?

JIM: Sports! [*He glances at it.*] Ole Dizzy Dean is on his bad behavior.

TOM [*uninterested*]: Yeah? [*He lights a cigarette and goes over to the fire-escape door.*]

JIM: Where are *you* going?

TOM: I'm going out on the terrace.

JIM [*going after him*]: You know, Shakespeare—I'm going to sell you a bill of goods!

TOM: What goods?

JIM: A course I'm taking.

TOM: Huh?

JIM: In public speaking! You and me, we're not the warehouse type.

TOM: Thanks—that's good news. But what has public speaking got to do with it?

JIM: It fits you for—executive positions!

TOM: Awww.

JIM: I tell you it's done a helluva lot for me.

[Image on screen: Executive at his desk.]

TOM: In what respect?

JIM: In every! Ask yourself what is the difference between you an' me and men in the office down front? Brains?—No!—Ability?—No! Then what? Just one little thing—

TOM: What is that one little thing?

JIM: Primarily it amounts to—social poise! Being able to square up to people and hold your own on any social level!

AMANDA [*from the kitchenette*]: Tom?

TOM: Yes, Mother?

AMANDA: Is that you and Mr. O'Connor?

TOM: Yes, Mother.

AMANDA: Well, you just make yourselves comfortable in there.

TOM: Yes, Mother.

AMANDA: Ask Mr. O'Connor if he would like to wash his hands.

JIM: Aw, no—no—thank you—I took care of that at the warehouse. Tom—

TOM: Yes?

JIM: Mr. Mendoza was speaking to me about you.

TOM: Favorably?

JIM: What do you think?

TOM: Well—

JIM: You're going to be out of a job if you don't wake up.

TOM: I am waking up—

JIM: You show no signs.

TOM: The signs are interior.

[Image on screen: The sailing vessel with the Jolly Roger again.]

TOM: I'm planning to change. [*He leans over the fire-escape rail, speaking with quiet exhilaration. The incandescent marquees and signs of the first-run movie houses light his face from across the alley. He looks like a voyager.*] I'm right at the point of committing myself to a future that doesn't include the warehouse and Mr. Mendoza or even a night-school course in public speaking.

JIM: What are you gassing about?

TOM: I'm tired of the movies.

JIM: Movies!

TOM: Yes, movies! Look at them—[*a wave toward the marvels of Grand Avenue*] All of those glamorous people—having adventures—hogging it all, gobbling the whole thing up! You know what happens? People go to the *movies* instead of *moving!* Hollywood characters are supposed to have all the adventures for everybody in America, while everybody in America sits in a dark room and watches them have them! Yes, until there's a war. That's when adventure becomes available to the masses! *Everyone's* dish, not only Gable's! Then the people in the dark room come out of the dark room to have some adventures themselves—goody, goody! It's our turn now, to go to the South Sea Island—to make a safari—to be exotic, far-off! But I'm not patient. I don't want to wait till then. I'm tired of the *movies* and I am *about* to *move!*

JIM [*incredulously*]: Move?

TOM: Yes.

JIM: When?

TOM: Soon!

JIM: Where? When?

[The music seems to answer the question, while Tom thinks it over. He searches in his pockets.]

TOM: I'm starting to boil inside. I know I seem dreamy, but inside—well, I'm boiling! Whenever I pick up a shoe, I shudder a little thinking how short life is and what I am doing! Whatever that means, I know it doesn't mean shoes—except as something to wear on a traveler's feet! [*He finds what he has been searching for in his pockets and holds out a paper to Jim.*] Look—

JIM: What?

TOM: I'm a member.

JIM [*reading*]: The Union of Merchant Seamen.

TOM: I paid my dues this month, instead of the light bill.

JIM: You will regret it when they turn the lights off.

TOM: I won't be here.

JIM: How about your mother?

TOM: I'm like my father. The bastard son of a bastard! Did you notice how he's grinning in his picture in there? And he's been absent going on sixteen years!

JIM: You're just talking, you drip. How does your mother feel about it?

TOM: Shhh! Here comes Mother! Mother is not acquainted with my plans!

AMANDA [*coming through the portieres*]: Where are you all?

TOM: On the terrace, Mother.

[They start inside. She advances to them. Tom is distinctly shocked at her appearance. Even Jim blinks a little. He is making his first contact with girlish Southern vivacity and in spite of the night-school course in public speaking is somewhat thrown off the beam by the unexpected outlay of social charm. Certain responses are attempted by Jim but are swept aside by Amanda's gay laughter and chatter. Tom is embarrassed but after the first shock Jim reacts very warmly. He grins and chuckles, is altogether won over.]

[Image on screen: Amanda as a girl.]

AMANDA [*coyly smiling, shaking her girlish ringlets*]: Well, well, well, so this is Mr. O'Connor. Introductions entirely unnecessary. I've heard so much about you from my boy. I finally said to him, Tom—good gracious!—why don't you bring this paragon to supper? I'd like to meet this nice young man at the warehouse!—instead of just hearing him sing your praises so much! I don't know why my son is so stand-offish—that's not Southern behavior!

Let's sit down and—I think we could stand a little more air in here! Tom, leave the door open. I felt a nice fresh breeze a moment ago. Where has it gone to? Mmm, so warm already! And not quite summer, even. We're going to burn up when summer really gets started. However, we're having—we're having a very light supper. I think light things are better fo' this time of year. The same as light clothes are. Light clothes an' light food are what warm weather calls fo'. You know our blood gets so thick during th' winter—it takes a while fo' us to *adjust* ou'selves—when the season changes . . . It's come so quick this year. I wasn't prepared. All of a sudden—heavens! Already summer! I ran to the trunk an' pulled out this light dress—terribly old! Historical almost! But feels so good—so good an' co-ol, y' know. . . .

TOM: Mother—

AMANDA: Yes, honey?

TOM: How about—supper?

AMANDA: Honey, you go ask Sister if supper is ready! You know that Sister is in full charge of supper! Tell her you hungry boys are waiting for it. [*to Jim*] Have you met Laura?

JIM: She—

AMANDA: Let you in? Oh, good, you've met already! It's rare for a girl as sweet an' pretty as Laura to be domestic! But Laura is, thank heavens, not only pretty but also very domestic. I'm not at all. I never was a bit. I never could make a thing but angel-food cake. Well, in the South we had so many servants. Gone, gone, gone. All vestiges of gracious living! Gone completely! I wasn't prepared for what the future brought me. All of my gentlemen callers were sons of planters and so of course I assumed that I would be married to one and raise my family on a large piece of land with plenty of servants. But man proposes—and woman accepts the proposal! To vary that old, old saying a little bit—I married no planter! I married a man who worked for the telephone company! That gallantly smiling gentleman over there! [*She points to the picture.*] A telephone man who—fell in love with long-distance! Now he travels and I don't even know where! But what am I going on for about my—tribulations? Tell me yours—I hope you don't have any! Tom?

TOM [*returning*]: Yes, Mother?

AMANDA: Is supper nearly ready?

TOM: It looks to me like supper is on the table.

AMANDA: Let me look—[*She rises prettily and looks through the portieres.*] Oh, lovely! But where is Sister?

TOM: Laura is not feeling well and says that she thinks she'd better not come to the table.

AMANDA: What? Nonsense! Laura? Oh, Laura!

LAURA [*from the kitchenette, faintly*]: Yes, Mother.

AMANDA: You really must come to the table. We won't be seated until you come to the table! Come in, Mr. O'Connor. You sit over there, and I'll. . . . Laura? Laura Wingfield! You're keeping us waiting, honey! We can't say grace until you come to the table!

[The kitchenette door is pushed weakly open and Laura comes in. She is obviously quite faint, her lips trembling, her eyes wide and staring. She moves unsteadily toward the table.]

[Screen legend: "Terror!"]

[Outside a summer storm is coming on abruptly. The white curtains billow inward at the windows and there is a sorrowful murmur from the deep blue dusk.]

[Laura suddenly stumbles; she catches at a chair with a faint moan.]

TOM: Laura!

AMANDA: Laura!

[There is a clap of thunder.]

[Screen legend: "Ah!"]

[despairingly] Why, Laura, you *are* ill, darling! Tom, help your sister into the living room, dear! Sit in the living room, Laura—rest on the sofa. Well! *[to Jim as Tom helps his sister to the sofa in the living room]* Standing over the hot stove made her ill! I told her that it was just too warm this evening, but—

[Tom comes back to the table.]

Is Laura all right now?

TOM: Yes.

AMANDA: What *is* that? Rain? A nice cool rain has come up! [*She gives Jim a frightened look.*] I think we may—have grace—now . . .

[Tom looks at her stupidly.] Tom, honey—you say grace!

TOM: Oh . . . "For these and all thy mercies—"

[They bow their heads, Amanda stealing a nervous glance at Jim. In the living room Laura, stretched on the sofa, clenches her hand to her lips, to hold back a shuddering sob.]

God's Holy Name be praised—

[The scene dims out.]

SCENE SEVEN

It is half an hour later. Dinner is just being finished in the dining room. Laura is still huddled upon the sofa, her feet drawn under her, her head resting on a pale blue pillow, her eyes wide and mysteriously watchful. The new floor lamp with its shade of rose-colored silk gives a soft, becoming light to her face, bringing out the fragile, unearthly prettiness which usually escapes attention. From outside there is a steady murmur of rain, but it is slackening and soon stops; the air outside becomes pale and luminous as the moon breaks through the clouds. A moment after the curtain rises, the lights in both rooms flicker and go out.

JIM: Hey, there, Mr. Light Bulb!

[Amanda laughs nervously.]

[Legend on screen: "Suspension of public service."]

AMANDA: Where was Moses when the lights went out? Ha-ha. Do you know the answer to that one, Mr. O'Connor?

JIM: No, Ma'am, what's the answer?

AMANDA: In the dark!

[Jim laughs appreciatively.]

Everybody sit still. I'll light the candles. Isn't it lucky we have them on the table? Where's a match? Which of you gentlemen can provide a match?

JIM: Here.

AMANDA: Thank you, Sir.

JIM: Not at all, Ma'am!

AMANDA [*as she lights the candles*]: I guess the fuse has burnt out. Mr. O'Connor, can you tell a burnt-out fuse? I know I can't and Tom is a total loss when it comes to mechanics.

[They rise from the table and go into the kitchenette, from where their voices are heard.]

Oh, be careful you don't bump into something. We don't want our gentleman caller to break his neck. Now wouldn't that be a fine howdy-do?

JIM: Ha-ha! Where is the fuse-box?

AMANDA: Right here next to the stove. Can you see anything?

JIM: Just a minute.

AMANDA: Isn't electricity a mysterious thing? Wasn't it Benjamin Franklin who tied a key to a kite? We live in such a mysterious universe, don't we? Some people say that science clears up all the mysteries for us. In my opinion it only creates more! Have you found it yet?

JIM: No, Ma'am. All these fuses look okay to me.

AMANDA: Tom!

TOM: Yes, Mother?

AMANDA: That light bill I gave you several days ago. The one I told you we got the notices about?

[Legend on screen: "Ha!"]

TOM: Oh—yeah.

AMANDA: You didn't neglect to pay it by any chance?

TOM: Why, I—

AMANDA: Didn't! I might have known it!

JIM: Shakespeare probably wrote a poem on that light bill, Mrs. Wingfield.

AMANDA: I might have known better than to trust him with it! There's such a high price for negligence in this world!

JIM: Maybe the poem will win a ten-dollar prize!

AMANDA: We'll just have to spend the remainder of the evening in the nineteenth century, before Mr. Edison made the Mazda lamp!

JIM: Candlelight is my favorite kind of light.

AMANDA: That shows you're romantic! But that's no excuse for Tom. Well, we got through dinner. Very considerate of them to let us get through dinner before they plunged us into everlasting darkness, wasn't it, Mr. O'Connor?

JIM: Ha-ha!

AMANDA: Tom, as a penalty for your carelessness you can help me with the dishes.

JIM: Let me give you a hand.

AMANDA: Indeed you will not!

JIM: I ought to be good for something.

AMANDA: Good for something? [*Her tone is rhapsodic.*] Why, Mr. O'Connor, nobody, *nobody's* given me this much entertainment in years—as you have!

JIM: Aw, now, Mrs. Wingfield!

AMANDA: I'm not exaggerating, not one bit! But Sister is all by her lonesome. You go keep her company in the parlor! I'll give you this lovely old candelabrum that used to be on the altar at the Church of the Heavenly Rest. It was melted a little out of shape when the church burnt down. Lightning struck it one spring. Gypsy Jones was holding a revival at the time and he intimated that the church was destroyed because the Episcopalians gave card parties.

JIM: Ha-ha.

AMANDA: And how about you coaxing Sister to drink a little wine? I think it would be good for her! Can you carry both at once?

JIM: Sure. I'm Superman!

AMANDA: Now, Thomas, get into this apron!

[Jim comes into the dining room, carrying the candelabrum, its candles lighted, in one hand and a glass of wine in the other. The door of the kitchenette swings closed on Amanda's gay laughter; the flickering light approaches the portieres. Laura sits up nervously as Jim enters. She can hardly speak from the almost intolerable strain of being alone with a stranger.]

[Screen legend: "I don't suppose you remember me at all!"]

[At first, before Jim's warmth overcomes her paralyzing shyness, Laura's voice is thin and breathless, as though she had just run up a steep flight of stairs. Jim's attitude is gently humorous. While the incident is apparently unimportant, it is to Laura the climax of her secret life.]

JIM: Hello there, Laura.

LAURA [*faintly*]: Hello.

[She clears her throat.]

JIM: How are you feeling now? Better?

LAURA: Yes. Yes, thank you.

JIM: This is for you. A little dandelion wine. [*He extends the glass toward her with extravagant gallantry.*]

LAURA: Thank you.

JIM: Drink it—but don't get drunk!

[He laughs heartily. Laura takes the glass uncertainly; she laughs shyly.]

Where shall I set the candles?

LAURA: Oh—oh, anywhere . . .

JIM: How about here on the floor? Any objections?

LAURA: No.

JIM: I'll spread a newspaper under to catch the drippings. I like to sit on the floor. Mind if I do?

LAURA: Oh, no.

JIM: Give me a pillow?

LAURA: What?

JIM: A pillow!

LAURA: Oh . . . [*She hands him one quickly.*]

JIM: How about you? Don't you like to sit on the floor?

LAURA: Oh—yes.

JIM: Why don't you, then?

LAURA: I—will.

JIM: Take a pillow!

[Laura does. She sits on the floor on the other side of the candelabrum. Jim crosses his legs and smiles engagingly at her.] I can't hardly see you sitting way over there.

LAURA: I can—see you.

JIM: I know, but that's not fair, I'm in the limelight.

[Laura moves her pillow closer.]

Good! Now I can see you! Comfortable?

LAURA: Yes.

JIM: So am I. Comfortable as a cow! Will you have some gum?

LAURA: No thank you.

JIM: I think that I will indulge, with your permission. [*He musingly unwraps a stick of gum and holds it up.*] Think of the fortune made by the guy that invented the first piece of chewing gum. Amazing, huh? The Wrigley Building is one of the sights of Chicago—I saw it when I went up to the Century of Progress. Did you take in the Century of Progress?

LAURA: No, I didn't.

JIM: Well, it was quite a wonderful exposition. What impressed me most was the Hall of Science. Gives you an idea of what the future will be in America, even more wonderful than the present time is! [*There is a pause. Jim smiles at her.*] Your brother tells me you're shy. Is that right, Laura?

LAURA: I—don't know.

JIM: I judge you to be an old-fashioned type of girl. Well, I think that's a pretty good type to be. Hope you don't think I'm being too personal—do you?

LAURA [*hastily, out of embarrassment*]: I believe I *will* take a piece of gum, if you—don't mind. [*clearing her throat*] Mr. O'Connor, have you—kept up with your singing?

JIM: Singing? Me?

LAURA: Yes. I remember what a beautiful voice you had.

JIM: When did you hear me sing?

[Laura does not answer, and in the long pause which follows a man's voice is heard singing offstage.]

VOICE :

O blow, ye winds, heigh-ho,
A-roving I will go!
I'm off to my love
With a boxing glove—
Ten thousand miles away!

JIM: You say you've heard me sing?

LAURA: Oh, yes! Yes, very often . . . I—don't suppose—you remember me—at all?

JIM [*smiling doubtfully*]: You know I have an idea I've seen you before. I had that idea as soon as you opened the door. It seemed almost like I was about to remember your name. But the name that I started to call you—wasn't a name! And so I stopped myself before I said it.

LAURA: Wasn't it—Blue Roses?

JIM [*springing up, grinning*]: Blue Roses! My gosh, yes—Blue Roses! That's what I had on my tongue when you opened the door! Isn't it funny what tricks your memory plays? I didn't connect you with high school somehow or other. But that's where it was; it was high school. I didn't even know you were Shakespeare's sister! Gosh, I'm sorry.

LAURA: I didn't expect you to. You—barely knew me!

JIM: But we did have a speaking acquaintance, huh?

LAURA: Yes, we—spoke to each other.

JIM: When did you recognize me?

LAURA: Oh, right away!

JIM: Soon as I came in the door?

LAURA: When I heard your name I thought it was probably you. I knew that Tom used to know you a little in high school. So when you came in the door—well, then I was—sure.

JIM: Why didn't you *say* something, then?

LAURA [*breathlessly*]: I didn't know what to say, I was—too surprised!

JIM: For goodness sakes! You know, this sure is funny!

LAURA: Yes! Yes, isn't it, though . . .

JIM: Didn't we have a class in something together?

LAURA: Yes, we did.

JIM: What class was that?

LAURA: It was—singing—chorus!

JIM: Aw!

LAURA: I sat across the aisle from you in the Aud.

JIM: Aw.

LAURA: Mondays, Wednesdays, and Fridays.

JIM: Now I remember—you always came in late.

LAURA: Yes, it was so hard for me, getting upstairs. I had that brace on my leg—it clumped so loud!

JIM: I never heard any clumping.

LAURA [*wincing at the recollection*]: To me it sounded like—thunder!

JIM: Well, well, well, I never even noticed.

LAURA: And everybody was seated before I came in. I had to walk in front of all those people. My seat was in the back row. I had to go clumping all the way up the aisle with everyone watching!

JIM: You shouldn't have been self-conscious.

LAURA: I know, but I was. It was always such a relief when the singing started.

JIM: Aw, yes, I've placed you now! I used to call you Blue Roses. How was it that I got started calling you that?

LAURA: I was out of school a little with pleurosis. When I came back you asked me what was the matter. I said I had pleurosis—you thought I said *Blue Roses.* That's what you always called me after that!

JIM: I hope you didn't mind.

LAURA: Oh, no—I liked it. You see, I wasn't acquainted with many—people. . . .
JIM: As I remember you sort of stuck by yourself.
LAURA: I—I—never have had much luck at—making friends.
JIM: I don't see why you wouldn't.
LAURA: Well, I—started out badly.
JIM: You mean being—
LAURA: Yes, it sort of—stood between me—
JIM: You shouldn't have let it!
LAURA: I know, but it did, and—
JIM: You were shy with people!
LAURA: I tried not to be but never could—
JIM: Overcome it?
LAURA: No, I—I never could!
JIM: I guess being shy is something you have to work out of kind of gradually.
LAURA [*sorrowfully*]: Yes—I guess it—
JIM: Takes time!
LAURA: Yes—
JIM: People are not so dreadful when you know them. That's what you have to remember! And everybody has problems, not just you, but practically everybody has got some problems. You think of yourself as having the only problems, as being the only one who is disappointed. But just look around you and you will see lots of people as disappointed as you are. For instance, I hoped when I was going to high school that I would be further along at this time, six years later, than I am now. You remember that wonderful write-up I had in *The Torch?*
LAURA: Yes! [*She rises and crosses to the table.*]
JIM: It said I was bound to succeed in anything I went into!
[Laura returns with the high school yearbook.]
Holy Jeez! *The Torch!*
[He accepts it reverently. They smile across the book with mutual wonder. Laura crouches beside him and they begin to turn the pages. Laura's shyness is dissolving in his warmth.]
LAURA: Here you are in *The Pirates of Penzance!*
JIM [*wistfully*]: I sang the baritone lead in that operetta.
LAURA [*raptly*]: So—*beautifully!*
JIM [*protesting*]: Aw—
LAURA: Yes, yes—beautifully—beautifully!
JIM: You heard me?
LAURA: All three times!
JIM: No!
LAURA: Yes!
JIM: All three performances?
LAURA [*looking down*]: Yes.
JIM: Why?
LAURA: I—wanted to ask you to—autograph my program.
[She takes the program from the back of the yearbook and shows it to him.]
JIM: Why didn't you ask me to?
LAURA: You were always surrounded by your own friends so much that I never had a chance to.
JIM: You should have just—
LAURA: Well, I—thought you might think I was—

JIM: Thought I might think you was—what?

LAURA: Oh—

JIM [*with reflective relish*]: I was beleaguered by females in those days.

LAURA: You were terribly popular!

JIM: Yeah—

LAURA: You had such a—friendly way—

JIM: I was spoiled in high school.

LAURA: Everybody—liked you!

JIM: Including you?

LAURA: I—yes, I—did, too—[*She gently closes the book in her lap.*]

JIM: Well, well, well! Give me that program, Laura.

[She hands it to him. He signs it with a flourish.]

There you are—better late than never!

LAURA: Oh, I—what a—surprise!

JIM: My signature isn't worth very much right now. But some day—maybe—it will increase in value! Being disappointed is one thing and being discouraged is something else. I am disappointed but I am not discouraged. I'm twenty-three years old. How old are you?

LAURA: I'll be twenty-four in June.

JIM: That's not old age!

LAURA: No, but—

JIM: You finished high school?

LAURA [*with difficulty*]: I didn't go back.

JIM: You mean you dropped out?

LAURA: I made bad grades in my final examinations. [*She rises and replaces the book and the program on the table. Her voice is strained.*] How is—Emily Meisenbach getting along?

JIM: Oh, that kraut-head!

LAURA: Why do you call her that?

JIM: That's what she was.

LAURA: You're not still—going with her?

JIM: I never see her.

LAURA: It said in the "Personal" section that you were—engaged!

JIM: I know, but I wasn't impressed by that—propaganda!

LAURA: It wasn't—the truth?

JIM: Only in Emily's optimistic opinion!

LAURA: Oh—

[Legend: "What have you done since high school?"]

[Jim lights a cigarette and leans indolently back on his elbows smiling at Laura with a warmth and charm which lights her inwardly with altar candles. She remains by the table, picks up a piece from the glass menagerie collection, and turns it in her hands to cover her tumult.]

JIM [*after several reflective puffs on his cigarette*]: What have you done since high school?

[She seems not to hear him.]

Huh?

[Laura looks up.]

I said what have you done since high school, Laura?

LAURA: Nothing much.

JIM: You must have been doing something these six long years.

LAURA: Yes.

JIM: Well, then, such as what?

LAURA: I took a business course at business college—

JIM: How did that work out?

LAURA: Well, not very—well—I had to drop out, it gave me—indigestion—[*Jim laughs gently.*]

JIM: What are you doing now?

LAURA: I don't do anything—much. Oh, please don't think I sit around doing nothing! My glass collection takes up a good deal of time. Glass is something you have to take good care of.

JIM: What did you say—about glass?

LAURA: Collection I said—I have one—[*She clears her throat and turns away again, acutely shy.*]

JIM [*abruptly*]: You know what I judge to be the trouble with you? Inferiority complex! Know what that is? That's what they call it when someone low-rates himself! I understand it because I had it, too. Although my case was not so aggravated as yours seems to be. I had it until I took up public speaking, developed my voice, and learned that I had an aptitude for science. Before that time I never thought of myself as being outstanding in any way whatsoever! Now I've never made a regular study of it, but I have a friend who says I can analyze people better than doctors that make a profession of it. I don't claim that to be necessarily true, but I can sure guess a person's psychology, Laura! [*He takes out his gum.*] Excuse me, Laura. I always take it out when the flavor is gone. I'll use this scrap of paper to wrap it in. I know how it is to get it stuck on a shoe. [*He wraps the gum in paper and puts it in his pocket.*] Yep—that's what I judge to be your principal trouble. A lack of confidence in yourself as a person. You don't have the proper amount of faith in yourself. I'm basing that fact on a number of your remarks and also on certain observations I've made. For instance that clumping you thought was so awful in high school. You say that you even dreaded to walk into class. You see what you did? You dropped out of school, you gave up an education because of a clump, which as far as I know was practically nonexistent! A little physical defect is what you have. Hardly noticeable even! Magnified thousands of times by imagination! You know what my strong advice to you is? Think of yourself as *superior* in some way!

LAURA: In what way would I think?

JIM: Why, man alive, Laura! Just look about you a little. What do you see? A world full of common people! All of 'em born and all of 'em going to die! Which of them has one-tenth of your good points! Or mine! Or anyone else's, as far as that goes—gosh! Everybody excels in some one thing. Some in many! [*He unconsciously glances at himself in the mirror.*] All you've got to do is to discover in *what!* Take me, for instance. [*He adjusts his tie at the mirror.*] My interest happens to lie in electro-dynamics. I'm taking a course in radio engineering at night school, Laura, on top of a fairly responsible job at the warehouse. I'm taking that course and studying public speaking.

LAURA: Ohhhh.

JIM: Because I believe in the future of television! [*turning his back to her.*] I wish to be ready to go up right along with it. Therefore I'm planning to get in on the ground floor. In fact I've already made the right connections and all that remains is for the industry itself to get under way! Full steam—[*His eyes are starry.*] *Knowledge*—Zzzzzp! *Money*—Zzzzzzp!—*Power!* That's the cycle democracy is built on!

[His attitude is convincingly dynamic. Laura stares at him, even her shyness eclipsed in her absolute wonder. He suddenly grins.]

I guess you think I think a lot of myself?

LAURA: No—o-o-o, I—

JIM: Now how about you? Isn't there something you take more interest in than anything else?

LAURA: Well, I do—as I said—have my—glass collection—

[A peal of girlish laughter rings from the kitchenette.]

JIM: I'm not right sure I know what you're talking about. What kind of glass is it?

LAURA: Little articles of it, they're ornaments mostly! Most of them are little animals made out of glass, the tiniest little animals in the world. Mother calls them the glass menagerie! Here's an example of one, if you'd like to see it! This one is one of the oldest. It's nearly thirteen.

[Music: "The Glass Menagerie."]

Oh, be careful—if you breathe, it breaks!

JIM: I'd better not take it. I'm pretty clumsy with things.

LAURA: Go on, I trust you with him! [*She places the piece in his palm.*] There now—you're holding him gently! Hold him over the light, he loves the light! You see how the light shines through him?

JIM: It sure does shine!

LAURA: I shouldn't be partial, but he is my favorite one.

JIM: What kind of a thing is this one supposed to be?

LAURA: Haven't you noticed the single horn on his forehead?

JIM: A unicorn, huh?

LAURA: Mmmm-hmmm!

JIM: Unicorns—aren't they extinct in the modern world?

LAURA: I know!

JIM: Poor little fellow, he must feel sort of lonesome.

LAURA [*smiling*]: Well, if he does, he doesn't complain about it. He stays on a shelf with some horses that don't have horns and all of them seem to get along nicely together.

JIM: How do you know?

LAURA [*lightly*]: I haven't heard any arguments among them!

JIM [*grinning*]: No arguments, huh? Well, that's a pretty good sign! Where shall I set him!

LAURA: Put him on the table. They all like a change of scenery once in a while!

JIM: Well, well, well, well—[*He places the glass piece on the table, then raises his arms and stretches.*] Look how big my shadow is when I stretch!

LAURA: Oh, oh, yes—it stretches across the ceiling!

JIM [*crossing to the door*]: I think it's stopped raining. [*He opens the fire-escape door and the background music changes to a dance tune.*] Where does the music come from?

LAURA: From the Paradise Dance Hall across the alley.

JIM: How about cutting the rug a little, Miss Wingfield?

LAURA: Oh, I—

JIM: Or is your program filled up? Let me have a look at it. [*He grasps an imaginary card.*] Why, every dance is taken! I'll just have to scratch some out.

[Waltz music: "La Golondrina."]

Ahhh, a waltz! [*He executes some sweeping turns by himself, then holds his arms toward Laura.*]

LAURA [*breathlessly*]: I—can't dance!

JIM: There you go, that inferiority stuff!

LAURA: I've never danced in my life!

JIM: Come on, try!

LAURA: Oh, but I'd step on you!

JIM: I'm not made out of glass.

LAURA: How—how—how do we start?

JIM: Just leave it to me. You hold your arms out a little.

LAURA: Like this?

JIM [*taking her in his arms*]: A little bit higher. Right. Now don't tighten up, that's the main thing about it—relax.

LAURA [*laughing breathlessly*]: It's hard not to.

JIM: Okay.

LAURA: I'm afraid you can't budge me.

JIM: What do you bet I can't? [*He swings her into motion.*]

LAURA: Goodness, yes, you can!

JIM: Let yourself go, now, Laura, just let yourself go.

LAURA: I'm—

JIM: Come on!

LAURA: —trying!

JIM: Not so stiff—easy does it!

LAURA: I know but I'm—

JIM: Loosen th' backbone! There now, that's a lot better.

LAURA: Am I?

JIM: Lots, lots better! [*He moves her about the room in a clumsy waltz.*]

LAURA: Oh, my!

JIM: Ha-ha!

LAURA: Oh, my goodness!

JIM: Ha-ha-ha!

[They suddenly bump into the table, and the glass piece on it falls to the floor. Jim stops the dance.]

What did we hit on?

LAURA: Table.

JIM: Did something fall off it? I think—

LAURA: Yes.

JIM: I hope that it wasn't the little glass horse with the horn!

LAURA: Yes. [*She stoops to pick it up.*]

JIM: Aw, aw, aw. It is broken?

LAURA: Now it is just like all the other horses.

JIM: It's lost its—

LAURA: Horn! It doesn't matter. Maybe it's a blessing in disguise.

JIM: You'll never forgive me. I bet that that was your favorite piece of glass.

LAURA: I don't have favorites much. It's no tragedy, Freckles. Glass breaks so easily. No matter how careful you are. The traffic jars the shelves and things fall off them.

JIM: Still I'm awfully sorry that I was the cause.

LAURA [*smiling*]: I'll just imagine he had an operation. The horn was removed to make him feel less—freakish!

[They both laugh.]

Now he will feel more at home with the other horses, the ones that don't have horns.

JIM: Ha-ha, that's very funny! [*Suddenly he is serious.*] I'm glad to see that you have a sense of humor. You know—you're—well—very different! Surprisingly different from anyone else I know! [*His voice becomes soft and hesitant with a genuine feeling.*] Do you mind me telling you that?

[Laura is abashed beyond speech.]

I mean it in a nice way—

[Laura nods shyly, looking away.]

You make me feel sort of—I don't know how to put it! I'm usually pretty good at expressing things, but—this is something that I don't know how to say!

[Laura touches her throat and clears it—turns the broken unicorn in her hands. His voice becomes softer.]

Has anyone ever told you that you were pretty?

[There is a pause, and the music rises slightly. Laura looks up slowly, with wonder, and shakes her head.]

Well, you are! In a very different way from anyone else. And all the nicer because of the difference, too.

[His voice becomes low and husky. Laura turns away, nearly faint with the novelty of her emotions.]

I wish that you were my sister. I'd teach you to have some confidence in yourself. The different people are not like other people, but being different is nothing to be ashamed of. Because other people are not such wonderful people. They're one hundred times one thousand. You're one times one! They walk all over the earth. You just stay here. They're common as—weeds, but—you—well, you're—*Blue Roses!*

[Image on screen: Blue Roses.]

[The music changes.]

LAURA: But blue is wrong for—roses. . . .

JIM: It's right for you! You're—pretty!

LAURA: In what respect am I pretty?

JIM: In all respects—believe me! Your eyes—your hair—are pretty! Your hands are pretty! [*He catches hold of her hand.*] You think I'm making this up because I'm invited to dinner and have to be nice. Oh, I could do that! I could put on an act for you, Laura, and say lots of things without being very sincere. But this time I am. I'm talking to you sincerely. I happened to notice you had this inferiority complex that keeps you from feeling comfortable with people. Somebody needs to build your confidence up and make you proud instead of shy and turning away and—blushing. Somebody—ought to—*kiss* you, Laura!

[His hand slips slowly up her arm to her shoulder as the music swells tumultuously. He suddenly turns her about and kisses her on the lips. When he releases her, Laura sinks on the sofa with a bright, dazed look. Jim backs away and fishes in his pocket for a cigarette.]

[Legend on screen: "A souvenir."]

Stumblejohn!

[He lights the cigarette, avoiding her look. There is a peal of girlish laughter from Amanda in the kitchenette. Laura slowly raises and opens her hand. It still contains the little broken glass animal. She looks at it with a tender, bewildered expression.]

Stumblejohn! I shouldn't have done that—that was way off the beam. You don't smoke, do you?

[She looks up, smiling, not hearing the question. He sits beside her rather gingerly. She looks at him speechlessly—waiting. He coughs decorously and moves a little farther aside as he considers the situation and senses her feelings, dimly, with perturbation. He speaks gently.]

Would you—care for a—mint?

[She doesn't seem to hear him but her look grows brighter even.]

Peppermint? Life Saver? My pocket's a regular drugstore—wherever I go. . . . [*He pops a mint in his mouth. Then he gulps and decides to make a clean breast of it. He speaks slowly and gingerly.*] Laura, you know, if I had a sister like you, I'd do the same thing as Tom. I'd bring out fellows and—introduce her to them. The right type of boys—of a type to—appreciate her. Only—well—he made a mistake about me. Maybe I've got no call to be saying this. That may not have been the idea in having me over. But what if it was? There's nothing wrong about that. The only trouble is that in my case—I'm not in a situation to—do the right thing. I can't take down your number and say I'll phone. I can't call up next week and—ask for a date. I thought I had better explain the situation in case you—misunderstood it and—I hurt your feelings. . . .

[There is a pause. Slowly, very slowly, Laura's look changes, her eyes returning slowly from his to the glass figure in her palm. Amanda utters another gay laugh in the kitchenette.]

LAURA [*faintly*]: You—won't—call again?

JIM: No, Laura, I can't. [*He rises from the sofa.*] As I was just explaining, I've—got strings on me. Laura, I've—been going steady! I go out all the time with a girl named Betty. She's a home-girl like you, and Catholic, and Irish, and in a great many ways we—get along fine. I met her last summer on a moonlight boat trip up the river to Alton, on the *Majestic*. Well—right away from the start it was—love!

[Legend: Love!]

[Laura sways slightly forward and grips the arm of the sofa. He fails to notice, now enrapt in his own comfortable being.]

Being in love has made a new man of me!

[Leaning stiffly forward, clutching the arm of the sofa, Laura struggles visibly with her storm. But Jim is oblivious; she is a long way off.]

The power of love is really pretty tremendous! Love is something that—changes the whole world, Laura!

[The storm abates a little and Laura leans back. He notices her again.]

It happened that Betty's aunt took sick, she got a wire and had to go to Centralia. So Tom—when he asked me to dinner—I naturally just accepted the invitation, not knowing that you—that he—that I—[*He stops awkwardly.*] Huh—I'm a stumblejohn!

[He flops back on the sofa. The holy candles on the altar of Laura's face have been snuffed out. There is a look of almost infinite desolation. Jim glances at her uneasily.]

I wish that you would—say something.

[She bites her lip which was trembling and then bravely smiles. She opens her hand again on the broken glass figure. Then she gently takes his hand and raises it level with her own. She carefully places the unicorn in the palm of his hand, then pushes his fingers closed upon it.]

What are you—doing that for? You want me to have him? Laura?

[She nods.]

What for?

LAURA: A—souvenir. . . .

[She rises unsteadily and crouches beside the Victrola to wind it up.]

[Legend on screen: "Things have a way of turning out so badly!" Or image: "Gentleman caller waving goodbye—gaily."]

[At this moment Amanda rushes brightly back into the living room. She bears a pitcher of fruit punch in an old-fashioned cut-glass pitcher, and a plate of macaroons. The plate has a gold border and poppies painted on it.]

AMANDA: Well, well, well! Isn't the air delightful after the shower! I've made you children a little liquid refreshment.

[She turns gaily to Jim.] Jim, do you know that song about lemonade?

"Lemonade, lemonade
Made in the shade and stirred with a spade—
Good enough for any old maid!"

JIM [*uneasily*]: Ha-ha! No—I never heard it.

AMANDA: Why, Laura! You look so serious!

JIM: We were having a serious conversation.

AMANDA: Good! Now you're better acquainted!

JIM [*uncertainly*]: Ha-ha! Yes.

AMANDA: You modern young people are much more serious-minded than my generation. I was so gay as a girl!

JIM: You haven't changed, Mrs. Wingfield.

AMANDA: Tonight I'm rejuvenated! The gaiety of the occasion, Mr. O'Connor! [*She tosses her head with a peal of laughter, spilling some lemonade.*] Oooo! I'm baptizing myself!

JIM: Here—let me—

AMANDA [*setting the pitcher down*]: There now. I discovered we had some maraschino cherries. I dumped them in, juice and all!

JIM: You shouldn't have gone to that trouble, Mrs. Wingfield.

AMANDA: Trouble, trouble? Why, it was loads of fun! Didn't you hear me cutting up in the kitchen? I bet your ears were burning! I told Tom how outdone with him I was for keeping you to himself so long a time! He should have brought you over much, much sooner! Well, now that you've found your way, I want you to be a very frequent caller! Not just occasional but all the time. Oh, we're going to have a lot of gay times together! I see them coming! Mmm, just breathe that air! So fresh, and the moon's so pretty! I'll skip back out—I know where my place is when young folks are having a—serious conversation!

JIM: Oh, don't go out, Mrs. Wingfield. The fact of the matter is I've got to be going.

AMANDA: Going, now? You're joking! Why, it's only the shank of the evening, Mr. O'Connor.

JIM: Well, you know how it is.

AMANDA: You mean you're a young workingman and have to keep workingmen's hours. We'll let you off early tonight. But only on the condition that next time you stay later. What's the best night for you? Isn't Saturday night the best night for you workingmen?

JIM: I have a couple of time-clocks to punch, Mrs. Wingfield. One at morning, another one at night!

AMANDA: My, but you *are* ambitious! You work at night, too?

JIM: No, Ma'am, not work but—Betty!

[He crosses deliberately to pick up his hat. The band at the Paradise Dance Hall goes into a tender waltz.]

AMANDA: Betty? Betty? Who's—Betty!

[There is an ominous cracking sound in the sky.]

JIM: Oh, just a girl. The girl I go steady with!

[He smiles charmingly. The sky falls.]

[Legend: "The Sky Falls."]

AMANDA [*a long-drawn exhalation*]: Ohhhh . . . Is it a serious romance, Mr. O'-Connor?

JIM: We're going to be married the second Sunday in June.

AMANDA: Ohhhh—how nice! Tom didn't mention that you were engaged to be married.

JIM: The cat's not out of the bag at the warehouse yet. You know how they are. They call you Romeo and stuff like that. [*He stops at the oval mirror to put on his hat. He carefully shapes the brim and the crown to give a discreetly dashing effect.*] It's been a wonderful evening, Mrs. Wingfield. I guess this is what they mean by Southern hospitality.

AMANDA: It really wasn't anything at all.

JIM: I hope it don't seem like I'm rushing off. But I promised Betty I'd pick her up at the Wabash depot, an' by the time I get my jalopy down there her train'll be in. Some women are pretty upset if you keep 'em waiting.

AMANDA: Yes, I know—the tyranny of women! [*She extends her hand.*] Good-bye, Mr. O'Connor. I wish you luck—and happiness—and success! All three of them, and so does Laura! Don't you, Laura?

LAURA: Yes!

JIM [*taking Laura's hand*]: Goodbye, Laura. I'm certainly going to treasure that souvenir. And don't you forget the good advice I gave you. [*He raises his voice to a cheery shout.*] So long, Shakespeare! Thanks again, ladies. Good night!

[He grins and ducks jauntily out. Still barely grimacing, Amanda closes the door on the gentleman caller. Then she turns back to the room with a puzzled expression. She and Laura don't dare to face each other. Laura crouches beside the Victrola to wind it.]

AMANDA [*faintly*]: Things have a way of turning out so badly. I don't believe that I would play the Victrola. Well, well—well! Our gentleman caller was engaged to be married! [*She raises her voice.*] Tom!

TOM [*from the kitchenette*]: Yes, Mother?

AMANDA: Come in here a minute. I want to tell you something awfully funny.

TOM [*entering with a macaroon and a glass of the lemonade*]: Has the gentleman caller gotten away already?

AMANDA: The gentleman caller has made an early departure. What a wonderful joke you played on us!

TOM: How do you mean?

AMANDA: You didn't mention that he was engaged to be married.

TOM: Jim? Engaged?

AMANDA: That's what he just informed us.

TOM: I'll be jiggered! I didn't know about that.

AMANDA: That seems very peculiar.

TOM: What's peculiar about it?

AMANDA: Didn't you call him your best friend down at the warehouse?

TOM: He is, but how did I know?

AMANDA: It seems extremely peculiar that you wouldn't know your best friend was going to be married!

TOM: The warehouse is where I work, not where I know things about people!

AMANDA: You don't know things anywhere! You live in a dream; you manufacture illusions!

[He crosses to the door.]

Where are you going?

TOM: I'm going to the movies.

AMANDA: That's right, now that you've had us make such fools of ourselves. The effort, the preparations, all the expense! The new floor lamp, the rug, the clothes for Laura! All for what? To entertain some other girl's fiancé! Go to the movies, go! Don't think about us, a mother deserted, an unmarried sister who's crippled and has no job! Don't let anything interfere with your selfish pleasure! Just go, go, go—to the movies!

TOM: All right, I will! The more you shout about my selfishness to me the quicker I'll go, and I won't go to the movies!

AMANDA: Go, then! Go to the moon—you selfish dreamer!

[Tom smashes his glass on the floor. He plunges out on the fire escape, slamming the door. Laura screams in fright. The dance-hall music becomes louder. Tom stands on the fire escape, gripping the rail. The moon breaks through the storm clouds, illuminating his face.]

[Legend on screen: "And so goodbye . . ."]

[Tom's closing speech is timed with what is happening inside the house. We see, as though through soundproof glass, that Amanda appears to be making a comforting speech to Laura, who is huddled upon the sofa. Now that we cannot hear the mother's speech, her silliness is gone and she has dignity and tragic beauty. Laura's hair hides her face until, at the end of the speech, she lifts her head to smile at her mother. Amanda's gestures are slow and graceful, almost dancelike, as she comforts her daughter. At the end of her speech she glances a moment at the father's picture—then withdraws through the portieres. At the close of Tom's speech, Laura blows out the candles, ending the play.]

TOM: I didn't go to the moon, I went much further—for time is the longest distance between two places. Not long after that I was fired for writing a poem on the lid of a shoe-box. I left Saint Louis. I descended the steps of this fire escape for a last time and followed, from then on, in my father's footsteps, attempting to find in motion what was lost in space. I traveled around a great deal. The cities swept about me like dead leaves, leaves that were brightly colored but torn away from the branches. I would have stopped, but I was pursued by something. It always came upon me unawares, taking me altogether by surprise. Perhaps it was a familiar bit of music. Perhaps it was only a piece of transparent glass. Perhaps I am walking along a street at night, in some strange city, before I have found companions. I pass the lighted window of a shop where perfume is sold. The window is filled with pieces of colored glass, tiny transparent bottles in delicate colors, like bits of a shattered rainbow. Then all at once my sister touches my shoulder. I turn around and look into her eyes. Oh, Laura, Laura, I tried to leave you behind me, but I am more faithful than I intended to be! I reach for a cigarette, I cross the street, I run into the movies or a bar, I buy a drink, I speak to the nearest stranger—anything that can blow your candles out!

[Laura bends over the candles.]

For nowadays the world is lit by lightning! Blow out your candles, Laura—and so goodbye. . . .

[She blows the candles out.]

1945

Theodore Roethke 1908–1963

Theodore Roethke died at the height of his creative powers, but fame and honor had come to him well before his death. After receiving Guggenheim Fellowships in 1946 and 1950, he was awarded a Pulitzer Prize in 1954 for The Waking: Poems, *1933–1953 (1953).* Words for the Wind *(1958) received a Bollingen Prize in 1958 and the Edna St. Vincent Millay Prize in 1959. And acclaim for his work continued after his death:* The Far Field, *published posthumously in 1964, won the National Book Award in 1965. Since the publication of his* Collected Poems *(1966), and as critics have looked more deeply into Roethke's poems, his reputation has continued to rise.*

Roethke was born in Saginaw, Michigan, where a dingy industrial atmosphere contrasted sharply with the loveliness of nearby lakes and streams, woods and farmlands—scenes that aroused in him a mystical reverence for nature. His father was a florist, and the strange paradoxes Roethke perceived in the plant world of his father's greenhouse—where death and life mingled in a weird, grotesque kind of beauty—helped shape his poetic sensibility and provided him with a rich source of imagery.

After taking his B.A. in 1929 at the University of Michigan, Roethke began a career in college and university teaching that took him first to Lafayette College in Pennsylvania, from 1931 to 1935, then, after he completed his M.A. at Michigan in 1936, to Pennsylvania State College, where he remained until 1943. During World War II he taught at Bennington College, and in 1947 he took a position at the University of Washington, Seattle, where he remained for the rest of his life.

Roethke's development as a poet began in his early twenties, soon after he graduated from the University of Michigan, but he was well into his thirties when his first volume, Open House, *appeared in 1941. His poems may be divided broadly into two groups: first, those that are orthodox in form, rational in theme, ironic in tone; and second, poems that utilize free forms, reflecting the influence of Whitman ("Be with me, Whitman, maker of catalogues") and the romantic transcendentalism of Emerson. He shared Emerson's belief in the inherent presence of spirit in nature, but he also saw the dark side of nature that Emerson tended to explain away. The impact of T. S. Eliot on Roethke was chiefly formal and technical, evident particularly in Roethke's efforts to effect "something other than the usual in old forms." From the whimsy of Roethke's delightful "Nonsense Poems" to the irony of the pieces in* The Far Field, *his vision of life and poetic style remained uniquely his own.*

FURTHER READING: *On the Poet and His Craft: Selected Prose of Theodore Roethke,* ed. R. Mills, 1965; *Selected Letters of Theodore Roethke,* ed. R. Mills, 1968; A. Seagar, *The Glass House: The Life of Theodore Roethke,* 1968; *Straw from Fire: From the Notebooks of Theodore Roethke,* ed. D. Wagoner, 1972; G. Wolff, *Theodore Roethke,* 1981; N. Chaney, *Theodore Roethke: The Poetics of Wonder,* 1981; L. Ross-Bryant, *Theodore Roethke: Poetry of the Earth,* 1981; N. Bowers, *Theodore Roethke: The Journey from I to Otherwise,* 1982; R. Stiffler, *Theodore Roethke: The Poet and His Critics,* 1986; W. Kalaidjian, *Understanding Theodore Roethke,* 1987; *Theodore Roethke,* ed. H. Bloom, 1988; P. Balakian, *Theodore Roethke's Far Fields: The Evolution of His Poetry,* 1989. D. Bogen, *A Necessary Order: Theodore Roethke and the Writing Process,* 1991; R. Kusch, *My Toughest Mentor: Theodore Roethke and William Carlos Williams,* 1999.

TEXT: *The Collected Poems of Theodore Roethke,* 1966.

DOLOR

I have known the inexorable sadness of pencils,
Neat in their boxes, dolor of pad and paper-weight,
All the misery of manila folders and mucilage,
Desolation in immaculate public places,
Lonely reception room, lavatory, switchboard,
The unalterable pathos of basin and pitcher,
Ritual of multigraph, paper-clip, comma,
Endless duplication of lives and objects.
And I have seen dust from the walls of institutions,
Finer than flour, alive, more dangerous than silica,
Sift, almost invisible, through long afternoons of tedium,
Dropping a fine film on nails and delicate eyebrows,
Glazing the pale hair, the duplicate grey standard faces.
1943, 1948

OPEN HOUSE

My secrets cry aloud.
I have no need for tongue.
My heart keeps open house,
My doors are widely swung.
An epic of the eyes
My love, with no disguise.

My truths are all foreknown,
This anguish self-revealed.
I'm naked to the bone,
With nakedness my shield.
Myself is what I wear:
I keep the spirit spare.

The anger will endure,
The deed will speak the truth
In language strict and pure.
I stop the lying mouth:
Rage warps my clearest cry
To witless agony.
1936 1936, 1941

CUTTINGS

Sticks-in-a-drowse droop over sugary loam,
Their intricate stem-fur dries;
But still the delicate slips keep coaxing up water;
The small cells bulge;

One nub of growth
Nudges a sand-crumb loose,
Pokes through a musty sheath
Its pale tendrilous horn.
1943–1944 1948

CUTTINGS (LATER)

This urge, wrestle, resurrection of dry sticks,
Cut stems struggling to put down feet,
What saint strained so much,
Rose on such lopped limbs to a new life?

I can hear, underground, that sucking and sobbing,
In my veins, in my bones I feel it,—
The small waters seeping upward,
The tight grains parting at last.
When sprouts break out,
Slippery as fish,
I quail, lean to beginnings, sheath-wet.
1943–1944 1948

ROOT CELLAR

Nothing would sleep in that cellar, dank as a ditch,
Bulbs broke out of boxes hunting for chinks in the dark,
Shoots dangled and drooped,
Lolling obscenely from mildewed crates,
Hung down long yellow evil necks, like tropical snakes.
And what a congress of stinks!—
Roots ripe as old bait,
Pulpy stems, rank, silo-rich,
Leaf-mold, manure, lime, piled against slippery planks.
Nothing would give up life:
Even the dirt kept breathing a small breath.
1943 1943, 1948

MY PAPA'S WALTZ

The whiskey on your breath
Could make a small boy dizzy;
But I hung on like death:
Such waltzing was not easy.

We romped until the pans
Slid from the kitchen shelf;
My mother's countenance
Could not unfrown itself.

The hand that held my wrist
Was battered on one knuckle;
At every step you missed
My right ear scraped a buckle.

You beat time on my head
With a palm caked hard by dirt,
Then waltzed me off to bed
Still clinging to your shirt.
1942 1942, 1948

IN A DARK TIME

I

In a dark time, the eye begins to see:
I meet my shadow in the deepening shade;
I hear my echo in the echoing wood,
A lord of nature weeping to a tree.
I live between the heron and the wren,
Beasts of the hill and serpents of the den.

II

What's madness but nobility of soul
At odds with circumstance? The day's on fire!
I know the purity of pure despair,
My shadow pinned against a sweating wall.
That place among the rocks—is it a cave
Or winding path? The edge is what I have.

III

A steady storm of correspondences!—
A night flowing with birds, a ragged moon,
And in broad day the midnight come again!
A man goes far to find out what he is—
Death of the self in a long tearless night,
All natural shapes blazing unnatural light.

IV

Dark, dark my light, and darker my desire.
My soul, like some heat-maddened fly,
Keeps buzzing at the sill. Which I is *I*?
A fallen man, I climb out of my fear.
The mind enters itself, and God the mind,
And one is One, free in the tearing wind.
1958 1960, 1963

Randall Jarrell 1914–1965

Randall Jarrell was renowned as a teacher, a critic, and a poet. He spent most of his adult life as a professor of literature and once remarked, "If I were a rich man, I would pay money for the privilege of being able to teach." His critical writings were renowned for their savage dissections of poetic mediocrity and their enthusiastic praise of poetic skill. Of Jarrell's own poetic talent, the American poet Robert Lowell observed: "His gifts, both by nature and by a lifetime of hard dedication and growth, were wit, pathos, and brilliance of intelligence. These qualities, in themselves, were often so well employed that he became, I think, the most heartbreaking English poet of his generation."

Jarrell spent his early years in California living with his paternal grandparents and great-grandparents. When he was twelve he moved to Tennessee, where he attended high school. Following his graduation, he was enrolled in a secretarial school to learn bookkeeping and shorthand in order to enter his uncle's candy firm. But Jarrell's indifference to business studies was so profound that his uncle finally agreed to send him to college instead. At Vanderbilt University he edited the literary magazine and studied under the poet-critic John Crowe Ransom. In 1939, Jarrell took an M.A. at Vanderbilt. He taught English at Kenyon College and at the University of Texas, and from 1942 to 1946 he served in the U.S. Army Air Force. From his military experiences came some of his finest writing, poems dealing with flying and the terrors of aerial warfare. In 1945, while still in the army, he published a volume of poems, Little Friend, Little Friend. *After his discharge from the Air Force, in 1946, he served for a short period as the literary editor of the* Nation. *In 1947, he accepted a position at the Women's College of the University of North Carolina, where he remained for the rest of his life.*

Jarrell wrote six volumes of poetry, a novel: Pictures from an Institution *(1954), and four volumes of critical essays:* Poetry and the Age *(1953),* A Sad Heart at the Supermarket *(1962),* The Third Book of Criticism *(1969), and* Kipling, Auden and Co., Essays and Reviews, 1935–1964 *(1980). Some of Jarrell's poetry was painfully realistic, some so extravagantly allusive as to resist interpretation. His dominant theme is change—change affecting women, children, and men in war and peace. His recurring motifs are journeys, dreams, fears, and death. He described human lives that fail to fulfill ideals, and he wrote of isolated people, suffering from loss and grieving at evil, men and women who could respond to life's agonies only by attempting, but failing, to escape them.*

FURTHER READING: *Randall Jarrell's Letters,* ed. M. Jarrell, 1985; *Randall Jarrell, 1914–1965,* ed. R. Lowell, P. Taylor, and R. Warren, 1967; K. Shapiro, *Randall Jarrell,* 1967; *The Achievement of Randall Jarrell,* ed. F. Hoffman, 1970; S. Ferguson, *The Poetry of Randall Jarrell,* 1971; M. Rosenthal, *Randall Jarrell,* 1972; H. Hagenbuchle, *The Black Goddess: A Study of the Archetypal Feminine in the Poetry of Randall Jarrell,* 1975; B. Quinn, *Randall Jarrell,* 1981; *Critical Essays on Randall Jarrell,* ed. S. Ferguson, 1983; J. Bryant, *Understanding Randall Jarrell,* 1986; W. Pritchard, *Randall Jarrell: A Literary Life,* 1990; M. Jarrell, *Remembering Randall: A Memoir of Poet, Critic, and Teacher Randall Jarrell,* 1999; S. Burt, *Randall Jarrell and His Age,* 2002; *Randall Jarrell on W. H. Auden,* ed. S. Burt, 2005.

TEXT: *The Complete Poems,* 1969.

LOSSES

It was not dying: everybody died.
It was not dying: we had died before
In the routine crashes—and our fields
Called up the papers, wrote home to our folks,
And the rates rose, all because of us.
We died on the wrong page of the almanac,[1]
Scattered on mountains fifty miles away;
Diving on haystacks, fighting with a friend,
We blazed up on the lines[2] we never saw.
We died like aunts or pets or foreigners.
(When we left high school nothing else had died
For us to figure we had died like.)

In our new planes, with our new crews, we bombed
The ranges by the desert or the shore,
Fired at towed targets, waited for our scores—
And turned into replacements and woke up
One morning, over England, operational.

[1]I.e., they crashed because they consulted the wrong page of *The Air Almanac* and thus used incorrect navigation data to establish their positions. Jarrell operated a training machine for navigators during World War II.
[2]Electric power lines.

It wasn't different: but if we died
It was not an accident but a mistake
(But an easy one for anyone to make).
We read our mail and counted up our missions—
In bombers named for girls, we burned
The cities we had learned about in school—
Till our lives wore out; our bodies lay among
The people we had killed and never seen.
When we lasted long enough they gave us medals;
When we died they said, "Our casualties were low."
They said, "Here are the maps": we burned the cities.
It was not dying—no, not ever dying;
But the night I died I dreamed that I was dead,
And the cities said to me: "Why are you dying?
We are satisfied, if you are; but why did I die?"

1944, 1945

THE DEATH OF THE BALL TURRET GUNNER[1]

From my mother's sleep I fell into the State,
And I hunched in its belly till my wet fur froze.
Six miles from earth, loosed from its dream of life,
I woke to black flak[2] and the nightmare fighters.
When I died they washed me out of the turret with a hose.

1945

A GIRL IN A LIBRARY[1]

An object among dreams, you sit here with your shoes off
And curl your legs up under you; your eyes
Close for a moment, your face moves toward sleep. . .

[1]"A ball turret was a plexiglass sphere set into the belly of a B-17 or B-24 and inhabited by two .50 caliber machine-guns and one man, a short small man. When this gunner tracked with his machine-guns a fighter attacking his bomber from below, he revolved with the turret; hunched upside-down in his little sphere, he looked like the foetus in the womb. The fighters which attacked him were armed with cannon firing explosive shells. The hose was a steam hose."—Jarrell's note.

[2]Anti-aircraft fire.

[1]"'A Girl in a Library' is a poem about the New World and the Old: about a girl, a student of Home Economics and Physical Education, who has fallen asleep in the library of a Southern college; about a woman who looks out of one book, Pushkin's *Eugene Onegin,* at this girl asleep among so many; and about the I of the poem, a man somewhere between the two. A *blind date* is an unknown someone you accompany to something; if he promises to come for you and doesn't, he has *stood you up.* The Corn King and the Spring Queen went by many names; in the beginning they were the man and woman who, after ruling for a time, were torn to pieces and scattered over the fields in order that the grain might grow. . . ."—Jarrell's note.

You are very human.
But my mind, gone out in tenderness,
Shrinks from its object with a thoughtful sigh.
This is a waist the spirit breaks its arm on.
The gods themselves, against you, struggle in vain.[2]
This broad low strong-boned brow; these heavy eyes;
These calves, grown muscular with certainties;
This nose, three medium-sized pink strawberries
—But I exaggerate. In a little you will leave:
I'll hear, half squeal, half shriek, your laugh of greeting—
Then, *decrescendo,*[3] bars of that strange speech
In which each sound sets out to seek each other,
Murders its own father, marries its own mother,
And ends as one grand transcendental vowel.

(Yet for all I know, the Egyptian Helen[4] spoke so.)
As I look, the world contracts around you:
I see Brünnhilde[5] had brown braids and glasses
She used for studying; Salome[6] straight brown bangs,
A calf's brown eyes, and sturdy light-brown limbs
Dusted with cinnamon, an apple-dumpling's . . .
Many a beast has gnawn a leg off and got free,
Many a dolphin curved up from Necessity[7]—
The trap has closed about you, and you sleep.
If someone questioned you, *What doest thou here?*[8]
You'd knit your brows like an orangoutang
(But not so sadly; not so thoughtfully)
And answer with a pure heart, guilelessly:
I'm studying. . . .[9]
If only you were not!
Assignments,
recipes,
the *Official Rulebook*
Of Basketball—ah, let them go; you needn't mind.
The soul has no assignments, neither cooks
Nor referees: it wastes its time.
It wastes its time.

[2]Jarrell's version of the phrase, "Against stupidity the very gods/Themselves contend in vain," from *The Maid of Orleans* (1801), by the German poet Johann Friedrich von Schiller (1759–1805).

[3]Decreasing in force or sound.

[4]According to one version of the legend, Helen of Troy was carried off to Egypt; it was her phantom that accompanied Paris to Troy.

[5]Daughter of the Teutonic god Wotan, portrayed in Richard Wagner's opera cycle, *The Ring of the Nibelungs* (1869–1874). She is put into a deep sleep until awakened by a kiss from the hero Siegfried.

[6]Temptress, niece of King Herod, who won the head of John the Baptist as a reward for her dancing (Matthew 14:6–11).

[7]The philosophical doctrine that the actions of all things are inevitably dictated by their being or nature.

[8]Words spoken by the Lord to Elijah, who is then moved to higher levels of perception (I Kings 19:9).

[9]Here and throughout the ellipsis points are Jarrell's.

Here in this enclave there are centuries
For you to waste: the short and narrow stream
Of Life meanders into a thousand valleys
Of all that was, or might have been, or is to be.
The books, just leafed through, whisper endlessly . . .
Yet it is hard. One sees in your blurred eyes
The "uneasy half-soul" Kipling[10] saw in dogs'.
One sees it, in the glass, in one's own eyes.
In rooms alone, in galleries, in libraries,
In tears, in searchings of the heart, in staggering joys
We memorize once more our old creation,
Humanity: with what yawns the unwilling
Flesh puts on its spirit, O my sister!

So many dreams! And not one troubles
Your sleep of life? no self stares shadowily
From these worn hexahedrons, beckoning
With false smiles, tears? . . .
                    Meanwhile Tatyana
Larina[11] (gray eyes nickel with the moonlight
That falls through the willows onto Lensky's tomb;
Now young and shy, now old and cold and sure)
Asks, smiling: "But what is she dreaming of, fat thing?"
I answer: She's not fat. She isn't dreaming.
She purrs or laps or runs, all in her sleep;
Believes, awake, that she is beautiful;
She never dreams.
                    Those sunrise-colored clouds
Around man's head—that inconceivable enchantment
From which, at sunset, we come back to life
To find our graves dug, families dead, selves dying:
Of all this, Tanya,[12] she is innocent.
For nineteen years she's faced reality:
They look alike already.
                    They say, man wouldn't be
The best thing in this world—and isn't he?—
If he were not too good for it. But she
—She's good enough for it.
                    And yet sometimes
Her sturdy form, in its pink strapless formal,
Is as if bathed in moonlight—modulated
Into a form of joy, a Lydian mode;[13]

[10]Rudyard Kipling (1865–1936), English poet and short story writer. His poem "Supplication of a Black Aberdeen" portrays a dog's "dim, distressed half-soul."

[11]A woman of beauty and sophistication in the verse drama *Eugene Onegin* (1833), by the Russian poet Alexander Pushkin (1799–1837), where she is saddened by the death of her friend Vladimir Lensky, killed in a duel.

[12]Diminutive form of "Tatyana."

[13]One of the modes of ancient Greek music, rich and sensual.

This Wooden Mean's[14] a kind, furred animal
That speaks, in the Wild of things, delighting riddles
To the soul that listens, trusting . . .
                                        Poor senseless Life:
When, in the last light sleep of dawn, the messenger
Comes with his message, you will not awake.
He'll give his feathery whistle, shake you hard,
You'll look with wide eyes at the dewy yard
And dream, with calm slow factuality:
"Today's Commencement. My bachelor's degree
In Home Ec., my doctorate of philosophy
In Phys. Ed.
                    [Tanya, they won't even *scan*]
Are waiting for me. . . ."
                                        Oh, Tatyana,
The Angel comes: better to squawk like a chicken
Than to say with truth, "But I'm a *good* girl,"
And Meet his Challenge with a last firm strange
Uncomprehending smile; and—then, then!—see
The blind date that has stood you up: your life.
(For all this, if it isn't perhaps, life,
Has yet, at least, a language of its own
Different from the books'; worse than the books'.)
And yet, the ways we miss our lives are life.
Yet . . . yet . . .
                    to have one's life add up to *yet!*

You sigh a shuddering sigh. Tatyana murmurs,
"Don't cry, little peasant"; leaves us with a swift
"Good-bye, good-bye . . . Ah, don't think ill of me . . ."
Your eyes open: you sit here thoughtlessly.
I love you—and yet—and yet—I love you.

Don't cry, little peasant. Sit and dream.
One comes, a finger's width beneath your skin,
To the braided maidens[15] singing as they spin;
There sound the shepherd's pipe, the watchman's rattle
Across the short dark distance of the years.
I am a thought of yours: and yet, you do not think . . .
The firelight of a long, blind, dreaming story
Lingers upon your lips; and I have seen
Firm, fixed forever in your closing eyes,
The Corn King beckoning to his Spring Queen.
                                        1951, 1955

[14]A contemptuous contrast to the Golden Mean, the philosophical doctrine that virtue is achieved through moderation and use of the intellect.

[15]The "braided maidens," and the shepherd and watchman alluded to on the following line, are minor characters in Wagnerian opera. Insignificant and dull-witted, they are unaware of what occurs around them.

IN MONTECITO

In a fashionable suburb of Santa Barbara,[1]
Montecito, there visited me one night at midnight
A scream with breasts. As it hung there in the sweet air
That was always the right temperature, the contractors
Who had undertaken to dismantle it, stripped off
The lips, let the air out of the breasts.
People disappear
Even in Montecito. Greenie Taliaferro,[2]
In her white maillot,[3] her good figure almost firm,
Her old pepper-and-salt hair stripped by the hairdresser
To nothing and dyed platinum—Greenie has left her Bentley.[4]
They have thrown away her electric toothbrush, someone else slips
The key into the lock of her safety-deposit box
At the Crocker-Anglo Bank; her seat at the cricket matches
Is warmed by buttocks less delectable than hers.
Greenie's girdle is empty.
A scream hangs there in the night:
They strip off the lips, let the air out of the breasts,
And Greenie has gone into the Greater Montecito
That surrounds Montecito like the echo of a scream.

1965

Elizabeth Bishop 1911–1979

Elizabeth Bishop was born in Worcester, Massachusetts, and raised in Nova Scotia, Canada, and Boston, Massachusetts. She attended Vassar College, where she majored in English literature, and in her graduation year, 1934, she met Marianne Moore, whose poetry of closely observed detail was a significant influence on Bishop's work. She traveled widely in Europe and South America (from 1952 to 1969 she lived in Brazil), and some of the themes and details of her poetry are responses to her travels and to her early childhood experiences in New England and Canada.

Her first volume, North and South, *appeared in 1946. For her* Poems *(1955) she received a Pulitzer Prize. A third volume of poetry,* Questions of Travel *(1965), was followed by* The Complete Poems *(1969), which received a National Book Award. Her last book of poems was* Geography III *(1976). In her poetry, Bishop often functioned as an impersonal observer capable of detachment and understanding at the same time. She used subtle rhythms, unlikely rhymes, and the impressionist's technique of implication and suggestion. She had a painter's eye for surfaces and appearances, yet her portrayals of the stark landscapes of the matter-of-fact world frequently evolved into dreamlike*

[1]In California. [2]Pronounced "Tolliver."
[3]A tight-fitting gymnastic suit of stretch-knit fabric. [4]An expensive, English automobile.

sequences, contrasting the commonsense world of everyday reality and the world of impressions and the imagination.

FURTHER READING: *Elizabeth Bishop and Her Art,* ed. L. Schwartz and S. Estes, 1983; *The Collected Prose,* 1984; T. Travisano, *Elizabeth Bishop: Her Artistic Development,* 1988; R. Parker, *The Unbeliever: The Poetry of Elizabeth Bishop,* 1988; B. Costello, *Elizabeth Bishop: Questions of Mastery,* 1991; L. Goldensohn, *Elizabeth Bishop: The Biography of a Poetry,* 1992; C. Doreski, *Elizabeth Bishop: The Restraints of Language,* 1993; *One Art: Letters by Elizabeth Bishop,* ed. R. Giroux, 1994; G. Fountain and B. Brazeau, *Remembering Elizabeth Bishop,* 1994; S. McCabe, *Elizabeth Bishop: Her Poetics of Loss,* 1994; M. Lombardi, *The Body and the Song,* 1995; D. Kalstone, *Becoming a Poet,* 1997; B. Miller, *Elizabeth Bishop: Life and the Memory of It,* 1997; *Divisions of the Heart: Elizabeth Bishop and the Art of Memory and Place,* ed. S. Barry, G. Davies, and P. Sanger, 2001; *Elizabeth Bishop,* ed. H. Bloom, 2002; K. Fortuny, *Elizabeth Bishop: The Art of Travel,* 2003.

TEXT: *Elizabeth Bishop: The Complete Poems, 1927–1979,* 1983.

A MIRACLE FOR BREAKFAST

At six o'clock we were waiting for coffee,
waiting for coffee and the charitable crumb
that was going to be served from a certain balcony,
—like kings of old, or like a miracle.
It was still dark. One foot of the sun
steadied itself on a long ripple in the river.

The first ferry of the day had just crossed the river.
It was so cold we hoped that the coffee
would be very hot, seeing that the sun
was not going to warm us; and that the crumb
would be a loaf each, buttered, by a miracle.
At seven a man stepped out on the balcony.

He stood for a minute alone on the balcony
looking over our heads toward the river.
A servant handed him the makings of a miracle,
consisting of one lone cup of coffee
and one roll, which he proceeded to crumb,
his head, so to speak, in the clouds—along with the sun.

Was the man crazy? What under the sun
was he trying to do, up there on his balcony!
Each man received one rather hard crumb,
which some flicked scornfully into the river,
and, in a cup, one drop of the coffee.
Some of us stood around, waiting for the miracle.

I can tell what I saw next; it was not a miracle.
A beautiful villa stood in the sun
and from its doors came the smell of hot coffee.

In front, a baroque white plaster balcony
added by birds, who nest along the river,
—I saw it with one eye close to the crumb—

and galleries and marble chambers. My crumb
my mansion, made for me by a miracle,
through ages, by insects, birds, and the river
working the stone. Every day, in the sun,
at breakfast time I sit on my balcony
with my feet up, and drink gallons of coffee.

We licked up the crumb and swallowed the coffee.
A window across the river caught the sun
as if the miracle were working, on the wrong balcony.

1937, 1946

THE FISH

I caught a tremendous fish
and held him beside the boat
half out of water, with my hook
fast in a corner of his mouth.
He didn't fight.
He hadn't fought at all.
He hung a grunting weight,
battered and venerable
and homely. Here and there
his brown skin hung in strips
like ancient wallpaper,
and its pattern of darker brown
was like wallpaper:
shapes like full-blown roses
stained and lost through age.
He was speckled with barnacles,
fine rosettes of lime,
and infested
with tiny white sea-lice,
and underneath two or three
rags of green weed hung down.
While his gills were breathing in
the terrible oxygen
—the frightening gills,
fresh and crisp with blood,
that can cut so badly—
I thought of the coarse white flesh
packed in like feathers,

the big bones and the little bones,
the dramatic reds and blacks
of his shiny entrails,
and the pink swim-bladder
like a big peony.
I looked into his eyes
which were far larger than mine
but shallower, and yellowed,
the irises backed and packed
with tarnished tinfoil
seen through the lenses
of old scratched isinglass.
They shifted a little, but not
to return my stare.
—It was more like the tipping
of an object toward the light.
I admired his sullen face,
the mechanism of his jaw,
and then I saw
that from his lower lip
—if you could call it a lip—
grim, wet, and weaponlike,
hung five old pieces of fish-line,
or four and a wire leader
with the swivel still attached,
with all their five big hooks
grown firmly in his mouth.
A green line, frayed at the end
where he broke it, two heavier lines,
and a fine black thread
still crimped from the strain and snap
when it broke and he got away
Like medals with their ribbons
frayed and wavering,
a five-haired beard of wisdom
trailing from his aching jaw.
I stared and stared
and victory filled up
the little rented boat,
from the pool of bilge
where oil had spread a rainbow
around the rusted engine
to the bailer rusted orange,
the sun-cracked thwarts,
the oarlocks on their strings,
the gunnels—until everything
was rainbow, rainbow, rainbow!
And I let the fish go.

1940, 1946

OVER 2,000 ILLUSTRATIONS AND A COMPLETE CONCORDANCE

Thus should have been our travels:
serious, engravable.
The Seven Wonders of the World are tired
and a touch familiar, but the other scenes,
innumerable, though equally sad and still,
are foreign. Often the squatting Arab,
or group of Arabs, plotting, probably,
against our Christian Empire,
while one apart, with outstretched arm and hand
points to the Tomb, the Pit, the Sepulcher.[1]
The branches of the date-palms look like files.
The cobbled courtyard, where the Well is dry,
is like a diagram, the brickwork conduits
are vast and obvious, the human figure
far gone in history or theology,
gone with its camel or its faithful horse.
Always the silence, the gesture, the specks of birds
suspended on invisible threads above the Site,
or the smoke rising solemnly, pulled by threads.
Granted a page alone or a page made up
of several scenes arranged in cattycornered rectangles
or circles set on stippled gray,
granted a grim lunette,[2]
caught in the toils of an initial letter,
when dwelt upon, they all resolve themselves.
The eye drops, weighted, through the lines
the burin[3] made, the lines that move apart
like ripples above sand,
dispersing storms, God's spreading fingerprint,
and painfully, finally, that ignite
in watery prismatic white-and-blue.
Entering the Narrows at St. Johns[4]
the touching bleat of goats reached to the ship.
We glimpsed them, reddish, leaping up the cliffs
among the fog-soaked weeds and butter-and-eggs.
And at St. Peter's[5] the wind blew and the sun shone madly.
Rapidly, purposefully, the Collegians marched in lines,
crisscrossing the great square with black,[6] like ants.

[1]The tomb, enclosed in the Church of the Holy Sepulcher in Jerusalem, where Jesus is said to have been buried.

[2]A crescent-shaped or semicircular form. [3]Engraver's tool.

[4]Entrance to St. John's Harbor in Newfoundland, Canada. [5]Church in Rome.

[6]I.e., files of seminary students, wearing black robes, crossing St. Peter's Square from their residential colleges to their university classrooms.

In Mexico the dead man lay
in a blue arcade; the dead volcanoes
glistened like Easter lilies.
The jukebox went on playing "Ay, Jalisco!"[7]
And at Volubilis[8] there were beautiful poppies
splitting the mosaics; the fat old guide made eyes.
In Dingle[9] harbor a golden length of evening
the rotting hulks held up their dripping plush.
The Englishwoman poured tea, informing us
that the Duchess was going to have a baby.
And in the brothels of Marrakesh[10]
the little pockmarked prostitutes
balanced their tea-trays on their heads
and did their belly-dances; flung themselves
naked and giggling against our knees,
asking for cigarettes. It was somewhere near there
I saw what frightened me most of all:
A holy grave, not looking particularly holy,
one of a group under a keyhole-arched stone baldaquin[11]
open to every wind from the pink desert.
An open, gritty, marble trough, carved solid
with exhortation, yellowed
as scattered cattle-teeth;
half-filled with dust, not even the dust
of the poor prophet paynim[12] who once lay there.
In a smart burnoose[13] Khadour looked on amused.

Everything only connected by "and" and "and."
Open the book. (The gilt rubs off the edges
of the pages and pollinates the fingertips.)
Open the heavy book. Why couldn't we have seen
this old Nativity[14] while we were at it?
—the dark ajar, the rocks breaking with light,
an undisturbed, unbreathing flame,
colorless, sparkless, freely fed on straw,
and, lulled within, a family with pets,
—and looked and looked our infant sight away.

1948, 1955

[7]Jalisco: state in Mexico where mariachi music originated.
[8]Ancient Roman city in North Africa, now a ruin.
[9]Town in southwest Ireland.
[10]City in Morocco.
[11]Ornamental structure, resembling a canopy, built over a sacred object.
[12]A pagan, a nonbeliever—a term sometimes used by Christians to refer to a Muslim.
[13]Hooded cloak worn by Arabs.
[14]The birth of Christ.

VISITS TO ST. ELIZABETHS[1]

1950

This is the house of Bedlam.

This is the man
that lies in the house of Bedlam.

This is the time
of the tragic man
that lies in the house of Bedlam.

This is a wristwatch
telling the time
of the talkative man
that lies in the house of Bedlam.

This is a sailor
wearing the watch
that tells the time
of the honored man
that lies in the house of Bedlam.

This is the roadstead all of board
reached by the sailor
wearing the watch
that tells the time
of the old, brave man
that lies in the house of Bedlam.

These are the years and the walls of the ward,
the winds and clouds of the sea of board
sailed by the sailor
wearing the watch
that tells the time
of the cranky man
that lies in the house of Bedlam.

This is a Jew in a newspaper hat
that dances weeping down the ward
over the creaking sea of board
beyond the sailor
winding his watch

[1]A hospital for the mentally ill in Washington, D.C., where the poet Ezra Pound was confined from 1946 to 1958.

that tells the time
of the cruel man
that lies in the house of Bedlam.

This is a world of books gone flat.
This is a Jew in a newspaper hat
that dances weeping down the ward
over the creaking sea of board
of the batty sailor
that winds his watch
that tells the time
of the busy man
that lies in the house of Bedlam.

This is a boy that pats the floor
to see if the world is there, is flat,
for the widowed Jew in the newspaper hat
that dances weeping down the ward
waltzing the length of a weaving board
by the silent sailor
that hears his watch
that ticks the time
of the tedious man
that lies in the house of Bedlam.

These are the years and the walls and the door
that shut on a boy that pats the floor
to feel if the world is there and flat.
This is a Jew in a newspaper hat
that dances joyfully down the ward
into the parting seas of board
past the staring sailor
that shakes his watch
that tells the time
of the poet, the man
that lies in the house of Bedlam.

This is the soldier home from the war.
These are the years and the walls and the door
that shut on a boy that pats the floor
to see if the world is round or flat.
This is a Jew in a newspaper hat
that dances carefully down the ward,
walking the plank of a coffin board
with the crazy sailor
that shows his watch
that tells the time
of the wretched man
that lies in the house of Bedlam.

1950 1950, 1965

SESTINA

September rain falls on the house.
In the failing light, the old grandmother
sits in the kitchen with the child
beside the Little Marvel Stove,
reading the jokes from the almanac,
laughing and talking to hide her tears.

She thinks that her equinoctial tears
and the rain that beats on the roof of the house
were both foretold by the almanac,
but only known to a grandmother.
The iron kettle sings on the stove.
She cuts some bread and says to the child,

It's time for tea now; but the child
is watching the teakettle's small hard tears
dance like mad on the hot black stove,
the way the rain must dance on the house.
Tidying up, the old grandmother
hangs up the clever almanac

on its string. Birdlike, the almanac
hovers half open above the child,
hovers above the old grandmother
and her teacup full of dark brown tears.
She shivers and says she thinks the house
feels chilly, and puts more wood in the stove.

It was to be, says the Marvel Stove.
I know what I know, says the almanac.
With crayons the child draws a rigid house
and a winding pathway. Then the child
puts in a man with buttons like tears
and shows it proudly to the grandmother.

But secretly, while the grandmother
busies herself about the stove,
the little moons fall down like tears
from between the pages of the almanac
into the flower bed the child
has carefully placed in the front of the house.

Time to plant tears, says the almanac.
The grandmother sings to the marvellous stove
and the child draws another inscrutable house.

1956, 1965

THE ARMADILLO

for ROBERT LOWELL[1]

This is the time of year
when almost every night
the frail, illegal fire balloons appear.
Climbing the mountain height,

rising toward a saint
still honored in these parts,[2]
the paper chambers flush and fill with light
that comes and goes, like hearts.

Once up against the sky it's hard
to tell them from the stars—
planets, that is—the tinted ones:
Venus going down, or Mars,

or the pale green one.[3] With a wind,
they flare and falter, wobble and toss;
but if it's still they steer between
the kite sticks of the Southern Cross,[4]

receding, dwindling, solemnly
and steadily forsaking us,
or, in the downdraft from a peak,
suddenly turning dangerous.

Last night another big one fell.
It splattered like an egg of fire
against the cliff behind the house.
The flame ran down. We saw the pair

of owls who nest there flying up
and up, their whirling black-and-white
stained bright pink underneath, until
they shrieked up out of sight.

The ancient owls' nest must have burned.
Hastily, all alone,
a glistening armadillo left the scene,
rose-flecked, head down, tail down,

[1]Compare Robert Lowell's "Skunk Hour" on pages 1763–1764.
[2]Rio de Janeiro, Brazil. [3]Uranus.
[4]A constellation visible in the southern hemisphere. Its stars are aligned in the form of a cross.

and then a baby rabbit jumped out,
short-eared, to our surprise.
So soft!—a handful of intangible ash
with fixed, ignited eyes.

Too pretty, dreamlike mimicry!
O falling fire and piercing cry
and panic, and a weak mailed fist
clenched ignorant against the sky!

1957, 1965

BRAZIL, JANUARY 1, 1502[1]

. . . embroidered nature . . . tapestried landscape.

—Landscape into Art, by SIR KENNETH CLARK[2]

Januaries, Nature greets our eyes
exactly as she must have greeted theirs:
every square inch filling in with foliage—
big leaves, little leaves, and giant leaves,
blue, blue-green, and olive,
with occasional lighter veins and edges,
or a satin underleaf turned over;
monster ferns
in silver-gray relief,
and flowers, too, like giant water lilies
up in the air—up, rather, in the leaves—
purple, yellow, two yellows, pink,
rust red and greenish white;
solid but airy; fresh as if just finished
and taken off the frame.

A blue-white sky, a simple web,
backing for feathery detail:
brief arcs, a pale-green broken wheel,
a few palms, swarthy, squat, but delicate;
and perching there in profile, beaks agape,
the big symbolic birds keep quiet,
each showing only half his puffed and padded,
pure-colored or spotted breast.

[1]The date on which Portuguese navigators first explored the present site of Rio de Janeiro, Brazil.
[2]A book on landscape painting, published in 1949, in which Clark asserts that medieval landscape painting showed nature, often depicted as though embroidered on a tapestry, as symbolic of "spiritual truths."

Still in the foreground there is Sin:
five sooty dragons near some massy rocks.
The rocks are worked with lichens, gray moonbursts
splattered and overlapping,
threatened from underneath by moss
in lovely hell-green flames,
attacked above
by scaling-ladder vines, oblique and neat,
"one leaf yes and one leaf no" (in Portuguese).
The lizards scarcely breathe; all eyes
are on the smaller, female one, back-to,
her wicked tail straight up and over,
red as a red-hot wire.

Just so the Christians, hard as nails,
tiny as nails, and glinting,
in creaking armor, came and found it all,
not unfamiliar:
no lovers' walks, no bowers,
no cherries to be picked, no lute music,
but corresponding, nevertheless,
to an old dream of wealth and luxury
already out of style when they left home—
wealth, plus a brand-new pleasure.
Directly after Mass, humming perhaps
L'Homme armé[3] or some such tune,
they ripped away into the hanging fabric,
each out to catch an Indian for himself—
those maddening little women who kept calling,
calling to each other (or had the birds waked up?)
and retreating, always retreating, behind it.

1959?, 1965

IN THE WAITING ROOM

In Worcester, Massachusetts,
I went with Aunt Consuelo
to keep her dentist's appointment
and sat and waited for her
in the dentist's waiting room.
It was winter, It got dark
early. The waiting room
was full of grown-up people,

[3]French: "The Armed Man," the name of a fifteenth-century melody often sung during a Roman Catholic mass.

arctics and overcoats,
lamps and magazines.
My aunt was inside
what seemed like a long time
and while I waited I read
the *National Geographic*
(I could read) and carefully
studied the photographs:
the inside of a volcano,
black, and full of ashes;
then it was spilling over
in rivulets of fire
Osa and Martin Johnson[1]
dressed in riding breeches,
laced boots, and pith helmets.
A dead man slung on a pole
—"Long Pig," the caption said.
Babies with pointed heads
wound round and round with string;
black, naked women with necks
wound round and round with wire
like the necks of light bulbs.
Their breasts were horrifying.
I read it right straight through.
I was too shy to stop.
And then I looked at the cover:
the yellow margins, the date.

Suddenly, from inside,
came an *oh!* of pain
—Aunt Consuelo's voice—
not very loud or long.
I wasn't at all surprised;
even then I knew she was
a foolish, timid woman.
I might have been embarrassed,
but wasn't. What took me
completely by surprise
was that it was *me:*
my voice, in my mouth.
Without thinking at all
I was my foolish aunt,
I—we—were falling, falling,
our eyes glued to the cover
of the *National Geographic,*
February, 1918.

[1]Husband and wife explorers and wildlife photographers, famous for their expeditions to the South Sea islands, Borneo, and Africa.

I said to myself: three days
and you'll be seven years old.
I was saying it to stop
the sensation of falling off
the round, turning world
into cold, blue-black space.
But I felt: you are an *I*,
you are an *Elizabeth*,
you are one of *them*.
Why should you be one, too?
I scarcely dared to look
to see what it was I was.
I gave a sidelong glance
—I couldn't look any higher—
at shadowy gray knees,
trousers and skirts and boots
and different pairs of hands
lying under the lamps.
I knew that nothing stranger
had ever happened, that nothing
stranger could ever happen.

Why should I be my aunt,
or me, or anyone?
What similarities—
boots, hands, the family voice
I felt in my throat, or even
the *National Geographic*
and those awful hanging breasts—
held us all together
or made us all just one?
How—I didn't know any
word for it—how "unlikely" . . .[2]
How had I come to be here,
like them, and overhear
a cry of pain that could have
got loud and worse but hadn't?

The waiting room was bright
and too hot. It was sliding
beneath a big black wave,
another, and another.

Then I was back in it.
The War was on. Outside,
in Worcester, Massachusetts,
were night and slush and cold,
and it was still the fifth
of February, 1918.

1971, 1976

[2]The ellipsis points are Bishop's.

ONE ART

The art of losing isn't hard to master;
so many things seem filled with the intent
to be lost that their loss is no disaster.

Lose something every day. Accept the fluster
of lost door keys, the hour badly spent.
The art of losing isn't hard to master.

Then practice losing farther, losing faster:
places, and names, and where it was you meant
to travel. None of these will bring disaster.

I lost my mother's watch. And look! my last, or
next-to-last, of three loved houses went.
The art of losing isn't hard to master.

I lost two cities, lovely ones. And, vaster,
some realms I owned, two rivers, a continent.
I miss them, but it wasn't a disaster.

—Even losing you (the joking voice, a gesture
I love) I shan't have lied. It's evident
the art of losing's not too hard to master
though it may look like (*Write* it!) like disaster.

1976

Robert Lowell 1917–1977

Robert Lowell was descended from distinguished New England families that included statesmen, soldiers, Mayflower colonists, and the poets James Russell Lowell and Amy Lowell. He was educated at a fashionable New England prep school, St. Mark's. For two years he attended Harvard, and then he transferred to Kenyon College in Ohio, where he studied under the distinguished poet and critic John Crowe Ransom.

In 1940, Lowell graduated from Kenyon as valedictorian of his class. Soon after the United States entered World War II, he tried to enlist, first in the army and then in the navy, but he was rejected. Later, as the war progressed, he became so opposed to the Allies' mass bombing of enemy civilian targets that he refused to serve when he was called for the draft. As a result, in 1943 he was convicted of draft evasion and sentenced to a year and a day in a federal prison.

After serving five months of his sentence, Lowell was paroled. Shortly afterward, he published Land of Unlikeness *(1944), his first book of poems. Two years later his fame as a poet was established with the publication of* Lord Weary's Castle, *for which he received a Pulitzer Prize for poetry. The volume deals with Lowell's New England background, his ancestry, and especially the moral and spiritual decline he saw in society. In both* Lord Weary's Castle *and his next book,* The Mills of the Kavanaughs *(1951), his despair is expressed in highly symbolic, richly allusive, rhetorical language.*

With the publication of Life Studies *(1959) a new direction in Lowell's poetry was confirmed. The poems are, in a painfully candid way, self-revelation. Their descriptions of personal disturbances and confinement in a hospital for the insane marked the advent of a new school of "confessional poets" who were given to intense self-examination and emotional self-exposure.* Life Studies, *Lowell's finest work and one of the most influential volumes of poetry of the age, also exhibits a less formal and less rhetorical manner than his earlier poems, for, as he said in an interview, he chose not to get his new "experience into tight metrical forms."*

*In his subsequent poetry (*For the Union Dead, *1964, is especially notable) Lowell partially moved away from personal revelation, just as he had moved away from his New England background as a subject for his writing. He also worked with a variety of literary forms, writing verse dramas and translating poems into English. As he grew older Lowell turned increasingly to political activity: In 1956, as a protest against America's foreign policy, he publicly refused to attend a White House Festival to promote the fine arts, and in 1967 he was arrested during a march on the Pentagon to protest the Vietnam War. In his final years he published* History *(1973), in which he attempted a new presentation of poems written in blank verse. His last work,* Day by Day, *was published in 1977, shortly before his death.*

Lowell's early work inspired vast and flattering praise—one fawning critic has been derisively described as falling "to his knees" in his reverent zeal to describe Lowell as the "king" of American poetry. But since his death, Lowell's glittering reputation has dimmed, yielding to the growing recognition of Sylvia Plath and Elizabeth Bishop as the finest poets of the age. Nevertheless, Lowell's work remains of great significance, in part because it embodies two of the major developments of modern poetry: the pursuit of the impersonal (the assumption of "masks," the reliance on allusion, reference, and translation) and its contrary, the open expression of self-revelation, the exposure of the "I."

Lowell's output was enormous: A recent edition of his collected poems totals almost twelve hundred pages. The poems are often dense, difficult, highly charged with "thrashing eloquence." Robert Frost judged that much of Lowell's early poetry lacked "compression," and some of his late work has been criticized as "trivia," as "organized jotting." For the demands that his writing often makes upon his readers, Lowell has been called the most "exacting poet of his time." But at its best, Lowell's work displays great technical craft and elegance. And for its descriptions of the instability of life, for its portrayals of death, sin, and furtive guilt, it stands with the finest American poetry of the twentieth century.

FURTHER READING: H. Staples, *Robert Lowell: The First Twenty Years,* 1962; C. Heymann, *American Aristocracy,* 1980; B. Raffel, *Robert Lowell,* 1981; I. Hamilton, *Robert Lowell: A Biography,* 1982; V. Bell, *Robert Lowell: Nihilist as Hero,* 1983; M. Rudman, *Robert Lowell: An Introduction to the Poetry,* 1983; N. Procopiow, *Robert Lowell: The Poet and His Critics,* 1984; J. Meyers, *Manic Power: Robert Lowell and His Circle,* 1987; *Robert Lowell,* ed. H. Bloom, 1987; *R. Lowell: Interviews and Memoirs,* ed. J. Meyers, 1988; P. Hobsbaum, *A Reader's Guide to Robert Lowell,* 1988; K. Wallingford, *Robert Lowell's Language of the Self,* 1988; *Robert Lowell: Essays on the Poetry,* ed. S. Axelrod and R. Deese, 1989; P. Mariani, *Lost Puritan: A Life of Robert Lowell,* 1994; R. Tillinghast, *Robert Lowell's Life and Work,* 1995; H. Hart, *Robert Lowell and the Sublime,* 1995; *Robert Lowell's Life and Work: Damaged Grandeur,* ed. R. Tillinghast, 1996; W. Doreski, *Robert Lowell's Shifting Colors: The Poetics of the Public and the Personal,* 1999; *The Critical Response to Robert Lowell,* ed. S. Axelrod, 1999.

TEXT: *Robert Lowell: Collected Poems,* ed. F. Bidart and D. Gewanter, 2003.

THE QUAKER GRAVEYARD IN NANTUCKET

(For Warren Winslow,[1] Dead at Sea)

Let man have dominion over the fishes of the sea and the fowls of the air and the beasts and the whole earth, and every creeping creature that moveth upon the earth.[2]

I

A brackish reach of shoal off Madaket,[3]—
The sea was still breaking violently and night
Had steamed into our north Atlantic Fleet,
When the drowned sailor clutched the drag-net. Light
Flashed from his matted head and marble feet,
He grappled at the net
With the coiled, hurdling muscles of his thighs:
The corpse was bloodless, a botch of reds and whites,
Its open, staring eyes
Were lustreless dead-lights[4]
Or cabin-windows on a stranded hulk
Heavy with sand. We weight the body, close
Its eyes and heave it seaward whence it came,
Where the heel-headed dogfish barks its nose
On Ahab's[5] void and forehead; and the name
Is blocked in yellow chalk.
Sailors, who pitch this portent at the sea
Where dreadnaughts shall confess
Its hell-bent deity,
When you are powerless
To sand-bag this Atlantic bulwark, faced
By the earth-shaker,[6] green, unwearied, chaste
In his steel scales: ask for no Orphean lute
To pluck life back.[7] The guns of the steeled fleet
Recoil and then repeat
The hoarse salute.

[1]The poet's cousin, killed during World War II.
[2]Genesis 1:26. Lowell quotes from the Douay Version of the Bible.
[3]Town and harbor at Nantucket Island, off the coast of Cape Cod.
[4]Heavy glass panes set into a ship's deck or side.
[5]The captain of the whaler *Pequod,* in Herman Melville's novel *Moby Dick* (1851), to which Lowell repeatedly alludes in the poem.
[6]Poseidon, Greek god of the sea and earthquakes.
[7]In Greek myth, Orpheus attempted to bring his bride, Eurydice, back from Hades by the power of his music.

II

Whenever winds are moving and their breath
Heaves at the roped-in bulwarks of this pier,
The terns and sea-gulls tremble at your death
In these home waters. Sailor, can you hear
The Pequod's sea wings, beating landward, fall
Headlong and break on our Atlantic wall
Off 'Sconset,[8] where the yawing S-boats[9] splash
The bellbuoy, with ballooning spinnakers,
As the entangled, screeching mainsheet clears
The blocks: off Madaket, where lubbers lash
The heavy surf and throw their long lead squids
For blue-fish? Sea-gulls blink their heavy lids
Seaward. The winds' wings beat upon the stones,
Cousin, and scream for you and the claws rush
At the sea's throat and wring it in the slush
Of this old Quaker graveyard where the bones
Cry out in the long night for the hurt beast
Bobbing by Ahab's whaleboats in the East.

III

All you recovered from Poseidon died
With you, my cousin, and the harrowed brine
Is fruitless on the blue beard of the god,
Stretching beyond us to the castles in Spain,
Nantucket's westward haven. To Cape Cod
Guns, cradled on the tide,
Blast the eelgrass about a waterclock
Of bilge and backwash, roil the salt and sand
Lashing earth's scaffold, rock
Our warships in the hand
Of the great God, where time's contrition blues
Whatever it was these Quaker sailors lost
In the mad scramble of their lives. They died
When time was open-eyed,
Wooden and childish; only bones abide
There, in the nowhere, where their boats were tossed
Sky-high, where mariners had fabled news
Of IS,[10] the whited monster. What it cost
Them is their secret. In the sperm-whale's slick
I see the Quakers drown and hear their cry:

[8]Siasconset, a town on Nantucket. [9]A class of racing yacht.
[10]Perhaps a reference to Revelation 17:8: "Behold the beast that was and is not and yet is."

"If God himself had not been on our side,
If God himself had not been on our side,
When the Atlantic rose against us, why,
Then it had swallowed us up quick."

IV

This is the end of the whaleroad[11] and the whale
Who spewed Nantucket bones on the thrashed swell
And stirred the troubled waters to whirlpools
To send the Pequod packing off to hell:
This is the end of them, three-quarters fools,
Snatching at straws to sail
Seaward and seaward on the turntail whale,
Spouting out blood and water as it rolls,
Sick as a dog to these Atlantic shoals:
Clamavimus,[12] O depths. Let the sea-gulls wail
For water, for the deep where the high tide
Mutters to its hurt self, mutters and ebbs.
Waves wallow in their wash, go out and out,
Leave only the death-rattle of the crabs,
The beach increasing, its enormous snout
Sucking the ocean's side.
This is the end of running on the waves;
We are poured out like water. Who will dance
The mast-lashed master of Leviathans[13]
Up from this field of Quakers in their unstoned graves?

V

When the whale's viscera go and the roll
Of its corruption overruns this world
Beyond tree-swept Nantucket and Wood's Hole[14]
And Martha's Vineyard,[15] Sailor, will your sword
Whistle and fall and sink into the fat?
In the great ash-pit of Jehoshaphat[16]
The bones cry for the blood of the white whale,
The fat flukes arch and whack about its ears,
The death-lance churns into the sanctuary, tears

[11]The sea.

[12]Latin: "We have cried out," an allusion to Psalms 130:1, "Out of the depths I have cried unto thee, O Lord."

[13]Old Testament sea monsters.

[14]Town on the Atlantic coast of Massachusetts, opposite Martha's Vineyard.

[15]Island near Nantucket.

[16]The "valley of decision," the scene of the Lord's judgment of the world (Joel 3:11–16).

The gun-blue swingle,[17] heaving like a flail,
And hacks the coiling life out: it works and drags
And rips the sperm-whale's midriff into rags,
Gobbets of blubber spill to wind and weather,
Sailor, and gulls go round the stoven timbers
Where the morning stars sing out together
And thunder shakes the white surf and dismembers
The red flag hammered in the mast-head.[18] Hide,
Our steel, Jonas Messias,[19] in Thy side.

VI

Our Lady of Walsingham[20]

There once the penitents took off their shoes
And then walked barefoot the remaining mile;
And the small trees, a stream and hedgerows file
Slowly along the munching English lane,
Like cows to the old shrine, until you lose
Track of your dragging pain.
The stream flows down under the druid tree,[21]
Shiloah's[22] whirlpools gurgle and make glad
The castle of God. Sailor, you were glad
And whistled Sion[23] by that stream. But see:

Our Lady, too small for her canopy,
Sits near the altar. There's no comeliness
At all or charm in that expressionless
Face with its heavy eyelids. As before,
This face, for centuries a memory,
Non est species, neque decor,[24]
Expressionless, expresses God: it goes
Past castled Sion. She knows what God knows,
Not Calvary's Cross nor crib at Bethlehem
Now, and the world shall come to Walsingham.

17A wooden, knifelike instrument.

18A reference to the flag nailed to the mast of the sinking *Pequod* at the end of *Moby Dick*.

19Jonah (Jonas) and the Messiah, Jesus, have frequently been compared in Christian writing, Jonah's experiences being considered prophetic of the Resurrection of Jesus.

20A shrine dedicated to the Virgin Mary, in Walsingham Priory, Norfolk, England.

21The oak tree held sacred among ancient pagan Celtic Druids.

22Shiloh, a town in ancient Palestine.

23Zion, a hill in Jerusalem that became a center of Hebrew government and life. Hence the term came later to be used to describe the Israelites, the church, and the heavenly city of God.

24Latin: There is no form nor comeliness (Isaiah 53:2 in the Latin Vulgate Bible).

VII

The empty winds are creaking and the oak
Splatters and splatters on the cenotaph,[25]
The boughs are trembling and a gaff
Bobs on the untimely stroke
Of the greased wash exploding on a shoal-bell
In the old mouth of the Atlantic. It's well;
Atlantic, you are fouled with the blue sailors,
Sea-monsters, upward angel, downward fish:
Unmarried and corroding, spare of flesh
Mart once of supercilious, wing'd clippers,
Atlantic, where your bell-trap guts its spoil
You could cut the brackish winds with a knife
Here in Nantucket, and cast up the time
When the Lord God formed man from the sea's slime
And breathed into his face the breath of life,
And blue-lung'd combers lumbered to the kill.
The Lord survives the rainbow of His will.

1945, 1946

MR. EDWARDS[1] AND THE SPIDER

I saw the spiders marching through the air,
Swimming from tree to tree that mildewed day
In latter August when the hay
Came creaking to the barn. But where
The wind is westerly,
Where gnarled November makes the spiders fly
Into the apparitions of the sky,
They purpose nothing but their ease and die
Urgently beating east to sunrise and the sea;

What are we in the hands of the great God?
It was in vain you set up thorn and briar
In battle array against the fire
And treason crackling in your blood;
For the wild thorns grow tame
And will do nothing to oppose the flame;
Your lacerations tell the losing game
You play against a sickness past your cure.
How will the hands be strong? How will the heart
endure?[2]

[25]A tomb monument built to honor one who is buried elsewhere.

[1]A reference to Jonathan Edwards (1703–1758), the last great defender of American Puritanism. The poem derives from Edwards' renowned essay "The Flying Spider" and from his sermons, among them "Sinners in the Hands of an Angry God."

[2]Can thine heart endure, or can thine hands be strong, in the days that I shall deal with thee? (Ezekiel 22:14). Edwards used this text for his sermon "Sinners in the Hands of an Angry God."

A very little thing, a little worm,
Or hourglass-blazoned spider,[3] it is said,
Can kill a tiger. Will the dead
Hold up his mirror and affirm
To the four winds the smell
And flash of his authority? It's well
If God who holds you to the pit of hell,
Much as one holds a spider, will destroy,
Baffle and dissipate your soul. As a small boy

On Windsor Marsh,[4] I saw the spider die
When thrown into the bowels of fierce fire:
There's no long struggle, no desire
To get up on its feet and fly—
It stretches out its feet
And dies. This is the sinner's last retreat;
Yes, and no strength exerted on the heat
Then sinews the abolished will, when sick
And full of burning, it will whistle on a brick.

But who can plumb the sinking of that soul?
Josiah Hawley,[5] picture yourself cast
Into a brick-kiln where the blast
Fans your quick vitals to a coal—
If measured by a glass,
How long would it seem burning! Let there pass
A minute, ten, ten trillion; but the blaze
Is infinite, eternal: this is death,
To die and know it. This is the Black Widow, death.

1946

MEMORIES OF WEST STREET AND LEPKE

Only teaching on Tuesdays, book-worming
in pajamas fresh from the washer each morning,
I hog a whole house on Boston's
"hardly passionate Marlborough Street,"[1]
where even the man
scavenging filth in the back alley trash cans,
has two children, a beach wagon, a helpmate,
and is a "young Republican."
I have a nine months' daughter,
young enough to be my granddaughter.
Like the sun she rises in her flame-flamingo infants' wear.

[3]The venomous female black widow spider has a red hourglass design on its underside.
[4]Near East Windsor, Connecticut, Edwards' boyhood home.
[5]A relative of Edwards and a suicide whose death Edwards attributed to the devil.
[1]A phrase by Henry James describing a street in an elegant section of Boston. Lowell lived in a house on Marlborough Street from 1955 to 1958.

These are the tranquillized *Fifties,*
and I am forty. Ought I to regret my seedtime?
I was a fire-breathing Catholic C.O.,[2]
and made my manic statement,
telling off the state and president, and then
sat waiting sentence in the bull pen
beside a Negro boy with curlicues
of marijuana in his hair.

Given a year,
I walked on the roof of the West Street Jail, a short
enclosure like my school soccer court,
and saw the Hudson River once a day
through sooty clothesline entanglements
and bleaching khaki tenements.
Strolling, I yammered metaphysics with Abramowitz,
a jaundice-yellow ("it's really tan")
and fly-weight pacifist,
so vegetarian,
he wore rope shoes and preferred fallen fruit.
He tried to convert Bioff and Brown,[3]
the Hollywood pimps, to his diet.
Hairy, muscular, suburban,
wearing chocolate double-breasted suits,
they blew their tops and beat him black and blue.

I was so out of things, I'd never heard
of the Jehovah's Witnesses.[4]
"Are you a C.O.?" I asked a fellow jailbird.
"No," he answered, "I'm a J.W."
He taught me the "hospital tuck,"[5]
and pointed out the T shirted back
of *Murder Incorporated's* Czar Lepke,[6]
there piling towels on a rack,
or dawdling off to his little segregated cell full
of things forbidden the common man:
a portable radio, a dresser, two toy American
flags tied together with a ribbon of Easter palm.

[2]In 1943 Lowell, a conscientious objector ("C.O."), was convicted of violating the Selective Service Act and sentenced to prison for a year and a day. While awaiting transfer to a federal prison he was held for ten days in the West Side Jail in New York City.

[3]William Bioff and George Browne, officials of a theatrical union, convicted in 1943 of extortion in Hollywood. In 1922 Browne had been convicted of pandering.

[4]Religious sect in the United States whose members refuse to participate in affairs of government or bear arms in wartime.

[5]Making a bed by tucking the loose ends of the bed clothes under the mattress tautly and forming a mitred corner at the foot of the bed.

[6]Louis "Lepke" Buchalter, a notorious racketeer convicted of murder in 1941. He had been the leader of "Murder Incorporated," a criminal assassination gang whose services were for hire. He was executed by electrocution in March 1944.

Flabby, bald, lobotomized,
he drifted in a sheepish calm,
where no agonizing reappraisal[7]
jarred his concentration on the electric chair—
hanging like an oasis in his air
of lost connections. . . .[8]

1958

SKUNK HOUR

for ELIZABETH BISHOP[1]

Nautilus Island's hermit
heiress still lives through winter in her Spartan cottage;
her sheep still graze above the sea.
Her son's a bishop. Her farmer
is first selectman[2] in our village;
she's in her dotage.

Thirsting for
the hierarchic privacy
of Queen Victoria's century,
she buys up all
the eyesores facing her shore,
and lets them fall.

The season's ill—
we've lost our summer millionaire,
who seemed to leap from an L. L. Bean[3]
catalogue. His nine-knot yawl[4]
was auctioned off to lobstermen.
A red fox stain covers Blue Hill.[5]

And now our fairy
decorator brightens his shop for fall;
his fishnet's filled with orange cork,
orange, his cobbler's bench and awl;
there is no money in his work,
he'd rather marry.

[7]In a speech given December 1953, John Foster Dulles, the U.S. Secretary of State, called for an "agonizing reappraisal" of American foreign policy.

[8]Here, and throughout, the ellipses are Lowell's.

[1]Lowell stated that "Skunk Hour" was modeled after Elizabeth Bishop's "The Armadillo" (see pages 1749–1750).

[2]An official elected to administer town affairs.

[3]Mail-order clothing and sporting goods store in Freeport, Maine.

[4]Sailboat. [5]A hill and coastal town near Bangor, Maine.

One dark night,
my Tudor Ford climbed the hill's skull;
I watched for love-cars. Lights turned down,
they lay together, hull to hull,
where the graveyard shelves on the town. . . .
My mind's not right.

A car radio bleats,
"Love, O careless Love. . . ."[6] I hear
my ill-spirit sob in each blood cell,
as if my hand were at its throat. . . .
I myself am hell;[7]
nobody's here—

only skunks, that search
in the moonlight for a bite to eat.
They march on their soles up Main Street:
white stripes, moonstruck eyes' red fire
under the chalk-dry and spar spire
of the Trinitarian Church.

I stand on top
of our back steps and breathe the rich air—
a mother skunk with her column of kittens swills the garbage pail.
She jabs her wedge-head in a cup
of sour cream, drops her ostrich tail,
and will not scare.
1957 1958, 1959

FOR THE UNION DEAD

"Relinquunt Omnia Servare Rem Publicam."[1]

The old South Boston Aquarium stands
in a Sahara of snow now. Its broken windows are boarded.
The bronze weathervane cod has lost half its scales.
The airy tanks are dry.

Once my nose crawled like a snail on the glass;
my hand tingled
to burst the bubbles
drifting from the noses of the cowed, compliant fish.

[6]A quotation from the lyrics of the folk song, "Careless Love."

[7]An adaptation of "Which way I fly is Hell; myself am Hell," the words of Satan in *Paradise Lost* (Book IV, line 75) by John Milton.

[1]Latin: "They give up everything to serve the republic."

My hand draws back. I often sigh still
for the dark downward and vegetating kingdom
of the fish and reptile. One morning last March,
I pressed against the new barbed and galvanized

fence on the Boston Common. Behind their cage,
yellow dinosaur steamshovels were grunting
as they cropped up tons of mush and grass
to gouge their underworld garage.

Parking spaces luxuriate like civic
sandpiles in the heart of Boston.
A girdle of orange, Puritan-pumpkin colored girders
braces the tingling Statehouse,

shaking over the excavations, as it faces Colonel Shaw[2]
and his bell-cheeked Negro infantry
on St. Gaudens' shaking Civil War relief,[3]
propped by a plank splint against the garage's earthquake.

Two months after marching through Boston,
half the regiment was dead;
at the dedication,
William James[4] could almost hear the bronze Negroes breathe.

Their monument sticks like a fishbone
in the city's throat.
Its Colonel is as lean
as a compass-needle.

He has an angry wrenlike vigilance,
a greyhound's gentle tautness;
he seems to wince at pleasure,
and suffocate for privacy.

He is out of bounds now. He rejoices in man's lovely,
peculiar power to choose life and die—
when he leads his black soldiers to death,
he cannot bend his back.
On a thousand small town New England greens,
the old white churches hold their air
of sparse, sincere rebellion; frayed flags
quilt the graveyards of the Grand Army of the Republic.[5]

[2]Colonel Robert Shaw (1837–1863), commander of a black regiment, the 54th Massachusetts, during the Civil War.

[3]A monument by the American sculptor Augustus Saint-Gaudens (1848–1907), on the Boston Common across from the Boston State House.

[4]American philosopher (1842–1910), brother of the novelist Henry James. In his "Oration at the Dedication of the Monument" (May 1897) William James said, "There on foot go the dark outcasts, so true to nature that one can almost hear them breathing as they march."

[5]Civil War veterans' organization of former members of the Union army and navy.

The stone statues of the abstract Union Soldier
grow slimmer and younger each year—
wasp-waisted they doze over muskets
and muse through their sideburns . . .

Shaw's father wanted no monument
except the ditch,
where his son's body was thrown
and lost with his "niggers."[6]

The ditch is nearer.
There are no statues for the last war[7] here;
on Boylston Street,[8] a commercial photograph
shows Hiroshima boiling

over a Mosler Safe, the "Rock of Ages"
that survived the blast. Space is nearer.
When I crouch to my television set,
the drained faces of Negro school-children rise like balloons.

Colonel Shaw
is riding on his bubble,
he waits
for the blessèd break.

The Aquarium is gone. Everywhere,
giant finned cars nose forward like fish;
a savage servility
slides by on grease.

1959, 1964

WAKING EARLY SUNDAY MORNING

O to break loose, like the chinook
salmon jumping and falling back,
nosing up to the impossible
stone and bone-crushing waterfall—
raw-jawed, weak-fleshed there, stopped by ten
steps of the roaring ladder, and then
to clear the top on the last try,
alive enough to spawn and die.

[6]The term used by a Confederate officer to describe Shaw's troops. Shaw and much of his regiment were killed in an assault on the Confederate Fort Wagner in South Carolina, 18 July 1863. They were buried in a common grave.

[7]World War II, 1939–1945. [8]A street in Boston.

Stop, back off. The salmon breaks
water, and now my body wakes
to feel the unpolluted joy
and criminal leisure of a boy—
no rainbow smashing a dry fly
in the white run is free as I,
here squatting like a dragon on
time's hoard before the day's begun!

Vermin run for their unstopped holes;
in some dark nook a fieldmouse rolls
a marble, hours on end, then stops;
the termite in the woodwork sleeps—
listen, the creatures of the night
obsessive, casual, sure of foot,
go on grinding, while the sun's
daily remorseful blackout dawns.

Fierce, fireless mind, running downhill.
Look up and see the harbor fill:
business as usual in eclipse
goes down to the sea in ships—
wake of refuse, dacron rope,
bound for Bermuda or Good Hope,
all bright before the morning watch
the wine-dark hulls of yawl and ketch.

I watch a glass of water wet
with a fine fuzz of icy sweat,
silvery colors touched with sky,
serene in their neutrality—
yet if I shift, or change my mood,
I see some object made of wood,
background behind it of brown grain,
to darken it, but not to stain.

O that the spirit could remain
tinged but untarnished by its strain!
Better dressed and stacking birch,
or lost with the Faithful at Church—
anywhere, but somewhere else!
And now the new electric bells,
clearly chiming, "Faith of our fathers,"
and now the congregation gathers.

O Bible chopped and crucified
in hymns we hear but do not read,
none of the milder subtleties
of grace or art will sweeten these
stiff quatrains shovelled out four-square—

they sing of peace, and preach despair;
yet they gave darkness some control,
and left a loophole for the soul.

No, put old clothes on, and explore
the corners of the woodshed for
its dregs and dreck: tools with no handle,
ten candle-ends not worth a candle,
old lumber banished from the Temple,
damned by Paul's precept and example,
cast from the kingdom, banned in Israel,
the wordless sign, the tinkling cymbal.

When will we see Him face to face?
Each day, He shines through darker glass.
In this small town where everything
is known, I see His vanishing
emblems, His white spire and flag-
pole sticking out above the fog,
like old white china doorknobs, sad,
slight, useless things to calm the mad.

Hammering military splendor,
top-heavy Goliath in full armor—
little redemption in the mass
liquidations of their brass,
elephant and phalanx moving
with the times and still improving,
when that kingdom hit the crash:
a million foreskins stacked like trash . . .

Sing softer! But what if a new
diminuendo brings no true
tenderness, only restlessness,
excess, the hunger for success,
sanity of self-deception
fixed and kicked by reckless caution,
while we listen to the bells—
anywhere, but somewhere else!

O to break loose. All life's grandeur
is something with a girl in summer . . .
elated as the President
girdled by his establishment
this Sunday morning, free to chaff
his own thoughts with his bear-cuffed staff,
swimming nude, unbuttoned, sick
of his ghost-written rhetoric!

No weekends for the gods now. Wars
flicker, earth licks its open sores,
fresh breakage, fresh promotions, chance
assassinations, no advance.
Only man thinning out his kind
sounds through the Sabbath noon, the blind
swipe of the pruner and his knife
busy about the tree of life . . .

Pity the planet, all joy gone
from this sweet volcanic cone;
peace to our children when they fall
in small war on the heels of small
war—until the end of time
to police the earth, a ghost
orbiting forever lost
in our monotonous sublime.

1967

WILL NOT COME BACK

[VOLVERAN][1]

Dark swallows will doubtless come back killing
the injudicious nightflies with a clack of the beak;
but these that stopped full flight to see your beauty
and my good fortune . . . as if they knew our names—
they'll not come back. The thick lemony honeysuckle,
climbing from the earthroot to your window,
will open more beautiful blossoms to the evening;
but these . . . like dewdrops, trembling, shining, falling,
the tears of day—they'll not come back. . . .
Some other love will sound his fireword for you
and wake your heart, perhaps, from its cool sleep;
but silent, absorbed, and on his knees,
as men adore God at the altar, as I love you—
don't blind yourself, you'll not be loved like that.

1970, 1973

[1]Spanish: they will return, the title given the poem in its first version, published in 1970.

Ann Petry 1908–1997

Although Ann Petry is distinguished as the first black woman writer to sell a million copies of a single work of fiction, she received relatively little critical attention during her most productive years in the 1940s and 1950s. Recently, however, her body of work, which consists of three novels, a collection of short stories, and four children's books, has garnered increased acclaim for its effectiveness in simultaneously considering issues of race and gender. Petry was born in Old Saybrook, Connecticut, in 1911, to a pair of successful professionals, her father a pharmacist and her mother a chiropodist. After briefly considering following in her father's footsteps, Petry chose instead to pursue a career as a writer. In the 1930s she worked for several small newspapers in Harlem, including The Amsterdam News *and* The People's Voice.

Petry published her first short story, "On Saturday the Siren Sounds at Noon," in 1943. Two years later she published "Like a Winding Sheet," a work that earned her national recognition after it was selected to appear in Best Short Stories of 1946. *As a result she received a fellowship from Houghton Mifflin that enabled her to complete her first novel,* The Street *(1946).* The Street *sold very well, and she followed up its success with* Country Place *(1947) and* The Narrows *(1953). The latter is generally regarded as her best novel. In the 1950s and 1960s, Petry turned her attention to writing children's books, such as* Harriet Tubman: Conductor on the Underground Railway *(1955) and* Tituba of Salem Village *(1964). In 1971 she collected and published her short fiction in* Miss Muriel and Other Stories. *Ann Petry died in 1997 at the age of 88.*

FURTHER READING: *Conjuring,* ed. M. Pryse and H. Spillers, 1985; H. Ervin, *Ann Petry: A Bio-Bibliography,* 1993; H. Holladay, *Ann Petry,* 1996.

TEXT: *Miss Muriel and Other Stories,* 1971.

SOLO ON THE DRUMS

The orchestra had a week's engagement at the Randlert Theater at Broadway and Forty-second Street. His name was picked out in lights on the marquee. The name of the orchestra and then his name underneath by itself.

There had been a time when he would have been excited by it. And stopped to let his mind and his eyes linger over it lovingly. Kid Jones. The name—his name—up there in lights that danced and winked in the brassy sunlight. And at night his name glittered up there on the marquee as though it had been sprinkled with diamonds. The people who pushed their way through the crowded street looked up at it and recognized it and smiled.

He used to eat it up. But not today. Not after what had happened this morning. He just looked at the sign with his name on it. There it was. Then he noticed that the sun had come out, and he shrugged and went on inside the theater to put on one of the cream-colored suits and get his music together.

After he had finished changing his clothes, he glanced in the long mirror in his dressing room. He hadn't changed any. Same face. No fatter and no thinner. No gray hair. Nothing. He frowned. Because he felt that the things that were eating him up inside ought to show. But they didn't.

When it was time to go out on the stage, he took his place behind the drums, not talking, just sitting there. The orchestra started playing softly. He made a mental note of the fact that the boys were working together as smoothly as though each one had been oiled.

The long gray curtains parted. One moment they were closed. And then they were open. Silently. Almost like magic. The high-powered spots flooded the stage with light. He could see specks of dust gliding down the wide beams of light. Under the bands of light the great space out front was all shadow. Faces slowly emerged out of it—disembodied heads and shoulders that slanted up and back, almost to the roof.

He hit the drums lightly. Regularly. A soft, barely discernible rhythm. A background. A repeated emphasis for the horns and the piano. The man with the trumpet stood up and the first notes came out sweet and clear and high.

Kid Jones kept up the drum accompaniment. Slow. Careful. Soft. And he felt his left eyebrow lift itself and start to twitch as the man played the trumpet. It happened whenever he heard the trumpet. The notes crept up, higher, higher, higher. So high that his stomach sucked in against itself. Then a little lower and stronger. A sound sustained. The rhythm of it beating against his ears until he was filled with it and sighing with it.

He wanted to cover his ears with his hands because he kept hearing a voice that whispered the same thing over and over again. The voice was trapped somewhere under the roof—caught and held there by the trumpet. "I'm leaving I'm leaving I'm leaving."

The sound took him straight back to the rain, the rain that had come with the morning. He could see the beginning of the day—raw and cold. He was at home. But he was warm because he was close to her, holding her in his arms. The rain and the wind cried softly outside the window.

And now—well, he felt as though he were floating up and up and up on that long blue note of the trumpet. He half closed his eyes and rode up on it. It had stopped being music. It was that whispering voice, making him shiver. Hating it and not being able to do anything about it. "I'm leaving it's the guy who plays the piano I'm in love with him and I'm leaving now today." Rain in the streets. Heat gone. Food gone. Everything gone because a woman's gone. It's everything you ever wanted, he thought. It's everything you never got. Everything you ever had, everything you ever lost. It's all there in the trumpet—pain and hate and trouble and peace and quiet and love.

The last note stayed up in the ceiling. Hanging on and on. The man with the trumpet had stopped playing but Kid Jones could still hear that last note. In his ears. In his mind.

The spotlight shifted and landed on Kid Jones—the man behind the drums. The long beam of white light struck the top of his head and turned him into a pattern of light and shadow. Because of the cream-colored suit and shirt, his body seemed to be encased in light. But there was a shadow over his face so that his features blended and disappeared. His hairline receded so far back that he looked like a man with a face that never ended. A man with a high, long face and dark, dark skin.

He caressed the drums with the brushes in his hands. They responded with a whisper of sound. The rhythm came over but it had to be listened for. It stayed that way for a long time. Low, insidious, repeated. Then he made the big bass drum growl and pick up the same rhythm.

The Marquis of Brund, pianist with the band, turned to the piano. The drums and the piano talked the same rhythm. The piano high. A little more insistent than the drums. The Marquis was turned sideways on the piano bench. His left foot tapped out the rhythm. His cream-colored suit sharply outlined the bulkiness of his body against the dark gleam of the piano. The drummer and the pianist were silhouetted in two separate brilliant shafts of light. The drums slowly dominated the piano.

The rhythm changed. It was faster. Kid Jones looked out over the crowded theater as he hit the drums. He began to feel as though he were the drums and the drums were he.

The theater throbbed with the excitement of the drums. A man, sitting near the front, shivered and his head jerked to the rhythm. A sailor put his arm around the girl sitting beside him, took his hand and held her face still and pressed his mouth close over hers. Close. Close. Close. Until their faces seemed to melt together. Her hat fell off and neither of them moved. His hand dug deep into her shoulder and still they didn't move.

A kid sneaked in through a side door and slid into an aisle seat. His mouth was wide open and he clutched his cap with both hands, tight and hard against his chest as he listened.

The drummer forgot he was in the theater. There was only him and the drums and they were far away. Long gone. He was holding Lulu, Helen, Susie, Mamie close in his arms. And all of them—all those girls blended into that one girl who was his wife. The one who said, "I'm leaving." She had said it over and over again, this morning, while rain dripped down the windowpanes.

When he hit the drums again it was with the thought that he was fighting with the piano player. He was choking the Marquis of Brund. He was putting a knife in clean between his ribs. He was slitting his throat with a long straight blade. Take my woman. Take your life.

The drums leaped with the fury that was in him. The men in the band turned their heads toward him—a faint astonishment showed in their faces.

He ignored them. The drums took him away from them, took him back, and back, and back, in time and space. He built up an illusion. He was sending out the news. Grandma died. The foreigner in the litter has an old disease and will not recover. The man from across the big water is sleeping with the chief's daughter. Kill. Kill. Kill. The war goes well with the men with the bad smell and the loud laugh. It goes badly with the chiefs with the round heads and the peacock's walk.

It is cool in the deep track in the forest. Cool and quiet. The trees talk softly. They speak of the dance tonight. The young girl from across the lake will be there. Her waist is slender and her thighs are rounded. Then the words he wanted to forget were all around Kid Jones again. "I'm leaving I'm leaving I'm leaving."

He couldn't help himself. He stopped hitting the drums and stared at the Marquis of Brund—a long malevolent look, filled with hate.

There was a restless, uneasy movement in the theater. He remembered where he was. He started playing again. The horn played a phrase. Soft and short. The drums answered. The horn said the same thing all over again. The drums repeated it. The next time it was more intricate. The phrase was turned around, it went back and forth and up and down. And the drums said it over, exactly the same.

He knew a moment of panic. This was where he had to solo again and he wasn't sure he could do it. He touched the drums lightly. They quivered and answered him.

And then it was almost as though the drums were talking about his own life. The woman in Chicago who hated him. The girl with the round, soft body who had been his wife and who had walked out on him, this morning, in the rain. The old woman who was his mother, the same woman who lived in Chicago, and who hated him because he looked like his father, his father who had seduced her and left her, years ago.

He forgot the theater, forgot everything but the drums. He was welded to the drums, sucked inside them. All of him. His pulse beat. His heart beat. He had become part of the drums. They had become part of him.

He made the big drum rumble and reverberate. He went a little mad on the big drum. Again and again he filled the theater with a sound like thunder. The sound seemed to come not from the drums but from deep inside himself; it was a sound that was being wrenched out of him—a violent, raging, roaring sound. As it issued from him he thought, This is the story of my love, this is the story of my hate, this is all there is left of me. And the sound echoed and reechoed far up under the roof of the theater.

When he finally stopped playing, he was trembling; his body was wet with sweat. He was surprised to see that the drums were sitting there in front of him. He hadn't become part of them. He was still himself. Kid Jones. Master of the drums. Greatest drummer in the world. Selling himself a little piece at a time. Every afternoon. Twice every evening. Only this time he had topped all his other performances. This time, playing like this after what had happened in the morning, he had sold all of himself—not just a little piece.

Someone kicked his foot. "Bow, you ape. Whassamatter with you?"

He bowed from the waist and the spotlight slid away from him, down his pants legs. The light landed on the Marquis of Brund, the piano player. The Marquis' skin glistened like a piece of black seaweed. Then the light was back on Kid Jones.

He felt hot and he thought, I stink of sweat. The talcum he had dabbed on his face after he shaved felt like a constricting layer of cement. A thin layer, but definitely cement. No air could get through to his skin. He reached for his handkerchief and felt the powder and the sweat mix as he mopped his face.

Then he bowed again. And again. Like a—like one of those things you pull the string and it jerks, goes through the motion of dancing. Pull it again and it kicks. Yeah, he thought, you were hot all right. The go-go gals ate you up and you haven't anyplace to go. Since this morning you haven't had anyplace to go. "I'm leaving it's the guy who plays the piano I'm in love with the Marquis of Brund he plays such sweet piano I'm leaving leaving leaving—"

He stared at the Marquis of Brund for a long moment. Then he stood up and bowed again. And again.

1971

Richard Wilbur 1921–

Although Richard Wilbur was born in New York City, he has belonged by training as well as by occupation to New England. He graduated from Amherst College in Massachusetts, took his M.A. at Harvard, and then began a teaching career that has included positions at Harvard, at Wellesley, and, since 1957, at Wesleyan University in Connecticut. Wilbur's poetry, with its careful skillfulness, verbal dexterity, and wide-ranging use of traditional forms, is more akin to that of Edwin Arlington Robinson, Robert Frost, and Robert Lowell than to the free verse effusiveness of Walt Whitman. Wilbur's concern with the puzzling tangle of appearance and reality, his belief in the power of imagination to perceive and create reality, and his love for and absorption with nature suggest a New England literary kinship with Emerson, Thoreau, and Emily Dickinson. Wilbur's first volumes of poetry, The Beautiful Changes *(1947) and* Ceremony *(1950), brought him immediate critical approval. His third,* Things of This World *(1956), won a Pulitzer Prize and a National Book Award. Other volumes have followed:* Advice to a Prophet *(1961);* The Poems of Richard Wilbur *(1963);* Walking to Sleep *(1969);* Opposites *(1973);* The Mind-Reader, *(1976); and* Responses *(1976), essays on poets and poetry.*

What most impresses Wilbur's readers, perhaps, is the freshness of his imagery, his mastery of a number of complex stanzaic forms, and the diversity of his themes. The rhythms of his poems are sometimes reminiscent of the hymn meters employed by Emily Dickinson, while his perceptions suggest her uses of the minutiae of nature and her fusion of images of life and death to convey a complex emotional experience. Wilbur's subjects range from the philosophical "Epistemology" to such down-to-earth pieces as "The Death of a Toad." He seeks "contact with the true sights and sounds of this world." In tone his poems vary from the light and comic to the tragic; in point of view they shift from the most subjectively lyrical to the detached and objective. But always within his admirable versatility and technical mastery lie a sharpness and freshness of figurative language that reveal his love of particularities, of colors and shapes and textures, and his conviction that the spirit is drawn to the actual things of the material world: "I like it," he has said, "when the ideas of a poem seem to be necessary aspects of the things or actions which it presents."

FURTHER READING: D. Hill, *Richard Wilbur,* 1967; H. Stevens, *Richard Wilbur,* 1977; *Richard Wilbur's Creation,* ed. W. Salinger, 1983; B. Michelson, *Conversations with Richard Wilbur,* ed. W. Butts, 1990; Bruce Michelson, *Wilbur's Poetry: Music in a Scattering Time,* 1991; R. Edgecombe, *A Reader's Guide to the Poetry of Richard Wilbur,* 1995; B. Hougen, *Ecstasy Within Discipline: The Poetry of Richard Wilbur,* 1995.

TEXT: *New and Collected Poems,* 1988.

MARGINALIA

Things concentrate at the edges; the pond-surface
Is bourne to fish and man and it is spread
In textile scum and damask light, on which
The lily-pads are set; and there are also
    Inlaid ruddy twigs, becalmed pine-leaves,
    Air-baubles, and the chain mail of froth.

Descending into sleep (as when the night-lift
Falls past a brilliant floor), we glimpse a sublime
Décor and hear, perhaps, a complete music,
But this evades us, as in the night meadows
    The crickets' million roundsong dies away
    From all advances, rising in every distance.

Our riches are centrifugal; men compose
Daily, unwittingly, their final dreams,
And those are our own voices whose remote
Consummate chorus rides on the whirlpool's rim,
    Past which we flog our sails, toward which we drift,
    Plying our trades, in hopes of a good drowning.

1954, 1956

LAMARCK[1] ELABORATED

"The environment creates the organ"

The Greeks were wrong who said our eyes have rays;
Not from these sockets or these sparkling poles
Comes the illumination of our days.
It was the sun that bored these two blue holes.

It was the song of doves begot the ear
And not the ear that first conceived of sound:
That organ bloomed in vibrant atmosphere,
As music conjured Ilium[2] from the ground.

The yielding water, the repugnant stone,
The poisoned berry and the flaring rose
Attired in sense the tactless finger-bone
And set the taste-buds and inspired the nose.

Out of our vivid ambiance came unsought
All sense but that most formidably dim.
The shell of balance rolls in seas of thought.
It was the mind that taught the head to swim.
Newtonian[3] numbers set in cosmic lyres
Whelmed us in whirling worlds we could not know,
And by the imagined floods of our desires
The voice of Sirens[4] gave us vertigo.

1956

[1]Jean Baptiste Lamarck (1744–1829), French biologist. His theory of evolution asserts that all life is shaped by a need to adapt to the environment.

[2]Troy. Described in the poetry of Homer.

[3]Sir Isaac Newton (1642–1727), English mathematician and physicist.

[4]Sea nymphs in Greek myth. Their alluring songs drew listeners to their death.

A HOLE IN THE FLOOR

for René Magritte[1]

The carpenter's made a hole
In the parlor floor, and I'm standing
Staring down into it now
At four o'clock in the evening,
As Schliemann[2] stood when his shovel
Knocked on the crowns of Troy.

A clean-cut sawdust sparkles
On the grey, shaggy laths,
And here is a cluster of shavings
From the time when the floor was laid.
They are silvery-gold, the color
Of Hesperian apple-parings.[3]

Kneeling, I look in under
Where the joists go into hiding.
A pure street, faintly littered
With bits and strokes of light,
Enters the long darkness
Where its parallels will meet.

The radiator-pipe
Rises in middle distance
Like a shuttered kiosk, standing
Where the only news is night.
Here it's not painted green,
As it is in the visible world.

For God's sake, what am I after?
Some treasure, or tiny garden?
Or that untrodden place,
The house's very soul,
Where time has stored our footbeats
And the long skein of our voices?

Not these, but the buried strangeness
Which nourishes the known:
That spring from which the floor-lamp
Drinks now a wilder bloom,
Inflaming the damask love-seat
And the whole dangerous room.

1961

[1]French surrealist painter (1898–1967).

[2]Heinrich Schliemann (1822–1890), German archeologist who discovered Troy.

[3]In Greek myth, one of the "labors" of Hercules was to obtain a golden apple from a tree guarded by a dragon and belonging to the Hesperides—"Daughters of the Evening."

TROLLING FOR BLUES

for John and Barbara

As with the dapper terns, or that sole cloud
Which like a slow-evolving embryo
Moils in the sky, we make of this keen fish
Whom fight and beauty have endeared to us
A mirror of our kind. Setting aside

His unreflectiveness, his flings in air,
The aberration of his flocking swerve
To spawning-grounds a hundred miles at sea,
How clearly, musing to the engine's thrum,
Do we conceive him as he waits below:

Blue in the water's blue, which is the shade
Of thought, and in that scintillating flux
Poised weightless, all attention, yet on edge
To lunge and seize with sure incisiveness,
He is a type of coolest intellect,

Or is so to the mind's blue eye until
He strikes and runs unseen beneath the rip,
Yanking imagination back and down
Past recognition to the unlit deep
Of the glass sponges, of chiasmodon,[1]

Of the old darkness of Devonian[2] dream,
Phase of a meditation not our own,
That long mêlée where selves were not, that life
Merciless, painless, sleepless, unaware,
From which, in time, unthinkably we rose.

1987

Shirley Jackson 1916–1965

Shirley Jackson, who today is remembered almost exclusively as the author of the short story "The Lottery," in fact enjoyed a prolific and varied career as a professional writer, producing a body of work that includes six novels, dozens of short stories, numerous essays, two memoirs, and several children's books. Jackson was born into a comfortable San Francisco middle-class family in 1916 (though she claimed to have been born in 1919).

[1]Small fish that lives at the deepest levels of the sea.
[2]A geologic period extending from 345 to 405 million years ago.

In 1934, while still in high school, she moved with her family to Rochester, New York. After graduating, she enrolled at the University of Rochester but dropped out during her first year. For the next several months, Jackson dedicated herself to developing her literary talents by writing poetry and fiction. In 1937 she entered Syracuse University, where she continued to pursue her interest in writing, editing a campus-wide literary magazine and placing second in a poetry contest. While at Syracuse, she also met future critic Stanley Edgar Hyman, whom she married and moved to New York with after graduation.

Jackson published her first story, "My Life with R. H. Macy," in late 1941. Two years later she placed for the first time a work of fiction in the influential New Yorker *magazine. The piece, titled "After You, My Dear Alphonse," inaugurated a long and beneficial relationship between Jackson and that important periodical. In 1945 Jackson and her husband relocated to Vermont after Hyman accepted a faculty position at Bennington College. Jackson published her first novel,* The Road Through the Wall, *in 1948. That was also the year* The New Yorker *published "The Lottery," the story that brought Jackson international recognition. The public's response to the piece was unprecedented, reportedly bringing* The New Yorker *more mail than any other story it had generated. Jackson also successfully employed the gothic style of "The Lottery" in novel-length works, including* The Haunting of Hill House *(1959) and the best-selling* We Have Always Lived in the Castle *(1962). Throughout the 1950s, at the height of her fame, she continued to produce novels as well as essays and fiction for many of country's most widely read magazines. In addition, Jackson wrote humorous books documenting the trials of her own domestic life, such as* Life Among the Savages *(1953) and* Raising Demons *(1957). Shirley Jackson died of heart failure in 1965 at the age of 48.*

FURTHER READING: *The Magic of Shirley Jackson,* ed. S. Hyman, 1966; L. Friedman, *Shirley Jackson,* 1975; J. Oppenheimer, *Private Demons: The Life of Shirley Jackson,* 1988; J. Hall, *Shirley Jackson: A Study of the Short Fiction,* 1993; P. Reinsch, *A Critical Bibliography of Shirley Jackson: American Writer (1919–1965),* 2001; D. Hattenhauer, *Shirley Jackson's American Gothic,* 2003; *Shirley Jackson: Essays on the Literary Legacy,* ed. B. Murphy, 2005.

TEXT: *The Magic of Shirley Jackson,* ed. S. Hyman, 1966.

THE LOTTERY

The morning of June 27th was clear and sunny, with the fresh warmth of a full-summer day; the flowers were blossoming profusely and the grass was richly green. The people of the village began to gather in the square, between the post office and the bank, around ten o'clock; in some towns there were so many people that the lottery took two days and had to be started on June 26th, but in this village, where there were only about three hundred people, the whole lottery took less than two hours, so it could begin at ten o'clock in the morning and still be through in time to allow the villagers to get home for noon dinner.

The children assembled first, of course. School was recently over for the summer, and the feeling of liberty sat uneasily on most of them; they tended to gather together quietly for a while before they broke into boisterous play, and their talk was still of the classroom and the teacher, of books and reprimands. Bobby Martin had already stuffed his pockets full of stones, and the other boys soon followed his example, selecting the smoothest and roundest stones; Bobby and Harry Jones and Dickie Delacroix—the villagers pronounced this name "Dellacroy"—eventually made a great pile of stones in one corner of the square and guarded it against the raids of the other boys. The girls stood aside, talking among themselves, looking over their shoulders at the boys, and the very small children rolled in the dust or clung to the hands of their older brothers or sisters.

Soon the men began to gather, surveying their own children, speaking of planting and rain, tractors and taxes. They stood together, away from the pile of stones in the corner, and their jokes were quiet and they smiled rather than laughed. The women, wearing faded house dresses and sweaters, came shortly after their menfolk. They greeted one another and exchanged bits of gossip as they went to join their husbands. Soon the women, standing by their husbands, began to call to their children, and the children came reluctantly, having to be called four or five times. Bobby Martin ducked under his mother's grasping hand and ran, laughing, back to the pile of stones. His father spoke up sharply, and Bobby came quickly and took his place between his father and his oldest brother.

The lottery was conducted—as were the square dances, the teen-age club, the Halloween program—by Mr. Summers, who had time and energy to devote to civic activities. He was a round-faced, jovial man and he ran the coal business, and people were sorry for him, because he had no children and his wife was a scold. When he arrived in the square, carrying the black wooden box, there was a murmur of conversation among the villagers, and he waved and called, "Little late today, folks." The postmaster, Mr. Graves, followed him, carrying a three-legged stool, and the stool was put in the center of the square and Mr. Summers set the black box down on it. The villagers kept their distance, leaving a space between themselves and the stool, and when Mr. Summers said, "Some of you fellows want to give me a hand?" there was a hesitation before two men, Mr. Martin and his oldest son, Baxter, came forward to hold the box steady on the stool while Mr. Summers stirred up the papers inside it.

The original paraphernalia for the lottery had been lost long ago, and the black box now resting on the stool had been put into use even before Old Man Warner, the oldest man in town, was born. Mr. Summers spoke frequently to the villagers about making a new box, but no one liked to upset even as much tradition as was represented by the black box. There was a story that the present box had been made with some pieces of the box that had preceded it, the one that had been constructed when the first people settled down to make a village here. Every year, after the lottery, Mr. Summers began talking again about a new box, but every year the subject was allowed to fade off without anything's being done. The black box grew shabbier each year; by now it was no longer completely black but splintered badly along one side to show the original wood color, and in some places faded or stained.

Mr. Martin and his oldest son, Baxter, held the black box securely on the stool until Mr. Summers had stirred the papers thoroughly with his hand. Because so much of the ritual had been forgotten or discarded, Mr. Summers had been successful in having slips of paper substituted for the chips of wood that had been used for generations. Chips of wood, Mr. Summers had argued, had been all very well when the village was tiny, but now that the population was more than three hundred and likely to keep on growing, it was necessary to use something that would fit more easily into the black box. The night before the lottery, Mr. Summers and Mr. Graves made up the slips of paper and put them in the box, and it was then taken to the safe of Mr. Summers's coal company and locked up until Mr. Summers was ready to take it to the square next morning. The rest of the year, the box was put away, sometimes one place, sometimes another; it had spent one year in Mr. Graves's barn and another year underfoot in the post office, and sometimes it was set on a shelf in the Martin grocery and left there.

There was a great deal of fussing to be done before Mr. Summers declared the lottery open. There were the lists to make up—of heads of families, heads of households in each family, members of each household in each family. There was the proper swearing-in of Mr. Summers by the postmaster, as the official of the lottery; at one time, some people remembered, there had been a recital of some sort, performed by the official of the lottery, a perfunctory, tuneless chant that had been rattled off duly each year; some people believed that the official of the lottery used to stand just so when he said or sang it, others believed that he was supposed to walk among the people, but years and years ago this part of the ritual had been allowed to lapse. There had been, also, a ritual salute, which the official of the lottery had had to use in addressing each person who came up to draw from the box, but this also had changed with time, until now it was felt necessary only for the official to speak to each person approaching. Mr. Summers was very good at all this; in his clean white shirt and blue jeans, with one hand resting carelessly on the black box, he seemed very proper and important as he talked interminably to Mr. Graves and the Martins.

Just as Mr. Summers finally left off talking and turned to the assembled villagers, Mrs. Hutchinson came hurriedly along the path to the square, her sweater thrown over her shoulders, and slid into place in the back of the crowd. "Clean forgot what day it was," she said to Mrs. Delacroix, who stood next to her, and they both laughed softly. "Thought my old man was out back stacking wood," Mrs. Hutchinson went on, "and then I looked out the window and the kids was gone, and then I remembered it was the twenty-seventh and came a-running." She dried her hands on her apron, and Mrs. Delacroix said, "You're in time, though. They're still talking away up there."

Mrs. Hutchinson craned her neck to see through the crowd and found her husband and children standing near the front. She tapped Mrs. Delacroix on the arm as a farewell and began to make her way through the crowd. The people separated good-humoredly to let her through; two or three people said, in voices just loud enough to be heard across the crowd, "Here comes your Missus, Hutchinson," and "Bill, she made it after all." Mrs. Hutchinson reached her husband, and Mr. Summers, who had been waiting, said cheerfully, "Thought we were going to have to get on without you, Tessie." Mrs. Hutchinson said, grinning, "Wouldn't have me leave m'dishes in the sink, now, would you, Joe?" and soft laughter ran through the crowd as the people stirred back into position after Mrs. Hutchinson's arrival.

"Well, now," Mr. Summers said soberly, "guess we better get started, get this over with, so's we can go back to work. Anybody ain't here?"

"Dunbar," several people said. "Dunbar, Dunbar."

Mr. Summers consulted his list. "Clyde Dunbar," he said. "That's right. He's broke his leg, hasn't he? Who's drawing for him?"

"Me, I guess," a woman said, and Mr. Summers turned to look at her. "Wife draws for her husband," Mr. Summers said. "Don't you have a grown boy to do it for you, Janey?" Although Mr. Summers and everyone else in the village knew the answer perfectly well, it was the business of the official of the lottery to ask such questions formally. Mr. Summers waited with an expression of polite interest while Mrs. Dunbar answered.

"Horace's not but sixteen yet," Mrs. Dunbar said regretfully. "Guess I gotta fill in for the old man this year."

"Right," Mr. Summers said. He made a note on the list he was holding. Then he asked, "Watson boy drawing this year?"

A tall boy in the crowd raised his hand. "Here," he said. "I'm drawing for m'-mother and me." He blinked his eyes nervously and ducked his head as several voices in the crowd said things like "Good fellow, Jack," and "Glad to see your mother's got a man to do it."

"Well," Mr. Summers said, "guess that's everyone. Old Man Warner make it?"

"Here," a voice said, and Mr. Summers nodded.

A sudden hush fell on the crowd as Mr. Summers cleared his throat and looked at the list. "All ready?" he called. "Now, I'll read the names—heads of families first—and the men come up and take a paper out of the box. Keep the paper folded in your hand without looking at it until everyone has had a turn. Everything clear?"

The people had done it so many times that they only half listened to the directions; most of them were quiet, wetting their lips, not looking around. Then Mr. Summers raised one hand high and said, "Adams." A man disengaged himself from the crowd and came forward. "Hi, Steve," Mr. Summers said, and Mr. Adams said, "Hi, Joe." They grinned at one another humorlessly and nervously. Then Mr. Adams reached into the black box and took out a folded paper. He held it firmly by one corner as he turned and went hastily back to his place in the crowd, where he stood a little apart from his family, not looking down at his hand.

"Allen," Mr. Summers said. "Anderson. . . . Bentham."

"Seems like there's no time at all between lotteries any more," Mrs. Delacroix said to Mrs. Graves in the back row. "Seems like we got through with the last one only last week."

"Time sure goes fast," Mrs. Graves said.

"Clark. . . . Delacroix."

"There goes my old man," Mrs. Delacroix said. She held her breath while her husband went forward.

"Dunbar," Mr. Summers said, and Mrs. Dunbar went steadily to the box while one of the women said, "Go on, Janey," and another said, "There she goes."

"We're next," Mrs. Graves said. She watched while Mr. Graves came around from the side of the box, greeted Mr. Summers gravely, and selected a slip of paper from the box. By now, all through the crowd there were men holding the small folded papers in their large hands, turning them over and over nervously. Mrs. Dunbar and her two sons stood together, Mrs. Dunbar holding the slip of paper.

"Harburt. . . . Hutchinson."

"Get up there, Bill," Mrs. Hutchinson said, and the people near her laughed.

"Jones."

"They do say," Mr. Adams said to Old Man Warner, who stood next to him, "that over in the north village they're talking of giving up the lottery."

Old Man Warner snorted. "Pack of crazy fools," he said. "Listening to the young folks, nothing's good enough for *them.* Next thing you know, they'll be wanting to go back to living in caves, nobody work any more, live *that* way for a while. Used to be a saying about 'Lottery in June, corn be heavy soon.' First thing you know, we'd all be eating stewed chickweed and acorns. There's *always* been a lottery," he added petulantly. "Bad enough to see young Joe Summers up there joking with everybody."

"Some places have already quit lotteries," Mrs. Adams said.

"Nothing but trouble in *that,*" Old Man Warner said stoutly. "Pack of young fools."

"Martin." And Bobby Martin watched his father go forward. "Overdyke. . . . Percy."

"I wish they'd hurry," Mrs. Dunbar said to her older son. "I wish they'd hurry."

"They're almost through," her son said.

"You get ready to run tell Dad," Mrs. Dunbar said.

Mr. Summers called his own name and then stepped forward precisely and selected a slip from the box. Then he called, "Warner."

"Seventy-seventh year I been in the lottery," Old Man Warner said as he went through the crowd. "Seventy-seventh time."

"Watson." The tall boy came awkwardly through the crowd. Someone said, "Don't be nervous, Jack," and Mr. Summers said, "Take your time, son."

"Zanini."

After that, there was a long pause, a breathless pause, until Mr. Summers, holding his slip of paper in the air, said, "All right, fellows." For a minute, no one moved, and then all the slips of paper were opened. Suddenly, all the women began to speak at once, saying, "Who is it?," "Who's got it?," "Is it the Dunbars?," "Is it the Watsons?" Then the voices began to say, "It's Hutchinson. It's Bill," "Bill Hutchinson's got it."

"Go tell your father," Mrs. Dunbar said to her older son.

People began to look around to see the Hutchinsons. Bill Hutchinson was standing quiet, staring down at the paper in his hand. Suddenly, Tessie Hutchinson shouted to Mr. Summers, "You didn't give him time enough to take any paper he wanted. I saw you. It wasn't fair!"

"Be a good sport, Tessie," Mrs. Delacroix called, and Mrs. Graves said, "All of us took the same chance."

"Shut up, Tessie," Bill Hutchinson said.

"Well, everyone," Mr. Summers said, "that was done pretty fast, and now we've got to be hurrying a little more to get done in time." He consulted his next list. "Bill," he said, "you draw for the Hutchinson family. You got any other households in the Hutchinsons?"

"There's Don and Eva," Mrs. Hutchinson yelled. "Make *them* take their chance!"

"Daughters draw with their husbands' families, Tessie," Mr. Summers said gently. "You know that as well as anyone else."

"It wasn't *fair,*" Tessie said.

"I guess not, Joe," Bill Hutchinson said regretfully. "My daughter draws with her husband's family, that's only fair. And I've got no other family except the kids."

"Then, as far as drawing for families is concerned, it's you," Mr. Summers said in explanation, "and as far as drawing for households is concerned, that's you, too. Right?"

"Right," Bill Hutchinson said.

"How many kids, Bill?" Mr. Summers asked formally.

"Three," Bill Hutchinson said. "There's Bill, Jr., and Nancy, and little Dave. And Tessie and me."

"All right, then," Mr. Summers said. "Harry, you got their tickets back?"

Mr. Graves nodded and held up the slips of paper. "Put them in the box, then," Mr. Summers directed. "Take Bill's and put it in."

"I think we ought to start over," Mrs. Hutchinson said, as quietly as she could. "I tell you it wasn't *fair.* You didn't give him time enough to choose. *Every*body saw that."

Mr. Graves had selected the five slips and put them in the box, and he dropped all the papers but those onto the ground, where the breeze caught them and lifted them off.

"Listen, everybody," Mrs. Hutchinson was saying to the people around her.

"Ready, Bill?" Mr. Summers asked, and Bill Hutchinson, with one quick glance around at his wife and children, nodded.

"Remember," Mr. Summers said, "take the slips and keep them folded until each person has taken one. Harry, you help little Dave." Mr. Graves took the hand of the little boy, who came willingly with him up to the box. "Take a paper out of the box, Davy," Mr. Summers said. Davy put his hand into the box and laughed. "Take just *one* paper," Mr. Summers said. "Harry, you hold it for him." Mr. Graves took the child's hand and removed the folded paper from the tight fist and held it while little Dave stood next to him and looked up at him wonderingly.

"Nancy next," Mr. Summers said. Nancy was twelve, and her school friends breathed heavily as she went forward, switching her skirt, and took a slip daintily from the box. "Bill, Jr.," Mr. Summers said, and Billy, his face red and his feet overlarge, nearly knocked the box over as he got a paper out. "Tessie," Mr. Summers said. She hesitated for a minute, looking around defiantly, and then set her lips and went up to the box. She snatched a paper out and held it behind her.

"Bill," Mr. Summers said, and Bill Hutchinson reached into the box and felt around, bringing his hand out at last with the slip of paper in it.

The crowd was quiet. A girl whispered, "I hope it's not Nancy," and the sound of the whisper reached the edges of the crowd.

"It's not the way it used to be," Old Man Warner said clearly. "People ain't the way they used to be."

"All right," Mr. Summers said. "Open the papers. Harry, you open little Dave's."

Mr. Graves opened the slip of paper and there was a general sigh through the crowd as he held it up and everyone could see that it was blank. Nancy and Bill, Jr., opened theirs at the same time, and both beamed and laughed, turning around to the crowd and holding their slips of paper above their heads.

"Tessie," Mr. Summers said. There was a pause, and then Mr. Summers looked at Bill Hutchinson, and Bill unfolded his paper and showed it. It was blank.

"It's Tessie," Mr. Summers said, and his voice was hushed. "Show us her paper, Bill."

Bill Hutchinson went over to his wife and forced the slip of paper out of her hand. It had a black spot on it, the black spot Mr. Summers had made the night before with the heavy pencil in the coal-company office. Bill Hutchinson held it up, and there was a stir in the crowd.

"All right, folks," Mr. Summers said. "Let's finish quickly."

Although the villagers had forgotten the ritual and lost the original black box, they still remembered to use stones. The pile of stones the boys had made earlier was ready; there were stones on the ground with the blowing scraps of paper that had come out of the box. Mrs. Delacroix selected a stone so large she had to pick it up with both hands and turned to Mrs. Dunbar. "Come on," she said. "Hurry up."

Mrs. Dunbar had small stones in both hands, and she said, gasping for breath, "I can't run at all. You'll have to go ahead and I'll catch up with you."

The children had stones already, and someone gave little Davy Hutchinson a few pebbles.

Tessie Hutchinson was in the center of a cleared space by now, and she held her hands out desperately as the villagers moved in on her. "It isn't fair," she said. A stone hit her on the side of the head.

Old Man Warner was saying, "Come on, come on, everyone." Steve Adams was in the front of the crowd of villagers, with Mrs. Graves beside him.

"It isn't fair, it isn't right," Mrs. Hutchinson screamed, and then they were upon her.

1948

Joseph Heller 1923–1999

Joseph Heller was born in Brooklyn, New York in 1923 to working-class Jewish American parents, Isaac and Lena Heller, who had immigrated to the United States from Russia. His father, who had worked driving a bakery truck, died when Heller was only four years old, after which his mother, with the help of the children, supported the family by working as a seamstress and laundress. In 1941 Heller graduated from high school and several months later enlisted in the Air Force. He spent World War II stationed in Corsica, where he flew sixty missions as a bomber pilot and developed a thorough distaste for war. After the war Heller married and, with the help of funding from the GI Bill, attended New York University, graduating Phi Beta Kappa with an English degree in 1948. He then enrolled at Columbia University, from which he took an M.A. in 1949. He spent the next year at Oxford University as a Fulbright Scholar and at about that time began writing short stories. Over the next decade, Heller first did low-level college teaching at Penn State and then worked at several national magazines, including Time, Look, *and* McCall's, *doing copywriting and promotions. In 1961 he returned to the academy to teach creative writing at Yale and at the University of Pennsylvania.*

During the 1950s Heller was also writing and publishing stories in such respected periodicals as Esquire *and* Atlantic Monthly. Catch-22, *his first novel, appeared in 1961, and was quickly recognized as a modern classic. Relying heavily on humor and satire, it influenced depictions of war in literature and film for a generation. Over the next ten years he wrote television plays and contributed to movie scripts. Thirteen years after* Catch-22, *Heller published his second novel,* Something Happened *(1974), which failed, most agree, to meet the public's expectations as a follow-up to the success of his first book. In the 1980s and 1990s he continued to write, publishing more than a half dozen novels and memoirs, including* Closing Time *(1994), a sequel to* Catch-22. *Joseph Heller died of a heart attack in 1999 at the age of 76.*

FURTHER READING: B. Keegan, *Joseph Heller: A Reference Guide,* 1978; *Critical Essays on Joseph Heller,* ed. J. Nagel, 1984; R. Merrill, *Joseph Heller,* 1987; D. Seed, *The Fiction of Joseph Heller,* 1989; J. Ruderman, *Joseph Heller,* 1991; S. Pinsker, *Understanding Joseph Heller,* 1991; *Conversations with Joseph Heller,* ed. A. Sorkin, 1993; M. Bruccoli and P. Bucker, *Joseph Heller: A Descriptive Bibliography,* 2002.

TEXT: *Catch-22,* 1995.

from *CATCH-22*

MAJOR MAJOR MAJOR MAJOR

Major major major major had had a difficult time from the start.

Like Miniver Cheevy,[1] he had been born too late—exactly thirty-six hours too late for the physical well-being of his mother, a gentle, ailing woman who, after a full day and a half's agony in the rigors of childbirth, was depleted of all resolve to pursue further the argument over the new child's name. In the hospital corridor, her husband moved ahead with the unsmiling determination of someone who knew what he was about. Major Major's father was a towering, gaunt man in heavy shoes and a black woolen suit. He filled out the birth certificate without faltering, betraying no emotion at all as he handed the completed form to the floor nurse. The nurse took it from him without comment and padded out of sight. He watched her go, wondering what she had on underneath.

Back in the ward, he found his wife lying vanquished beneath the blankets like a desiccated old vegetable, wrinkled, dry and white, her enfeebled tissues absolutely still. Her bed was at the very end of the ward, near a cracked window thickened with grime. Rain splashed from a moiling sky and the day was dreary and cold. In other parts of the hospital chalky people with aged, blue lips were dying on time. The man stood erect beside the bed and gazed down at the woman a long time.

'I have named the boy Caleb,' he announced to her finally in a soft voice. 'In accordance with your wishes.' The woman made no answer, and slowly the man smiled. He had planned it all perfectly, for his wife was asleep and would never know that he had lied to her as she lay on her sickbed in the poor ward of the county hospital.

[1]The protagonist of the poem "Miniver Cheevy," by Edwin Arlington Robinson.

From this meager beginning had sprung the ineffectual squadron commander who was now spending the better part of each working day in Pianosa[2] forging Washington Irving's[3] name to official documents. Major Major forged diligently with his left hand to elude identification, insulated against intrusion by his own undesired authority and camouflaged in his false mustache and dark glasses as an additional safeguard against detection by anyone chancing to peer in through the dowdy celluloid window from which some thief had carved out a slice. In between these two low points of his birth and his success lay thirty-one dismal years of loneliness and frustration.

Major Major had been born too late and too mediocre. Some men are born mediocre, some men achieve mediocrity, and some men have mediocrity thrust upon them. With Major Major it had been all three. Even among men lacking all distinction he inevitably stood out as a man lacking more distinction than all the rest, and people who met him were always impressed by how unimpressive he was.

Major Major had three strikes on him from the beginning—his mother, his father and Henry Fonda,[4] to whom he bore a sickly resemblance almost from the moment of his birth. Long before he even suspected who Henry Fonda was, he found himself the subject of unflattering comparisons everywhere he went. Total strangers saw fit to deprecate him, with the result that he was stricken early with a guilty fear of people and an obsequious impulse to apologize to society for the fact that he was *not* Henry Fonda. It was not an easy task for him to go through life looking something like Henry Fonda, but he never once thought of quitting, having inherited his perseverance from his father, a lanky man with a good sense of humor.

Major Major's father was a sober God-fearing man whose idea of a good joke was to lie about his age. He was a long-limbed farmer, a God-fearing, freedom-loving, law-abiding rugged individualist who held that federal aid to anyone but farmers was creeping socialism. He advocated thrift and hard work and disapproved of loose women who turned him down. His specialty was alfalfa, and he made a good thing out of not growing any. The government paid him well for every bushel of alfalfa he did not grow. The more alfalfa he did not grow, the more money the government gave him, and he spent every penny he didn't earn on new land to increase the amount of alfalfa he did not produce. Major Major's father worked without rest at not growing alfalfa. On long winter evenings he remained indoors and did not mend harness, and he sprang out of bed at the crack of noon every day just to make certain that the chores would not be done. He invested in land wisely and soon was not growing more alfalfa than any other man in the county. Neighbors sought him out for advice on all subjects, for he had made much money and was therefore wise. 'As ye sow, so shall ye reap,' he counseled one and all, and everyone said, 'Amen.'

Major Major's father was an outspoken champion of economy in government, provided it did not interfere with the sacred duty of government to pay farmers as much as they could get for all the alfalfa they produced that no one else wanted or for not producing any alfalfa at all. He was a proud and independent man who was opposed to unemployment insurance and never

[2]An island off the west coast of northern Italy, at whose air base the characters in the story are stationed in the midst of World War II.

[3]American writer (1783–1859). [4]Henry Fonda (1905–1982) was a famous movie actor.

hesitated to whine, whimper, wheedle, and extort for as much as he could get from whomever he could. He was a devout man whose pulpit was everywhere. 'The Lord gave us good farmers two strong hands so that we could take as much as we could grab with both of them,' he preached with ardor on the courthouse steps or in front of the A & P[5] as he waited for the bad-tempered gum-chewing young cashier he was after to step outside and give him a nasty look. 'If the Lord didn't want us to take as much as we could get,' he preached, 'He wouldn't have given us two good hands to take it with.' And the others murmured, 'Amen.'

Major Major's father had a Calvinist's faith in predestination and could perceive distinctly how everyone's misfortunes but his own were expressions of God's will. He smoked cigarettes and drank whiskey, and he thrived on good wit and stimulating intellectual conversation, particularly his own when he was lying about his age or telling that good one about God and his wife's difficulties in delivering Major Major. The good one about God and his wife's difficulties had to do with the fact that it had taken God only six days to produce the whole world, whereas his wife had spent a full day and a half in labor just to produce Major Major. A lesser man might have wavered that day in the hospital corridor, a weaker man might have compromised on such excellent substitutes as Drum Major, Minor Major, Sergeant Major, or C. Sharp Major, but Major Major's father had waited fourteen years for just such an opportunity, and he was not a person to waste it. Major Major's father had a good joke about opportunity. 'Opportunity only knocks once in this world,' he would say. Major Major's father repeated this good joke at every opportunity.

Being born with a sickly resemblance to Henry Fonda was the first of a long series of practical jokes of which destiny was to make Major Major the unhappy victim throughout his joyless life. Being born Major Major Major was the second. The fact that he had been born Major Major Major was a secret known only to his father. Not until Major Major was enrolling in kindergarten was the discovery of his real name made, and then the effects were disastrous. The news killed his mother, who just lost her will to live and wasted away and died, which was just fine with his father, who had decided to marry the bad-tempered girl at the A&P if he had to and who had not been optimistic about his chances of getting his wife off the land without paying her some money or flogging her.

On Major Major himself the consequences were only slightly less severe. It was a harsh and stunning realization that was forced upon him at so tender an age, the realization that he was not, as he had always been led to believe, Caleb Major, but instead was some total stranger named Major Major Major about whom he knew absolutely nothing and about whom nobody else had ever heard before. What playmates he had withdrew from him and never returned, disposed, as they were, to distrust all strangers, especially one who had already deceived them by pretending to be someone they had known for years. Nobody would have anything to do with him. He began to drop things and to trip. He had a shy and hopeful manner in each new contact, and he was always disappointed. Because he needed a friend so desperately, he never found one. He grew awkwardly into a tall, strange, dreamy boy with fragile eyes and a very delicate mouth whose tentative, groping smile collapsed instantly into hurt disorder at every fresh rebuff.

[5] A supermarket chain.

He was polite to his elders, who disliked him. Whatever his elders told him to do, he did. They told him to look before he leaped, and he always looked before he leaped. They told him never to put off until the next day what he could do the day before, and he never did. He was told to honor his father and his mother, and he honored his father and his mother. He was told that he should not kill, and he did not kill, until he got into the Army. Then he was told to kill, and he killed. He turned the other cheek on every occasion and always did unto others exactly as he would have had others do unto him. When he gave to charity, his left hand never knew what his right hand was doing. He never once took the name of the Lord his God in vain, committed adultery or coveted his neighbor's ass. In fact, he loved his neighbor and never even bore false witness against him. Major Major's elders disliked him because he was such a flagrant nonconformist.

Since he had nothing better to do well in, he did well in school. At the state university he took his studies so seriously that he was suspected by the homosexuals of being a Communist and suspected by the Communists of being a homosexual. He majored in English history, which was a mistake.

'*English* history!' roared the silver-maned senior Senator from his state indignantly. 'What's the matter with American history? American history is as good as any history in the world!'

Major Major switched immediately to American literature, but not before the F.B.I. had opened a file on him. There were six people and a Scotch terrier inhabiting the remote farmhouse Major Major called home, and five of them and the Scotch terrier turned out to be agents for the F.B.I. Soon they had enough derogatory information on Major Major to do whatever they wanted to with him. The only thing they could find to do with him, however, was take him into the Army as a private and make him a major four days later so that Congressmen with nothing else on their minds could go trotting back and forth through the streets of Washington, D.C., chanting, 'Who promoted Major Major? Who promoted Major Major?'

Actually, Major Major had been promoted by an I.B.M. machine with a sense of humor almost as keen as his father's. When war broke out, he was still docile and compliant. They told him to enlist, and he enlisted. They told him to apply for aviation cadet training, and he applied for aviation cadet training, and the very next night found himself standing barefoot in icy mud at three o'clock in the morning before a tough and belligerent sergeant from the Southwest who told them he could beat hell out of any man in his outfit and was ready to prove it. The recruits in his squadron had all been shaken roughly awake only minutes before by the sergeant's corporals and told to assemble in front of the administration tent. It was still raining on Major Major. They fell into ranks in the civilian clothes they had brought into the Army with them three days before. Those who had lingered to put shoes and socks on were sent back to their cold, wet, dark tents to remove them, and they were all barefoot in the mud as the sergeant ran his stony eyes over their faces and told them he could beat hell out of any man in his outfit. No one was inclined to dispute him.

Major Major's unexpected promotion to major the next day plunged the belligerent sergeant into a bottomless gloom, for he was no longer able to boast that he could beat hell out of any man in his outfit. He brooded for hours in his tent like Saul, receiving no visitors, while his elite guard of corporals stood discouraged watch outside. At three o'clock in the morning he found his solution, and Major Major and the other recruits were again shaken roughly awake and ordered to assemble barefoot in the drizzly glare at the administration tent, where the sergeant was already waiting, his fists clenched on his hips cockily, so eager to speak that he could hardly wait for them to arrive.

'Me and Major Major,' he boasted, in the same tough, clipped tones of the night before, 'can beat hell out of any man in my outfit.'

The officers on the base took action on the Major Major problem later that same day. How could they cope with a major like Major Major? To demean him personally would be to demean all other officers of equal or lesser rank. To treat him with courtesy, on the other hand, was unthinkable. Fortunately, Major Major had applied for aviation cadet training. Orders transferring him away were sent to the mimeograph room late in the afternoon, and at three o'clock in the morning Major Major was again shaken roughly awake, bidden Godspeed by the sergeant and placed aboard a plane heading west.

Lieutenant Scheisskopf turned white as a sheet when Major Major reported to him in California with bare feet and mudcaked toes. Major Major had taken it for granted that he was being shaken roughly awake again to stand barefoot in the mud and had left his shoes and socks in the tent. The civilian clothing in which he reported for duty to Lieutenant Scheisskopf was rumpled and dirty. Lieutenant Scheisskopf, who had not yet made his reputation as a parader, shuddered violently at the picture Major Major would make marching barefoot in his squadron that coming Sunday.

'Go to the hospital quickly,' he mumbled, when he had recovered sufficiently to speak, 'and tell them you're sick. Stay there until your allowance for uniforms catches up with you and you have some money to buy some clothes. And some shoes. Buy some shoes.'

'Yes, sir.'

'I don't think you have to call me "sir," sir,' Lieutenant Scheisskopf pointed out. 'You outrank me.'

'Yes, sir. I may outrank you, sir, but you're still my commanding officer.'

'Yes, sir, that's right,' Lieutenant Scheisskopf agreed. 'You may outrank me, sir, but I'm still your commanding officer. So you better do what I tell you, sir, or you'll get into trouble. Go to the hospital and tell them you're sick, sir. Stay there until your uniform allowance catches up with you and you have some money to buy some uniforms.'

'Yes, sir.'

'And some shoes, sir. Buy some shoes the first chance you get, sir.'

'Yes, sir. I will, sir.'

'Thank you, sir.'

Life in cadet school for Major Major was no different than life had been for him all along. Whoever he was with always wanted him to be with someone else. His instructors gave him preferred treatment at every stage in order to push him along quickly and be rid of him. In almost no time he had his pilot's wings and found himself overseas, where things began suddenly to improve. All his life, Major Major had longed for but one thing, to be absorbed, and in Pianosa, for a while, he finally was. Rank meant little to the men on combat duty, and relations between officers and enlisted men were relaxed and informal. Men whose names he didn't even know said 'Hi' and invited him to go swimming or play basketball. His ripest hours were spent in the day-long basketball games no one gave a damn about winning. Score was never kept, and the number of players might vary from one to thirty-five. Major Major had never played basketball or any other game before, but his great, bobbing height and rapturous enthusiasm helped make up for his innate clumsiness and lack of experience. Major Major found true happiness there on the lopsided basketball court with the officers and enlisted men who were almost his friends. If there were no winners, there were no losers, and Major Major enjoyed every gamboling moment right up till the day Colonel Cathcart roared up in his jeep after Major Duluth was killed and made it impossible for him ever to enjoy playing basketball there again.

'You're the new squadron commander,' Colonel Cathcart had shouted rudely across the railroad ditch to him. 'But don't think it means anything, because it doesn't. All it means is that you're the new squadron commander.'

Colonel Cathcart had nursed an implacable grudge against Major Major for a long time. A superfluous major on his rolls meant an untidy table of organization and gave ammunition to the men at Twenty-seventh Air Force Headquarters who Colonel Cathcart was positive were his enemies and rivals. Colonel Cathcart had been praying for just some stroke of good luck like Major Duluth's death. He had been plagued by one extra major; he now had an opening for one major. He appointed Major Major squadron commander and roared away in his jeep as abruptly as he had come.

For Major Major, it meant the end of the game. His face flushed with discomfort, and he was rooted to the spot in disbelief as the rain clouds gathered above him again. When he turned to his teammates, he encountered a reef of curious, reflective faces all gazing at him woodenly with morose and inscrutable animosity. He shivered with shame. When the game resumed, it was not good any longer. When he dribbled, no one tried to stop him; when he called for a pass, whoever had the ball passed it; and when he missed a basket, no one raced him for the rebound. The only voice was his own. The next day was the same, and the day after that he did not come back.

Almost on cue, everyone in the squadron stopped talking to him and started staring at him. He walked through life self-consciously with downcast eyes and burning cheeks, the object of contempt, envy, suspicion, resentment and malicious innuendo everywhere he went. People who had hardly noticed his resemblance to Henry Fonda before now never ceased discussing it, and there were even those who hinted sinisterly that Major Major had been elevated to squadron commander *because* he resembled Henry Fonda. Captain Black, who had aspired to the position himself, maintained that Major Major really *was* Henry Fonda but was too chickenshit to admit it.

Major Major floundered bewilderedly from one embarrassing catastrophe to another. Without consulting him, Sergeant Towser had his belongings moved into the roomy trailer Major Duluth had occupied alone, and when Major Major came rushing breathlessly into the orderly room to report the theft of his things, the young corporal there scared him half out of his wits by leaping to his feet and shouting '*Attention!*' the moment he appeared. Major Major snapped to attention with all the rest in the orderly room, wondering what important personage had entered behind him. Minutes passed in rigid silence, and the whole lot of them might have stood there at attention till doomsday if Major Danby had not dropped by from Group to congratulate Major Major twenty minutes later and put them all at ease.

Major Major fared even more lamentably at the mess hall, where Milo, his face fluttery with smiles, was waiting to usher him proudly to a small table he had set up in front and decorated with an embroidered tablecloth and a nosegay of posies in a pink cut-glass vase. Major Major hung back with horror, but he was not bold enough to resist with all the others watching. Even Havermeyer had lifted his head from his plate to gape at him with his heavy, pendulous jaw. Major Major submitted meekly to Milo's tugging and cowered in disgrace at his private table throughout the whole meal. The food was ashes in his mouth, but he swallowed every mouthful rather than risk offending any of the men connected with its preparation. Alone with Milo later, Major Major felt protest stir for the first time and said he would prefer to continue eating with the other officers. Milo told him it wouldn't work.

'I don't see what there is to work,' Major Major argued. 'Nothing ever happened before.'

'You were never the squadron commander before.'

'Major Duluth was the squadron commander and he always ate at the same table with the rest of the men.'

'It was different with Major Duluth, sir.'

'In what way was it different with Major Duluth?'

'I wish you wouldn't ask me that, sir,' said Milo.

'Is it because I look like Henry Fonda?' Major Major mustered the courage to demand.

'Some people say you *are* Henry Fonda,' Milo answered.

'Well, I'm not Henry Fonda,' Major Major exclaimed, in a voice quavering with exasperation. 'And I don't look the least bit like him. And even if I do look like Henry Fonda, what difference does that make?'

'It doesn't make any difference. That's what I'm trying to tell you, sir. It's just not the same with you as it was with Major Duluth.'

And it just wasn't the same, for when Major Major, at the next meal, stepped from the food counter to sit with the others at the regular tables, he was frozen in his tracks by the impenetrable wall of antagonism thrown up by their faces and stood petrified with his tray quivering in his hands until Milo glided forward wordlessly to rescue him, by leading him tamely to his private table. Major Major gave up after that and always ate at his table alone with his back to the others. He was certain they resented him because he seemed too good to eat with them now that he was squadron commander. There was never any conversation in the mess tent when Major Major was present. He was conscious that other officers tried to avoid eating at the same time, and everyone was greatly relieved when he stopped coming there altogether and began taking his meals in his trailer.

Major Major began forging Washington Irving's name to official documents the day after the first C.I.D. man showed up to interrogate him about somebody at the hospital who had been doing it and gave him the idea. He had been bored and dissatisfied in his new position. He had been made squadron commander but had no idea what he was supposed to *do* as squadron commander, unless all he was supposed to do was forge Washington Irving's name to official documents and listen to the isolated clinks and thumps of Major—de Coverley's horseshoes falling to the ground outside the window of his small office in the rear of the orderly-room tent. He was hounded incessantly by an impression of vital duties left unfulfilled and waited in vain for his responsibilities to overtake him. He seldom went out unless it was absolutely necessary, for he could not get used to being stared at. Occasionally, the monotony was broken by some officer or enlisted man Sergeant Towser referred to him on some matter that Major Major was unable to cope with and referred right back to Sergeant Towser for sensible disposition. Whatever he was supposed to get done as squadron commander apparently was getting done without any assistance from him. He grew moody and depressed. At times he thought seriously of going with all his sorrows to see the chaplain, but the chaplain seemed so overburdened with miseries of his own that Major Major shrank from adding to his troubles. Besides, he was not quite sure if chaplains were for squadron commanders.

He had never been quite sure about Major—de Coverley, either, who, when he was not away renting apartments or kidnaping foreign laborers, had nothing more pressing to do than pitch horseshoes. Major Major often paid strict attention to the horseshoes falling softly against the earth or riding down around the small steel pegs in the ground. He peeked out at Major—de Coverley for hours and marveled that someone so august had nothing more important to do. He was often tempted to join Major—de Coverley, but pitching horseshoes all day long seemed almost as dull as signing 'Major Major Major' to official documents, and Major—de Coverley's countenance was so forbidding that Major Major was in awe of approaching him.

Major Major wondered about his relationship to Major—de Coverley and about Major—de Coverley's relationship to him. He knew that Major—de Coverley was his executive officer, but he did not know what that meant, and he could not decide whether in Major—de Coverley he was blessed with a lenient superior or cursed with a delinquent subordinate. He did not want to ask Sergeant Towser, of whom he was secretly afraid, and there was no one else he could ask, least of all Major—de Coverley. Few people ever dared approach Major—de Coverley about anything and the only officer foolish enough to pitch one of his horseshoes was stricken the very next day with the worst case of Pianosan crud that Gus or Wes or even Doc Daneeka had ever seen or even heard about. Everyone was positive the disease had been inflicted upon the poor officer in retribution by Major—de Coverley, although no one was sure how.

Most of the official documents that came to Major Major's desk did not concern him at all. The vast majority consisted of allusions to prior communications which Major Major had never seen or heard of. There was never any need to look them up, for the instructions were invariably to disregard. In the space of a single productive minute, therefore, he might endorse twenty separate documents each advising him to pay absolutely no attention to any of the others. From General Peckem's office on the mainland came prolix bulletins each day headed by such cheery homilies as 'Procrastination is the Thief of Time' and 'Cleanliness is Next to Godliness.'

General Peckem's communications about cleanliness and procrastination made Major Major feel like a filthy procrastinator, and he always got those out of the way as quickly as he could. The only official documents that interested him were those occasional ones pertaining to the unfortunate second lieutenant who had been killed on the mission over Orvieto less than two hours after he arrived on Pianosa and whose partly unpacked belongings were still in Yossarian's tent. Since the unfortunate lieutenant had reported to the operations tent instead of to the orderly room, Sergeant Towser had decided that it would be safest to report him as never having reported to the squadron at all, and the occasional documents relating to him dealt with the fact that he seemed to have vanished into thin air, which, in one way, was exactly what did happen to him. In the long run, Major Major was grateful for the official documents that came to his desk, for sitting in his office signing them all day long was a lot better than sitting in his office all day long not signing them. They gave him something to do.

Inevitably, every document he signed came back with a fresh page added for a new signature by him after intervals of from two to ten days. They were always much thicker than formerly, for in between the sheet bearing his last endorsement and the sheet added for his new endorsement were the sheets bearing the most recent endorsements of all the other officers in scattered locations who were also occupied in signing their names to that same official document. Major Major grew despondent as he watched simple communications swell prodigiously into huge manuscripts. No matter how many times he signed one, it always came back for still another signature, and he began to despair of ever being free of any of them. One day—it was the day after the C.I.D. man's first visit—Major Major signed Washington Irving's name to one of the documents instead of his own, just to see how it would feel. He liked it. He liked it so much that for the rest of that afternoon he did the same with all the official documents. It was an act of impulsive frivolity and rebellion for which he knew afterward he would be punished severely. The next morning he entered his office in trepidation and waited to see what would happen. Nothing happened.

He had sinned, and it was good, for none of the documents to which he had signed Washington Irving's name ever came back! Here, at last, was progress, and Major Major threw himself into his new career with uninhibited gusto. Signing Washington Irving's name to official documents was not much of a career, perhaps, but it was less monotonous than signing 'Major Major Major.' When Washington Irving did grow monotonous, he could reverse the order and sign Irving Washington until that grew monotonous. And he was getting something done, for none of the documents signed with either of these names ever came back to the squadron.

What did come back, eventually, was a *second* C.I.D. man, masquerading as a pilot. The men knew he was a C.I.D. man because he confided to them he was and urged each of them not to reveal his true identity to any of the other men to whom he had already confided that he was a C.I.D. man.

'You're the only one in the squadron who knows I'm a C.I.D. man,' he confided to Major Major, 'and it's absolutely essential that it remain a secret so that my efficiency won't be impaired. Do you understand?'

'Sergeant Towser knows.'

'Yes, I know. I had to tell him in order to get in to see you. But I know he won't tell a soul under any circumstances.'

'He told me,' said Major Major. 'He told me there was a C.I.D. man outside to see me.'

'That bastard. I'll have to throw a security check on him. I wouldn't leave any top-secret documents lying around here if I were you. At least not until I make my report.'

'I don't get any top-secret documents,' said Major Major.

'That's the kind I mean. Lock them in your cabinet where Sergeant Towser can't get his hands on them.'

'Sergeant Towser has the only key to the cabinet.'

'I'm afraid we're wasting time,' said the second C.I.D. man rather stiffly. He was a brisk, pudgy, high-strung person whose movements were swift and certain. He took a number of photostats out of a large red expansion envelope he had been hiding conspicuously beneath a leather flight jacket painted garishly with pictures of airplanes flying through orange bursts of flak and with orderly rows of little bombs signifying fifty-five combat missions flown. 'Have you ever seen any of these?'

Major Major looked with a blank expression at copies of personal correspondence from the hospital on which the censoring officer had written 'Washington Irving' or 'Irving Washington.'

'No.'

'How about these?'

Major Major gazed next at copies of official documents addressed to him to which he had been signing the same signatures.

'No.'

'Is the man who signed these names in your squadron?'

'Which one? There are two names here.'

'Either one. We figure that Washington Irving and Irving Washington are one man and that he's using two names just to throw us off the track. That's done very often you know.'

'I don't think there's a man with either of those names in my squadron.'

A look of disappointment crossed the second C.I.D. man's face. 'He's a lot cleverer than we thought,' he observed. 'He's using a third name and posing as someone else. And I think . . . yes, I think I know what that third name is.' With excitement and inspiration, he held another photostat out for Major Major to study. 'How about this?'

Major Major bent forward slightly and saw a copy of the piece of V mail[6] from which Yossarian had blacked out everything but the name Mary and on which he had written, 'I yearn for you tragically. R. O. Shipman, Chaplain, U.S. Army.' Major Major shook his head.

'I've never seen it before.'

'Do you know who R. O. Shipman is?'

'He's the group chaplain.'

'That locks it up,' said the second C.I.D. man. 'Washington Irving is the group chaplain.'

Major Major felt a twinge of alarm. 'R. O. Shipman is the group chaplain,' he corrected.

'Are you sure?'

'Yes.'

'Why should the group chaplain write this on a letter?'

'Perhaps somebody else wrote it and forged his name.'

'Why should somebody want to forge the group chaplain's name?'

'To escape detection.'

'You may be right,' the second C.I.D. man decided after an instant's hesitation, and smacked his lips crisply. 'Maybe we're confronted with a gang, with two men working together who just happen to have opposite names. Yes, I'm sure that's it. One of them here in the squadron, one of them up

[6]A mail system used in World War II that involved censoring mail and reducing it in size by using microfilm, and then reprinting it later.

at the hospital and one of them with the chaplain. That makes three men, doesn't it? Are you absolutely sure you never saw any of these official documents before?'

'I would have signed them if I had.'

'With whose name?' asked the second C.I.D. man cunningly. 'Yours or Washington Irving's?'

'With my own name,' Major Major told him. 'I don't even know Washington Irving's name.'

The second C.I.D. man broke into a smile.

'Major, I'm glad you're in the clear. It means we'll be able to work together, and I'm going to need every man I can get. Somewhere in the European theater of operations is a man who's getting his hands on communications addressed to you. Have you any idea who it can be?'

'No.'

'Well, I have a pretty good idea,' said the second C.I.D. man, and leaned forward to whisper confidentially. 'That bastard Towser. Why else would he go around shooting his mouth off about me? Now, you keep your eyes open and let me know the minute you hear anyone even talking about Washington Irving. I'll throw a security check on the chaplain and everyone else around here.'

The moment he was gone, the first C.I.D. man jumped into Major Major's office through the window and wanted to know who the second C.I.D. man was. Major Major barely recognized him.

'He was a C.I.D. man,' Major Major told him.

'Like hell he was,' said the first C.I.D. man. 'I'm the C.I.D. man around here.'

Major Major barely recognized him because he was wearing a faded maroon corduroy bathrobe with open seams under both arms, linty flannel pajamas, and worn house slippers with one flapping sole. This was regulation hospital dress, Major Major recalled. The man had added about twenty pounds and seemed bursting with good health.

'I'm really a very sick man,' he whined. 'I caught cold in the hospital from a fighter pilot and came down with a very serious case of pneumonia.'

'I'm very sorry,' Major Major said.

'A lot of good that does me,' the C.I.D. man sniveled. 'I don't want your sympathy. I just want you to know what I'm going through. I came down to warn you that Washington Irving seems to have shifted his base of operations from the hospital to your squadron. You haven't heard anyone around here talking about Washington Irving, have you?'

'As a matter of fact, I have,' Major Major answered.

'That man who was just in here. He was talking about Washington Irving.'

'Was he really?' the first C.I.D. man cried with delight. 'This might be just what we needed to crack the case wide open! You keep him under surveillance twenty-four hours a day while I rush back to the hospital and write my superiors for further instructions.' The C.I.D. man jumped out of Major Major's office through the window and was gone.

A minute later, the flap separating Major Major's office from the orderly room flew open and the second C.I.D. man was back, puffing frantically in haste. Gasping for breath, he shouted, 'I just saw a man in red pajamas jumping out of your window and go running up the road! Didn't you see him?'

'He was here talking to me,' Major Major answered.

'I thought that looked mighty suspicious, a man jumping out the window in red pajamas.' The man paced about the small office in vigorous circles. 'At first I thought it was you, hightailing it for Mexico. But now I see it wasn't you. He didn't say anything about Washington Irving, did he?'

'As a matter of fact,' said Major Major, 'he did.'

'He did?' cried the second C.I.D. man. 'That's fine! This might be just the break we needed to crack the case wide open. Do you know where we can find him?'

'At the hospital. He's really a very sick man.'

'That's great!' exclaimed the second C.I.D. man. 'I'll go right up there after him. It would be best if I went incognito. I'll go explain the situation at the medical tent and have them send me there as a patient.'

'They won't send me to the hospital as a patient unless I'm sick,' he reported back to Major Major. 'Actually, I am pretty sick. I've been meaning to turn myself in for a checkup, and this will be a good opportunity. I'll go back to the medical tent and tell them I'm sick, and I'll get sent to the hospital that way.'

'Look what they did to me,' he reported back to Major Major with purple gums. His distress was inconsolable. He carried his shoes and socks in his hands, and his toes had been painted with gentian-violet solution, too. 'Who ever heard of a C.I.D. man with purple gums?' he moaned.

He walked away from the orderly room with his head down and tumbled into a slit trench and broke his nose. His temperature was still normal, but Gus and Wes made an exception of him and sent him to the hospital in an ambulance.

Major Major had lied, and it was good. He was not really surprised that it was good, for he had observed that people who did lie were, on the whole, more resourceful and ambitious and successful than people who did not lie. Had he told the truth to the second C.I.D. man, he would have found himself in trouble. Instead he had lied and he was free to continue his work.

He became more circumspect in his work as a result of the visit from the second C.I.D. man. He did all his signing with his left hand and only while wearing the dark glasses and false mustache he had used unsuccessfully to help him begin playing basketball again. As an additional precaution, he made a happy switch from Washington Irving to John Milton.[7] John Milton was supple and concise. Like Washington Irving, he could be reversed with good effect whenever he grew monotonous. Furthermore, he enabled Major Major to double his output, for John Milton was so much shorter than either his own name or Washington Irving's and took so much less time to write. John Milton proved fruitful in still one more respect. He was versatile, and Major Major soon found himself incorporating the signature in fragments of imaginary dialogues. Thus, typical endorsements on the official documents might read, 'John Milton is a sadist' or 'Have you seen Milton, John?' One signature of which he was especially proud read, 'Is anybody in the John, Milton?' John Milton threw open whole new vistas filled with charming, inexhaustible possibilities that promised to ward off monotony forever. Major Major went back to Washington Irving when John Milton grew monotonous.

[7]English poet (1608–1674).

Major Major had bought the dark glasses and false mustache in Rome in a final, futile attempt to save himself from the swampy degradation into which he was steadily sinking. First there had been the awful humiliation of the Great Loyalty Oath Crusade, when not one of the thirty or forty people circulating competitive loyalty oaths would even allow him to sign. Then, just when that was blowing over, there was the matter of Clevinger's plane disappearing so mysteriously in thin air with every member of the crew, and blame for the strange mishap centering balefully on him because he had never signed any of the loyalty oaths.

The dark glasses had large magenta rims. The false black mustache was a flamboyant organ-grinder's, and he wore them both to the basketball game one day when he felt he could endure his loneliness no longer. He affected an air of jaunty familiarity as he sauntered to the court and prayed silently that he would not be recognized. The others pretended not to recognize him, and he began to have fun. Just as he finished congratulating himself on his innocent ruse he was bumped hard by one of his opponents and knocked to his knees. Soon he was bumped hard again, and it dawned on him that they did recognize him and that they were using his disguise as a license to elbow, trip and maul him. They did not want him at all. And just as he did realize this, the players on his team fused instinctively with the players on the other team into a single, howling, bloodthirsty mob that descended upon him from all sides with foul curses and swinging fists. They knocked him to the ground, kicked him while he was on the ground, attacked him again after he had struggled blindly to his feet. He covered his face with his hands and could not see. They swarmed all over each other in their frenzied compulsion to bludgeon him, kick him, gouge him, trample him. He was pummeled spinning to the edge of the ditch and sent slithering down on his head and shoulders. At the bottom he found his footing, clambered up the other wall and staggered away beneath the hail of hoots and stones with which they pelted him until he lurched into shelter around a corner of the orderly room tent. His paramount concern throughout the entire assault was to keep his dark glasses and false mustache in place so that he might continue pretending he was somebody else and be spared the dreaded necessity of having to confront them with his authority.

Back in his office, he wept; and when he finished weeping he washed the blood from his mouth and nose, scrubbed the dirt from the abrasions on his cheek and forehead, and summoned Sergeant Towser.

'From now on,' he said, 'I don't want anyone to come in to see me while I'm here. Is that clear?'

'Yes, sir,' said Sergeant Towser. 'Does that include me?'

'Yes.'

'I see. Will that be all?'

'Yes.'

'What shall I say to the people who do come to see you while you're here?'

'Tell them I'm in and ask them to wait.'

'Yes, sir. For how long?'

'Until I've left.'

'And then what shall I do with them?'

'I don't care.'

'May I send them in to see you after you've left?'

'Yes.'

'But you won't be here then, will you?'

'No.'

'Yes, sir. Will that be all?'

'Yes.'

'Yes, sir.'

'From now on,' Major Major said to the middle-aged enlisted man who took care of his trailer, 'I don't want you to come here while I'm here to ask me if there's anything you can do for me. Is that clear?'

'Yes, sir,' said the orderly. 'When should I come here to find out if there's anything you want me to do for you?'

'When I'm not here.'

'Yes, sir. And what should I do?'

'Whatever I tell you to.'

'But you won't be here to tell me. Will you?'

'No.'

'Then what should I do?'

'Whatever has to be done.'

'Yes, sir.'

'That will be all,' said Major Major.

'Yes, sir,' said the orderly. 'Will that be all?'

'No,' said Major Major. 'Don't come in to clean, either. Don't come in for anything unless you're sure I'm not here.'

'Yes, sir. But how can I always be sure?'

'If you're not sure, just assume that I am here and go away until you are sure. Is that clear?'

'Yes, sir.'

'I'm sorry to have to talk to you in this way, but I have to. Goodbye.'

'Goodbye, sir.'

'And thank you. For everything.'

'Yes, sir.'

'From now on,' Major Major said to Milo Minderbinder, 'I'm not going to come to the mess hall any more. I'll have all my meals brought to me in my trailer.'

'I think that's a good idea, sir,' Milo answered. 'Now I'll be able to serve you special dishes that the others will never know about. I'm sure you'll enjoy them. Colonel Cathcart always does.'

'I don't want any special dishes. I want exactly what you serve all the other officers. Just have whoever brings it knock once on my door and leave the tray on the step. Is that clear?'

'Yes, sir,' said Milo. 'That's very clear. I've got some live Maine lobsters hidden away that I can serve you tonight with an excellent Roquefort salad and two frozen éclairs that were smuggled out of Paris only yesterday together with an important member of the French underground. Will that do for a start?'

'No.'

'Yes, sir. I understand.'

For dinner that night Milo served him broiled Maine lobster with excellent Roquefort salad and two frozen éclairs. Major Major was annoyed. If he sent it back, though, it would only go to waste or to somebody else, and Major Major had a weakness for broiled lobster. He ate with a guilty conscience. The next day for lunch there was terrapin Maryland with a whole quart of Dom Pérignon 1937,[8] and Major Major gulped it down without a thought.

After Milo, there remained only the men in the orderly room, and Major Major avoided them by entering and leaving every time through the dingy celluloid window of his office. The window unbuttoned and was low and large and easy to jump through from either side. He managed the distance between the orderly room and his trailer by darting around the corner of the tent when the coast was clear, leaping down into the railroad ditch and dashing along with head bowed until he attained the sanctuary of the forest. Abreast of his trailer, he left the ditch and wove his way speedily toward home through the dense underbrush, in which the only person he ever encountered was Captain Flume, who, drawn and ghostly, frightened him half to death one twilight by materializing without warning out of a patch of dewberry bushes to complain that Chief White Halfoat had threatened to slit his throat open from ear to ear.

'If you ever frighten me like that again,' Major Major told him, *'I'll* slit your throat open from ear to ear.'

Captain Flume gasped and dissolved right back into the patch of dewberry bushes, and Major Major never set eyes on him again.

When Major Major looked back on what he had accomplished, he was pleased. In the midst of a few foreign acres teeming with more than two hundred people, he had succeeded in becoming a recluse. With a little ingenuity and vision, he had made it all but impossible for anyone in the squadron to talk to him, which was just fine with everyone, he noticed, since no one wanted to talk to him anyway. No one, it turned out, but that madman Yossarian, who brought him down with a flying tackle one day as he was scooting along the bottom of the ditch to his trailer for lunch.

The last person in the squadron Major Major wanted to be brought down with a flying tackle by was Yossarian. There was something inherently disreputable about Yossarian, always carrying on so disgracefully about that dead man in his tent who wasn't even there and then taking off all his clothes after the Avignon[9] mission and going around without them right up to the day General Dreedle stepped up to pin a medal on him for his heroism over Ferrara[10] and found him standing in formation stark naked. No one in the world had the power to remove the dead man's disorganized effects from Yossarian's tent. Major Major had forfeited the authority when he permitted Sergeant Towser to report the lieutenant who had been killed over Orvieto less than two hours after he arrived in the squadron as never having arrived in the squadron at all. The only one with any right to remove his belongings from Yossarian's tent, it seemed to Major Major, was Yossarian himself, and Yossarian, it seemed to Major Major, had no right.

Major Major groaned after Yossarian brought him down with a flying tackle, and tried to wiggle to his feet. Yossarian wouldn't let him.

'Captain Yossarian,' Yossarian said, 'requests permission to speak to the major at once about a matter of life or death.'

[8] An expensive champagne. [9] A city in southern France.
[10] A city in northeastern Italy.

'Let me up, please,' Major Major bid him in cranky discomfort. 'I can't return your salute while I'm lying on my arm.

Yossarian released him. They stood up slowly. Yossarian saluted again and repeated his request.

'Let's go to my office,' Major Major said. 'I don't think this is the best place to talk.'

'Yes, sir,' answered Yossarian.

They smacked the gravel from their clothing and walked in constrained silence to the entrance of the orderly room.

'Give me a minute or two to put some mercurochrome on these cuts. Then have Sergeant Towser send you in.'

'Yes, sir.'

Major Major strode with dignity to the rear of the orderly room without glancing at any of the clerks and typists working at the desks and filing cabinets. He let the flap leading to his office fall closed behind him. As soon as he was alone in his office, he raced across the room to the window and jumped outside to dash away. He found Yossarian blocking his path. Yossarian was waiting at attention and saluted again.

'Captain Yossarian requests permission to speak to the major at once about a matter of life or death,' he repeated determinedly.

'Permission denied,' Major Major snapped.

'That won't do it.'

Major Major gave in. 'All right,' he conceded wearily. 'I'll talk to you. Please jump inside my office.'

'After you.'

They jumped inside the office. Major Major sat down, and Yossarian moved around in front of his desk and told him that he did not want to fly any more combat missions. *What could he do?* Major Major asked himself. All he could do was what he had been instructed to do by Colonel Korn and hope for the best.

'Why not?' he asked.

'I'm afraid.'

'That's nothing to be ashamed of,' Major Major counseled him kindly. 'We're all afraid.'

'I'm not ashamed,' Yossarian said. 'I'm just afraid.'

'You wouldn't be normal if you were never afraid. Even the bravest men experience fear. One of the biggest jobs we all face in combat is to overcome our fear.'

'Oh, come on, Major. Can't we do without that horseshit?'

Major Major lowered his gaze sheepishly and fiddled with his fingers. 'What do you want me to tell you?'

'That I've flown enough missions and can go home.'

'How many have you flown?'

'Fifty-one.'

'You've only got four more to fly.'

'He'll raise them. Every time I get close he raises them.'

'Perhaps he won't this time.'

'He never sends anyone home, anyway. He just keeps them around waiting for rotation orders until he doesn't have enough men left for the crews, and then raises the number of missions and throws them all back on combat status. He's been doing that ever since he got here.'

'You mustn't blame Colonel Cathcart for any delay with the orders,' Major Major advised. 'It's Twenty-seventh Air Force's responsibility to process the orders promptly once they get them from us.'

'He could still ask for replacements and send us home when the orders did come back. Anyway, I've been told that Twenty-seventh Air Force wants only forty missions and that it's only his own idea to get us to fly fifty-five.'

'I wouldn't know anything about that,' Major Major answered. 'Colonel Cathcart is our commanding officer and we must obey him. Why don't you fly the four more missions and see what happens?'

'I don't want to.'

What could you do? Major Major asked himself again. What could you do with a man who looked you squarely in the eye and said he would rather die than be killed in combat, a man who was at least as mature and intelligent as you were and who you had to pretend was not? What could you say to him?

'Suppose we let you pick your missions and fly milk runs,'[11] Major Major said. 'That way you can fly the four missions and not run any risks.'

'I don't want to fly milk runs. I don't want to be in the war any more.'

'Would you like to see our country lose?' Major Major asked.

'We won't lose. We've got more men, more money and more material. There are ten million men in uniform who could replace me. Some people are getting killed and a lot more are making money and having fun. Let somebody else get killed.'

'But suppose everybody on our side felt that way.'

'Then I'd certainly be a damned fool to feel any other way. Wouldn't I?'

What could you possibly say to him? Major Major wondered forlornly. One thing he could not say was that there was nothing he could do. To say there was nothing he could do would suggest he *would* do something if he could and imply the existence of an error of injustice in Colonel Korn's policy. Colonel Korn had been most explicit about that. He must never say there was nothing he could do.

'I'm sorry,' he said. 'But there's nothing I can do.'

1961

Allen Ginsberg 1926–1997

"I saw the best minds of my generation destroyed by madness, starving hysterical naked, / dragging themselves through the negro streets at dawn looking for an angry fix, / angelhead hipsters burning for the ancient heavenly connection. . . ." Thus, in his best-known work, Howl *(1956), Allen Ginsberg described the alienated Americans of the postwar 1950s whom his novelist friend Jack Kerouac named the "Beat Generation." Influenced chiefly by Walt Whitman and William Blake, Ginsberg bellowed his own "barbaric yawp," in lines far freer than Whitman's and with hallucinations far more frenzied than Blake's.*

[11]A mission that is routine and not dangerous.

Ginsberg's aim was to provide a rationale for the "disaffiliation" of all who protest against the official culture of the United States. His public readings, delivered in the style of the bardic chant and featuring a hirsute Ginsberg in the pose of an Old Testament prophet, were given behind and before the Iron Curtain, from the Ganges to Galilee to California, and his language of "extra vagance" made him one of the most widely known American poets of the age. He was born in Newark, New Jersey, the son of Louis Ginsberg, a teacher and lyric poet. After attending public schools in Paterson, New Jersey, Allen Ginsberg enrolled at Columbia University in 1943 at the age of seventeen. Two years later he was dismissed for allegedly scrawling an anti-Semitic obscenity on a classroom window and for making uncomplimentary remarks about the university president. After working at a number of odd jobs, Ginsberg was readmitted to Columbia, and following his graduation in 1948 he stayed on for graduate work.

Sometime during 1948–1949, he began to have mystical visions of William Blake, and later he spent eight months in a mental hospital undergoing psychiatric therapy. He worked for a time in 1950 as a book reviewer for Newsweek magazine and then took a job as a market research consultant. After a trip to Mexico in 1954 he settled in San Francisco, where, two years later, Lawrence Ferlinghetti's City Lights Books published Howl and Other Poems. *The enormous success of that small volume—enhanced greatly by a widely publicized trial that eventually cleared the book of charges of obscenity—helped bring Ginsberg great fame.*

The poems of Howl *have been characterized by Ginsberg's followers as prophetic in the same sense that much of the Bible is prophetic, denouncing evil and "pointing the way out. . . ." Ginsberg declared that his poetry was "adapted from prose seeds, journals, scratchings . . . according to ideas of measure of American speech picked up from W. C. Williams' imagist preoccupations." It exhibits Whitmanesque incantations and cataloging and is packed with stray thoughts and reflections on orgies and ecstasies. Although he was pacific in his social and political postures, he was militant in his wailing rhetoric. His poetry is uneven and effusive, and such volumes as* Empty Mirror *(1960),* Kaddish *(1960),* Reality Sandwiches *(1963), and* The Fall of America *(1973) are flooded with folly, rant, and spleen. But they are intense expressions of ideas passionately held and they made Ginsberg a pop hero and a cult leader of great popularity. A poster of Ginsberg, posed in an Uncle Sam suit, became one of the bestsellers of all time. His stature as a poet is still subject to debate, but that he exemplified a real tradition in American poetry is beyond dispute. And both his detractors and adherents can agree that his free verse and his intensity of expression clearly qualified him as the most conspicuous "sidewalk bard of America."*

FURTHER READING: *Selected Poems, 1947–1995,* 1996; *Spontaneous Mind: Selected Interviews, 1958–1996,* 2001; *Deliberate Prose: Selected Essays, 1952–1995,* 2001; T. Merrill, *Allen Ginsberg,* 1969, 1988; J. Kramer, *Allen Ginsberg in America,* 1970; *Allen Verbatim: Lectures on Poetry, Politics, Consciousness,* ed. G. Ball, 1974; J. Tytell, *Naked Angels: The Lives and Literature of the Beat Generation,* 1976; P. Portugés, *The Visionary Poetics of Allen Ginsberg,* 1978; *On the Poetry of Allen Ginsberg,* ed. L. Hyde, 1984; B. Miles, *Allen Ginsberg,* 1989; C. Cassidy, *Off the Road,* 1991; B. Miles, *Two Lectures on the Work of Allen Ginsberg,* 1993; B. Morgan, *The Works of Allen Ginsberg, 1941–1994: A Descriptive Bibliography,* 1995; B. Morgan, *The Response to Allen Ginsberg, 1926–1994: A Bibliography of Secondary Sources,* 1996; J. Kramer, *Allen Ginsberg in America,* 1969, 1997; G. Caveney, *Screaming With Joy: The Life of Allen Ginsberg,* 1999; J. Raskin, *American Scream: Allen Ginsberg's Howl and the Making of the Beat Generation,* 2004; C. Felver, *The Late Great Allen Ginsberg: A Photo Biography,* 2002; *The Poem That Changed America: "Howl" Fifty Years Later,* ed. Jason Shinder, 2006.

TEXT: *Collected Poems, 1947–1980,* 1984.

HOWL

for Carl Solomon[1]

I

I saw the best minds of my generation destroyed by madness, starving
hysterical naked,
dragging themselves through the negro streets at dawn looking for an
angry fix,
angelheaded hipsters burning for the ancient heavenly connection to the
starry dynamo in the machinery of night,
who poverty and tatters and hollow-eyed and high sat up smoking in the
supernatural darkness of cold-water flats floating across the tops of cities
contemplating jazz,
who bared their brains to Heaven under the El[2] and saw Mohammedan
angels staggering on tenement roofs illuminated,
who passed through universities with radiant cool eyes hallucinating
Arkansas and Blake-light[3] tragedy among the scholars of war,
who were expelled from the academies for crazy & publishing obscene odes
on the windows[4] of the skull,
who cowered in unshaven rooms in underwear, burning their money in
wastebaskets and listening to the Terror through the wall,
who got busted in their pubic beards returning through Laredo[5] with a belt
of marijuana for New York,
who ate fire in paint hotels or drank turpentine in Paradise Alley,[6] death,
or purgatoried their torsos night after night
with dreams, with drugs, with waking nightmares, alcohol and cock
and endless balls,
incomparable blind streets of shuddering cloud and lightning in the mind
leaping toward poles of Canada & Paterson,[7] illuminating all the
motionless world of Time between,
Peyote solidities of halls, backyard green tree cemetery dawns, wine
drunkenness over the rooftops, storefront boroughs of teahead
joyride neon blinking traffic light, sun and moon and tree vibrations
in the roaring winter dusks of Brooklyn, ashcan rantings and kind king
light of mind,
who chained themselves to subways for the endless ride from Battery
to holy Bronx[8] on benzedrine until the noise of wheels and children
brought them down shuddering mouth-wracked and battered bleak
of brain all drained of brilliance in the drear light of Zoo,

[1]A friend of Ginsberg and a fellow patient in a psychiatric hospital in 1949.

[2]Elevated railway in New York City.

[3]Ginsberg had had a mystical vision of the English poet William Blake (1757–1827).

[4]In 1945 Ginsberg was expelled from Columbia University for writing obscenities on university windows.

[5]City in Texas, on the border of Mexico.

[6]"A slum courtyard N. Y. Lower East Side, site of Kerouac's *Subterraneans*, 1958."—Ginsberg's note. Jack Kerouac (1922–1969), author of the Beat novel *The Subterraneans* (1958).

[7]Paterson, New Jersey, Ginsberg's hometown.

[8]The New York City subway line that runs north from the Battery at the south end of Manhattan Island, to the Bronx Zoo.

who sank all night in submarine light of Bickford's[9] floated out and sat
through the stale beer afternoon in desolate Fugazzi's,[10] listening to the
crack of doom on the hydrogen jukebox,
who talked continuously seventy hours from park to pad to bar to Bellevue[11]
to museum to the Brooklyn Bridge,
a lost battalion of platonic conversationalists jumping down the stoops
off fire escapes off windowsills off Empire State[12] out of the moon,
yacketayakking screaming vomiting whispering facts and memories and
anecdotes and eyeball kicks and shocks of hospitals and jails and wars,
whole intellects disgorged in total recall for seven days and nights with
brilliant eyes, meat for the Synagogue cast on the pavement,
who vanished into nowhere Zen New Jersey leaving a trail of ambiguous
picture postcards of Atlantic City Hall,
suffering Eastern sweats and Tangerian bone-grindings and migraines
of China[13] under junk-withdrawal in Newark's bleak furnished room,
who wandered around and around at midnight in the railroad yard
wondering where to go, and went, leaving no broken hearts,
who lit cigarettes in boxcars boxcars boxcars racketing through snow
toward lonesome farms in grandfather night,
who studied Plotinus[14] Poe St. John of the Cross[15] telepathy and bop
kabbalah[16] because the cosmos instinctively vibrated at their feet
in Kansas,
who loned it through the streets of Idaho seeking visionary indian angels
who were visionary indian angels,
who thought they were only mad when Baltimore gleamed in supernatural
ecstasy,
who jumped in limousines with the Chinaman of Oklahoma on the
impulse of winter midnight streetlight smalltown rain,
who lounged hungry and lonesome through Houston seeking jazz or sex
or soup, and followed the brilliant Spaniard to converse about America
and Eternity, a hopeless task, and so took ship to Africa,
who disappeared into the volcanoes of Mexico leaving behind nothing
but the shadow of dungarees and the lava and ash of poetry scattered
in fireplace Chicago,
who reappeared on the West Coast investigating the FBI in beards
and shorts with big pacifist eyes sexy in their dark skin passing out
incomprehensible leaflets,
who burned cigarette holes in their arms protesting the narcotic tobacco
haze of Capitalism,

[9]All-night cafeteria in New York City. [10]Bar in New York City's Greenwich Village.
[11]Public hospital in New York City that treats persons suffering from mental disorders.
[12]The Empire State Building in New York City.
[13]Tangiers and China, in Africa and Asia: sources of drugs imported into the United States.
[14]Roman philosopher (105–170) who advocated the pursuit of ecstatic, visionary experiences.
[15]Spanish religious mystic and poet (1542–1591).
[16]The mystical interpretation of Hebrew scriptures (the Kaballa) presented in the Bop jazz style of the late 1940s.

who distributed Supercommunist pamphlets in Union Square[17] weeping
and undressing while the sirens of Los Alamos[18] wailed them down,
and wailed down Wall, and the Staten Island ferry also wailed,
who broke down crying in white gymnasiums naked and trembling before
the machinery of other skeletons,
who bit detectives in the neck and shrieked with delight in policecars
for committing no crime but their own wild cooking pederasty
and intoxication,
who howled on their knees in the subway and were dragged off the roof
waving genitals and manuscripts,
who let themselves be fucked in the ass by saintly motorcyclists, and
screamed with joy,
who blew and were blown by those human seraphim, the sailors, caresses
of Atlantic and Caribbean love,
who balled in the morning in the evenings in rosegardens and the grass
of public parks and cemeteries scattering their semen freely to whomever
come who may,
who hiccuped endlessly trying to giggle but wound up with a sob behind
a partition in a Turkish Bath when the blond & naked angel came to
pierce them with a sword,
who lost their loveboys to the three old shrews of fate[19] the one eyed shrew
of the heterosexual dollar the one eyed shrew that winks out of the womb
and the one eyed shrew that does nothing but sit on her ass and snip
the intellectual golden threads of the craftsman's loom,
who copulated ecstatic and insatiate with a bottle of beer a sweetheart
a package of cigarettes a candle and fell off the bed, and continued along
the floor and down the hall and ended fainting on the wall with a vision
of ultimate cunt and come eluding the last gyzym of consciousness,
who sweetened the snatches of a million girls trembling in the sunset,
and were red eyed in the morning but prepared to sweeten the snatch
of the sunrise, flashing buttocks under barns and naked in the lake,
who went out whoring through Colorado in myriad stolen night-cars, N.C.,[20]
secret hero of these poems, cocksman and Adonis of Denver—joy to
the memory of his innumerable lays of girls in empty lots & diner
backyards, moviehouses' rickety rows, on mountaintops in caves or with
gaunt waitresses in familiar roadside lonely petticoat upliftings &
especially secret gas-station solipsisms[21] of johns, & hometown alleys too,
who faded out in vast sordid movies, were shifted in dreams, woke on a
sudden Manhattan, and picked themselves up out of basements hungover
with heartless Tokay[22] and horrors of Third Avenue iron dreams
& stumbled to unemployment offices,

[17] In New York City, a meeting place for radical speakers and protesters.

[18] Los Alamos, New Mexico, where the atom bomb was developed.

[19] In classical myth, the Fates are three goddesses of destiny. The first spins the individual's thread of life, the second determines its length, and the third cuts it off.

[20] Neal Cassady (1926–1968), Beat writer and friend of Ginsberg and Jack Kerouac.

[21] Solipsism: the philosophical theory that the self is the only thing that exists, and all experience is therefore subjective.

[22] A potent, fortified, inexpensive wine traditionally used by alcoholic derelicts.

who walked all night with their shoes full of blood on the snowbank docks
waiting for a door in the East River[23] to open to a room full of steamheat and opium,
who created great suicidal dramas on the apartment cliff-banks of the Hudson[24] under the wartime blue floodlight of the moon & their heads shall be crowned with laurel in oblivion,
who ate the lamb stew of the imagination or digested the crab at the muddy bottom of the rivers of Bowery,[25]
who wept at the romance of the streets with their pushcarts full of onions and bad music,
who sat in boxes breathing in the darkness under the bridge, and rose up to build harpsichords in their lofts,
who coughed on the sixth floor of Harlem crowned with flame under the tubercular sky surrounded by orange crates of theology,
who scribbled all night rocking and rolling over lofty incantations which in the yellow morning were stanzas of gibberish,
who cooked rotten animals lung heart feet tail borsht[26] & tortillas dreaming of the pure vegetable kingdom,
who plunged themselves under meat trucks looking for an egg,
who threw their watches off the roof to cast their ballot for Eternity outside of Time, & alarm clocks fell on their heads every day for the next decade,
who cut their wrists three times successively unsuccessfully, gave up and were forced to open antique stores where they thought they were growing old and cried,
who were burned alive in their innocent flannel suits on Madison Avenue[27] amid blasts of leaden verse & the tanked-up clatter of the iron regiments of fashion & the nitroglycerine shrieks of the fairies of advertising & the mustard gas of sinister intelligent editors, or were run down by the drunken taxicabs of Absolute Reality,
who jumped off the Brooklyn Bridge this actually happened and walked away unknown and forgotten into the ghostly daze of Chinatown soup alleyways & firetrucks, not even one free beer,
who sang out of their windows in despair, fell out of the subway window, jumped in the filthy Passaic,[28] leaped on negroes, cried all over the street, danced on broken wineglasses barefoot smashed phonograph records of nostalgic European 1930s German jazz finished the whiskey and threw up groaning into the bloody toilet, moans in their ears and the blast of colossal steamwhistles,
who barreled down the highways of the past journeying to each other's hotrod-Golgotha[29] jail-solitude watch or Birmingham jazz incarnation,
who drove crosscountry seventytwo hours to find out if I had a vision or you had a vision or he had a vision to find out Eternity,

[23]The river separating Brooklyn and Manhattan Island.
[24]The Hudson River, at New York City, lined with highrise apartment buildings.
[25]Slum area at the southern tip of Manhattan Island.
[26]A soup made of beets.
[27]In New York City, a center of advertising and publishing firms where, it is said, middle-class conformists traditionally wear look-alike gray flannel suits.
[28]River, renowned for its pollution, that flows through the industrial section of New Jersey.
[29]Hebrew for "Calvary," the site of the crucifixion of Jesus.

who journeyed to Denver, who died in Denver, who came back to Denver
& waited in vain, who watched over Denver & brooded & loned in Denver
and finally went away to find out the Time, & now Denver is lonesome
for her heroes,
who fell on their knees in hopeless cathedrals praying for each other's
salvation and light and breasts, until the soul illuminated its hair for
a second,
who crashed through their minds in jail waiting for impossible criminals
with golden heads and the charm of reality in their hearts
who sang sweet blues to Alcatraz,
who retired to Mexico to cultivate a habit,[30] or Rocky Mount[31] to tender
Buddha or Tangiers to boys or Southern Pacific[32] to the black locomotive
or Harvard to Narcissus[33] to Woodlawn[34] to the daisychain or grave,
who demanded sanity trials accusing the radio of hypnotism & were left with
their insanity & their hands & a hung jury,
who threw potato salad at CCNY[35] lecturers on Dadaism[36] and subsequently
presented themselves on the granite steps of the madhouse with shaven
heads and harlequin speech of suicide, demanding instantaneous
lobotomy.[37]
and who were given instead the concrete void of insulin Metrazol[38] electricity
hydrotherapy psychotherapy occupational therapy pingpong & amnesia,
who in humorless protest overturned only one symbolic pingpong table,
resting briefly in catatonia,[39]
returning years later truly bald except for a wig of blood, and tears and
fingers, to the visible madman doom of the wards of the madtowns
of the East,
Pilgrim State's Rockland's and Greystone's[40] foetid halls, bickering with
the echoes of the soul, rocking and rolling in the midnight
solitude-bench dolmen-realms of love, dream of life a nightmare,
bodies turned to stone as heavy as the moon,
with mother finally ******, and the last fantastic book flung out of the
tenement window, and the last door closed at 4 A.M. and the last telephone
slammed at the wall in reply and the last furnished room emptied down
to the last piece of mental furniture, a yellow paper rose twisted on a
wire hanger in the closet, and even that imaginary, nothing but a hopeful
little bit of hallucination—

[30]The homosexual Beat author and drug addict William S. Burroughs (1914–1997) had lived in Mexico and Tangiers in North Africa.

[31]Jack Kerouac (1922–1969) lived in Rocky Mount, North Carolina.

[32]Neal Cassady worked for the Southern Pacific Railroad.

[33]Figure in Greek myth who fell in love with his own reflection.

[34]Cemetery in the Bronx, New York. [35]The City College of New York.

[36]A movement in art and literature that advocated deliberate absurdity and irrationality.

[37]Surgical incisions that sever nerves in the frontal lobes of the brain, to relieve acute mental disorders.

[38]A drug used in shock treatment for medical therapy.

[39]Severe mental disorder in which the patient loses the ability or the will to move.

[40]Three hospitals for the insane, near New York City. Ginsberg's mother died at Greystone in 1956.

ah, Carl,[41] while you are not safe I am not safe, and now you're really in
the total animal soup of time—
and who therefore ran through the icy street obsessed with a sudden flash
of the alchemy of the use of the ellipse the catalog the meter & the
vibrating plane,
who dreamt and made incarnate gaps in Time & Space through images
juxtaposed, and trapped the archangel of the soul between visual images
and joined the elemental verbs and set the noun and dash of
consciousness together jumping with sensation of Pater Omnipotens
Aeterna Deus[42]
to recreate the syntax and measure of poor human prose and stand before
you speechless and intelligent and shaking with shame, rejected yet
confessing out the soul to conform to the rhythm of thought in his naked
and endless head,
the madman bum and angel beat in Time, unknown, yet putting down here
what might be left to say in time come after death,
and rose reincarnate in the ghostly clothes of jazz in the goldhorn shadow
of the band and blew the suffering of America's naked mind for love
into an eli eli lamma lamma sabacthani[43] saxophone cry that shivered
the cities down to the last radio
with the absolute heart of the poem of life butchered out of their own bodies
good to eat a thousand years.

II

What sphinx of cement and aluminum bashed open their skulls and ate up
their brains and imagination?
Moloch![44] Solitude! Filth! Ugliness! Ashcans and unobtainable dollars!
Children screaming under the stairways! Boys sobbing in armies!
Old men weeping in the parks! Moloch! Moloch! Nightmare of Moloch!
Moloch the loveless! Mental Moloch! Moloch the heavy judger of men!
Moloch the incomprehensible prison! Moloch the crossbone soulless
jailhouse and Congress of sorrows! Moloch whose buildings are judgment!
Moloch the vast stone of war! Moloch the stunned governments!
Moloch whose mind is pure machinery! Moloch whose blood is running
money! Moloch whose fingers are ten armies! Moloch whose breast is
a cannibal dynamo! Moloch whose ear is a smoking tomb!
Moloch whose eyes are a thousand blind windows! Moloch whose skyscrapers
stand in the long streets like endless Jehovahs! Moloch whose factories
dream and croak in the fog! Moloch whose smokestacks and antennae
crown the cities!

[41] Carl Solomon.

[42] Latin quotation taken from a letter written (April 1904) by the French impressionist painter Paul Cézanne (1839–1906): "Omnipotent Father, Eternal God." Ginsberg changed Cézanne's "Aeterne" ("Eternal") to "Aeterna," the feminine form of the word.

[43] An adaptation of the Aramaic "Eli, Eli, lama sabachthani?" "My God, my God, why hast thou forsaken me?" Jesus' last words on the cross (Matthew 27:46).

[44] "Or Molech, the Canaanite fire god, whose worship was marked by parents burning their children as propitiatory sacrifice. 'And thou shalt not let any of thy seed pass through the fire to Molech' (Leviticus 18:21)."—Ginsberg's note.

Moloch whose love is endless oil and stone! Moloch whose soul is electricity
and banks! Moloch whose poverty is the specter of genius! Moloch whose
fat is a cloud of sexless hydrogen! Moloch whose name is the Mind!
Moloch in whom I sit lonely! Moloch in whom I dream Angels! Crazy in
Moloch! Cocksucker in Moloch! Lacklove and manless in Moloch!
Moloch who entered my soul early! Moloch in whom I am a consciousness
without a body! Moloch who frightened me out of my natural ecstasy!
Moloch whom I abandon! Wake up in Moloch! Light streaming out
of the sky!
Moloch! Moloch! Robot apartments! invisible suburbs! skeleton treasuries!
blind capitals! demonic industries! special nations! invincible madhouses!
granite cocks! monstrous bombs!
They broke their backs lifting Moloch to Heaven! Pavements, trees, radios,
tons! lifting the city to Heaven which exists and is everywhere about us!
Visions! omens! hallucinations! miracles! ecstasies! gone down the
American river!
Dreams! adorations! illuminations! religions! the whole boatload of sensitive
bullshit!
Breakthroughs! over the river! flips and crucifixions! gone down the flood!
Highs! Epiphanies![45] Despairs! Ten years' animal screams and suicides!
Minds! New loves! Mad generation! down on the rocks of Time!
Real holy laughter in the river! They saw it all! the wild eyes! the holy yells!
They bade farewell! They jumped off the roof! to solitude! waving!
carrying flowers! Down to the river! into the street!

III

Carl Solomon! I'm with you in Rockland
where you're madder than I am
I'm with you in Rockland
where you must feel very strange
I'm with you in Rockland
where you imitate the shade of my mother
I'm with you in Rockland
where you've murdered your twelve secretaries
I'm with you in Rockland
where you laugh at this invisible humor
I'm with you in Rockland
where we are great writers on the same dreadful typewriter
I'm with you in Rockland
where your condition has become serious and is reported on the radio
I'm with you in Rockland
where the faculties of the skull no longer admit the worms of the senses
I'm with you in Rockland
where you drink the tea of the breasts of the spinsters of Utica
I'm with you in Rockland
where you pun on the bodies of your nurses the harpies of the Bronx

[45]The manifestations or appearances of a divine being.

I'm with you in Rockland
where you scream in a straightjacket that you're losing the game of
the actual pingpong of the abyss
I'm with you in Rockland
where you bang on the catatonic piano the soul is innocent and immortal
it should never die ungodly in an armed madhouse
I'm with you in Rockland
where fifty more shocks[46] will never return your soul to its body again
from its pilgrimage to a cross in the void
I'm with you in Rockland
where you accuse your doctors of insanity and plot the Hebrew socialist
revolution against the fascist national Golgotha
I'm with you in Rockland
where you will split the heavens of Long Island and resurrect your living
human Jesus from the superhuman tomb
I'm with you in Rockland
where there are twentyfive thousand mad comrades all together singing
the final stanzas of the Internationale[47]
I'm with you in Rockland
where we hug and kiss the United States under our bedsheets the
United States that coughs all night and won't let us sleep
I'm with you in Rockland
where we wake up electrified out of the coma by our own souls' airplanes
roaring over the roof they've come to drop angelic bombs the hospital
illuminates itself imaginary walls collapse O skinny legions run outside
O starry-spangled shock of mercy the eternal war is here O victory forget
your underwear we're free
I'm with you in Rockland
in my dreams you walk dripping from a sea-journey on the highway across
America in tears to the door of my cottage in the Western night

1955–1956 1956

A SUPERMARKET IN CALIFORNIA

What thoughts I have of you tonight, Walt Whitman, for I walked down the sidestreets under the trees with a headache self-conscious looking at the full moon.
In my hungry fatigue, and shopping for images, I went into the neon fruit supermarket, dreaming of your enumerations!
What peaches and what penumbras! Whole families shopping at night! Aisles full of husbands! Wives in the avocados, babies in the tomatoes!—and you, García Lorca,[1] what were you doing down by the watermelons?

[46]Electric shocks administered as treatment for mental disorders.
[47]National anthem of the Soviet Union from 1917 to 1944.
[1]Spanish poet and dramatist (1889–1937), author of "Ode to Walt Whitman."

I saw you, Walt Whitman, childless, lonely old grubber, poking among the
  meats in the refrigerator and eyeing the grocery boys.
I heard you asking questions of each: Who killed the pork chops? What price
  bananas? Are you my Angel?
I wandered in and out of the brilliant stacks of cans following you, and
  followed in my imagination by the store detective.
We strode down the open corridors together in our solitary fancy tasting
  artichokes, possessing every frozen delicacy, and never passing the cashier.

Where are we going, Walt Whitman? The doors close in an hour. Which way
  does your beard point tonight?
(I touch your book and dream of our odyssey in the supermarket and feel
  absurd.)
Will we walk all night through solitary streets? The trees add shade to shade,
  lights out in the houses, we'll both be lonely.
Will we stroll dreaming of the lost America of love past blue automobiles in
  driveways, home to our silent cottage?
Ah, dear father, graybeard, lonely old courage-teacher, what America did you
  have when Charon[2] quit poling his ferry and you got out on a smoking
  bank and stood watching the boat disappear on the black waters of
  Lethe?[3]

1955 1956

AMERICA

America I've given you all and now I'm nothing.
America two dollars and twentyseven cents January 17, 1956.
I can't stand my own mind.
America when will we end the human war?
Go fuck yourself with your atom bomb.
I don't feel good don't bother me.
I won't write my poem till I'm in my right mind.
America when will you be angelic?
When will you take off your clothes?
When will you look at yourself through the grave?
When will you be worthy of your million Trotskyites?[1]
America why are your libraries full of tears?
America when will you send your eggs to India?
I'm sick of your insane demands.
When can I go into the supermarket and buy what I need with my good
  looks?
America after all it is you and I who are perfect not the next world.
Your machinery is too much for me.

[2]Boatman, in classical myth, who ferried the dead across the river Styx to Hades.
[3]River of forgetfulness in Hades, where the dead drink and forget their previous lives.
[1]Followers of the Russian Communist Leon Trotsky (1877–1940).

You made me want to be a saint.
There must be some other way to settle this argument.
Burroughs[2] is in Tangiers I don't think he'll come back it's sinister.
Are you being sinister or is this some form of practical joke?
I'm trying to come to the point.
I refuse to give up my obsession.
America stop pushing I know what I'm doing.
America the plum blossoms are falling.
I haven't read the newspapers for months, everyday somebody goes on trial
    for murder.
America I feel sentimental about the Wobblies.[3]
America I used to be a communist when I was a kid I'm not sorry.
I smoke marijuana every chance I get.
I sit in my house for days on end and stare at the roses in the closet.
When I go to Chinatown I get drunk and never get laid.
My mind is made up there's going to be trouble.
You should have seen me reading Marx.[4]
My psychoanalyst thinks I'm perfectly right.
I won't say the Lord's Prayer.
I have mystical visions and cosmic vibrations.
America I still haven't told you what you did to Uncle Max after he came
    over from Russia.

I'm addressing you.
Are you going to let your emotional life be run by Time Magazine?
I'm obsessed by Time Magazine
I read it every week.
Its cover stares at me every time I slink past the corner candystore.
I read it in the basement of the Berkeley Public Library.
It's always telling me about responsibility. Businessmen are serious.
Movie producers are serious. Everybody's serious but me.
It occurs to me that I am America.
I am talking to myself again.

Asia is rising against me.
I haven't got a chinaman's chance.
I'd better consider my national resources.
My national resources consist of two joints of marijuana millions of genitals
    an unpublishable private literature that jetplanes 1400 miles an hour and
    twentyfive-thousand mental institutions.
I say nothing about my prisons nor the millions of underprivileged who live
    in my flowerpots under the light of five hundred suns.
I have abolished the whorehouses of France, Tangiers is the next to go.
My ambition is to be President despite the fact that I'm a Catholic.

[2]William S. Burroughs was then living in Morocco.

[3]Nickname for members of the Industrial Workers of the World, a radical organization of unions, established in 1905.

[4]Karl Marx (1818–1883), German social philosopher, major theorist of socialism and communism, author (with Friedrich Engels) of *The Communist Manifesto* (1848).

America how can I write a holy litany in your silly mood?
I will continue like Henry Ford my strophes are as individual as his automobiles more so they're all different sexes.
America I will sell you strophes $2500 apiece $500 down on your old strophe
America free Tom Mooney[5]
America save the Spanish Loyalists[6]
America Sacco & Vanzetti must not die[7]
America I am the Scottsboro boys.[8]
America when I was seven momma took me to Communist Cell meetings they sold us garbanzos[9] a handful per ticket a ticket costs a nickel and the speeches were free everybody was angelic and sentimental about the workers it was all so sincere you have no idea what a good thing the party was in 1935 Scott Nearing[10] was a grand old man a real mensch[11] Mother Bloor the Silk-strikers' Ewig-Weibliche[12] made me cry I once saw the Yiddish orator Israel Amter plain. Everybody must have been a spy.
America you don't really want to go to war.
America it's them bad Russians.
Them Russians them Russians and them Chinamen. And them Russians.
The Russia wants to eat us alive. The Russia's power mad. She wants to take our cars from out our garages.
Her wants to grab Chicago. Her needs a Red *Reader's Digest.* Her wants our auto plants in Siberia. Him big bureaucracy running our fillingstations.
That no good. Ugh. Him make Indians learn read. Him need big black niggers. Hah. Her makes us all work sixteen hours a day. Help.
America this is quite serious.
America this is the impression I get from looking in the television set.
America is this correct?
I'd better get right down to the job.
It's true I don't want to join the Army or turn lathes in precision parts factories, I'm nearsighted and psychopathic anyway.
America I'm putting my queer shoulder to the wheel.
1956

1956

[5]American labor leader imprisoned for murder in 1916 and pardoned in 1939.

[6]Supporters of the Spanish government against the insurgent armies of Francisco Franco in the Spanish Civil War (1936–1939).

[7]Nicola Sacco and Bartolomeo Vanzetti, political radicals convicted of robbery and murder in Massachusetts and executed in 1927. Their supporters argued that the two men were convicted because of their unpopular political beliefs.

[8]Nine blacks indicted in 1931 at Scottsboro, Alabama, for the rape of two white women. Their trials and convictions created a national uproar because of widespread belief that they were the victims of racial bigotry. Eventually all regained freedom.

[9]Chickpeas.

[10]Scott Nearing (1883–1983), Ella "Mother" Bloor (1862–1951), and Israel Amter (1881–1954), American socialist and communist leaders.

[11]German: human being.

[12]German: Eternal Female.

TO AUNT ROSE

Aunt Rose—now—might I see you
with your thin face and buck tooth smile and pain
of rheumatism—and a long black heavy shoe
for your bony left leg
limping down the long hall in Newark on the running carpet
past the black grand piano
in the day room
where the parties were
and I sang Spanish loyalist songs
in a high squeaky voice
(hysterical) the committee listening
while you limped around the room
collected the money—
Aunt Honey, Uncle Sam, a stranger with a cloth arm
in his pocket
and huge young bald head
of Abraham Lincoln Brigade[1]

—your long sad face
your tears of sexual frustration
(what smothered sobs and bony hips
under the pillows of Osborne Terrace)
—the time I stood on the toilet seat naked
and you powdered my thighs with calamine
against the poison ivy—my tender
and shamed first black curled hairs
what were you thinking in secret heart then
knowing me a man already—
and I an ignorant girl of family silence on the thin pedestal
of my legs in the bathroom—Museum of Newark.
Aunt Rose
Hitler is dead, Hitler is in Eternity; Hitler is with
Tamburlane and Emily Brontë
Though I see you walking still, a ghost on Osborne Terrace
down the long dark hall to the front door
limping a little with a pinched smile
in what must have been a silken
flower dress
welcoming my father, the Poet, on his visit to Newark
—see you arriving in the living room
dancing on your crippled leg
and clapping hands his book
had been accepted by Liveright

[1]A brigade of American volunteers who fought against Franco in the Spanish Civil War.

Hitler is dead and Liveright's gone out of business
The Attic of the Past and *Everlasting Minute*[2] are out of print
Uncle Harry sold his last silk stocking
Claire quit interpretive dancing school
Buba[3] sits a wrinkled monument in Old
Ladies Home blinking at new babies

last time I saw you was the hospital
pale skull protruding under ashen skin
blue veined unconscious girl
in an oxygen tent
the war in Spain has ended long ago
Aunt Rose

1958 1961

Gary Snyder 1930–

Poet Allen Ginsberg once said about himself and his friend Gary Snyder, "We are forest beatniks." Though he jokingly included himself in the comment, he was, in fact, accurately describing Snyder—a man from working-class origins who worked as a fire lookout, trail builder, and logger while developing a strong devotion to experimental poetics and avant-garde countercultural values. In his nineteen volumes of poetry and eight volumes of essays, Snyder merges these experiences and interests with meditations on his environment born out of long-standing interests in both Zen Buddhism and Native American tribal culture. The result is a distinctive blending of social and environmental activism with a powerful drive toward concise rendering of the moment's experience. Snyder says about his writing, "I try to hold both history and the wilderness in my mind, that my poems may approach the true measure of things and stand against the unbalance and ignorance of our time."

Born in San Francisco in 1930, at the beginning of the Great Depression, and growing up in Washington and Oregon, Snyder lived in poverty during his childhood years. But being gifted with both intelligence and a strong work ethic, he not only helped out financially with summer jobs while in high school but also won a scholarship to Reed College in Portland, Oregon. While in college, he still worked during the summers—first aboard a ship, then on a Park Service archaeological dig. After earning his bachelor's degree in anthropology and literature, Snyder spent a semester studying anthropology in Indiana University's graduate program and then studied Oriental culture and languages at the University of California, Berkeley. Never straying far from his pragmatic nature, he continued working intermittently in forestry-related jobs.

[2]Books of poetry written by Louis Ginsberg (1896–1976), the poet's father. *The Everlasting Minute* was published by the Horace Liveright Company.
[3]Yiddish: Grandmother.

In 1955 Snyder began translating the "Cold Mountain" poems of Han-shan—an eighth-century Chinese hermit-poet whose spare verse, mystical philosophy, and romantically antisocial "madman" persona were attractive to the young Snyder. In the same year he met Allen Ginsberg and participated with him and several other poets in a poetry reading in San Francisco. Ginsberg read an early version of his poem "Howl," and Snyder read "A Berry Feast." Still widely remembered today, the performance, known as "6 Poets at 6 Gallery," became identified as the inaugural event of the San Francisco Renaissance, an important poetic movement of which Snyder was a central figure. Also present, though not reading himself, was Beat novelist Jack Kerouac. Snyder and Kerouac became friends, and the two shared a cabin in the California mountains from 1955 to 1956. The experience provided material for Kerouac's novel The Dharma Bums *(1958), in which the character Japhy Ryder—an irrepressible, woods-loving, Zen-practicing poet—is clearly a portrait of Gary Snyder.*

Snyder's devotion to Buddhism and to Oriental culture in general led to a scholarship to study Zen and the Japanese language for a year in Japan. Except for a nine-month stint working as a seaman in the engine room of a tanker, he spent the next decade in Japan, including a period of residence in a Buddhist monastery. By the time he returned to live in the United States at the end of 1968, he had published six books of poetry and achieved a well-established reputation. In 1975 Snyder won the Pulitzer Prize for Poetry for Turtle Island*—a book of poems whose title is a Native American term for the North American continent and whose poems explore and celebrate a close relationship to the natural environment.*

Gary Snyder has often been compared to American essayist and naturalist Henry David Thoreau for the way both writers value a simple, direct contact with practical life and find profound meaning in seemingly ordinary events. His poetry, as one commentator has said, "gives you permission to use your senses." Poems such as "I Went into the Maverick Bar," "Soy Sauce," and "Poem Left in Sourdough Mountain Lookout" take everyday situations and expand them into moments of insight into the nature of things. In the same manner that poet William Carlos Williams's imagism expressed "no ideas but in things," much of Snyder's work focuses on the meaningfulness of concrete things and situations and avoids elaborate rhetoric. And the spareness and oriental flavor of Snyder's verse point to his early enthusiasm for the work of modernist poet Ezra Pound. Like Thoreau, Snyder emphasizes the connectedness of all things, but he goes beyond Thoreau to a more existential view of the nature of the self: "We are all composite beings, not only physically but intellectually, whose sole individual identifying feature is a particular form or structure changing in time." Poetry, for Snyder, makes that structure momentarily visible. "Riprap," the title poem for his first volume of poetry (published in 1959), is named for the material used to create stone paths for horses and humans in treacherous forest terrain. It articulates a view of poetry as words and images laid like solid objects, a kind of riprap of the mind, to provide firm footing on the uncertain path of human experience. It invites the reader to "Lay down these words / Before your mind like rocks. / . . . Before the body of the mind / In space and time."

Since the late 1960s, Gary Snyder has lived (in a house he built himself) in the Sierra Nevada Mountains of Northern California—writing, giving poetry readings and lectures, and teaching at the University of California, Davis. Never wavering from his naturalist leanings, he has also been working for environmental causes and advocating a more communal approach to living, which is based in family and friends.

FURTHER READING: *Riprap,* 1959; *Myths & Texts,* 1960; *Riprap & Cold Mountain Poems,* 1965; *A Range of Poems,* 1966; *Three Worlds, Three Realms, Six Roads,* 1966; *The Back Country,* 1967;

Regarding Wave, 1969; *The Blue Sky,* 1969; *Manzanita,* 1972; *Plute Creek,* 1972; *The Fudo Trilogy,* 1973; *Turtle Island,* 1974; *All in the Family,* 1975; *Smokey the Bear Sutra,* 1976; *Songs for Gaia,* 1979; *Axe Handles,* 1983; *Left Out in the Rain: New Poems 1947–1985,* 1986; *No Nature: New and Selected Poems,* 1992; *Mountains and Rivers without End,* 1996; *Earth House Hold: Technical Notes & Queries for Fellow Dharma Revolutionaries,* 1969; *The Old Ways: Six Essays,* 1977; *He Who Hunted Birds in His Father's Village: The Dimensions of a Haida Myth,* 1979; *The Real Work: Interviews & Talks, 1964–1979,* ed. S. McLean, 1980; *Passage through India,* 1983; *The Practice of the Wild,* 1990; *A Place in Space: Ethics, Aesthetics, and Watersheds: New and Selected Prose,* 1995; *The Gary Snyder Reader: Prose, Poetry, and Translations, 1952–1998,* 1999; G. Snyder et al., *The High Sierra of California,* 2002; B. Steuding, *Gary Snyder,* 1976; C. Molesworth, *Gary Snyder's Vision: Poetry and the Real Work,* 1983; B. Almon, *Gary Snyder,* 1979; K. McNeill, *Gary Snyder,* 1980; R. Schuler, *Journeys toward the Original Mind: The Long Poems of Gary Snyder,* 1994; D. Kherdian, *A Biographical Sketch and Descriptive Checklist of Gary Snyder,* 1965; H. McCord, *Some Notes to Gary Snyder's "Myths & Texts,"* 1971; L. Scigaj, ed., *Sustainable Poetry: Four American Ecopoets,* 1999; B. Cook, *The Beat Generation,* 1971; C. Altieri, *Enlarging the Temple: New Directions in American Poetry during the 1960s,* 1979; S. Charters, *Some Poems/Poets: Studies in American Underground Poetry since 1945,* 1971.

TEXTS: "Riprap," "Cold Mountain Is a House," and "Poem Left in Sourdough Mountain Lookout" are from *Riprap and Cold Mountain Poems,* 1990; "I Went into the Maverick Bar" is from *Turtle Island,* 1974; "Soy Sauce" is from *Axe Handles,* 1983.

RIPRAP[1]

Lay down these words
Before your mind like rocks.
          placed solid, by hands
In choice of place, set
Before the body of the mind
          in space and time:
Solidity of bark, leaf, or wall
          riprap of things:
Cobble of milky way,
          straying planets,
These poems, people,
          lost ponies with
Dragging saddles—
          and rocky sure-foot trails.
The worlds like an endless
          four-dimensional
Game of *Go.*[2]
          ants and pebbles
In the thin loam, each rock a word
          a creek-washed stone

[1]A rocky material used for rough paths, foundations, or retaining walls.
[2]An ancient Chinese board game.

Granite: ingrained
with torment of fire and weight
Crystal and sediment linked hot
all change, in thoughts,
As well as things.

1958

[TRANSLATION OF A POEM BY HAN-SHAN][1]

Cold Mountain is a house
Without beams or walls.
The six doors left and right are open
The hall is blue sky.
The rooms all vacant and vague
The east wall beats on the west wall
At the center nothing.

Borrowers don't bother me
In the cold I build a little fire
When I'm hungry I boil up some greens.
I've got no use for the kulak[2]
With his big barn and pasture—
He just sets up a prison for himself.
Once in he can't get out.
Think it over—
You know it might happen to you.

1958

POEM LEFT IN SOURDOUGH MOUNTAIN LOOKOUT[1]

I the poet Gary Snyder
Stayed six weeks in fifty-three
On this ridge and on this rock
& saw what every Lookout sees,
Saw these mountains shift about
& end up on the ocean floor
Saw the wind and waters break
The branched deer, the Eagle's eye,
& when pray tell, shall Lookouts die?

1958

[1]Han-shan was an eighth-century Chinese poet and religious figure, probably mythical. The name means "Cold Mountain."

[2]A wealthy farmer.

[1]Located in the Sourdough Mountain Range in the state of Washington.

I WENT INTO THE MAVERICK BAR

I went into the Maverick Bar
In Farmington, New Mexico.[1]
And drank double shots of bourbon
    backed with beer.
My long hair was tucked up under a cap
I'd left the earring in the car.

Two cowboys did horseplay
    by the pool tables,
A waitress asked us
    where are you from?
a country-and-western band began to play
"We don't smoke Marijuana in Muskokie"[2]
And with the next song,
    a couple began to dance.

They held each other like in High School dances
    in the fifties;
I recalled when I worked in the woods
    and the bars of Madras, Oregon.[3]
That short-haired joy and roughness—
    America—your stupidity.
I could almost love you again.

We left—onto the freeway shoulders—
    under the tough old stars—
In the shadow of bluffs
    I came back to myself,
To the real work, to
    "What is to be done."

1974

SOY SAUCE

for Bruce Boyd and Holly Tornheim

Standing on a stepladder
    up under hot ceiling
tacking on wire net for plaster,
a day's work helping Bruce and Holly on their house,
I catch a sour salt smell and come back
    down the ladder.

[1]A medium-size city in the northwest corner of New Mexico.
[2]A line from "Okie from Muskogee," a 1969 country-music song by Merle Haggard (1937–) that praised small-town (Muskogee, Oklahoma) American values and criticized "Hippie" culture.
[3]A small city in north-central Oregon.

"Deer lick it nights" she says,
and shows me the frame of the window she's planing,
clear redwood, but dark, with a smell.

"Scored a broken-up, two-thousand-gallon redwood
soy sauce tank from a company went out of business
down near San Jose."[1]

Out in the yard the staves are stacked:
I lean over, sniff them, ah! it's like Shinshu miso,
the darker saltier miso paste of the Nagano[2]
uplands, central main island, Japan—
it's like Shinshu pickles!

I see in mind my friend Shimizu Yasushi and me,
one October years ago, trudging through days of snow
crossing the Japan Alps and descending
the last night, to a farmhouse,
taking a late hot bath in the dark—and eating
        a bowl of chill miso radish pickles,
        nothing ever so good!

Back here, hot summer sunshine dusty yard,
        hammer in hand.

But I know how it tastes
        to lick those window frames
        in the dark,
                the deer.

1983

Adrienne Rich 1929–

Adrienne Rich was born into a privileged, white middle-class life in Baltimore, Maryland, where her father was a professor at Johns Hopkins University and her mother was a former concert pianist. Raised to be a conventional "dutiful daughter of the fathers," she reached outside those boundaries, eventually becoming one of the most acclaimed feminist poets and activists of the twentieth century.

Rich attended Radcliffe College where she was an excellent student. She graduated in 1951, the same year her first book of poetry, A Change of World, *was published and chosen for the Yale Series of Younger Poets by W. H. Auden. These early poems were conventional, formal verse, influenced by such older male poets as Robert Frost, Wallace*

[1]San Jose, California. [2]A city on the island of Honshu, Japan.

Stevens, William Butler Yeats, and Auden himself, who lauded her "intuitive grasp of much subtler and difficult matters like proportion, consistency of diction and tone, and matching of these with the subject at hand." Although Rich's first book of poetry revealed this skill with traditional forms, it also revealed, through such poems as "Aunt Jennifer's Tigers," a poet who was beginning to question aspects of tradition, particularly gender politics.

Soon after returning from a Guggenheim Fellowship in Europe, Rich followed conventional female scripts for a woman of her age and cultural position, marrying an economics professor at Harvard and having three children. In the late 1960s, Rich and her husband moved to New York, where they became activists against the war in Vietnam. However, Rich felt constrained by that domestic life—constraints that are signaled in her writing of that period, including The Diamond Cutters *(1955) and* Snapshots of a Daughter-in-Law *(1962)—and by 1970 she had separated from her husband.*

Remaining in New York City, she became an inner-city school teacher and expanded her political concerns, many of them emerging in the poems in her collection Diving into the Wreck *(1972), for which she won the 1974 National Book Award. Both the language and the verse of Rich's poetry of this time were much freer and more direct than those of her earlier work. In 1976, Rich announced her lesbian identity and articulated her very influential notion of the "lesbian continuum," which she defines as "a primary intensity between women." She describes the importance of lesbian identity for both heterosexual and homosexual females: "I believe it is the lesbian in every woman who is compelled by female energy . . . It is the lesbian in us who drives us to feel imaginatively, render in language, grasp, the full connection between woman and woman. It is the lesbian in us who is creative. . . ."*

Through over four decades of writing, Adrienne Rich's voice—as a poet, feminist, lesbian, and political writer—has strongly influenced and often inspired her readers. Rich is intensely personal and confessional, yet also publicly committed. Her series Twenty-One Love Poems *(1997) is intensely erotic and personal as well as formally and politically subversive. Her essays on motherhood, compulsory heterosexuality, racism, and global oppression have helped to define the current discussion on such topics. Her various dialogues with the black lesbian poet Audre Lorde have articulated many points of tension between white and black feminisms. Much of Rich's work, including poems in such volumes as* The Necessities of Life *(1966) and* An Atlas of the Difficult World *(1991), also reveals a commitment to heightening awareness of the symbols of power and privilege that, she believes, corrode modern society. Through her poetry, teaching, and activism, Adrienne Rich has encouraged men and women to strive for individual freedom and social wholeness. Rich builds on this theme and those that have characterized her extensive body of work in* Art of the Impossible *(2001), a collection of essays and a memoir, and* Fox: Poems 1998–2000 *(2001).*

FURTHER READING: *What Is Found There: Notebooks on Poets and Politics,* 1993; W. Martin, *An American Triptych: Anne Bradstreet, Emily Dickinson, Adrienne Rich,* 1984; M. Diaz-Diocaretz, *The Transforming Power of Language: The Poetry of Adrienne Rich,* 1984; *Reading Adrienne Rich: Reviews and Re-Visions, 1951–1981,* ed. J. Cooper, 1984; M. Diaz-Diocaretz, *Translating Poetic Discourse: Questions on Feminist Strategies in Adrienne Rich,* 1985; C. Keyes, *The Aesthetics of Power: The Poetry of Adrienne Rich,* 1986; C. Werner, *Adrienne Rich: The Poet and Her Critics,* 1988; A. Templeton, *The Dream and the Dialogue: Adrienne Rich's Feminist Poetics,* 1995; M. Dickie, *Stein, Bishop, and Rich: Lyrics of Love, War, and Place,* 1997; S. Sielke, *Fashioning the Female Subject: The Intertextual Networking of Dickinson, Moore, and Rich,* 1997; B. Estrin, *The American Love Lyric After Auschwitz and Hiroshima,* 2001; C. Langdell, *Adrienne Rich: The Moment of Change,* 2004.

TEXTS: "At a Bach Concert," "Living in Sin," and "Breakfast in a Bowling Alley in Utica, New York" are from *Collected Early Poems: 1950–1970,* 1970; "Divisions of Labor" is from *Time's Power: Poems 1985–1988,* 1989; "For This" and "1999" are from *Fox: Poems 1998–2000,* 2001.

AT A BACH CONCERT

Coming by evening through the wintry city
We said that art is out of love with life.
Here we approach a love that is not pity.

This antique discipline, tenderly severe,
Renews belief in love yet masters feeling,
Asking of us a grace in what we bear.

Form is the ultimate gift that love can offer—
The vital union of necessity
With all that we desire, all that we suffer.

A too-compassionate art is half an art.
Only such proud restraining purity
Restores the else-betrayed, too-human heart.

1951

LIVING IN SIN

She had thought the studio would keep itself;
No dust upon the furniture of love.
Half heresy, to wish the taps less vocal,
The panes relieved of grime. A plate of pears,
A piano with a Persian shawl, a cat
Stalking the picturesque amusing mouse
Had been her vision when he pleaded "Come."
Not that at five each separate stair would writhe
Under the milkman's tramp; that morning light
So coldly would delineate the scraps
Of last night's cheese and blank sepulchral bottles;
That on the kitchen shelf among the saucers
A pair of beetle-eyes would fix her own—
Envoy from some black village in the mouldings . . .[1]

[1]Here, and throughout, the ellipsis points are Rich's.

Meanwhile her night's companion, with a yawn
Sounded a dozen notes upon the keyboard,
Declared it out of tune, inspected whistling
A twelve hours' beard, went out for cigarettes;
While she, contending with a woman's demons,
Pulled back the sheets and made the bed and found
A fallen towel to dust the table-top,
And wondered how it was a man could wake
From night to day and take the day for granted.
By evening she was back in love again,
Though not so wholly but throughout the night
She woke sometimes to feel the daylight coming
Like a relentless milkman up the stairs.

1955

BREAKFAST IN A BOWLING ALLEY IN UTICA, NEW YORK

Smudged eyeballs,
mouth stale as air,
I'm newly dead, a corpse

so fresh the grave unnerves me.
Nobody here but me
and Hermes[1] behind the counter

defrosting sandwich steaks.
Paeans of *vox humana*[2]
sob from the walls. THIS LAND

IS MY LAND. . . . It sounds
mummified. Has no sex,
no liquor license.

I chew meat and bread
thinking of wheatfields—
a gold-beige ceinture[3]

and cattle like ghosts
of the buffalo, running
across plains, nearing

the abattoir.[4] Houses
dream old-fashionedly
in backwoods townships

[1]Greek god who conducted the dead to Hades. [2]Latin: the human voice.
[3]French: belt, sash. [4]French: slaughterhouse.

while the land glitters
with temporary life
stuck fast by choice:

trailers put out taproots
of sewage pipe, suckers
of TV aerial—

but in one of them,
perhaps, a man
alone with his girl

for the first time.

1963

DIVISIONS OF LABOR

The revolutions wheel, compromise, utter their statements:
a new magazine appears, mastheaded with old names,
an old magazine polishes up its act
with deconstructions[1] of the prose of Malcolm X
The women in the back rows of politics
are still licking thread to slip into the needle's
eye, trading bones for plastic, splitting pods
for necklaces to sell to the cruise-ships
producing immaculate First Communion dresses
with flatiron and irresolute hot water
still fitting the microscopic golden wires
into the silicon chips
still teaching, watching the children
quenched in the crossfire alleys, the flashflood gullies
the kerosene flashfires
—the women whose labor remakes the world
each and every morning
I have seen a woman sitting
between the stove and the stars
her fingers singed from snuffing out the candles
of pure theory Finger and thumb: both scorched:
I have felt that sacred wax blister my hand
1988

1989

[1]I.e., arcane critical examinations.

FOR THIS

If I've reached for your lines (I have)
  like letters from the dead that stir the nerves
dowsed you for a springhead
  to water my thirst
dug into my compost skeletons and petals
  you surely meant to catch the light:

—at work in my wormeaten wormwood-raftered
  stateless underground
    have I a plea?

If I've touched your finger
  with a ravenous tongue
    licked from your palm a rift of salt
if I've dreamt or thought you
  a pack of blood fresh-drawn
    hanging darkred from a hook
higher than my heart
  (you who understand transfusion)
    where else should I appeal?

A pilot light lies low
  while the gas jets sleep
    (a cat getting toed from stove
into nocturnal ice)
  language uncommon and agile as truth
    melts down the most intractable silence
A lighthouse keeper's ethics:
  you tend for all or none
    for this you might set your furniture on fire
A *this* we have blundered over
  as if the lamp could be shut off at will
    rescue denied for some

and still a lighthouse be

1999

1999

Before the acute
point of the severing
I wanted to see into my century's
hinged and beveled mirror
clear of smoke

eyes of coal and ruby
stunned neck the carrier of bricks and diamonds
brow of moonlit oyster shells
barbed wire lacework disgracing
the famous monument

Behind it spread the old
indigenous map landscape
before conquerors horizon ownless

1999

Denise Levertov 1923–1997

With the publication of her second volume of verse, Here and Now *(1957), Denise Levertov revealed a distinctiveness of style and observation that made her one of the most respected poets of her generation. She was born and raised in England and was educated at home. She wrote most of the poems in her first volume,* The Double Image *(1946), while working in London hospitals during World War II. In 1947, she married the American writer Mitchell Goodman and came to live in the United States, where she became a citizen in 1956.*

In America, Denise Levertov became interested in the poetry and prosody of such writers as Wallace Stevens, Ezra Pound, and William Carlos Williams, and during the interval between her first and second volumes of poetry her work underwent a transformation from the traditional versification of English poetry to the freer rhythms and colloquial diction of experimental American verse of the 1950s.

Her third volume of poems, Overland to the Islands, *appeared in 1958, and her fourth,* With Eyes at the Back of Our Heads, *two years later. In 1961, she became poetry editor for the* Nation, *and she published* The Jacob's Ladder. *In 1964,* O Taste and See *was published, followed by* The Sorrow Dance *(1967),* Relearning the Alphabet *(1970),* To Stay Alive *(1971),* Footprints *(1972),* The Freedom of the Dust *(1973), and* Life in the Forest, *(1979). Her collections of essays include* The Poet in the World *(1973) and* New and Selected Essays *(1992). She published her twentieth book of poems,* Evening Train, *in 1992 and* Tesserae, *a book of "memoirs and suppositions," in 1995.*

Denise Levertov's carefully controlled, exact lines and stanzas attest to the fact that she did not sacrifice form entirely for content in her poems. Although she rejected traditional accent and meter and such poetic devices as alliteration, she also avoided the opposite extreme of "spontaneous" writing. Her poems were constructed around the objects of this world at this time. Her aim was to render those objects in a fashion so precise that they conveyed at once the poet's innermost feelings and the moral and even political significance they suggested. The scope of Denise Levertov's themes was almost as broad as her range of imagery, and her emphasis on the essential identity of symbol and meaning was a conscious effort to give her poems a harmony "in utter contrast to the chaos in which they exist."

FURTHER READING: L. Wagner, *Denise Levertov,* 1967; *Denise Levertov: In Her Own Province,* ed. L. Wagner, 1979; H. Marten, *Understanding Denise Levertov,* 1988; *Critical Essays on Denise Levertov,* ed. L. Wagner-Martin, 1990; A. Rodgers, *Denise Levertov: The Poetry of Engagement,* 1993; *Conversations with Denise Levertov,* ed. J. Brooker, 1998; *The Letters of Denise Levertov and William Carlos Williams,* ed. C. MacGowan, 1998; *Denise Levertov: New Perspectives,* ed. A. Little and S. Paul, 2000; G. Macallister, *The Incarnational Poetics of Denise Levertov,* 2002; *The Letters of Robert Duncan and Denise Levertov,* ed. R. Bertholf and A. Gelpi, 2004.

TEXTS: "Beyond the End" is from *Here and Now,* 1957; "Pure Products" is from *Overland to the Islands,* 1958; "Come into Animal Presence" is from *The Jacob's Ladder,* 1961; "O Taste and See" and "The Ache of Marriage" are from *O Taste and See,* 1964; "Abel's Bride" is from *The Sorrow Dance,* 1967; "Zeroing In" is from *Breathing in the Water,* 1987; all other poems are from *Relearning the Alphabet,* 1970.

BEYOND THE END

In "nature" there's no choice—
                                        flowers
swing their heads in the wind, sun & moon
    are as they are. But we seem
almost to have it (not just
    available death)

It's energy: a spider's thread: not to
"go on living" but to quicken, to activate: extend:
    Some have it, they force it—
with work or laughter or even
    the act of buying, if that's
all they can lay hands on—

    the girls crowding the stores, where light,
        colour, solid dreams are—what gay
    desire! It's their festival,
        ring game, wassail, mystery.

It has no grace like that of
the grass, the humble rhythms, the
falling & rising of leaf and star;
it's barely
a constant. Like salt:
take it or leave it

The "hewers of wood"[1] & so on; every damn
craftsman has it while he's working

[1]"Let them live; but let them be hewers of wood and drawers of water" (Joshua 9:21).

but it's not
a question of work: some
shine with it, in repose. (Maybe it is
response, the will to respond—reason
can give nothing at all/like
the response to desire') maybe
a gritting of the teeth, to go
just that much further, beyond the end
beyond whatever ends: to begin, to be, to defy.
1953, 1957

PURE PRODUCTS

To the sea they came—
2000 miles in an old bus
fitted with brittle shelves and makeshift beds
and cluttered with U.S. canned goods
—to the Sea!
on which they paddle
innertubes —and the lowhovering Sun—
from which the old woman hides her head
under what looks like
a straw wastebasket.
"Yep, they cured me alright,
but see, it made my breasts grow like a woman's."
And she: "Something hurts him in his chest,
I think
maybe it's his heart,"—and hers
I can see beating at the withered throat.

To the Sea some force has driven them—
away from a lifetime.
And in this windless heat they purpose
to walk the 3 miles of shadeless beach to the shore
to ask in Spanish (of which they know
only yes and no) for wholewheat flour
(which is unknown in the region) that she
may bake their bread!
They are dying
in their gentleness, adorned
with wrinkled apple smiles—nothing
remains for them
but to live a little, invoking
the old powers.
1958

COME INTO ANIMAL PRESENCE

Come into animal presence.
No man is so guileless as
the serpent. The lonely white
rabbit on the roof is a star
twitching its ears at the rain.
The llama intricately
folding its hind legs to be seated
not disdains but mildly
disregards human approval.
What joy when the insouciant
armadillo glances at us and doesn't
quicken his trotting
across the track into the palm brush.

What is this joy? That no animal
falters, but knows what it must do?
That the snake has no blemish,
that the rabbit inspects his strange surroundings
in white star-silence? The llama
rests in dignity, the armadillo
has some intention to pursue in the palm-forest.
Those who were sacred have remained so,
holiness does not dissolve, it is presence
of bronze, only the sight that saw it
faltered and turned from it.
And old joy returns in holy presence.

1960, 1961

THE ACHE OF MARRIAGE

The ache of marriage:

thigh and tongue, beloved,
are heavy with it,
it throbs in the teeth

We look for communion
and are turned away, beloved,
each and each

It is leviathan and we
in its belly
looking for joy, some joy
not to be known outside it

two by two in the ark of
the ache of it.

1962, 1964

O TASTE AND SEE

The world is
not with us enough.[1]
O taste and see[2]

the subway Bible poster said,
meaning *The Lord,* meaning
if anything all that lives
to the imagination's tongue,

grief, mercy, language,
tangerine, weather, to
breathe them, bite,
savor, chew, swallow, transform

into our flesh our
deaths, crossing the street, plum, quince,
living in the orchard and being

hungry, and plucking
the fruit.

1963, 1964

ABEL'S BRIDE

Woman fears for man, he goes
out alone to his labors. No mirror
nests in his pocket. His face
opens and shuts with his hopes.
His sex hangs unhidden
or rises before him
blind and questing.

She thinks herself
lucky. But sad. When she goes out
she looks in the glass, she remembers
herself. Stones, coal,
the hiss of water upon the kindled
branches—her being
is a cave, there are bones at the hearth.

1966, 1967

[1]A reference to Wordsworth's sonnet "The World Is Too Much with Us" (1807).
[2]Psalms 34:8, "O taste and see that the Lord is good."

MAD SONG

My madness is dear to me.
I who was almost always the sanest among my friends,
one to whom others came for comfort,
now at my breasts (that look timid and ignorant,
        that don't look as if milk had flowed from them,
        years gone by)
cherish a viper.
                Hail, little serpent of useless longing
that may destroy me,
that bites me with such idle
needle teeth.

I who am loved by those who love me
for honesty,
to whom life was an honest breath
                taken in good faith,
I've forgotten how to tell joy from bitterness.

Dear to me, dear to me,
blue poison, green pain in the mind's veins.
How am I to be cured against my will?

1970

A HUNGER

Black beans, white sunlight.
These have sufficed.

Approval of mothers, of brothers,
of strangers—a plunge of the hands
in sifted flour, over the wrists.
It gives pleasure.

And being needed. Being loved for that.
Being forgiven.

What mountains there are
to border solitude and provide
limits, blue or
dark as raisins.

But hunger: a hunger there is
refuses. Refuses the earth.

1970

ZEROING IN

'I am a landscape,' he said,
'a landscape and a person walking in that landscape.
There are daunting cliffs there,
and plains glad in their way
of brown monotony. But especially
there are sinkholes, places
of sudden terror, of small circumference
and malevolent depths.'
'I know,' she said. 'When I set forth
to walk in myself, as it might be
on a fine afternoon, forgetting,
sooner or later I come to where sedge
and clumps of white flowers, rue perhaps,
mark the bogland, and I know
there are quagmires there that can pull you
down, and sink you in bubbling mud.'
'We had an old dog,' he told her, 'when I was a boy,
a good dog, friendly. But there was an injured spot
on his head, if you happened
just to touch it he'd jump up yelping
and bite you. He bit a young child,
they had to take him down to the vet's and destroy him.'
'No one knows where it is,' she said,
'and even by accident no one touches it.
It's inside my landscape, and only I, making my way
preoccupied through my life, crossing my hills,
sleeping on green moss of my own woods,
I myself without warning touch it,
and leap up at myself—'
'—or flinch back
just in time.'
'Yes, we learn that.
It's not terror, it's pain we're talking about:
those places in us, like your dog's bruised head,
that are bruised forever, that time
never assuages, never.'

1987

Anne Sexton 1928–1974

Anne Sexton was one of America's most notable confessional poets: "I tell so much truth in my poetry that I'm a fool if I say any more." She was born in Newton, Massachusetts, attended private and public schools, worked simultaneously as a librarian and a fashion model, and began writing poetry in 1957 when she studied at Boston University under Robert Lowell.

Her best work has the quality of a succinct short story in verse. It reads like a forced confession that is painfully direct and marked by witty irony, self-mockery, and sensitive meditation. The subject matter of her first volume, To Bedlam and Part Way Back *(1960), is apparent in the title—mental disturbance and psychic distress.* Bedlam *grew out of her own mental breakdown and her consequent commitment to an asylum, and it charts with painful honesty her journeys into madness and her visions of death. Her views of life and death were developed further in her second volume,* All My Pretty Ones *(1962), and in collections that followed:* Live or Die *(1967), which won a Pulitzer Prize,* Love Poems *(1969), and* Transformations *(1971), which offers macabre reappraisals of familiar fairy tales. In* The Book of Folly *(1972) and in works published after her death, such as* 45 Mercy Street *(1976), she continued her conversions of experience into harsh metaphors expressing an awareness of victimization, guilt, chaos. She was fascinated with death—with suicide as a rebuke of life and the living. Her later work sometimes was uneven, emotionally indulgent. Yet with its irrationalism and violence it was nonetheless compelling and piercing, just as she had wanted it to be. In an interview shortly before her death, by suicide, in 1974, she said of poetry: "I think it should be a shock to the senses. It should almost hurt."*

FURTHER READING: *Anne Sexton: A Self-Portrait in Letters,* ed. L. Sexton and L. Ames, 1977; *Anne Sexton: The Artist and Her Critics,* ed. J. McClatchy, 1978; *No Evil Star,* ed. S. Colburn, 1985; D. George, *Oedipus Anne,: The Poetry of Anne Sexton,* 1987; *Original Essays on the Poetry of Anne Sexton,* ed. F. Bixler, 1988; H. Bernard-King, *Anne Sexton,* 1989; D. Middlebrook, *Anne Sexton: A Biography,* 1991; G. Swiontkowski, *Imagining Incest: Sexton, Plath, Rich, and Olds on Life with Daddy,* 2003; P. McGowan, *Anne Sexton and Middle Generation Poetry: The Geography of Grief,* 2004.

TEXT: *The Complete Poems,* ed. L. Sexton, 1981.

THE FARMER'S WIFE

From the hodge porridge
of their country lust,
their local life in Illinois,
where all their acres look
like a sprouting broom factory,
they name just ten years now
that she has been his habit;
as again tonight he'll say
honey bunch let's go
and she will not say how there
must be more to living
than this brief bright bridge
of the raucous bed or even
the slow braille touch of him
like a heavy god grown light,
that old pantomime of love
that she wants although
it leaves her still alone,
built back again at last,

mind's apart from him, living
her own self in her own words
and hating the sweat of the house
they keep when they finally lie
each in separate dreams
and then how she watches him,
still strong in the blowzy bag
of his usual sleep while
her young years bungle past
their same marriage bed
and she wishes him cripple, or poet,
or even lonely, or sometimes,
better, my lover, dead.

1960

RINGING THE BELLS

And this is the way they ring
the bells in Bedlam
and this is the bell-lady
who comes each Tuesday morning
to give us a music lesson
and because the attendants make you go
and because we mind by instinct,
like bees caught in the wrong hive,
we are the circle of the crazy ladies
who sit in the lounge of the mental house
and smile at the smiling woman
who passes us each a bell,
who points at my hand
that holds my bell, E flat,
and this is the gray dress next to me
who grumbles as if it were special
to be old, to be old,
and this is the small hunched squirrel girl
on the other side of me
who picks at the hairs over her lip,
who picks at the hairs over her lip all day,
and this is how the bells really sound,
as untroubled and clean
as a workable kitchen,
and this is always my bell responding
to my hand that responds to the lady
who points at me, E flat;
and although we are no better for it,
they tell you to go. And you do.

1960

AND ONE FOR MY DAME

A born salesman,
my father made all his dough
by selling wool to Fieldcrest, Woolrich and Faribo.

A born talker,
he could sell one hundred wet-down bales
of that white stuff. He could clock the miles and sales

and make it pay.
At home each sentence he would utter
had first pleased the buyer who'd paid him off in butter.

Each word
had been tried over and over, at any rate,
on the man who was sold by the man who filled my plate.

My father hovered
over the Yorkshire pudding and the beef:
a peddler, a hawker, a merchant and an Indian chief.

Roosevelt! Willkie! and war!
How suddenly gauche I was
with my old-maid heart and my funny teenage applause.

Each night at home
my father was in love with maps
while the radio fought its battles with Nazis and Japs.

Except when he hid
in his bedroom on a three-day drunk,
he typed out complex itineraries, packed his trunk,

his matched luggage
and pocketed a confirmed reservation,
his heart already pushing over the red routes of the nation.

I sit at my desk
each night with no place to go,
opening the wrinkled maps of Milwaukee and Buffalo,

the whole U.S.,
its cemeteries, its arbitrary time zones,
through routes like small veins, capitals like small stones.

He died on the road,
his heart pushed from neck to back,
his white hanky signaling from the window of the Cadillac.

My husband,
as blue-eyed as a picture book, sells wool:
boxes of card waste, laps and rovings he can pull

to the thread
and say *Leicester, Rambouillet, Merino,*[1]
a half-blood, it's greasy and thick, yellow as old snow.

And when you drive off, my darling,
Yes, sir! Yes, sir! It's one for my dame,
your sample cases branded with my father's name,

your itinerary open,
its tolls ticking and greedy,
its highways built up like new loves, raw and speedy.
1962 1966

THE ADDICT

Sleepmonger,
deathmonger,
with capsules in my palms each night,
eight at a time from sweet pharmaceutical bottles
I make arrangements for a pint-sized journey.
I'm the queen of this condition.
I'm an expert on making the trip
and now they say I'm an addict.
Now they ask why.
Why!

Don't they know
that I promised to die!
I'm keeping in practice.
I'm merely staying in shape.
The pills are a mother, but better,
every color and as good as sour balls.
I'm on a diet from death.

Yes, I admit
it has gotten to be a bit of a habit—
blows eight at a time, socked in the eye,
hauled away by the pink, the orange,
the green and the white goodnights.
I'm becoming something of a chemical
mixture.
That's it!

[1]Breeds of sheep.

My supply
of tablets
has got to last for years and years.
I like them more than I like me.
Stubborn as hell, they won't let go.
It's a kind of marriage.
It's a kind of war
where I plant bombs inside
of myself.

Yes
I try
to kill myself in small amounts,
an innocuous occupation.
Actually I'm hung up on it.
But remember I don't make too much noise.
And frankly no one has to lug me out
and I don't stand there in my winding sheet.
I'm a little buttercup in my yellow nightie
eating my eight loaves in a row
and in a certain order as in
the laying on of hands
or the black sacrament.

It's a ceremony
but like any other sport
its full of rules.
It's like a musical tennis match where
my mouth keeps catching the ball.
Then I lie on my altar
elevated by the eight chemical kisses.

What a lay me down this is
with two pink, two orange,
two green, two white goodnights.
Fee-fi-fo-fum—
Now I'm borrowed.
Now I'm numb.
1966 1966

US

I was wrapped in black
fur and white fur and
you undid me and then
you placed me in gold light
and then you crowned me,

while snow fell outside
the door in diagonal darts.
While a ten-inch snow
came down like stars
in small calcium fragments,
we were in our own bodies
(that room that will bury us)
and you were in my body
(that room that will outlive us)
and at first I rubbed your
feet dry with a towel
because I was your slave
and then you called me princess.
Princess!

Oh then
I stood up in my gold skin
and I beat down the psalms
and I beat down the clothes
and you undid the bridle
and you undid the reins
and I undid the buttons,
the bones, the confusions,
the New England postcards,
the January ten o'clock night,
and we rose up like wheat,
acre after acre of gold,
and we harvested,
we harvested.

1969

ROWING

A story, a story!
(Let it go. Let it come.)
I was stamped out like a Plymouth fender
into this world.
First came the crib
with its glacial bars.
Then dolls
and the devotion to their plastic mouths.
Then there was school,
the little straight rows of chairs,
blotting my name over and over,
but undersea all the time,
a stranger whose elbows wouldn't work.
Then there was life
with its cruel houses

and people who seldom touched—
though touch is all—
but I grew,
like a pig in a trenchcoat I grew,
and then there were many strange apparitions,
the nagging rain, the sun turning into poison
and all of that, saws working through my heart,
but I grew, I grew,
and God was there like an island I had not rowed to,
still ignorant of Him, my arms and my legs worked,
and I grew, I grew,
I wore rubies and bought tomatoes
and now, in my middle age,
about nineteen in the head I'd say,
I am rowing, I am rowing
though the oarlocks stick and are rusty
and the sea blinks and rolls
like a worried eyeball,
but I am rowing, I am rowing,
though the wind pushes me back
and I know that that island will not be perfect,
it will have the flaws of life,
the absurdities of the dinner table,
but there will be a door
and I will open it
and I will get rid of the rat inside of me,
the gnawing pestilential rat.
God will take it with his two hands
and embrace it.

As the African says:
This is my tale which I have told,
if it be sweet, if it be not sweet,
take somewhere else and let some return to me.
This story ends with me still rowing.

1975

Sylvia Plath 1932–1963

The work of Sylvia Plath represents a romanticism in extremis, intense private agonies made public with a grotesque clarity. Her poetry has been praised as a supreme example of the confessional mode in modern literature and disparaged as "the longest suicide note ever written."

She was born in Boston, Massachusetts, the daughter of a German father and an Austrian mother whose attitudes and personalities were relentlessly exposed in their daughter's writing. As a child Plath was brilliant and erratic. At seventeen she published her first poem and her first short story. She entered Smith College on a scholarship, but she became increasingly filled with apprehensions of horror and death and obsessed with a sense of isolation and entrapment: "I've gone around for most of my life as in the rarified atmosphere under a bell jar."

Unable to reconcile her inner and outer worlds, she was briefly hospitalized and underwent intense psychiatric therapy. The events of these years she later presented in The Bell Jar, *an autobiographical novel about personality disintegration, which she published in 1963 under the pseudonym Victoria Lucas.*

In 1955 she graduated from Smith with highest honors and received a fellowship to Cambridge University, where she took her M.A. degree in 1957. In England she met and married British poet Ted Hughes in 1956. After a temporary return to America she lived in England for the remainder of her life.

Plath's first book of poetry, The Colossus, *was published in 1960 and acclaimed by critics for its range of language and stylistic brilliance. She then began work on the poems that were later to appear in* Ariel, *but instead of writing in her usual laborious manner, she wrote poems at "top speed, as one might write an urgent letter." The* Ariel *poems composed during this period reflect her renewed sense of the ungovernable chaos of human experience and her frightening visions of violence and horror. On February 11, 1963, she committed suicide.*

The Ariel *poems, published posthumously in 1965, were followed by* Uncollected Poems *(1965),* Crossing the Water *(1971), and* Winter Trees *(1972), works that reveal the painful intensity and desperation of a mind seeking to express, in hideous clarity, the visions of one trapped "in The Bell Jar" for whom "the world itself is a bad dream."*

FURTHER READING: *Letters from Home by Sylvia Plath: Correspondence 1950–1963,* ed. A. Roth, 1975; *Journals of Sylvia Plath,* ed. F. McCullough and T. Hughes, 1982; S. Bassnet, *Sylvia Plath,* 1987, 2005; L. Wagner-Martin, *Sylvia Plath,* 1987; A. Stevenson, *Bitter Flame: A Life of Sylvia Plath,* 1989; P. Alexander, *Rough Magic: A Biography of Sylvia Plath,* 1990; R. Hayman, *The Death and Life of Sylvia Plath,* 1991; N. Steiner, *A Closer Look at Ariel: A Memory of Sylvia Plath,* 1973; D. Holbrook, *Sylvia Plath: Poetry and Existence,* 1987; P. Annas, *A Disturbance in Mirrors: The Poetry of Sylvia Plath,* 1988; *Sylvia Plath,* ed. H. Bloom, 1989; S. Axelrod, *Sylvia Plath: The Wound and the Cure of Words,* 1990; J. Rose, *The Haunting of Sylvia Plath,* 1993; S. Van Dyne, *Revising Life: Sylvia Plath's Ariel Poems,* 1993; C. Hall, *Sylvia Plath,* 1998; A. Strangeways, *The Shaping of Shadows,* 1998; E. Butscher, *Sylvia Plath, Method and Madness, A Biography,* 2004; D. Middlebrook, *Her Husband, Hughes and Plath,* 2004; E. Wagner, *Ariel's Gift,* 2000; T. Brain, *The Other Sylvia Plath,* 2001; S. Blosser, *A Poetics on Edge, The Poetry and Prose of Sylvia Plath,* 2001; B. Lindberg-Seyersted, *Sylvia Plath, Studies in Her Poetry and Her Personality,* 2002; S. Bassnet, *Sylvia Plath, An Introduction to the Poetry,* 2004.

TEXT: *The Collected Poems, Sylvia Plath,* ed. T. Hughes, 1981.

THE BEE MEETING

Who are these people at the bridge to meet me? They are the villagers——
The rector, the midwife, the sexton, the agent for bees.
In my sleeveless summery dress I have no protection,
And they are all gloved and covered, why did nobody tell me?
They are smiling and taking out veils tacked to ancient hats.

I am nude as a chicken neck, does nobody love me?
Yes, here is the secretary of bees with her white shop smock,
Buttoning the cuffs at my wrists and the slit from my neck to my knees.
Now I am milkweed silk, the bees will not notice.
They will not smell my fear, my fear, my fear.

Which is the rector now, is it that man in black?
Which is the midwife, is that her blue coat?
Everybody is nodding a square black head, they are knights in visors,
Breastplates of cheesecloth knotted under the armpits.
Their smiles and their voices are changing. I am led through a beanfield.

Strips of tinfoil winking like people,
Feather dusters fanning their hands in a sea of bean flowers,
Creamy bean flowers with black eyes and leaves like bored hearts.
Is it blood clots the tendrils are dragging up that string?
No, no, it is scarlet flowers that will one day be edible.

Now they are giving me a fashionable white straw Italian hat
And a black veil that molds to my face, they are making me one of them.
They are leading me to the shorn grove, the circle of hives.
Is it the hawthorn that smells so sick?
The barren body of hawthorn, etherizing its children.

Is it some operation that is taking place?
It is the surgeon my neighbors are waiting for,
This apparition in a green helmet,
Shining gloves and white suit.
Is it the butcher, the grocer, the postman, someone I know?

I cannot run, I am rooted, and the gorse hurts me
With its yellow purses, its spiky armory.
I could not run without having to run forever.
The white hive is snug as a virgin,
Sealing off her brood cells, her honey, and quietly humming.

Smoke rolls and scarves in the grove.
The mind of the hive thinks this is the end of everything.
Here they come, the outriders, on their hysterical elastics.
If I stand very still, they will think I am cow-parsley,
A gullible head untouched by their animosity,

Not even nodding, a personage in a hedgerow.
The villagers open the chambers, they are hunting the queen.
Is she hiding, is she eating honey? She is very clever.
She is old, old, old, she must live another year, and she knows it.
While in their fingerjoint cells the new virgins

Dream of a duel they will win inevitably,
A curtain of wax dividing them from the bride flight,

The upflight of the murderess into a heaven that loves her.
The villagers are moving the virgins, there will be no killing.
The old queen does not show herself, is she so ungrateful?

I am exhausted, I am exhausted——
Pillar of white in a blackout of knives.
I am the magician's girl who does not flinch.
The villagers are untying their disguises, they are shaking hands.
Whose is that long white box in the grove, what have they accomplished,
    why am I cold.

1962 1962

LADY LAZARUS

I have done it again.
One year in every ten
I manage it——

A sort of walking miracle, my skin
Bright as a Nazi lampshade,
My right foot

A paperweight,
My face a featureless, fine
Jew linen.

Peel off the napkin
O my enemy.
Do I terrify?——

The nose, the eye pits, the full set of teeth?
The sour breath
Will vanish in a day.

Soon, soon the flesh
The grave cave ate will be
At home on me

And I a smiling woman.
I am only thirty.
And like the cat I have nine times to die.

This is Number Three.
What a trash
to annihilate each decade.

What a million filaments.
The peanut-crunching crowd
Shoves in to see

Them unwrap me hand and foot——
The big strip tease.
Gentleman, ladies,

These are my hands,
My knees.
I may be skin and bone,

Nevertheless, I am the same, identical woman.
The first time it happened I was ten.
It was an accident.

The second time I meant
To last it out and not come back at all.
I rocked shut

As a seashell.
They had to call and call
And pick the worms off me like sticky pearls.

Dying
Is an art, like everything else.
I do it exceptionally well.

I do it so it feels like hell.
I do it so it feels real.
I guess you could say I've a call.

It's easy enough to do it in a cell.
It's easy enough to do it and stay put.
It's the theatrical

Comeback in broad day
To the same place, the same face, the same brute
Amused shout:

"A miracle!"
That knocks me out.
There is a charge

For the eyeing of my scars, there is a charge
For the hearing of my heart——
It really goes.

And there is a charge, a very large charge,
For a word or a touch
Or a bit of blood

Or a piece of my hair or my clothes.
So, so, Herr Doktor.[1]
So, Herr Enemy.

I am your opus,
I am your valuable,
The pure gold baby

That melts to a shriek.
I turn and burn.
Do not think I underestimate your great concern.

Ash, ash—
You poke and stir.
Flesh, bone, there is nothing there——

A cake of soap,
A wedding ring,
A gold filling.

Herr God, Herr Lucifer,
Beware
Beware.

Out of the ash
I rise[2] with my red hair
And I eat men like air.
1962 1963, 1965

ARIEL[1]

Stasis in darkness.
Then the substanceless blue
Pour of tor[2] and distances.
God's lioness,
How one we grow,
Pivot of heels and knees!—The furrow

Splits and passes, sister to
The brown arc
Of the neck I cannot catch,

[1]German: Mr. Doctor.

[2]In Near Eastern fable the Phoenix, a symbol of death and resurrection, is a red and gold bird that, at the end of life, burns itself to ashes on a funeral pyre and then rises from the ashes newly reborn.

[1]The horse Sylvia Plath rode while attending riding school in England. [2]A high hill.

Nigger-eye
Berries cast dark
Hooks——

Black sweet blood mouthfuls,
Shadows.
Something else

Hauls me through air——
Thighs, hair;
Flakes from my heels.

White
Godiva[3], I unpeel—
Dead hands, dead stringencies.

And now I
Foam to wheat, a glitter of seas.
The child's cry

Melts in the wall.
And I
Am the arrow,

The dew that flies
Suicidal, at one with the drive
Into the red

Eye, the cauldron of morning.
1962 1963, 1965

DADDY

You do not do, you do not do
Any more, black shoe
In which I have lived like a foot
For thirty years, poor and white,
Barely daring to breathe or Achoo.

Daddy, I have had to kill you.
You died before I had time——
Marble-heavy, a bag full of God,
Ghastly statue with one grey toe[1]
Big as a Frisco seal

[3]Lady Godiva, eleventh-century wife of an English earl, famous for her legendary ride naked through the city of Coventry, to win remission of heavy taxes on the people.
[1]The toe of Plath's father was swollen and discolored from diabetic gangrene.

And a head in the freakish Atlantic
Where it pours bean green over blue
In the waters off beautiful Nauset.[2]
I used to pray to recover you.[3]
Ach, du.[4]

In the German tongue, in the Polish town[5]
Scraped flat by the roller
Of wars, wars, wars.
But the name of the town is common.
My Polack friend

Says there are a dozen or two.
So I never could tell where you
Put your foot, your root,
I never could talk to you.
The tongue stuck in my jaw.

It stuck in a barb wire snare.
Ich, ich, ich, ich,[6]
I could hardly speak.
I thought every German was you.
And the language obscene

An engine, an engine
Chuffing me off like a Jew.
A Jew to Dachau, Auschwitz, Belsen.[7]
I began to talk like a Jew.
I think I may well be a Jew.
The snows of the Tyrol,[8] the clear beer of Vienna
Are not very pure or true.
With my gypsy ancestress and my weird luck
And my Taroc pack[9] and my Taroc pack
I may be a bit of a Jew.

I have always been scared of *you*,
With your Luftwaffe,[10] your gobbledygoo.
And your neat moustache
And your Aryan eye, bright blue.[11]
Panzer[12] man, panzer-man, O You——

[2]Beach and harbor on Cape Cod. [3]Plath's father died when she was a child.
[4]German: Ah, you. [5]Plath's father was born in Poland to German parents.
[6]German: I, I, I, I. [7]Nazi concentration camps in Germany and Poland.
[8]Mountain region of Austria. [9]Tarot cards, used in fortune-telling.
[10]The name of the German air force in World War II.
[11]Reference to the Nazi theory of the superiority of the blond, blue-eyed Aryan race.
[12]German: armored, tank.

Not God but a swastika
So black no sky could squeak through.
Every woman adores a Fascist,
The boot in the face, the brute
Brute heart of a brute like you.

You stand at the blackboard, daddy,
In the picture I have of you,
A cleft in your chin instead of your foot
But no less a devil for that, no not
Any less the black man who

Bit my pretty red heart in two.
I was ten when they buried you.
At twenty I tried to die
And get back, back, back to you.
I thought even the bones would do.

But they pulled me out of the sack,
And they stuck me together with glue.[13]
And then I knew what to do.
I made a model of you,
A man in black with a Meinkampf[14] look

And a love of the rack and the screw.
And I said I do, I do.
So daddy, I'm finally through.
The black telephone's off at the root,
The voices just can't worm through.
If I've killed one man, I've killed two—
The vampire who said he was you
And drank my blood for a year,
Seven years, if you want to know.
Daddy, you can lie back now.

There's a stake in your fat black heart
And the villagers never liked you.
They are dancing and stamping on you.
They always *knew* it was you.
Daddy, daddy, you bastard, I'm through.
1962 1963, 1965

[13]A reference to Plath's recovery from her first suicide attempt.
[14]German: My struggle, the title of Adolf Hitler's political manifesto.

FEVER 103°

Pure? What does it mean?
The tongues of hell
Are dull, dull as the triple

Tongues of dull, fat Cerberus[1]
Who wheezes at the gate. Incapable
Of licking clean

The aguey tendon, the sin, the sin.
The tinder cries.
The indelible smell

Of a snuffed candle!
Love, love, the low smokes roll
From me like Isadora's scarves,[2] I'm in a fright

One scarf will catch and anchor in the wheel.
Such yellow sullen smokes
Make their own element. They will not rise,

But trundle round the globe
Choking the aged and the meek,
The weak

Hothouse baby in its crib,
The ghastly orchid
Hanging its hanging garden in the air,
Devilish leopard!
Radiation turned it white
And killed it in an hour.

Greasing the bodies of adulterers
Like Hiroshima ash and eating in.
The sin. The sin.

Darling, all night
I have been flickering, off, on, off, on.
The sheets grow heavy as a lecher's kiss.

Three days. Three nights.
Lemon water, chicken
Water, water make me retch.

[1]In classical myth, the three-headed dog that guarded the entrance to Hades.

[2]Isadora Duncan (1878–1927), American dancer who was strangled when her long scarf caught in the wheel of the car in which she rode.

I am too pure for you or anyone.
Your body
Hurts me as the world hurts God. I am a lantern—

My head a moon
Of Japanese paper, my gold beaten skin
Infinitely delicate and infinitely expensive.

Does not my heat astound you. And my light.
All by myself I am a huge camellia
Glowing and coming and going, flush on flush.

I think I am going up,
I think I may rise—
The beads of hot metal fly, and I, love, I

Am a pure acetylene
Virgin
Attended by roses,

By kisses, by cherubim,[3]
By whatever these pink things mean.
Not you, nor him

Not him, nor him
(My selves dissolving, old whore petticoats)—
To Paradise.
1962 1965

James Dickey 1923–1997

James Dickey was everybody's notion of the muscular poet. A football player and track star in college, he was an avid outdoorsman, archery expert, and guitarist; he served as a fighter pilot in both World War II and the Korean War, and he gave up a successful business career in advertising to write poetry. He was born in Atlanta, Georgia, on Groundhog Day, as he liked to point out, a suggestion perhaps of his affinity with the wilderness, which was to Dickey "a subject of endless interest and rejoicing."

*Dickey came to poetry, in his own words, "comparatively late": He was twenty-four before he began writing seriously, and in his late thirties before the publication of his first book of poems. Most of the poems in his first three volumes of poetry (*Into the Stone, *1960;* Drowning with Others, *1962; and* Helmets, *1964) were written mainly in short, three-beat lines; the syntax is usually clear and precise; stanzas are organized around a cluster of images. The worlds of physicality, animals, and nature are frequent*

[3]One of the orders of heavenly angels.

subjects; the dominant themes are death and renewal and the transformation possible for all living things. Even though Dickey often described dreams, memories, or illusions—"hallucinatory" subjects, in the poet's phrase—his poetry was relatively straightforward.

Dickey's next book, Buckdancer's Choice *(1965), marked a shift to what he called the "conclusionless" poem, which would "involve the reader in it, in all its imperfections and impurities, rather than offering him a (supposedly) perfected work for contemplation, judgment, and evaluation." The "conclusionless" poems are more narrative in form, with irregular meter and with longer lines typographically set to replace conventional punctuation and denote accents. The style is lush, sometimes even "woolly." The sense of the grotesque remains strong.*

In 1977 Dickey published The Bible: A New Vision, *a series of prose poems based on biblical texts. He also wrote literary criticism and novels,* Deliverance *(1970), which was made into a successful motion picture, and* Alnilam *(1987), which parallels, as did* Deliverance, *ancient quest myths. Dickey taught at several colleges and universities and read his poetry and lectured throughout the country, and he served as Consultant in Poetry to the Library of Congress. Poetry always remained his primary vocation, and in such volumes as* Poems 1957–1967 *(1967),* The Eye-Beaters *(1970), and* The Zodiac, *(1974), he demonstrated remarkable verbal energy, intensity, sympathy, and a sense of reconciliation unique in contemporary American poetry.*

FURTHER READING: *Babel to Byzantium,* 1968; *Self Interviews,* 1970; *Sorties, Journals, and New Essays,* 1971; *Striking In: The Early Notebooks of James Dickey,* ed. G. Van Ness, 1996; *The Whole Motion: Collected Poems 1945–1992,* 1993; R. Calhoun, *James Dickey: the Expansive Imagination,* 1973; R. Calhoun and R. Hill, *James Dickey,* 1983; R. Baughman, *Understanding James Dickey,* 1985; R. Kirschsten, *James Dickey and the Gentle Ecstasy of Earth,* 1988; *The Voiced Connections of James Dickey,* ed. R. Baughman, 1989; E. Suarez, *James Dickey and the Politics of Canon,* 1993; "Struggling for Wings," *The Art of James Dickey,* ed. R. Kirschten, 1997; R. Kirschten, *James Dickey and the Gentle Ecstasy of Earth,* 1997; G. Van Ness, *The One Voice of James Dickey: His Letters and Life,* 2003; *Critical Essays on James Dickey,* ed. R. Kirschten, 1994; *James Dickey,* ed. J. Baughman, 1999.

TEXT: *Poems 1957–1967,* 1967.

THE LIFEGUARD

In a stable of boats I lie still,
From all sleeping children hidden.
The leap of fish from its shadow
Makes the whole lake instantly tremble.
With my foot on the water, I feel
The moon outside

Take on the utmost of its power.
I rise and go out through the boats.
I set my broad sole upon silver,
On the skin of the sky, on the moonlight,
Stepping outward from earth onto water
In quest of the miracle

This village of children believed
That I could perform as I dived
For one who had sunk from my sight.
I saw his cropped haircut go under.
I leapt, and my steep body flashed
Once, in the sun.

Dark drew all the light from my eyes.
Like a man who explores his death
By the pull of his slow-moving shoulders,
I hung head down in the cold,
Wide-eyed, contained, and alone
Among the weeds,

And my fingertips turned into stone
From clutching immovable blackness.
Time after time I leapt upward
Exploding in breath, and fell back
From the change in the children's faces
At my defeat.

Beneath them I swam to the boathouse
With only my life in my arms
To wait for the lake to shine back
At the risen moon with such power
That my steps on the light of the ripples
Might be sustained.

Beneath me is nothing but brightness
Like the ghost of a snowfield in summer.
As I move toward the center of the lake,
Which is also the center of the moon,
I am thinking of how I may be
The savior of one

Who has already died in my care.
The dark trees fade from around me.
The moon's dust hovers together.
I call softly out, and the child's
Voice answers through blinding water.
Patiently, slowly,

He rises, dilating to break
The surface of stone with his forehead.
He is one I do not remember
Having ever seen in his life.
The ground I stand on is trembling
Upon his smile.

I wash the black mud from my hands.
On a light given off by the grave
I kneel in the quick of the moon
At the heart of a distant forest
And hold in my arms a child
Of water, water, water.
1961 1962

REINCARNATION (I)

Still, passed through the spokes of an old wheel, on and around
The hub's furry rust in the weeds and shadows of the riverbank,
This one is feeling his life as a man move slowly away.
Fallen from that estate, he has gone down on his knees
And beyond, disappearing into the egg buried under the sand

And wakened the low world being born, consisting now
Of the wheel on its side not turning, but leaning to rot away
In the sun a few feet farther off than it is for any man.
The roots bulge directly under the earth beneath him;
With his tongue he can hear them in their concerted effort

To raise something, anything, out of the dark of the ground.
He has come by gliding, by inserting the head between stems.
Everything follows that as naturally as the creation
Of the world, leaving behind arms and legs, leaving behind
The intervals between tracks, leaving one long wavering step

In sand and none in grass: he moves through, moving nothing,
And the grass stands as never entered. It is in the new
Life of resurrection that one can come in one's own time
To a place like a rotting wheel, the white paint flaking from it,
Rust slowly emerging, and coil halfway through it, stopped

By a just administration of light and dark over the diamonds
Of the body. Here, also naturally growing, is a flat leaf
To rest the new head upon. The stem bends but knows the weight
And does not touch the ground, holding the snub, patterned face
Swaying with the roots of things. Inside the jaws, saliva

Has turned ice cold, drawn from bird eggs and thunderstruck rodents,
Dusty pine needles, blunt stones, horse dung, leaf mold,
But mainly, now, from waiting—all the time a symbol of evil—
Not for food, but for the first man to walk by the gentle river:
Minute by minute the head becomes more poisonous and poised.

Here in the wheel is the place to wait, with the eyes unclosable,
Unanswerable, the tongue occasionally listening, this time
No place in the body desiring to burn the tail away or to warn,
But only to pass on, handless, what yet may be transferred
In a sudden giving-withdrawing move, like a county judge striking a match.
1964 1965

IN THE MOUNTAIN TENT

I am hearing the shape of the rain
Take the shape of the tent and believe it,
Laying down all around where I lie
A profound, unspeakable law.
I obey, and am free-falling slowly

Through the thought-out leaves of the wood
Into the minds of animals.
I am there in the shining of water
Like dark, like light, out of Heaven.

I am there like the dead, or the beast
Itself, which thinks of a poem—
Green, plausible, living, and holy—
And cannot speak, but hears,
Called forth from the waiting of things,

A vast, proper, reinforced crying
With the sifted, harmonious pause,
The sustained intake of all breath
Before the first word of the Bible.

At midnight water dawns
Upon the held skulls of the foxes
And weasels and tousled hares
On the eastern side of the mountain.
Their light is the image I make
As I wait as if recently killed,
Receptive, fragile, half-smiling,
My brow watermarked with the mark
On the wing of a moth

And the tent taking shape on my body
Like ill-fitting, Heavenly clothes.
From holes in the ground comes my voice
In the God-silenced tongue of the beasts.
"I shall rise from the dead," I am saying.
1962

THE SHARK'S PARLOR

Memory: I can take my head and strike it on a wall   on Cumberland Island
Where the night tide came crawling under the stairs   came up the first
Two or three steps   and the cottage stood on poles all night
With the sea-sprawled under it   as we dreamed of the great fin circling
Under the bedroom floor. In daylight there was my first brassy taste of beer
And Payton Ford and I came back from the Glynn County slaughterhouse
With a bucket of entrails and blood. We tied one end of a hawser
To a spindling porch pillar and rowed straight out of the house
Three hundred yards into the vast front yard of windless blue water
The rope outslithering its coil   the two-gallon jug stoppered and sealed
With wax   and a ten-foot chain leader   a drop-forged shark hook nestling.
We cast our blood on the waters   the land blood easily passing
For sea blood   and we sat in it for a moment with the stain spreading
Out from the boat   sat in a new radiance   in the pond of blood in the sea
Waiting for fins,   waiting to spill our guts also in the glowing water.
We dumped the bucket, and baited the hook with a run-over collie pup. The jug
Bobbed, trying to shake off the sun as a dog would shake off the sea.
We rowed to the house   feeling the same water lift the boat a new way,
All the time seeing where we lived rise and dip with the oars.
We tied up and sat down in rocking chairs, one eye or the other responding
to the blue-eye wink of the jug. Payton got us a beer and we sat
All morning sat there with blood on our minds   the red mark out
In the harbor slowly failing us   then   the house groaned   the rope
Sprang out of the water   splinters flew   we leapt from our chairs
And grabbed the rope   hauled   did nothing   the house coming subtly
Apart   all around us   underfoot   boards beginning to sparkle like sand
With the glinting of the bright hidden parts of ten-year-old nails
Pulling out   the tarred poles we slept propped-up on   leaning to sea
As in land wind   crabs scuttling from under the floor   as we took turns about

Two more porch pillars   and looked out and saw   something   a
   fish-flash
An almighty fin in trouble   a moiling of secret forces   a false start
Of water   a round wave growing: in the whole of Cumberland
   Sound the one ripple.
Payton took off without a word   I could not hold him either
But clung to the rope anyway: it was the whole house bending
Its nails that held whatever it was   coming in a little and like a fool
I took up the slack on my wrist. The rope drew gently   jerked
   I lifted
Clean off the porch and hit the water   the same water it was in
I felt in blue blazing terror at the bottom of the stairs and
   scrambled
Back up looking desperately into the human house as deeply as I
   could
Stopping my gaze before it went out the wire screen of the back
   door
Stopped it on the thistled rattan   the rugs I lay on and read
On my mother's sewing basket with next winter's socks spilling
   from it
The flimsy vacation furniture   a bucktoothed picture of myself.
Payton came back with three men from a filling station   and
   glanced at me
Dripping water   inexplicable   then we all grabbed hold like a
   tug-of-war.

We were gaining a little   from us a cry went up   from everywhere
People came running. Behind us the house filled with men and
   boys.
On the third step from the sea I took my place   looking down the
   rope.
Going into the ocean, humming and shaking off drops. A houseful
Of people put their backs into it   going up the steps from me
Into the living room   through the kitchen   down the back stairs
Up and over a hill of sand   across a dust road   and onto a raised
   field
Of dunes   we were gaining   the rope in my hands began to be wet
With deeper water   all other haulers retreated through the house
But Payton and I on the stairs   drawing hand over hand on our
   blood
Drawing into existence by the nose   a huge body   becoming
A hammerhead   rolling in beery shallows   and I began to let up
But the rope still strained behind me   the town had gone
Pulling-mad in our house: far away in a field of sand they struggled
They had turned their backs on the sea   bent double   some on
   their knees
The rope over their shoulders like a bag of gold   they strove for
   the ideal

Esso station across the scorched meadow   with the distant fish coming up
The front stairs the   sagging boards   still coming in   up   taking
Another step   toward the empty house   where the rope stood straining
By itself through the rooms   in the middle of the air. "Pass the word,"
Payton said, and I screamed it: "Let up, good God, let up!" to no one there.
The shark flopped on the porch, grating with salt-sand   driving back in
The nails he had pulled out   coughing chunks of his formless blood.
The screen door banged and tore off   he scrambled on his tail slid
Curved   did a thing from another world   and was out of his element and in
Our vacation paradise   cutting all four legs from under the dinner table
With one deep-water move   he unwove the rugs in a moment throwing pints
Of blood over everything we owned   knocked the buck teeth out of my picture
His odd head full of crushed jelly-glass splinters and radio tubes thrashing
Among the pages of fan magazines   all the movie stars drenched in sea-blood.
Each time we thought he was dead   he struggled back and smashed
One more thing   in all coming back to die   three or four more times after death.
At last we got him out   log-rolling him   greasing his sandpaper skin
With lard to slide him   pulling on his chained lips as the tide came
Tumbled him down the steps as the first night wave went under the floor.
He drifted off   head back   belly white as the moon. What could I do but buy
That house   for the one black mark still there   against death   a forehead-
toucher in the room he circles beneath   and has been invited to wreck?
Blood hard as iron on the wall   black with time   still bloodlike
Can be touched whenever the brow is drunk enough: all changes: Memory:
Something like three-dimensional dancing in the limbs   with age
Feeling more in two worlds than one   in all worlds the growing encounters.

1965

W. S. Merwin 1927–

W. S. Merwin was born in New York, the son of a clergyman. He attended Princeton University, where he studied medieval literature and romance languages. In 1948 he made his way to Europe, where he lived in France, Spain, and Portugal, worked as a tutor to the children of a Portuguese nobleman, and studied writing in Majorca under the English poet Robert Graves. Since that time, he has become a prolific writer of poems, fiction, drama, essays, travel books, and translations. Working sometimes with other translators he has translated into English twenty-one volumes of works in Spanish, French, Latin, Italian, ancient Greek, and medieval English, among them the Spanish national epic The Poem of El Cid *(1959), the* Satires *of the Roman poet Persius (1960), and the medieval French* Song of Roland *(1963). In 1998 he published* East Windows, *translations of Asian poems and sayings, and in 2000 a translation of Dante's* Purgatorio *(2000). His prize-winning translation of the medieval English poem* Sir Gawain and the Green Knight, *a fourteenth-century tale of adventure and enchantment in King Arthur's Court, appeared in 2002.*

The range of his writing is also evident in his essays—his most recent collection, Ends of the Earth *(2004), treats subjects as varied as explorers, mountains, butterflies, and Neanderthal bones. But it is for his poetry that Merwin has received the greatest acclaim. His first volume of verse,* A Mask for Janus *(1952), won a Yale Younger Poets Award. He then published* The Dancing Bears *(1954),* The Drunk in the Furnace *(1960),* The Moving Target *(1963),* The Lice *(1967),* The Carriers of Ladders *(1970), which won a Pulitzer Prize,* The Compass Flower *(1977),* Finding the Islands *(1982),* Opening the Hand *(1983), and* Rain in the Trees *(1988). A collection of his poetry,* Selected Poems, *was published in 1988. Six more volumes of his poetry were published in the 1990s. Two more volumes,* The Pupil *and* Migration *(a collection of old and new poems) were published in 2001 and 2005.*

In his torrent of poetry (he has written a total of twenty-three volumes) Merwin has moved from the full discursiveness of his earlier poetry to an epigrammatic poetry of simple statement and "shrinking margins." Much of his poetry presents an unsentimental portrait of humankind and nature; the writing is spare, undecorated, devoid even of punctuation. Yet he draws on the rich universalities of myth, finds intricate emblems and messages in everyday objects and events. Merwin has been described as a writer of poems that are both urgent and lyrical, that attempt to evoke a mood rather than tell a direct story. And he has been described as a deeply contemplative poet, one drawn to a natural world that inspires both wishful dreams and lessons of lost hope.

FURTHER READING: *W. S. Merwin: The First Four Books of Poems,* 1975; C. Davis, *W. S. Merwin,* 1981; *Regions of Memory: Uncollected Prose, 1949–1982,* 1987; *W. S. Merwin: Essays on the Poetry,* ed. C. Nelson and E. Folsom, 1987; E. Brunner, *Poetry as Labor and Privilege: The Writings of W. S. Merwin,* 1991; *The Lost Upland, Stories of Southwest France,* 1992; *Travels,* 1993; H. Hix, *Understanding W. S. Merwin,* 1997; *W. S. Merwin,* ed. H. Bloom, 2004.

TEXTS: "Direction" is from *Opening the Hand,* 1983; all other poems are from *W. S. Merwin: Selected Poems,* 1988.

GRANDFATHER IN THE OLD MEN'S HOME

Gentle at last, and as clean as ever,
He did not even need drink any more,
And his good sons unbent and brought him
Tobacco to chew, both times when they came
To be satisfied he was well cared for.
And he smiled all the time to remember
Grandmother, his wife, wearing the true faith
Like an iron nightgown, yet brought to birth
Seven times and raising the family
Through her needle's eye while he got away
Down the green river, finding directions
For boats. And himself coming home sometimes
Well-heeled but blind drunk, to hide all the bread
And shoot holes in the bucket while he made
His daughters pump. Still smiled as kindly in
His sleep beside the other clean old men
To see Grandmother, every night the same,
Huge in her age, with her thumbed-down mouth, come
Hating the river, filling with her stare
His gliding dream, while he turned to water,
While the children they both had begotten,
With old faces now, but themselves shrunken
To child-size again, stood ranged at her side,
Beating their little Bibles till he died.

1960

THE DRUNK IN THE FURNACE

For a good decade
The furnace stood in the naked gully, fireless
And vacant as any hat. Then when it was
No more to them than a hulking black fossil
To erode unnoticed with the rest of the junk-hill
By the poisonous creek, and rapidly to be added
To their ignorance.

They were afterwards astonished
To confirm, one morning, a twist of smoke like a pale
Resurrection, staggering out of its chewed hole,
And to remark then other tokens that someone,
Cosily bolted behind the eye-holed iron
Door of the drafty burner, had there established
His bad castle.

Where he gets his spirits
It's a mystery. But the stuff keeps him musical:
Hammer-and-anvilling with poker and bottle
To his jugged bellowings, till the last groaning clang
As he collapses onto the rioting
Springs of a litter of car-seats ranged on the grates,
To sleep like an iron pig.

In their tar-paper church
On a text about stoke-holes that are sated never
Their Reverend lingers. They nod and hate trespassers.
When the furnace wakes, though, all afternoon
Their witless offspring flock like piped rats to its siren
Crescendo, and agape on the crumbling ridge
Stand in a row and learn.

1960

NOAH'S RAVEN[1]

Why should I have returned?
My knowledge would not fit into theirs.
I found untouched the desert of the unknown,
Big enough for my feet. It is my home.
It is always beyond them. The future
Splits the present with the echo of my voice.
Hoarse with fulfillment, I never made promises.

1963

THE DRY STONE MASON

The mason is dead the gentle drunk
Master of dry walls
What he made of his years crosses the slopes without wavering
Upright but nameless
Ignorant in the new winter
Rubbed by running sheep
But the age of mortar has come to him

[1]From the Ark, Noah sent forth a dove and a raven to learn if the Flood had subsided. The dove returned. The raven did not. Genesis 8:7–9.

Bottles are waiting like fallen shrines
Under different trees in the rain
And stones drip where his hands left them
Leaning slightly inwards
His thirst is past

As he had no wife
The neighbors found where he kept his suit
A man with no family they sat with him
When he was carried through them they stood by their own dead
And they have buried him among the graves of the stones

1967

FLY

I have been cruel to a fat pigeon
Because he would not fly
All he wanted was to live like a friendly old man

He had let himself become a wreck filthy and confiding
Wild for his food beating the cat off the garbage
Ignoring his mate perpetually snotty at the beak
Smelling waddling having to be
Carried up the ladder at night content

Fly I said throwing him into the air
But he would drop and run back expecting to be fed
I said it again and again throwing him up
As he got worse
He let himself be picked up every time
Until I found him in the dovecote dead
Of the needless efforts

So that is what I am

Pondering his eye that could not
Conceive that I was a creature to run from

I who have always believed too much in words

1967

STRAWBERRIES

When my father died I saw a narrow valley

it looked as though it began across the river
from the landing where he was born but there was no river

I was hoeing the sand   of a small vegetable plot
for my mother   in deepening twilight
and looked up in time   to see a farm wagon
dry and gray   horse already hidden
and no driver   going into the valley
carrying a casket

and another wagon
coming out of the valley   behind a gray horse
with a boy driving   and a high load
of two kinds of berries   one of them strawberries

that night when I slept   I dreamed of things
wrong in the house   all of them signs
the water of the shower   running brackish
and an insect of a kind   I had seen him kill
climbing around   the walls of his bathroom
up in the morning   I stopped on the stairs
my mother was awake   already and asked me
if I wanted a shower   before breakfast
and for breakfast she said   we have strawberries

1983

DIRECTION

All I remember of the long lecture
which is all I remember of one summer
are the veins of the old   old bald head
and the loose white sleeve   and bony finger pointing
beyond the listeners
over their heads

there was the dazzling   wall and the empty sunlight
and reaching out of his age he told them
for the last time
what to do when they got to the world
giving them his every breath   to take with them like water
as they vanished

nobody was coming back that way

1983

A. R. Ammons 1926–2001

Ammons's distinguishing characteristic is his awareness of the natural world, of the facts, forms, and conditions of existence. He entitled his first book Ommateum *(1955), meaning the compound eye of an insect—an appropriate metaphor for a poet whose vision of reality was of an "overwhelming multiplicity." With a background in science and an eye for minutiae—whether he was scrutinizing a spider web, strolling a beach, or considering a backyard elm tree—he approached his subject with the patience of a naturalist on a field trip. As he explained in one poem, ". . . the way I think is / I think what I see."*

A Southerner, Ammons grew up on a backwoods farm near Whiteville, North Carolina. During World War II he worked in a shipyard and then served in the navy in the South Pacific. He returned home to enter Wake Forest College, where he earned a Bachelor of Science degree. For a time he was an elementary school principal and then attended the University of California at Berkeley for three semesters. For the next twelve years he lived in New Jersey, where he became vice-president of a company manufacturing laboratory glass. His first book of poems, Ommateum, *went unnoticed, but his second,* Expressions of Sea Level *(1964), brought him a teaching appointment at Cornell University. Thereafter, a succession of books appeared:* Corsons Inlet *(1965);* Tape for the Turn of the Year *(1965);* Northfield Poems *(1966);* Selected Poems *(1968);* Uplands *(1970);* Briefings *(1971);* Collected Poems 1951–1971 *(1972), which received the National Book Award;* Sphere: The Form of a Motion *(1974), which won the Bollingen Prize;* Diversifications: Poems *(1975);* The Snow Poems *(1977);* The Selected Poems, 1951–1977 *(1977);* A Coast of Trees: Poems *(1981), and* Sumerian Vistas *(1987).*

The character of Ammons's poetry changed radically after his first book. In Ommateum, *he addressed the vast and indifferent forms of nature in rather melodramatic, figurative modes: He assumed the stance of the insignificant man who is longing to escape the finite and who is questing, like the poet Emerson, for an infinite "Beyond." In subsequent books, Ammons reversed directions, recognizing, as he says in the retrospective poem "Emerson," that Emerson needed "to get up and I down."*

Ammons's allegiance to reality meant an immersion in discrete particulars, often in the most lowly forms—an insect, a crab, a weed; and his best known poems are probably those in which, in the tradition of William Carlos Williams and Marianne Moore, he presents a single perception in short, free-verse lyrics. Much of his work, however, deals with larger configurations. He was fascinated with the mystery of identity, with life cycles from generation to death, with the persistence of forms and species. His themes evolved through a series of opposing abstractions: permanence and change, stasis and motion, form and formlessness, order and disorder. The early transcendental strain persists in a final opposition: the one and the many. Usually, he raised the subject only to dismiss it with the recognition that "the eternal will not lie down on any temporal hill," but there remains the tantalizing possibility of an ultimate unity existing behind the chaotic world of particulars.

Ammons's theories of poetry and language are recurrent subjects in his work. In the poem "Essay on Poetics," he offers a revision or expansion of the organic theory of poetry: He sees the poem as analogous to a living organism; it is both synthesis and process, changing, dissolving, reorganizing as it flows through time. Since it reflects reality best when it is open to the greatest possible complexity, without imposed restrictions, the poet's art becomes "the conscious preparation for the unconscious / event."

The emphasis on flow, or linear movement, is apparent in Ammons's preference for free verse, run-over lines, and light, ongoing rhythms. He usually prefers minimal punctuation, but he savors the colon (a mark of anticipatory pause). His style tends to be casual, flattened toward the norm of prose, often with the literalness and factual quality of a report. In his long, experimental poems, he was interested in opening poetry to less structured forms and broader ranges of subject.

Similarly, his book The Snow Poems *was an attempt to make the everyday life of car repairs and supermarket excursions into acceptable subject matter. Such poems might be described as a series of diary entries that range from the serious to the trivial and zany—to weather reports, shopping lists, menus, jingles, and word games. While there is some question as to when such "open" poetry becomes simply "non-poetry," Ammons's efforts to expand the acceptable limits of his art, to jar preconceptions, and to surprise, shock, and even bore his readers represent one of the most significant directions in contemporary poetry.*

FURTHER READING: *Collected Poems, 1951–1971,* 1972; R. Howard, *Alone With America,* 1969; A. Holder, *A. R. Ammons,* 1978; *A. R. Ammons,* ed. H. Bloom, 1986; S. Schneider, *A. R. Ammons and the Poetics of Widening Scope,* 1994; *Critical Essays on A. R. Ammons,* ed. R. Kirschten, 1997; R. Kirschten, *Approaching Prayer, Ritual and the Shape of Myth in A. R. Ammons and James Dickey,* 1998; *Considering the Radiance: Essays on the Poetry of A. R. Ammons,* ed. D. Burak and R. Gilbert, 2005.

TEXTS: "Sight Seed" is from *Sumerian Vistas,* 1987; "Motion Which Disestablishes Organizes Everything" is from *The Hudson Review,* Summer 1987; "The Damned" is from *The Yale Review,* Spring 1988.

SIGHT SEED

When the jay caught
the cicada midair, a fluffy,
rustling beakful, the
burr-song flooded dull but
held low: the jay perched and
holding the prey to the branch
as if to halt
indecorous song pecked
once, a plink that did it,
but in the noticeable silence
proceeded at ease
and expertly to
take this, then that eye.

1987

MOTION WHICH DISESTABLISHES ORGANIZES EVERYTHING

William James *(The Varieties of Religious Experience,* p. 84)[1] is to be
commended for penning out of our finest recommendations for the bright outlook:

he was so miserable himself he knew how to put a fine point on the exact
prescription: he knew that anybody who knows anything about human

existence knows it can be heavy; in fact, it can be so heavy it can undo
its own heaviness, the knees can crumple, the breath and heart beat,

not to mention the bowels, can become irregular, etc.: but the world,
William knew, sardonic and skeptical, can characterize sufferers of such

symptoms malingering wimps, a heaviness not to be welcomed by a person who
like me feels like one of those: weight begets weight and nature works as well

(and mindlessly) down as up; you have to put english of your own into
the act misleading the way into lightenings: brightness, however

desirable, is a losing battle, though, and James knew it can be depended on
more often than not that folks won't have spare brightnesses on them every

morning that they want your heaviness to cost them: so, in general, if
someone asks how you are, no matter how you are, say something nice: say,

"fine," or "marvelous morning," and, this way, hell gradually notches up

[1]American psychologist (1842–1910). In *The Varieties of Religious Experience* (1902) he set forth the psychological satisfactions to be derived from religious faith.

toward paradise, a misconstruction many conspire to forward because

nearly all, maybe all, prefer one to the other: oppositions make things costly:
crooked teeth encourage the symmetry of braces but as soon as everybody's

teeth are perfect, crooked teeth misalign: something is always working
the other way: if you let the other way go, you get more in Dutch for

while the other way at first may constitute an alternative mainstream,
pretty soon it breaks up into dispersive tributaries and splinters a

rondure of fine points into branches and brooklets till it becomes
impossible to get a hold on it, a river system running backwards:

be bright: that is a wish that can be stable: you can always think of
happiness because it's wished right out of any rubbings with reality, so

you can keep the picture pure and steady: I always imagine a hillock,
about as much as I can get up these days, with a lovely shade tree and under

the tree this beautiful girl, unnervingly young, who projects golden
worlds: this scene attracts me so much that even though I'm a little

scared by it it feels enlivening, a rosy, sweet enlivening: poets
can always prevent our hubris, reminding us how the coffin slats peel

cloth and crack in, how the onset of time strikes at birth, how love falters,
how past the past is, how the eyes of hungry children feed the flies.

1987

THE DAMNED

This fellow grazed his woolly goats
on a high ledge, a very high place
snowless in summer, but it was,

perhaps because of the fellow's loneliness,
a region in which the mountains talked,
it seemed, and over a miles-wide gulf,

summits forever white rose useless
in august assumptions the polish of
the wind and glare of the sun sanctified,

the fellow supposed, and he thought,
well, few know that kind of thing,
a rare condition, though not good for grass:

and the fellow, noting that the peaks
had really said nothing yet, went to
the ledge-edge and looked down on the

summits of sweet-green hills
and runoff rills so lowly and supposed,
again, that these damned came of being

near the sanctified, wherever one finds
one one finds the other, and he wondered
if the heights knew, somehow, that the energy

of their complacency came of
a differentiation imposed on the backs,
so to speak, of the lowly, and he

wondered if the sanctified would not
wish to remove themselves, somehow, if
they knew that, but then, he supposed,

knowing that would spoil the sanctification
anyhow, so maybe the peaks could shine
there, since it seemed they had to, as

wastelands of what it means to be way high:
but the mountains had said nothing and
the fellow supposed himself a supposition,

too, no one having agreed with him, the peaks
too taken aback, except for this longing
for the valleys roaring in his guts.

1988

James Baldwin 1924–1987

James Baldwin has been called the most important American black writer of the twentieth century. He was born in Harlem, the oldest of nine children. His childhood and adolescence were dominated by his father—a stern, authoritarian man who was the minister of a storefront church. When he was fourteen, Baldwin underwent a deep religious experience and began to preach in competition with his father, a conflict of personal as well as religious significance. At the same time he began writing, and after his graduation from high school he began supporting himself in a succession of menial jobs.

In the winter of 1944–1945, Baldwin met Richard Wright, who encouraged him in his literary ambitions. He was to become literally and figuratively Wright's successor—his "native son" and heir as an American black writer. Like Wright, to escape American racial injustice, Baldwin left the United States for Europe, where he lived for nine years. While he was in Europe, his books first began to be published in the United States. The novel Go Tell It on the Mountain *(1953), a thinly veiled account of his youth, is considered by many critics his best work. In 1955 he produced a collection of essays,* Notes of a Native Son, *and in 1956* Giovanni's Room, *the story of a young, white expatriate in France attempting to come to terms with his homosexuality, a frequent subject of Baldwin's work.*

In 1957 he returned to America and immediately became involved in the civil rights struggle. His essays in this period, Nobody Knows My Name, More Notes of a Native Son *(1961) and* The Fire Next Time *(1963), are written with a force and a perceptiveness that have led many to consider Baldwin one of the foremost essayists in recent American literature. His next novel,* Another Country *(1962), reflects an increasing anxiety about race relations in America, as does a subsequent collection of short stories,* Going to Meet the Man *(1965). A later novel,* Tell Me How Long the Train's Been Gone *(1968), continues his preoccupation with the subjects of homosexuality, interracial love, and racial conflict.*

In 1971 Baldwin published a collection of dialogues with the noted anthropologist Margaret Mead, under the title A Rap on Race, *and in 1972 a volume of observations,* No Name in the Street, *expressing a furious disillusionment with modern America and the world. In 1974 he published* If Beale Street Could Talk, *a bitter protest novel, and in 1979* Just Above My Head, *a long and angry novel that is set in Harlem and tells the story of a famous gospel singer. In 1985 he published a collection of his nonfiction,* The Price of a Ticket. *Although Baldwin was fiercely attacked as insufficiently militant, he was nonetheless a forceful, brilliant voice, warning white America of the explosions to come and cautioning black America against the self-destructive excesses of racial hatred. Baldwin insisted that the American "complex fate" (a phrase he took from Henry James) necessarily makes the lives and the concerns of blacks and whites inseparable in modern America.*

FURTHER READING: F. Eckman, *The Furious Passage of James Baldwin,* 1966; *James Baldwin,* ed. H. Bloom, 1986; *Critical Essays on James Baldwin,* ed. F. Standley and N. Burt, 1988; W. Weatherby, *James Baldwin: Artist on Fire,* 1989; H. Porter, *Stealing the Fire: The Art and Protest of James Baldwin,* 1989; L. Rosset, *James Baldwin,* 1990; R. Lee, *James Baldwin: Climbing to the Light,* 1991; *James Baldwin,* ed. J. Köllhofer, 1991; J. Campbell, *Talking at the Gates: A Life of James Baldwin,* 1991, 2002; D. Leeming, *James Baldwin: A Biography,* 1994; *James Baldwin Now,* ed. D. McBride, 1999; *Re-viewing James Baldwin: Things Not Seen,* ed. D. Miller, 2000; L. Scott, *Witness to the Journey: James Baldwin's Later Fiction,* 2002.

TEXT: *Going to Meet the Man,* 1965.

SONNY'S BLUES

I read about it in the paper, in the subway, on my way to work. I read it, and I couldn't believe it, and I read it again. Then perhaps I just stared at it, at the newsprint spelling out his name, spelling out the story. I stared at it in the swinging lights of the subway car, and in the faces and bodies of the people, and in my own face, trapped in the darkness which roared outside.

It was not to be believed and I kept telling myself that, as I walked from the subway station to the high school. And at the same time I couldn't doubt it. I was scared, scared for Sonny. He became real to me again. A great block of ice got settled in my belly and kept melting there slowly all day long, while I taught my classes algebra. It was a special kind of ice. It kept melting, sending trickles of ice water all up and down my veins, but it never got less. Sometimes it hardened and seemed to expand until I felt my guts were going to come spilling out or that I was going to choke or scream. This would always be at a moment when I was remembering some specific thing Sonny had once said or done.

When he was about as old as the boys in my classes his face had been bright and open, there was a lot of copper in it; and he'd had wonderfully direct brown eyes, and great gentleness and privacy. I wondered what he looked like now. He had been picked up the evening before, in a raid on an apartment downtown, for peddling and using heroin.

I couldn't believe it: but what I mean by that is that I couldn't find any room for it anywhere inside me. I had kept it outside me for a long time. I hadn't wanted to know. I had had suspicions, but I didn't name them, I kept putting them away. I told myself that Sonny was wild, but he wasn't crazy. And he'd always been a good boy, he hadn't ever turned hard or evil or disrespectful, the way kids can, so quick, especially in Harlem. I didn't want to believe that I'd ever see my brother going down, coming to nothing, all that light in his face gone out, in the condition I'd already seen so many others. Yet it had happened and here I was, talking about algebra to a lot of boys who might, every one of them for all I knew, be popping off needles every time they went to the head. Maybe it did more for them than algebra could.

I was sure that the first time Sonny had ever had horse,[1] he couldn't have been much older than these boys were now. These boys, now, were living as we'd been living then, they were growing up with a rush and their heads bumped abruptly against the low ceiling of their actual possibilities. They were filled with rage. All they really knew were two darknesses, the darkness of their lives, which was now closing in on them, and the darkness of the movies, which had blinded them to that other darkness, and in which they now, vindictively, dreamed, at once more together than they were at any other time, and more alone.

When the last bell rang, the last class ended, I let out my breath. It seemed I'd been holding it for all that time. My clothes were wet—I may have looked as though I'd been sitting in a steam bath, all dressed up all afternoon. I sat alone in the classroom a long time. I listened to the boys outside, downstairs, shouting and cursing and laughing. Their laughter struck me for perhaps the

[1]Heroin.

first time. It was not the joyous laughter which—God knows why—one associates with children. It was mocking and insular, its intent was to denigrate. It was disenchanted, and in this, also, lay the authority of their curses. Perhaps I was listening to them because I was thinking about my brother and in them I heard my brother. And myself.

One boy was whistling a tune, at once very complicated and very simple, it seemed to be pouring out of him as though he were a bird, and it sounded very cool and moving through all that harsh, bright air, only just holding its own through all those other sounds.

I stood up and walked over to the window and looked down into the courtyard. It was the beginning of the spring and the sap was rising in the boys. A teacher passed through them every now and again, quickly, as though he or she couldn't wait to get out of that courtyard, to get those boys out of their sight and off their minds. I started collecting my stuff. I thought I'd better get home and talk to Isabel.

The courtyard was almost deserted by the time I got downstairs. I saw this boy standing in the shadow of a doorway, looking just like Sonny. I almost called his name. Then I saw that it wasn't Sonny, but somebody we used to know, a boy from around our block. He'd been Sonny's friend. He'd never been mine, having been too young for me, and, anyway, I'd never liked him. And now, even though he was a grown-up man, he still hung around that block, still spent hours on the street corners, was always high and raggy. I used to run into him from time to time and he'd often work around to asking me for a quarter or fifty cents. He always had some real good excuse too, and I always gave it to him, I don't know why.

But now, abruptly I hated him. I couldn't stand the way he looked at me, partly like a dog, partly like a cunning child. I wanted to ask him what the hell he was doing in the school courtyard.

He sort of shuffled over to me, and he said, "I see you got the papers. So you already know about it."

"You mean about Sonny? Yes, I already know about it. How come they didn't get you?"

He grinned. It made him repulsive and it also brought to mind what he'd looked like as a kid. "I wasn't there. I stay away from them people."

"Good for you." I offered him a cigarette and I watched him through the smoke. "You come all the way down here just to tell me about Sonny?"

"That's right." He was sort of shaking his head and his eyes looked strange, as though they were about to cross. The bright sun deadened his damp dark brown skin and it made his eyes look yellow and showed up the dirt in his kinked hair. He smelled funky. I moved a little way away from him and I said, "Well, thanks. But I already know about it and I got to get home."

"I'll walk you a little ways," he said. We started walking. There were a couple of kids still loitering in the courtyard and one of them said goodnight to me and looked strangely at the boy beside me.

"What're you going to do?" he asked me. "I mean, about Sonny?"

"Look. I haven't seen Sonny for over a year. I'm not sure I'm going to do anything. Anyway, what the hell *can* I do?"

"That's right," he said quickly, "ain't nothing you can do. Can't much help old Sonny no more, I guess."

It was what I was thinking and so it seemed to me he had no right to say it.

"I'm surprised at Sonny, though," he went on—he had a funny way of talking, he looked straight ahead as though he were talking to himself—"I thought Sonny was a smart boy, I thought he was too smart to get hung."

"I guess he thought so too," I said sharply, "and that's how he got hung. And how about you? You're pretty goddamn smart, I bet."

Then he looked directly at me, just for a minute. "I ain't smart," he said. "If I was smart, I'd have reached for a pistol a long time ago."

"Look. Don't tell *me* your sad story, if it was up to me, I'd give you one." Then I felt guilty—guilty, probably, for never having supposed that the poor bastard *had* a story of his own, much less a sad one, and I asked, quickly, "What's going to happen to him now?"

He didn't answer this. He was off by himself some place. "Funny thing," he said, and from his tone we might have been discussing the quickest way to get to Brooklyn, "when I saw the papers this morning, the first thing I asked myself was if I had anything to do with it. I felt sort of responsible."

I began to listen more carefully. The subway station was on the corner, just before us, and I stopped. He stopped, too. We were in front of a bar and he ducked slightly, peering in, but whoever he was looking for didn't seem to be there. The juke box was blasting away with something black and bouncy and I half watched the barmaid as she danced her way from the juke box to her place behind the bar. And I watched her face as she laughingly responded to something someone said to her, still keeping time to the music. When she smiled one saw the little girl, one sensed the doomed, still struggling woman beneath the battered face of the semi-whore.

"I never *give* Sonny nothing," the boy said finally, "but a long time ago I come to school high and Sonny asked me how it felt." He paused, I couldn't bear to watch him, I watched the barmaid, and I listened to the music which seemed to be causing the pavement to shake. "I told him it felt great." The music stopped, the barmaid paused and watched the juke box until the music began again. "It did."

All this was carrying me some place I didn't want to go. I certainly didn't want to know how it felt. It filled everything, the people, the houses, the music, the dark, quicksilver barmaid, with menace, and this menace was their reality.

"What's going to happen to him now?" I asked again.

"They'll send him away some place and they'll try to cure him." He shook his head. "Maybe he'll even think he's kicked the habit. Then they'll let him loose"—he gestured, throwing his cigarette into the gutter. "That's all."

"What do you mean that's *all?*"

But I knew what he meant.

"I *mean,* that's *all.*" He turned his head and looked at me, pulling down the corners of his mouth. "Don't you know what I mean?" he asked, softly.

"How the hell *would* I know what you mean?" I almost whispered it, I don't know why.

"That's right," he said to the air, "how would *he* know what I mean?" He turned toward me again, patient and calm, and yet I somehow felt him shaking, shaking as though he were going to fall apart. I felt that ice in my guts again, the dread I'd felt all afternoon; and again I watched the barmaid, moving about the bar, washing glasses, and singing. "Listen. They'll let him out and then it'll just start all over again. That's what I mean."

"You mean—they'll let him out. And then he'll just start working his way back in again. You mean he'll never kick the habit. Is that what you mean?"

"That's right," he said cheerfully. "*You* see what I mean."

"Tell me," I said at last, "why does he want to die? He must want to die, he's killing himself, why does he want to die?"

He looked at me in surprise. He licked his lips. "He don't want to die. He wants to live. Don't nobody want to die, ever."

Then I wanted to ask him—too many things. He could not have answered, or if he had, I could not have borne the answers. I started walking. "Well, I guess it's none of my business."

"It's going to be rough on old Sonny," he said. We reached the subway station. "This is your station?" he asked. I nodded. I took one step down. "Damn!" he said suddenly. I looked up at him. He grinned again. "Damn it if I didn't leave all my money home. You ain't got a dollar on you, have you? Just for a couple of days, is all."

All at once something inside gave and threatened to come pouring out of me. I didn't hate him any more. I felt that in another moment I'd start crying like a child.

"Sure," I said. "Don't sweat." I looked in my wallet and didn't have a dollar, I only had a five. "Here." I said. "That hold you?"

He didn't look at it—he didn't want to look at it. A terrible closed look came over his face, as though he were keeping the number on the bill a secret from him and me. "Thanks," he said, and now he was dying to see me go. "Don't worry about Sonny. Maybe I'll write him or something."

"Sure," I said. "You do that. So long."

"Be seeing you," he said. I went on down the steps.

And I didn't write Sonny or send him anything for a long time. When I finally did, it was just after my little girl died, he wrote me back a letter which made me feel like a bastard.

Here's what he said:

Dear brother,

You don't know how much I needed to hear from you. I wanted to write you many a time but I dug how much I must have hurt you and so I didn't write. But now I feel like a man who's been trying to climb up out of some deep, real deep and funky hole and just saw the sun up there, outside. I got to get outside.

I can't tell you much about how I got here. I mean I don't know how to tell you. I guess I was afraid of something or I was trying to escape from something and you know I have never been very strong in the head (smile). I'm glad Mama and Daddy are dead and can't see what's happened to their son and I swear if I'd known what I was doing I would never have hurt you so, you and a lot of other fine people who were nice to me and who believed in me.

I don't want you to think it had anything to do with me being a musician. It's more than that. Or maybe less than that. I can't get anything straight in my head down here and I try not to think about what's going to happen to me when I get outside again. Sometime I think I'm going to flip and *never* get outside and sometime I think I'll come straight back. I tell you one thing, though, I'd rather blow my brains out than go through this again. But that's what they all say, so they tell me. If I tell you when I'm coming to New York and if you could meet me, I sure would appreciate it. Give my love to Isabel and the kids and I was sure sorry to hear about little Gracie. I wish I could be like Mama and say the Lord's will be done, but I don't know it seems to me that trouble is the one thing that never does get stopped and I don't know what good it does to blame it on the Lord. But maybe it does some good if you believe it.

Your brother,
Sonny

Then I kept in constant touch with him and I sent him whatever I could and I went to meet him when he came back to New York. When I saw him many things I thought I had forgotten came flooding back to me. This was because I had begun, finally, to wonder about Sonny, about the life that Sonny lived inside. This life, whatever it was, had made him older and thinner and it had deepened the distant stillness in which he had always moved. He looked very unlike my baby brother. Yet, when he smiled, when we shook hands, the baby brother I'd never known looked out from the depths of his private life, like an animal waiting to be coaxed into the light.

"How you been keeping?" he asked me.

"All right. And you?"

"Just fine." He was smiling all over his face. "It's good to see you again."

"It's good to see you."

The seven years' difference in our ages lay between us like a chasm: I wondered if these years would ever operate between us as a bridge. I was remembering, and it made it hard to catch my breath, that I had been there when he was born; and I had heard the first words he had ever spoken. When he started to walk, he walked from our mother straight to me. I caught him just before he fell when he took the first steps he ever took in this world.

"How's Isabel?"

"Just fine. She's dying to see you."

"And the boys?"

"They're fine, too. They're anxious to see their uncle."

"Oh, come on. You know they don't remember me."

"Are you kidding? Of course they remember you."

He grinned again. We got into a taxi. We had a lot to say to each other, far too much to know how to begin.

As the taxi began to move, I asked, "You still want to go to India?"

He laughed. "You still remember that. Hell, no. This place is Indian enough for me."

"It used to belong to them," I said.

And he laughed again. "They damn sure knew what they were doing when they got rid of it."

Years ago, when he was around fourteen, he'd been all hipped on the idea of going to India. He read books about people sitting on rocks, naked, in all kinds of weather, but mostly bad, naturally, and walking barefoot through hot coals and arriving at wisdom. I used to say that it sounded to me as though they were getting away from wisdom as fast as they could. I think he sort of looked down on me for that.

"Do you mind," he asked, "if we have the driver drive alongside the park? On the west side—I haven't seen the city in so long."

"Of course not," I said. I was afraid that I might sound as though I were humoring him, but I hoped he wouldn't take it that way.

So we drove along, between the green of the park and the stony, lifeless elegance of hotels and apartment buildings, toward the vivid, killing streets of our childhood. These streets hadn't changed, though housing projects jutted up out of them now like rocks in the middle of a boiling sea. Most of the houses in which we had grown up had vanished, as had the stores from which we had stolen, the basements in which we had first tried sex, the rooftops from which we had hurled tin cans and bricks. But houses exactly like the houses of our past yet dominated the landscape, boys exactly like the boys we once had been found themselves smothering in these houses, came down into the streets for light and air and found themselves encircled by disaster. Some escaped the trap, most didn't. Those who got out always left something of themselves behind, as some animals amputate a leg and leave it in the trap. It might be said, perhaps, that I had escaped, after all, I was a school teacher; or that Sonny had, he hadn't lived in Harlem for years. Yet, as the cab moved uptown through streets which seemed, with a rush, to darken with dark people, and as I covertly studied Sonny's face, it came to me that what we both were seeking through our separate cab windows was that part of ourselves which had been left behind. It's always at the hour of trouble and confrontation that the missing member aches.

We hit 110th Street and started rolling up Lenox Avenue. And I'd known this avenue all my life, but it seemed to me again, as it had seemed on the day I'd first heard about Sonny's trouble, filled with a hidden menace which was its very breath of life.

"We almost there," said Sonny.

"Almost." We were both too nervous to say anything more.

We live in a housing project. It hasn't been up long. A few days after it was up it seemed uninhabitably new, now, of course, it's already rundown. It looks like a parody of the good, clean, faceless life—God knows the people who live in it do their best to make it a parody. The beat-looking grass lying around isn't enough to make their lives green, the hedges will never hold out the streets, and they know it. The big windows fool no one, they aren't big enough to make space out of no space. They don't bother with the windows, they watch the TV screen instead. The playground is most popular with the children who don't play at jacks, or skip rope, or roller skate, or swing, and they can be found in it after dark. We moved in partly because it's not too far from where I teach, and partly for the kids; but it's really just like the houses in which Sonny and I grew up. The same things happen, they'll have the same things to remember. The moment Sonny and I started into the house I had the feeling that I was simply bringing him back into the danger he had almost died trying to escape.

Sonny has never been talkative. So I don't know why I was sure he'd be dying to talk to me when supper was over the first night. Everything went fine, the oldest boy remembered him, and the youngest boy liked him, and Sonny had remembered to bring something for each of them; and Isabel, who is really much nicer than I am, more open and giving, had gone to a lot of trouble about dinner and was genuinely glad to see him. And she's always been able to tease Sonny in a way that I haven't. It was nice to see her face so vivid again and to hear her laugh and watch her make Sonny laugh. She wasn't, or, anyway, she didn't seem to be, at all uneasy or embarrassed. She chatted as though there were no subject which had to be avoided and she got Sonny past his first, faint stiffness. And thank God she was there, for I was filled with that icy dread again. Everything I did seemed awkward to me, and everything I said sounded freighted with hidden meaning. I was trying to remember everything I'd heard about dope addiction and I couldn't help watching Sonny for signs. I wasn't doing it out of malice. I was trying to find out something about my brother. I was dying to hear him tell me he was safe.

"Safe!" my father grunted, whenever Mamma suggested trying to move to a neighborhood which might be safer for children. "Safe, hell! Ain't no place safe for kids, nor nobody."

He always went on like this, but he wasn't, ever, really as bad as he sounded, not even on weekends, when he got drunk. As a matter of fact, he was always on the lookout for "something a little better," but he died before he found it. He died suddenly, during a drunken weekend in the middle of the war, when Sonny was fifteen. He and Sonny hadn't ever got on too well. And this was partly because Sonny was the apple of his father's eye. It was because he loved Sonny so much and was frightened for him, that he was always fighting with him. It doesn't do any good to fight with Sonny. Sonny just moves back, inside himself, where he can't be reached. But the principal reason that they never hit it off is that they were so much alike. Daddy was big and rough and loud-talking, just the opposite of Sonny, but they both had—that same privacy.

Mama tried to tell me something about this, just after Daddy died. I was home on leave from the army.

This was the last time I ever saw my mother alive. Just the same, this picture gets all mixed up in my mind with pictures I had of her when she was younger. The way I always see her is the way she used to be on a Sunday afternoon, say, when the old folks were talking after the big Sunday dinner. I always see her wearing pale blue. She'd be sitting on the sofa. And my father would be sitting in the easy chair, not far from her. And the living room would be full of church folks and relatives. There they sit, in chairs all around the living room, and the night is creeping up outside, but nobody knows it yet. You can see the darkness growing against the window-panes and you hear the street noises every now and again, or maybe the jangling beat of a tambourine from one of the churches close by, but it's real quiet in the room. For a moment nobody's talking, but every face looks darkening, like the sky outside. And my mother rocks a little from the waist, and my father's eyes are closed. Everyone is looking at something a child can't see. For a minute they've forgotten the children. Maybe a kid is lying on the rug, half asleep. Maybe somebody's got a kid in his lap and is absent-mindedly stroking the kid's head. Maybe there's a kid, quiet and big-eyed, curled up in a big chair in the corner. The silence, the darkness coming, and the darkness in the faces frightens the child obscurely. He hopes that the hand which strokes his forehead will never stop—will never die. He hopes that there will never come a time when the old folks won't be sitting around the living room, talking about where they've come from, and what they've seen, and what's happened to them and their kinfolk.

But something deep and watchful in the child knows that this is bound to end, is already ending. In a moment someone will get up and turn on the light.

Then the old folks will remember the children and they won't talk any more that day. And when light fills the room, the child is filled with darkness. He knows that every time this happens he's moved just a little closer to that darkness outside. The darkness outside is what the old folks have been talking about. It's what they've come from. It's what they endure. The child knows that they won't talk any more because if he knows too much about what's happening to *them,* he'll know too much too soon, about what's going to happen to *him.*

The last time I talked to my mother, I remember I was restless. I wanted to get out and see Isabel. We weren't married then and we had a lot to straighten out between us.

There Mama sat, in black, by the window. She was humming an old church song, *Lord you brought me from a long ways off.* Sonny was out somewhere. Mama kept watching the streets.

"I don't know," she said, "if I'll ever see you again, after you go off from here. But I hope you'll remember the things I tried to teach you."

"Don't talk like that," I said, and smiled. "You'll be here a long time yet."

She smiled, too, but she said nothing. She was quiet for a long time. And I said, "Mama, don't you worry about nothing. I'll be writing all the time, and you be getting the checks. . . ."

"I want to talk to you about your brother," she said, suddenly. "If anything happens to me he ain't going to have nobody to look out for him."

"Mama," I said, "ain't nothing going to happen to you *or* Sonny. Sonny's all right. He's a good boy and he's got good sense."

"It ain't a question of his being a good boy," Mama said, "nor of his having good sense. It ain't only the bad ones, nor yet the dumb ones that gets sucked under." She stopped, looking at me. "Your Daddy once had a brother," she said, and she smiled in a way that made me feel she was in pain. "You didn't never know that, did you?"

"No," I said, "I never knew that," and I watched her face.

"Oh, yes," she said, "your Daddy had a brother. She looked out of the window again. "I know you never saw your Daddy cry. But *I* did—many a time, through all these years."

I asked her, "What happened to his brother? How come nobody's ever talked about him?"

This was the first time I ever saw my mother look old.

"His brother got killed," she said, "when he was just a little younger than you are now. I knew him. He was a fine boy. He was maybe a little full of the devil, but he didn't mean nobody no harm."

Then she stopped and the room was silent, exactly as it had sometimes been on those Sunday afternoons. Mama kept looking out into the streets.

"He used to have a job in the mill," she said, "and, like all young folks, he just liked to perform on Saturday nights. Saturday nights, him and your father would drift around to different places, go to dances and things like that, or just sit around with people they knew, and your father's brother would sing, he had a fine voice, and play along with himself on his guitar. Well, this particular Saturday night, him and your father was coming home from some place, and they were both a little drunk and there was a moon that night, it was bright like day. Your father's brother was feeling kind of good, and he was whistling to himself, and he had his guitar slung over his shoulder. They was coming down a hill and beneath them was a road that turned off from the highway.

Well, your father's brother, being always kind of frisky, decided to run down this hill, and he did, with that guitar banging and clanging behind him, and he ran across the road, and he was making water behind a tree. And your father was sort of amused at him and he was still coming down the hill, kind of slow. Then he heard a car motor and that same minute his brother stepped from behind the tree, into the road, in the moonlight. And he started to cross the road. And your father started to run down the hill, he says he don't know why. This car was full of white men. They was all drunk, and when they seen your father's brother they let out a great whoop and holler and they aimed the car straight at him. They was having fun, they just wanted to scare him, the way they do sometimes, you know. But they was drunk. And I guess the boy, being drunk, too, and scared, kind of lost his head. By the time he jumped it was too late. Your father says he heard his brother scream when the car rolled over him, and he heard the wood of that guitar when it give, and he heard them strings go flying, and he heard them white men shouting, and the car kept on a-going and it ain't stopped till this day. And, time your father got down the hill, his brother weren't nothing but blood and pulp."

Tears were gleaming on my mother's face. There wasn't anything I could say.

"He never mentioned it," she said, "because I never let him mention it before you children. Your Daddy was like a crazy man that night and for many a night thereafter. He says he never in his life seen anything as dark as that road after the lights of that car had gone away. Weren't nothing, weren't nobody on that road, just your Daddy and his brother and that busted guitar. Oh, yes. Your Daddy never did really get right again. Till the day he died he weren't sure but that every white man he saw was the man that killed his brother."

She stopped and took out her handkerchief and dried her eyes and looked at me.

"I ain't telling you all this," she said, "to make you scared or bitter or to make you hate nobody. I'm telling you this because you got a brother. And the world ain't changed."

I guess I didn't want to believe this. I guess she saw this in my face. She turned away from me, toward the window again, searching those streets.

"But I praise my Redeemer," she said at last, "that He called your Daddy home before me. I ain't saying it to throw no flowers at myself, but, I declare, it keeps me from feeling too cast down to know I helped your father get safely through this world. Your father always acted like he was the roughest, strongest man on earth. And everybody took him to be like that. But if he hadn't had *me* there—to see his tears!"

She was crying again. Still I couldn't move. I said, "Lord, Lord, Mama, I didn't know it was like that."

"Oh, honey," she said, "there's a lot that you don't know. But you are going to find it out." She stood up from the window and came over to me. "You got to hold on to your brother," she said, "and don't let him fall, no matter what it looks like is happening to him and no matter how evil you gets with him. You going to be evil with him many a time. But don't you forget what I told you, you hear?"

"I won't forget," I said. "Don't you worry, I won't forget. I won't let nothing happen to Sonny."

My mother smiled as though she were amused at something she saw in my face. Then, "You may not be able to stop nothing from happening. But you got to let him know you's *there.*"

Two days later I was married, and then I was gone. And I had a lot of things on my mind and I pretty well forgot my promise to Mama until I got shipped home on a special furlough for her funeral.

And, after the funeral, with just Sonny and me alone in the empty kitchen, I tried to find out something about him.

"What do you want to do?" I asked him.

"I'm going to be a musician," he said.

For he had graduated, in the time I had been away, from dancing to the juke box to finding out who was playing what, and what they were doing with it, and he had bought himself a set of drums.

"You mean, you want to be a drummer?" I somehow had the feeling that being a drummer might be all right for other people but not for my brother Sonny.

"I don't think," he said, looking at me very gravely, "that I'll ever be a good drummer. But I think I can play a piano."

I frowned. I'd never played the role of the older brother quite so seriously before, had scarcely ever, in fact, *asked* Sonny a damn thing. I sensed myself in the presence of something I didn't really know how to handle, didn't understand. So I made my frown a little deeper as I asked: "What kind of musician do you want to be?"

He grinned. "How many kinds do you think there are?"

"Be *serious,*" I said.

He laughed, throwing his head back, and then looked at me. "I *am* serious."

"Well, then, for Christ's sake, stop kidding around and answer a serious question. I mean, do you want to be a concert pianist, or want to play classical music and all that, or—or what?" Long before I finished he was laughing again. "For Christ's *sake,* Sonny!"

He sobered, but with difficulty. "I'm sorry. But you sound so—*scared!*" and he was off again.

"Well, you may think it's funny now, baby, but it's not going to be so funny when you have to make your living at it, let me tell you *that.*" I was furious because I knew he was laughing at me and I didn't know why.

"No," he said, very sober now, and afraid, perhaps, that he'd hurt me, "I don't want to be a classical pianist. That isn't what interests me. I mean"—he paused, looking hard at me, as though his eyes would help me to understand, and then gestured helplessly, as though perhaps his hand would help—"I mean, I'll have a lot of studying to do, and I'll have to study *everything,* but, I mean, I want to play *with*—jazz musicians." He stopped. "I want to play jazz," he said.

Well, the word had never before sounded as heavy, as real, as it sounded that afternoon in Sonny's mouth. I just looked at him and I was probably frowning a real frown by this time. I simply couldn't see why on earth he'd want to spend his time hanging around nightclubs, clowning around on bandstands, while people pushed each other around a dance floor. It seemed—beneath him, somehow. I had never thought about it before, had never been forced to, but I suppose I had always put jazz musicians in a class with what Daddy called "good-time people."

"Are you *serious?*"

"Hell, *yes,* I'm serious."

He looked more helpless than ever, and annoyed, and deeply hurt.

I suggested helpfully: "You mean—like Louis Armstrong?"

His face closed as though I'd struck him. "No. I'm not talking about none of that old-time, down home crap."

"Well, look Sonny, I'm sorry, don't get mad. I just don't altogether get it, that's all. Name somebody—you know, a jazz musician you admire."

"Bird."

"Who?"

"Bird! Charlie Parker! Don't they teach you nothing in the god-damn army?"

I lit a cigarette. I was surprised and then a little amused to discover that I was trembling. "I've been out of touch," I said. "You'll have to be patient with me. Now. Who's this Parker character?"

"He's just one of the greatest jazz musicians alive," said Sonny, sullenly, his hands in his pockets, his back to me. "Maybe *the* greatest," he added, bitterly, "that's probably why *you* never heard of him."

"All right," I said, "I'm ignorant. I'm sorry. I'll go out and buy all the cat's records right away, all right?"

"It don't," said Sonny, with dignity, "make any difference to me. I don't care what you listen to. Don't do me no favors."

I was beginning to realize that I'd never seen him so upset before. With another part of my mind I was thinking that this would probably turn out to be one of those things kids go through and that I shouldn't make it seem important by pushing it too hard. Still, I didn't think it would do any harm to ask: "Doesn't all this take a lot of time? Can you make a living at it?"

He turned back to me and half leaned, half sat, on the kitchen table. "Everything takes time," he said, "and—well, yes, sure, I can make a living at it. But what I don't seem to be able to make you understand is that it's the only thing I want to do."

"Well, Sonny," I said gently, "you know people can't always do exactly what they *want* to do—"

"*No,* I don't know that," said Sonny, surprising me. "I think people *ought* to do what they want to do, what else are they alive for?"

"You are getting to be a big boy," I said desperately, "it's time you started thinking about your future."

"I'm thinking about my future," said Sonny, grimly. "I think about it all the time."

I gave up. I decided, if he didn't change his mind, that we could always talk about it later. "In the meantime," I said, "you got to finish school." We had already decided that he'd have to move in with Isabel and her folks. I knew this wasn't the ideal arrangement because Isabel's folks are inclined to be dicty[2] and they hadn't especially wanted Isabel to marry me. But I didn't know what else to do. "And we have to get you fixed up at Isabel's."

There was a long silence. He moved from the kitchen table to the window. "That's a terrible idea. You know it yourself."

"Do you have a *better* idea?"

[2]Snobbish.

He just walked up and down the kitchen for a minute. He was as tall as I was. He had started to shave. I suddenly had the feeling that I didn't know him at all.

He stopped at the kitchen table and picked up my cigarettes. Looking at me with a kind of mocking, amused defiance, he put one between his lips. "You mind?"

"You smoking already?"

He lit the cigarette and nodded, watching me through the smoke. "I just wanted to see if I'd have the courage to smoke in front of you." He grinned and blew a great cloud of smoke to the ceiling. "It was easy." He looked at my face. "Come on, now. I bet you was smoking at my age, tell the truth."

I didn't say anything but the truth was on my face, and he laughed. But now there was something very strained in his laugh. "Sure. And I bet that ain't all you was doing."

He was frightening me a little. "Cut the crap," I said. "We already decided that you was going to go and live at Isabel's. Now what's got into you all of a sudden?"

"*You* decided it," he pointed out. "*I* didn't decide nothing." He stopped in front of me, leaning against the stove, arms loosely folded. "Look, brother. I don't want to stay in Harlem no more, I really don't." He was very earnest. He looked at me, then over toward the kitchen window. There was something in his eyes I'd never seen before, some thoughtfulness, some worry all his own. He rubbed the muscle of one arm. "It's time I was getting out of here."

"Where do you want to *go,* Sonny?"

"I want to join the army. Or the navy, I don't care. If I say I'm old enough, they'll believe me."

Then I got mad. It was because I was so scared. "You must be crazy. You goddamn fool, what the hell do you want to go and join the *army* for?"

"I just told you. To get out of Harlem."

"Sonny, you haven't even finished *school.* And if you really want to be a musician, how do you expect to study if you're in the *army?*"

He looked at me, trapped, and in anguish. "There's ways. I might be able to work out some kind of deal. Anyway, I'll have the G.I. Bill when I come out."

"*If* you come out." We stared at each other. "Sonny, please. Be reasonable. I know the setup is far from perfect. But we got to do the best we can."

"I ain't learning nothing in school," he said. "Even when I go." He turned away from me and opened the window and threw his cigarette out into the narrow alley. I watched his back. "At least, I ain't learning nothing you'd want me to learn." He slammed the window so hard I thought the glass would fly out, and turned back to me. "And I'm sick of the stink of these garbage cans!"

"Sonny," I said, "I know how you feel, but if you don't finish school now, you're going to be sorry later that you didn't." I grabbed him by the shoulders. "And you only got another year. It ain't so bad. And I'll come back and I swear I'll help you do *whatever* you want to do. Just try to put up with it till I come back. Will you please do that? For me?"

He didn't answer and he wouldn't look at me.

"Sonny. You hear me?"

He pulled away. "I hear you. But you never hear anything *I* say."

I didn't know what to say to that. He looked out of the window and then back at me. "OK," he said, and sighed. "I'll try."

Then I said, trying to cheer him up a little, "They got a piano at Isabel's. You can practice on it."

And as a matter of fact, it did cheer him up for a minute. "That's right," he said to himself. "I forgot that." His face relaxed a little. But the worry, the thoughtfulness, played on it still, the way shadows play on a face which is staring into the fire.

But I thought I'd never hear the end of that piano. At first, Isabel would write me, saying how nice it was that Sonny was so serious about his music and how, as soon as he came in from school, or wherever he had been when he was supposed to be at school, he went straight to that piano and stayed there until suppertime. And, after supper, he went back to that piano and stayed there until everybody went to bed. He was at the piano all day Saturday and all day Sunday. Then he bought a record player and started playing records. He'd play one record over and over again, all day long sometimes, and he'd improvise along with it on the piano. Or he'd play one section of the record, one chord, one change, one progression, then he'd do it on the piano. Then back to the record. Then back to the piano.

Well, I really don't know how they stood it. Isabel finally confessed that it wasn't like living with a person at all, it was like living with sound. And the sound didn't make any sense to her, didn't make any sense to any of them—naturally. They began, in a way, to be afflicted by this presence that was living in their home. It was as though Sonny were some sort of god, or monster. He moved in an atmosphere which wasn't like theirs at all. They fed him and he ate, he washed himself, he walked in and out of their door; he certainly wasn't nasty or unpleasant or rude, Sonny isn't any of those things; but it was as though he were all wrapped up in some cloud, some fire, some vision all his own; and there wasn't any way to reach him.

At the same time, he wasn't really a man yet, he was still a child, and they had to watch out for him in all kinds of ways. They certainly couldn't throw him out. Neither did they dare to make a great scene about that piano because even they dimly sensed, as I sensed, from so many thousands of miles away, that Sonny was at that piano playing for his life.

But he hadn't been going to school. One day a letter came from the school board and Isabel's mother got it—there had, apparently, been other letters but Sonny had torn them up. This day, when Sonny came in, Isabel's mother showed him the letter and asked where he'd been spending his time. And she finally got it out of him that he'd been down in Greenwich Village, with musicians and other characters, in a white girl's apartment. And this scared her and she started to scream at him and what came up, once she began—though she denies it to this day—was what sacrifices they were making to give Sonny a decent home and how little he appreciated it.

Sonny didn't play the piano that day. By evening, Isabel's mother had calmed down but then there was the old man to deal with, and Isabel herself. Isabel says she did her best to be calm but she broke down and started crying. She says she just watched Sonny's face. She could tell, by watching him, what was happening with him. And what was happening was that they penetrated his cloud, they had reached him. Even if their fingers had been a thousand times more gentle than human fingers ever are, he could hardly help feeling that they had stripped him naked and were spitting on that nakedness. For he also had to see that his presence, that music, which was life or death to him, had been torture for them and that they had endured it, not at all for his sake, but only for mine. And Sonny couldn't take that. He can take it a little better today than he could then but he's still not very good at it and, frankly, I don't know anybody who is.

The silence of the next few days must have been louder than the sound of all the music ever played since time began. One morning, before she went to work, Isabel was in his room for something and she suddenly realized that all of his records were gone. And she knew for certain that he was gone. And he was. He went as far as the navy would carry him. He finally sent me a postcard from some place in Greece and that was the first I knew that Sonny was still alive. I didn't see him any more until we were both back in New York and the war had long been over.

He was a man by then, of course, but I wasn't willing to see it. He came by the house from time to time, but we fought almost every time we met. I didn't like the way he carried himself, loose and dreamlike all the time, and I didn't like his friends, and his music seemed to be merely an excuse for the life he led. It sounded just that weird and disordered.

Then we had a fight, a pretty awful fight, and I didn't see him for months. By and by I looked him up, where he was living, in a furnished room in the Village, and I tried to make it up. But there were lots of other people in the room and Sonny just lay on his bed, and he wouldn't come downstairs with me, and he treated these other people as though they were his family and I weren't. So I got mad and then he got mad, and then I told him that he might just as well be dead as live the way he was living. Then he stood up and he told me not to worry about him any more in life, that he *was* dead as far as I was concerned. Then he pushed me to the door and the other people looked on as though nothing were happening, and he slammed the door behind me. I stood in the hallway, staring at the door. I heard somebody laugh in the room and then the tears came to my eyes. I started down the steps, whistling to keep from crying, I kept whistling to myself, *You going to need me, baby, one of these cold, rainy days.*

I read about Sonny's trouble in the spring. Little Grace died in the fall. She was a beautiful little girl. But she only lived a little over two years. She died of polio and she suffered. She had a slight fever for a couple of days, but it didn't seem like anything and we just kept her in bed. And we would certainly have called the doctor, but the fever dropped, she seemed to be all right. So we thought it had just been a cold. Then, one day, she was up, playing, Isabel was in the kitchen fixing lunch for the two boys when they'd come in from school, and she heard Grace fall down in the living room. When you have a lot of children you don't always start running when one of them falls, unless they start screaming or something. And, this time, Grace was quiet. Yet, Isabel says that when she heard that *thump* and then that silence, something happened in her to make her afraid. And she ran to the living room and there was little Grace on the floor, all twisted up, and the reason she hadn't screamed was that she couldn't get her breath. And when she did scream, it was the worst sound, Isabel says, that she'd ever heard in all her life, and she still hears it sometimes in her dreams. Isabel will sometimes wake me up with a low, moaning, strangled sound and I have to be quick to awaken her and hold her to me and where Isabel is weeping against me seems a mortal wound.

I think I may have written Sonny the very day that little Grace was buried. I was sitting in the living room in the dark, by myself, and I suddenly thought of Sonny. My trouble made his real.

One Saturday afternoon, when Sonny had been living with us, or, anyway, been in our house, for nearly two weeks, I found myself wandering aimlessly about the living room, drinking from a can of beer, and trying to work up the courage to search Sonny's room. He was out, he was usually out whenever I was home, and Isabel had taken the children to see their grandparents. Suddenly I was standing still in front of the living room window, watching Seventh Avenue. The idea of searching Sonny's room made me still. I scarcely dared to admit to myself what I'd be searching for. I didn't know what I'd do if I found it. Or if I didn't.

On the sidewalk across from me, near the entrance to a barbecue joint, some people were holding an old-fashioned revival meeting. The barbecue cook, wearing a dirty white apron, his conked hair reddish and metallic in the pale sun, and a cigarette between his lips, stood in the doorway, watching them. Kids and older people paused in their errands and stood there, along with some older men and a couple of very tough-looking women who watched everything that happened on the avenue, as though they owned it, or were maybe owned by it. Well, they were watching this, too. The revival was being carried on by three sisters in black, and a brother. All they had were their voices and their Bibles and a tambourine. The brother was testifying and while he testified two of the sisters stood together, seeming to say, amen, and the third sister walked around with the tambourine outstretched and a couple of people dropped coins into it. Then the brother's testimony ended and the sister who had been taking up the collection dumped the coins into her palm and transferred them to the pocket of her long black robe. Then she raised both hands, striking the tambourine against the air, and then against one hand, and she started to sing. And the two other sisters and the brother joined in.

It was strange, suddenly, to watch, though I had been seeing these street meetings all my life. So, of course, had everybody else down there. Yet, they paused and watched and listened and I stood still at the window. *"Tis the old ship of Zion,"* they sang, and the sister with the tambourine kept a steady, jangling beat, *"it has rescued many a thousand!"* Not a soul under the sound of their voices was hearing this song for the first time, not one of them had been rescued. Nor had they seen much in the way of rescue work being done around them. Neither did they especially believe in the holiness of the three sisters and the brother, they knew too much about them, knew where they lived, and how. The woman with the tambourine, whose voice dominated the air, whose face was bright with joy, was divided by very little from the woman who stood watching her, a cigarette between her heavy, chapped lips, her hair a cuckoo's nest, her face scarred and swollen from many beatings, and her black eyes glittering like coal. Perhaps they both knew this, which was why, when, as rarely, they addressed each other, they addressed each other as Sister. As the singing filled the air the watching, listening faces underwent a change, the eyes focusing on something within; the music seemed to soothe a poison out of them; and time seemed, nearly, to fall away from the sullen, belligerent, battered faces, as though they were fleeing back to their first condition, while dreaming of their last. The barbecue cook half shook his head and smiled, and dropped his cigarette and disappeared into his joint. A man fumbled in his pockets for change and stood holding it in his hand impatiently, as though he had just remembered a pressing appointment further up the avenue. He looked furious. Then I saw Sonny, standing on the edge of the crowd. He was carrying a wide, flat notebook with a green cover, and it made him look, from where I was standing, almost like a schoolboy. The coppery sun brought out the copper in his skin, he was very faintly smiling, standing very still. Then the singing stopped, the tambourine turned into a collection plate again. The furious man dropped in his coins and vanished, so did a couple of the women, and Sonny dropped some change in the plate, looking directly at the woman with a little smile. He started across the avenue, toward the house. He has a slow, loping walk, something like the way Harlem hipsters walk, only he's imposed on this his own half-beat. I had never really noticed it before.

I stayed at the window, both relieved and apprehensive. As Sonny disappeared from my sight, they began singing again. And they were still singing when his key turned in the lock.

"Hey," he said.

"Hey, yourself. You want some beer?"

"No. Well, maybe." But he came up to the window and stood beside me, looking out. "What a warm voice," he said.

They were singing *If I could only hear my mother pray again!*

"Yes," I said, "and she can sure beat that tambourine."

"But what a terrible song," he said, and laughed. He dropped his notebook on the sofa and disappeared into the kitchen. "Where's Isabel and the kids?"

"I think they went to see their grandparents. You hungry?"

"No." He came back into the living room with his can of beer. "You want to come some place with me tonight?"

I sensed, I don't know how, that I couldn't possibly say no. "Sure. Where?"

He sat down on the sofa and picked up his notebook and started leafing through it. "I'm going to sit in with some fellows in a joint in the Village."

"You mean, you're going to play, tonight?"

"That's right." He took a swallow of his beer and moved back, to the window. He gave me a sidelong look. "If you can stand it."

"I'll try," I said.

He smiled to himself and we both watched as the meeting across the way broke up. The three sisters and the brother, heads bowed, were singing *God be with you till we meet again.* The faces around them were very quiet. Then the song ended. The small crowd dispersed. We watched the three women and the lone man walk slowly up the avenue.

"When she was singing before," said Sonny, abruptly, "her voice reminded me for a minute of what heroin feels like sometimes—when it's in your veins. It makes you feel sort of warm and cool at the same time. And distant. And—and sure." He sipped his beer, very deliberately not looking at me. I watched his face. "It makes you feel—in control. Sometimes you've got to have that feeling."

"Do you?" I sat down slowly in the easy chair.

"Sometimes." He went to the sofa and picked up his notebook again. "Some people do."

"In order," I asked, "to play?" And my voice was very ugly, full of contempt and anger.

"Well"—he looked at me with great, troubled eyes, as though, in fact, he hoped his eyes would tell me things he could never otherwise say—"they *think* so. And *if* they think so—!"

"And what do *you* think?" I asked.

He sat on the sofa and put his can of beer on the floor. "I don't know," he said, and I couldn't be sure if he were answering my question or pursuing his thoughts. His face didn't tell me. "It's not so much to *play.* It's to *stand* it, to be able to make it at all. On any level." He frowned and smiled: "In order to keep from shaking to pieces."

"But these friends of yours," I said, "they seem to shake themselves to pieces pretty goddamn fast."

"Maybe." He played with the notebook. And something told me that I should curb my tongue, that Sonny was doing his best to talk, that I should listen. "But of course you only know the ones that've gone to pieces. Some don't—or at least they haven't *yet* and that's just about all *any* of us can say." He paused. "And then there are some who just live, really, in hell, and they know it and they see what's happening, and they go right on. I don't know." He sighed, dropped the notebook, folded his arms. "Some guys, you can tell from the way they play, they on something *all* the time. And you can see that, well, it makes something real for them. But of course," he picked up his beer from the floor and sipped it and put the can down again, "they *want* to, too, you've got to see that. Even some of them that say they don't—*some,* not all."

"And what about you?" I asked—I couldn't help it. "What about you? Do *you* want to?"

He stood up and walked to the window and remained silent for a long time. Then he sighed. "Me," he said. Then: "While I was downstairs before, on my way here, listening to that woman sing, it struck me all of a sudden how much suffering she must have had to go through—to sing like that. It's *repulsive* to think you have to suffer that much."

I said: "But there's no way not to suffer—is there, Sonny?"

"I believe not," he said and smiled, "but that's never stopped anyone from trying." He looked at me. "Has it?" I realized, with this mocking look, that there stood between us, forever, beyond the power of time or forgiveness, the fact that I had held silence—so long!—when he had needed human speech to help him. He turned back to the window. "No, there's no way not to suffer. But you try all kinds of ways to keep from drowning in it, to keep on top of it, and to make it seem—well, like *you.* Like you did something, all right, and now you're suffering for it. You know?" I said nothing. "Well you know," he said, impatiently, "why *do* people suffer? Maybe it's better to do something to give it a reason, *any* reason."

"But we just agreed," I said, "that there's no way not to suffer. Isn't it better, then, just to—take it?"

"But nobody just takes it," Sonny cried, "that's what I'm telling you! *Everybody* tries not to. You're just hung up on the *way* some people try—it's not *your* way!"

The hair on my face began to itch, my face felt wet. "That's not true," I said, "that's not true. I don't give a damn what other people do, I don't even care how they suffer. I just care how *you* suffer." And he looked at me. "Please believe me," I said. "I don't want to see you—die—trying not to suffer."

"I won't," he said, flatly, "die trying not to suffer. At least, not any faster than anybody else."

"But there's no need," I said, trying to laugh, "is there? in killing yourself."

I wanted to say more, but I couldn't. I wanted to talk about will power and how life could be—well, beautiful. I wanted to say that it was all within; but was it? or, rather, wasn't that exactly the trouble? And I wanted to promise that I would never fail him again. But it would all have sounded—empty words and lies.

So I made the promise to myself and prayed that I would keep it.

"It's terrible sometimes, inside," he said, "that's what's the trouble. You walk these streets, black and funky and cold, and there's not really a living ass to talk to, and there's nothing shaking, and there's no way of getting it out—that storm inside. You can't talk it and you can't make love with it, and when you finally try to get with it and play it, you realize *nobody's* listening. So *you've* got to listen. You got to find a way to listen."

And then he walked away from the window and sat on the sofa again, as though all the wind had suddenly been knocked out of him. "Sometimes you'll do *anything* to play, even cut your mother's throat." He laughed and looked at me. "Or your brother's." Then he sobered. "Or your own." Then: "Don't worry. I'm all right now and I think I'll *be* all right. But I can't forget—where I've been. I don't mean just the physical place I've been, I mean where I've *been*. And *what* I've been."

"What have you been, Sonny?" I asked.

He smiled—but sat sideways on the sofa, his elbow resting on the back, his fingers playing with his mouth and chin, not looking at me. "I've been something I didn't recognize, didn't know I could be. Didn't know anybody could be." He stopped, looking inward, looking helplessly young, looking old. "I'm not talking about it now because I feel *guilty* or anything like that—maybe it would be better if I did, I don't know. Anyway, I can't really talk about it. Not to you, not to anybody," and now he turned and faced me. "Sometimes, you know and it was actually when I was most *out* of the world. I felt that I was in it, that I was *with* it, really, and I could play or I didn't really have to *play*, it just came out of me, it was there. And I don't know how I played, thinking about it now, but I know I did awful things, those times, sometimes, to people. Or it wasn't that I *did* anything to them—it was that they weren't real." He picked up the beer can; it was empty; he rolled it between his palms: "And other times—well, I needed a fix, I needed to find a place to lean, I needed to clear a space to *listen*—and I couldn't find it, and I—went crazy, I did terrible things to *me*, I was terrible *for* me." He began pressing the beer can between his hands, I watched the metal begin to give. It glittered, as he played with it, like a knife, and I was afraid he would cut himself, but I said nothing. "Oh well. I can never tell you. I was all by myself at the bottom of something, stinking and sweating and crying and shaking, and I smelled it, you know? *my* stink, and I thought I'd die if I couldn't get away from it and yet, all the same, I knew that everything I was doing was just locking me in with it. And I didn't know," he paused, still flattening the beer can, "I didn't know, I still *don't* know, something kept telling me that maybe it was good to smell your own stink, but I didn't think that *that* was what I'd been trying to do—and—who can stand it?" and he abruptly dropped the ruined beer can, looking at me with a small, still smile, and then rose, walking to the window as though it were the lodestone rock. I watched his face, he watched the avenue. "I couldn't tell you when Mama died—but the reason I wanted to leave Harlem so bad was to get away from drugs. And then, when I ran away, that's what I was running from—really. When I came back, nothing had changed, *I* hadn't changed, I was just—older." And he stopped drumming with his fingers on the windowpane. The sun had vanished, soon darkness would fall. I watched his face. "It can come again," he said, almost as though speaking to himself. Then he turned to me. "It can come again," he repeated. "I just want you to know that."

"All right," I said, at last. "So it can come again. All right."

He smiled, but the smile was sorrowful. "I had to try to tell you," he said.

"Yes," I said. "I understand that."

"You're my brother," he said, looking straight at me, and not smiling at all.

"Yes," I repeated, "yes. I understand that."

He turned back to the window, looking out. "All that hatred down there," he said, "all that hatred and misery and love. It's a wonder it doesn't blow the avenue apart."

We went to the only nightclub on a short, dark street, downtown. We squeezed through the narrow, chattering, jam-packed bar to the entrance of the big room, where the bandstand was. And we stood there for a moment, for the lights were very dim in this room and we couldn't see. Then, "Hello, boy," said a voice and an enormous black man, much older than Sonny or myself, erupted out of all that atmospheric lighting and put an arm around Sonny's shoulder. "I been sitting right here," he said, "waiting for you."

He had a big voice, too, and heads in the darkness turned toward us.

Sonny grinned and pulled a little away, and said, "Creole, this is my brother. I told you about him."

Creole shook my hand. "I'm glad to meet you, son," he said, and it was clear that he was glad to meet me *there,* for Sonny's sake. And he smiled, "You got a real musician in *your* family," and he took his arm from Sonny's shoulder and slapped him, lightly, affectionately, with the back of his hand.

"Well. Now I've heard it all," said a voice behind us. This was another musician, and a friend of Sonny's, a coal-black, cheerful-looking man, built close to the ground. He immediately began confiding to me, at the top of his lungs, the most terrible things about Sonny, his teeth gleaming like a lighthouse and his laugh coming up out of him like the beginning of an earthquake. And it turned out that everyone at the bar knew Sonny, or almost everyone; some were musicians, working there, or nearby, or not working, some were simply hangers-on, and some were there to hear Sonny play. I was introduced to all of them and they were all very polite to me. Yet, it was clear that, for them, I was only Sonny's brother. Here, I was in Sonny's world. Or, rather: his kingdom. Here, it was not even a question that his veins bore royal blood.

They were going to play soon and Creole installed me, by myself, at a table in a dark corner. Then I watched them, Creole, and the little black man, and Sonny, and the others, while they horsed around, standing just below the bandstand. The light from the bandstand spilled just a little short of them and, watching them laughing and gesturing and moving about, I had the feeling that they, nevertheless, were being most careful not to step into that circle of light too suddenly: that if they moved into the light too suddenly, without thinking, they would perish in flame. Then, while I watched, one of them, the small, black man, moved into the light and crossed the bandstand and started fooling around with his drums. Then—being funny and being, also, extremely ceremonious—Creole took Sonny by the arm and led him to the piano. A woman's voice called Sonny's name and a few hands started clapping. And Sonny, also being funny and being ceremonious, and so touched, I think, that he could have cried, but neither hiding it nor showing it, riding it like a man, grinned, and put both hands to his heart and bowed from the waist.

Creole then went to the bass fiddle and a lean, very bright-skinned brown man jumped up on the bandstand and picked up his horn. So there they were, and the atmosphere on the bandstand and in the room began to change and tighten. Someone stepped up to the microphone and announced them. Then there were all kinds of murmurs. Some people at the bar shushed others. The waitress ran around, frantically getting in the last orders, guys and chicks got closer to each other, and the lights on the bandstand, on the quartet, turned to a kind of indigo. Then they all looked different there. Creole looked about him for the last time, as though he were making certain that all his chickens were in the coop, and then he—jumped and struck the fiddle. And there they were.

All I know about music is that not many people ever really hear it. And even then, on the rare occasions when something opens within, and the music enters, what we mainly hear, or hear corroborated, are personal, private, vanishing evocations. But the man who creates the music is hearing something else, is dealing with the roar rising from the void and imposing order on it as it hits the air. What is evoked in him, then, is of another order, more terrible because it has no words, and triumphant, too, for that same reason. And his triumph, when he triumphs, is ours. I just watched Sonny's face. His face was troubled, he was working hard, but he wasn't with it. And I had the feeling that, in a way, everyone on the bandstand was waiting for him, both waiting for him and pushing him along. But as I began to watch Creole, I realized that it was Creole who held them all back. He had them on a short rein. Up there, keeping the beat with his whole body, wailing on the fiddle, with his eyes half closed, he was listening to everything, but he was listening to Sonny. He was having a dialogue with Sonny. He wanted Sonny to leave the shoreline and strike out for the deep water. He was Sonny's witness that deep water and drowning were not the same thing—he had been there, and he knew. And he wanted Sonny to know. He was waiting for Sonny to do the things on the keys which would let Creole know that Sonny was in the water.

And, while Creole listened, Sonny moved, deep within, exactly like someone in torment. I had never before thought of how awful the relationship must be between the musician and his instrument. He has to fill it, this instrument, with the breath of life, his own. He has to make it do what he wants it to do. And a piano is just a piano. It's made out of so much wood and wires and little hammers and big ones, and ivory. While there's only so much you can do with it, the only way to find this out is to try; to try and make it do everything.

And Sonny hadn't been near a piano for over a year. And he wasn't on much better terms with his life, not the life that stretched before him now. He and the piano stammered, started one way, got scared, stopped; started another way, panicked, marked time, started again; then seemed to have found a direction, panicked again, got stuck. And the face I saw on Sonny I'd never seen before. Everything had been burned out of it, and, at the same time, things usually hidden were being burned in, by the fire and fury of the battle which was occurring in him up there.

Yet, watching Creole's face as they neared the end of the first set, I had the feeling that something had happened, something I hadn't heard. Then they finished, there was scattered applause, and then, without an instant's warning, Creole started into something else, it was almost sardonic, it was *Am I Blue.* And, as though he commanded, Sonny began to play. Something began to happen. And Creole let out the reins. The dry, low, black man said something awful on the drums, Creole answered, and the drums talked back. Then the horn insisted, sweet and high, slightly detached perhaps, and Creole listened, commenting now and then, dry, and driving, beautiful and calm and old. Then they all came together again, and Sonny was part of the family again. I could tell this from his face. He seemed to have found, right there beneath his fingers, a damn brand-new piano. It seemed that he couldn't get over it. Then, for awhile, just being happy with Sonny, they seemed to be agreeing with him that brand-new pianos certainly were a gas.

Then Creole stepped forward to remind them that what they were playing was the blues. He hit something in all of them, he hit something in me, myself, and the music tightened and deepened, apprehension began to beat the air. Creole began to tell us what the blues were all about. They were not about anything very new. He and his boys up there were keeping it new, at the risk of ruin, destruction, madness, and death, in order to find new ways to make us listen. For, while the tale of how we suffer, and how we are delighted, and how we may triumph is never new, it always must be heard. There isn't any other tale to tell, it's the only light we've got in all this darkness.

And this tale, according to that face, that body, those strong hands on those strings, has another aspect in every country, and a new depth in every generation. Listen, Creole seemed to be saying, listen. Now these are Sonny's blues. He made the little black man on the drums know it, and the bright, brown man on the horn. Creole wasn't trying any longer to get Sonny in the water. He was wishing him Godspeed. Then he stepped back, very slowly, filling the air with the immense suggestion that Sonny speak for himself.

Then they all gathered around Sonny and Sonny played. Every now and again one of them seemed to say, amen. Sonny's fingers filled the air with life, his life. But that life contained so many others. And Sonny went all the way back, he really began with the spare, flat statement of the opening phrase of the song. Then he began to make it his. It was very beautiful because it wasn't hurried and it was no longer a lament. I seemed to hear with what burning he had made it his, with what burning we had yet to make it ours, how we could cease lamenting. Freedom lurked around us and I understood, at last, that he could help us to be free if we would listen, that he would never be free until we did. Yet, there was no battle in his face now. I heard what he had gone through, and would continue to go through until he came to rest in earth. He had made it his: that long line, of which we knew only Mama and Daddy. And he was giving it back, as everything must be given back, so that, passing through death, it can live forever. I saw my mother's face again, and felt, for the first time, how the stones of the road she had walked on must have bruised her feet. I saw the moonlit road where my father's brother died. And it brought something else back to me, and carried me past it, I saw my little girl again and felt Isabel's tears again, and I felt my own tears begin to rise. And I was yet aware that this was only a moment, that the world waited outside, as hungry as a tiger, and that trouble stretched above us, longer than the sky.

Then it was over. Creole and Sonny let out their breath, both soaking wet, and grinning. There was a lot of applause and some of it was real. In the dark, the girl came by and I asked her to take drinks to the bandstand. There was a long pause, while they talked up there in the indigo light and after awhile I saw the girl put a Scotch and milk on top of the piano for Sonny. He didn't seem to notice it, but just before they started playing again he sipped from it and looked toward me, and nodded. Then he put it back on top of the piano. For me, then, as they began to play again, it glowed and shook above my brother's head like the very cup of trembling.[3]

1965

Flannery O'Connor 1925–1964

Flannery O'Connor's fiction presents what she called the "sacramental view of life," a perspective usually developed out of antitheses. Her characters confront a world of violence and unexplained evil, against which none of the traditional virtues of sincerity, hard work, and foresight avail.

Her style is noted for its simplicity, wit, and masterful reproduction of the colloquial speech of her native South. She was born in Savannah, Georgia, and grew up in the small town of Milledgeville, where she lived until she died, aged thirty-eight. She attended the Women's College of Georgia and while in college published a number of short stories. She then studied in the writer's program at the University of Iowa, receiving an M.F.A. in 1947.

O'Connor's fiction is peopled with characters who have been described as haunted and grotesque, physical and emotional freaks often embracing a single and ferocious truth. They play out their lives against the backgrounds of the deepest, darkest South, as in her novel Wise Blood *(1952), which uses the setting of rural Tennessee to examine the character of a backwoods preacher both innocent and demonic, victim and assailant, who has created a church without Christ, where violence substitutes for religious faith.*

O'Connor is best known for short stories that exhibit an ironic, unsentimental acceptance of the human condition. They are filled with wry comedy and examples of satanic evil, and they are often concerned with what she called "the redemptive act" and a pervading "sense of Mystery which cannot be accounted for by human formula."

FURTHER READING: *Flannery O'Connor: The Complete Stories,* 1971; *The Habit of Being: Letters of Flannery O'Connor,* ed. S. Fitzgerald, 1979; E. Kessler, *Flannery O'Connor and the Language of Apocalypse,* 1986; S. Paulson, *Flannery O'Connor,* 1988; J. Baumgartner, *Flannery O'Connor: A Proper Scaring,* 1988; B. Ragen, *A Wreck on the Road to Damascus: Innocence, Guilt and Conversion in Flannery O'Connor,* 1989; R. Brinkmeyer, *The Art and Vision of Flannery O'Connor,* 1990; A. Di Renzo, *American Gargoyles: Flannery O'Connor and the Medieval Grotesque,* 1993; S. Gordon, *Flannery O'Connor: The Obedient Imagination,* 2000; G.

[3]"Awake, Awake, stand up O Jerusalem, which hast drunk at the hand of the LORD the cup of his fury; thou hast drunken the dregs of the cup of trembling, and wrung them out" (Isaiah 51:17).

Kilcourse, *Flannery O'Connor's Religious Imagination*, 2001; C. Seel, *Ritual Performance in the Fiction of Flannery O'Connor*, 2001; H. Edmondson, *Return to Good and Evil: Flannery O'Connor's Response to Nihilism*, 2002.

TEXT: *Flannery O'Connor, The Complete Stories*, 1971.

A GOOD MAN IS HARD TO FIND

The grandmother didn't want to go to Florida. She wanted to visit some of her connections in east Tennessee and she was seizing at every chance to change Bailey's mind. Bailey was the son she lived with, her only boy. He was sitting on the edge of his chair at the table, bent over the orange sports section of the *Journal.* "Now look here, Bailey," she said, "see here, read this," and she stood with one hand on her thin hip and the other rattling the newspaper at his bald head. "Here this fellow that calls himself The Misfit is aloose from the Federal Pen and headed toward Florida and you read here what it says he did to these people. Just you read it. I wouldn't take my children in any direction with a criminal like that aloose in it. I couldn't answer to my conscience if I did."

Bailey didn't look up from his reading so she wheeled around then and faced the children's mother, a young woman in slacks, whose face was as broad and innocent as a cabbage and was tied around with a green head-kerchief that had two points on the top like rabbit's ears. She was sitting on the sofa, feeding the baby his apricots out of a jar. "The children have been to Florida before," the old lady said. "You ought to take them somewhere else for a change so they would see different parts of the world and be broad. They never have been to east Tennessee."

The children's mother didn't seem to hear but the eight-year-old boy, John Wesley, a stocky child with glasses, said, "If you don't want to go to Florida, why dontcha stay at home?" He and the little girl, June Star, were reading the funny papers on the floor.

"She wouldn't stay at home to be queen for a day," June Star said without raising her yellow head.

"Yes and what would you do if this fellow, The Misfit, caught you?" the grandmother asked.

"I'd smack his face," John Wesley said.

"She wouldn't stay at home for a million bucks," June Star said. "Afraid she'd miss something. She has to go everywhere we go."

"All right, Miss," the grandmother said. "Just remember that the next time you want me to curl your hair."

June Star said her hair was naturally curly.

The next morning the grandmother was the first one in the car, ready to go. She had her big black valise that looked like the head of a hippopotamus in one corner, and underneath it she was hiding a basket with Pitty Sing, the cat, in it. She didn't intend for the cat to be left alone in the house for three days because he would miss her too much and she was afraid he might brush against one of the gas burners and accidentally asphyxiate himself. Her son, Bailey, didn't like to arrive at a motel with a cat.

She sat in the middle of the back seat with John Wesley and June Star on either side of her. Bailey and the children's mother and the baby sat in front and they left Atlanta at eight forty-five with the mileage on the car at 55890. The grandmother wrote this down because she thought it would be interesting to say how many miles they had been when they got back. It took them twenty minutes to reach the outskirts of the city.

The old lady settled herself comfortably, removing her white cotton gloves and putting them up with her purse on the shelf in front of the back window. The children's mother still had on slacks and still had her head tied up in a green kerchief, but the grandmother had on a navy blue straw sailor hat with a bunch of white violets on the brim and a navy blue dress with a small white dot in the print. Her collars and cuffs were white organdy trimmed with lace and at her neckline she had pinned a purple spray of cloth violets containing a sachet. In case of an accident, anyone seeing her dead on the highway would know at once that she was a lady.

She said she thought it was going to be a good day for driving, neither too hot nor too cold, and she cautioned Bailey that the speed limit was fifty-five miles an hour and that the patrolmen hid themselves behind billboards and small clumps of trees and sped out after you before you had a chance to slow down. She pointed out interesting details of the scenery: Stone Mountain; the blue granite that in some places came up to both sides of the highway; the brilliant red clay banks slightly streaked with purple; and the various crops that made rows of green lace-work on the ground. The trees were full of silver-white sunlight and the meanest of them sparkled. The children were reading comic magazines and their mother had gone back to sleep.

"Let's go through Georgia fast so we won't have to look at it much," John Wesley said.

"If I were a little boy," said the grandmother, "I wouldn't talk about my native state that way. Tennessee has the mountains and Georgia has the hills."

"Tennessee is just a hillbilly dumping ground," John Wesley said, "and Georgia is a lousy state too."

"You said it," June Star said.

"In my time," said the grandmother, folding her thin veined fingers, "children were more respectful of their native states and their parents and everything else. People did right then. Oh look at the cute little pickaninny!" she said and pointed to a Negro child standing in the door of a shack. "Wouldn't that make a picture, now?" she asked and they all turned and looked at the little Negro out of the back window. He waved.

"He didn't have any britches on," June Star said.

"He probably didn't have any," the grandmother explained. "Little niggers in the country don't have things like we do. If I could paint, I'd paint that picture," she said.

The children exchanged comic books.

The grandmother offered to hold the baby and the children's mother passed him over the front seat to her. She set him on her knee and bounced him and told him about the things they were passing. She rolled her eyes and screwed up her mouth and stuck her leathery thin face into his smooth bland one. Occasionally he gave her a faraway smile. They passed a large cotton field with five or six graves fenced in the middle of it, like a small island. "Look at the graveyard!" the grandmother said, pointing it out. "That was the old family burying ground. That belonged to the plantation."

"Where's the plantation?" John Wesley asked.

"Gone With the Wind," said the grandmother. "Ha. Ha."

When the children finished all the comic books they had brought, they opened the lunch and ate it. The grandmother ate a peanut butter sandwich and an olive and would not let the children throw the box and the paper napkins out the window. When there was nothing else to do they played a game by choosing a cloud and making the other two guess what shape it suggested. John Wesley took one the shape of a cow and June Star guessed a cow and John Wesley said, no, an automobile, and June Star said he didn't play fair, and they began to slap each other over the grandmother.

The grandmother said she would tell them a story if they would keep quiet. When she told a story, she rolled her eyes and waved her head and was very dramatic. She said once when she was a maiden lady she had been courted by a Mr. Edgar Atkins Teagarden from Jasper, Georgia. She said he was a very good-looking man and a gentleman and that he brought her a watermelon every Saturday afternoon with his initials cut in it, E. A. T. Well, one Saturday, she said, Mr. Teagarden brought the watermelon and there was nobody at home and he left it on the front porch and returned in his buggy to Jasper, but she never got the watermelon, she said, because a nigger boy ate it when he saw the initials, E. A. T.! This story tickled John Wesley's funny bone and he giggled and giggled but June Star didn't think it was any good. She said she wouldn't marry a man that just brought her a watermelon on Saturday. The grandmother said she would have done well to marry Mr. Teagarden because he was a gentleman and had bought Coca-Cola stock when it first came out and that he had died only a few years ago, a very wealthy man.

They stopped at The Tower for barbecued sandwiches. The Tower was a part stucco and part wood filling station and dance hall set in a clearing outside of Timothy. A fat man named Red Sammy Butts ran it and there were signs stuck here and there on the building and for miles up and down the highway saying, TRY RED SAMMY'S FAMOUS BARBECUE. NONE LIKE FAMOUS RED SAMMY'S! RED SAM! THE FAT BOY WITH THE HAPPY LAUGH. A VETERAN! RED SAMMY'S YOUR MAN!

Red Sammy was lying on the bare ground outside The Tower with his head under a truck while a gray monkey about a foot high, chained to a small chinaberry tree, chattered nearby. The monkey sprang back into the tree and got on the highest limb as soon as he saw the children jump out of the car and run toward him.

Inside, The Tower was a long dark room with a counter at one end and tables at the other and dancing space in the middle. They all sat down at a board table next to the nickelodeon and Red Sam's wife, a tall burnt-brown woman with hair and eyes lighter than her skin, came and took their order. The children's mother put a dime in the machine and played "The Tennessee Waltz," and the grandmother said that tune always made her want to dance. She asked Bailey if he would like to dance but he only glared at her. He didn't have a naturally sunny disposition like she did and trips made him nervous. The grandmother's brown eyes were very bright. She swayed her head from side to side and pretended she was dancing in her chair. June Star said play something she could tap to so the children's mother put in another dime and played a fast number and June Star stepped out onto the dance floor and did her tap routine.

"Ain't she cute?" Red Sam's wife said, leaning over the counter. "Would you like to come be my little girl?"

"No I certainly wouldn't," June Star said. "I wouldn't live in a broken-down place like this for a million bucks!" and she ran back to the table.

"Ain't she cute?" the woman repeated, stretching her mouth politely.

"Aren't you ashamed?" hissed the grandmother.

Red Sam came in and told his wife to quit lounging on the counter and hurry up with these people's order. His khaki trousers reached just to his hip bones and his stomach hung over them like a sack of meal swaying under his shirt. He came over and sat down at a table nearby and let out a combination sigh and a yodel. "You can't win," he said. "You can't win," and he wiped his sweating red face off with a gray handkerchief. "These days you don't know who to trust," he said. "Ain't that the truth?"

"People are certainly not nice like they used to be," said the grandmother.

"Two fellers come in here last week," Red Sammy said, "driving a Chrysler. It was a old beat-up car but it was a good one and these boys looked all right to me. Said they worked at the mill and you know I let them fellers charge the gas they bought? Now why did I do that?"

"Because you're a good man!" the grandmother said at once.

"Yes'm, I suppose so," Red Sam said as if he were struck with this answer.

His wife brought the orders, carrying the five plates all at once without a tray, two in each hand and one balanced on her arm. "It isn't a soul in this green world of God's that you can trust," she said. "And I don't count nobody out of that, not nobody," she repeated, looking at Red Sammy.

"Did you read about that criminal, The Misfit, that's escaped?" asked the grandmother.

"I wouldn't be a bit surprised if he didn't attack this place right here," said the woman. "If he hears about it being here, I wouldn't be none surprised to see him. If he hears it's two cent in the cash register, I wouldn't be a tall surprised if he . . ."

"That'll do," Red Sam said. "Go bring these people their Co'-Colas," and the woman went off to get the rest of the order.

"A good man is hard to find," Red Sammy said. "Everything is getting terrible. I remember the day you could go off and leave your screen door unlatched. Not no more."

He and the grandmother discussed better times. The old lady said that in her opinion Europe was entirely to blame for the way things were now. She said the way Europe acted you would think we were made of money and Red Sam said it was no use talking about it, she was exactly right. The children ran outside into the white sunlight and looked at the monkey in the lacy chinaberry tree. He was busy catching fleas on himself and biting each one carefully between his teeth as if it were a delicacy.

They drove off again into the hot afternoon. The grandmother took cat naps and woke up every few minutes with her own snoring. Outside of Toombsboro she woke up and recalled an old plantation that she had visited in this neighborhood once when she was a young lady. She said the house had six white columns across the front and that there was an avenue of oaks leading up to it and two little wooden trellis arbors on either side in front where you sat down with your suitor after a stroll in the garden. She recalled exactly which road to turn off to get to it. She knew that Bailey would not be willing to lose any time looking at an old house, but the more she talked about it, the more she wanted to see it once again and find out if the little twin arbors were still standing. "There was a secret panel in this house," she said craftily, not telling the truth but wishing that she were, "and the story went that all the family silver was hidden in it when Sherman[1] came through but it was never found . . ."

"Hey!" John Wesley said. "Let's go see it! We'll find it! We'll poke all the woodwork and find it! Who lives there? Where do you turn off at? Hey Pop, can't we turn off there?"

"We never have seen a house with a secret panel!" June Star shrieked. "Let's go to the house with the secret panel! Hey Pop, can't we go see the house with the secret panel!"

"It's not far from here, I know," the grandmother said. "It wouldn't take over twenty minutes."

Bailey was looking straight ahead. His jaw was as rigid as a horseshoe. "No," he said.

The children began to yell and scream that they wanted to see the house with the secret panel. John Wesley kicked the back of the front seat and June Star hung over her mother's shoulder and whined desperately into her ear that they never had any fun even on their vacation, that they could never do what THEY wanted to do. The baby began to scream and John Wesley kicked the back of the seat so hard that his father could feel the blows in his kidney.

"All right!" he shouted and drew the car to a stop at the side of the road. "Will you all shut up? Will you all just shut up for one second? If you don't shut up, we won't go anywhere."

"It would be very educational for them," the grandmother murmured.

"All right," Bailey said, "but get this: this is the only time we're going to stop for anything like this. This is the one and only time."

"The dirt road that you have to turn down is about a mile back," the grandmother directed. "I marked it when we passed."

"A dirt road," Bailey groaned.

After they had turned around and were headed toward the dirt road, the grandmother recalled other points about the house, the beautiful glass over the front doorway and the candle-lamp in the hall. John Wesley said that the secret panel was probably in the fireplace.

"You can't go inside this house," Bailey said. "You don't know who lives there."

"While you all talk to the people in front, I'll run around behind and get in a window," John Wesley suggested.

"We'll all stay in the car," his mother said.

They turned onto the dirt road and the car raced roughly along in a swirl of pink dust. The grandmother recalled the times when there were no paved roads and thirty miles was a day's journey. The dirt road was hilly and there were sudden washes in it and sharp curves on dangerous embankments. All at once they would be on a hill, looking down over the blue tops of trees for miles around,

[1]William Tecumseh Sherman (1820–1891), Union general in the American Civil War. His famous "March to the Sea" from Atlanta to Savannah, Georgia, in 1864 was marked by widespread plundering and destruction by Union troops.

then the next minute, they would be in a red depression with the dustcoated trees looking down on them.

"This place had better turn up in a minute," Bailey said, "or I'm going to turn around."

The road looked as if no one had traveled on it in months.

"It's not much farther," the grandmother said and just as she said it, a horrible thought came to her. The thought was so embarrassing that she turned red in the face and her eyes dilated and her feet jumped up, upsetting her valise in the corner. The instant the valise moved, the newspaper top she had over the basket under it rose with a snarl and Pitty Sing, the cat, sprang onto Bailey's shoulder.

The children were thrown to the floor and their mother, clutching the baby, was thrown out the door onto the ground; the old lady was thrown into the front seat. The car turned over once and landed right-side-up in a gulch off the side of the road. Bailey remained in the driver's seat with the cat—gray-striped with a broad white face and an orange nose—clinging to his neck like a caterpillar.

As soon as the children saw they could move their arms and legs, they scrambled out of the car, shouting, "We've had an ACCIDENT!" The grandmother was curled up under the dashboard, hoping she was injured so that Bailey's wrath would not come down on her all at once. The horrible thought she had had before the accident was that the house she had remembered so vividly was not in Georgia but in Tennessee.

Bailey removed the cat from his neck with both hands and flung it out the window against the side of a pine tree. Then he got out of the car and started looking for the children's mother. She was sitting against the side of a red gutted ditch, holding the screaming baby, but she only had a cut down her face and a broken shoulder. "We've had an ACCIDENT!" the children screamed in a frenzy of delight.

"But nobody's killed," June Star said with disappointment as the grandmother limped out of the car, her hat still pinned to her head but the broken front brim standing up at a jaunty angle and the violet spray hanging off the side. They all sat down in the ditch, except the children, to recover from the shock. They were all shaking.

"Maybe a car will come along," said the children's mother hoarsely.

"I believe I have injured an organ," said the grandmother, pressing her side, but no one answered her. Bailey's teeth were clattering. He had on a yellow sport shirt with bright blue parrots designed in it and his face was as yellow as the shirt. The grandmother decided that she would not mention that the house was in Tennessee.

The road was about ten feet above and they could see only the tops of the trees on the other side of it. Behind the ditch they were sitting in there were more woods, tall and dark and deep. In a few minutes they saw a car some distance away on top of a hill, coming slowly as if the occupants were watching them. The grandmother stood up and waved both arms dramatically to attract their attention. The car continued to come on slowly, disappeared around a bend and appeared again, moving even slower, on top of the hill they had gone over. It was a big black battered hearse-like automobile. There were three men in it.

It came to a stop just over them and for some minutes, the driver looked down with a steady expressionless gaze to where they were sitting, and didn't speak. Then he turned his head and muttered something to the other two and they got out. One was a fat boy in black trousers and a red sweat shirt with a silver stallion embossed on the front of it. He moved around on the right side of them and stood staring, his mouth partly open in a kind of loose grin. The other had on khaki pants and a blue striped coat and a gray hat pulled down very low, hiding most of his face. He came around slowly on the left side. Neither spoke.

The driver got out of the car and stood by the side of it, looking down at them. He was an older man than the other two. His hair was just beginning to gray and he wore silver-rimmed spectacles that gave him a scholarly look. He had a long creased face and didn't have on any shirt or undershirt. He had on blue jeans that were too tight for him and he was holding a black hat and a gun. The two boys also had guns.

"We've had an ACCIDENT!" the children screamed.

The grandmother had the peculiar feeling that the bespectacled man was someone she knew. His face was as familiar to her as if she had known him all her life but she could not recall who he was. He moved away from the car and began to come down the embankment, placing his feet carefully so that he wouldn't slip. He had on tan and white shoes and no socks, and his ankles were red and thin. "Good afternoon," he said. "I see you all had you a little spill."

"We turned over twice!" said the grandmother.

"Oncet," he corrected. "We seen it happen. Try their car and see will it run, Hiram," he said quietly to the boy with the gray hat.

"What you got that gun for?" John Wesley asked. "Whatcha gonna do with that gun?"

"Lady," the man said to the children's mother, "would you mind calling them children to sit down by you? Children make me nervous. I want all you all to sit down right together there where you're at."

"What are you telling US what to do for?" June Star asked.

Behind them the line of woods gaped like a dark open mouth. "Come here," said the mother.

"Look here now," Bailey began suddenly, "we're in a predicament! We're in . . ."

The grandmother shrieked. She scrambled to her feet and stood staring. "You're The Misfit!" she said. "I recognized you at once!"

"Yes'm," the man said, smiling slightly as if he were pleased in spite of himself to be known, "but it would have been better for all of you, lady, if you hadn't reckernized me."

Bailey turned his head sharply and said something to his mother that shocked even the children. The old lady began to cry and The Misfit reddened.

"Lady," he said, "don't you get upset. Sometimes a man says things he don't mean. I don't reckon he meant to talk to you that-away."

"You wouldn't shoot a lady, would you?" the grandmother said and removed a clean handkerchief from her cuff and began to slap at her eyes with it.

The Misfit pointed the toe of his shoe into the ground and made a little hole and then covered it up again. "I would hate to have to," he said.

"Listen," the grandmother almost screamed, "I know you're a good man. You don't look a bit like you have common blood. I know you must come from nice people!"

"Yes mam," he said, "finest people in the world." When he smiled he showed a row of strong white teeth. "God never made a finer woman than my mother and my daddy's heart was pure gold," he said. The boy with the red sweat shirt had come around behind them and was standing with his gun at his hip. The Misfit squatted down on the ground. "Watch them children, Bobby Lee," he said. "You know they make me nervous." He looked at the six of them huddled together in front of him and he seemed to be embarrassed as if he couldn't think of anything to say. "Ain't a cloud in the sky," he remarked, looking up at it. "Don't see no sun but don't see no cloud neither."

"Yes, it's a beautiful day," said the grandmother. "Listen," she said, "you shouldn't call yourself The Misfit because I know you're a good man at heart. I can just look at you and tell."

"Hush!" Bailey yelled. "Hush! Everybody shut up and let me handle this!" He was squatting in the position of a runner about to sprint forward but he didn't move.

"I pre-chate that, lady," The Misfit said and drew a little circle in the ground with the butt of his gun.

"It'll take a half a hour to fix this here car," Hiram called, looking over the raised hood of it.

"Well, first you Bobby Lee get him and that little boy to step over yonder with you," The Misfit said, pointing to Bailey and John Wesley. "The boys want to ast you something," he said to Bailey. "Would you mind stepping back in them woods there with them?"

"Listen," Bailey began, "we're in a terrible predicament! Nobody realizes what this is," and his voice cracked. His eyes were as blue and intense as the parrots in his shirt and he remained perfectly still.

The grandmother reached up to adjust her hat brim as if she were going to the woods with him but it came off in her hand. She stood staring at it and after a second she let it fall on the ground. Hiram pulled Bailey up by the arm as if he were assisting an old man. John Wesley caught hold of his father's hand and Bobby Lee followed. They went off toward the woods and just as they reached the dark edge, Bailey turned and supporting himself against a gray naked pine trunk, he shouted, "I'll be back in a minute, Mamma, wait on me!"

"Come back this instant!" his mother shrilled but they all disappeared into the woods.

"Bailey Boy!" the grandmother called in a tragic voice but she found she was looking at The Misfit squatting on the ground in front of her. "I just know you're a good man," she said desperately. "You're not a bit common!"

"Nome, I ain't a good man," The Misfit said after a second as if he had considered her statement carefully, "but I ain't the worst in the world neither. My daddy said I was a different breed of dog from my brothers and sisters. 'You know,' Daddy said, 'it's some that can live their whole life without asking about it and it's others has to know why it is, and this boy is one of the latters. He's going to be into everything!'" He put on his black hat and looked up suddenly and then away deep into the woods as if he were embarrassed again. "I'm sorry I don't have on a shirt before you ladies," he said, hunching his shoulders slightly. "We buried our clothes that we had on when we escaped and we're just making do until we can get better. We borrowed these from some folks we met," he explained.

"That's perfectly all right," the grandmother said. "Maybe Bailey has an extra shirt in his suitcase."

"I'll look and see terrectly," The Misfit said.

"Where are you taking him?" the children's mother screamed.

"Daddy was a card himself," The Misfit said. "You couldn't put anything over on him. He never got in trouble with the Authorities though. Just had the knack of handling them."

"You could be honest too if you'd only try," said the grandmother. "Think how wonderful it would be to settle down and live a comfortable life and not have to think about somebody chasing you all the time."

The Misfit kept scratching in the ground with the butt of his gun as if he were thinking about it. "Yes'm, somebody is always after you," he murmured.

The grandmother noticed how thin his shoulder blades were just behind his hat because she was standing up looking down on him. "Do you ever pray?" she asked.

He shook his head. All she saw was the black hat wiggle between his shoulder blades. "Nome," he said.

There was a pistol shot from the woods, followed closely by another. Then silence. The old lady's head jerked around. She could hear the wind move through the tree tops like a long satisfied insuck of breath. "Bailey Boy!" she called.

"I was a gospel singer for a while," The Misfit said. "I been most everything. Been in the arm service, both land and sea, at home and abroad, been twict married, been an undertaker, been with the railroads, plowed Mother Earth, been in a tornado, seen a man burnt alive oncet," and he looked up at the children's mother and the little girl who were sitting close together, their faces white and their eyes glassy. "I even seen a woman flogged," he said.

"Pray, pray," the grandmother began, "pray, pray . . ."

"I never was a bad boy that I remember of," The Misfit said in an almost dreamy voice, "but somewheres along the line I done something wrong and got sent to the penitentiary. I was buried alive," and he looked up and held her attention to him by a steady stare.

"That's when you should have started to pray," she said, "What did you do to get sent to the penitentiary that first time?"

"Turn to the right, it was a wall," The Misfit said, looking up again at the cloudless sky. "Turn to the left, it was a wall. Look up it was a ceiling, look down it was a floor. I forget what I done, lady. I set there and set there, trying to remember what it was I done and I ain't recalled it to this day. Oncet in a while, I would think it was coming to me, but it never come."

"Maybe they put you in by mistake," the old lady said vaguely.

"Nome," he said. "It wasn't no mistake. They had the papers on me."

"You must have stolen something," she said.

The Misfit sneered slightly. "Nobody had nothing I wanted," he said. "It was a head-doctor at the penitentiary said what I had done was kill my daddy but I know that for a lie. My daddy died in nineteen ought nineteen of the epidemic flu and I never had a thing to do with it. He was buried in the Mount Hopewell Baptist churchyard and you can go there and see for yourself."

"If you would pray," the old lady said, "Jesus would help you."

"That's right," The Misfit said.

"Well then, why don't you pray?" she asked trembling with delight suddenly.

"I don't want no hep," he said. "I'm doing all right by myself."

Bobby Lee and Hiram came ambling back from the woods. Bobby Lee was dragging a yellow shirt with bright blue parrots in it.

"Thow me that shirt, Bobby Lee," The Misfit said. The shirt came flying at him and landed on his shoulder and he put it on. The grandmother couldn't name what the shirt reminded her of. "No, lady," The Misfit said while he was buttoning it up, "I found out the crime don't matter. You can do one thing or you can do another, kill a man or take a tire off his car, because sooner or later you're going to forget what it was you done and just be punished for it."

The children's mother had begun to make heaving noises as if she couldn't get her breath. "Lady," he asked, "would you and that little girl like to step off yonder with Bobby Lee and Hiram and join your husband?"

"Yes, thank you," the mother said faintly. Her left arm dangled helplessly and she was holding the baby, who had gone to sleep, in the other. "Hep that lady up, Hiram," The Misfit said as she struggled to climb out of the ditch, "and Bobby Lee, you hold onto that little girl's hand."

"I don't want to hold hands with him," June Star said, "He reminds me of a pig."

The fat boy blushed and laughed and caught her by the arm and pulled her off into the woods after Hiram and her mother.

Alone with The Misfit, the grandmother found that she had lost her voice. There was not a cloud in the sky nor any sun. There was nothing around her but woods. She wanted to tell him that he must pray. She opened and closed her mouth several times before anything came out. Finally she found herself saying, "Jesus. Jesus," meaning, Jesus will help you, but the way she was saying it, it sounded as if she might be cursing.

"Yes'm," The Misfit said as if he agreed. "Jesus thown everything off balance. It was the same case with Him as with me except He hadn't committed any crime and they could prove I had committed one because they had the papers on me. Of course," he said, "they never shown me my papers. That's why I sign myself now. I said long ago, you get you a signature and sign everything you do and keep a copy of it. Then you'll know what you done and you can hold up the crime to the punishment and see do they match and in the end you'll have something to prove you ain't been treated right. I call myself The Misfit," he said, "because I can't make what all I done wrong fit what all I gone through in punishment."

There was a piercing scream from the woods, followed closely by a pistol report. "Does it seem right to you, lady, that one is punished a heap and another ain't punished at all?"

"Jesus!" the old lady cried. "You've got good blood! I know you wouldn't shoot a lady! I know you come from nice people! Pray! Jesus, you ought not to shoot a lady. I'll give you all the money I've got!"

"Lady," The Misfit said, looking beyond her far into the woods, "there never was a body that give the undertaker a tip."

There were two more pistol reports and the grandmother raised her head like a parched old turkey hen crying for water and called, "Bailey Boy, Bailey Boy!" as if her heart would break.

"Jesus was the only One that ever raised the dead," The Misfit continued, "and He shouldn't have done it. He thown everything off balance. If He did what He said, then it's nothing for you to do but thow away everything and follow Him, and if He didn't, then it's nothing for you to do but enjoy the few minutes you got left the best way you can—by killing somebody or burning down his house or doing some other meanness to him. No pleasure but meanness," he said and his voice had become almost a snarl.

"Maybe He didn't raise the dead," the old lady mumbled, not knowing what she was saying and feeling so dizzy that she sank down in the ditch with her legs twisted under her.

"I wasn't there so I can't say He didn't," The Misfit said. "I wisht I had of been there," he said, hitting the ground with his fist. "It ain't right I wasn't there because if I had been there I would of known. Listen lady," he said in a high voice, "if I had of been there I would of known and I wouldn't be like I am now." His voice seemed about to crack and the grandmother's head cleared for an instant. She saw the man's face twisted close to her own as if he were going to cry and she murmured, "Why you're one of my babies. You're one of my own children!" She reached out and touched him on the shoulder. The Misfit sprang back as if a snake had bitten him and shot her three times through the chest. Then he put his gun down on the ground and took off his glasses and began to clean them.

Hiram and Bobby Lee returned from the woods and stood over the ditch, looking down at the grandmother who half sat and half lay in a puddle of blood with her legs crossed under her like a child's and her face smiling up at the cloudless sky.

Without his glasses, The Misfit's eyes were red-rimmed and pale and defenseless-looking. "Take her off and thow her where you thown the others," he said, picking up the cat that was rubbing itself against his leg.

"She was a talker, wasn't she?" Bobby Lee said, sliding down the ditch with a yodel.

"She would of been a good woman," The Misfit said, "if it had been somebody there to shoot her every minute of her life."

"Some fun!" Bobby Lee said.

"Shut up, Bobby Lee," The Misfit said. "It's no real pleasure in life."

1955

John Updike 1932–

John Updike was born in Shillington, Pennsylvania, the son of a junior high school mathematics teacher. Growing up in what seemed to be a world of narrow horizons, he came to an early awareness that he could escape only through his own wits. Encouraged by his ambitious mother, he wrote his first short story at the age of eight. In school he was an honor student, edited his school newspaper, and was president of his high school class. When he graduated from high school, he entered Harvard, the college selected by his mother because she believed that it nurtured writers.

Updike graduated from Harvard summa cum laude *in 1954. Later that year he sold his first short story to the* New Yorker, *the magazine in which he would establish his reputation as a writer of short fiction in the 1950s and 1960s. He spent a year on a fellowship studying art in England, and then became a staff writer for the* New Yorker, *where he turned out poems, sketches, essays, short stories, and reviews. He became known as "The Brilliant Young Writer," a title that has since stirred critics to argue that in his later work he has failed to fulfill his early promise.*

In 1957 Updike left the New Yorker, *moved to Ipswich, Massachusetts, and became an independent writer. His first book,* The Carpentered Hen, *a collection of poems, appeared the next year. His first novel,* The Poorhouse Fair, *and his first collection of short stories,* The Same Door, *were published in 1959. In the years that have followed, Updike has become one of the most prolific writers in modern American literature, publishing numerous novels, as well as an opera libretto, a play, his memoirs (*Self-Consciousness, *1989), and many volumes of poetry, short stories, and essays.*

Updike won his first widespread, popular recognition with Couples *(1968), a novel of suburban life that is filled with descriptions of compulsive adulteries. To readers hardened by the extravagant carnality of today's books and movies, the eroticism of* Couples *seems mild indeed, but to many critics and reviewers in the 1960s the novel was shocking, lurid, "unredeemed pornography" and "obsessively venereal," judgments that proved to be powerfully tempting to the book-buying public and helped to make the novel a vast commercial success. Of greater artistic significance was* Centaur *(1963), a highly symbolic and allusive novel, drawing heavily on classical myth, that won the National Book Award.*

In 1978 Updike published the novel The Coup, *a dark comedy set in modern Africa and reporting the reminiscences of a one-time dictator of a newly emerged African nation. But he most frequently has set his fiction in small-town America—rural villages and prosperous suburbia—a landscape described in many of his short stories, in four "Rabbit novels":* Rabbit Run *(1960),* Rabbit Redux *(1971),* Rabbit Is Rich *(1981),* Rabbit at Rest *(1990), and in* The Witches of Eastwick *(1984), a satirical story of witchcraft and demonic possession that was made into a comic, and lucrative, movie.* Villages *(2004), Updike's twenty-first novel, returns to the world of small-town sex, mostly clandestine, which he portrayed thirty-six years before in* Couples, *and sustains his reputation as "troubadour in the melancholy poetics of adultery."*

Updike has said that "plain realism has never seemed to me to be enough," and in order to scrutinize what he sees as the "intricacy and opacity of the real world," he often turns to fantasy and illusion. In three recent novels, he has reworked themes and re-created characters from Nathaniel Hawthorne's The Scarlet Letter, *in order to portray the loves and follies of affluent "spiritual seekers" in today's America.*

Updike's America is often a drab world of middle- and lower-class materialism, a land of trivial lives centered on TV, movies, and fan magazines for the riff raff—a brand-name America whose inhabitants are sunk in installment buying, whose stomachs are bloated with franchised food, and whose minds are dulled by soap operas and by trashy tabloids sold at checkout stands. And while Updike's characters often search for spiritual and religious meaning, they usually discover that sentimental love is a trap, that their happiness is brief, and that their lives are as dull as their prepackaged meals.

Nevertheless, Updike's finest work has always come from his exploration of ordinary America and from his use of elegant prose, rich with metaphor, to portray the public and private feelings of Americans, their daily rounds of life, their language, clothes, food, houses, cars, boyfriends, and girlfriends. And he celebrates America as a place, with all its ugliness, where people hold on—enduring, if not heroically, at least doggedly.

FURTHER READING: A. K. Hamilton, *The Elements of John Updike,* 1970; L. Taylor, *Pastoral and Anti-Pastoral Patterns in John Updike's Fiction,* 1971; R. Burchard, *John Updike: Yea Sayings,* 1971; R. Detewiler, *John Updike,* 1972; J. Markle, *John Updike's Fiction,* 1973; S. Uphaus, *John Updike,* 1980; P. Vaughan, *John Updike's Images of America,* 1981; *Critical Essays on John Updike,* ed. W. Macnaughton, 1982; D. Greiner, *The Other John Updike,* 1982; D. Greiner, *John Updike's Novels,* 1984; *John Updike,* ed. H. Bloom, 1987; J. Newman, *John Updike,* 1988; D. Ristoff, *John Updike's America,* 1988; R. Luscher, *John Updike,* 1993; *Conversations with John Updike,* ed. J. Plath, 1994; J. Schiff, *John Updike Revisited,* 1998; W. Pritchard, *Updike: America's Man of Letters,* 2000; J. De Bellis, *The John Updike Encyclopedia,* 2000; D. Miller, *John Updike and the Cold War: Drawing the Iron Curtain,* 2001; *John Updike: The Critical Responses to the "Rabbit" Saga,* ed. J. De Bellis, 2005.

TEXT: *Pigeon Feathers and Other Stories,* 1962.

A & P[1]

In walks these three girls in nothing but bathing suits. I'm in the third check-out slot, with my back to the door, so I don't see them until they're over by the bread. The one that caught my eye first was the one in the plaid green two-piece. She was a chunky kid, with a good tan and a sweet broad soft-looking can with those two crescents of white just under it, where the sun never seems to hit, at the top of the backs of her legs. I stood there with my hand on a box of HiHo crackers trying to remember if I rang it up or not. I ring it up again and the customer starts giving me hell. She's one of these cash-register-watchers, a witch about fifty with rouge on her cheekbones and no eyebrows, and I know it made her day to trip me up. She'd been watching cash registers for fifty years and probably never seen a mistake before.

By the time I got her feathers smoothed and her goodies into a bag—she gives me a little snort in passing, if she'd been born at the right time they would have burned her over in Salem—by the time I get her on her way the girls had circled around the bread and were coming back, without a pushcart, back my way along the counters, in the aisle between the checkouts and the Special bins. They didn't even have shoes on. There was this chunky one, with the two-piece—it was bright green and the seams on the bra were still sharp and her belly was still pretty pale so I guessed she just got it (the suit)—there was this one, with one of those chubby berry-faces, the lips all bunched together under her nose, this one, and a tall one, with black hair that hadn't quite frizzed right, and one of these sunburns right across under the eyes, and a chin that was too long—you know, the kind of girl other girls think is very "striking" and "attractive" but never quite makes it, as they very well know, which is why they like her so much—and then the third one, that wasn't quite so tall. She was the queen. She kind of led them, the other two peeking around and making their shoulders round. She didn't look around, not this queen, she just walked straight on slowly, on these long white prima-donna legs. She came down a little hard on her heels, as if she didn't walk in her bare feet that much, putting down her heels and then letting the weight move along to her toes as if she

[1]A & P was the name of the nationwide supermarket chain whose full name was the Great Atlantic and Pacific Tea Company.

was testing the floor with every step, putting a little deliberate extra action into it. You never know for sure how girls' minds work (do you really think it's a mind in there or just a little buzz like a bee in a glass jar?) but you got the idea she had talked the other two into coming in here with her, and now she was showing them how to do it, walk slow and hold yourself straight.

She had on a kind of dirty-pink—beige, maybe, I don't know—bathing suit with a little nubble all over it and, what got me, the straps were down. They were off her shoulders looped loose around the cool tops of her arms, and I guess as a result the suit had slipped a little on her, so all around the top of the cloth there was this shining rim. If it hadn't been there you wouldn't have known there could have been anything whiter than those shoulders. With the straps pushed off, there was nothing between the top of the suit and the top of her head except just *her*, this clean bare plane of the top of her chest down from the shoulder bones like a dented sheet of metal tilted in the light. I mean, it was more than pretty.

She had sort of oaky hair that the sun and salt had bleached, done up in a bun that was unraveling, and a kind of prim face. Walking into the A & P with your straps down, I suppose it's the only kind of face you *can* have. She held her head so high her neck, coming up out of those white shoulders, looked kind of stretched, but I didn't mind. The longer her neck was, the more of her there was.

She must have felt in the corner of her eye me and over my shoulder Stokesie in the second slot watching, but she didn't tip. Not this queen. She kept her eyes moving across the racks, and stopped, and turned so slow it made my stomach rub the inside of my apron, and buzzed to the other two, who kind of huddled against her for relief, and then they all three of them went up the cat-and-dog-food-breakfast-cereal-macaroni-rice-raisins-seasonings-spreads-spaghetti-soft-drinks-crackers-and-cookies aisle. From the third slot I look straight up this aisle to the meat counter, and I watched them all the way. The fat one with the tan sort of fumbled with the cookies, but on second thought she put the package back. The sheep pushing their carts down the aisle—the girls were walking against the usual traffic (not that we have one-way signs or anything)—were pretty hilarious. You could see them, when Queenie's white shoulders dawned on them, kind of jerk, or hop, or hiccup, but their eyes snapped back to their own baskets and on they pushed. I bet you could set off dynamite in an A & P and the people would by and large keep reaching and checking oatmeal off their lists and muttering "Let me see, there was a third thing, began with A, asparagus, no ah, yes, applesauce!" or whatever it is they do mutter. But there was no doubt, this jiggled them. A few houseslaves in pin curlers even looked around after pushing their carts past to make sure what they had seen was correct.

You know, it's one thing to have a girl in a bathing suit down on the beach, where what with the glare nobody can look at each other much anyway, and another thing in the cool of the A & P, under the fluorescent lights, against all those stacked packages, with her feet paddling along naked over our checkerboard green-and-cream rubber-tile floor.

"Oh Daddy," Stokesie said beside me. "I feel so faint."

"Darling," I said. "Hold me tight." Stokesie's married, with two babies chalked up on his fuselage already, but as far as I can tell that's the only difference. He's twenty-two, and I was nineteen this April.

"Is it done?" he asks, the responsible married man finding his voice. I forgot to say he thinks he's going to be manager some sunny day, maybe in 1990 when it's called the Great Alexandrov and Petrooshki[2] Tea Company or something.

What he meant was, our town is five miles from the beach, with a big summer colony out on the Point, but we're right in the middle of town, and the women generally put on a shirt or shorts or something before they get out of the car into the street. And anyway these are usually women with six children and varicose veins mapping their legs and nobody, including them, could care less. As I say, we're right in the middle of town, and if you stand at our front doors you can see two banks and the Congregational church and the newspaper store and three real-estate offices and about twenty-seven old freeloaders tearing up Central Street because the sewer broke again. It's not as if we're on the Cape,[3] we're north of Boston and there's people in this town haven't seen the ocean for twenty years.

The girls had reached the meat counter and were asking McMahon something. He pointed, they pointed, and they shuffled out of sight behind a pyramid of Diet Delight peaches. All that was left for us to see was old McMahon patting his mouth and looking after them sizing up their joints. Poor kids, I began to feel sorry for them, they couldn't help it.

Now here comes the sad part of the story, at least my family says it's sad, but I don't think it's so sad myself. The store's pretty empty, it being Thursday afternoon, so there was nothing much to do except lean on the register and wait for the girls to show up again. The whole store was like a pinball machine and I didn't know which tunnel they'd come out of. After a while they come around out of the far aisle, around the light bulbs, records at discount of the Caribbean Six or Tony Martin Sings or some such gunk you wonder they waste the wax on, sixpacks of candy bars, and plastic toys done up in cellophane that fall apart when a kid looks at them anyway. Around they come, Queenie still leading the way, and holding a little gray jar in her hand. Slots Three through Seven are unmanned and I could see her wondering between Stokes and me, but Stokesie with his usual luck draws an old party in baggy gray pants who stumbles up with four giant cans of pineapple juice (what do these bums *do* with all that pineapple juice? I've often asked myself) so the girls come to me. Queenie puts down the jar and I take it into my fingers icy cold. Kingfish Fancy Herring Snacks in Pure Sour Cream: 49¢. Now her hands are empty, not a ring or a bracelet, bare as God made them, and I wonder where the money's coming from. Still with that prim look she lifts a folded dollar bill out of the hollow at the center of her nubbed pink top. The jar went heavy in my hand. Really, I thought that was so cute.

Then everybody's luck begins to run out. Lengel comes in from haggling with a truck full of cabbages on the lot and is about to scuttle into that door marked MANAGER behind which he hides all day when the girls touch his eye. Lengel's pretty dreary, teaches Sunday school and the rest, but he doesn't miss that much. He comes over and says, "Girls, this isn't the beach."

[2]Updike's story takes place during the Cold War, when it was possible to imagine that if the USSR prevailed in that struggle, it might control the United States—in which case A & P might come to stand for Alexandrov and Petrooshki.

[3]Cape Cod, in southern Massachusetts.

Queenie blushes, though maybe it's just a brush of sunburn I was noticing for the first time, now that she was so close. "My mother asked me to pick up a jar of herring snacks." Her voice kind of startled me, the way voices do when you see the people first, coming out so flat and dumb yet kind of tony, too, the way it ticked over "pick up" and "snacks." All of a sudden I slid right down her voice into her living room. Her father and the other men were standing around in ice-cream coats and bow ties and the women were in sandals picking up herring snacks on toothpicks off a big glass plate and they were all holding drinks the color of water with olives and sprigs of mint in them. When my parents have somebody over they get lemonade and if it's a real racy affair Schlitz in tall glasses with "They'll Do It Every Time"[4] cartoons stenciled on.

"That's all right," Lengel said. "But this isn't the beach." His repeating this struck me as funny, as if it had just occurred to him, and he had been thinking all these years the A & P was a great big dune and he was the head lifeguard. He didn't like my smiling—as I say he doesn't miss much—but he concentrates on giving the girls that sad Sunday-school-superintendent stare.

Queenie's blush is no sunburn now, and the plump one in plaid, that I liked better from the back—a really sweet can—pipes up, "We weren't doing any shopping. We just came in for the one thing."

"That makes no difference," Lengel tells her, and I could see from the way his eyes went that he hadn't noticed she was wearing a two-piece before. "We want you decently dressed when you come in here."

"We *are* decent," Queenie says suddenly, her lower lip pushing, getting sore now that she remembers her place, a place from which the crowd that runs the A & P must look pretty crummy. Fancy Herring Snacks flashed in her very blue eyes.

"Girls, I don't want to argue with you. After this come in here with your shoulders covered. It's our policy." He turns his back. That's policy for you. Policy is what the kingpins want. What the others want is juvenile delinquency.

All this while, the customers had been showing up with their carts but, you know, sheep, seeing a scene, they had all bunched up on Stokesie, who shook open a paper bag as gently as peeling a peach, not wanting to miss a word. I could feel in the silence everybody getting nervous, most of all Lengel, who asks me, "Sammy, have you rung up their purchase?"

I thought and said "No" but it wasn't about that I was thinking. I go through the punches, 4, 9, GROC, TOT—it's more complicated than you think, and after you do it often enough, it begins to make a little song, that you hear words to, in my case "Hello (*bing*) there, you (*gung*) hap-py *pee*-pul (*splat*)!"—the *splat* being the drawer flying out. I uncrease the bill, tenderly as you may imagine, it just having come from between the two smoothest scoops of vanilla I had ever known were there, and pass a half and a penny into her narrow pink palm, and nestle the herrings in a bag and twist its neck and hand it over, all the time thinking.

The girls, and who'd blame them, are in a hurry to get out, so I say "I quit" to Lengel quick enough for them to hear, hoping they'll stop and watch me, their unsuspected hero. They keep right on going, into the electric eye; the door flies open and they flicker across the lot to their car, Queenie and Plaid

[4]The name of a popular comic strip of the time.

and Big Tall Goony-Goony (not that as raw material she was so bad), leaving me with Lengel and a kink in his eyebrow.

"Did you say something, Sammy?"

"I said I quit."

"I thought you did."

"You didn't have to embarrass them."

"It was they who were embarrassing us."

I started to say something that came out "Fiddle-de-doo." It's a saying of my grandmother's, and I know she would have been pleased.

"I don't think you know what you're saying," Lengel said.

"I know you don't," I said. "But I do." I pull the bow at the back of my apron and start shrugging it off my shoulders. A couple customers that had been heading for my slot begin to knock against each other, like scared pigs in a chute.

Lengel sighs and begins to look very patient and old and gray. He's been a friend of my parents for years. "Sammy, you don't want to do this to your Mom and Dad," he tells me. It's true, I don't. But it seems to me that once you begin a gesture it's fatal not to go through with it. I fold the apron, "Sammy" stitched in red on the pocket, and put it on the counter, and drop the bow tie on top of it. The bow tie is theirs, if you've ever wondered. "You'll feel this for the rest of your life," Lengel says, and I know that's true, too, but remembering how he made that pretty girl blush makes me so scrunchy inside I punch the No Sale tab and the machine whirs "pee-pul" and the drawer splats out. One advantage to this scene taking place in summer, I can follow this up with a clean exit, there's no fumbling around getting your coat and galoshes, I just saunter into the electric eye in my white shirt that my mother ironed the night before, and the door heaves itself open, and outside the sunshine is skating around on the asphalt.

I look around for my girls, but they're gone, of course. There wasn't anybody but some young married screaming with her children about some candy they didn't get by the door of a powder-blue Falcon station wagon. Looking back in the big windows, over the bags of peat moss and aluminum lawn furniture stacked on the pavement, I could see Lengel in my place in the slot, checking the sheep through. His face was dark gray and his back stiff, as if he'd just had an injection of iron, and my stomach kind of fell as I felt how hard the world was going to be to me hereafter.

1961

Philip Roth 1933–

Controversies swirl around Philip Roth and his work. He is seen as a major figure in the Jewish American school of writers (along with Bernard Malamud and Saul Bellow), but his repeated emphasis on Jews and Jewish culture in America has been questioned both by literary critics, who feel that Roth has narrowly limited his literary range, and by many members of the Jewish community, who find Roth's satirical treatment of Judaism and Jews to be superficial—even demeaning.

Like the hero of his novel Goodbye, Columbus, *Roth was born and raised in Newark, New Jersey, and attended the Newark branch of Rutgers University. Later Roth transferred to Bucknell University, where he graduated* magna cum laude *in English. He moved on to graduate study at the University of Chicago, receiving an M.A. degree but never completing his doctoral studies. His short stories began to appear in the mid-1950s, and after the publication of* Goodbye, Columbus *(1959), awards, honors, and fellowships followed in rapid succession. They include a Guggenheim fellowship, a Jewish Book Council award, a* Paris Review *award. And in 1960* Goodbye, Columbus *earned for Roth the National Book Award as the most distinguished work of fiction published in 1959. Few literary careers have begun with such immediate, widespread, positive response.*

Letting Go *(1962), a novel focusing on graduate school experiences, confirmed Roth's reputation as a writer of stature. The theme of the perils and rewards of human commitment—nearly always present in Roth's work—is central to that novel as it is to* When She Was Good *(1967), a novel of American domestic manners and one of Roth's few works not centered on the lives of American Jews. With the sensational* Portnoy's Complaint *(1969), he not only received nationwide attention (often from those who assumed that Roth was describing his own triumphs as a sexual acrobat), he also entered into a new stage: realistic novels of manners were replaced by a series of works that were highly comic, inventive, mythic, even surrealistic—but still controversial.* Portnoy's Complaint *was followed by* Our Gang *(1971), a timely but heavy-handed satire of the Nixon administration. In 1972, Roth published* The Breast, *a Kafka-like tale of a man who is transformed into a giant breast. In the next year* The Great American Novel *appeared, a "comic extravaganza" that uses baseball as a metaphor to describe much of American culture. Later works have included* My Life as a Man *(1974),* The Professor of Desire *(1977), and a collection of illuminating critical essays,* Reading Myself and Others *(1975).* Zuckerman Unbound *(1981), his autobiographical novel, tells of the trials of a writer who seeks literary distinction but whose works are read merely for their steamy carnality. Continuing the saga of his fictional counterpart, Nathan Zuckerman, Roth published* Zuckerman Bound *(1985) and* Deception *(1990), describing the remaining life, and finally the death, of Zuckerman the writer. In* Operation Shylock, A Confession *(1993), Roth's subject was once again his favorite one, a writer, the moral shadow of himself. And in* Sabbath's Theater *(1995), judged by the critics to be a "hyperintelligent" and "splendidly wicked book," Roth's protagonist is a randy con man whose main purpose in life, even in his old age, is the pursuit of sex. Roth's recent novel,* I Married a Communist, *1998, a bitter yet funny story of a man whose wife has written a corrosive book about him, draws on the details of his own tempestuous and broken marriage.*

Roth is a master of satiric and unsparing wit, exploring the comic possibilities of subjects as diverse as low-comic lust and high-minded religion. He has a highly developed talent for presenting events that are both grotesque and funny. He writes of Jews struggling in Jewish and gentile worlds that threaten to suffocate them. He satirizes America's swollen prosperity and the puzzled young men who wander confusedly amid the glut of its riches. Although his works are humorous, his view of life is often harsh. Lives are surrounded by predictable miseries. Rapture is brief. Love is blunted. Even the act of sex declines into a form of protest—against parents and propriety.

Roth is at his best in revealing the varieties of life in cities like Newark and the New York suburbs, where the poor overflow the urban centers and struggle to catch even a glimpse of beauty while the moneyed suburbanites wallow complacently in shallow materialism. It is the world that Roth dissects satirically by depicting crass parents and spoiled children, by presenting memorable scenes of vulgar display, and by revealing the anguish and confusion of true believers and puzzled doubters whose best advice is, "You should never hit anybody about God."

FURTHER READING: *A Philip Roth Reader,* 1980; J. McDaniel, *The Fiction of Philip Roth,* 1974; S. Pinsker, *The Comedy that "Hoits,"* 1975; B. Rodgers, *Philip Roth,* 1978; J. Jones and G. Nance, *Philip Roth,* 1981; *Critical Essays on Philip Roth,* ed. S. Pinsker, 1982; H. Lee, *Philip Roth,* 1982; G. Searles, *The Fiction of Philip Roth and John Updike,* 1984; *Philip Roth,* ed. H. Bloom, 1986; *Reading Philip Roth,* ed. Z. Milbauer and D. Watson, 1988, M. Baumgartner, *Understanding Philip Roth,* 1990; *Conversations with Philip Roth,* ed. G. Searles, 1992; J. Halio, *Philip Roth Revisited,* 1992; A. Appelfeld, *Beyond Despair: Three Lectures and a Conversation with Philip Roth,* 1994; A. Cooper, *Philip Roth and the Jews,* 1996; S. Wade, *The Imagination in Transit, The Fiction of Philip Roth,* 1996; S. Milowitz, *Philip Roth Considered: The Concentrationary Universe of the American Writer,* 2000; *Philip Roth,* ed. H. Bloom, 2003; M. Shechner, *Up Society's Ass: Copper, Rereading Philip Roth,* 2003; D. Shostak, *Philip Roth—Countertexts, Counterlives,* 2004; *Philip Roth's Portnoy's Complaint,* ed. H. Bloom, 2004; *Philip Roth: New Perspectives on an American Author,* ed. D. Royal, 2005.

TEXT: *Goodbye, Columbus,* 1959.

THE CONVERSION OF THE JEWS

"You're a real one for opening your mouth in the first place," Itzie said. "What do you open your mouth all the time for?"

"I didn't bring it up, Itz, I didn't," Ozzie said.

"What do you care about Jesus Christ for anyway?"

"I didn't bring up Jesus Christ. He did. I didn't even know what he was talking about. Jesus is historical, he kept saying. Jesus is historical." Ozzie mimicked the monumental voice of Rabbi Binder.

"Jesus was a person that lived like you and me," Ozzie continued. "That's what Binder said—"

"Yeah? . . . So what! What do I give two cents whether he lived or not. And what do you gotta open your mouth!" Itzie Lieberman favored closed-mouthedness, especially when it came to Ozzie Freedman's questions. Mrs. Freedman had to see Rabbi Binder twice before about Ozzie's questions and this Wednesday at four-thirty would be the third time. Itzie preferred to keep *his* mother in the kitchen; he settled for behind-the-back subtleties such as gestures, faces, snarls and other less delicate barnyard noises.

"He was a real person, Jesus, but he wasn't like God, and we don't believe he is God." Slowly, Ozzie was explaining Rabbi Binder's position to Itzie, who had been absent from Hebrew School the previous afternoon.

"The Catholics," Itzie said helpfully, "they believe in Jesus Christ, that he's God." Itzie Lieberman used "the Catholics" in its broadest sense—to include the Protestants.

Ozzie received Itzie's remark with a tiny head bob, as though it were a footnote, and went on. "His mother was Mary, and his father probably was Joseph," Ozzie said. "But the New Testament says his real father was God."

"His *real* father?"

"Yeah," Ozzie said, "that's the big thing, his father's supposed to be God."

"Bull."

"That's what Rabbi Binder says, that it's impossible—"

"Sure it's impossible. That stuff's all bull. To have a baby you gotta get laid," Itzie theologized. "Mary hadda get laid."

"That's what Binder says: 'The only way a woman can have a baby is to have intercourse with a man.'"

"He said *that,* Ozz?" For a moment it appeared that Itzie had put the theological question aside. "He said that, intercourse?" A little curled smile shaped itself in the lower half of Itzie's face like a pink mustache. "What you guys do, Ozz, you laugh or something?"

"I raised my hand."

"Yeah? Whatja say?"

"That's when I asked the question."

Itzie's face lit up. "Whatja ask about—intercourse?"

"No, I asked the question about God, how if He could create the heaven and earth in six days, and make all the animals and the fish and the light in six days—the light especially, that's what always gets me, that He could make the light. Making fish and animals, that's pretty good—"

"That's damn good." Itzie's appreciation was honest but unimaginative: it was as though God had just pitched a one-hitter.

"But making light . . . I mean when you think about it, it's really something," Ozzie said. "Anyway, I asked Binder if He could make all that in six days, and He could *pick* the six days he wanted right out of nowhere, why couldn't He let a woman have a baby without having intercourse."

"You said intercourse, Ozz, to Binder?"

"Yeah."

"Right in class?"

"Yeah."

Itzie smacked the side of his head.

"I mean, no kidding around," Ozzie said, "that'd really be nothing. After all that other stuff, that'd practically be nothing."

Itzie considered a moment. "What'd Binder say?"

"He started all over again explaining how Jesus was historical and how he lived like you and me but he wasn't God. So I said I under*stood* that. What I wanted to know was different."

What Ozzie wanted to know was always different. The first time he had wanted to know how Rabbi Binder could call the Jews "The Chosen People" if the Declaration of Independence claimed all men to be created equal. Rabbi Binder tried to distinguish for him between political equality and spiritual legitimacy, but what Ozzie wanted to know, he insisted vehemently, was different. That was the first time his mother had to come.

Then there was the plane crash. Fifty-eight people had been killed in a plane crash at La Guardia. In studying a casualty list in the newspaper his mother had discovered among the list of those dead eight Jewish names (his grandmother had nine but she counted Miller as a Jewish name); because of the eight she said the plane crash was "a tragedy." During free-discussion time on Wednesday Ozzie had brought to Rabbi Binder's attention this matter of "some of his relations" always picking out the Jewish names. Rabbi Binder had begun to explain cultural unity and some other things when Ozzie stood up at his seat and said that what he wanted to know was different. Rabbi Binder insisted that he sit down and it was then that Ozzie shouted that he wished all fifty-eight were Jews. That was the second time his mother came.

"And he kept explaining about Jesus being historical, and so I kept asking him. No kidding, Itz, he was trying to make me look stupid."

"So what he finally do?"

"Finally he starts screaming that I was deliberately simple-minded and a wise guy, and that my mother had to come, and this was the last time. And that I'd never get bar-mitzvahed[1] if he could help it. Then, Itz, then he starts talking in that voice like a statue, real slow and deep, and he says that I better think over what I said about the Lord. He told me to go to his office and think it over." Ozzie leaned his body towards Itzie. "Itz, I thought it over for a solid hour, and now I'm convinced God could do it."

Ozzie had planned to confess his latest transgression to his mother as soon as she came home from work. But it was a Friday night in November and already dark, and when Mrs. Freedman came through the door she tossed off her coat, kissed Ozzie quickly on the face, and went to the kitchen table to light the three yellow candles, two for the Sabbath and one for Ozzie's father.

When his mother lit the candles she would move her two arms slowly towards her, dragging them through the air, as though persuading people whose minds were half made up. And her eyes would get glassy with tears. Even when his father was alive Ozzie remembered that her eyes had gotten glassy, so it didn't have anything to do with his dying. It had something to do with lighting the candles.

As she touched the flaming match to the unlit wick of a Sabbath candle, the phone rang, and Ozzie, standing only a foot from it, plucked it off the receiver and held it muffled to his chest. When his mother lit candles Ozzie felt there should be no noise; even breathing, if you could manage it, should be softened. Ozzie pressed the phone to his breast and watched his mother dragging whatever she was dragging, and he felt his own eyes get glassy. His mother was a round, tired, gray-haired penguin of a woman whose gray skin had begun to feel the tug of gravity and the weight of her own history. Even when she was dressed up she looked like a chosen person. But when she lit candles she looked like something better; like a woman who knew momentarily that God could do anything.

After a few mysterious minutes she was finished. Ozzie hung up the phone and walked to the kitchen table where she was beginning to lay the two places for the four-course Sabbath meal. He told her that she would have to see Rabbi Binder next Wednesday at four-thirty, and then he told her why. For the first time in their life together she hit Ozzie across the face with her hand.

All through the chopped liver and chicken soup parts of the dinner Ozzie cried; he didn't have any appetite for the rest.

On Wednesday, in the largest of the three basement classrooms of the synagogue, Rabbi Marvin Binder, a tall, handsome, broad-shouldered man of thirty with thick strong-fibered black hair, removed his watch from his pocket and saw that it was four o'clock. At the rear of the room Yakov Blotnik, the seventy-one-year-old custodian, slowly polished the large window, mumbling

[1] I.e., he would be denied the ceremony of bar mitzvah that initiates a Jewish boy of thirteen to his religious duties.

to himself, unaware that it was four o'clock or six o'clock, Monday or Wednesday. To most of the students Yakov Blotnik's mumbling, along with his brown curly beard, scythe nose, and two heel-trailing black cats, made him an object of wonder, a foreigner, a relic, towards whom they were alternately fearful and disrespectful. To Ozzie the mumbling had always seemed a monotonous, curious prayer; what made it curious was that old Blotnik had been mumbling so steadily for so many years, Ozzie suspected he had memorized the prayers and forgotten all about God.

"It is now free-discussion time," Rabbi Binder said. "Feel free to talk about any Jewish matter at all—religion, family, politics, sports—"

There was silence. It was a gusty, clouded November afternoon and it did not seem as though there ever was or could be a thing called baseball. So nobody this week said a word about that hero from the past, Hank Greenberg[2]—which limited free discussion considerably.

And the soul-battering Ozzie Freeman had just received from Rabbi Binder had imposed its limitation. When it was Ozzie's turn to read aloud from the Hebrew book the rabbi had asked him petulantly why he didn't read more rapidly. He was showing no progress. Ozzie said he could read faster but that if he did he was sure not to understand what he was reading. Nevertheless, at the rabbi's repeated suggestion Ozzie tried, and showed a great talent, but in the midst of a long passage he stopped short and said he didn't understand a word he was reading, and started in again at a drag-footed pace. Then came the soul-battering.

Consequently when free-discussion time rolled around none of the students felt too free. The rabbi's invitation was answered only by the mumbling of feeble old Blotnik.

"Isn't there anything at all you would like to discuss?" Rabbi Binder asked again, looking at his watch. "No questions or comments?"

There was a small grumble from the third row. The rabbi requested that Ozzie rise and give the rest of the class the advantage of his thought.

Ozzie rose. "I forget it now," he said, and sat down in his place.

Rabbi Binder advanced a seat towards Ozzie and poised himself on the edge of the desk. It was Itzie's desk and the rabbi's frame only a dagger's-length away from his face snapped him to sitting attention.

"Stand up again, Oscar," Rabbi Binder said calmly, "and try to assemble your thoughts."

Ozzie stood up. All his classmates turned in their seats and watched as he gave an unconvincing scratch to his forehead.

"I can't assemble any," he announced, and plunked himself down.

"Stand up!" Rabbi Binder advanced from Itzie's desk to the one directly in front of Ozzie; when the rabbinical back was turned Itzie gave it five-fingers off the tip of his nose, causing a small titter in the room. Rabbi Binder was too absorbed in squelching Ozzie's nonsense once and for all to bother with titters. "Stand up, Oscar. What's your question about?"

Ozzie pulled a word out of the air. It was the handiest word. "Religion."

"Oh, now you remember?"

"Yes."

"What is it?"

[2]American baseball player (1911–1986).

Trapped, Ozzie blurted the first thing that came to him. "Why can't He make anything He wants to make!"

As Rabbi Binder prepared an answer, a final answer, Itzie, ten feet behind him, raised one finger on his left hand, gestured it meaningfully towards the rabbi's back, and brought the house down.

Binder twisted quickly to see what had happened and in the midst of the commotion Ozzie shouted into the rabbi's back what he couldn't have shouted to his face. It was a loud, toneless sound that had the timbre of something stored inside for about six days.

"You don't know! You don't know anything about God!"

The rabbi spun back towards Ozzie. "What?"

"You don't know—you don't—"

"Apologize, Oscar, apologize!" It was a threat.

"You don't—"

Rabbi Binder's hand flicked out at Ozzie's cheek. Perhaps it had only been meant to clamp the boy's mouth shut, but Ozzie ducked and the palm caught him squarely on the nose.

The blood came in a short, red spurt on to Ozzie's shirt front.

The next moment was all confusion. Ozzie screamed, "You bastard, you bastard!" and broke for the classroom door. Rabbi Binder lurched a step backwards, as though his own blood had started flowing violently in the opposite direction, then gave a clumsy lurch forward and bolted out the door after Ozzie. The class followed after the rabbi's huge blue-suited back, and before old Blotnik could turn from his window, the room was empty and everyone was headed full speed up the three flights leading to the roof.

If one should compare the light of day to the life of man: sunrise to birth; sunset—the dropping down over the edge—to death; then as Ozzie Freedman wiggled through the trapdoor of the synagogue roof, his feet kicking backwards bronco-style at Rabbi Binder's outstretched arms—at that moment the day was fifty years old. As a rule, fifty or fifty-five reflects accurately the age of late afternoons in November, for it is in that month, during those hours, that one's awareness of light seems no longer a matter of seeing, but of hearing: light begins clicking away. In fact, as Ozzie locked shut the trapdoor in the rabbi's face, the sharp click of the bolt into the lock might momentarily have been mistaken for the sound of the heavier gray that had just throbbed through the sky.

With all his weight Ozzie kneeled on the locked door; any instant he was certain that Rabbi Binder's shoulder would fling it open, splintering the wood into shrapnel and catapulting his body into the sky. But the door did not move and below him he heard only the rumble of feet, first loud then dim, like thunder rolling away.

A question shot through his brain. "Can this be *me?*" For a thirteen-year-old who had just labeled his religious leader a bastard, twice, it was not an improper question. Louder and louder the question came to him—"Is it me? Is it me?"—until he discovered himself no longer kneeling, but racing crazily towards the edge of the roof, his eyes crying, his throat screaming, and his arms flying everywhichway as though not his own.

"Is it me? Is it me ME ME ME ME! It has to be me—but is it!"

It is the question a thief must ask himself the night he jimmies open his first window, and it is said to be the question with which bridegrooms quiz themselves before the altar.

In the few wild seconds it took Ozzie's body to propel him to the edge of the roof, his self-examination began to grow fuzzy. Gazing down at the street, he became confused as to the problem beneath the question: was it, is-it-me-who-called-Binder-a-bastard? or, is-it-me-prancing-around-on-the-roof? However, the scene below settled all, for there is an instant in any action when whether it is you or somebody else is academic. The thief crams the money in his pockets and scoots out the window. The bridegroom signs the hotel register for two. And the boy on the roof finds a streetful of people gaping at him, necks stretched backwards, faces up, as though he were the ceiling of the Hayden Planetarium.[3] Suddenly you know it's you.

"Oscar! Oscar Freedman!" A voice rose from the center of the crowd, a voice that, could it have been seen, would have looked like the writing on a scroll. "Oscar Freedman, get down from there. Immediately!" Rabbi Binder was pointing one arm stiffly up at him; and at the end of that arm, one finger aimed menacingly. It was the attitude of a dictator, but one—the eyes confessed all—whose personal valet had spit neatly in his face.

Ozzie didn't answer. Only for a blink's length did he look towards Rabbi Binder. Instead his eyes began to fit together the world beneath him, to sort out people from places, friends from enemies, participants from spectators. In little jagged starlike clusters his friends stood around Rabbi Binder, who was still pointing. The topmost point on a star compounded not of angels but of five adolescent boys was Itzie. What a world it was, with those stars below, Rabbi Binder below . . . Ozzie, who a moment earlier hadn't been able to control his own body, started to feel the meaning of the word control: he felt Peace and he felt Power.

"Oscar Freedman, I'll give you three to come down."

Few dictators give their subjects three to do anything; but, as always, Rabbi Binder only looked dictatorial.

"Are you ready, Oscar?"

Ozzie nodded his head yes, although he had no intention in the world—the lower one or the celestial one he'd just entered—of coming down even if Rabbi Binder should give him a million.

"All right then," said Rabbi Binder. He ran a hand through his black Samson hair as though it were the gesture prescribed for uttering the first digit. Then, with his other hand cutting a circle out of the small piece of sky around him, he spoke. "One!"

There was no thunder. On the contrary, at that moment, as though "one" was the cue for which he had been waiting, the world's least thunderous person appeared on the synagogue steps. He did not so much come out the synagogue door as lean out, onto the darkening air. He clutched at the doorknob with one hand and looked up at the roof.

"Oy!"

[3]Building in New York City that houses a device that projects a representation of the heavens onto a domed ceiling for viewing by spectators.

Yakov Blotnik's old mind hobbled slowly, as if on crutches, and though he couldn't decide precisely what the boy was doing on the roof, he knew it wasn't good—that is, it wasn't-good-for-the-Jews. For Yakov Blotnik life had fractionated itself simply: things were either good-for-the-Jews or no-good-for-the-Jews.

He smacked his free hand to his in-sucked cheek, gently. "Oy, Gut!" And then quickly as he was able, he jacked down his head and surveyed the street. There was Rabbi Binder (like a man at an auction with only three dollars in his pocket, he had just delivered a shaky "Two!"); there were the students, and that was all. So far it-wasn't-so-bad-for-the-Jews. But the boy had to come down immediately, before anybody saw. The problem: how to get the boy off the roof?

Anybody who has ever had a cat on the roof knows how to get him down. You call the fire department. Or first you call the operator and you ask her for the fire department. And the next thing there is great jamming of brakes and clanging of bells and shouting of instructions. And then the cat is off the roof. You do the same thing to get a boy off the roof.

That is, you do the same thing if you are Yakov Blotnik and you once had a cat on the roof.

When the engines, all four of them, arrived, Rabbi Binder had four times given Ozzie the count of three. The big hook-and-ladder swung around the corner and one of the firemen leaped from it, plunging headlong towards the yellow fire hydrant in front of the synagogue. With a huge wrench he began to unscrew the top nozzle. Rabbi Binder raced over to him and pulled at his shoulder.

"There's no fire . . ."

The fireman mumbled back over his shoulder and, heatedly, continued working at the nozzle.

"But there's no fire, there's no fire . . ." Binder shouted. When the fireman mumbled again, the rabbi grasped his face with both hands and pointed it up at the roof.

To Ozzie it looked as though Rabbi Binder was trying to tug the fireman's head out of his body, like a cork from a bottle. He had to giggle at the picture they made: it was a family portrait—rabbi in black skullcap, fireman in red fire hat, and the little yellow hydrant squatting beside like a kid brother, bareheaded. From the edge of the roof Ozzie waved at the portrait, a one-handed, flapping, mocking wave; in doing it his right foot slipped from under him. Rabbi Binder covered his eyes with his hands.

Firemen work fast. Before Ozzie had even regained his balance, a big, round, yellowed net was being held on the synagogue lawn. The firemen who held it looked up at Ozzie with stern, feelingless faces.

One of the firemen turned his head towards Rabbi Binder. "What, is the kid nuts or something?"

Rabbi Binder unpeeled his hands from his eyes, slowly, painfully, as if they were tape. Then he checked: nothing on the sidewalk, no dents in the net.

"Is he gonna jump, or what?" the fireman shouted.

In a voice not at all like a statue, Rabbi Binder finally answered. "Yes. Yes, I think so . . . He's been threatening to . . ."

Threatening to? Why, the reason he was on the roof, Ozzie remembered, was to get away; he hadn't even thought about jumping. He had just run to get away, and the truth was that he hadn't really headed for the roof as much as he'd been chased there.

"What's his name, the kid?"

"Freedman," Rabbi Binder answered. "Oscar Freedman."

The fireman looked up at Ozzie. "What is it with you, Oscar? You gonna jump, or what?"

Ozzie did not answer. Frankly, the question had just arisen.

"Look, Oscar, if you're gonna jump, jump—and if you're not gonna jump, don't jump. But don't waste our time, willya?"

Ozzie looked at the fireman and then at Rabbi Binder. He wanted to see Rabbi Binder cover his eyes one more time.

"I'm going to jump."

And then he scampered around the edge of the roof to the corner, where there was no net below, and he flapped his arms at his sides, swishing the air and smacking his palms to his trousers on the downbeat. He began screaming like some kind of engine,"Wheeeee . . . wheeeeee," and leaning way out over the edge with the upper half of his body. The firemen whipped around to cover the ground with the net. Rabbi Binder mumbled a few words to somebody and covered his eyes. Everything happened quickly, jerkily, as in a silent movie. The crowd, which had arrived with the fire engines, gave out a long, Fourth-of-July fireworks oooh-aahhh. In the excitement no one had paid the crowd much heed, except, of course, Yakov Blotnik, who swung from the doorknob counting heads. "Fier und tsvansik . . . finf und tsvantsik[4] . . . Oy, Gut!" It wasn't like this with the cat.

Rabbi Binder peeked through his fingers, checked the sidewalk and net. Empty. But there was Ozzie racing to the other corner. The firemen raced with him but were unable to keep up. Whenever Ozzie wanted to he might jump and splatter himself on the sidewalk, and by the time the firemen scooted to the spot all they could do with their net would be to cover the mess.

"Wheeeee . . . wheeeee . . ."

"Hey, Oscar," the winded fireman yelled. "What the hell is this, a game or something?"

"Wheeeee . . . wheeeee . . ."

"Hey, Oscar—"

But he was off now to the other corner, flapping his wings fiercely. Rabbi Binder couldn't take it any longer—the fire engines from nowhere, the screaming suicidal boy, the net. He fell to his knees, exhausted, and with his hands curled together in front of his chest like a little dome, he pleaded, "Oscar, stop it, Oscar. Don't jump, Oscar. Please come down . . . Please don't jump."

And further back in the crowd a single voice, a single young voice, shouted a lone word to the boy on the roof.

"Jump!"

It was Itzie. Ozzie momentarily stopped flapping.

"Go ahead, Ozz—jump!" Itzie broke off his point of the star and courageously, with the inspiration not of a wise-guy but of a disciple, stood alone. "Jump, Ozz, jump!"

[4]Yiddish: twenty-four . . . twenty-five.

Still on his knees, his hands still curled, Rabbi Binder twisted his body back. He looked at Itzie, then, agonizingly, back to Ozzie.

"OSCAR, DON'T JUMP! PLEASE, DON'T JUMP . . . please please . . ."

"Jump!" This time it wasn't Itzie but another point of the star. By the time Mrs. Freedman arrived to keep her four-thirty appointment with Rabbi Binder, the whole little upside down heaven was shouting and pleading for Ozzie to jump, and Rabbi Binder no longer was pleading with him not to jump, but was crying into the dome of his hands.

Understandably Mrs. Freedman couldn't figure out what her son was doing on the roof. So she asked.

"Ozzie, my Ozzie, what are you doing? My Ozzie, what is it?"

Ozzie stopped wheeeeeing and slowed his arms down to a cruising flap, the kind birds use in soft winds, but he did not answer. He stood against the low, clouded, darkening sky—light clicked down swiftly now, as on a small gear—flapping softly and gazing down at the small bundle of a woman who was his mother.

"What are you doing, Ozzie?" She turned towards the kneeling Rabbi Binder and rushed so close that only a paper-thickness of dusk lay between her stomach and his shoulders.

"What is my baby doing?"

Rabbi Binder gaped at her but he too was mute. All that moved was the dome of his hands; it shook back and forth like a weak pulse.

"Rabbi, get him down! He'll kill himself. Get him down, my only baby . . ."

"I can't," Rabbi Binder said, "I can't . . ." and he turned his handsome head towards the crowd of boys behind him. "It's them. Listen to them."

And for the first time Mrs. Freedman saw the crowd of boys, and she heard what they were yelling.

"He's doing it for them. He won't listen to me. It's them." Rabbi Binder spoke like one in a trance.

"For them?"

"Yes."

"Why for them?"

"They want him to . . ."

Mrs. Freedman raised her two arms upward as though she were conducting the sky. "For them he's doing it!" And then in a gesture older than pyramids, older than prophets and floods, her arms came slapping down to her sides. "A martyr I have. Look!" She tilted her head to the roof. Ozzie was still flapping softly. "My martyr."

"Oscar, come down, *please,*" Rabbi Binder groaned.

In a startling even voice Mrs. Freedman called to the boy on the roof. "Ozzie, come down, Ozzie. Don't be a martyr."

"Gawhead, Ozz—*be* a Martin!" It was Itzie. "Be a Martin, be a Martin," and all the voices joined in singing for Martindom, whatever *it* was. "Be a Martin, be a Martin . . ."

Somehow when you're on a roof the darker it gets the less you can hear. All Ozzie knew was that two groups wanted two new things: his friends were spirited and musical about what they wanted; his mother and the rabbi were even-toned, chanting, about what they didn't want. The rabbi's voice was without tears now and so was his mother's.

The big net stared up at Ozzie like a sightless eye. The big, clouded sky pushed down. From beneath it looked like a gray corrugated board. Suddenly, looking up into that unsympathetic sky, Ozzie realized all the strangeness of what these people, his friends, were asking: they wanted him to jump, to kill himself; they were singing about it now—it made them that happy. And there was an even greater strangeness: Rabbi Binder was on his knees, trembling. If there was a question to be asked now it was not "Is it me?" but rather "Is it us? . . . Is it us?"

Being on the roof, it turned out, was a serious thing. If he jumped would the singing become dancing? Would it? What would jumping stop? Yearningly, Ozzie wished he could rip open the sky, plunge his hands through, and pull out the sun; and on the sun, like a coin, would be stamped Jump or Don't Jump.

Ozzie's knees rocked and sagged a little under him as though they were setting him for a dive. His arms tightened, stiffened, froze, from shoulders to fingernails. He felt as if each part of his body were going to vote as to whether he should kill himself or not—and each part as though it were independent of *him.*

The light took an unexpected click down and the new darkness, like a gag, hushed the friends singing for this and the mother and rabbi chanting for that.

Ozzie stopped counting votes, and in a curiously high voice, like one who wasn't prepared for speech, he spoke.

"Mamma?"

"Yes, Oscar."

"Mamma, get down on your knees, like Rabbi Binder."

"Oscar—"

"Get down on your knees," he said, "or I'll jump."

Ozzie heard a whimper, then a quick rustling, and when he looked down where his mother had stood he saw the top of a head beneath that circle of dress. She was kneeling beside Rabbi Binder.

He spoke again. "Everybody kneel." There was the sound of everybody kneeling.

Ozzie looked around. With one hand he pointed towards the synagogue entrance. "Make *him* kneel."

There was a noise, not of kneeling, but of body-and-cloth stretching. Ozzie could hear Rabbi Binder saying in a gruff whisper, ". . . or he'll *kill* himself," and when next he looked there was Yakov Blotnik off the doorknob and for the first time in his life upon his knees in the Gentile posture of prayer.

As for the firemen—it is not as difficult as one might imagine to hold a net taut while you are kneeling.

Ozzie looked around again; and then he called to Rabbi Binder.

"Rabbi?"

"Yes, Oscar."

"Rabbi Binder, do you believe in God?"

"Yes."

"Do you believe God can do Anything?" Ozzie leaned his head out into the darkness. "Anything?"

"Oscar, I think—"

"Tell me you believe God can do Anything."

There was a second's hesitation. Then: "God can do Anything."

"Tell me you believe God can make a child without intercourse."

"He can."

"Tell me!"

"God," Rabbi Binder admitted, "can make a child without intercourse."

"Mamma, you tell me."

"God can make a child without intercourse," his mother said.

"Make *him* tell me." There was no doubt who *him* was.

In a few moments Ozzie heard an old comical voice say something to the increasing darkness about God.

Next, Ozzie made everybody say it. And then he made them all say they believed in Jesus Christ—first one at a time, then all together.

When the catechizing was through it was the beginning of evening. From the street it sounded as if the boy on the roof might have sighed.

"Ozzie?" A woman's voice dared to speak. "You'll come down now?"

There was no answer, but the woman waited, and when a voice finally did speak it was thin and crying, and exhausted as that of an old man who has just finished pulling the bells.

"Mamma, don't you see—you shouldn't hit me. He shouldn't hit me. You shouldn't hit me about God, Mamma. You should never hit anybody about God—"

"Ozzie, please come down now."

"Promise me, promise me you'll never hit anybody about God."

He had asked only his mother, but for some reason everyone kneeling in the street promised he would never hit anybody about God.

Once again there was silence.

"I can come down now, Mamma," the boy on the roof finally said. He turned his head both ways as though checking the traffic lights. "Now I can come down . . ."

And he did, right into the center of the yellow net that glowed in the evening's edge like an overgrown halo.

1959

Bernard Malamud 1914–1986

Bernard Malamud was a recorder of the Jewish experience, with all its despair, possibility, and hope for redemption. He was born in Brooklyn, the son of Russian immigrant parents. After graduating from the City College of New York in 1936, he attended Columbia University, from which he received an M.A. in 1942. He taught in a high school and then at Oregon State University from 1949 to 1961. While there he published The Natural *(1952), a comic novel that ironically mythologizes the American passion for "the national pastime," baseball. In 1957 he published* The Assistant, *a tragi-comedy of a young Italian American living in the midst of a Jewish family, which many critics consider to be his most successful novel.* The Magic Barrel *(1958), a collection of short stories for which he received a National Book Award, similarly reveals the tragedy and comedy inherent in human life. In* A New Life *(1961), one of Malamud's bestselling works, he concentrated on the spiritual rebirth of a comically suffering and despairing English teacher trapped in an academic wilderness.*

In 1963 Malamud published Idiots First, *a collection of short stories that was followed by* The Fixer *(1966), a parable of the plight of Russian Jews. In* Pictures of Fidelman *(1969), he presented a comic novel of a painter who travels to Europe and tries his hand at art criticism, imitation, forgery, and creation.* The Tenants *(1971) depicts the life of a middle-aged man living in a run-down tenement house and struggling to find mercy in a hostile world. In 1979, Malamud published his seventh and most ambitious novel,* Dubin's Lives, *a story of marriage and infidelity. The novel's hero, an aging writer, seeks rejuvenation and escape from a stale world. He finds, instead, a portion of the moral insight that can be gained from painful experience.*

Malamud's works often display the search for meaning made by a bereft, bewildered wanderer who yearns, but fails, to find the secret of life and happiness. Malamud revealed the relationships of comedy and terror, failure and success, weakness and courage; and he presented the individual as an emblem of modern humanity, confused, clinging to shattered dreams, and struggling for love and self-understanding in the midst of folly and threatening doom.

FURTHER READING: J. Helterman, *Understanding Bernard Malamud,* 1985; *Bernard Malamud,* ed. H. Bloom, 1986; *Critical Essays on Bernard Malamud,* ed. J. Salzberg, 1987; K. Ochshorn, *The Heart's Essential Landscape: Bernard Malamud's Hero,* 1990; *Conversations with Bernard Malamud,* ed. L. Lasher, 1991; E. Abramson, *Bernard Malamud Revisited,* 1993; *Talking Horse: Bernard Malamud on Life and Work,* ed. A. Cheuse and N. Delbanco, 1996; *The Complete Stories,* ed. R. Giroux, 1997; B. Sío-Castiñeira, *The Short Stories of Bernard Malamud: in Search of Jewish Post-Immigrant Identity,* 1998; M. Shaw, *Ethnic Identities in Bernard Malamud's Fiction,* 2000; J. Smith, *My Father Is a Book: A Memoir of Bernard Malamud,* 2006.

TEXT: *The Magic Barrel,* 1958.

THE MAGIC BARREL

Not long ago there lived in uptown New York, in a small, almost meager room, though crowded with books, Leo Finkle, a rabbinical student in the Yeshivah University. Finkle, after six years of study, was to be ordained in June and had been advised by an acquaintance that he might find it easier to win himself a congregation if he were married. Since he had no present prospects of marriage, after two tormented days of turning it over in his mind, he called in Pinye Salzman, a marriage broker whose two-line advertisement he had read in the *Forward.*[1]

The matchmaker appeared one night out of the dark fourth-floor hallway of the graystone rooming house where Finkle lived, grasping a black, strapped portfolio that had been worn thin with use. Salzman, who had been long in the business, was of slight but dignified build, wearing an old hat, and an overcoat too short and tight for him. He smelled frankly of fish, which he loved to eat, and although he was missing a few teeth, his presence was not displeasing, because of an amiable manner curiously contrasted with mournful eyes. His voice, his lips, his wisp of beard, his bony fingers were animated, but give him

[1] *The Jewish Daily Forward,* Yiddish newspaper in New York City.

a moment of repose and his mild blue eyes revealed a depth of sadness, a characteristic that put Leo a little at ease although the situation, for him, was inherently tense.

He at once informed Salzman why he had asked him to come, explaining that his home was in Cleveland, and that but for his parents, who had married comparatively late in life, he was alone in the world. He had for six years devoted himself almost entirely to his studies, as a result of which, understandably, he had found himself without time for a social life and the company of young women. Therefore he thought it the better part of trial and error—of embarrassing fumbling—to call in an experienced person to advise him on these matters. He remarked in passing that the function of the marriage broker was ancient and honorable, highly approved in the Jewish community, because it made practical the necessary without hindering joy. Moreover, his own parents had been brought together by a matchmaker. They had made, if not a financially profitable marriage—since neither had possessed any worldly goods to speak of—at least a successful one in the sense of their everlasting devotion to each other. Salzman listened in embarrassed surprise, sensing a sort of apology. Later, however, he experienced a glow of pride in his work, an emotion that had left him years ago, and he heartily approved of Finkle.

The two went to their business. Leo had led Salzman to the only clear place in the room, a table near a window that overlooked the lamp-lit city. He seated himself at the matchmaker's side but facing him, attempting by an act of will to suppress the unpleasant tickle in his throat. Salzman eagerly unstrapped his portfolio and removed a loose rubber band from a thin packet of much-handled cards. As he flipped through them, a gesture and sound that physically hurt Leo, the student pretended not to see and gazed steadfastly out the window. Although it was still February, winter was on its last legs, signs of which he had for the first time in years begun to notice. He now observed the round white moon, moving high in the sky through a cloud menagerie, and watched with half-open mouth as it penetrated a huge hen, and dropped out of her like an egg laying itself. Salzman, though pretending through eyeglasses he had just slipped on, to be engaged in scanning the writing on the cards, stole occasional glances at the young man's distinguished face, noting with pleasure the long, severe scholar's nose, brown eyes heavy with learning, sensitive yet ascetic lips, and a certain, almost hollow quality of the dark cheeks. He gazed around at shelves upon shelves of books and let out a soft, contented sigh.

When Leo's eyes fell upon the cards, he counted six spread out in Salzman's hand.

"So few?" he asked in disappointment.

"You wouldn't believe me how much cards I got in my office," Salzman replied. "The drawers are already filled to the top, so I keep them now in a barrel, but is every girl good for a new rabbi?"

Leo blushed at this, regretting all he had revealed of himself in a curriculum vitae he had sent to Salzman. He had thought it best to acquaint him with his strict standards and specifications, but in having done so, he felt he had told the marriage broker more than was absolutely necessary.

He hesitantly inquired, "Do you keep photographs of your clients on file?"

"First comes family, amount of dowry, also what kind promises," Salzman replied, unbuttoning his tight coat and settling himself in the chair. "After comes pictures, rabbi."

"Call me Mr. Finkle. I'm not yet a rabbi."

Salzman said he would, but instead called him doctor, which he changed to rabbi when Leo was not listening too attentively.

Salzman adjusted his horn-rimmed spectacles, gently cleared his throat and read in an eager voice the contents of the top card:

"Sophie P. Twenty four years. Widow one year. No children. Educated high school and two years college. Father promises eight thousand dollars. Has wonderful wholesale business. Also real estate. On the mother's side comes teachers, also one actor. Well known on Second Avenue."

Leo gazed up in surprise. "Did you say a widow?"

"A widow don't mean spoiled, rabbi. She lived with her husband maybe four months. He was a sick boy she made a mistake to marry him."

"Marrying a widow has never entered my mind."

"This is because you have no experience. A widow, especially if she is young and healthy like this girl, is a wonderful person to marry. She will be thankful to you the rest of her life. Believe me, if I was looking now for a bride, I would marry a widow."

Leo reflected, then shook his head.

Salzman hunched his shoulders in an almost imperceptible gesture of disappointment. He placed the card down on the wooden table and began to read another:

"Lily H. High school teacher. Regular. Not a substitute. Has savings and new Dodge car. Lived in Paris one year. Father is successful dentist thirty-five years. Interested in professional man. Well Americanized family. Wonderful opportunity."

"I knew her personally," said Salzman. "I wish you could see this girl. She is a doll. Also very intelligent. All day you could talk to her about books and theater and what not. She also knows current events."

"I don't believe you mentioned her age?"

"Her age?" Salzman said, raising his brows. "Her age is thirty-two years."

Leo said after a while, "I'm afraid that seems a little too old."

Salzman let out a laugh. "So how old are you, rabbi?"

"Twenty-seven."

"So what is the difference, tell me, between twenty-seven and thirty-two? My own wife is seven years older than me. So what did I suffer?—Nothing. If Rothschild's daughter wants to marry you, would you say on account of her age, no?"

"Yes," Leo said dryly.

Salzman shook off the no in the yes. "Five years don't mean a thing. I give you my word that when you will live with her for one week you will forget her age. What does it mean five years—that she lived more and knows more than somebody who is younger? On this girl, God bless her, years are not wasted. Each one that it comes makes better the bargain."

"What subject does she teach in high school?"

"Languages. If you heard the way she speaks French, you will think it is music. I am in the business twenty-five years, and I recommend her with my whole heart. Believe me, I know what I'm talking, rabbi."

"What's on the next card?" Leo said abruptly.

Salzman reluctantly turned up the third card:

"Ruth K. Nineteen years. Honor student. Father offers thirteen thousand cash to the right bridegroom. He is a medical doctor. Stomach specialist with marvelous practice. Brother in law owns own garment business. Particular people."

Salzman looked as if he had read his trump card.

"Did you say nineteen?" Leo asked with interest.

"On the dot."

"Is she attractive?" He blushed. "Pretty?"

Salzman kissed his finger tips. "A little doll. On this I give my word. Let me call the father tonight and you will see what means pretty."

But Leo was troubled. "You're sure she's that young?"

"This I am positive. The father will show you the birth certificate."

"Are you positive there isn't something wrong with her?" Leo insisted.

"Who says there is wrong?"

"I don't understand why an American girl her age should go to a marriage broker."

A smile spread over Salzman's face.

"So for the same reason you went, she comes."

Leo flushed. "I am pressed for time."

Salzman, realizing he had been tactless, quickly explained. "The father came, not her. He wants she should have the best, so he looks around himself. When we will locate the right boy he will introduce him and encourage. This makes a better marriage than if a young girl without experience takes for herself. I don't have to tell you this."

"But don't you think this young girl believes in love?" Leo spoke uneasily.

Salzman was about to guffaw but caught himself and said soberly, "Love comes with the right person, not before."

Leo parted dry lips but did not speak. Noticing that Salzman had snatched a glance at the next card, he cleverly asked, "How is her health?"

"Perfect," Salzman said, breathing with difficulty. "Of course, she is a little lame on her right foot from an auto accident that it happened to her when she was twelve years, but nobody notices on account she is so brilliant and also beautiful."

Leo got up heavily and went to the window. He felt curiously bitter and upbraided himself for having called in the marriage broker. Finally, he shook his head.

"Why not?" Salzman persisted, the pitch of his voice rising.

"Because I detest stomach specialists."

"So what do you care what is his business? After you marry her do you need him? Who says he must come every Friday night in your house?"

Ashamed of the way the talk was going, Leo dismissed Salzman, who went home with heavy, melancholy eyes.

Though he had felt only relief at the marriage broker's departure, Leo was in low spirits the next day. He explained it as arising from Salzman's failure to produce a suitable bride for him. He did not care for his type of clientele. But when Leo found himself hesitating whether to seek out another matchmaker, one more polished than Pinye, he wondered if it could be—his protestations to the contrary, and although he honored his father and mother—that he did not, in essence, care for the match-making institution? This thought he quickly put out of mind yet found himself still upset. All day he ran around in the woods—missed an important appointment, forgot to give out his laundry, walked out of a Broadway cafeteria without paying and had to run back with the ticket in his hand; had even not recognized his landlady in the street when she passed with a friend and courteously called out, "A good evening to you, Doctor Finkle." By nightfall, however, he had regained sufficient calm to sink his nose into a book and there found peace from his thoughts.

Almost at once there came a knock on the door. Before Leo could say enter, Salzman, commercial cupid, was standing in the room. His face was gray and meager, his expression hungry, and he looked as if he would expire on his feet. Yet the marriage broker managed, by some trick of the muscles, to display a broad smile.

"So good evening. I am invited?"

Leo nodded, disturbed to see him again, yet unwilling to ask the man to leave.

Beaming still, Salzman laid his portfolio on the table. "Rabbi, I got for you tonight good news."

"I've asked you not to call me rabbi. I'm still a student."

"Your worries are finished. I have for you a first-class bride."

"Leave me in peace concerning this subject." Leo pretended lack of interest.

"The world will dance at your wedding."

"Please, Mr. Salzman, no more."

"But first must come back my strength," Salzman said weakly. He fumbled with the portfolio straps and took out of the leather case an oily paper bag, from which he extracted a hard, seeded roll and a small, smoked white fish. With a quick motion of his hand he stripped the fish out of its skin and began ravenously to chew. "All day in a rush," he muttered.

Leo watched him eat.

"A sliced tomato you have maybe?" Salzman hesitantly inquired.

"No."

The marriage broker shut his eyes and ate. When he had finished he carefully cleaned up the crumbs and rolled up the remains of the fish, in the paper bag. His spectacled eyes roamed the room until he discovered, amid some piles of books, a one-burner gas stove. Lifting his hat he humbly asked, "A glass tea you got, rabbi?"

Conscience-stricken, Leo rose and brewed the tea. He served it with a chunk of lemon and two cubes of lump sugar, delighting Salzman.

After he had drunk his tea, Salzman's strength and good spirits were restored.

"So tell me, rabbi," he said amiably, "you considered some more the three clients I mentioned yesterday?"

"There was no need to consider."

"Why not?"

"None of them suits me."

"What then suits you?"

Leo let it pass because he could give only a confused answer.

Without waiting for a reply, Salzman asked, "You remember this girl I talked to you—the high school teacher?"

"Age thirty-two?"

But, surprisingly, Salzman's face lit in a smile. "Age twenty-nine."

Leo shot him a look. "Reduced from thirty-two?"

"A mistake," Salzman avowed. "I talked today with the dentist. He took me to his safety deposit box and showed me the birth certificate. She was twenty-nine years last August. They made her a party in the mountains where she went for her vacation. When her father spoke to me the first time I forgot to write the age and I told you thirty-two, but now I remember this was a different client, a widow."

"The same one you told me about? I thought she was twenty-four?"

"A different. Am I responsible that the world is filled with widows?"

"No, but I'm not interested in them, nor for that matter, in school teachers."

Salzman pulled his clasped hands to his breast. Looking at the ceiling he devoutly exclaimed, "Yiddishe kinder,[2] what can I say to somebody that he is not interested in high school teachers? So what then you are interested?"

Leo flushed but controlled himself.

"In what else will you be interested," Salzman went on, "if you not interested in this fine girl that she speaks four languages and has personally in the bank ten thousand dollars? Also her father guarantees further twelve thousand. Also she has a new car, wonderful clothes, talks on all subjects, and she will give you a first-class home and children. How near do we come in our life to paradise?"

"If she's so wonderful, why wasn't she married ten years ago?"

"Why?" said Salzman with a heavy laugh. "—Why? Because she is *partikiler.* This is why. She wants the *best.*"

Leo was silent, amused at how he had entangled himself. But Salzman had aroused his interest in Lily H., and he began seriously to consider calling on her. When the marriage broker observed how intently Leo's mind was at work on the facts he had supplied, he felt certain they would soon come to an agreement.

Late Saturday afternoon, conscious of Salzman, Leo Finkle walked with Lily Hirschorn along Riverside Drive. He walked briskly and erectly, wearing with distinction the black fedora that he had that morning taken with trepidation out of the dusty hat box on his closet shelf, and the heavy black Saturday coat he had thoroughly whisked clean. Leo also owned a walking stick, a present from a distant relative, but quickly put temptation aside and did not use it. Lily, petite and not unpretty, had on something signifying the approach of spring. She was au courant,[3] animatedly, with all sorts of subjects, and he weighed her words and found her surprisingly sound—score another for Salzman, whom he uneasily sensed to be somewhere around, hiding perhaps high in a tree along the street, flashing the lady signals with a pocket mirror; or perhaps a cloven-hoofed Pan, piping nuptial ditties as he danced his invisible way before them, strewing wild buds on the walk and purple grapes in their path, symbolizing fruit of a union, though there was of course still none.

Lily startled Leo by remarking, "I was thinking of Mr. Salzman, a curious figure, wouldn't you say?"

Not certain what to answer, he nodded.

She bravely went on, blushing, "I for one am grateful for his introducing us. Aren't you?"

[2]Yiddish: Yiddish children. [3]Informed, up-to-date.

He courteously replied, "I am."

"I mean," she said with a little laugh—and it was all in good taste, or at least gave the effect of being not in bad—"do you mind that we came together so?"

He was not displeased with her honesty, recognizing that she meant to set the relationship aright, and understanding that it took a certain amount of experience in life, and courage, to want to do it quite that way. One had to have some sort of past to make that kind of beginning.

He said that he did not mind. Salzman's function was traditional and honorable—valuable for what it might achieve, which, he pointed out, was frequently nothing.

Lily agreed with a sigh. They walked on for a while and she said after a long silence, again with a nervous laugh, "Would you mind if I asked you something a little bit personal? Frankly, I find the subject fascinating." Although Leo shrugged, she went on half embarrassedly, "How was it that you came to your calling? I mean was it a sudden passionate inspiration?"

Leo, after a time, slowly replied, "I was always interested in the Law."

"You saw revealed in it the presence of the Highest?"

He nodded and changed the subject. "I understand that you spent a little time in Paris, Miss Hirschorn?"

"Oh, did Mr. Salzman tell you, Rabbi Finkle?" Leo winced but she went on, "It was ages ago and almost forgotten. I remember I had to return for my sister's wedding."

And Lily would not be put off. "When," she asked in a trembly voice, "did you become enamored of God?"

He stared at her. Then it came to him that she was talking not about Leo Finkle, but of a total stranger, some mystical figure, perhaps even passionate prophet that Salzman had dreamed up for her—no relation to the living or dead. Leo trembled with rage and weakness. The trickster had obviously sold her a bill of goods, just as he had him, who'd expected to become acquainted with a young lady of twenty-nine, only to behold, the moment he laid eyes upon her strained and anxious face, a woman past thirty-five and aging rapidly. Only his self control had kept him this long in her presence.

"I am not," he said gravely, "a talented religious person," and in seeking words to go on, found himself possessed by shame and fear. "I think," he said in a strained manner, "that I came to God not because I loved Him, but because I did not."

This confession he spoke harshly because its unexpectedness shook him.

Lily wilted. Leo saw a profusion of loaves of bread go flying like ducks high over his head, not unlike the winged loaves by which he had counted himself to sleep last night. Mercifully, then, it snowed, which he would not put past Salzman's machinations.

He was infuriated with the marriage broker and swore he would throw him out of the room the minute he reappeared. But Salzman did not come that night, and when Leo's anger had subsided, an unaccountable despair grew in its place. At first he thought this was caused by his disappointment in Lily, but before long it became evident that he had involved himself with Salzman without a true knowledge of his own intent. He gradually realized—with an emptiness that seized him with six hands—that he had called in the broker to find him a bride because he was incapable of doing it himself. This terrifying insight he had derived as a result of his meeting and conversation with Lily Hirschorn. Her probing questions had somehow irritated him into revealing—to himself more than her—the true nature of his relationship to God, and from that it had come upon him, with shocking force, that apart from his parents, he had never loved anyone. Or perhaps it went the other way, that he did not love God so well as he might, because he had not loved man. It seemed to Leo that his whole life stood starkly revealed and he saw himself for the first time as he truly was—unloved and loveless. This bitter but somehow not fully unexpected revelation brought him to a point of panic controlled only by extraordinary effort. He covered his face with his hands and cried.

The week that followed was the worst of his life. He did not eat and lost weight. His beard darkened and grew ragged. He stopped attending seminars and almost never opened a book. He seriously considered leaving the Yeshivah, although he was deeply troubled at the thought of the loss of all his years of study—saw them like pages torn from a book, strewn over the city—and at the devastating effect of this decision upon his parents. But he had lived without knowledge of himself, and never in the Five Books and all the Commentaries—mea culpa[4]—had the truth been revealed to him. He did not know where to turn, and in all this desolating loneliness there was no *to whom,* although he often thought of Lily but not once could bring himself to go downstairs and make the call. He became touchy and irritable, especially with his landlady, who asked him all manner of personal questions; on the other hand, sensing his own disagreeableness, he waylaid her on the stairs and apologized abjectly, until mortified, she ran from him. Out of this, however, he drew the consolation that he was a Jew and that a Jew suffered. But gradually, as the long and terrible week drew to a close, he regained his composure and some idea of purpose in life: to go on as planned. Although he was imperfect, the ideal was not. As for his quest of a bride, the thought of continuing afflicted him with anxiety and heartburn, yet perhaps with this new knowledge of himself he would be more successful than in the past. Perhaps love would now come to him and a bride to that love. And for this sanctified seeking who needed a Salzman?

The marriage broker, a skeleton with haunted eyes, returned that very night. He looked, withal, the picture of frustrated expectancy—as if he had steadfastly waited the week at Miss Lily Hirschorn's side for a telephone call that never came.

Casually coughing, Salzman came immediately to the point: "So how did you like her?"

Leo's anger rose and he could not refrain from chiding the matchmaker: "Why did you lie to me, Salzman?"

Salzman's pale face went dead white, the world had snowed on him.

"Did you not state that she was twenty-nine?" Leo insisted.

"I gave you my word—"

"She was thirty-five, if a day. *At least* thirty-five."

"Of this don't be too sure. Her father told me—"

"Never mind. The worst of it was that you lied to her."

"How did I lie to her, tell me?"

[4]Latin: my fault, a ritual phrase traditionally spoken by those confessing their sins.

"You told her things about me that weren't true. You made me out to be more, consequently less than I am. She had in mind a totally different person, a sort of semimystical Wonder Rabbi."

"All I said, you was a religious man."

"I can imagine."

Salzman sighed. "This is my weakness that I have," he confessed. "My wife says to me I shouldn't be a salesman, but when I have two fine people that they would be wonderful to be married, I am so happy that I talk too much." He smiled wanly. "This is why Salzman is a poor man."

Leo's anger left him. "Well, Salzman, I'm afraid that's all."

The marriage broker fastened hungry eyes on him.

"You don't want any more a bride?"

"I do," said Leo, "but I have decided to seek her in a different way. I am no longer interested in an arranged marriage. To be frank, I now admit the necessity of premarital love. That is, I want to be in love with the one I marry."

"Love?" said Salzman, astounded. After a moment he remarked "For us, our love is our life, not for the ladies. In the ghetto they—"

"I know, I know," said Leo. "I've thought of it often. Love, I have said to myself, should be a by-product of living and worship rather than its own end. Yet for myself I find it necessary to establish the level of my need and fulfill it."

Salzman shrugged but answered, "Listen, rabbi, if you want love, this I can find for you also. I have such beautiful clients that you will love them the minute your eyes will see them."

Leo smiled unhappily. "I'm afraid you don't understand."

But Salzman hastily unstrapped his portfolio and withdrew a manila packet from it.

"Pictures," he said, quickly laying the envelope on the table.

Leo called after him to take the pictures away, but as if on the wings of the wind, Salzman had disappeared.

March came. Leo had returned to his regular routine. Although he felt not quite himself yet—lacked energy—he was making plans for a more active social life. Of course it would cost something, but he was an expert in cutting corners; and when there were no corners left he would make circles rounder. All the while Salzman's pictures had lain on the table, gathering dust. Occasionally as Leo sat studying, or enjoying a cup of tea, his eyes fell on the manila envelope, but he never opened it.

The days went by and no social life to speak of developed with a member of the opposite sex—it was difficult, given the circumstances of his situation. One morning Leo toiled up the stairs to his room and stared out the window at the city. Although the day was bright his view of it was dark. For some time he watched the people in the street below hurrying along and then turned with a heavy heart to his little room. On the table was the packet. With a sudden relentless gesture he tore it open. For a half-hour he stood by the table in a state of excitement, examining the photographs of the ladies Salzman had included. Finally, with a deep sigh he put them down. There were six, of varying degrees of attractiveness, but look at them long enough and they all became Lily Hirschorn; all past their prime, all starved behind bright smiles, not a true personality in the lot. Life, despite their frantic yoohooings, had passed them by; they were pictures in a brief case that stunk of fish. After a while, however, as Leo attempted to return the photographs into the envelope, he found in it another, a snapshot of the type taken by a machine for a quarter. He gazed at it a moment and let out a cry.

Her face deeply moved him. Why, he could at first not say. It gave him the impression of youth—spring flowers, yet age—a sense of having been used to the bone, wasted; this came from the eyes, which were hauntingly familiar, yet absolutely strange. He had a vivid impression that he had met her before, but try as he might he could not place her although he could almost recall her name, as if he had read it in her own handwriting. No, this couldn't be; he would have remembered her. It was not, he affirmed, that she had an extraordinary beauty—no, though her face was attractive enough; it was that *something* about her moved him. Feature for feature, even some of the ladies of the photographs could do better; but she leaped forth to his heart—had *lived,* or wanted to—more than just wanted, perhaps regretted how she had lived—had somehow deeply suffered: it could be seen in the depths of those reluctant eyes, and from the way the light enclosed and shone from her, and within her, opening realms of possibility: this was her own. Her he desired. His head ached and eyes narrowed with the intensity of his gazing, then as if an obscure fog had blown up in the mind, he experienced fear of her and was aware that he had received an impression, somehow, of evil. He shuddered, saying softly, it is thus with us all. Leo brewed some tea in a small pot and sat sipping it without sugar, to calm himself. But before he had finished drinking, again with excitement he examined the face and found it good: good for Leo Finkle. Only such a one could understand him and help him seek whatever he was seeking. She might, perhaps, love him. How she had happened to be among the discards in Salzman's barrel he could never guess, but he knew he must urgently go find her.

Leo rushed downstairs, grabbed up the Bronx telephone book, and searched for Salzman's home address. He was not listed, nor was his office. Neither was he in the Manhattan book. But Leo remembered having written down the address on a slip of paper after he had read Salzman's advertisement in the "personals" column of the *Forward.* He ran up to his room and tore through his papers, without luck. It was exasperating. Just when he needed the matchmaker he was nowhere to be found. Fortunately Leo remembered to look in his wallet. There on a card he found his name written and a Bronx address. No phone number was listed, the reason—Leo now recalled—he had originally communicated with Salzman by letter. He got on his coat, put a hat on over his skull cap and hurried to the subway station. All the way to the far end of the Bronx he sat on the edge of his seat. He was more than once tempted to take out the picture and see if the girl's face was as he remembered it, but he refrained, allowing the snapshot to remain in his coat pocket, content to have her so close. When the train pulled into the station he was waiting at the door and bolted out. He quickly located the street Salzman had advertised.

The building he sought was less than a block from the subway, but it was not an office building, nor even a loft, nor a store in which one could rent office space. It was a very old tenement house. Leo found Salzman's name in pencil on a soiled tag under the bell and climbed three dark flights to his apartment. When he knocked, the door was opened by a thin, asthmatic, gray-haired woman, in felt slippers.

"Yes?" she said, expecting nothing. She listened without listening. He could have sworn he had seen her, too, before but knew it was an illusion.

"Salzman—does he live here? Pinye Salzman," he said, "the matchmaker?"

She stared at him a long minute. "Of course."

He felt embarrassed. "Is he in?"

"No." Her mouth, though left open, offered nothing more.

"The matter is urgent. Can you tell me where his office is?"

"In the air." She pointed upward.

"You mean he has no office?" Leo asked.

"In his socks."

He peered into the apartment. It was sunless and dingy, one large room divided by a half-open curtain, beyond which he could see a sagging metal bed. The near side of a room was crowded with rickety chairs, old bureaus, a three-legged table, racks of cooking utensils, and all the apparatus of a kitchen. But there was no sign of Salzman or his magic barrel, probably also a figment of the imagination. An odor of frying fish made Leo weak to the knees.

"Where is he?" he insisted. "I've got to see your husband."

At length she answered, "So who knows where he is? Every time he thinks a new thought he runs to a different place. Go home, he will find you."

"Tell him Leo Finkle."

She gave no sign she had heard.

He walked downstairs, depressed.

But Salzman, breathless, stood waiting at his door.

Leo was astounded and overjoyed. "How did you get here before me?"

"I rushed."

"Come inside."

They entered. Leo fixed tea, and a sardine sandwich for Salzman. As they were drinking he reached behind him for the packet of pictures and handed them to the marriage broker.

Salzman put down his glass and said expectantly, "You found somebody you like?"

"Not among these."

The marriage broker turned away.

"Here is the one I want." Leo held forth the snapshot.

Salzman slipped on his glasses and took the picture into his trembling hand. He turned ghastly and let out a groan.

"What's the matter?" cried Leo.

"Excuse me. Was an accident this picture. She isn't for you."

Salzman frantically shoved the manila packet into his portfolio. He thrust the snapshot into his pocket and fled down the stairs.

Leo, after momentary paralysis, gave chase and cornered the marriage broker in the vestibule. The landlady made hysterical outcries but neither of them listened.

"Give me back the picture, Salzman."

"No." The pain in his eyes was terrible.

"Tell me who she is then."

"This I can't tell you. Excuse me."

He made to depart, but Leo, forgetting himself, seized the matchmaker by his tight coat and shook him frenziedly.

"Please," sighed Salzman. "*Please.*"

Leo ashamedly let him go. "Tell me who she is," he begged. "It's very important for me to know."

"She is not for you. She is a wild one—wild, without shame. This is not a bride for a rabbi."

"What do you mean wild?"

"Like an animal. Like a dog. For her to be poor was a sin. This is why to me she is dead now."

"In God's name, what do you mean?"

"Her I can't introduce to you," Salzman cried.

"Why are you so excited?"

Why, he asks," Salzman said, bursting into tears. "This is my baby, my Stella, she should burn in hell."

Leo hurried up to bed and hid under the covers. Under the covers he thought his life through. Although he soon fell asleep he could not sleep her out of his mind. He woke, beating his breast. Though he prayed to be rid of her, his prayers went unanswered. Through days of torment he endlessly struggled not to love her; fearing success, he escaped it. He then concluded to convert her to goodness, himself to God. The idea alternately nauseated and exalted him.

He perhaps did not know that he had come to a final decision until he encountered Salzman in a Broadway cafeteria. He was sitting alone at a rear table, sucking the bony remains of a fish. The marriage broker appeared haggard, and transparent to the point of vanishing.

Salzman looked up at first without recognizing him. Leo had grown a pointed beard and his eyes were weighted with wisdom.

"Salzman," he said, "love has at last come to my heart."

"Who can love from a picture?" mocked the marriage broker.

"It is not impossible."

"If you can love her, then you can love anybody. Let me show you some new clients that they just sent me their photographs. One is a little doll."

"Just her I want," Leo murmured.

"Don't be a fool, doctor. Don't bother with her."

"Put me in touch with her, Salzman," Leo said humbly. "Perhaps I can be of service."

Salzman had stopped eating and Leo understood with emotion that it was now arranged.

Leaving the cafeteria, he was, however, afflicted by a tormenting suspicion that Salzman had planned it all to happen this way.

Leo was informed by letter that she would meet him on a certain corner, and she was there one spring night, waiting under a street lamp. He appeared, carrying a small bouquet of violets and rosebuds. Stella stood by the lamp post, smoking. She wore white with red shoes, which fitted his expectations, although in a troubled moment he had imagined the dress red, and only the shoes white. She waited uneasily and shyly. From afar he saw that her eyes—clearly her father's—were filled with desperate innocence. He pictured, in her, his own redemption. Violins and lit candles revolved in the sky. Leo ran forward with flowers outthrust.

Around the corner, Salzman, leaning against a wall, chanted prayers for the dead.

1954, 1958

Tillie Olsen 1913–

Although she has published only a slight body of writing, Tillie Olsen has gained wide critical attention as a prose stylist and as a spokeswoman for the poor, the oppressed, the "despised people" of America. She has written of the lives of immigrants, western coal miners, midwestern farm laborers, sewer workers, slaughterhouse workers, merchant seamen, people she has known and lived with. She was born in Nebraska to Russian immigrant parents. Her formal education stopped at the eleventh grade, but she educated herself at the public library, and by the time she was eighteen she had begun to write. In her early twenties she had already won recognition as a writer of poems and short fiction about the difficult lives of workers, blacks, women, vagrants, strikers, and the poor.

She began work on her novel, Yonnondio, *in 1932, when she was only nineteen. But while she was still in her twenties, her career was interrupted as she married, raised children, and was forced to work at numerous jobs to help support her family. Her book* Silences *(1978) describes the interruptions imposed on her writing career and the burdens that some women suffer in their efforts to give expression to their lives, how even the daily tasks of housekeeping and child-rearing can smother women's artistic creativity and breed "silences."*

Finally published in 1974, Yonnondio, *the story of a coal miner's family and its long struggle to endure, was praised as one of the best works of the proletarian movement in American literature. But her greatest fame came with the publication of* Tell Me a Riddle *(1978). Its stories, including "I Stand Here Ironing," have frequently been reprinted, adapted for readings, and presented in stage productions. Tillie Olsen has frequently been praised as a prose stylist, but her greatest achievement has been to catch "the downward movement of life," to portray eloquently the working-class men and women of America struggling to understand one another and to find lives of dignity and fulfillment.*

FURTHER READING: E. Orr, *Tillie Olsen and a Feminist Spiritual Vision,* 1987; M. Faulkner, *Protest and Possibility in the Writing of Tillie Olsen,* 1993; N. Roberts, *Three Radical Women Writers: Class and Gender in Meridel Le Sueur, Tillie Olsen, and Josephine Herbst,* 1996; M. Weber, *Consuming Silences: How We Read Authors Who Don't Publish,* 2005.

TEXT: *Tell Me a Riddle,* 1956.

I STAND HERE IRONING

I stand here ironing, and what you asked me moves tormented back and forth with the iron.

"I wish you would manage the time to come in and talk with me about your daughter. I'm sure you can help me understand her. She's a youngster who needs help and whom I'm deeply interested in helping."

"Who needs help." . . . Even if I came, what good would it do? You think because I am her mother I have a key, or that in some way you could use me as a key? She has lived for nineteen years. There is all that life that has happened outside of me, beyond me.

And when is there time to remember, to sift, to weigh, to estimate, to total? I will start and there will be an interruption and I will have to gather it all together again. Or I will become engulfed with all I did or did not do, with what should have been and what cannot be helped.

She was a beautiful baby. The first and only one of our five that was beautiful at birth. You do not guess how new and uneasy her tenancy in her now-loveliness. You did not know her all those years she was thought homely, or see her poring over her baby pictures, making me tell her over and over how beautiful she had been—and would be, I would tell her—and was now, to the seeing eye. But the seeing eyes were few or nonexistent. Including mine.

I nursed her. They feel that's important nowadays. I nursed all the children, but with her, with all the fierce rigidity of first motherhood, I did like the books then said. Though her cries battered me to trembling and my breasts ached with swollenness, I waited till the clock decreed.

Why do I put that first? I do not even know if it matters, or if it explains anything.

She was a beautiful baby. She blew shining bubbles of sound. She loved motion, loved light, loved color and music and textures. She would lie on the floor in her blue overalls patting the surface so hard in ecstasy her hands and feet would blur. She was a miracle to me, but when she was eight months old I had to leave her daytimes with the woman downstairs to whom she was no miracle at all, for I worked or looked for work and for Emily's father, who "could no longer endure" (he wrote in his good-bye note) "sharing want with us."

I was nineteen. It was the pre-relief, pre-WPA world of the depression. I would start running as soon as I got off the streetcar, running up the stairs, the place smelling sour, and awake or asleep to startle awake, when she saw me she would break into a clogged weeping that could not be comforted, a weeping I can hear yet.

After a while I found a job hashing at night so I could be with her days, and it was better. But it came to where I had to bring her to his family and leave her.

It took a long time to raise the money for her fare back. Then she got chicken pox and I had to wait longer. When she finally came, I hardly knew her, walking quick and nervous like her father, looking like her father, thin, and dressed in a shoddy red that yellowed her skin and glared at the pockmarks. All the baby loveliness gone.

She was two. Old enough for nursery school they said, and I did not know then what I know now—the fatigue of the long day, and the lacerations of group life in the kinds of nurseries that are only parking places for children.

Except that it would have made no difference if I had known. It was the only place there was. It was the only way we could be together, the only way I could hold a job.

And even without knowing, I knew. I knew the teacher that was evil because all these years it has curdled into my memory, the little boy hunched in the corner, her rasp, "why aren't you outside, because Alvin hits you? that's no reason, go out, scaredy." I knew Emily hated it even if she did not clutch and implore "don't go Mommy" like the other children, mornings.

She always had a reason why we should stay home. Momma, you look sick. Momma, I feel sick. Momma, the teachers aren't there today, they're sick. Momma, we can't go, there was a fire there last night. Momma, it's a holiday today, no school, they told me.

But never a direct protest, never rebellion. I think of our others in their three-, four-year-oldness—the explosions, the tempers, the denunciations, the demands—and I feel suddenly ill. I put the iron down. What in me demanded that goodness in her? And what was the cost, the cost to her of such goodness?

The old man living in the back once said in his gentle way: "You should smile at Emily more when you look at her." What *was* in my face when I looked at her? I loved her. There were all the acts of love.

It was only with the others I remembered what he said, and it was the face of joy, and not of care or tightness or worry I turned to them—too late for Emily. She does not smile easily, let alone almost always as her brothers and sisters do. Her face is closed and sombre, but when she wants, how fluid. You must have seen it in her pantomimes, you spoke of her rare gift for comedy on the stage that rouses a laughter out of the audience so dear they applaud and applaud and do not want to let her go.

Where does it come from, that comedy? There was none of it in her when she came back to me that second time, after I had had to send her away again. She had a new daddy now to learn to love, and I think perhaps it was a better time.

Except when we left her alone nights, telling ourselves she was old enough.

"Can't you go some other time, Mommy, like tomorrow?" she would ask. "Will it be just a little while you'll be gone? Do you promise?"

The time we came back, the front door open, the clock on the floor in the hall. She rigid awake. "It wasn't just a little while. I didn't cry. Three times I called you, just three times, and then I ran downstairs to open the door so you could come faster. The clock talked loud. I threw it away, it scared me what it talked."

She said the clock talked loud again that night I went to the hospital to have Susan. She was delirious with the fever that comes before red measles, but she was fully conscious all the week I was gone and the week after we were home when she could not come near the new baby or me.

She did not get well. She stayed skeleton thin, not wanting to eat, and night after night she had nightmares. She would call for me, and I would rouse from exhaustion to sleepily call back: "You're all right, darling, go to sleep, it's just a dream," and if she still called, in a sterner voice, "now go to sleep, Emily, there's nothing to hurt you." Twice, only twice, when I had to get up for Susan anyhow, I went in to sit with her.

Now when it is too late (as if she would let me hold and comfort her like I do the others) I get up and go to her at once at her moan or restless stirring. "Are you awake, Emily? Can I get you something?" And the answer is always the same: "No, I'm all right, go back to sleep, Mother."

They persuaded me at the clinic to send her away to a convalescent home in the country where "she can have the kind of food and care you can't manage for her, and you'll be free to concentrate on the new baby." They still send children to that place. I see pictures on the society page of sleek young women planning affairs to raise money for it, or dancing at the affairs, or decorating Easter eggs or filling Christmas stockings for the children.

They never have a picture of the children so I do not know if the girls still wear those gigantic red bows and the ravaged looks on the every other Sunday when parents can come to visit "unless otherwise notified"—as we were notified the first six weeks.

Oh it is a handsome place, green lawns and tall trees and fluted flower beds. High up on the balconies of each cottage the children stand, the girls in their red bows and white dresses, the boys in white suits and giant red ties. The parents stand below shrieking up to be heard and the children shriek down to be heard, and between them the invisible wall "Not To Be Contaminated by Parental Germs or Physical Affection."

There was a tiny girl who always stood hand in hand with Emily. Her parents never came. One visit she was gone. "They moved her to Rose Cottage" Emily shouted in explanation. "They don't like you to love anybody here."

She wrote once a week, the labored writing of a seven-year-old. "I am fine. How is the baby. If I write my leter nicly I will have a star. Love." There never was a star. We wrote every other day, letters she could never hold or keep but only hear read—once. "We simply do not have room for children to keep any personal possessions," they patiently explained when we pieced one Sunday's shrieking together to plead how much it would mean to Emily, who loved so to keep things, to be allowed to keep her letters and cards.

Each visit she looked frailer. "She isn't eating," they told us.

(They had runny eggs for breakfast or mush with lumps. Emily said later, I'd hold it in my mouth and not swallow. Nothing ever tasted good, just when they had chicken.)

It took us eight months to get her released home, and only the fact that she gained back so little of her seven lost pounds convinced the social worker.

I used to try to hold and love her after she came back, but her body would stay stiff, and after a while she'd push away. She ate little. Food sickened her, and I think much of life too. Oh she had physical lightness and brightness, twinkling by on skates, bouncing like a ball up and down up and down over the jump rope, skimming over the hill; but these were momentary.

She fretted about her appearance, thin and dark and foreign-looking at a time when every little girl was supposed to look or thought she should look a chubby blonde replica of Shirley Temple. The doorbell sometimes rang for her, but no one seemed to come and play in the house or be a best friend. Maybe because we moved so much.

There was a boy she loved painfully through two school semesters. Months later she told me how she had taken pennies from my purse to buy him candy. "Licorice was his favorite and I brought him some every day, but he still liked Jennifer better'n me. Why, Mommy?" The kind of question for which there is no answer.

School was a worry to her. She was not glib or quick in a world where glibness and quickness were easily confused with ability to learn. To her overworked and exasperated teachers she was an overconscientious "slow learner" who kept trying to catch up and was absent entirely too often.

I let her be absent, though sometimes the illness was imaginary. How different from my now-strictness about attendance with the others. I wasn't working. We had a new baby, I was home anyhow. Sometimes, after Susan grew old enough, I would keep her home from school, too, to have them all together.

Mostly Emily had asthma, and her breathing, harsh and labored, would fill the house with a curiously tranquil sound. I would bring the two old dresser mirrors and her boxes of collections to her bed. She would select beads and single earrings, bottle tops and shells, dried flowers and pebbles, old postcards and scraps, all sorts of oddments; then she and Susan would play Kingdom, setting up landscapes and furniture, peopling them with action.

Those were the only times of peaceful companionship between her and Susan. I have edged away from it, that poisonous feeling between them, that terrible balancing of hurts and needs I had to do between the two, and did so badly, those earlier years.

Oh there are conflicts between the others too, each one human, needing, demanding, hurting, taking—but only between Emily and Susan, no, Emily toward Susan that corroding resentment. It seems so obvious on the surface, yet it is not obvious. Susan, the second child, Susan, golden- and curly-haired and chubby, quick and articulate and assured, everything in appearance and manner Emily was not; Susan, not able to resist Emily's precious things, losing or sometimes clumsily breaking them; Susan telling jokes and riddles to company for applause while Emily sat silent (to say to me later: that was *my* riddle, Mother, I told it to Susan); Susan, who for all the five years' difference in age was just a year behind Emily in developing physically.

I am glad for that slow physical development that widened the difference between her and her contemporaries, though she suffered over it. She was too vulnerable for that terrible world of youthful competition, of preening and parading, of constant measuring of yourself against every other, of envy, "If I had that copper hair," "If I had that skin. . . ." She tormented herself enough about not looking like the others, there was enough of the unsureness, the having to be conscious of words before you speak, the constant caring—what are they thinking of me? without having it all magnified by the merciless physical drives.

Ronnie is calling. He is wet and I change him. It is rare there is such a cry now. That time of motherhood is almost behind me when the ear is not one's own but must always be racked and listening for the child cry, the child call. We sit for a while and I hold him, looking out over the city spread in charcoal with its soft aisles of light. *"Shoogily,"* he breathes and curls closer. I carry him back to bed, asleep. *Shoogily.* A funny word, a family word, inherited from Emily, invented by her to say: *comfort.*

In this and other ways she leaves her seal, I say aloud. And startle at my saying it. What do I mean? What did I start to gather together, to try and make coherent? I was at the terrible, growing years. War years. I do not remember them well. I was working, there were four smaller ones now, there was not time for her. She had to help be a mother, and housekeeper, and shopper. She had to set her seal. Mornings of crisis and near hysteria trying to get lunches packed, hair combed, coats and shoes found, everyone to school or Child Care on time, the baby ready for transportation. And always the paper scribbled on by a smaller one, the book looked at by Susan then mislaid, the homework not done. Running out to that huge school where she was one, she was lost, she was a drop; suffering over the unpreparedness, stammering and unsure in her classes.

There was so little time left at night after the kids were bedded down. She would struggle over books, always eating (it was in those years she developed her enormous appetite that is legendary in our family) and I would be ironing, or preparing food for the next day, or writing V-mail to Bill, or tending the baby. Sometimes, to make me laugh, or out of her despair, she would imitate happenings or types at school.

I think I said once: "Why don't you do something like this in the school amateur show?" One morning she phoned me at work, hardly understandable through the weeping: "Mother, I did it. I won, I won; they gave me first prize; they clapped and clapped and wouldn't let me go."

Now suddenly she was Somebody, and as imprisoned in her difference as she had been in anonymity.

She began to be asked to perform at other high schools, even in colleges, then at city and statewide affairs. The first one we went to, I only recognized her that first moment when thin, shy, she almost drowned herself into the curtains. Then: Was this Emily? The control, the command, the convulsing and deadly clowning, the spell, then the roaring, stamping audience, unwilling to let this rare and precious laughter out of their lives.

Afterwards: You ought to do something about her with a gift like that—but without money or knowing how, what does one do? We have left it all to her, and the gift has as often eddied inside, clogged and clotted, has been used and growing.

She is coming. She runs up the stairs two at a time with her light graceful step, and I know she is happy tonight. Whatever it was that occasioned your call did not happen today.

"Aren't you ever going to finish the ironing, Mother? Whistler painted his mother in a rocker. I'd have to paint mine standing over an ironing board." This is one of her communicative nights and she tells me everything and nothing as she fixes herself a plate of food out of the icebox.

She is so lovely. Why did you want me to come in at all? Why were you concerned? She will find her way.

She starts up the stairs to bed. "Don't get me up with the rest in the morning." "But I thought you were having midterms." "Oh, those," she comes back in, kisses me, and says quite lightly, "in a couple of years when we'll all be atom-dead they won't matter a bit."

She has said it before. She *believes* it. But because I have been dredging the past, and all that compounds a human being is so heavy and meaningful in me, I cannot endure it tonight.

I will never total it all. I will never come in to say: She was a child seldom smiled at. Her father left me before she was a year old. I had to work her first six years when there was work, or I sent her home and to his relatives. There were years she had care she hated. She was dark and thin and foreign-looking in a world where the prestige went to blondeness and curly hair and dimples, she was slow where glibness was prized. She was a child of anxious, not proud, love. We were poor and could not afford for her the soil of easy growth. I was a young mother, I was a distracted mother. There were the other children pushing up, demanding. Her younger sister seemed all that she was not. There were years she did not want me to touch her. She kept too much in herself, her life was such she had to keep too much in herself. My wisdom came too late. She has much to her and probably nothing will come of it. She is a child of her age, of depression, of war, of fear.

Let her be. So all that is in her will not bloom—but in how many does it? There is still enough left to live by. Only help her to know—help make it so there is cause for her to know—that she is more than this dress on the ironing board, helpless before the iron.

1953–1954 1956

Tomás Rivera 1935–1984

Tomás Rivera was a pioneer in the development of modern Mexican American literature. His writing drew on his life as a Chicano in the United States, where he was born in the small farm-town of Crystal City, Texas, in 1935. His parents were migrant farm laborers who traveled, seasonally, through the Midwestern United States, following the crop harvests.

Rivera received his earliest formal education in Spanish-speaking schools, and he did not become fluent in English until he was in the fifth grade. He attended a junior college in Texas and later graduated from Southwest Texas State University. Rivera then enrolled in the graduate program in literature at the University of Oklahoma, from which he received a Ph.D. in 1969. Ten years later, after a career of teaching and administrative jobs in high schools and colleges in the Southwest, he was appointed Chancellor of the University of California at Riverside, a post he held until his death in 1984.

In his writing Rivera attempted to record the lives, the culture, and the heritage of Chicano men, women, and children in the United States. He wrote of migrant farmworkers and of those who live in urban barrios. His poems and stories record the stresses of life of the kind that he himself experienced as a young Chicano isolated from the dominant "Anglo" world of affluence and position.

But Rivera's primary aim was not to write social protest literature or propaganda for social causes. He wrote to portray realistically the lives of Mexican Americans who are simultaneously linked to the ancient traditions of Mexico and confronted by the English-speaking world of North America. He wrote of the collective faults and strengths and of the individual misperceptions and apprehensions of a cultural minority that must struggle to understand its own traditions while living in the midst of a dominant "Anglo" culture from which it often stands alienated and apart.

FURTHER READING: *Introduction to Chicano Studies,* ed. L. Duran and B. Russell, 1973; C. Tatum, *Chicano Literature,* 1982; *Tomás Rivera: The Complete Works,* 1991; *Hispanic-American Writers,* ed. H. Bloom, 1998; M. Martínez, *Countering the Counterculture: Rereading Postwar American Dissent from Jack Kerouac to Tomás Rivera,* 2003.

TEXT: . . . *And the Earth Did Not Part,* 1971.

. . . AND THE EARTH DID NOT PART

The first time he felt hate and anger was when he saw his mother cry for his uncle and for his aunt. They had both gotten tuberculosis and each of them had been sent to different sanitoriums. The children had then been parceled out among their aunts and uncles and they had taken care of them as best they could. His aunt had later died and shortly afterward his uncle had been brought home from the sanitorium, but he was already spitting blood every time he coughed. It was then that he saw his mother crying all the time. He had become angry because he couldn't strike back at anyone. He felt the same way now. But this time it was on account of his father.

"You should have left right away, son. Couldn't you see that your father was sick? All of you knew very well that he had been sunstruck before. Why didn't you come home?"

"Well, I don't know. Since the rest of us were soaking wet with sweat we didn't realize it was so hot, but I guess when one has been sunstruck it's different. Anyway, I told him to sit under the tree that's at the end of the rows but he didn't want to. It was then that he started to vomit. Then we saw that he couldn't hoe and we had to drag him to get him under the tree. He didn't struggle anymore. He simply let us take him. He didn't put up a fuss or anything.

"Poor man, my poor husband. He hardly slept last night. Didn't you hear him outside the house? He was twisting and turning all night; it must be painful. God, how I pray he gets well. I've been giving him cool lemonade all day but his eyes are still glassy. If I had been in the field yesterday I assure you that he would not have had a sunstroke. Poor man, he'll have spasms all over his body for at least three days and three nights. Now all of you take care of yourselves. If it gets too hot, rest. Don't overwork yourselves. Don't pay attention to the boss if he hurries you. Since he is not the one breaking his back, he thinks its easy."

He became angrier when he heard his father moan outside the shack. His father didn't stay inside because he said that he was overcome with anxiety whenever he did. He had to be outside where he could get fresh air. There he could stretch out on the grass and roll around when the spasms hit him. Then he thought about whether his father was going to die from the sunstroke. From time to time he would hear his father pray and ask God for help. At first he had hoped that he would get well soon but the following day he felt his anger increase. And he felt it increase more when his mother or his father clamored for the mercy of God. And their father's moans had awakened them that night and also at dawn and their mother had gotten up and had taken off his scapularies[1] from around his neck and had washed them for him. She had then lighted some small candles. But to no avail. It was the same as with his uncle and his aunt.

"What do you gain by doing that, mother? Don't tell me that you believe that sort of thing helped my uncle and my aunt? Why is it that we are here on earth as though buried alive? Either the germs eat us from the inside or the sun from the outside. Always some illness. And work, work, day in and day out. And for what? Poor father, he works just as hard as the rest of us, perhaps harder. He was born working, as he says. Barely five years old and he was already out there planting corn with his father. After feeding the earth and the sun for such a long time, . . . one day unexpectedly he is felled by the sun. And powerless to do anything. And to top it off, praying to God. God doesn't even remember us . . . There must not be a God. . . . No, better not to say it, what if father should worsen? Poor man, at least that must give him some hope."

His mother noticed how furious he was and in the morning she told him to calm down, that everything was in the hands of God and that his father would get well with God's help.

"Come now, do you really believe that? God, I am sure, doesn't give a damn about us. Look, can you tell me if father is mean or without love? You tell me if he has ever hurt anyone?"

[1]Two small pieces of cloth worn over the shoulders as a token of religious devotion.

"Well, no."

"There you are. See? And my uncle and my aunt? You tell me. And now their poor children not knowing their parents. Why did He have to take them? So you see, God doesn't give a damn about us poor people. Look, why do we have to live under these conditions? Are we hurting anybody? You're such a good person and yet you have to suffer so much. Can't you see? Tell me!"

"Oh, son, don't talk like that. Don't question the will of God. The ground might open up and devour you for talking like that. One must resign oneself to the will of God. Please don't talk like that, son. You frighten me. It seems that already the devil is in your very blood."

"Well, perhaps. At least that way I could release my anger. I'm tired of asking, why? Why you? Why father? Why my uncle? Why my aunt? Why their children? Can you tell me why? Why should we always be tied to the dirt, half buried in the earth like animals without any hope of any kind? You know that the only thing we can look forward to is coming over here every year. And as you yourself say, one does not rest until one dies. I guess that is the way my uncle and my aunt felt, and that's the way father will eventually feel!"

"That's the way it is, son. Only death can bring us rest."

"But, why us?"

"Well, it is said that. . . ."

"Don't say it! Don't tell me anything! I know what you're going to tell me!—that the poor will go to heaven."

The day started out cloudy and he felt the cool morning breeze brush his eyelashes as he and his brothers and sisters started to work. His mother had had to stay at home to take care of her husband. Thus he felt responsible for encouraging his brothers and sisters. In the morning, at least during the early hours, they were able to withstand the sun, but by ten-thirty the sun had suddenly completely cleared the sky and penetrated everything and everyone. They worked much slower because they would feel weakness and suffocation overcome them if they worked at a hurried pace. They then had to wipe the sweat from their eyes every few minutes because their eyes would become blurry.

"When you kids see blurry, stop working or slow down. When we get to the end of the rows we'll rest awhile to regain our strength. It's going to be hot today. I wish it would remain cloudy, as it was this morning. No one would complain then. But no, once the sun bears down not even a tiny cloud dares show itself out of sheer fright. The hell of it is, we'll be finished here by two and then we have to go to that field that is nothing but hills. It's ok on the top of the hill but when we're in the low parts it's suffocating. Not even the slightest breeze blows through there. Air almost doesn't enter. Remember?

"Yes."

"That's where we'll spend the hottest part of the day. Just drink a lot of water every few minutes even if the boss gets angry. If not you'll get sick. And if you can't take it any longer, tell me right away, ok? We'll go home. You saw what happened to father for holding out. The sun can suck the life out of you."

Just as they had thought, they had had to move to the other field by early afternoon. By three o'clock they were already sopping wet with sweat. Not a single part of their clothing remained dry. Every few minutes they stopped. Sometimes they gasped for breath, then everything became blurred and the fear of sunstroke creeped into them, but they continued.

"How do you feel?"

"Man, it's hot! But we have to keep going. At least until six. Only thing is that the water we have is no longer good for our thirst. How I wish I had a glass of cool water, real cold, just pulled up from the well, or an icy coke."

"You're crazy, you'd sure get sunstroke that way. Just don't work too fast. Let's see if we can hold up until six. Can you take it?"

At four o'clock the youngest became sick. He was only nine years old but since he was paid as an adult he tried to keep up with the others. He started to vomit and sat down, then he lay down. Fear stricken they all rushed over to him. He appeared to have fainted and when they opened his eyelids they found his eyes turned around. The one next to him in age started to cry but he told him immediately to shut up and help take him home. Spasms were moving over his small body. He then threw him on his back and carried him by himself. Once again he began asking why?

"Why my father, and now my little brother? He is barely nine years old. Why? He has to work like an animal, tied to the ground. Father, Mother, and he, my little brother, how could they possibly be guilty of anything?"

Each step that he took toward the house brought forth the echo of the question "why?" Half way down the road he became furious and then he started to cry out of despair. His other brothers and sisters didn't know what to do and they also started to cry, but out of fear. He then began to swear. And he didn't know when, but what he said he had been wanting to say for a long time. He cursed God. Upon doing it he felt the fear instilled in him by time and by his parents. For a split second he saw the earth open up to devour him. But, although he didn't look down, he then felt himself walking on very solid ground; *it was harder than he had ever felt it.* Anger swelled up in him again and he released it by cursing God. Then he noticed that his little brother no longer appeared quite so ill. He didn't know if his other little brothers and sisters realized how serious his curse had been.

That evening he didn't go to sleep until very late. He was experiencing a peace that he had never known before. It seemed to him that he had completely detached himself from everything. He was no longer worried about his father nor about his brother. All that he looked forward to was the new day, the coolness of the morning. By dawn his father was better. He was on his way to recovery. His little brother was also almost completely free of spasms. Time after time he felt surprised at what he had done the previous afternoon. He had cursed God and the earth had not parted. He was going to tell his mother but he decided to keep it a secret. He only told her that the earth didn't devour anyone, and that the sun didn't destroy anyone either.

He left for work and he was faced with a very cool morning. There were clouds and for the first time he felt himself capable of doing and undoing whatever he chose. He looked toward the ground and he kicked it and said to it,

"Not yet, you can't eat me yet. Someday. But I won't know."

1971

Amiri Baraka (LeRoi Jones)
1934–

He was born LeRoi Jones in Newark, New Jersey. In 1966, when he was thirty-two, he returned to Newark to serve as a leader, known as Imamu Amiri Baraka, of Spirit House, an African culture center. Jones had graduated from high school and attended Rutgers University in Newark. Later he transferred to Howard University, in Washington, D.C., from which he received a degree in English literature. For two years he served in the Air Force, stationed much of the time in Puerto Rico. Following his discharge he returned to the United States, to New York City, where he studied at Columbia University and at the New School for Social Research, from which he received an M.A. in German literature.

Jones taught at Columbia and at the New School, wrote newspaper and magazine articles, and in 1961 published his first collection of poems, Preface to a Twenty Volume Suicide Note. *Three years later he published his second volume of poems,* The Dead Lecturer. *He has also written volumes of plays, fiction, and essays, including* Dutchman and The Slave *(1964);* The System of Dante's Hell *(1965), a partially autobiographical novel;* Home, Social Essays *(1966);* Tales *(1967); and two books on music:* Blues People, Negro Music in White America *(1963) and* Black Music *(1967). In 1971 he published* Raise Race Rays Raze, Essays Since 1965 *and in 1978* The Motion of History and Other Plays.

Jones's early poetry shows the influence of such poets as Ezra Pound and, especially, William Carlos Williams, whose "quantitative verse" Jones sought to duplicate. He wanted to bring his poems close to the rhythms of spoken English by relating line lengths, pauses, phrasings, and the arrangements of stanzas to the rhythms of breathing, thus giving the poet a measure of control over the voicing of verse in a manner similar to that of a director of a musical score.

Jones's growing interest in the black revolution has made his later poetry increasingly nonformal and nontraditional. He has sought to write authentically of his own experiences in a vital street style, free of orthodox diction, images, and received ideas—a rejection of what he considers to be "white" poetic tradition. His views are evident in his drama Dutchman, *a fierce portrait of racial betrayal and cynical violence. As Amiri Baraka he is both a Black Power advocate and a black visionary writer. He wants, in his words, to "reach some people, move some people"—not with mere "skin drama," the black Broadway plays that lack revolutionary ideology, but with propaganda that is art: writing that unites art and politics; literature with a "clear revolutionary edge to it."*

FURTHER READING: T. Hudson, *From LeRoi Jones to Amiri Baraka,* 1973; *The Selected Plays and Prose,* 1979; *Selected Poetry,* 1979; L. Brown, *Amiri Baraka,* 1980; *The Autobiography of LeRoi Jones,* 1984; W. Harris, *The Poetry and Poetics of Amiri Baraka,* 1985; B. Bernotas, *Amiri Baraka,* 1991; H. Elam, *Taking It to the Streets: The Social Protest Theater of Luis Valdez and Amiri Baraka,* 1997; J. Watts, *Amiri Baraka: The Politics and Art of a Black Intellectual,* 2001.

TEXTS: "In Memory of Radio," "The Bridge," and "Notes for a Speech" are from *Preface to a Twenty Volume Suicide Note,* 1961; A Poem for Democrats is from *The Dead Lecturer,* 1964; all other poems are from *Black Magic,* 1969.

IN MEMORY OF RADIO

Who has ever stopped to think of the divinity of Lamont Cranston?[1]
(Only Jack Kerouac, that I know of: & me.
The rest of you probably had on WCBS and Kate Smith,
Or something equally unattractive.)

What can I say?
It is better to have loved and lost
Than to put linoleum in your living rooms?
Am I a sage or something?
Mandrake's hypnotic gesture of the week?[2]
(Remember, I do not have the healing powers of Oral Roberts . . .[3]
I cannot, like F. J. Sheen,[4] tell you how to get saved & *rich!*
I cannot even order you to gaschamber satori[5] like Hitler or
    Goody Knight[6]

& Love is an evil word.
Turn it backwards/see, see what I mean?
An evol word. & besides
who understands it?
I certainly wouldn't like to go out on that kind of limb.

Saturday mornings we listened to *Red Lantern* & his undersea folk.
At 11, *Let's Pretend*/& we did/& I, the poet, still do, Thank God!

What was it he used to say (after the transformation, when he was
safe & invisible & the unbelievers couldn't throw stones?) "Heh,
    heh, heh,
Who knows what evil lurks in the hearts of men? The Shadow
    knows."[7]

O, yes he does
O, yes he does.
An evil word it is,
This Love.

1961

[1]The hero of the radio serial "The Shadow" (1931–1954), who had "the power to cloud men's minds" and make himself invisible.

[2]The comic-strip hero Mandrake the Magician used magic hypnotic powers to overcome evil.

[3]Here, and throughout, the ellipsis points are Baraka's.

[4]Bishop Fulton J. Sheen (1895–1979), renowned for his radio sermons in the 1930s and 1940s.

[5]A state of sudden enlightenment in Zen Buddhism.

[6]Goodwin Knight, Governor of California (1953–1959) during controversies over the use of the gas chamber for capital punishment.

[7]Repeated signature phrase of "The Shadow."

THE BRIDGE

(# for wieners & mcclure)

I have forgotten the head
of where I am. Here at the bridge. 2
bars, down the street, seeming
to warp themselves around my fingers, the day,
screams in me; pitiful like a little girl
you sense will be dead before the winter
is over.

I can't see the bridge now, I've past
it, its shadow, we drove through, headed out
along the cold insensitive roads to what
we wanted to call "ourselves."
"How does the bridge go?" Even tho
you find yourself in its length
strung out along its breadth, waiting
for the cold sun to tear out your eyes. Enamoured
of its blues, spread out in the silk clubs of
this autumn tune. The changes are difficult, when
you hear them, & know they are all in you, the chords

of your disorder meddle with your would be disguises.
Sifting in, down, upon your head, with the sun & the insects.

(Late feeling) Way down till it barely, after that rush of
wind & odor reflected from hills you have forgotten the color
when you touch the water, & it closes, slowly, around your head.

The bridge will be behind you, that music you know, that place,
you feel when you look up to say, it is me, & I have forgotten,
all the things, you told me to love, to try to understand, the
bridge will stand, high up in the clouds & the light, & you,

(when you have let the song run out) will be sliding through
unmentionable black.

1961

NOTES FOR A SPEECH

African blues
does not know me. Their steps, in sands
of their own
land. A country
in black & white, newspapers

blown down pavements
of the world. Does
not feel
what I am.
                    Strength
in the dream, an oblique
suckling of nerve, the wind
throws up sand, eyes
are something locked in
hate, of hate, of hate, to
walk abroad, they conduct
their deaths apart
from my own. Those
heads, I call
my "people."
(And who are they. People. To concern
myself, ugly man. Who
you, to concern
the white flat stomachs
of maidens, inside houses
dying. Black, Peeled moon
light on my fingers
move under
her clothes. Where
is her husband. Black
words throw up sand
to eyes, fingers of
their private dead. Whose
soul, eyes, in sand. My color
is not theirs. Lighter, white man
talk. They shy away. My own
dead souls, my, so called
people. Africa
is a foreign place. You are
as any other sad man here
american.

1961

AN AGONY, AS NOW

I am inside someone
who hates me. I look
out from his eyes. Smell
what fouled tunes come in
to his breath. Love his
wretched women.

Slits in the metal, for sun. Where
my eyes sit turning, at the cool air
the glance of light, or hard flesh
rubbed against me, a woman, a man,
without shadow, or voice, or meaning.

This is the enclosure (flesh,
where innocence is a weapon. An
abstraction. Touch. (Not mine.
Or yours, if you are the soul I had
and abandoned when I was blind and had
my enemies carry me as a dead man
(if he is beautiful, or pitied.

It can be pain. (As now, as all his
flesh hurts me.) It can be that. Or
pain. As when she ran from me into
that forest.
                    Or pain, the mind
silver spiraled whirled against the
sun, higher than even old men thought
God would be. Or pain. And the other. The
yes. (Inside his books, his fingers. They
are withered yellow flowers and were never
beautiful.) The yes. You will, lost soul, say
'beauty.' Beauty, practiced, as the tree. The
slow river. A white sun in its wet sentences.

Or, the cold men in their gale. Ecstasy. Flesh
or soul. The yes. (Their robes blown. Their bowls
empty. They chant at my heels, not at yours.) Flesh
or soul, as corrupt. Where the answer moves too quickly.
Where the God is a self, after all.)

Cold air blown through narrow blind eyes. Flesh,
white hot metal. Glows as the day with its sun.
It is human love, I live inside. A bony skeleton
you recognize as words or simple feeling.

But it has no feeling. As the metal, is hot, it is not,
given to love.

It burns the thing
inside it. And that thing
screams.

1964

A POEM FOR DEMOCRATS

the city rises

in color, our sad
ness, blanket this wood place, single drop
of rain, blue image of
someone's love.
Net of rain. Crystal ice
glass strings, smash
(on such repertoire of memory
as:
baskets
the long walk up harbor
& the insistence, rain, as they build
City, is wicked. Not
this one, where I am, where they
still move, go to, out of
(transporting your loved one
across the line is death
by drowning.

Drowned love
hanged man, swung, cement on his feet.)
But
the small filth of the small mind
short structures of
newark, baltimore, cincinnati, omaha. Distress,
europe has passed we are alone. Europe
frail woman dead, we are alone

1964

A POEM FOR SPECULATIVE HIPSTERS

He had got, finally,
to the forest
of motives. There were no
owls, or hunters. No Connie Chatterleys[1]
resting beautifully
on their backs, having casually
brought socialism
to England.
Only ideas,
and their opposites.
Like,
he was *really*
nowhere.

1964

[1]The heroine of D. H. Lawrence's novel *Lady Chatterley's Lover* (1928).

A POEM SOME PEOPLE WILL HAVE TO UNDERSTAND

Dull unwashed windows of eyes
and buildings of industry. What
industry do I practice? A slick
colored boy, 12 miles from his
home. I practice no industry.
I am no longer a credit
to my race. I read a little,
scratch against silence slow spring
afternoons.
        I had thought, before, some years ago
that I'd come to the end of my life.
        Watercolor ego. Without the preciseness
a violent man could propose.
        But the wheel, and the wheels,
won't let us alone. All the fantasy
        and justice, and dry charcoal winters
All the pitifully intelligent citizens
        I've forced myself to love.

        We have awaited the coming of a natural
        phenomenon. Mystics and romantics, knowledgeable
        workers
        of the land.

        But none has come.
        (Repeat)
                        but none has come.
Will the machinegunners please step forward?

1969

A POEM FOR HALF-WHITE COLLEGE STUDENTS

Who are you, listening to me, who are you
listening to yourself? Are you white or
black, or does that have anything to do
with it? Can you pop your fingers to no
music, except those wild monkies go on
in your head, can you jerk, to no melody,
except finger poppers get it together
when you turn from starchecking to checking
yourself? How do you sound, your words, are they
yours? The ghost you see in the mirror, is it really
you, can you swear you are not an imitation greyboy,
can you look right next to you in that chair, and swear,
that the sister you have your hand on is not really
so full of Elizabeth Taylor, Richard Burton is

coming out of her ears. You may even have to be Richard
with a white shirt and face, and four million negroes
think you cute, you may have to be Elizabeth Taylor, old lady,
if you want to sit up in your crazy spot dreaming about dresses,
and the sway of certain porters' hips. Check yourself, learn who it is
speaking, when you make some ultrasophisticated point, check yourself
when you find yourself gesturing like Steve McQueen, check it out, ask
in your black heart who it is you are, and is that image black or white,
you might be surprised right out the window, whistling dixie on the way

1969

BIOGRAPHY

Hangs.
whipped
blood
striped
meat pulled
clothes ripped
slobber
feet dangled
pointing
noised
noise
churns
face
black sky
and moon
leather night
red
bleeds
drips
ground
sucks
blood
hangs
life wetting
sticky
mud

laughs
bonnets
wolfmoon
crazyteeth

hangs

hangs

granddaddy

granddaddy, they tore

his
neck
1969

Sonia Sanchez 1934–

The writing of Sonia Sanchez, like her lectures and readings, often shocks her audiences with its fierce rancor. She uses the street speech of big-city America, language that is deliberately nonstandard, that smolders with anger and contempt, that sometimes calls for violent retaliation against those she sees as oppressors of minorities, women, the poor. Her writing is marked by profanity, by hyperbole and double meanings (where "badddd" is good), by black English suited to "playing the dozens" and "signifying" (trading insults, using verbal jabs and wisecracks to gain an advantage).

Although she writes of life in the cities of the North, she was born in Alabama and spent her early childhood in the South. When she was nine, she was taken by her father to New York City, to Harlem. There, she went to public school and later attended New York City's Hunter College, graduating in 1955 with a degree in political science. For a year she did graduate work in literature at New York University. One of her teachers was the celebrated poet Louise Bogan, whose poetry reflected the classical ideals of restraint, regularity, detachment, and allegiance to literary tradition.

But Sonia Sanchez had absorbed the culture and the ideals of the streets of New York City, of black Harlem; as a result, her poetry is unrestrained, irregular, socially committed, devoted to making revolutionary changes in traditions that she believes are defunct. And while her stories and poems sometimes attempt to echo the galvanizing rhythms of the native speech of rural Africa, the language and subjects she has chosen are from the world of urban America.

Although she is an outspoken critic of America's traditional institutions, she has maintained a long association with American colleges and universities. Since the 1960s, she has taught at San Francisco State University, the University of Pittsburgh, Rutgers, Amherst College, and the University of Pennsylvania. At present she is a professor of English at Temple University in Philadelphia.

Nevertheless, her writing is purposely nonintellectual, opposed to the European-centered traditions and ideals of the white American establishment. She has been part of the black literary movement of protest that began in the 1960s and 1970s, formidable voices that have cried out not for reform but for revolution. In 1972, she became a Black Muslim, a member of Elijah Muhammad's Nation of Islam, whose doctrines are reflected in her writings of the 1970s, as in her Blues Book for Blue Black Magical Women *(1974).*

In 1975, Sonia Sanchez withdrew from the Nation of Islam, and in the 1980s and 1990s her poems, plays, and stories have become less scathing. But she remains devoted to changing what she sees as the uncaring, white-dominated culture of America, and her writing continues to reflect her concern for the oppressed and her desire to encourage black Americans to maintain their individuality and refuse to "wear the white mask."

FURTHER READING: J. Joyce, *Ijala: Sonia Sanchez and the African Poetic Tradition,* 1996; *Black American Women Poets and Dramatists,* ed. H. Bloom, 1996; E. Frost, *The Feminist Avant-garde in American Poetry,* 2003.

TEXTS: "the final solution/" and "to blk/record/buyers" are from *Homecoming,* 1969; "Womanhood" is from *A Blues Book for Blue Black Magical Women,* 1974; "Masks" and "Just Don't Never Give Up on Love" are from *Homegirls and Handgrenades,* 1984.

the final solution/

the leaders speak
america
land of free/
dom
land of im/mi/grant
wh/ites
and slave/
blacks. there is
no real problem here.
we the
lead/ers of free
a/mer/ica
say. give us your
hungry/
illiterates/
criminals/
dropouts/
(in other words)
your blacks
and we will
let them fight
in vietnam
defending america's honor.
we will make responsible
citi/
zens out of them or
kill them trying.
america
land of free/dom
free/
enter/
prise and de/mo/
cracy.

bring us your problems.
we your lead/ers
always find a solution.
after all
what else are
we get/
ting pd for?
1969

to blk/record/buyers

don't play me no
righteous bros.
white people
ain't rt bout nothing
no mo.
don't tell me bout
foreign dudes
cuz no blk/
people are grooving on a
sunday afternoon.
they either
making out/
signifying/[1]
drinking/
making molotov cocktails/
stealing
or rather more taking their goods
from the honky thieves who
ain't hung up
on no pacifist/jesus/
cross/ but.
play blk/songs
to drown out the
shit/screams of honkies. AAAH.
AAAH. AAAH. yeah. brothers.
andmanymoretogo.
1969

[1]Boasting, showing off, bantering with others.

WOMANHOOD

Moving. constantly.
some destiny calling
out to me
to explore the sea
and the sky.
to talk against
sleeping on our knees.

and i moved.
eldest daughter of the womb.
eldest daughter of the world.

open to all Blackness
making the country keep in step
to these our new sounds.
to the music of a
million Black souls.

and i called out to prophesy
to make me a woman
of the beginning tribe
to make me a woman of
tyrannical love to
cover our wounds.

and
Blackness was the
order of the day.
all who looked were
enchanted and
chanted who they once were

and we fell down upon
the earth and became ourselves.

and
Blackness was the
order of the day
and the voice of Elijah[1] was
heard opening the
door of the world
and all who came
after him,
poets and soothsayers
rappers and raconteurs

[1]Elijah Muhammad (1897–1975), leader of the Nation of Islam (Black Muslims), 1934–1975.

politicians and activists,
writers and teachers,
sang his wisdom.
and we fell down
upon the earth and
became ourselves.
and
i gave birth to myself,
twice. in one hour.
i became like Maat,[2]
unalterable in my
love of Black self and
righteousness.
and i heard the
trumpets of a new age
and i fell down
upon the earth
and became myself.

1974

MASKS

(blacks don't have the intellectual capacity to succeed.)

—WILLIAM COORS

the river runs toward day
and never stops.
so life receives the lakes
patrolled by one-eyed pimps
who wash their feet in our blue whoredom

the river floods
the days grow short
we wait to change our masks
we wait for warmer days and
fountains without force
we wait for seasons without power.

today
ah today
only the shrill sparrow seeks the sky
our days are edifice.
we look toward temples that give birth to sanctioned flesh.

[2]Ancient Near Eastern goddess of cosmic and moral order.

o bring the white mask
full of the chalk sky.

entering the temple
on this day of sundays
i hear the word spoken
by the unhurried speaker
who speaks of unveiled eyes.

o bring the chalk mask
full of attitudes.

straight in this chair
tall in an unrehearsed role
i rejoice
and the spirit sinks in twilight of
distant smells.

o bring the mask
full of drying blood.

fee, fie, fo, fum,
i smell the blood
of an englishman

o my people
wear the white masks
for they speak without speaking
and hear words of forgetfulness.

o my people.

1984

"JUST DON'T NEVER GIVE UP ON LOVE"

Feeling tired that day, I came to the park with the children. I saw her as I rounded the corner, sitting old as stale beer on the bench, ruminating on some uneventful past. And I thought, "Hell. No rap from the roots today. I need the present. On this day. This Monday. This July day buckling me under her summer wings, I need more than old words for my body to squeeze into."

I sat down at the far end of the bench, draping my legs over the edge, baring my back to time and time unwell spent. I screamed to the children to watch those curves threatening their youth as they rode their 10-speed bikes against mid-western rhythms.

I opened my book and began to write. They were coming again, those words insistent as his hands had been, pounding inside me, demanding their time and place. I relaxed as my hands moved across the paper like one possessed.

I wasn't sure just what it was I heard. At first I thought it was one of the boys calling me so I kept on writing. They knew the routine by now. Emergencies demanded a presence. A facial confrontation. No long distance screams across trees and space and other children's screams. But the sound pierced the pages and I looked around, and there she was inching her bamboo-creased body toward my back, coughing a beaded sentence off her tongue.

"Guess you think I ain't never loved, huh girl? Hee. Hee. Guess that what you be thinking, huh?"

I turned. Startled by her closeness and impropriety, I stuttered, "I, I, I, Whhhaat dooooo you mean?"

"Hee. Hee. Guess you think I been old like this fo'ever, huh?" She leaned toward me, "Huh? I was so pretty that mens brought me breakfast in bed. Wouldn't let me hardly do no work at all."

"That's nice ma'am. I'm glad to hear that." I returned to my book. I didn't want to hear about some ancient love that she carried inside her. I had to finish a review for the journal. I was already late. I hoped she would get the hint and just sit still. I looked at her out of the corner of my eyes.

"He could barely keep hisself in changing clothes. But he was pretty. My first husband looked like the sun. I used to say his name over and over again 'til it hung from my ears like diamonds. Has you ever loved a pretty man, girl?"

I raised my eyes, determined to keep a distance from this woman disturbing my day.

"No ma'am. But I've seen many a pretty man. I don't like them though cuz they keep their love up high in a linen closet and I'm too short to reach it."

Her skin shook with laughter.

"Girl you gots some spunk about you after all. C'mon over here next to me. I wants to see yo' eyes up close. You looks so uneven sittin' over there."

Did she say uneven? Did this old buddah splintering death say uneven? Couldn't she see that I had one eye shorter than the other; that my breath was painted on porcelain; that one breast crocheted keloids under this white blouse?

I moved toward her though. I scooped up the years that had stripped me to the waist and moved toward her. And she called to me to come out, come out wherever you are young woman, playing hide and go seek with scarecrow men. I gathered myself up at the gateway of her confessionals.

"Do you know what it mean to love a pretty man, girl?" She crooned in my ear. "You always running behind a man like that girl while he cradles his privates. Ain't no joy in a pretty yellow man, cuz he always out pleasurin' and givin' pleasure."

I nodded my head as her words sailed in my ears. Here was the pulse of a woman whose black ass shook the world once.

She continued. "A woman crying all the time is pitiful. Pitiful I says. I wuz pitiful sitting by the window every night like a cow in the fields chewin' on cud. I wanted to cry out, but not even God hisself could hear me. I tried to cry out til my mouth wuz split open at the throat. I 'spoze there is a time all womens has to visit the slaughter house. My visit lasted five years."

Touching her hands, I felt the summer splintering in prayer; touching her hands, I felt my bones migrating in red noise. I asked, "When did you see the butterflies again?"

Her eyes wandered like quicksand over my face. Then she smiled, "Girl don't you know yet that you don't never give up on love? Don't you know you has in you the pulse of winds? The noise of dragon flies?" Her eyes squinted close and she said, "One of them mornings he woke up callin' me and I wuz gone. I wuz gone running with the moon over my shoulders. I looked no which way at all. I had inside me 'nough knives and spoons to cut/scoop out the night. I wuz a tremblin' as I met the mornin'."

She stirred in her 84-year-old memory. She stirred up her body as she talked. "They's men and mens. Some good. Some bad. Some breathing death. Some breathing life. William wuz my beginnin'. I come to my second husband spittin' metal and he just pick me up and fold me inside him. I wuz christen' with his love."

She began to hum. I didn't recognize the song; it was a prayer. I leaned back and listened to her voice rustling like silk. I heard cathedrals and sonnets; I heard tents and revivals and a black woman spilling black juice among her ruins.

"We all gotta salute death one time or 'nother girl. Death be waitin' out doors trying to get inside. William died at his job. Death just turned 'round and snatched him right off the street."

Her humming became the only sound in the park. Her voice moved across the bench like a mutilated child. And I cried. For myself. For this woman talkin' about love. For all the women who have ever stretched their bodies out anticipating civilization and finding ruins.

The crashing of the bikes was anticlimactic. I jumped up, rushed toward the accident. Man. Little man. Where you bicycling to so very fast? Man. Second little man. Take it slow. It all passes so fast any how.

As I walked the boys and their bikes toward the bench, I smiled at this old woman waiting for our return.

"I want you to meet a great lady, boys."

"Is she a writer, too, ma?"

"No honey. She's a lady who has lived life instead of writing about it."

"After we say hello can we ride a little while longer? Please!"

"Ok. But watch your manners now and your bones afterwards."

"These are my sons, Ma'am."

"How you do sons? I'm Mrs. Rosalie Johnson. Glad to meet you."

The boys shook her hand and listened for a minute to her words. Then they rode off, spinning their wheels on a city neutral with pain.

As I stood watching them race the morning, Mrs. Johnson got up.

"Don't go," I cried. "You didn't finish your story."

"We'll talk by-and-by. I comes out here almost everyday. I sits here on the same bench everyday. I'll probably die sittin' here one day. As good a place as any I 'magine."

"May I hug you, ma'am? You've helped me so much today. You've given me strength to keep on looking."

"No. Don't never go looking for love girl. Just wait. It'll come. Like the rain fallin' from the heaven, it'll come. Just don't never give up on love."

We hugged; then she walked her 84-year-old walk down the street. A black woman. Echoing gold. Carrying couplets from the sky to crease the ground.

1984

Black Fire

An Anthology of Afro-American Writing 1968

The critical treatment of and artistic consciousness behind the literature written by black Americans underwent significant changes during the twentieth century. These changes were anchored by the publication of two seminal anthologies, The New Negro *(1925) and* Black Fire *(1968), the former associated with the Harlem Renaissance, the latter with the Black Arts Movement (BAM).*

The Black Fire *anthology, edited by LeRoi Jones (Amiri Baraka) and Larry Neal, and modeled after* The New Negro *(Alain Locke, editor), reoriented the political and artistic thinking of an emerging generation of black American writers, directing them away from the traditional forms that had characterized the Harlem Renaissance and toward a fusion of poetry and jazz that eventually gave birth to hip-hop. A selection of poems from that volume is included here.*

TEXT: *Black Fire,* 1968.

POEM

James T. Stewart

We drank Thunderbird[1] all night,
and rode the subway from Snyder to Olney
and back,
and made occasional love.
We went for a whole day through the white stores: Gimbels,
    Sterns and Wanamakers,[2]
and to Robin's bookstore on Thirteenth street;
and rubbernecked at sweazy faggots we chance to see,
and I thought while I stroked your legs
about the sweet hype,
the sweet smell of pot
    through the El[3] window along Market around 56th
and how we sat sedately
while a toilet flushed somewhere.
Oh and the revolutionary sheets
        and your calibrated belly
            (the children came too soon
            You'll never wear a Bikini
            at Coney Island)[4]
        where seasons of hairs make a steeple
        in your thighs—

[1]A cheap wine. [2]Major department stores in New York City.
[3]The elevated train. [4]A large amusement park and beach in Brooklyn.

a whole day.
A whole day to go reconnoitering
the rummage sales (you bought me a pair of pants and we
saw a silver casserole you wanted)
down the brittled pavements,
to see our tar-baby jesus
in the Moorish Temple window,
and saw a floor where black arabesques
flowered at your feet as you stepped out of bed.
Fully I see you now,
before footlights, in a lineup,
for some greedy hustler's game
and I drink Sterno[5]
and quietly die.

1968

NEON DIASPORA[1]

David Henderson

For the famous rhythm and blues quartet, the Drifters

The Drifters are in Harlem
The Drifters are at the Theresa
Staring over the soot-stained ghetto
Just as Castro did in '60[2]
The Drifter's suite—just as Castro's was—is directly
Over Chock Full O'Nuts,[3] the distinction being twelve stories
of elevation, of stained brick and crevices.

These fine slickheaded ghetto boys have wheeled
their agony through streets of iron, beast, blood
and fire singing *their* songs of freedom to the blackbelted
bucks of our America.
There Goes My Baby[4] through Atlanta, *Let the Music*
Play
Through Birmingham, Jackson, *Up On the Roof* through
Los Angeles, Jacksonville, *On Broadway, The Rat Race*

[5]A substance sometimes drunk for its alcoholic content, but likely to cause physical harm or death as a result.

[1]A diaspora is a migration of an ethnic group. In reference to African Americans, it particularly refers to the post-slavery migration from the South to the North.

[2]Fidel Castro became president of Cuba as a result of a military coup in 1959. He visited the United States the next year.

[3]A brand of coffee and a chain of stores that sell that brand.

[4]The first of several Drifters songs mentioned in the poem.

Chicago, Illinois, Manhattan—the Theresa built upon
base of Chock Full O' Nuts—*Let The Music Play just*
a little longer.
The Drifters are in the foul auricle of the city
walking no freedom orgasm to wave of biblical firehose.
The Drifters are in the Palm Café strutting for the
aristocracy
the Post Office Employees, the Parks Department truck
drivers, the
Transit Railroad Clerks and policemen. The nurses, the Fish
and
Chips' shack owners
The fully employed, steady working hands of Harlem. The
Drifters
are in the Palm Café to wave and shout, stomp and lead the
privileged, the responsibles
to the Apollo[5]
along with the rest.

II

The Drifters are in the fetid bosom of Manhattan
Rocking the Apollo like an exploding battleship:
The bobbing black crowd reach long upwards,
The short-skirted young girls dog in the aisles . . .
The Drifters are in the big Apple tonight
Sing us a song . . . SANG!

I see the enigmas of our Neon Diaspora

The Drifter's lashing gleaming red and black hair elongated
Crushed in waves like a murky manic sea. White hand-kerchiefs
billowing outward draw gasp from the crowd, mop brightly
brown faces and then are released above the orchestra to be
ripped to pieces in terms of love.
I see the lead singer of the Drifters (his teeth too big for
his mouth), react to his plasmic nickname. The Drifters
are legs encased in silver, they are pop-collared shirts
flowing
outward at the breast, they are blazing orange jackets exact
in tightness from shoulder to buttocks—holding all in
along the aorta line.
These hightop demons of the Quarter strip
do not dance

[5]A popular music theater in New York City.

These incantators of neon disasters
    do not clown
These imbibers of barbecue and Gordon's Gin

    are not from Liverpool

When I see them strut to the footlights, faintly
smiling amongst themselves, giving measured "cool" response
to the screaming, the dancing, the reaching, and then looking
into the crowd and darkness, swagger a retreat with that
Elemental sexuality (that has been our only hope for so long)
I love those black bastards with all the heart I dare.

1968

when my uncle willie saw

Carol Freeman

when
my uncle willie saw
aunt mimmies new baby he
look at his big cracked black hands the thick
pink nails split then
he looked at black mimmie with her gold teeth flashing and
he look at the baby
    then
later on he brag to everybody how he
got indin blood from his grand mama
    thenwhen
my uncle willie and aunt tee mimmie had
nother baby he
look at auntee then he
look out the window he
look at the midwife who smiling a little
shaking her head a little
and he say it albinodentyall member us get albinirs on mah cudin
    Tim side?
Aunt tee she grinsome then she laugh then she say willie-sherrif
    merriweather
say of this a boy if ah names him merriweather he gon give you fi'
    dollars?
then!
i seen uncle willie cry some.

1968

FOR THE TRUTH

(BECAUSE IT IS NECESSARY)

Edward Spriggs

in the tea rooms
of our revolution
we blatantly debate
our knowledge of world revolts
—our anxious ears only half-listened
to the songs of the martinique
who sings in muffled tones
from beneath a mechanized tombstone
built by the pulp of greedy merchants
who got stoned on the juices of our servitude
& who write prefaces to our "negritude"

from the tea rooms
of our revolution we emerge
to pamphleteer
the anticipatory designs
of our dead
& exiled poets
—without sanctions
from our unsuspecting brothers
whose death we so naively plot
(we engage in a hypothetical revolt
against a not-so-hypothetical enemy)

what kind of man are you
black revolutionary, so-called?
what kind of man are you trying to be
ultra-hip-revolutionary-nationalist-
quasi-strategist-ego-centric-phony
intellectual romantic black prima donna child
—screaming, "revolution means change . . ."
never finishing the sentence
or the thought
talking about "para-military"
strategy and techniques
publicizing a so-called underground program
wearing your military garb
as if you never heard of camouflage
so in love with intrigue
you have no thoughts
about the post-revolution life
that the total destruction
you talk about assumes . . .

you leave me quite confused
brother
i don't know who the enemy is
anymore
perhaps it is me, myself, because
i have these thoughts
in the tea rooms of our revolution.
1968

"OH SHIT A RIOT!"

Jacques Wakefield

"Oh shit a riot!"
"Get A.J. Lesters!" Pink Pants . . . 20.00 knit.
"Oh shit gonna get me some gator tops."
"WATCH OUT THE BLUECOATS ARE COMING!"
"Shit man get the match to this shoe!"
"They killed Martin Luther King."
    "THAT'S RIGHT"
    "UH, HUH"
    "DAMN RIGHT"
Hey, why don't y'all get some jew'ry stores.
    "I'M DOWN"
"COME ON!" They killed Martin Luther thingabob"
1968

June Jordan 1936–2002

Once described by feminist writer Adrienne Rich as "one of the most musically and lyrically gifted poets of the late twentieth century," African American writer June Jordan became best known for her poetry, written in the dialect of black English, that explored such themes as race relations, love, homosexuality, children's vulnerability and loss of innocence, and domestic violence.

Jordan was born on July 9, 1936, in Harlem, New York. She was the only child of Jamaican immigrants who worked, respectively, as a postal clerk and a nurse. When Jordan was age five, her parents purchased a brownstone on Hancock Street in the Bedford-Stuyvesant area of Brooklyn, and there she came of age. Her childhood years, paralleling the experiences of many blacks in poor, urban neighborhoods, were often difficult. "Throughout my growing up," she recalled, "my parents worked as hard as they could devise, and yet we never had a car, my parents never had a vacation, our family never knew what it was to feel satisfied, or proud, or basically secure."

The Jordans recognized the challenges their daughter faced and believed that if she had a "high quality" education, she would overcome many obstacles. From an early age, Jordan's father "pushed upon" her the "poets of the Scriptures, Shakespeare, Edgar Allen Poe, along with Paul Laurence Dunbar." Her parents also enrolled her in the Northfield School for Girls in Massachusetts, an elite New England Preparatory School. She graduated at age sixteen and shortly afterward entered Barnard College, then the women's division of Columbia University. As there were few blacks at either school, Jordan found the educational experiences culturally stifling. Later she would write, "No one ever presented me with a single black author, poet, historian, personage, or idea, for that matter. Nor was I ever assigned a single woman to study as a thinker, or writer, or poet, or life force." After two years she chose to leave Barnard because of the predominantly white environment, a decision she details in her 1975 essay, "Notes of a Barnard Dropout."

In 1955, Jordan married a white Columbia University student, and three years later gave birth to their son. But the marriage eventually unraveled, in part due to the many insults and threats Jordan and her husband encountered as an interracial couple. They divorced in 1965, and Jordan, then twenty-nine years old, became a single mother.

Fueled by the injustices she had seen and experienced, Jordan became interested in the Black Arts Movement and also turned more intimately to her writing. Her first book-length work, Who Look at Me, *appeared in 1969. An epic poem, accompanied by paintings, it explored her frustrations with racism and offered a vivid glimpse of her experiences as a single working mother. Following was a novel, written in black English, which portrayed two teenage lovers coming of age in Harlem. Titled* His Own Where, *the novel won a 1972 National Book Award nomination. Next were three well-received poetry collections,* Some Changes *(1971),* New Days: Poems of Exile and Return *(1973), and* Things I Do in the Dark *(1977). These volumes deftly explore the musical potential of language, and they also boldly address several contemporary social and political issues, such as police violence, rape, militarism, civil rights rollbacks, and the constraints of race, class, and gender. For instance, in "Uhuru in the O.R.," the poet proclaims, "The only successful heart transplant, of the first five attempts, / meant that a black heart kept alive a white man—a white / man who upheld apartheid."*

While reviewers generally praised these early works, some found her political views too strident, a charge leveled against several black writers of the sixties and seventies. That Jordan was undeterred by the negative criticism can be gleaned from "A New Politics of Sexuality," her landmark 1992 essay. Throughout the work she openly celebrates her bisexuality, insisting upon "the equal validity of all of the components of social/sexual complexity," and she calls for a continued struggle for justice, equality, and freedom.

June Jordan is now celebrated as a poet-activist and as one of the century's most prolific writers. In three decades, she published over twenty-five books in a variety of genres—short fiction, novels, children's books, operettas, biography, essays, and drama. Yet it was poetry, which she began writing at age seven, that remained her first love and, as well, the form of her most critically praised work. In her 1981 essay collection, Civil Wars, *she commented: "'Greatness' figured as a deeply motivating notion for me, throughout my childhood. I wanted to be 'a great poet'; indeed, anything less than greatness, anything less than acknowledged excellence did not interest me."*

Jordan's final work, Some of Us Did Not Die: New and Selected Essays *(2002), is a fitting tribute to her love of excellence and aspiration to greatness. Posthumously published, the book combines writings from her four previous essay collections with eight newer, previously unpublished pieces. One of the more poignant of these, "Besting a Worst Case Scenario," details her decade-long struggle with breast cancer, the disease that finally took her life. At her death in June 2002, Jordan was a professor of African American Studies at the University of California at Berkeley.*

FURTHER READING: *Passion: New Poems,* 1980; D. Davenport, *Four Contemporary Black Women Poets: Lucille Clifton, June Jordan, Audre Lorde, and Sherley Anne Williams,* 1987; A. Garrett and H. McCue, *Authors and Artists for Young Adults,* 1989; *Diverse Voices: Essays on Twentieth-Century Women Writers in English,* ed. H. Jump, 1991; W. White, *Dissonant Hu(e)-Manity: Another Way to Be Differently in the Work of Audre Lorde and June Jordan,* 2001.

TEXT: *Naming Our Own Destiny: New and Selected Poems,* 1989.

POEM ABOUT MY RIGHTS

Even tonight and I need to take a walk and clear
my head about this poem about why I can't
go out without changing my clothes my shoes
my body posture my gender identity my age
my status as a woman alone in the evening/
alone on the streets / alone not being the point/
the point being that I can't do what I want
to do with my own body because I am the wrong
sex the wrong age the wrong skin and
suppose it was not here in the city but down on the beach/
or far into the woods and I wanted to go
there by myself thinking about god/or thinking
about children or thinking about the world/all of it
disclosed by the stars and the silence:
I could not go and I could not think and I could not
stay there
alone
as I need to be
alone because I can't do what I want to do with my own
body and
who in the hell set things up
like this
and in France they say if the guy penetrates
but does not ejaculate then he did not rape me
and if after stabbing him if after screams if
after begging the bastard and if even after smashing
a hammer to his head if even after that if he
and his buddies fuck me after that

then I consented and there was
no rape because finally you understand finally
they fucked me over because I was wrong I was
wrong again to be me being me where I was/wrong
to be who I am
which is exactly like South Africa
penetration into Namibia penetrating into
Angola and does that mean I mean how do you know if
Pretoria ejaculates what will the evidence look like the
proof of the monster jackboot ejaculation on Blackland
and if
after Namibia and if after Angola and if after Zimbabwe
and if after all of my kinsmen and women resist even to
self-immolation of the villages and if after that
we lose nevertheless what will the big boys say will they
claim my consent:
Do You Follow Me: We are the wrong people of
the wrong skin on the wrong continent and what
in the hell is everybody being reasonable about
and according to the *Times* this week
back in 1966 the C.I.A. decided that they had this problem
and the problem was a man named Nkrumah[1] so they
killed him and before that it was Patrice Lumumba[2]
and before that it was my father on the campus
of my Ivy League school and my father afraid
to walk into the cafeteria because he said he
was wrong the wrong age the wrong skin the wrong
gender identity and he was paying my tuition and
before that
it was my father saying I was wrong saying that
I should have been a boy because he wanted one/a
boy and that I should have been lighter skinned and
that I should have had straighter hair and that
I should not be so boy crazy but instead I should
just be one/a boy and before that
it was my mother pleading plastic surgery for
my nose and braces for my teeth and telling me
to let the books loose to let them loose in other
words
I am very familiar with the problems of the C.I.A.
and the problems of South Africa and the problems
of Exxon Corporation and the problems of white
America in general and the problems of the teachers

[1]President of Ghana from 1960 to 1966.

[2]Prime minister of the Congo from 1960 until his assassination in 1961. He was president of the Congolese National Movement against the colonial power of Belgium and is regarded as a martyr.

and the preachers and the F.B.I. and the social
workers and my particular Mom and Dad/I am very
familiar with the problems because the problems
turn out to be
me
I am the history of rape
I am the history of the rejection of who I am
I am the history of the terrorized incarceration of
my self
I am the history of battery assault and limitless
armies against whatever I want to do with my mind
and my body and my soul and
whether it's about walking out at night
or whether it's about the love that I feel or
whether it's about the sanctity of my vagina or
the sanctity of my national boundaries
of the sanctity of my leaders or the sanctity
of each and every desire
that I know from my personal and idiosyncratic
and indisputably single and singular heart
I have been raped
be-
cause I have been wrong the wrong sex the wrong age
the wrong skin the wrong nose the wrong hair the
wrong need the wrong dream the wrong geographic
the wrong sartorial I
I have been the meaning of rape
I have been the problem everyone seeks to
eliminate by forced
penetration with or without the evidence of slime and/
but let this be unmistakable this poem
is not consent I do not consent
to my mother to my father to the teachers to
the F.B.I. to South Africa to Bedford-Stuy[3]
to Park Avenue to American Airlines to the hardon
idlers on the corners to the sneaky creeps in cars
I am not wrong: Wrong is not my name
My name is my own my own my own
and I can't tell you who the hell set things up like this
but I can tell you that from now on my resistance
my simple and daily and nightly self-determination
may very well cost you your life

1980

[3]Abbreviation for the Brooklyn section Bedford Stuyvesant, the largest concentration of blacks in New York City.

POEM FOR GUATEMALA

Dedicated to Rigoberto Manchú[1]

(With thanks to Journey to the Depths, *the testimony of Rigoberto Manchú, translated into English by Patricia Goedicke, October, 1982)*

No matter how loudly I call you the sound of your name
makes the day soft
Nothing about it sticks to my throat
Guatemala
syllables that lilt into twilight and lust
Guatemala
syllables to melt bullets

They call you Indian
They called me West Indian
You learned to speak Spanish when I did
We were thirteen
I wore shoes
I ate rice and peas
The beans and the rice in your pot
brought the soldiers
to hack off your arms

"Walk like that into the kitchen!
Walk like that into the clearing!
Girl with no arms!"
I had been playing the piano

Because of the beans and the rice in your pot
the soldiers arrived with an axe
to claim you guerrilla
girl with no arms

An Indian is not supposed to own a pot of food
An Indian is too crude
An Indian covers herself with dirt so the cold
times will not hurt her

Cover yourself with no arms!

They buried my mother in New Jersey.
Black cars carried her there.
She wore flowers and a long dress.

[1]Noble Peace Prize awardee for her work on behalf of the indigenous people of the Americas.

Soldiers pushed into your mother
and tore out her tongue
and whipped her under a tree
and planted a fly in the bleeding
places so that worms
spread through the flesh
then the dogs
then the buzzards
then the soldiers laughing
at the family of the girl
with no arms
guerrilla girl
with no arms

You go with no arms
among the jungle treacheries
You go with no arms
into the mountains hunting
revenge

I watch you
walk like that
into the kitchen
walk like that
into the clearing
girl with no arms

I am learning new syllables
of revolution

Guatemala
Guatemala
Girl with no arms

1989

Rita Dove 1952–

When asked what made her want to write, Poet Laureate Rita Dove always remarks, "Books. First and foremost, now, then, and always, I have been passionate about books." Dove's enthusiasm for the written word developed early in life as she devoured books of all kinds, including an outdated, multivolume encyclopedia set that her father bought at a flea market for $5. Science fiction tales particularly sparked the young girl's imagination, and it wasn't long before she had written her own sci-fi novel about robots taking control of the earth. Using each week's spelling list as the foundation for each *chapter, the clever, ambitious young writer penned forty-three chapters (one for each of the forty-three spelling lists of the school year). Supported by this interest in books and reading, Dove consistently excelled in school, winning two scholarships (one a Fulbright) that facilitated her studies in modern European literature at Germany's University of Tübingen and creative writing in the prestigious writers' program at the University of Iowa.*

After finishing her education, Rita Dove first received widespread attention with the publication of The Yellow House on the Corner *(1980) and* Museum *(1983). Poems from these collections such as "The House Slave" and "Parsley" show Dove's precision and supple use of layered language. Powerful emotions arise from restrained lines and carefully controlled diction. Her third volume of poetry,* Thomas and Beulah *(1986) told of the lives of her two maternal grandparents, who moved from the South to Akron, Ohio, where they met, married, and raised a family. Critics have remarked on Dove's "ability to draw real characters holding jobs, raising families, drinking beer, playing music. . .," and Dove demonstrated this skill in* Thomas and Beulah *as she wove autobiographical detail, historical event, and poetic inspiration into a coherent narrative sequence. Dove's talent was formally recognized when* Thomas and Beulah *won her the 1987 Pulitzer Prize in American Poetry. In the decade following the publication of* Thomas and Beulah, *Dove published two more books of poems:* Grace Notes *(1989) and* Selected Poems *(1993). Dove's lyric poetry shows a facility with drama and narrative that has served her well when she turns to other forms. She has written a collection of short stories,* Fifth Sunday *(1985); a novel,* Through the Ivory Gate *(1992); and a verse drama,* The Darker Face of the Earth *(1994), about a white woman in the pre–Civil-War South who falls in love with a black slave.*

Like American poets Melvin Tolson and Ralph Ellison, Dove embraces a full range of European, American, and African American traditions and influences. Well traveled, Dove has often set her poems in diverse places, including Europe, Israel, the American South, and her own hometown. She is willing to draw on both Greek mythology and African diasporic history. And like poets Claude McKay or Countee Cullen, Dove is at home with traditional European poetic forms, often using them to express contemporary American themes. To Dove, "language is everything" and "it is the sounds of the language, the way of telling something, that makes a poem." She has further expressed that she is "profoundly fascinated by the ways in which language can change your perceptions" and does not subscribe to writing poems that "feel good on the first reading because they stroke your preconceptions." Dove candidly reveals that she makes her poetry out of the words spoken around her, collecting them from her daily life and setting them down in colored folders where they can work together to shape themselves into poetic form.

In 1993, Rita Dove became the first black American poet (and the youngest) to be named Poet Laureate of the United States and was reappointed in 1994. Since 1989, she has been professor of English at the University of Virginia at Charlottesville, where she teaches creative writing.

FURTHER READING: E. Ingersol, *Conversations with Rita Dove,* 2003; M. Pereira, *Rita Dove's Cosmopolitanism,* 2003; T. Steffen, *Crossing Color: Transcultural Space and Place in Rita Doves' Poetry, Fiction, and Drama,* 2001; *African American Poets: Robert Hayden Through Rita Dove,* ed. H. Bloom, 2003; P. Righelato, *Understanding Rita Dove,* 2006.

TEXT: *Selected Poems,* 1993.

KENTUCKY, 1833

It is Sunday, day of roughhousing. We are let out in the woods. The young boys wrestle and butt their heads together like sheep—a circle forms; claps and shouts fill the air. The women, brown and glossy, gather round the banjo player, or simply lie in the sun, legs and aprons folded. The weather's an odd monkey—any other day he's on our backs, his cotton eye everywhere; today the light sifts down like the finest cornmeal, coating our hands and arms with a dust. God's dust, old woman Acker says. She's the only one who could read to us from the Bible, before Massa forbade it. On Sundays, something hangs in the air, a hallelujah, a skitter of brass, but we can't call it by name and it disappears.

Then Massa and his gentlemen friends come to bet on the boys. They guffaw and shout, taking sides, red-faced on the edge of the boxing ring. There is more kicking, butting, and scuffling—the winner gets a dram of whiskey if he can drink it all in one swig without choking.

Jason is bucking and prancing about—Massa said his name reminded him of some sailor, a hero who crossed an ocean, looking for a golden cotton field. Jason thinks he's been born to great things—a suit with gold threads, vest and all. Now the winner is sprawled out under a tree and the sun, that weary tambourine, hesitates at the rim of the sky's green light. It's a crazy feeling that carries through the night; as if the sky were an omen we could not understand, the book that, if we could read, would change our lives.

1980

ADOLESCENCE—I

In water-heavy nights behind grandmother's porch
We knelt in the tickling grasses and whispered:
Linda's face hung before us, pale as a pecan,
And it grew wise as she said:
    "A boy's lips are soft,
    As soft as baby's skin."
The air closed over her words.
A firefly whirred near my ear, and in the distance
I could hear streetlamps ping
Into miniature suns
Against a feathery sky.

1980

ADOLESCENCE—II

Although it is night, I sit in the bathroom, waiting.
Sweat prickles behind my knees, the baby-breasts are alert.
Venetian blinds slice up the moon; the tiles quiver in pale strips.

Then they come, the three seal men with eyes as round
As dinner plates and eyelashes like sharpened tines.
They bring the scent of licorice. One sits in the washbowl,

One on the bathtub edge; one leans against the door.
"Can you feel it yet?" they whisper.
I don't know what to say, again. They chuckle,

Patting their sleek bodies with their hands.
"Well, maybe next time." And they rise,
Glittering like pools of ink under moonlight,

And vanish. I clutch at the ragged holes
They leave behind, here at the edge of darkness.
Night rests like a ball of fur on my tongue.

1980

ADOLESCENCE—III

With Dad gone, Mom and I worked
The dusky rows of tomatoes.
As they glowed orange in sunlight
And rotted in shadow, I too
Grew orange and softer, swelling out
Starched cotton slips.

The texture of twilight made me think of
Lengths of Dotted Swiss. In my room
I wrapped scarred knees in dresses
That once went to big-band dances;
I baptized my earlobes with rosewater.
Along the window-sill, the lipstick stubs
Glittered in their steel shells.

Looking out at the rows of clay
And chicken manure, I dreamed how it would happen:
He would meet me by the blue spruce,
A carnation over his heart, saying,
"I have come for you, Madam;

I have loved you in my dreams."
At his touch, the scabs would fall away.
Over his shoulder, I see my father coming toward us:
He carries his tears in a bowl,
And blood hangs in the pine-soaked air.

1980

BANNEKER[1]

What did he do except lie
under a pear tree, wrapped in
a great cloak, and meditate
on the heavenly bodies?
Venerable, the good people of Baltimore
whispered, shocked and more than
a little afraid. After all it was said
he took to strong drink.
Why else would he stay out
under the stars all night
and why hadn't he married?
But who would want him! Neither
Ethiopian nor English, neither
lucky nor crazy, a capacious bird
humming as he penned in his mind
another enflamed letter
to President Jefferson—he imagined
the reply, polite and rhetorical.
Those who had been to Philadelphia
reported the statue
of Benjamin Franklin
before the library

his very size and likeness.
A wife? No, thank you.
At dawn he milked
the cows, then went inside
and put on a pot to stew
while he slept. The clock
he whittled as a boy
still ran. Neighbors
woke him up
with warm bread and quilts.
At nightfall he took out

[1]"Benjamin Banneker (1731–1806), first black man to devise an almanac and predict a solar eclipse accurately, was also appointed to the commission that surveyed and laid out what is now Washington, D.C."—Dove's note.

his rifle—a white-maned
figure stalking the darkened
breast of the Union—and
shot at the stars, and by chance
one went out. Had he killed?
I assure thee, my dear Sir!
Lowering his eyes to fields
sweet with the rot of spring, he could see
a government's domed city
rising from the morass and spreading
in a spiral of lights. . . .[2]

1983

JIVING[1]

Heading North, straw hat
cocked on the back of his head,

tight curls gleaming
with brilliantine, he didn't stop

until the nights of chaw
and river-bright

had retreated, somehow
into another's life. He landed

in Akron, Ohio
1921,

on the dingy beach
of a man-made lake.

Since what he'd been through
he was always jiving, gold hoop

from the right ear jiggling
and a glass stud, bright blue

in his left. The young ladies
saying *He sure plays*

[2]Ellipses, here and throughout, are Dove's.

[1]"Jiving" and the poems that follow first appeared in book form in *Thomas and Beulah* (1986), a sequence of poems loosely based on the lives of Dove's grandparents.

that tater bug
like the devil!

sighing their sighs
and dimpling.
1986

THE ZEPPELIN FACTORY[1]

The zeppelin factory
needed workers, all right—
but, standing in the cage
of the whale's belly, sparks
flying off the joints
and noise thundering,
Thomas wanted to sit
right down and cry.

That spring the third
largest airship was dubbed
the biggest joke
in town, though they all
turned out for the launch.
Wind caught,
"The Akron" floated
out of control,

three men in tow—
one dropped
to safety, one
hung on but the third,
muscles and adrenaline
failing, fell
clawing
six hundred feet.[2]

Thomas at night
in the vacant lot:
Here I am, intact
and faint-hearted.

[1]In a "Chronology" included in her volume of poems *Thomas and Beulah,* Dove's entry for 1929 reads, "The Goodyear Zeppelin Airdock is built—the largest building in the world without interior supports." Zeppelins, named for their inventor Ferdinand von Zeppelin (1838–1917), were rigid airships, dirigibles, similar in appearance to but much larger than modern-day blimps.

[2]"1931: The airship *Akron* disaster."—Dove's "Chronology" entry.

Thomas hiding
his heart with his hat
at the football game, eyeing
the Goodyear blimp overhead:
Big boy I know
you're in there.

1986

UNDER THE VIADUCT, 1932

He avoided the empty millyards,
the households towering
next to the curb. It was dark
where he walked, although above him
the traffic was hissing.

He poked a trail in the mud
with his tin-capped stick.
If he had a son this time
he would teach him how to step
between his family and the police,
the mob bellowing
as a kettle of communal soup
spilled over a gray bank of clothes. . . .

The pavement wobbled, loosened by rain.
He liked it down here
where the luck of the mighty
had tumbled,

black suit and collarbone.
He could smell the worms stirring in their holes.
He could watch the white sheet settle
while all across the North Hill Viaduct

tires slithered to a halt.

1986

ROAST POSSUM

The possum's a greasy critter
that lives on persimmons and what
the Bible calls carrion.

So much from the 1909 Werner
Encyclopedia,[1] three rows of deep green
along the wall. A granddaughter
propped on each knee,
Thomas went on with his tale—

but it was for Malcolm,[2] little
Red Delicious, that he invented
embellishments: *We shined that possum*
with a torch and I shinnied up,
being the smallest,
to shake him down. He glared at me,
teeth bared like a shark's
in that torpedo snout.
Man he was tough but no match
for old-time know-how.

Malcolm hung back, studying them
with his gold hawk eyes. When the girls
got restless, Thomas talked horses:
Strolling Jim, who could balance
a glass of water on his back
and trot the village square
without spilling a drop. Who put
Wartrace on the map and was buried
under a stone, like a man.

They like that part.
He would have gone on to tell them
that the Werner admitted Negro children
to be intelligent, though briskness
clouded over at puberty, bringing
indirection and laziness. Instead,
he added: *You got to be careful*
with a possum when he's on the ground;
he'll turn on his back and play dead
till you give up looking. That's
what you'd call sullin'.

Malcolm interrupted to ask
who owned Strolling Jim,
and who paid for the tombstone.

[1]A reprint of the Ninth Edition of the *Encyclopaedia Britannica* (with an "American Supplement"), in twenty-five volumes, published by the Werner Press of Akron, Ohio.

[2]Thomas's grandson.

They stared each other down
man to man, before Thomas,
as a grandfather, replied:
Yessir,
we enjoyed that possum. We ate him
real slow, with sweet potatoes.

1986

WEATHERING OUT

She liked mornings the best—Thomas gone
to look for work, her coffee flushed with milk,

outside autumn trees blowsy and dripping.
Past the seventh month she couldn't see her feet

so she floated from room to room, houseshoes flapping,
navigating corners in wonder. When she leaned

against a door jamb to yawn, she disappeared entirely.

Last week they had taken a bus at dawn
to the new airdock. The hangar slid open in segments

and the zeppelin nosed forward in its silver envelope.
The men walked it out gingerly, like a poodle,

then tied it to a mast and went back inside.
Beulah felt just that large and placid, a lake;

she glistened from cocoa butter smoothed in
when Thomas returned every evening nearly

in tears. He'd lean an ear on her belly
and say: *Little fellow's really talking,*

though to her it was more the *pok-pok-pok*
of a fingernail tapping a thick cream lampshade.

Sometimes during the night she woke and found him
asleep there and the child sleeping, too.

The coffee was good but too little. Outside
everything shivered in tinfoil—only the clover

between the cobblestones hung stubbornly on,
green as an afterthought. . . .

1986

DAYSTAR

She wanted a little room for thinking:
but she saw diapers steaming on the line,
a doll slumped behind the door.

So she lugged a chair behind the garage
to sit out the children's naps.

Sometimes there were things to watch—
the pinched armor of a vanished cricket,
a floating maple leaf. Other days
she stared until she was assured
when she closed her eyes
she'd see only her own vivid blood.

She had an hour, at best, before Liza appeared
pouting from the top of the stairs.
And just *what* was mother doing
out back with the field mice? Why,

building a palace. Later
that night when Thomas rolled over and
lurched into her, she would open her eyes
and think of the place that was hers
for an hour—where
she was nothing,
pure nothing, in the middle of the day.

1986

Maxine Hong Kingston 1940–

The writing of Maxine Hong Kingston is renowned for its fusion of myth and legend, fact and realistic fiction that portrays the lives and the heritage of Chinese immigrants in the United States and their American-born descendants. It is a world she knows well. Her parents were born in China. In the 1920s, her father emigrated to the United States, where he labored as an agricultural field hand, worked in a laundry, and managed a gambling house. Finally, after fifteen years, he earned enough to bring his wife to America, where their daughter Maxine Hong was born in 1940.

She was raised in Chinese American communities in California. A shy child, she began at an early age to express herself in writing. At the University of California at Berkeley she studied journalism and trained to be a teacher. After graduation she married Earl Kingston, a fellow student, and in 1965 she began teaching English in high schools, first in California and then in Hawaii. In 1977, she joined the faculty of the University of Hawaii, and in the 1980s, now a famous and award-winning writer, she returned to

California. Since 1990, she has been a member of the English Department at the University of California at Berkeley, where she teaches creative writing.

Her first book, The Woman Warrior *(1976), was chosen as the best nonfiction book of the year by the National Book Critics Circle. In 1978,* Time *magazine named it one of the ten best nonfiction books of the previous decade. It had been created out of Maxine Kingston's childhood memories and out of myths, legends, and stories of the lives of women told to her by family members and by the Chinese American "story-talkers" she had known as a child.*

In 1980, she published a companion volume, China Men, *which won the 1980 National Book Award for nonfiction. It, too, describes the lives of several generations on two continents and blends autobiography, history, and legend. It tells the experiences of Chinese American men, their struggles to emigrate to America, their hard physical labor building railroads and sugar plantations in the mainland United States and in Hawaii, their pursuit of success, and the dilemmas faced today by the young men who have grown up in the Chinese American culture of the contemporary United States.*

In her third book, the novel Tripmaster Monkey *(1989), Kingston moved from the recasting of history, autobiography, and legends to the writing of fiction. She told the story of a Chinese American beatnik questing for truth, moving—in the words of one critic—"like a giant tattered kite on the rampage" in a 1960s world of social activists, street philosophers, and eccentrics.*

Tripmaster Monkey *was judged to be, at its best, dazzling, at its worst, ranting and frenzied. As a result, Kingston's most highly praised writing remains the blend of fiction, history, and legend that she achieved in* The Woman Warrior *and* China Men. *She has called the two works "one big book" because they form a single story of Chinese Americans living in two different, often conflicting worlds. The books vividly describe the origins and the dimensions of life in those conflicting worlds, but Kingston's books are most memorable for the characters she describes, many of them lost to history and many of them—like the heroine of "No Name Woman"—victims of alienation, brutal violence, and antagonisms that cannot be resolved.*

FURTHER READING: *American Dragons: Twenty-Five Asian-American Voices,* ed. Laurence Yep, 1993; K. Cheung, *Articulate Silences: Hisaye Yamamoto, Maxine Hong Kingston, Joy Kogawa,* 1993; D. Simmons, *Maxine Hong Kingston,* 1999; D. Madsen, *Maxine Hong Kingston,* 2000; E. Huntley, *Maxine Hong Kingston,* A Critical Companion, 2001.

TEXT: *The Woman Warrior,* 1976.

NO NAME WOMAN

"You must not tell anyone," my mother said, "what I am about to tell you. In China your father had a sister who killed herself. She jumped into the family well. We say that your father has all brothers because it is as if she had never been born.

"In 1924 just a few days after our village celebrated seventeen hurry-up weddings—to make sure that every young man who went 'out on the road' would responsibly come home—your father and his brothers and your grandfather and his brothers and your aunt's new husband sailed for America, the Gold Mountain. It was your grandfather's last trip. Those lucky enough to get contracts waved goodbye from the decks. They fed and guarded the stowaways and helped them off in Cuba, New York, Bali, Hawaii. 'We'll meet in California next year,' they said. All of them sent money home.

"I remember looking at your aunt one day when she and I were dressing; I had not noticed before that she had such a protruding melon of a stomach. But I did not think, 'She's pregnant,' until she began to look like other pregnant women, her shirt pulling and the white tops of her black pants showing. She could not have been pregnant, you see, because her husband had been gone for years. No one said anything. We did not discuss it. In early summer she was ready to have the child, long after the time when it could have been possible.

"The village had also been counting. On the night the baby was to be born the villagers raided our house. Some were crying. Like a great saw, teeth strung with lights, files of people walked zigzag across our land, tearing the rice. Their lanterns doubled in the disturbed black water, which drained away through the broken bunds.[1] As the villagers closed in, we could see that some of them, probably men and women we knew well, wore white masks. The people with long hair hung it over their faces. Women with short hair made it stand up on end. Some had tied white bands around their foreheads, arms, and legs.

"At first they threw mud and rocks at the house. Then they threw eggs and began slaughtering our stock. We could hear the animals scream their deaths—the roosters, the pigs, a last great roar from the ox. Familiar wild heads flared in our night windows; the villagers encircled us. Some of the faces stopped to peer at us, their eyes rushing like searchlights. The hands flattened against the panes, framed heads, and left red prints.

"The villagers broke in the front and the back doors at the same time, even though we had not locked the doors against them. Their knives dripped with the blood of our animals. They smeared blood on the doors and walls. One woman swung a chicken, whose throat she had slit, splattering blood in red arcs about her. We stood together in the middle of our house, in the family hall with the pictures and tables of the ancestors around us, and looked straight ahead.

"At that time the house had only two wings. When the men came back, we would build two more to enclose our courtyard and a third one to begin a second courtyard. The villagers pushed through both wings, even your grandparents' rooms, to find your aunt's, which was also mine until the men returned. From this room a new wing for one of the younger families would grow. They ripped up her clothes and shoes and broke her combs, grinding them underfoot. They tore her work from the loom. They scattered the cooking fire and rolled the new weaving in it. We could hear them in the kitchen breaking our bowls and banging the pots. They overturned the great waist-high earthenware jugs; duck eggs, pickled fruits, vegetables burst out and mixed in acrid torrents. The old woman from the next field swept a broom through the air and loosed the spirits-of-the-broom over our heads. 'Pig.' 'Ghost.' 'Pig,' they sobbed and scolded while they ruined our house.

"When they left, they took sugar and oranges to bless themselves. They cut pieces from the dead animals. Some of them took bowls that were not broken and clothes that were not torn. Afterward we swept up the rice and sewed it back up into sacks. But the smells from the spilled preserves lasted. Your aunt

[1]Embankments built to control the flow of irrigation water.

gave birth in the pigsty that night. The next morning when I went for the water, I found her and the baby plugging up the family well.

"Don't let your father know that I told you. He denies her. Now that you have started to menstruate, what happened to her could happen to you. Don't humiliate us. You wouldn't like to be forgotten as if you had never been born. The villagers are watchful."

Whenever she had to warn us about life, my mother told stories that ran like this one, a story to grow up on. She tested our strength to establish realities. Those in the emigrant generations who could not reassert brute survival died young and far from home. Those of us in the first American generations have had to figure out how the invisible world the emigrants built around our childhoods fit in solid America.

The emigrants confused the gods by diverting their curses, misleading them with crooked streets and false names. They must try to confuse their offspring as well, who, I suppose, threaten them in similar ways—always trying to get things straight, always trying to name the unspeakable. The Chinese I know hide their names; sojourners take new names when their lives change and guard their real names with silence.

Chinese-Americans, when you try to understand what things in you are Chinese, how do you separate what is peculiar to childhood, to poverty, insanities, one family, your mother who marked your growing with stories, from what is Chinese? What is Chinese tradition and what is the movies?

If I want to learn what clothes my aunt wore, whether flashy or ordinary, I would have to begin, "Remember Father's drowned-in-the-well sister?" I cannot ask that. My mother has told me once and for all the useful parts. She will add nothing unless powered by Necessity, a riverbank that guides her life. She plants vegetable gardens rather than lawns; she carries the odd-shaped tomatoes home from the fields and eats food left for the gods.

Whenever we did frivolous things, we used up energy; we flew high kites. We children came up off the ground over the melting cones our parents brought home from work and the American movie on New Year's Day—*Oh, You Beautiful Doll* with Betty Grable one year, and *She Wore a Yellow Ribbon* with John Wayne another year. After the one carnival ride each, we paid in guilt; our tired father counted his change on the dark walk home.

Adultery is extravagance. Could people who hatch their own chicks and eat the embryos and the heads for delicacies and boil the feet in vinegar for party food, leaving only the gravel, eating even the gizzard lining—could such people engender a prodigal aunt? To be a woman, to have a daughter in starvation time was a waste enough. My aunt could not have been the lone romantic who gave up everything for sex. Women in the old China did not choose. Some man had commanded her to lie with him and be his secret evil. I wonder whether he masked himself when he joined the raid on her family.

Perhaps she encountered him in the fields or on the mountain where the daughters-in-law collected fuel. Or perhaps he first noticed her in the marketplace. He was not a stranger because the village housed no strangers. She had to have dealings with him other than sex. Perhaps he worked an adjoining field, or he sold her the cloth for the dress she sewed and wore. His demand must have surprised, then terrified her. She obeyed him; she always did as she was told.

When the family found a young man in the next village to be her husband, she stood tractably beside the best rooster, his proxy, and promised before they met that she would be his forever. She was lucky that he was her age and she would be the first wife, an advantage secure now. The night she first saw him, he had sex with her. Then he left for America. She had almost forgotten what he looked like. When she tried to envision him, she only saw the black and white face in the group photograph the men had had taken before leaving.

The other man was not, after all, much different from her husband. They both gave orders: she followed. "If you tell your family, I'll beat you. I'll kill you. Be here again next week." No one talked sex, ever. And she might have separated the rapes from the rest of living if only she did not have to buy her oil from him or gather wood in the same forest. I want her fear to have lasted just as long as rape lasted so that the fear could have been contained. No drawn-out fear. But women at sex hazarded birth and hence lifetimes. The fear did not stop but permeated everywhere. She told the man, "I think I'm pregnant." He organized the raid against her.

On nights when my mother and father talked about their life back home, sometimes they mentioned an "outcast table" whose business they still seemed to be settling, their voices tight. In a commensal tradition,[2] where food is precious, the powerful older people made wrongdoers eat alone. Instead of letting them start separate new lives like the Japanese, who could become samurais and geishas, the Chinese family, faces averted but eyes glowering sideways, hung on to the offenders and fed them leftovers. My aunt must have lived in the same house as my parents and eaten at an outcast table. My mother spoke about the raid as if she had seen it, when she and my aunt, a daughter-in-law to a different household, should not have been living together at all. Daughters-in-law lived with their husbands' parents, not their own; a synonym for marriage in Chinese is "taking a daughter-in-law." Her husband's parents could have sold her, mortgaged her, stoned her. But they had sent her back to her own mother and father, a mysterious act hinting at disgraces not told me. Perhaps they had thrown her out to deflect the avengers.

She was the only daughter; her four brothers went with her father, husband, and uncles "out on the road" and for some years became western men. When the goods were divided among the family, three of the brothers took land, and the youngest, my father, chose an education. After my grandparents gave their daughter away to her husband's family, they had dispensed all the adventure and all the property. They expected her alone to keep the traditional ways, which her brothers, now among the barbarians, could fumble without detection. The heavy, deep-rooted women were to maintain the past against the flood, safe for returning. But the rare urge west had fixed upon our family, and so my aunt crossed boundaries not delineated in space.

The work of preservation demands that the feelings playing about in one's guts not be turned into action. Just watch their passing like cherry blossoms. But perhaps my aunt, my forerunner, caught in a slow life, let dreams grow and fade and after some months or years went toward what persisted. Fear at the enormities of the forbidden kept her desires delicate, wire and bone. She looked at a man because she liked the way the hair was tucked behind his ears, or she

[2]Eating together at the same dining table.

liked the question-mark line of a long torso curving at the shoulder and straight at the hip. For warm eyes or a soft voice or a slow walk—that's all—a few hairs, a line, a brightness, a sound, a pace, she gave up family. She offered us up for a charm that vanished with tiredness, a pigtail that didn't toss when the wind died. Why, the wrong lighting could erase the dearest thing about him.

It could very well have been, however, that my aunt did not take subtle enjoyment of her friend, but, a wild woman, kept rollicking company. Imagining her free with sex doesn't fit, though. I don't know any women like that, or men either. Unless I see her life branching into mine, she gives me no ancestral help.

To sustain her being in love, she often worked at herself in the mirror, guessing at the colors and shapes that would interest him, changing them frequently in order to hit on the right combination. She wanted him to look back.

On a farm near the sea, a woman who tended her appearance reaped a reputation for eccentricity. All the married women blunt-cut their hair in flaps about their ears or pulled it back in tight buns. No nonsense. Neither style blew easily into heart-catching tangles. And at their weddings they displayed themselves in their long hair for the last time. "It brushed the backs of my knees," my mother tells me. "It was braided, and even so, it brushed the backs of my knees."

At the mirror my aunt combed individuality into her bob. A bun could have been contrived to escape into black streamers blowing in the wind or in quiet wisps about her face, but only the older women in our picture album wear buns. She brushed her hair back from her forehead, tucking the flaps behind her ears. She looped a piece of thread, knotted into a circle between her index fingers and thumbs, and ran the double strand across her forehead. When she closed her fingers as if she were making a pair of shadow geese bite, the string twisted together catching the little hairs. Then she pulled the thread away from her skin, ripping the hairs out neatly, her eyes watering from the needles of pain. Opening her fingers, she cleaned the thread, then rolled it along her hairline and the tops of her eyebrows. My mother did the same to me and my sisters and herself. I used to believe that the expression "caught by the short hairs" meant a captive held with a depilatory string. It especially hurt at the temples, but my mother said we were lucky we didn't have to have our feet bound when we were seven. Sisters used to sit on their beds and cry together, she said, as their mothers or their slaves removed the bandages for a few minutes each night and let the blood gush back into their veins. I hope that the man my aunt loved appreciated a smooth brow, that he wasn't just a tits-and-ass man.

Once my aunt found a freckle on her chin, at a spot that the almanac said predestined her for unhappiness. She dug it out with a hot needle and washed the wound with peroxide.

More attention to her looks than these pullings of hairs and pickings at spots would have caused gossip among the villagers. They owned work clothes and good clothes, and they wore good clothes for feasting the new seasons. But since a woman combing her hair hexes beginnings, my aunt rarely found an occasion to look her best. Women looked like great sea snails—the corded wood, babies, and laundry they carried were the whorls on their backs. The Chinese did not admire a bent back; goddesses and warriors stood straight. Still there must have been a marvelous freeing of beauty when a worker laid down her burden and stretched and arched.

Such commonplace loveliness, however, was not enough for my aunt. She dreamed of a lover for the fifteen days of New Year's, the time for families to exchange visits, money, and food. She plied her secret comb. And sure enough she cursed the year, the family, the village, and herself.

Even as her hair lured her imminent lover, many other men looked at her. Uncles, cousins, nephews, brothers would have looked, too, had they been home between journeys. Perhaps they had already been restraining their curiosity, and they left, fearful that their glances, like a field of nesting birds, might be startled and caught. Poverty hurt, and that was their first reason for leaving. But another, final reason for leaving the crowded house was the never-said.

She may have been unusually beloved, the precious only daughter, spoiled and mirror gazing because of the affection the family lavished on her. When her husband left, they welcomed the chance to take her back from the inlaws; she could live like the little daughter for just a while longer. There are stories that my grandfather was different from other people, "crazy ever since the little Jap bayoneted him in the head." He used to put his naked penis on the dinner table, laughing. And one day he brought home a baby girl, wrapped up inside his brown western-style greatcoat. He had traded one of his sons, probably my father, the youngest, for her. My grandmother made him trade back. When he finally got a daughter of his own, he doted on her. They must have all loved her, except perhaps my father, the only brother who never went back to China, having once been traded for a girl.

Brothers and sisters, newly men and women, had to efface their sexual color and present plain miens. Disturbing hair and eyes, a smile like no other threatened the ideal of five generations living under one roof. To focus blurs, people shouted face to face and yelled from room to room. The immigrants I know have loud voices, unmodulated to American tones even after years away from the village where they called their friendships out across the fields. I have not been able to stop my mother's screams in public libraries or over telephones. Walking erect (knees straight, toes pointed forward, not pigeon-toed, which is Chinese-feminine) and speaking in an inaudible voice, I have tried to turn myself American-feminine. Chinese communication was loud, public. Only sick people had to whisper. But at the dinner table, where the family members came nearest one another, no one could talk, not the outcasts nor any eaters. Every word that falls from the mouth is a coin lost. Silently they gave and accepted food with both hands. A preoccupied child who took his bowl with one hand got a sideways glare. A complete moment of total attention is due everyone alike. Children and lovers have no singularity here, but my aunt used a secret voice, a separate attentiveness.

She kept the man's name to herself throughout her labor and dying; she did not accuse him that he be punished with her. To save her inseminator's name she gave silent birth.

He may have been somebody in her own household, but intercourse with a man outside the family would have been no less abhorrent. All the village were kinsmen, and the titles shouted in loud country voices never let kinship be forgotten. Any man within visiting distance would have been neutralized as a lover—"brother," "younger brother," "older brother"—one hundred and fifteen relationship titles. Parents researched birth charts probably not so much to assure good fortune as to circumvent incest in a population that has but one hundred surnames. Everybody has eight million relatives. How useless then sexual mannerisms, how dangerous.

As if it came from an atavism deeper than fear, I used to add "brother" silently to boys' names. It hexed the boys, who would or would not ask me to dance, and made them less scary and as familiar and deserving of benevolence as girls.

But, of course, I hexed myself also—no dates. I should have stood up, both arms waving, and shouted out across libraries, "Hey, you! Love me back." I had no idea, though, how to make attraction selective, how to control its direction and magnitude. If I made myself American-pretty so that the five or six Chinese boys in the class fell in love with me, everyone else—the Caucasian, Negro, and Japanese boys—would too. Sisterliness, dignified and honorable, made much more sense.

Attraction eludes control so stubbornly that whole societies designed to organize relationships among people cannot keep order, not even when they bind people to one another from childhood and raise them together. Among the very poor and the wealthy, brothers married their adopted sisters, like doves. Our family allowed some romance, paying adult brides' prices and providing dowries so that their sons and daughters could marry strangers. Marriage promises to turn strangers into friendly relatives—a nation of siblings.

In the village structure, spirits shimmered among the live creatures, balanced and held in equilibrium by time and land. But one human being flaring up into violence could open up a black hole, a maelstrom that pulled in the sky. The frightened villagers, who depended on one another to maintain the real, went to my aunt to show her a personal, physical representation of the break she had made in the "roundness." Misallying couples snapped off the future, which was to be embodied in true offspring. The villagers punished her for acting as if she could have a private life, secret and apart from them.

If my aunt had betrayed the family at a time of large grain yields and peace, when many boys were born, and wings were being built on many houses, perhaps she might have escaped such severe punishment. But the men—hungry, greedy, tired of planting in dry soil, cuckolded—had had to leave the village in order to send food-money home. There were ghost plagues, bandit plagues, wars with the Japanese, floods. My Chinese brother and sister had died of an unknown sickness. Adultery, perhaps only a mistake during good times, became a crime when the village needed food.

The round moon cakes and round doorways, the round tables of graduated size that fit one roundness inside another, round windows and rice bowls—these talismen had lost their power to warn this family of the law: a family must be whole, faithfully keeping the descent line by having sons to feed the old and the dead, who in turn look after the family. The villagers came to show my aunt and her lover-in-hiding a broken house. The villagers were speeding up the circling of events because she was too shortsighted to see that her infidelity had already harmed the village, that waves of consequences would return unpredictably, sometimes in disguise, as now, to hurt her. This roundness had to be made coin-sized so that she would see its circumference: punish her at the birth of her baby. Awaken her to the inexorable. People who refused fatalism because they could invent small resources insisted on culpability. Deny accidents and wrest fault from the stars.

After the villagers left, their lanterns now scattering in various directions toward home, the family broke their silence and cursed her. "Aiaa, we're going to die. Death is coming. Death is coming. Look what you've done. You've killed us. Ghost! Dead ghost! Ghost! You've never been born." She ran out into the fields, far enough from the house so that she could no longer hear their voices, and pressed herself against the earth, her own land no more. When she felt the birth coming, she thought that she had been hurt. Her body seized together. "They've hurt me too much," she thought. "This is gall, and it will kill me." Her forehead and knees against the earth, her body convulsed and then released her onto her back. The black well of sky and stars went out and out and out forever; her body and her complexity seemed to disappear. She was one of the stars, a bright dot in blackness, without home, without a companion, in eternal cold and silence. An agoraphobia[3] rose in her, speeding higher and higher, bigger and bigger; she would not be able to contain it; there would be no end to fear.

Flayed, unprotected against space, she felt pain return, focusing her body. This pain chilled her—a cold, steady kind of surface pain. Inside, spasmodically, the other pain, the pain of the child, heated her. For hours she lay on the ground, alternately body and space. Sometimes a vision of normal comfort obliterated reality: she saw the family in the evening gambling at the dinner table, the young people massaging their elders' backs. She saw them congratulating one another, high joy on the mornings the rice shoots came up. When these pictures burst, the stars drew yet further apart. Black space opened.

She got to her feet to fight better and remembered that old-fashioned women gave birth in their pigsties to fool the jealous, pain-dealing gods, who do not snatch piglets. Before the next spasms could stop her, she ran to the pigsty, each step a rushing out into emptiness. She climbed over the fence and knelt in the dirt. It was good to have a fence enclosing her, a tribal person alone.

Laboring, this woman who had carried her child as a foreign growth that sickened her every day, expelled it at last. She reached down to touch the hot, wet, moving mass, surely smaller than anything human, and could feel that it was human after all—fingers, toes, nails, nose. She pulled it up on to her belly, and it lay curled there, butt in the air, feet precisely tucked one under the other. She opened her loose shirt and buttoned the child inside. After resting, it squirmed and thrashed and she pushed it up to her breast. It turned its head this way and that until it found her nipple. There, it made little snuffling noises. She clenched her teeth at its preciousness, lovely as a young calf, a piglet, a little dog.

She may have gone to the pigsty as a last act of responsibility: she would protect this child as she had protected its father. It would look after her soul, leaving supplies on her grave. But how would this tiny child without family find her grave when there would be no marker for her anywhere, neither in the earth nor the family hall? No one would give her a family hall name. She had taken the child with her into the wastes. At its birth the two of them had felt the same raw pain of separation, a wound that only the family pressing tight could

[3]Pathological fear of open space.

close. A child with no descent line would not soften her life but only trail after her, ghost-like, begging her to give it purpose. At dawn the villagers on their way to the fields would stand around the fence and look.

Full of milk, the little ghost slept. When it awoke, she hardened her breasts against the milk that crying loosens. Toward morning she picked up the baby and walked to the well.

Carrying the baby to the well shows loving. Otherwise abandon it. Turn its face into the mud. Mothers who love their children take them along. It was probably a girl; there is some hope of forgiveness for boys.

"Don't tell anyone you had an aunt. Your father does not want to hear her name. She has never been born." I have believed that sex was unspeakable and words so strong and fathers so frail that "aunt" would do my father mysterious harm. I have thought that my family, having settled among immigrants who had also been their neighbors in the ancestral land, needed to clean their name, and a wrong word would incite the kinspeople even here. But there is more to this silence: they want me to participate in her punishment. And I have.

In the twenty years since I heard this story I have not asked for details nor said my aunt's name; I do not know it. People who can comfort the dead can also chase after them to hurt them further—a reverse ancestor worship. The real punishment was not the raid swiftly inflicted by the villagers, but the family's deliberately forgetting her. Her betrayal so maddened them, they saw to it that she would suffer forever, even after death. Always hungry, always needing, she would have to beg food from other ghosts, snatch and steal it from those whose living descendants give them gifts. She would have to fight the ghosts massed at crossroads for the buns a few thoughtful citizens leave to decoy her away from village and home so that the ancestral spirits could feast unharassed. At peace, they could act like gods, not ghosts, their descent lines providing them with paper suits and dresses, spirit money, paper houses, paper automobiles, chicken, meat, and rice[4] into eternity—essences delivered up in smoke and flames, steam and incense rising from each rice bowl. In an attempt to make the Chinese care for people outside the family, Chairman Mao[5] encourages us now to give our paper replicas to the spirits of outstanding soldiers and workers, no matter whose ancestors they may be. My aunt remains forever hungry. Goods are not distributed evenly among the dead.

My aunt haunts me—her ghost drawn to me because now, after fifty years of neglect, I alone devote pages of paper to her, though not origamied[6] into houses and clothes. I do not think she always means me well. I am telling on her, and she was a spite suicide, drowning herself in the drinking water. The Chinese are always very frightened of the drowned one, whose weeping ghost, wet hair hanging and skin bloated, waits silently by the water to pull down a substitute.

1976

[4]Offerings traditionally left at the graves of dead ancestors.

[5]Mao Tse-tung (1893–1976), Chairman of the Chinese Communist Party and leader of China (1949–1959, 1969–1976).

[6]Origami: the art of folding paper into aesthetic forms.

Edward Albee 1928–

In 1962, responding to critical reviews linking him to the traditions of the European Theatre of the Absurd, Edward Albee remarked, "Which theatre is the absurd one?" He was pointing scornfully at the commercial Broadway theater, which had fallen on dismal days and stood in sharp contrast to the vitality of Off-Broadway theater, the milieu from which Albee himself had come and for which he has written his finest work.

Edward Franklin Albee III was a foundling, adopted in infancy by a wealthy theatrical family. Expelled from two private schools, he did better at a third, where he had the opportunity to spend many hours writing poetry and fiction. Much of his real learning, as with Eugene O'Neill, came later from odd jobs: office boy, restaurant counterman, Western Union messenger. Except for one juvenile experiment, a three-act farce composed when he was twelve, Zoo Story *was Albee's first play. Written in 1958, it was first produced in September 1959 in Berlin; the first American staging was Off-Broadway in 1960. Like most Off-Broadway plays,* Zoo Story *is short, has a small cast, and deals with human encounter and the search for communion. Its author's structural pattern is revealed: normal opening, increasing emotional tangle, peak of intensity, quick drop-off.*

Following Zoo Story *came a series of one-act plays:* The Death of Bessie Smith *(1960), a drama of social ostracism based on the life of a famous African American jazz singer;* The Sandbox *(1960); and* The American Dream *(1961), which displayed a situation increasingly familiar in Albee's plays: the middle-class American family living on illusion and dominated by an overbearing woman.*

Albee's first full-length play, and his greatest hit, was Who's Afraid of Virginia Woolf? *(1962), which ran on Broadway for two years, won many awards, and was made into a memorable and successful film. Notable plays followed:* Tiny Alice *(1964),* A Delicate Balance *(1966), for which Albee won his first Pulitzer Prize for Drama, and* Seascape *(1975), his second Pulitzer Prize winner. Albee's work continued to appear on Broadway and continued to startle and agitate his audiences, earning him the dubious title of "Shockmeister."*

Critics of Albee's plays argued that he made dubious excursions into metaphysics. He was said to "abhor plots," to rely overmuch on the psychological games and linguistic skirmishes of his characters to carry the action. As his plays became more cerebral and less conventionally dramatic, his audience dwindled. In 1983, his play The Man Who Had 3 Arms *was savaged by the New York critics and ignored by playgoers. A financial disaster, it closed after only sixteen performances, and for more than a decade, no new Albee play was presented on Broadway; no producer was willing to risk money on a playwright who seemed to have lost touch with his audience.*

Undaunted, Albee blamed his Broadway failures on New York's super-sensitive, "skirt-hiking" critics and on theatergoers who were, he said, incapable of understanding serious drama and wanted merely a "literate middle-browism." In an interview in 1991, he pointed out that he was only one of a number of illustrious "playwrights who are not performed on Broadway now: Sophocles, Aristophanes, Shakespeare. . . ." And he continued his prolific writing of plays, averaging almost one a year. He directed productions of his works in regional theaters in the United States and began teaching drama at the University of Houston. In Europe, where his reputation as a playwright remained high, he directed productions of his plays that attracted large audiences.

Albee once proclaimed, "I am not a Broadway playwright," but in 1994 he made a triumphal return to New York with a production of Three Tall Women. *Highly autobiographical, the play is centered on his adoptive mother in her old age as she confronts her past and a menacing future. For one play, at least, Albee had turned from the concentrated abstractions that had made his work inaccessible to audiences.* Three Tall Women *partially re-established his reputation with critics and playgoers, and it won for him his third Pulitzer Prize for Drama.*

Over the years, as public tastes and standards have altered, Albee's plays have come to seem far less licentious than they were first thought to be: In 1961 The Zoo Story *was denounced on the floor of the U.S. Senate as an example of dramatic "filth." Thirty-five years later President Clinton praised Albee for his radical dramas, saying, "In your rebellion the American theater was reborn." Nevertheless, critical reaction to Albee's work can still be sharply divided. When his* The Play About the Baby *opened in New York in 2001, it was praised as truly "accomplished" and panned as being "not merely awful, it is offal."*

Albee, now the most notable living American dramatist, continues to teach, to direct, and to take new directions in his writing. But his best work remains, as it has always been, iconoclastic and abstract—dramas of physical and psychological violence that strip men and women of their comforting illusions and repudiate cozy pieties about the modern world that is, to Albee, chaotic, brutal, and lost to hope.

FURTHER READING: *Edward Albee: An Interview and Essays,* ed. J. Wasserman, 1983; *Critical Essays on Edward Albee,* ed. P. Kolin and J. Davis, 1986; *Edward Albee,* ed. H. Bloom, 1987; G. McCarthy, *Edward Albee,* 1987; M. Roudané, *Understanding Edward Albee,* 1987; *Conversations with Edward Albee,* ed. P. Kolin, 1988; Mel Gussow, *Edward Albee: A Singular Journey,* 1999; A. Paolucci, *From Tension to Tonic: The Plays of Edward Albee* 2000; *Edward Albee: A Casebook,* ed. B. Mann, 2003; B. Horn, *Edward Albee: A Research and Production Sourcebook,* 2003; *The Collected Plays of Edward Albee,* 2 vols., 2004, 2005; *The Cambridge Companion to Edward Albee,* ed. S. Bottom, 2005.

TEXT: *The Zoo Story,* 1960, 1999.

THE ZOO STORY[1]

CHARACTERS

PETER: *A man in his early forties, neither fat nor gaunt, neither handsome nor homely. He wears tweeds, smokes a pipe, carries hornrimmed glasses. Although he is moving into middle age, his dress and his manner would suggest a man younger.*

JERRY: *A man in his late thirties, not poorly dressed, but carelessly. What was once a trim and lightly muscled body has begun to go to fat; and while he is no longer handsome, it is evident that he once was. His fall from physical grace should not suggest debauchery; he has, to come closest to it, a great weariness.*

[1]"This edition of *The Zoo Story* contains revisions to the original text. These revisions were made by the author in 1999, during rehearsals for his production of the play at the Alley Theatre in Houston, Texas."—Albee's note.

THE SCENE

It is Central Park; a Sunday afternoon in summer; the present. There are two park benches, one toward either side of the stage; they both face the audience. Behind them: foliage, trees, sky. At the beginning, PETER *is seated on one of the benches.*

As the curtain rises, PETER *is seated on the bench stage-right. He is reading a book. He stops reading, cleans his glasses, goes back to reading.* JERRY *enters.*

JERRY: I've been to the zoo. [PETER *doesn't notice*] I said, I've been to the zoo. MISTER, I'VE BEEN TO THE ZOO!

PETER: Hm? . . .[2] What? . . . I'm sorry, were you talking to me?

JERRY: I went to the zoo, and then I walked until I came here. Have I been walking north?

PETER: [*Puzzled*] North? Why . . . I . . . I think so. Let me see.

JERRY: [*Pointing past the audience*] Is that Fifth Avenue?

PETER: Why yes; yes, it is.

JERRY: And what is that cross street there; that one, to the right?

PETER: That? Oh, that's Seventy-fourth Street.

JERRY: And the zoo is around Sixty-fifth Street; so I've been walking north.

PETER: [*Anxious to get back to his reading*] Yes; it would seem so.

JERRY: Good old north.

PETER: [*Lightly, by reflex*] Ha, ha.

JERRY: [*After a slight pause*] But not due north.

PETER: I . . . well, no, not due north; but, we . . . call it north. It's northerly.

JERRY: [*Watches as* PETER, *anxious to dismiss him, prepares his pipe*] Well, boy; *you're* not going to get lung cancer, are you?

PETER: [*Looks up, a little annoyed, then smiles*] No, sir. Not from this.

JERRY: No, sir. What you'll probably get is cancer of the mouth, and then you'll have to wear one of those things Freud wore after they took one whole side of his jaw away. What do they call those things?

PETER: [*Uncomfortable*] A prosthesis?

JERRY: The very thing! A prosthesis. You're an educated man, aren't you? Are you a doctor?

PETER: Oh, no; no. I read about it somewhere; *Time* magazine, I think. [*He turns to his book*]

JERRY: Well, *Time* magazine isn't for blockheads.

PETER: No, I suppose not.

JERRY: [*After a pause*] Boy, I'm glad that's Fifth Avenue there.

PETER: [*Vaguely*] Yes.

JERRY: I don't like the west side of the park much.

PETER: Oh? [*Then, slightly wary, but interested*] Why?

JERRY: [*Offhand*] I don't know.

PETER: Oh. [*He returns to his book*]

JERRY: [*He stands for a few seconds, looking at* PETER, *who finally looks up again, puzzled*] Do you mind if we talk?

PETER: [*Obviously minding*] Why . . . no, no.

JERRY: Yes you do; you do.

[2]Here, and throughout, the ellipsis points are Albee's.

PETER: [*Puts his book down, his pipe out and away, smiling*] No, really; I don't mind.

JERRY: Yes you do.

PETER: [*Finally decided*] No; I don't mind at all, really.

JERRY: It's . . . it's a nice day.

PETER: [*Stares unnecessarily at the sky*] Yes. Yes, it is; lovely.

JERRY: I've been to the zoo.

PETER: Yes, I think you said so . . . didn't you?

JERRY: I bet you've got TV, huh?

PETER: Why yes, we have two; one for the children.

JERRY: You're married!

PETER: [*With pleased emphasis*] Why, certainly.

JERRY: It isn't a law, for God's sake.

PETER: No . . . no, of course not.

JERRY: And you have a wife.

PETER: [*Bewildered by the seeming lack of communication*] Yes!

JERRY: And you have children.

PETER: Yes; two.

JERRY: Boys?

PETER: No, girls . . . both girls.

JERRY: But you wanted boys.

PETER: Well . . . naturally, every man wants a son, but . . .

JERRY: [*Lightly mocking*] But that's the way the cookie crumbles?

PETER: [*Annoyed*] I wasn't going to say that.

JERRY: And you're not going to have any more kids, are you?

PETER: [*A bit distantly*] No. No more. [*Then back, and irksome*] Why did you say that? How would you know about that?

JERRY: The way you cross your legs, perhaps; something in the voice. Or maybe I'm just guessing. Is it your wife?

PETER: [*Furious*] That's none of your business! [*A silence*] Do you understand? [JERRY *nods.* PETER *is quiet now*] Well, you're right. We'll have no more children.

JERRY: [*Softly*] That *is* the way the cookie crumbles.

PETER: [*Forgiving*] Yes . . . I guess so.

JERRY: Do you mind if I ask you questions?

PETER: Oh, not really.

JERRY: I'll tell you why I do it; I don't talk to many people—except to say like: give me a beer, or where's the john, or what time does the feature go on, or keep your hands to yourself, buddy. You know—things like that.

PETER: I must say I don't . . .

JERRY: But every once in a while I like to talk to somebody, really *talk;* like to get to know somebody, know all about him.

PETER: [*Lightly laughing, still a little uncomfortable*] And am I the guinea pig for today?

JERRY: On a sun-drenched afternoon like this? Who better than a nice married man with two daughters and . . . uh . . . a dog? [PETER *shakes his head*] No? Two dogs. [PETER *shakes his head again*] Hm. No dogs? [PETER *shakes his head, sadly*] Oh, that's a shame. But you look like an animal man. CATS? [PETER *nods his head, ruefully*] Cats! But, that can't be your idea. No, sir. Your wife and daughters? [PETER *nods his head*] Is there anything else I should know?

PETER: [*He has to clear his throat*] There are . . . there are two parakeets. One . . . uh . . . one for each of my daughters.

JERRY: Birds.

PETER: My daughters keep them in a cage in their bedroom.

JERRY: Do they carry disease? The birds?

PETER: I don't believe so.

JERRY: That's too bad. If they did you could set them loose in the house and the cats could eat them and die, maybe. [PETER *looks blank for a moment, then laughs*] And what else? What do you do to support your enormous household?

PETER: I . . . uh . . . I have an executive position with a . . . a small publishing house. We . . . uh . . . we publish textbooks.

JERRY: That sounds nice; very nice. What do you make?

PETER: [*Still cheerful*] Now look here!

JERRY: Oh, come on.

PETER: Well, I make around 200,000 a year, but I don't carry more than forty dollars at any one time . . . in case you're a . . . a holdup man . . . ha, ha, ha.

JERRY: [*Ignoring the above*] Where do you live? [PETER *is reluctant*] Oh, look; I'm not going to rob you, and I'm not going to kidnap your parakeets, your cats, or your daughters.

PETER: [*Too loud*] I live between Lexington and Third Avenue, on Seventy-fourth Street.

JERRY: That wasn't so hard, was it?

PETER: I didn't mean to seem . . . ah . . . it's that you don't really carry on a conversation; you just ask questions. And I'm . . . I'm normally . . . uh . . . reticent. Why do you just stand there?

JERRY: I'll start walking around in a little while, and maybe later I'll sit down. Say, what's the dividing line between upper-middle-class and lower-upper-middle-class?

PETER: My dear fellow, I . . .

JERRY: Don't my dear fellow me.

PETER: [*Unhappily*] Was I patronizing? I believe I was; I'm sorry. But, you see, your question about the classes bewildered me.

JERRY: And when you're bewildered you become patronizing?

PETER: I . . . I don't express myself too well, sometimes. [*He attempts a joke on himself*] I'm in publishing, not writing.

JERRY: [*Amused, but not at the humor*] So be it. The truth *is: I* was being patronizing.

PETER: Oh, now; you needn't say that. [*It is at this point that* JERRY *may begin to move about the stage with slowly increasing determination and authority, but pacing himself, so that the long speech about the dog comes at the high point of the arc*]

JERRY: All right. Who are your favorite writers? Baudelaire and Stephen King?[3]

PETER: [*Wary*] Well, I like a great many writers; I have a considerable . . . catholicity of taste, if I may say so. Those two men are fine, each in his way. [*Warming up*] Baudelaire, of course . . . uh . . . is by far the finer of the two, but Stephen King has a place . . . in our . . . uh . . . national . . .

[3]Charles Baudelaire (1821–1867), French poet. His *Les Fleurs du mal* (*The Flowers of Evil*), published in 1857, describes his sense of despair, sin, and the degradation of life. Stephen King (1947–), best-selling American writer of macabre, fantastic, and supernatural tales.

JERRY: Skip it.

PETER: I . . . sorry.

JERRY: Do you know what I did before I went to the zoo today? I walked all the way up Fifth Avenue from Washington Square; all the way.

PETER: Oh; you live in the Village! [*This seems to enlighten* PETER]

JERRY: No, I don't. I took the subway down to the Village so I could walk all the way up Fifth Avenue to the zoo. It's one of those things a person has to do; sometimes a person has to go a very long distance out of his way to come back a short distance correctly.

PETER: [*Almost pouting*] Oh, I thought you lived in Greenwich Village.

JERRY: What were you trying to do? Make sense out of things? Bring order? The old pigeonhole bit? Well, that's easy; I'll tell you. I live in a four-story brownstone rooming-house on the upper West Side between Columbus Avenue and Central Park West. I live on the top floor; rear; west. It's a laughably small room, and one of my walls is made of beaverboard; this beaverboard separates my room from another laughably small room, so I assume that the two rooms were once one room, a small room, but not necessarily laughable. The room beyond my beaverboard wall is occupied by a black queen who always keeps his door open; well, not always but *always* when he's plucking his eyebrows, which he does with Buddhist concentration. This black queen has rotten teeth, which is rare, and he has a Japanese kimono, which is also pretty rare; and he wears this kimono to and from the john in the hall, which is pretty frequent. I mean, he goes to the john a lot. He never bothers me, and he never brings anyone up to his room. All he does is pluck his eyebrows, wear his kimono and go to the john. Now, the two front rooms on my floor are a little larger, I guess; but they're pretty small, too. There's a Puerto Rican family in one of them, a husband, a wife, and some kids; I don't know how many. These people entertain a lot. And in the other front room, there's somebody living there, but I don't know who it is. I've never seen who it is. Never. Never ever.

PETER: [*Embarrassed*] Why . . . why do you live there?

JERRY: [*From a distance*] I don't know.

PETER: It doesn't sound like a very nice place . . . where you live.

JERRY: Well, no; it isn't an apartment in the East Seventies. But, then again, I don't have one wife, two daughters, two cats and two parakeets. What I do have, I have toilet articles, a few clothes, a hot plate that I'm not supposed to have, a can opener, one that works with a key, you know; a knife, two forks, and two spoons, one small, one large; three plates, a cup, a saucer, a drinking glass, two picture frames, both empty, eight or nine books, a pack of pornographic playing cards, regular deck, and old Western Union typewriter that prints nothing but capital letters, and a small strongbox without a lock which has in it . . . what? Rocks! Some rocks . . . sea-rounded rocks I picked up on the beach when I was a kid. Under which . . . weighed down . . . are some letters . . . please letters . . . please why don't you do this, and please why do you do that letters. And when letters, too. When will you write? When will you come? When? These letters are from more recent years.

PETER: [*Stares glumly at his shoes, then*] About those two empty picture frames . . .?

JERRY: I don't see why they need any explanation at all. Isn't it clear? I don't have pictures of anyone to put in them.

PETER: Your parents . . . perhaps . . . a girl friend . . .

JERRY: You're a very sweet man, and you're possessed of a truly enviable innocence. But good old Mom and good old Pop are dead . . . you know? . . . I'm broken up about it, too . . . I mean really. BUT. That particular vaudeville act is playing the cloud circuit now, so I don't see how I can look at them, all neat and framed. Besides, or, rather, to be pointed about it, good old Mom walked out on good old Pop when I was ten and a half years old; she embarked on an adulterous turn of our southern states . . . a journey of a year's duration . . . and her most constant companion . . . among others, among many others . . . was a Mr. Barleycorn.[4] At least, that's what good old Pop told me after he went down . . . came back . . . brought her body north. We'd received the news between Christmas and New Year's, you see, that good old Mom had parted with the ghost in some dump in Alabama. And, without the ghost . . . she was less welcome. I mean, what was she? A stiff . . . a northern stiff. At any rate, good old Pop celebrated the New Year for an even two weeks and then slapped into the front of a somewhat moving city omnibus,[5] which sort of cleaned things out family-wise. Well no; then there was Mom's sister, who was given neither to sin nor the consolations of the bottle. I moved in on her, and my memory of her is slight excepting I remember still that she did all things dourly: sleeping, eating, working, praying. She dropped dead on the stairs to her apartment, my apartment then, too, on the afternoon of my high school graduation. A terribly middle-European joke, if you ask me.

PETER: Oh, my; oh, my.

JERRY: Oh, your what? But that was a long time ago, and I have no feeling about any of it that I care to admit to myself. Perhaps you can see, though, why good old Mom and good old Pop are frameless. What's your name? Your first name?

PETER: I'm Peter.

JERRY: I'd forgotten to ask you. I'm Jerry.

PETER: [*With a slight, nervous laugh*] Hello, Jerry.

JERRY: [*Nods his hello*] And let's see now; what's the point of having a girl's picture, especially in two frames? I have two picture frames, you remember. I never see the pretty little ladies more than once, and most of them wouldn't be caught in the same room with a camera. It's odd, and I wonder if it's sad.

PETER: The girls?

JERRY: No. I wonder if it's sad that I never see the little ladies more than once. I've never been able to have sex with, or, how is it put? . . . make love to anybody more than once. Once; that's it. . . . Oh, wait; for a week and a half, when I was fifteen . . . and I hang my head in shame that puberty was late . . . I was a h-o-m-o-s-e-x-u-a-l. I mean, I was queer . . . [*Very fast*] . . . queer, queer, queer . . . with bells ringing, banners snapping in the wind. And for those eleven days, I met at least twice a day with the park superintendent's son . . . a Greek boy, whose birthday was the same as mine, except he was a year older. I think I was very much in love . . . maybe just with sex. But that was the jazz of a very special hotel, wasn't it? And now; oh, do I love the little ladies; really, I love them. For about an hour.

PETER: Well, it seems perfectly simple to me. . . .

[4]I.e., John Barleycorn, a slang term for alcoholic drink.
[5]A public passenger bus.

JERRY: [*Angry*] Look! Are you going to tell me to get married and have parakeets?

PETER: [*Angry himself*] Forget the parakeets! And stay single if you want to. It's no business of mine. I didn't start this conversation in the . . .

JERRY: All right, all right. I'm sorry. All right? You're not angry?

PETER: [*Laughing*] No, I'm not angry.

JERRY: Good. Interesting that you asked me about the picture frames. I would have thought that you would have asked me about the pornographic playing cards.

PETER: [*With a knowing smile*] Oh, I've seen those cards.

JERRY: That's not the point. [*Laughs*] I suppose when you were a kid you and your pals passed them around, or you had a pack of your own.

PETER: Well, I guess a lot of us did.

JERRY: And you threw them away just before you got married.

PETER: Oh, now; look here. I didn't *need* anything like that when I got older.

JERRY: No?

PETER: [*Embarrassed*] I'd rather not talk about these things.

JERRY: So? Don't. Besides, I wasn't trying to plumb your postadolescent sexual life and hard times; what I wanted to get at is the value difference between pornographic playing cards when you're a kid, and pornographic playing cards when you're older. It's that when you're a kid you use the cards as a substitute for a real experience, and when you're older you use real experience as a substitute for the fantasy. But I imagine you'd rather hear about what happened at the zoo.

PETER: [*Enthusiastic*] Oh, yes; the zoo [*Then, awkward*] That is . . . if you. . . .

JERRY: Let me tell you about why I went . . . well, let me tell you some things. I've told you about the fourth floor of the roominghouse where I live. I think the rooms are better as you go down, floor by floor. I guess they are; I don't know. I don't know any of the people on the third and second floors. Oh, wait! I do know that there's a lady living on the third floor, in the front. I know because she cries all the time. Whenever I go out or come back in, whenever I pass her door I always hear her crying, muffled, but . . . very determined. Very determined indeed. But the one I'm getting to, and all about the dog, is the landlady. I don't like to use words that are too harsh in describing people. I don't like to. But the landlady is a fat, ugly, mean, stupid, unwashed, misanthropic, cheap, drunken bag of garbage. And you may have noticed that I very seldom use profanity, so I can't describe her as well as I might.

PETER: You describe her . . . vividly.

JERRY: Well, thanks. Anyway, she has a dog, and she and her dog are the gatekeepers of my dwelling. The woman is bad enough; she leans around in the entrance hall, spying to see that I don't bring in things or people, and when she's had her midafternoon pint of lemon-flavored gin she always stops me in the hall and grabs ahold of my coat or my arm, and she presses her disgusting body up against me to keep me in a corner so she can talk to me. The smell of her body and her breath . . . you can't imagine it . . . and somewhere, somewhere in the back of that pea-sized brain of hers, an organ developed just enough to let her eat, drink, and emit, she has some foul parody of sexual desire. And I, Peter, I am the object of her sweaty lust.

PETER: That's disgusting. That's . . . horrible.

JERRY: But I have found a way to keep her off. When she talks to me, when she presses herself to my body and mumbles about her room and how I should come there, I merely say: but, Love; wasn't yesterday enough for you, and the day before? Then she puzzles, she makes slits of her tiny eyes, she sways a little, and then, Peter . . . and it is at this moment that I think I might be doing some good in that tormented house . . . a simpleminded smile begins to form on her unthinkable face, and she giggles and groans as she thinks about yesterday and the day before; as she believes and relives what never happened. Then, she motions to that black monster of a dog she has, and she goes back to her room. And I am safe until our next meeting.

PETER: It's so. . . . I find it hard to believe that people such as that really *are*.

JERRY: [*Lightly mocking*] It's for reading about, isn't it?

PETER: [*Seriously*] Yes.

JERRY: And fact is better left to fiction. You're right, Peter. Well, what I have been meaning to tell you about is the dog; I shall, now.

PETER: [*Nervously*] Oh, yes; the dog.

JERRY: Don't go. You're not thinking of going, are you?

PETER: Well . . . no, I don't think so.

JERRY: [*As if to a child*] Because after I tell you about the dog, do you know what then? Then . . . then I'll tell you about what happened at the zoo.

PETER: [*Laughing faintly*] You're . . . you're full of stories, aren't you?

JERRY: You don't *have* to listen. Nobody is holding you here; remember that. Keep that in your mind.

PETER: [*Irritably*] I know that.

JERRY: You do? Good. [*The following long speech, it seems to me, should be done with a great deal of action, to achieve a hypnotic effect on* PETER, *and on the audience, too. Some specific actions have been suggested, but the director and the actor playing* JERRY *might best work it out for themselves*] ALL RIGHT. [*As if reading from a huge billboard*] THE STORY OF JERRY AND THE DOG! [*Natural again*] What I am going to tell you has something to do with how sometimes it's necessary to go a long distance out of the way in order to come back a short distance correctly; or, maybe I only think that it has something to do with that. But, it's why I went to the zoo today, and why I walked north . . . northerly, rather . . . until I came here. All right. The dog, I think I told you, is a black monster of a beast: an oversized head, tiny, tiny ears, and eyes . . . bloodshot, infected, maybe; and a body you can see the ribs through the skin. The dog is black, all black; all black except for the bloodshot eyes, and . . . yes . . . and open sore on its . . . *right* forepaw; that is red, too. And, oh yes; the poor monster, and I do believe it's an old dog . . . it's certainly a misused one . . . almost always has an erection . . . of sorts. That's red, too. And . . . what else? . . . oh, yes; there's a gray-yellow-white color, too, when he bares his fangs. Like this: Grrrrrr! Which is what he did when he saw me for the first time . . . the day I moved in. I worried about that animal the very first minute I met him. Now, animals don't take to me like Saint Francis had birds hanging off him all the time. What I mean is: animals are indifferent to me . . . like people [*He smiles slightly*] . . . most of the time. But this dog wasn't indifferent. From the very beginning he'd snarl and then go for me, to get one of my legs. Not like he was rabid, you know; he was sort of a stumbly dog, but he wasn't half-assed, either. It was a good, stumbly run; but I always got away. He got a piece of my trouser leg, look, you can see right here, where it's mended; he got that the second day I lived there; but, I kicked free and got upstairs fast, so that was that. [*Puzzles*] I still don't know to this day how the other roomers manage it, but you know what I *think:* I think it had to do only with me. Cozy. So. Anyway, this went on for over a week, whenever I came in; but never when I went out. That's funny. Or, it *was* funny. I could pack up and live in the street for all the dog cared. Well, I thought about it up in my room one day, one of the times after I'd bolted upstairs, and I made up my mind. I decided: First, I'll kill the dog with kindness, and if that doesn't work . . . I'll just kill him. [PETER *winces*] Don't react, Peter; just listen. So, the next day I went out and bought a bag of hamburgers, medium rare, no catsup, no onion; and on the way home I threw away the rolls and kept just the meat. [*Action for the following perhaps*] When I got back to the roominghouse the dog was waiting for me. I half-opened the door that led into the entrance hall, and there he was; waiting for me. It figured. I went in, very cautiously, and I had the hamburgers, you remember; I opened the bag, and I set the meat down about twelve feet from where the dog was snarling at me. Like so! He snarled; stopped snarling; sniffed; moved slowly; then faster; then faster toward the meat. Well, when he got to it he stopped, and he looked at me. I smiled; but tentatively, you understand. He turned his face back to the hamburgers, smelled, sniffed some more, and then . . . RRRAAAAGGGGGHHHH, like that . . . he tore into them. It was as if he had never eaten anything in his life before, except like garbage. Which might very well have been the truth. I don't think the landlady ever eats anything but garbage. But. He ate all the hamburgers, almost all at once, making sounds in his throat like a woman. *Then,* when he'd finished the meat, the hamburger, and tried to eat the paper, too, he sat down and smiled. I think he smiled; I know cats do. It was a very gratifying few moments. Then, BAM, he snarled and made for me again. He didn't get me this time, either. So, I got upstairs, and I lay down on my bed and started to think about the dog again. To be truthful, I was offended, and I was damn mad, too. It was six perfectly good hamburgers with not enough pork in them to make it disgusting. I was offended. But, after a while, I decided to try it for a few more days. If you think about it, this dog had what amounted to an antipathy toward me; really. And, I wondered if I mightn't overcome this antipathy. So, I tried it for five more days, but it was always the same: snarl, sniff: move; faster; stare: gobble; RAAGGGHHH; smile; snarl; BAM. Well, now; by this time Columbus Avenue was strewn with hamburger rolls and I was less offended than disgusted. So, I decided to kill the dog. [PETER *raises a hand in protest*] Oh, don't be so alarmed, Peter; I didn't succeed. The day I tried to kill the dog I bought only one hamburger and what I thought was a murderous portion of rat poison. When I bought the hamburger I asked the man not to bother with the roll, all I wanted was the meat. I expected some reaction from him, like: we don't sell no hamburgers without rolls; or, wha' d'ya wanna do, eat it out'a ya han's? But no; he smiled benignly, wrapped up the hamburger in waxed paper, and said: A bite for ya pussy-cat? I wanted to say: No, not really; it's part of a plan to poison a dog I know. But, you can't say "a dog I know" without sounding funny; so I said, a little too loud, I'm afraid, and too formally: YES, A BITE FOR MY PUSSY-CAT. People looked up. It always happens when I try to simplify things; people look up. But that's neither hither nor thither. So. On my way back to the roominghouse, I kneaded the hamburger and the rat poison together between my hands, at that point feeling as much sadness as disgust. I opened the door to the entrance hall, and there the monster was, waiting to take the offering and then jump me. Poor bastard; he never learned that the moment he took to smile before he went for me gave me time enough to get out of range. BUT, there he was; malevolence with an erection, waiting. I put the poison patty down, moved toward the stairs and watched. The poor animal gobbled the food down as usual, smiled, which made me almost sick, and then, BAM. But, I sprinted up the stairs, as usual, and the dog didn't get me, as usual. AND IT CAME TO PASS THAT THE BEAST WAS DEATHLY ILL. I knew this because he no longer attended me, and because the landlady sobered up. She stopped me in the hall the same evening of the attempted murder and confided the information that God had struck her puppy-dog a surely fatal blow. She had forgotten her bewildered lust, and her eyes were wide open for the first time. They looked like the dog's eyes. She sniveled and implored me to pray for the animal. I wanted to say to her: Madam, I have myself to pray for, the black queen, the Puerto Rican family, the person in the front room whom I've never seen, the woman who cries deliberately behind her closed door, and the rest of the people in all roominghouses, everywhere; besides, Madam, I don't understand how to pray. But . . . to simplify things . . . I told her I would pray. She looked up. She said that I was a liar, and that I probably wanted the dog to die. I told her, and there was so much truth here, that I didn't want the dog to die. I didn't, and not just because I'd poisoned him. I'm afraid that I must tell you I wanted the dog to live so that I could see what our new relationship might come to. [PETER *indicates his increasing displeasure and slowing growing antagonism*] Please understand, Peter; that sort of thing is important. You must believe me; it *is* important. We have to know the effect of our actions. [*Another deep sigh*] Well, anyway; the dog recovered. I have no idea why, unless he was a descendant of the puppy that guarded the gates of hell or some such resort. I'm not up on my mythology. [*He pronounces the word myth-o-logy*] Are you? [PETER *sets to thinking, but* JERRY *goes on*] At any rate, and you've missed the eight-thousand-dollar question, Peter; at any rate, the dog recovered his health and the landlady recovered her thirst, in no way altered by the bow-wow's deliverance. When I came home from a movie that was playing on Forty-second Street, a movie I'd seen, or one that was very much like one or several I'd seen, after the landlady told me puppykins was better, I was so hoping for the dog to be waiting for me. I was . . . well, how would you put it . . . enticed? . . . fascinated? . . . no, I don't think so . . . heart-shatteringly anxious, that's it; I was heart-shatteringly anxious to confront my friend again. [PETER *reacts scoffingly*] Yes, Peter; friend. That's the only word for it. I was heart-shatteringly et cetera to confront my doggy friend again. I came in the door and advanced, unafraid, to the center of the entrance hall. The beast was there . . . looking at me. And, you know, he looked better for his scrape with the nevermind. I stopped; I looked at him; he looked at me. I think . . . I think we stayed a long time that way . . . still, stone-statue . . . just looking at one another. I looked more into his face than he looked into mine. I mean, I can concentrate longer at looking into a dog's face than a dog can concentrate at looking into mine, or into anybody else's face, for that matter. But during that twenty seconds or two hours that we looked into each other's face, we made contact. Now, here is what I had wanted to happen: I loved the dog now, and I wanted him to love me. I had tried to love, and I had tried to kill, and both had been unsuccessful by themselves. I hoped . . . and I don't really know why I expected the dog to understand anything, much less my motivations . . . I hoped that the dog would understand. [PETER *seems to be hypnotized*] It's just . . .

it's just that . . . [JERRY *is abnormally tense, now*] . . . *it*'s just that if you can't deal with people, you have to make a start somewhere. WITH ANIMALS! [*Much faster now, and like a conspirator*] Don't you see? A person has to have some way of dealing with SOMETHING. If not with people . . . if not with people . . . SOMETHING. With a bed, with a cockroach, with a mirror . . . no, that's too hard, that's one of the last steps. With a cockroach, with a . . . with a . . . carpet, a roll of toilet paper . . . no, not that, either . . . that's a mirror, too; always check bleeding. You see how hard it is to find things? With a street corner, and too many lights, all colors reflecting on the oily-wet streets . . . with a wisp of smoke, a wisp . . . of smoke . . . with . . . with pornographic playing cards, with a strongbox . . . WITHOUT A LOCK . . . with love, with vomiting, with crying, with fury because the pretty little ladies aren't pretty little ladies, with making money with your body which is an act of love and I could prove it, with howling because you're alive; with God. How about that? WITH GOD WHO IS A BLACK QUEEN WHO WEARS A KIMONO AND PLUCKS HIS EYEBROWS, WHO IS A WOMAN WHO CRIES WITH DETERMINATION BEHIND HER CLOSED DOOR . . . with God who, I'm told, turned his back on the whole thing some time ago . . . with . . . some day, with people. [JERRY *sighs the next word heavily*] People. With an idea; a concept. And where better, where ever better in this humiliating excuse for a jail, where better to communicate one single, simple-minded idea than in an entrance hall? Where? It would be A START! Where better to make a beginning . . . to understand and just possibly be understood . . . a beginning of an understanding, that with . . . [*Here* JERRY *seems to fall into almost grotesque fatigue*] . . . than with A DOG. Just that; a dog. [*Here there is a silence that might be prolonged for a moment or so; then* JERRY *wearily finishes his story*] A dog. It seemed like a perfect sensible idea. Man is a dog's best friend, remember. So: the dog and I looked at each other. I longer than the dog. And what I saw then has been the same ever since. Whenever the dog and I see each other we both stop where we are. We regard each other with a mixture of sadness and suspicion, and then we feign indifference. We walk past each other safely; we have an understanding. It's very sad, but you'll have to admit that it is an understanding. We had made many attempts at contact, and we had failed. The dog has returned to garbage, and I to solitary but free passage. I have not returned. I mean to say, I have *gained* solitary free passage, if that much further loss can be said to be gain. I have learned that neither kindness nor cruelty by themselves, independent of each other, creates any effect beyond themselves; and I have learned that the two combined, together, at the same time, are the teaching emotion. And what is gained is loss. And what has been the result: the dog and I have attained a compromise; more of a bargain, really. We neither love nor hurt because we do not try to reach each other. And, *was* trying to feed the dog an act of love? And, perhaps, was the dog's attempt to bite me *not* an act of love? If we can so misunderstand, well then, why have we invented the word love in the first place? [*There is silence.*] The Story of Jerry and the Dog; the end. [PETER *is silent*] Well, Peter? [JERRY *is suddenly cheerful*] Well, Peter? Do you think I could sell that story to the *Reader's Digest* and make a couple of hundred bucks for *The Most Unforgettable Character I've Ever Met?* Huh? [JERRY *is animated, but* PETER *is disturbed*] Oh, come on now, Peter; tell me what you think.

PETER: [*Numb*] I . . . I don't understand what . . . I don't think I . . . [*Now, almost tearfully*] Why did you tell me all of this?

JERRY: Why not?

PETER: I DON'T UNDERSTAND!

JERRY: [*Furious, but whispering*] That's a lie.

PETER: No. No, it's not.

JERRY: [*Quietly*] I tried to explain it to you as I went along. I went slowly; it all has to do with . . .

PETER: I DON'T WANT TO HEAR ANY MORE. I don't understand you, or your landlady, or her dog . . .

JERRY: *Her* dog! I thought it was my . . . No. No, you're right. It *is* her dog. [*Looks at* PETER *intently, shaking his head*] I don't know what I was thinking about; of course you don't understand. [*In a monotone, wearily*] I don't live in your block; I'm not married to two parakeets, or whatever your setup is. I am a *permanent transient,* and my home is the sickening roominghouses on the West Side of New York City, which is the greatest city in the world. Amen.

PETER: I'm . . . I'm sorry; I didn't mean to . . .

JERRY: Forget it. I suppose you don't quite know what to make of me, eh?

PETER: [*A joke*] We get all kinds in publishing. [*Chuckles*]

JERRY: You're a funny man. [*He forces a laugh*] You know that? You're a very . . . a richly comic person.

PETER: [*Modestly, but amused*] Oh, now, not really. [*Still chuckling*]

JERRY: Peter, do I annoy you, or confuse you?

PETER: [*Lightly*] Well, I must confess that this wasn't the kind of afternoon I'd anticipated.

JERRY: You mean, I'm not the gentleman you were expecting.

PETER: I wasn't expecting anybody.

JERRY: No, I don't imagine you were. But I'm here, and I'm not leaving.

PETER: [*Consulting his watch*] Well, you may not be, but I must be getting home soon.

JERRY: Oh, come on; stay a while longer.

PETER: I really should get home; you see . . .

JERRY: [*Tickles* PETER'S *ribs with his fingers*] Oh, come on.

PETER: [*He is very ticklish; as* JERRY *continues to tickle him his voice becomes falsetto*] No, I . . . OHHHHH! Don't do that. Stop, Stop. Ohhh, no, no.

JERRY: Oh, come on.

PETER: [*As* JERRY *tickles*] Oh, hee, hee, hee. I must go. I . . . hee, hee, hee. After all, stop, stop, hee, hee, hee, after all, the parakeets will be getting dinner ready soon. Hee, hee. And the cats are setting the table. Stop, stop, and, and . . . [PETER *is beside himself now*] . . . and we're having . . . hee, hee . . . uh . . . ho, ho, ho. [JERRY *stops tickling* PETER, *but the combination of the tickling and his own mad whimsy has* PETER *laughing almost hysterically. As his laughter continues, then subsides,* JERRY *watches him, with a curious fixed smile*]

JERRY: Peter?

PETER: Oh, ha, ha, ha, ha, ha. What? What?

JERRY: Listen, now.

PETER: Oh, ho, ho. What . . . what is it, Jerry? Oh, my.

JERRY: [*Mysteriously*] Peter, do you want to know what happened at the zoo?

PETER: Ah, ha, ha. The what? Oh, yes; the zoo. Oh, ho, ho. Well, I had my own zoo there for a moment with . . . hee, hee, the parakeets getting dinner ready, and the . . ha, ha, whatever it was, the . . .

JERRY: [*Calmly*] Yes, that was very funny, Peter. I wouldn't have expected it. But do you want to hear about what happened at the zoo, or not?

PETER: Yes. Yes, by all means; tell me what happened at the zoo. Oh, my. I don't know what happened to me.

JERRY: Now I'll let you in on what happened at the zoo; but first, I should tell you why I went to the zoo. I went to the zoo to find out more about the way people exist with animals, and the way animals exist with each other, and with people too. It probably wasn't a fair test, what with everyone separated by bars from everyone else, the animals for the most part from each other, and always the people from the animals. But, if it's a zoo, that's the way it is. [*He pokes* PETER *on the arm*] Move over.

PETER: [*Friendly*] I'm sorry, haven't you enough room? [*He shifts a little*]

JERRY: [*Smiling slightly*] Well, all the animals are there, and all the people are there, and it's Sunday and all the children are there. [*He pokes* PETER *again*] Move over.

PETER: [*Patiently, still friendly*] All right. [*He moves some more, and* JERRY *has all the room he might need*]

JERRY: And it's a hot day, so all the stench is there, too, and all the balloon sellers, and all the ice cream sellers, and all the seals are barking, and all the birds are screaming. [*Pokes* PETER *harder*] Move over!

PETER: [*Beginning to be annoyed*] Look here, you have more than enough room! [*But he moves more, and is now fairly cramped at one end of the bench*]

JERRY: And I am there, and it's feeding time at the lions' house, and the lion keeper comes into the lion cage, one of the lion cages, to feed one of the lions. [*Punches* PETER *on the arm, hard*] MOVE OVER!

PETER: [*Very annoyed*] I can't move over any more, and stop hitting me. What's the matter with you?

JERRY: Do you want to hear the story? [*Punches* PETER's *arm again*]

PETER: [*Flabbergasted*] I'm not so sure! I certainly don't want to be punched in the arm.

JERRY: [*Punches* PETER's *arm again*] Like that?

PETER: Stop it! What's the matter with you?

JERRY: I'm crazy, you bastard.

PETER: That isn't funny.

JERRY: Listen to me, Peter. I want this bench. You go sit on the bench over there, and if you're good I'll tell you the rest of the story.

PETER: [*Flustered*] But . . . whatever for? What *is* the matter with you? Besides, I see no reason why I should give up this bench. I sit on this bench almost every Sunday afternoon, in good weather. It's secluded here; there's never anyone sitting here, so I have it all to myself.

JERRY: [*Softly*] Get off this bench, Peter; I want it.

PETER: [*Almost whining*] No.

JERRY: I said I want this bench, and I'm going to have it. Now get over there.

PETER: People can't have everything they want. You should know that; it's a rule; people can have some of the things they want, but they can't have everything.

JERRY: [*Laughs*] Imbecile! You're slow-witted!

PETER: Stop that!

JERRY: You're a vegetable! Go lie down on the ground.

PETER: [*Intense*] Now *you* listen to me. I've put up with you all afternoon.

JERRY: Not really.

PETER: LONG ENOUGH. I've put up with you long enough. I've listened to you because you seemed . . . well, because I thought you wanted to talk to somebody.

JERRY: You put things well; economically, and, yet . . . oh, what is the word I want to put justice to your . . . JESUS, you make me sick . . . get off here and give me my bench.

PETER: MY BENCH!

JERRY: [*Pushes* PETER *almost, but not quite, off the bench*] Get out of my sight.

PETER: [*Regarding his position*] God da . . . mn you. That's enough! I've had enough of you. I will not give up this bench; you can't have it, and that's that. Now, go away [JERRY *snorts but does not move*] Go away, I said. [JERRY *does not move*] Get away from here. If you don't move on . . . you're a bum . . . that's what you are. . . . If you don't move on, I'll get a policeman here and make you go. [JERRY *laughs, stays*] I warn you. I'll call a policeman.

JERRY: [*Softly*] You won't find a policeman around here; they're all over the west side of the park chasing fairies down from trees or out of the bushes. That's all they do. That's their function. So scream your head off; it won't do you any good.

PETER: POLICE! I warn you, I'll have you arrested. POLICE! [*Pause*] I said POLICE! [*Pause*] I feel ridiculous.

JERRY: You look ridiculous: a grown man screaming for the police on a bright Sunday afternoon in the park with nobody harming you. If a policeman *did* fill his quota and come sludging over this way he'd probably take you in as a nut.

PETER: [*With disgust and impotence*] Great God, I just came here to read, and now you want me to give up the bench. You're mad.

JERRY: Hey, I got news for you, as they say. I'm on your precious bench, and you're never going to have it for yourself again.

PETER: [*Furious*] Look, you; get off my bench. I don't care if it makes any sense or not. I want this bench to myself; I want you OFF IT!

JERRY: [*Mocking*] Aw . . . look who's mad.

PETER: GET OUT!

JERRY: No.

PETER: I WARN YOU!

JERRY: Do you know how ridiculous you look *now?*

PETER: [*His fury and self-consciousness have possessed him*] It doesn't matter. [*He is almost crying*] GET AWAY FROM MY BENCH!

JERRY: Why? You have everything in the world you want; you've told me about your home, and your family, and *your own* little zoo. You have everything, and now you want this bench. Are these the things men fight for? Tell me, Peter, is this bench, this iron and this wood, is this your honor? Is this the thing in the world you'd fight for? Can you think of anything more absurd?

PETER: Absurd? Look, I'm not going to talk to you about honor, or even try to explain it to you. Besides, it isn't a question of honor; but even if it were, you wouldn't understand.

JERRY: [*Contemptuously*] You don't even know what you're saying, do you? This is probably the first time in your life you've had anything more trying to face than changing your cats' toilet box. Stupid! Don't you have any idea, not even the slightest, what other people *need?*

PETER: Oh, boy, listen to you; well, you don't need this bench. That's for sure.

JERRY: Yes; yes, I do.

PETER: [*Quivering*] I've come here for years; I have hours of great pleasure, great satisfaction, right here. And that's important to a man. I'm a responsible person, and I'm a GROWNUP. This is my bench, and you have no right to take it away from me.

JERRY: Fight for it, then. Defend yourself; defend your bench.

PETER: You've *pushed* me to it. Get up and fight.

JERRY: Like a man?

PETER: [*Still angry*] Yes, like a man, if you insist on mocking me even further.

JERRY: I'll have to give you credit for one thing; you *are* a vegetable, and a slightly nearsighted one, I think . . .

PETER: THAT'S ENOUGH.

JERRY: . . . but, you know, as they say on TV all the time—you know—and I mean this, Peter, you have a certain dignity; it surprises me. . . .

PETER: STOP!

JERRY: [*Rises lazily*] Very well, Peter, we'll battle for the bench, but we're not evenly matched. [*He takes out and clicks open an ugly-looking knife*]

PETER: [*Suddenly awakening to the reality of the situation*] You *are* mad! You're stark raving mad! YOU'RE GOING TO KILL ME? [*But before* PETER *has time to think what to do* JERRY *tosses the knife at* PETER'S *feet*]

JERRY: There you go. Pick it up. You have the knife and we'll be more evenly matched.

PETER: [*Horrified*] No!

JERRY: [*Rushes over to* PETER, *grabs him by the collar;* PETER *rises; their faces almost touch*] Now you pick up that knife and you fight with me. You fight for your self-respect; you fight for that goddamned bench.

PETER: [*Struggling*] No! Let . . . let go of me! He . . . Help!

JERRY: [*Slaps* PETER *on each "fight"*] You fight, you miserable bastard; fight for that bench; fight for your manhood, you pathetic little vegetable. [*Spits in* PETER'S *face*] You couldn't even get your wife with a male child.

PETER: [*Breaks away, enraged*] It's a matter of genetics, not manhood, you . . . you monster. [*He darts down, picks up the knife and backs off a little; he is breathing heavily*] I'll give you one last chance; get out of here and leave me alone! [*He holds the knife with a firm arm, but far in front of him, not to attack, but to defend*]

JERRY: [*Sighs heavily*] So be it! [*With a rush he charges* PETER *and impales himself on the knife. Tableau: For just a moment, complete silence,* JERRY *impaled on the knife at the end of* PETER'S *still firm arm. Then* PETER *screams, pulls away, leaving the knife in* JERRY. JERRY *is motionless, on point. Then he, too, screams, and it must be the sound of an infuriated and fatally wounded animal. With the knife in him, he stumbles back to the bench that* PETER *had vacated. He crumbles there, sitting facing* PETER, *his eyes wide in agony, his mouth open*]

PETER: [*Whispering*] Oh my God, oh my God, oh my God. . . . [*He repeats these words many times, very rapidly*]

JERRY: [JERRY *is dying; but now his expression seems to change. His features relax, and while his voice varies, sometimes wrenched with pain, for the most part he seems removed from his dying. He smiles*] Peter, thank you, Peter. I mean that, now; thank you very much. [PETER'S *mouth drops open. He cannot move; he is transfixed*] I came unto you [*He laughs, so faintly*] and you have comforted me. Dear Peter.

PETER: [*Almost fainting*] Oh my God!

JERRY: You'd better go now. Somebody might come by, and you don't want to be here when anyone comes.

PETER: [*Does not move, but begins to weep*] Oh my God, oh my God.

JERRY: And Peter, I'll tell you something now; you're not really a vegetable; it's all right, you're an animal. You're an animal, too. But you'd better hurry now, Peter. Hurry, you'd better go . . . . [JERRY *takes a handkerchief and with great effort and pain wipes the knife handle clean of finger prints*] Hurry away, Peter. [PETER *begins to stagger away*] Wait . . . wait, Peter. Take your book . . . book. Right here . . . beside me . . . on your bench . . . my bench, rather. Come . . . take your book. [PETER *starts for the book, but retreats*] Hurry . . . Peter. [PETER *rushes to the bench, grabs the book, retreats*] Very good, Peter . . . very good. Now . . . hurry away. [PETER *hesitates for a moment, then flees, stage-left*] Hurry away . . . [*His eyes are closed now.*]

PETER: OH MY GOD!

JERRY: Hurry away, your parakeets are making the dinner . . . the cats . . . are setting the table . . .

PETER: [*Off stage. A pitiful howl*] OH MY GOD!

JERRY: [*His eyes still closed, he shakes his head and speaks; a combination of scornful mimicry and supplication*] Oh . . . my . . . God. [*He is dead*]

CURTAIN

1958 1959, 1960, 1999

Saul Bellow 1915–2005

The work of Saul Bellow is dominated by the figure of the marginal man, an alienated and absurd character caught between his own inadequacies and those imposed on him by his friends and society. Bellow's major themes were evident in his first novel, Dangling Man *(1944), which was based in part on the experiences of his early life. He was born in a small town in Quebec, Canada, of Russian immigrant parents who gave him the name Solomon Bellows. Later, when he was in his twenties and had begun to publish his writing, he omitted the final "s" from his last name and changed his first name from Solomon to Saul. When he was still a child, his parents moved to the United States, to Chicago, Illinois, where he grew up in a multilingual (English, French, Yiddish, and Hebrew), Orthodox Jewish household, an environment he later recalled as deeply religious, almost superstitious. In 1937 he graduated from Northwestern University, with honors in anthropology and sociology, and entered the University of Wisconsin on a graduate scholarship, but he soon withdrew to follow his consuming interest, fiction writing. For four years he supported himself by teaching in a Chicago teachers' college; he then served briefly in the Merchant Marine in World War II and later worked on the editorial staff of* Encyclopedia Britannica.

Dangling Man *was published when he was twenty-nine. Three years later he published his second novel,* The Victim. *In 1953 his picaresque novel,* The Adventures of Augie March, *appeared. Bellow's first best-seller, it firmly established him as a writer of national significance and won the first of his three National Book Awards. Bellow's fourth novel,* Seize the Day *(1956), was followed by* Henderson the Rain

King *(1958),* Herzog *(1964), and* Mr. Sammler's Planet *(1970), a grim novel of social turmoil. Bellow also wrote numerous short stories, some of which are collected in* Mosby's Memories *(1968), and a number of plays, including* The Last Analysis, *which was produced in 1964. In 1975 he published* Humboldt's Gift, *a "comedy of success and failure" that is his most humorous book. In the following year he became the seventh American to receive the Nobel Prize for Literature.*

In More Die of Heartbreak *(1987), Bellow again dealt with the dilemmas and follies of intellectuals struggling to flourish in materialist and mechanical America. In a short novel,* The Bellarosa Connection *(1989), he presented a sardonic exploration of a memory expert, a man who remembers everything but whose consciousness (Bellow's abiding subject) is too shallow to allow him to understand himself. In 1994 Bellow published* It All Adds Up, *a collection of his essays. They summarize his views on what ails America and what he sees as the causes of a deteriorating culture.*

For many years Bellow taught at the University of Chicago. In 1993 he moved to Boston University, where, though he was world famous and distinguished as a Nobel Prize winner, he sometimes taught freshman-level classes in literature. It is often thought that because he portrayed them so well, Bellow must have resembled his most memorable heroes: dreamy, bumbling, rumpled, hopelessly mired in their own problems and struggling with their "ideals." Bellow himself believed that he most resembled the hero of Henderson the Rain King, *a "quixotic violinist and pig farmer who vainly sought a higher truth and moral purpose in life." But to those around him, including his students, Bellow was a man of high intellect and wide learning, a man of certainties and often of sarcastic and withering wit. He did not suffer fools gladly, and in his last long novel,* Ravelstein *(2000), he portrayed the final days of a university professor whose aim in life was to expose the "creeping boobism and vulgarity" that surrounded him in America.*

Although he seemed to grow more irascible over the years, his outlook darker, Bellow did not abandon the hope and compassion for humankind that are fundamental to his work. The citation for Bellow's Nobel Prize praised his "exuberant ideas, flashing irony, hilarious comedy, and burning compassion." That compassion found its expression in his creation of vivid characters who, in Bellow's words, struggled against the necessity of living life "in a mass. Transformed by Science. Under organized power. Subject to tremendous controls. In a condition caused by mechanization." His vivid characters ranged from the highest intellectuals to the lowly: "the cheapies, the stingies, the hypochondriacs, the family bores, humanoids." But his greatest achievement was his depiction of the modern antihero, the contemporary man "who keeps on trying to find a foothold during his wanderings in our tottering world, one who can never relinquish his faith that the value of life depends on its dignity, not its success."

FURTHER READING: R. Kiernan, *Saul Bellow,* 1988; *Saul Bellow in the 1980s,* ed. G. Cronin and L. Goldman, 1989; M. Glenday, *Saul Bellow and the Decline of Humanism,* 1990; E. Pifer, *Saul Bellow against the Grain,* 1990; R. Miller, *Saul Bellow: A Biography of the Imagination,* 1991; *Saul Bellow at Seventy-Five: A Collection of Critical Essays,* ed. G. Bach, 1991; P. Hyland, *Saul Bellow,* 1992; *Saul Bellow,* A Mosaic, ed. L. Goldman, 1992; M. Friedrich, *Character and Narration in the Short Fiction of Saul Bellow,* 1995; *Saul Bellow and the Struggle at the Center,* ed. E. Hollahan, 1996; J. Atlas, *Bellow,* 2000; *Small Planets: Saul Bellow and the Art of Short Fiction,* ed. G. Bach and G. Cronin, 2000; M. Quayum, *Saul Bellow and American Transcendentalism,* 2004.

TEXT: *Him with His Foot in His Mouth,* 1984.

A SILVER DISH

What do you do about death—in this case, the death of an old father? If you're a modern person, sixty years of age, and a man who's been around, like Woody Selbst, what do you do? Take this matter of mourning, and take it against a contemporary background. How, against a contemporary background, do you mourn an octogenarian father, nearly blind, his heart enlarged, his lungs filling with fluid, who creeps, stumbles, gives off the odors, the moldiness or gassiness, of old men. I *mean!* As Woody put it, be realistic. Think what times these are. The papers daily give it to you—the Lufthansa pilot in Aden[1] is described by the hostages on his knees, begging the Palestinian terrorists not to execute him, but they shoot him through the head. Later they themselves are killed. And still others shoot others, or shoot themselves. That's what you read in the press, see on the tube, mention at dinner. We know now what goes daily through the whole of the human community, like a global death-peristalsis.

Woody, a businessman in South Chicago, was not an ignorant person. He knew more such phrases than you would expect a tile contractor (offices, lobbies, lavatories) to know. The kind of knowledge he had was not the kind for which you get academic degrees. Although Woody had studied for two years in a seminary, preparing to be a minister. Two years of college during the Depression was more than most high-school graduates could afford. After that, in his own vital, picturesque, original way (Morris, his old man, was also, in his days of nature, vital and picturesque), Woody had read up on many subjects, subscribed to *Science* and other magazines that gave real information, and had taken night courses at De Paul and Northwestern in ecology, criminology, existentialism. Also he had traveled extensively in Japan, Mexico, and Africa, and there was an African experience that was especially relevant to mourning. It was this: on a launch near the Murchison Falls in Uganda,[2] he had seen a buffalo calf seized by a crocodile from the bank of the White Nile.[3] There were giraffes along the tropical river, and hippopotamuses, and baboons, and flamingos and other brilliant birds crossing the bright air in the heat of the morning, when the calf, stepping into the river to drink, was grabbed by the hoof and dragged down. The parent buffaloes couldn't figure it out. Under the water the calf still threshed, fought, churned the mud. Woody, the robust traveler, took this in as he sailed by, and to him it looked as if the parent cattle were asking each other dumbly what had happened. He chose to assume that there was pain in this, he read brute grief into it. On the White Nile, Woody had the impression that he had gone back to the pre-Adamite past, and he brought reflections on this impression home to South Chicago. He brought also a bundle of hashish from Kampala.[4] In this he took a chance with the customs inspectors, banking perhaps on his broad build, frank face, high color. He didn't look like a wrongdoer, a bad guy; he looked like a good guy. But he liked taking chances. Risk was a wonderful stimulus. He threw down his trenchcoat on the customs counter. If the inspectors searched the pockets, he was prepared to say that the

[1]In October 1977, a Lufthansa airliner was hijacked by terrorists and flown to Aden, South Yeman, where the pilot was murdered. German commandos then stormed the airliner, killed the terrorists, and freed the passenger hostages.

[2]Nation in east central Africa.

[3]A chief—and remote—tributary of the Nile River in Africa.

[4]Capital city of Uganda.

coat wasn't his. But he got away with it, and the Thanksgiving turkey was stuffed with hashish. This was much enjoyed. That was practically the last feast at which Pop, who also relished risk or defiance, was present. The hashish Woody had tried to raise in his backyard from the Africa seeds didn't take. But behind his warehouse, where the Lincoln Continental was parked, he kept a patch of marijuana. There was no harm at all in Woody, but he didn't like being entirely within the law. It was simply a question of self-respect.

After that Thanksgiving, Pop gradually sank as if he had a slow leak. This went on for some years. In and out of the hospital, he dwindled, his mind wandered, he couldn't even concentrate enough to complain, except in exceptional moments on the Sundays Woody regularly devoted to him. Morris, an amateur who once was taken seriously by Willie Hoppe, the great pro himself, couldn't execute the simplest billiard shots anymore. He could only conceive shots; he began to theorize about impossible three-cushion combinations. Halina, the Polish woman with whom Morris had lived for over forty years as man and wife, was too old herself now to run to the hospital. So Woody had to do it. There was Woody's mother, too—a Christian convert—needing care; she was over eighty and frequently hospitalized. Everybody had diabetes and pleurisy and arthritis and cataracts and cardiac pacemakers. And everybody had lived by the body, but the body was giving out.

There was Woody's two sisters as well, unmarried, in their fifties, very Christian, very straight, still living with Mama in an entirely Christian bungalow. Woody, who took full responsibility for them all, occasionally had to put one of the girls (they had become sick girls) in a mental institution. Nothing severe. The sisters were wonderful women, both of them gorgeous once, but neither of the poor things was playing with a full deck. And all the factions had to be kept separate—Mama, the Christian convert; the fundamentalist sisters; Pop, who read the Yiddish paper as long as he could still see print; Halina, a good Catholic. Woody, the seminary forty years behind him, described himself as an agnostic. Pop had no more religion than you could find in the Yiddish paper, but he made Woody promise to bury him among Jews, and that was where he lay now, in the Hawaiian shirt Woody had bought for him at the tilers' convention in Honolulu. Woody would allow no undertaker's assistant to dress him, but came to the parlor and buttoned the stiff into the shirt himself, and the old man went down looking like Ben-Gurion[5] in a simple wooden coffin, sure to rot fast. That was how Woody wanted it all. At the graveside, he had taken off and folded his jacket, rolled up his sleeves on thick freckled biceps, waved back the little tractor standing by, and shoveled the dirt himself. His big face, broad at the bottom, narrowed upward like a Dutch house. And, his small good lower teeth taking hold of the upper lip in his exertion, he performed the final duty of a son. He was very fit, so it must have been emotion, not the shoveling, that made him redden so. After the funeral, he went home with Halina and her son, a decent Polack like his mother, and talented, too—Mitosh played the organ at hockey and basketball games in the Stadium,[6] which took a smart man because it was a rabble-rousing kind of occupation—and they had some drinks and comforted the old girl. Halina was true blue, always one hundred percent for Morris.

[5]David Ben-Gurion (1886–1973), Zionist leader and Israel's first prime minister.
[6]Chicago sports arena.

Then for the rest of the week Woody was busy, had jobs to run, office responsibilities, family responsibilities. He lived alone; as did his wife; as did his mistress: everybody in a separate establishment. Since his wife, after fifteen years of separation, had not learned to take care of herself, Woody did her shopping on Fridays, filled her freezer. He had to take her this week to buy shoes. Also, Friday night he always spent with Helen—Helen was his wife de facto. Saturday he did his big weekly shopping. Saturday night he devoted to Mom and his sisters. So he was too busy to attend to his own feelings except, intermittently, to note to himself, "First Thursday in the grave." "First Friday, and fine weather." "First Saturday; he's got to be getting used to it." Under his breath he occasionally said, "Oh, Pop."

But it was Sunday that hit him, when the bells rang all over South Chicago—the Ukrainian, Roman Catholic, Greek, Russian, African Methodist churches, sounding off one after another. Woody had his offices in his warehouse, and there had built an apartment for himself, very spacious and convenient, in the top story. Because he left every Sunday morning at seven to spend the day with Pop, he had forgotten by how many churches Selbst Tile Company was surrounded. He was still in bed when he heard the bells, and all at once he knew how heartbroken he was. This sudden big heartache in a man of sixty, a practical, healthy-minded, and experienced man, was deeply unpleasant. When he had an unpleasant condition, he believed in taking something for it. So he thought: What shall I take? There was plenty of remedies available. His cellar was stocked with cases of Scotch whisky, Polish vodka, Armagnac, Moselle, Burgundy. There were also freezers with steaks and with game and with Alaskan King crab. He bought with a broad hand—by the crate and by the dozen. But in the end, when he got out of bed, he took nothing but a cup of coffee. While the kettle was heating, he put on his Japanese judo-style suit and sat down to reflect.

Woody was moved when things were *honest*. Bearing beams were honest, undisguised concrete pillars inside high-rise apartments were honest. It was bad to cover up anything. He hated faking. Stone was honest. Metal was honest. These Sunday bells were very straight. They broke loose, they wagged and rocked, and the vibrations and the banging did something for him—cleansed his insides, purified his blood. A bell was a one-way throat, had only one thing to tell you and simply told it. He listened.

He had had some connections with bells and churches. He was after all something of a Christian. Born a Jew, he was a Jew facially, with a hint of Iroquois or Cherokee, but his mother had been converted more than fifty years ago by her brother-in-law, the Reverend Doctor Kovner. Kovner, a rabbinical student who had left the Hebrew Union College in Cincinnati to become a minister and establish a mission, had given Woody a partly Christian upbringing. Now, Pop was on the outs with these fundamentalists. He said that the Jews came to the mission to get coffee, bacon, canned pineapple, day-old bread, and dairy products. And if they had to listen to sermons, that was okay—this was the Depression[7] and you couldn't be too particular—but he knew they sold the bacon.

The Gospels said it plainly: "Salvation is from the Jews."

Backing the Reverend Doctor were wealthy fundamentalists, mainly Swedes, eager to speed up the Second Coming by converting all Jews. The foremost of

[7]The Great Depression of the 1930s in the United States.

Kovner's backers was Mrs. Skoglund, who had inherited a large dairy business from her late husband. Woody was under her special protection.

Woody was fourteen years of age when Pop took off with Halina, who worked in his shop, leaving his difficult Christian wife and his converted son and his small daughters. He came to Woody in the backyard one spring day and said, "From now on you're the man of the house." Woody was practicing with a golf club, knocking off the heads of dandelions. Pop came into the yard in his good suit, which was too hot for the weather, and when he took off his fedora[8] the skin of his head was marked with a deep ring and the sweat was sprinkled over his scalp—more drops than hairs. He said, "I'm going to move out." Pop was anxious, but he was set to go—determined. "It's no use. I can't live a life like this." Envisioning the life Pop simply *had* to live, his free life, Woody was able to picture him in the billiard parlor, under the El tracks in a crap game, or playing poker at Brown and Koppel's upstairs. "You're going to be the man of the house," said Pop. "It's okay. I put you all on welfare. I just got back from Wabansia Avenue, from the relief station." Hence the suit and the hat. "They're sending out a caseworker." Then he said, "You got to lend me money to buy gasoline—the caddie money you saved."

Understanding that Pop couldn't get away without his help, Woody turned over to him all he had earned at the Sunset Ridge Club in Winnetka.[9] Pop felt that the valuable life lesson he was transmitting was worth far more than these dollars, and whenever he was conning his boy a sort of high-priest expression came down over his bent nose, his ruddy face. The children, who got their finest ideas at the movies, called him Richard Dix.[10] Later, when the comic strip came out, they said he was Dick Tracy.

As Woody now saw it, under the tumbling bells, he had bankrolled his own desertion. Ha ha! He found this delightful; and especially Pop's attitude of "That'll teach you to trust your father." For this was a demonstration on behalf of real life and free instincts, against religion and hypocrisy. But mainly it was aimed against being a fool, the disgrace of foolishness. Pop had it in for the Reverend Doctor Kovner, not because he was an apostate (Pop couldn't have cared less), not because the mission was a racket (he admitted that the Reverend Doctor was personally honest), but because Doctor Kovner behaved foolishly, spoke like a fool, and acted like a fiddler. He tossed his hair like a Paganini[11] (this was Woody's addition; Pop had never even heard of Paganini). Proof that he was not a spiritual leader was that he converted Jewish women by stealing their hearts. "He works up all those broads," said Pop. "He doesn't even know it himself, I swear he doesn't know how he gets them."

From the other side, Kovner often warned Woody, "Your father is a dangerous person. Of course, you love him; you should love him and forgive him, Voodrow, but you are old enough to understand he is leading a life of wice."

It was all petty stuff: Pop's sinning was on a boy level and therefore made a big impression on a boy. And on Mother. Are wives children, or what? Mother

[8]A man's felt hat with the crown creased lengthwise.

[9]Upper-middle-class suburb north of Chicago, as is Evanston, mentioned later in the story.

[10]American movie actor (1894–1949) of the 1920s and 1930s, famous for his heroic roles in movie westerns.

[11]Niccolò Paganini (1782–1840), Italian violin virtuoso whose performances were marked by his dramatic gestures.

often said, "I hope you put that brute in your prayers. Look what he has done to us. But only pray for him, don't see him." But he saw him all the time. Woodrow was leading a double life, sacred and profane. He accepted Jesus Christ as his personal redeemer. Aunt Rebecca took advantage of this. She made him work. He had to work under Aunt Rebecca. He filled in for the janitor at the mission and settlement house.[12] In winter, he had to feed the coal furnace, and on some nights he slept near the furnace room, on the pool table. He also picked the lock of the storeroom. He took canned pineapple and cut bacon from the flitch[13] with his pocketknife. He crammed himself with uncooked bacon. He had a big frame to fill out.

Only now, sipping Melitta coffee, he asked himself: Had he been so hungry? No, he loved being reckless. He was fighting Aunt Rebecca Kovner when he took out his knife and got on a box to reach the bacon. She didn't know, she couldn't prove that Woody, such a frank, strong, positive boy, who looked you in the eye, so direct, was a thief also. But he was also a thief. Whenever she looked at him, he knew that she was seeing his father. In the curve of his nose, the movements of his eyes, the thickness of his body, in his healthy face, she saw that wicked savage Morris.

Morris, you see, had been a street boy in Liverpool—Woody's mother and her sister were British by birth. Morris's Polish family, on their way to America, abandoned him in Liverpool because he had an eye infection and they would all have been sent back from Ellis Island.[14] They stopped awhile in England, but his eyes kept running and they ditched him. They slipped away, and he had to make out alone in Liverpool at the age of twelve. Mother came of better people. Pop, who slept in the cellar of her house, fell in love with her. At sixteen, scabbing during a seamen's strike, he shoveled his way[15] across the Atlantic and jumped ship in Brooklyn. He became an American, and America never knew it. He voted without papers, he drove without a license, he paid no taxes, he cut every corner. Horses, cards, billiards, and women were his lifelong interests, in ascending order. Did he love anyone (he was so busy)? Yes, he loved Halina. He loved his son. To this day, Mother believed that he had loved her most and always wanted to come back. This gave her a chance to act the queen, with her plump wrists and faded Queen Victoria face. "The girls are instructed never to admit him," she said. The Empress of India speaking.

Bell-battered Woodrow's soul was whirling this Sunday morning, indoors and out, to the past, back to this upper corner of the warehouse, laid out with such originality—the bells coming and going, metal on naked metal, until the bell circle expanded over the whole of steel-making, oil-refining, power-producing mid-autumn South Chicago, and all its Croatians, Ukrainians, Greeks, Poles, and respectable blacks heading for their churches to hear Mass or to sing hymns.

Woody himself had been a good hymn singer. He still knew the hymns. He had testified, too. He was often sent by Aunt Rebecca to get up and tell a churchful of Scandihoovians that he, a Jewish lad, accepted Jesus Christ. For this she paid him fifty cents. She made the disbursement. She was the bookkeeper, fiscal chief,

[12]An institution established to provide community service to the poor and newly arrived immigrants.
[13]A slab or side of meat.
[14]Now a national monument in New York Bay, Ellis Island was, from 1892 to 1943, the main immigration center for immigrants entering the United States.
[15]I.e., worked his way as a coal stoker on a transatlantic steamship.

general manager of the mission. The Reverend Doctor didn't know a thing about the operation. What the Doctor supplied was the fervor. He was genuine, a wonderful preacher. And what about Woody himself? He also had fervor. He was drawn to the Reverend Doctor. The Reverend Doctor taught him to lift up his eyes, gave him his higher life. Apart from this higher life, the rest was Chicago—the ways of Chicago, which came so natural that nobody thought to question them. So, for instance, in 1933 (what ancient, ancient times!), at the Century of Progress World's Fair, when Woody was a coolie and pulled a rickshaw, wearing a peaked straw hat and trotting with powerful, thick legs, while the brawny red farmers—his boozing passengers—were laughing their heads off and pestered him for whores, he, although a freshman at the seminary, saw nothing wrong, when girls asked him to steer a little business their way, in making dates and accepting tips from both sides. He necked in Grant Park with a powerful girl who had to go home quickly to nurse her baby. Smelling of milk, she rode beside him on the streetcar to the West Side, squeezing his rickshaw puller's thigh and wetting her blouse. This was the Roosevelt Road car. Then, in the apartment where she lived with her mother, he couldn't remember that there were any husbands around. What he did remember was the strong milk odor. Without inconsistency, next morning he did New Testament Greek: The light shineth in darkness—*to fos en te skotia fainei*—and the darkness comprehended it not.

And all the while he trotted between the shafts on the fairgrounds he had one idea, nothing to do with these horny giants having a big time in the city: that the goal, the project, the purpose was (and he couldn't explain why he thought so; all evidence was against it)—God's idea was that this world should be a love world, that it should eventually recover and be entirely a world of love. He wouldn't have said this to a soul, for he could see himself how stupid it was—personal and stupid. Nevertheless, there it was at the center of his feelings. And at the same time, Aunt Rebecca was right when she said to him, strictly private, close to his ear even, "You're a little crook, like your father."

There was some evidence for this, or what stood for evidence to an impatient person like Rebecca. Woody matured quickly—he had to—but how could you expect a boy of seventeen, he wondered, to interpret the viewpoint, the feelings, of a middle-aged woman, and one whose breast had been removed? Morris said that if titties were not fondled and kissed, they got cancer in protest. It was a cry of the flesh. And this had seemed true to Woody. When his imagination tried the theory on the Reverend Doctor, it worked out—he couldn't see the Reverend Doctor behaving in that way to Aunt Rebecca's breasts! Morris's theory kept Woody looking from bosoms to husbands and from husbands to bosoms. He still did that. It's an exceptionally smart man who isn't marked forever by the sexual theories he hears from his father, and Woody wasn't all that smart. He knew this himself. Personally, he had gone far out of his way to do right by women in this regard. What nature demanded. He and Pop were common, thick men, but there's nobody too gross to have ideas of delicacy.

The Reverend Doctor preached, Rebecca preached, rich Mrs. Skoglund preached from Evanston, Mother preached. Pop also was on a soapbox. Everyone was doing it. Up and down Division Street, under every lamp, almost, speakers were giving out: anarchists, Socialists, Stalinists, single-taxers,[16] Zionists,

[16]Radical reformers who seek to replace all taxes with a single tax levied on land holdings.

Tolstoyans, vegetarians, and fundamentalist Christian preachers—you name it. A beef, a hope, a way of life or salvation, a protest. How was it that the accumulated gripes of all the ages took off so when transplanted to America?

And that fine Swedish immigrant Aase (Osie, they pronounced it), who had been the Skoglunds' cook and married the eldest son, to become his rich, religious widow—she supported the Reverend Doctor. In her time she must have been built like a chorus girl. And women seem to have lost the secret of putting up their hair in the high basketry fence of braid she wore. Aase took Woody under her special protection and paid his tuition at the seminary. And Pop said . . . But on this Sunday, at peace as soon as the bells stopped banging, this velvet autumn day when the grass was finest and thickest, silky green: before the first frost, and the blood in your lungs is redder than summer air can make it and smarts with oxygen, as if the iron in your system was hungry for it, and the chill was sticking it to you in every breath . . . Pop, six feet under, would never feel this blissful sting again. The last of the bells still had the bright air streaming with vibrations.

On weekends, the institutional vacancy of decades came back to the warehouse and crept under the door of Woody's apartment. It felt as empty on Sundays as churches were during the week. Before each business day, before the trucks and the crews got started, Woody jogged five miles in his Adidas suit. Not on this day still reserved for Pop, however. Although it was tempting to go out and run off the grief. Being alone hit Woody hard this morning. He thought: Me and the world; the world and me. Meaning that there always was some activity to interpose, an errand or a visit, a picture to paint (he was a creative amateur), a massage, a meal—a shield between himself and that troublesome solitude which used the world as its reservoir. But Pop! Last Tuesday, Woody had gotten into the hospital bed with Pop because he kept pulling out the intravenous needles. Nurses stuck them back, and then Woody astonished them all by climbing into bed to hold the struggling old guy in his arms. "Easy, Morris, Morris, go easy." But Pop still groped feebly for the pipes.

When the tolling stopped, Woody didn't notice that a great lake of quiet had come over his kingdom, the Selbst Tile warehouse. What he heard and saw was an old red Chicago streetcar, one of those trams the color of a stockyard steer. Cars of this type went out before Pearl Harbor—clumsy, big-bellied, with tough rattan seats and brass grips for the standing passengers. Those cars used to make four stops to the mile, and ran with a wallowing motion. They stank of carbolic or ozone and throbbed when the air compressors were being charged. The conductor had his knotted signal cord to pull, and the motorman beat the foot gong with his mad heel.

Woody recognized himself on the Western Avenue line and riding through a blizzard with his father, both in sheepskins and with hands and faces raw, the snow blowing in from the rear platform when the doors opened and getting into the longitudinal cleats of the floor. There wasn't warmth enough inside to melt it. And Western Avenue was the longest car line in the world, the boosters said, as if it was a thing to brag about. Twenty-three miles long, made by a draftsman with a T square, lined with factories, storage buildings, machine shops, used-car lots, trolley barns, gas stations, funeral parlors, six-flats, utility buildings, and junkyards, on and on from the prairies on the south to Evanston on the north. Woodrow and his father were going north to Evanston, to Howard Street, and then some, to see Mrs. Skoglund. At the end of the line they would still have about five blocks to hike. The purpose of the trip? To raise money for Pop. Pop had talked him into this. When they found out, Mother and Aunt Rebecca would be furious, and Woody was afraid, but he couldn't help it.

Morris had come and said, "Son, I'm in trouble. It's bad."

"What's bad, Pop?"

"Halina took money from her husband for me and has to put it back before old Bujak misses it. He could kill her."

"What did she do it for?"

"Son, you know how the bookies collect? They send a goon. They'll break my head open."

"Pop! You know I can't take you to Mrs. Skoglund."

"Why not? You're my kid, aren't you? The old broad wants to adopt you, doesn't she? Shouldn't I get something out of it for my trouble? What am I—outside? And what about Halina? She puts her life on the line, but my own kid says no."

"Oh, Bujak wouldn't hurt her."

"Woody, he'd beat her to death."

Bujak? Uniform in color with his dark-gray work clothes, short in the legs, his whole strength in his tool-and-die-maker's forearms and black fingers; and beat-looking—there was Bujak for you. But, according to Pop, there was big, big violence in Bujak, a regular boiling Bessemer[17] inside his narrow chest. Woody could never see the violence in him. Bujak wanted no trouble. If anything, maybe he was afraid that Morris and Halina would gang up on him and kill him, screaming. But Pop was no desperado murderer. And Halina was a calm, serious woman. Bujak kept his savings in the cellar (banks were going out of business). The worst they did was to take some of his money, intending to put it back. As Woody saw him, Bujak was trying to be sensible. He accepted his sorrow. He set minimum requirements for Halina: cook the meals, clean the house, show respect. But at stealing Bujak might have drawn the line, for money was different, money was vital substance. If they stole his savings he might have had to take action, out of respect for the substance, for himself—self-respect. But you couldn't be sure that Pop hadn't invented the bookie, the goon, the theft—the whole thing. He was capable of it, and you'd be a fool not to suspect him. Morris knew that Mother and Aunt Rebecca had told Mrs. Skoglund how wicked he was. They had painted him for her in poster colors—purple for vice, black for his soul, red for Hell flames: a gambler, smoker, drinker, deserter, screwer of women, and atheist. So Pop was determined to reach her. It was risky for everybody. The Reverend Doctor's operating costs were met by Skoglund Dairies. The widow paid Woody's seminary tuition; she bought dresses for the little sisters.

Woody, now sixty, fleshy and big, like a figure for the victory of American materialism, sunk in his lounge chair, the leather of its armrests softer to his fingertips than a woman's skin, was puzzled and, in his depths, disturbed by certain blots within him, blots of light in his brain, a blot combining pain and amusement in his breast (how did *that* get there?). Intense thought puckered the skin between his eyes with a strain bordering on headache. Why had he let

[17]Large container in which iron ore is heated. When oxygen is pumped through the molten iron, steel is produced, with a shower of sparks and a blast of heat.

Pop have his way? Why did he agree to meet him that day, in the dim rear of the poolroom?

"But what will you tell Mrs. Skoglund?"

"The old broad? Don't worry, there's plenty to tell her, and it's all true. Ain't I trying to save my little laundry-and-cleaning shop? Isn't that bailiff coming for the fixtures next week?" And Pop rehearsed his pitch on the Western Avenue car. He counted on Woody's health and his freshness. Such a straightforward-looking body was perfect for a con.

Did they still have such winter storms in Chicago as they used to have? Now they somehow seemed less fierce. Blizzards used to come straight down from Ontario, from the Arctic, and drop five feet of snow in an afternoon. Then the rusty green platform cars, with revolving brushes at both ends, came out of the barns to sweep the tracks. Ten or twelve streetcars followed in slow processions, or waited, block after block.

There was a long delay at the gates of Riverview Park, all the amusements covered for the winter, boarded up—the dragon's-back high-rides, the Bobs, the Chute, the Tilt-a-Whirl, all the fun machinery put together by mechanics and electricians, men like Bujak the tool-and-die maker, good with engines. The blizzard was having it all its own way behind the gates, and you couldn't see far inside; only a few bulbs burned behind the palings. When Woody wiped the vapor from the glass, the wire mesh of the window guards was stuffed solid at eye level with snow. Looking higher, you saw mostly the streaked wind horizontally driving from the north. In the seat ahead, two black coal heavers, both in leather Lindbergh flying helmets, sat with shovels between their legs, returning from a job. They smelled of sweat, burlap sacking, and coal. Mostly dull with black dust, they also sparkled here and there.

There weren't many riders. People weren't leaving the house. This was a day to sit legs stuck out beside the stove, mummified by both the outdoor and the indoor forces. Only a fellow with an angle, like Pop, would go and buck such weather. A storm like this was out of the compass, and you kept the human scale by having a scheme to raise fifty bucks. Fifty soldiers! Real money in 1933.

"That woman is crazy for you," said Pop.

"She's just a good woman, sweet to all of us."

"Who knows what she's got in mind. You're a husky kid. Not such a kid, either."

"She's a religious woman. She really has religion."

"Well, your mother isn't your only parent. She and Rebecca and Kovner aren't going to fill you up with their ideas. I know your mother wants to wipe me out of your life. Unless I take a hand, you won't even understand what life is. Because they don't know—those silly Christers."

"Yes, Pop."

"The girls I can't help. They're too young. I'm sorry about them, but I can't do anything. With you it's different."

He wanted me like himself, an American.

They were stalled in the storm, while the cattle-colored car waited to have the trolley[18] reset in the crazy wind, which boomed, tingled, blasted. At Howard Street they would have to walk straight into it, due north.

[18]Upward extending arm that conducts electricity from an overhead wire to the electric motors of a streetcar. When the trolley breaks loose from the overhead wire, the conductor must reconnect the trolley before the streetcar can move.

"You'll do the talking at first," said Pop.

Woody had the makings of a salesman, a pitchman. He was aware of this when he got to his feet in church to testify before fifty or sixty people. Even though Aunt Rebecca made it worth his while, he moved his own heart when he spoke up about his faith. But occasionally, without notice, his heart went away as he spoke religion and he couldn't find it anywhere. In its absence, sincere behavior got him through. He had to rely for delivery on his face, his voice—on behavior. Then his eyes came closer and closer together. And in this approach of eye to eye he felt the strain of hypocrisy. The twisting of his face threatened to betray him. It took everything he had to keep looking honest. So, since he couldn't bear the cynicism of it, he fell back on mischievousness. Mischief was where Pop came in. Pop passed straight through all those divided fields, gap after gap, and arrived at his side, bent-nosed and broad-faced. In regard to Pop, you thought of neither sincerity nor insincerity. Pop was like the man in the song: He wanted what he wanted when he wanted it. Pop was physical; Pop was digestive, circulatory, sexual. If Pop got serious, he talked to you about washing under the arms or in the crotch or of drying between your toes or of cooking supper, of baked beans and fried onions, of draw poker or of a certain horse in the fifth race at Arlington. Pop was elemental. That was why he gave such relief from religion and paradoxes, and things like that. Now, Mother *thought* she was spiritual, but Woody knew that she was kidding herself. Oh, yes, in the British accent she never gave up she was always talking to God or about Him—please God, God willing, praise God. But she was a big substantial bread-and-butter down-to-earth woman, with down-to-earth duties like feeding the girls, protecting, refining, keeping pure the girls. And those two protected doves grew up so overweight, heavy in the hips and thighs, that their poor heads looked long and slim. And mad. Sweet but cuckoo—Paula cheerfully cuckoo, Joanna depressed and having episodes.

"I'll do my best by you, but you have to promise, Pop, not to get me in Dutch with Mrs. Skoglund."

"You worried because I speak bad English? Embarrassed? I have a mockie accent?"

"It's not that. Kovner has a heavy accent, and she doesn't mind."

"Who the hell are those freaks to look down on me? You're practically a man and your dad has a right to expect help from you. He's in a fix. And you bring him to her house because she's bighearted, and you haven't got anybody else to go to."

"I got you, Pop."

The two coal trimmers stood up at Devon Avenue. One of them wore a woman's coat. Men wore women's clothing in those years, and women men's when there was no choice. The fur collar was spiky with the wet, and sprinkled with soot. Heavy, they dragged their shovels and got off at the front. The slow car ground on, very slow. It was after four when they reached the end of the line, and somewhere between gray and black, with snow spouting and whirling under the street lamps. In Howard Street, autos were stalled at all angles and abandoned. The sidewalks were blocked. Woody led the way into Evanston, and Pop followed him up the middle of the street in the furrows made earlier by trucks. For four blocks they bucked the wind and then Woody broke through the drifts to the snowbound mansion, where they both had to push the wrought-iron gate because of the drift behind it. Twenty rooms or more in this dignified house and nobody in them but Mrs. Skoglund and her servant Hjordis, also religious.

As Woody and Pop waited, brushing the slush from their sheepskin collars and Pop wiping his big eyebrows with the ends of his scarf, sweating and freezing, the chains began to rattle and Hjordis uncovered the air holes of the glass storm door by turning a wooden bar. Woody called her "monkfaced." You no longer see women like that, who put no female touch on the face. She came plain, as God made her. She said, "Who is it and what do you want?"

"It's Woodrow Selbst. Hjordis? It's Woody."

"You're not expected."

"No, but we're here."

"What do you want?"

"We came to see Mrs. Skoglund."

"What for do you want to see her?"

"Just tell her we're here."

"I have to tell her what you came for, without calling up first."

"Why don't you say it's Woody with his father, and we wouldn't come in a snowstorm like this if it wasn't important."

The understandable caution of women who live alone. Respectable old-time women, too. There was no such respectability now in those Evanston houses, with their big verandas and deep yards and with a servant like Hjordis, who carried at her belt keys to the pantry and to every closet and every dresser and every padlocked bin in the cellar. And in High Episcopal Christian Science Women's Temperance[19] Evanston, no tradespeople rang at the front door. Only invited guests. And here, after a ten-mile grind through the blizzard, came two tramps from the West Side. To this mansion where a Swedish immigrant lady, herself once a cook and now a philanthropic widow, dreamed, snowbound, while frozen lilac twigs clapped at her storm windows, of a new Jerusalem and a Second Coming and a Resurrection and a Last Judgment. To hasten the Second Coming, and all the rest, you had to reach the hearts of these scheming bums arriving in a snowstorm.

Sure, they let us in.

Then in the heat that swam suddenly up to their mufflered chins Pop and Woody felt the blizzard for what it was; their cheeks were frozen slabs. They stood beat, itching, trickling in the front hall that *was* a hall, with a carved newel post staircase and a big stained-glass window at the top. Picturing Jesus with the Samaritan woman. There was a kind of Gentile closeness to the air. Perhaps when he was with Pop, Woody made more Jewish observations than he would otherwise. Although Pop's most Jewish characteristic was that Yiddish was the only language he could read a paper in. Pop was with Polish Halina, and Mother was with Jesus Christ, and Woody ate uncooked bacon from the flitch. Still, now and then he had a Jewish impression.

Mrs. Skoglund was the cleanest of women—her fingernails, her white neck, her ears—and Pop's sexual hints to Woody all went wrong because she was so intensely clean, and made Woody think of a waterfall, large as she was, and grandly built. Her bust was big. Woody's imagination had investigated this. He thought she kept things tied down tight, very tight. But she lifted both arms once

[19]Women's Christian Temperance Union, an organization devoted to the prohibition of alcoholic beverages. Its headquarters is in Evanston, Illinois.

to a raise a window and there it was, her bust, beside him, the whole unbindable thing. Her hair was like the raffia you had to soak before you could weave with it in a basket class—pale, pale. Pop, as he took his sheepskin off, was in sweaters, no jacket. His darting looks made him seem crooked. Hardest of all for these Selbsts with their bent noses and big, apparently straightforward faces was to look honest. All the signs of dishonesty played over them. Woody had often puzzled about it. Did it go back to the muscles, was it fundamentally a jaw problem—the projecting angles of the jaws? Or was it the angling that went on in the heart? The girls called Pop Dick Tracy, but Dick Tracy was a good guy. Whom could Pop convince? Here Woody caught a possibility as it flitted by. Precisely because of the way Pop looked, a sensitive person might feel remorse for condemning unfairly or judging unkindly. Just because of a face? Some must have bent over backward. Then he had them. Not Hjordis. She would have put Pop into the street then and there, storm or no storm. Hjordis was religious but she was wised up, too. She hadn't come over in steerage and worked forty years in Chicago for nothing.

Mrs. Skoglund, Aase (Osie), led the visitors into the front room. This, the biggest room in the house, needed supplementary heating. Because of fifteen-foot ceilings and high windows, Hjordis had kept the parlor stove burning. It was one of those elegant parlor stoves that wore a nickel crown, or miter, and this miter, when you moved it aside, automatically raised the hinge of an iron stove lid. Into this hole you tipped the scuttle and the anthracite chestnut rattled down. It made a cake or dome of fire visible through the small isinglass frames. It was a pretty room, threequarters paneled in wood. The stove was plugged into the flue of the marble fireplace, and there were parquet floors and Axminster carpets and cranberry colored tufted Victorian upholstery, and a kind of Chinese étagère,[20] inside a cabinet, lined with mirrors and containing silver pitchers, trophies won by Skoglund cows, fancy sugar tongs and cut-glass pitchers and goblets. There were Bibles and pictures of Jesus and the Holy Land and that faint Gentile odor, as if things had been rinsed in a weak vinegar solution.

"Mrs. Skoglund, I brought my dad to you. I don't think you ever met him," said Woody.

"Yes, Missus, that's me, Selbst."

Pop stood short but masterful in the sweaters, and his belly sticking out, not soft but hard. He was a man of the hard-bellied type. Nobody intimidated Pop. He never presented himself as a beggar. There wasn't a cringe in him anywhere. He let her see at once by the way he said "Missus" that he was independent and that he knew his way around. He communicated that he was able to handle himself with women. Handsome Mrs. Skoglund, carrying a basket woven out of her own hair, was in her fifties—eight, maybe ten years his senior.

"I asked my son to bring me because I know you do the kid a lot of good. It's natural you should know both his parents."

"Mrs. Skoglund, my dad is in a tight corner and I don't know anybody else to ask for help."

This was all the preliminary Pop wanted. He took over and told the widow his story about the laundry-and-cleaning business and payments overdue, and explained about the fixtures and attachment notice, and the bailiff's office and

[20]A cabinet that holds a tier of shelves.

what they were going to do to him; and he said, "I'm a small man trying to make a living."

"You don't support your children," said Mrs. Skoglund.

"That's right," said Hjordis.

"I haven't got it. If I had it, wouldn't I give it? There's bread lines and soup lines all over town. Is it just me? What I have I divvy with. I give the kids. A bad father? You think my son would bring me if I was a bad father into your house? He loves his dad, he trusts his dad, he knows his dad is a good dad. Every time I start a little business going I get wiped out. This one is a good little business, if I could hold on to that little business. Three people work for me, I meet a payroll, and three people will be on the street, too, if I close down. Missus, I can sign a note and pay you in two months. I'm a common man, but I'm a hard worker and a fellow you can trust."

Woody was startled when Pop used the word "trust." It was as if from all four corners a Sousa band[21] blew a blast to warn the entire world: "Crook! This is a crook!" But Mrs. Skoglund, on account of her religious preoccupations, was remote. She heard nothing. Although everybody in this part of the world, unless he was crazy, led a practical life, and you'd have nothing to say to anyone, your neighbors would have nothing to say to you, if communications were not of a practical sort, Mrs. Skoglund, with all her money, was unworldly—two-thirds out of this world.

"Give me a chance to show what's in me," said Pop, "and you'll see what I do for my kids."

So Mrs. Skoglund hesitated, and then she said she'd have to go upstairs, she'd have to go to her room and pray on it and ask for guidance—would they sit down and wait. There were two rocking chairs by the stove. Hjordis gave Pop a grim look (a dangerous person) and Woody a blaming one (he brought a dangerous stranger and disrupter to injure two kind Christian ladies). Then she went out with Mrs. Skoglund.

As soon as they left, Pop jumped up from the rocker and said in anger, "What's this with the praying? She has to ask God to lend me fifty bucks?"

Woody said, "It's not you, Pop, it's the way these religious people do."

"No," said Pop. "She'll come back and say that God wouldn't let her."

Woody didn't like that; he thought Pop was being gross and he said, "No, she's sincere. Pop, try to understand: she's emotional, nervous, and sincere, and tries to do right by everybody."

And Pop said, "That servant will talk her out of it. She's a toughie. It's all over her face that we're a couple of chiselers."

"What's the use of us arguing," said Woody. He drew the rocker closer to the stove. His shoes were wet through and would never dry. The blue flames fluttered like a school of fishes in the coal fire. But Pop went over to the Chinese-style cabinet or étagère and tried the handle, and then opened the blade of his penknife and in a second had forced the lock of the curved glass door. He took out a silver dish.

"Pop, what is this?" said Woody.

[21] A band led by "The March King," John Philip Sousa (1854–1932), renowned for playing loud, military march music.

Pop, cool and level, knew exactly what this was. He relocked the étagère, crossed the carpet, listened. He stuffed the dish under his belt and pushed it down into his trousers. He put the side of his short thick finger to his mouth.

So Woody kept his voice down, but he was all shook up. He went to Pop and took him by the edge of his hand. As he looked into Pop's face, he felt his eyes growing smaller and smaller, as if something were contracting all the skin on his head. They call it hyperventilation when everything feels tight and light and close and dizzy. Hardly breathing, he said, "Put it back, Pop."

Pop said, "It's solid silver; it's worth dough."

"Pop, you said you wouldn't get me in Dutch."

"It's only insurance in case she comes back from praying and tells me no. If she says yes, I'll put it back."

"How?"

"It'll get back. If I don't put it back, you will."

"You picked the lock. I couldn't. I don't know how."

"There's nothing to it."

"We're going to put it back now. Give it here."

"Woody, it's under my fly, inside my underpants. Don't make such a noise about nothing."

"Pop, I can't believe this."

"For cry-ninety-nine, shut your mouth. If I didn't trust you I wouldn't have let you watch me do it. You don't understand such a thing. What's with you?"

"Before they come down, Pop, will you dig that dish out of your long johns."

Pop turned stiff on him. He became absolutely military. He said, "Look, I order you!"

Before he knew it, Woody had jumped his father and begun to wrestle with him. It was outrageous to clutch your own father, to put a heel behind him, to force him to the wall. Pop was taken by surprise and said loudly, "You want Halina killed? Kill her! Go on, you be responsible." He began to resist, angry, and they turned about several times, when Woody, with a trick he had learned in a Western movie and used once on the playground, tripped him and they fell to the ground. Woody, who already outweighed the old man by twenty pounds, was on top. They landed on the floor beside the stove, which stood on a tray of decorated tin to protect the carpet. In this position, pressing Pop's hard belly, Woody recognized that to have wrestled him to the floor counted for nothing. It was impossible to thrust his hand under Pop's belt to recover the dish. And now Pop had turned furious, as a father has every right to be when his son is violent with him, and he freed his hand and hit Woody in the face. He hit him three or four times in midface. Then Woody dug his head into Pop's shoulder and held tight only to keep from being struck and began to say in his ear, "Jesus, Pop for Christ sake remember where you are. Those women will be back!" But Pop brought up his short knee and fought and butted him with his chin and rattled Woody's teeth. Woody thought the old man was about to bite him. And because he was a seminarian, he thought: Like an unclean spirit. And held tight. Gradually Pop stopped threshing and struggling. His eyes stuck out and his mouth was open, sullen. Like a stout fish. Woody released him and gave him a hand up. He was then overcome with many many bad feelings of a sort he knew the old man never suffered. Never, never. Pop never had these groveling emotions. There was his whole superiority. Pop had no such feelings. He was like a horseman from Central Asia, a bandit from China. It was Mother, from Liverpool, who had the refinement, the English manners. It was the preaching Reverend Doctor in his black suit. You have refinement, and all they do is oppress you? The hell with that.

The long door opened and Mrs. Skoglund stepped in, saying "Did I imagine, or did something shake the house?"

"I was lifting the scuttle to put coal on the fire and it fell out of my hand. I'm sorry I was so clumsy," said Woody.

Pop was too huffy to speak. With his eyes big and sore and the thin hair down over his forehead, you could see by the tightness of his belly how angrily he was fetching his breath, though his mouth was shut.

"I prayed," said Mrs. Skoglund.

"I hope it came out well," said Woody.

"Well, I don't do anything without guidance, but the answer was yes, and I feel right about it now. So if you'll wait, I'll go to my office and write a check. I asked Hjordis to bring you a cup of coffee. Coming in such a storm."

And Pop, consistently a terrible little man, as soon as she shut the door, said, "A check? Hell with a check. Get me the greenbacks."

"They don't keep money in the house. You can cash it in her bank tomorrow. But if they miss that dish, Pop, they'll stop the check, and then where are you?"

As Pop was reaching below the belt, Hjordis brought in the tray. She was very sharp with him. She said, "Is this a place to adjust clothing, Mister? A men's washroom?"

"Well, which way is the toilet, then?" said Pop.

She had served the coffee in the seamiest mugs in the pantry, and she bumped down the tray and led Pop down the corridor, standing guard at the bathroom door so that he shouldn't wander about the house.

Mrs. Skoglund called Woody to her office and after she had given him the folded check said that they should pray together for Morris. So once more he was on his knees, under rows and rows of musty marbled-cardboard files, by the glass lamp by the edge of the desk, the shade with flounced edges, like the candy dish. Mrs. Skoglund, in her Scandinavian accent—an emotional contralto—raising her voice to Jesus-uh Christ-uh, as the wind lashed the trees, kicked the side of the house, and drove the snow seething on the windowpanes, to send light-uh, give guidance-uh, put a new heart-uh in Pop's bosom. Woody asked God only to make Pop put the dish back. He kept Mrs. Skoglund on her knees as long as possible. Then he thanked her, shining with candor (as much as knew how), for her Christian generosity and he said, "I know that Hjordis has a cousin who works at the Evanston YMCA. Could she please phone him and try to get us a room tonight so that we don't have to fight the blizzard all the way back? We're almost as close to the Y as to the car line. Maybe the cars have even stopped running."

Suspicious Hjordis, coming when Mrs. Skoglund called to her, was burning now. First they barged in, made themselves at home, asked for money, had to have coffee, probably left gonorrhea on the toilet seat. Hjordis, Woody remembered, was a woman who wiped the doorknobs with rubbing alcohol after guests had left. Nevertheless, she telephoned the Y and got them a room with two cots for six bits.

Pop had plenty of time, therefore, to reopen the étagère, lined with reflecting glass or German silver (something exquisitely delicate and tricky), and as soon as the two Selbsts had said thank you and goodbye and were in midstreet again up to the knees in snow, Woody said, "Well, I covered for you. Is that thing back?"

"Of course it is," said Pop.

They fought their way to the small Y building, shut up with wire grille and resembling a police station—about the same dimensions. It was locked, but they made a racket on the grille, and a small black man let them in and shuffled them upstairs to a cement corridor with low doors. It was like the small-mammal house in Lincoln Park.[22] He said there was nothing to eat, so they took off their wet pants, wrapped themselves tightly in the khaki army blankets, and passed out on their cots.

First thing in the morning, they went to the Evanston National Bank and got the fifty dollars. Not without difficulties. The teller went to call Mrs. Skoglund and was absent a long time from the wicket. "Where the hell has he gone?" said Pop.

But when the fellow came back, he said "How do you want it?"

Pop said, "Singles." He told Woody, "Bujak stashes it in one-dollar bills."

But by now Woody no longer believed Halina had stolen the old man's money.

Then they went into the street, where the snow-removal crews were at work. The sun shone broad, broad, out of the morning blue, and all Chicago would be releasing itself from the temporary beauty of those vast drifts.

"You shouldn't have jumped me last night, Sonny."

"I know, Pop, but you promised you wouldn't get me in Dutch."

"Well, it's okay. We can forget it, seeing you stood by me."

Only, Pop had taken the silver dish. Of course he had, and in a few days Mrs. Skoglund and Hjordis knew it, and later in the week they were all waiting for Woody in Kovner's office at the settlement house. The group included the Reverend Doctor Crabbie, head of the seminary, and Woody, who had been flying along, level and smooth, was shot down in flames. He told them he was innocent. Even as he was falling, he warned that they were wronging him. He denied that he or Pop had touched Mrs. Skoglund's property. The missing object—he didn't even know what it was—had probably been misplaced, and they would be very sorry on the day it turned up. After the others were done with him, Dr. Crabbie said that until he was able to tell the truth he would be suspended from the seminary, where his work had been unsatisfactory anyway. Aunt Rebecca took him aside and said to him, "You are a little crook, like your father. The door is closed to you here."

To this Pop's comment was "So what, kid?"

"Pop, you shouldn't have done it."

"No? Well, I don't give a care, if you want to know. You can have the dish if you want to go back and square yourself with all those hypocrites."

"I didn't like doing Mrs. Skoglund in the eye, she was so kind to us."

"Kind?"

"Kind."

"Kind has a price tag."

[22]Chicago park and site of the city zoo.

Well, there was no winning such arguments with Pop. But they debated it in various moods and from various elevations and perspectives for forty years and more, as their intimacy changed, developed, matured.

"Why did you do it, Pop? For the money? What did you do with the fifty bucks?" Woody, decades later, asked him that.

"I settled with the bookie, and the rest I put in the business."

"You tried a few more horses."

"I maybe did. But it was a double, Woody, I didn't hurt myself, and at the same time did you a favor."

"It was for me?"

"It was too strange of a life. That life wasn't *you,* Woody. All those women . . . Kovner was no man, he was an in-between. Suppose they made you a minister? Some Christian minister! First of all, you wouldn't have been able to stand it, and second, they would throw you out sooner or later."

"Maybe so."

"And you wouldn't have converted the Jews, which was the main thing they wanted."

"And what a time to bother the Jews," Woody said, "At least *I* didn't bug them."

Pop had carried him back to his side of the line, blood of his blood, the same thick body walls, the same coarse grain. Not cut out for a spiritual life. Simply not up to it.

Pop was no worse than Woody, and Woody was no better than Pop. Pop wanted no relation to theory, and yet he was always pointing Woody toward a position—a jolly, hearty, natural, likable, unprincipled position. If Woody had a weakness, it was to be unselfish. This worked to Pop's advantage, but he criticized Woody for it, nevertheless. "You take too much on yourself," Pop was always saying. And it's true that Woody gave Pop his heart because Pop was so selfish. It's usually the selfish people who are loved the most. They do what you deny yourself, and you love them for it. You give them your heart.

Remembering the pawn ticket for the silver dish, Woody startled himself with a laugh so sudden that it made him cough. Pop said to him after his expulsion from the seminary and banishment from the settlement house, "You want in again? Here's the ticket. I hocked that thing. It wasn't so valuable as I thought."

"What did they give?"

"Twelve-fifty was all I could get. But if you want it you'll have to raise the dough yourself, because I haven't got it anymore."

"You must have been sweating in the bank when the teller went to call Mrs. Skoglund about the check."

"I was a little nervous," said Pop. "But I didn't think they could miss the thing so soon."

That theft was part of Pop's war with Mother. With Mother, and Aunt Rebecca, and the Reverend Doctor. Pop took his stand on realism. Mother represented the forces of religion and hypochondria. In four decades, the fighting never stopped. In the course of time, Mother and the girls turned into welfare personalities and lost their individual outlines. Ah, the poor things, they became dependents and cranks. In the meantime, Woody, the sinful man, was their dutiful and loving son and brother. He maintained the bungalow—this took in roofing, painting, wiring, insulation, air-conditioning—and he paid for heat and light and food, and dressed them all out of Sears, Roebuck and Wieboldt's, and bought them a TV, which they watched as devoutly as they prayed. Paula took courses to learn skills like macramé-making and needlepoint, and sometimes got a little job as recreational worker in a nursing home. But she wasn't steady enough to keep it. Wicked Pop spent most of his life removing stains from people's clothing. He and Halina in the last years ran a Cleanomat in West Rogers Park—a so-so business resembling a laundromat—which gave him leisure for billiards, the horses, rummy and pinochle. Every morning he went behind the partition to check out the filters of the cleaning equipment. He found amusing things that had been thrown into the vats with the clothing—sometimes, when he got lucky, a locket chain or a brooch. And when he had fortified the cleaning fluid, pouring all that blue and pink stuff in from plastic jugs, he read the *Forward*[23] over a second cup of coffee, and went out, leaving Halina in charge. When they needed help with the rent, Woody gave it.

After the new Disney World was opened in Florida, Woody treated all his dependents to a holiday. He sent them down in separate batches, of course. Halina enjoyed this more than anybody else. She couldn't stop talking about the address given by an Abraham Lincoln automaton. "Wonderful, how he stood up and moved his hands, and his mouth. So real! And how beautiful he talked." Of them all, Halina was the soundest, the most human, the most honest. Now that Pop was gone, Woody and Halina's son, Mitosh, the organist at the Stadium, took care of her needs over and above Social Security, splitting expenses. In Pop's opinion, insurance was a racket. He left Halina nothing but some out-of-date equipment.

Woody treated himself, too. Once a year, and sometimes oftener, he left his business to run itself, arranged with the trust department at the bank to take care of his gang, and went off. He did that in style, imaginatively, expensively. In Japan, he wasted little time on Tokyo. He spent three weeks in Kyoto and stayed at the Tawaraya Inn, dating from the seventeenth century or so. There he slept on the floor, the Japanese way, and bathed in scalding water. He saw the dirtiest strip show on earth, as well as the holy places and the temple gardens. He visited also Istanbul, Jerusalem, Delphi, and went to Burma and Uganda and Kenya on safari, on democratic terms with drivers, Bedouins, bazaar merchants. Open, lavish, familiar, fleshier and fleshier but (he jogged, he lifted weights) still muscular—in his naked person beginning to resemble a Renaissance courtier in full costume—becoming ruddier every year, an outdoor type with freckles on his back and spots across the flaming forehead and the honest nose. In Addis Ababa he took an Ethiopian beauty to his room from the street and washed her, getting into the shower with her to soap her with his broad, kindly hands. In Kenya he taught certain American obscenities to a black woman so that she could shout them out during the act. On the Nile, below Murchison Falls, those fever trees rose huge from the mud, and hippos on the sandbars belched at the passing launch, hostile. One of them danced on his spit of sand, springing from the ground and coming down heavy, on all fours. There Woody saw the buffalo calf disappear, snatched by the crocodile.

[23] *The Jewish Forward,* a Yiddish-language newspaper.

Mother, soon to follow Pop, was being lightheaded these days. In company, she spoke of Woody as her boy—"What do you think of my Sonny?"—as though he was ten years old. She was silly with him, her behavior was frivolous, almost flirtatious. She just didn't seem to know the facts. And behind her all the others, like kids at the playground, were waiting their turn to go down the slide: one on each step, and moving toward the top.

Over Woody's residence and place of business there had gathered a pool of silence of the same perimeter as the church bells while they were ringing, and he mourned under it, this melancholy morning of sun and autumn. Doing a life survey, taking a deliberate look at the gross side of his case—of the other side as well, what there was of it. But if this heartache continued, he'd go out and run it off. A three-mile job—five, if necessary. And you'd think that this jogging was an entirely physical activity, wouldn't you? But there was something else in it. Because, when he was a seminarian, between the shafts of his World's Fair rickshaw, he used to receive, pulling along (capable and stable), his religious experiences while he trotted. Maybe it was all a single experience repeated. He felt truth coming to him from the sun. He received a communication that was also light and warmth. It made him very remote from his horny Wisconsin passengers, those farmers whose whoops and whore cries he could hardly hear when he was in one of his states. And again out of the flaming of the sun would come to him a secret certainty that the goal set for this earth was that it should be filled with good, saturated with it. After everything preposterous, after dog had eaten dog, after crocodile death had pulled everyone into his mud. It wouldn't conclude as Mrs. Skoglund, bribing him to round up the Jews and hasten the Second Coming, imagined it, but in another way. This was his clumsy intuition. It went no further. Subsequently, he proceeded through life as life seemed to want him to do it.

There remained one thing more this morning, which was explicitly physical, occurring first as a sensation in his arms and against his breast and, from the pressure, passing into him and going into his breast.

It was like this: When he came into the hospital room and saw Pop with the sides of his bed raised, like a crib, and Pop, so very feeble, and writhing, and toothless, like a baby, and the dirt already cast into his face, into the wrinkles—Pop wanted to pluck out the intravenous needles and he was piping his weak death noise. The gauze patches taped over the needles were soiled with dark blood. Then Woody took off his shoes, lowered the side of the bed, and climbed in and held him in his arms to soothe and still him. As if he were Pop's father, he said to him, "Now, Pop. Pop." Then it was like the wrestle in Mrs. Skoglund's parlor, when Pop turned angry like an unclean spirit and Woody tried to appease him, and warn him, saying, "Those women will be back!" Beside the coal stove, when Pop hit Woody in the teeth with his head and then became sullen, like a stout fish. But this struggle in the hospital was weak—so weak! In his great pity, Woody held Pop, who was fluttering and shivering. From those people, Pop had told him, you'll never find out what life is, because they don't know what it is. Yes, Pop—well, what is it, Pop? Hard to comprehend that Pop, who was dug in for eighty-three years and had done all he could to stay, should now want nothing but to free himself. How could Woody allow the old man to pull the intravenous needles out? Willful Pop, he wanted what he wanted when he wanted it. But what he wanted at the very last Woody failed to follow, it was such a switch.

After a time, Pop's resistance ended. He subsided and subsided. He rested against his son, his small body curled there. Nurses came and looked. They disapproved, but Woody, who couldn't spare a hand to wave them out, motioned with his head toward the door. Pop, whom Woody thought he had stilled, only had found a better way to get around him. Loss of heat was the way he did it. His heat was leaving him. As can happen with small animals while you hold them in your hand, Woody presently felt him cooling. Then, as Woody did his best to restrain him, and thought he was succeeding, Pop divided himself. And when he was separated from his warmth, he slipped into death. And there was his elderly, large, muscular son, still holding and pressing him when there was nothing anymore to press. You could never pin down that self-willed man. When he was ready to make his move, he made it—always on his own terms. And always, always, something up his sleeve. That was how he was.

1978, 1984

Kurt Vonnegut 1922–

Kurt Vonnegut burst upon the American consciousness in 1969 with his overwhelmingly popular novel Slaughterhouse-Five*—a treatment of the horrific and possibly pointless Allied bombing of Dresden in World War II that made Vonnegut an instant hero of the 1960s anti-war movement and an icon of postmodern art. Reaching mass audiences with his simple, readable prose style, he nonetheless appealed to more sophisticated readers through experimentation with narrative structure and point of view. Over the next three decades—as novelist, short-story writer, playwright, essayist, and public personality—he became one of the most familiar figures in the late twentieth-century American literary landscape, a figure critic James Woods once called, "a kind of de-solemnized Emerson, at once arguer, doubter, sermonizer and gossip."*

Kurt Vonnegut was born on Armistice Day in Indianapolis to a successful architect and the daughter of a wealthy brewer. Both parents were of German descent and spoke German but, in reaction to the anti-German sentiment resulting from World War I, did not teach the language to Kurt. The Vonneguts were affluent during the 1920s, and Kurt's older brother and sister received expensive private educations. However, with the arrival of the Great Depression in 1929, Kurt's father's architectural business evaporated. Consequently, the family had to move to a smaller house, and young Kurt was switched to a public school. His father became withdrawn and depressed, and his mother became increasingly anxious. During this period Kurt became emotionally estranged from his parents, and instead found parental figures in the family's African American housekeeper, Ida Young, and his uncle Alex, a socialist whose dislike of the idle rich strongly influenced Kurt's thinking.

In 1940, Vonnegut entered Cornell University, majoring in chemistry (at his father's behest) but giving more attention to working on the student newspaper than to his studies. Meanwhile, World War II had begun to rage overseas, which disturbed Vonnegut, who was not only a pacifist but self-conscious about his German descent. He at first wrote editorials denouncing the war in the school newspaper, but as the conflict wore on, he later decided it was justified. Like many proud Americans of his day, he left school to enlist without earning his bachelor's degree. His mother, appalled by the war and now dismayed by her son's involvement in it, committed suicide in May 1944—on the night before he was to arrive home on leave.

While serving in Europe, Vonnegut was captured by the Germans at the Battle of the Bulge and taken to Dresden, where he was quartered in the underground meat locker of a slaughterhouse. Thanks to the subterranean location, he and many of the other prisoners survived the Allied firebombing of Dresden in February 1945, but the city, with its many architectural treasures, was destroyed, and approximately 135,000 people, nearly all of them civilians, were killed. Vonnegut and the other prisoners were then given the gruesome task of digging corpses out of the debris and cremating them.

After the war Vonnegut married his high school sweetheart, Jane Marie Cox. They lived in Chicago, where he was employed as a police reporter and worked toward a master's degree in anthropology at the University of Chicago. When his master's thesis, titled "Fluctuations Between Good and Evil in Simple Tales," was rejected, he left the university, again without earning a degree. With only a high school diploma in hand, he took a job in public relations with General Electric. Meanwhile, he wrote short stories at night, and eventually sold one to Collier's *magazine. In 1951, after four years with GE, he quit his job in order to write full-time. From that time until 1965 he supported a large family on meager earnings from short stories sold to magazines like* Collier's *and* Saturday Evening Post *and from novels that brought in not much money and little critical recognition.*

In search of more financial stability, Vonnegut accepted a teaching job with the University of Iowa's Writers' Workshop in 1965. For the first time in his life he found himself in an academic literary community in which he could converse with creative writers and literary scholars and broaden his exposure to great works of literature. At last he was able to find the appropriate treatment for the subject that had been simmering for over twenty years: the bombing of Dresden. In Slaughterhouse-Five *he places the memory of this very real traumatic event in the hands of a befuddled, anti-heroic narrator named Billy Pilgrim, and confuses the chronology by having Billy kidnapped by space aliens who are able to move freely among past, present, and future. Having dealt in* Slaughterhouse-Five *with the monumental trauma of his war experience, Vonnegut suffered such a psychological letdown that he momentarily felt he might give up writing fiction; however, writing itself seems to have been effective therapy. In the succeeding decades he has continued to publish actively and to be regarded as one of America's most important living writers.*

Vonnegut's novels and short stories combine satirical elements in the tradition of Mark Twain and Jonathan Swift with science-fictional settings and plot twists reminiscent of the sci-fi novels of H. G. Wells and Aldous Huxley. Vonnegut's work presents what critic Robert Group has described as "a mixture of wistful humanism and cynical existentialism." Emphasizing the dangerously dehumanizing and isolating effects of modern technology, Vonnegut portrays an inherently meaningless universe in which each human being must find or create his or her own sort of meaningfulness. At the same time, many of his works display a core of solidly middle-class values—such as the importance of family and the value of a quiet, even conventional existence—presented in a narrative voice that, as he says in Palm Sunday *(1981), works best when it sounds "like a person from Indianapolis, which is what I am." In other stories, such as "Welcome to the Monkey House," he accentuates the interdependence of human beings—the need to reach out to others and be conscious and concerned about their needs and problems. Vonnegut sees the writer's function as subversive, but in a very wholesome way. As he said in a 1971 interview, the function of the novelist is to "catch people before they become generals and senators and presidents, and . . . poison their minds with humanity."*

FURTHER READING: D. Goldsmith, *Kurt Vonnegut: Fantasist of Fire and Ice,* 1972; P. Reed, *Kurt Vonnegut, Jr.,* 1972; *The Vonnegut Statement: Original Essays on the Life and Work of Kurt Vonnegut,* ed. J. Klinkowitz and J. Somer, 1973; C. Mayo, *Kurt Vonnegut: The Gospel from Outer Space, or Yes, We Have No Nirvanas,* 1973; R. Short, *Something to Believe in: Is Kurt Vonnegut Exorcist of Jesus Christ Superstar?,* 1976; S. Schatt, *Kurt Vonnegut, Jr.,* 1976; R. Giannone, *Vonnegut: A Preface to His Novels,* 1977; J. Lundquist, *Kurt Vonnegut,* 1977; *Vonnegut in America: An Introduction to the Life and Work of Kurt Vonnegut,* ed. J. Klinkowitz and D. Lawler, 1977; M. Loeb, *Vonnegut's Duty-Dance with Death: Theme and Structure in Slaughterhouse-Five,* 1979; *Happy Birthday, Kurt Vonnegut: A Festschrift for Kurt Vonnegut on His Sixtieth Birthday,* ed. J. Krementz, 1982; J. Klinkowitz, *Kurt Vonnegut,* 1982; W. Bly, *Kurt Vonnegut's Slaughterhouse-Five,* 1985; *Kurt Vonnegut: A Comprehensive Bibliography,* ed. A. Pieratt, J. Huffman-Klinkowitz, and J. Klinkowitz, 1987; *Conversations with Kurt Vonnegut,* ed. R. Allen, 1988; *Draftings in Vonnegut: The Paradox of Hope,* ed. L. Rackstraw, 1988; J. Klinkowitz, *Slaughterhouse-Five: Reforming the Novel and the World,* 1990; *Critical Essays on Kurt Vonnegut,* ed. R. Merrill, 1990; R. Allen, *Understanding Kurt Vonnegut,* 1991; L. Mustazza, *Forever Pursuing Genesis: The Myth of Eden in the Novels of Kurt Vonnegut,* 1991; D. Morse, *Kurt Vonnegut,* 1992; *The Critical Response to Kurt Vonnegut,* ed. L. Mustazza, 1994; B. Pettersson, *The World According to Kurt Vonnegut: Moral Paradox and Narrative Form,* 1994; *Sanity Plea: Schizophrenia in the Novels of Kurt Vonnegut,* ed. L. Broer, 1994; M. Leeds, *The Vonnegut Encyclopedia: An Authorized Compendium,* 1995; *The Vonnegut Chronicles: Interviews and Essays,* ed. P. Reed and M. Leeds, 1996; P. Reed, *The Short Fiction of Kurt Vonnegut,* 1997; K. Boon, *Chaos Theory and the Interpretation of Literary Texts: The Case of Kurt Vonnegut,* 1997; J. Klinkowitz, *Vonnegut in Fact: The Public Spokesmanship of Personal Fiction,* 1998; *Kurt Vonnegut,* ed. H. Bloom, 2000; T. Marvin, *Kurt Vonnegut: A Critical Companion,* 2002.

TEXT: *Welcome to the Monkey House,* 1968.

WELCOME TO THE MONKEY HOUSE

So Pete Crocker, the sheriff of Barnstable County, which was the whole of Cape Cod, came into the Federal Ethical Suicide Parlor in Hyannis one May afternoon—and he told the two six-foot Hostesses there that they weren't to be alarmed, but that a notorious nothinghead named Billy the Poet was believed headed for the Cape.

A nothinghead was a person who refused to take his ethical birth-control pills three times a day. The penalty for that was $10,000 and ten years in jail.

This was at a time when the population on Earth was 17 billion human beings. That was far too many mammals that big for a planet that small. The people were virtually packed together like drupelets.

Drupelets are the pulpy little knobs that compose the outside of a raspberry.

So the World Government was making a two-pronged attack on overpopulation. One pronging was the encouragement of ethical suicide, which consisted of going to the nearest Suicide Parlor and asking a Hostess to kill you painlessly while you lay on a Barcalounger. The other pronging was compulsory ethical birth control.

The sheriff told the Hostesses, who were pretty, tough-minded, highly intelligent girls, that roadblocks were being set up and house-to-house searches were being conducted to catch Billy the Poet. The main difficulty was that the police didn't know what he looked like. The few people who had seen him and known him for what he was were women—and they disagreed fantastically as to his height, his hair color, his voice, his weight, the color of his skin.

"I don't need to remind you girls," the sheriff went on, "that a nothinghead is very sensitive from the waist down. If Billy the Poet somehow slips in here and starts making trouble, one good kick in the right place will do wonders."

He was referring to the fact that ethical birth-control pills, the only legal form of birth control, made people numb from the waist down.

Most men said their bottom halves felt like cold iron or balsawood. Most women said their bottom halves felt like wet cotton or stale ginger ale. The pills were so effective that you could blindfold a man who had taken one, tell him to recite the Gettysburg Address, kick him in the balls while he was doing it, and he wouldn't miss a syllable.

The pills were ethical because they didn't interfere with a person's ability to reproduce, which would have been unnatural and immoral. All the pills did was take every bit of pleasure out of sex.

Thus did science and morals go hand in hand.

The two Hostesses there in Hyannis were Nancy McLuhan and Mary Kraft. Nancy was a strawberry blonde. Mary was a glossy brunette. Their uniforms were white lipstick, heavy eye makeup, purple body stockings with nothing underneath, and black-leather boots. They ran a small operation—with only six suicide booths. In a really good week, say the one before Christmas, they might put sixty people to sleep. It was done with a hypodermic syringe.

"My main message to you girls," said Sheriff Crocker, "is that everything's well under control. You can just go about your business here."

"Didn't you leave out part of your main message?" Nancy asked him.

"I don't get you."

"I didn't hear you say he was probably headed straight for us."

He shrugged in clumsy innocence. "We don't know that for sure."

"I thought that was all anybody *did* know about Billy the Poet: that he specializes in deflowering Hostesses in Ethical Suicide Parlors." Nancy was a virgin. All Hostesses were virgins. They also had to hold advanced degrees in psychology and nursing. They also had to be plump and rosy, and at least six feet tall.

America had changed in many ways, but it had yet to adopt the metric system.

Nancy McLuhan was burned up that the sheriff would try to protect her and Mary from the full truth about Billy the Poet—as though they might panic if they heard it. She told the sheriff so.

"How long do you think a girl would last in the E. S. S.," she said, meaning the Ethical Suicide Service, "if she scared that easy?"

The sheriff took a step backward, pulled in his chin. "Not very long, I guess."

"That's very true," said Nancy, closing the distance between them and offering him a sniff of the edge of her hand, which was poised for a karate chop. All Hostesses were experts at judo and karate. "If you'd like to find out how helpless we are, just come toward me, pretending you're Billy the Poet."

The sheriff shook his head, gave her a glassy smile. "I'd rather not."

"That's the smartest thing you've said today," said Nancy, turning her back on him while Mary laughed. "We're not scared—we're *angry*. Or we're not even *that*. He isn't *worth* that. We're *bored*. How boring that he should come a great distance, should cause all this fuss, in order to——" She let the sentence die there. "It's just too absurd."

"I'm not as mad at *him* as I am at the women who let him do it to them without a struggle"—said Mary—"who let him do it and then couldn't tell the police what he looked like. Suicide Hostesses at that!"

"Somebody hasn't been keeping up with her karate," said Nancy.

It wasn't just Billy the Poet who was attracted to Hostesses in Ethical Suicide Parlors. All nothingheads were. Bombed out of their skulls with the sex madness that came from taking nothing, they thought the white lips and big eyes and body stocking and boots of a Hostess spelled *sex, sex, sex.*

The truth was, of course, that sex was the last thing any Hostess ever had in mind.

"If Billy follows his usual M. O.," said the sheriff, "he'll study your habits and the neighborhood. And then he'll pick one or the other of you and he'll send her a dirty poem in the mail."

"Charming," said Nancy.

"He has also been known to use the telephone."

"How brave," said Nancy. Over the sheriff's shoulder, she could see the mailman coming.

A blue light went on over the door of a booth for which Nancy was responsible. The person in there wanted something. It was the only booth in use at the time.

The sheriff asked her if there was a possibility that the person in there was Billy the Poet, and Nancy said, "Well, if it is, I can break his neck with my thumb and forefinger."

"Foxy Grandpa," said Mary, who'd seen him, too. A Foxy Grandpa was any old man, cute and senile, who quibbled and joked and reminisced for hours before he let a Hostess put him to sleep.

Nancy groaned. "We've spent the past two hours trying to decide on a last meal."

And then the mailman came in with just one letter. It was addressed to Nancy in smeary pencil. She was splendid with anger and disgust as she opened it, knowing it would be a piece of filth from Billy.

She was right. Inside the envelope was a poem. It wasn't an original poem. It was a song from olden days that had taken on new meanings since the numbness of ethical birth control had become universal. It went like this, in smeary pencil again:

We were walking through the park,
A-goosing statues in the dark.
If Sherman's horse can take it,
So can you.

When Nancy came into the suicide booth to see what he wanted, the Foxy Grandpa was lying on the mint-green Barcalounger, where hundreds had died so peacefully over the years. He was studying the menu from the Howard Johnson's next door and beating time to the Muzak coming from the loudspeaker on the lemon-yellow wall. The room was painted cinder block. There was one barred window with a Venetian blind.

There was a Howard Johnson's next door to every Ethical Suicide Parlor, and vice versa. The Howard Johnson's had an orange roof and the Suicide Parlor had a purple roof, but they were both the Government. Practically everything was the Government.

Practically everything was automated, too. Nancy and Mary and the sheriff were lucky to have jobs. Most people didn't. The average citizen moped around home and watched television, which was the Government. Every fifteen minutes his television would urge him to vote intelligently or consume intelligently, or worship in the church of his choice, or love his fellowmen, or obey the laws—or pay a call to the nearest Ethical Suicide Parlor and find out how friendly and understanding a Hostess could be.

The Foxy Grandpa was something of a rarity, since he was marked by old age, was bald, was shaky, had spots on his hands. Most people looked twenty-two, thanks to anti-aging shots they took twice a year. That the old man looked old was proof that the shots had been discovered after his sweet bird of youth had flown.

"Have we decided on a last supper yet?" Nancy asked him. She heard peevishness in her own voice, heard herself betray her exasperation with Billy the Poet, her boredom with the old man. She was ashamed, for this was unprofessional of her. "The breaded veal cutlet is very good."

The old man cocked his head. With the greedy cunning of second childhood, he had caught her being unprofessional, unkind, and he was going to punish her for it. "You don't sound very friendly. I thought you were all supposed to be friendly. I thought this was supposed to be a pleasant place to come."

"I beg your pardon," she said. "If I seem unfriendly, it has nothing to do with you."

"I thought maybe I bored you."

"No, no," she said gamely, "not at all. You certainly know some very interesting history." Among other things, the Foxy Grandpa claimed to have known J. Edgar Nation, the Grand Rapids druggist who was the father of ethical birth control.

"Then *look* like you're interested," he told her. He could get away with that sort of impudence. The thing was, he could leave any time he wanted to, right up to the moment he asked for the needle—and he had to *ask* for the needle. That was the law.

Nancy's art, and the art of every Hostess, was to see that volunteers didn't leave, to coax and wheedle and flatter them patiently every step of the way.

So Nancy had to sit down there in the booth, to pretend to marvel at the freshness of the yarn the old man told, a story everybody knew, about how J. Edgar Nation happened to experiment with ethical birth control.

"He didn't have the slightest idea his pills would be taken by human beings someday," said the Foxy Grandpa. "His dream was to introduce morality into the monkey house at the Grand Rapids Zoo. Did you realize that?" he inquired severely.

"No. No, I didn't. That's very interesting."

"He and his eleven kids went to church one Easter. And the day was so nice and the Easter service had been so beautiful and pure that they decided to take a walk through the zoo, and they were just walking on clouds."

"Um." The scene described was lifted from a play that was performed on television every Easter.

The Foxy Grandpa shoehorned himself into the scene, had himself chat with the Nations just before they got to the monkey house. "'Good morning, Mr. Nation,' I said to him. 'It certainly is a nice morning.' 'And a good morning to *you,* Mr. Howard,' he said to me. 'There is nothing like an Easter morning to make a man feel clean and reborn and at one with God's intentions.'"

"Um." Nancy could hear the telephone ringing faintly, naggingly, through the nearly soundproof door.

"So we went on to the monkey house together, and what do you think we saw?"

"I can't imagine." Somebody had answered the phone.

"We saw a monkey playing with his private parts!"

"No!"

"Yes! And J. Edgar Nation was so upset he went straight home and he started developing a pill that would make monkeys in the springtime fit things for a Christian family to see."

There was a knock on the door.

"Yes——?" said Nancy.

"Nancy," said Mary, "telephone for you."

When Nancy came out of the booth, she found the sheriff choking on little squeals of law-enforcement delight. The telephone was tapped by agents hidden in the Howard Johnson's. Billy the Poet was believed to be on the line. His call had been traced. Police were already on their way to grab him.

"Keep him on, keep him on," the sheriff whispered to Nancy, and he gave her the telephone as though it were solid gold.

"Yes—?" said Nancy.

"Nancy McLuhan?" said a man. His voice was disguised. He might have been speaking through a kazoo. "I'm calling for a mutual friend."

"Oh?"

"He asked me to deliver a message."

"I see."

"It's a poem."

"All right."

"Ready?"

"Ready." Nancy could hear sirens screaming in the background of the call.

The caller must have heard the sirens, too, but he recited the poem without any emotion. It went like this:

"Soak yourself in Jergen's Lotion.
Here comes the one-man population
explosion."

They got him. Nancy heard it all—the thumping and clumping, the argle-bargle and cries.

The depression she felt as she hung up was glandular. Her brave body had prepared for a fight that was not to be.

The sheriff bounded out of the Suicide Parlor, in such a hurry to see the famous criminal he'd helped catch that a sheaf of papers fell from the pocket of his trench coat.

Mary picked them up, called after the sheriff. He halted for a moment, said the papers didn't matter any more, asked her if maybe she wouldn't like to come along. There was a flurry between the two girls, with Nancy persuading Mary to go, declaring that she had no curiosity about Billy. So Mary left, irrelevantly handing the sheaf to Nancy.

The sheaf proved to be photocopies of poems Billy had sent to Hostesses in other places. Nancy read the top one. It made much of a peculiar side effect of ethical birth-control pills: They not only made people numb—they also made people piss blue. The poem was called *What the Somethinghead Said to the Suicide Hostess,* and it went like this:

I did not sow, I did not spin,
And thanks to pills I did not sin.
I loved the crowds, the stink, the noise.
And when I peed, I peed turquoise.

I ate beneath a roof of orange;
Swung with progress like a door hinge.
'Neath purple roof I've come today
To piss my azure life away.

Virgin hostess, death's recruiter,
Life is cute, but you are cuter.
Mourn my pecker, purple daughter—
All it passed was sky-blue-water.

"You never heard that story before—about how J. Edgar Nation came to invent ethical birth control?" the Foxy Grandpa wanted to know. His voice cracked.

"Never did," lied Nancy.

"I thought everybody knew that."

"It was news to me."

"When he got through with the monkey house, you couldn't tell it from the Michigan Supreme Court. Meanwhile, there was this crisis going on in the United Nations. The people who understood science said people had to quit reproducing so much, and the people who understood morals said society would collapse if people used sex for nothing but pleasure."

The Foxy Grandpa got off his Barcalounger, went over to the window, pried two slats of the blind apart. There wasn't much to see out there. The view was blocked by the backside of a mocked-up thermometer twenty feet high, which faced the street. It was calibrated in billions of people on Earth, from zero to twenty. The make-believe column of liquid was a strip of translucent red plastic. It showed how many people there were on Earth. Very close to the bottom was a black arrow that showed what the scientists thought the population ought to be.

The Foxy Grandpa was looking at the setting sun through that red plastic, and through the blind, too, so that his face was banded with shadows and red.

"Tell me—" he said, "when I die, how much will that thermometer go down? A foot?"

"No."

"An inch?"

"Not quite."

"You know what the answer is, don't you?" he said, and he faced her. The senility had vanished from his voice and eyes. "One inch on that thing equals 83,333 people. You knew that, didn't you?"

"That—that might be true," said Nancy, "but that isn't the right way to look at it, in my opinion."

He didn't ask her what the right way was, in her opinion. He completed a thought of his own, instead. "I'll tell you something else that's true: I'm Billy the Poet, and you're a very good-looking woman."

With one hand, he drew a snub-nosed revolver from his belt. With the other, he peeled off his bald dome and wrinkled forehead, which proved to be rubber. Now he looked twenty-two.

"The police will want to know exactly what I look like when this is all over," he told Nancy with a malicious grin. "In case you're not good at describing people, and it's surprising how many women aren't:

I'm five foot two,
With eyes of blue,
With Brown hair to my shoulders—
A manly elf
So full of self
The ladies say he smolders."

Billy was ten inches shorter than Nancy was. She had about forty pounds on him. She told him he didn't have a chance, but Nancy was much mistaken. He had unbolted the bars on the window the night before and he made her go out the window and then down a manhole that was hidden from the street by the big thermometer.

He took her down into the sewers of Hyannis. He knew where he was going. He had a flashlight and a map. Nancy had to go before him along the narrow catwalk, her own shadow dancing mockingly in the lead. She tried to guess where they were, relative to the real world above. She guessed correctly when they passed under the Howard Johnson's, guessed from noises she heard. The machinery that processed and served the food there was silent. But, so people wouldn't feel too lonesome when eating there, the designers had provided sound effects for the kitchen. It was these Nancy heard—a tape recording of the clashing of silverware and the laughter of Negroes and Puerto Ricans.

After that she was lost. Billy had very little to say to her other than "Right," or, "Left," or "Don't try anything funny, Juno, or I'll blow your great big fucking head off."

Only once did they have anything resembling a conversation. Billy began it, and ended it, too. "What in hell is a girl with hips like yours doing selling death?" he asked her from behind.

She dared to stop. "I can answer that," she told him. She was confident that she could give him an answer that would shrivel him like napalm.

But he gave her a shove, offered to blow her fucking head off again.

"You don't even want to hear my answer," she taunted him. "You're afraid to hear it."

"I never listen to a woman till the pills wear off," sneered Billy. That was his plan, then—to keep her a prisoner for at least eight hours. That was how long it took for the pills to wear off.

"That's a silly rule."

"A woman's not a woman till the pills wear off."

"You certainly manage to make a woman feel like an object rather than a person."

"Thank the pills for that," said Billy.

There were 80 miles of sewers under Greater Hyannis, which had a population of 400,000 drupelets, 400,000 souls. Nancy lost track of the time down there. When Billy announced that they had at last reached their destination, it was possible for Nancy to imagine that a year had passed.

She tested this spooky impression by pinching her own thigh, by feeling what the chemical clock of her body said. Her thigh was still numb.

Billy ordered her to climb iron rungs that were set in wet masonry. There was a circle of sickly light above. It proved to be moonlight filtered through the plastic polygons of an enormous geodesic dome. Nancy didn't have to ask the traditional victim's question, "Where am I?" There was only one dome like that on Cape Cod. It was in Hyannis Port and it sheltered the ancient Kennedy Compound.[1]

It was a museum of how life had been lived in more expansive times. The museum was closed. It was open only in the summertime.

The manhole from which Nancy and then Billy emerged was set in an expanse of green cement, which showed where the Kennedy lawn had been. On the green cement, in front of the ancient frame houses, were statues representing the fourteen Kennedys who had been Presidents of the United States or the World. They were playing touch football.

The President of the World at the time of Nancy's abduction, incidentally, was an ex-Suicide Hostess named "Ma" Kennedy. Her statue would never join this particular touch-football game. Her name was Kennedy, all right, but she wasn't the real thing. People complained of her lack of style, found her vulgar. On the wall of her office was a sign that said, YOU DON'T HAVE TO BE CRAZY TO WORK HERE, BUT IT SURE HELPS, and another one that said THINK!, and another one that said, SOME DAY WE'RE GOING TO HAVE TO GET ORGANIZED AROUND HERE.

Her office was in the Taj Mahal.

Until she arrived in the Kennedy Museum, Nancy McLuhan was confident that she would sooner or later get a chance to break every bone in Billy's little body, maybe even shoot him with his own gun. She wouldn't have minded doing those things. She thought he was more disgusting than a blood-filled tick.

It wasn't compassion that changed her mind. It was the discovery that Billy had a gang. There were at least eight people around the manhole, men and women in equal numbers, with stockings pulled over their heads. It was the women who laid firm hands on Nancy, told her to keep calm. They were all at least as tall as Nancy and they held her in places where they could hurt her like hell if they had to.

Nancy closed her eyes, but this didn't protect her from the obvious conclusion: These perverted women were sisters from the Ethical Suicide Service.

[1]The family home of Joseph Kennedy (1888–1969) and his family, which included three sons who were major political figures: President John F. Kennedy (1917–1963), Senator Robert F. Kennedy (1925–1968), and Senator Edward M. Kennedy (1932–).

This upset her so much that she asked loudly and bitterly, "How can you violate your oaths like this?"

She was promptly hurt so badly that she doubled up and burst into tears.

When she straightened up again, there was plenty more she wanted to say, but she kept her mouth shut. She speculated silently as to what on Earth could make Suicide Hostesses turn against every concept of human decency. Nothingheadedness alone couldn't begin to explain it. They had to be drugged besides.

Nancy went over in her mind all the terrible drugs she'd learned about in school, persuaded herself that the women had taken the worst one of all. That drug was so powerful, Nancy's teachers had told her, that even a person numb from the waist down would copulate repeatedly and enthusiastically after just one glass. That had to be the answer: The women, and probably the men, too, had been drinking gin.

They hastened Nancy into the middle frame house, which was dark like all the rest, and Nancy heard the men giving Billy the news. It was in this news that Nancy perceived a glint of hope. Help might be on its way.

The gang member who had phoned Nancy obscenely had fooled the police into believing that they had captured Billy the Poet, which was bad for Nancy. The police didn't know yet that Nancy was missing, two men told Billy, and a telegram had been sent to Mary Kraft in Nancy's name, declaring that Nancy had been called to New York City on urgent family business.

That was where Nancy saw the glint of hope: Mary wouldn't believe that telegram. Mary knew Nancy had no family in New York. Not one of the 63,000,000 people living there was a relative of Nancy's.

The gang had deactivated the burglar-alarm system of the museum. They had also cut through a lot of the chains and ropes that were meant to keep visitors from touching anything of value. There was no mystery as to who and what had done the cutting. One of the men was armed with brutal lopping shears.

They marched Nancy into a servant's bedroom upstairs. The man with the shears cut the ropes that fenced off the narrow bed. They put Nancy into the bed and two men held Nancy while a woman gave her a knockout shot.

Billy the Poet had disappeared.

As Nancy was going under, the woman who had given her the shot asked her how old she was.

Nancy was determined not to answer, but discovered that the drug had made her powerless not to answer. "Sixty-three," she murmured.

"How does it feel to be a virgin at sixty-three?"

Nancy heard her own answer through a velvet fog. She was amazed by the answer, wanted to protest that it couldn't possibly be hers. "Pointless," she'd said.

Moments later, she asked the woman thickly, "What was in that needle?"

"What was in the needle, honey bunch? Why, honey bunch, they call that 'truth serum.'"

The moon was down when Nancy woke up—but the night was still out there. The shades were drawn and there was candlelight. Nancy had never seen a lit candle before.

What awakened Nancy was a dream of mosquitoes and bees. Mosquitoes and bees were extinct. So were birds. But Nancy dreamed that millions of insects were swarming about her from the waist down. They didn't sting. They fanned her. Nancy was a nothinghead.

She went to sleep again. When she awoke next time, she was being led into a bathroom by three women, still with stockings over their heads. The bathroom was already filled with the steam from somebody else's bath. There were somebody else's wet footprints crisscrossing the floor and the air reeked of pine-needle perfume.

Her will and intelligence returned as she was bathed and perfumed and dressed in a white nightgown. When the women stepped back to admire her, she said to them quietly, "I may be a nothinghead now. But that doesn't mean I have to think like one or act like one."

Nobody argued with her.

Nancy was taken downstairs and out of the house. She fully expected to be sent down a manhole again. It would be the perfect setting for her violation by Billy, she was thinking—down in a sewer.

But they took her across the green cement, where the grass used to be, and then across the yellow cement, where the beach used to be, and then out onto the blue cement, where the harbor used to be. There were twenty-six yachts that had belonged to various Kennedys, sunk up to their water lines in blue cement. It was to the most ancient of these yachts, the Marlin, once the property of Joseph P. Kennedy, that they delivered Nancy.

It was dawn. Because of the high-rise apartments all around the Kennedy Museum, it would be an hour before any direct sunlight would reach the microcosm under the geodesic dome.

Nancy was escorted as far as the companionway to the forward cabin of the Marlin. The women pantomimed that she was expected to go down the five steps alone.

Nancy froze for the moment and so did the women. And there were two actual statues in the tableau on the bridge. Standing at the wheel was a statue of Frank Wirtanen, once skipper of the Marlin. And next to him was his son and first mate, Carly. They weren't paying any attention to poor Nancy. They were staring out through the windshield at the blue cement.

Nancy, barefoot and wearing a thin white nightgown, descended bravely into the forward cabin, which was a pool of candlelight and pine-needle perfume. The companionway hatch was closed and locked behind her.

Nancy's emotions and the antique furnishings of the cabin were so complex that Nancy could not at first separate Billy the Poet from his surroundings, from all the mahogany and leaded glass. And then she saw him at the far end of the cabin, with his back against the door to the forward cockpit. He was wearing purple silk pajamas with a Russian collar. They were piped in red, and writhing across Billy's silken breast was a golden dragon. It was belching fire.

Anticlimactically, Billy was wearing glasses. He was holding a book.

Nancy poised herself on the next-to-the-bottom step, took a firm grip on the handholds in the companionway. She bared her teeth, calculated that it would take ten men Billy's size to dislodge her.

Between them was a great table. Nancy had expected the cabin to be dominated by a bed, possibly in the shape of a swan, but the Marlin was a day boat. The cabin was anything but a seraglio. It was about as voluptuous as a lower-middle-class dining room in Akron, Ohio, around 1910.

A candle was on the table. So were an ice bucket and two glasses and a quart of champagne. Champagne was as illegal as heroin.

Billy took off his glasses, gave her a shy, embarrassed smile, said, "Welcome."

"This is as far as I come."

He accepted that. "You're very beautiful there."

"And what am I supposed to say—that you're stunningly handsome? That I feel an overwhelming desire to throw myself into your manly arms?"

"If you wanted to make me happy, that would certainly be the way to do it." He said that humbly.

"And what about *my* happiness?"

The question seemed to puzzle him. "Nancy—that's what this is all about."

"What if my idea of happiness doesn't coincide with yours?"

"And what do you think my idea of happiness is?"

"I'm not going to throw myself into your arms, and I'm not going to drink that poison, and I'm not going to budge from here unless somebody makes me," said Nancy. "So I think your idea of happiness is going to turn out to be eight people holding me down on that table, while you bravely hold a cocked pistol to my head—and do what you want. That's the way it's going to have to be, so call your friends and get it over with!"

Which he did.

He didn't hurt her. He deflowered her with a clinical skill she found ghastly. When it was all over, he didn't seem cocky or proud. On the contrary, he was terribly depressed, and he said to Nancy, "Believe me, if there'd been any other way—"

Her reply to this was a face like stone—and silent tears of humiliation.

His helpers let down a folding bunk from the wall. It was scarcely wider than a bookshelf and hung on chains. Nancy allowed herself to be put to bed in it, and she was left alone with Billy the Poet again. Big as she was, like a double bass wedged on that narrow shelf, she felt like a pitiful little thing. A scratchy, war-surplus blanket had been tucked in around her. It was her own idea to pull up a corner of the blanket to hide her face.

Nancy sensed from sounds what Billy was doing, which wasn't much. He was sitting at the table, sighing occasionally, sniffing occasionally, turning the pages of a book. He lit a cigar and the stink of it seeped under the blanket. Billy inhaled the cigar, then coughed and coughed and coughed.

When the coughing died down, Nancy said loathingly through the blanket, "You're so strong, so masterful, so healthy. It must be wonderful to be so manly."

Billy only sighed at this.

"I'm not a very typical nothinghead," she said. "I hated it—hated everything about it."

Billy sniffed, turned a page.

"I suppose all the other women just loved it—couldn't get enough of it."

"Nope."

She uncovered her face. "What do you mean, 'Nope'?"

"They've all been like you."

This was enough to make Nancy sit up and stare at him. "The women who helped you tonight—"

"What about them?"

"You've done to them what you did to me?"

He didn't look up from his book. "That's right."

"Then why don't they kill you instead of helping you?"

"Because they understand." And then he added mildly, "They're *grateful*."

Nancy got out of bed, came to the table, gripped the edge of the table, leaned close to him. And she said to him tautly, "I am not grateful."

"You will be."

"And what could possibly bring about that miracle?"

"Time," said Billy.

Billy closed his book, stood up. Nancy was confused by his magnetism. Somehow he was very much in charge again.

"What you've been through, Nancy," he said, "is a typical wedding night for a strait-laced girl of a hundred years ago, when everybody was a nothinghead. The groom did without helpers, because the bride wasn't customarily ready to kill him. Otherwise, the spirit of the occasion was much the same. These are the pajamas my great-great-grandfather wore on his wedding night in Niagara Falls.

"According to his diary, his bride cried all that night, and threw up twice. But, with the passage of time, she became a sexual enthusiast."

It was Nancy's turn to reply by not replying. She understood the tale. It frightened her to understand so easily that, from gruesome beginnings, sexual enthusiasm could grow and grow.

"You're a very typical nothinghead," said Billy. "If you dare to think about it now, you'll realize that you're angry because I'm such a bad lover, and a funny-looking shrimp besides. And what you can't help dreaming about from now on is a really suitable mate for a Juno like yourself.

"You'll find him, too—tall and strong and gentle. The nothinghead movement is growing by leaps and bounds."

"But——" said Nancy, and she stopped there. She looked out a porthole at the rising sun.

"But what?"

"The world is in the mess it is today because of the nothingheadedness of olden times. Don't you see?" She was pleading weakly. "The world can't afford sex anymore."

"Of course it can afford sex," said Billy. "All it can't afford anymore is reproduction."

"Then why the laws?"

"They're bad laws," said Billy. "If you go back through history, you'll find that the people who have been most eager to rule, to make the laws, to enforce the laws and to tell everybody exactly how God Almighty wants things here on Earth—those people have forgiven themselves and their friends for anything and everything. But they have been absolutely disgusted and terrified by the natural sexuality of common men and women.

"Why this is, I do not know. That is one of the many questions I wish somebody would ask the machines. I do know this: The triumph of that sort of disgust and terror is now complete. Almost every man and woman looks and feels like something the cat dragged in. The only sexual beauty that an ordinary human being can see today is in the woman who will kill him. Sex is death. There's a short and nasty equation for you: 'Sex is death. Q. E. D.'

"So you see, Nancy," said Billy, "I have spent this night, and many others like it, attempting to restore a certain amount of innocent pleasure to the world, which is poorer in pleasure than it needs to be."

Nancy sat down quietly and bowed her head.

"I'll tell you what my grandfather did on the dawn of his wedding night," said Billy.

"I don't think I want to hear it."

"It isn't violent. It's—it's meant to be tender."

"Maybe that's why I don't want to hear it."

"He read his bride a poem." Billy took the book from the table, opened it. "His diary tells which poem it was. While we aren't bride and groom, and while we may not meet again for many years, I'd like to read this poem to you, to have you know I've loved you."

"Please—no. I couldn't stand it."

"All right, I'll leave the book here, with the place marked, in case you want to read it later. It's the poem beginning:

How do I love thee? Let me count the ways.
I love thee to the depth and breadth and height
My soul can reach, when feeling out of sight
For the ends of Being and ideal Grace."[1]

Billy put a small bottle on top of the book. "I am also leaving you these pills. If you take one a month, you will never have children. And still you'll be a nothinghead."

And he left. And they all left but Nancy.

When Nancy raised her eyes at last to the book and bottle, she saw that there was a label on the bottle. What the label said was this: WELCOME TO THE MONKEY HOUSE.

1968

William Styron 1925–

William Styron was born in Newport News, Virginia, in 1925 to a Northern mother, Pauline Abraham Styron, and a Southern father, William Styron, a shipyard engineer who, though descended from slave-owners, embraced politically liberal ideas. The community of Newport News, on the other hand, was thoroughly racially segregated. Young Styron grew up in an atmosphere that he later described as "semi-upper-middle class." He demonstrated an aptitude for writing at an early age, publishing several stories in his high school newspaper. In 1942 he enrolled at Davidson College, where he continued to publish his work in student periodicals. In 1943, however, Styron withdrew from Davidson to enlist in the Marines and then entered Duke University as an officer candidate. In 1944 he began active service as a lieutenant in the Marines, but before he could be shipped out from California for Okinawa, Japan had surrendered. As a result he saw no action in World War II. After his discharge, he returned to Duke and earned his B.A. in English.

[1]The opening lines of the poem "How Do I Love Thee?" by English poet Elizabeth Barrett Browning (1806–1861).

In 1947 Styron took an editing position in New York with the publishing company McGraw-Hill, but was fired after only a year. He began writing his first novel, set in the Tidewater region of Virginia in which he had grown up, in 1948, and published it in 1951 under the title Lie Down in Darkness. *The book brought him immediate critical acclaim. After being recalled into the Marines briefly during the Korean War, Styron relocated to Paris, France, where he lived among a group of intellectual American expatriates. In 1953 he co-founded the renowned* Paris Review *and married poet Rose Burgunder. He published his second novel,* Set This House on Fire, *in 1960. Eight years later he published the highly controversial novel* The Confessions of Nat Turner *(1968), for which he was awarded the Pulitzer Prize in 1969. Critic Albert Murray, writing in the* New Leader, *complained that Styron's novel suffered from "the same old failure of sensibility that plagues most other fiction about black people,' but Philip Rahv, writing for the* New York Review of Books, *praised the novel for "bringing home to us the monstrous reality of slavery in a psychodynamic manner that at the same time does not in the least neglect social or economic aspects." His next novel,* Sophie's Choice, *appeared in 1979, and was made into the 1982 Academy-Award-winning film starring Meryl Streep. William Styron currently resides in Roxbury, Connecticut, where he continues to write.*

FURTHER READING: J. Bryer, *William Styron: A Reference Guide,* 1978; P. Leon, *William Styron: An Annotated Bibliography of Criticism,* 1978; *The Achievement of William Styron,* ed. R. Morris, 1981; *Critical Essays on William Styron,* ed. A. Casciato and J. West III, 1982; J. Ruderman, *William Styron,* 1987; M. Laxmana, *Violence and Compassion in the Novels of William Styron: A Study in Tragic Humanism,* 1988; R. Sirlin, *William Styron's* Sophie's Choice, *Crime and Self-Punishment,* 1990; G. Cologne-Brookes, *The Novels of William Styron: From Harmony to History,* 1995; *The Critical Response to William Styron,* ed. D. Ross, 1995; D. Hadaller, *Gynicide: Women in the Novels of William Styron,* 1996; J. West, *William Styron: A Life,* 1998.

TEXT: *The Confessions of Nat Turner,* 1967.

from *THE CONFESSIONS OF NAT TURNER*[1]

For some reason I date the events of 1831 from this summer, five years earlier to the very month. I say this because I had my first vision then, the first intimation of my bloody mission, and these were both somehow intricately bound up with the drought and the fires. For on account of the dryness, brushfires had burned unchecked all summer throughout the woods and the swamps and the abandoned fields of the ruined plantations. They were all distant fires—Moore's wood lot was not threatened—but the smell of their burning was constantly in the air. In the old days, when dwellings might have been in danger, white men with their slaves would have gone out and fought these fires with shovel and ax, setting backfires and creating long swaths of cleared land as defense against the encroaching flames. But now most of that remote land was in spindly second-growth timber and great tracts of bramble-choked red earth gone fallow and worthless, and thus the fires smoldered night and day, filling the air with a perpetual haze and the scorched bittersweet odor of burnt undergrowth and charred pine. At times, after a spell of feeble rain, this haze would disappear and

[1]Styron's novel is narrated in the first person by Nat Turner, a slave who in 1831 led what came to be known as the Nat Turner Slave Rebellion.

the sunlight would become briefly clean, radiant; shortly thereafter the drought would set in again, interrupted by vagrant thunderstorms more wind and fury than rain, and the sawdust mist would begin its pungent domination of the air, causing the stars at night to lose their glitter and the sun to move day after day like a dulled round shimmering ember across the smoky sky. During that summer I commenced to be touched by a chill, a feeling of sickness, fright, an apprehension—as if these signs in the heavens might portend some great happening far more searing and deadly than the fires that were their earthly origin. In the woods I prayed often and searched ceaselessly in my Bible for some key, brooding long upon the Prophet Joel, who spoke of how *the sun and the moon shall be darkened and the stars shall withdraw their shining*,[2] and whose spirit—like mine now, stirred, swept as if by hot winds, trembling upon discovery—was so constantly shaken with premonitions and auguries of a terrible war.

Then late that summer I had the opportunity to go on a five-day fast. Hark[3] and I had together chopped several wagonloads of wood, because of the drought there was nothing to be done in the fields; and so Moore[4] gave us five days of absence—a fairly common dispensation during August. Later we would cart the wood into Jerusalem.[5] Having just stolen a plump little shoat from the Francis farm nearby, Hark declared that he would have nothing to do with fasting himself. But he said he was eager to accompany me to the woods and hoped that the odor of barbecued pork would not prove too much of a trial for my spirit or stomach. I assented to his company, adding only that he must let me have time for prayer and meditation, and to this he was cheerfully agreeable: he knew the fishing was good along the little stream I had discovered and he said that while I prayed he'd catch a mess of bass. Thus we passed the long hours—I secluded within my little thicket of trees, fasting and praying and reading from Isaiah while Hark splashed happily in the distance and warbled to himself or went off for hours in search of wild grapes and blackberries. One night as we lay beneath the smoky stars Hark spoke of his disappointment with God. "Hit do seem to me, Nat," he said in a measured voice, "dat de Lawd sho must be a white man. On'y a God dat was white could figger out how to make niggers so lonesome." He paused, then said: "On'y maybe he's a big black driver. An' if de Lawd is black he sho is de meanest black nigger bastid ever was born." I was too tired, too drained of strength, to try to answer.

On the morning of the fifth day I awoke feeling sickly and strange, with an aching emptiness at the pit of my belly and a giddiness swirling about in my brain. Never had a fast affected me with such weakness. It had grown wickedly hot. Smoke from the distant wildfires hung sulphurous in the air, so thick that the myriad shifting piney motes of it were nearly visible like dust, all but obliterating the round unwinking eye of a malign and yellow sun. Tree frogs in the oaks and pines joined with great legions of cicadas to set up an ominous shrilling, and my eardrums throbbed at the demented choir. I felt too exhausted to rise from my pine-needle bed and so stayed there reading and praying as the hot morning lengthened. When Hark came up from the creek I bade him

[2]Joel 3:15 (King James Version, as are the other biblical quotations that follow). Turner was very religious, and although a slave, he was literate.

[3]A fellow slave. [4]Turner's owner.

[5]The nearby town of Jerusalem, Virginia, today known as Courtland. Turner and his co-conspirators were later tried and executed in Jerusalem.

go back to the house since I wanted to remain alone. He was reluctant to leave. He tried to force me to eat and said I looked like a black ha'nt and clucked over me and fussed; but he finally did go, looking morose and apprehensive. After he had left I must have dropped off again into a deep slumber, for when I awoke I had lost all sense of time: great oily clouds of smoke coursed across the heavens and the sun had disappeared as if behind a rack of flaxen haze, leaving me with no notion of the hour of day. A languor like the onset of death had begun to invade my bones, an uncontrollable trembling seized my limbs; it was as if my spirit had slithered out of my body, letting the flesh sink away like a crumpled rag on the ground, all but lifeless, ready to be shivered, flayed, blown apart by divine remorseless winds.

"Lord," I said aloud, "give me a sign. Give me the first sign."

I rose to my feet with infinite difficulty and lassitude, clutching at a tree trunk, but hoisted myself no more than a foot or so from the ground when the sky began to whirl and spots of fire like minute blossoms danced before my eyes. Suddenly a calamitous roaring sound filled the heavens, touching me with awe and fright, and I slid to the earth again. As I did so, lifting my gaze upward, it was plain that a vast rent appeared in the boiling clouds above the treetops. I had become drenched in sweat and the droplets swarmed in my eyes yet I was unable to turn away from the great fissure yawning in the sky, seeming to throb now in rhythm to the roaring noise overwhelming all, drowning out even the shrilling forest din. Then swiftly in the very midst of the rent in the clouds I saw a black angel clothed in black armor with black wings outspread from east to west; gigantic, hovering, he spoke in a thunderous voice louder than anything I had ever heard: "*Fear God and give glory to Him for the hour of His judgment is come, and worship Him that made heaven and earth and the sea and the fountains of waters.*"[6] Then there appeared in the midst of the rent in the clouds another angel, also black, armored like the first, and his wings too compassed the heavens from east to west as he called out: "*If any man worship the beast and his image and receive his mark in his forehead, or in his hand, the same shall drink of the wine of the wrath of God, and he shall be tormented with fire and brimstone in the presence of the Lamb, and the smoke of their torment ascendeth up forever and ever.*"[7]

I started to cry out in terror, but at this moment the second black angel seemed to pour back into the clouds, faded, vanished, and in his place came still another angel—this angel white yet strangely faceless and resembling no living white being I had ever known. Silent, in glittering silver armor, he smote the remaining black angel with his sword, yet as in a dream I saw the sword noiselessly shatter and break in two; now the black angel raised his shield to face down his white foe, and the two spirits were locked in celestial battle high above the forest. The sun suddenly became dark and the blood ran in streams against the churning firmament. For a long time, or no time—what time?—the two angels struggled on high amid the blood-streaked billows and the noise of their battle mingled with the roaring sound within my senses like a hot wind until, half fainting, I felt as if I were about to be blown heavenward like a twig. Yet so quickly that it seemed but a heartbeat in space, the white angel was vanquished and his body was cast down through the outermost edges of the sky. Still I gazed upward where the black angel rode triumphant among the clouds, saying aloud now, and to me: "*Wherefore didst thou marvel? These shall make war with the Lamb*

[6]A quotation from Revelation 14:7. [7]Revelation 14:9–11.

and the Lamb shall overcome them, for he is Lord of lords and King of kings, and they that are with him are called, and chosen, and faithful.[8] *Such is your luck, such you are called to see, and let it come rough or smooth you must surely bear it."*

Instantly then the black angel was swallowed up into the empyrean and the great rent in the clouds melted at the edges and became one, leaving the sky murky and sulphurous as it had been before. An odor of burnt pine scorched and seared my nostrils, I felt surrounded by the flames of hell. I pitched forward on my hands and knees and vomited into the pine needles, vomiting without issue, retching in prolonged pained spasms that brought up only spittle and green strings of bile. Sparks as if from some satanic forge blew in endless windrows before my eyes, a million million pinpricks of catastrophic light.

"Lord," I whispered, "hast Thou truly called me to this?"

There was no answer, no answer at all save the answer in my brain: *This is the fast that I have chosen, to loose the bonds of wickedness, to undo the heavy burdens, to let the oppressed go free, and that ye break every yoke.*[9]

. . .

It was a Saturday, market day, and as usual the gallery was thronged with Negroes from the country who were generally allowed a few idle hours to fritter away while their masters attended to business in the town. After we unloaded the last logs Moore and Wallace went off on some errand and Hark and I retired—he with his pine-strip banjo, I with my Bible—to a shady corner of the gallery where I could meditate on a certain passage in Job which had attracted my curiosity. Hark strummed softly, humming a tune. Quite a few of the Negroes loitering about I had become acquainted with by now, largely because of these market days. Daniel, Joe, Jack, Henry, Cromwell, Marcus Aurelius, Nelson, half a dozen more—they had arrived with their masters from all over the county, had helped load or unload their owners' produce, and now stood about with nothing to do but ogle the passing bottoms or breasts of the Negro girls of the town, jabbering the while loudly about poontang and pussy, goosing each other and scuffling around in the dust. One or two succeeded with the girls and stole off with them into a field of alfalfa. Others played mumbletypeg with rusty stolen jackknives, or simply drowsed in the sunlight, waking now and then to exchange their sorry belongings: a straw hat bartered for a homemade jew's-harp, a lucky hairball from a cow's belly for a bag of pilfered snuff. I looked at them briefly, then returned to Job's racking, imponderable vision. But I found it difficult to concentrate, for although I had recovered some-what from my fever I could not dislodge the sensation that I had somehow been utterly changed and now dwelt at a distance from myself, in a new world apart. It was noon and Hark offered me a biscuit from a panful he had spirited out of the kitchen of one of Moore's customers, but I had no stomach for food. Even here in town the air was hazy, smelling of far-off fires.

Suddenly I became aware of a commotion—laughter and shouts from a cluster of white men behind the blacksmith's stable perhaps fifty yards away across the road. The bare earthen plot at the rear of the stable was the Saturday gathering place for the poor whites of the county just as the market gallery had become the social focus for the Negroes. These white idlers were the rogues and dregs of the community: penniless drunks and cripples, scroungers,

[8]Revelation 17:14. [9]A slightly altered version of Isaiah 58:6.

handymen, ex-overseers, vagabonds from North Carolina, harelipped roustabouts, squatters on pineland barrens, incorrigible loafers, cretins, rapscallions, and dimwits of every description, they made my present owner by comparison appear to possess the wisdom and dignity of King Solomon. There by the stable each Saturday with straw hats and cheap denim overalls they gathered in a shiftless mob, cadging from each other quarter-plugs of chewing tobacco or snorts of rotgut brandy, palavering endlessly (like the Negroes) about pussy and cooze, scheming out ways to make a dishonest half-dollar, tormenting stray cats and dogs, and allowing the slaves from their market promontory a bracing glimpse of white men worse off—in certain important respects at least—than themselves. Now when I looked up to find the source of the disturbance among them I saw that they had assembled in a rough circle. In the midst of the circle, perched upon a horse, was the squat, hunched form of Nathaniel Francis, roaring drunk, his round face besotted with swollen pleasure as he gazed down at something taking place on the ground. I was only mildly curious, thinking at first that it was a white man's wrestling match or drunken fist fight: hardly a Saturday passed without one or the other. But through the baggy pants' legs of one of the bystanders I saw what appeared to be two Negroes moving about, engaged in doing what I could not tell. Cackles of glee went up from the crowd, wild hoots and cries. They seemed to be egging the Negroes on, and Francis drunk in the saddle caused the horse to stamp and prance at the space within the encircling mob, raising an umbrella of dust. Hark had risen to his feet to gawk and I told him that he had better go find out what was happening; he moved slowly off.

After a minute or so Hark came back to the gallery, and the sheepish half-smile on his face—I will never forget that expression, its mixed quality of humor and gentle bewilderment—filled me with a sad foreboding, as if I had known, sensed what he was going to say the instant before his mouth opened to say it.

"Ole Francis he puttin' on a show fo' dem white trash," he proclaimed, loud enough for most all of the other Negroes to hear. "He drunker dan a scritch owl and he makin' dem two niggers Will and Sam fight each other. Don't neither of 'em want to fight but ev'y time one of 'em draw back an' *don't* whop de other, ole Francis he give dat nigger a stroke wid his whip. So dem niggers dey *got* to fight and Sam he done raised a bleedin' whelp on Will's face and Will I do believe he done broke off one of Sam's front teeth. Hit sho is some kind of cock fight."

At this, all the Negroes within hearing began to laugh—there was indeed something oddly comical about Hark's *way* of describing things—but at the same time my heart seemed to shrivel and die within me. This was *all* All! Of the indignities and wrongs that a Negro might endure—blistering toil and deprivation, slights and slurs and insults, beatings, chains, exile from beloved kin—none seemed more loathsome, at that minute, than this: that he be pitted in brutal combat against his own kind for the obscene amusement of human beings of any description—but especially those so mean and reptilian in spirit, so worthless, so likewise despised in the scheme of things and saved from the final morass only by the hairline advantage of a lighter skin. Not since the day years before when I was first sold had I felt such rage, intolerable rage, rage that echoed a memory of Isham's fury as he howled at Moore, rage that was a culmination of all the raw buried anguish and frustration growing inside me since the faraway dusk of childhood, on a murmuring veranda, when I first understood that I was a slave and a slave forever. My heart, as I say, shrank inside me, died, disappeared, and rage like a newborn child exploded there to fill the void: it was at this instant that I knew beyond doubt or danger that—whatever the place, whatever the appointed time, whoever the gentle young girl now serenely plucking blossoms within a bower or the mistress knitting in the coolness of a country parlor or the innocent lad seated contemplating the cobwebbed walls of an outhouse in a summery field—the whole world of white flesh would someday founder and split apart upon my retribution, would perish by my design and at my hands. My stomach heaved and I restrained the urge to vomit on the boards where I sat.

But now the commotion across the road dwindled, the shouts fell away, and the circle of white men broke up as they turned their attention to other pleasures. Aslant to one side in the saddle, Francis rode off at a lurching pace down the street, exhausted by his sport, smiling a smile of gratification and conquest. And at this moment I saw Will and Sam—battered-looking, bruised, and dusty—cross the road together, weaving toward the market. Will was muttering to himself as he stroked a swollen jaw and Sam shivered while he walked, trembling in pain, misery, and in the throes of grievous shame and abasement—a short, wiry little mulatto neither too old yet nor too calloused by suffering to be prevented from sobbing bitterly like a child as he wiped the blood away from a jagged cut across his lips. Still unperceiving of anything at all, still witlessly amused by Hark's account of the fray, the Negroes on the gallery watched Sam and Will approach and kept laughing. It was then that I rose to face them.

"My brothers!" I cried. "Stop yo' laughin' and listen to me! Leave off from that laughin', brothers, and listen to a minister of the Holy Word!" A hush fell over the Negroes and they stirred restlessly, turned toward me, puzzlement and wonder in their eyes. "Come closer!" I commanded them. "This here is no time for laughin'! This is a time for weepin', for *lamentation!* For rage! You is *men,* brothers, *men* not beasts of the field! You ain't no four-legged dogs! You is *men,* I say! Where oh where, my brothers, is yo' pride?"

Slowly, one by one, the Negroes drew near, among them Will and Sam, who climbed up from the road and stood gazing at me as they mopped their faces with gray slimy wads of waste cotton. Still other shuffled closer—young men mostly, along with a few older slaves; they scratched themselves out of nervousness, some eyes darted furtively across the road. But all were silent now, and with a delicious chill I could feel the way in which they had responded to the fury in my words, like blades of sawgrass bending to a sudden wind. And I began to realize, far back in the remotest corner of my mind, that I had commenced the first sermon I had ever preached. They became still. Brooding, motionless, the Negroes gazed at me with watchful and reflective concern, some of them hardly drawing a breath. My language was theirs, I spoke it as if it were a second tongue. My rage had captured them utterly, and I felt a thrill of power course out from myself to wrap them round, binding us for this moment as one.

"My brothers," I said in a gentler tone, "many of you has been to church with yo' mastahs and mist'esses at the Whitehead church or up Shiloh way or down at Nebo or Mount Moriah. Most of you hasn't got no religion. That's awright. White man's religion don't teach nothin' to black folk except to obey ole mastah and live humble—walk light and talk small. That's awright. But them of you that recollects they Bible teachin' knows about Israel in Egypt an' the peoples that was kept in bondage. Them peoples was Jewish peoples an' they had names just like us black folk—like you right there, Nathan, an' you, Joe—Joe is a Jewish name—an' you there, Daniel. Them Jews was just like the black folk. They had to sweat they fool asses off fo' ole Pharaoh. That white man had them Jews haulin' wood an' pullin' rock and thrashin' corn an' makin' bricks until they was near 'bout dead an' didn't git ary penny for none of it neither, like ev'y livin' mothah's son of us, them Jews was in *bondage.* They didn't have enough to eat neither, just some miser'ble cornmeal with weevils in it an' sour milk an' a little fatback that done got so high it would turn a buzzard's stomach. Drought an' hunger run throughout the land, just like now. Oh, my brothers, that was a sad time in Egypt fo' them Jews! It was a time fo' weepin' an' lamentation, a time of toil an' hunger, a time of *pain!* Pharaoh he whupped them Jews until they had red whelps on 'em from head to toe an' ev'y night they went to bed cryin', 'Lord, Lord, when is you goin' to make that white man set us free?'"

There was a stirring among the Negroes and I heard a voice in the midst of them say, "Yes, yes," faint and plaintive, and still another voice: "Mm-huh, dat's *right!*" I stretched out an arm slowly, as if to embrace them, and some of the crowd moved nearer still.

"Look aroun' you, brothers," I said, "what does you see? What does you see in the air? What does you see blowin' in the air?" The Negroes turned their faces toward the town, raised their eyes skyward: there in amber translucent haze the smoke from the distant fires swam through the streets, touching the gallery, even as I spoke, with its acrid and apple-sweet taste of scorched timber, its faint smell of corruption.

"That there is the smoke of *pestilence,* brothers," I went on, "the smoke of pestilence an' death. The same smoke that hanged over the Jews in bondage down there in Egypt land. The same smoke of pestilence an' death that hanged over them Jews in Egypt hangs over all black folk, all men whose skin is black, yo' skin and mine. An' we got a tougher row to hoe even than them Jews. Joseph he was at least a man, not no four-legged dog. My brothers, laughter is good, laughter is bread and salt and buttermilk and a balm for pain. But they is a time for ev'ything. They is a time for weepin' too. A time for rage! And in bondage black folk like you an' me must weep in they rage. *Leave off* from such dumb laughter like just now!" I cried, my voice rising. "When a white man he lift a hand against one of us'ns we must not laugh but rage and weep! 'By the rivers of Babylon, there we sat down, yea, we wept when we remembered Zion!'"[10] That's right!" ("Mm-huh, dat's right!" came the voice again, joined by another.) "'We hanged our harps upon the willows, for they that carried us away captive required of us a song. How shall we sing the Lord's song in a strange land?'[11] *That's right!*" I said, the words bitter on my tongue. "White man make you sing an' dance, make you shuffle, do the buck-an'-wing, play 'Ole Zip Coon'[12] on the banjo and the fiddle. 'They that carried us away captive required of us a song.' Yes! Leave off from that singin', leave off from that banjo,

[10]Psalm 137:1. [11]Psalm 137:2–4.

[12]A song popular in "blackface" entertainments; its tune was the same as that of "Turkey in the Straw."

leave off from that buck-an'-wing! They is a time for ev'ything. This is no time fo' singin', fo' laughter. Look aroun' you, my brothers, look into each other's eyes! You jest seen a white man pit brother 'gainst brother! Ain't none of you no four-legged beasts what can be whupped an' hurt like some flea-bit cur dog. You is men! You is *men,* my dear brothers, look at yo'selves, look to yo' *pride!*"

As I spoke, I saw two older black men at the rear of the crowd mutter to each other and shake their heads. Glances of puzzlement and worry crossed their faces and they sidled off, disappeared. The others still listened, intent, brooding, nearly motionless. I heard a soft sigh and a gentle "Amen." I raised my arms to either side of me and extended my hands, palms outward, as if in benediction. I felt the sweat pouring from my face.

"In the visions of the night, brothers," I continued, "God spoke to Jacob an' He said, 'I am God, the God of thy father: fear not to go down into Egypt, for I will there make of thee a great nation.'[13] An' Jacob went down into Egypt an' the peoples of Israel multiplied an' Moses was born. Moses he was born in the bulrushers an' he delivered the Jews out of Egypt an' into the Promised Land. Well, there they had a powerful lot of troubles too. But in the Promised Land them Jewish peoples they could stand up an' live like *men.* They become a great nation. No more fatback, no more pint of salt, no more peck of corn fo' them Jews; no more overseers, no more auction blocks; no more horn blow at sunrise fo' them mothahs' sons. They had chicken with pot likker an' spoonbread an' sweet cider to drink in the shade. They done got paid an honest dollar. Them Jews become *men.* But oh, my brothers, black folk ain't never goin' to be led from bondage without they has *pride!* Black folk ain't goin' to be free, they ain't goin' to have no spoonbread an' sweet cider less'n they studies to love they own *selves.* Only then will the first be last, and the last first. Black folk ain't never goin' to be no great nation until they studies to love they own black skin an' the beauty of that skin an' the beauty of them black hands that toils so hard and black feet that trods so weary on God's earth. And when white men in they hate an' wrath an' meanness fetches blood from that beautiful black skin then, oh *then,* my brothers, it is time not fo' laughing but fo' weeping an' rage an' lamentation! *Pride!*" I cried after a pause, and let my arms descend. "Pride, pride, *everlasting* pride, pride will make you free!"

I ceased speaking and gazed at the rapt black faces. Then I finished slowly and in a soft voice: "Arise, shine; for thy light is come, an' the glory of the Lord is risen upon thee.[14] Amen."

The Negroes were silent. Far off in Jerusalem, through the hot afternoon, a church bell let fall a single chime, striking the half-hour. Then the Negroes one by one straggled away across the gallery, some with troubled looks, some stupid and uncomprehending, some fearful. Others drew toward me, radiant; and Henry, who was deaf, who had read my lips, came up close to me and silently clasped my arm. I heard Nelson say, "You done spoke de truth," and he too drew near, and I felt their warmth and their brotherhood and hope and knew then what Jesus must have known when upon the shores of Galilee he said: "*Follow me, and I will make you fishers of men.*"[15]

1967

[13]Genesis 46:3. [14]Genesis 60:1. [15]Matthew 4:19.

N. Scott Momaday 1934–

Recognized as a founding artist of the "Native American Renaissance," N. Scott Momaday is celebrated today as one of the most distinguished living American writers. He was born Navarre Scott Mammedaty in southwest Oklahoma in 1934 to Native American parents who were artists and teachers. His father, Al Momaday, a Kiowa artist, and his mother, Natachee Scott, a part-Cherokee who was a teacher and writer, relocated with Momaday in 1946 to Jemez Pueblo, New Mexico, where they accepted positions at a small Indian day school. During Momaday's adolescence, his parents exposed him to a variety of educational experiences, including both reservation schools and the public schools of Albuquerque. He graduated from high school at a Virginia military academy and then enrolled at the University of New Mexico, where he earned a B.A. in political science. In 1960 he took an M.A. in English from Stanford University, and three years later received a Ph.D. in English from the same institution.

In 1968 Momaday made a remarkable beginning as a novelist, publishing his first novel, House Made of Dawn, *which was awarded the Pulitzer Prize for fiction. The following year his acclaimed autobiographical work* The Way to Rainy Mountain, *meditating especially on his Kiowa heritage, appeared and solidified his reputation as an authentic literary talent. In addition to numerous other novels and autobiographical works, he has published several volumes of poetry, including* Angle of Geese and Other Poems *(1974),* The Gourd Dancer *(1976), and* In the Presence of the Sun *(1992). N. Scott Momaday has taught at Berkeley, Stanford, and the University of Moscow, and is currently Regents Professor of Humanities at the University of Arizona.*

FURTHER READING: A. Velie, *Four American Indian Literary Masters: N. Scott Momaday, James Welch, Leslie Marmon Silko, and Gerald Vizenor,* 1982; M. Schubnell, *N. Scott Momaday: The Cultural and Literary Background,* 1985; *Ancestral Voice: Conversations with N. Scott Momaday,* ed. C. Woodard, 1989; *Conversations with N. Scott Momaday,* ed. M. Schubnell, 1997; L. Schweninger, *N. Scott Momaday,* 2001.

TEXTS: *The Way to Rainy Mountain,* 1996; *The Man Made of Words,* 1996.

from *THE WAY TO RAINY MOUNTAIN*

A single knoll rises out of the plain in Oklahoma, north and west of the Wichita Range.[1] For my people, the Kiowas,[2] it is an old landmark, and they gave it the name Rainy Mountain. The hardest weather in the world is there. Winter brings blizzards, hot tornadic winds arise in the spring, and in summer the prairie is an anvil's edge. The grass turns brittle and brown, and it

[1]A mountain range in southwestern Oklahoma.
[2]A Native American people located in southwestern Oklahoma and adjoining portions of Texas and New Mexico.

cracks beneath your feet. There are green belts along the rivers and creeks, linear groves of hickory and pecan, willow and witch hazel. At a distance in July or August the steaming foliage seems almost to writhe in fire. Great green and yellow grasshoppers are everywhere in the tall grass, popping up like corn to sting the flesh, and tortoises crawl about on the red earth, going nowhere in the plenty of time. Loneliness is an aspect of the land. All things in the plain are isolate; there is no confusion of objects in the eye, but one hill or one tree or one man. To look upon that landscape in the early morning, with the sun at your back, is to lose the sense of proportion. Your imagination comes to life, and this, you think, is where Creation was begun.

I returned to Rainy Mountain in July. My grandmother had died in the spring, and I wanted to be at her grave. She had lived to be very old and at last infirm. Her only living daughter was with her when she died, and I was told that in death her face was that of a child.

I like to think of her as a child. When she was born, the Kiowas were living the last great moment of their history. For more than a hundred years they had controlled the open range from the Smoky Hill River to the Red, from the headwaters of the Canadian to the fork of the Arkansas and Cimarron.[3] In alliance with the Comanches, they had ruled the whole of the southern Plains. War was their sacred business, and they were among the finest horsemen the world has ever known. But warfare for the Kiowas was preeminently a matter of disposition rather than of survival, and they never understood the grim, unrelenting advance of the U.S. Cavalry. When at last, divided and ill-provisioned, they were driven onto the Staked Plains[4] in the cold rains of autumn, they fell into panic. In Palo Duro Canyon[5] they abandoned their crucial stores to pillage and had nothing then but their lives. In order to save themselves, they surrendered to the soldiers at Fort Sill[6] and were imprisoned in the old stone corral that now stands as a military museum. My grandmother was spared the humiliation of those high gray walls by eight or ten years, but she must have known from birth the affliction of defeat, the dark brooding of old warriors.

Her name was Aho, and she belonged to the last culture to evolve in North America. Her forebears came down from the high country in western Montana nearly three centuries ago. They were a mountain people, a mysterious tribe of hunters whose language has never been positively classified in any major group. In the late seventeenth century they began a long migration to the south and east. It was a journey toward the dawn, and it led to a golden age. Along the way the Kiowas were befriended by the Crows,[7] who gave them the culture and religion of the Plains. They acquired horses, and their ancient nomadic spirit was suddenly free of the ground. They acquired Tai-me, the sacred Sun Dance doll, from that moment the object and symbol of their worship, and so shared in the divinity of the sun. Not least, they acquired the

[3]Two rivers that flow together near Tulsa, Oklahoma.
[4]A mesa area of Texas and New Mexico. [5]A large canyon in western Texas.
[6]A U.S. Army post in southwestern Oklahoma.
[7]A Native American people located in Montana.

sense of destiny, therefore courage and pride. When they entered upon the southern Plains they had been transformed. No longer were they slaves to the simple necessity of survival; they were a lordly and dangerous society of fighters and thieves, hunters and priests of the sun. According to their origin myth, they entered the world through a hollow log. From one point of view, their migration was the fruit of an old prophecy, for indeed they emerged from a sunless world.

Although my grandmother lived out her long life in the shadow of Rainy Mountain, the immense landscape of the continental interior lay like memory in her blood. She could tell of the Crows, whom she had never seen, and of the Black Hills,[8] where she had never been. I wanted to see in reality what she had seen more perfectly in the mind's eye, and traveled fifteen hundred miles to begin my pilgrimage.

Yellowstone,[9] it seemed to me, was the top of the world, a region of deep lakes and dark timber, canyons and waterfalls. But, beautiful as it is, one might have the sense of confinement there. The skyline in all directions is close at hand, the high wall of the woods and deep cleavages of shade. There is a perfect freedom in the mountains, but it belongs to the eagle and the elk, the badger and the bear. The Kiowas reckoned their stature by the distance they could see, and they were bent and blind in the wilderness.

Descending eastward, the highland meadows are a stairway to the plain. In July the inland slope of the Rockies is luxuriant with flax and buckwheat, stonecrop and larkspur. The earth unfolds and the limit of the land recedes. Clusters of trees, and animals grazing far in the distance, cause the vision to reach away and wonder to build upon the mind. The sun follows a longer course in the day, and the sky is immense beyond all comparison. The great billowing clouds that sail upon it are shadows that move upon the grain like water, dividing light. Farther down, in the land of the Crows and Blackfeet,[10] the plain is yellow. Sweet clover takes hold of the hills and bends upon itself to cover and seal the soil. There the Kiowas paused on their way; they had come to the place where they must change their lives. The sun is at home on the plains. Precisely there does it have the certain character of a god. When the Kiowas came to the land of the Crows, they could see the dark lees of the hills at dawn across the Bighorn River,[11] the profusion of light on the grain shelves, the oldest deity ranging after the solstices. Not yet would they veer southward to the caldron of the land that lay below; they must wean their blood from the northern winter and hold the mountains a while longer in their view. They bore Tai-me in procession to the east.

A dark mist lay over the Black Hills, and the land was like iron. At the top of a ridge I caught sight of Devil's Tower[12] upthrust against the gray sky as if

[8]A mountain range in South Dakota and Wyoming.

[9]A region of Wyoming, Idaho, and Montana where Yellowstone National Park is now located.

[10]A Native American people who, like the Crows, are located in Montana.

[11]A river in Wyoming and Montana.

[12]A tower of volcanic rock that forms a distinctive landmark in eastern Wyoming.

in the birth of time the core of the earth had broken through its crust and the motion of the world was begun. There are things in nature that engender an awful quiet in the heart of man; Devil's Tower is one of them. Two centuries ago, because they could not do otherwise, the Kiowas made a legend at the base of the rock. My grandmother said:

> Eight children were there at play, seven sisters and their brother. Suddenly the boy was struck dumb; he trembled and began to run upon his hands and feet. His fingers became claws, and his body was covered with fur. Directly there was a bear where the boy had been. The sisters were terrified; they ran, and the bear after them. They came to the stump of a great tree, and the tree spoke to them. It bade them climb upon it, and as they did so it began to rise into the air. The bear came to kill them, but they were just beyond its reach. It reared against the tree and scored the bark all around with its claws. The seven sisters were borne into the sky, and they became the stars of the Big Dipper.

From the moment, and so long as the legend lives, the Kiowas have kinsmen in the night sky. Whatever they were in the mountains, they could be no more. However tenuous their well-being, however much they had suffered and would suffer again, they had found a way out of the wilderness.

My grandmother had a reverence for the sun, a holy regard that now is all but gone out of mankind. There was a wariness in her, and an ancient awe. She was a Christian in her later years, but she had come a long way about, and she never forgot her birthright. As a child she had been to the Sun Dances; she had taken part in those annual rites, and by them she had learned the restoration of her people in the presence of Tai-me. She was about seven when the last Kiowa Sun Dance was held in 1887 on the Washita River[13] above Rainy Mountain Creek. The buffalo were gone. In order to consummate the ancient sacrifice—to impale the head of a buffalo bull upon the medicine tree—a delegation of old men journeyed into Texas, there to beg and barter for an animal from the Goodnight herd. She was ten when the Kiowas came together for the last time as a living Sun Dance culture. They could find no buffalo; they had to hang an old hide from the sacred tree. Before the dance could begin, a company of soldiers rode out from Fort Sill under orders to disperse the tribe. Forbidden without cause the essential act of their faith, having seen the wild herds slaughtered and left to rot upon the ground, the Kiowas backed away forever from the medicine tree. That was July 20, 1890, at the great bend of the Washita. My grandmother was there. Without bitterness, and for as long as she lived, she bore a vision of deicide.[14]

Now that I can have her only in memory, I see my grandmother in the several postures that were peculiar to her: standing at the wood stove on a winter morning and turning meat in a great iron skillet; sitting at the south

[13] A river in western Texas. [14] The killing of a god.

window, bent above her beadwork, and afterwards, when her vision failed, looking down for a long time into the fold of her hands; going out upon a cane, very slowly as she did when the weight of age came upon her; praying. I remember her most often at prayer. She made long, rambling prayers out of suffering and hope, having seen many things. I was never sure that I had the right to hear, so exclusive were they of all mere custom and company. The last time I saw her she prayed standing by the side of her bed at night, naked to the waist, the light of a kerosene lamp moving upon her dark skin. Her long, black hair, always drawn and braided in the day, lay upon her shoulders and against her breasts like a shawl. I do not speak Kiowa, and I never understood her prayers, but there was something inherently sad in the sound, some merest hesitation upon the syllables of sorrow. She began in a high and descending pitch, exhausting her breath to silence; then again and again—and always the same intensity of effort, of something that is, and is not, like urgency in the human voice. Transported so in the dancing light among the shadows of her room, she seemed beyond the reach of time. But that was illusion; I think I knew then that I should not see her again.

Houses are like sentinels in the plain, old keepers of the weather watch. There, in a very little while, wood takes on the appearance of great age. All colors wear soon away in the wind and rain, and then the wood is burned gray and the grain appears and the nails turn red with rust. The windowpanes are black and opaque; you imagine there is nothing within, and indeed there are many ghosts, bones given up to the land. They stand here and there against the sky, and you approach them for a longer time than you expect. They belong in the distance; it is their domain.

Once there was a lot of sound in my grandmother's house, a lot of coming and going, feasting and talk. The summers there were full of excitement and reunion. The Kiowas are a summer people; they abide the cold and keep to themselves, but when the season turns and the land becomes warm and vital they cannot hold still; an old love of going returns upon them. The aged visitors who came to my grandmother's house when I was a child were made of lean and leather, and they bore themselves upright. They wore great black hats and bright ample shirts that shook in the wind. They rubbed fat upon their hair and wound their braids with strips of colored cloth. Some of them painted their faces and carried the scars of old and cherished enmities. They were an old council of warlords, come to remind and be reminded of who they were. Their wives and daughters served them well. The women might indulge themselves; gossip was at once the mark and compensation of their servitude. They made loud and elaborate talk among themselves, full of jest and gesture, fright and false alarm. They went abroad in fringed and flowered shawls, bright beadwork and German silver. They were at home in the kitchen, and they prepared meals that were banquets.

There were frequent prayer meetings, and great nocturnal feasts. When I was a child I played with my cousins outside, where the lamplight fell upon the ground and the singing of the old people rose up around us and carried away into the darkness. There were a lot of good things to eat, a lot of laughter and surprise. And afterwards, when the quiet returned, I lay down with my grandmother and could hear the frogs away by the river and feel the motion of the air.

Now there is a funeral silence in the rooms, the endless wake of some final word. The walls have closed in upon my grandmother's house. When I returned to it in mourning, I saw for the first time in my life how small it was. It was late at night, and there was a white moon, nearly full. I sat for a long time on the stone steps by the kitchen door. From there I could see out across the land; I could see the long row of trees by the creek, the low light upon the rolling plains, and the stars of the Big Dipper. Once I looked at the moon and caught sight of a strange thing. A cricket had perched upon the handrail, only a few inches away from me. My line of vision was such that the creature filled the moon like a fossil. It had gone there, I thought, to live and die, for there, of all places, was its small definition made whole and eternal. A warm wind rose up and purled[15] like the longing within me.

The next morning I awoke at dawn and went out on the dirt road to Rainy Mountain. It was already hot, and the grasshoppers began to fill the air. Still, it was early in the morning, and the birds sang out of the shadows. The long yellow grass on the mountain shone in the bright light, and a scissortail[16] hied[17] above the land. There, where it ought to be, at the end of a long and legendary way, was my grandmother's grave. Here and there on the dark stones were ancestral names. Looking back once, I saw the mountain and came away.

1967, 1969

THE ARROWMAKER

The story of the arrowmaker, the "man made of words," is perhaps the first story I was told. My father loved to tell it to me, and I loved to hear it. It remains for me one of the most intensely vital stories in my experience, not only because it is a supernal example of the warrior idea—an adventure story in the best sense—but because it is a story about story, about the efficacy of language and the power of words. One does not come to the end of such a story. I have lived with the story of the arrowmaker for many years, and I am sure that I do not yet understand it in all of its consequent meanings. Nor do I expect to understand it so. The stories I keep close to me, day by day, are those that yield more and more of their spirit in time.

[15]Swirled, eddied. [16]A kind of bird: the scissor-tailed flycatcher.
[17]Flew quickly.

If an arrow is well made, it will have tooth marks upon it. That is how you know. The Kiowas made fine arrows and straightened them in their teeth. Then they drew them to the bow to see that they were straight.

Once there was a man and his wife. They were alone at night in their tepee. By the light of a fire the man was making arrows. After a while he caught sight of something. There was a small opening in the tepee where two hides had been sewn together. Someone was there on the outside, looking in. The man went on with his work, but he said to his wife, "Someone is standing outside. Do not be afraid. Let us talk easily, as of ordinary things." He took up an arrow and straightened it in his teeth; then, as it was right for him to do, he drew it to the bow and took aim, first in this direction and then in that. And all the while he was talking, as if to his wife. But this is how he spoke: "I know that you are there on the outside, for I can feel your eyes upon me. If you are a Kiowa, you will understand what I am saying, and you will speak your name." But there was no answer, and the man went on in the same way, pointing the arrow all around. At last his aim fell upon the place where his enemy stood, and he let go of the string. The arrow went straight to the enemy's heart.

Until very recently the story of the arrowmaker has been the private possession of a few, a tenuous link in that most ancient chain of language which we call the oral tradition; tenuous because the tradition itself appears to be so, for as many times as the story has been told, it has always been but one generation removed from extinction. That is to say, it has been neither more nor less durable than the human voice, and neither more nor less concerned to express the meaning of the human condition.

The story of the arrowmaker is a remarkable act of the imagination, a realization of words and meanings that is altogether simple and direct, yet nonetheless rare and profound, and it illustrates more clearly than anything else in my own experience something of the essential character of the imagination—and in particular of that personification which in this instance emerges from it: the man made of words.

It is important that the story of the arrowmaker returns in a special way upon itself. It is about language, after all, and it is therefore part and parcel of its own subject. Virtually, there is no difference between the telling and that which is told. The point of the story lies not so much in what the arrowmaker does, but in what he says—and, indeed, *that* he says it. The principal fact is that he speaks, and in so doing he places his very life in the balance.

It is this aspect of the story which interests me most, for it is here that the language becomes most conscious of itself; here we are very close to the origin and object of literature; here our sense of the verbal dimension is very keen, and we are aware of something in the nature of language that is at once perilous and compelling. "If you are a Kiowa, you will understand what I am saying, and you will speak your name." Everything is ventured in this simple declaration, which is also a question and a plea.

Precisely at this moment is the arrowmaker realized completely, and his reality consists in language. Implicit in his simple speech is all of his definition and all of his destiny, and by implication all of ours. He ventures to speak because he must; language is the repository of his whole knowledge, and it represents the only chance he has for survival. Instinctively and with great care he deals in the most honest and basic way with words. "Let us talk easily, as of ordinary things," he says. And of the ominous unknown he asks only the utterance of a name, only the most nominal sign that he is understood, that a word or a syllable is returned to him on the sheer edge of meaning. But there is no answer, and the arrowmaker knows at once what he has not known before: that his enemy is, and is present, and that he, the arrowmaker, has gained a crucial advantage over him. Make no mistake, the words of the arrowmaker reveal his peril clearly. The presence outside is decidedly an enemy; twice the storyteller tells us so. The venture is complete and irrevocable, and it ends in the restoration of order and well-being.

The story is meaningful. It is so because it is in the nature of language that it proceeds to the formulation of meaning. Moreover, the story of the arrowmaker especially centers upon this procession of words toward meaning. It seems in fact to turn upon the very idea that language involves the elements of risk and responsibility; and in this it seeks to confirm itself. In a word, it seems to say, everything is a risk. That may well be true, and it may also be that the whole of literature rests upon that truth.

The story of the arrowmaker is supremely metaphorical; indeed it is acutely and incisively a story about story; it is both an example and a definition of literature. It is complex, and yet it is clear; it seems to give more and more of itself in time. Clear it is, and yet there is a kind of resistance in it, as in a riddle; it is the richer for that. It is a kind of prism.

The arrowmaker is preeminently the man made of words. He has consummate being in language; it is the world of his origin and of his posterity, and there is no other. But it is a world of definite reality and of infinite possibility. I have come to believe that there is a sense in which the arrowmaker has a quality of being that is more viable than that of men in general—he has nearly a perfect right to be. We can imagine him, and he imagines himself, whole and vital, going on into the unknown darkness and beyond.

And yet the story has it that he is cautious and alone, and we are given to understand that his peril is great and immediate, and that he confronts it in the only way he can. I have no doubt that this is true. Language determines the arrowmaker, and his story determines our literary experience.

A word, then, on an essential irony which marks the story and gives peculiar substance to the man made of words. The storyteller is nameless and unlettered. We know very little about him, except that in the story is his presence and his mask. And that is enough. He tells of his life in language, and of the risk involved. It occurs to us that he is one with the arrowmaker, and that he has survived, by word of mouth, beyond other men. For the storyteller, for the arrowmaker, language does indeed represent the only chance for survival. It is appropriate that he survives in our time and that he has survived over a period of untold generations.

1967, 1997

Thomas Pynchon 1937–

Thomas Pynchon is one of the most critically celebrated yet physically invisible authors of our time. Acclaimed as a new, innovative literary voice soon after his work first appeared in the 1950s, he has been reclusive as a hermit. He never appears on television; he refuses to reveal his whereabouts; he even changes his name and address to confuse those who would pursue him.

His obsession with privacy has implications for his fiction, which he believes should be an exclusive communication with the reader, and from which the biographical details of the author's life should be absent. The facts known of his life are few and ordinary. He was born in 1937 in Glen Cove, Long Island, the descendant of a family that traces its roots back to the eleventh century. He graduated from high school at the age of sixteen and entered Cornell University the following fall, majoring in engineering physics. After a two-year stint in the U.S. Navy he returned to Cornell and changed his major to English. In 1959 he graduated, having taken, along the way, a course in European fiction from the famous novelist Vladimir Nabokov.

After graduation from Cornell, Pynchon lived briefly in Greenwich Village in New York City. From 1960 to 1962 he worked in Seattle as a technical writer for Boeing Corporation and wrote his novel V *(1963). His stories had begun to appear in literary journals as early as 1959, and in 1960 he published his famous story "Entropy," in which he uses the second law of thermodynamics as an analogy for the decline of western civilization.*

Pynchon's readers have found his apocalyptic messages and his richly varied, often whimsical prose well suited to their growing sense that western civilization is winding down, that old social orthodoxies will have to be discarded and replaced, perhaps, by the "overlooked" values of the poor and the oppressed, the down-and-outers who live with "a mind at peace" in the decayed cities of America.

Fanciers of all things redolent of "counterculture" welcomed his challenges to authority. Serious readers found significance in his social satire, in the religious overtones of his stories, and in the mythic quests of his protagonists. Readers have also found Pynchon's writing difficult, his style too decorative, too complex, laced as it is with foreign words and phrases, allusions to science, historical events, popular songs, classical music, and art.

The influence of T. S. Eliot, especially of Eliot's The Waste Land *and "The Hollow Men," has been seen in Pynchon's short stories and in the novel* V. *The theme of cultural decline is also notably present in* Gravity's Rainbow *(1973) and in Pynchon's recent novel,* Vineland *(1990), which continue his emphasis on the diminishing energy, the inevitable movement toward entropy, that seems to be the fate of life and culture in the western, technological world. Yet Pynchon is not wholly absorbed by a hopeless view of life, concerned as he is with the saving value of humane gestures (such as the protection of the small bird in "Entropy"), which "may"—he emphasizes only the possibility—ultimately hold the key to human survival and regeneration.*

FURTHER READING: J. Slade, *Thomas Pynchon,* 1974; *Mindful Pleasures: Essays on Thomas Pynchon,* ed. G. Levine and D. Leverenz, 1976; *Pynchon: A Collection of Critical Essays,* E. Mendelson, ed., 1978; D. Cowart, *Thomas Pynchon and the Art of Allusion,* 1980; T. Schaub, *Thomas Pynchon: The Voice of Ambiguity,* 1981; P. Cooper, *Signs and Symptoms: Thomas Pynchon and the Contemporary World,* 1983; M. Hite, *Ideas of Order in the Novels of Thomas Pynchon,* 1983; R. Newman, *Understanding Thomas Pynchon,* 1986; *Thomas Pynchon,* ed. H. Bloom, 1987; P. Seed, *The Fictional Labyrinths of Thomas Pynchon,* 1988; V. Price, *Christian Allusions in the Novels of Thomas Pynchon,* 1989; D. Eddins, *The Gnostic Pynchon,* 1990; J.

Dugdale, *Thomas Pynchon: Allusive Parables of Power,* 1990; J. Chambers, *Thomas Pynchon,* 1992; H. Berressem, *Pynchon's Poetics: Interfacing Theory and Text,* 1993; *Pynchon and Mason & Dixon,* ed. B. Horvath and I. Malin, 2000; *Thomas Pynchon: Reading from the Margins,* ed. N. Abbas, 2003; *Thomas Pynchon,* ed. H. Bloom, 2003.

TEXT: *Slow Learner,* 1984.

ENTROPY[1]

Boris has just given me a summary of his views. He is a weather prophet. The weather will continue bad, he says. There will be more calamities, more death, more despair. Not the slightest indication of a change anywhere. . . . We must get into step, a lockstep toward the prison of death. There is no escape. The weather will not change.

—*Tropic of Cancer*[2]

Downstairs, Meatball Mulligan's lease-breaking party was moving into its 40th hour. On the kitchen floor, amid a litter of empty champagne fifths, were Sandor Rojas and three friends, playing spit in the ocean and staying awake on Heidseck[3] and benzedrine pills. In the living room Duke, Vincent, Krinkles and Paco sat crouched over a 15-inch speaker which had been bolted into the top of a wastepaper basket, listening to 27 watts' worth of *The Heroes' Gate at Kiev.*[4] They all wore hornrimmed sunglasses and rapt expressions, and smoked funny-looking cigarettes which contained not, as you might expect, tobacco, but an adulterated form of *cannabis sativa.*[5] This group was the Duke di Angelis quartet. They recorded for a local label called Tambú and had to their credit one 10" LP entitled *Songs of Outer Space.*[6] From time to time one of them would flick the ashes from his cigarette into the speaker cone to watch them dance around. Meatball himself was sleeping over by the window, holding an empty magnum[7] to his chest as if it were a teddy bear. Several government girls, who worked for people like the State Department and NSA,[8] had passed out on couches, chairs and in one case the bathroom sink.

[1]A term used in several scientific fields to describe a state of chaos toward which all things inevitably degrade. In theoretical physics, entropy is reached when all matter has degraded to the same temperature and no heat energy is available for conversion to mechanical work. At that point the universe is said to have reached a state of "heat death." In communication theory, entropy is reached when communication ceases because the excessive flow of information overwhelms the ability to understand. In social theory, entropy is the state of chaos into which any society inevitably declines.

[2]Novel (1934) by the American writer Henry Miller (1891–1980).

[3]French champagne.

[4]"The Great Gate at Kiev," musical composition by the Russian composer Modest Petrovich Mussorgsky (1831–1881). In its orchestral version it portrays a triumphal procession accompanied by musical instruments, including bells and drums.

[5]Marijuana.

[6]An ironic title: In outer space, where there is no air to carry sound waves (the "airless void" cited later in the text), there can be no sound and therefore no songs.

[7]A large (1.5 liter) wine bottle.

[8]National Security Agency, intelligence-gathering agency of the U.S. government.

This was in early February of '57 and back then there were a lot of American expatriates around Washington, D.C., who would talk, every time they met you, about how someday they were going to go over to Europe for real but right now it seemed they were working for the government. Everyone saw a fine irony in this. They would stage, for instance, polyglot parties where the newcomer was sort of ignored if he couldn't carry on simultaneous conversations in three or four languages. They would haunt Armenian delicatessens for weeks at a stretch and invite you over for bulghour and lamb[9] in tiny kitchens whose walls were covered with bullfight posters. They would have affairs with sultry girls from Andalucía or the Midi[10] who studied economics at Georgetown. Their Dôme[11] was a collegiate Rathskeller out on Wisconsin Avenue called the Old Heidelberg and they had to settle for cherry blossoms instead of lime trees when spring came, but in its lethargic way their life provided, as they said, kicks.

At the moment, Meatball's party seemed to be gathering its second wind. Outside there was rain. Rain splatted against the tar paper on the roof and was fractured into a fine spray off the noses, eyebrows and lips of wooden gargoyles under the eaves, and ran like drool down the windowpanes. The day before, it had snowed and the day before that there had been winds of gale force and before that the sun had made the city glitter bright as April, though the calendar read early February. It is a curious season in Washington, this false spring. Somewhere in it are Lincoln's Birthday and the Chinese New Year, and a forlornness in the streets because cherry blossoms are weeks away still and, as Sarah Vaughan[12] has put it, spring will be a little late this year. Generally crowds like the one which would gather in the Old Heidelberg on weekday afternoons to drink Würtzburger[13] and to sing Lili Marlene[14] (not to mention The Sweetheart of Sigma Chi) are inevitably and incorrigibly Romantic. And as every good Romantic knows, the soul (*spiritus, ruach, pneuma*)[15] is nothing, substantially, but air; it is only natural that warpings in the atmosphere should be recapitulated in those who breathe it. So that over and above the public components—holidays, tourist attractions—there are private meanderings, linked to the climate as if this spell were a *stretto*[16] passage in the year's fugue: haphazard weather, aimless loves, unpredicted commitments: months one can easily spend *in* fugue, because oddly enough, later on, winds, rains, passions of February and March are never remembered in that city, it is as if they had never been.

The last bass notes of *The Heroes' Gate* boomed up through the floor and woke Callisto from an uneasy sleep. The first thing he became aware of was a small bird he had been holding gently between his hands, against his body. He turned his head sidewise on the pillow to smile down at it, at its blue hunched-down head and sick, lidded eyes, wondering how many more nights he would have to give it warmth before it was well again. He had been holding the bird

[9]Lamb cooked with bulgur (boiled) wheat, a dish of the Middle East.

[10]Andalucía: region of southern Spain; Midi: the south of France.

[11]Le Dôme, a Paris café, gathering place of writers, artists, and expatriate Americans in the 1920s.

[12]American jazz singer (1924–1990). She recorded the song "Spring Will Be a Little Late This Year" in 1953.

[13]Beer brewed in Würzburg, Germany.

[14]Sentimental German song, popular with German and Allied troops in World War II.

[15]"Soul" in Latin, Hebrew, and Greek.

[16]Italian: narrow, close. In music, the overlapping of musical statement and response in a fugue, when voices closely follow one another.

like that for three days: it was the only way he knew to restore its health. Next to him the girl stirred and whimpered, her arm thrown across her face. Mingled with the sounds of the rain came the first tentative, querulous morning voices of the other birds, hidden in philodendrons and small fan palms: patches of scarlet, yellow and blue laced through this Rousseau-like[17] fantasy, this hothouse jungle it had taken him seven years to weave together. Hermetically sealed, it was a tiny enclave of regularity in the city's chaos, alien to the vagaries of the weather, of national politics, of any civil disorder. Through trial-and-error Callisto had perfected its ecological balance, with the help of the girl its artistic harmony, so that the swayings of its plant life, the stirrings of its birds and human inhabitants were all as integral as the rhythms of a perfectly-executed mobile. He and the girl could no longer, of course, be omitted from that sanctuary; they had become necessary to its unity. What they needed from outside was delivered. They did not go out.

"Is he all right," she whispered. She lay like a tawny question mark facing him, her eyes suddenly huge and dark and blinking slowly. Callisto ran a finger beneath the feathers at the base of the bird's neck; caressed it gently. "He's going to be well, I think. See: he hears his friends beginning to wake up." The girl had heard the rain and the birds even before she was fully awake. Her name was Aubade: she was part French and part Annamese,[18] and she lived on her own curious and lonely planet, where the clouds and the odor of poincianas, the bitterness of wine and the accidental fingers at the small of her back or feathery against her breasts came to her reduced inevitably to the terms of sound: of music which emerged at intervals from a howling darkness of discordancy. "Aubade," he said, "go see." Obedient, she arose; padded to the window, pulled aside the drapes and after a moment said: "It is 37. Still 37." Callisto frowned. "Since Tuesday, then," he said. "No change." Henry Adams,[19] three generations before his own, had stared aghast at Power; Callisto found himself now in much the same state over Thermodynamics,[20] the inner life of that power, realizing like his predecessor that the Virgin and the dynamo stand as much for love as for power; that the two are indeed identical; and that love therefore not only makes the world go round but also makes the boccie ball spin, the nebula precess.[21] It was this latter or sidereal[22] element which disturbed him. The cosmologists had predicted an eventual heat-death for the universe (something like Limbo:[23] form and motion abolished, heat-energy identical at every point in it); the meteorologists, day-to-day, staved it off by contradicting with a reassuring array of varied temperatures.

[17]I.e., as in the exotic jungle scenes portrayed by the French artist Henri Rousseau (1844–1910). His jungle scenes were often painted in the hothouses of the Paris Botanical Gardens.

[18]From Annama, a region of Vietnam. [19]American historian (1838–1918).

[20]The three laws of thermodynamics state that energy in the world is constant and can neither be created nor destroyed; that heat must inevitably degrade to an equilibrium of uniform temperature (entropy); that there is an absolute zero temperature.

[21]A body of gas or dust (in interstellar space) that spins on an axis that itself rotates in a cone-shaped pattern, as the body of a top spins while at the same time its head also rotates in a wider circle.

[22]Relating to stars and constellations, astronomical.

[23]In theology, a place for the souls of the dead who are barred from heaven but do not deserve hell—a state of oblivion.

But for three days now, despite the changeful weather, the mercury had stayed at 37 degrees Fahrenheit. Leery at omens of apocalypse,[24] Callisto shifted beneath the covers. His fingers pressed the bird more firmly, as if needing some pulsing or suffering assurance of an early break in the temperature.

It was that last cymbal crash that did it. Meatball was hurled wincing into consciousness as the synchronized wagging of heads over the wastebasket stopped. The final hiss remained for an instant in the room, then melted into the whisper of rain outside. "Aarrgghh," announced Meatball in the silence, looking at the empty magnum. Krinkles, in slow motion, turned, smiled and held out a cigarette. "Tea time,[25] man," he said. "No, no," said Meatball. "How many times I got to tell you guys. Not at my place. You ought to know, Washington is lousy with Feds." Krinkles looked wistful. "Jeez, Meatball," he said, "you don't want to do nothing no more." "Hair of dog," said Meatball. "Only hope. Any juice left?" He began to crawl toward the kitchen. "No champagne, I don't think," Duke said. "Case of tequila behind the icebox." They put on an Earl Bostic[26] side. Meatball paused at the kitchen door, glowering at Sandor Rojas. "Lemons," he said after some thought. He crawled to the refrigerator and got out three lemons and some cubes, found the tequila and set about restoring order to his nervous system. He drew blood once cutting the lemons and had to use two hands squeezing them and his foot to crack the ice tray but after about ten minutes he found himself, through some miracle, beaming down into a monster tequila sour. "That looks yummy," Sandor Rojas said. "How about you make me one." Meatball blinked at him. "*Kitchi lofass a shegitbe,*"[27] he replied automatically, and wandered away into the bathroom. "I say," he called out a moment later to no one in particular. "I say, there seems to be a girl or something sleeping in the sink." He took her by the shoulders and shook. "Wha," she said. "You don't look too comfortable," Meatball said. "Well," she agreed. She stumbled to the shower, turned on the cold water and sat down crosslegged in the spray. "That's better," she smiled.

"Meatball," Sandor Rojas yelled from the kitchen. "Somebody is trying to come in the window. A burglar, I think. A second-story man." "What are you worrying about," Meatball said. "We're on the third floor." He loped back into the kitchen. A shaggy woebegone figure stood out on the fire escape, raking his fingernails down the windowpane. Meatball opened the window. "Saul," he said.

"Sort of wet out," Saul said. He climbed in, dripping. "You heard, I guess."

"Miriam left you," Meatball said, "or something, is all I heard."

There was a sudden flurry of knocking at the front door. "Do come in," Sandor Rojas called. The door opened and there were three coeds from George Washington, all of whom were majoring in philosophy. They were each holding a gallon of Chianti. Sandor leaped up and dashed into the living room. "We heard there was a party," one blonde said. "Young blood," Sandor shouted. He was an ex-Hungarian freedom fighter who had easily the worst chronic case of what certain critics of the middle class have called Don Giovannism[28] in

[24]A cosmic cataclysm that brings the end of the world. [25]I.e., Marijuana time.

[26]American jazz saxophonist and musical arranger (1913–1965).

[27]Hungarian slang: "Up yours."

[28]Compulsive woman-chasing, named for the licentious Don Juan (Italian: Don Giovanni) of Spanish legend.

the District of Columbia. *Purche porti la gonnella, voi sapete quel che fa.*[29] Like Pavlov's dog:[30] a contralto voice or a whiff of Arpège and Sandor would begin to salivate. Meatball regarded the trio blearily as they filed into the kitchen; he shrugged. "Put the wine in the icebox," he said "and good morning."

Aubade's neck made a golden bow as she bent over the sheets of foolscap, scribbling away in the green murk of the room. "As a young man at Princeton," Callisto was dictating, nestling the bird against the gray hairs of his chest, "Callisto had learned a mnemonic device for remembering the Laws of Thermodynamics: you can't win, things are going to get worse before they get better, who says they're going to get better. At the age of 54, confronted with Gibbs' notion of the universe,[31] he suddenly realized that undergraduate cant had been oracle, after all. That spindly maze of equations became, for him, a vision of ultimate, cosmic heat-death. He had known all along, of course, that nothing but a theoretical engine or system ever runs at 100% efficiency; and about the theorem of Clausius,[32] which states that the entropy of an isolated system always continually increases. It was not, however, until Gibbs and Boltzmann[33] brought to this principle the methods of statistical mechanics that the horrible significance of it all dawned on him: only then did he realize that the isolated system—galaxy, engine, human being, culture, whatever—must evolve spontaneously toward the Condition of the More Probable. He was forced, therefore, in the sad dying fall of middle age, to a radical reevaluation of everything he had learned up to then; all the cities and seasons and casual passions of his days had now to be looked at in a new and elusive light. He did not know if he was equal to the task. He was aware of the dangers of the reductive fallacy[34] and, he hoped, strong enough not to drift into the graceful decadence of an enervated fatalism. His had always been a vigorous, Italian sort of pessimism: like Machiavelli,[35] he allowed the forces of *virtù* and *fortuna*[36] to be about 50/50; but the equations now introduced a random factor which pushed the odds to some unutterable and indeterminate ratio which he found himself afraid to calculate." Around him loomed vague hothouse shapes; the pitifully small heart fluttered against his own. Counterpointed against his words the girl heard the chatter of birds and fitful car honkings scattered along the wet morning and Earl Bostic's alto rising in occasional wild peaks through the floor. The architectonic purity of her world was constantly threatened by such hints of anarchy: gaps and excrescences and skew lines, and a shifting or tilting of planes to

[29]Italian: If she wears a skirt, you know what he'll do, from the servant Leporello's catalogue of Don Giovanni's sexual conquests, in Act I of the opera *Don Giovanni* (1787) by Wolfgang Amadeus Mozart (1756–1791).

[30]The Russian physiologist Ivan Petrovich Pavlov (1849–1936) created in his dog a conditioned reflex that caused it automatically to salivate at the sound of a bell.

[31]Josiah Willard Gibbs (1839–1903), American physicist who formulated statistical equations to show how matter degrades toward entropy.

[32]Rudolph Clausius (1822–1888), German physicist who developed the idea of entropy (1865).

[33]Ludwig Boltzmann (1844–1906), Austrian physicist who developed a scientific law stating the ratio of a molecule's temperature to its energy: the higher the temperature, the higher the energy.

[34]The error of oversimplifying, reducing complex matters to easy simplicities.

[35]Niccolò Machiavelli (1469–1527), Italian diplomat and author of *The Prince* (1532), a book of political theorizing that gave advice to rulers and expressed a pessimistic view of humankind.

[36]Italian: virtue and chance.

which she had continually to readjust lest the whole structure shiver into a disarray of discrete and meaningless signals. Callisto had described the process once as a kind of "feedback": she crawled into dreams each night with a sense of exhaustion, and a desperate resolve never to relax that vigilance. Even in the brief periods when Callisto made love to her, soaring above the bowing of taut nerves in haphazard double-stops[37] would be the one singing string of her determination.

"Nevertheless," continued Callisto, "he found in entropy or the measure of disorganization for a closed system an adequate metaphor to apply to certain phenomena in his own world. He saw, for example, the younger generation responding to Madison Avenue with the same spleen his own had once reserved for Wall Street: and in American 'consumerism' discovered a similar tendency from the least to the most probable, from differentiation to sameness, from ordered individuality to a kind of chaos. He found himself, in short, restating Gibbs' prediction in social terms, and envisioned a heat-death for his culture in which ideas, like heat-energy, would no longer be transferred, since each point in it would ultimately have the same quantity of energy; and intellectual motion would, accordingly, cease." He glanced up suddenly. "Check it now," he said. Again she rose and peered out at the thermometer. "37," she said. "The rain has stopped." He bent his head quickly and held his lips against a quivering wing. "Then it will change soon," he said, trying to keep his voice firm.

Sitting on the stove Saul was like any big rag doll that a kid has been taking out some incomprehensible rage on. "What happened," Meatball said. "If you feel like talking, I mean."

"Of course I feel like talking," Saul said. "One thing I did, I slugged her."

"Discipline must be maintained."

"Ha, ha. I wish you'd been there. Oh Meatball, it was a lovely fight. She ended up throwing a *Handbook of Chemistry and Physics* at me, only it missed and went through the window, and when the glass broke I reckon something in her broke too. She stormed out of the house crying, out in the rain. No raincoat or anything."

"She'll be back."

"No."

"Well." Soon Meatball said: "It was something earth-shattering, no doubt. Like who is better, Sal Mineo or Ricky Nelson."

"What it was about," Saul said, "was communication theory. Which of course makes it very hilarious."

"I don't know anything about communication theory."

"Neither does my wife. Come right down to it, who does? That's the joke."

When Meatball saw the kind of smile Saul had on his face he said: "Maybe you would like tequila or something."

"No. I mean, I'm sorry. It's a field you can go off the deep end in, is all. You get where you're watching all the time for security cops: behind bushes, around corners. MUFFET is top secret."

"Wha."

"Multi-unit factorial field electronic tabulator."

[37]Playing two notes simultaneously on adjacent strings of a musical instrument such as a violin.

"You were fighting about that."

"Miriam has been reading science fiction again. That and *Scientific American.* It seems she is, as we say, bugged at this idea of computers acting like people. I made the mistake of saying you can just as well turn that around, and talk about human behavior like a program fed into an IBM machine."

"Why not," Meatball said.

"Indeed, why not. In fact it is sort of crucial to communication, not to mention information theory. Only when I said that she hit the roof. Up went the balloon. And I can't figure out *why*. If anybody should know why, I should. I refuse to believe the government is wasting taxpayers' money on me, when it has so many bigger and better things to waste it on."

Meatball made a moue.[38] "Maybe she thought you were acting like a cold, dehumanized amoral scientist type."

"My god," Saul flung up an arm. "Dehumanized. How much more human can I get? I worry, Meatball, I do. There are Europeans wandering around North Africa these days with their tongues torn out of their heads because those tongues have spoken the wrong words. Only the Europeans thought they were the right words."

"Language barrier," Meatball suggested.

Saul jumped down off the stove. "That," he said, angry, "is a good candidate for sick joke of the year. No, ace, it is *not* a barrier. If it is anything it's a kind of leakage. Tell a girl: 'I love you.' No trouble with two-thirds of that, it's a closed circuit. Just you and she. But that nasty four-letter word in the middle, *that's* the one you have to look out for. Ambiguity. Redundance. Irrelevance, even. Leakage. All this is noise. Noise screws up your signal, makes for disorganization in the circuit."

Meatball shuffled around. "Well, now, Saul," he muttered, "you're sort of, I don't know, expecting a lot from people. I mean, you know. What it is is, most of the things we say, I guess, are mostly noise."

"Ha! Half of what you just said, for example."

"Well, you do it too."

"I know," Saul smiled grimly. "It's a bitch, ain't it."

"I bet that's what keeps divorce lawyers in business. Whoops."

"Oh I'm not sensitive. Besides," frowning, "you're right. You find I think that most 'successful' marriages—Miriam and me, up to last night—are sort of founded on compromises. You never run at top efficiency, usually all you have is a minimum basis for a workable thing. I believe the phrase is Togetherness."

"Aarrgghh."

"Exactly. You find that one a bit noisy, don't you. But the noise content is different for each of us because you're a bachelor and I'm not. Or wasn't. The hell with it."

"Well sure," Meatball said, trying to be helpful, "you were using different words. By 'human being' you meant something that you can look at like it was a computer. It helps you think better on the job or something. But Miriam meant something entirely—"

"The hell with it."

Meatball fell silent. "I'll take that drink," Saul said after a while.

[38]A grimace.

The card game had been abandoned and Sandor's friends were slowly getting wasted on tequila. On the living room couch, one of the coeds and Krinkles were engaged in amorous conversation. "No," Krinkles was saying, "no, I can't put Dave[39] *down*. In fact I give Dave a lot of credit, man. Especially considering his accident and all." The girl's smile faded. "How terrible," she said. "What accident?" "Hadn't you heard?" Krinkles said. "When Dave was in the army, just a private E-2, they sent him down to Oak Ridge[40] on special duty. Something to do with the Manhattan Project. He was handling hot stuff one day and got an overdose of radiation. So now he's got to wear lead gloves all the time." She shook her head sympathetically. "What an awful break for a piano-player."

Meatball had abandoned Saul to a bottle of tequila and was about to go to sleep in a closet when the front door flew open and the place was invaded by five enlisted personnel of the U.S. Navy, all in varying stages of abomination. "This is the place," shouted a fat, pimply seaman apprentice who had lost his white hat. "This here is the hoorhouse that chief was telling us about." A stringy-looking 3rd class boatswain's mate pushed him aside and cased the living room. "You're right, Slab," he said. "But it don't look like much, even for Stateside. I seen better tail in Naples, Italy." "How much, hey," boomed a large seaman with adenoids, who was holding a Mason jar full of white lightning.[41] "Oh, my god," said Meatball.

Outside the temperature remained constant at 37 degrees Fahrenheit. In the hothouse Aubade stood absently caressing the branches of a young mimosa, hearing a motif of sap-rising, the rough and unresolved anticipatory theme of those fragile pink blossoms which, it is said, insure fertility. That music rose in a tangled tracery: arabesques of order competing fugally with the improvised discords of the party downstairs, which peaked sometimes in cusps and ogees of noise. That precious signal-to-noise ratio, whose delicate balance required every calorie of her strength, seesawed inside the small tenuous skull as she watched Callisto, sheltering the bird. Callisto was trying to confront any idea of the heat-death now, as he nuzzled the feathery lump in his hands. He sought correspondences. Sade,[42] of course. And Temple Drake,[43] gaunt and hopeless in her little park in Paris, at the end of *Sanctuary*. Final equilibrium. *Nightwood*.[44] And the tango.[45] Any tango, but more than any perhaps the sad sick dance in Stravinsky's *L'Histoire du Soldat*.[46] He

[39]The American jazz pianist Dave Brubeck (1920–). Krinkles's story is a farcical explanation of the "heavy hands" said to characterize Brubeck's playing.

[40]Oak Ridge, Tennessee, where radioactive materials were prepared for the Manhattan Project, the program to produce the atom bomb.

[41]Illicit whiskey, "moonshine."

[42]The Marquis de Sade (1740–1814), French writer associated with sadism and other sexual perversions.

[43]Character in the lurid novel *Sanctuary* (1931) by William Faulkner (1897–1962). At the end of the novel she is sitting, morally debased, in the Luxembourg Gardens of Paris.

[44]Psychological novel (1937) about decadent American expatriates living in Paris in the 1920s, by Djuna Barnes (1892–1982).

[45]Argentine ballroom dance introduced to Europe in 1912. Thought to be licentious and corrupting, it nevertheless became widely popular by the 1920s.

[46]French: "The Story of a Soldier," a musical composition by Igor Stravinsky (1882–1971), avant-garde Russian composer.

thought back: what had tango music been for them after the war, what meanings had he missed in all the stately coupled automatons in the *cafés-dansants,*[47] or in the metronomes which had ticked behind the eyes of his own partners? Not even the clean constant winds of Switzerland could cure the *grippe espagnole:*[48] Stravinsky had had it, they all had had it. And how many musicians were left after Passchendaele, after the Marne?[49] It came down in this case to seven: violin, double-bass. Clarinet, bassoon. Cornet, trombone. Tympani. Almost as if any tiny troupe of saltimbanques[50] had set about conveying the same information as a full pit-orchestra.[51] There was hardly a full complement left in Europe. Yet with violin and tympani Stravinsky had managed to communicate in that tango the same exhaustion, the same airlessness one saw in the slicked-down youths who were trying to imitate Vernon Castle,[52] and in their mistresses, who simply did not care. *Ma maîtresse.*[53] Celeste. Returning to Nice after the second war he had found that café replaced by a perfume shop which catered to American tourists. And no secret vestige of her in the cobblestones or in the old pension[54] next door; no perfume to match her breath heavy with the sweet Spanish wine she always drank. And so instead he had purchased a Henry Miller novel and left for Paris, and read the book on the train so that when he arrived he had been given at least a little forewarning. And saw that Celeste and the others and even Temple Drake were not all that had changed. "Aubade," he said, "my head aches." The sound of his voice generated in the girl an answering scrap of melody. Her movement toward the kitchen, the towel, the cold water, and his eyes following her formed a weird and intricate canon; as she placed the compress on his forehead his sigh of gratitude seemed to signal a new subject, another series of modulations.

"No," Meatball was still saying, "no, I'm afraid not. This is not a house of ill repute. I'm sorry, really I am." Slab was adamant. "But the chief said," he kept repeating. The seaman offered to swap the moonshine for a good piece. Meatball looked around frantically, as if seeking assistance. In the middle of the room, the Duke di Angelis quartet were engaged in a historic moment. Vincent was seated and the others standing: they were going through the motions of a group having a session, only without instruments. "I say," Meatball said. Duke moved his head a few times, smiled faintly, lit a cigarette, and eventually caught sight of Meatball. "Quiet, man," he whispered. Vincent began to fling his arms around, his fists clenched; then, abruptly, was still, then repeated the performance. This went on for a few minutes while Meatball sipped his drink moodily. The navy had withdrawn to the kitchen. Finally at some invisible signal the group stopped tapping their feet and Duke grinned and said, "At least we ended together."

[47]French: dance halls, nightclubs.
[48]French: Spanish flu, name given the worldwide influenza epidemic of 1918.
[49]Passchendaele in Belgium and the Marne in France, battlefields of World War I.
[50]French: performers, buffoons.
[51]Orchestra that plays in the orchestra pit of a theater or opera house.
[52]English ballroom dancer (1887–1918), widely popular in the United States and Europe before World War I.
[53]French: My mistress. [54]Boardinghouse.

Meatball glared at him. "I say," he said. "I have this new conception, man," Duke said. "You remember your namesake. You remember Gerry."[55]

"No," said Meatball. "I'll remember April, if that's any help."

"As a matter of fact," Duke said, "it was Love for Sale. Which shows how much you know. The point is, it was Mulligan, Chet Baker and that crew, way back then, out yonder. You dig?"

"Baritone sax," Meatball said. "Something about a baritone sax."

"But no piano, man. No guitar. Or accordion. You know what that means."

"Not exactly," Meatball said.

"Well first let me just say, that I am no Mingus, no John Lewis.[56] Theory was never my strong point. I mean things like reading were always difficult for me and all—"

"I know," Meatball said drily. "You got your card[57] taken away because you changed key on Happy Birthday at a Kiwanis Club picnic."

"Rotarian. But it occurred to me, in one of these flashes of insight, that if that first quartet of Mulligan's had no piano, it could only mean one thing."

"No chords," said Paco, the baby-faced bass.

"What he is trying to say," Duke said, "is no root chords.[58] Nothing to listen to while you blow a horizontal line. What one does in such a case is, one *thinks* the roots."

A horrified awareness was dawning on Meatball. "And the next logical extension," he said.

"Is to think everything," Duke announced with simple dignity. "Roots, line, everything."

Meatball looked at Duke, awed. "But," he said.

"Well," Duke said modestly, "there are a few bugs to work out."

"But," Meatball said.

"Just listen," Duke said. "You'll catch on." And off they went again into orbit, presumably somewhere around the asteroid belt.[59] After a while Krinkles made an embouchure[60] and started moving his fingers and Duke clapped his hand to his forehead. "Oaf!" he roared. "The new head[61] we're using, you remember, I wrote last night?" "Sure," Krinkles said, "the new head. I come in on the bridge. All your heads I come in then." "Right," Duke said. "So why—" "Wha," said Krinkles, "16 bars, I wait, I come in—" "16?" Duke said. "No. No, Krinkles. Eight you waited. You want me to sing it? A cigarette that bears a lipstick's traces, an airline ticket to romantic places." Krinkles scratched his head. "These Foolish Things, you mean." "Yes," Duke said, "yes, Krinkles. Bravo." "Not I'll Remember April," Krinkles said. "*Minghe morte,*"[62] said Duke, "I *figured* we were playing it a little slow," Krinkles said. Meatball chuckled. "Back to the old drawing board," he said. "No, man," Duke said, "back to the airless void." And they took

[55]Gerry Mulligan (1927–1996), jazz saxophonist and arranger. In the 1950s he led a "piano-less" jazz quartet that included the trumpeter Chet Baker (1929–1988).

[56]Charlie Mingus: bass player and composer (1929–1979); John Lewis (1920–2001), pianist and composer.

[57]Musicians' union card.

[58]The harmonic base of a musical piece, a takeoff point from which improvisation can develop.

[59]Distant belt of small planets and fragments that circles Earth between the orbits of Mars and Jupiter.

[60]The form of the lips in playing a wind instrument.

[61]The beginning of a piece of music, the lead-in.

[62]Italian vulgar slang: "Dead prick."

off again, only it seemed Paco was playing in G sharp while the rest were in E flat, so they had to start all over.

In the kitchen two of the girls from George Washington and the sailors were singing Let's All Go Down and Piss on the Forrestal.[63] There was a two-handed, bilingual *morra*[64] game on over by the icebox. Saul had filled several paper bags with water and was sitting on the fire escape, dropping them on passersby in the street. A fat government girl in a Bennington sweatshirt, recently engaged to an ensign attached to the Forrestal, came charging into the kitchen, head lowered, and butted Slab in the stomach. Figuring this was as good an excuse for a fight as any, Slab's buddies piled in. The *morra* players were nose-to-nose, screaming *trois, sette*[65] at the tops of their lungs. From the shower the girl Meatball had taken out of the sink announced that she was drowning. She had apparently sat on the drain and the water was now up to her neck. The noise in Meatball's apartment had reached a sustained, ungodly crescendo.

Meatball stood and watched, scratching his stomach lazily. The way he figured, there were only about two ways he could cope: (a) lock himself in the closet and maybe eventually they would all go away, or (b) try to calm everybody down, one by one. (a) was certainly the more attractive alternative. But then he started thinking about that closet. It was dark and stuffy and he would be alone. He did not feature being alone. And then this crew off the good ship Lollipop or whatever it was might take it upon themselves to kick down the closet door, for a lark. And if that happened he would be, at the very least, embarrassed. The other way was more a pain in the neck, but probably better in the long run.

So he decided to try and keep his lease-breaking party from deteriorating into total chaos: he gave wine to the sailors and separated the *morra* players; he introduced the fat government girl to Sandor Rojas, who would keep her out of trouble; he helped the girl in the shower to dry off and get into bed; he had another talk with Saul; he called a repairman for the refrigerator, which someone had discovered was on the blink. This is what he did until nightfall, when most of the revellers had passed out and the party trembled on the threshold of its third day.

Upstairs Callisto, helpless in the past, did not feel the faint rhythm inside the bird begin to slacken and fail. Aubade was by the window, wandering the ashes of her own lovely world; the temperature held steady, the sky had become a uniform darkening gray. Then something from downstairs—a girl's scream, an overturned chair, a glass dropped on the floor, he would never know what exactly—pierced that private time-warp and he became aware of the faltering, the constriction of muscles, the tiny tossings of the bird's head; and his own pulse began to pound more fiercely, as if trying to compensate. "Aubade," he called weakly, "he's dying." The girl, flowing and rapt, crossed the hothouse to gaze down at Callisto's hands. The two remained like that, poised, for one minute, and two, while the heartbeat ticked a graceful diminuendo down at last into stillness. Callisto raised his head slowly. "I held him," he protested, impotent with the wonder of it, "to give him the warmth of my body. Almost as if I were communicating life to him, or a sense of life. What has happened? Has the transfer of heat ceased to work? Is there no more. . . ." He did not finish.

[63]U.S. Navy aircraft carrier named after James Forrestal (1892–1949), U.S. secretary of defense (1947–1949).

[64]Italian game in which one player guesses the number of fingers raised by another player.

[65]*Trois,* French: three; *sette,* Italian: seven.

"I was just at the window," she said. He sank back, terrified. She stood a moment more, irresolute; she had sensed his obsession long ago, realized somehow that that constant 37 was now decisive. Suddenly then, as if seeing the single and unavoidable conclusion to all this she moved swiftly to the window before Callisto could speak; tore away the drapes and smashed out the glass with two exquisite hands which came away bleeding and glistening with splinters; and turned to face the man on the bed and wait with him until the moment of equilibrium was reached, when 37 degrees Fahrenheit should prevail both outside and inside, and forever, and the hovering, curious dominant of their separate lives should resolve into a tonic of darkness[66] and the final absence of all motion.

1958–1959 1960, 1984

James Welch 1940–2003

James Welch is considered both an early central figure in the "Native American Renaissance" and a major contributor to late twentieth-century American literature. He was born in 1940 in Browning, Montana, on the Blackfoot Reservation in the northwest corner of the state, to a Gros Ventre mother and a Blackfeet father. He attended reservation schools as a child before graduating from high school in Minneapolis, Minnesota. Welch then studied as an undergraduate at the University of Minnesota, Northern Montana College, and the University of Montana, where he earned his B.A. in 1965. Having decided to pursue a writing career, he enrolled in the M.F.A. program at the University of Montana and apprenticed under acclaimed poet Richard Hugo, who encouraged him to turn to his Native American culture for the subject matter of his writing.

In 1971 Welch published his first book, a volume of poems titled Riding the Earthboy 40. *It brought him widespread recognition almost immediately. His next two works,* Winter in the Blood *(1974) and* The Death of Jim Loney *(1979), both novels, earned him international critical attention. Both novels deal with the difficulty of Native Americans facing the cultural conflict of living in the late twentieth-century United States while at the same time feeling the pull of their heritage as Native Americans. In 1986 he solidified his standing as an important writer with the publication of his third novel* Fools Crow, *which shifted from the contemporary scene of the previous novels to a nineteenth-century historical context.* Fools Crow *was an enormous commercial success and also won numerous major awards, including the American Book Award and the Los Angeles Times Book Prize. In the 1990s he produced the novel* The Indian Lawyer *(1990) and the nonfiction book* Killing Custer: The Battle of Little Bighorn and the Fate of the Plains Indians *(1994), which he co-authored with documentary filmmaker Paul Stekler. His last novel,* The Heartsong of Charging Elk, *again set in nineteenth-century America, appeared in 2000. James Welch died of cancer in 2003 at the age of 62.*

[66]I.e., a return to the original darkness. A musical tonic is the beginning note to which a piece of music typically returns (resolves)

FURTHER READING: A. Velie, *Four American Indian Literary Masters: N. Scott Momaday, James Welch, Leslie Marmon Silko, and Gerald Vizenor,* 1982; L. Coltelli, *Winged Words: American Indian Writers Speak,* 1990; R. Gish, *Beyond Bounds: Cross-Cultural Essays on Anglo, American Indian, and Chicano Literature,* 1996; R. McFarland, *Understanding James Welch,* 2000; B. Schorcht, *Storied Voices in Native American Texts: Harry Robinson, Thomas King, James Welch, and Leslie Marmon Silko,* 2003; M. Lupton, *James Welch: A Critical Companion,* 2004.

TEXT: *The Death of Jim Loney,* 1987.

from *THE DEATH OF JIM LONEY*

[Jim Loney, a man of white and Native American parentage, lives in the small town of Harlem, Montana. He has, as the narrator puts it, "become something of a non-person, as one only can in a small town." Disconnected from tribal life and white culture, Loney searches memories of the parents who abandoned him and his odd dreams for a way to make sense of his life, descending into an alcoholism driven by resignation. As the holidays approach, his sister, a successful Washington D.C. businessperson, and his girlfriend, a schoolteacher from Texas, are scheming to rescue him by getting him out of Harlem.]

17

"You don't talk much anymore. Used to be we couldn't shut you up. What the hell's the matter with you?"

"Cat's got my tongue."

"Well, something's sure funny here. When I saw you coming out of the liquor store, I thought, Hey, what the hell's going on, me and Loney used to be the best of friends, he used to be the best friend I ever had. . . ." Pretty Weasel shook a cigarette out of Loney's pack.

"Times have changed," Loney said and he said it deliberately, for his own benefit. He felt small beside Pretty Weasel, as though they had been growing physically apart, he smaller, Pretty Weasel bigger.

"We can remedy that in a damn hurry."

"Yes," said Loney and he almost laughed.

Pretty Weasel lit the cigarette from Loney's and watched the smoke go away from him. He didn't smoke, ever, but he thought of the cigarette as a kind of offering. "I'm in with the old man. You knew that, didn't you?" He would start with this.

And Loney said, "That's what you came back for."

"Naw—you think that? I'll tell you why I came back—because I couldn't stand those people down there. You know why. Because they put the pressure on me, all this Indian bullshit. You know what they called me in the newspaper? Super Chief."

"That's what we used to call you."

"That was different. Up here it didn't mean anything."

"What did it mean down there?"

"Indian play basketball good, Indian friend of the white man. I don't mean maybe, either."

Loney thought about this. In the service they had called *him* Chief and he was only half Indian. It always startled Loney that when he stepped out of his day-to-day existence he was considered an Indian. He never felt Indian. Indians were people like the Cross Guns, the Old Chiefs—Amos After Buffalo. They lived an Indian way, at least tried. When Loney thought of Indians, he thought of the reservation families, all living under one roof, the old ones passing down the wisdom of their years, of their family's years, of their tribe's years, and the young ones soaking up their history, their places in their history, with a wisdom that went beyond age.

He remembered when the Cross Guns family used to come to town. The car would be full of adults and kids, and when they scattered to their various appointments, only old Emil Cross Guns would be left, sitting in the back seat in his black suit coat and black hat, black neckerchief knotted around his ropy old neck. Loney recalled going up to the window and touching his hand and the old man saying something in Gros Ventre.[1] All the kids used to touch his hand because he was a medicine man. It was Pretty Weasel who had told Loney that Emil had cured his older sister of infantile paralysis.

Emil was dead now and those days were gone to Loney. Everything was changed and the old ones did not exist. Even Pretty Weasel came from a different kind of family. Both his father and his mother had gone to college, back in the days when Indians didn't go to college. And his father had been tribal chairman for a number of years. There was a picture in their house of him shaking hands with President Eisenhower. Now he was old, but in a white man way, thrown away. Not like Emil Cross Guns.

Loney thought this and he grew sad, not for Pretty Weasel's father, nor for Emil Cross Guns, but for himself. He had no family and he wasn't Indian or white. He remembered the day he and Rhea had driven out to the Little Rockies. She had said he was lucky to have two sets of ancestors. In truth he had none.

"Pheasant, my man," said Pretty Weasel. "We're going after those wily ones tomorrow."

Loney looked up and beyond Pretty Weasel and was astonished to see Rhea hurry by him.

18

Once outside, Rhea ran the half block to her car. The stores were still open but the street was virtually deserted. She ran and the air was cold and she felt her eyes fill with tears. For a brief practical moment she felt that she should have said goodbye, but to whom? This is crazy, she thought, and she started her car and backed out into the street. She put the car into forward gear and it jumped forward, then stalled. "Damn you," she said. "Damn you." She glanced toward Kennedy's and she saw a figure standing in the light. At first she thought it was the college boy, but when the figure stepped off the curb and walked toward

[1]The language of the Gros Ventre Native American people.

the car, she recognized Loney. She wiped the tears from the corners of her eyes with a gloved hand.

She rolled down her window and said, "Hello." Then she said, "Get in." She said it almost coyly and the anger returned. She didn't need to be coy anymore.

Loney walked around the car and got in. He seemed wary and he closed and locked the door behind him as if to shut out a threatening crowd. But the street was virtually deserted as Rhea started the car and put it in gear. Neither of them looked in the store windows and she felt as though they were the only souls out in Harlem. She drove past her street and then past his street and soon they were on the outskirts of town where the main street met the new highway. Rhea turned left onto the highway and drove slowly toward the agency and the reservation. She didn't know what else to do.

Finally she said, "What is it that troubles you?"

Loney looked down at his hands and he discovered that he still had the bottle of wine in the paper sack. Without thinking, he twisted the top and he heard the paper tear and the metal cap break free. "I've been bad to you," he said. "Partly that—I've been very bad to you." He tightened the cap and he looked out the window and saw the lights of the agency twinkling through the dark cottonwoods along the Milk River. "I think you should never have met me." The fields were covered with an old snow.

"But what is it that really troubles you? For pity's sake, don't you know I want to help you?"

"It's not something . . . I don't even know myself. It has to do with the past." But Loney realized this wasn't good enough. He had thought and said it too often to believe it anymore. "It has to do with certain things. I know it has to do with my mother and father, but there are other things. It has to do with an aunt I lived with when I was a kid. I loved her and she died. That's okay. It was enough to love her. But I would like to know who she really was and how she died and why. I don't know."

Rhea felt her hands loosen on the steering wheel. She hadn't realized how tense she had been. But Loney was talking finally and she held her breath, in her mind urging him on.

"I know this is kind of strange, but I see a bird—I don't know what kind of bird it is—but I see it every night. Sometimes it flies slowly enough so that I can almost study it, but even then . . . it is a bird I've never seen in real life. I don't know. It comes and I look at it and then it fades away."

"Is it a dream?"

"It comes when I'm awake, but late at night when I'm tired—or drunk." Loney was silent for a moment. Then he said, "I don't know what this has to do with anything, certainly it has nothing to do with my aunt. It just comes every night, and every night I think, This must have some meaning. Sometimes I think it is a vision sent by my mother's people. I must interpret it, but I don't know how."

Loney paused again, then sighed. "There is a Bible phrase. It's crazy. It popped into my mind a couple of months ago at a football game. 'Turn away from man in whose nostrils is breath, for of what account is he?'[2] I haven't looked it up because I'm afraid I will find it and it will be bad."

[2]Isaiah 2:22: "Cease ye from man, whose breath is in his nostrils: for wherein is he to be accounted of?"

"It's from Isaiah," said Rhea.

Loney looked at her. "I think of it quite a bit. It just pops into my mind and I don't know how I know it. I went to a Catholic boarding school, and then I lived in a minister's house—it must come from one or the other. The minister was kind of a screwball. Maybe he put it in my mind. The point is, it's there and it bothers me. I want to make a little sense out of my life and all I get are crazy visions and Bible phrases. They're like puzzles."

By now they were almost to the bridge that spanned the Milk River. A few hundred yards beyond stood the entrance to the agency. Rhea had never actually been to the agency, but she knew there was a hospital back in there, along with some office buildings and a community of government houses. One of her best students, Arlene Small, lived out here with her mother. Arlene, like most of her Indian students, was shy, and Rhea had often wished she could take the girl home with her, to get to know her, but there were barriers. There were always barriers, some artificial, some natural.

She heard the tires hum as they crossed the bridge and she heard herself say, "You have decided not to come to Seattle."

"I can't. Not yet."

And Rhea heard herself again: "Did it ever occur to you that if you left you would leave these . . . visions behind? You might become so involved with a new life that your past would fade away—that bird would fade away for good."

"I don't know that I want that to happen."

Rhea slowed the car and turned off at the entrance to the agency. She held her wrist close to the illuminated dash panel. Her watch said 8:30. It felt more like midnight. She drove the lane back into the agency and as she neared the hospital, she said, "I'm going home first. I'll gather myself together, then I'll make a decision." She watched a dog trot past them on the other side of the road. Its tongue was hanging out and it ignored them. Rhea said, "What did you offer me? No, I'm talking to myself. What did you offer me?" She turned right at the hospital, toward some buildings. There was a moon, a half moon, and it struck the snow and the white buildings and Rhea could see the small rectangular houses beyond. "I think you offered me love. Is that correct? Not an all-consuming love, by any means, but a love I wasn't familiar with, without obligation, without pretense. An unpretentious love. A year's worth. More than I deserved, less than fulfilling. But love."

Loney wasn't used to that word. He said, "Yes," but he looked out his window.

Rhea looked past him and they were in the small housing project. Most of the picture windows were bare, without curtains, without lamps or light. But a couple had Christmas trees in them; the blues and reds and yellows of their ornaments and lights seemed festive and otherworldly. She wondered vaguely which house Arlene Small lived in. "It's almost Christmas," she said softly. And she thought, Why am I off the track? What is there about us that puts me off the track so easily? And she said, "We're finished. . . ."

"It would be for the best."

"It seems so simple."

"It's not."

"No, of course not. This is your country, isn't it? It means a great deal to you."

Loney thought for a moment. "I've never understood it. Once in a while I look around and I see things familiar and I think I will die here. It's my country then. Other times I want to leave, to see other things, to meet people, to die elsewhere."

"Why must you think of it in terms of dying?" Rhea turned the car around the small square. "Is it just a matter of dying?

Don't you want other things? It seems so limiting."

For the first time in a long time Loney laughed. "I'm sorry," he said. "I'm sorry."

"Don't be. Please laugh some more. It sounds so good after so long. It was a dumb thing to say, wasn't it?"

"I wish it was. It wasn't, though. Dying *is* limiting. Thinking about it is even more so, in a way."

"I hate to think of me leaving and you thinking about dying. It seems so pointless, our having been together."

"I won't think of it anymore." Loney looked at Rhea in the half light of the moonlit car. "It was the wrong thing. I don't want you to go, but I don't have enough in me to make you want to stay."

The hospital was dark brick and serene and Rhea turned again onto the lane that led to the entrance to the agency. "I won't stay," she said. The moonlight got brighter off the snow and she said, "I will not stay here." She felt dry inside and she said, "Nothing can make me stay here without you."

19

Loney couldn't sleep because if he slept he would dream, so he stared into the blackness of the small bedroom. From time to time he would roll over onto his side and grope for the bottle of wine beside the bed. He tried to think of nothing, but many thoughts came out of the dark and left him bewildered. He thought he had not blinked in a long time and so he blinked. He thought he heard Swipesy moan in the kitchen but the dog had been dead since Thanksgiving. And he thought it strange that he hadn't missed Swipesy at all, and yet he never thought of him as being dead. Just as he didn't think of Sandra as being dead. Or Kate as being gone for good. Or Rhea as leaving for good. He had wiped the slate clean, but it didn't occur to him.

He lay in bed and dreaded dawn. Pretty Weasel would come to take him hunting and he had no desire to hunt or to see Pretty Weasel. And he thought, After tomorrow I will have no future. Everybody and everything will be gone out of my life. Kate was right—I have nothing left, no conviction, no spirit. After tomorrow's slim purpose I will simply exist.

He lit another cigarette and smoked for a moment without thinking. Suddenly an image of his father as a younger man drifted into his mind. He saw the slick hair and the slightly too large ears and the white shirt. He was carrying a shotgun and Loney recognized it as his father's sixteen-gauge. He carried it against his chest as though he were posing for a picture and Loney remembered that picture from out of his past. Then the vision Loney had had a month before exploded in the darkness and his father was covered with snow and ice and he was grinning as he pressed the gun into Loney's hands.

Loney sat up and swung his legs off the bed. He was sweating and he felt sick. His father was still here. He was the last one left to Loney.

He hurried into the kitchen, across the cold linoleum, and switched on the light above the sink. He looked at the clock beside the refrigerator. Three thirty-five. Swipesy growled and Loney whirled around, but there was no dog.

He turned on the lamp on the kitchen table and then he looked out the window and he saw his father grinning in at him. He wasn't covered with snow and ice, but his face was blue.

Loney opened his mouth. Then he motioned for his father to come in, but his father only grinned. "Get out of here, you sonofabitch!" he yelled. And his father moved back into the darkness. Loney ran outside and stood at the corner of the house. He looked toward the street but he saw no movement. He saw nothing until he looked toward his window and he saw the large flakes falling against the yellow light. His feet began to burn and he realized he was barefoot.

Three or four inches of new snow lay on the frozen ground. As his eyes adjusted, Loney found that it was not dark; the snow had lit the night to a dull clear gray. He looked out into the backyard toward the garage and he saw Swipesy sniffing the base of a cottonwood tree. He whistled and the dog looked up. For an instant it seemed to recognize Loney. Then it took off, disappearing beyond the garage.

"No pheasant today!" Loney called after the dog.

Back in his bedroom, he dressed himself. As he pulled the warm socks over his burning feet he wondered why Pretty Weasel would want to hunt together after all these years. When Pretty Weasel first suggested it, Loney thought it must be a test. But a test of what? Guts? Ability? It didn't make sense. Pretty Weasel had the drop on him in both departments. Friendship? How could that be? Pretty Weasel didn't need friends. Loney reached for his wine and his eyes got wet. A kind of hopelessness burned through the early morning hangover. He was hung over most of the time now. It had nothing to do with headaches and bad stomach. It was more a general numbness and a general forgetfulness of all but the most whimsical detail, the most random thought. Now he thought of the day Pretty Weasel went away to college. Loney and George Yellow Eyes had driven him to Billings to catch the plane to the University of Wyoming. They missed his plane because they were two days late. They had spent the days in Lewistown with some girls they had met during the state tournament the winter before. Later, at the airport, Pretty Weasel had said to Loney, "You should be going to college instead of me." Then he said, "You're my best friend," and Loney and Yellow Eyes watched him get on the plane to Laramie.

20

Myron Pretty Weasel walked around to the back of Loney's small asbestos-brick house. Although it was still snowing a little, there was a hint of yellow on the eastern horizon. Pretty Weasel didn't drink much anymore and the five or six beers he had had with Loney the night before had thickened his mind. He didn't like that. Mornings were his best time and he didn't like his mind to be fucked up.

He pounded on the back door, his leather mittens muffling the noise in the false dawn. Then he pushed the door open and he saw Loney leaning over the table, his head raised as though he had just woken up. And he heard Loney say,

"But it's snowing." And as he stepped into the kitchen he smelled the faint sourness of a man who lives alone.

"I've changed our plans," he said, glancing around the wreck of the kitchen. He walked to the sink and turned on the water. The fact that the tap worked seemed to interest him. "You got any coffee?"

"Not made."

"Then I'll make some. Where is it?"

Loney pointed to a cupboard to the left of the sink. Pretty Weasel opened it and took out a jar. "Instant," he said:

"Flavor crystals," said Loney.

Pretty Weasel found on the stove a saucepan that had never been scoured. The mineral deposits on the bottom resembled a satellite picture of the moon. But it looked faintly sanitary.

As he waited for the water to boil, he rinsed two cups and set them on the table. He looked at Loney and was about to ask for sugar, but Loney shook his head.

Pretty Weasel walked through the hallway to the front of the house. To his surprise, the living room was orderly and clean. The furniture was tawdry, but there were pictures on the walls and curtains on the windows. There was a photograph in a gold frame on a knickknack shelf in one corner of the room. Pretty Weasel studied it in the light from the hallway. Although he had never seen her grown up, he figured it must be Kate. She was a beautiful woman, but she had been a beautiful, if skinny, girl. He looked around the room again and decided that Loney was a kitchen drunk.

As he poured the coffee he said, "We're going after deer. Get us a couple of those whitetails down by McFarland's. The snow's perfect."

"Why don't we hunt at your place?"

"No sport."

"Are you feeding them?"

"My private stock."

"I don't have a gun."

"I've got two. You can use my old thirty-thirty. I brought it."

"Get yourself a glass," Loney said, nodding toward the wine bottle.

"You always were a horse's ass. Have you had anything to eat? No, you wouldn't have. We'll drive into Dodson when we're done and eat lunch at Irene's." He circled the kitchen. "What the hell am I looking for?" Then he said, "What's Kate up to these days?"

"She's a big shot—education—in Washington, D.C. She was back here a couple of weeks ago. She asked about you."

"I doubt that." Pretty Weasel found a glass in the cupboard over the sink and poured himself some wine. He had had a crush on her as a boy, even though she was five years older. She was cold to him. She was cold to all of Loney's friends. They called her Ice Woman. She couldn't have been more than fifteen at the time. He hadn't seen her since. "I doubt it very much."

Loney said, "Shithead."

Pretty Weasel took a swallow of wine, then grimaced. "This stuff is real bad for you. Are you aware of that?"

"How do you propose to get to McFarland's?"

"We'll cross the river from the reservation side."

"But it's not frozen."

"Where have you been? Besides pickling your fucking brain with this stuff."

"Where have *you* been?" said Loney, and he was serious.

Pretty Weasel laughed suddenly and loudly. In the yellow kitchen the laughter seemed disjointed, as out of place as Loney's soundless bird. He laughed again, this time the bird turning gray in the chill beyond the walls.

"Where *have* you been?"

"Staying away from you juicers. Don't worry about it."

And in the next quiet seconds Loney realized that Pretty Weasel had come back only for this hunt. He had left the sad same life of Harlem, but he didn't know that Loney had left it too. They had gone opposite directions, Pretty Weasel to his father's ranch, Loney to his life of more absolute isolation. And now they were to hunt together.

For those seconds Loney felt a sense of knowledge without knowing what he had learned. Or the worth of it. Then it was gone.

1987

Joyce Carol Oates 1938–

Joyce Carol Oates is one of the most prolific of modern American writers. Since the appearance of her first book, By the North Gate *(1963), a collection of short stories, she has published more than one hundred volumes—short stories, novels, poems, plays, and essays. She began telling stories at an early age: "Before I could write," she has said, "I drew pictures to tell my stories." Her first published fiction appeared in* Mademoiselle *magazine in 1959, when she was twenty-one. Since that time her writing has gained wide critical acclaim. She has received awards from the Guggenheim Foundation and the National Institute of Arts and Letters, and her novel* them *(1969) won a National Book Award.*

Oates has said that "all art is autobiographical," but nothing in the outward events of her own life parallels the terror-filled and violent lives that exist in her fiction. She was born in Lockport, New York, and raised in a middle-class family. She attended Syracuse University on a scholarship, and after her graduation in 1960 she received a fellowship at the University of Wisconsin. One year later she graduated with an M.A., and for the next six years she taught literature at the University of Detroit. In 1967 she moved to Canada, where she was a faculty member of the University of Windsor, in Ontario. In recent years she has been teaching at Princeton University.

As a writer Oates is praised not only for her phenomenal productivity and wide-ranging talents, but also for her power to depict the torments and frightening derangements suffered by ordinary people in the modern world. She writes of factory workers, school girls, businessmen, teachers, preachers. They live in a middle-class world centered on their houses, large and small, and on backyard barbecues, shopping centers, drive-in restaurants, automobiles, and television. Outwardly her characters seem commonplace and predictable. Inwardly they are complex, often terrorized by others, by cruel fate, or by their own corrosive fears. Her works often portray frightening violence: murder, suicide, rape, riots, arson, beatings. Her use of sudden horrors and grotesque experiences has been described as "gothic," like tales by Washington Irving, Edgar Allan Poe, and their contemporaries who wrote of graveyards, ancient ruins, and mysterious forces of demonic evil. To Oates, today's "gothic" world is not one of ghosts in ancient ruined castles but of haunted lives in modern ruined cities. To perceive our situation as fundamentally grotesque and "gothic," she has said, is nothing more than to make "a fairly realistic assessment of modern life."

Oates's writing has been compared with that of Flannery O'Connor and William Faulkner, whose characters also confront violence and enigmatic malice, yet Oates has been accused of taking excessive delight in showing only the frightening destinies that await us. For the unrelieved sense of dread that pervades much of her writing, for the gloomy view of life it expresses, she has been called "The Dark Lady of American Letters." But from the brutal eruptions that she describes there often comes an affirmation, a revelation of the world behind—or beneath—the apparent world, a redeeming insight imposed on characters and readers alike by the very nightmarish experiences that she describes.

At a time when modern literature increasingly seems to move toward antirealism, away from depiction of the world of everyday things seen and heard and felt, Joyce Carol Oates continues to write primarily in the realistic tradition, rejecting the fragmentary and surrealistic quality of much avant-garde fiction. At times she does use narrative techniques common to experimental writers, but from her early work to her most recent, the impact of her writing has depended not as much on the mode of storytelling as on her ability to reveal the extraordinary behind the façade of the ordinary and on her compelling vision of urban America as a swirling, nightmarish world of obsessions, neurotic fears, and grotesque brutality.

FURTHER READING: *Joyce Carol Oates,* ed. H. Bloom, 1987; E. Bender, *Artist in Residence: The Phenomenon of Joyce Carol Oates;* 1987; G. Johnson, *Understanding Joyce Carol Oates,* 1987; *Conversations with Joyce Carol Oates,* ed. L. Milazzo, 1989; M. Wesley, *Refusal and Transgression in Joyce Carol Oates' Fiction,* 1993; B. Daly, *Lavish Self-Divisions: The Novels of Joyce Carol Oates,* 1996; M. Loeb, *Literary Marriages: A Study of Intertextuality in a Series of Short Stories by Joyce Carol Oates,* 2001; G. Cologne-Brookes, *Dark Eyes on America: The Novels of Joyce Carol Oates,* 2004.

TEXT: *The Wheel of Love and Other Stories,* 1970.

HOW I CONTEMPLATED THE WORLD FROM THE DETROIT HOUSE OF CORRECTION AND BEGAN MY LIFE OVER AGAIN

NOTES FOR AN ESSAY FOR AN ENGLISH CLASS
AT BALDWIN COUNTRY DAY SCHOOL;
POKING AROUND IN DEBRIS; DISGUST AND CURIOSITY;
A REVELATION OF THE MEANING OF LIFE; A HAPPY ENDING . . .

I EVENTS

1. The girl (myself) is walking through Branden's, that excellent store. Suburb of a large famous city that is a symbol for large famous American cities. The event sneaks up on the girl, who believes she is herding it along with a small fixed smile, a girl of fifteen, innocently experienced. She dawdles in a certain style by a counter of costume jewelry. Rings, earrings, necklaces. Prices

from $5 to $50, all within reach. All ugly. She eases over to the glove counter, where everything is ugly too. In her close-fitted coat with its black fur collar she contemplates the luxury of Branden's, which she has known for many years: its many mild pale lights, easy on the eye and the soul, its elaborate tinkly decorations, its women shoppers with their excellent shoes and coats and hairdos, all dawdling gracefully, in no hurry.

2. The girl seated at home. A small library, paneled walls of oak. Someone is talking to me. An earnest, husky, female voice drives itself against my ears, nervous, frightened, groping around my heart, saying, "If you wanted gloves, why didn't you say so? Why didn't you ask for them?" That store, Branden's is owned by Raymond Forrest who lives on Du Maurier Drive. We live on Sioux Drive. Raymond Forrest. A handsome man? An ugly man? A man of fifty or sixty, with gray hair, or a man of forty with earnest, courteous eyes, a good golf game; who is Raymond Forrest, this man who is my salvation? Father has been talking to him. Father is not his physician; Dr. Berg is his physician. Father and Dr. Berg refer patients to each other. There is a connection. Mother plays bridge with . . . On Mondays and Wednesdays our maid Billie works at . . . The strings draw together in a cat's cradle, making a net to save you when you fall. . . .

3. *Harriet Arnold's.* A small shop, better than Branden's. Mother in her black coat, I in my close-fitted blue coat. Shopping. Now look at this, isn't this cute, do you want this, why don't you want this, try this on, take this with you to the fitting room, take this also, what's wrong with you, what can I do for you, why are you so strange . . .? "I wanted to steal but not to buy," I don't tell her. The girl droops along in her coat and gloves and leather boots, her eyes scan the horizon, which is pastel pink and decorated like Branden's, tasteful walls and modern ceilings with graceful glimmering lights.

4. Weeks later, the girl at a bus stop. Two o'clock in the afternoon, a Tuesday; obviously she has walked out of school.

5. The girl stepping down from a bus. Afternoon, weather changing to colder. Detroit. Pavement and closed-up stores; grill-work over the windows of a pawnshop. What is a pawnshop, exactly?

II CHARACTERS

1. The girl stands five feet five inches tall. An ordinary height. Baldwin Country Day School draws them up to that height. She dreams along the corridors and presses her face against the Thermoplex glass. No frost or steam can ever form on that glass. A smudge of grease from her forehead . . . could she be boiled down to grease? She wears her hair loose and long and straight in suburban teen-age style, 1968. Eyes smudged with pencil, dark brown. Brown hair. Vague green eyes. A pretty girl? An ugly girl? She sings to herself under her breath, idling in the corridor, thinking of her many secrets (the thirty dollars she once took from the purse of a friend's mother, just for fun, the basement window she smashed in her own house just for fun) and thinking of her

brother who is at Susquehanna Boys' Academy, an excellent preparatory school in Maine, remembering him unclearly . . . he has long manic hair and a squeaking voice and he looks like one of the popular teen-age singers of 1968, one of those in a group. *The Certain Forces, The Way Out, The Maniacs Responsible.* The girl in her turn looks like one of those fieldsful of girls who listen to the boys' singing, dreaming and mooning restlessly, breaking into high sullen laughter, innocently experienced.

2. The mother. A Midwestern woman of Detroit and suburbs. Belongs to the Detroit Athletic Club. Also the Detroit Golf Club. Also the Bloomfield Hills Country Club. The Village Women's Club at which lectures are given each winter on Genet and Sartre[1] and James Baldwin,[2] by the Director of the Adult Education Program at Wayne State University. . . . The Bloomfield Art Association. Also the Founders Society of the Detroit Institute of Arts. Also . . . Oh, she is in perpetual motion, this lady, hair like blown-up gold and finer than gold, hair and fingers and body of inestimable grace. Heavy weighs the gold on the back of her hairbrush and hand mirror. Heavy heavy the candlesticks in the dining room. Very heavy is the big car, a Lincoln, long and black, that on one cool autumn day split a squirrel's body in two unequal parts.

3. The father. Dr.   . He belongs to the same clubs as #2. A player of squash and golf; he has a golfer's umbrella of stripes. Candy stripes. In his mouth nothing turns to sugar, however; saliva works no miracles here. His doctoring is of the slightly sick. The sick are sent elsewhere (to Dr. Berg?), the deathly sick are sent back for more tests and their bills are sent to their homes, the unsick are sent to Dr. Coronet (Isabel, a lady), an excellent psychiatrist for unsick people who angrily believe they are sick and want to do something about it. If they demand a male psychiatrist, the unsick are sent by Dr. (my father) to Dr. Lowenstein, a male psychiatrist, excellent and expensive, with a limited practice.

4. Clarita. She is twenty, twenty-five, she is thirty or more? Pretty, ugly, what? She is a woman lounging by the side of a road, in jeans and a sweater, hitchhiking, or she is slouched on a stool at a counter in some roadside diner. A hard line of jaw. Curious eyes. Amused eyes. Behind her eyes processions move, funeral pageants, cartoons. She says, "I never can figure out why girls like you bum around down here. What are you looking for anyway?" An odor of tobacco about her. Unwashed underclothes, or no underclothes, unwashed skin, gritty toes, hair long and falling into strands, not recently washed.

5. Simon. In this city the weather changes abruptly, so Simon's weather changes abruptly. He sleeps through the afternoon. He sleeps through the morning. Rising, he gropes around for something to get him going, for a cigarette or a pill to drive him out to the street, where the temperature is hovering around 35°. Why doesn't it drop? Why, why doesn't the cold clean air come down from Canada; will he have to go-up into Canada to get it? Will he have to leave the Country of his Birth and sink into Canada's frosty fields . . .? Will the

[1]Jean Genet (1910–1986), French dramatist; Jean-Paul Sartre (1905–1980), French philosopher and novelist.
[2]American novelist (1924–1987).

F.B.I. (which he dreams about constantly) chase him over the Canadian border on foot, hounded out in a blizzard of broken glass and horns . . .?

"Once I was Huckleberry Finn," Simon says, "but now I am Roderick Usher."[3] Beset by frenzies and fears, this man who makes my spine go cold, he takes green pills, yellow pills, pills of white and capsules of dark blue and green . . . he takes other things I may not mention, for what if Simon seeks me out and climbs into my girl's bedroom here in Bloomfield Hills and strangles me, what then . . .? (As I write this I begin to shiver. Why do I shiver? I am now sixteen and sixteen is not an age for shivering.) It comes from Simon, who is always cold.

III WORLD EVENTS

Nothing.

IV PEOPLE & CIRCUMSTANCES CONTRIBUTING TO THIS DELINQUENCY

Nothing.

V SIOUX DRIVE

George, Clyde G. 240 Sioux. A manufacturer's representative; children, a dog, a wife. Georgian with the usual columns. You think of the White House, then of Thomas Jefferson, then your mind goes blank on the white pillars and you think of nothing. Norris, Ralph W. 246 Sioux. Public relations. Colonial Bay window, brick, stone, concrete, wood, green shutters, sidewalk, lantern, grass, trees, blacktop drive, two children, one of them my classmate Esther (Esther Norris) at Baldwin. Wife, cars. Ramsey, Michael D. 250 Sioux. Colonial. Big living room, thirty by twenty-five, fireplaces in living room, library, recreation room, paneled walls wet bar five bathrooms five bedrooms two lavatories central air conditioning automatic sprinkler automatic garage door three children one wife two cars a breakfast room a patio a large fenced lot fourteen trees a front door with a brass knocker never knocked. Next is our house. Classic contemporary. Traditional modern. Attached garage, attached Florida room, attached patio, attached pool and cabana, attached roof. A front door mail slot through which pour *Time Magazine, Fortune, Life, Business Week,* the *Wall Street Journal,* the *New York Times,* the *New Yorker,* the *Saturday Review, M.D., Modern Medicine, Disease of the Month* . . . and also. . . . And in addition to all this, a quiet sealed letter from Baldwin saying: *Your daughter is not doing work compatible with her performance on the Stanford-Binet.*[4] . . . And your son is not doing

[3]Tormented character in "The Fall of the House of Usher," by Edgar Allan Poe.
[4]An intelligence test.

well, not well at all, very sad. Where is your son anyway? Once he stole trick-and-treat candy from some six-year-old kids, he himself being a robust ten. The beginning. Now your daughter steals. In the Village Pharmacy she made off with, yes she did, don't deny it, she made off with a copy of *Pageant Magazine* for no reason, she swiped a roll of Life Savers in a green wrapper and was in no need of saving her life or even in need of sucking candy; when she was no more than eight years old she stole, don't blush, she stole a package of Tums only because it was out on the counter and available, and the nice lady behind the counter (now dead) said nothing. . . . Sioux Drive. Maples, oaks, elms. Diseased elms cut down. Sioux Drive runs into Roosevelt Drive. Slow, turning lanes, not streets, all drives and lanes and ways and passes. A private police force. Quiet private police, in unmarked cars. Cruising on Saturday evenings with paternal smiles for the residents who are streaming in and out of houses, going to and from parties, a thousand parties, slightly staggering, the women in their furs alighting from automobiles bought of Ford and General Motors and Chrysler, very heavy automobiles. No foreign cars. Detroit. In 275 Sioux, down the block in that magnificent French-Normandy mansion, lives himself, who has the C account itself, imagine that! Look at where he lives and look at the enormous trees and chimneys, imagine his many fireplaces, imagine his wife and children, imagine his wife's hair, imagine her fingernails, imagine her bathtub of smooth clean glowing pink, imagine their embraces, his trouser pockets filled with odd coins and keys and dust and peanuts, imagine their ecstasy on Sioux Drive, imagine their income tax returns, imagine their little boy's pride in his experimental car, a scaled-down C, as he roars around the neighborhood on the sidewalks frightening dogs and Negro maids, oh imagine all these things, imagine everything, let your mind roar out all over Sioux Drive and Du Maurier Drive and Roosevelt Drive and Ticonderoga Pass and Burning Bush Way and Lincolnshire Pass and Lois Lane.

When spring comes, its winds blow nothing to Sioux Drive, no odors of hollyhocks or forsythia, nothing Sioux Drive doesn't already possess, everything is planted and performing. The weather vanes, had they weather vanes, don't have to turn with the wind, don't have to contend with the weather. There is no weather.

VI DETROIT

There is always weather in Detroit. Detroit's temperature is always 32°. Fast-falling temperatures. Slow-rising temperatures. Wind from the north-northeast four to forty miles an hour, small craft warnings, partly cloudy today and Wednesday changing to partly sunny through Thursday . . . small warnings of frost, soot warnings, traffic warnings, hazardous lake conditions small craft and swimmers, restless Negro gangs, restless cloud formations, restless temperatures aching to fall out the very bottom of the thermometer or shoot up over the top and boil everything over in red mercury.

Detroit's temperature is 32°. Fast-falling temperatures. Slow-rising temperatures. Wind from the north-northeast four to forty miles an hour. . . .

VII EVENTS

1. The girl's heart is pounding. In her pocket is a pair of gloves! In a plastic bag! Airproof breathproof plastic bag, gloves selling for twenty-five dollars on Branden's counter! In her pocket! Shoplifted! . . . In her purse is a blue comb, not very clean. In her purse is a leather billfold (a birthday present from her grandmother in Philadelphia) with snapshots of the family in clean plastic windows, in the billfold are bills, she doesn't know how many bills. . . . In her purse is an ominous note from her friend Tykie *What's this about Joe H. and the kids hanging around at Louise's Sat. night? You heard anything?* . . . passed in French class. In her purse is a lot of dirty yellow Kleenex, her mother's heart would break to see such very dirty Kleenex, and at the bottom of her purse are brown hairpins and safety pins and a broken pencil and a ballpoint pen (blue) stolen from somewhere forgotten and a purse-size compact of Cover Girl Make-Up, Ivory Rose. . . . Her lipstick is Broken Heart, a corrupt pink; her fingers are trembling like crazy; her teeth are beginning to chatter; her insides are alive; her eyes glow in her head; she is saying to her mother's astonished face *I want to steal but not to buy.*

2. At Clarita's Day or night? What room is this? A bed, a regular bed, and a mattress on the floor nearby. Wallpaper hanging in strips. Clarita says she tore it like that with her teeth. She was fighting a barbaric tribe that night, high from some pills; she was battling for her life with men wearing helmets of heavy iron and their faces no more than Christian crosses to breathe through, every one of those bastards looking like her lover Simon, who seems to breathe with great difficulty through the slits of mouth and nostrils in his face. Clarita has never heard of Sioux Drive. Raymond Forrest cuts no ice with her, nor does the C account and its millions; Harvard Business School could be at the corner of Vernor and 12th Street[5] for all she cares, and Vietnam might have sunk by now into the Dead Sea under its tons of debris, for all the amazement she could show . . . her face is overworked, overwrought, at the age of twenty (thirty?) it is already exhausted but fanciful and ready for a laugh. Clarita says mournfully to me *Honey somebody is going to turn you out let me give you warning.* In a movie shown on late television Clarita is not a mess like this but a nurse, with short neat hair and a dedicated look, in love with her doctor and her doctor's patients and their diseases, enamored of needles and sponges and rubbing alcohol. . . . Or no: she is a private secretary. Robert Cummings is her boss. She helps him with fantastic plots, the canned audience laughs, no, the audience doesn't laugh because nothing is funny, instead her boss is Robert Taylor and they are not boss and secretary but husband and wife, she is threatened by a young starlet, she is grim, handsome, wifely, a good companion for a good man. . . . She is Claudette Colbert. Her sister too is Claudette Colbert. They are twins, identical. Her husband Charles Boyer is a very rich handsome man and her sister, Claudette Colbert, is plotting her death in order to take her place as the rich man's wife, no one will know because they are *twins*. . . . All these marvelous lives Clarita might have lived, but she fell out the bottom at the age of thirteen. At the age when

[5]Downtown Detroit.

I was packing my overnight case for a slumber party at Toni Deshield's she was tearing filthy sheets off a bed and scratching up a rash on her arms. . . . Thirteen is uncommonly young for a white girl in Detroit, Miss Brock of the Detroit House of Correction said in a sad newspaper interview for the *Detroit News;* fifteen and sixteen are more likely. Eleven, twelve, thirteen are not surprising in colored . . . they are more precocious. What can we do? Taxes are rising and the tax base is falling. The temperature rises slowly but falls rapidly. Everything is falling out the bottom, Woodward Avenue is filthy, Livernois Avenue[6] is filthy! Scraps of paper flutter in the air like pigeons, dirt flies up and hits you right in the eye, oh Detroit is breaking up into dangerous bits of newspaper and dirt, watch out. . . .

Clarita's apartment is over a restaurant. Simon her lover emerges from the cracks at dark. Mrs. Olesko, a neighbor of Clarita's, an aged white wisp of a woman, doesn't complain but sniffs with contentment at Clarita's noisy life and doesn't tell the cops, hating cops, when the cops arrive. I should give more fake names, more blanks, instead of telling all these secrets. I myself am a secret; I am a minor.

3. My father reads a paper at a medical convention in Los Angeles. There he is, on the edge of the North American continent, when the unmarked detective put his hand so gently on my arm in the aisle of Branden's and said, "Miss, would you like to step over here for a minute?"

And where was he when Clarita put her hand on my arm, that wintry dark sulphurous aching day in Detroit, in the company of closed-down barber shops, closed-down diners, closed-down movie houses, homes, windows, basements, faces . . . she put her hand on my arm and said, "Honey, are you looking for somebody down here?"

And was he home worrying about me, gone for two weeks solid, when they carried me off . . .? It took three of them to get me in the police cruiser, so they said, and they put more than their hands on my arm.

4. I work on this lesson. My English teacher is Mr. Forest, who is from Michigan State. Not handsome, Mr. Forest, and his name is plain, unlike Raymond Forrest's, but he is sweet and rodentlike, he has conferred with the principal and my parents, and everything is fixed . . . treat her as if nothing has happened, a new start, begin again, only sixteen years old, what a shame, how did it happen?—nothing happened, nothing could have happened, a slight physiological modification known only to a gynecologist or to Dr. Coronet. I work on my lesson. I sit in my pink room. I look around the room with my sad pink eyes. I sigh, I dawdle, I pause, I eat up time, I am limp and happy to be home, I am sixteen years old suddenly, my head hangs heavy as a pumpkin on my shoulders, and my hair has just been cut by Mr. Faye at the Crystal Salon and is said to be very becoming.

(Simon too put his hand on my arm and said, "Honey, you have got to come with me," and in his six-by-six room we got to know each other. Would I go back to Simon again? Would I lie down with him in all that filth and craziness? Over and over again.

[6]Main streets in Detroit.

a Clarita is being betrayed as in front of a Cunningham Drug Store she is nervously eyeing a colored man who may or may not have money, or a nervous white boy of twenty with side-burns and an Appalachian look, who may or may not have a knife hidden in his jacket pocket, or a husky red-faced man of friendly countenance who may or may not be a member of the Vice Squad out for an early twilight walk.)

I work on my lesson for Mr. Forest. I have filled up eleven pages. Words pour out of me and won't stop. I want to tell everything . . . what was the song Simon was always humming, and who was Simon's friend in a very new trench coat with an old high school graduation ring on his finger . . .? Simon's bearded friend? When I was down too low for him, Simon kicked me out and gave me to him for three days, I think, on Fourteenth Street in Detroit, an airy room of cold cruel drafts with newspapers on the floor. . . . Do I really remember that or am I piecing it together from what they told me? Did they tell the truth? Did they know much of the truth?

VIII CHARACTERS

1. Wednesdays after school, at four; Saturday mornings at ten. Mother drives me to Dr. Coronet. Ferns in the office, plastic or real, they look the same. Dr. Coronet is queenly, an elegant nicotine-stained lady who would have studied with Freud had circumstances not prevented it, a bit of a Catholic, ready to offer you some mystery if your teeth will ache too much without it. Highly recommended by Father! Forty dollars an hour, Father's forty dollars! Progress! Looking up! Looking better! That new haircut is so becoming, says Dr. Coronet herself, showing how normal she is for a woman with an I.Q. of 180 and many advanced degrees.

2. Mother. A lady in a brown suede coat. Boots of shiny black material, black gloves, a black fur hat. She would be humiliated could she know that of all the people in the world it is my ex-lover Simon who walks most like her . . . self-conscious and unreal, listening to distant music, a little bow-legged with craftiness. . . .

3. Father. Tying a necktie. In a hurry. On my first evening home he put his hand on my arm and said, "Honey, we're going to forget all about this."

4. Simon. Outside, a plane is crossing the sky, in here we're in a hurry. Morning. It must be morning. The girl is half out of her mind, whimpering and vague; Simon her dear friend is wretched this morning . . . he is wretched with morning itself . . . he forces her to give him an injection with that needle she knows is filthy, she has a dread of needles and surgical instruments and the odor of things that are to be sent into the blood, thinking somehow of her father. . . . This is a bad morning, Simon says that his mind is being twisted out of shape, and so he submits to the needle that he usually scorns and bites his lip with his yellowish teeth, his face going very pale. *Ah baby!* he says in his soft mocking voice, which with all women is a mockery of love, *do it like this—Slowly—* And the girl, terrified, almost drops the precious needle but manages to turn

it up to the light from the window . . . is it an extension of herself then? She can give him this gift then? *I wish you wouldn't do this to me,* she says, wise in her terror, because it seems to her that Simon's danger—in a few minutes he may be dead—is a way of pressing her against him that is more powerful than any other embrace. She has to work over his arm, the knotted corded veins of his arm, her forehead wet with perspiration as she pushes and releases the needle, staring at that mixture of liquid now stained with Simon's bright blood. . . . When the drug hits him she can feel it herself, she feels that magic that is more than any woman can give him, striking the back of his head and making his face stretch as if with the impact of a terrible sun. . . . She tries to embrace him but he pushes her aside and stumbles to his feet. *Jesus Christ,* he says. . . .

5. Princess, a Negro girl of eighteen. What is her charge? She is closed-mouthed about it, shrewd and silent, you know that no one had to wrestle her to the sidewalk to get her in here; she came with dignity. In the recreation room she sits reading *Nancy Drew and the Jewel Box Mystery,* which inspires in her face tiny wrinkles of alarm and interest: what a face! Light brown skin, heavy shaded eyes, heavy eyelashes, a serious sinister dark brow, graceful fingers, graceful wristbones, graceful legs, lips, tongue, a sugar-sweet voice, a leggy stride more masculine than Simon's and my mother's, decked out in a dirty white blouse and dirty white slacks; vaguely nautical is Princess' style. . . . At breakfast she is in charge of clearing the table and leans over me, saying, *Honey you sure you ate enough?*

6. The girl lies sleepless, wondering. Why here, why not there? Why Bloomfield Hills and not jail? Why jail and not her pink room? Why downtown Detroit and not Sioux Drive? What is the difference? Is Simon all the difference? The girl's head is a parade of wonders. She is nearly sixteen, her breath is marvelous with wonders, not long ago she was coloring with crayons and now she is smearing the landscape with paints that won't come off and won't come off her fingers either. She says to the matron *I am not talking about anything,* not because everyone has warned her not to talk but because, because she will not talk; because she won't say anything about Simon, who is her secret. And she says to the matron, *I won't go home,* up until that night in the lavatory when everything was changed. . . . "No, I won't go home I want to stay here," she says, listening to her own words with amazement, thinking that weeds might climb everywhere over that marvelous $180,000 house and dinosaurs might return to muddy the beige carpeting, but never never will she reconcile four o'clock in the morning in Detroit with eight o'clock breakfasts in Bloomfield Hills. . . . oh, she aches still for Simon's hands and his caressing breath, though he gave her little pleasure, he took everything from her (five-dollar bills, ten-dollar bills, passed into her numb hands by men and taken out of her hands by Simon) until she herself was passed into the hands of other men, police, when Simon evidently got tired of her and her hysteria. . . . *No, I won't go home, I don't want to be bailed out.* The girl thinks as a *Stubborn and Wayward Child* (one of several charges lodged against her), and the matron understands her crazy white-rimmed eyes that are seeking out some new violence that will keep her in jail, should someone threaten to let her out. Such children try to strangle the matrons, the attendants, or one another . . . they want the locks locked forever, the doors nailed shut . . . and this girl is no different up until that night her mind is changed for her. . . .

IX THAT NIGHT

Princess and Dolly, a little white girl of maybe fifteen, hardy however as a sergeant and in the House of Correction for armed robbery, corner her in the lavatory at the farthest sink and the other girls look away and file out to bed, leaving her. God, how she is beaten up! Why is she beaten up? Why do they pound her, why such hatred? Princess vents all the hatred of a thousand silent Detroit winters on her body, this girl whose body belongs to me, fiercely she rides across the Midwestern plains on this girls' tender bruised body . . . revenge on the oppressed minorities of America! revenge on the slaughtered Indians! revenge on the female sex, on the male sex, revenge on Bloomfield Hills, revenge revenge. . . .

X DETROIT

In Detroit, weather weighs heavily upon everyone. The sky looms large. The horizon shimmers in smoke. Downtown the buildings are imprecise in the haze. Perpetual haze. Perpetual motion inside the haze. Across the choppy river is the city of Windsor, in Canada. Part of the continent has bunched up here and is bulging outward, at the tip of Detroit; a cold hard rain is forever falling on the expressways. . . . Shoppers shop grimly, their cars are not parked in safe places, their windshields may be smashed and graceful ebony hands may drag them out through their shatterproof smashed windshields, crying *Revenge for the Indians!* Ah, they all fear leaving Hudson's[7] and being dragged to the very tip of the city and thrown off the parking roof of Cobo Hall,[8] that expensive tomb, into the river. . . .

XI CHARACTERS WE ARE FOREVER ENTWINED WITH

1. Simon drew me into his tender rotting arms and breathed gravity into me. Then I came to earth, weighed down. He said, *You are such a little girl,* and he weighed me down with his delight. In the palms of his hands were teeth marks from his previous life experiences. He was thirty-five, they said. Imagine Simon in this room, in my pink room: he is about six feet tall and stoops slightly, in a feline cautious way, always thinking, always on guard, with his scuffed light suede shoes and his clothes that are anyone's clothes, slightly rumpled ordinary clothes that ordinary men might wear to not-bad jobs. Simon has fair long hair, curly hair, spent languid curls that are like . . . exactly like the curls of wood shavings to the touch, I am trying to be exact . . . and he smells of unheated mornings and coffee and too many pills coating his tongue with a faint green-white scum. . . . Dear Simon, who would be panicked in this room and in this house (right now Billie is vacuuming next door in my parents' room; a vacuum cleaner's roar is a sign of all good things), Simon who is said to have

[7]Detroit department store. [8]Exhibition hall in Detroit.

come from a home not much different from this, years ago, fleeing all the carpeting and the polished banisters . . . Simon has a deathly face, only desperate people fall in love with it. His face is bony and cautious, the bones of his cheeks prominent as if with the rigidity of his ceaseless thinking, plotting, for he has to make money out of girls to whom money means nothing, they're so far gone they can hardly count it, and in a sense money means nothing to him either except as a way of keeping on with his life. *Each Day's Proud Struggle,* the title of a novel we could read at jail. . . . Each day he needs a certain amount of money. He devours it. It wasn't love he uncoiled in me with his hollowed-out eyes and his courteous smile, that remnant of a prosperous past, but a dark terror that needed to press itself flat against him, or against another man . . . but he was the first, he came over to me and took my arm, a claim. We struggled on the stairs and I said, *Let me loose, you're hurting my neck, my face,* it was such a surprise that my skin hurt where he rubbed it, and afterward we lay face to face and he breathed everything into me. In the end I think he turned me in.

2. Raymond Forrest. I just read this morning that Raymond Forrest's father, the chairman of the board at   , died of a heart attack on a plane bound for London. I would like to write to Raymond Forrest a note of sympathy. I would like to thank him for not pressing charges against me one hundred years ago, saving me, being so generous . . . well, men like Raymond Forrest are generous men, not like Simon. I would like to write him a letter telling of my love, or of some other emotion that is positive and healthy. Not like Simon and his poetry, which he scrawled down when he was high and never changed a word . . . but when I try to think of something to say, it is Simon's language that comes back to me, caught in my head like a bad song, it is always Simon's language:

There is no reality only dreams
Your neck may get snapped when you wake
My love is drawn to some violent end
She keeps wanting to get away
My love is heading downward
And I am heading upward
She is going to crash on the sidewalk
And I am going to dissolve into the clouds

XII EVENTS

1. Out of the hospital, bruised and saddened and converted, with Princess' grunts still tangled in my hair . . . and Father in his overcoat looking like a prince himself, come to carry me off. Up the expressway and out north to home. Jesus Christ, but the air is thinner and cleaner here. Monumental houses. Heartbreaking sidewalks, so clean.

2. Weeping in the living room. The ceiling is two stories high and two chandeliers hang from it. Weeping, weeping, though Billie the maid is *probably listening.* I will never leave home again. Never. Never leave home. Never leave this home again, never.

3. Sugar doughnuts for breakfast. The toaster is very shiny and my face is distorted in it. Is that my face?

4. The car is turning in the driveway. Father brings me home. Mother embraces me. Sunlight breaks in movieland patches on the roof of our traditional-contemporary home, which was designed for the famous automotive stylist whose identity, if I told you the name of the famous car he designed, you would all know, so I can't tell you because my teeth chatter at the thought of being sued . . . or having someone climb into my bedroom with a rope to strangle me. . . . The car turns up the blacktop drive. The house opens to me like a doll's house, so lovely in the sunlight, the big living room beckons to me with its walls falling away in a delirium of joy at my return. Billie the maid is *no doubt* listening from the kitchen as I burst into tears and the hysteria Simon got so sick of. Convulsed in Father's arms, I say I will never leave again, never, why did I leave, where did I go, what happened, my mind is gone wrong, my body is one big bruise, my backbone was sucked dry, it wasn't the men who hurt me and Simon never hurt me but only those girls . . . my God, how they hurt me . . . I will never leave home again. . . . The car is perpetually turning up the drive and I am perpetually breaking down in the living room and we are perpetually taking the right exit from the expressway (Lahser Road) and the wall of the rest room is perpetually banging against my head and perpetually are Simon's hands moving across my body and adding everything up and so too are Father's hands on my shaking bruised back, far from the surface of my skin on the surface of my good blue cashmere coat (dry-cleaned for my release). . . . I weep for all the money here, for God in gold and beige carpeting, for the beauty of chandeliers and the miracle of a clean polished gleaming toaster and faucets that run both hot and cold water, and I tell them, *I will never leave home, this is my home, I love everything here, I am in love with everything here. . . .*

I am home.

1970

James Alan McPherson 1943–

James Alan McPherson was born in 1943 in Savannah, Georgia, the son of Mabel Smalls, a domestic worker, and James Allen McPherson, the state's only black licensed master electrician. As a child he developed a love of reading that began with comic books and then moved into classic works of short fiction. He attended Morgan State College in Baltimore and Morris Brown College in Atlanta, from which he earned a B.A. in English and history in 1965. That same year he entered a story he had written, titled "Gold Coast," in a short fiction competition sponsored by Atlantic *magazine among United Negro College Fund institutions, and it won first prize. He entered Harvard Law School in the fall of 1965 and graduated with an LL.B. in 1968. McPherson then studied at the University of Iowa's acclaimed Writers Workshop and took his M.F.A. in 1969. He published his first collection of stories,* Hue and Cry, *in 1968, and its critical success placed him among the leading writers of his generation. His second book of short fiction,*

Elbow Room, *appeared in 1977 and earned McPherson a Pulitzer Prize, making him the first African American to receive the award for fiction. In addition to his two short story collections, he has contributed articles and fiction to major magazines and written two memoirs,* Crabcakes *(1998) and* A Region Not Home: Reflections from Exile *(2000).*

McPherson is known especially for his portrayals of working-class characters, often caught in desperate circumstances. Although the situations he portrays are frequently specific to African American experience, he is concerned to go beyond particular societal considerations to the universally human. He says about his own writing: "Certain of these people happen to be black, and certain of them happen to be white; but I have tried to keep the color part of most of them far in the background, where these things should rightly be kept." McPherson currently teaches at the University of Iowa, where he has worked with the Writers Workshop since 1981.

FURTHER READING: *Crabcakes,* 1998; *A Region not Home: Reflections from Exile,* 2000; *Ancestral House: The Black Short Story in the Americas and Europe,* ed. C. Rowell, 1995; H. Beavers, *Wrestling Angels into Song: The Fictions of Ernest J. Gaines and James Alan McPherson,* 1995.
TEXT: *Elbow Room,* 1977.

THE FAITHFUL

There is John Butler, a barber, looking out his shop window on a slow Monday morning. Impeccable, as usual, in his starched white jacket, he stands and surveys the procession of colors blending into the avenue, a living advertisement for his profession. The colors are blurred because the window needs a cleaning; the red lettering has been allowed to fade, almost to a mere outline. Some of the passing faces he cannot recognize. But some recognize him behind the window and wave as they hurry past. Others, wanting to avoid all contact with the shop, pretend that he is not there. They ease out of view without acknowledging his nodding head. Still, he stands in his usual place between the edge of the window and the door; and when a familiar face moves by the window without glancing toward the shop, he shares the embarrassment and turns his own eyes away. In his mind he forgives the workers; but the shiftless, the workless, the timeless strollers up and down the avenue he does not spare.

"They still tryin' to starve us out," he says, turning to the members of his shop. Today they consist of Ray Powell, the second barber; Mickey Norris, who has again played hooky from school in order to earn a few dollars shining shoes; and two loafers, who have come in for a game of checkers and a chance to enjoy it. All wince to hear him start again.

"Maybe I'll go on down the block a minute," Mickey says, moving toward the door.

"Maybe you better go on to school." Butler tells him. "There ain't go'n be no work in here today."

Mickey, a sly boy, does not stray far from the green metal chair.

Butler gives him a severe look. "Not tomorrow either," he adds.

Mickey slinks back to the chair and sits, his hands going into his pockets for coins to toss.

Ray, a fat brown man who likes to give the impression of habitual efficiency, runs the edge of a hand towel between the teeth of his own black comb and puckers his lips in an exaggeration of effort. "It's just the first of the week, Reverend," he says. "Things are bound to pick up."

One of the loafers, Norm Tyson from the Projects,[1] knows better: he allows his opponent an advantage on the board and, before the man can incorporate it, says: "Looks like it's yours."

And then the two of them leave.

Just after noon, when Ray has gone across the street for lunch and Mickey has wandered off until evening, a young man looks in the door. A massive black tiara of hair encircles his head; his matching light green shirt and bell-bottom trousers advertise his wealth. Butler flashes his most hospitable smile and rises from his chair.

"How much for a quick one?" the young man asks from the door.

"For all that, two-fifty, maybe three dollars," Butler says.

The young man snorts and throws back his arms in playful amazement. "Just for a *trim?* You wouldn't wanna mess up my vibrations, would you?"

Butler loosens the smile and lowers his voice. "No," he says. "Better go somewheres else. I got me some heavy hands."

The young man laughs. "A heavy hand make a rusty register in your business, don't it?" And backs out the door before the barber can form an answer.

At the end of the day some regulars do come in; but they are losing more hairs than Butler clips. Still, they lower their heads, more from respect than necessity, and allow him limited operations around the edges. These balding faithfuls—John Gilmore or Dick Kendricks or Willie Russell—the backbone of his Sunday congregation, fold their hands beneath the white sheet-square and abide, in their turn, his wandering frustrations. "These whites have bullshitted our young men," he says. "Now, me, I'm as proud as the next man. But our boys didn't stop gettin' haircuts until these white boys started that mess. That's a fact. Wasn't no more than a couple years ago, they'd be lined up against that wall on a Saturday night, laughin' at the white boys. But soon as they see these white kids runnin' round wild, all at once they hair ain't long enough no more."

John Gilmore keeps his head lowered, his lips tight, his eyes watching his hands work beneath the sheet.

Ray, sitting in his own chair, looks up from the paper he has been reading and says: "Hey, I see where they arrested a big shot for tax evasion. First of the year they bound to hamstring *one* for example." But no one picks it up. Ray rattles and folds the paper, and eases back into his reading.

Once, there had been violent betting and spit-infested verbal battles and crowded-round checker games and hot clothes and numbers passing through; once, Butler would hum radio spirituals as he went about his work, or else trade righteous homilies with Ray, busy in the other chair. The men who remember those days—Gilmore, Kendricks, and the others—would like to have them back; but there is an unspoken fear of being too possessive about the past, and a determination not to allow the present to slip out of focus. They recognize another world outside the shop door, and find it much easier to pay up and walk away when Butler is done with his work.

[1]Low-income public housing.

"If it wasn't for you belonging to his church," John Gilmore tells his wife after each visit, "I wouldn't go in there."

"Now don't you be no trouble to him," Marie Gilmore reminds her husband. "He ain't got much longer to go."

On Sundays Butler now converts his sermons. The themes still resemble something familiar to his congregation, but lately the images have been doing different work. The relative few who still come into the church to hear it are growing bored. Some have already visited Reverend Tarwell and his more magical thumpings over on 138th. They like what they hear. There is talk that Tarwell plans to have himself crucified next month at Easter Sunrise Service and preach the entire sermon from the cross. Such resurrected remnants of the South appeal to them; the oldest have ever been homesick. Besides, Butler seems to have an obsession with a single theme: "I was walkin' down here this mornin', brothers and sisters," he begins, his rising voice mellowing into a comfortable chant, "thinkin' about the rift there is these days between father and son; thinkin' about the breach there is between son and son and daughter and daughter. I'm thinkin' this mornin' about old bloody Cain and his guiltless brother; about old man Abraham castin' his son out into the wilderness; about that old rascal, Saul, lettin' his *wine* turn him against young David. I see little Joseph tossed in the dark pit, strip naked of his garment by his brothers. And hungry Esau, just a-droolin' at the mouth, sellin' his birthright for a mess of *pottage*. There's old slick Jacob now, a-crawlin' in to blind Isaac's bedside underneath the *fleece* of a wild and woolly animal; and Esau standin' outside the door, just a-weepin' away. Next to him is old rebellious Absalom, up in an *oak* tree, swingin' by his hair with Joab ridin' *down* on him.[2] Just look at that boy cuss. I want to cut him down, Church, but I ain't got the strength. My arm is raised up to him, but my *razor's* kind of rusty. So can I git an *amen* over here . . .?"

Some of the people on his left say a weak "a-men."

"Can I hear an *a-men* over there . . .?"

Some few on the right say "a-men."

"My razor growin' *sharper* by the second . . ."

"You better lay off that stuff," Ella, his wife, tells him at Sunday dinner. "The church done got tired of that one record you keep playin'." They have not been invited out for Sunday dinner in over five months.

"They ain't got no cause to complain," Butler tells her. "I give them a good service. Besides, most of them don't even listen to nothin' but the names."

"Just the same you better lay off it for a while. It ain't their fault you goin' out of business."

Butler looks over at her. She is chewing with a deliberation calculated to enrage him into an argument. "Whose fault you reckon it is?" he demands.

She continues chewing, looking wise.

Butler looks at his own food. "All right," he says. "It's *my* fault."

"It ain't that you *have* to do Afros. Ray could do that and you could do your old customers. There ain't nothin' wrong with dividin' up the work thataway."

[2]A series of allusions to biblical stories of conflicts between brothers or between fathers (or father-figures) and sons.

"Ray ain't go'n do fancy cuts in *my* place. First thing you know, these young fellows come hangin' round there and drive the old customers away."

She chews for a while, sips her coffee, and watches him. She takes her time in swallowing, smacks her lips, and then says: "Then you won't have a place for much longer."

He scrapes at his own plate, trying to avoid her eyes.

"And the way *you* goin'," she adds, "you won't be preachin' much longer either."

This thought he takes to bed with him, while she lingers in the kitchen and sips, with irritating emphasis, another cup of coffee.

On another slow Monday morning, Ray, shaping his own mustache at the mirror, says: "You know, Reverend, I been thinking. Maybe we ought to go into processes. Nobody can say *now* that's imitating the white man. And there's guys on the block still wearing them."

Butler turns from the window, his face twitching. Images of winos and hustlers flash through his mind. "That's what you been thinkin', huh?" he says to Ray.

"Yeah, Reverend," Ray says, laughing to himself in the mirror. "Since the white folks always imitating us, maybe we could even process some of them."

"I don't process," Butler answers.

"It's work," Ray says, dropping the laugh and looking serious.

"It's devil's work," Butler says.

"Right now, I'd say we ain't got much of a choice."

Butler stands behind him. They exchange looks in the mirror. Ray works the scissors in his right hand, shaking off the hairs. Then he begins to clip his mustache again, drawing in his chin. Butler watches. After a while he says: "Ray, I know you think I'm a fool. I can't help that. But when you get to be my age, change is just hard. You can shape a boy's life by what you do to his hair," he says, looking over at Mickey tossing coins against the wall. "Now everybody can't do that, but I'm proud to say I done it more than once in my lifetime. And I want to do it some more. But scrapin' a few loose hairs off every Tom, Dick, and Harry that come in here, just to get the money, why anybody can do that. You understand what I'm sayin'?"

Ray lowers the scissors but does not answer.

"You, Mickey? You understand?"

Mickey thinks it over, tossing another coin to the wall. After a while he says, "Naw, suh," and nods his head.

Butler walks back to the window. "That's what I figured," he finally says, looking out.

A little after one o'clock John Gilmore comes in for a quick shave during his lunch hour. Lying almost horizontal in the chair, his rust brown lips and eyelids showing through the lather, he makes careful conversation while Butler exercises the repressed magic in his hands. "Times being what they is in religion and all," he says, "I been wonderin' what you been plannin' to do."

"About what?" Butler says, not pausing in his work.

"Well," Gilmore begins, "Marie say Second Calvary ain't drawin' no stronger membership. In fact, a lot of folks thinkin' about plain quittin'."

"That's their business," he answers, holding back Gilmore's ear. "They git what they pay for."

Gilmore waits until his ear is allowed to fall back into place. Then he says: "I hear Reverend Tarwell thinkin' 'bout *you* for assistant pastor of his place. Times bein' good for the colored like they is, he thinkin' 'bout goin' into politics in a few years. When he step down, there sure go'n be a crowd over at his place for somebody."

Butler paused to wipe the razor. "Ain't most of his people from South Carolina?" he asks.

"Some."

"Well, most of mine from Alabama. There's two different styles."

Gilmore licks some lather off his lip with a delicate flicker of his tongue. He moistens both lips in the process. "That don't make a difference no more," he says. "People thinkin' 'bout *unity* these days. All of us in the same boat no matter where we from."

"Guess so," Butler says lightly. But after cleaning his razor again he says: "Where you from?"

"Alabama."

"Then why you worryin' about Tarwell's church? Why don't he bring his people over to *mine?*"

Gilmore tightens his lips.

"He's the one plannin' to leave the community, not me."

"I'll tell him that," Gilmore says, closing his eyes tight and easing into a resolved silence.

Late on Thursday afternoon, Ray, his eyes averted, says he has to go. "It was a good shop, Reverend," he says, "but I got me a family to support."

"Where you goin' to?" Butler asks.

"This new parlor over on 145th."

"It's all set up, huh?"

Ray says, "Yeah."

"Well," Butler says, forcing a smile, "maybe my luck will change some now with you gone."

Ray looks sad. His fat jaws break out in sweat. He wipes it away, turning up the edge of his mustache. Lately he has taken to wearing his hair long about his ears: a steady warning, but of unsuspected proportions. "It ain't nothing to do with *luck,* Reverend," he sighs. "God*damn!* Everybody done switched over but *us.* Even the *barber schools* don't teach them old down-home cuts no more. You just *plain stubborn!*" Now he pauses, checking a great part of what has been building up in him. "Look, you want to get in on the money? It's easy as pie. There ain't no work involve in it. All you have to do is trim. *Trim!*" He sighs, smoothing down his ruffled mustache while stroking his face again. "You getting to be an old man, Reverend. You should be looking ahead. That's what I'm doing. That's *all* I'm doing."

"I'll take over your regulars."

"What regulars?" Ray says. "There ain't no regulars to divide. I cut your hair, you cut mine. Sometime Willie Russell or Jack Gilmore come in here out of guilt and let you burn their ears. What's gonna happen when they get tired? Who you go'n cut then, *yourself?*"

"You can take your stuff with you," Butler tells him, oblivious of Ray's exasperation. "But mind you don't take the goodwill over there to 145th."

Ray, locking his mouth against more hot words, sprawls into his own chair, penitent and brooding. Mickey, smoking a cigarette and listening in the john, blows a stream of smoke into the air and thinks his own thoughts.

"Now old Isaac," he tells his people on another Sunday morning, "he's a-layin' down to die. He done followed out God's directions and now ain't worried about but one thing: makin' his dyin' bed comfortable. He done married to Rebekah, accordin' to his *father's* will; he done planted, in his old age, the *seed* of a great nation in her womb. But now he's tired, Church, his eyesight is a-failin' and he's hungry for *red meat.* He's just about ready to lay his blessin' on anybody, just as long as he can get a taste of venison steak. But God—Glory, Glory—is a-workin' against him, as he always works against the *unwise.* He can't run the risk of that blessin' fallin' on Esau, who is all covered with hair. So he has to make Rebekah his instrument, one more time, to see that his work gits done. I want you to picture old Isaac now, just layin' in his darkness, pantin' for meat. And Jacob, God's beloved, sneakin' in to blind Isaac's bedside, a goatskin on his head, a service tray in his hand.[3] But look here, Church: yonder, over there, runnin' up from the woods with his hair holdin' him down, here come old Esau just a-hustlin' home. It's gonna be a close one, Church; both these boys is *movin' fast.* Now who go'n put money down on Esau? I say who go'n *bet* on Jacob? Both these boys is hustlin' on in. Who go'n lay somethin' on Esau this mornin' now . . .?"

No one responds.

"Well, then, who go'n *bet* on Jacob . . .?"

Most of them are confused. But some of the oldest, and most faithful, lay uninspired "a-mens" on Jacob.

"The race is gettin' closer by the minute . . ."

Marie Gilmore, dressed in her best white usher's uniform, gets up and leaves the room.

There is John Butler, the barber, on another Monday morning; again loitering by the window, again considering the rhythm of the street. He has not housed a complete checker game for almost a month.

"How do you do one of these Afros?" he asks Mickey, turning from the window.

"Nothin' to it, Rev," says Mickey, a careful boy who bears the jokings of his buddies concerning his own close-cut hair in order to keep some steady work. "Nothin' to it," he repeats, anticipation in his wise eyes. "You just let it grow, put some stuff on it, and keep it even all the time."

"What kind of stuff? Sound like a process to me."

"Naw, Rev," Mickey says.

"What is this *stuff?*"

"It's just to keep dandruff out."

"You think I could do one?"

"Hell, Rev, *any*body can do it."

Butler thinks a bit. "Mickey, what does it do for these kids?"

Mickey looks up at him, his face suggesting the fire of deeply held knowledge. "What *don't* it do for you?" is his answer.

Butler considers this.

[3]The story of Jacob and Esau is told in Genesis 27.

Just before closing time that same day John Gilmore comes in. He does not need a shave or even a trim. Nor does he offer much conversation. Butler waits. Finally Gilmore musters sufficient courage.

"Marie says she ain't comin' back to Second Calvary no more."

"Gone over to Tarwell, I bet."

Gilmore nods. His large hands dangle between his legs as he sits on the green metal chair across from Butler.

"She was a fine usher," Butler says. "Now Tarwell done beat me out of somethin' fine."

"You beat *yourself*," Gilmore says. "She didn't no more want to go over there than I want to stop comin' in here."

Butler looks at him. Gilmore looks down at his hands.

"So that's how it is?"

Gilmore nods again.

"And you call yourself a *Alabama* boy."

"That's been over a long time ago. Things change."

"I suppose you fixin' to grow yourself an Afro too, with that bald spot on your head."

Gilmore grows irritated. He gets up and moves toward the door. "I ain't fixin' to do *nothin'*," he says. "But if I was you I'd be fixin' to close up shop for a while so's I could reread my Bible for a spell."

"I know the Good Book," Butler says. "Thank you kindly."

Gilmore turns at the door, his long right hand holding it open. "Or maybe give up the Good Book and go back down home where you can cut the kind of hair you want."

"Maybe *all* of us ought to go back," Butler calls after him. But John Gilmore has already closed the door.

Through the ebb of the afternoon Butler slumps in his chair, taking inventory of his situation. He is not a poor man: the title to the shop is clear; the upper floor of his duplex is rented out to a schoolteacher; and there is, besides, a little money in the bank. But there is Mickey to consider if Butler were to close up shop; the boy's salary comes to three-fifty a week. He would not like to see Mickey leave, too. He would not like to see Mickey over on 145th, picking up ideas that have always been alien to his shop. He thinks some more about Mickey. Then he thinks about the South. Closing time comes, and goes. Mickey, passing down the street, sees him there and comes in. Butler sends him for coffee and then leans back again and closes his eyes. He thinks about going home, but again he thinks about the South. His feet braced against the footrest, the chair swinging around on its own, he recalls the red dirt roads of Alabama.

"Gimme a 'fro."

Having lost all sense of direction, he has to raise himself before the sound can be connected.

"Gimme a 'fro, please?"

A boy is standing next to his chair. He is Tommy Gilmore, youngest son of his former customer. Butler once baptized him during the heat of a summer revival. Tommy's hair is gray black and tightly curled, his mouth is open, his dungarees faded and torn at the knee; a dollar bill is held up to Butler in the edge of his fist.

"What you want?"

"A haircut."

"It's after closing time," Butler tells him. Then he sees the dollar. "And anyway, it's gonna cost you one-fifty. You got that much?"

The boy hands up the dollar.

"That ain't enough," Butler says, handing it back. "What else you got in your pocket? How much Marie give you?"

"Ain't got no more," the boy mumbles.

Greed lifts its thumb, but charity quickly waves it away. "You sure that's all you got?"

"Yes, sir."

Butler moves over to the hot-water heater and takes the board from behind it. He lays it across the armrests of his chair, takes a fresh cloth from the drawer and gives it a decisive snap. "Sit down, mister," he tells the boy. "I'm gonna give you the nicest schoolboy you ever seen."

Tommy does not move. His fist tightens around the dollar. Part of it disappears into the vise. His eyes narrow cynically. "A schoolboy ain't no 'fro," he states.

"Git up on the board, son."

"You go'n *gimme* one?"

"I'm a barber, ain't I?"

The boy mounts.

Butler secures him, and then ties the cloth.

Mickey comes in with the coffee, surveys the room, and then sets the steaming cup on the counter below the mirror.

Butler fastens the safety pin in the knot behind the boy's neck. "Now look here, Mickey, and you'll learn something," he says, as Mickey stands back to inspect the boy in the chair.

Mickey's eyes flicker over the scene, the curiosity in him slowly changing to doubt. "How you go'n do it, Rev? You ain't got no *comb,* you ain't got no *stuff,* and it ain't even *long* enough yet."

The boy begins to wiggle in the chair. The board shifts under him. "It is *too* long enough," he says.

"Naw, it ain't," says Mickey, malice in his eyes, his eyes on the younger boy's face, his head solemnly swaggering. "You got to go four, five months before you get enough. And you ain't got but one or two yet."

"Shut your trap, Mickey," Butler orders. He straightens the board with one hand and places the other on the struggling boy's shoulder. "I'm goin' to work on it now," he says, pressing down.

"But it ain't go'n do no *good!*"

"Shut up or go on home!" Butler says.

Mickey struts over to his own green chair at the end of the row, his face beaming the detachment of a protected bettor on a fixed poker game. He sits, watching with great intensity. The boy sees him and begins to squirm again.

"Quiet down, now," the barber says, this time pressing down on the boy's head. "I know what I'm doin'."

The boy obeys, whimpering some. Butler begins to use his shears. The hair is hard and thick, tightly curled and matted; but, deep inside it, near the scalp, he sees red dust rising. He is furious in his work, a starved man: turning and clipping and holding and brushing and shaping and holding and looking and seeing, beyond it all, the red dust rising. In ten minutes it is done. He stands back for a final look, then opens the pin, undoes the knot. Again he shapes the white sheet-square; again he brushes. The boy steps down, still whimpering softly. The board goes back behind the hot-water tank. And Butler lifts him up to the long mirror. The last whiffs of steam curl out from the cooling coffee. Mickey tightens his mouth and reaches into his pocket for a coin to toss against the wall. The boy looks into the mirror.

There is the barber, under the single bulb that sends light out through the windows of his shop. Gesturing, mouthing, making swift movements with his hands in the face of the shouting John Gilmore, who stands between him and the window. The boy is clinging to the man, crying softly. There is Mickey, still in his green chair against the wall, his own eyes, his open mind deciding.

"If you didn't call yourself a minister of God, I'd *kick your ass!*" the tightfisted John Gilmore is saying. His bottom lip is pushed far out from his face.

"Didn't you ever have a schoolboy when you was his age? Just answer me that."

"I went to a different school. But my son ain't no *plantation* Negro."[4]

"He didn't have nothin' but a dollar anyhow."

"Then you should of send him somewheres else!"

Tommy's mouth is open. He is crying without sound.

"*Look* at him! You can't *tell* me he don't look better now."

"We go'n close you down, old man. You hear what I'm sayin'? We go'n close this joint down and your church, *too!*"

"You go'n close us *all* down."

"We go'n run all you Toms[5] from the community . . ."

Mickey slides his hand into his pocket, rattling the coins.

On still another Sunday morning he stands, tired now, old, facing the last few strays of a scattered flock. It is almost Easter. Word is going around that Tarwell has already nailed the cross together in the basement of his church. Some say they have seen it. Others, some of those who are sitting here, are still reserving judgment. Marie Gilmore is back; but she has not come for the sermon. She sits at the back of the room in a purple dress, her eyes cast down. Butler, looking fierce and defensive, stares at the six or so faces peering up at him. Some look sheepish, some impatient; some look numb as always, waiting to be moved. He stands before them, his two hands gripping the edges of the pulpit. They wait. Several plump ladies fan themselves, waiting. One, Betty Jessup, sitting on the front pew, leans forward and whispers: "You fixin' to preach, or what?"

He does not answer.

Now the people begin to murmur among themselves: "What's wrong with him?" "When's he gonna start?"

"We are a stiff-necked people," he begins, his voice unusually steady, the music gone. "Our heads turn thisaway and thataway, but only in one direction at a time." He pauses. "We'll be judged for it."

"Who go'n judge us?" Marie Gilmore suddenly fires from the back of the room. They all turn, their mouths hanging loose. Marie Gilmore rises. "Who's to say what's to be judged and what ain't?" she says through trembling lips.

[4] I.e., a slave.

[5] Uncle Toms; black men who base their behavior on the expectations of whites—so called after the title character in Harriet Beecher Stowe's *Uncle Tom's Cabin.*

"Who's left to say for certain he knows the rules or can show us where they written down?" she says.

The people are amazed. Several of them wave their hands and nod their heads to quiet her. Marie Gilmore does not notice. Her eyes are fixed on Butler.

He stands behind the pulpit and does not say anything.

At Sunday dinner Ella says: "Well, what you go'n do *now?*"

"Send that truant officer after Mickey," Butler says quietly.

"What else?"

He shifts his eyes about the room, looking for something.

Ella sighs and strikes her chest. "Lord, why I had to marry a man with a *hard head?*"

Butler looks her in the face. "Because you couldn't do no better," he tells her.

1977

Alice Walker 1944–

Alice Walker was born in Georgia, the eighth child of impoverished black sharecroppers. Encouraged by her mother, who supported her desire to gain an education and become a writer, Walker graduated at the top of her high school class and received a scholarship to Spelman College for women in Atlanta. After two years at Spelman, she transferred to Sarah Lawrence College in New York, graduating with a B.A. in 1965.

Returning to the South, to Mississippi, she taught writing and black literature and joined in efforts to improve welfare rights and increase voter registration among Southern blacks. Her first publication appeared in 1966, an essay on the civil rights movement. Two years later she published her first book, Once *(1968), a collection of poems. Her first collection of short fiction,* In Love and Trouble *(1973), won an award from the National Institute of Arts and Letters for its unflinching portrayals of black women who exist as the wretched victims of racial and sexual oppression. Her second volume of stories,* You Can't Keep a Good Woman Down *(1981), brought her additional recognition as a short-story writer, but her greatest recognition has come as a writer of novels.*

The Third Life of Grange Copeland *(1970), Walker's first novel, presented themes that appear in much of her writing: the dehumanizing racism and sexism that black women experience at the hands of whites and blacks alike. Her second novel,* Meridian *(1976), won praise as the finest novel of the 1960s civil rights movement. Her third novel,* The Color Purple *(1982), received worldwide acclaim. Set in the first half of the twentieth century and written in the black English of the American South, the novel covers thirty years in the life of a semiliterate, downtrodden black woman who triumphs over black male oppression and demonstrates the power of women to join together and liberate themselves from sexual abuse and violence.* The Color Purple *won for its author a Pulitzer Prize and was made into an award-winning motion picture. By 1988 the novel had been translated into twenty-two languages and had sold more than six million copies.* The Same River Twice *(1996), a compilation of passages drawn from Walker's journals and letters, describes her experiences during the writing of the novel and the production of the movie* The Color Purple *and reports the difficulties that came with the fame and riches the movie brought.*

Walker has dealt unflinchingly with violence and sexuality, abortion, sadism, rape, pornography, and the impact of racial and sexual stereotypes on the relations of black men and women. Some critics have objected that her stories are too often melodramatic, that her characterizations are simplistic, a repetitious portrayal of good women suffering at the hands of bad men. And Walker has acknowledged that as a black feminist (she prefers the word "womanist"), her sympathies lie almost entirely with black women.

But in her collection of essays titled Living by the Word: Selected Writings, 1973–1987 *(1988), in a film documentary on her life and work,* Visions of the Spirit *(1988), and in the novels* The Temple of My Familiar *(1990),* Possessing the Secret of Joy *(1992),* By the Light of My Father's Smile *(1998), and* The Way Forward Is with a Broken Heart *(2000), Walker reveals a vision that has grown beyond black feminism to a sympathy for all living things on a planet filled with greed, ignorance, and the threat of nuclear war. Nevertheless, her greatest achievement remains her portrayal of the lives of black women, often grotesque and inarticulate, who struggle to deliver themselves from what Alice Walker has described as the black woman's demeaning life as "the mule of the world."*

FURTHER READING: *Alice Walker,* ed. H. Bloom, 1990; D. Winchell, *Alice Walker,* 1992; *Critical Essays on Alice Walker,* ed. I. Dieke, 1999; M. Lauret, *Alice Walker,* 2000; E. White, *Alice Walker: A Life,* 2004; G. Bates, *Alice Walker: A Critical Companion,* 2005.

TEXTS: *In Love and Trouble,* 1973; "Burial" from *Revolutionary Petunias and other Poems,* 1973.

EVERYDAY USE

for your grandmama

I will wait for her in the yard that Maggie and I made so clean and wavy yesterday afternoon. A yard like this is more comfortable than most people know. It is not just a yard. It is like an extended living room. When the hard clay is swept clean as a floor and the fine sand around the edges lined with tiny, irregular grooves, anyone can come and sit and look up into the elm tree and wait for the breezes that never come inside the house.

Maggie will be nervous until after her sister goes: she will stand hopelessly in corners, homely and ashamed of the burn scars down her arms and legs, eying her sister with a mixture of envy and awe. She thinks her sister has held life always in the palm of one hand, that "no" is a word the world never learned to say to her.

You've no doubt seen those TV shows where the child who has "made it" is confronted, as a surprise, by her own mother and father, tottering in weakly from backstage. (A pleasant surprise, of course: What would they do if parent and child came on the show only to curse out and insult each other?) On TV mother and child embrace and smile into each other's faces. Sometimes the mother and father weep, the child wraps them in her arms and leans across the table to tell how she would not have made it without their help. I have seen these programs.

Sometimes I dream a dream in which Dee and I are suddenly brought together on a TV program of this sort. Out of a dark and soft-seated limousine I am ushered into a bright room filled with many people. There I meet a smiling, gray, sporty man like Johnny Carson who shakes my hand and tells me what a fine girl I have. Then we are on the stage and Dee is embracing me with tears in her eyes. She pins on my dress a large orchid, even though she has told me once that she thinks orchids are tacky flowers.

In real life I am a large, big-boned woman with rough, man-working hands. In the winter I wear flannel nightgowns to bed and overalls during the day. I can kill and clean a hog as mercilessly as a man. My fat keeps me hot in zero weather. I can work outside all day, breaking ice to get water for washing; I can eat pork liver cooked over the open fire minutes after it comes steaming from the hog. One winter I knocked a bull calf straight in the brain between the eyes with a sledge hammer and had the meat hung up to chill before nightfall. But of course all this does not show on television. I am the way my daughter would want me to be: a hundred pounds lighter, my skin like an uncooked barley pancake. My hair glistens in the hot bright lights. Johnny Carson has much to do to keep up with my quick and witty tongue.

But that is a mistake. I know even before I wake up. Who ever knew a Johnson with a quick tongue? Who can even imagine me looking a strange white man in the eye? It seems to me I have talked to them always with one foot raised in flight, with my head turned in whichever way is farthest from them. Dee, though. She would always look anyone in the eye. Hesitation was no part of her nature.

"How do I look, Mama?" Maggie says, showing just enough of her thin body enveloped in pink skirt and red blouse for me to know she's there, almost hidden by the door.

"Come out into the yard," I say.

Have you ever seen a lame animal, perhaps a dog run over by some careless person rich enough to own a car, sidle up to someone who is ignorant enough to be kind to him? That is the way my Maggie walks. She has been like this, chin on chest, eyes on ground, feet in shuffle, ever since the fire that burned the other house to the ground.

Dee is lighter than Maggie, with nicer hair and a fuller figure. She's a woman now, though sometimes I forget. How long ago was it that the other house burned? Ten, twelve years? Sometimes I can still hear the flames and feel Maggie's arms sticking to me, her hair smoking and her dress falling off her in little black papery flakes. Her eyes seemed stretched open, blazed open by the flames reflected in them. And Dee. I see her standing off under the sweet gum tree she used to dig gum out of; a look of concentration on her face as she watched the last dingy gray board of the house fall in toward the red-hot brick chimney. Why don't you do a dance around the ashes? I'd wanted to ask her. She had hated the house that much.

I used to think she hated Maggie, too. But that was before we raised the money, the church and me, to send her to Augusta to school. She used to read to us without pity; forcing words, lies, other folks' habits, whole lives upon us two, sitting trapped and ignorant underneath the sound of her voice. She washed us in a river of make-believe, burned us with a lot of knowledge we didn't necessarily need to know. Pressed us to her with the serious way she read, to shove us away at just the moment, like dimwits, we seemed about to understand.

Dee wanted nice things. A yellow organdy dress to wear to her graduation from high school; black pumps to match a green suit she'd made from an old suit somebody gave me. She was determined to stare down any disaster in her efforts. Her eyelids would not flicker for minutes at a time. Often I fought off the temptation to shake her. At sixteen she had a style of her own: and knew what style was.

I never had an education myself. After second grade the school was closed down. Don't ask me why: in 1927 colored asked fewer questions than they do now. Sometimes Maggie reads to me. She stumbles along good-naturedly but can't see well. She knows she is not bright. Like good looks and money, quickness passed her by. She will marry John Thomas (who has mossy teeth in an earnest face) and then I'll be free to sit here and I guess just sing church songs to myself. Although I never was a good singer. Never could carry a tune. I was always better at a man's job. I used to love to milk till I was hooked in the side in '49. Cows are soothing and slow and don't bother you, unless you try to milk them the wrong way.

I have deliberately turned my back on the house. It is three rooms, just like the one that burned, except the roof is tin; they don't make shingle roofs any more. There are no real windows, just some holes cut in the sides, like the portholes in a ship, but not round and not square, with rawhide holding the shutters up on the outside. This house is in a pasture, too, like the other one. No doubt when Dee sees it she will want to tear it down. She wrote me once that no matter where we "choose" to live, she will manage to come see us. But she will never bring her friends. Maggie and I thought about this and Maggie asked me, "Mama, when did Dee ever *have* any friends?"

She had a few. Furtive boys in pink shirts hanging about on washday after school. Nervous girls who never laughed. Impressed with her they worshiped the well-turned phrase, the cute shape, the scalding humor that erupted like bubbles in lye. She read to them.

When she was courting Jimmy T she didn't have much time to pay to us, but turned all her faultfinding power on him. He *flew* to marry a cheap city girl from a family of ignorant flashy people. She hardly had time to recompose herself.

When she comes I will meet—but there they are!

Maggie attempts to make a dash for the house, in her shuffling way, but I stay her with my hand. "Come back here," I say. And she stops and tries to dig a well in the sand with her toe.

It is hard to see them clearly through the strong sun. But even the first glimpse of leg out of the car tells me it is Dee. Her feet were always neat-looking, as if God himself had shaped them with a certain style. From the other side of the car comes a short, stocky man. Hair is all over his head a foot long and hanging from his chin like a kinky mule tail. I hear Maggie suck in her breath. "Uhnnnh," is what it sounds like. Like when you see the wriggling end of a snake just in front of your foot on the road. "Uhnnnh."

Dee next. A dress down to the ground, in this hot weather. A dress so loud it hurts my eyes. There are yellows and oranges enough to throw back the light of the sun. I feel my whole face warming from the heat waves it throws out. Earrings gold, too, and hanging down to her shoulders. Bracelets dangling and making noises when she moves her arm up to shake the folds of the dress out of her armpits. The dress is loose and flows, and as she walks closer, I like it. I hear Maggie go "Uhnnnh" again. It is her sister's hair. It stands straight up like the wool on a sheep. It is black as night and around the edges are two long pigtails that rope about like small lizards disappearing behind her ears.

"Wa-su-zo-Tean-o!" she says, coming on in that gliding way the dress makes her move. The short stocky fellow with the hair to his naval is all grinning and he follows up with "Asalamalakim, my mother and sister!" He moves to hug Maggie but she falls back, right up against the back of my chair. I feel her trembling there and when I look up I see the perspiration falling off her chin.

"Don't get up," says Dee. Since I am stout it takes something of a push. You can see me trying to move a second or two before I make it. She turns, showing white heels through her sandals, and goes back to the car. Out she peeks next with a Polaroid. She stoops down quickly and lines up picture after picture of me sitting there in front of the house with Maggie cowering behind me. She never takes a shot without making sure the house is included. When a cow comes nibbling around the edge of the yard she snaps it and me and Maggie *and* the house. Then she puts the Polaroid in the back seat of the car, and comes up and kisses me on the forehead.

Meanwhile Asalamalakim is going through motions with Maggie's hand. Maggie's hand is as limp as a fish, and probably as cold, despite the sweat, and she keeps trying to pull it back. It looks like Asalamalakim wants to shake hands but wants to do it fancy. Or maybe he don't know how people shake hands. Anyhow, he soon gives up on Maggie.

"Well," I say. "Dee."

"No, Mama," she says. "Not 'Dee,' Wangero Leewanika Kemanjo!"

"What happened to 'Dee'?" I wanted to know.

"She's dead," Wangero said. "I couldn't bear it any longer, being named after the people who oppress me."

"You know as well as me you was named after your aunt Dicie," I said. Dicie is my sister. She named Dee. We called her "Big Dee" after Dee was born.

"But who was *she* named after?" asked Wangero.

"I guess after Grandma Dee," I said.

"And who was she named after?" asked Wangero.

"Her mother," I said, and saw Wangero was getting tired. "That's about as far back as I can trace it," I said. Though, in fact, I probably could have carried it back beyond the Civil War through the branches.

"Well," said Asalamalakim, "there you are."

"Uhnnnh," I heard Maggie say.

"There I was not," I said, "before 'Dicie' cropped up in our family, so why should I try to trace it that far back?"

He just stood there grinning, looking down on me like somebody inspecting a Model A car. Every once in a while he and Wangero sent eye signals over my head.

"How do you pronounce this name?" I asked.

"You don't have to call me by it if you don't want to," said Wangero.

"Why shouldn't I?" I asked. "If that's what you want us to call you, we'll call you."

"I know it might sound awkward at first," said Wangero.

"I'll get used to it," I said. "Ream it out again."

Well, soon we got the name out of the way. Asalamalakim had a name twice as long and three times as hard. After I tripped over it two or three times he told me to just call him Hakim-a-barber. I wanted to ask him was he a barber, but I didn't really think he was, so I didn't ask.

"You must belong to those beef-cattle peoples down the road," I said. They said "Asalamalakim" when they met you, too, but they didn't shake hands. Always too busy: feeding the cattle, fixing the fences, putting up salt-lick shelters, throwing down hay. When the white folks poisoned some of the herd the men stayed up all night with rifles in their hands. I walked a mile and a half just to see the sight.

Hakim-a-barber said, "I accept some of their doctrines, but farming and raising cattle is not my style." (They didn't tell me, and I didn't ask, whether Wangero (Dee) had really gone and married him.)

We sat down to eat and right away he said he didn't eat collards and pork was unclean. Wangero, though, went on through the chitlins and corn bread, the greens and everything else. She talked a blue streak over the sweet potatoes. Everything delighted her. Even the fact that we still used the benches her daddy made for the table when we couldn't afford to buy chairs.

"Oh, Mama!" she cried. Then turned to Hakim-a-barber. "I never knew how lovely these benches are. You can feel the rump prints," she said, running her hands underneath her and along the bench. Then she gave a sigh and her hand closed over Grandma Dee's butter dish. "That's it!" she said. "I knew there was something I wanted to ask you if I could have." She jumped up from the table and went over in the corner where the churn stood, the milk in it clabber by now. She looked at the churn and looked at it.

"This churn top is what I need," she said. "Didn't Uncle Buddy whittle it out of a tree you all used to have?"

"Yes," I said.

"Uh huh," she said happily. "And I want the dasher, too."

"Uncle Buddy whittle that, too?" asked the barber.

Dee (Wangero) looked up at me.

"Aunt Dee's first husband whittled the dash," said Maggie so low you almost couldn't hear her. "His name was Henry, but they called him Stash."

"Maggie's brain is like an elephant's," Wangero said, laughing. "I can use the churn top as a centerpiece for the alcove table," she said, sliding a plate over the churn, "and I'll think of something artistic to do with the dasher."

When she finished wrapping the dasher the handle stuck out. I took it for a moment in my hands. You didn't even have to look close to see where hands pushing the dasher up and down to make butter had left a kind of sink in the wood. In fact, there were a lot of small sinks; you could see where thumbs and fingers had sunk into the wood. It was beautiful light yellow wood, from a tree that grew in the yard where Big Dee and Stash had lived.

After dinner Dee (Wangero) went to the trunk at the foot of my bed and started rifling through it. Maggie hung back in the kitchen over the dishpan. Out came Wangero with two quilts. They had been pieced by Grandma Dee and then Big Dee and me had hung them on the quilt frames on the front porch and quilted them. One was in the Lone Star pattern. The other was Walk Around the Mountain. In both of them were scraps of dresses Grandma Dee had worn fifty and more years ago. Bits and pieces of Grandpa Jarrell's Paisley shirts. And one teeny faded blue piece, about the size of a penny matchbox, that was from Great Grandpa Ezra's uniform that he wore in the Civil War.

"Mama," Wangero said sweet as a bird. "Can I have these old quilts?"

I heard something fall in the kitchen, and a minute later the kitchen door slammed.

"Why don't you take one or two of the others?" I asked. "These old things was just done by me and Big Dee from some tops your grandma pieced before she died."

"No," said Wangero. "I don't want those. They are stitched around the borders by machine."

"That'll make them last better," I said.

"That's not the point," said Wangero. "These are all pieces of dresses Grandma used to wear. She did all this stitching by hand. Imagine!" She held the quilts securely in her arms, stroking them.

"Some of the pieces, like those lavender ones, come from old clothes her mother handed down to her," I said, moving up to touch the quilts. Dee (Wangero) moved back just enough so that I couldn't reach the quilts. They already belonged to her.

"Imagine!" she breathed again, clutching them closely to her bosom.

"The truth is," I said, "I promised to give them quilts to Maggie, for when she marries John Thomas."

She gasped like a bee had stung her.

"Maggie can't appreciate these quilts!" she said. "She'd probably be backward enough to put them to everyday use."

"I reckon she would," I said. "God knows I been saving 'em for long enough with nobody using 'em. I hope she will!" I didn't want to bring up how I had offered Dee (Wangero) a quilt when she went away to college. Then she had told me they were old-fashioned, out of style.

"But they're *priceless!*" she was saying now, furiously; for she has a temper. "Maggie would put them on the bed and in five years they'd be in rags. Less than that!"

"She can always make some more," I said. "Maggie knows how to quilt."

Dee (Wangero) looked at me with hatred. "You just will not understand. The point is these quilts, *these* quilts!"

"Well," I said, stumped. "What would *you* do with them?"

"Hang them," she said. As if that was the only thing you *could* do with quilts.

Maggie by now was standing in the door. I could almost hear the sound her feet made as they scraped over each other.

"She can have them, Mama," she said, like somebody used to never winning anything, or having anything reserved for her. "I can 'member Grandma Dee without the quilts."

I looked at her hard. She had filled her bottom lip with checkerberry snuff and it gave her face a kind of dopey, hangdog look. It was Grandma Dee and Big Dee who taught her how to quilt herself. She stood there with her scarred hands hidden in the folds of her skirt. She looked at her sister with something like fear but she wasn't mad at her. This was Maggie's portion. This was the way she knew God to work.

When I looked at her like that something hit me in the top of my head and ran down to the soles of my feet. Just like when I'm in church and the spirit of God touches me and I get happy and shout. I did something I never had done before: hugged Maggie to me, then dragged her on into the room, snatched the quilts out of Miss Wangero's hands and dumped them into Maggie's lap. Maggie just sat there on my bed with her mouth open.

"Take one or two of the others," I said to Dee.

But she turned without a word and went out to Hakim-a-barber.

"You just don't understand," she said, as Maggie and I came out to the car.

"What don't I understand?" I wanted to know.

"Your heritage," she said. And then she turned to Maggie, kissed her, and said, "You ought to try to make something of yourself, too, Maggie. It's really a new day for us. But from the way you and Mama still live you'd never know it."

She put on some sunglasses that hid everything above the tip of her nose and her chin.

Maggie smiled; maybe at the sunglasses. But a real smile, not scared. After we watched the car dust settle I asked Maggie to bring me a dip of snuff. And then the two of us sat there just enjoying, until it was time to go in the house and go to bed.

1973

BURIAL

I

They have fenced in the dirt road
that once led to Wards Chapel
A.M.E. church,
and cows graze
among the stones that
mark my family's graves.
The massive oak is gone
from out the church yard,
but the giant space is left
unfilled;
despite the two-lane blacktop
that slides across
the old, unalterable
roots.

II

Today I bring my own child here;
to this place where my father's
grandmother rests undisturbed
beneath the Georgia sun,

above her the neatstepping hooves
of cattle.
Here the graves soon grow back into the land.
Have been known to sink. To drop open without
warning. To cover themselves with wild ivy,
blackberries. Bittersweet and sage.
No one knows why. No one asks.
When Burning Off Day comes, as it does
some years,
the graves are haphazardly cleared and snakes
hacked to death and burned sizzling
in the brush. . . . The odor of smoke, oak
leaves, honeysuckle.
Forgetful of geographic resolutions as birds,
the farflung young fly South to bury
the old dead.

III

The old women move quietly up
and touch Sis Rachel's face.
"Tell Jesus I'm coming," they say.
"Tell Him I ain't goin' to *be*
long."

My grandfather turns his creaking head
away from the lavender box.
He does not cry. But looks afraid.
For years he called her "Woman";
shortened over the decades to
"'Oman."
On the cut stone for "'Oman's" grave
he did not notice
they had misspelled her name.
(The stone reads *Racher Walker*—not "Rachel"—
Loving Wife, Devoted Mother.)

IV

As a young woman, who had known her? Tripping
eagerly, "loving wife," to my grandfather's
bed. Not pretty, but serviceable. A hard
worker, with rough, moist hands. Her own two
babies dead before she came.
Came to seven children.
To aprons and sweat.

Came to quiltmaking.
Came to canning and vegetable gardens
big as fields.
Came to fields to plow.
Cotton to chop.
Potatoes to dig.
Came to multiple measles, chickenpox,
and croup.
Came to water from springs.
Came to leaning houses one story high.
Came to rivalries. Saturday night battles.
Came to straightened hair, Noxzema, and
feet washing at the Hardshell Baptist church.[1]
Came to zinnias around the woodpile.
Came to grandchildren not of her blood
whom she taught to dip snuff without
sneezing.
Came to death blank, forgetful of it all.

When he called her "'Oman" she no longer
listened. Or heard, or knew, or felt.

V

It is not until I see my first grade teacher
review her body that I cry.
Not for the dead, but for the gray in my
first grade teacher's hair. For memories
of before I was born, when teacher and
grandmother loved each other; and later
above the ducks made of soap and the orange-legged
chicks Miss Reynolds drew over
my own small hand
on paper with wide blue lines.

VI

Not for the dead, but for memories. None of
them sad. But seen from the angle of her
death.

1973

[1]A fundamentalist church in which members of the congregation wash the feet of others in a literalist imitation of Jesus' actions in John 13.

Amy Tan 1952–

Amy Tan's parents emigrated from China to California, where she was born and has spent most of her life. In 1973, after graduating from college, she spent three years in postgraduate study and then worked as a reporter, as an editor, and as a technical writer for computer companies.

In 1989 she published The Joy Luck Club, *a collection of interwoven stories about four Chinese women and their Chinese American daughters. It was an immediate success and soon was followed by her second novel,* The Kitchen God's Wife *(1991), the story of her grandmother and mother and of their lives in China. In her third novel,* The Hundred Secret Senses *(1995), Tan moved from the subject of mothers and daughters to a story of two half-sisters, one American, one Chinese, who make a pilgrimage to a remote mountain village in China where the American sister grows into an understanding of the mystical and spiritual wisdom of her Chinese half-sister. Tan has also written a children's book,* The Moon Lady *(1992). In her recent novel,* The Bonesetter's Daughter *(2001), as in much of her best fiction, Tan examines layers of family relationships and the shared and often anguished experiences of mothers from an ancient civilization and their modern Chinese American daughters living in today's America. A collection of Tan's autobiographical essays,* The Opposite of Fate, A Book of Musings, *was published in 2003.*

FURTHER READING: E. Huntley, *Amy Tan: A Critical Companion,* 1998; *Amy Tan,* ed. H. Bloom, 2000; M. Snodgrass, *Amy Tan: A Literary Companion,* 2004.

TEXT: *The Joy Luck Club,* 1989.

from *THE JOY LUCK CLUB*

HALF AND HALF

As proof of her faith, my mother used to carry a small leatherette Bible when she went to the First Chinese Baptist Church every Sunday. But later, after my mother lost her faith in God, that leatherette Bible wound up wedged under a too-short table leg, a way for her to correct the imbalances of life. It's been there for over twenty years.

My mother pretends that Bible isn't there. Whenever anyone asks her what it's doing there, she says, a little too loudly, "Oh, this? I forgot." But I know she sees it. My mother is not the best housekeeper in the world, and after all these years that Bible is still clean white.

Tonight I'm watching my mother sweep under the same kitchen table, something she does every night after dinner. She gently pokes her broom around the table leg propped up by the Bible. I watch her, sweep after sweep, waiting for the right moment to tell her about Ted and me, that we're getting divorced. When I tell her, I know she's going to say, "This cannot be."

And when I say that it is certainly true, that our marriage is over, I know what else she will say: "Then you must save it."

And even though I know it's hopeless—there's absolutely nothing left to save—I'm afraid if I tell her that, she'll still persuade me to try.

I think it's ironic that my mother wants me to fight the divorce. Seventeen years ago she was chagrined when I started dating Ted. My oldest sisters had dated only Chinese boys from church before getting married.

Ted and I met in a politics of ecology class when he leaned over and offered to pay me two dollars for the last week's notes. I refused the money and accepted a cup of coffee instead. This was during my second semester at UC Berkeley, where I had enrolled as a liberal arts major and later changed to fine arts. Ted was in his third year in pre-med, his choice, he told me, ever since he dissected a fetal pig in the sixth grade.

I have to admit that what I initially found attractive in Ted were precisely the things that made him different from my brothers and the Chinese boys I had dated; his brashness; the assuredness in which he asked for things and expected to get them; his opinionated manner; his angular face and lanky body; the thickness of his arms; the fact that his parents immigrated from Tarrytown, New York, not Tientsin, China.

My mother must have noticed these same differences after Ted picked me up one evening at my parents' house. When I returned home, my mother was still up, watching television.

"He is American," warned my mother, as if I had been too blind to notice. "A *waigoren*."[1]

"I'm American too," I said, "And it's not as if I'm going to marry him or something."

Mrs. Jordan also had a few words to say. Ted had casually invited me to a family picnic, the annual clan reunion held by the polo fields in Golden Gate Park. Although we had dated only a few times in the last month—and certainly had never slept together, since both of us lived at home—Ted introduced me to all his relatives as his girlfriend, which, until then, I didn't know I was.

Later, when Ted and his father went off to play volleyball with the others, his mother took my hand, and we started walking along the grass, away from the crowd. She squeezed my palm warmly but never seemed to look at me.

"I'm so glad to meet you *finally*," Mrs. Jordan said. I wanted to tell her I wasn't really Ted's girlfriend, but she went on. "I think it's nice that you and Ted are having such a lot of fun together. So I hope you won't misunderstand what I have to say."

And then she spoke quietly about Ted's future, his needs to concentrate on his medical studies, why it would be years before he could even think about marriage. She assured me she had nothing whatsoever against minorities; she and her husband, who owned a chain of office-supply stores, personally knew many fine people who were Oriental, Spanish, and even black. But Ted was going to be in one of those professions where he would be judged by a different standard, by patients and other doctors who might not be as understanding as the Jordans were. She said it was so unfortunate the way the rest of the world was, how unpopular the Vietnam War was.

"Mrs. Jordan, I am not Vietnamese," I said softly, even though I was on the verge of shouting. "And I have no intention of marrying your son."

[1]Chinese: "foreigner."

When Ted drove me home that day, I told him I couldn't see him anymore. When he asked me why, I shrugged. When he pressed me, I told him what his mother had said, verbatim, without comment.

"And you're just going to sit there! Let my mother decide what's right?" he shouted, as if I were a co-conspirator who had turned traitor. I was touched that Ted was so upset.

"What should we do?" I asked, and I had a pained feeling I thought was the beginning of love.

In those early months, we clung to each other with a rather silly desperation, because, in spite of anything my mother or Mrs. Jordan could say, there was nothing that really prevented us from seeing one another. With imagined tragedy hovering over us, we became inseparable, two halves creating the whole: yin and yang.[2] I was victim to his hero. I was always in danger and he was always rescuing me. I would fall and he would lift me up. It was exhilarating and draining. The emotional effect of saving and being saved was addicting to both of us. And that, as much as anything we ever did in bed, was how we made love to each other: conjoined where my weaknesses needed protection.

"What should we do?" I continued to ask him. And within a year of our first meeting we were living together. The month before Ted started medical school at UCSF[3] we were married in the Episcopal church, and Mrs. Jordan sat in the front pew, crying as was expected of the groom's mother. When Ted finished his residency in dermatology, we bought a run-down three-story Victorian with a large garden in Ashbury Heights. Ted helped me set up a studio downstairs so I could take in work as a free-lance production assistant for graphic artists.

Over the years, Ted decided where we went on vacation. He decided what new furniture we should buy. He decided we should wait until we moved into a better neighborhood before having children. We used to discuss some of these matters, but we both knew the question would boil down to my saying, "Ted, you decide," After a while, there were no more discussions. Ted simply decided. And I never thought of objecting. I preferred to ignore the world around me, obsessing only over what was in front of me: my T-square, my X-acto knife, my blue pencil.

But last year Ted's feelings about what he called "decision and responsibility" changed. A new patient had come to him asking what she could do about the spidery veins on her cheeks. And when he told her he could suck the red veins out and make her beautiful again, she believed him. But instead, he accidentally sucked a nerve out, and the left side of her smile fell down and she sued him.

After he lost the malpractice lawsuit—his first, and a big shock to him I now realize—he started pushing me to make decisions. Did I think we should buy an American car or a Japanese car? Should we change from whole-life to term insurance? What did I think about that candidate who supported the contras? What about a family?

I thought about things, the pros and the cons. But in the end I would be so confused, because I never believed there was ever any one right answer, yet there were many wrong ones. So whenever I said, "You decide," or "I don't

[2]Chinese philosophical principle of opposites, whose union and interactions shape the destiny of all things.

[3]University of California at San Francisco.

care," or "Either way is fine with me," Ted would say in his impatient voice, "No, *you* decide. You can't have it both ways, none of the responsibility, none of the blame."

I could feel things changing between us. A protective veil had been lifted and Ted now started pushing me about everything. He asked me to decide on the most trivial matters, as if he were baiting me. Italian food or Thai. One appetizer or two. Which appetizer. Credit card or cash. Visa or Master-Card.

Last month, when he was leaving for a two-day dermatology course in Los Angeles, he asked if I wanted to come along and then quickly, before I could say anything, he added, "Never mind, I'd rather go alone."

"More time to study," I agreed.

"No, because you can never make up your mind about anything," he said.

And I protested, "But it's only with things that aren't important."

"Nothing is important to you, then," he said in a tone of disgust.

"Ted, if you want me to go, I'll go."

And it was as if something snapped in him. "How the hell did we ever get married? Did you just say 'I do' because the minister said 'repeat after me'? What would you have done with your life if I had never married you? Did it ever occur to you?"

This was such a big leap in logic, between what I said and what he said, that I thought we were like two people standing apart on separate mountain peaks, recklessly leaning forward to throw stones at one another, unaware of the dangerous chasm that separated us.

But now I realize Ted knew what he was saying all along. He wanted to show me the rift. Because later that evening he called from Los Angeles and said he wanted a divorce.

Ever since Ted's been gone, I've been thinking. Even if I had expected it, even if I had known what I was going to do with my life, it still would have knocked the wind out of me.

When something that violent hits you, you can't help but lose your balance and fall. And after you pick yourself up, you realize you can't trust anybody to save you—not your husband, not your mother, not God. So what can you do to stop yourself from tilting and falling all over again?

My mother believed in God's will for many years. It was as if she had turned on a celestial faucet and goodness kept pouring out. She said it was faith that kept all these good things coming our way, only I thought she said "fate," because she couldn't pronounce that "th" sound in "faith."

And later, I discovered that maybe it was fate all along, that faith was just an illusion that somehow you're in control. I found out the most I could have was hope, and with that I was not denying any possibility, good or bad. I was just saying, If there is a choice, dear God or whatever you are, here's where the odds should be placed.

I remember the day I started thinking this, it was such a revelation to me. It was the day my mother lost her faith in God. She found that things of unquestioned certainty could never be trusted again.

We had gone to the beach, to a secluded spot south of the city near Devil's Slide. My father had read in *Sunset* magazine that this was a good place to catch ocean perch. And although my father was not a fisherman but a pharmacist's assistant who had once been a doctor in China, he believed in his *nengkan,* his ability to do anything he put his mind to. My mother believed she had *nengkan* to cook anything my father had a mind to catch. It was this belief in their *nengkan* that had brought my parents to America. It had enabled them to have seven children and buy a house in the Sunset district with very little money. It had given them the confidence to believe their luck would never run out, that God was on their side, that the house gods had only benevolent things to report and our ancestors were pleased, that life-time warranties meant our lucky streak would never break, that all the elements were in balance, the right amount of wind and water.

So there we were, the nine of us: my father, my mother, my two sisters, four brothers, and myself, so confident as we walked along our first beach. We marched in single file across the cool gray sand, from oldest to youngest. I was in the middle, fourteen years old. We would have made quite a sight, if anyone else had been watching, nine pairs of bare feet trudging, nine pairs of shoes in hand, nine black-haired heads turned toward the water to watch the waves tumbling in.

The wind was whipping the cotton trousers around my legs and I looked for some place where the sand wouldn't kick into my eyes. I saw we were standing in the hollow of a cove. It was like a giant bowl, cracked in half, the other half washed out to sea. My mother walked toward the right, where the beach was clean, and we all followed. On this side, the wall of the cove curved around and protected the beach from both the rough surf and the wind. And along this wall, in its shadow, was a reef ledge that started at the edge of the beach and continued out past the cove where the waters became rough. It seemed as though a person could walk out to sea on this reef, although it looked very rocky and slippery. On the other side of the cove, the wall was more jagged, eaten away by the water. It was pitted with crevices, so when the waves crashed against the wall, the water spewed out of these holes like white gulleys.

Thinking back, I remember that this beach cove was a terrible place, full of wet shadows that chilled us and invisible specks that flew into our eyes and made it hard for us to see the dangers. We were all blind with the newness of this experience: a Chinese family trying to act like a typical American family at the beach.

My mother spread out an old striped bedspread, which flapped in the wind until nine pairs of shoes weighed it down. My father assembled his long bamboo fishing pole, a pole he had made with his own two hands, remembering its design from his childhood in China. And we children sat huddled shoulder to shoulder on the blanket, reaching into the grocery sack full of bologna sandwiches, which we hungrily ate salted with sand from our fingers.

Then my father stood up and admired his fishing pole, its grace, its strength. Satisfied, he picked up his shoes and walked to the edge of the beach and then onto the reef to the point just before it was wet. My two older sisters, Janice and Ruth, jumped up from the blanket and slapped their thighs to get the sand off. Then they slapped each other's back and raced off down the beach shrieking. I was about to get up and chase them, but my mother nodded toward my four brothers and reminded me: "*Dangsying tamende shenti,*" which means "Take care of them," or literally, "Watch out for their bodies." These bodies were the anchors of my life: Matthew, Mark, Luke, and Bing. I fell back onto the sand, groaning as my throat grew tight, as I made the same lament: "Why?" Why did I have to care for them?

And she gave me the same answer: "*Yiding*."

I must. Because they were my brothers. My sisters had once taken care of me. How else could I learn responsibility? How else could I appreciate what my parents had done for me?

Matthew, Mark, and Luke were twelve, ten, and nine, old enough to keep themselves loudly amused. They had already buried Luke in a shallow grave of sand so that only his head stuck out. Now they were starting to pat together the outlines of a sand-castle wall on top of him.

But Bing was only four, easily excitable and easily bored and irritable. He didn't want to play with the other brothers because they had pushed him off to the side, admonishing him, "No, Bing, you'll just wreck it."

So Bing wandered down the beach, walking stiffly like an ousted emperor, picking up shards of rock and chunks of driftwood and flinging them with all his might into the surf. I trailed behind, imagining tidal waves and wondering what I would do if one appeared. I called to Bing every now and then, "Don't go too close to the water. You'll get your feet wet." And I thought how much I seemed like my mother, always worried beyond reason inside, but at the same time talking about the danger as if it were less than it really was. The worry surrounded me, like the wall of the cove, and it made me feel everything had been considered and was now safe.

My mother had a superstition, in fact, that children were predisposed to certain dangers on certain days, all depending on their Chinese birthdate. It was explained in a little Chinese book called *The Twenty-Six Malignant Gates*. There, on each page, was an illustration of some terrible danger that awaited young innocent children. In the corners was a description written in Chinese, and since I couldn't read the characters, I could only see what the picture meant.

The same little boy appeared in each picture: climbing a broken tree limb, standing by a falling gate, slipping in a wooden tub, being carried away by a snapping dog, fleeing from a bolt of lightning. And in each of these pictures stood a man who looked as if he were wearing a lizard costume. He had a big crease in his forehead, or maybe it was actually that he had two round horns. In one picture, the lizard man was standing on a curved bridge, laughing as he watched the little boy flying forward over the bridge rail, his slippered feet already in the air.

It would have been enough to think that even one of these dangers could befall a child. And even though the birthdates corresponded to only one danger, my mother worried about them all. This was because she couldn't figure out how the Chinese dates, based on the lunar calendar, translated into American dates. So by taking them all into account, she had absolute faith she could prevent every one of them.

The sun had shifted and moved over the other side of the cove wall. Everything had settled into place. My mother was busy keeping sand from blowing onto the blanket, then shaking sand out of shoes, and tacking corners of blankets back down again with the now clean shoes. My father was still standing at the end of the reef, patiently casting out, waiting for *nengkan* to manifest itself as a fish. I could see small figures farther down on the beach, and I could tell they were my sisters by their two dark heads and yellow pants. My brothers' shrieks were mixed with those of seagulls. Bing had found an empty soda bottle and was using this to dig sand next to the dark cove wall. And I sat on the sand, just where the shadows ended and the sunny part began.

Bing was pounding the soda bottle against the rock, so I called to him, "Don't dig so hard. You'll bust a hole in the wall and fall all the way to China." And I laughed when he looked at me as though he thought what I said was true. He stood up and started walking toward the water. He put one foot tentatively on the reef, and I warned him, "Bing."

"I'm gonna see Daddy," he protested.

"Stay close to the wall, then, away from the water," I said. "Stay away from the mean fish."

And I watched as he inched his way along the reef, his back hugging the bumpy cove wall. I still see him, so clearly that I almost feel I can make him stay there forever.

I see him standing by the wall, safe, calling to my father, who looks over his shoulder toward Bing. How glad I am that my father is going to watch him for a while! Bing starts to walk over and then something tugs on my father's line and he's reeling as fast as he can.

Shouts erupt. Someone has thrown sand in Luke's face and he's jumped out of his sand grave and thrown himself on top of Mark, thrashing and kicking. My mother shouts for me to stop them. And right after I pull Luke off Mark, I look up and see Bing walking alone to the edge of the reef. In the confusion of the fight, nobody notices. I am the only one who sees what Bing is doing.

Bing walks one, two, three steps. His little body is moving so quickly, as if he spotted something wonderful by the water's edge. And I think, *He's going to fall in.* I'm expecting it. And just as I think this, his feet are already in the air, in a moment of balance, before he splashes into the sea and disappears without leaving so much as a ripple in the water.

I sank to my knees watching that spot where he disappeared, not moving, not saying anything. I couldn't make sense of it. I was thinking, Should I run to the water and try to pull him out? Should I shout to my father? Can I rise on my legs fast enough? Can I take it all back and forbid Bing from joining my father on the ledge?

And then my sisters were back, and one of them said, "Where's Bing?" There was silence for a few seconds and then shouts and sand flying as everyone rushed past me toward the water's edge. I stood there unable to move as my sisters looked by the cove wall, as my brothers scrambled to see what lay behind pieces of driftwood. My mother and father were trying to part the waves with their hands.

We were there for many hours. I remember the search boats and the sunset when dusk came. I had never seen a sunset like that: a bright orange flame touching the water's edge and then fanning out, warming the sea. When it became dark, the boats turned their yellow orbs on and bounced up and down on the dark shiny water.

As I look back, it seems unnatural to think about the colors of the sunset and boats at a time like that. But we all had strange thoughts. My father was calculating minutes, estimating the temperature of the water, readjusting his estimate of when Bing fell. My sisters were calling, "Bing! Bing!" as if he were hiding in some bushes high above the beach cliffs. My brothers sat in the car, quietly reading comic books. And when the boats turned off their yellow orbs, my mother went for a swim. She had never swum a stroke in her life, but her faith in her own *nengkan* convinced her that what these Americans couldn't do, she could. She could find Bing.

And when the rescue people finally pulled her out of the water, she still had her *nengkan* intact. Her hair, her clothes, they were all heavy with the cold water, but she stood quietly, calm and regal as a mermaid queen who had just arrived out of the sea. The police called off the search, put us all in our car, and sent us home to grieve.

I had expected to be beaten to death, by my father, by my mother, by my sisters and brothers. I knew it was my fault. I hadn't watched him closely enough, and yet I saw him. But as we sat in the dark living room, I heard them, one by one whispering their regrets.

"I was selfish to want to go fishing," said my father.

"We shouldn't have gone for a walk," said Janice, while Ruth blew her nose yet another time.

"Why'd you have to throw sand in my face?" moaned Luke. "Why'd you have to make me start a fight?"

And my mother quietly admitted to me, "I told you to stop their fight. I told you to take your eyes off him."

If I had had any time at all to feel a sense of relief, it would have quickly evaporated, because my mother also said, "So now I am telling you, we must go and find him, quickly, tomorrow morning." And everybody's eyes looked down. But I saw it as my punishment: to go out with my mother, back to the beach, to help her find Bing's body.

Nothing prepared me for what my mother did the next day. When I woke up, it was still dark and she was already dressed. On the kitchen table was a thermos, a teacup, the white leatherette Bible, and the car keys.

"Is Daddy ready?" I asked.

"Daddy's not coming," she said.

"Then how will we get there? Who will drive us?"

She picked up the keys and I followed her out the door to the car. I wondered the whole time as we drove to the beach how she had learned to drive overnight. She used no map. She drove smoothly ahead, turning down Geary, then the Great Highway, signaling at all the right times, getting on the Coast Highway and easily winding the car around the sharp curves that often led inexperienced drivers off and over the cliffs.

When we arrived at the beach, she walked immediately down the dirt path and over to the end of the reef ledge, where I had seen Bing disappear. She held in her hand the white Bible. And looking out over the water, she called to God, her small voice carried up by the gulls to heaven. It began with "Dear God" and ended with "Amen," and in between she spoke in Chinese.

"I have always believed in your blessings," she praised God in that same tone she used for exaggerated Chinese compliments. "We knew they would come. We did not question them. Your decisions were our decisions. You rewarded us for our faith.

"In return we have always tried to show our deepest respect. We went to your house. We brought you money. We sang your songs. You gave us more blessings. And now we have misplaced one of them. We were careless. This is true. We had so many good things, we couldn't keep them in our mind all the time.

"So maybe you hid him from us to teach us a lesson, to be more careful with your gifts in the future. I have learned this. I have put it in my memory. And now I have come to take Bing back."

I listened quietly as my mother said these words, horrified. And I began to cry when she added, "Forgive us for his bad manners. My daughter, this one standing here, will be sure to teach him better lessons of obedience before he visits you again."

After her prayer, her faith was so great that she saw him, three times, waving to her from just beyond the first wave. "*Nale!*"—There! And she would stand straight as a sentinel, until three times her eyesight failed her and Bing turned into a dark spot of churning seaweed.

My mother did not let her chin fall down. She walked back to the beach and put the Bible down. She picked up the thermos and teacup and walked to the water's edge. Then she told me that the night before she had reached back into her life, back when she was a girl in China, and this is what she had found.

"I remember a boy who lost his hand in a firecracker accident," she said. "I saw the shreds of this boy's arm, his tears, and then I heard his mother's claim that he would grow back another hand, better than the last. This mother said she would pay back an ancestral debt ten times over. She would use a water treatment to soothe the wrath of Chu Jung, the three-eyed god of fire. And true enough, the next week this boy was riding a bicycle, both hands steering a straight course past my astonished eyes!"

And then my mother became very quiet. She spoke again in a thoughtful, respectful manner.

"An ancestor of ours once stole water from a sacred well. Now the water is trying to steal back. We must sweeten the temper of the Coiling Dragon who lives in the sea. And then we must make him loosen his coils from Bing by giving him another treasure he can hide."

My mother poured out tea sweetened with sugar into the teacup, and threw this into the sea. And then she opened her fist. In her palm was a ring of watery blue sapphire, a gift from her mother, who had died many years before. This ring, she told me, drew coveting stares from women and made them inattentive to the children they guarded so jealously. This would make the Coiling Dragon forgetful of Bing. She threw the ring into the water.

But even with this, Bing did not appear right away. For an hour or so, all we saw was seaweed drifting by. And then I saw her clasp her hands to her chest, and she said in a wondrous voice, "See, it's because we were watching the wrong direction." And I too saw Bing trudging wearily at the far end of the beach, his shoes hanging in his hand, his dark head bent over in exhaustion. I could feel what my mother felt. The hunger in our hearts was instantly filled. And then the two of us, before we could even get to our feet, saw him light a cigarette, grow tall, and become a stranger.

"Ma, let's go," I said as softly as possible.

"He's there," she said firmly. She pointed to the jagged wall across the water. "I see him. He is in a cave, sitting on a little step above the water. He is hungry and a little cold, but he has learned now not to complain too much."

And then she stood up and started walking across the sandy beach as though it were a solid paved path, and I was trying to follow behind, struggling and stumbling in the soft mounds. She marched up the steep path to where the car was parked, and she wasn't even breathing hard as she pulled a large inner tube from the trunk. To this lifesaver, she tied the fishing line from my father's bamboo pole. She walked back and threw the tube into the sea, holding onto the pole.

"This will go where Bing is. I will bring him back," she said fiercely. I had never heard so much *nengkan* in my mother's voice.

The tube followed her mind. It drifted out, toward the other side of the cove where it was caught by stronger waves. The line became taut and she strained to hold on tight. But the line snapped and then spiraled into the water.

We both climbed toward the end of the reef to watch. The tube had now reached the other side of the cove. A big wave smashed it into the wall. The bloated tube leapt up and then it was sucked in, under the wall and into a cavern. It popped out. Over and over again, it disappeared, emerged, glistening black, faithfully reporting it had seen Bing and was going back to try to pluck him from the cave. Over and over again, it dove and popped back up again, empty but still hopeful. And then, after a dozen or so times, it was sucked into the dark recess, and when it came out, it was torn and lifeless.

At that moment, and not until that moment, did she give up. My mother had a look on her face that I'll never forget. It was one of complete despair and horror, for losing Bing, for being so foolish as to think she could use faith to change fate. And it made me angry—so blindingly angry—that everything had failed us.

I know now that I had never expected to find Bing, just as I know now I will never find a way to save my marriage. My mother tells me, though, that I should still try.

"What's the point?" I say. "There's no hope. There's no reason to keep trying."

"Because you must," she says, "This is not hope. Not reason. This is your fate. This is your life, what you must do."

"So what can I do?"

And my mother says, "You must think for yourself, what you must do. If someone tells you, then you are not trying." And then she walks out of the kitchen to let me think about this.

I think about Bing, how I knew he was in danger, how I let it happen. I think about my marriage, how I had seen the signs, really I had. But I just let it happen. And I think now that fate is shaped half by expectation, half by inattention. But somehow, when you lose something you love, faith takes over. You have to pay attention to what you lost. You have to undo the expectation.

My mother, she still pays attention to it. That Bible under the table, I know she sees it. I remember seeing her write in it before she wedged it under.

I lift the table and slide the Bible out. I put the Bible on the table, flipping quickly through the pages, because I know it's there. On the page before the New Testament begins, there's a section called "Deaths," and that's where she wrote "Bing Hsu" lightly, in erasable pencil.

1989

Bobbie Ann Mason 1940–

Bobbie Ann Mason writes about blue-collar people in small-town and rural America—store clerks, waitresses, truck drivers—men and women who, she says, believe in "progress," but who "are kind of naive and optimistic, for the most part: they think better times are coming." They are, she says, a "shopping mall generation," people adrift in a high-tech world that controls their jobs and their desires, that gives them fast foods that gratify their taste and television sitcoms that fill their empty hours.

Mason came to know the lives of small-town working people and the world of mass culture while growing up in Kentucky, on a farm outside the small town of Mayfield. She spent her youth doing farm chores, reading stories of the Bobbsey Twins and the girl detective Nancy Drew, listening to rock music on the radio, and following the lives of celebrities. In the 1950s, she became the teenage president of the national fan club of a popular singing quartet, The Hilltoppers, *and followed them on concert tours through midwest America.*

Her youthful experiences at the edge of the world of entertainment glitz and glamour made her want to be a journalist, and when she was eighteen, she entered the University of Kentucky. Four years later she graduated and moved to New York, where she earned her living by writing articles on teen idols such as Fabian and Annette Funicello for "fan mags" like Movie Stars, Movie Life, *and* T. V. Star Parade.

But her university courses had stirred her interest in literature, and she entered the State University of New York at Binghamton, where she earned an M.A. in 1966. She then went to the University of Connecticut, where she graduated with a Ph.D. in English in 1972. She wrote her doctoral dissertation on Vladimir Nabokov, and in 1974 it was published as Nabokov's Garden. *From 1972 to 1979, she taught at Mansfield State College in Pennsylvania, and she published her second book,* The Girl Sleuth: A Feminist Guide to the Bobbsey Twins, Nancy Drew, and Their Sisters *(1975), a scholarly study of the popular books she had enjoyed when she was young.*

In her late thirties Mason began to write short stories, and she soon discovered that her best subjects for fiction were the working-class people of her native western Kentucky. Her stories began to appear in the New Yorker, Atlantic Monthly, Paris Review, Mother Jones, *and* Harper's. *In 1982 her first collection,* Shiloh and Other Stories, *appeared. Her next book was a novel,* In Country *(1985), which was made into a successful motion picture. A second collection of her short stories,* Love Life, *appeared in 1989. Her novel* Feather Crowns *(1993) sympathetically examines a pair of ordinary Americans to whom fate brings instant fame as curiosities in the carnival and freak-show world of the early twentieth century, foreboding antecedents of the grotesque simpletons who display themselves on today's TV talk shows before audiences fascinated by prurience and abnormality.* Midnight Magic, Selected Stories of Bobbie Ann Mason *appeared in 1998, and in 1999 she published* Clear Springs, A Memoir, *describing her origins in Kentucky and the stern and often numbing life on farms and in small towns that shaped her view of men and women and the lives they struggle to endure. Her most recent collection of short stories is* Zigzagging Down a Wild Trail *(2002).*

Mason's writing is peeled and terse. Her flat diction, direct sentences, and references to common, everyday things, to brand names, to the icons of pop culture, convey the sparseness and the pathos of her characters' lives. Her women shop at K mart, wear Dr. Scholl's sandals, and eat "tasty" food prepackaged for the microwave. They have frosted curls, like the heroine of "Shiloh," who works on her pectorals with dumbbells and reminds her husband of Wonder Woman. The men are vague. They sit, waiting, amid the wreckage of their lives. They have ill-fated plans for triumphs and exploits, like the hero of "Shiloh," who creates a log cabin out of Popsicle sticks and has noble dreams of building a real log cabin—from a kit. Drugged by American consumerism, they are fascinated by America's materialistic trivia and the higher sleaze exhibited by their moneyed betters, the rich and famous.

Mason's stories have been called "Grit Lit" and "Shopping Mall Realism." Her fiction is the kind, it is said, that "her own characters would never read" even if they were to "turn off the television long enough to look at a book at all." She is resolutely unsentimental, a regional writer in the tradition of William Faulkner, Flannery O'Connor, and Eudora Welty, and like them she has created characters who are recognizable anywhere in America.

FURTHER READING: A. Wilhelm, *Bobbie Ann Mason,* 1998; J. Price, *Understanding Bobbie Ann Mason,* 2000.

TEXT: *Shiloh and Other Stories,* 1982.

SHILOH

Leroy Moffitt's wife, Norma Jean, is working on her pectorals. She lifts three-pound dumbbells to warm up, then progresses to a twenty-pound barbell. Standing with her legs apart, she reminds Leroy of Wonder Woman.

"I'd give anything if I could just get these muscles to where they're real hard," says Norma Jean. "Feel this arm. It's not as hard as the other one."

"That's 'cause you're right-handed," says Leroy, dodging as she swings the barbell in an arc.

"Do you think so?"

"Sure."

Leroy is a truckdriver. He injured his leg in a highway accident four months ago, and his physical therapy, which involves weights and a pulley, prompted Norma Jean to try building herself up. Now she is attending a body-building class. Leroy has been collecting temporary disability since his tractor-trailer jackknifed in Missouri, badly twisting his left leg in its socket. He has a steel pin in his hip. He will probably not be able to drive his rig again. It sits in the backyard, like a gigantic bird that has flown home to roost. Leroy has been home in Kentucky for three months, and his leg is almost healed, but the accident frightened him and he does not want to drive any more long hauls. He is not sure what to do next. In the meantime, he makes things from craft kits. He started by building a miniature log cabin from notched Popsicle sticks. He varnished it and placed it on the TV set, where it remains. It reminds him of a rustic Nativity scene. Then he tried string art (sailing ships on black velvet), a macramé owl kit, a snap-together B-17 Flying Fortress, and a lamp made out of a model truck, with a light fixture screwed in the top of the cab. At first the kits were diversions, something to kill time, but now he is thinking about building a full-scale log house from a kit. It would be considerably cheaper than building a regular house, and besides, Leroy has grown to appreciate how things are put together. He has begun to realize that in all the years he was on the road he never took time to examine anything. He was always flying past scenery.

"They won't let you build a log cabin in any of the new subdivisions," Norma Jean tells him.

"They will if I tell them it's for you," he says, teasing her. Ever since they were married, he has promised Norma Jean he would build her a new home one day. They have always rented, and the house they live in is small and nondescript. It does not even feel like a home, Leroy realizes now.

Norma Jean works at the Rexall drugstore, and she has acquired an amazing amount of information about cosmetics. When she explains to Leroy the three stages of complexion care, involving creams, toners, and moisturizers, he thinks happily of other petroleum products—axle grease, diesel fuel. This is a connection between him and Norma Jean. Since he has been home, he has felt unusually tender about his wife and guilty over his long absences. But he can't tell what she feels about him. Norma Jean has never complained about his traveling; she has never made hurt remarks, like calling his truck a "widow-maker." He is reasonably certain she has been faithful to him, but he wishes she would celebrate his permanent homecoming more happily. Norma Jean is often startled to find Leroy at home, and he thinks she seems a little disappointed about it. Perhaps he reminds her too much of the early days of their marriage, before he went on the road. They had a child who died as an infant, years ago. They never speak about their memories of Randy, which have almost faded, but now that Leroy is home all the time, they sometimes feel awkward around each other, and Leroy wonders if one of them should mention the child. He has the feeling that they are waking up out of a dream together—that they must create a new marriage, start afresh. They are lucky they are still married. Leroy has read that for most people losing a child destroys the marriage—or else he heard this on *Donahue.* He can't always remember where he learns things anymore.

At Christmas, Leroy bought an electric organ for Norma Jean. She used to play the piano when she was in high school. "It don't leave you," she told him once. "It's like riding a bicycle."

The new instrument had so many keys and buttons that she was bewildered by it at first. She touched the keys tentatively, pushed some buttons, then pecked out "Chopsticks." It came out in an amplified fox-trot rhythm, with marimba sounds.

"It's an orchestra!" she cried.

The organ had a pecan-look finish and eighteen preset chords, with optional flute, violin, trumpet, clarinet, and banjo accompaniments. Norma Jean mastered the organ almost immediately. At first she played Christmas songs. Then she bought *The Sixties Songbook* and learned every tune in it, adding variations to each with the rows of brightly colored buttons.

"I didn't like these old songs back then," she said. "But I have this crazy feeling I missed something."

"You didn't miss a thing," said Leroy.

Leroy likes to lie on the couch and smoke a joint and listen to Norma Jean play "Can't Take My Eyes Off You" and "I'll Be Back." He is back again. After fifteen years on the road, he is finally settling down with the woman he loves. She is still pretty. Her skin is flawless. Her frosted curls resemble pencil trimmings.

Now that Leroy has come home to stay, he notices how much the town has changed. Subdivisions are spreading across western Kentucky like an oil slick. The sign at the edge of town says "Pop: 11,500"—only seven hundred more than it said twenty years before. Leroy can't figure out who is living in all the new houses. The farmers who used to gather around the courthouse square on Saturday afternoons to play checkers and spit tobacco juice have gone. It has been years since Leroy has thought about the farmers, and they have disappeared without his noticing.

Leroy meets a kid named Stevie Hamilton in the parking lot at the new shopping center. While they pretend to be strangers meeting over a stalled car, Stevie tosses an ounce of marijuana under the front seat of Leroy's car. Stevie is wearing orange jogging shoes and a T-shirt that says CHATTAHOOCHEE SUPER-RAT. His father is a prominent doctor who lives in one of the expensive subdivisions in a new white-columned brick house that looks like a funeral parlor. In the phone book under his name there is a separate number, with the listing "Teenagers."

"Where do you get this stuff?" asks Leroy. "From your pappy?"

"That's for me to know and you to find out," Stevie says. He is slit-eyed and skinny.

"What else you got?"

"What you interested in?"

"Nothing special. Just wondered."

Leroy used to take speed on the road. Now he has to go slowly. He needs to be mellow. He leans back against the car and says, "I'm aiming to build me a log house, soon as I get time. My wife, though, I don't think she likes the idea."

"Well, let me know when you want me again," Stevie says. He has a cigarette in his cupped palm, as though sheltering it from the wind. He takes a long drag, then stomps it on the asphalt and slouches away.

Stevie's father was two years ahead of Leroy in high school. Leroy is thirty-four. He married Norma Jean when they were both eighteen, and their child Randy was born a few months later, but he died at the age of four months and three days. He would be about Stevie's age now. Norma Jean and Leroy were at the drive-in, watching a double feature (*Dr. Strangelove* and *Lover Come Back*), and the baby was sleeping in the back seat. When the first movie ended, the baby was dead. It was the sudden infant death syndrome. Leroy remembers handing Randy to a nurse at the emergency room, as though he were offering her a large doll as a present. A dead baby feels like a sack of flour. "It just happens sometimes," said the doctor, in what Leroy always recalls as a nonchalant tone. Leroy can hardly remember the child anymore, but he still sees vividly a scene from *Dr. Strangelove* in which the President of the United States was talking in a folksy voice on the hot line to the Soviet premier about the bomber accidentally headed toward Russia. He was in the War Room, and the world map was lit up. Leroy remembers Norma Jean standing catatonically beside him in the hospital and himself thinking: Who is this strange girl? He had forgotten who she was. Now scientists are saying that crib death is caused by a virus. Nobody knows anything, Leroy thinks. The answers are always changing.

When Leroy gets home from the shopping center, Norma Jean's mother, Mabel Beasley, is there. Until this year, Leroy has not realized how much time she spends with Norma Jean. When she visits, she inspects the closets and then the plants, informing Norma Jean when a plant is droopy or yellow. Mabel calls the plants "flowers," although there are never any blooms. She always notices if Norma Jean's laundry is piling up. Mabel is a short, overweight woman whose tight, brown-dyed curls look more like a wig than the actual wig she sometimes wears. Today she has brought Norma Jean an off-white dust ruffle she made for the bed; Mabel works in a custom-upholstery shop.

"This is the tenth one I made this year," Mabel says. "I got started and couldn't stop."

"It's real pretty," says Norma Jean.

"Now we can hide things under the bed," says Leroy, who gets along with his mother-in-law primarily by joking with her. Mabel has never really forgiven him for disgracing her by getting Norma Jean pregnant. When the baby died, she said that fate was mocking her.

"What's that thing?" Mabel says to Leroy in a loud voice, pointing to a tangle of yarn on a piece of canvas.

Leroy holds it up for Mabel to see. "It's my needlepoint," he explains. "This is a *Star Trek* pillow cover."

"That's what a woman would do," says Mabel. "Great day in the morning!"

"All the big football players on TV do it," he says.

"Why, Leroy, you're always trying to fool me. I don't believe you for one minute. You don't know what to do with yourself—that's the whole trouble. Sewing!"

"I'm aiming to build us a log house," says Leroy. "Soon as my plans come."

"Like *heck* you are," says Norma Jean. She takes Leroy's needlepoint and shoves it into a drawer. "You have to find a job first. Nobody can afford to build now anyway."

Mabel straightens her girdle and says, "I still think before you get tied down y'all ought to take a little run to Shiloh."

"One of these days, Mama," Norma Jean says impatiently.

Mabel is talking about Shiloh, Tennessee. For the past few years, she has been urging Leroy and Norma Jean to visit the Civil War battleground there. Mabel went there on her honeymoon—the only real trip she ever took. Her husband died of a perforated ulcer when Norma Jean was ten, but Mabel, who was accepted into the United Daughters of the Confederacy in 1975, is still preoccupied with going back to Shiloh.

"I've been to kingdom come and back in that truck out yonder," Leroy says to Mabel, "but we never yet set foot in that battleground. Ain't that something? How did I miss it?"

"It's not even that far," Mabel says.

After Mabel leaves, Norma Jean reads to Leroy from a list she has made. "Things you could do," she announces. "You could get a job as a guard at Union Carbide, where they'd let you set on a stool. You could get on at the lumberyard. You could do a little carpenter work, if you want to build so bad. You could—"

"I can't do something where I'd have to stand up all day."

"You ought to try standing up all day behind a cosmetics counter. It's amazing that I have strong feet, coming from two parents that never had strong feet at all." At the moment Norma Jean is holding on to the kitchen counter, raising her knees one at a time as she talks. She is wearing two-pound ankle weights.

"Don't worry," says Leroy. "I'll do something."

"You could truck calves to slaughter for somebody. You wouldn't have to drive any big old truck for that."

"I'm going to build you this house," says Leroy. "I want to make you a real home."

"I don't want to live in any log cabin."

"It's not a cabin. It's a house."

"I don't care. It looks like a cabin."

"You and me together could lift those logs. It's just like lifting weights."

Norma Jean doesn't answer. Under her breath, she is counting. Now she is marching through the kitchen. She is doing goose steps.

Before his accident, when Leroy came home he used to stay in the house with Norma Jean, watching TV in bed and playing cards. She would cook fried chicken, picnic ham, chocolate pie—all his favorites. Now he is home alone much of the time. In the mornings, Norma Jean disappears, leaving a cooling place in the bed. She eats a cereal called Body Buddies, and she leaves the bowl on the table, with the soggy tan balls floating in a milk puddle. He sees things about Norma Jean that he never realized before. When she chops onions, she stares off into a corner, as if she can't bear to look. She puts on her house slippers almost precisely at nine o'clock every evening and nudges her jogging shoes under the couch. She saves bread heels for the birds. Leroy watches the birds at the feeder. He notices the peculiar way goldfinches fly past the window. They close their wings, then fall, then spread their wings to catch and lift themselves. He wonders if they close their eyes when they fall. Norma Jean closes her eyes when they are in bed. She wants the lights turned out. Even then, he is sure she closes her eyes.

He goes for long drives around town. He tends to drive a car rather carelessly. Power steering and an automatic shift make a car feel so small and inconsequential that his body is hardly involved in the driving process. His injured leg stretches out comfortably. Once or twice he has almost hit something, but even the prospect of an accident seems minor in a car. He cruises the new subdivisions, feeling like a criminal rehearsing for a robbery. Norma Jean is probably right about a log house being inappropriate here in the new subdivisions. All the houses look grand and complicated. They depress him.

One day when Leroy comes home from a drive he finds Norma Jean in tears. She is in the kitchen making a potato and mushroom-soup casserole, with grated-cheese topping. She is crying because her mother caught her smoking.

"I didn't hear her coming. I was standing here puffing away pretty as you please," Norma Jean says, wiping her eyes.

"I knew it would happen sooner or later," says Leroy, putting his arm around her.

"She don't know the meaning of the word 'knock,'" says Norma Jean. "It's a wonder she hadn't caught me years ago."

"Think of it this way," Leroy says. "What if she caught me with a joint?"

"You better not let her!" Norma Jean shrieks. "I'm warning you, Leroy Moffitt!"

"I'm just kidding. Here, play me a tune. That'll help you relax."

Norma Jean puts the casserole in the oven and sets the timer. Then she plays a ragtime tune, with horns and banjo, as Leroy lights up a joint and lies on the couch, laughing to himself about Mabel's catching him at it. He thinks of Stevie Hamilton—a doctor's son pushing grass. Everything is funny. The whole town seems crazy and small. He is reminded of Virgil Mathis, a boastful policeman Leroy used to shoot pool with. Virgil recently led a drug bust in a back room at a bowling alley, where he seized ten thousand dollars' worth of marijuana. The newspaper had a picture of him holding up the bags of grass and grinning widely. Right now, Leroy can imagine Virgil breaking down the door and arresting him with a lungful of smoke. Virgil would probably have been alerted to the scene because of all the racket Norma Jean is making. Now she sounds like a hard-rock band. Norma Jean is terrific. When she switches to a Latin-rhythm version of "Sunshine Superman," Leroy hums along. Norma Jean's foot goes up and down, up and down.

"Well, what do you think?" Leroy says, when Norma Jean pauses to search through her music.

"What do I think about what?"

His mind has gone blank. Then he says, "I'll sell my rig and build us a house." That wasn't what he wanted to say. He wanted to know what she thought—what she *really* thought—about them.

"Don't start in on that again," says Norma Jean. She begins playing "Who'll Be the Next in Line?"

Leroy used to tell hitchhikers his whole life story—about his travels, his hometown, the baby. He would end with a question: "Well, what do you think?" It was just a rhetorical question. In time, he had the feeling that he'd been telling the same story over and over to the same hitchhikers. He quit talking to hitchhikers when he realized how his voice sounded—whining and self-pitying, like some teenage-tragedy song. Now Leroy has the sudden impulse to tell Norma Jean about himself, as if he had just met her. They have known each other so long they have forgotten a lot about each other. They could become reacquainted. But when the oven timer goes off and she runs to the kitchen, he forgets why he wants to do this.

The next day, Mabel drops by. It is Saturday and Norma Jean is cleaning. Leroy is studying the plans of his log house, which have finally come in the mail. He has them spread out on the table—big sheets of stiff blue paper, with diagrams and numbers printed in white. While Norma Jean runs the vacuum, Mabel drinks coffee. She sets her coffee cup on a blueprint.

"I'm just waiting for time to pass," she says to Leroy, drumming her fingers on the table.

As soon as Norma Jean switches off the vacuum, Mabel says in a loud voice, "Did you hear about the datsun dog that killed the baby?"

Norma Jean says, "The word is 'dachshund.'"

"They put the dog on trial. It chewed the baby's legs off. The mother was in the next room all the time." She raises her voice. "They thought it was neglect."

Norma Jean is holding her ears. Leroy manages to open the refrigerator and get some Diet Pepsi to offer Mabel. Mabel still has some coffee and she waves away the Pepsi.

"Datsuns are like that," Mabel says. "They're jealous dogs. They'll tear a place to pieces if you don't keep an eye on them."

"You better watch out what you're saying, Mabel," says Leroy.

"Well, facts is facts."

Leroy looks out the window at his rig. It is like a huge piece of furniture gathering dust in the backyard. Pretty soon it will be an antique. He hears the vacuum cleaner. Norma Jean seems to be cleaning the living room rug again.

Later, she says to Leroy, "She just said that about the baby because she caught me smoking. She's trying to pay me back."

"What are you talking about?" Leroy says, nervously shuffling blueprints.

"You know good and well," Norma Jean says. She is sitting in a kitchen chair with her feet up and her arms wrapped around her knees. She looks small and helpless. She says, "The very idea, her bringing up a subject like that! Saying it was neglect."

"She didn't mean that," Leroy says.

"She might not have *thought* she meant it. She always says things like that. You don't know how she goes on."

"But she didn't really mean it. She was just talking."

Leroy opens a king-sized bottle of beer and pours it into two glasses, dividing it carefully. He hands a glass to Norma Jean and she takes it from him mechanically. For a long time, they sit by the kitchen window watching the birds at the feeder.

Something is happening. Norma Jean is going to night school. She has graduated from her six-week body-building course and now she is taking an adult-education course in composition at Paducah Community College. She spends her evenings outlining paragraphs.

"First you have a topic sentence," she explains to Leroy. "Then you divide it up. Your secondary topic has to be connected to your primary topic."

To Leroy, this sounds intimidating. "I never was any good in English," he says.

"It makes a lot of sense."

"What are you doing this for, anyhow?"

She shrugs. "It's something to do." She stands up and lifts her dumbbells a few times.

"Driving a rig, nobody cared about my English."

"I'm not criticizing your English."

Norma Jean used to say, "If I lose ten minutes' sleep, I just drag all day." Now she stays up late, writing compositions. She got a B on her first paper—a how-to theme on soup-based casseroles. Recently Norma Jean has been cooking unusual foods—tacos, lasagna, Bombay chicken. She doesn't play the organ anymore, though her second paper was called "Why Music Is Important to Me." She sits at the kitchen table, concentrating on her outlines, while Leroy plays with his log house plans, practicing with a set of Lincoln Logs. The thought of getting a truckload of notched, numbered logs scares him, and he wants to be prepared. As he and Norma Jean work together at the kitchen table, Leroy has the hopeful thought that they are sharing something, but he knows he is a fool to think this. Norma Jean is miles away. He knows he is going to lose her. Like Mabel, he is just waiting for time to pass.

One day, Mabel is there before Norma Jean gets home from work, and Leroy finds himself confiding in her. Mabel, he realizes, must know Norma Jean better than he does.

"I don't know what's got into that girl," Mabel says. "She used to go to bed with the chickens. Now you say she's up all hours. Plus her a-smoking. I like to died."

"I want to make her this beautiful home," Leroy says, indicating the Lincoln Logs. "I don't think she even wants it. Maybe she was happier with me gone."

"She don't know what to make of you, coming home like this."

"Is that it?"

Mabel takes the roof off his Lincoln Log cabin. "You couldn't get *me* in a log cabin," she says. "I was raised in one. It's no picnic, let me tell you."

"They're different now," says Leroy.

"I tell you what," Mabel says, smiling oddly at Leroy.

"What?"

"Take her on down to Shiloh. Y'all need to get out together, stir a little. Her brain's all balled up over them books."

Leroy can see traces of Norma Jean's features in her mother's face. Mabel's worn face has the texture of crinkled cotton, but suddenly she looks pretty. It occurs to Leroy that Mabel has been hinting all along that she wants them to take her with them to Shiloh.

"Let's all go to Shiloh," he says. "You and me and her. Come Sunday."

Mabel throws up her hands in protest. "Oh, no, not me. Young folks want to be by theirselves."

When Norma Jean comes in with groceries, Leroy says excitedly, "Your mama here's been dying to go to Shiloh for thirty-five years. It's about time we went, don't you think?"

"I'm not going to butt in on anybody's second honeymoon," Mabel says.

"Who's going on a honeymoon, for Christ's sake?" Norma Jean says loudly.

"I never raised no daughter of mine to talk that-a-way," Mabel says.

"You ain't seen nothing yet," says Norma Jean. She starts putting away boxes and cans, slamming cabinet doors.

"There's a log cabin at Shiloh," Mabel says. "It was there during the battle. There's bullet holes in it."

"When are you going to *shut up* about Shiloh, Mama?" asks Norma Jean.

"I always thought Shiloh was the prettiest place, so full of history," Mabel goes on. "I just hoped y'all could see it once before I die, so you could tell me about it." Later, she whispers to Leroy, "You do what I said. A little change is what she needs."

"Your name means 'the king,'" Norma Jean says to Leroy that evening. He is trying to get her to go to Shiloh, and she is reading a book about another century.

"Well, I reckon I ought to be right proud."

"I guess so."

"Am I still king around here?"

Norma Jean flexes her biceps and feels them for hardness. "I'm not fooling around with anybody, if that's what you mean," she says.

"Would you tell me if you were?"

"I don't know."

"What does *your* name mean?"

"It was Marilyn Monroe's real name."

"No kidding!"

"Norma comes from the Normans. They were invaders," she says. She closes her book and looks hard at Leroy. "I'll go to Shiloh with you if you'll stop staring at me."

On Sunday, Norma Jean packs a picnic and they go to Shiloh. To Leroy's relief, Mabel says she does not want to come with them. Norma Jean drives, and Leroy, sitting beside her, feels like some boring hitchhiker she has picked up. He tries some conversation, but she answers him in monosyllables. At Shiloh, she drives aimlessly through the park, past bluffs and trails and steep ravines. Shiloh is an immense place, and Leroy cannot see it as a battleground. It is not what he expected. He thought it would look like a golf course. Monuments are everywhere, showing through the thick clusters of trees. Norma Jean passes the log cabin Mabel mentioned. It is surrounded by tourists looking for bullet holes.

"That's not the kind of log house I've got in mind," says Leroy apologetically.

"I know *that*."

"This is a pretty place. Your Mama was right."

"It's O.K.," says Norma Jean. "Well, we've seen it. I hope she's satisfied."

They burst out laughing together.

At the park museum, a movie on Shiloh is shown every half hour, but they decide that they don't want to see it. They buy a souvenir Confederate flag for Mabel, and then they find a picnic spot near the cemetery. Norma Jean has brought a picnic cooler, with pimiento sandwiches, soft drinks, and Yodels. Leroy eats a sandwich and then smokes a joint, hiding it behind the picnic cooler. Norma Jean has quit smoking altogether. She is picking cake crumbs from the cellophane wrapper, like a fussy bird.

Leroy says, "So the boys in gray ended up in Corinth. The Union soldiers zapped 'em finally. April 7, 1862."

They both know that he doesn't know any history. He is just talking about some of the historical plaques they have read. He feels awkward, like a boy on a date with an older girl. They are still just making conversation.

"Corinth is where Mama eloped to," says Norma Jean.

They sit in silence and stare at the cemetery for the Union dead and, beyond, at a tall cluster of trees. Campers are parked nearby, bumper to bumper, and small children in bright clothing are cavorting and squealing. Norma Jean wads up the cake wrapper and squeezes it tightly in her hand. Without looking at Leroy, she says, "I want to leave you."

Leroy takes a bottle of Coke out of the cooler and flips off the cap. He holds the bottle poised near his mouth but cannot remember to take a drink. Finally he says, "No, you don't."

"Yes, I do."

"I won't let you."

"You can't stop me."

"Don't do me that way."

Leroy knows Norma Jean will have her own way. "Didn't I promise to be home from now on?" he says.

"In some ways, a woman prefers a man who wanders," says Norma Jean. "That sounds crazy, I know."

"You're not crazy."

Leroy remembers to drink from his Coke. Then he says, "Yes, you *are* crazy. You and me could start all over again. Right back at the beginning."

"We *have* started all over again," says Norma Jean. "And this is how it turned out."

"What did I do wrong?"

"Nothing."

"Is this one of those women's lib things?" Leroy asks.

"Don't be funny."

The cemetery, a green slope dotted with white markers, looks like a subdivision site. Leroy is trying to comprehend that his marriage is breaking up, but for some reason he is wondering about white slabs in a graveyard.

"Everything was fine till Mama caught me smoking," says Norma Jean, standing up. "That set something off."

"What are you talking about?"

"She won't leave me alone—*you* won't leave me alone." Norma Jean seems to be crying, but she is looking away from him. "I feel eighteen again. I can't face that all over again." She starts walking away. "No, it *wasn't* fine. I don't know what I'm saying. Forget it."

Leroy takes a lungful of smoke and closes his eyes as Norma Jean's words sink in. He tries to focus on the fact that thirty-five hundred soldiers died on the grounds around him. He can only think of that war as a board game with plastic soldiers. Leroy almost smiles, as he compares the Confederates' daring attack on the Union camps and Virgil Mathis's raid on the bowling alley. General Grant, drunk and furious, shoved the Southerners back to Corinth, where Mabel and Jet Beasley were married years later, when Mabel was still thin and good-looking. The next day, Mabel and Jet visited the battleground, and then Norma Jean was born, and then she married Leroy and they had a baby, which they lost, and now Leroy and Norma Jean are here at the same battleground. Leroy knows he is leaving out a lot. He is leaving out the insides of history. History was always just names and dates to him. It occurs to him that building a house out of logs is similarly empty—too simple. And the real inner workings of a marriage, like most of history, have escaped him. Now he sees that building a log house is the dumbest idea he could have had. It was clumsy of him to think Norma Jean would want a log house. It was a crazy idea. He'll have to think of something else, quickly. He will wad the blueprints into tight balls and fling them into the lake. Then he'll get moving again. He opens his eyes. Norma Jean has moved away and is walking through the cemetery, following a serpentine brick path.

Leroy gets up to follow his wife, but his good leg is asleep and his bad leg still hurts him. Norma Jean is far away, walking rapidly toward the bluff by the river, and he tries to hobble toward her. Some children run past him, screaming noisily. Norma Jean has reached the bluff, and she is looking out over the Tennessee River. Now she turns toward Leroy and waves her arms. Is she beckoning to him? She seems to be doing an exercise for her chest muscles. The sky is unusually pale—the color of the dust ruffle Mabel made for their bed.

1980, 1982

David Bradley 1950–

Critically acclaimed as a consummate literary craftsman, David Bradley emerged at an early age as one of the foremost literary stylists of his generation. Bradley's novels deal with subjects related to both the historical subjugation of African Americans and the current difficulties of their existence in American society, yet he regards himself as a novelist with traditional novelistic concerns and attitudes. He says about his own writing, "I am interested in the basics of plot and character, less concerned with abstract ideas. It is my belief that writers of novels should have no belief, that the idea of what is true is something that emerges from the writing, rather than being placed into it."

Bradley was born in Bedford, a small town in rural southeastern Pennsylvania, in 1950, the only son of a minister, David Henry Bradley, Sr., and a local historian, Harriette Jackson Bradley. In 1968 he graduated from high school and enrolled at the University of Pennsylvania, where he excelled as a student. As an undergraduate he was named a Benjamin Franklin Scholar, a National Achievement Scholar, and a Presidential Scholar. Bradley graduated summa cum laude in 1972 with a degree in English and creative writing and received a General Honors Certificate and a Thouron British-American Exchange Scholarship. He attended King's College in London and took his M.A. in 1974.

Bradley wrote his first novel, South Street *(1975), set in the black urban ghetto of Philadelphia, while still a student at the University of Pennsylvania. It received only passing critical attention; however, with his second novel, he established a national reputation.* The Chaneysville Incident *(1981) was praised by the* New York Times Book Review *as one of the best novels of 1981 and was cited by other major reviewers as "the most significant work by a new male black author since James Baldwin," and "the best novel about the black experience in America since Ellison's* Invisible Man.*"* The Chaneysville Incident *was selected as a Book of the Month Club alternative and earned Bradley both the Pen/Faulkner Prize for 1982 and an Academy Award from the American Academy and Institute of Arts and Letters. Bradley was a professor of Creative Writing at Temple University from 1976 to 1996, and now teaches in the Creative Writing program at the University of Oregon. He continues to write fiction as well as essays and reviews for numerous publications, including* Esquire, Redbook, The New Yorker, *and the* New York Times Book Review.

FURTHER READING: *Crossroads Modernism: Descent and Emergence in African American Literary Culture,* 2002; *When Race Becomes Real: Black and White Writers Confront Their Personal Histories,* ed. B. Singley, 2002.

TEXT: *The Chaneysville Incident,* 1981.

from *THE CHANEYSVILLE INCIDENT*

[The narrator of *The Chaneysville Incident* is John Washington, a young African American history professor. In this excerpt he is visiting Jack Crawley, an old man who became a surrogate father for John after his real father, Moses Washington, died when John was twelve years old. Jack is now very ill, evidently close to death. The scene takes place at Jack's ramshackle house near the town in western Pennsylvania where John lived as a child and adolescent.]

197903042100

(SUNDAY)

LATER THAT NIGHT, when the fire was roaring in the chimney and the cold came slicing through the cabin's walls, Old Jack taught me another lesson: if you would bend a man, abandon all the usual means. Do not bother with psychology or diplomacy or even war; if you would bend a man, not just influence him or sway him or even convince him but *bend* him, do it with ritual. For even if he claims to have no belief, no religion, no adherence to any formal or informal order of service, there is, somewhere within him, a hidden agenda. And he will respond to it without hesitation, without thought, almost without knowledge, certainly without will. All you need to do is to guess the beginning of it. With me, Old Jack did not even have to guess—he knew. He had created it.

And so, when the meal was finished and the dishes washed, when the fire was stoked and the mugs of warmed and sweetened whiskey were in our hands, he did not hesitate; he did not even ask. He just said: "You want a story."

No, I did not want a story. I wanted to sit and drink hot whiskey and pray that we would make it through the night, and later fall into a drugged and dreamless sleep. And so I did not give him the response he wanted; I did not give him a response at all.

But he spoke as though I had: "Then fetch the candle."

I didn't move. I just sat there with the cup held tight against my belly, trying to keep the cold at bay. For a while we struggled, and then I knew that I would win, even if he was a weak old man. I must have relaxed a little then, and he must have sensed it. Because he said:

"Bring the matches too. Can't have light without strikin' fire." And I found myself moving, getting up and going to the shelf, taking down the candle and the matches, the motions so familiar they were almost painful. But when I came back to the table it changed. Because he was lying on his cot, not sitting in his chair. And so it was not precisely the same as it had been, not precisely as he would have had it. Now it was I who struck the match and lit the wick and set the candle in a pool of wax, a prisoner of its own substance, I who blew the lamp out. And so it might have been all right. But then he said:

"Put the matches back." He did not need to say the rest of it.

"Time was," he said, "when folks figured I was one a the orneriest bastards alive. An' they figgered Josh was another. Tell the truth, I suspect as how we was; we was pert near as ornery as Mose.

"Now, could be you don't know what I'm sayin' when I say we was ornery. You probly think bein' ornery is jest like bein' mean, or stubborn, an' that's on account a you found out about it from lookin' in some damn book. Well, bein' ornery is bein' stubborn, an' it is bein' mean, but that ain't the best part of it.

What ornery comes down to is how you act 'roun' white folks. Now, I recall old Charlie DeCharmes, don't know if you recollect him, but if Charlie wasn't mean an' stubborn, I don't know who was. Nasty too. You coulda said to him, Charlie, we got us a barrel a whiskey an' a pot a venison stew, come on an' help us do it in, an' you had a good chance a comin' away without him. But if you was to say to him, Charlie, we're goin' down here to the field an' beat the livin' daylights outa each other with two-by-fours jest for the pure pain of it, why, you'd be lucky if he didn't get there ahead a you an' start in an' beat hell outa his ownself. He was married to a girl from down McConnellsburg way, an' folks down there couldn't understand why didn't nobody up here try to stop him from beatin' on her all the time, but the way we figured it, she musta knowed what she was gettin' into when she married him, on accounta the night she met him he was poundin' the hell outa three fellas down to Hawley's. She knowed Charlie was mean; *everybody* knowed Charlie was mean. But every mornin' 'cept Sunday he went to work down to Heckerman's, an' he always got there on time. When he went to town he always put on a necktie, an' he always called the white folks mister an' ma'am. He was meanern a snake an' nastiern garlicky milk, but he weren't ornery.

"Me and Josh, we didn't beat on nobody much; there was more times than not that we'd go outa our way to steer clear of a fight, lessen there was whiskey or money in question. But we was ornery. Me, why, I'd been knowed to make fun a white folks right to their faces, which was ornery. I'd been knowed to come right out an' tell 'em to buy their butt a ticket on the express train to hell, which was surely ornery. An' Josh? He went so far beyond that . . . Well, lemme tell you, what he done ain't the kinda thing folks is gonna quit talkin' about, an' it ain't the kinda thing folks is gonna still be talkin' about, neither; it's the kinda thing they won't ever talk about at all.

"It first come out one Saturday night, when we was all settin' around to Hawley's, which me an' Josh an' Mose done jest for the company, seein' as what we was drinkin' was Mose's whiskey marked up to make a profit for Hawley. Only Josh wasn't there that night, which wasn't hardly usual; only time Josh missed a Saturday night at Hawley's was when we was all three off somewheres. So as you might expect, somebody sooner or later wanted to know where he was, an' somebody else said they seen him ridin' down the Springs Road, an' swore he was wearin' a suit. Now, everybody knowed better. I questioned the fella perty close—I forget now who it was 'xactly, but I made him get mighty particular 'bout what he seen, an' what he only thought he seen, an' what he only wisht he seen. An' what it come down to was, he seen somebody *looked* like Josh ridin' hard down the Springs Road. An' soon as I got him to stop bein' so sure, I was perty certain it wasn't Josh, an' I said so. Mose, he shook his head. 'Jack,' he says, 'you shoulda been a white man. Fella come along an' says he seen somethin' an' you hound him till he admits it might not a been that he saw, only somethin' that looks jest like it, an' from there you say he couldn'ta seen what he said he seen.'

"'Well, damn,' I says. 'There's a big diff—' But 'fore I could say much, in through the door comes Josh hisself, and he was dressed in overhauls jest like always. 'There,' I says, 'ya see?' 'See what?' Mose says. He looks at Josh an' says to him, 'What the hell was you doin' on the Springs Road in a suit?' 'Who, me?' Josh says. 'I wasn't on no Springs Road, an' I don't have no suit.' Mose looks at him real close, an' he wrinkles his nose up a couple a times. 'You lyin',' he says.

'I ain't,' says Josh. 'You is,' says Mose. 'You callin' me a liar?' Josh says. Well, the whole place got real quiet; folks was figurin' out how to get a bet down an' get out the way at the same time. Woulda been a fair fight—Mose had the muscle, but Josh was fastern a blue racer—but it never come off, on accounta Mose says, 'No, I ain't callin' you a liar. Way I figure it,' he says, 'you jest forgot all 'bout buyin' a suit an' borrowin' a horse an' ridin' down to wherever. Ain't your fault; fellas forgets all the time, 'specially when they been sniffin' bay rum. You know what I mean?' Well, I started sniffin' too, like I shoulda been all along, an' I was startin' to see what Mose meant when I seen that Josh knowed what he meant. You could tell sure, 'cause Josh, bein' so damn white an' all, Josh could blush. An' he was blushin' then. Looked like a cross 'tween a raspberry an' a McIntosh.

"'Goddamn!' I says. 'This nigger's in love.' Mose looks at me an' grins. 'Damn, Jack,' he says, 'you ain't so dumb after all.' But Josh wasn't havin' none a that. 'Naw,' he says, 'naw, he ain't dumb. He's jest a damn fool that don't know his butt from a bung hole.' But I knowed I was on the right track, an' Mose did too. 'I don't know, Josh,' Mose says. 'Jack seems to be perty sure you been out cattin' around. . . .' 'Nawsir,' I says. 'He ain't been cattin' no place. We ain't talkin' 'bout pussy-snatchin'. This here is *love* we're talkin' about.' Mose shook his head—Josh was jest too busy splutterin' an' blushin' to say anythin'—an' he says, 'Now, how you know all that, Jack? I can't see it.' Well, he was lyin'; half the time Mose acted dumb, but you didn't need to know him too well to know he was always one step ahead a you, sometimes two, an' half the time he was leadin' you by the nose. But he liked to let things come out their own way. So I went straight on. 'Well,' I says, 'he done shaved on Saturday afternoon, an' that means women is in there somewheres.' Mose nods. 'An',' I says, 'he was wearin' a suit. . . .' 'Hold up there,' Mose says. 'I thought you didn't believe that.' 'I didn't,' I says. 'Reason I didn't was that it woulda been mighty strange. But when you got a woman stuck in the middle of somethin', actin' mighty strange is reglar.' Mose considers that for a minute, an' then he says, 'Good point. Continue, sir, if you please.' Sounded jest like a white man. Jest 'bout everybody there started grinnin', 'cause they seen Mose's 'white man' act before. As for me, I knowed how to play too.

"'Certainly, Mr. Washington,' I says. 'Well,' I says, 'we're sure about the woman. We're sure about the suit, on accounta women makes strange things reglar, an' if that ain't enough, you can take a whiff a Mr. White an' you'll sniff the stink a bay rum, which sure as hell ain't no more reglarn a suit, an' if one unreglar thing is goin' on, then why not another one?' 'Indeed,' Mose says. 'Continue, sir.' An' I was glad to keep goin' too, on accounta I was havin' a real good time turnin' Josh into a cherry. Every time I'd say somethin' else, he'd turn red someplace else. By that time I had his face red an' his neck red. So I pulled up ma socks an' went to work on the backs of his hands.

"'Certainly, sir,' I says. 'Now, this here woman must be a mighty special woman. Man don't put on a suit an' stinkwater jest to lay out in the brier patch with some country girl. She's so special, Mr. White is in love with her. He *respects* her.' 'An' how do you know that, Mr. Crawley?' says Mose. 'Well, my dear Mr. Washington,' I says, 'it ain't but midnight, which is jest about the time willin' women is crawlin' out their windows, or leastways throwin' up the sashes, an' Mr. White is here among us, which means the lady is not willin', on accounta if she was, Mr. White would be elsewhere. On the other hand, he didn't come in cussin' an' swearin' an' goin' on 'bout bitches what gets a man to dress up an' put on stinkwater an' gets his nose open an' then don't wanna do nothin' 'cept sit on a porch swing an' hold hands. An' that must mean that Mr. White don't mind jest settin' on a porch swing an' holdin' hands. An' *that* means he's in love.'

"Now, about this time Josh was 'bout the shade of a barn door, an' I was ready to ease up some. But Mose, he looks at me an' he says, 'Well, I'll tell you, Jack, you reason that there out jest like a white man. Onliest problem with it is you left out one thing: man said he seen Josh here headin' down the Springs Road, an' that road don't go nowheres but south, an' as I know don't nobody know bettern you, there ain't nary a colored family that way 'fore you get clean to Cumberland. An' lessen Josh done stole hisself somebody's racehorse, ain't no way he could get clean to Cumberland an' back in that little piece a time, let alone doin' any courtin'. So I wisht you'd think like a white man a while more an' tell me jest 'xactly who this lady is.' Well, he surely had a point, an' I knowed he did, an' if I hadn't a knowed it I woulda been able to figure it out pert quick by the way old Josh jest quieted down an' looked at me. Quit blushin', quit chompin' at the bit; he jest looked, 'sif to say, there, you smart-butted bastard, let's us see who gonna be laughin' at who in 'bout three minutes. Everybody else was lookin' at me too, seein' what I was gonna do. An' I didn't know, but I did know if I didn't do somethin' I was gonna look like God's own fool, an' the only thing I could figure was to make a joke outa it, so I says, 'Thinkin' like a white man, the answer's clearern air: Josh's been a courtin' a white woman.'

"Well, nobody said nothin' for a second, an' then for 'bout five minutes you couldn't hear nothin' but folks laughin'. Hawley was laughin'. Charlie DeCharmes was laughin' fit to bust his gut. Mose, he was damn near rollin' on the floor. Me, I was perty happy gettin' outa that little tight spot I'd jawed ma way into, an' I was laughin' perty good for a minute. But then I looked at Josh, an' I seen somethin' knocked the chuckle clean outa me: Josh, he wasn't laughin' at all. He wasn't even smilin'. He was lookin' at 'em all laughin', lookin' real hard. An' then he spun around on his heel an' stomped out. The rest of 'em was so damn busy laughin' they didn't even know he was gone. But I knowed, an' it didn't take a whole lotta figurin' to see that there wasn't nothin' good gonna come of it.

"Well, the next day, I went huntin' him. It took me a load a huntin', too. It was sundown 'fore I come on him, settin' on a rock by the side a the road, up on Blackoak Ridge, watchin' the sun go down. I come up on him from behind an' he didn't even hear me come; he was that far gone with starin'. So I walked right up behind him—didn't try to be quiet, but it didn't make no difference—an' I grabbed his arms real tight. Had to do that; you don't walk up on a man like that an' say somethin'—it's a fast way to get your head took off. So I grabbed him, an' I swear to God he didn't hardly notice that. He just turns an' looks up at me an' grins. Dumbest damn grin I ever seen. I left him go. 'Lissen here,' I says. 'I come lookin' for you to tell you I didn't mean to ram them spurs in like I done—' Now, usually Josh woulda made you beg him to leave you apologize, but this time he jest waved it off. 'Why, Jack,' he says, 'that wasn't nothin'.' An' he goes right back to lookin' at the sunset. 'Naw,' I says, 'I don't think there was no harm done; wouldn't nobody believe it 'cept me.' That there got his attention. 'What?' he says. 'What the hell you sayin'?' I jest shrugged at him. 'I ain't sayin' nothin' 'cept that your secret's safe.' 'Ain't no secret,' Josh says. 'Ain't gonna be for long,' I says, 'if you keep on settin' out in the middle of a God-damn field in plain sight a the main road, moonin' over a sunset. Everybody gonna know what you doin'.' 'Damn if they are,' says Josh. 'Damn if they ain't,' says I. 'Hell, you act like you the first sorry soul ever fell in love. I'll lay you five to one you an' this girl decided you was gonna watch the damn sun go down every night an' think sweet thoughts an' . . .' I let up there, 'cause he was turnin' so red I figured he was gonna bust somethin'. So I says, 'Josh,' I says, 'lemme tell you somethin'.' I says, 'You recall when I was all het up 'bout that Berry girl, one lives out near Pleasantville? The one you an' Mose kept actin' like you was sniffin' around jest to get me goin'? You remember all that, Josh? Well, I'm gonna tell you what me an' that girl useta do. We went to town one day an' we bought us each a colored candle. Blue ones. An' every night at eight o'clock, she'd be in her house an' I'd be wherever I was, an' we'd light up them candles an' stare at 'em an' think 'bout each other jest as hard as we could. So you go back to your sunset, 'fore it's all gone.'

"Well, I moved off a ways an' waited there till the last piece a pink was gone outa the sky. Wasn't bored waitin'. I had me a couple things to think about. First thing was that Berry girl. Lord, she was somethin'! Long strong legs an' eyes like gooseberries an' skin that felt like hot whiskey on a raw throat, an' that damn candle-starin' was damn near as good as bein' right inside her, an' I swear to God I mighta married her if it hadn't been for the fact that I went out there one day an' seen where she had a yellow candle an' a green candle an' a red candle right upside the blue one, an' every one a them others was shorter. But she was still somethin'. But then I started thinkin' 'bout what was sure to happen when the word got out. An' that's what I was thinkin' 'bout when the sky got dark an' Josh stood up an' shook hisself like a hound dog comin' outa a crick, an' come over to me.

"'I guess,' he says, 'if I'da knowed how you was feelin', I wouldn'ta give you such a hard time 'bout that Berry girl.' An' then he told me the whole damned story: how he was drivin' down to the railway depot in Cumberland to pick up a load a stuff for some white man, an' how he saw this girl walkin' along the road, an' he offered her a ride, even though she was white an' it was the middle a the South County, on accounta she smiled at him jest like he was anybody else, an' how she talked to him jest like a woman oughta talk to a man, how she wasn't puttin' herself above him. An' he told me how he quit hurryin' the horses along, jest so he could stretch out talkin' to her. An' he told me how he finely drove her right up to her door an' she ast him to get down an' have a taste a cider, an' how he done it, an' how she poured it for him an' set with him at the table, an' how that girl had walked him out to the wagon an' told him how much she had liked talkin' to him, an' how much she had always dreamed about talkin' to somebody the way they talked to each other, an' that she hoped he'd come back. He told me how he kissed her, with his heart beatin' hell outa his chest half from excitement an' half from fear. An' he told me how he whipped them horses over them mountains, half the time thinkin' like a colored man that jest finished kissin' a white girl, wonderin' if maybe hadn't somebody seen it, or if maybe it wasn't some kinda trap, an' the other half thinkin' like a man oughta think about a woman, never mind what color she was. He told me he knowed that last didn't make no sense, on accounta he knowed he was down there in the South County, an' headin' into what useta be slave territory, an' he knowed he shoulda been hatin' jest as hard as he could, but all it took was a glass a cider an' a young girl's kiss, an' he was ready to forget everything he knowed. He told me all that, an' I listened to him. An' when he was done tellin' me we went over an' got on the road an' walked on back. An' we never spoke of any of it again. Not never.

"Well, if it hadda been up to me, wouldn't nobody a spoke about it, on accounta this wasn't jest a little piece a trouble Josh was fixin' to get hisself into. An' it was surely the wrong time to do it—I don't guess there's ever been a right one, but this surely was the wrong one. Folks don't recall too good anymore, or they don't want to, but 'round here the Klu Klux Klan was a perty big thing. Jest about then the Republicans an' the Klan was the big parties, an' the Klan managed to elect the sheriff. So if it hadda been up to me the whole thing woulda stayed mighty quiet. But it wasn't up to me. The word got out someways. An' once it was out, wasn't no question how it spread; them biddies up to the church done it. Them bitches'd spread anything 'ceptin' their legs for their husbands. I swear, you want to keep somethin' quiet, the onliest way to do it is to pass a law against sewin' circles an' tea parties. Better yet, get rid a the women. Anyways, they spread it.

"Truth was, when it come out it wasn't all that bad. They thought Josh was foolin' with some piece a white trash, which scandalized the women, but hell, none a us woulda give a damn, an' sure wasn't nobody tellin' the white folks, so when I heard that story, I done all I could to keep folks thinkin' it; tole 'em the truth. Said Josh wasn't cattin' around, he'd found hisself a white girl that had a good family an' went to church an' didn't have no mustache nor harelip nor gimp leg or nothin' an' she loved him. Well, didn't nobody believe it, an' I figured if the truth ever did come out they still wouldn't believe it. Only problem was Mose. He was liable to catch on to the truth. An' that was gonna be trouble, 'cause Mose didn't have no love for white folks. He'd sell to 'em, an' he'd buy from 'em when he had to, an' he'd talk to 'em if there wasn't no way around it, but he sure as hell wasn't goin' to think too much a Josh fallin' in love with one of 'em. But as it turned out, what Josh was up to was so far offa Mose's line a thinkin' he couldn't even guess at it. An' I sure as hell didn't want to tell him. But the time come when I had to.

"Way it fell out was like this. The whole thing went on clean through the summer. The talk was gettin' louder an' Josh was gettin' moonier. Mostly he wasn't around. When he was, he'd show up down to Hawley's an' lose his money an' grin like a fool. He'd carry Mose's 'shine aroun' an' deliver it an' never take a taste. Three different times I knowed about, gals he'd been carryin' on with up the country someplace come a huntin' for him, so fired up they come up the Hill walkin' bowlegged, an' they left the same way—he wouldn't have nothin' to do with 'em. It was sad. Went on like that through the hot months, into the fall. Then things got a little easier. The talk started to die down a little bit—some girl's belly started to show 'fore they got her to the altar, an' them biddies had that to go on about—an' I figgered maybe it was gonna turn out okay, Josh'd come to his senses 'fore the dam busted loose. But jest about the time the first frost hit the ground he come to see me, an' when he tole me why he come, I knowed that dam was gonna be bustin' mighty quick, an' it wasn't no millpond it was holdin' back, it was a Goddamned cesspool.

"He come in the mornin' an' we set out there underneath the oak tree drinkin' spring water an' eatin' cold chicken by way a breakfast, an' he told me how what he'd been doin' was goin' down there to the South County to work for that girl's daddy, helpin' in the fields an' forkin' manure an' I don't know what all, jest so's he'd have a chance to see her, an' how they'd had their chances, but they hadn't done nothin' but talk, she jest loved to talk, an' he didn't want nothin' else from her, on accounta there'd be time enough for that. That there made me set up, on accounta I could see it comin' but I couldn't believe it. So I left him tell me about how he'd spent three months stayin' away from other women an' cleanin' everything he owned, an' cleanin' up his mind—gettin' hisself worthy, was the way he put it—an' then he'd gone down there one night an' asted that girl to marry him, an' how she said she would, an' how he figured that maybe, since her daddy had seen how he could work, an' had always treated him fair, maybe it would be all right with him. An' how he was fixin' to go down there an ast the man if he could marry his daughter.

"I tell you, Johnny, I jest set there. Finely I says to him—an' I knowed I was walkin' on marshy ground, but the way I seen it, he was fixin' to go marchin' over quicksand—'Josh, does this girl know you ain't as white as you look?' But he didn't get all huffy like he usually done whenever somebody made mention of the fact that he wasn't 'xactly what you'd call dark-skinned. He said, yeah, she knew; matter of fact, that was jest about the first thing she ast him, on accounta he looked colored, 'cept for his skin. So I says to him, 'You mean you let her talk to you like that? Like you was some kinda funny-lookin' animal?' An' he says, 'It wasn't like that. She was jest . . . curious.' Well, I knowed then he was too far gone for me to hope to talk sense into him, but I knowed I had to try, so I said to him, 'Josh, I don't know. I ain't said nothin' 'bout none a this, mostly on accounta so far as I can see it ain't done nobody no harm, 'ceptin' a couple country girls. But what you're talkin' about now . . .' He held up his hand an' says, 'I know what I'm sayin'.' I looked at him, an' I says, 'I ain't sure you do. You're settin' there happiern a pig in a garbage pile on accounta you love the girl an' the girl loves you, an' you think maybe her daddy ain't gonna get too upset at the thought of a colored man for a son-in-law an' pickaninnies for grandchildren. You figure you found somebody white that's worth takin' serious. Well, maybe you have. Maybe that girl ain't never gonna look at you an' think nigger, an' maybe her family ain't neither. But you talkin' 'bout the South County, an' you an' me both know ain't nothin' good come outa the South County—' 'I know that,' he says, 'I been knowin' it. An' I tell you, Jack, it ain't too much different from the North County.' Well, he had a point there, but not much a one, an' I says, 'North, south, east, west, any way from Sunday. What you think is gonna happen when the neighbors find out?' He was quiet there for a minute; he hadn't taken that into account. 'Well,' he says finely, 'maybe we'll have to move away.' 'Yeah,' I says. 'Take her away from the folks she loves. She's gonna end up hatin' you, for sure. She will think nigger, for sure. An' where you gonna go? East? West? North? Clear to Goddamn Canada? Same damn story. Colored man an' a white woman, an' sooner or later somebody's gonna say somethin', an' it'll set her to thinkin'. Or maybe you'll have babies by that time; somebody'll say somethin' to them. An' you know you—you can't let nothin' like that go by 'thout you say somethin' too, an' that's jest how the end's gonna start.' He thought about that for a while, an' then he looks at me an' says, 'I'll tell you, Jack, from the day I was born I hated everything white, jest on accounta I couldn't see good an' didn't look right. An' you know how folks has treated me over the years. Well, I got even now, 'cause if there's one thing I can sure do, it's pass for white.'

"I jest set there. I couldn't say nothin'. I couldn't even think. What the man was talkin' 'bout doin' jest plain turned ma stomach. Finely I said, 'If this girl's so good, how come you don't get her to pass for colored?' He jest looked at me; he couldn't even begin to see what I was gettin' at. 'Damnit,' I says, 'you listen to me—' An' he put up his hand again an' stopped me. 'Jack,' he says, 'I made up ma mind. I'm gonna go down there an' get this thing set up decent an' formal an' proper, an' when we get that done good an' right we'll set down an' we'll figure out what to do about the rest of it.' An' he got up an' walked away.

"Well, I set there a long time, thinkin' 'bout how you could grow up right 'side a man an' not know a damn thing about what made him do what he done, an' how any way you cut it, Josh had a right to go to hell any damn way he wanted. By the time I got done thinkin' 'bout that, it was time to go to work. So I did.

"Shined me quite a few shoes that day; it was the dusty time a the year an' fellas'd come down from the courthouse three an' four times a day, jest to get the dust knocked off. There was a lot more of 'em than usual too, on accounta the boots was in town. The reglar fellas, see, the judge an' the sheriff an' the county commissioners an' the lawyers an' whatnot, them was what I called the shoes, on accounta that's what they wore. They was always around, on accounta most of 'em had offices in the courthouse or on the Square, or somewheres. But what I called the boots—on accounta that's what *they* wore—didn't have no offices. They was the ones that went out to the townships an' made sure things got done the way the shoes wanted 'em done. Some of 'em was around as much as the shoes was—a couple of 'em hung around the Alliquippa, settin' up in the lobby, an' every oncet in a while somebody'd come in an' give 'em somethin' to take to somebody else, if you get ma meanin'—but most of 'em stayed clear a town, lessen there was somethin' goin' on. But I knowed 'em all anyways, on accounta I might forget a face, but I don't never forget a pair a shoes. Or a pair a boots.

"So between the shoes gettin' dust knocked off 'em an' the boots—which was there, I figgered, on accounta elections was comin' up—there was a lot more shinin' to do, an' that was fine with me, on accounta there ain't nothin' like workin' hard an' steady to make your mind work. An' I needed to work mine. On accounta oncet I quit thinkin' 'bout stoppin' Josh I started thinkin' 'bout the South County.

"I knowed the South County. I had reason to know it. If there was anyplace in this whole part a the country a colored man would want to steer clear of, the South County was it. All them folks down there had come up from Maryland an' Virginia, an' some of 'em didn't know the Civil War was over, or, leastways, didn't know which side won. Anyways, I was thinkin' maybe I oughta get maself together an' go on down there with Josh. An' I was thinkin', too, that maybe I ought to let Mose in on what was goin' on, 'cause sure God if there was gonna be any kinda trouble, we was gonna need Mose. But on the other hand, I more or less give Josh ma word that I wasn't gonna say nothin' to nobody, least of all Mose. So I polished an' I pondered. Wasn't payin' too much attention to what them fellas was sayin'; most times it didn't amount to a hill a beans anyways, an' when it did, I usually knowed it 'fore they did. But 'long 'bout one o'clock, one a the fools that worked in some damn office or other, shufflin' papers in between takin' bribes, come over an' set his butt up there an' tells me to shine, but 'fore I can get started good he leans over an' gives me that fishy-eyeball look white folks toss at you when they're tryin' to act dangerous. I can't recall his name now; I do recollect that he bought his shoes outa the Montgomery Ward catalog, an' his heels was always run over, an' I recall he was so damn stupid they caught him takin' bribes. Now I think on it, he mighta been so damn dumb he wasn't takin' bribes, so the rest a them crooks had to make it look like he was, jest to get shut a him. Anyways, he leans over an' he says to me, 'Jack,' he says, 'I want you to know you're a good fella. You're a credit to your race.' Well, I thanked him kindly an' kept on shinin'; when they start with that it's best to jest ignore 'em; they don't mean no harm. But he wasn't through. 'Jack,' he says, 'I want you to know some folks come to me today, astin' 'bout you. Seems they heard some colored boy was nosin' 'round with a young lady down in Southampton.' *That* made me stop polishin'. But I managed to play dumb. 'Southampton?' I says. 'Why, I wouldn't be seein' no gal down there. Ain't a colored family—' 'I said a young *lady,* Jack,' he says. 'Well, like I was sayin' . . . Oh,' I says. Like I jest caught on. 'Well, you ain't got to worry none, Jack,' he says. 'I told them folks that you was too much a credit to your race to be actin' that way towards a young lady. Now ain't that the truth?' Well, I was about ready to fall offa ma stool, but leastways I could keep ma head down an' shine, so I says, 'Yes, sir, that surely is the truth.' He says, 'Well, I'm glad to hear it. On accounta these folks was mighty upset. Bad enough, boy even thinkin' 'bout interferin' with a young lady, but the way they tell it, he's been bein' perty slick, goin' down there to Southampton an' actin' like he was workin' for the young lady's father, an' then hangin' 'round down there, tryin' to talk that young lady into doin' unspeakable things. You wouldn't know any niggers that slick, would you, Jack?' Well, there was enough trouble brewin' 'thout me startin' a pot, but I wasn't about to take that crap from nobody. So I put the polish down an' I stood up an' I looked him right in the eye an' I said, 'Mister, I don't *know* no niggers.' Well, he faded clean to pale white, jest like a catfish's belly. That's when white folks scare me; when they gets that fishbelly white color. Unpredictable as a copperhead, an' could be the bite's poison too; I couldn't say. But he got up an' he didn't say a damn thing. He jest looked at me, 'sif to say, If I had me a book, your name would sure God be in it, an' then he went away.

"Well, in a way it was good that it happened like it done, on accounta it settled ma mind on jest about everything. So as soon as I could get outa there I set out lookin' for Mose.

"Now, Mose wasn't the easiest fella to find, 'specially that time a year. What he'd be was holed up somewheres cleanin' his equipment so he'd be ready when they harvested the corn, or he'd be trampin' over half the County lookin' for God knows what. He done that all the time. I don't know why; he already knowed the County bettern God knowed Creation. Anyways, you couldn't find him if he was holed up; places where he kept his worms an' his kettles an' whatnot was the closest-kept secret this side a Eleanor Roosevelt's underwear. You couldn't track him if he was explorin'; wasn't a man alive could track Mose 'thout a bloodhound, an' maybe not then. But what we done a long time 'fore all this was to set up a couple signs; I had ma signs an' Mose had his an' Josh had his. So the first thing I done was to head for a old hollow tree about two mile northwest, out towards Wolfsburg, an' when I got there I felt around inside it for a while an' come up with an acorn. Which meant that he wasn't holed up—in which case he wouldn'ta left nothin' an' ma butt woulda been busted—an' that he had headed south from there. Which may not sound like a whole lotta help, but if you know where a man started an' which direction he headed in, you oughta be able to find him 'thout too much trouble. So I found me a creek, an' I followed that upstream—which was what Mose woulda done jest in case somebody decided to track him with some dogs—lookin' for high ground, an' when I found some I headed south again, right up over Kintons Knob.

"I was halfways to Manns Choice when I heard him comin'. He was singin'. He always done that. May sound strange for a man to take all that trouble hidin' his trail from dogs that ain't even there an' then go around makin' noise like that, but Mose claimed that it didn't make no difference, on accounta what he sung was spirituals an' couldn't nobody but colored folks hear 'em, an' even they couldn't hear 'em too far. Well, he musta been right, 'cause I could hear him comin'—well, more like I could feel him, on accounta his voice was so low—an' it wasn't moren five seconds later that I seen him. I tell you, it was always a sight to see Mose movin' through the woods. You'd see him in town, or even up to Hawley's, an' you'd start to think maybe he wasn't so much, nothin' moren any other man. But you see him in the woods, movin' along over dry leaves without makin' a sound, movin' in big long strides that done to distance what a flame does to wax, you'd jest about want to head for town an' streetlights an' sidewalks 'cause you'd know you never had no more business in the woods than a catfish in a foot race.

"I stopped an' he come up to me. Says, 'Hey, Jack, what you doin' out here with your pants wet?' I still hadn't dried off from wadin' in that damn creek. 'I been pissin' in 'em,' I says, 'an' you gonna be pissin' in yours when you hear what I got to say. Siddown.' An' he done it, an' I told it all to him. Well, not all of it. I didn't tell him about the sunset-starin' an' whatnot, on accounta he wouldn'ta understood it; Mose wasn't never crazy enough over a woman to do anything like that. He had a hard enough time understandin' it as it was.

"'Damnation,' he says when I'd done finished tellin' him. Says, 'I can't see why a man'd want to go an' get messed up with a white woman for.' 'Hell,' I says. 'You can't see what a man'd want to get messed up with any kinda woman for. But this here ain't no time to be gettin' into that. This here's the time to be catchin' up to Josh.' Well, he seen the sense a that, even if he didn't see the sense a nothin' else, an' we set out.

"Well, it was 'bout four o'clock when we got back; Mose coulda made it faster, I imagine, but I held him back a bit. So we was too late. When we come up the Hill—we come up the back way, a course—we could jest about smell the fact that old Josh'd already lit out; you could hear his dogs a yippin' an' yappin' like they only done when they'd got fed recent an' knowed they wasn't gonna get left out to run nothin'. But we stopped by Josh's place anyways, jest to make sure. Well, he was gone, all right, an' it didn't look like he'd done changed his mind about what he was gonna do—you could see where he'd took a bath an' shaved, an' his overhauls was hung up on a nail, so he musta been wearin' that suit didn't nobody believe he owned. Mose looked the place over for a minute or two an' then he looks at me. 'I ain't never seen this fool this neat,' he says. 'Me neither,' I says. 'This place don't smell a nothin' 'sides pine tar soap,' he says. 'Surely don't,' I says. 'He ain't had a woman in here, 'cause you can't smell that,' he says. 'Surely can't,' I says. He shook his head. 'You mean to tell me some little old pasty woman can do all that to a man?' 'Mose,' I says, 'I think what's important here is that she's a woman. Now, we know white men ain't worth dog dung, but it strikes me that *any* kinda woman is a mighty powerful thing to fool with.' Mose shook his head again an' went outside. I knowed where he was goin', so I jest waited. He come back in about a minute. 'Sonofabitch,' he says. 'The sonofabitch limed his sonofabitchin' outhouse!' You could tell he was struck with it. 'Hell,' he says, 'maybe he is fool enough to go down there an' ast a white man can he marry his daughter.' 'Well, damn,' I says, 'I tole you that. Tole you he was fixin' to get his butt busted.' Mose looks at me real sharp. '*His* butt? *Your* butt. Every black butt this side a Pittsburgh. You think they gonna let it go at his butt? Why, the first damn thing them white folks is gonna get to thinkin' is if one nigger can quit sneakin' in the back winda an' start knockin' at the front door, we all gonna be linin' up on the porch. What you think they gonna do?'

"Well, Mose may not a been the smartest fella when it come to men an' women, but he sure knowed a good bit about politics. I tell you, I had never even thought that far, but I seen he was dead right. I heard 'bout the riots they had right down in Philadelphia an' out there to St. Louis maybe two, three years before this all went on. Way I heard it, that St. Louis thing started on accounta some little boy went swimmin' in the white folks' water, an' they throwed rocks at him till he drowned, an' if they done that to a little boy that went swimmin' in the wrong swimmin' hole, I hated to think what they was gonna do to a full-growed man that started tryin' to marry somebody's white daughter. So I thought about that for a half a second, an' then I says, 'Well, we best not be settin' 'round here talkin' about outhouses, then. We best find that fool an' pound some sense into his head.' Mose nods. 'Yeah,' he says, 'only we gonna have a damn hard time, seein' as the way I judge it he's got about a half-hour lead, an' he's gonna be on horseback.' I thought hard, an' then I says, 'Would be, 'ceptin' he's gonna be ridin' slow, on accounta the road'll be dusty an' he won't wanna mess up his suit. An' we can borrow a horse from Hawley. An' you know every shortcut for thirty miles, so we shouldn't have no problem.' 'Well,' says Mose, 'we do got one. We don't know where he's goin'.'

"Which was true. So there we was; half an hour behind already, an' we didn't even know where the finish line was. All I could do was stand there. 'Come on,' Mose says, an' he starts out the door. 'Come on where?' I says. 'Well, hell, Jack,' he says, 'we know he's headed south. We'll head that way an' maybe we'll get an idea.'

"So we lit out. Went chargin' down to Hawley's, but he wasn't there, so we jest told his missus we was borrowin' the horse. Turned out he took the horse with him. So we hotfooted it down the west side a the Hill, headin' for the swingin' bridge into town—that was standin' then—so's we could hit the Springs Road, but then, jest like Mose said, an idea hit me. Well, all it was was me recallin' what that white fella had said 'bout Southampton Township; but I guess you could call it an idea. Anyways, I jest says, 'We go east,' an' Mose didn't even bother to say what the hell or give me a funny look; he jest swung off an' we went hightailin' it down towards the Narrows. I tried to get up enough breath to tell him what was happenin', but he waved me off. I was grateful for it too, on accounta travelin' with Mose on foot was somethin' that took all the breath you could spare, leastways till you caught your second wind. So I didn't try to explain nothin' else, I jest kept movin', an' pretty soon it come to me what we was doin': we was trailin'. Not trackin', now; trailin'. Anybody that's spent jest a little bit a time in the woods knows there's a world a difference. Maybe you got a pack a dogs, an' they'll all take after a bear, an' every one of 'em will head off one way, followin' the scent. Trackin'. But there'll be one old hound—mostly it's an old hound, though I seen a couple pups that could do it—an' he'll circle around an' whine an' sniff an' whine some more, an' then he'll take off in some damn-fool direction that don't make no sense. He won't act like he's got a scent, on accounta he don't; he'll jest act like he knowed right where he was goin', an' jest what he was doin'. An' if you're out for the exercise, you follow the pack, but if you want bear meat, you follow that hound, on accounta what he done is put hisself right into that old bear's head. Started thinkin' jest like him. Knows where that bear is goin' an' what he's gonna do, jest as soon as the bear knows.

"Now, Mose, he wasn't no fool. He knowed I'd knowed Josh a sight longern him, an' he knowed we was still a sight closer, an' he figured I knowed, jest *knowed,* what the man'd do. An' I started to tell him he was wrong, but then I says to maself, Jack, maybe you do know. So I forgot about where I was goin'; I jest let the spirit move me, so to speak, an' old Mose come whippin' along beside me, never sayin' a word, never astin' a question. We was trailin'.

"An' we was movin' too, I mean to tell you. We covered some ground in the next hour or so. 'Bout a mile, mile an' a half down, we cut off from the river an' headed south on that road, runs down that side a the mountain, down towards Charlesville, an' we went on down there lickety-split. Might not a been too hard on Mose, but it was a pace that shoulda been gettin' to me. Only it wasn't, on accounta I had that knowin' feelin'. I seen old hound dogs that'll go like that all night, long as they got a scent. An' I had it, so we kept on. Musta covered seven, eight mile in that hour, all told. But then the feelin' left me. Jest like that, an' soon as it did, the strength went outa me too, an' I stopped dead.

"Or anyways, I tried to. Mose wouldn't let me. We dropped back to walk, but he made me keep movin'. He knowed jest what had happened, too. 'Lost it?' he says. I was too outa breath to do nothin' but nod. An' then, 'thout knowin' why, I looked up in the sky, an' I seen the sun.

"I stopped dead in ma tracks. I says, 'Mose, if you was to want to get up on top a mountain to watch the sun go down, which one would you pick?' Well, I think that shook his faith, a little bit anyways, on accounta he says, 'Jest what the hell would I be wantin' to watch the sun go down for?' Well, I didn't want to tell him. I didn't know *how* to tell him. So I says, 'Look, you're on your way to see this fella about marryin' his daughter, an' you figure seein' as he's white an' you're colored it might be the last damn sunset you're ever gonna see, so you want to get a good long look, an' the fella you got to see is down in Southampton Township.' Mose shook his head. 'Well,' he says, 'if I had me a horse, an' I was comin' down this way—' I stopped him there, on accounta the fella that said he seen Josh said he seen him on the Springs Road. 'Naw,' I says, 'you're comin' down—' 'The Springs Road,' Mose says. An' I knowed I didn't have to say no more. 'Yeah,' Mose says, an' he was starin' up at the sky, which was a mite dangerous on accounta we was pacin' along perty good again. 'I come down the Springs Road. Reason I'm on the Springs Road is so won't nobody know where I'm headed—' 'An' on accounta you couldn't borrow no horse from Hawley an' the onliest other place for a colored man to get one is to pay Les down to the Springs for one a them ridin'-stable nags.' 'Uh huh,' Mose says. 'So it takes me a while to get down there an' pay Les his dime an' ride out—' 'Saddle up an' ride out, on accounta Les ain't gonna be saddlin' up no horse for no damn dime.' 'Uh huh, an' I ride on down the valley as fast as I can go—' 'No, not that fast, on accounta it's dusty an' I'm wearin' ma suit.' 'Uh huh, an' I get to Patience an' cut off an' head up over the mountain, then I come down through Rainsburg an' head up over the mountain again, an' jest about sundown . . .' An' he looked at me an' I looked at him, 'cause now we knowed where Josh was gonna be. He was either gonna be goin' so slow he'd be on Evitts Mountain, west a Rainsburg, or he was gonna be pushin' to get to the top a Tussey Mountain, east a Rainsburg, an' all we had to do was get up on that east mountain 'fore the sun was clean down, an' either we'd catch him or we'd be ahead of him. So we lit out.

"Now, I don't recall too much more 'bout that part of it, mainly on accounta the fact that Mose wasn't 'xactly human when it come to coverin' ground in a hurry. I seen him run moren one dog into the ground, an' there was stories that he'd outdistanced a pair of fellas that was after him on horseback. You may not believe it, but I sure as hell do, on accounta that night was like the Goddamn trottin' races at the county fair, so far as I'm concerned. I won't say the trees went flyin' by, but there sure wasn't no time to be carvin' your name into the bark. An' I know we passed up moren one farmer's wagon. Don't know how many; couldn't count an' move at the same time. But it was a lot. An' jest 'bout the time the sun started touchin' the tree-tops, we seen some smudges a smoke an' 'fore we knowed it we was in Rainsburg. Wasn't much of a town—still ain't. Couple houses, a genral store, an' a couple churches. Well, for a small town there was a goodly amount of commotion goin' on; bunch a farmers at the store, settin', but we didn't have no time to stop an' pass the time a day. We jest hightailed it to the south end a town, an' we cut up over the ridge, an' we had to slow down, but we made the best time we could, an' even Mose was puffin' a shade when we hit the top. Me, I was damn near dead. An' I damn near died for real when we got there, 'cause the sun was gone, an' so was Josh. There was enough light for us to find the place where Josh'd tied the horse.

"We headed off again; there was a chance we might catch him 'fore he got to the fork in the road at the bottom of the mountain. We mighta too, if it hadn't been so damn dark an' that road hadn't been so damn windy. Time we got to the bottom I felt like I jest come through a prizefight with three dozen pine trees. So we sat at the bottom an' caught our breath; wasn't nothin' more to do till the moon come up.

"Soon as we caught our breath Mose says, 'I don't like this. I don't like all them farmers back there, an' I don't like all them wagons on the road.' Well, I told him I didn't like it neither, but I had worse things to worry about. 'Like what?' he says. 'Well, for one thing,' I says, 'you an' me figured out somethin' that ain't gonna make us too damn comfortable is likely to happen if we don't catch up to Josh.' 'Yeah,' says Mose. 'Now, jest what do you think that might be?' Well, I hadn't really thought 'bout *'xactly* what it might be, an' I said so. 'Well,' Mose says, 'jest 'xactly what you think is gonna make us any more uncomfortable than a bunch a redneck farmers with shotguns in their hands an' likker in their guts, 'cept maybe a bunch a redneck farmers with shotguns an' full a whiskey that's got wind of a colored boy tryin' to marry up with a white girl?'

"Well, then it hit me. An' I was jest about to start gettin' religion real quick when two things happened, right at the same time. First thing was, the moon come pokin' over Warrior Ridge; a big, full orangey moon, looked like it was swole up like a blood blister. Second was, we heard harness jinglin' an' hoofbeats comin' from up the mountain, on the road we jest come down. Lots a harness.

Lots a hoofbeats. An' voices, the way drunk men sound when they think they're bein' sneaky. I looked at Mose, an' I swear to Jesus, it was the onliest time up till then I ever seen that man scared. Wasn't scared when that damnfool Langford Beegle hired us to kill a bear for him an' didn't bother to tell us he'd winged the sonofabitch already, so when we got there the bear come chargin' out of a thicket maddern Joseph after Mary said she was interfered with by an angel. Wasn't scared when the sheriff took his money an' then tried to kill us an' take the whiskey. But he was scared that night, let me tell you. Me, I wasn't scared, I was pure terrified. An' I looked at him an' he looked at me, an' the same damn thought come to us both at the same damn time: headin' for trouble like we knowed we was, an' hadn't neither one of us thought to bring a gun. All we had was Mose's huntin' knife.

"Course, even if we hada had a gun, we wasn't gonna do nothin' right then, 'cept what we did, which was slink off into the woods aside of the road, an' set there, waitin' for 'em to come past, hopin' to God they wouldn't see us, or smell the fear comin' offa us, which was a damn sight more likely. 'Jesus, Mose,' I says, 'I hope they ain't got dogs.' 'Dogs?' Mose says. 'What the hell would they want dogs for?' 'Why, to try . . .' an' I stopped. 'Cause I seen somethin'. They wasn't gonna need no dogs, 'cause they knowed where Josh was goin' even if we didn't. All we had to do was follow 'em. 'Mose,' I says, 'Mose, all we got to do—' 'Is follow 'em. Yeah, I know that. But since you're so smart, what the hell we gonna do after we follow 'em?' Well, I didn't have the answer to that one, an' it didn't matter anyways, on accounta they was damn near on top a us by then.

"They come by us, ridin' slow. I wanted to be 'bout six miles away, downwind, but where we was 'bout four feet from the edge a the road, sucked up right to a birch log. We couldn't half breathe. What we could do was watch, an' what we seen was 'bout thirty old white farmers with faces that looked like somebody shoulda made shoes outa 'em. They was likkered—they was *well* likkered—you could smell it. But you couldn't see it in their faces. Those faces was set. An' they set in their saddles, them that had saddles to set in, straightern hell. Every one of 'em had a shotgun or a rifle. An' I could moren see 'em. I could smell 'em—smell the whiskey an' the horses an' the sweat an' all that, but mostly I could smell the angry. Maybe you don't think angry has a smell, but it does. Smells just like hot iron, only it's jest a shade softern that, jest a touch more fleshy. In a funny way, it's like a woman's smell. A woman, first thing, when she's fresh an' young, she smells sweet an' tangy. You can let her be for a while, couple years, maybe, an' she's still got that sweetness, maybe a little more salt to her, but that don't hurt. But you let her set for too long 'thout touchin' her an' it all turns sour. Not lemon sour; rotten sour, like the way milk tastes if you take it atop a maple syrup. An' that's what happens to the angry smell. An' that's what'd happened down there, 'cause the angry I was smellin' was an old-smellin' angry, an' I knowed soon as I smelled it somebody was gonna die that night.

"We waited till they passed, then we straightened up a shade. I looked at Mose, an' Mose looked at me, an' I knowed he'd been sniffin' the angry same as I done. But there wasn't nothin' to do 'cept light out after 'em, so I stood. Or I tried to; jest 'bout the time I got to ma knees, Mose hauls me back down. I wasn't fool enough to say nothin'; I jest looked around till I seen what he seen. An' presently I did. They had a rear guard; one fella on horseback, with canvas tied 'round his horseshoes so's they wouldn't make no noise. He had hisself a shotgun, jest like the rest. But that wasn't all. He was all dressed up, wearin' a hood, made outa some kinda white cloth, came to a point at the top an' hung clean down to his chest, an' a kinda sheet over the rest of him that hung down to his knees. He rode by slow an' quiet. An' we watched him till he was near outa sight, then we crawled out onto the road an' set off after him.

"We didn't have to worry 'bout him seein' us. Fool runs around in a white sheet on a moonlit night is gonna stay in sight to you a damn sight longer than you're gonna stay in sight to him. What we had to worry 'bout was stayin' outa earshot. So we couldn't talk. An' that was a problem, on accounta I wanted to tell Mose somethin'. Which was that I knowed who that last fella was. Could tell him by his boots. Pair I shined damn near every day for years. Belonged to Parker Adams. Parker, he'd been round the courthouse longern the man on the monument. You wanted somethin' done, you went to see Parker, an' Parker knowed who to talk to, an' he'd talk to 'em, an' he'd tell you yes or no, an' how much it was gonna cost. Parker took the money, an' I guess if any of it had ever come out, it woulda been Parker that went to jail, only none of it never did. Thing was, Parker wasn't no free lance. He done what he done on accounta it worked both ways, an' come election time he was right out there twistin' arms for the party. I wouldn't say they owned him, but wasn't no question a whose side he was on, an' who he took orders from. Which jest let you know 'xactly how far the whole thing had gone. 'Cause havin' Parker Adams there, dressed up in a sheet, was 'bout the same thing as havin' a speech by the mayor, an' the Presbyterian preacher handy to lead the prayer. Whatever they was gonna do to Josh, it wasn't gonna be no lynchin'. It was gonna be damn near as official as the Fourth of July.

"So we followed quiet. We knowed how to do that, an' you can bet we never done it no better. 'Bout two miles from the forks, or maybe it's closer to three, we come up to Chaneysville, which ain't much of a town, but there was likely to be somebody to see us, an' maybe call out or somethin', an' tip off Parker. Thing was, we couldn't take a chance on goin' around, on accounta the road splits off three different ways that I know of, an' maybe a couple more. So I was worryin', but it turned out that town was shut down tightern I don't know what. All the porches was empty an' all the curtains was drawn, an' there wasn't no lights showin' behind 'em. Wasn't nobody in that town takin' a chance on seein' something they wasn't wanted to see. Which was fine, since it meant they wasn't gonna be seein' us.

"Parker took the left-hand fork, or maybe it was the middle one, I don't recall too good, but anyways we followed him down the road an' past a few farmhouses, an' up over a couple hills, an' we was gettin' a little tired on accounta we couldn't hardly breathe right for fear a makin' noise, but we stuck to him. Had to. An' finely he stopped.

"I don't know how close he come to spottin' us. He jest stopped dead an' whirled that horse around an' looked over his backtrail, an' wasn't time for us to take cover; wasn't time for us to do nothin' 'cept freeze an' hope to God that whatever was behind us was dark enough to keep us hid. I swear I don't know how it was he didn't see us. But he didn't, 'cause after a long minute he turned off on a lane, an' that was that.

"I wanted to set there for a second an' shake, but we didn't have no time. Mose lit off through the woods fastern a scalded hound dog, an' I knowed he musta knowed a shortcut, so I jest tucked in close to Mose's butt an' kept ma head down, an' we went tearin' through them woods for maybe a quarter mile, an' then we come out into some old loggin' road, wasn't much moren a track but it was a hell of a lot clearer than the woods, an' we started runnin'. I don't know how we managed it—ma feet was 'bout ready to pack up any second, but I'll tell you, I knowed how bad things was gonna get an' a set of blistered-up toes was hardly gonna be the worst of it. So we run, an about ten minutes later that track widened up a bit, an' Mose quit runnin' an' took to the woods again an' circled us around, an' we busted up onto some open fields, a pasture, a couple cornfields, an' then we slipped into a little ring a woods, an' come up back of a farmhouse.

"''Zis it?' I says. 'Better be,' Mose says. 'We beat 'em?' I says. 'How the hell do I know?' says Mose. Well, I didn't see nobody. The house was jest a big old two-story white farmhouse, with white curtains in the windows with yellow lamp-light comin' through, an' a old glider swing on the porch. There was a front yard an' a back yard an' a barn an' a outhouse an' what looked like mighta been a separate stable. There was a faint odor a hog, but the pens musta been a good ways off 'cause I couldn't see no hogs or hear 'em grunt. What it all come down to was a perty picture of a country farmhouse, an' not a livin' soul in it.

"Mose waved his hand an' we backed outa there a ways. 'Whad we back out for?' I says. 'We busted our guts gettin' down here 'fore them peckerwoods, an' we ain't 'xactly got time to spare.' 'Yeah,' Mose says. 'We ain't got a lotta things. We ain't got no guns an' we ain't got no horse an' we ain't got the love a nobody this side a hell, so we sure God better have ourselves a plan.' Well, that's the way Mose was. 'Mose,' I says, 'this here ain't the kinda thing you want to go make a prayer meetin' outa. All we got to do is nip up to the back door there an' knock an' get in an' get Josh out, an' hightail it 'fore them bastards get here.' Mose shook his head. 'Jack, you ain't thought it—' 'Mose,' I says, 'I ain't got to think nothin' through, an' if I do, I'll do it when I has to. Now, I know you ain't really got that much love for Josh, or nobody else for that matter, but he's like a brother to me, so you all jest set on your butt here an' plan, an' when I bring him back you tell us both about it.'

"Now, maybe I wasn't as careful as Mose, but I wasn't no hot-headed fool. I took a good look around 'fore I done nothin', an' I waited two seconds while the moon went behind a cloud, but once it did I didn't waste no time with sneakin' an' crawlin'. I busted right outa cover an' hightailed it across the back yard, prayin' whatever dog them folks had wouldn't start in to barkin'. I come up to the back door an' opened her up an' went in. Wasn't no time to be polite—if them farmers rode up I sure God didn't want to be outside.

"Soon as I come in I could see 'em settin' there, 'round the table. Josh was there, an' an old rawboned-lookin' fella had to be the father, an' two big dumb-lookin' country boys had to be the brothers. Wasn't no woman in sight.

"I hadn't made a whole lotta noise, an' I guess I come in so fast they didn't have no time to do nothin' about what I did make, so I took 'em all by surprise. I says, ''xcuse me, gentlemen, I hate to bust up the meetin', but I got some business to discuss with Mr. White here,' an' I jest reached right over an' grabbed old Josh by the shoulder an' tried to jest haul him away. An' when I pulled him he come all right, but the chair came with him. On accounta he was tied to it. Whole thing fell on the floor an' there he was, layin' on his side, lookin' up at me with his eyes widern the sky. I looked at him for a second, an' then I looked up an' I seen three pistols pointed at me, an' jest like I told Mose, I thought it through when I had to. An' then I put ma hands up, real slow.

"The old man looks at me an' he grins real wide, an' I could see where his teeth was goin' green. 'Why, boys,' he says, 'I guess we went to a whole lotta trouble for nothin'. We wouldn'ta had to work on this one so hard if we'da knowed these fools was jest gonna come droppin' by.' The two boys laughed real good at that one. Real deep belly laughs; went 'Wheeyoo, wheeyoo.' 'That's enough now,' the old man says, an' the two of 'em shut up 'sif they was switched. He waves the gun at me, an' he nods toward the chair. 'Siddown, boy.' I sat. 'Merle,' he says, 'Merle, you come 'round behind me now an' go over there an' tie him up.' One a them fools come around, an' I damn near seen ma chance, 'cause he started to cut in 'tween us, but at the last minute he recollected what the old man told him ten seconds back an' went behind. He come around an' rummaged around in a cupboard for a while, with his behind stickin' up in the air, lookin' like a mountain covered over with denim. After a while he backs outa the cupboard. 'Pa,' he says, 'we done used up all the rope on that un there,' an' he gives a nod at Josh, who was still layin' there on the floor. The other lunk hadn't said nothin' up till then, but he chimes in on that, an' he says, 'That's right, Pa, we used her all up on this un here,' an' jest in case Pa didn't know which un where he was talkin' about, he fetched poor Josh a kick in the kidneys. I was lookin' right at him when it landed, an' it wasn't no love tap, neither, but Josh didn't show it. His eyes was blank, an' he hardly even winced. Well, up till then I hadn't really been thinkin'. But lookin' at Josh, seein' him hardly even wince when that dumb ox kicked him, well, I did start thinkin' 'bout how in hell we was gonna get outa there. An' the first thing I seen was we wasn't gonna get outa there. I had maybe an outside chance, 'cause I wasn't tied yet, an' with three of 'em there they was gonna have to be mighty careful how they fired them pistols, an' if Josh coulda maybe kicked one in the shins or somethin' to give me half a second's start, well, maybe I coulda made it. An' if I coulda got clear, maybe me an' Mose together could do somethin'. But none a that looked likely, on accounta Josh wasn't gonna be kickin' nobody to give nobody else half a second's nothin'. It didn't take much figurin' to know what had happened. His mind was ruint. On accounta he figgered out—too late, jest like I figgered out too late—that that girl had been settin' him up all along. Maybe he even figgered out that there was folks comin' to lynch him. An' if he figgered that far, he was surely gonna have figgered that when he swung she was gonna be right there, watchin' an' grinnin' an' fixin' to go gushy in her bloomers when he started jerkin' around. Anyways, I knowed I couldn't 'xpect no help from Josh. Meanwhile, Pa was tellin' the second one to take it easy, he didn't want Josh to die 'fore they was ready. 'Wayne,' he says, 'you go on out to the spring porch an' see if there ain't none a that there chain left hangin'.' 'Hey, Pa,' the first one says, 'there's a whole heap more rope out in the barn.' 'I know that, Merle,' the old man says, 'but I don't want nobody outside jest now.' Well, it turned out there was some chain, an' the two of 'em, Merle an' Wayne, they chained me to the chair, an' the old man never once took his eyes off me, so I didn't have a chance to do nothin'. When they was done, Wayne says, 'Pa, we finished on this un here,' an' he slaps me upside the head jest so's there wasn't no mistake. 'You want I should set that un there on his feet?' 'You do that, Wayne,' the old man says, 'but stay outa ma line a fire. This un looks like he's got some run in him.' Wayne looks at me. 'This un here?' he says, an' he went to give me another crack. Onliest thing I could move was ma head, but I twisted around an' took the slap flush on the mouth, an' I got a mouthful a finger an' bit as hard as I could an' twisted ma head as sharp as I could, an' I heard the bone go snap jest 'fore Wayne started bellerin'. Sounded awful. An' it was an awful sight, let me tell you, a two-hundred-an'-fifty-pound farm boy starin' down at his pinkie finger that was pointin' south when the rest a his fingers was pointin' east, cryin' like a baby. The old man jest shook his head. 'Yeah, Wayne,' he says, 'that un there.'

"Well, I can't say what they mighta done to me—I suspect as how that wasn't ma smartest move—but they never got the chance, on accounta there come a knock on the front door. The old man told Merle to set Josh an' me aloose from the chairs, which he done, an' they herded us both down the hallway towards the parlor. Josh jest walked along, calm as you please, lookin' dead. I suspect it wouldn'ta mattered if they hadn'ta tied his hands. It was harder for me; them chains was the heaviest damn things you can imagine. They wasn't even tied to me, jest wrapped around, an' it woulda been easiern hell to whip 'em off if it hadn'ta been for the fact that ma arms was inside next to ma chest. There wasn't nothin' I could do, so I jest clanked along.

"Jest 'fore we got to the door I heard a sound. Funny sound. Like a dog makes when you hit it all the time. I stopped an' I turned around an' looked, an' then I seen her. The girl. She was standin' up to the top a the steps, lookin' down at us. She was a little bit of a thing, with long dark hair an' skin the color a snow an' these big black eyes; I could see 'em starin' at us. She was dressed all in white, in a dress that went clear to the floor, an' the wall behind her was white, an' there wasn't no light up there to speak of, so all you could see was the hair an' the eyes an' the size of her. But you could hear her voice; that was the sound.

"Well, the old man looked up at her an' he says, 'Clydette, I told you to get outa sight an' stay outa sight.' But she didn't pay him no attention. She says, 'Joshua? Joshua?' I looked at Josh, but it was like he didn't hear her. I didn't blame him for not turnin' his head, I wouldn'ta turned my head for her no more neither, but it was like he didn't even hear her. But the old man heard her, an' went flyin' up them steps and fetched her a good clean slap an' knocked her sprawlin'. Then he come back, an' him an' Wayne an' Merle hauled us out inta the yard.

"They was waitin' out in the yard, all them farmers an' Parker Adams in his sheet, laid out in a half circle. They was all carryin' torches, an' the whole yard was lit up brightern day. Soon as they seen Josh, the whole bunch of 'em left out a roar like a mangled she-bear, an' for the first time it come to me jest how bad it was. I had perty much figured out I was gonna die, but I'd been too close to that too many times to let it spook me. But hearin' that roar, I got to thinkin' 'bout what they might do to me 'forehand, things that, well, once they happen to a man, he'd jest as soon die, an' if you come along an' save his life afterwards, it ain't no kindness.

"Well, Parker waited till they quieted down, an' then he waved his hand an' some a them farmers come up on the porch an' laid hold a Josh. Then Merle gives me a shove an' I come out in the torchlight. I seen old Parker give a start, 'cause I knowed he recognized me. 'What the hell you got there, Mr. McElfish?' he says. Only he made his voice all high an' whispery, an' it come to me that didn't nobody else there know 'xactly who he was. 'Don't rightly know,' the old man says. 'He come bustin' into the party so's me an' the boys give him these chains for a door prize. Figger he must be hooked up with that un there. But

I don't see it matters none; a nigger's a nigger, an' if you gonna have a lynchin', two's as good as one.' 'Maybe,' says Parker, 'but these two runs with a third one, an' if they're both here, third one can't be far off. You, Jack,' he says, 'where's Moses at?' I give ma voice a good shake, on accounta I seen a chance an' I wanted Parker to think I was scaredern I was, an' I says, 'He was right here, but he went to get the sheriff, an' when they get here you gonna be in some kinda trouble, an' if I was you I'd turn tail an' head back to Maryland fast as I could.' I wanted old Parker to get it in his head that I didn't know who he was. Only it damn near backfired. 'Mr. McElfish,' Parker says in that high whispery voice, 'you told this man where I was from?' 'No, sir,' says the old man. 'He musta been listenin' for a while 'fore he come bustin' in.' So I was safe; Parker musta let on to 'em he was from Maryland, which made all kindsa sense. ''Sides,' the old man says, 'we gonna kill him anyways, so it don't make no diff—' 'Listen here, McElfish,' Parker says. 'You bear in mind who's runnin' this lynchin'. Now, maybe we'll kill 'em both, an' maybe we'll let this one watch so he can go back an' tell the rest. I ain't decided.' Well, jest about then Wayne perks up a little, an' he says, 'If we only gonna lynch that un there, kin we mess this un here up a little 'fore we leave him go?' Parker looks at him. 'McElfish,' he says, 'you shut this lump of pork fat up 'fore I decide to lynch him too.' 'Shup, Wayne,' the old man says, an' Wayne shut up.

"They put us up in front of a bunch of 'em an' they made us march. Josh coulda run, maybe, but he looked deadern a two-day-old catfish, an' I wasn't gonna get too far wearin' eighty pounds a chain. So we jest walked along, me keepin' ma eyes peeled for a sign a Mose. I figgered he had to be doin' somethin', an' I knowed it wasn't goin' for no sheriff. But he didn't show hisself, an' nothin' happened. So all I could do was march.

"Well, they took us back down the lane to the main road, an' they marched us south for maybe a mile or so. It musta been a sight: two colored men walkin' along with ropes around their necks like they was dogs an' thirty men with guns on horseback an' wagons, an' what all. I got to thinkin' it musta looked jest like somebody goin' huntin'. We was the dogs an' they was the hunters, an' the onliest thing we needed was a coon, only we was the coons, an' they sure as damnit was gonna tree us, or one of us anyways, an' that got all mixed up in ma head, an' I started to laugh, real soft like, an' the chains started to clinkin' a little when ma chest moved, not much, jest a little *clink, clink, clink,* an' that was funny too, an' I started laughin' a little more, an' I marched right along while we turned off the main road an' went up over a hill, chucklin' an' clinkin', an' I mighta turned right into the jolliest bastard in hell if it wasn't for the fact that when we got to the other side a that hill there was a clearin' an' 'leven more fellas in sheets an' a big oak tree an' underneath of it a pile a wood, an' it come to me that when I said lynch I thought about hangin', but didn't everybody think that way, some thought about burnin'. An' I stopped chucklin'. I'm shamed to say it, but when them chains stopped clinkin' I heard a funny sound, like hoofbeats far off. An' Wayne, he sings out, 'Looky, Pa, looky, that un there wet hisself.' An' I looked down an' I seen he was right. But I couldn't feel it. Even when I seen it, I couldn't feel it.

"But nobody was payin' no attention. The 'leven sheets come trottin' up an' the farmers come up closer with the torches, an' they looked us over. Didn't say nothin'; didn't nobody say nothin'. It was so quiet all you could hear was a horse snort now an' again. They jest set there lookin'. After a minute Parker come up an' nods to the other sheets, an' they nodded to him, an' one of 'em says, 'Where'd *he* come from?' Said it in that same high whispery voice, so's wouldn't nobody know him. But I knowed him. I knowed 'em all. Knowed 'em by their boots. I'd shined every damn pair, that very day. Parker tole 'em how I'd come into the party, an' then he tole 'em how Mose was goin' to get the sheriff, an' they all chuckled a little, an' I knowed why: if he *hadda* gone to get the sheriff, you coulda bet dollars to double eagles there was least two deputies that wasn't gonna be handy. But after they was done chucklin' they stirred a little like they was uneasy. An' I seen why, right away: they wasn't sure they could kill me. If Josh was to disappear wouldn't nobody much know, or care. Me, I was another matter. Folks would miss me. An' somebody was maybe gonna look for me. An' the only way they was gonna be able to make folks stop lookin' was by tellin' 'em the truth, or somethin' like it, an' that wasn't gonna go down too easy. On accounta folks is funny; they'll get off their porches an' pull the shades an' keep their eyes screwed shut, but sometimes if you tell 'em what it is they ain't seein', they take notice.

"Well, Parker an' the rest a them sheets trotted aside to try an' figger out what to do. Me, I was feelin' mighty guilty, on accounta Josh was gonna die, an' I was feelin' good knowin' that I maybe wasn't. An' that's the way it was lookin', 'cause when the conference was over they hauled me over to the edge of the clearin' an' chained me to a tree an' they set Wayne to keep an eye on me, an' then they dismounted an' set about lynchin' Josh.

"It's funny how you see things. Why, a day before all that, if you was to a tole me I could set there an' watch the Klan lynch ma best friend an' not feel a thing, I woulda laughed in your face. But the truth is I can get more riled about it layin' here than I was then. It was jest like watchin' somebody butcher a hog. First they pulled his clothes off him—coat, vest, tie, shirt, pants, long johns, everything—an' they tossed the free end of a rope over the limb a that oak tree an' looped the noose end 'round below his armpits, an' they hoisted him up. Then Parker commenced to make some kinda speech. I couldn't hear what he was sayin' but I knowed what he was gettin' at, on accounta he kept pointin' to Josh's privates an' every time he done it them farmers would grumble. An' then he pulled out a knife an' held it right upside Josh's parts, an' they left out a roar. But Josh didn't. He jest hung there. An' that started gettin' to 'em; I guess it don't make no sense to lynch a man that don't pay you no mind. So Parker said somethin', an' one of them farmers went to his horse an' come back with a whip. I guess they figured to get old Josh's attention.

"They sure as hell had Wayne's. He could barely keep his eyes off 'em while they was uncoilin' that whip an' gettin' people moved around to give the sheet that had it enough room to swing. He started closer an' closer so's he could get a good look at what was goin' on. Matter a fact, one a the sheets seen how far from me Wayne was gettin' to be, an' he come over to take care a that. That was what I figgered, anyways. Only when that sheet came up to Wayne, he walked right on by him. Or looked to. Then he stopped an' turned, an' went back t'other way. An' I couldn't figger what *that* was all about, until all the sudden Wayne goes 'Wheeyoo,' real soft like, an' falls on his face. The sheet kept right on walkin'. It was too dark for me to see the boots, but it wasn't too dark for me to count, an' when he got back to the middle a the clearin' there was thirteen sheets there.

"I didn't waste no time.

"They hadn't bothered to chain me good, jest wrapped 'bout eighty pounds a chain round me an' a tree. So I wriggled around as much as I dared, made a little noise, but there wasn't nobody near enough to hear 'sides Wayne, an' I was perty certain Wayne wasn't listenin'. I twisted an' turned, an' I bruised maself on that chain, but I was gettin' a little play when they started in to whippin' Josh.

"The first crack made me jerk ma head up. Now, you gotta understand, that there wasn't no ridin' crop. It was a bullwhip. If it'd been me I woulda screamed when the first one caught me, but Josh didn't make a sound. The sheet that was whippin' him started windin' up for another go; they was set on gettin' sound outa Josh. Only you don't bullwhip a man too long—it ain't sound that comes out; it's his guts to come out. I had to do somethin' fast. All I could think about was Wayne's pistol. I wanted that pistol so bad I could taste it. An' I started twistin' harder, an' pert soon I could see ma way out. I needed to give three good jerks, that was all. Trouble was, I was gonna have to make noise, lotsa noise. But if they heard that there chain clinkin', that was gonna be the end of everything. So I had to time it. I jest hoped Josh could take three more cracks.

"The second one come. Whip went slappin' through the air an' I twisted them chains. They give a little. Not enough. Josh, he didn't give at all. He jest swung there, his face jest as blank as a whitewashed board.

"The third one come. I got so close to bein' aloose I coulda cried. Close, but close ain't there. Josh still wasn't sayin' nothin'. I could see blood startin' to drip on the wood underneath him, but he didn't make a sound, he jest swung back an' forth like a scarecrow in the wind.

"The fourth one come. I got it that time, an' I left them chains fall easy as I could, an' I dropped an' scooted across the ground to where good old Wayne was layin' in the dust. It took a minute to work his pistol out from under him, but 'fore they was ready to give Josh another crack I was lined up. I waited. Sights was lined up perfect. That sheet wound up an' let the whip go, an' jest about the time it was halfways to Josh I squeezed that trigger jest as gentle as I could. I was aimin' for the chest but the slug dropped moren I'd figgered an' took the bastard in the hip. Blowed him halfways into the woods. Well, they stood there for a second, like they didn't know what the hell happened. I lined up on Parker. Coulda taken a closer shot, but I couldn't be sure about 'xactly who the others was, you see. Well, I was hurried an' the shot went high, but that second shot sure attracted some attention. One a them sheets looks over an' shouts, 'The nigger's loose,' an' one a the other sheets shouts, 'You all get him, I'll watch this sonofabitch.' An' then they come.

"Those bastards was stupid. Farmers can't do nothin' in the woods at night, an' them sheets was even worse—they was all the time gettin' their hems caught. I backed away real fast, an' soon as I was in the woods I left off the other three shots in the pistol to slow 'em down, an' then I lit out. I coulda got shed of 'em in two or three minutes, but I pulled 'em along for a good ten, lettin' 'em catch sight a me—they couldn't read sign worth a damn—takin' 'em uphill all the damn time so they'd wind theyselves good. After about a mile an' a half a dodgin' tree trunks an' playin' peekaboo, I cut back downhill an' left 'em play tag with theyselves.

"By the time I got back to the clearin', Mose had got his knife outa Wayne an' had Josh cut down from the tree an' tied onto a horse. Josh wasn't blank-lookin' no more. I guess that whip had cut loose a lotta things. He jest set there, cryin' like I ain't never seen a man cry. I don't know if it was the pain or the fear or the way that girl done him, but he wasn't good for nothin'. Soon as I was on horse-back—Mose had picked out three good ones, an' run off the other horses—we rode out.

"We rode as hard as we could, but we couldn't make no time on accounta we couldn't keep Josh in the saddle. He wouldn't hold on. He wouldn't do nothin', 'cept cry. I wasn't too happy with him, but Mose was downright disgusted, an' he commenced to cussin' Josh three ways from Sunday. 'Damnit,' Mose says, 'we go through hell an' high water to rescue his pasty hind end an' all he wants to do is cry. Goddamn you, you mutilated sonofabitch, if you don't quit that cryin' an' start to ridin' I'm gonna lynch you ma own self.' 'Mose,' I says, 'go easy on him.' 'Easy, hell,' Mose says. 'You think them bastards are gonna go easy on us when they catch up? Which they gonna be doin' perty quick if we don't start ridin' hard. We got maybe ten minutes start in a two-hour ride outa this damn place, an' God knows what kinda fancy steppin' when we get back to someplace where we can hide, an' we can't do none a that with a Goddamn dead man to cart around.' He reins in right there an' he says, 'Now, Josh, you listen to me. I know you been through a lot, but I swear 'fore God if you don't straighten yourself up an' start ridin' I'm gonna leave you here an' leave the bastards lynch you. I ain't entirely sure you ain't got it comin'.'

"Well, he was right in a way, an' he was wrong in a way, but 'fore I could say nothin' Josh looks up an' says, 'Leave me. I don't give a damn.' Mose jest stared at him. Then he says, 'All right. I got a life, an' I aim to keep it. Come on, Jack.'

"I says, 'Now wait a minute. Let me talk to him. Looka here, Josh,' I says, 'I know how you feel. I swear I do. But you dyin' ain't the way to do things. Why, what you oughta do is go back there an' take that bitch out in the woods an' beat her till there's no tomorrow. Kill her if you want to, I'll help you. But lettin' 'em kill you, that don't make no sense. That's what they wanted to begin with.'

"Mose looks at me an' he looks at Josh. ''Zat it? 'Zat *all?*' 'What you mean, 'zat all?' I says. 'The man was in love with that girl. He worked honest labor all damn summer jest to stay close to her. He give up other women to stay clean for her. He was fixin' to marry her. He trusted her. He was ready to pass for white, for *white*, so's he could be with her. Then she turns around an' tries to get him kilt, an' then you come along an' say 'zat all? Yeah, that's all. Damn near all there is, anywhere. But what the hell would you know about that? You don't love nobody. You don't trust nobody. You don't give up nothin' for nobody. Well, maybe he was wrong, an' maybe he shoulda knowed better, an' maybe I think he's a damn fool too, but I tell you, I can't be real certain that if I was in his shoes I'd be too wild about stayin' alive maself. Now you ride on if you want. I'm gonna stay here an' talk to him, an' if I have to leave him, I swear, I'm gonna kill me a white girl.'

"Well, Mose, he looks at me, an' he shakes his head, an' he says, 'Jack, I swear, you as simple-minded as this here fool. Where you think I got this here sheet?' I couldn't think a nothin' to say, on accounta I didn't know where he got that sheet. So he told us. Told us how he'd gone on in that house, lookin' for a sheet, an' found that girl all beat an' bloodied, an' how she claimed she didn't have nothin' to do with it, that they musta been watchin' her an' Josh all along, an' waitin' for the right time, an' when they was ready they wanted her to tell 'em when he was comin' down to see her, an' she seen they didn't have nothin' good in mind, so they beat her an' made her tell, an' then they beat her again when they caught her tryin' to make some kinda signal to warn Josh off, an' how she begged him to save Josh somehow, an' give him the sheet, an' told him where they was takin' us.

"Well, I'll tell you, sometimes I useta get a little hot with Mose, on accounta the way he could lie easiern most folks breathe, but I was glad he could make stuff up that quick right then—or maybe he didn't have to make it up, maybe that was the guff she give him when he went in there to steal that sheet, to keep him from killin' her right then. I don't know. All I know is, Josh was whipped enough to believe it, an' he started ridin' better.

"Mose knowed a trail that ran along the top a Polish Mountain, an' we followed it almost to Evert. I was all for comin' on into town, but Mose kept sayin' he wasn't satisfied as to what was happenin'. I says to him, 'We know what's happenin', on accounta we jest finished puttin' a stop to it,' but Mose wouldn't listen. We finely holed up way up near dumb-butted town Mose called Oppenheimer. I hadn't never heard of it. It was a Godforsaken place to hole up, too; dry as dust, not a stream for miles. But Mose knowed a spring, an' he knowed a cave, an' it turned out he had some food cached up there, an' bandages an' some horse liniment, an' we cleaned Josh's back up an' bandaged him, an' then we ate an' then we had some whiskey, an' by the time the sun come up we was feelin' pretty good, most ways. 'Cept I could see that Josh wasn't comin' around the way he shoulda. He didn't say mucha anything. I knowed what it was, too; he finely seen through the lyin' Mose'd been doin' about that girl. I tried to tell Mose that, but he wouldn't listen. He jest wanted to go on an' on about politics, an' what them sheets was hopin' to accomplish by lynchin' Josh. I swear, Mose could make things about ten times as confusin' as they needed to be. An' I told him that. Said, 'Hell, Mose, we know what they was tryin' to accomplish.' 'Yeah,' Mose says, 'but why?'

"'Why?' I says. 'Hell, why ain't even a question. They done it on accounta white folks ain't noted for feelin' kindly towards colored folks, that's why. They're doin' the same damn thing all over the country all the damn time.' Well, Mose says, 'I know that, Jack. But there's more to why than jest that. There's "Why here?" an' there's "Why now?" an' there's—' 'Yeah,' I says, 'I know you know all the letters in the whatchemacallit, but I don't give a damn.' Well, he says, 'Jack, don'tcha see, we gotta figger out them whys so we can figger out who done it an' then begin to do somethin' about 'em. We can't jest go in there an' start beatin' on everybody white.' Well, I said, I didn't see why we couldn't, it sounded like they wasn't too particular about which nigger they started in on, but anyways, I already knowed who they was. An' I told 'em how I knowed, an' I told him who they was. An' Mose got real thoughtful.

"Well, we holed up that day an' the next, which was Sunday. Josh got so's he could move around pretty good, but his mind jest wasn't there. He still wasn't talkin'. Jest set there, sippin' whiskey, sayin' nothin'. By Sunday night, I was beginnin' to think we was gonna have to shoot him, like you do a horse with a busted leg—he was that bad. Finely Mose sets down with him an' he says, 'Looka-here, Josh,' he says, 'we had about enough a this moonin' around. If you worryin' about that girl—' 'Hell with her,' Josh says, an' I begun to think that maybe that there whippin' was a good thing some ways; it got some sense in his head anyways. 'All right,' Mose says, 'hell with her. I ain't got no time to be huntin' down women anyways; we got twelve men to lay for.' Well, there he was, lyin' again, but I didn't mind it this time, neither, on accounta I seen that he was tryin' to get Josh's juices flowin'. Course there wasn't no way we was gonna ambush them twelve without causin' a whole lot a stir, but maybe we coulda done one or two, which mighta been enough to get Josh back whatever it was he left down there in the South County. So I says, 'That's right, Josh, we got twelve sheets that needs to be taken to the scrub board an' hung out to dry. An' if that ain't enough, we can go get that farmer an' the one fool son he's got left—' Well, to tell you the truth, I was beginnin' to warm to the idea. But Josh cut me off right there. 'Leave it be,' he says. That was all he said. But he said it in a voice that was lowern a mole's belly an' deadern Thursday night. An' that took the starch right outa me. An' I left it be.

"I left it be the next day when I come on in an' took to shinin' shoes. I shined every pair a shoes in the courthouse. An' I shined every pair a boots that was down there in Southampton—'cept one. Story was a tree fell an' busted up that one's hip. They told me that. Othern that, didn't nobody say nothin'. I didn't neither. I left it be.

"Next day Josh come on into town an' went down to Hawkin's an' bought hisself some Mail Pouch an' walked around town half the day, chewin' tobacco an' spittin' juice on the sidewalk, jest like Mose told him to do. Didn't nobody say nothin' to him; they was leavin' it be.

"An' the next day Mose come down, leadin' two horses an' ridin' the third, an' he hitched 'em to the post in front a the courthouse. Half the Town seen him doin' it but didn't nobody say nothin', an' an hour later them horses was gone, an' didn't nobody say nothin' 'bout that, neither. They left it be.

"That's the way it was. They left it all be. Course, Josh, he wasn't never the same. I don't think he ever did say moren three words at a time to anybody again. He'd walk aroun' town silent as the grave. He'd go into Hawkin's an' half the time he'd say what he wanted, an' the rest a the time he'd jest point. I guess he was so mad he didn't want to start talkin', 'fraid it would all come out. He left it be, too.

"But somebody didn't leave it be, on accounta every month or so something bad would happen to one a them sheets. One went blind from drinkin' leaded shine. One fell in a ditch an' broke his leg an' caught pneumonia an' died. 'Nother one's wife left him. On like that. Jest bad news. Not too much at any one time, but steady; somethin' got every one of 'em. An' inside a 'bout three years wasn't none of 'em around here no more. Some moved on. 'Bout half was dead. Somebody didn't leave it be. . . ."

And then he started to cough. Long, racking coughs, as if he had been holding it all in while he told the tale, and now it had to come out. When he was finished the rag was bloody and his body was shaking with chills. I blew the candle out, got up and lit the lamp. When the light was steady I busied myself with stoking the fire and stirring the grate, with making the hot gases roar in the flue. I boiled water and made him a strong toddy. He could barely drink it but I got it down him, along with more of the penicillin. He swallowed and coughed. When the toddy was gone I let him lie back. He lay perfectly straight on the cot, but the chills made him shiver. He tried to talk. "Hush now," I said.

I sat up through the night. I fed the fire and drank hot whiskey and tried to stay awake. He slept a sleep that was closer to coma, from time to time rousing to something close to consciousness to call a name or mumble bits of tales. The stories were breaking up inside him; he coughed out fragments. I listened to him, sitting by the roaring stove, sipping whiskey and feeding the fire.

1981

Gloria Naylor 1950–

Gloria Naylor has won wide recognition for her portrayal of the world of black women. She knows the lives of black women in both the urban North and the rural South. She was born and grew up in New York City, but from her late teens to her mid-twenties she served as a missionary for the Jehovah's Witnesses in North Carolina and Florida. She then returned to New York, where she worked her way through Brooklyn College as a telephone operator in a New York City hotel. After graduation, in 1981, she entered Yale University, from which she received an M.A. in 1983.

She has written five novels, The Women of Brewster Place *(1982),* Linden Hills *(1985),* Mama Day *(1988),* Bailey's Cafe *(1992), and* The Men of Brewster Place *(1998). They explore the experience of black women and men in America as they themselves see it. Naylor shows their experiences of oppression, their strength of spirit, their sense of communion, and their awareness of the riches of their culture.*

The Women of Brewster Place *won the American Book Award as the year's best first novel, and in 1989 it was made into a motion picture. In seven chapters, one of them "Lucielia Louise Turner," it presents a panorama of the lives of seven different women who live on a dead-end street, Brewster Place. It is Naylor's attempt to present a revealing "microcosm" of the life of black women in the United States, showing their independence, their resilience, their sexuality, and the strategies they "have employed historically for their psychic health and survival."* Linden Hills *and* Mama Day *continue the same themes and with some of the same characters, showing the dangers of middle-class life in the suburbs, where black men and women are separated from their unique culture and their sense of identity. In* The Men of Brewster Place *Naylor returns to the inner-city neighborhood but now writes from the viewpoint of husbands and sons.*

Gloria Naylor has taught at Princeton, George Washington University, New York University, and Boston University; and she has lectured in India as a part of a cultural exchange program sponsored by the U.S. government. Yet she has retained a strong sense of her origins and an appreciation of the unique richness those origins have brought to her work. She argues that writers cannot escape their heritage, cannot escape the fact that the material of literature must be "filtered through the mind of the writer . . . and that filter can only be what he or she is." What the writer produces, she says, "is always rooted in a specific body politic, both personal and historical."

FURTHER READING: *Gloria Naylor: Critical Perspectives Past and Present,* ed. H. Gates and K. Appiah, 1993; V. Fowler, *Gloria Naylor: In Search of Sanctuary,* 1996; *The Critical Response to Gloria Naylor,* ed. S. Felton and M. Loris, 1997; *Gloria Naylor's Early Novels,* ed. M. Kelley, 1999; M. Whitt, *Understanding Gloria Naylor,* 1999; C. Wilson, *Gloria Naylor: A Critical Companion,* 2001; *Gloria Naylor: Strategy and Technique, Magic and Myth,* ed. S. Stave, 2001; *Conversations with Gloria Naylor,* ed. M. Montgomery, 2004.

TEXT: *The Women of Brewster Place,* 1982.

from *THE WOMEN OF BREWSTER PLACE*

LUCIELIA LOUISE TURNER

The sunlight was still watery as Ben trudged into Brewster Place, and the street had just begun to yawn and stretch itself. He eased himself onto his garbage can, which was pushed against the sagging brick wall that turned Brewster into a dead-end street. The metallic cold of the can's lid seeped into the bottom of his thin trousers. Sucking on a piece of breakfast sausage caught in his back teeth, he began to muse. Mighty cold, these spring mornings. The old days you could build a good trash fire in one of them barrels to keep warm. Well, don't want no summons now, and can't freeze to death. Yup, can't freeze to death.

His daily soliloquy completed, he reached into his coat pocket and pulled out a crumpled brown bag that contained his morning sun. The cheap red liquid moved slowly down his throat, providing immediate justification as the blood began to warm in his body. In the hazy light a lean dark figure began to make its way slowly up the block. It hesitated in front of the stoop at 316, but looking around and seeing Ben, it hurried over.

"Yo, Ben."

"Hey, Eugene, I thought that was you. Ain't seen ya round for a coupla days."

"Yeah." The young man put his hands in his pockets, frowned into the ground, and kicked the edge of Ben's can. "The funeral's today, ya know."

"Yeah."

"You going?" He looked up into Ben's face.

"Naw, I ain't got no clothes for them things. Can't abide 'em no way—too sad—it being a baby and all."

"Yeah. I was going myself, people expect it, ya know?"

"Yeah."

"But, man, the way Ciel's friends look at me and all—like I was filth or something. Hey, I even tried to go see Ciel in the hospital, heard she was freaked out and all."

"Yeah, she took it real bad."

"Yeah, well, damn, I took it bad. It was my kid, too, ya know. But Mattie, that fat, black bitch, just standin' in the hospital hall sayin' to me—to me, now, 'Whatcha want?' Like I was a fuckin' germ or something. Man, I just turned and left. You gotta be treated with respect, ya know?"

"Yeah."

"I mean, I should be there today with my woman in the limo and all, sittin' up there, doin' it right. But how you gonna be a man with them ball-busters tellin' everybody it was my fault and I should be the one dead? Damn!"

"Yeah, a man's gotta be a man." Ben felt the need to wet his reply with another sip. "Have some?"

"Naw, I'm gonna be heading on—Ciel don't need me today. I bet that frig, Mattie, rides in the head limo, wearing the pants. Shit—let 'em." He looked up again. "Ya know?"

"Yup."

"Take it easy, Ben." He turned to go.

"You too, Eugene."

"Hey, you going?"

"Naw."

"Me neither. Later."

"Later, Eugene."

Funny, Ben thought, Eugene ain't stopped to chat like that for a long time—near on a year, yup, a good year. He took another swallow to help him bring back the year-old conversation, but it didn't work; the second and third one didn't either. But he did remember that it had been an early spring morning like this one, and Eugene had been wearing those same tight jeans. He had hesitated outside of 316 then, too. But that time he went in . . .

Lucielia had just run water into the tea kettle and was putting it on the burner when she heard the cylinder turn. He didn't have to knock on the door; his key still fit the lock. Her thin knuckles gripped the handle of the kettle, but she didn't turn around. She knew. The last eleven months of her life hung compressed in the air between the click of the lock and his "Yo, baby."

The vibrations from those words rode like parasites on the air waves and came rushing into her kitchen, smashing the compression into indistinguishable days and hours that swirled dizzily before her. It was all there: the frustration of being left alone, sick, with a month-old baby; her humiliation reflected in the caseworker's blue eyes for the unanswerable "you can find him to have it, but can't find him to take care of it" smile; the raw urges that crept, uninvited, between her thighs on countless nights; the eternal whys all meshed with the explainable hate and unexplainable love. They kept circling in such a confusing pattern before her that she couldn't seem to grab even one to answer him with. So there was nothing in Lucielia's face when she turned it toward Eugene, standing in her kitchen door holding a ridiculously pink Easter bunny, nothing but sheer relief. . . .

"So he's back." Mattie sat at Lucielia's kitchen table, playing with Serena. It was rare that Mattie ever spoke more than two sentences to anybody about anything. She didn't have to. She chose her words with the grinding precision of a diamond cutter's drill.

"You think I'm a fool, don't you?"

"I ain't said that."

"You didn't have to," Ciel snapped.

"Why you mad at me, Ciel? It's your life, honey."

"Oh, Mattie, you don't understand. He's really straightened up this time. He's got a new job on the docks that pays real good, and he was just so depressed before with the new baby and no work. You'll see. He's even gone out now to buy paint and stuff to fix up the apartment. And, and Serena needs a daddy."

"You ain't gotta convince me, Ciel."

No, she wasn't talking to Mattie, she was talking to herself. She was convincing herself it was the new job and the paint and Serena that let him back into her life. Yet, the real truth went beyond her scope of understanding. When she laid her head in the hollow of his neck there was a deep musky scent to his body that brought back the ghosts of the Tennessee soil of her childhood. It reached up and lined the inside of her nostrils so that she inhaled his presence almost every minute of her life. The feel of his sooty flesh penetrated the skin of her fingers and coursed through her blood and became one, somewhere, wherever it was, with her actual being. But how do you tell yourself, let alone this practical old woman who loves you, that he was back because of that. So you don't.

You get up and fix you both another cup of coffee, calm the fretting baby on your lap with her pacifier, and you pray silently—very silently—behind veiled eyes that the man will stay.

Ciel was trying to remember exactly when it had started to go wrong again. Her mind sought for the slender threads of a clue that she could trace back to—perhaps—something she had said or done. Her brow was set tightly in concentration as she folded towels and smoothed the wrinkles over and over, as if the answer lay concealed in the stubborn creases of the terry cloth.

The months since Eugene's return began to tick off slowly before her, and she examined each one to pinpoint when the nagging whispers of trouble had begun in her brain. The friction on the towels increased when she came to the month that she had gotten pregnant again, but it couldn't be that. Things were different now. She wasn't sick as she had been with Serena, he was still working—no it wasn't the baby. It's not the baby, it's not the baby—the rhythm of those words sped up the motion of her hands, and she had almost yanked and folded and pressed them into a reality when, bewildered, she realized that she had run out of towels.

Ciel jumped when the front door slammed shut. She waited tensely for the metallic bang of his keys on the coffee table and the blast of the stereo. Lately that was how Eugene announced his presence home. Ciel walked into the living room with the motion of a swimmer entering a cold lake.

"Eugene, you're home early, huh?"

"You see anybody else sittin' here?" He spoke without looking at her and rose to turn up the stereo.

He wants to pick a fight, she thought, confused and hurt. He knows Serena's taking her nap, and now I'm supposed to say, Eugene, the baby's asleep, please cut the music down. Then he's going to say, you mean a man can't even relax in his own home without being picked on? I'm not picking on you, but you're going to wake up the baby. Which is always supposed to lead to: You don't give a damn about me. Everybody's more important than me—that kid, your friends, everybody. I'm just chickenshit around here, huh?

All this went through Ciel's head as she watched him leave the stereo and drop defiantly back down on the couch. Without saying a word, she turned and went into the bedroom. She looked down on the peaceful face of her daughter and softly caressed her small cheek. Her heart became full as she realized, this is the only thing I have ever loved without pain. She pulled the sheet gently over the tiny shoulders and firmly closed the door, protecting her from the music. She then went into the kitchen and began washing the rice for their dinner.

Eugene, seeing that he had been left alone, turned off the stereo and came and stood in the kitchen door.

"I lost my job today," he shot at her, as if she had been the cause.

The water was turning cloudy in the rice pot, and the force of the stream from the faucet caused scummy bubbles to rise to the surface. These broke and sprayed tiny starchy particles onto the dirty surface. Each bubble that broke seemed to increase the volume of the dogged whispers she had been ignoring for the last few months. She poured the dirty water off the rice to destroy and silence them, then watched with a malicious joy as they disappeared down the drain.

"So now, how in the hell I'm gonna make it with no money, huh? And another brat comin' here, huh?"

The second change of the water was slightly clearer, but the starch-speckled bubbles were still there, and this time there was no way to pretend deafness to their message. She had stood at that sink countless times before, washing rice, and she knew the water was never going to be totally clear. She couldn't stand there forever—her fingers were getting cold, and the rest of the dinner had to be fixed, and Serena would be waking up soon and wanting attention. Feverishly she poured the water off and tried again.

"I'm fuckin' sick of never getting ahead. Babies and bills, that's all you good for."

The bubbles were almost transparent now, but when they broke they left light trails of starch on top of the water that curled around her fingers. She knew it would be useless to try again. Defeated, Ciel placed the wet pot on the burner, and the flames leaped up bright red and orange, turning the water droplets clinging on the outside into steam.

Turning to him, she silently acquiesced. "All right, Eugene, what do you want me to do?"

He wasn't going to let her off so easily. "Hey, baby, look, I don't care what you do. I just can't have all these hassles on me right now, ya know?"

"I'll get a job. I don't mind, but I've got no one to keep Serena, and you don't want Mattie watching her."

"Mattie—no way. That fat bitch'll turn the kid against me. She hates my ass, and you know it."

"No, she doesn't, Eugene." Ciel remembered throwing that at Mattie once. "You hate him, don't you?" "Naw, honey," and she had cupped both hands on Ciel's face. "Maybe I just loves you too much."

"I don't give a damn what you say—she ain't minding my kid."

"Well, look, after the baby comes, they can tie my tubes—I don't care." She swallowed hard to keep down the lie.

"And what the hell we gonna feed it when it gets here, huh—air? With two kids and you on my back, I ain't never gonna have nothin'." He came and grabbed her by the shoulders and was shouting into her face. "Nothin', do you hear me, nothin'!"

"Nothing to it, Mrs. Turner." The face over hers was as calm and antiseptic as the room she lay in. "Please, relax. I'm going to give you a local anesthetic and then perform a simple D & C, or what you'd call a scraping to clean out the uterus. Then you'll rest here for about an hour and be on your way. There won't even be much bleeding." The voice droned on in its practiced monologue, peppered with sterile kindness.

Ciel was not listening. It was important that she keep herself completely isolated from these surroundings. All the activities of the past week of her life were balled up and jammed on the right side of her brain, as if belonging to some other woman. And when she had endured this one last thing for her, she would push it up there, too, and then one day give it all to her—Ciel wanted no part of it.

The next few days Ciel found it difficult to connect herself up again with her own world. Everything seemed to have taken on new textures and colors. When she washed the dishes, the plates felt peculiar in her hands, and she was more conscious of their smoothness and the heat of the water. There was a disturbing split second between someone talking to her and the words penetrating sufficiently to elicit a response. Her neighbors left her presence with slight frowns of puzzlement, and Eugene could be heard mumbling, "Moody bitch."

She became terribly possessive of Serena. She refused to leave her alone, even with Eugene. The little girl went everywhere with Ciel, toddling along on plump uncertain legs. When someone asked to hold or play with her, Ciel sat nearby, watching every move. She found herself walking into the bedroom several times when the child napped to see if she was still breathing. Each time she chided herself for this unreasonable foolishness, but within the next few minutes some strange force still drove her back.

Spring was slowly beginning to announce itself at Brewster Place. The arthritic cold was seeping out of the worn gray bricks, and the tenants with apartment windows facing the street were awakened by six o'clock sunlight. The music no longer blasted inside of 3C, and Ciel grew strong with the peacefulness of her household. The playful laughter of her daughter, heard more often now, brought a sort of redemption with it.

"Isn't she marvelous, Mattie? You know she's even trying to make whole sentences. Come on, baby, talk for Auntie Mattie."

Serena, totally uninterested in living up to her mother's proud claims, was trying to tear a gold-toned button off the bosom of Mattie's dress.

"It's so cute. She even knows her father's name. She says, my da da is Gene."

"Better teach her your name," Mattie said, while playing with the baby's hand. "She'll be using it more."

Ciel's mouth flew open to ask her what she meant by that, but she checked herself. It was useless to argue with Mattie. You could take her words however you wanted. The burden of their truth lay with you, not her.

Eugene came through the front door and stopped short when he saw Mattie. He avoided being around her as much as possible. She was always polite to him, but he sensed a silent condemnation behind even her most innocent words. He constantly felt the need to prove himself in front of her. These frustrations often took the form of unwarranted rudeness on his part.

Serena struggled out of Mattie's lap and went toward her father and tugged on his legs to be picked up. Ignoring the child and cutting short the greetings of the two women, he said coldly, "Ciel, I wanna talk to you."

Sensing trouble, Mattie rose to go. "Ciel, why don't you let me take Serena downstairs for a while. I got some ice cream for her."

"She can stay right here," Eugene broke in. "If she needs ice cream, I can buy it for her."

Hastening to soften his abruptness, Ciel said, "That's okay, Mattie, it's almost time for her nap. I'll bring her later—after dinner."

"All right. Now you all keep good." Her voice was warm. "You too, Eugene," she called back from the front door.

The click of the lock restored his balance to him. "Why in the hell is she always up here?"

"You just had your chance—why didn't you ask her yourself? If you don't want her here, tell her to stay out," Ciel snapped back confidently, knowing he never would.

"Look, I ain't got time to argue with you about that old hag. I got big doings in the making, and I need you to help me pack." Without waiting for a response, he hurried into the bedroom and pulled his old leather suitcase from under the bed.

A tight, icy knot formed in the center of Ciel's stomach and began to melt rapidly, watering the blood in her legs so that they almost refused to support her weight. She pulled Serena back from following Eugene and sat her in the middle of the living room floor.

"Here, honey, play with the blocks for Mommy—she has to talk to Daddy." She piled a few plastic alphabet blocks in front of the child, and on her way out of the room, she glanced around quickly and removed the glass ashtrays off the coffee table and put them on a shelf over the stereo.

Then, taking a deep breath to calm her racing heart, she started toward the bedroom.

Serena loved the light colorful cubes and would sometimes sit for an entire half-hour, repeatedly stacking them up and kicking them over with her feet. The hollow sound of their falling fascinated her, and she would often bang two of them together to re-create the magical noise. She was sitting, contentedly engaged in this particular activity, when a slow dark movement along the baseboard caught her eye.

A round black roach was making its way from behind the couch toward the kitchen. Serena threw one of her blocks at the insect, and, feeling the vibrations of the wall above it, the roach sped around the door into the kitchen. Finding a totally new game to amuse herself, Serena took off behind the insect with a block in each hand. Seeing her moving toy trying to bury itself under the linoleum by the garbage pail she threw another block, and the frantic roach now raced along the wall and found security in the electric wall socket under the kitchen table.

Angry at losing her plaything, she banged the block against the socket, attempting to get it to come back out. When that failed, she unsuccessfully tried to poke her chubby finger into the thin horizontal slit. Frustrated, tiring of the game, she sat under the table and realized she had found an entirely new place in the house to play. The shiny chrome of the table and chair legs drew her attention, and she experimented with the sound of the block against their smooth surfaces.

This would have entertained her until Ciel came, but the roach, thinking itself safe, ventured outside of the socket. Serena gave a cry of delight and attempted to catch her lost playmate, but it was too quick and darted back into the wall. She tried once again to poke her finger into the slit. Then a bright slender object, lying dropped and forgotten, came into her view. Picking up the fork, Serena finally managed to fit the thin flattened prongs into the electric socket.

Eugene was avoiding Ciel's eyes as he packed. "You know, baby, this is really a good deal after me bein' out of work for so long." He moved around her still figure to open the drawer that held his T-shirts and shorts. "And hell, Maine ain't far. Once I get settled on the docks up there, I'll be able to come home all the time."

"Why can't you take us with you?" She followed each of his movements with her eyes and saw herself being buried in the case under the growing pile of clothes.

"'Cause I gotta check out what's happening before I drag you and the kid up there."

"I don't mind. We'll make do. I've learned to live on very little."

"No, it just won't work right now. I gotta see my way clear first."

"Eugene, please." She listened with growing horror to herself quietly begging.

"No, and that's it!" He flung his shoes into the suitcase.

"Well, how far is it? Where did you say you were going?" She moved toward the suitcase.

"I told ya—the docks in Newport."

"That's not in Maine. You said you were going to Maine."

"Well, I made a mistake."

"How could you know about a place so far up? Who got you the job?"

"A friend."

"Who?"

"None of your damned business!" His eyes were flashing with the anger of a caged animal. He slammed down the top of the suitcase and yanked it off the bed.

"You're lying, aren't you? You don't have a job, do you? Do you?"

"Look, Ciel, believe whatever the fuck you want to. I gotta go." He tried to push past her.

She grabbed the handle of the case. "No, you can't go."

"Why?"

Her eyes widened slowly. She realized that to answer that would require that she uncurl that week of her life, pushed safely up into her head, when she had done all those terrible things for that other woman who had wanted an abortion. She and she alone would have to take responsibility for them now. He must understand what those actions had meant to her, but somehow, he had meant even more. She sought desperately for the right words, but it all came out as—

"Because I love you."

"Well, that ain't good enough."

Ciel had let the suitcase go before he jerked it away. She looked at Eugene, and the poison of reality began to spread through her body like gangrene. It drew his scent out of her nostrils and scraped the veil from her eyes, and he stood before her just as he really was—a tall, skinny black man with arrogance and selfishness twisting his mouth into a strange shape. And, she thought, I don't feel anything now. But soon, very soon, I will start to hate you. I promise—I will hate you. And I'll never forgive myself for not having done it sooner—soon enough to have saved my baby. Oh, dear God, my baby.

Eugene thought the tears that began to crowd into her eyes were for him. But she was allowing herself this one last luxury of brief mourning for the loss of something denied to her. It troubled her that she wasn't sure exactly what that something was, or which one of them was to blame for taking it away. Ciel began to feel the overpowering need to be near someone who loved her. I'll get Serena and we'll go visit Mattie now, she thought in a daze.

Then they heard the scream from the kitchen.

The church was small and dark. The air hung about them like a stale blanket. Ciel looked straight ahead, oblivious to the seats filling up behind her. She didn't feel the damp pressure of Mattie's heavy arm or the doubt that invaded the air over Eugene's absence. The plaintive Merciful Jesuses, lightly sprinkled with sobs, were lost on her ears. Her dry eyes were locked on the tiny pearl-gray casket, flanked with oversized arrangements of red-carnationed bleeding hearts and white-lilied eternal circles. The sagging chords that came loping out of the huge organ and mixed with the droning voice of the black-robed old man behind the coffin were also unable to penetrate her.

Ciel's whole universe existed in the seven feet of space between herself and her child's narrow coffin. There was not even room for this comforting God whose melodious virtues floated around her sphere, attempting to get in. Obviously, He had deserted or damned her, it didn't matter which. All Ciel knew was that her prayers had gone unheeded—that afternoon she had lifted her daughter's body off the kitchen floor, those blank days in the hospital, and now. So she was left to do what God had chosen not to.

People had mistaken it for shock when she refused to cry. They thought it some special sort of grief when she stopped eating and even drinking water unless forced to; her hair went uncombed and her body unbathed. But Ciel was not grieving for Serena. She was simply tired of hurting. And she was forced to slowly give up the life that God had refused to take from her.

After the funeral the well-meaning came to console and offer their dog-eared faith in the form of coconut cakes, potato pies, fried chicken, and tears. Ciel sat in the bed with her back resting against the headboard; her long thin fingers, still as midnight frost on a frozen pond, lay on the covers. She acknowledged their kindnesses with nods of her head and slight lip movements, but no sound. It was as if her voice was too tired to make the journey from the diaphragm through the larynx to the mouth.

Her visitors' impotent words flew against the steel edge of her pain, bled slowly, and returned to die in the senders' throats. No one came too near. They stood around the door and the dressing table, or sat on the edges of the two worn chairs that needed upholstering, but they unconsciously pushed themselves back against the wall as if her hurt was contagious.

A neighbor woman entered in studied certainty and stood in the middle of the room. "Child, I know how you feel, but don't do this to yourself. I lost one, too. The Lord will . . ." And she choked, because the words were jammed down into her throat by the naked force of Ciel's eyes. Ciel had opened them fully now to look at the woman, but raw fires had eaten them worse than lifeless—worse than death. The woman saw in that mute appeal for silence the ragings of a personal hell flowing through Ciel's eyes. And just as she went to reach for the girl's hand, she stopped as if a muscle spasm had overtaken her body and, cowardly, shrank back. Reminiscences of old, dried-over pains were no consolation in the face of this. They had the effect of cold beads of water on a hot iron—they danced and fizzled up while the room stank from their steam.

Mattie stood in the doorway, and an involuntary shudder went through her when she saw Ciel's eyes. Dear God, she thought, she's dying, and right in front of our faces.

"Merciful Father, no!" she bellowed. There was no prayer, no bended knee or sackcloth supplication in those words, but a blasphemous fireball that shot forth and went smashing against the gates of heaven, raging and kicking, demanding to be heard.

"No! No! No!" Like a black Brahman cow, desperate to protect her young, she surged into the room, pushing the neighbor woman and the others out of her way. She approached the bed with her lips clamped shut in such force that the muscles in her jaw and the back of her neck began to ache.

She sat on the edge of the bed and enfolded the tissue-thin body in her huge ebony arms. And she rocked. Ciel's body was so hot it burned Mattie when she first touched her, but she held on and rocked. Back and forth, back and forth—she had Ciel so tightly she could feel her young breasts flatten against the buttons of her dress. The black mammoth gripped so firmly that the slightest increase of pressure would have cracked the girl's spine. But she rocked.

And somewhere from the bowels of her being came a moan from Ciel, so high at first it couldn't be heard by anyone there, but the yard dogs began an unholy howling. And Mattie rocked. And then, agonizingly slow, it broke its way through the parched lips in a spaghetti-thin column of air that could be faintly heard in the frozen room.

Ciel moaned. Mattie rocked. Propelled by the sound, Mattie rocked her out of that bed, out of that room, into a blue vastness just underneath the sun and above time. She rocked her over Aegean seas so clean they shone like crystal, so clear the fresh blood of sacrificed babies torn from their mother's arms and given to Neptune could be seen like pink froth on the water. She rocked her on and on, past Dachau, where soul-gutted Jewish mothers swept their children's entrails off laboratory floors. They flew past the spilled brains of Senegalese infants whose mothers had dashed them on the wooden sides of slave ships. And she rocked on.

She rocked her into her childhood and let her see murdered dreams. And she rocked her back, back into the womb, to the nadir of her hurt, and they found it—a slight silver splinter, embedded just below the surface of the skin. And Mattie rocked and pulled—and the splinter gave way, but its roots were deep, gigantic, ragged, and they tore up flesh with bits of fat and muscle tissue clinging to them. They left a huge hole, which was already starting to pus over, but Mattie was satisfied. It would heal.

The bile that had formed a tight knot in Ciel's stomach began to rise and gagged her just as it passed her throat. Mattie put her hand over the girl's mouth and rushed her out the now-empty room to the toilet. Ciel retched yellowish-green phlegm, and she brought up white lumps of slime that hit the seat of the toilet and rolled off, splattering onto the tiles. After a while she heaved only air, but the body did not seem to want to stop. It was exorcising the evilness of pain.

Mattie cupped her hands under the faucet and motioned for Ciel to drink and clean her mouth. When the water left Ciel's mouth, it tasted as if she had been rinsing with a mild acid. Mattie drew a tub of hot water and undressed Ciel. She let the nightgown fall off the narrow shoulders, over the pitifully thin breasts and jutting hipbones. She slowly helped her into the water, and it was like a dried brown autumn leaf hitting the surface of a puddle.

And slowly she bathed her. She took the soap, and, using only her hands, she washed Ciel's hair and the back of her neck. She raised her arms and cleaned the armpits, soaping well the downy brown hair there. She let the soap slip between the girl's breasts, and she washed each one separately, cupping it in her hands. She took each leg and even cleaned under the toenails. Making Ciel rise and kneel in the tub, she cleaned the crack in her behind, soaped her pubic hair, and gently washed the creases in her vagina—slowly, reverently, as if handling a newborn.

She took her from the tub and toweled her in the same manner she had been bathed—as if too much friction would break the skin tissue. All of this had been done without either woman saying a word. Ciel stood there, naked, and felt the cool air play against the clean surface of her skin. She had the sensation of fresh mint coursing through her pores. She closed her eyes and the fire was gone. Her tears no longer fried within her, killing her internal organs with their steam. So Ciel began to cry—there, naked, in the center of the bathroom floor.

Mattie emptied the tub and rinsed it. She led the still-naked Ciel to a chair in the bedroom. The tears were flowing so freely now Ciel couldn't see, and she allowed herself to be led as if blind. She sat on the chair and cried—head erect. Since she made no effort to wipe them away, the tears dripped down her chin and landed on her chest and rolled down to her stomach and onto her dark pubic hair. Ignoring Ciel, Mattie took away the crumpled linen and made the bed, stretching the sheets tight and fresh. She beat the pillows into a virgin plumpness and dressed them in white cases.

And Ciel sat. And cried. The unmolested tears had rolled down her parted thighs and were beginning to wet the chair. But they were cold and good. She put out her tongue and began to drink in their saltiness, feeding on them. The first tears were gone. Her thin shoulders began to quiver, and spasms circled her body as new tears came—this time, hot and stinging. And she sobbed, the first sound she'd made since the moaning.

Mattie took the edges of the dirty sheet she'd pulled off the bed and wiped the mucus that had been running out of Ciel's nose. She then led her freshly wet, glistening body, baptized now, to the bed. She covered her with one sheet and laid a towel across the pillow—it would help for a while.

And Ciel lay down and cried. But Mattie knew the tears would end. And she would sleep. And morning would come.

1980, 1982

Leslie Marmon Silko 1948–

In 1872, Robert Marmon came as a trader to the Indian Pueblo at Laguna in New Mexico Territory, fifty miles west of Albuquerque. He married a Laguna woman and settled at the Pueblo, and there his great-granddaughter was born three-quarters of a century later. Because of her mixed ancestry—Laguna Indian, Hispanic, and white—Leslie Marmon Silko was an outsider, yet she was raised with the children of the Pueblo and absorbed the tales and myths told to her by her great-grandmother, from whom she took her interest in becoming a storyteller herself.

Silko attended the Indian school in Laguna until the fifth grade, at which time she was sent to study in Albuquerque. There she graduated from high school, entered the University of New Mexico, and graduated with honors in 1969. Afterward, she briefly attended law school at the University of New Mexico with the intention of preparing herself to defend the legal rights of Native Americans, but her fascination with storytelling and literature prompted her to transfer to the graduate school to study English. Propelled by her love of literature, she chose creative writing as her avocation and subsequently taught English and fiction writing at the University of New Mexico, Vassar College, and the University of Arizona.

Silko has said, "I am of mixed-breed ancestry, but what I know is Laguna." Most of her poetry and fiction is set at Laguna, and, following the tradition of the storyteller of the Pueblo culture, her narrative style is spare. Her writing displays a strong sense of the weather and the landscape: the mountains, streams, and valleys of the region. She concentrates on the everyday life of the people she knows, the distinct mythical, historical, and present-day worlds in which they simultaneously exist.

Silko wrote her first published story "The Man to Send Rain Clouds" (1969) for a class in creative writing at the University of New Mexico. Her first book, Laguna Woman *(1974), traces the close relationship of the people to the landscape around the Laguna Pueblo. Her first novel and most critically praised work,* Ceremony *(1977), tells of the experiences of a World War II veteran named Tayo, who returns from the war and must struggle to readjust to the Native American life and customs he had left. The novel employs a series of flashbacks to render the horrors Tayo experienced while incarcerated in a Japanese prisoner-of-war camp. On his release he is initially sent to a veterans' hospital in Los Angeles, where the doctors prove unable to diagnose or cure his illness. Back in Laguna, however, with the help of Old Betonie, a tribal elder, and Ts'eh, a medicine woman, his lengthy quest for healing and identity succeeds. Tayo comes to terms with both his identity and his wartime experiences, and he begins his growth into manhood.*

Silko has also written plays and filmscripts and a collection of short stories, poems, and photographs about the Laguna people, published under the title Storyteller *in 1981. In 1986, an edited version of her correspondence with the poet James Wright appeared, under the title* Delicacy and the Strength of Lace. *Her most controversial work,* The Almanac of the Dead, *was published in 1991. A scathing novel, it describes the rage of Native Americans in the United States whose lives are dominated by the transplanted European culture that Silko portrays as a lethal disease. Believing that white culture and society are septic and doomed, Silko's Native Americans join similarly oppressed African Americans in setting out to retake North America with the force of modern firearms and with hexes and ancient witchcraft.*

Silko's recent novel, Gardens in the Dunes *(1999), is a mixture of myth, allegory, and Southwestern history. The reader watches as Indigo, the novel's child-heroine, unwittingly embarks on an exhilarating journey across America, throughout Europe and Brazil, and finally back to her native Southwest America. Repeatedly torn between competing cultures, in the end Indigo remains true to the traditions and values of her own tribe. As with* Storyteller *and* Ceremony, Gardens in the Dunes *confirms Silko's skill as a storyteller, portraying Native Americans today, living at the same time in the contemporary world of technology and materialism and in a separate world of traditions and ideals of America's first people.*

FURTHER READING: P. Seyersted, *Leslie Marmon Silko,* 1980; G. Sayler, *Leslie Marmon Silko,* 1997; H. Jaskowski, *Leslie Marmon Silko,* 1998; *Conversations with Leslie Marmon Silko,* ed. E. Arnold, 2000; A. Aldama, *Disrupting Savagism: Intersecting Chicana/o, Mexican Immigrant, and Native American Struggles for Self-Representation,* 2001; *Leslie Marmon Silko's Ceremony: A Casebook,* ed. A. Chavkin, 2002.

TEXT: *Storyteller,* 1981.

THE MAN TO SEND RAIN CLOUDS

They found him under a big cottonwood tree. His Levi jacket and pants were faded light blue so that he had been easy to find. The big cottonwood tree stood apart from a small grove of winterbare cottonwoods which grew in the wide, sandy arroyo. He had been dead for a day or more, and the sheep had wandered and scattered up and down the arroyo. Leon and his brother-in-law, Ken, gathered the sheep and left them in the pen at the sheep camp before they returned to the cottonwood tree. Leon waited under the tree while Ken drove the truck through the deep sand to the edge of the arroyo. He squinted up at the sun and unzipped his jacket—it sure was hot for this time of year. But high and northwest the blue mountains were still in snow. Ken came sliding down the low, crumbling bank about fifty yards down, and he was bringing the red blanket.

Before they wrapped the old man, Leon took a piece of string out of his pocket and tied a small gray feather in the old man's long white hair. Ken gave him the paint. Across the brown wrinkled forehead he drew a streak of white and along the high cheekbones he drew a strip of blue paint. He paused and watched Ken throw pinches of corn meal and pollen into the wind that fluttered the small gray feather. Then Leon painted with yellow under the old man's broad nose, and finally, when he had painted green across the chin, he smiled.

"Send us rain clouds, Grandfather." They laid the bundle in the back of the pickup and covered it with a heavy tarp before they started back to the pueblo.

They turned off the highway onto the sandy pueblo road. Not long after they passed the store and post office they saw Father Paul's car coming toward them. When he recognized their faces he slowed his car and waved for them to stop. The young priest rolled down the car window.

"Did you find old Teofilo?" he asked loudly.

Leon stopped the truck. "Good morning, Father. We were just out to the sheep camp. Everything is O.K. now."

"Thank God for that. Teofilo is a very old man. You really shouldn't allow him to stay at the sheep camp alone."

"No, he won't do that any more now."

"Well, I'm glad you understand. I hope I'll be seeing you at Mass this week—we missed you last Sunday. See if you can get old Teofilo to come with you." The priest smiled and waved at them as they drove away.

Louise and Teresa were waiting. The table was set for lunch, and the coffee was boiling on the black iron stove. Leon looked at Louise and then at Teresa.

"We found him under a cottonwood tree in the big arroyo near sheep camp. I guess he sat down to rest in the shade and never got up again." Leon walked toward the old man's bed. The red plaid shawl had been shaken and spread carefully over the bed, and a new brown flannel shirt and pair of stiff new Levi's were arranged neatly beside the pillow. Louise held the screen door open while Leon and Ken carried in the red blanket. He looked small and shriveled, and after they dressed him in the new shirt and pants he seemed more shrunken.

It was noontime now because the church bells rang the Angelus. They ate the beans with hot bread, and nobody said anything until after Teresa poured the coffee.

Ken stood up and put on his jacket. "I'll see about the gravediggers. Only the top layer of soil is frozen. I think it can be ready before dark."

Leon nodded his head and finished his coffee. After Ken had been gone for a while, the neighbors and clanspeople came quietly to embrace Teofilo's family and to leave food on the table because the gravediggers would come to eat when they were finished.

The sky in the west was full of pale yellow light. Louise stood outside with her hands in the pockets of Leon's green army jacket that was too big for her. The funeral was over, and the old men had taken their candles and medicine bags and were gone. She waited until the body was laid into the pickup before she said anything to Leon. She touched his arm, and he noticed that her hands were still dusty from the corn meal that she had sprinkled around the old man. When she spoke, Leon could not hear her.

"What did you say? I didn't hear you."

"I said that I had been thinking about something."

"About what?"

"About the priest sprinkling holy water for Grandpa. So he won't be thirsty."

Leon stared at the new moccasins that Teofilo had made for the ceremonial dances in the summer. They were nearly hidden by the red blanket. It was getting colder, and the wind pushed gray dust down the narrow pueblo road. The sun was approaching the long mesa where it disappeared during the winter. Louise stood there shivering and watching his face. Then he zipped up his jacket and opened the truck door. "I'll see if he's there."

Ken stopped the pickup at the church, and Leon got out; and then Ken drove down the hill to the graveyard where people were waiting. Leon knocked at the old carved door with its symbols of the Lamb. While he waited he looked up at the twin bells from the king of Spain with the last sunlight pouring around them in their tower.

The priest opened the door and smiled when he saw who it was. "Come in! What brings you here this evening?"

The priest walked toward the kitchen, and Leon stood with his cap in his hand, playing with the earflaps and examining the living room—the brown sofa, the green armchair, and the brass lamp that hung down from the ceiling by links of chain. The priest dragged a chair out of the kitchen and offered it to Leon.

"No thank you, Father. I only came to ask you if you would bring your holy water to the graveyard."

The priest turned away from Leon and looked out the window at the patio full of shadows and the dining-room windows of the nuns' cloister across the patio. The curtains were heavy, and the light from within faintly penetrated; it was impossible to see the nuns inside eating supper. "Why didn't you tell me he was dead? I could have brought the Last Rites anyway."

Leon smiled. "It wasn't necessary, Father."

The priest stared down at his scuffed brown loafers and the worn hem of his cassock. "For a Christian burial it was necessary."

His voice was distant, and Leon thought that his blue eyes looked tired.

"It's O.K. Father, we just want him to have plenty of water."

The priest sank down into the green chair and picked up a glossy missionary magazine. He turned the colored pages full of lepers and pagans without looking at them.

"You know I can't do that, Leon. There should have been the Last Rites and a funeral Mass at the very least."

Leon put on his green cap and pulled the flaps down over his ears. "It's getting late, Father. I've got to go."

When Leon opened the door Father Paul stood up and said, "Wait." He left the room and came back wearing a long brown overcoat. He followed Leon out the door and across the dim churchyard to the adobe steps in front of the church. They both stooped to fit through the low adobe entrance. And when they started down the hill to the graveyard only half of the sun was visible above the mesa.

The priest approached the grave slowly, wondering how they had managed to dig into the frozen ground; and then he remembered that this was New Mexico, and saw the pile of cold loose sand beside the hole. The people stood close to each other with little clouds of steam puffing from their faces. The priest looked at them and saw a pile of jackets, gloves, and scarves in the yellow, dry tumbleweeds that grew in the graveyard. He looked at the red blanket, not sure that Teofilo was so small, wondering if it wasn't some perverse Indian trick—something they did in March to ensure a good harvest—wondering if maybe old Teofilo was actually at sheep camp corraling the sheep for the night. But there he was, facing into a cold dry wind and squinting at the last sunlight, ready to bury a red wool blanket while the faces of his parishioners were in shadow with the last warmth of the sun on their backs.

His fingers were stiff, and it took him a long time to twist the lid off the holy water. Drops of water fell on the red blanket and soaked into dark icy spots. He sprinkled the grave and the water disappeared almost before it touched the dim, cold sand; it reminded him of something—he tried to remember what it was, because he thought if he could remember he might understand this. He sprinkled more water; he shook the container until it was empty, and the water fell through the light from sundown like August rain that fell while the sun was still shining, almost evaporating before it touched the wilted squash flowers.

The wind pulled at the priest's brown Franciscan robe and swirled away the corn meal and pollen that had been sprinkled on the blanket. They lowered the bundle into the ground, and they didn't bother to untie the stiff pieces of new rope that were tied around the ends of the blanket. The sun was gone, and over on the highway the eastbound lane was full of headlights. The priest walked away slowly. Leon watched him climb the hill, and when he had disappeared within the tall, thick walls, Leon turned to look up at the high blue mountains in the deep snow that reflected a faint red light from the west. He felt good because it was finished, and he was happy about the sprinkling of the holy water; now the old man could send them big thunder-clouds for sure.

1981

COYOTE HOLDS A FULL HOUSE IN HIS HAND

He wasn't getting any place with Mrs. Sekakaku, he could see that. She was warming up leftover chili beans for lunch and when her niece came over they left him alone on the red plastic sofa and talked at the kitchen table. Aunt Mamie was still sick that's what her niece was telling her and they were all so worried because the doctors at Keams Canyon said they'd tried everything already and old man Ko'ite had come over from Oraibi and still Aunt Mamie was having dizzy spells and couldn't get out of bed. He was looking at the same *Life* magazine he'd already looked at before and it didn't have any pictures of high school girls twirling batons or plane crashes or anything he wanted to look at more than twice, but he didn't want to listen to them because then he'd know just what kind of gossip Mrs. Sekakaku found more important than him and his visit. He set the magazine down on his lap and traced his finger over the horse head embossed on the plastic cushion. It was always like that. When he didn't expect it, it always came to him, but when he wanted something to happen, like with Mrs. Sekakaku, then it shied away. Mrs. Sekakaku's letters had made the corner of the trading post where the mailboxes were smell like the perfume counter at Woolworth's. The Mexican woman with the fat arms was the postmaster and ran the trading post. She didn't approve of perfumed letters and she used to pretend the letters weren't there even when he could smell them and see their pastel edges sticking out of the pile in the general delivery slot.

The Mexican woman thought Pueblo men were great lovers—he knew this because he heard her say so to another Mexican woman one day while he was finishing his strawberry soda on the other side of the dry goods section. In the summer he spent a good number of hours there watching her because she wore sleeveless blouses that revealed her fat upper arms, full and round, and the tender underarm creases curving to her breasts. They had not noticed he was still there leaning on the counter behind a pile of overalls; ". . . the size of a horse" was all that he had heard, but he knew what she was talking about. They were all like that, those Mexican women. That was all they talked about when they were alone. "As big as a horse"—he knew that much Spanish and more too, but she had never treated him nice, not even when he brought her the heart-shaped box of candy, carried it on the bus all the way from Albuquerque. He didn't think it was being older than her because she was over thirty herself—it was because she didn't approve of men who drank. That was the last thing he did before he left town; he did it because he had to, because liquor was illegal on the reservation. So the last thing he did was have a few drinks to carry home with him the same way other people stocked up on lamb nipples or extra matches. She must have smelled it on his breath when he handed her the candy because she didn't say anything and she left the box under the counter by the old newspapers and balls of string. The cellophane was never opened and the fine gray dust that covered everything in the store finally settled on the pink satin bow. The postmaster was jealous of the letters that were coming, but she was the one who had sent him into the arms of Mrs. Sekakaku.

In her last two letters Mrs. Sekakaku had been hinting around for him to come see her at Bean Dance time. This was after Christmas when he had sent a big poinsettia plant all the way to the Second Mesa on the mail bus. Up until then she had never answered the part in his letters where he said he wished he could see the beautiful Hopi mesas with snow on them. But that had been the first time a potted plant ever rode into Hopi on the mail bus and Mrs. Sekakaku finally realized the kind of man he was. All along that had been the trouble at Laguna, nobody understood just what kind of man he was. They thought he was sort of good for nothing, he knew that, but for a long time he kept telling himself to keep on trying and trying. But it seemed like people would never forget the time the whole village was called out to clean up for feast day and he sent his mother to tell them he was sick with liver trouble. He was still hurt because they didn't understand that with liver trouble you can walk around and sometimes even ride the bus to Albuquerque. Everyone was jealous of him and they didn't stop to think how much it meant to his mother to have someone living with her in her old age. All they could talk about was the big C.O.D. that came to the post office in his name and she cashed her pension check to pay for it. But she was the one who told him, "Sonny Boy, if you want that jacket, you go ahead and order it." It was made out of brown vinyl resembling leather and he still wore it whenever he went to town. Even on the day she had the last stroke his two older brothers had been telling her to quit paying his bills for him and to make him get out and live on his own. But she always stood up for him in front of the others even if she did complain privately at times to her nieces who then scolded him about the bills from the record club and the correspondence school. He always knew he could be a lawyer—he had listened to the lawyers in the courtrooms of the Federal Building on those hot summer afternoons when he needed a cool place to sit while he waited for the bus to Laguna. He listened and he knew he could be a lawyer because he was so good at making up stories to justify why things happened the way they did. He thought correspondence school would be different from Indian school which had given him stomach aches and made him run away all through his seventh grade year. Right after that he had cut his foot pretty bad chopping wood for his older brother's wife, the one who kept brushing her arm across his shoulders whenever she poured coffee at the supper table. The foot had taken so long to heal that his mother agreed he shouldn't go back to Indian School or chop wood anymore. A few months after that they were all swimming at the river and he hurt his back in a dive off the old wooden bridge so it was no wonder he couldn't do the same work as the other young men.

When Mildred told him she was marrying that Hopi, he didn't try to stop her although she stood there for a long time like she was waiting for him to say something. He liked things just the way they were down along the river after dark. Her mother and aunts owned so many fields they expected a husband to hoe and he had already promised his mother he wouldn't leave her alone in her old age. He thought it would be easier this way but after Mildred's wedding, people who had seen him and Mildred together started joking about how he had lost out to a Hopi.

Hopi men were famous for their fast hands and the way they could go on all night. Some of the jokes hinted that he was as lazy at lovemaking as he was with his shovel during Spring ditch cleaning and that he took his girl friends to the deep sand along the river so he could lie on the bottom while they worked on top. But later on, some of the older men took him aside and told him not to feel bad about Mildred and told him about women they'd lost to Hopis when they were all working on the railroad together in Winslow. Women believe those stories about Hopi men, they told him, because women like the sound of those stories, and they don't care if it's the Hopi men who are making up the stories in the first place. So when he finally found himself riding the Greyhound bus into Winslow on his way to see Mrs. Sekakaku and the Bean Dance he got to thinking about those stories about Hopi men. It had been years since Mildred had married that Hopi and her aunts and her mother kept the man working in their fields all year round. Even Laguna people said "poor thing" whenever they saw that Hopi man walking past with a shovel on his shoulder. So he knew he wasn't going because of that—he was going because of Mrs. Sekakaku's letters and because it was lonely living in a place where no one appreciates you even when you keep trying and trying. At Hopi he could get a fresh start; he could tell people about himself while they looked at the photos in the plastic pages of his wallet.

He waited for the mail bus and drank a cup of coffee in the café across the street from the pink stucco motel with a cowboy on its neon sign. He had a feeling something in his life was about to change because of this trip, but he didn't know if it would be good for him or bad. Sometimes he was able to look at what he was doing and to see himself clearly two or three weeks into the future. But this time when he looked, he only saw himself getting off the bus on the sandy shoulder of the highway below Second Mesa. He stared up at the Hopi town on the sandrock and thought that probably he would get married.

The last hundred feet up the wagon trail seemed the greatest distance to him and he felt an unaccustomed tightness in his lungs. He knew it wasn't old age—it was something else—something that wanted him to work for it. A short distance past the outside toilets at the edge of the mesa top he got his breath back and their familiar thick odor reassured him. He saw that one of the old toilets had tipped over and rolled down the side of the mesa to the piles of stove ashes, broken bottles and corn shucks on the slope below. He'd get along all right. Like a lot of people, at one time he believed Hopi magic could outdo all the other Pueblos but now he saw that it was all the same from time to time and place to place. When Hopi men got tired of telling stories about all-nighters in Winslow motels then probably the old men brought it around to magic and how they rigged the Navajo tribal elections one year just by hiding some little painted sticks over near Window Rock. Whatever it was he had come for, he was ready.

He checked his reflection in the window glass of Mrs. Sekakaku's front door before he knocked. Gray hair made him look dignified, that is what she had written after he sent her the photographs. He believed in photographs to show people as you were telling them about yourself and the things you'd done and the places you'd been. He always carried a pocket camera and asked people passing by to snap one of him outside the fancy bars and restaurants in the Heights where he walked after he had a few drinks in the Indian bars downtown. He didn't tell her he'd never been inside those places, that he didn't think Indians were welcome there. Behind him he could hear a dog barking. It sounded like a small dog but it also sounded very upset and little dogs were the first ones to bite. So he turned and at first he thought it was a big rat crawling out the door of Mrs. Sekakaku's bread oven but it was a small gray wire-haired dog that wouldn't step out any further. Only lonely widows let their dogs sleep in the bread oven although they always pretend otherwise and scold the dogs whenever relatives or guests come. It must have known it was about to be replaced because it almost choked on its own barking. "Not much longer little doggy," he was saying softly while he knocked on the door. He was beginning to wonder if she had forgotten he was coming and he could feel his confidence lose its footing just a little. She walked up from behind while he was knocking—something he always dreaded because it made the person knocking look so foolish—knocking and waiting while the one you wanted wasn't inside the house at all but was standing right behind you. The way the little dog was barking probably all the neighbors had seen him and were laughing. He managed to smile and would have shaken hands but she was bending over petting the little dog running around and around her ankles. "I hope you haven't been waiting too long! My poor Aunt Mamie had one of her dizzy spells and I was over helping." She was still looking down at the dog while she said this and he noticed she wasn't wearing her perfume. At first he thought his understanding of the English language must be failing, that really she had only invited him over to Bean Dance, that he had misread her letters when she said that a big house like hers was lonely and that she did not like walking alone in the evenings from the water faucet outside the village. Maybe all this had only meant she was afraid a bunch of Navajos might jump out from the shadows of the mesa rocks to take turns on top of her. But when she warmed up the leftover chili beans and went on talking to her niece about the dizzy spells he began to suspect what was going on. She was one of those kinds of women who wore Evening in Paris to Laguna feast and sprinkled it on letters but back at Hopi she pretended she was somebody else. She had lured his letters and snapshots and the big poinsettia plant to show off to her sisters and aunts, and now his visit so she could pretend he had come uninvited, overcome with desire for her. He should have seen it all along, but the first time he met her at Laguna feast a gust of wind had shown him the little roll of fat above her garter and left him dreaming of a plunge deep into the crease at the edge of the silk stocking. The old auntie and the dizzy spells gave her the perfect excuse and a story to protect her respectability. It was only 2:30 but already she was folding a flannel nightgown while she talked to her niece. And here he had been imagining the night together the whole bus ride from Laguna—fingering the creases and folds and the little rolls while she squeezed him with both hands. Their night together had suddenly lifted off and up like a butterfly moving away from him, and the breathlessness he had felt coming up the mesa returned. He was feeling bitter—if that's all it took then he'd find a way to get that old woman out of bed. He said it without thinking—the words just found his mouth and he said "excuse me ladies," straightening his belt buckle as he walked across the room, "but it sounds to me like your poor auntie is in bad shape." Mrs. Sekakaku's niece looked at him for the first time all afternoon. "Is he a medicine man?" she asked her aunt and for an instant he could see Mrs. Sekakaku hesitate and he knew he had to say "Yes, it's something I don't usually mention myself. Too many of those guys just talk about it to attract women. But this is a serious case." It was sounding so good that he was afraid he would start thinking about the space between the cheeks of the niece's ass and be unable to go on. But the next thing he said was they had a cure they did at Laguna for dizzy spells like Aunt Mamie was having. He could feel a momentum somewhere inside himself—it wasn't hope, because he knew Mrs. Sekakaku had tricked him—but whatever it was it was going for broke. He imagined the feel of grabbing hold of the tops of the niece's thighs which were almost as fat and would feel almost as good as the tops of Mrs. Sekakaku's thighs. "There would be no charge. This is something I want to do especially for you." That was all it took because these Hopi ladies were like all the other Pueblo women he ever knew, always worrying about saving money, and nothing made them enemies for longer than selling them the melon or mutton leg they felt they should get for free as a love gift. Because all of them, even the thin ones and the old ones, believed he was after them. "Oh, that would be so kind of you! We are so worried about her!" "Well, not so fast," he said even though his heart was racing. "It won't work unless everything is just so. All her clanswomen must come to her house but there can't be any men there, not even outside." He paused. He knew exactly what to say. "This is very important. Otherwise the cure won't work." Mrs. Sekakaku let out her breath suddenly and tightened her lips and he knew that any men or boys not in the kivas preparing for Bean Dance would be sent far away from Aunt Mamie's house. He looked over at the big loaf of fresh oven bread the niece had brought when she came; they hadn't offered him any before, but now after she served him a big bowl of chili beans she cut him a thick slice. It was all coming back to him now about how good medicine men get treated and he wasn't surprised at himself anymore. Once he got started he knew just how it should go. It was getting it started that gave him trouble sometimes. Mrs. Sekakaku and her niece hurried out to contact all the women of the Snow Clan to bring them to Aunt Mamie's for the cure. There were so many of them sitting in rows facing the sickbed—on folding chairs and little canvas stools they'd brought just like they did for a kiva ceremony or a summer dance. He had never stopped to think how many Snow Clan women there might be, and as he walked across the room he wondered if he should have made some kind of age limit. Some of the women sitting there were pretty old and bony but then there were all these little girls—one squatted down in front of him to play jacks and he could see the creases and dimples of her legs below her panties. The initiated girls and the women sat serious and quiet with the ceremonial presence the Hopis are famous for. Their eyes were full of the power the clanswomen shared whenever they gathered together. He saw it clearly and he never doubted its strength. Whatever he took, he'd have to run with it, but the women would prevail as they always had.

He sat on the floor by the fireplace and asked them to line up. He reached into the cold white juniper ashes and took a handful and told the woman standing in front of him to raise her skirt above her knees. The ashes were slippery and carried his hands up and around each curve each fold each roll of flesh on her thighs. He reached high but his fingers never strayed above the edge of the panty leg. They stepped in front of him one after the other and he worked painstakingly with each one—the silvery white ashes billowing up like clouds above skin dusted like early snow on brown hills, and he lost all track of time. He closed his eyes so he could feel them better—the folds of skin and flesh above the knee, little crevices and creases like a hawk feels canyons and arroyos while he is soaring. Some thighs he gripped as if they were something wild and fleet like antelope and rabbits, and the women never flinched or hesitated because they believed the recovery of their clansister depended on them. The dimple and pucker at the edge of the garter and silk stockings brought him back, and he gave special attention to Mrs. Sekakaku, the last one before Aunt Mamie. He traced the ledges and slopes with all his fingers pressing in the ashes. He was out of breath and he knew he could not stand up to get to Aunt Mamie's bed so he bowed his head and pretended he was praying. "I feel better already. I'm not dizzy," the old woman said, not letting anyone help her out of bed or walk with her to the fireplace. He rubbed her thighs as carefully as he had rubbed the others, and he could tell by the feel she'd probably live a long time.

The sun was low in the sky and the bus would be stopping for the outgoing mail pretty soon. He was quitting while he was ahead, while the Hopi men were still in the kivas for Bean Dance. He graciously declined any payment but the women insisted they wanted to do something so he unzipped his jacket pocket and brought out his little pocket camera and a flash cube. As many as they could stood with him in front of the fireplace and someone snapped the picture. By the time he left Aunt Mamie's house he had two shopping bags full of pies and piki bread.

Mrs. Sekakaku was acting very different now—when they got back to her house she kicked the little gray dog and blocked up the oven door with an orange crate. But he told her he had to get back to Laguna right away because he had something important to tell the old man. It was something they'd been trying and trying to do for a long time. At sundown the mail bus pulled onto the highway below Second Mesa but he was tasting one of the pumpkin pies and forgot to look back. He set aside a fine-looking cherry pie to give to the postmaster. Now that they were even again with the Hopi men maybe this Laguna luck would hold out a little while longer.

1980 1981

Raymond Carver 1938–1988

"A long time ago," Raymond Carver once recalled, "my wife and I and our two baby children moved from Yakima, Washington, to a little town outside of Chico, California. There we found an old house and paid twenty-five dollars a month rent. In order to finance this move, I'd had to borrow a hundred and twenty-five dollars from a druggist I'd delivered prescriptions for. . . ." They were "stone broke," he added, but he had wanted to be a writer as long as he could remember, and he knew that he needed an education.

He enrolled at Chico State College and signed up for "Creative Writing 101," a course taught by John Gardner, who was soon to become famous as a novelist. Gardner encouraged Carver, introduced him to the works of major writers such as Flaubert, James Joyce, and Isak Dinesen. Gardner also introduced Carver to the small literary magazines that published the best fiction and poetry in the United States—a "revelation" to Carver, whose reading and aspirations as a writer had been confined to such publications as Sports Afield, True, Argosy, *and* Rogue. *Gardner advised Carver to "Read all the Faulkner you can get your hands on, and then read all of Hemingway to clean Faulkner out of your system."*

The influence of Hemingway is evident in the undecorated prose and the conversational tone of Carver's fiction, but Carver drew the events and characters for his stories from his own working-class background. He was born in Clatskanie, Oregon, and grew up in Yakima, Washington, where his father worked in a sawmill. At the age of eighteen Carver married and was forced to work, he later reported, at "some crap job or other" to support his family. Like many of his characters, he and his family seemed condemned to live a life of bare subsistence, but he managed to graduate from college in 1963 and to continue studying writing at the University of Iowa and at Stanford.

Carver's first published works were volumes of poems, and he published poetry and essays all his life, but his reputation rests on his short fiction. In 1967, one of his stories, "Will You Please Be Quiet, Please?" was included in Best American Short Stories, *and it provided the title for a collection of his stories published in 1976. Three other collections,* What We Talk about When We Talk about Love *(1981),* Cathedral *(1983), and* Where I'm Calling from *(1988) have been received enthusiastically not only by critics but by numerous writers who have been strongly influenced by his work.*

Carver has been called a "minimalist" for his flat diction, his spare plots, his faceless characters. He often writes of men and women who are culturally impoverished, small-town people who are physical and spiritual cripples, alcoholics, insomniacs, men without jobs, couples in failed marriages—people who dwell in trailer camps and spend their evenings in laundromats. Carver said, "I admit I hold to the dark view of things," and the meager lives of his characters seem to be wholly vacuous, barren of hope, yet they are portrayed by a narrative voice that speaks with profound compassion for ordinary men and women even while showing their flaws with a relentless force.

FURTHER READING: *All of Us: The Collected Poems,* 1998; A. Saltzman, *Understanding Raymond Carver,* 1988; *Conversations with Raymond Carver,* ed. M. Gentry and W. Stull, 1990; *Carver Country,* ed. T. Gallagher, 1990; P. Runyon, *Reading Raymond Carver,* 1992; E. Campbell, *Raymond Carver: A Study of the Short Fiction,* 1992; S. Halpert, *Raymond Carver: An Oral Biography,* 1993, 1995; A. Meyer, *Raymond Carver,* 1995; K. Nesset, *The Stories of Raymond Carver,* 1995; A. Bethea, *Techniques and Sensibility in the Fiction and Poetry of Raymond Carver,* 2001; H. Bloom, *Raymond Carver: Comprehensive Research and Study Guide,* 2002; G. Lainsbury, *The Carver Chronotope,* 2003; M. Carver, *What It Used to Be Like,* 2005.

TEXT: *Cathedral,* 1983.

CATHEDRAL

This blind man, an old friend of my wife's, he was on his way to spend the night. His wife had died. So he was visiting the dead wife's relatives in Connecticut. He called my wife from his in-laws'. Arrangements were made. He would come by train, a five-hour trip, and my wife would meet him at the station. She hadn't seen him since she worked for him one summer in Seattle ten years ago. But she and the blind man had kept in touch. They made tapes and mailed them back and forth. I wasn't enthusiastic about his visit. He was no one I knew. And his being blind bothered me. My idea of blindness came from the movies. In the movies, the blind moved slowly and never laughed. Sometimes they were led by seeing-eye dogs. A blind man in my house was not something I looked forward to.

That summer in Seattle she had needed a job. She didn't have any money. The man she was going to marry at the end of the summer was in officers' training school. He didn't have any money, either. But she was in love with the guy, and he was in love with her, etc. She'd seen something in the paper: HELP WANTED—*Reading to Blind Man,* and a telephone number. She phoned and went over, was hired on the spot. She'd worked with this blind man all summer. She read stuff to him, case studies, reports, that sort of thing. She helped him organize his little office in the county social-service department. They'd become good friends, my wife and the blind man. How do I know these things? She told me. And she told me something else. On her last day in the office, the blind man asked if he could touch her face. She agreed to this. She told me he touched his fingers to every part of her face, her nose—even her neck! She never forgot it. She even tried to write a poem about it. She was always trying to write a poem. She wrote a poem or two every year, usually after something really important had happened to her.

When we first started going out together, she showed me the poem. In the poem, she recalled his fingers and the way they had moved around over her face. In the poem, she talked about what she had felt at the time, about what went through her mind when the blind man touched her nose and lips. I can remember I didn't think much of the poem. Of course, I didn't tell her that. Maybe I just don't understand poetry. I admit it's not the first thing I reach for when I pick up something to read.

Anyway, this man who'd first enjoyed her favors, the officer-to-be, he'd been her childhood sweetheart. So okay. I'm saying that at the end of the summer she let the blind man run his hands over her face, said goodbye to him, married her childhood etc., who was now a commissioned officer, and she moved away from Seattle. But they'd kept in touch, she and the blind man. She made the first contact after a year or so. She called him up one night from an Air Force base in Alabama. She wanted to talk. They talked. He asked her to send him a tape and tell him about her life. She did this. She sent the tape. On the tape, she told the blind man about her husband and about their life together in the military. She told the blind man she loved her husband but she didn't like it where they lived and she didn't like it that he was a part of the military-industrial thing. She told the blind man she'd written a poem and he was in it. She told him that she was writing a poem about what it was like to be an Air Force officer's wife. The poem wasn't finished yet. She was still writing it. The blind man made a tape. He sent her the tape. She made a tape. This went on for years. My wife's officer was posted to one base and then another. She sent tapes from Moody AFB, McGuire, McConnell, and finally Travis, near Sacramento, where one night she got to feeling lonely and cut off from people she kept losing in that moving-around life. She got to feeling she couldn't go it another step. She went in and swallowed all the pills and capsules in the medicine chest and washed them down with a bottle of gin. Then she got into a hot bath and passed out.

But instead of dying, she got sick. She threw up. Her officer—why should he have a name? he was the childhood sweetheart, and what more does he want?—came home from somewhere, found her, and called the ambulance. In time, she put it all on a tape and sent the tape to the blind man. Over the years, she put all kinds of stuff on tapes and sent the tapes off lickety-split. Next to writing a poem every year, I think it was her chief means of recreation. On one tape, she told the blind man she'd decided to live away from her officer for a time. On another tape, she told him about her divorce. She and I began going out, and of course she told her blind man about it. She told him everything, or so it seemed to me. Once she asked me if I'd like to hear the latest tape from the blind man. This was a year ago. I was on the tape, she said. So I said okay, I'd listen to it. I got us drinks and we settled down in the living room. We made ready to listen. First she inserted the tape into the player and adjusted a couple of dials. Then she pushed a lever. The tape squeaked and someone began to talk in this loud voice. She lowered the volume. After a few minutes of harmless chitchat, I heard my own name in the mouth of this stranger, this blind man I didn't even know! And then this: "From all you've said about him, I can only conclude—" But we were interrupted, a knock at the door, something, and we didn't ever get back to the tape. Maybe it was just as well. I'd heard all I wanted to.

Now this same blind man was coming to sleep in my house.

"Maybe I could take him bowling," I said to my wife. She was at the draining board doing scalloped potatoes. She put down the knife she was using and turned around.

"If you love me," she said, "you can do this for me. If you don't love me, okay. But if you had a friend, any friend, and the friend came to visit, I'd make him feel comfortable." She wiped her hands with the dish towel.

"I don't have any blind friends," I said.

"You don't have *any* friends," she said. "Period. Besides," she said, "god-damn it, his wife's just died! Don't you understand that? The man's lost his wife!"

I didn't answer. She'd told me a little about the blind man's wife. Her name was Beulah. Beulah! That's a name for a colored woman.

"Was his wife a Negro?" I asked.

"Are you crazy?" my wife said. "Have you just flipped or something?" She picked up a potato. I saw it hit the floor, then roll under the stove. "What's wrong with you?" she said. "Are you drunk?"

"I'm just asking," I said.

Right then my wife filled me in with more detail than I cared to know. I made a drink and sat at the kitchen table to listen. Pieces of the story began to fall into place.

Beulah had gone to work for the blind man the summer after my wife had stopped working for him. Pretty soon Beulah and the blind man had themselves a church wedding. It was a little wedding—who'd want to go to such a wedding in the first place?—just the two of them, plus the minister and the minister's wife. But it was a church wedding just the same. It was what Beulah had wanted, he'd said. But even then Beulah must have been carrying the cancer in her glands. After they had been inseparable for eight years—my wife's word, *inseparable*—Beulah's health went into a rapid decline. She died in a Seattle hospital room, the blind man sitting beside the bed and holding on to her hand. They'd married, lived and worked together, slept together—had sex, sure—and then the blind man had to bury her. All this without his having ever seen what the goddamned woman looked like. It was beyond my understanding. Hearing this, I felt sorry for the blind man for a little bit. And then I found myself thinking what a pitiful life this woman must have led. Imagine a woman who could never see herself as she was seen in the eyes of her loved one. A woman who could go on day after day and never receive the smallest compliment from her beloved. A woman whose husband could never read the expression on her face, be it misery or something better. Someone who could wear makeup or not—what difference to him? She could, if she wanted, wear green eye-shadow around one eye, a straight pin in her nostril, yellow slacks and purple shoes, no matter. And then to slip off into death, the blind man's hand on her hand, his blind eyes streaming tears—I'm imagining now—her last thought maybe this: that he never even knew what she looked like, and she on an express to the grave. Robert was left with a small insurance policy and half of a twenty-peso Mexican coin. The other half of the coin went into the box with her. Pathetic.

So when the time rolled around, my wife went to the depot to pick him up. With nothing to do but wait—sure, I blamed him for that—I was having a drink and watching the TV when I heard the car pull into the drive. I got up from the sofa with my drink and went to the window to have a look.

I saw my wife laughing as she parked the car. I saw her get out of the car and shut the door. She was still wearing a smile. Just amazing. She went around to the other side of the car to where the blind man was already starting to get out. This blind man, feature this, he was wearing a full beard! A beard on a blind man! Too much, I say. The blind man reached into the back seat and dragged out a suitcase. My wife took his arm, shut the car door, and, talking all the way, moved him down the drive and then up the steps to the front porch. I turned off the TV. I finished my drink, rinsed the glass, dried my hands. Then I went to the door.

My wife said, "I want you to meet Robert. Robert, this is my husband. I've told you all about him." She was beaming. She had this blind man by his coat sleeve.

The blind man let go of his suitcase and up came his hand.

I took it. He squeezed hard, held my hand, and then he let it go.

"I feel like we've already met," he boomed.

"Likewise," I said. I didn't know what else to say. Then I said, "Welcome. I've heard a lot about you." We began to move then, a little group, from the porch into the living room, my wife guiding him by the arm. The blind man was carrying his suitcase in his other hand. My wife said things like, "To your left here, Robert. That's right. Now watch it, there's a chair. That's it. Sit down right here. This is the sofa. We just bought this sofa two weeks ago."

I started to say something about the old sofa. I'd liked that old sofa. But I didn't say anything. Then I wanted to say something else, small-talk, about the scenic ride along the Hudson. How going *to* New York, you should sit on the right-hand side of the train, and coming *from* New York, the left-hand side.

"Did you have a good train ride?" I said. "Which side of the train did you sit on, by the way?"

"What a question, which side!" my wife said. "What's it matter which side?" she said.

"I just asked," I said.

"Right side," the blind man said. "I hadn't been on a train in nearly forty years. Not since I was a kid. With my folks. That's been a long time. I'd nearly forgotten the sensation. I have winter in my beard now," he said. "So I've been told, anyway. Do I look distinguished, my dear?" the blind man said to my wife.

"You look distinguished, Robert," she said. "Robert," she said. "Robert, it's just so good to see you."

My wife finally took her eyes off the blind man and looked at me. I had the feeling she didn't like what she saw. I shrugged.

I've never met, or personally known, anyone who was blind. This blind man was late forties, a heavy-set, balding man with stooped shoulders, as if he carried a great weight there. He wore brown slacks, brown shoes, a light-brown shirt, a tie, a sports coat. Spiffy. He also had this full beard. But he didn't use a cane and he didn't wear dark glasses. I'd always thought dark glasses were a must for the blind. Fact was, I wished he had a pair. At first glance, his eyes looked like anyone else's eyes. But if you looked close, there was something different about them. Too much white in the iris, for one thing, and the pupils seemed to move around in the sockets without his knowing it or being able to stop it. Creepy. As I stared at his face, I saw the left pupil turn in toward his nose while the other made an effort to keep in one place. But it was only an effort, for that eye was on the roam without his knowing it or wanting it to be.

I said, "Let me get you a drink. What's your pleasure? We have a little of everything. It's one of our pastimes."

"Bub, I'm a Scotch man myself," he said fast enough in this big voice.

"Right," I said. Bub! "Sure you are. I knew it."

He let his fingers touch his suitcase, which was sitting alongside the sofa. He was taking his bearings. I didn't blame him for that.

"I'll move that up to your room," my wife said.

"No, that's fine," the blind man said loudly. "It can go up when I go up."

"A little water with the Scotch?" I said.

"Very little," he said.

"I knew it," I said.

He said, "Just a tad. The Irish actor, Barry Fitzgerald? I'm like that fellow. When I drink water, Fitzgerald said, I drink water. When I drink whiskey, I drink whiskey."[1] My wife laughed. The blind man brought his hand up under his beard. He lifted his beard slowly and let it drop.

I did the drinks, three big glasses of Scotch with a splash of water in each. Then we made ourselves comfortable and talked about Robert's travels. First the long flight from the West Coast to Connecticut, we covered that. Then from Connecticut up here by train. We had another drink concerning that leg of the trip.

I remembered having read somewhere that the blind didn't smoke because, as speculation had it, they couldn't see the smoke they exhaled. I thought I knew that much and that much only about blind people. But this blind man smoked his cigarette down to the nubbin and then lit another one. This blind man filled his ashtray and my wife emptied it.

When we sat down at the table for dinner, we had another drink. My wife heaped Robert's plate with cube steak, scalloped potatoes, green beans. I buttered him up two slices of bread. I said, "Here's bread and butter for you." I swallowed some of my drink. "Now let us pray," I said, and the blind man lowered his head. My wife looked at me, her mouth agape. "Pray the phone won't ring and the food doesn't get cold," I said.

We dug in. We ate everything there was to eat on the table. We ate like there was no tomorrow. We didn't talk. We ate. We scarfed. We grazed that table. We were into serious eating. The blind man had right away located his foods, he knew just where everything was on his plate. I watched with admiration as he used his knife and fork on the meat. He'd cut two pieces of meat, fork the meat into his mouth, and then go all out for the scalloped potatoes, the beans next, and then he'd tear off a hunk of buttered bread and eat that. He'd follow this up with a big drink of milk. It didn't seem to bother him to use his fingers once in a while, either.

We finished everything, including half a strawberry pie. For a few moments, we sat as if stunned. Sweat beaded on our faces. Finally, we got up from the table and left the dirty plates. We didn't look back. We took ourselves into the living room and sank into our places again. Robert and my wife sat on the sofa. I took the big chair. We had us two or three more drinks while they talked about the major things that had come to pass for them in the past ten years. For the most part, I just listened. Now and then I joined in. I didn't want him to think I'd left the room, and I didn't want her to think I was feeling left out. They talked of things that had happened to them—to them!—these past ten years. I waited in vain to hear my name on my wife's sweet lips: "And then my dear husband came into my life"—something like that. But I heard nothing of the sort. More talk of Robert. Robert had done a little of everything, it seemed, a regular blind jack-of-all-trades. But most recently he and his wife had had an Amway distributorship, from which, I gathered, they'd earned their living, such as it was. The blind man was also a ham radio operator. He talked in his loud voice about conversations he'd had with fellow operators in Guam, in the Philippines, in Alaska, and even in Tahiti. He said he'd have a lot of friends there if he ever

[1]An approximation of words spoken by the Irish actor Barry Fitzgerald in the motion picture *The Quiet Man* (1952).

wanted to go visit those places. From time to time, he'd turn his blind face toward me, put his hand under his beard, ask me something. How long had I been in my present position? (Three years.) Did I like my work? (I didn't.) Was I going to stay with it? (What were the options?) Finally, when I thought he was beginning to run down, I got up and turned on the TV.

My wife looked at me with irritation. She was heading toward a boil. Then she looked at the blind man and said, "Robert, do you have a TV?"

The blind man said, "My dear, I have two TVs. I have a color set and a black-and-white thing, an old relic. It's funny, but if I turn the TV on, and I'm always turning it on, I turn on the color set. It's funny, don't you think?"

I didn't know what to say to that. I had absolutely nothing to say to that. No opinion. So I watched the news program and tried to listen to what the announcer was saying.

"This is a color TV," the blind man said. "Don't ask me how, but I can tell."

"We traded up a while ago," I said.

The blind man had another taste of his drink. He lifted his beard, sniffed it, and let it fall. He leaned forward on the sofa. He positioned his ashtray on the coffee table, then put the lighter to his cigarette. He leaned back on the sofa and crossed his legs at the ankles.

My wife covered her mouth, and then she yawned. She stretched. She said, "I think I'll go upstairs and put on my robe. I think I'll change into something else. Robert, you make yourself comfortable," she said.

"I'm comfortable," the blind man said.

"I want you to feel comfortable in this house," she said.

"I am comfortable," the blind man said.

After she'd left the room, he and I listened to the weather report and then to the sports roundup. By that time, she'd been gone so long I didn't know if she was going to come back. I thought she might have gone to bed. I wished she'd come back downstairs. I didn't want to be left alone with a blind man. I asked him if he wanted another drink, and he said sure. Then I asked if he wanted to smoke some dope with me. I said I'd just rolled a number. I hadn't, but I planned to do so in about two shakes.

"I'll try some with you," he said.

"Damn right," I said. "That's the stuff."

I got our drinks and sat down on the sofa with him. Then I rolled us two fat numbers. I lit one and passed it. I brought it to his fingers. He took it and inhaled.

"Hold it as long as you can," I said. I could tell he didn't know the first thing.

My wife came back downstairs wearing her pink robe and her pink slippers.

"What do I smell?" she said.

"We thought we'd have us some cannabis," I said.

My wife gave me a savage look. Then she looked at the blind man and said, "Robert, I didn't know you smoked."

He said, "I do now, my dear. There's a first time for everything. But I don't feel anything yet."

"This stuff is pretty mellow," I said. "This stuff is mild. It's dope you can reason with," I said. "It doesn't mess you up."

"Not much it doesn't, bub," he said, and laughed.

My wife sat on the sofa between the blind man and me. I passed her the number. She took it and toked and then passed it back to me. "Which way is this going?" she said. Then she said, "I shouldn't be smoking this. I can hardly keep my eyes open as it is. That dinner did me in. I shouldn't have eaten so much."

"It was the strawberry pie," the blind man said. "That's what did it," he said, and he laughed his big laugh. Then he shook his head.

"There's more strawberry pie," I said.

"Do you want some more, Robert?" my wife said.

"Maybe in a little while," he said.

We gave our attention to the TV. My wife yawned again. She said, "Your bed is made up when you feel like going to bed, Robert. I know you must have had a long day. When you're ready to go to bed, say so." She pulled his arm. "Robert?"

He came to and said, "I've had a real nice time. This beats tapes, doesn't it?"

I said, "Coming at you," and I put the number between his fingers. He inhaled, held the smoke, and then let it go. It was like he'd been doing it since he was nine years old.

"Thanks, bub," he said. "But I think this is all for me. I think I'm beginning to feel it," he said. He held the burning roach out for my wife.

"Same here," she said. "Ditto. Me, too." She took the roach and passed it to me. "I may just sit here for a while between you two guys with my eyes closed. But don't let me bother you, okay? Either one of you. If it bothers you, say so. Otherwise, I may just sit here with my eyes closed until you're ready to go to bed," she said. "Your bed's made up, Robert, when you're ready. It's right next to our room at the top of the stairs. We'll show you up when you're ready. You wake me up now, you guys, if I fall asleep." She said that and then she closed her eyes and went to sleep.

The news program ended. I got up and changed the channel. I sat back down on the sofa. I wished my wife hadn't pooped out. Her head lay across the back of the sofa, her mouth open. She'd turned so that her robe had slipped away from her legs, exposing a juicy thigh. I reached to draw her robe back over her, and it was then that I glanced at the blind man. What the hell! I flipped the robe open again.

"You say when you want some strawberry pie," I said.

"I will," he said.

I said, "Are you tired? Do you want me to take you up to your bed? Are you ready to hit the hay?"

"Not yet," he said. "No, I'll stay up with you, bub. If that's all right. I'll stay up until you're ready to turn in. We haven't had a chance to talk. Know what I mean? I feel like me and her monopolized the evening." He lifted his beard and he let it fall. He picked up his cigarettes and his lighter.

"That's all right," I said. Then I said, "I'm glad for the company."

And I guess I was. Every night I smoked dope and stayed up as long as I could before I fell asleep. My wife and I hardly ever went to bed at the same time. When I did go to sleep, I had these dreams. Sometimes I'd wake up from one of them, my heart going crazy.

Something about the church and the Middle Ages was on the TV. Not your run-of-the-mill TV fare. I wanted to watch something else. I turned to the other channels. But there was nothing on them, either. So I turned back to the first channel and apologized.

"Bub, it's all right," the blind man said. "It's fine with me. Whatever you want to watch is okay. I'm always learning something. Learning never ends. It won't hurt me to learn something tonight. I got ears," he said.

We didn't say anything for a time. He was leaning forward with his head turned at me, his right ear aimed in the direction of the set. Very disconcerting. Now and then his eyelids drooped and then they snapped open again. Now and then he put his fingers into his beard and tugged, like he was thinking about something he was hearing on the television.

On the screen, a group of men wearing cowls was being set upon and tormented by men dressed in skeleton costumes and men dressed as devils. The men dressed as devils wore devil masks, horns, and long tails. This pageant was part of a procession. The Englishman who was narrating the thing said it took place in Spain once a year. I tried to explain to the blind man what was happening.

"Skeletons," he said. "I know about skeletons," he said, and he nodded.

The TV showed this one cathedral. Then there was a long, slow look at another one. Finally, the picture switched to the famous one in Paris, with its flying buttresses, and its spires reaching up to the clouds. The camera pulled away to show the whole of the cathedral rising above the skyline.

There were times when the Englishman who was telling the thing would shut up, would simply let the camera move around over the cathedrals. Or else the camera would tour the countryside, men in fields walking behind oxen. I waited as long as I could. Then I felt I had to say something. I said, "They're showing the outside of this cathedral now. Gargoyles. Little statues carved to look like monsters. Now I guess they're in Italy. Yeah, they're in Italy. There's paintings on the walls of this one church."

"Are those fresco paintings, bub?" he asked, and he sipped from his drink.

I reached for my glass. But it was empty. I tried to remember what I could remember. "You're asking me are those frescoes?" I said. "That's a good question. I don't know."

The camera moved to a cathedral outside Lisbon. The differences in the Portuguese cathedral compared with the French and Italian were not that great. But they were there. Mostly the interior stuff. Then something occurred to me, and I said, "Something has occurred to me. Do you have any idea what a cathedral is? What they look like, that is? Do you follow me? If somebody says cathedral to you, do you have any notion what they're talking about? Do you know the difference between that and a Baptist church, say?"

He let the smoke dribble from his mouth. "I know they took hundreds of workers fifty or a hundred years to build," he said. "I just heard the man say that, of course. I know generations of the same families worked on a cathedral. I heard him say that, too. The men who began their life's work on them, they never lived to see the completion of their work. In that wise, bub, they're no different from the rest of us, right?" He laughed. Then his eyelids drooped again. His head nodded. He seemed to be snoozing. Maybe he was imagining himself in Portugal. The TV was showing another cathedral now. This one was in Germany. The Englishman's voice droned on. "Cathedrals," the blind man said. He sat up and rolled his head back and forth. "If you want the truth, bub, that's about all I know. What I just said. What I heard him say. But maybe you could describe one to me? I wish you'd do it. I'd like that. If you want to know, I really don't have a good idea."

I stared hard at the shot of the cathedral on the TV. How could I even begin to describe it? But say my life depended on it. Say my life was being threatened by an insane guy who said I had to do it or else.

I stared some more at the cathedral before the picture flipped off into the countryside. There was no use. I turned to the blind man and said, "To begin with, they're very tall." I was looking around the room for clues. "They reach way up. Up and up. Toward the sky. They're so big, some of them, they have to have these supports. To help hold them up, so to speak. These supports are called buttresses. They remind me of viaducts, for some reason. But maybe you don't know viaducts, either? Sometimes the cathedrals have devils and such carved into the front. Sometimes lords and ladies. Don't ask me why this is," I said.

He was nodding. The whole upper part of his body seemed to be moving back and forth.

"I'm not doing so good, am I?" I said.

He stopped nodding and leaned forward on the edge of the sofa. As he listened to me, he was running his fingers through his beard. I wasn't getting through to him, I could see that. But he waited for me to go on just the same. He nodded, like he was trying to encourage me. I tried to think what else to say. "They're really big," I said. "They're massive. They're built of stone. Marble, too, sometimes. In those olden days, when they built cathedrals, men wanted to be close to God. In those olden days, God was an important part of everyone's life. You could tell this from their cathedral-building. I'm sorry," I said, "but it looks like that's the best I can do for you. I'm just no good at it."

"That's all right, bub," the blind man said. "Hey, listen. I hope you don't mind my asking you. Can I ask you something? Let me ask you a simple question, yes or no. I'm just curious and there's no offense. You're my host. But let me ask if you are in any way religious? You don't mind my asking?"

I shook my head. He couldn't see that, though. A wink is the same as a nod to a blind man. "I guess I don't believe in it. In anything. Sometimes it's hard. You know what I'm saying?"

"Sure, I do," he said.

"Right," I said.

The Englishman was still holding forth. My wife sighed in her sleep. She drew a long breath and went on with her sleeping.

"You'll have to forgive me," I said. "But I can't tell you what a cathedral looks like. It just isn't in me to do it. I can't do any more than I've done."

The blind man sat very still, his head down, as he listened to me.

I said, "The truth is, cathedrals don't mean anything special to me. Nothing. Cathedrals. They're something to look at on late-night TV. That's all they are."

It was then that the blind man cleared his throat. He brought something up. He took a handkerchief from his back pocket. Then he said, "I get it, bub. It's okay. It happens. Don't worry about it," he said. "Hey, listen to me. Will you do me a favor? I got an idea. Why don't you find us some heavy paper? And a pen. We'll do something. We'll draw one together. Get us a pen and some heavy paper. Go on, bub, get the stuff," he said.

So I went upstairs. My legs felt like they didn't have any strength in them. They felt like they did after I'd done some running. In my wife's room, I looked around. I found some ballpoints in a little basket on her table. And then I tried to think where to look for the kind of paper he was talking about.

Downstairs, in the kitchen, I found a shopping bag with onion skins in the bottom of the bag. I emptied the bag and shook it. I brought it into the living room and sat down with it near his legs. I moved some things, smoothed the wrinkles from the bag, spread it out on the coffee table.

The blind man got down from the sofa and sat next to me on the carpet.

He ran his fingers over the paper. He was blind. He went up and down the sides of the paper. The edges, even the edges. He fingered the corners.

"All right," he said. "All right, let's do her."

He found my hand, the hand with the pen. He closed his hand over my hand. "Go ahead, bub, draw," he said. "Draw. You'll see. I'll follow along with you. It'll be okay. Just begin now like I'm telling you. You'll see. Draw," the blind man said.

So I began. First I drew a box that looked like a house. It could have been the house I lived in. Then I put a roof on it. At either end of the roof, I drew spires. Crazy.

"Swell," he said. "Terrific. You're doing fine," he said. "Never thought anything like this could happen in your lifetime, did you, bub? Well, it's a strange life, we all know that. Go on now. Keep it up."

I put in windows with arches. I drew flying buttresses. I hung great doors. I couldn't stop. The TV station went off the air. I put down the pen and closed and opened my fingers. The blind man felt around over the paper. He moved the tips of his fingers over the paper, all over what I had drawn, and he nodded.

"Doing fine," the blind man said.

I took up the pen again, and he found my hand. I kept at it. I'm no artist. But I kept drawing just the same.

My wife opened up her eyes and gazed at us. She sat up on the sofa, her robe hanging open. She said, "What are you doing? Tell me, I want to know."

I didn't answer her.

The blind man said, "We're drawing a cathedral. Me and him are working on it. Press hard," he said to me. "That's right. That's good," he said. "Sure. You got it, bub. I can tell. You didn't think you could. But you can, can't you? You're cooking with gas now. You know what I'm saying? We're going to really have us something here in a minute. How's the old arm?" he said. "Put some people in there now. What's a cathedral without people?"

My wife said, "What's going on? Robert, what are you doing? What's going on?"

"It's all right," he said to her. "Close your eyes now," the blind man said to me.

I did it. I closed them just like he said.

"Are they closed?" he said. "Don't fudge."

"They're closed," I said.

"Keep them that way," he said. He said, "Don't stop now. Draw."

So we kept on with it. His fingers rode my fingers as my hand went over the paper. It was like nothing else in my life up to now.

Then he said, "I think that's it. I think you got it," he said. "Take a look. What do you think?"

But I had my eyes closed. I thought I'd keep them that way for a little longer. I thought it was something I ought to do.

"Well?" he said. "Are you looking?"

My eyes were still closed. I was in my house. I knew that. But I didn't feel like I was inside anything.

"It's really something," I said.

1981, 1983

Don DeLillo 1936–

Don DeLillo has written eleven novels; the first, Americana, *was published in 1971, the eleventh,* Underworld, *twenty-six years later. They present an alarming world of catastrophe and violence from which his characters often find relief in the narcotic of their televisions and in the resplendent abundance of their supermarkets. His novels link the ordinary to the exotic and absurd. In* End Zone *(1972) the game of football is made analogous to thermonuclear warfare.* Great Jones Street *(1973) describes America's music/drug culture and the malevolent lives of rock stars and their parasitical groupies. The hero of* Ratner's Star *(1976), a mathematical genius and Nobel Prize winner, attempts to create a language to answer mysterious radio signals from outer space. He is fourteen years old.* Running Dog *(1978) portrays a writer and military authorities jointly questing for a pornographic movie made in Hitler's bunker at the end of World War II. The narrator of* White Noise *(1985), Jack Gladney, is an academic wheeler-dealer who is chairman of a college department of Hitler studies and teaches a course in Advanced Nazism to Hitler majors. His latest novel,* Underworld *(1997), dissects the last half-century of American life. For DeLillo it was a time dominated by the events of the Cold War and the threat of nuclear destruction, a threat that he sees as the source of spectacular discontinuities that characterize contemporary life in the United States.*

DeLillo's characters seem frequently to exist at the outer edge of life, unaware that they are about to tumble into chaos. They are usually intelligent, thoughtful, and troubled. And they are established, middle-class. The women are "crisp and alert, in diet trim," and there is something about the husbands "suggesting massive insurance coverage." Yet their world is cheapened by advertising and ersatz "convenience" products. They live amid "open cartons, crumpled tinfoil, shiny bags of potato chips, bowls of pasty substances covered with plastic wrap, flip-top rings and twist ties, individually wrapped slices of orange cheese." Packages with "Day-Glo sale stickers" give them a "sense of well-being." They decorate themselves with "Dacron, Orlon, Lycra, Spandex." Though it leaks and kills, they have grown to revere the technology that both serves and dominates them: the automated bank-teller machine that reports Jack Gladney's bank balance stirs in him "waves of relief and gratitude. . . . The system had blessed my life."

According to DeLillo, the technology that most dominates America is television: "for most people there are only two places in the world. Where they live and their TV set." In DeLillo's world, "the narcotic undertow and eerie diseased brain-sucking power" of television creates "brain fade." His characters grow habituated to horror, addicted to viewing catastrophe: "Only a catastrophe gets our attention. We want them, we need them, we depend on them."

DeLillo's prose style is matched to his characters and their plight. It is satirical, corrosive, dazzling, and witty. Critics praise it for being piercing: "hard-edged, pre-stressed, sheet metalled." He salts his writing with puns, wry nudges, and arcane allusions. He uses bits and pieces of commercials, quotations from worn-out pieties and political slogans. He is fascinated by jargon, especially the euphemistic language used by "the media" and advertising for vague explanations and arousal of desire and greed. Jargon, DeLillo has said, is "a language that almost holds off reality. . . . The interesting thing about jargon is that if it lives long enough, it stops being jargon and becomes part of natural speech, and we all find ourselves using it. . . ."

DeLillo first came to the attention of the broad reading public with the publication of White Noise *(1985), which won the year's American Book Award for fiction. Recognition came slowly in part because he has shunned the literary limelight, avoiding radio interviews and guest spots on TV talk shows. He also rejects invitations to lecture and teach at universities, remarking, "I never liked school. Why go back now?"*

Like most satirists, DeLillo is a moralist, hoping to "expose fools and lash knaves." He presents a dark and ominous world seldom understood by those who dwell in it. He shows a culture drowning in information and "things." He indicts its shallowness, its self-deceptions, ugliness, venality, and carnal excesses, its meltdowns, toxic gases, riots, savage beatings, and casual murders. That indictment has brought him criticism and praise. He has been called unpatriotic, a "bad citizen," a "literary vandal." He has also been praised for his ability to see the nation's "sinister ambiguities," and he has been compared to Mark Twain, another moralist who found satire and comedy the best weapons to use against derangements of life that seem impervious to the force of ordinary prose.

FURTHER READING: T. LeClair, *In the Loop: Don DeLillo and the Systems Novel,* 1987; *Introducing Don DeLillo,* ed. F. Lentricchia, 1991; D. Keesey, *Don DeLillo,* 1993; *Critical Essays on Don DeLillo,* ed. H. Ruppersburg and T. Engles, 2000; *Don DeLillo,* ed. H. Bloom, 2003; *Don DeLillo's White Noise,* ed. H. Bloom; 2003; J. Kavadlo, *Don DeLillo: Balance at the Edge of Belief,* 2004.

TEXT: *White Noise,* 1985.

from *WHITE NOISE*

1

The station wagons arrived at noon, a long shining line that coursed through the west campus. In single file they eased around the orange I-beam sculpture and moved toward the dormitories. The roofs of the station wagons were loaded down with carefully secured suitcases full of light and heavy clothing; with boxes of blankets, boots and shoes, stationery and books, sheets, pillows, quilts; with rolled-up rugs and sleeping bags; with bicycles, skis, rucksacks, English and Western saddles, inflated rafts. As cars slowed to a crawl and stopped, students sprang out and raced to the rear doors to begin removing the objects inside; the stereo sets, radios, personal computers; small refrigerators and table ranges; the cartons of phonograph records and cassettes; the hairdryers and styling irons; the tennis rackets, soccer balls, hockey and lacrosse sticks, bows and arrows; the controlled substances, the birth control pills and devices; the junk food still in shopping bags—onion-and-garlic chips, nacho thins, peanut creme patties, Waffelos and Kabooms, fruit chews and toffee popcorn; the Dum-Dum pops, the Mystic mints.

I've witnessed this spectacle every September for twenty-one years. It is a brilliant event, invariably. The students greet each other with comic cries and gestures of sodden collapse. Their summer has been bloated with criminal pleasures, as always. The parents stand sun-dazed near their automobiles, seeing images of themselves in every direction. The conscientious suntans. The well-made faces and wry looks. They feel a sense of renewal, of communal recognition. The women crisp and alert, in diet trim, knowing people's names. Their husbands content to measure out the time, distant but ungrudging, accomplished in parenthood, something about them suggesting massive insurance coverage. This assembly of station wagons, as much as anything they might do in the course of the year, more than formal liturgies or laws, tells the parents they are a collection of the like-minded and the spiritually akin, a people, a nation.

I left my office and walked down the hill and into town. There are houses in town with turrets and two-story porches where people sit in the shade of ancient maples. There are Greek revival and Gothic churches. There is an insane asylum with an elongated portico, ornamented dormers and a steeply pitched roof topped by a pineapple finial. Babette and I and our children by previous marriages live at the end of a quiet street in what was once a wooded area with deep ravines. There is an expressway beyond the backyard now, well below us, and at night as we settle into our brass bed the sparse traffic washes past, a remote and steady murmur around our sleep, as of dead souls babbling at the edge of a dream.

I am chairman of the department of Hitler studies at the College-on-the-Hill. I invented Hitler studies in North America in March of 1968. It was a cold bright day with intermittent winds out of the east. When I suggested to the chancellor that we might build a whole department around Hitler's life and work, he was quick to see the possibilities. It was an immediate and electrifying success. The chancellor went on to serve as adviser to Nixon, Ford and Carter before his death on a ski lift in Austria.

At Fourth and Elm, cars turn left for the supermarket. A policewoman crouched inside a boxlike vehicle patrols the area looking for cars parked illegally, for meter violations, lapsed inspection stickers. On telephone poles all over town there are homemade signs concerning lost dogs and cats, sometimes in the handwriting of a child.

2

Babette is tall and fairly ample; there is a girth and heft to her. Her hair is a fanatical blond mop, a particular tawny hue that used to be called dirty blond. If she were a petite woman, the hair would be too cute, too mischievous and contrived. Size gives her tousled aspect a certain seriousness. Ample women do not plan such things. They lack the guile for conspiracies of the body.

"You should have been there," I said to her.

"Where?"

"It's the day of the station wagons."

"Did I miss it again? You're supposed to remind me."

"They stretched all the way down past the music library and onto the interstate. Blue, green, burgundy, brown. They gleamed in the sun like a desert caravan."

"You know I need reminding, Jack."

Babette, disheveled, has the careless dignity of someone too preoccupied with serious matters to know or care what she looks like. Not that she is a gift-bearer of great things as the world generally reckons them. She gathers and tends the children, teaches a course in an adult education program, belongs to a group of volunteers who read to the blind. Once a week she reads to an elderly man named Treadwell who lives on the edge of town. He is known as Old Man Treadwell, as if he were a landmark, a rock formation or brooding swamp. She reads to him from the *National Enquirer,* the *National Examiner,* the *National Express,* the *Globe,* the *World,* the *Star.* The old fellow demands his weekly dose of cult mysteries. Why deny him? The point is that Babette, whatever she is doing, makes me feel sweetly rewarded, bound up with a full-souled woman, a lover of daylight and dense life, the miscellaneous swarming air of families. I watch her all the time doing things in measured sequence, skillfully, with seeming ease, unlike my former wives, who had a tendency to feel estranged from the objective world—a self-absorbed and high-strung bunch, with ties to the intelligence community.

"It's not the station wagons I wanted to see. What are the people like? Do the women wear plaid skirts, cable-knit sweaters? Are the men in hacking jackets?[1] What's a hacking jacket?"

"They've grown comfortable with their money," I said. "They genuinely believe they're entitled to it. This conviction gives them a kind of rude health. They glow a little."

"I have trouble imagining death at that income level," she said.

"Maybe there is no death as we know it. Just documents changing hands."

"Not that we don't have a station wagon ourselves."

"It's small, it's metallic gray, it has one whole rusted door."

"Where is Wilder?" she said, routinely panic-stricken, calling out to the child, one of hers, sitting motionless on his tricycle in the backyard.

Babette and I do our talking in the kitchen. The kitchen and the bedroom are the major chambers around here, the power haunts, the sources. She and I are alike in this, that we regard the rest of the house as storage space for furniture, toys, all the unused objects of earlier marriages and different sets of children, the gifts of lost in-laws, the hand-me-downs and rummages. Things, boxes. Why do these possessions carry such sorrowful weight? There is a darkness attached to them, a foreboding. They make me wary not of personal failure and defeat but of something more general, something large in scope and content.

She came in with Wilder and seated him on the kitchen counter. Denise and Steffie came downstairs and we talked about the school supplies they would need. Soon it was time for lunch. We entered a period of chaos and noise. We milled about, bickered a little, dropped utensils. Finally we were all satisfied with what we'd been able to snatch from the cupboards and refrigerator or swipe from each other and we began quietly plastering mustard or

[1]Stylish jackets with a fitted waist and a flared skirt, tailored to be worn while horseback riding (hacking).

mayonnaise on our brightly colored food. The mood was one of deadly serious anticipation, a reward hard-won. The table was crowded and Babette and Denise elbowed each other twice, although neither spoke. Wilder was still seated on the counter surrounded by open cartons, crumpled tinfoil, shiny bags of potato chips, bowls of pasty substances covered with plastic wrap, flip-top rings and twist ties, individually wrapped slices of orange cheese. Heinrich came in, studied the scene carefully, my only son, then walked out the back door and disappeared.

"This isn't the lunch I'd planned for myself," Babette said. "I was seriously thinking yogurt and wheat germ."

"Where have we heard that before?" Denise said.

"Probably right here," Steffie said.

"She keeps buying that stuff."

"But she never eats it," Steffie said.

"Because she thinks if she keeps buying it, she'll have to eat it just to get rid of it. It's like she's trying to trick herself."

"It takes up half the kitchen."

"But she throws it away before she eats it because it goes bad," Denise said. "So then she starts the whole thing all over again."

"Wherever you look," Steffie said, "there it is."

"She feels guilty if she doesn't buy it, she feels guilty if she buys it and doesn't eat it, she feels guilty when she sees it in the fridge, she feels guilty when she throws it away."

"It's like she smokes but she doesn't," Steffie said.

Denise was eleven, a hard-nosed kid. She led a more or less daily protest against those of her mother's habits that struck her as wasteful or dangerous. I defended Babette. I told her I was the one who needed to show discipline in matters of diet. I reminded her how much I liked the way she looked. I suggested there was an honesty inherent in bulkiness if it is just the right amount. People trust a certain amount of bulk in others.

But she was not happy with her hips and thighs, walked at a rapid clip, ran up the stadium steps at the neoclassical high school. She said I made virtues of her flaws because it was my nature to shelter loved ones from the truth. Something lurked inside the truth, she said.

The smoke alarm went off in the hallway upstairs, either to let us know the battery had just died or because the house was on fire. We finished our lunch in silence.

3

Department heads wear academic robes at the College-on-the-Hill. Not grand sweeping full-length affairs but sleeveless tunics puckered at the shoulders. I like the idea. I like clearing my arm from the folds of the garment to look at my watch. The simple act of checking the time is transformed by this flourish. Decorative gestures add romance to a life. Idling students may see time itself as a complex embellishment, a romance of human consciousness, as they witness the chairman walking across campus, crook'd arm emerging from his medieval robe, the digital watch blinking in late summer dusk. The robe is black, of course, and goes with almost anything.

There is no Hitler building as such. We are quartered in Centenary Hall, a dark brick structure we share with the popular culture department, known officially as American environments. A curious group. The teaching staff is composed almost solely of New York émigrés, smart, thuggish, movie-mad, trivia-crazed. They are here to decipher the natural language of the culture, to make a formal method of the shiny pleasures they'd known in their Europe-shadowed childhoods—an Aristotelianism of bubble gum wrappers and detergent jingles. The department head is Alfonse (Fast Food) Stompanato, a broad-chested glowering man whose collection of pre-war soda pop bottles is on permanent display in an alcove. All his teachers are male, wear rumpled clothes, need haircuts, cough into their armpits. Together they look like teamster officials assembled to identify the body of a mutilated colleague. The impression is one of pervasive bitterness, suspicion and intrigue.

An exception to some of the above is Murray Jay Siskind, an ex-sportswriter who asked me to have lunch with him in the dining room, where the institutional odor of vaguely defined food aroused in me an obscure and gloomy memory. Murray was new to the Hill, a stoop-shouldered man with little round glasses and an Amish beard. He was a visiting lecturer on living icons and seemed embarrassed by what he'd gleaned so far from his colleagues in popular culture.

"I understand the music, I understand the movies, I even see how comic books can tell us things. But there are full professors in this place who read nothing but cereal boxes."

"It's the only avant-garde we've got."

"Not that I'm complaining. I like it here. I'm totally enamored of this place. A small-town setting. I want to be free of cities and sexual entanglements. Heat. This is what cities mean to me. You get off the train and walk out of the station and you are hit with the full blast. The heat of air, traffic and people. The heat of food and sex. The heat of tall buildings. The heat that floats out of the subways and the tunnels. It's always fifteen degrees hotter in the cities. Heat rises from the sidewalks and falls from the poisoned sky. The buses breathe heat. Heat emanates from crowds of shoppers and office workers. The entire infrastructure is based on heat, desperately uses up heat, breeds more heat. The eventual heat death of the universe that scientists love to talk about is already well underway and you can feel it happening all around you in any large or medium-sized city. Heat and wetness."

"Where are you living, Murray?"

"In a rooming house. I'm totally captivated and intrigued. It's a gorgeous old crumbling house near the insane asylum. Seven or eight boarders, more or less permanent except for me. A woman who harbors a terrible secret. A man with a haunted look. A man who never comes out of his room. A woman who stands by the letter box for hours, waiting for something that never seems to arrive. A man with no past. A woman with a past. There is a smell about the place of unhappy lives in the movies that I really respond to."

"Which one are you?" I said.

"I'm the Jew. What else would I be?"

There was something touching about the fact that Murray was dressed almost totally in corduroy. I had the feeling that since the age of eleven in his crowded plot of concrete he'd associated this sturdy fabric with higher learning in some impossibly distant and tree-shaded place.

"I can't help being happy in a town called Blacksmith," he said. "I'm here to avoid situations. Cities are full of situations, sexually cunning people. There are parts of my body I no longer encourage women to handle freely. I was in a situation with a woman in Detroit. She needed my semen in a divorce suit. The irony is that I love women. I fall apart at the sight of long legs, striding, briskly, as a breeze carries up from the river, on a week-day, in the play of morning light. The second irony is that it's not the bodies of women that I ultimately crave but their minds. The mind of a woman. The delicate chambering and massive unidirectional flow, like a physics experiment. What fun it is to talk to an intelligent woman wearing stockings as she crosses her legs. That little staticky sound of rustling nylon can make me happy on several levels. The third and related irony is that it's the most complex and neurotic and difficult women that I am invariably drawn to. I like simple men and complicated women."

Murray's hair was tight and heavy-looking. He had dense brows, wisps of hair curling up the sides of his neck. The small stiff beard, confined to his chin and unaccompanied by a mustache, seemed an optional component, to be stuck on or removed as circumstances warranted.

"What kind of lectures do you plan giving?"

"That's exactly what I want to talk to you about," he said. "You've established a wonderful thing here with Hitler. You created it, you nurtured it, you made it your own. Nobody on the faculty of any college or university in this part of the country can so much as utter the word Hitler without a nod in your direction, literally or metaphorically. This is the center, the unquestioned source. He is now your Hitler, Gladney's Hitler. It must be deeply satisfying for you. The college is internationally known as a result of Hitler studies. It has an identity, a sense of achievement. You've evolved an entire system around this figure, a structure with countless substructures and interrelated fields of study, a history within history. I marvel at the effort. It was masterful, shrewd and stunningly preemptive. It's what I want to do with Elvis."

Several days later Murray asked me about a tourist attraction known as the most photographed barn in America. We drove twenty-two miles into the country around Farmington. There were meadows and apple orchards. White fences trailed through the rolling fields. Soon the signs started appearing. THE MOST PHOTOGRAPHED BARN IN AMERICA. We counted five signs before we reached the site. There were forty cars and a tour bus in the makeshift lot. We walked along a cowpath to the slightly elevated spot set aside for viewing and photographing. All the people had cameras; some had tripods, telephoto lenses, filter kits. A man in a booth sold postcards and slides—pictures of the barn taken from the elevated spot. We stood near a grove of trees and watched the photographers. Murray maintained a prolonged silence, occasionally scrawling some notes in a little book.

"No one sees the barn," he said finally.

A long silence followed.

"Once you've seen the signs about the barn, it becomes impossible to see the barn."

He fell silent once more. People with cameras left the elevated site, replaced at once by others.

"We're not here to capture an image, we're here to maintain one. Every photograph reinforces the aura. Can you feel it, Jack? An accumulation of nameless energies."

There was an extended silence. The man in the booth sold postcards and slides.

"Being here is a kind of spiritual surrender. We see only what the others see. The thousands who were here in the past, those who will come in the future. We've agreed to be part of a collective perception. This literally colors our vision. A religious experience in a way, like all tourism."

Another silence ensued.

"They are taking pictures of taking pictures," he said.

He did not speak for a while. We listened to the incessant clicking of shutter release buttons, the rustling crank of levers that advanced the film.

"What was the barn like before it was photographed?" he said. "What did it look like, how was it different from other barns, how was it similar to other barns? We can't answer these questions because we've read the signs, seen the people snapping the pictures. We can't get outside the aura. We're part of the aura. We're here, we're now."

He seemed immensely pleased by this.

4

When times are bad, people feel compelled to overeat. Blacksmith is full of obese adults and children, baggy-pantsed, short-legged, waddling. They struggle to emerge from compact cars; they don sweatsuits and run in families across the landscape; they walk down the street with food in their faces; they eat in stores, cars, parking lots, on bus lines and movie lines, under the stately trees.

Only the elderly seem exempt from the fever of eating. If they are sometimes absent from their own words and gestures, they are also slim and healthy-looking, the women carefully groomed, the men purposeful and well dressed, selecting shopping carts from the line outside the supermarket.

I crossed the high school lawn and walked to the rear of the building and toward the small open stadium. Babette was running up the stadium steps. I sat across the field in the first row of stone seats. The sky was full of streaking clouds. When she reached the top of the stadium she stopped and paused, putting her hands to the high parapet and leaning into it to rest diagonally. Then she turned and walked back down, breasts chugging. The wind rippled her oversized suit. She walked with her hands on her hips, fingers spread. Her face was tilted up, catching the cool air, and she didn't see me. When she reached the bottom step she turned to face the seats and did some kind of neck stretching exercise. Then she started running up the steps.

Three times she ascended the steps, walked slowly down. There was no one around. She worked hard, hair floating, legs and shoulders working. Every time she reached the top she leaned into the wall, head down, upper body throbbing. After the last descent I met her at the edge of the playing field and embraced her, putting my hands inside the sweatband of her gray cotton pants. A small plane appeared over the trees. Babette was moist and warm, emitting a creaturely hum.

She runs, she shovels snow, she caulks the tub and sink. She plays word games with Wilder and reads erotic classics aloud in bed at night. What do I do? I twirl the garbage bags and twist-tie them, swim laps in the college pool. When I go walking, joggers come up soundlessly behind me, appearing at my side, making me jump in idiotic fright. Babette talks to dogs and cats. I see colored spots out of the corner of my right eye. She plans ski trips that we never take, her face bright with excitement. I walk up the hill to school, noting the whitewashed stones that line the driveways of newer homes.

Who will die first?

This question comes up from time to time, like where are the car keys. It ends a sentence, prolongs a glance between us. I wonder if the thought itself is part of the nature of physical love, a reverse Darwinism that awards sadness and fear to the survivor. Or is it some inert element in the air we breathe, a rare thing like neon, with a melting point, an atomic weight? I held her in my arms on the cinder track. Kids came running our way, thirty girls in bright shorts, an improbable bobbing mass. The eager breathing, the overlapping rhythms of their footfalls. Sometimes I think our love is inexperienced. The question of dying becomes a wise reminder. It cures us of our innocence of the future. Simple things are doomed, or is that a superstition? We watched the girls come round again. They were strung out now, with faces and particular gaits, almost weightless in their craving, able to land lightly.

The Airport Marriott, the Downtown Travelodge, the Sheraton Inn and Conference Center.

On our way home I said, "Bee wants to visit at Christmas. We can put her in with Steffie."

"Do they know each other?"

"They met at Disney World. It'll be all right."

"When were you in Los Angeles?"

"You mean Anaheim."

"When were you in Anaheim?"

"You mean Orlando. It's almost three years now."

"Where was I?" she said.

My daughter Bee, from my marriage to Tweedy Browner, was just starting seventh grade in a Washington suburb and was having trouble readjusting to life in the States after two years in South Korea. She took taxis to school, made phone calls to friends in Seoul and Tokyo. Abroad she'd wanted to eat ketchup sandwiches with Trix sticks. Now she cooked fierce sizzling meals of scallion bushes and baby shrimp, monopolizing Tweedy's restaurant-quality range.

That night, a Friday, we ordered Chinese food and watched television together, the six of us. Babette had made it a rule. She seemed to think that if kids watched television one night a week with parents or stepparents, the effect would be to de-glamorize the medium in their eyes, make it wholesome domestic sport. Its narcotic undertow and eerie diseased brain-sucking power would be gradually reduced. I felt vaguely slighted by this reasoning. The evening in fact was a subtle form of punishment for us all. Heinrich sat silent over his egg rolls. Steffie became upset every time something shameful or humiliating seemed about to happen to someone on the screen. She had a vast capacity for being embarrassed on other people's behalf. Often she would leave the room until Denise signaled to her that the scene was over. Denise used these occasions to counsel the younger girl on toughness, the need to be mean in the world, thick-skinned.

It was my own formal custom on Fridays, after an evening in front of the TV set, to read deeply in Hitler well into the night.

On one such night I got into bed next to Babette and told her how the chancellor had advised me, back in 1968, to do something about my name and appearance if I wanted to be taken seriously as a Hitler innovator. Jack Gladney would not do, he said, and asked me what other names I might have at my disposal. We finally agreed that I should invent an extra initial and call myself J. A. K. Gladney, a tag I wore like a borrowed suit.

The chancellor warned against what he called my tendency to make a feeble presentation of self. He strongly suggested I gain weight. He wanted me to "grow out" into Hitler. He himself was tall, paunchy, ruddy, jowly, big-footed and dull. A formidable combination. I had the advantages of substantial height, big hands, big feet, but badly needed bulk, or so he believed—an air of unhealthy excess, of padding and exaggeration, hulking massiveness. If I could become more ugly, he seemed to be suggesting, it would help my career enormously.

So Hitler gave me something to grow into and develop toward, tentative as I have sometimes been in the effort. The glasses with thick black heavy frames and dark lenses were my own idea, an alternative to the bushy beard that my wife of the period didn't want me to grow. Babette said she liked the series J. A. K. and didn't think it was attention-getting in a cheap sense. To her it intimated dignity, significance and prestige.

I am the false character that follows the name around.

5

Let's enjoy these aimless days while we can, I told myself, fearing some kind of deft acceleration.

At breakfast, Babette read all our horoscopes aloud, using her storytelling voice. I tried not to listen when she got to mine, although I think I wanted to listen, I think I sought some clues.

After dinner, on my way upstairs, I heard the TV say: "Let's sit half lotus and think about our spines."

That night, seconds after going to sleep, I seemed to fall through myself, a shallow heart-stopping plunge. Jarred awake, I stared into the dark, realizing I'd experienced the more or less normal muscular contraction known as the myoclonic jerk. Is this what it's like, abrupt, peremptory? Shouldn't death, I thought, be a swan dive, graceful, white-winged and smooth, leaving the surface undisturbed?

Blue jeans tumbled in the dryer.

We ran into Murray Jay Siskind at the supermarket. His basket held generic food and drink, nonbrand items in plain white packages with simple labeling. There was a white can labeled CANNED PEACHES. There was a white package of bacon without a plastic window for viewing a representative slice. A jar of roasted nuts had a white wrapper bearing the words IRREGULAR PEANUTS. Murray kept nodding to Babette as I introduced them.

"This is the new austerity," he said. "Flavorless packaging. It appeals to me. I feel I'm not only saving money but contributing to some kind of spiritual consensus. It's like World War III. Everything is white. They'll take our bright colors away and use them in the war effort."

He was staring into Babette's eyes, picking up items from our cart and smelling them.

"I've bought these peanuts before. They're round, cubical, pock-marked, seamed. Broken peanuts. A lot of dust at the bottom of the jar. But they taste good. Most of all I like the packages themselves. You were right, Jack. This is the last avant-garde. Bold new forms. The power to shock."

A woman fell into a rack of paperback books at the front of the store. A heavyset man emerged from the raised cubicle in the far corner and moved warily toward her, head tilted to get a clearer sightline. A checkout girl said, "Leon, parsley," and he answered as he approached the fallen woman, "Seventy-nine." His breast pocket was crammed with felt-tip pens.

"So then you cook at the rooming house," Babette said.

"My room is zoned for a hot plate. I'm happy there. I read the TV listings, I read the ads in *Ufologist Today.* I want to immerse myself in American magic and dread. My seminar is going well. The students are bright and responsive. They ask questions and I answer them. They jot down notes as I speak. It's quite a surprise in my life."

He picked up our bottle of extra-strength pain reliever and sniffed along the rim of the child-proof cap. He smelled our honeydew melons, our bottles of club soda and ginger ale. Babette went down the frozen food aisle, an area my doctor had advised me to stay out of.

"Your wife's hair is a living wonder," Murray said, looking closely into my face as if to communicate a deepening respect for me based on this new information.

"Yes, it is," I said.

"She has important hair."

"I think I know what you mean."

"I hope you appreciate that woman."

"Absolutely."

"Because a woman like that doesn't just happen."

"I know it."

"She must be good with children. More than that, I'll bet she's great to have around in a family tragedy. She'd be the type to take control, show strength and affirmation."

"Actually she falls apart. She fell apart when her mother died."

"Who wouldn't?"

"She fell apart when Steffie called from camp with a broken bone in her hand. We had to drive all night. I found myself on a lumber company road. Babette weeping."

"Her daughter, far away, among strangers, in pain. Who wouldn't?"

"Not her daughter. My daughter."

"Not even her own daughter."

"No."

"Extraordinary. I have to love it."

The three of us left together, trying to maneuver our shopping carts between the paperback books scattered across the entrance. Murray wheeled one of our carts into the parking lot and then helped us heave and push all our double-bagged merchandise into the back of the station wagon. Cars entered and exited. The policewoman in her zippered minicab scouted the area for red flags on the parking meters. We added Murray's single lightweight bag of white items to our load and headed across Elm in the direction of his rooming house. It seemed to me that Babette and I, in the mass and variety of our purchases, in the sheer plenitude those crowded bags suggested, the weight and size and number, the familiar package designs and vivid lettering, the giant sizes, the family bargain packs with Day-Glo sale stickers, in the sense of replenishment we felt, the sense of well-being, the security and contentment these products brought to some snug home in our souls—it seemed we had achieved a fullness of being that is not known to people who need less, expect less, who plan their lives around lonely walks in the evening.

Murray took Babette's hand on leaving.

"I'd ask you to visit my room but it's too small for two people unless they're prepared to be intimate."

Murray is able to produce a look that is sneaky and frank at the same time. It is a look that gives equal credence to disaster and lecherous success. He says that in the old days of his urban entanglements he believed there was only one way to seduce a woman, with clear and open desire. He took pains to avoid self-depreciation, self-mockery, ambiguity, irony, subtlety, vulnerability, a civilized world-weariness and a tragic sense of history—the very things, he says, that are most natural to him. Of these he has allowed only one element, vulnerability, to insert itself gradually into his program of straightforward lust. He is trying to develop a vulnerability that women will find attractive. He works at it consciously, like a man in a gym with weights and a mirror. But his efforts so far have produced only this half sneaky look, sheepish and wheedling.

He thanked us for the lift. We watched him walk toward the lopsided porch, propped with cinder blocks, where a man in a rocker stared into space.

6

Heinrich's hairline is beginning to recede. I wonder about this. Did his mother consume some kind of gene-piercing substance when she was pregnant? Am I at fault somehow? Have I raised him, unwittingly, in the vicinity of a chemical dump site, in the path of air currents that carry industrial wastes capable of producing scalp degeneration, glorious sunsets? (People say the sunsets around here were not nearly so stunning thirty or forty years ago.) Man's guilt in history and in the tides of his own blood has been complicated by technology, the daily seeping falsehearted death.

The boy is fourteen, often evasive and moody, at other times disturbingly compliant. I have a sense that his ready yielding to our wishes and demands is a private weapon of reproach. Babette is afraid he will end up in a barricaded room, spraying hundreds of rounds of automatic fire across an empty mall before the SWAT teams come for him with their heavy-barreled weapons, their bullhorns and body armor.

"It's going to rain tonight."

"It's raining now," I said.

"The radio said tonight."

I drove him to school on his first day back after a sore throat and fever. A woman in a yellow slicker held up traffic to let some children cross. I pictured her in a soup commercial taking off her oilskin hat as she entered the cheerful kitchen where her husband stood over a pot of smoky lobster bisque, a smallish man with six weeks to live.

"Look at the windshield," I said. "Is that rain or isn't it?"

"I'm only telling you what they said."

"Just because it's on the radio doesn't mean we have to suspend belief in the evidence of our senses."

"Our senses? Our senses are wrong a lot more often than they're right. This has been proved in the laboratory. Don't you know about all those theorems that say nothing is what it seems? There's no past, present or future outside our own mind. The so-called laws of motion are a big hoax. Even sound can trick the mind. Just because you don't hear a sound doesn't mean it's not out there. Dogs can hear it. Other animals. And I'm sure there are sounds even dogs can't hear. But they exist in the air, in waves. Maybe they never stop. High, high, high-pitched. Coming from somewhere."

"Is it raining," I said, "or isn't it?"

"I wouldn't want to have to say."

"What if someone held a gun to your head?"

"Who, you?"

"Someone. A man in a trenchcoat and smoky glasses. He holds a gun to your head and says, 'Is it raining or isn't it? All you have to do is tell the truth and I'll put away my gun and take the next flight out of here.'"

"What truth does he want? Does he want the truth of someone traveling at almost the speed of light in another galaxy? Does he want the truth of someone in orbit around a neutron star? Maybe if these people could see us through a telescope we might look like we were two feet two inches tall and it might be raining yesterday instead of today."

"He's holding the gun to *your* head. He wants your truth."

"What good is my truth? My truth means nothing. What if this guy with the gun comes from a planet in a whole different solar system? What we call rain he calls soap. What we call apples he calls rain. So what am I supposed to tell him?"

"His name is Frank J. Smalley and he comes from St. Louis."

"He wants to know if it's raining *now*, at this very minute?"

"Here and now. That's right."

"Is there such a thing as now? 'Now' comes and goes as soon as you say it. How can I say it's raining now if your so-called 'now' becomes 'then' as soon as I say it?"

"You said there was no past, present, or future."

"Only in our verbs. That's the only place we find it."

"Rain is a noun. Is there rain here, in this precise locality, at whatever time within the next two minutes that you choose to respond to the question?"

"If you want to talk about this precise locality while you're in a vehicle that's obviously moving, then I think that's the trouble with this discussion."

"Just give me an answer, okay, Heinrich?"

"The best I could do is make a guess."

"Either it's raining or it isn't," I said.

"Exactly. That's my whole point. You'd be guessing. Six of one, half dozen of the other."

"But you *see* it's raining."

"You see the sun moving across the sky. But is the sun moving across the sky or is the earth turning?"

"I don't accept the analogy."

"You're so sure that's rain. How do you know it's not sulfuric acid from factories across the river? How do you know it's not fallout from a war in China? You want an answer here and now. Can you prove, here and now, that this stuff is rain? How do I know that what you call rain is really rain? What *is* rain anyway?"

"It's the stuff that falls from the sky and gets you what is called wet."

"I'm not wet. Are you wet?"

"All right," I said. "Very good."

"No, seriously, are you wet?"

"First-rate," I told him. "A victory for uncertainty, randomness and chaos. Science's finest hour."

"Be sarcastic."

"The sophists and the hairsplitters enjoy their finest hour."

"Go ahead, be sarcastic, I don't care."

Heinrich's mother lives in an ashram[2] now. She has taken the name Mother Devi and runs the business end of things. The ashram is located on the outskirts of the former copper-smelting town of Tubb, Montana, now called Dharamsalapur. The usual rumors abound of sexual freedom, sexual slavery, drugs, nudity, mind control, poor hygiene, tax evasion, monkey-worship, torture, prolonged and hideous death.

I watched him walk through the downpour to the school entrance. He moved with deliberate slowness, taking off his camouflage cap ten yards from the doorway. At such moments I find I love him with an animal desperation, a need to take him under my coat and crush him to my chest, keep him there, protect him. He seems to bring a danger to him. It collects in the air, follows him from room to room. Babette bakes his favorite cookies. We watch him at his desk, an unpainted table covered with books and magazines. He works well into the night, plotting chess moves in a game he plays by mail with a convicted killer in the penitentiary.

It was warm and bright the next day and students on the Hill sat on lawns and in dorm windows, playing their tapes, sunbathing. The air was a reverie of wistful summer things, the last languorous day, a chance to go bare-limbed once more, smell the mown clover. I went into the Arts Duplex, our newest building, a winged affair with a facade of anodized aluminum, sea-green, cloud-catching. On the lower level was the movie theater, a sloped and dark-carpeted space with two hundred plush seats. I sat in shallow light at the end of the first row and waited for my seniors to arrive.

They were all Hitler majors, members of the only class I still taught, Advanced Nazism, three hours a week, restricted to qualified seniors, a course of study designed to cultivate historical perspective, theoretical rigor and mature insight into the continuing mass appeal of fascist tyranny, with special emphasis on parades, rallies and uniforms, three credits, written reports.

Every semester I arranged for a screening of background footage. This consisted of propaganda films, scenes shot at party congresses, outtakes from mystical epics featuring parades of gymnasts and mountaineers—a collection

[2]Hindu religious retreat.

I'd edited into an impressionistic eighty-minute documentary. Crowd scenes predominated. Close-up jostled shots of thousands of people outside a stadium after a Goebbels speech, people surging, massing, bursting through the traffic. Halls hung with swastika banners, with mortuary wreaths and death's-head insignia. Ranks of thousands of flagbearers arrayed before columns of frozen light, a hundred and thirty anti-aircraft searchlights aimed straight up—a scene that resembled a geometric longing, the formal notation of some powerful mass desire. There was no narrative voice. Only chants, songs, arias, speeches, cries, cheers, accusations, shrieks.

I got to my feet and took up a position at the front of the theater, middle aisle, facing the entranceway.

They came in out of the sun in their poplin walk shorts and limited-edition T-shirts, in their easy-care knits, their polo styling and rugby stripes. I watched them take their seats, noting the subdued and reverent air, the uncertain anticipation. Some had notebooks and pencil lights; some carried lecture material in bright binders. There were whispers, rustling paper, the knocking sound of seats dropping as one by one the students settled in. I leaned against the front of the apron, waiting for the last few to enter, for someone to seal the doors against our voluptuous summer day.

Soon there was a hush. It was time for me to deliver the introductory remarks. I let the silence deepen for a moment, then cleared my arms from the folds of the academic robe in order to gesture freely.

When the showing ended, someone asked about the plot to kill Hitler. The discussion moved to plots in general. I found myself saying to the assembled heads, "All plots tend to move deathward. This is the nature of plots. Political plots, terrorist plots, lovers' plots, narrative plots, plots that are part of children's games. We edge nearer death every time we plot. It is like a contract that all must sign, the plotters as well as those who are the targets of the plot."

Is this true? Why did I say it? What does it mean?

7

Two nights a week Babette goes to the Congregational church at the other end of town and lectures to adults in the basement on correct posture. Basically she is teaching them how to stand, sit and walk. Most of her students are old. It isn't clear to me why they want to improve their posture. We seem to believe it is possible to ward off death by following rules of good grooming. Sometimes I go with my wife to the church basement and watch her stand, turn, assume various heroic poses, gesture gracefully. She makes references to yoga, kendo,[3] trance-walking. She talks of Sufi dervishes,[4] Sherpa mountaineers.[5] The old folks nod and listen. Nothing is foreign, nothing too remote to apply.

[3]Yoga: Hindu philosophy that teaches mental and physical exercises; kendo: Japanese ritualized fencing with bamboo staves.

[4]Members of a Muslim religious sect who whirl and dance to achieve religious ecstasy.

[5]Nepalese who serve as porters on mountain-climbing expeditions in the Himalayas.

I am always surprised at their acceptance and trust, the sweetness of their belief. Nothing is too doubtful to be of use to them as they seek to redeem their bodies from a lifetime of bad posture. It is the end of skepticism.

We walked home under a marigold moon. Our house looked old and wan at the end of the street, the porch light shining on a molded plastic tricycle, a stack of three-hour colored-flame saw-dust-and-wax logs. Denise was doing her homework in the kitchen, keeping an eye on Wilder, who had wandered downstairs to sit on the floor and stare through the oven window. Silence in the halls, shadows on the sloping lawn. We closed the door and disrobed. The bed was a mess. Magazines, curtain rods, a child's sooty sock. Babette hummed something from a Broadway show, putting the rods in a corner. We embraced, fell sideways to the bed in a controlled way, then repositioned ourselves, bathing in each other's flesh, trying to kick the sheets off our ankles. Her body had a number of long hollows, places the hand might stop to solve in the dark, tempo-slowing places.

We believed something lived in the basement.

"What do you want to do?" she said.

"Whatever you want to do."

"I want to do whatever's best for you."

"What's best for me is to please you," I said.

"I want to make you happy, Jack."

"I'm happy when I'm pleasing you."

"I just want to do what you want to do."

"I want to do whatever's best for you."

"But you please me by letting me please you," she said.

"As the male partner I think it's my responsibility to please."

"I'm not sure whether that's a sensitive caring statement or a sexist remark."

"Is it wrong for the man to be considerate toward his partner?"

"I'm your partner when we play tennis, which we ought to start doing again, by the way. Otherwise I'm your wife. Do you want me to read to you?"

"First-rate."

"I know you like me to read sexy stuff."

"I thought you liked it too."

"Isn't it basically the person being read to who derives the benefit and the satisfaction? When I read to Old Man Treadwell, it's not because I find those tabloids stimulating."

"Treadwell's blind, I'm not. I thought you liked to read erotic passages."

"If it pleases you, then I like to do it."

"But it has to please you too, Baba. Otherwise how would I feel?"

"It pleases me that you enjoy my reading."

"I get the feeling a burden is being shifted back and forth. The burden of being the one who is pleased."

"I want to read, Jack. Honestly."

"Are you totally and completely sure? Because if you're not, we absolutely won't."

Someone turned on the TV set at the end of the hall, and a woman's voice said: "If it breaks easily into pieces, it is called shale. When wet, it smells like clay."

We listened to the gently plummeting stream of nighttime traffic.

I said, "Pick your century. Do you want to read about Etruscan[6] slave girls, Georgian rakes?[7] I think we have some literature on flagellation brothels.[8] What about the Middle Ages? We have incubi and succubi.[9] Nuns galore."

"Whatever's best for you."

"I want you to choose. It's sexier that way."

"One person chooses, the other reads. Don't we want a balance, a sort of give-and-take? Isn't that what makes it sexy?"

"A tautness, a suspense. First-rate. I will choose."

"I will read," she said. "But I don't want you to choose anything that has men inside women, quote-quote, or men entering women. 'I entered her.' 'He entered me.' We're not lobbies or elevators. 'I wanted him inside me,' as if he could crawl completely in, sign the register, sleep, eat, so forth. Can we agree on that? I don't care what these people do as long as they don't enter or get entered."

"Agreed."

"'I entered her and began to thrust.'"

"I'm in total agreement," I said.

"'Enter me, enter me, yes, yes.'"

"Silly usage, absolutely."

"'Insert yourself, Rex. I want you inside me, entering hard, entering deep, yes, now, oh.'"

I began to feel an erection stirring. How stupid and out of context. Babette laughed at her own lines. The TV said: "Until Florida surgeons attached an artificial flipper."

Babette and I tell each other everything. I have told everything, such as it was at the time, to each of my wives. There is more to tell, of course, as marriages accumulate. But when I say I believe in complete disclosure I don't mean it cheaply, as anecdotal sport or shallow revelation. It is a form of self-renewal and a gesture of custodial trust. Love helps us develop an identity secure enough to allow itself to be placed in another's care and protection. Babette and I have turned our lives for each other's thoughtful regard, turned them in the moonlight in our pale hands, spoken deep into the night about fathers and mothers, childhood, friendships, awakenings, old loves, old fears (except fear of death). No detail must be left out, not even a dog with ticks or a neighbor's boy who ate an insect on a dare. The smell of pantries, the sense of empty afternoons, the feel of things as they rained across our skin, things as facts and passions, the feel of pain, loss, disappointment, breathless delight. In these night recitations we create a space between things as we felt them at the time and as we speak them now. This is the space reserved for irony, sympathy and fond amusement, the means by which we rescue ourselves from the past.

I decided on the twentieth century. I put on my bathrobe and went down the hall to Heinrich's room to find a trashy magazine Babette might read from, the type that features letters from readers detailing their sexual experiences. This struck me as one of the few things the modern imagination has contributed

[6]Of Etruria, ancient region of Italy north of Rome (modern Tuscany).
[7]Dissolute men (rakehells) of eighteenth- and early-nineteenth-century England.
[8]Houses of prostitution for those who find gratification in being whipped.
[9]Incubi: demons who attack sleeping women; succubi: female demons who attack sleeping men.

to the history of erotic practices. There is a double fantasy at work in such letters. People write down imagined episodes and then see them published in a national magazine. Which is the greater stimulation?

Wilder was in there watching Heinrich do a physics experiment with steel balls and a salad bowl. Heinrich wore a terry cloth robe, a towel around his neck, another towel on his head. He told me to look downstairs.

In a stack of material I found some family photo albums, one or two of them at least fifty years old. I took them up to the bedroom. We spent hours going through them, sitting up in bed. Children wincing in the sun, women in sun hats, men shading their eyes from the glare as if the past possessed some quality of light we no longer experience, a Sunday dazzle that caused people in their churchgoing clothes to tighten their faces and stand at an angle to the future, somewhat averted it seemed, wearing fixed and fine-drawn smiles, skeptical of something in the nature of the box camera.

Who will die first?

8

My struggle with the German tongue began in mid-October and lasted nearly the full academic year. As the most prominent figure in Hitler studies in North America, I had long tried to conceal the fact that I did not know German. I could not speak or read it, could not understand the spoken word or begin to put the simplest sentence on paper. The least of my Hitler colleagues knew some German; others were either fluent in the language or reasonably conversant. No one could major in Hitler studies at the College-on-the-Hill without a minimum of one year of German. I was living, in short, on the edge of a landscape of vast shame.

The German tongue. Fleshy, warped, spit-spraying, purplish and cruel. One eventually had to confront it. Wasn't Hitler's own struggle to express himself in German the crucial subtext of his massive ranting autobiography, dictated in a fortress prison in the Bavarian hills? Grammar and syntax. The man may have felt himself imprisoned in more ways than one.

I'd made several attempts to learn German, serious probes into origins, structures, roots. I sensed the deathly power of the language. I wanted to speak it well, use it as a charm, a protective device. The more I shrank from learning actual words, rules and pronunciation, the more important it seemed that I go forward. What we are reluctant to touch often seems the very fabric of our salvation. But the basic sounds defeated me, the harsh spurting northernness of the words and syllables, the command delivery. Something happened between the back of my tongue and the roof of my mouth that made a mockery of my attempts to sound German words.

I was determined to try again.

Because I'd achieved high professional standing, because my lectures were well attended and my articles printed in the major journals, because I wore an academic gown and dark glasses day and night whenever I was on campus, because I carried two hundred and thirty pounds on a six-foot three-inch frame and had big hands and feet, I knew my German lessons would have to be secret.

I contacted a man not affiliated with the college, someone Murray Jay Siskind had told me about. They were fellow boarders in the green-shingled house on

Middlebrook. The man was in his fifties, a slight shuffle in his walk. He had thinning hair, a bland face and wore his shirtsleeves rolled up to his forearms, revealing thermal underwear beneath.

His complexion was of a tone I want to call flesh-colored. Howard Dunlop was his name. He said he was a former chiropractor but didn't offer a reason why he was no longer active and didn't say when he'd learned German, or why, and something in his manner kept me from asking.

We sat in his dark crowded room at the boarding house. An ironing board stood unfolded at the window. There were chipped enamel pots, trays of utensils set on a dresser. The furniture was vague, foundling. At the borders of the room were the elemental things. An exposed radiator, an army-blanketed cot. Dunlop sat at the edge of a straight chair, intoning generalities of grammar. When he switched from English to German, it was as though a cord had been twisted in his larynx. An abrupt emotion entered his voice, a scrape and gargle that sounded like the stirring of some beast's ambition. He gaped at me and gestured, he croaked, he verged on strangulation. Sounds came spewing from the base of his tongue, harsh noises damp with passion. He was only demonstrating certain basic pronunciation patterns but the transformation in his face and voice made me think he was making a passage between levels of being.

I sat there taking notes.

The hour went quickly. Dunlop managed a scant shrug when I asked him not to discuss the lessons with anyone. It occurred to me that he was the man Murray had described in his summary of fellow boarders as the one who never comes out of his room.

I stopped at Murray's room and asked him to come home with me for dinner. He put down his copy of *American Transvestite* and slipped into his corduroy jacket. We stopped on the porch long enough for Murray to tell the landlord, who was sitting there, about a dripping faucet in the second-floor bathroom. The landlord was a large florid man of such robust and bursting health that he seemed to be having a heart attack even as we looked on.

"He'll get around to fixing it," Murray said, as we set out on foot in the direction of Elm. "He fixes everything eventually. He's very good with all those little tools and fixtures and devices that people in cities never know the names of. The names of these things are only known in outlying communities, small towns and rural areas. Too bad he's such a bigot."

"How do you know he's a bigot?"

"People who can fix things are usually bigots."

"What do you mean?"

"Think of all the people who've ever come to your house to fix things. They were all bigots, weren't they?"

"I don't know."

"They drove panel trucks, didn't they, with an extension ladder on the roof and some kind of plastic charm dangling from the rearview mirror?"

"I don't know, Murray."

"It's obvious," he said.

He asked me why I'd chosen this year in particular to learn German, after so many years of slipping past the radar. I told him there was a Hitler conference scheduled for next spring at the College-on-the-Hill. Three days of lectures, workshops and panels. Hitler scholars from seventeen states and nine foreign countries. Actual Germans would be in attendance.

At home Denise placed a moist bag of garbage in the kitchen compactor. She started up the machine. The ram stroked downward with a dreadful wrenching sound, full of eerie feeling. Children walked in and out of the kitchen, water dripped in the sink, the washing machine heaved in the entranceway. Murray seemed engrossed in the incidental mesh. Whining metal, exploding bottles, plastic smashed flat. Denise listened carefully, making sure the mangling din contained the correct sonic elements, which meant the machine was operating properly.

Heinrich said to someone on the phone, "Animals commit incest all the time. So how unnatural can it be?"

Babette came in from running, her outfit soaked through. Murray walked across the kitchen to shake her hand. She fell into a chair, scanned the room for Wilder. I watched Denise make a mental comparison between her mother's running clothes and the wet bag she'd dumped in the compactor. I could see it in her eyes, a sardonic connection. It was these secondary levels of life, these extrasensory flashes and floating nuances of being, these pockets of rapport forming unexpectedly, that made me believe we were a magic act, adults and children together, sharing unaccountable things.

"We have to boil our water," Steffie said.

"Why?"

"It said on the radio."

"They're always saying boil your water," Babette said. "It's the new thing, like turn your wheel in the direction of the skid. Here comes Wilder now. I guess we can eat."

The small child moved in a swaying gait, great head wagging, and his mother made faces of delight, happy and outlandish masks, watching him approach.

"Neutrinos go right through the earth," Heinrich said into the telephone.

"Yes yes yes," said Babette.

9

They had to evacuate the grade school on Tuesday. Kids were getting headaches and eye irritations, tasting metal in their mouths. A teacher rolled on the floor and spoke foreign languages. No one knew what was wrong. Investigators said it could be the ventilating system, the paint or varnish, the foam insulation, the electrical insulation, the cafeteria food, the rays emitted by microcomputers, the asbestos fireproofing, the adhesive on shipping containers, the fumes from the chlorinated pool, or perhaps something deeper, finer-grained, more closely woven into the basic state of things.

Denise and Steffie stayed home that week as men in Mylex suits and respirator masks made systematic sweeps of the building with infrared detecting and measuring equipment. Because Mylex is itself a suspect material, the results tended to be ambiguous and a second round of more rigorous detection had to be scheduled.

The two girls and Babette, Wilder and I went to the supermarket. Minutes after we entered, we ran into Murray. This was the fourth or fifth time I'd seen him in the supermarket, which was roughly the number of times I'd seen him on campus. He clutched Babette by the left bicep and sidled around her, appearing to smell her hair.

"A lovely dinner," he said, standing directly behind her. "I like to cook myself, which doubles my appreciation of someone who does it well."

"Come any time," she said, turning in an effort to find him.

We moved together into the ultra-cool interior. Wilder sat in the shopping cart trying to grab items off the shelves as we went by. It occurred to me that he was too old and too big to be sitting in supermarket carts. I also wondered why his vocabulary seemed to be stalled at twenty-five words.

"I'm happy to be here," Murray said.

"In Blacksmith?"

"In Blacksmith, in the supermarket, in the rooming house, on the Hill. I feel I'm learning important things every day. Death, disease, afterlife, outer space. It's all much clearer here. I can think and see."

We moved into the generic food area and Murray paused with his plastic basket to probe among the white cartons and jars. I wasn't sure I understood what he was talking about. What did he mean, much clearer? He could think and see what?

Steffie took my hand and we walked past the fruit bins, an area that extended about forty-five yards along one wall. The bins were arranged diagonally and backed by mirrors that people accidentally punched when reaching for fruit in the upper rows. A voice on the loudspeaker said: "Kleenex Softique, your truck's blocking the entrance." Apples and lemons tumbled in twos and threes to the floor when someone took a fruit from certain places in the stacked array. There were six kinds of apples, there were exotic melons in several pastels. Everything seemed to be in season, sprayed, burnished, bright. People tore filmy bags off racks and tried to figure out which end opened. I realized the place was awash in noise. The toneless systems, the jangle and skid of carts, the loudspeaker and coffee-making machines, the cries of children. And over it all, or under it all, a dull and unlocatable roar, as of some form of swarming life just outside the range of human apprehension.

"Did you tell Denise you were sorry?"

"Maybe later," Steffie said. "Remind me."

"She's a sweet girl and she wants to be your older sister and your friend if you'll let her."

"I don't know about friend. She's a little bossy, don't you think?"

"Aside from telling her you're sorry, be sure to give her back her *Physicians' Desk Reference.*"

"She reads that thing all the time. Don't you think that's weird?"

"At least she reads something."

"Sure, lists of drugs and medicines. And do you want to know why?"

"Why?"

"Because she's trying to find out the side effects of the stuff that Baba uses."

"What does Baba use?"

"Don't ask me. Ask Denise."

"How do you know she uses anything?"

"Ask Denise."

"Why don't I ask Baba?"

"Ask Baba," she said.

Murray came out of an aisle and walked alongside Babette, just ahead of us. He took a twin roll of paper towels out of her cart and smelled it. Denise had found some friends and they went up front to look at the paperback books in spindly racks, the books with shiny metallic print, raised letters, vivid illustrations of cult violence and windswept romance. Denise was wearing a green visor. I heard Babette tell Murray she'd been wearing it fourteen hours a day for three weeks now. She would not go out without it, would not even leave her room. She wore it in school, when there was school, wore it to the toilet, the dentist's chair, the dinner table. Something about the visor seemed to speak to her, to offer wholeness and identity.

"It's her interface with the world," Murray said.

He helped Babette push her loaded cart. I heard him say to her, "Tibetans believe there is a transitional state between death and rebirth. Death is a waiting period, basically. Soon a fresh womb will receive the soul. In the meantime the soul restores to itself some of the divinity lost at birth." He studied her profile as if to detect a reaction. "That's what I think of whenever I come in here. This place recharges us spiritually, it prepares us, it's a gateway or pathway. Look how bright. It's full of psychic data."

My wife smiled at him.

"Everything is concealed in symbolism, hidden by veils of mystery and layers of cultural material. But it is psychic data, absolutely. The large doors slide open, they close unbidden. Energy waves, incident radiation. All the letters and numbers are here, all the colors of the spectrum, all the voices and sounds, all the code words and ceremonial phrases. It is just a question of deciphering, rearranging, peeling off the layers of unspeakability. Not that we would want to, not that any useful purpose would be served. This is not Tibet. Even Tibet is not Tibet anymore."

He studied her profile. She put some yogurt in her cart.

"Tibetans try to see death for what it is. It is the end of attachment to things. This simple truth is hard to fathom. But once we stop denying death, we can proceed calmly to die and then go on to experience uterine rebirth or Judeo-Christian afterlife or out-of-body experience or a trip on a UFO or whatever we wish to call it. We can do so with clear vision, without awe or terror. We don't have to cling to life artificially, or to death for that matter. We simply walk toward the sliding doors. Waves and radiation. Look how well-lighted everything is. The place is sealed off, self-contained. It is timeless. Another reason why I think of Tibet. Dying is an art in Tibet. A priest walks in, sits down, tells the weeping relatives to get out and has the room sealed. Doors, windows sealed. He has serious business to see to. Chants, numerology, horoscopes, recitations. Here we don't die, we shop. But the difference is less marked than you think."

He was almost whispering now and I tried to get up closer without ramming my cart into Babette's. I wanted to hear everything.

"Supermarkets this large and clean and modern are a revelation to me. I spent my life in small steamy delicatessens with slanted display cabinets full of trays that hold soft wet lumpy matter in pale colors. High enough cabinets so you had to stand on tiptoes to give your order. Shouts, accents. In cities no one notices specific dying. Dying is a quality of the air. It's everywhere and nowhere. Men shout as they die, to be noticed, remembered for a second or two. To die in an apartment instead of a house can depress the soul, I would imagine, for several lives to come. In a town there are houses, plants in bay windows. People notice dying better. The dead have faces, automobiles. If you don't know a name, you know a street name, a dog's name. 'He drove an orange Mazda.' You know a couple of useless things about a person that become major facts of identification and cosmic placement when he dies suddenly, after a short illness, in his own bed, with a comforter and matching pillows, on a rainy Wednesday afternoon, feverish, a little congested in the sinuses and chest, thinking about his dry cleaning."

Babette said, "Where is Wilder?" and turned to stare at me in a way that suggested ten minutes had passed since she'd last seen him. Other looks, less pensive and less guilty, indicated greater time spans, deeper seas of inattention. Like: "*I didn't know whales were mammals.*" The greater the time span, the blanker the look, the more dangerous the situation. It was as if guilt were a luxury she allowed herself only when the danger was minimal.

"How could he get out of the cart without my noticing?"

The three adults each stood at the head of an aisle and peered into the traffic of carts and gliding bodies. Then we did three more aisles, heads set forward, weaving slightly as we changed our sightlines. I kept seeing colored spots off to the right but when I turned there was nothing there. I'd been seeing colored spots for years but never so many, so gaily animated. Murray saw Wilder in another woman's cart. The woman waved at Babette and headed toward us. She lived on our street with a teenage daughter and an Asian baby, Chun Duc. Everyone referred to the baby by name, almost in a tone of proud proprietorship, but no one knew who Chun belonged to or where he or she had come from.

"Kleenex Softique, Kleenex Softique."

Steffie was holding my hand in a way I'd come to realize, over a period of time, was not meant to be gently possessive, as I'd thought at first, but reassuring. I was a little astonished. A firm grip that would help me restore confidence in myself, keep me from becoming resigned to whatever melancholy moods she thought she detected hovering about my person.

Before Murray went to the express line he invited us to dinner, a week from Saturday.

"You don't have to let me know till the last minute."

"We'll be there," Babette said.

"I'm not preparing anything major, so just call beforehand and tell me if something else came up. You don't even have to call. If you don't show up, I'll know that something came up and you couldn't let me know."

"Murray, we'll be there."

"Bring the kids."

"No."

"Great. But if you decide to bring them, no problem. I don't want you to feel I'm holding you to something. Don't feel you've made an ironclad commitment. You'll show up or you won't. I have to eat anyway, so there's no major catastrophe if something comes up and you have to cancel. I just want you to know I'll be there if you decide to drop by, with or without kids. We have till next May or June to do this thing so there's no special mystique about a week from Saturday."

"Are you coming back next semester?" I said.

"They want me to teach a course in the cinema of car crashes."

"Do it."

"I will."

I rubbed against Babette in the checkout line. She backed into me and I reached around her and put my hands on her breasts. She rotated her hips and I nuzzled her hair and murmured, "Dirty blond." People wrote checks, tall boys bagged the merchandise. Not everyone spoke English at the cash terminals, or near the fruit bins and frozen foods, or out among the cars in the lot. More and more I heard languages I could not identify much less understand, although the tall boys were American-born and the checkout women as well, short, fattish in blue tunics, wearing stretch slacks and tiny white espadrilles. I tried to fit my hands into Babette's skirt, over her belly, as the slowly moving line edged toward the last purchase point, the breath mints and nasal inhalers.

It was out in the parking lot that we heard the first of the rumors about a man dying during the inspection of the grade school, one of the masked and Mylex-suited men, heavy-booted and bulky. Collapsed and died, went the story that was going around, in a classroom on the second floor.

10

Tuition at the College-on-the-Hill is fourteen thousand dollars, Sunday brunch included. I sense there is a connection between this powerful number and the way the students arrange themselves physically in the reading areas of the library. They sit on broad cushioned seats in various kinds of ungainly posture, clearly calculated to be the identifying signs of some kinship group or secret organization. They are fetal, splayed, knock-kneed, arched, square-knotted, sometimes almost upside-down. The positions are so studied they amount to a classical mime. There is an element of overrefinement and inbreeding. Sometimes I feel I've wandered into a Far Eastern dream, too remote to be interpreted. But it is only the language of economic class they are speaking, in one of its allowable outward forms, like the convocation of station wagons at the start of the year.

Denise watched her mother pull the little cellophane ribbon on a bonus pack of sixteen individually wrapped units of chewing gum. Her eyes narrowed as she turned back to the address books on the kitchen table before her. The eleven-year-old face was an expert mask of restrained exasperation.

She waited a long moment, then said evenly, "That stuff causes cancer in laboratory animals in case you didn't know."

"You wanted me to chew sugarless gum, Denise. It was your idea."

"There was no warning on the pack then. They put a warning, which I would have a hard time believing you didn't see."

She was transcribing names and phone numbers from an old book to a new one. There were no addresses. Her friends had phone numbers only, a race of people with a seven-bit analog consciousness.

"I'm happy to do it either way," Babette said. "It's totally up to you. Either I chew gum with sugar and artificial coloring or I chew sugarless and colorless gum that's harmful to rats."

Steffie got off the phone. "Don't chew at all," she said. "Did you ever think of that?"

Babette was breaking eggs into a wooden salad bowl. She gave me a look that wondered how the girl could talk on the phone and listen to us at the same time. I wanted to say because she finds us interesting.

Babette said to the girls, "Look, either I chew gum or I smoke. If you want me to start smoking again, take away my chewing gum and my Mentho-Lyptus."

"Why do you have to do one or the other?" Steffie said. "Why not do neither one?"

"Why not do both?" Denise said, the face carefully emptying itself of expression. "That's what you want, isn't it? We all get to do what we want, don't we? Except if we want to go to school tomorrow we can't because they're fumigating the place or whatever."

The phone rang; Steffie grabbed it.

"I'm not a criminal," Babette said. "All I want to do is chew a pathetic little tasteless chunk of gum now and then."

"Well it's not that simple," Denise said.

"It's not a crime either. I chew about two of those little chunks a day."

"Well you can't anymore."

"Well I can, Denise. I want to. Chewing happens to relax me. You're making a fuss over nothing."

Steffie managed to get our attention by the sheer pleading force of the look on her face. Her hand was over the mouthpiece of the phone. She did not speak but only formed the words.

The Stovers want to come over.

"Parents or children?" Babette said.

My daughter shrugged.

"We don't want them," Babette said.

"Keep them out," Denise said.

What do I say?

"Say anything you want."

"Just keep them out of here."

"They're boring."

"Tell them to stay home."

Steffie retreated with the phone, appearing to shield it with her body, her eyes full of fear and excitement.

"A little gum can't possibly hurt," Babette said.

"I guess you're right. Never mind. Just a warning on the pack."

Steffie hung up. "Just hazardous to your health," she said.

"Just rats," Denise said. "I guess you're right. Never mind."

"Maybe she thinks they died in their sleep."

"Just useless rodents, so what's the difference?"

"What's the difference, what's the fuss?" Steffie said.

"Plus I'd like to believe she chews only two pieces a day, the way she forgets things."

"What do I forget?" Babette said.

"It's all right," Denise said. "Never mind."

"What do I forget?"

"Go ahead and chew. Never mind the warning. I don't care."

I scooped Wilder off a chair and gave him a noisy kiss on the ear and he shrank away in delight. Then I put him on the counter and went upstairs to find Heinrich. He was in his room studying the deployment of plastic chessmen.

"Still playing with the fellow in prison? How's it going?"

"Pretty good. I think I got him cornered."

"What do you know about this fellow? I've been meaning to ask."

"Like who did he kill? That's the big thing today. Concern for the victim."

"You've been playing chess with the man for months. What do you know about him except that he's in jail for life, for murder? Is he young, old, black, white? Do you communicate at all except for chess moves?"

"We send notes sometimes."

"Who did he kill?"

"He was under pressure."

"And what happened?"

"It kept building and building."

"So he went out and shot someone. Who did he shoot?"

"Some people in Iron City."

"How many?"

"Five."

"Five people."

"Not counting the state trooper, which was later."

"Six people. Did he care for his weapons obsessively? Did he have an arsenal stashed in his shabby little room off a six-story concrete car park?"

"Some handguns and a bolt-action rifle with a scope."

"A telescopic sight. Did he fire from a highway overpass, a rented room? Did he walk into a bar, a washette, his former place of employment and start firing indiscriminately? People scattering, taking cover under tables. People out on the street thinking they heard firecrackers. 'I was just waiting for the bus when I heard this little popping noise like firecrackers going off.'"

"He went up to a roof."

"A rooftop sniper. Did he write in his diary before he went up to the roof? Did he make tapes of his voice, go to the movies, read books about other mass murderers to refresh his memory?"

"Made tapes."

"Made tapes. What did he do with them?"

"Sent them to people he loved, asking for forgiveness."

"'I can't help myself, folks.' Were the victims total strangers? Was it a grudge killing? Did he get fired from his job? Had he been hearing voices?"

"Total strangers."

"Had he been hearing voices?"

"On TV."

"Talking just to him? Singling him out?"

"Telling him to go down in history. He was twenty-seven, out of work, divorced, with his car up on blocks. Time was running out on him."

"Insistent pressuring voices. How did he deal with the media? Give lots of interviews, write letters to the editor of the local paper, try to make a book deal?"

"There is no media in Iron City. He didn't think of that till it was too late. He says if he had to do it all over again, he wouldn't do it as an ordinary murder, he would do it as an assassination."

"He would select more carefully, kill one famous person, get noticed, make it stick."

"He now knows he won't go down in history."

"Neither will I."

"But you've got Hitler."

"Yes, I have, haven't I?"

"What's Tommy Roy Foster got?"

"All right, he's told you all these things in the letters he sends. What do you say when you respond?"

"I'm losing my hair."

I looked at him. He wore a warmup suit, a towel around his neck, sweatbands on both wrists.

"You know what your mother would say about this chess by mail relationship."

"I know what you would say. You're saying it."

"How is your mother? Hear from her lately?"

"She wants me to go out to the ashram this summer."

"Do you want to go?"

"Who knows what I want to do? Who knows what anyone wants to do? How can you be sure about something like that? Isn't it all a question of brain chemistry, signals going back and forth, electrical energy in the cortex? How do you know whether something is really what you want to do or just some kind of nerve impulse in the brain? Some minor little activity takes place somewhere in this unimportant place in one of the brain hemispheres and suddenly I want to go to Montana or I don't want to go to Montana. How do I know I really want to go and it isn't just some neurons firing or something? Maybe it's just an accidental flash in the medulla and suddenly there I am in Montana and I find out I really didn't want to go there in the first place. I can't control what happens in my brain, so how can I be sure what I want to do ten seconds from now, much less Montana next summer? It's all this activity in the brain and you don't know what's you as a person and what's some neuron that just happens to fire or just happens to misfire. Isn't that why Tommy Roy killed those people?"

In the morning I walked to the bank. I went to the automated teller machine to check my balance. I inserted my card, entered my secret code, tapped out my request. The figure on the screen roughly corresponded to my independent estimate, feebly arrived at after long searches through documents, tormented arithmetic. Waves of relief and gratitude flowed over me. The system had blessed my life. I felt its support and approval. The system hardware, the mainframe sitting in a locked room in some distant city. What a pleasing interaction. I sensed that something of deep personal value, but not money, not that at all, had been authenticated and confirmed. A deranged person was escorted from the bank by two armed guards. The system was invisible, which made it all the more impressive, all the more disquieting to deal with. But we were in accord, at least for now. The networks, the circuits, the streams, the harmonies.

11

I woke in the grip of a death sweat. Defenseless against my own racking fears. A pause at the center of my being. I lacked the will and physical strength to get out of bed and move through the dark house, clutching walls and stair rails. To feel my way, reinhabit my body, re-enter the world. Sweat trickled down my ribs. The digital reading on the clock-radio was 3:51. Always odd numbers at times like this. What does it mean? Is death odd-numbered? Are there life-enhancing numbers, other numbers charged with menace? Babette murmured in her sleep and I moved close, breathing her heat.

Finally I slept, to be awakened by the smell of burning toast. That would be Steffie. She burns toast often, at any hour, intentionally. She loves the smell, she is addicted; it's her treasured scent. It satisfies her in ways wood smoke cannot, or snuffed candles, or the odor of explosive powder drifting down the street from firecrackers set off on the Fourth. She has evolved orders of preference. Burnt rye, burnt white, so on.

I put on my robe and went downstairs. I was always putting on a bathrobe and going somewhere to talk seriously to a child. Babette was with her in the kitchen. It startled me. I thought she was still in bed.

"Want some toast?" Steffie said.

"I'll be fifty-one next week."

"That's not old, is it?"

"I've felt the same for twenty-five years."

"Bad. How old is my mother?"

"She's still young. She was only twenty when we were married the first time."

"Is she younger than Baba?"

"About the same. Just so you don't think I'm one of those men who keeps finding younger women."

I wasn't sure whether my replies were meant for Steffie or Babette. This happens in the kitchen, where the levels of data are numerous and deep, as Murray might say.

"Is she still in the CIA?" Steffie said.

"We're not supposed to talk about that. She's just a contract agent anyway."

"What's that?"

"That's what people do today for a second income."

"What exactly does she do?" Babette said.

"She gets a phone call from Brazil. That activates her."

"Then what?"

"She carries money in a suitcase the length and breadth of Latin America."

"That's all? I could do that."

"Sometimes they send her books to review."

"Have I met her?" Babette said.

"No."

"Do I know her name?"

"Dana Breedlove."

Steffie's lips formed the words as I spoke them.

"You're not planning to eat that, are you?" I said to her.

"I always eat my toast."

The phone rang and I picked it up. A woman's voice delivered a high-performance hello. It said it was computer-generated, part of a marketing survey aimed at determining current levels of consumer desire. It said it would ask a series of questions, pausing after each to give me a chance to reply.

I gave the phone to Steffie. When it became clear that she was occupied with the synthesized voice, I spoke to Babette in low tones.

"She liked to plot."

"Who?"

"Dana. She liked to get me involved in things."

"What kind of things?"

"Factions. Playing certain friends against other friends. Household plots, faculty plots."

"Sounds like ordinary stuff."

"She spoke English to me, Spanish or Portuguese to the telephone."

Steffie twisted around, used her free hand to pull her sweater away from her body, enabling her to read the label.

"Virgin acrylic," she said into the phone.

Babette checked the label on her sweater. A soft rain began to fall.

"How does it feel being nearly fifty-one?" she said.

"No different from fifty."

"Except one is even, one is odd," she pointed out.

That night, in Murray's off-white room, after a spectacular meal of Cornish hen in the shape of a frog, prepared on a two-burner hot plate, we moved from our metal folding chairs to the bunk bed for coffee.

"When I was a sportswriter," Murray said, "I traveled constantly, lived in planes and hotels and stadium smoke, never got to feel at home in my own apartment. Now I have a place."

"You've done wonders," Babette said, her gaze sweeping desperately across the room.

"It's small, it's dark, it's plain," he said in a self-satisfied way. "A container for thought."

I gestured toward the old four-story building on several acres across the street. "Do you get any noise from the insane asylum?"

"You mean beatings and shrieks? It's interesting that people still call it the insane asylum. It must be the striking architecture, the high steep roof, the tall chimneys, the columns, the little flourishes here and there that are either quaint or sinister—I can't make up my mind. It doesn't look like a rest home or psychiatric facility. It looks like an insane asylum."

His trousers were going shiny at the knees.

"I'm sorry you didn't bring the kids. I want to get to know small kids. This is the society of kids. I tell my students they're already too old to figure importantly in the making of society. Minute by minute they're beginning to diverge from each other. 'Even as we sit here,' I tell them, 'you are spinning out from the core, becoming less recognizable as a group, less targetable by advertisers and mass-producers of culture. Kids are a true universal. But you're well beyond that, already beginning to drift, to feel estranged from the products you consume. Who are they designed for? What is your place in the marketing scheme? Once you're out of school, it is only a matter of time before you experience the vast loneliness and dissatisfaction of consumers who have lost their group identity.' Then I tap my pencil on the table to indicate time passing ominously."

Because we were seated on the bed, Murray had to lean well forward, looking past the coffee cup poised in my hand, in order to address Babette.

"How many children do you have, all told?"

She appeared to pause.

"There's Wilder, of course. There's Denise."

Murray sipped his coffee, trying to look at her, sideways, with the cup at his lower lip.

"There's Eugene, who's living with his daddy this year in Western Australia. Eugene is eight. His daddy does research in the outback. His daddy is also Wilder's daddy."

"The boy is growing up without television," I said, "which may make him worth talking to, Murray, as a sort of wild child, a savage plucked from the bush, intelligent and literate but deprived of the deeper codes and messages that mark his species as unique."

"TV is a problem only if you've forgotten how to look and listen," Murray said. "My students and I discuss this all the time. They're beginning to feel they ought to turn against the medium, exactly as an earlier generation turned against their parents and their country. I tell them they have to learn to look as children again. Root out content. Find the codes and messages, to use your phrase, Jack."

"What do they say to that?"

"Television is just another name for junk mail. But I tell them I can't accept that. I tell them I've been sitting in this room for more than two months, watching TV into the early hours, listening carefully, taking notes. A great and humbling experience, let me tell you. Close to mystical."

"What's your conclusion?"

He crossed his legs primly and sat with the cup in his lap, smiling straight ahead.

"Waves and radiation," he said. "I've come to understand that the medium is a primal force in the American home. Sealed-off, timeless, self-contained, self-referring. It's like a myth being born right there in our living room, like something we know in a dream-like and preconscious way. I'm very enthused, Jack."

He looked at me, still smiling in a half sneaky way.

"You have to learn how to look. You have to open yourself to the data. TV offers incredible amounts of psychic data. It opens ancient memories of world birth, it welcomes us into the grid, the network of little buzzing dots that make up the picture pattern. There is light, there is sound. I ask my students, 'What more do you want?' Look at the wealth of data concealed in the grid, in the bright packaging, the jingles, the slice-of-life commercials, the products hurtling out of darkness, the coded messages and endless repetitions, like chants, like mantras.[10] '*Coke is it, Coke is it, Coke is it.*' The medium practically overflows with sacred formulas if we can remember how to respond innocently and get past our irritation, weariness and disgust."

"But your students don't agree."

"Worse than junk mail. Television is the death throes of human consciousness, according to them. They're ashamed of their television past. They want to talk about movies."

He got up and refilled our cups.

"How do you know so much?" Babette said.

"I'm from New York."

"The more you talk, the sneakier you look, as if you're trying to put something over on us."

"The best talk is seductive."

"Have you ever been married?" she said.

[10]Hindu religious incantations or prayers.

"Once, briefly. I was covering the Jets, the Mets and the Nets. How odd a figure I must seem to you now, a solitary crank who maroons himself with a TV set and dozens of stacks of dust-jacketed comic books. Don't think I wouldn't appreciate a dramatic visit between two and three in the morning," he told her, "from an intelligent woman in spike heels and a slit skirt, with high-impact accessories."

It was drizzling as we walked home, my arm around her waist. The streets were empty. Along Elm all the stores were dark, the two banks were dimly lit, the neon spectacles in the window of the optical shop cast a gimmicky light on the sidewalk.

Dacron, Orlon, Lycra Spandex.

"I know I forget things," she said, "but I didn't know it was so obvious."

"It isn't."

"Did you hear Denise? When was it, last week?"

"Denise is smart and tough. No one else notices."

"I dial a number on the phone and forget who I'm calling. I go to the store and forget what to buy. Someone will tell me something, I'll forget it, they'll tell me again, I'll forget it, they'll tell me again, showing a funny-looking smile."

"We all forget," I said.

"I forget names, faces, phone numbers, addresses, appointments, instructions, directions."

"It's something that's just been happening, more or less to everyone."

"I forget that Steffie doesn't like to be called Stephanie. Sometimes I call her Denise. I forget where I've parked the car and then for a long, long moment I forget what the car looks like."

"Forgetfulness has gotten into the air and water. It's entered the food chain."

"Maybe it's the gum I chew. Is that too farfetched?"

"Maybe it's something else."

"What do you mean?"

"You're taking something besides chewing gum."

"Where did you get that idea?"

"I got it secondhand from Steffie."

"Who did Steffie get it from?"

"Denise."

She paused, conceding the possibility that if Denise is the source of a rumor or theory, it could very well be true.

"What does Denise say I'm taking?"

"I wanted to ask you before I asked her."

"To the best of my knowledge, Jack, I'm not taking anything that could account for my memory lapses. On the other hand I'm not old, I haven't suffered an injury to the head and there's nothing in my family background except tipped uteruses."

"You're saying maybe Denise is right."

"We can't rule it out."

"You're saying maybe you're taking something that has the side effect of impairing memory."

"Either I'm taking something and I don't remember or I'm not taking something and I don't remember. My life is either/or. Either I chew regular gum or I chew sugarless gum. Either I chew gum or I smoke. Either I smoke or I gain weight. Either I gain weight or I run up the stadium steps."

"Sounds like a boring life."

"I hope it lasts forever," she said.

Soon the streets were covered with leaves. Leaves came tumbling and scraping down the pitched roofs. There were periods in every day when a stiff wind blew, baring the trees further, and retired men appeared in the backyards, on the small lawns out front, carrying rakes with curved teeth. Black bags were arrayed at the curbstone in lopsided rows.

A series of frightened children appeared at our door for their Halloween treats.

12

I went to German lessons twice a week, in the late afternoon, darkness crowding in earlier with each succeeding visit. It was Howard Dunlop's working rule that we sit facing each other during the full length of the lesson. He wanted me to study his tongue positions as he demonstrated the pronunciation of consonants, diphthongs, long and short vowels. He in turn would look closely into my mouth as I attempted to reproduce the unhappy sounds.

His was a mild and quiet face, an oval surface with no hint of distinctiveness until he started his vocal routines. Then the warping began. It was an eerie thing to see, shamefully fascinating, as a seizure might be if witnessed in a controlled environment. He tucked his head into his trunk, narrowed his eyes, made grimacing humanoid faces. When it was time for me to repeat the noises I did likewise, if only to please the teacher, twisting my mouth, shutting my eyes completely, conscious of an overarticulation so tortured it must have sounded like a sudden bending of the natural law, a stone or tree struggling to speak. When I opened my eyes he was only inches from my mouth, leaning in to peer. I used to wonder what he saw in there.

There were strained silences before and after each lesson. I tried to make small talk, get him to discuss his years as a chiropractor, his life before German. He would look off into the middle distance, not angry or bored or evasive—just detached, free of the connectedness of events, it seemed. When he did speak, about the other boarders or the landlord, there was something querulous in his voice, a drawn-out note of complaint. It was important for him to believe that he'd spent his life among people who kept missing the point.

"How many students do you have?"

"For German?"

"Yes."

"You're the only one I have for German. I used to have others. German has fallen off. These things go in cycles, like everything else."

"What else do you teach?"

"Greek, Latin, ocean sailing."

"People come here to learn ocean sailing?"

"Not so much anymore."

"It's amazing how many people teach these days," I said. "There is a teacher for every person. Everyone I know is either a teacher or a student. What do you think it means?"

He looked off toward a closet door.

"Do you teach anything else?" I said.

"Meteorology."

"Meteorology. How did that come about?"

"My mother's death had a terrible impact on me. I collapsed totally, lost my faith in God. I was inconsolable, withdrew completely into myself. Then one day by chance I saw a weather report on TV. A dynamic young man with a glowing pointer stood before a multicolored satellite photo, predicting the weather for the next five days. I sat there mesmerized by his self-assurance and skill. It was as though a message was being transmitted from the weather satellite through that young man and then to me in my canvas chair. I turned to meteorology for comfort. I read weather maps, collected books on weather, attended launchings of weather balloons. I realized weather was something I'd been looking for all my life. It brought me a sense of peace and security I'd never experienced. Dew, frost and fog. Snow flurries. The jet stream. I believe there is a grandeur in the jet stream. I began to come out of my shell, talk to people in the street. 'Nice day.' 'Looks like rain.' 'Hot enough for you?' Everyone notices the weather. First thing on rising, you go to the window, look at the weather. You do it, I do it. I made a list of goals I hoped to achieve in meteorology. I took a correspondence course, got a degree to teach the subject in buildings with a legal occupancy of less than one hundred. I've taught meteorology in church basements, in trailer parks, in people's dens and living rooms. They came to hear me in Millers Creek, Lumberville, Watertown. Factory workers, housewives, merchants, members of the police and the fire. I saw something in their eyes. A hunger, a compelling need."

There were little holes in the cuffs of his thermal undershirt. We were standing in the middle of the room. I waited for him to go on. It was the time of year, the time of day, for a small insistent sadness to pass into the texture of things. Dusk, silence, iron chill. Something lonely in the bone.

When I got home, Bob Pardee was in the kitchen practicing his golf swing. Bob is Denise's father. He said he was driving through town on his way to Glassboro to make a presentation and thought he'd take us all to dinner.

He swung his locked hands in slow motion over his left shoulder, following through smoothly. Denise eyed him from a stool by the window. He wore a half shaggy cardigan with sleeves that draped over the cuffs.

"What kind of presentation?" she said.

"Oh, you know. Charts, arrows. Slap some colors on a wall. It's a basic outreach tool, sweetheart."

"Did you change jobs again?"

"I'm raising funds. Busy as hell, too, better believe."

"What kind of funds?"

"Just whatever's out there, you know? People want to give me food stamps, etchings. Hey, great, I don't mind."

He was bent over a putt. Babette leaned on the refrigerator door with her arms folded, watching him. Upstairs a British voice said: "There are forms of vertigo that do not include spinning."

"Funds for what?" Denise said.

"There's a little thing you might have had occasion to hear of, called the Nuclear Accident Readiness Foundation. Basically a legal defense fund for the industry. Just in case kind of thing."

"Just in case what?"

"Just in case I faint from hunger. Let's sneak up on some ribs, why don't we? You got your leg men, you got your breast men. Babette, what do you say? I'm about semiprepared to slaughter my own animal."

"How many jobs is this anyway?"

"Don't pester me, Denise."

"Never mind, I don't care, do what you want."

Bob took the three older kids to the Wagon Wheel. I drove Babette to the river-edge house where she would read to Mr. Treadwell, the blind old man who lived there with his sister. Wilder sat between us, playing with the supermarket tabloids that Treadwell favored as reading matter. As a volunteer reader to the blind, Babette had some reservations about the old gent's appetite for the unspeakable and seamy, believing that the handicapped were morally bound to higher types of entertainment. If we couldn't look to them for victories of the human spirit, who could we look to? They had an example to set just as she did as a reader and morale-booster. But she was professional in her duty, reading to him with high earnestness, as to a child, about dead men who leave messages on answering machines.

Wilder and I waited in the car. The plan was that after the reading the three of us would meet the Wagon Wheel group at the Dinky Donut, where they would have dessert and we would have dinner. I'd brought along a copy of *Mein Kampf*[11] for that segment of the evening.

The Treadwell house was an old frame structure with rotting trellises along the porch. Less than five minutes after she'd entered, Babette came out, walked uncertainly to the far end of the porch and peered across the dim yard. Then she walked slowly toward the car.

"Door was open. I went in, nobody. I looked around, nothing, nobody. I went upstairs, no sign of life. There doesn't seem to be anything missing."

"What do you know about his sister?"

"She's older than he is and probably in worse shape if you disregard the fact that he's blind and she isn't."

The two nearest houses were dark, both up for sale, and no one at four other houses in the area knew anything about the Treadwells' movements over the past few days. We drove to the state trooper barracks and talked to a female clerk who sat behind a computer console. She told us there was a disappearance every eleven seconds and taped everything we said.

At the Dinky Donut, outside town, Bob Pardee sat quietly as the family ate and talked. The soft pink golfer's face had begun to droop from his skull. His flesh seemed generally to sag, giving him the hangdog look of someone under strict orders to lose weight. His hair was expensively cut and layered, a certain amount of color combed in, a certain amount of technology brought to bear, but it seemed to need a more dynamic head. I realized Babette was looking at him carefully, trying to grasp the meaning of the four careening years they'd spent as man and wife. The panoramic carnage. He drank, gambled, drove his car down embankments, got fired, quit, retired, traveled in disguise to Coaltown where he paid a woman to speak Swedish to him as they screwed. It was the Swedish that enraged Babette, either that or his need to confess it, and she hit out at him—hit out with the backs of her hands, with her elbows and wrists. Old

[11]German: *My Struggle* (1925–1927), title of the autobiography of Adolf Hitler.

loves, old fears. Now she watched him with a tender sympathy, a reflectiveness that seemed deep and fond and generous enough to contain all the magical counterspells to his current run of woe, although I knew, of course, as I went back to my book, that it was only a passing affection, one of those kindnesses no one understands.

By noon the next day they were dragging the river.

13

The students tend to stick close to campus. There is nothing for them to do in Blacksmith proper, no natural haunt or attraction. They have their own food, movies, music, theater, sports, conversation and sex. This is a town of dry cleaning shops and opticians. Photos of looming Victorian homes decorate the windows of real estate firms. These pictures have not changed in years. The homes are sold or gone or stand in other towns in other states. This is a town of tag sales and yard sales, the failed possessions arrayed in driveways and tended by kids.

Babette called me at my office in Centenary Hall. She said Heinrich had been down at the river, wearing his camouflage cap and carrying an Instamatic, to watch them drag for the bodies, and while he was there word came that the Treadwells had been found alive but shaken in an abandoned cookie shack at the Mid-Village Mall, a vast shopping center out on the interstate. Apparently they'd been wandering through the mall for two days, lost, confused and frightened, before taking refuge in the littered kiosk. They spent two more days in the kiosk, the weak and faltering sister venturing out to scavenge food scraps from the cartoon-character disposal baskets with swinging doors. It was sheer luck that their stay at the mall coincided with a spell of mild weather. No one knew at this point why they didn't ask for help. It was probably just the vastness and strangeness of the place and their own advanced age that made them feel helpless and adrift in a landscape of remote and menacing figures. The Treadwells didn't get out much. In fact no one yet knew how they'd managed to get to the mall. Possibly their grandniece had dropped them off in her car and then forgotten to pick them up. The grandniece could not be reached, Babette said, for comment.

The day before the happy discovery, the police had called in a psychic to help them determine the Treadwells' whereabouts and fate. It was all over the local paper. The psychic was a woman who lived in a mobile home in a wooded area outside town. She wished to be known only as Adele T. According to the paper, she and the police chief, Hollis Wright, sat in the mobile home while she looked at photos of the Treadwells and smelled articles from their wardrobe. Then she asked the chief to leave her alone for an hour. She did exercises, ate some rice and *dahl,*[12] proceeded to trance in. During this altered state, the report went on, she attempted to put a data trace on whatever distant physical systems she wished to locate, in this case Old Man Treadwell and his sister. When chief Wright re-entered the trailer, Adele T. told him to forget the river and to

[12]Lentils mixed with spices, an East Indian dish.

concentrate on dry land with a moonscape look about it, within a fifteen-mile radius of the Treadwell home. The police went at once to a gypsum processing operation ten miles down river, where they found an airline bag that contained a handgun and two kilos of uncut heroin.

The police had consulted Adele T. on a number of occasions and she had led them to two bludgeoned bodies, a Syrian in a refrigerator and a cache of marked bills totaling six hundred thousand dollars, although in each instance, the report concluded, the police had been looking for something else.

The American mystery deepens.

14

We crowded before the window in Steffie's small room, watching the spectacular sunset. Only Heinrich stayed away, either because he distrusted wholesome communal pleasures or because he believed there was something ominous in the modern sunset.

Later I sat up in bed in my bathrobe studying German. I muttered words to myself and wondered whether I'd be able to restrict my German-speaking at the spring conference to brief opening remarks or whether the other participants would expect the language to be used throughout, in lectures, at meals, in small talk, as a mark of our seriousness, our uniqueness in world scholarship.

The TV said: "And other trends that could dramatically impact your portfolio."

Denise came in and sprawled across the foot of the bed, her head resting on her folded arms, facing away from me. How many codes, countercodes, social histories were contained in this simple posture? A full minute passed.

"What are we going to do about Baba?" she said.

"What do you mean?"

"She can't remember anything."

"Did she ask you whether she's taking medication?"

"No."

"No she's not or no she didn't ask?"

"She didn't ask."

"She was supposed to," I said.

"Well she didn't."

"How do you know she's taking something?"

"I saw the bottle buried in the trash under the kitchen sink. A prescription bottle. It had her name and the name of the medication."

"What is the name of the medication?"

"Dylar. One every three days. Which sounds like it's dangerous or habit-forming or whatever."

"What does your drug reference say about Dylar?"

"It's not in there. I spent hours. There are four indexes."

"It must be recently marketed. Do you want me to double-check the book?"

"I already looked. I *looked*."

"We could always call her doctor. But I don't want to make too much of this. Everybody takes some kind of medication, everybody forgets things occasionally."

"Not like my mother."

"I forget things all the time."

"What do you take?"

"Blood pressure pills, stress pills, allergy pills, eye drops, aspirin. Run of the mill."

"I looked in the medicine chest in your bathroom."

"No Dylar?"

"I thought there might be a new bottle."

"The doctor prescribed thirty pills. That was it. Run of the mill. Everybody takes something."

"I still want to know," she said.

All this time she'd been turned away from me. There were plot potentials in this situation, chances for people to make devious maneuvers, secret plans. But now she shifted position, used an elbow to prop her upper body and watched me speculatively from the foot of the bed.

"Can I ask you something?"

"Sure," I said.

"You won't get mad?"

"You know what's in my medicine chest. What secrets are left?"

"Why did you name Heinrich Heinrich?"

"Fair question."

"You don't have to answer."

"Good question. No reason why you shouldn't ask."

"So why did you?"

"I thought it was a forceful name, a strong name. It has a kind of authority."

"Is he named after anyone?"

"No. He was born shortly after I started the department and I guess I wanted to acknowledge my good fortune. I wanted to do something German. I felt a gesture was called for."

"Heinrich Gerhardt Gladney?"

"I thought it had an authority that might cling to him. I thought it was forceful and impressive and I still do. I wanted to shield him, make him unafraid. People were naming their children Kim, Kelly and Tracy."

There was a long silence. She kept watching me. Her features, crowded somewhat in the center of her face, gave to her moments of concentration a puggish and half-belligerent look.

"Do you think I miscalculated?"

"It's not for me to say."

"There's something about German names, the German language, German *things*. I don't know what it is exactly. It's just there. In the middle of it all is Hitler, of course."

"He was on again last night."

"He's always on. We couldn't have television without him."

"They lost the war," she said. "How great could they be?"

"A valid point. But it's not a question of greatness. It's not a question of good and evil. I don't know what it is. Look at it this way. Some people always wear a favorite color. Some people carry a gun. Some people put on a uniform and feel bigger, stronger, safer. It's in this area that my obsessions dwell."

Steffie came in wearing Denise's green visor. I didn't know what this meant. She climbed up on the bed and all three of us went through my German-English dictionary, looking for words that sound about the same in both languages, like orgy and shoe.

Heinrich came running down the hall, burst into the room. "Come on, hurry up, plane crash footage." Then he was out the door, the girls were off the bed, all three of them running along the hall to the TV set.

I sat in bed a little stunned. The swiftness and noise of their leaving had put the room in a state of molecular agitation. In the debris of invisible matter, the question seemed to be, What is happening here? By the time I got to the room at the end of the hall, there was only a puff of black smoke at the edge of the screen. But the crash was shown two more times, once in stopaction replay, as an analyst attempted to explain the reason for the plunge. A jet trainer in an air show in New Zealand.

We had two closet doors that opened by themselves.

That night, a Friday, we gathered in front of the set, as was the custom and the rule, with take-out Chinese. There were floods, earthquakes, mud slides, erupting volcanoes. We'd never before been so attentive to our duty, our Friday assembly. Heinrich was not sullen, I was not bored. Steffie, brought close to tears by a sitcom husband arguing with his wife, appeared totally absorbed in these documentary clips of calamity and death. Babette tried to switch to a comedy series about a group of racially mixed kids who build their own communications satellite. She was startled by the force of our objection. We were otherwise silent, watching houses slide into the ocean, whole villages crackle and ignite in a mass of advancing lava. Every disaster made us wish for more, for something bigger, grander, more sweeping.

I walked into my office on Monday to find Murray sitting in the chair adjacent to the desk, like someone waiting for a nurse to arrive with a blood-pressure gauge. He'd been having trouble, he said, establishing an Elvis Presley power base in the department of American environments. The chairman, Alfonse Stompanato, seemed to feel that one of the other instructors, a three-hundred-pound former rock 'n' roll bodyguard named Dimitrios Cotsakis, had established prior right by having flown to Memphis when the King died, interviewed members of the King's entourage and family, been interviewed himself on local television as an Interpreter of the Phenomenon.

A more than middling coup, Murray conceded. I suggested that I might drop by his next lecture, informally, unannounced, simply to lend a note of consequence to the proceedings, to give him the benefit of whatever influence and prestige might reside in my office, my subject, my physical person. He nodded slowly, fingering the ends of his beard.

Later at lunch I spotted only one empty chair, at a table occupied by the New York émigrés. Alfonse sat at the head of the table, a commanding presence even in a campus lunchroom. He was large, sardonic, dark-staring, with scarred brows and a furious beard fringed in gray. It was the very beard I would have grown in 1969 if Janet Savory, my second wife, Heinrich's mother, hadn't argued against it. "Let them see that bland expanse," she said, in her tiny dry voice. "It is more effective than you think."

Alfonse invested everything he did with a sense of all-consuming purpose. He knew four languages, had a photographic memory, did complex mathematics in his head. He'd once told me that the art of getting ahead in New York was based on learning how to express dissatisfaction in an interesting way. The air was full of rage and complaint. People had no tolerance for your particular hardship unless you knew how to entertain them with it. Alfonse himself was occasionally entertaining in a pulverizing way. He had a manner that enabled him to absorb and destroy all opinions in conflict with his. When he talked about popular culture, he exercised the closed logic of a religious zealot, one who kills for his beliefs. His breathing grew heavy, arrhythmic, his brows seemed to lock. The other émigrés appeared to find his challenges and taunts a proper context for their endeavor. They used his office to pitch pennies to the wall.

I said to him, "Why is it, Alfonse, that decent, well-meaning and responsible people find themselves intrigued by catastrophe when they see it on television?"

I told him about the recent evening of lava, mud and raging water that the children and I had found so entertaining.

"We wanted more, more."

"It's natural, it's normal," he said, with a reassuring nod. "It happens to everybody."

"Why?"

"Because we're suffering from brain fade. We need an occasional catastrophe to break up the incessant bombardment of information."

"It's obvious," Lasher said. A slight man with a taut face and slicked-back hair.

"The flow is constant," Alfonse said. "Words, pictures, numbers, facts, graphics, statistics, specks, waves, particles, motes. Only a catastrophe gets our attention. We want them, we need them, we depend on them. As long as they happen somewhere else. This is where California comes in. Mud slides, brush fires, coastal erosion, earthquakes, mass killings, et cetera. We can relax and enjoy these disasters because in our hearts we feel that California deserves whatever it gets. Californians invented the concept of life-style. This alone warrants their doom."

Cotsakis crushed a can of Diet Pepsi and threw it at a garbage pail.

"Japan is pretty good for disaster footage," Alfonse said. "India remains largely untapped. They have tremendous potential with their famines, monsoons, religious strife, train wrecks, boat sinkings, et cetera. But their disasters tend to go unrecorded. Three lines in the newspaper. No film footage, no satellite hookup. This is why California is so important. We not only enjoy seeing them punished for their relaxed life-style and progressive social ideas but we know we're not missing anything. The cameras are right there. They're standing by. Nothing terrible escapes their scrutiny."

"You're saying it's more or less universal, to be fascinated by TV disasters."

"For most people there are only two places in the world. Where they live and their TV set. If a thing happens on television, we have every right to find it fascinating, whatever it is."

"I don't know whether to feel good or bad about learning that my experience is widely shared."

"Feel bad," he said.

"It's obvious," Lasher said. "We all feel bad. But we can enjoy it on that level."

Murray said, "This is what comes from the wrong kind of attentiveness. People get brain fade. This is because they've forgotten how to listen and look as children. They've forgotten how to collect data. In the psychic sense a forest fire on TV is on a lower plane than a ten-second spot for Automatic Dishwasher All. The commercial has deeper waves, deeper emanations. But we have reversed the relative significance of these things. This is why people's eyes, ears, brains and nervous systems have grown weary. It's a simple case of misuse."

Grappa casually tossed half a buttered roll at Lasher, hitting him on the shoulder. Grappa was pale and baby-fattish and the tossed roll was an attempt to get Lasher's attention.

Grappa said to him, "Did you ever brush your teeth with your finger?"

"I brushed my teeth with my finger the first time I stayed overnight at my wife's parents' house, before we were married, when her parents spent a weekend at Asbury Park. They were an Ipana family."

"Forgetting my toothbrush is a fetish with me," Cotsakis said. "I brushed my teeth with my finger at Woodstock, Altamont, Monterey, about a dozen other seminal events."

Grappa looked at Murray.

"I brushed my teeth with my finger after the Ali-Foreman fight in Zaire," Murray said. "That's the southernmost point I've ever brushed my teeth with my finger at."

Lasher looked at Grappa.

"Did you ever crap in a toilet bowl that had no seat?"

Grappa's response was semi-lyrical. "A great and funky men's room in an old Socony Mobil station on the Boston Post Road the first time my father took the car outside the city. The station with the flying red horse. You want the car? I can give you car details down to the last little option."

"These are the things they don't teach," Lasher said. "Bowls with no seats. Pissing in sinks. The culture of public toilets. All those great diners, movie houses, gas stations. The whole ethos of the road. I've pissed in sinks all through the American West. I've slipped across the border to piss in sinks in Manitoba and Alberta. This is what it's all about. The great western skies. The Best Western motels. The diners and drive-ins. The poetry of the road, the plains, the desert. The filthy stinking toilets. I pissed in a sink in Utah when it was twenty-two below. That's the coldest I've ever pissed in a sink in."

Alfonse Stompanato looked hard at Lasher.

"Where were you when James Dean died?" he said in a threatening voice.

"In my wife's parents' house before we were married, listening to 'Make Believe Ballroom' on the old Emerson table model. The Motorola with the glowing dial was already a thing of the past."

"You spent a lot of time in your wife's parents' house, it seems, screwing," Alfonse said.

"We were kids. It was too early in the cultural matrix for actual screwing."

"What were you doing?"

"She's my wife, Alfonse. You want me to tell a crowded table?"

"James Dean is dead and you're groping some twelve-year-old."

Alfonse glared at Dimitrios Cotsakis.

"Where were you when James Dean died?"

"In the back of my uncle's restaurant in Astoria, Queens, vacuuming with the Hoover."

Alfonse looked at Grappa.

"Where the hell were you?" he said, as if the thought had just occurred to him that the actor's death was not complete without some record of Grappa's whereabouts.

"I know exactly where I was, Alfonse. Let me think a minute."

"Where were you, you son of a bitch?"

"I always know these things down to the smallest detail. But I was a dreamy adolescent. I have these gaps in my life."

"You were busy jerking off. Is that what you mean?"

"Ask me Joan Crawford."

"September thirty, nineteen fifty-five. James Dean dies. Where is Nicholas Grappa and what is he doing?"

"Ask me Gable, ask me Monroe."

"The silver Porsche approaches an intersection, going like a streak. No time to brake for the Ford sedan. Glass shatters, metal screams. Jimmy Dean sits in the driver's seat with a broken neck, multiple fractures and lacerations. It is five forty-five in the afternoon, Pacific Coast Time. Where is Nicholas Grappa, the jerk-off king of the Bronx?"

"Ask me Jeff Chandler."

"You're a middle-aged man, Nicky, who trafficks in his own childhood. You have an obligation to produce."

"Ask me John Garfield, ask me Monty Clift."

Cotsakis was a monolith of thick and wadded flesh. He'd been Little Richard's personal bodyguard and had led security details at rock concerts before joining the faculty here.

Elliot Lasher threw a chunk of raw carrot at him, then asked, "Did you ever have a woman peel flaking skin from your back after a few days at the beach?"

"Cocoa Beach, Florida," Cotsakis said. "It was very tremendous. The second or third greatest experience of my life."

"Was she naked?" Lasher said.

"To the waist," Cotsakis said.

"From which direction?" Lasher said.

I watched Grappa throw a cracker at Murray. He skimmed it backhand like a Frisbee.

15

I put on my dark glasses, composed my face and walked into the room. There were twenty-five or thirty young men and women, many in fall colors, seated in armchairs and sofas and on the beige broadloom. Murray walked among them, speaking, his right hand trembling in a stylized way. When he saw me, he smiled sheepishly. I stood against the wall, attempting to loom, my arms folded under the black gown.

Murray was in the midst of a thoughtful monologue.

"Did his mother know that Elvis would die young? She talked about assassins. She talked about the life. The life of a star of this type and magnitude. Isn't the life structured to cut you down early? This is the point, isn't it? There are rules, guidelines. If you don't have the grace and wit to die early, you are forced to vanish, to hide as if in shame and apology. She worried about his sleepwalking. She thought he might go out a window. I have a feeling about mothers. Mothers really do know. The folklore is correct."

"Hitler adored his mother," I said.

A surge of attention, unspoken, identifiable only in a certain convergence of stillness, an inward tensing. Murray kept moving, of course, but a bit more deliberately, picking his way between the chairs, the people seated on the floor. I stood against the wall, arms folded.

"Elvis and Gladys liked to nuzzle and pet," he said. "They slept in the same bed until he began to approach physical maturity. They talked baby talk to each other all the time."

"Hitler was a lazy kid. His report card was full of unsatisfactorys. But Klara loved him, spoiled him, gave him the attention his father failed to give him. She was a quiet woman, modest and religious, and a good cook and housekeeper."

"Gladys walked Elvis to school and back every day. She defended him in little street rumbles, lashed out at any kid who tried to bully him."

"Hitler fantasized. He took piano lessons, made sketches of museums and villas. He sat around the house a lot. Klara tolerated this. He was the first of her children to survive infancy. Three others had died."

"Elvis confided in Gladys. He brought his girlfriends around to meet her."

"Hitler wrote a poem to his mother. His mother and his niece were the women with the greatest hold on his mind."

"When Elvis went into the army, Gladys became ill and depressed. She sensed something, maybe as much about herself as about him. Her psychic apparatus was flashing all the wrong signals. Foreboding and gloom."

"There's not much doubt that Hitler was what we call a mama's boy."

A note-taking young man murmured absently, "*Muttersöhnchen*."[13] I regarded him warily. Then, on an impulse, I abandoned my stance at the wall and began to pace the room like Murray, occasionally pausing to gesture, to listen, to gaze out a window or up at the ceiling.

"Elvis could hardly bear to let Gladys out of his sight when her condition grew worse. He kept a vigil at the hospital."

"When his mother became severely ill, Hitler put a bed in the kitchen to be closer to her. He cooked and cleaned."

"Elvis fell apart with grief when Gladys died. He fondled and petted her in the casket. He talked baby talk to her until she was in the ground."

"Klara's funeral cost three hundred and seventy kronen. Hitler wept at the grave and fell into a period of depression and self-pity. He felt an intense loneliness. He'd lost not only his beloved mother but also his sense of home and hearth."

"It seems fairly certain that Gladys's death caused a fundamental shift at the center of the King's world view. She'd been his anchor, his sense of security. He began to withdraw from the real world, to enter the state of his own dying."

"For the rest of his life, Hitler could not bear to be anywhere near Christmas decorations because his mother had died near a Christmas tree."

"Elvis made death threats, received death threats. He took mortuary tours and became interested in UFOs. He began to study the *Bardo Thödol*, commonly known as *The Tibetan Book of the Dead*. This is a guide to dying and being reborn."

"Years later, in the grip of self-myth and deep remoteness, Hitler kept a portrait of his mother in his spartan quarters at Obersalzberg. He began to hear a buzzing in his left ear."

Murray and I passed each other near the center of the room, almost colliding. Alfonse Stompanato entered, followed by several students, drawn perhaps

[13]German: "Momma's boy."

by some magnetic wave of excitation, some frenzy in the air. He settled his surly bulk in a chair as Murray and I circled each other and headed off in opposite directions, avoiding an exchange of looks.

"Elvis fulfilled the terms of the contract. Excess, deterioration, self-destructiveness, grotesque behavior, a physical bloating and a series of insults to the brain, self-delivered. His place in legend is secure. He bought off the skeptics by dying early, horribly, unnecessarily. No one could deny him now. His mother probably saw it all, as on a nineteen-inch screen, years before her own death."

Murray, happily deferring to me, went to a corner of the room and sat on the floor, leaving me to pace and gesture alone, secure in my professional aura of power, madness and death.

"Hitler called himself the lonely wanderer out of nothingness. He sucked on lozenges, spoke to people in endless monologues, free-associating, as if the language came from some vastness beyond the world and he was simply the medium of revelation. It's interesting to wonder if he looked back from the *führerbunker,*[14] beneath the burning city, to the early days of his power. Did he think of the small groups of tourists who visited the little settlement where his mother was born and where he'd spent summers with his cousins, riding in ox carts and making kites? They came to honor the site, Klara's birthplace. They entered the farmhouse, poked around tentatively. Adolescent boys climbed on the roof. In time the numbers began to increase. They took pictures, slipped small items into their pockets. Then crowds came, mobs of people overrunning the courtyard and singing patriotic songs, painting swastikas on the walls, on the flanks of farm animals. Crowds came to his mountain villa, so many people he had to stay indoors. They picked up pebbles where he'd walked and took them home as souvenirs. Crowds came to hear him speak, crowds erotically charged, the masses he once called his only bride. He closed his eyes, clenched his fists as he spoke, twisted his sweat-drenched body, remade his voice as a thrilling weapon. 'Sex murders,' someone called these speeches. Crowds came to be hypnotized by the voice, the party anthems, the torchlight parades."

I stared at the carpet and counted silently to seven.

"But wait. How familiar this all seems, how close to ordinary. Crowds come, get worked up, touch and press—people eager to be transported. Isn't this ordinary? We *know* all this. There must have been something different about those crowds. What was it? Let me whisper the terrible word, from the Old English, from the Old German, from the Old Norse. *Death.* Many of those crowds were assembled in the name of death. They were there to attend tributes to the dead. Processions, songs, speeches, dialogues with the dead, recitations of the names of the dead. They were there to see pyres and flaming wheels, thousands of flags dipped in salute, thousands of uniformed mourners. There were ranks and squadrons, elaborate backdrops, blood banners and black dress uniforms. Crowds came to form a shield against their own dying. To become a crowd is to keep out death. To break off from the crowd is to risk death as an individual, to face dying alone. Crowds came for this reason above all others. They were there to be a crowd."

[14]German: *leader's underground fortification*—the name given the secret underground headquarters from which Adolf Hitler directed German forces at the end of World War II and in which he committed suicide in 1945.

Murray sat across the room. His eyes showed a deep gratitude. I had been generous with the power and madness at my disposal, allowing my subject to be associated with an infinitely lesser figure, a fellow who sat in La-Z-Boy chairs and shot out TVs. It was not a small matter. We all had an aura to maintain, and in sharing mine with a friend I was risking the very things that made me untouchable.

People gathered round, students and staff, and in the mild din of half heard remarks and orbiting voices I realized we were now a crowd. Not that I needed a crowd around me now. Least of all now. Death was strictly a professional matter here. I was comfortable with it, I was on top of it. Murray made his way to my side and escorted me from the room, parting the crowd with his fluttering hand.

1985

Gloria Anzaldúa 1942–2004

Gloria Anzaldúa is a writer whose work explores many "borderlands": Mexico/United States, Spanish/English, poetry/prose, male/female, poor/rich, homosexual/heterosexual. Anzaldúa was born into poverty, the child of migrant farm workers, in 1942, in a farming community in south Texas known as Jesus Maria of the Valley. Her father, Urbano Anzaldúa, decided when she and her siblings were still young that working the migrant farmer routes would mean that his children would miss too much school. He brought some stability to their lives, which facilitated his children's uninterrupted education for several years, by relocating the family to Hargill, Texas, where he and his family worked as sharecroppers. However, her father died when Anzaldúa was fifteen, making it necessary for her, her mother (Amalia García Anzaldúa), and her brothers and sister to return to migrant farming, working the fields between south Texas and Arkansas. Nevertheless, Anzaldúa managed to complete high school and earn a B.A. from Pan American University in 1969. After receiving a master's degree from the University of Texas in 1973, she began teaching summer high school classes to the children of migrant families working in the Midwest. From 1974 to 1977 she studied as a doctoral student at the University of Texas, but when her dissertation topic was not approved, she left without her degree. For the next several years she supported herself by teaching at the University of California, Santa Cruz, where she continued her doctoral studies, and at San Francisco State University. During this time she also began to write professionally.

Throughout the 1980s Anzaldúa contributed essays, stories, and poems to various edited collections and periodicals. She gained attention in feminist and literary circles in 1981 with the publication of This Bridge Called My Back: Writings by Radical Women of Color, *which she coedited with Cherrie Moraga. Anzaldúa spent two years, 1984–1986, teaching at Norwich Academy in Vermont, and her awareness of her ethnic isolation in that environment helped to stimulate the creation of her multi-genre* Borderlands/La Frontera: The New Mestiza *(1987), which most critics, and Anzaldúa herself, have considered to be her major work. In the 1990s she continued to write and publish essays, poetry, and short fiction, as well as several children's books and a novel,* La Prieta, *which appeared in 1995. Anzaldúa had only recently completed her long-delayed Ph.D. dissertation at the University of California, Santa Cruz when she died of complications from diabetes in 2004.*

FURTHER READING: A. Cheatham, *This Way Daybreak Comes: Women's Values and the Future,* 1986; *Critical Essays: Gay and Lesbian Writers of Color,* ed. E. Nelson, 1993; A. Keating, *Women Reading Women Writing: Self-invention in Paula Gunn Allen, Gloria Anzaldúa, and Audre Lorde,* 1996; C. Steele, *We Heal from Memory: Sexton, Lorde, Anzaldúa, and the Poetry of Witness,* 2000; B. Trigo, *Remembering Maternal Bodies: Melancholy in Latina and Latin American Women's Writing,* 2006; *Identity Politics Reconsidered,* ed. L. Alcoff et al., 2006.

TEXT: *Borderlands/La Frontera, The New Mestiza,* 1987.

from *BORDERLANDS/LA FRONTERA: THE NEW MESTIZA*

[One of the borderlands traversed in Anzaldúa's text is the border region between Spanish and English. In order to preserve the full impact of her movement between, and mixing of, the two languages, no translations are given here other than those provided by Anzaldúa herself—contrary to the practice otherwise followed in the *Anthology of American Literature* of translating foreign words and phrases and providing definitions for unfamiliar ones. All the footnotes for these selections are Anzaldúa's. Anzaldúa's text as originally published also includes scholarly citations, but those are omitted here.]

THE HOMELAND, AZTLÁN

EL OTRO MÉXICO

El otro México que acá hemos construido
el espacio es lo que ha sido
territorio nacional.
Esté el esfuerzo de todos nuestros hermanos
y latinoamericanos que han sabido
progressar.

—*Los Tigres del Norte*[1]

"The *Aztecas del norte* . . . compose the largest single tribe or nation of Anishinabeg (Indians) found in the United States today. . . . Some call themselves Chicanos and see themselves as people whose true homeland is Aztlán [the U.S. Southwest]."

Wind tugging at my sleeve
feet sinking into the sand
I stand at the edge where earth touches ocean

[1]Los Tigres del Norte is a *conjunto* band.

where the two overlap
a gentle coming together
at other times and places a violent clash.

Across the border in Mexico
stark silhouette of houses gutted by waves,
cliffs crumbling into the sea,
silver waves marbled with spume
gashing a hole under the border fence.
Miro el mar atacar
la cerca en Border Field Park
con sus buchones de agua,
an Easter Sunday resurrection
of the brown blood in my veins.

Oigo el llorido del mar, el respiro del aire,
my heart surges to the beat of the sea.
In the gray haze of the sun
the gulls' shrill cry of hunger,
the tangy smell of the sea seeping into me.

I walk through the hole in the fence
to the other side.
Under my fingers I feel the gritty wire
rusted by 139 years
of the salty breath of the sea.

Beneath the iron sky
Mexican children kick their soccer ball across,
run after it, entering the U.S.

I press my hand to the steel curtain—
chainlink fence crowned with rolled barbed wire—
rippling from the sea where Tijuana touches San Diego
unrolling over mountains
and plains
and deserts,
this "Tortilla Curtain" turning into *el río Grande*
flowing down to the flatlands
of the Magic Valley of South Texas
its mouth emptying into the Gulf.

1,950 mile-long open wound
dividing a *pueblo,* a culture,
running down the length of my body,
staking fence rods in my flesh,
splits me splits me
me raja me raja

This is my home
this thin edge of
barbwire.

But the skin of the earth is seamless.
The sea cannot be fenced,
el mar does not stop at borders.
To show the white man what she thought of his
arrogance,
Yemaya blew that wire fence down.

This land was Mexican once,
was Indian always
and is.
And will be again.

Yo soy un puente tendido
del mundo gabacho al del mojado,
lo pasado me estirá pa' 'trás
y lo presente pa' 'delante.
Que la Virgen de Guadalupe me cuide
Ay ay ay, soy mexicana de este lado.

The U.S.-Mexican border *es una herida abierta* where the Third World grates against the first and bleeds. And before a scab forms it hemorrhages again, the lifeblood of two worlds merging to form a third country—a border culture. Borders are set up to define the places that are safe and unsafe, to distinguish *us* from *them*. A border is a dividing line, a narrow strip along a steep edge. A borderland is a vague and undetermined place created by the emotional residue of an unnatural boundary. It is in a constant state of transition. The prohibited and forbidden are its inhabitants. *Los atravesados* live here: the squint-eyed, the perverse, the queer, the troublesome, the mongrel, the mulato, the half-breed, the half dead; in short, those who cross over, pass over, or go through the confines of the "normal." Gringos in the U.S. Southwest consider the inhabitants of the borderlands transgressors, aliens—whether they possess documents or not, whether they're Chicanos, Indians or Blacks. Do not enter, trespassers will be raped, maimed, strangled, gassed, shot. The only "legitimate" inhabitants are those in power, the whites and those who align themselves with whites. Tension grips the inhabitants of the borderlands like a virus. Ambivalence and unrest reside there and death is no stranger.

In the fields, *la migra*. My aunt saying, "*No corran*, don't run. They'll think you're *del otro lao*." In the confusion, Pedro ran, terrified of being caught. He couldn't speak English, couldn't tell them he was fifth generation American. *Sin papeles*—he did not carry his birth certificate to work in the fields. *La migra* took him away while we watched. *Se lo llevaron*. He tried to smile when he looked back at us, to raise his fist. But I saw the shame pushing his head down, I saw the terrible weight of shame hunch his shoulders. They deported him to Guadalajara by plane. The furthest he'd ever been to Mexico was Reynosa, a small border town opposite Hidalgo, Texas, not far from McAllen. Pedro walked all the way to the Valley. *Se lo llevaron sin un centavo al pobre. Se vino andando desde Guadalajara.*

During the original peopling of the Americas, the first inhabitants migrated across the Bering Straits and walked south across the continent. The oldest evidence of humankind in the U.S.—the Chicanos' ancient Indian ancestors—was found in Texas and has been dated to 35000 B.C.. In the Southwest United States archeologists have found 20,000-year-old campsites of the Indians who migrated through, or permanently occupied, the Southwest, Aztlán—land of the herons, land of whiteness, the Edenic place of origin of the Azteca.

In 1000 B.C., descendants of the original Cochise people migrated into what is now Mexico and Central America and became the direct ancestors of many of the Mexican people. (The Cochise culture of the Southwest is the parent culture of the Aztecs. The Uto-Aztecan languages stemmed from the language of the Cochise people.)[2] The Aztecs (the Nahuatl word for people of Aztlán) left the Southwest in 1168 A.D.

Now let us go.
Tihueque, tihueque,
Vámonos, vámonos.
Un pájaro cantó.
Con sus ocho tribus salieron
de la "cueva del origen."
los aztecas siguieron al dios
Huitzilopochtli.

Huitzilopochtli, the God of War, guided them to the place (that later became Mexico City) where an eagle with a writhing serpent in its beak perched on a cactus. The eagle symbolizes the spirit (as the sun, the father); the serpent symbolizes the soul (as the earth, the mother). Together, they symbolize the struggle between the spiritual/celestial/male and the underworld/earth/feminine. The symbolic sacrifice of the serpent to the "higher" masculine powers indicates that the patriarchal order had already vanquished the feminine and matriarchal order in pre–Columbian America.

At the beginning of the 16th century, the Spaniards and Hernán Cortés invaded Mexico and, with the help of tribes that the Aztecs had subjugated, conquered it. Before the Conquest, there were twenty-five million Indian people in Mexico and the Yucatán. Immediately after the Conquest, the Indian population had been reduced to under seven million. By 1650, only one-and-a-half-million pure-blooded Indians remained. The *mestizos* who were genetically equipped to survive small pox, measles, and typhus (Old World diseases to

[2]Besides the Aztecs, the Ute, Gabrillino of California, Pima of Arizona, some Pueblo of New Mexico, Comanche of Texas, Opata of Sonora, Tarahumara of Sinaloa and Durango, and the Huichol of Jalisco speak Uto-Aztecan languages and are descended from the Cochise people.

which the natives had no immunity), founded a new hybrid race and inherited Central and South America. *En 1521 nacio una nueva raza, el mestizo, el mexicano* (people of mixed Indian and Spanish blood), a race that had never existed before. Chicanos, Mexican-Americans, are the offspring of those first matings.

Our Spanish, Indian, and *mestizo* ancestors explored and settled parts of the U.S. Southwest as early as the sixteenth century. For every gold-hungry *conquistador* and soul-hungry missionary who came north from Mexico, ten to twenty Indians and *mestizos* went along as porters or in other capacities. For the Indians, this constituted a return to the place of origin, Aztlán, thus making Chicanos originally and secondarily indigenous to the Southwest. Indians and *mestizos* from central Mexico intermarried with North American Indians. The continual intermarriage between Mexican and American Indians and Spaniards formed an even greater *mestizaje*.

EL DESTIERRO/THE LOST LAND

Entonces corré la sangre
no sabe el indio que hacer,
le van a quitar su tierra,
la tiene que defender,
el indio se cae muerto,
y el afuerino de pie.
Levántate, Manquilef.

Arauco tiene una pena
más negra que su chamal,
ya no son los españoles
los que les hacen llorar,
hoy son los propios chilenos
los que les quitan su pan.
Levántate, Pailahuan.

—Violeta Parra, "*Arauco tiene una pena*"

In the 1800s, Anglos migrated illegally into Texas, which was then part of Mexico, in greater and greater numbers and gradually drove the *tejanos* (native Texans of Mexican descent) from their lands, committing all manner of atrocities against them. Their illegal invasion forced Mexico to fight a war to keep its Texas territory. The Battle of the Alamo, in which the Mexican forces vanquished the whites, became, for the whites, the symbol for the cowardly and villainous character of the Mexicans. It became (and still is) a symbol that legitimized the white imperialist takeover. With the capture of Santa Anna later in 1836, Texas became a republic. *Tejanos* lost their land and, overnight, became the foreigners.

Ya la mitad del terreno
les vendió el traidor Santa Anna,
con lo que se ha hecho muy rica
la nación americana.

¿Qué acaso no se conforman
con el oro de las minas?
Ustedes muy elegantes
y aquí nosotros en ruinas.
—from the Mexican corrido,
"Del peligro de la Intervención"

In 1846, the U.S. incited Mexico to war. U.S. troops invaded and occupied Mexico, forcing her to give up almost half of her nation, what is now Texas, New Mexico, Arizona, Colorado and California.

With the victory of the U.S. forces over the Mexican in the U.S.-Mexican War, *los norteamericanos* pushed the Texas border down 100 miles, from *el río Nueces* to *el río Grande*. South Texas ceased to be part of the Mexican state of Tamaulipas. Separated from Mexico, the Native Mexican-Texan no longer looked toward Mexico as home; the Southwest became our homeland once more. The border fence that divides the Mexican people was born on February 2, 1848 with the signing of the Treaty of Guadalupe-Hidalgo. It left 100,000 Mexican citizens on this side, annexed by conquest along with the land. The land established by the treaty as belonging to Mexicans was soon swindled away from its owners. The treaty was never honored and restitution, to this day, has never been made.

The justice and benevolence of God
will forbid that . . . Texas should again
become a howling wilderness
trod only by savages, or . . . benighted
by the ignorance and superstition,
the anarchy and rapine of Mexican misrule.
The Anglo-American race are destined
to be forever the proprietors of
this land of promise and fulfillment.
Their laws will govern it,
their learning will enlighten it,
their enterprise will improve it.
Their flocks range its boundless pastures,
for them its fertile lands will yield . . .
luxuriant harvests . . .
The wilderness of Texas has been redeemed
by Anglo-American blood & enterprise.
—William H. Wharton

The Gringo, locked into the fiction of white superiority, seized complete political power, stripping Indians and Mexicans of their land while their feet were still rooted in it. *Con el destierro y el exilo fuimos desuñados, destroncados, destripados*—we were jerked out by the roots, truncated, disemboweled, dispossessed, and separated from our identity and our history. Many, under the threat of Anglo terrorism, abandoned homes and ranches and went to Mexico. Some stayed and protested. But as the courts, law enforcement officials, and government officials not only ignored their pleas but penalized them for their efforts, *tejanos* had no other recourse but armed retaliation.

After Mexican-American resisters robbed a train in Brownsville, Texas on October 18, 1915, Anglo vigilante groups began lynching Chicanos. Texas Rangers would take them into the brush and shoot them. One hundred Chicanos were killed in a matter of months, whole families lynched. Seven thousand fled to Mexico, leaving their small ranches and farms. The Anglos, afraid that the *mexicanos*[3] would seek independence from the U.S., brought in 20,000 army troops to put an end to the social protest movement in South Texas. Race hatred had finally fomented into an all out war.

My grandmother lost all her cattle,
they stole her land.

"Drought hit South Texas," my mother tells me. "*La tierra se puso bien secaylos animales comenzaron a morrirse de se'. Mi papáse murío de un* heart attack *dejando a mamá* pregnant *y con ocho huercos,* with eight kids and one on the way. *Yo fuí la mayor, tenía diez años.* The next year the drought continued *y el ganado* got hoof and mouth. *Se calleron* in droves *en las pastas y el* brushland, *pansas blancas* ballooning to the skies. *El siguiente año* still no rain. *Mi pobre madre viuda perdió* two-thirds of her *ganado.* A smart *gabacho* lawyer took the land away *mamá* hadn't paid taxes. *No hablaba inglés,* she didn't know how to ask for time to raise the money." My father's mother, Mama Locha, also lost her *terreno.* For a while we got $12.50 a year for the "mineral rights" of six acres of cemetery, all that was left of the ancestral lands. Mama Locha had asked that we bury her there beside her husband. *El cemeterio estaba cercado.* But there was a fence around the cemetery, chained and padlocked by the ranch owners of the surrounding land. We couldn't even get in to visit the graves, much less bury her there. Today, it is still padlocked. The sign reads: "Keep out. Trespassers will be shot."

In the 1930s, after Anglo agribusiness corporations cheated the small Chicano landowners of their land, the corporations hired gangs of *mexicanos* to pull out the brush, chaparral and cactus and to irrigate the desert. The land they toiled over had once belonged to many of them, or had been used communally by them. Later the Anglos brought in huge machines and root plows and had the Mexicans scrape the land clean of natural vegetation. In my childhood I saw the end of dryland farming. I witnessed the land cleared; saw the huge pipes connected to underwater sources sticking up in the air. As children, we'd go fishing in some of those canals when they were full and hunt for snakes in them when they were dry. In the 1950s I saw the land, cut up into thousands of neat rectangles and squares, constantly being irrigated. In the 340-day growth season, the seeds of any kind of fruit or vegetable had only to be stuck in the ground in order to grow. More big land corporations came in and bought up the remaining land.

[3]The Plan of San Diego, Texas, drawn up on January 6, 1915, called for the independence and segregation of the states bordering Mexico: Texas, New Mexico, Arizona, Colorado, and California. Indians would get their land back, Blacks would get six states from the south and form their own independent republic.

To make a living my father became a sharecropper. Rio Farms Incorporated loaned him seed money and living expenses. At harvest time, my father repaid the loan and forked over 40% of the earnings. Sometimes we earned less than we owed, but always the corporations fared well. Some had major holdings in vegetable trucking, livestock auctions and cotton gins. Altogether we lived on three successive Rio farms; the second was adjacent to the King Ranch and included a dairy farm; the third was a chicken farm. I remember the white feathers of three thousand Leghorn chickens blanketing the land for acres around. My sister, mother and I cleaned, weighed and packaged eggs. (For years afterwards I couldn't stomach the sight of an egg.) I remember my mother attending some of the meetings sponsored by well-meaning whites from Rio Farms. They talked about good nutrition, health, and held huge barbeques. The only thing salvaged for my family from those years are modern techniques of food canning and a food-stained book they printed made up of recipes from Rio Farms' Mexican women. How proud my mother was to have her recipe for *enchiladas coloradas* in a book.

El cruzar del mojado/Illegal Crossing

> *"Ahora si ya tengo una tumba para llorar,"*
> *dice Conchita,* upon being reunited with
> her unknown mother just before the mother dies
> —from Ismael Rodriguez' film,
> *Nosotros los pobres*[4]

La crisis. Los gringos had not stopped at the border. By the end of the nineteenth century, powerful landowners in Mexico, in partnership with U.S. colonizing companies, had dispossessed millions of Indians of their lands. Currently, Mexico and her eighty million citizens are almost completely dependent on the U.S. market. The Mexican government and wealthy growers are in partnership with such American conglomerates as American Motors, IT&T and Du Pont which own factories called *maquiladoras.* One-fourth of all Mexicans work at *maquiladoras;* most are young women. Next to oil, *maquiladoras* are Mexico's second greatest source of U.S. dollars. Working eight to twelve hours a day to wire in backup lights of U.S. autos or solder miniscule wires in TV sets is not the Mexican way. While the women are in the *maquiladoras,* the children are left on their own. Many roam the street, become part of *cholo* gangs. The infusion of the values of the white culture, coupled with the exploitation by that culture, is changing the Mexican way of life.

The devaluation of the *peso* and Mexico's dependency on the U.S. have brought on what the Mexicans call *la crisis. No hay trabajo.* Half of the Mexican people are unemployed. In the U.S. a man or woman can make eight times what they can in Mexico. By March, 1987, 1,088 pesos were worth one U.S. dollar. I remember when I was growing up in Texas how we'd cross the border at Reynosa or Progreso to buy sugar or medicines when the dollar was worth eight *pesos* and fifty *centavos.*

[4]*Nosotros los pobres* was the first Mexican film that was truly Mexican and not an imitation European film. It stressed the devotion and love that children should have for their mother and how its lack would lead to the dissipation of their character. This film spawned a generation of mother-devotion/ungrateful-sons films.

La travesía. For many *mexicanos del otro lado,* the choice is to stay in Mexico and starve or move north and live. *Dicen que cada mexicano siempre sueña de la conquista en los brazos de cuatro gringas rubias, la conquista del país poderoso del norte, los Estados Unidos. En cada Chicano y mexicano vive el mito del tesoro territorial perdido.* North Americans call this return to the homeland the silent invasion.

> "A la cueva volverán"
> —El Puma *en la cancion "Amalia"*

South of the border, called North America's rubbish dump by Chicanos, *mexicanos* congregate in the plazas to talk about the best way to cross. Smugglers, *coyotes, pasadores, enganchadores* approach these people or are sought out by them. "*¿Qué dicen muchachos a echársela de mojado?*"

> "Now among the alien gods with
> weapons of magic am I."
> —Navajo protection song,
> sung when going into battle.

We have a tradition of migration, a tradition of long walks. Today we are witnessing *la migración de los pueblos mexicanos,* the return odyssey to the historical/mythological Aztlán. This time, the traffic is from south to north.

El retorno to the promised land first began with the Indians from the interior of Mexico and the *mestizos* that came with the *conquistadores* in the 1500s. Immigration continued in the next three centuries, and, in this century, it continued with the *braceros* who helped to build our railroads and who picked our fruit. Today thousands of Mexicans are crossing the border legally and illegally; ten million people without documents have returned to the Southwest.

Faceless, nameless, invisible, taunted with "Hey cucaracho" (cockroach). Trembling with fear, yet filled with courage, a courage born of desperation. Barefoot and uneducated, Mexicans with hands like boot soles gather at night by the river where two worlds merge creating what Reagan calls a frontline, a war zone. The convergence has created a shock culture, a border culture, a third country, a closed country.

Without benefit of bridges, the "*mojados*" (wetbacks) float on inflatable rafts across *el río Grande,* or wade or swim across naked, clutching their clothes over their heads. Holding onto the grass, they pull themselves along the banks with a prayer to *Virgen de Guadalupe* on their lips: *Ay virgencita morena, mi madrecita, dame tu bendición.*

The Border Patrol hides behind the local McDonalds on the outskirts of Brownsville, Texas or some other border town. They set traps around the river beds beneath the bridge. Hunters in army-green uniforms stalk and track these economic refugees by the powerful nightvision of electronic sensing devices planted in the ground or mounted on Border Patrol vans. Cornered by flashlights, frisked while their arms stretch over their heads, *los mojados* are handcuffed, locked in jeeps, and then kicked back across the border.

One out of every three is caught. Some return to enact their rite of passage as many as three times a day. Some of those who make it across undetected fall prey to Mexican robbers such as those in Smugglers' Canyon on the American side of the border near Tijuana. As refugees in a homeland that does not want them, many find a welcome hand holding out only suffering, pain, and ignoble death.

Those who make it past the checking points of the Border Patrol find themselves in the midst of 150 years of racism in Chicano *barrios* in the Southwest and in big northern cities. Living in a no-man's-borderland, caught between being treated as criminals and being able to eat, between resistance and deportation, the illegal refugees are some of the poorest and the most exploited of any people in the U.S. It is illegal for Mexicans to work without green cards. But big farming combines, farm bosses and smugglers who bring them in make money off the "wetbacks"' labor—they don't have to pay federal minimum wages, or ensure adequate housing or sanitary conditions.

The Mexican woman is especially at risk. Often the *coyote* (smuggler) doesn't feed her for days or let her go to the bathroom. Often he rapes her or sells her into prostitution. She cannot call on county or state health or economic resources because she doesn't know English and she fears deportation. American employers are quick to take advantage of her helplessness. She can't go home. She's sold her house, her furniture, borrowed from friends in order to pay the *coyote* who charges her four or five thousand dollars to smuggle her to Chicago. She may work as a live-in maid for white, Chicano or Latino households for as little as $15 a week. Or work in the garment industry, do hotel work. Isolated and worried about her family back home, afraid of getting caught and deported, living with as many as fifteen people in one room, the *mexicana* suffers serious health problems. *Se enferma de los nervios, de alta presión.*

La mojada, la mujer indocumentada, is doubly threatened in this country. Not only does she have to contend with sexual violence, but like all women, she is prey to a sense of physical helplessness. As a refugee, she leaves the familiar and safe homeground to venture into unknown and possibly dangerous terrain.

This is her home
this thin edge of
barbwire.

1987

Jamaica Kincaid 1949–

In her lifetime journey from the Caribbean island of Antigua, where she was born, to the rural town of Bennington, Vermont, where she now lives and teaches, Jamaica Kincaid has created a distinctive body of work that has earned both praise and perplexity from her readers. The lyrical prose of her early short stories and novels eloquently describes the pain of adolescent longing for maternal love and a childish bewilderment with the adult world of work and relationship, as well as the natural world of death. Her work has been praised by the writer Susan Sontag for its "emotional truthfulness" and by the novelist and short-story writer David Leavitt for "its potent imagination." But other reviewers have focused on what they perceive as Kincaid's unforgiving rage at both her mother and her homeland

and questioned her unending bitterness. None of it seems to matter to Kincaid, who once said in an interview, "I never think of the audience. I never think of people reading. I never think of people, period."

Kincaid's writing is grounded in autobiographical roots, and her language sings with the rhythms of her island upbringing. "For me, everything passes through the self," she has said. Born Elaine Potter Richardson on May 25, 1949, she was her parents' only child until the age of nine. The special intimacy of that solitary relationship with her mother, and the ensuing tensions within that bond as Kincaid grew older and as three other children entered the family, set up the themes of stories like "Girl" and "Wingless" and of novels like Annie John *(1983) and* The Autobiography of My Mother *(1996). Kincaid explores again and again how her mother's controlling and cruel behavior ultimately destroyed any love between them. She also expands on that matriarchal theme, dissecting with searing insight the relationship between an abusive maternal power and the power wielded by the mother country of England as it dominated and disciplined its island colony. In her book-length essay,* A Small Place *(1988), Kincaid condemns England for its "criminal" oppression of her people and criticizes Antigua for its acquiescence to that crime. Some reviewers were shocked by the harshness of her critique, but Kincaid made no apologies. In a 1997 interview in* Mother Jones, *she remarked: "I think in many ways the problem that my writing would have with an American reviewer is that Americans find difficulty very hard to take. They are inevitably looking for a happy ending. Perversely, I will not give the happy ending. I think life is difficult and that's that. I am not at all—absolutely not at all—interested in the pursuit of happiness."*

Kincaid came to America at the age of seventeen to work as an au pair *and send money back to her impoverished family in Antigua. The experience shaped the central plot and emotional themes of her novel* Lucy *(1990). But feeling like a servant and depressed by the isolation, Kincaid left that position to live in New York City, where she held several jobs and enrolled in community college and photography courses. Though she won a scholarship to Franconia College in New Hampshire, she stayed only one year, returning to New York and finding work as a writer for the* Village Voice *and* Ingenue. *These various experiences honed the skills of lucid observation and evocative description that would characterize her future writing. They also put greater distance between her and her homeland, and when she changed her name to Jamaica Kincaid in 1973, it was, she says, "a way for me to do things without being the same person who couldn't do them—the same person who had all these weights."*

Her big break as a writer came in 1976 when an editor from the New Yorker *saw her work and hired her. Kincaid's writing for the magazine's feature column "Talk of the Town," collected in her* Talk Stories *(2001), served as her "apprenticeship," she says. In 1978, the* New Yorker *published her first short story, "Girl," and by the time her first collection, the award-winning* At the Bottom of the River, *was published five years later, her talent had come into full bloom.*

Since then, Kincaid has received numerous accolades for her passionate and emotionally powerful prose. Like the writers Toni Morrison, Sandra Cisneros, and Maxine Hong Kingston, she has been the recipient of an Anisfield Wolf Book Award (1997), which honors work that exposes racism and explores the richness of human diversity. Those early haunting themes of loss and longing continue to characterize Kincaid's work, especially her painful 1997 narrative of her relationship with a brother dying of AIDS, and her most recent novel, Mr. Potter *(2002), in which she once again travels to her childhood home to explore the patterns of family and national history.*

But other works, like My Garden (Book) *(1999), a collection of Kincaid's many meditations on one of her most passionate hobbies, convey a deepening sense of contentment and security: "The garden is for me an exercise in memory, a way of remembering my own immediate past, a way of getting to a past that is my own (the Caribbean sea) and the past as it is indirectly related to me (the conquest of Mexico and its surroundings)." Married and the mother of two children, Kincaid seems to have made peace with her memories, even if it is the peace of an exile in a new home.*

FURTHER READING: *Annie John,* 1983; *A Small Place,* 1988; *Lucy,* 1990; *Autobiography of My Mother,* 1996; *My Brother,* 1997; *My Garden (Book)*,1999; *Talk Stories,* 2001; M. Ferguson, *Jamaica Kincaid: Where the Land Meets the Body,* 1994; L. Paravisini Gebert, *Jamaica Kincaid: A Critical Companion,* 1994; D. Simmons, *Jamaica Kincaid,* 1994; *Jamaica Kincaid,* ed. H. Bloom, 1998; A. MacDonald-Smythe, *Making Homes in the West/Indies: Constructions of Subjectivity in the Writings of Michelle Cliff and Jamaica Kincaid,* 2001; J. Bouson, *Jamaica Kincaid: Writing Memory, Writing Back to the Mother,* 2005.

TEXT: *At the Bottom of the River,* 1983.

GIRL

Wash the white clothes on Monday and put them on the stone heap; wash the color clothes on Tuesday and put them on the clothesline to dry; don't walk barehead in the hot sun; cook pumpkin fritters in very hot sweet oil; soak your little cloths right after you take them off; when buying cotton to make yourself a nice blouse, be sure that it doesn't have gum on it, because that way it won't hold up well after a wash; soak salt fish overnight before you cook it; is it true that you sing benna in Sunday school?; always eat your food in such a way that it won't turn someone else's stomach; on Sundays try to walk like a lady and not like the slut you are so bent on becoming; don't sing benna in Sunday school; you mustn't speak to wharf-rat boys, not even to give directions; don't eat fruits on the street—flies will follow you; *but I don't sing benna on Sundays at all and never in Sunday school*; this is how to sew on a button; this is how to make a button-hole for the button you have just sewed on; this is how to hem a dress when you see the hem coming down and so to prevent yourself from looking like the slut I know you are so bent on becoming; this is how you iron your father's khaki shirt so that it doesn't have a crease; this is how you iron your father's khaki pants so that they don't have a crease; this is how you grow okra—far from the house, because okra tree harbors red ants; when you are growing dasheen, make sure it gets plenty of water or else it makes your throat itch when you are eating it; this is how you sweep a corner; this is how you sweep a whole house; this is how you sweep a yard; this is how you smile to someone you don't like too much; this is how you smile to someone you don't like at all; this is how you smile to someone you like completely; this is how you set a table for tea; this is how you set a table for dinner; this is how you set a table for dinner with an important guest; this is how you set a table for lunch; this is how you set a table for breakfast; this is how to behave in the presence of men who don't know you very well, and this way they won't recognize immediately the slut I have warned you against becoming; be sure to wash every day, even if it is with your own spit; don't squat down to play marbles—you are not a boy, you know; don't pick people's flowers—you might catch something; don't throw stones at blackbirds, because it might not be a blackbird at all; this is how to make a bread pudding;

this is how to make doukona; this is how to make pepper pot; this is how to make a good medicine for a cold; this is how to make a good medicine to throw away a child before it even becomes a child; this is how to catch a fish; this is how to throw back a fish you don't like, and that way something bad won't fall on you; this is how to bully a man; this is how a man bullies you; this is how to love a man, and if this doesn't work there are other ways, and if they don't work don't feel too bad about giving up; this is how to spit up in the air if you feel like it, and this is how to move quick so that it doesn't fall on you; this is how to make ends meet; always squeeze bread to make sure it's fresh; *but what if the baker won't let me feel the bread?*; you mean to say that after all you are really going to be the kind of woman who the baker won't let near the bread?

1978 1983

WINGLESS

The small children are reading from a book filled with simple words and sentences.

"'Once upon a time there was a little chimney-sweep, whose name was Tom.'"

"'He cried half his time, and laughed the other half.'"

"'You would have been giddy, perhaps, at looking down: but Tom was not.'"

"'You, of course, would have been very cold sitting there on a September night, without the least bit of clothes on your wet back; but Tom was a water-baby, and therefore felt cold no more than a fish.'"

The children have already learned to write their names in beautiful penmanship. They have already learned how many farthings make a penny, how many pennies make a shilling, how many shillings make a pound, how many days in April, how many stone in a ton. Now they singsong here and tumble there, tearing skirts with swift movements. Must Dulcie really cry after thirteen of her play chums have sat on her? There, Dulcie, there. I myself have been kissed by many rude boys with small, damp lips, on their way to boys' drill. I myself have humped girls under my mother's house. But I swim in a shaft of light, upside down, and I can see myself clearly, through and through, from every angle. Perhaps I stand on the brink of a great discovery, and perhaps after I have made my great discovery I will be sent home in chains. Then again, perhaps my life is as predictable as an insect's and I am in my pupa stage. How low can I sink, then? That woman over there, that large-bottomed woman, is important to me. It's for her that I save up my sixpences instead of spending for sweets. Is this a love like no other? And what pain have I caused her? And does she love me? My needs are great, I can see. But there are the children again (of which I am one), shrieking, whether in pain or pleasure I cannot tell. The children, who are beautiful in groupings of three, and who only last night pleaded with their mothers to sing softly to them, are today maiming each other. The children at the end of the day have sour necks, frayed hair, dirt under their fingernails, scuffed shoes, torn clothing. And why? First they must be children.

I shall grow up to be a tall, graceful, and altogether beautiful woman, and I shall impose on large numbers of people my will and also, for my own amusement, great pain. But now. I shall try to see clearly. I shall try to tell differences. I shall try to distinguish the subtle gradations of color in fine cloth, of fingernail length, of manners. That woman over there. Is she cruel? Does she love me? And if not, can I make her? I am not yet tall, beautiful, graceful, and able to impose my will. Now I swim in a shaft of light and can see myself clearly. The schoolhouse is yellow and stands among big green-leaved trees. Inside are our desks and a woman who wears spectacles, playing the piano. Is a girl who can sing "Gaily the troubadour plucked his guitar" in a pleasing way worthy of being my best friend? There is the same girl, unwashed and glistening, setting traps for talking birds. Is she to be one of my temptations? Oh, this must be a love like no other. But how can my limbs that hate be the same limbs that love? How can the same limbs that make me blind make me see? I am defenseless and small. I shall try to see clearly. I shall try to separate and divide things as if they were sums, as if they were drygoods on the grocer's shelves. Is this my mother? Is she here to embarrass me? What shall I say about her behind her back, when she isn't there, long after she has gone? In her smile lies her goodness. Will I always remember that? Am I horrid? And if so, will I always be that way? Not getting my own way causes me to fret so, I clench my fist. My charm is limited, and I haven't learned to smile yet. I have picked many flowers and then deliberately torn them to shreds, petal by petal. I am so unhappy, my face is so wet, and still I can stand up and walk and tell lies in the face of terrible punishments. I can see the great danger in what I am—a defenseless and pitiful child. Here is a list of what I must do. So is my life to be like an apprenticeship in dressmaking, a thorny path to carefully follow or avoid? Inside, standing around the spectacled woman playing the piano, the children are singing a song in harmony. The children's voices: pinks, blues, yellows, violets, all suspended. All is soft, all is embracing, all is comforting. And yet I myself, at my age, have suffered so. My tears, big, have run down my cheeks in uneven lines—my tears, big, and my hands too small to hold them. My tears have been the result of my disappointments. My disappointments stand up and grow ever taller. They will not be lost to me. There they are. Let me pin tags on them. Let me have them registered, like newly domesticated animals. Let me cherish my disappointments, fold them up, tuck them away, close to my breast, because they are so important to me.

But again I swim in a shaft of light, upside down, and I can see myself clearly, through and through, from every angle. Over there, I stand on the brink of a great discovery, and it is possible that like an ancient piece of history my presence will leave room for theories. But who will say? For days my body has been collecting water, but still I won't cry. What is that to me? I am not yet a woman with a terrible and unwanted burden. I am not yet a dog with a cruel and unloving master. I am not yet a tree growing on barren and bitter land. I am not yet the shape of darkness in a dungeon.

Where? What? Why? How then? Oh, that!

I am primitive and wingless.

"Don't eat the strings on bananas—they will wrap around your heart and kill you."

"Oh. Is that true?"

"No."

"Is that something to tell children?"

"No. But it's so funny. You should see how you look trying to remove all the strings from the bananas with your monkey fingernails. Frightened?"

"Frightened. Very frightened."

Today, keeping a safe distance, I followed the woman I love when she walked on a carpet of pond lilies. As she walked, she ate some black nuts, pond-lily black nuts. She walked for a long time, saying what must be wonderful things to herself. Then in the middle of the pond she stopped, because a man had stood up suddenly in front of her. I could see that he wore clothes made of tree bark and sticks in his ears. He said things to her and I couldn't make them out, but he said them to her so forcefully that drops of brown water sprang from his mouth. The woman I love put her hands over her ears, shielding herself from the things he said. Then he put wind in his cheeks and blew himself up until in the bright sun he looked like a boil, and the woman I love put her hands over her eyes, shielding herself from the way he looked. Then, instead of removing her cutlass from the folds of her big and beautiful skirt and cutting the man in two at the waist, she only smiled—a red, red smile—and like a fly he dropped dead.

The sea, the shimmering pink-colored sand, the swimmers with hats, two people walking arm in arm, talking in each other's face, dots of water landing on noses, the sea spray on ankles, on over-developed calves, the blue, the green, the black, so deep, so smooth, a great and swift undercurrent, glassy, the white wavelets, a storm so blinding that the salt got in our eyes, the sea turning inside out, shaking everything up like a bottle with sediment, a boat with two people heaving a brown package overboard, the mystery, the sharp teeth of that yellow spotted eel, the wriggle, the smooth lines, open mouths, families of great noisy birds, families of great noisy people, families of biting flies, the sea, following me home, snapping at my heels, all the way to the door, the sea, the woman.

"I have frightened you? Again, you are frightened of me?"

"You have frightened me. I am very frightened of you."

"Oh, you should see your face. I wish you could see your face. How you make me laugh."

And what are my fears? What large cows! When I see them coming, shall I run and hide face down in the gutter? Are they really cows? Can I stand in a field of tall grass and see nothing for miles and miles? On the other hand, the sky, which is big and blue as always, has its limits. This afternoon the wind is loud as in a hurricane. There isn't enough light. There is a noise—I can't tell where it is coming from. A big box has stamped on it "Handle Carefully." I have been in a big white building with curving corridors. I have passed a dead person. There is the woman I love, who is so much bigger than me.

That mosquito . . . now a stain on the wall. That lizard, running up and down, up and down . . . now so still. That ant, bloated and sluggish, a purseful of eggs in its jaws . . . now so still. That blue-and-green bird, head held aloft, singing . . . now so still. That land crab, moving slowly, softly, even beautifully, sideways . . . but now so still. That cricket, standing on a tree stem, so ugly, so revolting, I am made so unhappy . . . now so still. That mongoose, now asleep in its hole, now stealing the sleeping chickens, moving so quickly, its eyes like two grains of light . . . now so still. That fly, moving so contentedly from tea bun to tea bun . . . now so still. That butterfly, moving contentedly from beautiful plant to beautiful plant in the early-morning sun . . . now so still. That tadpole, swimming playfully in the shallow water . . . now so still.

I shall cast a shadow and I shall remain unaware.

My hands, brown on this side, pink on this side, now indiscriminately dangerous, now vagabond and prodigal, now cruel and careless, now without remorse or forgiveness, but now innocently slipping into a dress with braided sleeves, now holding an ice-cream cone, now reaching up with longing, now clasped in prayer, now feeling for reassurance, now pleading my desires, now pleasing, and now, even now, so still in bed, in sleep.

1978 1983

Louise Erdrich 1954–

Louise Erdrich has received wide critical acclaim for her novels portraying the lives of Indians and whites living in North Dakota over the past century. The first novel, Love Medicine *(1984, 1993), a series of interconnected stories, follows members of two Chippewa families living on the Turtle Mountain Reservation in North Dakota from the 1930s to the 1980s. A great critical success, the novel was translated into eighteen languages and became an international bestseller. The next in the series,* The Beet Queen *(1986), deals with Native Americans only indirectly while concentrating on the lives of Americans of Polish and German descent living in the small-town world of North Dakota. In her third novel,* Tracks *(1988), set at the turn of the century, and her fourth novel,* The Bingo Palace *(1994), set in the present day, Erdrich returns to the Indian characters introduced in* Love Medicine, *completing her account of the lives of small-town whites and three generations of Native Americans.*

Erdrich's narratives exist both as independent short stories and as extended tales in a loosely connected fictional cycle, a form that is traditional in Indian storytelling. Erdrich, of Chippewa descent, describes herself as "half German American and half French-Indian," but insists that her stories are not simply autobiographical. Rather, her work has developed out of the narrative traditions and storytelling cycles of the Native American people with whom she was raised. She was born in Little Falls, Minnesota, and spent her childhood in the small town of Wahpeton, North Dakota. Her mother and father were teachers in an Indian school run by the U.S. Bureau of Indian Affairs. They told her stories of the Indian and white communities of which she was a part and encouraged her to read and to write her own stories. She often visited her maternal grandparents on the Turtle Mountain Reservation in North Dakota, and she later acknowledged that "the people in our families made everything into a story. They love to tell a good story. . . . people just sit and the stories start coming, one after another."

When she was eighteen Erdrich won a scholarship to Dartmouth College, which had just instituted a new program in Native American studies. At Dartmouth she won prizes for her short stories and poetry and saw her writing published for the first time, in college literary magazines. After graduation she worked as a school teacher, waitress, short-order cook, even as a flagger on a construction site, absorbing the experiences that would later appear as illuminating details in her fiction. In 1979 she entered the creative writing program at Johns Hopkins University, graduating with a master's degree in 1980. She then worked as an editor of an Indian council newspaper in Boston, and in 1981 was appointed writer-in-residence at Dartmouth. In that same year she married Michael Dorris, an anthropologist and writer who was a professor of Native American studies at Dartmouth. Until his death, the couple worked in a collaboration that resulted in the publication of more than twenty volumes.

Erdrich's novel Tales of Burning Love *(1996) revisits the people and the scenes of middle-western America that she portrayed in her most noted work of fiction,* Love Medicine. *Her sixth novel,* The Antelope Wife *(1998), portrays the agonies and complexities of life for Native Americans living in the foreign world of Big City America. One of Erdrich's most recent works,* The Last Report on the Miracles at Little No Horse *(2001)—a tale about a woman who lives most of her life as a Catholic mission priest—is again set in the same fictional town as* Love Medicine. *One of the most prolific of American writers, Erdrich has published three additional novels since 2001:* The Master Butcher's Singing Club *(2003),* Four Souls *(2004), and* The Painted Drum *(2005). Recently, in addition to fiction, she has published* The Blue Jay's Dance, A Birth Year *(1995), a yearlong journal mixed with nature essays and meditations on motherhood, and several volumes of poetry, including* Jacklight *(1984),* Baptism of Desire *(1998), and* Original Fire, Selected and New Poems *(2003).*

Erdrich has acknowledged a desire to "undermine" the stereotypical images of the Indian so strongly embedded in American popular culture: the oversimplified visions of Native Americans as picture-gallery oddities and exotics, the noble savages, dying braves, and love-torn Indian maidens of romantic novels, motion pictures, and television. She attempts to portray the strengths and weaknesses of Native American culture as it exists on reservations where the intrusion of the non-Indian world creates cross-cultural confusions and controversies. Her characters show all the strengths and the weaknesses of Native Americans living in complex relationships with each other and with an outside world of sometimes overwhelming dimensions.

Erdrich has been criticized for lacking "political commitment" and for failing to use her writing to advance constantly the cause of Indian rights in the United States. Her response is that she has no desire to be "polemical" in her fiction, that she is not solely an "ethnic writer," and does not write exclusively about American Indians, adding, "I really consider myself a writer first. Then an Indian, or a woman, or a mother." Nonetheless, her greatest achievement has been to convey, with noteworthy humor and stylistic grace, the excitements and the bleak sadness of a people who must live in an uncertain world of shifting traditions, a people who are being altered by the urbanizing force of American industrial society but are at the same time sustaining a vital resistance to that external world, which with all its electronic and cultural potency has not yet silenced the many voices of native America.

FURTHER READING: J. Fleischner, *A Reader's Guide to the Fiction of Louise Erdrich,* 1994; P. Beidler and G. Barton, *A Reader's Guide to the Novels of Louise Erdrich,* 1999; *The Chippewa Landscape of Louise Erdrich,* ed. A. Chavkin, 1999; L. Stookey, *Louise Erdrich: A Critical Companion,* 1999; H. Wong, *Louise Erdrich's Love Medicine: A Casebook,* 2000; C. Jacobs, *The Novels of Louise Erdrich: Stories of Her People,* 2001; P. Hafen, *Reading Louise Erdrich's Love Medicine,* 2003.

TEXT: *Love Medicine,* 1993.

from *LOVE MEDICINE*

THE RED CONVERTIBLE (1974)

LYMAN LAMARTINE

I was the first one to drive a convertible on my reservation. And of course it was red, a red Olds. I owned that car along with my brother Henry Junior. We owned it together until his boots filled with water on a windy night and he bought out my share. Now Henry owns the whole car, and his younger brother Lyman (that's myself), Lyman walks everywhere he goes.

How did I earn enough money to buy my share in the first place? My one talent was I could always make money. I had a touch for it, unusual in a Chippewa. From the first I was different that way, and everyone recognized it. I was the only kid they let in the American Legion Hall to shine shoes, for example, and one Christmas I sold spiritual bouquets for the mission door to door. The nuns let me keep a percentage. Once I started, it seemed the more money I made the easier the money came. Everyone encouraged it. When I was fifteen I got a job washing dishes at the Joliet Café, and that was where my first big break happened.

It wasn't long before I was promoted to busing tables, and then the short-order cook quit and I was hired to take her place. No sooner than you know it I was managing the Joliet. The rest is history. I went on managing. I soon became part owner, and of course there was no stopping me then. It wasn't long before the whole thing was mine.

After I'd owned the Joliet for one year, it blew over in the worst tornado ever seen around here. The whole operation was smashed to bits. A total loss. The fryalator was up in a tree, the grill torn in half like it was paper. I was only sixteen. I had it all in my mother's name, and I lost it quick, but before I lost it I had every one of my relatives, and their relatives, to dinner, and I also bought that red Olds I mentioned, along with Henry.

The first time we saw it! I'll tell you when we first saw it. We had gotten a ride up to Winnipeg, and both of us had money. Don't ask me why, because we never mentioned a car or anything, we just had all our money. Mine was cash, a big bankroll from the Joliet's insurance. Henry had two checks—a week's extra pay for being laid off, and his regular check from the Jewel Bearing Plant.

We were walking down Portage anyway, seeing the sights, when we saw it. There it was, parked, large as life. Really as *if* it was alive. I thought of the word *repose,* because the car wasn't simply stopped, parked, or whatever. That car reposed, calm and gleaming, a FOR SALE sign in its left front window. Then, before we had thought it over at all, the car belonged to us and our pockets were empty. We had just enough money for gas back home.

We went places in that car, me and Henry. We took off driving all one whole summer. We started off toward the Little Knife River and Mandaree in Fort Berthold and then we found ourselves down in Wakpala somehow, and then suddenly we were over in Montana on the Rocky Boy, and yet the summer was not even half over. Some people hang on to details when they travel, but we didn't let them bother us and just lived our everyday lives here to there.

I do remember this one place with willows. I remember I laid under those trees and it was comfortable. So comfortable. The branches bent down all around me like a tent or a stable. And quiet, it was quiet, even though there was a powwow close enough so I could see it going on. The air was not too still, not too windy either. When the dust rises up and hangs in the air around the dancers like that, I feel good. Henry was asleep with his arms thrown wide. Later on, he woke up and we started driving again. We were somewhere in Montana, or maybe on the Blood Reserve—it could have been anywhere. Anyway it was where we met the girl.

All her hair was in buns around her ears, that's the first thing I noticed about her. She was posed alongside the road with her arm out, so we stopped. That girl was short, so short her lumber shirt looked comical on her, like a nightgown. She had jeans on and fancy moccasins and she carried a little suitcase.

"Hop on in," says Henry. So she climbs in between us.

"We'll take you home," I says. "Where do you live?"

"Chicken," she says.

"Where the hell's that?" I ask her.

"Alaska."

"Okay," says Henry, and we drive.

We got up there and never wanted to leave. The sun doesn't truly set there in summer, and the night is more a soft dusk. You might doze off, sometimes, but before you know it you're up again, like an animal in nature. You never feel like you have to sleep hard or put away the world. And things would grow up there. One day just dirt or moss, the next day flowers and long grass. The girl's name was Susy. Her family really took to us. They fed us and put us up. We had our own tent to live in by their house, and the kids would be in and out of there all day and night. They couldn't get over me and Henry being brothers, we looked so different. We told them we knew we had the same mother, anyway.

One night Susy came in to visit us. We sat around in the tent talking of this and that. The season was changing. It was getting darker by that time, and the cold was even getting just a little mean. I told her it was time for us to go. She stood up on a chair.

"You never seen my hair," Susy said.

That was true. She was standing on a chair, but still, when she unclipped her buns the hair reached all the way to the ground. Our eyes opened. You couldn't tell how much hair she had when it was rolled up so neatly. Then my brother Henry did something funny. He went up to the chair and said, "Jump on my shoulders." So she did that, and her hair reached down past his waist, and he started twirling, this way and that, so her hair was flung out from side to side.

"I always wondered what it was like to have long pretty hair," Henry says. Well we laughed. It was a funny sight, the way he did it. The next morning we got up and took leave of those people.

On to greener pastures, as they say. It was down through Spokane and across Idaho then Montana and very soon we were racing the weather right along under the Canadian border through Columbus, Des Lacs, and then we were in Bottineau County and soon home. We'd made most of the trip, that summer, without putting up the car hood at all. We got home just in time, it turned out, for the army to remember Henry had signed up to join it.

I don't wonder that the army was so glad to get my brother that they turned him into a Marine. He was built like a brick outhouse anyway. We liked to tease him that they really wanted him for his Indian nose. He had a nose big and sharp as a hatchet, like the nose on Red Tomahawk, the Indian who killed Sitting Bull, whose profile is on signs all along the North Dakota highways. Henry went off to training camp, came home once during Christmas, then the next thing you know we got an overseas letter from him. It was 1970, and he said he was stationed up in the northern hill country. Whereabouts I did not know. He wasn't such a hot letter writer, and only got off two before the enemy caught him. I could never keep it straight, which direction those good Vietnam soldiers were from.

I wrote him back several times, even though I didn't know if those letters would get through. I kept him informed all about the car. Most of the time I had it up on blocks in the yard or half taken apart, because that long trip did a hard job on it under the hood.

I always had good luck with numbers, and never worried about the draft myself. I never even had to think about what my number was. But Henry was never lucky in the same way as me. It was at least three years before Henry came home. By then I guess the whole war was solved in the government's mind, but for him it would keep on going. In those years I'd put his car into almost perfect shape. I always thought of it as his car while he was gone, even though when he left he said, "Now it's yours," and threw me his key.

"Thanks for the extra key," I'd said. "I'll put it up in your drawer just in case I need it." He laughed.

When he came home, though, Henry was very different, and I'll say this: the change was no good. You could hardly expect him to change for the better, I know. But he was quiet, so quiet, and never comfortable sitting still anywhere but always up and moving around. I thought back to times we'd sat still for whole afternoons, never moving a muscle, just shifting our weight along the ground, talking to whoever sat with us, watching things. He'd always had a joke, then, too, and now you couldn't get him to laugh, or when he did it was more the sound of a man choking, a sound that stopped up the throats of other people around him. They got to leaving him alone most of the time, and I didn't blame them. It was a fact: Henry was jumpy and mean.

I'd bought a color TV set for my mom and the rest of us while Henry was away. Money still came very easy. I was sorry I'd ever bought it though, because of Henry. I was also sorry I'd bought color, because with black-and-white the pictures seem older and farther away. But what are you going to do? He sat in front of it, watching it, and that was the only time he was completely still. But it was the kind of stillness that you see in a rabbit when it freezes and before it will bolt. He was not easy. He sat in his chair gripping the armrests with all his might, as if the chair itself was moving at a high speed and if he let go at all he would rocket forward and maybe crash right through the set.

Once I was in the room watching TV with Henry and I heard his teeth click at something. I looked over, and he'd bitten through his lip. Blood was going down his chin. I tell you right then I wanted to smash that tube to pieces. I went over to it but Henry must have known what I was up to. He rushed from his chair and shoved me out of the way, against the wall. I told myself he didn't know what he was doing.

My mom came in, turned the set off real quiet, and told us she had made something for supper. So we went and sat down. There was still blood going down Henry's chin, but he didn't notice it and no one said anything, even though every time he took a bite of his bread his blood fell onto it until he was eating his own blood mixed in with the food.

While Henry was not around we talked about what was going to happen to him. There were no Indian doctors on the reservation, and my mom couldn't come around to trusting the old man, Moses Pillager, because he courted her long ago and was jealous of her husbands. He might take revenge through her son. We were afraid that if we brought Henry to a regular hospital they would keep him.

"They don't fix them in those places," Mom said; "they just give them drugs."

"We wouldn't get him there in the first place," I agreed, "so let's just forget about it."

Then I thought about the car.

Henry had not even looked at the car since he'd gotten home, though like I said, it was in tip-top condition and ready to drive. I thought the car might bring the old Henry back somehow. So I bided my time and waited for my chance to interest him in the vehicle.

One night Henry was off somewhere. I took myself a hammer. I went out to that car and I did a number on its underside. Whacked it up. Bent the tail pipe double. Ripped the muffler loose. By the time I was done with the car it looked worse than any typical Indian car that has been driven all its life on reservation roads, which they always say are like government promises—full of holes. It just about hurt me, I'll tell you that! I threw dirt in the carburetor and I ripped all the electric tape off the seats. I made it look just as beat up as I could. Then I sat back and waited for Henry to find it.

Still, it took him over a month. That was all right, because it was just getting warm enough, not melting, but warm enough to work outside.

"Lyman," he says, walking in one day, "that red car looks like shit."

"Well it's old," I says. "You got to expect that."

"No way!" says Henry. "That car's a classic! But you went and ran the piss right out of it, Lyman, and you know it don't deserve that. I kept that car in A-one shape. You don't remember. You're too young. But when I left, that car was running like a watch. Now I don't even know if I can get it to start again, let alone get it anywhere near its old condition."

"Well you try," I said, like I was getting mad, "but I say it's a piece of junk."

Then I walked out before he could realize I knew he'd strung together more than six words at once.

After that I thought he'd freeze himself to death working on that car. He was out there all day, and at night he rigged up a little lamp, ran a cord out the window, and had himself some light to see by while he worked. He was better than he had been before, but that's still not saying much. It was easier for him to do the things the rest of us did. He ate more slowly and didn't jump up and down during the meal to get this or that or look out the window. I put my hand in the back of the TV set, I admit, and fiddled around with it good, so that it was almost impossible now to get a clear picture. He didn't look at it very often anyway. He was always out with that car or going off to get parts for it. By the time it was really melting outside, he had it fixed.

I had been feeling down in the dumps about Henry around this time. We had always been together before. Henry and Lyman. But he was such a loner now that I didn't know how to take it. So I jumped at the chance one day when Henry seemed friendly. It's not that he smiled or anything. He just said, "Let's take that old shitbox for a spin." Just the way he said it made me think he could be coming around.

We went out to the car. It was spring. The sun was shining very bright. My only sister, Bonita, who was just eleven years old, came out and made us stand together for a picture. Henry leaned his elbow on the red car's windshield, and he took his other arm and put it over my shoulder, very carefully, as though it was heavy for him to lift and he didn't want to bring the weight down all at once.

"Smile," Bonita said, and he did.

That picture. I never look at it anymore. A few months ago, I don't know why, I got his picture out and tacked it on the wall. I felt good about Henry at the time, close to him. I felt good having his picture on the wall, until one night when I was looking at television. I was a little drunk and stoned. I looked up at the wall and Henry was staring at me. I don't know what it was, but his smile had changed, or maybe it was gone. All I know is I couldn't stay in the same room with that picture. I was shaking. I got up, closed the door, and went into the kitchen. A little later my friend Ray came over and we both went back into that room. We put the picture in a brown bag, folded the bag over and over tightly, then put it way back in a closet.

I still see that picture now, as if it tugs at me, whenever I pass that closet door. The picture is very clear in my mind. It was so sunny that day Henry had to squint against the glare. Or maybe the camera Bonita held flashed like a mirror, blinding him, before she snapped the picture. My face is right out in the sun, big and round. But he might have drawn back, because the shadows on his face are deep as holes. There are two shadows curved like little hooks around the ends of his smile, as if to frame it and try to keep it there—that one, first smile that looked like it might have hurt his face. He has his field jacket on and the worn-in clothes he'd come back in and kept wearing ever since. After Bonita took the picture, she went into the house and we got into the car. There was a full cooler in the trunk. We started off, east, toward Pembina and the Red River because Henry said he wanted to see the high water.

The trip over there was beautiful. When everything starts changing, drying up, clearing off, you feel like your whole life is starting. Henry felt it, too. The top was down and the car hummed like a top. He'd really put it back in shape, even the tape on the seats was very carefully put down and glued back in layers. It's not that he smiled again or even joked, but his face looked to me as if it was clear, more peaceful. It looked as though he wasn't thinking of anything in particular except the bare fields and windbreaks and houses we were passing.

The river was high and full of winter trash when we got there. The sun was still out, but it was colder by the river. There were still little clumps of dirty snow here and there on the banks. The water hadn't gone over the banks yet, but it would, you could tell. It was just at its limit, hard swollen, glossy like an old gray scar. We made ourselves a fire, and we sat down and watched the current go. As I watched it I felt something squeezing inside me and tightening and trying to let go all at the same time. I knew I was not just feeling it myself; I knew I was feeling what Henry was going through at that moment. Except that I couldn't stand it, the closing and opening. I jumped to my feet. I took Henry by the shoulders and I started shaking him. "Wake up," I says, "wake up, wake up, wake up!" I didn't know what had come over me. I sat down beside him again.

His face was totally white and hard. Then it broke, like stones break all of a sudden when water boils up inside them.

"I know it," he says. "I know it. I can't help it. It's no use."

We start talking. He said he knew what I'd done with the car. It was obvious it had been whacked out of shape and not just neglected. He said he wanted to give the car to me for good now, it was no use. He said he'd fixed it just to give it back and I should take it.

"No way," I says. "I don't want it."

"That's okay," he says, "you take it."

"I don't want it, though," I says back to him, and then to emphasize, just to emphasize, you understand, I touch his shoulder. He slaps my hand off.

"Take that car," he says.

"No," I say. "Make me," I say, and then he grabs my jacket and rips the arm loose. That jacket is a class act, suede with tags and zippers. I push Henry backwards, off the log. He jumps up and bowls me over. We go down in a clinch and come up swinging hard, for all we're worth, with our fists. He socks my jaw so hard I feel like it swings loose. Then I'm at his rib cage and land a good one under his chin so his head snaps back. He's dazzled. He looks at me and I look at him and then his eyes are full of tears and blood and at first I think he's crying. But no, he's laughing. "Ha! Ha!" he says. "Ha! Ha! Take good care of it."

"Okay," I says. "Okay, no problem. Ha! Ha!"

I can't help it, and I start laughing, too. My face feels fat and strange, and after a while I get a beer from the cooler in the trunk, and when I hand it to Henry he takes his shirt and wipes my germs off. "Hoof-and-mouth disease," he says. For some reason this cracks me up, and so we're really laughing for a while, and then we drink all the rest of the beers one by one and throw them in the river and see how far, how fast, the current takes them before they fill up and sink.

"You want to go on back?" I ask after a while. "Maybe we could snag a couple of nice Kashpaw girls."

He says nothing. But I can tell his mood is turning again.

"They're all crazy, the girls up here, every damn one of them."

"You're crazy too," I say, to jolly him up. "Crazy Lamartine boys!"

He looks as though he will take this wrong at first. His face twists, then clears, and he jumps up on his feet. "That's right!" he says. "Crazier 'n hell. Crazy Indians!"

I think it's the old Henry again. He throws off his jacket and starts springing his legs up from the knees like a fancy dancer. He's down doing something between a grass dance and a bunny hop, no kind of dance I ever saw before, but neither has anyone else on all this green growing earth. He's wild. He wants to pitch whoopee! He's up and at me and all over. All this time I'm laughing so hard, so hard my belly is getting tied up in a knot.

"Got to cool me off!" he shouts all of a sudden. Then he runs over to the river and jumps in.

There's boards and other things in the current. It's so high. No sound comes from the river after the splash he makes, so I run right over. I look around. It's getting dark. I see he's halfway across the water already, and I know he didn't swim there but the current took him. It's far. I hear his voice, though, very clearly across it.

"My boots are filling," he says.

He says this in a normal voice, like he just noticed and he doesn't know what to think of it. Then he's gone. A branch comes by. Another branch. And I go in.

By the time I get out of the river, off the snag I pulled myself onto, the sun is down. I walk back to the car, turn on the high beams, and drive it up the bank. I put it in first gear and then I take my foot off the clutch. I get out, close the door, and watch it plow softly into the water. The headlights reach in as they go down, searching, still lighted even after the water swirls over the back end. I wait. The wires short out. It is all finally dark. And then there is only the water, the sound of it going and running and going and running and running.

1984 1993

Tina Howe 1937–

Tina Howe's plays are recurrently autobiographical, which she has acknowledged with the cryptic observation, "All of the events are true, but none of them happened." Painting Churches, *her most autobiographical play, and her best, has characters and events that reflect her own experiences, but they are not simply replicas of the characters and experiences of her actual life. Her father, Quincy Howe, was not a famous poet, like the aging parent Gardner Church in* Painting Churches, *but a nationally famous journalist and radio and TV news analyst of the 1940s and 1950s. And her mother's eccentricities, noteworthy as they may have been (she decorated the family home with the skeletons of small animals), are reflected in her daughter's plays only in their vehemence.*

Howe's childhood was steeped in discussions of intellectual issues, books, writing, and politics. She was led to an interest in the stage because she was, in her own words, "tall and goofy-looking as a child" and became a mimic as "the ultimate defense: Get them to laugh with you before they laugh at you. So all through school and college I was the class clown." She went to private schools and to Sarah Lawrence College in New York. There she studied the writing of fiction, and when she had difficulty in writing a short story, she turned instead to writing a short play, Closing Time. *Its subject was the end of the world, and its diversity of actors played the roles of kings, queens, and talking pigeons. The success of her play, when it was first staged at the college, caused the audience to break into applause at the final curtain and to shout, "Author, author!" The response to her work astonished her, and once she heard it, she later acknowledged, "I was hooked."*

After graduating from college, she taught English in high schools and worked as a drama coach. And she began the struggle to establish herself as a serious playwright. She first wrote two strongly feminist plays about the life of women: The Nest *(1969) and* Birth and After Birth *(1977). The reviews of* The Nest *were so harshly critical that the play closed after only a single performance.* Birth and After Birth *presented such unrelenting details of women giving birth and in language so explicit that no producer has ever been willing to bring it to the stage.*

Her next play, Museum *(1976), had a lighter touch and received more complimentary reviews. It was a satirical examination of the products of modern art seen through the eyes and described in the conversations of visitors to exhibits of modern art. Next came* The Art of Dining *(1979). It was about the complexities of life revealed in the way men and women eat, and it was marked by an on-stage food fight, perhaps the first ever seen on the legitimate stage in America.* Appearances *and* Painting Churches *followed in 1982 and 1983. Her next play,* Coastal Disturbances *(1986), presented the love stories of several couples whose passions and recriminations were sounded out from the sand dunes in which they lay under a summer sun on a New England beach, which required, for its recreation on a theater stage, the importation of twenty tons of sand. Other works include* Approaching Zanzibar *(1989),* One Shoe Off *(1993),* Pride's Crossing *(1997),* Women in Flames *(1999),* Rembrandt's Gift *(1999),* Agog in the Galapagos *(2002), and* Water Music *(2003).*

Howe has said, "I am motivated very strongly by esthetics," and in Painting Churches, *as in a number of her plays, she has a character of artistic temperament confronting a world of conventionality and encountering the subtle complexities amid which one must live and die. Howe's plays also express a feminist viewpoint, although she argues that her work challenges the conformist ideal of a single, unitary feminist point of view in art or in life: "We all have our own pasts, and we all have our own points of view, and our own intentions. . . . I don't think there's such a thing as a woman's voice. I think there are women's voices and that all our voices are very distinct from each other."*

FURTHER READING: *Feminine Focus: The New Women Playwrights,* ed. E. Brater, 1989; *A Search for a Postmodern Theater: Interviews with Contemporary Playwrights,* ed. J. DiGaetani, 1991; *Speaking on Stage: Interviews with Contemporary American Playwrights,* ed. C. Kullman, 1996; C. Bigsby, *Contemporary American Playwrights,* 2000.

TEXT: *Painting Churches* from *Contemporary Plays by Women,* ed. E. Kilgore, 1991.

PAINTING CHURCHES

CHARACTERS

FANNY SEDGWICK CHURCH, a Bostonian from a fine old family, in her sixties.
GARDNER CHURCH, her husband, an eminent New England poet from a finer family, in his seventies.
MARGARET CHURCH (MAGS), their daughter, a painter, in her early thirties.

TIME: Several years ago.

PLACE: Boston, Massachusetts.

ACT I

SCENE 1

The living room of the Churches' townhouse on Beacon Hill one week before everything will be moved to Cape Cod. Empty packing cartons line the room and all the furniture has been tagged with brightly colored markers. At first glance it looks like any discreet

Boston interior, but on closer scrutiny one notices a certain flamboyance. Oddities from secondhand stores are mixed in with the fine old furniture, and exotic handmade curios vie with tasteful family objets d'art. What makes the room remarkable, though, is the play of light that pours through three soaring arched windows. At one hour it's hard edged and brilliant; the next, it's dappled and yielding. It transforms whatever it touches, giving the room a distinct feeling of unreality. It's several years ago, a bright spring morning.

FANNY *is sitting on the sofa, wrapping a valuable old silver coffee service. She's wearing a worn bathrobe and fashionable hat. As she works, she makes a list of everything on a yellow legal pad.* GARDNER *can be heard typing in his study down the hall.*

FANNY (*Picks up a coffee pot*): God, this is good-looking! I'd forgotten how handsome Mama's old silver was! It's probably worth a fortune. It certainly weighs enough! (*Calling*) GARRRRRRRRRRRRRRRRRDNERRRRRRRRRRRR? . . . Well, it should bring us a pretty penny, that's for sure: (*Wraps it, places it in a carton, and then picks up the tray that goes with it. She holds it up like a mirror and adjusts her hat. Louder in another register*) OH, GARRRRRRRRRRRRRRRRDNERRRRR? (GARDNER *continues typing. She then reaches for a small box and opens it with reverence*) Grandma's Paul Revere teaspoons![1] . . . (*She takes out several and fondles them*) I don't care how desperate things get, these will never go! One has to maintain some standards! (*She writes on her list*) Grandma's Paul Revere teaspoons, Cotuit![2] WASN'T IT THE AMERICAN WING OF THE METROPOLITAN MUSEUM OF ART[3] THAT WANTED GRANDMA'S PAUL REVERE TEASPOONS SO BADLY? . . . (*She looks at her reflection in the tray again*) This is a very good-looking hat, if I do say so. I was awfully smart to grab it up. (*Silence*)
DON'T YOU REMEMBER A DISTINGUISHED-LOOKING MAN COMING TO THE HOUSE AND OFFERING US FIFTY THOUSAND DOLLARS FOR GRANDMA'S PAUL REVERE TEASPOONS? . . . HE HAD ON THESE MARVELOUS SHOES! THEY WERE SO POINTED AT THE ENDS WE COULDN'T IMAGINE HOW HE EVER GOT THEM ON AND THEY WERE SHINED TO WITHIN AN INCH OF THEIR LIVES AND I REMEMBER HIM SAYING HE CAME FROM THE . . . AMERICAN WING OF THE METROPOLITAN MUSEUM OF ART! . . . HELLO? . . . GARDNER? . . . ARE YOU THERE! (*The typing stops*) YOO-HOOOOOOO . . . (*Like a foghorn*) GARRRRRRRRRRDNERRRRRRR?

GARDNER (*Offstage; from his study*): YES, DEAR . . . IS THAT YOU?

FANNY: OF COURSE IT'S ME! WHO ELSE COULD IT POSSIBLY BE? . . . DARLING, PLEASE COME HERE FOR A MINUTE. (*The typing resumes*) FOR GOD'S SAKE, WILL YOU STOP THAT DREADFUL TYPING BEFORE YOU SEND ME STRAIGHT TO THE NUT HOUSE? . . . (*In a new register*) GARRRRRRRRRRRRRRDNERRRRRR?

[*He stops.*]

GARDNER (*Offstage*): WHAT'S THAT? MAGS IS BACK FROM THE NUT HOUSE?

FANNY: I SAID . . . Lord, I hate this yelling. . . . PLEASE . . . COME . . . HERE!

[*Brief silence.*]

[1]Because of his fame as an American Revolutionary War hero, the silverware of the Boston silversmith Paul Revere (1735–1818) is highly prized and valuable.
[2]Seaside village, on the Cape Cod Peninsula, sixty miles southeast of Boston.
[3]Museum in New York City. Its American Wing houses a collection of American art from colonial times to the present.

GARDNER (*Offstage*): I'LL BE WITH YOU IN A MOMENT, I DIDN'T HEAR HER RING. (*Starts singing*) "Nothing could be finer than to be in Carolina."

FANNY: It's a wonder I'm not in a straight-jacket already. Actually, it might be rather nice for a change . . . peaceful. DARLING . . . I WANT TO SHOW YOU MY NEW HAT!

[*Silence.* GARDNER *enters, still singing. He's wearing mismatched tweeds and is holding a stack of papers which keep drifting to the floor.*]

GARDNER: Oh, don't you look nice! Very attractive, very attractive!

FANNY: But I'm still in my bathrobe.

GARDNER (*Looking around the room, leaking more papers*): Well, where's Mags?

FANNY: Darling, you're dropping your papers all over the floor.

GARDNER (*Spies the silver tray*): I remember this! Aunt Alice gave it to us, didn't she? (*He picks it up*) Good Lord, it's heavy. What's it made of? Lead?!

FANNY: No, Aunt Alice did *not* give it to us. It was Mama's.

GARDNER: Oh, yes . . . (*He starts to exit with it*)

FANNY: Could I have it back, please?

GARDNER (*Hands it to her, dropping more papers*): Oh, sure thing. . . . Where's Mags? I thought you said she was here.

FANNY: I didn't say Mags was here, I asked *you* to come here.

GARDNER (*Papers spilling*): Damned papers keep falling . . .

FANNY: I wanted to show you my new hat. I bought it in honor of Mags' visit. Isn't it marvelous?

GARDNER (*Picking up the papers as more drop*): Yes, yes, very nice . . .

FANNY: Gardner, you're not even looking at it!

GARDNER: Very becoming . . .

FANNY: You don't think it's too bright, do you? I don't want to look like a traffic light. Guess how much it cost?

GARDNER (*A whole sheaf of papers slides to the floor; he dives for them*): OH, SHIT!

FANNY (*Gets to them first*): It's all right, I've got them, I've got them. (*She hands them to him*)

GARDNER: You'd think they had wings on them . . .

FANNY: Here you go . . .

GARDNER: . . . damned things won't hold still!

FANNY: Gar . . .?

GARDNER (*Engrossed in one of the pages*): Mmmmm?

FANNY: HELLO?

GARDNER (*Startled*): What's that?

FANNY (*In a whisper*): My hat. Guess how much it cost.

GARDNER: Oh, yes. Let's see . . . ten dollars?

FANNY: Ten dollars . . . IS THAT ALL?

GARDNER: Twenty?

FANNY: GARDNER, THIS HAPPENS TO BE A DESIGNER HAT! DESIGNER HATS START AT FIFTY DOLLARS . . . SEVENTY-FIVE!

GARDNER (*Jumps*): Was that the door bell?

FANNY: No, it wasn't the door bell. Though it's high time Mags were here. She was probably in a train wreck!

GARDNER (*Looking through his papers*): I'm beginning to get fond of Wallace Stevens[4] again.

FANNY: This damned move is going to kill me! Send me straight to my grave!

GARDNER (*Reading from a page*):

> "The mules that angels ride come slowly down
> The blazing passes, from beyond the sun.
> Descensions of their tinkling bells arrive.
> These muleteers are dainty of their way . . ."

(*Pause*) Don't you love that! "These muleteers are *dainty* of their way"!?

FANNY: Gar, the hat. How much? (GARDNER *sighs*) Darling . . .?

GARDNER: Oh, yes. Let's see . . . fifty dollars? Seventy-five?

FANNY: It's French.

GARDNER: Three hundred!

FANNY (*Triumphant*): No, eighty-five cents.

GARDNER: Eighty-five cents! . . . I thought you said . . .

FANNY: That's right . . . eighty . . . five . . . *cents!*

GARDNER: Well, you sure had me fooled!

FANNY: I found it at the thrift shop.

GARDNER: I thought it cost at least fifty dollars or seventy-five. You know, designer hats are very expensive!

FANNY: It was on the markdown table. (*She takes it off and shows him the label*) See that? Lily Daché![5] When I saw that label, I nearly keeled over right into the fur coats!

GARDNER (*Handling it*): Well, what do you know, that's the same label that's in my bathrobe.

FANNY: Darling, Lily Daché designed hats, not men's bathrobes!

GARDNER: Yup . . . Lily Daché . . . same name . . .

FANNY: If you look again, I'm sure you'll see . . .

GARDNER: . . . same script, same color, same size. I'll show you. (*He exits*)

FANNY: Poor lamb can't keep anything straight anymore. (*Looks at herself in the tray again*) God, this is a good-looking hat!

GARDNER (*Returns with a nondescript plaid bathrobe. He points to the label*): See that? . . . What does it say?

FANNY (*Refusing to look at it*): Lily Daché was a *hat* designer! She designed ladies' *hats!*

GARDNER: What . . . does . . . it . . . say?

FANNY: Gardner, you're being ridiculous.

GARDNER (*Forcing it on her*): Read . . . the label!

FANNY: Lily Daché did *not* design this bathrobe, I don't care what the label says!

GARDNER: READ! (FANNY *reads it*) ALL RIGHT, NOW WHAT DOES IT SAY!

FANNY (*Chagrined*): Lily Daché.

GARDNER: I told you!

[4]Wallace Stevens (1879–1955), American poet. The following quotation is from his poem "Le Monocle de Mon Oncle."

[5]Renowned American fashion designer (1892–1989).

FANNY: Wait a minute, let me look at that again. (*She does; then throws the robe at him in disgust*) Gar, Lily Daché never designed a bathrobe in her life! Someone obviously ripped the label off one of her hats and then sewed it into the robe.

GARDNER (*Puts it on over his jacket*): It's damned good-looking. I've always loved this robe. I think you gave it to me. . . . Well, I've got to get back to work. (*He abruptly exits*)

FANNY: Where did you get that robe anyway? . . . I didn't give it to you, did I . . .?

[*Silence.* GARDNER *resumes typing.*]

FANNY (*Holding the tray up again and admiring herself*): You know, I think I *did* give it to him. I remember how excited I was when I found it at the thrift shop . . . fifty cents and never worn! *I* couldn't have sewn that label in to impress him, could I? . . . I can't be that far gone! . . . The poor lamb wouldn't even notice it, let alone understand its cachet.[6] . . . Uuuuuuh, this damned tray is even heavier than the coffee pot. They must have been amazons in the old days! (*Writes on her pad*) "Empire tray, Parke-Bernet Galleries," and good riddance! (*She wraps it and drops it into the carton with the coffee pot*) Where *is* that wretched Mags? It would be just like her to get into a train wreck! She was supposed to be here hours ago. Well, if she doesn't show up soon, I'm going to drop dead of exhaustion. God, wouldn't that be wonderful? . . . Then they could just cart me off into storage with all the old chandeliers and china . . .

[*The doorbell rings.*]

FANNY: It's Mags, it's Mags! (*A pause. Dashing out of the room, colliding into* GARDNER) Good god, look at me! I'm still in my bathrobe!

GARDNER (*Offstage*): Coming, coming . . . I've got it . . . coming! (*Dashing into the room, colliding into* FANNY) I've got it . . . hold on . . . coming . . . coming . . .

FANNY (*Offstage*): Mags is here! It's Mags . . . she's finally here!

[GARDNER *exits to open the front door.* MAGS *comes staggering in carrying a suitcase and an enormous duffel bag. She wears wonderfully distinctive clothes and has very much her own look. She's extremely out of breath and too wrought up to drop her heavy bags.*]

MAGS: I'm sorry. . . . I'm sorry I'm so late. . . . Everything went wrong! A passenger had a heart attack outside of New London[7] and we had to stop. . . . It was terrifying! All these medics and policemen came swarming onto the train and the conductor kept running up and down the aisles telling everyone not to leave their seats under any circumstances. . . . Then the New London fire department came screeching down to the tracks, sirens blaring, lights whirling,

[6]Prestigious, esteemed quality.
[7]City in southeast Connecticut, on the rail line between New York City and Boston.

and all these men in black rubber suits started pouring through the doors. . . . *That* took two hours . . .

FANNY (*Offstage*): Darling . . . darling . . . where are you?

MAGS: *Then,* I couldn't get a cab at the station. There just weren't any! I must have circled the block fifteen times. Finally I just stepped out into the traffic with my thumb out, but no one would pick me up . . . so I walked . . .

FANNY (*Offstage*): Damned zipper's stuck . . .

GARDNER: You walked all the way from the South Station?[8]

MAGS: Well actually, I ran . . .

GARDNER: You had poor Mum scared to death.

MAGS (*Finally puts the bags down with a deep sigh*): I'm sorry. . . . I'm really sorry. It was a nightmare.

[FANNY *reenters the room, her dress over her head. The zipper's stuck; she staggers around blindly.*]

FANNY: Damned zipper! Gar, will you please help me with this?

MAGS: I sprinted all the way up Beacon Hill.

GARDNER (*Opening his arms wide*): Well come here and let's get a look at you. (*He hugs her*) Mags!

MAGS (*Squeezing him tight*): Oh, Daddy . . . Daddy!

GARDNER: My Mags!

MAGS: I never thought I'd get here! . . . Oh, you look wonderful!

GARDNER: Well, you don't look so bad yourself!

MAGS: I love your hair. It's gotten so . . . white!

FANNY (*Still lost in her dress, struggling with the zipper*): This is *so* typical . . . just as Mags arrives, my zipper has to break! (*She grunts and struggles*)

MAGS (*Waves at her*): Hi, Mum . . .

FANNY: Just a minute, dear, my zipper's . . .

GARDNER (*Picks up* MAGS' *bags*): Well, sit down and take a load off your feet . . .

MAGS: I was so afraid I'd never make it . . .

GARDNER (*Staggering under the weight of the bags*): What have you got in here? Lead weights?

MAGS: I can't believe you're finally letting me do you.

[FANNY *flings her arms around* MAGS, *practically knocking her over.*]

FANNY: Oh, darling . . . my precious Mags, you're here at last.

GARDNER (*Lurching around in circles*): Now let's see . . . where should I put these. . .?

FANNY: I was sure your train had derailed and you were lying dead in some ditch!

MAGS (*Pulls away from* FANNY *to come to* GARDNER'S *rescue*): Daddy, please, let me . . . these are much too heavy.

FANNY (*Finally noticing* MAGS): GOOD LORD, WHAT HAVE YOU DONE TO YOUR HAIR?!

[8]Boston railroad station.

MAGS (*Struggling to take the bags from* GARDNER): Come on, give them to me . . . please? (*She sets them down by the sofa*)

FANNY (*As her dress starts to slide off one shoulder*): Oh, not again! . . . Gar, would you give me a hand and see what's wrong with this zipper. One minute it's stuck, the next it's falling to pieces.

[GARDNER *goes to her and starts fussing with it.*]

MAGS (*Pacing*): I don't know, it's been crazy all week. Monday, I forgot to keep an appointment I'd made with a new model. . . . Tuesday, I overslept and stood up my advanced painting students. . . . Wednesday, the day of my meeting with Max Zoll, I forgot to put on my underpants . . .

FANNY: GODDAMMIT, GAR, CAN'T YOU DO ANYTHING ABOUT THIS ZIPPER?!

MAGS: I mean, there I was, racing down Broome Street in this gauzy Tibetan skirt when I tripped and fell right at his feet . . . SPLATTT! My skirt goes flying over my head and there I am . . . everything staring him in the face . . .

FANNY: COME ON GAR, USE A LITTLE MUSCLE!

MAGS (*Laughing*): Oh, well, all that matters is that I finally got here. . . . I mean . . . there you are . . .

GARDNER (*Struggling with the zipper*): I can't see it, it's too small!

FANNY (*Whirls away from* GARDNER, *pulling her dress off altogether*): OH, FORGET IT! JUST FORGET IT! The trolley's[9] probably missing half its teeth, just like someone else I know. (*To* MAGS) I grind my teeth in my sleep now, I've worn them all down to stubs. Look at that! (*She flings open her mouth and points*) Nothing left but the gums!

GARDNER: I never hear you grind your teeth . . .

FANNY: That's because I'm snoring so loud. How could you hear anything through all that racket? It even wakes me up. It's no wonder poor Daddy has to sleep downstairs.

MAGS (*Looking around*): Jeez, look at the place! So, you're finally doing it . . . selling the house and moving to Cotuit year round. I don't believe it. I just don't believe it!

GARDNER: Well, how about a drink to celebrate Mags' arrival?

MAGS: You've been here so long. Why move now?

FANNY: Gardner, what are you wearing that bathrobe for?

MAGS: You can't move. I won't let you!

FANNY (*Softly to* GARDNER): Really, darling, you ought to pay more attention to your appearance.

MAGS: You love this house. *I* love this house . . . the room . . . the light.

GARDNER: So, Mags, how about a little . . . (*He drinks from an imaginary glass*) to wet your whistle?

FANNY: We can't start drinking now, it isn't even noon yet!

MAGS: I'm starving. I've got to get something to eat before I collapse! (*She exits toward the kitchen*)

FANNY: What *have* you done to you hair, dear? The color's so queer and all your nice curl is gone.

GARDNER: It looks to me as if she dyed it.

[9]Zipper track.

FANNY: Yes, that's it. You're absolutely right! It's a completely different color. She dyed it bright red!

[MAGS *can be heard thumping and thudding through the icebox.*]

FANNY: NOW, MAGS, I DON'T WANT YOU FILLING UP ON SNACKS. . . . I'VE MADE A PERFECTLY BEAUTIFUL LEG OF LAMB FOR LUNCH! . . . HELLO? . . . DO YOU HEAR ME? . . . (*To* GARDNER) No one in our family has *ever* had red hair, it's so common looking.

GARDNER: I like it. It brings out her eyes.

FANNY: WHY ON EARTH DID YOU DYE YOUR HAIR *RED*, OF ALL COLORS?!

MAGS (*Returns, eating Saltines out of the box*): I didn't dye my hair, I just added some highlight.

FANNY: I suppose that's what your arty friends in New York do . . . dye their hair all the colors of the rainbow!

GARDNER: Well, it's damned attractive if you asked me . . . damned attractive!

[MAGS *unzips her duffel bag and rummages around in it while eating the Saltines.*]

FANNY: Darling, I told you not to bring a lot of stuff with you. We're trying to get rid of things.

MAGS (*Pulls out a folding easel and starts setting it up*): AAAAAHHHHHH, here it is. Isn't it a beauty? I bought it just for you!

FANNY: Please don't get crumbs all over the floor. Crystal was just here yesterday. It was her last time before we move.

MAGS (*At her easel*): God, I can hardly wait! I can't believe you're finally letting me do you.

FANNY: *Do* us? . . . What *are* you talking about?

GARDNER (*Reaching for the Saltines*): Hey, Mags, could I have a couple of those?

MAGS (*Tosses him the box*): Sure! (*To* FANNY) Your portrait.

GARDNER: Thanks. (*He starts munching on a handful*)

FANNY: You're planning to paint our portrait now? While we're trying to move . . .?

GARDNER (*Sputtering Saltines*): Mmmmm, I'd forgotten just how delicious Saltines are!

MAGS: It's a perfect opportunity. There'll be no distractions; you'll be completely at my mercy. Also, you promised.

FANNY: I did?

MAGS: Yes, you did.

FANNY: Well, I must have been off my rocker.

MAGS: No, you said, "You can paint us, you can dip us in concrete, you can do anything you want with us just so long as you help us get out of here!"

GARDNER (*Offering the box of Saltines to* FANNY): You really ought to try some of these, Fan, they're absolutely delicious!

FANNY (*Taking a few*): Why, thank you.

MAGS: I figure we'll pack in the morning and you'll pose in the afternoons. It'll be a nice diversion.

FANNY: These *are* good!

GARDNER: Here, dig in . . . take some more.

MAGS: I have some wonderful news . . . amazing news! I wanted to wait till I got here to tell you.

[GARDNER *and* FANNY *eat their Saltines, passing the box back and forth as* MAGS *speaks.*]

MAGS: You'll die! Just fall over into the packing cartons and die! Are you ready? . . . BRACE YOURSELVES . . . OKAY, HERE GOES. . . . I'm being given a one-woman show at one of the most important galleries in New York this fall. Me, Margaret Church, exhibited at Castelli's, 420 West Broadway. . . . Can you believe it?! . . . MY PORTRAITS HANGING IN THE SAME ROOMS THAT HAVE SHOWN RAUSCHENBERG, JOHNS, WARHOL, KELLY, LICHTENSTEIN, STELLA, SERRA, ALL THE HEAVIES.[10] . . . It's incredible, beyond belief . . . I mean, at my age. . . . Do you know how good you have to be to get in there? It's a miracle . . . an honest-to-God, star-spangled miracle!

[*Pause.*]

FANNY (*Mouth full*): Oh, darling, that's wonderful. We're so happy for you!

GARDNER (*Mouth full*): No one deserves it more, no one deserves it more!

MAGS: Through some fluke, some of Castelli's people showed up at our last faculty show at Pratt[11] and were knocked out . . .

FANNY (*Reaching for the box of Saltines*): More, more . . .

MAGS: They said they hadn't seen anyone handle light like me since the French Impressionists. They said I was this weird blend of Pierre Bonnard, Mary Cassatt and David Hockney . . .[12]

GARDNER (*Swallowing his mouthful*): I told you they were good.

MAGS: Also, no one's doing portraits these days. They're considered passé. I'm so out of it, I'm in.

GARDNER: Well, you're loaded with talent and always have been.

FANNY: She gets it all from Mama, you know. Her miniature of Henry James is still one of the main attractions at the Atheneum.[13] Of course no woman of breeding could be a professional artist in her day. It simply wasn't done. But talk about talent . . . that woman had talent to burn!

MAGS: I want to do one of you for the show.

FANNY: Oh, do Daddy, he's the famous one.

MAGS: No, I want to do you both. I've always wanted to do you and now I've finally got a good excuse.

FANNY: It's high time somebody painted Daddy again! I'm sick to death of that dreadful portrait of him in the National Gallery[14] they keep reproducing. He looks like an undertaker!

GARDNER: Well, I think you should just do Mum. She's never looked handsomer.

FANNY: Oh, come on, I'm a perfect fright and you know it.

[10]Famous twentieth-century painters of abstract, experimental, and "Pop" art.

[11]School in Brooklyn, New York, for training in professions and the arts.

[12]David Hockney (1937–), British "Pop" artist; Pierre Bonnard (1867–1947), French Neo-Impressionist and Expressionist painter; Mary Cassatt (1844–1926), Impressionist American painter.

[13]Private library founded in Boston in 1807.

[14]National Gallery of Art, in Washington, D.C., a branch of the Smithsonian Institution.

MAGS: I want to do you both. Side by side. In this room. Something really classy. You look so great. Mum with her crazy hats and everything and you with that face. If I could just get you to hold still long enough and actually pose.

GARDNER (*Walking around, distracted*): Where are those papers I just had? Goddammit, Fanny . . .

MAGS: I have the feeling it's either now or never.

GARDNER: I can't hold on to anything around here. (*He exits to his study*)

MAGS: I've always wanted to do you. It would be such a challenge.

FANNY (*Pulling* MAGS *onto the sofa next to her*): I'm so glad you're finally here, Mags. I'm very worried about Daddy.

MAGS: Mummy, please. I just got here.

FANNY: He's getting quite gaga.

MAGS: Mummy . . .!

FANNY: You haven't seen him in almost a year. Two weeks ago he walked through the front door of the Codman's house, kissed Emily on the cheek and settled down in the maid's room, thinking he was home!

MAGS: Oh, come on, you're exaggerating.

FANNY: He's as mad as a hatter and getting worse every day! It's this damned new book of his. He works on it around the clock. I've read some of it, and it doesn't make one word of sense, it's all at sixes and sevens . . .

GARDNER (*Pokes his head back in the room, spies some of his papers on a table and grabs them*): Ahhh, here they are. (*He exits*)

FANNY (*Voice lowered*): Ever since this dry spell with his poetry, he's been frantic, absolutely . . . frantic!

MAGS: I hate it when you do this.

FANNY: I'm just trying to get you to face the facts around here.

MAGS: There's nothing wrong with him! He's just as sane as the next man. Even saner, if you ask me.

FANNY: You know what he's doing now? You couldn't guess in a million years! . . . He's writing criticism! Daddy! (*She laughs*) Can you believe it? The man doesn't have one analytic bone in his body. His mind is a complete jumble and always has been!

[*There's a loud crash from* GARDNER*'s study.*]

GARDNER (*Offstage*): SHIT!

MAGS: He's abstracted. . . . That's the way he is.

FANNY: He doesn't spend any time with me anymore. He just holes up in that filthy study with Toots. God, I hate that bird! Though actually they're quite cunning together. Daddy's teaching him Gray's *Elegy*. You ought to see them in there, Toots perched on top of Daddy's head, spouting out verse after verse . . . Daddy, tap-tap-tapping away on his typewriter. They're quite a pair.

GARDNER (*Pokes his head back in*): Have you seen that Stevens' poem I was reading before?

FANNY (*Long-suffering*): NO, I HAVEN'T SEEN THAT STEVENS' POEM YOU WERE READING BEFORE! . . . Things are getting very tight around here, in case you haven't noticed. Daddy's last Pulitzer[15] didn't even cover our real estate tax, and now

[15] Pulitzer Prize, one of the annual awards for achievements in American journalism and in prose and poetry.

that he's too doddery to give readings anymore, that income is gone . . . (*Suddenly handing* MAGS *the sugar bowl she'd been wrapping*) Mags, *do* take this sugar bowl. You can use it to serve tea to your students at that wretched art school of yours . . . .

MAGS: It's called Pratt! The Pratt Institute.

FANNY: Pratt, Splatt, whatever . . .

MAGS: And I don't serve tea to my students, I teach them how to paint.

FANNY: Well, I'm sure none of them has ever seen a sugar bowl as handsome as this before.

GARDNER (*Reappearing again*): You're sure you haven't seen it?

FANNY (*Loud and angry*): YES, I'M SURE I HAVEN'T SEEN IT! I JUST TOLD YOU I HAVEN'T SEEN IT!

GARDNER (*Retreating*): Right you are, right you are. (*He exits*)

FANNY: God!

[*Silence.*]

MAGS: What do you have to yell at him like that for?

FANNY: Because the poor thing's as deaf as an adder![16]

[MAGS *sighs deeply; silence.* FANNY, *suddenly exuberant, leads her over to a lamp.*]

FANNY: Come, I want to show you something.

MAGS (*Looking at it*): What is it?

FANNY: Something I made. (MAGS *is about to turn it on*) WAIT, DON'T TURN IT ON YET! It's got to be dark to get the full effect. (*She rushes to the windows and pulls down the shades*)

MAGS: What *are* you doing?

FANNY: Hold your horses a minute. You'll see . . . (*As the room gets darker and darker*) Poor me, you wouldn't believe the lengths I go to to amuse myself these days . . . .

MAGS (*Touching the lampshade*): What is this? It looks like a scene of some sort.

FANNY: It's an invention I made . . . a kind of magic lantern.

MAGS: Gee . . . it's amazing . . .

FANNY: What I did was buy an old engraving of the Grand Canal . . .[17]

MAGS: You *made* this?

FANNY: . . . and then color it in with crayons. Next, I got out my sewing scissors and cut out all the street lamps and windows . . . anything that light would shine through. Then I pasted it over a plain lampshade, put the shade on this old horror of a lamp, turned on the switch and . . . (*She turns it on*) VOILA . . . VENICE TWINKLING AT DUSK! It's quite effective, don't you think . . .?

MAGS (*Walking around it*): Jeez . . .

FANNY: And see, I poked out all the little lights on the gondolas with a straight pin.

MAGS: Where on earth did you get the idea?

[16]According to ancient proverbial belief, the adder (a venomous snake) cannot hear.
[17]Largest of the canals in the city of Venice, Italy.

FANNY: Well you know, idle minds . . . (*She spins the shade, making the lights whirl*)

MAGS: It's really amazing. I mean, you could sell this in a store!

GARDNER (*Enters*): Here it is. It was right on top of my desk the whole time. (*He crashes into a table*) OOOOOWWWWW!

FANNY: LOOK OUT, LOOK OUT!

MAGS (*Rushes over to* GARDNER): Oh, Daddy, are you all right?

FANNY: Watch where you're going, watch where you're going!

GARDNER (*Hopping up and down on one leg*): GODDAMMIT! . . . I HIT MY SHIN.

FANNY: I was just showing Mags my lamp . . .

GARDNER (*Limping over to it*): Oh, yes, isn't that something? Mum is awfully clever with that kind of thing. . . . It was all her idea. Buying the engraving, coloring it in, cutting out all those little dots.

FANNY: Not "dots" . . . lights and windows, lights and windows!

GARDNER: Right, right . . . lights and windows.

FANNY: Well, we'd better get some light back in here before someone breaks their neck. (*She zaps the shades back up*)

GARDNER (*Puts his arm around* MAGS): Gee, it's good to have you back.

MAGS: It's good to be back.

GARDNER: And I like that new red hair of yours. It's very becoming.

MAGS: But I told you, I hardly touched it . . .

GARDNER: Well, something's different. You've got a glow. So . . . how do you want us to pose for this grand portrait of yours . . .? (*He poses self-consciously*)

MAGS: Oh, Daddy, setting up a portrait takes a lot of time and thought. You've got to figure out the background, the lighting, what to wear, the sort of mood you want to—

FANNY: OOOOH, LET'S DRESS UP, LET'S DRESS UP! (*She grabs a packing blanket, drapes it around herself and links arms with* GARDNER, *striking an elegant pose*) This *is* going to be fun. She was absolutely right! Come on, Gar, look distinguished!

MAGS: Mummy, please, it's not a game!

FANNY (*More and more excited*): You still have your tuxedo, don't you? And I'll wear my marvelous long black dress that makes me look like that fascinating woman in the Sargent painting![18] (*She strikes the famous profile pose*)

MAGS: MUMMY?!

FANNY: I'm sorry, we'll behave, just tell us what to do.

[FANNY *and* GARDNER *settle down next to each other.*]

GARDNER: That's right, you're the boss.

FANNY: Yes, you're the boss.

MAGS: But I'm not ready yet; I haven't set anything up.

FANNY: Relax, darling, we just want to get the hang of it . . .

[18] The portrait entitled "Madame X" (now in the Metropolitan Museum of Art) by the American painter John Singer Sargent (1856–1925) shows a beautiful woman dressed in a long black gown and posed as a symbol of fashionable elegance and high social status.

[FANNY *and* GARDNER *stare straight ahead, trying to look like suitable subjects, but they can't hold still. They keep making faces, lifting an eyebrow, wriggling a nose, twitching a lip. Nothing big and grotesque, just flickering changes; a half-smile here, a self-important frown there. They steal glances at each other every so often.*]

GARDNER: How am I doing, Fan?

FANNY: Brilliantly, absolutely brilliantly!

MAGS: But you're making faces.

FANNY: *I'm* not making faces. (*Turning to* GARDNER *and making a face*) Are *you* making faces, Gar?

GARDNER (*Instantly making one*): Certainly not! I'm the picture of restraint!

[*Without meaning to,* FANNY *and* GARDNER *get sillier and sillier. They start giggling, then laughing.*]

MAGS (*Can't help but join in*): You two are impossible . . . completely impossible! I was crazy to think I could ever pull this off! (*Laughing away*) Look at you . . . just . . . look at you!

[*Blackout.*]

SCENE 2

Two days later, around five in the afternoon. Half of the Church household has been dragged into the living room for packing. Overflowing cartons are everywhere. They're filled with pots and pans, dishes and glasses, and the entire contents of two linen closets. MAGS *has placed a stepladder under one of the windows. A pile of tablecloths and curtains is flung beneath it. Two side chairs are in readiness for the eventual pose.*

MAGS *has just pulled a large crimson tablecloth out of a carton. She unfurls it with one shimmering toss.*

MAGS: PERFECT . . . PERFECT!

FANNY (*Seated on the sofa, clutches an old pair of galoshes to her chest*): Look at these old horrors; half the rubber is rotted away and the fasteners are falling to pieces. . . . GARDNER? . . . OH, GARRRRRRRRRDNERRRRR?

MAGS (*Rippling out the tablecloth with shorter snapping motions*): Have you ever seen such a color?

FANNY: I've found your old sledding galoshes in with the pots and pans. Do you still want them?

MAGS: It's like something out of a Rubens![19]

[MAGS *slings the tablecloth over a chair and then sits on a footstool to finish the Sara Lee banana cake she started. As she eats, she looks at the tablecloth, making happy grunting sounds.* FANNY *lovingly puts the galoshes on over her shoes and wiggles her feet.*]

[19]I.e., like the richly ornate scenes painted by the Flemish artist Peter Paul Rubens (1577–1640).

FANNY: God, these bring back memories! There were real snowstorms in the old days. Not these pathetic little two-inch droppings we have now. After a particularly heavy one, Daddy and I used to go sledding on the Common.[20] This was way before you were born.... God, it was a hundred years ago! ... Daddy would stop writing early, put on these galoshes and come looking for me, jingling the fasteners like castanets. It was a kind of mating call, almost ... (*She jingles them*) The Common was always deserted after a storm; we had the whole place to ourselves. It was so romantic.... We'd haul the sled up Beacon Street, stop under the State House,[21] and aim it straight down to the Park Street Church, which was much further away in those days.... Then Daddy would lie down on the sled, I'd lower myself on top of him, we'd rock back and forth a few times to gain momentum and then ...

WHOOOOOOOOSSSSSSSHHHHH ... down we'd plunge like a pair of eagles locked in a spasm of lovemaking. God, it was wonderful! ... The city whizzing past us at ninety miles an hour ... the cold ... the darkness ... Daddy's hair in my mouth ... GAR ... REMEMBER HOW WE USED TO GO SLEDDING IN THE OLD DAYS? ...

Sometimes he'd lie on top of me. That was fun. I liked that even more. (*In her foghorn voice*) GARRRRRRRRRDNERRRRR?

MAGS: Didn't he say he was going out this afternoon?

FANNY: Why, so he did! I completely forgot. (*She takes off the galoshes*) I'm getting just as bad as him. (*She drops them into a different carton—wistful*) Gar's galoshes, Cotuit.

[*A pause.* MAGS *picks up the tablecloth again, holds it high over her head.*]

MAGS: Isn't this fabulous? ... (*She then wraps* FANNY *in it*) It's the perfect backdrop. Look what it does to your skin.

FANNY: Mags, what *are* you doing?

MAGS: It makes you glow like a pomegranate ... (*She whips it off her*) Now all I need is a hammer and nails ... (*She finds them*) YES! (*She climbs up the stepladder and starts hammering a corner of the cloth into the molding of one of the windows*) This is going to look so great! ... I've never seen such color!

FANNY: Darling, what is going on ...?

MAGS: Rembrandt, eat your heart out! You seventeenth-century Dutch has-been, you. (*She hammers more furiously*)

FANNY: MARGARET, THIS IS NOT A CONSTRUCTION SITE.... PLEASE ... STOP IT ... YOO-HOOOOO ... DO YOU HEAR ME?

[GARDNER *suddenly appears, dressed in a raincoat.*]

GARDNER: Yes, dear, here I am. I just stepped out for a walk down Chestnut Street. Beautiful afternoon, absolutely beautiful! ... Why, that looks very nice, Mags, very nice indeed ...

FANNY (*To* MAGS): You're going to ruin the walls to say nothing of mama's best tablecloth.... Mags, do you hear me? ... yoo-hoo! ... darling, I must insist you stop that dreadful ...

[20]Public park in central Boston.

[21]The Massachusetts State House, seat of the state legislature, adjacent to the Boston Common.

MAGS (*Steps down; stands back and looks at the tablecloth*): That's it. That's IT!
FANNY (*To* GARDNER, *worried*): Where have *you* been?

[MAGS *kisses her fingers at the backdrop and settles back into her banana cake.*]

GARDNER (*To* FANNY): You'll never guess who I ran into on Chestnut Street . . . Pate Baldwin!

[GARDNER *takes his coat off and drops it on the floor. He sits in one of the posing chairs.*]

MAGS (*Mouth full of cake*): Oh, Daddy, I'm nowhere near ready for you yet.

FANNY (*Picks up* GARDNER'S *coat and hands it to him*): Darling, coats do *not* go on the floor.

GARDNER (*Rises, but forgets where he's supposed to go*): He was in terrible shape. I hardly recognized him. Well, it's the Parkinson's disease . . .

FANNY: You mean, Hodgkin's disease . . .

GARDNER: Hodgkin's disease . . .?

MAGS (*Leaves her cake and returns to the tablecloth*): Now to figure out exactly how to use this gorgeous light . . .

FANNY: Yes, Pate has Hodgkin's disease, not Parkinson's disease. Sammy Bishop has Parkinson's disease. In the closet . . . your coat goes . . . in the closet!

GARDNER: You're absolutely right! Pate has Hodgkin's disease. (*He stands motionless, the coat over his arm*)

FANNY: And Goat Davis has Addison's disease.

GARDNER: I always get them confused.

FANNY (*Pointing towards the closet*): That way . . .

[GARDNER *exits to the closet;* FANNY *calls after him.*]

FANNY: Grace Phelps has it too, I think. Or, it might be Hodgkin's, like Pate. I can't remember.

GARDNER (*Returns with a hanger*): Doesn't The Goat have Parkinson's disease?

FANNY: No, that's Sammy Bishop.

GARDNER: God, I haven't seen The Goat in ages! (*The coat still over his arm, he hands* FANNY *the hanger*)

FANNY: He hasn't been well.

GARDNER: Didn't Heppy . . . *die?*!

FANNY: What are you giving me this for? . . . Oh, Heppy's been dead for years. She died on the same day as Luster Bright, don't you remember?

GARDNER: I always liked her.

FANNY (*Gives* GARDNER *back the hanger*): Here, I don't want this.

GARDNER: She was awfully attractive.

FANNY: Who?

GARDNER: Heppy!

FANNY: Oh, yes, Heppy had real charm.

MAGS (*Keeps adjusting the tablecloth*): Better . . . better . . .

GARDNER: Which is something The Goat is short on, if you ask me. He has Hodgkin's disease, doesn't he? (*Puts his raincoat back on and sits down*)

FANNY: Darling, what *are* you doing? I thought you wanted to hang up your coat!

GARDNER (*After a pause*): OH, YES, THAT'S RIGHT!

[GARDNER *goes back to the closet; a pause.*]

FANNY: Where were we?

GARDNER (*Returns with yet another hanger*): Let's see . . .

FANNY (*Takes both hangers from him*): FOR GOD'S SAKE, GAR, PAY ATTENTION!

GARDNER: It was something about The Goat . . .

FANNY (*Takes the coat from* GARDNER): HERE, LET ME DO IT! . . . (*Under her breath to* MAGS) See what I mean about him? You don't know the half of it!

[FANNY *hangs the raincoat up in the closet.*]

FANNY: Not the half.

MAGS (*Still tinkering with the backdrop*): Almost . . . almost . . .

GARDNER (*Sitting back down in one of the posing chairs*): Oh, Fan, did I tell you, I ran into Pate Baldwin just now. I'm afraid he's not long for this world.

FANNY (*Returning*): Well, it's that Hodgkin's disease . . . (*She sits on the posing chair next to him*)

GARDNER: God, I'd hate to see him go. He's one of the great editors of our times. I couldn't have done it without him. He gave me everything, everything!

MAGS (*Makes a final adjustment*): Yes, that's it! (*She stands back and gazes at them*) You look wonderful!

FANNY: Isn't it getting to be . . . (*She taps at an imaginary watch on her wrist and drains an imaginary glass*) cocktail time?!

GARDNER (*Looks at his watch*): On the button, on the button! (*He rises*)

FANNY: I'll have the usual, please. Do join us, Mags! Daddy bought some Dubonnet[22] especially for you!

MAGS: Hey. I was just getting some ideas.

GARDNER (*To* MAGS, *as he exits for the bar*): How about a little . . . Dubonnet to wet your whistle?

FANNY: Oh, Mags, it's like old times having you back with us like this!

GARDNER (*Offstage*): THE USUAL FOR YOU, FAN?

FANNY: I wish we saw more of you. . . . PLEASE! . . . Isn't he darling? Have you ever known anyone more darling than Daddy?

GARDNER (*Offstage; hums Jolson's "You Made Me Love You"*)[23]: MAGS, HOW ABOUT YOU? . . . A LITTLE . . . DUBONNET?

FANNY: Oh, *do* join us! MAGS (*To* GARDNER): No, nothing, thanks.

FANNY: Well, what do you think of your aged parents picking up and moving to Cotuit year round? Pretty crazy, eh what? . . . Nothing but the gulls, oysters and us!

GARDNER (*Returns with* FANNY'S *drink*): Here you go . . .

[22]Brand of alcoholic drink, taken as an appetizer before meals.

[23]Al Jolson (1888–1950), American musical theater and movie star. He first sang "You Made Me Love You" in the Broadway musical *Honeymoon Express* (1913). Interest in Jolson and his rendition of the song was revived in the 1940s with the production of the motion picture *The Jolson Story* (1945).

FANNY: Why thank you, Gar. (*To* MAGS) You sure you won't join us?

GARDNER (*Lifts his glass towards* FANNY *and* MAGS): Cheers!

[GARDNER *and* FANNY *take that first lifesaving gulp.*]

FANNY: Aaaaahhhhh! GARDNER: Hits the spot, hits the spot!

MAGS: Well, I certainly can't do you like that!

FANNY: Why not? I think we look very . . . *comme il faut!*

[FANNY *slouches into a rummy pose;* GARDNER *joins her.*]

FANNY: WAIT . . . I'VE GOT IT! I'VE GOT IT! (*She whispers excitedly to* GARDNER)

MAGS: Come on, let's not start this again!

GARDNER: What's that? . . . Oh, yes . . . yes, yes . . . I know the one you mean. Yes, right, right . . . of course.

[*A pause.*]

FANNY: How's . . . *this?!*

[FANNY *grabs a large serving fork and she and* GARDNER *fly into an imitation of Grant Wood's American Gothic.*][24]

MAGS: And I wonder why it's taken me all these years to get you to pose for me. You just don't take me seriously! Poor old Mags and her ridiculous portraits . . .

FANNY: Oh, darling, your portraits aren't *ridiculous!* They may not be all that one *hopes* for, but they're certainly not—

MAGS: Remember how you behaved at my first group show in Soho? . . . Oh, come on, you remember. It was a real circus! Think back. . . . It was about six years ago. . . . Daddy had just been awarded some presidential medal of achievement and you insisted he wear it around his neck on a bright red ribbon, and you wore this . . . *huge* feathered hat to match! I'll never forget it! It was the size of a giant pizza with twenty-inch red turkey feathers shooting straight up into the air. . . . Oh, come on, you remember, don't you?

FANNY (*Leaping to her feet*): HOLD EVERYTHING! THIS IS IT! THIS IS REALLY IT! Forgive me for interrupting, Mags darling, it'll just take a minute. (*She whispers excitedly to* GARDNER)

MAGS: I had about eight portraits in the show, mostly of friends of mine, except for this old one I'd done of Mrs. Crowninshield.

GARDNER: All right, all right . . . let's give it a whirl.

[*A pause; then they mime Michelangelo's* Pietà[25] *with* GARDNER *lying across* FANNY'S *lap as the dead Christ.*]

[24]Title of a painting by Grant Wood (1892–1942), American artist. One of the most recognizable pieces of American art ever created, it shows a stern-faced woman and man standing before a framed house built in American gothic style, the man holding a pitchfork upright.

[25]Statue of the Virgin Mary holding the body of the dead Jesus, created by the Italian artist Michelangelo Buonarroti (1475–1561).

MAGS (*Depressed*): The *Pietà*. Terrific!

FANNY (*Jabbing* GARDNER *in the ribs*): Hey, we're getting good at this.

GARDNER: Of course it would help if we didn't have all these modern clothes on.

MAGS: AS I WAS SAYING . . .

FANNY: Sorry, Mags . . . sorry . . .

[*Huffing and creaking with the physical exertion of it all,* FANNY *and* GARDNER *return to their seats.*]

MAGS: As soon as you stepped foot in the gallery you spotted it and cried out, "MY GOD, WHAT'S MILLICENT CROWNINSHIELD DOING HERE?" Everyone looked up, what with Daddy's clanking medal and your amazing hat which I was sure would take off and start flying around the room. A crowd gathered. . . . Through some utter fluke, you latched on to *the* most important critic in the city, I mean . . . Mr. Modern Art himself, and you hauled him over to the painting, trumpeting out for all to hear, "THAT'S MILLICENT CROWNINSHIELD! I GREW UP WITH HER. SHE LIVES RIGHT DOWN THE STREET FROM US IN BOSTON. BUT IT'S A VERY POOR LIKENESS, IF YOU ASK ME! HER NOSE ISN'T NEARLY THAT LARGE AND SHE DOESN'T HAVE SOMETHING QUEER GROWING OUT OF HER CHIN! THE CROWNINSHIELDS ARE REALLY QUITE GOOD-LOOKING, STUFFY, BUT GOOD-LOOKING NONETHELESS!"

GARDNER (*Suddenly jumps up, ablaze*): WAIT, WAIT . . . IF IT'S MICHELANGELO YOU WANT . . . I'm sorry, Mags. . . . One more . . . just one more . . . please?

MAGS: Sure, why not? Be my guest.

GARDNER: Fanny, prepare yourself!

[*More whispering.*]

FANNY: But I think *you* should be God.

GARDNER: Me? . . . Really?

FANNY: Yes, it's much more appropriate.

GARDNER: Well, if you say so . . .

[FANNY *and* GARDNER *ease down to the floor with some difficulty and lie on their sides,* FANNY *as Adam,* GARDNER *as God, their fingers inching closer and closer in the attitude of Michelangelo's The Creation.*[26] *Finally they touch.* MAGS *cheers, whistles, applauds.*]

MAGS: THREE CHEERS . . . VERY GOOD . . . NICELY DONE, NICELY DONE!

[FANNY *and* GARDNER *hold the pose a moment more, flushed with pleasure; then rise, dust themselves off and grope back to their chairs.*]

MAGS: So, there we were . . .

FANNY: Yes, *do* go on!

MAGS: . . . huddled around Millicent Crowninshield, when you whipped into your pocketbook and suddenly announced, "HOLD EVERYTHING! I'VE GOT A PHOTOGRAPH OF HER RIGHT HERE, THEN YOU CAN SEE WHAT SHE REALLY LOOKS

[26]The name given a section of Michelangelo's painting on the ceiling of the Sistine Chapel in the Vatican. It shows the finger of God reaching out to touch and give life to Adam.

LIKE!" . . . You then proceeded to crouch down to the floor and dump everything out of your bag, and I mean . . . *everything!* . . . leaking packets of sequins and gummed stars, seashells, odd pieces of fur, crochet hooks, a monarch butterfly embedded in plastic, dental floss, antique glass buttons, small jingling bells, lace . . . I thought I'd die! Just sink to the floor and quietly die! . . . You couldn't find it, you see. I mean, you spent the rest of the afternoon on your hands and knees crawling through this ocean of junk, muttering, "It's *got* to be here somewhere; I know I had it with me!" . . . Then Daddy pulled me into the thick of it all and said, "By the way, have you met our daughter Mags yet? She's the one who did all these pictures . . . paintings . . . portraits . . . whatever you call them." (*She drops to her hands and knees and begins crawling out of the room*) By this time, Mum had somehow crawled out of the gallery and was lost on another floor. She began calling for me . . . "YOO-HOO, MAGS . . . WHERE ARE YOU? . . . OH, MAGS, DARLING . . . HELLO? . . . ARE YOU THERE?" (*She reenters and faces them*) This was at my *first* show.

[*Blackout.*]

SCENE 3

Twenty-four hours later. The impact of the impending move has struck with hurricane force. FANNY *has lugged all their clothing into the room and dumped it in various cartons. There are coats, jackets, shoes, skirts, suits, hats, sweaters, dresses, the works. She and* GARDNER *are seated on the sofa, going through it all.* FANNY, *wearing a different hat and dress, holds up a ratty overcoat.*

FANNY: What about this gruesome old thing?

[GARDNER *is wearing several sweaters and vests, a Hawaiian holiday shirt, and a variety of scarves and ties around his neck. He holds up a pair of shoes.*]

GARDNER: God . . . remember these shoes? Pound[27] gave them to me when he came back from Italy. I remember it vividly.

FANNY: *Do* let me give it to the thrift shop! (*She stuffs the coat into the appropriate carton*)

GARDNER: He bought them for me in Rome. Said he couldn't resist; bought himself a pair too since we both wore the same size. God, I miss him! (*Pause*) HEY, WHAT ARE YOU DOING WITH MY OVERCOAT?!

FANNY: Darling, it's threadbare!

GARDNER: But that's my overcoat! (*He grabs it out of the carton*) I've been wearing it every day for the past thirty-five years!

FANNY: That's just my point: it's had it.

GARDNER (*Puts it on over everything else*): There's nothing wrong with this coat!

FANNY: I trust you remember that the cottage is an eighth the size of this place and you simply won't have room for half this stuff! (*She holds up a sports jacket*) This dreary old jacket, for instance. You've had it since Hector was a pup!

[27]Ezra Pound (1885–1972), American poet.

GARDNER (*Grabs the jacket and puts it on over his coat*): Oh, no, you don't . . .
FANNY: And this God-awful hat . . .
GARDNER: Let me see that.

[GARDNER *stands next to* FANNY *and they fall into a lovely tableau.* MAGS *suddenly pops out from behind a wardrobe carton with a flash camera and takes a picture of them.*]

MAGS: PERFECT!

FANNY (*Hands flying to her face*): GOOD GOD, WHAT WAS THAT . . . ?

GARDNER (*Hands flying to his heart*): JESUS CHRIST, I'VE BEEN SHOT!

MAGS (*Walks to the center of the room, advancing the film*): That was terrific. See if you can do it again.
FANNY: What *are* you doing . . . ?
GARDNER (*Feeling his chest*): Is there blood?
FANNY: I see lace everywhere . . .
MAGS: It's all right, I was just taking a picture of you. I often use a Polaroid at this stage.
FANNY (*Rubbing her eyes*): Really, Mags, you might have given us some warning!
MAGS: But that's the whole point: to catch you unawares!
GARDNER (*Rubbing his eyes*): It's the damndest thing . . . I see lace everywhere.
FANNY: Yes, so do I . . .
GARDNER: It's rather nice, actually. It looks as if you're wearing a veil.
FANNY: I *am* wearing a veil!

[*The camera spits out the photograph.*]

MAGS: OH GOODY, HERE COMES THE PICTURE!
FANNY (*Grabs the partially developed print out of her hands*): Let me see, let me see . . .
GARDNER: Yes, let's have a look.

[GARDNER *and* FANNY *have another quiet moment together looking at the photograph.* MAGS *tiptoes away from them and takes another picture.*]

MAGS: YES!

FANNY: NOT AGAIN! PLEASE, DARLING!

GARDNER: WHAT WAS THAT? . . . WHAT HAPPENED?

[FANNY *and* GARDNER *stagger towards each other.*]

MAGS: I'm sorry, I just couldn't resist. You looked so—
FANNY: WHAT ARE YOU TRYING TO DO . . . *BLIND* US?!
GARDNER: Really, Mags, enough is enough . . .

[GARDNER *and* FANNY *keep stumbling about kiddingly.*]

FANNY: Are you still there, Gar?

GARDNER: Right as rain, right as rain!

MAGS: I'm sorry; I didn't mean to scare you. It's just a photograph can show you things you weren't aware of. Here, have a look. (*She gives them to* FANNY) Well, I'm going out to the kitchen to get something to eat. Anybody want anything? (*She exits*)

FANNY (*Looking at the photos, half-amused, half-horrified*): Oh, Gardner, have you ever . . . ?

GARDNER (*Looks at the photos and laughs*): Good grief . . .

MAGS (*Offstage; from the kitchen*): IS IT ALL RIGHT IF I TAKE THE REST OF THIS TAPIOCA FROM LAST NIGHT?

FANNY: IT'S ALL RIGHT WITH ME. How about you, Gar?

GARDNER: Sure, go right ahead. I've never been that crazy about tapioca.

FANNY: What are you talking about, tapioca is one of your favorites.

MAGS (*Enters, slurping from a large bowl*): Mmmmmmmm . . .

FANNY: Really, Mags, I've never seen anyone eat as much as you.

MAGS (*Takes the photos back*): It's strange. I only do this when I come home.

FANNY: What's the matter, don't I feed you enough?

GARDNER: Gee, it's hot in here! (*Starts taking off his coat*)

FANNY: God knows, you didn't eat anything as a child! I've never seen such a fussy eater. Gar, what *are* you doing?

GARDNER (*Shedding clothes to the floor*): Taking off some of these clothes. It's hotter than Tophet[28] in here!

MAGS (*Looking at her photos*): Yes, I like you looking at each other like that . . .

FANNY (*To* GARDNER): Please watch where you're dropping things; I'm trying to keep some order around here.

GARDNER (*Picks up what he dropped, dropping even more in the process*): Right, right . . .

MAGS: Now all I've got to do is figure out what you should wear.

FANNY: Well, I'm going to wear my long black dress, and you'd be a fool not to do Daddy in his tuxedo. He looks so distinguished in it, just like a banker!

MAGS: I haven't really decided yet.

FANNY: Just because you walk around looking like something the cat dragged in, doesn't mean Daddy and I want to, do we Gar?

[GARDNER *is making a worse and worse tangle of his clothes.*]

FANNY: HELLO . . . ?

GARDNER (*Looks up at* FANNY): Oh, yes, awfully attractive, awfully attractive!

FANNY (*To* MAGS): If you don't mind me saying so, I've never seen you looking so forlorn. You'll never catch a husband looking that way. Those peculiar clothes, that God-awful hair . . . really, Mags, it's very distressing!

MAGS: I don't think my hair's so bad, not that it's terrific or anything . . .

FANNY: Well, I don't see other girls walking around like you. I mean, girls from your background. What would Lyman Wigglesworth think if he saw you in the street?

MAGS: Lyman Wigglesworth?! . . . Uuuuuuughhhhhhh! (*She shudders*)

[28] In the Bible, a place for the punishment of the wicked after death.

FANNY: All right then, that brilliant Cabot boy . . . what *is* his name?

GARDNER: Sammy.

FANNY: No, not Sammy . . .

GARDNER: Stephen . . . Stanley . . . Stuart . . . Sheldon . . . Sherlock . . . Sherlock! It's *Sherlock!*

MAGS: Spence!

FANNY: SPENCE, THAT'S IT! HIS NAME IS SPENCE!

GARDNER: THAT'S IT . . . SPENCE! SPENCE CABOT!

FANNY: Spence Cabot was first in his class at Harvard.

MAGS: Mum, he has no facial hair.

FANNY: He has his own law firm on Arlington Street.

MAGS: Spence Cabot has six fingers on his right hand!

FANNY: So, he isn't the best-looking thing in the world. Looks isn't everything. He can't help it if he has extra fingers. Have a little sympathy!

MAGS: But the extra one has this weird nail on it that looks like a talon . . . It's long and black and . . . (*She shudders*)

FANNY: No one's perfect, darling. He has lovely handwriting and an absolutely saintly mother. Also, he's as rich as Croesus![29] He's a lot more promising than some of those creatures you've dragged home. What was the name of that dreadful Frenchman who smelled like sweaty socks? . . . Jean Duke of Scripto?

MAGS (*Laughing*): Jean-Luc Zichot!

FANNY: And that peculiar little Oriental fellow with all the teeth! Really, Mags, he could have been put on display at the circus!

MAGS: Oh, yes, Tsu Chin. He was strange, but very sexy . . .

FANNY (*Shudders*): He had such tiny . . . feet! Really, Mags, you've got to bear down. You're not getting any younger. Before you know it, all the nice young men will be taken and then where will you be? . . . All by yourself in that grim little apartment of yours with those peculiar clothes and that bright red hair . . .

MAGS: MY HAIR IS NOT BRIGHT RED!

FANNY: I only want what's best for you, you know that. You seem to go out of your way to look wanting. I don't understand it. . . . Gar, what *are* you putting your coat on for? . . . You look like some derelict out on the street. We don't wear coats in the house. (*She helps him out of it*) That's the way. . . . I'll just put this in the carton along with everything else . . . (*She drops it into the carton, then pauses*) Isn't it about time for . . . *cocktails!*

GARDNER: What's that?

[FANNY *taps her wrist and mimes drinking.*]

GARDNER (*Looks at his watch*): Right you are, right you are! (*Exits to the bar*) THE USUAL . . .?

FANNY: *Please!*

GARDNER (*Offstage*): HOW ABOUT SOMETHING FOR YOU MAGS?

[29]Ancient king of Lydia (560–546 B.C.), noted for his immense wealth.

MAGS: SURE, WHY NOT? . . . LET'ER RIP!

GARDNER (*Offstage*): WHAT'S THAT . . .?

FANNY: SHE SAID YES. SHE SAID YES! MAGS: I'LL HAVE SOME DUBONNET! YES!

GARDNER (*Poking his head back in*): How about a little Dubonnet?

FANNY: That's just what she said. . . . She'd like some . . . Dubonnet!

GARDNER (*Goes back to the bar and hums another Jolson tune*): GEE, IT'S GREAT HAVING YOU BACK LIKE THIS, MAGS . . . IT'S JUST GREAT! (*More singing*)

FANNY (*Leaning closer to* MAGS): You have such *potential,* darling! It breaks my heart to see how you've let yourself go. If Lyman Wigglesworth . . .

MAGS: Amazing as it may seem, I don't *care* about Lyman Wigglesworth!

FANNY: From what I've heard, he's quite a lady killer!

MAGS: But with whom? . . . Don't think I haven't heard about his fling with . . . Hopie Stonewall!

FANNY (*Begins to laugh*): Oh, God, let's not get started on Hopie Stonewall again . . . ten feet tall with spots on her neck . . . (*To* GARDNER) OH, DARLING, DO HURRY BACK! WE'RE TALKING ABOUT PATHETIC HOPIE STONEWALL!

MAGS: It's not so much her incredible height and spotted skin; it's those tiny pointed teeth and the size eleven shoes!

FANNY: I love it when you're like this!

[MAGS *starts clomping around the room making tiny pointed-teeth nibbling sounds.*]

FANNY: GARDNER . . . YOU'RE MISSING EVERYTHING! (*Still laughing*) Why is it Boston girls are always so . . . tall?

MAGS: Hopie Stonewall isn't a Boston girl; she's a giraffe. (*She prances around the room with an imaginary dwarf-sized Lyman*) She's perfect for Lyman Wigglesworth!

GARDNER (*Returns with* FANNY'S *drink, which he hands her*): Now, where were we . . .?

FANNY (*Trying not to laugh*): HOPIE STONEWALL . . .!

GARDNER: Oh, yes, she's the very tall one, isn't she?

[FANNY *and* MAGS *burst into gales.*]

MAGS: The only hope for us . . . "Boston girls" is to get as far away from our kind as possible.

FANNY: She always asks after you, darling. She's very fond of you, you know.

MAGS: Please, I don't want to hear!

FANNY: Your old friends are *always* asking after you.

MAGS: It's not so much how creepy they all are, as how much they remind me of myself!

FANNY: But you're not "creepy," darling . . . just . . . shabby!

MAGS: I mean, give me a few more inches and some brown splotches here and there, and Hopie and I could be sisters!

FANNY (*In a whisper to* GARDNER): Don't you love it when Mags is like this? I could listen to her forever!

MAGS: I mean . . . look at me!

FANNY (*Gasping*): Don't stop, don't stop!

MAGS: Awkward . . . plain . . . I don't know how to dress, I don't know how to talk. When people find out Daddy's my father, they're always amazed. . . . "Gardner Church is YOUR father?! Aw, come on, you're kidding?!"

FANNY (*In a whisper*): Isn't she divine . . .?

MAGS: Sometimes I don't even tell them. I pretend I grew up in the Midwest somewhere . . . farming people . . . we work with our hands.

GARDNER (*To* MAGS): Well, how about a little refill . . .?

MAGS: No, no more thanks.

[*Pause.*]

FANNY: What did you have to go and interrupt her for? She was just getting up a head of steam . . .

MAGS (*Walking over to her easel*): The great thing about being a portrait painter, you see, is it's the *other* guy that's exposed; you're safely hidden behind the canvas and easel. (*Standing behind it*) You can be as plain as a pitchfork, as inarticulate as mud, but it doesn't matter because you're completely concealed: your body, your face, your intentions. Just as you make your most intimate move, throw open your soul . . . they stretch and yawn, remembering the dog has to be let out at five. . . . To be so invisible while so enthralled . . . it takes your breath away!

GARDNER: Well put, Mags. Awfully well put!

MAGS: That's why I've always wanted to paint you, to see if I'm up to it. It's quite a risk. Remember what I went through as a child with my great masterpiece . . .?

FANNY: You painted a masterpiece when you were a child . . .?

MAGS: Well, it was a masterpiece to me.

FANNY: I had no idea you were precocious as a child. Gardner, do you remember Mags painting a masterpiece as a child?

MAGS: I didn't paint it. It was something I made!

FANNY: Well, this is all news to me! Gar, *do* get me another drink! I haven't had this much fun in years! (*She hands him her glass and reaches for* MAGS'S) Come on, darling, join me . . .

MAGS: No, no more, thanks. I don't really like the taste.

FANNY: Oh, come on, kick up your heels for once!

MAGS: No, nothing . . . really.

FANNY: Please? Pretty please? . . . To keep me company?!

MAGS (*Hands* GARDNER *her glass*): Oh, all right, what the hell . . .

FANNY: That's a good girl!

GARDNER (*Exiting*): Coming right up, coming right up!

FANNY (*Yelling after* GARDNER): DON'T GIVE ME TOO MUCH NOW. THE LAST ONE WAS AWFULLY STRONG . . . AND HURRY BACK SO YOU DON'T MISS ANYTHING! . . . Daddy's so cunning, I don't know what I'd do without him. If anything should happen to him, I'd just . . .

MAGS: Mummy, nothing's going to happen to him . . .!

FANNY: Well, wait till you're our age, it's no garden party. Now . . . where were we . . .?

MAGS: My first masterpiece . . .

FANNY: Oh, yes, but *do* wait till Daddy gets back so he can hear it too: . . . YOO-HOO . . . GARRRRRRDNERRRRRR? . . . ARE YOU COMING? (*Silence*) Go and check on him will you?

[GARDNER *enters with both drinks. He's very shaken.*]

GARDNER: I couldn't find the ice.

FANNY: Well, *finally!*

GARDNER: It just up and disappeared . . . (*Hands* FANNY *her drink*) There you go. (FANNY *kisses her fingers and takes a hefty swig*) Mags. (*He hands* MAGS *her drink*)

MAGS: Thanks, Daddy.

GARDNER: Sorry about the ice.

MAGS: No problem, no problem.

[GARDNER *sits down; silence.*]

FANNY (*To* MAGS): Well, drink up, drink up! (MAGS *downs it in one gulp*) GOOD-GIRL! . . . Now, what's all this about a masterpiece . . .?

MAGS: I did it during that winter you sent me away from the dinner table. I was about nine years old.

FANNY: We sent you from the dinner table?

MAGS: I was banished for six months.

FANNY: You *were?* . . . How extraordinary!

MAGS: Yes, it *was* rather extraordinary!

FANNY: But why?

MAGS: Because I played with my food.

FANNY: You did?

MAGS: I used to squirt it out between my front teeth.

FANNY: Oh, I remember that! God, it used to drive me crazy, absolutely . . . crazy! (*Pause*) "MARGARET, STOP THAT OOZING RIGHT THIS MINUTE, YOU ARE NOT A TUBE OF TOOTHPASTE!"

GARDNER: Oh, yes . . .

FANNY: It was perfectly disgusting!

GARDNER: I remember. She used to lean over her plate and squirt it out in long runny ribbons . . .

FANNY: That's enough, dear.

GARDNER: They were quite colorful, actually; decorative almost. She made the most intricate designs. They looked rather like small, moist Oriental rugs . . .

FANNY (*To* MAGS): But why, darling? What on earth possessed you to do it?

MAGS: I couldn't swallow anything. My throat just closed up. I don't know, I must have been afraid of choking or something.

GARDNER: I remember one in particular. We'd had chicken fricassee and spinach. . . . She made the most extraordinary—

FANNY (*To* GARDNER): WILL YOU PLEASE SHUT UP?! (*Pause*) Mags, what *are* you talking about? You never choked in your entire life! This is the most distressing conversation I've ever had. Don't you think it's distressing, Gar?

GARDNER: Well, that's not quite the word I'd use.

FANNY: What word *would* you use, then?

GARDNER: I don't know right off the bat, I'd have to think about it.

FANNY: THEN, THINK ABOUT IT!

[*Silence.*]

MAGS: I guess I was afraid of making a mess. I don't know; you were awfully strict about table manners. I was always afraid of losing control. What if I started to choke and began spitting up over everything . . .?

FANNY: All right, dear, that's enough.

MAGS: No, I was really terrified about making a mess; you always got so mad whenever I spilled. If I just got rid of everything in neat little curlicues beforehand, you see. . .

FANNY: I SAID: THAT'S ENOUGH!

[*Silence.*]

MAGS: I thought it was quite ingenious, but you didn't see it that way. You finally sent me from the table with, "When you're ready to eat like a human being, you can come back and join us!" . . . So, it was off to my room with a tray. But I couldn't seem to eat there either. I mean, it was so strange settling down to dinner in my *bedroom*. . . . So I just flushed everything down the toilet and sat on my bed listening to you: clinkity-clink, clatter clatter, slurp, slurp . . . but that got pretty boring after a while, so I looked around for something to do. It was wintertime, because I noticed I'd left some crayons on top of my radiator and they'd melted down into these beautiful shimmering globs, like spilled jello, trembling and pulsing . . .

GARDNER (*Overlapping; eyes closed*):
"This luscious and impeccable fruit of life
Falls, it appears, of its own weight to earth . . ."

MAGS: Naturally, I wanted to try it myself, so I grabbed a red one and pressed it down against the hissing lid. It oozed and bubbled like raspberry jam!

GARDNER:
"When you were Eve, its acrid juice was sweet,
Untasted, in its heavenly, orchard air . . ."

MAGS: I mean, that radiator was really hot! It took incredible will power not to let go, but I held on, whispering, "Mags, if you let go of this crayon, you'll be run over by a truck on Newberry Street, so help you God!" . . . So I pressed down harder, my fingers steaming and blistering . . .

FANNY: I had no idea about any of this, did you, Gar?

MAGS: Once I'd melted one, I was hooked! I finished off my entire supply in one night, mixing color over color until my head swam! . . . The heat, the smell, the brilliance that sank and rose . . . I'd never felt such exhilaration! . . . Every week I spent my allowance on crayons. I must have cleared out every box of Crayolas in the city!

GARDNER (*Gazing at* MAGS): You know, I don't think I've ever seen you looking prettier! You're awfully attractive when you get going!

FANNY: Why, what a lovely thing to say.

MAGS: AFTER THREE MONTHS THAT RADIATOR WAS . . . SPECTACULAR! I MEAN, IT LOOKED LIKE SOME COLOSSAL FRUITCAKE, FIVE FEET TALL . . .!

FANNY: It sounds perfectly hideous.

MAGS: It was a knockout; shimmering with pinks and blues, lavenders, and maroons, turquoise and golds, oranges and creams. . . . For every color, I imagined a taste . . . YELLOW: lemon curls dipped in sugar . . . RED: glazed cherries laced with rum . . . GREEN: tiny peppermint leaves veined with chocolate . . . PURPLE:—

FANNY: That's quite enough!

MAGS: And then the frosting . . . ahhhh, the frosting! A satiny mix of white and silver . . . I kept it hidden under blankets during the day. . . . My huge . . . (*She starts laughing*) looming . . . teetering sweet—

FANNY: I ASKED YOU TO STOP! GARDNER, WILL YOU PLEASE GET HER TO STOP!

GARDNER: See here, Mags, Mum asked you to—

MAGS: I was so . . . *hungry* . . . losing weight every week. I looked like a scarecrow what with the bags under my eyes and bits of crayon wrapper leaking out of my clothes. It's a wonder you didn't notice. But finally you came to my rescue . . . if you could call what happened rescue. It was more like a rout!

FANNY: Darling . . . *please!*	GARDNER: Now, look, young lady—

MAGS: The winter was almost over . . . It was very late at night. . . . I must have been having a nightmare because suddenly you and Daddy were at my bed, shaking me. . . . I quickly glanced towards the radiator to see if it was covered. . . . *It wasn't!* It glittered and towered in the moonlight like some . . . gigantic Viennese pastry! You followed my gaze and saw it. Mummy screamed . . . "WHAT HAVE YOU GOT IN HERE? . . . MAGS, WHAT HAVE YOU BEEN DOING?" . . . She crept forward and touched it, and then jumped back. "IT'S FOOD!" she cried . . . "IT'S ALL THE FOOD SHE'S BEEN SPITTING OUT! OH, GARDNER, ITS A MOUNTAIN OF ROTTING GARBAGE!"

FANNY (*Softly*): Yes . . . it's coming back . . . it's coming back . . .

MAGS: Daddy exited as usual; left the premises. He fainted, just keeled over onto the floor . . .

GARDNER: Gosh, I don't remember any of this . . .

MAGS: My heart stopped! I mean, I knew it was all over. My lovely creation didn't have a chance. Sure enough . . . out came the blowtorch. Well, it couldn't have *really* been a blowtorch, I mean, where would you have ever gotten a blowtorch? . . . I just have this very strong memory of you standing over my bed, your hair streaming around your face, aiming this . . . flamethrower at my confection . . . my cake . . . my tart . . . my strudel. . . . "IT'S GOT TO BE DESTROYED IMMEDIATELY! THE THING'S ALIVE WITH VERMIN! . . . JUST LOOK AT IT! . . . IT'S PRACTICALLY CRAWLING ACROSS THE ROOM!" . . . Of course in a sense you were right. It *was* a monument of my castoff dinners, only I hadn't built it with food. . . . I found my own materials. I was languishing with hunger, but oh, dear Mother . . . I FOUND MY OWN MATERIALS . . .!

FANNY: Darling . . . *please?!*

MAGS: I tried to stop you, but you wouldn't listen. . . . OUT SHOT THE FLAME! . . . I remember these waves of wax rolling across the room and Daddy coming to, wondering what on earth was going on. . . . Well, what did you know about my abilities? . . . You see, I had . . . I mean, I *have* abilities . . . (*Struggling to say it*) I have abilities. I have . . . strong abilities. I have . . . very strong abilities. They are very strong . . . very, very strong . . .

[MAGS *rises and runs out of the room overcome as* FANNY *and* GARDNER *watch, speechless. The curtain falls.*]

ACT II

SCENE 1

Three days later. Miracles have been accomplished. Almost all of the Churches' furniture has been moved out, and the cartons of dishes and clothing are gone. All that remains are odds and ends. MAGS'S *tableau looms, impregnable.* FANNY *and* GARDNER *are dressed in their formal evening clothes, frozen in their pose. They hold absolutely still.* MAGS *stands at her easel, her hands covering her eyes.*

FANNY: All right, you can look now.

MAGS (*Removes her hands*): Yes! . . . I told you you could trust me on the pose.

FANNY: Well, thank God you let us dress up. It makes all the difference. Now we really look like something.

MAGS (*Starts to sketch them*): I'll say . . .

[*A silence as she sketches.*]

GARDNER (*Recites Yeats's "The Song of Wandering Aengus"*[30] *in a wonderfully resonant voice as they pose*):

"I went out to the hazel wood,
Because a fire was in my head,
And cut and peeled a hazel wand,
And hooked a berry to a thread,
And when white moths were on the wing,
And moth-like stars were flickering out,
I dropped the berry in a stream
And caught a little silver trout.

When I had laid it on the floor
I went to blow the fire a-flame,
But something rustled on the floor,
And someone called me by my name:
It had become a glimmering girl
With apple blossoms in her hair
Who called me by my name and ran
And faded through the brightening air.

[30]Gardner quotes the complete text of "The Song of the Wandering Aengus" by the Irish poet William Butler Yeats (1865–1939).

Though I am old with wandering
Through hollow lands and hilly lands,
I will find out where she has gone,
And kiss her lips and take her hands;
And walk among long dappled grass,
And pluck till time and times are done,
The silver apples of the moon,
The golden apples of the sun."

FANNY: That's lovely, dear. Just lovely. Is it one of yours?

GARDNER: No, no, it's Yeats. I'm using it in my book.

FANNY: Well, you recited it beautifully, but then you've always recited beautifully. That's how you wooed me, in case you've forgotten. . . . You must have memorized every love poem in the English language! There was no stopping you when you got going . . . your Shakespeare, Byron, and Shelley . . . you were shameless . . . *shameless!*

GARDNER (*Eyes closed*):

"I will find out where she has gone,
And kiss her lips and take her hands . . ."

FANNY: And then there was your own poetry to do battle with; your sonnets and quatrains. When you got going with them, there was nothing left of me! You could have had your pick of any girl in Boston! Why you chose me, I'll never understand. I had no looks to speak of and nothing much in the brains department. . . . Well, what did you know about women and the world? . . . What did any of us know . . .?

[*Silence.*]

FANNY: GOD, MAGS, HOW LONG ARE WE SUPPOSED TO SIT LIKE THIS? . . . IT'S AGONY!

MAGS (*Working away*): You're doing fine . . . just fine . . .

FANNY (*Breaking her pose*): It's so . . . boring!

MAGS: Come on, don't move. You can have a break soon.

FANNY: I had no idea it would be so boring!

GARDNER: Gee, I'm enjoying it.

FANNY: You would . . .!

[*A pause.*]

GARDNER (*Begins reciting more Yeats, almost singing it*):

"He stood among a crowd at Drumahair;
His heart hung all upon a silken dress,
And he had known at last some tenderness,
Before earth made of him her sleepy care;
But when a man poured fish into a pile,
It seemed they raised their little silver heads . . ."[31]

[31]A quotation from Yeats's "The Man Who Dreamed of Faeryland."

FANNY: Gar . . . PLEASE! (*She lurches out of her seat*) God, I can't take this anymore!

MAGS (*Keeps sketching* GARDNER): I know it's tedious at first, but it gets easier . . .

FANNY: It's like a Chinese water torture! (*Crosses to* MAGS *and looks at* GARDNER *posing*) Oh, darling, you look marvelous, absolutely marvelous! Why don't you just do Daddy!?

MAGS: Because you look marvelous too. I want to do you both!

FANNY: Please! . . . I have one foot in the grave and you know it! Also, we're way behind in our packing. There's still one room left which everyone seems to have forgotten about!

GARDNER: Which one is that?

FANNY: You know perfectly well which one it is!

GARDNER: I do . . .?

FANNY: Yes, you do!

GARDNER: Well, it's news to me.

FANNY: I'll give you a hint. It's in . . . *that* direction. (*She points*)

GARDNER: The dining room?

FANNY: No.

GARDNER: The bedroom?

FANNY: No.

GARDNER: Mags' room?

FANNY: No.

GARDNER: The kitchen?

FANNY: *Gar?!*

GARDNER: The guest room?

FANNY: Your God-awful study!

GARDNER: Oh, shit!

FANNY: That's right, "Oh, shit!" It's books and papers up to the ceiling! If you ask me, we should just forget it's there and quietly tiptoe away . . .

GARDNER: My study . . .!

FANNY: Let the new owners dispose of everything . . .

GARDNER (*Gets out of his posing chair*): Now, just one minute . . .

FANNY: You never look at half the stuff in there!

GARDNER: I don't want you touching those books! They're mine!

FANNY: Darling, we're moving to a cottage the size of a handkerchief! Where, pray tell, is there room for all your books?

GARDNER: I don't know. We'll just have to make room!

MAGS (*Sketching away*): RATS!

FANNY: I don't know what we're doing fooling around with Mags like this when there's still so much to do . . .

GARDNER (*Sits back down, overwhelmed*): My study . . .!

FANNY: You can stay with her if you'd like, but one of us has got to tackle those books! (*She exits to his study*)

GARDNER: I'm not up to this.

MAGS: Oh, good, you're staying!

GARDNER: There's a lifetime of work in there . . .

MAGS: Don't worry, I'll help. Mum and I will be able to pack everything up in no time.

GARDNER: God . . .

MAGS: It won't be so bad . . .

GARDNER: I'm just not up to it.

MAGS: We'll all pitch in . . .

[GARDNER *sighs, speechless. A silence as* FANNY *comes staggering in with an armload of books, which she drops to the floor with a crash.*]

GARDNER: WHAT WAS THAT?! MAGS: GOOD GRIEF!

FANNY (*Sheepish*): Sorry, sorry . . . (*She exits for more*)

GARDNER: I don't know if I can take this . . .

MAGS: Moving is awful . . . I know . . .

GARDNER (*Settling back into his pose*): Ever since Mum began tearing the house apart, I've been having these dreams. . . . I'm a child again back at 16 Louisberg Square[32] . . . and this stream of moving men is carrying furniture into our house . . . van after van of tables and chairs, sofas and love seats, desks and bureaus . . . rugs, bathtubs, mirrors, chiming clocks, pianos, iceboxes, china cabinets . . . but what's amazing is that all of it is familiar . . .

[FANNY *comes in with another load, which she drops on the floor. She exits for more.*]

GARDNER: No matter how many items appear, I've seen every one of them before. Since my mother is standing in the midst of it directing traffic, I ask her where it's all coming from, but she doesn't hear me because of the racket . . . so finally I just scream out . . . "WHERE IS ALL THIS FURNITURE COMING FROM?" . . . Just as a moving man is carrying Toots into the room, she looks at me and says, "Why, from the land of Skye!" . . . The next thing I know, *people* are being carried in along with it . . .

[FANNY *enters with her next load; drops it and exits.*]

GARDNER: People I've never seen before are sitting around our dining-room table. A group of foreigners is going through my books, chattering in a language I've never heard before. A man is playing a Chopin polonaise on Aunt Alice's piano. Several children are taking baths in our tubs from Cotuit . . .

MAGS: It sounds marvelous.

GARDNER: Well, it isn't marvelous at all because all of these perfect strangers have taken over our things . . .

[FANNY *enters, hurls down another load and exits.*]

MAGS: How odd . . .

GARDNER: Well, it *is* odd, but then something even odder happens . . .

MAGS (*Sketching away*): Tell me, tell me!

GARDNER: Well, our beds are carried in. They're all made up with sheets and everything, but instead of all these strange people in them, *we're* in them . . .!

MAGS: What's so odd about that?

[32]Louisberg Square, elegant residential district in Boston.

GARDNER: Well, you and Mum are brought in, both sleeping like angels . . . Mum snoring away to beat the band . . .

MAGS: Yes . . .

[FANNY *enters with another load, lets it fall.*]

GARDNER: But there's no one in mine. It's completely empty, never even been slept in! It's as if I were dead or had never even existed . . .

[FANNY *exits.*]

GARDNER: "HEY . . . WAIT UP!" I yell to the moving men . . . "THAT'S MY BED YOU'VE GOT THERE!" But they don't stop; they don't even acknowledge me. . . . "HEY, COME BACK HERE . . . I WANT TO GET INTO MY BED!" I cry again and I start running after them . . . down the hall, through the dining room, past the library. . . . Finally I catch up to them and hurl myself right into the center of the pillow. Just as I'm about to land, the bed suddenly vanishes and I go crashing down to the floor like some insect that's been hit by a fly swatter!

[FANNY *staggers in with her final load; she drops it with a crash and then collapses in her posing chair.*]

FANNY: THAT'S IT FOR ME! I'M DEAD!

[*Silence.*]

FANNY: Come on, Mags, how about you doing a little work around here.

MAGS: That's all I've been doing! This is the first free moment you've given me!

FANNY: You should see all the books in there . . . and papers! There are enough loose papers to sink a ship!

GARDNER: Why is it we're moving, again . . .?

FANNY: Because life is getting too complicated here.

GARDNER (*Remembering*): Oh, yes . . .

FANNY: And we can't afford it anymore.

GARDNER: That's right, that's right . . .

FANNY: We don't have the . . . *income* we used to!

GARDNER: Oh, yes . . . *income!*

FANNY (*Assuming her pose again*): Of course, we have our savings and various trust funds, but I wouldn't dream of touching those!

GARDNER: No, no, you must never dip into capital!

FANNY: I told Daddy I'd be perfectly happy to buy a gun and put a bullet through our heads so we could avoid all this, but he wouldn't hear of it!

MAGS (*Sketching away*): No, I shouldn't think so.

[*Pause.*]

FANNY: I've always admired people who kill themselves when they get to our stage of life. Well, no one can touch my Uncle Edmond in that department . . .

MAGS: I know, I know . . .

FANNY: The day before his seventieth birthday he climbed to the top of the Old North Church and hurled himself face down into Salem Street! They had to scrape him up with a spatula! God, he was a remarkable man . . . state senator, president of Harvard . . .

GARDNER (*Rises and wanders over to his books*): Well, I guess I'm going to have to do something about all of these . . .

FANNY: Come on Mags, help Daddy! Why don't you start bringing in his papers . . .

[GARDNER *sits on the floor; he picks up a book and soon is engrossed in it.* MAGS *keeps sketching, oblivious. Silence.*]

FANNY (*To* MAGS): Darling? . . . HELLO? . . . God, you two are impossible! Just look at you . . . heads in the clouds! No one would ever know we've got to be out of here in two days. If it weren't for me, nothing would get done around here . . . (*She starts stacking* GARDNER'S *books into piles*) There! That's all the maroon ones!

GARDNER (*Looks up*): What do you mean, *maroon* ones?!

FANNY: All your books that are maroon are in *this* pile . . . and your books that are green in *that* pile! . . . I'm trying to bring some order into your life for once. This will make unpacking so much easier.

GARDNER: But, my dear Fanny, it's not the color of a book that distinguishes it, but what's *inside* it!

FANNY: This will be a great help, you'll see. Now what about this awful striped thing? (*She picks up a slim, aged volume*) Can't it go . . . ?

GARDNER: No!

FANNY: But it's as queer as Dick's hatband! There are no others like it.

GARDNER: Open it and read. Go on . . . open it!

FANNY: We'll get nowhere at this rate.

GARDNER: I said . . . READ!

FANNY: Really, Gar, I—

GARDNER: Read the dedication!

FANNY (*Opens and reads*): "To Gardner Church, you led the way. With gratitude and affection, Robert Frost.[33] (*She closes it and hands it to him*)

GARDNER: It was published the same year as my *Salem Gardens.*

FANNY (*Picking up a very worn book*): Well, what about this dreadful thing? It's filthy. (*She blows off a cloud of dust*)

GARDNER: Please . . . *please?!*

FANNY (*Looking through it*): It's all in French.

GARDNER (*Snatching it away from her*): André Malraux[34] gave me that . . .!

FANNY: I'm just trying to help.

GARDNER: It's a first edition of Baudelaire's *Fleurs du mal.*[35]

FANNY (*Giving it back*): Well, pardon me for living!

GARDNER: Why do you have to drag everything in here in the first place . . . ?

[33]Robert Frost (1874–1963), American poet.

[34]André Malraux (1901–1976), French literary and political figure.

[35]Charles Baudelaire (1821–1867). His collected poems were published as *Les Fleurs du mal* (*The Flowers of Evil*) in 1857.

FANNY: Because there's no room in your study. You ought to see the mess in there! . . . WAKE UP, MAGS, ARE YOU GOING TO PITCH IN OR NOT?!

GARDNER: I'm not up to this.

FANNY: Well, you'd better be unless you want to be left behind!

MAGS (*Stops her sketching*): All right, all right . . . I just hope you'll give me some more time later this evening.

FANNY (*To* MAGS): Since you're young and in the best shape, why don't you bring in the books and I'll cope with the papers. (*She exits to the study*)

GARDNER: Now just a minute . . .

FANNY (*Offstage*): WE NEED A STEAM SHOVEL FOR THIS!

MAGS: Okay, what do you want me to do?

GARDNER: Look, I don't want you messing around with my—

[FANNY *enters with an armful of papers, which she drops into an empty carton.*]

GARDNER: HEY, WHAT'S GOING ON HERE?!

FANNY: I'm packing up your papers. COME ON, MAGS, LET'S GET CRACKING! (*She exits for more papers*)

GARDNER (*Plucks several papers out of the carton*): What is this . . .?

MAGS (*Exits into his study*): GOOD LORD, WHAT HAVE YOU DONE IN HERE?!

GARDNER (*Reading*): This is my manuscript.

[FANNY *enters with another batch, which she tosses on top of the others.*]

GARDNER: What *are* you doing?!

FANNY: Packing, darling . . . PACKING! (*She exits for more*)

GARDNER: SEE HERE, YOU CAN'T MANHANDLE MY THINGS THIS WAY!

[MAGS *enters, staggering under a load of books, which she sets down on the floor.*]

GARDNER: *I* PACK MY MANUSCRIPT! I KNOW WHERE EVERYTHING IS!

FANNY (*Offstage*): IF IT WERE UP TO YOU, WE'D NEVER GET OUT OF HERE! WE'RE UNDER A TIME LIMIT, GARDNER. KITTY'S PICKING US UP IN TWO DAYS . . . TWO . . . DAYS! (*She enters with a larger batch of papers and heads for the carton*)

GARDNER (*Grabbing* FANNY'S *wrist*): NOW, HOLD IT! . . . JUST . . . HOLD IT RIGHT THERE!

FANNY: OOOOOWWWWWWW!

GARDNER: *I* PACK MY THINGS!

FANNY: LET GO, YOU'RE HURTING ME!

GARDNER: THAT'S MY MANUSCRIPT! GIVE IT TO ME!

FANNY (*Lifting the papers high over her head*): I'M IN CHARGE OF THIS MOVE, GARDNER! WE'VE GOT TO GET CRACKING!

GARDNER: I said . . . GIVE IT TO ME!

MAGS: Come on, Mum, let him have it.

[FANNY *and* GARDNER *struggle.*]

GARDNER (*Finally wrenches the pages from* FANNY): LET . . . ME . . . HAVE IT! . . . THAT'S MORE LIKE IT!

FANNY (*Soft and weepy*): You see what he's like? . . . I try and help with his packing and what does he do . . .?

GARDNER (*Rescues the rest of his papers from the carton*): YOU DON'T JUST THROW EVERYTHING INTO A BOX LIKE A PILE OF GARBAGE! THIS IS A BOOK, FANNY. SOMETHING I'VE BEEN WORKING ON FOR TWO YEARS! (*Trying to assemble his papers, but only making things worse, dropping them all over the place*) You show a little respect for my things. . . . You don't just throw them around every which way. . . . It's tricky trying to make sense of poetry; it's much easier to write the stuff . . . that is, if you've still got it in you . . .

MAGS: Here, let me help . . . (*Taking some of the papers*)

GARDNER: Criticism is tough sledding. You can't just dash off a few images here, a few rhymes there . . .

MAGS: Do you have these pages numbered in any way?

FANNY (*Returning to her posing chair):* HA!

GARDNER: This is just the introduction.

MAGS: I don't see any numbers on these.

GARDNER (*Exiting to his study*): The important stuff is in my study . . .

FANNY (*To* MAGS): You don't know the half of it . . . *not the half* . . . !

GARDNER (*Offstage; thumping around*): HAVE YOU SEEN THOSE YEATS POEMS I JUST HAD . . . ?

MAGS (*Reading over several pages*): What is this? . . . It doesn't make sense. It's just fragments . . . pieces of poems.

FANNY: That's it, honey! That's his book. His great critical study! Now that he can't write his own poetry, he's trying to explain other people's. The only problem is, he can't get beyond typing them out. The poor lamb doesn't have the stamina to get beyond the opening stanzas, let alone trying to make sense of them.

GARDNER (*Thundering back with more papers, which keep falling*): GODDAMMIT, FANNY, WHAT DID YOU DO IN THERE? I CAN'T FIND ANYTHING!

FANNY: I just took the papers that were on your desk.

GARDNER: Well, the entire beginning is gone. (*He exits*)

FANNY: I'M TRYING TO HELP YOU, DARLING!

GARDNER (*Returns with another armload*): SEE THAT? . . . NO SIGN OF CHAPTER ONE OR TWO . . . (*He flings it all down to the floor*)

FANNY: Gardner . . . PLEASE?!

GARDNER (*Kicking through the mess*): I TURN MY BACK FOR ONE MINUTE AND WHAT HAPPENS? . . . MY ENTIRE STUDY IS TORN APART! (*He exits*)

MAGS: Oh, Daddy . . . don't . . . please . . . Daddy . . . *please?!*

GARDNER (*Returns with a new batch of papers, which he tosses up into the air*): THROWN OUT! . . . THE BEST PART IS THROWN OUT! . . . lost . . . (*He starts to exit again*)

MAGS (*Reads one of the fragments to steady herself*):

> "I have known the inexorable sadness of pencils,
> Neat in their boxes, dolor of pad and paperweight,
> All the misery of manila folders and mucilage . . ."[36]

They're beautiful . . . just beautiful.

[36]From the poem "Dolor" by the American poet Theodore Roethke (1908–1963). Among the following quotations are selections from the poetry of Roethke, Robert Frost, James Dickey, and Emily Dickinson.

GARDNER (*Stops*): Hey, what's that you've got there?

FANNY: It's your manuscript, darling. You see, it's right where you left it.

GARDNER (*To* MAGS): Read that again.

MAGS:

"I have known the inexorable sadness of pencils,
Neat in their boxes, dolor of pad and paperweight,
All the misery of manila folders and mucilage . . ."

GARDNER: Well, well, what do you know . . .

FANNY (*Hands him several random papers*): You see . . . no one lost anything. Everything's here, still intact.

GARDNER (*Reads*):

"I knew a woman, lovely in her bones,
When small birds sighed, she would sigh back at them;
Ah, when she moved, she moved more ways than one:
The shapes a bright container can contain! . . ."

FANNY (*Hands him another*): And . . .

GARDNER (*Reads*): Ahh . . . Frost . . .

"Some say the world will end in fire,
Some say in ice.
From what I've tasted of desire
I hold with those who favor fire."

FANNY (*Under her breath to* MAGS): He can't give up the words. It's the best he can do. (*Handing him another*) Here you go, here's more.

GARDNER:

"Farm boys wild to couple
With anything with soft-wooded trees
With mounds of earth mounds
Of pinestraw will keep themselves off
Animals by legends of their own . . ."

MAGS (*Eyes shut*): Oh, Daddy, I can't bear it . . . I . . .

FANNY: Of course no one will ever publish this.

GARDNER: Oh, here's a marvelous one. Listen to this!

"There came a Wind like a Bugle—
It quivered through the Grass
And a Green Chill upon the Heat
So ominous did pass
We barred the Windows and the Doors
As from an Emerald Ghost—
The Doom's electric Moccasin . . ."

SHIT, WHERE DID THE REST OF IT GO . . . ?

FANNY: Well, don't ask *me.*

GARDNER: It just stopped in mid-air!

FANNY: Then go look for the original.

GARDNER: Good idea, good idea! (*He exits to his study*)

FANNY (*To* MAGS): He's incontinent now, too. He wets his pants, in case you haven't noticed. (*She starts laughing*) You're not laughing. Don't you think it's funny? Daddy needs diapers. . . . I don't know about you, but I could use a drink! GAR . . . WILL YOU GET ME A SPLASH WHILE YOU'RE OUT THERE . . . ?

MAGS: STOP IT!

FANNY: It means we can't go out anymore. I mean, what would people say . . . ?

MAGS: Stop it. Just stop it.

FANNY: My poet laureate can't hold it in! (*She laughs harder*)

MAGS: That's enough . . . STOP IT . . . Mummy . . . I beg of you . . . *please stop it!*

[GARDNER *enters with a book and indeed a large stain has blossomed on his trousers. He plucks it away from his leg.*]

GARDNER: Here we go . . . I found it . . .

FANNY (*Pointing at it*): See that? See? . . . He just did it again! (*Goes off into a shower of laughter*)

MAGS: (*Looks, turns away*): SHUT . . . UP! . . . (*Building to a howl*) WILL YOU PLEASE JUST . . . SHUT . . . UP!

FANNY (*To* GARDNER): Hey, what about that drink?

FANNY: Never mind, I'll get it, I'll get it.

[FANNY *exits, convulsed. Silence.*]

GARDNER: Well, where were we?

MAGS (*Near tears*): Your poem.

GARDNER: Oh yes . . . the Dickinson. (*He shuts his eyes, reciting from memory, holding the book against his chest*)

"There came a Wind like a Bugle—
It quivered through the Grass
And a Green Chill upon the Heat
So ominous did pass
We barred the Windows and the Doors
As from an Emerald Ghost—"

(*Opens the book and starts riffling through it*) Let's see now, where's the rest? . . . (*He finally finds it*) Ahhh, here we go . . . !

FANNY (*Reenters, drink in hand*): I'm back! (*Takes one look at* GARDNER *and bursts out laughing again*)

MAGS: I don't believe you! How you can laugh at him?!

[*They all speak simultaneously as* MAGS *gets angrier and angrier.*]

FANNY: I'm sorry, I wish I could stop, but there's really nothing else to do. Look at him . . . just . . . look at him . . . !

MAGS: It's so cruel . . . You're so . . . incredibly cruel to him . . . I mean, YOUR DISDAIN REALLY TAKES MY BREATH AWAY! YOU'RE IN A CLASS BY YOURSELF WHEN IT COMES TO HUMILIATION!

GARDNER (*Reading*):

"The Doom's electric Moccasin
That very instant passed—
On a strange Mob of panting Trees
And Fences fled away
And Rivers where the Houses ran
Those looked that lived—that Day—
The Bell within the steeple wild
The flying tidings told—
How much can come
And much can go,
And yet abide the World!"

(*He shuts the book with a bang, pauses and looks around the room, confused*) Now, where was I . . . ?

FANNY: Safe and sound in the middle of the living room with Mags and me.

GARDNER: But I was looking for something, wasn't I . . . ?

FANNY: Your manuscript.

GARDNER: THAT'S RIGHT! MY MANUSCRIPT! My manuscript!

FANNY: And here it is all over the floor. See, you're standing on it.

GARDNER (*Picks up a few pages and looks at them*): Why so I am . . .

FANNY: Now all we have to do is get it up off the floor and packed neatly into these cartons!

GARDNER: Yes, yes, that's right. Into the cartons!

FANNY (*Kicks a carton over to him*): Here, you use this one and I'll start over here . . . (*She starts dropping papers into a carton nearby*) BOMBS AWAY! . . . Hey . . . this is fun!

GARDNER (*Picks up his own pile, lifts it high over his head and flings it down into the carton*): BOMBS AWAY . . . This is fun!

FANNY: I told you! The whole thing is to figure out a system!

GARDNER: I don't know what I'd do without you, Fan. I thought I'd lost everything.

FANNY (*Makes dive-bomber noises and machine-gun explosions as she wheels more and more papers into the carton*): TAKE THAT AND THAT AND THAT!

GARDNER (*Joins in the fun, outdoing her with dips, dives, and blastings of his own*): BLAM BLAM BLAM BLAM! . . . ZZZZZZZZRAAAAAAFOOM! . . . BLATTY-DE-BLATTY-DE-BLATTY-DE-KABOOOOOOOOM! . . .
WHAAAAAAA . . . DA-DAT-DAT-DAT-DAT-DAT . . .
WHEEEEEEEE AAAAAAAAAAAAA . . . FOOOOOO . . .

[*They get louder and louder as papers fly every which way.*]

FANNY (*Mimes getting hit with a bomb*): AEEEEEEEIIIIIIIIIIIII! YOU GOT ME RIGHT IN THE GIZZARD! (*She collapses on the floor and starts going through death throes, having an absolute ball*)

GARDNER: TAKE THAT AND THAT AND THAT AND THAT . . . (*A series of explosions follow*)

MAGS (*Furious*): This is how you help him? . . . THIS IS HOW YOU PACK HIS THINGS?

FANNY: I keep him company. I get involved . . . which is a hell of a lot more than you do!

MAGS (*Wild with rage*): BUT YOU'RE MAKING A MOCKERY OF HIM. . . . YOU TREAT HIM LIKE A CHILD OR SOME DIMWITTED SERVING BOY. HE'S JUST AN AMUSEMENT TO YOU!

FANNY (*Fatigue has finally overtaken her. She's calm, almost serene*): And to you who see him once a year, if that . . . what is he to *you?* . . . I mean, what do you give him from yourself that costs you something? . . . Hmmmmmm? . . . (*Imitating* MAGS) "Oh, hi Daddy, it's great to see you again. How have you been? . . . Gee, I love your hair. It's gotten so . . . *white!*" . . . What color do you expect it to get when he's this age? . . . I mean, if you care so much how he looks, why don't you come and see him once in a while? . . . But oh, no . . . you have your paintings to do and your shows to put on. You just come and see us when the whim strikes. (*Imitating* MAGS) "Hey, you know what would be really great? . . . To do a portrait of you! I've always wanted to paint you, you're such great subjects!" . . . *Paint* us?! . . . What about opening your eyes and really *seeing* us? . . . Noticing what's going on around here for a change! It's all over for Daddy and me. This is it! "Finita la commedia!" . . . All I'm trying to do is exit with a little flourish; have some fun. . . . What's so terrible about that? . . . It can get pretty grim around here, in case you haven't noticed . . . Daddy, tap-tap-tapping out his nonsense all day; me traipsing around to the thrift shops trying to amuse myself. . . . He never keeps me company anymore; never takes me out anywhere. . . . I'd put a bullet through my head in a minute, but then who'd look after him? . . . What do you think we're moving to the cottage for? . . . So I can watch him like a hawk and make sure he doesn't get lost. Do you think that's anything to look forward to? . . . Being Daddy's nursemaid out in the middle of nowhere? I'd much rather stay here in Boston with the few friends I have left, but you can't always do what you want in this world! "L'homme propose, Dieu dispose!"[37] . . . If you want to paint us so badly, you ought to paint us as we really are. There's your picture."

[FANNY *points to* GARDNER, *who's quietly playing with a paper glider.*]

FANNY: Daddy spread out on the floor with all his toys and me hovering over him to make sure he doesn't hurt himself! (*She goes over to him*) YOO-HOO . . . GAR? . . . HELLO?

GARDNER (*Looks up at her*): Oh, hi there, Fan. What's up?

FANNY: How's the packing coming . . .?

GARDNER: Packing . . .?

FANNY: Yes, you were packing your manuscript, remember? (*She lifts up a page and lets it fall into a carton*)

GARDNER: Oh, yes . . .

[37]French: Man proposes, God disposes.

FANNY: Here's your picture, Mags. Face over this way . . . turn your easel over here . . . (*She lets a few more papers fall*) Up, up . . . and away . . .

[*Blackout.*]

SCENE 2

The last day. All the books and boxes are gone. The room is completely empty except for MAGS'S *backdrop. Late afternoon light dapples the walls; it changes from pale peach to deeper violet. The finished portrait sits on the easel, covered with a cloth.* MAGS *is taking down the backdrop.*

FANNY (*Offstage to* GARDNER): DON'T FORGET TOOTS!

GARDNER (*Offstage; from another part of the house*): WHAT'S THAT?

FANNY (*Offstage*): I SAID: DON'T FORGET TOOTS! HIS CAGE IS SITTING IN THE MIDDLE OF YOUR STUDY!

[*Silence.*]

FANNY (*Offstage*): HELLO? . . . ARE YOU THERE?

GARDNER (*Offstage*): I'LL BE RIGHT WITH YOU; I'M JUST GETTING TOOTS!

GARDNER (*Offstage*): WHAT'S THAT? I CAN'T HEAR YOU?

FANNY (*Offstage*): I'M GOING THROUGH THE ROOMS ONE MORE TIME TO MAKE SURE WE DIDN'T FORGET ANYTHING . . . KITTY'S PICKING US UP IN FIFTEEN MINUTES, SO PLEASE BE READY. . . . SHE'S DROPPING MAGS OFF AT THE STATION AND THEN IT'S OUT TO ROUTE 3 AND THE CAPE HIGHWAY . . .

GARDNER (*Enters, carrying* TOOTS *in his cage*): Well, this is it. The big moment has finally come, eh what, Toots? (*He sees* MAGS) Oh, hi there, Mags, I didn't see you . . .

MAGS: Oh, hi, Daddy, I'm just taking this down . . . (*She does and walks over to* TOOTS) Oh, Toots, I'll miss you. (*She makes little chattering noises into his cage*)

GARDNER: Come on, recite a little Gray's *Elegy* for Mags before we go.

MAGS: Yes, Mum said he was really good at it now.

GARDNER: Well, the whole thing is to keep at it every day. (*Slowly to* TOOTS)

> "The curfew tolls the knell of parting day,
> The lowing herd wind slowly o'er the lea . . ."[38]

Come on, show Mags your stuff! (*Slower*)

> "The curfew tolls the knell of parting day,
> The lowing herd wind slowly o'er the lea . . ."

[*Silence;* GARDNER *makes little chattering sounds.*]

[38] The opening lines from "Elegy in a Country Churchyard" (1751) by the English poet Thomas Gray (1716–1771).

GARDNER: Come on, Toots, old boy . . .
MAGS: How does it go?
GARDNER (*To* MAGS):

"The curfew tolls the knell of parting day,
The lowing herd wind slowly o'er the lea . . ."

MAGS (*Slowly to* TOOTS):

The curfew tolls for you and me,
As quietly the herd winds down . . .

GARDNER: No, no, it's "The curfew tolls the knell of parting *day* . . ."!
MAGS (*Repeating after him*): "The curfew tolls the knell of parting day . . ."
GARDNER: "The lowing herd wind slowly o'er the lea . . ."
MAGS (*With a deep breath*):

The curfew tolls at parting day,
The herd low slowly down the lea . . . no, *knell!*
They come winding down the *knell!*

GARDNER: Listen, Mags . . . *listen!*

[*A pause.*]

TOOTS (*Loud and clear with* GARDNER'S *inflection*):

"The curfew tolls the knell of parting day,
The lowing herd wind slowly o'er the lea,
The ploughman homeward plods his weary way,
And leaves the world to darkness and to me."

MAGS: HE SAID IT. . . . HE SAID IT! . . . AND IN YOUR VOICE . . . OH, DADDY, THAT'S AMAZING!

GARDNER: Well, Toots is very smart, which is more than I can say for a lot of people I know . . .

MAGS (*To* TOOTS): Polly want a cracker? Polly want a cracker?

GARDNER: You can teach a parakeet to say anything; all you need is patience . . .

MAGS: But *poetry* . . . that's so hard . . .

[FANNY *enters carrying a suitcase and* GARDNER'S *typewriter in its case. She's dressed in her traveling suit, wearing a hat to match.*]

FANNY: WELL, THERE YOU ARE! I THOUGHT YOU'D DIED!

MAGS (*To* FANNY): HE SAID IT! I FINALLY HEARD TOOTS RECITE GRAY'S *ELEGY*. (*She makes silly clucking sounds into the cage*)

FANNY: Isn't it uncanny how much he sounds like Daddy? Sometimes when I'm alone here with him, I've actually thought he *was* Daddy and started talking to him. Oh, yes, Toots and I have had quite a few meaty conversations together!

[FANNY *wolf-whistles into the cage; then draws back.* GARDNER *covers the cage with a traveling cloth. Silence.*]

FANNY (*Looking around the room*): God, the place looks so bare.

MAGS: I still can't believe it . . . Cotuit, year round. I wonder if there'll be any phosphorus when you get there?

FANNY: What on earth are you talking about? (*She carries the discarded backdrop out into the hall*)

MAGS: Remember that summer when the ocean was full of phosphorus?

GARDNER (*Taking* TOOTS *out into the hall*): Oh, yes . . .

MAGS: It was a great mystery where it came from or why it settled in Cotuit. But one evening when Daddy and I were taking a swim, suddenly it was there!

GARDNER (*Returns*): I remember.

MAGS: I don't know where Mum was . . .

FANNY (*Reentering*): Probably doing the dishes!

MAGS (*To* GARDNER): As you dove into the water, this shower of silvery green sparks erupted all around you. It was incredible! I thought you were turning into a saint or something; but then you told me to jump in too and the same thing happened to me . . .

GARDNER: Oh, yes, I remember that . . . the water smelled all queer.

MAGS: What *is* phosphorus, anyway?

GARDNER: Chemicals, chemicals . . .

FANNY: No, it isn't. Phosphorus is a green liquid inside insects. Fireflies have it. When you see sparks in the water it means insects are swimming around . . .

GARDNER: Where on earth did you get that idea . . .?

FANNY: If you're bitten by one of them, it's fatal!

MAGS: And the next morning it was still there . . .

GARDNER: It was the damndest stuff to get off! We'd have to stay in the shower a good ten minutes. It comes from chemical waste, you see . . .

MAGS: Our bodies looked like mercury as we swam around . . .

GARDNER: It stained all the towels a strange yellow green.

MAGS: I was in heaven, and so were you for that matter. You'd finished your day's poetry and would turn somersaults like some happy dolphin . . .

FANNY: Damned dishes . . . why didn't I see any of this?!

MAGS: I remember one night in particular. . . . We sensed the phosphorus was about to desert us; blow off to another town. We were chasing each other under water. At one point I lost you, the brilliance was so intense . . . but finally your foot appeared . . . then your leg. I grabbed it! . . . I remember wishing the moment would hold forever; that we could just be fixed there, laughing and iridescent. . . . Then I began to get panicky because I knew it would pass; it was passing already. You were slipping from my grasp. The summer was almost over. I'd be going back to art school; you'd be going back to Boston. . . . Even as I was reaching for you, you were gone. We'd never be like that again.

[*Silence.* FANNY *spies* MAGS's *portrait covered on the easel.*]

FANNY: What's that over there? Don't tell me we forgot something!

MAGS: It's your portrait. I finished it.

FANNY: You finished it? How on earth did you manage that?

MAGS: I stayed up all night.

FANNY: You did? . . . *I* didn't hear you, did you hear her, Gar . . .?

GARDNER: Not a peep, not a peep!

MAGS: Well, I wanted to get it done before you left. You know, see what you thought. It's not bad, considering . . . I mean, I did it almost completely from memory. The light was terrible and I was trying to be quiet so I wouldn't wake you. It was hardly an ideal situation. . . . I mean, you weren't the most cooperative models . . . (*She suddenly panics and snatches the painting off the easel. She hugs it to her chest and starts dancing around the room with it*) Oh, God, you're going to hate it! You're going to hate it! How did I ever get into this? . . . Listen, you don't really want to see it . . . it's nothing . . . just a few dabs here and there. . . . It was awfully late when I finished it. The light was really impossible and my eyes were hurting like crazy. . . . Look, why don't we just go out to the sidewalk and wait for Kitty so she doesn't have to honk—

GARDNER (*Snatches the painting out from under her grasp*): WOULD YOU JUST SHUT UP A MINUTE AND LET US SEE IT?

MAGS (*Laughing and crying*): But it's nothing, Daddy . . . *really!* . . . I've done better with my eyes closed! It was so late I could hardly see anything and then I spilled a whole bottle of thinner into my palette . . .

GARDNER (*Sets the portrait down on the easel and stands back to look at it*): THERE!

MAGS (*Dancing around them in a panic*): Listen, it's just a quick sketch. . . . It's still wet. . . . I didn't have enough time. . . . It takes at least forty hours to do a decent portrait . . .

[*Suddenly it's very quiet as* FANNY *and* GARDNER *stand back to look at the painting. More and more beside herself,* MAGS *keeps leaping around the room wrapping her arms around herself, making little whimpering sounds.*]

MAGS: Please don't . . . no . . . don't . . . oh, please! . . . Come on, don't look. . . . Oh, God, don't . . . please . . .

[*An eternity passes as* FANNY *and* GARDNER *gaze at their portrait.*]

GARDNER: Well . . .

FANNY: Well . . .

[*More silence.*]

FANNY: I think it's perfectly dreadful!	GARDNER: Awfully clever, awfully clever!

FANNY: What on earth did you do to my face . . . ?

GARDNER: I particularly like Mum!

FANNY: Since when do I have purple skin?!

MAGS: I told you it was nothing, just a silly—

GARDNER: She looks like a million dollars!

FANNY: AND WILL YOU LOOK AT MY HAIR . . . IT'S BRIGHT ORANGE!

GARDNER (*Views the painting from another angle*): It's really very good!

FANNY (*Pointing*): That doesn't look anything like me!

GARDNER: First-rate!

FANNY: Since when do I have purple skin and bright orange hair?

MAGS (*Trying to snatch the painting off the easel*): Listen, you don't have to worry about my feelings . . . really . . . I—

GARDNER (*Blocking her way*): NOT SO FAST . . .

FANNY: And look at how I'm sitting! I've never sat like that in my life!

GARDNER (*Moving closer to the painting*): Yes, yes, it's awfully clever . . .

FANNY: I HAVE NO FEET!

GARDNER: The whole thing is quite remarkable!

FANNY: And what happened to my legs, pray tell? . . . They just vanish below the knees! . . . At least my dress is presentable. I've always loved that dress.

GARDNER: It sparkles somehow . . .

FANNY (*To* GARDNER): Don't you think it's becoming?

GARDNER: Yes, very becoming, awfully becoming . . .

FANNY (*Examining it at closer range*): Yes, she got the dress very well, how it shows off what's left of my figure . . . My smile is nice too.

GARDNER: Good and wide . . .

FANNY: I love how the corners of my mouth turn up . . .

GARDNER: It's very clever . . .

FANNY: They're almost quivering . . .

GARDNER: Good lighting effects!

FANNY: Actually, I look quite . . . *young,* don't you think?

GARDNER (*To* MAGS): You're awfully good with those highlights.

FANNY (*Looking at it from different angles*): And you look darling . . . !

GARDNER: Well, I don't know about that . . .

FANNY: No, you look absolutely darling. Good enough to eat.

MAGS (*In a whisper*): They like it. . . . They like it!

[*A silence as* FANNY *and* GARDNER *keep gazing at their portrait.*]

FANNY: You know what it is? The wispy brush stroke makes us look like a couple in a French Impressionist painting.

GARDNER: Yes, I see what you mean . . .

FANNY: A Manet or Renoir[39] . . .

GARDNER: It's very evocative.

FANNY: There's something about the light . . .

[*They back up to survey the picture from a distance.*]

FANNY: You know those Renoir café scenes . . . ?

[39] Edouard Manet (1832–1883) and Pierre August Renoir (1841–1919), French Impressionist painters.

GARDNER: She doesn't lay on the paint with a trowel; it's just touches here and there . . .

MAGS: They *like* it . . . !

FANNY: You know the one with the couple dancing? . . . Not that we're dancing. There's just something similar in the mood . . . a kind of gaiety, almost. . . . The man has his back to you and he's swinging the woman around. . . . OH, GAR, YOU'VE SEEN IT A MILLION TIMES! IT'S HANGING IN THE MUSEUM OF FINE ARTS! . . . They're dancing like this . . .

[FANNY *goes up to* GARDNER *and puts an arm on his shoulders.*]

MAGS: They like it. . . . They like it!

FANNY: She's got on this wonderful flowered dress with ruffles at the neck and he's holding her like this. . . . That's right . . . and she's got the most rhapsodic expression on her face . . .

[*Getting into the spirit of it,* GARDNER *takes* FANNY *in his arms and slowly begins to dance around the room.*]

GARDNER: Oh, yes . . . I know the one you mean. . . . They're in a sort of haze . . . and isn't there a little band playing off to one side . . . ?

FANNY: Yes, that's it!

[KITTY'S *horn honks outside.* MAGS *is the only one who hears it.*]

MAGS: There's Kitty! (*She's torn and keeps looking towards the door, but finally gives in to their stolen moment*)

FANNY: And there's a man in a dark suit playing the violin and someone's conducting, I think. . . . And aren't Japanese lanterns strung up . . . ?

[FANNY *and* GARDNER *pick up speed, dipping and whirling around the room. Strains of a faraway Chopin waltz are heard.*]

GARDNER: Oh, yes! There are all these little lights twinkling in the trees . . .

FANNY: And doesn't the woman have a hat on? . . . A big red hat . . . ?

GARDNER: . . . and lights all over the dancers, too. Everything shimmers with this marvelous glow. Yes, yes . . . I can see it perfectly! The whole thing is absolutely extraordinary!

[*The lights become dreamy and dappled as* FANNY *and* GARDNER *dance around the room.* MAGS *watches them, moved to tears as slowly the curtain falls.*]

END

1983

Toni Morrison 1931–

Through her fiction and her essays, Toni Morrison has become a powerful force speaking out on issues of race and gender in modern America. Born in Lorain, Ohio, as Chloe Anthony Wofford, she was an honor student in high school and attended Howard University, graduating in 1953. She enrolled in graduate school at Cornell University, and in 1955 received an M.A. in English, writing her master's thesis on modern writers, including novelist William Faulkner, whose rhythmic prose she admires and sometimes emulates. Morrison has also expressed her admiration for the characterizations achieved by Faulkner, who "seemed to me the only writer who took black people seriously." After graduation from Cornell, Morrison began a teaching career, first at Texas Southern University and then at Howard. During that time she married Harold Morrison and had two children. From 1965 to 1984, she worked as an editor for Random House, and continued teaching: at Yale, Bard, SUNY–Albany, and, since 1989, at Princeton. In recent years, she has also traveled extensively and has given readings of her work, sometimes in joint recitals where her reading is interpreted on the stage by the choreographer and dancer Bill Jones to the rhythmic accompaniment of jazz drummer Max Roach.

Morrison published her first novel, The Bluest Eye, *in 1970. It was followed by* Sula *in 1974. Her third novel,* Song of Solomon *(1977), won the Fiction Award of the National Book Critics Circle. It was followed by her fourth novel,* Tar Baby *(1981), and by her highly successful fifth novel,* Beloved *(1987), which won a Pulitzer Prize for Fiction and was produced as a movie in 1998. In 1992 a collection of lectures she gave at Harvard on racism in literature was published under the title* Playing in the Dark, Whiteness and the Literary Imagination, *and in the same year her sixth novel,* Jazz, *appeared. Her novel* Paradise *(1998) was criticized for being "heavy-handed" and lacking in "novelistic magic." Nevertheless, Morrison has been hailed as "the best writer in America," and her works are read throughout the world. Her greatest single distinction came in 1993 when she became the first African American and the eighth woman to win a Nobel Prize for Literature. In 2003 she published her eighth novel,* Love.

Morrison stands prominently in the line of black writers that includes Douglass, Toomer, Cullen, Hughes, Wright, and Ellison. She directly confronts issues of race and oppression, especially the oppression of women. She rarely focuses on male characters; Song of Solomon *is her only novel with a male protagonist. From the beginning of her career she has written about the crushing effect of racism on "the most vulnerable unit in society—a black female and a child." Morrison's writing is strewn with descriptions of sexual violence against women, and her novels are alive with characters who are victims and scapegoats, made grotesque and stunted by racism and poverty. Her characters experience rejection and degradation that cause them to turn on themselves with self-loathing, and Morrison does not flinch from showing lives of stunning brutality. In* Beloved, *an escaped slave mother kills her baby daughter to keep her from the clutches of slave catchers; in* Jazz *a middle-aged, married man heedlessly murders his teenage lover, and at her funeral his rejected wife attempts to disfigure the girl's corpse with a kitchen knife. In* Paradise, *a careless mother leaves her infant twins to die of heat in a Cadillac that has its windows closed. Pain and the anguish of loneliness dominate the lives of her characters, yet she also writes of their love and endurance, in a contrasting prose that is measured and smooth flowing.*

Morrison upbraids blacks who abandon their black heritage for the alluring materialism of the United States, a nation that she has described as "Star spangled. Race strangled." Of Morrison it has been said that "There is not an angrier writer in the

United States today. . . . She has unleashed a firestorm of vituperation against white America for the ongoing suffering of black slaves and their descendants." It has also been said that Morrison is "a great novelist and the closest thing the country has to a national writer. The fact that she speaks as a woman and a black only enhances her ability to speak as an American." Morrison herself says that her fictions are meant to show all readers "how to survive whole in a world where we are all of us, in some measure, victims of something." Morrison's fiction shows not only how people can survive, but also how they can, through their suffering and resistance to repression, move toward a redeeming understanding of their true selves.

FURTHER READING: K. Carmean, *Toni Morrison's World of Fiction,* 1993; *Toni Morrison: Critical Perspectives Past and Present,* ed. H. Gates and K. Appiah, 1994; *Conversations with Toni Morrison,* ed. D. Taylor-Guthrie, 1994; L. Peach, *Toni Morrison,* 1995; J. Furman, *Toni Morrison's Fiction,* 1996; *Toni Morrison's Fiction,* ed. D. Middleton, 1997; *Toni Morrison: Critical and Theoretical Approaches,* ed. N. Peterson, 1997; A. Mori, *Toni Morrison and Womanist Discourse,* 1999; J. Duvall, *The Identifying Fictions of Toni Morrison: Modernist Authenticity and Postmodern Blackness,* 2000; T. Higgins, *Religiosity, Cosmology, and Folklore: The African Influence in the Novels of Toni Morrison,* 2002; L. Fulti, *Toni Morrison: Playing with Difference,* 2003; *The Toni Morrison Encyclopedia,* ed. E. Beaulieu, 2003.

TEXT: *Beloved,* 1997.

from *BELOVED*

I am beloved and she is mine. I see her take flowers away from leaves   she puts them in a round basket   the leaves are not for her   she fills the basket   she opens the grass   I would help her but the clouds are in the way   how can I say things that are pictures   I am not separate from her   there is no place where I stop   her face is my own and I want to be there in the place where her face is and to be looking at it too   a hot thing

All of it is now   it is always now   there will never be a time when I am not crouching and watching others who are crouching too   I am always crouching   the man on my face is dead   his face is not mine   his mouth smells sweet but his eyes are locked   some who eat nasty themselves   I do not eat   the men without skin bring us their morning water to drink   we have none   at night I cannot see the dead man on my face   daylight comes through the cracks and I can see his locked eyes   I am not big   small rats do not wait for us to sleep   someone is thrashing but there is no room to do it in   if we had more to drink we could make tears   we cannot make sweat or morning water so the men without skin bring us theirs   one time they bring us sweet rocks to suck   we are all trying to leave our bodies behind   the man on my face has done it   it is hard to make yourself die forever   you sleep short and then return   in the beginning we could vomit   now we do not   now we cannot   his teeth are pretty white points   someone is trembling   I can feel it over here   he is fighting hard to leave his body which is a small bird trembling   there is no room to tremble so he is not able to die   my own dead man is pulled away from my face   I miss his pretty white points

We are not crouching now   we are standing but my legs are like my dead man's eyes   I cannot fall because there is no room to   the men without skin are making loud noises   I am not dead   the bread is sea-colored   I am too hungry to eat it   the sun closes my eyes   those able to die are in a pile   I cannot find my man   the one whose teeth I have loved   a hot thing   the little hill of dead people   a hot thing   the men without skin push them through with poles   the woman is there with the face I want   the face that is mine   they fall into the sea which is the color of the bread   she has nothing in her ears   if I had the teeth of the man who died on my face I would bite the circle around her neck   bite it away   I know she does not like it   now there is room to crouch and to watch the crouching others   it is the crouching that is now always now   inside   the woman with my face is in the sea   a hot thing

In the beginning I could see her   I could not help her because the clouds were in the way   in the beginning I could see her   the shining in her ears   she does not like the circle around her neck   I know this   I look hard at her so she will know that the clouds are in the way   I am sure she saw me   I am looking at her see me   she empties out her eyes   I am there in the place where her face is and telling her the noisy clouds were in my way   she wants her earrings   she wants her round basket   I want her face   a hot thing   in the beginning the women are away from the men and the men are away from the women   storms rock us and mix the men into the women and the women into the men   that is when I begin to be on the back of the man   for a long time I see only his neck and his wide shoulders above me   I am small   I love him because he has a song   when he turned around to die I see the teeth he sang through   his singing was soft   his singing is of the place where a woman takes flowers away from their leaves and puts them in a round basket   before the clouds   she is crouching near us   but I do not see her until he locks his eyes and dies on my face   we are that way   there is no breath coming from his mouth and the place where breath should be is sweet-smelling   the others do not know he is dead   I know his song is gone   now I love his pretty little teeth instead

I cannot lose her again   my dead man was in the way like the noisy clouds   when he dies on my face I can see hers   she is going to smile at me   she is going to   her sharp earrings are gone   the men without skin are making loud noises   they push my own man through   they do not push the woman with my face through   she goes in   they do not push her   she goes in   the little hill is gone   she was going to smile at me   she was going to   a hot thing

They are not crouching now   we are   they are floating on the water   they break up the little hill and push it through   I cannot find my pretty teeth   I see the dark face that is going to smile at me   it is my dark face that is going to smile at me   the iron circle is around our neck   she does not have sharp earrings in her ears or a round basket   she goes in the water   with my face

I am standing in the rain falling   the others are taken   I am not taken   I am falling like the rain is   I watch him eat   inside I am crouching to keep from falling with the rain   I am going to be in pieces   he hurts where I sleep   he puts his finger there   I drop the food and break into pieces   she took my face away   there is no one to want me   to say me my name   I wait on the bridge because she is under it   there is night and there is day   again   again   night day   night day   I am waiting   no iron circle is around my neck   no boats go on this water   no men without skin   my dead man is not floating here   his teeth are down there where the blue is and the grass   so is the face I want   the face that is going to smile at me   it is going to   in the day diamonds are in the water where she is and turtles   in the night I hear chewing and swallowing and laughter   it belongs to me   she is the laugh   I am the laugher   I see her face which is mine   it is the face that was going to smile at me in the place where we crouched   now she is going to   her face comes through the water   a hot thing   her face is mine   she is not smiling   she is chewing and swallowing   I have to have my face   I go in   the grass opens   she opens it   I am in the water and she is coming   there is no round basket   no iron circle around her neck   she goes up where the diamonds are   I follow her   we are in the diamonds which are her earrings now   my face is coming   I have to have it   I am looking for the join   I am loving my face so much   my dark face is close to me   I want to join   she whispers to me   she whispers   I reach for her   chewing and swallowing she touches me   she knows I want to join   she chews and swallows me   I am gone   now I am her face   my own face has left me   I see me swim away   a hot thing   I see the bottoms of my feet   I am alone   I want to be the two of us   I want the join

I come out of blue water   after the bottoms of my feet swim away from me   I come up   I need to find a place to be   the air is heavy   I am not dead   I am not   there is a house   there is what she whispered to me   I am where she told me   I am not dead   I sit   the sun closes my eyes   when I open them I see the face I lost   Sethe's is the face that left me   Sethe sees me see her and I see the smile   her smiling face is the place for me   it is the face I lost   she is my face smiling at me   doing it at last   a hot thing   now we can join   a hot thing

1997

August Wilson 1945–2005

August Wilson was a major figure in American drama of the last two decades of the twentieth century and the beginning of the twenty-first. He won numerous New York Drama Critics Circle Awards, American Theatre Critics' Association Awards, and Tony Awards, and was awarded Bush and Guggenheim Fellowships. Wilson is one of only seven American authors to win two Pulitzer Prizes for Drama. His plays are predominantly realistic dramas focusing on the difficulties of African American life in the twentieth century.

Wilson was born Frederick August Kittel, Jr., the son of a German-born baker, Frederick August Kittel, and an African American woman, Daisy Wilson Kittel. He was the fourth of six children. His birthplace and the city in which he grew up was Pittsburgh, Pennsylvania, which later became the principal setting for his plays. His father gave the family little support, either financial or emotional, and the mother and six children lived in poverty in a two-bedroom apartment in one of the poorer sections of Pittsburgh. She supported the family by working as a cleaning woman. Eventually Daisy Wilson married a second time, to David Bedford, and the family moved to a mostly white suburban neighborhood, where they suffered racial discrimination and abuse. Young August attended Gladstone High School as one of its few non-white students. There he encountered racial animosity that culminated in a confrontation with a white teacher who had accused him of plagiarism. He dropped out of high school and instead spent his days at the public library educating himself.

In 1965 Wilson moved into a rooming house in Pittsburgh; he supported himself with menial jobs while writing poetry in his free time. He became interested in such radical political movements as Black Power and the Nation of Islam. But perhaps more important to his development as a writer was his encounter with blues and jazz music. One night in his room he put onto his phonograph the song "Nobody in Town Can Bake a Sweet Jellyroll Like Mine," by Bessie Smith. He later called that moment "a birth, a baptism, a resurrection, and a redemption all rolled up in one." He recalled that "the universe stuttered and everything fell to a new place." It was, in his words, "the beginning of my consciousness that I was a representative of a culture and the carrier of some very valuable antecedents." He also became entranced with the visual art of Romare Bearden, who attempted in his paintings to capture the texture of African American existence in the twentieth century. Wilson found in this another "moment of privilege and exaltation that comes from recognizing yourself as a vital part of a much larger world than you had imagined." At the same time he began to have a sense of the twentieth-century American dramatic tradition—of such dramatists as Eugene O'Neill, Tennessee Williams, and Arthur Miller—as something of which he wanted to be a part. Still more pertinently, he was influenced by African American dramatists of the 1960s like Amiri Baraka and Ed Bullins.

By the late 1960s Wilson had begun to play an active role in the dramatic life of Pittsburgh by helping to establish the Hill Theatre and the Black Horizons on the Hill theatre company. By the early 1970s he had decided to drop the surname of his father, who had died several years earlier, and use instead his mother's birth name, thus rechristening himself August Wilson. In 1978 he moved to St. Paul, Minnesota, where he worked as a writer for the Science Museum of Minnesota and developed his dramatic art through work with the Playwrights' Center in Minneapolis. Wilson's big professional breakthrough came in 1982, when his play Ma Rainey's Black Bottom *led to his being invited to participate in the prestigious National Playwrights Conference at the Eugene O'Neill Theatre Center in Waterford, Connecticut. There he met Lloyd Richards, the Director of the Center, who was also the Dean of the Yale School of Drama. Richards, seeing Wilson's potential, helped him fuse his already considerable verbal mastery with a greater technical virtuosity in the art of plotting and dramatic effects. With the help of Richards, whom Wilson gratefully termed "my guide, my mentor, and my provocateur,"* Ma Rainey's Black Bottom *was revised and successfully performed first by the Yale Repertory Theatre and then on Broadway (1985), for which it earned the first of Wilson's many New York Drama Critics Circle Awards. That success was quickly followed (1986) by the even more spectacularly successful* Fences*, which, among many other honors, received a Pulitzer Prize in 1987. When* Joe Turner's Come and Gone *opened on Broadway while* Fences *was still running, Wilson became the first African American to have two plays being performed* *on Broadway at the same time. In 1990 his* The Piano Lesson *earned a second Pulitzer Prize, and it was followed by* Two Trains Running *(1992) and* Seven Guitars *(1996), both of which received considerable acclaim. He also adapted* The Piano Lesson *for a made-for-television movie that aired as part of the Hallmark Hall of Fame series.*

In his Preface to Three Plays *(in which he published* Ma Rainey's Black Bottom, Fences, *and* Joe Turner's Come and Gone*), Wilson remarked that "writing a play is for me like walking down the landscape of the self, unattended, unadorned, exploring what D. H. Lawrence called 'the dark forest of the soul.' It is a place rife with shadows, a place of suspect quality and occasional dazzling brightness." Aside from the individual success of his plays, he was conscious of producing a total body of work, a ten-play cycle, which would document the trials and the consolations of African American life in the twentieth century. Each play represents one decade of that century*—Ma Rainey's Black Bottom *the twenties,* Fences *the fifties,* Joe Turner's Come and Gone *the teens, and so on. Thus, each play is itself a work of dramatic art and also functions as part of a comprehensive chronicle of the twentieth-century African American odyssey.*

August Wilson died in October 2005 in Seattle, Washington of liver cancer. At the time of his death plans were underway to rename the Virginia Theatre in New York City the August Wilson Theatre, an event that he called "the capstone of my career"; it would, he said, help to ease his dying. The renaming took place on October 17, 2005, approximately two weeks after his death.

FURTHER READING: *May All Your Fences Have Gates: Essays on the Drama of August Wilson*, ed. A. Nadel, 1994; K. Pereira, *August Wilson and the African American Odyssey*, 1995; S. Shannon, *The Dramatic Vision of August Wilson*, 1995; M. Bogumil, *Understanding August Wilson*, 1998; P. Wolfe, *August Wilson*, 1999; H. Elam, *The Past as Present in the Drama of August Wilson*, 2004; *Conversations with August Wilson*, ed. J. Bryer and M. Hartig, 2006.

TEXT: *Three Plays*, 1991.

FENCES

for Lloyd Richards, who adds to whatever he touches

When the sins of our fathers visit us
We do not have to play host.
We can banish them with forgiveness
As God, in His Largeness and Laws.

—AUGUST WILSON

LIST OF CHARACTERS

TROY MAXSON
JIM BONO, Troy's friend
ROSE, Troy's wife
LYONS, Troy's oldest son by previous marriage
GABRIEL, Troy's brother
CORY, Troy's and Rose's Son
RAYNELL, Troy's daughter

SETTING

The setting is the yard which fronts the only entrance to the Maxson household, an ancient two-story brick house set back off a small alley in a big-city neighborhood. The entrance to the house is gained by two or three steps leading to a wooden porch badly in need of paint.

A relatively recent addition to the house and running its full width, the porch lacks congruence. It is a sturdy porch with a flat roof. One or two chairs of dubious value sit at one end where the kitchen window opens onto the porch, An old-fashioned icebox stands silent guard at the opposite end.

The yard is a small dirt yard, partially fenced, except for the last scene, with a wooden saw horse, a pile of lumber, and other fence-building equipment set off to the side. Opposite is a tree from which hangs a ball made of rags. A baseball bat leans against the tree. Two oil drums serve as garbage receptacles and sit near the house at right to complete the setting.

THE PLAY

Near the turn of the century, the destitute of Europe sprang on the city with tenacious claws and an honest and solid dream. The city devoured them. They swelled its belly until it burst into a thousand furnaces and sewing machines, a thousand butcher shops and bakers' ovens, a thousand churches and hospitals and funeral parlors and money-lenders. The city grew. It nourished itself and offered each man a partnership limited only by his talent, his guile and his willingness and capacity for hard work. For the immigrants of Europe, a dream dared and won true.

The descendants of African slaves were offered no such welcome or participation. They came from places called the Carolinas and the Virginias, Georgia, Alabama, Mississippi, and Tennessee. They came strong, eager searching. The city rejected them and they fled and settled along the riverbanks and under bridges in shallow, ramshackle houses made of sticks and tarpaper. They collected rags and wood. They sold the use of their muscles and their bodies. They cleaned houses and washed clothes, they shined shoes, and in quiet desperation and vengeful pride, they stole, and lived in pursuit of their own dream. That they could breathe free, finally, and stand to meet life with the force of dignity and whatever eloquence the heart could call upon.

By 1957, the hard-won victories of the European immigrants had solidified the industrial might of America. War had been confronted and won with new energies that used loyalty and patriotism as its fuel. Life was rich, full, and flourishing. The Milwaukee Braves won the World Series, and the hot winds of change that would make the sixties a turbulent, racing, dangerous, and provocative decade had not yet begun to blow full.

ACT 1

SCENE 1

It is 1957. TROY *and* BONO *enter the yard, engaged in conversation.* TROY *is fifty-three years old, a large man with thick, heavy hands; it is this largeness that he strives to fill out and make an accommodation with. Together with his blackness, his largeness informs his sensibilities and the choices he has made in his life.*

Of the two men, BONO *is obviously the follower. His commitment to their friendship of thirty-odd years is rooted in his admiration of* TROY*'s honesty, capacity for hard work, and his strength, which* BONO *seeks to emulate.*

It is Friday night, payday, and the one night of the week the two men engage in a ritual of talk and drink. TROY *is usually the most talkative and at times he can be crude and almost vulgar, though he is capable of rising to profound heights of expression. The men carry lunch buckets and wear or carry burlap aprons and are dressed in clothes suitable to their jobs as garbage collectors.*

BONO. Troy, you ought to stop that lying!

TROY. I ain't lying! The nigger had a watermelon this big. [*He indicates with his hands.*] Talking about . . . "What watermelon, Mr. Rand?" I liked to fell out! "What watermelon, Mr. Rand?" . . . And it sitting there big as life.

BONO. What did Mr. Rand say?

TROY. Ain't said nothing. Figure if the nigger too dumb to know he carrying a watermelon, he wasn't gonna get much sense out of him. Trying to hide that great big old watermelon under his coat. Afraid to let the white man see him carry it home.

BONO. I'm like you . . . I ain't got no time for them kind of people.

TROY. Now what he look like getting mad cause he see the man from the union talking to Mr. Rand?

BONO. He come to me talking about . . . "Maxson gonna get us fired," I told him to get away from me with that. He walked away from me calling you a troublemaker. What Mr. Rand say?

TROY. Ain't said nothing. He told me to go down the Commissioner's office next Friday. They called me down there to see them.

BONO. Well, as long as you got your complaint filed, they can't fire you. That's what one of them white fellows tell me.

TROY. I ain't worried about them firing me. They gonna fire me cause I asked a question? That's all I did. I went to Mr. Rand and asked him, "Why? Why you got the white mens driving and the colored lifting?" Told him, "What's the matter, don't I count? You think only white fellows got sense enough to drive a truck. That ain't no paper job! Hell, anybody can drive a truck. How come you got all whites driving and the colored lifting?" He told me "take it to the union." Well, hell, that's what I done! Now they wanna come up with this pack of lies.

BONO. I told Brownie if the man come and ask him any questions . . . just tell the truth! It ain't nothing but something they done trumped up on you cause you filed a complaint on them.

TROY. Brownie don't understand nothing. All I want them to do is change the job description. Give everybody a chance to drive the truck. Brownie can't see that. He ain't got that much sense.

BONO. How you figure he be making out with that gal be up at Taylor's all the time . . . that Alberta gal?

TROY. Same as you and me. Getting just as much as we is. Which is to say nothing.

BONO. It is, huh? I figure you doing a little better than me . . . and I ain't saying what I'm doing.

TROY. Aw, nigger, look here . . . I know you. If you had got anywhere near that gal, twenty minutes later you be looking to tell somebody. And the first one you gonna tell . . . that you gonna want to brag to . . . is me.

BONO. I ain't saying that, I see where you be eyeing her.

TROY. I eye all the women. I don't miss nothing. Don't never let nobody tell you Troy Maxson don't eye the women.

BONO. You been doing more than eyeing her. You done bought her a drink or two.

TROY. Hell yeah, I bought her a drink! What that mean? I bought you one, too. What that mean cause I buy her a drink? I'm just being polite.

BONO. It's all right to buy her one drink. That's what you call being polite. But when you wanna be buying two or three . . . that's what you call eyeing her.

TROY. Look here, as long as you known me . . . you ever known me to chase after women?

BONO. Hell yeah! Long as I done known you. You forgetting I knew you when.

TROY. Naw, I'm talking about since I been married to Rose?

BONO. Oh, not since you been married to Rose. Now, that's the truth, there, I can say that.

TROY. All right then! Case closed.

BONO. I see you be walking up around Alberta's house. You supposed to be at Taylors' and you be walking up around there.

TROY. What you watching where I'm walking for? I ain't watching after you.

BONO. I seen you walking around there more than once.

TROY. Hell, you liable to see me walking anywhere! That don't mean nothing cause you see me walking around there.

BONO. Where she come from anyway? She just kinda showed up one day.

TROY. Tallahassee. You can look at her and tell she one of them Florida gals. They got some big healthy women down there. Grow them right up out the ground. Got a little bit of Indian in her. Most of them niggers down in Florida got some Indian in them.

BONO. I don't know about that Indian part. But she damn sure big and healthy. Women wear some big stockings. Got them great big old legs and hips as wide as the Mississippi River.

TROY. Legs don't mean nothing. You don't do nothing but push them out of the way. But them hips cushion the ride!

BONO. Troy, you ain't got no sense.

TROY. It's the truth! Like you riding on Goodyears!

ROSE *enters from the house. She is ten years younger than* TROY, *her devotion to him stems from her recognition of the possibilities of her life without him: a succession of abusive men and their babies, a life of partying and running the streets, the Church, or aloneness with its attendant pain and frustration. She recognizes* TROY'S *spirit as a fine and illuminating one and she either ignores or forgives his faults, only some of which she recognizes. Though she doesn't drink, her presence is an integral part of the Friday night rituals. She alternates between the porch and the kitchen, where supper preparations are under way.*

ROSE. What you all out here getting into?

TROY. What you worried about what we getting into for? This is men talk, woman.

ROSE. What I care what you all talking about? Bono, you gonna stay for supper?

BONO. No, I thank you, Rose. But Lucille say she cooking up a pot of pigfeet.

TROY. Pigfeet! Hell, I'm going home with you! Might even stay the night if you got some pigfeet. You got something in there to top them pigfeet, Rose?

ROSE. I'm cooking up some chicken. I got some chicken and collard greens.

TROY. Well, go on back in the house and let me and Bono finish what we was talking about. This is men talk. I got some talk for you later. You know what kind of talk I mean. You go on and powder it up.

ROSE. Troy Maxson, don't you start that now!

TROY [*puts his arm around her*]. Aw, woman . . . come here. Look here. Bono . . . when I met this woman . . . I got out that place, say, "Hitch up my pony, saddle up my mare . . . there's a woman out there for me somewhere. I looked here. Looked there. Saw Rose and latched on to her." I latched on to her and told her—I'm gonna tell you the truth—I told her, "Baby, I don't wanna marry, I just wanna be your man." Rose told me . . . tell him what you told me, Rose.

ROSE. I told him if he wasn't the marrying kind, then move out the way so the marrying kind could find me.

TROY. That's what she told me. "Nigger, you in my way. You blocking the view! Move out the way so I can find me a husband." I thought it over two or three days, Come back—

ROSE. Ain't no two or three days nothing. You was back the same night.

TROY. Come back, told her . . . "Okay, baby . . . but I'm gonna buy me a banty rooster and put him out there in the backyard . . . and when he see a stranger come, he'll flap his wings and crow . . . ." Look here, Bono, I could watch the front door by myself . . . it was that back door I was worried about.

ROSE. Troy, you ought not talk like that. Troy ain't doing nothing but telling a lie.

TROY. Only thing is . . . when we first got married . . . forget the rooster . . . we ain't had no yard!

BONO. I hear you tell it. Me and Lucille was staying down there on Logan Street. Had two rooms with the outhouse in the back. I ain't mind the outhouse none. But when that goddamn wind blow through there in the winter . . . that's what I'm talking about! To this day I wonder why in the hell I ever stayed down there for six long years. But see, I didn't know I could do no better. I thought only white folks had inside toilets and things.

ROSE. There's a lot of people don't know they can do no better than they doing now. That's just something you got to learn. A lot of folks still shop at Bella's.

TROY. Ain't nothing wrong with shopping at Bella's. She got fresh food.

ROSE. I ain't said nothing about if she got fresh food. I'm talking about what she charge. She charge ten cents more than the A&P.

TROY. The A&P ain't never done nothing for me. I spends my money where I'm treated right. I go down to Bella, say, "I need a loaf of bread, I'll pay you Friday." She give it to me. What sense that make when I got money to go and spend it somewhere else and ignore the person who done right by me? That ain't in the Bible.

ROSE. We ain't talking about what's in the Bible. What sense it make to shop there when she overcharge?

TROY. You shop where you want to. I'll do my shopping where the people been good to me.

ROSE. Well, I don't think it's right for her to overcharge. That's all I was saying.

BONO. Look here . . . I got to get on. Lucille going be raising all kind of hell.

TROY. Where you going, nigger? We ain't finished this pint. Come here, finish this pint.

BONO. Well, hell, I am . . . if you ever turn the bottle loose.

TROY [*hands him the bottle*]. The only thing I say about the A&P is I'm glad Cory got that job down there. Help him take care of his school clothes and things. Gabe done moved out and things getting tight around here. He got that job . . . . He can start to look out for himself.

ROSE. Cory done went and got recruited by a college football team.

TROY. I told that boy about that football stuff. The white man ain't gonna let him get nowhere with that football. I told him when he first come to me with it. Now you come telling me he done went and got more tied up in it. He ought to go and get recruited in how to fix cars or something where he can make a living.

ROSE. He ain't talking about making no living playing football. It's just something the boys in school do. They gonna send a recruiter by to talk to you. He'll tell you he ain't talking about making no living playing football. It's a honor to be recruited.

TROY. It ain't gonna get him nowhere. Bono'll tell you that.

BONO. If he be like you in the sports . . . he's gonna be all right. Ain't but two men ever played baseball as good as you. That's Babe Ruth and Josh Gibson. Them's the only two men ever hit more home runs than you.

TROY. What it ever get me? Ain't got a pot to piss in or a window to throw it out of.

ROSE. Times have changed since you was playing football, Troy. That was before the war. Times have changed a lot since then.

TROY. How in hell they done changed?

ROSE. They got lots of colored boys playing ball now. Baseball and football.

BONO. You right about that, Rose. Times have changed, Troy. You just come along too early.

TROY. There ought not never have been no time called too early! Now you take that fellow . . . What's that fellow they had playing right field for the Yankees back then? You know who I'm talking about, Bono. Used to play right field for the Yankees.

ROSE. Selkirk?

TROY. Selkirk! That's it! Man batting .269, understand? .269. What kind of sense that make? I was hitting .432 with thirty-seven home runs! Man batting .269 and playing right field for the Yankees! I saw Josh Gibson's daughter yesterday. She walking around with raggedy shoes on her feet. Now I bet you Selkirk's daughter ain't walking around with raggedy shoes on the feet! I bet you that!

ROSE. They got a lot of colored baseball players now. Jackie Robinson was the first. Folks had to wait for Jackie Robinson.

TROY. I done seen a hundred niggers play baseball better than Jackie Robinson. Hell, I know some teams Jackie Robinson couldn't even make! What you talking about Jackie Robinson. Jackie Robinson wasn't nobody. I'm talking about if you could play ball then they ought to have let you play. Don't care what color you were. Come telling me I come along too early. If you could play . . . then they ought to have let you play.

TROY *takes a long drink from the bottle.*

ROSE. You gonna drink yourself to death. You don't need to be drinking like that.

TROY. Death ain't nothing. I done seen him. Done wrassled with him. You can't tell me nothing about death. Death ain't nothing but a fastball on the outside corner. And you know what I'll do to that! Lookee here, Bono . . . am I lying? You get one of them fastballs, about waist high, over the outside corner of the plate where you can get the meat of the bat on it . . . and good god! You can kiss it goodbye. Now, am I lying?

BONO. Naw, you telling the truth there. I seen you do it.

TROY. If I'm lying . . . that 450 feet worth of lying! [*Pause.*] That's all death is to me. A fastball on the outside corner.

ROSE. I don't know why you want to get on talking about death.

TROY. Ain't nothing wrong with talking about death. That's part of life. Everybody gonna die. You gonna die, I'm gonna die. Bono's gonna die. Hell, we all gonna die.

ROSE. But you ain't got to talk about it. I don't like to talk about it.

TROY. You the one brought it up. Me and Bono was talking about baseball . . . you tell me I'm gonna drink myself to death. Ain't that right, Bono's You know I don't drink this but one night out of the week. That's Friday night. I'm gonna drink just enough to where I can handle it. Then I cuts it loose. I leave it alone. So don't you worry about me drinking myself to death. Cause I ain't worried about Death. I done seen him. I done wrestled with him.

Look here, Bono . . . I looked up one day and Death was marching straight at me. Like Soldiers on Parade! The Army of Death was marching straight at me. The middle of July, 1941. It got real cold just like it be winter. It seem like Death himself reach out and touched me on the shoulder. He touched me just like I touch you. I got cold as ice and Death standing there grinning at me.

ROSE. Troy, why don't you hush that talk.

TROY. I say . . . what you want, Mr. Death? You be wanting me? You done brought your army to be getting me? I looked him dead in the eye. I wasn't fearing nothing. I was ready to tangle. Just like I'm ready to tangle now. The Bible say be ever vigilant. That's why I don't get but so drunk. I got to keep watch.

ROSE. Troy was right down there in Mercy Hospital. You remember he had pneumonia? Laying there with a fever talking plumb out of his head.

TROY. Death standing there staring at me . . . carrying that sickle in his hand. Finally he say, "You want bound over for another year?" See, just like that . . . "You want bound over for another year?" I told him, "Bound over hell! Let's settle this now!"

It seem like he kinda fell back when I said that, and all the cold went out of me. I reached down and grabbed that sickle and threw it just as far as I could throw it . . . and me and him commenced to wrestling.

We wrestled for three days and three nights. I can't say where I found the strength from. Everytime it seemed like he was gonna get the best of me, I'd reach way down deep inside myself and find the strength to do him one better.

ROSE. Everytime Troy tell that story he find different ways to tell it. Different things to make up about it.

TROY. I ain't making up nothing. I'm telling you the facts of what happened. I wrestled with Death for three days and three nights and I'm standing here to tell you about it. [*Pause.*] All right. At the end of the third night we done weakened each other to where we can't hardly move. Death stood up, throwed on his robe . . . had him a white robe with a hood on it. He throwed on that robe and went off to look for his sickle. Say, "I'll be back." Just like that. "I'll be back." I told him, say, "Yeah, but . . . you gonna have to find me!" I wasn't no fool. I wasn't going looking for him. Death ain't nothing to play with. And I know he's gonna get me. I know I got to join his army . . . his camp followers. But as long as I keep my strength and see him coming . . . as long as I keep up my vigilance . . . he's gonna have to fight to get me. I ain't going easy.

BONO. Well, look here, since you got to keep up your vigilance . . . let me have the bottle.

TROY. Aw hell, I shouldn't have told you that part. I should have left out that part.

ROSE. Troy be talking that stuff and half the time don't even know what he be talking about.

TROY. Bono know me better than that.

BONO. That's right. I know you. I know you got some Uncle Remus in your blood. You got more stories than the devil got sinners.

TROY. Aw hell, I done seen him too! Done talked with the devil.

ROSE. Troy, don't nobody wanna be hearing all that stuff.

LYONS *enters the yard from the street. Thirty-four years old,* TROY'S *son by a previous marriage, he sports a neatly trimmed goatee, sport coat, white shirt, tieless and buttoned at the collar. Though he fancies himself a musician, he is more caught up in the rituals and "idea" of being a musician than in the actual practice of the music. He has come to borrow money from* TROY, *and while he knows he will be successful, he is uncertain as to what extent his lifestyle will be held up to scrutiny and ridicule.*

LYONS. Hey, Pop.

TROY. What you come "Hey, Popping" me for?

LYONS. How you doing, Rose? [*He kisses her.*] Mr. Bono. How you doing?

BONO. Hey, Lyons . . . how you been?

TROY. He must have been doing all right. I ain't seen him around here last week.

ROSE. Troy, leave your boy alone. He come by to see you and you wanna start all that nonsense.

TROY. I ain't bothering Lyons. [*Offers him the bottle.*] Here . . . get you a drink. We got an understanding. I know why he come by to see me and he know I know.

LYONS. Come on, Pop . . . I just stopped by to say hi . . . see how you was doing.

TROY. You ain't stopped by yesterday.

ROSE. You gonna stay for supper, Lyons? I got some chicken cooking in the oven.

LYONS. No, Rose . . . thanks. I was just in the neighborhood and thought I'd stop by for a minute.

TROY. You was in the neighborhood all right, nigger. You telling the truth there. You was in the neighborhood cause it's my payday.

LYONS. Well, hell, since you mentioned it . . . let me ave ten dollars.

TROY. I'll be damned! I'll die and go to hell and play blackjack with the devil before I give you ten dollars.

BONO. That's what I wanna know about . . . that devil you done seen.

LYONS. What . . . Pop done seen the devil? You too much, Pops.

LYONS. Well . . . hell, since you mentioned it . . . let me have ten dollars.

TROY. Yeah, I done seen him. Talked to him too!

ROSE. You ain't seen no devil. I done told you that man ain't had nothing to do with the devil. Anything you can't understand, you want to call it the devil.

TROY. Look here, Bono . . . I went down to see Hertzberger about some furniture. Got three rooms for two-ninety-eight. That what it say on the radio. "Three rooms . . . two-ninety-eight." Even made up a little song about it. Go down there . . . man tell me I can't get no credit. I'm working every day and can't get no credit. What to do? I got an empty house with some raggedy furniture in it. Cory ain't got no bed. He's sleeping on a pile of rags on the floor. Working every day and can't get no credit. Come back here—Rose'll tell you—madder than hell. Sit down . . . try to figure what I'm gonna do. Come a knock on the door. Ain't been living here but three days. Who know I'm here? Open the door . . . devil standing there bigger than life. White fellow . . . White fellow . . . got on good clothes and everything. Standing there with a clipboard in his hand. I ain't had to say nothing. First words come out of his mouth was . . . "I understand you need some furniture and can't get no credit." I liked to fell over. He say, "I'll give you all the credit you want, but you got to pay the interest on it." I told him, "Give me three rooms worth and charge whatever you want." Next day a truck pulled up here and two men unloaded them three rooms. Man what drove the truck give me a book. Say send ten dollars, first of every month to the address in the book and every thing will be all right. Say if I miss a payment the devil was coming back and it'll be hell to pay. That was fifteen years ago. To this day . . . the first of the month I send my ten dollars, Rose'll tell you.

ROSE. Troy lying.

TROY. I ain't never seen that man since. Now you tell me who else that could have been but the devil? I ain't sold my soul or nothing like that, you understand. Naw, I wouldn't have truck with the devil about nothing like that. I got my furniture and pays my ten dollars the first of the month just like clockwork.

BONO. How long you say you been paying this ten dollars a month?

TROY. Fifteen years!

BONO. Hell, ain't you finished paying for it yet? How much the man done charged you?

TROY. Ah hell, I done paid for it. I done paid for it ten times over! The fact is I'm scared to stop paying it.

ROSE. Troy lying. We got that furniture from Mr. Glickman. He ain't paying no ten dollars a month to nobody.

TROY. Aw hell, woman. Bono know I ain't that big a fool.

LYONS. I was just getting ready to say . . . I know where there's a bridge for sale.

TROY. Look here, I'll tell you this . . . it don't matter to me if he was the devil. It don't matter if the devil give credit. Somebody has got to give it.

ROSE. It ought to matter. You going around talking about having truck with the devil . . . God's the one you gonna have to answer to. He's the one gonna be at the Judgment.

LYONS. Yeah, well, look here, Pop . . . Let me have that ten dollars. I'll give it back to you. Bonnie got a job working at the hospital.

TROY. What I tell you, Bono? The only time I see this nigger is when he wants something. That's the only time I see him.

LYONS. Come on, Pop, Mr. Bono don't want to hear all that. Let me have the ten dollars. I told you Bonnie working.

TROY. What that mean to me? "Bonnie working." I don't care if she working. Go ask her for the ten dollars if she working. Talking about "Bonnie working." Why ain't you working?

LYONS. Aw, Pop, you know I can't find no decent job. Where am I gonna get a job at? You know I can't get no job.

TROY. I told you I know some people down there. I can get you on the rubbish if you want to work. I told you that the last time you came by here asking me for something.

LYONS. Naw, Pop . . . thanks. That ain't for me. I don't wanna be carrying nobody's rubbish. I don't wanna be punching nobody's time clock.

TROY. What's the matter, you too good to carry people's rubbish? Where you think that ten dollars you talking about come from? I'm just supposed to haul people's rubbish and give my money to you cause you too lazy to work. You too lazy to work and wanna know why you ain't got what I got.

ROSE. What hospital Bonnie working at? Mercy?

LYONS. She's down at Passavant working in the laundry.

TROY. I ain't got nothing as it is. I give you that ten dollars and I got to eat beans the rest of the week. Naw . . . you ain't getting no ten dollars here.

LYONS. You ain't got to be eating no beans. I don't know why you wanna say that.

TROY. I ain't got no extra money. Gabe done moved over to Miss Pearl's paying her the rent and things done got tight around here. I can't afford to be giving you every payday.

LYONS. I ain't asked you to give me nothing. I asked you to loan me ten dollars. I know you got ten dollars.

TROY. Yeah, I got it. You know why I got it? Cause I don't throw my money away out there in the streets. You living the fast life . . . wanna be a musician . . . running around in them clubs and things . . . then, you learn to take care of yourself. You ain't gonna find me going and asking nobody for nothing. I done spent too many years without.

LYONS. You and me is two different people, Pop.

TROY. I done learned my mistake and learned to do what's right by it. You still trying to get something for nothing. Life don't owe you nothing. You owe it to yourself. Ask Bono. He'll tell you I'm right.

LYONS. You got your way of dealing with the world . . . I got mine. The only thing that matters to me is the music.

TROY. Yeah, I can see that! It don't matter how you gonna eat . . . where your next dollar is coming from. You telling the truth there.

LYONS. I know I got to eat. But I got to live too. I need something that gonna help me to get out of the bed in the morning. Make me feel like I belong in the world. I don't bother nobody. I just stay with the music cause that's the only way I can find to live in the world. Otherwise there ain't no telling what I might do. Now I don't come criticizing you and how you live. I just come by to ask you for ten dollars. I don't wanna hear all that about how I live.

TROY. Boy, your mamma did a hell of a job raising you.

LYONS. You can't change me, Pop. I'm thirty-four years old. If you wanted to change me, you should have been there when I was growing up. I come by to see you . . . ask for ten dollars and you want to talk about how I was raised. You don't know nothing about how I was raised.

ROSE. Let the boy have ten dollars, Troy.

TROY [*to* LYONS]. What the hell you looking at me for? I ain't got no ten dollars. You know what I do with my money. [*To* ROSE.] Give him ten dollars if you want him to have it.

ROSE. I will. Just as soon as you turn it loose.

TROY [*handing* ROSE *the money*]. There it is. Seventy-six dollars and forty-two cents. You see this, Bono? Now, I ain't gonna get but six of that back.

ROSE. You ought to stop telling that lie. Here, Lyons. [*She hands him the money.*]

LYONS. Thanks, Rose. Look . . . I got to run . . . I'll see you later.

TROY. Wait a minute. You gonna say, "Thanks, Rose" and ain't gonna look to see where she got that ten dollars from? See how they do me, Bono?

LYONS. I know she got it from you, Pop. Thanks. I'll give it back to you.

TROY. There he go telling another lie. Time I see that ten dollars . . . he'll be owing me thirty more.

LYONS. See you, Mr. Bono.

BONO. Take care, Lyons!

LYONS. Thanks, Pop. I'll see you again.

LYONS *exits the yard.*

TROY. I don't know why he don't go and get him a decent job and take care of that woman he got.

BONO. He'll be all right, Troy. The boy is still young.

TROY. The boy is thirty-four years old.

ROSE. Let's not get off into all that.

BONO. Look here . . . I got to be going. I got to be getting on. Lucille gonna be waiting.

TROY [*puts his arm around* ROSE]. See this woman, Bono? I love this woman. I love this woman so much it hurts. I love her so much . . . I done run out of ways of loving her. So I got to go back to basics. Don't you come by my house Monday morning talking about time to go to work . . . 'cause I'm still gonna be stroking!

ROSE. Troy! Stop it now!

BONO. I ain't paying him no mind, Rose. That ain't nothing but gin-talk. Go on, Troy. I'll see you Monday.

TROY. Don't you come by my house, nigger! I done told you what I'm gonna be doing.

The lights go down to black.

SCENE 2

The lights come up on ROSE *hanging up clothes. She hums and sings softly to herself. It is the following morning.*

ROSE [*sings*].

Jesus, be a fence all around me every day
Jesus, I want you to protect me as I travel on my way.
Jesus, be a fence all around me every day.

TROY *enters from the house.*

Jesus, I want you to protect me
As I travel on my way.

[*To* TROY.] Morning. You ready for breakfast? I can fix it soon as I finish hanging up these clothes.

TROY. I got the coffee on. That'll be all right. I'll just drink some of that this morning.

ROSE. That 651 hit yesterday. That's the second time this month. Miss Pearl hit for a dollar . . . seem like those that need the least always get lucky. Poor folks can't get nothing.

TROY. Them numbers don't know nobody. I don't know why you fool with them. You and Lyons both.

ROSE. It's something to do.

TROY. You ain't doing nothing but throwing your money away.

ROSE. Troy, you know I don't play foolishly. I just play a nickel here and a nickel there.

TROY. That's two nickels you done thrown away.

ROSE. Now I hit sometimes . . . that makes up for it. It always comes in handy when I do hit. I don't hear you complaining then.

TROY. I ain't complaining now. I just say it's foolish. Trying to guess out of six hundred ways which way the number gonna come. If I had all the money niggers, these Negroes, throw away on numbers for one week—just one week—I'd be a rich man.

ROSE. Well, you wishing and calling it foolish ain't gonna stop folks from playing numbers. That's one thing for sure. Besides . . . some good things come from playing numbers. Look where Pope done bought him that restaurant off of numbers.

TROY. I can't stand niggers like that. Man ain't had two dimes to rub together. He walking around with his shoes all run over bumming money for cigarettes. All right. Got lucky there and hit the numbers . . .

ROSE. Troy, I know all about it.

TROY. Had good sense, I'll say that for him. He ain't throwed his money away. I seen niggers hit the numbers and go through two thousand dollars in four days. Man bought him that restaurant down there . . . fixed it up real nice . . . and then didn't want nobody to come in it! A Negro go in there and can't get no kind of service. I seen a white fellow come in there and order a bowl of stew. Pope picked all the meat out of the pot for him. Man ain't had nothing but a bowl of meat!

Negro come behind him and ain't got nothing but the potatoes and carrots. Talking about what numbers do for people, you picked a wrong example. Ain't done nothing but make a worser fool out of him than he was before.

ROSE. Troy, you ought to stop worrying about what happened at work yesterday.

TROY. I ain't worried. Just told me to be down there at the Commissioner's office on Friday. Everybody think they gonna fire me. I ain't worried about them firing me. You ain't got to worry about that. [*Pause.*] Where's Cory? Cory in the house? [*Calls.*] Cory?

ROSE. He gone out.

TROY. Out, huh? He gone out he know I want him to help me with this fence. I know how he is. That boy scared of work.

GABRIEL *enters. He comes halfway down the alley and, hearing* TROY*'s voice, stops.*

TROY [*continues*]. He ain't done a lick of work in his life.

ROSE. He had to go to football practice. Coach wanted them to get in a little extra practice before the season start.

TROY. I got his practice . . . running out of here before he get his chores done.

ROSE. Troy, what is wrong with you this morning? Don't nothing set right with you. Go on back in there and go to bed . . . get up on the other side.

TROY. Why something got to be wrong with me? I ain't said nothing wrong with me.

ROSE. You got something to say about everything. First it's the numbers . . . then it's the way the man runs his restaurant . . . then you done got on Cory. What's it gonna be next? Take a look up there and see if the weather suits you . . . or is it gonna be how you gonna put up the fence with the clothes hanging in the yard.

TROY. You hit the nail on the head then.

ROSE. I know you like I know the back of my hand. Go on in there and get you some coffee . . . see if that straighten you up. 'Cause you ain't right this morning.

TROY *starts into the house and sees* GABRIEL. GABRIEL *starts singing.* TROY*'s brother, he is seven years younger than* TROY. *Injured in World War II, he has a metal plate in his head. He carries an old trumpet tied around his waist and believes with every fiber of his being that he is the Archangel Gabriel. He carries a chipped basket with an assortment of discarded fruits and vegetables he has picked up in the strip district and which he attempts to sell.*

GABRIEL [*singing*].

Yes, ma'am I got plums
You ask me how I sell them
Oh ten cents apiece
Three for a quarter
Come and buy now
'Cause I'm here today
And tomorrow I'll be gone

GABRIEL *enters.*

Hey, Rose!

ROSE. How you doing Gabe?

GABRIEL. There's Troy . . . Hey, Troy!

TROY. Hey, Gabe.

Exit into kitchen.

ROSE [*to* GABRIEL]. What you got there?

GABRIEL. You know what I got, Rose. I got fruits and vegetables.

ROSE [*looking in basket*]. Where's all these plums you talking about?

GABRIEL. I ain't got no plums today, Rose. I was just singing that. Have some tomorrow. Put me in a big order for plums. Have enough plums tomorrow for St. Peter and everybody.

TROY *reenters from kitchen, crosses to steps.*

[*To* ROSE.] Troy's mad at me.

TROY. I ain't mad at you. What I got to be mad at you about? You ain't done nothing to me.

GABRIEL. I just moved over to Miss Pearl's to keep out from in your way. I ain't mean no harm by it.

TROY. Who said anything about that? I ain't said anything about that.

GABRIEL. You ain't mad at me, is you?

TROY. Naw . . . I ain't mad at you, Gabe. If I was mad at you I'd tell you about it.

GABRIEL. Got me two rooms. In the basement. Got my own door too. Wanna see my key? [*He holds up a key.*] That's my own key! My two rooms!

TROY. Well, that's good, Gabe. You got your own key . . . that's good.

ROSE. You hungry, Gabe? I was just fixing to cook Troy his breakfast.

GABRIEL. I'll take some biscuits. You got some biscuits? Did you know when I was in heaven . . . every morning me and St. Peter would sit down by the gate and eat some big fat biscuits? Oh, yeah! We had us a good time. We'd sit there and eat us them biscuits and then St. Peter would go off to sleep and tell me to wake him up when it's time to open the gates for the judgment.

ROSE. Well, come on . . . I'll make up a batch of biscuits.

ROSE *exits into the house.*

GABRIEL. Troy . . . St. Peter got your name in the book. I seen it. It say . . . Troy Maxson. I say . . . I know him! He got the same name like what I got. That's my brother!

TROY. How many times you gonna tell me that, Gabe?

GABRIEL. Ain't got my name in the book. Don't have to have my name. I done died and went to heaven. He got your name though. One morning St. Peter was looking at his book . . . marking it up for the judgment . . . and he let me see your name. Got it in there under M. Got Rose's name . . . I ain't seen it like I seen yours . . . but I know it's in there. He got a great big book. Got everybody's name what was ever been born. That's what he told me. But I seen your name. Seen it with my own eyes.

TROY. Go on in the house there. Rose going to fix you something to eat.

GABRIEL. Oh, I ain't hungry. I done had breakfast with Aunt Jemimah. She come by and cooked me up a whole mess of flapjacks. Remember how we used to eat them flapjacks?

TROY. Go on in the house and get you something to eat now.

GABRIEL. I got to sell my plums. I done sold some tomatoes. Got me two quarters. Wanna see? [*He shows* TROY *his quarters.*] I'm gonna save them and buy me a new horn so St. Peter can hear me when it's time to open the gates. [GABRIEL *stops suddenly. Listens.*] Hear that? That's the hellhounds. I got to chase them out of here. Go on get out of here! Get out!

GABRIEL *exits singing.*

Better get ready for the judgment
Better get ready for the judgment
My Lord is coming down

ROSE *enters from the house.*

TROY. He's gone off somewhere.

GABRIEL [*offstage*].

Better get ready for the judgment
Better get ready for the judgment morning
Better get ready for the judgment
My God is coming down

ROSE. He ain't eating right. Miss Pearl say she can't get him to eat nothing.

TROY. What you want me to do about it, Rose? I done did everything I can for the man. I can't make him get well. Man got half his head blown away . . . what you expect?

ROSE. Seem like something ought to be done to help him.

TROY. Man don't bother nobody. He just mixed up from that metal plate he got in his head. Ain't no sense for him to go back into the hospital.

ROSE. Least he be eating right. They can help him take care of himself.

TROY. Don't nobody wanna be locked up, Rose. What you wanna lock him up for? Man go over there and fight the war . . . messin' around with them Japs, get half his head blow off . . . and they give him a lousy three thousand dollars. And I had to swoop down on that.

ROSE. Is you fixing to go into that again?

TROY. That's the only way I got a roof over my head . . . cause of that metal plate.

ROSE. Ain't no sense you blaming yourself for nothing. Gabe wasn't in no condition to manage that money. You done what was right by him. Can't nobody say you ain't done what was right by him. Look how long you took care of him . . . till he wanted to have his own place and moved over there with Miss Pearl.

TROY. That ain't what I'm saying woman! I'm just stating the facts. If my brother didn't have that metal plate in his head . . . I wouldn't have a pot to piss in or a window to throw it out of. And I'm fifty-three years old. Now see if you can understand that!

TROY *gets up from the porch and starts to exit the yard.*

ROSE. Where you going off to? You been running out of here every Saturday for weeks. I thought you was gonna work on this fence?

TROY. I'm gonna walk down to Taylors'. Listen to the ball game. I'll be back in a bit. I'll work on it when I get back.

He exits the yard. The lights go to black.

SCENE 3

The lights come up on the yard. It is four hours later. ROSE *is taking down the clothes from the line.* CORY *enters carrying his football equipment.*

ROSE. Your daddy like to had a fit with you running out of here this morning without doing your chores.

CORY. I told you I had to go to practice.

ROSE. He say you were supposed to help him with this fence.

CORY. He been saying that the last four or five Saturdays, and then he don't never do nothing, but go down to Taylors'. Did you tell him about the recruiter?

ROSE. Yeah, I told him.

CORY. What he say?

ROSE. He ain't said nothing too much. You get in there and get started on your chores before he gets back. Go on and scrub down them steps before he gets back here hollering and carrying on.

CORY. I'm hungry. What you got to eat, Mama?

ROSE. Go on and get started on your chores. I got some meat loaf in there. Go on and make you a sandwich . . . and don't leave no mess in there.

CORY *exits into the house.* ROSE *continues to take down the clothes.* TROY *enters the yard and sneaks up and grabs her from behind.*

Troy! Go on, now. You liked to scared me to death. What was the score of the game? Lucille had me on the phone and I couldn't keep up with it.

TROY. What I care about the game? Come here, woman.

[*He tries to kiss her.*]

ROSE. I thought you went down Taylors' to listen to the game. Go on, Troy! You supposed to be putting up this fence.

TROY [*attempting to kiss her again*]. I'll put it up when I finish with what is at hand.

ROSE. Go on, Troy. I ain't studying you.

TROY [*chasing after her*]. I'm studying you . . . fixing to do my homework!

ROSE. Troy, you better leave me alone.

TROY. Where's Cory? That boy brought his butt home yet?

ROSE. He's in the house doing his chores.

TROY [*calling*]. Cory! Get your butt out here, boy!

ROSE *exits into the house with the laundry.*
TROY *goes over to the pile of wood, picks up a board, and starts sawing.*
CORY *enters from the house.*

TROY. You just now coming in here from leaving this morning?

CORY. Yeah, I had to go to football practice.

TROY. Yeah, what?

CORY. Yessir.

TROY. I ain't but two seconds off you noway. The garbage sitting in there overflowing . . . you ain't done none of your chores . . . and you come in here talking about "Yeah."

CORY. I was just getting ready to do my chores now, Pop . . .

TROY. Your first chore is to help me with this fence on Saturday. Everything else come after that. Now get that saw and cut them boards.

CORY *takes the saw and begins cutting the boards.*
TROY *continues working. There is a long pause.*

CORY. Hey, Pop . . . why don't you buy a TV?

TROY. What I want with a TV? What I want one of them for?

CORY. Everybody got one. Earl, Ba Bra . . . Jesse!

TROY. I ain't asked you who had one. I say what I want with one?

CORY. So you can watch it. They got lots of things on TV. Baseball games and everything. We could watch the World Series.

TROY. Yeah . . . and how much this TV cost?

CORY. I don't know. They got them on sale for around two hundred dollars.

TROY. Two hundred dollars, huh?

CORY. That ain't that much, Pop.

TROY. Naw, it's just two hundred dollars. See that roof you got over your head at night? Let me tell you something about that roof. It's been over ten years since that roof was last tarred. See now . . . the snow come this winter and sit up there on that roof like it is . . . and it's gonna seep inside. It's just gonna be a little bit . . . ain't gonna hardly notice it. Then the next thing you know, it's gonna be leaking all over the house. Then the wood rot from all that water and you gonna need a whole new roof. Now, how much you think it cost to get that roof tarred?

CORY. I don't know.

TROY. Two hundred and sixty-four dollars . . . cash money. While you thinking about a TV, I got to be thinking about the roof . . . and whatever else go wrong here. Now if you had two hundred dollars, what would you do . . . fix the roof or buy a TV?

CORY. I'd buy a TV. Then when the roof started to leak . . . when it needed fixing . . . I'd fix it.

TROY. Where you gonna get the money from? You done spent it for a TV. You gonna sit up and watch the water run all over your brand new TV.

CORY. Aw, Pop. You got money. I know you do.

TROY. Where I got it at, huh?

CORY. You got it in the bank.

TROY. You wanna see my bankbook? You wanna see that seventy-three dollars and twenty-two cents I got sitting up in there?

CORY. You ain't got to pay for it all at one time. You can put a down payment on it and carry it on home with you.

TROY. Not me. I ain't gonna owe nobody nothing if I can help it. Miss a payment and they come and snatch it right out of your house. Then what you got? Now, soon as I get two hundred dollars clear, then I'll buy a TV. Right now, as soon as I get two hundred and sixty-four dollars, I'm gonna have this roof tarred.

CORY. Aw . . . Pop!

TROY. You go on and get you two hundred dollars and buy one if ya want it. I got better things to do with my money.

CORY. I can't get no two hundred dollars. I ain't never seen two hundred dollars.

TROY. I'll tell you what . . . you get you a hundred dollars and I'll put the other hundred with it.

CORY. All right, I'm gonna show you.

TROY. You gonna show me how you can cut them boards right now.

CORY *begins to cut the boards. There is a long pause.*

CORY. The Pirates won today. That makes five in a row.

TROY. I ain't thinking about the Pirates. Got an all-white team. Got that boy . . . that Puerto Rican boy . . . Clemente. Don't even half-play him. That boy could be something if they give him a chance, Play him one day and sit him on the bench the next.

CORY. He gets a lot of chances to play.

TROY. I'm talking about playing regular. Playing every day so you can get your timing. That's what I'm talking about.

CORY. They got some white guys on the team that don't play every day. You can't play everybody at the same time.

TROY. If they got a white fellow sitting on the bench . . . you can bet your last dollar he can't play! That colored guy got to be twice as good before he get on the team. That's why I don't want you to get all tied up in them sports. Man on the team and what it get him? They got colored on the team and don't use them. Same as not having them. All them teams the same.

CORY. The Braves got Hank Aaron and Wes Covington. Hank Aaron hit two home runs today. That makes forty-three.

TROY. Hank Aaron ain't nobody. That what you supposed to do. That's how you supposed to play the game. Ain't nothing to it. It's just a matter of timing . . . getting the right follow-through. Hell, I can hit forty-three home runs right now!

CORY. Not off no major-league pitching, you couldn't.

TROY. We had better pitching in the Negro leagues. I hit seven home runs off of Satchel Paige. You can't get no better than that!

CORY. Sandy Koufax. He's leading the league in strikeouts.

TROY. I ain't thinking of no Sandy Koufax.

CORY. You got Warren Spahn and Lew Burdette. I bet you couldn't hit no home runs off of Warren Spahn.

TROY. I'm through with it now. You go on and cut them boards. [*Pause.*] Your mama tell me you done got recruited by a college football team? Is that right?

CORY. Yeah. Coach Zellman say the recruiter gonna be coming by to talk to you. Get you to sign the permission papers.

TROY. I thought you supposed to be working down there at the A&P. Ain't you suppose to be working down there after school?

CORY. Mr. Stawicki say he gonna hold my job for me until after the football season. Say starting next week I can work weekends.

TROY. I thought we had an understanding about this football stuff? You suppose to keep up with your chores and hold that job down at the A&P. Ain't been around here all day on a Saturday. Ain't none of your chores done . . . and now you telling me you done quit your job.

CORY. I'm going to be working weekends.

TROY. You damn right you are! And ain't no need for nobody coming around here to talk to me about signing nothing.

CORY. Hey, Pop . . . you can't do that. He's coming all the way from North Carolina.

TROY. I don't care where he coming from. The white man ain't gonna let you get nowhere with that football noway. You go on and get your book-learning so you can work yourself up in that A&P or learn how to fix cars or build houses or something, get you a trade. That way you have something can't nobody take away from you. You go on and learn how to put your hands to some good use. Besides hauling people's garbage.

CORY. I get good grades, Pop. That's why the recruiter wants to talk with you. You got to keep up your grades to get recruited. This way I'll be going to college. I'll get a chance . . .

TROY. First you gonna get your butt down there to the A&P and get your job back.

CORY. Mr. Stawicki done already hired somebody else 'cause I told him I was playing football.

TROY. You a bigger fool than I thought . . . to let somebody take away your job so you can play some football. Where you gonna get your money to take out your girlfriend and whatnot? What kind of foolishness is that to let somebody take away your job?

CORY. I'm still gonna be working weekends.

TROY. Naw . . . naw. You getting your butt out of here and finding you another job.

CORY. Come on, Pop! I got to practice. I can't work after school and play football too. The team needs me. That's what Coach Zellman say . . .

TROY. I don't care what nobody else say. I'm the boss . . . you understand? I'm the boss around here. I do the only saying what counts.

CORY. Come on, Pop!

TROY. I asked you . . . did you understand?

CORY. Yeah . . .

TROY. What?!

CORY. Yessir.

TROY. You go on down there to that A&P and see if you can get your job back. If you can't do both . . . then you quit the football team. You've got to take the crookeds with the straights.

CORY. Yessir. [*Pause.*] Can I ask you a question?

TROY. What the hell you wanna ask me? Mr. Stawicki the one you got the questions for.

CORY. How come you ain't never liked me?

TROY. Liked you? Who the hell say I got to like you? What law is there say I got to like you? Wanna stand up in my face and ask a damn foolass question like that. Talking about liking somebody. Come here, boy, when I talk to you.

CORY *comes over to where* TROY *is working. He stands slouched over and* TROY *shoves him on his shoulder.*

Straighten up, goddammit! I asked you a question . . . what law is there say I got to like you?

CORY. None.

TROY. Well, all right then! Don't you eat every day? [*Pause.*] Answer me when I talk to you! Don't you eat every day?

CORY. Yeah.

TROY. Nigger, as long as you in my house, you put that sir on the end of it when you talk to me.

CORY. Yes . . . sir.

TROY. You eat every day.

CORY. Yessir!

TROY. Got a roof over your head.

CORY. Yessir!

TROY. Got clothes on your back.

CORY. Yessir.

TROY. Why you think that is?

CORY. Cause of you.

TROY. Ah, hell I know it's cause of me . . . but why do you think that is?

CORY [*hesitant*]. Cause you like me.

TROY. Like you? I go out of here every morning . . . bust my butt . . . putting up with them crackers every day . . . cause I like you? You are the biggest fool I ever saw. [*Pause.*] It's my job. It's my responsibility! You understand that? A man got to take care of his family. You live in my house . . . sleep you behind on my bedclothes . . . fill you belly up with my food . . . cause you my son. You my flesh and blood. Not cause I like you! Cause it's my duty to take care of you. I owe a responsibility to you! Let's get this straight right here . . . before it go along any further . . . I ain't got to like you. Mr. Rand don't give me my money come payday cause he likes me. He gives me cause he owe me. I done give you everything I had to give you. I gave you your life! Me and your mama worked that out between us. And liking your black ass wasn't part of the bargain. Don't you try and go through life worrying about if somebody like you or not. You best be making sure they doing right by you. You understand what I'm saying boy?

CORY. Yessir.

TROY. Then get the hell out of my face, and get on down to that A&P.

ROSE *has been standing behind the screen door for much of the scene. She enters as* CORY *exits.*

ROSE. Why don't you let the boy go ahead and play football, Troy? Ain't no harm in that. He's just trying to be like you with the sports.

TROY. I don't want him to be like me! I want him to move as far away from my life as he can get. You the only decent thing that ever happened to me. I wish him that. But I don't wish him a thing else from my life. I decided seventeen years ago that boy wasn't getting involved in no sports. Not after what they did to me in the sports.

ROSE. Troy, why don't you admit you was too old to play in the major leagues? For once . . . why don't you admit that?

TROY. What do you mean too old? Don't come telling me I was too old. I just wasn't the right color. Hell, I'm fifty-three years old and can do better than Selkirk's .269 right now!

ROSE. How's was you gonna play ball when you were over forty? Sometimes I can't get no sense out of you.

TROY. I got good sense, woman. I got sense enough not to let my boy get hurt over playing no sports. You been mothering that boy too much. Worried about if people like him.

ROSE. Everything that boy do . . . he do for you. He wants you to say "Good job, son." That's all.

TROY. Rose, I ain't got time for that. He's alive. He's healthy. He's got to make his own way. I made mine. Ain't nobody gonna hold his hand when he get out there in that world.

ROSE. Times have changed from when you was young, Troy. People change. The world's changing around you and you can't even see it.

TROY [*slow, methodical*]. Woman . . . I do the best I can do. I come in here every Friday. I carry a sack of potatoes and a bucket of lard. You all line up at the door with your hands out. I give you the lint from my pockets. I give you my sweat and my blood. I ain't got no tears. I done spent them. We go upstairs in that room at night . . . and I fall down on you and try to blast a hole into forever. I get up Monday morning . . . find my lunch on the table. I go out. Make my way. Find my strength to carry me through to the next Friday. [*Pause.*] That's all I got, Rose. That's all I got to give. I can't give nothing else.

TROY *exits into the house. The lights go down to black.*

SCENE 4

It is Friday. Two weeks later. CORY *starts out of the house with his football equipment. The phone rings.*

CORY [*calling*]. I got it! [*He answers the phone and stands in the screen door talking.*] Hello? Hey, Jesse. Naw . . . I was just getting ready to leave now.

ROSE [*calling*]. Cory!

CORY. I told you, man, them spikes is all tore up. You can use them if you want, but they ain't no good. Earl got some spikes.

ROSE [*calling*]. Cory!

CORY [*calling to* ROSE]. Mam? I'm talking to Jesse. [*Into phone.*] When she say that? [*Pause.*] Aw, you lying, man. I'm gonna tell her you said that.

ROSE [*calling*]. Cory, don't you go nowhere!

CORY. I got to go to the game, Ma! [*Into the phone.*] Yeah, hey, look, I'll talk to you later. Yeah, I'll meet you over Earl's house. Later. Bye, Ma.

CORY *exits the house and starts out the yard.*

ROSE. Cory, where you going off to? You got that stuff all pulled out and thrown all over your room.

CORY [*in the yard*]. I was looking for my spikes. Jesse wanted to borrow my spikes.

ROSE. Get up there and get that cleaned up before your daddy get back in here.

CORY. I got to go to the game! I'll clean it up when I get back.

CORY *exits.*

ROSE. That's all he need to do is see that room all messed up.

ROSE *exits into the house.* TROY *and* BONO *enter the yard.* TROY *is dressed in clothes other than his work clothes.*

BONO. He told him the same thing he told you. Take it to the union.

TROY. Brownie ain't got that much sense. Man wasn't thinking about nothing. He wait until I confront them on it . . . then he wanna come crying seniority. [*Calls.*] Hey, Rose!

BONO. I wish I could have seen Mr. Rand's face when he told you.

TROY. He couldn't get it out of his mouth! Liked to bit his tongue! When they called me down there to the Commissioner's office . . . he thought they was gonna fire me. Like everybody else.

BONO. I didn't think they was gonna fire you. I thought they was gonna put you on the warning paper.

TROY. Hey, Rose! [*To* BONO.] Yeah, Mr. Rand like to bit his tongue.

TROY *breaks the seal on the bottle, takes a drink, and hands it to* BONO.

BONO. I see you run right down to Taylors' and told that Alberta gal.

TROY [*calling*]. Hey Rose! [*To* BONO.] I told everybody. Hey, Rose! I went down there to cash my check.

ROSE [*entering from the house*]. Hush all that hollering, man! I know you out here. What they say down there at the Commissioner's office?

TROY. You supposed to come when I call you, woman. Bono'll tell you that. [*To* BONO.] Don't Lucille come when you call her?

ROSE. Man, hush your mouth. I ain't no dog . . . talk about "come when you call me."

BONO [*puts his arm around* ROSE]. You hear this, Bono? I had me an old dog used to get uppity like that. You say, "C'mere, Blue!" . . . and he just lay there and look at you. End up getting a stick and chasing him away trying to make him come.

ROSE. I ain't studying you and your dog. I remember you used to sing that old song.

TROY [*he sings*].

> Hear it ring! Hear it ring!
> I had a dog his name was Blue.

ROSE. Don't nobody wanna hear you sing that old song.

TROY [*sings*]. You know Blue was mighty true.

ROSE. Used to have Cory running around here singing that song.

BONO. Hell, I remember that song myself.

TROY [*sings*].

> You know Blue was a good old dog.
> Blue treed a possum in a hollow log.

That was my daddy's song. My daddy made up that song.

ROSE. I don't care who made it up. Don't nobody wanna hear you sing it.

TROY [*makes a song like calling a dog*]. Come here, woman.

ROSE. You come in here carrying on, I reckon they ain't fired you. What they say down there at the Commissioner's office?

TROY. Look here, Rose . . . Mr. Rand called me into his office today when I got back from talking to them people down there . . . it come from up top . . . he called me in and told me they was making me a driver.

ROSE. Troy, you kidding!

TROY. No I ain't. Ask Bono.

ROSE. Well, that's great, Troy. Now you don't have to hassle them people no more.

LYONS *enters from the street.*

TROY. Aw hell, I wasn't looking to see you today. I thought you was in jail. Got it all over the front page of the Courier about them raiding Sefus's place . . . where you be hanging out with all them thugs.

LYONS. Hey, Pop . . . that ain't got nothing to do with me. I don't go down there gambling. I go down there to sit in with the band. I ain't got nothing to do with the gambling part. They got some good music down there.

TROY. They got some rogues . . . is what they got.

LYONS. How you been, Mr. Bono? Hi, Rose.

BONO. I see where you playing down at the Crawford Grill tonight.

ROSE. How come you ain't brought Bonnie like I told you? You should have brought Bonnie with you, she ain't been over in a month of Sundays.

LYONS. I was just in the neighborhood . . . thought I'd stop by.

TROY. Here he come . . .

BONO. Your daddy got a promotion on the rubbish. He's gonna be the first colored driver. Ain't got to do nothing but sit up there and read the paper like them white fellows.

LYONS. Hey, Pop . . . if you knew how to read you'd be all right.

BONO. Naw . . . naw . . . you mean if the nigger knew how to drive he'd be all right. Been fighting with them people about driving and ain't even got a license. Mr. Rand know you ain't got no driver's license?

TROY. Driving ain't nothing. All you do is point the truck where you want it to go. Driving ain't nothing.

BONO. Do Mr. Rand know you ain't got no driver's license? That's what I'm talking about. I ain't asked if driving was easy. I asked if Mr. Rand know you ain't got no driver's license.

TROY. He ain't got to know. The man ain't got to know my business. Time he find out, I have two or three driver's licenses.

LYONS [*going into his pocket*]. Say, look here, Pop . . .

TROY. I knew it was coming. Didn't I tell you, Bono? I know what kind of "Look here, Pop" that was. The nigger fixing to ask me for some money. It's Friday night. It's my payday. All them rogues down there on the avenue . . . the ones that ain't in jail . . . and Lyons is hopping in his shoes to get down there with them.

LYONS. See, Pop . . . if you give somebody else a chance to talk sometimes, you'd see that I was fixing to pay you back your ten dollars like I told you. Here . . . I told you I'd pay you when Bonnie got paid.

TROY. Naw . . . you go ahead and keep that ten dollars. Put it in the bank. The next time you feel like you wanna come by here and ask me for something . . . you go on down there and get that.

LYONS. Here's your ten dollars, Pop. I told you I don't want you to give me nothing. I just wanted to borrow ten dollars.

TROY. Naw . . . you go on and keep that for the next time you want to ask me.

LYONS. Come on, Pop . . . here go your ten dollars.

ROSE. Why don't you go on and let the boy pay you back, Troy?

LYONS. Here you go, Rose. If you don't take it I'm gonna have to hear about it for the next six months. [*He hands her the money.*]

ROSE. You can hand yours over here too, Troy.

TROY. You see this, Bono. You see how they do me.

BONO. Yeah, Lucille do me the same way.

GABRIEL *is heard singing off stage. He enters.*

GABRIEL. Better get ready for the Judgment! Better get ready for . . . Hey! . . . Hey! . . . There's Troy's boy!

LYONS. How are you doing, Uncle Gabe?

GABRIEL. Lyons . . . The King of the Jungle! Rose . . . hey, Rose. Got a flower for you. [*He takes a rose from his pocket.*] Picked it myself. That's the same rose like you is!

ROSE. That's right nice of you, Gabe.

LYONS. What you been doing, Uncle Gabe?

GABRIEL. Oh, I been chasing hellhounds and waiting on the time to tell St. Peter to open the gates.

LYONS. You been chasing hellhounds, huh? Well . . . you doing the right thing, Uncle Gabe. Somebody got to chase them.

GABRIEL. Oh, yeah . . . I know it. The devil's strong. The devil ain't no pushover. Hellhounds snipping at everybody's heels. But I got my trumpet waiting on the Judgment time.

LYONS. Waiting on the Battle of Armageddon, huh?

GABRIEL. Ain't gonna be too much of a battle when God get to waving that Judgment sword. But the people's gonna have a hell of a time trying to get into heaven if them gates ain't open.

LYONS [*putting his arm around* GABRIEL]. You hear this, Pop. Uncle Gabe, you all right!

GABRIEL [*laughing with* LYONS]. Lyons! King of the Jungle.

ROSE. You gonna stay for supper, Gabe? Want me to fix you a plate?

GABRIEL. I'll take a sandwich, Rose. Don't want no plate. Just wanna eat with my hands. I'll take a sandwich.

ROSE. How about you, Lyons? You staying? Got some short ribs cooking.

LYONS. Naw, I won't eat nothing till after we finished playing. [*Pause.*] You ought to come down and listen to me play, Pop.

TROY. I don't like that Chinese music. All that noise.

ROSE. Go on in the house and wash up, Gabe . . . I'll fix you a sandwich.

GABRIEL [*to* LYONS, *as he exits*]. Troy's mad at me.

LYONS. What you made at Uncle Gabe for, Pop?

ROSE. He thinks Troy's mad at him cause he moved over to Miss Pearl's.

TROY. I ain't mad at the man. He can live where he want to live at.

LYONS. What he move over there for? Miss Pearl don't like nobody.

ROSE. She don't mind him none. She treats him real nice. She just don't allow all that singing.

TROY. She don't mind that rent he be Paying . . . That's what she don't mind.

ROSE. Tory, I ain't going through that with you no more. He's over there cause he want to have his own place. He can come and go as he please.

TROY. Hell, he could come and go as he please here. I wasn't stopping him. I ain't put no rules on him.

ROSE. It ain't the same thing, Troy. And you know it.

GABRIEL *comes to the door.*

Now, that's the last I wanna hear about that. I don't wanna hear nothing else about Gabe and Miss Pearl. And next week . . .

GABRIEL. I'm ready for my sandwich, Rose.

ROSE. And next week . . . when that recruiter come from that school . . . I want you to sign that paper and go on and let Cory play football. Then that'll be the last I have to hear about that.

TROY [*to* ROSE *as she exits in to the house*]. I ain't thinking about Cory nothing.

LYONS. What . . . Cory got recruited? What school he going to?

TROY. That boy walking around here smelling his piss . . . thinking he's grown. Thinking he's gonna do what he want, irrespective of what I say. Look here, Bono . . . I left the Commissioner's office and went down to the A&P . . . that boy ain't working down there. He lying to me. Telling me he got his job back . . . telling me he working weekends . . . telling me he working after school . . . Mr. Stawicki tell me he ain't working down there at all!

LYONS. Cory just growing up. He's just busting at the seams trying to fill out your shoes.

TROY. I don't care what he's doing. When he get to the point where he wanna disobey me . . . then it's time for him to move on. Bono'll tell you that. I bet he ain't never disobeyed his daddy without paying the consequences.

BONO. I ain't never had a chance. My daddy came on through . . . but I ain't never knew him to see him . . . or what he had on his mind or where he went. Just moving on through. Searching out the New Land. That's what the old folks used to call it. See a fellow moving around from place to place . . . woman to woman . . . called it searching out the New Land. I can't say if he ever found it. I come along, didn't want no kids. Didn't know if I was gonna be in one place long enough to fix on them right as their daddy. I figured I was going searching too. As it turned out I been hooked up with Lucille near about as long as your daddy been with Rose. Going on sixteen years.

TROY. Sometimes I wish I hadn't known my daddy. He ain't cared nothing about no kids. A kid to him wasn't nothing. All he wanted was for you to learn how to walk so he could start you to working. When it come time for eating . . . he ate first. If there was anything left over, that's what you got. Man would sit down and eat two chickens and give you the wing.

LYONS. You ought to stop that, Pop. Every dad feed their kids. No matter how hard times is . . . everybody care about their kids. Make sure they have something to eat.

TROY. The only thing my daddy cared about was getting them bales of cotton in to Mr. Lubin. That's the only thing that mattered to him. Sometimes I used to wonder why he was living. Wonder why the devil hadn't come and got him. "Get them bales of cotton in to Mr. Lubin" and find out he owe him money . . . .

LYONS. He should have just went on and left when he saw he couldn't get nowhere. That's what I would have done.

TROY. How he gonna leave with eleven kids? And where he gonna go? He ain't knew how to do nothing but farm. No, he was trapped and I think he knew it. But I'll say this for him . . . he felt a responsibility toward us. Maybe he ain't treated us the way I felt he should have . . . but without that responsibility he could have walked off and left us . . . made his own way.

BONO. A lot of them did. Back in those days what you talking about . . . they walk out their front door and just take on down one road or another and keep on walking.

LYONS. There you go! That's what I'm talking about.

BONO. Just keep on walking till you come to something else. Ain't you never heard of nobody having the walking blues? Well, that's what you call it when you just take off like that.

TROY. My daddy ain't had them walking blues! What you talking about? He stayed right there with his family. But he was just as evil as he could be. My mama couldn't stand him. Couldn't stand that evilness. She run off when I was about eight. She sneaked off one night after he had gone to sleep. Told me she was coming back for me. I ain't never seen her no more. All his women run off and left him. He wasn't good for nobody.

When my turn come to head out, I was fourteen and got to sniffing around Joe Canewell's daughter. Had us an old mule we called Greyboy. My daddy sent me out to do some plowing and I tied up Greyboy and went to fooling around with Joe Canewell's daughter. We done found us a nice little spot, got real cozy with each other. She about thirteen and we done figured we was grown anyway . . . so we down there enjoying ourselves . . . ain't thinking about nothing. We didn't know Greyboy had got loose and wandered back to the house and my daddy was looking for me. We down there by the creek enjoying ourselves when my daddy come up on us. Surprised us. He had them leather straps off the mule and commenced to whupping me like there was no tomorrow. I jumped up, mad and embarrassed. I was scared of my daddy. When he commenced to whupping on me . . . quite naturally I run to get out of the way. [*Pause.*] Now I thought he was mad cause I ain't done my work. But I see where he was chasing me off so he could have the gal for himself. When I see what the matter of if was, I lost all fear of my daddy. Right there is where I become a man . . . at fourteen years of age. [*Pause.*] Now it was my turn to run him off. I picked up them same reins that he had used on me. I picked up them reins and commenced to whupping on him. The gal jumped up and run off . . . and when my daddy turned to face me. I could see why the devil had never come to get him . . . cause he was the devil himself. I don't know what happened. When I woke up, I was laying right there by the creek, and Blue . . . this old dog we had . . . was licking my face. I thought I was blind. I couldn't see nothing. Both my eyes were swollen shut. I laid there and cried. I didn't know what I was gonna do. The only thing I knew was the time had come for me to leave my daddy's house. And right there the world suddenly got big. And it was a long time before I could cut it down to where I could handle it.

Part of that cutting down was when I got to the place where I could feel him kicking in my blood and knew that the only thing that separated us was the matter of a few years.

GABRIEL *enters from the house with a sandwich.*

LYONS. What you got there. Uncle Gabe?

GABRIEL. Got me a ham sandwich. Rose gave me a ham sandwich.

TROY. I don't know what happened to him. I done lost touch with everybody except Gabriel. But I hope he's dead. I hope he found some peace.

LYONS. That's a heavy story, Pop. I didn't know you left home when you was fourteen.

TROY. And didn't know nothing. The only part of the world I knew was the forty-two acres of Mr. Lubin's land. That's all I knew about life.

LYONS. Fourteen's kinda young to be out on your own. [*Phone rings.*] I don't even think I was ready to be out on my own at fourteen. I don't know what I would have done.

TROY. I got up from the creek and walked on down to Mobile. I was through with farming. Figured I could do better in the city. So I walked the two hundred miles to Mobile.

LYONS. Wait a minute . . . you ain't walked no two hundred miles, Pop. Ain't nobody gonna walk no two hundred miles. You talking about some walking there.

BONO. That's the only way you got anywhere back in them days.

LYONS. Shhh. Damn if I wouldn't have hitched a ride with someday!

TROY. Who you gonna hitch it with? They ain't had no cars and things like they got now. We talking about 1918.

ROSE [*entering*]. What you all out here getting into?

TROY [*to* ROSE]. I'm telling Lyons how good he got it. He don't know nothing about this I'm talking.

ROSE. Lyons, that was Bonnie on the phone. She say you supposed to pick her up.

LYONS. Yeah, okay Rose.

TROY. I walked on down to Mobile and hitched up with some of them fellows that was heading this way. Got up here and found out . . . not only couldn't you get a job . . . you couldn't find no place to live. I thought I was in freedom.

Shhh. Colored folks living down there on the river banks in whatever kind of shelter they could find for themselves. Right down there under the Brady Street Bridge. Living in shacks made of sticks and tarpaper. Messed around there and went from bad to worse. Started stealing. First it was food. Then I figured, hell, if I steal money I can buy me some food. Buy me some shoes too! One thing led to another. Met your mama. I was young and anxious to be a man. Met your mama and had you. What I do that for? Now I got to worry about feeding you and her. Got to steal three times as much. Went out one day looking for somebody to rob . . . that's what I was, a robber. I'll tell you the truth. I'm ashamed of it today. But it's the truth. Went to rob this fellow . . . pulled out my knife . . . and he pulled out a gun. Shot me in the chest. I felt just like somebody had taken a hot branding iron and laid it on me. When he shot me I jumped at him with knife. They told me I killed him and they put me in the penitentiary and locked me up for fifteen years. That's where I met Bono. That's where I learned how to play baseball. Got out that place and your mama had taken you and went on to make life without me. Fifteen years was a long time for her to wait. But that fifteen years cured me of that robbing stuff. Rose'll tell you, She asked me when I met her if I had gotten all that foolishness out of my system. And I told her, "Baby, it's you and baseball all what count with me." You hear me, Bono? I meant it too. She say, "Which one comes first?" I told her, "Baby, ain't no doubt it's baseball . . . but you stick and get old with me and we'll both outlive this baseball." Am I right, Rose? And it's true.

ROSE. Man, hush your mouth. You ain't said no such thing. Talking about, "Baby you know you'll always be number one with me." That's what you was talking.

TROY. You hear that, Bono. That's why I love her.

BONO. Rose'll keep you straight. You get off the track, she'll straighten you up.

ROSE. Lyons, you better get on up and get Bonnie. She waiting on you.

LYONS [*get up to go*]. Hey, Pop, why don't you come on down to the Grill and hear me play?

TROY. I ain't going down there. I'm too old to be sitting around in them clubs.

BONO. You got to be good to play down at the Grill.

LYONS. Come on, Pop . . .

TROY. I got to get up in the morning.

LYONS. You ain't got to stay long.

TROY. Naw, I'm gonna get my supper and go on to bed.

LYONS. Well, I got to go. I'll see you again.

TROY. Don't you come around my house on my payday.

ROSE. Pick up the phone and let somebody know you coming. And bring Bonnie with you. You know I'm always glad to see her.

LYONS. Yeah, I'll do that, Rose. You take care now. See you, Pop, See you, Mr. Bono. See you, Uncle Gabe.

GABRIEL. Lyons! King of the Jungle!

LYONS *exits.*

TROY. Is supper ready, woman? Me and you got some business to take care of. I'm gonna tear it up too.

ROSE. Troy, I done told you now!

TROY [*puts his arm around* BONO]. Aw hell, woman . . . this is Bono. Bono like family. I done known this nigger since . . . how long I done know you?

BONO. It's been a long time.

TROY. I done know this nigger since Skippy was a pup. Me and him done been through some times.

BONO. You sure right about that.

TROY. Hell, I done know him longer than I known you. And we still standing shoulder to shoulder. Hey look here, Bono . . . a man can't ask for no more than that. [*Drinks to him.*] I love you, nigger.

BONO. Hell, I love you too . . . I got to get home see my woman. You got yours in hand. I got to get mine.

BONO *starts to exit as* CORY *enters the yard, dressed in his football uniform. He gives* TROY *a hard, uncompromising look.*

CORY. What you do that for, Pop?

He throws his helmet down in the direction of TROY.

ROSE. What's the matter? Cory . . . What's the matter?

CORY. Papa done went up to the school and told Coach Zellman I can't play football no more. Wouldn't even let me play the game. Told him to tell the recruiter not to come.

ROSE. Troy . . .

TROY. What you Troying me for. Yeah, I did it. And the boy know why I did it.

CORY. Why you wanna do that to me? That was the one chance I had.

ROSE. Ain't nothing wrong with Cory playing football, Troy.

TROY. The boy lied to me. I told the nigger if he wanna play football . . . to keep up his chores and hold down that job at the A&P. That was the conditions. Stopped down there to see Mr. Stawicki . . .

CORY. I can't work after school during the football season, Pop! I tried to tell you that Mr. Stawicki's holding my job for me. You don't never want to listen to nobody. And then you wanna go and do this to me!

TROY. I ain't done nothing to you. You done it to yourself.

CORY. Just cause you didn't have a chance! You just scared I'm gonna be better than you, that's all.

TROY. Come here.

ROSE. Troy . . .

CORY *reluctantly crosses over to* TROY.

TROY. All right! See. You done made a mistake.

CORY. I didn't even do nothing!

TROY. I'm gonna tell you what your mistake was. See . . . you swung at the ball and didn't hit it. That's strike one. See, you in the batter's box now. You swung and you missed. That's strike one. Don't you strike out!

Lights fade to black.

ACT 2

SCENE 1

The following morning. CORY *is at the tree hitting the ball with the bat. He tries to mimic* TROY, *but his swing is awkward, less sure.* ROSE *enters from the house.*

ROSE. Cory, I want to help me with this cupboard.

CORY. I ain't quitting the team. I don't care what Poppa say.

ROSE. I'll talk to him when he gets back. He had to go see about your Uncle Gabe. The police done arrested him. Say he was disturbing the peace. He'll be back directly. Come on in here and help me clean out the top of this cupboard.

CORY *exits into the house.*
ROSE *sees* TROY *and* BONO *coming down the alley.*

Troy . . . what they say down there?

TROY. Ain't said nothing. I give them fifty dollars and they let him go. I'll talk to you about it. Where's Cory?

ROSE. He's in there helping me clean out these cupboards.

TROY. Tell him to get his butt out here.

TROY *and* BONO *go over to the pile of wood.* BONO *picks up the saw and begins sawing.*

TROY [*to* BONO]. All they want is the money. That makes six or seven times I done went down there and got him. See me coming they stick out their hands.

BONO. Yeah. I know what you mean. That's all they care about . . . that money. They don't care about what's right. [*Pause.*] Nigger, why you got to go and get some hard wood?. You ain't doing nothing but building a little old fence. Get you some soft pine wood. That's all you need.

TROY. I know what I'm doing. This is outside wood. You put pine wood inside the house. Pine wood is inside wood. This here is outside wood. Now you tell me where the fence is gonna be?

BONO. You don't need this wood. You can put it up with pine wood and it'll stand as long as you gonna be here looking at it.

TROY. How you know how long I'm gonna be here, nigger? Hell, I might just live forever. Live longer than old man Horsely.

BONO. That's what Magee used to say.

TROY. Magee's damn fool. Now you tell me who you ever heard of gonna pull their own teeth with a pair of rusty pliers.

BONO. The old folks . . . my granddaddy used to pull his teeth with pliers. They ain't had no dentists for the colored folks back then.

TROY. Get clean pliers! You understand? Clean pliers! Sterilize them! Besides we ain't living back then. All Magee had to do was walk over to Doc Goldblum's.

BONO. I see where you and that Tallahassee gal . . . that Alberta . . . I see where you all done got tight.

TROY. What you mean "got tight"?

BONO. I see where you be laughing and joking with her all the time.

TROY. I laughs and jokes with all of them, Bono. You know me.

BONO. That ain't the kind of laughing and joking I'm talking about.

CORY *enters from the house.*

CORY. How you doing, Mr. Bono?

TROY. Cory? Get that saw from Bono and cut some wood. He talking about the wood's too hard to cut. Stand back there, Jim, and let that young boy show you how it's done.

BONO. He's sure welcome to it.

CORY *takes the saw and begins to cut the wood.*

Whew-e-e! Look at that. Big old strong boy. Look like Joe Louis. Hell, must be getting old the way I'm watching that boy whip through that wood.

CORY. I don't see why Mama want a fence around the yard noways.

TROY. Damn if I know either. What the hell she keeping out with it? She ain't got nothing nobody want.

BONO. Some people build fences to keep people out . . . and other people build fences to keep people in. Rose wants to hold on to you all. She loves you.

TROY. Hell, nigger, I don't need nobody to tell me my wife loves me. Cory . . . go on in the house and see if you can find that other saw.

CORY. Where's it at?

TROY. I said find it! Look for it till you find it!

CORY *exits into the house.*

What's that supposed to mean? Wanna keep us in?

BONO. Troy . . . I done known you seem like damn near my whole life. You and Rose both. I done know both of you all for a long time. I remember when you met Rose. When you was hitting them baseballs out the park. A lot of them old gals was after you then. You had the pick of the litter. When you picked Rose, I was happy for you. That was the first time I knew you had any sense. I said . . . My man Troy knows what he's doing . . . I'm gonna follow this nigger . . . he might take me somewhere. I been following you too. I done learned a whole heap of things about life watching you. I done learned how to tell where the shit lies. How to tell it from the alfalfa. You done learned me a lot of things. You showed me how to not make the same mistakes . . . to take life as it comes along and keep putting one foot in front of the other. [*Pause.*] Rose a good woman, Troy.

TROY. Hell, nigger, I know she a good woman. I been married to her for eighteen years. What you got on your mind, Bono?

BONO. I just say she a good woman, Just like I say anything. I ain't got to have nothing on my mind.

TROY. You just gonna say she a good woman and leave it hanging out there like that? Why you telling me she a good woman?

BONO. She loves you, Troy. Rose loves you.

TROY. You saying I don't measure up. That's what you trying to say. I don't measure up cause I'm seeing this other gal. I know what you trying to say.

BONO. I know what Rose means to you, Troy. I'm just trying to say I don't want to see you mess up.

TROY. Yeah, I appreciate that, Bono. If you was messing around on Lucille I'd be telling you the same thing.

BONO. Well, that's all I got to say. I just say that because I love you both.

TROY. Hell, you know me . . . I wasn't out there looking for nothing. You can't find a better woman than Rose. I know that. But seems like this woman just stuck onto me where I can't shake her loose. I done wrestled with it, tried to throw her off me . . . but she just stuck on tighter. Now she's stuck on for good.

BONO. You's in control . . . that's what you tell me all the time. You responsible for what you do.

TROY. I ain't ducking the responsibility of it. As long as it sets right in my heart . . . then I'm okay. Cause that's all I listen to. It'll tell me right from wrong every time. And I ain't talking about doing Rose no bad turn. I love Rose. She done carried me a long ways and I love and respect her for that.

BONO. I know you do. That's why I don't want to see you hurt her. But what you gonna do when she find out? What you got then? If you try and juggle both of them . . . sooner or later you gonna drop one of them. That's common sense.

TROY. Yeah, I hear what you saying, Bono. I been trying to figure a way to work it out.

BONO. Work it out right, Troy. I don't want to be getting all up between you and Rose's business . . . but work it so it come out right.

TROY. Ah hell, I get all up between you and Lucille's business. When you gonna get that woman that refrigerator she been wanting? Don't tell me you ain't got no money now. I know who your banker is. Mellon don't need that money bad as Lucille want that refrigerator. I'll tell you that.

BONO. Tell you what I'll do . . . when you finish building this fence for Rose . . . I'll buy Lucille that refrigerator.

TROY. You done stuck your foot in your mouth now!

TROY *grabs up a board and begins to saw.* BONO *starts to walk out the yard.*

Hey, nigger . . . where you going?

BONO. I'm going home. I know you don't expect me to help you now. I'm protecting my money. I wanna see you put that fence up by yourself. That's what I want to see. You'll be here another six months without me.

TROY. Nigger, you ain't right.

BONO. When it comes to my money . . . I'm right as fireworks on the Fourth of July.

TROY. All right, we gonna see now. You better get out your bankbook.

BONO *exits, and* TROY *continues to work.*
ROSE *enters from the house.*

ROSE. What they say down there? What's happening with Gabe?

TROY. I went down there and got him out. Cost me fifty dollars. Say he was disturbing the peace. Judge set up a hearing for him in three weeks. Say to show cause why he shouldn't be recommitted.

ROSE. What was he doing that cause them to arrest him?

TROY. Some kids was teasing him and he run them off home. Say he was howling and carrying on. Some folks seen him and called the police. That's all it was.

ROSE. Well, what's you say? What'd you tell the judge?

TROY. Told him I'd look after him. It didn't make no sense to recommit the man. He stuck out his big greasy palm and told me to give him fifty dollars and take him on home.

ROSE. Where's he at now? Where'd he go off to?

TROY. He's gone about his business. He don't need nobody to hold his hand.

ROSE. Well, I don't know. Seem like that would be the best place for him if they did put him into the hospital. I know what you're gonna say. But that's what I think would be best.

TROY. The man done had his life ruined fighting for what? And they wanna take and lock him up. Let him be free. He don't bother nobody.

ROSE. Well, everybody got their own way of looking at it I guess. Come on and get your lunch. I got a bowl of lima beans and some cornbread in the oven. Come and get something to eat. Ain't no sense you fretting over Gabe.

ROSE *turns to go into the house.*

TROY. Rose . . . got something to tell you.

ROSE. Well, come on . . . wait till I get this food on the table.

TROY. Rose!

She stops and turns around.

I don't know how to say this. [*Pause.*] I can't explain it none. It just sort of grows on you till it gets out of hand. It starts out like a little bush . . . and the next thing you know it's a whole forest.

ROSE. Troy . . . what is you talking about?

TROY. I'm talking, woman, let me talk. I'm trying to find a way to tell you . . . I'm gonna be a daddy. I'm gonna be somebody's daddy.

ROSE. Troy . . . you're not telling me this? You're gonna be . . . what?

TROY. Rose . . . no . . . see . . .

ROSE. You telling me you gonna be somebody's daddy? You telling your wife this?

GABRIEL *enters from the street. He carries a rose in his hand.*

GABRIEL. Hey, Troy! Hey, Rose!

ROSE. I have to wait eighteen years to hear something like this.

GABRIEL. Hey, Rose . . . I got a flower for you. [*He hands it to her.*] That's a rose. Same rose like you is.

ROSE. Thanks, Gabe.

GABRIEL. Troy, you ain't mad at me is you? Them bad mens come and put me away. You ain't mad at me is you?

TROY. Naw, Gabe, I ain't mad at you.

ROSE. Eighteen years and you wanna come with this.

GABRIEL [*takes a quarter out of his pocket*]. See what I got? Got a brand new quarter.

TROY. Rose . . . it's just . . .

ROSE. Ain't nothing you can say, Troy. Ain't no way of explaining that.

GABRIEL. Fellow that give me this quarter had a whole mess of them. I'm gonna keep this quarter till it stop shining.

ROSE. Gabe, go on in the house there. I got some watermelon in the Frigidaire. Go on and get you a piece.

GABRIEL. Say, Rose . . . you know I was chasing hellhounds and them bad mens come and get me and take me away. Troy helped me. He come down there and told them they better let me go before he beat them up. Yeah, he did!

ROSE. You go on and get you a piece of watermelon, Gabe. Them bad mens is gone now.

GABRIEL. Okay, Rose . . . gonna get me some watermelon. The kind with the stripes on it.

GABRIEL *exits into the house.*

ROSE. Why, Troy? Why? After all these years to come dragging this in to me now. It don't make no sense at your age. I could have expected this ten or fifteen years ago, but not now.

TROY. Age ain't got nothing to do with it, Rose.

ROSE. I done tried to be everything a wife should be. Everything a wife could be. Been married eighteen years and I got to live to see the day you tell me you been seeing another woman and done fathered a child by her. And you know I ain't never wanted no half nothing in my family. My whole family is half. Everybody got different fathers and mothers . . . my two sisters and my brother. Can't hardly tell who's who. Can't never sit down and talk about Papa and Mama. It's your papa and your mama and my papa and my mama . . .

TROY. Rose . . . stop it now.

ROSE. I ain't never wanted that for none of my children. And now you wanna drag your behind in here and tell me something like this.

TROY. You ought to know. It's time for you to know.

ROSE. Well, I don't want to know, goddamn it!

TROY. I can't just make it go away. It's done now. I can't wish the circumstance of the thing away.

ROSE. And you don't want to either. Maybe you want to wish me and my boy away. Maybe that's what you want? Well, you can't wish us away. I've got eighteen years of my life invested in you. You ought to have stayed upstairs in my bed where you belong.

TROY. Rose . . . now listen to me . . . we can get a handle on this thing. We can talk this out . . . come to an understanding.

ROSE. All of a sudden it's "we." Where was "we" at when you was down there rolling around with some godforsaken woman? "We" should have come to an understanding before you started making a damn fool of yourself. You're a day late and a dollar short when it comes to an understanding with me.

TROY. It's just . . . She gives me a different idea . . . a different understanding about myself. I can step out of this house and get away from the pressures and problems . . . be a different man. I ain't got to wonder how I'm gonna pay the bills or get the roof fixed. I can just be a part of myself that I ain't never been.

ROSE. What I want to know . . . is do you plan to continue seeing her. That's all you can say to me.

TROY. I can sit up in her house and laugh. Do you understand what I'm saying. I can laugh out loud . . . and it feels goods. It reaches all the way down to the bottom of my shoes. [*Pause.*] Rose, I can't give that up.

ROSE. Maybe you ought to go on and stay down there with her . . . if she's a better woman than me.

TROY. It ain't about nobody being a better woman or nothing. Rose, you ain't the blame. A man couldn't ask for no woman to be a better wife than you've been. I'm responsible for it. I done locked myself into a pattern trying to take care of you all that I forgot about myself.

ROSE. What the hell was I there for? That was my job, not somebody else's.

TROY. Rose, I done tried all my life to live decent . . . to live a clean . . . hard . . . useful life. I tried to be a good husband to you. In every way I knew how. Maybe I come into the world backwards, I don't know. But . . . you born with two strikes on you before you come to the plate. You got to guard it closely . . . always looking for the curve ball on the inside corner. You can't afford to let none get past you. You can't afford a call strike. If you going down . . . you going down swinging. Everything lined up against you. What you gonna do. I fooled them, Rose. I bunted. When I found you and Cory and a halfway decent job . . . I was safe. Couldn't nothing touch me. I wasn't gonna strike out no more. I wasn't going back to the penitentiary. I wasn't gonna lay in the streets with a bottle of wine. I was safe. I had me a family. A job. I wasn't gonna get that last strike. I was on first looking for one of them boys to knock me in. To get me home.

ROSE. You should have stayed in my bed, Troy.

TROY. Then when I saw that gal . . . she firmed up my backbone. And I got to thinking that if I tried . . . I just might be able to steal second. Do you understand after eighteen years I wanted to steal second.

ROSE. You should have held me tight. You should have grabbed me and held on.

TROY. I stood on first base for eighteen years and I thought . . . well, goddamn it . . . go on for it!

ROSE. We're not talking about baseball! We're talking about you going off to lay in bed with another woman . . . and then bring it home to me. That's what we're talking about. We ain't talking about no baseball.

TROY. Rose, you're not listening to me. I'm trying the best I can to explain it to you. It's not easy for me to admit that I been standing in the same place for eighteen years.

ROSE. I been standing with you! I been right here with you, Troy. I got a life too. I gave eighteen years of my life to stand in the same spot with you. Don't you think I ever wanted other things? Don't you think I had dreams and hopes? What about my life? What about me? Don't you think it ever crossed my mind to want to know other men? That I wanted to lay up somewhere and forget about my responsibilities? That I wanted someone to make me laugh so I could feel good? You not the only one who's got wants and needs. But I held on to you, Troy. I took all my feelings, my wants and needs, my dreams . . . and I buried them inside you. I planted a seed and watched and prayed over it. I planted myself inside you and waited to bloom. And it didn't take me no eighteen years to find out the soil was hard and rocky and it wasn't never gonna bloom.

But I held on to you, Troy. I held you tighter. You was my husband. I owed you everything I had. Every part of me I could find to give you. And upstairs in that room . . . with the darkness falling in on me . . . I gave everything I had to try and erase the doubt that you wasn't the finest man in the world. And wherever you was going . . . I wanted to be there with you. Cause you was my husband. Cause that's the only way I was gonna survive as your wife. You always talking about what you give . . . and what you don't have to give. But you take too. You take . . . and don't even know nobody's giving!

ROSE *turns to exit into the house;* TROY *grabs her arm.*

TROY. You say I take and don't give!
ROSE. Troy! You're hurting me!
TROY. You say I take and don't give!
ROSE. Troy . . . you're hurting my arm! Let go!
TROY. I done give you everything I got. Don't you tell that lie on me.
ROSE. Troy!
TROY. Don't you tell that lie on me!
CORY *enters from the house.*

CORY. Mama!

ROSE. Troy. You're hurting me.
TROY. Don't you tell me about no taking and giving.

CORY *comes up behind* TROY *and grabs him.* TROY, *surprised, is thrown off balance just as* CORY *throws a glancing blow that catches him on the chest and knocks him down.* TROY *is stunned, as is* CORY.

ROSE. Troy. Troy. No!

TROY *gets to his feet and starts at* CORY

Troy . . . no. Please! Troy!

ROSE *pulls on* TROY *to hold him back.* TROY *stops himself.*

TROY [*to* CORY]. All right. That's strike two. You stay away from around me, boy. Don't you strike out. You living with a full count. Don't you strike out.

TROY *exits out the yard as the lights go down.*

SCENE 2

It is six months later, early afternoon. TROY *enters from the house and starts to exit the yard.* ROSE *enters from the house.*

ROSE. Troy, I want to talk to you.

TROY. All of a sudden, after all this time, you want to talk to me, huh? You ain't wanted to talk to me for months. You ain't wanted to talk to me last night. You ain't wanted no part of me then. What you wanna talk to me about now?

ROSE. Tomorrow's Friday.

TROY. I know what day tomorrow is. You think I don't know tomorrow's Friday? My whole life I ain't done nothing but look to see Friday coming and you got to tell me it's Friday.

ROSE. I want to know if you're coming home.

TROY. I always come home, Rose. You know that. There ain't never been a night I ain't come home.

ROSE. That ain't what I mean . . . and you know it. I want to know if you're coming straight home after work.

TROY. I figure I'd cash my check . . . hang out at Taylors' with the boys . . . maybe play a game of checkers . . .

ROSE. Troy, I can't live like this. I won't live like this. You livin' on borrowed time with me. It's been going on six months now you ain't been coming home.

TROY. I be here every night. Every night of the year. That's 365 days.

ROSE. I want you to come home tomorrow after work.

TROY. Rose . . . I don't mess up my pay. You know that now. I take my pay and I give it to you. I don't have no money but what you give me back. I just want to have little time to myself . . . a little time to enjoy life.

ROSE. What about me? When's my time to enjoy life?

TROY. I don't know what to tell you, Rose. I'm doing the best I can.

ROSE. You ain't been home from work but time enough to change your clothes and run out . . . and you wanna call that the best you can do?

TROY. I'm going over to the hospital to see Alberta. She went into the hospital this afternoon. Look like she might have the baby early. I won't be gone long.

ROSE. Well, you ought to know. They went over to Miss Pearl's and got Gabe today. She said you told them to go ahead and lock him up.

TROY. I ain't said no such thing. Whoever told you that is telling a lie. Pearl ain't doing nothing but telling a big fat lie.

ROSE. She ain't had to tell me. I read it on the papers.

TROY. I ain't told them nothing of the kind.

ROSE. I saw it right there on the papers.

TROY. What it say, huh?

ROSE. It said you told them to take him.

TROY. Then they screwed that up, just the way they screw up everything. I ain't worried about what they got on the paper.

ROSE. Say the government sent part of his check to the hospital and the other part to you.

TROY. I ain't got nothing to do with that if that's the way it works. I ain't made up the rules about how it work.

ROSE. You did Gabe just like you did Cory. You wouldn't sign the paper for Cory . . . but you signed for Gabe. You signed that paper.

The telephone is heard ringing inside the house.

TROY. I told you I ain't signed nothing, woman! The only thing I signed was the release form. Hell, I can't read, I don't know what they had on that paper! I ain't signed nothing about sending Gabe away.

ROSE. I said send him to the hospital . . . you said let him be free . . . now you done went down there and signed him to the hospital for half his money. You went back on yourself, Troy. You gonna have to answer for that.

TROY. See now . . . you been over there talking to Miss Pearl. She done got mad cause she ain't getting Gabe's rent money. That's all it is. She's liable to say anything.

ROSE. Troy, I seen where you signed the paper.

TROY. You ain't seen nothing I signed. What she doing got papers on my brother anyway? Miss Pearl telling a big fat lie. And I'm gonna tell her about it too! You ain't seen nothing I signed. Say . . . you ain't seen nothing I signed.

ROSE *exits into the house to answer the telephone. Presently she returns.*

ROSE. Troy . . . that was the hospital. Alberta had the baby.

TROY. What she have? What is it?

ROSE. It's a girl.

TROY. I better get on down to the hospital to see her.

ROSE. Troy . . .

TROY. Rose . . . I got to go see her now. That's only right . . . what's the matter . . . the baby's all right, ain't it?

ROSE. Alberta died having the baby.

TROY. Died . . . you say she's dead? Alberta's dead?

ROSE. They said they done all they could. They couldn't do nothing for her.

TROY. The baby? How's the baby?

ROSE. They say it's healthy. I wonder who's gonna bury her.

TROY. She had family, Rose. She wasn't living in the world by herself.

ROSE. I know she wasn't living in the world by herself.

TROY. Next thing you gonna want to know if she had any insurance.

ROSE. Troy, you ain't got to talk like that.

TROY. That's the first thing that jumped out your mouth. "Who's gonna bury her?" Like I'm fixing to take on that task for myself.

ROSE. I am your wife. Don't push me away.

TROY. I ain't pushing nobody away. Just give me some space. That's all. Just give me some room to breathe.

ROSE *exits into the house.* TROY *walks about the yard.*

TROY [*with a quiet rage that threatens to consume him*]. All right . . . Mr. Death. See now . . . I'm gonna tell you what I'm gonna do. I'm gonna take and build me a fence around this yard. See? I'm gonna build me a fence around what belongs to me. And then I want you to stay on the other side. See? You stay over there until you're ready for me. Then you come on. Bring your army. Bring your sickle. Bring your wrestling clothes. I ain't gonna fall down on my vigilance this time. You ain't gonna sneak up on me no more. When you ready for me . . . when the top of your list say Troy Maxson . . . that's when you come around here. You come up and knock on the front door. Ain't nobody else got nothing to do with this. This is between you and me. Man to man. You stay on the other side of that fence until you ready for me. Then you come up and knock on the front door. Anytime you want. I'll be ready for you.

The lights go down to black.

SCENE 3

The lights come up on the porch. It is late evening three days later. ROSE *sits listening to the ball game waiting for* TROY. *The final out of the game is made and* ROSE *switches off the radio.* TROY *enters the yard carrying an infant wrapped in blankets. He stands back from the house and calls.*

ROSE *enters and stands on the porch. There is a long, awkward silence, the weight of which grows heavier with each passing second.*

TROY. Rose . . . I'm standing here with my daughter in my arms. She ain't but a wee bittie little old thing. She don't know nothing about grownups' business. She innocent . . . and she ain't got no mama.

ROSE. What you telling me for, Troy?

She turns and exits into the house.

TROY. Well . . . I guess we'll just sit out here on the porch.

He sits down on the porch. There is an awkward indelicateness about the way be handles the body. His largeness engulfs and seems to swallow it. He speaks loud enough for ROSE *to hear.*

A man's got to do what's right for him. I ain't sorry for nothing I done. It felt right in my heart. [*To the baby.*] What you smiling at? Your daddy's a big man. Got these great big old hands. But sometimes he's scared. And right now your daddy's scared cause we sitting out here and ain't got no home. Oh, I been homeless before. I ain't had no little baby with me. But I been homeless. You just be out on the road by your lonesome and you see one of them trains coming and you just kinda go like this . . .

He sings as a lullaby.

Please, Mr. Engineer let a man ride the line
Please, Mr. Engineer let a man ride the line
I ain't got no ticket please let me ride the blinds.

ROSE *enters from the house.* TROY, *hearing her steps behind him, stands and faces her.*

She's my daughter, Rose. My own flesh and blood. I can't deny her no more than I can deny them boys. [*Pause.*] You and them boys is my family. You and them and this child is all I got in the world. So I guess what I'm saying is . . . I'd appreciate it if you'd help me take care of her.

ROSE. Okay, Troy . . . you're right. I'll take care of your baby for you . . . cause . . . like you say . . . she's innocent . . . and you can't visit the sins of the father upon the child. A motherless child has got a hard time. [*She takes the baby from him.*] From right now . . . this child got a mother. But you a womanless man.

ROSE *turns and exits into the house with the baby.*
Lights go down to black.

SCENE 4

It is two months later. LYONS *enters the street. He knocks on the door and calls.*

LYONS. Hey, Rose! [*Pause.*] Rose!

ROSE [*from inside the house*]. Stop that yelling. You gonna wake up Raynell. just got her to sleep.

LYONS. I just stopped by to pay Papa this twenty dollars I owe him. Where's Papa at?

ROSE. He should be here in a minute. I'm getting ready to go down to the church. Sit down and wait on him.

LYONS. I got to go pick up Bonnie over her mother's house.

ROSE. Well, sit it down there on the table. He'll get it.

LYONS [*enters the house and sets the money on the table*]. Tell Papa I said thanks. I'll see you again.

ROSE. All right, Lyons. We'll see you.

LYONS *starts to exit as* CORY *enters.*

CORY. Hey, Lyons.

LYONS. What's happening, Cory? Say man, I'm sorry I missed your graduation. You know I had a gig and couldn't get away. Otherwise, I would have been there, man. So what you doing?

CORY. I'm trying to find a job.

LYONS. Yeah I know how that go, man. It's rough out here. Jobs are scarce.

CORY. Yeah, I know.

LYONS. Look here, I got to run. Talk to Papa . . . he know some people. He'll be able to help get you a job. Talk to him . . . see what he say.

CORY. Yeah . . . all right, Lyons.

LYONS. You take care. I'll talk to you soon. We'll find some time to talk.

LYONS *exits the yard.*
CORY *wanders over to the tree, picks up the bat, and assumes a batting stance.*
He studies an imaginary pitcher and swings.
Dissatisfied with the result, he tries again.
TROY *enters. They eye each other for a beat.*
CORY *puts the bat down and exits the yard.*
TROY *starts into the house as* ROSE *exits with* RAYNELL.
She is carrying a cake.

TROY. I'm coming in and everybody's going out.

ROSE. I'm taking this cake down to the church for the bake sale. Lyons was by to see you. He stopped by to pay you your twenty dollars. It's laying in there on the table.

TROY [*going into his pocket*]. Well . . . here go this money.

ROSE. Put it in there on the table, Troy. I'll get it.

TROY. What time you coming back?

ROSE. Ain't no use in you studying me. It don't matter what time I come back.

TROY. I just asked you a question, woman. What's the matter . . . can't I ask you a question?

ROSE. Troy, I don't want to go into it. Your dinner's in there on the stove. All you got to do is heat it up. And don't you be eating the rest of them cakes in there. I'm coming back for them. We having a bake sale at the church tomorrow.

ROSE *exits the yard.*
TROY *sits down on the steps, takes a pint bottle from his pocket, opens it, and drinks. He begins to sing.*

TROY.

Hear it ring! Hear it ring!
Had an old dog his name was Blue
You know Blue was mighty true
You know Blue as a good old dog
Blue trees a possum in a hollow log
You know from that he was a good old dog.

BONO *enters the yard.*

BONO. Hey, Troy.

TROY. Hey, what's happening, Bono?

BONO. I just thought I'd stop by to see you.

TROY. What you stop by and see me for? You ain't stopped by in a mouth of Sundays. Hell, I must owe you money or something.

BONO. Since you got your promotion I can't keep up with you. Used to see you every day. Now I don't even know what route you working.

TROY. They keep switching me around. Got me out in Greentree now . . . hauling white folks' garbage.

BONO. Greentree, huh? You lucky, at least you ain't got to be lifting them barrels. Damn if they ain't getting heavier. I'm gonna put in my two years and call it quits.

TROY. I'm thinking about retiring myself.

BONO. You got it easy. You can drive for another five years.

TROY. It ain't the same, Bono. It ain't like working the back of the truck. Ain't got nobody to talk to . . . feel like you working by yourself. Naw, I'm thinking about retiring. How's Lucille?

BONO. She all right. Her arthritis get to acting up on her sometime. Saw Rose on my way in. She going down to the church, huh?

TROY. Yeah, she took up going down there. All them preachers looking for somebody to fatten their pockets. [*Pause.*] Got some gin here.

BONO. Naw, thanks. I just stopped by to say hello.

TROY. Hell, nigger . . . you can take a drink. I ain't never known you to say no to a drink. You ain't got to work tomorrow.

BONO. I just stopped by. I'm fixing to go over to Skinner's. We got us a domino game going over his house every Friday.

TROY. Nigger, you can't play no dominoes. I used to whup you four games out of five.

BONO. Well, that learned me. I'm getting better.

TROY. Yeah? Well, that's all right.

BONO. Look here . . . I got to be getting on. Stop by sometime, huh?

TROY. Yeah, I'll do that, Bono. Lucille told Rose you bought her a new refrigerator.

BONO. Yeah, Rose told Lucille you had finally built your fence . . . so I figured we'd call it even.

TROY. I knew you would.

BONO. Yeah . . . okay. I'll be talking to you.

TROY. Yeah, take care, Bono. Good to see you. I'm gonna stop over.

BONO. Yeah. Okay, Troy.

BONO *exits.* TROY *drinks from the bottle.*

TROY.

Old Blue died and I dig his grave
Let him down with a golden chain
Every night when I hear old Blue bark
I know Blue treed a possum in Noah's Ark
Hear it ring! Hear it ring!

CORY *enters the yard. They eye each other for a beat.* TROY *is sitting in the middle of the steps.* CORY *walks over.*

CORY. I got to get by.

TROY. Say what? What's you say?

CORY. You in my way. I got to get by.

TROY. You got to get by where? This is my house. Bought and paid for. In full. Took me fifteen years. And if you wanna go in my house and I'm sitting on the steps . . . you say excuse me. Like your mama taught you.

CORY. Come on, Pop . . . I got to get by.

CORY *starts to maneuver his way past* TROY. TROY *grabs his leg and shoves him back.*

TROY. You just gonna walk over top of me?

CORY. I live here too!

TROY [*advancing toward him*]. You just gonna walk over top of me in my own house?

CORY. I ain't scared of you.

TROY. I ain't asked if you was scared of me. I asked you if you was fixing to walk over top of me in my own house? That's the question. You ain't gonna say excuse me? You just gonna walk over top of me?

CORY. If you wanna put it like that.

TROY. How else am I gonna put it?

CORY. I was walking by you to go into the house cause you sitting on the steps drunk, singing to yourself. You can put it like that.

TROY. Without saying excuse me???

CORY *doesn't respond.*

I asked you a question. Without saying excuse me???

CORY. I ain't got to say excuse me to you. You don't count around here no more.

TROY. Oh, I see . . . I don't count around here no more. You ain't got to say excuse me to your daddy. All of a sudden you done got so grown that your daddy don't count around here no more . . . Around here in his own house and yard that he done paid for with the sweat of his brow. You done got so grown to where you gonna take over. You gonna take over my house. Is that right? You gonna wear my pants. You gonna go in there and stretch out on my bed. You ain't got to say excuse me cause I don't count around here no more. Is that right?

CORY. That's right. You always talking this dumb stuff. Now, why don't you just get out my way?

TROY. I guess you got someplace to sleep and something to put in your belly. You got that, huh? You got that? That's what you need. You got that, huh?

CORY. You don't know what I got. You ain't got to worry about what I got.

TROY. You right! You one hundred percent right! I done spent the last seventeen years worrying about what you got. Now it's your turn, see? I'll tell you what to do. You grown . . . we done established that. You a man. Now, let's see you act like one. Turn your behind around and walk out this yard. And when you get out there in the alley . . . you can forget about this house. See? Cause this is my house. You go on and be a man and get your own house. You can forget about this. Cause this is mine. You go on and get yours cause I'm through with doing for you.

CORY. You talking about what you did for me . . . what'd you ever give me?

TROY. Them feet and bones! That pumping heart, nigger! I give you more than anybody else is ever gonna give you.

CORY. You ain't never gave me nothing! You ain't never done nothing but hold me back. Afraid I was gonna be better than you. All you ever did was try and make me scared of you. I used to tremble every time you called my name. Every time I heard your footsteps in the house. Wondering all the time . . . what's Papa gonna say if I do this? . . . What's he gonna say if I do that? . . . What's Papa gonna say if I turn on the radio? And mama, too . . . she tries . . . but she's scared of you.

TROY. You leave your mama out of this. She ain't got nothing to do with this.

CORY. I don't know how she stand you . . . after what you did to her.

TROY. I told you to leave your mama out of this!

He advances toward CORY.

CORY. What you gonna do . . . give me a whupping? You can't whup me no more. You're too old. You just an old man.

TROY [*shoves him on his shoulder*]. Nigger! That's what you are. You just another nigger on the street to me!

CORY. You crazy! You know that?

TROY. Go on now! You got the devil in you. Get on away from me!

CORY. You just a crazy old man . . . talking about I got the devil in me.

TROY. Yeah, I'm crazy! If you don't get on the other side of that yard . . . I'm gonna show you how crazy I am! Go on . . . get the hell out of my yard.

CORY. It ain't your yard. You took Uncle Gabe's money he got from the army to buy this house and then you put him out.

TROY [*advances on* CORY]. Get your black ass out of my yard!

TROY*'s advance backs* CORY *up against the tree.* CORY *grabs up the bat.*

CORY. I ain't going nowhere! Come on . . . put me out! I ain't scared of you.

TROY. That's my bat!

CORY. Come on!

TROY. Put my bat down!

CORY. Come on, put me out.

CORY *swings at* TROY, *who backs across the yard.*

What's the matter? You so bad . . . put me out!

TROY *advances toward* CORY.

CORY [*backing up*]. Come on! Come on!

TROY. You're gonna have to use it! You wanna draw that bat back on me . . . you're gonna have to use it.

CORY. Come on! . . . Come on!

CORY *swings the bat at* TROY *a second time. He misses.* TROY *continues to advances toward him.*

TROY. You're gonna have to kill me! You wanna draw that bat back on me. You're gonna have to kill me.

CORY, *backed up against the tree, can go no farther.* TROY *taunts him. He sticks out his head and offers him a target.*

Come on! Come on!

CORY *is unable to swing the bat.* TROY *grabs it.*

TROY. Then I'll show you.

CORY *and* TROY *struggle over the bat. The struggle is fierce and fully engaged.* TROY *ultimately is the stronger and takes the bat from* CORY *and stands over him ready to swing. He stops himself.*

Go on and get away from around my house.

CORY, *stung by his defeat, picks himself up, walks slowly out of the yard and up the alley.*

CORY. Tell Mama I'll be back for my things.
TROY. They'll be on the other side of that fence.

CORY *exits.*

I can't taste nothing. Helluljah! I can't taste nothing no more. [TROY *assumes a batting posture and begins to taunt Death, the fastball on the outside corner.*] Come on! It's between you and me now! Come on! Anytime you want! Come on! I be ready for you . . . but I ain't gonna be easy.

The lights go down on the scene.

SCENE 5

The time is 1965. The lights come up in the yard. It is the morning of TROY'S *funeral. A funeral plaque with a light hangs beside the door. There is a small garden plot off to the side. There is noise and activity in the house as* ROSE, LYONS, *and* BONO *have gathered. The door opens and* RAYNELL, *seven years old, enters dressed in a flannel nightgown. She crosses to the garden and pokes around with a stick.* ROSE *calls from the house.*

ROSE. Raynell!
RAYNELL. Mam?
ROSE. What you doing out there?
RAYNELL. Nothing.
ROSE *comes to the door.*
ROSE. Girl, get in here and get dressed. What you doing?
RAYNELL. Seeing if my garden growed.
ROSE. I told you it ain't gonna grow overnight. You got to wait.
RAYNELL. It don't look like it never gonna grow. Dag!
ROSE. I told you a watched pot never boils. Get in here and get dressed.
RAYNELL. This ain't even no pot, Mama.
ROSE. You just have to give it a chance. It'll grow. Now you come on and do what I told you. We got to be getting ready. This ain't no morning to be playing around. You hear me?
RAYNELL. Yes, mam.

ROSE *exits into the house.*

RAYNELL *continues to poke at her garden with a stick.*

CORY *enters. He is dressed in a Marine corporal's uniform, and carries a duffelbag. His posture is that of a military man, and his speech has a clipped sternness.*

CORY [*to* RAYNELL]. Hi. [*Pause.*] I bet your name is Raynell.
RAYNELL. Uh huh.

CORY. Is your mama home?

RAYNELL *runs up on the porch and calls through the screen door.*

RAYNELL. Mama . . . there's some man out here. Mama?

ROSE *comes to the door.*

ROSE. Cory? Lord have mercy! Look here, you all!

ROSE *and* CORY *embrace in a tearful reunion as* BONO *and* LYONS *enters from the house dressed in funeral clothes.*

BONO. Aw, looka here . . .
ROSE. Done got all grown up!
CORY. Don't cry, Mama. What you crying about?
ROSE. I'm just so glad you made it.
CORY. Hey Lyons. How you doing, Mr. Bono.

LYONS *goes to embrace* CORY.

LYONS. Look at you, man. Look at you. Don't he look good, Rose. Got them Corporal stripes.

ROSE. What took you so long?

CORY. You know how the Marines are, Mama. They got to get all their paperwork straight before they let you do anything.

ROSE. Well, I'm sure glad you made it. They let Lyons come. Your Uncle Gabe's still in the hospital. They don't know if they gonna let him out or not. I just talked to them a little while ago.

LYONS. A Corporal in the United States Marines.

BONO. Your daddy knew you had it in you. He used to tell me all the time.

LYONS. Don't he look good, Mr. Bono?

BONO. Yeah, he remind me of Troy when I first met him. [*Pause.*] Say, Rose, Lucille's down at the church with the choir. I'm gonna go down and get the pallbearers lined up. I'll be back to get you all.

ROSE. Thanks, Jim.

CORY. See you, Mr. Bono.

LYONS [*with his arm around* RAYNELL]. Cory . . . look at Raynell. Ain't she precious? She gonna break a whole lot of hearts.

ROSE. Raynell, come and say hello to your brother. This is your brother, Cory. You remember Cory.

RAYNELL. No, Mam.

CORY. She don't remember me, Mama.

ROSE. Well, we talk about you. She heard us talk about you. [*To* RAYNELL.] This is your brother, Cory. Come on and say hello.

RAYNELL. Hi.

CORY. Hi. So you're Raynell. Mama told me a lot about you.

ROSE. You all come on into the house and let me fix you some breakfast. Keep up your strength.

CORY. I ain't hungry, Mama.

LYONS. You can fix me something, Rose. I'll be in there in a minute.

ROSE. Cory, you sure you don't want nothing? I know they ain't feeding you right.

CORY. No, Mama . . . thanks. I don't feel like eating. I'll get something later.

ROSE. Raynell . . . get on upstairs and get that dress on like I told you.

ROSE *and* RAYNELL *exit into the house.*

LYONS. So . . . I hear you thinking about getting married.

CORY. Yeah, I done found the right one, Lyons. It's about time.

LYONS. Me and Bonnie been split up about four years now. About the time Papa retired. I guess she just got tired of all them changes I was putting her through. [*Pause.*] I always knew you was gonna make something out yourself. Your head was always in the right direction. So . . . you gonna stay in . . . make it a career . . . put in your twenty years?

CORY. I don't know. I got six already, I think that's enough.

LYONS. Stick with Uncle Sam and retire early. Ain't nothing out here. I guess Rose told you what happened with me. They got me down the workhouse. I thought I was being slick cashing other people's checks.

CORY. How much time you doing?

LYONS. They give me three years. I got that beat now. I ain't got but nine more months. It ain't so bad. You learn to deal with it like anything else. You got to take the crookeds with the straights. That's what Papa used to say. He used to say that when he struck out. I seen him strike out three times in a row . . . and the next time up he hit the ball over the grandstand. Right out there in Homestead Field. He wasn't satisfied hitting in the seats . . . he want to hit it over everything! After the game he had two hundred people standing around waiting to shake his hand. You got to take the crookeds with the straights. Yeah, Papa was something else.

CORY. You still playing?

LYONS. Cory . . . you know I'm gonna do that. There's some fellows down there we got us a band . . . we gonna try and stay together when we get out . . . but yeah, I'm still playing. It still helps me to get out of bed in the morning. As long as it do that I'm gonna be right there playing and trying to make some sense out of it.

ROSE [*calling*]. Lyons, I got these eggs in the pan.

LYONS. Let me go on and get these eggs, man. Get ready to go bury Papa. [*Pause.*] How you doing? You doing all right?

CORY *nods.*

LYONS *touches him on the shoulder and they share a moment of silent grief.*

LYONS *exits into the house.* CORY *wanders about the yard.*

RAYNELL *enters.*

RAYNELL. Hi.

CORY. Hi.

RAYNELL. Did you used to sleep in my room?

CORY. Yeah . . . that used to be my room.

RAYNELL. That's what Papa call it. "Cory's room." It got your football in the closet.

ROSE *comes to the door.*

ROSE. Raynell, get in there and get them good shoes on.

RAYNELL. Mama, can't I wear these? Them other one hurt my feet.

ROSE. Well, they just gonna have to hurt your feet for a while. You ain't said they hurt your feet when you went down to the store and got them.

RAYNELL. They didn't hurt then. My feet done got bigger.

ROSE. Don't you give me no backtalk now. You get in there and get them shoes on.

RAYNELL *exits into the house.*

Ain't too much changed. He still got that piece of rag tied to that tree. He was out here swinging that bat. I was just ready to go back in the house. He swung that bat and then he just fell over. Seem like he swung it and stood there with this grin on his face . . . and then he just fell over. They carried him on down to the hospital, but I knew there wasn't no need . . . why don't you come on in the house?

CORY. Mama . . . I got something to tell you. I don't know how to tell you this . . . but I've got to tell you . . . I'm not going to Papa's funeral.

ROSE. Boy, hush your month. That's your daddy you talking about. I don't want hear that kind of talk this morning. I done raised you to come to this? You standing there all healthy and grown talking about you ain't going to your daddy's funeral?

CORY. Mama . . . listen . . .

ROSE. I don't want to hear it, Cory. You just get that thought out of your head.

CORY. I can't drag Papa with me everywhere I go. I've got to say no to him. One time in my life I've got to say no.

ROSE. Don't nobody have to listen to nothing like that. I know you and your daddy ain't seen eye to eye, but I ain't got to listen to that kind of talk this morning. Whatever was between you and your daddy . . . the time has come to put it aside. Just take it and set it over there on the shelf and forget about it. Disrespecting your daddy ain't gonna make you a man, Cory. You got to find a way to come to that on your own. Not going to your daddy's funeral ain't gonna make you a man.

CORY. The whole time I was growing up . . . living in his house . . . Papa was like a shadow that followed you everywhere. It weighted on you and sunk into your flesh. It would wrap around you and lay there until you couldn't tell which one was you anymore. That shadow digging in your flesh. Trying to crawl in. Trying to live through you. Everywhere I looked, Troy Maxson was staring back at me . . . hiding under the bed . . . in the closet. I'm just saying I've got to find a way to get rid of that shadow, Mama.

ROSE. You just like him. You got him in you good.

CORY. Don't tell me that, Mama.

ROSE. You Troy Maxson all over again.

CORY. I don't want to be Troy Maxson. I want to be me.

ROSE. You can't be nobody but who you are, Cory. That shadow wasn't nothing but you growing into yourself. You either got to grow into it or cut it down to fit you. But that's all you got to make life with. That's all you got to measure yourself against that world out there. Your daddy wanted you to be everything he wasn't . . . and at the same time he tried to make you into everything he was. I don't know if he was right or wrong . . . but I do know he meant to do more good than he meant to do harm. He wasn't always right. Sometimes when he touched he bruised. And sometimes when he took me in his arms he cut.

When I first met your daddy I thought . . . Here is a man I can lay down with and make a baby. That's the first thing I thought when I seen him. I was thirty years old and had done seen my share of men. But when he walked up to me and said, "I can dance a waltz that'll make you dizzy," I thought, Rose Lee, here is a man that you can open yourself up to and be filled to bursting. Here is a man that can fill all them empty spaces you been tipping around the edges of. One of them empty spaces was being somebody's mother.

I married your daddy and settled down to cooking his supper and keeping clean sheets on the bed. When your daddy walked through the house he was so big he filled it up. That was my first mistake. Not to make him leave some room for me. For my part in the matter. But at that time I wanted that. I wanted a house that I could sing in. And that's what your daddy gave me. I didn't know to keep up his strength I had to give up little pieces of mine. I did that. I took on his life as mine and mixed up the pieces so that you couldn't hardly tell which was which anymore. It was my choice. It was my life and I didn't have to live it like that. But that's what life offered me in the way of being a woman and I took it. I grabbed hold of it with both hands.

By the time Raynell came into the house, me and your daddy had done lost touch with one another. I didn't want to make my blessing off of nobody's misfortune . . . but I took on to Raynell like she was all them babies I had wanted and never had.

The phone rings.

Like I'd been blessed to relive a part of my life. And if the Lord see fit to keep up my strength . . . I'm gonna do her just like your daddy did you . . . I'm gonna give her the best of what's in me.

RAYNELL [*entering, still with her old shoes*]. Mama . . . Reverend Tollivier on the phone.

ROSE *exits into the house.*

RAYNELL. Hi.
CORY. Hi.
RAYNELL. You in the Army or the Marines?
CORY. Marines.
RAYNELL. Papa said it was the Army. Did you know Blue?
CORY. Blue? Who's Blue?
RAYNELL. Papa's dog what he sing about all the time.
CORY [*singing*].

Hear it ring! Hear it ring!
I had a dog his name was Blue
You know Blue was mighty true
You know Blue was a good old dog

Blue treed a possum in a hollow log
You know from that he was a good old dog.
Hear it ring! Hear it ring!

RAYNELL *joins in singing.*

CORY AND RAYNELL.

Blue treed a possum out on a limb
Blue looked at me and I looked at him
Grabbed that possum and put him in a sack
Blue stayed there till I came back
Old Blue's feets was big and round
Never allowed a possum to touch the ground.
Old Blue died and I dug his grave
I dug his grave with a silver spade
Let him down with a golden chain
Any every night I call his name
Go on Blue, you good dog you
Go on Blue, you good dog you.

RAYNELL.

Blue laid down and died like a man
Blue laid down and died . . .

BOTH.

Blue laid down and died like a man
Now he's treeing possums in the Promised Land
I'm gonna tell you this to let you know
Blue's gone where the good dogs go
When I hear old Blue bark
When I hear old Blue bark
Blue treed a possum in Noah's Ark
Blue treed a possum in Noah's Ark.

ROSE *comes to the screen door.*

ROSE. Cory, we gonna be ready to go in a minute.
CORY [*to* RAYNELL]. You go on in the house and change them shoes like Mama told you so we can go to Papa's funeral.
RAYNELL. Okay, I'll be back.

RAYNELL *exits into the house.* CORY *gets up and crosses over to the tree.* ROSE *stands in the screen door watching him.* GABRIEL *enters from the alley.*

GABRIEL [*calling*]. Hey, Rose!
ROSE. Gabe?

GABRIEL. I'm here, Rose. Hey Rose, I'm here!

ROSE *enters from the house.*

ROSE. Lord . . . Look here, Lyons!
LYONS. See, I told you, Rose . . . I told you they'd let him come.
CORY. How you doing, Uncle Gabe?
LYONS. How you doing, Uncle Gabe?
GABRIEL. Hey, Rose. It's time. It's time to tell St. Peter to open the gates. Troy, you ready? You ready, Troy. I'm gonna tell St. Peter to open the gates. You get ready now.

GABRIEL, *with great fanfare, braces himself to blow. The trumpet is without a mouthpiece. He puts the end of it into his mouth and blows with great force, like a man who has been waiting some twenty-odd years for this single moment. No sound comes out of the trumpet. He braces himself and blows again with the same results. A third time he blows. There is a weight of impossible description that falls away and leaves him bare and exposed to a frightful realization. It is a trauma that a sane and normal mind would be unable to withstand. He begins to dance. A slow, strange dance, eerie and life-giving. A dance of atavistic signature and ritual.* LYONS *attempts to embrace him.* GABRIEL *pushes* LYONS *away. He begins to bawl in what is an attempt at song, or perhaps a song turning back into itself in an attempt at speech. He finishes his dance and the gates of heaven stand open as wide as God's closet.*

That's the way that go!

(BLACKOUT)

1987

Frederick Busch 1941–2006

Frederick Busch was a prolific and wide-ranging author of fiction—including historical novels, novels with contemporary settings, and several collections of short stories. He said about his own writing, "I write about characters I want to matter more than my own theories and more than my own delights. The great problem is to face the fullest implications of one's insights and fears—and to sustain the energy to make a usable shape from them." Though his writings did not attract a great popular following, they achieved significant critical recognition, earning Busch a reputation as a "writer's writer."

Busch was born in Brooklyn, New York, in 1941 to Benjamin Busch, an attorney, and Phyllis Schnell Busch, a teacher and author. He attended Muhlenberg College, in Allentown, Pennsylvania, earning his B.A. degree in 1962, then studied at Columbia University as a Woodrow Wilson fellow in 1962–1963. After a period of working as a writer and editor for magazines in New York City and Greenwich, Connecticut, he returned to Columbia and earned a Master's degree in 1967. In the meantime he had begun teaching as an instructor at Colgate University, where he remained as a faculty member throughout his career, becoming Fairchild Professor of Literature in 1987. He also spent a year as acting director of the program in creative writing at the University of Iowa in 1978–1979.

Busch's first novel was I Wanted a Year without Fall *(1970), which he followed with* Manual Labor *(1974)—about which Joyce Carol Oates, writing for the* New York Times Book Review, *remarked, "Stylistically, it is very 'contemporary,' that is, its sentences are terse, cautious, precise, at times mildly ironic, but never do they veer into abstraction." In all, Busch published fifteen novels, six collections of short stories, and several volumes of nonfiction writings. His major recognitions included a National Jewish Book Award for Fiction in 1985, an American Academy of Arts and Letters Fiction Award in 1986, and a PEN/Malamud Award (for his achievement as a writer of short stories) in 1991. He was particularly admired as, in the words of critic Howard Frank Mosher, "a shrewd and sympathetic chronicler of modern American family life." Frederick Busch died in New York of a heart attack in February 2006.*

FURTHER READING: D. Greiner, *Domestic Particulars: The Novels of Frederick Busch,* 1988; *Writers and Their Craft: Short Stories and Essays on the Narrative,* ed. N. Delbanco and L. Goldstein, 1991.

TEXT: *The Children in the Woods,* 1994.

BRING YOUR FRIENDS TO THE ZOO

Because many of them did not know when or how to say no and ate too much and the wrong kind of food—sometimes fatally. They spent the day begging and lost health, too, through lack of exercise. The NO FEEDING RULE has enabled us to establish balanced diets for them, preserve their health and encourage breeding. In one year, while visitors were offering food, the elephants seized no less than fourteen coats, twelve handbags, ten cameras, eight gloves and six return tickets to Leicester,[1] damaging them beyond repair. In the same year one hundred eighty visitors were bitten by other animals—monkeys, parrots, cockatoos and ponies. We want it to be a happy day for you and all the animals.

Present yourself at nine-thirty in the morning as the cashier slides his window up. It is advised that when you ask for two tickets, at eight shillings apiece, you calculate that there are twenty shillings in a pound and you are asking him to change a ten-pound note before he's done any business. Check your fly and clear your throat and look at all the bus stops while he turns his head away and then, because it is an English zoo, offers you apologies, and then commits revenge, smiling: nine pounds four in coin—half-pound pieces, two-shilling pieces, one-shilling pieces, a clanking lump in your sport coat pocket. You should at this point sound like a sack of chains. Watch the bus stops.

Take twenty-four thousand customers on an average summer's day—and one in four brought food for the animals. Six thousand paper bags of food was a *very* large "extra," seven days a week! We want it to be a happy day for you and all the animals. Please Do Not Feed. Them, for we want it to be a happy day for you and all the animals. Please.

[1]A city in central England.

Then close the guide and say, "Good morning. Hi."

At this time of year she wears a light tan raincoat that is stiff and clean. Her Liberty scarf, a bright blue paisley, shows at the throat. Her hem is too long for fashion and her slender legs are not shown to her best advantage. Her hair blows in the harsh autumn wind that has risen in August, a warning of what the year is to be, but her hair is heavy and it settles about her as the wind wavers, and she still looks composed. She wears her hair simply and does not look stylish; she looks as if she cares to look no other way, and so she carries an air of threat: she is too much her own construction, insufficiently swayed by London modes, or winds of summer, you. Greet her by saying, "Good morning. Hi."

Once through the gate, face right. The Deer House, the Camel House, the Giraffe House, the Cattle and Zebra House and the Antelope House will all be found on your left across the canal and a wild ravine. Water Bus rides on the artificial river start at ten. And for the *little* children there is riding in the Children's Zoo too, on the tiny Shetland Ponies and the diminutive donkeys. As you face your right you see a path before you. Take it. The Cranes and Goose Paddock on your immediate left; you pass, on your right, the Owls' Aviary and the Pheasantry. All of the pheasants have gone away and you can count up fourteen empty cages, waiting. You can listen to the wind across the Reptile House, the Reptiliary, the Gentlemen's Toilets, the Charles Clore Pavilion for Mammals, and Moonlight World. Ahead of you a great fence of wide-mesh wire catches the wind; it is a huge crazy sail that is warped to the ground like a tent and has a door of brushed aluminum. It peaks in twenty places, this mad enclosure, it bulges at its sides; thick steel pipes at strange angles jut like spars and when you walk inside, saying, "You go first. You come first, you always came first for me. You know that," the noise that she makes for you by listening in silence, saying nothing, even when you smirk your sudden words away, is lost. For you are in the Snowdon Aviary, opened in 1965, the first out-of-doors walk-through aviary in the London Zoo, which houses many birds from a variety of natural habitats. The Aviary was designed by Lord Snowdon[2] in association with Mr. Cedric Price and Mr. Frank Newby. A special leaflet about the Aviary is available from the Zoo Shop (price one shilling). Lost, because the wind is constantly a high sighing human voice inside this cage. The ground slopes sharply and the steep bank is cut by a narrow concrete walk. A wide-barred railing keeps you from falling down, as the waterfall goes down, roaring, onto rocks and wet bright vegetation, but you must be cautious at the dangerous rail not to drop like the water down on the rocks and tangled bushes below, very far. There are trees and creepers, everything is twined and seizing and moist and you must take care in the constant wind in which the bellow of her silence is lost.

Shapes and colors move in the transplanted brush, something always is moving off the edge of your vision near a pool or in the shadow of a twisted tree or under something green. Over one hundred forty birds of every color are housed here, and below there are egrets ignoring you, herons and spoonbills, teal and ibises, turacos, kestrel—all were here this morning, will remain tonight, in the breathing wind and faintest rattle, as if chains were shaken, that the fence must always make.

[2]Antony Armstrong-Jones (1930–). From 1960 until their divorce in 1978, he was the husband of Princess Margaret, the sister of England's Queen Elizabeth II.

Plans to make the London Zoo the most beautiful and modern zoo in the world have been moving forward. Moving forward, out the final door, leaving you in the Aviary, she will face a wooden wall and large white sign: UNDER REDEVELOPMENT. Beyond and left she should see the West Bridge. Call her and the wind will crush your words. No birds will rise in fright at the sound of your voice. Move along the rail at which you must take care and leave this unique and justly famous structure.

Say to her, waiting at the Regent's Canal before the bridge, "Did you want to leave me there with the other funny birds?"

"No. No. You aren't a funny bird."

"I thought maybe that's why you weren't talking to me."

"I am talking to you."

"Right, yes, you are talking to me. Right. What are you saying?"

"Nothing, I suppose. I don't know. Am I being cruel?"

"What's your best guess?"

"I'm not here to be cruel. I don't want anything bad to happen to you."

"Me neither."

"That's not why I'm here."

"I wonder if I could ask you why you *are*."

"Why I am?"

"Not in general, I mean. We could work out all the metaphysics later, how come you exist, et cetera. I mean why did—no. Dammit. You see? I'm a vicious man. I didn't come here, I didn't ask you to come here, so I could be nasty. Honest."

"No. I know."

"Now *I* don't."

"What?"

"I swear I all of a sudden have no idea why we're doing this. I think I would have stood in front of the gate on Prince Albert Road all day, waiting. I would have called your mother's house, I would have *gone* there and lied my way in. I mean it was crucial, understand? It was essential. Absolutely necessary to see you. Except I don't know why now. Why did you come?"

"Because you cabled me. It was very dramatic. You asked me to."

"But why did you *want* to come?"

"Because you wanted me to. Stupid. Because in America—"

"Please: what happened in America? What did we do? What was it?"

"Oh, that's an easy one. It was a scandal at your university. It was a humiliation to my husband. His students talked about it, your students talked about it. I shouldn't be surprised if you and I didn't manage to talk about it publicly every chance we'd had. Do you remember that oaf of a gibbering something-in-administration of yours, the one with the yellow plastic teeth? 'Ah, the benefits of exchange professorships,' he said. 'Hands and everything else across the waters.' What a pig he was."

"So is that what it was? An embarrassment?"

"You never should whine. I wish you wouldn't."

"But I need to *know* this!"

"You're spoiling your leave what-you-may-call-it."

"Leave of absence. I'm not on leave."

"Why are you in England, then? Your cable said sudden leave or something."

"Guess why I'm here. And I left very suddenly."

"Oh not me. You didn't come all the way over on account of me, that's *hideous!*"

"All right."

"You *didn't.*"

"All right."

"Yes you did."

"I don't want to discuss the mechanics of it."

"But all those miles!"

"Why did *you* fly over all those miles in the first place?"

"But it was end of term. The job was over, we had to come home."

"*He* had to come home."

"This is an ancient conversation."

"And how come you live at your mother's house?"

"Yes. How did you know that?"

"I called your husband on the phone."

"You rang my husband? You made my husband *talk* to you?"

"I'm sorry. You want me to be sorry?"

"I want you to feel like the through-and-through child that you are."

You should not miss the Crane and Goose Paddocks. Cranes fly with outstretched neck and legs trailing behind them. They feed on seeds and small animal life, and nest on the ground.

The London Zoo is now doing its best to correct this lack of breeding by setting up a large colony of chimpanzees at Regent's Park. Here it is hoped to breed enough baby chimps to make it unnecessary to take any further specimens from the wild.

To mention only a few of the fascinating exhibits, there are the stick insects which are masters of protective camouflage. The praying mantis, which preys on other insects, stalking them and finally pouncing upon them with its powerful, sharply spined, grasping forelegs, is a fascinating, sinister exhibit. Many of them have been reared in the zoo from eggs sent in masses from warmer lands.

The bactrian camel has two humps. The dromedary has one hump.

While a sparrow has fourteen joints to its neck a giraffe has only seven. Giraffes rarely utter any sound.

Keep to the left on entering the Reptile House; it will help you to make the most of these notes. They store their poison in glands in their head. When they bite. The cobra's hood is produced by the spreading of certain ribs near the neck. Rattlesnakes warn by. Green mamba. Kirtland's tree snake looks like the bark of a tree. Then outside to the Broad Walk, directly ahead. Few people realize there are so many kinds of monkeys and apes. And the Charles Clore Pavilion for Mammals, opened in May of 1967.

Stand facing the door while she looks through its glass at the glass-faced cages where one can ascertain the waking/sleeping rhythms, burrowing habits and jumping capacities of small mammals on display, each in its natural habitat. When she turns from the binturongs and tree kangaroos, by glass twice removed, and the sound of your wordless shout rains onto visitors and the brownish cement of the building, the Otter Pool to your right, the Staff Car Park to your left, the Outer Circle Walk will be at your back. Say, "Why don't you live with your husband now? Why didn't you tell me when you left him? Why don't you let me *love* you?" Noting the stiffness of her stance, the sense she gives, like a smell of imminent flight in wild things, ask her lower, say more secretly, "Why?"

"My husband hates me."

"Did he hit you?"

"*Hate.* Not hit. He doesn't hit."

"Do you hate me?"

"No. I don't know. No."

"I guess I ruined your life."

"Perhaps you did. And if you did you've no need really to be proud. That's simple enough to do. What could be more fragile?"

"Did you love me in America?"

"Please stop asking me questions like that."

"But you don't love me now."

"Now it doesn't matter if I do."

"Oh yes it does."

"I'm sorry. I mean now it makes no difference. No, not that either. I can't really say things cleverly, can I?"

"You can say. You do fine."

"I'm not trying to injure you, you see. I'm trying *not* to injure you.

I'm trying—listen to me as if I were a student. A stupid student. A stupid child. Which I am."

"Would you understand what I meant if I started to cry now?"

"Oh, American men don't cry, though, do they? Please?"

"Of course not. You know how I keep forgetting things. Forgive me."

"You me."

"Well, *talk,* talk, tell me. Tell me."

"Have you ever read the personal page of the *Times?* Our *Times,* over here?"

"Sherlock Holmes called that page the agony columns."

"Yes. There's a section headed *In Memoriam.*"

"Yes."

"And on the anniversary of someone's death—this always comes directly after *Marriages,* you know."

"Doesn't it."

"On the anniversary of death the family place a message. Usually it's one sentence, headed with the dead person's last name in very dark letters. Sort of '*Smith, W. A.—To the loving memory of William Albert Smith, felled whilst on duty in Bosnia, August 11, 1913, perishing bravely at his Embassy post, ever remembered by all, sacred to the memory of his loving family.*' That sort of thing. I suppose people do read them. I sometimes read them when I've nothing better to do."

"You've recently been having nothing better to do."

"I've spent some time alone."

"I guess you have."

"Most often I feel spooky, sort of, you know, *peeping.* Looking at that sorrow or make-believe sorrow, all of it out on display, like a show or something. Of course it might be real agony, sometimes I think so. And how ghoulish it is of me to finger it and then go away. It's so morbid of me, isn't it? But I do it sometimes."

"And you saw this ad put in by your husband, announcing his death and how he mourned it."

"No."

"I apologize for saying that."

"We both used to say things like that."

"Mostly me, I had less to lose. I used to think like that."

"What I want to tell you is during the time—I mean when my husband threw me out, as soon as we were home, really, and I lived in a room at my mother's. My old room. Lord. Why do you think things always work out like *that?*"

"You can come and live in my room."

"Anyway I read a lot of *In Memoriams.* I suppose I was thinking of writing my own. But do you know, the history of England is there, in those little drizzly horrible squibs of formal language. Things that happened before I was born, or when I was too young to remember. Sacred to the memory of so-and-so, he was shot down thus-and-such, France, 1942. Killed at sea, 1918. On and on. All those people dead, all those people remembering them. And then the little nonhistorical people. Killed in a tragic accident. Felled by a premature stroke. Dead before her tenth year. So *much!* And all those people remembering. Everything is gone, but they keep on remembering. The history is still left. The families are still left. Something is left. Death didn't kill it all, there is such *sadness* left. Like bones in a body when the skin is corrupted and gone all to powders. There *is* something left of what there was and the sad people keep it here."

"I'm trying to marry a widow, you mean?"

"I suppose. I'm so—"

"Well, widows don't mourn at the zoo. They don't stay faithful to some kind of memories—after being *un*faithful—by coming to meet their memories' cuckold that they're supposed to be faithful to after dishonoring what they're honoring *now.*"

"I don't—I'm sorry, really, I really didn't get that. I don't understand what you said. Would you say it again?"

"No. I can't even remember it."

The Pavilion, designed to house the Zoological Society's large collection of small mammals, is a new building with one hundred cages and three outside enclosures, accommodating some two hundred burrowing, jumping, running and climbing animals—marmots, martens, civets, mongooses, lemurs, marmosets, squirrel monkeys, ocelots, wallabies, wombats, porcupines and acouchies. When you follow her inside you can skirt the upper-floor exhibits and walk directly to the stairs that go down. Observe the sign that says DO NOT SPEAK LOUDLY and BEWARE PICKPOCKETS. Put your hand on your wallet, check your fly, walk downstairs with your change adrift in your pocket, rattling.

You will see that this hot wandering chamber is dark, lighted only by tiny red bulbs. A rail divides each crypt of the chamber in half, and each wall is windowed. Several different worlds have been placed side by side, sealed off from one another and discrete, in each glass wall. Follow the wall, keep to the left of the rail. Such creatures as bats, kinkajous,[3] flying squirrels, douroucoulis[4] and bush babies are normally active from dusk to dawn. In this large nocturnal section, known as the Moonlight World, special lighting has been installed, based on a study of these creatures' individual habits. This reverses their days and nights so that they are most active during public visiting hours. When the visitors leave, the lighting gradually increases and the animals fall asleep. They read the *Times* before retiring, and the angwantibos[5] sing at the mouth of the

[3]A small, tree-dwelling mammal that lives in rainforests.
[4]A kind of New World monkey. [5]A small African primate.

gerbils' burrow as the light bulbs buzz. Visacha. Mouse lemurs. Seldom seen in movement. Seldom seen. For safety a dimly lit green sign on the ceiling warns the visitors to STAND IN PLACE UNTIL YOUR EYES ARE USED TO THE DARK.

Call to her that your eyes are not used to the dark yet.

"Hush, will you? Listen, I have to go now."

She will have moved around several bends of the chamber by now, for her eyes have grown used to the dark. Call to her again. If she silences you, remain silent, for rare Allen's bush babies live here and we want it to be a happy day for you and all the animals.

Still, you should call once more. Note that on the walls around you there are eyes, open eyes, blinking eyes, eyes that flee and return. Note that as you shout, as your feet shuffle, clanking the chains in your pocket, as your hands are held before you while you lurch, always to the left of your rail in the Moonlight World, how you frighten the eyes. They retreat. But they come back. The eyes in silence are the animals awake. When the visitors leave, the lighting gradually increases and the animals fall asleep. This reverses their days and their nights.

Now it is day. This is night to them, they are awake. As long as it is dark they are awake, for their eyes have grown used to the dark. And somewhere in the turnings of the Moonlight World she should say, "We have to go. I have to go."

"I don't want to go unless you come with me."

"No."

"Please."

"No. Hush."

"What about *my* history? Whose memory is that supposed to be sacred to? Who's remembering me? What about me? What good does loving you do *me?*"

But there is so much to see at the London Zoo. Take twenty-four thousand visitors on an average summer's day. As they enter the Moonlight World they obey the sign that tells them to STAND IN PLACE UNTIL YOUR EYES ARE USED TO THE DARK. When you flee them as they enter, you should keep to the left of the rail. The tiny animal eyes are open, of course, as you shuffle, jangling, for the eyes have grown used to the dark. This nighttime is their day. Take twenty-four thousand visitors. Come again and bring your friends to the Zoo. Beware pickpockets. Flee. Climb the stairs slowly and try to find her waiting for you at the top. When the visitors leave it is raw golden daylight. Come up blinking, blind.

1994

Billy Collins 1941–

A serious poet who has also achieved wide-ranging popular success in his lifetime, Billy Collins is indeed a rare literary figure. Named Poet Laureate Consultant in Poetry in 2001 and 2002, he often entertains poetry lovers with readings of his work on National Public Radio and at venues around the world.

Born and raised in New York, Collins received his Ph.D in Romantic Poetry from the University of California, Riverside, and embarked on an academic career that brought him to Lehman College, where he has taught since the 1970s. Since his first work was published in obscure journals like Oink, *Collins's poems have regularly appeared in the* New Yorker, Harper's, Poetry, TriQuarterly, American Poetry Review, *and* The Paris Review. *He first gained widespread recognition with his second book,* Questions about Angels, *which was selected for the National Poetry Series. His subsequent books have garnered many awards, including the Beth Hokin Prize, and fellowships from the National Endowment for the Arts and the Guggenheim Foundation.*

The New Yorker *once praised Collins for his ability to "turn an apparently simple phrase into a numinous moment." He is a metaphysical poet of ideas, who has an unusual ability to evoke popular response through humor and commonplace experience. About his writing process, Collins claims it is unstructured and that his "pen is an instrument of discovery rather than just a recording implement." And in talking about poetry and his own work, he once cited Robert Frost's "Stopping by Woods on a Snowy Evening," explaining that "the poet is willing to stop anywhere" and that "it's this willingness to slow down and examine the serious bits of fluff in our lives that is the poet's interest."*

To date, Collins has published eight books of poetry, three of which have surpassed sales records for poetry: Pokerface *(1977),* Video Poems *(1980),* The Apple That Astonished Paris *(1988),* Questions about Angels *(1991),* The Art of Drowning *(1995),* Picnic, Lightning *(1998),* Sailing Alone around the Room *(2001), and* Nine Horses *(2002). Collins continues his long-time affiliation with Lehman College, CUNY, and in recent years has also conducted poetry workshops at University College, Galway, and served as poet-in-residence at Burren College of Art in Ireland.*

FURTHER READING: *The Apple That Astonished Paris: Poems by Billy Collins,* 1988; *The Art of Drowning,* 1995; *Taking Off Emily Dickinson's Clothes,* 2000; *Heresy and the Ideal: On Contemporary Poetry,* ed. D. Baker, 2000; *Nine Horses: Poems,* 2002; *Poetry 180: A Turning Back to Poetry,* ed. B. Collins, 2003; *The Eye of the Poet: Six Views of the Art and Craft of Poetry,* ed. D. Citino, B. Collins, Y. Komunyakaa; *Daddy's Little Boy,* 2004.

TEXT: *Sailing Alone around the Room,* 2001.

WINTER SYNTAX

A sentence starts out like a lone traveler
heading into a blizzard at midnight,
tilting into the wind, one arm shielding his face,
the tails of his thin coat flapping behind him.

There are easier ways of making sense,
the connoisseurship of gesture, for example.
You hold a girl's face in your hands like a vase.
You lift a gun from the glove compartment
and toss it out the window into the desert heat.
These cool moments are blazing with silence.

The full moon makes sense. When a cloud crosses it
it becomes as eloquent as a bicycle leaning
outside a drugstore or a dog who sleeps all afternoon
in a corner of the couch.

Bare branches in winter are a form of writing.
The unclothed body is autobiography.
Every lake is a vowel, every island a noun.

But the traveler persists in his misery,
struggling all night through the deepening snow,
leaving a faint alphabet of bootprints
on the white hills and the white floors of valleys,
a message for field mice and passing crows.

At dawn he will spot the vine of smoke
rising from your chimney, and when he stands
before you shivering, draped in sparkling frost,
a smile will appear in the beard of icicles,
and the man will express a complete thought.

2001

BOOKS

From the heart of this dark, evacuated campus
I can hear the library humming in the night,
a choir of authors murmuring inside their books
along the unlit, alphabetical shelves,
Giovanni Pontano next to Pope, Dumas next to his son,
each one stitched into his own private coat,
together forming a low, gigantic chord of language.

I picture a figure in the act of reading,
shoes on a desk, head tilted into the wind of a book,
a man in two worlds, holding the rope of his tie
as the suicide of lovers saturates a page,
or lighting a cigarette in the middle of a theorem.
He moves from paragraph to paragraph
as if touring a house of endless, paneled rooms.

I hear the voice of my mother reading to me
from a chair facing the bed, books about horses and dogs,
and inside her voice lie other distant sounds,
the horrors of a stable ablaze in the night,
a bark that is moving toward the brink of speech.

I watch myself building bookshelves in college,
walls within walls, as rain soaks New England,
or standing in a bookstore in a trench coat.

I see all of us reading ourselves away from ourselves,
straining in circles of light to find more light

until the line of words becomes a trail of crumbs
that we follow across a page of fresh snow;

when evening is shadowing the forest
and small birds flutter down to consume the crumbs,
we have to listen hard to hear the voices
of the boy and his sister receding into the woods.

2001

INTRODUCTION TO POETRY

I ask them to take a poem
and hold it up to the light
like a color slide

or press an ear against its hive.

I say drop a mouse into a poem
and watch him probe his way out,

or walk inside the poem's room
and feel the walls for a light switch.

I want them to water-ski
across the surface of a poem
waving at the author's name on the shore.

But all they want to do
is tie the poem to a chair with rope
and torture a confession out of it.

They begin beating it with a hose
to find out what it really means.

2001

Simon Ortiz 1941–

Simon Ortiz is unique among major contemporary Native American writers for having been reared in a thoroughly traditional home, where his tribal tongue, not English, was the first language of his youth. He was born in 1941 in Albuquerque, New Mexico, to Acoma Pueblo parents: Joe L. Ortiz, a railroad worker and tribal elder, and Mamie Toribio Ortiz, a potter. He spent his childhood in McCartys, an Acoma community located in west New Mexico, attending schools operated by the Bureau of

Indian Affairs. When he was twelve, his parents sent him to Santa Fe to attend St. Catherine's Indian School, an environment in which learning was encouraged but attachment to Native traditions was discouraged. He returned home after a year and eventually graduated from an integrated high school near McCartys. After short stints as a worker at a uranium mine and a student at Fort Lewis College, Ortiz served in the U.S. Army from 1963 to 1966, then enrolled at the University of New Mexico, from which he earned a B.A. in 1968. He then entered the University of Iowa's M.F.A. program and took his degree in 1969.

Ortiz published his first collection of poems, Naked in the Wind, *in 1971, but it was his second book of verse,* Going for the Rain *(1976), that established him as a significant poet. Since the late 1970s Ortiz has published more than a dozen volumes of poetry, fiction, essays, and children's literature, including the 1992* Woven Stone, *which collects poems from three of his earlier volumes. Ortiz has said about his own work, "As a writer, I've tried to consider most importantly my life as a Native American who is absolutely related to the land and all that that means culturally, politically, personally. Nothing is separate from me in that sense, and I am included with the earth and all its aspects and details." He has taught at colleges in Arizona, California, Oregon, and South Dakota, but has continued for the most part to live in and near the Acoma Pueblo homeland. He currently resides in McCartys, New Mexico.*

FURTHER READING: A. Wiget, *Simon Ortiz,* 1986; L. Coltelli, *Winged Words: American Indian Writers Speak,* 1990; K. Peiffer, *Coyote at Large: Humor in American Nature Writing,* 2000.

TEXTS: *A Good Journey,* 1977; *Woven Stone,* 1992.

A DESIGNATED NATIONAL PARK

Montezuma Castle in the Verde Valley, Arizona.

DESIGNATED FEDERAL RECREATION FEE AREA
ENTREE FEES
$1.00 FOR 1 DAY PERMIT
MONTEZUMA CASTLE ONLY INCLUDES PURCHASER
OR OTHERS WITH HIM
IN PRIVATE NON-COMMERCIAL VEHICLE
$0.50 FOR 1 DAY PERMIT
MONTEZUMA CASTLE ONLY INCLUDES PURCHASER
ON COMMERCIAL VEHICLE

AUTHORIZED
BY THE LAND AND WATER
CONSERVATION FUND ACT OF 1965

This morning,
I have to buy a permit to get back home.

Birds,
they must have been,
these people,
"Thank you for letting me come to see you."
I tell them that.

Secreted in my cave,
look at the sun.
Shadows on sycamore,
a strange bird and a familiar bird.
River, hear the river.
What it must be,
that pigeon sound.
Hear
in my cave, sacred song.
Morning feeling, sacred song.
We shall plant today.
PRESS BUTTON
(on a wooden booth)
"For a glimpse into the lives
of these people who lived here."
Pressing the button, I find
painted sticks and cloth fragments
in a child's hand,
her eyelashes still intact.
Girl, my daughter, my mother,
softly asleep.
They have unearthed you.

59TH CONGRESS OF THE UNITED STATES OF AMERICA
AT THE FIRST SESSION,
BEGUN AND HELD AT THE CITY OF WASHINGTON
ON MONDAY, THE FOURTH DAY OF DECEMBER,
ONE THOUSAND, NINE HUNDRED AND FIVE.

AN ACT
FOR THE PRESERVATION OF AMERICAN ANTIQUITIES.

And a last sign post quote:

BUILT SOMETIME BETWEEN
1200 AD AND 1350 AD
ABANDONED BY AD 1450.

s/ The Sinagua Indians

SEE MUSEUM FOR MORE INFORMATION

1977

CANYON DE CHELLY[1]

Lie on your back on stone,
the stone carved to fit
the shape of yourself.
Who made it like this,
knowing that I would be along
in a million years and look
at the sky being blue forever?

My son is near me. He sits
and turns on his butt
and crawls over to stones,
picks one up and holds it,
and then puts it into his mouth.
The taste of stone.
What is it but stone,
the earth in your mouth.
You, son, are tasting forever.

We walk to the edge of the cliff
and look down into the canyon.
On this side, we cannot see
the bottom cliffedge but looking
further out, we see fields,
sand furrows, cottonwoods.
In winter, they are softly gray.
The cliffs' shadows are distant,
hundreds of feet below;
we cannot see our own shadows.
The wind moves softly into us.
My son laughs with the wind;
he gasps and laughs.

We find gray root, old wood,
so old, with curious twists
in it, curving back into curves,
juniper, pinon, or something
with hard, red berries in spring.
You taste them, and they are sweet
and bitter, the berries a delicacy
for bluejays. The plant rooted
fragilely into a sandy place
by a canyon wall, the sun bathing
shiny, pointed leaves.

[1]A large canyon located in northeastern Arizona at its border with New Mexico. Since 1931 it has been the Canyon de Chelly National Monument, operated by the National Park Service but within the boundaries of the Navajo Tribal Trust Land.

My son touches the root carefully,
aware of its ancient quality.
He lays his soft, small fingers on it
and looks at me for information.
I tell him: wood, an old root,
and around it, the earth, ourselves.

1977

FINAL SOLUTION: JOBS, LEAVING

They would leave
on Sundays from the depot in Grants.[1]
It seemed always, always, so final.
Goodbye. Goodbye Daddy. Daddy,
please come back. Please don't go.
Daddy. But they would leave.

Winslow.
Flagstaff.
Seligman.
Barstow.[2]

We had to buy groceries,
had to have clothes, homes, roofs,
windows. Surrounded by the United States,
we had come to need money.

The solution was to change,
to leave, to go to jobs.

Utah.
California.
Idaho.
Oregon.

The children would cry.
The women would be so angry.
So angry.
Silent, we left.
We didn't want to leave, but
we left.

[1]Grants, New Mexico
[2]Winslow, Arizona; Flagstaff, Arizona; Seligman, Arizona; Barstow, California.

"I don't want you and your brothers
to ever have to work for the railroad."
They kept the railroad repaired,
and the trains raced through
their land. Hearts. Blood. Bones
and skin. Wrenched muscles.
"You ever pick up a rail?
With your bare hands." Your sweat
burning in your eyes. Blood. Heart.
Skin. Bones. And they died too.
"I hope." How much they hated,
how much they hoped. How much.

American Fork, Utah, February, 1959.
Dear Mama & Children,
I hope you are all well
as I am. Children, help your mother
and take care of each others
and around our home. Remember
that you must always love
your mothers. Think of the prayers
for the land. Mama, I wish
I was home with all of you.
I will be home in a few weeks.
I love you all. Make sure
you feed the horses. My love
and hugs to each of you and Mama,
Daddy.

Saw him in Seligman.
Or was it Valentine. Or Phoenix.
Or somewhere. "He step off
the train. That was the last time
I saw him. My friend." Tears.
Wine doesn't work. They died too.

One week, two weeks, three weeks,
months, we waited. Years.
Train. O Daddy, O Daddy. Train
would come thundering, thundering
thundering toward us. Hearts.
Blood. Bones and skin. Love
and hope. O Daddy. Please train.

The children would laugh or cry
or be so silent.
The women were so angry.

Yes, we would wait again. Weeks, weeks, months, but not
those years again. O Daddy, never those years. Never again
those years. Our own solution will be strength: hearts,
blood, bones, skin, hope and love. The woman anger and
courage risen as the People's voice again

1992

Sherman Alexie 1966–

Sherman Alexie represents a second generation of critically and commercially successful Native American writers to emerge in the last decades of the twentieth century. His long list of accomplishments, much of which he achieved before he was thirty years old, includes numerous awards and recognitions for his work in verse, fiction, and film. Alexie was born in 1966 in Spokane, Washington, the son of a Spokane father, Sherman Joseph Alexie, and a part-Coeur d'Alene mother, Lillian Cox Alexie. He was reared and educated on the Spokane reservation in Wellpinit, Washington. After completing the eighth grade, he decided to leave the reservation to attend an integrated high school. He graduated with honors and received a scholarship to Gonzaga University, where he enrolled in 1985. Two years later he transferred to Washington State University in Pullman, but left three credits shy of his degree, which the university eventually awarded him in 1995. While at Washington State, Alexie apprenticed under writer Alex Kuo, who encouraged his young student to read and write poetry.

Alexie published his first book, I Would Steal Horses, *in 1992, and it won several minor awards. Later that year he released his second collection,* The Business of Fancydancing: Stories and Poems, *which received national attention. In quick succession he published three more books before the end of 1993, including the acclaimed* The Lone Ranger and Tonto Fistfight in Heaven, *winner of the PEN/Hemingway Award for First Book of Fiction. In 1995 he published* Reservation Blues, *his first novel. Three years later, he wrote the screenplay for the film* Smoke Signals, *based on one of the stories from* The Lone Ranger and Tonto Fistfight in Heaven. *It won several awards at the 1998 Sundance Film Festival and was released nationwide later that year by Miramax Studios. In recent years Alexie has continued to write award-winning poetry and fiction. His short story "What You Pawn I Will Redeem," from the story collection* Ten Little Indians *(2003), was awarded an O. Henry Prize in 2005. Novelist Christina García, one of the O. Henry Prize jurors, commented about Alexie's narrative, "He does not preen or try to impress. He has nothing to prove to his reader, only something to tell them. Like me, Sherman Alexie is in love with his homeless Spokane Indian narrator and so he simply steps aside to let his character have every inch of the stage." Sherman Alexie currently resides in Wellpinit, Washington.*

FURTHER READING: S. Brill de Ramírez, *Contemporary American Indian Literatures and the Oral Tradition,* 1999; *Here First: Autobiographical Essays by Native American Writers,* ed. A. Krupat and B. Swann, 2000; D. Grassian, *Understanding Sherman Alexie,* 2005.

TEXTS: *Ten Little Indians,* 2003; *Beloit Poetry Journal,* Fall 1995.

WHAT YOU PAWN I WILL REDEEM

NOON

One day you have a home and the next you don't, but I'm not going to tell you my particular reasons for being homeless, because it's my secret story, and Indians have to work hard to keep secrets from hungry white folks.

I'm a Spokane Indian boy, an Interior Salish,[1] and my people have lived within a one-hundred-mile radius of Spokane, Washington, for at least ten thousand years. I grew up in Spokane, moved to Seattle twenty-three years ago for college, flunked out within two semesters, worked various blue- and bluer-collar jobs for many years, married two or three times, fathered two or three kids, and then went crazy. Of course, "crazy" is not the official definition of my mental problem, but I don't think "asocial disorder" fits it, either, because that makes me sound like I'm a serial killer or something. I've never hurt another human being, or at least not physically. I've broken a few hearts in my time, but we've all done that, so I'm nothing special in that regard. I'm a boring heartbreaker, at that, because I've never abandoned one woman for another. I never dated or married more than one woman at a time. I didn't break hearts into pieces overnight. I broke them slowly and carefully. I didn't set any land-speed records running out the door. Piece by piece, I disappeared. And I've been disappearing ever since. But I'm not going to tell you any more about my brain or my soul.

I've been homeless for six years. If there's such a thing as being an effective homeless man, I suppose I'm effective. Being homeless is probably the only thing I've ever been good at. I know where to get the best free food. I've made friends with restaurant and convenience-store managers who let me use their bathrooms. I don't mean the public bathrooms, either. I mean the employees' bathrooms, the clean ones hidden in the back of the kitchen or the pantry or the cooler. I know it sounds strange to be proud of, but it means a lot to me, being truthworthy enough to piss in somebody else's clean bathroom. Maybe you don't understand the value of a clean bathroom, but I do.

Probably none of this interests you. I probably don't interest you much. Homeless Indians are everywhere in Seattle. We're common and boring, and you walk right on by us, with maybe a look of anger or disgust or even sadness at the terrible fate of the noble savage. But we have dreams and families. I'm friends with a homeless Plains Indian man whose son is the editor of a big-time newspaper back east. That's his story, but we Indians are great storytellers and liars and mythmakers, so maybe that Plains Indian hobo is a plain old everyday Indian. I'm kind of suspicious of him, because he describes himself only as Plains Indian, a generic term, and not by a specific tribe. When I asked him why he wouldn't tell me exactly what he is, he said, "Do any of us know exactly what we are?" Yeah, great, a philosophizing Indian. "Hey," I said, "you got to have a home to be that homely." He laughed and flipped me the eagle and walked away. But you probably want to know more about the story I'm really trying to tell you.

[1]A member of a Native American group that speaks the Interior Salishan language.

I wander the streets with a regular crew, my teammates, my defenders, and my posse. It's Rose of Sharon, Junior, and me. We matter to one another if we don't matter to anybody else. Rose of Sharon is a big woman, about seven feet tall if you're measuring overall effect, and about five feet tall if you're talking about the physical. She's a Yakama Indian of the Wishram variety. Junior is a Colville, but there are about 199 tribes that make up the Colville, so he could be anything. He's good-looking, though, like he just stepped out of some "Don't Litter the Earth" public-service advertisement. He's got those great big cheekbones that are like planets, you know, with little moons orbiting around them. He gets me jealous, jealous, and jealous. If you put Junior and me next to each other, he's the Before Columbus Arrived Indian, and I'm the After Columbus Arrived Indian. I am living proof of the horrible damage that colonialism has done to us Skins. But I'm not going to let you know how scared I sometimes get of history and its ways. I'm a strong man, and I know that silence is the best way of dealing with white folks.

This whole story started at lunchtime, when Rose of Sharon, Junior, and I were panning the handle down at Pike Place Market. After about two hours of negotiating, we earned five dollars, good enough for a bottle of fortified courage from the most beautiful 7–Eleven in the world. So we headed over that way, feeling like warrior drunks, and we walked past this pawnshop I'd never noticed before. And that was strange, because we Indians have built-in pawnshop radar. But the strangest thing was the old powwow-dance regalia I saw hanging in the window.

"That's my grandmother's regalia," I said to Rose of Sharon and Junior.

"How do you know for sure?" Junior asked.

I didn't know for sure, because I hadn't seen that regalia in person ever. I'd seen only photographs of my grandmother dancing in it. And that was before somebody stole it from her fifty years ago. But it sure looked like my memory of it, and it had all the same colors of feathers and beads that my family always sewed into their powwow regalia.

"There's only one way to know for sure," I said.

So Rose of Sharon, Junior, and I walked into the pawnshop and greeted the old white man working behind the counter.

"How can I help you?" he asked.

"That's my grandmother's powwow regalia in your window," I said. "Somebody stole it from her fifty years ago, and my family has been looking for it ever since."

The pawnbroker looked at me like I was a liar. I understood. Pawnshops are filled with liars.

"I'm not lying," I said. "Ask my friends here. They'll tell you."

"He's the most honest Indian I know," Rose of Sharon said.

"All right, honest Indian," the pawnbroker said. "I'll give you the benefit of the doubt. Can you prove it's your grandmother's regalia?"

Because they don't want to be perfect, because only God is perfect, Indian people sew flaws into their powwow regalia. My family always sewed one yellow bead somewhere on their regalia. But we always hid it where you had to search hard to find it.

"If it really is my grandmother's," I said, "there will be one yellow bead hidden somewhere on it."

"All right, then," the pawnbroker said. "Let's take a look."

He pulled the regalia out of the window, laid it down on his glass counter, and we searched for that yellow bead and found it hidden beneath the armpit.

"There it is," the pawnbroker said. He didn't sound surprised. "You were right. This is your grandmother's regalia."

"It's been missing for fifty years," Junior said.

"Hey, Junior," I said. "It's my family's story. Let me tell it."

"All right," he said. "I apologize. You go ahead."

"It's been missing for fifty years," I said.

"That's his family's sad story," Rose of Sharon said. "Are you going to give it back to him?"

"That would be the right thing to do," the pawnbroker said. "But I can't afford to do the right thing. I paid a thousand dollars for this. I can't give away a thousand dollars."

"We could go to the cops and tell them it was stolen," Rose of Sharon said.

"Hey," I said to her, "don't go threatening people."

The pawnbroker sighed. He was thinking hard about the possibilities.

"Well, I suppose you could go to the cops," he said. "But I don't think they'd believe a word you said."

He sounded sad about that. Like he was sorry for taking advantage of our disadvantages.

"What's your name?" the pawnbroker asked me.

"Jackson," I said.

"Is that first or last?" he asked.

"Both."

"Are you serious?"

"Yes, it's true. My mother and father named me Jackson Jackson. My family nickname is Jackson Squared. My family is funny."

"All right, Jackson Jackson," the pawnbroker said. "You wouldn't happen to have a thousand dollars, would you?"

"We've got five dollars total," I said.

"That's too bad," he said and thought hard about the possibilities. "I'd sell it to you for a thousand dollars if you had it. Heck, to make it fair, I'd sell it to you for nine hundred and ninety-nine dollars. I'd lose a dollar. It would be the moral thing to do in this case. To lose a dollar would be the right thing."

"We've got five dollars total," I said again.

"That's too bad," he said again and thought harder about the possibilities. "How about this? I'll give you twenty-four hours to come up with nine hundred and ninety-nine dollars. You come back here at lunchtime tomorrow with the money, and I'll sell it back to you. How does that sound?"

"It sounds good," I said.

"All right, then," he said. "We have a deal. And I'll get you started. Here's twenty bucks to get you started."

He opened up his wallet and pulled out a crisp twenty-dollar bill and gave it to me. Rose of Sharon, Junior, and I walked out into the daylight to search for nine hundred and seventy-four more dollars.

1:00 P.M.

Rose of Sharon, Junior, and I carried our twenty-dollar bill and our five dollars in loose change over to the 7–Eleven and spent it to buy three bottles of imagination. We needed to figure out how to raise all that money in one day. Thinking hard, we huddled in an alley beneath the Alaska Way Viaduct and finished off those bottles one, two, and three.

2:00 P.M.

Rose of Sharon was gone when I woke. I heard later she had hitchhiked back to Toppenish[2] and was living with her sister on the reservation.

Junior was passed out beside me, covered in his own vomit, or maybe somebody else's vomit, and my head hurt from thinking, so I left him alone and walked down to the water. I loved the smell of ocean water. Salt always smells like memory.

When I got to the wharf, I ran into three Aleut[3] cousins who sat on a wooden bench and stared out at the bay and cried. Most of the homeless Indians in Seattle come from Alaska. One by one, each of them hopped a big working boat in Anchorage or Barrow or Juneau, fished his way south to Seattle, jumped off the boat with a pocketful of cash to party hard at one of the highly sacred and traditional Indian bars, went broke and broker, and has been trying to find his way back to the boat and the frozen north ever since.

These Aleuts smelled like salmon, I thought, and they told me they were going to sit on that wooden bench until their boat came back.

"How long has your boat been gone?" I asked.

"Eleven years," the elder Aleut said.

I cried with them for a while.

"Hey," I said. "Do you guys have any money I can borrow?"

They didn't.

3:00 P.M.

I walked back to Junior. He was still passed out. I put my face down near his mouth to make sure he was breathing. He was alive, so I dug around in his blue-jean pockets and found half a cigarette. I smoked it all the way down and thought about my grandmother.

Her name was Agnes, and she died of breast cancer when I was fourteen. My father thought Agnes caught her tumors from the uranium mine on the reservation. But my mother said the disease started when Agnes was walking back from the powwow one night and got run over by a motorcycle. She broke three ribs, and my mother said those ribs never healed right, and tumors always take over when you don't heal right.

[2]A small city in south-central Washington.
[3]A Native American from the Aleutian Islands, in Alaska.

Sitting beside Junior, smelling the smoke and salt and vomit, I wondered if my grandmother's cancer had started when somebody stole her powwow regalia. Maybe the cancer started in her broken heart and then leaked out into her breasts. I know it's crazy, but I wondered if I could bring my grandmother back to life if I bought back her regalia.

I needed money, big money, so I left Junior and walked over to the Real Change office.

4:00 P.M.

"Real Change is a multifaceted organization that publishes a newspaper, supports cultural projects that empower the poor and homeless, and mobilizes the public around poverty issues. Real Change's mission is to organize, educate, and build alliances to create solutions to homelessness and poverty. They exist to provide a voice to poor people in our community."

I memorized Real Change's mission statement because I sometimes sell the newspaper on the streets. But you have to stay sober to sell it, and I'm not always good at staying sober. Anybody can sell the newspaper. You buy each copy for thirty cents and sell it for a dollar and keep the net profit.

"I need one thousand four hundred and thirty papers," I said to the Big Boss.

"That's a strange number," he said. "And that's a lot of papers."

"I need them."

The Big Boss pulled out the calculator and did the math. "It will cost you four hundred and twenty-nine dollars for that many," he said.

"If I had that kind of money, I wouldn't need to sell the papers."

"What's going on, Jackson-to-the-Second-Power?" he asked. He is the only one who calls me that. He is a funny and kind man.

I told him about my grandmother's powwow regalia and how much money I needed to buy it back.

"We should call the police," he said.

"I don't want to do that," I said. "It's a quest now. I need to win it back by myself."

"I understand," he said. "And to be honest, I'd give you the papers to sell if I thought it would work. But the record for most papers sold in a day by one vendor is only three hundred and two."

"That would net me about two hundred bucks," I said.

The Big Boss used his calculator. "Two hundred and eleven dollars and forty cents," he said.

"That's not enough," I said.

"The most money anybody has made in one day is five hundred and twenty-five. And that's because somebody gave Old Blue five hundred-dollar bills for some dang reason. The average daily net is about thirty dollars."

"This isn't going to work."

"No."

"Can you lend me some money?"

"I can't do that," he said. "If I lend you money, I have to lend money to everybody."

"What can you do?"

"I'll give you fifty papers for free. But don't tell anybody I did it."

"Okay," I said.

He gathered up the newspapers and handed them to me. I held them to my chest. He hugged me. I carried the newspapers back toward the water.

5:00 P.M.

Back on the wharf, I stood near the Bainbridge Island Terminal and tried to sell papers to business commuters walking onto the ferry.

I sold five in one hour, dumped the other forty-five into a garbage can, and walked into the McDonald's, ordered four cheeseburgers for a dollar each, and slowly ate them.

After eating, I walked outside and vomited on the sidewalk. I hated to lose my food so soon after eating it. As an alcoholic Indian with a busted stomach, I always hope I can keep enough food in my stomach to stay alive.

6:00 P.M.

With one dollar in my pocket, I walked back to Junior. He was still passed out, so I put my ear to his chest and listened for his heartbeat. He was alive, so I took off his shoes and socks and found one dollar in his left sock and fifty cents in his right sock. With two dollars and fifty cents in my hand, I sat beside Junior and thought about my grandmother and her stories.

When I was sixteen, my grandmother told me a story about World War II. She was a nurse at a military hospital in Sydney, Australia. Over the course of two years, she comforted and healed U.S. and Australian soldiers.

One day, she tended to a wounded Maori soldier.[4] He was very dark-skinned. His hair was black and curly, and his eyes were black and warm. His face with covered with bright tattoos.

"Are you Maori?" he asked my grandmother.

"No," she said. "I'm Spokane Indian. From the United States."

"Ah, yes," he said. "I have heard of your tribes. But you are the first American Indian I have ever met."

"There's a lot of Indian soldiers fighting for the United States," she said. "I have a brother still fighting in Germany, and I lost another brother on Okinawa."[5]

"I am sorry," he said. "I was on Okinawa as well. It was terrible." He had lost his legs to an artillery attack.

"I am sorry about your legs," my grandmother said.

"It's funny, isn't it?" he asked.

"What's funny?"

"How we brown people are killing other brown people so white people will remain free."

[4]The Maori are the pre-European inhabitants of New Zealand.

[5]A Japanese island chain that was the site of a major battle between American and Japanese forces in World War II.

"I hadn't thought of it that way."

"Well, sometimes I think of it that way. And other times, I think of it the way they want me to think of it. I get confused."

She fed him morphine.

"Do you believe in heaven?" he asked.

"Which heaven?" she asked.

"I'm talking about the heaven where my legs are waiting for me."

They laughed.

"Of course," he said, "my legs will probably run away from me when I get to heaven. And how will I ever catch them?"

"You have to get your arms strong," my grandmother said. "So you can run on your hands."

They laughed again.

Sitting beside Junior, I laughed with the memory of my grandmother's story. I put my hand close to Junior's mouth to make sure he was still breathing. Yes, Junior was alive, so I took his two dollars and fifty cents and walked to the Korean grocery store over in Pioneer Square.

7:00 P.M.

In the Korean grocery store, I bought a fifty-cent cigar and two scratch lottery tickets for a dollar each. The maximum cash prize was five hundred dollars a ticket. If I won both, I would have enough money to buy back the regalia.

I loved Kay, the young Korean woman who worked the register. She was the daughter of the owners and sang all day.

"I love you," I said when I handed her the money.

"You always say you love me," she said.

"That's because I will always love you."

"You are a sentimental fool."

"I'm a romantic old man."

"Too old for me."

"I know I'm too old for you, but I can dream."

"Okay," she said. "I agree to be a part of your dreams, but I will only hold your hand in your dreams. No kissing and no sex. Not even in your dreams."

"Okay," I said. "No sex. Just romance."

"Good-bye, Jackson Jackson, my love, I will see you soon."

I left the store, walked over to Occidental Park, sat on a bench, and smoked my cigar all the way down.

Ten minutes after I finished the cigar, I scratched my first lottery ticket and won nothing. So I could win only five hundred dollars now, and that would be just half of what I needed.

Ten minutes later, I scratched my other lottery ticket and won a free ticket, a small consolation and one more chance to win money.

I walked back to Kay.

"Jackson Jackson," she said. "Have you come back to claim my heart?"

"I won a free ticket," I said.

"Just like a man," she said. "You love money and power more than you love me."

"It's true," I said. "And I'm sorry it's true."

She gave me another scratch ticket, and I carried it outside. I liked to scratch my tickets in private. Hopeful and sad, I scratched that third ticket and won real money. I carried it back inside to Kay.

"I won a hundred dollars," I said.

She examined the ticket and laughed. "That's a fortune," she said and counted out five twenties. Our fingertips touched as she handed me the money. I felt electric and constant.

"Thank you," I said and gave her one of the bills.

"I can't take that," she said. "It's your money."

"No, it's tribal. It's an Indian thing. When you win, you're supposed to share with your family."

"I'm not your family."

"Yes, you are."

She smiled. She kept the money. With eighty dollars in my pocket, I said good-bye to my dear Kay and walked out into the cold night air.

8:00 P.M.

I wanted to share the good news with Junior. I walked back to him, but he was gone. I later heard he had hitchhiked down to Portland, Oregon, and died of exposure in an alley behind the Hilton Hotel.

9:00 P.M.

Lonely for Indians, I carried my eighty dollars over to Big Heart's in South Downtown. Big Heart's is an all-Indian bar. Nobody knows how or why Indians migrate to one bar and turn it into an official Indian bar. But Big Heart's has been an Indian bar for twenty-three years. It used to be way up on Aurora Avenue, but a crazy Lummi Indian burned that one down, and the owners moved to the new location, a few blocks south of Safeco Field.

I walked inside Big Heart's and counted fifteen Indians, eight men and seven women. I didn't know any of them, but Indians like to belong, so we all pretended to be cousins.

"How much for whiskey shots?" I asked the bartender, a fat white guy.

"You want the bad stuff or the badder stuff?"

"As bad as you got."

"One dollar a shot."

I laid my eighty dollars on the bar top.

"All right," I said. "Me and all my cousins here are going to be drinking eighty shots. How many is that apiece?"

"Counting you," a woman shouted from behind me, "that's five shots for everybody."

I turned to look at her. She was a chubby and pale Indian sitting with a tall and skinny Indian man.

"All right, math genius," I said to her and then shouted for the whole bar to hear. "Five drinks for everybody!"

All of the other Indians rushed the bar, but I sat with the mathematician and her skinny friend. We took our time with our whiskey shots.

"What's your tribe?" I asked them.

"I'm Duwamish," she said. "And he's Crow."

"You're a long way from Montana," I said to him.

"I'm Crow," he said. "I flew here."

"What's your name?" I asked them.

"I'm Irene Muse," she said. "And this is Honey Boy."

She shook my hand hard, but he offered his hand like I was supposed to kiss it. So I kissed it. He giggled and blushed as well as a dark-skinned Crow can blush.

"You're one of them two-spirits, aren't you?" I asked him.

"I love women," he said. "And I love men."

"Sometimes both at the same time," Irene said.

We laughed.

"Man," I said to Honey Boy. "So you must have about eight or nine spirits going on inside of you, enit?"

"Sweetie," he said, "I'll be whatever you want me to be."

"Oh, no," Irene said. "Honey Boy is falling in love."

"It has nothing to do with love," he said.

We laughed.

"Wow," I said. "I'm flattered, Honey Boy, but I don't play on your team."

"Never say never," he said.

"You better be careful," Irene said. "Honey Boy knows all sorts of magic. He always makes straight boys fall for him."

"Honey Boy," I said, "you can try to seduce me. And Irene, you can try with him. But my heart belongs to a woman named Kay."

"Is your Kay a virgin?" Honey Boy asked.

We laughed.

We drank our whiskey shots until they were gone. But the other Indians bought me more whiskey shots because I'd been so generous with my money. Honey Boy pulled out his credit card, and I drank and sailed on that plastic boat.

After a dozen shots, I asked Irene to dance. And she refused. But Honey Boy shuffled over to the jukebox, dropped in a quarter, and selected Willie Nelson's "Help Me Make It Through the Night." As Irene and I sat at the table and laughed and drank more whiskey, Honey Boy danced a slow circle around us and sang along with Willie.

"Are you serenading me?" I asked him.

He kept singing and dancing.

"Are you serenading me?" I asked him again.

"He's going to put a spell on you," Irene said.

I leaned over the table, spilling a few drinks, and kissed Irene hard. She kissed me back.

10:00 P.M.

Irene pushed me into the women's bathroom, into a stall, shut the door behind us, and shoved her hand down my pants. She was short, so I had to lean over to kiss her. I grabbed and squeezed her everywhere I could reach, and she was wonderfully fat, and every part of her body felt like a large, warm, and soft breast.

MIDNIGHT

Nearly blind with alcohol, I stood alone at the bar and swore I'd been standing in the bathroom with Irene only a minute ago.

"One more shot!" I yelled at the bartender.

"You've got no more money!" he yelled.

"Somebody buy me a drink!" I shouted.

"They've got no more money!"

"Where's Irene and Honey Boy?"

"Long gone!"

2:00 A.M.

"Closing time!" the bartender shouted at the three or four Indians still drinking hard after a long hard day of drinking. Indian alcoholics are either sprinters or marathon runners.

"Where's Irene and Honey Bear?" I asked.

"They've been gone for hours," the bartender said.

"Where'd they go?"

"I told you a hundred times, I don't know."

"What am I supposed to do?"

"It's closing time. I don't care where you go, but you're not staying here."

"You are an ungrateful bastard. I've been good to you."

"You don't leave right now, I'm going to kick your ass."

"Come on, I know how to fight."

He came for me. I don't remember what happened after that.

4:00 A.M.

I emerged from the blackness and discovered myself walking behind a big warehouse. I didn't know where I was. My face hurt. I touched my nose and decided it might be broken. Exhausted and cold, I pulled a plastic tarp from a truck bed, wrapped it around me like a faithful lover, and fell asleep in the dirt.

6:00 A.M.

Somebody kicked me in the ribs. I opened my eyes and looked up at a white cop.

"Jackson," said the cop. "Is that you?"

"Officer Williams," I said. He was a good cop with a sweet tooth. He'd given me hundreds of candy bars over the years. I wonder if he knew I was diabetic.

"What the hell are you doing here?" he asked.

"I was cold and sleepy," I said. "So I laid down."

"You dumb-ass, you passed out on the railroad tracks."

I sat up and looked around. I was lying on the railroad tracks. Dockworkers stared at me. I should have been a railroad-track pizza, a double Indian pepperoni with extra cheese. Sick and scared, I leaned over and puked whiskey.

"What the hell's wrong with you?" Officer Williams asked. "You've never been this stupid."

"It's my grandmother," I said. "She died."

"I'm sorry, man. When did she die?"

"1972."

"And you're killing yourself now?"

"I've been killing myself ever since she died."

He shook his head. He was sad for me. Like I said, he was a good cop.

"And somebody beat the hell out of you," he said. "You remember who?"

"Mr. Grief and I went a few rounds."

"It looks like Mr. Grief knocked you out."

"Mr. Grief always wins."

"Come on," he said, "let's get you out of here."

He helped me stand and led me over to his squad car. He put me in the back. "You throw up in there," he said, "and you're cleaning it up."

"That's fair," I said.

He walked around the car and sat in the driver's seat. "I'm taking you over to detox," he said.

"No, man, that place is awful," I said. "It's full of drunk Indians."

We laughed. He drove away from the docks.

"I don't know how you guys do it," he said.

"What guys?" I asked.

"You Indians. How the hell do you laugh so much? I just picked your ass off the railroad tracks, and you're making jokes. Why the hell do you do that?"

"The two funniest tribes I've ever been around are Indians and Jews, so I guess that says something about the inherent humor of genocide."

We laughed.

"Listen to you, Jackson. You're so smart. Why the hell are you on the streets?"

"Give me a thousand dollars, and I'll tell you."

"You bet I'd give you a thousand dollars if I knew you'd straighten up your life."

He meant it. He was the second-best cop I'd ever known.

"You're a good cop," I said.

"Come on, Jackson," he said. "Don't blow smoke up my ass."

"No, really, you remind me of my grandfather."

"Yeah, that's what you Indians always tell me."

"No, man, my grandfather was a tribal cop. He was a good cop. He never arrested people. He took care of them. Just like you."

"I've arrested hundreds of scumbags, Jackson. And I've shot a couple in the ass."

"It don't matter. You're not a killer."

"I didn't kill them. I killed their asses. I'm an ass-killer."

We drove through downtown. The missions and shelters had already released their overnighters. Sleepy homeless men and women stood on corners and stared up at the gray sky. It was the morning after the night of the living dead.

"Did you ever get scared?" I asked Officer Williams.

"What do you mean?"

"I mean, being a cop, is it scary?"

He thought about that for a while. He contemplated it. I liked that about him.

"I guess I try not to think too much about being afraid," he said. "If you think about fear, then you'll be afraid. The job is boring most of the time. Just driving and looking into dark corners, you know, and seeing nothing. But then things get heavy. You're chasing somebody or fighting them or walking around a dark house and you just know some crazy guy is hiding around a corner, and hell yes, it's scary."

"My grandfather was killed in the line of duty," I said.

"I'm sorry. How'd it happen?"

I knew he'd listen closely to my story.

"He worked on the reservation. Everybody knew everybody. It was safe. We aren't like those crazy Sioux or Apache or any of those other warrior tribes. There's only been three murders on my reservation in the last hundred years."

"That is safe."

"Yeah, we Spokane, we're passive, you know? We're mean with words. And we'll cuss out anybody. But we don't shoot people. Or stab them. Not much, anyway."

"So what happened to your grandfather?"

"This man and his girlfriend were fighting down by Little Falls."

"Domestic dispute. Those are the worst."

"Yeah, but this guy was my grandfather's brother. My great-uncle."

"Oh, no."

"Yeah, it was awful. My grandfather just strolled into the house. He'd been there a thousand times. And his brother and his girlfriend were all drunk and beating on each other. And my grandfather stepped between them just like he'd done a hundred times before. And the girlfriend tripped or something. She fell down and hit her head and started crying. And my grandfather knelt down beside her to make sure she was all right. And for some reason, my great-uncle reached down, pulled my grandfather's pistol out of the holster, and shot him in the head."

"That's terrible. I'm sorry."

"Yeah, my great-uncle could never figure out why he did it. He went to prison forever, you know, and he always wrote these long letters. Like fifty pages of tiny little handwriting. And he was always trying to figure out why he did it. He'd write and write and write and try to figure it out. He never did. It's a great big mystery."

"Do you remember your grandfather?"

"A little bit. I remember the funeral. My grandmother wouldn't let them bury him. My father had to drag her away from the grave."

"I don't know what to say."

"I don't, either."

We stopped in front of the detox center.

"We're here," Officer Williams said.

"I can't go in there," I said.

"You have to."

"Please, no. They'll keep me for twenty-four hours. And then it will be too late."

"Too late for what?"

I told him about my grandmother's regalia and the deadline for buying it back.

"If it was stolen," he said, "then you need to file reports. I'll investigate it myself. If that thing is really your grandmother's, I'll get it back for you. Legally."

"No," I said. "That's not fair. The pawnbroker didn't know it was stolen. And besides, I'm on a mission here. I want to be a hero, you know? I want to win it back like a knight."

"That's romantic crap."

"It might be. But I care about it. It's been a long time since I really cared about something."

Officer Williams turned around in his seat and stared at me. He studied me.

"I'll give you some money," he said. "I don't have much. Only thirty bucks. I'm short until payday. And it's not enough to get back the regalia. But it's something."

"I'll take it," I said.

"I'm giving it to you because I believe in what you believe. I'm hoping, and I don't know why I'm hoping it, but I hope you can turn thirty bucks into a thousand somehow."

"I believe in magic."

"I believe you'll take my money and get drunk on it."

"Then why are you giving it to me?"

"There ain't no such thing as an atheist cop."

"Sure there is."

"Yeah, well, I'm not an atheist cop."

He let me out of the car, handed me two fives and a twenty, and shook my hand. "Take care of yourself, Jackson," he said. "Stay off the railroad tracks."

"I'll try," I said.

He drove away. Carrying my money, I headed back toward the water.

8:00 A.M.

On the wharf, those three Aleut men still waited on the wooden bench.

"Have you seen your ship?" I asked.

"Seen a lot of ships," the elder Aleut said. "But not our ship."

I sat on the bench with them. We sat in silence for a long time. I wondered whether we would fossilize if we sat there long enough.

I thought about my grandmother. I'd never seen her dance in her regalia. More than anything, I wished I'd seen her dance at a powwow.

"Do you guys know any songs?" I asked the Aleuts.

"I know all of Hank Williams,"[6] the elder Aleut said.

"How about Indian songs?"

"Hank Williams is Indian."

"How about sacred songs?"

[6]American singer and songwriter (1923–1953).

"Hank Williams is sacred."

"I'm talking about ceremonial songs, you know, religious ones. The songs you sing back home when you're wishing and hoping."

"What are you wishing and hoping for?"

"I'm wishing my grandmother was still alive."

"Every song I know is about that."

"Well, sing me as many as you can."

The Aleuts sang their strange and beautiful songs. I listened. They sang about my grandmother and their grandmothers. They were lonely for the cold and snow. I was lonely for everybody.

10:00 A.M.

After the Aleuts finished their last song, we sat in silence. Indians are good at silence.

"Was that the last song?" I asked.

"We sang all the ones we could," the elder Aleut said. "All the others are just for our people."

I understood. We Indians have to keep our secrets. And these Aleuts were so secretive that they didn't refer to themselves as Indians.

"Are you guys hungry?" I asked.

They looked at one another and communicated without talking.

"We could eat," the elder Aleut said.

11:00 A.M.

The Aleuts and I walked over to Mother's Kitchen, a greasy diner in the International District. I knew they served homeless Indians who'd lucked in to money.

"Four for breakfast?" the waitress asked when we stepped inside.

"Yes, we're very hungry," the elder Aleut said.

She sat us in a booth near the kitchen. I could smell the food cooking. My stomach growled.

"You guys want separate checks?" the waitress asked.

"No, I'm paying for it," I said.

"Aren't you the generous one," she said.

"Don't do that," I said.

"Do what?" she asked.

"Don't ask me rhetorical questions. They scare me."

She looked puzzled, and then she laughed.

"Okay, Professor," she said. "I'll only ask you real questions from now on."

"Thank you."

"What do you guys want to eat?"

"That's the best question anybody can ask anybody," I said.

"How much money you got?" she asked.

"Another good question," I said. "I've got twenty-five dollars I can spend. Bring us all the breakfast you can, plus your tip."

She knew the math.

"All right, that's four specials and four coffees and fifteen percent for me."

The Aleuts and I waited in silence. Soon enough, the waitress returned and poured us four coffees, and we sipped at them until she returned again with four plates of food. Eggs, bacon, toast, hash-brown potatoes. It is amazing how much food you can buy for so little money.

Grateful, we feasted.

NOON

I said farewell to the Aleuts and walked toward the pawnshop. I later heard the Aleuts had waded into the saltwater near Dock 47 and disappeared. Some Indians said the Aleuts walked on the water and headed north. Other Indians saw the Aleuts drown. I don't know what happened to them.

I looked for the pawnshop and couldn't find it. I swear it wasn't located in the place where it had been before. I walked twenty or thirty blocks looking for the pawnshop, turned corners and bisected intersections, looked up its name in the phone books, and asked people walking past me if they'd ever heard of it. But that pawnshop seemed to have sailed away from me like a ghost ship. I wanted to cry. Right when I'd given up, when I turned one last corner and thought I might die if I didn't find that pawnshop, there it was, located in a space I swore it hadn't been filling up a few minutes before.

I walked inside and greeted the pawnbroker, who looked a little younger than he had before.

"It's you," he said.

"Yes, it's me," I said.

"Jackson Jackson."

"That is my name."

"Where are your friends?"

"They went traveling. But it's okay. Indians are everywhere."

"Do you have my money?"

"How much do you need again?" I asked and hoped the price had changed.

"Nine hundred and ninety-nine dollars."

It was still the same price. Of course it was the same price. Why would it change?

"I don't have that," I said.

"What do you have?"

"Five dollars."

I set the crumpled Lincoln on the countertop. The pawnbroker studied it.

"Is that the same five dollars from yesterday?"

"No, it's different."

He thought about the possibilities.

"Did you work hard for this money?" he asked.

"Yes," I said.

He closed his eyes and thought harder about the possibilities. Then he stepped into his back room and returned with my grandmother's regalia.

"Take it," he said and held it out to me.

"I don't have the money."

"I don't want your money."

"But I wanted to win it."

"You did win it. Now, take it before I change my mind."

Do you know how many good men live in this world? Too many to count!

I took my grandmother's regalia and walked outside. I knew that solitary yellow bead was part of me. I knew I was that yellow bead in part. Outside, I wrapped myself in my grandmother's regalia and breathed her in. I stepped off the sidewalk and into the intersection. Pedestrians stopped. Cars stopped. The city stopped. They all watched me dance with my grandmother. I was my grandmother, dancing.

2003

DEFENDING WALT WHITMAN

Basketball is like this for young Indian boys, all arms and legs
and serious stomach muscles. Every body is brown!
These are the twentieth-century warriors who will never kill,
although a few sat quietly in the deserts of Kuwait,
waiting for orders to do something, to do something.

God, there is nothing as beautiful as a jumpshot
on a reservation summer basketball court
where the ball is moist with sweat,
and makes a sound when it swishes through the net
that causes Walt Whitman to weep because it is so perfect.

There are veterans of foreign wars here
although their bodies are still dominated
by collarbones and knees, although their bodies still respond
in the ways that bodies are supposed to respond when we are young.
Every body is brown! Look there, that boy can run
up and down this court forever. He can leap for a rebound
with his back arched like a salmon, all meat and bone
synchronized, magnetic, as if the court were a river,
as if the rim were a dam, as if the air were a ladder
leading the Indian boy toward home.

Some of the Indian boys still wear their military hair cuts
while a few have let their hair grow back.
It will never be the same as it was before!
One Indian boy has never cut his hair, not once, and he braids it
into wild patterns that do not measure anything.
He is just a boy with too much time on his hands.
Look at him. He wants to play this game in bare feet.

God, the sun is so bright! There is no place like this.
Walt Whitman stretches his calf muscles

on the sidelines. He has the next game.
His huge beard is ridiculous on the reservation.
Some body throws a crazy pass and Walt Whitman catches it
with quick hands. He brings the ball close to his nose
and breathes in all of its smells: leather, brown skin, sweat,
black hair, burning oil, twisted ankle, long drink of warm water,
gunpowder, pine tree. Walt Whitman squeezes the ball tightly.
He wants to run. He hardly has the patience to wait for his turn.
"What's the score?" he asks. He asks, "What's the score?"

Basketball is like this for Walt Whitman. He watches these Indian boys
as if they were the last bodies on earth. Every body is brown!
Walt Whitman shakes because he believes in God.
Walt Whitman dreams of the Indian boy who will defend him,
trapping him in the corner, all flailing arms and legs
and legendary stomach muscles. Walt Whitman shakes
because he believes in God. Walt Whitman dreams
of the first jumpshot he will take, the ball arcing clumsily
from his fingers, striking the rim so hard that it sparks.
Walt Whitman shakes because he believes in God.
Walt Whitman closes his eyes. He is a small man and his beard
is ludicrous on the reservation, absolutely insane.
His beard makes the Indian boys righteously laugh. His beard
frightens the smallest Indian boys. His beard tickles the skin
of the Indian boys who dribble past him. His beard, his beard!

God, there is beauty in every body. Walt Whitman stands
at center court while the Indian boys run from basket to basket.
Walt Whitman cannot tell the difference between
offense and defense. He does not care if he touches the ball.
Half of the Indian boys wear t-shirts damp with sweat
and the other half are bareback, skin slick and shiny.
There is no place like this. Walt Whitman smiles.
Walt Whitman shakes. This game belongs to him.

1995

Reference Works, Bibliographies

Abrahams, Roger, and Szwed, John. *Afro-American Folk Culture,* 1978.

Alexander, Harriet. *American and British Poetry: A Guide to the Criticism, 1979–1990,* 1996.

Andrews, William L., and others, eds. *The Oxford Companion to African American Literature,* 1997.

Altick, Richard D., and Wright, Andrew. *Selective Bibliography for the Study of English and American Literature,* 6th edition, 1979.

Bain, Robert, and Flora, Joseph M. *Fifty Southern Writers Before 1900,* 1987.

———. *Fifty Southern Writers After 1900,* 1987.

Beidler, Peter G., and Egge, Marion F. *The American Indian in Short Fiction: An Annotated Bibliography,* 1979.

Bercovitch, Sacvan, ed. *The Cambridge History of American Literature,* 2 vols., 1994.

Benardete, Jane, ed. *American Realism,* 1972.

Biblowitz, Iris, ed. *Women and Literature: An Annotated Bibliography of Women Writers,* 3rd edition, 1976.

Blanck, Jacob. *Bibliography of American Literature,* Vols. I–, 1955–.

Bordman, Gerald. *The Oxford Companion to American Theatre,* 1984.

Brown, Julie, ed. *American Short Story Writers,* 1995.

Bryer, J. R., ed. *Sixteen Modern American Authors: A Survey of Research and Criticism,* 1973.

Burke, W. J., and Howe, W. D. *American Authors and Books,* revised by Irving Weiss, 1962.

Charters, Ann, ed. *The Beats: Literary Bohemians in Postwar America,* 2 parts, 1983.

Clark, H. H. *American Literature: Poe Through Garland,* 1971.

Colonnese, Tom, and Owens, Louise, eds. *American Indian Novelists: An Annotated Critical Bibliography,* 1985.

Davidson, Cathy, and others, eds. *The Oxford Companion to Women's Writing in the United States,* 1995.

Davis, R. B. *American Literature Through Bryant,* 1969.

Davis, Thadious M., and Harris, Trudier, eds. *Afro-American Fiction Writers after 1955,* 1984.

———. *Afro-American Writers after 1955: Dramatists and Prose Writers,* 1985.

Duke, Maurice, and others, eds. *American Women Writers: Bibliographical Essays,* 1983.

Erisman, Fred, and Etulain, Richard, eds. *Fifty Western Writers: A Bio-Bibliographical Sourcebook,* 1982.

Etheridge, James M., and Kapala, Barbara, eds. *Contemporary Authors: A Bio-Bibliographical Guide . . .,* 1962– (a continuing series).

Etulain, Richard. *A Bibliographical Guide to the Study of Western American Literature,* 1982.

Fabre, Genevieve. *Afro-American Poetry and Drama, 1760–1975,* 1979.

Flora, Joseph M. and Bain, Robert. *Contemporary Fiction Writers of the South: A Bio-Bibliographical Sourcebook,* 1993.

French, William P., ed. *Afro-American Poetry and Drama, 1760–1975,* 1979.
Frye, Northrop, and others, eds. *The Harper Handbook to Literature,* 2nd edition, 1997.
Gerstenberger, Donna, and Hendrick, George. *The American Novel: A Checklist of Twentieth-Century Criticism on Novels Written Since 1789,* 2 vols., 1961, 1970.
Gohdes, Clarence. *Literature and Theater in the States and Regions of the U.S.A.: An Historical Bibliography,* 1967.
Gohdes, Clarence, and Marovitz, Sanford. *Bibliographical Guide to the Study of the Literature of the U.S.A.,* 5th edition, 1983.
Gossin, Pamela. *Encyclopedia of Literature and Science,* 2002.
Gray, Jeffrey, McCorkle, James, and Balkun, Mary McAleer, eds. *The Greenwood Encyclopedia of American Poets and Poetry,* 5 vols., 2006.
Greiner, Donald J., ed. *American Poets Since World War II,* 2 parts, 1980.
Gwynn, R. S., ed. *American Poets Since World War II,* Second Series, 1991.
Handlin, Oscar, and others. *Harvard Guide to American History,* 1954.
Hanna, Archibald. *A Mirror for the Nation: An Annotated Bibliography of American Social Fiction,* 1901–1950, 1985.
Harnes, James. *Literary Research Guide: An Annotated Listing of Reference Sources in English Literary Studies,* 4th edition, 2002.
Harold, Jan. *American Folklore: An Encyclopedia,* 1996.
Harris, Trudier, and Davis, Thadious M., eds. *Afro-American Poets Since 1955,* 1985.
Harris, Trudier, ed. *Afro-American Writers Before the Harlem Renaissance,* 1986.
———. *Afro-American Writers from the Harlem Renaissance to 1940,* 1987.
Hart, J. D., and Leininger, Philip. *The Oxford Companion to American Literature,* 6th edition, 1995.
Hatch, James V., and Abdullah, Omanii. *Black Playwrights, 1823–1977,* 1977.
Havelice, Patricia. *Index to American Author Bibliographies,* 1971.
Hawkins-Dady, Mark. *Reader's Guide to Literature in English,* 1996.
Helterman, Jeffrey, and Layman, Richard, eds. *American Novelists Since World War II,* 1978.
Herzberg, M. J., and others. *The Reader's Encyclopedia of American Literature,* 1961.
Hoffman, Daniel, ed. *Harvard Guide to Contemporary American Writing,* 1979.
Holman, C. H. *The American Novel Through Henry James,* 1966.
Holman, C. H., and Harmon, William, eds. *A Handbook to Literature,* 6th edition, 1992.
Howard, Sharon M. *African American Women Fiction Writers, 1859–1986,* 1989.
Inge, M. Thomas, and others, eds. *Black American Writers,* 2 vols., 1978.
Jackson, Blyden, and Rubin, Louis D., Jr., eds. *Black Poetry in America,* 1974.
Jehlen, Myra, and Warner, Michael, eds. *The English Literatures of America, 1500–1800,* 1997.
Jones, H. M., and Ludwig, R. M. *Guide to American Literature and Its Backgrounds Since 1890,* 4th edition, 1972.
Jordan, Casper LeRoy. *Bibliographical Guide to African-American Women Writers,* 1993.
Kanellos, Nicolás. *Biographical Dictionary of Hispanic Literature in the United States,* 1989.
Kibler, James E., Jr., ed. *American Novelists Since World War II,* Second Series, 1980.
Kimbel, Bobby Ellen, ed. *American Short-Story Writers Before 1880,* 1988.

———. *American Short-Story Writers, 1880–1910,* 1988.
———. *American Short-Story Writers, 1910–1945,* Second Series, 1991.
Kolb, Harold. *A Field Guide to the Study of American Literature,* 1976.
Koster, Donald. *American Literature and Language: A Guide to Information Sources,* 1974.
Kunitz, S. J., and Haycraft, Howard, eds. *American Authors, 1600–1900,* 1944.
———. *Twentieth Century Authors,* 1942. 1st supplement, 1955.
Kuntz, Joseph. *Poetry Explication,* 1953. Revised 1962.
———. *American Literature: A Study and Research Guide,* 1976.
Larchman, Marvin. *A Reader's Guide to the American Novel of Detection,* 1993.
Leary, Lewis. *Articles on American Literature, 1900–1950,* 1954.
———. *Articles on American Literature, 1950–1967,* 1970.
———. *Articles on American Literature, 1968–1975,* 1979.
Littlefield, Daniel L., ed. *A Biobibliography of Native American Writers, 1771–1924,* 1981.
———. *A Biobibliography of Native American Writers, 1772–1924: A Supplement,* 1985.
Lomeli, Francisco A. and Shirley, Carl R., eds. *Chicano Writers,* First Series, 1989.
Long, E. H. *American Drama from Its Beginning to the Present,* 1970.
Ludwig, Richard M., ed. *Bibliographical Supplement, Literary History of the United States,* 4th edition, revised, 1974.
Ludwig, Richard M., and Nault, Clifford A., Jr. *Annals of American Literature, 1602–1983,* 1986.
MacNicholas, John, ed. *Twentieth-Century American Dramatists,* 2 parts, 1981.
Mainiero, Lina. *American Women Writers: A Critical Reference Guide from Colonial Times to the Present,* 4 vols., 1979–1982.
Malkoff, Karl. *Crowell's Handbook of Contemporary American Poetry,* 1973.
Margolies, Edward, and Bakish, David. *Afro-American Fiction, 1853–1976,* 1979.
Martine, James J., ed. *American Novelists, 1910–1945,* 3 parts, 1981.
Martinez, Julio A., and Lomeli, Francisco A., eds. *Chicano Literature, A Reference Guide,* 1985.
Millet, F. B. *Contemporary American Authors: A Critical Survey and 219 Biographies,* 1940.
Morris, R. B., ed. *Encyclopedia of American History,* 1953.
Myerson, Joel, ed. *The American Renaissance in New England,* 1978.
Myerson, Joel, and Helterman, J., eds. *Dictionary of Literary Biography,* 9 vols., 1978–1983.
Nadel, I. B. *Jewish Writers of North America: A Guide to Information Sources,* 1981.
Nevius, Blake. *The American Novel: Sinclair Lewis to the Present,* 1970.
Nilon, Charles. *Bibliography of Bibliographies of American Literature,* 1970.
Page, James, and Min Roh, Joe. *Selected Black American, African, and Caribbean Authors: A Bio-Bibliography,* 1985.
Palmer, Helen, and Dyson, Jane. *American Drama Criticism,* 1967. Supplement 1970.
Parini, Jay, ed. *The Columbia History of American Poetry,* 1993.
Parker, Patricia. *Early American Fiction: A Reference Guide,* 1984.
Perkins, George, and others, eds. *Benét's Reader's Encyclopedia of American Literature,* 1991.
Perry, Margaret. *The Harlem Renaissance: An Annotated Bibliography,* 1982.
Pizer, Donald, ed. *Documents of American Realism and Naturalism,* 1998.

Pizer, Donald, ed. *The Cambridge Companion to American Realism and Naturalism, Howells to London,* 1995.
Pizer, Donald, and Harbert, Earl N., eds. *American Realists and Naturalists,* 1982.
Quartermain, Peter, ed. *American Poets, 1880–1945,* First Series, 1986.
———. *American Poets, 1880–1945,* Second Series, 1986.
———. *American Poets, 1880–1945,* Third Series, 1987.
Rawlings, Peter, ed. *Americans on Fiction, 1776–1900,* 3 vols., 2002.
Reardon, Joan, and Thorsen, Kristine A. *Poetry by American Women, 1900–1975,* 1979.
Rees, Robert, and Harbert, Earl, eds. *Fifteen American Authors Before 1900,* 1984.
Rock, Roger. *The Native American in American Literature: A Selectively Annotated Bibliography,* 1985.
Rogal, Samuel. *A Chronological Outline of American Literature,* 1987.
Rood, Karen L., and others, eds. *Dictionary of Literary Biography Yearbook: 1980,* 1981– (a continuing annual series).
Rubin, Louis, ed. *A Bibliographical Guide to the Study of Southern Literature,* 1969.
Ruoff, A. LaVonne Brown. *American Indian Literatures: An Introduction, Bibliographic Review, and Selected Bibliography,* 1990.
Rush, T. G., and others, eds. *Black American Writers Past and Present: A Biographical and Bibliographical Dictionary,* 1975.
Sabin, Joseph, and others. *A Dictionary of Books Relating to America from Its Discovery to the Present Time,* 29 vols., 1868–1936.
Salzman, Jack, ed. *Cambridge Handbook of American Literature,* 1986.
Schweik, Robert, and Riesner, Dieter. *Reference Sources in English and American Literature,* 1977.
Sternlicht, Sanford. *A Reader's Guide to Modern American Drama,* 2002.
Stringer, Jenny, ed. *Oxford Companion to Twentieth-Century Literature in English,* 1996.
Thurston, Jarvis, and others. *Short Fiction Criticism,* 1960.
Tompkins, Jane. *Sensational Designs: The Cultural Work of American Fiction, 1790–1860,* 1985.
Trachtenberg, Stanley, ed. *American Humorists, 1800–1950,* 2 parts, 1982.
Turner, Darwin. *Afro-American Writers,* 1970.
Tyler, Gary. *Drama Criticism,* 1966.
Ungar, Leonard. *American Writers: A Collection of Literary Biographies,* 8 vols., 1974–1981.
Vinson, James, ed. *Contemporary Dramatists,* 2nd edition, 1977.
———. *Contemporary Novelists,* 3rd edition, 1980.
———. *Contemporary Poets,* 3rd edition, 1980.
Vinson, James, and Kirkpatrick, D. L. *Twentieth-Century Western Writers,* 1982.
Vrana, Stan. *Interviews and Conversations with Twentieth-Century Authors Writing in English: An Index,* 1982.
Walker, Warren, *Twentieth-Century Short Story Explication,* 3rd edition, 1977; Supplement I, 1980; Supplement II, 1983.
Weixlmann, Joe. *American Short-Fiction Criticism and Scholarship, 1959–1977,* 1982.
White, Barbara A. *American Women Writers: An Annotated Bibliography of Criticism,* 1977.
William, Jerry. *Southern Literature, 1968–1975: A Checklist of Scholarship,* 1978.

Wilmeth, Don B., and Miller, Tice, eds. *Cambridge Guide to American Theatre,* 1993.

Wolfreys, Julian, and others. *The Continuum Encyclopedia of Modern Criticism and Theory,* 2002.

Woodress, James. *Dissertations in American Literature, 1891–1966,* 1968.

———. ed. *Eight American Authors: A Review of Research and Criticism,* revised edition, 1971.

Woodress, James, and others, eds. *American Literary Scholarship: An Annual,* 1965–.

Wright, Lyle. *American Fiction, 1774–1850,* 1948. 2nd edition, 1969.

———. *American Fiction, 1851–1875,* 1957.

———. *American Fiction, 1876–1900,* 1966.

Criticism, Literary and Cultural History

Aaron, Daniel. *Writers on the Left: Episodes in American Literary Communism,* 1961.

———. *The Unwritten War: American Writers and the Civil War,* 1973.

Ahnebrink, Lars. *The Beginnings of Naturalism in American Fiction,* 1961.

Aldridge, John. *After the Lost Generation: A Critical Study of the Writers of Two Wars,* 1951.

Aldridge, Owen. *Early American Literature: A Comparatist Approach,* 1983.

Allen, G. W. *American Prosody,* 1935.

Altieri, Charles. *Enlarging the Temple: New Directions in American Poetry During the 1960s,* 1979.

Anderson, Quentin. *The Imperial Self,* 1971.

Auchincloss, Louis. *Pioneers and Caretakers: A Study of Nine American Women Novelists,* 1965.

Baumbach, Jonathan. *The Landscape of Nightmare: Studies in the Contemporary American Novel,* 1965.

Baym, Nina. *American Women Writers and the Work of History,* 1995.

Beach, J. W. *American Fiction: 1920–1940,* 1941.

Bell, Bernard W. *The Afro-American Novel and Its Tradition,* 1988.

Bercovitch, Sacvan, ed. *The Revaluation of Puritanism,* 1974.

———. *The Puritan Origins of the American Self,* 1975.

Berthoff, Warner. *The Ferment of Realism: American Literature, 1884–1919,* 1965.

———. *A Literature Without Qualities: American Writing Since 1945,* 1979.

Bewley, Marius. *The Complex Fate,* 1954.

———. *The Eccentric Design,* 1959.

Bigsby, C. W. E. *A Critical Introduction to Twentieth-Century American Drama,* Vol. I, 1900–1940, 1982.

Blair, Walter, ed. *Native American Humor,* 2nd edition, 1960.

Bogan, Louise. *Achievement in American Poetry, 1900–1950,* 1951.

Bone, R. A. *The Negro Novel in America,* revised edition, 1965.

Bradbury, John. *Renaissance in the South,* 1963.

Bradbury, Malcolm. *The Modern American Novel,* 1983.

Breslin, James. *From Modern to Contemporary American Poetry, 1945–1965,* 1984.

Bridgman, Richard. *The Colloquial Style in America,* 1966.

Brooks, Peter. *Reading for the Plot: Design and Intention in Narrative,* 1985.

Brooks, Van Wyck. *The Flowering of New England, 1815–1865,* 1937.

———. *New England: Indian Summer, 1865–1915,* 1940.

———. *The Times of Melville and Whitman,* 1947.

———. *The Confident Years: 1885–1915,* 1955.

Brown, H. R. *The Sentimental Novel in America, 1789–1860,* 1940.

Brown, Sterling. *Negro Poetry and Drama,* 1937.

Buell, Lawrence. *Literary Transcendentalism,* 1973.

———. *New England Literary Culture,* 1986.
Byerman, Keith. *Fingering the Jagged Grain: Tradition and Form in Recent Black Fiction,* 1985.
Cady, E. H. *The Light of Common Day: Realism in American Fiction,* 1971.
Canby, H. S. *Classic Americans,* 1958.
Cargill, Oscar. *Intellectual America: Ideas on the March,* 1941.
Carter, Everett. *The American Idea,* 1977.
Cassuto, Leonard. *The Inhuman Race: The Racial Grotesque in American Literature,* 1996.
Chase, Richard. *The American Novel and Its Tradition,* 1957.
Clark, H. H., ed. *Transitions in American Literary History,* 1954.
Commager, H. S. *The American Mind,* 1950.
Cowie, Alexander. *The Rise of the American Novel,* 1948.
Cowley, Malcolm. *After the Genteel Tradition: American Writers, 1910–1930,* revised edition, 1964.
———. *A Second Flowering: Works and Days of the Lost Generation,* 1973.
Cunliffe, Marcus. *The Literature of the United States,* 1967, 1984.
Curti, Merle. *The Growth of American Thought,* 3rd edition, 1964.
Davidson, Cathy. *Revolution and the Word: The Rise of the Novel in America,* 1986; 2nd edition, 2004.
Davis, Richard. *Intellectual Life in the Colonial South, 1585–1763,* 1977.
Davis, Thadious, and Harris, Trudier. *Afro-American Literary Critics: An Introduction,* 1984.
Dekker, George. *The American Historical Romance,* 1988.
Dembo, L. S. *Conceptions of Reality in Modern American Poetry,* 1966.
Drake, William. *The First Wave: Women Poets in America, 1915–1945,* 1987.
Edel, Leon. *The Psychological Novel, 1900–1950,* 1955.
Eisdein, Gregory, *Literature and Humanitarian Reform in the Civil War Era,* 1996.
Eisinger, Chester. *Fiction of the Forties,* 1963.
Elder, John. *Imagining the Earth: Poetry and the Vision of Nature,* 1985.
Elliott, Emory. *American Colonial Writers, 1735–1781,* 1984.
———. *American Writers of the Early Republic,* 1984.
———. *Colonial Writers, 1606–1734,* 1984.
———. *The Columbia History of the American Novel: New Views,* 1991.
———. *The Cambridge Introduction to Early American Literature,* 2002.
Elliott, Emory, and others, eds. *Columbia Literary History of the United States,* 1988.
Emerson, Everett, ed. *Major Writers of Early American Literature,* 1972.
———. ed. *American Literature, 1764–1789: The Revolutionary Years,* 1977.
———. *Puritanism in America, 1620–1750,* 1977.
Fabre, Genevieve. *Afro-American Poetry and Drama, 1760–1975,* 1979.
Falk, Robert. *The Victorian Mode in American Fiction, 1865–1885,* 1965.
Feidelson, Charles. *Symbolism and American Literature,* 1959.
Feller, Daniel. *The Jacksonian Promise: America 1815–1840,* 1995.
Felperin, Howard. *Beyond Deconstruction: The Uses and Abuses of Literary Theory,* 1985.
Ferguson, Robert. *Reading the Early Republic,* 2004.
Fiedler, Leslie. *Love and Death in the American Novel,* 1960.
Fisher, Philip. *Hard Facts: Setting and Form in the American Novel,* 1985.

Fishkin, Shelley Fisher. *From Fact to Fiction: Journalism and Imaginative Writing in America,* 1985.
Fletcher, Angus. *A New Theory for American Poetry: Democracy, the Environment, and the Future of the Imagination,* 2004.
French, Warren. *The Social Novel at the End of an Era,* 1966.
Frohock, W. M. *The Novel of Violence in America,* revised edition, 1957.
Fryer, Judith. *The Faces of Eve: Women in the Nineteenth-Century American Novel,* 1976.
Fussell, Edwin. *Frontier: American Literature and the American West,* 1965.
Gabler-Hover, Janet, and Sattelmeyer, Robert, eds. *American History Through Literature, 1820–1870,* 3 vols., 2006.
Galloway, David. *The Absurd Hero in American Fiction,* 1966.
Gates, Henry Louis. *Figures in Black: Words, Signs, and the Racial Self,* 1987.
———. *The Signifying Monkey: A Theory of African-American Literary Criticism,* 1989.
Geismar, Maxwell. *Writers in Crisis: The American Novel Between Two Wars,* 1942.
———. *The Last of the Provincials: The American Novel, 1915–1925,* 1947.
———. *Rebels and Ancestors: The American Novel, 1890–1915,* 1953.
———. *American Moderns: From Rebellion to Conformity,* 1958.
Gelpi, Albert. *The Tenth Muse: The Psyche of the American Poet,* 1975.
Gould, Jean. *American Women Poets: Pioneers of Modern Poetry,* 1980.
Gould, Philip. *Covenant and Republic: Historical Romance and the Politics of Puritanism,* 1996.
Gray, Richard. *A History of American Literature,* 2004.
———. *The Literature of Memory: Modern Writers of the American South,* 1977.
———. *Writing the South,* 1986, 1998.
Gregory, Horace, and Zaturenska, Marya. *A History of American Poetry, 1900–1940,* 1946, 1969.
Gross, S. L., and Hardy, J. E., eds. *Images of the Negro in American Literature,* 1966.
Grossman, Jay. *Reconstituting the American Renaissance, Emerson, Whitman, and the Politics of Representation,* 2005.
Hart, J. D. *The Popular Book: A History of America's Literary Taste,* 1950.
Hassan, Ihab. *Radical Innocence, Studies in the Contemporary American Novel,* 1961.
———. *Contemporary American Literature, 1945–1972,* 1973.
Hoffman, Daniel. *Form and Fable in American Fiction,* 1961.
———. *Harvard Guide to American Writing,* 1979.
Hoffman, Frederick. *The Twenties: American Writing in the Postwar Decade,* 1955.
———. *The Art of Southern Fiction,* 1967.
Horton, R. W., and Edwards, Herbert. *Backgrounds of American Literary Thought,* 1952.
Howard, Leon. *Literature and the American Tradition,* 1960.
Hubbell, Jay B. *The South in American Literature, 1607–1900,* 1954.
Huggins, R. I. *Harlem Renaissance,* 1971.
Jackson, Blyden. *A History of African American Literature,* Volume I, 1989.
Jameson, Fredric. *Postmodernism, or, The Cultural Logic of Late Capitalism,* 1991.
Jaskoski, Helen. *Early Native American Writing,* 1996.
Jones, Howard Mumford. *O Strange New World: American Culture, The Formative Years,* 1964.
———. *The Theory of American Literature,* 2nd edition, 1965.
———. *The Age of Energy: Varieties of American Experience, 1865–1915,* 1971.
Kammer, Michael. *A Season of Youth,* 1978.

Kartiganer, Donald M., and Griffith, Malcolm A. *Theories of American Literature,* 1972.
Kaul, A. N. *The American Vision: Actual and Ideal Society in Nineteenth-Century Fiction,* 1963.
Kazin, Alfred. *On Native Grounds: An Interpretation of Modern American Prose Literature,* 1942.
———. *Bright Book of Life: American Novelists and Storytellers from Hemingway to Mailer,* 1973.
Kenner, Hugh. *A Homemade World: The American Modernist Writers,* 1975.
Kermode, Frank. *The Uses of Error,* 1991.
Klein, Marcus. *After Alienation: American Novels in Mid-Century,* 1964.
Knight, Grant. *The Critical Period in American Literature, 1890–1900,* 1951.
———. *The Strenuous Age in American Literature, 1900–1910,* 1954.
Kolb, Harold. *The Illusion of Life: American Realism as a Literary Form,* 1970.
Kramer, Dale. *Chicago Renaissance: The Literary Life in the Midwest, 1900–1930,* 1966.
Krutch, J. W. *The American Drama Since 1918,* 1939.
Kupperman, Karen, ed. *America in European Consciousness,* 1995.
Lawrence, D. H. *Studies in Classic American Literature,* 1923.
Lee, Robert Edson. *From West to East: Studies in the Literature of the American West,* 1966.
Leisy, E. E. *The American Historical Novel,* 1950.
Levin, David. *In Defense of Historical Literature,* 1967.
Levin, Harry. *The Power of Blackness: Hawthorne, Poe, Melville,* 1958.
Lewis, R. W. B. *The American Adam; Innocence, Tragedy, and Tradition in the Nineteenth Century,* 1955.
Lively, Robert. *Fiction Fights the Civil War,* 1956.
Long, Eugene Hudson. *American Drama from Its Beginnings to the Present,* 1970.
Loving, Jerome. *Lost in the Customhouse: Authorship in the American Renaissance,* 1993.
Lynen, J. F. *The Design of the Present: Essays on Time and Form in American Literature,* 1969.
Lynn, Kenneth S. *The Dream of Success: A Study of the Modern American Imagination,* 1955.
McGiffert, Michael. *Puritanism and the American Experience,* 1969.
Malin, Irving. *New American Gothic,* 1962.
Margolies, Edward. *Native Sons: A Critical Study of Twentieth-Century Negro American Authors,* 1968.
Martin, Jay. *Harvests of Change: American Literature, 1865–1914,* 1967.
Marx, Leo. *The Machine in the Garden: Technology and the Pastoral Ideal in America,* 1964.
Matthiessen, F. O. *American Renaissance: Art and Expression in the Age of Emerson and Whitman,* 1941.
May, Henry. *The End of American Innocence: The First Years of Our Own Time, 1912–1917,* 1959.
———. *The Enlightenment in America,* 1976.
Mazzaro, Jerome. *Postmodern American Poetry,* 1980.
McWilliams, John. *New England's Crises and Cultural Memory: Literature, Politics, History, Religion, 1620–1860,* 2004.
Menand, Louis. *The Metaphysical Club: A Story of Ideas in America,* 2001.

Mencken, H. L. *The American Language: An Inquiry into the Development of English in the United States,* revised edition, 1936. Supplement I, 1945; Supplement II, 1948.
Meserve, Walter. *An Emerging Entertainment: The Drama of the American People from the Beginnings to 1828,* 1977.
Miller, Jordan, and Frazer, Winifred. *American Drama Between the Wars,* 1991.
Miller, Perry. *The New England Mind: The Seventeenth Century,* 1939.
———. *The New England Mind: From Colony to Province,* 1953.
———. *The Raven and the Whale: The War of Words and Wits in the Era of Poe and Melville,* 1956.
Miller, Ruth. *Backgrounds to Black American Literature,* 1971.
Millgate, Michael. *American Social Fiction,* 1967.
Moers, Ellen. *Literary Women,* 1976.
Moffitt, John, and Sebastián, Santiago. *O Brave New People: The European Invention of the American Indian,* 1996.
Mordden, Ethan. *The American Theatre,* 1981.
Morgan, E. S. *Visible Saints: The History of a Puritan Idea,* 1963.
Morison, S. E. *The Intellectual Life of Colonial New England,* 1956.
Mott, F. L. *Golden Multitudes: The Story of Best Sellers in the United States,* 1947.
———. *American Journalism: A History of Newspapers in the United States Through 250 Years. 1690 to 1940,* 1941, revised 1951.
———. *A History of American Magazines,* 4 vols., 1938–1957.
Mumford, Lewis. *The Golden Day,* 1926.
Murdock, K. B. *Literature and Theology in Colonial New England,* 1949.
Myerson, Joel, ed. *The Transcendentalists: A Review of Research and Criticism,* 1984.
Newman, Charles. *The Post-Modern Aura: The Act of Fiction in an Age of Inflation,* 1985.
Nye, Russel. *The Cultural Life of the New Nation,* 1960.
Olderman, Raymond. *Beyond the Wasteland: The American Novel in the 1960s,* 1972.
Parrington, V. L. *Main Currents in American Thought: An Interpretation of American Literature from the Beginnings to 1920,* 3 vols., 1927–1930.
Pattee, F. L. *A History of American Literature Since 1870,* 1915, 1968.
———. *The Development of the American Short Story,* 1923, 1966.
Pearce, R. H. *The Continuity of American Poetry,* 1961.
Peden, William. *The American Short Story: Continuity and Change, 1940–1975,* 2nd edition, 1975.
Perkins, David. *A History of Modern Poetry,* 2 vols., 1976, 1987.
Person, Stow. *American Minds: A History of Ideas,* 1958.
Phillips, Robert. *The Confessional Poets,* 1963.
Pinsky, Robert. *The Situation of Poetry: Contemporary Poetry and Its Traditions,* 1977.
Pizer, Donald. *Realism and Naturalism in Nineteenth-Century American Literature,* 1966.
———, and Harbert, Earl. *American Realists and Naturalists,* 1982.
Poirier, Richard. *A World Elsewhere: The Place of Style in American Literature,* 1966.
———. *Poetry and Pragmatism,* 1991.
Porte, Joel. *The Romance in America,* 1969.
Quinn, A. H. *A History of the American Drama from the Civil War to the Present Day,* revised edition, 1936.
———. *American Fiction: An Historical and Critical Survey,* 1936.

———. *A History of the American Drama from the Beginning to the Civil War,* revised edition, 1943.
———, and others. *The Literature of the American People,* 1951.
Quinones, Ricardo. *Mapping Literary Modernism: Time and Development,* 1985.
Quirk, Tom, and Scharnhorst, Gary, eds. *American History Through Literature, 1870–1920,* 3 vols., 2006.
Reising, Russell. *The Unusable Past: Theory and Study of American Literature,* 1986.
Rideout, Walter. *The Radical Novel in the United States, 1900–1954,* 1956.
Ridgely, J. V. *Nineteenth-Century Southern Literature,* 1980.
Riley, I. W. *American Thought from Puritanism to Pragmatism and Beyond,* 1923, 1959.
Rosenblatt, Roger. *Black Fiction,* 1974.
Rourke, Constance. *American Humor: A Study of the National Character,* 1931.
Rubin, Louis. *The Faraway Country: Writers of the Modern South,* 1963.
———, ed. *The History of Southern Literature,* 1985.
Ruland, Richard. *The Rediscovery of American Literature: Premises of Critical Taste, 1900–1940,* 1967.
———, ed. *The Native Muse: Theories of American Literature,* Vol. I, 1972.
———, ed. *A Storied Land: Theories of American Literature.* Vol. II, 1976.
Ruland, Richard, and Bradbury, Malcolm. *From Puritanism to Modernism, A History of American Literature,* 1991.
Ruoff, LaVonne Brown, and Ward, Jerry W., eds. *Redefining American Literary History,* 1990.
Samuels, Shirley. *Romances of the Republic,* 1996.
Schneider, H. W. *The Puritan Mind,* 1930, 1958.
Shafer, Yvonne. *American Women Playwrights: 1900–1950,* 1996.
Seed, Patricia. *Ceremonies of Possession in Europe's Conquest of the New World,* 1996.
Seelye, John. *Prophetic Waters: The River in Early American Life and Literature,* 1977.
Silverman, Kenneth. *A Cultural History of the American Revolution,* 1976.
Slotkin, Richard, *Regeneration Through Violence: The Mythology of the American Frontier, 1600–1860,* 1973.
Smith, H. N. *Virgin Land: The American West as Symbol and Myth,* 1950.
———. *Democracy and The Novel,* 1979.
Spencer, Benjamin. *The Quest for Nationality: An American Literary Campaign,* 1957.
Spengermann, William C. *The Adventurous Muse: The Poetics of American Fiction: 1789–1900,* 1977.
Spiller, R. E. *The Cycle of American Literature,* 1951, 1967.
———, and others. *Literary History of the United States,* 4th edition, revised, 1974.
Stepanchev, Stephen. *American Poetry Since 1945,* 1965.
Stewart, Randall. *American Literature and the Christian Tradition,* 1958.
Stipes, Emily. *The Poetry of American Women from 1632 to 1945,* 1977.
Straumann, Heinrich. *American Literature in the Twentieth Century,* 1965.
Sundquist, Eric. *To Wake the Nations: Race in the Making of American Literature,* 1993.
Tanner, Tony. *The Reign of Wonder,* 1965.
Taubmann, Howard. *The Making of the American Theatre,* 1965.
Tompkins, Jane. *Sensational Designs: The Cultural Work of American Fiction, 1790–1860,* 1985.

Trachtenberg, Stanley. *American Humorists, 1800–1950,* 1982.
———. *Colonial Writers, 1606–1734,* 1984.
Trent, W. P., and others. *Cambridge History of American Literature,* 4 vols., 1917–1933.
Tuttleton, James W. *The Novel of Manners in America,* 1972.
Tyler, Alice Felt. *Freedom's Ferment: Phases of American Social History to 1860,* 1970.
Tyler, M. C. *A History of American Literature, 1607–1765,* 2 vols., 1878.
Van Doren, Carl. *The American Novel, 1789–1939,* 1940.
Vendler, Helen. *Part of Nature, Part of Us: Modern American Poets,* 1980.
Vogel, Dan. *The Three Masks of American Tragedy,* 1976.
von Hallberg, Robert. *American Poetry and Culture, 1945–1980,* 1985.
Wagenknecht, Edward. *Cavalcade of the American Novel,* 1952.
Waggoner, H. H. *American Poets: From the Puritans to the Present Day,* 1968.
Walcutt, C. C. *American Literary Nationalism, A Divided Stream,* 1956.
Weales, Gerald. *American Drama Since World War II,* 1962.
———. *The Jumping-Off Place: American Drama in the 1960s,* 1969.
Weaver, Gordon, ed. *The American Short Story, 1945–1980: A Critical History,* 1983.
West, Ray. *The Short Story in America, 1900–1950,* 1952.
White, Peter, ed. *Puritan Poets and Poetics: Seventeenth-Century Poetry in Theory and Practice,* 1985.
Wiget, Andrew *Native American Literature,* 1985.
Williams, S. T. *The Spanish Background of American Literature,* 1955.
Wilson, Edmund. *Patriotic Gore: Studies in the Literature of the American Civil War,* 1962.
Wood, James. *Magazines in the United States,* 2nd edition, 1956.
Ziff, Larzer. *The American 1890's,* 1966.
———. *Puritanism in America: New Culture in a New World,* 1973.

Acknowledgments

EDWARD ALBEE, *The Zoo Story.* Copyright © 1960 by Edward Albee. Reprinted by permission of The Putnam Publishing Group. *The Zoo Story* is the sole property of the author and is fully protected by copyright. It may not be acted either by professionals or amateurs without written consent. Public readings, radio and television broadcasts are likewise forbidden. All inquiries concerning these rights should be addressed to the William Morris Agency, 1350 Avenue of the Americas, NYC 10019.

SHERMAN ALEXIE, "What You Pawn I Will Redeem," from *Ten Little Indians* (Grove Press, 2003). Reprinted by permission of Grove Press. "Defending Walt Whitman," from *The Summer of Black Widows.* Copyright © 1996 by Sherman Alexie. Reprinted by permission of Hanging Loose Press.

A. R. AMMONS, "Sight Seed," from *Sumerian Vistas.* Copyright © 1987 by A. R. Ammons. Used by permission of W. W. Norton & Company, Inc. "Motion Which Disestablishes Organizes Everything," from *The Hudson Review* XL, no. 2 (summer 1987). Copyright © 1987 by A. R. Ammons. Reprinted with the permission of *The Hudson Review.* "The Damned," from *Brink Road.* Copyright © 1996 by A. R. Ammons. Used by permission of W. W. Norton & Company, Inc.

GLORIA ANZALDÚA, "The Homeland, Aztlán," from *Borderlands/La Frontera: The New Mestiza.* Copyright © 1987, 1999 by Gloria Anzaldúa. Reprinted by permission of Aunt Lute Books.

JAMES BALDWIN, "Sonny's Blues" was originally published in *Partisan Review.* Collected in *Going to Meet the Man,* © 1965 by James Baldwin. Copyright renewed. Published by Vintage Books. Reprinted by arrangement with the James Baldwin Estate.

IMANU AMIRI BARAKA (LEROI JONES), "In Memory of Radio," "The Bridge," and "Notes for a Speech," from *Preface to a Twenty Volume Suicide Note.* Copyright © 1961 by Amiri Baraka. "An Agony, As Now," "A Poem for Democrats," and "A Poem for Speculative Hipsters," from *The Dead Lecturer* (New York: Grove Press, 1964). Copyright © 1964 by Amiri Baraka. "A Poem Some People Will Have to Understand," "A Poem for Half-White College Students," and "Biography," from *Black Magic.* Copyright © 1969 by Amiri Baraka. All reprinted with the permission of Sterling Lord Literistic, Inc.

SAUL BELLOW, "A Silver Dish," from *Him with His Foot in His Mouth and Other Stories.* Copyright © 1974, 1978, 1982, 1984 by Saul Bellow, Ltd. Reprinted by permission of HarperCollins Publishers, Inc.

Elizabeth Bishop, "A Miracle for Breakfast," "The Fish," "Over 2,000 Illustrations and a Complete Concordance," "Visits to St. Elizabeth's," "Sestina," "The Armadillo," "Brazil, January 1, 1502," "In the Waiting Room," and "One Art," from *The Complete Poems 1927–1979.* Copyright © 1979, 1983 by Alice Helen Methfessel. Reprinted by permission of Farrar, Straus & Giroux, LLC.

David Bradley, "197903042100 (Sunday)," from *The Chaneysville Incident.* Copyright © 1981 by David H. Bradley, Jr. Reprinted by permission of HarperCollins Publishers.

Frederick Busch, "Bring Your Friends to the Zoo," from *The Children in the Woods: New and Selected Stories.* Copyright © 1994 by Frederick Busch. Reprinted by permission of Houghton Mifflin Company. All rights reserved.

Raymond Carver, "Cathedral," from *Cathedral.* Reprinted by permission of International Creative Management, Inc. Copyright © 1981 by Raymond Carver, 1989 by Tess Gallagher.

Billy Collins, "Winter Syntax," "Books," and "Introduction to Poetry," from *Sailing Alone Around the Room: New and Selected Poems.* Reprinted by permission of The University of Arkansas Press. Copyright © 1988 by Billy Collins.

Countée Cullen, "Harlem Wine," from *The New Negro*; "From the Dark Tower," from *Copper Sun*; "Yet Do I Marvel," "For a Lady I Know," "Incident," "A Brown Girl Dead," and "Heritage," from *Color*; "Scottsboro, Too, Is Worth Its Song," from *Medea and Some Poems.* Copyrights held by Amistad Research Center Administered by Thompson and Thompson, Brooklyn, NY.

E. E. Cummings, "the Cambridge ladies who live in furnished souls," "next to of course god america i," "my sweet old etcetera," "somewhere i have never travelled,gladly beyond," "r-p-o-p-h-e-s-s-a-g-r," "anyone lived in a pretty how town," "pity this busy monster,manunkind," "when serpents bargain for the right to squirm," and "l(a," from *Complete Poems 1904–1962,* edited by George J. Firmage. Copyright 1923, 1925, 1926, 1931, 1935, 1938, 1939, 1940, 1944, 1945, 1946, 1947, 1948, 1949, 1950, 1951, 1952, 1953, 1954, © 1955, 1956, 1957, 1958, 1959, 1960, 1961, 1962, 1963, 1966, 1967, 1968, 1972, 1973, 1974, 1975, 1976, 1977, 1978, 1979, 1980, 1981, 1982, 1983, 1984, 1985, 1986, 1987, 1988, 1989, 1990, 1991 by the Trustees for the E. E. Cummings Trust. Copyright © 1973, 1976, 1978, 1979, 1981, 1983, 1985, 1991 by George James Firmage. Used by permission of Liveright Publishing Company.

Don DeLillo, excerpt from *White Noise.* Copyright © 1985 by Don DeLillo. Reprinted with the permission of Penguin Putnam, Inc.

James Dickey, "The Lifeguard," "Reincarnation (I)," "In the Mountain Tent," and "The Shark's Parlor," from *James Dickey's Poems 1957–1967* (Middletown, CT: Wesleyan University Press, 1967). Reprinted by permission of Wesleyan University Press.

Emily Dickinson, selected poems reprinted by permission of the publishers and the Trustees of Amherst College from *The Poems of Emily Dickinson,* edited by Thomas H. Johnson (Cambridge, MA: The Belknap Press of Harvard University Press). Copyright © 1951, 1955, 1979, 1983 by the President and

Fellows of Harvard College. Selected letters to T. W. Higginson reprinted by permission of the publishers from *The Letters of Emily Dickinson,* edited by Thomas H. Johnson (Cambridge, MA: The Belknap Press of Harvard University Press). Copyright © 1958, 1986 by the President and Fellows of Harvard College.

DINÉ BAHANE', excerpts from *Diné bahane': The Navajo Creation Story,* ed. Paul G. Zolbrod (Albuquerque, NM: University of New Mexico Press, 1984). Reprinted by permission of the University of New Mexico Press.

JOHN DOS PASSOS, "Preface" to *U.S.A.*, "Proteus," from *The 42nd Parallel,* "Newsreel XLIII" and "The Body of an American," from *1919,* "Newsreel LXVI" and "The Camera Eye (50)," from *The Big Money,* and "Vag," from *U.S.A.* All selections from *U.S.A.* (Boston: Houghton Mifflin Company, 1938). Reprinted with the permission of Elizabeth H. Dos Passos.

RITA DOVE, "Kentucky, 1833," "Adolescence—I," "Adolescence—II," "Adolescence—III," "Banneker," "Jiving," "The Zeppelin Factory," "Under the Viaduct, 1932," "Roast Possum," "Weathering Out," and "Daystar," from *Selected Poems.* Copyright © 1980, 1983, 1986, 1993 by Rita Dove. Reprinted with the permission of the author.

W. E. B. DU BOIS, "On Being Crazy" from *The Crisis.* Pearson Prentice Hall wishes to thank The Crisis Publishing Co., Inc., the publisher of the magazine of the National Association for the Advancement of Colored People, for the use of this material first published in the June 1923 issue of *The Crisis.*

T. S. ELIOT, "Journey of the Magi," from *Collected Poems 1909–1962.* Copyright 1936 by Harcourt, Inc., copyright © 1964, 1963 by T. S. Eliot. Reprinted by permission of the publisher. "Gerontion," "The Waste Land," "Notes on 'The Waste Land'," "Journey of the Magi," "Preludes I–IV," and "The Love Song of J. Alfred Prufrock," from *Collected Poems 1909–1962.* Reprinted in Canada by permission of Faber and Faber, Ltd. "Tradition and the Individual Talent," from *Selected Essays* (New York: Harcourt Brace, 1950). Reprinted in Canada by permission of Faber and Faber, Ltd.

RALPH ELLISON, Chapter 1 from *Invisible Man.* Copyright 1947, 1948, 1952 by Ralph Ellison. Copyright renewed 1975, 1976, 1980 by Ralph Ellison. Used by permission of Random House, Inc.

LOUISE ERDRICH, "The Red Convertible," from *Love Medicine,* New and Expanded Edition. Copyright © 1984, 1993 by Louise Erdrich. Reprinted by permission of Henry Holt and Company, LLC.

WILLIAM FAULKNER, "That Evening Sun," from *Collected Stories of William Faulkner.* Copyright 1931 and renewed 1959 by William Faulkner. Used by permission of Random House, Inc. Excerpt from *Intruder in the Dust.* Copyright 1929 and renewed 1957 by William Faulkner. Copyright © 1973 by Random House, Inc. Used by permission of Random House, Inc.

CAROL FREEMAN, "when my uncle willie saw," from *Black Fire,* ed. LeRoi Jones and Larry Neal (William Morrow, 1968), p. 331. Originally published in *Soulbook.*

ROBERT FROST, "Design," "Nothing Gold Can Stay," "Stopping by Woods on a Snowy Evening," "Acquainted with the Night," "West-Running Brook," "Desert Places," "Neither out Far Nor in Deep," "Directive," and "In Winter in the Woods Alone," from *The Poetry of Robert Frost* (New York: Henry Holt, 1969).

ALLEN GINSBERG, "Howl," "A Supermarket in California," "America," and "To Aunt Rose," from *Collected Poems 1947–1980.* Copyright © 1955, 1956, 1958, 1959, 1974 by Allen Ginsberg. Reprinted with the permission of HarperCollins Publishers, Inc.

ELLEN GLASGOW, "The Difference," from *The Shadowy Third and Other Stories.* Copyright 1923 by Doubleday, Page & Co., Inc., and renewed 1951 by First and Merchants National Bank of Richmond, Virginia. Reprinted by permission of Harcourt, Inc.

JOSEPH HELLER, "Major Major Major Major," from *Catch-22.* Copyright © 1955, 1961 by Joseph Heller. Copyright © renewed 1989 by Joseph Heller. All rights reserved. Reprinted with the permission of Simon & Schuster Adult Publishing Group.

ERNEST HEMINGWAY, "Big Two-Hearted River," from *The Short Stories of Ernest Hemingway.* Copyright 1925 by Charles Scribner's Sons. Copyright renewed 1953 by Ernest Hemingway. Reprinted with the permission of Scribner, an imprint of Simon & Schuster Adult Publishing Group.

DAVID HENDERSON, "Neon Diaspora," from *Black Fire,* ed. LeRoi Jones and Larry Neal (William Morrow, 1968), pp. 230–232.

TINA HOWE, "Painting Churches," from *Coastal Disturbances: Four Plays.* Copyright © 1982 by Tina Howe.

LANGSTON HUGHES, "The Negro Speaks of Rivers," copyright 1926 by Alfred A. Knopf, Inc. and renewed 1954 by Langston Hughes, "The Weary Blues," copyright 1926 by Alfred A. Knopf and renewed 1954 by Langston Hughes, "Young Gal's Blues," copyright 1927 by Alfred A. Knopf and renewed 1955 by Langston Hughes, "I, Too," copyright 1926 by Alfred A. Knopf, Inc. and renewed 1954 by Langston Hughes, "Note on Commercial Theatre," from *Selected Poems of Langston Hughes,* copyright 1927 by Alfred A. Knopf, Inc. and renewed 1955 by Langston Hughes. Used by permission of Alfred A. Knopf, a division of Random House, Inc. "Dream Boogie," "Dream Deferred (Harlem)," and "Theme for English B," from *The Collected Poems of Langston Hughes.* Copyright © by The Estate of Langston Hughes. Used by permission of Alfred A. Knopf, a division of Random House, Inc. "On the Road," from *Short Stories.* Copyright © 1996 by Ramona Bass and Arnold Rampersad. Reprinted by permission of Hill and Wang, a division of Farrar, Straus and Giroux, LLC.

ZORA NEALE HURSTON, "How It Feels to Be Colored Me," from *The Complete Stories of Zora Neale Hurston.* Reprinted by permission of the Victoria Sanders Literary Agency. "The Gilded Six-Bits," from *The Complete Stories of Zora Neale Hurston.* Introduction copyright © 1995 by Henry Louis Gates, Jr. and Sieglinde Lemke. Compilation copyright © 1995 by Vivian Bowden, Lois J.

Hurston Gaston, Clifford Hurston, Lucy Ann Hurston, Winifred Hurston Clark, Zora Mack Goins, Edgar Hurston, Sr., and Barbara Hurston Lewis. Afterword and Bibliography copyright © 1995 by Henry Louis Gates, Jr. Reprinted by permission of HarperCollins Publishers, Inc. "The Gilded Six-Bits" was originally published in *Story*, August 1933.

SHIRLEY JACKSON, "The Lottery," from *The Lottery and Other Stories.* Copyright © 1948, 1949 by Shirley Jackson. Copyright renewed 1976, 1977 by Laurence Hyman, Barry Hyman, Mrs. Sarah Webster, and Mrs. Joanne Schnurer. Reprinted by permission of Farrar, Straus and Giroux, LLC.

RANDALL JARRELL, "Losses," "The Death of the Ball Turret Gunner," "A Girl in a Library," and "In Montecito," from *The Complete Poems.* Copyright © 1969, renewed 1997 by Mary von S. Jarrell. Reprinted by permission of Farrar, Straus and Giroux, LLC.

ROBINSON JEFFERS, "Boats in a Fog," copyright 1925 and renewed 1953 by Robinson Jeffers, "Hurt Hawks," copyright 1927 and renewed 1955 by Robinson Jeffers, and "Shine, Perishing Republic," copyright 1934 and renewed 1962 by Donnan Jeffers and Garth Jeffers, from *The Selected Poetry of Robinson Jeffers.* Used by permission of Random House, Inc.

JAMES WELDON JOHNSON, "Lift Every Voice and Sing," from *Saint Peter Relates an Incident.* Copyright 1917, 1921, 1935 by James Weldon Johnson, copyright renewed © 1963 by Grace Nail Johnson. Used by permission of Viking Penguin, a division of Penguin Group (USA) Inc.

JUNE JORDAN, "Poem about My Rights" and "Poem for Guatemala," from *Naming Our Destiny: New and Selected Poems.* Copyright © 1989 by June Jordan. Appears by permission of the publisher, Thunder's Mouth Press.

JAMAICA KINCAID, "Girl" and "Wingless," from *At the Bottom of the River.* Copyright © 1983 by Jamaica Kincaid. Reprinted by permission of Farrar, Straus and Giroux, LLC.

MARTIN LUTHER KING, JR., "I Have a Dream," from *The Peaceful Warrior.* Copyright 1963 Martin Luther King, Jr., copyright renewed 1991 Coretta Scott King. Reprinted by arrangement with the Estate of Martin Luther King, Jr., c/o Writers House as agent for the proprietor, New York, NY.

MAXINE HONG KINGSTON, "No Name Woman," from *The Woman Warrior.* Copyright © 1975, 1976 by Maxine Hong Kingston. Used by permission of Alfred A. Knopf, a division of Random House, Inc.

DENISE LEVERTOV, "Beyond the End" and "Pure Products," from *Collected Earlier Poems: 1940–1960.* Copyright © 1957 by Denise Levertov. "Mad Song" and "A Hunger," from *Relearning the Alphabet.* Copyright © 1970 by Denise Levertov Goodman. "Zeroing In," from *Breathing the Water.* Copyright © 1987 by Denise Levertov Goodman. "Come into Animal Presence," "Abel's Bride," "O Taste and See," and "The Ache of Marriage," from *Poems 1960–1967.* Copyright © 1966 by Denise Levertov. All reprinted with the permission of New Directions Publishing Corporation.

Alain Locke, "Foreword," from *The New Negro.* Copyright 1925 Albert & Charles Boni, Inc. Reprinted with the permission of Scribner, an imprint of Simon and Schuster Adult Publishing Group.

Robert Lowell, "Memories of West Street and Lepke," "Skunk Hour," "For the Union Dead," "Waking Early Sunday Morning," and "Will Not Come Back," from *Selected Poems.* Copyright © 1976 by Robert Lowell. Reprinted with the permission of Farrar, Straus & Giroux, LLC. "The Quaker Graveyard in Nantucket" and "Mr. Edwards and the Spider," from *Lord Weary's Castle.* Copyright 1946 and renewed 1974 by Robert Lowell. Reprinted by permission of Harcourt, Inc.

Bernard Malamud, "The Magic Barrel," from *The Magic Barrel and Other Stories.* Copyright © 1950, 1958, renewed 1977, 1986 by Bernard Malamud. Reprinted by permission of Farrar, Straus and Giroux, LLC.

Bobbie Ann Mason, "Shiloh," from *Shiloh and Other Stories.* Copyright © 1982 by Bobbie Ann Mason. Reprinted by permission of International Creative Management, Inc.

James Alan McPherson, "The Faithful," from *Elbow Room.* Reprinted by permission of the author.

W. S. Merwin, "Grandfather in the Old Men's Home" and "The Drunk in the Furnace" © 1959 by W. S. Merwin, "Strawberries" and "Direction" © 1983 by W. S. Merwin, "The Dry Stone Mason" and "Fly" © 1966 by W. S. Merwin, "Noah's Raven" © 1963 by W. S. Merwin, reprinted with the permission of the Wylie Agency.

Edna St. Vincent Millay, "Euclid alone has looked on Beauty bare," from *Collected Poems* (HarperCollins). Copyright © 1923, 1951 by Edna St. Vincent Millay and Norma Milla Ellis. All rights reserved. Reprinted by permission.

N. Scott Momaday, excerpt from *The Way to Rainy Mountain.* Reprinted by permission. "The Arrowmaker," from *The Man Made of Words.* Copyright © 1997 by the author and reprinted by permission of St. Martin's Press, LLC.

Marianne Moore, "To a Steam Roller," "The Fish," "Poetry," "No Swan So Fine," from *The Collected Poems of Marianne Moore.* Copyright © 1935 by Marianne Moore; copyright renewed © 1963 by Marianne Moore and T. S. Eliot. "The Mind Is an Enchanting Thing" and "In Distrust of Merits," from *The Collected Poems of Marianne Moore.* Copyright © 1944 by Marianne Moore; copyright renewed © 1972 by Marianne Moore. All reprinted with the permission of Scribner, an imprint of Simon & Schuster Adult Publishing Group.

Toni Morrison, excerpt from *Beloved.* Copyright © 1997 by Toni Morrison. Used by permission of Alfred A. Knopf, a division of Random House, Inc.

Gloria Naylor, "Lucielia Louise Turner," from *The Women of Brewster Place.* Copyright © 1980, 1982 by Gloria Naylor. Used by permission of Viking Penguin, a division of Penguin Group (USA), Inc.

JOYCE CAROL OATES, "How I Contemplated the World from the Detroit House of Correction and Began My Life Over Again," from *The Wheel of Love.* Copyright © 1970 by Joyce Carol Oates. Reprinted by permission of John Hawkins & Associates, Inc.

TIM O'BRIEN, "On the Rainy River," from *The Things They Carried.* Copyright © 1990 by Tim O'Brien. Reprinted by permission of Houghton Mifflin Company. All rights reserved.

FLANNERY O'CONNOR, "A Good Man Is Hard to Find," from *A Good Man Is Hard to Find and Other Stories.* Copyright © 1953 by Flannery O'Connor and renewed 1981 by Regina O'Connor. Reprinted by permission of Harcourt, Inc.

TILLIE OLSEN, "I Stand Here Ironing," copyright © 1956, 1957, 1960, 1961 by Tillie Olson, from *Tell Me a Riddle,* Introduction by John Leonard. Used by permission of Dell Publishing, a division of Random House, Inc.

SIMON ORTIZ, "A Designated National Park" and "Canyon de Chelly," from *A Good Journey.* Reprinted by permission of the author. "Final Solution: Jobs, Leaving," from *Woven Stone.* Reprinted by permission of the author.

ANN PETRY, "Solo on the Drums," from *Miss Muriel and Other Stories.* Copyright © 1971 by Ann Petry. Copyright renewed 1999 by Ann Petry. Reprinted by the permission of Russell & Volkening as agents for the author.

SYLVIA PLATH, "The Bee Meeting," "Lady Lazarus," "Ariel," "Daddy," and "Fever 103°," from *Ariel.* Copyright © 1961, 1962, 1963, 1964, 1965, 1966 by Ted Hughes. Reprinted by permission of HarperCollins Publishers, Inc. Reprinted in Canada by permission of Faber & Faber, Ltd.

KATHERINE ANNE PORTER, "Flowering Judas," from *Flowering Judas and Other Stories.* Copyright © 1930 and renewed 1958 by Katherine Anne Porter. Reprinted by permission of Harcourt, Inc.

EZRA POUND, "A Retrospect," from *The Literary Essays of Ezra Pound.* Copyright 1935 by Ezra Pound. "I [And then went down to the ship]," "II [Hang it all, Robert Browning]," "XLV [With Usura]," and "LXXXI [What thou lovest well remains]," from *The Cantos.* Copyright © 1934, 1938, 1948 by Ezra Pound. "Portrait d'une Femme," "Salutation," "A Pact," "In a Station of the Metro," and "The River-Merchant's Wife," from *Personae.* "I [E. P. Ode pour l'Election de Son Sepulchre]," "II [The age demanded an image]," "III [The tea-rose tea-gown, etc.]," "IV [These fought in any case]," and "V [There died a myriad]," from "Hugh Selwyn Mauberley" from *Personae.* Copyright 1926 by Ezra Pound. All reprinted with the permission of New Directions Publishing Corporation.

THOMAS PYNCHON, "Entropy," from *Slow Learner.* Copyright © 1984 by Thomas Pynchon. Reprinted with the permission of Little, Brown and Company.

ADRIENNE RICH, "At a Bach Concert," copyright © 1993, 1951 by Adrienne Rich, "Living in Sin," copyright © 1993, 1955 by Adrienne Rich, "Breakfast in a Bowling Alley in Utica, New York," copyright © 1993 by Adrienne Rich, copyright © 1966 by W. W. Norton & Company, Inc., from *Collected Early Poems: 1950–1970.* Used by permission of the author and W. W. Norton & Company, Inc. "Divisions of Labor," from *Time's Power: Poems 1985–1988.* Copyright © 1989 by Adrienne Rich. Used by permission of the author and W. W. Norton & Company, Inc. "For This," and "1999" from *Fox: Poems 1998–2000.* Copyright © 2001 by Adrienne Rich. Used by permission of the author and W. W. Norton & Company, Inc.

Tomás Rivera, ". . . And the Earth Did Not Part." Reprinted with permission from the publisher of ". . . y no se lo tragó la tierra/. . . And the Earth Did Not Devour Him" (Houston: Arte Publico Press, University of Houston, 1987).

Theodore Roethke, "Dolor," copyright 1943 by Modern Poetry Association, Inc., "Open House," copyright 1941 by Theodore Roethke, "Cuttings," copyright 1948 by Theodore Roethke, "Cuttings (Later)," copyright 1948 by Theodore Roethke, "Root Cellar," copyright 1943 by Modern Poetry Association, Inc., "My Papa's Waltz," copyright 1942 by Hearst Magazines, Inc., and "In a Dark Time," copyright © 1960 by Beatrice Roethke, Administratix of the Estate of Theodore Roethke, from *The Collected Poems of Theodore Roethke.* Used by permission of Doubleday, a division of Random House, Inc.

Philip Roth, "The Conversion of the Jews," from *Goodbye, Columbus.* Copyright © 1959, renewed 1987 by Philip Roth. Reprinted by permission of Houghton Mifflin Co. All rights reserved.

Sonia Sanchez, "the final solution/" and "to blk/record/buyers," from *Homecoming.* Reprinted by permission of Broadside Press. "Womanhood," from *A Blues Book for Blue Black Magical Women.* Reprinted by permission of Broadside Press. "Masks" and "Just Don't Never Give Up on Love," from *homegirls and handgrenades.* Copyright © 1984 by Sonia Sanchez. Appears by permission of the publisher, Thunder's Mouth Press.

Anne Sexton, "The Farmer's Wife" and "Ringing the Bells," from *Bedlam and Part Way Back.* Copyright © 1960 by Anne Sexton, renewed 1988 by Linda G. Sexton. "Us," from *Love Poems.* Copyright © 1967, 1968, 1969 by Anne Sexton. "Rowing," from *The Awful Rowing Toward God.* Copyright © 1975 by Loring Conant, Jr., Executor of the Estate of Anne Sexton. "And One for My Dame" and "The Addict," from *Live or Die.* Copyright © 1966 by Anne Sexton. All reprinted by permission of Houghton Mifflin Company. All rights reserved.

Leslie Marmon Silko, "The Man to Send Rain Clouds" and "Coyote Holds a Full House in His Hand," from *Storyteller.* Copyright © 1981 by Leslie Marmon Silko. Reprinted with the permission of The Wylie Agency.

Gary Snyder, "Riprap" and "Poem Left in Sourdough Mountain Lookout," from *Riprap and Cold Mountain Poems.* Copyright © 1958 by Gary Snyder. "Soy Sauce," from *Axe Handles.* Copyright © 1983 by Gary Snyder. "I Went into the Maverick Bar," from *Turtle Island.* Copyright © 1974 by Gary Snyder. Reprinted by permission of New Directions Publishing Corp.

EDWARD SPRIGGS, "For the Truth," from *Black Fire.* Copyright © by Edward Spriggs.

JOHN STEINBECK, "The Snake" and "The Vigilante," from *The Long Valley.* Copyright 1936, renewed © 1964 by John Steinbeck. Used by permission of Viking Penguin.

WALLACE STEVENS, "Peter Quince at the Clavier," "Disillusionment of Ten O'Clock," "Sunday Morning," "Domination of Black," "The Death of a Soldier," "Anecdote of the Jar," "A High-Toned Old Christian Woman," "The Emperor of Ice-Cream," "The Idea of Order at Key West," "Of Modern Poetry," "Final Soliloquy of the Interior Paramour," "The Plain Sense of Things," and "Of Mere Being," from *The Collected Poems of Wallace Stevens.* Copyright 1954 by Wallace Stevens and renewed 1982 by Holly Stevens. Used by permission of Alfred A. Knopf, a division of Random House, Inc.

JAMES T. STEWART, "Poem," from *Black Fire,* ed. LeRoi Jones and Larry Neal (William Morrow, 1968), pp. 203–204.

WILLIAM STYRON, excerpt from *The Confessions of Nat Turner.* Copyright © 1966, 1967 by William Styron. Used by permission of Random House, Inc.

AMY TAN, "Half and Half," from *The Joy Luck Club.* Copyright © 1989 by Amy Tan. Used by permission of G. P. Putnam's Sons, a division of Penguin Group (USA), Inc.

JEAN TOOMER, "Blood-Burning Moon," "Cotton Song," "Carma," and "Song of the Son," from *Cane.* Copyright 1923 by Boni & Liveright, renewed 1951 by Jean Toomer. Used by permission of Liveright Publishing Corporation.

JOHN UPDIKE, "A & P," from *Pigeon Feathers and Other Stories.* Copyright © 1962 and renewed 1990 by John Updike. Used by permission of Alfred A. Knopf, a division of Random House, Inc.

KURT VONNEGUT, "Welcome to the Monkey House," from *Welcome to the Monkey House.* Copyright © 1961 by Kurt Vonnegut, Jr. Used by permission of Dell Publishing, a division of Random House, Inc.

JACQUES WAKEFIELD, "oh shit a riot!" from *Black Fire,* ed. LeRoi Jones and Larry Neal (William Morrow, 1968), p. 440.

ALICE WALKER, "Everyday Use," from *In Love and Trouble: Stories of Black Women.* Copyright © 1973 by Alice Walker. Reprinted by permission of Harcourt, Inc. "Burial," from *Revolutionary Petunias and Other Poems.* Copyright © 1972 and renewed 2000 by Alice Walker. Reprinted by permission of Harcourt, Inc.

JAMES WELCH, excerpt from *The Death of Jim Loney.* Reprinted by permission.

EUDORA WELTY, "Powerhouse," from *A Curtain of Green and Other Stories.* Copyright © 1941 and renewed 1969 by Eudora Welty. Reprinted by permission of Harcourt, Inc.

RICHARD WILBUR, "Marginalia" and "Lamarck Elaborated," from *Things of This World.* Copyright © 1956 and renewed 1984 by Richard Wilbur. "A Hole in the Floor," from *Advice to a Prophet and Other Poems.* Copyright © 1961 and renewed 1989 by Richard Wilbur. "Trolling for Blues," from *New and Collected Poems.* Copyright © 1987 by Richard Wilbur. All reprinted by permission of Harcourt, Inc.

TENNESSEE WILLIAMS, *The Glass Menagerie.* Copyright 1945 by Tennessee Williams. Reprinted by permission of Georges Borchardt, Inc., for the author.

WILLIAM CARLOS WILLIAMS, "Seafarer" and "Landscape with the Fall of Icarus" from *The Collected Poems of William Carlos Williams: Volume II, 1939–1962,* edited by Christopher MacGowan. Copyright 1953, © 1962 by William Carlos Williams. "Con Brio," "The Young Housewife," "Pastoral," "Tract," "Danse Russe," "Queen-Ann's-Lace," "Spring and All," "To Elsie," "The Red Wheelbarrow," "At the Ball Game," "Between Walls," "This Is Just to Say," "The Yachts," and "These" from *The Collected Poems of William Carlos Williams: Volume I, 1909–1939,* edited by Christopher MacGowan. Copyright 1938, 1944, 1945 by William Carlos Williams. All reprinted with the permission of New Directions Publishing Corporation.

AUGUST WILSON, *Fences.* Copyright © 1986 by August Wilson. Used by permission of Dutton Signet, a division of Penguin Group (USA) Inc.

THOMAS WOLFE, "Only the Dead Know Brooklyn" and "The Far and the Near," from *From Death to Morning.* Copyright © 1935 by Charles Scribner's Sons; copyright renewed © 1963 by Paul Gitlin Administrator, C.T.A. Reprinted with the permission of Scribner, an imprint of Simon & Schuster Adult Publishing Group.

RICHARD WRIGHT, excerpt from *Native Son.* Copyright 1940 by Richard Wright. Copyright © renewed 1968 by Ellen Wright. Reprinted by permission of HarperCollins Publishers.

Index to Authors, Titles, and First Lines

Note: First lines are set in roman type; all titles are italicized except titles of short works when listed under the main title of the works or under authors' names.

G

H

I

J

N

Q

R

T

Y

Z